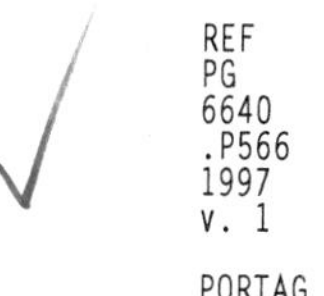
REF
PG
6640
.P566
1997
v. 1

PORTAG

Chicago Public Library
W9-DEI-222
Unabridged Polish-English dictionar

Chicago Public Library
REF
PG
6640
.P566
1997
V.1
R0125630562
C
P
L
REFERENCE
Form 178 rev. 1-94

UNABRIDGED

POLISH-ENGLISH

DICTIONARY

Volume I

A - N

UNABRIDGED

POLISH-ENGLISH

DICTIONARY

Volume I

A - N

Iwo Cyprian Pogonowski

HIPPOCRENE BOOKS
New York

Other Books by Iwo Cyprian Pogonowski

POLISH-ENGLISH/ENGLISH-POLISH
PRACTICAL DICTIONARY (Completely Revised)
ISBN 0-7818-0085-4 $11.95 pb

POLISH-ENGLISH/ENGLISH-POLISH
CONCISE DICTIONARY (Completely Revised)
With Complete Phonetics
ISBN 0-7818-0133-8 $9.95 pb

POLISH-ENGLISH/ENGLISH-POLISH
COMPACT DICTIONARY
ISBN 0-7818-0496-4 $8.95 pb

POLISH-ENGLISH/ENGLISH-POLISH
STANDARD DICTIONARY
Revised Edition with Business Terms
ISBN 0-7818-0282-2 $19.95 pb

POLISH PHRASEBOOK AND DICTIONARY (New Edition)
ISBN 0-7818-0134-0 $9.95 pb

POLISH PHRASEBOOK AND DICTIONARY
COMPANION CASSETTES
Volume I 2 cassettes
ISBN 0-7818-0340-3 $12.95
Volume II 2 cassettes
ISBN 0-7818-0384-5 $12.95

ENGLISH CONVERSATIONS FOR POLES (New Edition)
ISBN 0-87052-873-4 $9.95 pb

UNIWERSALNY

POLSKO-ANGIELSKI

SŁOWNIK

Tom I

A - N

Iwo Cyprian Pogonowski

HIPPOCRENE BOOKS

New York

For information, address:
HIPPOCRENE BOOKS, INC.
17 1 Madison Avenue
New York, NY 10016

Library of Congress Cataloging-in-Publication Data
Pogonowski, Iwo, 1921-
Unabridged Polish-English dictionary / Iwo Cyprian Pogonowski.
p. cm.
Added title page title: Polsko-angielski słownik.
ISBN 0-7818-0441-8
1. Polish language--Dictionaries--English. 2. English language--Dictionaries--Polish. I. Title: Polsko-angielski słownik
PG6640.P566 1997
491/8'5321--dc21 97-14300
CIP

Printed in the United States of America.

DEDICATION

In memory of my father,
Professor Jerzy Pogonowski,
who cultivated my interest
in languages and history

ADVISORY COMMITTEE

Joanna Banach, Philologist

Robert B. Frary, Ph.D. Professor and Director of the Learning Resources Center at Virginia Polytechnic Institute and State University

Armin Kargol, Ph.D. Mathematician

Zbigniew A. Kruszewski, Ph.D. Chairman of Political Science, Univ. of Texas in El Paso

Ewa Kurek, Ph.D, Professor, Catholic University of Lublin

Thomas O. MacAdoo, Ph.D. Professor of Classical Languages Virginia Polytechnic Institute and State University

Remigiusz Paczkowski, Ph.D. Economist

Richard Pipes Ph.D., Professor of History, Harvard University

Magdalena Pogonowska, MD. Radiologist

Andrzej Pogonowski, Lawyer

Joanna Radwańska-Williams, Ph.D. Philologist

Emil Skibiński, Pharmacist

Kazimierz Sowiński, MD.

Ewa Thompson, Ph.D. Professor of Slavic Studies, Rice University, Houston, Texas

Jolanta Wawrzycka, Ph.D. Professor of English at Radford University, Radford Virginia

Joseph Wiencko, Telecommunications Management Consultant

Jerzy Żemajtis, Ph.D. Civil Engineer

Ździslaw Żygulski, Ph.D. Professor, Art Historian, Curator of Polish National Museum, Czartoryski Collection in Kraków, Poland

TABLE OF CONTENTS

SPIS RZECZY

INTRODUCTION

It is a known fact that most Poles interested in the English language think about the United States rather than Great Britain as the country they would like to visit, or where they have relatives. For this reason Iwo Pogonowski has based his dictionary on the American usage of the English language. Thus, common American expressions are used in translations from the Polish.

While serving as an Adjunct Professor at Virginia Polytechnic Institute and State University, Pogonowski collected and discussed American expressions with a number of his colleagues. For instance, the English language contains many everyday expressions that originate from Anglo-Saxon and French; where there are two similar expressions, one often acquires a negative meaning. On the other hand, in the Polish language, like Latin, an expression can have both a positive and a negative sense. The determination of the proper translation into English of such Polish expressions required consultations with American linguists. Particular entries give idioms, as well as definitions in various contexts, making this dictionary a valuable reference for understanding the Polish culture and language.

This Polish-English Unabridged Dictionary follows the dictionaries of Jan Stanisławski at the turn of the century, Tadeusz Grzebieniowski in the 1920s and Kazimierz Bulas in 1962. Its nearly 4,000 pages contain about 200,000 entries, including technical and scientific terms, that reflect Professor Pogonowski's enormous knowledge: he is as comfortable in the fields of science and technology as he is in the fields of history and culture.

As with his previous dictionaries this one relies upon Professor Pogonowski's unique phonetic system -- and I should add, that Professor Pogonowski's dictionaries are still the only Polish-English dictionaries that employ a phonetic system of any sort for English speakers. This system enables English speakers to learn to pronounce Polish sounds through rules of pronunciation with which they are familiar. It is a dictionary that can be used by specialists as well as readers who already know some Polish and want to develop and enrich their competence in the field. And, lastly, Poles in Poland, for whom knowledge of English is now a basic element of education, will find it useful, as they did Professor Pogonowski's earlier dictionaries.

Zdzisław Mach Ph.D.
Dean of the College of Philosophy
Jagiellonian University
Cracow, Poland

WSTĘP

Istnieje kilka słowników polsko-angielskich i angielsko-polskich różnej wielkości i różnej klasy. Jest ich jednak ciagle za mało, biorąc pod uwagę, stale zwiekszającą się ruchliwość Polaków i ich obecność w światowym życiu gospodarczym i kulturalnym, a także otwarcie się Polski na świat. Szczególnie w Stanach Zjednoczonych potrzeba większej ilości i rozmaitości slowników jest bardzo widoczna. Rynek amerykański jest jednak bardzo specificzny. Polonia w USA jest bardzo zróżnicowana. Potomkowie emigrantów sprzed kilku pokoleń, ludzie często dobrze wyksztalceni i znający języki obce, uczą się języka przodków aby poznać ich kulturę, i odkryć swoje "korzenie". Proces poszukiwania źródeł swojej kultury i tożsamości jest charakterystyczną cechą współczesnych społeczeństw, szczególnie tych, które, jak społeczeństwo amerykańskie, złożone jest z emigrantów. Dla tych ludzi słownik jest narzędziem umożliwiającym dostęp do tekstów kulturowych, przede wszystkim do literatury, a także ułatwiającym kontakty ze starym krajem, łatwiejsze teraz niż przed laty, kiedy Polska była zdominowana przez wpływy sowieckie. Są też inni potomkowie emigrantów, ludzie niewykształceni i nie nawykli do uczenia się języków obcych. Ci też potrzebują słowników aby opanować elementy języka przodków w stopniu wystarczającym dla nawiązania kontaktów z krewnymi w Polsce. Słowniki muszą odpowiadać oczekiwaniom i potrzebom wszystkich grup potencjalnych użytkowników. Są jeszcze inni Amerykanie, którzy potrzebują polsko-angielskiego i angielsko-polskiego słownika. Myślę, tu o osobach nie mających rodzinnych związków z Polską ale z powodów zawodowych czy prywatnych zainteresowań chcących uczyć się języka polskiego. Im potrzebny jest słownik praktyczny, łatwy w użyciu. Są wreszcie studenci i intelektualiści - ludzie studiujący języki i literaturę słowiańską. Im potrzebny jest słownik obszerny, erudycyjny, pozwalający na opanowanie niuansów językowych.

Uniwersalny słownik Iwa C. Pogonowskiego wypełni lukę na amerykańskim rynku słowników. Co prawda luka ta nie jest już tak duża jak kilka lat temu, kiedy to trudno było kupić w księgarniach słownik polsko-angielski czy angielsko-polski. Jeśli dziś jest lepiej, to niemała w tym zasługa samego Iwa Pogonowskiego. W roku 1979 ukazał się jego słownik wydany przez Hippocrene Books, Inc. Był to jedyny słownik w którym były podane wskazówki fonetyczne przy każdym haśle polskim w przeciwieństwie do wszystkich innych słowników, w których podawano jedynie informacje o zasadach wymowy polskiej. Tak więc amerykański lub angielski użytkownik musiał sam rekonstruować polską wymowę wdług przepisu załączonego daleko od miejsca gdzie interesujące go hasło znajdowałoby się. Ważną cechą słownika Pogonowskiego jest zastosowanie głównie amerykańskiej wersji języka angielskiego i amerykańskich wyrażeń. Jako adjunct professor Virginia Politechnical Institute and State University Pogonowski zaczągromadzić przez szereg lat bieżące wyrażenia amerykańskie, które sprawdzał ze swoimi kolegami wykładowcami na tej właśnie uczelni. Język angielski zawiera wiele równoznacznych wyrażeń pochodzenia francuskiego, germańskiego lub celtyckiego, ponadto są one zwyczajowo używane w sensie pozytywnym lub negatywnym. Ustalenie tego zjawiska wymagało wielu konsultacji z amerykńskimi językoznawcami. W języku polskim, podobnie jak i w łacinie, zazwyczaj używa się jednego tylko ogólnego wyrażenia, które można stosować lub w znaczeniu pozytywnym albo negatywnym. Podstawowe zastosowanie wersji amerykańskiej raczej niż brytyjskiej odpowiada zainteresowaniom większości Polaków, którzy mają znacznie więcej powiązań ze Stanami Zjednoczonymi niż z Wielką Brytanią. Znany jest również fakt że Brytyjczycy subsydiują słowniki angielskie wydawane w Europie pod warunkiem zastosowania w nich brytyjskiej wersji ortografii i wyrażeń języka angielskiego, które to wyrażenia często bardzo się różnią od ich odpowiedników amerykańskich.

Pierwszy słownik Pogonowskiego był niezwykły, co najmniej z dwóch jeszcze powodów. Po pierwsze zawierał aneks, w którym Autor przedstawił zarys historii Polski i na okładce załączył kolorową ilustrację rynku krakowskiego. Po drugie Iwo Pogonowski zastosował oryginalną transkrypcję fonetyczną słów zamiast zwykle spotykanych znaków fonetycznych sporządził swój własny system polegający z grubsza biorąc na zapisie wymowy polskiej przy pomocy zwykłego alfabetu, przy czym anglojęzyczni użytkownicy słownika mogli wymawiać głoski według tych samych zasad, jakie obowiazują w języku angielskim. Dzięki temu, argumentował Autor, amerykański użytkownik słownika uczący się języka polskiego nie musi opanowywać specjalnego systemu międzynarodowych znaków fonetycznych (czego znaczna większość ludzi nie ma ochoty czynić), lecz może uczyć się poprawnej wymowy polskich słów korzystając ze znanych sobie reguł fonetycznych. Co prawda pomysl Pogonowskiego był dla wielu specjalistów - jezykoznawców kontrowersyjny, ale jego słowniki były za to "user friendly" - przyjazne dla użytkownika, a o to przede wszystkim chodziło Autorowi. Wieloletni pobyt w USA nauczył bowiem Pogonowskiego, że bardzo wielu Amerykanów, szczególnie polskiego pochodzenia, zniechęca się trudnościami fonetycznymi polskiego języka i zapisem fonetycznym, który trudno im opanować.

Zarys historii Polski w aneksie do słownika to też pomysł niezwykły, niespotykany w tego rodzaju publikacjach. I znowu aby go zrozumieć trzeba odnieść się do specyficznego środowiska, do społeczności Amerykanów polskiego pochodzenia lub Amerykanów bez polskich koneksji ale zainteresowanych Polska. Słownik miał być w zamyśle Autora wprowadzeniem do wiedzy o Polsce, jej historii, kultury i języka. Miałem przed laty możność dowiedzieć się o powstawaniu słownika i mogłem często rozmawiać z Autorem o powodach, które skłonily go do nadania mu takiego właśnie kształtu. Historia Polski zajmuje, najdelikatniej mówiąc, marginalne miejsce w nauczaniu historii powszechnej w szkołach amerykańskich, gdzie nacisk kładzie się na epokę porozbiorową. Dostęp do wiedzy na temat Polski jest, szczególnie dla niespecjalistów, w Ameryce dość trudny. Jest to specjalnie ważne w dzisiejszej epoce rewolucyjnie szybkiej wymiany informacji, w epoce, w której wszelka izolacja Polski przyczynia się do niewiedzy o naszej ojczyźnie i często czyni antypolską propagandę jedynym źródłem wiedzy o nas i o naszej historii i kulturze. Toteż pierwszy słownik Pogonowskiego pomyślany został jako klucz do zrozumienia Polski i jej kultury.

W krótkim czasie po opublikowaniu pierwszego słownika Pogonowski opracował szereg mniejszych słowników polsko-angielskich, w tym jedną wersję kieszonkową, zawsze zaopatrując wszystkie polskie hasła we wskazówki fonetyczne dla użytkowników mówiących po angielsku. W rezultacie pierwsze wydania słowników Pogonowskiego zostały rozpowszechnione w ponad 100,000 egzemplarzy. Sam Autor nawiasem mówiac nie poprzestał na pisaniu słowników. Jest znany także dzięki swojemu atlasowi *Poland: a Historical Atlas*, w którym opisał, oraz na 200 mapach i wykresach zilustrował, historię i prahistorię Polski, jak również dzięki encyklopedycznej książce *Jews in Poland: The Rise of Jews as a Nation from Congressus Judaicus in Poland to the Knesset in Israel*. Wraca jednak stale do kolejnych, udoskonalonych wersji słownika.

Slownik Pogonowskiego z 1979 roku byl podręczny. Obecny uniwersalny słownik polsko-angielski jest dziełem o znacznie większej skali - trzytomowe dzieło zawiera około 200 000 haseł na blisko 4000 stronach. Poszczególne hasła wzbogacone są o idiomy i przykłady kontekstowego zastosowania słów, co pozwala użytkownikowi na znacznie pełniejsze poznanie bogactwa języka i jego "ducha". Uniwersalny słownik Pogonowskiego ma nowoczesny charakter w tym że nie pomija wyraźnie zaznaczonych wyrażeń wulgarnych i gwarowych. Przy wyliczaniu znaczeń wielu haseł dodane są też ich znaczenia w gwarze przestępczej. Ten rzeczywiście uniwersalny słownik jest jednocześnie równie "user friendly" jak jego pierwsi dużo skromniejsi poprzednicy.

Słowniki Pogonowskiego są pierwszymi nowymi słownikami polsko-angielskimi od prac Jana Stanisławskiego sprzed pierwszej wojny światowej, Tadeusza Grzebieniowskiego w latach dwudziestych i Kazimierza Bulasa z 1962go roku. Iwo Pogonowski stworzył słowniki nowego typu. Zastosował on tę samą co poprzednio, choć udoskonaloną formę zapisu fonetycznego. Zadbał o to, aby słownik zawierał ogólne wskazówki fonetyczne oraz informacje o języku polskim. Słowniki Pogonowskiego udostępniły i udostępniają szerokim rzeszom Polaków wymowę angielską bez rażących błędów omówionych poniżej. Dowodzi tego duże zapotrzebowanie na jego słowniki. Ponieważ zapis fonetyczny Pogonowskiego składa się ze zwykłych liter polskiego i angielskiego alfabetu, co dla użytkowników jest bez porównania bardziej przystępne niż międzynarodowe symbole fonetyczne, które niestety zawierają w polskich słownikach wiele błędów. Autor uważa, że w nieprzystępny sposób jest opisana w nich angielska spółgłoska "sepleniona", 'th'. Pominięty jest fakt, że dla szerokiej rzeszy Polaków uczących się angielskiego, oznacza ona pięć różnych "seplenionych" dźwięków (spółgłoski dźwięczne "d", "dz" i "z" oraz spółgłoski bezdźwięczne "s" i "t"). Również w opisie samogłosek angielskich dotychczasowe polskie słowniki nie uwzględniły faktu, że polski dźwięk "y" ma bliski odpowiednik w języku angielskim. W ten sposób przyjął się np. wyraz "biznes", którego angielska wymowa może być w przybliżeniu zapisana po polsku jako słowo "byznys". Niestety wszystkie dotychczasowe polskie słowniki sugerują Polakom, żeby wymawiali polski dźwięk "i" [ee] tam gdzie powinien być znany im dźwięk "y". Tak więc do wszystkich trudności w kontaktach Polaków z Anglikami i Amerykanami dochodzą jeszcze zupełnie nieuzasadnione i śmieszne błędy w wymowie. Ten stan rzeczy spowodowany był wpływem francuskim na fonetyczny zapis stosowany przez Stanisławskiego, Grzebieniowskiego i Bulasa. Francuzi, podobnie jak Włosi i Hiszpanie, wymawiają i zapisują niedokładnie angielski dźwięk podobny do polskiego "y" jako dźwięk zbliżony do polskiego "i" [ee]. Czynią to dlatego, że nie mają w swoim własnym języku dźwięku pobodnego do polskiego "y". Do pojawienia się słowników Pogonowskiego, Polacy nie korzystali z podobieństwa swego rodzimego dźwięku "y" do zbliżonego dźwięku angielskiego i powtarzali nagminny błąd zachodnich Europejczyków, dla których polski dźwięk "y" i jego angielski odpowiednik jest trudny do wypowiedzenia. Tak więc z powodu tego, że Stanisławski skorzystał z zachodnio-europejskiej interpretacji wymowy angielskiej przy tworzeniu pierwszego wielkiego słownika polsko-angielskiego utrwalił on w języku polskim błędną wymowę w wielu słowach zapożyczonych z języka angielskiego. Dla Amerykanów i Anglików dotychczasowe słowniki polskie podają tylko ogólne wskazówki wymowy, tak że przy każdym haśle polskim nie ma w nawiasie pouczenia jak dane hasło wymawiać. Nawet jeżeli ktoś przeczyta ogólne wskazówki fonetyczne dotyczące języka polskiego to i tak ich nie zapamięta. Zwłaszcza tyczy się to ludzi, których szkoły amerykańskie nie przygotowały do kontaktu z obcymi językami.

W celu przełamania trudności porozumiewania się między Polakami i Amerykanami Pogonowski napisał również rozmówki polskie (Polish Phrasebook and Dictionary) dla Amerykanów, które zostały zaopatrzone w nagrania dźwiękowe polskich aktorów i wydane przez Hippocrene Books, Inc. Poza zapisem fonetycznym omówionym powyżej zastosował on w rozmówkach zapis obrazkowy określający stopień poufałości i rodzaje męski, żeński i nijaki odpowiadający wymogom polskiej gramatyki i etykiety.

Iwo Pogonowski zanalizował szczegółowo wymowę polską i angielską w oparciu o przekroje narządów mowy i ustalił różnice w używaniu tych narządów przez ludzi mówiących po polsku i po angielsku. W ten sposób wypracował uproszczony zapis fonetyczny. Wielką zasługą Pogonowskiego jest to że ulepszył możliwości porozumienia się ludzi mówiących po polsku i po angielsku. Słownik Pogonowskiego odzwierciedla też ogromną i wielostronną erudycję Autora, poprzez to, że zawiera wysoce specjalistyczne hasła zarówno z zakresu historii i kultury jak też najnowszej termnologii technicznej i naukowej.

Polish-English Unabridged Dictionary lub Uniwersalny Słownik Polsko-Angielski to wielki slownik, po który sięgną zapewne specjaliści i ludzie znający już język polski. Polacy którzy interesują się amerykańską wersją języka angielskiego znajdą w nim bogaty materiał w postaci tłumaczeń potocznych wyrażeń polskich na ich amerykańskie odpowiedniki. Nowy uniwersalny słownik Pogonowskiego będzie też użyteczny dla początkującego użytkownika, dzięki swojej przystępności. Jest dostosowany do rynku amerykańskiego, ale oczywiście będzie równie pożyteczny dla Polonii w innych częściach świata. Z pewnością znajdzie też użytkowników w Polsce, gdzie poprzednie słowniki Pogonowskiego, mimo ograniczonej dostępności, spotykały się niejednokrotnie z wdzięcznym przyjęciem.

Aleksander Gella
Professor of Sociology
State University of New York at Buffalo

FOREWORD

Thoughts and ideas are formulated in a different way in each language. Languages which belong to the same group are not simply equivalent. This is true of Polish and English, both of which are members of the same Indo-European group. For this reason I have tried to give an adequate translation of each entry so that it would reflect both its meaning and its spirit. Thus, each Polish word, phrase, or expression was translated using American literary, colloquial, vulgar, or "street language," which I have referred to as "mob jargon." British examples were marked: (Brit.).

Words in the Polish language have numerous grammatical forms, each spelled differently. If each of these grammatical cases was explained as a separate entry, there would be several million of such entries. The present Unabridged Polish-English Dictionary contains about 200,000 Polish entries, each followed by a phonetic transcription. Other comparable Polish-English dictionaries contain up to 180,000 entries. The present dictionary contains words, phrases, and expressions from the general Polish vocabulary as well as large number of medical, legal, technical and other scientific terms. Important regional and historic entries are included. Words which have a secondary vulgar meaning or are used differently in the street language are properly explained and identified. An attempt was made to arrange English translation in order of the frequency of their use.

The great wealth and variety of Polish grammatical forms does not exist in the English language. This is because Polish is an inflective language and English is an isolating or positional language. These characteristics are discussed at the end of the third volume on pages

3891 -- 3901. The polish type of declension of nouns and adjectives through seven grammatical cases with the corresponding changes in the spelling does not exist in the English language. Diminutives and augmentatives play an important descriptive role in the Polish language; they are much less numerous and less important in English. Some diminutives and augmentatives became a part of Polish literary and colloquial vocabulary. Many Polish diminutive and augmentative forms are used only sporadically as explained at the end of the third volume of this dictionary. The difficulties of translating Polish diminutives and augmentatives into English are discussed there. While the Polish language contains such a wealth of grammatical forms, the English language is richer in idiomatic expressions, pronouns, and prepositions.

The Polish perfect and imperfect forms of verbs differ in spelling and pronunciation. Each is presented as a separate entry and the imperfect form is marked: (*repeatedly*). The corresponding verbal noun, or a gerund, is marked: (*repeated*). Perfect and imperfect forms of verbs are not used in the English language.

Adjectival nouns and adverbs are included as separate entries (each with corresponding phonetic transcription) in order to make the Unabridged Polish-English Dictionary truly user-friendly. In the translation of the infinitive form of verbs the preposition "to" was omitted for the sake of simplicity. However, in the translation of phrases and expressions the preposition "to" was included as were the articles.

There are two plural forms in the Polish language. The small plural (for qantities of 2, 3, and 4) differs from the large plural (for quantities 5 or more). Since in the English language there is only one plural form the examples of Polish plural forms of nouns, adjectives, and verbes are shown in the third volume on pages 3931 -- 3950.

The Polish reflexive form contains indirect meanings between passive and active forms used in both Polish and English languages. While some of the English intransitive verbs are reflexive, generally Polish reflexive verbs can not be literally translated into the English language.

Polish reflexive verbs are listed as separate entries each with the particle "się" at the end.

English speakers usually experience difficulties in the pronunciation of Polish palatal consonants which are explained in this dictionary by the use of diagrams of speech organs. Such palatal consonants do not exist in the English language. The frequent changing of Polish voiced consonants into unvoiced consonants presents another difficulty. For this reason, a detailed phonetic transcription is included with each Polish phrase and expression. The phonetic symbols used in this dictionary are summarized on the inside of the front and back covers of each volume. A detailed Pronunciation Guide for English speakers is on pages 29a -- 42a of the first volume of this dictionary. Polish pronunciation is given as in common, everyday speech. Accented syllables are shown in bold print in the transcription of the pronunciation.

All grammatical forms such as nouns, adjectives, verbs, adverbs, pronouns, prepositions, prefixes, and expressions of the entries were marked with symbols shown on the list of abbreviations

Generally, the Polish language contains more numerous substantival, adjectival and verbal forms, than English, with each form spelled differently. In English, on the other hand, each noun may be used as a verb without any change in its spelling. Polish rules of grammar and phonetics may be stated using the expression "always, with a few exceptions, while corresponding English rules are less clear and are described using such words as "often, "sometimes," and "frequently." English phonetics and idioms conform to the rules less often than their Polish counterparts.

The spelling and hyphenation used in this dictionary was checked against current basic dictionaries in both languages. Unfortunately the hyphenation shown in the current dictionaries is not often observed in the press. When two Polish words constituted an adjectival, adverbial, or substantival expression they were marked as the abbreviation: exp.:. Often such Polish two-word expressions are translated with a single English word. All expressions were listed as separate secondary entries, each followed by a detailed phonetic transcription.

The author is greatly indebted to all the scholars and specialists, both those in the advisory committee and those outside of it, who supplied the information about the usage of specific terms in their fields.

Iwo Cyprian Pogonowski

PRZEDMOWA

Pojęcia i myśli formuje się w poszczególnych językach w różny sposób. Nawet języki należące do tej samej grupy (jak np polski i angielski do grupy indo-europejskiej) nie są równoznaczne. Z tego też powodu starałem się dawać przy każdym słowie i zwrocie dokładne odpowiedniki zarówno w znaczeniu pojęciowym jak pod względem zabarwienia uczuciowego. Każdy wyraz i zwrot polski był tłumaczony odpowiednim wyrazem i zwrotem angielskim literackim, potocznym, wulgarnym czy gwarowym (slangowym) używanym w Ameryce. Przykłady brytyjskie były załączone z dopiskiem: (Brit.).

Język polski zawiera liczne formy gramatyczne poszczególnych słów i gdyby wprowadzić każdą z nich jako odrębne hasło słownika to takich haseł byłoby kilka milionów. Niniejszy Uniwersalny Słownik Polsko-Angielski zawiera ponad 200 000 objaśnionych haseł. Jest to większa ilość niż w porównywalnych słownikach polsko-angielskich. Słownik zawiera wyrazy, wyrażenia i zwroty z zakresu ogólnego słownictwa polskiego jak również znaczną ilośc terminów medycznych, prawniczych, technicznych, przyrodniczych. Podano niektóre regionalizmy i wyrazy historyczne. Słowa, które zawierają znaczenia specjalne używane w gwarach przestępczych zostały zaopatrzone w przypisek (mob jargon). Znaczenia haseł były podane według częstości użycia.

Bogactwo polskich form gramatycznych nie ma odpowiednika w angielskim. Odmiana rzeczowników i przymiotników przez siedem przypadków przez wszystkie możliwe osoby z odpowiednimi zmianami końcówek, typowymi dla języka polskiego, nie istnieje w angielskim. Ważną rolę w jezyku polskim odgrywają zdrobnienia i zgrubienia z ich nieodłącznym zabarwieniem uczuciowym. Ich rola w języku angielskim jest znacznie mniejsza. Niektóre polskie zdrobnienia i zgrubienia są częścią polskiego języka tak literackiego jak i potocznego. Znaczna część polskich zdrobnień i zgrubień jest używana tylko sporadycznie, niemniej odpowiednie ich przykłady są załączone w tomie trzecim, gdzie są też pokazane trudności w ich tłumaczeniu na język angielski, który z koleii jest bogatszy w wyrażenia zwyczajowo-idiomatyczne; więcej jest w nim przyimków i zaimków.

Polska forma niedokonana czasowników została oznaczona słowem (*repeatedly*), a rzeczowników pochodnych słowem (*repeated*) dla haseł często używanych, zwłaszcza takich, które powstały przez dodanie przyrostka to podstawowego czasownika. Czasowniki angielskie nie mają oddzielnych form dokonanych i niedokonanych jak to ma miejsce w języku polskim.

Dla wygody użytkowników zostały załączone również przysłówki i rzeczowniki pochodne od przymiotników włącznie z ich wymowa. Natomiast opuszczono cechę angielskiego bezokolicznika "to" w tłumaczeniu bezokoliczników polskich w przeciwieństwie do podanych wyrażeń gdzie tą cechę zachowano. W tłumaczeniu wyrażeń załączono odpowiednie rodzajniki określone i nieokreślone. Podano liczbę mnogą rzeczowników w wypadkach trudnych dla użytkownika mówiącego po angielsku.

Specjalną cechą charakterystyczną języka polskiego jest odróżnienie małej liczby mnogiej (2, 3 i 4) od dużej (5 i więcej); tego rozróżnienia nie ma w języku angielskim. Z tego powodu podano przykłady liczenia po polsku uwzględniając wszelkiego rodzaju rzeczowniki i przymiotniki włącznie ze zdrobnieniami (strony 3933 do 3949 w tomie trzecim).

Polska forma zwrotna zawiera określenia pośrednie między formami czynną i bierną charakterystycznymi dla obu języków. Tej formy nie można dosłownie przetłumaczyć na język angielski. Na przykład powiedzenie "wzruszyłem się" nie znaczy dokładnie "I am touched," co równa się polskiemu "jestem wzruszony." "I touched muself" natomiast wcale nie znaczy "wzruszyłem się." Forma zwrotna polskich czasowników została podana jako oddzielne hasło ze względu na różnicę w znaczeniu i wymowie.

Wymowa języka polskiego stwarza wiele trudności ludziom mówiącym po angielsku. Polskie palatalne spółgłoski nie mają odpopwiednika w języku angielskim sostały one wyjaśnione za pomocą rysunku przekroju narządów mowy. Trudny dla cudzoziemców jest przechodni charakter polskich spółgłosek dzwięcznych, które przechodzą w bezdźwięczne zależnie od położenia w danym słowie. Z tego też powodu podano wymowę nie tylko podstawowych haseł ale również wszystkich wyrażeń. Skrócony system wymowy podano na początku in na końcu każdego tomu bezpośrednio pod okładką. Szczegółowe wyjaśnienie systemu wymowy słów polskich dla użytkowników mówiących po angielsku podano na stronach 29a -- 42a tomu pierwszego. Zastosowano codzienną, zwykłą wymowę. Akcentowane sylaby zaznaczono tłustą czcinką. Niniejszy Uniwersalny Słownik Polsko-Angielski zawiera system transkrypcji fonetycznej opracowany przez autora.

Oznaczono formy gramatyczne poszczególnych haseł: rzeczowniki, przymiotniki, czasowniki, przysłówki, zaimki, przyimki, przedrostki, i zwroty.

Ogólnie biorąc język polski ma więcej form rzeczownikowych, przymiotnikowych oraz czasownikowych. W angielskim natomiast prawie każdy rzeczownik bez zmiany pisowni może być użyty jako czasownik a nieraz także jako przymiotnik. Polskie zasady gramatyczne i fonetyczne można wyrazić słowami "zawsze z kilkoma wyjątkami", angielskie zasady gramatyczne i fonetyczne są bardziej płynne -- mówi się w nich: "często", "czasem" i "nieraz". W angielskim przeważają wyrażenia i fonetyka zwyczajowe.

Ortografia polska i angielska zostały sprawdzone z podstawowymi słownikami w bierzących wydaniach. Podstawą Universalnego Słownika Polsko-Angielskiego była ortografia amerykańska. Myślniki (czasem nazywane łącznikami) stosowane w słownikach standartowych języka angielskiego zastosowano w przygotowaniu niniejszego uniwersalnego słownika. Trzeba zwrócic uwage na to że stosowanie myślników w prasie anglo-językcznej często odbiega od przykładów zamieszczonych w słownikach. Wyrazy złożone pisane z łącznikiem lub bez, często jako dwa oddzielne wyrazy, dla prostoty podano jako wyrażenia oznaczone skrótem: exp.:. Często zdarza się że takie dwa oddzielne wyrazy tłumaczy się jednym wyrazem angielskim. Wszystkie zwroty podano jako oddzielne drugorzędne hasła, każde zaopatrzone w dokładną wskazówkę jak ma być ono wymawiane.

Pragnę wyrazić wdzięczność naukowcom i fachowcom wymienionym i nie wymienionym na liście doradców, którzy udzielali porad w zakresie słownictwa ze swoich specjalności.

Iwo Cyprian Pogonowski

Phonetic Guide

Fonetyka

POGONOWSKI

PHONETIC NOTATION

POLISH PRONUNCIATION FOR ENGLISH SPEAKERS

Pronunciation related to familiar English sounds
Pronunciation explained with speech organ diagrams

GUIDE TO PRONUNCIATION
IN COMMON, EVERYDAY SPEECH

Pogonowski Phonetic Symbols

Polish vowels:

A, a as in: father, car;
  in the phonetic guide: a

E, e as in: let, met, get;
  in the phonetic guide: e

I, i as in: feel, keel;
  in the phonetic guide: ee

O, o as in: bought, not;
  in the phonetic guide: o

U,u,Ó,ó as in: hook, too;
  in the phonetic guide: oo

Y, y as in: it, big, bib;
  in the phonetic guide: i

Polish Palatal Consonants

Speech organ diagram for Polish palatal consonants:

ś = śh, ź = źh
ć = ćh, dź = dźh

The two Polish nasalized vowels:

Ą, ą as in: *French sound of "on"*;
  in the phonetic guide: <u>own</u>

Ę, ę as in: *French sound of "vin"*;
  in the phonetic guide: <u>an</u>

POLISH FOR ENGLISH SPEAKERS

Note in the text when voiced consonants become unvoiced

Polish consonants:

unvoiced:		*voiced*:	
p	= p	b	= b
t	= t	d	= d
k	= k	g	= g as in "go"
k in kie	= k	g in gie	= g
f	= f	w	= v
s	= s	z	= z
ś	= śh	ź	= źh
sz	= sh	ż & rz	= zh
c	= ts	dz	= dz
ć	= ćh	dź	= dźh
cz	= ch	dż	= dzh
h & ch	= kh	l	= l
h in hie	= kh		

Glides:		*Nasals:*	
r	= r	m	= m
j	= y	n	= n
ł	= w	ń & ni	= ń

(Polish ń = Spanish ñ)

The phonetic transcription follows all entries.
It is subdivided into syllables.
In multi-syllable words the stressed syllables are printed in bold letters.
Polish vowels are pure and consist of one sound only.
Polish vowels are never drawn out or extended as often happens in English.

Schematic Ellipse of the Tip of the Tongue Positions Of Six Basic Polish Vowels

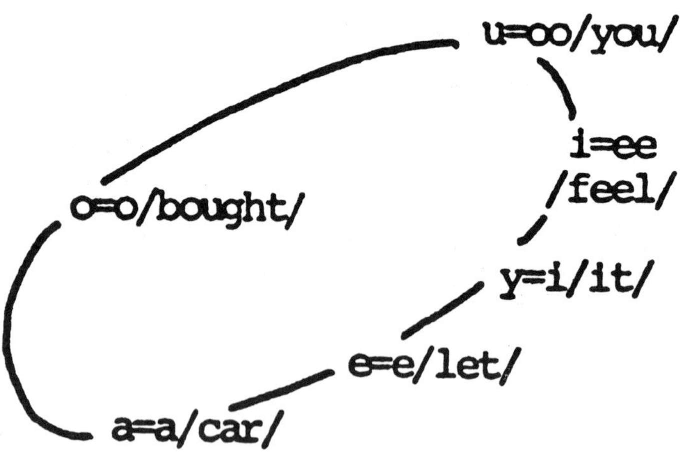

Polish nasalized vowels "ą" and "ę" are discussed on the next pages

Polish vowels:

A, a as in: father, car; in the phonetic guide: a

E, e, as in: let, met, get; in the phonetic guide: e

I, i, as in: feel, keel; in the phonetic guide: ee

O, o, as in: bought, not; in the phonetic guide: o

U, u, Ó, ó as in: tooth, too; in the phonetic guide: oo

Y, y, as in: it, big, bib; in the phonetic guide: i

The two *Polish nasalized vowels: ą and ę* cannot be exactly described by English sounds.

The two Polish nasalized vowels:

Ą, ą, shown in the phonetic guide as: <u>own</u> =
French sound of "on"
it is a single nasalized sound composed of:
a clear "o" as in "bought" followed by "w"
and the ending with a trace of "n"

Ę, ę, shown in the phonetic guide as: <u>an</u> =
French sound in ("vin")
it is a single nasalized sound composed of:
a clear "e" as in "pen" and the ending with
a trace of "n"

POLISH CONSONANTS

Most Polish consonants are to be read as in English. However, voiced consonants often become unvoiced at the end of a Polish word and immediately in front or behind of any unvoiced consonant. The phonetic guide at each entry shows this feature of the Polish language.

There are *no silent* Polish letters, except "c" in "ch" which is pronounced as [kh].

UNVOICED CONSONANTS: (without sounding the vocal cords)	VOICED CONSONANTS: (with sounding the vocal cords)
p = p	b = b
t = t	d = d
k = k	g = g
k in kie = <u>k</u>	g in gie = <u>g</u>
f = f	w = v
s = s	z = z
ś = śh	ź = źh
sz = sh	ż = zh
(sz = sh	rz = zh)

UNVOICED CONSONANTS: (without vibration of vocal cords) (cont.)

ć = ćh
cz = ch
h & ch = kh
h in hie = kh

VOICED CONSONANTS: (with vibration of vocal cords) (cont.)

dź = dźh
dż = dzh

l = l

GLIDES:

r = r
j = y
ł = w

NASALS:

m = m
n = n
ń & ni = ń

PRONUNCIATION OF POLISH CONSONANTS

SPELLED OR VOICED DIFFERENTLY THAN IN ENGLISH

cz = ch in the phonetic guide - it is pronounced exactly like "ch" in English.

sz = sh in the phonetic guide - it is pronounced exactly like "sh" in English.

szcz = shch in the phonetic guide - it is pronounced exactly like in "fresh cheese" in English.

h & ch = kh in the phonetic guide - it is pronounced like in Scottish "loch."

ń & ni = ń with an apostrophe in the phonetic guide - it is a nasal consonant as in "onion," or Spanish "n" as in"mañana". It also occurs in Polish when "n" is followed by the vowel "i."

ni = ń when the "i" is followed by a vowel

ni = ń + "ee" when the "i" is followed by a consonant.

j = y - a gliding consonant - pronounced exactly like "y" in the English word "yes."

ł = w - a gliding consonant - pronounced like "w" in English.

r = r - a gliding consonant - it is trilled with the tip of the tongue

g = g - in Polish it is always pronounced as in the English word "good."

gie = g underlined indicates a trace of an "ee" sound after "g" and before the sound of "e" as in "let."

hie = kh underlined indicates a trace of an "ee" sound after "kh" and before the "e" sound, as in "get."

kie = k underlined indicates a trace of an "ee" sound after "k" and before the "e" sound, as in "pet."

PRONUNCIATION OF POLISH PALATAL CONSONANTS

Polish palatal consonants are pronounced by touching the upper palate with the tongue.

They are:

ć = ćh with an apostrophe over the "c"

ci = ćh when the "i" is followed by a vowel

ci = ć + "ee" when the "i" is followed by a consonant

ć = ts, it is pronounced like "t" in nature.

dź = dźh with an apostrophe over the "z" - pronounced like "dz" while touching the tooth ridge.

dż = dzh - pronounced like "dzh" while touching the upper palate.

ś = śh with an apostrophe over the "s" - pronounced like "sh" while touching the tooth ridge.

si = śh when the "i" is followed by a vowel

si = śh + "ee" when the "i" is followed by a consonant

ź = źh with an apostrophe over the "z" - pronounced like "zh" while touching the upper palate.

zi = ź when the "i" is followed by a vowel

zi = ź + "ee" when the "i" is followed by a consonant

(ż = rz) = zh (note: a dot over the "z"). It is pronounced like the "s" in measure.

ść = śhćh with apostrophes over "s" and "c" - - two consonants produced by touching the ridge of the teeth ridge with the tongue while pronouncing each consonant separately.

SPEECH ORGAN DIAGRAM

for Polish palatal consonants
not used in the English language.

Explosives: air compressed behind lips and teeth,
then suddenly released:
dź, dzi, [dźh] and ć, ci, [ćh]

Fricatives: air flow with a continuous friction:
ź, zi, [źh], and ś, si, [śh].
The tip of the tongue is at the tooth ridge.

POLISH SOUND "R"

is fluttered and may be pronounced like the Scottish "r"

The mouth is slightly open; the tip of the tongue is raised; it vibrates on the exhaling impulse and strikes the tooth-ridge; the sides of the tongue touch back teeth. The tongue does not glide as far back as is needed in the English "r."

ABBREVIATIONS -- SKRÓTY

adj. exp.:	adjectival expression	wyrażenie przymiotnikowe
adj.f.	feminine adjective	przymiotnik żeński
adj.m.	masculine adjective	przymiotnik męski
adj.n.	neuter adjective	przymiotnik męski
adv.	adverb	przysłówek
adv. exp.:	adverbial expression	wyrażenie przysłówkow
am.	American	amerykański
Brit.	British	brytyjski
chem.	chemistry; chemical	chemia; chemiczny
colloq:	colloquialism	kolokwializm; wyrażenie potoczne, gwarowe
conj.	conjunction	spójnik
constr.	construction	budowa; budowlany
cont.	continued	ciąg dalszy
etc.	et cetera; and so on; and so forth; and others	et cetera; i tak dalej; i inni
excl.	exclamation	wykrzyknik
exp.:	expression; phrase	wyrażenie; zwrot
ext.	extinct	zanikły; wygasły
f.	feminine noun	rzeczownik żeński
geol.	geology; geological	geologia; geologiczny
gram.	grammar; grammatical	gramatyka; gramatyczny
hist.	history; historic; rare; (not current)	historia; historyczny; rzadki archaiczny (nie bieżący)
hyp.	hyphen	myślnik; łącznik
indecl.	indeclinable	nieodmienny
inf.	infinitive	bezokolicznik
m.	masculine noun	rzeczownik męski
m.in.	among others	między innymi

n.	neuter noun	rzeczownik nijaki
numb.	number, numeral	numer; liczba; liczebnik
part.	particle	partykuła
pl.	plural	liczba mnoga
poet.	poetry; poetical	poezja; poetyczny
pref.	prefix	przedrostek
polit.	politics; political	polityka; polityczny
p.p.	past participle	imiesłów czasu przeszłego
prep.	preposition	przyimek
pron.	pronoun	zaimek
s.	substantive; noun	rzeczownik
sb.	somebody; someone	ktoś
slang	slang; jargon	gwara; żargon
soc.	social	społeczny
suf.	suffix	przyrostek
v.	verb	czasownik
v.exp.:	verbal expression	wyrażenie czasownikowe
vulg.	vulgarity; vulgar	ordynarność; ordynarny
wg	according to	według
W.W.II	World War II	druga wojna światowa

VOLUME I

TOM I

A - N

A

a [ah](as"a" in car) conj. and; or; but; then; at that time; excl.: **a!** [ah] oh!; well!; well, well!
a conto [ah **kon**-to] adv. (commercial) on account
a jakże! [ah **yahg**-zhe] excl.: oh yes... ; yes indeed!
a to [ah to] conj. and so
a- [ah] prefix: a-; not- without
abak [ah-bahk] = **abakus** m. abacus
abaka [ah-**bah**-kah] f. Manilla hemp
abakan [ah-**bah**-kahn] m. monumental wall hanging (made by M. Abakanowicz)
abandon [ah-**bahn**-don] m. abandonment (in insurance)
abandonatariusz [ah-bahn-do-nah-**tah**-ryoosh] m. abandonee (in insurance procedures)
abat [ah-baht] m. abbot
abazja [ah-**bah**-zyah] f. abasia; inability to stand up and walk
abazyjny [ah-bah-**ziy**-ni] adj.m. abasic; of inability to walk and stand up
abażur [ah-**bah**-zhoor] m. lamp shade; a device to screen light
abażurek [ah-bah-**zhoo**-rek] m. small lamp shade; a small device to screen light
ABC [ah-be-tse] n. ABC, rudiments
abcug [**ahp**-tsoog] m. colloq: exp.: **w krótkich abcugach** [f **kroot**-keekh ahp-**tsoo**-gahkh] exp.: in a short time; quickly
abderyta [ahb-de-**ri**-tah] m. fool; simpleton; primitive person
abduktor [ahb-**doo**-ktor] m. abductor (muscle)
abdykacja [ahb-di-**kah**-tsyah] f. abdication; renunciation; surrender
abdykacyjny [ahb-di-kah-**tsiy**-ni] adj.m. of abdication
abdykować [ahb-di-ko-vahćh] v. abdicate, abdicate the throne (*repeatedly*)
abdykowanie [ahb-di-ko-**vah**-ńe] n. abdication (of)
abecadło [ah-be-**tsah**-dwo] n. A.B.C., alphabet; rudiment
abecadłowy [ah-be-tsah-**dwo**-vi] adj.m. alphabetical
abedryta [ah-be-**dri**-tah] m. fool; simpleton
aberracja [ah-ber-**rah**-tsyah] f. aberration; mental derangement; deviation from what is right, true, normal
abietyna [ah-bye-**ti**-nah] f. pine resin
abietynowy [ah-bye-ti-**no**-vi] adj.m. of pine resin
abiogeneza [ah-byo-ge-**ne**-zah] f. abiogenesis
abiogenik [ah-byo-**ge**-ńeek] m. abiogenist
abiogennie [ah-byo-**gen**-ńe] adv. abiogenetically
abiogenny [ah-byo-**gen**-ni] adj.m. abiogenetic; abiogenetical
abiologia [ah-byo-**lo**-gyah] f. abiology; the study of inanimate things
abiologicznie [ah-byo-lo-**geech**-ńe] adv. abiologically
abiologiczny [ah-byo-lo-**geech**-ni] adj.m. abiological
Abisynka [ah-bee-**sin**-kah] f. (woman) Abyssinian; native of Abyssinia
abiotyczny [ah-byo-**tich**-ni] adj.m. abiotic
abioza [ah-**byo**-zah] f. abiosis
abisal [ah-**bee**-sahl] m. abyss (sea depth below 1700 meters and lake depth below 400 meters below reach of light)
abisalny [ah-bee-**sahl**-ni] adj.m. abyssal; abysmal
abisobiont [ah-bee-**so**-byont] m. abyssobiont; creature of abysmal depth
abisofil [ah-bee-**so**-feel] m. abyssphyle; creature of abysmal depth
Abisyńczyk [ah-bee-**siń**-chik] m. Abyssinian; native of Abyssinia
abisyński [ah-bee-**siń**-skee] adj.m. Abyssinian; of Abyssinia
abiturient [ah-bee-**too**-ryent] m. school-leaving pupil; graduate

abiturientka [ah-bee-too-**ryen**-tkah] f. (woman) school-leaving pupil; graduate
abiudykacja [ah-byoo-di-**kah**-tsyah] f. legal denial of property rights
abiuracja [ah-byoo-**rah**-tsyah] f. abjuration; giving up under oath; renunciation (of a right, etc.)
ablacja [ahb-**lah**-tsyah] f. ablation
ablacyjny [ahb-lah-**tsiy**-ni] adj.m. of ablation
ablaktacja [ahb-lahk-**tah**-tsyah] f. ablactation
ablaktować [ahb-lahk-**to**-vahćh] v. ablactate; wean (*repeatedly*)
ablaktowanie [ahb-lahk-to-**vah**-ńe] n. ablactation
ablatiwus [ahb-lah-**tee**-voos] m. ablative
ablegat [ahb-**le**-gaht] m. ablegate; envoy
ablegier [ahb-**le**-ger] m. layer
ablegrować [ahb-le-**gro**-vahćh] v. layer a shoot (*repeatedly*)
ablucja [ahb-**loo**-tsyah] f. ablution; a washing of the body (as a ceremony, etc.)
abnegacja [ahb-ne-**gah**-tsyah] f. abnegation; self-denial
abnegat [ahb-**ne**-gaht] m. man living a life of abnegation; man practicing self-denial; slovenly person; untidy person
abo [**ah**-bo] conj. see: **albo**
abolicja [ah-bo-**lee**-tsyah] f. abolition; annulment; amnesty for certain offenses
abolicjonista [ah-bo-lee-tsyo-**ńee**-stah] m. abolitionist
abolicjonizm [ah-bo-lee-**tsyo**-ńeezm] m. abolitionism
abominacja [ah-bo-mee-**nah**-tsyah] f. abomination of; disgust for
mieć abominację do [myećh ah-bo-mee-**nah**-tsyan do] exp.: to hold in abomination; to have in abomination; to hold in disgust
wzbudzać abominację [**vzboo**-dzahćh ah-bo-mee-**nah**-tsyan] exp.: to sicken; to disgust; to revolt
abonament [ah-bo-**nah**-ment] m. subscription (to a paper, etc.); season ticket
abonamentowy [ah-bo-nah-men-**to**-vi] adj.m. subscription (fee, term, etc.)
abonencki [ah-bo-**nen**-tskee] adj.m. subscriber's (fee, etc.)
abonent [ah-**bo**-nent] m. subscriber; holder of a season ticket; contract passenger
abonent telefonu [ah-**bo**-nent te-le-**fo**-noo] exp.: telephone subscriber
abonentka [ah-bo-**nen**-tkah] f. (woman) subscriber; holder of a season ticket; contract passenger
abonować [ah-bo-**no**-vahćh] v. subscribe (to a periodical, etc.) (*repeatedly*)
abonować się [ah-bo-**no**-vahćh śhan] v. take out a season-ticket (*repeatedly*)
abonowanie [ah-bo-no-**vah**-ńe] n. subscription
aborcja [ah-**bor**-tsyah] f. abortion
abordaż [ah-**bor**-dahsh] m. boarding (of a ship as an act of war, etc.)
abordażowy [ah-bor-dah-**zho**-vi] adj.m. boarding (a ship) (as an act of war, etc.)
aborygen [ah-bo-**ri**-gen] m. an aboriginal
aborygeni [ah-bo-ri-**ge**-ńee] pl. aborigines
abradować [ah-brah-**do**-vahćh] v. cause abrasion (*repeatedly*)
Abraham [ah-**brah**-khahm] m. Abraham
łono Abrahama [**wo**-no ah-brah-**khah**-mah] exp.: death (bed)
abrakadabra [ah-brah-kah-**dah**-brah] f. abracadabra; nonsense
abrazja [ah-**brah**-zyah] f. (geological) abrasion
abrazyjnie [ah-brah-**ziy**-ńe] adv. abrasively
abrazyjny [ah-brah-**ziy**-ni] adj.m. abrasive
abrewiacja [ah-bre-**vyah**-tsyah] f. abbreviation
abrewiatura [ah-bre-vyah-**too**-rah] f. abbreviation
abrogacja [ah-bro-**gah**-tsyah] f. abrogation
abrogować [ah-bro-**go**-vahćh] v. abrogate; abolish; repeal; annul

(*repeatedly*)
abrogowanie [ah-bro-go-**vah**-ńe] n. abrogation
abrupcja [ah-**broo**-ptsyah] f. sudden interruption (of music)
abrys [**ah**-bris] m. design; sketch; project
absces [**ahp**-stses] m. abscess
absencja [ahp-**sen**-tsyah] f. absence; non-attendance; absenting oneself (from school, etc.); truancy
absencja chorobowa [ahp-**sen**-tsyah kho-ro-**bo**-vah] exp.: sick-leave
absenteizm [ahp-sen-**te**-eezm] m. absenteeism
absentować się [ahp-sen-**to**-vahćh śhan] v. absent oneself (from school, etc.); play truant (*repeatedly*)
absolucja [ahp-so-**loo**-tsyah] f. absolution; freeing of guilt; forgiveness; remission of sins
absolut [ahp-**so**-loot] m. absolute; perfect; complete; pure; not mixed; not limited (power)
absolutnie [ahp-so-**loot**-ńe] adv. absolutely; definitely
absolutnie nic [ahp-so-**loot**-ńe ńeets] exp.: absolutely nothing
absolutnie nie [ahp-so-**loot**-ńe ńe] exp.: definitely not
absolutnie nikt [ahp-so-**loot**-ńe ńeekt] exp.: not a soul
absolutnie najlepsza rzecz [ahp-so-**loot**-ńe nahy-**lep**-shah zhech] exp.: the very best thing
wierzyć absolutnie [**vye**-zhićh ahp-so-**loot**-ńe] exp.: to believe implicitly
absolutność [ahp-so-**loot**-nośhćh] f. absoluteness
absolutny [ahp-so-**loot**-ni] adj.m. absolute; complete; pure; not mixed; of unlimited power
absolutna bzdura [ahp-so-**loot**-nah **bzdoo**-rah] exp.: utter nonsense
absolutny nonsens [ahp-so-**loot**-ni **non**-sens] exp: absolute nonsense
absolutne szaleństwo [ahp-so-**loot**-ne shah-**leń**-stfo] exp.: stark madness
absolutna władza [ahp-so-**loot**-nah **vwah**-dzah] exp.: absolute power
zero absolutne [**ze**-ro ahp-so-**loot**-ne] exp.: absolute zero
absolutorium [ahp-so-loo-**to**-ryoom] n. absolution; release; school-leaving (university-leaving) certificate; completion of university studies
otrzymać absolutorium [o-**tshi**-mahćh ahp-so-loo-**to**-ryoom] exp.: to complete one's university studies
absolutysta [ahp-so-loo-**tis**-tah] m. absolutist; advocate of absolutism
absolutystyczny [ahp-so-loo-tis-**tich**-ni] adj.m. absolutist (principles, laws, etc.)
absolutyzacja [ahp-so-loo-ti-**zah**-tsyah] f. making (something) absolute
absolutyzm [ahp-so-**loo**-tizm] m. absolutism; absolute monarchy
absolutyzować [ahp-so-loo-ti-**zo**-vahćh] v. absolutize; make (something) absolute (*repeatedly*)
absolwent [ahp-**sol**-vent] m. school-leaving student (pupil); alumnus; former pupil; old boy; graduate of a school
absolwentka [ahp-sol-**vent**-kah] f. (girl) school-leaving student (pupil); alumnus; former pupil; graduate of a school
absorbat [ahp-**sor**-baht] m. absorbable gas
absorbent [ahp-**sor**-bent] m. absorbent
absorber [ahp-**sor**-ber] m. absorber
absorbować [ahp-sor-**bo**-vahćh] v. absorb; suck up; assimilate; interest greatly; engross; pay for; take in (a shock) without recoil; take in and not reflect (light or sound); imbibe (moisture, etc.); be preoccupied with; occupy one's mind entirely (*repeatedly*)
absorbowanie [ahp-sor-bo-**vah**-ńe] n. absorption; imbibition; being absorbed
absorpcja [ahp-**sorp**-tsyah] f. absorption; imbibition; great interest; being absorbed
absorpcyjny [ahp-sorp-**tsiy**-ni] adj.m. absorptive; capable of absorbing moisture; absorbing

abstrahować [ahp-strah-**kho**-vahćh] v. abstract; take no account of; take away from; pass over; omit; not to mention; absorb (moisture) (*repeatedly*)
abstrahując od [ahp-strah-**khoo**-yownts ot] exp.: to say nothing of...; to make no mention of; quite apart from...; setting aside; putting aside; taking no account of; passing over in silence
abstrahując od tego, że...[ahp-strah-**khoo**-yownts ot **te**-go zhe] exp.: without counting that...; to say nothing of; to make no mention of; apart from; putting aside; setting aside; taking no account of (something, etc.)

abstrahowanie [ahp-strah-kho-**vah**-ńe] n. abstraction

abstrakcja [ahp-**strah**-ktsyah] f. abstraction; abstract; removal; an abstract idea, thing, etc.; an abstract painting, etc.; mental withdrawal

abstrakcjonista [ahp-strahk-tsyo-**ńee**-stah] m. abstractionist

abstrakcjonistyczny [ahp-strahk-tsyo-ńees-**tich**-ni] adj.m. of abstractionism

abstrakcjonizm [ahp-strahk-**tsyo**-ńeezm] m. abstractionism

abstrakcyjnie [ahp-strahk-**tsiy**-ńe] adv. using abstraction; by abstractive thinking; abstractly
myśleć abstrakcyjnie [**miśh**-lećh ahp-strahk-**tsiy**-ńe] exp.: to think theoretically or abstractly

abstrakcyjność [ahp-strahk-**tsiy**-nośhćh] f. abstractness

abstrakcyjny [ahp-strahk-**tsiy**-ni] adj.m. abstract; (phil.) discrete

abstrakt [**ahp**-strahkt] m. abstract; abstraction; absentminded person; (organ keys) tracker

abstynencja [ahp-sti-**nen**-tsyah] f. abstinence (from liquor, etc.); temperance; teetotalism
abstynencja całkowita [ahp-sti-**nen**-tsyah tsahw-ko-**vee**-tah] exp. teetotalism; total abstinence (from liquor, etc.)

abstynent [ahp-**sti**-nent] m. abstainer; teetotaller

abstynentka [ahp-sti-**nen**-tkah] f. (woman) abstainer; teetotaller

absurd [**ahp**-soort] m. the absurd; absurdity; nonsense
sprowadzić do absurdu [spro-**vah**-dźheećh do ahp-**soor**-doo] exp.: to reduce to absurdity; to make so unreasonable as to be ridiculous

absurdalnie [ahp-soor-**dahl**-ńe] adv. absurdly; so unreasonably as to be ridiculous

absurdalność [ahp-soor-**dahl**-nośhćh] f. absurdity; nonsense; preposterousness; irrationality

absurdalny [ahp-soor-**dahl**-ni] adj.m. absurd; nonsensical; incongruous; preposterous; irrational

absyda [ahp-**si**-dah] f. apsis; apse

absynt [**ahp**-sint] m. absinth

absztyfikant [ahp-shti-**fee**-kahnt] m. slang: suitor; wooer; sweetheart

absztyfikować się [ahp-shti-fee-**ko**-vahćh śhan] v. slang: court; woo; spoon (a girl) (*repeatedly*)

abulia [ah-**boo**-lyah] f. abulia

abuliczny [ah-boo-**leech**-ni] adj.m. abulic

abulik [ah-**boo**-leek] m. (an) abulic

abwilski [ahb-**veel**-skee] adj.m. of Abeville

aby [**ah**-bi] conj. to; in order to; in order that; only to; that
aby wrócić wcześniej [**ah**-bi **vroo**-ćheećh **fcheśh**-ńey] exp.: in order to come back earlier (home, etc.)
aby wrócić wnet [**ah**-bi **vroo**-ćheećh vnet] exp.: in order to come back soon (home, etc.)
aby nie [**ah**-bi ńe] exp.: lest; in order not to
aby nie kawał? [ah-bi ńe **kah**-vahw] exp.: isn't that a joke by any chance?
abym mógł [**ah**-bim moogw] exp.: so that I could...; so that I may
abyśmy nie zginęli [ah-**biśh**-mi ńe zgee-ne-lee] exp.: lest we perish
czy aby zapłaci? [chi **ah**-bi zah-**pwah**-ćhee] exp.: will he pay I wonder?

acan [ah-tsahn] m. Sir; see: **asan**

acani [ah-**tsah**-ńee] f. Madam; see: **asani**
a capella [ah kah-**pe**-lah] exp.: (music) without instruments
acefalia [ah-tse-**fah**-lyah] f. acephalia
acefaliczny [ah-tse-fah-**leech**-ni] adj.m. acephalous
acetal [ah-**tse**-tahl] m. (chem.) acetal
acetamid [ah-tse-**tah**-meet] m. acetamide
acetanilid [ah-tse-tah-**ńee**-leet] m. acetanilide
acetofenon [ah-tse-to-**fe**-non] m. acetophenone
acetometr [ah-tse-**to**-metr] m. acetimeter; acetometer
aceton [ah-**tse**-ton] m. (chem.) acetone (inflammable liquid)
acetonemia [ah-tse-to-**ne**-myah] f. acetonemia
acetonowy [ah-tse-to-**no**-vi] adj.m. (chem.) acetonic
acetylen [ah-tse-**ti**-len] m. (chem.) acetylene (a gas)
acetylenek [ah-tse-**ti**-le-nek] m. chem. acetylene salt
acetylenowy [ah-tse-ti-le-**no**-vi] adj.m. (chem.) acetylene (lamp, gas, etc.)
spawanie acetylenowo-tlenowe [spah-**vah**-ńe ah-tse-ti-le-**no**-vo tle-**no**-ve] exp.: oxacetylene welding
acetoceluloza [ah-tse-to-tse-loo-**lo**-zah] f. acetic-cellulose
acetosalicylowy [ah-tse-to-sah-lee-tsi-**lo**-vi] adj.m. acetylsalicylic
acyl [**ah**-tsil] m. acyl
ach! [ahkh] excl.: oh! ah!
achać [ah-khahćh] v. colloq: marvel (at) (*repeatedly*)
Achilles [ah-**kheel**-les] m. Achilles
achillesowy [ah-kheel-le-**so**-vi] adj.m. of Achilles
pięta achillesowa [**pyan**-tah ah-kheel-le-**so**-vah] exp.: tendon of Achilles; a weak point
achromatyczność [ah-khro-mah-**tich**-nośhćh] f. achromatism
achromatyczny [ah-khro-mah-**tich**-ni] adj.m. achromatic
acpan [**ahts**-pahn] m. colloq: Mister
acz [ahch] conj. albeit; though; tho; although; as; see: **aczkolwiek**
aczkolwiek [ahch-**kol**-vyek] conj. though; although; albeit; as
adadżio [ah-**dah**-dzhyo] n. slower than andante (in music)
adagio [ah-**dah**-dzhyo] n. slower than andante (in music)
adamaszek [ah-dah-**mah**-shek] m. damask (a reversible fabric)
adamaszkowy [ah-dah-mahsh-**ko**-vi] adj.m. damask (reversible fabric, etc.)
adamellit [ah-dah-**mel**-leet] m. adamite rock
adamita [ah-dah-**mee**-tah] m. Adamite
adamowy [ah-dah-**mo**-vi] adj.m. Adam's (apple, etc.)
adamowe plemię [ah-dah-**mo**-ve **ple**-myan] exp.: the human race
adamowy strój [ah-dah-**mo**-vi strooy] exp.: birthday suit
jabłko adamowe [**yahp**-ko ah-dah-**mo**-ve] exp.: Adam's apple
adamsyt [ah-**dahm**-sit] m. variety of poison gas
adaptabilność [ah-dahp-tah-**beel**-nośhćh] f. adaptability
adaptacja [ah-dahp-**tah**-tsyah] f. adaptation; adjusting to
adaptacyjny [ah-dahp-tah-**tsiy**-ni] adj.m. of adaptation
adaptator [ah-dahp-**tah**-tor] m. adaptor (of a book, play, etc.)
adaptatorka [ah-dahp-tah-**tor**-kah] f. (woman) adaptor (of a book, play, etc.)
adaptatorski [ah-dahp-tah-**tor**-skee] adj.m. adaptational; adaptative; adaptive
adaptatorsko [ah-dahp-tah-**tor**-sko] adv. adaptationally
adapter [ah-**dahp**-ter] m. record player; adapter; pick-up
adapterowy [ah-dahp-te-**ro**-vi] adj.m. of a record player; of an adapter; of a pick-up
adaptować [ah-dahp-**to**-vahćh] v. adapt; make suitable; adjust to new circumstances; arrange (music, etc.) (*repeatedly*)
adaptować się [ah-dahp-**to**-vahćh śhan] v. adapt oneself; make

oneself suitable; adjust oneself to new circumstances (*repeatedly*)
adaptowanie się [ah-dahp-to-**vah**-ńe śhan] n. adapting oneself
addent [**ahd**-dent] m. addent
addenda [ahd-**den**-dah] pl. addenda
addukcja [ahd-**doo**-ktsyah] f. adduction
adduktor [ahd-**dook**-tor] m. adductor
addycja [ahd-**di**-tsyah] f. atomic addition without side products
addycyjny [ahd-di-**tsiy**-ni] adj.m. of atomic addition (without side products)
addytywność [ahd-di-**tiv**-nośhćh] f. additive character; additivity
addytywnie [ahd-di-**tiv**-ńe] adv. additively
addytywny [ahd-di-**tiv**-ni] adj.m. additive
adekwatnie [ah-de-**kfaht**-ńe] adv. adequately
adekwatność [ah-de-**kfaht**-nośhćh] f. adequacy
adekwatny [ah-de-**kfaht**-ni] adj.m. adequate
adenina [ah-de-**ńee**-nah] f. adenine
adenopatia [ah-de-no-**pah**-tyah] f. adenopathy
adenotomia [ah-de-no-**to**-myah] f. adenotomy
adept [**ah**-dept] m. pupil; student; adherent; votary
adeptka [ah-**dep**-tkah] f. (female) pupil; student; adherent; votary
adherent [aht-**khe**-rent] m. follower, adherent; partisan; votary
adhezja [aht-**khe**-zyah] f. adhesion
adhezyjny [aht-khe-**ziy**-ni] adj.m. adhesion
adiabata [ah-dyah-**bah**-tah] f. adiabatic curve
adiabatyczny [ah-dyah-bah-**tich**-ni] adj.m. adiabatic
adiafora [ah-dyah-**fo**-rah] f. adiaphoron
adiantyt [ah-**dyahn**-tit] m. Adiantum
adidas [ah-**dee**-dahs] m. Adidas; slang: AIDS; Acquired Immune Deficiency Syndrome
adidasy [ah-dee-**dah**-si] pl. colloq: Adidas shoes
adideacja [ah-dee-de-**ah**-tsyah] f. interpretation of the meaning of a word by association with a similar word
adiektywizacja [ah-dye-kti-vee-**zah**-tsyah] f. changing words into adjective form
adiudykacja [ah-dyoo-di-**kah**-tsyah] f. adjudication; rejection by judicial sentence
adiunkt [**ah**-dyoonkt] m. tutor; lecturer
adiunktura [ah-dyoonk-**too**-rah] f. lecturer's position (function)
adiustacja [ah-dyoo-**stah**-tsyah] f. revision (of a manuscript); editorial preparation; adjustment
adiustacyjny [ah-dyoo-stah-**tsiy**-ni] adj.m. revision (of a manuscript); editorial (preparation, etc.); of an adjustment
adiustator [ah-dyoo-**stah**-tor] m. reviser of a manuscript
adiustatorka [ah-dyoo-stah-**tor**-kah] f. (woman) reviser of a manuscript
adiustować [ah-dyoos-**to**-vahćh] v. revise a manuscript; edit a manuscript preparation; adjust (*repeatedly*)
adiustowanie [ah-dyoos-to-**vah**-ńe] n. revision (of a manuscript); editorial preparation; adjustment
adiutancki [ah-dyoo-**tahn**-tskee] adj.m. of aide-de-camp; aid-de-camp's (functions, duties, etc.)
adiutant [ah-**dyoo**-tahnt] m. aide-de-camp; aid-de-camp; a military officer serving as an assistant to a superior
adleryzm [ahd-**le**-rizm] m. Adlerian form of psychoanalysis
administracja [ahd-mee-ńee-**strah**-tsyah] f. administration; management; authorities; executive officials of a government, etc. (and their policy); board of trustees
administracyjnie [ahd-mee-ńee-strah-**tsiy**-ńe] adv. administratively
administracyjny [ahd-mee-ńee-strah-**tsiy**-ni] adj.m. administrative
administrator [ahd-mee-ńee-**strah**-tor] m. administrator; manager; steward (of an estate, etc.)

administratorka [ahd-mee-ńee-strah-tor-kah] f. (female) administrator; manager; steward (of an estate, etc.)
administratorski [ahd-mee-ńee-strah-tor-skee] adj.m. administrative
administrować [ahd-mee-ńee-stro-vahćh] v. administer, manage something; direct (*repeatedly*)
administrowanie [ahd-mee-ńee-stro-vah-ńe] n. administration; management (of an estate, etc.)
admiracja [ahd-mee-rah-tsyah] f. admiration
admiralicja [ahd-mee-rah-lee-tsyah] f. admiralty
admiralski [ahd-mee-rahl-skee] adj.m. admiral's; of an admiral
admiralstwo [ahd-mee-rahl-stfo] n. admiralship
admirał [ahd-mee-rahw] m. admiral
admirator [ahd-mee-rah-tor] m. colloq: admirer
admiratorka [ahd-mee-rah-tor-kah] f. colloq: (female) admirer
admirować [ahd-mee-ro-vahćh] v. colloq: admire (*repeatedly*)
admonicja [ahd-mo-ńee-tsyah] f. admonition; warning; reproving
adnominalnie [ahd-no-mee-nahl-ńe] adv. adnominally
adnominalny [ahd-no-mee-nahl-ni] adj.m. adnominal
adnotacja [ahd-no-tah-tsyah] f. annotation; note; reference; an explanatory note for ...
adnotować [ahd-no-to-vahćh] v. annotate; note; reference; add an explanatory note (for) (*repeatedly*)
adolescencja [ah-do-les-tsen-tsyah] f. adolescence
adoniczny [ah-do-ńeech-ni] adj.m. Adonic (verse, etc.)
adonijski [ah-do-ńeey-skee] adj.m. Adonic (verse, etc.)
adonik [ah-do-ńeek] m. an Adonic verse
adonis [ah-do-ńees] m. an Adonis; philanderer; flirt
adopcja [ah-dop-tsyah] f. adoption (of a child, an idea, an animal, a building, etc.)
adopcyjny [ah-dop-tsiy-ni] adj.m. adoptive
adoptować [ah-dop-to-vahćh] v. adopt; take legally into one's family and rise as one's own child; take as one's own (*repeatedly*)
adoptowanie [ah-dop-to-vah-ńe] n. adoption
adoptowany [ah-dop-to-vah-ni] adj.m. adopted; adoptive
adoracja [ah-do-rah-tsyah] f. adoration; worshipping; worship as divine; devotion; great love
adorator [ah-do-rah-tor] m. adorer; worshipper; admirer; courter; wooer; one who loves greatly
adoratorka [ah-do-rah-tor-kah] f. (female) adorer; worshipper; admirer; courter; wooer; one who loves greatly
adorować [ah-do-ro-vahćh] v. adore; admire; like very much; love greatly; worship as divine (*repeatedly*)
adorowanie [ah-do-ro-vah-ńe] n. adoration; worshipping; worship as divine; devotion; great love
adra [ah-drah] f. grain (in wood, etc.); vain (in rock, etc.)
adrenalina [ah-dre-nah-lee-nah] f. adrenalin
adres [ah-dres] m. address
adresarka [ah-dre-sahr-kah] f. addressing machine; Addressograph
adresat [ah-dre-saht] m. addressee; the person to whom mail, etc. is addressed; receiver; recipient; drawee of a check
adresatka [ah-dre-saht-kah] f. (female) addressee; the person to whom mail, etc. is addressed; receiver; recipient; drawee of a check
adresograf [ah-dre-so-grahf] m. addressing machine; Addressograph
adresografia [ah-dre-so-grah-fyah] f. the use of an addressograph
adresować [ah-dre-so-vahćh] v. address; write the destination (*repeatedly*)
adresowanie [ah-dre-so-vah-ńe] n. addressing; writing the destination

adresowy [ah-dre-so-vi] adj.m. of address
adria [ah-dryah] f. variety of woolen yarn
adriatycki [ah-dryah-ti-tskee] adj.m. of Adriatic; Adriatic (sea, etc.)
adsorbat [aht-sor-baht] m. adsorbate
adsorbent [aht-sor-bent] m. adsorbent
adsorber [aht-sor-ber] m. adsorption device; adsorption apparatus
adsorbować [aht-sor-bo-vahćh] v. adsorb (on the surface) (*repeatedly*)
adsorbowanie [aht-sor-bo-vah-ńe] n. adsorption (on the surface)
adsorpcja [aht-sorp-tsyah] f. adsorption
adsorpcyjny [aht-sorp-tsiy-ni] adj.m. adsorptive
adwekcja [ahd-vek-tsyah] f. advection; horizontal movement of masses of air
adwekcyjny [ahd-vek-tsiy-ni] adj.m. advective; of horizontal movement of masses of air
adwent [ahd-vent] m. advent; a coming; period including four Sundays before Christmas
adwentowy [ahd-ven-to-vi] adj.m. of the Advent; Advent (time, etc.)
adwentysta [ahd-ven-tis-tah] m. Adventist
adwerbalny [ahd-ver-bahl-ni] adj.m. adverbial
adwerbialny [ahd-ver-byahl-ni] adj.m. adverbial
adwersarz [ahd-ver-sahsh] m. colloq: adversary
adwokacina [ahd-vo-kah-ćhee-nah] m. second-rate lawyer; shabby lawyer
adwokacki [ahd-vo-kah-tskee] adj.m. lawyer's; barrister's; solicitor's; attorney's
adwokat [ahd-vo-kaht] m. lawyer; attorney; solicitor; counsel; advocate; one who pleads another's cause or is in support of something
adwokatka [ahd-vo-kah-tkah] f. (woman) lawyer; attorney; solicitor; counsel; advocate; one who pleads another's cause or is in support of something
adwokatowa [ahd-vo-kah-to-vah] f. lawyer's wife
adwokatować [ahd-vo-kah-to-vahćh] v. advocate (*repeatedly*)
adwokatowanie [ahd-vo-kah-to-vah-ńe] n. advocacy
adwokatura [ahd-vo-kah-too-rah] f. legal profession; bar
aelowiec [ah-e-lo-vyets] m. soldier of Peoples' (Communist) Army (in World War II)
aelowski [ah-e-lof-skee] adj.m. of Peoples' (Communist) Army (in World War II)
aeracja [ah-e-rah-tsyah] f. aeration
aerator [ah-e-rah-tor] m. aerator
aero- [ah-e-ro] prefix: aero-
aerob [ah-e-rop] m. aerobe
aerobik [ah-e-ro-beek] m. aerobic exercise
aerobiont [ah-e-ro-byont] m. aerobian
aerobioza [ah-e-ro-byo-zah] f. aerobiosis; life in air (oxygen)
aerobowo [ah-e-ro-bo-vo] adv. aerobically
aerobowy [ah-e-ro-bo-vi] adj.m. aerobic
aerobus [ah-e-ro-boos] m. airbus
aerocasco [ah-e-ro-kah-sko] n. flight insurance
aerodrom [ah-e-ro-drom] m. aerodrome; airport
aerodyna [ah-e-ro-di-nah] f. aircraft heavier than air
aerodynamiczny [ah-e-ro-di-nah-meech-ni] adj.m. aerodynamic
aerodynamik [ah-e-ro-di-nah-meek] m. specialist in aerodynamics
aerodynamika [ah-e-ro-di-nah-mee-kah] f. aerodynamics
aeroelastyczność [ah-e-ro-e-lah-stich-nośhćh] f. elastic reactions of flying object to aerodynamic forces and inertia
aeroembolizm [ah-e-ro-em-bo-leezm] m. aeroembolism
aeroenergetyka [ah-e-ro-e-ner-ge-ti-kah] f. study of wind energy
aerofagia [ah-e-ro-fah-gyah] f. aerophagia
aerofobia [ah-e-ro-fo-byah] f. aerophobia

aerofon [ah-e-ro-fon] m. aerophone
aerofotografia [ah-e-ro-fo-to-**grah**-fyah] f. aerophotography
aerofotogrametria [ah-e-ro-fo-to-grah-**me**-tryah] f. photogrammetry based on aerial photography
aerograf [ah-e-**ro**-grahf] m. pressurized spray gun with paint
aerografia [ah-e-ro-**grah**-fyah] f. painting with spray gun
aeroklub [ah-e-**ro**-kloop] m. flying club; aero-club
aerolit [ah-e-**ro**-leet] m. aerolite; stony meteorite
aerolog [ah-e-**ro**-log] m. aerologist
aerologia [ah-e-ro-**lo**-gyah] f. aerology
aerologiczny [ah-e-ro-lo-**geech**-ni] adj.m. aerologic; aerological
aeromechanika [ah-e-ro-me-**khah**-ńee-kah] f. aeromechanics
aerometr [ah-e-**ro**-metr] m. aerometer; air gauge
aeronauta [ah-e-ro-**nahw**-tah] m. aeronaut; air (space) traveler
aeronautyczny [ah-e-ro-nahw-**tich**-ni] adj.m. aeronautic
aeronautyka [ah-e-ro-**nahw**-ti-kah] f. aeronautics; the science of making and flying aircraft
aeronawigacja [ah-e-ro-nah-vee-**gah**-tsyah] f. aerial navigation
aeronomia [ah-e-ro-**no**-myah] f. aeronomy
aeroplan [ah-e-**ro**-plahn] m. airplane; plane; aeroplane (Brit.)
aeroplankton [ah-e-ro-**plahnk**-ton] m. aerial plankton
aeroport [ah-e-**ro**-port] m. airport
aerosanie [ah-e-ro-**sah**-ńe] pl. snowmobile
aeroskop [ah-e-**ro**-skop] m. aeroscope; prototype of movie camera
aerosprężystość [ah-e-ro-spr<u>an</u>-**zhi**-stośhćh] f. elastic reactions of flying object to aerodynamic forces and inertia
aerosol [ah-e-**ro**-zol] m. aerosol spray; deodorant
aerostat [ah-e-**ro**-staht] m. aerostat
aerostatyczny [ah-e-ro-stah-**tich**-ni] adj.m. aero-static; stable in the air, in flight, etc.
aerostatyka [ah-e-ro-**stah**-ti-kah] f. aerostatics
aeroterapia [ah-e-ro-te-**rah**-pyah] f. aerotherapy
aerotriangulacja [ah-e-ro-tryahn-goo-**lah**-tsah] f. triangulation made on the basis of aerial photographs
aerozol [ah-e-**ro**-zol] m. = **aerosol**
aerozolować [ah-e-ro-zo-**lo**-vahćh] v. spray aerosol (*repeatedly*)
aerozolowanie [ah-e-ro-zo-lo-**vah**-ńe] n. spraying aerosol
aerozolowy [ah-e-ro-zo-**lo**-vi] adj.m. of aerosol
afabularność [ah-fah-boo-**lahr**-nośhćh] f. lack of a plot
afabularny [ah-fah-boo-**lahr**-ni] adj.m. lacking the plot
afatyk [ah-**fah**-tik] m. man who lost his speech; aphasic
afazja [ah-**fah**-zyah] f. loss of speech; aphasia
afekcja [ah-**fek**-tsyah] f. love; affection (hist.)
afekt [**ah**-fekt] m. affection; emotion; affect
działać w afekcie [**dźhah**-wahćh v ah-**fek**-ćhe] exp.: to act in severe mental strain; to act under severe provocation
afektacja [ah-fek-**tah**-tsyah] f. affectation; artificial behavior; a pretending to like, have, etc.; pose; primness (hist.)
afektować [ah-fek-**to**-vahćh] v. act unnaturally; pretend; exaggerate (*repeatedly*)
afektowanie [ah-fek-to-**vah**-ńe] adv. with affect; emotionally; lackadaisically
afektowany [ah-fek-to-**vah**-ni] adj.m. affected; afflicted; influenced; emotionally moved; mincing; prim; lackadaisical
afektywnie [ah-fek-**tiv**-ńe] adv. affectively
afektywny [ah-fek-**tiv**-ni] adj.m. affective
afelium [ah-**fe**-lyoom] n. aphelion
afera [ah-**fe**-rah] f. swindle; shabby business; dirty business; love affair; an amorous episode
afereza [ah-fe-**re**-zah] f. aphaeresis; aphesis

aferowy [ah-fe-**ro**-vi] adj.m. of a swindle; of shady dealing
aferzysta [ah-fe-**zhi**-stah] m. swindler; confidence man; schemer; machinator; shady speculator; con-artist
aferzystka [ah-fe-**zhi**-stkah] f. (woman) swindler; confidence woman; schemer; machinator; shady speculator; con-artist
afgan [**ahf**-gahn] m. Afghan rug
Afgańczyk [ahf-**gahń**-chik] m. Afghan; native of Afghanistan
afgański [ahf-**gahń**-skee] adj.m. Afghan; of Afghanistan
afiks [**ah**-feeks] m. affix
afiksacja [ah-feek-**sah**-tsyah] f. affixation
afiliacja [ah-feel-**yah**-tsyah] f. affiliation
afiliować [ah-feel-**yo**-vahćh] v. affiliate (*repeatedly*)
afiliowanie [ah-feel-yo-**vah**-ńe] n. affiliation
afinacja [ah-fee-**nah**-tsyah] f. selection (of silver, gold, etc.) by washing
afirmacja [ah-feer-**mah**-tsyah] f. affirmation; affirmative statement
afirmatywnie [ah-feer-mah-**tiv**-ńe] adv. affirmatively
afirmatywny [ah-feer-mah-**tiv**-ni] adj.m. affirmative
afirmować [ah-feer-**mo**-vahćh] v. affirm; validate; confirm (*repeatedly*)
afirmowanie [ah-feer-mo-**vah**-ńe] n. affirmation; validation; confirmation
afisz [**ah**-feesh] m. poster; bill board; bill; placard
afiszować [ah-fee-**sho**-vahćh] v. advertise; flaunt; parade; make a show (of) (*repeatedly*)
afiszować się [ah-fee-**sho**-vahćh śhan] v. show off; flaunt oneself; go about (with); show (off)
afiszowanie [ah-fee-sho-**vah**-ńe] n. advertising; showing off
afiszowy [ah-fee-**sho**-vi] adj.m. advertising (print, etc.)
aflaston [ah-**flah**-ston] m. ornament on ship's bow
afleksyjność [ah-flek-**siy**-nośhćh] f. lack of inflexion (in English, etc.)
afleksyjny [ah-flek-**siy**-ni] adj.m. lacking inflexion
afonia [ah-**fo**-ńyah] f. aphonia; loss of voice
afoniczny [ah-fo-**ńeech**-ni] adj.m. aphonic
aforysta [ah-fo-**ris**-tah] m. aphorist
aforystyczny [ah-fo-ris-**tich**-ni] adj.m. of aphorism; of adage; of maxim; aphoristic
aforystka [ah-fo-**ris**-tkah] f. (female) aphorist
aforystyka [ah-fo-**ri**-sti-kah] f. writing of aphorisms
aforyzm [ah-**fo**-rizm] m. aphorism; adage; maxim
aforyzmowy [ah-fo-riz-**mo**-vi] adj.m. aphoristic
afotyczny [ah-fo-**tich**-ni] adj.m. aphotic; without light
afrikaans [ahf-ree-**kahns**] m. Afrikaans; Dutch dialect in South Africa; second official language in South Africa
afro [**ah**-fro] n. Afro hair style (shaped in a round and bushy mass)
Afrodyta [ah-fro-**di**-tah] f. Aphrodite
afrodyzjak [ah-fro-**di**-zyahk] m. aphrodisiac drug; drug exciting sexual desire
afront [**ah**-front] m. affront; an open insult
zrobić afront [**zro**-beećh **ah**-front] exp.: to affront; to insult openly
afrontować [ah-fron-**to**-vahćh] v. insult (to the face by behavior of language); deliberately offend (*repeatedly*)
Afrykaner [ah-fri-**kah**-ner] m. Afrikaner; descendent of Dutch colonists in South Africa
Afrykanin [ah-fri-**kah**-ńeen] m. African; native of Africa
afrykanista [ah-fri-kah-**ńee**-stah] m. Africanist
afrykanistyczny [ah-fri-kah-ńee-**stich**-ni] adj.m. of African studies
afrykanistyka [ah-fri-kah-**ńee**-sti-kah] f. African studies
afrykanizacja [ah-fri-kah-ńee-**zah**-tsyah] f. Africanization
Afrykanka [ah-fri-**kahn**-kah] f.

(female) African; native of Africa
afrykanologia [ah-fri-kah-no-**lo**-gyah] f. African studies
afrykański [ah-fri-**kahń**-skee] adj.m. African; of Africa
afrykata [ah-fri-**kah**-tah] f. affricative; affricate (of a non-syllabic consonant)
afty [**ahf**-ti] pl. viral ulceration of oral cavity; aphthae
aga [**ah**-gah] m. Muslim polite title; frog (Bufo marinus, 10 inch long)
agama [ah-**gah**-mah] f. Agama lizard
agalmatolit [ah-gahl-mah-**to**-leet] m. agalmatolite (mineral)
agamia [ah-**gah**-myah] f. agamic condition
agamicznie [ah-gah-**meech**-ńe] adv. agamically
agamiczny [ah-gah-**meech**-ni] adj.m. agamic
agamospermia [ah-gah-mo-**sper**-myah] f. asexual reproduction
agapa [ah-**gah**-pah] f. love feast; agape
agapant [ah-**gah**-pahnt] m. (ornamental plant) Agapanthus
agar [**ah**-gahr] m. agar, agar-agar
agarowy [ah-gah-**ro**-vi] adj.m. agar (jelly, etc.); of agar-agar
agat [**ah**-gaht] m. miner. agate
agatowy [ah-gah-**to**-vi] adj.m. agat (ring, etc.)
agawa [ah-**gah**-vah] f. agave
agencja [ah-**gen**-tsyah] f. agency; a firm empowered to act for another; office
agencja prasowa [ah-**gen**-tsyah prah-**so**-vah] exp.: news agency
agencyjny [ah-gen-**tsiy**-ni] adj.m. of agency; agency (contract, etc.)
agenda [ah-**gen**-dah] f. branch of business; department; agenda; a list of things to be done or dealt with at a meeting, etc.; memorandum book; diary
agens [**ah**-gens] m. active subject of a sentence
agent [**ah**-gent] m. agent empowered to act for another; a representative; deputy; broker
agent giełdowy [**ah**-gent gew-**do**-vi] exp.: broker; stock market broker
agent obcego wywiadu [**ah**-gent op-**tse**-go vi-**vyah**-doo] exp.: foreign spy; intelligencer; foreign secret agent
agent podróżujący [**ah**-gent po-droo-zhoo-**yown**-tsi] exp.: travelling salesman; commercial traveller
agentka [ah-**gen**-tkah] f. (woman) agent empowered to act for another; a representative; deputy; broker
agentura [ah-gen-**too**-rah] f. agency body of agents; branch office
agentura wywiadu [ah-gen-**too**-rah vi-**vyah**-doo] exp.: intelligence agency
agenturalny [ah-gen-too-**rahl**-ni] adj.m. agency (shop, etc.)
agio [**ah**-zhyo] n. increment of trading value (of stocks and bonds) above the nominal value
agitacja [ah-gee-**tah**-tsyah] f. agitation; canvassing; propaganda; campaigning; electioneering; excitement; nervousness
agitacja wyborcza [ah-gee-**tah**-tsyah vi-**bor**-chah] exp.: canvassing; election campaign
agitacyjność [ah-gee-tah-**tsiy**-nośhćh] f. agitational character
agitacyjny [ah-gee-tah-**tsiy**-ni] adj.m. agitator's (activities, etc.); propaganda (speech, text, etc.); canvassing; electioneering; slang: stump (oratory, etc.)
agitator [ah-gee-**tah**-tor] m. agitator; propagandist; canvasser; electioneer; stump orator
agitator wyborczy [ah-gee-**tah**-tor vi-**bor**-chi] exp.: electioneer; canvasser
agitatorka [ah-gee-tah-**tor**-kah] f. (female) agitator; propagandist; canvasser; electioneer; colloq: stump orator; door-bell pusher
agitatorski [ah-gee-tah-**tor**-skee] adj.m. agitator's; propagandist's; canvasser's; electioneer's
agitka [ah-**gee**-tkah] f. colloq: propaganda leaflet; propaganda speech; propaganda slogan, etc.
agitować [ah-gee-**to**-vahćh] v.

agitate; canvass; electioneer; be on the stump; advocate (*repeatedly*)
agitować w wyborach [ah-gee-**to**-vahćh v vi-**bo**-rahkh] exp.: to canvass; to campaign
agitowanie [ah-gee-to-**vah**-ńe] n. agitation; canvassing; electioneering; advocacy
aglikon [ah-**glee**-kon] m. genin
aglomeracja [ah-glo-me-**rah**-tsyah] f. agglomeration
aglomeracyjny [ah-glo-me-rah-**tsiy**-ni] adj.m. agglomerate; agglomerative
aglomerat [ah-glo-**me**-raht] m. agglomerate
aglomerować [ah-glo-me-**ro**-vahćh] v. agglomerate (*repeatedly*)
aglomerowanie [ah-glo-me-ro-**vah**-ńe] n. agglomeration
aglomerownia [ah-glo-me-**ro**-vńah] f. agglomeration plant
aglutynacja [ah-gloo-ti-**nah**-tsyah] f. agglutination; adhesion
aglutynacyjny [ah-gloo-ti-nah-**tsiy**-ni] adj.m. of agglutination; of adhesion; agglutinative
aglutynina [ah-gloo-ti-**ńee**-nah] f. agglutinin
aglutynować [ah-gloo-ti-**no**-vahćh] v. agglutinate (*repeatedly*)
aglutynować się [ah-gloo-ti-**no**-vahćh śhan] v. become agglutinated (*repeatedly*)
aglutynowanie [ah-gloo-ti-no-**vah**-ńe] n. agglutination
agnacja [ahg-**nah**-tsyah] f. agnation; kinship; alliance
agnacki [ahg-**nah**-tskee] adj.m. agnate; agnatic; of kinship
agnacyjny [ahg-nah-**tsiy**-ni] adj.m. agnate; of kinship
agnat [**ahg**-naht] m. agnate
agnatka [ahg-**nah**-tkah] f. (female) agnate
agnostyczny [ah-gno-**sti**-chni] adj.m. agnostic; nescient
agnostycyzm [ah-gno-**sti**-tsizm] m. agnosticism
agnostyk [ah-**gno**-stik] m. agnostic; one who believes that it is impossible to know if God exists
agnozja [ah-**gno**-zyah] f. agnosia
agogiczny [ah-go-**geech**-ni] adj.m. agogic (accent, etc.)
agogika [ah-go-**gee**-kah] f. agoge
agon [**ah**-gon] m. agon; contest
agonalny [ah-go-**nahl**-ni] adj.m. of agony; of the state of agony
agonia [ah-**go**-ńyah] f. agony of death; death-struggle; great mental or physical pain; death pangs; death throes
agoniczny [ah-go-**ńeech**-ni] adj.m. agonic; of agony; of the state of agony
agonistyka [ah-go-**ńee**-sti-kah] f. agonistics; (athletic) contest
agora [ah-**go**-rah] f. agora; gathering place
agorafobia [ah-go-rah-**fo**-byah] f. agoraphobia
agradacja [ah-grah-**dah**-tsyah] f. accumulation of sediments in water
agrafa [ah-**grah**-fah] f. large safety pin
agrafia [ah-**grah**-fyah] f. agraphia; loss of the ability to write
agrafka [ah-**grahf**-kah] f. safety pin; hist.: buckle; brooch
agramatyczny [ah-grah-mah-**tich**-ni] adj.m. non-grammatical
agramatyzm [ah-grah-**mah**-tizm] m. lack of grammaticalness; lack of grammaticality
agranulocyt [ah-grah-noo-**lo**-tsit] m. agranulocyte
agranulocytoza [ah-grah-noo-lo-tsi-**to**-zah] f. agranulocytosis
agrariusz [ah-**grah**-ryoosh] m. big landowner; agrarian (politician)
agrarny [ah-**grahr**-ni] adj.m. agrarian
reforma agrarna [re-**for**-mah ah-**grahr**-nah] exp.: land reform
agrarysta [ah-grah-**ri**-stah] m. follower of agrarianism
agrarystyczny [ah-grah-ri-**stich**-ni] adj.m. of agrarianism
agraryzm [ah-**grah**-rizm] m. agrarianism
agrawacja [ah-grah-**vah**-tsyah] f. aggravation (of disease)
agregacja [ah-gre-**gah**-tsyah] f. aggregation
agregat [ah-**gre**-gaht] m. aggregate (of homogenous particles, etc.);

unit
agregatownia [ah-gre-gah-**tov**-ńah] f. aggregate sorting plant
agregatowy [ah-gre-gah-**to**-vi] adj.m. aggregate; aggregational
agremant [ah-gre-**mah**] n. acceptance of an envoy
agresja [ah-**gre**-syah] f. aggression; unprovoked attack or warlike act; act of aggression
agresor [ah-**gre**-sor] m. aggressor
agrest [**ah**-grest] m. gooseberry
agrestnik [ah-**gre**-stńeek] m. gooseberry stone; gooseberry moth
agrestowy [ah-gre-**sto**-vi] adj.m. gooseberry (bush, wine, etc.)
agresyjny [ah-gre-**siy**-ni] adj.m. (war; etc.) of aggression
agresyjność [ah-gre-**siy**-nośhćh] f. aggressiveness; truculence
agresywnie [ah-gre-**siv**-ńe] adv. aggressively; in a boldly hostile manner; in warlike manner
agresywność [ah-gre-**siv**-nośhćh] f. aggressiveness; truculence; offensiveness
agresywny [ah-gre-**siv**-ni] adj.m. aggressive; boldly hostile; quarrelsome; bold and active; truculent; offensive; enterprising
agreściak [ah-**gre**-śhćhahk] m. gooseberry moth
agro- [**ah**-gro] prefix: agro-; of fields
agrobiolog [ah-gro-**byo**-log] m. agrobiologist
agrobiologia [ah-gro-byo-**lo**-gyah] f. agrobiology
agrobiologiczny [ah-gro-byo-lo-**geech**-ni] adj.m. agrobiologic
agrocenoza [ah-gro-tse-**no**-zah] f. biocoenose
agrochemia [ah-gro-**khe**-myah] f. agricultural chemistry
agrochemiczny [ah-gro-khe-**meech**-ni] adj.m. of agricultural chemistry
agrochemik [ah-gro-**khe**-meek] m. agricultural chemist
agroekologia [ah-gro-e-ko-**lo**-gyah] f. agricultural ecology
agrogaz [ah-**gro**-gahs] m. manure-gas (60% methane)
agroklimatolog [ah-gro-klee-mah-**to**-log] m. specialist in agricultural climatology
agroklimatologia [ah-gro-klee-mah-to-**lo**-gyah] f. agricultural climatology
agrolotnictwo [ah-gro-lot-**ńee**-tstfo] n. aviation serving agriculture
agrolotniczy [ah-gro-lot-**ńee**-chi] adj.m. of aircraft used in agriculture
agromelioracja [ah-gro-me-lyo-**rah**-tsyah] f. agricultural reclamation (drainage)
agromelioracyjny [ah-gro-me-lyo-rah-**tsiy**-ni] adj.m. of agricultural reclamation (drainage)
agromeliorant [ah-gro-me-**lyo**-rahnt] m. specialist in agricultural reclamation (drainage)
agrometeorolog [ah-gro-me-te-o-**ro**-log] m. specialist in agricultural meteorology
agrometeorologia [ah-gro-me-te-o-ro-**lo**-gyah] f. agricultural meteorology
agrometeorologiczny [ah-gro-me-te-o-ro-lo-**geech**-ni] adj.m. of agricultural meteorology
agrominimum [ah-gro-**mee**-ńee-moom] n. minimum conditions for agricultural activity
agronom [ah-**gro**-nom] m. agronomist; specialist in science and economy of crop production
agronomia [ah-gro-**no**-myah] f. agronomy; crop production science and economy
agronomiczny [ah-gro-no-**meech**-ni] adj.m. agronomic; of agronomy
agronomka [ah-gro-**nom**-kah] f. (female) agronomist; specialist in science and economy of crop production
agronomówka [ah-gro-no-**moof**-kah] f. agronomist's office and laboratory
agrotechnik [ah-gro-**tekh**-ńeek] m. specialist in crop production
agrotechnika [ah-gro-**tekh**-ńee-kah] f. technique of crop production
aguti [ah-**goo**-tee] n. agouti; agouty (mammal)
aha! [ah-**khah**] excl.: oh yes...
ahistorycznie [ah-khee-sto-**rich**-ńe]

adv. not historically
ahistoryczność [ah-khee-sto-**rich**-nośhćh] f. lack of historicity
ahistoryczny [ah-khee-sto-**rich**-ni] adj.m. not historical
ahistoryzm [ah-khee-**sto**-rizm] m. absence of historical approach
ahoj [**ah**-khoy] excl.: ahoy (used in hailing)
ahumanisticzny [ah-khoo-mah-ńees-**tich**-ni] adj.m. not humanistic
AIDS [eyds] m. AIDS (Acquired Immune Deficiency Syndrome)
aikido [ahy-**kee**-do] n. Japanese martial art
ailant [**ahy**-lahnt] m. Ailanthus tree
aintelektualizm [ah-een-te-lek-too-**ah**-leezm] m. negation of reason in (understanding of) life
aintelektualny [ah-een-te-lek-too-**ahl**-ni] adj.m. of negation of reason in (understanding of) life
ais [ahys] m. sound "a" raised by one half tone
aj! [ahy] excl.: oh!
aj aj aj! [ah-yah-**yahy**] excl.: dear, dear!; dear me!
ajatollah [ah-yah-**tol**-lahkh] m. ayatollah
ajencja [ah-**yen**-tsyah] f. agency; see: **agencja**
ajencyjny [ah-yen-**tsiy**-ni] adj.m. of agency; agency (contract, etc.)
ajent [**ah**-yent] m. agent; one that acts for another; see: **agent**
ajentka [ah-**yen**-tkah] f. agent; see: **agentka**
ajentura [ah-yen-**too**-rah] f. agency; a firm empowered to act for another; office
ajer [**ah**-yer] m. sweet flag; sweet rush; calamus
ajerkoniak [ah-yer-**ko**-ńahk] m. liqueur (made of eggs beaten up with spirit, sugar, and vanilla); eggnog
ajerowy [ah-ye-**ro**-vi] adj.m. of sweet flag; of sweet rush; of calamus
ajerówka [ah-ye-**roof**-kah] f. vodka flavored with sweet-sedge
ajuści! [ah-**yoośh**-ćhee] excl.: of course!; my eye!; not so!
AK [ah-**kah**] f. Polish Home Army (W.W.II) (Armia Krajowa)
akacja [ah-**kah**-tsyah] f. acacia; locust tree; locust shrub
akacjowy [ah-kah-**tsyo**-vi] adj.m. acacia (tree, shrub); locust (tree, shrub)
akademia [ah-kah-**de**-myah] f. academy; college; fellow; celebration; session of celebration, commemorative meeting
akademicki [ah-kah-de-**mee**-tskee] adj.m. academical; academic; student's; orthodox
dom akademicki [dom ah-kah-de-**mee**-tskee] exp.: students' hostel; students' dormitory
akademicko [ah-kah-de-**mee**-tsko] adv. academically
akademiczka [ah-kah-de-**mee**-chkah] f. (female) academician; (university) student
akademiczny [ah-kah-de-**mee**-chni] adj.m. academic; colloq: conventional
akademik [ah-kah-**de**-meek] m. academician; (students') dormitory; (university) student
akademizacja [ah-kah-de-mee-**zah**-tsyah] f. academization
akademizm [ah-kah-**de**-meezm] m. academism; formalism
akademizować [ah-kah-de-mee-**zo**-vahćh] v. academize (*repeatedly*)
akanie [ah-**kah**-ńe] n. Russian and Belorus pronunciation of "o" like "a"
akant [**ah**-kahnt] m. acanthus; brank ursine; bear's breech
akantowy [ah-kahn-**to**-vi] adj.m. acanthus (shrub, etc.)
akapit [ah-**kah**-peet] m. paragraph; section
akapitowy [ah-kah-pee-**to**-vi] adj.m. paragraph (indent, etc.)
akataleksa [ah-kah-tah-**le**-ksah] f. lack of acatalectic characteristic
akatalektyczny [ah-kah-tah-le-**ktich**-ni] adj.m. acatalectic
akatolicki [ah-kah-to-**lee**-tskee] adj.m. non-catholic
akaustobiolit [ah-kahw-sto-**byo**-leet] m. sedimentary rock of organic origin

akceleracja [ahk-tse-le-**rah**-tsyah] f. acceleration
akcelerator [ahk-tse-le-**rah**-tor] m. accelerator
akcelerograf [ahk-tse-le-**ro**-grahf] m. accelerograph
akcelerometr [ahk-tse-le-**ro**-metr] m. accelerometer
akcencik [ahk-**tsen**-ćheek] m. (nice, small) accent; stress; emphasis; ton; feature; element
akcent [**ahk**-tsent] m. accent; stress; emphasis; ton; feature; element
akcentacja [ahk-tsen-**tah**-tsyah] f. accentuation (of a syllable, etc.)
akcentacyjny [ahk-tsen-tah-**tsiy**-ni] adj.m. of accentuation (of a syllable, etc.)
akcentolog [ahk-tsen-**to**-log] m. specialist in accentuation
akcentologia [ahk-tsen-to-**lo**-gyah] f. study of accentuation
akcentować [ahk-tsen-**to**-vahćh] v. accent; accentuate; stress; emphasize (*repeatedly*)
akcentowanie [ahk-tsen-to-**vah**-ńe] n. accentuation
akcentowy [ahk-tsen-**to**-vi] adj.m. accent (system, rule, etc.)
akcentuacja [ahk-tsen-too-**ah**-tsyah] f. accentuation (of a syllable, of a fact, etc.) see: **akcentacja**
akcentuacyjny [ahk-tsen-too-ah-**tsiy**-ni] adj.m. accentual; of accent
akcept [**ahk**-tsept] m. commercial: acceptance; accepted draft
akceptacja [ahk-tsep-**tah**-tsyah] f. acceptance (of a bill)
akceptant [ahk-**tsep**-tahnt] m. acceptant (of a bill)
akceptor [ahk-**tsep**-tor] m. accepter (of a bill)
akceptować [ahk-tse-**pto**-vahćh] v. accept; approve; agree (*repeatedly*)
akceptowanie [ahk-tse-pto-**vah**-ńe] n. acceptance (of a bill, etc.)
akceptowy [ahk-tse-**pto**-vi] adj.m. of direct bank payment; accepted
akces [**ahk**-tses] m. accession
zgłosić akces do [**zgwo**-śheećh ahk-tses do] exp.: to accede to; to join (a party, etc.)
akcesja [ahk-**tse**-syah] f. accession; collection and registration of books in a library
akcesorium [ahk-tse-**so**-ryoom] n. accessory
akcesoria [ahk-tse-**so**-ryah] pl. accessories; appendages; appliance; accompaniments; garnitures; subsidiaries
akcesoryczny [ahk-tse-so-**rich**-ni] adj.m. accessory; subsidiary
akcesoryjny [ahk-tse-so-**riy**-ni] adj.m. accessory; subsidiary
akcesyjny [ahk-tse-**siy**-ni] adj.m. joining; of accession
akcja [**ahk**-tsyah] f. action; share; plot; campaign (for, against); operation; suit; law suit
akcja ratunkowa [**ahk**-tsyah rah-toon-**ko**-vah] exp.: rescue action; life-saving action or operation
akcja powieści [**ahk**-tsyah po-**vye**-śhćhee] exp.: plot; action
akcja sztuki [**ahk**-tsyah **shtoo**-kee] exp.: plot; action
akcja wyborcza [**ahk**-tsyah vi-**bor**-chah] exp.: election campaign
prowadzić akcję [pro-**vah**-dźheećh **ahk**-tsyan] exp.: to carry on a campaign
wszcząć akcję [fshchownćh **ahk**-tsyan] exp.: to launch a campaign
akcjonariat [ahk-tsyo-**nah**-ryaht] m. an enterprise in which employees hold in common part of its stock
akcjonariusz [ahk-tsyo-**nah**-ryoosh] m. shareholder; investor; stockholder
akcjonariuszka [ahk-tsyo-nah-**ryoosh**-kah] f. (woman) shareholder; investor; stockholder
akcydens [ahk-**tsi**-dens] m. incidental printing; accidental element; casual profit; job-printing; job-work; profits on the side; slang: perk
akcydencja [ahk-tsi-**den**-tsyah] f. additional custom duty
akcydensista [ahk-tsi-den-**śhee**-stah] m. printer of incidental items
akcydensowy [ahk-tsi-den-**so**-vi] adj.m. job (work); incidental (printing); accidental (element); casual (leaflet, etc.)

akcydentalny [ahk-tsi-den-**tahl**-ni] adj.m. of accessory; incidental; accidental; casual; of unimportant characteristic (traits, etc.)
akcyjnie [ahk-**tsiy**-ńe] adv. actively
akcyjność [ahk-**tsiy**-nośhćh] f. incorporation; joint-stock ownership
akcyjny [ahk-**tsiy**-ni] adj.m. of (business) incorporation; joint-stock-...; of shares
bank akcyjny [bahnk ahk-**tsiy**-ni] exp.: joint-stock bank
kapitał akcyjny [kah-**pee**-tahw ahk-**tsiy**-ni] exp.: joint stock; capital stock
spółka akcyjna [**spoow**-kah ahk-**tsiy**-nah] exp.: joint-stock company; incorporated company
akcyza [ahk-**tsi**-zah] f. excise tax; toll (tax); excise office
akcyzowy [ahk-tsi-**zo**-vi] adj.m. excise (tax, duty, office, etc.); toll (tax, etc.)
akcyźnik [ahk-**tsi**-źhńeek] m. excise officer; exciseman (Brit.)
akefaliczny [ah-ke-fah-**leech**-ni] adj.m. headless; (verse etc.) without title
akinezja [ah-kee-**ne**-zyah] f. akinesia; disturbance of motion in a muscle
aklamacja [ah-klah-**mah**-tsyah] f. an approving vote by loud voice rather than by ballot; acclamation; loud applause
przez aklamację [pshes ah-klah-**mah**-tsyan] exp.: by acclamation
uchwalić przez aklamację [oo-**khfah**-leećh pshes ah-klah-**mah**-tsyan] exp.: to carry by acclamation
aklamować [ah-klah-**mo**-vahćh] v. approve by voice vote; acclaim; praise; applause (*repeatedly*)
aklimatyzacja [ah-klee-mah-ti-**zah**-tsyah] f. acclimatization; becoming accustomed to a new climate or environment; naturalization; domestication; acclimatization; air-conditioning
aklimatyzacyjny [ah-klee-mah-ti-zah-**tsiy**-ni] adj.m. of acclimatization; of acclimation; of naturalization; of domestication
czynnik aklimatyzacyjny [**chin**-ńeek ah-klee-mah-ti-zah-**tsiy**-ni] exp.: acclimatizer
aklimatyzować [ah-klee-mah-ti-**zo**-vahćh] v. acclimatize; acclimate; naturalize; domesticate (*repeatedly*)
aklimatyzować się [ah-klee-mah-ti-**zo**-vahćh śhan] v. become accustomed to a new climate or environment; become acclimatized (*repeatedly*)
aklimatyzowanie się [ah-klee-mah-ti-zo-**vah**-ńe śhan] n. becoming accustomed to a new climate or environment; becoming acclimatized
aklina [ah-**klee**-nah] f. aclinic line
akliniczny [ah-klee-**ńeech**-ni] adj.m. aclinic
akmeista [ahk-me-**ee**-stah] m. Russian poet opposed to symbolism
akmeistyczny [ahk-me-ee-**stich**-ni] adj.m. of Russian poetry opposed to symbolism (beginning of 20th cent.)
akmeizm [ahk-**me**-eezm] m. Russian poetry opposed to symbolism (beginning of 20th cent.)
akolada [ah-ko-**lah**-dah] f. accolade; brace (in music notation)
akolita [ah-ko-**lee**-tah] m. acolyte
akomodacja [ah-ko-mo-**dah**-tsyah] f. accommodation; adjustment (of the eye)
akomodacyjny [ah-ko-mo-dah-**tsiy**-ni] adj.m. accommodational (force of an eye, etc.)
akomodować [ah-ko-mo-**do**-vahćh] v. accommodate; adjust (to); do a favor (for); have space (for); make comfortable; adapt (to something) (*repeatedly*)
akomodować się [ah-ko-mo-**do**-vahćh śhan] v. accommodate oneself; adjust oneself (to); make oneself comfortable; adapt oneself (*repeatedly*)
akomodowanie [ah-ko-mo-do-**vah**-ńe] n. accommodation
akompaniament [ah-kom-pah-**ńyah**-ment] m. accompaniment
przy akompaniamencie [pshi ah-

kom-pah-ńyah-**men**-ćhe] exp.: accompanied by
akompaniator [ah-kom-pah-**ńyah**-tor] m. accompanist
akompaniatorka [ah-kom-pah-ńyah-**tor**-kah] f. (female) accompanist
akompaniować [ah-kom-pah-**ńyo**-vahćh] v. accompany; go with; add to; play or sing an accompaniment (for or to) (*repeatedly*)
akompaniowanie [ah-kom-pah-ńyo-**vah**-ńe] n. accompaniment (for or to)
akonit [ah-**ko**-ńeet] m. aconite
akonityna [ah-ko-ńee-**ti**-nah] f. aconitine
akonto [ah-**kon**-to] n. payment on account; deposit
akord [**ah**-kort] m. chord; job-work; work by the job; piece-work; contract work
praca na akord [**prah**-tsah nah **ah**-kort] exp.: piece-work; job-work
pracować na akord [prah-**tso**-vahćh nah **ah**-kort] exp.: to do piece-work; to work by the job
akordeon [ah-kor-**de**-on] m. accordion (musical instrument)
akordeonista [ah-kor-de-o-**ńee**-stah] m. accordion-player
akordnik [ah-**kord**-ńeek] m. piece-worker; contract-worker
akordowiec [ah-kor-**do**-vyets] m. piece-worker; contract-worker
akordowo [ah-kor-**do**-vo] adv. by piece (work); by contract (work)
akordowy [ah-kor-**do**-vi] adj.m. (music) chordal; piece (work); contract (work)
praca akordowa [**prah**-tsah ah-kor-**do**-vah] exp.: piece-work; job-work
robotnik akordowy [ro-**bot**-ńeek ah-kor-**do**-vi] exp.: piece-worker; job-worker
akordyka [ah-**kor**-di-kah] f. introduction to chordal music
akowiec [ah-**ko**-vyets] m. soldier of the Polish Home Army (World War II)
akowski [ah-**kof**-skee] adj.m. of the Polish Home Army (World War II)
akr [ahkr] m. acre
akrania [ah-**krah**-ńyah] f. partial or total lack of cranial bone; Acrania
akredytacja [ah-kre-di-**tah**-tsyah] f. accreditation
akredytacyjny [ah-kre-di-tah-**tsiy**-ni] adj.m. of accreditation
akredytować [ah-kre-di-**to**-vahćh] v. accredit (to a government); believe in; attribute (*repeatedly*)
akredytowanie [ah-kre-di-to-**vah**-ńe] n. accreditation; sanctioning; authorization; providing with credentials; official vouching for
akredytowany [ah-kre-di-to-**vah**-ni] adj.m. accredited; sanctioned; authorized; provided with credentials; officially vouched for
akredytywa [ah-kre-di-**ti**-vah] f. fin. letter of credit
akrobacja [ah-kro-**bah**-tsyah] f. acrobatics; acrobatic (tricks, etc.)
akrobacyjny [ah-kro-bah-**tsiy**-ni] adj.m. acrobatic; of acrobatics
akrobata [ah-kro-**bah**-tah] m. acrobat; gymnast
akrobatka [ah-kro-**bah**-tkah] f. (woman) acrobat; gymnast
akrobatycznie [ah-kro-bah-**tich**-ńe] adv. acrobatically
akrobatyczny [ah-kro-bah-**tich**-ni] adj.m. acrobatic; of acrobatics
akrobatyka [ah-kro-**bah**-ti-kah] f. acrobatics; acrobatic tricks
akrofobia [ah-kro-**fo**-byah] f. acrophobia
akroleina [ah-kro-le-**ee**-nah] f. acrolein
akrolit [ah-**kro**-leet] m. acrolith
akromegalia [ah-kro-me-**gahl**-yah] f. acromegaly; acromegalia; morbid enlargement of parts of the body
akromonogram [ah-kro-mo-**no**-grahm] m. Greek verse with repeating syllables
akronim [ah-**kro**-ńeem] m. acronym
akronimowo [ah-kro-ńee-**mo**-vo] adv. acronymically
akronimowy [ah-kro-ńee-**mo**-vi] adj.m. acronymic
akropol [ah-**kro**-pol] m. Acropolis
akrostych [ah-**kro**-stikh] m. acrostic
akroter [ah-**kro**-ter] m. acroterium; akroterion
akroterion [ah-kro-**te**-ryon] m.

acroterium; akroterion
akroterium [ah-kro-**te**-ryoom] n. acroterium; akroterion
akrybia [ah-**kri**-byah] f. colloq: exactitude; thoroughness; accuracy; exactness; precision (in philology, etc.)
akrydyna [ah-kri-**di**-nah] f. acridine
akrydynowy [ah-kri-di-**no**-vi] adj.m. of acridine; acridinic
akryl [**ah**-kril m. acrylic resin
akrylan [ah-**kri**-lahn] m. acrylic acid
akrylowy [ah-kri-**lo**-vi] adj.m. acrylic
aksamit [ahk-**sah**-meet] m. velvet
aksamitek [ahk-sah-**mee**-tek] m. (nice, small) velvet
aksamitka [ahk-sah-**mee**-tkah] f. velvet ribbon
aksamitnie [ahk-sah-**meet**-ńe] adv. like velvet; in a silky manner; in a mellow (voice, etc.)
aksamitność [ahk-sah-**meet**-nośhćh] f. quality of velvet; silkiness; mellowness (of voice)
aksamitny [ahk-sah-**meet**-ni] adj.m. velvety; silky; mellow (of voice); peachy; dowdy; of velvet; velvet (garment, etc.)
aksamitowiec [ahk-sah-mee-**to**-vyets] m. Maranta (a herb)
akselbant [**ahk**-sel-bahnt] m. aglet; aiglet; aiguilette; epaulette made of gold or silver cord
aksjologia [ahk-syo-**lo**-gyah] f. axiology
aksjologicznie [ahk-syo-lo-**geech**-ńe] adv. axiologically
aksjologiczny [ahk-syo-lo-**geech**-ni] adj.m. axiological
aksjomat [ahk-**syo**-maht] m. axiom
aksjomatycznie [ahk-syo-mah-**tich**-ńe] adv. axiomatically
aksjomatyczny [ahk-syo-mah-**tich**-ni] adj.m. axiomatic (projection); axiom (of parallels, continuity, order, etc.)
aksjomatyka [ahk-syo-**mah**-ti-kah] f. study of axioms
aksjomatyzacja [ahk-syo-mah-ti-**zah**-tsyah] f. axiomatization
aksjomatyzować [ahk-syo-mah-ti-**zo**-vahćh] v. axiomatize (*repeatedly*)
aksjomatyzowanie [ahk-syo-mah-ti-zo-**vah**-ńe] n. axiomatization
aksoida [ahk-**soy**-dah] f. axoid
akson [**ahk**-son] m. axon; axone
aksonometria [ahk-so-no-**me**-tryah] f. axonometry
aksonometryczny [ahk-so-no-me-**trich**-ni] adj.m. axonometric (projection, etc.)
aksynit [ahk-**si**-ńeet] m. axinite
akt [ahkt] m. deed; act; a doing; a law; a main division of a drama or opera; certificate; legal document; action; proof in writing; painting of a nude
akt kupna [ahkt **koop**-nah] exp.: purchase deed; deed
akt oskarżenia [ahkt os-kahr-**zhe**-ńah] exp.: bill of indictment
akt zgonu [ahkt **zgo**-noo] exp.: death certificate
akta [**ahk**-tah] pl. documents; deeds; dossier; files; records
aktor [**ahk**-tor] m. actor
aktoreczka [ahk-to-**rech**-kah] f. young actress; starlet; actress of no standing
aktorka [ahk-**tor**-kah] f. actress
aktorski [ahk-**tor**-skee] adj.m. of actors; theatrical; stagy; histrionic; showy; affected
zespół aktorski [**zes**-poow ahk-**tor**-skee] exp.: troupe; company of actors
aktorsko [ahk-**tor**-sko] adv. stage-like; like an actor
aktorstwo [ahk-**tor**-stfo] n. stage-playing; histrionics; theatrical art; staging; make belief; theatrical profession; the actors; the performers
aktorzyca [ahk-to-**zhi**-tsah] f. nasty actress; actress of poor standing; actress of bad reputation
aktorzyna [ahk-to-**zhi**-nah] m. mean actor; actor of poor standing; actor of bad reputation; pitiful actor
aktowy [ahk-**to**-vi] adj.m. of an act; of acts; of documents
aktówka [ahk-**toof**-kah] f. briefcase; portfolio
aktualia [ahk-too-**ah**-lyah] pl. current events; actualities
aktualista [ahk-too-ah-**lee**-stah] m.

follower of actualism
aktualistyczny [ahk-too-ah-lee-**stich**-ni] adj.m. actualistic
aktualizacja [ahk-too-ah-lee-**zah**-tsyah] f. bringing up to date; modernization
aktualizm [ahk-too-**ah**-leezm] m. actualism
aktualizować [ahk-too-ah-lee-**zo**-vahćh] v. bring up to date; modernize *(repeatedly)*
aktualizować się [ahk-too-ah-lee-**zo**-vahćh śhan] v. become a reality *(repeatedly)*
aktualizowanie się [ahk-too-ah-lee-zo-**vah**-ńe śhan] n. becoming a reality
aktualnie [ahk-too-**ahl**-ńe] adv. at the moment; at the present moment; actually
aktualność [ahk-too-**ahl**-nośhćh] f. reality; present-day interest
aktualności dnia [ahk-too-ahl-**nośh**-ćhee dńah] exp.: current events; an actual thing
aktualny [ah-ktoo-**ahl**-ni] adj.m. timely; current; up to date; topical; of the moment; opportune; seasonable; now going on; of the present time
być nie aktualnym [bićh ńe ah-ktoo-**ahl**-nim] exp.: to be no longer feasible
rzecz aktualna [zhech ahk-too-**ahl**-nah] exp.: news item; current issue; a live issue; issue of the day
aktyn [**ahk**-tin] m. actinium (atomic number 89)
aktynicznie [ahk-ti-**ńeech**-ńe] adv. actinically
aktyniczność [ahk-ti-**ńeech**-nośhćh] f. degree of actinic radiation
aktyniczny [ahk-ti-**ńeech**-ni] adj.m. actinic
aktynograf [ahk-ti-**no**-grahf] m. actinograph
aktynometria [ahk-ti-no-**me**-tryah] f. actinometry
aktynometryczny [ahk-ti-no-me-**trich**-ni] adj.m. actinometric
aktynoterapia [ahk-ti-no-te-**rah**-pyah] f. actinotherapy
aktynowiec [ahk-ti-**no**-vyets] m. actinide
aktynowy [ahk-ti-**no**-vi] adj.m. actinic
aktyw [**ahk**-tif] m. active body; action group; active members
aktywa [ahk-**ti**-vah] pl. holdings; assets; anything owned that has value; a durable thing
aktywacja [ahk-ti-**vah**-tsyah] f. activation
aktywacyjny [ahk-ti-vah-**tsiy**-ni] adj.m. of activation
aktywator [ahk-ti-**vah**-tor] m. activator
aktywista [ahk-ti-**vees**-tah] m. active member; activist
aktywistka [ahk-ti-**vees**-tkah] f. (woman) active member; activist
aktywistyczny [ahk-ti-vees-**tich**-ni] adj.m. of activism
aktywizacja [ahk-ti-vee-**zah**-tsyah f. activation
aktywizować [ahk-ti-vee-**zo**-vahćh] v. activate; stimulate to activity; make active; put on active (military) duty *(repeatedly)*
aktywizacyjny [ahk-ti-vee-zah-**tsiy**-ni] adj.m. of activation
aktywizator [ahk-ti-vee-**zah**-tor] m. activator
aktywizm [ahk-**ti**-veezm] m. activism; advocacy of a policy of action
aktywizować [ahk-ti-vee-**zo**-vahćh] v. activate; activize; stimulate to activity *(repeatedly)*
aktywizowanie [ahk-ti-vee-zo-**vah**-ńe] n. activeness; activation; stimulation to activity
aktywizująco [ahk-ti-vee-zoo-**yown**-tso] adv. stimulating to activity
aktywnie [ahk-**tiv**-ńe] adv. actively
aktywność [ahk-**tiv**-nośhćh] f. activity; being active; liveliness; go; a specific action
aktywny [ahk-**tiv**-ni] adj.m. active; snappy; acting; working; lively; agile; causing motion or change; (chem., phys.) active
aktywować [ahk-ti-**vo**-vahćh] v. activate *(repeatedly)*
aktywowanie [ahk-ti-vo-**vah**-ńe] n. activation

akulturacja [ah-kool-too-**rah**-tsyah] f. acculturation; intercultural borrowing; process of acquiring culture starting at infancy
akumulacja [ah-koo-moo-**lah**-tsyah] f. accumulation; cumulativeness; cumulation
akumulacja pierwotna [ah-koo-moo-**lah**-tsyah pyer-**vot**-nah] exp.: primary (primitive) accumulation
akumulacyjnie [ah-koo-moo-lah-**tsiy**-ńe] adv. accumulatively; cumulatively
akumulacyjny [ah-koo-moo-lah-**tsiy**-ni] adj.m. accumulative; cumulative
akumulator [ah-koo-moo-**lah**-tor] m. battery; storage battery; secondary battery; accumulator
akumulatorek [ah-koo-moo-lah-**to**-rek] m. small-sized battery; little battery
akumulatornia [ah-koo-moo-lah-**tor**-ńah] f. battery shed; battery storage space; battery room; accumulator plant
akumulatorowy [ah-koo-moo-lah-to-**ro**-vi] adj.m. of a storage battery; storage-battery (poles, etc.)
akumulować [ah-koo-moo-**lo**-vahćh] v. accumulate; collect; pile up; amass; cumulate (*repeatedly*)
akumulować się [ah-koo-moo-**lo**-vahćh śhan] v. accumulate; amass; collect (*repeatedly*)
akumulowanie [ah-koo-moo-lo-**vah**-ńe] n. accumulation; collection; cumulation
akupresura [ah-koo-pre-**soo**-rah] f. acupressure
akupunktura [ah-koo-poon-**ktoo**-rah] f. acupuncture
akurat [ah-**koo**-raht] adv. just; exactly; no less than; at the very moment that ...; just as; negative usage: nothing of the kind; nothing doing; what else?; what next?
akuratnie [ah-koo-**raht**-ńe] adv. accurately; carefully and exactly
akuratność [ah-koo-**raht**-nośhćh] f. accuracy; exactness; correctness
akuratny [ah-koo-**raht**-ni] adj.m. accurate; careful and exact; free from errors; precise; meticulous; scrupulous; punctual
akustycznie [ah-koo-**stich**-ńe] adv. acoustically
akustyczność [ah-koo-**stich**-nośhćh] f. acoustic quality (of a room, etc.)
akustyczny [ah-koo-**stich**-ni] adj.m. acoustic; resonant; phonic; having to do with hearing or acoustics
akustyk [ah-**koo**-stik] m. acoustician; specialist in acoustics
akustyka [ah-**koo**-sti-kah] f. acoustics; resonance
akuszer [ah-**koo**-sher] m. obstetrician; accoucheur
akuszeria [ah-koo-**sher**-yah] f. obstetrics; midwifery
akuszerka [ah-koo-**sher**-kah] f. midwife; accoucheuse
akuszerski [ah-koo-**sher**-skee] adj.m. of obstetrics; of midwifery; obstetric; obstetrical
akuszerstwo [ah-koo-**sher**-stfo] n. obstetrics; midwifery
akuszeryjny [ah-koo-she-**riy**-ni] adj.m. of obstetrics; of midwifery; obstetric; obstetrical
akutowy [ah-koo-**to**-vi] adj.m. acute (sound by the end of a vowel)
akuzator [ah-koo-**zah**-tor] m. colloq: accuser
akuzatyw [ah-koo-**zah**-tif] m. accusative case
akwadukt [ahk-**fah**-dookt] m. aqueduct; see: **akwedukt**
akwaforcista [ahk-fah-for-**ćhee**-stah] m. aquafortist; etcher
akwaforta [ahk-fah-**for**-tah] f. etching; a print made from an etched plate; art of etching
akwafortowy [ahk-fah-for-**to**-vi] adj.m. of (aquafortis, nitric acid) etching
akwakultura [ahk-fah-kool-**too**-rah] f. aquaculture; aquiculture; hydroponics; growing of plants in nutrient solution
akwalung [ahk-**fah**-loong] m. breathing equipment used in scuba diving
akwalunger [ahk-fah-**loon**-ger] m. scuba diver

akwamaryn [ahk-fah-**mah**-rin] m. aquamarine
akwamaryna [ahk-fah-mah-**ri**-nah] f. aquamarine
akwanauta [ahk-fah-**nahw**-tah] m. student of sea bottom and deep water
akwanautyka [ahk-fah-**nahw**-ti-kah] f. study of sea bottom and deep water
akwarela [ahk-fah-**re**-lah] f. a watercolor; painting in (with) watercolors; the watercolors
akwarelista [ahk-fah-re-**lee**-stah] m. watercolorist; painter in (with) watercolors
akwarelistka [ahk-fah-re-**lee**-stkah] f. (woman) watercolorist; painter in (with) watercolors
akwarelka [ahk-fah-**rel**-kah] f. a nice watercolor; small painting in (with) watercolors
akwarelowy [ahk-fah-re-**lo**-vi] adj.m. watercolor (painting, etc.)
akwariarstwo [ahk-fahr-**yahr**-stfo] n. study of aquarium plants and organisms
akwariarz [ahk-**fahr**-yahsh] m. specialist of aquarium plants and organisms
akwariowy [ahk-fahr-**yo**-vi] adj.m. of an aquarium; aquarium (fish, water, etc.)
akwarium [ahk-**fahr**-yoom] n. aquarium; fish bowl
akwarysta [ahk-fah-**ri**-stah] m. specialist of aquarium plants and organisms
akwarystyczny [ahk-fah-ri-**stich**-ni] adj.m. of the study of aquarium plants and organisms
akwarystyka [ahk-fah-ri-sti-kah] f. study of aquarium plants and organisms
akwatinta [ahk-fah-**teen**-tah] f. aquatint; etching by aquatint
akwatynta [ahk-fah-**tin**-tah] f. aquatint (technique and etchings)
trawić akwatyntą [**trah**-veećh ahk-fah-**tin**-town] exp.: to etch with aquatint; to aquatint
akwawita [ahk-fah-**vee**-tah] f. acquavitae; alcohol; vodka
akwedukt [ahk-**fe**-dookt] m. aqueduct; large pipe or structure for bringing water
akwen [**ahk**-fen] m. body of water
akwilon [ahk-**fee**-lon] m. cutting North wind; biting North wind
akwizycja [ahk-fee-**zi**-tsyah] f. acquisition; solicitation; canvassing; acting as a travelling-agent
akwizycyjnie [ahk-fee-zi-**tsiy**-ńe] adv. acquisitively
akwizycyjność [ahk-fee-zi-**tsiy**-nośhćh] f. acquisitiveness
akwizycyjny [ahk-fee-zi-**tsiy**-ni] adj.m. acquisitive
akwizytor [ahk-fee-**zi**-tor] m. solicitor; travelling buyer
akwizytor ubezpieczeniowy [ahk-fee-**zi**-tor oo-bes-pye-che-**ńo**-vi] exp.: insurance agent
akwizytorka [ahk-fee-zi-**tor**-kah] f. (female) solicitor; travelling buyer
akwizytorski [ahk-fee-zi-**tor**-skee] adj.m. solicitor's; travelling buyer's
alabarda [ah-lah-**bahr**-dah] f. halberd; bill; pole-axe
alabaster [ah-lah-**bah**-ster] m. alabaster; translucent gypsum
alabastrowo [ah-lah-bah-**stro**-vo] adv. (white, etc.) like alabaster; like translucent gypsum
alabastrowość [ah-lah-bah-**stro**-vośhćh] f. quality of alabaster; alabastrine nature
alabastrowy [ah-lah-bah-**stro**-vi] adj.m. of alabaster; of translucent gypsum; alabastrine; alabaster (statue, etc.)
Aladyn [ahl-**lah**-din] m. Aladdin; Aladdin's lamp
lampa Aladyna [**lahm**-pah ahl-lah-**di**-nah] exp.: Aladdin's lamp
alalia [ah-**lah**-lyah] f. alalia; inability to speak
alanina [ah-lah-**ńee**-nah] f. alanine
alarm [**ah**-lahrm] m. alarm; alert; commotion; stir; a sudden call to arms; a warning of danger; fear caused by danger
uderzyć na alarm [oo-**de**-zhićh nah **ah**-lahrm] exp.: to sound the alarm; to warn of danger
narobić alarmu [nah-ro-beećh ah-

lahr-moo] exp.: to raise the alarm
odwołanie alarmu [od-vo-**wah**-ńe ah-lahr-moo] exp.: all clear
alarmista [ah-lahr-**mee**-stah] m. alarmist; panic-monger
alarmistycznie [ah-lahr-mee-**stich**-ńe] adv. with alarm; with panic
alarmistyczny [ah-lahr-mee-**stich**-ni] adj.m. alarmist; panicky
alarmować [ah-lahr-**mo**-vahćh] v. alarm; give alarm; frighten; startle; terrify (*repeatedly*)
alarmować się [ah-lahr-**mo**-vahćh śhan] v. take alarm (*repeatedly*)
alarmowanie [ah-lahr-mo-**vah**-ńe] n. alarm; giving alarm; frightening; startling; terrifying
alarmowo [ah-lahr-**mo**-vo] adv. with alarm
alarmowy [ah-lahr-**mo**-vi] adj.m. alarm (bell, etc.); of alarm
dzwonek alarmowy [**dzvo**-nek ah-lahr-**mo**-vi] exp.: alarm-bell; call-bell
alarmująco [ah-lahr-moo-**yown**-tso] adv. alarmingly
alasz [**ah**-lahsh] m. kummel-flavored liqueur, Allasch
alba [**ahl**-bah] f. alb; alba (song)
Albańczyk [ahl-**bahń**-chik] m. Albanian; a native of Albania
Albanka [ahl-**bahn**-kah] f. (woman) Albanian; a native of Albania
albański [ahl-**bahń**-skee] adj.m. Albanian; of Albania
albatros [ahl-**bah**-tros] m. (zool.) albatross (bird)
albertyn [ahl-**ber**-tin] m. monk of the order founded by Brother Albert of Cracow (for the care of the homeless and tending of the sick)
albertyzm [ahl-**ber**-tizm] m. adaptation of Aristotle's philosophy to Christian theology
albigens [ahl-**bee**-gens] m. Albigense
albinizm [ahl-**bee**-ńeezm] m. albinism; albinoism
albinos [ahl-**bee**-nos] m. albino
albinoska [ahl-bee-**no**-skah] f. albino (woman)
albinotyczny [ahl-bee-no-**tich**-ni] adj.m. of albinism
albit [**ahl**-beet] m. albite (mineral)
albityzacja [ahl-bee-ti-**zah**-tsyah] f. albitization
albo [**ahl**-bo] conj. or; else
jedno albo drugie [**yed**-no ahl-bo **droo**-ge] exp.: one or the other; either of the two
albo ... albo [**ahl**-bo **ahl**-bo] exp.: either ... or
albo albo [**ahl**-bo **ahl**-bo] exp.: there is no alternative; there is only one way out; you can't have it both ways (have your cake and eat it)
albo ten, albo tamten [**ahl**-bo ten **ahl**-bo **tahm**-ten] exp.: either of them (of the two)
albo tędy, albo tamtędy [**ahl**-bo **tan**-di, **ahl**-bo tahm-**tan**-di] exp.: this way or that; either way
albo też [**ahl**-bo tesh] exp.: or else
albo ci to źle tu? [**ahl**-bo ćhee to źhle too] exp.: are you unhappy here?
albowiem [ahl-**bo**-vyem] conj. for; as; since; because; on account of
alboż [**ahl**-bosh] (particle) = **albo**
alboż ci to źle? [**ahl**-bosh ćhee to źhle] exp.: you aren't doing badly, are you?
album [**ahl**-boom] m. album; sketch-book
album do znaczków [**ahl**-boom do **znahch**-koof] exp.: stamp collector's album; stamp-album
albumik [ahl-**boo**-meek] m. (nice, small) album; sketch-book
albumina [ahl-boo-**mee**-nah] f. albumin
albuminoid [ahl-boo-mee-**no**-eed] m. albuminoid
albuminoidowy [ahl-boo-mee-no-ee-**do**-vi] adj.m. albuminoidal
albuminowy [ahl-boo-mee-**no**-vi] adj.m. of albumin; albuminous
albuminoza [ahl-boo-mee-**no**-zah] f. albuminosis
albuminuria [ahl-boo-mee-**noor**-yah] f. albuminuria
albumowo [ahl-boo-**mo**-vo] adv. in form of an album
albumowy [ahl-boo-**mo**-vi] adj.m. album (paper, etc.); of an album
alcejski [ahl-**tsey**-skee] adj.m. Alcaic (verse, etc.)

alchemia [ahl-**khe**-myah] f. alchemy; alchemistry
alchemicznie [ahl-khe-**meech**-ńe] adv. alchemically
alchemiczny [ahl-khe-**meech**-ni] adj.m. alchemical; alchemic; alchemistical
alchemik [ahl-**khe**-meek] m. alchemist (of the Middle Ages)
alchemizować [ahl-khe-mee-**zo**-vahćh] v. alchemize; transmute (*repeatedly*)
alcista [ahl-**ćhee**-stah] m. alto; singer with alto voice
alcistka [ahl-**ćhee**-stkah] f. (woman) alto; singer with alto voice
aldehyd [ahl-**de**-khit] m. aldehyde
aldehydowy [ahl-de-khi-**do**-vi] adj.m. aldehydic
aldosteron [ahl-do-**ste**-ron] m. aldosterone
aldosteronizm [ahl-do-ste-**ro**-ńeezm] m. aldosteronism
aldoza [ahl-**do**-zah] f. aldose
aldrowanda [ahl-dro-**vahn**-dah] f. Aldrovanda
ale [**ah**-le] conj. however; but; still; yet; not at all; oh!; well, well!; n. defect; weak point; hitch; flaw
ale ale [**ah**-le **ah**-le] exp.: oh! I say...; oh, look here; I mustn't forget; I object!
ale ścisk! [**ah**-le śhćheesk] exp.: what a crowd!
alegat [ah-**le**-gaht] m. annex; voucher
aleatorycznie [ah-le-ah-to-**rich**-ńe] adv. in an aleatoric manner
aleatoryczny [ah-le-ah-to-**rich**-ni] adj.m. aleatoric; improvisatory; random
aleatoryzm [ah-le-ah-**to**-rizm] m. aleatory condition
alegoria [ah-le-**go**-ryah] f. allegory; a story in which people, things, and events have a symbolic meaning (often instructive)
alegorycznie [ah-le-go-**rich**-ńe] adv. allegorically
alegoryczność [ah-le-go-**rich**-nośhćh] f. allegoricalness
alegoryczny [ah-le-go-**rich**-ni] adj.m. allegoric; allegorical
alegoryka [ah-le-**go**-ri-kah] f. allegorisms; allegoric elements (in a book, etc.)
alegoryzm [ah-le-**go**-rizm] m. allegorism
alegoryzować [ah-le-go-ri-**zo**-vahćh] v. allegorize (*repeatedly*)
alegoryzownie [ah-le-go-ri-zo-**vah**-ńe] n. allegorizing; allegorization
aleja [ah-**le**-yah] f. avenue; alley; walk; vista; ride; boulevard; parade rout; path; lane; drive
alejka [ah-**ley**-kah] f. lane
aleksandryczny [ah-lek-sahn-**drich**-ni] adj.m. Alexandrine (verse)
aleksandryjski [ah-lek-sahn-**driy**-skee] adj.m. Alexandrian (period)
aleksandryn [ah-lek-**sahn**-drin] m. Alexandrian (verse)
aleksandryt [ah-lek-**sahn**-drit] m. alexandrite (mineral)
aleksja [ah-**le**-ksyah] f. alexia; aphasia
aleksykalizm [ah-le-ksi-**kah**-leezm] m. aphasia; loss of the ability to name object
aleksyna [ah-le-**ksi**-nah] f. alexin (a substance which destroys bacteria)
alembik [ah-**lem**-beek] m. alembic; pure vodka; distillation flask
alembikować [ah-lem-bee-**ko**-vahćh] v. distill; distil (Brit.) (*repeatedly*)
alembikowy [ah-lem-bee-**ko**-vi] adj.m. of alembic (vodka, etc.)
alergen [ah-**ler**-gen] m. substance causing allergy
alergenny [ah-ler-**gen**-ni] adj.m. causing allergy
alergia [ah-**ler**-gyah] f. allergy
alergicznie [ah-ler-**geech**-ńe] adv. disagreeably sensitive; inducing allergy
alergiczny [ah-ler-**geech**-ni] adj.m. allergic; of, caused by, or having an allergy
alergik [ah-**ler**-geek] m. an allergic person
alergolog [ah-ler-**go**-log] m. allergist; a doctor who specializes in treating allergies
alergologia [ah-ler-go-**lo**-gyah] f. specialty in treating allergies
alergologiczny [ah-ler-go-lo-**geech**-ni] adj.m. of the specialty in treating

allergies
alergometria [ah-ler-go-**me**-tryah] f. determination of the level of allergy in an individual
alert [**ah**-lert] m. alert; signal of danger; the state of readiness (for an emergency, etc.)
aleucki [ah-le-**oo**-tskee] adj.m. Aleutian
aleukemia [ah-lew-**ke**-myah] f. variety of leukemia
aleuron [ah-**lew**-ron] m. aleuron
aleuronowy [ah-lew-ro-**no**-vi] adj.m. aleuron (grains, layer, etc.)
Aleut [ah-le-oot] m. Aleut
ależ [**ah**-lesh] conj. why (yes)
ależ tak! [**ah**-lesh tahk] exp.: why yes!; why of course; by all means!
ależ nie! [ah-lesh **ńe**!] exp.: why not?; nothing of the kind!
czy wolno? Ależ proszę bardzo! [chi **vol**-no? ah-lesh **pro**-shan **bahr**-dzo] exp.: by all means, do!
alfa [**ahl**-fah] f. (Greek letter) alpha
alfa i omega [**ahl**-fah ee o-**me**-gah] exp.: the alpha and omega
alfaaktywny [ahl-fah-ahk-**tiv**-ni] adj.m. emitting alpha rays
alfabet [ahl-**fah**-bet] m. alphabet; the ABC; the abc
według alfabetu [**ve**-dwoog ahl-fah-**be**-too] exp.: alphabetically; in alphabetical order
alfabetycznie [ahl-fah-be-**tich**-ńe] adv. alphabetically; in alphabetical order
alfabetyczny [ahl-fah-be-**tich**-ni] adj.m. alphabetical (order)
alfabetyzacja [ahl-fah-be-ti-**zah**-tsyah] f. alphabetization
alfabetyzować [ahl-fah-be-ti-**zo**-vahćh] v. alphabetize (*repeatedly*)
alfabetyzowanie [ahl-fah-be-ti-zo-**vah**-ńe] n. alphabetization
alfanumerycznie [ahl-fah-noo-me-**rich**-ńe] adv. alphanumerically
alfanumeryczny [ahl-fah-noo-me-**rich**-ni] adj.m. alphanumerical; alphanumeric
alfapromieniotwrórczy [ahl-fah-pro-mye-**ńo**-**tfoor**-chi] adj.m. emitting alpha rays
alfons [**ahl**-fons] m. pimp; cadet; prostitute's bully
alfresko [ahl-**fre**-sko] adv. in fresco
alga [**ahl**-gah] f. alga; algae
algebra [ahl-**ge**-brah] f. algebra
algebraicznie [ahl-ge-brah-**eech**-ńe] adv. algebraically
algebraiczny [ahl-ge-brah-**eech**-ni] adj.m. algebraic
algebraik [ahl-ge-**brah**-eek] m. algebraist
algebrarzysta [ahl-ge-brah-**zhi**-stah] m. algebraist
algezja [ahl-**ge**-zyah] f. algesia; sensitiveness to pain
algezymetr [ahl-ge-**zi**-metr] m. algesimeter; device for measuring the intensity of pain
Algierczyk [ahl-**ger**-chik] m. Algerian
algierka [ahl-**ger**-kah] f. Algerian fur coat
Algierka [ahl-**ger**-kah] f. Algerian (woman)
algierski [ahl-**ger**-skee] adj.m. Algerian
algina [ahl-**gee**-nah] f. algin; algine
alginowy [ahl-gee-**no**-vi] adj.m. alginic (acid, etc.)
algofilia [ahl-go-**fee**-lyah] f. algophilia; pleasure of inflicting pain
algofobia [ahl-go-**fo**-byah] f. algophobia; fear of pain
algol [**ahl**-gol] m. Algol; ALGOL; algebraic and logical language for programming computer
algolog [ahl-**go**-log] m. algologist
algologia [ahl-go-**lo**-gyah] f. algology
algologicznie [ahl-go-lo-**geech**-ńe] adv. algologically
algologiczny [ahl-go-lo-**geech**-ni] adj.m. algological
algoncki [ahl-**gon**-tskee] adj.m. Algonkian (language, etc.)
Algonkian [ahl-**gon**-kyahn] m. Algonquin tribe
algonkiński [ahl-gon-**keeń**-skee] adj.m. Algonkian
algoński [ahl-**goń**-skee] adj.m. Algonkian
algorytm [ahl-**go**-ritm] m. algorithm; algorism
algorytmiczny [ahl-go-rit-**meech**-ni] adj.m. algorithmic; algorismic
algorytmizacja [ahl-go-rit-mee-**zah**-

tsyah] f. making algorithmic; setting up of a step by step procedure for solving a problem
algrafia [ahl-**grah**-fyah] f. a printing technique
aliancki [ahl-**yahn**-tskee] adj.m. allied (forces, etc.); of the allied states
alians [ahl-yahns] m. alliance
aliant [ahl-yahnt] m. ally
alianci [ahl-**yahn**-ćhee] pl. the allies; the Allied Nations of World War II
aliantka [ahl-**yahn**-tkah] f. (woman) ally
alias [ahl-yahs] m. alias; an assumed name; adv. otherwise named
aliaż [ahl-yahsh] m. colloq: mixture (of metals, etc.); alloy
alibi [ah-**lee**-bee] n. alibi
udowodnić swoje alibi [oo-do-**vod**-ńeećh **sfo**-ye ah-**lee**-bee] exp.: to establish one's alibi; to set up an alibi
alicykliczny [ah-lee-tsi-**kleech**-ni] adj.m. alicyclic
alidada [ah-lee-**dah**-dah] f. alidada; alidade
alienacja [ah-lye-**nah**-tsyah] f. alienation; feeling strange; feeling not accepted
alienacyjny [ah-lye-nah-**tsiy**-ni] adj.m. of alienation
alienować [ah-lye-**no**-vahćh] v. alienate; transfer ownership of property to another; make unfriendly or withdrawn; cause transference of (affection) (*repeatedly*)
alienować się [ah-lye-**no**-vahćh śhan] v. become alienated; isolate oneself (socially) (*repeatedly*)
alienowanie [ah-lye-no-**vah**-ńe] n. alienation
alifatyczny [ah-lee-fah-**tich**-ni] adj.m. aliphatic
aligacja [ah-lee-**gah**-tsyah] f. alligation (of ingredients, etc.)
aligator [ah-lee-**gah**-tor] m. (zool.) alligator
alikant [ah-**lee**-kahnt] m. Alicant (wine)
alikwot [ah-**lee**-kfot] m. aliquot tone
alimenta [ah-lee-**men**-tah] pl. alimony
alimentacja [ah-lee-men-**tah**-tsyah] f. feeding (of a boiler, etc.); obligation to pay alimony
alimentacyjny [ah-lee-men-tah-**tsiy**-ni] adj.m. feed (pump, etc.); of alimony
alimentator [ah-lee-men-**tah**-tor] m. feed-pump
alimentować [ah-lee-men-**to**-vahćh] v. pay alimony (*repeatedly*)
alimentowanie [ah-lee-men-to-**vah**-ńe] n. paying of alimony
alimenty [ah-lee-**men**-ti] pl. alimony (for separated wife)
alinearny [ah-lee-ne-**ahr**-ni] adj.m. out of line; discontinuous
aliści [ah-**leeśh**-ćhee] conj. but; however; yet; still; nevertheless; exp.: lo; behold; lo and behold
alit [**ah**-leet] m. alite
aliteracja [ah-lee-te-**rah**-tsyah] f. alliteration; head rhyme; initial rhyme
aliteracki [ah-lee-te-**rah**-tskee] adj.m. not literary
aliteracyjnie [ah-lee-te-rah-**tsiy**-ńe] adv. alliteratively
aliteracyjność [ah-lee-te-rah-**tsiy**-nośhćh] f. alliterativeness
aliteracyjny [ah-lee-te-rah-**tsiy**-ni] adj.m. alliterative; marked by alliteration
alizaryna [ah-lee-zah-**ri**-nah] f. alizarin
alizarynowy [ah-lee-zah-ri-**no**-vi] adj.m. alizarin (dye, black, red, etc.)
alka [**ahl**-kah] f. Alca; auk (bird)
alkacymetria [ahl-kah-tsi-**me**-tryah] f. a volumetric chemical analysis
alkad [**ahl**-kaht] m. alcaide; mayor
alklaliczny [ahl-kah-**leech**-ni] adj.m. Alcaic
alkalia [ahl-**kah**-lyah] pl. chem. alkalies
alkaliceluloza [ahl-kah-lee-tse-loo-**lo**-zah] f. alkali cellulose
alkalicznie [ahl-kah-**leech**-ńe] adv. chem. (to react, etc.) as an alkali
alkaliczność [ahl-kah-**leech**-nośhćh] f. chem. alkalinity

alkaliczny [ahl-kah-**leech**-ni] adj.m. chem. alkaline
alkalifil [ahl-**kah**-lee-feel] m. alkaline water (and soil) organism
alkalifilny [ahl-kah-lee-**feel**-ni] adj.m. of alkaline water (and soil) organism
alkalimetr [ahl-kah-**lee**-metr] m. chem. alkalimeter
alkalimetria [ahl-kah-lee-**me**-tryah] f. chem. alkalimetry
alkalizować [ahl-kah-lee-**zo**-vahćh] v. chem. alkalize; alkalinize (*repeatedly*)
alkalizowanie [ahl-kah-lee-zo-**vah**-ńe] n. chem. alkalization
alkalizujący [ahl-kah-lee-zoo-**yown**-tsi] adj.m. chem. alkalescent
alkaloid [ahl-kah-**lo**-eet] m. alkaloid
alkaloza [ahl-kah-**lo**-zah] f. alkalosis; excessive alkalinity of the blood
alkan [**ahl**-kahn] m. paraffin
alkanna [ahl-**kahn**-nah] f. alkanet
alkazar [ahl-**kah**-zahr] m. alcazar
alken [**ahl**-ken] m. alkene; olefin
alkiermes [ahl-**ker**-mes] m. alkermes; kermes (insect, dyestuff); pokeberry; pokeweed
alkierz [**ahl**-kesh] m. alcove; recess
alkierzyk [ahl-**ke**-zhik] m. (small, nice) alcove; recess
alkil [**ahl**-keel] m. chem. alkyl
alkilacja [ahl-kee-**lah**-tsyah] f. alkylation
alkilowy [ahl-kee-**lo**-vi] adj.m. alkyl (group, halide, etc.)
alkohol [ahl-**ko**-khol] m. alcohol; spirit; liquor; alcoholics; drinks; slang: booze; hooch; rum
alkohol skażony [ahl-**ko**-khol skah-**zho**-ni] exp.: denaturated alcohol
alkoholan [ahl-ko-**kho**-lahn] m. alcoholate
alkoholiczka [ahl-ko-kho-**leech**-kah] f. (woman) alcoholic; heavy drinker; inveterate drunkard
alkoholiczny [ahl-ko-kho-**leech**-ni] adj.m. alcoholic; alcoholic's
alkoholik [ahl-ko-**kho**-leek] m. alcoholic; heavy drinker; inveterate drunkard
alkoholiza [ahl-ko-kho-**lee**-zah] f. alcoholysis
alkoholizacja [ahl-ko-kho-lee-**zah**-tsyah] f. alcoholization
alkoholizm [ahl-ko-**kho**-leezm] m. alcoholism; alcoholic disease
alkoholizować [ahl-ko-kho-lee-**zo**-vahćh] v. alcoholize; load (wine) (*repeatedly*)
alkoholometr [ahl-ko-kho-**lo**-metr] m. alcoholometer
alkoholometria [ahl-ko-kho-lo-**me**-tryah] f. alcoholometry
alkoholometryczny [ahl-ko-kho-lo-me-**tri**-chni] adj.m. alcoholometric
alkoholomierz [ahl-ko-kho-**lo**-myesh] m. alcoholometer
alkoholowy [ahl-ko-kho-**lo**-vi] adj.m. alcoholic; spirituous; intoxicating
alkoran [ahl-**ko**-rahn] m. Alcoran
alkowa [ahl-**ko**-vah] f. alcove; recess; bedchamber
tajemnice alkowy [tah-yem-**ńee**-tse ahl-**ko**-vi] exp.: the privacies of the bedchamber
alkowiany [ahl-ko-**vyah**-ni] adj.m. of alcove
alkówka [ahl-**koof**-kah] f. (small) alcove; recess
Allach [**ahl**-lahkh] m. Allah; the Supreme Being of the Muslims
Allah [**ahl**-lahkh] m. Allah; the Supreme Being of the Muslims
allegretto [ahl-le-**gret**-to] n. allegretto
allegro [ahl-**le**-gro] n. allegro
alleluja [ahl-le-**loo**-yah] n. alleluia; hallelujah; hallelujah
allen [**ahl**-len] m. allene
allil [**ahl**-leel] m. allyl
allilowy [ahl-lee-**lo**-vi] adj.m. allylic
Alma Mater [**ahl**-mah **mah**-ter] exp.: Alma Mater
almanach [ahl-**mah**-nahkh] m. almanac; a calendar with astronomical data, weather forecasts, etc.
almanachowy [ahl-mah-nah-**kho**-vi] adj.m. of almanac
almanak [ahl-**mah**-nahk] m. almanac; a calendar with astronomical data, weather forecasts, etc.
almandyn [ahl-**mahn**-din] m. almandine; almandite (mineral)
almawiwa [ahl-mah-**vee**-vah] f. (a

type of) coat; wrap
almeja [ahl-**me**-yah] f. alme; almeh (Egyptian singing and dancing girl)
alniko [ahl-**ńee**-ko] n. alnico
alo- [**ah**-lo] prefix: other-
alochromatyczny [ah-lo-khro-mah-**tich**-ni] adj.m. allochromatic; allochroous; changing colors; variable in colors
alochromatyzm [ah-lo-khro-**mah**-tizm] m. allochromatic condition
alochton [ah-**lokh**-ton] m. an alochthonous man (not native)
alochtoniczny [ah-lokh-to-**ńeech**-ni] adj.m. alochthonous
alodialnie [ah-lo-**dyahl**-ńe] adv. alodially; allodially
alodialny [ah-lo-**dyahl**-ni] adj.m. of alodium (property); alodial
alodium [ah-**lo**-dyoom] n. alodium
alodynować [ah-lo-di-**no**-vahćh] v. treat aluminum surface in acid (*repeatedly*)
alodynowanie [ah-lo-di-no-**vah**-ńe] n. treatment of aluminum surface in acid (for protection against corrosion)
aloes [ah-**lo**-es] m. aloe
aloesowy [ah-lo-e-**so**-vi] adj.m. aloetic (medicine, leaf, etc.)
alofan [ah-**lo**-fahn] m. allophane
alofon [ah-**lo**-fon] m. allophone
alofoniczny [ah-lo-fo-**ńeech**-ni] adj.m. allophonic
alogamia [ah-lo-**gah**-myah] f. allogamy; cross-fertilization
alogamiczny [ah-lo-gah-**meech**-ni] adj.m. allogamous; cross-fertilized
alogeniczny [ah-lo-ge-**ńeech**-ni] adj.m. allogenic
alogicznie [ah-lo-**geech**-ńe] adv. illogically
alogiczność [ah-lo-**geech**-nośhćh] f. illogical situation; illogical condition
alogiczny [ah-lo-**geech**-ni] adj.m. illogical; outside of logic
alogizm [ah-**lo**-geezm] m. illogicalness
aloina [ah-lo-**ee**-nah] f. aloin
aloksyt [ah-**lo**-ksit] m. aloxite
alokacja [ah-lo-**kah**-tsyah] f. allocation; bookkeeping designation
alokucja [ah-lo-**koo**-tsyah] f. allocution; formal speech; hortatory address
alomorf [ah-**lo**-morf] m. allomorph
alonim [ah-**lo**-ńeem] m. allonym
alonimowy [ah-lo-ńee-**mo**-vi] adj.m. allonymous
alonż [**ah**-lonsh] m. rider (to a bill); adapter; adaptor; lengthening tube
alonżka [ah-**lonsh**-kah] f. rider (to a bill); adapter; adaptor; lengthening tube
alopat [ah-**lo**-paht] m. allopath; allopathist
alopata [ah-lo-**pah**-tah] m. allopath; allopathist
alopatia [ah-lo-**pah**-tyah] f. allopathy
alopatycznie [ah-lo-pah-**tich**-ńe] adv. allopathically
alopatyczny [ah-lo-pah-**tich**-ni] adj.m. allopathic
aloploid [ah-lo-**plo**-eet] m. plant with two sets of chromosomes
aloploidalność [ah-lo-plo-ee-**dahl**-nośhćh] f. occurrence of two sets of chromosomes in the nucleus of a somatic cell
alosaur [ah-**lo**-zahwr] m. allosaur; Allosaurus
alosom [ah-**lo**-som] m. allosome
alotropowo [ah-lo-tro-**po**-vo] adv. allotropically
alotropowy [ah-lo-tro-**po**-vi] adj.m. allotropic; allotropous
alowiec [ah-**lo**-vyets] m. member of the Polish People's Army (W.W.II)
alowski [ah-**lof**-skee] adj.m. of the Polish People's Army (W.W.II)
aloza [ah-**lo**-zah] f. shad
alpaga [ahl-**pah**-gah] f. alpaca
alpagowy [ahl-pah-**go**-vi] adj.m. alpaca (coat, etc.); of alpaca
alpaka [ahl-**pah**-kah] f. alpaca
alpakowy [ahl-pah-**ko**-vi] adj.m. alpaca (coat, etc.); of alpaca; German silver (spoon, etc.); nickel-silver (fork, etc.); of German silver; of nickel-silver
alpaks [**ahl**-pahks] m. alpax; silumin; italsil
al pari [ahl **pah**-ree] adv. (commercial) at par

alpejczyk [ahl-**pey**-chik] m. Alpine skier
alpejka [ahl-**pey**-kah] f. (female) Alpine skier
alpejski [ahl-**pey**-skee] adj.m. Alpine; of the Alps
fiołek alpejski [**fyo**-wek ahl-**pey**-skee] exp.: cyclamen
alpidy [ahl-**pee**-di] pl. Alpids
alpinarium [ahl-pee-**nahr**-yoom] n. alpine garden
alpinada [ahl-pee-**nah**-dah] f. Alpine competition (sporting events)
alpinista [ahl-pee-**ńee**-stah] m. Alpine climber; mountain climber
alpinistka [ahl-pee-**ńee**-stkah] f. (female) Alpine climber; mountain climber
alpinistyczny [ahl-pee-ńee-**stich**-ni] adj.m. of Alpinism; mountain climbing (achievement, etc.); for (of) mountain-climbing
alpinistyka [ahl-pee-**ńee**-sti-kah] f. Alpinism; Alpine mountain-climbing; mountaineering
alpinizm [ahl-**pee**-ńeezm] m. Alpinism; Alpine mountain-climbing; mountaineering
al seco [ahl **se**-ko] n. wall painting on dry plaster
alstrometria [ahl-stro-**me**-tryah] f. Alstroemetria (herb)
alt [ahlt] m. (music) alto
altana [ahl-**tah**-nah] f. bower; arbor; summer-house
altanka [ahl-**tahn**-kah] f. (small, nice) bower; arbor; summer-house
altannik [ahl-**tahn**-ńeek] m. bower-bird; gardener bird
altarysta [ahl-tah-**ri**-stah] m. altarist; chaplain; vicar; acolyte; altar boy
altarzysta [ahl-tah-**zhi**-stah] m. altarist; chaplain; vicar; acolyte; altar boy
altazymut [ahl-tah-**zi**-moot] m. altazimuth
altembas [ahl-**tem**-bahs] m. cloth of gold; brocade
altembasowy [ahl-tem-bah-**so**-vi] adj.m. of cloth of gold; brocade (tapestry, etc.)
alteracja [ahl-te-**rah**-tsyah] f. inflection (of a note); irritation; excitement; (legal) alteration
alternacja [ahl-ter-**nah**-tsyah] f. alternation; alternate system
alternacyjnie [ahl-ter-nah-**tsiy**-ńe] adv. alternatively
alternacyjność [ahl-ter-nah-**tsiy**-nośhćh] f. alternativeness
alternacyjny [ahl-ter-nah-**tsiy**-ni] adj.m. alternate; alternative
alternat [ahl-**ter**-naht] m. (legal) alternate; rotation in precedence
alternator [ahl-ter-**nah**-tor] m. alternator
alternatywa [ahl-ter-nah-**ti**-vah] f. alternative; option; choice between things; variant; one of the things to be chosen; something left to choose
alternatywnie [ahl-ter-nah-**tiv**-ńe] adv. optionally
alternatywność [ahl-ter-nah-**tiv**-nośhćh] f. alternation; optional character; alternativeness
alternatywny [ahl-ter-nah-**tiv**-ni] adj.m. alternative; optional
alternować [ahl-ter-**no**-vahćh] v. alternate (*repeatedly*)
alternowanie [ahl-ter-no-**vah**-ńe] n. alternation
alterocentryczny [ahl-te-ro-tsen-**trich**-ni] adj.m. altruistic
alterocentryzm [ahl-te-ro-**tsen**-trizm] m. altruism
alterować [ahl-te-**ro**-vahćh] v. inflect (a note); alter the tune; worry (*repeatedly*)
alterować się [ahl-te-**ro**-vahćh śhan] v. get irritated; become irritated; get excited (*repeatedly*)
alterowanie [ahl-te-ro-**vah**-ńe] n. inflecting (a note); altering the tune; worry
altocumulus [ahl-to-koo-**moo**-loos] m. alto-cumulus
altostratus [ahl-to-**strah**-toos] m. alto-stratus
altowiolinista [ahl-to-vyo-lee-**ńee**-stah] m. viola player
altowiolinistka [ahl-to-vyo-lee-**ńee**-stkah] f. (female) viola player
altowiolista [ahl-to-vyo-**lee**-stah] m. viola player
altowiolistka [ahl-to-vyo-**lee**-stkah] f. (female) viola player
altowy [ahl-**to**-vi] adj.m. (music) alto

(voice, etc.)
altówka [ahl-**toof**-kah] f. (music) viola; alto; alt horn
altruista [ahl-troo-**ee**-stah] m. altruist
altruistycznie [ahl-troo-ee-**stich**-ńe] adv. altruistically; unselfishly; selflessly
altruistyczny [ahl-troo-ees-**tich**-ni] adj.m. altruistic; unselfish; selfless; concerned for the welfare of others
altruizm [ahl-**troo**-eezm] m. altruism; unselfishness; selflessness
altymetr [ahl-**ti**-metr] m. altimeter
altymetria [ahl-ti-**me**-tryah] f. altimetry
altysta [ahl-**ti**-stah] m. alto; singer with alto voice; viola player
altystka [ahl-**ti**-stkah] f. (female) alto; singer with alto voice; viola player
aluminiować [ah-loo-mee-**ńyo**-vahćh] v. plate with aluminum (*repeatedly*)
aluminiowanie [ah-loo-mee-ńyo-**vah**-ńe] n. plating with aluminum
aluminiowy [ah-loo-mee-**ńyo**-vi] adj.m. of aluminum; aluminum (alloy, etc.)
aluminium [ah-loo-**mee**-ńyoom] n. aluminum; aluminium (Brit.)
aluminografia [ah-loo-mee-no-**grah**-fyah] f. a printing technique
aluminotermia [ah-loo-mee-no-**ter**-myah] f. aluminothermy; aluminothermics
alumn [**ah**-loomn] m. alumnus
alumnat [ah-**loom**-naht] m. seminary
alumożel [ah-loo-**mo**-zhel] m. aluminum gel
aluwialny [ah-loo-**vyahl**-ni] adj.m. alluvial; deposited by flowing water (clay, sand)
aluwium [ah-**loo**-vyoom] n. alluvium
aluzja [ah-**loo**-zyah] f. hint; allusion; insinuation; reference to; innuendo; dig
delikatna aluzja [de-lee-**kaht**-nah ah-**loo**-zyah] exp.: insinuation; innuendo
robić aluzję [ro-beećh ah-**loo**-zyan] exp.: to allude (to something); to hint (at); to drop a hint; to insinuate; to imply (that)
aluzyjnie [ah-loo-**ziy**-ńe] adv. allusively; by way of allusion
aluzyjność [ah-loo-**ziy**-nośhćh] f. allusiveness
aluzyjny [ah-loo-**ziy**-ni] adj.m. allusive
alweolarnie [ahl-ve-o-**lahr**-ńe] adv. alveolarly
alweolarny [ahl-ve-o-**lahr**-ni] adj.m. alveolar; of alveolus; of teethridge
alzacki [ahl-**zah**-tskee] adj.m. Alsatian (wolf-hound, etc.)
Alzatczyk [ahl-**zaht**-chik] m. Alsatian; native of Alsace
ałła [**ahw**-wah] not declined: Turkish war cry "Allah"
ałłachować [ahw-wah-**kho**-vahćh] v. to shout Turkish war cry "Allah" (*repeatedly*)
ałtajski [ahw-**tahy**-skee] adj.m. Altaic
ałun [**ah**-woon] m. alum
ałunować [ah-woo-**no**-vahćh] v. alum; impregnate with alum (*repeatedly*)
ałunowy [ah-woo-**no**-vi] adj.m. aluminous; alum (flower, etc.)
ałycza [ah-**wi**-chah] f. thorny plum tree (or shrub)
ałyczowy [ah-wi-**cho**-vi] adj.m. thorny plum (hedge, etc.)
amagnetyczny [ah-mahg-ne-**tich**-ni] adj.m. non-magnetic
amalgam [ah-**mahl**-gahm] m. amalgam; alloy including mercury
amalgamacja [ah-mahl-gah-**mah**-tsyah] f. amalgamation
amalgamat [ah-mahl-**gah**-maht] m. amalgam; merger (of societies, etc.); amalgamation; fusion
amalgamować [ah-mahl-gah-**mo**-vahćh] v. amalgamate (*repeatedly*)
amalgamować się [ah-mahl-gah-**mo**-vahćh śhan] v. amalgamate; merge; fuse (*repeatedly*)
amalgamowanie [ah-mahl-gah-mo-**vah**-ńe] n. amalgamation
amant [**ah**-mahnt] m. lover; beau; paramour
amantka [ah-**mahn**-tkah] f. lover; paramour; belle
amarant [ah-**mah**-rahnt] m. amaranth; the color of amaranth

amarantowaty [ah-mah-rahn-to-**vah**-ti] adj.m. amaranthine
amarantowieć [ah-mah-rahn-**to**-vyećh] v. take amaranthine hue; turn amaranth (color) (*repeatedly*)
amarantowo [ah-mah-rahn-**to**-vo] adv. in amaranth; in amaranth-purple
amarantowy [ah-mah-rahn-**to**-vi] adj.m. amaranth; amaranth-purple
amarylek [ah-mah-**ri**-lek] m. amaryllis
amarylis [ah-mah-**ri**-lees] m. amaryllis
amarylkowaty [ah-mah-ril-ko-**vah**-ti] adj.m. amaryllidaceous; of the amaryllis family
amatol [ah-**mah**-tol] m. amatol (an explosive)
amator [ah-**mah**-tor] m. amateur; fancier; lover; nonprofessional; dilettante; somewhat unskillful; dabbler; bidder; prospective buyer; candidate (for)
amatorka [ah-mah-**tor**-kah] f. (woman) amateur; fancier; lover; nonprofessional; dilettante; somewhat unskillful; dabbler; bidder; prospective buyer; candidate (for)
amatorski [ah-mah-**tor**-skee] adj.m. amateurish; amateur; unprofessional; made by (performed by) amateurs
teatr amatorski [**te**-ahtr ah-mah-**tor**-skee] exp.: amateur theater
po amatorsku [po ah-mah-**tor**-skoo] exp.: amateurishly; like an amateur; unprofessionally
amatorsko [ah-mah-**tor**-sko] adv. amateurishly; as an amateur; unprofessionally; in dilettante fashion; for a hobby
amatorskość [ah-mah-**tor**-skośhćh] f. amateurism; doing for fun; doing as a hobby; dilettantism; lack of professionalism
amatorstwo [ah-mah-**tor**-stfo] n. amateurism; love of; fondness for; doing for fun; doing as a hobby; dilettantism; lack of professionalism; amateur sport (boxing, etc,)
amatorszczyzna [ah-mah-tor-**shchiz**-nah] f. amateurish execution; lack of professional finish
amazonit [ah-mah-**zo**-ńeet] m. amazonite; amazonstone
amazonka [ah-mah-**zon**-kah] f. Amazon; (woman's) riding-habit; horsewoman; lady's riding outfit
amazoński [ah-mah-**zoń**-skee] adj.m. of Amazon; of (woman's) riding-habit; of horsewoman
ambaje [ahm-**bah**-ye] pl. nonsense; absurd ideas; absurdities
ambaras [ahm-**bah**-rahs] m. embarrassment; perplexity; awkward situation; a fix
być w ambarasie [bićh v ahm-bah-**rah**-śhe] exp.: colloq: to be in a fix; to be in a quandary
wprawić w ambaras [**fprah**-veećh v ahm-**bah**-rahs] exp.: to embarrass (somebody)
ambarasować [ahm-bah-rah-**so**-vahćh] v. embarrass; perplex; puzzle; disconcert; trouble; disturb; put in a fix (*repeatedly*)
ambarasować się [ahm-bah-rah-**so**-vahćh śh<u>an</u>] v. become embarrassed; trouble oneself (*repeatedly*)
ambasada [ahm-bah-**sah**-dah] f. embassy; ambassador and his staff; the embassy building
ambasador [ahm-bah-**sah**-dor] m. ambassador; the highest ranking representative of one country in another
ambasador w Polsce [ahm-bah-**sah**-dor f **pol**-stse] exp.: ambassador to Poland
ambasadorka [ahm-bah-sah-**dor**-kah] f. woman ambassador; ambassadress
ambasadorostwo [ahm-bah-sah-do-**ro**-stfo] n. ambassador and his wife
ambasadorowa [ahm-bah-sah-do-**ro**-vah] f. ambassador's wife
ambasadorować [ahm-bah-sah-do-**ro**-vahćh] v. be an ambassador (*repeatedly*)
ambasadorowanie [ahm-bah-sah-do-ro-**vah**-ńe] n. being an ambassador
ambasadorski [ahm-bah-sah-**dor**-

skee] adj.m. ambassadorial (functions, etc.); ambassador's; of an ambassador
ambasadorstwo [ahm-bah-sah-**dor**-stfo] n. office (post, etc.) of an ambassador
ambasadzki [ahm-bah-**sah**-tskee] adj.m. of an embassy
ambicja [ahm-**bee**-tsyah] f. ambition; aspiration; self-esteem; pride; self-respect; dignity; haughtiness; arrogance; a strong desire for fame; the thing so desired
ambicjonalnie [ahm-bee-tsyo-**nahl**-ńe] adv. ambitiously
ambicjonalność [ahm-bee-tsyo-**nahl**-nośhćh] f. ambitiousness
ambicjonalny [ahm-bee-tsyo-**nahl**-ni] adj.m. dictated by ambition; of ambition; ambitious
ambicyjka [ahm-bee-**tsiy**-kah] f. petty ambition
ambicyjny [ahm-bee-**tsiy**-ni] adj.m. dictated by ambition; of ambition; ambitious
ambilogia [ahm-bee-**lo**-gyah] f. double meaning; ambiguousness
ambiofonia [ahm-byo-**fo**-ńyah] f. electro-acoustic control of acoustic properties of a hall
ambiofoniczny [ahm-byo-fo-**ńeech**-ni] adj.m. of electro-acoustic control of acoustic properties of a hall
ambit [**ahm**-beet] m. mettle; spirit of ambition; aisle of a church
wziąć na ambit [vźhownćh nah **ahm**-beet] exp.: to be on one's mettle
ambitnie [ahm-**beet**-ńe] adv. ambitiously
ambitny [ahm-**beet**-ni] adj.m. ambitious; showing great effort; proud; self-respecting; aspiring
ambitus [ahm-**bee**-toos] m. ambitus; the compass of a melody
ambiwalencja [ahm-bee-vah-**len**-tsyah] f. ambivalence; ambivalency
ambiwalentnie [ahm-bee-vah-**lent**-ńe] adv. ambivalently
ambiwalentny [ahm-bee-vah-**lent**-ni] adj.m. ambivalent
ambliopia [ahm-**blyo**-pyah] f. amblyopia; dimness of sight
ambona [ahm-**bo**-nah] f. pulpit; hunter's point of vintage (built on trees or piles)
ambonka [ahm-**bon**-kah] f. small pulpit; naintop (on a ship); crew's nest
ambra [**ahm**-brah] f. ambergris (of whales used in perfumery)
ambrazura [ahm-brah-**zoo**-rah] f. embrasure
ambrowiec [ahm-**bro**-vyets] m. liquidambar; balsam tree
ambrowy [ahm-**bro**-vi] adj.m. ambergris (wax, etc.)
ambrozja [ahm-**bro**-zyah] f. ambrosia; ragweed
ambrozjański [ahm-bro-**zyahń**-skee] adj.m. ambrosial (song, chant, etc.); Ambrosian
ambrozyjski [ahm-bro-**ziy**-skee] adj.m. ambrosial; worthy of the gods; delicious
ambulakralny [ahm-boo-lah-**krahl**-ni] adj.m. ambulacral (foot, system, etc.)
ambulakrum [ahm-boo-**lah**-kroom] n. ambulacrum
ambulans [ahm-**boo**-lahns] m. ambulance; first-aid station; mail-coach; mail-cart
ambulansowy [ahm-boo-lahn-**so**-vi] adj.m. ambulance (transportation, service, etc.); first-aid (station, etc.)
ambulatorium [ahm-boo-lah-**to**-ryoom] n. out-patients' department of a hospital; dispensary; infirmary
ambulatoryjnie [ahm-boo-lah-to-**riy**-ńe] adv. (treat or examine) in an out-patient's clinic
ambulatoryjny [ahm-boo-lah-to-**riy**-ni] adj.m. ambulant; ambulatory; for out-patients; for out-patient treatment
pacjent ambulatoryjny [**pah**-tsyent ahm-boo-lah-to-**riy**-ni] exp.: out-patient
ameba [ah-**me**-bah] f. ameba
amebocyt [ah-me-**bo**-tsit] m. amebocyte
ameboidalny [ah-me-bo-ee-**dahl**-ni] adj.m. of an amoeboid; amoeban;

amoebic; amebic (abscess, etc.)
amebowaty [ah-me-bo-**vah**-ti] adj.m. amoebic; amoebian; amoebiform
ameboza [ah-me-**bo**-zah] f. amebiasis
amelioracja [ah-mel-yo-**rah**-tsyah] f. amelioration; improvement
amelioracyjny [ah-mel-yo-rah-**tsiy**-ni] adj.m. ameliorative
amen [**ah**-men] m. amen; be it so; aye; the end; for certain
na amen [nah **ah**-men] exp.: completely; most surely; altogether; utterly; for good; for good and all
już amen [yoosh **ah**-men] exp.: it's finished; it is the last of it
pewne jak amen w pacierzu [**pev**-ne yahk **ah**-men f pah-**ćhe**-zhoo] exp.: as sure as fate; dead sure; for certain; without fail; as sure as...
amencja [ah-**men**-tsyah]] f. amentia; temporary confusional insanity
ameryk [ah-**me**-rik] m. americium (atomic number 95)
amerykan [ah-me-**ri**-kahn] m. type of two-wheel carriage
amerykany [ah-me-ri-**kah**-ni] pl. (exp.:) variety of potatoes
Amerykanin [ah-me-ri-**kah**-ńeen] m. American; a native of America
amerykanista [ah-me-ri-kah-**ńee**-stah] m. specialist in American studies
amerykanistyka [ah-me-ri-kah-**ńees**-ti-kah] f. American studies
amerykanizacja [ah-me-ri-kah-ńee-**zah**-tsyah] f. Americanization
amerykanizm [ah-me-ri-**kah**-ńeezm] m. Americanism; American idiom
polskie amerykanizmy [**pol**-sk͟e ah-me-ri-kah-**ńeez**-mi] exp.: American idioms adapted to Polish language by immigrants from Poland
amerykanizować [ah-me-ri-kah-ńee-**zo**-vahćh] v. Americanize (*repeatedly*)
amerykanizować się [ah-me-ri-kah-ńee-**zo**-vahćh śh͟a͟n] v. develop American characteristics; Americanize (oneself)(*repeatedly*)
amerykanizowanie [ah-me-ri-kah-ńee-zo-**vah**-ńe] n. Americanization
Amerykanka [ah-me-ri-**kahn**-kah] f. American; American woman
amerykanka [ah-me-ri-**kahn**-kah] f. sofa-bed; double-entry book-keeping; job-press (print.); catch-as-catch-can wrestling; type of racing skate
amerykański [ah-me-ri-**kahń**-skee] adj.m. American; of America
amerykańskość [ah-me-ri-**kahń**-skośhćh] f. American character
ametaboliczny [ah-me-tah-bo-**leech**-ni] adj.m. ametabolic; ametabolous
ametabolizm [ah-me-tah-**bo**-leezm] m. ametabolism
ametodycznie [ah-me-to-**dich**-ńe] adv. amethodically; not methodically
ametodyczny [ah-me-to-**dich**-ni] adj.m. amethodical; not methodical
ametropia [ah-me-**tro**-pyah] f. ametropia; myopia or astigmatism
ametropowy [ah-me-tro-**po**-vi] adj.m. ametropic
ametyst [ah-**me**-tist] m. amethyst
ametystowo [ah-me-ti-**sto**-vo] adv. (to shine like) amethyst
ametystowy [ah-me-ti-**sto**-vi] adj.m. of amethysts; amethystine; of the color of amethyst
amfetamina [ahm-fe-tah-**mee**-nah] f. amphetamine
amfibia [ahm-**fee**-byah] f. zool.: amphibian; amphibious tank; amphibious aircraft; amphibion
amfibijny [ahm-fee-**beey**-ni] adj.m. amphibian; amphibious (tank, aircraft, etc.)
amfibiotyczny [ahm-fee-byo-**tich**-ni] adj.m. amphibiotic
amfibol [ahm-**fee**-bol] m. amphibole; hornblende
amfibolia [ahm-fee-**bol**-yah] f. ambiguity caused by misspelling or bad punctuation; amphibology; amphibolia; amphibolic fever
amfiboliczny [ahm-fee-bo-**leech**-ni] adj.m. ambiguous because of misspelling or bad punctuation;

amphibolous; amphibolic
amfibolit [ahm-fee-**bo**-leet] m. amphibolite
amfibologia [ahm-fee-bo-**lo**-gyah] f. ambiguity caused by misspelling or bad punctuation; amphibology; amphibolia
amfibologiczny [ahm-fee-bo-lo-**geech**-ni] adj.m. ambiguous because of misspelling or bad punctuation; amphibolous; amphibolic
amfibrach [ahm-**fee**-brahkh] m. amphibrach
amfibrachiczny [ahm-fee-brah-**kheech**-ni] adj.m. amphibrachic
amfigonia [ahm-fee-**go**-ńyah] f. amphigony
amfilada [ahm-fee-**lah**-dah] f. suite of rooms; succession; series; row; enfilade; raking fire
amfiladowy [ahm-fee-lah-**do**-vi] adj.m. en suite (of rooms); enfilade; raking (artillery fire)
amfimacer [ahm-fee-**mah**-tser] m. amphimacer (verse)
amfimakr [ahm-**fee**-mahkr] m. amphimacer (verse)
amfimaksja [ahm-fee-**mah**-ksyah] f. amphimixis
amfiploid [ahm-fee-**plo**-eet] m. organism with two sets of chromosomes; amphiploid
amfiploidalność [ahm-fee-plo-ee-**dahl**-nośhćh] f. occurrence of two sets of chromosomes in nucleus of somatic cells in two species
amfisben [ahm-**fees**-ben] m. amphisbaena lizard
amfiteatr [ahm-fee-**te**-ahtr] m. amphitheater; rising gallery
amfiteatralnie [ahm-fee-te-ah-**trahl**-ńe] adv. amphitheatrically; with rising rows of seats; in rising tiers
amfiteatralność [ahm-fee-te-ah-**trahl**-nośhćh] f. amphitheatrical character
amfiteatralny [ahm-fee-te-ah-**trahl**-ni] adj.m. amphitheatrical
amfitrion [ahm-**fee**-tryon] m. Amphitryon; host; entertainer
amfolit [ahm-**fo**-leet] m. ampholyte
amfora [ahm-**fo**-rah] f. amphora; amphorae
amforyczny [ahm-fo-**rich**-ni] adj.m. of amphora
amfoteryczność [ahm-fo-te-**rich**-nośhćh] f. amphoteric character
amfoteryczny [ahm-fo-te-**rich**-ni] adj.m. amphoteric
amia [**ah**-myah] f. bowfin fish
amid [**ah**-meet] m. amide
amidaza [ah-mee-**dah**-zah] f. amidase
amidowy [ah-mee-**do**-vi] adj.m. amide (compound, etc.); amidic; amic
amigdalina [ah-meeg-dah-**lee**-nah] f. amygdaline; almond kernel taste and aroma component
amimia [ah-**mee**-myah] f. amimia; loss of ability to communicate with gestures and facial expressions
amina [ah-**mee**-nah] f. amine
aminek [ah-**mee**-nek] m. herb of the genus Ammi
aminobenzen [ah-mee-no-**ben**-zen] m. aniline; aniline oil
aminobenzoesowy [ah-mee-no-ben-zo-e-**so**-vi] adj.m. aminobenzoic (acid)
aminocukier [ah-mee-no-**tsoo**-k̲er] m. amino-sugar
aminokwas [ah-mee-**no**-kfahs] m. amino acid
aminoplast [ah-mee-**no**-plahst] m. light color plastic
aminować [ah-mee-**no**-vahćh] v. introduce amino acid into organic compounds (*repeatedly*)
aminowanie [ah-mee-no-**vah**-ńe] n. introduction of amino acid into organic compounds
aminowy [ah-mee-**no**-vi] adj.m. aminic; of the amino group
aminotrofia [ah-mee-no-**tro**-fyah] f. muscular atrophy
amitotycznie [ah-mee-to-**tich**-ńe] adv. amitotically
amitotyczny [ah-mee-to-**tich**-ni] adj.m. amitotic
amitoza [ah-mee-**to**-zah] f. amitosis
amnestia [ahm-**ne**-styah] f. amnesty; act of pardon; act of oblivion
amnestionować [ahm-ne-styo-**no**-

vahćh] v. amnesty; grant amnesty; give amnesty (*repeatedly*)
amnestionowanie [ahm-ne-styo-no-**vah**-ńe] n. granting amnesty; giving amnesty
amnestiować [ahm-ne-**styo**-vahćh] v. amnesty; grant amnesty; give amnesty (*repeatedly*)
amnestiowanie [ahm-ne-styo-**vah**-ńe] n. granting amnesty; giving amnesty
amnestyczny [ahm-ne-**stich**-ni] adj.m. of amnesty; of pardon
amnestyjny [ahm-ne-**stiy**-ni] adj.m. of amnesty; of pardon; of oblivion
amnezja [ahm-**ne**-zyah] f. amnesia; loss of memory
amnezyjny [ahm-ne-**ziy**-ni] adj.m. amnesic; amnestic
amok [**ah**-mok] m. amok; murderous frenzy
amon [**ah**-mon] m. (chem.) ammonium
amonal [ah-**mo**-nahl] m. ammonal
amonek [ah-**mo**-nek] m. amomum
amoniak [ah-**mo**-ńyahk] m. (chem.) ammonia
amoniakalnia [ah-mo-ńyah-**kahl**-ńah] f. ammonia plant
amoniakalny [ah-mo-ńyah-**kahl**-ni] adj.m. ammonia (water, etc.); ammoniacal
amoniakat [ah-mo-**ńyah**-kaht] m. (chem.) ammonia salt
amoniakować [ah-mo-ńyah-**ko**-vahćh] v. purify water with ammonia (ammonia salt) (*repeatedly*)
amoniakowanie [ah-mo-ńyah-ko-**vah**-ńe] n. water purification with ammonia (ammonia salt)
amoniakownia [ah-mo-ńyah-**kov**-ńah] f. ammonia refining plant (from cocking gas)
amonifikacja [ah-mo-ńee-fee-**kah**-tsyah] f. ammonification
amonit [ah-**mo**-ńeet] m. ammonite (explosive); shell of cephalopods Ammonidea
amonitowy [ah-mo-ńee-**to**-vi] adj.m. ammonitic
amonowy [ah-mo-**no**-vi] adj.m. ammonium (sulfate, etc.)
amor [**ah**-mor] m. Cupid; Amor
jego amory z nią [**ye**-go ah-**mo**-ri z ńown] exp.: his courtship to her; his courting her; his liaison with her
amoralista [ah-mo-rah-**lee**-stah] m. advocate of amorality
amoralizm [ah-mo-**rah**-leezm] m. amoralism; amorality; lack of morality
amoralność [ah-mo-**rahl**-nośhćh] f. amorality; lack of morality
amoralny [ah-mo-**rahl**-ni] adj.m. amoral; non-moral
amorek [ah-**mo**-rek] m. cupid
amorficzność [ah-mor-**feech**-nośhćh] f. amorphism; formlessness
amorficzny [ah-mor-**feech**-ni] adj.m. amorphous; uncrystallized; formless
amorfizm [ah-**mor**-feezm] m. amorphism; formlessness
amorka [ah-**mor**-kah] f. a variety of viola
amorowy [ah-mo-**ro**-vi] adj.m. colloq: erotic; of love
amortyzacja [ah-mor-ti-**zah**-tsyah] f. depreciation; amortization; shock absorption; shock absorbing
amortyzacyjny [ah-mor-ti-zah-**tsiy**-ni] adj.m. sinking (fund); shock-absorbing (device)
amortyzator [ah-mor-ti-**zah**-tor] m. shock-absorber; damper
amortyzować [ah-mor-ti-**zo**-vahćh] v. amortize; sink; absorb (shocks, etc.); extinguish; damp; deaden; break a fall (*repeatedly*)
amortyzować się [ah-mor-ti-**zo**-vahćh śhan] v. become amortized; be paid off; be redeemed; be extinguished (*repeatedly*)
amortyzowanie się [ah-mor-ti-zo-**vah**-ńe śhan] n. becoming amortized; being paid off
amory [ah-**mo**-ri] pl. flirtation; courting; love affairs
ampeks [**ahm**-peks] m. sound and picture recording device
ampeksowy [ahm-pek-**so**-vi] adj.m. (tape) of sound and picture recording device

amper [ahm-per] m. ampere; amp
amperogodzina [ahm-pe-ro-go-**dźhee**-nah] f. ampere-hour
amperomierz [ahm-pe-**ro**-myesh] m. ammeter; meter of amperes; amperemeter
amperosekunda [ahm-pe-ro-se-**koon**-dah] f. ampere-second
amperozwój [ahm-**pe**-ro-zvooy] m. ampere turn
ampla [**ahm**-plah] f. indirect-light lamp
amplidyna [ahm-plee-**di**-nah] f. direct-current amplifying generator
amplifikacja [ahm-plee-fee-**kah**-tsyah] f. amplification; exaggeration
amplifikator [ahm-plee-fee-**kah**-tor] m. amplifier; intensifier
amplifikatornia [ahm-plee-fee-kah-**tor**-ńah] f. (radio, etc.) control-room
amplifikować [ahm-plee-fee-**ko**-vahćh] v. amplify; magnify; enlarge; intensify; exaggerate (*repeatedly*)
amplifikowanie [ahm-plee-fee-ko-**vah**-ńe] n. amplification
amplituda [ahm-plee-**too**-dah] f. amplitude; swing (of a pendulum)
ampuła [ahm-**poo**-wah] f. big ampoule; large ampul; a large glass container for one dose of...
ampułka [ahm-**poow**-kah] f. ampoule; ampul; a small sealed strilized glass container (for an injection) for one dose of ...
amputacja [ahm-poo-**tah**-tsyah] f. amputation
amputacyjny [ahm-poo-tah-**tsiy**-ni] adj.m. of amputation
amputować [ahm-poo-**to**-vahćh] v. amputate; to cut off (*repeatedly*)
amputowanie [ahm-poo-to-**vah**-ńe] n. amputation
amulet [ah-**moo**-let] m. amulet; talisman; charm
amunicja [ah-moo-**ńee**-tsyah] f. ammunition; munition; munitions
amunicyjny [ah-moo-ńee-**tsiy**-ni] adj.m. ammunition (box, etc.); munition (worker); m. munition carrier
amur [**ah**-moor] m. variety of carp fish
amurski [ah-**moor**-skee] adj.m. Amur (phellodendron, cork tree, etc.)
amuzja [ah-**moo**-zyah] f. amusia; loss of ability to follow and appreciate music
amylaza [ah-mi-**lah**-zah] f. amylase
an- [ahn] prefix : a-; an-; not-
anabaptysta [ah-nah-bahp-**tis**-tah] m. anabaptist; dipper
anabaptyzm [ah-nah-**bahp**-tizm] m. anabaptism
anabena [ah-nah-**be**-nah] f. Anabaena algae
anabiotyczny [ah-nah-byo-**tich**-ni] adj.m. anabiotic
anabioza [ah-nah-**byo**-zah] f. anabiosis; resuscitation
anaboliczny [ah-nah-bo-**leech**-ni] adj.m. of anabolism; anabolic
anbolik [ah-nah-**bo**-leek] m. anabolic
anabolizm [ah-nah-**bo**-leezm] m. anabolism; constructive metabolism
anachoreta [ah-nah-kho-**re**-tah] m. hermit; anchoret; anchorite
anachoretka [ah-nah-kho-**re**-tkah] f. (woman) hermit; anchoret; anchorite
anachoretyzm [ah-nah-kho-**re**-tizm] m. anchoretism; anchoritism; anchoritic mode of life
anachronicznie [ah-nah-khro-**ńeech**-ńe] adv. anachronistically; anachronously; in an out-of-date manner
anachroniczność [ah-nah-khro-**ńeech**-nośhćh] f. anachronism
anachroniczny [ah-nah-khro-**ńeech**-ni] adj.m. anachronistical; anachronic; anachronistic; anachronous; out of date; outdated; out of its proper historical time
anachronizm [ah-nah-**khro**-ńeezm] m. anachronism
anadiploza [ah-nah-dee-**plo**-zah] f. anadiplosis
anadromiczny [ah-nah-dro-**meech**-ni] adj.m. anadromous
anaerob [ah-nah-e-rop] m. anaerobe
anaerobiont [ah-nah-e-**ro**-byont] m. anaerobe

anaerobioza [ah-nah-e-ro-**byo**-zah] f. anaerobiosis
anaerobowo [ah-nah-e-ro-**bo**-vo] adv. anaerobically
anaerobowy [ah-nah-e-ro-**bo**-vi] adj.m. anaerobic
anafilaksja [ah-nah-fee-**lah**-ksyah] f. excessive susceptibility; anaphylaxis
anafilaktyczny [ah-nah-fee-lahk-**tich**-ni] adj.m. excessively susceptible; anaphylactic
anafora [ah-nah-**fo**-rah] f. anaphora
anaforeza [ah-nah-fo-**re**-zah] f. movement of negative particles towards the positive electrode
anaforyczny [ah-nah-fo-**rich**-ni] adj.m. of the movement of negative particles towards the positive electrode
anaglif [ah-**nah**-gleef] m. stereoscopic picture
anagnoryzm [ah-nah-**gno**-rizm] m. anagnorisis
anagram [ah-**nah**-grahm] m. anagram; change by transposition of letters
anagramowo [ah-nah-grah-**mo**-vo] adv. anagrammatically
anagramowy [ah-nah-grah-**mo**-vi] adj.m. anagrammatical; anagrammatic
anakolut [ah-nah-**ko**-loot] m. anacoluthon; syntactical inconsistency
anakolutycznie [ah-nah-ko-loo-**tich**-ńe] adv. anacoluthically; with syntactical inconsistency
anakolutyczny [ah-nah-ko-loo-**tich**-ni] adj.m. anacoluthic; syntactically inconsistent
anakonda [ah-nah-**kon**-dah] f. anaconda
anakreontyczny [ah-nah-kre-on-**tich**-ni] adj.m. anacreontic (poem, drinking song, etc.)
anakreontyk [ah-nah-kre-**on**-tik] m. anacreontic verse
anakruza [ah-nah-**kroo**-zah] f. anacrusis; light lyric music
analekta [ah-nah-**lek**-tah] f. analecta; literary gleanings
analeptyk [ah-nah-**lep**-tik] m. analeptic
analfabeta [ah-nahl-fah-**be**-tah] m. illiterate; an ignorant
analfabetka [ah-nahl-fah-**bet**-kah] f. (woman) illiterate; an ignorant
analfabetyczny [ah-nahl-fah-be-**tich**-ni] adj.m. analphabetic
analfabetyzm [ah-nahl-fah-**be**-tizm] m. illiteracy; complete ignorance
analgetyczny [ah-nahl-ge-**tich**-ni] adj.m. analgetic; analgesic
analgetyk [ah-nahl-**ge**-tik] m. analgetic
analgezja [ah-nahl-**ge**-zyah] f. analgesia; analgia; analgesis; absence of sensibility to pain
analitycznie [ah-nah-lee-**tich**-ńe] adv. analytically
analityczny [ah-nah-lee-**tich**-ni] adj.m. analytical; analytic; of analysis
analityk [ah-nah-**lee**-tik] m. analyst
analityka [ah-nah-**lee**-ti-kah] f. analytics
analiza [ah-nah-**lee**-zah] f. analysis; parsing; analysis of a sentence; detailed examination (by parts) of something
analizator [ah-nah-lee-**zah**-tor] m. analyzer
analizować [ah-nah-lee-**zo**-vahćh] v. analyze; resolve (into constituent parts, elements, etc.); anatomize; parse (into parts of speech) (*repeatedly*)
analizowanie [ah-nah-lee-zo-**vah**-ńe] n. analysis; resolution (into constituent parts, elements, etc.)
analny [ah-**nahl**-ni] adj.m. anal; of the anus; near the anus
analog [ah-**nah**-log] m. analogue; (a) parallel; analog computer; analogist
analogia [ah-nah-**lo**-gyah] f. analogy; parallelism; parallel; parity; similarity in some way; analogue; likness in some way
przez analogię [pshes ah-nah-**lo**-gyan] exp.: by (way of) analogy
przeprowadzić analogię [pshe-pro-**vah**-dźheećh ah-nah-**lo**-gyan] exp.: to analogize
analogicznie [ah-nah-lo-**geech**-ńe] adv. analogically
analogiczność [ah-nah-lo-**geech**-

nośhćh] f. analogy; similarity in some way; parallelism; parity
analogiczny [ah-nah-lo-**geech**-ni] adj.m. analogous; similar in some way; analogical; analogic; parallel; based on analogy; implying analogy; analogistic
analogizm [ah-nah-**lo**-geezm] m. analogism
analogizować [ah-nah-lo-gee-**zo**-vahćh] v. analogize; reason by analogy (*repeatedly*)
analogizowanie [ah-nah-lo-gee-zo-**vah**-ńe] n. reasoning by analogy
analogon [ah-nah-**lo**-gon] m. analogue; analogon; (a) parallel
analogowy [ah-nah-lo-**go**-vi] adj.m. analog (computer, etc.)
anamnestyczny [ah-nahm-ne-**stich**-ni] adj.m. anamnestic (discussion of medical history, etc.)
anamneza [ah-nahm-**ne**-zah] f. anamnesis; recollection
anamorfoza [ah-nah-mor-**fo**-zah] f. anamorphosis
ananas [ah-**nah**-nahs] m. pineapple; rascal; rogue; blighter; trouble maker
ananasarnia [ah-nah-nah-**sahr**-ńah] f. pinery; pineapple plantation
ananasowaty [ah-nah-nah-so-**vah**-ti] adj.m. of the pineapple family
ananasowy [ah-nah-nah-**so**-vi] adj.m. pineapple (shrub, oil, etc.)
ananasówka [ah-nah-nah-**soof**-kah] f. pineapple-flavored vodka
ananim [ah-**nah**-ńeem] m. ananym; pseudonym consisting of real name written backwards
ananke [ah-**nahn**-ke] n. fate; destiny
anapest [ah-**nah**-pest] m. anapest
anapestyczny [ah-nah-pes-**tich**-ni] adj.m. anapestic
anarchia [ah-**nahr**-khyah] f. anarchy; lawlessness; confusion; political disorder and violence; the absence or failure of government
anarchicznie [ah-nahr-**kheech**-ńe] adv. anarchically
anarchiczny [ah-nahr-**kheech**-ni] adj.m. anarchic(al); lawless
anarchista [ah-nahr-**khees**-tah] m. anarchist; undisciplined person; a person who believes that governments are unnecessary or undesirable
anarchistka [ah-nahr-**khee**-stkah] f. (woman) anarchist; undisciplined person; a person who believes that governments are unnecessary or undesirable
anarchistyczny [ah-nahr-khee-**stich**-ni] adj.m. anarchistic; anarchist
anarchizacja [ah-nahr-khee-**zah**-tsyah] f. advocacy of anarchy; causing of anarchy; anarchism
anarchizm [ah-**nahr**-kheezm] m. anarchism
anarchizować [ah-nahr-khee-**zo**-vahćh] v. make anarchistic; promote anarchy; cause anarchy; anarchize; reduce to anarchy (*repeatedly*)
anarchizować się [ah-nahr-khee-**zo**-vahćh śh<u>an</u>] v. abandon oneself to anarchy; abandon oneself to lawlessness (*repeatedly*)
anastatyczny [ah-nah-stah-**tich**-ni] adj.m. anastatic
anastrofa [ah-nah-**stro**-fah] f. anastrophe
anastygmat [ah-nah-**stig**-maht] m. anastigmat; anastigmatic lens
anatema [ah-nah-**te**-mah] f. anathema; curse
anatoksyna [ah-nah-tok-**si**-nah] f. anatoxin; a toxoid
anatolijski [ah-nah-to-**leey**-skee] adj.m. of Anatolia
anatom [ah-**nah**-tom] m. anatomist; a person who specializes in the structure of organisms of plants and animals
anatomia [ah-nah-**to**-myah] f. anatomy; science of the structure of organisms of plants and animals; any analysis (of a crime, scheme, etc.)
anatomicznie [ah-nah-to-**meech**-ńe] adv. anatomically; with respect to anatomy
anatomiczny [ah-nah-to-**meech**-ni] adj.m. anatomical; of anatomy
model anatomiczny [mo-del ah-nah-to-**meech**-ni] exp.: manikin
anatomik [ah-nah-**to**-meek] m. anatomist
anatomista [ah-nah-to-**mee**-stah] m.

anatomist
anatomizować [ah-nah-to-mee-**zo**-vahćh] v. anatomize (*repeatedly*)
anatomopatolog [ah-nah-to-mo-pah-**to**-log] m. anatomicopathologist
anatomopatologiczny [ah-nah-to-mo-pah-to-lo-**geech**-ni] adj.m. anatomicopathologic
ancestralny [ahn-tse-**strahl**-ni] adj.m. ancestral
anchois [ahn-**shwah**] n. can of anchovies
ancymonek [ahn-tsi-**mo**-nek] m. colloq: slyboots; artful kid
andabata [ahn-dah-**bah**-tah] m. andabata (in Rome)
andaluzyjski [ahn-dah-loo-**ziy**-skee] adj.m. Andalusian; of Andalusia
andaluzyt [ahn-dah-**loo**-zit] m. andalusite (mineral)
andante [ahn-**dahn**-te] n. andante (music)
andantino [ahn-dahn-**tee**-no] n. andantino (music)
andegaweński [ahn-de-gah-**veń**-skee] adj.m. Andegavin; Andegavine; of Anjou
andezyn [ahn-**de**-zin] m. andesin (mineral)
andezyt [ahn-**de**-zit] m. andesite (mineral)
andradyt [ahn-**drah**-dit] m. andradite (mineral)
andragogika [ahn-drah-**go**-gee-kah] f. education of grownups
androdiecja [ahn-dro-**dye**-tsyah] f. androdioecism
androfobia [ahn-dro-**fo**-byah] f. homophobia; phobia of men
androgen [ahn-**dro**-gen] m. androgen; male sex hormone
androgenny [ahn-dro-**gen**-ni] adj.m. androgenic
androginia [ahn-dro-**gee**-ńyah] f. androgynism; hermaphroditism
android [ahn-**dro**-eet] m. android; automaton of human form
androlog [ahn-**dro**-log] m. medical specialist of male sex organs
andrologia [ahn-dro-**lo**-gyah] f. andrology; science of male sex hormons and related problems
andrologiczny [ahn-dro-lo-**geech**-ni] adj.m. andrologic; of andrology
androny [ahn-**dro**-ni] pl. foolish talk; nonsense; bosh; poppycock
pleść androny [pleśhćh ahn-**dro**-ni] exp.: to talk nonsense; to talk through one's hat
andrus [**ahn**-droos] m. rough kid; a mischievous boy; street-boy; urchin
andrusowato [ahn-droo-so-**vah**-to] adv. roguishly; prankishly; in prankish manner; with pranks
andrusowaty [ahn-droo-so-**vah**-ti] adj.m. roguish; prankish; full of pranks
andrusowski [ahn-droo-**sof**-skee] adj.m. roguish; prankish; full of pranks
andrut [**ahn**-droot] m. wafer; gofer
andrzejki [ahn-**dzhey**-kee] pl. St. Andrew's night party and horoscopes
andrzejkowy [ahn-dzhey-**ko**-vi] adj.m. of St. Andrew's night party and horoscopes
andynista [ahn-di-**ńee**-stah] m. Andean mountain climber
andynizm [ahn-**di**-ńeezm] m. Andean mountain climbing
anegdociarstwo [ah-ne-gdo-**ćhahr**-stfo] m. story-telling; anecdotage
anegdociarz [ah-ne-**gdo**-ćhahsh] m. story-teller; anecdotist
anegdota [ah-ne-**gdo**-tah] f. anecdote; a story; theme; subject matter (of a book, etc.); yarn
anegdotka [ah-ne-**gdo**-tkah] f. a short amusing story (about celebrities, etc.)
anegdotycznie [ah-ne-gdo-**tich**-ńe] adv. anecdotically; with the use of anecdotic (usually undocumented) material
anegdotyczny [ah-ne-gdo-**tich**-ni] adj.m. anecdotic; anecdotal; thematic; pertaining to the theme or subject matter; imaginary; fabulous
anegdotyzm [ah-ne-**gdo**-tizm] m. anecdotic nature; anecdotal character
aneks [**ah**-neks] m. annex; appendix; a section, usually containing extra information added at the end of a book or

document; a wing added to a building; something annexed, esp. to a building
aneksja [ah-**ne**-ksyah] f. annexation; incorporation into a state a territory of another state (usually associated with an aggression against a country)
aneksjonista [ah-ne-ksyo-**ńee**-stah] m. annexationist; politician favoring annexation
aneksjonistyczny [ah-ne-ksyo-ńee-**stich**-ni] adj.m. annexational
aneksjonizm [ah-ne-**ksyo**-ńeezm] m. policy of annexation
aneksyjny [ah-ne-**ksiy**-ni] adj.m. annexational; annexive
anektować [ah-nek-**to**-vahćh] v. annex; attach esp. to something larger; incorporate into a state (usually by force) the territory of another state (*repeatedly*)
anektowanie [ah-nek-to-**vah**-ńe] n. annexation
anekumena [ah-ne-koo-**me**-nah] f. land not inhabited permanently and not used economically
anemia [ah-**ne**-myah] f. anaemia; a medical condition caused by not having enough red cells in the blood
anemiczka [ah-ne-**meech**-kah] f. anaemic female
anemicznie [ah-ne-**meech**-ńe] adv. weakly; faintly; feebly
anemiczny [ah-ne-**meech**-ni] adj.m. anaemic; suffering from anaemia; weak; faint; feeble; pale; lacking hemoglobin
anemik [ah-**ne**-meek] m. anaemic male
anemizować [ah-ne-mee-**zo**-vahćh] v. exsanguinate (*repeatedly*)
anemochor [ah-ne-**mo**-khor] m. plant depending on wind fertilization
anemochoria [ah-ne-mo-**khor**-yah] f. wind fertilization
anemochoryczny [ah-ne-mo-kho-**rich**-ni] adj.m. of wind fertilization
anemogam [ah-ne-**mo**-gahm] m. plant pollinated by wind
anemogamia [ah-ne-mo-**gah**-myah] f. plant pollination by wind
anemogamiczny [ah-ne-mo-gah-**meech**-ni] adj.m. of pollination by wind
anemograf [ah-ne-**mo**-grahf] m. recording anemometer
anemometr [ah-ne-**mo**-metr] m. anemometer
anemon [ah-**ne**-mon] m. anemone; wind-flower
anemonowy [ah-ne-mo-**no**-vi] adj.m. anemone (flower, etc.)
anemoplankton [ah-ne-mo-**plahnk**-ton] m. plankton carried by wind
anemoskop [ah-ne-**mo**-skop] m. anemoscope
anepigraf [ah-ne-**pee**-grahf] m. anepigraphic work; literary work without title
anergia [ah-**ner**-gyah] f. anergy; anergia; lack of energy
aneroid [ah-ne-**ro**-eet] m. aneroid barometer (bending of a thin plate instead of rise and fall of mercury)
aneroidowy [ah-ne-roy-**do**-vi] adj.m. aneroid (barometer, etc.)
anestetycznie [ah-ne-ste-**tich**-ńe] adv. under anaesthesia
anestetyczny [ah-ne-ste-**tich**-ni] adj.m. anaesthetic (used in surgery, causing a lack of feeling in a part of the body or unconsciousness); insensible
anestetyk [ah-ne-**ste**-tik] m. a drug causing a loss of feeling or unconsciousness; anaesthetic
anestetyka [ah-ne-**ste**-ti-kah] f. anesthetics
anestetysta [ah-ne-ste-**tis**-tah] m. anesthetist
anestezja [ah-ne-**ste**-zyah] f. a loss of consciousness or of feeling caused by an anaesthetic; anaesthesia
anestezja miejscowa [ah-ne-**ste**-zyah myeys-**tso**-vah] exp.: local anaesthesia
anestezja ogólna [ah-ne-**ste**-zyah o-**gool**-nah] exp.: general anaesthesia
poddawać anestezji [pod-**dah**-vahćh ah-ne-**ste**-zyee] exp.: to anaesthetize; to subject to anaesthesia
anestezjolog [ah-ne-ste-**zyo**-log] m.

anaesthetist; anesthesiologist; a physician responsible for giving anaesthesia during surgery
anestezjologia [ah-ne-ste-zyo-**lo**-gyah] f. anesthesiology (the science)
anestezjologicznie [ah-ne-ste-zyo-lo-**geech**-ńe] adv. anesthetically
anestezjologiczny [ah-ne-ste-zyo-lo-**geech**-ni] adj.m. anaesthetic
anestezyjny [ah-ne-ste-**ziy**-ni] adj.m. (local) anaesthetic
anestezyna [ah-ne-ste-**zi**-nah] f. anaesthetic
anewryzm [ah-**ne**-vrizm] m. aneurism; aneurysm
anfelcja [ahn-**fel**-tsyah] f. cartilaginous red algae
angaria [ahn-**gahr**-yah] f. angary; seizure of property of neutrals
angaż [**ahn**-gahsh] m. work-contract (of an actor, etc.)
angażować [ahn-gah-**zho**-vahćh] v. engage; undertake; hire; bind; pledge oneself; bind by a promise of marriage; employ; involve; occupy with; attract and hold attention; enter into (conflict, conversation, etc.); book (an actor); entangle; give employment; give job (*repeatedly*)
angażować się [ahn-gah-**zho**-vahćh śhan] v. engage oneself (to do); take employment; take a job; commit oneself; get involved; become entangled; embark upon (an enterprise, etc.) (*repeatedly*)
angażowanie [ahn-gah-zho-**vah**-ńe] n. engaging or being engaged; engagement
angażowanie się [ahn-gah-zho-**vah**-ńe śhan] n. commitment; engaging oneself (also in a conflict); taking employment
angelologia [ahn-ge-lo-**lo**-gyah] f. theology of angels; colloq: unreality; daydreaming
Angielka [ahn-**gel**-kah] f. English woman; mare of English breed; wine glass; a type of kitchen stove; variety of wheat
młoda Angielka [**mwo**-dah ahn-**gel**-kah] exp.: young English woman; English girl
angielski [ahn-**gel**-skee] adj.m. English; English language
angielska choroba [ahn-**gel**-skah kho-**ro**-bah] exp.: rickets; rachitis see: **krzywica** [kshi-**vee**-tsah]
angielska flegma [ahn-**gel**-skah **fleg**-mah] exp.: coolness; stolidity; imperturbability; impassivity; un-excitability
angielski pieprz [ahn-**gel**-skee pyepsh] exp.: pimento; green pepper
mówić po angielsku [moo-veećh po ahn-**gel**-skoo] exp.: to speak English
mówić z angielska [**moo**-veećh z ahn-**gel**-skah] exp.: speak with an English accent
po angielsku [po ahn-**gel**-skoo] exp.: in English
ulotnić się po angielsku [oo-**lot**-ńeećh śhan po ahn-**gel**-skoo] exp.: to take a French leave (without saying goodbye)
angielszczyć [ahn-**gel**-shchićh] v. Anglicize (*repeatedly*)
angielszczyć się [ahn-**gel**-shchićh śhan] v. become Anglicized (*repeatedly*)
angielszczyzna [ahn-gel-**shchiz**-nah] f. English language; English; things English; English way of life
angielszczyzna żargonowa [ahn-gel-**shchiz**-nah zhahr-go-**no**-vah] exp.: pidgin English
łamana angielszczyzna [wah-**mah**-nah ahn-gel-**shchiz**-nah] exp.: broken English
poprawna angielszczyzna [po-**prahv**-nah ahn-gel-**shchiz**-nah] exp.: correct English
angina [ahn-**gee**-nah] f. angina; quinsy; inflammation of the throat
angiochirurgia [ahn-gyo-khee-**roor**-gyah] f. vascular surgery
angiografia [ahn-gyo-**grah**-fyah] f. angiography
angiocardiografia [ahn-gyo-kahr-dyo-**grah**-fyah] f. angiocardiography
angiologia [ahn-gyo-**lo**-gyah] f. angiology; study of blood vessels and lymph
anglez [**ahn**-gles] m. a lively dance; frock-coat; ringlet; curl; English

type (printed letters)
anglezować [ahn-gle-**zo**-vahćh] v. Anglicize; dock a horses tail and hog its mane; post in rhythm with horse's trot (*repeatedly*)
anglezowanie [ahn-gle-zo-**vah**-ńe] n. posting in rhythm with horse's trot
anglezyt [ahn-**gle**-zit] m. anglesite (mineral)
Anglia [**ahn**-glyah] f. England
anglicyzm [ahn-**glee**-tsizm] m. Anglicism; Briticism
Anglik [**ahn**-gleek] m. Englishman; Britisher; Briton
młody Anglik [**mwo**-di **ahn**-gleek] exp.: an English boy; young Englishman
anglikanin [ahn-glee-**kah**-ńeen] m. Anglican; adherent of the Church of England
anglikański [ahn-glee-**kahń**-skee] adj.m. Anglican
kościół anglikański [**kośh**-ćhoow ahn-glee-**kahń**-skee] exp.: Church of England
anglista [ahn-**glee**-stah] m. student of English; Anglicist; student of English philology
anglistyka [ahn-**glee**-sti-kah] f. English studies; English philology
anglizować [ahn-glee-**zo**-vahćh] v. post in the rhythm of the trot of a horse (*repeatedly*)
anglizowanie [ahn-glee-zo-**vah**-ńe] n. posting in rhythm with horse's trot
Anglo-Amerykanin [**ahn**-glo ah-me-ri-**kah**-ńeen] m. Anglo-American; an American of English birth or ancestry
anglo-amerykański [ahn-glo ah-me-ri-**kahń**-skee] adj.m. Anglo-American (relations, etc.)
angloarab [ahn-glo-**ah**-rahb] m. horse of anglo-arab breed
anglofil [ahn-**glo**-feel] m. Anglophile; an admirer of the English way of life; an admirer of things English
anglofilizm [ahn-glo-**fee**-leezm] m. anglophile attitude
anglofilstwo [ahn-glo-**feel**-stfo] n. anglophile attitude
anglofob [ahn-**glo**-fop] m. anglophobe
anglofobia [ahn-glo-**fo**-byah] f. anglophobia
anglojęzyczny [ahn-glo-y<u>an</u>-**zich**-ni] adj.m. English-language (press, etc.); English-speaking (people, persons, etc.)
angloman [ahn-**glo**-mahn] m. Anglomaniac
anglomania [ahn-glo-**mah**-ńyah] f. Anglomania
anglosaksoński [ahn-glo-sahk-**soń**-skee] adj.m. Anglo-Saxon
Anglosas [ahn-**glo**-sahs] m. Anglo-Saxon
anglosaski [ahn-glo-**sah**-skee] adj.m. Anglo-Saxon
angoba [ahn-**go**-bah] f. high quality clay
Angola [ahn-**go**-lah] f. Angola
Angora [ahn-**go**-rah] f. Angora; former name for Ankara
angora [ahn-**go**-rah] f. angora cat (goat, rabbit, sheep); angora wool
angorski [ahn-**gor**-skee] adj.m. angora (cat, goat, sheep, wool)
angoryzm [ahn-**go**-rizm] m. angora-hair characteristics
angstrem [**ahng**-strem] m. angstrom
anheliczny [ahn-khe-**leech**-ni] adj.m. good-natured; self-sacrificing
anhelliczny [ahn-khel-**leech**-ni] adj.m. good-natured; self-sacrificing
anhydryt [ahn-**khi**-drit] m. anhydrite (mineral)
anhydrytowy [ahn-khi-dri-**to**-vi] adj.m. anhydrite (cement, etc.)
ani [ah-ńee] conj. neither; nor; not; not even; not as much; or
ani nawet [**ah**-ńee **nah**-vet] exp.: not even
ani razu [ah-ńee **rah**-zoo] exp.: not even once; not even one time
ani to, ani tamto [**ah**-ńee to **ah**-ńee **tahm**-to] exp.: neither this nor that
ani więcej, ani mniej [**ah**-ńee **vy<u>an</u>**-tsey **ah**-ńee mńey] exp.: neither more nor less
ani żywej duszy [**ah**-ńee **zhi**-vey **doo**-shi] exp.: not a living soul
ani jeden człowiek nie widział [**ah**-ńee **ye**-den **chwo**-vyek ńe **vee**-dźhahw] exp.: not a man saw

(something or somebody)
ani mi się śni [ah-ńee mee śh<u>an</u> śhńee] exp.: never in my life
ani mi się waż! [ah-ńee mee śh<u>an</u> vahsh] exp.: don't you dare!
ani się (nie) umywa [ah-ńee śh<u>an</u> ńe oo-**mi**-vah] exp.: nowhere near; totally unlike
anielica [ah-ńe-**lee**-tsah] f. (female) angel; an angelic woman
anielski [ah-**ńel**-skee] adj.m. angelic; cherubic; angelical
anielsko [ah-**ńel**-sko] adv. angelically; like an angel
anielskość [ah-**ńel**-skośhćh] f. angelic sweetness
anihilacja [ah-ńee-khee-**lah**-tsyah] f. annihilation
anihilacyjny [ah-ńee-khee-lah-**tsiy**-ni] adj.m. annihilative; annihilatory
anilana [ah-ńee-**lah**-nah] f. variety of synthetic fiber
anilanowy [ah-ńee-lah-**no**-vi] adj.m. synthetic fiber (sweater, etc.)
anilina [ah-ńee-**lee**-nah] f. aniline
anilinowy [ah-ńee-lee-**no**-vi] adj.m. aniline (toxin, dye, etc.)
animacja [ah-ńee-**mah**-tsyah] f. animation
animacyjny [ah-ńee-mah-**tsiy**-ni] adj.m. animation (technique, training, etc.)
animadwersja [ah-ńe-mahd-**ver**-syah] f. animadversion; remonstrance; censure
animalistyczny [ah-ńe-mah-lee-**stich**-ni] adj.m. animalistic; like an animal
animalistyka [ah-ńe-mah-**lee**-sti-kah] f. animal themes in art
animalizm [ah-ńe-**mah**-leezm] m. animalism
animalny [ah-ńee-**mahl**-ni] adj.m. animalistic
animator [ah-ńee-**mah**-tor] m. animator
animatorka [ah-ńee-mah-**tor**-kah] f. (female) animator
animista [ah-ńee-**mee**-stah] m. animist
animistycznie [ah-ńee-mee-**stich**-ńe] adv. in animistic manner
animistyczny [ah-ńee-mee-**stich**-ni] adj.m. animistic
animizacja [ah-ńee-mee-**zah**-tsyah] f. animism
animizm [ah-**ńee**-meezm] m. animism
animizować [ah-ńee-mee-**zo**-vahćh] v. attribute conscious life to nature or natural objects (*repeatedly*)
animizowanie [ah-ńee-mee-zo-**vah**-ńe] n. attribution of conscious life to nature or natural objects
animować [ah-ńee-**mo**-vahćh] v. animate; stimulate; enliven (*repeatedly*)
animować się [ah-ńee-**mo**-vahćh śh<u>an</u>] v. become animated; grow stimulated (*repeatedly*)
animowanie się [ah-ńee-mo-**vah**-ńe śh<u>an</u>] n. becoming animated
animowany [ah-ńee-mo-**vah**-ni] adj.m. animated; stimulated
animozja [ah-ńee-**mo**-zyah] f. animosity; feeling of strong dislike; hatred; hostility; rancor; ill blood; ill will; ill-feeling
animusz [ah-**ńee**-moosh] m. courage; verve; vigor; zest; spirit; high spirits; keenness; gusto; pep
anioł [**ah**-ńow] m. angel
aniołeczek [ah-ńo-**we**-chek] m. cherub; little angel; little darling
aniołek [ah-**ńo**-wek] m. cherub; little angel; darling
aniołkowaty [ah-ńow-ko-**vah**-ti] m. like a cherub; like an angel
anion [**ah**-ńyon] m. anion
anionit [ah-**ńyo**-ńeet] m. anionic compound
anionowy [ah-ńyo-**no**-vi] adj.m. anionic
aniwersarz [ah-ńee-**ver**-sahsh] m. anniversary
anizogameta [ah-ńee-zo-gah-**me**-tah] f. anisogamete
anizogamia [ah-ńee-zo-**gah**-myah] f. anisogamy
anizotropia [ah-ńee-zo-**tro**-pyah] f. anisotropy; anisotropism
anizotropowo [ah-ńee-zo-tro-**po**-vo] adv. anisotropically
anizotropowy [ah-ńee-zo-tro-**po**-vi] adj.m. anisotropic
aniżeli [ah-ńee-**zhe**-lee] part.: rather;

then; rather then
inaczej aniżeli [ee-nah-chey ah-ńee-zhe-lee] exp.: otherwise than; differently from
inny aniżeli [een-ni ah-ńee-zhe-lee] exp.: other than; different from
wolę "A" aniżeli "B" [vo-lan ah ah-ńee-zhe-lee be] exp.: I prefer A to B
aniżeliby [ah-ńee-zhe-lee-bi] part.: rather should; rather would
ankier [ahn-ker] m. anchor-iron
ankieta [ahn-ke-tah] f. poll; inquiry; questionnaire; survey form
ankieter [ahn-ke-ter] m. poll taker; inquirer
ankieterka [ahn-ke-ter-kah] f. (female) poll taker; inquirer
ankietować [ahn-ke-to-vahćh] v. poll; send out questionnaires; collect survey (*repeatedly*)
ankietowanie [ahn-ke-to-vah-ńe] n. poll; inquiry; sending out questionnaires; survey
ankietowany [ahn-ke-to-vah-ni] adj.m. polled (person, etc.); m. polled person
ankietowy [ahn-ke-to-vi] adj.m. of poll; of inquiry; of questionnaire; of survey form
ankietyzacja [ahn-ke-ti-zah-tsyah] f. poll; inquiry; sending out questionnaires; survey
ankietyzować [ahn-ke-ti-zo-vahćh] v. poll; send out questionnaires; collect survey (*repeatedly*)
ankietyzowanie [ahn-ke-ti-zo-vah-ńe] n. poll; inquiry; sending out questionnaires; survey
ankiloza [ahn-kee-lo-zah] f. ankylosis
ankrować [ahn-kro-vahćh] v. to fasten with anchor-iron (or with cramp-iron); fix; cast anchor; secure firmly (*repeatedly*)
ankrowanie [ahn-kro-vah-ńe] n. fastening with anchor
ankrowy [ahn-kro-vi] adj.m. anchor (iron, etc.); of an anchor; of anchors
annalina [ahn-nah-lee-nah] f. annaline
annalista [ahn-nah-lee-stah] m. annalist; historian
annalistyczny [ahn-nah-lee-stich-ni] adj.m. annalistic
annalistyka [ahn-nah-lee-sti-kah] f. annalism
annały [ahn-nah-wi] pl. annals
Annasz [ahn-nahsh] m. Annas
grób Annasza [groob ahn-nah-shah] exp.: the grave of Annas (with a Greek rather than Hebrew inscription)
od Annasza do Kajfasza [od ahn-nah-shah do kahy-fah-shah] exp.: (drive somebody) from pillar to post; from Annas to Caiaphas
annaty [ahn-nah-ti] pl. annual payments
annominacja [ahn-no-mee-nah-tsyah] f. allusion based on similarity of words
ano [ah-no] part. well then; now then
ano tak [ah-no tahk] exp.: well yes
ano to tak [ah-no to tahk] exp.: well it's like this; that's the way it is
ano trudno [ah-no trood-no] exp.: it can't be helped; dear me!
anoda [ah-no-dah] f. anode
anodować [ah-no-do-vahćh] v. anodize (*repeatedly*)
anodowanie [ah-no-do-vah-ńe] n. anodization
anodowo [ah-no-do-vo] adv. anodically; anodally
anodowy [ah-no-do-vi] adj.m. of anode; anodic; anodal
anodyna [ah-no-di-nah] f. anodyne
anodyzacja [ah-no-di-zah-tsyah] f. anodization
anodyzować [ah-no-di-zo-vahćh] v. anodize; cover with a protective oxide film a metal which serves as an anode (*repeatedly*)
anoksemia [ah-no-kse-myah] f. anoxemia
anoksemiczny [ah-no-kse-meech-ni] adj.m. anoxemic
anoksja [ah-no-ksyah] f. anoxia
anoksyjny [ah-no-ksiy-ni] adj.m. anoxic
anoksybiont [ah-no-ksi-byont] m. anaerobe
anoksybioza [ah-no-ksi-byo-zah] f.

anaerobiosis; life without oxygen
anomalia [ah-no-**mah**-lyah] pl. anomaly; abnormality; anything anomalous
anomalistyczny [ah-no-mah-lees-**tich**-ni] adj.m. anomalistic
anomalnie [ah-no-**mahl**-ńe] adv. anomalously
anomalność [ah-no-**mahl**-nośhćh] f. anomalousness
anomalny [ah-no-**mahl**-ni] adj.m. abnormal; anomalous
anonim [ah-**no**-ńeem] m. anonym; anonymous (letter); (work, poem, letter, etc.) without the name of the author; anonymous author; anonymous writer
anonimat [ah-no-**ńee**-maht] m. anonymity
anonimowo [ah-no-ńee-**mo**-vo] adv. anonymously; withholding author's name
anonimowość [ah-no-ńee-**mo**-vośhćh] f. anonymity
anonimowy [ah-no-ńee-**mo**-vi] adj.m. without the name of the author; anonymous; with no name known; lacking individuality
anons [**ah**-nons] m. advertisement (in a newspaper); ad
anonsować [ah-non-**so**-vahćh] v. announce; advertise; promise; declare publicly; make known publicly; be an announcer; serve as an announcer (*repeatedly*)
anonsować się [ah-non-**so**-vahćh śh<u>an</u>] v. proclaim one's presence; promise (*repeatedly*)
anonsowanie [ah-non-so-**vah**-ńe] n. announcement
anorak [ah-**no**-rahk] m. Eskimo diving gear
anoreksja [ah-no-**re**-ksyah] f. anorexia; obsession with weight loss (anorexia nervosa)
anormalnie [ah-nor-**mahl**-ńe] adv. abnormally; irregularly
anormalność [ah-nor-**mahl**-nośhćh] f. anomaly; abnormality; anything abnormal
anormalny [ah-nor-**mahl**-ni] adj.m. abnormal; irregular; anomalous; unnatural; odd; inconsistent; strange
anormatywność [ah-nor-mah-**tiv**-nośhćh] f. lack of norms
anormatywny [ah-nor-mah-**tiv**-ni] adj.m. lacking of norms
anorogeniczny [ah-no-ro-ge-**ńeech**-ni] adj.m. anorogenic
anortozyt [ah-nor-**to**-zit] m. anorthosite (igneous rock)
anortyt [ah-**nor**-tit] m. anorthite (feldspar in igneous rocks)
anosmia [ah-**nos**-myah] f. loss of smell
ansa [**ahn**-sah] f. grudge; resentment; animosity; ill will; dislike; hatred; hostility
czuć ansę do kogoś [choośh ahn-s<u>an</u> do ko-gośh] exp.: to bear somebody ill will; to have a grudge against somebody
nie mam ansy do niego [ńe mahm **ahn**-si do **ńe**-go] exp.: I have no grudge against him
ansambl [ahn-**sahmbl**] m. theater company (of actors and actresses); ensemble (music)
ansamblowy [ahn-sahm-**blo**-vi] adj.m. of a theater company
anszlus [**ahn**-shloos] m. Anschluss; annexation of Austria by Germany (1938-1945)
anta [**ahn**-tah] f. rectangular column
antaba [ahn-**tah**-bah] f. iron bar (door closing); bolt; door handle
antabka [ahn-**tahp**-kah] f. (small) iron bar (door closing); bolt; door handle
antabus [ahn-**tah**-boos] m. a medication used against alcoholism
antagonista [ahn-tah-go-**ńee**-stah] m. antagonist; opponent; adversary; (medical term) counteracting muscle
antagonistka [ahn-tah-go-**ńee**-stkah] f. (woman) antagonist; opponent; adversary
antagonistycznie [ahn-tah-go-ńee-**stich**-ńe] adv. antagonistically
antagonistyczny [ahn-tah-go-ńee-**stich**-ni] adj.m. antagonistic; hostile; conflicting
antagonizm [ahn-tah-**go**-ńeezm] m. antagonism; hostility; adversary position or attitude

antagonizować [ahn-tah-go-ńee-**zo**-vahćh] v. antagonize; incur the dislike of (*repeatedly*)
antał [ahn-tahw] m. barrel; cask
antałek [ahn-**tah**-wek] m. (small) barrel; cask
antarktyczny [ahn-tahr-**ktich**-ni] adj.m. Antarctic; of, or near the South Pole
antecedencje [ahn-te-tse-**den**-tsye] pl. antecedents; (personal) past history
antecedens [ahn-te-**tse**-dens] m. (phil.) antecedent
antecedentnie [ahn-te-tse-**den**-tńe] adv. antecedently
antecedentny [ahn-te-tse-**den**-tni] adj.m. antecedental
antedatować [ahn-te-dah-**to**-vahćh] v. antedate; precede in time (*repeatedly*)
antefiks [ahn-**te**-feeks] m. antefix; antefixal ornament
antefiksowy [ahn-te-fee-**kso**-vi] adj.m. antefixal
antek [**ahn**-tek] m. street-boy; urchin; mischievous boy
antekliza [ahn-te-**klee**-zah] f. bowing of continental plate
antena [ahn-**te**-nah] f. antenna; (exterior) aerial (Brit.); feeler
antena pokojowa [ahn-**te**-nah po-ko-**yo**-vah] exp.: indoor antenna
antena satelitarna [ahn-**te**-nah sah-te-lee-**tahr**-nah] exp.: satellite dish; directional microwave antenna; parabolic reflector
antenacki [ahn-te-**nah**-tskee] adj.m. ancestor's
antenat [ahn-**te**-naht] m. ancestor; forefather; forebear; progenitor; forerunner
antenatka [ahn-te-**nah**-tkah] f. ancestress; forebear
antenowy [ahn-te-**no**-vi] adj.m. antennal; aerial- (Brit.); antenna-; of an aerial (Brit.); of antenna
anteriora [ahn-te-**ryo**-rah] pl. earlier events
antidotum [ahn-tee-**do**-toom] n. antidote; remedy to counteract a poison; anything that works against an evil; neutralizer
antocyjan [ahn-to-**tsi**-yahn] m. anthocyan (pigment)
antocyjanowy [ahn-to-tsi-yah-**no**-vi] adj.m. anthocyan (pigment)
antofyllit [ahn-to-**fil**-leet] m. antophylite (mineral)
antologia [ahn-to-**lo**-gyah] f. anthology; collection of poems, stories, etc.
antologicznie [ahn-to-lo-**geech**-ńe] adv. anthologically
antologiczny [ahn-to-lo-**geech**-ni] adj.m. anthological
antologista [ahn-to-lo-**gee**-stah] m. anthologist
antonim [ahn-**to**-ńeem] m. antonym; a word meaning the opposite of another word
antonimia [ahn-to-**ńee**-myah] f. antonymy
antonimiczny [ahn-to-ńee-**meech**-ni] adj.m. antonymic
antonomazja [ahn-to-no-**mah**-zyah] f. antonomasia; the use of a title rather than the proper name
antonówka [ahn-to-**noof**-kah] f. a variety of apple
antracen [ahn-**trah**-tsen] m. anthracene
antracenowy [ahn-trah-tse-**no**-vi] adj.m. anthracene (oil, etc.)
antrachion [ahn-**trah**-khyon] m. anthraquinone
antrachionowy [ahn-trah-khyo-**no**-vi] adj.m. of anthraquinone
antracyt [ahn-**trah**-tsit] m. anthracite; hard natural coal
antracytowy [ahn-trah-tsi-**to**-vi] adj.m. anthracitic
antraknoza [ahn-trah-**kno**-zah] f. anthracnosis; anthracnose
antraks [**ahn**-trahks] m. anthrax; carbuncle
antrakt [**ahn**-trahkt] m. interval; interact; interlude; entr'acte
antraktowy [ahn-trah-**kto**-vi] adj.m. of interval; interval (music, etc.)
antreprener [ahn-tre-**pre**-ner] m. entrepreneur in the show business
antrepryza [ahn-tre-**pri**-zah] f. enterprise; undertaking
antresola [ahn-tre-**so**-lah] f. entresol; mezzanine
antropo- [ahn-**tro**-po] prefix:

anthrop-; anthropo-; human being
antropocentrycznie [ahn-tro-po-tsen-**trich**-ńe] adv. anthropocentrically
antropocentryczny [ahn-tro-po-tsen-**trich**-ni] adj.m. anthropocentric; centering one's view of everything around man
antropofag [ahn-**tro**-po-fahg] m. anthropophagous
antropofagia [ahn-tro-po-**fah**-gyah] f. anthropophagy
antropogeneza [ahn-tro-po-ge-**ne**-zah] f. anthropogenesis
antropogeniczny [ahn-tro-po-ge-**ńeech**-ni] adj.m. anthropogenic
antropogeograf [ahn-tro-po-ge-**o**-grahf] m. anthropogeographer
antropogeografia [ahn-tro-po-ge-o-**grah**-fyah] f. anthropogeography
antropogeograficzny [ahn-tro-po-ge-o-grah-**feech**-ni] adj.m. anthropogeographical
antropoid [ahn-tro-**po**-eet] m. anthropoid; any of several large tailless semierect apes
antropoidalny [ahn-tro-po-ee-**dahl**-ni] adj.m. anthropoid (ape, etc.)
antropolog [ahn-tro-**po**-log] m. anthropologist
antropologia [ahn-tro-po-**lo**-gyah] f. anthropology (the study of the characteristics, customs, etc. of mankind)
antropologicznie [ahn-tro-po-lo-**geech**-ńe] adv. anthropologically
antropologiczny [ahn-tro-po-lo-**geech**-ni] adj.m. anthropological
antropologizm [ahn-tro-po-**lo**-geezm] m. anthropology
antropometr [ahn-tro-**po**-metr] m. device for measuring body height or location of anthropometric points; anthropometer
antropometria [ahn-tro-po-**me**-tryah] f. anthropometry; study of human body measurements
antropomorficznie [ahn-tro-po-mor-**feech**-ńe] adv. anthropomorphically
antropomorficzny [ahn-tro-po-mor-**feech**-ni] adj.m. attributing human characteristics to gods, objects, etc.; anthropomorphic
antropomorfizacja [ahn-tro-po-mor-fee-**zah**-tsyah] f. anthropomorphization
antropomorfizacyjny [ahn-tro-po-mor-fee-zah-**tsiy**-ni] adj.m. of anthropomorphization
antropomorfizm [ahn-tro-po-**mor**-feezm] m. attribution of human characteristics to gods, objects, etc.; anthropomorphism
antropomorfizować [ahn-tro-po-mor-fee-**zo**-vahćh] v. attribute a human form or personality (to); anthropomorphize (*repeatedly*)
antroponimia [ahn-tro-po-**ńee**-myah] f. onomastics; the science of names; onomatology
antroponimiczny [ahn-tro-po-ńee-**meech**-ni] adj.m. onomastic; of the science of names
antroposkopia [ahn-tro-po-**sko**-pyah] f. method of describing human physical characteristics
antropotechnika [ahn-tro-po-**tekh**-ńee-kah] f. ergonomics; biotechnology
antropozofia [ahn-tro-po-**zo**-fyah] f. anthroposophy
antropozoonoza [ahn-tro-po-zo-o-**no**-zah] f. antropo-zoonosis
antrykot [ahn-**tri**-kot] m. entrecote; steak
anturium [ahn-**toor**-yoom] n. Anthurium (plant)
anty- [**ahn**-ti] prefix: anti-
antyalkoholizm [ahn-ti-ahl-ko-**kho**-leezm] m. anti-alcoholism; teetotalism; temperance movement
antyalkoholowy [ahn-ti-ahl-ko-kho-**lo**-vi] adj.m. anti-alcoholic; prohibitory (laws, etc.)
antyapeks [ahn-ti-**ah**-peks] m. antapex; solar apex
antyatom [ahn-ti-**ah**-tom] m. hypothetical atom with negatively charged nucleus
antyatomowy [ahn-ti-ah-to-**mo**-vi] adj.m. of the hypothetical atom with negatively charged nucleus; of the opposition to nuclear weapons; anti-atom-bomb (shelter, etc.)
antybakch [ahn-**ti**-bahkkh] m. form of three-syllable verse in antiquity

antybiogram [ahn-ti-**byo**-grahm] m. laboratory test result on the resistance of bacteria to antibiotics, etc.
antybiotyczny [ahn-ti-byo-**tich**-ni] adj.m. antibiotic
antybiotyki [ahn-ti-byo-**ti**-kee] pl. antibiotics
antybioza [ahn-ti-**byo**-zah] f. antibiosis
antybka [ahn-**tip**-kah] f. pipe-stem
antybodziec [ahn-ti-**bo**-dźhets] m. anti-stimulant; tranquilizer
antybodźcowo [ahn-ti-boćh-**tso**-vo] adv. as anti-stimulant; like tranquilizer
antybodźcowy [ahn-ti-boćh-**tso**-vi] adj.m. of anti-stimulant; of tranquilizer
antybohater [ahn-ti-bo-**khah**-ter] m. anti-hero
antybohaterski [ahn-ti-bo-khah-**ter**-skee] adj.m. anti-heroic; of an anti-hero
antybroń [ahn-ti-**broń**] f. device neutralizing a particular weapon
antycentrum [ahn-ti-**tsen**-troom] n. point on Earth surface located symmetrically with respect to the epicenter on the opposed hemisphere
antycesarz [ahn-ti-**tse**-sahsh] m. anti-Caesar
antychlor [ahn-ti-**khlor**] m. antichlor
antychryst [ahn-**ti**-khrist] m. antichrist; the Antichrist; Satan; great opponent of Christ; hooligan
antycyklon [ahn-ti-**tsi**-klon] m. anticyclone
antycyklonalny [ahn-ti-tsi-klo-**nahl**-ni] adj.m. anticyclonic
antycyklonowy [ahn-ti-tsi-klo-**no**-vi] adj.m. anticyclonic
antycypacja [ahn-ti-tsi-**pah**-tsyah] f. anticipation; the act of looking forward; pleasurable expectations; anticipation chords
antycypować [ahn-ti-tsi-**po**-vahćh] v. anticipate; expect; forestall; foresee (*repeatedly*)
antycypowanie [ahn-ti-tsi-po-**vah**-ńe] n. anticipation
antycząstka [ahn-ti-**ch<u>own</u>**-stkah] f. anti-particle; particle with opposite charge
antycznie [ahn-**tich**-ńe] adv. in antiquity; in ancient times; in past ages
antyczny [ahn-**tich**-ni] adj.m. antique; archaic; old-fashioned; of ancient times; outmoded; out-of-date; antiquated
antydaktyl [ahn-ti-**dahk**-til] m. antidactyl (verse)
antydatować [ahn-ti-dah-**to**-vahćh] v. antedate; put an earlier than the actual date; predate; come before in time (*repeatedly*)
antydatowanie [ahn-ti-dah-to-**vah**-ńe] n. antedating
antydemokratyczny [ahn-ti-de-mo-krah-**tich**-ni] adj.m. antidemocratic; antidemocratical
antydepresyjny [ahn-ti-de-pre-**siy**-ni] adj.m. antidepressant; antidepressive
antydetonator [ahn-ti-de-to-**nah**-tor] m. antiknock agent; anti-detonator
antydeuteron [ahn-ti-dew-**te**-ron] m. anti-deuteron
antydiuretyna [ahn-ti-dyoo-re-**ti**-nah] f. antidiuretic hormone
antydogmatyczny [ahn-ti-dog-mah-**tich**-ni] adj.m. antidogmatic
antydogmatyzm [ahn-ti-dog-**mah**-tizm] m. antidogmatism
antydopingowy [ahn-ti-do-peen-**go**-vi] adj.m. enforcing athletic regulations against stimulants, dope, and narcotics
antydramat [ahn-ti-**drah**-maht] m. anti-drama; grotesque and paradoxical drama
antydynastyczny [ahn-ti-di-nah-**stich**-ni] adj.m. anti-dynastic
antyelektron [ahn-ti-e-**lek**-tron] m. anti-electron
antyempiryzm [ahn-ti-em-**pee**-rizm] m. antiempirical theory stating that reason and not experience of the senses should be the basis of knowledge
antyenzym [ahn-ti-**en**-zim] m. antienzyme
antyestetyzm [ahn-ti-es-**te**-tizm] m. anti-aestheticism; lack of good taste

antyfaszysta [ahn-ti-fah-**shi**-stah] m. antifascist
antyfaszystowski [ahn-ti-fah-shi-**stof**-skee] adj.m. antifascist
antyfebryna [ahn-ti-fe-**bri**-nah] f. antifebrin
antyfeminista [ahn-ti-fe-mee-**ńee**-stah] m. anti-feminist; woman-hater
antyfeministyczny [ahn-ti-fe-mee-ńee-**stich**-ni] adj.m. anti-feminist (attitude, etc.)
antyfeminizm [ahn-ti-fe-**mee**-ńeezm] m. anti-feminism
antyferromagnetyczny [ahn-ti-fer-ro-mah-gne-**tich**-ni] adj.m. anti-ferromagnetic
antyferromagnetyzm [ahn-ti-fer-ro-mah-**gne**-tizm] m. anti-ferromagnetism
antyfeudalizm [ahn-ti-fe-oo-**dah**-leezm] m. anti-feudalism
antyfilm [ahn-ti-**feelm**] m. anti-film
antyfonał [ahn-ti-**fo**-nahw] m. antiphonal
antyfonarz [ahn-ti-**fo**-nahsh] m. antiphonal
antyfona [ahn-ti-**fo**-nah] f. antiphon
antyfraza [ahn-ti-**frah**-zah] f. antiphrasis; use of words in opposite senses (for irony, etc.)
antyfrykcyjny [ahn-ti-frik-**tsiy**-ni] adj.m. antifrictional
antyfryz [ahn-**ti**-friz] m. anti-freeze
antygen [ahn-**ti**-gen] m. antigen
antygenowy [ahn-ti-ge-**no**-vi] adj.m. antigenic
antygoryt [ahn-ti-**go**-rit] m. antigorite (mineral)
antygradacja [ahn-ti-grah-**dah**-tsyah] f. anti-gradation
antygrypina [ahn-ti-gri-**pee**-nah] f. colloq: flu (grippe) medicine
antygrypowy [ahn-ti-gri-**po**-vi] adj.m. against-flu (medicine, etc.)
antyhitlerowiec [ahn-ti-khee-tle-**ro**-vyets] m. enemy of Hitlerism; enemy of Nazism
antyhitlerowski [ahn-ti-khee-tle-**rof**-skee] adj.m. anti-Hitlerite (plot, etc.); anti-Nazi
antyhormon [ahn-ti-**hor**-mon] m. anti-hormone
antyhumanistyczny [ahn-ti-khoo-mah-ńee-**stich**-ni] adj.m. anti-humanistic
antyhumanitarny [ahn-ti-khoo-mah-ńee-**tahr**-ni] adj.m. anti-humanitarian
antyimperialistyczny [ahn-ti-eem-per-yah-lee-**stich**-ni] adj.m. anti-imperialistic
antyimplozyjny [ahn-ti-eem-plo-**ziy**-ni] adj.m. anti-implosive
antyimportowy [ahn-ti-eem-por-**to**-vi] adj.m. anti-import (measures, duties, etc.)
antyinflacyjny [ahn-ti-een-flah-**tsiy**-ni] adj.m. anti-inflation (measures, etc.)
antyintelektualista [ahn-ti-een-te-le-ktoo-ah-**lee**-stah] m. an anti-intellectual
antyintelektualizm [ahn-ti-een-te-le-ktoo-**ah**-leezm] m. anti-intellectualism
antyintelektualny [ahn-ti-een-te-lek-too-**ahl**-ni] adj.m. anti-intellectual
antyk [**ahn**-tik] m. antique; curio; Greco-Latin civilization; the Greco-Latin world; antiquity; ancient object of art; antique piece of furniture; an old-fashioned person; back number
antykadencja [ahn-ti-kah-**den**-tsyah] f. the part of intonational phrase which is increasing in strength
antykapitalistyczny [ahn-ti-kah-pee-tah-lee-**stich**-ni] adj.m. anti-capitalistic; anticapitalist
antykatoda [ahn-ti-kah-**to**-dah] f. anticathode
antykatolicki [ahn-ti-kah-to-**lee**-tskee] adj.m. anti-Catholic
antykizować [ahn-ti-kee-**zo**-vahćh] v. stylize to appear like an antique (*repeatedly*)
antyklerykalizm [ahn-ti-kle-ri-**kah**-leezm] m. anti-clericalism
antyklerykalny [ahn-ti-kle-ri-**kahl**-ni] adj.m. anticlerical
antyklerykał [ahn-ti-kle-**ri**-kahw] m. an anticlerical
antyklina [ahn-ti-**klee**-nah] f. anticline
antyklinalny [ahn-ti-klee-**nahl**-ni] adj.m. anticlinal
antyklinorium [ahn-ti-klee-**nor**-yoom]

n. anticlinal terrain
antykolizyjny [ahn-ti-ko-lee-**ziy**-ni] adj.m. avoiding collision
antykolonializm [ahn-ti-ko-lo-**ńyah**-leezm] m. anti-colonialism
antykolonialny [ahn-ti-ko-lo-**ńyahl**-ni] adj.m. anti-colonial
antykomunistyczny [ahn-ti-ko-moo-ńee-**stich**-ni] adj.m. anti-communist (opposition, etc.)
antykomunizm [ahn-ti-ko-**moo**-ńeezm] m. anti-communism
antykoncepcja [ahn-ti-kon-**tsep**-tsyah] f. contraception
antykoncepcyjny [ahn-ti-kon-tsep-**tsiy**-ni] adj.m. contraceptive
środki antykoncepcyjne [**śhrot**-kee ahn-ti-kon-tsep-**tsiy**-ne] exp.: contraceptives
antykonstytucyjny [ahn-ti-kon-sti-too-**tsiy**-ni] adj.m. anti-constitutional
antykorodal [ahn-ti-ko-**ro**-dahl] m. anti-corrosive alloy of aluminum, silicon, magnesium, manganese, and titanium
antykorozyjny [ahn-ti-ko-ro-**ziy**-ni] adj.m. anti-corrosive
antykwa [ahn-**tik**-fah] f. Roman type print (font)
antykwariat [ahn-ti-**kfahr**-yaht] m. old curiosity shop; antique-dealer's shop
antykwariat książkowy [ahn-ti-**kfahr**-yaht kśh<u>own</u>-**shko**-vi] exp.: shop dealing with out-of-print books; second-hand book-shop
antykwariusz [ahn-ti-**kfahr**-yoosh] m. antiquary; second-hand bookseller
antykwarnia [ahn-ti-**kfahr**-ńah] f. old curiosity shop; antique-dealer's shop
antykwarski [ahn-ti-**kfahr**-skee] adj.m. antiquarian; antique-dealer's...
antykwarstwo [ahn-ti-**kfahr**-stfo] n. trade in antiquities; trade in antiques; second-hand book trade
antykwarycznie [ahn-ti-kfah-**rich**-ńe] adv. (to buy or get) second-hand
antykwaryczny [ahn-ti-kfah-**rich**-ni] adj.m. antiquarian; antique-dealer's
książka antykwaryczna [**kśh<u>own</u>sh**-kah ahn-ti-kfah-**rich**-nah] exp.: second-hand book
antylogarytm [ahn-ti-lo-**gah**-ritm] m. antilogarithm
antylogia [ahn-ti-**lo**-gyah] f. antilogy
antylogizm [ahn-ti-**lo**-geezm] m. antilogism
antylopa [ahn-ti-**lo**-pah] f. antelope
antylopi [ahn-ti-**lo**-pee] adj.m. of antelope; antelopian; antelope (leather, etc.)
antyludowy [ahn-ti-loo-**do**-vi] adj.m. anti-social
antymagnetyczny [ahn-ti-mahg-ne-**tich**-ni] adj.m. antimagnetic
antymateria [ahn-ti-mah-**ter**-yah] f. antimatter
antymetabolia [ahn-ti-me-tah-**bol**-yah] f. anti-metabolism
antymetabolit [ahn-ti-me-tah-**bo**-leet] m. antimetabolite
antymieszczański [ahn-ti-mye-**shchahń**-skee] m. anti-bourgeoisie (policy, etc.)
antymilitarystyczny [ahn-ti-mee-lee-tah-ri-**stich**-ni] adj.m. antimilitarist
antymilitaryzm [ahn-ti-mee-lee-**tah**-rizm] m. antimilitarism
antymolowy [ahn-ti-mo-**lo**-vi] adj.m. moth-killing; anti-moth (spray, etc.)
antymon [ahn-**ti**-mon] m. antimony; stibnite (mineral); stibium
antymonarchistyczny [ahn-ti-mo-nahr-khee-**stich**-ni] adj.m. anti-monarchy (plot, etc.); anti-monarchistic (conspiracy, etc.)
antymonek [ahn-ti-**mo**-nek] m. antimonic compound
antymonit [ahn-ti-**mo**-ńeet] m. stibnite (mineral)
antymonowy [ahn-ti-mo-**no**-vi] adj.m. antimonic; antimonious (acid, oxide, etc.); antimony (compound, etc.)
antymonyl [ahn-ti-**mo**-nil] m. antimonyl
antynarodowy [ahn-ti-nah-ro-**do**-vi] adj.m. anti-national; contrary to national interest; antinational
antynaturalistyczny [ahn-ti-nah-too-rah-lee-**stich**-ni] adj.m. against naturalism

antynaturalizm [ahn-ti-nah-too-**rah**-leezm] m. opposition to naturalism
antynaukowo [ahn-ti-nah-oo-**ko**-vo] adv. anti-scientifically
antynaukowy [ahn-ti-nah-oo-**ko**-vi] adj.m. anti-scientific; anti-scholarly; anti-academic
antyneutron [ahn-ti-ne-**oo**-tron] m. antineutron
antynikotynowy [ahn-ti-ńee-ko-ti-**no**-vi] adj.m. anti-nicotine; against smoking of cigarettes; against smoking tobacco; against chewing tobacco
antynomia [ahn-ti-**no**-myah] f. contradiction in terms; antinomy
antynomiczność [ahn-ti-no-**meech**-nośhćh] f. contradiction in terms; antinomy
antynomiczny [ahn-ti-no-**meech**-ni] adj.m. of contradiction in terms; antinomic; antinomical
antynomijny [ahn-ti-no-**meey**-ni] adj.m. of contradiction in terms; antinomic; antinomical
antynuklearny [ahn-ti-noo-kle-**ahr**-ni] adj.m. against nuclear weapons
antypaństwowy [ahn-ti-pahń-**stfo**-vi] adj.m. anti-national; anti-state (activities, etc.); detrimental to the state; subversive
antypapieski [ahn-ti-pah-**pye**-skee] adj.m. anti-papal
antypapież [ahn-ti-**pah**-pyesh] m. antipope
antypasat [ahn-ti-**pah**-saht] m. anti-trade winds
antypasatowy [ahn-ti-pah-sah-**to**-vi] adj.m. anti-trade (wind, etc.)
antypatia [ahn-ti-**pah**-tyah] f. antipathy; dislike; aversion; object of dislike; object of aversion; object of repugnance
antypatycznie [ahn-ti-pah-**tich**-ńe] adv. in a distasteful manner; repulsively
antypatyczność [ahn-ti-pah-**tich**-nośhćh] f. repugnancy; repulsiveness
antypatyczny [ahn-ti-pah-**tich**-ni] adj.m. repugnant; repulsive; loathsome; unlikable; unpleasant; having distasteful manners
antyperystaltyka [ahn-ti-pe-ri-**stahl**-ti-kah] f. anti-peristalsis
antypiryna [anh-ti-pee-**ri**-nah] f. antipyrine (used to relieve pain, fever, or infection)
antypka [ahn-**tip**-kah] f. a variety of rose bush
antypoda [ahn-ti-**po**-dah] f. person living on the opposite side of the globe
antypody [ahn-ti-**po**-di] pl. antipodes
antypodowy [ahn-ti-po-**do**-vi] adj.m. antipodal
antypodycznie [ahn-ti-po-**dich**-ńe] adv. in antipodal position
antypodyczny [ahn-ti-po-**dich**-ni] adj.m. antipodal
antypokojowy [ahn-ti-po-ko-**yo**-vi] adj.m. endangering the peace; detrimental to peace; bellicose; warmongering
antypolski [ahn-ti-**pol**-skee] adj.m. anti-Polish; endangering Poland; detrimental to the Poles; filled with hatred against Poles
antypostępowy [anh-ti-po-st<u>an</u>-**po**-vi] adj.m. hostile to progress; backward; retrograde
antypowieść [anh-ti-**po**-vyeśhćh] f. an anti-novel; a multi-plot novel
antyproton [anh-ti-**pro**-ton] m. antiproton
antypsychologiczny [ahn-ti-psi-kho-lo-**geech**-ni] adj.m. in opposition to psychologism
antypsychologizm [ahn-ti-psi-kho-**lo**-geezm] m. opposition to psychologism
antyradiolokacja [ahn-ti-rah-dyo-lo-**kah**-tsyah] f. technology used against radiolocation; radar jamming
antyradiolokacyjny [ahn-ti-rah-dyo-lo-kah-**tsiy**-ni] adj.m. of the technology used against radiolocation
antyradziecki [ahn-ti-rah-**dźhe**-tskee] adj.m. hostile to the Soviet Union
antyrakieta [ahn-ti-rah-**<u>k</u>e**-tah] f. anti-missile; anti-rocket
antyrakietowy [ahn-ti-rah-<u>k</u>e-**to**-vi] adj.m. anti-missile (defense, etc.); anti-rocket (system, etc.)

antyrealistyczny [ahn-ti-re-ah-lee-**stich**-ni] adj.m. against realism
antyrealizm [ahn-ti-re-**ah**-leezm] m. anti-realism
antyrepublikański [ahn-ti-re-poob-lee-**kahń**-skee] adj.m. anti-Republican
antyreumatyczny [ahn-ti-rew-mah-**tich**-ni] adj.m. antirheumatic
antyrewolucyjny [ahn-ti-re-vo-loo-**tsiy**-ni] adj.m. antirevolutionary
antyrezonans [ahn-ti-re-**zo**-nahns] m. anti-resonance
antyreżimowy [ahn-ti-re-zhee-**mo**-vi] adj.m. anti-governmental; in opposition to a political regime
antyreżymowy [ahn-ti-re-zhi-**mo**-vi] adj.m. anti-governmental; in opposition to a political regime
antyrobotniczy [ahn-ti-ro-bot-**ńee**-chi] adj.m. hostile to the working class
antyrojalistyczny [ahn-ti-ro-yah-lee-**stich**-ni] adj.m. antiroyal; antiroyalist; hostile to monarchy
antyrządowy [ahn-ti-zhown-**do**-vi] adj.m. hostile to the government in power
antysanitarny [ahn-ti-sah-ńee-**tahr**-ni] adj.m. unsanitary
antysemicki [ahn-ti-se-**mee**-tskee] adj.m. anti-Semitic; anti-Jewish; having prejudice against Jews; discriminating against or persecuting Jews
antysemita [ahn-ti-se-**mee**-tah] m. anti-Semite
antysemitka [ahn-ti-se-**mee**-tkah] f. (woman) anti-Semite
antysemityzm [ahn-ti-se-**mee**-tizm] m. anti-Semitism
antyseptyczny [ahn-ti-sep-**tich**-ni] adj.m. antiseptic; preventing infection, decay, etc.; sterile; disinfecting; preservative
antyseptyk [ahn-ti-**sep**-tik] m. antiseptic; any antiseptic substance, as alcohol
antyseptyka [ahn-ti-**sep**-ti-kah] f. antisepsis
antyserum [ahn-ti-**se**-room] n. antiserum
antysocjalistyczny [ahn-ti-so-tsyah-lee-**stich**-ni] adj.m. in opposition to socialism; anti-socialist; antisocialistic
antyspołecznie [ahn-ti-spo-**wech**-ńe] adv. antisocially
antyspołeczny [ahn-ti-spo-**wech**-ni] adj.m. antisocial; not sociable; harmful to the welfare of people
antystrofa [ahn-ti-**stro**-fah] f. antistrophe
antyszambrować [ahn-ti-shahm-**bro**-vahćh] v. cool one's heels in waiting-rooms (*repeatedly*)
antytalent [ahn-ti-**tah**-lent] m. complete lack of ability (to do something); person lacking ability (to do something)
antytetyczny [ahn-ti-te-**tich**-ni] adj.m. antithetic; antithetical
antyteza [ahn-ti-**te**-zah] f. antithesis; the exact opposite; a contrast or opposition as of ideas, etc.
antytoksycznie [ahn-ti-tok-**sich**-ńe] adv. anti-toxically
antytoksyczny [ahn-ti-tok-**sich**-ni] adj.m. antitoxic (against a specific toxin)
antytoksyna [ahn-ti-tok-**si**-nah] f. antitoxin; a substance formed in the blood to act against a specific toxin; a serum containing an antitoxin, injected into a person to prevent a disease
antytradycjonalizm [ahn-ti-trah-di-tsyo-**nah**-leezm] m. anti-traditionalism
antytrynitariusz [ahn-ti-tri-ńee-**tahr**-yoosh] m. sectarian rejecting Holy Trinity; anti-Trinitarian
antytrynitarski [ahn-ti-tri-ńee-**tahr**-skee] adj.m. anti-Trinitarian
antytrynitarz [ahn-ti-tri-**ńee**-tahsh] m. sectarian rejecting Holy Trinity; anti-Trinitarian
antyutleniacz [ahn-ti-oo-**tle**-ńahch] m. antioxidant
antywibracyjny [ahn-ti-vee-brah-**tsiy**-ni] adj.m. anti-vibratory
antywitamina [ahn-ti-vee-tah-**mee**-nah] f. antivitamin
antywojenny [ahn-ti-vo-**yen**-ni] adj.m. antiwar
anulować [ah-noo-**lo**-vahćh] v. annul; cancel (an order, etc.); nullify; repeal; revoke; rescind (a

law, etc.); render void; do away with; deprive (of legal force); abate (a writ, etc.) (*repeatedly*)
anulowanie [ah-noo-lo-**vah**-ńe] n. annulment; nullification; cancellation; rescission; defeasance; abatement
anyż [**ah**-nish] m. anise; plant of the parsley family; its fragrant seed, used for flavoring
anyżek [ah-**ni**-zhek] m. aniseed cake
anyżelka [ah-ni-**zhel**-kah] f. angelica root
anyżkowy [ah-nish-**ko**-vi] adj.m. anise (oil, etc.); aniseed (flavor, etc.); anisic (acid, etc.)
anyżowy [ah-ni-**zho**-vi] adj.m. anise (oil, etc.); aniseed (flavor, etc.); anisic (acid, etc.)
anyżówka [ah-ni-**zhoof**-kah] f. aniseed vodka
aojda [ah-**oy**-dah] m. ballad singer
aorta [ah-**or**-tah] f. aorta; the main artery of the body carrying blood from the heart
aoryst [ah-**o**-rist] m. aorist
aorystyczny [ah-o-ri-**stich**-ni] adj.m. aoristic
apagogiczny [ah-pah-go-**geech**-ni] adj.m. apagogic
apanaż [ah-**pah**-nahsh] m. appanage; a dependency; loosely, any property appropriated to or by a person as his share or perquisite; a provision made under condition of renunciation of any future inheritance
apanażowy [ah-pah-nah-**zho**-vi] adj.m. appanage (dependency, etc.)
aparacik [ah-pah-**rah**-ćheek] m. (small) apparatus; appliance; camera; gadget; device; mechanism
aparat [ah-**pah**-raht] m. apparatus; appliance; camera; gadget; device; mechanism; machinery; any complex machine, device, or system
aparat fotograficzny [ah-**pah**-raht fo-to-grah-**feech**-ni] exp.: camera
aparat nadawczy [ah-**pah**-raht nah-**dahf**-chi] exp.: transmitter; broadcasting apparatus
aparat odbiorczy [ah-**pah**-raht od-**byor**-chi] exp.: receiver; receiving set
aparat radiowy [ah-**pah**-raht rah-**dyo**-vi] exp.: wireless (set); radio set
aparat terroru [ah-**pah**-raht ter-**ro**-roo] exp.: terror apparatus (used by a state as security forces)
aparatczyk [ah-pah-**raht**-chik] m. apparatchik; highly disciplined communist bureucrat; member of a communist apparatus
aparatownia [ah-pah-rah-**tov**-ńah] f. storage space for appliances
aparatura [ah-pah-rah-**too**-rah] f. apparatus; gear; machinery; tackle; instrumentation
apartamencik [ah-pahr-tah-**men**-ćheek] m. (small, nice) residence; apartment
apartament [ah-pahr-**tah**-ment] m. residence; suite of rooms; elegant set of rooms (private or in a hotel)
apartheid [ah-**pahrt**-hahyt] m. apartheid
aparycja [ah-pah-**ri**-tsyah] f. apparition; presence; carriage; bearing; anything that appears unexpectedly or strangely; a ghost; phantom; becoming visible
apasz [**ah**-pahsh] m. apache; street ruffian; hoodlum; bully
apaszka [ah-**pahsh**-kah] f. woman's colored triangular neckerchief
apaszowski [ah-pah-**shof**-skee] adj.m. ruffianly
apatia [ah-**pah**-tyah] f. apathy; lack of emotion; indifference; listlessness; dullness; torpidity; torpor
apatycznie [ah-pah-**tich**-ńe] adv. apathetically; listlessly; with indifference
apatyczny [ah-pah-**tich**-ni] adj.m. apathetic; listless; indifferent; dull; torpid
apatyt [ah-**pah**-tit] m. apatite (mineral)
apatytowy [ah-pah-ti-**to**-vi] adj.m. apatite (mineral, etc.)
apedagogiczny [ah-pe-dah-go-**geech**-ni] adj.m. anti-educational

apeks [ah-peks] m. apex; the highest point; tip; summit; a climax

apel [ah-pel] m. appeal; muster; roll-call; roll; parade; the assembly; an urgent request; request for help; dodge (in fencing); breaking in (of a dog)
stanąć do apelu [stah-nownćh do ah-pe-loo] exp.: to turn out for roll-call; to answer the appeal; (military:) to assembly; to muster; to parade
apel poległych [ah-pel po-leg-wikh] exp.: reading of the roll of the dead (soldiers)
pies ma dobry apel [pyes mah dob-ri ah-pel] exp.: the dog is well broken in

apelacja [ah-pe-lah-tsyah] f. appeal; Court of Appeal; appeal lodged with a higher tribunal; the right of appeal
bez apelacji [bez ah-pe-lah-tsyee] exp.: without appeal; beyond recall; decisively; finally; irrevocably
wnieść apelację do sądu [vńeśhćh ah-pe-lah-tsyan do sown-doo] exp.: to enter an appeal to a court; to submit an appeal to a court

apelacyjny [ah-pe-lah-tsiy-ni] adj.m. appellate; (jurisdiction) of appeal
sąd apelacyjny [sownt ah-pe-lah-tsiy-ni] exp.: appellate court; court of appeals; court that can review appeals and reverse the decisions of lower courts

apelant [ah-pe-lahnt] m. appellant; a person who appeals (to a higher court); appealer

apelatywny [ah-pe-lah-tiv-ni] adj.m. (gram.) appellative

apelować [ah-pe-lo-vahćh] v. appeal; make an appeal (*repeatedly*)

apelowy [ah-pe-lo-vi] adj.m. of appeal
plac apelowy [plahts ah-pe-lo-vi] exp.: parade-ground

apendyks [ah-pen-diks] m. appendix; additional material at the end of a book

apepcja [ah-pep-tsyah] f. indigestion

apercepcja [ah-per-tsep-tsyah] f. introspective; self-consciousness; mental perception; apperception

apercepcyjny [ah-per-tsep-tsiy-ni] adj.m. apperceptive

apercypować [ah-per-tsi-po-vahćh] v. have apperception of; apperceive (*repeatedly*)

apercypowanie [ah-per-tsi-po-vah-ńe] n. apperception

aperiodyczny [ah-per-yo-dich-ni] adj.m. aperiodic

aperitif [ah-pe-ree-teef] m. aperitif

apertura [ah-per-too-rah] f. aperture; an opening; hole

apertyzacja [ah-per-ti-zah-tsyah] f. preservation of food in hermetically closed containers

apetycik [ah-pe-ti-ćheek] m. hearty appetite; gusto for food

apetycznie [ah-pe-tich-ńe] adv. appetizingly

apetyczny [ah-pe-tich-ni] adj.m. appetizing; stimulating the appetite; savory; delicious

apetyt [ah-pe-tit] m. appetite; desire for food; craving; any strong desire; relish
mam apetyt na to [mahm ah-pe-tit nah to] exp.: I would love to eat it; I would eat it with relish; I would enjoy that

aphelium [ahp-hel-yoom] n. aphelion

apikalny [ah-pee-kahl-ni] adj.m. apical; of the tip of the tongue

aplanat [ah-plah-naht] m. aplanat; aplanatic lens

aplanatyczny [ah-plah-nah-tich-ni] adj.m. aplanatic; free from or corrected for spherical aberration

aplaudować [ah-plahw-do-vahćh] v. applaud; express approval for (*repeatedly*)

aplauz [ah-plahws] m. applause; plaudits; approval, esp. as shown by clapping hands, shouting, etc.
przyjąć z aplauzem [pshi-yownćh z ah-plahw-zem] exp.: to applaud; to receive with (an enthusiastic) applause
spotkać się z aplauzem [spot-kahćh śhan z ah-plahw-zem] exp.: to meet with applause

aplika [ah-**plee**-kah] f. an applied ornament (on a wall or furniture)
aplikacja [ah-plee-**kah**-tsyah] f. application; internship; probation; practice; applique; decoration made of one material attached to another
aplikacyjny [ah-plee-kah-**tsiy**-ni] adj.m. applicative; applicable
aplikant [ah-**plee**-kahnt] m. intern; probationer; apprentice (in legal profession, crafts, and trade); applicant; one who applies (for employment, help, etc.); petitioner; novice
aplikantura [ah-plee-kahn-**too**-rah] f. internship; apprenticeship
aplikatura [ah-plee-kah-**too**-rah] f. proper position of fingers on musical instruments
aplikować [ah-plee-**ko**-vahćh] v. apply; practice; undergo training; put to practical or specific use; make a request; give (medication, etc.) (*repeatedly*)
aplikowanie [ah-plee-ko-**vah**-ńe] n. application; practicing
aplit [**ah**-pleet] m. aplite (mineral)
aplomb [**ah**-plomp] m. aplomb; self-assurance
apochromat [ah-po-**khro**-maht] m. apochromat; apochromatic lens
apochromatyczny [ah-po-khro-mah-**tich**-ni] adj.m. apochromatic
apodyktycznie [ah-po-dik-**tich**-ńe] adv. peremptorily; dogmatically; positively and arrogantly; imperviously; pragmatically
apodyktyczność [ah-po-dik-**tich**-nośhćh] f. peremptoriness; dogmatic tone; imperious manner; pragmatic approach
apodyktyczny [ah-po-dik-**tich**-ni] adj.m. peremptory; dogmatic; imperious; barring further action; final; that cannot be denied, delayed, etc. (as a command); opinionated
człowiek apodyktyczny [chwo-vyek ah-po-dik-**tich**-ni] exp.: man who lays down the law
apodżiatura [ah-po-dzhyah-**too**-rah] f. appogiatura
apoenzym [ah-po-**en**-zim] m. apoenzyme
apoferment [ah-po-**fer**-ment] m. fermented apoenzyme
apofilit [ah-po-**fee**-leet] m. apophylite (mineral)
apofiza [ah-po-**fee**-zah] f. apophysis
apofonia [ah-po-**fo**-ńyah] f. apophony; ablaut; vowel gradation
apofoniczny [ah-po-fo-**ńeech**-ni] adj.m. apophonic
apoftegma [ah-pof-**teg**-mah] f. apophthegm; aphorism; maxim
apoftegmat [ah-pof-**teg**-maht] m. apophthegm; aphorism; maxim
apogeum [ah-po-**ge**-oom] n. culminating point; height; zenith; an apogee
apograf [ah-**po**-grahf] m. apograph; copy (of an original)
apokalipsa [ah-po-kah-**leep**-sah] f. apocalypse; any revelation of a violent struggle in which evil will be destroyed; symbolic imagery, and expectation of an imminent cosmic cataclysm; vision
apokaliptycznie [ah-po-kah-leep-**tich**-ńe] adv. apocalyptically
apokaliptyczny [ah-po-kah-leep-**tich**-ni] adj.m. apocalyptic; relating to, or resembling an apocalypse; forecasting the ultimate destiny of the world; foreboding imminent doom; ultimately decisive
apokopa [ah-po-**ko**-pah] f. apocope
apokryf [ah-**po**-krif] m. apocrypha; apocryphal writing
apokryficzny [ah-po-kri-**feech**-ni] adj.m. apocryphal (writing, etc.)
apokryfowy [ah-po-kri-**fo**-vi] adj.m. apocryphal (writing, etc.)
apoliński [ah-po-**leeń**-skee] adj.m. of Apollo; Apolline; Apollinian; Apollonistic
apolitycznie [ah-po-lee-**tich**-ńe] adv. apolitically; with political disengagement
apolityczność [ah-po-lee-**tich**-nośhćh] f. non-political attitude, character, etc.; political disengagement
apolityczny [ah-po-lee-**tich**-ni] adj.m. non-political; apolitical; not concerned with political matters;

disengaged politically
apollo [ah-**pol**-lo] m. Apollo; apollo (butterfly)
apolog [ah-**po**-log] m. apologue
apologeta [ah-po-lo-**ge**-tah] m. apologist; one who defends or attempts to justify (a doctrine, faith, action, etc.); vindicator; defender (of a faith, a cause, or an institution)
apologetycznie [ah-po-lo-ge-**tich**-ńe] adv. apologetically
apologetyczny [ah-po-lo-ge-**tich**-ni] adj.m. apologetic; showing apology; expressing regret (about something)
apologetyk [ah-po-lo-**ge**-tik] m. an apologetic; apology
apologetyka [ah-po-lo-**ge**-ti-kah] f. apologetics
apologia [ah-po-**lo**-gyah] f. apology; formal defense (of some idea, doctrine, etc.); an expression of regret (for a fault, insult etc.); vindication
apologizować [ah-po-lo-gee-**zo**-vahćh] v. make apologies (for theories, etc.); praise (ideas, etc.); rationalize (*repeatedly*)
apomorfina [ah-po-mor-**fee**-nah] f. apomorphine
aponeuroza [ah-po-new-**ro**-zah] f. aponeurosis
apopleksja [ah-po-**plek**-syah] f. apoplexy; sudden paralysis (caused by the breaking or obstruction of a blood vessel in the brain)
apoplektycznie [ah-po-plek-**tich**-ńe] adv. apoplectically
apoplektyczny [ah-po-plek-**tich**-ni] adj.m. apoplectic
atak apoplektyczny [**ah**-tahk ah-po-plek-**tich**-ni] exp.: apoplectic seizure or stroke
apoplektyk [ah-po-**plek**-tik] m. apoplectic; person liable to apoplexy
aporia [ah-**po**-ryah] f. aporia
aport [ah-port] m. apport; contribution (of capital, etc.); initial share; act of apporting; retrieving; excl.: seek dead! (to a dog)
aporter [ah-**por**-ter] m. retriever
aportować [ah-por-**to**-vahćh] v. retrieve; get (something) back; recover; restore; produce an object by spiritualistic medium; find and bring back (by a trained dog) (*repeatedly*)
aportowanie [ah-por-to-**vah**-ńe] n. retrieving
aportowy [ah-por-**to**-vi] adj.m. retrieving
apostata [ah-pos-**tah**-tah] m. apostate; a person guilty of apostasy; turncoat
apostatyczny [ah-pos-tah-**tich**-ni] adj.m. apostatical
apostazja [ah-pos-**tah**-zyah] f. apostasy
aposteriorycznie [ah-pos-te-ryo-**rich**-ńe] adv. a posteriori
aposterioryczny [ah-pos-te-ryo-**rich**-ni] adj.m. a posteriori (reasoning, demonstration, etc.)
aposterioryzm [ah-pos-te-**ryo**-rizm] m. methodological empiricism
apostolat [ah-pos-**to**-laht] m. mission; apostolate; apostleship; bishopric
apostolski [ah-po-**stol**-skee] adj.m. apostolic; missionary
Stolica Apostolska [sto-**lee**-tsah ah-po-**stol**-skah] exp.: Apostolic See; Holy See; Vatican
apostolstwo [ah-po-**stol**-stfo] n. apostolate
apostoł [ah-**po**-stow] m. apostle; leader of a new movement; preacher; advocate
apostołka [ah-po-**stow**-kah] f. (woman) apostle; leader of a new movement; preacher; advocate
apostołować [ah-po-sto-**wo**-vahćh] v. evangelize; preach the Gospel; preach; advocate (*repeatedly*)
apostrof [ah-**po**-strof] m. apostrophe
apostrofa [ah-po-**stro**-fah] f. apostrophe
apostroficzny [ah-po-stro-**feech**-ni] adj.m. apostrophic
apostrofować [ah-po-stro-**fo**-vahćh] v. apostrophize (*repeatedly*)
apotema [ah-po-**te**-mah] f. apothem
apoteoza [ah-po-te-**o**-zah] f. apotheosis; the glorifying (of a

person or thing)
apoteozować [ah-po-te-o-**zo**-vahćh] v. apotheosize; glorify; deify (*repeatedly*)
apoteozowanie [ah-po-te-o-zo-**vah**-ńe] n. glorification
apotropaiczny [ah-po-tro-pah-**eech**-ni] adj.m. apotropaic; designed to avert evil
apotropaizm [ah-po-tro-**pah**-eezm] m. apotropaism; the magic of averting evil
apozycja [ah-po-**zi**-tsyah] f. apposition (grammatical apposition)
apozycyjny [ah-po-zi-**tsiy**-ni] adj.m. of apposition
apraksja [ah-**prah**-ksyah] f. apraxia; loss of coordinated movements
apreter [ah-**pre**-ter] m. dresser; finisher (of fabrics, leather, etc.)
apretować [ah-pre-**to**-vahćh] v. dress; finish (textures, etc.) (*repeatedly*)
apretura [ah-pre-**too**-rah] f. dressing; finishing; putting within margins
apreturować [ah-pre-too-**ro**-vahćh] v. dress; finish (*repeatedly*)
apreturowanie [ah-pre-too-ro-**vah**-ńe] n. finishing (textures, etc.)
a priori [ah **pryo**-ree] exp.: see: **aprioryczny**
argument a priori [ahr-**goo**-ment ah **pryo**-ree] exp.: apriori (presumptive) argument
apriorycznie [ah-pryo-**rich**-ńe] adv. a priori
aprioryczność [ah-pryo-**rich**-nośhćh] f. a priority
aprioryczny [ah-pryo-**rich**-ni] adj.m. a priori; from cause to effect; based on theory instead of experience
apriorysta [ah-pryo-**ri**-stah] m. apriorist
apriorystyczny [ah-pryo-ri-**stich**-ni] adj.m. a priori (argument, etc.)
aprioryzm [ah-**pryo**-rizm] m. apriorism
aprobacja [ah-pro-**bah**-tsyah] f. approval; approbation
aprobata [ah-pro-**bah**-tah] f. approval; approbation; sanction; applause; favorable attitude or opinion; formal consent
spotkać się z aprobatą [**spot**-kahćh śhan z ah-pro-**bah**-town] exp.: to meet with approval
wyrazić aprobatę [vi-**rah**-źheećh ah-pro-**bah**-tan] exp.: to express one's approval of...
aprobatywnie [ah-pro-bah-**tiv**-ńe] adv. with approval
aprobatywny [ah-pro-bah-**tiv**-ni] adj.m. giving approval
aprobować [ah-pro-**bo**-vahćh] v. approve (of); endorse; sanction (*repeatedly*)
aprobowanie [ah-pro-bo-**vah**-ńe] n. applause; sanction; approval
aprobująco [ah-pro-boo-**yown**-tso] adv. approvingly; with approval
kiwnąć głową aprobująco [**keev**-nownćh **gwo**-vown ah-pro-boo-**yown**-tso] exp.: to nod approvingly; to nod approval
aproksymacja [ah-pro-ksi-**mah**-tsyah] f. approximation
aproksymatywny [ah-pro-ksi-mah-**tiv**-ni] adj.m. approximate
aprosza [ah-**pro**-shah] f. sap; covered siege-trench
aprowidować [ah-pro-vee-**do**-vahćh] v. provide; supply (food or commodities); purvey (for the army, etc.) (*repeatedly*)
aprowidować się [ah-pro-vee-**do**-vahćh śhan] v. provide for oneself; supply oneself (with food or commodities) (*repeatedly*)
aprowidowanie [ah-pro-vee-do-**vah**-ńe] n. food supply; bringing provisions
aprowizacja [ah-pro-vee-**zah**-tsyah] f. food supply; provisions; the providing of provisions; supplies
aprowizacyjny [ah-pro-vee-zah-**tsiy**-ni] adj.m. provision (merchant, system, etc.)
artykuły aprowizacyjne [ahr-ti-**koo**-wi ah-pro-vee-zah-**tsiy**-ne] exp.: provisions
braki aprowizacyjne [**brah**-kee ah-pro-vee-zah-**tsiy**-ne] exp.: scarcity of provisions
kartki aprowizacyjne [**kahr**-tkee ah-pro-vee-zah-**tsiy**-ne] exp.: food cards; ration cards; coupons

aprowizator [ah-pro-vee-**zah**-tor] m. purveyor
a psik! [ah pśheek] exp.: (imitation of the sound of a sneeze)
apsyda [ah-**psi**-dah] f. apse; apses
apsydalny [ah-psi-**dahl**-ni] adj.m. apsidal
apsydowy [ah-psi-**do**-vi] adj.m. apsidal
apteczka [ahp-**tech**-kah] f. medicine chest
apteczka podróżna [ahp-**tech**-kah po-**droozh**-nah] exp.: first aid kit
apteczny [ahp-**tech**-ni] adj.m. pharmaceutic; pharmaceutical
punkt apteczny [poonkt ahp-**tech**-ni] exp.: dispensary
skład apteczny [skwaht ahp-**tech**-ni] exp.: drug-store
zapach apteczny [**zah**-pahkh ahp-**tech**-ni] exp.: a smell of medicines
apteka [ahp-**te**-kah] f. pharmacy; drug-store
aptekarka [ahp-te-**kahr**-kah] f. (woman) chemist; druggist
aptekarski [ahp-te-**kahr**-skee] adj.m. chemist's; drugist's; pharmaceutic
po aptekarsku [po ahp-te-**kahr**-skoo] exp.: like a chemist; colloq: with utmost accuracy
waga aptekarska [**vah**-gah ahp-te-**kahr**-skah] exp.: dispensing balance; pharmacist's scales
aptekarstwo [ahp-te-**kahr**-stfo] n. pharmacy; pharmaceutics; dispensing; preparation of drugs and medicines
aptekarz [ahp-**te**-kahsh] m. chemist; druggist
aptekarzowa [ahp-te-kah-**zho**-vah] f. druggist's wife
aptekarzyna [ahp-te-kah-**zhi**-nah] m. despicable druggist
ar [ahr] m. are; 100 square meters
ara [**ah**-rah] f. macaw (bird); arrara; ara
Arab [**ah**-rahp] m. Arab; a native of Arabia; Arabian horse
arabczyk [ah-**rahp**-chik] m. Arabian horse
arabesk [ah-**rah**-besk] m. arabesque
arabeska [ah-rah-**bes**-kah] f. arabesque
arabeskowy [ah-rah-bes-**ko**-vi] adj.m. arabesque
arabista [ah-rah-**bee**-stah] m. Arabist; specialist in Arabic; student of Arabic
arabistyczny [ah-rah-bee-**stich**-ni] adj.m. of the Arabic studies
arabistyka [ah-rah-**bee**-sti-kah] f. Arabic philology
arabizm [ah-**rah**-beezm] m. Arab style; Arabic borrowing
arabizować [ah-rah-bee-**zo**-vahćh] v. arabianize; arabize (*repeatedly*)
arabizować się [ah-rah-bee-**zo**-vahćh śhan] v. acquire Arabic culture, style, etc. (*repeatedly*)
Arabka [ah-**rahp**-kah] f. Arabian woman; Arabian mare
arabski [ah-**rahp**-skee] adj.m. Arabian (horse; desert, etc.); Arabic (language, etc.)
awantura arabska [ah-vahn-**too**-rah ah-**rahp**-skah] exp.: fantastic adventure; slang: noisy quarrel
język arabski [**yan**-zik ah-**rahp**-skee] exp.: Arabic language
po arabsku [po ah-**rahp**-skoo] exp.: in Arabic; in Arabian fashion; after the Arabian manner
arabszczyzna [ah-rahp-**shchiz**-nah] f. Arabic, the Arabic language
arachid [ah-**rah**-kheet] m. peanut
arachidowy [ah-rah-khee-**do**-vi] adj.m. peanut (oil, etc.)
arachnolog [ah-rah-**khno**-log] m. aranchologist; specialist in the study of spiders
arachnologia [ah-rah-khno-**lo**-gyah] f. arachnology; the study of spiders and other arachnids
aragonit [ah-rah-**go**-ńeet] m. aragonite (mineral)
aragonitowy [ah-rah-go-ńee-**to**-vi] adj.m. aragonitic
arak [**ah**-rahk] m. arrack; rack
arakowy [ah-rah-**ko**-vi] adj.m. arrack (smell, taste, punch, etc.)
aralia [ah-**rah**-lyah] f. aralia (plant); araliaceous plant
araliowaty [ah-rah-lyo-**vah**-ti] adj.m. araliaceous (plant, etc.)
aramejski [ah-rah-**mey**-skee] adj.m. Aramaic; Aramean; Aramaean; the original language of the Bible

aranż [ah-rahnsh] m. (musical) arrangement; adaptation
aranżacja [ah-rahn-**zhah**-tsyah] f. (musical) arrangement; adaptation
aranżer [ah-**rahn**-zher] m. organizer; arranger; schemer; dance leader
aranżerka [ah-rahn-**zher**-kah] f. (female) organizer; arranger; schemer; dance leader
aranżować [ah-rahn-**zho**-vahćh] v. organize; arrange; put in the correct order; classify; prepare; arrive at agreement about (something); scheme; plan (*repeatedly*)
aranżowanie [ah-rahn-zho-**vah**-ńe] n. arrangement
arara [ah-**rah**-rah] f. macaw (bird); arrara; ara
araukaria [ah-rahw-**kahr**-yah] f. araucarian pine tree
arbalet [ahr-**bah**-let] m. arbalest; arbalester; cross-bow; cross-bow man; cross-bow bolt
arbiter [ahr-**bee**-ter] m. arbitrator; moderator; judge; umpire; mediator
arbitralnie [ahr-bee-**trahl**-ńe] adv. arbitrarily; despotically
arbitralność [ahr-bee-**trahl**-nośhćh] f. arbitrariness; despotic (high-handed, masterly, etc.) manner of acting
arbitralny [ahr-bee-**trahl**-ni] adj.m. arbitrary; despotic; absolute; discretionary
arbitraż [ahr-**bee**-trahsh] m. arbitration (of exchange); judgment (settlement) of a dispute by an arbiter; arbitrage
arbitrażować [ahr-bee-trah-**zho**-vahćh] v. arbitrate; mediate (*repeatedly*)
arbitrażowanie [ahr-bee-trah-zho-**vah**-ńe] n. arbitration; mediation; arbitrament
arbitrażowy [ahr-bee-trah-**zho**-vi] adj.m. arbitral; of arbitration; resulting from arbitration
arboretum [ahr-bo-**re**-toom] n. arboretum; botanical garden of trees
arbuz [**ahr**-boos] m. watermelon; slang: refusal; rebuff; head; pate
arcaby [ahr-**tsah**-bi] pl. checkers; draughts (Brit.); see: **warcaby**
archaicznie [ahr-khah-**eech**-ńe] adv. in archaic way; in archaic language
archaiczność [ahr-khah-**eech**-nośhćh] f. characteristic of being archaic; archaism; archaicism
archaiczny [ahr-khah-**eech**-ni] adj.m. archaic; ancient; old-fashioned; no longer used
archaik [ahr-**khah**-eek] m. archaic
archaista [ahr-khah-**ee**-stah] m. archaist
archaistyczny [ahr-khah-ee-**stich**-ni] adj.m. archaistic
archaizacja [ahr-khah-ee-**zah**-tsyah] f. imitation of the archaic usage, or style
archaizator [ahr-khah-ee-**zah**-tor] m. imitator of the archaic
archaizm [ahr-**khah**-eezm] m. archaism; an archaic word; obsolete expression
archaizować [ahr-khah-ee-**zo**-vahćh] v. make look archaic; imitate (*repeatedly*)
archaizowanie [ahr-khah-ee-zo-**vah**-ńe] n. imitation of the archaic
archanielski [ahr-khah-**ńel**-skee] adj.m. archangelic
archanielstwo [ahr-khah-**ńel**-stfo] n. archangelic nature; archangelic character
archanioł [ahr-**khah**-ńow] m. archangel; an angel of a high rank
archeocjaty [ahr-khe-o-**tsyah**-ti] pl. Archeocyathi (Cambrian fossils)
archeograf [ahr-khe-**o**-grahf] m. archeographer; scholar of antique scripts
archeografia [ahr-khe-o-**grah**-fyah] f. archeography; study of antique scripts
archeolog [ahr-khe-**o**-log] m. archeologist
archeologia [ahr-khe-o-**lo**-gyah] f. archaeology; the study of the life of ancient peoples; archeology
archeologicznie [ahr-khe-o-lo-**geech**-ńe] adv. archaeologically; as regards archaeology (archeology)
archeologiczny [ahr-khe-o-lo-**geech**-ni] adj.m. archaeological (studies,

research, excavations, etc.)
archeopteryks [ahr-khe-o-**pte**-riks] m. archaeopteryx (pigeon-like bird
archeozoiczny [ahr-khe-o-zo-**eech**-ni] adj.m. Archeozoic (era, etc.)
archeozoik [ahr-khe-o-**zo**-eek] m. Archeozoic era
archetyp [ahr-**khe**-tip] m. archetype; prototype
archetypowo [ahr-khe-ti-**po**-vo] adv. as a prototype
archetypowy [ahr-khe-ti-**po**-vi] adj.m. archetypal; prototype (model, etc.)
archi- [ahr-khee-] prefix: principal
archidiakon [ahr-khee-**dyah**-kon] m. archdeacon
archidiakonalny [ahr-khee-dyah-ko-**nahl**-ni] adj.m. archidiaconal
archidiakonat [ahr-khee-dyah-**ko**-naht] m. archdeaconship; archdeaconry; archdeacon's district
archidiakonia [ahr-khee-dyah-**ko**-ńyah] f. archdeacon's residence; archdeaconship; archdeaconry; archdeacon's district
archidiecezja [ahr-khee-dye-**tse**-zyah] f. archdiocese
archigonia [ahr-khee-**go**-ńyah] f. archegonia; spontaneous generation
archijerej [ahr-khee-**ye**-rey] m. Orthodox metropolitan
archikatedra [ahr-khee-kah-**te**-drah] f. archbishop's see; archsee
archikatedralny [ahr-khee-kah-te-**drahl**-ni] adj.m. of archbishop's cathedral (church, etc.)
archikonfraternia [ahr-khee-kon-frah-**ter**-ńah] f. archconfraternity
archimandria [ahr-khee-**mahn**-dryah] f. office of a superior of Greek monastery
archimandryta [ahr-khee-mahn-**dri**-tah] m. archimandrite; honorary title of an abbot, patriarch, etc.
archimedesowy [ahr-khee-me-de-**so**-vi] adj.m. Archimedean (principle, screw, etc.)
archipelag [ahr-khee-**pe**-lahg] m. archipelago; a group of many islands
archiprezbiter [ahr-khee-prez-**bee**-ter] m. archpriest; archipresbyter
archirej [ahr-**khee**-rey] m. Orthodox metropolitan
architekt [ahr-**khee**-tekt] m. architect; planer; builder; organizer; creator
architektka [ahr-khee-**tek**-tkah] f. (female) architect; planer; builder; organizer; creator
architektonicznie [ahr-khee-te-kto-**ńeech**-ńe] adv. architecturally; structurally
architektoniczny [ahr-khee-te-kto-**ńeech**-ni] adj.m. architectonic; architectural; structural; tectonic
architektonika [ahr-khee-te-**kto**-ńee-kah] f. architectonics; the science of architecture; structural design
architektura [ahr-khee-te-**ktoo**-rah] f. architecture; the science or profession of designing and constructing buildings; a style of construction; structure; construction
architektura wnętrz [ahr-khee-te-**ktoo**-rah vnantsh] exp.: interior design; interior decoration
architektura ogrodnicza [ahr-khee-te-**ktoo**-rah o-grod-**ńee**-chah] exp.: landscaping; garden designing
architraw [ahr-**khee**-trahf] m. architrave
archiwalia [ahr-khee-**vahl**-yah] pl. archives; records; archival material; files; rolls
archiwalnie [ahr-khee-**vahl**-ńe] adv. on the basis of archival records
archiwalny [ahr-khee-**vahl**-ni] adj.m. archival
archiwariusz [ahr-khee-**vahr**-yoosh] m. archivist; keeper of archives, records, or files; registrar; university registrar
archiwista [ahr-khee-**vee**-stah] m. archivist
archiwistka [ahr-khee-**vee**-stkah] f. (female) archivist
archiwistyka [ahr-khee-**vee**-sti-kah] f. science of archives; science of record keeping
archiwizować [ahr-khee-vee-**zo**-vahćh] v. organize archives; keep records; keep files; file

(*repeatedly*)
archiwolta [ahr-khee-**vol**-tah] f. archivolt
archiwoznawstwo [ahr-khee-vo-**znahf**-stfo] n. see: **archiwistyka**
archiwum [ahr-**khee**-voom] n. family or public archive(s) or records; files; Record Office; registry; register office
archont [**ahr**-khont] m. archon
archozaur [ahr-**kho**-zahwr] m. archosaurus (reptile)
arcy- [**ahr**-tsi] prefix: arch-; most; exceedingly; extremely; supremely; tremendously; awfully (interesting, etc.)
arcybanalny [ahr-tsi-bah-**nahl**-ni] adj.m. very banal; lacking originality
arcybiskup [ahr-tsi-**bee**-skoop] m. archbishop
arcybiskupi [ahr-tsi-bee-**skoo**-pee] adj.m. archiepiscopal; of archbishop
arcybiskupstwo [ahr-tsi-bee-**skoop**-stfo] n. archbishopric
arcybogaty [ahr-tsi-bo-**gah**-ti] adj.m. very rich; luxurious
arcybractwo [ahr-tsi-**brahts**-tfo] n. archconfraternity
arcychrześcijański [ahr-tsi-khshe-śhćhee-**yahń**-skee] adj.m. staunch; (title:) Most Christian
arcyciekawy [ahr-tsi-ćhe-**kah**-vi] adj.m. most interesting
arcydelikatny [ahr-tsi-de-lee-**kaht**-ni] adj.m. meticulously delicate
arcydiakon [ahr-tsi-**dyah**-kon] m. archdeacon
arcydobry [ahr-tsi-**do**-bri] adj.m. unusually good
arcydziełko [ahr-tsi-**dźhew**-ko] n. (small, nice) masterpiece
arcydzieło [ahr-tsi-**dźhe**-wo] n. masterpiece
arcydzięgiel [ahr-tsi-**dźhan**-gel] m. angelica (a herb)
arcydzięglowy [ahr-tsi-dźhan-**glo**-vi] adj.m. angelica (herb, etc.)
arcydziwny [ahr-tsi-**dźheev**-ni] adj.m. very strange
arcygroźny [ahr-tsi-**groźh**-ni] adj.m. very threatening
arcykapłan [ahr-tsi-**kah**-pwahn] m. high priest
arcykapłanka [ahr-tsi-kah-**pwahn**-kah] f. high priestess
arcykapłański [ahr-tsi-kah-**pwahń**-skee] adj.m. high-priestly
arcykatedra [ahr-tsi-kah-**te**-drah] f. archsee; archbishop's see
arcykomtur [ahr-tsi-**kom**-toor] m. Grand Commander (of the armed monks of the Teutonic Order)
arcykosztowny [ahr-tsi-kosh-**tov**-ni] adj.m. very expensive
arcyksiążę [ahr-tsi-**kśhown**-zhan] m. archduke
arcyksiążęcy [ahr-tsi-kśhown-**zhan**-tsi] adj.m. archducal; of the archduchy
arcyksięstwo [ahr-tsi-**kśhan**-stfo] n. archduchy; archducal family
arcyksiężna [ahr-tsi-**kśhan**-zhnah] f. archduchess
arcyksiężniczka [ahr-tsi-kśhanzh-**ńeech**-kah] f. archduchess; archduke's daughter
arcyłgarz [ahr-**tsi**-wgahsh] m. the greatest liar
arcyłotr [ahr-**tsi**-wotr] m. arch-knave
arcymiły [ahr-tsi-**mee**-wi] adj.m. extremely nice
arcymistrz [ahr-**tsi**-meestsh] m. past master (in, of); absolute master of (a subject, sport, etc.)
arcynudny [ahr-tsi-**nood**-ni] adj.m. most boring
arcypasterz [ahr-tsi-**pah**-stesh] m. arch-prelate; arch-pastor
arcypięknie [ahr-tsi-**pyank**-ńe] adv. most beautifully
arcypiękny [ahr-tsi-**pyank**-ni] adj.m. most beautiful
arcyskromnie [ahr-tsi-**skrom**-ńe] adv. very modestly; most frugally
arcyskromny [ahr-tsi-**skrom**-ni] adj.m. very modest; most frugal
arcyśmieszny [ahr-tsi-**śhmyesh**-ni] adj.m. very funny; most comical
arcytrudny [ahr-tsi-**trood**-ni] adj.m. of very difficult (disposition, etc.); most difficult
arcyważny [ahr-tsi-**vahzh**-ni] adj.m. very important; most important
arcyzabawny [ahr-tsi-zah-**bah**-vni] adj.m. very funny; most amusing
arden [**ahr**-den] m. heavy draw

horse of the Ardennes
ardeński [ahr-**deń**-skee] adj.m. Ardennes (population, forests, climate, etc.)
arealny [ah-re-**ahl**-ni] adj.m. unreal; not realistic (plans, ideas, etc.)
areał [ah-**re**-ahw] m. acreage
areka [ah-**re**-kah] f. areca; catechu (nuts)
arekowy [ah-re-**ko**-vi] adj.m. of areca; catechu (nuts, etc.)
areligijny [ah-re-lee-**geey**-ni] adj.m. non-religious; of an agnostic
arena [ah-**re**-nah] f. arena; stage; scene; the center of an ancient Roman amphitheater, where contests were held; any place or sphere of struggle
arena międzynarodowa [ah-**re**-nah myan-dzi-nah-ro-**do**-vah] exp.: the arena of international politics; the international scene
arena wojenna [ah-**re**-nah vo-**yen**-nah] exp.: the theater of war; the arena of war
arena polityczna [ah-**re**-nah po-lee-**tich**-nah] exp.: arena of politics
wkraczać na arenę [fkrah-chahćh nah ah-**re**-nan] exp.: to come into prominence
zejść z areny [zeyśhćh z ah-**re**-ni] exp.: to quit the scene
arenal [ah-**re**-nahl] m. wet coastal sands
arenda [ah-**ren**-dah] f. lease (out); rent; inn; leased property or rights
arendarz [ah-**ren**-dahsh] m. lease-holder; inn-keeper (hist.); publican; lessee
arendować [ah-ren-**do**-vahćh] v. lease (out); put out to lease; take on a lease; take lease of; take lease to (property, etc.) (*repeatedly*)
arendowy [ah-ren-**do**-vi] adj.m. of lease
arenga [ah-**ren**-gah] f. arenga palm; preamble
arenowy [ah-re-**no**-vi] adj.m. sandy; of sand
areografia [ah-re-o-**grah**-fyah] f. study of the planet Mars
areograficzny [ah-re-o-grah-**feech**-ni] adj.m. of study of the planet Mars
areola [ah-re-**o**-lah] f. areola; a small pit or cavity; heavenly crown; aureole
areolog [ah-re-**o**-log] m. areologist
areologia [ah-re-o-**lo**-gyah] f. areology; study of the planet Mars
areologicznie [ah-re-o-lo-**geech**-ńe] adv. areologically
areologiczny [ah-re-o-lo-**geech**-ni] adj.m. areological
areometr [ah-**re**-o-metr] m. hydrometer; areometer
areometryczny [ah-re-o-me-**trich**-ni] adj.m. of hydrometer; aerometric
areopag [ah-re-**o**-pahg] m. Areopagus
areopagita [ah-re-o-pah-**gee**-tah] m. Areopagite; member of the Areopagus
areszt [**ah**-resht] m. arrest; jail; custody; confinement; detention; prison; gaol; house of detention; slang: cooler
areszt domowy [**ah**-resht do-**mo**-vi] exp.: house arrest; open arrest
areszt koszarowy [**ah**-resht ko-shah-**ro**-vi] exp.: confinement to barracks
areszt prewencyjny [**ah**-resht pre-ven-**tsiy**-ni] exp.: detention of suspicion
być zaaresztowanym [bićh zah-ah-re-shto-**vah**-nim] exp.: to be under arrest
położyć areszt na coś [po-**wo**-zhićh **ah**-resht nah tsośh] exp.: to seize something
aresztancki [ah-re-**shtahn**-tskee] adj.m. prisoner's; convict's
aresztant [ah-**re**-shtahnt] m. prisoner; convict; slang: jail-bird
aresztantka [ah-re-**shtahn**-tkah] f. (female) prisoner; convict; slang: jail-bird; lag (Brit.)
aresztować [ah-re-**shto**-vahćh] v. arrest; imprison; apprehend; take into custody; impound; confiscate; seize (*repeatedly*)
aresztowanie [ah-re-shto-**vah**-ńe] n. arrest; imprisonment; detention; seizure

nakaz aresztowania [nah-kahs ah-re-shto-**vah**-ńah] exp.: writ of arrest; capias
aresztowany [ah-re-shto-**vah**-ni] adj.m. arrested; jailed (person)
arfa [**ahr**-fah] f. sieve; winnower; harp
arfować [ahr-**fo**-vahćh] v. sieve; use winnower; sift (*repeatedly*)
argentan [ahr-**gen**-tahn] m. nickel silver
argentometria [ahr-gen-to-**me**-tryah] f. argentometry
Argentyńczyk [ahr-gen-**tiń**-chik] m. Argentine
Argentynka [ahr-gen-**tin**-kah] f. Argentine (woman)
argentyński [ahr-gen-**tiń**-skee] adj.m. Argentine
argentyt [ahr-**gen**-tit] m. argentite (mineral)
arginina [ahr-gee-**ńee**-nah] f. arginine
argon [**ahr**-gon] m. argon (atomic number 18)
argona [ahr-**go**-nah] f. fabric of artificial fiber and wool of sheep
Argonauta [ahr-go-**nahw**-tah] m. Argonaut
argonowy [ahr-go-**no**-vi] adj.m. argon (laser, etc.)
argot [**ahr**-got] m. slang
argument [ahr-**goo**-ment] m. argument for; argument against; reason; plea; contention; point
ostateczny argument [o-stah-**tech**-ni ahr-**goo**-ment] exp.: clinching argument; final argument; decisive argument
pokonać argumentami [po-**ko**-nahćh ahr-goo-men-**tah**-mee] exp.: to defeat with arguments; to argue somebody down
przytaczać argumenty [pshi-**tah**-chahćh ahr-goo-**men**-ti] exp.: to put forward arguments (for something)
wysuwać argumenty [vi-**soo**-vahćh ahr-goo-**men**-ti] exp.: to put forward arguments (for something)
zbić argument [zbeećh ahr-**goo**-ment] exp.: to knock the bottom out of an argument
argumentacja [ahr-goo-men-**tah**-tsyah] f. reasoning; argumentation; motivation
argumentacyjnie [ahr-goo-men-tah-**tsiy**-ńe] adv. argumentatively
argumentacyjny [ahr-goo-men-tah-**tsiy**-ni] adj.m. argumentative
argumentator [ahr-goo-men-**tah**-tor] m. argumentator; conversationalist
argumentować [ahr-goo-men-**to**-vahćh] v. argue; contend; give reasons for or against; dispute; quarrel; debate; maintain; persuade by giving reasons (*repeatedly*)
argumentowanie [ahr-goo-men-to-**vah**-ńe] n. arguing; argumentation
argus [**ahr**-goos] m. argus pheasant
argusowy [ahr-goo-**so**-vi] adj.m. argus (pheasant, etc.)
aria [**ahr**-yah] f. aria (in an opera) song in an opera (especially for solo voice)
Aria [**ahr**-yah] m. see: Aryjczyk
Ariadna [ahr-**yahd**-nah] f. Ariadna
nić Ariadny [ńeećh ahr-**yahd**-ni] exp.: clue; clew
Arian [**ahr**-yahn] m. Arian; Aryan
Arianin [ahr-**yah**-ńeen] m. Arian
arianizm [ahr-**yah**-ńeezm] m. Arianism
Arianka [ahr-**yahn**-kah] f. (female) Arian; Aryan
ariański [ahr-**yahń**-skee] adj.m. Arian; Aryan
ariergarda [ahr-yer-**gahr**-dah] f. rear guard
arierscena [ahr-yer-**stse**-nah] f. back of the stage
arieta [ahr-**ye**-tah] f. arieta
arietka [ahr-**ye**-tkah] f. (small) arieta
arion [**ahr**-yon] m. garden snail
arioso [ahr-**yo**-zo] n. arioso
ariostowy [ahr-yo-**sto**-vi] adj.m. in the style of Ariosto
arka [**ahr**-kah] f. ark
arkabuz [ahr-**kah**-boos] m. harquebus; arquebus
arkada [ahr-**kah**-dah] f. arcade; covered passageway (lined with shops); arcaded passageway; line of arches and their supporting columns

Arkadia [ahr-**kah**-dyah] f. ideal rustic paradise
arkadka [ahr-**kah**-tkah] f. (small) arcade
arkadkowy [ahr-kah-**tko**-vi] adj.m. arcade (wall paintings, etc.)
arkadowanie [ahr-kah-do-**vah**-ńe] n. arcading; arcade; arcades
arkadowy [ahr-kah-**do**-vi] adj.m. arcaded (passage, courtyard, etc.)
arkadyjski [ahr-kah-**diy**-skee] adj.m. Arcadian
arkan [**ahr**-kahn] m. lasso; lariat
arkana [ahr-**kah**-nah] pl. arcana; secrets; esoteric mysteries; slang: the ropes
arkatura [ahr-kah-**too**-rah] f. arcade part of a structure
arkebuz [ahr-**ke**-boos] m. harquebus; arquebus
arkebuza [ahr-ke-**boo**-zah] f. harquebus; arquebus
arkebuzer [ahr-ke-**boo**-zer] m. harquebusier; arquebusier
arkosolium [ahr-ko-**so**-lyoom] n. arch-like grave in catacombs
arkoza [ahr-**ko**-zah] f. a variety of sandstone
arktogea [ahr-kto-**ge**-ah] f. Eurasia, North America, and Africa as a zoological unit
arktyczny [ahr-**ktich**-ni] adj.m. Arctic; of or near the North Pole
arkusik [ahr-**koo**-śheek] m. small sheet of paper
arkusz [**ahr**-koosh] m. sheet (of paper, metal, etc.); (business) form
arkuszowy [ahr-koo-**sho**-vi] adj.m. in-folio; sheet (metal, etc.)
arlekin [ahr-**le**-keen] m. harlequin
arlekinada [ahr-le-kee-**nah**-dah] f. harlequinade; buffoonery; horseplay
arlekinowy [ahr-le-kee-**no**-vi] adj.m. harlequin (colors, etc.)
arlekiński [ahr-le-**keeń**-skee] adj.m. harlequin (coat, etc.)
armada [ahr-**mah**-dah] f. armada; fleet of warships; fleet of airplanes
armadyl [ahr-**mah**-dil] m. armadillo
armagnac [ahr-mah-**ńahk**] m. armagnac (a French brandy similar to: cognac)
armata [ahr-**mah**-tah] f. cannon
armatka [ahr-**mah**-tkah] f. small caliber gun
armatni [ahr-**maht**-ńee] adj.m. of cannon; gun (fire, etc.)
ogień armatni [**o**-geń ahr-**maht**-ńee] exp.: gun-fire; artillery fire
mięso armatnie [**my**an-so ahr-**maht**-ńe] exp.: cannon fodder
armatnik [ahr-**maht**-ńeek] m. gunner
armator [ahr-**mah**-tor] m. ship owner; skipper; charterer
armatorski [ahr-mah-**tor**-skee] adj.m. shipowner's; skipper's; charterer's; chartering
armatura [ahr-mah-**too**-rah] f. fittings; fitments; mountings; fixtures; tackle; armature
Armenka [ahr-**men**-kah] f. Armenian (woman)
armenoidalny [ahr-me-no-ee-**dahl**-ni] adj.m. Armenoid
Armeńczyk [ahr-**meń**-chik] m. Armenian
armeński [ahr-**meń**-skee] adj.m. Armenian
armia [**ahr**-myah] f. army; array; field army; vast host; multitude (of unemployed, etc.)
Armia Czerwona [**ahr**-myah cher-**vo**-nah] exp.: Red Army of the USSR
Armia Krajowa [**ahr**-myah krah-**yo**-vah] exp.: the Home Army (the Polish underground army of the Resistance Movement in World War II with its Commander-in-Chief in Great Britain)
Armia Zbawienia [**ahr**-myah zbah-**vye**-ńah] exp.: the Salvation Army
armijny [ahr-**meey**-ni] adj.m. army's
armila [ahr-**mee**-lah] f. armila
armilarny [ahr-mee-**lahr**-ni] adj.m. armillary
arminianin [ahr-mee-**ńyah**-ńeen] m. believer in Arminianism
arminianizm [ahr-mee-**ńyah**-ńeezm] m. Arminianism
armistycjum [ahr-mee-**sti**-tsyoom] n. armistice; truce; cease-fire
arnika [ahr-**ńee**-kah] f. arnica; mountain tobacco; tincture of

arnica
arnikowy [ahr-ńee-**ko**-vi] adj.m. of arnica; of mountain tobacco; arnica (oil, etc.)
arnota [ahr-**no**-tah] f. archiote (tree)
arogancja [ah-ro-**gahn**-tsyah] f. arrogance; insolence; conceit; overweening behavior; contumely; presumption
arogancki [ah-ro-**gahn**-tskee] adj.m. arrogant; haughty; insolent; conceited; presumptuous; contumelious
arogancko [ah-ro-**gahn**-tsko] adv. arrogantly; with arrogance; haughtily; insolently; with insolence; conceitedly; contumeliously
arogant [ah-**ro**-gahnt] m. arrogant person; conceited person; insolent man; overweening man
arogantka [ah-ro-**gahn**-tkah] f. arrogant woman; conceited woman; insolent woman; overweening woman
aromacik [ah-ro-**mah**-ćheek] m. (nice, little) aroma; flavor; fragrance; sweet smell
aromat [ah-**ro**-maht] m. aroma; flavor; fragrance; sweet smell; redolence; aromatic substance; aromatic compound
aromatycznie [ah-ro-mah-**tich**-ńe] adv. aromatically; fragrantly
aromatyczny [ah-ro-mah-**tich**-ni] adj.m. aromatic; fragrant; sweet-smelling; with aromatic flavor
aromatyzacja [ah-ro-mah-ti-**zah**-tsyah] f. aromatization
aromatyzer [ah-ro-mah-**ti**-zer] m. aromatizer
aromatyzować [ah-ro-mah-ti-**zo**-vahćh] v. aromatize (*repeatedly*)
aromatyzowanie [ah-ro-mah-ti-zo-**vah**-ńe] n. aromatization
aron [**ah**-ron] m. arum (plant)
arpedżio [ahr-**pe**-dzhyo] n. arpeggio
arpedżiowy [ahr-pe-**dzhyo**-vi] adj.m. arpeggio (rhythm, etc.)
arpeggio [ahr-**pe**-dzhyo] n. arpeggio
arras [**ahr**-rahs] m. arras (tapestry)
arrasowy [ahr-rah-**so**-vi] adj.m. arras (tapestry, etc.)
arsen [ahr-sen] m. arsenic
arsenalik [ahr-se-**nah**-leek] m. (small) arsenal
arsenał [ahr-**se**-nahw] m. arsenal; armory; assemblage (of arguments, tricks, objects, etc.); stock-in-trade (of catch-words, etc.)
arsenawy [ahr-se-**nah**-vi] adj.m. arsenious
arsenek [ahr-**se**-nek] m. arsenide
arseniak [ahr-**se**-ńahk] m. arseno-hydrogen
arsenian [ahr-**se**-ńyahn] m. arsenate
arsenin [ahr-**se**-ńeen] m. arsenite
arsenit [ahr-**se**-ńeet] m. arsenolite; white arsenic
arsenoorganiczny [ahr-se-no-or-gah-**ńeech**-ni] adj.m. arseno-organic (compound, etc.)
arsenopiryt [ahr-se-no-**pee**-rit] m. arsenopyrite; arsenical pyrite; mispickel (mineral)
arsenowodór [ahr-se-no-**vo**-door] m. arseno-hydrogen
arsenowy [ahr-se-**no**-vi] adj.m. arsenic
arsonwalizacja [ahr-son-vah-lee-**zah**-tsyah] f. high-frequency electrical treatment; arsonvalization
arsyna [ahr-**si**-nah] f. arsine
arszenik [ahr-**she**-ńeek] m. arsenic trioxide; arsenic (poison)
arszenikowy [ahr-she-ńee-**ko**-vi] adj.m. arsenical
zatrucie arszenikowe [zah-**troo**-ćhe ahr-she-ńee-**ko**-ve] exp.: arsenical poisoning; arsenicism; arsenism
arszyn [**ahr**-shin] m. arshin (= 28 inches) (Russian measure)
artefakt [ahr-**te**-fahkt] m. artefact; artifact
artel [**ahr**-tel] m. artel (work and minor producer's cooperative in Russia)
arteria [ahr-**ter**-yah] f. artery; thoroughfare; highway; waterway
arterialny [ahr-ter-**yahl**-ni] adj.m. arterial
arteriografia [ahr-ter-yo-**grah**-fyah] f. arteriography
arteriograficzny [ahr-ter-yo-grah-**feech**-ni] adj.m. arteriographic
arteriosklerotyczny [ahr-ter-yo-skle-

ro-tich-ni] adj.m. arteriosclerotic
arterioskleroza [ahr-ter-yo-skle-ro-zah] f. arteriosclerosis
arteriotomia [ahr-ter-yo-to-myah] f. arteriotomy
arteroskleroza [ahr-te-ro-skle-ro-zah] f. arteriosclerosis
arteryna [ahr-te-ri-nah] f. arterin
artezyjska studnia [ahr-te-ziy-skah stood-ńah] exp.: artisan well
artretyczka [ahr-tre-tich-kah] f. an arthritic woman; a gouty woman
artretyczny [ahr-tre-tich-ni] adj.m. arthritic; gouty
guz artretyczny [gooz ahr-tre-tich-ni] exp.: gouty concretion; tophus
artretyk [ahr-tre-tik] m. an arthritic person; a gouty person
artretyzm [ahr-tre-tizm] m. arthritis; gout
artrologia [ahr-tro-lo-gyah] f. arthrology
artropatia [ahr-tro-pah-tyah] f. joint disease; arthropathy
artroza [ahr-tro-zah] f. arthrosis
artyficjalizm [ahr-ti-fee-tsyah-leezm] m. artificialness
artykulacja [ahr-ti-koo-lah-tsyah] f. articulation; (dent.) occlusion; (arch.) arrangement (of the elevation); disposition
artykulacyjnie [ahr-ti-koo-lah-tsiy-ńe] adv. articulately; with articulation
artykulacyjny [ahr-ti-koo-lah-tsiy-ni] adj.m. articulatory; occlusal
artykulik [ahr-ti-koo-leek] m. short article; paragraph on a newspaper
artykuł [ahr-ti-koow] m. article; entry; clause; commodity; staple; (grammatical:) article
artykuł wstępny [ahr-ti-koow fstanp-ni] exp.: leader; editorial; leading article
artykuły codziennego użytku [ahr-ti-koo-wi tso-dźhen-ne-go oo-zhit-koo] exp.: articles of daily use
artykuły gopodarstwa domowego [ahr-ti-koo-wi go-spo-dahr-stfah do-mo-ve-go] exp.: household goods; household supplies
artykuły przemysłowe [ahr-ti-koo-wi pshe-mi-swo-ve] exp.: manufactured goods
artykuły skórzane [ahr-ti-koo-wi skoo-zhah-ne] exp.: leather-ware
artykuły spożywcze [ahr-ti-koo-wi spo-zhif-che] exp.: articles of food; articles of consumption; groceries
artykuły żelazne [ahr-ti-koo-wi zhe-lah-zne] exp.: hardware articles; ironware
artykułować [ahr-ti-koo-wo-vahćh] v. articulate; divide (a facade, elevation, etc.); vocalize; formulate (opinions, etc.) (*repeatedly*)
artykułowanie [ahr-ti-koo-wo-vah-ńe] n. articulation; division (of a facade, elevation, etc.); vocalization
artykułowany [ahr-ti-koo-wo-vah-ni] adj.m. articulate (speech, etc.)
artykułowy [ahr-ti-koo-wo-vi] adj.m. (theme, etc.) for an article; of an article
artyleria [ahr-ti-ler-yah] f. artillery; gunnery; ordnance
artyleria lekka [ahr-ti-ler-yah lek-kah] exp.: light artillery
artyleria polowa [ahr-ti-ler-yah po-lo-vah] exp.: field artillery
artyleria przeciwlotnicza [ahr-ti-ler-yah pshe-ćheef-lot-ńee-chah] exp.: antiaircraft artillery; flak
artyleryjski [ahr-ti-le-riy-skee] adj.m. artillery (shell, etc.)
artylerzysta [ahr-ti-le-zhis-tah] m. artillerist; gunner; artillery officer
artysta [ahr-ti-stah] m. artist; performer
artysta filmowy [ahr-ti-stah feel-mo-vi] exp.: movie actor; film star; cinema actor
artystka [ahr-ti-stkah] f. actress; woman artist; performer; woman graphic artist
artystostwo [ahr-ti-sto-stfo] n. formalism
artystowski [ahr-ti-stof-skee] adj.m. formalistic (in art)
artystycznie [ahr-ti-stich-ńe] adv. artistically; in a masterly way; skillfully; sensitively to beauty
artystyczność [ahr-ti-stich-nośhćh] f. artistic character; gracefulness; elegance
artystyczny [ahr-ti-stich-ni] adj.m.

artistic; graceful; elegant
rzemiosło artystyczne [zhe-**myo**-swo ahr-ti-**stich**-ne] exp.: artistic handicraft
artyzm [ahr-tizm] m. artistry; artistic skill
arum [ah-room] m. arum
Aryjczyk [ah-**riy**-chik] m. Aryan; Indo-European
Aryjka [ah-**riy**-kah] f. Aryan; Indo-European (woman)
aryjski [ah-**riy**-skee] adj. Aryan
aryjskość [ah-**riy**-skośhćh] f. Aryan character
aryl [ah-ril] m. aryl; aromatic radical
arylować [ah-ri-**lo**-vahćh] v. arilate (*repeatedly*)
arylowanie [ah-ri-lo-**vah**-ńe] n. arylation
arylowy [ah-ri-**lo**-vi] adj.m. aryl (group, etc.)
arymaż [ah-**ri**-mahsh] m. trimming of a ship
arystokracja [ah-ri-sto-**krah**-tsyah] f. aristocracy
arystokrata [ah-ri-sto-**krah**-tah] m. aristocrat
arystokratka [ah-ri-sto-**krah**-tkah] f. (female) aristocrat
arystokratycznie [ah-ri-sto-krah-**tich**-ńe] adv. aristocratically
arystokratyczność [ah-ri-sto-krah-**tich**-nośhćh] f. aristocratic character
arystokratyczny [ah-ri-sto-krah-**tich**-ni] adj.m. aristocratic
arystokratyzm [ah-ri-sto-**krah**-tizm] m. aristocratic descent; aristocratic birth
aryston [ah-**ri**-ston] m. a mechanical-musical instrument
arystotelesowski [ah-ri-sto-te-le-**sof**-skee] adj.m. Aristotelian; Aristotle's (experiment, etc.)
arystotelesowy [ah-ri-sto-te-le-**so**-vi] adj.m. Aristotelian; Aristotle's
arystoteliczny [ah-ri-sto-te-**leech**-ni] adj.m. Aristotelian; Aristotle's
arystotelik [ah-ri-sto-te-leek] m. Aristotelian; follower of Aristotle's theories
arystotelizm [ah-ri-sto-te-leezm] m. Aristotelianism
arytmetycznie [ah-rit-me-**tich**-ńe] adv. arithmetically; by arithmetic; colloq: numerically
arytmetyczny [ah-rit-me-**tich**-ni] adj.m. arithmetical; arithmetic
średnia arytmetyczna [**śhred**-ńah ah-rit-me-**tich**-nah] exp.: arithmetic mean
postęp arytmetyczny [pos-tanp ah-rit-me-**tich**-ni] exp.: arithmetic progression
arytmetyk [ah-rit-**me**-tik] m. arithmetician
arytmetyka [ah-rit-**me**-ti-kah] f. arithmetic
arytmetyzacja [ah-rit-me-ti-**zah**-tsyah] f. arithmetization
arytmia [ah-**rit**-myah] f. arrhythmia; want of rhythm; irregularity; (medical) arrhythmia
arytmicznie [ah-rit-**meech**-ńe] adv. arrhythmically; not rhythmically
arytmiczność [ah-rit-**meech**-nośhćh] f. arrhythmia; lack of rhythm; irregularity (med.)
arytmiczny [ah-rit-**meech**-ni] adj.m. arrhythmic; not rhythmic
arytmograf [ah-rit-**mo**-grahf] m. arithmometer; calculating machine; calculator
arytmogryf [ah-rit-**mo**-grif] m. arrhythmogram; arithmetical charade
arytmometr [ah-rit-**mo**-metr] m. arithmometer; calculator; calculating machine
arywista [ah-ri-**vee**-stah] m. careerist; (social) climber; upstart
arywistka [ah-ri-**vee**-stkah] f. (female) careerist; (social) climber; upstart
arywizm [ah-**ri**-veezm] m. careerism; the art of getting on; unscrupulous ambition
as [ahs] m. ace; A flat
as nad asy [ahs naht **ah**-si] exp.: the ace of aces
asafetyda [ah-sah-fe-**ti**-dah] f. asafetida
asan [ah-sahn] m. Sir
asani [ah-**sah**-ńee] f. Madam
asauł [ah-**sah**-oow] m. officer of Cossack cavalry
ascendent [ah-**stsen**-dent] m. ancestor (hist.)

ascensyjny [ah-stsen-**siy**-ni] adj.m. ascensive
asceta [ah-**stse**-tah] m. ascetic; one who leads a life of strict self-denial; austere man (in appearance, manner, or attitude)
ascetka [ah-**stse**-tkah] f. ascetic (woman)
ascetycznie [ah-stse-**tich**-ńe] adv. ascetically; austerely
ascetyczność [ah-stse-**tich**-nośhćh] f. ascetism; self-denial; austerity
ascetyczny [ah-stse-**tich**-ni] adj.m. ascetic(al) self-denying; austere
ascetyka [ah-**stse**-ti-kah] f. ascetic theology; asceticism
ascetyzm [ah-**stse**-tizm] m. ascetic habits; self-discipline
asceza [ahs-**tse**-zah] f. ascesis; asceticism; Spartan life; self-discipline
asejsmiczny [ah-sey-**smeech**-ni] adj.m. free of seismic movements
asekuracja [ah-se-koo-**rah**-tsyah] f. insurance; insurance policy; assurance; security; safeguard (against); insurance brokers
asekuracyjny [ah-se-koo-rah-**tsiy**-ni] adj.m. insurance (fee, agency, policy, etc.); security (belt. etc.); safeguarding (device, etc.); protective
asekurancki [ah-se-koo-**rahn**-tskee] adj.m. securing oneself against responsibility for one's own decisions
asekurancko [ah-se-koo-**rahn**-tsko] adv. by way of securing oneself against responsibility for one's own decisions
asekuranctwo [ah-se-koo-**rahn**-tstfo] n. tactics of securing oneself against responsibility for one's own decisions
asekurant [ah-se-**koo**-rahnt] m. insurance broker; underwriter; one who secures himself against responsibility for his own decisions
asekurantyzm [ah-se-koo-**rahn**-tizm] m. tactics of securing oneself against responsibility for one's own decisions
asekurator [ah-se-koo-**rah**-tor] m. insurance broker; underwriter
asekurować [ah-se-koo-**ro**-vahćh] v. insure against; secure; safeguard; protect; belay (*repeatedly*)
asekurować się [ah-se-koo-**ro**-vahćh śhan] v. insure (oneself); take out an insurance against; protect oneself; play safe (*repeatedly*)
asekurowanie [ah-se-koo-ro-**vah**-ńe] n. providing insurance (against)
asekurowanie się [ah-se-koo-ro-**vah**-ńe śhan] n. providing oneself with insurance (against)
asemantyczność [ah-se-mahn-**tich**-nośhćh] f. lacking of semantic quality
asemantyczny [ah-se-mahn-**tich**-ni] adj.m. not semantic
asenizacja [ah-se-ńee-**zah**-tsyah] f. garbage removal; improvement of sanitation
asenizacyjny [ah-se-ńee-zah-**tsiy**-ni] adj.m. garbage (collector, transport, etc.)
asenizator [ah-se-ńee-**zah**-tor] m. garbage collector
asenizować [ah-se-ńee-**zo**-vahćh] v. improve the sanitation (of a town, etc.) (*repeatedly*)
asenizowanie [ah-se-ńee-zo-**vah**-ńe] n. improvement of sanitation
asenterunek [ah-sen-te-**roo**-nek] m. conscription; compulsory recruitment
aseptycznie [ah-sep-**tich**-ńe] adv. in a way free of germs; aseptically
aseptyczny [ah-sep-**tich**-ni] adj.m. aseptic; sterile; sterilized
aseptyka [ah-**sep**-ti-kah] f. sterilization; asepsis
asercja [ah-**ser**-tsyah] f. assertion
asertoryczny [ah-ser-to-**rich**-ni] adj.m. assertive
asesor [ah-**se**-sor] m. assessor; associate judge
asesoria [ah-se-**sor**-yah] f. appellate court (in Kingdom of Poland)
asesorski [ah-se-**sor**-skee] adj.m. assessory; assessorial
asesorstwo [ah-se-**sor**-stfo] n. assesor's office; assesor and his wife

asesura [ah-se-**soo**-rah] f. assessor's office
asfalciarski [ah-sfahl-**ćhahr**-skee] adj.m. of asphalt worker
asfalciarz [ah-**sfahl**-ćhahsh] m. asphalt worker
asfalt [**ah**-sfahlt] m. asphalt; mineral pitch
asfalten [ah-**sfahl**-ten] m. asphaltene
asfaltobeton [ah-sfahl-to-**be**-ton] m. asphalt macadam; asphaltic concrete; asphalt cement; asphalt grout; bituminous concrete
asfaltobetonowy [ah-sfahl-to-be-to-**no**-vi] adj.m. of asphalt macadam; of asphaltic concrete
asfaltoguma [ah-sfahl-to-**goo**-mah] f. asphalt-rubber mix (for coating of pavement)
asfaltować [ah-sfahl-**to**-vahćh] v. asphalt (a road, etc.) (*repeatedly*)
asfaltowanie [ah-sfahl-to-**vah**-ńe] n. paving with asphalt
asfaltownia [ah-sfahl-**tov**-ńah] f. asphalt-mixing plant
asfaltowy [ah-sfahl-**to**-vi] adj.m. asphalt (road, etc.)
asfaltyt [ah-**sfahl**-tit] m. asphaltite
asfiksja [ah-**sfee**-ksyah] f. asphyxia
asfodel [ah-**sfo**-del] m. asphodel
asfodelowy [ah-sfo-de-**lo**-vi] adj.m. asphodel (meadow, etc.)
asindziej [ah-**śheen**-dźhey] m. colloq: Sir
askaryda [ah-skah-**ri**-dah] f. ascarid (parasite)
askarydoza [ah-skah-ri-**do**-zah] f. ascaridiasis
asklepiadejski [ah-skle-pyah-**dey**-skee] adj.m. (verse, etc.) of Asclepiades
askorbinowy [ah-skor-bee-**no**-vi] adj.m. against scurvy (vitamin C, acid, etc.)
asocjacja [ah-so-**tsyah**-tsyah] f. association (of ideas, molecules, notions, etc.)
asocjacjonista [ah-so-tsyah-tsyo-**ńee**-stah] m. associationist; a Fourierist
asocjacjonistyczny [ah-so-tsyah-tsyo-ńee-**stich**-ni] adj.m. associationist
asocjacjonizm [ah-so-tsyah-**tsyo**-ńeezm] m. associationism; Fourierism
asocjacyjnie [ah-so-tsyah-**tsiy**-ńe] adv. through association
asocjacyjny [ah-so-tsyah-**tsiy**-ni] adj.m. associatory; associative (reflex, etc.)
asocjatywnie [ah-so-tsyah-**tiv**-ńe] adv. associatively
asocjatywność [ah-so-tsyah-**tiv**-nośhćh] f. associativeness
asocjatywny [ah-so-tsyah-**tiv**-ni] adj.m. associative
asocjować [ah-so-**tsyo**-vahćh] v. associate (*repeatedly*)
asocjować się [ah-so-**tsyo**-vahćh śhan] v. be associated (*repeatedly*)
asomatyczny [ah-so-mah-**tich**-ni] adj.m. asomatous; incorporeal; immaterial
asonacja [ah-so-**nah**-tsyah] f. assonance; partial correspondence of sound
asonancja [ah-so-**nahn**-tsyah] f. assonance; partial correspondence of sound
asonans [ah-**so**-nahns] m. assonance; partial correspondence of sound
asonansowy [ah-so-nahn-**so**-vi] adj.m. assonant; assonantal
asonoryzacja [ah-so-no-ri-**zah**-tsyah] f. elimination of noises and sounds
asortyment [ah-sor-**ti**-ment] m. assortment; variety; choice; stock
asortyment czcionek [ah-sor-**ti**-ment **chćho**-nek] exp.: font; set of type
asortymentowo [ah-sor-ti-men-**to**-vo] adv. by assortment; by variety; by choice
asortymentowy [ah-sor-ti-men-**to**-vi] adj.m. assorted; classified; made up of various sorts; miscellaneous
aspan [**ah**-spahn] m. Sir
aspani [ahs-**pah**-ńee] f. Madam
asparagina [ahs-pah-rah-**gee**-nah] f. asparagine
asparaginowy [ahs-pah-rah-gee-**no**-vi] adj.m. asparagine (acid, etc.)
asparagus [ahs-pah-**rah**-goos] m. asparagus

aspekt [ah-spekt] m. aspect; bearing; face; complexion; feature; the way one appears; the appearance of a thing or idea from specific point of view
rozważyć coś we wszystkich aspektach [roz-**vah**-zhićh tsośh ve **fshist**-keekh ah-**spek**-tahkh] exp.: to consider a thing in all its bearings or from all sides
sprawa ma inny aspekt [**sprah**-vah mah **een**-ni **ah**-spekt] exp.: the problem has a different complexion (a different character)
aspektowy [ah-spe-**kto**-vi] adj.m. aspectual
aspergiloza [ah-sper-gee-**lo**-zah] f. aspergillosis; infection by mold fungus of the genus Aspergillus
aspermia [ah-**sper**-myah] f. aspermia; aspermatism
aspidistra [ah-spee-**dee**-strah] f. Aspidistra (herbs)
aspiracja [ah-spee-**rah**-tsyah] f. aspiration (for, after); ambition to; pretension to; inhalation; breathing; drawing out by suction; removal by an aspirator
aspiracyjny [ah-spee-rah-**tsiy**-ni] adj.m. of ambition; of aspiration; of industrial vacuum cleaning (of grain, etc.)
aspirancki [ah-spee-**rahn**-tskee] adj.m. post-graduate (studies, etc.)
aspirant [ah-**spee**-rahnt] m. candidate to a post (in the legal profession, in the civil service, etc.); post-graduate student; midshipman; reefer
aspirantka [ah-spee-**rahn**-tkah] f. (woman) candidate to a post (in the legal profession, in the civil service, etc.); post-graduate student; midshipman; reefer
aspirantura [ah-spee-rahn-**too**-rah] f. functions (term of office, etc.) of a candidate to a post (in the legal profession, in the civil service, etc.); post-graduate studies
aspirata [ah-spee-**rah**-tah] f. aspirate
aspirator [ah-spee-**rah**-tor] m. aspirator
aspirować [ah-spee-**ro**-vahćh] v. aspirate; aspire (to, after) (*repeatedly*)
aspirować do czegoś [ah-spee-**ro**-vahćh do **che**-gośh] exp.: to aspire to (after) something
aspirowanie [ah-spee-ro-**vah**-ńe] n. aspiration
aspiryna [ah-spee-**ri**-nah] f. aspirin
aspołecznie [ah-spo-**wech**-ńe] adv. not socially; in a reclusive way; selfishly
aspołeczność [ah-spo-**wech**-nośhćh] f. indifference to social matters
aspołeczny [ah-spo-**wech**-ni] adj.m. asocial; indifferent to social matters; avoiding contact with others; selfish; non-social; contrary to the dictates of social life; antisocial; unsocial; not social; reclusive (attitude)
astat [**ah**-staht] m. astatine (atomic number 85)
astatyczny [ah-stah-**tich**-ni] adj.m. astatic
astazja [ah-**stah**-zyah] f. astasa
astenia [ah-**ste**-ńyah] f. asthenia; debility
asteniczny [ah-ste-**ńeech**-ni] adj.m. asthenic; debilitating; weal; slender built
astenik [ah-**ste**-ńeek] m. an asthenic; person of slender build
astenopia [ah-ste-**no**-pyah] f. asthenopia; weakening of sight
astenosfera [ah-ste-no-**sfe**-rah] f. asthenosphere
astenotymia [ah-ste-no-**ti**-myah] f. fearful disposition
astenotymik [ah-ste-no-**ti**-meek] m. person of fearful disposition
aster [**ah**-ster] m. aster (a plant)
astereognozja [ah-ste-re-o-**gno**-zyah] f. agnosia related to the sense of touch
asteroida [ah-ste-**roy**-dah] f. asteroid
asteronim [ah-ste-**ro**-ńeem] m. cryptonym composed of asterisks
asterysk [ah-**ste**-risk] m. asterisk (*)
asteryzm [ah-**ste**-rizm] m. asterism
astma [**ahst**-mah] f. asthma; chronic disorder of coughing and difficult breathing, etc.
astmatyczka [ahst-mah-**tich**-kah] f.

asthmatic; woman affected with asthma
astmatycznie [ahst-mah-**tich**-ńe] adv. asthmatically
astmatyczny [ahst-mah-**tich**-ni] adj.m. asthmatic
astmatyk [ahst-**mah**-tik] m. asthmatic; person affected with asthma
astragal [ahs-**trah**-gahl] m. ball of ankle-joint; astragalus
astragalowy [ahs-trah-gah-**lo**-vi] adj.m. of the ball of ankle-joint; astragalar
astralnie [ahs-**trahl**-ńe] adv. astrally
astralny [ahs-**trahl**-ni] adj.m. astral; of form or like the stars
astrefowy [ahs-tre-**fo**-vi] adj.m. not included in a zone (region, belt)
astro- [**ahs**-tro] prefix: astro-; astr-
astrobiologia [ahs-tro-byo-**lo**-gyah] f. astrobiology
astrobotanika [ahs-tro-bo-**tah**-ńee-kah] f. astrobotany
astrochemia [ahs-tro-**khe**-myah] f. astrochemistry
astrofizyczny [ahs-tro-fee-**zich**-ni] adj.m. astrophysical
astrofizyk [ahs-tro-**fee**-zik] m. astrophysicist
astrofizyka [ahs-tro-**fee**-zi-kah] f. astrophysics
astrofotografia [ahs-tro-fo-to-**grah**-fyah] f. astrophotography
astrofotometr [ahs-tro-fo-**to**-metr] m. astrophotometer
astrofotometria [ahs-tro-fo-to-**me**-tryah] f. astrophotometry
astrognozja [ahs-tro-**gno**-zyah] f. ability to name the stars in the sky
astrograf [ahs-**tro**-grahf] m. astrograph; photographic telescope
astrografia [ahs-tro-**grah**-fyah] f. astrophotography
astrokompas [ahs-tro-**kom**-pahs] m. astronavigation instrument
astrokopuła [ahs-tro-ko-**poo**-wah] f. astrodome; translucent dome (copula) of an airplane navigator
astrolabium [ahs-tro-**lah**-byoom] n. astrolabe
astrolatria [ahs-tro-**lah**-tryah] f. worship of the stars
astrolog [ahs-**tro**-log] m. astrologer
astrologia [ahs-tro-**lo**-gyah] f. astrology; colloq: pseudo-science claiming to foretell the future by the supposed influence of the stars, planets, etc. on human life
astrologicznie [ahs-tro-lo-**gich**-ńe] adv. astrologically
astrologiczny [ahs-tro-lo-**gich**-ni] adj.m. astrological
astrometeorologia [ahs-tro-me-te-o-ro-**lo**-gyah] f. astrometeorology
astrometr [ahs-**tro**-metr] m. astrometer
astrometria [ahs-tro-**me**-tryah] f. astrometry; determination of the location of celestial bodies
astrometryczny [ahs-tro-me-**trich**-ni] adj.m. astrometric
astronauta [ahs-tro-**nahw**-tah] m. astronaut; one trained to make flights in outer space
astronautycznie [ahs-tro-nahw-**tich**-ńe] adv. astronautically
astronautyczny [ahs-tro-nahw-**tich**-ni] adj.m. astronautic; space (flight, etc.)
astronautyka [ahs-tro-**nahw**-ti-kah] f. astronautics
astronawigacja [ahs-tro-nah-vee-**gah**-tsyah] f. astronavigation
astronawigacyjny [ahs-tro-nah-vee-gah-**tsiy**-ni] adj.m. of astronavigation; astronavigational
astronom [ahs-**tro**-nom] m. astronomer
astronomia [ahs-tro-**no**-myah] f. astronomy
astronomicznie [ahs-tro-no-**meech**-ńe] adv. astronomically; enormously; colossally
astronomiczny [ahs-tro-no-**meech**-ni] adj.m. astronomic(al); colloq: enormous; colossal; dizzy
astronomka [ahs-tro-**nom**-kah] f. (woman) astronomer
astroorientacja [ahs-tro-or-yen-**tah**-tsyah] f. location of a spaceship by the stars; astronavigation
astrospektroskop [ahs-tro-spek-**tro**-skop] m. astrospectroscope
astrospektroskopia [ahs-tro-spek-tro-**sko**-pyah] f. astrospectroscopy

astygmat [ahs-**ti**-gmaht] m. astigmatic camera lens
astygmatycznie [ahs-ti-gmah-**tich**-ńe] adv. astigmatically
astygmatyczny [ahs-ti-gmah-**tich**-ni] adj.m. astigmatic
astygmatyk [ahs-ti-**gmah**-tik] m. an astigmatic person
astygmatyzm [ahs-ti-**gmah**-tizm] m. astigmatism
asumpt [**ah**-soompt] m. inducement; prompting
asybilacja [ah-si-bee-**lah**-tsyah] f. assibilation (in poetry)
asygnacja [ah-sig-**nah**-tsyah] f. order (of payment); transfer of funds; an early check used in Poland (in the 15th-18th centuries)
asygnacyjny [ah-sig-nah-**tsiy**-ni] adj.m. paper (money)
asygnata [ah-sig-**nah**-tah] f. order (of payment); cash order; voucher; paper money; banknote
asygnować [ah-sig-**no**-vahćh] v. assign; allot; allocate; bestow upon; appropriate for; budget; allow; transfer money; give an order of payment; issue orders of payment (*repeatedly*)
asygnowanie [ah-sig-no-**vah**-ńe] n. assignment; allotment; allocation; bestowal (upon); appropriation (for); budgeting; allowance; transfer (of money); the giving out of an order of payment; issuing orders of payment
asylabiczny [ah-si-lah-**beech**-ni] adj.m. of asyllabia
asylabizm [ah-si-**lah**-beezm] m. asyllabia
asymetria [ah-si-**me**-tryah] f. asymmetry; lack of symmetry; want of symmerty; the lack of correspondence of opposite parts in size, shape, and position
asymetrycznie [ah-si-me-**trich**-ńe] adv. asymmetrically
asymetryczność [ah-si-me-**trich**-nośhćh] f. asymmetry
asymetryczny [ah-si-me-**trich**-ni] adj.m. asymmetrical; asymmetric
asymilacja [ah-si-mee-**lah**-tsyah] f. assimilation; assimilative process; absorption; animalization of food; incorporation; making like or alike
asymilacyjnie [ah-si-mee-lah-**tsiy**-ńe] adv. by assimilation
asymilacyjny [ah-si-mee-lah-**tsiy**-ni] adj.m. assimilative; digestive; absorbing
asymilant [ah-si-**mee**-lahnt] m. assimilationist; advocate of the assimilation of races
asymilat [ah-si-**mee**-laht] m. assimilative substance or agent
asymilator [ah-si-mee-**lah**-tor] m. assimilationist; advocate of the assimilation of races
asymilować [ah-si-mee-**lo**-vahćh] v. assimilate; absorb; liken; absorb and incorporate; digest; make like or alike; imbibe (*repeatedly*)
asymilować się [ah-si-mee-**lo**-vahćh śh<u>an</u>] v. assimilate; become assimilated; go native; become like; be absorbed and incorporated (*repeatedly*)
asymilowanie [ah-si-mee-lo-**vah**-ńe] n. assimilation; absorption
asymptota [ah-sim-**pto**-tah] f. asymptote
asymptotyczny [ah-sim-pto-**tich**-ni] adj.m. asymptotic (curve, etc.)
asynchronia [ah-sin-**khro**-ńyah] f. asynchronism; lack of concurrence in time
asynchroniczny [ah-sin-khro-**ńeech**-ni] adj.m. asynchronous; not concurring in time
asynchronizm [ah-sin-**khro**-ńeezm] m. asynchronism
asyndeton [ah-sin-**de**-ton] m. asyndeton
asyndetyczny [ah-sin-de-**tich**-ni] adj.m. asyndetic; not joined by a conjunction
asynergia [ah-si-**ner**-gyah] f. asynergy; asynergia
asyriolog [ah-sir-**yo**-log] m. Assyriologist
asyriologia [ah-sir-yo-**lo**-gyah] f. Assyriology
Asyryjczyk [ah-si-**riy**-chik] m. Assyrian
Asyryjka [ah-si-**riy**-kah] f. Assyrian (woman)
asyryjski [ah-si-**riy**-skee] adj.m. Assyrian

asysta [ah-**si**-stah] f. attendance; escort; assistance; company; suite (or train) of (followers, admirers, etc.); an instance (or act) of helping; act of aiding
w asyście [v ah-**si**-śhćhe] exp.: attended by; accompanied by; escorted by
dla asysty [dlah ah-**si**-sti] exp.: in order to escort; in order to accompany or attend
asystencja [ah-si-**sten**-tsyah] f. assistance
asystencki [ah-si-**sten**-tskee] adj.m. assistant's (functions, etc.)
asystent [ah-**si**-stent] m. assistant; one who assists; helper; aid
asystentka [ah-si-**stent**-kah] f. (woman) assistant; one who assists; helper; aid
asystentura [ah-sis-ten-**too**-rah] f. post (term of office, etc.) of professor's assistant
asystować [ah-si-**sto**-vahćh] v. help; aid; accompany; attend; court; assist; escort; wait upon; assist at; be present at (*repeatedly*)
asystowanie [ah-si-sto-**vah**-ńe] n. help; aid; attendance; escort; company; assistance; assisting; courtship
aszelski [ah-**shel**-skee] adj.m. Acheulean (period)
aszmość [**ahsh**-mośhćh] m. Sir
aść [ahśhćh] m. Sir
aśćka [**aśhćh**-kah] f. Madam
at! [aht] excl.: oh! phooey! pshaw! pish!
atak [**ah**-tahk] m. attack; charge (fit); spasm; offensive; assault; onslaught; onset; (med.) fit; spasm; access; bout; line of scrimmage; the rush line
atak bombowy [**ah**-tahk bom-**bo**-vi] exp.: attack from the air; air raid; bombing attack
atak czołowy [**ah**-tahk cho-**wo**-vi] exp.: frontal attack
atak gazowy [**ah**-tahk gah-**zo**-vi] exp.: gas attack
atak lotniczy [**ah**-tahk lot-**ńee**-chi] exp.: air raid
atak na bagnety [**ah**-tahk nah bahg-**ne**-ti] exp.: bayonet charge
atak serca [**ah**-tahk **ser**-tsah] exp.: heart attack
gwałtowny atak [gvahw-**tov**-ni **ah**-tahk] exp.: assault; onslaught; onset
iść do ataku [eeśhćh do ah-**tah**-koo] exp.: to rush to the attack; to charge
ruszyć do ataku [**roo**-shićh do ah-**tah**-koo] exp.: to take the offensive; to assume the offensive
atakamit [ah-tah-**kah**-meet] m. atacamite (mineral)
atakować [ah-tah-**ko**-vahćh] v. attack; assault; charge; assail; (chem.) act on; use force against in order to harm; speak or write against; undertake vigorously; begin acting upon harmfully (*repeatedly*)
atakowanie [ah-tah-ko-**vah**-ńe] n. attack
ataksja [ah-**tah**-ksyah] f. ataxia; confusion
ataksyjny [ah-tahk-**siy**-ni] adj.m. ataxic
atalia [ah-**tahl**-yah] f. Attalea palm tree
ataman [ah-**tah**-mahn] m. Cossack chieftain
ataraksja [ah-tah-**rah**-ksyah] f. ataraxia; confusion; lack of order
ataszat [ah-**tah**-shaht] m. office of an attache (at an embassy, etc.)
atawistycznie [ah-tah-vee-**stich**-ńe] adv. atavistically
atawistyczny [ah-tah-vee-**stich**-ni] adj.m. atavistic
atawizm [ah-**tah**-veezm] m. atavism; recurrence of a form typical of ancestors more remote than the parents, usually due to genetic recombination; an individual or character manifesting atavism; reversion (to an earlier type, etc.); throwback
ateista [ah-te-**ee**-stah] m. atheist; unbeliever; one who denies the existence of God
ateistka [ah-te-**ee**-stkah] f. (woman) atheist; unbeliever; woman who denies the existence of God

ateistycznie [ah-te-ee-**stich**-ńe] adv. atheistically
ateistyczny [ah-te-ee-**stich**-ni] adj.m. atheistic
ateizacja [ah-te-ee-**zah**-tsyah] f. propagation of atheism; acceptance of atheism
ateizm [ah-**te**-eezm] m. atheism; a disbelief in the existence of deity; the doctrine that there is no deity; ungodliness; wickedness
atelier [ah-te-**lye**] n. atelier; a studio or workshop, as of an artist or couturier
atelier filmowe [ah-te-**lye** feel-**mo**-ve] exp.: film studio
atelierowy [ah-tel-ye-**ro**-vi] adj.m. atelier (pictures, etc.)
atematyczny [ah-te-mah-**tich**-ni] adj.m. athematic; having no theme; without a theme
atencja [ah-**ten**-tsyah] f. deference
okazywać atencję [o-kah-**zi**-vahćh ah-**ten**-tsyan] exp.: to pay deference to (somebody)
robić atencje [**ro**-beećh ah-**ten**-tsye] exp.: to pay deference
z atencją [z ah-**ten**-tsyown] exp.: with deference; with marks of respect
Atenka [ah-**ten**-kah] f. Athenian woman
atentat [ah-**ten**-taht] m. attempt on somebody's life
Ateńczyk [ah-**teń**-chik] m. Athenian
ateński [ah-**teń**-skee] adj.m. Athenian; of Athens
atest [**ah**-test] m. attest; inspection sticker; certificate
atestacja [ah-tes-**tah**-tsyah] f. attestation; certificate (of quality, etc.); testimonial
atestat [ah-**tes**-taht] m. attestation; certificate; testimonial; verification
atestować [ah-tes-**to**-vahćh] v. attest; certify (quality); verify (the usage, etc.); testify (to the truth, etc.); be a proof of; manifest; authenticate (officially, by signing, etc.) (*repeatedly*)
ateusz [ah-**te**-oosh] m. atheist
ateuszostwo [ah-te-oo-**sho**-stfo] n. atheism; see: **ateism**
atlant [**ah**-tlahnt] m. atlas; architectural column in shape of man's statue
Atlantyk [ah-**tlahn**-tik] m. Atlantic
atlantycki [ah-tlahn-**ti**-tskee] adj.m. Atlantic
sojusz atlantycki [**so**-yoosh ah-tlahn-**ti**-tskee] exp.: Atlantic Alliance; North Atlantic Treaty Organization; NATO
atlas [**ah**-tlahs] m. atlas (of maps, statue, vertebrae, etc.); a book of maps, etc.
atlas historyczny [ah-tlahs khee-sto-**reech**-ni] exp.: historical atlas (showing geopolitical changes with respect to time)
atlas geograficzny [**ah**-tlahs ge-o-grah-**feech**-ni] exp.: geographical atlas
atlasik [ah-**tlah**-śheek] m. (small, nice) atlas
atleta [ah-**tle**-tah] m. athlete; wrestler; a person trained or skilled to contend for a prize (in exercises or games requiring physical strength, agility, skill, stamina, etc.)
atletka [ah-**tle**-tkah] f. (female) athlete
atletycznie [ah-tle-**tich**-ńe] adv. athletically
atletycznie zbudowany [ah-tle-**tich**-ńe zboo-do-**vah**-ni] exp.: of athletic build
atletyczny [ah-tle-**tich**-ni] adj.m. athletic; vigorous; active; used by athletes
zawody atletyczne [zah-**vo**-di ah-tle-**tich**-ne] exp.: athletic contest
atletyka [ah-**tle**-ti-kah] f. athletics
lekka atletyka [**lek**-kah ah-**tle**-ti-kah] exp.: track-and-field competitive athletic events (such as running, jumping, and weight, disc, and javelin throwing, etc.)
uprawiać atletykę [oo-**prah**-vyahćh ah-**tle**-ti-kan] exp.: to go in for athletics
atłas [**ah**-twahs] m. satin
szkoda czasu i atłasu [**shko**-dah **chah**-soo ee ah-**twah**-soo] exp.: it's a waste of time; it isn't worth it; it isn't worth the trouble; it

isn't worth your (my, etc.) while
w atłasach [v ah-**twah**-sahkh] exp.: in silks
atłasek [ah-**twah**-sek] m. threads of floss silk; raised embroidery
atłaskowy [ah-twah-**sko**-vi] adj.m. satin-; satiny; silky; silken (texture, luster, etc.)
atłasowo [ah-twah-**so**-vo] adv. very smoothly
atłasowy [ah-twah-**so**-vi] adj.m. satin-; satiny; silky; silken (texture, luster, etc.)
atłasowa skóra [ah-twah-**so**-vah **skoo**-rah] exp.: soft skin
atłasowe dotknięcie [ah-twah-**so**-ve do-**tkńan**-ćhe] exp.: soft touch
atłasowe spojrzenie [ah-twah-**so**-ve spoy-**zhe**-ńe] exp.: tender look
atmofilny [ah-tmo-**feel**-ni] adj.m. gaseous (chemicals in the air, etc.)
atmoliza [ah-tmo-**lee**-zah] f. atmolysis; atmolyzation
atmometr [ah-**tmo**-metr] m. atmometer
atmometria [ah-tmo-**me**-tryah] f. atmometry
atmometryczny [ah-tmo-me-**trich**-ni] adj.m. atmometric
atmosfera [ah-tmo-**sfe**-rah] f. atmosphere; air; climate; all the air surrounding the earth; pervading mood or spirit; ambiance; the general tone or effect; a unit of pressure equal to 14.69 pounds per square inch
atmosfera dostatku [ah-tmo-**sfe**-rah do-**stah**-tkoo] exp.: an air of wealth
atmosfera komfortu [ah-tmo-**sfe**-rah kom-**for**-too] exp.: an air of comfort
atmosfera pokoju [ah-tmo-**sfe**-rah po-**ko**-yoo] exp.: the air in the room
atmosfera spokoju [ah-tmo-**sfe**-rah spo-**ko**-yoo] exp.: an air of peace
atmosfera zaufania [ah-tmo-**sfe**-rah zah-oo-**fah**-ńah] exp.: an atmosphere of mutual trust; an environment of mutual trust
atmosfera ziemska [ah-tmo-**sfe**-rah **źhem**-skah] exp.: the earth atmosphere
miła atmosfera [**mee**-wah ah-tmo-**sfe**-rah] exp.: a pleasant atmosphere
napięta atmosfera [nah-**pyan**-tah ah-tmo-**sfe**-rah] exp.: a feeling of tenseness
nieskrępowana atmosfera [ńe-skran-po-**vah**-nah ah-tmo-**sfe**-rah] exp.: a relaxed atmosphere
stworzyć miłą atmosferę [**stfo**-zhićh **mee**-wown ah-tmo-**sfe**-ran] exp.: to create a pleasant atmosphere; to put people at ease
swobodna atmosfera [sfo-**bod**-nah ah-tmo-**sfe**-rah] exp.: a relaxed atmosphere
atmosferka [ah-tmo-**sfer**-kah] f. colloq: (nice, little) atmosphere
atmosferycznie [ah-tmo-sfe-**rich**-ńe] adv. atmospherically
atmosferyczny [ah-tmo-sfe-**rich**-ni] adj.m. atmospheric(al)
ciepły front atmosferyczny [**ćhe**-pwi front ah-tmo-sfe-**rich**-ni] exp.: warm (atmospheric) front
ciśnienie atmosferyczne [ćhee-**śhńe**-ńe ah-tmo-sfe-**rich**-ne] exp.: atmospheric pressure; barometric pressure
front atmosferyczny [front ah-tmo-sfe-**rich**-ni] exp.: atmospheric front
niż atmosferyczny [ńeesh ah-tmo-sfe-**rich**-ni] exp.: atmospheric low (pressure)
opady atmosferyczne [o-**pah**-di ah-tmo-sfe-**rich**-ne] exp.: fall of rain or snow
przeszkody atmosferyczne [pshe-**shko**-di ah-tmo-sfe-**rich**-ne] exp.: static; atmospherics
warunki atmosferyczne [vah-**roon**-kee ah-tmo-sfe-**rich**-ne] exp.: weather conditions
wyż atmosferyczny [vish ah-tmo-sfe-**rich**-ni] exp.: atmospheric high (pressure)
zimny front atmosferyczny [**źheem**-ni front ah-tmo-sfe-**rich**-ni] exp.: cold (atmospheric) front
atofan [ah-**to**-fahn] m. atophan;

Atophan
atoksycznie [ah-to-**ksich**-ńe] adv. non-toxically
atoksyczny [ah-to-**ksich**-ni] adj.m. non-toxic
atoksyl [ah-**to**-ksil] m. atoxyl, Atoxyl
atol [**ah**-tol] m. atoll; a coral island consisting of a reef surrounding a lagoon
atoli [ah-**to**-lee] conj. however; still; nevertheless
atom [**ah**-tom] m. atom; a tiny particle; bit
jądro atomu [yown-dro ah-**to**-moo] exp.: atomic nucleus
rozbicie atomu [roz-**bee**-ćhe ah-**to**-moo] exp.: smashing of the atom
rozszczepienie jądra atomu [ros-shche-**pye**-ńe yown-drah ah-**to**-moo] exp.: nuclear fission
atomista [ah-to-**mee**-stah] m. atomist
atomistyczny [ah-to-mee-**stich**-ni] adj.m. atomistic; atomic
atomistyka [ah-to-**mee**-sti-kah] f. atomistics; atomism
atomizacja [ah-to-mee-**zah**-tsyah] f. atomization; reduction to atoms or minute particles; subjection to atomic bombing
atomizator [ah-to-mee-**zah**-tor] m. atomizer; spray; sprayer
atomizer [ah-to-**mee**-zer] m. atomizer; spray; sprayer
atomizm [ah-**to**-meezm] m. (phil.) a doctrine that the universe is composed of simple indivisible minute particles
atomizować [ah-to-mee-**zo**-vahćh] v. atomize; reduce to minute particles or to a fine spray; subject to atomic bombing (*repeatedly*)
atomizowanie [ah-to-mee-zo-**vah**-ńe] n. atomization
atomowo [ah-to-**mo**-vo] adv. atomically
atomowy [ah-to-**mo**-vi] adj.m. atomic; nuclear
bomba atomowa [**bom**-bah ah-to-**mo**-vah] exp.: atomic bomb; A-bomb
broń atomowa [broń ah-to-**mo**-vah] exp.: nuclear weapon
ciężar atomowy [ćhan-zhahr ah-to-**mo**-vi] exp.: atomic weight
elektrownia atomowa [e-lek-**trov**-ńah ah-to-**mo**-vah] exp.: atomic power plant
energia atomowa [e-**ner**-gyah ah-to-**mo**-vah] exp.: atomic energy
liczba atomowa [**leedzh**-bah ah-to-**mo**-vah] exp.: atomic number
mieszanka atomowa [mye-**shahn**-kah ah-to-**mo**-vah] exp.: atomic cocktail; a radioactive substance (as iodide of sodium) dissolved in water and administered orally to patients sick with cancer
stos atomowy [stos ah-to-**mo**-vi] exp.: atomic pile
zegar atomowy [**ze**-gahr ah-to-**mo**-vi] exp.: atomic clock
atomówka [ah-to-**moof**-kah] f. colloq: A-bomb; atomic power plant
atonalizm [ah-to-**nah**-leezm] m. atonality; absence of tonality; atonalism
atonalnie [ah-to-**nahl**-ńe] adv. atonally
atonalność [ah-to-**nahl**-nośhćh] f. atonality; absence of tonality; atonalism
atonalny [ah-to-**nahl**-ni] adj.m. atonal (music)
atonia [ah-**to**-ńyah] f. atony; lack of physiological tone; atonality; atonalism
atoniczny [ah-to-**ńeech**-ni] adj.m. atonic (without sound, without accent); lacking physiological tone
atrakcja [ah-**trah**-ktsyah] f. attraction; attractiveness; high light
główna atrakcja [**gwoov**-nah ah-**trah**-ktsyah] exp.: main attraction; chief attraction
pozbawiony wszelkich atrakcji [poz-bah-**vyo**-ni **fshel**-keekh ah-**trah**-ktsyee] exp.: utterly unattractive
atrakcyjnie [ah-trahk-**tsiy**-ńe] adv. attractively; charmingly; arousing interest or pleasure
atrakcyjność [ah-trahk-**tsiy**-

nośhćh] f. attractiveness; lure; fascination
atrakcyjny [ah-trahk-**tsiy**-ni] adj.m. attractive; having or relating to the power to attract; inviting; alluring
atrament [ah-**trah**-ment] m. ink
plama od atramentu [**plah**-mah od ah-trah-**men**-too] exp.: ink-stain
atramentowy [ah-trah-men-**to**-vi] adj.m. ink-; inky; inky black
ołówek atramentowy [o-**woo**-vek ah-trah-men-**to**-vi] exp.: ink-pencil
plamy atramentowe [**plah**-mi ah-trah-men-**to**-ve] exp.: ink-stains
atrapa [ah-**trah**-pah] f. show-window imitation (of an article); dummy; catch; fake object
atrepsja [ah-**tre**-psyah] f. athrepsia
atrepsyjny [ah-tre-**psiy**-ni] adj.m. athreptic
atrezja [ah-**tre**-zyah] f. atresia
atrium [**ah**-tryoom] n. atrium
atrofia [ah-**tro**-fyah] f. atrophy; wasting away or progressive decline; degeneration
atroficzny [ah-tro-**feech**-ni] adj.m. atrophic
atropina [ah-tro-**pee**-nah] f. atropine
atropinowy [ah-tro-pee-**no**-vi] adj.m. atropine (poison, drops, etc.)
atropizm [ah-**tro**-peezm] m. atropism
atrybucja [ah-tri-**boo**-tsyah] f. attribution; competence; powers
atrybut [ah-**tri**-boot] m. attribute; an inherent characteristic; an accidental quality; a word ascribing a quality; adjective
atrybutywny [ah-tri-boo-**tiv**-ni] adj.m. attributive
attache [ah-tah-**she**] m. attache (military, commercial, etc.)
attycki [aht-**ti**-tskee] adj.m. of Attica; Attic (salt, wit, etc.)
attycyzm [aht-**ti**-tsizm] m. Atticism; colloq: wit; subtlety of taste; purity of language
attyk [**aht**-tik] m. attic
attyka [**aht**-ti-kah] f. attic (wall shielding the roof from the street)
attykowy [aht-ti-**ko**-vi] adj.m. attic
atu [**ah**-too] n. trump; trump card
bez atu [bez **ah**-too] exp.: no trump
atut [**ah**-toot] m. trump; trump card
atutować [ah-too-**to**-vahćh] v. play trump (*repeatedly*)
atutowy [ah-too-**to**-vi] adj.m. trump (play, etc.)
atypia [ah-**ti**-pyah] f. not typical disease
atypowo [ah-ti-**po**-vo] adv. not typically
atypowość [ah-ti-**po**-vośhćh] f. not typical condition
atypowy [ah-ti-**po**-vi] adj.m. not typical
au! [ahw] excl.: ow!
audialny [ahw-**dyahl**-ni] adj.m. audible; of hearing
audiencja [ahw-**dyen**-tsyah] f. audience
przyjąć na audiencję [**pshi**-yownćh nah ahw-**dyen**-tsyan] exp.: to receive in audience
udzielić audiencji [oo-**dźhe**-leećh ahw-**dyen**-tsyee] exp.: to grant (give) an audience
uzyskać audiencję [oo-**zis**-kahćh ahw-**dyen**-tsyan] exp.: to obtain an audience
audiencjonalny [ahw-dyen-tsyo-**nahl**-ni] adj.m. of audience
audiencyjny [ahw-dyen-**tsiy**-ni] adj.m. of audience
audioamator [ahw-dyo-ah-**mah**-tor] m. audiophile
audiogeniczny [ahw-dyo-ge-**ńeech**-ni] adj.m. audiogenic
audiogram [ahw-**dyo**-grahm] m. audiogram; plot of audiometric readings
audiolog [ahw-**dyo**-log] m. audiologist
audiologia [ahw-dyo-**lo**-gyah] f. audiology
audiologiczny [ahw-dyo-lo-**geech**-ni] adj.m. audiological
audiometr [ahw-**dyo**-metr] m. audiometer
audiometria [ahw-dyo-**me**-tryah] f. audiometry
audion [**ahw**-dyon] m. Audion
audiotaśma [ahw-dyo-**tahśh**-mah] f. audiotape
audiowizualnie [ahw-dyo-vee-zoo-**ahl**-ńe] adv. in audiovisual manner

audiowizualny [ahw-dyo-vee-zoo-**ahl**-ni] adj.m. audiovisual
audiowizualne nagrania [ahw-dyo-vee-zoo-**ahl**-ne nah-**grah**-ńah] exp.: audiovisuals
audycja [ahw-**di**-tsyah] f. broadcast; program; popular concert; pop
nadać audycję [**nah**-dahćh ahw-di-tsyan] exp.: to broadcast a program
audytor [ahw-**di**-tor] m. auditor; judicial assessor
audytorium [ahw-di-**to**-ryoom] n. auditorium; lecture-room; audience; attendance
audytoryjny [ahw-di-to-**riy**-ni] adj.m. auditorium (building, etc.)
audytywny [ahw-di-**tiv**-ni] adj.m. auditory
auerowski [ah-we-**rof**-skee] adj.m. Auer (metal, etc.)
Augiasz [**ahw**-gyahsh] m. Augeas (a king of Elis)
augiaszowy [ahw-gyah-**sho**-vi] adj.m. Augean (stables, etc.)
augit [**ahw**-geet] m. augite (mineral)
augment [**ahw**-gment] m. augment (of a vowel)
augmentacja [ahw-gmen-**tah**-tsyah] f. augmentation
augmentatyw [ahw-gmen-**tah**-tif] m. augmentative expression
augmentatywnie [ahw-gmen-tah-**tiv**-ńe] adv. in augmentative way
augmentatywny [ahw-gmen-tah-**tiv**-ni] adj.m. augmentative (suffix)
augsburski [ahwks-**boor**-skee] adj.m. Augsburg (confession, etc.)
augur [**ahw**-goor] m. augur; prophet
augustianin [ahw-goo-**styah**-ńeen] m. an Augustianian
augustianizm [ahw-goo-**styah**-ńeezm] m. Augustianism
augustiański [ahw-goo-**styahń**-skee] adj.m. Augustinian (order, church, etc.)
augustowski [ahw-goo-**stof**-skee] adj.m. Augustan (era, etc.)
augustynizm [ahw-goo-**sti**-ńeezm] m. Augustinianism
aukcja [**ahwk**-tsyah] f. auction; sale at auction; sale by auction
aukcyjny [ahwk-**tsiy**-ni] adj.m. auction (sale, room, etc.)
auksyna [ahwk-**si**-nah] f. growth hormone
auksynowo [ahwk-si-**no**-vo] adv. with growth hormone
auksynowy [ahwk-si-**no**-vi] adj.m. of growth hormone
aula [**ahw**-lah] f. hall; assembly hall; aula
aulos [**ahw**-los] m. (Greek) oboe
auł [**ah**-oow] m. Asiatic village
aura [**ahw**-rah] f. weather; weather conditions; atmosphere; climate; aura
auramina [ahw-rah-**mee**-nah] f. a synthetic dye; an antiseptic
aureola [ahw-re-**o**-lah] f. halo; aureole; radiant light around head or body; corona; nimbus (of victory, etc.); glory
aureomycyna [ahw-re-o-mi-**tsi**-nah] f. Aureomycin
aurykuł [ahw-**ri**-koow] m. auricula; bear's ear (a primrose)
aurypigment [ahw-ri-**pee**-gment] m. orpiment; auripigment
auskultacja [ahw-skool-**tah**-tsyah] f. auscultation
auskultować [ahw-skool-**to**-vahćh] v. auscultate; stethoscope (*repeatedly*)
auskultowanie [ahw-skool-to-**vah**-ńe] n. auscultation; stethoscopic examination
auspicje [ahw-**spee**-tsye] pl. auspices; prophetic sign; kindly patronage and guidance; protection
pod auspicjami [pot ahw-spee-**tsyah**-mee] exp.: under the auspices of
austenit [ahw-**ste**-ńeet] m. austenite
austenityczny [ahw-ste-ńee-**tich**-ni] adj.m. asthenic
austeria [ahw-**ster**-yah] f. inn
australoidalny [ahw-strah-lo-ee-**dahl**-ni] adj.m. Australoid
Australijczyk [ahw-strah-**leey**-chik] m. Australian
Australijka [ahw-strah-**leey**-kah] f. Australian (female)
australijski [ahw-strah-**leey**-skee] adj.m. Australian
australopitek [ahw-strah-lo-**pee**-tek] m. Australopithecus

austriacki [ahw-stri-**yah**-stkee] adj.m. Austrian
austriackie gadanie [ahw-stri-**yah**-stke gah-**dah**-ńe] exp.: silly talk; balderdash; fiddle-faddle; drivel; fiddlesticks!
Austriaczka [ahw-stri-**yah**-chkah] f. Austrian (woman or girl)
Austriak [ahw-**stri**-yahk] m. Austrian
austrofil [ahw-**stro**-feel] m. Austrophile
austrofilski [ahw-stro-**feel**-skee] adj.m. Austrophile (activity, etc.)
austrofilizm [ahw-stro-**fee**-leezm] m. Austrophilism; friendliness to Austria
austrofilstwo [ahw-stro-**feel**-stfo] n. Austrophilism; friendliness to Austria
austro-węgierski [**ahw**-stro van-**ger**-skee] adj.m. Austro-Hungarian
auszpik [**ahw**-shpeek] m. aspic; meat jelly
aut [ahwt] m. ball out of court; out
autarcha [ahw-**tahr**-khah] m. despot; absolute ruler
autarchia [ahw-**tahr**-khyah] f. autarchy; autarky; absolute sovereignty; self-sufficiency
autarkia [ahw-**tahr**-kyah] f. self-sufficiency; autarky; economic independence
autarkiczny [ahw-tahr-**keech**-ni] adj.m. self-sufficient; autarkical
autarkizm [ahw-**tahr**-keezm] m. self-sufficiency; autarky
autekologia [ahw-te-ko-**lo**-gyah] f. autecology; ecology of individual plant
autekologiczny [ahw-te-ko-lo-**geech**-ni] adj.m. autecological
autentycznie [ahw-ten-**tich**-ńe] adv. authentically; genuinely
autentyczność [ahw-ten-**tich**-nośhćh] f. authenticity; conformation to fact or reality; trustworthiness
autentyczny [ahw-ten-**tich**-ni] adj.m. authentic; authenticated; genuine; authoritative; trustworthy; conforming to fact or reality; worthy of acceptance or belief; real; true
autentyk [ahw-**ten**-tik] m. authentic (genuine) object or specimen; an original
autentyzm [ahw-**ten**-tizm] m. conformity with facts; authenticity; genuineness
autko [**ahw**-tko] n. toy motorcar; toy car; a very small car
auto [**ahw**-to] n. car; automobile; motorcar
auto ciężarowe [**ahw**-to ćhan-zhah-**ro**-ve] exp.: truck; lorry
auto pancerne [**ahw**-to pahn-**tser**-ne] exp.: armored car
auto sportowe [**ahw**-to spor-**to**-ve] exp.: sports car
auto wyścigowe [**ahw**-to viśh-ćhee-**go**-ve] exp.: racing car
auto osobowe [**ahw**-to o-so-**bo**-ve] exp.: passenger car; private car
pojechać autem [po-**ye**-khahćh **ahw**-tem] exp.: to go by car; to take a ride; to go for a drive
auto- [**ahw**-to] prefix: auto-; self-
autoafirmacja [ahw-to-ah-feer-**mah**-tsyah] f. self-affirmation
autoagresja [ahw-to-ah-**gre**-syah] f. self-aggression; allergy
autoagresyjny [ahw-to-ah-gre-**siy**-ni] adj.m. allergic
autoalarm [ahw-to-**ah**-lahrm] m. automatic radio receiver of distress signals on ships; automatic alarm device (for cars, homes, etc.)
autoanaliza [ahw-to-ah-nah-**lee**-zah] f. self-analysis; auto-analysis
autobiograf [ahw-to-**byo**-grahf] m. autobiographer
autobiografia [ahw-to-byo-**grah**-fyah] f. autobiography
autobiograficznie [ahw-to-byo-grah-**feech**-ńe] adv. autobiographically
autobiograficzny [ahw-to-byo-grah-**feech**-ni] adj.m. autobiographical
autobiografizm [ahw-to-byo-**grah**-feezm] m. autobiographic tendency; autobiographic touch
autobus [ahw-**to**-boos] m. bus; coach; motorbus; motor coach
jechać autobusem [**ye**-khahćh ahw-to-**boo**-sem] exp.: to go by bus; to take a bus
autobusowy [ahw-to-boo-**so**-vi]

adj.m. bus (stop, etc.)
przystanek autobusowy [pshi-**stah**-nek ahw-to-boo-**so**-vi] exp.: bus stop
połączenie autobusowe [po-wown-**che**-ńe ahw-to-boo-**so**-ve] exp.: bus connection
autocamping [ahw-to-**kem**-peeng] m. auto-camping; tourist-camping
autocasco [ahw-to-**kahs**-ko] n. autocasco; car insurance
autocefalia [ahw-to-tse-**fah**-lyah] f. autocephaly; independence
autocenzura [ahw-to-tsen-**zoo**-rah] f. self-censorship
autocharakterystyka [ahw-to-khah-rahk-te-**ri**-sti-kah] f. self-characterization
autochromia [ahw-to-**khro**-myah] f. color printing
autochromowy [ahw-to-khro-**mo**-vi] adj.m. autochrome
autochton [ahw-**to**-khton] m. native; aboriginal; autochthonous person; original inhabitant
autochtonicznie [ahw-to-khto-**ńeech**-ńe] adv. indigenously; autochthonously
autochtoniczny [ahw-to-khto-**ńeech**-ni] adj.m. autochthonous; indigenous; native
autochtonka [ahw-to-**khton**-kah] f. (woman) aboriginal; autochthonous woman; original inhabitant
autochtoński [ahw-to-**khtoń**-skee] adj.m. autochthonous; indigenous; native
autodafe [ahw-to-dah-**fe**] n. auto-da-fe
autocross [ahw-**to**-kros] m. cross-country auto race
autodestrukcja [ahw-to-de-**strook**-tsyah] f. self-destruction
autodrabina [ahw-to-drah-**bee**-nah] f. truck-mounted fireman's ladder
autodrezyna [ahw-to-dre-**zi**-nah] f. motor-trolley (on rails)
autodrom [ahw-**to**-drom] m. autodrome; racing course for motorcars
autodydakta [ahw-to-di-**dahk**-tah] m. self-taught person (without a teacher)
autodydaktyka [ahw-to-di-**dahk**-ti-kah] f. self-instruction
autoerotyzm [ahw-to-e-**ro**-tizm] m. autoerotism; narcissism
autoerotycznie [ahw-to-e-ro-**tich**-ńe] adv. autoerotically
autoerotyczny [ahw-to-e-ro-**tich**-ni] adj.m. autoerotic
autofilia [ahw-to-**feel**-yah] f. selfishness; self-adulation
autogamia [ahw-to-**gah**-myah] f. self-fertilization; autogamy
autogamiczny [ahw-to-gah-**meech**-ni] adj.m. self-fertilized; autogamous; autogamic
autogeneza [ahw-to-ge-**ne**-zah] f. autogenesis; spontaneous generation
autogenetycznie [ahw-to-ge-ne-**tich**-ńe] adv. autogenetically
autogenetyczny [ahw-to-ge-ne-**tich**-ni] adj.m. autogenetic
autogen [ahw-**to**-gen] m. autogenous welding
autogeniczny [ahw-to-ge-**ńeech**-ni] adj.m. self-generated; autogenous
autogenny [ahw-to-**gen**-ni] adj.m. self-generated; autogenous
autogenowy [ahw-to-ge-**no**-vi] adj.m. self-generated; autogenous
autograf [ahw-**to**-grahf] m. autograph
autografia [ahw-to-**grah**-fyah] f. autography
autograficzny [ahw-to-grah-**feech**-ni] adj.m. autographic; signed with one's own hand
autohemoterapia [ahw-to-khe-mo-te-**rah**-pyah] f. autohemotherapy
autohipnoza [ahw-to-kheep-**no**-zah] f. autohypnosis
autohipnotyczny [ahw-to-kheep-no-**tich**-ni] adj.m. autohypnotic
autoimitacja [ahw-to-ee-mee-**tah**-tsyah] f. self-imitation
autoimmunizacja [ahw-to-eem-moo-ńee-**zah**-tsyah] f. autoimmunization; autoimmunity
autoinfekcja [ahw-to-een-**fe**-ktsyah] f. self-infection; autoinfection
autointoksykacja [ahw-to-een-to-ksi-**kah**-tsyah] f. autointoxication
autoironia [ahw-to-ee-**ro**-ńyah] f. self-irony

autojonizacja [ahw-to-yo-ńee-**zah**-tsyah] f. atomic self-ionization
autokar [ahw-**to**-kahr] m. (motor) coach; touring car
autokarawan [ahw-to-kah-**rah**-vahn] m. motor hearse
autokarowy [ahw-to-kah-**ro**-vi] adj.m. (excursion, etc.) by motor coach; by touring car
autokarykatura [ahw-to-kah-ri-kah-**too**-rah] f. self-portrait in caricature
autokatalityczny [ahw-to-kah-tah-lee-**tich**-ni] adj.m. autocatalytic (process; reaction, etc.)
autokataliza [ahw-to-kah-tah-**lee**-zah] f. autocatalysis; self-catalysis
autokefalia [ahw-to-ke-**fah**-lyah] f. autocephaly; independence
autokefaliczny [ahw-to-ke-fah-**leech**-ni] adj.m. autocephalous; independent; self-governing
autokemping [ahw-to-**kem**-peeng] m. auto-camping; tourist camping site
autoklaw [ahw-**to**-klahf] m. autoclave; sterilizing vessel
autokod [ahw-**to**-kod] m. automatic computer-code
autokomentarz [ahw-to-ko-**men**-tahsh] m. commentary on one's own work
autokontrola [ahw-to-kon-**tro**-lah] f. self-control
autokracja [ahw-to-**krah**-tsyah] f. autocracy; rule by one person; absolute government
autokrata [ahw-to-**krah**-tah] m. autocrat
autokrator [ahw-to-**krah**-tor] m. autocrator; autocrat
autokratycznie [ahw-to-krah-**tich**-ńe] adv. autocratically
autokratyczny [ahw-to-krah-**tich**-ni] adj.m. autocratic; autocratical
autokratyzm [ahw-to-**krah**-tizm] m. autocracy; rule by one person; absolute government; autocratic disposition
autokros [ahw-**to**-kros] m. cross-country auto-race
autokrytycyzm [ahw-to-kri-**ti**-tsizm] m. self-criticism
autokrytyka [ahw-to-**kri**-ti-kah] f. self-criticism
autol [**ahw**-tol] m. kind of lubricant
autolitografia [ahw-to-lee-to-**grah**-fyah] f. lithographic drawing made directly on the stone by the artist
autolityczny [ahw-to-lee-**tich**-ni] adj.m. autolytic
autoliza [ahw-to-**lee**-zah] f. autolysis
autolizować [ahw-to-lee-**zo**-vahćh] v. autolyze; undergo autolysis (*repeatedly*)
autolizowanie [ahw-to-lee-zo-**vah**-ńe] n. autolysis
automacik [ahw-to-**mah**-ćheek] m. colloq: small automatic gun
automasaż [ahw-to-**mah**-sahsh] m. massaging oneself; self-massage; giving oneself a massage
automat [ahw-**to**-maht] m. automatic device (machine); automatic apparatus; automaton
  automat do gry hazardowej [ahw-**to**-maht do gri khah-zahr-**do**-vey] exp.: slot-machine; coin operated gambling machine; "one-armed bandit"
  automat hamulcowy [ahw-**to**-maht khah-mool-**tso**-vi] exp.: automatic brake
  automat do sprzedaży [ahw-**to**-maht do spshe-**dah**-zhi] exp.: vending-machine
  automat do sprzedaży jedzenia [ahw-**to**-maht do spshe-**dah**-zhi ye-**dze**-ńah] exp.: automat; vending machine with coin operated food compartments
  automat do sprzedaży za monety [ahw-**to**-maht do spshe-**dah**-zhi zah mo-**ne**-ti] exp.: slot-machine; coin operated machine
  automat telefoniczny [ahw-**to**-maht te-le-fo-**ńeech**-ni] exp.: public telephone
automatowy [ahw-to-mah-**to**-vi] adj.m. of an automaton
automatycznie [ahw-to-mah-**tich**-ńe] adv. automatically; by means (with the help) of an automatic device
automatyczność [ahw-to-mah-**tich**-nośhćh] f. automatic behavior; automatic response

automatyczny [ahw-to-mah-**tich**-ni] adj.m. automatic; self-acting; self-operated; acting or done spontaneously or unconsciously; having self-acting or self-regulating mechanism
automatyk [ahw-to-**mah**-tik] m. automation-engineer; automation specialist
automatyka [ahw-to-**mah**-ti-kah] f. automation; automatically controlled operation; automatization
automatyzacja [ahw-to-mah-ti-**zah**-tsyah] f. automation; automatically controlled operation; automatization
automatyzm [ahw-to-**mah**-tizm] m. automatic action; automatism; instinctive reaction
automatyzować [ahw-to-mah-ti-**zo**-vahćh] v. automatize (*repeatedly*)
automatyzowanie [ahw-to-mah-ti-zo-**vah**-ńe] n. automatization
automobil [ahw-to-**mo**-beel] m. car; automobile; motor-car; see: **auto**
automobilista [ahw-to-mo-bee-**lee**-stah] m. motorist; automobilist
automobilistka [ahw-to-mo-bee-**lee**-stkah] f. (woman) motorist; automobilist
automobilizm [ahw-to-mo-**bee**-leezm] m. motoring
automobilklub [ahw-to-mo-**beel**-kloop] m. automobile club
automobilowy [ahw-to-mo-bee-**lo**-vi] adj.m. motor (show, rally, traffic, etc.); of automobile
jazda automobilowa [**yahz**-dah ahw-to-mo-bee-**lo**-vah] exp.: motoring
klub automobilowy [kloop ahw-to-mo-bee-**lo**-vi] exp.: automobile club
rajd automobilowy [rahyt ahw-to-mo-bee-**lo**-vi] exp.: motor rally
ruch automobilowy [rookh ahw-to-mo-bee-**lo**-vi] exp.: car traffic
transport automobilowy [**trahn**-sport ahw-to-mo-bee-**lo**-vi] exp.: motor transport
wypadek automobilowy [vi-**pah**-dek ahw-to-mo-bee-**lo**-vi] exp.: car accident; car crash
wystawa automobilowa [vi-**stah**-vah ahw-to-mo-bee-**lo**-vah] exp.: motor-show; car-show
wyścigi automobilowe [vi-**śhćhee**-gee ahw-to-mo-bee-**lo**-ve] exp.: motor-race; car-race; motor-racing; car-racing
automorfizm [ahw-to-**mor**-feezm] m. automorphism
autonaprawa [ahw-to-nah-**prah**-vah] f. car repair; car repair shop; garage; automobile repairing and service
autonomia [ahw-to-**no**-myah] f. autonomy; self-government; the right to self-government
autonomicznie [ahw-to-no-**meech**-ńe] adv. autonomously; independently; through self-government
autonomiczność [ahw-to-no-**meech**-nośhćh] f. autonomy; autonomic character
autonomiczny [ahw-to-no-**meech**-ni] adj.m. autonomous; self-governing; independent; autonomic
autonomista [ahw-to-no-**mee**-stah] m. advocate of autonomy; autonomist
autonomistyczny [ahw-to-no-mee-**stich**-ni] adj.m. advocating autonomy; independent
autonomizacja [ahw-to-no-mee-**zah**-tsyah] f. granting of autonomy
autonomizm [ahw-to-**no**-meezm] m. autonomy; independence
autonomizować [ahw-to-no-mee-**zo**-vahćh] v. grant autonomy; make independent (*repeatedly*)
autonomizować się [ahw-to-no-mee-**zo**-vahćh śh<u>an</u>] v. obtain autonomy; make oneself independent (*repeatedly*)
autooksydacja [ahw-to-o-ksi-**dah**-tsyah] f. autoxidation
autoparodia [ahw-to-pah-**ro**-dyah] f. travesty of one's own work
autopilot [ahw-to-**pee**-lot] m. autopilot; automatic pilot
autoplastyka [ahw-to-**plah**-sti-kah] f. autoplasty; autoplastic operation; autoplastic grafting
autoploid [ahw-to-**plo**-eed] m.

autoploid
autoploidalność [ahw-to-plo-ee-dahl-nośhćh] f. autoploid condition
autopompa [ahw-to-pom-pah] f. truck mounted and operated fire-department pump
autopoprawka [ahw-to-po-prahf-kah] f. author's correction of his own text (of a new law, etc.)
autoportret [ahw-to-por-tret] m. self-portrait
autopsja [ahw-to-psyah] f. autopsy; personal inspection; personal witnessing; necropsy; dissection of a dead body; post-mortem examination
autopsyjny [ahw-too-psiy-ni] adj.m. of autopsy
autor [ahw-tor] m. author; writer; man of letters; originator; promoter; maker
autoradiografia [ahw-to-rah-dyo-grah-fyah] f. autoradiography
autoradiogram [ahw-to-rah-dyo-grahm] m. autoradiogram
autorament [ahw-to-rah-ment] m. class; type; sort; hist.: contingent; troops
autoreferat [ahw-to-re-fe-raht] m. review of work by the author himself
autorefleksja [ahw-to-re-fle-ksyah] f. self-reflection; taking stock of oneself
autoregeneracja [ahw-to-re-ge-ne-rah-tsyah] f. spontaneous regeneration
autoregulacja [ahw-to-re-goo-lah-tsyah] f. self-regulation; build-in automatic regulation
autoreklama [ahw-to-re-klah-mah] f. self-advertising; self-advertisement
autoreklamiarski [ahw-to-re-klah-myahr-skee] adj.m. self-advertising
autorka [ahw-tor-kah] f. authoress; female author; woman of letters; writer
autorski [ahw-tor-skee] adj.m. author's; writer's
chroniony prawem autorskim [khro-ńo-ni prah-vem ahw-tor-skeem] exp.: copyrighted
egzemplarz autorski [eg-zem-plahsh ahw-tor-skee] exp.: complimentary copy (of a book)
honorarium autorskie [kho-no-rah-ryoom ahw-tor-ske] exp.: royalty; author's fee
naruszyć prawo autorskie [nah-roo-shićh prah-vo ahw-tor-ske] exp.: to pirate
prawo autorskie [prah-vo ahw-tor-ske] exp.: copyright
wolny od prawa autorskiego [vol-ni ot prah-vah ahw-tor-ske-go] exp.: out of copyright
autorstwo [ahw-tor-stfo] n. authorship; paternity
autorytarny [ahw-to-ri-tahr-ni] adj.m. based on an absolute obedience; authoritarian (model of family, government, etc.); dictatorial
autorytatywnie [ahw-to-ri-tah-tiv-ńe] adv. authoritatively; on good authority; from a reliable source
autorytatywny [ahw-to-ri-tah-tiv-ni] adj.m. authoritative; reliable; certain; authoritarian; dictatorial; peremptory
autorytet [ahw-to-ri-tet] m. authority; influence; control (over); a recognized authority
posiadać autorytet [po-śhah-dahćh ahw-to-ri-tet] exp.: to have influence
zdobyć autorytet [zdo-bićh ahw-to-ri-tet] exp.: to establish one's influence
autoryzacja [ahw-to-ri-zah-tsyah] f. authorization; permission; sanction
autoryzować [ahw-to-ri-zo-vahćh] v. authorize (*repeatedly*)
autoryzowanie [ahw-to-ri-zo-vah-ńe] n. permission; adaptation; sanction; authorization
autosanie [ahw-to-sah-ńe] pl. snowmobile
autoserwis [ahw-to-ser-vees] m. garage; auto-service; auto repair
autostop [ahw-to-stop] m. hitch-hiking; travel by hitch-hiking; hitching a ride
podróżować autostopem [po-droo-zho-vahćh ahw-to-sto-pem]

exp.: to hitch-hike
autostopowicz [ahw-to-sto-**po**-veech] m. hitch-hiker
autostopowiczka [ahw-to-sto-po-**veech**-kah] f. (female) hitch-hiker
autostopowy [ahw-to-sto-**po**-vi] adj.m. hitch-hiker's (record book, etc.)
autostrada [ahw-to-**strah**-dah] f. superhighway; freeway; speedway; highway
autostradowy [ahw-to-strah-**do**-vi] adj.m. superhighway (traffic, etc.); freeway (access ramp, etc.); speedway (sign, etc.)
autosugestia [ahw-to-soo-**ge**-styah] f. autosuggestion; self-suggestion; faith-cure; self-hypnosis
autosyfon [ahw-to-**si**-fon] m. home device for mixing carbon-dioxide with water
autoszczepionka [ahw-to-shche-**pyon**-kah] f. auto-vaccination
autotematyczny [ahw-to-te-mah-**tich**-ni] adj.m. (writing) centered on oneself
autotematyzm [ahw-to-te-**mah**-tizm] m. writing centered on oneself and one's works
autoterapeutyczny [ahw-to-te-rah-pew-**tich**-ni] adj.m. autotherapeutic
autoterapia [ahw-to-te-**rah**-pyah] f. autotherapy; self-treatment; spontaneous cure
autotomia [ahw-to-**to**-myah] f. autotomy; self-division
autotransformer [ahw-to-trahn-**sfor**-mer] m. autotransformer
autotransfuzja [ahw-to-trahn-**sfoo**-zyah] f. autotransfusion
autotransplantacja [ahw-to-trahns-plahn-**tah**-tsyah] f. autotransplantation
autotrof [ahw-**to**-trof] m. autotroph
autotrofia [ahw-to-**tro**-fyah] f. autotrophic condition
autotroficznie [ahw-to-tro-**feech**-ńe] adv. autotrophically
autotroficzny [ahw-to-tro-**feech**-ni] adj.m. autotrophic
autotrofizm [ahw-to-**tro**-feezm] m. autotrophic condition
autotypia [ahw-to-**ti**-pyah] f. autotype
autotypografia [ahw-to-ti-po-**grah**-fyah] f. autotypography
autotypowy [ahw-to-ti-**po**-vi] adj.m. autotypic
autoutleniacz [ahw-to-oo-**tle**-ńahch] m. self-oxidizing compound
autoutlenianie [ahw-to-oo-tle-**ńah**-ńe] n. autoxidation
autowy [ahw-**to**-vi] adj.m. of touch line; out-of-touch-line (shot, ball, etc.)
autożyro [ahw-to-**zhi**-ro] n. autogiro; Autogiro
autsajder [ahwt-**sahy**-der] m. outsider
autsajderstwo [ahwt-sahy-**der**-stfo] n. being an outsider
autunit [ahw-**too**-ńeet] m. autunite (mineral)
autystyczny [ahw-ti-**stich**-ni] adj.m. autistic; absorbed in self-centered subjective mental activity (as delusions, hallucinations, etc.); withdrawn from reality
autyzm [**ahw**-tizm] m. autism
awal [**ah**-vahl] m. endorsement (of a note or check)
awalista [ah-vah-**lee**-stah] m. endorser (of a note or check)
awalansza [ah-vah-**lahn**-shah] f. avalanche; a large mass of snow, earth, etc. sliding down a mountain; an overwhelming amount; see: **lawina**
awangarda [ah-vahn-**gahr**-dah] f. vanguard; van; advance-guard; forefront
awangardowo [ah-vahn-gahr-**do**-vo] adv. as a vanguard
awangardowość [ah-vahn-gahr-**do**-vośhćh] f. being a vanguard
awangardowy [ah-vahn-gahr-**do**-vi] adj.m. vanguard (artist, etc.)
awangardysta [ah-vahn-gahr-**di**-stah] m. vanguard artist; forerunner; precursor
awangardyzm [ah-vahn-**gahr**-dizm] m. vanguard movement in art
awangardzista [ah-vahn-gahr-**dźhee**-stah] m. vanguard artist; forerunner; precursor
awangardzizm [ah-vahn-**gahr**-

dźheezm] m. vanguard movement in art
awanport [ah-**vahn**-port] m. roadstead; ship parking area outside port; see: **reda**
awanpost [ah-**vahn**-post] m. outpost
awans [**ah**-vahns] m. promotion; advancement; preferment
awanse [ah-**vahn**-se] pl. advances; overtures; promotions; advance payments
dać awans [dahćh **ah**-vahns] exp.: to promote
dostać awans [**do**-stahćh **ah**-vahns] exp.: to be promoted; to get moved up
awans społeczny [**ah**-vahns spo-**wech**-ni] exp.: social advancement
wpłacić awansem [**fpwah**-ćheećh ah-**vahn**-sem] exp.: to pay in advance; to pay on account
awanscena [ah-vahn-**stse**-nah] f. proscenium; stage strip in front of the curtain
awansować [ah-vahn-**so**-vahćh] v. promote; be promoted; pay in advance; make progress; advance (*repeatedly*)
awansować na wyższe stanowisko [ah-vahn-**so**-vahćh nah **vish**-she stah-no-**vee**-sko] exp.: to promote to a higher rank; to be promoted to a higher rank
awansowanie [ah-vahn-so-vah-ńe] n. promotion
awansowy [ah-vahn-**so**-vi] adj.m. advance (payment, etc.)
awantaż [ah-**vahn**-tahsh] m. advantage
awantura [ah-vahn-**too**-rah] f. brawl; fuss; row; scandal; disturbance
zrobić awanturę [**zro**-beećh ah-vahn-**too**-ran] exp.: to make a scene
awanturka [ah-vahn-**toor**-kah] f. slight row; something of a fuss; an affair
awanturnica [ah-vahn-toor-**ńee**-tsah] f. adventuress; intriguer; libertine; shrew; vixen
awanturnictwo [ah-vahn-toor-**ńee**-tstfo] n. fussiness; roisterly behavior; rowdiness; rashness; venturesomeness
awanturniczo [ah-vahn-toor-**ńee**-cho] adv. with fuss; with rowdiness; with love of adventure
awanturniczość [ah-vahn-toor-**ńee**-chośhćh] f. love of adventure; fussiness; rowdiness; rashness; venturesomeness
awanturniczy [ah-vahn-toor-**ńee**-chi] adj.m. adventurous; stormy; rowdyish; roistering; quarrelsome; rackety; venturesome; rash; risky; disposed to seek adventure
awanturnik [ah-vahn-**toor**-ńeek] m. brawler; rowdy man; trouble maker; adventurer; man living by his wits
awanturować się [ah-vahn-too-**ro**-vahćh śhan] v. fuss; storm; brawl; make a row; wrangle; racket; engage in ventures (*repeatedly*)
awanturowanie się [ah-vahn-too-ro-**vah**-ńe śhan] n. fuss; storm; brawl; making a row
awanturin [ah-vahn-**too**-reen] m. aventurine (mineral)
awaria [ah-**vahr**-yah] f. damage; injury; average (or damage to ship and cargo); break-down;
powstała awaria [pof-**stah**-wah ah-**vah**-ryah] exp.: there was a break-down; there was damage
awaryjnie [ah-vah-**riy**-ńe] adv. with damage
awaryjność [ah-vah-**riy**-nośhćh] f. damage risk; accident occurrence
awaryjny [ah-vah-**riy**-ni] adj.m. damage (report, etc.)
wyjście awaryjne [**viy**-śhćhe ah-vah-**riy**-ne] exp.: emergency exit
awerroista [ah-ver-ro-ee-stah] m. (an) Averroist
awerroistyczny [ah-ver-ro-ee-**stich**-ni] adj.m. Averroist; Averroistic
awerroizm [ah-ver-**ro**-eezm] m. Averroism; 13th cent. philosophy of Ibn Rushd Averroes of Cordoba
awers [**ah**-vers] m. obverse (of a coin); face (of embroidery, etc.)
awersja [ah-**ver**-syah] f. aversion; intense dislike; the object of an intense dislike; repulsion;

repugnance
mieć awersję [myech ah-ver-syan] exp.: detest (something); dislike (somebody)
poczuć awersję [po-chooch ah-ver-syan] exp.: to take a dislike to (somebody or something)
wzbudzić awersję [vzboo-dźheech ah-ver-syan] exp.: to arouse a feeling of repulsion in somebody
awiacja [ah-vyah-tsyah] f. aviation
awifauna [ah-vee-fahw-nah] f. avian (bird) population of an epoch and territory
awinioński [ah-vee-ńyoń-skee] adj.m. Avignonese
awiofon [ah-vyo-fon] m. intercom (intercommunication) on board of an aircraft
awiomatka [ah-vyo-mah-tkah] f. aircraft carrier
awionetka [ah-vyo-ne-tkah] f. light plane; sports plane; light airplane
awionika [ah-vyo-ńee-kah] f. aviation electronics; avionics
awiotechnika [ah-vyo-tekh-ńee-kah] f. aircraft technology
awista [ah-vees-tah] f. indication on a check that it may be cashed upon identification of the payee
awitaminoza [ah-vee-tah-mee-no-zah] f. disease (as pellagra) resulting from vitamin deficiency; avitaminosis
awiz [ah-vees] m. advice; notification; notice
awizacja [ah-vee-zah-tsyah] f. letter of advice; notification; notice; monitory note
awizacyjny [ah-vee-zah-tsiy-ni] adj.m. notification (letter, etc.)
awizo [ah-vee-zo] n. advice; notification; notice; see: **awiz**; advice-boat; dispatch-boat
awizować [ah-vee-zo-vahćh] v. notify (*repeatedly*)
awizować się [ah-vee-zo-vahćh śhan] v. announce one's arrival (*repeatedly*)
awizowanie [ah-vee-zo-vah-ńe] n. notification; announcement
awizowiec [ah-vee-zo-vyets] m. advice-boat; dispatch-boat
awokado [ah-vo-kah-do] n. avocado
axel [ah-ksel] m. figure skating jump and spin
potrójny axel [po-trooy-ni ah-ksel] exp.: triple spin
azali [ah-zah-lee] conjunction: does not have an exact English equivalent; if; whether
azalia [ah-zah-lyah] f. azalea (flower)
azaliż [ah-zah-leesh] = **azali**; conj. does not have an exact English equivalent; if; whether
azard [ah-zahrt] m. hazard
azbest [ahz-best] m. asbestos
azbestocement [ahz-be-sto-tse-ment] m. asbestos-cement
azbestowy [ahz-be-sto-vi] adj.m. of asbestos
azbestoza [ahz-be-sto-zah] f. asbestosis
azeotrop [ah-ze-o-trop] m. azeotrope
azeotropia [ah-ze-o-tro-pyah] f. azeotropy
azeotropizm [ah-ze-o-tro-peezm] m. azeotropism
azeotropowy [ah-ze-o-tro-po-vi] adj.m. azeotropic
Azerbejdżanin [ah-zer-bey-dzhah-ńeen] m. Azerbaijani
azerbejdżański [ah-zer-bey-dzhahń-skee] adj.m. Azerbaijani (oil, etc.); Azerbaijanese (language, etc.)
Azjata [ahz-yah-tah] m. Asian; Asiatic (sometimes taken to be offensive)
Azjatka [ahz-yah-tkah] f. Asian (woman); Asiatic (woman)
azjatycki [ahz-yah-ti-tskee] adj.m. Asian; Oriental; of, relating to, or characteristic of the continent of Asia or its people; Asiatic
azobenzen [ah-zo-ben-zen] m. azobenzene
azoiczny [ah-zo-eech-ni] adj.m. azoic; having no life
azoik [ah-zo-eek] m. azoic era (before there was life on earth)
azoospermia [ah-zo-o-sper-myah] f. azoospermia
azot [ah-zot] m. nitrogen
azot atmosferyczny [ah-zot aht-mo-sfe-rich-ni] exp.: atmospheric nitrogen

azotan [ah-**zo**-tahn] m. nitrate
azotan srebra [ah-**zo**-tahn **sreb**-rah] exp.: silver nitrate; silver bath (used in photography)
azotanowy [ah-zo-tah-**no**-vi] adj.m. of nitrate
azotawy [ah-zo-**tah**-vi] adj. nitrous
azotek [ah-**zo**-tek] m. nitride
azotniak [ah-**zot**-ńahk] m. lime nitrogen; calcium cyamide
azotobakter [ah-zo-**to**-bahk-ter] m. soil bacteria able to react with nitrogen from the air
azotobakteryna [ah-zo-to-bahk-te-**ri**-nah] f. culture of soil bacteria able to react with nitrogen from the air
azotometr [ah-zo-**to**-metr] m. nitrometer
azotować [ah-zo-**to**-vahćh] v. nitrify (*repeatedly*)
azotowanie [ah-zo-to-**vah**-ńe] n. nitrification
azotowce [ah-zo-**tof**-tse] pl. the nitrogen family
azotowodorowy [ah-zo-to-vo-do-**ro**-vi] adj.m. of nitro-hydrogen
azotowy [ah-zo-**to**-vi] adj.m. nitrogenous; nitric
kwas azotowy [kfahs ah-zo-**to**-vi] exp.: nitric acid
nawóz azotowy [**nah**-voos ah-zo-**to**-vi] exp.: lime nitrogen fertilizer
sól kwasu azotowego [sool **kfah**-soo ah-zo-to-**ve**-go] exp.: nitrite
związek azotowy [**zvyown**-zek ah-zo-**to**-vi] exp.: nitrogen compound
azotyn [ah-**zo**-tin] m. nitrite
azotyn amonu [ah-**zo**-tin ah-**mo**-noo] exp.: ammonium nitrite
azotyn potasu [ah-**zo**-tin po-**tah**-soo] exp.: potassium nitrite
azotyn sodu [ah-**zo**-tin **so**-doo] exp.: sodium nitrite
azowy [ah-**zo**-vi] adj.m. of azo
barwniki azowe [bahrv-**ńee**-kee ah-**zo**-ve] exp.: azo dyes
azozwiązek [ah-zo-**zvyown**-zek] m. azo compound
azulan [ah-**zoo**-lahn] m. alcoholic extract of camomile
azulen [ah-**zoo**-len] m. azulene
azuryt [ah-**zoo**-rit] m. azurite
azydek [ah-**zi**-dek] m. azide
azyl [**ah**-zil] m. asylum; refuge; sanctuary; harbor
prawo azylu [**prah**-vo ah-**zi**-loo] exp.: right of asylum
prosić o azyl [**pro**-śheećh o **ah**-zil] exp.: to ask for political asylum
skorzystać z prawa azylu [sko-**zhis**-tahćh s **prah**-vah ah-**zi**-loo] exp.: to take refuge
szukać azylu [**shoo**-kahćh ah-**zi**-loo] exp.: to seek refuge
udzielić azylu [oo-**dźhe**-leećh ah-**zi**-loo] exp.: to grant asylum; to grant safe refuge
azylum [ah-**zi**-loom] n. (political) asylum
azymut [ah-**zi**-moot] m. azimuth; distance clockwise in degrees from the north point or, in the Southern Hemisphere, south point
azymutalnie [ah-zi-moo-**tahl**-ńe] adv. using azimuthal projection
azymutalny [ah-zi-moo-**tahl**-ni] adj.m. azimuth-; of azimuth
koło azymutalne [**ko**-wo ah-zi-moo-**tahl**-ne] exp.: azimuth-circle used in azimuthal equidistant projection map of the surface of the earth so centered at any given point that a straight line radiating from the center to any other point represents the shortest distance and can be measured to scale
aż [ahsh] particle: as much; up to; as late as; till; until; as far as; as far back as; down to; all the way; conjunction: till; until; so that; so much so that
aż do [ahsh do] exp.: till; until; as far as; all the way (up to, down to, to the end, top, death, etc.)
aż do czubka [ahsh do **choop**-kah] exp.: to the very top
aż do końca [ahsh do **koń**-tsah] exp.: till the end; until the very end
aż do następnego roku [ahsh do nahs-**tanp**-ne-go **ro**-koo] exp.: till the next year; as late as the next year
aż do portu [ahsh do **por**-too] exp.: all the way down to the

harbor
aż do skutku [ahsh do **skoot**-koo] exp.: till the end; until the result is attained
aż do stóp [ahsh do stoop] exp.: right down to the feet
aż do stycznia [ahsh do **stich**-ńah] exp.: till January; as late as in January
aż do szczytu [ahsh do **shchi**-too] exp.: all the way to the summit
aż dotąd [ahsh **do**-townt] exp.: till now; up to now; up to here
aż mąciło się w głowie [ahsh mown-**ćhee**-wo śhan v **gwo**-vye] exp.: till one's head reeled
aż na dachu [ahsh nah **dah**-khoo] exp.: as high as on the roof
aż po szyję [ahsh po **shi**-yan] exp.: right up to the neck
aż tak daleko [ahsh tahk dah-**le**-ko] exp.: excessively far
aż w średniowieczu [ahsh f śhred-ńo-**vye**-choo] exp.: as far back as the Middle Ages
aż za dużo [ahsh zah **doo**-zho] exp.: only too much
aż zaklął [ahsh **zah**-klow] exp.: he actually swore; he swore, would you believe it?
dobroć sięgająca aż naiwności [**do**-broćh śhan-gah-**yown**-tsah ahsh nah-eev-**nośh**-ćhee] exp.: kind-heartedness even bordering on naivete
od króla aż do szewca [ot **kroo**-lah ahsh do **shef**-tsah] exp.: from the king down to the cobbler
hotel był przyzwoity, aż wystawny [**kho**-tel biw pshi-zvo-ee-ti ahsh vi-**stahv**-ni] exp.: the hotel was decent, I should even say luxurious; the hotel was decent, even luxurious
wejść aż na setne piętro [veyśhćh ahsh nah **set**-ne **pyan**-tro] exp.: to walk as far up as the 100th floor
ażeby [ah-**zhe**-bi] conj. that; in order that; so that; to
ażeby go cholera! [ah-**zhe**-bi go kho-le-rah] excl.: to hell with him!; curse the man!; confound him!
ażio [**ah**-zhyo] n. agio; premium (over and above the official rate of exchange)
ażiotaż [ah-**zhyo**-tahsh] m. speculation in stock-market or in stocks; stock-jobbing; agiotage
ażur [**ah**-zhoor] m. open (pierced) work; ornamental work (in masonry); transparent texture (in cloth); lace
ażurek [ah-**zhoo**-rek] m. hemstitch
ażurować [ah-zhoo-**ro**-vahćh] v. ornament with open-work; provide with open-work ornamentation; pink (*repeatedly*)
ażurowanie [ah-zhoo-ro-**vah**-ńe] n. ornamentation with open-work
ażurowo [ah-zhoo-**ro**-vo] adv. in open work; transparently
ażurowy [ah-zhoo-**ro**-vi] adj.m. lace-like; transparent
ażurowa robota [ah-zhoo-**ro**-vah ro-**bo**-tah] exp.: open work

Ą

Ą, ą [own] the letter "ą"; Polish nasal vowel

B

B, b [be] n. the letter "b"; the sound of the letter "b"
duże "b" [**doo**-zhe be] exp.: capital "b" or "B"
ba [bah] excl.: hey?!; nay; yes; and; indeed...; and even; what more; or rather; more than that; of course; that's all very well; easier said than done; he has, has he?; you do; do you?
baba [**bah**-bah] f. woman (old, simple); grandmother; ram; rammer; beetle; slang: female
baba z niego [**bah**-bah z **ńe**-go] exp.: he is a coward

Herod baba [**he**-rod **bah**-bah] exp.: an overbearing, shrewish woman; virago; scold
ubijać babą [oo-**bee**-yahćh **bah**-bown] exp.: to compact with a ram; to ram; to beetle
wiejska baba [**vyey**-skah **bah**-bah] exp.: country woman; peasant woman; gammer
babbit [**bahb**-beet] m. Babbitt-metal
babbityzm [bahb-**bee**-tizm] m. antifriction characteristic
babcia [**bahp**-ćhah] f. grandmother; grannie; grandmamma; grandma; old woman
jak babcię kocham [yahk **bahp**-ćhan **ko**-khahm] exp.: believe me; truly; honestly; in all conscience; upon my word; well, I never!
babcin [**bahp**-ćheen] adj.m. grandmother's; grandma's
babciny [bahp-**ćhee**-ni] adj.m. grandmother's; grandma's
babeczka [bah-**bech**-kah] f. cake; mud pie; bun
Babel [**bah**-bel] f. Babel; a babel; pandemonium; confusion of sounds and voices
Wieża Babel [**vye**-zhah **bah**-bel] exp.: Tower of Babel
babi [**bah**-bee] adj.m. woman's; old woman's; country woman's; peasant woman's
babie lato [**bah**-bye **lah**-to] exp.: Indian Summer; gossamer thread; gossamer; air-thread
babiarstwo [bah-**byahr**-stfo] n. gossiping; gossipy disposition; gossipy nature
babiarz [**bah**-byahsh] m. lady chaser; ladies' man; womanizer
babieć [**bah**-byećh] v. turn into an old woman; age; become womanish; loose virility; become effeminate; get sissy; get softy (*repeatedly*)
Babilończyk [bah-bee-**loń**-chik] m. Babylonian
babiloński [bah-bee-**loń**-skee] adj.m. Babylonian
niewola babilońska [ńe-**vo**-lah bah-bee-**loń**-skah] exp.: Babylonian Captivity
babimór [bah-**bee**-moor] m. club-moss; wolf's-claw
babina [bah-**bee**-nah] f. old woman; paltry cake; cake of sorts
babiniec [bah-**bee**-ńets] m. gathering of women; hen party; Queen's maids of honor; servant girl's quarter; church porch
babinka [bah-**been**-kah] f. poor little old woman
babińska [bah-**beeń**-skah] adj.f.
Rzeczpospolita Babińska [zhech-pos-po-**lee**-tah bah-**beeń**-skah] exp.: 16th cent. association of humorists
babiogórzec [bah-byo-**goo**-zhets] m. inhabitant of the Western foothills of Babia Góra, a peak in West Beskids (Carpathian range)
babirusa [bah-bee-**roo**-sah] f. variety of wild pig
babka [**bahp**-kah] f. grandmother; lass; chick; cake; flat hammer with two identical square faces and no peen; little anvil for beating a scythe on; dragon fly; slang: lass; lassie; a bit of skirt; a bit of fluff; flapper; girlie
na dwoje babka wróżyła [nah **dvo**-ye **bahp**-kah vroo-**zhi**-wah] exp.: there is no telling how things will turn out; there is no telling what the outcome will be
babkarstwo [bahp-**kahr**-stfo] n. unskilled village midwifery
babkowate [bhap-ko-**vah**-te] pl. the plantaginaceous family of plants; the gobid family of fishes
babkowaty [bahp-ko-**vah**-ti] adj.m. old-wifish; old woman's
babrać [**bah**-brahćh] v. smear; stain; dabble; soil; fumble (*repeatedly*)
babrać na papierze [**bah**-brahćh nah pah-**pye**-zhe] exp.: to write or draw hastily, carelessly, often illegibly; to scrawl all over a sheet of paper
babrać się [**bah**-brahćh śhan] v. puddle; dabble in something; smear (stain, soil) one's fingers; mess about; muddle; potter; fumble at; fumble with (*repeatedly*)
babrała [bah-**brah**-wah] m. scribbler;

fumbler; daubster
babranie [bahb-**rah**-ńe] n. smearing; smudging; fumbling
babranie się [bahb-**rah**-ńe śhan] n. getting dirty; messing about
babranina [bah-brah-**ńee**-nah] f. mess; muddle; bungle; messing about; bungling; fumbling; pottering; scrawling; scribbling
babski [**bahp**-skee] adj.m. woman's; old woman's; womanish; womanly; womanlike
babskie gadanie [**bahp**-ske gah-**dah**-ńe] exp.: old wives' tales
po babsku [po **bahp**-skoo] exp.: in a feminine way
babsko [**bahp**-sko] n. hag; an ugly, often vicious old woman; shrew
babskość [**bahp**-skośhćh] f. womanish nature
babsztyl [**bahp**-shtil] m. = **babsko**
babuin [bah-**boo**-een] m. baboon; African ape
babula [bah-**boo**-lah] f. granny; grandma; (nice) old woman
babuleńka [bah-boo-**leń**-kah] f. dear grannie
babunia [bah-**boo**-ńah] f. = **babcia**
babus [**bah**-boos] m. hag; big, fat woman with masculine features
babusia [bah-**boo**-śhah] f. grandmother
babuwista [bah-boo-**vees**-tah] m. Babouvist
babuwizm [bah-**boo**-veezm] m. Babouvism; 18th cent. French revolutionary doctrine of equality and communism of all property (by F.N. Babeuf)
baby-sitter [**bey**-bee **see**-ter] m. baby-sitter
bac [bahts] (not declined:) slap; plump; thump; wang
baca [**bah**-tsah] m. flock-master; shepherd in charge
bach [bahkh] (not decl.:) flop; plop
bachanalia [bah-khah-**nah**-lyah] pl. drunken revel; carousal; orgy; revelry; carousing
bachancki [bah-**khahn**-tskee] adj.m. Bacchantic
bachant [**bah**-khahnt] m. drunken reveller; carouser
bachantka [bah-**khahnt**-kah] f. (woman) drunken reveller; carouser; Bacchante; Maenad
bachiczny [bah-**kheech**-ni] adj.m. drunken; riotous
uczta bachiczna [**ooch**-tah bah-**kheech**-nah] exp.: carousal; orgy; revel
bachmat [**bahkh**-maht] m. Tartar horse; steed
bachnąć [**bahkh**-nownćh] v. colloq: hit; strike; thwack
bachnąć się [**bahkh**-nownćh śhan] v. colloq: drop heavily (on a bed, etc.); slump (suddenly); throw oneself at (suddenly); slouch; collapse
bachor [**bah**-khor] m. kid; brat; child; bantling; whipster; tyke
bachorek [bah-**kho**-rek] m. small kid; brat; small child
bachorza [bah-**kho**-zhah] f. marsh
bachorze [bah-**kho**-zhe] f. marsh
bachusowy [bah-khoo-**so**-vi] adj.m. Bacchanal; Bacchic
baciar [**bah**-ćhahr] m. colloq: rogue; knave; thief; swindler; street kid
bacik [**bah**-ćheek] m. small whip
backhand [**bek**-hend] m. backhand; a stroke as in tennis (with the bach of the hand turned in the direction of movement)
bacnąć [**bahts**-nownćh] v. strike; thwack; swat; fall flat; fall plop; tumble down; slang: come a cropper
bacować [bah-**tso**-vahćh] v. tend a flock of sheep; shepherd (*repeatedly*)
bacowanie [bah-tso-**vah**-ńe] n. tending a flock of sheep
bacowski [bah-**tsof**-skee] adj.m. flock-master's
bacówka [bah-**tsoof**-kah] f. flock-master's hut
baczek [**bah**-chek] m. side-whisker; one of the sideburns; sideburn
baczenie [bah-**che**-ńe] n. attention; care; vigilance; alertness
bacznie [**bahch**-ńe] adv. attentively; with care; keenly; eagerly; intently; closely; with close attention
baczność [**bahch**-nośhćh] f. attention; watchfulness; care

baczność! [**bahch**-nośhćh] exp.: attention! (military command)
mieć się na baczności [myećh śhan nah bahch-**nośh**-ćhee] exp.: to look out; to be on the look-out; to be on alert; to be watchful; to watch one's step; to be careful; to be on guard
stać na baczność [stahćh nah **bahch**-nośhćh] exp.: to stand at attention
baczny [**bahch**-ni] adj.m. attentive (to); watchful (for); wide awake; intent; careful (of); open-eyed; open-eared
baczna uwaga [**bahch**-nah oo-**vah**-gah] exp.: undivided attention
bądź baczniejszy [bowndźh bahch-**ńey**-shi] exp.: be more attentive; be more watchful!
baczyć [**bah**-chićh] v. look; observe; survey; keep an eye (on); watch; pay attention (to); take care (of); mind; pay regard (to); have regard (to) (*repeatedly*)
bać się [bahćh śhan] v. fear; be afraid (of); be frightened (at, of); stand in awe (of); dread; be scared (of); be anxious; be apprehensive (*repeatedly*)
bać się śmiertelnie [bahćh śhan śhmyer-**tel**-ńe] exp.: to be scared out of one's wits; to be terrified
bój się Boga! [booy śhan **bo**-gah] excl.: compose yourself!; man alive!; for heaven's sake!; what?!; really?!
nie bać się zimna [ńe bahćh śhan **źheem**-nah] exp.: to be proof against cold; to withstand cold
badacz [**bah**-dahch] m. researcher; scholar; man of learning; explorer; student (of); research worker; investigator
badacz przyrody [**bah**-dahch pshi-**ro**-di] exp.: naturalist; scientist; scientific investigator
badaczka [bah-**dahch**-kah] f. (female) research worker; scholar; investigator; researcher
badać [**bah**-dahćh] v. investigate; examine; research; do research work (on); make researches (of); survey; search; view; see into; study; inspect; explore; probe; test; inquire; go into; look into; take up a question; sound out; interrogate; reconnoitre; question; submit to an inquiry (*repeatedly*)
badać rachunki [**bah**-dahćh rah-**khoon**-kee] exp.: to audit accounts
badać wzrokiem [**bah**-dahćh **vzro**-kem] exp.: to observe; to scan; to scrutinize; to take stock; to peer (into)
badać się [**bah**-dahćh śhan] v. undergo medical examination; scrutinize each other (*repeatedly*)
badający [bah-dah-**yown**-tsi] adj.m. investigating; m. investigator
badan [**bah**-dahn] m. saxifrage (herb)
badanie [bah-**dah**-ńe] n. inquiry; study; examination; search; survey; investigation; scrutiny; probe; exploration; audit; inspection; test; proof; interrogation; questioning
badanie lekarskie [bah-**dah**-ńe le-**kahr**-ske] exp.: medical examination
badanie naukowe [bah-**dah**-ńe nah-oo-**ko**-ve] exp.: scientific research; research work
badany [bah-**dah**-ni] m. the person under examination; the person being examined; adj.m. examined
badawczo [bah-**dahf**-cho] adv. searchingly; scrutinizingly
badawczy [bah-**dahf**-chi] adj.m. questioning; scrutinizing; searching; interrogative; investigative
praca badawcza [**prah**-tsah bah-**dahf**-chah] exp.: research work; investigation; inquiry
badian [**bah**-dyahn] m. star anise; variety of magnolia tree
badminton [bahd-**meen**-ton] m. badminton (a court game)
badmintonista [bahd-meen-to-**ńees**-tah] m. badminton player
badyl [**bah**-dil] m. stem; stalk; plant; herb; (wild) flower; weed
badylarka [bah-di-**lahr**-kah] f. slang: (woman) marketing gardener;

owner of a vegetable garden
badylarski [bah-di-**lahr**-skee] adj.m. of suburban vegetable gardening; of a suburban vegetable gardner
badylarstwo [bah-di-**lahr**-stfo] n. suburban vegetable gardening
badylarz [bah-**di**-lahsh] m. slang: marketing gardener; greengrocer; owner of a vegetable garden
badylasty [bah-di-**lahs**-ti] adj.m. stalky
badylkowaty [bah-dil-ko-**vah**-ti] adj.m. stalky; slender
badylowaty [bah-di-lo-**vah**-ti] adj.m. stalky; slender
bagatela [bah-gah-**te**-lah] f. trifle; easy matter; a mere trifle; bagatelle
o, to bagatela [o to bah-gah-**te**-lah] exp.: it's no matter; it is all right; never mind; it's a trifle; it's quite easy; excl.: well, well!; a trifle!
bagatelizować [bah-gah-te-lee-**zo**-vahćh] v. belittle; minimize; make light of; set no store by; ignore; underestimate; trifle (*repeatedly*)
bagatelizowanie [bah-gah-te-lee-zo-**vah**-ńe] n. belittling; minimizing; underestimating
bagatelka [bah-gah-**tel**-kah] f. trifle; a small matter; a mere trifle
bagatelny [bah-gah-**tel**-ni] adj.m. trivial; trifling; of no importance
bagaż [**bah**-gahsh] m. luggage; baggage
bagaż nauki [**bah**-gahsh nah-**oo**-kee] exp.: mental outfit; mental equipment
bagaż ręczny [**bah**-gahsh ranch-ni] exp.: hand-luggage; hand-baggage
nadać bagaż [nah-dahćh **bah**-gahsh] exp.: to check in luggage; to have one's baggage registered
odbiór bagażu [**od**-byoor bah-**gah**-zhoo] exp.: baggage claim area
przechowalnia bagażu [pshe-kho-**vahl**-ńah bah-**gah**-zhoo] exp.: left-luggage office; baggage cloak-room
bagażnik [bah-**gahzh**-ńeek] m. car-trunk; bike-carrier; luggage boot
bagażowe [bah-gah-**zho**-ve] n. fee for carrying baggage; carriage fee
bagażownia [bah-gah-**zhov**-ńah] f. baggage claim area; left-luggage room
bagażowy [bah-gah-**zho**-vi] m. porter; adj.m. baggage-; luggage-
bagażówka [bah-gah-**zhoof**-kah] f. luggage car; luggage taxi; luggage railroad car
bagdady [bahg-**dah**-di] pl. sheep's fur coat
bagienko [bah-**gen**-ko] n. (small) bog; swamp; marsh
bagienny [bah-**gen**-ni] adj.m. boggy; marshy; swampy
bagier [**bah**-ger] m. dredge; drag; digger; dredger
bagieta [bah-**ge**-tah] f. molding
bagietka [bah-**ge**-tkah] f. glass rod; wheat roll
bagnecik [bahg-**ne**-ćheek] m. small bayonet
bagnet [**bahg**-net] m. bayonet; (soil) cutter
bagnetowy [bahg-ne-**to**-vi] adj.m. bayonet (cap, etc.)
bagnica [bahg-**ńee**-tsah] f. a bog herb; scheuchzeria
bagnicowaty [bahg-nee-tso-**vah**-ti] adj.m. of a bog herb; of scheuchzeria family of herbs
bagnicowate [bahg-ńee-tso-**vah**-te] pl. plants of the scheuchzeria family (of herbs)
bagnisko [bahg-**ńees**-ko] n. (big) swamp; fen; morass; marsh; bog; quagmire
bagnistość [bahg-**ńees**-tośhćh] f. bogginess; marshiness
bagnisty [bahg-**ńees**-ti] adj.m. swampy; fenny; boggy; marshy; paludal; quaggy; sloughy; morassy
teren bagnisty [**te**-ren bahg-**ńees**-ti] exp.: swampy ground; marshlands
bagno [**bahg**-no] n. swamp; fen; morass; marsh; bog; quagmire; slough; quag; (moral) sewer; cesspool of inequity
ugrząść w bagnie [oo-gzhownśhćh v **bahg**-ńe] exp.: to get bogged (down)
bagnoznawstwo [bahg-no-znahf-

stfo] n. study of evolution of marshes
bagrować [bah-**gro**-vahćh] v. dredge (up, out, away); drag (*repeatedly*)
bagrowanie [bah-gro-**vah**-ńe] n. dredging; dragging
bagrowisko [bah-gro-**vees**-ko] n. pile of dredged out material
bagrownica [bah-grov-**ńee**-tsah] f. dredge; drag; digger
bagrowy [bah-**gro**-vi] adj.m. dredge; (of, for) dredging
bagrzysta [bah-**gzhis**-tah] m. dredge operator; dredger
bainit [bah-**ee**-ńeet] m. variety of perlite (volcanic glass)
baj [bahy] m. story teller
baja [**bah**-yah] f. baize; colloq: story; tale; fib; lie
baje [**bah**-ye] pl. colloq: humbug; bunkum; claptrap
bajacz [**bah**-yahch] m. blabberer; twaddler; tale teller
bajaczka [bah-**yahch**-kah] f. (woman) blabberer; twaddler; tale teller
bajać [**bah**-yahćh] v. tell tales; tell stories; prattle; blabber; twaddle; talk nonsense (*repeatedly*)
bajadera [bah-yah-**de**-rah] f. Hindu entertaining dancer; bayadere; fabric with horizontal stripes and contrasting colors
bajaderka [bah-yah-**der**-kah] f. kind of cake
bajan [**bah**-yahn] m. variety of accordion
bajanie [bah-**yah**-ńe] n. colloq: tales; stories; prattle; blabber; twaddle; nonsense
bajarka [bah-**yahr**-kah] f. (woman) blabberer; twaddler; tale teller
bajarstwo [bah-**yahr**-stfo] n. story telling
bajarz [**bah**-yahsh] m. blabberer; twaddler; tale teller; fibster; liar; teller of lies
bajcować [bahy-**tso**-vahćh] v. colloq: brag; exaggerate; bluff; mislead (*repeatedly*)
bajcowanie [bahy-tso-**vah**-ńe] n. colloq: bragging; exaggeration; bluffing; misleading
bajczarka [bahy-**chahr**-kah] f. (woman) gossip; tabby; busybody; trouble-maker; scandalmonger
bajczarski [bahy-**chahr**-skee] adj.m. gossipy
bajczarstwo [bahy-**chahr**-stfo] n. gossip; gossipry
bajczarz [**bahy**-chahsh] m. gossip; liar; teller of lies; busybody; trouble-maker; scandalmonger
bajczyć [**bahy**-chićh] v. gossip; prattle; blabber (*repeatedly*)
bajda [**bahy**-dah] f. piece of gossip; fictitious story; nonsense; prattle; bosh; claptrap; cock-and-bull story; rigmarole; balderdash
bajdak [**bahy**-dahk] m. flat-bottom boat in the Ukraine
bajduła [bahy-**doo**-wah] m. blabberer; twaddler; tale teller
bajdurzenie [bahy-doo-**zhe**-ńe] n. nonsensical talk; drivel; prattle; blabber
bajdurzyć [bahy-**doo**-zhićh] v. talk nonsense; prate; blabber; drivel (*repeatedly*)
bajduś [**bahy**-doośh] exp.: (only in) **klituś-bajduś** [klee-toośh **bahy**-doośh] exp.: nonsense; silly talk; rubbish; drivel
bajdziarski [bahy-**dźhahr**-skee] adj.m. fictitious; gossipy
bajdziarstwo [bahy-**dźhahr**-stfo] n. gossiping; scandalmongering; prattle; twaddle; humbug
bajeczka [bah-**yech**-kah] f. fairy tale; story; nursery tale; piece of gossip; rumor; yarn
bajecznie [bah-**yech**-ńe] adv. fabulously; admirably; magnificently; incredibly; unbelievably; enormously; prodigiously; extremely; awfully
to brzmi bajecznie [to bzhmee bah-**yech**-ńe] exp.: it sounds improbable
bajeczność [bah-**yech**-nośhćh] f. myth; legend; mythical character; prodigy
bajeczny [bah-**yech**-ni] adj.m. mythic; legendary; mythical; fabulous; prodigious; stupendous; unheard of; enormous; immense

bajeczne dzieje [bah-**yech**-ne **dźhe**-ye] exp.: legendary times
bajer [**bah**-yer] m. slang: confidence game on a small scale; bamboozlement
bajerować [bah-ye-**ro**-vahćh] v. play a petty confidence game; hoax; spoof; take in a customer (*repeatedly*)
bajerowanie [bah-ye-ro-**vah**-ńe] n. slang: hoax; spoof
bajgieł [**bahy**-gew] m. Jewish cracknel
bajgiełe [bahy-**ge**-we] not declined: Jewish cracknel
bajka [**bahy**-kah] f. fairy-tale; gossip; scandal; story; fable
bajka! [**bahy**-kah] exp.: it's a pack of lies!; it's not to the point!; it's nonsense!; that's fiction!
jak z bajki [yahk z **bahy**-kee] exp.: fairy-like; wonderful; marvelous
kraina z bajki [krah-ee-nah z **bahy**-kee] exp.: fairyland; wonderland
roznosić bajki [roz-**no**-śheećh **bahy**-kee] exp.: to gossip; to go scandalmongering
włożyć między bajki [**vwo**-zhićh **myan**-dzi **bahy**-kee] exp.: not to believe
bajkopis [bahy-**ko**-pees] m. writer of fables; composer of fables
bajkopisarstwo [bahy-ko-pee-**sahr**-stfo] n. writing of fables
bajkopisarz [bahy-ko-**pee**-sahsh] m. writer of fables; fabulist
bajkowo [bahy-**ko**-vo] adv. fabulously; wonderfully
bajkowość [bahy-**ko**-vośhćh] f. wonderfulness; marvelousness; magnificence; fairyland-quality
bajkowy [bahy-**ko**-vi] adj.m. wonderful; marvelous; magnificent; fairyland-
bajoński [bah-**yoń**-skee] adj.m. vast (sums of money, etc.)
bajopis [bah-**yo**-pees] m. writer of fables; fabulist
bajorek [bah-**yo**-rek] m. bullion; gold thread; silver thread
bajorko [bah-**yor**-ko] n. (small) puddle; slough; quag; morass; mire
bajoro [bah-**yo**-ro] n. puddle; slough; quag; morass; mire
bajowy [bah-**yo**-vi] adj.m. like a coarse, felt-like woolen cloth; baize; of baize
bajówka [bah-**yoof**-kah] f. baize coat
bajram [**bahy**-rahm] m. Muslim feast at the end of Ramadan
bajronicznie [bahy-ro-**ńeech**-ńe] adv. in Byronic style
bajroniczny [bahy-ro-**ńeech**-ni] adj.m. Byronic; Byronian
bajronista [bahy-ro-**ńees**-tah] m. Byronist
bajronistyczny [bahy-ro-ńees-**tich**-ni] adj.m. Byronic; Byronian
bajronizm [bahy-**ro**-ńeezm] m. Byronism
bajronizować [bahy-ro-ńee-**zo**-vahćh] v. imitate Byron's style (*repeatedly*)
bajronowski [bahy-ro-**nof**-skee] adj.m. Byronic; Byronian
bajroński [bahy-**roń**-skee] adj.m. Byronic; Byronian
bajt [bahyt] m. byte; an 8-bit; a group of adjacent binary digits often shorter than a word that a computer processes as a unit; when used to store text in a computer, a single byte may be used to designate one character from a field of 256 different characters; see: **bit**
bajtlować [bahy-**tlo**-vahćh] v. colloq: talk nonsense; tell lies; hoax; prattle; drivel; prate; fib; bamboozle (*repeatedly*)
bajtlowanie [bahy-tlo-**vah**-ńe] n. colloq: nonsense; prattle; drivel; twaddle
bajzel [**bahy**-zel] m. vulg.: whorehouse; brothel; mess; jumble
bajzelmama [bahy-zel-**mah**-mah] f. vulg.: owner of a whorehouse; owner of a brothel (woman)
bak [bahk] m. gasoline tank; can; side-whisker; sideburn
baka [**bah**-kah] f. beacon; buoy
bakalarski [bah-kah-**lahr**-skee] adj.m. school-teacher's
bakalarstwo [bah-kah-**lahr**-stfo] n. school-teaching
bakalaureat [bah-kah-lahw-**re**-aht]

m. baccalaureate; bachelor's degree
bakalie [bah-**kah**-lye] pl. delicacies; dainties; sweet almonds, raisins, nuts, and figs, etc.
bakalijki [bah-kah-**leey**-kee] pl. delicacies; dainties; sweet almonds, raisins, nuts, figs, etc.
bakaliowy [bah-kah-**lyo**-vi] adj.m. of delicacies
bakałarz [bah-**kah**-wahsh] m. colloq: school-teacher (of old); B.S.; B.A.
bakałarzować [bah-kah-wah-**zho**-vahćh] v. be a school-teacher; teach school children (*repeatedly*)
bakałarzyć [bah-kah-**wah**-zhićh] v. be a school-teacher; teach school children (*repeatedly*)
bakałarzyna [bah-kah-wah-**zhi**-nah] m. paltry school-teacher
bakan [**bah**-kahn] m. beacon; buoy
bakarat [bah-**kah**-raht] m. crystal (made at Baccarat); baccarat (game)
bakaratowy [bah-kah-rah-**to**-vi] adj.m. baccarat (glass, etc.)
bakbort [**bahk**-bort] m. port side of a ship; left side of a ship
bakburta [bahk-**boor**-tah] f. port side of a ship; left side of a ship
bakchanalia [bahk-khah-**nah**-lyah] pl. drunken revel; carousal; orgy; revelry; carousing; bacchanalia
bakcyl [**bahk**-tsil] m. microbe; germ
bakczysz [**bahk**-chish] m. baksheesh
bakelit [bah-**ke**-leet] m. bakelite
bakelitowy [bah-ke-lee-**to**-vi] adj.m. bakelite (tray, etc.)
baken [**bah**-ken] m. beacon; buoy
bakier [**bah**-ker] adv. slantways
na bakier [nah **bah**-ker] exp.: tilted; awry; slantwise; being cross with somebody
bakierować [bah-ke-**ro**-vahćh] v. warp; distort; twist (*repeatedly*)
bakierować się [bah-ke-**ro**-vahćh śhan] v. go crooked (*repeatedly*)
bakłaszka [bah-**kwahsh**-kah] f. (soldier's) canteen (water vessel)
bakłażan [bah-**kwah**-zhahn] m. eggplant; guineasquash; eggfruit
bakonista [bah-ko-**ńees**-tah] m. (a) Baconian
bakonizm [bah-**ko**-ńeezm] m. Baconian philosophy
baksztag [**bahk**-shtahg] m. guy wire; backstay; guy
bakszysz [**bahk**-shish] m. baksheesh
bakteremia [bahk-te-**re**-myah] f. presence of bacteria in blood
bakteria [bahk-**te**-ryah] f. germ; microbe; bacterium
bakterie [bahk-**ter**-ye] pl. bacteria; germs
bakteriemia [bahk-ter-**ye**-myah] f. bacteriolysis by body's defense mechanism
bakteriobójczo [bahk-ter-yo-**booy**-cho] adv. (act) as a germicide
bakteriobójczy [bahk-ter-yo-**booy**-chi] adj.m. destroying germs
bakteriocyd [bahk-ter-**yo**-tsit] m. bactericide
bakteriocydy [bahk-ter-yo-**tsi**-di] pl. germicides
bakteriofag [bahk-ter-**yo**-fahg] m. bacteriophage; bacteria-destroying agent
bakteriofagi [bahk-ter-yo-**fah**-gee] pl. bacteriophages
bakteriolitycznie [bahk-ter-yo-lee-**tich**-ńe] adv. in a bacteriolytic manner
bakteriolityczny [bahk-ter-yo-lee-**tich**-ni] adj.m. bacteriolytic
bakterioliza [bahk-ter-yo-**lee**-zah] f. bacteriolysis
bakteriolizyna [bahk-ter-yo-lee-**zi**-nah] f. bacteriolysin
bakteriolizyny [bahk-ter-yo-lee-**zi**-ni] pl. bacteriolysins
bakteriolog [bahk-ter-**yo**-log] m. bacteriologist
bakteriologia [bahk-ter-yo-**lo**-gyah] f. bacteriology
bakteriologicznie [bahk-ter-yo-lo-**geech**-ńe] adv. bacteriologically
bakteriologiczny [bahk-ter-yo-lo-**geech**-ni] adj.m. bacteriological
wojna bakteriologiczna [**voy**-nah bahk-ter-yo-lo-**geech**-nah] exp.: germ warfare; bacteriological warfare
bakterioryza [bahk-ter-yo-**ri**-zah] f. bacterial nitrogen fixation in soil
bakterioskopia [bahk-ter-yo-**sko**-pyah] f. bacterioscopy
bakteriostatycznie [bahk-ter-yo-stah-

tich-ńe] adv. bacteriostatically
bakteriostatyczny [bahk-ter-yo-stah-tich-ni] adj.m. bacteriostatic
bakterioterapia [bahk-te-ryo-te-rah-pyah] f. bacteriotherapy
bakterioza [bahk-te-ryo-zah] f. bacteriosis
bakteryjnie [bahk-te-riy-ńe] adv. bacterially
bakteryjny [bahk-te-riy-ni] adj.m. bacterial
baktrian [bahk-tryahn] m. Bactrian (two hump) camel
bal [bahl] m. ball; dance; treat; bale (of merchandise); log used in construction
balans [bah-lahns] m. balancing movement; balancing pole; balance-wheel (of a watch)
balansista [bah-lahn-śhee-stah] m. tight-rope walker; acrobat; juggler
balansjer [bah-lahn-syer] m. scale-beam; balancing pole; balance-wheel (of a watch)
balansować [bah-lahn-so-vahćh] v. balance; oscillate; bob up and down (on water) (*repeatedly*)
balansowanie [bah-lahn-so-vah-ńe] n. balancing; oscillation
balansowy [bah-lahn-so-vi] adj.m. balancing (movement, etc.)
balansówka [bah-lahn-soof-kah] f. hand-operated small press
balas [bah-lahs] m. baluster; banister; rail-post; rail
balasa [bah-lah-sah] f. baluster; banister; rail post; rail
balasek [bah-lah-sek] m. altar-rail
balast [bah-lahst] m. ballast; kentledge; dead-wood
balastować [bah-lah-sto-vahćh] v. ballast (*repeatedly*)
balastowanie [bah-lah-sto-vah-ńe] n. using (placing, etc.) a ballast
balastowy [bah-lah-sto-vi] adj.m. ballast (port, etc.)
balata [bah-lah-tah] f. balata; bully tree; balata gum
baldach [bahl-dahkh] m. baldaquin; baldachin; umbel (a rich fabric)
baldachim [bahl-dah-kheem] m. canopy; baldachin
baldachimowy [bahl-dah-khee-mo-vi] adj.m. canopy (fabric, etc.)
baldachogrono [bahl-dah-kho-gro-no] n. corymb (species of inflorescence)
baldaszek [bahl-dah-shek] m. umbellate; canopy; baldachin
baldaszkogrono [bahl-dahsh-ko-gro-no] n. corymb (species of inflorescence)
baldaszkowaty [bahl-dahsh-ko-vah-ti] m. umbellate; umbellar; umbelliform
baldszkowate [bahl-dahsh-ko-vah-te] pl. the Umbelliferae
balenit [bah-le-ńeet] m. artificial whalebone
balerina [bah-le-ree-nah] f. ballerina
balerinka [bah-le-reen-kah] f. (small, girl) ballerina
baleron [bah-le-ron] m. ham (boned, enclosed in a bladder, boiled and smoked)
baleryna [bah-le-ri-nah] f. ballerina
balet [bah-let] m. ballet
baletka [bah-let-kah] f. ballet slipper
baletmistrz [bah-let-meestsh] m. ballet master
baletmistrzowski [bah-let-mees-tshof-skee] adj.m. ballet-master's
baletmistrzyni [bah-let-mees-tshi-ńee] f. (female) ballet director
baletnica [bah-let-ńee-tsah] f. ballet dancer; ballet girl
baletniczka [bah-let-ńeech-kah] f. (small) ballet dancer; ballet girl
baletniczy [bah-let-ńee-chi] adj.m. of a ballet dancer; ballet (dress, slippers, etc.)
baletowy [bah-le-to-vi] adj.m. of ballet; ballet (performance, etc.)
balia [bah-lyah] f. wash tub; tub
balijka [bah-leey-kah] f. (small) wash tub; tub
balista [bah-lees-tah] f. catapult (an ancient military engine); ballista
balistokardiograf [bah-lees-to-kahr-dyo-grahf] m. ballistocardiograph
balistokardiografia [bah-lees-to-kahr-dyo-grah-fyah] f. ballistocardiography
balistokardiograficzny [bah-lees-to-kahr-dyo-grah-feech-ni] f. ballistocardiographic
balistokardiogram [bah-lees-to-

kahr-**dyo**-grahm] m. ballistocardiogram
balistol [bah-**lees**-tol] m. a kind of grease
balistycznie [bah-lees-**tich**-ńe] adv. ballistically
balistyczny [bah-lees-**tich**-ni] adj.m. ballistic
krzywa balistyczna [**kshi**-vah bah-lees-**tich**-nah] exp.: ballistic curve
rakieta balistyczna [rah-k̲e-tah bah-lees-**tich**-nah] exp.: ballistic missile
balistyka [bah-**lee**-sti-kah] f. ballistics
balkon [**bahl**-kon] m. balcony
balkonik [bahl-**ko**-ńeek] m. (small, nice) balcony; gallery
balkonowy [bahl-ko-**no**-vi] adj.m. balcony (seats, etc.)
drzwi balkonowe [dzhvee bahl-ko-**no**-ve] exp.: French window
ballada [bahl-**lah**-dah] f. ballad
balladowo [bahl-lah-**do**-vo] adv. in style of a ballad
balladowość [bahl-lah-**do**-vośhćh] f. ballad style
balladowy [bahl-lah-**do**-vi] adj.m. ballad (poetry)
balladyczność [bahl-lah-**dich**-nośhćh] f. ballad style
balladyczny [bahl-lah-**dich**-ni] adj.m. balladic
balladysta [bahl-lah-**dis**-tah] m. ballad writer; ballad composer
balladystka [bahl-lah-**dist**-kah] f. (female) ballad writer; ballad composer
balladzista [bahl-lah-**dźhees**-tah] m. ballad writer; author of ballads
balladzistka [bahl-lah-**dźheest**-kah] f. (woman) ballad writer; author of ballads
balneoklimatyczny [bahl-ne-o-klee-mah-**tich**-ni] adj.m. balneoclimatic
balneolog [bahl-ne-**o**-log] m. balneologist
balneologia [bahl-ne-o-**lo**-gyah] f. balneology; therapeutic use of bath
balneologiczny [bahl-ne-o-lo-**geech**-ni] adj.m. balneologic
balneoterapeutyczny [bahl-ne-o-te-rah-pew-**tich**-ni] adj.m. of balneotherapy
balneoterapia [bahl-ne-o-te-**rah**-pyah] f. balneotherapy (treatment of diseases by bath)
balon [**bah**-lon] m. balloon; sphere
balon próbny [**bah**-lon **proob**-ni] exp.: trial balloon; feeler
robić z kogoś balona [ro-beećh s **ko**-gośh bah-**lo**-nah] exp.: to make a fool of somebody; to make somebody look silly; colloq: to pull somebody's leg
balonet [bah-**lo**-net] m. ballonet; air compartment filled with atmospheric air for maintaining the shape of a flying balloon
balonfok [**bah**-lon-fok] m. balloon sail
baloniarski [bah-lo-**ńahr**-skee] adj.m. of balloon (sport, etc.)
baloniarstwo [bah-lo-**ńahr**-stfo] n. ballooning
baloniarz [bah-**lo**-ńahsh] m. balloonist
balonik [bah-**lo**-ńeek] m. small balloon
balonikowy [bah-lo-ńe-**ko**-vi] adj.m. (small) balloon (test)
balonkliwer [bah-lon-**klee**-ver] m. (type of) balloon sail
balonowy [bah-lo-**no**-vi] adj.m. balloon (flight, barrage, tire, gas, etc.)
lot balonowy [lot bah-lo-**no**-vi] exp.: balloon flight
balot [**bah**-lot] m. small bale
balotada [bah-lo-**tah**-dah] f. leap of a horse; balotade
balotaż [bah-**lo**-tahsh] m. voting by ballot; ballot
balotować [bah-lo-**to**-vahćh] v. ballot; vote by ballot (for, against) (*repeatedly*)
balotowanie [bah-lo-to-**vah**-ńe] n. ballot; balloting
balować [bah-**lo**-vahćh] v. attend balls; junket; dance away one's time (*repeatedly*)
balowanie [bah-lo-**vah**-ńe] n. attending balls; dancing away one's time
balowicz [bah-**lo**-veech] m. frequent (dancing) party participant
balowo [bah-**lo**-vo] adv. in ball-

dress; in evening dress; in decoration
balowy [bah-**lo**-vi] adj.m. ball-
sala balowa [**sah**-lah bah-**lo**-vah] exp.: ball-room; dance-hall
balsa [**bahl**-sah] f. balsa (tree, wood, etc.)
balsam [**bahl**-sahm] m. balm; balsam; fragrant healing ointment or oil; anything healing or soothing
balsamicznie [bahl-sah-**meech**-ńe] adv. like balm; with the fragrance of balm; with a balmy fragrance
balsamiczny [bahl-sah-**meech**-ni] adj.m. balmy; balsamic; soothing, mild, etc.; aromatic
balsamina [bahl-sah-**mee**-nah] f. garden balsam
balsaminka [bah-sah-**meen**-kah] f. (nice, little) garden balsam
balsamista [bahl-sah-**mees**-tah] m. balsamer
balsamka [bahl-**sahm**-kah] f. balsam apple
balsamować [bahl-sah-**mo**-vahćh] v. embalm (a corpse); protect (a dead body) from decay; perfume; fill with balmy fragrance; preserve a dead body with various chemicals (*repeatedly*)
balsamowanie [bahl-sah-mo-**vah**-ńe] n. embalmment
balsamowy [bahl-sah-**mo**-vi] adj.m. balmy; balsamic
balsowy [bahl-**so**-vi] adj.m. of balsa (very light in weight) wood
baltolog [bahl-**to**-log] m. philologist of Baltic languages
baltologia [bahl-to-**lo**-gyah] f. philology of Baltic languages
balustrada [bah-loos-**trah**-dah] f. railing; hand rail; guard rail
balustradka [bah-loos-**traht**-kah] f. (small) railing; hand rail; guard rail
balustradowy [bah-loos-trah-**do**-vi] adj.m. of a balustrade; balustrade (enclosure, etc.)
balwiernia [bahl-**vyer**-ńah] f. barber shop
balwierstwo [bahl-**vyer**-stfo] n. barber's trade
balwierz [**bahl**-vyesh] m. barber; barber-surgeon (of old)
balzakiana [bahl-zah-**kyah**-anh] pl. study (of life, style, etc.) of Balzac
balzakista [bahl-zah-**kees**-tah] m. student (of life, style, etc.) of Balzac
balzakowski [bahl-zah-**kof**-skee] adj.m. in the style of Balzac
bałabajka [bah-wah-**bahy**-kah] f. balalaika
bałabuch [bah-**wah**-bookh] m. homemade "sweetmeat" cake
bałagan [bah-**wah**-gahn] m. mess; disorder; disarray; confusion; untidiness; muddle; puddle; muss
narobić bałaganu [nah-**ro**-beećh bah-wah-**gah**-noo] exp.: to make a mess; to bungle up; to jumble up
bałaganiara [bah-wah-gah-**ńah**-rah] f. messy, untidy, disorderly woman; slut; slattern
bałaganiarka [bah-wah-gah-**ńahr**-kah] f. messy, untidy, disorderly woman; slut; slattern
bałaganiarski [bah-wah-gah-**ńahr**-skee] adj.m. disorderly; untidy; messy; chaotic
bałaganiarsko [bah-wah-gah-**ńahr**-sko] adv. in a disorderly manner; chaotically
bałaganiarstwo [bah-wah-gah-**ńahr**-stfo] n. disorderliness; untidiness; topsy-turvy condition
bałaganiarz [bah-wah-**gah**-ńahsh] m. disorderly, untidy, messy, chaotic person; bungler; muddler
bałaganić [bah-wah-**gah**-ńeećh] v. make a mess; throw things into confusion; be disorderly, untidy, messy, chaotic, etc.; waste one's time; loiter; idle time away (*repeatedly*)
bałaganienie [bah-wah-gah-**ńe**-ńe] n. disorderliness; untidiness; messiness
bałaganik [bah-wah-**gah**-ńeek] m. perfect mess; precious mess
bałałajka [bah-wah-**wahy**-kah] f. balalaika
bałamucenie [bah-wah-moo-**tse**-ńe] n. deception; coaxing; misleading
bałamucić [bah-wah-**moo**-ćheećh] v. lead astray; loiter; flirt; coax;

seek to seduce; philander; mislead; wheedle; vamp; trifle (with); dally (with); carry on a flirtation (*repeatedly*)
bałamucić się [bah-wah-**moo**-ćheećh śh<u>an</u>] v. flirt; coquet; delude oneself; let oneself be deceived (*repeatedly*)
bałamuctwo [bah-wah-**moo**-tstfo] n. deception; falsehood; misleading statement; deceit; delusion; flirting; flirtation; deception; coaxing; wheedling; coquetry; vagueness; obscurity; fogginess
bałamut [bah-**wah**-moot] m. flirt; seducer; person inclined to flirt; person spreading confusion
bałamutka [bah-wah-**moot**-kah] f. flirt; seducer; coquette; trifler
bałamutnie [bah-wah-**moot**-ńe] adv. delusively; in a confusing manner; deludingly
bałamutność [bah-wah-**moot**-nośhćh] f. flirtatious disposition; misleading character or nature
bałamutny [bah-wah-**moot**-ni] adj.m. misleading; confusing; delusive; evasive; deceptive; flirtatious
bałkański [bahw-**kahń**-skee] adj.m. Balkan; of the Balkans
bałtolog [bahw-**to**-log] m. student of Balto-Slavic languages, and culture
bałtologia [bah-to-**lo**-gyah] f. study of Balto-Slavic languages, and cultures
bałto-słowiański [**bahw**-to swo-**vyahń**-skee] adj.m. Balto-Slavic (languages, culture, etc.)
bałtycki [bahw-**tits**-kee] adj.m. Baltic
bałtysta [bahw-**tis**-tah] m. philologist (of Baltic languages)
bałtystyka [bahw-**tis**-ti-kah] f. philology (of Baltic languages)
bałuch [**bah**-wookh] m. goggle eye
bałuchy [bah-**woo**-khi] pl. goggle eyes
bałwan [**bahw**-vahn] m. snowman; ass; breaking wave crest; blockhead; fool; nitwit; fetish; idol; lump; block; snow-mass; swelling mass of smoke, etc.
bałwanek [bahw-**vah**-nek] m. idol; fetish; small snowman; decoy-duck
bałwaniasty [bahw-vah-**ńahs**-ti] adj.m. surging; swelling; billowy
bałwanica [bahw-vah-**ńee**-tsah] f. vulg.: stupid woman; imbecile; moron; cretin; idiot; nitwit
bałwanić [bahw-**vah**-ńeećh] v. agitate; toss; disturb (*repeatedly*)
bałwanić się [bahw-**vah**-ńeećh śh<u>an</u>] v. bulge; billow; surge; swell; act the fool; play a fool; fool around; fool about (*repeatedly*)
bałwanieć [bahw-**vah**-ńećh] v. become confused; grow stupid (*repeatedly*)
bałwanienie [bahw-vah-**ńe**-ńe] n. stupefaction
bałwanisty [bahw-vah-**ńees**-ti] adj.m. surging; swelling; billowy
bałwanowaty [bahw-vah-no-**vah**-ti] adj.m. dull-brained; stupid; doltish
bałwański [bahw-**vahń**-skee] adj.m. stupid; silly; brainless
bałwaństwo [bahw-**vahń**-stfo] n. stupidity; foolishness
bałwochwalca [bahw-vo-**khfahl**-tsah] m. idolater; idolatrous admirer; idolizer; worshiper of idols
bahłwochwalczo [bahw-vo-**khfahl**-cho] adv. with idolatrous admiration; blindly; slavishly; loving (or admiring) excessively
bałwochwalczy [bahw-vo-**khfahl**-chi] adj.m. idolatrous; slavish; blind
bałwochwalczyni [bahw-vo-khfahl-**chi**-ńee] f. idolatress; idolizer
bałwochwalstwo [bahw-vo-**khfahl**-stfo] n. worship of idols; image worship; idolizing of; excessive devotion to or reverence for some person or thing
bałyk [**bah**-wik] m. colloq: crawl
na bałyku [nah bah-**wi**-koo] exp.: on all fours
bam [bahm] m. ding; dong
bamber [**bahm**-ber] m. colloq: German farmer
bambetle [bahm-**bet**-le] pl. slang: lumber; rubbish; odds and ends; trash
bambocjada [bahm-bots-**yah**-dah] f. bambocciade
bambosz [**bahm**-bosh] m. soft

slipper
bamboszek [bahm-**bo**-shek] m. soft child's slipper
bambus [**bahm**-boos] m. bamboo (plant, rod, etc.); vulg.: nigger
bambusowy [bahm-boo-**so**-vi] adj.m. bamboo (chair, etc.)
ban [bahn] m. Hungarian governor
banalizować [bah-nah-lee-**zo**-vahćh] v. trivialize; render commonplace; hackney (*repeatedly*)
banalizowanie [bah-nah-lee-zo-**vah**-ńe] n. trivialization
banalnie [bah-**nahl**-ńe] adv. without imagination; in an unoriginal fashion; tritely; in a commonplace fashion
banalność [bah-**nahl**-nośhćh] f. banality; triviality; commonplace saying; truism; unimportant matter
banalny [bah-**nahl**-ni] adj.m. without significance; unimportant; banal; commonplace; trite; trivial; humdrum; unoriginal; tame; uninspired; threadbare (joke, etc.)
banał [**bah**-nahw] m. stock phrase; tag; banality; truism; triviality
banały [bah-**nah**-wi] pl. banalities; trivia; trifles; exp.: small talk
pleść banały [pleśhćh bah-**nah**-wi] exp.: to utter platitudes
banan [**bah**-nahn] m. banana; the banana plant
bananojad [bah-nah-**no**-yaht] m. touraco; Musophaga
bananowaty [bah-nah-no-**vah**-ti] adj.m. of banana-shape
bananowiec [bah-nah-**no**-vyets] m. banana plant; plantain
bananownia [bah-nah-**nov**-ńah] f. banana ripening plant
bananowy [bah-nah-**no**-vi] adj.m. of banana; banana (leaf, etc.)
banat [bah-naht] m. region under administration of Hungarian ban
banatka [bah-**naht**-kah] f. variety of wheat
band [bend] m. jazz band; an informal orchestra
banda [**bahn**-dah] f. band; gang; bunch (of friends, etc.); company; pack (of fools, etc.); multitude; swarm; host; army
cała banda [**tsah**-wah **bahn**-dah] exp.: the whole lot of you (us, etc.); multitude; swarm; host; army
bandaż [**bahn**-dahsh] m. bandage
bandażować [bahn-dah-**zho**-vahćh] v. put a bandage on; swathe; dress (a wound, etc.); parcel (a rope) (*repeatedly*)
bandażowanie [bahn-dah-zho-**vah**-ńe] n. putting on a bandage
bandażownictwo [bahn-dah-zhov-**neets**-tfo] n. proper method of putting on a bandage
bandera [bahn-**de**-rah] f. flag; jack; ensign; colors
banderia [bahn-**de**-ryah] f. escort of honor of horsemen in regional costumes
banderilla [bahn-de-**reel**-lah] f. banderilla (used in bullfights)
banderillero [bahn-de-reel-**le**-ro] m. banderillero (in a bullfight)
banderka [bahn-**de**-rkah] f. pennon
banderola [bahn-de-**ro**-lah] f. banderole
banderolka [bahn-de-**rol**-kah] f. small banderole; excise band; (mail) wrapper
banderolować [bahn-de-ro-**lo**-vahćh] v. banderole; secure with a banderole (*repeatedly*)
banderolowanie [bahn-de-ro-lo-**vah**-ńe] n. putting on banderoles
banderowiec [bahn-de-**ro**-vyets] m. member of an Ukrainian military organization during World War II and till 1947 (which was led by Stefan Bandera, 1908-59, and committed massive extermination of Poles in Volhynia and Galicia. Bandera was assassinated by a Soviet agent in West Germany.)
bandolet [bahn-**do**-let] m. shoulder-belt
bandolier [bahn-**dol**-yer] m. bandoleer; bandolier
bandos [**ban**-dos] m. seasonal farm worker
bandura [bahn-**doo**-rah] f. Ukrainian musical instrument with strings
bandurka [bahn-**door**-kah] f. (small, nice) Ukrainian musical instrument with strings

bandy [bahn-di] n. variety of hockey
bandycki [bahn-**dits**-kee] adj.m. of a bandit; of a robber; ruffianly; bandit's
napad bandycki [**nah**-pahd bahn-**dits**-kee] exp.: hold-up; robbery; act of banditry
bandyta [bahn-**di**-tah] m. bandit; robber; ruffian; gangster; thug
bandytyzm [bahn-**di**-tizm] m. banditry; banditism; robbery
bandzior [**bahn**-dźhor] m. slang: bandit; robber; gangster; thug
bandżo [**bahn**-dzho] n. banjo; four-string African musical instrument
bandżola [bahn-**dzho**-lah] f. banjo; four-string African musical instrument
bania [**bah**-ńah] f. container; bulgy object; bulb; sphere; globe; dome; blister; bubble; balloon
baniak [**bah**-ńahk] m. laundry boiler
banialuk [bah-**ńah**-look] m. nonsense; rot; rubbish; bosh
pleść banialuki [pleśhćh bah-ńah-**loo**-kee] exp.: to talk nonsense
banialuka [bah-ńah-**loo**-kah] f. nonsense; rot; rubbish; bosh
banian [**bah**-ńyahn] m. banyan tree
baniasto [bah-**ńahs**-to] adv. spherically; like a globe
baniasty [bah-**ńahs**-ti] adj.m. spherical; globular; dome-shaped; bulging; bulbous
banicja [bah-**ńee**-tsyah] f. deportation; banishment; exile
banicyjny [bah-ńe-**tsiy**-ni] adj.m. of exile; of deportation; of banishment
banieczka [bah-**ńech**-kah] f. (small) container; bulgy object; bulb; sphere; globe; dome; blister; bubble; balloon
banie się [**bah**-ńe śhan] n. being afraid; fearing; fear
baniopień [bah-**ńo**-pyeń] m. iodine-producing algae
banita [bah-**ńee**-tah] m. outlaw; outcast; exile
banitka [bah-**ńeet**-kah] f. (woman) outlaw; outcast; exile
banjo [**bahn**-dżho] n. banjo
banjola [bahn-**dżho**-lah] f. banjo
bank [bahnk] m. bank; pool; computer data base
bank hipoteczny [bahnk khee-po-**tech**-ni] exp.: mortgage bank
bank kredytowy [bahnk kre-di-**to**-vi] exp.: loan bank
bankier [**bahn**-ker] m. banker
bankierski [bahn-**ker**-skee] adj.m. banker's; banking
bankierstwo [bahn-**ker**-stfo] n. banking; banking business; banking circles
bankiet [**bahn**-ket] m. banquet
bankieta [bahn-**ke**-tah] f. bank (of earth, etc.); wall footing
ława bankietowa [**wah**-vah bahn-ke-**to**-vah] exp.: earth bank; wall footing
bankietować [bahn-ke-**to**-vahćh] v. carouse; banquet (*repeatedly*)
bankietowy [bahn-ke-**to**-vi] adj.m. banquet (speech, etc.); banqueting (guests, etc.)
bankiwa [bahn-**kee**-vah] f. variety of pheasant (bird)
banknot [**bahnk**-not] m. banknote; bill; note; greenback
banknotowy [bahnk-no-**to**-vi] adj.m. banknote (paper, etc.)
banko [**bahn**-ko] indecl. banco
grać banko [grahćh **bahn**-ko] exp.: to go banco
bankowiec [bahn-**ko**-vyets] m. bank employee; bank clerk; bank employees' vacation center
bankowość [bahn-**ko**-vośhćh] f. banking; banking business
bankowy [bahn-**ko**-vi] adj.m. bank-
dom bankowy [dom bahn-**ko**-vi] exp.: banking-house
rachunek bankowy [rah-**khoo**-nek bahn-**ko**-vi] exp.: bank-account
transakcje bankowe [trahn-**zahk**-tsye bahn-**ko**-ve] exp.: banking transactions
bankructwo [bahn-**kroots**-tfo] n. bankruptcy; insolvency; failure; smash
ogłosić bankructwo [o-**gwo**-śheećh bahn-**kroots**-tfo] exp.: to declare insolvency; to declare bankruptcy
bankrut [**bahn**-kroot] m. bankrupt; a person legally declared unable to

pay his debts
bankrutka [bahn-**kroot**-kah] f. bankrupt; a woman legally declared unable to pay her debts
bankrutować [bahn-kroo-**to**-vahćh] v. go bankrupt; fail; become insolvent (*repeatedly*)
bankrutowanie [bahn-kroo-to-**vah**-ńe] n. bankruptcy; insolvency; failure
banksja [**bahnk**-syah] f. banksia; Australian honeysuckle
bant [bahnt] m. band; clip; hinge
bantamka [bahn-**tahm**-kah] f. variety of small size chicken
Bantu [**bahn**-too] m. (African languages) Bantu
bantustan [bahn-**too**-stahn] m. Negro reservation in South Africa
bańczasty [bahń-**chah**-sti] adj.m. spherical; globular; bulby; bubbly; blistery
bańka [**bahń**-kah] f. bulb; can; container; milk-can; glass ball; bubble; nipple (in glass, metal, etc.); cupping-glass; colloq: one million zloty
bańka mydlana [**bahń**-kah mid-**lah**-nah] exp.: soap-bubble
baobab [bah-**o**-bahp] m. baobab (tree, fruit)
baon [**bah**-on] m. battalion; see: **batalion**
baptysta [bahp-**tis**-tah] m. baptist
baptysterium [bahp-tis-**ter**-yoom] n. baptistery; baptismal font
bar [bahr] m. bar; bar-room; restaurant; tap-room; gin-shop; saloon; buffet; refreshment bar; barium; bar (unit of pressure)
bar mleczny [bahr **mlech**-ni] exp.: milk bar
bar samoobsługowy [bahr sah-mo-op-swoo-**go**-vi] exp.: self-service bar; cafeteria
baraban [bah-**rah**-bahn] m. large drum used by Turkish Janissary units
barachło [bah-rah-**khwo**] n. colloq: useless junk; rabble; riff-raff; bunch of drunks (Russ.)
barak [**bah**-rahk] m. barrack; frame-house; hut
barakowóz [bah-rah-**ko**-voos] m. mobile home; mobile store; trailer
barakowy [bah-rah-**ko**-vi] adj.m. barrack-like
barakuda [bah-rah-**koo**-dah] f. barracuda
barakudowaty [bah-rah-koo-do-**vah**-ti] adj.m. barracuda-shaped; of the barracuda family of fish
barakudowate [bah-rah-koo-do-**vah**-te] pl. the barracuda family of fish
baran [**bah**-rahn] m. ram; tup; sheep; Aries (astrol.); battering ram; colloq: blockhead; idiot
baranek [bah-**rah**-nek] m. lamb; gentle lamb; cosset; cirrose cloud
barani [bah-**rah**-ńee] adj.m. sheep's (wool, etc.); mutton (chop, etc.)
baranica [bah-rah-**ńee**-tsah] f. sheepskin; woolfel; astrakhan cap; fur cap; sheepskin coat
baranieć [bah-**rah**-ńećh] v. be stupefied; be bewildered; be dumbfounded; stand aghast; be taken aback (*repeatedly*)
baranienie [bah-rah-**ńe**-ńe] n. being stupefied; being bewildered; being dumbfounded
baranina [bah-rah-**ńee**-nah] f. mutton
barankowaty [bah-rahn-ko-**vah**-ti] adj.m. like a lamb; sheepish
barankowy [bah-rahn-**ko**-vi] adj.m. sheepskin (fur, etc.); astrakhan (coat, cap, etc.)
baraszki [bah-**rahsh**-kee] pl. frolics; gambols; romps; pranks
stroić baraszki [**stro**-eećh bah-**rahsh**-kee] exp.: to frolic; to gambol; to romp; to caper (*repeatedly*)
baraszkować [bah-rahsh-**ko**-vahćh] v. frolic; gambol; romp; caper (*repeatedly*)
baraszkowanie [bah-rahsh-ko-**vah**-ńe] n. frolics; gambols; romps; pranks
barat [**bah**-raht] m. drum
baraż [**bah**-rahsh] m. playing-off (a tie); play-off (after a tie)
barażowy [bah-rah-**zho**-vi] adj.m. of playing-off (a tie); of play-off (after a tie)
barbakan [bahr-**bah**-kahn] m.

barbican
barbaria [bahr-**bah**-ryah] f. barbarity; savageness; savagery; barbarians; savages; barbarous land; savage lands
barbarka [bahr-**bahr**-kah] f. St. Barbara's day (Dec. 4th.) miners' festival
barbarkowy [bahr-bahr-**ko**-vi] adj.m. of St. Barbara's day (Dec. 4th.) miners' festival
barbarus [bahr-**bah**-roos] m. barbarian; savage; vandal
barbaryt [bahr-**bah**-rit] m. variety of nitroglycerin explosive
barbaryzacja [bahr-bah-ri-**zah**-tsyah] f. barbarization; barbarizing
barbaryzm [bahr-**bah**-rizm] m. barbarism
barbaryzować [bahr-bah-ri-**zo**-vahćh] v. barbarize (a country, a language, etc.) (*repeatedly*)
barbaryzować się [bahr-bah-ri-**zo**-vahćh śhan] v. barbarize oneself; become barbarous (*repeatedly*)
barbaryzowanie [bahr-bah-ri-zo-**vah**-ńe] n. barbarization
barbaryzowanie się [bahr-bah-ri-zo-**vah**-ńe śhan] n. becoming barbarous
barbarzyńca [bahr-bah-**zhiń**-tsah] m. barbarian; savage; vandal
barbarzyński [bahr-bah-**zhiń**-skee] adj.m. savage; barbaric; uncivilized; barbarous; vandalic
po barbarzyńsku [po bahr-bah-**zhiń**-skoo] exp.: in a savage way; like a barbarian; in an uncivilized manner
barbarzyńsko [bahr-bah-**zhiń**-sko] adv. barbarously; like a savage
barbarzyństwo [bahr-bah-**zhiń**-stfo] n. barbarity; savagery; vandalism; barbarous age
barbet [**bahr**-bet] m. barb (of a nun's head-dress)
barbituran [bahr-bee-**too**-rahn] m. sleeping medication
barbituranowy [bahr-bee-too-rah-**no**-vi] adj.m. barbituric (acid, tranquilizer, etc.)
barbiturat [bahr-bee-**too**-raht] m. barbiturate; salt or ester of a barbituric acid
barbiturowy [bahr-bee-too-**ro**-vi] adj.m. barbituric
barbórka [bahr-**boor**-kah] f. St. Barbara's day (Dec. 4th.) miners' festival
barbórkowy [bahr-boor-**ko**-vi] adj.m. of St. Barbara's day (Dec. 4th.) miners' festival
barchan [**bahr**-khan] m. fustian; thick-set (fabric); sickle-shaped dune
barchanka [bahr-**khahn**-kah] f. fustian shirt
barchanowy [bahr-khah-**no**-vi] adj.m. fustian (shirt, etc.); of fustian
barciak [**bahr**-ćhahk] m. wax-moth
barciel [**bahr**-ćhel] m. beehive beetle
barciowy [bahr-**ćho**-vi] adj.m. of a wild beehive
miód barciowy [myoot bahr-**ćho**-vi] exp.: wild honey
barczatka [bahr-**chaht**-kah] f. variety of moth
barczatki [bahr-**chaht**-kee] pl. the Lasiocampidae moth family
barczystość [bahr-**chis**-tośhćh] f. broad shoulders; sturdy build
barczysty [bahr-**chis**-ti] adj.m. broad-shouldered; square built
barć [bahrćh] f. wild beehive
bard [bahrt] m. bard; poet
bardo [**bahr**-do] n. weaver's reed
bardon [**bahr**-don] m. musical instrument with strings
bardotka [bahr-**dot**-kah] f. low-cut brassiere
bardziej [**bahr**-dźhey] adv. more; (emphatic "bardzo"); worse
tym bardziej [tim **bahr**-dźhey] exp.: all the more (reason)
bardzo [**bahr**-dzo] adv. very; ever so; very much; greatly; vastly; great deal; a lot
bardzo proszę [**bahr**-dzo **pro**-shan] exp.: please; if you please; by all means
jak bardzo [yahk **bahr**-dzo] exp.: how much; how very; how
nie bardzo [ńe **bahr**-dzo] exp.: not quite; not altogether; hardly
nie bardzo wiem [ńe **bahr**-dzo vyem] exp.: I hardly know; I don't quite know

za bardzo [zah **bahr**-dzo] exp.: too much; badly; sorely
barek [**bah**-rek] m. small bar on casters; small bar (on shelves, etc.); drinking paraphernalia
barelief [bah-**re**-lyef] m. bas-relief; bass-relief
baretka [bah-**ret**-kah] f. (medal) ribbon
bargiel [**bahr**-gel] m. nuthatch; sparrow-like bird
baribal [bah-**ree**-bahl] m. American black bear
bariera [bahr-**ye**-rah] f. rail; barrier; hand rail; obstacle; dike; dyke; starting-gate; hindrance; gateway
bariera dźwięku [bahr-**ye**-rah **dźhvyan**-koo] exp.: sonic barrier; sound barrier
barierka [bahr-**yer**-kah] f. small railing
bark [bahrk] m. shoulder girdle; bark; barque (three-masted vessel)
barki [**bahr**-kee] pl. shoulders
barka [**bahr**-kah] f. river boat; barge
barkantyna [bahr-kahn-**ti**-nah] f. bark; barque
barkarola [bahr-kah-**ro**-lah] f. barcarole
barkarz [**bahr**-kahsh] m. barge-master; boatman; bargeman
barkas [**bahr**-kahs] m. long-boat; lighter; fishing sailboat; small service ship
barkasa [bahr-**kah**-sah] f. long-boat; lighter
barkentyna [bahr-ken-**ti**-nah] f. bark; barque; barkentine (a three-masted ship)
barki [**bahr**-kee] pl. shoulders; back; three-masted ships; barges
barkowiec [bahr-**ko**-vyets] m. ship built to handle unitized floating cargo
barkowy [bahr-**ko**-vi] adj.m. shoulder (strap, slip, etc.); humeral; acromial; of the acromion; of river boat; barge (transport, traffic, etc.)
barłożenie [bahr-wo-**zhe**-ńe] n. littering; scattering rubbish; littering down (a stable)
barłożyć [bahr-**wo**-zhićh] v. litter; scatter rubbish; litter down (a stable) (*repeatedly*)
barłóg [**bahr**-woog] m. litter bed; bed of straw; pallet; litter; bed of misery
barman [**bahr**-mahn] m. barman; tapster
barmanka [bahr-**mahn**-kah] f. barmaid
barn [bahrn] m. unit of area used in nuclear physics; barn
barobus [bah-**ro**-boos] m. bar on wheels; mobile bar
barocyklonometr [bah-ro-tsik-lo-**no**-metr] m. device indicating the approach and direction of a tornado or hurricane
barograf [bah-**ro**-grahf] m. barograph (self-registering barometer)
barogram [bah-**ro**-grahm] m. barogram
barok [**bah**-rok] m. baroque
barokowo [bah-ro-**ko**-vo] adv. in baroque style
barokowość [bah-ro-**ko**-vośhćh] f. baroque characteristics
barokowy [bah-ro-**ko**-vi] adj.m. baroque; grotesque; whimsical; bizarre
barometr [bah-**ro**-metr] m. barometer; weather-glass
barometryczny [bah-ro-me-**trich**-ni] adj.m. barometric (pressure, etc.); barometer (glass, etc.)
niż barometryczny [ńeesh bah-ro-me-**trich**-ni] exp.: barometric low (pressure)
wyż barometryczny [vish bah-ro-me-**trich**-ni] exp.: barometric high (pressure)
baron [**bah**-ron] m. baron (noble)
baronat [bah-**ro**-naht] m. barony
baronet [bah-**ro**-net] m. baronet
baronia [bah-**ro**-ńyah] f. barony; the barons
baronostwo [bah-ro-**nos**-tfo] n. baron and baroness; the title of baron; barony
baronowa [bah-ro-**no**-vah] f. baroness
baronowski [bah-ro-**nof**-skee] adj.m. baronial (title, etc.)
baronówna [bah-ro-**noov**-nah] f. baron's daughter

barować się [bah-ro-vahćh śhan] v. slang: scuffle (*repeatedly*)
barowóz [bah-ro-voos] m. bar on wheels; mobile bar
barowy [bah-ro-vi] adj.m. bar (parlour, etc.); of barium; barium; baric
dania barowe [dah-ńah bah-ro-ve] exp.: dishes from the buffet
lokal barowy [lo-kahl bah-ro-vi] exp.: bar-room; bar
stołek barowy [sto-wek bah-ro-vi] exp.: bar stool
barrakuda [bahr-rah-koo-dah] f. barracuda
barrakudowaty [bahr-rah-koo-do-vah-ti] adj.m. barracuda-shape; of barracuda family
barranco [bahr-rahn-ko] n. barranco; barranca (geology)
barszcz [bahrshch] m. borscht soup
tani jak barszcz [tah-ńee yahk bahrshch] exp.: dirt cheap
barszczowiny [bahrsh-cho-vee-ni] pl. sediment of borscht ferment (used in poultice's medication, etc.)
barszczowy [bahrsh-cho-vi] adj.m. borscht (color, etc.); the color of red borscht; amaranth pink
barszczyk [bahrsh-chik] m. (tasty) borscht; good little borscht
barta [bahr-tah] f. battle-axe
bartłomiejówka [bahr-two-mye-yoof-kah] f. summer-time swelling of rivers in Poland
bartne [bahr-tne] n. bee-keeping tax; honey tax (collected in kind)
bartnica [bahr-tńee-tsah] f. instrument for scooping holes in bee-hives
bartnicki [bahr-tńeets-kee] adj.m. of wild-bee rearing
bartnictwo [bahr-tńeets-tfo] n. wild-bee rearing
bartniczy [bahr-tńee-chi] adj.m. bee-keeper's; of keeping of wild forest bees; rich in bee-hives
bartnik [bahr-tńeek] m. wild-bee keeper; honey-eating bear
bartny [bahr-tni] adj.m. bee-keeping-; bee-keeper's; m. keeper of wild forest bees; overseer of apiary of wild bees
bartne [bahrt-ne] exp.: bee-keeper's rent payment in kind
barwa [bahr-vah] f. color; hue; tint; tinge; dye; tone; timbre; stamp; colors (of a club, etc.); bloom (on grapes, etc.); the blood of wounded game; tone-coloring; quality
barwiarka [bahr-vyahr-kah] f. (woman) dyer; dye tank
barwiarski [bahr-vyahr-skee] adj.m. dyer's; dyeing; tinctorial
barwiarstwo [bahr-vyahr-stfo] n. dyeing; dyer's craft
barwiarz [bahr-vyahsh] m. dyer
barwica [bahr-vee-tsah] f. golden red color; padding; rouge; woodruff (herb); discoloration of wood (by fungus)
barwiczka [bahr-veech-kah] f. golden red color; woodruff (an herb)
barwić [bahr-veećh] v. color; dye; tinge; stain; paint; embellish (a narrative, etc.); bleed; leave traces of blood (*repeatedly*)
barwić się [bahr-veećh śhan] v. color oneself; assume a different color; change color; show changing colors; emit a play of colors; exhibit a play of colors (*repeatedly*)
barwidło [bahr-veed-wo] n. dye; dye-stuff; coloring stuff; coloring substance; pigment; rouge
barwienie [bahr-vye-ńe] n. coloration
barwienie się [bahr-vye-ńe śhan] n. acquiring coloration
barwierski [bahr-vyer-skee] adj.m. dyer's; dyeing; tinctorial
barwinek [bahr-vee-nek] m. myrtle; cutfinger; periwinkle
barwinkowy [bahr-veen-ko-vi] adj.m. of a myrtle; of a cutfinger; of a periwinkle
barwiony [bahr-vyo-ni] adj.m. colored; dyed; stained
barwistość [bahr-vees-tośhćh] f. bright colors; colorfulness
barwisty [bahr-vees-ti] adj.m. colorful; bright-colored; gorgeous; glaring; ostensible
barwiście [bahr-veeśh-ćhe] adv.

colorfully; in bright colors
barwnie [**bahrv**-ńe] adv. in colors; colorfully; in different colors; gorgeously
barwnik [**bahrv**-ńeek] m. dye; stain; tincture; coloring substance; pigment
barwnikowy [bahrv-ńee-**ko**-vi] adj.m. tinctorial; dyeing; staining; pigmental
barwność [**bahrv**-nośhćh] f. colorfulness; variegation; gaudiness; vividness
barwny [**bahrv**-ni] adj.m. in colors; bright-colored; many-colored; vivid; variegated; colorful; florid; gaudy; vivid with color; many-colored; varicolored
barwoczułość [bahr-vo-**choo**-wośhćh] f. panchromatism; sensitiveness to light of all colors
barwoczuły [bahr-vo-**choo**-wi] adj.m. panchromatic; sensitive to light of all colors
barworodny [bahr-vo-**rod**-ni] adj.m. chromogenic; producing color
barwoślepota [bahr-vo-śhle-**po**-tah] f. color-blindness
bary [**bah**-ri] pl. large shoulders; broad shoulders; parallel bars
baryczny [bah-**rich**-ni] adj.m. of atmospheric pressure
barykada [bah-ri-**kah**-dah] f. barricade; barrier; obstacle
barykadować [bah-ri-kah-**do**-vahćh] v. barricade; block; bolt; bar; fence off; rise barricade; erect barricade; obstruct (*repeatedly*)
barykadować się [bah-ri-kah-**do**-vahćh śhan] v. barricade oneself; bar oneself in; fence oneself in (*repeatedly*)
barykadowanie się [bah-ri-kah-do-**vah**-ńe śhan] n. barricading oneself
barykadowy [bah-ri-kah-**do**-vi] adj.m. (defense, etc.) of barricade
baryła [bah-ri-wah] f. barrel; cask; tun; big-bellied person; pot-bellied man; tubby man; paunchy person
baryłeczka [bah-ri-**wech**-kah] f. short and fat person; dumpling; small barrel; small cask
baryłeczkowaty [bah-ri-wech-ko-**vah**-ti] adj.m. rotund; tubby; plump (man, etc.)
baryłka [bah-**riw**-kah] f. small barrel; small cask; barrel of oil (159 l.)
baryłkarz [bah-**riw**-kahsh] m. braconid (insect)
baryłkowatość [bah-riw-ko-**vah**-tośhćh] f. rotundity
baryłkowaty [bah-riw-ko-**vah**-ti] adj.m. rotund; tubby; plump (man, etc.)
barymetria [bah-ri-**met**-ryah] f. estimate of animal's body weight based of exterior measurements
barysfera [bah-ri-**sfe**-rah] f. central part of the earth
baryt [**bah**-rit] m. barite; heavy spar
baryton [bah-**ri**-ton] m. baritone
barytonista [bah-ri-to-**ńees**-tah] m. baritone (singer and instrument)
barytonowy [bah-ri-to-**no**-vi] adj.m. baritone (voice, etc.)
barytowy [bah-ri-**to**-vi] adj.m. barium-sulfate; baryta white
bas [bahs] m. bass; bass-viol; double bass; bass clarinet; bass tuba
basałyk [bah-**sah**-wik] m. brat; stripling; kid; Turkish whip with a lead ball at the end; flogging; thrashing
basarunek [bah-sah-**roo**-nek] m. compensation for loss; thrashing; hiding
baseball [**beyz**-bol] m. baseball
baseballista [beyz-bo-**lees**-tah] m. baseball player
baseballowy [beyz-bo-**lo**-vi] adj.m. baseball (game, bat, etc.)
Basedowa choroba [bah-se-**do**-vah kho-**ro**-bah] exp.: exophthalmic goitre; Grave's disease
basek [**bah**-sek] m. lowest sounding violin string
baselista [bah-se-**lees**-tah] m. double-bass player
basen [**bah**-sen] m. pool; tank; swimming pool; reservoir; basin; bed-pan
basenowy [bah-se-**no**-vi] adj.m. pool-; tank-; swimming pool; reservoir (water, etc.); of a basin; of a reservoir; of a pool; of a tank
baserunek [bah-se-**roo**-nek] m.

compensation for loss; thrashing; hiding
basetla [bah-**set**-lah] f. double-bass; blockhead; fat lady
basetlista [bah-set-**lees**-tah] m. double-bass player
basior [**bah**-śhor] m. male wolf
basiora [bah-**śho**-rah] f. female wolf; she-wolf
basista [bah-**śhees**-tah] m. bass-player; bass-singer
basiur [**bah**-śhoor] m. male wolf
Bask [bahsk] m. Basque
baskerwil [bahs-**ker**-veel] m. baroque-style English lettering
Baskijka [bahs-**keey**-kah] f. Basque woman or girl; (Basque) beret
baskijski [bah-**skeey**-skee] adj.m. Basque
baskina [bah-**skee**-nah] f. basque bodice
baskinka [bahs-**keen**-kah] f. Spanish style jacket; basque bodice
basklarnet [bahs-**klahr**-net] m. bass clarinet
baskwil [**bahs**-kfeel] m. casement bolt; double-door bolt
baskwilowy [bahs-kfee-**lo**-vi] adj.m. of casement bolt; of double-door bolt
basować [bah-**so**-vahćh] v. sing the bass part; sing in a bass voice; play the bass; chime in (with); cringe (to); fawn (upon) (*repeatedly*)
basowanie [bah-so-**vah**-ńe] n. singing the bass part; singing in a bass voice; playing the bass; chiming in (with); cringing (to); fawning (upon)
basowy [bah-**so**-vi] adj.m. bass (voice, etc.); low (voice); deep-sounding (voice); deep-mouthed (bark of a dog)
bas-relief [bahs **re**-lyef] m. bas-relief; sculptural relief; sculpture executed in bas-relief
basset [**bah**-set] m. basset hound
basta [**bahs**-tah] excl.: enough!; no more!; that will do!; that's it!
bastard [**bahs**-tahrt] m. bastard; hybrid; mongrel
bastarda [bahs-**tahr**-dah] f. 16th cent. printing font
bastardowy [bahs-tahr-**do**-vi] adj.m. bastard (child, etc.); cross-bred
bastardyzacja [bahs-tahr-di-**zah**-tsyah] f. bastardization; cross-breeding
bastardyzować [bahs-tahr-di-**zo**-vahćh] v. bastardize; cross-breed; debase (*repeatedly*)
basteja [bahs-**te**-yah] f. semi-circular small bastion
bastion [**bahs**-tyon] m. bastion; bulwark; rampart
bastionik [bahs-**tyo**-ńeek] m. small bastion; turret
bastionowy [bahs-tyo-**no**-vi] adj.m. bastion (system, etc.); bulwark (structure, etc.); rampart (fortification, etc.)
bastinado [bahs-tee-**nah**-dn] n. bastinado (punishment by repeated blows)
bastonada [bahs-to-**nah**-dah] f. bastinado (punishment by repeated blows)
bastylia [bahs-**ti**-lyah] f. small castle built outside city wall
basy [**bah**-si] pl. double-bass
basza [**bah**-shah] m. pasha
baszłyk [**bahsh**-wik] m. cowl; hood
baszostwo [bah-**shost**-fo] n. pashalik; pashadom
baszowski [bah-**shof**-skee] adj.m. pasha's (rule, etc.); of a pasha
baszta [**bahsh**-tah] f. tower; turret; water tower
basztowy [bahsh-**to**-vi] adj.m. of a tower; of a turret; of a water tower
baśka [**bahśh**-kah] f. (wooden hammer) pile driver; colloq: pate; head
baśniowo [bah-**śhńo**-vo] adv. mythically; fabulously; as in a fairy tale
baśniowość [bah-**śhńo**-vośhćh] f. mythical character (of writing, tale, etc.)
baśniowy [bah-**śhńo**-vi] adj.m. mythical; fabulous; fairy-tale
baśń [bahśhń] f. fable; myth; legend; story; tall story; rumor; report; gossip
bat [baht] m. whip; lash; the lash
baty [**bah**-ti] pl. whipping; lashing;

beating; licking; slang: whacking
batalia [bah-**tah**-lyah] f. battle; fight; contest; struggle
batalion [bah-**tah**-lyon] m. battalion; host; army
batalionowy [bah-tah-lyo-**no**-vi] adj.m. battalion (commander, headquarters, etc.)
batalista [bah-tah-**lees**-tah] m. battle-scenes painter (artist)
batalityczny [bah-tah-lees-**tich**-ni] adj.m. battle (painting, etc.)
batalistyka [bah-tah-**lees**-ti-kah] f. the painting of battle scenes
batat [**bah**-taht] m. batata; Spanish sweet potato
bateria [bah-**ter**-yah] f. battery; storage battery; percussion section; set (of bottles, boilers, etc.); array (of bottles, etc.)
bateriowy [bah-ter-**yo**-vi] adj.m. battery (cell, etc.)
bateryjka [bah-te-**riy**-kah] f. small battery
bateryjny [bah-te-**riy**-ni] adj.m. of battery; battery (unit, etc.)
batial [**bah**-tyahl] m. continental shelf (200 m. to 1700 m. sea depth)
batialny [bah-**tyahl**-ni] adj.m. of continental shelf
batiar [**bah**-tyahr] m. colloq: street-boy; swindler; rouge; thief; knave
batik [**bah**-teek] m. batik (printing of colored designs); color designs printed
batikarski [bah-tee-**kahr**-skee] adj.m. batik (shop, etc.)
batikować [bah-tee-**ko**-vahćh] v. batik (*repeatedly*)
batikowanie [bah-tee-ko-**vah**-ńe] n. making of batiks
batikowy [bah-tee-**ko**-vi] adj.m. batik (method, printing, etc.)
batiuszka [bah-**tyoosh**-kah] m. colloq: Russian orthodox priest
batog [**bah**-tog] m. (big) whip; cord (of a loom)
batolit [bah-**to**-leet] m. batholith (igneous rock)
batometr [bah-**to**-metr] m. bathometer
batometria [bah-to-**met**-ryah] f. analysis of water samples collected by bathometer
baton [**bah**-ton] m. chocolate bar
batonik [bah-**to**-ńeek] m. small chocolate bar
batorówka [bah-to-**roof**-kah] f. visorless cap; sword of a model used in the days of King Stefan Batory
batożek [bah-**to**-zhek] m. small whip
batożenie [bah-to-**zhe**-ńe] n. whipping; flogging
batożyć [bah-**to**-zhićh] v. whip; lash; flog (*repeatedly*)
batożysko [bah-to-**zhis**-ko] n. whip handle; whip stick
battledress [**betl**-dres] m. battle dress (short coat)
batut [**bah**-toot] m. trampoline; web supported by springs inside metal frame; springboard for tumbling
batuta [bah-**too**-tah] f. baton; conductor's wand
batybental [bah-ti-**ben**-tahl] m. sea-bottom outside the continental shelf
batybiont [bah-**ti**-byont] m. deep-water animal
batybionty [bah-ti-**byon**-ti] pl. deep-water animals
batygraficzny [bah-ti-grah-**feech**-ni] adj.m. bathymetric (curve, etc.)
batymetr [bah-**ti**-metr] m. bathometer; bathymeter
batymetria [bah-ti-**met**-ryah] f. bathymetry
batymetryczny [bah-ti-me-**trich**-ni] adj.m. bathymetric
batypelagial [bah-ti-pe-**lah**-gyahl] m. water depth below the penetration of sunlight
batysfera [bah-ti-**sfe**-rah] f. bathy sphere; diving sphere for deep-sea observation
batyskaf [bah-**ti**-skahf] m. submarine for deep-sea diving and observation; bathyscaph
batyst [**bah**-tist] m. batiste; cambric
batystat [bah-**tis**-taht] m. diving cylinder for underwater observation (to 1,000 ft. depth)
batystowy [bah-tis-**to**-vi] adj.m. batiste (blouse, etc.)
bauer [**bah**-wer] m. colloq: rich German farmer

bauksyt [**bahwk**-sit] m. bauxite (mineral)
baumkuchen [**bahwm**-koo-khen] m. pyramidal cake (made to resemble a tree)
Bawar [**bah**-vahr] m. Bavarian; Bavarian beer
Bawarka [bah-**vahr**-kah] f. Bavarian (woman); drink of hot milk and tea (or water) with sugar
bawarski [bah-**vahr**-skee] adj.m. Bavarian
bawełna [bah-**vew**-nah] f. cotton; the cotton plant; cotton yarn; darning cotton; cotton cloth
owijać w bawełnę [o-**vee**-yahćh v bah-**vew**-nan] exp.: to beat about the bush; to mince the truth; to equivocate; to mince matters
bawełniak [bah-**vew**-ńahk] m. garment of cotton cloth
bawełnianka [bah-vew-**ńahn**-kah] f. shoddy cotton cloth; shoddy garment
bawełniany [bah-vew-**ńah**-ni] adj.m. cotton- (fiber, etc.)
bawełniarski [bah-vew-**ńahr**-skee] adj.m. cotton (industry, etc.)
bawełniasty [bah-vew-**ńah**-sti] adj.m. cottony
bawełnica [bah-vew-**ńee**-tsah] f. byssinosis; chronic industrial disease resulting from inhalation of cotton dust (causing bronchitis, emphysema, and asthma)
bawełniczka [bah-vew-**ńeech**-kah] f. cotton yarn
bawełnisty [bah-vew-**ńee**-sti] adj.m. cottony
bawełnopodobny [bah-vew-no-po-**dob**-ni] adj.m. cotton-like
bawet [**bah**-vet] m. bib (of an apron)
bawialnia [bah-**vyahl**-ńah] f. sitting room; parlor; drawing room
bawialniany [bah-vyahl-**ńah**-ni] adj.m. of sitting room; of parlor; of drawing room
bawić [**bah**-veećh] v. entertain; recreate; stay; play; cheer; amuse; have fun; enjoy oneself; have a good time; make merry; take (a vacation, etc.) (*repeatedly*)
bawić na wakacjach [**bah**-veećh nah vah-**kah**-tsyahkh] exp.: to be on vacation
bawić towarzystwo [**bah**-veećh to-vah-**zhis**-tfo] exp.: to entertain one's company
długo bawić [**dwoo**-go **bah**-veećh] exp.: to stay a long time
przestać bawić [**pshe**-stahćh **bah**-veećh] exp.: to tire (of); to stop to amuse; to be fed up with
bawić się [**bah**-veećh śhan] v. play (at, or with); toy; dabble; twiddle; trifle; fiddle; amuse oneself; make merry; have fun; enjoy oneself; have a good time; revel; dissipate; be on the spree (*repeatedly*)
bawić się myślą [**bah**-veećh śhan **mi**-śhlown] exp.: to toy with an idea
jak się bawiłeś? [yahk śhan bah-**vee**-weśh] exp.: how did you enjoy yourself?
nie bawić się w ... [ńe bah-veećh śhan v ...] exp.: to lose no time over (something)
bawidamek [bah-vee-**dah**-mek] m. colloq: ladies' man; gallant
bawidełko [bah-vee-**dew**-ko] n. plaything; toy; trifle; bauble
bawienie [bah-**vye**-ńe] n. playing; entertainment; amusement
bawolica [bah-vo-**lee**-tsah] f. female buffalo
bawół [**bah**-voow] m. buffalo; slang: clumsy person; slow-poke
baza [**bah**-zah] f. base; basis; ground-work; support; milliary base
bazalt [**bah**-zahlt] m. basalt
bazaltołom [bah-zahl-**to**-wom] m. basalt quarry
bazaltowy [bah-zahl-**to**-vi] adj.m. basalt (rock, etc.); of basalt; basaltic (formation, etc.)
bazar [**bah**-zahr] m. bazaar
bazgracz [**bahz**-grahch] m. scribbler; scrawler; dauber; daubster
bazgrać [**bahz**-grahćh] v. scribble; scrawl; scratch; daub; splotch (*repeatedly*)

bazgrała [bahz-**grah**-wah] m. scribbler; scrawler; dauber; daubster
bazgranie [bahz-**grah**-ńe] n. scrawl; scrawls; scribble; scribbling; daub
bazgranina [bahz-grah-**ńee**-nah] f. scrawl; scrawls; scribble; scribbling; daub
bazgrolić [bahz-**gro**-leećh] v. colloq: scrawl; scribble; daub (*repeatedly*)
bazgroły [bahz-**gro**-wi] pl. scrawls; scribble; scribbling; daub
bazia [**bah**-źhah] f. catkin; ament; pet lamb; cosset
bazooka [bah-**zoo**-kah] f. bazooka; portable smoothbore firing tube that launches armor-piercing rockets
bazować [bah-**zo**-vahćh] v. base oneself (on); be based (on, upon); establish (*repeatedly*)
bazowanie [bah-zo-**vah**-ńe] n. basing; establishing
bazowy [bah-**zo**-vi] adj.m. of a base; base (supplies, etc.)
bazuna [bah-**zoo**-nah] f. long Kashubian trumpet
bazyleus [bah-zi-**le**-oos] m. basileus; achron basileus
bazylia [bah-**zi**-lyah] f. sweet basil (an aromatic herb)
bazylianin [bah-zil-**yah**-ńeen] m. Basilian monk
bazyliański [bah-zil-**yahń**-skee] adj.m. Basilian (order, etc.)
bazylika [bah-zi-**lee**-kah] f. basilica
bazyliki [bah-zi-**lee**-kee] pl. Basilicae
bazylikalny [bah-zi-lee-**kahl**-ni] adj.m. of a basilica
bazylikowy [bah-zi-lee-**ko**-vi] adj.m. of basilica
bazyliszek [bah-zi-**lee**-shek] m. basilisk; cockatrice
bazyliszkowaty [bah-zi-leesh-ko-**vah**-ti] adj.m. like basilisk; like cockatrice
bazyliszkowy [bah-zi-leesh-**ko**-vi] adj.m. basilisk (glance, etc.)
baźka [**bahśh**-kah] f. catkin; ament; pet lamb; cosset
bażanciarnia [bah-zhahn-**ćhahr**-ńah] f. pheasantry
bażancik [bah-**zhahn**-ćheek] m. young pheasant; poult
bażant [**bah**-zhahnt] m. pheasant
bażantarnia [bah-zhahn-**tahr**-ńah] f. pheasantry
bażantnik [bah-**zhahnt**-ńeek] m. owner of a pheasantry; pheasant rearer
bażyna [bah-**zhi**-nah] f. crowberry
bażynowate [bah-zhi-no-**vah**-te] pl. the crowberry family of shrubs
bąbel [**bown**-bel] m. blister; bleb; bubble; nipple
bąbelek [bown-**be**-lek] m. (small) blister; bleb; bubble; nipple
bąblasty [bown-**blah**-sti] adj.m. blistery; blistered
bąblowica [bown-blo-**vee**-tsah] f. disease caused by tape warm
bąblowiec [bown-**blo**-vyets] m. tape worm; hydatid
bączasty [bown-**chah**-sti] adj.m. bulbous
bączek [**bown**-chek] m. chit; chick; mite; little top; little bittern (bird); (small) row-boat
bączywie [bown-**chi**-vye] n. nuphar; yellow water-lily
bądź [bownćh] v. be this; conj. either-or; anyhow; at any rate; particle: any
bądź co bądź [**bownćh** tso **bownćh**] exp.: however; though; tho'; anyhow; at any rate; anyway; all the same
bądź gotów [bownćh **go**-toof] exp.: be ready
bądź grzeczny [bownćh **gzhech**-ni] exp.: be good
bądź grzeczny wobec [bownćh **gzhech**-ni **vo**-bets] exp.: be polite to (towards)
bądź miły [bownćh **mee**-wi] exp.: be nice
bądź taki dobry [bownćh **tah**-kee **do**-bri] exp.: be so kind
bądź to, bądź tamto [bownćh to bownćh **tahm**-to] exp.: either this or that; either ... or ...
co bądź [**tso** bownćh] exp.: anything; any old thing
gdzie bądź [gdźhe bownćh] exp.: anywhere
jak bądź [yahk bownćh] exp.: anyhow; sloppily; slipshod

jaki bądź [yah-kee bownćh] exp.: of any kind; of whatever kind; large or small; good or bad
kto bądź [kto bownćh] exp.: anybody
który bądź [ktoo-ri bownćh] exp.: any one (of ...)
bąk [bownk] m. horse fly; mistake; blunder; bloomer; howler; (bird) bittern; gadfly (Tabanus); breeze; tot; mite; sprat; brat; peg-top; rowboat; vulg. fart
bąkać [bown-kahćh] v. mumble; hint; mutter; hum; allude (to) (*repeatedly*)
bąkanie [bown-kah-ńe] n. mumbling; alluding
bąkanina [bown-kah-ńee-nah] f. mumble; mutter
bąknąć [bownk-nownćh] v. mumble; hint; mutter; hum; allude
bąknięcie [bownk-ńan-ćhe] n. mumble; hint; hum
bąkojad [bown-ko-yaht] m. passerine bird; perching bird
bąkowaty [bown-ko-vah-ti] adj.m. tabanid (blood-eating insect)
bąkowate [bown-ko-vah-te] pl. the family Tabanidae
be [be] indecl.: the letter "b"; sheep's bleat "baa"; excl. fie!; fie-fie!; no!; nasty!
ani be ani me [ah-ńee be ah-ńee me] exp.: not a word; not a sound
beat [beet] m. beat; rhythm (in jazz and rock music)
beatles [bee-tels] m. see: **bitels**
beatnik [beet-ńeek] m. see: **bitnik**
beatyfikacja [be-ah-ti-fee-kah-tsyah] f. beatification
beatyfikacyjny [be-ah-ti-fee-kah-tsiy-ni] adj.m. of beatification
beatyfikować [be-ah-ti-fee-ko-vahćh] v. beatify (*repeatedly*)
beatyfikowanie [be-ah-ti-fee-ko-vah-ńe] n. beatification
bebech [be-bekh] m. colloq: bowel; gut; entrails; traps; chattels; lumber; odds and ends
bebechy [be-be-khi] pl. guts; bowels; entrails; traps; chattels; odds and ends
chłop z bebechami [khwop z be-be-khah-mee] exp.: gutty guy
z bebechami [z be-be-khah-mee] exp.: with bag and baggage
bebeszenie [be-be-she-ńe] n. gutting (an animal); cleaning (a fish)
bebeszyć [be-be-shićh] v. gut (an animal); clean (a fish) (*repeatedly*)
bebłać [beb-wahćh] v. throw about; rummage; smear (*repeatedly*)
bebłać się [beb-wahćh śhan] v. rummage (in); smear oneself (*repeatedly*)
bebop [bee-bop] m. bop; bebop jazz
bech [bekh] m. brat
bechowiec [be-kho-vyets] m. colloq: member of Polish Rural Battalions during World War II (Bataliony Chłopskie; BCh)
bechowski [be-khof-skee] adj.m. of Polish Rural Battalions
becić [be-ćheećh] v. make (somebody) lose (a card game) (*repeatedly*)
becić się [be-ćheećh śhan] v. lose (a card game) (*repeatedly*)
becik [be-ćheek] m. infant wrap padded with dawn
bechtać [bekh-tahćh] v. instigate (*repeatedly*)
bechtać kogoś [bekh-tahćh ko-gośh] exp.: to hound somebody on; to set somebody on; to embitter; to arouse ill will in somebody
beczeć [be-chećh] v. bleat; yell; bellow; moan; cry; blubber (*repeatedly*)
beczek [be-chek] m. cry-baby; blubberer
beczenie [be-che-ńe] n. bleat; bleating; caterwaul; caterwauling; moaning (of an instrument, etc.); (baby's) cry; crying; blubbering
beczka [bech-kah] f. barrel; keg; cask; piece; pipe; butt; hogshead; barrel-volt; barrel-roll
beczka bez dna [bech-kah bez dnah] exp.: bottomless barrel; an endless task; a hopeless task; spendthrift (man)
beczka wina [bech-kah vee-nah] exp.: barrel full of vine
piwo z beczki [pee-vo z bech-kee]

exp.: draft beer; beer on tap
robić beczkę [ro-beećh **bech**-kan] exp.: to roll (a plane)
zacząć z innej beczki [zah-chownćh z **een**-ney **bech**-kee] exp.: to change the subject; to shift one's ground
beczkarnia [bech-**kahr**-ńah] f. coopery
beczkować [bech-**ko**-vahćh] v. barrel (wine, herrings, etc.) (*repeatedly*)
beczkowanie [bech-ko-**vah**-ńe] n. the barrelling (of wine, herrings, etc.); barrelling
beczkowaty [bech-ko-**vah**-ti] adj.m. bulgy; barrel-like; rotund
beczkowo [bech-**ko**-vo] adv. barrel (vaulted, etc.); like a barrel
beczkowóz [bech-**ko**-voos] m. water-cart; water-wagon; watering-cart
beczkowy [bech-**ko**-vi] adj.m. bulgy; barrel-like; rotund
lot beczkowy [lot bech-**ko**-vi] exp.: barrel roll (by a plane)
ogórek beczkowy [o-**goo**-rek bech-**ko**-vi] exp.: barrel-pickled cucumber
sklepienie beczkowe [skle-**pye**-ńe bech-**ko**-ve] exp.: barrel vault
beczułka [be-**choow**-kah] f. small barrel; small cask; tub
beczułkowaty [be-choow-ko-**vah**-ti] adj.m. bulgy; barrel-bellied; rotund
bedeker [be-**de**-ker] m. tourist guide book
bedliszka [bed-**leesh**-kah] f. fungus-eating ant
bedliszki [bed-**leesh**-kee] pl. fungus-eating ants
bedłka [**bedw**-kah] f. agaric (fungus)
bedłkowaty [bedw-ko-**vah**-ti] adj.m. agaricaceous; of the gill fungi
bedłkowate [bedw-ko-**vah**-te] pl. the family Agaricaceae
bednarczyk [bed-**nahr**-chik] m. cooper's apprentice; cooper's son
bednarka [bed-**nahr**-kah] f. cooperage; coopering; cooper's craft; cooper's wife; woman cooper; band-iron; stave
bednarnia [bed-**nahr**-ńah] f. coopery; cooper's workshop
bednarski [bed-**nahr**-skee] adj.m. cooper's (ware, etc.)
bednarstwo [bed-**nahr**-stfo] n. cooperage; coopering; cooper's craft
bednarz [**bed**-nahsh] m. cooper
bednarzowa [bed-nah-**zho**-vah] f. cooper's wife
bednarzyć [bed-**nah**-zhićh] v. cooper (*repeatedly*)
bednia [**bed**-ńah] f. vat
Beduin [be-**doo**-een] m. Bedouin
beduina [be-doo-**ee**-nah] f. opera cloak
beduinka [be-doo-**een**-kah] f. opera cloak
Beduinka [be-doo-**een**-kah] f. Bedouin (woman)
befsztyk [**bef**-shtik] m. beef-steak (broiled or fried); steak
befsztykowy [bef-shti-**ko**-vi] adj.m. of beef-steak (broiled or fried); of a steak
begonia [be-**go**-ńyah] f. begonia
behapowiec [be-khah-**po**-vyets] m. agent of the office of work-place safety and hygiene
behapowski [be-khah-**pof**-skee] adj.m. of the office of work-place safety and hygiene
behawiorysta [bee-khe-vyo-**ris**-tah] m. behaviorist
behawiorystyczny [bee-khe-vyo-ris-**tich**-ni] adj.m. behavioristic; behavioral
behawioryzm [bee-khe-**vyo**-rizm] m. behaviorism; a doctrine that psychology must be based on the evidence of behavior and exclude consciousness and mind as impossible to study; behavioral science
bej [bey] m. (Turkish) bey
bejca [**bey**-tsah] f. stain; mordant; ooze; pickle; fungicide
bejcować [bey-**tso**-vahćh] v. stain; imbue with mordant; steep in ooze; curry (hides); pickle (*repeatedly*)
bejcówka [bey-**tsoof**-kah] f. (tanner's) ooze
bejcowanie [bey-tso-**vah**-ńe] n. staining
bejram [**bey**-rahm] m. Bairam; the

end of Ramadan (Muslim festival)
bek [bek] m. bleat; blubber; cry; colloq: back (of a soccer team)
beka [**be**-kah] f. large barrel
bekać [**be**-kahćh] v. belch; squall; burp (*repeatedly*)
bekać się [**be**-kahćh śhan] v. rut; slang: belch; burp (*repeatedly*)
bekadło [be-**kahd**-wo] n. primitive fire-alarm horn
bekanie [be-**kah**-ńe] n. belching
bekanie się [be-**kah**-ńe śhan] n. being in (sexual) heat
bekas [**be**-kahs] m. (bird) snipe
bekasi [be-**kah**-śhee] adj.m. of a snipe
bekasik [be-**kah**-śheek] m. small snipe
bekhend [**bek**-hent] m. backhand (in tennis)
bekiesza [be-**ke**-shah] f. (Hungarian) frogged coat; man's fur-wrap
bekieszka [be-**kesh**-kah] f. (small, nice) (Hungarian) frogged coat; man's fur-wrap
bekliwy [bek-**lee**-vi] adj.m. bleating; whimpering; blubbering
beknąć [**bek**-nownćh] v. colloq: burp; pay (too much); foot the bill; pay a lot; fork out; pay dearly
beknąć za to [**bek**-nownćh zah to] exp.: colloq: to pay a lot for it
grubo beknąć [**groo**-bo **bek**-nownćh] exp.: colloq: to pay a lot of money
beknięcie [bek-**ńan**-ćhe] n. colloq: paying too much; paying a lot
bekon [**be**-kon] m. bacon; bacon hog; beckoner
bekoniarnia [be-ko-**ńahr**-ńah] f. bacon factory
bekoniarstwo [be-ko-**ńahr**-stfo] n. bacon curing
bekonowy [be-ko-**no**-vi] adj.m. bacon (hog, etc.)
bekowisko [be-ko-**vees**-ko] n. rut; rutting time; rutting season; rutting ground
beksa [**bek**-sah] f. cry baby
beksiwy [bek-**śhee**-vi] adj.m. tearful; blubbering
bekwarek [bek-**fah**-rek] m. variety of nightingale (bird)
bel [bel] m. bel (electr.)
bela [**be**-lah] f. log; beam; bale (of cloth, etc.); pack
bela papieru [**be**-lah pah-**pye**-roo] exp.: ten reams of paper
belcanto [bel-**kahn**-to] n. bel canto
beleczka [be-**lech**-kah] f. small beam; bar (on a uniform, sleeve, shoulder, etc.)
beleczkowy [be-lech-**ko**-vi] adj.m. beamlike; trabecular
beletrysta [be-le-**tris**-tah] m. fiction-writer; fictionist; belletrist
beletrystka [be-le-**trist**-kah] f. (female) fiction-writer; fictionist; belletrist
beletrystyczny [be-le-tris-**tich**-ni] adj.m. of fiction; belletristic
beletrystyka [be-le-**tris**-ti-kah] f. fiction; belles-letters; light literature; letters; polite letters
beletryzacja [be-le-tri-**zah**-tsyah] f. fictionalization
beletryzator [be-le-tri-**zah**-tor] m. writer specializing in fictionalization (of historic events, etc.)
beletryzować [be-le-tri-**zo**-vahćh] v. write works of fiction; write light literature; fictionalize; treat as a fiction (*repeatedly*)
beletryzowanie [be-le-tri-zo-**vah**-ńe] n. writing works of fiction; writing light literature; fictionalizing; treating as a fiction
belfer [**bel**-fer] m. colloq: school-teacher; schoolmaster; usher; slang: teach
belferka [bel-**fer**-kah] f. colloq: school-teaching; school-mistress
belferować [bel-fe-**ro**-vahćh] v. teach school (*repeatedly*)
belferski [bel-**fer**-skee] adj.m. school-teacher's; schoolmaster's; usher's
belferstwo [bel-**fer**-stfo] n. colloq: school-teaching
belferzyna [bel-fe-**zhi**-nah] m. slang: contemptible school-teacher; paltry school-teacher
belfrować [bel-**fro**-vahćh] v. teach; be a school-teacher (*repeatedly*)
belfrowanie [bel-fro-**vah**-ńe] n. colloq: school-teaching
Belg [belg] m. Belgian

Belgijka [bel-**geey**-kah] f. Belgian (woman)
belgijka [bel-**geey**-kah] f. (garden) cold frame; hotbed; hooded blouse
belgijski [bel-**geey**-skee] adj.m. Belgian
belka [**bel**-kah] f. beam; bar; girder
belka stropowa [**bel**-kah stro-**po**-vah] exp.: tie-beam
belkować [bel-**ko**-vahćh] v. joist (*repeatedly*)
belkowanie [bel-ko-**vah**-ńe] n. entablature; carpentry; structural beams
belkowaty [bel-ko-**vah**-ti] adj.m. beamy; massive; broad
belkowina [bel-ko-**vee**-nah] f. (beam) timber
belkowy [bel-**ko**-vi] adj.m. of beams
strop belkowy [strop bel-**ko**-vi] exp.: beam ceiling
belladona [bel-lah-**do**-nah] f. belladonna (poison plant)
belona [be-**lo**-nah] f. garfish; horn fish; garpike; needlefish; snook
belotka [be-**lot**-kah] f. a card game
belować [be-**lo**-vahćh] v. bale; make up into bales (*repeatedly*)
belowanie [be-lo-**vah**-ńe] n. baling
beluarda [be-loo-**ahr**-dah] f. boulevard; bulwark
belweder [bel-**ve**-der] m. belvedere
belwederczyk [bel-ve-**der**-chik] m. one who took part in the capture of the Warsaw Belvedere at the outbreak of Rising in 1830
belwederski [bel-ve-**der**-skee] adj.m. belvedere (architecture, etc.)
Belzebub [bel-**ze**-boop] m. Belzebub; colloq: Old Nick
belzebubi [bel-ze-**boo**-bee] adj.m. Belzebubian
bełgot [**bew**-got] m. mumbling; mumble; stammer; gibber; jabber; sputter; murmur
bełk [bewk] m. gulf; abyss; whirlpool
bełkot [**bew**-kot] m. mumbling; mumble; stammer; gibber; jabber; sputter; murmur (of water, etc.)
bełkotać [bew-**ko**-tahćh] v. mumble; stammer; gibber; jabber; sputter; murmur (*repeatedly*)
bełkotanie [bew-ko-**tah**-ńe] n. mumbling; stammering; jabbering
bełkotka [bew-**kot**-kah] f. jabbering woman; sputtering woman; instrument for mixing gas into fluid
bełkotliwie [bew-ko-**tlee**-vye] adv. mumbling; stammeringly; jabbering
bełkotliwość [bew-ko-**tlee**-vośhćh] f. habit of mumbling
bełkotliwy [bew-ko-**tlee**-vi] adj.m. mumbling; stammering; gibbering; jabbering; sputtering
bełkowisko [bew-ko-**vees**-ko] n. whirlpool
bełt [bewt] m. murmur; arrow butt; (geogr.) strait; crossbow bolt; colloq: tasteless cheap wine
bełtać [**bew**-tahćh] v. stir; stir up; mix up; beat up (eggs, etc.); whisk; scramble (*repeatedly*)
bełtać się [**bew**-tahćh śh<u>an</u>] v. gurgle; splash; dangle (*repeatedly*)
bełtanie [bew-**tah**-ńe] n. stirring; gurgling
bełtanina [bew-tah-**ńee**-nah] f. stirred liquid; gurgling liquid
bemol [**be**-mol] m. (music) flat
bemolowy [be-mo-**lo**-vi] adj.m. (music) flat (sign, etc.)
benedyktyn [be-ne-**dik**-tin] m. Benedictine; black monk
benedyktynka [be-ne-dik-**tin**-kah] f. Benedictine nun; benedictine (flavored) liqueur
benedyktyński [be-ne-dik-**tiń**-skee] adj.m. Benedictine (rule, monk, nun, etc.); painstaking; laborious; wearisome (work, etc.)
benefaktor [be-ne-**fahk**-tor] m. benefactor
beneficjalny [be-ne-fee-**tsyahl**-ni] adj.m. beneficiary
beneficjant [be-ne-**fee**-tsyahnt] m. incumbent; payee; assignee
beneficjent [be-ne-**fee**-tsyent] m. beneficiary
beneficjum [be-ne-**feets**-yoom] n. benefice; incumbency; church preferment; hist. ecclesiastic living
benefis [be-**ne**-fees] m. benefit; actor's benefit; ticket night

na jego benefis [nah **ye**-go be-**ne**-fees] exp.: for his benefit; on his account; to his profit
benefisant [be-ne-**fee**-sahnt] m. actor for whose benefit a performance is given; actor's benefit night (hist.)
benefisantka [be-ne-fee-**sahnt**-kah] f. actress for whose benefit a performance is given
benefisowy [be-ne-fee-**so**-vi] adj.m. benefit (performance, etc.)
benetyt [be-**ne**-tit] m. bennetite
Bengalczyk [ben-**gahl**-chik] m. Bengali
Bengalka [ben-**gahl**-kah] f. (woman) Bengali
bengalski [ben-**gahl**-skee] adj.m. Bengal; Bengali
beniamin [beń-**yah**-meen] m. benjamin; favorite; darling pet
benthamizm [ben-**tah**-meezm] m. Benthamism; philosophy of Bentham
beniaminek [beń-yah-**mee**-nek] m. precious favorite; darling pet
bental [**ben**-tahl] m. environment at the bottom of a body of water
bentoniczny [ben-to-**ńeech**-ni] adj.m. (organisms) of the environment at the bottom of a body of water
bentonit [ben-**to**-ńeet] m. bentonite
bentonitowy [ben-to-ńee-**to**-vi] adj.m. bentonitic
bentos [**ben**-tos] m. benthos
bentosowy [ben-to-**so**-vi] adj.m. benthonic; benthic
benzen [**ben**-zen] m. benzene; bemzol (Brit.)
benzenowy [ben-ze-**no**-vi] adj.m. benzene (series, etc.)
benzochinon [ben-zo-**khee**-non] m. benzoquinone (used in dyes)
benzoes [ben-**zo**-es] m. benzoic acid
benzoesowy [ben-zo-e-**so**-vi] adj.m. of benzoic acid
benzofenantren [ben-zo-fe-**nahn**-tren] m. pyrone
benzol [**ben**-zol] m. benzene
benzolowy [ben-zo-**lo**-vi] adj.m. benzene (series, etc.)
benzyna [ben-**zi**-nah] f. gasoline; petrol (Brit.); gas; slang: juice
benzynomierz [ben-zi-**no**-myesh] m. gasoline meter (attached to pump used to measure the volume sold)
benzynowy [ben-zi-**no**-vi] adj.m. benzine; gasoline (can, etc.); petrol (price, etc.) (Brit.)
stacja benzynowa [**stah**-tsyah ben-zi-**no**-vah] exp.: gasoline station; gas station; service station; filling station
ber [ber] m. foxtail (grass); Hungarian millet
bera [**be**-rah] f. butter pear
berbeć [**ber**-bećh] m. colloq: small kid; toddler; brat; dot
berberyjski [ber-be-**riy**-skee] adj.m. Berber (language, etc.)
berberys [ber-**be**-ris] m. barberry (fruit, shrub)
berberysowaty [ber-be-ri-so-**vah**-ti] adj.m. of the barberry family
berberysowate [ber-be-ri-so-**vah**-te] pl. the barberry family
berberysowy [ber-be-ri-**so**-vi] adj.m. barberry (hedge, etc.)
berceuse [ber-tse-**oo**-se] f. cradle-song; berceuse
berdysz [**ber**-dish] m. battle-axe; pol-axe; broad-axe
berecik [be-**re**-ćheek] m. small beret
berek [**be**-rek] m. tag play
bereka [be-**re**-kah] f. service-tree
beret [**be**-ret] m. beret; academic cap
bereziak [be-**re**-źhahk] m. former inmate of Bereza Kartuska prison camp
bergamot [ber-**gah**-mot] m. bergamot
bergamota [ber-gah-**mo**-tah] f. bergamot (a mixture of lemon and pear); variety of pear tree
bergamotka [ber-gah-**mot**-kah] f. bergamot (a mixture of lemon and pear); variety of pear tree
bergamotowy [ber-gah-mo-**to**-vi] adj.m. bergamot (pear-shaped orange, fragrance, etc.)
bergsonista [berk-so-**ńees**-tah] m. Bergsonian
bergsonizm [berk-**so**-ńeezm] m. Bergsonism
beri-beri [be-**ree** be-**ree**] indecl. beriberi (deficiency disease)

berkel [ber-kel] m. berkelium (atomic number 97)
berkeleizm [ber-ke-le-eezm] m. Berkeleianism
berkszyr [berk-shir] m. Berkshire swine
berkut [ber-koot] m. golden eagle
berlacz [ber-lahch] m. felt overshoe
berlinka [ber-leen-kah] f. barge
Berlinka [ber-leen-kah] f. (female) Berliner
berlinkarz [ber-leen-kahsh] m. barge-master; bargee
Berlińczyk [ber-leeń-chik] m. Berliner
berliński [ber-leeń-skee] adj.m. Berlin (wall, etc.); of Berlin
berło [ber-wo] n. scepter; an emblem of royal authority; staff of office; wand; mace; bishop's verge; bauble
dzierżyć berło [dźher-zhićh ber-wo] exp.: to wield the specter; to hold the specter
bermudy [ber-moo-di] pl. Bermuda shorts
bermudzki [ber-moots-kee] adj.m. of Bermuda; Bermudian (sail, etc.)
bermyca [ber-mi-tsah] f. bearskin cap; furry cap
bernard [ber-nahrt] m. Saint Bernard dog
bernardyn [ber-nahr-din] m. Bernardine monk
bernardynek [ber-nahr-di-nek] m. (medical) scraper
bernardynka [ber-nahr-din-kah] f. Bernardine nun; a species of snuff
bernardyński [ber-nahr-diń-skee] adj.m. Bernardine (order, etc.)
bernikla [ber-ńeek-lah] f. variety of goose
berso [ber-so] n. walkway enclosed with arch of climbing plants
berta [ber-tah] f. Big Bertha gun
bertram [ber-trahm] m. pyrethrum
berwiono [ber-vyo-no] n. log; stump; raft-timber (hist.)
beryl [be-ril] m. beryl (mineral); beryllium; glucinum
berylowy [be-ri-lo-vi] adj.m. beryllium (bronze, etc.); glucinum (bronze, etc.)
berżera [ber-zhe-rah] f. variety of armchair
berżeretka [ber-zhe-ret-kah] f. 18th cent. light French sentimental song; 16th cent. French dance
besemerować [be-se-me-ro-vahćh] v. produce steel in the Bessemer converter (*repeatedly*)
besemerowanie [be-se-me-ro-vah-ńe] n. production of steel in the Bessemer converter
besemerownia [be-se-me-rov-ńah] f. plant producing steel in the Bessemer converter
besemerowski [be-se-me-rof-skee] adj.m. Bessemer (steel, etc.)
besować [be-so-vahćh] v. stain wood; mordant; fix colors (in dyeing) (*repeatedly*)
bessa [bes-sah] f. slump in prices; fall, drop, decline in prices
bestia [bes-tyah] f. beast; brute; colloq: rogue; knave; rapscallion; scamp; scapegrace
bestializm [bes-tyah-leezm] m. bestiality
bestialski [bes-tyahl-skee] adj.m. bestial; brutish; brutal; savage; inhuman; atrocious
bestialskie czyny [bes-tyahl-ske chi-ni] exp.: atrocities
po bestialsku [po bes-tyahl-skoo] exp.: bestially; brutally; savagely
bestialsko [bes-tyahl-sko] adv. bestially; brutally; savagely
bestialstwo [bes-tyahl-stfo] n. bestiality; inhumane behavior; brutishness; brutality; savagery; inhumanity; atrocities
bestiarium [bes-tyahr-yoom] n. medieval didactic tales with animal motives
bestiariusz [bes-tyahr-yoosh] m. medieval Christian didactic tale with animal motives
bestseller [best-se-ler] m. bestseller
bestwić [best-feećh] v. bait; goad; worry (somebody) (*repeatedly*)
bestwić się [best-feećh śhan] v. torment; worry (somebody) (*repeatedly*)
bestwić się nad kimś [best-feećh śhan naht keemśh] exp.: to torment somebody
bestyjka [bes-tiy-kah] f. rascal;

rogue; a mischievous child, etc.
beszamel [be-**shah**-mel] m. sauce made of egg yolks and milk
beszamelowy [be-shah-me-**lo**-vi] adj.m. bechamel (sauce, etc.)
besztać [**besh**-tahćh] v. scold; rebuke; chide; trounce; come down (upon somebody); row (*repeatedly*)
besztanie [besh-**tah**-ńe] n. a scolding; a rebuke; a trouncing; a trimming
besztanina [besh-tah-**ńee**-nah] f. a scolding; a rebuke; a trouncing; a trimming
bet [bet] m. bedding; pillows; blankets and quilts; feather bed
wyłazić z betów [vi-**wah**-źheećh z **be**-toof] exp.: to get out of bed; to tear oneself away from one's feather bed
beta [**be**-tah] f. Greek letter beta
promienie beta [pro-**mye**-ńe **be**-tah] exp.: beta rays
betaaktywny [be-tah-ahk-**tiv**-ni] adj.m. radiating beta-rays
betabion [be-**tah**-byon] m. betabion; betaxin
betatron [be-**tah**-tron] m. betatron
betaina [be-tah-**ee**-nah] f. betaine
betapromieniotwórczy [be-tah-pro-mye-ńo-**tfoor**-chi] adj.m. radiating beta rays
betatron [be-**tah**-tron] m. betatron (electron accelerator)
betel [**be**-tel] m. betel (pepper)
betelowy [be-te-**lo**-vi] adj.m. betel (pepper, pan, etc.)
beton [**be**-ton] m. concrete; beton; colloq: the conservative politicians
beton drzewny [**be**-ton **dzhev**-ni] exp.: sawdust concrete
beton lekki [**be**-ton **lek**-kee] exp.: lightweight concrete; framed concrete
beton natryskiwany [**be**-ton nah-tris-kee-**vah**-ni] exp.: sprayed concrete
beton wibrowany [**be**-ton vee-bro-**vah**-ni] exp.: vibrated concrete
beton wodoodporny [**be**-ton vo-do-ot-**por**-ni] exp.: watertight concrete
beton zbrojony [**be**-ton zbro-**yo**-ni] exp.: reinforced concrete
mur-beton [moor **be**-ton] exp.: colloq: dead sure; dead certain
natryskiwać mur betonem [nah-tris-**kee**-vahćh moor be-**to**-nem] exp.: to spray a wall with concrete grout
to jest mur-beton [to yest moor **be**-ton] exp.: it's a sure thing; it's dead certain
betoniarka [be-to-**ńahr**-kah] f. concrete-mixer
betoniarnia [be-to-**ńahr**-ńah] f. concrete-mixing plant
betoniarski [be-to-**ńahr**-skee] adj.m. concrete worker's (tools, etc.)
betoniarz [be-**to**-ńahsh] m. concrete worker; concreter (Brit.)
betonit [be-**to**-ńeet] m. concrete slab; concrete block
betonka [be-**ton**-kah] f. concreted runway
betonoskop [be-to-**nos**-kop] m. ultrasound device for measuring the quality of concrete
betonować [be-to-**no**-vahćh] v. concrete; pour concrete (*repeatedly*)
betonowanie [be-to-no-**vah**-ńe] n. pouring concrete
betonownia [be-to-**nov**-ńah] f. concrete-mixing plant
betonowy [be-to-**no**-vi] adj.m. of concrete; concrete (floor, etc.)
bety [**be**-ti] pl. colloq: bedding
bewatron [be-**vah**-tron] m. variety of particle accelerator
bez [bes] prep. without
bez butów [bez **boo**-toof] exp.: barefoot; without shoes; with shoes off
bez czci i wiary [bes **chćhee** ee **vyah**-ri] exp.: lost to shame; dead to honor
bez kapelusza [bes kah-pe-**loo**-shah] exp.: with hat off; bare-head
bez kompromisu [bes kom-pro-**mee**-soo] exp.: uncompromisingly
bez marynarki [bez mah-ri-**nahr**-kee] exp.: in short sleeves; with (my, his) coat off
bez obawy [bez o-**bah**-vi] exp.:

without fear
bez ogródek [bez o-**groo**-dek] exp.: off the bat
bez przesady! [bes pshe-**sah**-di] excl.: let's not exaggerate!
bez pytania [bes pi-**tah**-ńah] exp.: without (asking) permission
bez zadawania pytań [bez zah-dah-**vah**-ńah **pi**-tahń] exp.: no questions asked
bez żartów! [bez **zhahr**-toof] exp.: no nonsense
bez [bes] m. lilac
bez- [bes] prefix: "un" (also used as the suffix "less" is in English)
beza [**be**-zah] f. meringue; kiss
bezakcentowy [bez-ahk-tsen-**to**-vi] adj.m. unaccented (one-syllable words, etc.); unaccentuated; unstressed
bezalkoholowy [bez-ahl-ko-kho-**lo**-vi] adj.m. non-alcoholic; soft (drink); dry (day, town, etc.)
bezan [**be**-zahn] m. mizzen-sail
bezanmaszt [be-zahn-**mahsht**] m. mizzen-mast
bezapelacyjnie [bez-ah-pe-lah-**tsiy**-ńe] adv. authoritatively; decisively; irrevocably; without appeal; for good and all
bezapelacyjność [bez-ah-pe-lah-**tsiy**-nośhćh] f. peremptoriness; authoritativeness; finality; irrevocable character (of a step, etc.); decisive character
bezapelacyjny [bez-ah-pe-lah-**tsiy**-ni] adj.m. peremptory; authoritative; undisputable; without appeal; final; decisive; irrevocable
bezatomowy [bez-ah-to-**mo**-vi] adj.m. atom-free (zone, etc.)
bezatutowy [bez-ah-too-**to**-vi] adj.m. no-trump (game, etc.)
bezawaryjnie [bez-ah-vah-**riy**-ńe] adv. without hindrance; in an accident free manner
bezawaryjny [bez-ah-vah-**riy**-ni] adj.m. without hindrance; accident free (work, etc.)
bezbarwnie [bez-**bahrv**-ńe] adv. without color; blankly; without expression; dully; uneventfully
bezbarwność [bez-**bahrv**-nośhćh] f. lack of color; dullness; drabness; monotony (of landscape, etc.); tonelessness (of voice)
bezbarwny [bez-**bahrv**-ni] adj.m. colorless; plain; drab; dull; toneless (voice, etc.); flat (tone, etc.); monotonous (life, etc.); devoid of color; insipid (style, etc.)
bezbiałkowy [bez-byahw-**ko**-vi] adj.m. protein-free
bezbłędnie [bez-**bwand**-ńe] adv. faultlessly; correctly; perfectly; accurately
bezbłędność [bez-**bwand**-nośhćh] f. faultlessness; perfection
bezbłędny [bez-**bwand**-ni] adj.m. faultless; correct; flawless
bezbolesność [bez-bo-**les**-nośhćh] f. painlessness; absence of pain
bezbolesny [bez-bo-**les**-ni] adj.m. painless; without pain
bezboleśnie [bez-bo-**leśh**-ńe] adv. painlessly
bezbożnica [bez-bozh-**ńee**-tsah] f. atheist; godless woman; ungodly woman; anti-religious woman
bezbożnictwo [bez-bozh-**ńeets**-tfo] n. atheism; godlessness; impiety
bezbożniczy [bez-bozh-**ńee**-chi] adj.m. atheistic; godless; impious
bezbożnie [bez-**bozh**-ńe] adv. godlessly; impiously; irreligiously
bezbożnik [bez-**bozh**-ńeek] m. atheist; godless man; ungodly person; unbelieving person; anti-religious person; irreligious man
bezbożność [bez-**bozh**-nośhćh] f. atheism; godlessness; impiety
bezbożny [bez-**bozh**-ni] adj.m. atheistic; godless; impious
bezbożny czyn [bez-**bozh**-ni chin] exp.: wickedness; impiety
bezbrakowy [bez-brah-**ko**-vi] adj.m. free of waste; showing no waste
bezbramkowy [bez-brahm-**ko**-vi] adj.m. scoreless
bezbramkowo [bez-brahm-**ko**-vo] adv. with no goals scored
bezbrody [bez-**bro**-di] adj.m. beardless
bezbronnie [bez-**bron**-ńe] adv. defenselessly; helplessly; without weapons; without arms; carrying

no arms
bezbronność [bez-**bron**-nośhćh] f. lack of defense; helplessness; armlessness
bezbronny [bez-**bron**-ni] adj.m. defenseless; unprotected; helpless; unarmed; weaponless
bezbrzeże [bez-**bzhe**-zhe] n. infinity; immensity; boundlessness
bezbrzeżnie [bez-**bzhezh**-ńe] adv. immensely; infinitely; boundlessly
bezbrzeżność [bez-**bzhezh**-nośhćh] f. infinity; immensity; boundlessness
bezbrzeżny [bez-**bzhezh**-ni] adj.m. immense; infinite; unlimited; boundless
bezcel [**bes**-tsel] m. aimlessness; pointlessness; uselessness
bezcelowo [bes-tse-**lo**-vo] adv. aimlessly; pointlessly; uselessly; vainly; to no avail; in vain; to no end; to no purpose
bezcelowość [bes-tse-**lo**-vośhćh] f. aimlessness; pointlessness; uselessness
bezcelowy [bes-tse-**lo**-vi] adj.m. aimless; pointless; useless; purposeless; futile; vain; unavailing
to jest bezcelowe [to yest bes-tse-**lo**-ve] exp.: it is of no avail; it is to no purpose; it is in vain; it won't work; it isn't worthwhile
nie jest to bezcelowe [ńe yest to bes-tse-**lo**-ve] exp.: it is not for nothing
bezcen [**bes**-tsen] in exp.:
za bezcen [zah **bes**-tsen] exp.: dirt cheap; very cheap
bezcenność [bes-**tsen**-nośhćh] f. pricelessness; inestimable value
bezcenny [bes-**tsen**-ni] adj.m. priceless; invaluable; inestimable; beyond price
bezceremonialnie [bes-tse-re-mo-**ńyahl**-ńe] adv. in a free and easy way; in a familiar way; roughly; off-hand
bezceremonialność [bes-tse-re-mo-**ńyahl**-nośhćh] f. free and easy way; a familiar way; bluntness; unceremonious treatment; informality
bezceremonialny [bes-tse-re-mo-**ńyahl**-ni] adj.m. free and easy; familiar; rough; informal; blunt; downright; off-hand
bezchmurnie [bes-**khmoor**-ńe] adv. cloudlessly; serenely; clearly
bezchmurny [bes-**khmoor**-ni] adj.m. cloudless; serene; clear
bezcielesność [bes-će-**les**-nośhćh] f. immateriality; impalpability; bodilessness
bezcielesny [bes-će-**les**-ni] adj.m. immaterial; impalpable; bodiless; incorporeal; disembodied
bezcieleśnie [bes-će-**leśh**-ńe] adv. immaterially; impalpably
bezcieniowy [bes-će-**ńo**-vi] adj.m. shadeless; shadowless
bezcierniowy [bes-ćher-**ńo**-vi] adj.m. thornless
bezcłowo [bes-**tswo**-vo] adv. in a duty-free manner
bezcłowy [bes-**tswo**-vi] adj.m. duty-free
bezczasowo [bes-chah-**so**-vo] adv. timelessly
bezczasowość [bes-chah-**so**-vośhćh] f. timelessness
bezczasowy [bes-chah-**so**-vi] adj.m. timeless
bezczaszkowiec [bes-chahsh-**ko**-vyets] m. acraniate (without skull)
bezczaszkowce [bes-chahsh-**kof**-tse] pl. Acrania; Cephalochorda (without skull)
bezczelnie [bes-**chel**-ńe] adv. insolently; impudently; brazenly; shamelessly; unblushingly
bezczelnie odpowiadać [bes-**chel**-ńe ot-po-**vyah**-dahćh] exp.: to answer back
bezczelnik [bes-**chel**-ńeek] m. brazen-faced fellow; insolent man; shameless individual
bezczelność [bes-**chel**-nośhćh] f. insolence; impudence; audacity; impertinence; brazenness; effrontery; rankness; slang: cheek
co za bezczelność! [tso zah bes-**chel**-nośhćh] exp.: what nerve!; what impudence!
bezczelny [bes-**chel**-ni] adj.m. insolent; impudent; brazen-faced; brassy; shameless; unblushing;

colloq: cool; nervy; cheeky; rank
bezczeszczenie [bes-chesh-**che**-ńe] n. profanation; violation; desecration; defilement; outrage (against)
bezcześcić [bes-**cheśh**-ćheećh] v. profane; violate; desecrate; defile; pollute; outrage (*repeatedly*)
bezczyn [**bes**-chin] m. passivity; inactivity
bezczynnie [bes-**chin**-ńe] adv. idly; inactively
stać bezczynnie [stahćh bes-**chin**-ńe] exp.: to lie idle; to stand idly by; to lookon with folded arms
bezczynność [bes-**chin**-nośhćh] f. idleness; inactivity; inaction; inertia
bezczynny [bes-**chin**-ni] adj.m. idle; inactive
bezdarnie [bez-**dahr**-ńe] adv. clumsily; awkwardly (hist.)
bezdarny [bez-**dahr**-ni] adj.m. untalented; clumsy; awkward
bezdech [**bez**-dekh] m. apnoea; apnea; transient cessation of respiration
bezdennie [bez-**den**-ńe] adv. abysmally; hopelessly (stupid, dull, clumsy, etc.)
bezdenność [bez-**den**-nośhćh] f. abyss; chasm
bezdenny [bez-**den**-ni] adj.m. bottomless; fathomless; abysmal; hopeless (fool, etc.); infinite (despair, etc.)
bezdeń [**bez**-deń] f. abyss; chasm
bezdeszczowy [bez-desh-**cho**-vi] adj.m. rainless; dry
bezdewizowo [bez-de-vee-**zo**-vo] adv. without paying in foreign currency
bezdewizowy [bez-de-vee-**zo**-vi] adj. m. not paid in foreign currency
bezdętkowy [bez-dant-**ko**-vi] adj.m. tubeless; without an inner-tube
bezdna [**bez**-dnah] f. abyss; chasm
bezdnia [**bez**-dńah] f. abyss; chasm
bezdno [**bez**-dno] n. abyss; chasm
bezdogmatyzm [bez-dog-**mah**-tizm] m. rejection of all dogmas; negation of all dogmas
bezdomnie [bez-**dom**-ńe] adv. without a roof above one's head
bezdomność [bez-**dom**-nośhćh] f. homelessness
bezdomny [bez-**dom**-ni] adj.m. homeless; houseless; shelterless; m.: wanderer; vagrant; outcast; homeless person
dziecko bezdomne [**dźhets**-ko bez-**dom**-ne] exp.: waif
bezdotykowo [bez-do-ti-**ko**-vo] adv. without touching
bezdotykowy [bez-do-ti-**ko**-vi] adj.m. touch-free (procedure, etc.)
bezdowodowy [bez-do-vo-**do**-vi] adj.m. unwarranted; groundless
bezdrganiowo [bez-drgah-**ńo**-vo] adv. without vibration
bezdroże [bez-**dro**-zhe] n. pathless wilderness; devious paths
sprowadzić na bezdroże [spro-**vah**-dźheećh nah bez-**dro**-zhe] exp.: to lead astray; to mislead; to misguide; to deprave; to pervert
zejść na bezdroże [zeyśhćh nah bez-**dro**-zhe] exp.: to go astray; to fall into error; to go wrong
bezdrożnie [bez-**dro**-zhńe] adv. deviously; pathlessly
bezdrożność [bez-**dro**-zhnośhćh] f. lack of roads; pathlessness; tracklessness; devious path; impropriety; wrongdoing; act of lawlessness
bezdrożny [bez-**dro**-zhni] adj.m. wayless; pathless; trackless; having no road
bezdrzewie [bez-**dzhe**-vye] n. lack of trees; woodless tract
bezdrzewny [bez-**dzhev**-ni] adj.m. treeless; woodless
bezdrzewny papier [bez-**dzhev**-ni **pah**-pyer] exp.: rag paper
bezdusznie [bez-**doosh**-ńe] adv. soullessly; spiritlessly; dully; stiffly; formally; in a stereotyped manner; in a cut and dry manner; in a spiritless manner
bezduszność [bez-**doosh**-nośhćh] f. soullessness; lack of spirit; formal and stiff treatment; stereotyped treatment
bezduszny [bez-**doosh**-ni] adj.m. soulless; insensate; unfeeling;

spiritless; dull; formal; stiff; stereotyped; cut and dried
bezdymnie [bez-**dim**-ńe] adv. without smoke
bezdymny [bez-**dim**-ni] adj.m. smokeless
bezdyskusyjnie [bez-dis-koo-**siy**-ńe] adv. without any need for reconsideration
bezdyskusyjny [bez-dis-koo-**siy**-ni] adj.m. out of question
bezdziedziczny [bez-dźhe-**dźheech**-ni] adj.m. heirless
bezdzietnie [bez-**dźhet**-ńe] adv. without offspring
umarł bezdzietnie [oo-mahrw bez-**dźhet**-ńe] exp.: he died childless
bezdzietność [bez-**dźhet**-nośhćh] f. childlessness; lack of offspring
bezdzietny [bez-**dźhet**-ni] adj.m. childless; without offspring
bezdźwięcznie [bez-**dźhvyanch**-ńe] adv. soundlessly; without sound; (sounded) with the breath
bezdźwięczność [bez-**dźhvyanch**-nośhćh] f. soundlessness; voiceless pronunciation
bezdźwięczny [bez-**dźhvyanch**-ni] adj.m. soundless; voiceless; sounded with the breath; unvoiced; surd; breathed
głoska bezdźwięczna [**gwos**-kah bez-**dźhvyanch**-nah] exp.: tenuis; (a) surd; (a) media; surd mute (k, p, t); voiceless stop
beze mnie [be-**ze** mńe] adv. without me; in my absence; exp.: count me out!; leave me out!
bezeceństwo [be-ze-**tseń**-stfo] n. iniquity; infamy; ignominy; wickedness; atrocity; outrage; shameful deed
bezechowy [bez-e-**kho**-vi] adj.m. echoless; anechoic
bezecnica [be-zets-**ńee**-tsah] f. shameless woman
bezecnie [be-**zets**-ńe] adv. wickedly; infamously; ignominiously; shamelessly
bezecnik [be-**zets**-ńeek] m. shameless man; scoundrel
bezecność [be-**zets**-nośhćh] f. wickedness; infamy; ignominy; shamelessness; outrage; villainy; atrocity
bezecny [be-**zets**-ni] adj.m. wicked; infamous; ignominious
bezgarażowy [bez-gah-rah-**zho**-vi] adj.m. lacking a garage
postój bezgarażowy [**pos**-tooy bez-gah-rah-**zho**-vi] exp.: open-air parking
bezgarbny [bez-**gahrb**-ni] adj.m. humpless; flat; even; plane
bezgłos [**bez**-gwos] m. loss of voice; aphonia
bezgłosy [bez-**gwo**-si] adj.m. voiceless; dumb
bezgłośnie [bez-**gwośh**-ńe] adv. noiselessly; silently
bezgłośny [bez-**gwośh**-ni] adj.m. noiseless; silent; voiceless; dumb; still
bezgłowie [bez-**gwo**-vye] n. chaos; lack of organization or leadership
bezgłowy [bez-**gwo**-vi] adj.m. acephalous; with head cut off; (nail, etc.) without a head; headless; brainless; stupid
bezgorączkowy [bez-go-rownch-**ko**-vi] adj.m. without fever; feverless
bezgoryczkowy [bez-go-rich-**ko**-vi] adj.m. without bitterness; devoid of bitter principle
bezgotówkowy [bez-go-toof-**ko**-vi] adj.m. without cash; settled by check; by bank transfer; non-cash (payment, etc.)
bezgranicze [bez-grah-**ńee**-che] n. immensity; boundlessness
bezgranicznie [bez-grah-**ńeech**-ńe] adv. without limits; boundlessly; infinitely; immensely; extremely; exceedingly
bezgraniczność [bez-grah-**ńeech**-nośhćh] f. boundlessness; immensity; infinity; infinitude
bezgraniczny [bez-grah-**ńeech**-ni] adj.m. without bounds; boundless; infinite; unlimited; unconfined; immeasurable; immense
bezgrzebieniowiec [bez-gzhe-bye-**ńo**-vyets] m. ratite bird
bezgrzebieniowce [bez-gzhe-bye-**ńof**-tse] pl. the ratite birds
bezgrzesznie [bez-**gzhesh**-ńe] adv. sinlessly; innocently

bezgrzeszny [bez-**gzhesh**-ni] adj.m. sinless; innocent; chaste; undefiled by sin; pure
bezgrzywy [bez-**gzhi**-vi] adj.m. with hogged mane; (horse) without mane
bezguście [bez-**goośh**-ćhe] n. lack of good taste; trash
bezgwiezdny [bez-**gvyezd**-ni] adj.m. starless (sky, etc.)
bezgwieździsty [bez-gvyeźh-**dźhees**-ti] adj.m. starless
bezhołowie [bes-kho-**wo**-vye] n. colloq: confusion; mess; chaos
bezideowiec [bez-ee-de-**o**-vyets] m. person devoid of ideals; person devoid of guiding principles
bezideowość [bez-ee-de-**o**-vośhćh] f. lack of ideals; lack of guiding principles
bezideowy [bez-ee-de-**o**-vi] adj.m. devoid of ideals
bezik [**be**-źheek] m. bezique (a card game)
bezimiennie [bez-ee-**myen**-ńe] adv. anonymously; namelessly
bezimienność [bez-ee-**myen**-nośhćh] f. anonymity
bezimienny [bez-ee-**myen**-ni] adj.m. anonymous; nameless; unnamed
bezinteresownie [bez-een-te-re-**sov**-ńe] adv. disinterestedly; unselfishly; free of charge
bezinteresowność [bez-een-te-re-**sov**-nośhćh] f. unselfishness; disinterestedness
bezinteresowny [bez-een-te-re-**sov**-ni] adj.m. disinterested; unselfish; cost-free; free of charge; unpaid
bezinwestycyjny [bez-een-ves-ti-**tsiy**-ni] adj.m. not requiring additional investment
bezkarnie [bes-**kahr**-ńe] adv. with impunity
ujść bezkarnie [ooyśhćh bes-**kahr**-ńe] exp.: to go unpunished; to get off scot-free; to get away with it
bezkarność [bes-**kahr**-nośhćh] f. impunity; exemption from punishment
bezkarny [bes-**kahr**-ni] adj.m. unpunished; unchastised; exempt from punishment
pozostać bezkarnym [po-**zo**-stahćh bes-**kahr**-nim] exp.: to go unpunished
bezkastowy [bes-kahs-**to**-vi] adj.m. having no castes; classless
bezkierunkowo [bes-k̲e-roon-**ko**-vo] adv. aimlessly
bezkierunkowy [bes-k̲e-roon-**ko**-vi] adj.m. undirected
bezklasowy [bes-klah-**so**-vi] adj.m. classless; without class distinction
społeczeństwo bezklasowe [spo-we-**cheń**-stfo bes-klah-**so**-ve] exp.: classless society
bezkłopotliwy [bes-kwo-po-**tlee**-vi] adj.m. trouble free; easy going
bezkłowy [bes-**kwo**-vi] adj.m. having no fangs; without fangs
bezkofeinowy [bes-ko-fe-ee-**no**-vi] adj.m. decaffeinated (coffee)
bezkolankowy [bes-ko-lahn-**ko**-vi] adj.m. jointless; unarticulated
bezkolczasty [bes-kol-**chahs**-ti] adj.m. thornless; thorn free
bezkoleśny [bes-ko-**leśh**-ni] adj.m. without wheels
bezkolizyjnie [bes-ko-lee-**ziy**-ńe] adv. in a way free from the possibility of collisions
bezkolizyjność [bes-ko-lee-**ziy**-nośhćh] f. freedom from collisions; vertical separation
bezkolizyjny [bes-ko-lee-**ziy**-ni] adj.m. free from the possibility of collisions
skrzyżowanie bezkolizyjne [skshi-zho-**vah**-ńe bes-ko-lee-**ziy**-ne] exp.: multi-level intersection
bezkolorowo [bes-ko-lo-**ro**-vo] adv. colorlessly; dully
bezkolorowy [bes-ko-lo-**ro**-vi] adj.m. colorless
bezkompromisowo [bes-kom-pro-mee-**so**-vo] adv. uncompromisingly; with intransigence
bezkompromisowość [bes-kom-pro-mee-**so**-vośhćh] f. uncompromising attitude; intransigence
bezkompromisowy [bes-kom-pro-mee-**so**-vi] adj.m. uncompromising; intransigent;

thoroughgoing; colloq: hard-shell
bezkonduktorski [bes-kon-dook-**tor**-skee] adj.m. not requiring the presence of a conductor
bezkonfliktowo [bes-kon-fleek-**to**-vo] adv. in a conflict-free fashion; peacefully; neutrally; indifferently
bezkonfliktowość [bes-kon-fleek-**to**-vośhćh] f. conflict-free condition; peacefulness; neutrality; indifference
bezkonfliktowy [bes-kon-fleek-**to**-vi] adj.m. conflict-free; peaceful; neutral; indifferent
bezkonkurencyjnie [bes-kon-koo-ren-**tsiy**-ńe] adv. matchlessly; peerlessly; uniquely; outrunning all competition
bezkonkurencyjny [bes-kon-koo-ren-**tsiy**-ni] adj.m. unrivaled; matchless; peerless; unique; beyond competition; unattainable by any competitor
bezkonny [bes-**kon**-ni] adj.m. horseless; without horses
bezkońcówkowy [bes-koń-tsoof-**ko**-vi] adj.m. (gram.) uninflected
bezkopytny [bes-ko-**pit**-ni] adj.m. unhoofed
bezkorbowy [bes-kor-**bo**-vi] adj.m. crankless
bezkoronowy [bes-ko-ro-**no**-vi] adj.m. apetalous (plant, etc.)
bezkoronowe [bes-ko-ro-**no**-ve] pl. the apetalous plants
bezkorzystny [bes-ko-**zhist**-ni] adj.m. profitless; unprofitable
bezkres [**bes**-kres] m. immensity; infinity; infinitude; boundlessness
bezkresność [bes-**kres**-nośhćh] f. immensity; infinity; infinitude; boundlessness
bezkresny [bes-**kres**-ni] adj.m. boundless; endless; infinite (space, magnitude, etc); unlimited
bezkreśnie [bes-**kreśh**-ńe] adv. boundlessly; endlessly; infinitely; without limits; without bounds
bezkrewny [bes-**krev**-ni] adj.m. anemic; anaemic; bloodless; colorless; without vitality
bezkręgowiec [bes-kran-**go**-vyets] m. invertebrate; spineless animal
bezkręgowce [bes-kran-**gof**-tse] pl. invertebrates
bezkręgowy [bes-kran-**go**-vi] adj.m. invertebrate; spineless
bezkręgowe [bes-kran-**go**-ve] pl. invertebrate animals
bezkrólewie [bes-kroo-**le**-vye] n. interregnum
bezkrwawo [bes-**krfah**-vo] adv. bloodlessly; without bloodshed
bezkrwawy [bes-**krfah**-vi] adj.m. bloodless; free of bloodshed
bezkrwistość [bes-**krfees**-tośhćh] f. anemia; anaemia; lack of blood; lack of vitality
bezkrwisty [bes-**krfees**-ti] adj.m. anemic; anaemic; bloodless; colorless; without vitality
bezkrytycyzm [bes-kri-**ti**-tsizm] m. lack of criticism; lack of discrimination
bezkrytycznie [bes-kri-**tich**-ńe] adv. uncritically; indiscriminately; credulously; gullibly
bezkrytyczność [bes-kri-**tich**-nośhćh] f. lack of criticism; lack of discrimination
bezkrytyczny [bes-kri-**tich**-ni] adj.m. uncritical; indiscriminate
bezkryzysowo [bes-kri-zi-**so**-vo] adv. without crises
bezkryzysowy [bes-kri-zi-**so**-vi] adj.m. without crises; without upheavals
bezksiężycowy [bes-kśhan-zhi-**tso**-vi] adj.m. moonless (night, etc.)
bezkształtnie [bes-**kshtahwt**-ńe] adv. shapelessly; formlessly
bezkształtność [bes-**kshtahwt**-nośhćh] f. shapelessness
bezkształtny [bes-**kshtahwt**-ni] adj.m. shapeless; formless
bezkwiatowy [bes-kfyah-**to**-vi] adj.m. flowerless; without flowers
bezkwietny [bes-**kfyet**-ni] adj.m. flowerless; without flowers
bezlampowy [bez-lahm-**po**-vi] adj.m. tubeless; valveless (Brit.)
bezlesie [bez-**le**-śhe] n. woodless region; deforested track
bezleśność [bez-**leśh**-nośhćh] f. absence of forest (in a region)
bezleśny [bez-**leśh**-ni] adj.m. woodless; deforested; timberless
bezlik [**bez**-leek] m. multitude; host;

swarm
bezlik kłopotów [**bez**-leek kwo-**po**-toof] exp.: a sea of troubles; a world of trouble
bez liku [bez **lee**-koo] adv. no end
bezlistny [bez-**leest**-ni] adj.m. leafless; aphyllous
bezliścieniowy [bez-leeśh-ćhe-**ńo**-vi] adj.m. acotyledonous; with no distinct seed-lobes
bezliściowate [bez-leeśh-ćho-**vah**-te] pl. the family Buxbaumiaceae
bezlitosność [bez-lee-**tos**-nośhćh] f. mercilessness; ruthlessness; inflexibility
bezlitosny [bez-lee-**tos**-ni] adj.m. merciless; ruthless
bezlitośnie [bez-lee-**tośh**-ńe] adv. mercilessly; ruthlessly; without pity; without mercy; inexorably; inflexibly; relentlessly
bezlotek [bez-**lo**-tek] m. penguin
bezlotki [bez-**lot**-kee] pl. penguins
bezludnie [bez-**lood**-ńe] adv. desolately; in seclusion
bezludność [bez-**lood**-nośhćh] f. desolateness; seclusion; isolation
bezludny [bez-**lood**-ni] adj.m. desolate; uninhabited; deserted; solitary; secluded; isolated
bezludzie [bez-**loo**-dźhe] n. wilderness; waste; isolated spot
bezład [**bez**-waht] m. disorder; confusion; chaos; incoherence; welter; promiscuity; pell-mell; helter-skelter; hurry-scurry
bezładnie [bez-**wahd**-ńe] adv. in confusion; in disorderly fashion; chaotically; incoherently; pell-mell; helter-skelter
bezładność [bez-**wahd**-nośhćh] f. confusion; chaos; disorder; incoherence; pell-mell; helter-skelter; hurry-scurry
bezładny [bez-**wahd**-ni] adj.m. confused; chaotic; disorderly; disconnected; incoherent; pell-mell; helter-skelter
bezłodygowy [bez-wo-di-**go**-vi] adj.m. stemless
bezłożyskowiec [bez-wo-zhis-**ko**-vyets] m. aplacental animal; implacental animal
bezłożyskowy [bez-wo-zhis-**ko**-vi] adj.m. aplacental; implacental; having no placenta
bezłożyskowce [bez-wo-zhis-**kof**-tse] pl. aplacental animals; implacental animals
bezłuski [bez-**woos**-kee] adj.m. scaleless; not covered with scales
bez mała [bez **mah**-wah] adv. nearly; almost; all but
bezmelodyjność [bez-me-lo-**diy**-nośhćh] f. lack of melody; unmelodiousness
bezmian [**bez**-myahn] m. steelyard scales; spring balance
bezmiar [**bez**-myahr] m. immensity; boundlessness; no end of; vastness; host; swarm; multitude; countless number
bezmiar zagadnień [**bez**-myahr zah-**gahd**-ńeń] exp.: countless problems; countless questions; countless issues; a hundred and one problems; zillion problems; no end of problems; zillion questions
bezmiernie [bez-**myer**-ńe] adv. immensely; infinitely; immeasurably; without bounds
bezmierność [bez-**myer**-nośhćh] f. boundlessness; immensity; infinity
bezmierny [bez-**myer**-ni] adj.m. immense; infinite; immeasurable; boundless
bezmiesięczny [bez-mye-**śhanch**-ni] adj.m. moonless
bezmięsny [bez-**myan**-sni] adj.m. fleshless; emaciated; meatless
bezmiłosierny [bez-mee-wo-**śher**-ni] adj.m. merciless; pitiless; ruthless; inexorable
bezmleczność [bez-**mlech**-nośhćh] f. morbid absence of milk in a female
bezmocz [**bez**-moch] m. absence of urine; anuria
bezmogilny [bez-mo-**geel**-ni] adj.m. graveless; tombless; deprived of a grave
bezmotorowy [bez-mo-to-**ro**-vi] adj.m. motorless
bezmowność [bez-**moov**-nośhćh] f. loss of speech; aphasia
bezmowny [bez-**mov**-ni] adj.m. speechless; dumb
bezmózgi [bez-**mooz**-gee] adj.m.

brainless; idle-brained; stupid; idiotic
bezmroźny [bez-**mroźh**-ni] adj.m. frost-free
bezmyślnie [bez-**miśhl**-ńe] adv. blankly; carelessly; wantonly; inconsiderately; thoughtlessly
bezmyślność [bez-**miśhl**-nośhćh] f. thoughtlessness; wantonness; lack of consideration
bezmyślny [bez-**miśhl**-ni] adj.m. blank; thoughtless; vacant; unthinking; unreasoning; careless; silly; inconsiderate
beznadzieja [bez-nah-**dźhe**-yah] f. hopelessness; desperate state; forlornness
beznadziejnie [bez-nah-**dźhey**-ńe] adv. hopelessly; beyond hope
beznadziejna sprawa [bez-nah-**dźhey**-nah **sprah**-vah] exp.: hopeless case
beznadziejność [bez-nah-**dźhey**-nośhćh] f. hopelessness; desperate state; forlornness
beznadziejny [bez-nah-**dźhey**-ni] adj.m. hopeless; desperate; crass; wretched (weather, etc.)
stan beznadziejny [stahn bez-nah-**dźhey**-ni] exp.: a hopeless condition
beznadziejny idiota [bez-nah-**dźhey**-ni ee-**dyo**-tah] exp.: a hopeless fool
beznamiętnie [bez-nah-**myan**-tńe] adv. dispassionately; impassively; without feeling; without emotion
beznamiętność [bez-nah-**myant**-nośhćh] f. impassiveness; lack of feeling; absence of emotions
beznamiętny [bez-nah-**myan**-tni] adj.m. dispassionate; impassive; passionless
beznasienny [bez-nah-**śhen**-ni] adj.m. seedless
beznikotynowy [bez-ńee-ko-ti-**no**-vi] adj.m. nicotine-free
beznogi [bez-**no**-gee] adj.m. legless; lame; footless; m. footless cripple; legless cripple
beznosy [bez-**no**-si] adj.m. noseless; without a nose
beznożny [bez-**nozh**-ni] adj.m. legless; lame; footless; m. footless cripple; legless cripple
bezoar [be-**zo**-ahr] m. bazoar
bezoarowy [be-zo-ah-**ro**-vi] adj.m. bazoar (poison, etc.)
bezobjawowo [bez-o-byah-**vo**-vo] adv. asymptomatically
bezobjawowość [bez-o-byah-**vo**-vośhćh] f. absence of morbid symptoms
bezobjawowy [bez-o-byah-**vo**-vi] adj.m. asymptomatic; without morbid symptoms
bezobłoczny [bez-o-**bwoch**-ni] adj.m. cloudless
bezodblaskowy [bez-od-blahs-**ko**-vi] adj.m. gleam free; glare free (car headlight, etc.); non-dazzle
bezodpływowy [bez-ot-pwi-**vo**-vi] adj.m. without outflow; with no outlet
bezodpryskowy [bez-ot-pris-**ko**-vi] adj.m. shatterproof (glass, etc.)
bezodrzutowy [bez-od-zhoo-**to**-vi] adj.m. recoilless (rifle, etc.)
bezogonowiec [bez-o-go-**no**-vyets] m. tailless plane
bezogonowy [bez-o-go-**no**-vi] adj.m. tailless (planes, gliders, apes, etc.); anurous; ecaudate
bez ogródek [bez o-**groo**-dek] adv. bluntly; unequivocally; off the bat; in plain terms; plainly; without mincing words
bez ogródki [bez o-**groot**-kee] adv. bluntly; unequivocally; off the bat; in plain terms; plainly; without mincing words
bezokolicznik [bez-o-ko-**leech**-ńeek] m. infinitive; infinitive mood
bezokolicznikowy [bez-o-ko-leech-ńee-**ko**-vi] adj.m. infinitive; of infinitive
tryb bezokolicznikowy [trib bez-o-ko-leech-ńee-**ko**-vi] exp.: the infinitive; infinitive mood
bezokoliczny [bez-o-ko-**leech**-ni] adj.m. infinitive (hist.)
bezopadowy [bez-o-pah-**do**-vi] adj.m. without precipitation (of rain, snow, etc.)
bezosobisty [bez-o-so-**bees**-ti] adj.m. impersonal; non-subjective
bezosobowo [bez-o-so-**bo**-vo] adv. impersonally

bezosobowość [bez-o-so-**bo**-vośhćh] f. impersonality
bezosobowy [bez-o-so-**bo**-vi] adj.m. impersonal
forma bezosobowa [**for**-mah bez-o-so-**bo**-vah] exp.: impersonal form
bezostny [bez-**ost**-ni] adj.m. awnless (wheat, etc.)
bezowocnie [bez-o-**vots**-ńe] adv. fruitlessly; in vain; unsuccessfully; to no end; to no purpose; without results; with no result; vainly
bezowocność [bez-o-**vots**-nośhćh] f. futility; fruitlessness; uselessness
bezowocny [bez-o-**vots**-ni] adj.m. futile; fruitless; vain; unfruitful; unsuccessful; abortive
bezowocowy [bez-o-vo-**tso**-vi] adj.m. producing no fruits; acarpous
bezowodniowiec [bez-o-vod-**ńo**-vyets] m. animal without fetal (foetal) membrane
bezowodniowce [bez-o-vod-**ńof**-tse] pl. animals without fetal (foetal) membrane
bezpamiętnie [bes-pah-**myant**-ńe] adv. passionately; desperately; madly; deliriously
bezpamiętny [bes-pah-**myant**-ni] adj.m. passionate; absent-minded; abstracted; delirious
bezpański [bes-**pahń**-skee] adj.m. ownerless; unowned; unclaimed; stray (dog, etc.); derelict (ship, etc.); nobody's
bezpański pies [bes-**pahń**-skee pyes] exp.: stray dog
ziemia bezpańska [**źhe**-myah bes-**pahń**-skah] exp.: no man's land
bezpańskość [bes-**pahń**-skośhćh] f. ownerless condition
bezpaństwowiec [bes-pahń-**stfo**-vyets] m. stateless person
bezpaństwowość [bes-pahń-**stfo**-vośhćh] f. statelessness
bezpaństwowy [bes-pahń-**stfo**-vi] adj.m. stateless
bezpańszczyźniany [bes-pahń-shchiźh-**ńah**-ni] adj.m. free of vassal's corvee; free of villein service; free of duty to perform unpaid labor
bezpardonowo [bes-pahr-do-**no**-vo] adv. pitilessly; mercilessly; ruthlessly; relentlessly
bezpardonowy [bes-pahr-do-**no**-vi] adj.m. pitiless; merciless; ruthless; relentless
bezpartyjnik [bes-pahr-**tiy**-ńeek] m. an independent; person with no party adherence (affiliation)
bezpartyjność [bes-pahr-**tiy**-nośhćh] f. non-party status; freedom of party adherence
bezpartyjny [bes-pahr-**tiy**-ni] adj.m. non-party; independent; m. person with no party affiliation
bezpestkowy [bes-pest-**ko**-vi] adj.m. stoneless (cherry, etc.); seedless (grapes, etc.)
bezpiecze [bes-**pye**-che] n. safe place
bezpieczeństwo [bes-pye-**cheń**-stfo] n. security; safety; safeness; protection
zawór (klapa) bezpieczeństwa [zah-voor (**klah**-pah) bes-pye-**cheń**-stfah] exp.: safety valve
środki bezpieczeństwa [**śrot**-kee bes-pye-**cheń**-stfah] exp.: precautionary measures; measures of precaution
Rada Bezpieczeństwa [**rah**-dah bes-pye-**cheń**-stfah] exp.: Security Council (UN)
bezpiecznie [bes-**pyech**-ńe] adv. safely; securely
bezpieczniak [bes-**pyech**-ńahk] m. slang: member of security forces
bezpiecznik [bes-**pyech**-ńeek] m. safety-cock; safety-tap; fuse; circuit breaker; safety valve
bezpiecznikowy [bes-pyech-ńee-**ko**-vi] adj.m. of a safety-cock; of a safety-tap; of a fuse; of a circuit breaker; of a safety valve
bezpieczny [bes-**pyech**-ni] adj.m. safe; secure; protected; sheltered; harmless
bezpieka [bes-**pye**-kah] f. slang: security forces
bezpieniężny [bes-pye-**ńan**-zhni] adj.m. moneyless; money-free
bezpieńka [bes-**pyeń**-kah] f. stemless tree seedling

bezpióry [bes-**pyoo**-ri] adj.m. unfledged; featherless
bezplanowo [bes-plah-**no**-vo] adv. withat a plan; haphazard
bezplanowość [bes-plah-**no**-vośhćh] f. absence of plan
bezplanowy [bes-plah-**no**-vi] adj.m. planless; haphazard; incoherent; chaotic; random
bezpłatkowy [bes-pwaht-**ko**-vi] adj.m. having no petals; apetalous
bezpłatnie [bes-**pwaht**-ńe] adv. free of charge; gratuitously; gratis
bezpłatność [bes-**pwaht**-nośhćh] f. free use (of education, etc.)
bezpłatny [bes-**pwaht**-ni] adj.m. free (ticket, instruction, etc.); gratuitous; cost-free; free of cost; complimentary; unpaid; unsalaried; rent-free; tax-free; postage-free
bezpłciowo [bes-**pwćho**-vo] adv. asexually (generated, etc.)
bezpłciowość [bes-**pwćho**-vośhćh] f. asexuality; sexlessness; featurelessness (of literary work)
bezpłciowy [bes-**pwćho**-vi] adj.m. asexual; sexless; neutral; insipid
bezpłodnie [bes-**pwod**-ńe] adv. barrenly; unproductively
bezpłodność [bes-**pwod**-nośhćh] f. sterility; barrenness; infertility; futility
bezpłodny [bes-**pwod**-ni] adj.m. sterile; ineffectual; barren; fruitless; unproductive; neuter; futile (efforts, etc.); academic (discussion, etc.)
bezpodmiotowo [bes-pod-myo-**to**-vo] adv. without subject (in a sentence, etc.)
bezpodmiotowy [bes-pod-myo-**to**-vi] adj.m. without subject; having no subject; infinite
bezpodstawnie [bes-pot-**stahv**-ńe] adv. groundlessly; baselessly; without reason; without cause
bezpodstawność [bes-pot-**stahv**-nośhćh] f. groundlessness; baselessness; idleness; flimsiness (of charges, etc.)
bezpodstawny [bes-pot-**stahv**-ni] adj.m. groundless; baseless; causeless; ungrounded; unfounded; unwarranted; idle (accusation, etc.); flimsy; without foundation
bezpopiołowy [bes-po-pyo-**wo**-vi] adj.m. cinderless
bezpostaciowość [bes-po-stah-**ćho**-vośhćh] f. amorphism; shapelessness
bezpostaciowy [bes-po-stah-**ćho**-vi] adj.m. amorphous; shapeless; formless; anomalous; uncrystallized (chemical, etc.)
bezpostojowy [bes-pos-to-**yo**-vi] adj.m. non-stop
bezpośredni [bes-po-**śhred**-ńee] adj.m. direct; immediate; straightforward; point-blank; frank; open; artless; close; nearest
bezpośrednia przyczyna [bes-po-**śhred**-ńah pshi-**chi**-nah] exp.: the direct cause; the immediate cause
bieg bezpośredni [byeg bes-po-**śhred**-ńee] exp.: direct gear
pociąg bezpośredni [po-ćhowng bes-po-**śhred**-ńee] exp.: through train
bezpośrednio [bes-po-**śhred**-ńo] adv. immediately; point-blank; directly; personally; in person
bezpośrednio po [bes-po-**śhred**-ńo po] exp.: immediately after
bezpośrednio przed [bes-po-**śhred**-ńo pshet] exp.: immediately before
bezpośredniość [bes-po-**śhred**-ńośhćh] f. directness; immediacy; direct contact; frankness; openness; artlessness
bezpotomnie [bes-po-**tom**-ńe] adv. without issue; without offspring
bezpotomny [bes-po-**tom**-ni] adj.m. heirless; issueless
bezpowietrznie [bes-po-**vyetsh**-ńe] adv. without air
bezpowietrzny [bes-po-**vyetsh**-ni] adj.m. airless
bezpowrotnie [bes-po-**vrot**-ńe] adv. irretrievably; beyond recall; irrevocably; never to return
bezpowrotny [bes-po-**vrot**-ni] adj.m. irretrievable; irredeemable; gone beyond return; irreparable
bezpożytecznie [bes-po-zhi-**tech**-ńe]

adv. unprofitably; profitlessly; uselessly
bezpożyteczny [bes-po-zhi-**tech**-ni] adj.m. unprofitable; profitless; useless
bezprawie [bes-**prah**-vye] n. chaos; lawlessness; illegal action; anarchy; abuse of authority; wrongdoing; wrongful act
bezprawnie [bes-**prahv**-ńe] adv. lawlessly; illegally; illicitly; by force; forcibly; wrongfully
bezprawność [bes-**prahv**-nośhćh] f. illegality; illicitness
bezprawny [bes-**prahv**-ni] adj.m. lawless; illegal; illicit; unlawful; forcible; wrongful
bezprecedensowy [bes-pre-tse-den-**so**-vi] adj.m. without precedent
bezprefiksalny [bes-pre-feek-**sahl**-ni] adj.m. without prefix
bezpretensjonalnie [bes-pre-ten-syo-**nahl**-ńe] adv. unpretentiously; unassumingly; without pretense (pretence); modestly; genuinely
bezpretensjonalność [bes-pre-ten-syo-**nahl**-nośhćh] f. unpretentiousness; unpretending disposition; unassuming disposition
bezpretensjonalny [bes-pre-ten-syo-**nahl**-ni] adj.m. unpretentious; unpretending; unassuming; of modest disposition; genuine; devoid of pretense (pretence)
bezproblemowo [bes-pro-ble-**mo**-vo] adv. problem-free
bezproblemowość [bes-pro-ble-**mo**-vośhćh] f. problem-free condition
bezproblemowy [bes-pro-ble-**mo**-vi] adj.m. free of problems; devoid of problems
bezprocentowo [bes-pro-tsen-**to**-vo] adv. free of interest
bezprocentowy [bes-pro-tsen-**to**-vi] adj.m. without interest; bearing no interest
bezprodukcyjnie [bes-pro-dook-**tsiy**-ńe] adv. unproductively; unprofitably
bezprodukcyjny [bes-pro-dook-**tsiy**-ni] adj.m. unproductive; unprofitable
bezproduktywnie [bes-pro-dook-**tiv**-ńe] adv. unproductively; unprofitably
bezproduktywny [bes-pro-dook-**tiv**-ni] adj.m. unproductive; unprofitable
bezprogramowość [bes-pro-grah-**mo**-vośhćh] f. lack of program; lack of plan; casualness; off-handedness
bezprogramowy [bes-pro-grah-**mo**-vi] adj.m. with no program; unplanned; casual; off-hand
bezpromienny [bes-pro-**myen**-ni] adj.m. rayless; emitting no rays
bezprzedmiotowo [bes-pshed-myo-**to**-vo] adv. aimlessly; to no purpose; uselessly; without definite purpose
bezprzedmiotowość [bes-pshed-myo-**to**-vośhćh] f. aimlessness
bezprzedmiotowy [bes-pshed-myo-**to**-vi] adj.m. aimless; useless; objectless
bezprzedrostkowy [bes-pshed-rost-**ko**-vi] adj.m. without prefix
bezprzestankowy [bes-pshes-tahn-**ko**-vi] adj.m. incessantly; without intermission; without stopping; ceaseless; endless; unending; continual; for ever; perpetual; never ending
bezprzestanny [bes-pshes-**tahn**-ni] adj.m. incessant; without intermission; without stopping; ceaseless; endless; unending; continual; for ever; perpetual; never ending
bezprzewodowy [bes-pshe-vo-**do**-vi] adj.m. wireless (communication, transmission, etc.)
bezprzyciskowy [bes-pshi-ćhees-**ko**-vi] adj.m. without accent; unstressed; unaccented
bezprzyczynowość [bes-pshi-chi-**no**-vośhćh] f. groundlessness; baselessness; lack of foundation
bezprzyczynowy [bes-pshi-chi-**no**-vi] adj.m. groundless; baseless; unfounded
bezprzykładnie [bes-pshi-**kwahd**-ńe] adv. exceptionally; without precedent; uncommonly
bezprzykładny [bes-pshi-**kwahd**-ni] adj.m. unprecedented;

unparalleled; unheard of; exceptional; uncommon; without precedent
bezprzyrostkowy [bes-pshi-ro-**stko**-vi] adj.m. without suffix
bezprzytomnie [bes-pshi-**tom**-ńe] adv. unconsciously; haggardly; vacantly; absent-mindedly; frantically; franticly; madly
bezprzytomność [bes-pshi-**tom**-nośhćh] f. unconsciousness; haggardness; vacancy; absent-mindedness; frenzy; listlessness
bezprzytomny [bes-pshi-**tom**-ni] adj.m. unconscious; haggard; vacant; absent-minded; frantic; mad
bezpylny [bes-**pil**-ni] adj.m. dust-free
bezpyłowy [bes-pi-**wo**-vi] adj.m. dust-free
bezradnie [bez-**rahd**-ńe] adv. helplessly
bezradnieć [bez-**rahd**-ńećh] v. become helpless; grow shiftless; become resourceless (*repeatedly*)
bezradność [bez-**rahd**-nośhćh] f. helplessness; perplexity
bezradny [bez-**rahd**-ni] adj.m. helpless; baffled; at a loss; resourceless; at one's wit's end; shiftless
bezradosny [bez-rah-**dos**-ni] adj.m. joyless
bezrdzeniowy [bez-rdze-**ńo**-vi] adj.m. spineless
bezrdzenny [bez-**rdzen**-ni] adj.m. without core
bezrękawnik [bez-ran-**kahv**-ńeek] m. sleeveless jacket; vest; jumper
bezręki [bez-**ran**-kee] adj.m. armless; handless (cripple)
bezrobocie [bez-ro-**bo**-ćhe] n. unemployment
bezrobotny [bez-ro-**bo**-tni] adj.m. unemployed; out of work; m. an unemployed
bezrobotni [bez-ro-**bo**-tńee] pl. the unemployed
zasiłek dla bezrobotnych [zah-**śhee**-wek dlah bez-ro-**bo**-tnikh] exp.: unemployment compensation
bezrogi [bez-**ro**-gee] adj.m. hornless
bezrolność [bez-**rol**-nośhćh] f. lack of farmland
bezrolny [bez-**rol**-ni] adj.m. landless; with no land; m. dispossessed farmer; man without farmland of his own
bezrozumnie [bez-ro-**zoom**-ńe] adv. madly; crazily; senselessly; like one demented
bezrozumny [bez-ro-**zoom**-ni] adj.m. bereft of reason; mad; crazy; senseless; demented
bezrożny [bez-**rozh**-ni] adj.m. hornless; colloq: without corners
bezrtęciowy [bes-rtan-**ćho**-vi] adj.m. without mercury
bezruch [**bez**-rookh] m. immobility; standstill; stagnation; inertness; quiescence; akinesia; absence of motion in a muscle
w bezruchu [v bez-**roo**-khoo] exp.: at a standstill
bezrunny [bez-**roon**-ni] adj.m. without fleece
bezrybie [bez-**ri**-bye] n. lack of fish
na bezrybiu i rak ryba [nah bez-**ri**-byoo ee rahk **ri**-bah] exp.: half a loaf is better than no bread; any port is good in a storm; do the best you can
bezrybny [bez-**rib**-ni] adj.m. lacking of fish; deprived of fish
bezrymny [bez-**rim**-ni] adj.m. lacking of rhyme; unrhymed (verse)
bezrymowość [bez-ri-mo-**vośhćh**] f. lack of rhyme; unrhymed manner
bezrymowy [bez-ri-**mo**-vi] adj.m. lacking rhyme; unrhymed (verse); without rhyme
bezrząd [**bez**-zhownt] m. absence of authority; lack of government; anarchy; chaos
bezrzęsy [bez-**zhan**-si] adj.m. without eyelashes
bezsennie [bes-**sen**-ńe] adv. sleeplessly; without sleep
bezsenność [bes-**sen**-nośhćh] f. sleeplessness; insomnia; wakefulness
bezsenny [bes-**sen**-ni] adj.m. sleepless; restless; wakeful
bezsens [**bes**-sens] m. nonsense
bezsensownie [bes-sen-**sov**-ńe] adv. absurdly; nonsensically

bezsensowność [bes-sen-**sov**-nośhćh] f. absurdity; nonsense; preposterousness; senselessness; stupidity; emptiness (of words, etc.); lack of sense
bezsensowny [bes-sen-**sov**-ni] adj.m. absurd; nonsensical; wanton (destruction, etc.) preposterous; senseless; stupid; incongruous; insensate; vacuous
bezsensowy [bes-sen-**so**-vi] adj.m. absurd; nonsensical; preposterous; senseless; stupid; incongruous; insensate; vacuous
bezsercowy [bes-ser-**tso**-vi] adj.m. acardiac; without a heart
bezsęczny [bes-**sanch**-ni] adj.m. without knots; without knars
bezsęki [bes-**san**-kee] adj.m. without knots; without knars
bezsękowy [bes-san-**ko**-vi] adj.m. without knots; without knars
bezsilnie [bes-**śheel**-ńe] adv. powerlessly; weakly; helplessly
bezsilnikowiec [bes-śheel-ńee-**ko**-vyets] m. glider; motorless plane
bezsilnikowy [bes-śheel-ńee-**ko**-vi] adj.m. motorless
bezsilność [bes-**śheel**-nośhćh] f. impotence; lack of strength; weakness; helplessness
bezsilny [bes-**śheel**-ni] adj.m. powerless; weak; helpless; without strength; forceless; impotent
bezsiła [bes-**śhee**-wah] f. impotence; lack of strength; weakness; helplessness
bezskorupowy [bes-sko-roo-**po**-vi] adj.m. shell-less
bezskrzydlaty [bes-skshi-**dlah**-ti] adj.m. wingless; apterous
bezskrzydły [bes-**skshi**-dwi] adj.m. wingless; apterous
bezskutecznie [bes-skoo-**tech**-ńe] adv. ineffectively; in vain; without success; vainly; without result; to no purpose; unsuccessfully
bezskuteczność [bes-skoo-**tech**-nośhćh] f. inefficiency; futility
bezskuteczny [bes-skoo-**tech**-ni] adj.m. to no avail; futile; ineffective; nugatory; inefficient; unavailing; slang: no good
bezsławny [bes-**swahv**-ni] adj.m. inglorious; unglorious
bezsłoneczny [bes-swo-**nech**-ni] adj.m. sunless
bezsłownie [bes-**swov**-ńe] adv. wordlessly
bezsłowny [bes-**swov**-ni] adj.m. wordless
bezsmak [**bes**-smahk] m. lack of taste
bezsmarowy [bes-smah-**ro**-vi] adj.m. greaseless
bezsoczność [bes-**soch**-nośhćh] f. achylia (deficiency of secretion of acids in the stomach)
bezsolny [bes-**sol**-ni] adj.m. saltless; insipid; salt free (diet, etc.)
bezspornie [bes-**spor**-ńe] adv. admittedly; undeniably; beyond dispute; clearly; unquestionably; indisputably; incontestably
bezsporność [bes-**spor**-nośhćh] f. incontestability; indisputability
bezsporny [bes-**spor**-ni] adj.m. beyond controversy; clear; incontestable; undebatable; unquestionable; beyond dispute
bezspójnikowy [bes-spooy-ńee-**ko**-vi] adj.m. not joined by a conjunction; asyndic
bezsprężarkowy [bes-spran-zhahr-**ko**-vi] adj.m. airless-injection (engine, etc.); without air-compressor (operation, etc.)
bezsprzecznie [bes-**spshech**-ńe] adv. indisputably; evidently; undeniably; admittedly
bezsprzeczność [bes-**spshech**-nośhćh] f. indisputability; incontestability
bezsprzeczny [bes-**spshech**-ni] adj.m. indisputable; self-evident; irrefutable; beyond dispute
bezstanowy [bes-stah-**no**-vi] adj.m. classless (society, etc.); without distinction of rank
bezstawowy [bes-stah-**vo**-vi] adj.m. jointless; without joints; anarthrous
bezstopniowy [bes-stop-**ńo**-vi] adj.m. smoothly working; conic-gear (transmission, etc.) **przekładnia bezstopniowa** [pshe-**kwahd**-ńah bes-stop-**ńo**-vah]

exp.: conic-gear transmission
bezstronnie [bes-**stron**-ńe] adv. impartially; dispassionately; fairly; in all fairness; without prejudice; without bias; disinterestedly; without fear or favor
bezstronność [bes-**stron**-nośhćh] f. impartiality; fairness; open-mindedness; candor
bezstronny [bes-**stron**-ni] adj.m. impartial; dispassionate; fair-minded; candid; unbiased; even-handed; open-minded; neutral
bezstykowy [bes-sti-**ko**-vi] adj.m. jointless; not touching
bezstylowy [bes-sti-**lo**-vi] adj.m. devoid of style; without style
bezszczękowy [bes-shchan-**ko**-vi] adj.m. jawless
bezszelestnie [bes-she-**lest**-ńe] adv. noiselessly; without a sound
bezszelestny [bes-she-**lest**-ni] adj.m. noiseless; silent; still
bezszkieletowy [bes-shke-le-**to**-vi] adj.m. frameless (building, etc.)
bezszkolny [bes-**shkol**-ni] adj.m. without a school
bezszmerowo [bes-shme-**ro**-vo] adv. noiselessly; silently
bezszmerowy [bes-shme-**ro**-vi] adj.m. noiseless; silent
bezsznurowy [bes-shnoo-**ro**-vi] adj.m. wireless
bezszumowy [bes-shoo-**mo**-vi] adj.m. noiseless; silent
bezszumnie [bes-**shoom**-ńe] adv. noiselessly; silently
bezszumny [bes-**shoom**-ni] adj.m. noiseless; silent (motor, etc.)
bezszwowo [bes-**shfo**-vo] adv. without seams; without welds
bezszwowy [bes-**shfo**-vi] adj.m. seamless; weldless
bezszyjkowy [bes-shiy-**ko**-vi] adj.m. styleless; without a neck
bezszynowy [bes-shi-**no**-vi] adj.m. trackless
bezśnieżnie [bes-**śhńezh**-ńe] adv. without snow
bezśnieżny [bes-**śhńezh**-ni] adj.m. without snow
bezśpiewny [bes-**śhpyev**-ni] adj.m. songless
bezśrednikowy [bes-śhred-ńee-**ko**-vi] adj.m. without semicolons
bezświadomy [bes-śhfyah-**do**-mi] adj.m. unaware; ignorant; involuntary; unconscious
bezświetlny [bes-**śhfyetl**-ni] adj.m. unlit; without light
beztalencie [bes-tah-**len**-ćhe] n. lack of talent; talentless person
beztematyczny [bes-te-mah-**tich**-ni] adj.m. devoid of a theme; without a theme
bezterminowo [bes-ter-mee-**no**-vo] adv. without time-limit; with no date fixed; with no term stated; of unlimited duration; in (for, to) perpetuity
bezterminowy [bes-ter-mee-**no**-vi] adj.m. termless; without time-limit; with no date fixed; with no term stated; of unlimited duration; in (for, to) perpetuity
beztestamentowy [bes-tes-tah-men-**to**-vi] adj.m. without a testament
beztlenowiec [bes-tle-**no**-vyets] m. anaerobe (organism able to live without oxygen)
beztlenowy [bes-tle-**no**-vi] adj.m. anaerobic (reaction, etc.)
beztłuszczowy [bes-twoosh-**cho**-vi] adj.m. fatless; devoid of fat
beztreściowy [bes-treśh-**ćho**-vi] adj.m. void of substance; empty; insipid; vapid; making no sense
beztreściwie [bes-treśh-**ćhee**-vye] adv. emptily; without nutritive elements; insipidly; vapidly
beztreściwy [bes-treśh-**ćhee**-vi] adj.m. containing no nutritive elements; not nutritive; void of substance; empty; insipid; vapid; making no sense
beztroska [bes-**tros**-kah] f. unconcern; light-heartedness; jauntiness; absence of cares; carelessness; don't care attitude
beztroski [bes-**tros**-kee] adj.m. carefree; careless; jaunty; happy-go-lucky; devil-may-care; airy; indifferent
beztrosko [bes-**tros**-ko] adv. light-heartedly; jauntily; airily; carelessly; with unconcern
beztrwożnie [bes-**trfozh**-ńe] adv. fearlessly

bezuchy [bez-**oo**-khi] adj.m. without an ear; without ears
bezuczuciowość [bez-oo-choo-**ćho**-vośhćh] f. insensibility; lack of feeling
bez ustanku [bez oo-**stahn**-koo] adv. incessantly; without intermission; without stopping; ceaselessly; endlessly; unendingly; continually; for ever; perpetually
bezustannie [bez-oo-**stahn**-ńe] adv. incessantly; without intermission; ceaselessly; endlessly; unendingly; continually; for ever; perpetually
bezustanny [bez-oo-**stahn**-ni] adj.m. ceaseless; endless; unending; continual; for ever; perpetual; everlasting; uninterrupted
bezusterkowo [bez-oo-ster-**ko**-vo] adv. faultlessly; flawlessly
bezusterkowy [bez-oo-ster-**ko**-vi] adj.m. faultless; flawless
bezustnikowy [bez-oost-ńee-**ko**-vi] adj.m. without mouthpiece
bezużytecznie [bez-oo-zhi-**tech**-ńe] adv. uselessly; idly; unnecessarily
bezużyteczność [bez-oo-zhi-**tech**-nośhćh] f. uselessness; inutility
bezużyteczny [bez-oo-zhi-**tech**-ni] adj.m. useless; idle; unprofitable; unnecessary; unserviceable
bezwapienny [bez-vah-**pyen**-ni] adj.m. decalcified
bezwargowy [bez-vahr-**go**-vi] adj.m. without lips; achilous
bezwartościowość [bez-vahr-to-**śhćho**-vośhćh] f. worthlessness; trashiness; lack of artistic value
bezwartościowo [bez-vahr-to-**śhćho**-vo] adv. worthlessly
bezwartościowy [bez-vahr-to-**śhćho**-vi] adj.m. worthless; of no value; measly; trashy; drossy; of no artistic value
bezwarunkowo [bez-vah-roon-**ko**-vo] adv. unconditionally; absolutely; utterly; without qualification; implicitly
bezwarunkowy [bez-vah-roon-**ko**-vi] adj.m. unconditional; utter; absolute; complete; implicit
bezwąsy [bez-v<u>own</u>-si] adj.m. without moustache
bezwęzełkowy [bez-v<u>an</u>-zew-**ko**-vi] adj.m. without burls
bezwęzłowy [bez-w<u>an</u>z-**wo**-vi] adj.m. without knots
bezwibracyjny [bez-vee-brah-**tsiy**-ni] adj.m. vibrationless; without vibration
bezwiednie [bez-**vye**-dńe] adv. unknowingly; involuntarily; unconsciously; automatically; mechanically; unintentionally; unwittingly; unawares
bezwiedny [bez-**vye**-dni] adj.m. unknowing; unconscious; involuntary; automatic; mechanical; unintentional; unwitting
bezwietrznie [bez-**vyetsh**-ńe] adv. without wind
bezwietrzny [bez-**vyetsh**-ni] adj.m. windless; airless
bezwitaminowy [bez-vee-tah-mee-**no**-vi] adj.m. devoid of vitamins
bezwiórowo [bez-vyoo-**ro**-vo] adv. without shavings
bezwiórowy [bez-vyoo-**ro**-vi] adj.m. without shavings (or cuttings)
bezwizowy [bez-vee-**zo**-vi] adj.m. not requiring an entry visa; having no visa; lacking entry visa; without visa
bezwład [**bez**-vwaht] m. inertia; inertness; torpor; torpidity; palsy; decline; paralysis
bezwładnie [bez-**vwah**-dńe] adv. inertly; torpidly
bezwładnościowy [bez-vwahd-no-**śhćho**-vi] adj.m. inertial
bezwładność [bez-**vwahd**-nośhćh] f. inertia; torpor; decline; palsy; inertness
siła bezwładności [**śhee**-wah bez-vwahd-**nośh**-ćhee] exp.: force of inertia
bezwładny [bez-**vwahd**-ni] adj.m. inert; disable; palsied; in a decline; torpid
bezwłasnościowy [bez-vwah-sno-**śhćho**-vi] adj.m. devoid of property
bezwłasnowolny [bez-vwah-sno-**vol**-ni] adj.m. legally incapable; with no will of one's own; automatic
bezwłosowy [bez-vwo-**so**-vi] adj.m.

hairless; free from hair; smooth-skinned
bezwłosy [bez-**vwo**-si] adj.m. hairless; free from hair; smooth-skinned
bezwłókniasty [bez-vwook-**ńahs**-ti] adj.m. fiberless
bezwłóknisty [bez-vwook-**ńees**-ti] adj.m. fiberless
bezwodnik [bez-**vod**-ńeek] m. anhydride
bezwodny [bez-**vod**-ni] adj.m. waterless; without water; anhydrous; dry; exsiccated
bezwodzie [bez-**vo**-dźhe] n. waterless region; waterless tract
bezwodzikowy [bez-vo-dźhee-**ko**-vi] adj.m. of piston rod made of a pipe
bezwola [bez-**vo**-lah] f. indifference; lack of volition
bezwolnie [bez-**vol**-ńe] adv. involuntarily; passively; undecidedly; inertly; resignedly; with resignation; with abandon; without will power; unresisting
bezwolność [bez-**vol**-nośhćh] f. passivity; inertia; torpidity
bezwolny [bez-**vol**-ni] adj.m. involuntary; passive; undecided; inert; volitionless; torpid
bezwonnie [bez-**von**-ńe] adv. without odor; without scent
bezwonność [bez-**von**-nośhćh] f. lack of odor; absence of scent
bezwonny [bez-**von**-ni] adj.m. without odor; fragrance free; scentless; emitting no scent
bezwrażliwy [bez-vrah-**zhlee**-vi] adj.m. insensible (to, of); insensitive (to)
bezwrzecionowy [bez-vzhe-ćho-**no**-vi] adj.m. having no spindle
bezwstyd [**bes**-fstit] m. impudence; shamelessness; brazenness; effrontery; lewdness; immodesty; unchastity; licentiousness; debauchery; meretriciousness; audacity; hardihood
bezwstydnica [bes-fstid-**ńee**-tsah] f. impudent woman; shameless woman; lewd woman; licentious woman; profligate; strumpet
bezwstydnie [bes-**fstid**-ńe] adv. impudently; shamelessly; brazenly; immodestly; lewdly
bezwstydnik [bes-**fstid**-ńeek] m. impudent person; shameless man; lewd man; licentious man; profligate
bezwstydność [bes-**fstid**-nośhćh] f. impudence; shamelessness; brazenness; lewdness; immodesty
bezwstydny [bes-**fstid**-ni] adj.m. shameless; lewd; flagrant; impudent; shamelessly; brazen; immodest; unchaste; rank; flagrant; glaring
bezwyjątkowo [bez-vi-yown-**tko**-vo] adv. without exception
bezwyjątkowy [bez-vi-yown-**tko**-vi] adj.m. without exception; having no exception; exceptionless; absolute
bezwyjściowy [bez-viy-**śhćho**-vi] adj.m. without exit; with no way out; hopeless
bezwymiarowy [bez-vi-myah-**ro**-vi] adj.m. dimensionless; not dimensional
bezwymienny [bez-vi-**myen**-ni] adj.m. exchangeless; not exchangeable
bezwyrazowy [bez-vi-rah-**zo**-vi] adj.m. expressionless; devoid of expression
bez wyrazu [bez vi-**rah**-zoo] adv. devoid of expression; expressionless(ly)
bezwyznaniowiec [bez-vi-znah-**ńo**-vyets] m. person without denomination; unbeliever; irreligious man
bezwyznaniowo [bez-vi-znah-**ńo**-vo] adv. without denomination
bezwyznaniowy [bez-vi-znah-**ńo**-vi] adj.m. nonsectarian; undenominational; non-religious
bezwzględnie [bez-**vzgland**-ńe] adv. ruthlessly; cruelly; despotically; utterly; with utmost severity; with an iron hand; without fail; without reserve; completely; without exception; positively; certainly; implicitly; arbitrarily **to jest bezwzględnie pewne** [to yest bez-**vzgland**-ńe **pev**-ne] exp.: it's a dead certainty (dead sure)

bezwzględnie warto [bez-**vzgland**-ńe **vahr**-to] exp.: certainly worthwhile; (it was) well worthwhile

bezwzględność [bez-**vzgland**-nośhćh] f. absoluteness; peremptoriness; positiveness; relentlessness; high-handed conduct; severity; completeness; tyrannical nature

bezwzględny [bez-**vzgland**-ni] adj.m. ruthless; despotic; severe; tyrannical; high-handed; utter; complete; unreserved; absolute; positive; implicit; emphatic
bezwzględna temperatura [bez-**vzgland**-nah tem-pe-rah-**too**-rah] exp.: absolute temperature
zero bezwzględne [**ze**-ro bez-**vzgland**-ne] exp.: absolute zero

bezwzrokowy [bez-vzro-**ko**-vi] adj.m. blind; sightless

bezzałogowy [bez-zah-wo-**go**-vi] adj.m. (operated, etc.) without a crew

bezzasadnie [bez-zah-**sah**-dńe] adv. without foundation

bezzasadność [bez-zah-**sah**-dnośhćh] f. groundlessness; lack of foundation (motivation)

bezzasadny [bez-zah-**sah**-dni] adj.m. baseless; groundless; unfounded; unwarranted; ungrounded

bezzawiasowce [bez-zah-vyah-**sof**-tse] pl. the inarticulate animals (lacking shell-hinge); the brachiopods; brachiopodans; brachiopodous animals

bezzaworowy [bez-zah-vo-**ro**-vi] adj.m. valveless

bezzębie [bez-**zan**-bye] n. lack of teeth (caused by a disease, old age, etc.)

bezzębny [bez-**zanb**-ni] adj.m. toothless; edentate

bezznaczeniowy [bez-znah-che-**ńo**-vi] adj.m. meaningless; not semantic

bezzwłocznie [bez-**zvwoch**-ńe] adv. immediately; instantly; without delay; right away; straight away; promptly; speedily; at once

bezzwłoczny [bez-**zvwoch**-ni] adj.m. immediate; prompt; speedy; hasty; without delay; not delayed

bezzwrotnie [bez-**zvrot**-ńe] adv. not to be reclaimed; not to be returned; not to be repaid

bezzwrotny [bez-**zvrot**-ni] adj.m. not to be refunded; not returnable; not repayable

bezżennie [bez-**zhen**-ńe] adv. in celibacy
umrzeć bezżennie [**oom**-zhećh bez-**zhen**-ńe] exp.: to die unmarried (single)
żyć bezżennie [zhićh bez-**zhen**-ńe] exp.: to live unmarried

bezżenność [bez-**zhen**-nośhćh] f. bachelorhood; singleness; celibacy; the single state

bezżenny [bez-**zhen**-ni] adj.m. celibate; single; unmarried; m. bachelor

bezżeństwo [bez-**zheń**-stfo] n. celibacy

bezżuchwowiec [bez-zhookh-**fo**-vyets] m. animal without mandible; jawless animal

beż [besh] m. beige

beżowy [be-**zho**-vi] adj.m. beige

bęben [**ban**-ben] m. drum; side-drum; tom-tom; barrel; cylinder; tumbler; tumbling-wheel; fusee (in a watch); tambour; colloq: kid; kiddie; brat; tot

bębenek [ban-**be**-nek] m. tambourine; tympanum; eardrum

bębenkowiec [ban-ben-**ko**-vyets] m. revolver; gun with a revolving cylinder

bębenkowy [ban-ben-**ko**-vi] adj.m. drum (membrane, etc.); tympanic; barrel (shape); of a cylinder; equipped with a little drum
błona bębenkowa [**bwo**-nah ban-ben-**ko**-vah] exp.: tympanic membrane inside the ear, that vibrates when struck by sound waves; ear-drum

bębnica [banb-**ńee**-tsah] f. flatulence; tympanites; meteorism

bębnić [**banb**-bńeećh] v. beat the drum; thump; rattle; rataplan; tattoo; pelt; patter; go pit-a-pat; rattle off (lessons) (*repeatedly*)
bębnić na alarm [**ban**-bńeećh nah **ah**-lahrm] exp.: to sound the alarm

bębnić na odwrót [ban-bńeećh nah **od**-vroot] exp.: to sound a retreat
bębnić w drzwi [ban-bńeećh v dzhvee] exp.: to batter at the door
bębnienie [banb-**ńe**-ńe] n. sounding the alarm
bębnować [banb-**no**-vahćh] v. tumble (castings); polish (castings) in a tumbling box (*repeatedly*)
bębnowanie [banb-no-**vah**-ńe] n. tumbling (castings); polishing (castings) in a tumbling box
bębnowy [banb-**no**-vi] adj.m. equipped with a drum
bęc [bants] interjection: bounce!; flop!; bang!; smack!; plunk!
bęcnąć [**bants**-nownćh] v. flop down; come down with a smack; bang against; drop down
bęcwał [**bants**-fahw] m. nincompoop; dullard; jolt-head; dolt
bękarci [ban-**kahr**-ćhee] adj.m. bastard (birth, etc.); of illegitimate birth; inferior; sham
bękarcie szczęście [ban-**kahr**-ćhe shchanśh-ćhe] exp.: the devils own luck
bękarcieć [ban-**kahr**-ćhećh] v. degenerate (*repeatedly*)
bękart [ban-kahrt] m. colloq: bastard
biada [**byah**-dah] excl.: woe!
biada ci! [**byah**-dah ćhee] exp.: you will be sorry!
biadać [**byah**-dahćh] v. moan (for, over); complain; lament; whine; slang: bellyache (*repeatedly*)
biadanie [byah-**dah**-ńe] n. lamentations; complaints
biadolenie [byah-do-**le**-ńe] n. lamentations; complaints; whimpering; whining; snivelling; squeals; squealing
biadolić [byah-**do**-leećh] v. complain; whimper; whine; snivel; squeal (*repeatedly*)
bialuchny [byah-**lookh**-ni] adj.m. very white
bialuteńki [byah-loo-**teń**-kee] adj.m. very nicely white
bialutki [byah-**loot**-kee] adj.m. perfectly white; beautifully white; as white as snow
białaczka [byah-**wahch**-kah] f. leukemia; leukaemia
białaczkowy [byah-wahch-**ko**-vi] adj.m. leukemia (symptoms, etc.)
białawo [byah-**wah**-vo] adv. whitishly; in shade of white; in whitish color
białawy [byah-**wah**-vi] adj.m. whitish
białko [**byahw**-ko] n. egg white; protein; white of the eye; the white of an egg; glair; albumen; albumin
reakcja na białko [re-**ahk**-tsyah nah **byahw**-ko] exp.: protein test
białkomocz [byahw-**ko**-moch] m. albuminuria; albumin in the urine
białkować [byahw-**ko**-vahćh] v. whitewash (*repeatedly*)
białkowanie [byahw-ko-**vah**-ńe] n. whitewashing
białkowaty [byahw-ko-**vah**-ti] adj.m. proteinaceous; albuminoidal
białkowość [byahw-**ko**-vośhćh] f. protein content
białkowy [byahw-**ko**-vi] adj.m. glairy; albuminous; proteinaceous; protein (rich, free, etc.)
białkówka [byahw-**koof**-kah] f. white of the eye
biało [**byah**-wo] adv. in white
biało ubrany [**byah**-wo oo-**brah**-ni] exp.: dressed in white
biało-czerwony [**byah**-wo cher-**vo**-ni] exp.: white-red (Polish flag, etc.)
białobrody [byah-wo-**bro**-di] adj.m. white-bearded
białodrzew [byah-**wo**-dzhef] m. white poplar; abele
białogłowa [byah-wo-**gwo**-vah] adj. f. white-haired (woman); f. woman; the fair sex
białogłowy [byah-wo-**gwo**-vi] adj.m. white-haired (man)
białogon [byah-**wo**-gon] m. erne; golden eagle; sea eagle; wheatear
białogrzbiety [byah-wo-**gzhbye**-ti] adj.m. (cattle) having white stripe along the spine
białogrzywy [byah-wo-**gzhi**-vi] adj.m. white-maned

białogwardyjski [byah-wo-gvahr-**diy**-skee] adj.m. White Guardist
białogwardzista [byah-wo-gvahr-**dźhees**-tah] m. soldier of the White Guard (organized in Russia in 1917)
białokory [byah-wo-**ko**-ri] adj.m. white-bark (birch, etc.)
białolicy [byah-wo-**lee**-tsi] adj.m. white-complexioned
Białorusin [biah-wo-**roo**-śheen] m. Byelorussian; Belorussian
białoruski [byah-wo-**roos**-kee] adj.m. Byelorussian; Belorus (state, etc.)
białorusycyzm [byah-wo-roo-**si**-tsizm] m. borrowing from Belorus language
białoruszczyzna [byah-wo-roosh-**chiz**-nah] f. the language of Belorus; Belorus culture
białoryb [byah-**wo**-rip] m. whitefish
białorzęsy [byah-wo-**zhan**-si] adj.m. having albino eyelashes; having white eyelashes
białorzytka [byah-wo-**zhit**-kah] f. variety of thrush (bird)
białosęp [byah-**wo**-sanp] m. white vulture
białoskórnictwo [byah-wo-skoor-**ńeets**-tfo] n. soft-leather industry; tawery
białoskórniczy [byah-wo-skoor-**ńee**-chi] adj.m. of soft leather (for gloves, etc.); tawer's (craft, etc.); of a dresser of white leather
białoskórnik [byah-wo-**skoor**-ńeek] m. soft-leather worker (merchant); tawer
białoskóry [byah-wo-**skoo**-ri] adj.m. white-skinned; m. white man
białoskrzydły [byah-wo-**skshid**-wi] adj.m. white-winged
białosz [**byah**-wosh] m. white horse; white stone
białoszyi [byah-wo-**shi**-yee] adj.m. white-necked
białościenny [byah-wo-**śhćhen**-ni] adj.m. white-walled
białość [**byah**-wośhćh] f. whiteness
rozpalony do białości [ros-pah-**lo**-ni do byah-**wośh**-ćhee] exp.: white-hot
białowłosy [byah-wo-**vwo**-si] adj.m. white-haired
białozór [byah-**wo**-zoor] m. gerafalcon
biały [**byah**-wi] adj.m. white; fair (skinned, etc.); pure; chaste; reactionary (politician, etc.); retrograde; m. white man
biała broń [**byah**-wah broń] exp.: side arms; cutting weapons
biały dzień [**byah**-wi dźheń] exp.: broad daylight
biały wiersz [**byah**-wi vyersh] exp.: blank verse
czarno na białym [**chahr**-no nah **byah**-wim] exp.: in black and white; black and white
do białego rana [do byah-**we**-go **rah**-nah] exp.: till dawn; till daylight
biandria [bee-**ahn**-dryah] f. second marriage by a woman not divorced from her first husband
biatlon [**byah**-tlon] m. biathlon (cross country skiing and sharpshooting competition)
biatlonista [byah-tlo-**ńees**-tah] m. competitor in biathlon
biatlonowy [byah-tlo-**no**-vi] adj.m. biatholon (competition, etc.)
biba [**bee**-bah] f. drinking spree; razzle-dazzle; carousal
bibelot [bee-**be**-lot] m. trinket; knick-knack
bibka [**bee**-pkah] f. (small) drinking spree; razzle-dazzle; carousal
Biblia [**beeb**-lyah] f. Bible; colloq: the gospel
biblijnie [bee-**bleey**-ńe] adv. biblically; scripturally
biblijny [bee-**bleey**-ni] adj.m. biblical
bibliobus [bee-**blyo**-boos] m. mobile-library bus
bibliofag [bee-**blyo**-fahg] m. bibliophagic insect (worm); book-devouring animal
bibliofil [bee-**blyo**-feel] m. bibliophile
bibliofilski [bee-blyo-**feel**-skee] adj.m. bibliophilic
bibliofilstwo [bee-blyo-**feel**-stfo] n. bibliophilism; love of books
bibliograf [bee-**blyo**-grahf] m. bibliographer
bibliografia [bee-blyo-**grah**-fyah] f. bibliography

bibliograficznie [bee-blyo-grah-**feech**-ńe] adv. bibliographically
bibliograficzny [bee-blyo-grah-**feech**-ni] adj.m. bibliographic
bibliografka [bee-blyo-**grahf**-kah] f. (woman) bibliographer
bibliolog [bee-**blyo**-log] m. bibliologist
bibliologia [bee-blyo-**lo**-gyah] f. bibliology
bibliologiczny [bee-blyo-lo-**geech**-ni] adj.m. of bibliology; bibliologic
biblioman [bee-**blyo**-mahn] m. bibliomaniac; bibliomane
bibliomania [bee-blyo-**mahń**-yah] f. extreme preoccupation with collecting books; bibliomania
bibliomanka [bee-blyo-**mahn**-kah] f. (female) bibliomaniac; bibliomane
biblioteczka [bee-blyo-**tech**-kah] f. small library; bookcase
biblioteczny [bee-blyo-**tech**-ni] adj.m. library (building, edition, etc.)
biblioteka [bee-blyo-**te**-kah] f. library; bookcase; book series
  biblioteka podręczna [bee-blyo-**te**-kah pod-**ranch**-nah] exp.: reference library
bibliotekarka [bee-blyo-te-**kahr**-kah] f. (woman) librarian
bibliotekarski [bee-blyo-te-**kahr**-skee] adj.m. librarian's
bibliotekarstwo [bee-blyo-te-**kahr**-stfo] n. library science; library management (administration)
bibliotekarz [bee-blyo-**te**-kahsh] m. (man) librarian
bibliotekarzować [bee-blyo-te-kah-**zho**-vahćh] v. colloq: run a library (*repeatedly*)
bibliotekoznawca [bee-blyo-te-ko-**znahf**-tsah] m. library specialist
bibliotekoznawczy [bee-blyo-te-ko-**znahf**-chi] adj.m. of library science
bibliotekoznawstwo [bee-blyo-te-ko-**znahf**-stfo] n. library science
bibliowóz [bee-**blyo**-voos] m. mobile library bus
biblioznawczy [bee-blyo-**znahf**-chi] adj.m. of library science
biblista [bee-**blees**-tah] m. student of the Bible; Biblicist
biblistyka [bee-**blees**-ti-kah] f. study of the Bible
biblot [**beeb**-lot] m. trinket; knick-knack
bibosz [**bee**-bosh] m. bibber; one addicted to drinking; tipper
bibrety [beeb-**re**-ti] pl. dyed rabbit furs
bibularz [bee-**boo**-lahsh] m. blotting-pad; writing pad
bibulasty [bee-boo-**lahs**-ti] adj.m. spongy; absorbent
bibuła [bee-**boo**-wah] f. blotting paper; illegal political publication; literary trash (garbage)
bibułka [bee-**boow**-kah] f. cigarette paper; sheet of blotting paper
bibułkowy [bee-boow-**ko**-vi] adj.m. of tissue-paper
bibułowy [bee-boo-**wo**-vi] adj.m. of blotting paper
biceps [**bee**-tseps] m. biceps; upperarm flexor muscle
bicie [**bee**-ćhe] n. beating; thrashing; flogging; lashing; slaughtering; minting; breaking; striking; stroking
  bicie serca [**bee**-ćhe **ser**-tsah] exp.: heartbeat
  bicie w bębny [**bee**-ćhe v **banb**-ni] exp.: drum-beat; the beating of drums
  bicie w drzwi [**bee**-ćhe v dzhvee] exp.: knocking at the door
  bicie w dzwony [**bee**-ćhe v **dzvo**-ni] exp.: the ringing of bells
bicie się [**bee**-ćhe śhan] n. fighting with each other
bicykl [**bee**-tsikl] m. bicycle with one set of sprockets
bicz [beech] m. whip; lash; whiplash
  bicz boży [beech **bo**-zhi] exp.: scourge
  strzelać z bicza [stshe-lahćh z bee-chah] exp.: to crack a whip
biczować [bee-**cho**-vahćh] v. lash; whip; flagellate; colloq: scourge (*repeatedly*)
biczować się [bee-**cho**-vahćh śhan] v. flagellate oneself; practice self-flagellation (*repeatedly*)
biczowanie [bee-cho-**vah**-ńe] n. flagellation
biczowanie się [bee-cho-**vah**-ńe

śhan] n. self-flagellation
biczyk [**bee**-chik] m. small whip
biczysko [bee-**chis**-ko] n. whipstock; whip handle; crop
bić [beećh] v. defeat; strike; hit; thump; smite; slaughter; kill; mint; coin; print; churn; whip; drive (piles); stud; lash (*repeatedly*)
bić czołem [beećh **cho**-wem] exp.: to bow humbly; to kowtow
bić głową o mur [beećh **gwo**-vown o moor] exp.: to hit one's head against a (stone) wall
bić skrzydłami [beećh skshi-**dwah**-mee] exp.: to flutter (bird's) wings
bić zadem [beećh **zah**-dem] exp.: to kick with the hind legs
bić się [beećh śhan] v. hit oneself; exchange blows (*repeatedly*)
bić się w piersi [beećh śhan f **pyer**-śhee] exp.: to beat one's breast; to repent
bić się z myślami [beećh śhan z mi-**ślah**-mee] exp.: to hesitate; to waver; to be undecided
bidet [**bee**-det] m. bidet
bidetowy [bee-de-**to**-vi] adj.m. of bidet; bidet (bowl, etc.)
bidło [**beed**-wo] n. a moving part of a loom
bidon [**bee**-don] m. bicycle mounted drinking bottle
bidula [bee-**doo**-lah] f. colloq: poor soul; poor thing; poor devil; poor little darling; poor dear
biec [byets] v. run; trot; speed; sail; glide; flow; pass; fleet; fly (*repeatedly*)
bieda [**bye**-dah] f. poverty; want; trouble; distress; evil days; fix; bother; dilemma; quandary; the poor; the needy; the indigent; two-wheel one-horse carriage; gig; trap
biedactwo [bye-**dah**-tstfo] n. poor devil (soul, thing)
biedaczek [bye-**dah**-chek] m. poor devil (soul, thing)
biedaczka [bye-**dach**-kah] f. poor woman; beggar woman
biedaczyna [bye-dah-**chi**-nah] m. poor devil (soul, thing); run-down pauper
biedaczysko [bye-dah-**chis**-ko] m. or n. poor devil (soul, thing); run-down pauper
biedak [**bye**-dahk] m. poor man; pauper; poor beggar
biedaszyb [bye-**dah**-ship] m. primitive surface mine in which the needy dig coal for their own use
biedermeier [bee-der-**mah**-yer] m. Bierdermeier furniture style
biedermeierowski [bee-der-mah-ye-**rof**-skee] adj.m. Bierdermeier (furniture, etc.)
biedka [**byet**-kah] f. two-wheel one-horse carriage; gig; trap
biedniacki [byed-**ńah**-tskee] adj.m. destitute villager's
biedniaczka [byed-**ńahch**-kah] f. destitute country woman
biedniak [**byed**-ńahk] m. destitute country man; poor villager
biednie [**byed**-ńe] adv. poorly; wretchedly
biednieć [**byed**-ńećh] v. grow poor; decline; be on the downward path (*repeatedly*)
biednienie [byed-**ńe**-ńe] n. growing poorer; becoming poor
biedniutki [byed-**ńoot**-kee] adj.m. poor little (darling, etc.)
biedny [**byed**-ni] adj.m. poor; indigent; needy; unhappy; wretched; modest worthless; contemptible; miserable; mean; m. beggar
biedota [bye-**do**-tah] f. poor people; the poor; the destitute; the needy; poverty; indigence; miserable possessions
biedować [bye-**do**-vahćh] v. suffer want; eke out one's existence; live in poverty; be in want; live from hand to mouth (*repeatedly*)
biedowanie [bye-do-**vah**-ńe] n. a life of misery
biedronka [bye-**dron**-kah] f. ladybird
biedrzyniec [bye-**dzhi**-ńets] m. anise
biedrzyga [bye-**dzhi**-gah] f. May apple (a herb)
biedrzynek [bye-**dzhi**-nek] m. red valerian (a herb)
biedula [bye-**doo**-lah] f. poor devil

(soul, thing)
biedulka [bye-**dool**-kah] f. (little) poor devil (soul, thing)
biedzenie się [bye-**dze**-ńe śhan] n. taking pains; exerting oneself
biedzić się [**bye**-dźheećh śhan] v. take pains (over); toil (at); exert oneself; sweat (over); drudge (over) (*repeatedly*)
bieg [byeg] m. run; running pace; gait (of a horse); race; round; course; motion; (piston) travel; process; progress; sequence; order; drift; trend; current; gear; speed; flight (of stairs)
bieg konia [byek **ko**-ńah] exp.: a horse's gait
biegiem! [**bye**-gem] exp.: at the double!; double-quick
biegacz [**bye**-gahch] m. runner; racer; bishop (in chess); a variety of (dark, shiny) beetle; traveller (in a spinning machine)
biegaczka [bye-**gahch**-kah] f. (female) runner; racer
biegaczowaty [bye-gah-cho-**vah**-ti] adj.m. of (dark, shiny) beetle
biegaczowate [bye-gah-cho-**vah**-te] pl. the family of (dark, shiny) beetles
biegać [**bye**-gahćh] v. run; race; run a race; circulate; flit; whisk; be current (gossip, etc.) (*repeatedly*)
biegać się [**bye**-gahćh śhan] v. be in heat (animals) (*repeatedly*)
biegający [bye-gah-**yown**-tsi] adj.m. running (man, bird, etc.)
bieganie [bye-**gah**-ńe] n. running
bieganina [bye-gah-**ńee**-nah] f. comings and goings; agitation; bustle; excitement; running about (for errands, etc.)
biegle [**bye**-gle] adv. fluently; competently; efficiently; smoothly; with ease
biegłościowy [byeg-wośh-**ćho**-vi] adj.m. skill (level, etc.); proficiency (level, etc.)
biegłość [**bye**-gwośhćh] f. fluency (in); skill (for); dexterity; routine; proficiency; efficiency (in); mastery (of); conversance (with); competence (for)
biegły [**bye**-gwi] adj.m. skilful; skilled; fluent; efficient; expert (in, at); proficient (in, at); m. expert; connoisseur
biegnąć [**bye**-gnownćh] v. run; race; run a race; circulate; flit; whisk; be current (gossip, etc.); see: **biegać**
biegnięcie [byeg-**ńan**-ćhe] n. running (around, etc.)
biegnik [**byeg**-ńeek] m. (music) run; rapid scale passage
biegnikowy [byeg-ńee-**ko**-vi] adj.m. of rapid scale passage (music)
biegowy [bye-**go**-vi] adj.m. running (exercise, shoes, gear, etc.)
biegówka [bye-**goof**-kah] f. a type of cross-country ski
biegówki [bye-**goof**-kee] pl. skis for cross-country runs
biegun [**bye**-goon] m. pole; rocker; spindle; trunnion; steed
biegun południowy [**bye**-goon po-wood-**ńo**-vi] exp.: South Pole
biegun północny [**bye**-goon poow-**nots**-ni] exp.: North Pole
biegunecznik [bye-goo-**nech**-ńeek] m. mountain damson; paradise tree; Simarouba tree
biegunecznikowaty [bye-goo-nech-ńee-ko-**vah**-ti] adj.m. simaroubaceous
biegunecznikowate [bye-goo-nech-ńee-ko-**vah**-te] pl. the family of Simarouba trees
biegunka [bye-**goon**-kah] f. diarrhea; dysentery
biegunowo [bye-goo-**no**-vo] adv. diametrically
biegunowość [bye-goo-**no**-vośhćh] f. polarity; reverse (of)
biegunowy [bye-goo-**no**-vi] adj.m. polar; rocking (chair, etc.)
biegus [**bye**-goos] m. variety of domesticated duck; variety of shore inhabiting bird
biel [byel] f. whiteness; white color; white hair; white
bielactwo [bye-**lahts**-tfo] n. albinism
bielak [**bye**-lahk] m. albino; mountain hare
bielarka [bye-**lahr**-kah] f. bleacher; bleaching-machine
bielarnia [bye-**lahr**-ńah] f. bleachers;

bleaching-plant
bielawa [bye-**lah**-vah] f. marsh
bielec [**bye**-lets] m. termite
bieleć [**bye**-lećh] v. whiten; turn white; appear white; go white; become white (*repeatedly*)
bielejący [bye-le-**yown**-tsi] adj.m. reflecting white color
bielenie [bye-**le**-ńe] n. whitening; turning white
bielica [bye-**lee**-tsah] f. mugwort
bielicować [bye-lee-**tso**-vahćh] v. turn soil into mugwort (*repeatedly*)
bielicowanie [bye-lee-tso-**vah**-ńe] n. development of mugwort soil
bielicowy [bye-lee-**tso**-vi] adj.m. mugwort (herb, etc.)
bielić [**bye**-leećh] v. whiten; tin; whitewash; bleach; blanch; refine; filter; colloq: show (somebody) in a favorable light (*repeatedly*)
bielić się [**bye**-leećh śhan] v. whiten; show oneself in a favorable light; grow white; turn white; become whiter; colloq: show oneself in a favorable light (*repeatedly*)
bielidło [bye-**lee**-dwo] n. whitewash
bielik [**bye**-leek] m. erne; golden eagle; sea eagle
bielikrasa [bye-lee-**krah**-sah] f. calla lily; Arum lily
bielinek [bye-**lee**-nek] m. cabbage butterfly
bieliniak [bye-**lee**-ńahk] m. pierid butterfly
bielistki [bye-**lee**-stkee] pl. squirrel fur
bielizna [bye-**leez**-nah] f. linen; tablecloth; clothes; laundry; underwear; colloq: undies
bielizna damska [bye-**leez**-nah dahm-skah] exp.: lingerie
bielizna trykotowa [bye-**leez**-nah tri-ko-**to**-vah] exp.: hosiery
bieliźniany [bye-lee-**źhńah**-ni] adj.m. linen (fabric, etc.); lingerie (department, etc.)
bieliźniarka [bye-lee-**źhńahr**-kah] f. dresser; chest of drawers (Brit.); shirt-maker (woman)
bieliźniarski [bye-lee-**źhńahr**-skee] adj.m. shirt-making; shirt-maker's (shop, etc.)
bieliźniarstwo [bye-lee-**źhńahr**-stfo] n. shirt-making
bielmo [**byel**-mo] n. cataract; web-eye; film over the eye; leucoma; albugo; endosperm
bielmowy [byel-**mo**-vi] adj.m. endospermic
bielnica [byel-**ńee**-tsah] f. vitiligo; skin disorder (caused by diabetes, antibiotics, etc.); smooth white skin spots
bielnik [**byel**-ńeek] m. bleachery
bielony [bye-**lo**-ni] adj.m. whitened; bleached
bieluchny [bye-**loo**-khni] adj.m. nice and white; beautifully white; very, very white
bieluń [**bye**-looń] m. jimsonweed; stramonium; thorn apple
bielusieńki [bye-loo-**śheń**-kee] adj.m. very, very white; beautifully white; nice and white
bieluśki [bye-**loośh**-kee] adj.m. very white; nicely white
bieluteńki [bye-loo-**teń**-kee] adj.m. very, very white; beautifully white; nice and white
bielutki [bye-**loot**-kee] adj.m. very white; nicely white
białuga [bye-**woo**-gah] f. beluga; white whale
biennale [byen-**nah**-le] n. biannual artistic event
bierka [**byer**-kah] f. chessman; pawn
biernie [**byer**-ńe] adv. passively; with indifference
biernie się zachowywać [**byer**-ńe śhan zah-kho-**vi**-vahćh] exp.: to stand by; to watch and wait
biernik [**byer**-ńeek] m. accusative
biernikowy [byer-ńee-**ko**-vi] adj.m. accusative (form, etc.)
bierność [**byer**-nośhćh] f. passivity
biernota [byer-**no**-tah] f. passivity
bierny [**byer**-ni] adj.m. passive; indifferent; listless; inactive; neutral (chemical, etc.); resistless; adverse; negative (balance of an account)
bierwiono [byer-**vyo**-no] n. log; stump
bierzmować [byezh-**mo**-vahćh] v.

administer the sacrament of confirmation; confirm (*repeatedly*)
bierzmowanie [byezh-mo-**vah**-ńe] n. the sacrament of confirmation; Confirmation
bies [byes] m. the devil; Satan; fiend; the deuce
biesiada [bye-**śhah**-dah] f. feast; convivial gathering; (dinner-) party; banquet; entertainment; revel; revelry
biesiadniczy [bye-śhah-**dńee**-chi] adj.m. convivial; festive; jovial
biesiadnik [bye-**śhah**-dńeek] m. feaster; convivial guest
biesiadny [bye-**śhah**-dni] adj.m. convivial; festive
biesiadować [bye-śhah-**do**-vahćh] v. feast; banquet; revel (*repeatedly*)
biesiadowanie [bye-śhah-do-**vah**-ńe] n. feasting; banqueting
biesić się [**bye**-śheećh śhan] v. rave; rage; storm (*repeatedly*)
biesowski [bye-**sof**-skee] adj.m. devilish; devil's
bieżąco [bye-**zhown**-tso] adv. currently; day by day
bieżący [bye-**zhown**-tsi] adj.m. current; flowing; running; present; actual
bieżący rachunek [bye-**zhown**-tsi rah-**khoo**-nek] exp.: current account
bieżący rok [bye-**zhown**-tsi rok] exp.: current year
bieżący stan [bye-**zhown**-tsi stahn] exp.: current condition
bieżeć [**bye**-zhećh] v. run; trot; speed; sail; glide; flow; pass; fleet; fly (*repeatedly*); see: **biec**
bieżnia [**byezh**-ńah] f. runway; track; racecourse; tire tread
bieżnik [**byezh**-ńeek] m. tire tread
bieżnikować [byezh-ńee-**ko**-vahćh] v. retread (tires) (*repeatedly*)
bieżnikowanie [byezh-ńee-ko-**vah**-ńe] n. retreading of tires
bieżnikownia [byezh-ńee-**kov**-ńah] f. tire retreading plant
bieżny [**byezh**-ni] adj.m. racing (contest, tread, etc.)
bifacjalny [bee-fahts-**yahl**-ni] adj.m. dorsoventral; dorsiventral
bifilarny [bee-fee-**lahr**-ni] adj.m. bifilar (micrometer, etc.); with two threads (or wires)
bifilarne uzwojenie [bee-fee-**lahr**-ne ooz-vo-**ye**-ńe] exp.: bifilar winding
bifurkacja [bee-foor-**kah**-tsyah] f; forking (of the roads); bifurcation
bigamia [bee-**gah**-myah] f. bigamy
bigamicznie [bee-gah-**meech**-ńe] adv. bigamously
bigamiczny [bee-gah-**meech**-ni] adj.m. bigamous
bigamista [bee-gah-**mees**-tah] m. bigamist (man)
bigamistka [bee-gah-**mees**-tkah] f. bigamist (woman)
big-band [**beeg**-bend] m. big band; jazz orchestra (in 1960-1970)
bigbandowy [beeg-ben-**do**-vi] adj.m. of jazz orchestra
big-beat [**beeg**-beet] m. heavy persistent beat; rock 'n' roll music (in use in 1960-70)
bigbit [**beeg**-beet] m. heavy persistent beat; rock 'n' roll music (in use in 1960-70)
bigbitowy [beeg-bee-**to**-vi] adj.m. of rock 'n' roll
bigiel [**bee**-gel] m. colloq: verve; animation; vivacity; vitality; energy
bigos [**bee**-gos] m. hashed meat and cabbage dish (traditional Polish food); jumble; hotch-potch; mish-mash
narobić bigosu [nah-**ro**-beećh bee-**go**-soo] exp.: to mess things up
bigosik [bee-**go**-śheek] m. (nice little) bigos
bigot [**bee**-got] m. bigot; churchy man
bigoteria [bee-go-**te**-ryah] f. bigotry; religionism; religiosity
bigoteryjny [bee-go-te-**riy**-ni] adj.m. bigoted; religiose; excessively religious
bigotka [bee-**got**-kah] f. bigot; bigoted woman
bigować [bee-**go**-vahćh] v. groove (cardboard) (*repeatedly*)
bigowanie [bee-go-**vah**-ńe] n. making (bending) grooves (in a cardboard)

bigówka [bee-**goof**-kah] f. device for making bending-grooves in a cardboard
bijać [**bee**-yahćh] v. defeat; strike; hit, etc. see: **bić** (*repeatedly*)
bijać się [**bee**-yahćh śhan] v. take part in brawls (*repeatedly*)
bijak [**bee**-yahk] m. hammer's face; carpenter's wooden hammer; the face of a hammer
bijakowy [bee-yah-**ko**-vi] adj.m. of hammer's face
bijatyka [bee-yah-**ti**-kah] f. fight; brawl; tussle; scrimmage
bikini [bee-**kee**-ńee] n. bikini; woman's scanty two-piece bathing suit
bikiniarski [bee-kee-**ńahr**-skee] adj.m. of flashy dresser
bikiniarstwo [bee-kee-**ńahr**-stfo] n. wearing flashy clothes; living like a Teddy boy
bikiniarz [bee-**kee**-ńahsh] m. Teddy boy; a silly, vain man; fob
bikolateralny [bee-ko-lah-te-**rahl**-ni] adj.m. alike on both sides; bicollateral
bikwadratowy [bee-kfah-drah-**to**-vi] adj.m. biquadratic (equation, etc.)
bil [beel] m. billiard cue; pork fat
bila [**bee**-lah] f. billiard ball; winning stroke
zrobić bilę [**zro**-beećh **bee**-lan] exp.: to score; to play a winning game (hazard)
bilabialny [bee-lah-**byahl**-ni] adj.m. bilabiate; having two lips
bilans [**bee**-lahns] m. balance sheet; balance; rest; outcome; result
bilansista [bee-lahn-**śhees**-tah] m. accountant
bilansować [bee-lahn-**so**-vahćh] v. balance accounts; equalize; compare; take stock of (*repeatedly*)
bilansować się [bee-lahn-**so**-vahćh śhan] v. balance (*repeatedly*)
bilansowanie [bee-lahn-so-**vah**-ńe] n. balancing (of books, etc.)
bilansowanie się [bee-lahn-so-**vah**-ńe śhan] n. coming to an exact balance; balancing each other
bilansowy [bee-lahn-**so**-vi] adj.m. balance (sheet, etc.)
zestawienie bilansowe [ze-stah-**vye**-ńe bee-lahn-**so**-ve] exp.: balance sheet
bilansoznawstwo [bee-lahn-so-**znahf**-stfo] n. accountancy; profession of accounting
bilard [**bee**-lahrt] m. billiards; billiard table; billiard room; colloq: pills
bilardowy [bee-lahr-**do**-vi] adj.m. billiard (balls, etc.)
bilardzista [bee-lahr-**dźhees**-tah] m. billiard player
bilateralizm [bee-lah-te-**rah**-leezm] m. bilateralism
bilateralny [bee-lah-te-**rahl**-ni] adj.m. bilateral
bilbokiet [beel-**bo**-ket] m. cup-and-ball (a toy)
bileciarka [bee-le-**ćhahr**-kah] f. ticket printing machine; ticket puncturing device
bilecik [bee-**le**-ćheek] m. scribble
bilecik miłosny [bee-**le**-ćheek mee-**wos**-ni] exp.: love-letter
bilet [**bee**-let] m. note; ticket
bilet bankowy [**bee**-let bahn-**ko**-vi] exp.: bank-note
bilet lotniczy [**bee**-let lot-ńee-chi] exp.: airplane ticket
bilet wizytowy [**bee**-let vee-zi-**to**-vi] exp.: business card; visiting card
bileter [bee-**le**-ter] m. ticket-collector; usher; attendant
bileterka [bee-le-**ter**-kah] f. usherette; attendant
biletować [bee-le-**to**-vahćh] v. sell tickets (*repeatedly*)
biletowy [bee-le-**to**-vi] adj.m. ticket (office, etc.)
biliard [**beel**-yahrt] m. thousand billions (Brit.); quadrillion (USA)
bilingwizm [bee-**leeng**-veezm] m. bilingualism; the constant oral use of two languages
bilion [**bee**-lyon] m. billion (a million millions in Europe; trillion in the USA) (10 to the ninth power)
bilionowy [beel-yo-**no**-vi] adj.m. billionth (Brit.); trillionth (USA)
bilirubina [bee-lee-roo-**bee**-nah] f. bilirubin (reddish yellow pigment)
biliterowy [bee-lee-te-**ro**-vi] adj.m. of two letters

biliwerdyna [bee-lee-ver-**di**-nah] f. biliverdin (green pigment)
bill [beel] m. bill (draft of proposed act of parliament)
bilon [**bee**-lon] m. coins; small change
bim- [beem] exp.: tic (tack); ding (dong)
bimbać [**beem**-bahćh] v. make light of something, somebody (*repeatedly*)
bimbać sobie [**beem**-bahćh **so**-bye] exp.: to take it easy
bim-bam [beem-bahm] exp.: ding-dong
bimber [**beem**-ber] m. illegally distilled liquor; moonshine; hooch
bimbrarstwo [beem-**brahr**-stfo] n. illicit distilling of liquor
bimbrarz [**beem**-brahsh] m. maker of illicit liquor; seller of illicit liquor; moonshiner
bimbrownia [beem-**brov**-ńah] f. illegal distilling of liquor
bimbrownictwo [beem-brov-**ńee**-tstfo] n. illegal distilling of liquor
bimbrowniczy [beem-brov-**nee**-chi] adj.m. moonshine (liquor, etc.)
bimbrownik [beem-**brov**-ńeek] m. maker of illicit liquor; seller of illicit liquor; moonshiner
bimetal [bee-**me**-tahl] m. bimetallic plate (sheet, ribbon, wire, etc.)
bimetalistyczny [bee-me-tah-lees-**tich**-ni] adj.m. bimetallic
bimetalizm [bee-me-**tah**-leezm] m. system of coins using gold and silver; bimetallism
bimetalowy [bee-me-tah-**lo**-vi] adj.m. bimetallic; bimetal; bimetallistic
bimorficzny [bee-mor-**feech**-ni] adj.m. bimorphemic
bimorfizm [bee-**mor**-feezm] m. bimorphemic condition
bims [beems] m. (ship) beam
binarny [bee-**nahr**-ni] adj.m. binary
binaryzacja [bee-nah-ri-**zah**-tsyah] f. expressing in a binary form
bindaż [**been**-dahsh] m. walkway covered with climbing wines, etc.
binduga [been-**doo**-gah] f. a raft making place on a river near shore
bingo [**been**-go] n. bingo; game of chance played with cards
binistor [bee-**ńees**-tor] m. semiconductor used in computer memory
binokle [bee-**no**-kle] pl. eyeglasses
binokular [bee-no-**koo**-lahr] m. field glass
binokularny [bee-no-koo-**lahr**-ni] adj.m. binocular (vision, etc.); adapted to the use of both eyes
binominalny [bee-no-mee-**nahl**-ni] adj.m. two-terms (biological species name)
bio- [byo] prefix: bio-; life-; tissue-
bioastronautyka [byo-ahs-tro-**nahw**-ti-kah] f. bioastronautics; medical and biological aspect of astronautics
biocenologia [byo-tse-no-**lo**-gyah] f. study of biocoenosis
biocenotyczny [byo-tse-no-**tich**-ni] adj.m. biocoenotic; biocenotic
biocenotyka [byo-tse-**no**-ti-kah] f. study of biocoenosis
biocenoza [byo-tse-**no**-zah] f. biocoenosis; biocenosis; an ecological (self-regulating) community
biochemia [byo-**khe**-myah] f. biochemistry
biochemiczny [byo-khe-**meech**-ni] adj.m. biochemical
biochemik [byo-**khe**-meek] m. biochemist
biocybernetyczny [byo-tsi-ber-ne-**tich**-ni] adj.m. biocybernetic
biocybernetyk [byo-tsi-ber-**ne**-tik] m. biocyberneticist
biocybernetyka [byo-tsi-ber-**ne**-ti-kah] f. biocybernetics
biodegradacja [byo-de-grah-**dah**-tsyah] f. biodegradation
biodra [**byod**-rah] pl. loins; hips
biodro [**byod**-ro] n. hip; huckle; coxa; haunch
biodrowy [byo-**dro**-vi] adj.m. hip-; huckle-; huckle (bone, etc.); coxal
kość biodrowa [kośhćh byo-**dro**-vah] exp.: hip-bone; huckle-bone
staw biodrowy [stahv byo-**dro**-vi] exp.: hip-joint
biodrówka [byo-**droof**-kah] f. colloq: pork meat with a part of hip-bone; pants (hip-high, not up to

the waist)
biodrzasty [byo-**dzhah**-sti] adj.m. broad-hipped
biodynamika [byo-di-**nah**-mee-kah] f. biodynamics
bioelektronika [byo-e-lek-tro-**ńee**-kah] f. bionics
bioelektryczny [byo-e-lek-**trich**-ni] adj.m. bionic; bioelectric
bioenergetyka [byo-e-ner-**ge**-ti-kah] f. bioenergetics
bioenergoterapia [byo-e-ner-go-te-**rah**-pyah] f. therapy based on bioenergetics
biofiltracja [byo-feel-**trah**-tsyah] f. biological sewer treatment
biofizyczny [byo-fee-**zich**-ni] adj.m. biophysical
biofizyk [byo-**fee**-zik] m. biophysicist
biofizyka [byo-**fee**-zi-kah] f. biophysics
biogaz [**byo**-gahs] m. methane
biogenetyczny [byo-ge-ne-**tich**-ni] adj.m. biogenetic
biogeneza [byo-ge-**ne**-zah] f. biogenetics; biogenesis
biogeniczny [byo-ge-**ńeech**-ni] adj.m. biogenic
biogeochemia [byo-ge-o-**khe**-myah] f. biochemistry
biogeografia [byo-ge-o-**grah**-fyah] f. biogeography
biogeograficzny [byo-ge-o-grah-**feech**-ni] adj.m. biogeographic
biograf [**byo**-grahf] m. biographer
biografia [byo-**grah**-fyah] f. biography
biograficznie [byo-grah-**feech**-ńe] adv. biographically
biograficzny [byo-grah-**feech**-ni] adj.m. biographic(al)
biografistyka [byo-grah-**fees**-ti-kah] f. biographic literature
biografizm [byo-**grah**-feezm] m. study of literature from the biographic point of view
biografka [byo-**grahf**-kah] f. biographer (woman)
biogram [**byo**-grahm] m. short biographical note
bioinżynieria [byo-een-zhi-**ńe**-ryah] f. bioengineering
biokataliza [byo-kah-tah-**lee**-zah] f. biocatalysis
biokatalizator [byo-kah-tah-lee-**zah**-tor] m. biocatalyst
biokatalizatory [byo-kah-tah-lee-zah-**to**-ri] pl. biocatalysts
bioklimat [byo-**klee**-maht] m. bioclimate
bioklimatologia [byo-klee-mah-to-**lo**-gyah] f. bioclimatology
bioklimatologiczny [byo-klee-mah-to-lo-**geech**-ni] adj.m. bioclimatologic
bioklimatyczny [byo-klee-mah-**tich**-ni] adj.m. bioclimatic
biokorozja [byo-ko-**ro**-zyah] f. biocorrosion
biokosmonautyka [byo-kos-mo-**nahw**-ti-kah] f. bioastronautics
biolit [**byo**-leet] m. biolith; rock of biologic origin
biolog [**byo**-log] m. biologist
biologia [byo-**lo**-gyah] f. biology
biologicznie [byo-lo-**geech**-ńe] adv. biologically
wyniszczyć biologicznie [vi-**ńeesh**-chićh byo-lo-**geech**-ńe] exp.: to exterminate
biologiczny [byo-lo-**geech**-ni] adj.m. biologic(al)
wyniszczenie biologiczne [vi-ńeesh-**che**-ńe byo-lo-**geech**-ne] exp.: extermination
biologistyczny [byo-lo-gees-**tich**-ni] adj.m. biologistic
biologizm [byo-**lo**-geezm] m. biologism
biologizować [byo-lo-gee-**zo**-vahćh] v. give biological explanations (to social events, etc.) (*repeatedly*)
bioluminescencja [byo-loo-mee-nes-**tsen**-tsyah] f. bioluminescence
bioluminescencyjny [byo-loo-mee-nes-tsen-**tsiy**-ni] adj.m. bioluminescent
biom [byom] m. biome
biomasa [byo-**mah**-sah] f. biomass
biomechanika [byo-me-**khah**-ńee-kah] f. biomechanics (of the movements of animals)
biometeorolog [byo-me-te-o-**ro**-log] m. biometeorologist
biometeorologia [byo-me-te-o-ro-**lo**-gyah] f. biometeorology
biometeorologiczny [byo-me-te-o-ro-lo-**geech**-ni] adj.m. biometeorologic

biometria [byo-**me**-tryah] f. biometrics; biometry
biomotor [byo-**mo**-tor] m. mechanical resuscitation device
bionik [**byo**-ńeek] m. specialist in bionics
bionika [**byo**-ńee-kah] f. bionics
bionomia [byo-**no**-myah] f. bionomy; ecology, physiology; bionomics
biopolimer [byo-po-**lee**-mer] m. biopolymer
biopotencjał [byo-po-**ten**-tsyahw] m. electrical potential in living tissue (of the brain, etc.)
bioprąd [**byo**-prownt] m. bioelectric current
biopreparat [byo-pre-**pah**-raht] m. serum vaccine
bioproteza [byo-pro-**te**-zah] f. artificial limb actuated by bioelectric current of the user
biopsja [**byo**-psyah] f. biopsy
biopsychiczny [byo-psi-**kheech**-ni] adj.m. biopsychic; biopsychical
biopsychologia [byo-psi-kho-**lo**-gyah] f. biopsychology
biorący [byo-**rown**-tsi] m. taker
biorca [**byor**-tsah] m. patient being subjected to transfusion
biorytm [**byo**-ritm] m. biorhythm
bios [byos] m. bios
biosfera [byo-**sfe**-rah] f. biosphere
biostratygrafia [byo-strah-ti-**grah**-fyah] f. biostratigraphy
biosynteza [byo-sin-**te**-zah] f. biosynthesis
biotechnika [byo-**tekh**-ńee-kah] f. biotechnology
biotechnologia [byo-tekh-no-**lo**-gyah] f. biotechnology
bioterapia [byo-te-**rah**-pyah] m. therapy based on bioenergetics
biotrop [**byo**-trop] m. biotrope
biotyczny [byo-**tich**-ni] adj.m. biotic
biotyna [byo-**ti**-nah] f. biotin; vitamin H
biotyp [**byo**-tip] m. biotype
biotyt [**byo**-tit] m. biotite
bioza [**byo**-zah] f. boise
biplan [**bee**-plahn] m. biplane; two-planed airplane
bipolarność [bee-po-**lahr**-nośhćh] f. bipolarity
bipolarny [bee-po-**lahr**-ni] adj.m. bipolar
birbancki [beer-**bahnts**-kee] adj.m. carousing; revelling; merry-making (company, etc.)
birbant [**beer**-bahnt] m. carouser; reveller; merry-maker; rake
birbantka [beer-**bahnt**-kah] f. (woman) carouser; reveller; merry-maker; rake
birbantować [beer-bahn-**to**-vahćh] v. carouse; revel; make merry; dissipate; be on the spree (*repeatedly*)
birema [bee-**re**-mah] f. bireme (Roman galley)
biret [**bee**-ret] m. beret; biretta; cap
birkut [**beer**-koot] m. golden eagle
Birmanka [beer-**mahn**-kah] f. Burmeese woman
Birmańczyk [beer-**mahń**-chik] m. Burmeese; a Burmeese
birmański [beer-**mahń**-skee] adj.m. Burmeese
bis [bees] m. encore
biseksualizm [bee-se-ksoo-**ah**-leezm] m. bisexualism
biseksualnie [bee-se-ksoo-**ahl**-ńe] adv. bisexually
biseksualny [bee-se-ksoo-**ahl**-ni] adj.m. bisexual
bisior [**bee**-śhor] m. byssus; delicate fabric
bisiorka [bee-**śhor**-kah] f. bead
bisiorki [bee-**śhor**-kee] pl. beads
biskajski [bees-**kahy**-skee] adj.m. of Biscay
biskup [**bees**-koop] m. bishop
biskupi [bee-**skoo**-pee] adj.m. bishop's
biskupstwo [bee-**skoop**-stfo] n. bishopric; episcopate
biskwit [**bees**-kfeet] m. biscuit; cracker
biskwitować [bees-kfee-**to**-vahćh] v. make a bisque; fire (ceramics, china, clay, etc.) at 900 degrees centigrade (*repeatedly*)
biskwitowanie [bees-kfee-to-**vah**-ńe] n. making a bisque; firing (ceramics, china, clay, etc.) at 900 degrees centigrade
biskwitowy [bees-kfee-**to**-vi] adj.m. biscuit (china, clay, oven, etc.)

bisować [bee-**so**-vahćh] v. encore (*repeatedly*)
bisowanie [bee-so-**vah**-ńe] n. encoring
bisowy [bee-**so**-vi] adj.m. played as an encore
bissus [**bees**-soos] m. byssus (weave, fabric); fine fabric
bistr [beestr] m. bistre (brown pigment)
bistro [**bees**-tro] n. bistro; French quick service wine shop or restaurant; small bar or tavern; (the Russian word "bystro," meaning "quickly," was brought to France after the defeat of Napoleon)
bisurman [bee-**soor**-mahn] m. vulg.: Mussulman; Muslim; blusterer; brawler; swaggerer; roisterer
bisurmanić [bee-soor-**mah**-ńeećh] v. convert to Islam (*repeatedly*)
bisurmanić się [bee-soor-**mah**-ńeećh śhan] v. convert oneself to Islam; live in poverty; dissipate; carouse; revel; frolic; play pranks (*repeatedly*)
bisurmanin [bee-soor-**mah**-ńeen] m. colloq: Mussulman; Muslim
bisurmański [bee-soor-**mahń**-skee] adj.m. vulg.: Muslim; blustering; swaggering; roistering; brawling
po bisurmańsku [po bee-soor-**mahń**-skoo] exp.: like a blusterer; like a swaggerer
biszkopcik [beesh-**kop**-ćheek] m. (small, nice) sponge cake
biszkopt [**beesh**-kopt] m. biscuit; sponge cake; cracker
biszkoptowy [beesh-kop-**to**-vi] adj.m. sponge cake (dough)
bit [beet] m. beat
bit [beet] m. bit; a unit of computer information equivalent to the result of a choice between two alternatives: 0 or 1, yes or no, on or off; the physical representation in a computer memory of a bit by an electrical pulse; a magnetized spot; or a hole whose presence or absence indicates data
bitels [**bee**-tels] m. one of The Beatles (English rock group)
bitelsowski [bee-tel-**sof**-skee] adj.m. Beatles' (hairdo, etc.)
bitewny [bee-**tev**-ni] adj.m. battle (cry, etc.); of the battle field
bitka [**beet**-kah] f. scuffle; scrimmage; pounded cutlet (of veal, beef, etc.)
bitnie [**beet**-ńe] adv. valiantly
bitnik [**beet**-ńeek] m. beatnik
bitnikowski [beet-ńee-**kof**-skee] adj.m. beatnik's; of a beatnik
bitność [**beet**-nośhćh] f. valor; daring; warlike spirit; pugnacity
bitny [**beet**-ni] adj.m. valiant
bitonalność [bee-to-**nahl**-nośhćh] f. bitonality
bitonalny [bee-to-**nahl**-ni] adj.m. bitonal
bitowy [bee-**to**-vi] adj.m. of the rock n' roll music; of the computer bit
bitum [**bee**-toom] m. bitumen; mineral pitch
bitumen [bee-**too**-men] m. bitumen; mineral pitch
bitumiczny [bee-too-**meech**-ni] adj.m. bituminous (coal, etc.); pitch (paper, etc.)
bitumin [bee-**too**-meen] m. bitumen; mineral pitch; crude oil; asphalt; natural gas
bituminować [bee-too-mee-**no**-vahćh] v. bituminize; cover with bitumen; impregnate with bitumen (*repeatedly*)
bituminizacja [bee-too-mee-ńee-**zah**-tsyah] f. bituminization
bituminowanie [bee-too-mee-no-**vah**-ńe] n. bituminization
bituminowy [bee-too-mee-**no**-vi] adj.m. bitumen (rich area, etc.)
bitumizacja [bee-too-mee-**zahts**-yah] f. bituminization
bitwa [**beet**-fah] f. battle; fight; combat; (military) action; slang: brawl
pole bitwy [po-le **beet**-fi] exp.: battlefield
bity [**bee**-ti] adj.m. beaten; full; close
bite dwie godziny [**bee**-te dvye go-**dźhee**-ni] exp.: two full hours
bite cztery strony [**bee**-te **chte**-ri **stro**-ni] exp.: four closely written pages
droga bita [**dro**-gah **bee**-tah] exp.:

beaten track; highway
biuletyn [byoo-**le**-tin] m. bulletin
biuletyn meteorologiczny [byoo-le-tin me-te-o-ro-lo-**geech**-ni] exp.: weather report
biuralista [byoo-rah-**lees**-tah] m. official; clerk
biuralistka [byoo-rah-**leest**-kah] f. (woman) official; clerk
biureczko [byoo-**rech**-ko] n. (nice) writing table; desk; writing desk
biureta [byoo-**re**-tah] f. burette
biurko [**byoor**-ko] n. writing table; desk; writing desk
biurkowy [byoor-**ko**-vi] adj.m. desk (telephone, etc.)
biuro [**byoo**-ro] n. office; bureau; office hours
biuro informacyjne [**byoo**-ro een-for-mah-**tsiy**-ne] exp.: information office
biuro podróży [**byoo**-ro pod-**roo**-zhi] exp.: travel agency
główne biuro [**gwoov**-ne **byoo**-ro] exp.: headquarters; head office
po biurze [po **byoo**-zhe] exp.: after office hours
biurokracja [byoo-ro-**krah**-tsyah] f. bureaucracy; red tape; officialism; officialdom
biurokrata [byoo-ro-**krah**-tah] m. bureaucrat; red-tapist
biurokratka [byoo-ro-**kraht**-kah] f. (woman) bureaucrat; red-tapist
biurokratycznie [byoo-ro-krah-**tich**-ńe] adv. bureaucratically; with plenty of red tape
biurokratyczny [byoo-ro-krah-**tich**-ni] adj.m. bureaucratic; official; fond of red tape
biurokratyzm [byoo-ro-**krah**-tizm] m. bureaucracy; red tape; officialism; bureaucratism; red-tapism
biurokratyzować [byoo-ro-krah-ti-**zo**-vahćh] v. spread red tape; implant the spirit of officialism (*repeatedly*)
biurokratyzować się [byoo-ro-krah-ti-**zo**-vahćh shan] v. favor red-tapism; favor official procedure marked by excessive complexity which results in delay or inaction (*repeatedly*)
biurokratyzowanie [byoo-ro-krah-ti-zo-**vah**-ńe] n. bureaucratization
biurowiec [byoo-**ro**-vyets] m. office building
biurowość [byoo-**ro**-vośhćh] f. clerical work
biurowy [byoo-**ro**-vi] adj.m. office; clerk's; official's; clerical
godziny biurowe [go-**dźhee**-ni byoo-**ro**-ve] exp.: office hours
kolega biurowy [ko-**le**-gah byoo-**ro**-vi] exp.: office mate
materiały biurowe [mah-ter-**yah**-wi byoo-**ro**-ve] exp.: stationery
siła biurowa [**śhee**-wah byoo-**ro**-vah] exp.: clerk; office worker
skład materiałów biurowych [skwaht mah-te-**ryah**-woof byoo-**ro**-vikh] exp.: office supplies; stationer's shop
zajęcie biurowe [zah-**yan**-ćhe byoo-**ro**-ve] exp.: office work; white-collar work
biurwa [**byoor**-vah] f. vulg.: slang: stupid (nasty) office-bitch
biust [byoost] m. bust; breast; bosom
biustonosz [byoos-**to**-nosh] m. brassiere; bra; bust-bodice
biwak [**bee**-vahk] m. bivouac; bivouacking; encampment
biwakować [bee-vah-**ko**-vahćh] v. bivouac; encamp (*repeatedly*)
biwakowanie [bee-vah-ko-**vah**-ńe] n. encamping
biwakowy [bee-vah-**ko**-vi] adj.m. bivouac; camp (fire, etc.)
bizantyjski [bee-zahn-**tiy**-skee] adj.m. Byzantine (art, cross, mosaic, etc.)
bizantynista [bee-zahn-ti-**ńees**-tah] m. Byzantinist
bizantynistka [bee-zahn-ti-**ńeest**-kah] f. (woman) Byzantinist
bizantynizm [bee-zahn-ti-**ńeezm**] m. Byzantinism
bizantynolog [bee-zahn-ti-**no**-log] m. Byzantinist
bizantynologia [bee-zahn-ti-no-**lo**-gyah] f. Byzantine studies
bizantyński [bee-zahn-**tiń**-skee] adj.m. Byzantine (art, etc.)
bizmut [**beez**-moot] m. bismuth (mineral)
bizmutowy [beez-moo-**to**-vi] adj.m.

bismuth; bismuthic
bizmutyn [beez-**moo**-tin] m. bismuthine (mineral)
biznes [**beez**-nes] m. business
biznesmen [beez-**nes**-men] m. businessman
bizon [**bee**-zon] m. bison; colloq: great lout; sluggard; lazybones; oaf
bizun [**bee**-zoon] m. cowhide; thong; strap; lash; colloq: oaf; lazybones; great lout; sluggard
biżuteria [bee-zhoo-**te**-ryah] f. jewelry; jewels
biżuteryjny [bee-zhoo-te-**riy**-ni] adj.m. jewel (gold, etc.)
blacha [**blah**-khah] f. sheet metal; cook top; the range; tinware; baking-pan; (music) the brass
blacharnia [blah-**khahr**-ńah] f. sheet-iron works (shop); tinsmith's workshop
blacharski [blah-**khahr**-skee] adj.m. tinsmith's
wyroby blacharskie [vi-**ro**-bi blah-**khahr**-ske] exp.: tinware
blacharstwo [blah-**khahr**-stfo] n. tinsmith's work
blacharz [**blah**-khahsh] m. tinsmith
blachowkręt [blah-**kho**-fkrant] m. sheet metal screw; self-threading screw; thread-cutting screw
blachownia [blah-**khov**-ńah] f. sheet-iron works (shop)
blachownica [blah-khov-**ńee**-tsah] f. rolling mill; plate girder; armored breast-plate
blacik [**blah**-ćheek] m. (small) table-top
bladaczka [blah-**dahch**-kah] f. chlorosis; greensickness
bladawo [blah-**dah**-vo] adv. palishly; rather palely; somewhat palely
bladawy [blah-**dah**-vi] adj.m. palish; rather pale; somewhat pale; wan; paly; pallid
bladnąć [**blahd**-nownćh] v. grow pale; turn white; go white; fade; blanch; pale (before, beside) (*repeatedly*)
blado [**blah**-do] adv. palely; weakly; feebly; faintly; wanly
to blado wypadło [to **blah**-do vi-**pahd**-wo] exp.: it was colorless; it was tame; it was nerveless; colloq: it was poor; it was not very good
wyglądać blado [vi-**glown**-dahćh **blah**-do] exp.: to look pale
blado- [**blah**-do] prefix: pale (green, etc.); pale-pink; pinkish
bladoczerwony [blah-do-cher-**vo**-ni] adj.m. pale-red
bladolicy [blah-do-**lee**-tsi] adj.m. pale-faced; pale-looking
bladoróżowy [blah-do-roo-**zho**-vi] adj.m. pale-pink; pinkish
bladość [**blah**-dośhćh] f. pallor; paleness; faintness; dimness; lack of distinctness; weakness; tameness; lack of color; lack of nerve; wanness
bladożółty [blah-do-**zhoow**-ti] adj.m. pale-yellow; primrose yellow; daffodil
blady [**blah**-di] adj.m. pale; pallid; grey; gray; wan; white; bloodless; dim; bleak; lurid; faint; indistinct; weak; tame; colorless; nerveless; flimsy; poor
bladziuchny [blah-**dźhookh**-ni] adj.m. very pale
bladziuteńki [blah-dźhoo-**teń**-kee] adj.m. very, very pale
bladziutki [blah-**dźhoot**-kee] adj.m. very pale
blaga [**blah**-gah] f. lie; bluff; boasting; bluster; blague; humbug; claptrap; raillery
blagier [**blah**-ger] m. liar; hoaxer; boaster; braggart; bluffer; blusterer (man)
blagierka [blah-**ger**-kah] f. liar; hoaxer; boaster; braggart; bluffer; blusterer (woman)
blagierski [blah-**ger**-skee] adj.m. hoaxing; boasting; bragging; bluffing; blustering
blagierstwo [blah-**ger**-stfo] n. lie; bluff; boasting; bluster; blague; humbug; claptrap
blagować [blah-**go**-vahćh] v. hoax; boast; brag; bluff; talk big (*repeatedly*)
blagowanie [blah-go-**vah**-ńe] n. hoax; boast; brag; bluff; talking big; humbug; claptrap; raillery
blak [blahk] m. (a) shallow (water);

shoal
blaknąć [blahk-nownćh] v. discolor; fade; grow dim; pale (*repeatedly*)
nie blaknący [ńe blahk-**nown**-tsi] exp.: unfading
blakmanaż [**blahk**-mah-nahsh] m. blancmange; variety of white dessert
blaknięcie [blahk-**ńan**-ćhe] n. paling; growing dim
blamaż [**blah**-mahsh] m. discredit; disgrace; shame; loss of face; humiliation; mortification
blamować się [blah-**mo**-vahćh śhan] v. disgrace oneself; bring shame on oneself; bring discredit on oneself; put oneself open to ridicule; lose face; cut a sorry figure; suffer a humiliation; be mortified (*repeatedly*)
blamowanie się [blah-mo-**vah**-ńe śhan] n. disgracing oneself; bringing shame on oneself
blanco [blahn-ko] exp.:
podpisać in blanco [pot-**pee**-sahćh een **blahn**-ko] exp.: to sign a blank (check, etc.)
blank [blahnk] m. battlement; blank leather
blanka [**blahn**-kah] f. crenelated battlements
blankiet [**blahn**-ket] m. blank form; printed form; blank (check, etc.)
blankista [blahn-**kees**-tah] m. adherent to L. Blanqui (French) revolutionary movement
blankistowski [blahn-kees-**tof**-skee] adj.m. of the 19th cent. critique of capitalism
blankizm [**blahn**-keezm] m. 19th cent. critique of capitalism
blanko [blahn-ko] exp.:
podpisać in blanko [pot-**pee**-sahćh een **blahn**-ko] exp.: to sign a blank (check, etc.)
blankowy [blahn-**ko**-vi] adj.m. short (stock market transaction, etc.)
blansz [blahnsh] m. white face-powder
blanszować [blahn-**sho**-vahćh] v. scold (fruit, vegetables, etc.); whiten (hides, etc.) (*repeatedly*)
blanszować się [blahn-**sho**-vahćh śhan] v. powder one's face (*repeatedly*)
blanszowanie [blahn-sho-**vah**-ńe] n. scolding (of fruits, etc.); whitening (hides, etc.)
blanszowanie się [blahn-sho-**vah**-ńe śhan] n. powdering one's face
blanszownik [blahn-**shov**-ńeek] m. device for scolding (of fruits, etc.)
blask [blahsk] m. flush; brightness; brilliance; radiance; sheen; refulgence; glitter; polish; glossiness; shine; luster; glamor; garishness; glory; grandeur; gleam
bez blasku [bes **blahs**-koo] exp.: lusterless; dead
blaski i cienie [**blah**-skee ee **ćhe**-ńe] exp.: ups and downs (of)
blask księżyca [blahsk kśhan-**zhi**-tsah] exp.: moonlight
blask słoneczny [blahsk swo-**nech**-ni] exp.: sunlight; sunshine
fałszywy blask [fahw-**shi**-vi blahsk] exp.: gloss; false glitter
łagodny blask [wah-**god**-ni blahsk] exp.: shimmer; lambency
blaskowy [blahs-**ko**-vi] adj.m. radiant; shining; gleaming; of gleam; of glory; of grandeur
blastema [blahs-**te**-mah] f. blastema
blastocel [blah-**sto**-tsel] m. blastocoele; blastocoel
blastoderma [blahs-to-**der**-mah] f. blastoderm
blastoidea [blahs-to-ee-**de**-ah] pl. Blastoidea
blastomer [blahs-**to**-mer] m. blastomere
blastula [blahs-**too**-lah] f. blastula
blaszanka [blah-**shahn**-kah] f. can; tin can; tin (Brit.)
blaszanka na mleko [blah-**shahn**-kah nah **mle**-ko] exp.: milk-can
blaszany [blah-**shah**-ni] adj.m. tin
instrumenty blaszane [een-stroo-**men**-ti blah-**shah**-ne] exp.: brass instruments
wyroby blaszane [vi-**ro**-bi blah-**shah**-ne] exp.: tinware
blaszka [**blahsh**-kah] f. metal plate; lamina; blade; lamella; tin plate; badge; gill; identity plate; identity disc; identity tag
dzielić na blaszki [**dźhe**-leećh nah **blahsh**-kee] exp.: to foliate

blaszkodzioby [blahsh-ko-**dźho**-bi] adj.m. lamellirostal (bird)
blaszkodziobe [blahsh-ko-**dźho**-be] pl. Lamellirostres
blaszkorogi [blahsh-ko-**ro**-gee] adj.m. lamellicornous (beetle)
blaszkorogie [blahsh-ko-**ro**-ge] pl. Lamellicornia
blaszkoskrzelny [blahsh-ko-**skshel**-ni] adj.m. lamellibranchiate
blaszkoskrzelne [blahsh-ko-**skshel**-ne] pl. Lamellibranchiata
blaszkowaty [blahsh-ko-**vah**-ti] adj.m. lamellar; lamellate; composed of thin plates
blaszkowy [blahsh-**ko**-vi] adj.m. foliate
blaszkowe złoto [blahsh-**ko**-ve **zwo**-to] exp.: gold foil
blat [blaht] m. sheet; plate; colloq: tabletop; desk top; dresser top
blat stołu [blaht **sto**-woo] exp.: tabletop
blech [blekh] m. bleachery
blednąć [**bled**-nownćh] v. grow pale; turn white; go white; fade; blanch; pale (beside) (*repeatedly*)
blednica [bled-**ńee**-tsah] f. chlorosis; greensickness
blednieć [**bled**-ńećh] v. grow pale; turn white; go white; fade; blanch; pale (before, beside); see: **blednąć** (*repeatedly*)
bledniẹcie [bled-**ńan**-ćhe] n. growing pale; fading
bledszy [**blet**-shi] adj.m. more pale; augmentative form of: **"blady"**
bledziuchny [ble-**dźhookh**-ni] adj.m. faintly pale
bledziuteńki [ble-dźhoo-**teń**-kee] adj.m. very, very pale
bledziutki [ble-**dźhoot**-kee] adj.m. very pale; awfully pale
blef [blef] m. bluff; bluffing
blefiarz [**ble**-fyahsh] m. bluff
blefować [**ble-fo**-vahćh] v. bluff (*repeatedly*)
blefowanie [ble-fo-**vah**-ńe] n. bluffing
blejtram [**bley**-trahm] m. stretcher (of canvas)
blejtramowy [bley-trah-**mo**-vi] adj.m. stretcher (canvas, etc.)
blejwas [**bley**-vahs] m. white lead; ceruse
blekot [**ble**-kot] m. fool's parsley (a poisonous weed)
blenda [**blen**-dah] f. blank (window); (photographic) diaphragm; (black) blende (mineral); (pitch) blende (of uranium)
bleskotka [bles-**kot**-kah] f. chalcid; chalcid fly
blezer [**ble**-zer] m. blazer (jacket)
blich [bleekh] m. bleachery
blicharz [**blee**-khahsh] m. bleacher
blichować [blee-**kho**-vahćh] v. bleach; put a coating of calcium sulphate plaster (on a wall) (*repeatedly*)
blichowanie [blee-kho-**vah**-ńe] n. bleaching; coating (a wall) with calcium sulphate plaster
blichtr [bleekhtr] m. tinsel; false show; glare; trumpery; sham brilliance
blik [bleek] m. bright spot in a picture imitating light
blin [bleen] m. (kind of) pancake
blindaż [**bleen**-dahsh] m. blindage; armor-plating; timbering; sheeting
blindgafel [bleend-**gah**-fel] m. bowsprit extension
bliski [**blees**-kee] adj.m. near; imminent; nearby; close; impending; at hand; in sight; recent; not far away; at short range; m. close relative
bliski znajomy [**blees**-kee znah-**yo**-mi] exp.: close (intimate) acquaintance; colloq: good friend
pozostawać w bliskich stosunkach [po-zo-**stah**-vahćh v **blees**-keekh sto-**soon**-kahkh] exp.: to be in close (intimate) relations
bliskie podobieństwo [**blees**-ke po-do-**byeń**-stfo] exp.: close resemblance
z bliska [z **blees**-kah] exp.: from close range; from near; adv. carefully; in detail
blisko [**blees**-ko] adv. near(ly); close(ly); nearby; close by; just by; within call; at hand; almost pretty nearly; approximately; practically; very nearly
blisko spokrewniony [**blees**-ko spo-kre-**vńo**-ni] exp.: closely

related
blisko dwa miesiące [**blees**-ko dvah mye-**śhown**-tse] exp.: nearly two months
blisko końca [**blees**-ko **koń**-tsah] exp.: towards the end
być blisko czegoś [bićh **blees**-ko **che**-gośh] exp.: to be quite close to something
daleko i blisko [dah-**le**-ko ee **blees**-ko] exp.: far and near
blisko rzeki [**blees**-ko **zhe**-kee] exp.: near the river
blisko siebie [**blees**-ko **śhe**-bye] exp.: close to each other
bliskoś ć [**blees**-kośhćh] f. nearness; proximity; imminence; impendence; impendency; instancy; coming (of dawn, of death, etc.); close friendship; intimacy; family ties; close relationship
bliskoznacznik [blees-ko-**znahch**-ńeek] m. synonym; synonymous word
bliskoznacznoś ć [blees-ko-**znahch**-nośhćh] f. synonymity
bliskoznaczny [blees-ko-**znahch**-ni] adj.m. synonymous
bliziutki [blee-**źhoot**-kee] adj.m. very near; close by; round the corner
bliziutko [blee-**źhoot**-ko] adv. very near; close by; round the corner
blizna [**bleez**-nah] f. scar; gash; mark; seam; cicatrice; cicatrix
z blizną na twarzy [z **bleez**-nown nah **tfah**-zhi] exp.: with a scarred face
bliznowacenie [bleez-no-vah-**tse**-ńe] n. healing over; forming cicatrices; cicatrization
bliznowacieć [bleez-no-**vah**-ćhećh] v. heal over; skin over; scar (*repeatedly*)
bliznowaty [bleez-no-**vah**-ti] adj.m. cicatricial
bliźni [**bleeźh**-ńee] m. fellow man; fellow creature; neighbor; adj.m. identical; twin (brother)
bliźniactwo [bleeźh-**ńah**-tstfo] n. the phenomenon of double birth; being a twin
bliźniaczek [blee-**źhńah**-chek] m. baby twin
bliźniaczka [bleeźh-**ńahch**-kah] f. twin sister; mat-weed; the matgrass (Nardus stricta)
bliźniaczo [bleeźh-**ńah**-cho] adv. identically; similarly
bliźniaczy [bleeźh-**ńah**-chi] adj.m. twin; identical; similar; of one pattern; twin-born
ciąża bliźniacza [**ćhown**-zhah bleeźh-**ńah**-chah] exp.: twin pregnancy
domek bliźniaczy [**do**-mek bleeźh-**ńah**-chi] exp.: duplex; semi-detached house; a house consisting of two separate family units
pług bliźniaczy [pwoog bleeźh-**ńah**-chi] exp.: turn-over plow
statek bliźniaczy [**stah**-tek bleeźh-**ńah**-chi] exp.: sister ship
bliźniak [**bleeźh**-ńahk] m. twin; twin brother; twin sister; twin child; twin crystal; macle (mineral)
bliźniaki [bleeźh-**ńah**-kee] exp.: twins; duplex; semi-detached hause; double pot
bliźniarka [bleeźh-**ńahr**-kah] f. rambutan (Indian tree)
bliźniczka [bleeźh-**ńeech**-kah] f. mat-weed (a grass)
bliźnić się [**bleeźh**-ńeećh śhan] v. scar; heal over; cicatrize (*repeatedly*)
bliźnię [**bleeźh**-ńan] n. twin baby
bliźnięta [bleeźh-**ńan**-tah] pl. twins; twin children; Gemini (astrol.)
bliżej [**blee**-zhey] adv. nearer by; closer; more nearly (closely, exactly, precisely, in detail)
coraz bliżej [**tso**-rahs **blee**-zhey] exp.: nearer and nearer
znać bliżej [znahćh **blee**-zhey] exp.: be closely acquainted with
bliższoś ć [**bleesh**-shośhćh] f. greater (more pronounced) nearness
bliższy [**bleesh**-shi] adj.m. nearer; closer; direct
bliższe dane [**bleesh**-she **dah**-ne] exp.: more definite data; further particulars
bloczek [**blo**-chek] m. pad; (small) notebook; miniature sheet; small

pulley for rising weights or transmitting power; trochlea
blok [blok] m. block; pulley; block of buildings; barrack in a German-Nazi concentration camp; writing-pad
blok mieszkalny [blok myesh-**kahl**-ni] exp: block of flats
blok partyjny [blok pahr-**tiy**-ni] exp.: party faction
blok rysunkowy [blok ri-soon-**ko**-vi] exp.: drawing-block
blokada [blo-**kah**-dah] f. blockade; (railroad) block system; (printing) turning of letters
blokdiagram [blok-**dyah**-grahm] m. block diagram
bloking [**blo**-keeng] m. blocking in volleyball; blockage
blokować [blo-**ko**-vahćh] v. block; blockade; obstruct; stall; take up space; interlock; sidetrack (a question, etc.) (*repeatedly*)
blokowanie [blo-ko-**vah**-ńe] n. blockage; obstruction; stalling
blokowisko [blo-ko-**vees**-ko] n. colloq: gloomy group of large multistory apartment buildings
blokownik [blo-**kov**-ńeek] m. blocking element in a steering mechanism
blokowy [blo-**ko**-vi] adj.m. block (of lava, etc.); of a bloc; m. barrack chief in a German-Nazi concentration camp; railroad signal-box operator
pismo blokowe [**pees**-mo blo-**ko**-ve] exp.: block letters; sanskrit
blokówka [blo-**koof**-kah] f. bookbinding machine for sewing with thin wire
blond [blont] not declined: fair(-haired); blond
blondas [**blon**-dahs] m. slang: blond (man)
blondyn [**blon**-din] m. blond (man)
blondyneczka [blon-di-**nech**-kah] f. nice little blonde (girl); fair-haired girl
blondynek [blon-**di**-nek] m. blond (boy); nice blond boy
blondynka [blon-**din**-kah] f. blonde (woman); fair-haired girl
blotka [**blot**-kah] f. low card; girlie
blues [bloos] m. early jazz music; sad Negro music; blues
bluesowy [bloo-**so**-vi] adj.m. of blues; in blues (style, etc.)
bluetka [bloo-**et**-kah] f. short one-act play
bluff [blef] m. bluff; bluffing
bluffiarz [**ble**-fyahsh] m. bluff
bluffować [ble-**fo**-vahćh] v. bluff (*repeatedly*)
bluszcz [blooshch] m. ivy
bluszczowaty [bloo-shcho-**vah**-ti] adj.m. ivy-like; shaped like an ivy
bluszczowość [bloo-**shcho**-vośhćh] f. colloq: ivy-style
bluszczowy [bloosh-**cho**-vi] adj.m. ivy-covered; ivied
bluszczyk [**bloosh**-chik] m. ground-ivy
bluza [**bloo**-zah] f. blouse; tunic; smock; billiard pocket
bluzczarka [bloos-**chahr**-kah] f. blouse seamstress
bluzeczka [bloo-**zech**-kah] f. (nice, little) blouse
bluzg [bloozg] m. gush; spirt; jet
bluzgać [**blooz**-gahćh] v. spout; spurt; squirt; gush; spirt; jet (*repeatedly*)
bluzganie [blooz-**gah**-ńe] n. jetting; spouting; gushing (a liquid)
bluzgnąć [**blooz**-gnownćh] v. spout; squirt; gush; spirt; jet
bluzgnięcie [bloozg-**ńan**-ćhe] n. spout; squirt; gush; jet
bluzka [**bloos**-kah] f. blouse
bluzkowy [bloos-**ko**-vi] adj.m. blouse (fabric, etc.)
bluznąć [**blooz**-nownćh] v. spout; squirt; gush; spirt; jet
bluźnić [**bloożh**-ńeećh] v. curse; blaspheme; colloq: talk nonsense; revile; profane; utter absurdities (*repeatedly*)
bluźnierca [bloożh-**ńer**-tsah] m. blasphemer
bluźnierczo [bloożh-**ńer**-cho] adv. blasphemously
bluźnierczy [bloożh-**ńer**-chi] adj.m. blasphemous
bluźnierski [bloożh-**ńer**-skee] adj.m. blasphemous
bluźnierstwo [bloożh-**ńer**-stfo] n. blasphemy

bluźnięcie [bloożh-ńan-ćhe] n. spouting; squirting; gushing
błagać [**bwah**-gahćh] v. beseech (for); invoke; implore; entreat; crave (for); supplicate (for) (*repeatedly*)
błagająco [bwah-gah-**yown**-tso] adv. beseechingly; imploringly; entreatingly
błagalnie [bwah-**gahl**-ńe] adv. beseechingly; imploringly
błagalny [bwah-**gahl**-ni] adj.m. imploring; beseeching; suppliant
błaganie [bwah-**gah**-ńe] n. imploration; entreaty; humble request; invocation; appeal
błaho [**bwah**-kho] adv. in a trifling manner; insignificantly
błahostka [bwah-**khost**-kah] f. trifle; trivial matter; frivolity; trinket
błahość [**bwah**-khośhćh] f. triviality; futility; insignificance; unimportance; inconsequence; flimsiness; immateriality
błahy [**bwah**-khi] adj.m. trifling; futile; insignificant; immaterial; unimportant; trivial; flimsy; inconsequential; nugatory
błam [bwahm] m. fur lining (texture); length of cloth; piece of cloth
błamować [bwah-**mo**-vahćh] v. sew (skins) together for a fur lining (*repeatedly*)
bławat [**bwah**-vaht] m. blue silk texture; blue cornflower; bluebottle
bławatek [bwah-**vah**-tek] m. blue cornflower; bluebottle
bławatkowy [bwah-vah-**tko**-vi] adj.m. blue (eyes, etc.)
bławatnik [bwah-**vaht**-ńeek] m. mercer; dealer in textile fabrics; Cotinga passerine bird; cotingid
bławatny [bwah-**vaht**-ni] adj.m. mercer's (shop, etc.) of a blue silk texture; blue (color)
bławatowy [bwah-vah-**to**-vi] adj.m. blue
bławy [**bwah**-vi] adj.m. light-blue
błazen [**bwah**-zen] m. clown; zany; buffoon; fool; tomfool; low comedian; court jester
wyjść na błazna [viyśhćh nah **bwahz**-nah] exp.: to look silly
błazenada [bwah-ze-**nah**-dah] f. foolery; buffoonery
błazeński [bwah-**zeń**-skee] adj.m. clownish; tomfool; scurrilous
błazeńsko [bwah-**zeń**-sko] adv. clownishly
błazeństwo [bwah-**zeń**-stfo] n. foolery; buffoonery
błaznować [bwah-**zno**-vahćh] v. clown; play the clown; buffoon; colloq: tomfool; monkey; droll; fool around (*repeatedly*)
błaznowanie [bwahz-no-**vah**-ńe] n. foolery; buffoonery
błaźnić [**bwahźh**-ńeećh] v. make the fool (of somebody) (*repeatedly*)
błaźnić się [**bwahźh**-ńeećh śhan] v. make the fool of oneself; make an ass of oneself; discredit oneself (*repeatedly*)
błaźnienie się [bwahźh-**ńe**-ńe śhan] n. discrediting oneself
błąd [bwownt] m. error; mistake; lapse; slip-up; fallacy; fault; defect; incorrectness; slip; misstatement; misconception; misapprehension
błąd gramatyczny [bwownt grah-mah-**tich**-ni] exp.: grammatical error; mistake in grammar
błąd w pisowni [bwownt f pee-**sov**-ńee] exp.: mistake in spelling
być w błędzie [bićh v **bwan**-dźhe] exp.: to be wrong; to be mistaken; to err; to be under a delusion (misconception)
wprowadzić w błąd [fpro-**vah**-dźheećh v bwownt] exp.: to lead into error; to lead astray; to mislead; to misguide; to misinform; to deceive
wyprowadzić z błędu [vi-pro-**vah**-dźheećh z **bwan**-doo] exp.: to correct (somebody's) misunderstanding; to set (somebody) straight
błądzący [bwown-**dzown**-tsi] adj.m. vagrant; wandering; truant; stray
błądzenie [bwown-**dze**-ńe] n. wandering (in the dark); being lost
błądzić [**bwown**-dźheećh] v. make

a mistake; make mistakes; be mistaken; be wrong; err; do wrong; go astray; stumble; blunder; wander; roam; rove; travel; ramble; grope (*repeatedly*)

błąkać się [**bwown**-kahćh śhan] v. wander (about); stray; roam; rove; be on the rove; vagabondize (*repeatedly*)

błąkający się [bwown-kah-**yown**-tsi śhan] adj.m. vagrant; stray; unclaimed

błąkanie się [bwown-**kah**-ńe śhan] n. wandering about; losing the way; being disoriented

błąkanina [bwown-kah-**ńee**-nah] f. wandering; wanderings; ramble; rambles; roving; journey; journeys; peregrination; peregrinations

błędnie [**bwand**-ńe] adv. mistakenly; by mistake; aimlessly; like a stray sheep

błędnie obliczyć [**bwand**-ńe ob-**lee**-chićh] exp.: to miscalculate

błędnie osądzić [**bwand**-ńe o-**sown**-dźheećh] exp.: to misjudge

błędnik [**bwand**-ńeek] m. labyrinth (of the ear)

błędnikowy [bwand-ńee-**ko**-vi] adj.m. of ear-labyrinth

błędnodruk [bwand-no-**drook**] m. misprint of a postal stamp

błędność [**bwand**-nośhćh] f. faultiness; incorrectness; erroneousness; fallacy (of an opinion, etc.); unsoundness (of a statement, etc.)

błędny [**bwand**-ni] adj.m. faulty; incorrect; erroneous; wrong; wild; false; fallacious; mistaken; unsound; misjudged; improper; wandering; roving; roaming; vagrant; stray; vague; far-away; truant

błędna odpowiedź [**bwand**-nah ot-po-vyećh] exp.: wrong answer

błędne koło [**bwand**-ne **ko**-wo] exp.: vicious circle

błędny rycerz [**bwand**-ni **ri**-tsesh] exp.: knight errant

błędne oczy [**bwan**-dne **o**-chi] exp.: wild look; fishy eyes

błędny ognik [**bwand**-ni **o**-gńeek] exp.: fen-fire; jack-o'-lantern; will-o'-the-wisp

błękit [**bwan**-keet] m. blue (color); azure; blue pigment; sky

błękitnawo [bwan-keet-**nah**-vo] adv. bluishly

błękitnawy [bwan-keet-**nah**-vi] adj.m. bluish

błękitnie [bwan-**keet**-ńe] adv. with a blue tint

błękitnieć [bwan-**keet**-ńećh] v. turn blue; become blue; grow blue; assume a blue color (*repeatedly*)

błękitno [bwan-**keet**-no] adv. bluishly

błękitnooki [bwan-keet-no-**o**-kee] adj.m. blue-eyed

błękitność [bwan-**keet**-nośhćh] f. (the) blue

błękitny [bwan-**keet**-ni] adj.m. sky-blue; azure; celeste; blue in hue, of low saturation and medium brilliance

błękitna krew [bwan-**keet**-nah kref] exp.: blue blood

błocenie [bwo-**tse**-ńe] n. muddying up; spattering with mud

błocić [**bwo**-ćheećh] v. get muddy; soil with mud; spatter with mud; smear with mud (*repeatedly*)

błocić się [**bwo**-ćheećh śhan] v. get (oneself) muddy; get soiled with mud; get spattered with mud; get smeared with mud (*repeatedly*)

błocisko [bwo-**ćhees**-ko] n. nasty mud; heavy mud

błocko [**bwots**-ko] n. muddy light clay

błogi [**bwo**-gee] adj.m. blissful; delightful; sweet; rapturous; salutary

błogi stan [**bwo**-gee stahn] exp.: bliss

błogo [**bwo**-go] adv. blissfully; delightfully; rapturously

jak to błogo! [yahk to **bwo**-go] exp.: how delightful!

błogosławić [bwo-go-**swah**-veećh] v. bless; praise; exalt; thank (heaven, etc.); commend; glorify; give one's blessing (*repeatedly*)

błogosławienie [bwo-go-swah-**vye**-ńe] n. benediction

błogosławieństwo [bwo-go-swah-**vyeń**-stfo] n. (a) blessing; benediction
błogosławiony [bwo-go-swah-**vyo**-ni] adj.m. blessed; happy
błogosławiony stan [bwo-go-swah-**vyo**-ni stahn] exp.: pregnancy
błogostan [bwo-**go**-stahn] m. blissfulness; felicity; happiness
błogość [**bwo**-gośhćh] f. bliss; felicity; happiness; well-being; comfort; snugness
błona [**bwo**-nah] f. membrane; coat; film; tunic; velum; web; integument; pellicle
błona dziewicza [**bwo**-nah dźhe-**vee**-chah] exp.: hymen; a fold of mucous membrane of the vagina
błona śluzowa [**bwo**-nah śhloo-**zo**-vah] exp.: mucous membrane
błoniasty [bwo-**ńahs**-ti] adj.m. filmy; membranaceous; membranous (wings, etc.)
błonica [bwo-**ńee**-tsah] f. diphtheria
błonicowy [bwo-ńee-**tso**-vi] adj.m. diphtherial; diphtheric; diphtheritic; diphtherian; diphtheroid; resembling diphtheria
błoniczy [bwo-**ńee**-chi] adj.m. diphtheria (bacillus, toxin, etc.)
błonie [**bwo**-ńe] n. meadow; plain; public grassy land; village green
błonka [**bwon**-kah] f. pellicle; film; fine membrane; cuticle
błonkoskrzydlaty [bwon-ko-skshid-**lah**-ti] adj.m. hymenopterous (nocturnal bat, etc.)
błonkoskrzydły [bwon-ko-**skshid**-wi] adj.m. hymenopterous
błonkoskrzydłe [bwon-ko-**skshid**-we] pl. Hymenoptera
błonkowaty [bwon-ko-**vah**-ti] adj.m. membranous; scarious
błonkówka [bwon-**koof**-kah] f. hymenopteron (insect)
błonnik [**bwon**-ńeek] m. cellulose
błonnikowy [bwon-ńee-**ko**-vi] adj.m. cellulose (varnish, etc.)
błonotwórczy [bwo-no-**tfoor**-chi] adj.m. surface membrane forming
błonowy [bwo-**no**-vi] adj.m. membranous (bone, etc.); membrane (tissue, etc.)
błotko [**bwot**-ko] n. nasty thin mud
błotniak [**bwot**-ńahk] m. harrier
błotniarka [bwot-**ńahr**-kah] f. press-filter; fresh-water snail
błotnik [**bwot**-ńeek] m. (car) fender; mudguard; splash-board; front end fender
błotnistość [bwot-**ńees**-tośhćh] f. swampiness; marshiness; mire; sloppiness
błotnisty [bwot-**ńees**-ti] adj.m. muddy; swampy; splashy; sloppy; boggy; paludal
błotny [**bwot**-ni] adj.m. muddy; miry; marshy; marsh (gas, etc.); swamp
kąpiel błotna [**k<u>own</u>**-pyel **bwot**-nah] exp.: mud-bath
gaz błotny [gahz **bwot**-ni] exp.: marsh-gas
ptactwo błotne [**ptahts**-tfo **bwot**-ne] exp.: water fowl
błoto [**bwo**-to] n. mud; muck; dirt
błota [**bwo**-tah] pl. swamp; swamps; marshlands; marshes; bogs
grząskie błoto [gzh<u>own</u>s-<u>k</u>e **bwo**-to] exp.: slush
mieszać z błotem [**mye**-shahćh z **bwo**-tem] exp.: to abuse; to revile
ugrząść w błocie [oo-gzh<u>own</u>śhćh v **bwo**-ćhe] exp.: to get stuck in the mud
błysk [bwisk] m. flash; flare; sparkle; glint; glance; glimmer (of hope, etc.); spoon-bait (fishing)
błysk dowcipu [bwisk dof-**ćhee**-poo] exp.: flight of fancy (wit)
błyskać [**bwis**-kahćh] v. flash; glitter; lighten; glint; sparkle; flicker; fulminate; fulgurate; gleam; shine (*repeatedly*)
błyskać się [**bwis**-kahćh śh<u>an</u>] v. lighten (*repeatedly*)
błyska się i grzmi [**bwis**-kah śh<u>an</u> ee gzhmee] exp.: it lightens and thunders
błysnęło się [bwis-**ne**-wo śh<u>an</u>] exp.: it lightened; there was a flash of lightning
błyskanie [bwis-**kah**-ńe] n. flashes of lightning
błyskanie się [bwis-**kah**-ńe śh<u>an</u>] n. flashes of lightning

błyskawica [bwi-skah-**vee**-tsah] f. (flash, shaft, bolt, or stroke of) lightning; posted news sheet
błyskawicowy [bwi-skah-vee-**tso**-vi] adj.m. of lightning; lightning (speed, etc.)
błyskawicznie [bwi-skah-**veech**-ńe] adv. like lightning; in no time at all; like a streak; with lightning speed; in a flash; as quick as thought
błyskawiczność [bwi-skah-**veech**-nośhćh] f. flashiness; glitter; sparkle; immediate response
błyskawiczny [bwi-skah-**veech**-ni] adj.m. swift; rapid; quick as a lightning; blitz (krieg, war, etc.)
wojna błyskawiczna [**voy**-nah bwis-kah-**veech**-nah] exp.: blitz
zamek błyskawiczny [**zah**-mek bwi-skah-**veech**-ni] exp.: zipper; zip fastener
błyskotać [bwi-**sko**-tahćh] v. sparkle; glitter; flicker (*repeatedly*)
błyskotanie [bwi-sko-**tah**-ńe] n. sparkle; glitter; flicker
błyskotka [bwi-**skot**-kah] f. gewgaw; tinsel; trinket; gaud; spangle; paillette
błyskotliwie [bwi-sko-**tlee**-vye] adv. glitteringly; showily; gaudily; brilliantly; with sprightly wit; with sharp wit
błyskotliwość [bwi-sko-**tlee**-vośhćh] f. glitter; sparkle; tinsel; showiness; brightness; gaudiness; brilliance; sharp wit; sprightliness; lambency
błyskotliwy [bwi-sko-**tlee**-vi] adj.m. flashy; gaudy; shiny; glittery; sparkling; tinsel; showy; witty; brilliant; bright; gaudy; lambent; with a sharp wit; sprightly; pointed; smart; nimble-witted
błyskotny [bwi-**skot**-ni] adj.m. flashy; gaudy; shiny; glittery = **błyskotliwy** [bwi-sko-**tlee**-vi]
błyskowy [bwi-**sko**-vi] adj.m. flash-; flash (light, spectrum, etc.)
błysnąć [**bwis**-nownćh] v. flash
błysnęło [bwis-**ne**-wo] exp.: it lightened; there was a flash of lightning
błystka [**bwist**-kah] f. troll; trolling-spoon (for fishing)
błyszcz [bwishch] m. (iron, silver, antimony, etc.) glance
błyszcząco [bwi-**shchown**-tso] adv. brilliantly
błyszczący [bwi-**shchown**-tsi] adj.m. shining; brilliant; shiny; sparkling; lustrous; sheeny; radiant; refulgent; polished; orient (pearls, etc.)
błyszczeć [**bwish**-chećh] v. shine; glitter; gleam; glisten; shimmer; scintillate; cut a dash; make a brilliant figure (*repeatedly*)
błyszczeć się [**bwish**-chećh śhan] v. emphatic: shine; glitter; gleam; glisten; shimmer; scintillate; cut a dash; make a brilliant figure (*repeatedly*)
błyszczenie [bwish-**che**-ńe] n. shining; glittering; sparkling
błyszczenie się [bwish-**che**-ńe śhan] n. shining; glittering; sparkling
błyszczka [**bwishch**-kah] f. troll; trolling-spoon (for fishing)
błyszczyk [**bwish**-chik] m. troll; trolling-spoon (for fishing)
błyśnięcie [bwiśh-**ńan**-ćhe] n. a flash of lightning
bo [bo] conjunction: because; for; or; or else; as; since; but then; particle: to be sure; true; such as it is
bo i [bo ee] exp.: but then
bo ja wiem? [bo yah vyem] exp.: how should I know?; how can I tell?; I have no idea
bo przecież [bo **pshe**-ćhesh] exp.: but then
boa [**bo**-ah] m. boa; boa-constrictor
boazeria [bo-ah-**ze**-ryah] f. wainscot(ing); (wall) paneling
bobak [**bo**-bahk] m. Polish marmot; a burrowing squirrel
bobas [**bo**-bahs] m. tiny tot; little dot; toddler
bobasek [bo-**bah**-sek] m. very tiny tot; sweet little dot; toddler
bobek [**bo**-bek] m. laurel; sheep-droppings; goat-droppings
bober [**bo**-ber] m. broad bean
bobik [**bo**-beek] m. vetch; hairy vetch (Vicia faba minor)

bobina [bo-bee-nah] f. bobbin; narrow roll of paper
bobiniarka [bo-bee-ńahr-kah] f. machine for cutting narrow rolls of paper
bobkowy [bop-ko-vi] adj.m. bay-
liść bobkowy [leeśhćh bop-ko-vi] exp.: bay leaf
bobo [bo-bo] n. babe; kiddy
bobowniczek [bo-bov-ńee-chek] m. brooklime
bobownik [bo-bov-ńeek] m. bog-bean; buck-bean
bobowy [bo-bo-vi] adj.m. bean (seeds, soup, etc.)
ruda bobowa [roo-dah bo-bo-vah] exp.: bean ore
bobówka [bo-boof-kah] f. bean soup; pupa of a fly
bobrek [bob-rek] m. bog-bean; buck-bean
bobrkowaty [bobr-ko-vah-ti] adj.m. of the buck-bean family of plants
bobrkowate [bobr-ko-vah-te] pl. the buck-bean family of plants; the Menyanthaceae
bobroszczur [bob-ro-shchoor] m. coypu; nutria
bobrować [bob-ro-vahćh] v. wade; dive; rummage (for); ferret (for) (*repeatedly*)
bobrowanie [bo-bro-vah-ńe] n. wading; ferreting
bobrowisko [bo-bro-vees-ko] n. beaver's marshy forest
bobrownia [bo-brov-ńah] f. beavery
bobrowy [bo-bro-vi] adj.m. beaver (hat, fur, etc.); beaver's
bobrowa czapka [bo-bro-vah chahp-kah] exp.: beaver hat
bobrowe futro [bo-bro-ve foot-ro] exp.: beaver fur
bobsleista [bop-sle-ees-tah] m. bobsleigh racer
bobslej [bop-sley] m. bob-sleigh; bobsled
bobslejowy [bop-sle-yo-vi] adj.m. bob-sleigh (competition, track, etc.); bob-sled (race, etc.)
bochen [bo-khen] m. big loaf of bread; big lump
bochenek [bo-khe-nek] m. loaf; lump
bochenkowaty [bo-khen-ko-vah-ti] adj.m. loaflike; resembling a loaf of bread
bocian [bo-ćhahn] m. stork; colloq: self-styled reformer
bocianek [bo-ćhah-nek] m. young stork
bociani [bo-ćhah-ńee] adj.m. stork's (nest, etc.)
bocianiątko [bo-ćhah-ńownt-ko] n. stork's chick
bocianica [bo-ćhah-ńee-tsah] f. female stork
bocianicha [bo-ćhah-ńee-khah] f. (old, big) female stork
bocianiec [bo-ćhah-ńets] m. ship's lookout; crow's nest
bocianię [bo-ćhah-ńan] n. small stork's chick
bocianiucha [bo-ćhah-ńoo-khah] f. (old, big) female stork
bocianowaty [bo-ćhah-no-vah-ti] adj.m. stork-like; resembling a stork
bocianowy [bo-ćhah-no-vi] adj.m. stork's; of a stork
bociek [bo-ćhek] m. (nice) stork
boczasty [bo-chahs-ti] adj.m. broad-hipped
boczek [bo-chek] m. flank; side; flitch of bacon
na boczku [nah boch-koo] exp.: on the side; dishonestly; illegally
boczenie się [bo-che-ńe śhan] n. being angry; being cross; frowning (on, upon)
boczkiem [boch-kem] adv. sideways; stealthily; on the sly
bocznia [boch-ńah] f. palmetto
bocznica [boch-ńee-tsah] f. siding (track)
bocznik [boch-ńeek] m. (electric) shunt
bocznikować [boch-ńee-ko-vahćh] v. shunt (electrically) (*repeatedly*)
bocznikowy [boch-ńee-ko-vi] adj.m. shunt (circuit, motor, etc.)
bocznościan [bo-chno-śhćhahn] m. hovercraft with air skirt
boczny [boch-ni] adj.m. lateral; side (track, etc.); collateral (line)
boczna droga [boch-nah dro-gah] exp.: secondary road
boczna ulica [boch-nah oo-lee-tsah] exp.: by-street; off street

boczne drzwi [boch-ne dzhvee] exp.: side door
boczne światło [boch-ne śhfyaht-wo] exp.: sidelight
boczny tor [boch-ni tor] exp.: sidetrack
nawa boczna [nah-vah boch-nah] exp.: side aisle (in a church etc.)
puścić na boczny tor [poośh-ćheećh nah boch-ni tor] exp.: to sidetrack (something or somebody)
boczyć [bo-chićh] v. deviate (*repeatedly*)
boczyć się [bo-chićh śhan] v. sulk; be angry (with); be sulky; frown (on, upon); look askance (at) (*repeatedly*)
boć [boćh] conj. (emphatic) because; for; as; since
boćwina [boćh-fee-nah] f. red-beet leaves; red-beet soup
boćwinka [boćh-fee-nkah] f. red-beet leaves; red-beet soup
bodaj [bo-dahy] part. I wish; may be; should be...; would be...; just; at least; if only; maybe even; very likely; unless I am mistaken
bodajże [bo-dahy-zhe] part. = (emphatic) **bodaj**
bodiak [bo-dyahk] m. musk-thistle
bodiakowy [bo-dyah-ko-vi] adj.m. musk-thistle (thorn, etc.)
bodliwy [bod-lee-vi] adj.m. apt to gore; apt to horn; apt to toss
bodmeria [bod-mer-yah] f. bottomry (hypothecated ship as security for a loan)
bodnąć [bod-nownćh] v. gore; toss; horn; butt; prick; sting; nettle
bodnąć się [bod-nownćh śhan] v. gore each other; horn one another
bodnięcie [bod-ńan-ćhe] n. gore; goring
bodoni [bo-do-ńee] m. type of font
bodot [bo-dot] m. telegraph of J.M.E. Baudot
bodzenie [bo-dze-ńe] n. goring; horning
bodziak [bo-dźhahk] m. musk-thistle
bodziec [bo-dźhets] m. stimulus; impulse; incentive; incitement; urge; motive; mainspring; goad; spur; motivation
bodziszek [bo-dźhee-shek] m. geranium; crane's bill
bodziszkowaty [bo-dźheesh-ko-vah-ti] adj.m. of the Geraniacae herb
bodziszkowate [bo-dźheesh-ko-vah-te] pl. the Geraniacae family of herbs
bodźcowy [boćh-tso-vi] adj.m. incentive (system, etc.)
bogacenie się [bo-gah-tse-ńe śhan] n. enriching oneself; improving oneself
bogacić [bo-gah-ćheećh] v. enrich; improve; cultivate (*repeatedly*)
bogacić się [bo-gah-ćheećh śhan] v. get rich; grow rich; enrich oneself; make money; increase in number (quantity) (*repeatedly*)
bogacieć [bo-gah-ćhećh] v. = **bogacić się** (*repeatedly*)
bogactwo [bo-gahts-tfo] n. riches; wealth; means; fortune; plenty; opulence; great number; great quantity; great variety; money-bags; mammon; shekels
bogactwa [bo-gahts-tfah] pl. riches; fortunes; resources; wealth; plenty; great number; copiousness; variety
bogacz [bo-gahch] m. rich man; wealthy person; man of means
bogacze [bo-gah-che] pl. the rich; the wealthy; men of means
bogaczka [bo-gahch-kah] f. rich woman; wealthy woman; woman of means
Bogarodzica [bo-gah-ro-dźhee-tsah] f. the Mother of Christ; the Virgin Mary; Our Lady; ancient hymn to St. Mary
bogatek [bo-gah-tek] m. buprestid (beetle)
bogatka [bo-gaht-kah] f. tit; greater titmouse
bogatkowaty [bo-gaht-ko-vah-ti] adj.m. of buprestid beetle
bogatkowate [bo-gaht-ko-vah-te] pl. the Buprestid family of beetles
bogato [bo-gah-to] adv. richly; lavishly; gorgeously; generously; in great numbers; in great plenty; in great quantity
bogato żyć [bo-gah-to zhićh]

exp.: to live in affluence; slang: to live high on the hog
bogaty [bo-**gah**-ti] adj.m. rich; wealthy; opulent; well-off; costly; ample; copious; fertile (soil)
bogaci i biedni [bo-**gah**-ćhee ee **byed**-ńee] exp.: the rich and the poor; the haves and have-nots
bogdanka [bog-**dahn**-kah] f. lady-love; inamorata
bogini [bo-**gee**-ńee] f. goddess; idol
boginka [bo-**geen**-kah] f. nymph
bogobojna [bo-go-**boy**-nah] adj.f. pious; devout; church going (woman)
bogobojnie [bo-go-**boy**-ńe] adv. piously; religiously
bogobojność [bo-go-**boy**-nośhćh] f. godliness; piety; the fear of God; religious feelings
bogobojny [bo-go-**boy**-ni] adj.m. pious; devout; church-going; godly
bogoburczy [bo-go-**boor**-chi] adj.m. iconoclastic
bogoburstwo [bo-go-**boor**-stfo] n. iconoclasm
bogoojczyźniany [bo-go-oy-chi-**źhńah**-ni] adj.m. jingoistic
bogożerca [bo-go-**zher**-tsah] m. iconoclast
Bogurodzica [bo-goo-ro-**dźhee**-tsah] f. the Mother of Christ; the Virgin Mary; Our Lady; ancient hymn to St. Mary
boguwola [bo-goo-**vo**-lah] f. oriole
bohater [bo-**khah**-ter] m. hero
kult bohaterów [koolt bo-khah-**te**-roof] exp.: hero-worship
bohaterka [bo-khah-**ter**-kah] f. heroine
bohaterski [bo-khah-**ter**-skee] adj.m. heroic
po bohatersku [po bo-khah-**ter**-skoo] exp.: heroically; stoutly; with heroism; with gallantry
bohatersko [bo-khah-**ters**-ko] adv. heroically; stoutly; with heroism
bohaterstwo [bo-khah-**ter**-stfo] n. heroism
bohaterszczyzna [bo-khah-tersh-**chiz**-nah] f. false heroism; unnecessary heroism
bohema [bo-**khe**-mah] f. Bohemia
bohemista [bo-khe-**mees**-tah] m. Bohemian studies' specialist; Czech studies' specialist
bohemistyczny [bo-khe-mees-**tich**-ni] adj.m. of Bohemian studies; of Czech studies
bohemistyka [bo-khe-**mees**-ti-kah] f. Bohemian studies; Czech studies
bohemizm [bo-**khe**-meezm] m. Bohemism; Czech borowing
bohomaz [bo-**kho**-mahs] m. daub; daubster
boiken [**boy**-ken] m. cold-resistant apple tree
boisko [bo-**ees**-ko] n. stadium; field; threshing floor; gridiron; sports field; court
boiskowy [bo-ees-**ko**-vi] adj.m. field (events, etc.)
boj [boy] m. colloq: funk; dread
mieć boja [myećh **bo**-yah] exp.: colloq: to have the funk; to be funky; to funk; to be afraid; to be paralysed with fear; to dread
boja [**bo**-yah] f. buoy; beacon
boja dzwonna [**bo**-yah **dzvon**-nah] exp.: bell-buoy
boja kotwiczna [**bo**-yah kot-**feech**-nah] exp.: mooring buoy
bojar [**bo**-yahr] m. boyar (member of eastern Balto-Slavic gentry)
bojarski [bo-**yahr**-skee] adj.m. boyar's; boyars'
bojarzyn [bo-**yah**-zhin] m. boyar (member of eastern Balto-Slavic gentry)
bojaźliwie [bo-yah-**źhlee**-vye] adv. shyly; timidly; coyly; faint-heartedly; without guts; timorously; without grit; skittishly (acting horse)
bojaźliwość [bo-yah-**źhlee**-vośhćh] f. shyness; timidity; faint-heartedness; coyness
bojaźliwy [bo-yah-**źhlee**-vi] adj.m. shy; timid; coy; without guts; cowardly; skittish (horse)
bojaźliwy człowiek [bo-yah-**źhlee**-vi **chwo**-vyek] exp.: shirker; flincher
bojaźliwy koń [bo-yah-**źhlee**-vi koń] exp.: shyer
bojaźń [**bo**-yahźhń] f. fear; fright; anxiety; terror

bojer [bo-yer] m. ice (sail) boat
bojerowiec [bo-ye-ro-vyets] m. ice-boat sailor
bojerowy [bo-ye-ro-vi] adj.m. ice-boat (sport, competition, etc.)
bojka [boy-kah] f. (small) buoy; beacon
bojkot [boy-kot] m. boycott
bojkotować [boy-ko-to-vahćh] v. boycott; cold shoulder; black list (*repeatedly*)
bojkotowanie [boy-ko-to-vah-ńe] n. boycott; non-cooperation; boycotting
bojler [boy-ler] m. boiler
bojować [bo-yo-vahćh] v. fight; wage war; war (*repeatedly*)
bojowiec [bo-yo-vyets] m. fighter; member of a storming party
bojowniczka [bo-yov-ńeech-kah] f. (female) fighter; militant; combatant; champion (of a cause)
bojownik [bo-yov-ńeek] m. fighter; militant; combatant; champion
bojownik o pokój [bo-yov-ńeek o po-kooy] exp.: fighting pacifist
bojowo [bo-yo-vo] adv. aggressively; pugnaciously; combatively; in fighting readiness
wyglądać bojowo [vi-glown-dahćh bo-yo-vo] exp.: to look aggressive; to look warlike
bojowość [bo-yo-vośhćh] f. aggressiveness; pugnaciousness; combativeness; fighting readiness; militancy; fighting spirit; bellicosity
bojowy [bo-yo-vi] adj.m. pugnacious; combative; warlike; bellicose; aggressive; truculent; dashing; daring; venturesome; fighting; war-; combat-; battle (cry, etc.); militant; operational
gotowość bojowa [go-to-vośhćh bo-yo-vah] exp.: alert; combat readiness
okrzyk bojowy [ok-shik bo-yo-vi] exp.: war-cry; battle-cry
szyk bojowy [shik bo-yo-vi] exp.: battle-array; order of battle
siły bojowe [śhee-wi bo-yo-ve] exp.: striking force(s)
bojówka [bo-yoof-kah] f. fighting group; armed band; storming party
bojówkarski [bo-yoof-kahr-skee] adj.m. armed band (attack, etc.)
bojówkarz [bo-yoof-kahsh] m. member of a fighting group (armed band, storming party)
bojówkowy [bo-yoof-ko-vi] adj.m. of armed band
bojrep [boy-rep] m. anchor-marking line (rope)
bok [bok] m. side; flank
kłucie w boku [kwoo-ćhe v bo-koo] exp.: stitch in the side; sharp pain in the side
na boku [nah bo-koo] exp.: aside; apart; on one side
po bokach [po bo-kahkh] exp.: on both sides; on either side
pod bokiem [pod bo-kem] exp.: near by; at hand
podpierać się pod bokami [pot-pye-rahćh śhan pod bo-kah-mee] exp.: to be with arms akimbo
przy czyimś boku [pshi chi-eemśh bo-koo] exp.: at somebody's side
robić bokami [ro-beećh bo-kah-mee] exp.: to pant; to be on one's last legs (in difficulties)
stać na boku [stahćh nah bo-koo] exp.: to stand aloof
to mi bokiem wychodzi [to mee bo-kem vi-kho-dźhee] exp.: I'm fed up with it
u boku [oo bo-koo] exp.: at one side
uderzenie z boku [oo-de-zhe-ńe z bo-koo] exp.: side-blow; by-blow
uwaga na boku [oo-vah-gah nah bo-koo] exp.: side note
w bok [v bok] exp.: to one side; aside
widok z boku [vee-dok z bo-koo] exp.: side-view
zarobić coś na boku [zah-ro-beećh tsośh nah bo-koo] exp.: to earn something on the side
z boku [z bo-koo] exp.: from the side; from one side; in confidence; aloof
zrywać boki ze śmiechu [zri-vahćh bo-kee ze śhmye-khoo] exp.: to split one's sides with laughter

żarty na bok [zhahr-ti nah bok] exp.: speaking seriously; no joke!
bokobrody [bo-ko-**bro**-di] pl. whiskers; sideburns
boks [boks] m. boxing (sport); (horse's) stall; boxcalf (leather)
bokser [**bok**-ser] m. boxer; pugilist; small bulldog; Boston terrier
bokser zawodowy [**bok**-ser zah-vo-**do**-vi] exp.: prize-fighter
bokserka [bok-**ser**-kah] f. female (dog) boxer
bokserski [bok-**ser**-skee] adj.m. boxing (gloves, etc.); boxing (bout, etc.); pugilistic
mecz bokserski [mech bok-**ser**-skee] exp.: boxing match; spar; prize-fight
rękawice bokserskie [ran-kah-**vee**-tse bok-**ser**-ske] exp.: boxing gloves
waga bokserska [**vah**-gah bok-**ser**-skah] exp.: boxing-weight
boksować [bok-**so**-vahćh] v. box (*repeatedly*)
boksować się [bok-**so**-vahćh śhan] v. box; spar (*repeatedly*)
boksowanie [bok-so-**vah**-ńe] n. boxing
boksowanie się [bok-so-**vah**-ńe śhan] n. boxing bout
boksowy [bok-**so**-vi] adj.m. of boxcalf; boxcalf (leather, etc.)
boksyt [**bo**-ksit] m. bauxite (mineral)
bola [**bo**-lah] f. bola; hurling and entangling weapon
bolak [**bo**-lahk] m. tumor
bolas [**bo**-lahs] m. bolas (missile weapon for catching animals)
boląco [bo-**lown**-tso] adv. painfully
bolący [bo-**lown**-tsi] adj.m. painful; aching; sore
bolączka [bo-**lown**-chkah] f. pain; grief; sore place; tender spot; weak point; complaint
bolec [**bo**-lets] m. pin; bolt; cotter
boleć [**bo**-lećh] v. pain; ache; hurt; smart; suffer; regret; grieve (at, for); be sorry; mourn (over a dead person) (*repeatedly*)
boli mnie głowa [**bo**-lee mńe **gwo**-vah] exp.: I have a headache
boleję że muszę...[bo-**le**-yan zhe **moo**-shan] exp.: it gives me pain to have to (do something)
bolejący [bo-le-**yown**-tsi] adj.m. dismal; piteous; melancholy; mournful
boleń [**bo**-leń] m. predatory silver carp
bolerko [bo-**ler**-ko] n. (small, nice) bolero (jacket, dance, etc.)
bolero [bo-**le**-ro] n. bolero (jacket, dance, etc.)
bolesność [bo-**les**-nośhćh] f. pain; feeling of pain
bolesny [bo-**les**-ni] adj.m. sore; painful; sad; woeful; acute; dismal; agonizing; severe; hurtful; distressing; trying (pain, etc.)
bolesna mina [bo-**les**-nah **mee**-nah] exp.: vinegar countenance; colloq: sourpuss; grouch; killjoy
boleściwie [bo-leśh-**ćhee**-vye] adv. sorrowfully; mournfully; with pain
boleściwy [bo-leśh-**ćhee**-vi] adj.m. sorrowful; mournful
boleść [**bo**-leśhćh] f. grief; pain; sorrow; tribulation; anguish
mieć boleści [myećh bo-**leśh**-ćhee] exp.: to be in pain; to suffer pains
boleśnie [bo-**leśh**-ńe] adv. sorely; painfully; acutely; badly; heavily; sorrowfully; mournfully; woefully
bolid [**bo**-leet] m. bolide (meteorite)
bolimuszka [bo-lee-**moosh**-kah] f. stable-fly
boliwar [bo-**lee**-vahr] m. Venezuelan monetary unit (100 cents or 100 Venezuelan centavos)
Boliwijczyk [bo-lee-**veey**-chik] m. Bolivian
Boliwijka [bo-lee-**veey**-kah] f. Bolivian
boliwijski [bo-lee-**veey**-skee] adj.m. Bolivian
bolometr [bo-**lo**-metr] m. bolometer
bolometrycznie [bo-lo-met-**rich**-ńe] adv. bolometrically
bolometryczny [bo-lo-met-**rich**-ni] adj.m. bolometric
bolończyk [bo-**loń**-chik] m. Bolognese; native of Bologna
bolszewicki [bol-she-**veets**-kee] adj.m. Bolshevist; Bolshevik (party)
bolszewik [bol-**she**-veek] m.

Bolshevik
bolszewizm [bol-**she**-veezm] m. Bolshevism
bolus [**bo**-loos] m. bole (clay)
bom [bom] m. boom; derrick; exp.: bang!; boom!
bomba [**bom**-bah] f. bomb; bomb shell; sphere; a sensation; beer-mug; bombe (of ice cream)
bomba atomowa [**bom**-bah ah-to-mo-vah] exp.: atom bomb; atomic bomb; A-bomb
bomba szklana [**bom**-bah **shklah**-nah] exp.: glass ball
bomba wodorowa [**bom**-bah vo-do-ro-vah] exp.: hydrogen bomb; H-bomb
jak bomba [yahk **bom**-bah] exp.: like a whirlwind
wpaść jak bomba [fpahśhćh yahk **bom**-bah] exp.: to rush in; to burst in
bombajka [bom-**bahy**-kah] f. short-sleeved cloth jacket
bombarda [bom-**bahr**-dah] f. catapult
bombardier [bom-**bahr**-dyer] m. bombardier
bombardierski [bom-bahr-**dyer**-skee] adj.m. bombardier's
bombardon [bom-**bahr**-don] m. bombardon; a bass tuba
bombardować [bom-bahr-**do**-vahćh] v. bombard; raid; shell; bomb (*repeatedly*)
bombardowanie [bom-bahr-do-**vah**-ńe] n. bombardment; raid
bombast [**bom**-bahst] m. bombast; turgidity; tumidity
bombastycznie [bom-bah-**stich**-ńe] adv. with bombast; bombastically
bombastyczność [bom-bah-**stich**-nośhćh] f. bombast; turgidity; tumidity
bombastyczny [bom-bah-**stich**-ni] adj.m. bombastic; turgid; tumid; orotund; mouth-filling; high-flown
bombazyna [bom-bah-**zi**-nah] f. bombazine (weave)
bombaż [**bom**-bahsh] m. making concave shape; dishing (of tin cans, etc.)
bombiasty [bom-**byahs**-ti] adj.m. spherical
bombka [**bomp**-kah] f. small sphere; sphere-shape skirt
bombka piwa [**bomp**-kah **pee**-vah] exp.: small beer; glass of beer
bomblerka [bom-**bler**-kah] f. drinking bout; spree
bomblować [bom-**blo**-vahćh] v. go on a drinking bout; be on a spree; have a good time; have some fun (*repeatedly*)
bomblowanie [bom-blo-**vah**-ńe] n. drinking bout; spree
bombonierka [bom-bo-**ńer**-kah] f. chocolate box; fancy box of bonbons; snug little apartment; love-nest
bomboszczelny [bom-bo-**shchel**-ni] adj.m. bombproof; safe from the force of bombs
bombowiec [bom-**bo**-vyets] m. bomber; bombing plane; bomb-carrier; raider
bombowiec nurkujący [bom-**bo**-vyets noor-koo-**yown**-tsi] exp.: dive-bomber; diving bomber
bombowy [bom-**bo**-vi] adj.m. of a bomb; bomb (release, etc.); colloq: sensational; bombshell (sensation, upset, etc.)
nalot bombowy [**nah**-lot bom-**bo**-vi] exp.: air raid
bombramreja [bom-brahm-**re**-yah] f. fifth boom above deck
bombramstenga [bom-brahm-**sten**-gah] f. jib-boom
bombramżagiel [bom-brahm-**zhah**-gel] m. fifth sail above deck
bombramżaglowy [bom-brahm-zhahg-**lo**-vi] adj.m. (pull, etc.) of the fifth sail above deck
bomkliwer [bom-**klee**-ver] m. extension of boom
bomstenga [bom-**sten**-gah] f. jib boom
bomsztenga [bom-**shten**-gah] f. jib boom
bon [bon] m. bill; bond; ticket; coupon; debenture; free meal ticket
bon skarbowy [bon skahr-**bo**-vi] exp.: Treasury note; Treasury bill; Treasury bond
bona [**bo**-nah] f. nursery maid
bonanza [bo-**nahn**-zah] f. bonanza;

rich vein of gold ore; colloq: something valuable, profitable, or rewarding
bonapartysta [bo-nah-pahr-**tis**-tah] m. Bonapartist
bonapartystyczny [bo-nah-pahr-tis-**tich**-ni] adj.m. Bonapartist
bonapartyzm [bo-nah-**pahr**-tizm] m. Bonapartism
bondar [**bon**-dahr] m. cooper
bonderyzacja [bon-de-ri-**zah**-tsyah] f. bonderizing
bongo [**bon**-go] n. bongo antelope; bongo drum
bonia [**bo**-ńah] f. ornamental groove on elevations of buildings
bonifikata [bo-ńee-fee-**kah**-tah] f. compensation; indemnity; indemnification; allowance; rebate; discount; reduction of price; bonus
bonifikować [bo-ńee-fee-**ko**-vahćh] v. compensate; indemnify (for); give a discount; allow a rebate; take a percentage off a price (*repeatedly*)
bonifikowanie [bo-ńee-fee-ko-**vah**-ńe] n. compensation; indemnity; indemnification; allowance; rebate; discount; reduction of price; bonus
bonifrater [bo-ńee-**frah**-ter] m. brother of the Order of St. John of God
boniować [bo-**ńo**-vahćh] v. rusticate (a wall) (*repeatedly*)
boniowanie [bo-ńo-**vah**-ńe] n. rustication
bonitacja [bo-ńee-**tahts**-yah] f. appraisal and classification (of soil, forest, etc.)
bonitacyjny [bo-ńee-tah-**tsiy**-ni] adj.m. of appraisal and classification (soil, forest, etc.)
bonitować [bo-ńee-**to**-vahćh] v. appraise and classify (of soil, forest, etc.) (*repeatedly*)
bonitowanie [bo-ńee-to-**vah**-ńe] n. appraisal and bonification
bonkreta [bon-**kre**-tah] f. variety of pear
bon mot [b<u>own</u> mo] (French) exp.: clever turn of speech; short, straight to the point expression
bono [**bo**-no] n. (mine) gallery; platform
bonować [bo-**no**-vahćh] v. build a gallery; build a platform (in a mine); go on a drinking bout; be on a spree; have a good time; have some fun (*repeatedly*)
bonowy [bo-**no**-vi] adj.m. of bond; of debenture; of coupon
bont [bont] m. finger-board (of a string instrument); king post; center-post of a triangular truss
bon ton [b<u>own</u> t<u>own</u>] (French) exp.: m. good taste; fashionable style; proper thing
bon vivant [b<u>own</u> vee-**vahn**] exp.: m. person having sociable tastes; frivolous person; playboy
bon viveur [b<u>own</u> vee-**ver**] exp.: m. person having sociable tastes; frivolous person; playboy
bonza [**bon**-zah] m. bonze; Buddhist priest; pompous personage
bonżurka [bon-**zhoor**-kah] f. warm and soft house jacket
boogie-woogie [**boo**-gee **woo**-gee] n. boogie-woogie; percussion blues
bookmacher [book-**mah**-kher] m. bookmaker
boom [boom] m. boom (market, etc.)
bor [bor] m. boron (atomic number 5); drill; borer
bora [**bo**-rah] f. bora (wind)
boracyt [bo-**rah**-tsit] m. boracite (mineral)
boraks [**bo**-rahks] m. borax
boraksowy [bo-rahk-**so**-vi] adj.m. boraceous
boran [**bo**-rahn] m. borate
boratynka [bo-rah-**tin**-kah] f. Polish 17th. cent coin (1/3 of a grosz)
borazol [bo-**rah**-zol] m. borazole (inflammable fluid)
borazon [bo-**rah**-zon] m. borazon
bordel [**bor**-del] m. vulg.: brothel; whorehouse; bawdy-house; see: **burdel**
bordiura [bor-**dyoo**-rah] f. fringe; border; edge; rim; verge
bordiurka [bor-**dyoor**-kah] f. (nice, little) fringe; border; edge; rim; verge
bordiurowy [bor-dyoo-**ro**-vi] adj.m.

edge (decoration, etc.); border (line, etc.)

bordo [**bor**-do] n. crimson-dark red; Bordeaux color; Bordeaux wine; claret; adj.m. deep-red; crimson

bordoski [bor-**do**-skee] adj.m. Bordeaux (wine, mixture, etc.)

bordowy [bor-**do**-vi] adj.m. deep-red; crimson (color, etc.)

bordun [**bor**-doon] m. bourdon (in organ and in bagpipes); a drone bass

borealny [bo-re-**ahl**-ni] adj.m. boreal; northern (wind)

zorza borealna [**zo**-zhah bo-re-**ahl**-nah] exp.: aurora borealis; northern lights; northern aurora

boreasz [bo-**re**-ahsh] m. Boreas; north wind

borecznik [bo-**rech**-ńeek] m. small membrane-wing insect (harmful to coniferous trees)

borecznikowaty [bo-rech-ńee-ko-**vah**-ti] adj.m. of a membrane-wing insect

borecznikowate [bo-rech-ńee-ko-**vah**-te] pl. the family of membrane-wing insects

borek [**bo**-rek] m. small forest

borg [borg] m. credit

na borg [nah borg] exp.: colloq: on credit

borgis [**bor**-gees] m. bourgeois font (type)

borgować [bor-**go**-vahćh] v. sell on credit; sell on tick; give on loan; loan; buy on credit; buy on tick; take a loan; take loans (*repeatedly*)

bormaszyna [bor-mah-**shi**-nah] f. drill; borer; boring machine

bornaski [bor-**nahs**-kee] adj.m. of a viral animal infection of the central nervous system

borneol [bor-**ne**-ol] m. borneol (acrystalline cyclic acid)

bornica [bor-**ńee**-tsah] f. Compsilura parasitic fly

bornit [**bor**-ńeet] m. bornite (mineral)

borny [**bor**-ni] adj.m. boric; boracic

kwas borny [kfahs **bor**-ni] exp.: boric acid

borodziej [bo-**ro**-dźhey] m. variety of cermabycid beetle whose larva damages pine and spruce trees

borować [bo-**ro**-vahćh] v. drill; bore (*repeatedly*)

borowanie [bo-ro-**vah**-ńe] n. drilling

borowiaczek [bo-ro-**vyah**-chek] m. variety of nocturnal bat

borowiec [bo-**ro**-vyets] m. variety of nocturnal bat; one of the boron group elements

borowik [bo-**ro**-veek] m. boletus (a fungus)

borowikowaty [bo-ro-vee-ko-**vah**-ti] adj.m. like a boletus mushroom

borowikowate [bo-ro-vee-ko-**vah**-te] pl. the boletus family of mushrooms

borowina [bo-ro-**vee**-nah] f. bilberry shrubs; whortleberry shrubs; huckleberry shrubs; therapeutic mud; variety of peat

borowinowy [bo-ro-vee-**no**-vi] adj.m. mud (bath, etc.)

borowisko [bo-ro-**vees**-ko] n. clearing (in a forest)

borowodorek [bo-ro-vo-**do**-rek] m. borohydride; variety of rocket fuel (undergoing spontaneous combustion on contact with air)

borowodór [bo-ro-**vo**-door] m. borane; boron hydride (fuel)

borowy [bo-**ro**-vi] adj.m. sylvan; of the woods; forest (trees, road, etc.); boronic; boric; boron (oxide, etc.); m. forester; forest ranger; game warden

borówczany [bo-roof-**chah**-ni] adj.m. bilberry (juice, etc.); whorlteberry (juice, etc.)

borówka [bo-**roof**-kah] f. bilberry; whortleberry; huckleberry; hunting horn; cask (barrel)

borówka brusznica [bo-**roof**-kah broosh-**ńee**-tsah] exp.: red berry; fenberry; cranberry

borówkowaty [bo-roof-ko-**vah**-ti] adj.m. of the vacciniaceous family of plants

borówkowate [bo-roof-ko-**vah**-te] pl. the vacciniaceous family of plants

borówkowy [bo-roof-**ko**-vi] adj.m. bilberry (forest); whortleberry (jar, etc.); huckleberry (dish, jar, etc.)

borsalino [bor-sah-lee-no] n. broad-trimmed felt hat of Italian make
borsuczę [bor-**soo**-chan] n. badger's young
borsuczy [bor-**soo**-chi] adj.m. badger's (skin, hair, etc.)
borsuczyca [bor-soo-**chi**-tsah] f. female badger
borsuk [**bor**-sook] m. badger
borsukowaty [bor-soo-ko-**vah**-ti] adj.m. bearish (man)
bort [bort] m. variety of diamond
borta [**bor**-tah] f. border; edging; trimming; braid; braiding; galloon
Boruta [bo-**roo**-tah] m. evil spirit
borykać się [bo-**ri**-kahćh śhan] v. cope; struggle; wrestle; grapple; battle; be at grips (*repeatedly*)
borykanie się [bo-ri-**kah**-ńe śhan] n. struggle; fight; battle
bosak [**bo**-sahk] m. boat hook; crampon; grapnel; sandal; sled with unshod runners; cart with unrimmed wheels
na bosaka [nah bo-**sah**-kah] exp.: barefoot; with no shoes on
boski [**bos**-kee] adj.m. divine; godlike; of God
oddawać cześć boską [od-dah-vahćh cheśhćh **bos**-kown] exp.: to worship
na litość boską! [nah **lee**-tośhćh **bos**-kown] exp.: for goodness' sake!
niech ręka boska broni! [ńekh **ran**-kah **bos**-kah **bro**-ńee] exp.: God forbid!
rany boskie [**rah**-ni **bos**-ke] exp.: good heavens!
bosko [**bos**-ko] adv. divinely; admirably; heavenly
boskość [**bos**-kośhćh] f. divinity; godhead; divine nature
bosman [**bos**-mahn] m. boatswain; bosun; bos'n
bosmanat [bos-**mah**-naht] m. boatswain's functions
bosmanmat [**bos**-mahn-**maht**] m. boatswain's mate
bosmański [bos-**mahń**-skee] adj.m. boatswain's
sprzęt bosmański [spshant bos-**mahń**-skee] exp.: naval stores
boso [**bo**-so] adv. barefoot; with no shoes on; with one's shoes off
bosonogi [bo-so-**no**-gee] adj.m. barefoot; bare-footed
boss [bos] m. boss; chief; master
bossa nova [**bo**-sah **no**-vah] f. bossa nova (Brazilian dance)
boston [**bos**-ton] m. hesitation waltz
bostonowy [bos-to-**no**-vi] adj.m. boston (dancing figure, etc.)
bosy [**bo**-si] adj.m. barefoot; with no shoes on; with one's shoes off; unshod; with not rimmed wheels; with unshod (sleigh) runners
bose nogi [**bo**-se **no**-gee] exp.: bare feet
bose buty [**bo**-se **boo**-ti] exp.: sandals
bośniacki [bośh-**ńah**-tskee] adj.m. Bosnian
bot [bot] m. snow-shoe
botanicznie [bo-tah-**ńeech**-ńe] adv. botanically; in respect of botany; from the botanical point of view
botaniczny [bo-tah-**ńeech**-ni] adj.m. botanical
botanik [bo-**tah**-ńeek] m. botanist
botanika [bo-**tah**-ńee-kah] f. botany
botek [**bo**-tek] m. shoe with felt upper
botfort [**bot**-fort] m. riding boot
botriomykoza [bot-ryo-mi-**ko**-zah] f. fungus disease of horses
botticellowski [bot-tee-chel-**lof**-skee] adj.m. Botticellian
botulizm [bo-**too**-leezm] m. botulism; sausage poisoning
botwina [bot-**fee**-nah] f. young beet leaves; garden beet
botwinka [bot-**feen**-kah] f. young beet leaves; soup of young beet leaves; garden beet = (**boćwina**)
boucle [boo-**kle**] (French) not declined: loop-weaved cloth
boulle [bool] n. buhl (style, furniture, etc.); buhlwork (inlaid decoration of A.C. Boulle, 1642-1732)
bowiem [**bo**-vyem] conj. for; because; since; as; hence
boy [boy] m. page (in a hotel, restaurant, etc.)
Bozia [**bo**-źhah] f. God (child's expression)

bożątko [bo-zhownt-ko] n. mythical good imp
bożek [bo-zhek] m. idol; pagan god; divinity; graven image; colloq: ruler; dictator; autocrat
bożodrzew [bo-zho-dzhef] m. simarouba tree
bożonarodzeniowy [bo-zho-nah-ro-dze-ńo-vi] adj.m. Christmas (festivities, etc.); Yuletide
bożnica [bozh-ńee-tsah] f. synagogue; temple; prayer house; see: **bóżnica**
boży [bo-zhi] adj.m. God's; divine
Boże Ciało [bo-zhe ćhah-wo] exp.: Corpus Christi
Boże Narodzenie [bo-zhe nah-ro-dze-ńe] exp.: Christmas; X-mas
po bożemu [po bo-zhe-moo] exp.: honestly
bożyszcze [bo-zhish-che] n. idol; pagan god
bób [boop] m. broad bean
dać bobu [dahćh bo-boo] exp.: to beat (somebody); to punish (an opponent, a competitor, etc.)
bóbr [boobr] m. beaver
płakać jak bóbr [pwah-kahćh yahk boobr] exp.: to melt into tears
bobry [bob-ri] (pl.) exp.: beaver fur
Bóg [boog] m. God
mój Boże! [mooy bo-zhe] exp.: good God!
chwała Bogu! [khfah-wah bo-goo] exp.: thank God!
nie daj Boże! [ńe dahy bo-zhe] exp.: God forbid!
szczęść Boże! [shchanśhćh bo-zhe] exp.: God speed you!
z Bogiem! [z bo-gem] exp.: may God keep you in His care
bój [booy] m. fight; battle; combat; struggle
bójka [booy-kah] f. tussle; scrimmage; scuffle; fight; row; scrap
ból [bool] m. pain; ache; sore; soreness; suffering
ból głowy [bool gwo-vi] exp.: headache
ból gardła [bool gahr-dwah] exp.: sore throat
ból serca [bool ser-tsah] exp.: heartache; a heavy heart
ból zębów [bool zan-boof] exp.: toothache
zadać ból [zah-dahćh bool] exp.: to cause pain; to cause suffering; to hurt; to give pain
złagodzić ból [zwah-go-dźheećh bool] exp.: to soothe the pain
bólowy [boo-lo-vi] adj.m. of pain; of suffering
bór [boor] m. forest; wood
bóstwo [boos-tfo] n. deity; idol; pagan god; Divinity
bóść [boośhćh] v. gore; sting; toss; horn; butt; nettle (*repeatedly*)
bóść się [boośhćh śhan] v. gore each other; horn one another (*repeatedly*)
bóżnica [boozh-ńee-tsah] f. synagogue; house of prayer; temple
brabancki [brah-bahn-tskee] adj.m. Brabant (lace, etc.)
brabanckie koronki [brah-bahn-tske ko-ron-kee] exp.: (Brabant) Mechlin lace
brach [brahkh] m. slang: brother
brachiosaurus [brah-khyo-zahw-roos] m. Brachiosaurus
brachycefal [brah-khi-tse-fahl] m. brachycephal; short-headed (broad-headed) person
brachycefalia [brah-khi-tse-fahl-yah] f. brachycephaly
brachygrafia [brah-khi-grah-fyah] f. brachygraphia; shorthand; stenography
brachygraficzny [brah-khi-grah-feech-ni] adj.m. written in abbreviations; coded; stenographic; written in shorthand
bracia [brah-ćhah] pl. brothers; brethren
bracia szlachta [brah-ćhah shlahkh-tah] exp.: noblemen's fellowship
bracia zakonni [brah-ćhah zah-kon-ńee] exp.: religious community; community of monks
bracić się [brah-ćheećh śhan] v. unite with ties of brotherhood;

see: **bratać się** (*repeatedly*)
braciszek [brah-**ćhee**-shek] m. younger brother; friar; lay brother
braciszkowie [brah-ćheesh-**ko**-vye] (pl.) exp.: friars; brothers; brethren; brotherhood; community
bracki [**brahts**-kee] adj.m. brotherly (love, etc.) = **bratni**
bractwo [**brah**-tstfo] n. fraternity; brotherhood; guild; gild; sodality
całe bractwo [**tsah**-we **brah**-tstfo] exp.: the whole lot (of them, you, etc.)
brać [brahćh] v. take; hold; catch hold; take possession; take over; capture; seize; enlist; commandeer; derive; provide oneself; engage; invite; buy; purchase; lease; undertake; get; receive; charge; put on; take in; imbibe; negotiate; clear; jump (a ditch); round (a corner); swallow; have; submit (to); take away; use; use up; employ; make use; understand; treat; misunderstand; take upon oneself; set in; be deceived; swallow the bait; resort to; find means; arise; spring; make for (*repeatedly*)
brać do wojska [brahćh do **voy**-skah] exp.: to enlist
brać górę [brahćh **goo**-ran] exp.: to get the upper hand
brać na serio [brahćh nah **se**-ryo] exp.: to take seriously
brać na siebie obowiązek [brahćh nah **śhe**-bye o-bo-**vyown**-zek] exp.: to take on duty
brać pod uwagę [brahćh pod oo-**vah**-gan] exp.: to take into consideration
brać ślub [brahćh śhloop] exp.: to get married; to wed
brać udział [brahćh **oo**-dźhahw] exp.: to take part
brać w rachubę [brahćh v rah-**khoo**-ban] exp.: to take to account; to consider
brać za dobrą monetę [brahćh zah **do**-brown mo-**ne**-tan] exp.: to take in good part
brać za złe [brahćh zah zwe] exp.: to take amiss
bierze mnie chęć [**bye**-zhe mńe khanćh] exp.: I feel inclined; I have a mind; I would like (to)
bierze mróz [**bye**-zhe mroos] exp.: it begins to freeze
brać się do dzieła [brahćh śhan do **dźhe**-wah] exp.: to set about one's work; to start on a project
brać [brahćh] f. gang; band; company; tribe (of actors, etc.)
bradykardia [brah-di-**kahr**-dyah] f. bradycardia; slow action of the heart
bradziażyć [brah-**dźhah**-zhićh] v. colloq: dissipate; carouse; run wild; draggle; loiter (*repeatedly*)
bradziażyć się [brah-**dźhah**-zhićh śhan] v. indulge oneself; go wenching; tramp (*repeatedly*)
brahman [**brahkh**-mahn] m. brahman; brahmin
brahmanizm [brahkh-**mah**-ńeezm] m. brahmanism; brahminism
braja [**brah**-yah] f. mash; pulp; slush (of wet snow); see: **breja**
brajl [brahyl] m. braille; system of printing for the blind
brajlowski [brahy-**lof**-skee] adj.m. braille (system, printing, etc.)
brajtszwanc [**brahyt**-shfahnts] m. broadtail (fur)
brak [brahk] m. lack; need; want; scarcity; shortage; absence; fault; defect; weakness; deficiency; disadvantage; privation; hardship; poverty; reject; wastage; choice
bez braku [bez **brah**-koo] exp.: regardless of choice; indiscriminately; irrespective of everything
cierpieć na brak czegoś [**ćher**-pyećh nah brahk **che**-gośh] exp.: to lack something; to suffer from the lack of something
nie brak mu odwagi [ńe brahk moo od-**vah**-gee] exp.: he abounds in courage
z braku czasu [z **brah**-koo **chah**-soo] exp.: for lack of time
zaspokoić brak [zah-spo-ko-eećh brahk] exp.: to supply a want
brakarka [brah-**kahr**-kah] f. (woman) sorter
brakarnia [brah-**kahr**-ńah] f. sorting-house

brakarski [brah-**kahr**-skee] adj.m. sorting (house, etc.)
brakarstwo [brah-**kahr**-stfo] n. sorting; sorter's work
brakarz [brah-kahsh] m. sorter
braknąć [**brahk**-nownćh] v. cast off; reject; sort; be wanting; be missing; be deficient; see: **brakować**
brakorób [brah-**ko**-roop] m. defective worker; bungler
brakoróbstwo [brah-ko-**roop**-stfo] n. defective work; bungling
brakować [brah-**ko**-vahćh] v. cast off; reject; sort; be wanting; be missing; be deficient (*repeatedly*)
brakuje wielu książek [brah-**koo**-ye **vye**-loo **kśhown**-zhek] exp.: many books are missing
brakuje pieniędzy [brah-**koo**-ye pye-ńan-dzi] exp.: there is lack of money; money is lacking
brakuje mi słów [brah-**koo**-ye mee swoof] exp.: words fail me
brakuje mi sił [brah-**koo**-ye mee śheew] exp.: my power fails me
czy brakuje ci czego? [chi brah-**koo**-ye ćhee **che**-go] exp.: are you all right?; are you O.K.?; Are you missing anything?
kogo brakuje? [**ko**-go brah-**koo**-ye] exp.: who is absent?
nic mi nie brakuje [ńeets mee ńe brah-**koo**-ye] exp.: nothing is the matter with me; I am O.K.
brakowanie [brah-ko-**vah**-ńe] n. sorting; controlling the quality (of products, etc.)
brakownia [brah-**kov**-ńah] f. sorting-house
brakowny [brah-**kov**-ni] adj.m. defective; faulty
brakteat [brahk-**te**-aht] m. medieval one-sided coin
brakujący [brah-koo-**yown**-tsi] adj.m. missing; absent
brakujące ogniwo [brah-koo-**yown**-tse og-**ńee**-vo] exp.: the missing link
bralka [**brahl**-kah] f. stove tile
brama [**brah**-mah] f. gate; gateway; front door; sluice gate; wicket gate; port; (glacier's) snout
brama triumfalna [**brah**-mah tryoom-**fahl**-nah]] exp.: triumphal arch; arch of triumph
bramin [**brah**-meen] m. brahmin; brahman
braminizm [brah-**mee**-ńeezm] m. brahminism; brahmanism
braminka [brah-**meen**-kah] f. brahminee (woman)
bramiński [brah-**meeń**-skee] adj.m. brahminee (theory, belief, etc.)
bramka [**brahm**-kah] f. goal; gate; gateway; front gate; wicket-gate
obronić bramkę [ob-**ro**-ńeećh **brahm**-kan] exp.: to save the goal
zdobyć bramkę [**zdo**-bićh **brahm**-kan] exp.: to score a goal
bramkarka [brahm-**kahr**-kah] f. woman goalkeeper
bramkarski [brahm-**kahr**-skee] adj.m. goalkeeper's
bramkarz [**brahm**-kahsh] m. goalkeeper; colloq: goalie
bramkowy [brahm-**ko**-vi] adj.m. goal (line, pole)
bramować [brah-**mo**-vahćh] v. border; edge; fringe (*repeatedly*)
bramować się [brah-**mo**-vahćh śhan] v. be bordered (with); be edged (with); be fringed (with) (*repeatedly*)
bramowanie [brah-mo-**vah**-ńe] n. border; edge; edging; fringe
bramownica [brah-mov-**ńee**-tsah] f. gantry crane; crane mounted on a frame with two rails spanning the work place
bramowy [brah-**mo**-vi] adj.m. gate (structure, etc.)
bramreja [brahm-**re**-yah] f. topgallant yard
bramsel [**brahm**-sel] m. topgallant sail
bramstenga [brahm-**sten**-gah] f. topgallant mast
bramżagiel [brahm-**zhah**-gel] m. topgallant sail
branchiosaurus [brahn-khyo-**zahw**-roos] m. branchiosaurus
brander [**brahn**-der] m. fire-ship
brandmur [**brahnd**-moor] m. fire wall; fire partition
brandy [**bren**-di] f. brandy
brandzel [**brahn**-dzel] m. insole; inner-sole (of a shoe)

brandzlowy [brahn-**dzlo**-vi] adj.m. insole (leather, etc.); of the insole
branie [**brah**-ńe] n. the taking (from the verb: **brać**)
braniec [**brah**-ńets] m. prisoner of war; captive; recruit
branka [**brahn**-kah] f. recruitment; enlistment; impressment into the czarist army; captive (woman)
brankard [**brahn**-kahrt] m. brake-van; luggage-van; baggage cart; freight car; merchandise truck
bransoleta [brahn-so-**le**-tah] f. bracelet; wristlet; bangle
bransoletka [brahn-so-**let**-kah] f. bracelet; wristlet; bangle; colloq: handcuffs
brant [brahnt] m. pure gold
branża [**brahn**-zhah] f. line (of business); branch; craft
branżowiec [brahn-**zho**-vyets] m. specialist of a (particular) trade
branżowo [brahn-**zho**-vo] adv. within the trade
branżowy [brahn-**zho**-vi] adj.m. belonging to the trade; of the trade
bras [brahs] m. brace (rope)
brasować [brah-**so**-vahćh] v. brace (horizontal turning of sail's boom) (*repeatedly*)
brat [braht] m. brother; mate; comrade; companion; associate; colleague; chum; brother in arms; friar; member of a fraternity; fellow (doctor, countryman, worker, officer, etc.)
brat cioteczny [braht ćho-**tech**-ni] exp.: first cousin
brat przyrodni [braht pshi-**rod**-ńee] exp.: stepbrother
być za pan brat [bićh zah pahn braht] exp.: to be on easy terms
bratać [**brah**-tahćh] v. unite; bind with ties of brotherhood (*repeatedly*)
bratać się [**brah**-tahćh śhan] v. fraternize; chum up (*repeatedly*)
bratanek [brah-**tah**-nek] m. nephew
bratanica [brah-tah-**ńee**-tsah] f. niece (brother's daughter)
bratanie się [brah-tah-ńe śhan] n. fraternization
bratanka [brah-**tahn**-kah] f. niece (brother's daughter)
bratek [**brah**-tek] m. pansy
braterski [brah-**ter**-skee] adj.m. brotherly (love, etc.); fraternal
po bratersku [po brah-**ter**-skoo] exp.: in a brotherly manner; like a brother; as a brother would; as a brother does; as brothers do; as brothers are; as brothers want to do
bratersko [brah-**ter**-sko] adv. in a brotherly manner; like a brother; as a brother would
braterstwo [brah-**ter**-stfo] n. brotherhood; fraternity; brother and his wife; kinship; blood relationship
bratni [**braht**-ńee] adj.m. brotherly
bratniak [**braht**-ńahk] m. alumni association; former university students' corporation
bratobójca [brah-to-**booy**-tsah] m. fratricide; murderer of one's brother; colloq: Cain
bratobójczy [brah-to-**booy**-chi] adj.m. fratricidal; civil (war); domestic (war)
bratobójstwo [brah-to-**booy**-stfo] n. fratricide; murder of one's brother
bratowa [brah-**to**-vah] f. sister-in-law
bratszpil [**braht**-shpeel] m. windlass
brauning [**brahw**-ńeeng] m. Browning automatic pistol
braunit [**brahw**-ńeet] m. manganese oxide (in mineral form)
braunsztyn [**brahwn**-shtin] m. manganese dioxide (in mineral form)
bravissimo! [brah-**vees**-see-mo] excl.: very fine!; splendid!
brawo [**brah**-vo] interjection: bravo; applause; clapping of hands; cheers; acclamation
bić brawo [beećh **brah**-vo] exp.: to applaud
brawo! [**brah**-vo] excl.: bravo!; well done!; hear-hear!
brawura [brah-**voo**-rah] f. gallantry; bravery; bravura; bravado; daring; dash; rashness; heroics
brawurowo [brah-voo-**ro**-vo] adv. dashingly; with bravado
brawurowy [brah-voo-**ro**-vi] adj.m.

daring; done with bravura; brilliantly played
Brazylijczyk [brah-zi-**leey**-chik] m. Brazilian
Brazylijka [brah-zi-**leey**-kah] f. Brazilian (woman)
brazylijski [brah-zi-**leey**-skee] adj.m. Brazilian
brąz [browns] m. bronze; brown; the color of bronze; colloq: bronze statue
epoka brązu [e-**po**-kah **brown**-zoo] exp.: the bronze age
brązal [**brown**-zahl] m. aluminum bronze
brązować [brown-**zo**-vahćh] v. bronze (*repeatedly*)
brązowanie [brown-zo-**vah**-ńe] n. coating with bronze
brązowić [brown-**zo**-veećh] v. bronze; brown; tan (*repeatedly*)
brązowić się [brown-**zo**-veećh śhan] v. bronze; brown; tan; become bronze-like; acquire a bronze color (*repeatedly*)
brązowieć [brown-**zo**-vyećh] v. bronze; brown; tan; become bronze-like; acquire a bronze color; show brown (*repeatedly*)
brązowienie [brown-zo-**vye**-ńe] n. acquiring bronze color
brązowienie się [brown-zo-**vye**-ńe śhan] n. putting bronze color on oneself
brązownia [brown-**zov**-ńah] f. braziery; bronze-foundry
brązownictwo [brown-zov-**ńeets**-tfo] n. brazier's work; bronzing; brazier's trade
brązowniczy [brown-zov-**ńee**-chi] adj.m. brazier's (shop, etc.); bronze-founder's
brązownik [brown-**zov**-ńeek] m. brazier; bronze-founder
brązowo [brown-**zo**-vo] adv. of bronze color; in brown color
brązowooki [brown-zo-vo-**o**-kee] adj.m. brown-eyed
brązowowłosy [brown-zo-vo-**vwo**-si] adj.m. brown-haired
brązowy [brown-**zo**-vi] adj.m. bronze (medal, age, etc.); brown; of brown color; tawny; tanned; colloq: statuesque; unreal
break [breyk] (Engl.) m. short interruption of boxing match
brechacz [**bre**-khahch] m. colloq: fibber; liar
brechać [**bre**-khahćh] v. colloq: fib; lie (*repeatedly*)
brednia [**bred**-ńah] f. nonsense; rubbish; drivel; fudge; balderdash; fidle-faddle; twaddle
brednie [**bred**-ńe] pl. nonsense
pleść brednie [pleśhćh **bred**-ńe] exp.: to talk nonsense
bredzenie [bre-**dze**-ńe] n. ravings; maundering; talking nonsense
bredzić [**bre**-dźheećh] v. rave; talk nonsense; talk rubbish; drivel; be absurd; be preposterous; be nonsensical; talk gibberish; twaddle; maunder; jabber (*repeatedly*)
breja [**bre**-yah] f. slush; mash; pulp
brek [brek] m. brake-van; brake; wagonette
brekcja [**brek**-tsyah] f. breccia (mineral)
brekinia [bre-**kee**-ńah] f. variety of sorb tree; service-tree
brekowy [bre-**ko**-vi] m. brakeman (railroad worker)
breloczek [bre-**lo**-chek] m. (nice, little) trinket
brelok [**bre**-lok] m. trinket
bretnal [**bret**-nahl] m. board-nail
Bretonka [bre-**ton**-kah] f. Breton
Breton [**bre**-ton] m. Breton
bretoński [bre-**toń**-skee] adj.m. Breton
brew [bref] f. eyebrow; brow
marszczyć brwi [**marsh**-chićh brvee] exp.: to frown; to contract the brows; to knit one's brows; to show displeasure (with, on, or upon)
brewe [**bre**-ve] indecl. (Pope's) brief (breve)
brewerie [bre-**ver**-ye] pl. brawl; row; uproar; disturbance; commotion; wrangle
wyprawiać brewerie [vi-**prah**-vyahćh bre-**ver**-ye] exp.: to make a row; to roister; to brawl; to wrangle; colloq: to kick up a raw
brewiarz [**bre**-vyahsh] m. breviary
brewka [**bref**-kah] f. (small, nice)

eyebrow; brow
brewny [**brev**-ni] adj.m. superciliary
brezent [**bre**-zent] m. tarpaulin; (waterproof) canvas
brezentowy [bre-zen-**to**-vi] adj.m. tarpaulin; canvas (tilt, bucket, etc.)
brezylia [bre-**zil**-yah] f. Brazil-wood
brezylka [bre-**zil**-kah] f. Brazil-wood
bridż [brich] m. see: **brydż** (bridge game)
bridżowy [bri-**dzho**-vi] adj.m. bridge (game, etc.)
brie [bree] m. Brie cheese
briefing [**bree**-feeng] (Engl.) m. briefing of newsmen
briofil [**bryo**-feel] m. organism living in moss on bogs
briologia [bryo-**log**-yah] f. study of the phylum Bryophyta
brizol [**bree**-zol] m. brisol; see: **bryzol**
brnąć [brnownćh] v. wade; flounder; colloq: blunder along; work one's way; fight one's way; struggle one's way (*repeatedly*)
brnąć w długi [brnownćh v **dwoo**-gee] exp.: to have run into debt; to incur debts over head and ears
brnięcie [brńan-ćhe] n. wading; struggling through
broczyć [**bro**-chićh] v. bleed; shed blood; soak with blood (*repeatedly*)
broczyć krwią [**bro**-chićh krfyown] exp.: to bleed; to drip with blood
broczyć się [**bro**-chićh śhan] v. bleed (*repeatedly*)
broczyć się krwią [**bro**-chićh śhan krfyown] exp.: to bleed; to drip with blood
broda [**bro**-dah] f. beard; chin
zapuścić brodę [zah-**poośh**-ćheećh **bro**-dan] exp.: to grow a beard
druga broda [**droo**-gah **bro**-dah] exp.: double chin
brodacz [**bro**-dahch] m. bearded man; man with a beard
brodaczka [bro-**dahch**-kah] f. usnea (a lichen)
brodaty [bro-**dah**-ti] adj.m. bearded
brodawczak [bro-**dahf**-chahk] m. variety of (benign) tumor
brodawka [bro-**dahf**-kah] f. wart; nipple; mamilla; pap; teat; papilla; verruca
brodawkowaty [bro-dahf-ko-**vah**-ti] adj.m. mammilliform; verrucal; verrucous
brodawkowate [bro-dahf-ko-**vah**-te] pl. verrucose plants; verrucated plants
brodawkowy [bro-dahf-**ko**-vi] adj.m. mammillary; papillary; papillate
brodawnik [bro-**dav**-ńeek] m. Leontodon of the chicory family; dandelion; blow-ball; Taraxacum
broderia [bro-**der**-yah] f. embroidery
brodnia [**brod**-ńah] f. small dragnet
brodnik [**brod**-ńeek] m. small dragnet
brodzący [bro-**dzown**-tsi] adj.m. wading (bird, etc.)
brodzenie [bro-**dze**-ńe] n. wading; floundering
brodzić [**bro**-dźheećh] v. wade; flounder; work one's way (through thicket, etc.); fight one's way (*repeatedly*)
brodziec [**bro**-dźhets] m. tattler; wader; wading bird
brodzik [**bro**-dźheek] m. small shallow swimming pool for children
brogować [bro-**go**-vahćh] v. stack (corn sheaves) (*repeatedly*)
broić [**bro**-eećh] v. make mischief; frolic; romp; gambol; do mischief (*repeatedly*)
brojenie [bro-**ye**-ńe] n. making mischief; frolicking; romp; gambol; doing mischief
brojler [**broy**-ler] m. broiler (chicken)
brokat [**bro**-kaht] m. brocade; gold-cloth
brokatowy [bro-kah-**to**-vi] adj.m. of brocade; brocade (tapestry, etc.)
broker [**bro**-ker] m. stock broker
brokuły [bro-**koo**-wi] pl. broccoli (type of cauliflower)
brom [brom] m. bromine; bromide
bromatologia [bro-mah-to-lo-gyah] f. food science (concerned with food chemistry, digestibility, nutrition value, hygiene of food

production, and food handling)
bromek [**bro**-mek] m. bromide
bromian [**bro**-myahn] m. bromate
bromianometria [bro-myah-no-**metr**-yah] f. bromometry
bromianometrycznie [bro-myah-no-met-**rich**-ńe] adv. bromometrically
bromianometryczny [bro-myah-no-met-**rich**-ni] adj.m. bromometric
bromoaceton [bro-mo-ah-**tse**-ton] m. bromoacetone
bromoform [bro-**mo**-form] m. bromoform
bromolej [bro-**mo**-ley] m. bromoil process of making copies
bromosrebrowy [bro-mo-sreb-**ro**-vi] adj.m. bromide (paper, gas-light, etc.)
bromować [bro-**mo**-vahćh] v. bromate; brominate (*repeatedly*)
bromowanie [bro-mo-**vah**-ńe] n. bromination
bromowodorowy [bro-mo-vo-do-**ro**-vi] adj.m. hydrobromic (acid, etc.)
bromowodór [bro-mo-**vo**-door] m. hydrobromide
bromowy [bro-**mo**-vi] adj.m. bromic
bromural [bro-**moo**-rahl] m. bromural (a tranquilizer)
brona [**bro**-nah] f. harrow; portcullis (on city gate)
brona talerzowa [**bro**-nah tah-le-**zho**-vah] exp.: disk harrow
bronchit [**bron**-kheet] m. bronchitis; (animal) husk
bronchitowy [bron-khee-**to**-vi] adj.m. bronchitis (cough, etc.); husk (cow disease, etc.)
bronchoskop [bron-**kho**-skop] m. bronchoscope
bronchoskopia [bron-kho-**sko**-pyah] f. bronchoscopy
broniak [**bro**-ńahk] m. harrow tooth
broniący [bro-**ńown**-tsi] adj.m. defending; vindictive; vindicatory
bronić [**bro**-ńeećh] v. defend; protect; guard; shield; interdict; prohibit; forbid; deny; refuse (*repeatedly*)
bronić czyjejś sprawy [**bro**-ńeećh **chi**-yeyśh **sprah**-vi] exp.: to plead somebody's cause
bronić swych pozycji [**bro**-ńeećh sfikh po-**zits**-yee] exp.: to stick to one's guns
bronić się [**bro**-ńeećh śhan] v. to defend oneself (*repeatedly*)
bronienie [bro-**ńe**-ńe] n. defense; protection; vindication; prohibition
bronienie się [bro-**ńe**-ńe śhan] n. protecting oneself; vindicating oneself
bronować [bro-**no**-vahćh] v. harrow; drag (*repeatedly*)
bronowanie [bro-no-**vah**-ńe] n. harrowing; dragging
brontozaur [bron-**to**-zahwr] m. Brontosaurus
bronzyt [**bron**-zit] m. bronzite (mineral)
broń [broń] f. weapon; arm; arms; branch of service
broń biała [broń **byah**-wah] exp.: cutting weapons; cold steel (Brit.)
broń boczna [broń **boch**-nah] exp.: side arms; cold steel (Brit.)
broń palna [broń **pahl**-nah] exp.: fire arms
pod bronią [pod **bro**-ńown] exp.: in arms; under arms
chwycić za broń [**khfi**-ćheećh zah broń] exp.: to take up arms
składać broń [**skwah**-dahćh broń] exp.: to lay down (one's) arms
brosza [**bro**-shah] f. breast pin
broszeczka [bro-**shech**-kah] f. (nice, small) pin; brooch
broszka [**brosh**-kah] f. brooch
broszura [bro-**shoo**-rah] f. pamphlet; folder; booklet; brochure
broszurka [bro-**shoo**-rkah] f. (small) pamphlet; folder; booklet; brochure
broszurować [bro-shoo-**ro**-vahćh] v. wire-stitch (a pamphlet, etc.) (*repeatedly*)
broszurowanie [bro-shoo-ro-**vah**-ńe] n. wire-stitching
broszurowany [bro-shoo-ro-**vah**-ni] adj.m. unbound; paper-backed
broszurowy [bro-shoo-**ro**-vi] adj.m. in pamphlet form; paper-backed
browar [**bro**-vahr] m. brewery
browarniany [bro-vahr-**ńah**-ni] adj.m. brewer's; brewing
browarnictwo [bro-vahr-**ńeets**-tfo] n. beer making; brewing; the

brewing trade
browarniczy [bro-vahr-ńee-chi] adj.m. of a brewery
browarny [bro-**vahr**-ni] adj.m. brewer's; brewing
browarowy [bro-vah-**ro**-vi] adj.m. of a brewery
browning [**brahw**-ńeeng] m. browning gun
brozma [**broz**-mah] f. torsk (codfish)
brożyna [bro-**zhi**-nah] f. center post in a rick (hayrick, haystack, stack, straw-stack, etc.)
bród [broot] m. ford; wading place
w bród [v broot] exp.: in profusion; galore
bródka [**broot**-kah] f. little beard; tuft
kozia bródka [ko-źhah **broot**-kah] exp.: goatee
bródkowy [broot-**ko**-vi] adj.m. genial
bróg [broog] m. haystack; rick; hayrick; stack; straw-stack
brr [brr] excl. denotes: a shudder of disgust; feeling of cold, fear, etc.
brucela [broo-**tse**-lah] f. brucella
bruceloza [broo-tse-**lo**-zah] f. brucellosis
brucyt [**broo**-tsit] m. brucite (mineral)
brud [broot] m. dirt; filth; squalor; uncleanness; squalidity; grime; grubbiness; muck; vileness; sordidness; piggishness
brudy [**broo**-di] pl. refuse; dirty linen; dirty clothes
brudy kanałowe [**broo**-di kah-nah-**wo**-ve] exp.: sewage; sullage; excrements
brudas [**broo**-dahs] m. dirty person; grub; colloq: slut; slattern; drab; trollop; muckworm
brudasek [broo-**dah**-sek] m. piggywiggy
bruderszaft [**broo**-der-shahft] m. drinking as a pledge of friendship, with arms linked, as a start of calling each other by first names
brudnawy [brood-**nah**-vi] adj.m. soiled; not very clean
brudniak [**brood**-ńahk] m. soiled clothes basket
brudnica [brood-**ńee**-tsah] f. tussock moth
brudno- [**brood**-no] prefix: brownish; grayish
brudnoczerwony [brood-no-cher-**vo**-ni] exp.: brownish red
brudnożółty [brood-no-**zhoow**-ti] exp.: brownish gray
brudnobiały [brood-no-**byah**-wi] exp.: grayish white
brudno [**brood**-no] adv. dirtily; in a dirty manner
pisać na brudno [**pee**-sahćh nah **brood**-no] exp.: to make a rough copy; make a rough draft
brudnobiały [brood-no-**byah**-wi] adj.m. dirty-white
brudnopis [brood-**no**-pees] m. rough copy; draft (of a letter, document, etc.)
brudnoszary [brood-no-**shah**-ri] adj.m. dirty-gray
brudnożółty [brood-no-**zhoow**-ti] adj.m. dirty-yellow
brudny [**brood**-ni] adj.m. dirty; filthy; mucky; nasty; shabby; sordid; scurvy; piggish; grimy; squalid; grubby; slatternly; sluttish; unclean; uncleanly
brudne myśli [**brood**-ne **miśh**-lee] exp.: obscene thoughts
brudne pieniądze [**brood**-ne pye-**ńown**-dze] exp.: dirty money; ill-gotten money; dishonorable gain
brudzenie [broo-**dze**-ńe] n. soiling; making a mess
brudzenie się [broo-**dze**-ńe śhan] n. soiling oneself; becoming dirty
brudzić [**broo**-dźheećh] v. soil; make dirty (*repeatedly*)
brudzić sobie twarz, ręce [**broo**-dźheećh **so**-bye tfahsh **ran**-tse] exp.: to soil one's face, hands
brudzić się [**broo**-dźheećh śhan] v. get soiled; become dirty; soil one's hands; soil one's clothes; show the dirt (*repeatedly*)
brudzio [**broo**-dźho] m. slang: see: **bruderszaft**
bruk [brook] m. pavement; paving stones; flagstones; paved surface
szlifować bruki [shlee-**fo**-vahćh **broo**-kee] exp.: to loaf about in the streets
wyrzucić na bruk [vi-**zhoo**-ćheećh nah brook] exp.: to turn

out into the street
brukać [**broo**-kahćh] v. soil; make dirty; smear; stain (*repeatedly*)
brukać się [**broo**-kahćh śhan] v. soil oneself; make oneself dirty; smear oneself; stain oneself (*repeatedly*)
brukanie [broo-**kah**-ńe] n. soiling; making dirty; smearing; staining
brukanie się [broo-**kah**-ńe śhan] n. soiling oneself; making oneself dirty; smearing oneself; staining oneself
brukarski [broo-**kahr**-skee] adj.m. paver's; paving (contractor, stones, etc.)
brukarstwo [broo-**kahrs**-tfo] n. paver's work; paving (of streets, etc.)
brukarz [**broo**-kahsh] m. paver
brukiew [**broo**-kef] f. turnip-rooted cabbage; rutabaga
brukować [broo-**ko**-vahćh] v. pave; cobble (*repeatedly*)
brukowanie [broo-ko-**vah**-ńe] n. paving
brukowiec [broo-**ko**-vyets] m. paving-stone; cobble-stone; tabloid; gutter paper; colloq: rag; loafer; gutter-paper; tabloid
brukowy [broo-**ko**-vi] adj.m. paving (stones, etc.); of the street; from the gutter
prasa brukowa [**prah**-sah broo-**ko**-vah] exp.: tabloids; gutter press
wyrażenie brukowe [vi-rah-**zhe**-ńe broo-**ko**-ve] exp.: vulgar expression
brukselka [broo-**ksel**-kah] f. Brussels sprouts
brukselski [broo-**ksel**-skee] adj.m. Brussels; of Brussels
brukwiany [broo-**kfyah**-ni] adj.m. of turnip-rooted cabbage
brukwiowy [broo-**kfyo**-vi] adj.m. of turnip-rooted cabbage; of rutabaga
brulion [**brool**-yon] m. rough draft copy; notebook; exercise book; preliminary draft
brulionowość [brool-yo-**no**-vośhćh] f. drafting; rough-copying
brulionowy [brool-yo-**no**-vi] adj.m. written in form of a rough draft; (paper) for making notes
brulot [**broo**-lot] m. fire-ship
brunat [**broo**-naht] m. the color brown (hist.)
brunatnawy [broo-naht-**nah**-vi] adj.m. brownish
brunatnica [broo-naht-**ńee**-tsah] f. alga containing a brown pigment
brunatnić [broo-**naht**-ńeećh] v. color brown; to give brown hues (*repeatedly*)
brunatnić się [broo-**naht**-ńeećh śhan] v. show brown hues; form brown patches (*repeatedly*)
brunatnieć [broo-**naht**-ńećh] v. acquire a brown tint; turn brown; become brown (*repeatedly*)
brunatnienie [broo-naht-**ńe**-ńe] n. acquiring a brown tint; turning brown; becoming brown
brunatnienie się [broo-naht-**ńe**-ńe śhan] n. putting brown color on oneself
brunatno [broo-**nah**-tno] adv. in brown color
brunatność [broo-**nah**-tnośhćh] f. the color brown
brunatnożółty [broo-naht-no-**zhoow**-ti] adj.m. ocher
brunatny [broo-**nah**-tni] adj.m. brown; tawny; tan-colored; russet
węgiel brunatny [**van**-gel broo-**nah**-tni] exp.: lignite
brunecik [broo-**ne**-ćheek] m. dark-haired boy
brunet [**broo**-net] m. dark-haired man; black-haired man
brunetka [broo-**net**-kah] f. brunette; dark-haired woman; slang: flea
brus [broos] m. hone; whetstone; Turkey-stone; wooden beam; match board; plank pile; colloq: boorish man; boor
brusić [**broo**-śheećh] v. sharpen (on a hone, on a whetstone); hone (*repeatedly*)
brusznica [broosh-**ńee**-tsah] f. cranberry; red whortleberry; cowberry
brusznicowy [broosh-ńee-**tso**-vi] adj.m. cranberry (jam, etc.)
brutal [**broo**-tahl] m. brute; bully; beast; savage
brutalizacja [broo-tah-lee-**zahts**-yah]

f. brutalization
brutalizm [broo-**tah**-leezm] m. brutality
brutalizować [broo-tah-lee-**zo**-vahćh] v. brutalize (*repeatedly*)
brutalizowanie [broo-tah-lee-zo-**vah**-ńe] n. brutalization
brutalnie [broo-**tahl**-ńe] adv. brutally; roughly; crudely
brutalność [broo-**tahl**-nośhćh] f. brutality; roughness; crudeness; savageness; ill-treatment
brutalny [broo-**tahl**-ni] adj.m. brutal; rough; crude; savage; tough
brutto [**broot**-to] not declined: gross
cena brutto [**tse**-nah **broot**-to] exp.: gross price
waga brutto [**vah**-gah **broot**-to] exp.: gross weight
dochód brutto [**do**-khoot **broot**-to] exp.: gross receipts
bruzda [**brooz**-dah] f. furrow; groove; deep wrinkle; streak; trench; rut; trail; fissure
bruzdka [**broost**-kah] f. small furrow
bruzdkować [broost-**ko**-vahćh] v. striate (*repeatedly*)
bruzdkowanie [broost-ko-**vah**-ńe] n. striation
bruzdkowany [broost-ko-**vah**-ni] adj.m. striated
bruzdkowy [broost-**ko**-vi] adj.m. of striation
bruzdnica [broozd-**ńee**-tsah] f. Dinoflagellata plant
bruzdobrzuch [brooz-**do**-bzhookh] m. solenogaster; alpacophora
bruzdobrzuchy [brooz-do-**bzhoo**-khi] pl. Alpacophora
bruzdogłowiec [brooz-do-**gwo**-vyets] m. the tapeworm Diphyllobothrium
bruzdować [brooz-**do**-vahćh] v. furrow; groove (*repeatedly*)
bruzdowanie [brooz-do-**vah**-ńe] n. making furrows; making grooves
bruzdowany [brooz-do-**vah**-ni] adj.m. grooved; channelled; sulcate
bruzdowaty [brooz-do-**vah**-ti] adj.m. furrowy
bruzdownica [brooz-dov-**ńee**-tsah] f. grooving machine
bruzdowy [brooz-**do**-vi] adj.m. of a furrow
bruździć [**broośh**-dźheećh] v. furrow; root (the ground); colloq: make difficulties; muddle; obstruct; hinder; impede; baffle; thwart; cross (plans, etc.); disrupt; throw a monkey wrench (into a peace negotiation, etc.) (*repeatedly*)
brużdżenie [broozh-**dzhe**-ńe] n. colloq: disruption; hindering; colloq: putting a spoke into somebody's wheel
brwi [brvee] pl. eyebrows
brwiowy [**brvyo**-vi] adj.m. superciliary
bryczesy [bri-**che**-si] pl. riding-breeches
bryczka [**brich**-kah] f. britzska; chaise; wagonette
bryczuszka [bri-**choosh**-kah] f. (small, nice) britzska; chaise; wagonette
brydż [brich] m. bridge (card game)
brydż według zapisu międzynarodowego [brich **ved**-woog zah-**pee**-soo my<u>an</u>-dzi-nah-ro-do-**ve**-go] exp.: contract bridge
dobrze grać w brydża [**dob**-zhe grahćh v **bri**-dzhah] exp.: to be a good hand at bridge
brydżyk [**bri**-dzhik] m. (nice, little) bridge (card game)
brydżowy [bri-**dzho**-vi] adj.m. bridge (player, table, etc.)
brydżysta [bri-**dzhis**-tah] m. bridge-player
brydżystka [bri-**dzhist**-kah] f. (woman) bridge-player
bryfok [**bri**-fok] m. rectangular sail
bryg [brig] m. brig
brygada [bri-**gah**-dah] f. brigade (a large body of troops); working gang; (working) party; squad
brygadier [bri-**gah**-dyer] m. brigadier; foreman; overseer; brigadier general
brygadierka [bri-gah-**dyer**-kah] f. (female) brigadier; foreman; overseer
brygadierski [bri-gah-**dyer**-skee] adj.m. brigadier's; foreman's; overseer's; brigadier general's
brygadowy [bri-gah-**do**-vi] adj.m. of a brigade; brigade (system, etc.)

brygadzista [bri-gah-**dźhees**-tah] m. foreman; overseer
brygadzistka [bri-gah-**dźheest**-kah] f. forewoman; (female) overseer
brygantyna [bri-gahn-**ti**-nah] f. brigantine
bryja [**bri**-yah] f. mash; pulp; slush
bryk [brik] m. crib; pony; slang: cab
bryk! [brik] excl.: crash!
posługiwać się brykiem [po-swoo-**gee**-vahćh śhan **bri**-kem] exp.: to crib; slang: to cab
bryka [**bri**-kah] f. break; cart; wagonette
brykać [**bri**-kahćh] v. prance; buck; gambol; caper; cut capers; frisk; skip; cut and run; make off; set off (by horse at a run); turn tail; decamp (*repeatedly*)
brykanie [bri-**kah**-ńe] n. gambols; capers; friskiness; escape; flight; decampment
brykieciarka [bri-ke-**ćhahr**-kah] f. briquette-making machine
brykieciarnia [bri-ke-**ćhahr**-ńah] f. briquette plant
brykiel [**bri**-kel] m. busk; baleen; whalebone
brykiet [**bri**-ket] m. briquette
brykietować [bri-ke-**to**-vahćh] v. form into briquettes (coal dust, saw dust, etc.) (*repeatedly*)
brykietowanie [bri-ke-to-**vah**-ńe] n. forming into briquettes (coal dust, saw dust, etc.)
brykietownia [bri-ke-**tov**-ńah] f. briquette factory
brykla [**brik**-lah] f. busk; baleen; whalebone
bryknąć [**bri**-knownćh] v. prance; buck; gambol; caper; cut capers; frisk; skip; cut and run; make off; set off (by horse at a run); turn tail; decamp
bryknięcie [brik-**ńan**-ćhe] n. (horse's) buck; escapade; frolic; gambol; escape; flight; decampment
brylancik [bri-**lahn**-ćheek] m. (nice, little) brilliant; diamond
brylant [**bri**-lahnt] m. brilliant; diamond
pierścionek z brylantem [pyerśh-ćho-nek z bri-**lahn**-tem] exp.: diamond ring
brylantowo [bri-lahn-**to**-vo] adv. (to sparkle, etc.) like diamonds
brylantowy [bri-lahn-**to**-vi] adj.m. diamond (ring, wedding, etc.)
brylantyna [bri-lahn-**ti**-nah] f. brilliantine
brylantynować [bri-lahn-ti-**no**-vahćh] v. put brilliantine (on one's hair) (*repeatedly*)
brylasty [bri-**lahs**-ti] adj.m. cloddy; massive; lumpish; nubby
brylok [**bri**-lok] m. colloq: pendant
brylować [bri-**lo**-vahćh] v. shine (in society) (*repeatedly*)
brylowanie [bri-lo-**vah**-ńe] n. shining (in society)
bryła [**bri**-wah] f. lump; mass; clod (of earth); solid body; a solid; external shape of a structure
bryła obrotowa [**bri**-wah ob-ro-**to**-vah] exp.: solid of revolution
bryłka [**briw**-kah] f. lump; clot; nodule (of stone, etc.); nub; nubble (of coal, etc.); slug (of metal, etc.); nugget (of gold, etc.)
bryłkowaty [briw-ko-**vah**-ti] adj.m. cloddy; lumpy
bryłowacieć [bri-wo-**vah**-ćhećh] v. cake; agglutinate (*repeatedly*)
bryłowatość [bri-wo-**vah**-tośhćh] f. massiveness
bryłowaty [bri-wo-**vah**-ti] adj.m. lumpy; massive; nubby; lumpish
bryłowy [bri-**wo**-vi] adj.m. of a lump; of a mass
góry bryłowe [**goo**-ri bri-**wo**-ve] exp.: faulted mountains
kąt bryłowy [kownt bri-**wo**-vi] exp.: solid angle
bryndza [**brin**-dzah] f. ewe's cheese; colloq: straits; straitened circumstances
u niego bryndza [oo ńe-go **brin**-dzah] exp.: he is broke; he is out of pocket; he is hard up; he is stony-broke
brysiowaty [bri-śho-**vah**-ti] adj.m. mastiff-like (dog); like a large deep-chested smooth-coated guard dog
brystol [**bris**-tol] m. Bristol board
brystolowy [bris-to-**lo**-vi] adj.m. of Bristol board

bryś [briśh] m. (small) mastiff; yard dog; chained dog
bryt [brit] m. gore (sewn into a garment)
brytan [**bri**-tahn] m. mastiff; yard dog; chained dog
brytania [bri-**tah**-ńyah] f. Britannia metal
brytfanka [brit-**fahn**-kah] f. (small) frying pan
brytfanna [brit-**fahn**-nah] f. frying pan
Brytyjczyk [bri-**tiy**-chik] m. Britisher; British subject
brytyjski [bri-**tiy**-skee] adj.m. British
bryza [**bri**-zah] f. breeze; sea breeze
bryzg [brisk] m. splash; spatter; plash
bryzgi wody [**briz**-gee **vo**-di] exp.: spray
bryzgać [**briz**-gahćh] v. splash; spatter; plash (*repeatedly*)
bryzgać błotem [**briz**-gahćh **bwo**-tem] exp.: to splash with mud; to spatter with mud
bryzganie [briz-**gah**-ńe] n. splashes; spatters
bryzgnąć [**brizg**-nownćh] v. splash; spatter; plash
bryzgnięcie [brizg-**ńan**-ćhe] n. splash; spatter
bryznąć [**briz**-nownćh] v. splash; spatter; plash
bryznięcie [briz-**ńan**-ćhe] n. splash; spatter
bryzol [**bri**-zol] m. brisol
brzana [**bzhah**-nah] f. barbel (fresh water fish); slang: girl; lassie
brzanka [**bzhah**-nkah] f. timothy (grass); barbel (fish)
brzany [**bzhah**-ni] adj.m. of millet; millet (seeds, etc.)
brzask [bzhahsk] m. dawn; daybreak; break of day; reflection of light; faint light
z brzaskiem [**z bzhahs**-kem] exp.: at daybreak
brząkać [**bzhown**-kahćh] v. strum; thrum; twang; thump (the piano); clank (*repeatedly*)
brząkadło [bzhown-**kah**-dwo] n. bad musical instrument; clanging object; rattling object
brząkanie [bzhown-**kah**-ńe] n. strumming; thrumming; twanging; thumping (the piano); clanking
brząknąć [**bzhownk**-nownćh] v. strum; thrum; twang; thump (the piano); clank
brząknięcie [bzhownk-**ńan**-ćhe] n. a clank; a strum; a thrum; a twang; a thump
brzdąc [bzhdownts] m. tot; brat
brzdąkać [**bzhdown**-kahćh] v. strum (*repeatedly*)
brzdąkanie [bzhdown-**kah**-ńe] n. a strum; strumming; thrumming
brzdąkanina [bzhdown-kah-**ńee**-nah] f. an objectional strum
brzdąknąć [**bzhdownk**-nownćh] v. strum; thrum; twang (a guitar)
brzdąknięcie [bzhdown-**kńan**-ćhe] n. a strum; strumming; thrumming
brzdęk [bzhdank] interjection: twang!; tang!; bang!; flop!; a bang; a twang; a tang; a flop
brzdękać [**bzhdan**-kahćh] v. strum; thrum; twang (a guitar) (*repeatedly*)
brzdękanie [bzhdan-**kah**-ńe] n. colloq: playing an instrument poorly
brzdęknąć [**bzhdank**-nownćh] v. fall flop; fall with a flop; fall plump (on the floor, to the ground, etc.)
brzdęknięcie [bzhdank-**ńan**-ćhe] n. flop; a fall with a flop
brzechwa [**bzhekh**-fah] f. the stabilizer in flight (of an arrow, bomb, etc.); shaft of an arrow
brzeczka [**bzhech**-kah] f. wort; sweetwort; mash; (tannery) liquor
brzeg [bzheg] m. shore; margin; bank; waterside; riverside; coast; brim; rim; edge; border; skirt; brink; verge; brow; flap; hem; fringe; selvage; selvedge
iść brzegiem lasu [eeśhćh **bzhe**-gem **lah**-soo] exp.: to skirt a forest; to walk on the edge of a forest
na brzeg [nah bzheg] exp.: ashore
na brzegu [nah **bzhe**-goo] exp.: ashore
wyrzucić na brzeg [vi-**zhoo**-ćheećh nah bzheg] exp.: to

strand
osiąść na brzegu [o-śhownśhćh nah **bzhe**-goo] exp.: to run ashore
brzegarka [bzhe-**gahr**-kah] f. veneer-edging machine; board-edging machine; router; routing plane
brzegowiec [bzhe-**go**-vyets] m. American manatee
brzegowy [bzhe-**go**-vi] adj.m. waterside
linia brzegowa [leeń-yah bzhe-**go**-vah] exp.: shore line
brzegowe [bzhe-**go**-ve] exp.: wharf charges; wharf dues; wharfage dues
brzegówka [bzhe-**goof**-kah] f. bank swallow; sand martin (a bird)
brzemienność [bzhe-**myen**-nośhćh] f. pregnancy
brzemienny [bzhe-**myen**-ni] adj.m. pregnant; heavy with; loaded with; colloq: big (with consequences, etc.); fraught (with danger, etc.); of far-reaching (consequences)
brzemię [**bzhe**-myan] n. burden; load; weight; onus
brzeszcze [**bzhesh**-che] n. (cutting) edge
brzeszczot [**bzhesh**-chot] m. blade (of a sword, a machete, etc.); web (of a saw, etc.)
brzezina [bzhe-**źhee**-nah] f. birch wood; birch (wood)
brzezinka [bzhe-**źhee**-nkah] f. (small) birch wood; birch (wood)
brzezinowy [bzhe-źhee-**no**-vi] adj.m. of a birch wood; of a birch thicket
brzeźniak [**bzheźh**-ńahk] m. birch thicket
brzeżek [**bzhe**-zhek] m. the very edge; a nice edge; the very border; the very brink; a glimmer (of hope)
brzeżny [**bzhezh**-ni] adj.m. border; marginal; skirting; coastal; riverside (wharf, etc.)
brzeżyca [bzhe-**zhi**-tsah] f. littorella; an aquatic shoreweed
brzęczeć [**bzhan**-chećh] v. ring; tinkle; clink; chink; jingle; buzz; hum; clatter; click; tang; twang; drum; zoom; drone; ping (*repeatedly*)
brzęcząca moneta [bzhan-**chown**-tsah mo-**ne**-tah] exp.: hard cash
brzęczek [**bzhan**-chek] m. buzzer
brzęczenie [bzhan-**che**-ńe] n. rattle; clang; tinkle; jingle; jangle; ring; chink; clank; click; clatter; tang; twang; buzz; hum; drum; zoom; drone; ping
brzęczka [**bzhanch**-kah] f. variety of whitethroat (bird) (Silvia)
brzęczyk [**bzhan**-chik] m. buzzer
brzęczykowy [bzhan-chi-**ko**-vi] adj.m. buzzer's; of a buzzer
brzęk [bzhank] m. clink; chink; rattle; ping; buzz; hum; drone
brzękać [**bzhan**-kahćh] v. strum; thrum; twang; thump (the piano); clank (*repeatedly*)
brzękadełko [bzhan-kah-**dew**-ko] n. rattling toy
brzękadło [bzhan-**kahd**-wo] n. rattling (object, etc.); clanging (bell, etc.); jingling (chain, etc.)
brzękanie [bzhan-**kah**-ńe] n. thumping (the piano); clanking
brzękliwie [bzhan-**klee**-vye] adv. with a clink; with a rattle; with clattering; with a ping; with a clatter; with a twang
brzękliwy [bzhan-**klee**-vi] adj.m. rattling; tinkling; clattering
brzęknąć [**bzhank**-nownćh] v. strum; thrum; twang; thump (the piano); clank
brzęknąć [**bzhank**-nownćh] v. swell (*repeatedly*)
brzęknięcie [bzhank-ńan-ćhe] n. clink; chink; rattle; ping; buzz; hum; drone; swelling
brzmiący [**bzhmyown**-tsi] adj.m. sounding; sonorous; vocal
mile brzmiący [**mee**-le **bzhmyown**-tsi] exp.: pleasing to the ear; euphonic; pleasant to the ear
niemile brzmiący [ńe-**mee**-le **bzhmyown**-tsi] exp.: offensive; jarring
brzmieć [bzhmyećh] v. sound; ring; purport; resound; blare; call; be heard; peal; swell; read; run; go (*repeatedly*)
dzwon brzmi [dzvon bzhmee] exp.: the bell peals; the bell rings

out; there is a peal of the bell
tekst brzmi jak następuje [tekst bzhmee yahk nah-stan-**poo**-ye] exp.: the text runs as follows; the text reads as follows; the text goes as follows
to brzmi dziwnie [to bzhmee **dźheev**-ńe] exp.: this sounds strange
brzmienie [**bzhmye**-ńe] n. sound (of a voice, etc.); purport; tenor; wording; rung (of a voice); tone (of a voice); reading (of a text, etc.); contents (of a letter, etc.); terms (of a contract, etc.)
brzmieniowo [bzhmye-**ńo**-vo] adv. of sound quality
brzmieniowy [bzhmye-**ńo**-vi] adj.m. sound (values, etc.)
brzona [**bzho**-nah] f. lavaret (a white fish)
brzoskiew [**bzhos**-kef] f. variety of cabbage
brzoskwinia [bzhos-**kfee**-ńah] f. peach; peach tree
brzoskwiniarnia [bzhos-kfee-**ńahr**-ńah] f. peachery
brzoskwiniowy [bzhos-kfee-**ńo**-vi] adj.m. peach (tree, brandy, etc.); peach-colored
brzoskwiniówka [bzhos-kfee-**ńoof**-kah] f. peach brandy; peach vodka
brzoskwinka [bzhos-**kfeen**-kah] f. (small, nice) peach (tree)
brzost [bzhost] m. Scotch elm; wych-elm; witch hazel
brzostowy [bzhos-**to**-vi] adj.m. of Scotch elm; Scotch elm (wood)
brzoza [**bzho**-zah] f. birch
brzozowaty [bzho-zo-**vah**-ti] adj.m. birch-like; betulaceous
brzozowy [bzho-**zo**-vi] adj.m. of birch; birch; birchen
brzózka [**bzhoos**-kah] f. (young, small) birch
brzuch [bzhookh] m. belly; abdomen; stomach; tummy; guts; abdomen (of an insect); vulg.: tripes; guts
ból brzucha [bool **bzhoo**-khah] exp.: stomach ache; colloq: belly ache
brzuchacz [**bzhoo**-khahch] m. potbelly; paunchy man
brzuchal [**bzhoo**-khahl] m. potbelly; paunchy man
brzuchaty [bzhoo-**khah**-ti] adj.m. big-bellied; corpulent; ventricose; potbellied; bulging (pot, etc.); bulgy (jar, etc.)
brzucho [**bzhoo**-kho] n. slang: belly; paunch
brzuchomówca [bzhoo-kho-**moof**-tsah] m. ventriloquist
brzuchomówstwo [bzhoo-kho-**moof**-stfo] n. ventriloquism
brzuchonóg [bzhoo-**kho**-noog] m. gastropod
brzuchorzęska [bzhoo-kho-**zhan**-skah] f. Gastrotricha (fresh-water tiny animal with scale on the belly)
brzuchorzęski [bzhoo-kho-**zhan**-skee] pl. the family of Gastrotricha (fresh-water animals 1.5 millimeter long)
brzusiec [**bzhoo**-śhets] m. belly; pad; ball (of a finger, etc.)
brzuszek [**bzhoo**-shek] m. tummy
brzuszny [**bzhoosh**-ni] adj.m. abdominal; ventral; of the belly
dur brzuszny [door **bzhoosh**-ni] exp.: enteric fever; typhoid fever
brzuszyna [bzhoo-**shi**-nah] f. colloq: little belly
brzuszysko [bzhoo-**shis**-ko] n. colloq: big belly
brzydactwo [bzhi-**dahts**-tfo] n. ugliness; ugly thing; ugly person; eyesore; unsightly man; hideous person; slang: fright; horror
brzydal [**bzhi**-dahl] m. ugly man; unsightly person; a fright; a horror
brzydki [**bzhit**-kee] adj.m. ugly; unsightly; hideous; foul; ill-looking; bad; nasty; mean; base; shabby; shameful; disgraceful; despicable; vile; rude; vulgar
płeć brzydka [pwećh **bzhit**-kah] exp.: the men; the sterner sex
brzydko [**bzhit**-ko] adv. in an ugly manner; hideously; in a naughty way; in a messy way
brzydnąć [**brzid**-nownćh] v. become ugly; grow ugly; lose one's looks; lose one's beauty

(*repeatedly*)
brzydnięcie [bzhid-ńan-ćhe] n. becoming ugly; growing ugly
brzydota [bzhi-**do**-tah] f. ugliness; unsightliness; ugly person; unsightly person; ugly thing; eyesore; monstrosity
brzydula [bzhi-**doo**-lah] f. ugly girl; unsightly girl; uncomely girl; an ugly dear thing; an ugly poor thing
brzydzenie [bzhi-**dze**-ńe] n. abhorrence; abomination; disgust
brzydzenie się [bzhi-**dze**-ńe śhan] n. feeling abhorrence; feeling abomination; feeling disgust
brzydzić [**bzhi**-dźheećh] v. inspire disgust; inspire abhorrence; sicken; repel (*repeatedly*)
brzydzić się [**bzhi**-dźheećh śhan] v. feel disgust; loathe; abhor; detest; hold in disgust (*repeatedly*)
brzytwa [**bzhit**-fah] f. razor
tonący brzytwy się chwyta [to-**nown**-tsi **bzhit**-fi śhan **khfi**-tah] exp.: a drowning man catches at a straw
brzytwodziób [bzhit-**fo**-dźhoop] m. variety of plover (bird)
bu! [boo] excl.: boo! (imitation of a weeping sound)
bubek [**boo**-bek] m. buck; whipper snapper; young fellow; dandy; fop; dude
bubel [**boo**-bel] m. unsalable item
bubkowaty [boop-ko-**vah**-ti] adj.m. foppish; like a dandy
buble [**boo**-ble] pl. unsalable goods
buc [boots] m. colloq: overbearing and arrogant man; puffed up man
bucefał [boo-**tse**-fahw] m. charger; slang: old hack; jade
buch [bookh] excl.: bang!; slap!; dash!; smack!; flump!; plump!;
buchać [**boo**-khahćh] v. squirt; flare; blaze; burst forth; flame out; gush; spout; flush forth; spurt; scurry; scuttle; scamper; hit; strike; knock; thump; thwack; snoop; pinch; steal; make away with; explode (*repeatedly*)
buchać dymem [**boo**-khahćh **di**-mem] exp.: to eject clouds of smoke
buchać płomieniem [**boo**-khahćh pwo-**mye**-ńem] exp.: to blaze forth
buchalter [boo-**khahl**-ter] m. bookkeeper
buchalteria [boo-khahl-**te**-ryah] f. bookkeeping
buchalteryjny [boo-khahl-te-**riy**-ni] adj.m. bookkeeping (department, etc.)
buchanie [boo-**khah**-ńe] n. bursting; flaring; gushing; spouting; colloq: stealing
buchaniec [boo-**khah**-ńets] m. knock; thump; thwack
buchnąć [**bookh**-nownćh] v. squirt; flare; blaze; burst forth; flame out; gush; spout; flush forth; spurt; scurry; scuttle; scamper; hit; strike; knock; thump; thwack; snoop; make away with; steal; explode
buchnięcie [bookh-**ńan**-ćhe] n. squirting; bursting; gushing; spouting; exploding; colloq: stealing
buchta [**bookh**-tah] f. ground rooted up by wild boars; coiled rope; dumpling with jam inside; bay; creek
buchtować [bookh-**to**-vahćh] v. root up (the soil by boars); coil (a rope, etc.) (*repeatedly*)
buchtowanie [bookh-to-**vah**-ńe] n. rooting up (soil by boars); coiling (a rope, etc.)
buchtowisko [bookh-to-**vees**-ko] n. ground rooted up by wild boars; coiled rope; dumpling with jam inside; bay; creek
buciczek [boo-**ćhee**-chek] m. small child's shoe
bucik [**boo**-ćheek] m. shoe; boot
bucior [**boo**-ćhor] m. big boot; beetle-crusher; big old shoe
bucisko [boo-**ćhees**-ko] n. big boot; beetle-crusher; big old shoe
buczeć [**boo**-chećh] v. boom; zoom; hum; buzz; drone; toot; scream; cipher; blubber; boohoo; weep noisily (*repeatedly*)
buczek [**boo**-chek] m. young beech; beech stick; hooter; siren; steam

whistle
buczenie [boo-**che**-ńe] n. boom; zoom; hum; buzz; drone; toot
buczyna [boo-**chi**-nah] f. beechood; beech-grove; beech mast
buda [**boo**-dah] f. shed; shanty; shack; hut; booth; kennel; hood; tilt; cover of a carriage; stall; slang: shop
buddaizm [bood-**dah**-eezm] m. buddhism
buddyjka [bood-**diy**-kah] f. buddhist woman
buddyjski [bood-**diy**-skee] adj.m. buddhist
buddysta [bood-**dis**-tah] m. a buddhist
buddyzm [**bood**-dizm] m. buddhism
budka [**boot**-kah] f. shelter; cabin; stall; booth; sentry-box; watch-box; cab; newsstand
budka telefoniczna [**boot**-kah te-le-fo-**ńeech**-nah] exp.: telephone (call) box; telephone booth
budleja [bood-**le**-yah] f. Buddleia shrub or tree
budnik [**bood**-ńeek] m. news-vendor
budowa [boo-**do**-vah] f. construction; erection; edifice; framework; structure; rising of (a structure, etc.); texture; fiber; formation; make; conformation; build; the build; constitution; figure; proportions; building
biuro budowy [**byoo**-ro boo-**do**-vi] exp.: building-office
plac budowy [plahts boo-**do**-vi] exp.: building-site
budowa ciała [boo-**do**-vah **ćhah**-wah] exp.: structure of the body; build; figure; proportions of the body; constitution
budowa dróg [boo-**do**-vah drook] exp.: road-building
budowa zdania [boo-**do**-vah **zdah**-ńah] exp.: sentence structure
budować [boo-**do**-vahćh] v. build; construct; edify; erect; rise; put up; elevate; inspire; exert good influence upon (*repeatedly*)
budować zamki na lodzie [boo-**do**-vahćh **zahm**-kee nah **lo**-dźhe] exp.: to build castles in the air; to build castles on ice
budować się [boo-**do**-vahćh śhan] v. build a house of one's own; be under construction; be in process of construction; be in course of construction (*repeatedly*)
budowanie [boo-do-**vah**-ńe] n. building; erecting; raising (of a structure, etc.)
budowanie się [boo-do-**vah**-ńe śhan] n. building one's own house (barn, etc.)
budowla [boo-**dov**-lah] f. building (large); edifice; house; structure; fabric; pile
budowlanka [boo-dov-**lahn**-kah] f. building trade school; building timber
budowlany [boo-dov-**lah**-ni] adj.m. building; structural; constructional; architectural
przedsiębiorca budowlany [pshet-śhan-**byor**-tsah boo-dov-**lah**-ni] exp.: builder; building contractor
przedsiębiorstwo budowlane [pshet-śhan-**byor**-stfo boo-dov-**lah**-ne] exp.: building enterprise
budownictwo [boo-dov-**ńeets**-tfo] n. colloq: architecture; tectonics; the building trade
budowniczy [boo-dov-**ńee**-chi] m. builder; master builder; architect; colloq: maker; adj.m. structural; constructional; architectural
budrys [**bood**-ris] m. slang: Lithuanian
budrysówka [bood-ri-**soof**-kah] f. long jacket with a hood
buduar [boo-**doo**-ahr] m. lady's chamber; boudoir
buduarek [boo-doo-**ah**-rek] m. (small, nice) lady's chamber; boudoir
buduarowy [boo-doo-ah-**ro**-vi] adj.m. of a boudoir; intimate; secret
buduarowe przygody [boo-doo-ah-**ro**-ve pshi-**go**-di] exp.: amorous adventures
budująco [boo-doo-**yown**-tso] adv. in edifying manner
budujący [boo-doo-**yown**-tsi] adj.m. edifying; elevating; moralizing; beneficial; exemplary
budulcowy [boo-dool-**tso**-vi] adj.m. of timber; of lumber; of building

material
budulec [boo-**doo**-lets] m. timber; lumber; building material; colloq: constructive element; matter; substance; stuff
budyneczek [boo-di-**ne**-chek] m. (nice, little) building
budynek [boo-**di**-nek] m. building; house; edifice
budyniowy [boo-di-**ńo**-vi] adj.m. pudding- (-cloth, etc.); of a pudding; for puddings
budyń [**boo**-diń] m. pudding
budzenie [boo-**dze**-ńe] n. awakening; arising; waking up
budzenie się [boo-**dze**-ńe śhan] n. awakening; arising; waking up
budziciel [boo-**dźhee**-ćhel] m. wakener
budzicielka [boo-dźhee-**ćhel**-kah] f. (woman) wakener
budzić [**boo**-dźheećh] v. wake up; wake; awake; waken; awaken; rouse; stir; arise; evoke; excite (feelings, etc.); arouse (envy, etc.); prompt (to) (*repeatedly*)
budzić się [**boo**-dźheećh śhan] v. wake (up); to awake; start up; spring up; arise (*repeatedly*)
budzik [**boo**-dźheek] m. alarm clock; alarm
budżet [**bood**-zhet] m. budget
budżetować [bood-zhe-**to**-vahćh] v. budget; prepare a budget (*repeatedly*)
budżetowanie [bood-zhe-to-**vah**-ńe] n. budgeting; preparing a budget
budżetowy [bood-zhe-**to**-vi] adj.m. budgetary; financial; fiscal; budget (law, etc.)
bufa [**boo**-fah] f. puff
bufy [**boo**-fi] pl. puffed sleeves
bufeciarz [boo-**fe**-ćhahsh] m. barman; bartender
bufecik [boo-**fe**-ćheek] m. (small, nice) sideboard; cupboard; bar; snack bar; quick-lunch bar; refreshment room; refreshments; refreshment table
bufet [**boo**-fet] m. sideboard; cupboard; bar; snack bar; quick-lunch bar; refreshment room; refreshments; refreshment table
bufetowa [boo-fe-**to**-vah] f. barmaid
bufetowy [boo-fe-**to**-vi] m. barman; bartender; adj.m. buffet (dish, etc.); bar (sales, etc.)
buffo [**boof**-fo] (not declined:) buffo; clown; buffoon; singer of comic roles on opera
bufiasto [boo-**fyah**-sto] adv. (sewn, etc.) in puffy folds
bufiasty [boo-**fyah**-sti] adj.m. puffed (up); puffy; full
bufka [**boo**-fkah] f. puff
bufon [**boo**-fon] m. buffoon; braggart; coxcomb; fop; clown; a ludicrous figure; a stupid man; a gross man; an uneducated man
bufonada [boo-fo-**nah**-dah] f. buffoonery; clownery; drollery; foppery; brag; coarse, loutish behavior; loutish practice
bufoneria [boo-fo-**ner**-yah] f. buffoonery; clownery; drollery; foppery; brag
bufoński [boo-**foń**-skee] adj.m. foppish; affected
bufor [**boo**-for] m. buffer
buforowy [boo-fo-**ro**-vi] adj.m. buffer (state, etc.)
bugaj [**boo**-gahy] m. cluster of sprouting trees and shrubs
buhaj [**boo**-khahy] m. bull (kept for breeding)
bujać [**boo**-yahćh] v. rock; lie; soar; fly about; float in the air; roam; rove; flit about; swing; dangle; gad about; daydream; be wool-gathering; indulge in daydreaming; grow rank; grow luxuriantly; fib; tell lies; tell stories (*repeatedly*)
bujać się [**boo**-yahćh śhan] v. rock; swing; dangle; be sweet on (somebody) (*repeatedly*)
bujak [**boo**-yahk] m. rocking chair
bujanie [boo-**yah**-ńe] n. rocking; lying; dangling; floating
bujanie się [boo-**yah**-ńe śhan] n. rocking oneself
bujanka [boo-**yahn**-kah] f. bee fly
bujda [**booy**-dah] f. colloq: hoax; fib; flam; humbug; slang: spoof
bujnąć [**booy**-nownćh] v. rock; lie; soar; fly about; float in the air; roam; rove; flit about; swing; dangle; gad about; daydream; be

woolgathering; indulge in daydreaming; grow rank; grow luxuriantly; fib; tell lies; tell stories
bujnąć się [**booy**-nownćh śhan] v. rock; swing; dangle; be sweet on (somebody)
bujnie [**booy**-ńe] adv. exuberantly; luxuriantly; rankly; wantonly
bujnięcie [booy-**ńan**-ćhe] n. rocking; swinging; dangling
bujnięcie się [booy-**ńan**-ćhe śhan] n. rocking oneself; swinging; dangling
bujność [**booy**-nośhćh] f. exuberance; abundance; rank growth; wanton growth; luxuriance; rankness
bujny [**booy**-ni] adj.m. exuberant; rich; abundant; luxuriant; bushy; fertile; gross; wanton; lush; rampant; active (imagination)
buk [book] m. beech (tree)
bukat [**boo**-kaht] m. calf past the vealer stage; calf's skin
bukatowy [boo-kah-**to**-vi] adj.m. of a calf; calf (leather, etc.)
bukieciarstwo [boo-ke-**ćhahr**-stfo] n. art of decorating with flowers; making bouquets, garlands, etc.
bukieciarz [boo-**ke**-ćhahsh] m. decorator using flowers; maker of bouquets, garlands, etc.
bukiecik [boo-**ke**-ćheek] m. posy; nosegay; small bouquet
bukiet [**boo**-ket] m. bouquet; bunch of flowers; cluster of trees; aroma of wine; raciness; tail of a doe
bukietowy [boo-ke-**to**-vi] adj.m. bouquet (flowers, etc.)
bukiew [**boo**-kef] f. beech mast
bukinista [boo-kee-**ńees**-tah] m. second-hand (sidewalk) bookseller
bukłak [**book**-wahk] m. wine-bag; wineskin; goatskin
bukmacher [book-**mah**-kher] m. bookmaker
bukmacherstwo [book-mah-**kher**-stfo] n. booking
bukolicznie [boo-ko-**leech**-ńe] adv. bucolically
bukoliczny [boo-ko-**leech**-ni] adj.m. bucolic; pastoral
bukolika [boo-**ko**-lee-kah] f. a bucolic; pastoral poem
bukować [boo-**ko**-vahćh] v. pair (sheep); mate; book; make a reservation (*repeatedly*)
bukowanie [boo-ko-**vah**-ńe] n. pairing; mating; booking; making reservations
bukowaty [boo-ko-**vah**-ti] adj.m. of the beech family (of trees)
bukowate [boo-ko-**vah**-te] pl. the beech family (of trees)
bukowina [boo-ko-**vee**-nah] f. beechwood
bukowisko [boo-ko-**vees**-ko] n. mating time of fallow dear
bukownik [boo-**kov**-ńeek] m. ram; tup
bukowy [boo-**ko**-vi] adj.m. beech; of beech; beechen
bukówka [boo-**koof**-kah] f. variety of apple
bukranion [boo-**krahń**-yon] m. bucranium (in architecture)
buks [books] m. wheel bearing; hub
buksa [**book**-sah] f. towline; hawser
buksować [book-**so**-vahćh] v. tow; trail; take in tow; have in tow; surge (of a wheel in a car) (*repeatedly*)
buksowanie [book-so-**vah**-ńe] n. towage; trackage
bukszpan [**book**-shpahn] m. box (tree); boxwood
bukszpanowaty [book-shpah-no-**vah**-ti] adj.m. buxaceous; of the box tree family
bukszpanowate [book-shpah-no-**vah**-te] pl. buxaceous trees; the box tree family
bukszpanowy [book-shpah-**no**-vi] adj.m. boxwood (engraving block, etc.); of boxwood
bukszpir [**book**-shpeer] m. bowsprit extension
bukszpryt [**book**-shprit] m. bowsprit (a spar projecting forward)
buksztel [**book**-shtel] m. centering (in construction)
bukwa [**book**-fah] f. beech mast
bukwica [book-**fee**-tsah] f. betony (plant)
bul, bul [bool bool] exp.: (bubbling sound)

bulaj [**boo**-lahy] m. bull's eye; illuminator
bulanżeryt [boo-lahn-**zhe**-rit] m. boulangerite (mineral)
buldeneż [bool-**de**-nesh] m. guelder rose; snowball-tree (Brit.)
buldog [**bool**-dog] m. bulldog; colloq: bulldog gun
buldogowaty [bool-do-go-**vah**-ti] adj.m. bulldogged; bulldoggy
buldożer [bool-**do**-zher] m. bulldozer
bulgot [**bool**-got] m. bubble; gurgle
bulgotać [bool-**go**-tahćh] v. bubble; gurgle; make bubbling sounds; colloq: mumble; splutter; spatter (*repeatedly*)
bulgotanie [bool-go-**tah**-ńe] n. bubbling; gargling; sputtering
bulić [**boo**-leećh] v. slang: fork out; shell out; cough up; stump up; plank down (*repeatedly*)
bulier [**bool**-yer] m. boiler
bulik [**boo**-leek] m. spot on ice where hockey game is resumed
bulimia [boo-**lee**-myah] f. bulimia
bulina [boo-**lee**-nah] f. bowline
bulion [**boo**-lyon] m. bouillon; broth; beef-tea; stock soup; clear soup
bulionowy [boo-lyo-**no**-vi] adj.m. bouillon (stock, soup, etc.)
bulla [**bool**-lah] f. papal edict; bulla
bulterier [bool-**ter**-yer] m. bullterier
bulwa [**bool**-vah] f. bulb; tuber; Jerusalem artichoke; colloq: protuberance; bump
bulwar [**bool**-vahr] m. boulevard; avenue; embankment; breakwater; bulwark
bulwarowy [bool-vah-**ro**-vi] adj.m. of the boulevards; colloq: of the street; unrefined
bulwarówka [bool-vah-**roof**-kah] f. light comedy; farce of small artistic value
bulwersować [bool-ver-**so**-vahćh] v. agitate; perturb; upset (*repeatedly*)
bulwiasty [bool-**vyahs**-ti] adj.m. bulbous; bulbiform; bulbiferous; tuberous; tuberiform; tuberiferous
bulwka [**boolf**-kah] f. (small, nice) bulb; tuber
bulwkowaty [boolf-ko-**vah**-ti] adj.m. tubercular (plant)
bulwocebula [bool-vo-tse-**boo**-lah] f. underground bulb (procreating vegetatively)
bulwowy [bool-**vo**-vi] adj.m. of a bulb
buła [**boo**-wah] f. large roll of bread; bread roll; bungler; fumbler; nodule; knot; gnarl
bułanek [boo-**wah**-nek] m. dun horse; sorrel horse; palomino
bułanka [boo-**wahn**-kah] f. dun mare; palomino mare
bułany [boo-**wah**-ni] adj.m. dun; palomino
bułat [**boo**-waht] m. sword; scimitar; falchion; Damascus steel
bułatowy [boo-wah-**to**-vi] adj.m. scimitar (blade, etc.); damask (steel, blade, etc.)
buława [boo-**wah**-vah] f. mace; truncheon; baton; staff of office; wand; club; warder; colloq: office; post
buławinka [boo-wah-**veen**-kah] f. ergot (fungus)
buławnik [boo-**wahv**-ńeek] m. phantom orchis; hetman
buławowaty [boo-wah-vo-**vah**-ti] adj.m. clavate; club-shaped
bułczak [**boow**-chahk] m. shelf fungus
bułczany [boow-**chah**-ni] adj.m. bread (flour, etc.)
bułczarka [boow-**chahr**-kah] f. woman trading in rolls of bread
bułczasty [boow-**chahs**-ti] adj.m. rounded; curved; like a loaf
bułeczka [boo-**wech**-kah] f. small bread roll
Bułgar [**boow**-gahr] m. Bulgarian
Bułgarka [boow-**gahr**-kah] f. Bulgarian (woman)
bułgarski [boow-**gahr**-skee] adj.m. Bulgarian (language)
po bułgarsku [po boow-**gahr**-skoo] exp.: in Bulgarian
bułgarszczyzna [boow-gahrsh-**chiz**-nah] f. things Bulgarian (language, culture, etc.)
bułgaryzować [boow-gah-ri-**zo**-vahćh] v. make Bulgarian; assimilate to Bulgaria (*repeatedly*)
bułka [**boow**-kah] f. roll (breakfast); bread roll; loaf

bułka tarta [**boow**-kah **tahr**-tah] exp.: bread crumbs
bułka z masłem [**boow**-kah z **mahs**-wem] exp.: bread and butter; easy work
słodka bułka [**swot**-kah **boow**-kah] exp.: bun
bułkowy [boow-**ko**-vi] adj.m. bread-roll (flour, etc.)
bułowaty [boo-wo-**vah**-ti] adj.m. nodular
bum [boom] excl.: bang!; boom!; m. boom (on a sail boat)
bumblerka [boom-**bler**-kah] f. drinking bout; spree
bumelanctwo [boo-me-**lahn**-tstfo] n. loafing; shirking; absenteeism
bumelant [boo-**me**-lahnt] m. loafer; shirker; absentee; bummer; sluggard; drone; colloq: slacker; slang: slouch; lazy bum
bumelować [boo-me-**lo**-vahćh] v. shirk; evade (a duty, etc.) (*repeatedly*)
bumelowanie [boo-me-lo-**vah**-ńe] n. loafing; shirking; wasting of time
bumerang [boo-**me**-rahng] m. boomerang
bumerangowy [boo-me-rahn-**go**-vi] adj.m. of a boomerang
buna [**boo**-nah] f. buna; synthetic rubber
bunda [**boon**-dah] f. sheepskin; sleeveless jerkin; (sleeveless) vest
bundowiec [boon-**do**-vyets] m. member of the Jewish (socialist) Bund
bundz [boonts] m. raw goat cheese
bungalow [boon-**gah**-lof] m. bungalow
bunkier [**boon**-ker] m. pillbox; bunker; underground isolated cell in German-Nazi concentration camp; ship's coal bin; storage bunker; coal bunker
bunkrować [boon-**kro**-vahćh] v. load fuel; coal; fuel (*repeatedly*)
bunkrowanie [boon-kro-**vah**-ńe] n. loading fuel; loading coal; fueling
bunkrowiec [boon-**kro**-vyets] m. fuel supply ship (near shore)
bunkrowy [boon-**kro**-vi] adj.m. bunker (coal, etc.)
bunowy [boo-**no**-vi] adj.m. of buna; buna (tires, etc.)
bunsenowski [boon-se-**nof**-skee] adj.m. Bunsen's (burner, battery, flame, etc.)
bunt [boont] m. mutiny; riot; sedition; revolt; rebellion; protest; dissent; bunch; cluster
podnieść bunt [**pod**-ńeśhćh boont] exp.: to rise in revolt
buntować [boon-**to**-vahćh] v. stir (up); rouse to revolt; instigate to insubordination; incite revolt; protest; rise; revolt (*repeatedly*)
buntować się [boon-**to**-vahćh śhan] v. revolt; rebel; mutiny; resist; protest (*repeatedly*)
buntowanie [boon-to-**vah**-ńe] n. incitement to revolt; incitement to insubordination
buntowanie się [boon-to-**vah**-ńe śhan] n. mutiny; rebellion; revolt; riot; resistance; defiance; protest; dissent
buntowniczo [boon-to-**vńee**-cho] adv. rebelliously; seditiously; mutinously; defiantly; in defiance; in rebellion; riotously
buntowniczość [boon-to-**vńee**-chośhćh] f. rebelliousness; defiance
buntowniczy [boon-to-**vńee**-chi] adj.m. rebellious; seditious; riotous; refractory; mutinous; turbulent; insubordinate
buntownicze nastroje [boon-to-**vńee**-che nahs-**tro**-ye] exp.: atmosphere of rebellion; seditiousness; riotousness; turbulence; insubordination
buntownik [boon-**tov**-ńeek] m. rebel; mutineer; rioter
buńczucznie [booń-**chooch**-ńe] adv. dashingly; with dash
buńczuczność [booń-**chooch**-nośhćh] f. dash; swagger; bluster; bounce; display; panache
buńczuczny [booń-**chooch**-ni] adj.m. cocky; perky; dashing; swaggering; blustery; bouncing; showy; gaudy; fond of display; m. standard-bearer of Ukrainian Cossacks (of old)
buńczuczyć się [booń-**choo**-chićh śhan] v. swagger; bluster; fume;

storm (*repeatedly*)
buńczuk [booń-chook] m. horse-tail ensign; panache (on a helmet)
bura [boo-rah] f. reprimand; talking-to; dressing-down; rating; wigging
dać burę [dahćh boo-ran] exp.: to reprimand; to give a scolding; to scold; to give it hot
dostać burę [dos-tahćh boo-ran] exp.: to get a scold; to get it hot
oberwać burę [o-ber-vahćh boo-ran] exp.: to get a scold; to get it hot; to get a dressing-down; to be hauled over the coals
buraczany [boo-rah-chah-ni] adj.m. beet (plant, etc.); of beetroot; reddish-violet; claret
buraczarnia [boo-rah-chahr-ńah] f. beet storage building
buraczek [boo-rah-chek] m. small beet
buraczki [boo-rahch-kee] pl. beets; beet greens; beetroot puree
buraczkowo [boo-rahch-ko-vo] adv. in reddish-violet color; in claret color
buraczkowy [boo-rahch-ko-vi] adj.m. in reddish-violet color; in claret color
buraczysko [boo-rah-chis-ko] n. beet field
burak [boo-rahk] m. beet; beetroot
burak cukrowy [boo-rahk tsoo-kro-vi] exp.: white beet; sugar beet
burak ćwikłowy [boo-rahk ćhfee-kwo-vi] exp.: red beet
burakowaty [boo-rah-ko-vah-ti] adj.m. beet-shaped
burakowy [boo-rah-ko-vi] adj.m. beet (sugar, etc.)
buran [boo-rahn] m. Siberian north-eastern wind
burawy [boo-rah-vi] adj.m. dunnish
burberry [bahr-be-ri] n. Burberry cloth (for outdoor use)
burczeć [boor-chećh] v. rumble; grumble; hum; drone; growl; nag; mutter; murmur (*repeatedly*)
burczenie [boor-che-ńe] n. rumble (in the belly); grumble; hum; nagging; drone; growl; mutter; murmur
burczymucha [boor-chi-moo-khah] m. colloq: growler; grumbler; nag; nagger
burda [boor-dah] f. scuffle; row; brawl; disturbance; wrangle; affray; shindy; fracas; uproar; slang: rumpus; kick-up; m. rough neck; hoodlum; brawler
wywołać burdę [vi-vo-wahćh boor-dan] exp.: to kick up a row; to rise Cain
burdel [boor-del] m. vulg. brothel; whorehouse; bawdy-house (Brit.)
burdon [boor-don] m. bourdon
burek [boo-rek] m. mongrel dog; tabby (cat)(Brit.)
bureta [boo-re-tah] f. shoddy silk
buretowy [boo-re-to-vi] adj.m. shoddy; of shoddy silk
burgos [boor-gos] m. bourgois (type, font)
burgrabia [boor-grah-byah] m. burgrave
burgrabiowski [boor-grah-byof-skee] adj.m. of a burgrave
burgund [boor-goont] m. burgundy wine
burgundzki [boor-goonts-kee] adj.m. Burgundian; burgundy (vintage)
buriacki [boor-yahts-kee] adj.m. Buriat; Buryat
Buriat [boor-yaht] m. Buriat; Buryat
Buriatka [boor-yaht-kah] f. (woman) Buriat; Buryat
burka [boor-kah] f. hooded greatcoat; hooded cloak
burkliwie [boor-klee-vye] adv. in a surly tone; gruffly; churlishly
burkliwy [boor-klee-vi] adj.m. surly; gruff; churlish
burkliwy ton [boor-klee-vi ton] exp.: gruffness; churlishness; surliness
burknąć [boor-knownćh] v. growl; grunt; snarl out (a remark, etc.)
burknięcie [boor-kńan-ćhe] n. surly utterance; gruff remark
burleska [boor-les-kah] f. burlesque; grotesque exaggeration; comic imitation; mockery by caricature; theatrical entertainment sometimes including striptease acts
burleskowy [boor-les-ko-vi] adj.m.

burlesque; comical; clownish
burłacki [boor-**wahts**-kee] adj.m. Russian river-hauler's (songs, villages, etc.)
burłak [**boor**-wahk] m. Russian hauler of river boats up-stream bound; colloq: pauper; vagabond
Burmanka [boor-**mahn**-kah] f. Burmese woman
Burmańczyk [boor-**mahń**-chik] m. Burmese
burmański [boor-**mahń**-skee] adj.m. Burmese
burmistrz [**boor**-meestsh] m. mayor
burmistrzostwo [boor-mee-**stsho**-stfo] n. mayoralty
burmistrzowa [boor-mee-**stsho**-vah] f. mayoress
burmistrzować [boor-mee-**stsho**-vahćh] v. mayor (a town) (*repeatedly*)
burmistrzowski [boor-mee-**stshof**-skee] adj.m. mayor's
burmistrzówna [boor-mee-**stshoov**-nah] f. mayor's daughter
burnonit [boor-**no**-ńeet] m. bournonite (mineral)
burnus [**boor**-noos] m. burnouse; burnous
buro [**boo**-ro] adv. in dun color
burozielony [boo-ro-źhe-**lo**-ni] adj.m. of greenish-dun color
buroziem [boo-**ro**-źhem] m. poor soil of the steppes
Burowie [boo-**ro**-vye] pl. Boers
bursa [**boor**-sah] f. boarding-school; stock-exchange; purse
bursiarz [**boor**-śhahsh] m. boarding-school pupil
bursz [boorsh] m. (obstreperous) member of a fraternity
burszowski [boor-**shof**-skee] adj.m. of misbehaving (arrogant) German university student
bursztówka [boor-**shtoof**-kah] f. variety of apple
bursztyn [**boor**-shtin] m. amber; succinite; amber jewelry or ornament
bursztynian [boor-**shti**-ńyahn] m. succinate
bursztyniarnia [boor-shti-**ńahr**-ńah] f. amber forest; amber quarry; amber workshop
bursztyniarstwo [boor-shti-**ńahr**-stfo] n. amber-quarry work
bursztyniarz [boor-**shti**-ńahsh] m. amber-quarry worker; amber jeweler; amber cutter
bursztynka [boor-**shtin**-kah] f. amber-color snail
bursztynodajny [boor-shti-no-**dahy**-ni] adj.m. amber-rich (area, forest, land, etc.)
bursztynowiec [boor-shti-**no**-vyets] m. liquidamber; liquidambar
bursztynowy [boor-shti-**no**-vi] adj.m. of amber; amber (brooch, etc.); amber-colored
kwas bursztynowy [kfahs boor-shti-**no**-vi] exp.: succinic acid
burt [boort] m. border; edging; trimming; braid; braising; galloon
burta [**boor**-tah] f. ship's side; boat's side; border; edge; rim; brim
człowiek za burtą! [**chwo**-vyek zah **boor**-town] exp.: man overboard!
lewa burta [le-vah **boor**-tah] exp.: port side
prawa burta [**prah**-vah **boor**-tah] exp.: starboard
wolna burta [**vol**-nah **boor**-tah] exp.: freeboard
wyrzucić za burtę [vi-**zhoo**-ćheećh zah **boor**-tan] exp.: to throw overboard
burtnica [boort-**ńee**-tsah] f. rowers' bench or seat
burtowy [boor-**to**-vi] adj.m. of ship's side; of boat's side
burtówka [boor-**toof**-kah] f. upper-deck storage closet at ship's side
burunduk [boo-**roon**-dook] m. Siberian squirrel
bury [**boo**-ri] adj.m. dark gray; dun; grizzly; m. colloq: bear
burza [**boo**-zhah] f. tempest; storm; wind storm; rain storm
burza gradowa [**boo**-zhah grah-**do**-vah] exp.: hailstorm
burza magnetyczna [**boo**-zhah mahg-ne-**tich**-nah] exp.: magnetic storm
burza oklasków [**boo**-zhah o-**klahs**-koof] exp.: a storm of applause

burza piaskowa [**boo**-zhah pyahs-**ko**-vah] exp.: sandstorm
burza śnieżna [**boo**-zhah **śhńezh**-nah] exp.: snowstorm
burza z piorunami [**boo**-zhah s pyo-roo-**nah**-mee] exp.: thunderstorm
burza w szklance wody [**boo**-zhah f shklahn-tse **vo**-di] exp.: a storm in a teacup
gwałtowna burza [gvahw-**tov**-nah **boo**-zhah] exp.: violent storm
cisza przed burzą [**ćhee**-shah pshet **boo**-zhown] exp.: the calm before the storm
ma się na burzę [mah śhan nah **boo**-zhan] exp.: a storm is brewing; a storm is coming
nadciąga burza [naht-**ćhown**-gah **boo**-zhah] exp.: a storm is approaching; a storm is coming
rozpoczęła się burza [ros-po-**che**-wah śhan **boo**-zhah] exp.: the storm broke (out)
strefa burz [**stre**-fah boosh] exp.: storm zone; storm belt
ściągnąć burzę [**śhćhowng**-nownćh **boo**-zhan] exp.: to stir up a hornets' nest
miotany burzą [myo-**tah**-ni **boo**-zhown] exp.: storm-tossed
unieruchomiony przez burzę [oo-ńe-roo-kho-**myo**-ni pshes **boo**-zhan] exp.: stormbound
rozpętać burzę [ros-**pan**-tahćh **boo**-zhan] exp.: to stir up a storm
wpaść jak burza [**fpaśhćh** yahk **boo**-zhah] exp.: to burst in
wywołać burzę [vi-**vo**-wahćh **boo**-zhan] exp.: to stir up a storm
zanosi się na burzę [zah-**no**-śhee śhan nah **boo**-zhan] exp.: there is thunder in the air

burzan [**boo**-zhahn] m. bent; bent grass

burzanka [boo-**zhahn**-kah] f. colocynth (vine)

burzący [boo-**zhown**-tsi] adj.m. destructive; causing destruction
bomba burząca [**bom**-bah boo-**zhown**-tsah] exp.: demolition bomb

burzeć [**boo**-zhećh] v. become dark gray; become grizzly; become dun (*repeatedly*)

burzenie [boo-**zhe**-ńe] n. ruin; destruction; wreck; overthrow; dislocation; becoming dark-gray; becoming grizzly

burzenie się [boo-**zhe**-ńe śhan] n. effervescence; fermentation; agitation; unrest

burzliwie [boo-**zhlee**-vye] adv. tempestuously; stormily; thunderously; boisterously; wildly; eventfully

burzliwość [boo-**zhlee**-vośhćh] f. storminess; tempestuousness; stormy state (of the weather, etc.); roughness (of the sea); uproariousness (of a meeting, etc.); boisterousness
burzliwość morza [boo-**zhlee**-vośhćh **mo**-zhah] exp.: heavy seas; high seas

burzliwy [boo-**zhlee**-vi] adj.m. stormy; tempestuous; turbulent; thunderous; wild; eventful; checkered (life); of ups and downs

burzowiec [boo-**zho**-vyets] m. storm sewer; storm-water drain

burzowy [boo-**zho**-vi] adj.m. stormy; storm (clouds, etc.)
chmura burzowa [**khmoo**-rah boo-**zho**-vah] exp.: storm-cloud; thunder-cloud

burzyciel [boo-**zhi**-ćhel] m. destroyer; wrecker; devastator; instigator

burzycielski [boo-zhi-**ćhel**-skee] adj.m. destructive; subversive

burzycielstwo [boo-zhi-**ćhel**-stfo] n. destructive tendencies; subversive tendencies

burzyć [**boo**-zhićh] v. destroy; demolish; pull down; stir up; raze; ruin; wreck; devastate; shatter; ruffle; dash; incite; ferment; effervesce (*repeatedly*)
burzyć krew [**boo**-zhićh kref] exp.: to stir the blood; to incite; to instigate

burzyć się [**boo**-zhićh śhan] v. rebel; rise in revolt; seethe; boil; surge; foam; eddy; be agitated; be mad; ferment; effervesce (*repeatedly*)

burzyk [boo-zhik] m. mutton-bird; shearwater
burzyny [boo-zhi-ni] pl. foam
burżuazja [boor-zhoo-ahz-yah] f. bourgeoisie; middle class
drobna burżuazja [drob-nah boor-zhoo-ahz-yah] exp.: tradespeople
burżuazyjny [boor-zhoo-ah-ziy-ni] adj.m. bourgeois
burżuj [boor-zhooy] m. slang: bourgeois
business [beez-nes] m. business
businessman [beez-nes-men] m. businessman
busola [boo-so-lah] f. compass
busolowy [boo-so-lo-vi] adj.m. of a compass
busz [boosh] m. the bush
buszel [boo-shel] m. bushel
Buszman [boosh-mahn] m. bushman
buszmański [boosh-mahń-skee] adj.m. bushman's; bushmen's
Buszmen [boosh-men] m. bushman
buszmeński [boosh-meń-skee] adj.m. bushman's; bushmen's
buszować [boo-sho-vahćh] v. rummage; pillage; ransack; plunder; loot; roister; romp; rampage (*repeatedly*)
buszowanie [boo-sho-vah-ńe] n. rummage; pillage; ransack; plunder
buszówka [boo-shoof-kah] f. rummage; pillage; ransack; plunder
but [boot] m. boot; shoe; sabot
bez butów [bes boo-toof] exp.: barefoot
buty z cholewami [boo-ti s kho-le-vah-mee] exp.: riding boots; knee boots
głupi jak but [gwoo-pee yahk boot] exp.: as dull as ditch water; stupid as an owl
umarł w butach [oo-mahrw v boo-tahkh] exp.: he's done for!
buta [boo-tah] f. arrogance; insolence; uppishness; pride; haughtiness; overbearing attitude
butadien [boo-tah-dyen] m. butadiene
butadienowy [boo-tah-dye-no-vi] adj.m. of butadiene
butan [boo-tahn] m. butane
butanol [boo-tah-nol] m. butanol
butanowy [boo-tah-no-vi] adj.m. of butane
butelczyna [boo-tel-chi-nah] f. slang: bottle of spirits
buteleczka [boo-te-lech-kah] f. small bottle; flask; vial
butelka [boo-tel-kah] f. bottle
nabić w butelkę [nah-beećh v boo-tel-kan] exp.: colloq: to deceive; to cheat; to take in; to hoodwink
pociągać z butelki [po-ćhown-gahćh z boo-tel-kee] exp.: colloq: to booze; to tipple; to soak
postawić butelkę [po-stah-veećh boo-tel-kan] exp.: colloq: to pay for a drink; to stand a drink; to treat to a drink (of beer, etc.)
butelkonosy [boo-tel-ko-no-si] adj.m. bottle-nosed (dolphin)
butelkować [boo-tel-ko-vahćh] v. bottle; bottle (of beer, etc.) (*repeatedly*)
butelkowanie [boo-tel-ko-vah-ńe] n. bottling (of wine, etc.)
butelkowaty [boo-tel-ko-vah-ti] adj.m. bottle-shaped
butelkowy [boo-tel-ko-vi] adj.m. bottle; bottled
buten [boo-ten] m. butene
butersznit [boo-ter-shńeet] m. sandwich (with sausage, cheese, cucumber, etc.)
butik [boo-teek] m. boutique; small fashionable shop
butikowy [boo-tee-ko-vi] adj.m. of a boutique; of a small fashionable shop; boutique (merchandise, clothing, jewelry, etc.)
butla [boo-tlah] f. demijohn; carboy; balloon; cylinder
butla gazowa [boo-tlah gah-zo-vah] exp.: gas cylinder
butnie [boot-ńe] adv. arrogantly; with arrogance; insolently; uppishly; overbearingly; haughtily
butny [boot-ni] adj.m. arrogant; insolent; overbearing; uppish; haughty; supercilious
butonierka [boo-to-ńer-kah] f. buttonhole
butwieć [boo-tfyećh] v. rot (away); moulder (away) (*repeatedly*)

butwienie [boo-**tfye**-ńe] n. rotting (away); moldering (away)
butwina [boot-**fee**-nah] f. decaying humus in a pine forest
butyl [**boo**-til] m. butyl
butylen [boo-**ti**-len] m. butylene
butylowy [boo-ti-**lo**-vi] adj.m. butyl (alcohol, rubber, etc.)
butyrometr [boo-**ti**-ro-metr] m. butyrometer
buza [**boo**-zah] f. refreshing oatmeal or ground millet beverage
buzdygan [booz-**di**-gahn] m. mace; spiked club
buzdyganek [booz-di-**gah**-nek] m. small mace; small spiked club; star-thistle
buzia [**boo**-źhah] f. face; mouth
dać buzi [dahćh **boo**-źhee] exp.: to give a kiss; to let somebody give one a kiss
rozdziawiać buzię [roz-**dźhah**-vyahćh **boo**-źhan] exp.: to open one's mouth wide
buziaczek [boo-**źhah**-chek] m. (child's, girl's) face; little kiss
buziak [**boo**-źhahk] m. (child's, girl's) face; kiss
dać buziaka [dahćh boo-**źhah**-kah] exp.: to give a kiss; to let somebody give one a kiss
buziuchna [boo-**źhookh**-nah] f. (child's, girl's) face
buziulka [boo-**źhool**-kah] f. (child's, girl's) face
buzować [boo-**zo**-vahćh] v. blaze away; burn brightly; flame; crackle; glare; stoke (a stove) (*repeatedly*)
buzować się [boo-**zo**-vahćh śhan] v. blaze away; burn brightly; flame; crackle; glare (*repeatedly*)
buzowanie [boo-zo-**vah**-ńe] n. burning brightly; stoking (a stove)
buzowanie się [boo-zo-**vah**-ńe śhan] n. burning brightly; stoking (a stove)
buźka [**boośh**-kah] f. (nice, little) face; mouth; colloq: kiss; diminutive of **buzia**
by [bi] conj. in order that; (conditional) as if; at least; even; though; like; see: conj. **aby**
chętnie bym [**khant**-ńe bim] exp.: I should willingly ...
może byś przestał [**mo**-zhe biśh **pshe**-stahw] exp.: I wish you would stop that
może byście przestali [**mo**-zhe **biśh**-ćhe pshe-**stah**-lee] exp.: I wish all of you would stop that
może byśmy wyszli [**mo**-zhe **biśh**-mi **vi**-shlee] exp.: perhaps we should go out
bycie [**bi**-ćhe] n. being; manner
byczek [**bi**-chek] m. bull calf; bullhead fish; miller's thumb fish; colloq: strapper; strapping man
byczki [**bich**-kee] pl. can of small freshwater fish
byczkowy [bich-**ko**-vi] adj.m. of a can of small freshwater fish
byczo [**bi**-cho] adv. stunningly; splendidly; first-rate
byczo! [**bi**-cho] slang excl.: fine!; swell!; righto!
byczy [**bi**-chi] adj.m. bull's; colloq: very good; glorious; swell
bycza mina [**bi**-chah **mee**-nah] exp.: forbidding look; forbidding aspect
byczy kark [**bi**-chi kahrk] exp.: bull neck
byczyć się [**bi**-chićh śhan] v. vulg.: fritter, loaf, loiter one's time away; hang about (*repeatedly*)
byczysko [bi-**chis**-ko] n. (big, old) bull; bullock; vulg.: lumpish man; blunderer; bloomer
być [**bićh**] v. be; exist; live (note: an irregular verb) (*repeatedly*)
być dobrej myśli [bićh **do**-brey **mi**-śhlee] exp.: to be of good cheer
być może [bićh **mo**-zhe] exp.: perhaps; maybe
być u siebie [bićh oo **śhe**-bye] exp.: be at home
był mróz [biw mroos] exp.: it was frosty; it was freezing; it froze
był w marynarce [biw v mah-ri-**nahr**-tse] exp.: he had a jacket on
byłbym przyszedł [**biw**-bim **pshi**-shedw] exp.: I was about to come; I would have come; I almost came
było nie było [**bi**-wo ńe **bi**-wo] exp.: come what may; whatever

the outcome I'll take the chance; be it as it may; none the less
czy kto był? [chi kto biw] exp.: did anybody stop by?
jakoś to będzie [**yah**-kośh to **ban**-dźhe] exp.: things will turn out well in the end; let's be hopeful; let's be of good cheer
będzie na niego [**ban**-dźhe nah **ńe**-go] exp.: colloq: he will get the blame; they'll say it's his fault
jest ciemno [yest **ćhem**-no] exp.: it is dark
jest mi głupio [yest mee **gwoo**-pyo] exp.: I am perplexed
jestem po robocie [**yes**-tem po ro-**bo**-ćhe] exp.: I am through with my work
jestem! [**yes**-tem] excl.: here! (I am present)
jestem do niczego [**yes**-tem do ńee-**che**-go] exp.: I feel rotten
nic z tego nie będzie [ńeets s **te**-go ńe **ban**-dźhe] exp.: it will come to nothing
nie może być! [ńe **mo**-zhe bićh] exp.: impossible!; you don't say! unbelievable!
nie bądź długo [ńe bownćh **dwoo**-go] exp.: don't be long
nie bądź dzieckiem [ńe bownćh **dźhets**-kem] exp.: don't be childish
niech będzie [ńekh **ban**-dźhe] exp.: very well; all right
niech tak będzie [ńekh tahk **ban**-dźhe] exp.: be it so; let it be as it is
skąd jesteś? [skownt **yes**-teśh] exp.: where are you from?
tak jest [tahk yest] exp.: that is so; that's how it is; excl.: yes! right!; good!; yes, sir!; right, sir!
to jest [to yest] exp.: that is; that is to say

bydełko [bi-**dew**-ko] n. (nice, one's own) cattle; livestock

bydlak [**bid**-lahk] m. vulg.: nasty beast; brute; savage; brutal man; dirty dog; skunk; wretch

bydlątko [bid-**lownt**-ko] n. (nice, one's own, young, small) head of cattle

bydleń [**bid**-leń] m. gadfly

bydlę [**bid**-lan] n. beast; animal; cow; bullock; calf; brute; vulg.: nasty beast; brute; brutal man; colloq: dirty dog; skunk; wretch
skończone bydlę [skoń-**cho**-ne **bid**-lan] exp.: perfect swine

bydlęcieć [bid-**lan**-ćhećh] v. to sink to the level of a beast (*repeatedly*)

bydlęcy [bid-**lan**-tsi] adj.m. of animal; animal; beastly; dirty; scurvy
bydlęcy nawóz [bid-**lan**-tsi **nah**-voos] exp.: dung

bydło [**bi**-dwo] n. cattle; livestock; vulg.: brutes; dirty pigs

bydłostan [bi-**dwo**-stahn] m. stock (of a farm); livestock

byk [bik] m. bull; bullock; colloq: bloomer; howler; mistake; butt (blow with the head); blunder; vulg: lubber; lumpish man; hulk; hulking man; a big hulk of a man
czyś ty z byka spadł? [chiśh ti z **bi**-kah spahdw] exp.: are you right in your head, man?; are you crazy?; are you out of your mind?
walka byków [**vahl**-kah **bi**-koof] exp.: bullfight
palnąć byka [**pahl**-nownćh **bi**-kah] exp.: to make a blunder

bykowiec [bi-**ko**-vyets] m. whip; cowhide; vulg.: pizzle

byle [**bi**-le] conj. in order to; so as to; on condition that; so long as; as long as; only; pron. any; slap-dash
byle co [**bi**-le tso] exp.: anything
byle czyj [**bi**-le chiy] exp.: anybody's; just anybody's
byle kto [**bi**-le kto] exp.: anybody
byle jak [**bi**-le yahk] exp.: anyhow; slap-dash; indifferently
byle gdzie [**bi**-le gdźhe] exp.: anywhere; no matter where; any old place; just anywhere
byle nie mnie [**bi**-le ńe mńe] exp.: only not me
byle jaki [**bi**-le **yah**-kee] exp.: any; whatever
nie byle jak [ńe **bi**-le yahk] exp.: in no mean fashion; splendidly; mightily
nie byle kto [ńe **bi**-le kto] exp.:

no small fry; not just anyone
byleby [**bi**-le-**bi**] conj. see: **byle**
bylejakość [bi-le-**yah**-kośhćh] f. negligence; shoddiness; poor quality
bylica [bi-**lee**-tsah] f. mugwort; motherwort
bylina [bi-**lee**-nah] f. (a) perennial (plant); ancient Russian epic song
bylinowy [bi-lee-**no**-vi] adj.m. perennial
były [**bi**-wi] adj.m. former; past (ages, etc.); old; ex-; one-time; late; quondam
bynajmniej [bi-**nahy**-mńey] adv. by no means; not at all; not a bit; not in the least; far from it; no indeed; rather not
bynajmniej nie [bi-**nahy**-mńey ńe] exp.: not at all; not a bit
bynajmniej nie bliżej [bi-**nahy**-mńey ńe **blee**-zhey] exp.: as far as ever
bynajmniej nieuprzejmy [bi-nahy-mńey ńe-oo-**pshey**-mi] exp.: anything but kind
byronista [bahy-ro-**ńees**-tah] m. Byronist
byronistka [bahy-ro-**ńeest**-kah] f. (female) Byronist
byronizm [bahy-**ro**-ńeezm] m. Byronism
byronowski [bahy-ro-**nof**-skee] adj.m. Byronic
byroński [bahy-**roń**-skee] adj.m. Byronic
po byrońsku [po bahy-**roń**-skoo] exp.: Byronically
bystro [**bis**-tro] adv. fast; swiftly; quick; quickly; rapidly; impetuously; sharply; keenly; with discernment; sagaciously; with sagacity; astutely; shrewdly; colloq: cutely
bystronogi [bis-tro-**no**-gee] adj.m. swift of foot
bystrooki [bis-tro-**o**-kee] adj.m. sharp-eyed; quick-sighted; keen-sighted; lynx-eyed
bystrość [**bis**-trośhćh] f. swiftness; shrewdness; fastness; quickness; speed; rapidity; promptness; impetuosity; sharpness; acuteness; sagacity; quick wits; keenness
bystrość wzroku [**bis**-trośhćh **vzro**-koo] exp.: keen sight
bystrość słuchu [**bis**-trośhćh **swoo**-khoo] exp.: sharpness of hearing; keenness of hearing
bystrotok [bis-**tro**-tok] m. swift current
bystry [**bi**-stri] adj.m. rapid; prompt; quick; swift; swift-flowing; impetuous; keen; keen-witted; acute; sharp; sharp-witted; clear-headed; discerning; quick of apprehension; smart; clever; nimble; wide awake; argute; bright; nice; subtle; discriminating; perspicacious; ready-witted; colloq: cute; as sharp as a needle
bystry sąd [**bi**-stri sownt] exp.: sagacity; shrewdness; discernment; discrimination; good head; long head
bystrz [bistsh] m. slang: rapids; shoot
mknąć po bystrzu [mknownćh po **bis**-tshoo] exp.: to shoot the rapids
bystrze [**bis**-tshe] n. swift current
bystrzyca [bis-**tshi**-tsah] f. rapids
bystrzyk [**bis**-tshik] m. South-American multicolored fish
bystrzyna [bis-**tshi**-nah] f. rapids; see: **bystrzyca**
byt [bit] m. existence; life; livelihood; survival; maintenance; well-being; entity; being
dobry byt [**dob**-ri bit] exp.: welfare; well-being; prosperity
mieć zapewniony byt [myećh zah-pev-**ńo**-ni bit] exp.: to have one's existence secured; to be provided for
racja bytu [**rahts**-yah **bi**-too] exp.: justification; raison d'etre; usefulness
rozpocząć byt [ros-**po**-chownćh bit] exp.: to come into being
stracić rację bytu [**strah**-ćheećh **rahts**-yan **bi**-too] exp.: to survive usefulness
walka o byt [**vahl**-kah o bit] exp.: struggle for existence; struggle for survival

zapewnić komuś byt [zah-pev-ńeećh ko-moośh bit] exp.: to provide for somebody; to make provisions for somebody
bytność [bit-nośhćh] f. stay; sojourn; visit; (social) call at (Brit.); presence; attendance
podczas jego bytności za granicą [pot-chahs ye-go bit-nośh-ćhee zah grah-ńee-tsown] exp.: when he was abroad; while he was abroad
za jej bytności [zah yey bit-nośh-ćhee] exp.: during her stay (at)
bytować [bi-to-vahćh] v. live; exist; dwell; be inherent (in) (*repeatedly*)
bytowanie [bi-to-vah-ńe] n. life; existence
warunki bytowania [vah-roon-kee bi-to-vah-ńah] exp.: living conditions
zwykłe bytowanie [zvik-we bi-to-vah-ńe] exp.: mere existence
bytowy [bi-to-vi] adj.m. existential; vital; of life; living (questions, etc.)
potrzeby bytowe [po-tshe-bi bi-to-ve] exp.: (the) necessities of life
sprawy bytowe [sprah-vi bi-to-ve] exp.: vital questions
warunki bytowe [vah-roon-kee bi-to-ve] exp.: living conditions
bywać [bi-vahćh] v. frequent; be often at; go often (to); attend; resort; be often present at; visit; go out; happen; occur; take place; be frequent; be of frequent occurrence; be sometimes the case (*repeatedly*)
bywaj! [bi-vahy] excl.: welcome!; come here!; come along!
bywaj zdrów! [bi-vahy zdroof] exp.: goodbye (and keep well)
bywał w ogniu [bi-vahw v og-ńoo] exp.: he was many times under fire
bywałem w opałach [bi-vah-wem v o-pah-wahkh] exp.: I was many a time in trouble
bywało [bi-vah-wo] exp.: often; sometimes; many times; many a time
bywało czasem [bi-vah-wo chahs-sem] exp.: it was sometimes (so hot, so cold, etc.)
on bywa w świecie [on bi-vah f śhfye-ćhe] exp.: he goes out a great deal
on często u nas bywa [on chans-to oo nahs bi-vah] exp.: he often comes to see us; he often comes to call on us; he often visits us
bywalczyni [bi-vahl-chi-ńee] f. woman frequenter (of theater, restaurant, etc.)
bywalec [bi-vah-lets] m. old-timer; experienced man; old hand; frequenter; habitual guest; habitue; patron; man of the world; old stager
bywały [bi-vah-wi] adj.m. experienced; knowledgeable; travelled
człowiek bywały [chwo-vyek bi-vah-wi] exp.: old-timer; experienced man; old hand; frequenter; habitual guest; habitue; patron; man of the world; old stager; see: **bywalec**
bywanie [bi-vah-ńe] n. frequenting; visiting; being habitually (at, in)
bzdet [bzdet] m. slang: disapproval; slight; disrespect; scorn; trash; rubbish; shoddy goods; nonsense
bzdura [bzdoo-rah] f. nonsense; rubbish; buncombe; bunkum; humbug; fiddle-faddle; flapdoodle; trash; trifle; bagatelle; triviality; matter of no importance; slang: tosh; rot; popycock; vulg.: bullshit
bzdury! [bzdoo-ri] pl. excl.: (stuff and) nonsense!; fiddle!; fiddlesticks!; fiddle-de-dee!; slang: skittles!
pleść bzdury [pleśhćh bzdoo-ri] exp.: to talk nonsense; to drivel; to talk drivel
bzdurnie [bzdoor-ńe] adv. colloq: nonsensically; absurdly
bzdurny [bzdoor-ni] adj.m. colloq: nonsensical; absurd; silly; preposterous; trivial; trifling; frivolous; paltry; slang: mushy; potty
bzdurstwo [bzdoor-stfo] n. nonsense; rubbish; humbug; fiddle-faddle; trash; trifle;

bagatelle; triviality; matter of no importance; see: **bzdura**
bzdurzenie [bzdoo-**zhe**-ńe] n. drivel; silly talk; stupid talk
bzdurzyć [**bzdoo**-zhićh] v. talk nonsense; talk bosh; indulge in bragging; indulge in blustering; indulge in idle talk; vapor; slang: rot; drivel (*repeatedly*)
bzdyczyć [**bzdi**-chićh] v. talk nonsense; talk bosh; indulge in bragging; indulge in blustering; indulge in idle talk; vapor; slang: rot; drivel (*repeatedly*)
bzdyczyć się [**bzdi**-chićh śhan] v. colloq: sulk; be sulky (*repeatedly*)
bzik [bźheek] m. crank; loony; crazy; fool; colloq: fad; craze; mania; pet notion; fixed idea; an eccentric; a crank
mieć bzika [myećh **bźhee**-kah] exp.: to be crazy; to be cracked; to have a screw loose; to be off one's rocker; to have a bee in one's bonnet; see: **bzikować**
mieć bzika na punkcie czegoś [myećh **bźhee**-kah nah **poonk**-ćhe **che**-gośh] exp.: to be crazy about something; to be mad on something; to have something on the brain; to be silly about something; to be enthusiastic about something; to be eccentric about something; to be keen about something; to be demented about something; to be mentally unbalanced about something; colloq: to be nuts (nutty) about something something
bzikować [bźhee-**ko**-vahćh] v. colloq: go bananas; lose one's cool; go off the deep end; crawl up the wall; go ape; be off one's rocker; go nuts; go bonkers; see: **mieć bzika** (*repeatedly*)
bzikowanie [bźhee-ko-**vah**-ńe] n. becoming crazy; getting off one's rocker
bzikowaty [bźhee-ko-**vah**-ti] adj.m. mentally unbalanced; eccentric; colloq: crazy; cracked; slang: barmy; nutty
bzowina [bzo-**vee**-nah] f. elder; elderberry tree or bush
bzowy [**bzo**-vi] adj.m. elder; elderberry (wine, flower water)
bzyczeć [**bzi**-chećh] v. whizz; buzz; hum; see: **bzykać** (*repeatedly*)
bzyczenie [bzi-**che**-ńe] n. humming; buzz; buzzing; drone; whiz; whizz (of a bullet)
bzyk [bzik] m. hum; humming; buzz; buzzing; drone; whiz; whizz (of a bullet)
bzykać [**bzi**-kahćh] v. buzz; hum; whiz; whizz; see: **bzyczeć** (*repeatedly*)
bzykanie [bzi-**kah**-ńe] n. hum; humming; buzz; buzzing; drone; whiz; whizz (of a bullet) see: **bzyk**
bzyknąć [**bzik**-nownćh] v. hum; buzz; whizz; sing (as a flying bullet); see: **bzykać**
bzyknięcie [bzik-**ńan**-ćhe] n. hum; humming; buzz; buzzing; drone; whiz; whizz (of a bullet) see: **bzyk**
bździć [bźhdźheećh] v. vulg.: fart (*repeatedly*)
bździna [**bźhdźhee**-nah] f. an expulsion of intestinal gas; vulg.: (a) fart

C

C, c [tse] n. the letter "c"; (music) C; **C-dur** C-major; **(C)moll** C-minor
brać górne C [brahćh **goor**-ne tse] exp.: to take the high C
cabernet [kah-ber-**ne**] m. variety of French red wine
caca [tsah-tsah] indecl. baby talk: lovely; nice
cacanie [tsah-**tsah**-ńe] adv. slang: first-rate; splendidly; in fine style
cacanka [tsah-**tsahn**-kah] f. good thing
cacany [tsah-**tsah**-ni] adj.m. slang: lovely; first-rate
cackać [**tsahts**-kahćh] v. fondle; pamper; humor; coddle (*repeatedly*)
cackać się [**tsahts**-kahćh śhan] v. handle delicately; be overly meticulous; be tactful; spare

(other's feelings) (*repeatedly*)
cackać dziecko [tsahts-kahćh dźhets-ko] exp.: to fondle a baby; to keep a baby amused
cackanie się [tsahts-kah-ńe śhan] n. humoring; being overly meticulous; handling delicately
cacko [tsahts-ko] n. jewel; trinket; plaything; toy; beauty; a beaut
cacy [tsah-tsi] adj. indecl. baby talk: lovely; nice; adv. nicely; charmingly; delightfully
cacy-cacy [tsah-tsi tsah-tsi] exp.: slang: all sweetness
cadyk [tsah-dik] m. revered leader of Jewish Hasidic commune
cafeteria [kah-fe-ter-yah] f. cafeteria
cajg [tsahyg] m. jean; work clothes' fabric
cajgowy [tsahy-go-vi] adj.m. jean (coat, pants, etc.)
cajgowe spodnie [tsahy-go-ve spod-ńe] exp.: jeans (pants)
cakiel [tsah-kel] m. Carpathian breed of sheep
cal [tsahl] m. inch
cal po calu [tsahl po tsah-loo] exp.: inch by inch
calec [tsah-lets] m. undisturbed ground below plowing; bedrock
calendarium [kah-len-dahr-yoom] n. (Latin) calendar; tabular register; orderly list of events
calizna [tsah-leez-nah] f. undisturbed strata (of bed-rock, coal, etc.)
call-girl [kol gerl] f. (Engl.) call girl; a prostitute with whom an appointment may be made by telephone
calowy [tsah-lo-vi] adj.m. one-inch (thick, high, long, deep, etc.)
deska calowa [des-kah tsah-lo-vah] exp.: a board one inch thick
calówka [tsah-loof-kah] f. folding inch-rule; one-inch (board, etc.)
calusieńki [tsah-loo-śheń-kee] adj.m. complete; entire; from top to bottom
calusieńko [tsah-loo-śheń-ko] adv. completely; entirely; from top to bottom
caluśki [tsah-loośh-kee] adj.m. nicely complete
caluteńki [tsah-loo-teń-kee] adj.m. complete; entire; from top to bottom
caluteńko [tsah-loo-teń-ko] adv. completely; entirely; from top to bottom
calutki [tsah-loot-kee] adj.m. nicely complete; a cool (one million, etc.)
calvados [kahl-vah-dos] m. French apple vodka
calypso [kah-leep-so] n. calypso music and dance of West Indies; ballad satirizing current events in the style of West Indies
cała [tsah-wah] adj.f. whole
cała naprzód [tsah-wah nah-pshoot] exp.: full steam forwards
całą parą [tsah-wown pah-rown] exp.: full steam (forwards)
całka [tsahw-kah] f. integral
całkiem [tsahw-kem] adv. quite; entirely; completely; totally; altogether; throughout; fully; utterly; wholly; absolutely; in all respects; in every respect
całkować [tsahw-ko-vahćh] v. integrate; colloq: generalize; treat as a whole (*repeatedly*)
całkować powtórnie [tsahw-ko-vahćh po-ftoor-ńe] exp.: to reintegrate (*repeatedly*)
całkowalność [tsahw-ko-vahl-nośhćh] f. existence of an integral of a function
całkowalny [tsahw-ko-vahl-ni] adj.m. integrable
całkowanie [tsahw-ko-vah-ńe] n. integration
całkowicie [tsahw-ko-vee-ćhe] adv. altogether; throughout; entirely; completely; fully; utterly; wholly; absolutely; in all respects; in every respect
całkowicie nagi [tsahw-ko-vee-ćhe nah-gee] exp.: stark naked
całkowicie osamotniony [tsahw-ko-vee-ćhe o-sah-mot-ńo-ni] exp.: all alone
całkowicie przytomny [tsahw-ko-vee-ćhe pshi-tom-ni] exp.: wide awake
całkowitość [tsahw-ko-vee-tośhćh] f. wholeness; completeness; integrality;

utterness

całkowity [tsahw-ko-**vee**-ti] adj.m. total; complete; full; utter; thorough; whole; absolute; plenary; out and out; unreserved (approval, etc.); undivided (attention, etc.); gross (ignorance, etc.); rank (injustice, etc.); dead (certainty, etc.); perfect (peace, etc.); downright (impossibility, etc.); stark (madness, etc.); strict (neutrality, etc.)
liczba całkowita [**leedzh**-bah tsahw-ko-**vee**-tah] exp.: integer; whole number

całkowy [tsahw-**ko**-vi] adj.m. integral
rachunek całkowy [rah-**khoo**-nek tsahw-**ko**-vi] exp.: integral calculus

cało [**tsah**-wo] adv. in one piece; safely; safe and sound
przybyć cało [**pshi**-bićh **tsah**-wo] exp.: to arrive safe and sound
wyjść cało [viyśhćh **tsah**-wo] exp.: to get off safe and sound; to get off scot-free

cało- [**tsah**-wo] prefix: whole-; full-; all-

całobrzegi [tsah-wo-**bzhe**-gee] adj.m. (leaf, etc.) having smooth edges

całodniowy [tsah-wo-**dńo**-vi] adj.m. full day's; daylong

całodobowy [tsah-wo-do-**bo**-vi] adj.m. a twenty-four hour (period, etc.); full day's; daily (output, etc.); day and night's (journey, march, etc.)

całodzienny [tsah-wo-**dźhen**-ni] adj.m. full day's; daylong

całogodzinny [tsah-wo-go-**dźheen**-ni] adj.m. a full hour's (walk, etc.); hour-long; hourly (supply, output, etc.)

całokształt [tsah-**wo**-kshtahwt] m. totality; the whole; entirety; the bulk; ensemble
całokształt sytuacji [tsah-**wo**-kshtahwt si-too-**ah**-tsyee] exp.: the situation as a whole; the entire situation; the situation in general

całomiesięczny [tsah-wo-mye-**śhanch**-ni] adj.m. a full month's (work, etc.); monthly uninterrupted (activity, etc.); the one month's (output, etc.)

całonocny [tsah-wo-**nots**-ni] adj.m. full night's; nightlong

całopalenie [tsah-wo-pah-**le**-ńe] n. holocaust; burnt-offering

całopalny [tsah-wo-**pahl**-ni] adj.m. holocaustal

całoroczny [tsah-wo-**roch**-ni] adj.m. full year's; yearly (output, etc.)

całosezonowy [tsah-wo-se-zo-**no**-vi] adj.m. of the whole season

całospektaklowy [tsah-wo-spek-tahk-**lo**-vi] adj.m. of an entire spectacle duration (play, program, music, etc.)

całostka [tsah-**wost**-kah] f. self-contained whole; separate whole

całostronicowy [tsah-wo-stro-ńee-**tso**-vi] adj.m. full-page (figure, advertisement, text, list, announcement, etc.)

całościowo [tsah-wo-**śhćho**-vo] adv. comprehensively; generally; in an overall manner; sweepingly

całościowość [tsah-wo-**śhćho**-vośhćh] f. comprehensibleness; generality; overall character

całościowy [tsah-wo-**śhćho**-vi] adj.m. comprehensive; general; overall; sweeping

całość [**tsah**-wośhćh] f. totality; entirety; the whole; a whole; bulk; (complete) body; integrity; wholeness; safety; integer; the whole lot; sum
całość sytuacji [**tsah**-wośhćh si-too-**ah**-tsyee] exp.: the situation as a whole
iść na całość [eeśhćh nah **tsah**-wośhćh] exp.: to commit oneself completely
jako jedna całość [yah-ko **yed**-nah **tsah**-wośhćh] exp.: as one unit; as one entity
połączyć w całość [po-**wown**-chićh f **tsah**-wośhćh] exp.: to integrate
w całości [f tsah-**wośh**-ćhee] exp.: on the whole; wholly; taken as a whole; by and large; in the aggregate; altogether

całotonowy [tsah-wo-to-**no**-vi] adj.m. of (musical) tones; of the scale of six complete tones
całotygodniowy [tsah-wo-ti-god-**ńo**-vi] adj.m. a full week's (work, etc.); a whole week's (stay, etc.); weekly (output, etc.)
całować [tsah-**wo**-vahćh] v. kiss; embrace; give a kiss (*repeatedly*)
całować na dobranoc [tsah-**wo**-vahćh nah dob-**rah**-nots] exp.: to kiss good-night
całować kogoś w usta [tsah-**wo**-vahćh **ko**-gośh v **oos**-tah] exp.: to kiss somebody on the lips
całować się [tsah-**wo**-vahćh śhan] v. to share a kiss; to kiss each other (*repeatedly*)
umieć się całować [**oo**-myećh śhan tsah-**wo**-vahćh] exp.: to know how to kiss
całowagonowy [tsah-wo-vah-go-**no**-vi] adj.m. of a full carload
całowanie [tsah-wo-**vah**-ńe] n. kisses; giving kisses
całowanie się [tsah-wo-**vah**-ńe śhan] n. kissing; sharing a kiss
całowieczny [tsah-wo-**vyech**-ni] adj.m. century-long
całowieczorny [tsah-wo-vye-**chor**-ni] adj.m. evening-long (spectacle, program, etc.)
całowieczorowy [tsah-wo-vye-cho-**ro**-vi] adj.m. evening-long (spectacle, program, etc.)
całun [**tsah**-woon] m. shroud
okryć całunem tajemnicy [**o**-krićh tsah-**woo**-nem tah-yem-**ńee**-tsi] exp.: to shroud in mystery
całunek [tsah-**woo**-nek] m. kiss; see: **pocałunek**
całus [**tsah**-woos] m. kiss
posłać całusa [**po**-swahćh tsah-**woo**-sah] exp.: to throw a kiss; to blow a kiss (to)
całusek [tsah-**woo**-sek] m. a sweet kiss; little honey cake
cały [**tsah**-wi] adj.m. whole; all; entire; safe; the whole of; full; total; complete; great; the greatest; only; intact; integrate; unhurt; unharmed; unscathed
cały rok [**tsah**-wi rok] exp.: all the year (round)
cała Europa [**tsah**-wah ew-**ro**-pah] exp.: all (the whole of) Europe
całą parą [**tsah**-wown **pah**-rown] exp.: full steam
całe szczęście! [**tsah**-we shchanśh-ćhe] exp.: thank goodness!
całymi godzinami [tsah-**wi**-mee go-dźhee-**nah**-mee] exp.: for hours and hours
cały i zdrów [**tsah**-wi ee zdroof] exp.: safe and sound
na całego [nah tsah-**we**-go] exp.: colloq: fully; decisively; the whole hog; with abandon; risking everything
na całe szczęście [nah **tsah**-we shchan-śhćhe] exp.: fortunately
iść na całego [eeśhćh nah tsah-**we**-go] exp.: to go the whole length; to go to all lengths; to go whole hog
przez cały dzień [pshes **tsah**-wi dźheń] exp.: all day long
to cały ojciec [to **tsah**-wi **oy**-ćhets] exp.: he is the very image of his father
camembert [kah-mem-**ber**] m. Camembert; a soft French cheese
campanilla [kem-pah-**ńeel**-lah] f. bell tower (free-standing); campanille
camping [**kem**-peeng] m. camping
campingować [kem-peen-**go**-vahćh] v. camp; go camping (*repeatedly*)
campingowiec [kem-peen-**go**-vyets] m. camping man
campingowy [kem-peen-**go**-vi] adj.m. camping (outfit, etc.)
campus [**kahm**-poos] m. university grounds and buildings (in USA, England, etc.); campus
canasta [kah-**nahs**-tah] f. canasta; card game using two full decks
candida [kahn-**dee**-dah] f. font based on antique letter shapes
canoe [**kah**-noo] n. canoe (a narrow boat propelled by paddles)
canotier [kah-**no**-tyer] m. canoe rider; canoeist
cantabile [kahn-tah-**bee**-le] adv. in a singing manner
canto [**kahn**-to] n. song; singing voice
canzona [kahn-**tso**-nah] f. canzone

(music)
canzonetta [kahn-tso-**net**-tah] f. canzonet (music)
cap [tsahp] m. billy goat; male goat; he-goat; buck; peg (holding two bales together); lifting hook (used in hand-drilling of wells); colloq: man with a goatee; nitwit; fool; gaby; excl.: snap!; smack!; slang: man; fool; exp.: to catch (something) suddenly
capi [**tsah**-pee] adj.m. billy goat's; goat's
capiga [tsah-**pee**-gah] f. plow-handle; plow-tail
capina [tsah-**pee**-nah] f. log-handling bar with a hook
capnąć [**tsahp**-nownćh] v. snap up; snatch up; catch; catch hold; pinch; filch; nab (a thief, etc.)
capriccio [kah-**preech**-yo] n. capriccio (music, drawing, etc.)
capriccioso [kah-preech-**yo**-zo] adv. jokingly; with fussiness; changing suddenly; inconstantly
capstrzyk [**tsahp**-stshik] m. tattoo (signal); torchlight tattoo (march); retreat; drumming; rapping; taps; last post (Brit.)
capu [**tsah**-poo] (only in) exp.:
na łapu capu [nah **wah**-poo **tsah**-poo] exp.: in a hurry; quickly; rushingly; carelessly; negligently; helter-skelter; pell-mell; haphazardly
car [tsahr] m. tsar; tzar; czar
carat [**tsah**-raht] m. tsarism; tsardom; czarism; czardom
caravaning [kah-rah-**vah**-ńeeng] m. caravaning; travel in a caravan
carewicz [tsah-**re**-veech] m. czarevitch; tsarevitch
cargo [**kahr**-go] n. cargo; freight
carioca [kahr-**yo**-kah] f. Latin-American dance; carioca music
carobójca [tsah-ro-**booy**-tsah] m. assassin of a tsar
carowa [tsah-**ro**-vah] f. tsarina; tzarina; czarina; see: **caryca**
carski [**tsahr**-skee] adj.m. czar's; tsar's
carstwo [**tsahr**-stfo] n. tsardom; czardom; tsar's empire (rule, state, authority, throne)
caryca [tsah-**ri**-tsah] f. tsarina; tzarina; czarina; see: **carowa**
caryzm [**tsah**-rizm] m. tsarism; tsardom; czarism; czardom; see: **carat**
casco [**kahs**-ko] n. travel and shipment insurance
cassate [kah-**sah**-te] n. Neapolitan ice ream
casus [**kah**-zoos] m. casus (belli)
casus belli [**kah**-zoos **bel**-lee] exp.: casus belli; event or action that (allegedly) justifies war
cążki [tsownsh-kee] pl. small tongs; pliers; pincers
ceber [**tse**-ber] m. bucket; wooden pail; slang: head (mob jargon)
leje jak z cebra [le-ye yahk s **tse**-brah] exp.: it rains cats and dogs
ceberek [tse-**be**-rek] m. (small, nice) bucket; wooden pail
cebertyzacja [tse-ber-ti-**zah**-tsyah] f. the Cebertowicz electrical method of ground stabilization; electrical petrification
cebion [**tse**-byon] m. types of vitamin C pills and injections
cebrzyk [**tseb**-zhik] m. small bucket; kit
cebula [tse-**boo**-lah] f. onion; onion-shaped dome; turnip (watch); slang: many layers of clothing (to be peeled off later)
cebulanka [tse-boo-**lahn**-kah] f. onion beetle
cebularz [tse-**boo**-lahsh] m. roll or pie topped with onion; onion farmer (seller)
cebulasty [tse-boo-**lah**-sti] adj.m. onion-shaped
cebulica [tse-boo-**lee**-tsah] f. squill; scillia (plant)
cebulka [tse-**bool**-kah] f. onion; bulb (of lily, tulip, etc.)
cebulkowaty [tse-bool-ko-**vah**-ti] adj.m. bulbous
cebulkowy [tse-bool-**ko**-vi] adj.m. onion (smell, etc.)
cebulowaty [tse-boo-lo-**vah**-ti] adj.m. bulbous
cebulowy [tse-boo-**lo**-vi] adj.m. onion (smell, etc.)
cech [tsekh] m. trade; guild
cecha [**tse**-khah] f. feature; mark;

characteristic; attribute; token; stamp; character; index (of a logarithm); tool for marking
cecha dodatnia [**tse**-khah do-**daht**-ńah] exp.: virtue; quality
cecha firmy [**tse**-khah **feer**-mi] exp.: trademark
cechmistrz [**tsekh**-meestsh] m. head officer of a trade guild
cechować [tse-**kho**-vahćh] v. be characteristic (of); be a feature (of); be an attribute (of); be a trait (of); be the main feature (of); distinguish; mark out; denote; characterize; brand; mark; stamp; gauge; graduate (a scale, etc.); calibrate; standardize (*repeatedly*)
cechować się [tse-**kho**-vahćh śhan] v. have a feature; have a characteristic (*repeatedly*)
cechowanie [tse-kho-**vah**-ńe] n. stamping; graduation; calibration; standardization
cechownia [tse-**khov**-ńah] f. stamping station; marking shop; miners' trade union hall
cechownica [tse-khov-**ńee**-tsah] f. stamp; marker (a tool)
cechownik [tse-**khov**-ńeek] m. marker; automatic telephone calls connecting and steering device
cechowy [tse-**kho**-vi] adj.m. guild's; guild (hall, etc)
cechówka [tse-**khoof**-kah] f. hammer-shape logger's tree marker; marking hammer
cechsztyn [**tsekh**-shtin] m. Permian limestone
cechsztyński [tsekh-**shtiń**-skee] adj.m. of Permian limestone
cechunek [tse-**khoo**-nek] m. stamping; graduation; calibration; standardization
cedent [**tse**-dent] m. transferrer
cedet [**tse**-det] m. Central Department Store (Centralny Dom Towarowy)
cedować [tse-**do**-vahćh] v. cede (to); transfer; release; give up (*repeatedly*)
cedowanie [tse-do-**vah**-ńe] n. cession; transfer; release
cedr [tsedr] m. cedar
cedrat [**tsed**-raht] m. citron
cedrowina [tsed-ro-**vee**-nah] f. cedar-wood
cedrowy [tsed-**ro**-vi] adj.m. of cedar; cedar (nuts, leaf, oil, wood, etc.)
cedrówka [tsed-**roof**-kah] f. cedar-wood; cedrela
cedrzyk [**tsed**-zhik] m. cedar-wood; cedrela; toon; toonwood
cedrzyniec [tsed-**zhi**-ńets] m. California cedar
ceduła [tse-**doo**-wah] f. (stock market) quotation; list of shares; consignment note
cedułka [tse-**doow**-kah] f. (small stock market) quotation; small list of shares; consignment note
cedzak [**tse**-dzahk] m. strainer; colander; drainer
cedzakowy [tse-dzah-**ko**-vi] adj.m. of draining
łyżka cedzakowa [**wish**-kah tse-dzah-**ko**-vah] exp.: skimmer (spoon)
cedzenie [tse-**dze**-ńe] n. straining; filtering; percolating; sipping; trickling
cedzić [**tse**-dźheećh] v. strain; filter; percolate; sip; trickle (*repeatedly*)
cedzić się [**tse**-dźheećh śhan] v. be filtered (*repeatedly*)
cedzidło [tse-**dźheed**-wo] n. strainer; percolator; filter; skimmer
cedzidłowy [tse-dźheed-**wo**-vi] adj.m. of a strainer; of a percolator; of a filter; of a skimmer
cedziny [tse-**dźhee**-ni] pl. sediment; dregs; grounds
cefal [**tse**-fahl] m. cephalopod (cuttlefish, octopus, squid, etc.)
cefeida [tse-**fey**-dah] f. Cepheid (a pulsating star)
cegielnia [tse-**gel**-ńah] f. brickyard; brick factory; brickkiln
cegielniany [tse-gel-**ńah**-ni] adj.m. brickyard (workers, etc.)
cegielnictwo [tse-gel-**ńeets**-tfo] n. brickmaking
cegielniczy [tse-gel-**ńee**-chi] adj.m. of brickmaking (industry, etc.)
cegielnik [tse-**gel**-ńeek] m.

brickmaker
cegiełka [tse-**gew**-kah] f. (little) brick; share; cake (of)
cegiełkować [tse-gew-**ko**-vahćh] v. rub clean (a deck, etc.) with bricks (*repeatedly*)
cegiełkowy [tse-gew-**ko**-vi] adj.m. of a small brick
ceglany [tse-**glah**-ni] adj.m. of bricks; brick (wall, etc.); brick-colored
ceglarka [tse-**glahr**-kah] f. brick press (for shaping of bricks out of clay)
ceglarski [tse-**glahr**-skee] adj.m. of brickmaking (industry, etc.)
ceglarstwo [tse-**glahr**-stfo] n. brickmaking
ceglarz [**tseg**-lahsh] m. brickyard worker; brickmaker
ceglasto [tse-**glahs**-to] adv. in color of bricks
ceglasty [tse-**glahs**-ti] adj.m. brick-colored; orange-red; made of bricks; made of ground bricks
cegła [**tse**-gwah] f. brick; unwanted book
ceik [**tse**-eek] m. variety of butterfly
Cejlończyk [tsey-**loń**-chik] m. Ceylonese; Sin(g)halese
cejloński [tsey-**loń**-skee] adj.m. Ceylon (tea, etc.)
cekaem [tse-**kah**-em] m. machinegun
cekaemista [tse-kah-e-**mees**-tah] m. machinegunner
cekaemowy [tse-kah-e-**mo**-vi] adj.m. of machinegun
cekin [**tse**-keen] m. punctured multi-colored metallic decorations (sown on dresses, etc.)
cekinowy [tse-kee-**no**-vi] adj.m. of punctured multi-colored metallic decorations (sown on dresses, regional costumes, etc.)
cerkopia [tser-**ko**-pyah] f. trumpet-tree
cel [tsel] m. purpose; aim; goal; end; ends; object (of ridicule, etc.); objective; design; butt; intent; view; point; drift (of words, etc.); destination; (shooting) target; bull's eye; (gun) sight
cel uświęca środki [tsel oo-**śhfyan**-tsah **śhrot**-kee] exp.: the end justifies the means
brać na cel [brahćh nah tsel] exp.: to take aim at
mieć na celu [myećh nah **tse**-loo] exp.: to have in view
osiągnąć swój cel [o-**śhowng**-nownćh sfooy tsel] exp.: to gain one's end
trafić do celu [**trah**-feećh do **tse**-loo] exp.: to hit the mark
chybić celu [**khi**-beećh **tse**-loo] exp.: to miss the mark
celem [**tse**-lem] exp.: for the purpose of
w tym celu [f tim **tse**-loo] exp.: for this purpose; with this end in view
to nie ma celu [to ńe mah **tse**-loo] exp.: that's of no avail
strzelanie do celu [stshe-**lah**-ńe do **tse**-loo] exp.: target practice
cel podróży [tsel po-**droo**-zhi] exp.: destination
cel pośmiewiska [tsel po-śhmye-**vees**-kah] exp.: laughingstock
cela [**tse**-lah] f. cell; ward
cela śmierci [**tse**-lah **śhmyer**-ćhee] exp.: death row cell
celebra [tse-**le**-brah] f. celebration (of a religious ceremony); solemn performance; pomp
celebracja [tse-le-**brah**-tsyah] f. celebration; pomp; see: **celebra**
celebrans [tse-**le**-brahns] m. officiating priest; officiant; celebrant
celebrant [tse-**le**-brahnt] m. officiating priest; officiant; celebrant
celebrować [tse-le-**bro**-vahćh] v. celebrate; officiate; perform an act (solemn duty, etc.) with pomp; solemnize; solemnify (*repeatedly*)
celebrowanie [tse-le-bro-**vah**-ńe] n. celebration
celesta [tse-**les**-tah] f. celesta (a keyboard instrument)
celestyn [tse-**les**-tin] m. Celestine (monk); celestite (mineral)
celibat [tse-**lee**-baht] m. celibacy; self-restraint; continence

celibatowy [tse-lee-bah-**to**-vi] adj.m. celibate
celka [**tsel**-kah] f. small (monastery) cell; battery cell; elementary cell (in a crystal, etc.)
cellon [**tsel**-lon] m. celluloid plastic
cellonowy [tsel-lo-**no**-vi] adj.m. celluloid-plastic (paint, film, etc.)
celnictwo [tsel-**ńeets**-tfo] n. custom house; the custom-house officials
celniczka [tsel-**ńeech**-kah] f. (woman) custom officer
celniczy [tsel-**ńee**-chi] adj.m. of the custom house; customs (office, etc.)
celnie [**tsel**-ńe] adv. accurately; with unerring aim; pointedly
celnie strzelać [**tsel**-ńe **stshe**-lahćh] exp.: to aim true; to shoot expertly
celnik [**tsel**-ńeek] m. customs inspector; customs officer
celność [**tsel**-nośhćh] f. accuracy (of aiming); precision; unerring aim; marksmanship; choice quality; selectness; prominence; notability
celny [**tsel**-ni] adj.m. accurate; well-aimed; of choice quality; select; splendid; excellent; eminent; prominent; foremost; notable; of the custom house; customs
opłata celna [o-**pwah**-tah **tsel**-nah] exp.: customs duty
deklaracja celna [de-klah-**rah**-tsyah **tsel**-nah] exp.: custom-house declaration
rewizja celna [re-**vee**-zyah **tsel**-nah] exp.: customs inspection
urząd celny [oo-zhownt **tsel**-ni] exp.: custom house
odprawa celna [ot-**prah**-vah **tsel**-nah] exp.: customs clearance
celna uwaga [**tsel**-nah oo-**vah**-gah] exp.: poignant remark; pointed remark
celna odpowiedź [**tsel**-nah ot-**po**-vyećh] exp.: poignant answer; pointed answer
celobioza [tse-lo-**byo**-zah] f. cellobiose
celofan [tse-**lo**-fahn] m. cellophane
celofanowy [tse-lo-fah-**no**-vi] adj.m. cellophane (wrapping, etc.)
celolit [tse-**lo**-leet] m. foam-concrete
celoma [tse-**lo**-mah] f. mesodermal cavity
celon [**tse**-lon] m. celluloid plastic
celonowy [tse-lo-**no**-vi] adj.m. celluloid-plastic (paint, film, etc.)
celostat [tse-**lo**-staht] m. Sun coelostat; observation device composed of mirrors
celoteks [tse-**lo**-teks] m. celotex; kind of fiber board
celować [tse-**lo**-vahćh] v. aim; take aim (at); excel (in); exceed (in); be very good (at); be noted (for); be great (at); distinguish oneself (by); excel (at); outdo (in); surpass (in) (*repeatedly*)
celowanie [tse-lo-**vah**-ńe] n. taking aim; distinguishing oneself
celownica [tse-lov-**ńee**-tsah] f. finder; viewfinder
celowniczy [tse-lov-**ńee**-chi] adj.m. sight (groove, opening, etc.); m. gun-layer; trainer
celownik [tse-**lov**-ńeek] m. dative (gram. case); gun sight; hindsight; back-sight; sight-vane; pinnule; viewfinder
celownikowy [tse-lov-ńee-**ko**-vi] adj.m. of dative case
celowo [tse-**lo**-vo] adv. on purpose; intentionally; purposely; with intent; by design; sensibly; usefully
celowościowy [tse-lo-vośh-**ćho**-vi] adj.m. of purposefulness; of expediency; of the sense of purpose
celowość [tse-**lo**-vośhćh] f. suitableness; purposefulness; expediency; sense of purpose; usefulness; advisability; propriety
celowy [tse-**lo**-vi] adj.m. suitable; purposeful; expedient; final; advisable; proper; intentional
celozja [tse-**lo**-zyah] f. celosia (tropical herb)
celsjan [**tsel**-syahn] m. celsian; barium feldspar (mineral)
Celsjusz [**tsel**-syoosh] m. Celsius
dwa stopnie Celsjusza [dvah **stop**-ńe tsel-**syoo**-shah] exp.: two degrees centigrade
Celt [tselt] m. Celt; Kelt; Gaelic

celta [tsel-tah] f. tarpaulin
celtolog [tsel-to-log] m. Celticist
celtologia [tsel-to-lo-gyah] f. Celtic studies; Keltic studies
celtowy [tsel-to-vi] adj.m. of tarpaulin; tarpaulin (cover, etc.)
celtycki [tsel-tits-kee] adj.m. Celtic; Keltic; Gaelic (art, language, etc.)
celująco [tse-loo-yown-tso] adv. perfectly; faultlessly
celujący [tse-loo-yown-tsi] adj.m. excellent; perfect
celularny [tse-loo-lahr-ni] adj.m. cellular; cellulose
celulaza [tse-loo-lah-zah] f. cellulase; an enzyme that hydrolyses cellulose
celuloid [tse-loo-loyt] m. celluloid
celuloidowy [tse-loo-loy-do-vi] adj.m. celluloid
celuloza [tse-loo-lo-zah] f. cellulose
celulozownia [tse-loo-lo-zov-ńah] f. cellulose plant
celulozownictwo [tse-loo-lo-zov-ńeets-tfo] n. cellulose industry
celulozowniczy [tse-loo-lo-zov-ńee-chi] adj.m. of cellulose making (machinery, etc.)
celulozowy [tse-loo-lo-zo-vi] adj.m. cellulose (paper, etc.); cellulosic
cembrowacz [tsem-bro-vahch] m. casing worker; timbering worker
cembrować [tsem-bro-vahćh] v. case (a well); timber (a shaft) (*repeatedly*)
cembrowanie [tsem-bro-vah-ńe] n. boarding; casing
cembrowina [tsem-bro-vee-nah] f. boarding
cembrzyna [tsem-bzhi-nah] f. boarding; casing
cemenciarz [tse-men-ćhahsh] m. cement worker; cementer (Brit.)
cement [tse-ment] m. cement
cementacja [tse-men-tah-tsyah] f. cementation
cementacyjny [tse-men-tah-tsiy-ni] adj.m. cementation (powder, water, etc.)
cementarka [tse-men-tahr-kah] f. concrete pipe making equipment
cementować [tse-men-to-vahćh] v. cement (bricks, etc.); colloq: cement (friendship, etc.); rivet; seal (a deal, etc.) (*repeatedly*)
cementować się [tse-men-to-vahćh śhan] v. be cemented; become cemented (*repeatedly*)
cementowanie [tse-men-to-vah-ńe] n. cementation
cementownia [tse-men-tov-ńah] f. cement plant; cement mill
cementownictwo [tse-men-tov-ńeets-tfo] n. cement manufacture
cementownik [tse-men-tov-ńeek] m. feeding pipe cement mix used in well-casing
cementowy [tse-men-to-vi] adj.m. of cement; cement (floor, etc.)
mleko cementowe [mle-ko tse-men-to-ve] exp.: cement grout
zaczyn cementowy [zah-chin tse-men-to-vi] exp.: cement paste
zaprawa cementowa [zah-prah-vah tse-men-to-vah] exp.: cement mortar
cementówka [tse-men-toof-kah] f. cement mix foundation; brick or block made of cement; water used in preparation of cement mix
cementyt [tse-men-tit] m. cementite
cena [tse-nah] f. price; value; cost; rate; worth; respect; respect for (somebody)
bez ceny [bes tse-ni] exp.: priceless
cena stała [tse-nah stah-wah] exp.: fixed price
cena zniżona [tse-nah zńee-zho-nah] exp.: reduced price
po tej cenie [po tey tse-ńe] exp.: at that price
w jakiej cenie jest...? [v yah-key tse-ńe yest] exp.: what is the price of ...?
za wszelką cenę [zah fshel-kown tse-nan] exp.: at any price
cenestetyczny [tse-nes-te-tich-ni] adj.m. kinesthetic; self-conscious (perception, etc.)
cenestezja [tse-nes-te-zyah] f. kinesthesia; kinesthesis; self-consciousness (based on perception)
cenić [tse-ńeećh] v. value; rate; put a price on; esteem; prize; appreciate; evaluate; respect; have a high opinion (of someone;

about something) (*repeatedly*)
drogo cenić [**dro**-go tse-ńeećh] exp.: to put a high price on
nisko cenić [**ńees**-ko tse-ńeećh] exp.: to put a low price on
wysoko cenić [vi-**so**-ko **tse**-ńeećh] exp.: to price highly

cenić się [**tse**-ńeećh śh<u>an</u>] v. value oneself; have a high opinion of oneself (of one's worth) (*repeatedly*)
nie cenić się [ńe **tse**-ńeećh śh<u>an</u>] exp.: to make oneself cheap

cenienie [tse-**ńe**-ńe] n. evaluation; estimation

cenienie się [tse-**ńe**-ńe śh<u>an</u>] n. self-esteem

ceniony [tse-**ńo**-ni] adj.m. esteemed; respected; priced; evaluated

cennik [**tsen**-ńeek] m. price list; price catalogue; price-current

cennikowy [tsen-ńee-**ko**-vi] adj.m. price-list (quotations, etc.)

cenny [**tsen**-ni] adj.m. valuable; precious; costly; esteemed

cenobita [tse-no-**bee**-tah] m. cenobite; a member of a religious order in a monastery or convent

cenocyt [tse-**no**-tsit] m. malaria germ

cenogenetycznie [tse-no-ge-ne-**tich**-ńe] adv. cenogenetically

cenogenetyczny [tse-no-ge-ne-**tich**-ni] adj.m. cenogenetic

cenogeneza [tse-no-ge-**ne**-zah] f. cenogenesis

cenotaf [tse-**no**-tahf] m. cenotaph; symbolic grave of persons buried elsewhere

cenotwórczy [tse-no-**tfoor**-chi] adj.m. price-setting (mechanism, etc.); price-shaping (process, etc.)

cenowy [tse-**no**-vi] adj.m. of price; price (stabilization, etc.)

cenoza [tse-**no**-zah] f. cenosis

cent [tsent] m. cent; slang: cubic centimeter of narcotizing fluid

centaur [tsen-**tah**-oor] m. centaur

center [**tsen**-ter] m. man in the center of attack in soccer game

centezymalny [tsen-te-zi-**mahl**-ni] adj.m. centesimal; of scales of one hundred divisions

centnar [**tsent**-nahr] m. 100 kg = 220 lb (hundredweight = 100 lb)

centra [**tsen**-trah] f. passing of the soccer ball to a player in front of the goal

centrala [tsen-**trah**-lah] f. head office; main office; exchange

centralista [tsen-trah-**lees**-tah] m. centralist

centralistyczny [tsen-trah-lees-**tich**-ni] adj.m. centralistic; centralist

centralizacja [tsen-trah-lee-**zah**-tsyah] f. centralization

centralizacyjny [tsen-trah-lee-zah-**tsiy**-ni] adj.m. centralizing

centralizator [tsen-trah-lee-**zah**-tor] m. centralizer

centralizm [tsen-**trah**-leezm] m. centralism

centralizować [tsen-trah-lee-**zo**-vahćh] v. centralize; concentrate (power, etc.) (*repeatedly*)

centralizować się [tsen-trah-lee-**zo**-vahćh śh<u>an</u>] v. be centralized; be concentrated (*repeatedly*)

centralizowanie [tsen-trah-lee-zo-**vah**-ńe] n. centralization

centralka [tsen-**trahl**-kah] f. small telephone exchange; small central exchange

centralkowy [tsen-trahl-**ko**-vi] adj.m. of small telephone exchange

centralnie [tsen-**trahl**-ńe] adv. centrally
umieścić centralnie [oo-**myeśh**-ćheećh tsen-**trahl**-ńe] exp.: to locate centrally (in the center)

centralny [tsen-**trahl**-ni] adj.m. central; middle; midmost; leading; main

centrodia [tsen-**tro**-dyah] f. centroid; center of rotating mass

centroida [tsen-**troy**-dah] f. centroid; center of rotating mass

centroidalny [tsen-tro-ee-**dahl**-ni] adj.m. centroidal

centrolew [tsen-**tro**-lef] m. coalition of center-left parties

centrolewica [tsen-tro-le-**vee**-tsah] f. coalition of center-left parties

centrolewicowy [tsen-tro-le-vee-**tso**-vi] adj.m. center-left (government, coalition, etc.)

centromer [tsen-**tro**-mer] m. centromere
centrosom [tsen-**tro**-som] m. centrosome
centrować [tsen-**tro**-vahćh] v. center; put on common centerline (*repeatedly*)
centrowanie [tsen-tro-**vah**-ńe] n. centering
centrowiec [tsen-**tro**-vyets] m. centrist; member of the political center
centrowy [tsen-**tro**-vi] adj.m. central; of the center
centrówka [tsen-**troof**-kah] f. centralizing lathe
centrum [**tsen**-troom] n. center; middle; hub; focus; ganglion; political center
centrum handlowe [**tsen**-troom khahn-**dlo**-ve] exp.: shopping center
centrum miasta [**tsen**-troom **myahs**-tah] exp.: city (town) center
centrycznie [tsen-**trich**-ńe] adv. centrically
centryczność [tsen-**trich**-nośhćh] f. centricity
centryczny [tsen-**trich**-ni] adj.m. centric
centryfuga [tsen-tri-**foo**-gah] f. centrifuge; centrifugal separator
centryfugować [tsen-tri-foo-go-vahćh] v. centrifuge; separate by means of a centrifuge (*repeatedly*)
centrysta [tsen-**tris**-tah] m. centrist
centrystowski [tsen-tris-**tof**-skee] adj.m. of centrist (parties, etc.)
centrystyczny [tsen-tri-**stich**-ni] adj.m. of centrist (programs, etc.)
centryzm [**tsen**-trizm] m. centrist views
centuria [tsen-**toor**-yah] f. century plant; Mexican agave; Roman unit
centurion [tsen-**toor**-yon] m. (Roman) centurion
centusiowski [tse-too-**śhof**-skee] adj.m. stingy (man, habit, etc.)
centuś [**tsen**-toośh] m. stingy man; miserly creature; one spending grudgingly
centyfolia [tsen-ti-**fol**-yah] f. cabbage rose
centygram [tsen-**ti**-grahm] m. centigram; 1/1000 gram
centylitr [tsen-**ti**-leetr] m. centiliter; 1/1000 liter
centym [**tsen**-tim] m. centime; 1/100 of the French franc; French cent
centymetr [tsen-**ti**-metr] m. centimeter
centymetrowy [tsen-ti-met-**ro**-vi] adj.m. of one centimeter length; centimeter (length, etc.)
centymetrówka [tsen-ti-met-**roof**-kah] f. measuring tape with scale in centimeters
cenzor [**tsen**-zor] m. censor
cenzorski [tsen-**zor**-skee] adj.m. censor's; censorial; licenser's
cenzura [tsen-**zoo**-rah] f. censorship; censure; school report
cenzuralnie [tsen-zoo-**rahl**-ńe] adv. correctly; decently; properly; not in a vulgar manner
cenzuralność [tsen-zoo-**rahl**-nośhćh] f. correctness; decency; propriety; decorum
cenzuralny [tsen-zoo-**rahl**-ni] adj.m. of the censorship; censorship (regulations, etc.); correct; decent; not vulgar
cenzurka [tsen-**zoor**-kah] f. report card (in grade school)
cenzurować [tsen-zoo-**ro**-vahćh] v. censor; censure; make excisions; block out; blue-pencil; criticize; find fault (*repeatedly*)
cenzurowanie [tsen-zoo-ro-**vah**-ńe] n. censoring; finding fault
cenzurowany [tsen-zoo-ro-**vah**-ni] adj.m. censored; m. a word game
siedzieć na cenzurowanym [śhe-dźhećh nah tsen-zoo-ro-**vah**-nim] exp.: to feel ill at ease; to be on the carpet
bawić się w cenzurowane [bah-veećh śhan f tsen-zoo-ro-**vah**-ne] exp.: to play the gossip game
cenzurowy [tsen-zoo-**ro**-vi] adj.m. of censorship
cenzus [**tsen**-zoos] m. census; qualification; requirement
cenzus naukowy [**tsen**-zoos nah-oo-**ko**-vi] exp.: degree of

education
cenzus majątkowy [tsen-zoos mah-yown-tko-vi] exp.: property requirement
cenzusowiec [tsen-zoo-so-vyets] m. person with high-school education
cenzusowy [tsen-zoo-so-vi] adj.m. of the census; having the qualifications
ceownik [tse-ov-ńeek] m. channel iron
cep [tsep] m. flail; colloq: blockhead
cepak [tse-pahk] m. slang: flail handle; swingle of a flail; cudgel
cepeliada [tse-pel-yah-dah] f. fair of the central organization of the folkloric art industry
cepeliowski [tse-pel-yof-skee] adj.m. of the central organization of the folkloric art industry
ceper [tse-per] m. man from lowlands; (unwelcome) stranger in the mountains
cepiga [tse-pee-gah] f. plow-handle; plow-tail
cepisko [tse-pees-ko] n. the long handle of a flail
cepowaty [tse-po-vah-ti] adj.m. hard-hitting; delivering heavy blows (like a flail)
cepowisko [tse-po-vees-ko] n. flailing floor; the long handle of a flail
cer [tser] m. cerium (atomic number 58)
cera [tse-rah] f. complexion; skin; mend; darn; darned place
ceramiczny [tse-rah-meech-ni] adj.m. ceramic; earthenware
ceramik [tse-rah-meek] m. ceramist; ceramicist; ceramic artist
ceramika [tse-rah-mee-kah] f. ceramics; pottery
ceramografia [tse-rah-mo-grah-fyah] f. painting on ceramic pottery
cerata [tse-rah-tah] f. oilcloth
ceratka [tse-raht-kah] f. waterproof sheet; jaconet (a cotton fabric)
ceratoryt [tse-rah-to-rit] m. decorative design on oilcloth
ceratowy [tse-rah-to-vi] adj.m. of oilcloth; oilcloth (covering, etc.)
ceratozaurus [tse-rah-to-zahw-roos] m. Ceratosaurus dinosaur
ceratyt [tse-rah-tit] m. ceratite
cerber [tser-ber] m. Cerberus; vigilant guardian; guardian dog
cerbet [tser-bet] m. wall built of ceramic elements connected with concrete mortar
cerebracja [tse-re-brah-tsyah] f. cerebration; thinking; using the mind; unconscious cerebration
cerebralny [tse-re-brahl-ni] adj.m. cerebral; of the brain; of the intellect; intellectual in nature; retroflex (consonant)
cerebrozyd [tse-re-bro-zit] m. cerebroside
ceregiele [tse-re-ge-le] pl. fuss; petty formalities; ceremony
robić ceregiele [ro-beećh tse-re-ge-le] exp.: stand on (upon) ceremony with somebody; make a fuss of somebody or of something
bez ceregieli [bes tse-re-ge-lee] exp.: unceremoniously; without ceremony
ceregielić się [tse-re-ge-leećh śhan] v. make a fuss; fuss; pretend to decline; be ceremonious (*repeatedly*)
ceregielować się [tse-re-ge-lo-vahćh śhan] v. make a fuss; fuss; pretend to decline; be ceremonious (*repeatedly*)
ceregielowanie się [tse-re-ge-lo-vah-ńe śhan] n. making a fuss; standing on ceremony
ceremonia [tse-re-mo-ńyah] f. ceremony; fuss; formalities; official function
ceremonialnie [tse-re-mo-ńyahl-ńe] adv. ceremonially; pompously; ceremoniously; with pomp and circumstance
ceremonialność [tse-re-mo-ńyahl-nośhćh] f. ceremonious behavior; ceremoniousness; punctiliousness
ceremonialny [tse-re-mo-ńyahl-ni] adj.m. ceremonial; ceremonious; solemn; pompous; formal; punctilious
ceremoniał [tse-re-mo-ńyahw] m. ceremonial; etiquette
ceremoniant [tse-re-mo-ńyahnt] m. ceremonious man

ceremoniantka [tse-re-mo-**ńyahnt**-kah] f. ceremonious woman
ceremoniować się [tse-re-mo-**ńyo**-vahćh śhan] v. be ceremonious; be formal; be punctilious; stand on ceremony (*repeatedly*)
ceres [**tse**-res] m. purified coconut oil used as butter substitute
cereus [tse-**re**-oos] m. night-blooming (Cereus) cactus
cerezyna [tse-re-**zi**-nah] f. ceresin
cerezyt [tse-**re**-zit] m. ingredient of waterproof concrete
cerka [**tser**-kah] f. small, invisible mending (on stockings, etc.)
cerkaria [tser-**kahr**-yah] f. cercaria; tadpole-shaped larva
cerkiew [**tser**-kef] f. Orthodox Church; Uniate Church
cerkiewizm [tser-**ke**-veezm] m. word or linguistic form of the Church Slavonic language
cerkiewka [tser-**kef**-kah] f. small rural Orthodox Church (or Uniate Church)
cerkiewny [tser-**kev**-ni] adj.m. of an Orthodox Church; of the Uniate Church
język cerkiewny [**yan**-zik tser-**kev**-ni] exp.: Church Slavonic (Slavic) language
pismo cerkiewne [**pees**-mo tser-**kev**-ne] exp.: the Church Slavonic (Slavic) alphabet
cerkiewszczyzna [tser-kef-**shchiz**-nah] f. language of an Slavic-Orthodox church; Church Slavonic
cermetal [tser-**me**-tahl] m. cer-met (for tools, blades, etc.)
cerograf [tse-**ro**-grahf] m. pledge; bond; formally signed document; see: **cyrograf**
cerografia [tse-ro-**grah**-fyah] f. cerography (printing)
ceroplastyka [tse-ro-**plahs**-ti-kah] f. ceroplastics; sculpturing in wax; wax sculptures
cerowaczka [tse-ro-**vahch**-kah] f. darner (woman)
cerować [tse-**ro**-vahćh] v. darn (*repeatedly*)
cerować artystycznie [tse-ro-vahćh ahr-tis-**tich**-ńe] exp.: to fine-draw; to mend invisibly
cerowalnia [tse-ro-**vahl**-ńah] f. darning shop; darning store
cerowanie [tse-ro-**vah**-ńe] n. darning; mending
cerownia [tse-**rov**-ńah] f. darning shop; darning store
cerowniczy [tse-rov-**ńee**-chi] adj.m. of mending (equipment, etc.)
cerowy [tse-**ro**-vi] adj.m. ceric; cerium (oxide, etc.)
cerówka [tse-**roof**-kah] f. mending needle
certa [**tser**-tah] f. a Black Sea fish
certacja [tser-**tah**-tsyah] f. insincere excuse; kidding; pampering
certepatria [tser-te-**pah**-tryah] f. charter party
certolić się [tser-**to**-leećh śhan] v. slang: be fussy; fuss; make a fuss; outdo each other in politeness (*repeatedly*)
certować się [tser-**to**-vahćh śhan] v. pretend; stand on ceremony; fuss; be ceremonious; pretend to decline (an invitation, etc.) (*repeatedly*)
certowanie się [tser-to-**vah**-ńe śhan] n. pretense; fuss; ceremoniousness; affected politeness
certówka [tser-**toof**-kah] f. net for carp fish
certyfikat [tser-ti-**fee**-kaht] m. certificate; affidavit; treasury bill
certyfikować [tser-ti-fee-**ko**-vahćh] v. give a certificate; make an affidavit (*repeatedly*)
cerusyt [tse-**roo**-sit] m. cerussite (mineral)
cerwidy [tser-**vee**-di] pl. the family Cervidae
ces [tses] m. C flat (music)
cesarka [tse-**sahr**-kah] f. guinea fowl; guinea hen; slang: delivery by cesarian operation; cesarian operation; cesarian section
cesarski [tse-**sahr**-skee] adj.m. imperial; emperor's; empress's
cesarskie cięcie [tse-**sahr**-ske **ćhan**-ćhe] exp.: cesarian section
cesarstwo [tse-**sahr**-stfo] n. empire
cesarz [**tse**-sahsh] m. emperor
cesarzewicz [tse-sah-**zhe**-veech] m.

cesarevitch
cesarzowa [tse-sah-**zho**-vah] f. empress
cesarzówna [tse-sah-**zhoov**-nah] f. emperor's daughter
cesja [**tse**-syah] f. cession; transfer
cesjonariusz [tse-syo-**nahr**-yoosh] m. cessionary; purchaser (of rights, titles, etc.)
cet [tset] m. even number
cetan [**tse**-tahn] m. cetane
cetanowy [tse-tah-**no**-vi] adj.m. cetane (rating, etc.)
cetnar [**tset**-nahr] m. centner; quintal; 100 kilogram
cetnarowy [tset-nah-**ro**-vi] adj.m. of centner; of hundredweight; of quintal; of 100 kilograms weight; weighing a hundred kilograms
cetnarówka [tset-nah-**roof**-kah] f. quintal cask
cetno [**tset**-no] n. even number
cetyna [tse-**ti**-nah] f. litter of conifer needles and branches
cetyniak [tse-**ti**-ńahk] m. conifer-beetle
cetyniec [tse-**ti**-ńets] m. bark beetle
cetynowy [tse-ti-**no**-vi] adj.m. of litter of conifer needles and branches (oil, etc.)
cewa [**tse**-vah] f. reel; bobbin
cewiacz [**tse**-vyahch] m. spooler
cewiaczka [tse-**vyahch**-kah] f. (woman) spooler
cewiarka [tse-**vyahr**-kah] f. (woman) spooler; winding machine
cewiarnia [tse-**vyahr**-ńah] f. spool department; winding section
cewiarski [tse-**vyahr**-skee] adj.m. winding (machine, worker, etc.)
cewić [**tse**-veećh] v. spool; reel; wind on a spool (*repeatedly*)
cewienie [tse-**vye**-ńe] n. spooling; reeling; winding on a spool
cewka [**tsef**-kah] f. reel; bobbin; spool; coil; duct; leg of a deer; snare; weaver's conical spool
cewka łzowa [**tsef**-kah **wzo**-vah] exp.: tear duct; lachrymal duct
cewka moczowa [**tsef**-kah mo-**cho**-vah] exp.: urethra
cewka zapłonowa [**tsef**-kah zah-**pwo**-no-vah] exp.: spark coil; sparking-coil
cewkowaty [tsef-ko-**vah**-ti] adj.m. tubular
cewkowy [tsef-**ko**-vi] adj.m. of (electric, magnetic, ignition, etc.) coil
cewnik [**tsev**-ńeek] m. catheter
cewnikować [tsev-ńee-**ko**-vahćh] v. catheterize (*repeatedly*)
cewnikowanie [tsev-ńee-ko-**vah**-ńe] n. catheterization
cez [tses] m. cesium (atomic number 55)
ceza [**tse**-zah] f. bag-shaped dragnet
cezar [**tse**-zahr] m. Caesar
cezalpinia [tse-zahl-**pee**-ńyah] f. Caesalpinia tree or bush; brasilwood
cezarianizm [tse-zahr-**yah**-ńeezm] m. caesarism
cezariański [tse-zahr-**yahń**-skee] adj.m. Caesar's (rule, etc.)
cezaropapizm [tse-zah-ro-**pah**-peezm] m. caesaropapism; caesaropapacy; papal supremacy
cezarowy [tse-zah-**ro**-vi] adj.m. Caesar's (edict, etc.)
cezaryjski [tse-zah-**riy**-skee] adj.m. Caesar's (rule, etc.)
cezarystyczny [tse-zah-ris-**tich**-ni] adj.m. Caesar-like
cezaryzm [tse-**zah**-rizm] m. caesarism
cezowy [tse-**zo**-vi] adj.m. of cesium; containing cesium
cezura [tse-**zoo**-rah] f. (music) turning point; caesura
cęgi [**tsan**-gee] pl. tongs; pliers; nippers; pincers; pipe-wrench
cęgowy [tsan-**go**-vi] adj.m. of tongs (decorative design, etc.)
cętka [**tsant**-kah] f. dot
cętkować [tsant-**ko**-vahćh] v. speckle; spot; dot; mottle; dapple (*repeatedly*)
cętkowanie [tsant-ko-**vah**-ńe] n. speckling; dotting; mottling
cętkowany [tsan-tko-**vah**-ni] adj.m. spotted; dotted; speckled
cętkowaty [tsan-tko-**vah**-ti] adj.m. spotted; dotted; speckled
ch [kh] (not declined) voiceless consonant "kh"
cha, cha [khah khah] excl.: ha! ha!
chabanina [khah-bah-**ńee**-nah] f.

slang: meat of inferior quality (partly spoiled)
chabaź [**khah**-bahśh] m. weed; nasty weed
chaber [**khah**-ber] m. cornflower
chabet [**khah**-bet] m. jade; rip
chabeta [khah-**be**-tah] f. jade; rip
chabrowy [khahb-**ro**-vi] adj.m. of the cornflower; cornflower blue; sky-blue; blue
chachar [**khah**-khahr] m. slang: tramp; loiterer (mob jargon)
chachmęcić [khahkh-**man**-ćheećh] v. slang: cloud; muddle; mix up; bungle; befuddle; confuse; tangle; entangle (mob jargon) (*repeatedly*)
chadecja [khah-**de**-tsyah] f. the Christian Democratic Party
chadecki [khah-**dets**-kee] adj.m. of the Christian Democratic Party
chadek [**khah**-dek] m. member of the Christian Democratic Party
chadzać [**khah**-dzahćh] v. be accustomed to go; be accustomed to wear (*repeatedly*)
chajtać się [**khahy**-tahćh śhan] v. slang: marry; get married (*rep.*)
chajtnięty [khahyt-**ńan**-ti] adj.m. married
chalazon [khah-**lah**-zon] m. chalaza; one yolk anchor inside an egg
chalaza [khah-**lah**-zah] pl. chalazas; (two) yolk anchors inside an egg
chalcedon [khahl-**tse**-don] m. chalcedony (precious stone)
Chaldejczyk [khahl-**dey**-chik] m. (a) Chaldean
chaldejski [khahl-**dey**-skee] adj.m. Chaldean
chalif [**khah**-leef] m. caliph
chalkantyt [khahl-**kahn**-tit] m. chalcanthite (mineral)
chalkofilny [khahl-ko-**feel**-ni] adj.m. chalcophyllite (compound)
chalkograf [khahl-**ko**-grahf] m. copper engraver; chalcographer
chalkografia [khahl-ko-**grah**-fyah] f. copper engraver's trade; chalcography
chalkopiryt [khahl-ko-**pee**-rit] m. chalcopyrite
chalkozyn [khahl-**ko**-zin] m. chalcosine; chalcocite (mineral)
challenge [**shah**-lanzh] m. international light aircraft competition (1928-1934) won by Poland in 1932 and 1934 (Challenge International de Tourisme)
chała [**khah**-wah] f. plaited white bread; colloq: literary garbage; muck; trash; second-rate literary work, play, concert, film, etc.; school slang: failing grade
chałaciarz [khah-**wah**-ćhahsh] m. gabardine-wearing Jew
chałacik [khah-**wah**-ćheek] m. small lab coat; laboratory coat; overalls; overall; Jewish boy's gabardine long coat
chałastra [khah-**wahs**-trah] f. mob
chałat [**khah**-waht] m. lab. coat; laboratory coat; overalls; overall; Jewish (oriental) gabardine long coat
chałatowy [khah-wah-**to**-vi] adj.m. (fabric) for overalls; gabardine-wearing (Jew); m. gabardine-wearing Jew
chałka [**khahw**-kah] f. plaited white bread
chałowaty [khah-wo-**vah**-ti] adj.m. colloq: like literary garbage; mucky; trashy; second-rate (literary work, play, concert, film, etc.)
chałowy [khah-**wo**-vi] adj.m. colloq: like literary garbage; mucky; trashy; second-rate (literary work, play, concert, film, etc.)
chałtura [khahw-**too**-rah] f. slang: musician's or singer's second-rate engagement to make extra income
chałturka [khahw-**toor**-kah] f. slang: (small) musician's or singer's second-rate engagement to make extra income
chałturnictwo [khahw-toor-**ńeets**-tfo] n. slang: musician's or singer's second-rate engagements (to make extra income)
chałturniczy [khahw-toor-**ńee**-chi] adj.m. slang: of musician's or singer's second-rate engagements
chałturnik [khahw-**toor**-ńeek] m. slang: musician or singer taking

(off and on) second-rate engagements
chałturowiec [khahw-too-**ro**-vyets] m. slang: musician or singer taking second-rate engagements
chałturowy [khahw-too-**ro**-vi] adj.m. slang: of musician's or singer's second-rate engagements
chałturzenie [khahw-too-**zhe**-ńe] n. slang: (the taking of) irregular second-rate artistic engagements
chałturzyć [khahw-**too**-zhićh] v. slang: take second-rate artistic engagements (*repeatedly*)
chałturzysta [khahw-too-**zhis**-tah] m. slang: musician or singer taking second-rate engagements
chałturzystka [khahw-too-**zhist**-kah] f. slang: (woman) musician or singer taking second-rate engagements
chałupa [khah-**woo**-pah] f. hut; cottage; colloq: shack; cabin; slang: home
chałupina [khah-woo-**pee**-nah] f. (small) hut; cottage; shack; cabin
chałupinka [khah-woo-**peen**-kah] f. (very small) hut; cottage; shack; cabin
chałupka [khah-**woop**-kah] f. (small) hut; cottage; shack; cabin
chałupnica [khah-woop-**ńee**-tsah] f. woman cottage-worker; landless peasant woman
chałupnictwo [khah-woop-**ńeets**-tfo] n. outwork; cottage-work; cottage-industry
chałupniczka [khah-woop-**ńeech**-kah] f. woman cottage-worker; landless peasant woman
chałupniczo [khah-woop-**ńee**-cho] adv. by means of cottage-work
chałupniczy [khah-woop-**ńee**-chi] adj.m. cottage-worker's (production, etc.)
chałupnik [khah-**woop**-ńeek] m. outworker; cottage-worker
chałupsko [khah-**woop**-sko] n. (nasty, run down) hut; cottage; shack; cabin
chałwa [**khahw**-vah] f. halva(h); oriental sweetmeat of ground walnuts and honey
cham [khahm] m. colloq: roughneck; boor; cad; tyke; cur; yokel; plebeian; slang: country man; brute
chamy [**khah**-mi] pl. colloq: rabble; riff-raff
chamica [khah-**mee**-tsah] f. vulg.: boorish woman; uneducated woman
chamicki [khah-**mee**-tskee] adj.m. Hamitic
chamidło [khah-**meed**-wo] n. rude, vulgar man
chamieć [**khah**-myećh] v. become rusticated; coarsen; roughen (*repeatedly*)
chamisko [khah-**mees**-ko] n. rude, vulgar man
chamka [**khahm**-kah] f. vulg.: boorish woman; uneducated woman
chamowaty [khah-mo-**vah**-ti] adj.m. boorish; churlish; intractable; vulgar
champion [**chem**-pyon] m. champion
championka [chem-**pyon**-kah] f. (woman) champion
chamsin [**khahm**-seen] m. khamsin; khamseen; desert wind
chamski [**khahm**-skee] adj.m. caddish; boorish; coarse; rustic
po chamsku [po **khahm**-skoo] exp.: caddishly; boorishly; coarsely; like a yokel; in rough manner
chamstwo [**khahm**-stfo] n. caddishness; boorishness; coarse behavior; rabble; riff-raff
chamsyn [**khahm**-sin] m. khamsin; khamseen; desert wind
chamuś [**khah**-moośh] m. (nasty, little) roughneck; boor; cad; tyke; cur; yokel
chan [khahn] m. khan
chanat [**khah**-naht] m. khanate
chandra [**khahn**-drah] f. doldrums; blues; despondency; dejection; spleen; blues; slang: the hip; the hump
mieć chandrę [myećh **khahn**-dran] exp.: to have (to get) the blues; to feel blue
chandryczyć się [khahn-**dri**-chićh śhan] v. slang: squabble; reprimand constantly; grumble all

the time; argue (*repeatedly*)
chanowy [khah-**no**-vi] adj.m. of a khan
chański [**khahń**-skee] adj.m. khan's (soldiers, etc.)
chanuka [khah-**noo**-kah] f. Hanukka; Hanukah
chaos [**khah**-os] m. chaos; confusion; disarray; muddle; mess; jumble (of opinions, etc.)
chaos w głowie [**khah**-os v **gwo**-vye] exp.: a state of bewilderment; the head in a state of turmoil; confusion
chaotycznie [khah-o-**tich**-ńe] adv. chaotically; confusedly; pell-mell; topsy-turvy; totally disordered
mówić chaotycznie [**moo**-veećh khah-o-**tich**-ńe] exp.: to speak incoherently, chaotically
chaotyczność [khah-o-**tich**-nośhćh] f. confusion; topsy-turvydom
chaotyczność mowy [khah-o-**tich**-nośhćh **mo**-vi] exp.: incoherence
chaotyczny [khah-o-**tich**-ni] adj.m. chaotic; disorderly; disjointed; desultory; confused; rigmarole; pell-mell; incoherent; rambling; disjointed; rough-and-tumble
chap! [khahp] excl.: (sudden grip with teeth, beak, etc.) got it!
chapać [**khah**-pahćh] v. snatch; snap at; snap up; grab; slang: steal (mob jargon) (*repeatedly*)
chapanie [khah-**pah**-ńe] n. snatching; grabbing; snapping
chapnąć [**khahp**-nownćh] v. snatch; snap at; snap up; grab
chaps! [khahps] excl.: (sudden grip with teeth, beak, etc.) got it!
chaps, znienacka [khahps zńe-**nahts**-kah] exp.: to grab unawares; to catch unexpectedly
charakter [khah-**rahk**-ter] m. disposition; character; moral nature; moral strength; fiber; mettle; backbone; guts; personality; capacity; function; office; quality; handwriting; letter; writing symbol
charakter pisma [khah-**rahk**-ter **pees**-mah] exp.: handwriting
człowiek z charakterem [**chwo**-vyek s khah-rahk-**te**-rem] exp.: man of character
brak charakteru [brahk khah-rahk-**te**-roo] exp.: lack of principle; lack of backbone
w charakterze dyrektora [f khah-rahk-**te**-zhe di-rek-**to**-rah] exp.: in the capacity of director
charakterek [khah-rahk-**te**-rek] m. petulant character; flippancy; self-willed person; restive person; slang: grumbler; groucher; grouser
charakterniak [khah-rahk-**ter**-ńahk] m. slang: strong-willed man; resolute man; assertive man
charakternik [khah-rahk-**ter**-ńeek] m. slang: strong-willed man; resolute man; assertive man
charakterny [khah-rahk-**ter**-ni] adj.m. slang: strong-willed; resolute; assertive; firm
charakterolog [khah-rahk-te-**ro**-log] m. characterologist
charakterologia [khah-rahk-te-ro-**lo**-gyah] f. characterology
charakterologicznie [khah-rahk-te-ro-lo-**geech**-ńe] adv. characterologically
charakterologiczny [khah-rahk-te-ro-lo-**geech**-ni] adj.m. characterological
charakteropata [khah-rahk-te-ro-**pah**-tah] m. characterologically deformed (brain damaged) individual
charakteropatia [khah-rah-kte-ro-**pah**-tyah] f. characterological deformation (caused by brain damage etc.)
charakteropatyczny [khah-rah-kte-ro-pah-**tich**-ni] adj.m. characterologically deformed
charakterotwórczy [khah-rah-kte-ro-**tfoor**-chi] adj.m. character-building; character-forming
charakterowy [khah-rah-kte-**ro**-vi] adj.m. of a character
charakterystycznie [khah-rah-kte-ri-**stich**-ńe] adv. characteristically; typically; distinctively; specifically; in a characteristic manner
charakterystyczność [khah-rah-kte-

ri-**stich**-nośhćh] f. characteristic nature (of folk songs, etc.)
charakterystyczny [khah-rah-kte-ri-**stich**-ni] adj.m. characteristic (of); typical; distinctive; specific
cecha charakterystyczna [tse-khah khah-rah-kte-ri-**stich**-nah] exp.: characteristic trait; distinctive feature
charakterystyka [khah-rah-kte-**ri**-sti-kah] f. description of the character; artistic representation of a personality; a characteristic; distinctive trait
charakteryzacja [khah-rah-kte-ri-**zah**-tsyah] f. characterization; make-up; disguise
charakteryzator [khah-rah-kte-ri-**zah**-tor] m. make-up man
charakteryzatorka [khah-rah-kte-ri-zah-**tor**-kah] f. makeup woman
charakteryzatorski [khah-rah-kte-ri-zah-**tor**-skee] adj.m. of a makeup; makeup (skill, etc.)
charakteryzować [khah-rah-kte-ri-**zo**-vahćh] v. characterize; describe; stamp; make up (a person's face); disguise (as) (*repeatedly*)
charakteryzować się [khah-rah-kte-ri-**zo**-vahćh śhan] v. be typified (by); be characterized (by); bear the stamp (of); make oneself up; disguise oneself (*repeatedly*)
charakteryzowanie [khah-rah-kte-ri-zo-**vah**-ńe] n. characterization; make-up; disguise
charchotać [khahr-**kho**-tahćh] v. colloq: wheeze; rattle in one's throat; grunt; speak in a hoarse voice (*repeatedly*)
charci [**khahr**-ćhee] adj.m. greyhound's
charcica [khahr-**ćhee**-tsah] f. greyhound bitch
charciczka [khahr-**ćheech**-kah] f. (nice, little) greyhound bitch
charcik [**khahr**-ćheek] m. miniature greyhound
charcząco [khahr-**chown**-tso] adv. wheezingly; hoarsely
charczący [khahr-**chown**-tsi] adj.m. wheezing; raucous; hoarse; stertorous
charczeć [**khahr**-chećh] v. wheeze; snort; be hoarse (*repeatedly*)
charczenie [khahr-**che**-ńe] n. wheeze; death-rattle
charge d'affaires [shahr-**zhe** dah-**fer**] m. charge d'affaires; a diplomat who substitutes for a minister or for an ambassador in his absence
chargot [**khar**-got] m. hoarse voice; raucous sounds
chark [khahrk] m. vulg.: gob; phlegm; mucus
charkać [**khahr**-kahćh] v. cough up phlegm; expectorate (*repeatedly*)
charkanie [khar-**kah**-ńe] n. coughing up (phlegm, blood, etc.)
charknąć [**khark**-nownćh] v. cough up phlegm; expectorate
charknięcie [khark-**ńan**-ćhe] n. coughing up (phlegm, blood, etc.)
charkot [**khahr**-kot] m. rattling in the throat; rattle; hoarse voice
charkotać [khahr-**ko**-tahćh] v. wheeze; snort; be hoarse (*repeatedly*)
charkotanie [khahr-ko-**tah**-ńe] n. wheezing; snorting; being hoarse
charkotliwie [khahr-kot-**lee**-vye] adv. in a hoarse voice; hoarsely
charkotliwy [khahr-kot-**lee**-vi] adj.m. hoarse, raucous (voice)
charleston [**chahrls**-ton] m. Charleston (dance)
charłacki [khahr-**wahts**-kee] adj.m. decrepit; wasted
charłactwo [khahr-**wahts**-tfo] n. decrepitude; cachexia; cachexy; general physical wasting and malnutrition
charłaczy [khahr-**wah**-chi] adj.m. decrepit; wasted
charłać [**khahr**-wahćh] v. be sickly; be frail; be decrepit (*repeatedly*)
charłak [**khahr**-wahk] m. decrepit person; wasted person; worn out person; starveling
chart [khahrt] m. greyhound; borzoi
charter [**chahr**-ter] m. charter
charterowy [chahr-te-**ro**-vi] adj.m. chartered; charter (flight, etc.)
charytatywnie [khah-ri-tah-**tiv**-ńe] adv. charitably; beneficently; benevolently
charytatywność [khah-ri-tah-**tiv**-

nośhćh] f. charity

charytatywny [khah-ri-tah-**tiv**-ni] adj.m. charitable; beneficent; benevolent
praca charytatywna [**prah**-tsah khah-ri-tah-**tiv**-nah] exp.: charity work; welfare work

charyzma [khah-**riz**-mah] f. charisma

charyzmat [khah-**riz**-maht] m. charismus

charyzmatyczny [khah-riz-mah-**tich**-ni] adj.m. charismatic

chasmogamiczny [khahs-mo-gah-**meech**-ni] adj.m. chasmogamous

chasyd [**khah**-sit] m. orthodox Jew; rabbinist; member of Hasidic sect

chasydyzm [khah-**si**-dizm] m. Hasidism

chasydzki [khah-**sits**-kee] adj.m. Hasidic

chaszcze [**khahsh**-che] pl. brushwood; thicket; scrub

chata [**khah**-tah] f. hut; cabin; slang: hide-out; hideout
chata wolna [**khah**-tah **vol**-nah] exp.: colloq: parents are not at home

chateńka [khah-**teń**-kah] f. very nice little hut; very small cabin

chatka [**khaht**-kah] f. small hut; small cabin

chatynka [khah-**tin**-kah] f. (small, nice) hut; small cabin

chcąc [khtsownts] p.p.: wanting
chcąc nie chcąc [khtsownts ńe khtsownts] exp.: willy-nilly; necessarily; of necessity

chcący [**khtsown**-tsi] adj.m. willing; ready; disposed (person); adv. on purpose
dla chcącego nie ma nic trudnego [dlah khtsown-**tse**-go ńe mah ńeets trood-**ne**-go] exp.: where there's a will there's a way

chcenie [**khtse**-ńe] n. willingness (to do); readiness (to do); inclination (to do); disposition (to do)

chcieć [khćhećh] v. want; be willing; intend; desire; like; please; wish; choose; care; be keen; will; have the will; try; attempt (*repeatedly*)
chce mi się spać [khtse mee śhan spahćh] exp.: I want to sleep
chce mi się pić [khtse mee śhan peećh] exp.: I am thirsty
chcę, żeby wrócił [khtsan **zhe**-bi **vroo**-ćheew] exp.: I want him to come back
on sam nie wie, czego chce [on sahm ńe vye **che**-go khtse] exp.: he does not know his own mind
pech chciał [pekh khćhahw] exp.: by ill luck; as ill luck would have it

chciejstwo [**khćhey**-stfo] n. wishful thinking

chciwie [**khćhee**-vye] adv. greedily; hungrily; keenly; avidly; rapaciously; with greed; with avidity

chciwiec [**khćhee**-vyets] m. greedy man; grasping man; covetous man

chciwość [**khćhee**-vośhćh] f. greed; covetousness; avidity; rapacity; cupidity; acquisitiveness

chciwy [**khćhee**-vi] adj.m. greedy; covetous; avid; eager for; rapacious; acquisitive

che, che, che [khe khe khe] excl.: ha! ha!

chebd [khept] m. dwarf elder

checza [**khe**-chah] f. Kashubian cottage

cheddar [**che**-dahr] m. cheddar cheese

cheder [**khe**-der] m. heder; cheder (Jewish school)

chelidonia [khe-lee-**do**-ńyah] f. tetterwort; celandine

chełbia [**khew**-byah] f. aurelia (a jellyfish)

chełbotać [khew-**bo**-tahćh] v. lap; splash (*repeatedly*)

chełbotanie [khew-bo-**tah**-ńe] n. lapping; splashing

chełmiak [**khew**-myahk] m. touraco bird; Musophaga

chełmiński [khew-**meeń**-skee] adj.m. of Chełmno

chełpić się [**khew**-peećh śhan] v. boast; brag; bluster; vaunt; swagger; glory; pride (*repeatedly*)

chełpienie się [khew-**pye**-ńe śhan] n. boastfulness; brag; bluster; vaunt; swagger; big words

chełpliwie [khew-**plee**-vye] adv. boastfully; swaggeringly; vaingloriously
chełpliwy [khew-**plee**-vi] adj.m. boastful; vainglorious
chemia [**khe**-myah] f. chemistry
chemiczka [khe-**meech**-kah] f. woman chemist (or chemistry student)
chemicznie [khe-**meech**-ńe] adv. chemically
chemicznofizyczny [khe-meech-no-fee-**zich**-ni] adj.m. of physical chemistry
chemiczny [khe-**meech**-ni] adj.m. chemical
chemiczno-fizyczny [khe-**meech**-no fee-**zich**-ni] exp.: physical-chemistry (course, etc.)
pralnia chemiczna [**prahl**-ńah khe-**meech**-nah] exp.: dry-cleaner's
wojna chemiczna [**voy**-ńah khe-**meech**-nah] exp.: gas warfare
związek chemiczny [**zvyown**-zek khe-**meech**-ni] exp.: chemical compound
chemigraf [khe-**mee**-grahf] m. zincograph
chemigrafia [khe-mee-**grah**-fyah] f. zincography; zincograph
chemigraficzny [khe-mee-grah-**feech**-ni] adj.m. zincographic
chemik [**khe**-meek] m. chemist (or chemistry student)
chemikalia [khe-mee-**kahl**-yah] pl. chemicals
chemikaliowiec [khe-mee-kahl-**yo**-vyets] m. ship transporting chemicals
chemiluminescencja [khe-mee-loo-mee-nes-**tsen**-tsyah] f. chemiluminescence
chemioterapeutyczny [khe-myo-te-rah-pew-**tich**-ni] adj.m. chemotherapeutic
chemioterapeutyk [khe-myo-te-rah-**pew**-tik] m. specialist in chemotherapy
chemioterapia [khe-myo-te-**rah**-pyah] f. chemotherapy
chemisorpcja [khe-mee-**sorp**-tsyah] f. chemical absorption
chemizacja [khe-mee-**zah**-tsyah] f. application of chemistry to agriculture, etc.
chemizacyjny [khe-mee-zah-**tsiy**-ni] adj.m. of chemical services (to agriculture, industry, etc.)
chemizator [khe-mee-**zah**-tor] m. specialist in the application of chemistry to agriculture, etc.
chemizować [khe-mee-**zo**-vahćh] v. introduce the products of chemistry (to agriculture, etc.) (*repeatedly*)
chemizować się [khe-mee-**zo**-vahćh śhan] v. accept the products of chemistry (in technology etc.) (*repeatedly*)
chemizowanie się [khe-mee-zo-**vah**-ńe śhan] n. the use of products of chemistry (in technology etc.)
chemizm [**khe**-meezm] m. chemism
chemoautotrof [khe-mo-ahw-**to**-trof] m. chemoautotroph; chemoautotrophic organism
chemoautotrofia [khe-mo-ahw-to-**tro**-fyah] f. chemoautotrophy
chemoautotroficznie [khe-mo-ahw-to-tro-**feech**-ńe] adv. chemoautotrophically
chemoautotroficzny [khe-mo-ahw-to-tro-**feech**-ni] adj.m. chemoautotrophic
chemogeniczny [khe-mo-ge-**ńeech**-ni] adj.m. (sedimentary deposits) originating from chemical reactions
chemolak [khe-**mo**-lahk] m. acid-resisting paint
chemoodporny [khe-mo-ot-**por**-ni] adj.m. resistant to chemicals
chemoreceptor [khe-mo-re-**tsep**-tor] m. receptor reacting to chemical signals
chemosterylant [khe-mo-ste-**ri**-lahnt] m. chemical causing infertility in insects; chemosterilant
chemosterylizacja [khe-mo-ste-ri-lee-**zah**-tsyah] f. chemical sterilization of insects
chemosyntetyczny [khe-mo-sin-te-**tich**-ni] adj.m. chemosynthetic
chemosynteza [khe-mo-sin-**te**-zah] f. chemosynthesis
chemotaksja [khe-mo-**tah**-ksyah] f. chemotaxis
chemotaktycznie [khe-mo-tahk-**tich**-

ńe] adv. chemotactically
chemotaktyczny [khe-mo-tahk-**tich**-ni] adj.m. chemotactic
chemoterapeutyczny [khe-mo-te-rah-pew-**tich**-ni] adj.m. chemotherapeutic
chemoterapeutyk [khe-mo-te-rah-**pew**-tik] m. specialist in chemotherapy
chemoterapia [khe-mo-te-**rah**-pyah] f. chemotherapy
chemotropiczny [khe-mo-tro-**peech**-ni] adj.m. chemotropic
chemotropizm [khe-mo-**tro**-peezm] m. chemotropism
cherlacki [kher-**lahts**-kee] adj.m. decrepit; sickly; frail; feeble
cherlactwo [kher-**lahts**-tfo] n. decrepitude; sickliness; debility
cherlać [**kher**-lahćh] v. be sickly; be frail; waste away (*repeatedly*)
cherlak [**kher**-lahk] m. weakling
cherlakowato [kher-lah-ko-**vah**-to] adv. sickishly
cherlakowaty [kher-lah-ko-**vah**-ti] adj.m. (chronically) sick; sickish; somewhat sick
cherlawiec [kher-**lah**-vyets] m. (chronic) weakling
cherlawo [kher-**lah**-vo] adv. in a sickly manner
cherlawy [kher-**lah**-vi] adj.m. (chronically) sickly; cachectic
cherry brandy [che-ri **bren**-di] f. cherry brandy
cherub [**khe**-roob] m. cherub
cherubin [khe-**roo**-been] m. cherub
cherubinek [khe-roo-**bee**-nek] m. (small, very nice) cherub
cherubinkowaty [khe-roo-been-ko-**vah**-ti] adj.m. cherubic
cherubinkowy [khe-roo-been-**ko**-vi] adj.m. cherubic
chevrolet [shev-**ro**-let] m. chevrolet (car, car make)
chęch [kh<u>an</u>kh] m. moss
chęchy [**kh<u>an</u>**-khi] pl. mossy swamps
chęć [kh<u>an</u>ćh] f. wish; desire; inclination
bez chęci [bes **kh<u>an</u>**-ćhee] exp.: reluctantly
chęć mnie bierze [kh<u>an</u>ćh mńe **bye**-zhe] exp.: I have a mind (for)
dobre chęci [**do**-bre **kh<u>an</u>**-ćhee] exp.: good intentions
mieć chęć na [myećh kh<u>an</u>ćh nah] exp.: to have a mind for; to want; to have fancy for (something)
z miłą chęcią [z **mee**-w<u>own</u> **kh<u>an</u>**-ćh<u>own</u>] exp.: with pleasure; very willingly
zrobię to z chęcią [**zro**-by<u>an</u> to s **kh<u>an</u>**-ćh<u>own</u>] exp.: I will do it with pleasure; I shall be glad to do it
chędogi [kh<u>an</u>-**do**-gee] adj.m. neat; clean; tidy; orderly
chędogo [kh<u>an</u>-**do**-go] adv. in neat fashion; neatly; clean; tidily; in an orderly fashion
chędożyć [kh<u>an</u>-**do**-zhićh] v. clean; put in order; vulg. slang: have sex (mob jargon) (*repeatedly*)
chętka [**kh<u>an</u>t**-kah] f. fancy; desire; itch for; itch to do; whim; caprice
nabrać chętki [nah-brahćh **kh<u>an</u>t**-kee] exp.: to take a fancy (to do); to take a fancy for (something)
mam chętkę [mahm **kh<u>an</u>t**-k<u>an</u>] exp.: I itch for; I itch to do
chętnie [**kh<u>an</u>t**-ńe] adv. willingly; readily; with a good grace; with pleasure; heartily
chętnie zrobić [**kh<u>an</u>t**-ńe **zro**-beećh] exp.: to be glad to do
chętniej [**kh<u>an</u>t**-ńey] adv. more willingly; more readily; with a better grace; with greater pleasure; preferably; rather; sooner
chętniej bym stracił [**kh<u>an</u>t**-ńey bim **strah**-ćheew] exp.: I would rather lose; I would as soon lose; I would sooner lose (Brit.)
chętny [**kh<u>an</u>t**-ni] adj.m. willing; ready; (prospective) buyer (or purchaser)
chętny do nauki [**kh<u>an</u>t**-ni do nah-**oo**-kee] exp.: eager to learn
czy są chętni? [chi s<u>own</u> **kh<u>an</u>t**-ńee] exp.: any volunteers?
chi! chi! [khee khee] excl.: ha! ha!
chiazma [**khyahz**-mah] f. (optic) chiasma
chibcik [**kheep**-ćheek] exp.:
na chibcika [nah kheep-**ćhee**-kah]

exp.: adv. colloq: quickly; in a hurry
chich [kheekh] m. suppressed giggle; stifled laughter; chuckle
chichot [**khee**-khot] m. giggle; laughter; cackle; chuckle; titter; snicker; snigger
chichotać [khee-**kho**-tahćh] v. chuckle; giggle; cackle; titter; snicker (*repeatedly*)
chichotać się [khee-**kho**-tahćh śhan] v. chuckle; giggle; cackle; titter; snicker (*repeatedly*)
chichotanie [khee-kho-**tah**-ńe] n. giggle; laughter; cackle; chuckle; titter; snicker; snigger
chichotek [khee-**kho**-tek] m. short and suppressed giggle
chichotka [khee-**khot**-kah] f. giggle
chichotliwie [khee-khot-**lee**-vye] adv. with a giggle; with a chuckle
chichotliwy [khee-khot-**lee**-vi] adj.m. giggling; chuckling; sniggering
chichrać się [**kheekh**-rahćh śhan] v. chuckle; giggle; cackle; titter; snicker (*repeatedly*)
chichy [**khee**-khi] pl. giggles; laughter; cackles; chuckles; titters
chief [cheef] m. chief mechanical engineer on a merchant ship
chili [**chee**-lee] n. chili; hot pepper; a thick sauce of meat and chilies
chiliasta [kheel-**yahs**-tah] m. believer in chiliasm
chiliastyczny [kheel-yahs-**tich**-ni] adj.m. chiliastic; of millennium
chiliazm [**kheel**-yahzm] m. chiliasm; millenniarism
Chilijczyk [chee-**leey**-chik] m. Chilean
Chilijka [chee-**leey**-kah] f. Chilean (woman)
chilijski [chee-**leey**-skee] adj.m. Chilean
chimera [khee-**me**-rah] f. whim; phantasm; illusion; fanciful notion; caprice; freak; chimera
miewać chimery [**mye**-vahćh khee-**me**-ri] exp.: to be capricious; to be freakish; to be wayward
chimeryczka [khee-me-**rich**-kah] f. freakish woman; erratic woman; chimerical woman
chimerycznie [khee-me-**rich**-ńe] adv. chimerically; capriciously; whimsically; fancifully
chimeryczność [khee-me-**rich**-nośhćh] f. chimerical nature; unreality
chimeryczny [khee-me-**rich**-ni] adj.m. chimerical; capricious; whimsical; fanciful
chimeryk [khee-**me**-rik] m. chimerical man (person); capricious man; whimsical man; fanciful man; freakish man
chimeryzm [khee-**me**-rizm] m. chimerism
chinidyna [khee-ńee-**di**-nah] f. quinidine
chinina [khee-**ńee**-nah] f. quinine
zatrucie chininą [zah-**troo**-ćhe khee-**ńee**-nown] exp.: quinine poisoning; cinchonism
chininowy [khee-ńee-**no**-vi] adj.m. quinine (poisoning, etc.)
Chinka [**kheen**-kah] f. Chinese woman
chinolina [khee-no-**lee**-nah] f. quinoline
chinolog [khee-**no**-log] m. sinologist
chinon [**khee**-non] m. quinone
chinowiec [khee-**no**-vyets] m. cinchona; quinquin
chinowy [khee-**no**-vi] adj.m. quinic
proszek chinowy [**pro**-shek khee-**no**-vi] exp.: quinine
chinozol [khee-**no**-zol] m. quinosol (used in agriculture)
Chińczyk [**kheeń**-chik] m. Chinese man
chiński [**kheeń**-skee] adj.m. Chinese; of China
chińszczyzna [kheeń-**shchiz**-nah] f. Chinese language; Chinese art; sinology; oriental ceremony
dla mnie to chińszczyzna [dlah mńe to kheeń-**shchiz**-nah] exp.: it's Greek to me; I don't get it; I don't know what it is
chionosfera [khyo-no-**sfe**-rah] f. region of accumulation of snow where glaciers are forming
chippendale [chi-**pen**-del] m. Chippendale
chips [cheeps] pl. potato chips
chiragra [khee-**rahg**-rah] f. chiragra; gouty affection of the hand

chirologia [khee-ro-**lo**-gyah] f. chiromancy; palmistry; sign language; gesture language
chiromancja [khee-ro-**mahn**-tsyah] f. chiromancy; palmistry
chiromanta [khee-ro-**mahn**-tah] m. chiromancer; palmist
chiromantka [khee-ro-**mahnt**-kah] f. (woman) chiromancer; palmist
chirotechnika [khee-ro-**tekh**-ńee-kah] f. science of hand-tools design for efficiency and esthetics
chirurg [**khee**-roorg] m. surgeon; slang: sawbones
chirurgia [khee-**roor**-gyah] f. surgery; colloq: surgical department
chirurgicznie [khee-roor-**geech**-ńe] adv. surgically
chirurgiczny [khee-roor-**geech**-ni] adj.m. surgical
chiton [**khee**-ton] m. chiton
chityna [khee-**ti**-nah] f. chitin
chitynowy [khee-ti-**no**-vi] adj.m. chitin (shell, etc.); chitinous
chiwian [**khee**-vyahn] m. ailanthus, Chinese sumac; tree of heaven
chlać [khlahćh] v. vulg.: booze; swig; swill; soak; guzzle (*repeatedly*)
chlamida [khlah-**mee**-dah] f. chlamys
chlamidospory [khlah-mee-dos-**po**-ri] pl. chlamydospores
chlanie [**khlah**-ńe] n. boozing; guzzling
chlańsko [**khlahń**-sko] n. slang: drinking bout
chlap [khlahp] excl.: splash!; flop!
chlapa [**khlah**-pah] f. foul weather; bad weather; nasty weather; a lewd woman; slattern
chlapać [**khlah**-pahćh] v. splash; soak; guzzle; blab; babble; blab out a secret (*repeatedly*)
chlapać się [**khlah**-pahćh śhan] v. splash; splash about (*repeatedly*)
chlapanie [khlah-**pah**-ńe] n. splashing
chlapanina [khlah-pah-**ńee**-nah] f. foul weather; bad weather; nasty weather
chlapawica [khlah-pah-**vee**-tsah] f. foul weather; bad weather; nasty weather
chlapnąć [**khlahp**-nownćh] v. splash; splash about; soak; guzzle; blab; babble; blab out a secret
chlapnięcie [khlahp-**ńan**-ćhe] n. splash; blabbing out a secret
chlapu, chlapu [**khlah**-poo **khlah**-poo] exp.: drip, drip (wading sound)
chlasnąć [**khlah**-snownćh] v. whack; flap; slap; slash; babble; babble out secrets
chlast! [khlahst] excl.: slap!; flap!
chlastać [**khlahs**-tahćh] v. whack; flap; slap; slash; babble; babble out secrets (*repeatedly*)
chlastać się [**khlahs**-tahćh śhan] v. whack oneself; flap oneself; slash oneself (*repeatedly*)
chlastanie [khlahs-**tah**-ńe] n. whacking; flapping; slapping; slashing; babbling; babbling out secrets
chlaśnięcie [khlahśh-**ńan**-ćhe] n. whacking; flapping; slapping; slashing; babbling; babbling out secrets
chleb [khlep] m. bread; loaf; livelihood; corn
chleb z masłem [khlep z **mah**-swem] exp.: bread and butter
chleb powszedni [khlep po-**fshed**-ńee] exp.: daily bread
o chlebie i wodzie [o **khle**-bye ee **vo**-dźhe] exp.: on a bread-and-water diet
zarabiać na chleb [zah-**rah**-byahćh nah khlep] exp.: to earn one's daily bread; to make a living
chlebak [**khle**-bahk] m. haversack
chlebek [**khle**-bek] m. small loaf of bread; (nice, little) bread
chlebny [**khleb**-ni] adj.m. of bread; bread (ticket, oven, etc.)
chlebodajny [khle-bo-**dahy**-ni] adj.m. fertile; bread-giving
chlebodawca [khle-bo-**dahf**-tsah] m. employer; master
chlebowiec [khle-**bo**-vyets] m. bread fruit (Artocarpus)
chlebowy [khle-**bo**-vi] adj.m. of bread; bread (ticket, oven, etc.)
chlebuś [**khle**-boośh] m. (dear, little) bread

chlew [khlef] m. pigsty; pigpen
trzoda chlewna [tsho-dah khlev-nah] exp.: pigs; hogs; swine
chlewek [khle-vek] m. small pigpen
chlewiarka [khle-vyahr-kah] f. (woman) hog-breeder
chlewiarnia [khle-vyahr-ńah] f. piggery; pigsties; pig farm
chlewiarz [khle-vyahsh] m. hog-breeder; piggery manager
chlewik [khle-veek] m. (small) pigsty; pigpen
chlewmistrz [khlev-meestsh] m. hog-breeder; piggery manager
chlewmistrzyni [khlev-meest-shi-ńee] f. (woman) hog-breeder; piggery manager
chlewnia [khlev-ńah] f. pigsty; pigpen; hogs; pigs; swine
chlewny [khlev-ni] adj.m. of pigsty; of pigpen; of hogs; of pigs; of swine
chlip! chlip! [khleep khleep] exp.: lap! lap!
chlipać [khlee-pahćh] v. lap up; sob; whimper (*repeatedly*)
chlipanie [khlee-pah-ńe] n. lapping up; sobbing; whimpering
chlipliwie [khleep-lee-vye] adv. with a snivel; with a whimper
chlipliwy [khleep-lee-vi] adj.m. snivelling; whimpering
chlipnąć [khleep-nownćh] v. lap up; sob; whimper
chloantyt [khlo-ahn-tit] m. chloanthite (mineral)
chlor [khlor] m. chlorine
chloral [khlo-rahl] m. chloral
chloran [khlo-rahn] m. chlorate
chlorargiryt [khlo-rahr-gee-rit] m. silver chloride (mineral)
chlorator [khlo-rah-tor] m. (water) chlorination device
chlorawy [khlo-rah-vi] adj.m. chlorous (acid, etc.)
chlorek [khlo-rek] m. chloride
chlorella [khlo-rel-lah] f. chlorella
chloretyl [khlo-re-til] m. chloroethane
chlorkować [khlor-ko-vahćh] v. bleach (*repeatedly*)
chlorkowanie [khlor-ko-vah-ńe] n. bleaching
chloroamina [khlo-ro-ah-mee-nah] f. chloramine
chlorobenzen [khlo-ro-ben-zen] m. chlorobenzene
chlorofil [khlo-ro-feel] m. chlorophyll; chlorophyl
chlorofilowy [khlo-ro-fee-lo-vi] adj.m. chlorophyll (tooth-paste, body, corpuscle, etc)
chloroform [khlo-ro-form] m. chloroform
chloroformować [khlo-ro-for-mo-vahćh] v. chloroform (*repeatedly*)
chloroformowy [khlo-ro-for-mo-vi] adj.m. chloroform (anesthesia, etc.)
chloroliza [khlo-ro-lee-zah] f. chlorinolysis
chloromierz [khlo-ro-myesh] m. chlorometer
chloroplast [khlo-ro-plahst] m. chloroplast
chloroplastyna [khlo-ro-plahs-ti-nah] f. chloroplast protein
chlorosrebrowy [khlo-ro-sre-bro-vi] adj.m. silver-chloride (electrode, paper, etc.)
chlorotetracyklina [khlo-ro-tet-rah-tsik-lee-nah] f. chlorotetracycline (an antibiotic)
chlorować [khlo-ro-vahćh] v. chlorinate (*repeatedly*)
chlorowanie [khlo-ro-vah-ńe] n. chlorination
chlorowcować [khlo-rof-tso-vahćh] v. halogenate; replace hydrogen atoms with chlorine in organic compounds (*repeatedly*)
chlorowcowanie [khlo-rof-tso-vah-ńe] n. halogenation; replacement of hydrogen atoms with chlorine in organic compounds
chlorowcowodór [khlo-rof-tso-vo-door] m. hydrochloride
chlorowiec [khlo-ro-vyets] m. halogen
chlorownia [khlo-rov-ńah] f. water chlorination equipment; water chlorination station
chlorownica [khlo-rov-ńee-tsah] f. chlorinator
chlorownik [khlo-rov-ńeek] m. water chlorinator
chlorowodorek [khlo-ro-vo-do-rek] m. hydrochloride

chlorowodorowy [khlo-ro-vo-do-**ro**-vi] adj.m. hydrochloric (acid)
chlorowodór [khlo-ro-**vo**-door] m. hydrogen chloride
chlorowy [khlo-**ro**-vi] adj.m. chloric
chloroza [khlo-**ro**-zah] f. chlorosis; iron deficiency anemia; greensickness
chloryn [**khlo**-rin] m. chlorite
chlorynowy [khlo-ri-**no**-vi] adj.m. chlorous-acid-salt (bleaching, etc.)
chloryt [**khlo**-rit] m. chlorite (mineral)
chlorytyzacja [khlo-ri-ti-**zah**-tsyah] f. chloritization
chluba [**khloo**-bah] f. glory; pride; credit
to mu przynosi chlubę [to moo pshi-**no**-shee **khloo**-ban] exp.: this does him credit; this is to his credit
chlubić się [**khloo**-beećh śhan] v. glory (in); take pride (in); boast (of); flatter oneself (on) (*repeatedly*)
chlubienie się [khloo-**bye**-ńe śhan] n. taking pride (in); boasting (of)
chlubnie [**khloob**-ńe] adv. with glory; commendably; in a praiseworthy manner; with credit
chlubny [**khloob**-ni] adj.m. glorious; honorable; excellent; creditable
chlup! [khloop] excl.: plash!; splash!; flop!; lap!
chlupać [**khloo**-pahćh] v. splash; gurgle; gulp down; drink at one gulp (*repeatedly*)
chlupanie [khloo-**pah**-ńe] n. lap; lapping; bubbling
chlupnąć [**khloop**-nownćh] v. splash; gurgle; gulp down; drink at one gulp
chlupnięcie [khloop-**ńan**-ćhe] n. splash; splashing
chlupki [**khloop**-kee] adj.m. drippy; gurgling; splashy
chlupot [**khloo**-pot] m. lap; lapping; bubbling
chlupotać [khloo-**po**-tahćh] v. splash; gurgle; gulp down; drink at one gulp (*repeatedly*)
chlupotanie [khloo-po-**tah**-ńe] n. lap; lapping; bubbling
chlupotliwie [khloo-pot-**lee**-vye] adv. with a lapping sound; with a bubbling sound
chlupotliwy [khloo-pot-**lee**-vi] adj.m. lapping (sound, etc.); bubbling
chlusnąć [**khloos**-nownćh] v. splash; fling; spout; spurt
on chluszcze [on **khloosh**-che] exp.: he is splashing
chlust [khloost] excl.: swish!; whizz!; m. sound of splashing
chlustać [**khloo**-stahćh] v. spout; spurt; plunge; fling; flush; gush; spirt; splash (*repeatedly*)
on chlusta [on **khloos**-tah] exp.: he is splashing
chlustanie [khloo-**stah**-ńe] n. spout; spurt; plunge; fling; flush; gush; spirt; splash; gust
chluśnięcie [khloośh-**ńan**-ćhe] n. spout; spurt; gush; spirt; splash; gust (of rain, etc.)
chłam [khwahm] m. junk; trash; scrap; rubbish; shoddy (goods)
chłapać [**khwah**-pahćh] v. colloq: gasp; lap up; lap down; swill (*repeatedly*)
chłapanie [khwah-**pah**-ńe] n. colloq: swilling; gasping; lapping up
chłapnąć [**khwahp**-nownćh] v. colloq: gasp; lap up; lap down; swill
chłapnięcie [khwahp-**ńan**-ćhe] n. gasp; swash; lapping up
chłeptać [**khwep**-tahćh] v. lap up; lap down; swill (*repeatedly*)
chłeptanie [khwep-**tah**-ńe] n. lapping up; lapping down; swilling
chłodek [**khwo**-dek] m. (nice) cool (of the night, etc.)
chłodnawo [khwod-**nah**-vo] adv. rather coolly; somewhat chilly; on the cool side
chłodnawy [khwod-**nah**-vi] adj.m. coldish; rather cool; fresh; somewhat chilly; coolish
chłodnąć [**khwod**-nownćh] v. cool; freshen; grow chilly; become coolish; cool down (*repeatedly*)
chłodnia [**khwod**-ńah] f. refrigerating machine; freezer; cold storage plant; cooler; meat-safe; cold storage
chłodniarz [**khwod**-ńahsh] m. refrigeration engineer

chłodnica [khwod-ńee-tsah] f. (car) radiator; cooler
chłodnica ulowa [khwod-ńee-tsah oo-lo-vah] exp.: cellular radiator; honeycomb radiator
chłodnicowiec [khwod-ńee-tso-vyets] m. refrigeration engineer (technician)
chłodnictwo [khwod-ńeets-tfo] n. refrigeration engineering
chłodniczy [khwod-ńee-chi] adj.m. refrigerating; cooling; refrigeration (equipment, etc.)
chłodnieć [khwod-ńećh] v. cool (down); become cool (*repeatedly*)
chłodnięcie [khwod-ńan-ćhe] n. cooling (down); becoming cool
chłodnik [khwod-ńeek] m. cold borscht; cold soup; cold beverage
chłodniowiec [khwod-ńo-vyets] m. refrigeration ship
chłodniowy [khwod-ńo-vi] adj.m. of a refrigerating machine; of cold storage
chłodno [khwod-no] adv. coolly; with reserve; reservedly
chłodno uprzejmy [khwod-no oo-pshey-mi] exp.: reservedly polite
jest chłodno [yest khwod-no] exp.: it is cool
jest mi chłodno [yest mee khwod-no] exp.: I am (I feel) cold
chłodnorost [khwod-no-rost] m. microtherm (plant)
chłodny [khwod-ni] adj.m. cool; reserved; tepid; wintry; chilly
chłodzący [khwo-dzown-tsi] adj.m. cooling; refrigerating; frigorific
chłodzenie [khwo-dze-ńe] n. cooling system; refrigeration
chłodziarka [khwo-dźhahr-kah] f. refrigerator; refrigerating machine
chłodzić [khwo-dźheećh] v. cool; chill; refresh; refrigerate; damp (*repeatedly*)
chłodzić się [khwo-dźheećh śhan] v. cool; be cooling; refresh oneself (*repeatedly*)
chłodziwo [khwo-dźhee-vo] n. cooling agent (fluid or gas); refrigerating agent; refrigerant; frigorific mixture
chłodzony [khwo-dzo-ni] adj.m. cooled
chłodzony wodą [khwo-dzo-ni vo-down] exp.: water-cooled
chłonąć [khwo-nownćh] v. absorb; devour; drink in; inhale; imbibe; take in; breathe in (*repeatedly*)
chłonięcie [khwo-ńan-ćhe] n. absorption; inhalation; imbibition
chłonka [khwon-kah] f. lymph
chłonnie [khwon-ńe] adv. absorbingly
chłonność [khwon-nośhćh] f. absorbency; power of absorption
chłonny [khwon-ni] adj.m. absorbent; absorptive; absorbing; receptive
chłop [khwop] m. peasant; country man; villager; man; slang: husband; fiance; lover; sweetheart
chłopi [khwo-pee] pl. exp.: the peasantry
chłopie! [khwo-pye] excl.: man!
równy chłop [roov-ni khwop] exp.: regular guy; a real good sort
sto chłopa [sto khwo-pah] exp.: a hundred men
chłopaczek [khwo-pah-chek] m. boy; kid
chłopaczkowaty [khwo-pahch-ko-vah-ti] adj.m. boyish
chłopaczyna [khwo-pah-chi-nah] m. laddie (Brit.); hapless boy
chłopaczysko [khwo-pah-chis-ko] m. or n. (big, tough) boy; lad; youth; young man; youngster; urchin
chłopak [khwo-pahk] m. boy; lad; youth; young man; youngster; urchin; office boy; slang: knave; jack
chłopak na posyłki [khwo-pahk nah po-siw-kee] exp.: errand-boy
mój chłopak [mooy khwo-pahk] exp.: my boyfriend
chłopcowaty [khwop-tso-vah-ti] adj.m. boyish
chłopczyca [khwop-chi-tsah] f. hoyden; tomboy; a bold, boisterous girl
chłopczyk [khwop-chik] m. (small, nice) boy; lad; youngster; stripling; urchin; young fellow; fiance; lover
chłopczykowaty [khwop-chi-ko-vah-ti] adj.m. boyish

chłopczyna [khwop-**chi**-nah] m. laddie (Brit.); hapless boy
chłopczyński [khwop-**chiń**-skee] adj.m. lad's; youngster's
chłopczysko [khwop-**chis**-ko] m. kid; lad; youngster
chłopeczka [khwo-**pech**-kah] f. wide peasant skirt
chłopek [**khwo**-pek] m. hapless peasant; yokel; countryman; (small, backwoods) farmer
chłopiątko [khwo-**pyownt**-ko] n. very pretty little kid
chłopiec [**khwo**-pyets] m. boy; lad; youngster; stripling; urchin; young fellow; fiance; lover
chłopieć [**khwo**-pyećh] v. become a peasant (*repeatedly*)
chłopię [**khwo**-pyan] n. boy; lad; youngster; stripling; urchin; young fellow; kid
chłopięco [khwo-**pyan**-tso] adv. like a boy
chłopięctwo [khwo-**pyants**-tfo] n. boyhood
chłopięcy [khwo-**pyan**-tsi] adj.m. boyish; boy's; boys'; puerile
po chłopięcemu [po khwo-pyan-**tse**-moo] exp.: like a young boy
wiek chłopięcy [vyek khwo-**pyan**-tsi] exp.: boyhood
chłopina [khwo-**pee**-nah] m. hapless peasant; yokel; countryman; (small, backwoods) farmer
chłopisko [khwo-**pees**-ko] n. poor guy; great big guy
chłopka [**khwop**-kah] f. peasant woman; country style dress with wide skirt and fitted bodice
chłopoman [khwo-**po**-mahn] m. exalted idealizer of the peasantry
chłopomania [khwo-po-**mah**-ńyah] f. exalted idealization of the peasantry
chłopomański [khwo-po-**mahń**-skee] adj.m. of exalted idealization of the peasantry
chłopomańsko [khwo-po-**mahń**-sko] adv. with exalted idealization of the peasantry
chłopomaństwo [khwo-po-**mahń**-stfo] n. an exalted idealization of the peasantry
chłoporobotnik [khwo-po-ro-**bot**-ńeek] m. part-time farmer and part-time industrial worker
chłopowina [khwo-po-**vee**-nah] m. poor, worn out man
chłop-robotnik [khwop ro-**bot**-ńeek] m. part-time farmer and part-time industrial worker
chłopski [**khwop**-skee] adj.m. peasant (household, etc.); rustic; boorish; peasant-like
chłopski rozum [**khwop**-skee **ro**-zoom] exp.: common sense
po chłopsku [po **khwop**-skoo] exp.: peasant fashion; like a boor; with the rudeness of a rustic
chłopskość [**khwop**-skośhćh] f. rusticity; peasant origin; the rudeness of a rustic
chłopstwo [**khwop**-stfo] n. peasantry
chłoptaś [**khwop**-tahśh] m. diminutive of boy; see: **chłopiec**
chłoptyś [**khwop**-tiśh] m. diminutive of boy; see: **chłopiec**
chłopyszek [khwo-**pi**-shek] m. diminutive of boy; see: **chłopiec**
chłopyś [**khwo**-piśh] m. diminutive of boy; see: **chłopiątko**
chłosnąć [**khwos**-nownćh] v. flog; lash; swish; castigate; scathe
chłosta [**khwos**-tah] f. lashing; flogging; whipping; the lash
kara chłosty [**kah**-rah **khwos**-ti] exp.: lash
chłostać [**khwos**-tahćh] v. flog; whip; lash; swish; castigate; scathe; lay on (*repeatedly*)
chłostanie [khwo-**stah**-ńe] n. lashing; flogging; whipping
chłód [khwoot] m. cold; freshness; coolness; iciness; shiver; chilly atmosphere; colloq: distance of manner; frigidness; tepidity
chłyst [khwist] m. young stag
chłystek [**khwis**-tek] m. squirt; whippersnapper; an insignificant but presumptuous person
chmara [**khmah**-rah] f. swarm; host; countless numbers
chmara komarów [**khmah**-rah ko-**mah**-roof] exp.: clouds of mosquitos
chmiel [khmyel] m. hop; hops; the vapors of liquor

chmielarnia [khmye-lahr-ńah] f. hop-field; hop-garden
chmielarski [khmye-**lahr**-skee] adj.m. of hop-growing
chmielarstwo [khmye-**lahr**-stfo] n. hop-growing
chmielarz [**khmye**-lahsh] m. hop-grower
chmielenie [khmye-**le**-ńe] n. flavoring with hop
chmielić [**khmye**-leećh] v. hop; flavor with hop (*repeatedly*)
chmielik [**khmye**-leek] m. self-heal (plant)
chmielina [khmye-**lee**-nah] f. hop-bine; bine; twining stem of hop
chmielnik [**khmyel**-ńeek] m. hop-field; hop-garden; see: **chmielarnia**
chmielny [**khmyel**-ni] adj.m. hop (kiln, etc.); drunk; m. drunkard; drunk
chmielobranie [khmye-lo-**brah**-ńe] n. harvest of hop
chmielograb [khmye-**lo**-grahp] m. variety of birch tree; Ostrya caprinifolia
chmielować [khmye-**lo**-vahćh] v. hop; flavor with hops (*repeatedly*)
chmielowanie [khmye-lo-**vah**-ńe] n. flavoring with hops
chmielowy [khmye-**lo**-vi] adj.m. of hops; of hop
chmura [**khmoo**-rah] f. cloud (of dust, etc.); swarm; swarms
chmury [**khmoo**-ri] pl. clouds; cloudscape
pod chmury [pot **khmoo**-ri] exp.: sky-high
z wielkiej chmury mały deszcz [z **vyel**-key **khmoo**-ri **mah**-wi deshch] exp.: much cry and little wool
chmureczka [khmoo-**rech**-kah] f. (nice, little) cloudlet
chmurka [**khmoor**-kah] f. cloudlet
chmurki [**khmoor**-kee] pl. fleecy clouds
chmurnawy [khmoor-**nah**-vi] adj.m. partly cloudy; somewhat gloom
chmurnie [**khmoor**-ńe] adv. cloudily; gloomily
chmurnieć [**khmoor**-ńećh] v. become overcast; darken; assume gloomy appearance (*repeatedly*)
chmurno [**khmoor**-no] adv. cloudily; gloomily
chmurny [**khmoor**-ni] adj.m. cloudy; clouded (sky, etc.); gloomy; sullen; dark; ominous; high-flown
chmurowy [khmoo-**ro**-vi] adj.m. of a cloud; (flight, etc.) in a cloud
chmurzyć [**khmoo**-zhićh] v. overcast; cloud; darken (*repeatedly*)
chmurzyć czoło [**khmoo**-zhićh **cho**-wo] exp.: frown; knit the brow
chmurzyć się [**khmoo**-zhićh śhan] v. become cloudy; become overcast; darken; cloud up; frown; scowl; assume a sullen look (*repeatedly*)
chmurzysko [khmoo-**zhis**-ko] n. (big, black) cloud
chmyz [khmis] m. midget; dwarf
chochelka [kho-**khel**-kah] f. (small, nice) ladle; dipper; scoop
chochla [**khokh**-lah] f. ladle; dipper; scoop
chochlik [**khokh**-leek] m. sprite; imp; brownie; gnome; hobgoblin
chochlik drukarski [**khokh**-leek droo-**kahr**-skee] exp.: the printer's imp; the demon of misprints
chochlikowaty [kho-khlee-ko-**vah**-ti] adj.m. impish; gnomish
chochoł [**kho**-khow] m. straw-cover of plants; capsheaf; tuft of hair
chociaż [kho-ćhahsh] conj. albeit; even if; though; tho'; while; at least; even if; at least; if only
choć [khoćh] conj. albeit; even if; though, tho'; while; at least; even if; at least; if only
choć do jutra [khoćh do **yoo**-trah] exp.: at least till tomorrow
choć nie wiem jak [khoćh ńe vyem yahk] exp.: no matter how
choć zginę [khoćh **zgee**-nan] exp.: even if I were to suffer the loss of my life; even if it comes (came) to losing my life; even if I were to die
choćby [**khodźh**-bi] conj. albeit; even if; though; tho'; while; as much as; at least; even
choćby nawet [**khodźh**-bi **nah**-vet] exp.: even though
chodaczek [kho-**dah**-chek] m. (small,

child's) clog; moccasin
chodaczkowy [kho-dahch-**ko**-vi] adj.m. clogs-wearing
szlachta chodaczkowa [shlahkh-tah kho-dahch-**ko**-vah] exp.: the minor nobility
chodak [**kho**-dahk] m. clog; moccasin
chodliwość [khod-**lee**-vośhćh] f. salability
chodliwy [khod-**lee**-vi] adj.m. saleable; salable
chodnica [khod-**ńee**-tsah] f. line stretched under sail's boom for support of sailor's feet
chodniczek [khod-**ńee**-chek] m. pathway in a garden; runner (carpet)
chodnik [**khod**-ńeek] m. sidewalk; pathway; carpet; stair carpet; footpath; pavement; boardwalk; gangway; entry (to a mine)
chodnikowiec [khod-ńee-**ko**-vyets] m. (mine) header
chodnikowy [khod-ńee-**ko**-vi] adj.m. pavement; paving; m. (mine) header
płyta chodnikowa [**pwi**-tah khod-ńee-**ko**-vah] exp.: flagstone
chodny [**khod**-ni] adj.m. (body parts) used for walking
chodu [**kho**-doo] excl.: run!; go away!; move!; get lost!
chodząco [kho-**dzown**-tso] adv. while walking
chodzący [kho-**dzown**-tsi] adj.m. walking
chodząca encyklopedia [kho-**dzown**-tsah en-tsi-klo-**pe**-dyah] exp.: walking encyclopedia
chodzenie [kho-**dze**-ńe] n. walking; running (errands, etc.)
chodzić [**kho**-dźheećh] v. go; walk; move; creep; pace; attend; come; tread; stalk (*repeatedly*)
chodzi o to, czy [**kho**-dźhee o to chi] exp.: the question is whether
chodzi o życie [**kho**-dźhee o **zhi**-ćhe] exp.: life is at stake
chodzić do szkoły [**kho**-dźheećh do **shko**-wi] exp.: to go to school
chodzić na wykłady [**kho**-dźheećh nah vi-**kwah**-di] exp.: to attend lectures
chodzić na medycynę [**kho**-dźheećh nah me-di-**tsi**-nan] exp.: to study medicine
chodzić koło czegoś [**kho**-dźheećh **ko**-wo **che**-gośh] exp.: to busy oneself with something
chodzić w czymś [**kho**-dźheećh f chimśh] exp.: to wear something
chodzić w tango [**kho**-dźheećh f **tahn**-go] exp.: slang: to cheat on one's husband (mob jargon)
chodzić za kimś [**kho**-dźheećh zah keemśh] exp.: to follow (to shadow) somebody; to keep an eye on somebody
chodź! [khoćh] exp.: come on!; let's go!
chodźcie! [**khoćh**-ćhe] exp.: pl. let's go!
nie o to chodzi [ńe o to **kho**-dźhee] exp.: that's beside the point; that's neither here nor there
o co chodzi? [o tso **kho**-dźhee] exp.: what is the matter? what is it? what's the trouble?
o ile o mnie chodzi [o ee-le o mńe **kho**-dźhee] exp.: as far as I am concerned
o to chodzi [o to **kho**-dźhee] exp.: that's the thing; that's the point; that's it; that's what I mean; that's the jest of it
o to właśnie chodzi [o to **vwahśh**-ńe **kho**-dźhee] exp.: that's the very thing; that's just the point
chodzik [**kho**-dźheek] m. loiterer; pendulum clock
chodzony [kho-**dzo**-ni] m. dance (at walking pace)
choina [kho-ee-nah] f. fir; pine; pine wood
choineczka [kho-ee-**nech**-kah] f. little spruce; young fir; nice Christmas tree
choinka [kho-een-kah] f. little spruce; young fir; Christmas tree; a party with a Christmas tree
choinkowy [kho-een-**ko**-vi] adj.m. of little spruce; of young fir; Christmas-tree (trimmings, etc.)
choinowy [khoy-**no**-vi] adj.m. of

spruce; of fir; of pine; pine (forest, etc.)
choinówka [khoy-**noof**-kah] f. pine-bud moth
choja [**kho**-yah] f. slang: spruce; pine tree
chojaczek [kho-**yah**-chek] m. small spruce; little pine tree
chojak [**kho**-yahk] m. spruce; pine tree
chojar [**kho**-yahr] m. big spruce tree; large pine tree
chojniak [**khoy**-ńahk] m. young spruce forest; young pine thicket
chojractwo [khoy-**rahts**-tfo] n. bluster; swagger; bounce
chojrak [**khoy**-rahk] m. daredevil
udawać chojraka [oo-**dah**-vahćh khoy-**rah**-kah] exp.: to swagger
chojrakować [khoy-rah-**ko**-vahćh] v. swagger; pretend to be brave (*repeatedly*)
cholekinaza [kho-le-kee-**nah**-zah] f. a medicine regulating metabolic processes
cholera [kho-**le**-rah] f. cholera; vulg.: rage; excl.: damn!; damn it! damnation!; hell! the devil!; son of a bitch!
do cholery z tym! [do kho-**le**-ri s tim] exp.: colloq: to hell with that!
idź do cholery! [eećh do kho-**le**-ri] exp.: colloq: go to hell!
jak cholera [yahk kho-**le**-rah] exp.: colloq: like sin; like the devil; jolly well
jak jasna cholera [yahk **yahs**-nah kho-**le**-rah] exp.: colloq: like the very devil
po jaką cholerę? [po **yah**-kown kho-**le**-ran] exp.: colloq: what the hell for?
cholernie [kho-**ler**-ńe] adv. vulg.: awfully; cursedly; like hell; like the devil; like the deuce
cholernik [kho-**ler**-ńeek] m. spitfire; vulg.: son of a bitch
cholerny [kho-**ler**-ni] adj.m. vulg.: bloody; damned; devilish; pesky; awful; terrible; thumping; thundering; strapping; mighty
cholerować [kho-le-**ro**-vahćh] v. slang: curse (using the word "cholera"); bitch; holler in a vulgar manner; complain in a nasty way (*repeatedly*)
cholerowy [kho-le-**ro**-vi] adj.m. cholera (symptoms, etc.)
cholerstwo [kho-**ler**-stfo] n. aggravation; irritant; nuisance
choleryczka [kho-le-**rich**-kah] f. woman spitfire; irascible woman
cholerycznie [kho-le-**rich**-ńe] adv. with anger; with fiery temper
choleryczny [kho-le-**rich**-ni] adj.m. choleric; fiery; choleraic; bilious; angry; irate; m. cholera patient
choleryk [kho-**le**-rik] m. spitfire; irascible man
choleryna [kho-le-**ri**-nah] f. cholerine (heavy bacterial infection)
cholesterol [kho-les-**te**-rol] m. cholesterol
cholesterolowy [kho-les-te-ro-**lo**-vi] adj.m. of cholesterol
cholesteryna [kho-les-te-**ri**-nah] f. cholesterol
cholewa [kho-**le**-vah] f. boot; top (of knee-boot)
buty z cholewami [**boo**-ti s kho-le-**vah**-mee] exp.: knee-boots; top boots
robić z gęby cholewę [**ro**-beećh z **gan**-bi kho-**le**-van] exp.: to fail to keep one's word; to make empty statements
cholewka [kho-**lef**-kah] f. shoe top; hose-top; leg of a stocking; small boot
cholewkarski [kho-lef-**kahr**-skee] adj.m. of leather-stitching
cholewkarstwo [kho-lef-**kahr**-stfo] n. leather-stitching; producing tops of knee-boot; boot making
cholewkarz [kho-**lef**-kahsh] m. leather-stitcher; producer tops of knee-boot
chołodziec [kho-**wo**-dźhets] m. cold borscht; cooling soup
chomątko [kho-**mownt**-ko] n. small horse-collar; clip; hanger
chomąto [kho-**mown**-to] n. horse-collar; clip; hanger; stirrup
chomik [**kho**-meek] m. hamster; slang: (man) pack rat
chomikarski [kho-mee-**kahr**-skee] adj.m. slang: saving unnecessary

junk
chomikarstwo [kho-mee-**kahr**-stfo] n. slang: gathering unnecessary junk
chomikować [kho-mee-**ko**-vahćh] v. slang: gather unnecessary junk (*repeatedly*)
chomikowaty [kho-mee-ko-**vah**-ti] adj.m. hamster-like; colloq: like a pack rat
chomikowate [kho-mee-ko-**vah**-te] pl. the Cricetidae family
chomikowy [kho-mee-**ko**-vi] adj.m. hamster's
chondra [**khon**-drah] f. chondrule; chondritic crystalline (limestone) structure
chondriom [**khon**-dryom] m. chondriome; chondrioma
chondriosom [khon-**dryo**-som] m. chondriosome; mitochondrion
chondroblast [khon-**dro**-blahst] m. chondroblast
chondrocyt [khon-**dro**-tsit] m. cell formed by chondroblasts
chondrologia [khon-dro-**lo**-gyah] f. study of cartilages; chondrology
chondryt [**khon**-drit] m. chondrite
chopinista [sho-pe-**ńees**-tah] m. pianist specializing in Chopin's music
chopinistka [sho-pe-**ńeest**-kah] f. (woman) pianist specializing in Chopin's music
chopinistyka [sho-pe-**ńees**-ti-kah] f. study and specialization in Chopin's music
chopinolog [sho-pe-**no**-log] m. student of Chopin's music
chopinologia [sho-pe-no-**lo**-gyah] f. study of Chopin's music
chopinologiczny [sho-pe-no-lo-**geech**-ni] adj.m. of (the study of) Chopin's music
chopinowski [sho-pe-**nof**-skee] adj.m. of Chopin; of Chopin's music; composed by Chopin
chora [**kho**-rah] adj. f. sick; ill; ailing; infirm; unwell; sore; lame; crazy; f. patient; invalid (woman)
chorał [**kho**-rahw] m. chorale
chorałowy [kho-rah-**wo**-vi] adj.m. chorale (tune, etc.)
chorągiew [kho-**rown**-gef] f. flag; standard; ensign; troop
chorągiewka [kho-rown-**gef**-kah] f. pennon; banderole; weathercock; paper flag; web of a feather
zwinąć chorągiewkę [**zvee**-nownćh kho-rown-**gef**-kan] exp.: to back out; to beat a retreat; to veer around; to change one's mind; to waver; to be inconsistent
chorągiewny [kho-rown-**gev**-ni] adj.m. of a flag (stitch)
chorągwiany [kho-rowng-**vyah**-ni] adj.m. of a flag; flag (staff, colors, etc.)
szlachta chorągwiana [**shlahkh**-tah kho-rowng-**vyah**-nah] exp.: yeomanry
chorążostwo [kho-rown-**zhos**-tfo] n. office of standard-bearer; the rank of ensign
chorąży [kho-**rown**-zhi] m. standard-bearer; ensign
chorążyna [kho-rown-**zhi**-nah] f. wife of standard-bearer; wife of ensign
chorea [kho-**re**-ah] f. chorea; St. Vitus's dance
chorej [**kho**-rey] m. choree; choreus
choreograf [kho-re-**o**-grahf] m. choreographer
choreografia [kho-re-o-**grah**-fyah] f. choreography
choreograficznie [kho-re-o-grah-**feech**-ńe] adv. for stage dancing; choreographically
choreograficzny [kho-re-o-grah-**feech**-ni] adj.m. choreographic(al)
choreografka [kho-re-o-**grahf**-kah] f. (woman) choreographer
choreolog [kho-re-**o**-log] m. student of science and history of choreography
choreologia [kho-re-o-**lo**-gyah] f. studies and history of choreography
choriamb [**khor**-yahmp] m. choriamb
chorion [**khor**-yon] m. chorion
choroba [kho-**ro**-bah] f. sickness; illness; disease; affection; complaint; slang: = **cholera**
choroba angielska [kho-**ro**-bah ahn-**gel**-skah] exp.: rickets
choroba morska [kho-**ro**-bah

mors-kah] exp.: seasickness
choroba umysłowa [kho-**ro**-bah oo-mi-**swo**-vah] exp.: mentaldeficiency; insanity; mental illness
choroba zawodowa [kho-**ro**-bah zah-vo-**do**-vah] exp.: occupational disease
złożony chorobą [zwo-**zho**-ni kho-**ro**-bown] exp.: bedridden
chorobliwie [kho-ro-**blee**-vye] adv. morbidly; sickly; unhealthily
chorobliwość [kho-ro-**blee**-vośhćh] f. morbidity; sickliness
chorobliwy [kho-ro-**blee**-vi] adj.m. morbid; sickly; pathological
chorobotwórczo [kho-ro-bo-**tfoor**-cho] adv. pathogenetically; morbifically
chorobotwórczość [kho-ro-bo-**tfoor**-chośhćh] f. pathogenesis; pathogenesy; pathogeny
chorobotwórczy [kho-ro-bo-**tfoor**-chi] adj.m. pathogenetic; pathogenic
chorobowe [kho-ro-**bo**-ve] n. sick benefit
chorobowo [kho-ro-**bo**-vo] adv. by sickness; because of sickness
chorobowość [kho-ro-**bo**-vośhćh] f. frequency of sickness
chorobowy [kho-ro-**bo**-vi] adj.m. morbid; sickness (leave, etc.)
być na chorobowym [bićh nah kho-ro-**bo**-vim] exp.: to be on sick leave
urlop chorobowy [**oor**-lop kho-ro-**bo**-vi] exp.: sick leave
zasiłek chorobowy [zah-**śhee**-wek kho-ro-**bo**-vi] exp.: sick benefit
chorografia [kho-ro-**grah**-fyah] f. chorography; art of mapping
chorograficzny [kho-ro-grah-**feech**-ni] adj.m. chorographic
chorolog [kho-**ro**-log] m. chorologist
chorologia [kho-ro-**lo**-gyah] f. chorology
chorologiczny [kho-ro-lo-**geech**-ni] adj.m. chorological
chorować [kho-**ro**-vahćh] v. be ill; be afflicted; be ailing; be laid up; be unwell; suffer (from); be crazy (about travelling, etc.) (*repeatedly*)
chorowanie [kho-ro-**vah**-ńe] n. illness; illnesses; sickness
chorowitość [kho-ro-**vee**-tośhćh] f. sickliness; sickly constitution
chorowity [kho-ro-**vee**-ti] adj.m. sickly; sickly-looking; cranky; pimping; unhealthy
choróbsko [kho-**roop**-sko] n. nasty and protracted sickness
chory [**kho**-ri] adj.m. sick; ill; ailing; infirm; unwell; sore; lame; crazy; m. patient; invalid
chory z miłości [**kho**-ri z mee-**wośh**-ćhee] exp.: lovesick
izba chorych [**eez**-bah **kho**-rikh] exp.: sick-ward; sick bay; infirmary
lista chorych [**lees**-tah **kho**-rikh] exp.: sick list
mieć chore gardło [myećh **kho**-re **gahrd**-wo] exp.: to have a sore throat
mieć chore płuca [myećh **kho**-re **pwoo**-tsah] exp.: to have bad lungs
obłożnie chory [ob-**wozh**-ńe **kho**-ri] exp.: seriously ill
chorzeć [**kho**-zhećh] v. be sick; be ill (*repeatedly*)
chowacz [**kho**-vahch] m. variety of beetle (Ceuthorrhynchus)
chować [**kho**-vahćh] v. hide; put away; tuck away; lay away; stow away; shove away; conceal; duck; bring up; educate; breed; rear; rise; keep; bury; entomb; preserve; maintain (*repeatedly*)
chować głowę w piasek [**kho**-vahćh **gwo**-van f **pyah**-sek] exp.: to hide one's head in the sand
chować się [**kho**-vahćh śhan] v. hide; hide oneself; remain in hiding; conceal oneself; keep out of sight; be brought up; be educated; be bred; be reared; be kept; be buried (*repeatedly*)
chować się w zbytku [**kho**-vahćh śhan v **zbit**-koo] exp.: to grow up in luxury; to be brought up in luxury
chowaj Boże! [**kho**-vahy **bo**-zhe] excl.: colloq: God forbid!
chowanie [kho-**vah**-ńe] n. concealment; education

chowanka [kho-**vahn**-kah] f. playing hide-and-seek
chowany [kho-**vah**-ni] adj.m. hidden; m. hide-and-seek
bawić się w chowanego [**bah**-veećh śhan f kho-vah-**ne**-go] exp.: to play hide-and-seek
chód [khoot] m. gait; walk; pace; movement; motion; move (of a figure on the chessboard)
chodu! [**kho**-doo] exp.: excl.: get lost!; run!; go away!; move!
chody [**kho**-di] pl. paths (of wild game); connections
na chodzie [nah **kho**-dźhe] exp.: in action; in working order
mieć chody [myećh **kho**-di] exp.: to have connections
chór [khoor] m. choir; choral society; chorus; host; organ-loft; gallery
chórem [**khoo**-rem] exp.: in chorus
chóralistyka [khoo-rah-**lee**-sti-kah] f. study of chorus' problems and arrangements
chóralnie [khoo-**rahl**-ńe] adv. in chorus
chóralny [khoo-**rahl**-ni] adj.m. choral; concerted
chórmistrz [**khoor**-meestsh] m. choirmaster; director of a choir
chórowy [khoo-**ro**-vi] adj.m. of a choir
chórzysta [khoo-**zhis**-tah] m. chorister
chórzystka [khoo-**zhis**-tkah] f. chorus-girl; chorine (a young woman who sings and dances)
chów [khoof] m. raising; breeding (of animals); growing (of plants)
domowego chowu [do-mo-**ve**-go **kho**-voo] exp.: home-grown; homebred
chrabąszcz [**khrah**-bownshch] m. beetle; May-bug; cockchafer
chram [khrahm] m. pagan temple
chrapa [**khrah**-pah] f. nostril
chrapać [**khrah**-pahćh] v. snore; snort; wheeze; rattle in one's throat (*repeatedly*)
chrapanie [khrah-**pah**-ńe] n. snore
chrapka [**khrahp**-kah] f. wish; desire; inclination
mieć chrapkę na [myećh **khrahp**-kan nah] exp.: to feel like; to want; to itch for
chrapliwie [khrah-**plee**-vye] adv. hoarsely; in a harsh voice; in a grating voice
chrapliwość [khrah-**plee**-vośhćh] f. hoarseness; croaking voice; asperity of a voice
chrapliwy [khrah-**plee**-vi] adj.m. raucous; hoarse; husky; grating
chrapnąć [**khrahp**-nownćh] v. snore; snort; wheeze; rattle in one's throat
chrapnięcie [khrahp-**ńan**-ćhe] n. snore; wheeze
chrapowaty [khrah-po-**vah**-ti] adj.m. raucous; hoarse; husky; grating
chrestomatia [khres-to-**mah**-tyah] f. chrestomathy
chrobot [**khro**-bot] m. scratching; scraping; creaking; grating
chrobotać [khro-**bo**-tahćh] v. creak; grate; scratch; scrape (*repeatedly*)
chrobotanie [khro-bo-**tah**-ńe] n. creaking; scratching; grating
chrobotliwie [khro-bo-**tlee**-vye] adv. creakingly; scratchingly
chrobotliwy [khro-bo-**tlee**-vi] adj.m. creaking; scratching; grating
chrobotnąć [khro-**bo**-tnownćh] v. creak; grate; scratch; scrape
chrobry [**khrob**-ri] adj.m. mighty; brave; valiant; gallant; intrepid
Bolesław Chrobry [bo-**les**-wahf **khrob**-ri] exp.: Boleslaus the Brave; Boleslaus the Great
chrom [khrom] m. metal: chrome; chromium (atomic number 24); colloq: leather: box-calf
chromać [**khro**-mahćh] v. limp; halt; hobble; be deficient (*repeatedly*)
chromal [**khro**-mahl] m. chromium alloy
chromanie [khro-**mah**-ńe] n. lameness; halt; hobble
chromatofor [khro-mah-**to**-for] m. chromatophore
chromatograf [khro-mah-**to**-grahph] m. chromatograph
chromatografia [khro-mah-to-**grah**-fyah] f. chromatography
chromatograficznie [khro-mah-to-

chromatographically
chromatograficzny [khro-mah-to-grah-**feech**-ni] adj.m. chromatographic
chromatoliza [khro-mah-to-**lee**-zah] f. chromatolysis
chromatopsja [khro-mah-**top**-syah] f. chromatopsia; ability to notice and distinguish colors
chromatotechnika [khro-mah-to-**tekh**-ńee-kah] f. chemical dyeing
chromatron [khro-**mah**-tron] m. color-picture tube in a television set
chromatycznie [khro-mah-**tich**-ńe] adv. chromatically
chromatyczny [khro-mah-**tich**-ni] adj.m. chromatic
skala chromatyczna [skah-lah khro-mah-**tich**-nah] exp.: chromatic scale
chromatyka [khro-**mah**-ti-kah] f. chromatology; science of colors
chromatyna [khro-mah-**ti**-nah] f. chromatin
chromatyzm [khro-**mah**-tizm] m. chromatism; chromatic harmony
chromian [**khro**-myahn] m. chromate
chromianować [khro-myah-**no**-vahćh] v. chromize (*repeatedly*)
chromianowanie [khro-myah-no-**vah**-ńe] n. chromate treatment; chromate coating (of metal)
chromieć [**khro**-myećh] v. become lame; limp; be poor and ineffectual (*repeatedly*)
chromit [**khro**-meet] m. chromite (mineral)
chromocynkografia [khro-mo-tsin-ko-**grah**-fyah] f. photo-mechanical method of making zinc plates for color printing
chromodruk [khro-**mo**-drook] m. color-print; color-printing
chromofor [khro-**mo**-for] m. chromophore
chromogen [khro-**mo**-gen] m. chromogen
chromogeniczny [khro-mo-ge-**ńeech**-ni] adj.m. chromogenic
chromolić [khro-**mo**-leećh] v. vulg.: slight; treat with disregard; disdain; scorn; depreciate; make light of; neglect; ignore (*repeatedly*)
chromolitografia [khro-mo-lee-to-**grah**-fyah] f. chromolithography; chromolithograph; chromo
chromonikiel [khro-mo-**ńee**-kel] m. chrome-nickel alloy
chromonikielina [khro-mo-ńee-ke-**lee**-nah] f. corrosion-resistent chrome-nickel alloy used in high temperatures
chromoniklowy [khro-mo-ńee-**klo**-vi] adj.m. chrome-nickel (alloy, etc.)
chromoplast [khro-**mo**-plahst] m. chromoplast
chromoproteid [khro-mo-pro-**te**-eet] m. chromoprotein
chromosfera [khro-mo-**sfe**-rah] f. chromosphere
chromosferyczny [khro-mo-sfe-**rich**-ni] adj.m. chromospheric
chromosom [khro-**mo**-som] m. chromosome
chromosomalny [khro-mo-so-**mahl**-ni] adj.m. chromosomal
chromosomowy [khro-mo-so-**mo**-vi] adj.m. chromosomal (characteristic number, etc.)
chromota [khro-**mo**-tah] f. lameness
chromotaksja [khro-mo-**tah**-ksyah] f. directional movement of an insect caused by a color-stimulus
chromotropizm [khro-mo-**tro**-peezm] m. chromotropism
chromotypia [khro-mo-**ti**-pyah] f. chromotypy; chromotypography
chromować [khro-**mo**-vahćh] v. chrome; plate with chromium; treat with chromium (*repeatedly*)
chromowanie [khro-mo-**vah**-ńe] n. chromium plating; treating with chromium
chromowany [khro-mo-**vah**-ni] adj.m. chromium-plated; treated with chromium
chromowiec [khro-**mo**-vyets] m. one of the heavy metals (chromium, molybdenum, tungsten)
chromowy [khro-**mo**-vi] adj.m. chromic; chromous
skóra chromowa [skoo-rah khro-**mo**-vah] exp.: box-calf
chromozom [khro-**mo**-zom] m. chromosome; see: **chromosom**
chromozomalny [khro-mo-zo-**mahl**-

ni] adj.m. chromosomal
chromozomowy [khro-mo-zo-**mo**-vi] adj.m. chromosomal
chromy [**khro**-mi] adj.m. limping; lame; m. lame man
chroma [**khro**-mah] adj. f. limping (woman); f. lame woman
chronicznie [khro-**ńeech**-ńe] adv. chronically
chroniczny [khro-**ńeech**-ni] adj.m. chronic; habitual
chronić [**khro**-ńeećh] v. shelter; protect; guard; shield; fence; give refuge; prevent (*repeatedly*)
chroniony patentem [khro-**ńo**-ni pah-**ten**-tem] exp.: patented
chronić się [**khro**-ńeećh śhan] v. shelter oneself (from); protect oneself (against); guard oneself (against); take refuge (from) (*repeatedly*)
chronienie [khro-**ńe**-ńe] n. sheltering; guarding
chronik [**khro**-ńeek] m. person chronically ill
chronograf [khro-**no**-grahf] m. chronograph
chronografia [khro-no-**grah**-fyah] f. chronography
chronograficznie [khro-no-grah-**feech**-ńe] adv. chronographically
chronograficzny [khro-no-grah-**feech**-ni] adj.m. chronographic
chronologia [khro-no-**lo**-gyah] f. chronology
chronologicznie [khro-no-lo-**geech**-ńe] adv. chronologically
chronologiczność [khro-no-lo-**geech**-nośhćh] f. chronology
chronologiczny [khro-no-lo-**geech**-ni] adj.m. chronological
chronologizacja [khro-no-lo-gee-**zah**-tsyah] f. arranging chronologically
chronologizować [khro-no-lo-gee-**zo**-vahćh] v. chronologize; arrange chronologically; chronicle (*repeatedly*)
chronologizowanie [khro-no-lo-gee-zo-**vah**-ńe] n. arranging chronologically; chronicling
chronometr [khro-**no**-metr] m. chronometer; timepiece
chronometraż [khro-no-**me**-trahsh] m. timing (of events)
chronometrażysta [khro-no-me-trah-**zhis**-tah] m. timekeeper; timer
chronometr [khro-**no**-metr] m. timepiece; chronometer
chronometria [khro-no-**met**-ryah] f. chronometry
chronometrować [khro-no-met-**ro**-vahćh] v. measure with a chronometer (*repeatedly*)
chronometrowy [khro-no-met-**ro**-vi] adj.m. of a chronometer
chronometrycznie [khro-no-met-**rich**-ńe] adv. chronometrically
chronometryczny [khro-no-met-**rich**-ni] adj.m. chronometrical; chronometric
chronoskop [khro-**no**-skop] m. chronoscope
chronostych [khro-**no**-stikh] m. chronostichon; chronogram written in a poetic form
chropawo [khro-**pah**-vo] adv. roughly; harshly; coarsely; unevenly; ruggedly; hoarsely; gratingly
chropawość [khro-**pah**-vośhćh] f. roughness; harshness; coarseness
chropawy [khro-**pah**-vi] adj.m. rough; harsh; coarse; hoarse; ragged; uneven; raucous
chropowacieć [khro-po-**vah**-ćhećh] v. roughen; coarsen; become uneven; grow rugged; become harsh; grow hoarse (*repeatedly*)
chropowacizna [khro-po-vah-**ćheez**-nah] f. rough surface; coarseness
chropowato [khro-po-**vah**-to] adv. roughly; callously; coarsely; harshly; unevenly; ruggedly
chropowatość [khro-po-**vah**-tośhćh] f. roughness; coarseness; harshness; unevenness (of a surface, etc.); ruggedness; asperity
chropowaty [khro-po-**vah**-ti] adj.m. rough; callous; coarse; harsh; uneven; rugged; hoarse; raucous
chroszcz [khroshch] m. shepherd's cress; rattle
chrumkać [**khroom**-kahćh] v. grunt (*repeatedly*)
chrup chrup [khroop khroop] exp.: crunch crunch
chrupać [**khroo**-pahćh] v. crunch;

munch; crack; champ (*repeatedly*)
chrupanie [khroo-**pah**-ńe] n. crunching; munching; cracking
chrupiący [khroo-**pyown**-tsi] adj.m. crisp
chrupka [**khroop**-kah] f. crisp sort of cake
chrupki [**khroop**-kee] adj.m. crisp; crusty; brittle
chrupko [**khroop**-ko] adv. crisply; with brittleness
chrupliwy [khroop-**lee**-vi] adj.m. brittle
chrupnąć [**khroop**-nownćh] v. crunch; munch; crack; champ
chrupnięcie [khroop-**ńan**-ćhe] n. crunch; crack
chrupot [**khroo**-pot] m. crunch; crackle
chrupotać [khroo-**po**-tahćh] v. crackle; crunch; munch; crack; champ (*repeatedly*)
chrupotanie [khroo-po-**tah**-ńe] n. crackling; cracking
chrusnąć [**khroos**-nownćh] v. clang; crunch; munch; eat up
chrust [khroost] m. kindling; cracknel; brushwood; dry twigs; dry biscuit (of fried paste)
chrustać [**khroos**-tahćh] v. clang; crunch; munch; eat up (*repeatedly*)
chrustniak [**khroost**-ńahk] m. brushwood fence; wattle fence; kindling; cracknel; brushwood; dry twigs; dry biscuit
chrustowy [khroos-**to**-vi] adj.m. brushwood (fence); wattle (fence)
chruściany [khroośh-**ćhah**-ni] adj.m. brushwood (fence); wattle (fence)
chruścić [**khroośh**-ćheećh] v. crack; crackle (*repeatedly*)
chruściel [**khroośh**-ćhel] m. wading bird; rail; corn crake
chruścik [**khroośh**-ćheek] m. caddisfly
chruśniak [**khroośh**-ńahk] m. brushwood fence; wattle fence; kindling; cracknel; brushwood; dry twigs; dry biscuit
chryja [**khri**-yah] f. row; shindy; brawl; (major) scandal; fracas; uproar
chrypa [**khri**-pah] f. bad hoarseness; sore throat
chrypieć [**khri**-pyećh] v. speak in a hoarse voice; grate; emit harsh sounds (*repeatedly*)
chrypienie [khri-**pye**-ńe] n. grating sounds; harsh sounds
chrypka [**khrip**-kah] f. hoarseness; sore throat
chrypliwie [khri-**plee**-vye] adv. hoarsely; huskily; with a grating sound; with a hoarse voice
chrypliwość [khri-**plee**-vośhćh] f. hoarseness; huskiness; grating sounds; harsh sounds
chrypliwy [khri-**plee**-vi] adj.m. hoarse; husky; grating; harsh
chrypły [**khrip**-wi] adj.m. hoarse; husky; grating; harsh
chrypnąć [**khrip**-nownćh] v. get hoarse (*repeatedly*)
chrystiania [khri-**styah**-ńyah] f. christiania (sport event)
chrystianizacja [khri-styah-ńee-**zah**-tsyah] f. Christianization
chrystianizacyjny [khri-styah-ńee-zah-**tsiy**-ni] adj.m. Christianizing
chrystianizm [khri-**styah**-ńeezm] m. Christianity
chrystianizować [khri-styah-ńee-**zo**-vahćh] v. Christianize (*repeated.*)
chrystianizować się [khri-styah-ńee-zo-vahćh śhan] v. become Christianized (*repeatedly*)
chrystianizowanie się [khri-styah-ńee-zo-**vah**-ńe śhan] n. becoming Christianized
chrystologia [khris-to-**lo**-gyah] f. Christology
Chrystus [**khris**-toos] m. Christ
chrystusowy [khris-too-**so**-vi] adj.m. Christlike; of Christ; Christ's
chryz- [khriz] prefix: chrys-; (gold-)
chryzalida [khri-zah-**lee**-dah] f. chrysalis
chryzantema [khri-zahn-**te**-mah] f. chrysanthemum
chryzmat [**khriz**-maht] m. chrismon; white baptismal robe
chryzmo [**khriz**-mo] n. chrism (consecrated oil)
chryzoberyl [khri-zo-**be**-ril] m. chrysoberyl (mineral)
chryzografia [khri-zo-**grah**-fyah] f.

chrysography
chryzolit [khri-**zo**-leet] m. chrysolite
chryzopraz [khri-**zo**-prahs] m. chrysoprasm (mineral)
chryzotyl [khri-**zo**-til] m. chrysotile (mineral, a kind of asbestos)
chryzotylowy [khri-zo-ti-**lo**-vi] adj.m. chrysotile (asbestos, etc.)
chrzan [khshahn] m. horseradish
do chrzanu [do **khshah**-noo] exp.: no good; useless; good for nothing
chrzanić [**khshah**-ńeećh] v. vulg.: talk nonsense; slang: cobble; fumble (*repeatedly*)
chrzanik [**khshah**-ńeek] m. (nice, little) horseradish
chrzanowy [khshah-**no**-vi] adj.m. of horseradish; horseradish (sauce, soup, etc.)
chrząkać [**khshown**-kahćh] v. hawk; clear one's throat; hem and haw; grunt (of a pig) (*repeatedly*)
chrząkanie [khshown-**kah**-ńe] n. clearing one's throat; grunt
chrząknąć [**khshown**-knownćh] v. hawk; clear one's throat; hem and haw; grunt (by a pig)
chrząknięcie [khshownk-**ńan**-ćhe] n. hawk; grunt
chrząsnąć [**khshown**-snownćh] v. clash; jangle; clatter; clang; grate; grit; crunch
chrząstka [**khshownst**-kah] f. cartilage; gristle; copula
chrząstkoszkieletowy [khshown-stko-shke-le-**to**-vi] adj.m. elasmobranch; of the class Elasmobranchii of fishes
chrząstkotwórczy [khshown-stko-**tfoor**-chi] adj.m. cartilage-making (cells, substance, etc.); gristle-making
chrząstkowacieć [khshown-stko-**vah**-ćhećh] v. chondrify (*repeatedly*)
chrząstkowaty [khshown-stko-**vah**-ti] adj.m. cartilaginous (fish, etc.); gristly
chrząstkowy [khshown-**stko**-vi] adj.m. cartilaginous; chondral
chrząstny [**khshownst**-ni] adj.m. cartilaginous; chondral
chrząszcz [khshownshch] m. May bug; beetle; cockchafer
chrząszczowaty [khshownsh-cho-**vah**-ti] adj.m. coleopterous; coleopteroid
chrząszczyk [**khshownsh**-chik] m. (little) May bug; beetle; cockchafer
chrząścica [khshownśh-**ćhee**-tsah] f. chondrus algae
chrzciciel [**khshćhee**-ćhel] m. baptizer; baptist
chrzcić [khshćheećh] v. baptize; christen; initiate (*repeatedly*)
chrzcić się [khshćheećh śhan] v. become baptized; get baptized (*repeatedly*)
chrzcielnica [khshćhel-**ńee**-tsah] f. baptismal font
chrzcielny [**khshćhel**-ni] adj.m. baptismal
chrzciny [**khshćhee**-ni] pl. baptism; christening-party
chrzczenie [**khshche**-ńe] n. baptism; christening
chrzest [khshest] m. baptism; christening; consecration; blessing
chrzest bojowy [khshest bo-**yo**-vi] exp.: baptism of fire
chrzestny [**khshest**-ni] adj.m. baptismal; fontal
ojciec chrzestny [**oy**-ćhets **khshest**-ni] exp.: godfather
matka chrzestna [**maht**-kah **khshest**-nah] exp.: godmother
rodzice chrzestni [ro-**dźhee**-tse **khshest**-ńee] exp.: godparents
chrześcijanin [khshe-śhćhee-**yah**-ńeen] m. Christian
chrześcijanka [khshe-śhćhee-**yahn**-kah] f. Christian woman
chrześcijański [khshe-śhćhee-**yahń**-skee] adj.m. Christian
po chrześcijańsku [po khshe-śhćhee-**yahń**-skoo] exp.: in a Christian way; as a Christian
chrześcijaństwo [khshe-śhćhee-**yahń**-stfo] n. Christianity; Christianism; Christendom
chrześniaczek [khsheśh-**ńah**-chek] m. (small) godson; a male godchild
chrześniaczka [khsheśh-**ńahch**-kah] f. goddaughter

chrześniak [**khsheśh**-ńahk] m. godson
chrześnica [khsheśh-**ńee**-tsah] f. goddaughter
chrzęsnąć [**khshans**-nownćh] v. clank; jangle; grate; crunch
chrzęst [khshanst] m. clatter; clang; clash; jangle; gritting sound
chrząstnoszkieletowy [khshanst-no-shke-le-**to**-vi] adj.m. elasmobranch; of the class Elasmobranchii of fishes
chrzęstny [**khshanst**-ni] adj.m. cartilaginous; chondral
chrzęścić [**khshan**-śhćheećh] v. clank; jangle; grate; crunch (*repeatedly*)
chuch [khookh] m. puff; huff (in checkers)
chuchać [**khoo**-khahćh] v. puff; breathe; nurse; pet; fondle (*repeatedly*)
chuchanie [khoo-**khah**-ńe] n. puffing; fondling
chucherko [khoo-**kher**-ko] n. small weakling; starveling
chucherkowaty [khoo-kher-ko-**vah**-ti] adj.m. weak; frail; faint
chuchnąć [**khookh**-nownćh] v. puff; breathe; nurse; pet; fondle
chuchnięcie [khookh-**ńan**-ćhe] n. puff
chuchrak [**khookh**-rahk] m. weakling; frail-bodied person; colloq: starveling
chuchro [**khookh**-ro] n. weakling; frail-bodied person
chuchrowato [khookh-ro-**vah**-to] adv. weakly; frailly; faintly
chuchrowaty [khookh-ro-**vah**-ti] adj.m. weak; frail; faint
chuć [khooćh] f. colloq: lust; sexual appetite; concupiscence
chuda [**khoo**-dah] adj.f. lean; thin (female)
chudawy [khoo-**dah**-vi] adj.m. rather thin; on the lean side
chuderlak [khoo-**der**-lahk] m. weakling; sickly man
chuderlawość [khoo-der-**lah**-vośhćh] f. weakness; sickliness; meagerness
chuderlawy [khoo-der-**lah**-vi] adj.m. weakly; sickly; meager
chudeusz [khoo-**de**-oosh] m. lean guy; scrag; starveling
chudnąć [**khood**-nownćh] v. lose weight; grow thin; lose flesh; become thin; thin (*repeatedly*)
chudnięcie [khood-**ńan**-ćhe] n. loss of flesh; thinning; loss of weight
chudo [**khoo**-do] adv. thinly; thin; scantily; sparingly; meagerly; poorly; without fat; with no fat
chudoba [khoo-**do**-bah] f. livestock; cattle; meager property; possessions; belongings; the poor; the needy; the indigent; poverty
chudopachołek [khoo-do-pah-**kho**-wek] m. poverty-stricken yeoman; commoner
chudość [**khoo**-dośhćh] f. thinnes; leanness; lankness; gauntness; scragginess; meagerness
chudy [**khoo**-di] adj.m. lean; thin (male); lank; gaunt; skinny; arid (soil); scraggy; meager; scrawny; poor; modest; without fat; barren
chudziaczek [khoo-**dźhah**-chek] m. (poor, little) lean guy; starveling
chudziak [**khoo**-dźhahk] m. lean guy; starveling
chudziec [**khoo**-dźhets] m. lean animal
chudzielec [khoo-**dźhe**-lets] m. skinny fellow; scrag; weed
chudzina [khoo-**dźhee**-nah] m. poor skinny guy; poor devil
chudziutki [khoo-**dźhoot**-kee] adj.m. very skinny (old) guy
chudzizna [khoo-**dźhee**-znah] f. lean person; scrag; starveling
chuj [khooy] m. vulg.: penis; mob slang: man; prick; cock; dick
chuj-dupa [khooy **doo**-pah] m. vulg.: idiot; lout; fumbler; obscene slang: stool-pigeon (mob jargon)
chujowo [khoo-**yo**-vo] adv. obscene slang: vulg.: very badly; like a penis; in a bad way
chujowy [khoo-**yo**-vi] adj.m. vulg.: fumbling; like a no good prick; vulg.: slang: no good (jargon)
chuligan [khoo-**lee**-gahn] m. hoodlum; ruffian; roughneck; hooligan
chuliganeria [khoo-lee-gah-**ner**-yah]

f. hooligans; hoodlums; roughnecks; hooliganism
chuliganić [khoo-lee-**gah**-ńeećh] v. roughhouse; brawl; behave like a hooligan; indulge in rowdy pranks (*repeatedly*)
chuliganka [khoo-lee-**gahn**-kah] f. (woman) hoodlum; ruffian; roughneck; hooligan
chuligański [khoo-lee-**gahń**-skee] adj.m. hooligan's; hoodlum's; roughneck's; hooligans'
po chuligańsku [po khoo-lee-**gahń**-skoo] exp.: like a hooligan; like a hoodlum
chuligaństwo [khoo-lee-**gahń**-stfo] n. hooliganism; rowdyism; ruffian behavior; hooligans' pranks
churał [**khoo**-rahw] m. Mongolian parliament
chusta [**khoos**-tah] f. wrap; shawl; plaid; rug; cloth
chustczyna [khoost-**chi**-nah] f. (old, little) wrap; shawl; plaid; rug; cloth
chusteczka [khoos-**tech**-kah] f. (nice) handkerchief; kerchief; (pretty) scarf
chusteczkowy [khoos-tech-**ko**-vi] adj.m. of a handkerchief
chustka [**khoost**-kah] f. handkerchief; kerchief; scarf; wrapper
chustkowy [khoost-**ko**-vi] adj.m. of a handkerchief; covered with a kerchief; wearing a scarf
chusyt [**khoo**-sit] m. see: **chasyd**
chuścina [khoośh-**ćhee**-nah] f. (worn out, old) scarf; kerchief
chutliwy [khoot-**lee**-vi] adj.m. lustful
chutor [**khoo**-tor] m. detached farmstead on the Polish-Ukrainian borderland
chwacki [**khfahts**-kee] adj.m. brave; plucky; gallant; rakish
chwacko [**khfahts**-ko] adv. bravely; pluckily; gallantly; rakishly
chwalba [**khfahl**-bah] f. praise; eulogy; exaltation; boasting; brag; boastfulness
chwalca [**khfahl**-tsah] m. admirer; praiser; eulogist; adulator; flatterer
chwalebnie [khfah-**leb**-ńe] adv. commendably; laudably; creditably; gloriously
chwalebny [khfah-**leb**-ni] adj.m. glorious; praiseworthy; creditable; laudable
chwalenie [khfah-**le**-ńe] n. praise; eulogy; exaltation; boasting; brag; boastfulness
chwalenie się [khfah-**le**-ńe śhan] n. self-praise; brag; boastfulness
chwalić [**khfah**-leećh] v. praise; commend; laud; extol; exalt; glorify (*repeatedly*)
chwalić sobie [**khfah**-leećh **so**-bye] exp.: to be (perfectly) satisfied with
chwalić się [**khfah**-leećh śhan] v. boat; brag; talk big; flatter oneself (on) (*repeatedly*)
chwalipięta [khfah-lee-**pyan**-tah] m. braggart; arrogant boaster
chwała [**khfah**-wah] f. praise; glory; splendor; pride of; a credit to
chwała Bogu [**khfah**-wah **bo**-goo] exp.: thank Goodness; thank God; thank heaven
chwast [khfahst] m. weed; tassel
chwastnica [khfahst-**ńee**-tsah] f. variety of grass; Echinochloa
chwastobójczo [khfah-sto-**booy**-cho] adv. weed-killing
chwastobójczy [khfah-sto-**booy**-chi] adj.m. weed-killing
chwastownik [khfah-**sto**-vńeek] m. harrow (used for weed control)
chwastowy [khfah-**sto**-vi] adj.m. of a weed
chwat [khfaht] m. valiant person; brick of a man; smart guy; fish of the family Cyprinidae
chwiać [khfyahćh] v. waver; toss; rock; agitate; shake; loosen (*repeatedly*)
chwiać się [khfyahćh śhan] v. shake; sway; totter; reel; rock; hesitate; fluctuate; be loose; be shaky; be rickety; be unsteady; be unsound; falter; vacillate; wane; decline (*repeatedly*)
chwianie [**khfyah**-ńe] n. rocking; faltering; tottering
chwiejba [**khfyey**-bah] f. swaying and reeling of a ship
chwiejnica [khfyey-**ńee**-tsah] f.

glider-flight training scaffold
chwiejnie [khfyey-ńe] adv. shakily; titteringly; unsteadily; with indecision
chwiejność [khfyey-nośhćh] f. shakiness; tottering position; unsteadiness; hesitation; indecision; fluctuation
chwiejny [khfyey-ni] adj.m. shaky; tottering; unsteady; hesitating; unstable; wavering; vacillating; labile; irresolute; wishy-washy
chwierutać [khfye-roo-tahćh] v. loosen (*repeatedly*)
chwila [khfee-lah] f. moment; while; instant; minute; time; spell; fit (of anger, etc.)
chwilami [khfee-lah-mee] exp.: from time to time; sometimes; not continuously; not always
co chwila [tso khfee-lah] exp.: every moment; every now and then; every now and again; very often
do tej chwili [do tey khfee-lee] exp.: up to this moment; until now
lada chwila [lah-dah khfee-lah] exp.: any moment
na chwilę [nah khfee-lan] exp.: for a moment
nie mieć wolnej chwili [ńe myećh vol-ney khfee-lee] exp.: not to have a moment to spare
od tej chwili [ot tey khfee-lee] exp.: from this time onward; from now on
przed chwilą [pshet khfee-lown] exp.: a while ago
przez chwilę [pshes khfee-lan] exp.: for a while
w danej chwili [v dah-ney khfee-lee] exp.: at the given moment
w jednej chwili [v yed-ney khfee-lee] exp.: at once
w ostatniej chwili [v o-staht-ńey khfee-lee] exp.: at the last moment
w tej chwili [f tey khfee-lee] exp.: even as we speak; now
w wolnych chwilach [v vol-nikh khfee-lahkh] exp.: at one's leisure; in leisure hours
za chwilę [zah khfee-lan] exp.: in a moment
z chwilą [s khfee-lown] exp.: on; upon
z chwilą jego przybycia [s khfee-lown ye-go pshi-bi-ćhah] exp.: on his arrival
chwile [khfee-le] pl. moments; time; times
chwileczka [khfee-lech-kah] f. a jiffy
chwileczkę! [khfee-lech-kan] exp.: just a minute!; just a moment!; let me see!
chwilka [khfeel-kah] f. short while; short spell; minute
chwilowo [khfee-lo-vo] adv. momentarily; temporarily; for the time being; for the present; at present; in the interim; ad interim
chwilowość [khfee-lo-vośhćh] f. temporariness; transitoriness
chwilowy [khfee-lo-vi] adj.m. momentary; temporary; short-lived; passing; fleeting; of short duration; instantaneous
chwilówka [khfee-loof-kah] f. slang: short-term loan
chwost [khfost] m. tail; tassel
chwycenie [khfi-tse-ńe] n. grasping; getting hold (of); catching
chwycić [khfi-ćheećh] v. grasp; seize; get hold; grip; catch; clutch; snatch; snap; clench; clip
chwycić się [khfi-ćheećh śhan] v. seize; catch hold; resort (to arms, etc.); grasp each other; let oneself be caught
chwyt [khfit] m. grasp; grip; hold; handgrip; clasp; handle; trick; catch; bite; tang
chwytacz [khfi-tahch] m. grasper; grab; holder; grip; lewis; claws
chwytać [khfi-tahćh] v. grasp; seize; get hold; grip; catch; clutch; snatch; snap; clench; clip (*repeatedly*)
chwytać się [khfi-tahćh śhan] v. seize; catch hold; resort (to arms, etc.); grasp each other; let oneself be caught (*repeatedly*)
chwytak [khfi-tahk] m. grasper; grab; holder; grip; lewis; claws
chwytakowy [khfi-tah-ko-vi] adj.m. grasping; grabbing; of a holder
chwytanie [khfi-tah-ńe] n. grasp;

clutch; snatch (at, of)
chwytanie powietrza [khfi-tah-ńe po-vyet-shah] exp.: gasp; gasping for air
chwytarka [khfi-tahr-kah] f. grasper; grab; holder; grip; lewis; claws
chwytliwie [khfit-lee-vye] adv. quickly; with a quick apprehension
chwytliwość [khfit-lee-vośhćh] f. quickness (of ear, etc.); quickness of apprehension
chwytliwy [khfit-lee-vi] adj.m. quick; quick of apprehension
chwytnik [khfit-ńeek] m. pincers
chwytność [khfit-nośhćh] f. ability to grasp; ability to catch
chwytny [khfit-ni] adj.m. prehensile; adapted for grasping
chyba [khi-bah] part. maybe; surely; I daresay; like enough; as like as not; I suppose; I imagine; I fancy; f. a miss (of a target, etc.)
chyba! [khi-bah] excl.: I should say so!; of course!; you bet!
chyba tak [khi-bah tahk] exp.: I (should) think so; I hope so; I suspect so
chyba nie! [khi-bah ńe] exp.: surely not; scarcely; hardly; I don't think so; don't tell me; I don't suppose so
chyba że [khi-bah zhe] exp.: unless
chybcikiem [khip-ćhee-kem] adv. in a hurry; with speed
chybiać [khi-byahćh] v. miss (a target, etc.); fail; miscarry; go wrong; go amiss; do no good (*repeatedly*)
chybianie [khi-byah-ńe] n. failure; missing
chybić [khi-beećh] v. miss (a target, etc.); fail; miscarry; go wrong; go amiss; do no good
na chybił trafił [nah khi-beew trah-feew] exp.: at random; at a venture; by trial and error; at a guess
ani chybi [ah-ńee khi-bee] exp.: for sure; without fail; for certain
chybienie [khi-bye-ńe] n. failure; missing
chybiony [khi-byo-ni] adj.m. abortive; pointless; ineffective; unsuccessful; ineffectual
chybiony cios [khi-byo-ni ćhos] exp.: a miss
chybki [khip-kee] adj.m. swift; fast; nimble; supple; pliant; shaky
chybko [khip-ko] adv. swiftly; fast
chybnąć [khib-nownćh] v. swing; reel; rock; sway
chybnąć się [khib-nownćh śhan] v. move; rock; lose balance
chybnięcie się [khib-ńan-ćhe śhan] n. loss of balance; rocking
chybot [khi-bot] m. wobble
chybotać [khi-bo-tahćh] v. rock; shake; wobble; swing (*repeatedly*)
chybotać się [khi-bo-tahćh śhan] v. rock; shake; wobble; swing (*repeatedly*)
chybotanie [khi-bo-tah-ńe] n. swing; swinging motion; rocking; wobble; wobbling
chybotliwie [khi-bot-lee-vye] adv. shakily
chybotliwość [khi-bot-lee-vośhćh] f. shaky condition; wobbly nature
chybotliwy [khi-bot-lee-vi] adj.m. shaky; wobbly
chycać [khi-tsahćh] v. jump; leap (*repeatedly*)
chychy [khi-khi] pl. giggle; giggling
chycić [khi-ćheećh] v. slang: grasp; grip; hold; see: **chwycić**
chylenie się [khi-le-ńe śhan] n. stooping; bending; being on the decline; being decrepit; being on the ebb
chylić [khi-leećh] v. bow; bend; incline (*repeatedly*)
chylić czoło [khi-leećh cho-wo] exp.: to do reverence
chylić się [khi-leećh śhan] v. bend; be bent; bend down; be inclined; droop; sink; stoop; decline; be decaying; be on the ebb; be decrepit; tend (towards) (*repeatedly*)
chył [khiw] m. bend; a bend
chyłkiem [khiw-kem] adv. stealthily; on the sly
chyłkiem wyjść [khiw-kem viyśhćh] exp.: to sneak out; to steal away; to sneak away
chyłomierz [khi-wo-myesh] m.

clinometer (for measuring of angles of elevation or inclination)
chytrość [khi-trośhćh] f. cunning; slyness; guile; craft; craftiness; wiliness; trickiness; shrewdness; astuteness; keenness on gain
chytrus [khit-roos] m. sly fox; slyboots; slick (Wily, etc.); sharp enough to cut himself; foxy guy
chytrusek [khit-roo-sek] m. little sly fox; slick kid; little slyboots
chytruska [khit-roos-kah] f. cunning woman; shrewd woman; stingy woman; greedy woman
chytry [khit-ri] adj.m. sly; artful; wily; crafty; tricky; shifty; keen on gain; stingy; covetous; knowing; politic; shifty; ferrety; profit-seeking; miserly
chytrze [khit-she] adv. slyly; artfully; with guile; trickily; knowingly; cunningly
chytrzejszy [khit-shey-shi] adj.m. craftier; slicker; see: **chytry**
chytrzenie [khit-she-ńe] n. scheming
chytrzyć [khit-shićh] v. be full of tricks; scheme; fox (*repeatedly*)
chyżo [khi-zho] adv. swiftly; fast; nimbly; fleetly; hot-foot
chyżość [khi-zhośhćh] f. swiftness; fastness; fleetness; nimbleness; speed; velocity; celerity; lightness of foot
chyży [khi-zhi] adj.m. swift; light on foot; nimble; eager; fast
ci [ćhee] pron. these; they; part.: for you; excl.: well!
ciach! [ćhahkh] excl.: bang!; crash!
ciachać [ćhah-khahćh] v. slash; cut; lash; bash; snip; thwack; chop; hack; hit (*repeatedly*)
ciachać się [ćhah-khahćh śhan] v. slash oneself; cut oneself; bash oneself; thwack oneself; hit oneself (*repeatedly*)
ciachnąć [ćhahkh-nownćh] v. slash; cut; lash; bash; snip; thwack; chop; hack; hit
ciachnąć się [ćhahkh-nownćh śhan] v. slash oneself; cut oneself; bash oneself; thwack oneself; hit oneself
ciachnięcie [ćhahkh-ńan-ćhe] n. slash; cut; lash; bash; snip; thwack
ciacho [ćhah-kho] n. slang: (big, tasty) cake
ciaćkać się [ćhahćh-kahćh śhan] v. handle delicately; handle with care; humor; be (especially) tactful (*repeatedly*)
ciałko [ćhahw-ko] n. little body; corpuscle
białe ciałko krwi [byah-we ćhahw-ko krfee] exp.: leukocyte
czerwone ciałko krwi [cher-vo-ne ćhahw-ko krfee] exp.: erythrocyte
ciało [ćhah-wo] n. body; substance; frame; anatomy; staff; flesh; aggregate; corpse; carcass; mortal remains
budowa ciała [boo-do-vah ćhah-wah] exp.: physique
ciało stałe [ćhah-wo stah-we] exp.: solid
ciało niebieskie [ćhah-wo ńe-byes-ke] exp.: celestial body
ciałopalenie [ćhah-wo-pah-le-ńe] n. (ritual) cremation
ciałopalny [ćhah-wo-pahl-ni] adj.m. crematory (rites, etc.)
ciamajda [ćhah-mahy-dah] f. & m. slouch; ninny; nincompoop; dolt
ciamajdowaty [ćhah-mahy-do-vah-ti] adj.m. slouchy; doltish
ciamcia [ćhahm-ćhah] f. & m. slouch; ninny; nincompoop; dolt
ciamkać [ćhahm-kahćh] v. eat noisily; splash (*repeatedly*)
ciamkanie [ćhahm-kah-ńe] n. smacking noises
ciap! [ćhahp] (not declined:) bang!
ciapa [ćhah-pah] m. & f. slouch; ninny; nincompoop; dolt
ciapać [ćhah-pahćh] v. chop; hack; splash; eat noisily (*repeatedly*)
ciapanie [ćhah-pah-ńe] n. splashing noises; hacking noises
ciap-ciap [ćhahp-ćhahp] exp.: pit-a-pat
ciapciak [ćhahp-ćhahk] m. slang: slouch; ninny; nincompoop; dolt
ciapka [ćhahp-kah] f. dot; splash (of color); spot
ciapkać [ćhahp-kahćh] v. slosh; squelch in the mud (*repeatedly*)
ciapnąć [ćhahp-nownćh] v. chop;

hack; splash; eat noisily
ciapnięcie [ćhahp-ńan-ćhe] n. splashing noises; hacking noises
ciapowaty [ćhah-po-vah-ti] adj.m. clumsy; lazy; doltish
ciarka [ćhahr-kah] f. gooseflesh
ciarki [ćhahr-kee] pl. shuddering; gooseflesh
przechodzą mnie ciarki [pshe-kho-dzown mńe ćhahr-kee] exp.: my flesh creeps; it makes my flesh creep; I shudder
ciasnawy [ćhahs-nah-vi] adj.m. rather tight; narrowish; rather confined
ciasno [ćhahs-no] adv. tightly; closely; close; tight; dangerously; parochially; narrow; narrow-mindedly; in an insular manner
ciasnota [ćhahs-no-tah] f. tightness; narrow-mindedness; lack of space
ciasny [ćhahs-ni] adj.m. narrow; tight; cramped; close; poky; close-fitting; strict; restricted; contracted; insular; parochial; narrow-minded; hidebound; niggling; groovy
ciasteczko [ćhahs-tech-ko] n. (nice, little) cake; pie; pastry
ciastkarnia [ćhahst-kahr-ńah] f. pastry shop; confectionery
ciastkarski [ćhahst-kahr-skee] adj.m. pastry (trade, shop, etc.)
ciastkarstwo [ćhahst-kahr-stfo] n. pastry trade; confectionery industry
ciastkarz [ćhahst-kahsh] m. pastry cook; owner of a pastry shop
ciastko [ćhahst-ko] n. cake; pie; pastry; confectionery
ciastkowy [ćhahst-ko-vi] adj.m. of cake; of pastry; of confectionery; confectioner's
ciasto [ćhahs-to] n. dough; paste; batter; cake; tart; plastic mixture
ciastowatość [ćhahs-to-vah-tośhćh] f. pastiness
ciastowaty [ćhahs-to-vah-ti] adj.m. doughy; pasty
ciąć [ćhownćh] v. cut; clip; snip; scissor; chop; hew; lash; whip; sting; slash; gash; pelt; play cards (*repeatedly*)
ciąć się [ćhownćh śhan] v. hack one another; slash one another; gash one another; exchange angry words; bandy words; play cards with great fervor (*repeatedly*)
ciąg [ćhowng] m. draught; draw; course; flight; sequence; duration; pathway; flow; discharge of fluid; migration of birds; train; fleet; series; row; set; run; pull; thrust
ciąg dalszy [ćhowng dahl-shi] exp.: continuation
ciąg dalszy nastąpi [ćhowng dahl-shi nah-stown-pee] exp.: to be continued
jednym ciągiem [yed-nim ćhown-gem] exp.: at a stretch
siła ciągu [śhee-wah ćhown-goo] exp.: thrust
w ciągu roku [f ćhown-goo ro-koo] exp.: in the course of the year; during the year
ciągacz [ćhown-gahch] m. wire maker; iron bar maker
ciągać [ćhown-gahćh] v. pull; draw; drag (*repeatedly*)
ciągać się [ćhown-gahćh śhan] v. be pulled; be drawn; be dragged; drag oneself (*repeatedly*)
ciągadło [ćhown-gahd-wo] n. wire-making tool; drawing tool
ciąganie [ćhown-gah-ńe] n. dragging
ciągarka [ćhown-gahr-kah] f. wire-making machine; drawing machine
ciągarnia [ćhown-gahr-ńah] f. wire-making section in a steel plant; drawing department
ciągarstwo [ćhown-gahr-stfo] n. wire-making; drawing
ciągle [ćhowng-le] adv. continually; constantly; endlessly; incessantly; all the time; forever; everlastingly; perpetually
ciągliwość [ćhowng-lee-vośhćh] f. ductility; malleability; plasticity
ciągliwy [ćhowng-lee-vi] adj.m. ductile; malleable; tenacious; stringy (fluid); plastic (flow)
ciągło [ćhowng-wo] n. drawbar
ciągłość [ćhowng-wośhćh] f. continuity; unbroken succession; uninterrupted sequence;

permanence; consecutiveness
ciągły [ćhowng-wi] adj.m. constant; unceasing; continuous; perpetual; uninterrupted; ceaseless; endless; everlasting; tough (clay)
ciągnąć [ćhowng-nownćh] v. pull; draw; tug; lug; drag; haul; have in tow; trail; obtain; pump; deduce; infer; suck; inhale; attract; stretch; expand; extend; continue; proceed; blow; sweep; run; tend; lean; dilate; wear on; draw out; lengthen; sweep; stream (*repeatedly*)
ciągnąć dalej [ćhowng-nownćh dah-ley] exp.: to carry on; to go on
ciągnąć się [ćhowng-nownćh śhan] v. last; pull one another; be dragged; be ductile; drag on; wear on; drift; stretch (*repeatedly*)
ciągnienie [ćhowng-ńe-ńe] n. drawing; pull; haul; draw; traction
ciągnięcie [ćhowng-ńan-ćhe] n. drawing; pulling; towing
ciągnik [ćhowng-ńeek] m. tractor; agrimotor; crawler; tractionengine
ciągnikowy [ćhowng-ńee-ko-vi] adj.m. tractor (plow, etc.); of a tractor; traction (wheels, etc.); of a crawler
ciągomierz [ćhown-go-myesh] m. gas-flow meter; fluid-flow meter
ciągota [ćhown-go-tah] f. slang: sex-urge; itch; inclination; shivers; disposition; proneness
ciągotki [ćhown-got-kee] pl. slang: sex-urge; itch; inclination; shivers; disposition; proneness
ciągoty [ćhown-go-ti] pl. slang: sex-urge; itch; inclination; shivers; disposition; proneness
ciągownictwo [ćhown-gov-ńeets-tfo] n. wire-making; drawing (wire, rod, bar, etc.)
ciągownik [ćhown-gov-ńeek] m. drawing die
ciągowy [ćhown-go-vi] adj.m. of draft; draft (chimney, etc.); of current of air
ciągutka [ćhown-goot-kah] f. stringy candy
ciąża [ćhown-zhah] f. pregnancy; cyesis
być w ciąży [bićh f ćhown-zhi] exp.: to be pregnant
ciążek [ćhown-zhek] m. (scale) weight
ciążki [ćhownsh-kee] pl. dumbbells
ciążenie [ćhown-zhe-ńe] n. gravitation; tendency; inclination; proclivity (to, towards)
ciążowy [ćhown-zho-vi] adj.m. of pregnancy; cyetic
ciążyć [ćhown-zhićh] v. weigh (heavy); lie heavy; be heavy; press heavily; gravitate (towards); lean (towards); be a burden (on); burden; brood (over); rest (with) (*repeatedly*)
ciąży na mnie obowiązek [ćhown-zhi nah mńe o-bo-vyown-zek] exp.: it is incumbent on me; it rests with me
ciąży na nim zarzut [ćhown-zhi nah ńeem zah-zhoot] exp.: he is charged with
cibora [ćhee-bo-rah] f. cyperus (plant)
cicerone [chee-che-ro-ne] m. professional guide
ciceronować [chee-che-ro-no-vahćh] v. act as a guide (*repeatedly*)
cichaczem [ćhee-khah-chem] adv. stealthily; on the quiet; by stealth; on the sly; in secret; secretly
cichcem [ćheekh-tsem] adv. slang: stealthily; see: **cichaczem**
cichnąć [ćheekh-nownćh] v. quiet down; subside; abate; calm down; lull; become silent; become quiet (*repeatedly*)
cichnięcie [ćheekh-ńan-ćhe] n. quieting down; subsiding; abating; calming down
cicho [ćhee-kho] adv. silently; noiselessly; softly; privately; gently; quietly; smoothly; modestly; without ostentation; on the quiet; privily; in secret
było cicho [bi-wo ćhee-kho] exp.: everything was quiet
cicho bądź! [ćhee-kho bownćh]

exp.: be quiet!
cicho! [**ćhee**-kho] excl.: hush!; not a sound!
cichobieżność [ćhee-kho-**byezh**-nośhćh] f. noiselessness (of operation, engine, etc.)
cichobieżny [ćhee-kho-**byezh**-ni] adj.m. noiseless (motor, etc.)
cichociemny [ćhee-kho-**ćhem**-ni] m. parachute commando operating in German occupied Poland during World War II
cichość [**ćhee**-khośhćh] f. silence; hush; quiet; tranquillity; calm; stillness; lull; see: **cisza**
cichusieńki [ćhee-khoo-**śheń**-kee] adj.m. very muffled; very still
cichuteńki [ćhee-khoo-**teń**-kee] adj.m. very still; see: **cichusieńki**
cichuteńko [ćhee-khoo-**teń**-ko] adv. very quietly; see: **cichutko**
cichutki [ćhee-**khoot**-kee] adj.m. (nicely) quiet; secluded
cichutko [ćhee-**khoot**-ko] adv. very quietly; very softly
cichy [**ćhee**-khi] adj.m. quiet; still; low; gentle (man); calm; serene; muffled; stifled; barely audible; silent; noiseless; smooth; soft, velvety (walk, etc.); stagnant (water, etc.); unruffled (air, etc.); modest (man); private; unofficial; tacit (agreement)
cicha woda brzegi rwie [**ćhee**-khah **vo**-dah **bzhe**-gee rvye] exp.: still waters run deep
po cichu [po **ćhee**-khoo] exp.: quietly; noiselessly; silently; tacitly; secretly; in secret; on the sly; privately; unofficially; without ostentation
z cicha pęk [s **ćhee**-khah pank] exp.: unexpectedly, suddenly with composure and coolness
ciebie [**ćhe**-bye] pron. (to, for, from, out of, instead of) you
ciec [ćhets] v. leak; flow; stream; run; drip; trickle; ooze; be leaky; leak (*repeatedly*)
krew mi cieknie z nosa [kref mee **ćhek**-ńe z **no**-sah] exp.: my nose is bleeding
ciecierzyca [ćhe-ćhe-**zhi**-tsah] f. gram (plant); chickpea; Cicer
cieciora [ćhe-**ćho**-rah] f. heathhen; black-hen; gray-hen
cieciorka [ćhe-**ćhor**-kah] f. heathhen; axseed; crown vetch (Coronilla varia)
ciecz [ćhech] f. liquid; fluid
ciecz doskonała [ćhech dos-ko-**nah**-wah] exp.: ideal liquid
ciecz nieściśliwa [ćhech ńe-śhćhee-**śhlee**-vah] exp.: incompressible liquid
ciecz nie zwilżająca [ćhech ńe zveel-zhah-yown-tsah] exp.: non-wetting liquid
miara dla cieczy [**myah**-rah dlah **ćhe**-chi] exp.: liquid measure
cieczenie [ćhe-**che**-ńe] n. escape by birds on foot; slow sliding of ground; viscous flow
cieczka [**ćhech**-kah] f. the period of sexual heat in animals; heat
cieczowy [ćhe-**cho**-vi] adj.m. of flowing fluid
cieć [ćhećh] m. slang: custodian; doorman
ciek [ćhek] m. flow of water
ciekać się [**ćhe**-kahćh śhan] v. be in the period of sexual excitement (of animals); be in heat (*repeatedly*)
ciekaw [**ćhe**-kahf] adj.m. curious; prying; interested; see: **ciekawy**
nie jestem ciekaw [ńe **yes**-tem **ćhe**-kahf] exp.: I am not interested (to know, etc.)
ciekaw jestem, czy [**ćhe**-kahf **yes**-tem chi] exp.: I wish to know if; I wish to know whether
ciekawić [ćhe-**kah**-veećh] v. interest; absorb (*repeatedly*)
ciekawić się [ćhe-**kah**-veećh śhan] v. take interest (in) (*repeatedly*)
ciekawie [ćhe-**kah**-vye] adv. curiously; with interest; pryingly; inquisitively; absorbingly
nadzwyczaj ciekawie [nahd-**zvi**-chahy ćhe-**kah**-vye] exp.: fascinatingly; thrillingly
ciekawostka [ćhe-kah-**vost**-kah] f. curious detail; piece of small gossip; interesting piece of information; (a) curiosity; curio
ciekawość [ćhe-**kah**-vośhćh] f. curiosity; interest; thirst for

knowledge; inquisitiveness; prying disposition; an interesting thing; (a) curiosity
ciekawska [ćhe-**kahf**-skah] adj.f. inquisitive; prying; peeping; f. (female) eaves-dropper
ciekawski [ćhe-**kahf**-skee] adj.m. inquisitive; prying; peeping; m. peeping Tom; eaves-dropper
ciekawy [ćhe-**kah**-vi] adj.m. cute; curious; quaint; interesting; of interest; prying; peeping; inquiring; inquisitive; m. onlooker; bystander; looker on
ciekawe! [ćhe-**kah**-ve] excl.: how curious!
jestem ciekawy [**yes**-tem ćhe-**kah**-vi] exp.: I wonder; I am curious; I would like to know; I am dying to know
cieki [**ćhe**-kee] pl. feet (of gallinaceous birds)
ciekły [**ćhek**-wi] adj.m. liquid; fluid; molten
ciekną́ć [**ćhek**-nownćh] v. leak; flow; stream; run; drip; trickle; ooze; be leaky; leak (*repeatedly*)
cieknięcie [ćhek-ńan-ćhe] n. leakage; flow
cielaczek [ćhe-**lah**-chek] m. (small) calf
cielak [**ćhe**-lahk] m. calf
cielątko [ćhe-**lownt**-ko] n. very small calf; very young calf
cielec [**ćhe**-lets] m. exp.: steer
złoty cielec [**zwo**-ti **ćhe**-lets] exp.: golden steer (of the Israelites); symbol of wealth
cielenie się [ćhe-le-ńe śhan] n. calving; fawning
cielesność [ćhe-**les**-nośhćh] f. lust; carnality; having physical existence
cielesny [ćhe-**les**-ni] adj.m. carnal; bodily; of the body; corporal; sexual; lustful; sensual; of the flesh; material; substantial
stosunek cielesny [sto-**soo**-nek ćhe-**les**-ni] exp.: sexual intercourse
cieleśnie [ćhe-**leśh**-ńe] adv. carnally; bodily; sexually; lustfully; sensually
cielę [**ćhe**-lan] n. calf; colloq: fool; simpleton; dolt; blockhead
cielęcina [ćhe-lan-**ćhee**-nah] f. veal; calf-leather; calfskin
cielęcy [ćhe-**lan**-tsi] adj.m. calf's; calf (leather, skin, etc.); like a calf; stupid; silly; veal (roast, etc.)
pieczeń cielęca [**pye**-cheń ćhe-**lan**-tsah] exp.: roast veal
skóra cielęca [**skoo**-rah ćhe-**lan**-tsah] exp.: calf skin
cielętnik [ćhe-**lant**-ńeek] m. calf-barn; calf-pen
cielica [ćhe-**lee**-tsah] f. heifer; cow-calf
cieliczka [ćhe-**leech**-kah] f. heifer up to three months of age
cielić się [**ćhe**-leećh śhan] v. calve; fawn (*repeatedly*)
cielistość [ćhe-**lees**-tośhćh] f. flesh-color; fleshiness; plumpness
cielisty [ćhe-**lees**-ti] adj.m. flesh-colored; fleshy; plump
cielna [**ćhel**-nah] adj.f. heavy with young; in calf; with calf; in fawn
cielsko [**ćhel**-sko] n. (big, old, ugly, etc.) body
ciemiączko [ćhe-**myownch**-ko] n. fontanel; fontanelle
ciemieniowy [ćhe-mye-**ńo**-vi] adj.m. parietal
ciemieniucha [ćhe-mye-**ńoo**-khah] f. parietal scab
ciemiernik [ćhe-**myer**-ńeek] m. hellebore; bear's foot (poisonous plant)
ciemiernikowy [ćhe-myer-ńee-**ko**-vi] adj.m. of hellebore; bear's-foot (leaves, plant, poison, etc.)
ciemierzyca [ćhe-mye-**zhi**-tsah] f. veratrum (poisonous plant)
ciemię [**ćhe**-myan] n. crown of the head; septum of the skull
on jest nie w ciemię bity [on yest ńe f **ćhe**-myan **bee**-ti] exp.: he is nobody's fool; he is no fool; he has his wits about him
ciemięga [ćhe-**myan**-gah] m. gawk; lout; thick-head; dullard; clumsy man; stupid fellow
ciemięski [ćhe-**myan**-skee] adj.m. tyrannical
ciemięstwo [ćhe-**myans**-tfo] n. tyranny; oppression

ciemiężca [ćhe-**myansh**-tsah] m. oppressor; taskmaster
ciemiężenie [ćhe-myan-**zhe**-ńe] n. oppression; subjugation
ciemiężony [ćhe-myan-**zho**-ni] adj.m. oppressed; subjugated
ciemiężyca [ćhe-myan-**zhi**-tsah] f. veratrum (poisonous plant)
ciemiężyciel [ćhe-myan-**zhi**-ćhel] m. oppressor
ciemiężycowy [ćhe-myan-zhi-**tso**-vi] adj.m. veratrum (poison, plant, medication, etc.)
ciemiężyć [ćhe-**myan**-zhićh] v. oppress; tread down; keep in subjugation (*repeatedly*)
ciemiężyk [ćhe-**myan**-zhik] m. swallowwort; vincentoxicum (plant)
ciemnawo [ćhem-**nah**-vo] adv. dimly
było ciemnawo [**bi**-wo ćhem-**nah**-vo] exp.: it was darkish
ciemnawy [ćhem-**nah**-vi] adj.m. dim; darkish
ciemnia [**ćhem**-ńah] f. darkroom; dark region; dark space
ciemniactwo [ćhem-**ńahts**-tfo] n. ignorance; dullness
ciemniak [**ćhem**-ńahk] m. slang: backward man; ignorant man; uneducated man
ciemnica [ćhem-**ńee**-tsah] f. dark cell; dungeon; darkness; the dark
ciemnić [**ćhem**-ńeećh] v. darken; grow dark; grow blind; grow dim; grow dusky; show as a dark patch (*repeatedly*)
ciemnieć [**ćhem**-ńećh] v. darken; grow dark; grow blind; grow dim; grow dusky; show as a dark patch (*repeatedly*)
ciemnienie [ćhem-**ńe**-ńe] n. dimming; darkening; getting dark
ciemniowy [ćhem-**ńo**-vi] adj.m. of darkroom; darkroom (equipment, etc.)
ciemniusieńki [ćhem-ńoo-**śheń**-kee] adj.m. (very nicely) dark or dim
ciemniuteńki [ćhem-ńoo-**teń**-kee] adj.m. (very nicely) dark or dim
ciemniutki [ćhem-**ńoot**-kee] adj.m. (nicely or pleasantly) dark or dim
ciemniutko [ćhem-**ńoot**-ko] adv. in a (nicely or pleasantly) dark (or dim) manner
ciemno- [**ćhem**-no] prefix: dark-
ciemno [**ćhem**-no] adv. darkly; dimly; obscurely; in dark color; n. darkness; the dark
było ciemno [**bi**-wo **ćhem**-no] exp.: it was dark; it was dusky
ciemno ubrany [**ćhem**-no oo-**brah**-ni] exp.: darkly dressed
jest ciemno [yest **ćhem**-no] exp.: it is dark
robi się ciemno [**ro**-bee śhan **ćhem**-no] exp.: it's getting dark; it's growing dark (dusky)
robi się ciemno w oczach [**ro**-bee śhan **ćhem**-no v **o**-chahkh] exp.: one's head reels; one's mind reels; one feels dizzy
ciemnobeżowy [ćhem-no-be-**zho**-vi] adj.m. dark-beige
ciemnoblond [**ćhem**-no-**blont**] adj.m. dark blond
ciemnobłękitny [ćhem-no-bwan-**keet**-ni] adj.m. dark-blue; slate blue
ciemnobrązowy [ćhem-no-brown-**zo**-vi] adj.m. dark-brown; dun
ciemnobrewy [ćhem-no-**bre**-vi] adj.m. dark-browed
ciemnofioletowy [ćhem-no-fyo-le-**to**-vi] adj.m. dark-violet; prune
ciemnogranatowy [ćhem-no-grah-nah-**to**-vi] adj.m. navy blue; mazarine blue
ciemnogród [ćhem-**no**-groot] m. colloq: ignorance; backwardness
ciemnolicy [ćhem-no-**lee**-tsi] adj.m. swarthy
ciemnoniebieski [ćhem-no-ńe-**byes**-kee] adj.m. dark-blue
ciemnooki [ćhem-no-**o**-kee] adj.m. dark-eyed
ciemnopomarańczowy [ćhem-no-po-mah-rahń-**cho**-vi] adj.m. dark-orange (color, etc.)
ciemnopąsowy [ćhem-no-pown-**so**-vi] adj.m. crimson
ciemnopopielaty [ćhem-no-po-pye-**lah**-ti] adj.m. dark-gray
ciemnosiny [ćhem-no-**śhee**-ni] adj.m. livid
ciemnoskóry [ćhem-no-**skoo**-ri]

adj.m. dark-skinned; swarthy
ciemnoszary [ćhem-no-**shah**-ri] adj.m. dark-gray
ciemność [**ćhem**-nośhćh] f. darkness; the dark; obscurity; gloom; shades of night; blackness; opaqueness; opacity; abstruseness
ciemności egipskie [**ćhem**-nośh-ćhee e-**geep**-ske] exp.: pitch-dark
w ciemnościach [f ćhem-**nośh**-ćhahkh] exp.: by night; in the dark; in pitch-darkness
ciemnota [ćhem-**no**-tah] f. obscurity; ignorance; illiteracy; colloq: ignorant, uneducated people
wciskać ciemnotę [**fćhees**-kahćh ćhem-**no**-tan] exp.: slang: cheat; lie; tell lies (mob jargon)
ciemnowiśniowy [ćhem-no-veeśh-**ńo**-vi] adj.m. cerise
ciemnowłosy [ćhem-no-**vwo**-si] adj.m. dark-haired
ciemnozielony [ćhem-no-źhe-**lo**-ni] adj.m. dark-green; rifle-green
ciemnożółty [ćhem-no-**zhoow**-ti] adj.m. dark-yellow
ciemny [**ćhem**-ni] adj.m. dark; dim; dusky; gloomy; somber; murky; pitch-dark; low pitched; unenlightened; ignorant; obscure; opaque; swarthy; abstruse; colloq: suspicious; dubious; doubtful; uncertain; shady; m. blind
ciemna masa [**ćhem**-nah mah-sah] exp.: the rubble; uneducated man
ciemny typ [**ćhem**-ni tip] exp.: person of shady (disreputable, unreliable) character
cienić [**ćhe**-ńeećh] v. shade; cast shade (*repeatedly*)
cienieć [**ćhe**-ńećh] v. thin; grow thin; grow shrill (*repeatedly*)
cienienie [ćhe-**ńe**-ńe] n. shading; thinning
cieniolubność [ćhe-ńo-**loob**-nośhćh] f. shade-seeking nature; shade-loving characteristic
cieniolubny [ćhe-ńo-**loob**-ni] adj.m. shade-seeking; shade-loving
cieniować [ćhe-**ńo**-vahćh] v. shade; modulate; grade; vary the tone (of voice) (*repeatedly*)
cieniować się [ćhe-**ńo**-vahćh śhan] v. show varying shades (of color, intensity, etc.) (*repeatedly*)
cieniowanie [ćhe-ńo-**vah**-ńe] n. varying shades (of color, etc.)
cienioznośność [ćhe-ńo-**znośh**-nośhćh] f. shadow tolerance; property of being unaffected by shadow; characteristic of growing in shadow
cienioznośny [ćhe-ńo-**znośh**-ni] adj.m. unaffected by shadow; growing in shadow
cienisto [ćhe-**ńees**-to] adv. shadily
cienistość [ćhe-**ńees**-tośhćh] f. shadiness
cienisty [ćhe-**ńees**-ti] adj.m. shady; shade-giving; shadowy; affording shade
cieniście [ćhe-**ńeeśh**-ćhe] adv. in a shadowy manner; shadily
cieniuchno [ćhe-**ńookh**-no] adv. very thinly; slenderly; fine; (in a very nice way) high-pitched
cieniuchny [ćhe-**ńookh**-ni] adj.m. very thin; slender; fine; (of a very nicely) high pitched (voice, etc.)
cieniujący [ćhe-ńoo-**yown**-tsi] adj.m. varying in shade
cieniusieńki [ćhe-ńoo-**śheń**-kee] adj.m. (very nicely or pleasantly) thin; the thinnest
cieniusieńko [ćhe-ńoo-**śheń**-ko] adv. thinly; slenderly; fine; (in a very nice way) shrill
cieniuteńki [ćhe-ńoo-**teń**-kee] adj.m. (very nicely or pleasantly) thin; the thinnest
cieniuteńko [ćhe-ńoo-**teń**-ko] adv. thinly; slenderly; fine; thin (in a very nice way)
cieniutki [ćhe-**ńoot**-kee] adj.m. (nicely) thin; very thin
cieniutko [ćhe-**ńoot**-ko] adv. thinly; slenderly (in a nice way); acutely
cienki [**ćhen**-kee] adj.m. thin; slender; slight; flimsy; finespun; delicate; weak; high-pitched; fluty; shrill
śpiewać cienkim głosem [**śhpye**-vahćh **ćhen**-keem **gwo**-sem] exp.: to feel small; to act meekly;

to live from hand to mouth; to come down a peg or two

cienko [**ćhen**-ko] adv. thinly; slenderly; slightly; flimsily; fine; shrilly; piercingly

cienko śpiewać [**ćhen**-ko **śhpye**-vahćh] exp.: to feel small; to act meekly; to live from hand to mouth; to come down a peg or two; to speak submissively

cienko- [**ćhen**-ko] prefix: thin-

cienkonogi [ćhen-ko-**no**-gee] adj.m. spindle-shanked

cienkoprzędny [ćhen-ko-**pshand**-ni] adj.m. of thin yarn; thinly spinnable

cienkorunny [ćhen-ko-**roon**-ni] adj.m. of thin wool; having thin wool

cienkościenny [ćhen-ko-**śhćhen**-ni] adj.m. of thin wall; thin-walled

cienkość [**ćhen**-kośhćh] f. thinness; fineness; slenderness; tenuity

cienkowargi [ćhen-ko-**vahr**-gee] adj.m. of thin lips; thin-lipped

cienkowarstwowy [ćhen-ko-vahr-**stfo**-vi] adj.m. of thin layers; thinly stratified

cienkowełnisty [ćhen-ko-vew-**ńees**-ti] adj.m. of thin wool

cienkowłóknisty [ćhen-ko-vwook-**ńees**-ti] adj.m. of thin fiber

cienkusz [**ćhen**-koosh] m. slang: watery beer; weak wine

ciennik [**ćhen**-ńeek] m. shader

cień [ćheń] m. shade; shadow; ghost; darkness;

chodzić za kimś jak cień [**kho**-dźheećh zah keemśh yahk ćheń] exp.: to shadow somebody; to tag somebody's heels; to stalk

cienie pod oczami [**ćhe**-ńe pod o-**chah**-mee] exp.: rings (shadows) under the eyes; circles under the eyes

cień prawdy [ćheń **prahv**-di] exp.: a particle of truth

pozostawać w cieniu [po-zo-**stah**-vahćh f **ćhe**-ńoo] exp.: to keep in the background

ciepać [**ćhe**-pahćh] v. fling (*repeatedly*)

ciepełko [ćhe-**pew**-ko] n. pleasant warmth; nice gentle heat

cieplak [**ćhe**-plahk] m. colloq: warming enclosure on a construction site

cieplarka [ćhe-**plahr**-kah] f. thermostat; incubator

cieplarnia [ćhe-**plahr**-ńah] f. greenhouse; hothouse; stove

cieplarniany [ćhep-lahr-**ńah**-ni] adj.m. of a greenhouse; of a hothouse

cieplica [ćhep-**lee**-tsah] f. hot spring; thermal spring

cieplicowy [ćhep-lee-**tso**-vi] adj.m. of a hot spring; thermal

cieplik [**ćhep**-leek] m. warmth

cieplnie [**ćhepl**-ńe] adv. in respect of heat

cieplny [**ćhepl**-ni] adj.m. thermic; thermal (insulation, etc.); caloric; calorific

energia cieplna [e-**ner**-gyah **ćhepl**-nah] exp.: thermal energy

izolacja cieplna [ee-zo-**lah**-tsyah **ćhepl**-nah] exp.: thermal insulation

przewodnictwo cieplne [pshe-vod-**ńeets**-tfo **ćhepl**-ne] exp.: thermal conductivity

ciepluchno [ćhep-**lookh**-no] adv. very nicely and warmly

ciepluchny [ćhep-**lookh**-ni] adj.m. very nice and warm

cieplutki [ćhep-**loot**-kee] adj.m. nice and warm

cieplutko [ćhep-**loot**-ko] adv. nice and warm

ciepławy [ćhep-**wah**-vi] adj.m. not enthusiastic; lukewarm; tepid

ciepło [**ćhep**-wo] adv. warmly; with warmth; n. warmth; heat

ciepło topnienia [**ćhep**-wo to-**pńe**-ńah] exp.: heat of fusion

trzymać w cieple [**tshi**-mahćh f **ćhep**-le] exp.: to keep warm

jest ciepło [yest **ćhep**-wo] exp.: it is warm

jest mi ciepło [yest mee **ćhep**-wo] exp.: I am warm

ubierać się ciepło [oo-**bye**-rahćh śhan **ćhep**-wo] exp.: to dress warmly

ciepłochłonny [ćhep-wo-**khwon**-ni]

adj.m. heat-absorbing
ciepłochronny [ćhep-wo-**khron**-ni] adj.m. heat-preserving; insulating
ciepłochwiejny [ćhep-wo-**khfyey**-ni] adj.m. heat-varying; of changing temperature
ciepłociąg [ćhep-**wo**-ćh<u>owng</u>] m. hot water and steam conduits for heating groups of buildings, etc.
ciepłokrwisty [ćhep-wo-**krfees**-ti] adj.m. warm-blooded
ciepłolecznictwo [ćhep-wo-lech-**ńeets**-tfo] n. thermotherapy
ciepłolubność [ćhep-wo-**loob**-nośhćh] f. stenothermy
ciepłolubny [ćhep-wo-**loob**-ni] adj.m. stenothermal
ciepłomierz [ćhep-**wo**-myesh] m. calorimeter
ciepłorodny [ćhep-wo-**rod**-ni] adj.m. calefacient; calefactory; calorific
ciepłorost [ćhep-**wo**-rost] m. mesotherm (plant requiring a moderate degree of heat)
ciepłostałość [ćhep-wo-**stah**-wośhćh] f. thermostability
ciepłostały [ćhep-wo-**stah**-wi] adj.m. thermostable
ciepłota [ćhep-**wo**-tah] f. temperature
ciepłownia [ćhep-**wov**-ńah] f. heating plant
ciepłownictwo [ćhep-wov-**ńeets**-tfo] n. heat energy production in form of steam or hot water
ciepłowniczy [ćhep-wov-**ńee**-chi] adj.m. heat-energy (transfer, conduits, etc.)
ciepłownik [ćhep-**wov**-ńeek] m. heating plant engineer
ciepłowodny [ćhep-wo-**vod**-ni] adj.m. warm water (fish, etc.)
ciepły [**ćhep**-wi] adj.m. warm; cordial; slang: rich (mob jargon)
ciepłe kluski [**ćhep**-we **kloos**-kee] exp.: sluggard; a habitually lazy person; slacker
ciepły gość [**ćhep**-wi gośhćh] exp.: slang: dupe; pigeon; easy prey (mob jargon)
ciepnąć [**ćhep**-n<u>own</u>ćh] v. fling
cierkać [**ćher**-kahćh] v. chirp (*repeatedly*)
cierkanie [ćher-**kah**-ńe] n. chirp; chirping
cierlica [ćher-**lee**-tsah] f. flax comb; hackle; scutcher
cierlik [**ćher**-leek] m. bunting; yellowhammer (bird)
cierniczek [ćher-**ńee**-chek] m. boxthorn; stickleback (fish) (Pungitilius)
ciernik [**ćher**-ńeek] m. boxthorn; stickleback (fish) (Gasterosteous aculeatus)
cierniopląt [ćher-**ńo**-pl<u>own</u>t] m. woody wine (Paullinia)
cierniowaty [ćher-ńo-**vah**-ti] adj.m. thorny
cierniowy [ćher-**ńo**-vi] adj.m. of thorns; thorny
cierniówka [ćher-**ńoof**-kah] f. whitethroat (bird); blackthorn; sloe (plant)
ciernistość [ćher-**ńees**-tośhćh] f. thorny nature; prickly character
ciernisty [ćher-**ńees**-ti] adj.m. thorny; prickly; spiky; spined
ciernićie [ćher-**ńeeśh**-ćhe] adv. with thorns; vexatiously
cierny [**ćher**-ni] adj.m. frictional; rubbing
cierń [ćherń] m. thorn; prickle; spike; thorny shrub; bramble; blackthorn
cierpiąco [ćher-**py<u>own</u>**-tso] adv. in pain
cierpiący [ćher-**py<u>own</u>**-tsi] adj.m. suffering; ailing; ill; indisposed; m. sufferer; patient; invalid
cierpieć [**ćher**-pyećh] v. suffer; be in pain; be afflicted; be in torment; endure; bear; stand; stomach; tolerate; put up with (*repeatedly*)
cierpieć głód [**ćher**-pyećh gwoot] exp.: to starve
cierpieć na ból zęba [**ćher**-pyećh nah bool **z<u>an</u>**-bah] exp.: to have a toothache
nie cierpię tego [ńe **ćher**-py<u>an</u> te-go] exp.: I cannot bear it
cierpieć się [**ćher**-pyećh śh<u>an</u>] v. (*repeatedly*) (only in) exp.:
nie cierpieć się [ńe **ćher**-pyećh śh<u>an</u>] exp.: to hate each other; to detest each other; to hate one another; to detest one another

cierpienie [ćher-**pye**-ńe] n. suffering; pain; ailment; torment; torture; misery; hardship; tribulations; disease; illness; sickness; infirmity; complaint; anguish; agony; grief; affliction
cierpiętnica [ćher-pyant-**ńee**-tsah] f. (woman) sufferer; martyr
cierpiętnictwo [ćher-pyant-**ńeets**-tfo] n. morbid pleasure in recollection of one's past sufferings
cierpiętniczy [ćher-pyant-**ńee**-chi] adj.m. of martyrdom
cierpiętnik [ćher-**pyant**-ńeek] m. (willing) sufferer; martyr
cierpkawy [ćherp-**kah**-vi] adj.m. tartish; somewhat acrid
cierpki [**ćherp**-kee] adj.m. tart; acid; surly; acrid; sour; harsh; vinegarish
cierpkie słowa [**ćherp**-ke **swo**-vah] exp.: harsh words
cierpko [**ćherp**-ko] adv. tartly; acridly; pungently; harshly; sourly
cierpkość [**ćherp**-kośhćh] f. tartness; acridness; harshness
cierpliwie [ćher-**plee**-vye] adv. with patience; patiently; with forbearance; forbearingly
cierpliwość [ćher-**plee**-vośhćh] f. patience; endurance; forbearance
straciłem cierpliwość [strah-**ćhee**-wem ćher-**plee**-vośhćh] exp.: I'm out of patience
cierpliwości! [ćher-plee-**vośh**-ćhee] excl.: have patience!; be patient!
cierpliwy [ćher-**plee**-vi] adj.m. enduring; patient; forbearing
cierpnąć [**ćherp**-nownćh] v. grow numb; creep; go to sleep (*repeatedly*)
cierpnie mi noga [**ćherp**-ńe mee no-gah] exp.: my leg goes numb; my leg goes to sleep
cierpnięcie [ćherp-**ńan**-ćhe] n. getting numb
ciesielka [ćhe-**śhel**-kah] f. carpentry; timberwork
ciesielnia [ćhe-**śhel**-ńah] f. carpenter's shop
ciesielski [ćhe-**śhel**-skee] adj.m. carpenters'; carpenter's
ciesielstwo [ćhe-**śhel**-stfo] n. carpentry (in construction)
ciesiołka [ćhe-**śhow**-kah] f. carpentry (in construction)
cieszenie [ćhe-**she**-ńe] n. rejoicing
cieszyć [**ćhe**-shićh] v. cheer; gladden; rejoice; gratify; please; delight; tickle; amuse (*repeatedly*)
cieszyć się [**ćhe**-shićh śhan] v. be glad; rejoice over; be pleased with; be happy about; enjoy; look forward to; anticipate (*repeatedly*)
cieszyć się dobrym zdrowiem [**ćhe**-shićh śhan **dob**-rim **zdro**-vyem] exp.: to enjoy good health; to bo robust
cieszynianka [ćhe-shi-**ńahn**-kah] f. woman inhabitant of Cieszyn
cieszynit [ćhe-**shi**-ńeet] m. teschinite (mineral)
cieszyński [ćhe-**shiń**-skee] adj.m. of Cieszyn; of Tesin
cieśla [**ćheśh**-lah] m. carpenter; woodworker; shipwright; wood construction worker
cieślarnia [ćheśh-**lahr**-ńah] f. carpenter's shop
cieślica [ćheśh-**lee**-tsah] f. carpenter's axe
cieśnina [ćheśh-**ńee**-nah] f. straits; narrows; sound; ravine
cieśń [ćheśhń] f. isthmus
cietrzew [**ćhe**-tshef] m. blackcock (male); black grouse; grey hen (female)
cietrzewi [ćhe-**tshe**-vee] adj.m. blackcock's; of the black grouse; greyhen's
cięcie [**ćhan**-ćhe] n. cut; gash; snip; lash; slash; cutting blow; stroke; scar; (forest) clearing
cesarskie cięcie [tse-**sahr**-ske **ćhan**-ćhe] exp.: caesarean section
cięciwa [ćhan-**ćhee**-vah] f. chord (in geometry); bowstring; string; tension member (in a truss, etc.)
cięgi [**ćhan**-gee] pl. lashing; flogging; thrashing; gashing
dostać cięgi [do-stahćh **ćhan**-gee] exp.: to get a licking
cięgiem [**ćhan**-gem] adv. colloq: constantly; endlessly; for ever; all the time; see: **ciągle**

ciągło [ćhang-wo] n. coupling bar; pull rod
ciągłowy [ćhang-wo-vi] adj.m. of coupling bar; of pull rod
ciągnik [ćhang-ńeek] m. drum-and-crank hoist
ciągno [ćhang-no] n. flexible connector; tension member; tie rod
ciągnowy [ćhang-no-vi] adj.m. of flexible connector; of tension member; of tie rod
ciągocić [ćhan-go-ćheećh] v. call (partridges while hunting) (*repeatedly*)
ciągotać [ćhan-go-tahćh] v. call (partridges while hunting) (*repeatedly*)
cięto [ćhan-to] adv. with a sharp tongue; bitingly; keenly; trenchantly; doggedly
ciętość [ćhan-tośhćh] f. cutting quality; sharpness; doggedness; incisiveness; keenness; trenchancy
cięty [ćhan-ti] adj.m. sharp-tongued; biting; dogged; incisive; keen-witted; ready; tipsy
być ciętym na [bićh ćhan-tim nah] exp.: to be dead set against
cięte kwiaty [ćhan-te kfyah-ti] exp.: cut flowers; bouquet of flowers
cięty dowcip [ćhan-ti dof-ćheep] exp.: ready wit; keen wit; biting wit
rana cięta [rah-nah ćhan-tah] exp.: cut; cut wound; knife wound; hack
ciężar [ćhan-zhahr] m. weight; burden; gravity; onus; duty; charge; task; encumbrance
ciężar właściwy [ćhan-zhahr vwah-śhćhee-vi] exp.: specific gravity
ciężar własny [ćhan-zhahr vwahs-ni] exp.: dead load
ciężar całkowity [ćhan-zhahr tsahw-ko-vee-ti] exp.: all-up weight; total weight
być ciężarem [bićh ćhan-zhah-rem] exp.: to encumber; to be a burden
ciężarek [ćhan-zhah-rek] m. plumb bob; weight; sinker; sounding-lead; plummet; plumb rule
ciężarki gimnastyczne [ćhan-zhahr-kee geem-nah-stich-ne] exp.: pl. dumbbells; free weights (see **hantle**)
ciężarkowy [ćhan-zhahr-ko-vi] adj.m. of (small) weight
zegar ciężarkowy [ze-gahr ćhan-zhahr-ko-vi] exp.: weight-driven clock
ciężarna [ćhan-zhahr-nah] adj.f. pregnant; with child; with young; f. expectant mother; pregnant woman; woman with child
ciężarny [ćhan-zhahr-ni] adj.m. weighty; heavy
ciężarowiec [ćhan-zhah-ro-vyets] m. weightlifter
ciężarowy [ćhan-zhah-ro-vi] adj.m. of weight; of weights
samochód ciężarowy [sah-mo-khoot ćhan-zhah-ro-vi] exp.: truck; lorry (Brit.)
ciężarówka [ćhan-zhah-roof-kah] f. truck; pickup truck; lorry (Brit.)
mała ciężarówka [mah-wah ćhan-zhah-roof-kah] exp.: pickup (truck)
ciężeć [ćhan-zhećh] v. grow heavy; become heavy; become a burden; encumber (*repeatedly*)
ciężkawo [ćhansh-kah-vo] adv. in somewhat heavy manner
ciężkawy [ćhansh-kah-vi] adj.m. rather heavy; somewhat heavy
ciężki [ćhansh-kee] adj.m. heavy; weighty; bulky; oppressive; clumsy; dull; inept; unwieldy; lumbering; uncouth; massive; stiff; troublesome; difficult; grave; severe; bad; grievous; sore; indigestible; hellish
ciężkie roboty [ćhansh-ke ro-bo-ti] exp.: hard labor
ciężki idiota [ćhansh-kee ee-dyo-tah] exp.: hopeless fool
ciężko [ćhansh-ko] adv. heavily; clumsily; ponderously; arduously; gloomily; sadly; seriously; gravely; severely; badly; with difficulty
ciężko pracować [ćhansh-ko prah-tso-vahćh] exp.: to work

hard
ciężko strawny [**ćhansh**-ko **strahv**-ni] exp.: hard to digest; indigestible
ciężko mi na sercu [**ćhansh**-ko mee nah **ser**-tsoo] exp.: I have a heavy heart
ciężko mu idzie w życiu [**ćhansh**-ko moo ee-dźhe v **zhi**-ćhoo] exp.: it goes hard with him
ciężko myślący [**ćhansh**-ko mi-**śhlown**-tsi] exp.: slow of wit
ciężko chory [**ćhansh**-ko **kho**-ri] exp.: seriously ill
ciężko zachorować [**ćhansh**-ko zah-kho-**ro**-vahćh] exp.: to fall gravely ill

ciężkość [**ćhansh**-kośhćh] f. heaviness; weight; ponderosity; difficulty
siła ciężkości [**śhee**-wah ćhansh-**keśh**-ćhee] exp.: gravity
środek ciężkości [**śhro**-dek ćhansh-**kośh**-ćhee] exp.: center of gravity

ciężkozbrojny [ćhansh-ko-**zbroy**-ni] adj.m. heavy-armed; m. heavy-armed soldier

ciężyć [**ćhan**-zhićh] v. weigh (heavy); see: ciążyć (*repeatedly*)

cinerama [see-ne-**rah**-mah] f. cinerama

ciocia [**ćho**-ćhah] f. auntie; aunt

ciocin [**ćho**-ćheen] adj.m. auntie's

ciociny [ćho-**ćhee**-ni] adj.m. auntie's

ciołek [**ćho**-wek] m. bull-calf; young bull

cios [ćhos] m. blow; stroke; hit; shock; in construction: ashlar; block; joint
cios ostateczny [ćhos os-tah-**tech**-ni] exp.: final blow
oddać cios [**od**-dahćh ćhos] exp.: to strike back
zadać cios [**zah**-dahćh ćhos] exp.: to strike a blow

ciosa [**ćho**-sah] f. a veriety of fish (pelecus cultratus)

ciosać [**ćho**-sahćh] v. hew; chop out; chop into shape; dress building stone (*repeatedly*)
grubo ciosany [**groo**-bo ćho-**sah**-ni] exp.: rough-hewn; primitive

ciosak [**ćho**-sahk] m. pick hammer; cavil

cioska [**ćhos**-kah] f. axe

ciosła [**ćhos**-wah] f. drawing knife (for cutting with two hands)

ciosowy [ćho-**so**-vi] adj.m. squared (timber); stone (column, etc.)

ciota [**ćho**-tah] f. witch; (bad) aunt; slang: homosexual; fag (jargon)

ciotczyn [**ćhot**-chin] adj.m. aunt's

ciotczyny [ćhot-**chi**-ni] adj.m. aunt's

ciotczysko [ćhot-**chis**-ko] n. (big, bad, dear, etc.) aunt
biedne ciotczysko [**byed**-ne ćhot-**chis**-ko] n. poor aunt

cioteczka [ćho-**tech**-kah] f. (dear) aunt

cioteczna siostra [ćho-**tech**-nah **śhost**-rah] exp.: (female) first cousin

cioteczny brat [ćho-**tech**-ni braht] exp.: (male) first cousin

ciotka [**ćhot**-kah] f. aunt; aunt; aunty

ciotuchna [ćho-**tookh**-nah] f. darling aunt; exp.: aunt darling!

cip-cip! [ćheep ćheep] excl.: chick! chick!

cipa [**ćhee**-pah] f. slang: vulg.: pussy; vulva; female partner in sexual intercourse (mob jargon)

cipka [**ćheep**-kah] f. small young hen; slang: vulg.: chick; pussy; vulva; female partner in sexual intercourse (mob jargon)

cirkarama [tseer-kah-**rah**-mah] f. panoramic (circular) film projection using eleven cameras

cirrocumulus [tseer-ro-koo-**moo**-loos] m. cirrocumulus (cloud)

cirrostratus [tseer-ro-**strah**-toos] m. cirrostratus (cloud)

cirrus [**tseer**-roos] m. cirrus (cloud)

cirykać [ćhee-ri-kahćh] v. call a partridge (while hunting) (*repeatedly*)

cis [ćhees] m. yew (tree)

cisak [**ćhee**-sahk] m. chestnut horse; sorrel

cisawica [ćhee-sah-**vee**-tsah] f. bronzed skin disease; Addison's disease

cisawiec [ćhee-**sah**-vyets] m.

chestnut horse; sorrel
cisawy [ćhee-**sah**-vi] adj.m. chestnut (horse)
cisina [ćhee-**śhee**-nah] f. yew trees
ciskacz [**ćhees**-kahch] m. hauler
ciskać [**ćhees**-kahćh] v. fling; cast; throw; hurl; sling; plunk; let fly (*repeatedly*)
ciskać gromy [**ćhees**-kahćh **gro**-mi] exp.: to thunder against; to invoke curses; to swear
ciskać się [**ćhees**-kahćh śhan] v. throw oneself (on a bed, on the ground, etc.); fret; fume; storm; rage; act agitated (*repeatedly*)
ciskanie się [ćhees-**kah**-ńe śhan] n. storming; raging; throwing one's weight around; acting agitated; vexing; acting with irritation
cisnąć [**ćhees**-nownćh] v. press; exert pressure (on); oppress; squeeze; clasp; fold; bear (on); urge; hurt; pinch; crowd; tighten; be tight; (*repeatedly*) fling; cast; throw; hurl; sling; plunk; let fly
cisnąć się [**ćhees**-nownćh śhan] v. press; crowd; push; throng; thrust oneself; force one's way; elbow one's way; press together (*repeatedly*); throw oneself (on a bed, on the ground, etc.) fret; fume; storm; rage; act with rage
cisowaty [ćhee-so-**vah**-ti] adj.m. taxaceous; of the yew family
cisowy [ćhee-**so**-vi] adj.m. of yew; yew (grove, etc.)
cisza [**ćhee**-shah] f. calm; silence; hush; quiet; tranquillity; stillness; lull
głęboka cisza [gwan-**bo**-kah **ćhee**-shah] exp.: dead silence
pas ciszy [pahs **ćhee**-shi] exp.: doldrums at sea; dead calm
proszę o ciszę! [pro-shan o **ćhee**-shan] exp.: silence, please!
cisza! [**ćhee**-shah] excl.: silence!; quiet!
cisza!, cisza! [**ćhee**-shah **ćhee**-shah] excl.: chair!, chair! (during a meeting)
ciszej! [**ćhee**-shey] excl.: quieter!; not so loud!
ciszkiem [**ćheesh**-kem] adv. on the quiet; stealthily; secretly
ciszyć [**ćhee**-shićh] v. still; appease; make quiet; calm down (*repeatedly*)
ciszyć się [**ćhee**-shićh śhan] v. calm oneself down (*repeatedly*)
ciśnienie [ćheeśh-**ńe**-ńe] n. pressure; blood pressure; thrust; stress
ciśnienie atmosferyczne [ćheeśh-**ńe**-ńe aht-mos-fe-**rich**-ne] exp.: atmospheric pressure
pod ciśnieniem [pot ćheeśh-**ńe**-ńem] exp.: under pressure; under stress
wysokie ciśnienie [vi-**so**-ke ćheeśh-**ńe**-ńe] exp.: high blood pressure; hypertension
ciśnieniomierz [ćheeśh-ńe-**ńo**-myesh] m. pressure gauge
ciśnieniowy [ćheeśh-ńe-**ńo**-vi] adj.m. pressure (gauge, recorder, chamber, etc.)
ciśnięcie [ćheeśh-**ńan**-ćhe] n. squeezing; pinching; stressing
cito [**tsee**-to] n. quickly; immediately (an inscription in medical prescriptions)
citroen [tsee-**tro**-en] m. Citroen (car)
ciucia [**ćhoo**-ćhah] f. colloq: puppy; piggy
ciuch [ćhookh] m. colloq: used clothing; slang: personal clothing
ciuchcia [**ćhookh**-ćhah] f. colloq: suburban narrow-gauge commuter railroad
ciuchowy [ćhoo-**kho**-vi] adj.m. colloq: used-clothing (store, etc.); slang: of personal clothing
ciuciubabka [ćhoo-ćhoo-**bahp**-kah] f. blindman's buff; colloq: to act blindly
ciućma [**ćhooćh**-mah] m. & f. sluggard; oaf; lout; duffer; incompetent man; awkward man
ciułactwo [ćhoo-**wahts**-tfo] n. money-grubbing
ciułacz [**ćhoo**-wahch] m. money-grubber
ciułać [**ćhoo**-wahćh] v. hoard; save; lay by; scrape together (*repeatedly*)
ciułanie [ćhoo-**wah**-ńe] n. hoarding; saving; laying by; scraping together

ciup [ćhoop] indecl. exp.:
ściągnąć usta w ciup [**śhćh**owng-nownćh **oo**-stah f ćhoop] exp.: to prim one's mouth; to prim one's lips
ciupa [**ćhoo**-pah] f. jail; clink; hovel; tiny dwelling
ciupać [**ćhoo**-pahćh] v. slang: strike; knock; hit; chop; vulg.: fuck; screw (*repeatedly*)
ciupaga [ćhoo-**pah**-gah] f. hatchet (in form of a decorated walking stick); alpenstock; Tatra mouintaineer's stick
ciupanie [ćhoo-**pah**-ńe] n. slang: strike; knock; hit; chop; vulg.: fuck; fucking; screwing
ciupas [**ćhoo**-pahs] m. transport of prisoners under guard
ciupasem [ćhoo-**pah**-sem] adv. under convoy; (transport) under an armed convoy
ciupka [**ćhoop**-kah] f. tiny room; very small dwelling; small hovel; tiny dwelling
ciupnąć [**ćhoop**-nownćh] v. slang: strike; knock; hit; chop; vulg.: fuck; screw
ciupnięcie [ćhoop-**ńan**-ćhe] n. slang: strike; knock; hit; chop; vulg.: fuck; fucking; screwing
ciur, ciur [ćhoor ćhoor] exp.: drip, drip
ciura [**ćhoo**-rah] m. colloq: lout; bumpkin; camp follower; a nobody
ciury [**ćhoo**-ri] pl. small fry
ciurczeć [**ćhoor**-chećh] v. trickle; drip; flow; stream; birds: chirp; sing (*repeatedly*)
ciurkać [**ćhoor**-kahćh] v. trickle; drip; flow; stream; birds: chirp; sing (*repeatedly*)
ciurkanie [ćhoor-**kah**-ńe] n. trickling; dripping; chirping
ciurkiem [**ćhoor**-kem] adv. in a trickle; with big drops; without interruption; one after another; in turns; without choice
ciurlikać [ćhoor-**lee**-kahćh] v. babble; murmur; trill (*repeatedly*)
ciurlikanie [ćhoor-lee-**kah**-ńe] n. babble (of a stream); murmur (of a brook); trill (of a bird)
ciuszek [**ćhoo**-shek] m. colloq: any part of attractive feminine attire
ciut ciut [ćhoot ćhoot] exp.: just a little bit (more, farther, better, earlier, etc.)
ciwun [**ćhee**-voon] m. bailiff of old
cizia [**ćhee**-źhah] f. colloq: pretty, elegant, sexy young woman
ciżba [**ćheezh**-bah] f. crowd; throng; squeeze; crush
ciżemka [ćhee-**zhem**-kah] f. Cracow-style 16th cent. shoe
ciżma [**ćheezh**-mah] f. Cracow-style 16th cent. footwear
cklić [tskleećh] v. feel sick (*repeatedly*)
ckliwica [tsklee-**vee**-tsah] f. sea onion
ckliwie [**tsklee**-vye] adv. sickeningly; sadly; with exaggerated sentimentality
ckliwo [**tsklee**-vo] adv. sickeningly; sadly
robi mu się ckliwo [**ro**-bee moo śhan **tsklee**-vo] exp.: he feels sad
ckliwość [**tsklee**-vośhćh] f. mawkishness; nausea; qualm; faintness; sloppiness; sentimentality
ckliwy [**tsklee**-vi] adj.m. sickly; faint; sloppy; sentimental; nauseous; nauseating; mawkish
clearing [**klee**-reeng] m. balancing accounts; exchanging checks
clearingowy [klee-reen-**go**-vi] adj.m. of clearing transactions
clenie [**tsle**-ńe] n. collection of customs duties
clerk [klerk] m. ivory-tower intellectual
clić [tsleećh] v. collect customs duty; lay a customs duty (*repeatedly*)
clochard [klo-**shahrt**] m. loiterer; homeless beggar; pauper
clou [kloo] (not declined:) high point; main attraction; clou
clown [klahwn] m. clown
clownada [klahw-**nah**-dah] f. clowning; acting as a clown; showing off
clownowski [klahw-**nof**-skee] adj.m. of a clown
cłapać [**tswah**-pahćh] v. colloq:

shuffle (along); amble; clack (one's slippers) (*repeatedly*)
cło [tswo] n. customs
podlegający cłu [pod-le-gah-yown-tsi tswoo] exp.: dutiable
wolny od cła [vol-ni ot tswah] exp.: duty-free
cmentarniany [tsmen-tahr-ńah-ni] adj.m. typical of a cemetery
cmentarnie [tsmen-tahr-ńe] adv. like in a cemetery (atmosphere, etc.)
cmentarny [tsmen-tahr-ni] adj.m. of the cemetery; cemetery (wall, landscaping, etc.)
cmentarz [tsmen-tahsh] m. cemetery; burial ground; churchyard; graveyard; necropolis
cmentarzyk [tsmen-tah-zhik] m. small cemetery; small burial ground; small graveyard
cmentarzysko [tsmen-tah-zhis-ko] n. prehistoric burial ground; big graveyard
cmokać [tsmo-kahćh] v. smack; click (a horse); suck (a pipe, candy, etc); kiss with a smack (*repeatedly*)
cmokanie [tsmo-kah-ńe] n. smacking; clicking (a horse); sucking (a pipe, etc.); kissing with a smack
cmokier [tsmo-ker] m. colloq: uncritical admirer; blind follower
cmoknąć [tsmok-nownćh] v. smack; click (a horse); suck (a pipe); kiss with a smack
cmoknięcie [tsmok-ńan-ćhe] n. smacking; clicking (a horse); sucking (a pipe); kissing with a smack
cmoktać [tsmok-tahćh] v. smack one's tongue; kiss with a smack; drink with lapping sounds; sip; suck (*repeatedly*)
cmoktanie [tsmok-tah-ńe] n. smacking; clicking (a horse); sucking (a pipe); kissing with a smack
cnić się [tsńeećh śhan] v. feel nostalgic; hanker (after) (*repeatedly*)
cnota [tsno-tah] f. virtue; righteousness; virginity; chastity
chodząca cnota [kho-dzown-tsah tsno-tah] exp.: model of virtue
cnoty [tsno-ti] pl. good qualities
pozbawić cnoty [poz-bah-veećh tsno-ti] exp.: to deflower; to deprive of virginity
zachować cnotę [zah-kho-vahćh tsno-tan] exp.: to remain chaste
cnotka [tsnot-kah] f. fictitious virtue; slang: virgin; would-be-virgin (mob jargon)
cnotliwie [tsno-tlee-vye] adv. virtuously
cnotliwość [tsno-tlee-vośhćh] f. virtue; righteousness; chastity
cnotliwy [tsno-tlee-vi] adj.m. virtuous; righteous; chaste
kobieta cnotliwa [ko-bye-tah tsno-tlee-vah] exp.: woman of virtue
cny [tsni] adj.m. worthy; noble
co [tso] pronoun & particle: what; which; who; that; as; the same as; how much; how many; as much as many; who?; at; conj.: every time; whenever
co bądź [tso bownćh] exp.: anything; whatever you like
co do [tso do] exp.: as regards
co do mnie [tso do mńe] exp.: as for me
co miesiąc [tso mye-śhownts] exp.: every month
co nieco [tso ńe-tso] exp.: just a little; just a bit; a trifle
co niemiara [tso ńe-myah-rah] exp.: great quantities; great numbers; lots; heaps; no end
dopiero co [do-pye-ro tso] exp.: just now
co mu jest? [tso moo yest] exp.: what's the matter with him?
co tylko [tso til-ko] exp.: just (a minute ago)
co więcej [tso vyan-tsey] exp.: what's more; more information will be given
co za pożytek z tego? [tso zah po-zhi-tek s te-go] exp.: what's the use of it?
co z tego? [tso s te-go] exp.: what of that?
co za widok! [tso zah vee-dok] excl.: what a sight!
co zacz? [tso zahch] exp.: who is the man?

czego [che-go] pron. why; what
czemu [che-moo] pron. why
czym [chim] pron. what with
po co [po tso] exp: why
przez co [pshes tso] exp.: whereby; and so; and thus
cobol [**ko**-bol] m. international computer language for economics
cochać [**tso**-khahćh] v. scratch; scrape; rub against (*repeatedly*)
cocker-spaniel [ko-ker **spah**-ńel] m. cocker spaniel
cocktail [**kok**-tahyl] m. cocktail
cocktail-bar [**kok**-tahyl bahr] m. cocktail bar
cocktailowy [kok-tahy-**lo**-vi] adj.m. of cocktail
kieliszek cocktailowy [ke-**lee**-shek kok-tahy-**lo**-vi] exp.: cocktail glass
coda [**ko**-dah] f. coda (in music)
codziennie [tso-**dźhen**-ńe] adv. every day; daily; day in day out; commonly
wyglądać codziennie [vi-**glown**-dahćh tso-**dźhen**-ńe] exp.: to look commonplace
codzienność [tso-**dźhen**-nośhćh] f. ordinariness; commonplaceness
codzienny [tso-**dźhen**-ni] adj.m. everyday; daily; ordinary; commonplace; workaday (clothes)
co dzień [tso dźheń] exp.: daily
na co dzień [nah tso dźheń] exp.: on weekdays
cofacz [**tso**-fahch] m. backspacer; backspace key
cofać [**tso**-fahćh] v. move back; remove; draw back; shift back; pull back; throw back; take back; recall; call off; revoke; go back (on a promise, etc.); restrain; check; keep back; retract; withhold (*repeatedly*)
cofać samochód [**tso**-fahćh sah-**mo**-khoot] exp.: to back a car
cofać słowo [**tso**-fahćh **swo**-vo] exp.: go back on one's word
cofać się [**tso**-fahćh śhan] v. back up; retreat; regress; retire; remove; return; withdraw; recoil; fall back; ebb away; step back; flinch; quail; abandon; forsake (*repeatedly*)
nie cofać się przed niczym [ńe **tso**-fahćh śhan pshed **ńee**-chim] exp.: to stop at nothing; to dare everything
cofanie [tso-**fah**-ńe] n. removal; withdrawal; retraction; recall; revocation; recantation
cofanie się [tso-**fah**-ńe śhan] n. retreat; recession
cofka [**tsof**-kah] f. water backed-up (behind a dam, etc.)
cofnąć [**tsof**-nownćh] v. move back; remove; draw back; shift back; pull back; throw back; take back; recall; call off; revoke; go back (on a promise, etc.); restrain; check; keep back; retract; withhold
cofnąć się [**tsof**-nownćh śhan] v. back up; retreat; regress; retire; remove; withdraw; recoil; fall back; ebb away; step back; flinch; quail; abandon; forsake
cofnięcie [tsof-**ńan**-ćhe] n. withdrawal; retraction; removal
cofnięty [tsof-**ńan**-ti] adj.m. standing back; retreating; underdeveloped
cofnięty w rozwoju [tsof-**ńan**-ti v roz-**vo**-yoo] exp.: underdeveloped
cogodzinny [tso-go-**dźhin**-ni] adj.m. hourly
cokolwieczek [tso-kol-**vye**-chek] adv. colloq: just a little; a trifle; a tiny bit
cokolwiek [tso-**kol**-vyek] pron. anything; anything you like; whatever; everything; adv. somewhat; just a little; just a trifle; a little bit; a tiny bit
cokolwiek bądź [tso-**kol**-vyek bownćh] exp.: no matter what
cokolwiek się stanie [tso-**kol**-vyek śhan **stah**-ńe] exp.: whatever may happen
cokolwiek za mały [tso-**kol**-vyek zah **mah**-wi] exp.: just a little bit too small; rather small; smallish
cokołowy [tso-ko-**wo**-vi] adj.m. of pedestal; of socle; of socket
cokołówka [tso-ko-**wooof**-kah] f. ceramic (bracket) socket
cokół [**tso**-koow] m. socle; base; socket (of a light bulb, etc.)
cola [**ko**-lah] f. coke; Coca-Cola

collage [ko-**lahzh**] m. collage
college [**ko**-leedzh] m. college
comber [**tsom**-ber] m. saddle (of mutton); rump; loin; haunch
comiesięczny [tso-mye-**śhanch**-ni] adj.m. monthly
cominutowy [tso-mee-noo-**to**-vi] adj.m. minutely
compact [**kom**-pahkt] m. compact disk
concertino [kon-cher-**tee**-no] n. a short concert; solo instruments in concerto grosso
confetti [kon-**fet**-tee] n. confetti; bits of colored paper
coniedzielny [tso-ńe-**dźhel**-ni] adj.m. every Sunday (regularly)
coniunctivus [koń-yoonk-**tee**-voos] m. conditional (mood)
conocny [tso-**nots**-ni] adj.m. nightly
conradysta [kon-rah-**dis**-tah] m. specialist in the works of Joseph Conrad (Tadeusz Józef Konrad Korzeniowski, 1857-1924)
consensus [kon-**sen**-soos] m. consensus (of opinion); agreement (in discussion)
contessa [kon-**tes**-sah] f. countess
continuum [kon-**tee**-noo-oom] n. continuum
contra [**kon**-trah] prep.: against; f. counterpunch; negative print
constans [**kons**-tahns] m. constant (factor, coefficient, etc.)
consulting [kon-**sahl**-teeng] m. consulting
consultingowy [kon-sahl-teen-**go**-vi] adj.m. consulting (firm, etc.)
copyright [ko-**pee**-rahyt] m. copyright
coraz [**tso**-rahs] adv. ever; repeatedly
coraz lepiej [**tso**-rahs **le**-pyey] exp.: better and better
coraz to [**tso**-rahs to] exp.: every now and again
coraz więcej [**tso**-rahs **vyan**-tsey] exp.: more and more
corocznie [tso-**roch**-ńe] adv. every year; yearly; annually
coroczny [tso-**roch**-ni] adj.m. yearly; annual
corrida [kor-**ree**-dah] f. corrida; bullfight
corso [**kor**-so] n. main street; street festival
cosecans [ko-**se**-kahns] m. cosecant
cosinus [ko-**see**-noos] m. cosine
cosinusoida [ko-see-noo-**soy**-dah] f. cosine curve
coś [tsośh] pron. something; something or other; a little; a smattering; some; somewhat; somehow
coś niecoś [tsośh **ńe**-tsośh] exp.: a little; something; somewhat
coś podobnego! [tsośh po-**dob**-**ne**-go] excl.: incredible!; is that so?!; you don't say!; well, well!; something of the kind
coś w tym rodzaju [tsośh f **tim** ro-**dzah**-yoo] exp.: something like that
i coś [ee tsośh] exp.: and some; odd
cośkolwiek [tsośh-**kol**-vyek] pron. = **cokolwiek**
cotangens [ko-**tahn**-gens] m. cotangent
cotygodniowo [tso-ti-god-**ńo**-vo] adv. weekly; every week; week in and week out
cotygodniowy [tso-ti-god-**ńo**-vi] adj.m. weekly
country [**kahn**-tri] adj.m. country (music, etc.)
coupe [koo-**pe**] n. two-door car
cowboy [**kov**-boy] m. cowboy
po cowboysku [po kov-**boy**-skoo] exp.: like a cowboy; cowboy fashion
cowboyski [kov-**boy**-skee] adj.m. of a cowboy
cowieczorny [tso-vye-**chor**-ni] adj.m. nightly
córa [**tsoo**-rah] f. daughter
córa Koryntu [**tsoo**-rah ko-**rin**-too] exp.: prostitute
córcia [**tsoor**-ćhah] f. (little, dear) daughter
córczyn [**tsoor**-chin] adj.m. daughter's
córeczka [tsoo-**rech**-kah] f. dim. dear daughter; little daughter
córeńka [tsoo-**reń**-kah] f. dimminutive: very dear daughter; sweet little daughter

córka [**tsoor**-kah] f. daughter
córka chrzestna [**tsoor**-kah **khshest**-nah] exp.: goddaughter
córuchna [tsoo-**rookh**-nah] f. dim. dear daughter; dear little daughter
córunia [tsoo-**roo**-ńah] f. darling daughter
córusia [tsoo-**roo**-śhah] f. (darling, sweet) daughter
cóż [tsoosh] pron.: what then
cóż to? [tsoosh to] exp.: what is it?
no i cóż? [no ee tsoosh] exp.: what now?
więc cóż z tego? [vyants tsoosh s **te**-go] exp.: well, what of it?
cóż z tego, że [tsoosh s **te**-go zhe] exp.: what if; what though
cóż z tego kiedy... [tsoosh s **te**-go ke-di] exp.: but then; only
cracoviana [krah-ko-**vyah**-nah] pl. literature, documents, and art pertaining to Cracow (Kraków)
crawl [krahwl] m. crawl; speed swimming stroke
credo [**kre**-do] n. credo
crescendo [kre-**shen**-do] adv. crescendo; with an increase in volume (of music, etc.)
cucenie [tsoo-**tse**-ńe] n. restoring consciousness; reviving
cucha [**tsoo**-khah] f. Tatra mountaineer's woolen overcoat
cuchnący [tsookh-**nown**-tsi] adj.m. ill-smelling; putrid; foul; rank; stinking; malodorous; fetid
cuchnąć [**tsookh**-nownćh] v. stink foul; smell foul; smell bad; have a nasty smell (*repeatedly*)
cuchnięcie [tsookh-**ńan**-ćhe] n. stench; fetor; offensive smell; stink; foul smell; fetid smell
cucić [**tsoo**-ćheećh] v. revive; restore to consciousness (*repeatedly*)
cucić się [**tsoo**-ćheećh śhan] v. regain consciousness (*repeatedly*)
cud [tsoot] m. wonder; miracle; marvel; prodigy
cudem [**tsoo**-dem] exp.: by a miracle; miraculously
jakim cudem?! [yah-keem **tsoo**-dem] excl.: how so?!
cudacki [tsoo-**dahts**-kee] adj.m. queer; odd; bizarre; whimsical
cudackość [tsoo-**dahts**-kośhćh] f. queerness; oddness; oddity; whimsicality
cudactwo [tsoo-**dahts**-tfo] n. queerness; oddness; oddity; whimsicality
cudacznie [tsoo-**dahch**-ńe] adv. queerly; oddly; whimsically
cudaczność [tsoo-**dahch**-nośhćh] f. queerness; oddness; oddity; whimsicality
cudaczny [tsoo-**dahch**-ni] adj.m. queer; odd
cudak [**tsoo**-dahk] m. odd man; crank; eccentric person; an original; oddity
cudeńka [tsoo-**deń**-kah] pl. (improbable) wonders
cudeńko [tsoo-**deń**-ko] n. (improbable) wonder
cudnie [**tsood**-ńe] adv. wonderfully; marvelously; beautifully
cudny [**tsood**-ni] adj.m. wonderfully fine; wonderful; beautiful
cudo [**tsoo**-do] n. wonder; marvel; prodigy; portent; freak; monstrosity
cudotwórca [tsoo-do-**tfoor**-tsah] m. miracle worker; thaumaturge; magician; wizard; sorcerer
cudotwórczy [tsoo-do-**tfoor**-chi] adj.m. miracle-working
cudotwórczyni [tsoo-do-tfoor-**chi**-ńee] f. (woman) miracle worker; thaumaturge; magician
cudotwórstwo [tsoo-do-**tfoor**-stfo] n. thaumaturgy; the working of miracles
cudować [tsoo-**do**-vahćh] v. wonder; fuss (*repeatedly*)
cudownie [tsoo-**dov**-ńe] adv. prodigiously; miraculously; wonderfully; marvelously
cudowność [tsoo-**dov**-nośhćh] f. wonderful nature (of); marvel; wander; prodigy
cudowny [tsoo-**dov**-ni] adj.m. prodigious; miraculous; wonderful; marvelous; adorable
cudowne dziecko [tsoo-**dov**-ne **dźhets**-ko] exp.: prodigy
cudowny obraz [tsoo-**dov**-ni **ob**-rahs] exp.: miraculous image;

miraculous painting
cudzołożnica [tsoo-dzo-wozh-**ńee**-tsah] f. adulteress
cudzołożnik [tsoo-dzo-**wozh**-ńeek] m. adulterer
cudzołożny [tsoo-dzo-**wozh**-ni] adj.m. adulterous
cudzołożyć [tsoo-dzo-**wo**-zhićh] v. commit adultery (*repeatedly*)
cudzołóstwo [tsoo-dzo-**woos**-tfo] n. adultery; misconduct
codzoziemiec [tsoo-dzo-**źhe**-myets] m. alien; foreigner
codzoziemka [tsoo-dzo-**źhem**-kah] f. (woman) foreigner; alien
cudzoziemski [tsoo-dzo-**źhem**-skee] adj.m. foreign; alien
po cudzoziemsku [po tsoo-dzo-**źhem**-skoo] exp.: after foreign fashion
z cudzoziemska [s tsoo-dzo-**źhem**-skah] exp.: after foreign fashion
cudzoziemszczyzna [tsoo-dzo-źhemsh-**chiz**-nah] f. foreign influence
cudzożywnie [tsoo-dzo-**zhiv**-ńe] adv. heterotrophically
cudzożywność [tsoo-dzo-**zhiv**-nośhćh] f. heterotrophy
cudzożywny [tsoo-dzo-**zhiv**-ni] adj.m. heterotrophic
cudze [**tsoo**-dze] n. someone else's property; another person's property; other peoples' property
cudzesy [tsoo-**dze**-si] pl. colloq: begged for cigarettes; someone else's cigarettes
cudzy [**tsoo**-dzi] adj.m. someone else's; another person's; other people's; alien; foreign
cudzysłów [tsoo-**dzi**-swoof] m. quotation marks; inverted commas
cug [tsoog] m. team of horses; current of air; chess move; slang: craving (cigarettes, alcohol, etc.)
cugant [**tsoo**-gahnt] m. team horse
cugiel [**tsoo**-gel] m. rein
cugle [**tsoog**-le] pl. reins
popuścić cugli [po-**poośh**-ćheećh **tsoog**-lee] exp.: to give reins; to let out reins; to let somebody have his fling
nie popuścić cugli [ńe po-**poośh**-ćheećh **tsoog**-lee] exp.: to keep tight reins; not to let out the reins; colloq: to enforce strict control
cugowiec [tsoo-**go**-vyets] m. team horse
cugowy [tsoo-**go**-vi] adj.m. team (horse); m. team horse
cukier [**tsoo**-ker] m. sugar
cukier buraczany [**tsoo**-ker boo-rah-**chah**-ni] exp.: beet sugar
cukier kryształowy [**tsoo**-ker kri-shtah-**wo**-vi] exp.: crystal sugar
cukier puder [**tsoo**-ker **poo**-der] exp.: powdered sugar
cukier w kostkach [**tsoo**-ker f **kost**-kahkh] exp.: lump sugar
cukry [**tsook**-ri] pl. sweets; sweetmeats; candied fruits
kostka cukru [**kost**-kah **tsoo**-kroo] exp.: lump of sugar
cukiereczek [tsoo-ke-**re**-chek] m. (attractive, pleasant) sweet; candy; sweetmeat
cukierek [tsoo-**ke**-rek] m. sweet; candy; sweetmeat
cukierenka [tsoo-ke-**ren**-kah] f. (small, nice) confectionery
cukierkowaty [tsoo-ker-ko-**vah**-ti] adj.m. nauseating; mawkish; sentimental; candy-like
cukierkowy [tsoo-ker-**ko**-vi] adj.m. of a sweet; of a candy; mawkish; treacly; sugary; commonplace (looks, etc.)
cukiernia [tsoo-**ker**-ńah] f. confectionery
cukierniany [tsoo-ker-**ńah**-ni] adj.m. cafe (atmosphere, etc.)
cukiernica [tsoo-ker-**ńee**-tsah] f. sugar basin (Brit.); sugar bowl
cukiernictwo [tsoo-ker-**ńets**-tfo] n. confectionery trade; confectionery business
cukierniczka [tsoo-ker-**ńeech**-kah] f. sugar basin (Brit.); sugar bowl
cukierniczy [tsoo-ker-**ńee**-chi] adj.m. confectioner's; pastry-cook's
cukiernik [tsoo-**ker**-ńeek] m. confectioner; pastry-cook
cukinia [tsoo-**kee**-ńah] f. green pumpkin
cukrodajny [tsoo-kro-**dahy**-ni] adj.m.

sacchariferous
cukromierz [tsoo-**kro**-myesh] m. saccharimeter
cukromocz [tsoo-**kro**-moch] m. glycosuria
cukrowacenie [tsoo-kro-vah-**tse**-ńe] n. saccharification
cukrowacieć [tsoo-kro-**vah**-ćhećh] v. saccharify (*repeatedly*)
cukrować [tsoo-**kro**-vahćh] v. sweeten; sugar (one's coffee, etc.); dust (a cake, etc.) with powdered sugar; ice (a cake, etc.) (*repeatedly*)
cukrować się [tsoo-**kro**-vahćh śhan] v. be converted into sugar; be saccharified (*repeatedly*)
cukrowanie [tsoo-kro-**vah**-ńe] n. sweetening
cukrowiec [tsoo-**kro**-vyets] m. sugar cane
cukrownia [tsoo-**krov**-ńah] f. sugar-works; sugar-mill
cukrowniany [tsoo-krov-**ńah**-ni] adj.m. sugar-mill (worker, etc.)
cukrownictwo [tsoo-krov-**ńeets**-tfo] n. sugar industry
cukrowniczy [tsoo-krov-**ńee**-chi] adj.m. sugar-mill (worker, etc.)
cukrownik [tsoo-**krov**-ńeek] m. sugar manufacturer; sugar refiner
cukrowość [tsoo-**kro**-vośhćh] f. sugar content (in sugar beets, sugar cane, etc.)
cukrowy [tsoo-**kro**-vi] adj.m. of sugar; sugar; saccharic; sugary
cukrówka [tsoo-**kroof**-kah] f. colloq: variety of summer cabbage; variety of early pear
cukrzan [**tsoo**-kshahn] m. saccharate
cukrzenie [tsook-**she**-ńe] n. saccharification
cukrzyca [tsoo-**kshi**-tsah] f. diabetes
cukrzycowy [tsoo-kshi-**tso**-vi] adj.m. diabetic
cukrzyć [**tsoo**-kshićh] v. sugar; sweeten; dust with sugar; ice (*repeatedly*)
cukrzyk [**tsook**-shik] m. sunbird; colloq: diabetic
cuma [**tsoo**-mah] f. mooring rope; hawser; bridle; spring
cumować [tsoo-**mo**-vahćh] v. moor (*repeatedly*)
cumowanie [tsoo-mo-**vah**-ńe] n. mooring
cumownica [tsoo-mov-**ńee**-tsah] f. bollard
cumowniczy [tsoo-mov-**ńee**-chi] adj.m. mooring (rope, line, etc.)
cumowy [tsoo-**mo**-vi] adj.m. mooring (buoy, etc.)
cumulonimbus [koo-moo-lo-**ńeem**-boos] m. cumulonimbus (anvil-shaped cloud)
cumulus [koo-**moo**-loos] m. cumulus (cloud)
cumulusowy [koo-moo-loo-**so**-vi] adj.m. of a cumulus (cloud)
cup! [tsoop] indecl. bang!
cupnąć [**tsoop**-nownćh] v. squat down
cupu [**tsoo**-poo] (only in) exp.: **łupu cupu** [**woo**-poo **tsoo**-poo] exp.: rub-a-dub; bang bang
curie [kyoo-**ree**] m. curie (a unit of radioactivity)
curieterapia [kyoo-ree-te-**rahp**-yah] f. curie-therapy; a variety of radiotherapy
curiosum [koor-**yo**-zoom] indecl.: curiosity; oddity; monstrosity
curry [ke-ree] n. curry powder
cwał [tsfahw] m. gallop; canter **cwałem** [**tsfah**-wem] exp.: at a gallop; in full speed; in full career; full tilt; posthaste; hotfoot; as hard as one can
cwałować [tsfah-**wo**-vahćh] v. ride at full career; gallop; canter (*repeatedly*)
cwałowanie [tsfah-wo-**vah**-ńe] n. gallop; galloping
cwałowy [tsfah-**wo**-vi] adj.m. of full gallop
cwaniacki [tsfah-**ńahts**-kee] adj.m. artful; sly; cunning; crafty
cwaniactwo [tsfah-**ńahts**-tfo] n. cunning; craft
cwaniaczek [tsfah-**ńah**-chek] m. colloq: (small) artful man (boy); dodger; fox; shrewish man
cwaniaczka [tsfah-**ńahch**-kah] f. colloq: artful woman; dodger; vixen; shrewish (ill-tempered) woman
cwaniak [**tsfah**-ńahk] m. city

slicker; sly dog; crafty guy; dodger; slang: cheat; swindler
cwaniara [tsfah-ńah-rah] f. colloq: artful woman; dodger; vixen; female fox; shrewish woman
cwany [tsfah-ni] adj.m. sly; cunning; crafty; artful; deep file
cwelich [tsfe-leekh] m. twill; tick; ticking
cwibak [tsfee-bahk] m. kind of plum-cake
cwikier [tsfee-ker] m. pince-nez; eyeglasses
cybernetyczny [tsi-ber-ne-tich-ni] adj.m. cybernetic
cybernetyk [tsi-ber-ne-tik] m. cyberneticist
cybernetyka [tsi-ber-ne-ti-kah] f. cybernetics
cybernetyzacja [tsi-ber-ne-ti-zah-tsyah] f. cybernation
cybernetyzować [tsi-ber-ne-ti-zo-vahćh] v. apply cybernetics; use cybernetic description (*repeatedly*)
cybet [tsi-bet] m. civet cat (skunk); musky-odored substance produced by the sexual organs of the civet cat (used in pefumes)
cybety [tsi-be-ti] pl. civets; civet fur
cybeta [tsi-be-tah] f. civet cat (skunk); musky-odored substance produced by the sexual organs of the civet cat (used in pefumes); civet fur
cyborg [tsi-borg] m. cyborg; man dependent on mechanical device for survival
cyborgizacja [tsi-bor-gee-zah-tsyah] f. replacement of living organ with mechanical device; steering of living organism by interference with biochemical and neurophysiological processes
cyborium [tsi-bor-yoom] n. ciborium; a goblet-shaped vessel for holding eucharistic bread; pyx
cybuch [tsi-bookh] m. pipestem; blowpipe
cybuszek [tsi-boo-shek] m. (small) pipe-stem; blow-pipe
cyc [tsits] m. printed (calico) cotton fabric; nipple; vulg.: teat
cycek [tsi-tsek] m. slang: nipple of woman's breast; pap; teat
cycełe [tsi-tse-we] indecl. zizith; fringes and tassels worn on ceremonial garments of Jewish males
cyckać [tsits-kahćh] v. slang: suck; suck in (*repeatedly*)
cycero [tsi-tse-ro] n. pica font
cyceroński [tsi-tse-roń-skee] adj.m. Ciceronian
cycowy [tsi-tso-vi] adj.m. of printed cotton (skirt, etc.)
cydr [tsidr] m. cider
cyferblat [tsi-fer-blaht] m. clock dial; vulg.: mug; face; phiz
cyferka [tsi-fer-kah] f. small number
cyfra [tsif-rah] f. number; initial; monogram; cipher; embroidered design (on Polish mountaineers's garments, etc.)
cyfry [tsif-ri] pl. numbers
cyfry arabskie [tsif-ri ah-rahp-ske] exp.: Arabic numerals
cyfry rzymskie [tsif-ri zhim-ske] exp.: Roman numerals
cyfrofonia [tsi-fro-foń-yah] f. ciphony; the electronic scrambling of voice transmission
cyfronik [tsi-fro-ńeek] m. specialist in computer electronics
cyfronika [tsi-fro-ńee-kah] f. electronics of computers
cyfrować [tsi-fro-vahćh] v. initial; embroider; cipher; write in code (*repeatedly*)
cyfrowanie [tsi-fro-vah-ńe] n. embroidered design (on Polish mountaineers's garments, etc.)
cyfrowany [tsi-fro-vah-ni] adj.m. embroidered with design
cyfrowo [tsi-fro-vo] adv. in figures; numerically
cyfrowy [tsi-fro-vi] adj.m. numeral; ciphered; written in code
cygaj [tsi-gahy] m. Polish mountain sheep
Cygan [tsi-gahn] m. Gypsy; Gipsy; Romany; Zingaro; Bohemian
cygan [tsi-gahn] m. colloq: cheat; swindler; liar; fibber
cyganeczka [tsi-gah-nech-kah] f. dark-haired pretty little girl; nice Gypsy girl
cyganek [tsi-gah-nek] m. pocket

knife with wooden handle; iron stove; a card game
cyganeria [tsi-gah-**ne**-ryah] f. Bohemia
cyganiak [tsi-**gah**-ńahk] m. slang: Gypsy boy; dark hair, dark boy
cyganiątko [tsi-gah-**ńownt**-ko] n. Gipsy child; dark hair, dark skin child
cyganicha [tsi-gah-**ńee**-khah] f. (big, old, bad) Gipsy woman; dark-haired, dark-skin (old, big) woman
cyganić [tsi-**gah**-ńeećh] v. cheat; trick; lie; fool; sharp; tell lies; fib (*repeatedly*)
cyganienie [tsi-gah-**ńe**-ńe] n. cheating; telling lies
Cyganka [tsi-**gahn**-kah] f. Gipsy woman; dark-haired, dark-skin woman
cygański [tsi-**gahń**-skee] adj.m. gipsy; Bohemian
po cygańsku [po tsi-**gahń**-skoo] adv. exp.: gipsy fashion; in Romany language; colloq: deceitfully; fraudulently; thievishly; trickily
cygaństwo [tsi-**gahń**-stfo] n. The Gipsies; the Romany; colloq: deceit; fraud; lie; fib; vagrancy; nomadism; Gipsy life
cygaretka [tsi-gah-**ret**-kah] f. thin (slim) cigar
cygarnica [tsi-gahr-**ńee**-tsah] f. cigar case; cigarette case; cigar holder; cigarette holder
cygarniczka [tsi-gahr-**ńeech**-kah] f. cigarette holder; mouthpiece
cygaro [tsi-**gah**-ro] n. cigar
w kształcie cygara [f **kshtahw**-ćhe tsi-**gah**-rah] exp.: cigar-shaped
cygarowy [tsi-gah-**ro**-vi] adj.m. cigar (tobacco, smoke, factory, box, etc.)
cyjan [**tsi**-yahn] m. cyanogen
cyjanamid [tsi-yah-**nah**-meed] m. cyanamide
cyjanek [tsi-**yah**-nek] m. cyanide
cyjanin [tsi-**yah**-ńeen] m. cyanine
cyjanit [tsi-**yah**-ńeet] m. cyanite
cyjankali [tsi-yahn-**kah**-lee] n. potassium cyanide
cyjankowy [tsi-yahn-**ko**-vi] adj.m. of cyanide; cyanide (process, etc.)
cyjanotypia [tsi-yah-no-**ti**-pyah] f. line-reproduction on light-sensitive paper
cyjanować [tsi-yah-**no**-vahćh] v. harden (toughen) steel surface with cyanide (*repeatedly*)
cyjanowanie [tsi-yah-no-**vah**-ńe] n. cyanide hardening
cyjanowodorowy [tsi-yah-no-vo-do-**ro**-vi] adj.m. hydrocyanic
cyjanowodór [tsi-yah-no-**vo**-door] m. prussic acid; hydrogen cyanide
cyjanowy [tsi-yah-**no**-vi] adj.m. cyanic
cyjanoza [tsi-yah-**no**-zah] f. cyanosis
cyk [tsik] indecl. tick; tick-tack; chirp; colloq: cheerio (invitation to drink)
cykać [**tsi**-kahćh] v. tick; chirp; colloq: sip slowly; supply grudgingly; pay by driblets; take sips (*repeatedly*)
cykada [tsi-**kah**-dah] f. cicada (homopterous insect)
cykanie [tsi-**kah**-ńe] n. tick-tack (of a clock, etc.); colloq: paying by driblets
cykas [**tsi**-kahs] m. sago palm; cycas; cycad
cykasowaty [tsi-kah-so-**vah**-ti] adj.m. cycad-like
cykasowate [tsi-kah-so-**vah**-te] pl. the family of sago palm; the Cycadaceae
cykata [tsi-**kah**-tah] f. candied peel (of oranges, lemons, melons, etc.)
cykl [tsikl] m. cycle; course; series; round; period
cykl słoneczny [tsikl swo-**nech**-ni] exp.: solar cycle
cyklamen [tsi-**klah**-men] m. cyclamen (of primarose family)
cyklamenowy [tsi-klah-me-**no**-vi] adj.m. cyclamen (smell, color, etc.)
cyklicznie [tsi-**kleech**-ńe] adv. cyclically; periodically
cykliczność [tsi-**kleech**-nośhćh] f. periodicity
cykliczny [tsi-**kleech**-ni] adj.m. cyclic; cyclical; periodic; periodical
cyklik [**tsi**-kleek] m. cyclic poet

cyklina [tsi-**klee**-nah] f. scraper (tool)
cykliniarka [tsi-klee-**ńahr**-kah] f. scraper-polisher machine
cykliniarski [tsi-klee-**ńahr**-skee] adj.m. of scraper-polisher
cykliniarz [tsi-**klee**-ńahsh] m. floor scraping and polishing worker
cyklinować [tsi-klee-**no**-vahćh] v. scrape (wood, floor) (*repeatedly*)
cyklinowanie [tsi-klee-no-**vah**-ńe] n. scraping (of wood, parquet floor)
cyklista [tsi-**klees**-tah] m. cyclist
cyklistówka [tsi-klees-**toof**-kah] f. cyclist cap
cyklodrom [tsi-**klo**-drom] m. cycle-racing track
cykloergometr [tsi-klo-er-**go**-metr] m. cyclometer for testing cyclists' endurance
cyklofrenia [tsi-klo-**fre**-ńyah] f. cyclic schizophrenia
cykloheksan [tsi-klo-**khe**-ksahn] m. cyclohexane
cykloida [tsi-**kloy**-dah] f. cycloid
cykloidalny [tsi-klo-ee-**dahl**-ni] adj.m. cycloid (movement, etc.)
cykloidowy [tsi-klo-ee-**do**-vi] adj.m. cycloid (shape, etc.)
cyklometr [tsi-**klo**-metr] m. cyclometer
cyklomorfoza [tsi-klo-mor-**fo**-zah] f. cyclic (seasonal) morphosis
cyklon [**tsi**-klon] m. cyclone; tornado; typhoon; hurricane; tropical cyclone; chem.: name of a poison gas used in German-Nazi gas chambers in concentration camps
cykloniczny [tsi-klo-**ńeech**-ni] adj.m. cyclonic
cyklop [**tsi**-klop] m. Cyclop
cyklopi [tsi-**klo**-pee] adj.m. Cyclopean; giant
cyklopowy [tsi-klo-**po**-vi] adj.m. Cyclopean; giant
cyklorama [tsi-klo-**rah**-mah] f. cyclorama
cyklostyl [tsi-**klos**-til] m. cyclostyle
cyklotron [tsi-**klo**-tron] m. cyclotron
cyklotronowy [tsi-klo-tro-**no**-vi] adj.m. of a cyclotron
cyklotymia [tsi-klo-**ti**-myah] f. cyclothymia
cyklotymiczny [tsi-klo-ti-**meech**-ni] adj.m. cyclothymic
cyklotymik [tsi-klo-**ti**-meek] m. cyclothymic person; cyclothyme
cyklowy [tsi-**klo**-vi] adj.m. cyclic
cykloza [tsi-**klo**-zah] f. cyclosis
cyknąć [**tsik**-nownćh] v. tick; chirp; colloq: sip slowly; supply grudgingly; pay by driblets; take sips
cyknięcie [tsik-**ńan**-ćhe] n. (a) tick; (a) chirp; colloq: payment (by driblets)
cykor [**tsi**-kor] m. colloq: fear; dread; anxiety; slang: coward
cykoria [tsi-**ko**-ryah] f. chicory; endive; slang: funk; fear
cykoriowate [tsi-kor-yo-**vah**-te] pl. the chicor family
cykoriowy [tsi-kor-**yo**-vi] adj.m. chicory (flower, etc.); endive (salad, etc.)
cykoriowe [tsi-kor-**yo**-ve] pl. the chicor family
cykot [**tsi**-kot] m. ticking (of a clock)
cykotać [tsi-**ko**-tahćh] v. tick (*repeatedly*)
cykotanie [tsi-ko-**tah**-ńe] n. ticking (of a clock)
cykuta [tsi-**koo**-tah] f. (water) hemlock; poison hemlock; cowbane
cylinder [tsi-**leen**-der] m. cylinder; barrel; (men's) top hat; silk hat; colloq: topper
cylindrowy [tsi-leen-**dro**-vi] adj.m. cylindric
cylindrycznie [tsi-leen-**drich**-ńe] adv. cylindrically; in barrel-shape
cylindryczny [tsi-leen-**drich**-ni] adj.m. cylindric; cylindrical; barrel-shaped; tubular
cym [tsim] (only in) exp.:
cym, cyrym, cym [tsim tsi-**rim** tism] (a refrain)
rym, cym, cym [rim tsim **tism**] exp.: (a refrain)
cyma [**tsi**-mah] f. cyma; shape formed by concave and convex lines; "s" shape molding
cymbalista [tsim-bah-**lees**-tah] m. dulcimer player
cymbał [**tsim**-bahw] m. dulcimer;

slang: dolt; bumpkin; chucklehead; booby; duffer; blockhead
cymbały [tsim-**bah**-wi] pl. dulcimer
cymbałki [tsim-**bahw**-kee] pl. dulcimer (child's toy)
cymelia [tsim-**mel**-yah] pl. cimelia; church treasures; heirlooms
cymelium [tsim-**mel**-yoom] n. rare and valuable manuscript
Cymeryjczyk [tsim-me-**riy**-chik] m. Cimmerian
Cymeryjski [tsim-me-**riy**-skee] adj.m. Cimmerian
cymes [**tsi**-mes] m. (Yiddish) slang: crackerjack; a first-rate thing; a super-duper thing; good merchandise
cyna [**tsi**-nah] f. tin; pewter; stannum
cynaderki [tsi-nah-**der**-kee] pl. (cooked animal's) kidneys
cynadry [tsi-**nah**-dri] pl. (animal's) kidneys
cynamon [tsi-**nah**-mon] m. cinnamon; spice of laurel bark
cynamonowiec [tsi-nah-mo-**no**-vyets] m. cinnamon tree
cynamonowo [tsi-nah-mo-**no**-vo] adv. colloq: (to smell, etc.) like a cinnamon
cynamonowy [tsi-nah-mo-**no**-vi] adj.m. cinnamon (bark, tree, etc.); the color of cynamon; cinnamic (acid)
cynawy [tsi-**nah**-vi] adj.m. stannous (compound, etc.)
cyneraria [tsi-ne-**rah**-ryah] f. cineraria (pot plant)
cynestetycznie [tsi-nes-te-**tich**-ńe] adv. kinesthetically
cynestetyczny [tsi-nes-te-**tich**-ni] adj.m. kinesthetic
cynestezja [tsi-nes-**te**-zyah] f. kinesthesia; kinesthesis
cynfolia [tsin-**fo**-lyah] f. tin foil fin foli wrapper
cyngiel [**tsin**-gel] m. trigger
cynia [**tsi**-ńah] f. zinnia (tropical herb or bush)
cynian [**tsi**-ńahn] m. salt of tin-acid
cynicki [tsi-**ńeets**-kee] adj.m. of the Cynics; Cynic
cynicznie [tsi-**ńeech**-ńe] adv. cynically; brazenly; unblushingly
cyniczność [tsi-**ńeech**-nośhćh] f. cynicism
cyniczny [tsi-**ńeech**-ni] adj.m. cynical; brazen; brazen-faced; unblushing
cynik [**tsi**-ńeek] m. cynic; Cynic
cynizm [**tsi**-ńeezm] m. cynicism; brazenness; Cynicism
cynk [tsink] m. zinc; tutenag; spelter; slang: tip; sign; warning
cynkarka [tsin-**kahr**-kah] f. zinc-socket making machine
cynkit [**tsin**-keet] m. zinc mineral
cynkografia [tsin-ko-**grah**-fyah] f. zincography
cynkograficznie [tsin-ko-grah-**feech**-ńe] adv. by means of zincography
cynkograficzny [tsin-ko-grah-**feech**-ni] adj.m. zincographic
cynkolit [tsin-**ko**-leet] m. Griffith's white
cynkotyp [tsin-**ko**-tip] m. zincotype; slang: zinco
cynkotypia [tsin-ko-**ti**-pyah] f. zincography
cynkować [tsin-**ko**-vahćh] v. zinc; coat with zinc; slang: give tips (mob jargon) (*repeatedly*)
cynkowajs [**tsin**-ko-vahys] m. colloq: zinc oxide; zinc white
cynkowanie [tsin-ko-**vah**-ńe] n. coating with zinc; slang: giving tips (mob jargon)
cynkowaty [tsin-ko-**vah**-ti] adj.m. zincky; zinky; zincy
cynkownia [tsin-**kov**-ńah] f. zinc-works
cynkowy [tsin-**ko**-vi] adj.m. of zinc; zinc (white, etc.); zincic
blenda cynkowa [**blen**-dah tsin-**ko**-vah] exp.: zinc blende
tlenek cynkowy [**tle**-nek tsin-**ko**-vi] exp.: zinc oxide
cynkwajs [**tsink**-fahys] m. colloq: zinc white; zinc oxide; flowers of zinc
cynober [tsi-**no**-ber] m. vermilion; cinnabar
cynobrowy [tsi-no-**bro**-vi] adj.m. vermilion; cinnabar (color)
cynować [tsi-**no**-vahćh] v. tin; coat with tin; tin-plate (*repeatedly*)
cynowanie [tsi-no-**vah**-ńe] n.

tinning; tin-plating
cynownia [tsi-**nov**-ńah] f. tinworks
cynowany [tsi-no-**vah**-ni] adj.m. tinned; tin-plated
cynowy [tsi-**no**-vi] adj.m. of tin; tin (ware, etc.); stannic
naczynia cynowe [nah-**chi**-ńah tsi-**no**-ve] exp.: pewter; tinware
cypel [**tsi**-pel] m. cape; tip; promontory; headland; foreland; spit
Cypryjczyk [tsi-**priy**-chik] m. Cypriote
cypryjski [tsi-**priy**-skee] adj.m. Cyprian
cyprys [**tsi**-pris] m. cypress
cyprysik [tsi-**pri**-śheek] m. variety of cypress tree
cyprysowaty [tsi-pri-so-**vah**-ti] adj.m. cypress-like
cyprysowate [tsi-pri-so-**vah**-te] pl. the family of cypress trees (Cupressaceae)
cyprysowy [tsi-pri-**so**-vi] adj.m. of cypress; cypress (hedge, etc.)
cypryśnik [tsi-**priśh**-ńeek] m. taxodium; cypress (large) swamp tree
cyraneczka [tsi-rah-**nech**-kah] f. (small, nice) garganey; teal
cyranka [tsi-**rahn**-kah] f. garganey; teal
cyrenaik [tsi-re-**nah**-eek] m. follower of Cyrenaicism
cyrenaizm [tsi-re-**nah**-eezm] m. Cyrenaicism
cyrk [tsirk] m. circus; slang: weird behavior; bizarre behavior
cyrkiel [**tsir**-kel] m. compass; rim; edge (of skirt, or dress)
cyrklować [tsir-**klo**-vahćh] v. describe a circle; calculate; reckon (Brit.) (*repeatedly*)
cyrklowanie [tsir-klo-**vah**-ńe] n. reckoning (Brit.); calculating
cyrklowy [tsir-**klo**-vi] adj.m. compass (point, etc.)
cyrkon [**tsir**-kon] m. zirconium (atomic number 40); zircon (mineral)
cyrkonowy [tsir-ko-**no**-vi] adj.m. zirconic
cyrkonówka [tsir-ko-**noof**-kah] f. Nernst lamp; Nernst glower
cyrkowiec [tsir-**ko**-vyets] m. circus performer; acrobat
cyrkowy [tsir-**ko**-vi] adj.m. circus (tent, etc.)
cyrkówka [tsir-**koof**-kah] f. circus actress
cyrkulacja [tsir-koo-**lah**-tsyah] f. circulation
cyrkulacyjny [tsir-koo-lah-**tsiy**-ni] adj.m. circulatory
cyrkularka [tsir-koo-**lahr**-kah] f. colloq: circular saw
cyrkulować [tsir-koo-**lo**-vahćh] v. circulate; be in circulation (*repeatedly*)
cyrkuł [**tsir**-koow] m. police precinct
cyrkumfleks [tsir-**koom**-fleks] m. circumflex accent
cyrkumfleksowy [tsir-koom-flek-**so**-vi] adj.m. circumflex (tonic accent, etc.)
cyrla [**tsir**-lah] f. mountain top; glen
cyrograf [tsi-**ro**-grahf] m. pledge; bond; formally signed document
cyrulik [tsi-**roo**-leek] m. barber; barber-surgeon (of old)
cyrylica [tsi-ri-**lee**-tsah] f. Cyrillic alphabet
pisać cyrylicą [**pee**-sahćh tsi-ri-**lee**-tsown] exp.: to use the Cyrillic alphabet
cyrylicki [tsi-ri-**leets**-kee] adj.m. Cyrillic (alphabet, print, etc.)
cysta [**tsi**-tah] f. cyst; saccule
cysteina [tsis-te-**ee**-nah] f. cystine
cysterka [tsis-**ter**-kah] f. Cystercian nun
cysterna [tsis-**ter**-nah] f. cistern; tank car; vat; storage tank
cysternowy [tsis-ter-**no**-vi] adj.m. tank (car, etc.)
cysters [**tsis**-ters] m. (a) Cystercian
cysterski [tsis-**ter**-skee] adj.m. Cystercian
cystofor [tsis-**to**-for] m. cystophore
cystografia [tsis-to-**grah**-fyah] f.X-ray examination of the bladder by means of a contrast; cystogrphy
cystogram [tsis-**to**-grahm] m. X-ray cystography; picture showing the bladder by means of a contrast
cystoskop [tsis-**to**-skop] m. cystoscope
cystoskopia [tsis-to-**sko**-pyah] f.

cystoscopy
cystotomia [tsis-to-to-myah] f. cystotomy (operation)
cystyda [tsis-ti-dah] f. cystid; fyngus spore
cystyna [tsis-ti-nah] f. cystine (in bladder stones, etc.)
cyt! [tsit] excl.: hush!; hist!; m. chirp
cytacja [tsi-tah-tsyah] f. citation
cytadela [tsi-tah-de-lah] f. citadel; fortress; stronghold
cytadelowy [tsi-tah-de-lo-vi] adj.m. of a citadel; of a fortress; of a stronghold
cytat [tsi-taht] m. quotation; citation; excerption
błędny cytat [bwand-ni tsi-taht] exp.: misquotation
cytata [tsi-tah-tah] f. quotation
cytatowy [tsi-tah-to-vi] adj.m. quotation (content, etc.)
cyto- [tsi-to] prefix: cyt-; cyto- (of a cell)
cytoblast [tsi-to-blahst] m. cytoblast
cytochemia [tsi-to-khe-myah] f. cytochemistry; chemistry of cells
cytodiagnostyka [tsi-to-dyahg-nos-ti-kah] f. diagnosis based on microscopic study of cell samples
cytofizjologia [tsi-to-feez-yo-lo-gyah] f. physiology of animal and plant cells (tissues)
cytogenetycznie [tsi-to-ge-ne-tich-ńe] adv. cytogenetically
cytogenetyczny [tsi-to-ge-ne-tich-ni] adj.m. cytogenetic
cytogenetyk [tsi-to-ge-ne-tik] m. cytogeneticist
cytogenetyka [tsi-to-ge-ne-ti-kah] f. cytogenetics
cytokinetyczny [tsi-to-kee-ne-tich-ni] adj.m. cytokinetic
cytokineza [tsi-to-kee-ne-zah] f. cytokinesis
cytokinina [tsi-to-kee-ńee-nah] f. cytokinin
cytolog [tsi-to-log] m. cytologist
cytologia [tsi-to-lo-gyah] f. cytology
cytologicznie [tsi-to-lo-geech-ńe] adv. cytologically
cytologiczny [tsi-to-lo-geech-ni] adj.m. cytologic
cytoplazma [tsi-to-plahz-mah] f. cytoplasm
cytować [tsi-to-vahćh] v. quote; cite; adduce; refer (to a source, etc.); summon (*repeatedly*)
błędnie cytować [bwand-ńe tsi-to-vahćh] exp.: to misquote
cytowanie [tsi-to-vah-ńe] n. quotation; citation
godny cytowania [god-ni tsi-to-vah-ńah] exp.: quoteworthy
cytra [tsi-trah] f. zither; zittern; cittern; cithern
cytron [tsi-tron] m. citronella bush or tree
cytronelowy [tsi-tro-ne-lo-vi] adj.m. citronella (oil, etc.)
cytrus [tsi-troos] m. citrus
cytrusowy [tsi-troo-so-vi] adj.m. citrus (thorny trees, shrubs, fruit, etc.)
cytryn [tsi-trin] m. citrine
cytryna [tsi-tri-nah] f. lemon; lemon tree; slang: Citroen car
cytrynada [tsi-tri-nah-dah] f. lemonade
cytrynek [tsi-tri-nek] m. brimstone butterfly
cytrynian [tsi-tri-ńyahn] m. cytrate
cytrynka [tsi-trin-kah] f. lemon; lemon tree (diminutive of **cytryna**)
cytrynowiec [tsi-tri-no-vyets] m. lemon tree
cytrynowy [tsi-tri-no-vi] adj.m. of the lemon tree; of lemon trees; lemon (color, taste, grove, etc.); citric (acid, etc.)
cytrynówka [tsi-tri-noof-kah] f. lemon-flavored vodka
cytrzysta [tsi-tshis-tah] m. zither player
cytrzystka [tsi-tshist-kah] f. (woman) zither player
cytwar [tsit-fahr] m. zedoary (plant)
cyweta [tsi-ve-tah] f. civet; civet cat
cywil [tsi-veel] m. civilian
w cywilu [f tsi-vee-loo] exp.: in civilian life; in plain clothes; slang: in civvies; in civies
cywilista [tsi-vee-lees-tah] m. civilian; practitioner of the civil law
cywilistyka [tsi-vee-lees-ti-kah] f. civil law

cywilizacja [tsi-vee-lee-**zah**-tsyah] f. civilization
ucieczka od cywilizacji [oo-ćhech-kah ot tsi-vee-lee-**zah**-tsyee] exp.: flight from civilization; the call of the wild
cywilizacyjnie [tsi-vee-lee-zah-**tsiy**-ńe] adv. in respect of civilization
cywilizacyjny [tsi-vee-lee-zah-**tsiy**-ni] adj.m. of civilization; civilizing (role, influence, etc.)
cywilizator [tsi-vee-lee-**zah**-tor] m. civilizer
cywilizatorski [tsi-vee-lee-zah-**tor**-skee] adj.m. civilizing; civilizatory
cywilizatorstwo [tsi-vee-lee-zah-**tor**-stfo] n. work of civilization; civilizing activities
cywilizować [tsi-vee-lee-**zo**-vahćh] v. civilize; reclaim (from barbarism) (*repeatedly*)
cywilizować się [tsi-vee-lee-**zo**-vahćh śhan] v. become civilized (*repeatedly*)
cywilizowanie się [tsi-vee-lee-zo-**vah**-ńe śhan] n. becoming civilized
cywilizowany [tsi-vee-lee-zo-**vah**-ni] adj.m. civilized
cywilnie [tsi-**veel**-ńe] adv. in civilian clothes (not in uniform)
cywilny [tsi-**veel**-ni] adj.m. civilian; civil
odwaga cywilna [od-**vah**-gah tsi-**veel**-nah] exp.: moral courage
po cywilnemu [po tsi-veel-**ne**-moo] exp.: in civilian clothes; in plain clothes
prawo cywilne [**prah**-vo tsi-**veel**-ne] exp.: civil law
śmierć cywilna [śhmyerćh tsi-**veel**-nah] exp.: civil death
urząd stanu cywilnego [oo-zhownt **stah**-noo tsi-veel-**ne**-go] exp.: office of vital statistics; registry; registrar's office
cyzelator [tsi-ze-**lah**-tor] m. engraver; carver; meticulous person
cyzelatorski [tsi-ze-lah-**tor**-skee] adj.m. engraving (apprentice, etc.); carving (work, etc.)
cyzelatorstwo [tsi-ze-lah-**tor**-stfo] n. engraving; carving
cyzelatura [tsi-ze-lah-**too**-rah] f. quality of engraving; engraving
cyzelernia [tsi-ze-**ler**-ńah] f. engraving shop; engraving section of a factory
cyzelować [tsi-ze-**lo**-vahćh] v. engrave; carve; file; smooth; elaborate to perfection (*repeatedly*)
cyzelowanie [tsi-ze-lo-**vah**-ńe] n. engraving; carving; filing; smoothing; elaborating to perfection
cyzelunek [tsi-ze-**loo**-nek] m. engraving work; carving; filing; smoothing
cyzjojan [tsiz-**yo**-yahn] m. rhymed Latin calendar
cza-cza [chah chah] f. cha-cha; dance (three steps and a shuffle)
czacha [**chah**-khah] f. slang: head; skull
czad [chaht] m. carbon monoxide; smell of burning; fumes
czadnia [**chahd**-ńah] f. blast-furnace gas exit
czadnica [chahd-**ńee**-tsah] f. gas generator
czadnicowy [chahd-ńee-**tso**-vi] adj.m. gas-generator (combustion, etc.)
czador [**chah**-dor] m. Muslim female veil covering the whole person and providing openings for eyes
czadowy [chah-**do**-vi] adj.m. of carbon monoxide; of the smell of burning; of fumes
czadra [**chahd**-rah] f. Muslim (female) veil covering the whole person and providing openings for eyes
czaić się [**chah**-eećh śhan] v. lie in wait; lurk; stalk; crouch; couch; cower; pursue stealthily (*repeatedly*)
czajenie się [chah-**ye**-ńe śhan] n. lying in wait; lurking; stalking; crouching; couching; cowering; pursuing stealthily
czajka [**chahy**-kah] f. gull; lapwing; pewit; Cossack canoe
czajniczek [chahy-**ńee**-chek] m. tea pot (diminutive)
czajnik [**chahy**-ńeek] m. tea pot;

kettle
nastawić czajnik [nah-**stah**-veećh **chahy**-ńeek] exp.: to put the kettle on
czako [**chah**-ko] n. shako
czamara [chah-**mah**-rah] f. old-fashioned Polish overcoat
czamarka [chah-**mahr**-kah] f. small, old-fashioned Polish overcoat
czambuł [**chahm**-boow] m. Tartar striking force; slang: head; face
w czambuł [f **chahm**-boow] exp.: altogether; wholesale; in a lump; bodily; sweepingly; root-and-branch; thread and thrump
czapa [**chah**-pah] f. large cap; slang: execution (mob jargon)
dać w czapę [dahćh f **chah**-pan] exp.: slang: to shoot dead; to execute by shooting (mob jargon)
dostać w czapę [**dos**-tahćh f **chah**-pan] exp.: slang: to be shot dead; to be executed by a firing squad (mob jargon)
czapeczka [chah-**pech**-kah] f. bonnet; root-cap; pileorhiza
czapeczkowaty [chah-pech-ko-**vah**-ti] adj.m. cap-like
czapierzyć się [chah-**pye**-zhićh śhan] v. bristle; stand out (*repeatedly*)
czapka [**chahp**-kah] f. cap; pileus
bez czapki [bes **chahp**-kee] exp.: bare-headed
futrzana czapka [foot-**shah**-nah **chahp**-kah] exp.: fur cap
lisia czapka [**lee**-śhah **chahp**-kah] exp.: fox-fur cap; halo round the moon (sign of coming rain)
czapkarski [chahp-**kahr**-skee] adj.m. cap-maker's (trade, etc.)
czapkarstwo [chahp-**kahr**-stfo] n. cap making
czapkarz [**chahp**-kahsh] m. cap maker
czapkować [chahp-**ko**-vahćh] v. cap with reverence; bow (to); truckle (to) (*repeatedly*)
czapkowanie [chahp-ko-**vah**-ńe] n. obsequiousness; exhibiting a servile attitude
czapla [**chahp**-lah] f. heron
czaplątko [chahp-**lownt**-ko] n. young heron
czapli [**chahp**-lee] adj.m. heron's
czapliniec [chahp-**lee**-ńets] m. heron preserve
czaplowaty [chahp-lo-**vah**-ti] adj.m. of the family of herons; heron-like
czaplowate [chahp-lo-**vah**-te] pl. the family of herons
czapnictwo [chahp-**ńeets**-tfo] n. cap making
czapniczy [chahp-**ńee**-chi] adj.m. cap (selling stand, etc.)
czapnik [**chahp**-ńeek] m. cap maker
czaprak [**chahp**-rahk] m. horse blanket; caparison; trappings
czar [chahr] m. spell; charm; sorcery; magic; witchcraft; enchantment; wizardry; fascination; lure; enticement; glamor; attraction
czar prysnął [chahr **pris**-now] exp.: the spell was broken
kraina czarów [krah-**ee**-nah **chah**-roof] exp.: fairyland; wonderland
czara [**chah**-rah] f. bowl; wine-cup; goblet
czarci [**chahr**-ćhee] adj.m. diabolical; devilish; devil's
czarcię [**chahr**-ćhan] n. (diminutive) the devil; the deuce
czarcikęs [chahr-**ćhee**-kans] m. blue scabious (Succisa parentis)
czarcikęsik [chahr-ćhee-**kan**-śheek] m. herb of teasel family (Succisella inflexa)
czarcio [**chahr**-ćho] adv. diabolically; devilishly
czarczaf [**chahr**-chahf] m. face veil of Muslim women
czardasz [**chahr**-dash] m. czardas (Hungarian dance)
czareczka [chah-**rech**-kah] f. (nice) very small bowl; small goblet
czarka [**chahr**-kah] f. small bowl; small goblet
czarleston [chahr-**les**-ton] m. Charleston (dance)
czarna [**chahr**-nah] adj.f. black; dark; dirty; villainous; wicked; slang: f. dark-skinned girl; Negro woman; black coffee
czarna dusza [**chahr**-nah **doo**-shah] exp.: wicked soul
czarna giełda [**chahr**-nah **gew**-dah] exp.: black market

czarna owca [chahr-nah **of**-tsah] exp.: black sheep
czarna kawa [**chahr**-nah **kah**-vah] exp.: black coffee; social evening
duża czarna [**doo**-zhah **chahr**-nah] exp.: black coffee (full portion)
mała czarna [**mah**-wah **char**-nah] exp.: small cup of black coffee
pół czarnej [poow **chahr**-ney] exp.: demi-tasse (small cup of black coffee)
czarniak [**chahr**-ńahk] m. dark variety of cod; coal-fish
czarniawa [chahr-**ńah**-vah] f. black mass; dark mass (of people, clouds, etc.)
czarniawy [chahr-**ńah**-vi] adj.m. blackish
czarnidło [chahr-**ńeed**-wo] n. black; blacking; black paint; black ink
czarnieć [**chahr**-ńećh] v. blacken; paint black; black (*repeatedly*)
czarnieć się [**chahr**-ńećh śhan] v. blacken; become black; grow black; turn black; go black; show black; loom black; appear like a black (shape, spot, stain, etc.) (*repeatedly*)
czarnina [chahr-**ńee**-nah] f. soup of blood (of pigs, ducks, geese, etc.)
czarniusieńki [chahr-ńoo-**śheń**-kee] adj.m. as black as coal; very nicely black
czarniutki [chahr-**ńoot**-kee] adj.m. as black as coal; nicely black
czarno [**chahr**-no] adv. in black; blackly
czarno na białym [**chahr**-no nah **byah**-wim] exp.: in black and white
czarnobrewa [chahr-no-**bre**-vah] f. black-browed woman
czarnobrewy [chahr-no-**bre**-vi] adj.m. black-browed
czarnobrody [chahr-no-**bro**-di] adj.m. black-bearded
czarnobrunatny [chahr-no-broo-**naht**-ni] adj.m. brownish black
czarnogiełdowy [chahr-no-gew-**do**-vi] adj.m. black-market (trader, etc.); of black market
czarnogiełdziarz [chahr-no-**gew**-dźhash] m. black-marketeer
czarnogłowy [chahr-no-**gwo**-vi] adj.m. black-haired
czarnogłówka [chahr-no-**gwoof**-kah] f. variety of black-headed sheep
czarnogórski [chahr-no-**goor**-skee] adj.m. Montenegrin
Czarnogórzec [chahr-no-**goo**-zhets] m. (a) Montenegrin
czarnogrzywy [chahr-no-**gzhi**-vi] adj.m. black-maned
czarnoksięski [chahr-no-**kśhans**-kee] adj.m. magic; conjuring; sorcerer's; wizard's; wizard (practices, etc.)
czarnoksięstwo [chahr-no-**kśhans**-tfo] n. magic; sorcery; wizardry; witchcraft; voodoo
czarnoksiężnik [chahr-no-**kśhanzh**-ńeek] m. sorcerer; wizard; magician; voodoo doctor
czarnolicy [chahr-no-**lee**-tsi] adj.m. black-faced; dark-faced
czarnooki [chahr-no-**o**-kee] adj.m. black-eyed
czarnooprawny [chahr-no-o-**prahv**-ni] adj.m. black-rimmed; in black binding
czarnopióry [chahr-no-**pyoo**-ri] adj.m. black-feathered
czarnopolowy [chahr-no-po-**lo**-vi] adj.m. of black squares on the chess board
czarnorogi [chahr-no-**ro**-gee] adj.m. black-horned
czarnorynkowy [chahr-no-rin-**ko**-vi] adj.m. black-market (deal, etc.)
czarnoseciniec [chahr-no-se-**ćhee**-ńets] m. member of the Black-Hundred; Black-Hundred reactionary (anti-Semite)
czarnoskóra [chahr-no-**skoo**-rah] f. black-skinned woman
czarnoskóry [chahr-no-**skoo**-ri] adj.m. black-skinned; m. black
czarnoskrzydlaty [chahr-no-skshi-**dlah**-ti] adj.m. black-winged
czarność [**chahr**-nośhćh] f. the black (of a paint, etc.); blackness (of the night, skin, hair, etc.); darkness; nigritude
czarnowidz [chahr-**no**-veets] m. pessimist
czarnowidztwo [chahr-no-**veets**-tfo] n. pessimism
czarnowłosy [chahr-no-**vwo**-si]

adj.m. black-haired
czarnowron [chahr-**no**-vron] m. black crow
czarnoziem [chahr-**no**-źhem] m. humus; (black) mould
czarnoziemny [chahr-no-**źhem**-ni] adj.m. humus (soil, etc.)
czarnuch [**chahr**-nookh] m. colloq: black-haired boy; Gipsy; swarthy-complexioned man; slang: Negro; darky; vulg.: Nigger
czarnucha [chahr-**noo**-khah] f. black-haired girl; Gipsy girl; swarthy-complexioned girl; slang: Negro girl; darky
czarnuchowaty [chahr-noo-kho-**vah**-ti] adj.m. of black-beetle variety
czarnuchowate [chahr-noo-kho-**vah**-te] pl. the family of a black-beetle variety (Tenebrionidae)
czarnula [chahr-**noo**-lah] f. black-haired darling
czarnulka [chahr-**nool**-kah] f. black-haired darling
czarnuszka [chahr-**noosh**-kah] f. black-haired darling
czarny [**chahr**-ni] adj.m. black; dark; dirty; villainous; wicked; m. dark-skinned; Negro; reactionary; slang: Catholic priest (mob jargon)
czarne myśli [**chahr**-ne **miśh**-lee] exp.: dejection; doldrums; wretchedness; blues
czarny charakter [**chahr**-ni khah-**rahk**-ter] exp.: mischief-maker; viper; villain; bad man
czarny rynek [**chahr**-ni **ri**-nek] exp.: black market
na czarną godzinę [nah **chahr**-nown go-**dźhee**-nan] exp.: against a rainy day
czarodziej [chah-**ro**-dźhey] m. wizard; sorcerer; magician; charmer; enchanter
czarodziejka [chah-ro-**dźhey**-kah] f. sorceress; charmer; enchantress
czarodziejski [chah-ro-**dźhey**-skee] adj.m. magic(al); fairy
różdżka czarodziejska [**rooshch**-kah chah-ro-**dźhey**-skah] exp.: magic wand
czarodziejsko [chah-ro-**dźhey**-sko] adv. magically; by magic
czarodziejstwo [chah-ro-**dźhey**-stfo] n. magic; sorcery; witchcraft
czarować [chah-**ro**-vahćh] v. charm; bewitch; work charms; perform marvels; beguile; ravish; enchant; delight; fascinate; captivate; entice; lure; mislead (*repeatedly*)
czarowanie [chah-ro-**vah**-ńe] n. sorcery; magic
czarownica [chah-rov-**ńee**-tsah] f. sorceress; witch; hag; harridan; a disreputable, shrewish old woman
czarowniczy [chah-rov-**ńee**-chi] adj.m. magic; bewitching
czarownie [chah-**rov**-ńe] adv. enchantingly; ravishingly; delightfully; with fascination; in a captivating way; enthrallingly; glamorously
czarownik [chah-**rov**-ńeek] m. sorcerer; wizard; magician; charmer; enchanter
czarowny [chah-**rov**-ni] adj.m. charming; enchanting; ravishing; delightful; fascinating; captivating; enthralling; glamorous; magic
czart [chahrt] m. devil; deuce
czartawa [chahr-**tah**-vah] f. evening primrose (Circacea); enchanter's nightshade
czarter [**chahr**-ter] m. charter
czarterować [chahr-te-**ro**-vahćh] v. charter (airplanes, ships, etc.) (*repeatedly*)
czarterowanie [chahr-te-ro-**vah**-ńe] n. charter; chartering
czarterowy [chahr-te-**ro**-vi] adj.m. charter (airplane, ship, etc.); of a charter
czarterpartia [chahr-ter-**pahr**-tyah] f. charter party
czartowski [chahr-**tof**-skee] adj.m. devil's; devilish; hellish
czartysta [chahr-**tis**-tah] m. follower of chartism
czartystowski [chahr-tis-**tof**-skee] adj.m. of chartism
czartyzm [**chahr**-tizm] m. chartism (labor movement, 1836-1848, Brit.)
czarująco [chah-roo-**yown**-tso] adv. enchantingly; in a bewitching way; charmingly; fascinatingly;

delightfully
czarujący [chah-roo-yown-tsi] adj.m. charming; fascinating; enchanting; bewitching; delightful
czaruś [**chah**-roośh] m. attentive, handsome young man
czas [chahs] m. time; duration; season; age; day; days; moment; while; space; bout; spell; grammatical tense; weather
co pewien czas [tso **pe**-vyen chahs] exp.: now and then; now and again; sometimes
czas przeszły [chahs **pshe**-shwi] exp.: past; past tense
czas przyszły [chahs **pshi**-shwi] exp.: future; future tense
czas teraźniejszy [chahs te-rahźh-**ńey**-shi] exp.: present; present tense
czas lokalny [chahs lo-**kahl**-ni] exp.: local time
czas słoneczny [chahs swo-**nech**-ni] exp.: solar time
czas środkowoeuropejski [chahs śhrot-**ko**-vo-ew-ro-**pey**-skee] exp.: Central-European Time
czas wolny [chahs **vol**-ni] exp.: spare time
do czasu aż [do **chah**-soo ahsh] exp.: till; until
lepsze czasy [**lep**-she **chah**-si] exp.: better days
na czasie [nah **chah**-śhe] exp.: timely; well-timed
na jakiś czas [nah **yah**-keeśh chahs] exp.: for a time
od czasu do czasu [ot **chah**-soo do **chah**-soo] exp.: from time to time
od czasu jak [ot chah-soo yahk] exp.: since
od jakiegoś czasu [ot yah-ke-gośh **chah**-soo] exp.: for some time now
od tego czasu [ot **te**-go **chah**-soo] exp.: ever since
po pewnym czasie [po **pev**-nim **chah**-śhe] exp.: after a while
przez cały ten czas [pshes **tsah**-wi ten chahs] exp.: all the time
z czasem [s **chah**-sem] exp.: in course of time
za czasów [zah **chah**-soof] exp.: at the time
za moich czasów [zah **mo**-eekh **chah**-soof] exp.: at my time
złe czasy [zwe **chah**-si] exp.: hard times
zmysł czasu [zmisw **chah**-soo] exp.: the sense of time
czasami [chah-**sah**-mee] adv. at times; occasionally; now and then; by chance; by any chance
czasem [**chah**-sem] adv. sometimes; occasionally; by any chance; now and then; by chance
z czasem [s **chah**-sem] exp.: in course of time
czasochłonnie [chah-so-**khwon**-ńe] adv. in a time-consuming way
czasochłonność [chah-so-**khwon**-nośhćh] f. time-consuming characteristic
czasochłonny [chah-so-**khwon**-ni] adj.m. time-consuming
czasomierz [chah-**so**-myesh] m. timer; timing device
czasopismo [chah-so-**pees**-mo] n. periodical; magazine; journal
czasopiśmiennictwo [chah-so-peeśh-myen-**ńeets**-tfo] n. periodical press
czasopiśmienniczy [chah-so-peeśh-myen-**ńee**-chi] adj.m. of the periodical press
czasoprzestrzenny [chah-so-pshes-**tshen**-ni] adj.m. of time-space system (in the theory of relativity)
czasoprzestrzeń [chah-so-**pshes**-tsheń] f. time-space system (in the theory of relativity)
czasownik [chah-**sov**-ńeek] m. verb
czasownikowo [chah-sov-ńee-**ko**-vo] adv. in form of a verb
czasownikowy [chah-sov-ńee-**ko**-vi] adj.m. verbal (form, etc.)
czasowo [chah-**so**-vo] adv. temporarily; for the time being; provisionally; in respect of time
czasowość [chah-**so**-vośhćh] f. transitoriness
czasowy [chah-**so**-vi] adj.m. temporal; temporary; of time; time; transient; transitory; provisional
bomba czasowa [**bom**-bah chah-**so**-vah] exp.: time bomb

czasza [**chah**-shah] f. bowl; canopy
czaszka [**chahsh**-kah] f. skull; cranium; brain pan; slang: head
trupia czaszka [troo-pyah **chahsh**-kah] exp.: death's-head
czaszkowiec [chahsh-**ko**-vyets] m. cranial animal
czaszkowce [chahsh-**kof**-tse] pl. cranial animals; Craniata
czaszkowy [chahsh-**ko**-vi] adj.m. cranial
czata [**chah**-tah] f. watch; outlook; wait; ambush; ambuscade; outpost
na czatach [nah **chah**-tahkh] exp.: lying in ambush; see: **czatować**
czatować [chah-**to**-vahćh] v. lurk; lie in wait (for); lie in ambush; be on the watch (*repeatedly*)
czatować na sposobność [chah-to-vahćh nah spo-**sob**-nośhćh] exp.: to watch one's opportunity
czatowanie [chah-to-**vah**-ńe] n. lurking; lying in wait (for); being on the watch; ambush
czatownik [chah-**tov**-ńeek] m. look-out man; watch; the watch
czaty [**chah**-ti] pl. watch; lookout; wait; ambush; outpost
być na czatach [bićh nah **chah**-tahkh] exp.: to be on the lookout; to keep (a good) watch
cząber [ch<u>own</u>-ber] m. savory (plant)
cząsteczka [ch<u>own</u>-**stech**-kah] f. particle; molecule; corpuscle; a very small part; tiny particle
cząsteczkowy [ch<u>own</u>-stech-**ko**-vi] adj.m. molecular; corpuscular
cząstka [ch<u>own</u>st-kah] f. particle; small part; share; portion; small segment
cząstkowo [ch<u>own</u>-**stko**-vo] adv. partially; fractionally; piece by piece; by piecemeal
cząstkowy [ch<u>own</u>-**stko**-vi] adj.m. partial; fractional; fragmentary
czchać [chkhahćh] v. sneeze; scamper (*repeatedly*)
czchnąć [chkhn<u>own</u>ćh] v. sneeze; scamper; run; go quickly
czchnięcie [chkhń<u>an</u>-ćhe] n. sneeze; a sneeze; a scampering
czciciel [**chćhee**-ćhel] m. adorer; worshipper; idolater; venerator; devotee; votary
czcicielka [chćhee-**ćhel**-kah] f. worshipper; idolatress; venerator; devotee; votary
czcić [chćheećh] v. adore; worship; idolize; venerate; revere; hold sacred; celebrate; observe (*repeatedly*)
czcigodnie [chćhee-**god**-ńe] adv. honorably; with veneration; with reverence
czcigodny [chćhee-**god**-ni] adj.m. honorable; revered; venerable
czcionka [**chćhon**-kah] f. type; character; letter in print
czcionkowy [chćhon-**ko**-vi] adj.m. type (shape, metal, etc.)
czcionnik [**chćhon**-ńeek] m. container (case) of type-characters
czczenie [**chche**-ńe] n. veneration; celebration
czczo [chcho] adv. empty (stomach); fasting; emptily; vainly; idly; futilely
jestem na czczo [**yes**-tem nah chcho] exp.: I have not had my breakfast; I have had nothing to eat; I have not had any breakfast
na czczo [nah chcho] exp.: on an empty stomach; unfed; fasting
czczość [chchośhćh] f. feeling of emptiness in the stomach; futility
czczy [chchi] adj.m. empty; vain; futile; idle
czcza formalność [chchah for-**mahl**-nośhćh] exp.: mere formality
czcza gadanina [chchah gah-dah-**ńee**-nah] exp.: idle talk; clap-trap; twaddle; blab; blah
czczy pretekst [chchi **pre**-tekst] exp.: flimsy pretext
Czech [chekh] m. Czech
czechista [che-**khees**-tah] m. student of Czech literature, language, and culture
czechizacja [che-khee-**zah**-tsyah] f. Czechization
czechizm [**che**-kheezm] m. borrowing from Czech language
czechizować [che-khee-**zo**-vahćh] v. submit to Czech influence

(*repeatedly*)
czechizować się [che-khee-zo-vahćh śhan] v. accept Czech influence; become Czech (*repeatedly*)
czechizowanie [che-khee-zo-**vah**-ńe] n. submission to Czech influence
czeczota [che-**cho**-tah] f. birch-wood prized as veneer material
czeczotka [che-**chot**-kah] f. redpoll (bird); birch-wood prized as veneer material
czeczotkowatość [che-chot-ko-**vah**-tośhćh] f. birch-wood characteristic (fibers, etc.)
czeczotkowy [che-chot-**ko**-vi] adj.m. birch-wood (table, etc.)
czego [che-go] conjunction: why?; what?; what; why
czegoś [che-gośh] conj. = **coś**
czegoż [che-gosh] conj. = **cóż**
czegóż [che-goosh] conj. = **cóż**
czek [chek] m. check (in banking); cheque (Brit.)
czek bez pokrycia [chek bes po-**kri**-ćhah] exp.: bad check; hot check; unsecured check
czek kasowy [chek kah-**so**-vi] exp.: cashier's check
książka czekowa [kśhownsh-kah che-**ko**-vah] exp.: check-book
obrót czekowy [**ob**-root che-**ko**-vi] exp.: check system; transactions in checks
rachunek czekowy [rah-**khoo**-nek che-**ko**-vi] exp.: checking account
czekać [che-kahćh] v. wait (for); await; stand by; expect; look forward (for); be ready for; waste time; be in store (for) (*repeatedly*)
kazać komuś czekać [kah-zahćh ko-moośh **che**-kahćh] exp.: to keep somebody waiting
tylko czekać! [til-ko **che**-kahćh] excl.: any moment!
czekan [che-kahn] m. pickhammer; ice-axe; pick; pickax; pickaxe; kind of a flute
czekanie [che-**kah**-ńe] n. wait
długie czekanie [**dwoo**-ge che-**kah**-ńe] exp.: a long wait
czekanista [che-kah-**ńees**-tah] m. flutist
czekolada [che-ko-**lah**-dah] f. chocolate; slab of chocolate
filiżanka czekolady [fee-lee-**zhahn**-kah che-ko-**lah**-di] exp.: cup of chocolate
czekoladka [che-ko-**laht**-kah] f. small chocolate; chocolate candy
czekoladowo [che-ko-lah-**do**-vo] adv. in (or of) chocolate brown color
czekoladowy [che-ko-lah-**do**-vi] adj.m. of chocolate; chocolate brown (color)
czekowy [che-**ko**-vi] adj.m. checking
książeczka czekowa [kśhown-**zhech**-kah che-**ko**-vah] exp.: checkbook; cheque-book (Brit.)
rachunek czekowy [rah-**khoo**-nek che-**ko**-vi] exp.: checking account
czeladka [che-**laht**-kah] f. slang: members of a household
czeladniczy [che-lahd-**ńee**-chi] adj.m. journeyman's; apprentice's
czeladnik [che-**lahd**-ńeek] m. journeyman; apprentice
czeladny [che-**lahd**-ni] adj.m. journeyman's; apprentice's
czeladź [**che**-lahćh] f. domestics; pl. household servants; retinue
czelesta [che-**les**-tah] f. celesta
czelista [che-**lees**-tah] m. cellist
czelnie [**chel**-ńe] adv. impudently; with effrontery; with nerve; with audacity; with self-assurance
czelność [**chel**-nośhćh] f. impudence; effrontery; nerve
czelny [**chel**-ni] adj.m. insolent; impudent; brazen-faced; cocky; arrogant; self-assured; outstanding
czeluść [**che**-loośhćh] f. abyss; gulf; precipice; depths
czemchać [**chem**-khahćh] v. chafe (*repeatedly*)
czemchanie [chem-**khah**-ńe] n. chafing
czempion [**chem**-pyon] m. champion; first place winner in competition
czempionat [chem-**pyo**-naht] m. championship
czempionka [chem-**pyon**-kah] f. (woman) champion; first place winner in competition
czemu [**che**-moo] part. why?; to what?; what to?; what for?

czemuż [che-moosh] part. = **cóż**

czep [chep] m. sticky thistle; colloq: velcro; woven interlock

czepeczek [che-pe-chek] m. (small, nice) bonnet; hood; night cap; caul; calyptra

czepek [che-pek] m. bonnet; hood; night cap; caul; calyptra

urodzić się w czepku [oo-ro-dźheećh śhan f chep-koo] exp.: to be born with a silver spoon in one's mouth

czepiać [che-pyahćh] v. molest; annoy; ask questions (*repeatedly*)

czepiać się [che-pyahćh śhan] v. adhere (to); stick (to); cling (to a hope, etc.); catch (at); hang (on); peck (at); depend on generosity; curry favor (with); find fault (with); pick holes (in); carp (at) (*repeatedly*)

czepiak [che-pyahk] m. spidermonkey

czepianie [che-pyah-ńe] n. molesting; annoying

czepianie się [che-pyah-ńe śhan] n. sticking; clinging; picking holes

czepić [che-peećh] v. coif; put coif on a bride (*repeatedly*)

czepić się [che-peećh śhan] v. adhere (to); stick (to); cling (to a hope, etc.); catch (at); hang (on); peck (at); depend on generosity; curry favor (with); find fault (with); pick holes (in); carp (at)

czepiec [che-pyets] m. hood; cap; coif; caul; slang: marriage

czepiga [che-pee-gah] f. plow-handle; plow-tail

czepiny [che-pee-ni] pl. sticky items; burrs

czepliwy [chep-lee-vi] adj.m. sticky; adhesive; cling; tenacious; tacky; bellicose; quarrelsome

czepny [chep-ni] adj.m. sticky; adhesive; cling; tenacious; tacky

czerecha [che-re-khah] f. (sour-sweet) cherry tree

czereda [che-re-dah] f. gang; throng; crowd; swarm; pack

czeremcha [che-rem-khah] f. bird cherry; bird's cherry; hagberry

czeremchowy [che-rem-kho-vi] adj.m. bird-cherry (wine, etc.); hagberry (wine, etc.)

czeremszyna [che-rem-shi-nah] f. bird-cherry blossom; bird-cherry grove; hagberry grove

czerep [che-rep] m. shell; skull; fragment; splinter; shard; potsherd; ruins; body of a pot

czereśnia [che-reśh-ńah] f. cherry; (sweet) cherry tree; gean

czereśniak [che-reśh-ńahk] m. slang: farmer

czereśniowy [che-reśh-ńo-vi] adj. m. of the cherry; cherry (juice)

Czerkies [cher-kes] m. Circassian

Czerkieska [cher-kes-kah] f. Circassian (woman)

czerkieska [cher-kes-kah] f. fur cap; Circassian coat

czermień [cher-myeń] f. poisonous marsh lily (Calla palustris)

czerniaczka [cher-ńahch-kah] f. melanosis; skin cancer

czerniaczkowy [cher-ńahch-ko-vi] adj.m. melanotic; of skin cancer

czerniak [cher-ńahk] m. melanosis; skin cancer

czernica [cher-ńee-tsah] f. blueberry; bilberry; whortleberry; blackberry; blueberry shrub

czernić [cher-ńeećh] v. blacken; black; paint black; loom black; stain black; show black (*repeatedly*)

czernić się [cher-ńeećh śhan] v. blacken; turn black; grow black; go black; stain black; loom black; show black (*repeatedly*)

czernidlak [cher-ńeed-lahk] m. variety of mushroom (Coprinus)

czernidło [cher-ńeed-wo] n. blacking; printing ink

czernidłowy [cher-ńee-dwo-vi] adj.m. of printing ink

czerniec [cher-ńets] m. Actaea herb and (poisonous) baneberry

czernieć [cher-ńećh] v. blacken; turn black; grow black; go black; stain black; loom black; show black (*repeatedly*)

czernienie [cher-ńe-ńe] n. blackening; turning black

czernina [cher-ńee-nah] f. black soup of blood (of pig, duck, or goose)

czernuszka [cher-**noosh**-kah] f. fennelflower (Nigella)
czerń [cherń] f. black color; black dress; black clothes; black pigment; blackness (of the night, etc.); riff-raff; rabble; populace
czerpaczka [cher-**pahch**-kah] f. ship-mounted dredge
czerpać [**cher**-pahćh] v. scoop; draw (water from a well, etc.); ladle; derive (benefit) (*repeatedly*)
czerpadło [cher-**pahd**-wo] n. scoop; bucket (mounted on a machine)
czerpak [**cher**-pahk] m. scoop; scooper; bail; bucket; ladle; dipper; (type of) fish net
czerpakowy [cher-pah-**ko**-vi] adj.m. of a scoop
czerpalniczy [cher-pahl-**ńee**-chi] adj.m. scoop (frame, etc.)
czerpanie [cher-**pah**-ńe] n. drawing (water, etc.); scooping (dirt, etc.)
czerparka [cher-**pahr**-kah] f. scoop; dredge; digger; excavator
czerpatka [cher-**paht**-kah] f. hydrophyllum (plant)
czerpatkowaty [cher-paht-ko-**vah**-ti] adj.m. of hydrophyllum family
czerpatkowate [cher-paht-ko-**vah**-te] pl. the hydrophyllum family; the water-leaf family of plants
czerpnia [**cherp**-ńah] f. (air, etc.) intake
czerstwieć [**cher**-stfyećh] v. become stale; become ruddy; grow vigorous; acquire strength (*repeatedly*)
czerstwienie [cher-**stfye**-ńe] n. becoming stale; becoming ruddy; growing vigorous; acquiring strength
czerstwo [**cher**-stfo] adv. healthily
czerstwo wyglądać [**cher**-stfo vig-lown-dahćh] exp.: to look healthy; to look hale and hearty
czerstwość [**cher**-stfośhćh] f. staleness; vigor; robustness
czerstwy [**cher**-stfi] adj.m. stale; robust (man); firm; hale and hearty; nimble; ruddy; fresh
czert [chert] m. chert (rock)
czerw [cherf] m. worm; grub; maggot; bee larva
czerwcowy [**cherf-tso**-vi] adj.m. in June; June (weather, etc.)
czerwczyk [**cherf**-chik] m. a species of May-bug
czerwica [cher-**vee**-tsah] f. wood-boring insect
czerwić [**cher**-veećh] v. lay bee eggs in a beehive (*repeatedly*)
czerwiec [**cher**-vyets] m. June; scleranth; knawel; nopal; cochineal cactus
czerwce [**cherf**-tse] pl. the scale insects; kermes dyestuff
czerwienica [cher-vye-**ńee**-tsah] f. polycythemia
czerwienić [cher-**vye**-ńeećh] v. redden; paint red; give a red color (to) (*repeatedly*)
czerwienić się [cher-**vye**-ńeećh śhan] v. blush; redden; turn crimson; show red; appear red (*repeatedly*)
czerwienieć [cher-**vye**-ńećh] v. blush; redden; turn crimson; show red; appear red (*repeatedly*)
czerwienienie [cher-vye-**ńe**-ńe] n. reddening; appearing red
czerwienienie się [cher-vye-**ńe**-ńe śhan] n. blushing
czerwienny [cher-**vyen**-ni] adj.m. of hearts (in a card game)
czerwień [**cher**-vyeń] f. red (color); redness; scarlet; crimson; red paint; red texture; red fabric; red garment; pl.: hearts (in a card game)
czerwik [**cher**-veek] m. coca; worm; grub; maggot; bee larva
czerwikowate [cher-vee-ko-**vah**-te] pl. erythroxylaceous family of plants
czerwioch [**cher**-vyokh] m. scolex
czerwiogubnie [cher-vyo-**goob**-ńe] adv. (to act, etc.) as a vermifuge
czerwiogubny [cher-vyo-**goob**-ni] adj.m. vermicidal; vermifugal; vermicide; anthelmintic
czerwionka [cher-**vyon**-kah] f. rudd
czerwiowy [cher-**vyo**-vi] adj.m. of a grub; of a maggot; of bee larva
czerwonak [cher-**vo**-nahk] m. flamingo
czerwonawo [cher-vo-**nah**-vo] adv. in reddish color
czerwonawy [cher-vo-**nah**-vi] adj.m.

reddish
czerwoniec [cher-**vo**-ńets] m. ten-ruble bill; ten-ruble coin in Russia and in Soviet Union
czerwonka [cher-**von**-kah] f. dysentery
czerwonkowy [cher-von-**ko**-vi] adj.m. dysenteric
czerwono [cher-**vo**-no] adv. in red; prefix: red- (brown, white, etc.)
czerwonoarmista [cher-vo-no-ahr-**mees**-tah] m. soldier of the Red Army
czerwonobrunatny [cher-vo-no-broo-**naht**-ni] adj.m. red-brown
czerwonogwardyjski [cher-vo-no-gvahr-**diy**-skee] adj.m. of the Red Army
czerwonogwardzista [cher-vo-no-gvahr-**dźhees**-tah] m. (a, the) Red Army soldier
czerwonokrzyski [cher-vo-no-**kshis**-kee] adj.m. of the Red Cross
czerwononogi [cher-vo-no-**no**-gee] adj.m. red-legged
czerwononosy [cher-vo-no-**no**-si] adj.m. red-nosed
czerwonoskórnictwo [cher-vo-no-skoor-**ńeets**-tfo] n. vegetable tanning
czerwonoskóry [cher-vo-no-**skoo**-ri] adj.m. red-skinned; copper-skin (Indian); m. redskin Indian
czerwonoskrzydły [cher-vo-no-**skshid**-wi] adj.m. red-winged
czerwoność [cher-**vo**-nośhćh] f. red color; redness
czerwoność twarzy [cher-**vo**-nośhćh **tfah**-zhi] exp.: ruddiness; floridity; erubescence
czerwony [cher-**vo**-ni] adj.m. red; scarlet; crimson; ruddy; m. red
czerwoni [cher-**vo**-ńee] pl. the reds
Czerwony Krzyż [cher-**vo**-ni kshish] exp.: the Red Cross
czerwony na twarzy [cher-**vo**-ni nah **tfah**-zhi] exp.: red-faced; ruddy; florid; erubescent; rubicund
czerwończyk [cher-**voń**-chik] m. variety of butterfly
czesać [che-sahćh] v. comb; brush; dress hair; do hair; hackle (flax) (*repeatedly*)
czesać się [**che**-sahćh śh<u>an</u>] v. comb one's hair; brush one's hair; dress one's hair; do one's hair; tidy one's hair (*repeatedly*)
czesak [**che**-sahk] m. urchin
czesalnia [che-**sahl**-ńah] f. combing mill; hackling room; hackler
czesalniczy [che-sahl-**ńee**-chi] adj.m. hackling (comb, etc.)
czesanie [che-**sah**-ńe] n. hairdressing; hackling (of flax)
czesanka [che-**sahn**-kah] f. worsted; carded wool; cheviot
czesankowy [che-sahn-**ko**-vi] adj.m. of worsted; worsted (fabric, etc.); of cheviot; cheviot (cloth, dress, etc.)
czesarka [che-**sahr**-kah] f. comber; hackling machine
czeski [**ches**-kee] adj.m. Czech
czesne [**ches**-ne] n. tuition
czester [**ches**-ter] m. Chester cheese
czesucza [che-**soo**-chah] f. fabric of raw silk
czesuczowy [che-soo-**cho**-vi] adj.m. of raw silk
czesuncza [che-**soon**-chah] f. fabric of raw silk
czeszczyzna [chesh-**chiz**-nah] f. Czech language; Czech culture
Czeszka [**chesh**-kah] f. Czech woman or girl
cześć [cheśhćh] f. honor; cult; worship; respect; adoration; reverence; veneration; good name; greeting: excl.: hi!; hello! cheerio! (Brit.)
ku czci [koo chćhee] exp.: in honor of; in commemoration of
na cześć [nah cheśhćh] exp.: in honor of; in praise of; in commemoration of
oddawać cześć [od-**dah**-vahćh cheśhćh] exp.: to honor; to venerate; to revere; to do honor; to pay reverence; to pay homage; to regard with veneration; to treat with respect
utrata czci [oo-**trah**-tah chćhee] exp.: infamy; loss of face; disgrace; outlawry
cześnik [**cheśh**-ńeek] m. cupbearer

cześnikostwo [cheśh-ńee-**kos**-tfo] n. cupbearer's dignity (function)
częstawo [chan-**stah**-vo] adv. not very frequently
częstawy [chan-**stah**-vi] adj.m. moderately frequent; not very frequent
często [**chan**-sto] adv. often; frequently; many times; again and again
często gęsto [**chans**-to **gan**-sto] exp.: colloq: more often than not
dość często [dośhćh **chan**-sto] exp.: now and again; now and then
częstochowski [chan-sto-**khof**-skee] adj.m. of Częstochowa
rymy częstochowskie [**ri**-mi chan-sto-**khof**-ske] exp.: doggerel rhymes
częstokół [chan-**sto**-koow] m. palisade
częstokroć [chan-**sto**-kroćh] adv. often; repeatedly; frequently; many a time; oftentimes; more often than not
częstokrotnie [chan-sto-**krot**-ńe] adv. often; repeatedly; frequently; many a time; oftentimes; more often than not
częstokrotny [chan-sto-**krot**-ni] adj.m. frequent; of frequent occurrence; repeated
częstomocz [chan-**sto**-moch] m. frequent urination
częstoskurcz [chan-**sto**-skoorch] m. tachycardia; rapid heart action
częstościomierz [chan-sto-**śhćho**-myesh] m. frequency meter
częstość [**chan**-stośhćh] f. frequency; frequent occurrence; recurrence
częstotliwie [chan-sto-**tlee**-vye] adv. repeatedly; in rapid succession
częstotliwościomierz [chan-sto-tlee-vośh-**ćho**-myesh] m. frequency meter
częstotliwość [chan-sto-**tlee**-vośhćh] f. frequency; recurrence; rapid occurrence
częstotliwy [chan-sto-**tlee**-vi] adj.m. repeated; recurring in rapid succession; gram.: frequentative; iterative
częstować [chan-**sto**-vahćh] v. treat (to something); regale (with) (*repeatedly*)
częstować się [chan-**sto**-vahćh śhan] v. treat oneself (to something); help oneself (to); regale one another (with) (*repeatedly*)
częstowanie [chan-sto-**vah**-ńe] n. a treat; treat
częstszy [**chans**-tshi] adj.m. more frequent; repeated more often
coraz częstszy [**tso**-rahs **chans**-tshi] exp.: more and more frequent; occurring more and more frequently
częsty [**chans**-ti] adj.m. frequent; repeated often; of frequent occurrence
częściej [**chan**-śhćhey] adv. more often; more frequently
coraz częściej [**tso**-rahs **chan**-śhćhey] exp.: more and more frequently; occurring with an increasing frequency
częściowo [chan-**śhćho**-vo] adv. partly; in part; partially
częściowo tak [chan-**śhćho**-vo tahk] exp.: yes, in a way
tylko częściowo [**til**-ko chan-**śhćho**-vo] exp.: not altogether; incompletely
częściowy [chan-**śhćho**-vi] adj.m. partial; fragmentary
część [chanśhćh] f. part; share; section; piece; portion; instalment; unit; quota
część składowa [chanśhćh skwah-**do**-vah] exp.: component
część zamienna [chanśhćh zah-**myen**-nah] exp.: spare part
lwia część [lvyah chanśhćh] exp.: the lion's share; the great majority; the vast majority
po części [po **chan**-śhćhee] exp.: partly; in part; as a part (of); in a sense; in a way; in a manner; in a manner of speaking
w części [f **chan**-śhćhee] exp.: partly; in part; part (ownership, etc.); in a sense; in a way; in a manner; in a manner of speaking
Czilijczyk [chi-**leey**-chik] m. (a) Chilean

czilijski [chi-**leey**-skee] adj.m. Chilean; of Chile; Chilian
czkać [chkahćh] v. hiccup (*repeatedly*)
czkanie [**chkah**-ńe] n. a hiccup; hiccups
czkawka [**chkahf**-kah] f. hiccups
czknąć [chkn<u>own</u>ćh] v. hiccup
czknięcie [**chkń**<u>an</u>-ćhe] n. a hiccup
człapać [**chwah**-pahćh] v. shuffle (along); amble; clack (one's shoes, etc.) (*repeatedly*)
człapak [**chwah**-pahk] m. ambler
człapanie [chwah-**pah**-ńe] n. shuffling (along); ambling; clacking (one's shoes, slippers, sandals, etc.)
człap-człap [chwahp chwahp] exp.: flop-flop; clip-clop
człapu-człapu [**chwah**-poo **chwah**-poo] exp.: flop-flop; clip-clop
człapy [**chwah**-pi] pl. old, worn-out shoes
człeczek [**chwe**-chek] m. diminutive person; undersized person; midge; midget; homunculus; manikin
człeczy [**chwe**-chi] adj.m. human
człeczyna [chwe-**chi**-nah] m. poor little fellow; bit of a man; whipper-snapper
człeczysko [chwe-**chi**-sko] n. great big man; great big guy
człek [chwek] m. man; fellow; guy; pron.: one; you; a guy
człekokształtny [chwe-ko-**kshtahwt**-ni] adj.m. anthropoidal; subhuman
człekokształtne [chwe-ko-**kshtahwt**-ne] pl. anthropoids
człon [chwon] m. element (of construction, etc.); segment; link; member; gram.: clause (of a sentence)
członek [**chwo**-nek] m. limb; member (of a party, family, etc.); man's sex organ; penis; vulg. cock; pl.: membership; constituency
członkowie towarzystwa [chwon-**ko**-vye to-vah-**zhist**-fah] exp.: members of an association
członiasty [chwo-**ńahs**-ti] adj.m. articulate; joined (limb, etc.)
członkini [chwon-**kee**-ńee] f. woman member (of a party, club, association, etc.)
członkonóg [chwon-**ko**-noog] n. arthropod
członkonogi [chwon-ko-**no**-gee] pl. Arthropoda
członkostwo [chwon-**ko**-stfo] n. membership
członkować [chwon-**ko**-vahćh] v. articulate; segment (*repeatedly*)
członkowanie [chwon-ko-**vah**-ńe] n. articulation
członkowaty [chwon-ko-**vah**-ti] adj.m. membered; jointed
członkowski [chwon-**kof**-skee] adj.m. member's; members'; membership (fee); party (dues)
członować [chwo-**no**-vahćh] v. segment; articulate (*repeatedly*)
członowanie [chwo-no-**vah**-ńe] n. articulation
członowiec [chwo-**no**-vyets] m. entromostracan
członowce [chwo-**nof**-tse] pl. the Entromostraca family
członowość [chwo-**no**-vośhćh] f. segmentation; cleavage
członowy [chwo-**no**-vi] adj.m. segmental; segmentary
człowieczek [chwo-**vye**-chek] m. little guy; homunculi
człowieczeństwo [chwo-vye-**cheń**-stfo] n. humanity; human nature; human dignity; mankind
człowieczy [chwo-**vye**-chi] adj.m. human
Syn Człowieczy [sin chwo-**vye**-chi] exp.: the Son of Man
człowieczyna [chwo-vye-**chi**-nah] m. bit of a man; poor little devil; whipper-snapper
człowieczysko [chwo-vye-**chi**-sko] m. great big guy; great big man
człowiek [**chwo**-vyek] m. man; a human being; individual; guy; somebody; someone; a one; you; a man; slang: bloke
bądź człowiekiem [b<u>own</u>ćh chwo-**vye**-<u>k</u>em] exp.: be a man; be human
jakiś człowiek do ciebie [yah-keeśh **chwo**-vyek do **ćhe**-bye] exp.: somebody to see you
ludzie [**loo**-dźhe] pl. people
niepewny człowiek [ńe-**pev**-ni

chwo-vyek] exp.: a dubious character
człowieku! [chwo-**vye**-koo] excl.: my good man!; man alive!; my dear!
człowiekowaty [chwo-vye-ko-**vah**-ti] adj.m. of the family Hominidae
człowiekowate [chwo-vye-ko-**vah**-te] pl. the family Hominidae
czmerać [**chme**-rahćh] v. rummage (*repeatedly*)
czmych! [chmikh] exclamation describing sudden escape from danger
czmychać [**chmi**-khahćh] v. flee; bolt; steal out; whisk away; whisk off; levant; sniff (in disdain) (*repeatedly*)
czmychanie [chmi-**khah**-ńe] n. flight; disdainful sniff
czmychnąć [**chmikh**-nownćh] v. flee; bolt; steal out; whisk away; whisk off; levant; sniff (in disdain)
czmychnięcie [chmikh-**ńan**-ćhe] n. flight; disdainful sniff
czochać [**cho**-khahćh] v. scratch; rub (*repeatedly*)
czochać się [**cho**-khahćh śhan] v. scratch oneself; rub oneself (*repeatedly*)
czochra [**chokh**-rah] f. ripple; hackle
czochrać [**chokh**-rahćh] v. tousle; ripple; hackle; scratch; rub; chafe (*repeatedly*)
czochrać się [**chokh**-rahćh śhan] v. scratch one's head; rub; chafe; rub oneself (against); fray (*repeatedly*)
czochranie [chokh-**rah**-ńe] n. scratching; rubbing; chafing
czołg [chowg] m. tank (military); reptile; crawler
czołgać się [**chow**-gahćh śhan] v. crawl; creep; trail; grovel; cringe; cower (*repeatedly*)
czołganie się [chow-**gah**-ńe śhan] n. crawling; creeping
czołgista [chow-**gees**-tah] m. tankman; member of a tank crew
czołgowy [chow-**go**-vi] adj.m. tank (gun, crew, etc.)
czoło [**cho**-wo] n. forehead; brow; head; face; boldness; impudence; front; forepart; forefront; front ranks; van; foreground; top; cream; flower; the pick
czołem! [**cho**-wem] excl.: hi!; hello!; cheerio! (Brit.)
marszczyć czoło [**mahrsh**-chićh **cho**-wo] exp.: to frown
na czele [nah **che**-le] adv. in the forefront; in the van; at the head; at the top
stać na czele [stahćh nah **che**-le] exp.: to manage (a business, etc.); to be in the forefront; to be in the van; to be at the head; to be at the top; to run the show
stawić czoło [**stah**-veećh **cho**-wo] exp.: to face; to brave
w pocie czoła [f **po**-ćhe **cho**-wah] exp.: in the sweat of one's brows
wysunąć się na czoło [vi-**soo**-nownćh śhan nah **cho**-wo] exp.: to come to the front
czołobitnie [cho-wo-**beet**-ńe] adv. servilely; subserviently; obsequiously; fawningly; with servility
czołobitność [cho-wo-**beet**-nośhćh] f. servility; subservience; obsequiousness; fawning
czołobitny [cho-wo-**beet**-ni] adj.m. servile; subservient; obsequious; fawning
czołowo [cho-**wo**-vo] adv. frontally; (to collide, etc.) head-on
czołowy [cho-**wo**-vi] adj.m. frontal; leading; chief; foremost; front-rank; advanced; leading; outstanding; prominent; principal; main
zderzenie czołowe [zde-**zhe**-ńe cho-**wo**-ve] exp.: frontal collision; head-on collision
czołówka [cho-**woof**-kah] f. forefront; spearhead; advance party; van; first ranks; leaders; front-page news; title section of a film; leading article
czop [chop] m. peg; plug; pin; bung; spigot; spile; pintle; stop; stub; stump; swivel; tenon; dowel; dovetail; wrist-pin; head (of an abscess, etc.)
czopek [**cho**-pek] m. small plug;

stopper; spigot; suppository
czopiarka [cho-**pyahr**-kah] f. tenon saw; tenon-cutting machine
czopować [cho-**po**-vahćh] v. stop up; plug; bung; tampon; obstruct; dowel (*repeatedly*)
czopowanie [cho-po-**vah**-ńe] n. stopping up; plugging; obstructing
czopowe [cho-**po**-ve] n. tax on the sale of liquor
czopownica [cho-pov-**ńee**-tsah] f. tenon saw
czopowy [cho-**po**-vi] adj.m. of tenon
otwór czopowy [ot-foor cho-**po**-vi] exp.: bunghole of a cask or barrel
czopuch [**cho**-pookh] m. chimney-flue; smoke-flue
czort [**chort**] m. the devil; the deuce
czort wie gdzie [chort vye gdźhe] exp.: Goodness knows where
co u czorta! [tso oo **chor**-tah] excl.: what the devil; what the hell
czosnaczek [chos-**nah**-chek] m. sauce-alone (plant smelling like garlic); Alliaria officinalis
czosnek [**chos**-nek] m. garlic; garlic bulb
czosnkowaty [chosn-ko-**vah**-ti] adj.m. garlicky
czosnkowy [chosn-**ko**-vi] adj.m. of garlic; alliaceous
czosnkowy zapach [chosn-**ko**-vi **zah**-pahkh] exp.: smell of garlic
czółeczko [choo-**wech**-ko] n. (small) child's forehead
czółenko [choo-**wen**-ko] n. small (open) boat; shuttle; top lever of a shotgun
czółko [**choow**-ko] n. (small, nice) forehead; head-dress in a woman's regional dress
czółno [**choow**-no] n. boat; canoe; skiff; dinghy; dingey; dugout
czterdziestka [chter-**dźhest**-kah] f. forty; forty years of age; quarter of a liter (bottle); number forty
czterdziestodniowy [chter-dźhes-to-**dńo**-vi] adj.m. forty days'; of forty days; forty-day (period); of forty days' duration; lasting forty days
czterdziestogodzinny [chter-dźhes-to-go-**dźheen**-ni] adj.m. forty-hour (workweek, etc.); of forty hours; lasting forty hours
czterdziestolatek [chter-dźhes-to-**lah**-tek] m. forty years old man
czterdziestolecie [chter-dźhes-to-**le**-ćhe] n. fortieth anniversary; period of forty years
czterdziestoletni [chter-dźhes-to-**let**-ńee] adj.m. forty years old; forty years'; forty-year; of forty years; of forty years' duration
czterdziestu [chter-**dźhes**-too] num. forty (men)
czterdziesty [chter-**dźhes**-ti] num.m. fortieth
jedna czterdziesta [**yed**-nah chter-**dźhes**-tah] exp.: one fortieth
czterdzieści [chter-**dźheśh**-ćhee] num. forty
czterdzieścioro [chter-dźheśh-**ćho**-ro] num. forty (people, children, etc.)
czterech [**chte**-rekh] num. four (men)
czterechsetlecie [chte-rekh-set-**le**-ćhe] n. four hundred years (period, etc.); four-hundredth anniversary; quatercentenary
czterechsetny [chte-rekh-**set**-ni] num.m. four-hundredth
czterej [**chte**-rey] num. four (men)
czternastak [chter-**nahs**-tahk] m. fourteen-point buck
czternastka [chter-**nahst**-kah] f. fourteen; (bus, room, etc.) number fourteen
czternastodniowy [chter-nahs-to-**dńo**-vi] adj.m. fourteen days' (work, etc.); fourteen-day (period, etc.); of fourteen days; lasting fourteen days; of fourteen days' duration
czternastolatek [chter-nahs-to-**lah**-tek] m. a boy of fourteen
czternastolatka [chter-nahs-to-**lah**-tkah] f. a girl of fourteen
czternastoletni [chter-nahs-to-**let**-ńee] adj.m. of fourteen years; of fourteen years' duration; fourteen years' (service, etc.); fourteen years old; fourteen-year-old
czternastowieczny [chter-nahs-to-**vyech**-ni] adj.m. of the fourteenth

century; dating back to the fourteenth century; fourteenth century (church, painting, etc.)
czternastozgłoskowiec [chter-nahs-to-zgwos-ko-vyets] m. verse of fourteen syllables
czternastozgłoskowy [chter-nahs-to-zgwos-ko-vi] adj.m. of fourteen syllables
czternastu [chter-nahs-too] num.m. fourteen (men)
czternasty [chter-nahs-ti] num.m. fourteenth; 14th
czternaście [chter-nahśh-ćhe] num. fourteen; 14
czternaścioro [chter-nahśh-ćho-ro] num. fourteen children; fourteen persons (of both sexes)
cztero- [chte-ro] pref. four-; tetra-; quadr-; quadri-
czteroaktowy [chte-ro-ahk-to-vi] adj.m. in four acts
czteroaktówka [chte-ro-ahk-toof-kah] f. play of four acts
czterobarwny [chte-ro-bahrv-ni] adj.m. of four colors
czteroboczny [chte-ro-boch-ni] adj.m. quadrilateral
czterochlorek [chte-ro-khlo-rek] m. tetrachloride
czterocyfrowy [chte-ro-tsif-ro-vi] adj.m. of four figures
czterocylindrowy [chte-ro-tsi-leen-dro-vi] adj.m. of four cylinders; four cylinder (engine, etc.)
czteroczęściowy [chte-ro-chanśh-ćho-vi] adj.m. of four parts
czterodniowy [chte-ro-dńo-vi] adj.m. of four days; lasting four days; four-day (period, etc.); of four days' duration
czterodźwięk [chte-ro-dźhvyank] m. a (musical) chord of four tones
czterofluorek [chte-ro-floo-o-rek] m. tetrafluoride
czterogodzinny [chte-ro-go-dźheen-ni] adj.m. four-hours'(work, etc.); four-hour (shifts, etc.); of four hours; lasting four hours; of four hours' duration
czteroklasowy [chte-ro-klah-so-vi] adj.m. four-grade (school, etc.)
czteroklasówka [chte-ro-klah-soof-kah] f. four-grade school
czterokołowy [chte-ro-ko-wo-vi] adj.m. four-wheeled (vehicle)
czterokonny [chte-ro-kon-ni] adj.m. four-horse, four-horsed; of four horses; four horsepower (engine)
czterokrotnie [chte-ro-krot-ńe] adv. four times
czterokrotność [chte-ro-krot-nośhćh] f. (the) quadruple
czterokrotny [chte-ro-krot-ni] adj.m. fourfold; quadruple
czterolecie [chte-ro-le-ćhe] n. four years; fourth anniversary
czteroletni [chte-ro-let-ńee] adj.m. four years old; four years'
czterolistny [chte-ro-leest-ni] adj.m. four-leaved; four-leaf (clover, etc.); four-leafed
czteromiesięczny [chte-ro-mye-śhanch-ni] adj.m. of four months; four months'; four-month (period); of four months' duration; four months old; four-month-old
czteromotorowy [chte-ro-mo-to-ro-vi] adj.m. four-engined; four-engine (aeroplane, etc.)
czteronogi [chte-ro-no-gee] adj.m. four-legged
czteronożny [chte-ro-nozh-ni] adj.m. four-legged
czteroosobowy [chte-ro-o-so-bo-vi] adj.m. four-people (car, etc.); four-person (compartment, etc.)
czteropiętrowy [chte-ro-pyan-tro-vi] adj.m. four stories high; four storied (building)
czteropłatkowy [chte-ro-pwaht-ko-vi] adj.m. tetrapetalous
czteropolówka [chte-ro-po-loof-kah] f. four-course rotation (of crops)
czteroskibowiec [chte-ro-skee-bo-vyets] m. four-furrow plow
czterospadowy [chte-ro-spah-do-vi] adj.m. slanting four ways
dach czterospadowy [dahkh chte-ro-spah-do-vi] exp.: hip roof
czterostronny [chte-ro-stron-ni] adj.m. quadrilateral; quadripartite
czterosuw [chte-ro-soof] m. four-stroke engine
czterosuwowy [chte-ro-soo-vo-vi] adj.m. four-stroke (engine)
czterotakt [chte-ro-tahkt] m. four-stroke engine

czterotaktowy [chte-ro-tahk-**to**-vi] adj.m. four-stroke (engine)
czterotygodniowy [chte-ro-ti-god-**ńo**-vi] adj.m. four-weeks' (stay, etc.); four week (periods, etc.); of four weeks; of four weeks' duration; four weeks old; four-week-old
czterowartościowy [chte-ro-vahr-tośh-**ćho**-vi] adj.m. quadrivalent; tetravalent
czterowiersz [chte-**ro**-vyersh] m. quatrain; tetrastich
czterowiosłówka [chte-ro-vyos-**woof**-kah] f. four-oar boat
czterozgłoskowy [chte-ro-zgwos-**ko**-vi] adj.m. of four syllables
czterozmianowy [chte-ro-zmyah-**no**-vi] adj.m. four-shift (work, etc.)
cztery [**chte**-ri] num. four; n. good mark (in school); B; grade of B
cztery litery [**chte**-ri lee-**te**-ri] exp.: four-letter word = **dupa** (vulg.)
w cztery oczy [f **chte**-ri **o**-chi] exp.: in private (between two people)
czterykroć [chte-**ri**-kroćh] adv. four times
czterykroć sto tysięcy [chte-**ri**-kroćh sto ti-**śh**an-tsi] exp.: four hundred thousand; 400,000 = **czterysta tysięcy**
czterysta [**chte**-ris-tah] num. four hundred; 400
czterystumetrowiec [chte-ris-too-met-**ro**-vyets] m. four-hundred-meter (race) runner
czterystumetrówka [chte-ris-too-met-**roof**-kah] f. four-hundred-meter race
czub [choop] m. tuft; crest; head; topknot; hair on the top of the head; tip; top; stem (of a ship)
brać się za czuby [brahćh śhan zah **choo**-bi] exp.: to come to blows; to pick up a fight
dostać po czubie [**dos**-tahćh po **choo**-bye] exp.: to be beaten up; to be hit on the head; slang: to be bopped on the noodle
mieć w czubie [myećh f **choo**-bye] exp.: to be tipsy; to be in liquor
łyżka z czubem [**wish**-kah s **choo**-bem] exp.: a heaped spoonful
czubajka [choo-**bahy**-kah] f. (Lepiota) mushroom
czubatka [choo-**baht**-kah] f. crested hen; crested titmouse
czubato [choo-**bah**-to] adv. with a tuft; with a crest; (filled) to overflowing
czubaty [choo-**bah**-ti] adj.m. tufted; tufty; crested; tapering; heaped (spoonful, cupful, plateful, etc.)
czubek [**choo**-bek] m. (small, nice) tuft; crest; head; topknot; hair on the top of the head; tip; top; stem (of a ship)
czubki [**choop**-kee] pl. the inmates of a lunatic asylum; the inmates of a psychiatric hospital
chodzić na czubkach palców [**kho**-dźheećh nah **choop**-kahkh **pahl**-tsoof] exp.: to walk on the tips of one's toes; to tiptoe
na czubku nosa [nah **choop**-koo **no**-sah] exp.: on the tip of one's nose
po czubek głowy [po **choo**-bek **gwo**-vi] exp.: from top to toe
czubiasto [choo-**byahs**-to] adv. in a tuft
czubiasty [choo-**byahs**-ti] adj.m. tufty
czubić się [choo-beećh śhan] v. scuffle; tussle; bickering; squabble; quarrel; peck one another (*repeatedly*)
czubienie się [choo-**bye**-ńe śhan] n. scuffling; tussling; bickering; squabbling; quarrelling
czubki [**choop**-kee] pl. the inmates of a lunatic asylum; the inmates of a psychiatric hospital
czucie [**choo**-ćhe] n. feeling; smelling; sense perception; sensation; sense (of dignity, etc.)
paść bez czucia [pahśhćh bes **choo**-ćhah] exp.: to fall senseless; to fall unconscious
czucie się [**choo**-ćhe śhan] n. feeling (about oneself)
czuciowy [choo-**ćho**-vi] adj.m. of feeling; sensitive; sensory; sensual; sensorial; sensuous
czuć [chooćh] v. feel; have the feeling; smell; scent; wind; taste;

be aware of; entertain a feeling of; be conscious of; feel by intuition; anticipate; sniff; have the sense of smell (*repeatedly*)
czuć pismo nosem [chooćh **pis**-mo **no**-sem] exp.: to smell a rat; to get wind of ...
czuć wolę Bożą [chooćh **vo**-lan **bo**-zhown] exp.: to feel the sex urge (to feel God's will)
tam czuć [tahm chooćh] exp.: there is a bad smell there; it stinks there

czuć się [chooćh śhan] v. feel; be (happy, etc.) (*repeatedly*)
czuć się dobrze [chooćh śhan **dob**-zhe] exp.: to feel well; to be well; to be at ease; to be OK
czuć się niedobrze [chooćh śhan ńe-**dob**-zhe] exp.: to feel unwell; to feel seedy; to be out of sorts; to be off color; to be below the mark
czuję się słabo [**choo**-yan śhan **swah**-bo] exp.: I feel weak; I am weak
jak się czujesz? [yahk śhan **choo**-yesh] exp.: how do you feel?; how are you?; are you well?
on się czuł artystą [on śhan choow ar-**tis**-town] exp.: at heart he was an artist

czuj [chooy] m. mob slang: intuition

czujka [**chooy**-kah] f. sentry; feeler; vedette

czujnie [**chooy**-ńe] adv. with vigilance; watchfully
czujnie spać [**chooy**-ńe spahćh] exp.: to sleep lightly; to be a light sleeper

czujnik [**chooy**-ńeek] m. sensor; gauge; pick up; dial indicator; fleximeter; deflection indicator; dial micrometer; sensing device

czujność [**chooy**-nośhćh] f. vigilance; watchfulness; alertness
zmylić czyjąś czujność [zmi-**leećh** chi-yownśh **chooy**-nośhćh] exp.: to throw somebody off his guard; to put somebody off his guard

czujny [**chooy**-ni] adj.m. vigilant; watchful; alert; wide awake; light (sleep)
być czujnym [bićh **chooy**-nim] exp.: to be alert; to be on the lookout; to keep one's eyes open; to keep one's ears open

czule [**choo**-le] adv. tenderly; affectionately; fondly; lovingly; with affection; with feeling

czulenie się [choo-**le**-ńe śhan] n. endearment; love-making; tenderness

czulić się [**choo**-leećh śhan] v. endear (oneself to); coax; cajole; wheedle; make love (to); fondle; pet (*repeatedly*)
czulić się do siebie [**choo**-leećh śhan do **śhe**-bye] exp.: to make love to each other; to fondle each other; to pet each other

czułek [**choo**-wek] m. mimosa; feeler; palp; tentacle; antena; horn (of an insect)

czułki [**choow**-kee] pl. tentacles

czułkowiec [choow-**ko**-vyets] m. tentaculate (water) animal
czułkowce [choow-**kof**-tse] pl. Tentaculata (water) animal

czułkowy [choow-**ko**-vi] adj.m. of tentacle; of tentacles

czułostka [choo-**wost**-kah] f. term of endearment; word of endearment

czułostkowo [choo-wost-**ko**-vo] adv. sentimentally; soft-heartedly; over-sensitively

czułostkowość [choo-wost-**ko**-vośhćh] f. sentimentality; soft-heartedness; oversensitivity; mawkishness

czułostkowy [choo-wost-**ko**-vi] adj.m. sentimental; soft-hearted; oversensitive; mawkish; slushy

czułość [choo-wośhćh] f. tenderness; affection; fondness; caress; endearment; words of love; sensitiveness; sensitivity; susceptibility; niceness (of an instrument); sharpness (of the senses); keenness (of the senses)

czuły [**choo**-wi] adj.m. tender; affectionate; sensitive; delicate; impressionable; acute; keen
czuła para [**choo**-wah **pah**-rah] exp.: loving couple

czumak [**choo**-mahk] m. Ukrainian

carter
czupiradło [choo-pee-**rahd**-wo] n. scarecrow; a fright
czupryna [choo-**pri**-nah] f. mop of hair; head of hair; shag
czuprynka [choo-**prin**-kah] f. (diminutive = nice, little) mop of hair; head of hair; shag
czupurnie [choo-**poor**-ńe] adv. pugnaciously; boastfully; defiantly; quarrelsomely; with bluster
czupurność [choo-**poor**-nośhćh] f. defiance; quarrelsomeness; pugnacity; bluster
czupurny [choo-**poor**-ni] adj.m. pugnacious; boastful; defiant; blustering
czupurzenie się [choo-poo-**zhe**-ńe śhan] n. being defiant; being quarrelsome; being pugnacious; blustering
czupurzyć się [choo-**poo**-zhićh śhan] v. be defiant; be quarrelsome; be pugnacious; bluster (*repeatedly*)
czuszka [**choosh**-kah] f. variety of paprika
czuszykanie [choo-shi-**kah**-ńe] n. call of the grouse at mating time
czuwać [**choo**-vahćh] v. watch; be vigilant; be watchful; be on the alert; nurse; look out; watch over; take care; stay up for; tend; see to; look after; sit up for; keep vigil (*repeatedly*)
czuwanie [choo-**vah**-ńe] n. watch; wakefulness; vigil
czuwaj! [**choo**-vahy] excl.: be prepared! (a boy-scout greeting)
czuwak [**choo**-vahk] m. dead man's control (electric train break)
czuwanie [choo-**vah**-ńe] n. vigil; watch; wakefulness
czwarta [**chfahr**-tah] f. four o'clock
czwartaczka [chfahr-**tahch**-kah] f. variety of malaria
czwartak [**chfahr**-tahk] m. soldier of the 4th regiment (in 1830)
czwartek [**chfahr**-tek] m. Thursday
Wielki Czwartek [**vyel**-kee **chfahr**-tek] exp.: Maundy Thursday (before Easter in commemoration of the institution of the Eucharist)
czwartkowy [chfahrt-**ko**-vi] adj.m. of Thursday
czwartnik [**chfahrt**-ńeek] m. quotation
czwartoklasista [chfahr-to-klah-**śhees**-tah] m. fourth grader
czwartorzęd [chfahr-**to**-zhant] m. Quaternary (geol. period when man first appeared)
czwartorzędny [chfahr-to-**zhand**-ni] adj.m. fourth-rate
czwartorzędowy [chfahr-to-zhan-**do**-vi] adj.m. quaternary; of the Quaternary period; m. member of the group fourth in rank or order
czwarty [**chfahr**-ti] num. fourth
co czwarty [tso **chfahr**-ti] exp.: every fourth (man, etc.)
czwarta [**chfahr**-tah] exp.: four o'clock
czwarta część [**chfahr**-tah chanśhćh] exp.: one fourth
jedna czwarta [**yed**-nah **chfahr**-tah] exp.: one fourth
pół do czwartej [poow do **chfahr**-tey] exp.: half past three
o czwartej [o **chfahr**-tey] exp.: at four
czworaczki [chfo-**rahch**-kee] pl. quadruplets; slang: quads
czworak [**chfo**-rahk] m. farm hands' living quarters; building consisting of four apartments
czworaki [chfo-**rah**-kee] adj.m fourfold; quadruple; pl. buildings consisting of four apartments
na czworakach [nah chfo-**rah**-kah] exp.: on all fours; on one's hands and knees
czwornik [**chfor**-ńeek] m. (pipe) cross; four-way piece (pipe joint)
czworo [**chfo**-ro] num. four
taniec we czworo [tah-ńets ve **chfo**-ro] exp.: square dance
czworoboczny [chfo-ro-**boch**-ni] adj.m. quadrilateral; quadrate
czworobok [chfo-**ro**-bok] m. quadrilateral; square; tetragon
czworogran [chfo-**ro**-grahn] m. quadrilateral; square; tetragon
czworograniasty [chfo-ro-grah-**ńahs**-ti] adj.m. quadrate; square
czworokanciasty [chfo-ro-kahn-**ćhahs**-ti] adj.m. quadrate; square;

four-cornered
czworokąt [chfo-ro-kownt] m. quadrangle; quad; tetragon
czworokątnie [chfo-ro-kownt-ńe] adv. in the form of a quadrangle
czworokątny [chfo-ro-kownt-ni] adj.m. quadrangular; quadrate; tetragonal; square
czworolist [chfo-ro-leest] m. quatrefoil; truelove; the herb of Paris
czworonogi [chfo-ro-no-gee] adj.m. quadrupedal; four-footed; quadruped
czworonożny [chfo-ro-nozh-ni] adj.m. quadrupedal; four-footed; quadruped
czworonóg [chfo-ro-noog] m. quadruped; four-footed animal
czworościan [chfo-ro-śhćhahn] m. tetrahedron
czwóra [chfoo-rah] f. slang: number four; B grade in school
czwórbojowy [chfoor-bo-yo-vi] adj.m. of four-category competition (in sport)
czwórbój [chfoor-booy] m. four-category competition (in sport)
czwórka [chfoor-kah] f. number four; foursome; formation four deep; crew of four; team of four (people, horses, etc.); B mark in school; four (-oared boat)
czwórkowy [chfoor-ko-vi] adj.m. of four; of fours
czwórmecz [chfoor-mech] m. four-team contest
czwórnasób [chfoor-nah-soop] adv. fourfold; quadruply; four times
powiększyć w czwórnasób [po-vyank-shićh f chfoor-nah-soop] exp.: to quadruple; to increase four times
czwórniak [chfoor-ńahk] m. variety of honey
czwórnik [chfoor-ńeek] m. four-way pipe fitting
czwórnóg [chfoor-noog] m. drilling-rig tower made of four pipes
czwórszereg [chfoor-she-reg] m. four-row formation
czy [chi] conj. if; whether
czy jesteś gotów? [chi yes-teśh go-toof] exp.: are you ready?
czy tu, czy tam [chi too chi tahm] exp.: whether here or there
czy widzisz? [chi vee-dźheesh] exp.: do you see?
tak czy inaczej [tahk chi ee-nah-chey] exp.: one way or the other
czyhać [chi-khahćh] v. lurk; lie in wait (for); be on the look-out (for) (*repeatedly*)
czyhanie [chi-khah-ńe] n. lurking; lying in wait (for); being on the lookout for
czyhitanie [chi-khee-tah-ńe] n. call of the grouse at mating time
czyj [chiy] pron. m. whose
czyja [chi-yah] pron. f. whose
czyje [chi-ye] pron. n. whose
czyjakolwiek [chi-yah-kol-vyek] pron. f. anybody's
czyjekolwiek [chi-ye-kol-vyek] pron. n. anybody's
czyjkolwiek [chiy-kol-vyek] pron. m. anybody's
czyjaś [chi-yahśh] pron. f. somebody's; anybody's; someone else's
czyjeś [chi-yeśh] pron. n. somebody's; anybody's; someone else's
czyjś [chiyśh] pron. m. somebody's; anybody's; someone else's
czyli [chi-lee] conj. or; otherwise; that is to say; in other words; (emphatic:) if; whether
czym? [chim] exp.: with what?
czym... tym... [chim tim] adv. the sooner... the; the more ... the; the less... the...
czyn [chin] m. act; action; deed; collective action in commemoration of an anniversary
czyn bohaterski [chin bo-khah-ter-skee] exp.: heroic deed; heroic feat
człowiek czynu [chwo-vyek chi-noo] exp.: man of action
czynel [chi-nel] m. percussion instrument made of metal plate
czynić [chi-ńeećh] v. do; make; render; act; amount; cause; give; form; constitute; make up (*repeatedly*)
czynić się [chi-ńeećh śhan] v. be

making oneself; become; make oneself (into); be under way; be in progress (*repeatedly*)
czynienie [chi-ńe-ńe] n. doing; acting; dealing
mieć coś do czynienia [myećh tsośh do chi-ńe-ńah] exp.: to have something to do; to have some business to settle
mieć z kimś do czynienia [myećh s keemśh do chi-**ńe**-ńah] exp.: to have to do with somebody
nie chcę mieć z nim nic do czynienia [ńe khtsan myećh z ńeem ńeets do chi-ńe-ńah] exp.: I do not want to have anything to do with him
czynienie się [chi-ńe-ńe śhan] n. being in progress; becoming
czynnie [**chin**-ńe] adv. actively
czynnie znieważyć [**chin**-ńe zńe-**vah**-zhićh] exp.: to strike (somebody) in the face; to commit an assault (on somebody, someone, etc.)
czynnik [**chin**-ńeek] m. factor; agent; element; medium
czynnik społeczny [**chin**-ńeek spo-**wech**-ni] exp.: a representative of the community
czynnik chłodzący [**chin**-ńeek khwo-**dzown**-tsi] exp.: cooling medium; cooling agent
czynnościowo [chin-nośh-**ćho**-vo] adv. functionally
czynnościowy [chin-nośh-**ćho**-vi] adj.m. functional
czynność [**chin**-nośhćh] f. activity; function; action; operation; act; work
czynny [**chin**-ni] adj.m. active; acting; in operation
być czynnym [bićh **chin**-nim] exp.: be active; be at work; be working; run (a business, etc.); be open (for business, etc.)
czynna zniewaga [**chin**-nah zńe-**vah**-gah] exp.: assault and battery
strona czynna [**stro**-nah **chin**-nah] exp.: active voice
w czynnej służbie [f **chin**-ney **swoozh**-bye] exp.: in active service; on the active list
czynownik [chi-**nov**-ńeek] m. state official in czarist Russia
czynsz [chinsh] m. rent; rental; rent-charge
czynszownik [chin-**shov**-ńeek] m. tenant farmer
czynszowy [chin-**sho**-vi] adj.m. rent; rental; tenement; m. copyholder
dom czynszowy [dom chin-**sho**-vi] exp.: tenement-house; apartment-house
właściciel domu czynszowego [vwahśh-**ćhee**-ćhel **do**-moo chin-sho-**ve**-go] exp.: landlord
właścicielka domu czynszowego [vwahśh-ćhee-**ćhel**-kah **do**-moo chin-sho-**ve**-go] exp.: landlady
czynszówka [chin-**shoof**-kah] f. tenement-house; apartment-house
czyraczność [chi-**rahch**-nośhćh] f. abcessed area; area covered with boils
czyraczny [chi-**rahch**-ni] adj.m. of a boil; of a furuncle; of an abscess
czyrak [**chi**-rahk] m. boil; furuncle; abscess; anbury; rising
czyrakowaty [chi-rah-ko-**vah**-ti] adj.m. furuncular; furunculous
czyrakowy [chi-rah-**ko**-vi] adj.m. furuncular; furunculous
czysta [**chis**-tah] f. pure vodka; bottle of pure vodka; pure-vodka drink
czystka [**chist**-kah] f. purge; comb-out; weeding out; expurgating
czysto [**chis**-to] adv. clean; clear; true; in tune; purely; correctly; entirely; exclusively; net
do czysta [do **chis**-tah] exp.: completely; altogether; cleanly; until it's very clean
dochód na czysto [**do**-khoot nah **chis**-to] exp.: net profit
przepisać na czysto [pshe-**pee**-sahćh nah **chis**-to] exp.: to make a fair copy; to make a final copy; to make a clean copy
wyjść na czysto [viyśhćh nah **chis**-to] exp.: to get off clear; to be square; to have neither gain nor loss; to break even
czystodruk [chis-**to**-drook] m. test-print of a printing machine
czystopis [chis-**to**-pees] m. final

copy; fair copy; clean copy
czystość [chis-tośhćh] f. purity; cleanness; tidiness; neatness; spruceness; nattiness; clarity; lucidity; limpidity (of a fluid); clearness; fineness; probity; integrity; rectitude; honesty; virtue; chastity; continence
wątpliwej czystości [vownt-plee-vey chis-tośh-ćhee] exp.: far from clean; anything but clean; soiled
czysty [chis-ti] adj.m. clean; unsoiled; tidy; neat; spruce; natty; free of guilt; free of sin; free of suspicion; clear; limpid; lucid; pure; fine; absolute; true; perfect; unadulterated; unmixed; sheer; net; free of debts; upright; honest; above board; clean-handed; unstained; untarnished; chaste; continent; virtuous; virginal; undefiled
czysta [chis-tah] exp.: colloq: pure vodka; raw vodka
czyste pole [chis-te po-le] exp.: the open country
czyste szaleństwo [chis-te shah-leń-stfo] exp.: sheer madness
czysty arkusz [chis-ti ahr-koosh] exp.: blank sheet
czysta prawda [chis-tah prahv-dah] exp.: plain truth
czyste sumienie [chis-te soo-mye-ńe] exp.: clear conscience
do czysta [do chis-tah] exp.: clean; completely
ogolony do czysta [o-go-lo-ni do chis-tah] exp.: clean-shaven
spłukany do czysta [spwoo-kah-ni do chis-tah] exp.: colloq: stony-broke; broke; without a penny
czyszczak [chish-chahk] m. purger; cleanout
czyszczalnia [chish-chahl-ńah] f. seed cleaning plant
czyszczący [chish-chown-tsi] adj.m. purgative
środek czyszczący [śhro-dek chish-chown-tsi] exp.: a purgative
czyszczenie [chish-che-ńe] n. cleaning; brushing; scouring; abstersion; scour; diarrhea
czyścibut [chiśh-ćhee-boot] m. shoeblack; colloq: shoeshine boy
czyścica [chiśh-ćhee-tsah] f. calamint
czyściciel [chiśh-ćhee-ćhel] m. cleaner; scourer
czyścić [chiśh-ćheećh] v. clean; scour; brush; rub; shine; purge; geld (*repeatedly*)
czyścić chemicznie [chiśh-ćheećh khe-meech-ńe] exp.: to dry-clean
czyścić się [chiśh-ćheećh śhan] v. clean one's clothes; brush one's shoes; be cleaned; be brushed; be shined; be polished; be scoured (*repeatedly*)
łatwo się czyścić [wah-tfo śhan chiśh-ćheećh] exp.: to be easy to clean
czyściec [chiśh-ćhets] m. purgatory
czyścioch [chiśh-ćhokh] m. stickler for cleanliness
czyściocha [chiśh-ćho-khah] f. (woman) stickler for cleanliness; slang: pure unflavored vodka
czyścioszek [chiśh-ćho-shek] m. (little) stickler for cleanliness
czyścioszka [chiśh-ćhosh-kah] f. (female, girl) stickler for cleanliness
czyściuchno [chiśh-ćhookh-no] adv. very clean; nicely clean
czyściuchny [chiśh-ćhookh-ni] adj.m. very clean; nicely clean
czyściusieńki [chiśh-ćhoo-śheń-kee] adj.m. unusually clean; very nicely clean
czyściusieńko [chiśh-ćhoo-śheń-ko] adv. unusually clean; very nicely clean
czyściuteńki [chiśh-ćhoo-teń-kee] adj.m. unusually clean; very nicely clean
czyściuteńko [chiśh-ćhoo-teń-ko] adv. unusually clean; very nicely clean
czyściutki [chiśh-ćhoot-kee] adj.m. unusually clean; very nicely clean
czyściutko [chiśh-ćhoot-ko] adv. unusually clean; very nicely clean
czyściwo [chiśh-ćhee-vo] n. cleaning supplies; detergent
czyśćcowy [chiśhćh-tso-vi] adj.m.

purgatorial
czytać [chi-tahćh] v. read (*repeatedly*)
błędnie czytać [bwand-ńe chi-tahćh] exp.: to misread
czy umie czytać? [chi oo-mye chi-tahćh] exp.: can he read?; can she read?
czyta się dużo o ... [chi-tah śhan doo-zho o] exp.: one reads a lot about ...; one reads a great deal about ...
czytać coś pobieżnie [chi-tahćh tsośh po-byezh-ńe] exp.: to go over something; to read something cursorily; to read superficially
czytać między wierszami [chi-tahćh myan-dzi vyer-shah-mee] exp.: to read between the lines
czytać nuty [chi-tahćh noo-ti] exp.: to read music
czytać po polsku [chi-tahćh po pol-skoo] exp.: to read Polish
czytać uważnie [chi-tahćh oo-vahzh-ńe] exp.: to read carefully; to study; to peruse; to scan; to scrutinize
czytać dalej [chi-tahćh dah-ley] exp.: to read on
czytaj dalej! [chi-tahy dah-ley] excl.: read on!
czytać z gwiazd [chi-tahćh z gvyahst] exp.: to read the stars; to read the sky
jest co czytać [yest tso chi-tahćh] exp.: there is plenty to read
czytać się [chi-tahćh śhan] v. read about; be easy to read (*repeatedly*)
czyta się o nim [chi-tah śhan o ńeem] exp.: he is in the news
przyjemnie się to czyta [pshi-yem-ńe śhan to chi-tah] exp.: it is pleasant reading
czytadło [chi-tahd-wo] n. colloq: easy, pleasant to read book
czytająca [chi-tah-yown-tsah] f. reader; adj.f. reading
czytający [chi-tah-yown-tsi] m. reader; adj.m. reading
czytanie [chi-tah-ńe] n. reading
lampa do czytania [lahm-pah do chi-tah-ńah] exp.: reading-lamp
umiejętność czytania i pisania [oo-mye-yant-nośhćh chi-tah-ńah ee pee-sah-ńah] exp.: literacy
czytanka [chi-tahn-kah] f. piece of reading-matter; reader
czytelnia [chi-tel-ńah] f. reading room; lending library
czytelniany [chi-tel-ńah-ni] adj.m. of a reading-room; of a lending library
czytelnictwo [chi-tel-ńeets-tfo] n. reading habit; reading
czytelniczka [chi-tel-ńeech-kah] f. (woman) reader; reading individual
czytelniczy [chi-tel-ńee-chi] adj.m. of reading habit; of readers
czytelnie [chi-tel-ńe] adv. legibly; readably
czytelnik [chi-tel-ńeek] m. reader; reading individual (male)
czytelnicy [chi-tel-ńee-tsi] pl. readers; reading public
czytelność [chi-tel-nośhćh] f. readability; legibility; literacy
czytelny [chi-tel-ni] adj.m. legible; readable
czytnik [chit-ńeek] m. microfilm reading glass; electronic transmitter of written text
czytywać [chi-ti-vahćh] v. read often; read sometimes; be wont to read (*repeatedly*)
czytywać w łóżku [chi-ti-vahćh v woosh-koo] exp.: to often read in bed; to have a habit of reading in bed; to have a custom to read in bed
czytywałem [chi-ti-vah-wem] exp.: I used to read; I would often read; I would sometimes read
czytywanie [chi-ti-vah-ńe] n. the habit of reading; the practice of reading
czyż [chish] part. if; whether
czyżby [chizh-bi] = (emphatic) **czy**
czyżby! [chizh-bi] exp.: excl.: oh?; really?; is that so?; you don't say so?; don't tell me!
czyżemka [chi-zhem-kah] f. sixteenth century footwear (hist.)
czyżyk [chi-zhik] m. siskin

Ć

Ć, ć [ćh] n. the letter "ć"; the sound ć [ćh]
ćma [ćhmah] f. obscurity; swarm; night butterfly; night moth; darkness; dark night; host; multitude
ćmić [ćhmeećh] v. obscure; dim; darken; eclipse; smoke; smolder; sicken; blind; dazzle; daze; shine faintly; glimmer; drizzle (rain) (*repeatedly*)
ćmić papierosy [ćhmeećh pah-pye-ro-si] exp.: to smoke one's cigarettes
ćmi w oczach [ćhmee v o-chahkh] exp.: one is blinded
ćmi w oczy [ćhmee v o-chi] exp.: one is dazzled; one is dazed
ćmić się [ćhmeećh śhan] v. be obscured; be dimmed; smolder; be blinded; be dazzled; glimmer; shine faintly (*repeatedly*)
ćmi mi się w oczach [ćhmee mee śhan v o-chahkh] exp.: my head swims
ćmi się w oczach [ćhmee śhan v o-chahkh] exp.: one is blinded; one is dazzled; one is dazed
ćmienie [ćhmye-ńe] n. dimming; shining faintly; obscuring
ćpach [ćhpahkh] m. vulg.: junkie; drug addict (mob jargon)
ćpać [ćhpahćh] v. vulg.: gobble; narcotize oneself (*repeatedly*)
ćpanie [ćhpah-ńe] n. gobbling; slang: taking drugs (mob jargon)
ćpun [ćhpoon] m. colloq: drug addict; mob slang: junkie; junky
ćwiarteczka [ćhfyahr-tech-kah] f. colloq: very small quarter
ćwiartka [ćhfyahrt-kah] f. one quarter; one fourth (of a liter, etc.); quarter (of a bushel, etc.); a quarter-liter bottle (of vodka, etc.); quarter paper (in printing)
ćwiartka koła [ćhfyahrt-kah ko-wah] exp.: quadrant
ćwiartka cytryny [ćhfyahrt-kah tsi-tri-ni] exp.: segment of a lemon
ćwiartka baraniny [ćhfyahrt-kah bah-rah-ńee-ni] exp.: leg of mutton; shoulder of mutton
ćwiartkowy [ćhfyahrt-ko-vi] adj.m. of one quarter (size, etc.)
ćwiartować [ćhfyahr-to-vahćh] v. quarter; divide into quarters; cut to pieces; tear to pieces (*repeatedly*)
ćwiartowanie [ćhfyahr-to-vah-ńe] n. dividing into quarters; cutting to pieces; tearing to pieces
ćwiartuchna [ćhfyahr-tookh-nah] f. slang: quarter-liter bottle of vodka
ćwiczebny [ćhfee-cheb-ni] adj.m. training (ground, field, etc.); schooling (program, etc.)
ćwiczenie [ćhfee-che-ńe] n. exercise; instruction; drill; training; practice; schooling
odbywać ćwiczenia ze studentami [od-bi-vahćh ćhfee-che-ńah ze stoo-den-tah-mee] exp.: to have a class
pójść na ćwiczenia ze studentami [pooyśhćh nah ćhfee-che-ńah ze stoo-den-tah-mee] exp.: to meet a class
ćwiczeniowy [ćhfee-che-ńo-vi] adj.m. training (hours, etc.); school (book, etc.)
ćwiczyć [ćhfee-chićh] v. exercice; drill; instruct; practice; train; flog; beat; lash (*repeatedly*)
ćwiczyć się [ćhfee-chićh śhan] v. practice oneself in; train oneself in; school oneself in (patience, endurance, etc.) (*repeatedly*)
ćwiczę się dalej [ćhfee-chan śhan dah-ley] exp.: I am keeping up my training
ćwieczek [ćhfye-chek] m. (small) nail; stud; hobnail; peg; clout-nail
ćwiek [ćhfyek] m. nail; stud; hobnail; peg; clout-nail; slang: imbecile; muff; bungler; slacker
zabić sobie ćwieka w głowę [zah-beećh so-bye ćhfye-kah v gwo-van] exp.: colloq: to put oneself out; to puzzle oneself; to perplex oneself

wybić sobie ćwieka z głowy [vi-beećh **so**-bye **ćhfye**-kah z **gwo**-vi] exp.: colloq: to argue oneself out (of something, etc.)
ćwiekować [ćhfye-**ko**-vahćh] v. stud; encrust (*repeatedly*)
ćwiekowanie [ćhfye-ko-**vah**-ńe] n. studding; encrustation
ćwierciowy [ćhfyer-**ćho**-vi] adj.m. of one quarter
ćwierć [ćhfyerćh] f. one fourth (of a liter, etc.); quarter (of a carcass, a bushel, etc.); (school) term; joint (of beef, veal, mutton, etc.); quarterly pay
jej trzy ćwierci do śmierci [yey tshi **ćhfyer**-ćhee do **śhmyer**-ćhee] exp.: colloq: she is more dead than alive; she is on her last leg
ćwierćarkuszowy [ćhfyerćh-ahr-koo-**sho**-vi] adj.m. (paper size) quarto
ćwierćfinalista [ćhfyerćh-fee-nah-**lees**-tah] m. player in a quarterfinal match; contender in a quarterfinal round
ćwierćfinał [ćhfyerćh-**fee**-nahw] m. quarterfinal match; quarterfinal round
ćwierćfinałowy [chfyerćh-fee-nah-**wo**-vi] adj.m. quarterfinal (match, etc.)
ćwierćinteligent [ćhfyerćh-een-te-**lee**-gent] m. colloq: man of a substandard education
ćwierćkolumna [ćhfyerćh-ko-**loom**-nah] f. quarter-column (used in architecture)
ćwierćnuta [ćhfyerćh-**noo**-tah] f. crotchet (in music)
ćwierćrocze [ćhfyerćh-**ro**-che] n. quarter of a year; three months; term (of school, etc.)
ćwierćton [**ćhfyerćh**-ton] m. quartertone
ćwierćwiecze [ćhfyerćh-**vye**-che] n. quarter of a century
ćwierćwiekowy [ćhfyerćh-vye-**ko**-vi] adj.m. of a quarter of a century
ćwierk [ćhfyerk] m. twitter; chirp; warble
ćwierkać [**ćhfyer**-kahćh] v. twitter; chirp; warble (*repeatedly*)
ćwierkanie [ćhfyer-**kah**-ńe] n. twitter; chirping; warble
ćwierkliwy [chfyer-**klee**-vi] adj.m. often chirping; sounding like a chirp
ćwierknąć [**ćhfyerk**-nownćh] v. twitter; chirp; warble
ćwierknięcie [ćhfyerk-**ńan**-ćhe] n. a twitter; a chirp; a warble
ćwik [ćhfeek] m. colloq: sly fox; deep file; capon
zdrów jak ćwik [zdroof yahk ćhfeek] exp.: colloq: bursting with health; as fit as a fiddle; sound as a bell
ćwikać [**ćhfee**-kahćh] v. colloq: lash; mob slang: steal (*repeatedly*)
ćwikła [**ćhfeek**-wah] f. red beet with horseradish (salad)
ćwikłowy [ćhfeek-**wo**-vi] adj.m. of red beet(s)
ćwiknąć [**ćhfeek**-nownćh] v. colloq: lash; mob slang: steal
ćwir! [ćhfeer] excl.: chirrup!
ćwok [ćhfok] m. slang: uneducated man; crude man; simpleton

D

D, d [de] n. the letter "d"
dach [dahkh] m. roof; shelter
bez dachu nad głową [bez **dah**-khoo naht **gwo**-vown] exp.: without shelter; homeless
być pod dachem [bićh pod **dah**-khem] exp.: to be sheltered; to have a roof above one's head; to be indoors
dach czterospadowy [dahkh chte-ro-**spah-do**-vi] exp.: hip roof
dach dwuspadowy [dahkh dvoo-spah-**do**-vi] exp.: gable roof; ridge roof
dach opuszczany [dahkh o-poosh-**chah**-ni] exp.: convertible top (of a car)
dach płaski [dahkh **pwahs**-kee] exp.: flat roof
mieć dach nad głową [myećh dahkh naht **gwo**-vown] exp.: to

have a shelter
pozbawili go dachu nad głową [poz-bah-**vee**-lee go **dah**-khoo naht **gwo**-vown] exp.: they made him homeless
dacha [**dah**-khah] f. fur covering (used in a sledge, etc.)
dacharz [**dah**-khahsh] m. roofer
dachowy [dah-**kho**-vi] adj.m. of a roof; of roofs; roof (tiles etc.)
dachówczarka [dah-khoof-**chahr**-kah] f. tile-forming machine
dachówczarnia [dah-khoof-**chahr**-ńah] f. tile-producing plant
dachówka [dah-**khoof**-kah] f. tile; roofing-tile
dachówkarz [dah-**khoof**-kahsh] m. tile maker
dachówkowato [dah-khoof-ko-**vah**-to] adv. like tiles
układać dachówkowato [oo-**kwah**-dahćh dah-khoof-ko-**vah**-to] exp.: to imbricate
dachówkowy [dah-khoof-**ko**-vi] adj.m. of tiles; tile [clay, etc.]
dacyt [**dah**-tsit] m. an igneous rock (used for paving)
dacza [**dah**-chah] f. suburban family house; summer house (especially in Russia)
dać [dahćh] v. give to; pay; result; bid; hand over; let have; set; have (done); perform (a play); provide with; supply with; afford; yield (milk, etc.); give for; bring in; produce
co to da? [tso to dah] exp.: what good is that? what will that do?
dać dochód [dahćh **do**-khoot] exp.: to bring income
dać do zrozumienia [dahćh do zro-zoo-**mye**-ńah] exp.: to give to understand
dać komuś spokój [dahćh ko-moośh **spo**-kooy] exp.: to let (leave) somebody alone
dać komuś w kość [dahćh ko-moośh f kośhćh] exp.: to drive somebody to make a great effort
dać komuś w twarz [dahćh ko-moośh f tfahsh] exp.: to slap somebody's (in the face)
dać możność [dahćh **mozh**-nośhćh] exp.: to enable somebody
dać w łapę [dahćh v **wah**-pan] exp.: slang: to bribe
dać wiarę [dahćh **vyah**-ran] exp.: to give credit
dać znać [dahćh znahćh] exp.: to give information; inform
dać przykład [dahćh **pshi**-kwahd] exp.: to set an example
dać ognia [dahćh **og**-ńah] exp.: to fire; to shoot
dać ognia do papierosa [**dahćh** og-ńah do pah-pye-**ro**-sah] exp.: to give a light
daj Boże! [dahy **bo**-zhe] excl.: Heaven grant it!; please God!
dajmy na to [**dahy**-mi nah to] exp.: let us suppose; suppose
dać się [dahćh śhan] v. let oneself be defeated; surrender; yield; be possible; be feasible
co się da [tso śhan dah] exp.: as much as one can; whatever one can
czym się da [chim śhan dah] exp.: with whatever possible
dać się komuś we znaki [dahćh śhan **ko**-moośh ve **znah**-kee] exp.: to make somebody suffer
ile się da [ee-le śhan dah] exp.: as much as one can; whatever one can
jak się tylko da [yahk śhan **til**-ko dah] exp.: if at all possible; as soon as possible; in any way possible; as soon as one can; somehow or other
gdzie się da [gdźhe śhan dah] exp.: wherever possible
nie da się tego przewidzieć [ńe dah śhan **te**-go pshe-**vee**-dźhećh] exp.: it's impossible to foresee; there's no telling
nie da się tego zrobić [ńe dah śhan **te**-go **zro**-beećh] exp.: it's impossible to do; it's impossible to make
nie mniej niż się da [ńe mńey ńeesh śhan dah] exp.: no less than possible
to się da zrobić [to śhan dah **zro**-beećh] exp.: it can be done; it is feasible
to się dało zrobić [to śhan **dah**-

wo **zro**-beećh] exp.: it was successfully done; it was feasible
z kim się da [s keem śh<u>an</u> dah] exp.: with whoever turns up
dadaista [dah-dah-**ees**-tah] m. dadaist
dadaistyczny [dah-dah-ees-**tich**-ni] adj.m. dadaistic
dadaizm [dah-**dah**-eezm] m. Dadaism (rebellion against war)
dafnia [**dahf**-ńah] f. daphnia
dagerotyp [dah-ge-**ro**-tip] m. daguerreotype
dagerotypia [dah-ge-ro-**ti**-pyah] f. daguerreotypy
dagerotypować [dah-ge-ro-ti-**po**-vahćh] v. daguerreotype (*repeatedly*)
dagerotypowy [dah-ge-ro-ti-**po**-vi] adj.m. of daguerreotype
daglezja [dah-**glez**-yah] f. Douglas spruce (pine, hemlock)
daglezjowy [dah-glez-**yo**-vi] adj.m. of Douglas spruce (pine, hemlock)
dahabilja [dah-khah-**beel**-yah] f. dahabeah (Nile houseboat)
daimonion [dahy-**mo**-ńyon] m. voice of conscience (according to Socrates)
dajk [dahyk] m. (geol.) dike; dyke
dajna [**dahy**-nah] f. Lithuanian folk song
dakron [**dah**-kron] m. Dacron; polyester textile fiber
dakronowy [dah-kro-**no**-vi] adj.m. of Dacron; of polyester textile fiber
daktyl [**dahk**-til] m. date (fruit); measure of syllables in a verse
daktylicznie [dahk-ti-**leech**-ni] adv. dactylically
daktyliczny [dahk-ti-**leech**-ni] adj.m. dactylic
daktylioteka [dahk-til-yo-**te**-kah] f. dactyliotheca
daktylografia [dahk-ti-lo-**grah**-fyah] f. dactylology; the art of communicating ideas by signs made with fingers
daktylogram [dah-kti-**lo**-grahm] m. dactylogram
daktyloskopia [dahk-ti-lo-**sko**-pyah] f. finger-printing; dactyloscopy
daktyloskopijny [dahk-ti-lo-sko-**peey**-ni] adj.m. of finger-printing; dactyloscopic
daktylowiec [dahk-ti-**lo**-vyets] m. date-palm
daktylowy [dahk-ti-**lo**-vi] adj.m. date (tree, etc.)
śliwa daktylowa [**śhlee**-vah dahk-ti-**lo**-vah] exp.: persimmon
dal [dahl] f. distance; remoteness; far away; aloof; distant
skok w dal [skok v dahl] exp.: long jump
w dal [v dahl] adv. far away; far off; into the distance
w dali [v **dah**-lee] adv. far; far away; far off; in the distance
z dala [z **dah**-lah] adv. from afar; from far away; from the distance
z dala od [z **dah**-lah ot] exp.: far away from (home, etc.)
dalajlama [dah-lahy-**lah**-mah] m. Dalai Lama
dalba [**dahl**-bah] f. pile cluster for mooring of ships and protection of the coast
dalece [dah-**le**-tse] adv. further; by far; so far; (so) much so
tak dalece [tahk dah-**le**-tse] exp.: so much so; to such a degree; so far; to the extent
dalej [**dah**-ley] moreover; further off; so on; later; further back; next; afterwards; after this; further back; then; furthermore
dalej za lasem [**dah**-ley zah **lah**-sem] exp.: beyond the forest
i tak dalej [ee tahk **dah**-ley] exp.: and so on
robić dalej [**ro**-beećh **dah**-ley] exp.: to keep on doing; to resume doing; to go on doing; to continue doing; to persist in doing
dalejże! [dah-ley-zhe] excl.: go on! keep on! stay with it! (emphatic **dalej**)
daleki [dah-**le**-kee] adj.m. distant; remote; far-away; strange; far; long
daleka meta [dah-**le**-kah **me**-tah] exp.: far ahead
z daleka [z dah-**le**-kah] exp.: from far away; from the distance; from afar
daleko [dah-**le**-ko] adv. far off; far away; a long way off; a long way

away; long time ahead; far back; long ago; a lot; a great deal
daleko ci do tego [dah-**le**-ko ćhee do **te**-go] exp.: you are nowhere near it; you are a long way off; not by a long shot
daleko idący [dah-**le**-ko ee-d**own**-tsi] exp.: far-reaching
daleko w dole [dah-**le**-ko v **do**-le] exp.: way down; low down
daleko w dół [dah-**le**-ko v doow] exp.: way down; low down
tak daleko, że [tahk dah-**le**-ko zhe] exp.: so far as
za daleko [zah dah-**le**-ko] exp.: too far
dalekobieżny [dah-le-ko-**byezh**-ni] adj.m. long-distance (bus, etc.)
dalekomierz [dah-le-**ko**-myesh] m. range-finder; telemeter
dalekomorski [dah-le-ko-**mor**-skee] adj.m. deep-sea; deep-water; sea going (ship, etc.)
dalekonośny [dah-le-ko-**nośh**-ni] adj.m. long-range (gun, etc.)
dalekopis [dah-le-**ko**-pees] m. teletype; teleprinter; telewriter; teleautograph
dalekopisowy [dah-le-ko-pee-**so**-vi] adj.m. teletype (network, etc.)
dalekosiężność [dah-le-ko-**śhanzh**-nośhćh] f. long reach
dalekosiężny [dah-le-ko-**śhanzh**-ni] adj.m. far-reaching
dalekość [dah-**le**-kośhćh] f. distance
dalekowidz [dah-le-**ko**-veets] m. far-sighted person; presbyope
dalekowzrocznie [dah-le-ko-**vzroch**-ńe] adv. in a far-sighted way; in long-sighted manner; sagaciously
dalekowzroczność [dah-le-ko-**vzroch**-nośhćh] f. far-sightedness; presbyopia; long sight; long-sightedness; foresight; sagacity
dalekowzroczny [dah-le-ko-**vzroch**-ni] adj.m. far-sighted; presbyopic; long-sighted; far-seeing; foreseeing; sagacious
człowiek dalekowzroczny [**chwo**-vyek dah-le-ko-**vzroch**-ni] exp.: man of vision; long-sighted man
dalia [**dah**-lyah] f. dahlia
dalibóg! [dah-**lee**-boog] excl.: upon my word!
Dalmatynka [dahl-mah-**tin**-kah] f. Dalmatian woman
dalmatyńczyk [dahl-mah-**tiń**-chik] m. Dalmatian dog
Dalmatyńczyk [dahl-mah-**tiń**-chik] m. Dalmatian man
dalmatyński [dahl-mah-**tiń**-skee] adj.m. Dalmatian
dalmierz [**dahl**-myesh] m. range finder; telemeter
dalocelownik [dah-lo-tse-**lov**-ńeek] m. range-finder and aiming device for ships' and coastal artillery
dalszoplanowy [dahl-sho-plah-**no**-vi] adj.m. of lesser urgency; ulterior; not immediate
dalszy [**dahl**-shi] adj.m. further; later; ulterior; subsequent; fresh; new (chapter, etc.); outlying; another; a further; continued; gram.: indirect (complement)
dalsze wysiłki [**dahl**-she vi-**śheew**-kee] exp.: further efforts
dalszy ciąg [**dahl**-shi ćh**owng**] exp.: continuation; sequel
dalszy ciąg nastąpi [**dahl**-shi ćh**owng** nahs-**town**-pee] exp.: to be continued; there will be a sequel; the matter will not end there; there is more to come
dalszy plan [**dahl**-shi plahn] exp.: background
w dalszym ciągu [v **dahl**-shim **ćhown**-goo] exp.: to continue to do (something, etc.); to continue (to talk, to write, to wait, etc.)
daltonista [dahl-to-**ńees**-tah] m. color-blind person; daltonist
daltonistyczny [dahl-to-ńees-**tich**-ni] adj.m. daltonic; color-blind
daltonizm [dahl-**to**-ńeezm] m. daltonism; color-blindness
daltoński [dahl-**toń**-skee] adj.m. Daltonian (system, etc.)
dama [**dah**-mah] f. lady; partner; (chess) queen
damara [dah-**mah**-rah] f. a natural resin
damarowy [dah-mah-**ro**-vi] adj.m. natural-resin (paint, etc.)
damascena [dah-mahs-**tse**-nah] f. damson plum

Damascenka [dah-mahs-**tsen**-kah] f. woman from Damascus
damasceńka [dah-mah-**stseń**-kah] f. damask sword; damask blade (made of Damascus steel)
damasceński [dah-mah-**stseń**-skee] adj.m. damask (steel, etc.); of Damascus
damaskinaż [dah-mahs-**kee**-nahsh] m. gold and silver ornamentation of weapons in Damascus style
damaszka [dah-**mahsh**-kah] f. damson (plum)
damka [**dahm**-kah] f. little lady; lady's bicycle; (checker') king
damoklesowy [dah-mo-kle-**so**-vi] adj.m. of Damocles
miecz damoklesowy [myech dah-mo-kle-**so**-vi] exp.: the sword of Damocles; an ever-present danger
damski [**dahm**-skee] adj.m. lady's; ladies'
po damsku [po **dahm**-skoo] exp.: ladylike; in lady's fashion
damski boks [**dahm**-skee boks] exp.: slang: wife beating; girl friend beating
damski bokser [**dahm**-skee **bok**-ser] exp.: slang: prison inmate serving time for wife beating (or girl friend or any other woman beating) (mob jargon)
damula [dah-**moo**-lah] f. pretentious (little) lady; see: **dama**
damulka [dah-**mool**-kah] f. (diminutive) **dama**
dana [**dah**-nah] adj. f. given (data); exp.: tra-la-la (song-sound expressing gaiety)
danaidowy [dah-nah-ee-**do**-vi] adj.m. Danaidean; fruitless; endless
dancing [**dahn**-seeng] m. dance; dancing party; dancing-hall
dancingowy [dahn-seen-**go**-vi] adj.m. dancing (hall, etc.)
dandy [**dahn**-di] m. colloq: dandys
dandys [**dahn**-dis] m. dandys
dandysowaty [dahn-di-so-**vah**-ti] adj.m. dandyish
dandyzm [**dahn**-dizm] m. dandyism
dane [**dah**-ne] pl. data; information; evidence; particulars; substance; stuff; makings; information processes in computers
baza danych [**bah**-zah **dah**-nikh] exp.: (computer) data base
bliższe dane [**bleesh**-she **dah**-ne] exp.: description
dane osobiste [**dah**-ne o-so-**bees**-te] exp.: personal data; personal details
mieć dane po temu [myećh **dah**-ne po **te**-moo] exp.: to be justified in (doing, saying etc.)
mieć wszelkie dane [myećh fshel-k̲e **dah**-ne] exp.: to have every chance; to have all facts
danie [**dah**-ńe] n. serving (of food); dish; course
danie się [**dah**-ńe śh̲a̲n̲] n. surrender (see: **poddanie się**)
daniel [**dah**-ńel] m. fallow deer
danina [dah-**ńee**-nah] f. tribute; compulsory loan; (capital) levy
danser [**dahn**-ser] m. dancer
danserka [dahn-**ser**-kah] f. dancer
dansing [**dahn**-seeng] m. dancing
dansingowy [dahn-seen-**go**-vi] adj.m. dancing (hall, etc.)
dantejski [dahn-**tey**-skee] adj.m. Dantean
dantejskie sceny [dahn-**tey**-sk̲e **stse**-ni] exp.: infernal scenes
dany [**dah**-ni] adj.m. given
w danych warunkach [v **dah**-nikh vah-**roon**-kahkh] exp.: under the given conditions
dań [dahń] f. gift; tax (an old expression)
dar [dahr] m. gift; present; faculty; ability; dower; dowry; talent
dar słowa [dahr **swo**-vah] exp.: eloquence; fluency of speech
w darze [v **dah**-zhe] exp.: as a gift
darcie [**dahr**-ćhe] n. tearing; rending; pains; shooting pain; picking
darczyńca [dahr-**chiń**-tsah] m. giver; giving person (legal term)
darć [dahrćh] f. slang: rheumatic aches and pains
darda [**dahr**-dah] f. javelin
dardanelski [dahr-dah-**nel**-skee] adj.m. of (Turkish) Dardanelles
osioł dardanelski [**o**-śhow dahr-dah-**nel**-skee] exp.: dumbell; dummy; fool; blockhead

daremnie [dah-**rem**-ńe] adv. in vain; without success; to no purpose; to no avail; idly; ineffectively; without result; without pay
daremność [dah-**rem**-nośhćh] f. futility; ineffectiveness
daremny [dah-**rem**-ni] adj.m. futile; vain; idle; ineffective; unavailing; unpaid
darmo [**dahr**-mo] adv. free; gratuitously; free of charge; for nothing; to no avail
dostać za darmo [**dos**-tahćh zah **dahr**-mo] exp.: to get free of charge
na darmo [nah **dahr**-mo] exp.: in vain; for nothing; to no avail
nie darmo [ńe **dahr**-mo] exp.: not for nothing; not in vain
darmocha [dahr-**mo**-khah] f. slang: charity; unpaid labor
darmowy [dahr-**mo**-vi] adj.m. gratuitous; free
darmozjad [dahr-**mo**-zyaht] m. sponger; parasite; scrounger; cadger; loafer
darnina [dahr-**ńee**-nah] f. turf; sward; sod
darniować [dahr-**ńo**-vahćh] v. sod; cover with sod (*repeatedly*)
darniowanie [dahr-ńo-**vah**-ńe] n. sodding; covering with sod
darniowy [dahr-**ńo**-vi] adj.m. soddy; turfy
darniówka [dahr-**ńoof**-kah] f. (common burrowing) mole
darń [dahrń] f. sod; turf
darować [dah-**ro**-vahćh] v. give; present; make a gift; overlook; excuse; pardon; condone; remit; forgive; spare
darować komuś dług [dah-**ro**-vahćh **ko**-moośh dwoog] exp.: to remit somebody's debt
darować komuś grzechy [dah-**ro**-vahćh **ko**-moośh **gzhe**-khi] exp.: to absolve somebody from sins
darować komuś winę [dah-**ro**-vahćh **ko**-moośh **vee**-n<u>an</u>] exp.: to absolve somebody from guilt
darować komuś życie [dah-**ro**-vahćh **ko**-moośh **zhi**-ćhe] exp.: to spare somebody's life
pan daruje, ale ...[pahn dah-**roo**-ye **ah**-le] exp.: I beg your pardon but...; excuse me but ...
darowanie [dah-ro-**vah**-ńe] n. remission; remittal; condonation
nie do darowania [ńe do dah-ro-**vah**-ńah] exp.: unforgivable; unpardonable; inexcusable
darowany [dah-ro-**vah**-ni] adj.m. gift (horse, watch, etc.)
darowizna [dah-ro-**veez**-nah] f. donation; gift; grant; demise; deed of gift
darowywać [dah-ro-**vi**-vahćh] v. give; present; make a gift; overlook; excuse; pardon; condone; remit; forgive; spare (*repeatedly*)
darsonwalizacja [dahr-son-vah-lee-**zahts**-yah] f. D'Arsonvalism; high-frequency electrical treatment
darujący [dah-roo-**y<u>own</u>**-tsi] adj.m. of forgiveness; of pardon; of remission; remissive; m. donor; granter
darwinista [dahr-vee-**ńees**-tah] m. Darwinian
darwinistka [dahr-vee-**ńeest**-kah] f. (female) Darwinian
darwinistyczny [dahr-vee-ńees-**tich**-ni] adj.m. Darwinian
darwinizm [dahr-**vee**-ńeezm] m. Darwinism
darwinowski [dahr-vee-**nof**-skee] adj.m. Darwinian; Darwin's (theory, etc.)
darzbór! [**dahzh**-boor] excl.: happy hunting! good hunting!
darzyć [**dah**-zhićh] v. present; bestow; show (favor, etc.); grant
darzyć kogoś zaufaniem [**dah**-zhićh **ko**-gośh zah-oo-**fah**-ńem] exp. : to put one's trust in somebody (*repeatedly*)
darzyć się [**dah**-zhićh śh<u>an</u>] v. thrive (*repeatedly*)
darzy mu się [**dah**-zhi moo śh<u>an</u>] exp.: he is thriving
daszek [**dah**-shek] m. rooflet; penthouse; hood; lamp-shade; screen; peak; visor; eye-shade; eye-shield; circumflex accent
daszkowy [dahs-**ko**-vi] adj.m. in shape of a roof; hooded
data [**dah**-tah] f. date

pod dobrą datą [pot **dob**-rown dah-town] exp.: tipsy; slang: screwed; squiffy; under the influence
starej daty [**stah**-rey **dah**-ti] exp.: old-fashioned; antiquated; of the old school; outmoded; out-of-date; out of fashion
świeżej daty [**śhfye**-zhey **dah**-ti] exp.: of recent date
datacja [dah-**tah**-tsyah] f. formal dating (of a document, etc.)
dataria [dah-**tah**-ryah] f. datary; dataria
datariusz [dah-**tah**-ryoosh] m. datary (schedule-calendar)
datek [**dah**-tek] m. small gift
datiwus [dah-**tee**-voos] m. a dative grammatical case
datować [dah-**to**-vahćh] v. date (*repeatedly*)
datować mylnie [dah-**to**-vahćh **mil**-ńe] exp.: to miss date
datować się [dah-**to**-vahćh śhan] v. date (oneself)(*repeatedly*)
datować się od [dah-**to**-vahćh śhan ot] exp.: to date from (a given period)
datownik [dah-**tov**-ńeek] m. date-stamp; dater; postmark; date-maker
datura [dah-**too**-rah] f. datura; Jimson weed; thorn apple
dawać [**dah**-vahćh] v. give (*repeatedly*); see: **dać**
dawaj! [**dah**-vahy] excl.: give it!
dawać się [**dah**-vahćh śhan] v. yield; surrender; be possible; be feasible (*repeatedly*)
dawać się lubić [**dah**-vahćh śhan **loo**-beećh] exp.: to make it easy to be liked
dawanie [dah-**vah**-ńe] n. giving
dawanie się [dah-**vah**-ńe śhan] n. yielding
dawca [**dahf**-tsah] m. giver; donor
dawca krwi [**dahf**-tsah krfee] exp.: blood donor
dawczyni [dahf-**chi**-ńee] f. (woman) giver; donor
dawien [**dah**-vyen] adj.n. = **dawny**
z dawien dawna [z **dah**-vyen **dahv**-nah] exp.: from times immemorial; for a very long time
dawka [**dahf**-kah] f. dose; portion
śmiertelna dawka [śhmyer-**tel**-nah **dahf**-kah] exp.: lethal dose
za duża dawka [zah **doo**-zhah **dahf**-kah] exp.: overdose
dawkomierz [dahf-**ko**-myesh] m. dosage measuring device
dawkować [dahf-**ko**-vahćh] v. dose (*repeatedly*)
dawkowanie [dahf-ko-**vah**-ńe] n. dosage; dosing
dawkownik [dahf-**kov**-ńeek] m. dosing device
dawniej [**dahv**-ńey] adv. formerly; in former times; at one time; in the past
jak dawniej [yahk **dahv**-ńey] exp.: as before; as of old
dawno [**dahv**-no] adv. long ago; in the past; once; once upon a time; in olden days; in olden times; in past ages; since a long time; long since
dawno po [**dahv**-no po] exp.: long after; long past
dawno temu [**dahv**-no **te**-moo] exp.: long ago; long since
jak dawno temu? [yahk **dahv**-no **te**-moo] exp.: how long ago?; how long since?
dawność [**dahv**-nośhćh] f. long duration; antiquity
dawny [**dahv**-ni] adj.m. old; old-time; former; ancient; pristine; one time; some time; ex-; previous; preceding; late; past; of long standing
od dawna [od **dahv**-nah] adv. since a long time; for a long time
od dawien dawna [od dah-vyen **dahv**-nah] adv. since a long time; since very long
po dawnemu [po dahv-**ne**-moo] adv. as formerly; as before; as previously; as of old; as in the past
z dawna [z **dahv**-nah] adv. long since; long before
z dawien dawna [z **dah**-vyen **dahv**-nah] adv. since a very long time; since times immemorial
za dawnych dni [zah **dahv**-nikh dńee] exp.: in the old days
dawstwo [**dahf**-stfo] n. the giving

(of blood, etc.)
dąb [downp] m. oak tree (wood)
stawać dęba [**stah**-vahćh **dan**-bah] exp.: to rear; to prance; to jib; to mutiny; to rebel
włosy stają mu dęba [**vwo**-si **stah**-yown moo **dan**-bah] exp: his hair stands on end
dąbczak [**downp**-chahk] m. young oak
dąbek [**down**-bek] m. young oak
dąbrowa [down-**bro**-vah] f. oak grove; oak forest; oak wood
dąbrowszczak [down-**brof**-shchahk] m. soldier of J. Dąbrowski international brigade in Spain (1936-39)
dąbrówka [down-**broof**-kah] f. ground-pine (Ajuga)
dąć [downćh] v. blow; resound; play Trumpet, etc. (*repeatedly*)
dąć się [downćh śhan] v. puff up; be proud; give oneself airs (*repeatedly*)
dąs [downs] m. sulk
dąsać się [**down**-sahćh śhan] v. sulk; be in the pouts; mump; be fussing; be moody (*repeatedly*)
dąsalska [down-**sahl**-skah] f. colloq: sulking girl; pout
dąsalski [down-**sahl**-skee] m. colloq: sulking boy; pout
dąsanie się [down-**sah**-ńe śhan] n. sulks; sulking; mumps; mumping
dąsy [**down**-si] pl. sulkiness; mumps; pouts
dążenie [down-**zhe**-ńe] n. aim; aspiration; endeavor; design; pursuit (of); eagerness (after, for); anxiety (to do); trend (towards); drift (towards)
dążność [**down**-zhnośhćh] f. tendency; eagerness; anxiety
dążyć [**down**-zhićh] v. aspire; tend; aim (at); be bound (for); be bent (for); make (for); steer (for); bend one's steps (for); trend (towards); be desirous (of doing); strain (after); strive (after) (*repeatedly*)
dążyć do celu [**down**-zhićh do **tse**-loo] exp.: to pursue one's ends
dbać [dbahćh] v. care; take care; look after; be careful of; mind; keep an eye on; bear in mind; fend for (oneself, etc.); attach importance to; set store by; be particular about (*repeatedly*)
dbać o siebie [dbahćh o **śhe**-bye] exp.: to take care of oneself; to fend for oneself
nie dbać o ...[ńe dbahćh o] exp.: to attach no importance to ...; to be heedless of ...
dbałość [**dbah**-wośhćh] f. care; solicitude; attentiveness; scrupulousness; conscientiousness
dbałość o swój wygląd [**dbah**-wośhćh o sfooy **vi**-glownt] exp.: tidiness; neatness
dbały [**dbah**-wi] adj.m. careful; solicitous; attentive; heedful; mindful; scrupulous; tidy; conscientious; neat; assiduous
dbanie [**dbah**-ńe] n. care; solicitude; attentiveness; scrupulousness; conscientiousness
de- [de] prefix: de-; from-; down-; partly-
dead-weight [ded weyt] exp.: (Engl.) dead-weight
dealer [**dee**-ler] m. dealer
dealerski [dee-**ler**-skee] adj.m. dealer's; of a dealer
debata [de-**bah**-tah] f. debate; discussion; disputation
debaty [de-**bah**-ti] pl. debate; debates; proceedings
debatować [de-bah-**to**-vahćh] v. debate; discuss; thrash out; deliberate; ponder (on, over) (*repeatedly*)
debatowanie [de-bah-to-**vah**-ńe] n. debates
debel [**de**-bel] m. double (in sport); four-oar boat
debet [**de**-bet] m. the debit side; debit (of an account)
debetować [de-be-**to**-vahćh] v. debit (an account, etc.) (*repeatedly*)
debetowanie [de-be-to-**vah**-ńe] n. debiting
debetowy [de-be-**to**-vi] adj.m. of debit; debit (account, etc.)
debil [**de**-beel] m. mentally retarded man (person)

debilizm [de-**bee**-leezm] m. (mild) mental retardation
debilka [de-**beel**-kah] f. mentally retarded (female)
debilny [de-**beel**-ni] adj.m. of mental retardation
debilowaty [de-bee-lo-**vah**-ti] adj.m. showing some mental retardation
debit [**de**-beet] m. the right to sell foreign newspapers and magazines
debiut [**de**-byoot] m. debut; opening (in chess)
debiutancki [de-byoo-**tahn**-tskee] adj.m. of debutant; debutant's
debiutant [de-**byoo**-tahnt] m. debutant
debiutantka [de-byoo-**tahnt**-kah] f. debutante
debiutować [de-byoo-**to**-vahćh] v. make one's debut (*repeatedly*)
debiutowanie [de-byoo-to-**vah**-ńe] n. making one's debut
deblista [deb-**lees**-tah] m. contestant in the doubles (sport)
deblistka [deb-**leest**-kah] f. (woman) contestant in the doubles (sport)
debrza [**deb**-zhah] f. ("v"-shape) steep valley
decemwir [de-**tsem**-veer] m. decemvir
decemwirat [de-tsem-**vee**-raht] m. decemvirate
decentralistycznie [de-tsen-trah-lees-**tich**-ńe] adv. by decentralization
decentralistyczny [de-tsen-trah-lees-**tich**-ni] adj.m. decentralizing
decentralizacja [de-tsen-trah-lee-**zah**-tsyah] f. decentralization
decentralizacyjny [de-tsen-trah-lee-zah-**tsiy**-ni] adj.m. decentralizing (tendency, etc.)
decentralizować [de-tsen-trah-lee-**zo**-vahćh] v. decentralize (*repeatedly*)
decentralizować się [de-tsen-trah-lee-**zo**-vahćh śhan] v. become decentralized (*repeatedly*)
dech [dekh] m. breath; breathing; panting; gasping; gust of wind; breath of air; Genetivus: **tchu** [tkhoo]
bez tchu [bes tkhoo] exp.: out of breath; breathless; panting; gasping; without respite; ceaselessly
co tchu [tso tkhoo] exp.: as fast as possible; in all possible haste; with all possible speed; as quick as one can
jednym tchem [**yed**-nim tkhem] exp.: at one time (to do)
nabrać tchu [nah-brahćh tkhoo] exp.: to draw breath; to pause for breath
póki tchu [**poo**-kee tkhoo] exp.: to the last gasp
stracić dech [**strah**-ćheećh dekh] exp.: to lose one's wind
wypić jednym tchem [**vi**-peećh **yed**-nim tkhem] exp.: to drink at one gulp
zaczerpnąć tchu [zah-**cherp**-nownćh tkhoo] exp.: to draw one's breath
decha [**de**-khah] f. (rough) board
pijany w dechę [pee-**yah**-ni v **de**-khan] exp.: slang: dead drunk
w dechę [v **de**-khan] exp.: slang: excellent; first-rate; topping; corking; scrumptious; scrummy; slang: hunky-dory
dechrystianizacja [de-khri-styah-ńee-**zah**-tsyah] f. campaign to remove the influence of Christianity
decy- [**de**-tsi] prefix: deci-; ten-; tenth-
decybel [de-**tsi**-bel] m. decibel
decybelowy [de-tsi-be-**lo**-vi] adj.m. of a decibel
decydencki [de-tsi-**dents**-kee] adj.m. of a decider; of a deciding person
decydent [de-**tsi**-dent] m. decider; deciding person
decydować [de-tsi-**do**-vahćh] v. decide; resolve; determine; make a decision; take a decision; make a resolution; make resolutions; (*repeatedly*)
decydować się [de-tsi-**do**-vahćh śhan] v. decide on; fix on; take a resolution; take a decision; make up one's mind; settle upon (*repeatedly*)
decydowanie [de-tsi-do-**vah**-ńe] n. decision; resolution; deciding
decydowanie się [de-tsi-do-**vah**-ńe śhan] n. making a decision;

making a resolution
decydująco [de-tsi-doo-yown-tso] adv. decisively; conclusively; vitally; finally; crucially
decydujący [de-tsi-doo-yown-tsi] adj.m. decisive; conclusive; vital; final; crucial
decydująca chwila [de-tsi-doo-yown-tsah khfee-lah] exp.: zero hour; decisive moment
decydujący moment [de-tsi-doo-yown-tsi mo-ment] exp.: decisive moment; the real issue; the pivot; the crucial issue
decygram [de-tsi-grahm] m. decigram; decigramme (Brit.)
decylitr [de-tsi-leetr] m. deciliter
decyma [de-tsi-mah] f. decimal musical measure
decymalny [de-tsi-mahl-ni] adj.m. decimal (system, etc.)
decymetr [de-tsi-metr] m. decimeter
decyzja [de-tsi-zyah] f. decision; ruling; resolve; resolution
powziąć decyzję [po-vźhownćh de-tsi-zyan] exp.: to come to a decision
decyzyjny [de-tsi-ziy-ni] adj.m. decisive
dederon [de-de-ron] m. an artificial fiber (made in East Germany)
dederonowy [de-de-ro-no-vi] adj.m. of an artificial fiber
dedukcja [de-dook-tsyah] f. deduction; inference
dedukcyjnie [de-dook-tsiy-ńe] adv. deductively; by way of deduction; inferentially; by inference
dedukcyjny [de-dook-tsiy-ni] adj.m. deductive; inferential
dedukować [de-doo-ko-vahćh] v. deduce; infer (*repeatedly*)
dedukowanie [de-doo-ko-vah-ńe] n. deduction; inference
dedykacja [de-di-kah-tsyah] f. dedication; inscription (of a book)
dedykacyjnie [de-di-kah-tsiy-ńe] adv. by way of dedication
dedykacyjny [de-di-kah-tsiy-ni] adj.m. dedicatory
dedykować [de-di-ko-vahćh] v. dedicate; inscribe (a book) (*repeatedly*)
dedykowanie [de-di-ko-vah-ńe] n. dedication; inscribing
defa [de-fah] f. colloq: defensive
defekacja [de-fe-kahts-yah] f. defecation; excretion of waste matter from the bowels
defekacyjny [de-fe-kah-tsiy-ni] adj.m. defecation (fertilizer, sediment, etc.)
defekt [de-fekt] m. defect; flaw; fault; damage; injury; reject; deficiency; imperfection; shortcoming; wastrel
defekty [de-fek-ti] pl. rejects; rejectamenta; faults
defektologia [de-fek-to-lo-gyah] f. study of physical and mental defects
defektoskop [de-fek-to-skop] m. defectoscope; flaw detector
defektoskopia [de-fek-to-sko-pyah] f. flaw detection
defektoskopowy [de-fek-to-sko-po-vi] adj.m. flaw-detection (procedure, etc.)
defektować [de-fek-to-vahćh] v. fail; break down; conk; blow out; go flat; puncture (a tire) (*repeatedly*)
defektowy [de-fek-to-vi] adj.m. defective
defektywnie [de-fek-tiv-ńe] adv. defectively
defektywny [de-fek-tiv-ni] adj.m. defective
defenestracja [de-fe-nes-trah-tsyah] f. "defenestration" (or throwing out of a window of the Castle Hradchany) of German dignitaries by Czech Protestants, in Prague in 1618 (the beginning of the Thirty Year War)
defensor [de-fen-sor] m. defensive (ball) player
defensywa [de-fen-si-vah] f. defensive; exp.: military security service
w defensywie [v de-fen-siv-ye] exp.: on the defensive
defensywnie [de-fen-siv-ńe] adv. defensively
defensywność [de-fen-si-vnośhćh] f. defensiveness
defensywny [de-fen-siv-ni] adj.m. defensive

defetysta [de-fe-**tis**-tah] m. defeatist; croaker
defetystyczny [de-fe-tis-**tich**-ni] adj.m. defeatist
defetyzm [de-**fe**-tizm] m. defeatism; resignation to defeat
defibracja [de-fee-**brah**-tsyah] f. grinding of wood fibers into pulp
defibracyjny [de-fee-brah-**tsiy**-ni] adj.m. of grinding of wood fibers
defibrator [de-fee-**brah**-tor] m. machine for grinding of wood fibers into pulp (for cardboard production, etc.)
defibrować [de-fee-**bro**-vahćh] v. defiber (*repeatedly*)
defibrowanie [de-fee-bro-**vah**-ńe] n. pulp making
defibrylacja [de-fee-bri-**lah**-tsyah] f. defibrillation; restoration of the rhythm of a fibrillating heart
defibrylator [de-fee-bri-**lah**-tor] m. defibrillator
defibrylować [de-fee-bri-**lo**-vahćh] v. defibrillate; restore the rhythm of a fibrillating heart (*repeatedly*)
deficyt [de-**fee**-tsit] m. deficit; deficiency; shortage; a loss in business operations
deficytowo [de-fee-tsi-**to**-vo] adv. in deficit; by way of deficit
deficytowość [de-fee-tsi-**to**-vośhćh] f. scarcity; short supply; unrenumerativeness; deficit (spending, etc.); excess of expenditure over revenue
deficytowy [de-fee-tsi-**to**-vi] adj.m. unremunerative; losing; scarce; in short supply; deficient (in amount, quality, etc.)
defiguracja [de-fee-goo-**rah**-tsyah] f. disfigurement
defilada [de-fee-**lah**-dah] f. march past; fly-past; organized procession; parade
defiladowy [de-fee-lah-**do**-vi] adj.m. parade (grounds, etc.)
defilować [de-fee-**lo**-vahćh] v. march past; rank past; defile; march in an organized procession; march in a parade (*repeatedly*)
defilowanie [de-fee-lo-**vah**-ńe] n. march past; fly-past; organized procession; parade; parading
definicja [de-fee-**ńee**-tsyah] f. definition; sharp demarcation (of outlines, limits, details, etc.)
definicyjny [de-fee-ńee-**tsiy**-ni] adj.m. of definition; definitional
definiendum [de-fee-**ńyen**-doom] n. definiendum; defined term
definiens [de-**fee**-ńyens] m. definiens; defining expression
definiować [de-fee-**ńyo**-vahćh] v. define; describe exactly; determine; give the definition (of); fix the limits of; make clear; make a definition (*repeatedly*)
definiowanie [de-fee-ńyo-**vah**-ńe] n. defining; determining
definitywnie [de-fee-ńee-**tiv**-ńe] adv. decisively; finally; conclusively; definitively
definitywność [de-fee-ńee-**tiv**-nośhćh] f. definitiveness
definitywny [de-fee-ńee-**tiv**-ni] adj.m. decisive; final; conclusive; definitive; authoritative
deflacja [de-**flah**-tsyah] f. deflation
deflacyjny [de-flah-**tsiy**-ni] adj.m. deflationary
deflagracja [de-flahg-**rah**-tsyah] f. deflagration
deflagrator [de-flahg-**rah**-tor] m. deflagrator
deflagrować [de-flahg-**ro**-vahćh] v. deflagrate; burn suddenly (*repeatedly*)
deflektometr [de-flek-**to**-metr] m. shipboard device for correction of magnetic deviation
deflektor [de-**fle**-ktor] m. deflector
defloracja [de-flo-**rah**-tsyah] f. defloration; rupture of the hymen
defoliacja [de-fol-**yah**-tsyah] f. defoliation
defoliacyjny [de-fol-yah-**tsiy**-ni] adj.m. of defoliation
defoliant [de-fo-lyahnt] m. defoliant
deformacja [de-for-**mah**-tsyah] f. deformation; disfiguration; malformation; deformity; set; strain (in materials); change for the worse
deformować [de-for-**mo**-vahćh] v. deform; disfigure; make hideous (or monstrous) (*repeatedly*)
deformować się [de-for-mo-vahćh

śhan] v. deform; be deformed; take a set; strain; become misshapen; become changed in shape (*repeatedly*)
deformowanie [de-for-mo-**vah**-ńe] n. deformation; disfiguration; malformation; deformity; straining (materials); changing for the worse
defraudacja [de-frahw-**dah**-tsyah] f. embezzlement; defalcation
defraudancki [de-frahw-**dahn**-tskee] adj.m. embezzling; of embezzlement
defraudant [de-**frahw**-dahnt] m. embezzler; defalcator
defraudantka [de-frahw-**dahnt**-kah] f. (woman) embezzler; defalcator
defraudować [de-frahw-**do**-vahćh] v. embezzle; defalcate (*repeatedly*)
defraudowanie [de-frahw-do-**vah**-ńe] n. embezzling; defalcating
degeneracja [de-ge-ne-**rah**-tsyah] f. degeneration; degeneracy; devolution
degeneracki [de-ge-ne-**rah**-tskee] adj.m. degenerate
degeneracyjny [de-ge-ne-rah-**tsiy**-ni] adj.m. degenerative
degenerat [de-ge-**ne**-raht] m. degenerate; a degenerate
degenerować [de-ge-ne-**ro**-vahćh] v. cause degeneration (*repeatedly*)
degenerować się [de-ge-ne-**ro**-vahćh śhan] v. degenerate; deteriorate (*repeatedly*)
deglomeracja [de-glo-me-**rah**-tsyah] f. deglomeration
deglomeracyjny [de-glo-me-rah-**tsiy**-ni] adj.m. of deglomeration
deglomerować [de-glo-me-**ro**-vahćh] v. cause deglomeration; undo conglomeration (*repeatedly*)
deglomerowanie [de-glo-me-ro-**vah**-ńe] n. deglomeration
degradacja [de-grah-**dah**-tsyah] f. degradation; reduction in rank
degradować [de-grah-**do**-vahćh] v. degrade; reduce in rank; cashier (an officer); disrate (*repeatedly*)
degradowanie [de-grah-do-**vah**-ńe] n. degradation; reduction in rank; degeneration; debasing
degrengolada [de-gren-go-**lah**-dah] f. downfall; tumbledown
degresja [de-**gre**-syah] f. degression; gradual decrease; gradual descend
degresywnie [de-gre-**siv**-ńe] adv. degressively
degresywny [de-gre-**siv**-ni] adj.m. degressive
degustacja [de-goos-**tah**-tsyah] f. tasting (of wine, etc. for commercial purposes)
degustacyjny [de-goos-tah-**tsiy**-ni] adj.m. tasting (of wine, etc. for commercial purposes); taster's
degustator [de-goo-**stah**-tor] m. taster (of wine, etc. for commercial purposes); wine-tester; tea-taster
degustować [de-goo-**sto**-vahćh] v. taste (of wine, etc. for commercial purposes) (*repeatedly*)
degustowanie [de-goo-sto-**vah**-ńe] n. wine tasting
dehumanizacja [de-khoo-mah-ńee-**zah**-tsyah] f. dehumanization
dehumanizować [de-khoo-mah-ńee-**zo**-vahćh] v. dehumanize (*repeatedly*)
dehumanizować się [de-khoo-mah-ńee-**zo**-vahćh śhan] v. become dehumanized (*repeatedly*)
dehydrator [de-khi-**drah**-tor] m. dehydrator
deifikacja [de-ee-fee-**kah**-tsyah] f. deification
deifikować [de-ee-fee-**ko**-vahćh] v. deify; make a god of; look upon as a god (*repeatedly*)
deifikowanie [de-ee-fee-ko-**vah**-ńe] n. deification
deiktyczny [de-ee-**ktich**-ni] adj.m. deictic; showing or pointing out directly
deista [de-**ee**-stah] m. deist
deistycznie [de-ee-**stich**-ńe] adv. deistically
deistyczny [de-ee-**stich**-ni] adj.m. deistic; deistical
deizm [**de**-eezm] m. deism
dejdwud [**deyd**-voot] m. dead-wood
dejman [**dey**-mahn] m. day-man; worker hired on a daily basis to

clean ship in a port
dejonizować [de-yo-ńee-**zo**-vahćh] v. deionize; remove ions (from water, gas, etc.) (*repeatedly*)
dejwud [**dey**-voot] m. dead-wood
dek [dek] m. (ship's) deck
deka [**de**-kah] f. blanket; horse-blanket; saddle-cloth; coverlet; housing; pot-lid; sternum; cover of violin-case; slang: decagram
dekabrysta [de-kah-**bris**-tah] m. Decembrist; Dekabrist
dekabrystowski [de-kah-bris-**tof**-skee] adj.m. Decembrist (movement, etc.); Dekabrist (conspiracy, etc.)
dekada [de-**kah**-dah] f. decade
dekadencja [de-kah-**den**-tsyah] f. decadence; decline; deterioration
dekadencki [de-kah-**den**-tskee] adj.m. decadent
dekadent [de-**kah**-dent] m. decadent
dekadentyzm [de-kah-**den**-tizm] m. decadentism
dekadowy [de-kah-**do**-vi] adj.m. of a decade
dekaedr [de-**kah**-edr] m. decahedron; polyhedron of ten faces
dekagon [de-**kah**-gon] m. decagon
dekagram [de-**kah**-grahm] m. decagram; decagramme (Brit.)
dekagramowy [de-kah-grah-**mo**-vi] adj.m. of a decagram
dekalitr [de-**kah**-leetr] m. decaliter; dekaliter
dekalitrowy [de-kah-lee-**tro**-vi] adj.m. decaliter (measure, etc.)
dekalkomania [de-kahl-ko-**mah**-ńyah] f. decalcomania
dekalog [de-**kah**-log] m. decalogue; Ten Commandments
dekalogowy [de-kah-lo-**go**-vi] adj.m. decalogue (authority, etc.)
dekametr [de-**kah**-metr] m. decameter
dekametrowy [de-kah-me-**tro**-vi] adj.m. of a decameter
dekanat [de-**kah**-naht] m. decanate; deanery
dekantacja [de-kahn-**tah**-tsyah] f. decantation
dekantator [de-kahn-**tah**-tor] m. (chemical) decanter (hist.)
dekanter [de-**kahn**-ter] m. decanter
dekantować [de-kahn-**to**-vahćh] v. decant (*repeatedly*)
dekapilator [de-kah-pee-**lah**-tor] m. hair remover
dekapitalizować [de-kah-pee-tah-lee-**zo**-vahćh] v. cause depreciation; use up the value (of buildings, investments, etc.) (*repeatedly*)
dekapitalizować się [de-kah-pee-tah-lee-**zo**-vahćh śhan] v. depreciate; use up; lose value (*repeatedly*)
dekapować [de-kah-**po**-vahćh] v. pickle (*repeatedly*)
dekarbonizacja [de-kahr-bo-ńee-**zahts**-yah] f. decarbonation
dekarbonizować [de-kahr-bo-ńee-**zo**-vahćh] v. decarbonize; remove carbon from (*repeatedly*)
dekarcha [de-**kahr**-khah] m. decarch; dekarch
dekarchia [de-**kahr**-khyah] f. decarchy; dekarchy
dekarski [de-**kahr**-skee] adj.m. roofer's; tiler's
dekarstwo [de-**kahr**-stfo] n. roofing; tiling
dekartelizacja [de-kahr-te-lee-**zah**-tsyah] f. subdividing of cartels into smaller economic units
dekartelizować [de-kahr-te-lee-**zo**-vahćh] v. subdivide a cartel into smaller economic units (*repeatedly*)
dekartelizować się [de-kahr-te-lee-**zo**-vahćh śhan] v. undergo division of a cartel (*repeatedly*)
dekarz [**de**-kahsh] m. roofer; tiler
dekatyzacja [de-kah-ti-**zah**-tsyah] f. shrinking of cloth; steaming of cloth
dekatyzarka [de-kah-ti-**zahr**-kah] f. machine for shrinking of cloth; machine for steaming of cloth
dekatyzować [de-kah-ti-**zo**-vahćh] v. shrink; steam (cloth) (*repeatedly*)
dekatyzowanie [de-kah-ti-zo-**vah**-ńe] adj.m. shrinking; steaming (of cloth)
dekiel [**de**-kel] m. lid (of a pot, etc.); piano top; fraternity cap
deklamacja [de-klah-**mah**-tsyah] f.

declamation; recitation; verse-reading; bombast; rant; pompous language (high sounding)
deklamacyjność [de-klah-mah-**tsiy**-nośhćh] f. theatrical declamation; bombast; rant; pompous language (of a speech, verse reading, etc.)
deklamacyjny [de-klah-mah-**tsiy**-ni] adj.m. of a theatrical declamation; of a bombast; of a pompous language (of a speech, verse reading, etc.)
deklamator [de-klah-**mah**-tor] m. reciter; slang: (insincere) reciter; ranter; bluffer; blusterer; humbug
deklamatorka [de-klah-mah-**tor**-kah] f. (female) reciter; (insincere) reciter; ranter; bluffer; blusterer; humbug
deklamatorski [de-klah-mah-**tor**-skee] adj.m. declamatory; of a declamation; of a recitation; of a verse-reading; bombastic; pompous; of a high sounding language
deklamatorsko [de-klah-mah-**tor**-sko] adv. like a declamation; like a recitation; bombastically; pompously
deklamatorstwo [de-klah-mah-**tor**-stfo] n. declamation; recitation; verse-reading; bombast; rant; pompous language; high sounding language
deklamatoryka [de-klah-mah-**to**-ri-kah] f. theory of declamation; rules of recitation
deklamować [de-klah-**mo**-vahćh] v. recite; declaim; give recitation; rant; talk big (*repeatedly*)
deklamowanie [de-klah-mo-**vah**-ńe] n. declamation; recitation; verse-reading; bombast; rant; pompous language; high sounding language
deklaracja [de-klah-**rah**-tsyah] f. declaration; proclamation; statement; pledge form; proposal (of marriage)
deklaracja podatkowa [de-klah-**rah**-tsyah po-dah-**tko**-vah] exp.: income-tax return
deklaracyjnie [de-klah-rah-**tsiy**-ńe] adv. declaratively
deklaracyjny [de-klah-rah-**tsiy**-ni] adj.m. declarative; declaratory; of a declaration; of a proclamation; of a statement; of a pledge form; of a proposal (of marriage)
deklaratywizm [de-klah-rah-**ti**-veezm] m. uncritical tendency to support something
deklaratywnie [de-klah-rah-**tiv**-ńe] adv. insincerely; giving empty promises etc.
deklaratywność [de-klah-rah-**tiv**-nośhćh] f. uncritical tendency to support something
deklaratywny [de-klah-rah-**tiv**-ni] adj.m. insincere; giving empty promises etc.
deklarować [de-klah-**ro**-vahćh] v. declare; commit oneself (to); pledge oneself (*repeatedly*)
deklarować się [de-klah-**ro**-vahćh śhan] v. declare; declare oneself (for, against); propose (*repeatedly*)
deklarować się przeciw [de-klah-**ro**-vahćh śhan **pshe**-ćheef] exp.: to declare oneself against
deklarować się za [de-klah-**ro**-vahćh śhan zah] exp.: to declare oneself for
deklarowanie [de-klah-ro-**vah**-ńe] n. declaration
deklarowanie się [de-klah-ro-**vah**-ńe śhan] n. declaring oneself (for)
deklasacja [de-klah-**sah**-tsyah] f. lowering in the social scale
deklasować [de-klah-**so**-vahćh] v. lower in the social scale (*repeatedly*)
deklasować się [de-klah-**so**-vahćh śhan] v. be lowered in the social scale; lose caste (*repeatedly*)
deklasowanie [de-klah-so-**vah**-ńe] n. degradation; assigning to a lower social status
deklasowanie się [de-klah-so-**vah**-ńe śhan] n. lowering oneself in social status
deklinacja [de-klee-**nah**-tsyah] f. declination; giving of inflected forms; declension; the inflection of nouns, pronouns, or adjectives
deklinacyjny [de-klee-nah-**tsiy**-ni] adj.m. declinational; declination

(compass, etc.); (in grammar:) declensional
deklinator [de-klee-nah-tor] m. magnetic needle
deklinometr [de-klee-**no**-metr] m. device for measuring magnetic declination
deklinować [de-klee-**no**-vahćh] v. (gram.) decline (*repeatedly*)
deklinować się [de-klee-**no**-vahćh śhan] v. (gram.) be declined (*repeatedly*)
deklinowanie [de-klee-no-**vah**-ńe] n. declination
deklinowanie się [de-klee-no-**vah**-ńe śhan] n. undergoing declination
dekoder [de-**ko**-der] m. decoding device; decoder
dekodować [de-ko-**do**-vahćh] v. decode; convert into intelligible language (*repeatedly*)
dekolonizacja [de-ko-lo-ńee-**zah**-tsyah] f. decolonization; freeing from colonial status
dekolonizacyjny [de-ko-lo-ńee-zah-**tsiy**-ni] adj.m. decolonizing (process, etc.)
dekolonizować [de-ko-lo-ńee-**zo**-vahćh] v. decolonize (*repeatedly*)
dekolt [**de**-kolt] m. low-cut neck; decolletage
dekoltować się [de-kol-**to**-vahćh śhan] v. wear low-necked dresses; wear a low-necked dress (*repeatedly*)
dekoltowanie się [de-kol-to-**vah**-ńe śhan] n. wearing of low-necked dresses
dekoltowany [de-kol-to-**vah**-ni] adj.m. low-necked (dress, etc.)
dekompletować [de-kom-ple-**to**-vahćh] v. render incomplete; break up (a set, etc.) (*repeatedly*)
dekomponować [de-kom-po-**no**-vahćh] v. change composition of something; decompose; rot (*repeatedly*)
dekomponowanie [de-kom-po-no-**vah**-ńe] n. decomposition; rot
dekompozycja [de-kom-po-**zi**-tsyah] f. decomposition; rot
dekompresja [de-kom-**pre**-syah] f. decompression
dekompresor [de-kom-**pre**-sor] m. decompressor
dekompresyjny [de-kom-pre-**siy**-ni] adj.m. decompressive
dekomunizacja [de-ko-moo-ńee-**zah**-tsyah] f. liquidation of the communist system
dekomunizować [de-ko-moo-ńee-**zo**-vahćh] v. liquidate the communist system (*repeatedly*)
dekomunizować się [de-ko-moo-ńee-**zo**-vahćh śhan] v. undergo the liquidation of the communist system (*repeatedly*)
dekoncentracja [de-kon-tsen-**trahts**-yah] f. decentralization
dekoncentracyjny [de-kon-tsen-trah-**tsiy**-ni] adj.m. decentralization (program, etc.)
dekoncentrować [de-kon-tsen-**tro**-vahćh] v. deconcentrate; decentralize (*repeatedly*)
dekoncentrować się [de-kon-tsen-**tro**-vahćh śhan] v. become decentralized (*repeatedly*)
dekoniunktura [de-ko-ńoon-**ktoo**-rah] f. crisis; bear market
dekonspiracja [de-kon-spee-**rah**-tsyah] f. unmasking; exposition; bringing out of hiding
dekonspirować [de-kon-spee-**ro**-vahćh] v. unmask; expose; bring out of hiding (*repeatedly*)
dekonspirować się [de-kon-spee-**ro**-vahćh śhan] v. throw off the mask; expose oneself; come out of hiding (*repeatedly*)
dekoracja [de-ko-**rah**-tsyah] f. decoration; adornment; ornament; trimming; garnishing (of a dish); scenery; setting; embellishment; window-dressing; badge of honor
dekoracyjnie [de-ko-rah-**tsiy**-ńe] adv. decoratively; ornamentally
dekoracyjność [de-ko-rah-**tsiy**-nośhćh] f. decorative value; decorative effect
dekoracyjny [de-ko-rah-**tsiy**-ni] adj.m. decorative; ornamental; pertaining to theater setting
dekorator [de-ko-**rah**-tor] m. decorator; (theater) scene-painter; interior decorator
dekoratorka [de-ko-rah-**tor**-kah] f. (female) decorator; (theater)

scene-painter; interior decorator
dekoratorski [de-ko-rah-**tor**-skee] adj.m. decorator's
dekoratorstwo [de-ko-rah-**tor**-stfo] n. interior design
dekoratywność [de-ko-rah-**tiv**-nośhćh] f. decorative value; decorative effect
dekoratywny [de-ko-rah-**tiv**-ni] adj.m. decorative; ornamental; pertaining to theater setting
dekorować [de-ko-**ro**-vahćh] v. decorate; adorn; embellish; trim; garnish (a dish); confer (a medal, an order, etc.) (*repeatedly*)
dekorować się [de-ko-**ro**-vahćh śhan] v. decorate oneself (*repeatedly*)
dekorowanie [de-ko-ro-**vah**-ńe] n. decoration
dekort [**de**-kort] m. deduction (from the price); discount
dekortykacja [de-kor-ti-**kah**-tsyah] f. decortication; peeling of the outer cover; removal of (the cortex, the bark, etc.)
dekortykować [de-kor-ti-**ko**-vahćh] v. decorticate (*repeatedly*)
dekować [de-**ko**-vahćh] v. help dodge military service during the war; roof (a house, etc.) (*repeatedly*)
dekować się [de-**ko**-vahćh śhan] dodge military service during the war; avoid doing compulsory work for an occupying enemy; slang: hide (*repeatedly*)
dekowanie [de-ko-**vah**-ńe] n. dodging military service during war; install roofing
dekownik [de-**kov**-ńeek] m. shirker; one who evades an imposed duty
dekret [**de**-kret] m. decree; edict; fiat
dekretacja [de-kre-**tah**-tsyah] f. instruction note on a margin of an application form, etc.
dekretalia [de-kre-**tah**-lyah] pl. archive of papal pronouncements on the Church-law; decretals
dekretować [de-kre-**to**-vahćh] v. decree; ordain by decree (*repeatedly*)
dekretowanie [de-kre-to-**vah**-ńe] n. issuing of decrees
dekretowy [de-kre-**to**-vi] adj.m. of decree; by decree
dekstroza [dek-**stro**-zah] f. dextrose
dekstryna [dek-**stri**-nah] f. dextrin
delabializować [de-lah-byah-lee-**zo**-vahćh] v. unround (a vowel by spreading the lips laterally)
delcredere [del-kre-**de**-re] n. del credere (of the statute of frauds)
deleatur [de-le-**ah**-toor] n. mark of deletion for printers
delegacja [de-le-**gah**-tsyah] f. delegation; commission; business trip; written order to go on a business trip
delegacyjny [de-le-gah-**tsiy**-ni] adj.m. delegation (order, etc.)
delegalizacja [de-le-gah-lee-**zahts**-yah] f. delegalization
delegalizować [de-le-gah-lee-**zo**-vahćh] v. delegalize (*repeatedly*)
delegat [de-**le**-gaht] m. delegate; commissioner; deputy; vicarial
delegatka [de-le-**gah**-tkah] f. (female) delegate; commissioner; deputy
delegatura [de-le-gah-**too**-rah] f. representation; office of a representative; delegacy
delegować [de-le-**go**-vahćh] v. delegate; depute; deputize; appoint as deputy (*repeatedly*)
delegowana [de-le-go-**vah**-nah] f. (woman) delegate
delegowanie [de-le-go-**vah**-ńe] n. delegation
delegowany [de-le-go-**vah**-ni] m. a delegate
deleksykalizacja [de-le-ksi-kah-lee-**zah**-tsyah] f. revival of lexicality of a word included in a lexicon
delektować [de-le-**kto**-vahćh] v. regale (*repeatedly*)
delektować się [de-le-**kto**-vahćh śhan] v. relish; delight (in); regale oneself; savor; feast (upon) (*repeatedly*)
delektowanie się [de-lek-to-**vah**-ńe śhan] n. regaling; feasting upon
delficki [del-**fee**-tskee] Delphian; Delphic
delfin [**del**-feen] m. dolphin; swimming style; dolphin as a

decorative motive; dauphin: colloq: the oldest son
delfiny [del-**fee**-ni] pl. dolphins; the family of toothed whales
delfiniak [del-**fee**-ńahk] m. dolphin-striker
delfinina [del-fee-**ńee**-nah] f. delphinine
delfinista [del-fee-**ńees**-tah] m. swimmer using the dolphin style
delft [delft] m. Delft china; delftware
delia [**del**-yah] f. Polish nobleman's fur-lined coat (of old)
deliberacja [de-lee-be-**rahts**-yah] f. deliberation; consideration of alternatives; meditation; debate
deliberować [de-lee-be-**ro**-vahćh] v. deliberate; consider alternatives; meditate; debate (*repeatedly*)
delicja [de-**lee**-tsyah] f. tidbit
delicje [de-**lee**-tsye] pl. delicacies; dainties; pleasures; tidbits; dainties
delikacić się [de-lee-**kah**-ćheećh śhan] v. become refined; acquire refinement (*repeatedly*)
delikacik [de-lee-**kah**-ćheek] m. tenderling; delicate person
delikates [de-lee-**kah**-tes] m. a dainty; a delicacy; tidbit
delikatesy [de-lee-kah-**te**-si] pl. dainties; delicatessen (grocery store)
delikatesowy [de-lee-kah-te-**so**-vi] adj.m. delicatessen (store, etc.)
delikatnie [de-lee-**kaht**-ńe] adv. delicately; subtly; gently; softly; daintily; with refinement; tactfully; considerately; thoughtfully; sensitively; tenderly; frailly; weakly; nicely; mildly; finely; ticklishly; trickily; in a slippery way
delikatnieć [de-lee-**kaht**-ńećh] v. soften; become smooth; become silky; become sleek (*repeatedly*)
delikatność [de-lee-**kaht**-nośhćh] f. delicacy; gentleness; softness; subtleness; daintiness; tact; consideration; thoughtfulness; sensitiveness; frailness; nicety; fragility
delikatność dotknięcia [de-lee-**kaht**-nośhćh dot-**kńan**-ćhah] exp.: lightness of touch
delikatny [de-lee-**kaht**-ni] adj.m. delicate; subtle; gentle; soft; dainty; refined; tactful; considerate; thoughtful; sensitive; tender; frail; weak; nice; fragile; mild; fine; queasy; ticklish; tricky; slippery; easily digestible
delikt [**de**-leekt] m. delict; transgression
delikwent [de-**lee**-kfent] m. delinquent; culprit; offender; colloq: poor fellow; person submitted to an ordeal
delikwentka [de-lee-**kfen**-tkah] f. (female) delinquent; culprit; offender; colloq: poor girl; woman submitted to an ordeal
delimitacja [de-lee-mee-**tah**-tsyah] f. delimitation
delimitacyjny [de-lee-mee-tah-**tsiy**-ni] adj.m. delimitative
delimitować [de-lee-mee-**to**-vahćh] v. delimit; delineate (*repeatedly*)
delirium [de-**lee**-ryoom] n. delirium
delirka [de-**leer**-kah] f. slang: a rage
deliryczny [de-lee-**rich**-ni] adj.m. of delirium
dell'arte [del-**ahr**-te] n. 16th cent. improvised comedy
dellartowski [del-ahr-**tof**-skee] adj.m. of 16th cent. improvised comedy
delta [**del**-tah] f. delta
delta rzeki [**del**-tah **zhe**-kee] exp.: river-delta
promienie delta [pro-**mye**-ńe **del**-tah] exp.: delta rays
deltoid [del-**to**-eet] m. deltoid
deltowy [del-**to**-vi] adj.m. delta-shaped
deluwialny [de-loo-**vyahl**-ni] adj.m. diluvial; diluvian
deluwium [de-**loo**-vyoom] n. diluvium; deluge
demagog [de-**mah**-gog] m. demagogue; ranter furthering his own interests
demagogia [de-mah-**go**-gyah] f. demagogy; rant
demagogicznie [de-mah-go-**geech**-ńe] adv. demagogically
demagogiczny [de-mah-go-**geech**-ni] adj.m. demagogic

demagogizować [de-mah-go-gee-**zo**-vahćh] v. act as a demagogue; use demagogy (*repeatedly*)
demarche [de-**mahrsh**] m. (French) demarche; maneuver; diplomatic move; diplomatic maneuver
demarkacja [de-mahr-**kah**-tsyah] f. demarcation
demarkacyjny [de-mahr-kah-**tsiy**-ni] adj.m. of demarcation; of boundary
linia demarkacyjna [**lee**-ńyah de-mahr-kah-**tsiy-nah**] exp.: demarcation line; boundary-line
demaskator [de-mah-**skah**-tor] m. exposer; whistle blower
demaskatorski [de-mah-skah-**tor**-skee] adj.m. exposing; whistle blowing
demaskatorsko [de-mah-skah-**tor**-sko] adv. in an exposing manner; like a whistle blower
demaskatorstwo [de-mah-skah-**tor**-stfo] n. unmasking; bringing to light; whistle blowing
demaskować [de-mah-**sko**-vahćh] v. unmask; uncover; denounce; uncloak; bring to light; expose (*repeatedly*)
demaskować się [de-mah-**sko**-vahćh śhan] v. throw off the mask; be unmasked; be denounced; be brought to light (*repeatedly*)
demaskowanie [de-mah-sko-**vah**-ńe] n. unmasking; bringing to light
demaskowanie się [de-mah-sko-**vah**-ńe śhan] n. unmasking oneself; exposing oneself
dematerializacja [de-mah-ter-yah-lee-**zah**-tsyah] f. dematerialization
dematerializować [de-mah-ter-yah-lee-**zo**-vahćh] v. cause to disappear (*repeatedly*)
dematerializować się [de-mah-ter-yah-lee-**zo**-vahćh śhan] v. cease to exist; disappear (*repeatedly*)
demencja [de-**men**-tsyah] f. dementia
dementi [de-**men**-tee] f. official denial; official correction
dementować [de-men-**to**-vahćh] v. deny; contradict; give the lie (to a statement, etc.) (*repeatedly*)
dementowanie [de-men-to-**vah**-ńe] n. denial; contradiction
demeszkować [de-mesh-**ko**-vahćh] v. damascene; ornament with wavy patterns (*repeatedly*)
demilitaryzacja [de-mee-lee-tah-ri-**zah**-tsyah] f. demilitarization
demilitaryzacyjny [de-mee-lee-tah-ri-zah-**tsiy**-ni] adj.m. of demilitarization
demilitaryzować [de-mee-lee-tah-ri-**zo**-vahćh] v. demilitarize (*repeatedly*)
demineralizacja [de-mee-ne-rah-lee-**zah**-tsyah] f. demineralization
demineralizacyjny [de-mee-ne-rah-lee-zah-**tsiy**-ni] adj.m. of demineralization
demineralizować [de-mee-ne-rah-lee-**zo**-vahćh] v. demineralize (*repeatedly*)
deminutiwum [de-mee-noo-**tee**-voom] n. diminutive
deminutyw [de-mee-**noo**-tif] m. diminutive
deminutywność [de-mee-noo-**tiv**-nośhćh] f. diminutiveness
deminutywny [de-mee-noo-**tiv**-ni] adj.m. diminutive (gram.)
deminutywum [de-mee-noo-**ti**-voom] n. diminutive
demistyfikacja [de-mees-ti-fee-**kah**-tsyah] f. demystification; clearing up of a mystery; unmasking
demistyfikator [de-mee-sti-fee-**kah**-tor] m. man clearing up of a mystery; whistle blower
demistyfikatorski [de-mee-sti-fee-kah-**tor**-skee] adj.m. of clearing up of a mystery; unmasking (deed, action, etc.)
demistyfikować [de-mee-sti-fee-**ko**-vahćh] v. demystify; explicate; unmask; uncover; denounce; uncloak; bring to light (*repeatedly*)
demistyfikować się [de-mee-sti-fee-**ko**-vahćh śhan] v. demystify oneself; throw off a mask; be unmasked; be denounced; be brought to light (*repeatedly*)
demitologizacja [de-mee-to-lo-gee-**zah**-tsyah] f. demythologization
demitologizować [de-mee-to-lo-gee-

zo-vahćh] v. demythologize
demiurg [**de**-myoorg] m. demiurge
demiurgicznie [de-myoor-**geech**-ńe] adv. demiurgically
demiurgiczny [de-myoor-**geech**-ni] adj.m. demiurgical; demiurgic
demobil [de-**mo**-beel] m. military equipment left over after demobilization and changes
demobilizacja [de-mo-bee-lee-**zah**-tsyah] f. demobilization; colloq: demob (Brit.)
demobilizacyjny [de-mo-bee-lee-zah-**tsiy**-ni] adj.m. of demobilization
demobilizować [de-mo-bee-lee-**zo**-vahćh] v. demobilize; disband (*repeatedly*)
demobilizować się [de-mo-bee-lee-**zo**-vahćh śhan] v. become demobilized; lose readiness (*repeatedly*)
demobilizująco [de-mo-bee-lee-zoo-**yown**-tso] adv. causing to disband; causing to lose readiness
demobilowy [de-mo-bee-**lo**-vi] adj.m. of military equipment left over after demobilization and changes
demodulacja [de-mo-doo-**lah**-tsyah] f. demodulation; detection (of a wave, a current, etc.)
demodulator [de-mo-doo-**lah**-tor] m. demodulator
demodulować [de-mo-doo-**lo**-vahćh] v. demodulate; extract the intelligence from a modulated signal (*repeatedly*)
demograf [de-**mo**-grahf] m. demographer
demografia [de-mo-**grah**-fyah] f. demography
demograficznie [de-mo-grah-**feech**-ńe] adv. demographically
demograficzny [de-mo-grah-**feech**-ni] adj.m. demographic; of vital statistics
demokracja [de-mo-**krah**-tsyah] f. democracy; rule by the people
demokrata [de-mo-**krah**-tah] m. democrat
demokratka [de-mo-**krah**-tkah] f. (female) democrat
demokratycznie [de-mo-krah-**tich**-ńe] adv. democratically
demokratyczność [de-mo-krah-**tich**-nośhćh] f. democratic character (of culture, etc.)
demokratyczny [de-mo-krah-**tich**-ni] adj.m. democratic
demokratyzacja [de-mo-krah-ti-**zah**-tsyah] f. democratization
demokratyzacyjny [de-mo-krah-ti-zah-**tsiy**-ni] adj.m. democratizing
demokratyzm [de-mo-**krah**-tizm] m. democratism
demokratyzować [de-mo-krah-ti-**zo**-vahćh] v. democratize (*repeatedly*)
demokratyzować się [de-mo-krah-ti-**zo**-vahćh śhan] v. become democratized (*repeatedly*)
demokratyzowanie [de-mo-krah-ti-zo-**vah**-ńe] n. democratizing
demokratyzowanie się [de-mo-krah-ti-zo-**vah**-ńe śhan] n. become democratized
demolka [de-**mol**-kah] f. demolition work; malicious tearing up (slang)
demolować [de-mo-**lo**-vahćh] v. demolish; destroy; smash; break to pieces; knock down (*repeatedly*)
demolowanie [de-mo-lo-**vah**-ńe] n. destruction
demolud [de-**mo**-loot] m. colloq: country ruled by Soviet-style people's democracy
demon [**de**-mon] m. demon; fiend
kobieta demon [ko-**bye**-tah **de**-mon] exp.: vamp
demonicznie [de-mo-**ńeech**-ńe] adv. demonically; devilishly
demoniczność [de-mo-**ńeech**-nośhćh] f. demoniac character (of an action, etc.)
demoniczny [de-mo-**ńeech**-ni] adj.m. demonic; demonical; devilish
demonizacja [de-mo-ńee-**zah**-tsyah] f. giving demoniac character
demonizm [de-**mo**-ńeezm] m. belief in evil spirits (ghosts); demonic character (of an action, etc.)
demonizować [de-mo-ńee-**zo**-vahćh] v. demonize (*repeatedly*)
demonizowanie [de-mo-ńee-zo-**vah**-ńe] n. demonization
demonokracja [de-mo-no-**krah**-tsyah] f. demonocracy; rule by demons
demonolog [de-mo-**no**-log] m.

demonologist
demonologia [de-mo-no-**lo**-gyah] f. demonology
demonologiczny [de-mo-no-lo-**geech**-ni] adj.m. of demonology
demonstracja [de-mon-**strah**-tsyah] f. demonstration; mass manifestation; showing by reasoning; proof
demonstracyjnie [de-mon-strah-**tsiy**-ńe] adv. demonstratively; conspicuously; ostentatiously
demonstracyjny [de-mon-strah-**tsiy**-ni] adj.m. demonstrative; conspicuous; ostentatious
demonstrant [de-**mon**-strahnt] m. demonstrant
demonstrantka [de-mon-**strahnt**-kah] f. (woman) demonstrant
demonstrator [de-mon-**strah**-tor] m. demonstrator; teacher's assistant
demonstrować [de-mon-**stro**-vahćh] v. demonstrate; show; make a show (of strength, etc.) (*repeatedly*)
demonstrowanie [de-mon-stro-**vah**-ńe] n. demonstration
demontaż [de-**mon**-tahsh] m. dismantling; disassembly; stripping
demontażowy [de-mon-tah-**zho**-vi] adj.m. stripping (operation, etc.); dismantling (crew, etc.)
demontować [de-mon-**to**-vahćh] v. dismantle; disassemble; strip (*repeatedly*)
demoralizacja [de-mo-rah-lee-**zah**-tsyah] f. demoralization; depravity; laxity of discipline
demoralizator [de-mo-rah-lee-**zah**-tor] m. perverter
demoralizatorka [de-mo-rah-lee-zah-**tor**-kah] f. (woman) perverter
demoralizować [de-mo-rah-lee-**zo**-vahćh] v. demoralize (*repeatedly*)
demoralizować się [de-mo-rah-lee-**zo**-vahćh śhan] v. become demoralized (*repeatedly*)
demoralizowanie [de-mo-rah-lee-zo-**vah**-ńe] n. demoralization; depravation; laxity of discipline
demoralizowanie się [de-mo-rah-lee-zo-**vah**-ńe śhan] n. become demoralized
demoralizująco [de-mo-rah-lee-zoo-**yown**-tso] adv. demoralizingly
demotyczny [de-mo-**tich**-ni] adj.m. demotic (writing, etc.)
denacjonalizacja [de-nah-tsyo-nah-lee-**zah**-tsyah] f. denationalization
denacjonalizować [de-nah-tsyo-nah-lee-**zo**-vahćh] v. denationalize (*repeatedly*)
denacyfikacja [de-nah-tsi-fee-**kah**-tsyah] f. denazification
denacyfikacyjny [de-nah-tsi-fee-kah-**tsiy**-ni] adj.m. of denazification
denar [**de**-nahr] m. denarius
denarowy [de-nah-**ro**-vi] adj.m. denarius (coin, silver, etc.)
denat [**de**-naht] m. defunct; deceased (in a murder); a suicide
denatka [de-**nah**-tkah] f. (female) defunct; deceased (in a murder); (woman) suicide
denaturacja [de-nah-too-**rah**-tsyah] f. denaturation
denaturalizacja [de-nah-too-rah-lee-**zahts**-yah] f. denaturalization; stripping of one's citizenship
denaturalizować [de-nah-too-rah-lee-**zo**-vahćh] v. denaturalize (*repeatedly*)
denaturalizować się [de-nah-too-rah-lee-**zo**-vahćh śhan] v. lose one's nationality (*repeatedly*)
denaturat [de-nah-**too**-raht] m. methanol; methyl alcohol
denaturator [de-nah-too-**rah**-tor] m. denaturing agent
denaturować [de-nah-too-**ro**-vahćh] v. denature; deprive of natural qualities (*repeatedly*)
denaturowanie [de-nah-too-ro-**vah**-ńe] n. denaturation
denazalizacja [de-nah-zah-lee-**zah**-tsyah] f. denasalization; loss of nasal sound
denazalizować [de-nah-zah-lee-**zo**-vahćh] v. denasalize; remove nasal sound (*repeatedly*)
denazyfikacja [de-nah-zi-fee-**kah**-tsyah] f. denazification
denazyfikacyjny [de-nah-zi-fee-kah-**tsiy**-ni] adj.m. denazification (program, etc.)
dendera [den-**de**-rah] f. thorn apple; Jimson weed

dendrarium [den-**drahr**-yoom] m. arboretum
dendrografia [den-dro-**grah**-fyah] f. dendrography
dendrolog [den-**dro**-log] m. dendrologist
dendrologia [den-dro-**lo**-gyah] f. dendrology; the study of trees
dendrologiczny [den-dro-lo-**geech**-ni] adj.m. dendrologic
dendrometria [den-dro-**me**-tryah] f. methods of measuring trees (content and products)
dendryt [**den**-drit] m. dendrite
dendrytowy [den-dri-**to**-vi] adj.m. dendritic
dendrytycznie [den-dri-**tich**-ńe] adv. dendritically
dendrytyczny [den-dri-**tich**-ni] adj.m. dendritical
denerwować [de-ner-**vo**-vahćh] v. bother; make nervous; make uneasy; make fidgety; vex; irritate; upset; exasperate; disturb (*repeatedly*)
denerwować się [de-ner-**vo**-vahćh śhan] v. be nervous; be uneasy; fret; be fidgety; be irritated; be upset; be exasperated; be disturbed; flutter; be jumpy; get excited (*repeatedly*)
nie denerwuj się [ńe de-**ner**-vooy śhan] exp.: don't be nervous; don't get excited; keep calm; slang: keep your shirt on
denerwowanie [de-ner-vo-**vah**-ńe] n. nervousness; irritation; exasperation; excitement; flutter
denerwowanie się [de-ner-vo-**vah**-ńe śhan] n. becoming nervous; become irritated
denerwująco [de-ner-voo-**yown**-tso] adv. irritatingly; exasperatingly; disturbingly; in a nerve-racking manner
denerwujący [de-ner-voo-**yown**-tsi] adj.m. vexing; irritating; exasperating; disturbing; trying; aggravating
denitryfikacja [de-ńee-tri-fee-**kah**-tsyah] f. denitrification; removal of nitrogen (from)
denitryfikacyjny [de-ńee-tri-fee-kah-**tsiy**-ni] adj.m. of denitrification; of removal of nitrogen
denitryfikator [de-ńee-tri-fee-**kah**-tor] m. denitrification agent
denitryfikatory [de-ńee-tri-fee-kah-**to**-ri] pl. denitrifying bacteria
denitryfikować [de-ńee-tri-fee-**ko**-vahćh] v. denitrify (*repeatedly*)
deniwelacja [de-ńee-ve-**lah**-tsyah] f. the difference between the highest and the lowest elevation in an area; drop; change of level
denko [**den**-ko] n. crown of a hat; small bottom of a bottle, glass, pot, etc.
dennica [den-**ńee**-tsah] f. structural element of the ship's bottom
denniak [**den**-ńahk] m. bottom layer (in a coal mine)
dennik [**den**-ńeek] m. structural element of the ship's bottom
dennikowaty [den-ńee-ko-**vah**-ti] adj.m. of deep-sea fish
dennikowate [den-ńee-ko-**vah**-te] pl. the family of deep-sea fishes (Liparidae)
denny [**den**-ni] adj.m. of the bottom (of the sea, of the river, etc.); ground (angling, etc.)
denotacja [de-no-**tah**-tsyah] f. denotation; denoting connotations
densymetr [den-**si**-metr] m. densimeter
dentalny [den-**tahl**-ni] adj.m. (consonant) pronounced with the use of upper teeth
dentyna [den-**ti**-nah] f. dentin; dentine; the principal material of a tooth
dentysta [den-**tis**-tah] m. dentist
dentystka [den-**tis**-tkah] f. (woman) dentist
dentystyczny [den-tis-**tich**-ni] adj.m. dental; dentist's
dentystyka [den-**tis**-ti-kah] f. dentistry
denudacja [de-noo-**dah**-tsyah] f. denudation; stripping of all cover
denudacyjny [de-noo-dah-**tsiy**-ni] adj.m. denudational
denuklearyzacja [de-noo-kle-ah-ri-**zah**-tsyah] f. denuclearization
denuklearyzacyjny [de-noo-kle-ah-ri-zah-**tsiy**-ni] adj.m. of denuclearization

denuklearyzować [de-noo-kle-ah-ri-**zo**-vahćh] v. denuclearize (*repeatedly*)
denuklearyzowanie [de-noo-kle-ah-ri-zo-**vah**-ńe] n. denuclearization
denuncjacja [de-noon-**tsyah**-tsyah] f. denunciation; information (against); delation; accusation
denuncjant [de-**noon**-tsyahnt] m. colloq: informer; denouncer; whistle blower; denuncitor
denuncjator [de-noon-**tsyah**-tor] m. informer; whistle blower; denouncer; denunciator
denuncjatorka [de-noon-tsyah-**tor**-kah] f. (woman) informer; whistle blower; denouncer
denuncjatorski [de-noon-tsyah-**tor**-skee] adj.m. informer's; whistle blower's; denouncer's; denunciative; denunciatory
denuncjować [de-noon-**tsyo**-vahćh] v. inform (against); denounce (*repeatedly*)
denuncjowanie [de-noon-tsyo-**vah**-ńe] n. informing (against); denunciation
deontologia [de-on-to-**lo**-gyah] f. deontology; science of ethics
deontologiczny [de-on-to-lo-**geech**-ni] adj.m. deontological
depalatalizacja [de-pah-lah-tah-lee-**zah**-tsyah] f. depalatalization; loss of the palatal sound of consonants
depalatalizować [de-pah-lah-tah-lee-**zo**-vahćh] v. lose the palatal sound (*repeatedly*)
depalatalizować się [de-pah-lah-tah-lee-**zo**-vahćh śhan] v. become a non-palatal (sound, etc.) (*repeatedly*)
departament [de-pahr-**tah**-ment] m. department (of state administration, etc.)
departamentalny [de-pahr-tah-men-**tahl**-ni] adj.m. departmental
depenalizacja [de-pe-nah-lee-**zah**-tsyah] f. removal of penalization
dependent [de-**pen**-dent] m. clerk (in a lawyer's office)
depersonalizacja [de-per-so-nah-lee-**zahts**-yah] f. depersonalization
depersonalizować [de-per-so-nah-lee-**zo**-vahćh] v. depersonalize; make impersonal (*repeatedly*)
depesza [de-**pe**-shah] f. wire; telegram; cable; dispatch
depesza radiowa [de-**pe**-shah rah-**dyo**-vah] exp.; radiogram
depeszować [de-pe-**sho**-vahćh] v. telegraph; wire; cable (*repeatedly*)
depeszowanie [de-pe-sho-**vah**-ńe] n. sending of a telegram; sending of a wire; sending by cable
depeszowiec [de-pe-**sho**-vyets] m. newsman editing wired-in information
depeszowy [de-pe-**sho**-vi] adj.m. telegram (form, etc.)
depilacja [de-pee-**lah**-tsyah] f. depilation; hair removal
depilacyjny [de-pee-lah-**tsiy**-ni] adj.m. of depilation; depilatory
depilator [de-pee-**lah**-tor] m. depilating agent; depilator
depilować [de-pee-**lo**-vahćh] v. depilate (*repeatedly*)
depo [**de**-po] n. locomotive shed
depolaryzacja [de-po-lah-ri-**zah**-tsyah] m. depolarization
depolaryzator [de-po-lah-ri-**zah**-tor] m. depolarizer
depolaryzować [de-po-lah-ri-**zo**-vahćh] v. depolarize (*repeatedly*)
depolonizacja [de-po-lo-ńee-**zah**-tsyah] f. loss of Polish identity
depolonizacyjny [de-po-lo-ńee-zah-**tsiy**-ni] adj.m. of the loss of Polish identity
depolonizować [de-po-lo-ńee-**zo**-vahćh] v. destroy Polish identity; do away with Polish characteristics (*repeatedly*)
depolonizować się [de-po-lo-ńee-**zo**-vahćh śhan] v. lose Polish identity; lose Polish characteristics (*repeatedly*)
deponent [de-**po**-nent] m. depositor
deponować [de-po-**no**-vahćh] v. deposit; put in safe keeping (*repeatedly*)
deponować się [de-po-**no**-vahćh śhan] v. be deposited; accumulate (*repeatedly*)
deponowanie [de-po-no-**vah**-ńe] n. deposits
depopulacja [de-po-poo-**lah**-tsyah] f.

depopulation
depopularyzacja [de-po-poo-lah-ri-**zah**-tsyah] f. loss of popularity
depopularyzować [de-po-poo-lah-ri-**zo**-vahćh] v. make unpopular; render unpopular (*repeatedly*)
depopularyzować się [de-po-poo-lah-ri-**zo**-vahćh śhan] v. lose popularity; become unpopular (*repeatedly*)
deportacja [de-por-**tah**-tsyah] f. deportation; transportation (to penal colony, etc.)
deportacyjny [de-por-tah-**tsiy**-ni] adj.m. of deportation
deportować [de-por-**to**-vahćh] v. deport; transport (to penal colony, etc.) (*repeatedly*)
deportowanie [de-por-to-**vah**-ńe] n. deportation
deportowany [de-por-to-**vah**-ni] m. deported person
depozyt [de-**po**-zit] m. deposit; bail; security; trust-money
depozyt bankowy [de-**po**-zit bahn-**ko**-vi] exp.: bank deposit; safe-deposit
depozytariusz [de-po-zi-**tahr**-yoosh] m. depositary
depozytor [de-po-**zi**-tor] m. depositor
depozytowy [de-po-zi-**to**-vi] adj.m. deposit (account, bank, etc.)
deprawacja [de-prah-**vah**-tsyah] f. depravation; depravity; corruption; viciousness
deprawator [de-prah-**vah**-tor] m. depraver
deprawować [de-prah-**vo**-vahćh] v. deprave; corrupt; pervert; debauch (*repeatedly*)
deprawować się [de-prah-**vo**-vahćh śhan] v. become deprave; become corrupt; become perverted (*repeatedly*)
deprawowanie [de-prah-vo-**vah**-ńe] n. depravation; corruption; perversion; depravement; depravedness
deprawowanie się [de-prah-vo-**vah**-ńe śhan] n. undergoing depravation; becoming corrupt
deprawująco [de-prah-voo-**yown**-tso] adv. depravedly
deprawujący [de-prah-voo-**yown**-tsi] adj.m. depraved
deprecjacja [de-pre-**tsyah**-tsyah] f. depreciation; debasement
deprecjonować [de-pre-tsyo-**no**-vahćh] v. depreciate; debase (of currency, etc.) (*repeatedly*)
deprecjonować się [de-pre-tsyo-**no**-vahćh śhan] v. depreciate oneself (*repeatedly*)
deprecjonowanie [de-pre-tsyo-no-**vah**-ńe] n. depreciation; debasement
deprecjonowanie się [de-pre-tsyo-no-**vah**-ńe śhan] n. self-depreciation; self-debasement
deprecjonująco [de-pre-tsyo-noo-**yown**-tso] adv. depreciatingly
deprecjonujący [de-pre-tsyo-noo-**yown**-tsi] adj.m. depreciative; depreciatory
depresja [de-**pre**-syah] f. depression; dejection; low spirits; dumps; low; low barometric pressure; (geological) depression
depresyjnie [de-pre-**siy**-ńe] adv. depressively
depresyjny [de-pre-**siy**-ni] adj.m. depressive
deprymować [de-pri-**mo**-vahćh] v. depress; dispirit; deject; dishearten (*repeatedly*)
deprymować się [de-pri-**mo**-vahćh śhan] v. become depressed; become dispirited; become dejected; become disheartened (*repeatedly*)
deprymowanie [de-pri-mo-**vah**-ńe] n. disheartening
deprymowanie się [de-pri-mo-**vah**-ńe śhan] n. becoming dispirited
deprymująco [de-pri-moo-**yown**-tso] adv. depressingly
deprymujący [de-pri-moo-**yown**-tsi] adj.m. depressing; chilling
deprymująca rada [de-pri-moo-**yown**-tsah **rah**-dah] exp.: cold comfort; cold counsel
deptać [**dep**-tahćh] v. trample (the soil); tread; pace up and down; stain; soil; muddy (*repeatedly*)
deptać koło czegoś [**dep**-tahćh **ko**-wo **che**-gośh] exp.: to bestir oneself for something; to bustle about something

deptać po piętach [**dep**-tahćh po **pyan**-tahkh] exp.: to tread on (somebody's) heels
nie deptać trawy [ńe **dep**-tahćh **trah**-vi] exp.: keep off the grass
deptać się [**dep**-tahćh śhan] v. trample on each other (*repeatedly*)
deptak [**dep**-tahk] m. promenade; walk; treadle; pedal; treadmill (of daily routine, etc.)
deptanie [dep-**tah**-ńe] n. trampling; muddying; soiling
deptanie się [dep-**tah**-ńe śhan] n. stepping on each other (toes, feet, etc.)
deputacja [de-poo-**tah**-tsyah] f. deputation; a group of representatives elected for a specific task
deputacki [de-poo-**tah**-tskee] adj.m. of a deputation
deputat [de-**poo**-taht] m. allowance; ration; payment in kind; member of deputation
deputatowy [de-poo-tah-**to**-vi] m. allowanced; of payment in kind
deputowany [de-poo-to-**vah**-ni] m. deputy
dera [**de**-rah] f. rug; blanket; horse blanket; saddle-cloth; horse cloth; bed-spread
deranżować [de-rahn-**zho**-vahćh] v. bother; trouble; inconvenience; disturb; give inconvenience (*repeatedly*)
deranżować się [de-rahn-**zho**-vahćh śhan] v. bother; trouble; trouble oneself (about); inconvenience oneself; give oneself inconvenience (*repeatedly*)
deratyzacja [de-rah-ti-**zah**-tsyah] f. extermination of rats
deratyzacyjny [de-rah-ti-zah-**tsiy**-ni] adj.m. of extermination of rats
derbista [der-**bee**-stah] m. horse participating in a derby; winner of a derby (horse race)
derbistka [der-**bee**-stkah] f. mare participating in a derby; winner of a derby (horse race)
derbowy [der-**bo**-vi] adj.m. horse-race (program, etc.)
derby [**der**-bi] n. horse race; match (sport competition)
dereniak [de-**re**-ńahk] m. dogberry vine
derenina [de-re-**ńee**-nah] f. dogwood (tree, shrub)
dereniowaty [de-re-ńo-**vah**-ti] adj.m. cornaceous
dereniowate [de-re-ńo-**vah**-te] pl. the dogwood family of trees
dereniowy [de-re-**ńo**-vi] adj.m. of dogwood; dogwood (grove, etc.); dogberry (syrup, etc.)
dereniówka [de-re-**ńoof**-kah] f. dogberry vodka
dereń [**de**-reń] m. dogwood; cornel; dogberry
deresz [**de**-resh] m. roan horse
dereszowaty [de-re-sho-**vah**-ti] adj.m. roan; m. roan horse
derka [**der**-kah] f. rug; blanket; horse blanket; saddle-cloth; horse cloth; bed-spread
derkacz [**der**-kahch] m. corncrake; landrail (bird)
derkać [**der**-kahćh] v. cracke (*repeatedly*)
derkanie [der-**kah**-ńe] n. crake's cry
derma [**der**-mah] f. dermatoid
dermatofit [der-mah-**to**-feet] m. dermatophyte
dermatofityd [der-mah-to-**fee**-tit] m. secondary dermatophyte
dermatoglif [der-mah-**to**-gleef] m. dermatoglyph
dermatoglifika [der-mah-to-**glee**-fee-kah] f. dermatoglyphics; science of identification by skin patterns on hands and feet
dermatoid [der-mah-**to**-eet] m. imitation leather; dermatoid
dermatoidowy [der-mah-to-ee-**do**-vi] adj.m. of imitation leather; of dermatoid
dermatol [der-**mah**-tol] m. dermatol
dermatolog [der-mah-**to**-log] m. dermatologist
dermatologia [der-mah-to-**lo**-gyah] f. dermatology
dermatologiczny [der-mah-to-lo-**geech**-ni] adj.m. dermatological
dermatomykoza [der-mah-to-mi-**ko**-zah] f. dermatomycosis
dermatoza [der-mah-**to**-zah] f. dermatosis

dermograf [der-**mo**-grahf] m. pencil for writing on skin for diagnostic purposes
dermografizm [der-mo-**grah**-feezm] m. dermographism
dermoplastyka [der-mo-**plahs**-ti-kah] f. plastic surgery
derogacja [de-ro-**gah**-tsyah] f. legal derogation
derogacyjny [de-ro-gah-**tsiy**-ni] adj.m. legally derogatory
derogować [de-ro-**go**-vahćh] v. legally derogate (*repeatedly*)
derogowanie [de-ro-go-**vah**-ńe] n. legal derogation; superceding of one law over another
derwisz [**der**-veesh] m. dervish
derwiszowski [der-vee-**shof**-skee] adj.m. dervish (abandonment, etc.)
derywacja [de-ri-**vah**-tsyah] f. derivation (of a word, etc.); deflection (of a bullet, etc.)
derywacyjny [de-ri-vah-**tsiy**-ni] adj.m. derivative
derywat [de-ri-vaht] m. derivative (word, etc.)
derywometr [de-ri-**vo**-metr] m. drift indicator
derywować [de-ri-**vo**-vahćh] v. create new words from existing basic words; derive (words, etc.) (*repeatedly*)
derywowanie [de-ri-vo-**vah**-ńe] n. derivation of new words
des [des] n. D flat (music)
desa [**de**-sah] f. art and antique store
desant [**de**-sahnt] m. descent; a sudden attack; landing; landing-operation; landing troops; raid
desantować [de-sahn-**to**-vahćh] v. raid; make a landing; attack (*repeatedly*)
desantowiec [de-sahn-**to**-vyets] m. commando-man; ranger; raiding ship
desantowy [de-sahn-**to**-vi] adj.m. of landing; landing (operation, etc.); raiding
oddział desantowy [od-dźhahw de-sahn-**to**-vi] exp.: landing party
descendent [des-**tsen**-dent] m. legal descendent; outdated product losing in competition
deseczka [de-**sech**-kah] f. slat; lath; small board
desegregacja [de-seg-re-**gah**-tsyah] f. desegregation (of races)
desemantyzacja [de-se-mahn-ti-**zah**-tsyah] f. loss of clarity of the meaning of a word
deseniarka [de-se-**ńahr**-kah] f. press for making leather ornaments
desenik [de-**se**-ńeek] m. (nice, small) pattern; design; decorative design
deseniować [de-se-**ńo**-vahćh] v. make a design; decorate with a pattern (*repeatedly*)
deseniowanie [de-se-ńo-**vah**-ńe] n. making decorative design
deseniowy [de-se-**ńo**-vi] adj.m. design (type, etc.)
deseń [**de**-seń] m. pattern; design; decorative design
w ten deseń [f ten **de**-seń] exp.: slang: like this; this way
deser [**de**-ser] m. dessert; sweets
na deser [nah **de**-ser] exp.: for dessert; by way of desert
deserowy [de-se-**ro**-vi] adj.m. dessert-; dessert (dish, etc.)
desinteressement [dez-an-te-**res**-mah] n. (French) no objections; lack of interest; neutral position
deska [**des**-kah] f. plank; board; ski; slang: surfing board
od deski do deski [od **des**-kee do **des**-kee] exp.: from cover to cover; from beginning to end
do grobowej deski [do gro-**bo**-vey **des**-kee] exp.: till death itself
deski [**des**-kee] pl.: (snow) skis
deski sceniczne [**des**-kee stse-**ńeech**-ne] pl.: the stage
deskonarciarstwo [des-ko-nahr-**ćhahr**-stfo] m. snowboarding
deskonarciarz [des-ko-**nahr**-ćhahsh] m. snowboarder
deskonarta [des-ko-**nahr**-tah] f. snowboard
deskorolka [des-ko-**rol**-kah] f. skateboard
deskorolkarstwo [des-ko-rol-**kahr**-stfo] m. skateboarding
deskorolkarz [des-ko-**rol**-kahsh] m. skateboarder

deskować [des-**ko**-vahćh] v. board up; plank (*repeatedly*)
deskowanie [des-ko-**vah**-ńe] n. boarding; planking
deskowy [des-**ko**-vi] adj.m. (made) out of boards
deskrypcja [des-**krip**-tsyah] f. description
deskrypcyjnie [des-krip-**tsiy**-ńe] adv. descriptively
deskrypcyjny [des-krip-**tsiy**-ni] adj.m. descriptive
descryptor [des-**krip**-tor] m. descriptor
deskryptywny [des-krip-**tiv**-ni] adj.m. descriptive
deskwamacja [des-kfah-**mah**-tsyah] f. desquamation; peeling off in scales
desman [**des**-mahn] m. desman (an aquatic mammal)
desorber [de-**sor**-ber] m. desorber
desorpcja [de-**sorp**-tsyah] f. desorption
despekt [**des**-pekt] m. disrespect
desperacja [des-pe-**rah**-tsyah] f. desperation; despair; loss of hope
desperacki [des-pe-**rahts**-kee] adj.m. desperate; very serious; rush or violent because of despair
po desperacku [po des-pe-**rahts**-koo] exp.: in despair
desperacko [des-pe-**rah**-tsko] adv. desperately
desperat [des-**pe**-raht] m. desperado; man moved by despair
desperatka [des-pe-**rah**-tkah] f. woman moved by despair
desperować [de-spe-**ro**-vahćh] v. despair; lose hope (*repeatedly*)
despota [des-**po**-tah] m. despot; tyrant; oppressor; bully
despotka [des-**po**-tkah] f. despot; tyrant; oppressor; bully
despotycznie [des-po-**tich**-ńe] adv. despotically; high-handedly
despotyczność [des-po-**tich**-nośhćh] f. despotism; tyranny; colloq: bullying
despotyczny [des-po-**tich**-ni] adj.m. despotic; high-handed; domineering; tyrannical; oppressive
despotyzm [de-**spo**-tizm] m. despotism; tyranny; colloq: bullying
dessous [de-**soo**] n. (French) lingerie
destabilizacja [de-stah-bee-lee-**zah**-tsyah] f. destabilization; instability
destabilizować [de-stah-bee-lee-**zo**-vahćh] v. destabilize; make unstable (*repeatedly*)
destrukcja [de-**strook**-tsyah] f. destruction; destroying; wreck; ruin
destrukcyjnie [de-strook-**tsiy**-ńe] adv. destructively
destrukcyjność [de-strook-**tsiy**-nośhćh] f. destructiveness
destrukcyjny [de-strook-**tsiy**-ni] adj.m. destructive; destroying
destrukt [**de**-strookt] m. paper damaged in printing; worn out banknote; badly damaged book
destruktor [de-**strook**-tor] m. destroyer
destruktywnie [de-strook-**tiv**-ńe] adv. destructively
destruktywność [de-strook-**tiv**-nośhćh] f. destructiveness
destruktywny [de-strook-**tiv**-ni] adj.m. destructive; destroying
destylacja [de-sti-**lah**-tsyah] f. distillation
destylacja frakcyjna [de-sti-lah-tsyah frahk-**tsiy**-nah] exp.: fractional distillation; fractionation
destylacja sucha drewna [de-sti-lah-tsyah **soo**-khah **drev**-nah] exp.: wood distillation
destylacja sucha węgla [de-sti-lah-tsyah **soo**-khah **van**-glah] exp.: coal carbonization
destylacyjny [de-sti-lah-**tsiy**-ni] adj.m. distillation (apparatus, etc.); distilling (flask, tube, etc.)
destylarka [de-sti-**lahr**-kah] f. small distiller; small still
destylarnia [de-sti-**lahr**-ńah] f. distillery; still-room
destylat [de-**sti**-laht] m. distillate
destylator [de-sti-**lah**-tor] m. distiller; still
destylować [de-sti-**lo**-vahćh] v. distil; concentrate (*repeatedly*)
destylować się [de-sti-**lo**-vahćh śhan] v. distil; be distilled; undergo distillation (*repeatedly*)

destylowanie [de-sti-lo-**vah**-ńe] n. distillation
destylowanie się [de-sti-lo-**vah**-ńe śhan] n. undergoing distillation
desu [**de**-soo] n. lingerie
desulfitacja [de-sool-fee-**tah**-tsyah] f. removal of sulphur from food products; desulfuration
desusy [de-**soo**-si] pl. colloq: panties
desygnacja [de-sig-**nah**-tsyah] f. designation
desygnat [de-**sig**-naht] m. referent; designation
desygnować [de-si-**gno**-vahćh] v. designate; appoint; nominate (to a post, etc.) (*repeatedly*)
desygnowanie [de-sig-no-**vah**-ńe] n. designation
desykant [de-**si**-kahnt] m. chemical agent used for drying leaves and stems (of potatoes, etc.) in preparation for harvesting machine
deszcz [deshch] m. rain
deszcz ze śniegiem [deshch ze **śhńe**-gem] exp.: sleet
drobny deszcz [**drob**-ni deshch] exp.: drizzle
na deszczu [nah **desh**-choo] exp.: in the rain
pada deszcz [**pah**-dah deshch] exp.: it rains
przelotny deszcz [pshe-**lot**-ni deshch] exp.: shower
spod deszczu [spod **desh**-choo] exp.: out of the rain
ulewny deszcz [oo-**lev**-ni deshch] exp.: downpour; heavy rain; driving rain
z deszczu pod rynnę [z **desh**-choo pod **rin**-nan] exp.: out of the frying pan into the fire; to swap bad for worse
deszczodajny [desh-cho-**dahy**-ni] adj.m. rain-making
deszczomierz [desh-**cho**-myesh] m. rain gauge
deszczoodporny [desh-cho-ot-**por**-ni] adj.m. rainproof; rain-tight
deszczować [desh-**cho**-vahćh] v. irrigate by spraying (*repeatedly*)
deszczowanie [desh-cho-**vah**-ńe] n. irrigation by spraying
deszczowiec [desh-**cho**-vyets] m. raincoat; galosh
deszczownia [desh-**chov**-ńah] f. equipment for irrigation by spraying
deszczownica [desh-chov-**ńee**-tsah] f. irrigation spraying equipment
deszczowo [desh-**cho**-vo] adv. rainy (day); likely to rain
jest deszczowo [yest desh-**cho**-vo] exp.: it is a rainy day
deszczowy [desh-**cho**-vi] adj.m. rainy; showery; drizzly; wet; rough
pora deszczowa [po-rah desh-**cho**-vah] exp.: rainy season; wet season
woda deszczowa [**vo**-dah desh-**cho**-vah] exp.: rain-water
deszczówka [desh-**choof**-kah] f. rain-water; rain-water drain; raincoat with hood
deszczułka [desh-**choow**-kah] f. lath; small board
deszczułkarka [desh-choow-**kahr**-kah] f. parquet-floor making machine
deszczułkarnia [desh-choow-**kahr**-ńah] f. parquet-floor making plant
deszczyk [**desh**-chik] m. small shower; little rain
deszyfracja [de-shi-**frah**-tsyah] f. decoding; deciphering
deszyfrator [de-shi-**frah**-tor] m. decoder
deszyfraż [de-**shi**-frahsh] m. decoding system; (military) decoding service
deszyfrować [de-shi-**fro**-vahćh] v. decode; decipher; convert into intelligible language (*repeatedly*)
detal [**de**-tahl] m. detail; trifling matter; retail trade
detalicznie [de-tah-**leech**-ńe] adv. by retail; at retail
sprzedawać detalicznie [spshe-**dah**-vahćh de-tah-**leech**-ńe] exp.: to sell by retail; to retail
detaliczny [de-tah-**leech**-ni] adj.m. retail-; of retail
handel detaliczny [**khahn**-del de-tah-**leech**-ni] exp.: retail trade
detalista [de-tah-**lees**-tah] m. retailer
detekcja [de-**tek**-tsyah] detection; demodulation

detektor [de-**tek**-tor] m. detector; coherer
detektorowy [de-tek-to-**ro**-vi] adj.m. of a detector
detektyw [de-**tek**-tif] m. detective
prywatny detektyw [pri-**vaht**-ni de-**tek**-tif] exp.: private eye; private investigator; sleuth
detektywistyczny [de-tek-ti-vee-**stich**-ni] adj.m. detective (novel, etc.)
detergent [de-**ter**-gent] m. detergent
deterioracja [de-ter-yo-**rah**-tsyah] f. deterioration; degeneration; decadence; decline
determinacja [de-ter-mee-**nah**-tsyah] f. determination; resoluteness; resignation; determinate growth; determinacy; exactness
determinant [de-ter-**mee**-nahnt] m. determinant
determinanta [de-ter-mee-**nahn**-tah] f. result of (mathematical, etc.) determination
determinista [de-ter-mee-**ńee**-stah] m. determinist; necessitarian
deterministyczny [de-ter-mee-ńee-**stich**-ni] adj.m. deterministic
determinizm [de-ter-**mee**-ńeezm] m. determinism; necessitarianism
determinować [de-ter-mee-**no**-vahćh] v. determine (*repeatedly*)
determinowanie [de-ter-mee-no-**vah**-ńe] n. determination
determinowany [de-ter-mee-no-**vah**-ni] adj.m. determinate; definitive; arbitrary; established
detoksykacja [de-tok-si-**kah**-tsyah] f. detoxication
detoksykacyjny [de-tok-si-kah-**tsiy**-ni] adj.m. detoxication (process, etc.); detoxifying (agent, etc.)
detonacja [de-to-**nah**-tsyah] f. detonation; explosion
detonacyjny [de-to-nah-**tsiy**-ni] adj.m. detonable; detonatable; detonative; detonational
detonator [de-to-**nah**-tor] m. detonator; detonating fuse; exploder
detonować [de-to-**no**-vahćh] v. detonate; explode; abash; disconcert; put out of countenance; sing out of tune (*repeatedly*)
detonować się [de-to-**no**-vahćh śhan] v. lose countenance; be disconcerted; be abashed (*repeatedly*)
detonowanie [de-to-no-**vah**-ńe] n. detonation
detonowanie się [de-to-no-**vah**-ńe śhan] n. loss of countenance
detronizacja [de-tro-ńee-**zah**-tsyah] f. dethronement; deposition (of a ruler)
detronizacyjny [de-tro-ńee-zah-**tsiy**-ni] adj.m. of a dethronement; of a deposition (of a ruler)
detronizować [de-tro-ńee-**zo**-vahćh] v. dethrone; depose (a monarch) (*repeatedly*)
detronizowanie [de-tro-ńee-zo-**vah**-ńe] n. dethronement
deuter [**dew**-ter] m. deuter
deuteron [dew-**te**-ron] m. deuteron
dewaloryzacja [de-vah-lo-ri-**zah**-tsyah] f. lowering the value
dewaloryzować [de-vah-lo-ri-**zo**-vahćh] v. lower the value of (something) (*repeatedly*)
dewaluacja [de-vah-loo-**ah**-tsyah] f. devaluation; lowering the exchange value of currency; colloq: depreciation
dewaluacyjny [de-vah-loo-ah-**tsiy**-ni] adj.m. of a devaluation; of a lowering the exchange value of currency
dewaluować [de-vah-loo-**o**-vahćh] v. devalue; depreciate; devaluate (*repeatedly*)
dewaluować się [de-vah-loo-**o**-vahćh śhan] v. lose value; become devaluated; become depreciated (*repeatedly*)
dewaluowanie [de-vah-loo-o-**vah**-ńe] n. devaluation
dewaluowanie się [de-vah-loo-o-**vah**-ńe śhan] n. (self) devaluation
dewastacja [de-vah-**stah**-tsyah] f. devastation; destruction; ravage; havoc
dewastacyjny [de-vah-stah-**tsiy**-ni] adj.m. of devastation; of destruction; of ravage; of havoc; devastating (blow, etc.); ravaging (management, etc.)

dewastator [de-vah-**stah**-tor] m. wrecker; spoiler; devastator
dewastatorski [de-vah-stah-**tor**-skee] adj.m. of wrecking; of ravaging; destruction (program, etc.)
dewastować [de-vah-**sto**-vahćh] v. devastate; ravage; lay waste; play havoc; make havoc; ruin (*repeatedly*)
dewastowanie [de-vah-sto-**vah**-ńe] n. devastation; destruction; ravage; havoc
dewerbalny [de-ver-**bahl**-ni] adj.m. (a noun) without a verb
dewetyna [de-ve-**ti**-nah] f. doeskin
dewiacja [de-**vyah**-tsyah] f. deviation; straying; deflexion
dewiacyjny [de-vyah-**tsiy**-ni] adj.m. of a deviation; deviate; deviant
dewiant [**de**-vyahnt] m. deviant; pervert
dewiator [de-**vyah**-tor] m. man who determines and corrects ship's magnetic deviation
dewitalizacja [de-vee-tah-lee-**zah**-tsyah] f. devitalization (of a nerve, etc.); depravation of vitality
dewiza [de-**vee**-zah] f. foreign money; motto; slogan; device
kurs dewiz [koors **de**-vees] exp.: rate of exchange of foreign currencies
dewizka [de-**vees**-kah] f. watch-chain
dewizowiec [de-vee-**zo**-vyets] m. colloq: foreigner paying with foreign currency; owner of bank account with foreign currency deposit
dewizowo [de-vee-**zo**-vo] adv. by means of foreign currency
dewizowy [de-vee-**zo**-vi] adj.m. foreign-currency (regulations, policy; etc.)
dewizówka [de-vee-**zoof**-kah] f. slang: prostitute paid with foreign money (mob jargon)
dewocja [de-**vo**-tsyah] f. devotion; piety; religionism; bigotry
dewocjonalia [de-vo-tsyo-**nah**-lyah] pl. devotional articles
dewocyjnie [de-vo-**tsiy**-ńe] adv. devotionally
dewocyjny [de-vo-**tsiy**-ni] adj.m. devotional
dewolucja [de-vo-**loo**-tsyah] f. devolution (a legal term)
dewolucyjny [de-vo-loo-**tsiy**-ni] adj.m. devolutionary
dewon [**de**-von] m. Devonian period
dewoński [de-**voń**-skee] adj.m. of the Devonian period
dewot [**de**-vot] m. bigot; devotee
dewotka [de-**vo**-tkah] f. devotee; (woman) bigot
dezabil [de-**zah**-beel] m. dishabille; the state of being partially dressed or in night clothes
dezaktualizacja [dez-ahk-too-ah-lee-**zah**-tsyah] f. loss of timeliness; loss of seasonableness
dezaktualizować [de-zahk-too-ah-lee-**zo**-vahćh] v. make no longer timely; put out of date; put out of consideration (*repeatedly*)
dezaktualizować się [de-zahk-too-ah-lee-**zo**-vahćh śh<u>an</u>] v. become no longer timely; being out of date; being out of consideration; being stale; lose one's immediate interest (*repeatedly*)
dezaktywacja [de-zahk-ti-**vah**-tsyah] f. deactivation; making inactive; making ineffective
dezaprobata [de-zah-pro-**bah**-tah] f. disapproval; depreciation; censure
dezaprobować [de-zah-pro-**bo**-vahćh] v. disapprove; deprecate; censure; pass a censure; condemn; reject; express an objection (*repeatedly*)
dezatomizacja [de-zah-to-mee-**zah**-tsyah] f. denuclearization
dezawuować [de-zah-voo-o-vahćh] v. disavow; disown; repudiate; disdain; disclaim; deny any knowledge of; deny any responsibility for (*repeatedly*)
dezawuowanie [de-zah-voo-o-**vah**-ńe] n. disavowal; disowning; repudiation
dezercja [de-**zer**-tsyah] f. desertion; defection
dezerter [de-**zer**-ter] m. deserter; fugitive; runaway
dezerterować [de-zer-te-**ro**-vahćh] v. desert; run away; fall away;

abandon (*repeatedly*)
dezerterowanie [de-zer-te-ro-**vah**-ńe] n. desertion
dezerterski [de-zer-**ter**-skee] adj.m. of a deserter
dezetka [de-**zet**-kah] f. ten-oar boat
deziluzja [dez-ee-**loo**-zyah] f. disillusion
dezinformacja [dez-een-for-**mah**-tsyah] f. disinformation
dezinformacyjny [dez-een-for-mah-**tsiy**-ni] adj.m. misleading
dezinformować [dez-een-for-**mo**-vahćh] v. mislead; give false information (*repeatedly*)
dezintegracja [dez-een-te-**grah**-tsyah] f. disintegration; break up
dezintegracyjny [dez-een-te-grah-**tsiy**-ni] adj.m. causing disintegration
dezintegralny [dez-een-te-**grahl**-ni] adj.m. not all-inclusive
dezintegrować [dez-een-te-**gro**-vahćh] v. disintegrate (*repeatedly*)
dezodorant [de-zo-**do**-rahnt] m. deodorant
dezodoryzacja [de-zo-do-ri-**zah**-tsyah] f. deodorization
dezodoryzator [de-zo-do-ri-**zah**-tor] m. deodorant; deodorizing equipment; deodorizer
dezodoryzować [de-zo-do-ri-**zo**-vahćh] v. deodorize (*repeatedly*)
dezodoryzowanie [de-zo-do-ri-zo-**vah**-ńe] n. deodorization
dezoksyrybonukleinowy [de-zo-ksi-ri-bo-noo-kle-ee-**no**-vi] adj.m. deoxyribonucleic (acid); DNA
dezorganizacja [de-zor-gah-ńee-**zah**-tsyah] f. disorganization; confusion; disorder; derangement
dezorganizacyjny [de-zor-gah-ńee-zah-**tsiy**-ni] adj.m. causing disorganization; causing confusion; disorderly
dezorganizować [de-zor-gah-ńee-**zo**-vahćh] v. disorganize; throw into confusion; throw into disorder; upset; derange; throw out of gear (*repeatedly*)
dezorganizować się [de-zor-gah-ńee-**zo**-vahćh śhan] v. become disorganized; fall into confusion; fall into disorder; go out of gear (*repeatedly*)
dezorganizowanie [de-zor-gah-ńee-zo-**vah**-ńe] n. disorganization
dezorientacja [de-zor-yen-**tah**-tsyah] f. disorientation; confusion; bewilderment; misconception
dezorientować [de-zor-yen-**to**-vahćh] v. disorient; confuse; cause to lose one's bearings (*repeatedly*)
dezorientować się [de-zor-yen-**to**-vahćh śhan] v. become confused; become bewildered; lose one's way; lose one's bearings (*repeatedly*)
dezorientowanie [de-zor-yen-to-**vah**-ńe] n. confusion; bewilderment
dezurbanizacja [de-zoor-bah-ńee-**zah**-tsyah] f. break up of urban congestion
dezyderat [de-zi-**de**-raht] m. clearly stated demand; desideratum
dezynfekcja [de-zin-**fek**-tsyah] f. disinfection; fumigation
dezynfekcyjny [de-zin-fek-**tsiy**-ni] adj.m. of disinfection; of fumigation
dezynfekować [de-zin-fe-**ko**-vahćh] v. disinfect; fumigate (*repeatedly*)
dezynfekowanie [de-zin-fe-ko-**vah**-ńe] n. disinfection; fumigation
dezynfektor [de-zin-**fek**-tor] m. disinfectant; fumigator; man conducting disinfection (fumigation)
dezynsekcja [de-zin-**sek**-tsyah] f. disinsection; disinsectization; removal of insects
dezynsekcyjny [de-zin-sek-**tsiy**-ni] adj.m. of disinsection
dezynsekować [de-zin-se-**ko**-vahćh] v. conduct disinsection; conduct disinsectization (*repeatedly*)
dezynsekowanie [de-zin-se-ko-**vah**-ńe] n. disinsection; disinsectization
dezyntegracja [de-zin-te-**grah**-tsyah] f. disintegration; break-up
dezyntegracyjny [de-zin-te-grah-**tsiy**-ni] adj.m. of disintegration; of a break-up; disintegrative
dezyntegralny [de-zin-te-**grahl**-ni] adj.m. of disintegration; of a

break-up; disintegrative
dezyntegrować [de-zin-te-**gro**-vahćh] v. disintegrate (*repeatedly*)
dezynwoltura [de-zin-vol-**too**-rah] f. lack of deference; off-hand manner; cheekiness; sauce
dębak [**dan**-bahk] m. acrid, dry wine
dębczak [**danp**-chahk] m. oak sapling; oak stick
dębianka [dan-**byahn**-kah] f. gall-nut; gall-fly
dębieć [**dan**-byećh] v. harden; become tough; be taken aback; stand dumbfounded; astounded; be flabbergasted (*repeatedly*)
dębienie [dan-**bye**-ńe] n. hardening astonishment; being flabbergasted
dębik [**dan**-beek] m. mountain avens
dębina [dan-**bee**-nah] f. oak wood; oak bark; oak stand
dębinka [dan-**been**-kah] f. oak grove; oak coppice; oak thicket; oak stick
dębniak [**danb**-ńahk] m. variety of mead; oak coppice
dębnik [**danb**-ńeek] m. tan
dębny [**danb**-ni] adj.m. of tan
skóra dębna [**skoo**-rah **danb**-nah] exp.: tanned leather
dębowy [dan-**bo**-vi] adj.m. of oak; oak (furniture, etc.)
dęciak [**dan**-ćhahk] m. slang: bowler (hat)
dęcie [**dan**-ćhe] n. blowing; resounding
dętka [**dant**-kah] f. pneumatic tire; tube; air chamber; (ball) bladder
dętologia [dan-to-**lo**-gyah] f. slang: empty boastful talk; bullshit
dęty [**dan**-ti] adj.m. blown; hollow; inflated; puffed up with pride; sham; faked
instrument dęty [een-**stroo**-ment **dan**-ti] exp.: wind-instrument
orkiestra dęta [or-**ke**-strah **dan**-tah] exp.: brass band
diabaz [**dyah**-bahs] m. diabase (mineral)
diabazowy [dyah-bah-**zo**-vi] adj.m. of diabase; diabase (quarry, etc.)
diabelec [dyah-**be**-lets] m. slang: a mean man; a pest; a nuisance of a man; bad man; a tease
diabelnie [dyah-**bel**-ńe] adv. diabolically; devilishly; infernally; confoundedly; cursedly; damnably
diabelny [dyah-**bel**-ni] adj.m. diabolical; devilish; infernal; confounded; deuced
diabelna awantura [dyah-**bel**-nah ah-vahn-**too**-rah] exp.: infernal row; awful row; slang: hell of a row
diabelny kłopot [dyah-**bel**-ni **kwo**-pot] exp.: the deuce of a mess; the deuce of a fix
diabelski [dyah-**bel**-skee] adj.m. diabolical; devilish; devil's; fiendish; hellish; infernal; confounded; deuced; slang: doggone; damned
diabelsko [dyah-**bel**-sko] adv. diabolically; devilishly; infernally; confoundedly; cursedly; damnably
diabelstwo [dyah-**bel**-stfo] n. deviltry; diabolism; devilishness; slang: nuisance
diabeł [**dyah**-bew] m. devil; fiend; demon; the deuce; the Evil One
diabełek [dyah-**be**-wek] m. devilkin; imp; little devil; an ancient card game
diabetolog [dyah-be-**to**-log] m. specialist in diabetes
diabetologia [dyah-be-to-**lo**-gyah] f. specialty of diabetes
diabetologiczny [dyah-be-to-lo-**geech**-ni] adj.m. diabetic
diabetyk [dyah-**be**-tik] m. diabetic
diablę [**dyah**-blan] m. little devil; imp
diabli [**dyah**-blee] adj.m. diabolical; devilish; devil's; fiendish; hellish; pl. devils; slang: doggone; damned
pal diabli! [pahl **dyah**-blee] exp.: never mind!; I don't give a damn; I don't care a damn!; come what may!
diablica [dyah-**blee**-tsah] f. shrew
to istna diablica [to **eest**-nah dyah-**blee**-tsah] exp.: she is a devil incarnate
diablik [**dyah**-bleek] m. little devil; imp
diablo [**dyah**-blo] adv. diabolically; devilishly; infernally; confoundedly; cursedly; damnably

diablo mało [**dyah**-blo **mah**-wo] exp.: precious little
diablotka [dyah-**blo**-tkah] f. cracker; biscuit
diabolicznie [dyah-bo-**leech**-ńe] adv. diabolically; devilishly; satanically
diaboliczność [dyah-bo-**leech**-nośhćh] f. diabolicalness; deviltry; witchcraft; wickedness; mischief
diaboliczny [dyah-bo-**leech**-ni] adj.m. diabolical; devilish; satanic
diachronia [dyah-**khro**-ńyah] f. diachrony
diachronicznie [dyah-khro-**ńeech**-ńe] adv. diachronic
diachroniczny [dyah-khro-**ńeech**-ni] adj.m. diachronic
diadem [**dyah**-dem] m. diadem; tiara; coronet
diafon [**dyah**-fon] m. diaphone; fog signal of two tones
diaforetyczny [dyah-fo-re-**tich**-ni] adj.m. diaphoretic
diaforeza [dyah-fo-**re**-zah] f. diaphoresis; induced (profuse) perspiration
diafragma [dyah-**frahg**-mah] f. diaphragm
diafragmowy [dyah-frahg-**mo**-vi] adj.m. diaphragmatic
diagenetyczny [dyah-ge-ne-**tich**-ni] adj.m. diagenetic
diageneza [dyah-ge-**ne**-zah] f. diagenesis
diagnoskop [dyah-**gno**-skop] m. diagnostic device for car engines
diagnosta [dyah-**gno**-stah] m. diagnostician
diagnostyczny [dyah-gno-**stich**-ni] adj.m. diagnostic
diagnostyk [dyah-**gno**-stik] m. diagnostician
diagnostyka [dyah-**gno**-sti-kah] f. diagnostics
diagnoza [dyah-**gno**-zah] f. diagnosis
postawić diagnozę [po-**stah**-veećh dyah-**gno**-zan] exp.: to diagnose; to make a diagnosis
diagnozować [dyah-gno-**zo**-vahćh] v. diagnose; make a diagnosis
diagonal [dyah-**go**-nahl] m. diagonal cloth; twill
diagonalizm [dyah-go-**nah**-leezm] adv. diagonally
diagonalnie [dyah-go-**nahl**-ńe] adv. diagonally
diagonalny [dyah-go-**nahl**-ni] adj.m. diagonal
diagram [**dyah**-grahm] m. diagram; graph
diak [dyahk] m. psalmist
diakon [**dyah**-kon] m. deacon
diakonat [dyah-**ko**-naht] m. deaconship; diaconate
diakonisa [dyah-ko-**ńee**-sah] f. (woman) deacon
diakrytyczny [dyah-kri-**tich**-ni] adj.m. diacritical; distinguishing
znak diakrytyczny [znahk dyah-kri-**tich**-ni] exp.: diacritical mark, as a macron, added to a letter or symbol to show pronunciation, etc.
dialekt [**dyah**-lekt] m. dialect; idiom
dialektalny [dyah-lek-**tahl**-ni] adj.m. dialectical; dialectal
dialektolog [dyah-lek-**to**-log] m. dialectologist
dialektologia [dyah-lek-to-**lo**-gyah] f. dialectology
dialektologicznie [dyah-lek-to-lo-**geech**-ńe] adv. dialectologically
dialektologiczny [dyah-lek-to-lo-**geech**-ni] adj.m. dialectological
dialektowo [dyah-lek-**to**-vo] adv. dialectally
dialektowy [dyah-lek-**to**-vi] adj.m. dialectal (atlas, etc.)
dialektycznie [dyah-lek-**tich**-ńe] adv. dialectally; dialectically; in accordance with the tenets of dialectical materialism
dialektyczny [dyah-lek-**tich**-ni] adj.m. dialectical; dialectal
materializm dialektyczny [mah-te-**ryah**-leezm dyah-lek-**tich**-ni] exp.: dialectical materialism
dialektyk [dyah-**lek**-tik] m. dialectician
dialektyka [dyah-**lek**-ti-kah] f. dialectics; logical debate; a logical test of ideas for validity
dialektyzacja [dyah-lek-ti-**zah**-tsyah] f. introduction of dialectic expressions into literary language
dialektyzm [dyah-**lek**-tizm] m. dialectal term; dialectal phrase

dialektyzować [dyah-lek-ti-**zo**-vahćh] v. bring dialectic expressions into literary language (*repeatedly*)
dializa [dyah-**lee**-zah] f. dialysis
dializacyjny [dyah-lee-zah-**tsiy**-ni] adj.m. dialytic
dializat [dyah-**lee**-zaht] m. dialysate; dialyzate
dializator [dyah-lee-**zah**-tor] m. dialyzer
dializować [dyah-lee-**zo**-vahćh] v. dialyze; subject to dialysis (*repeatedly*)
dializować się [dyah-lee-**zo**-vahćh śhan] v. dialyze oneself; undergo dialysis (*repeatedly*)
dialog [**dyah**-log] m. dialogue; interchange of ideas by open discussion; the passages of talk in a play, story, etc.
dialogować [dyah-lo-**go**-vahćh] v. take part in a dialogue; express in dialogue (*repeatedly*)
dialogowy [dyah-lo-**go**-vi] adj.m. of dialogue; dialogical
diamencik [dyah-**men**-ćheek] m. small diamond
diament [**dyah**-ment] m. diamond; cutting diamond; glass-cutter
diamentonośny [dyah-men-to-**nośh**-ni] adj.m. rich in diamonds
diamentować [dyah-men-**to**-vahćh] v. cut with diamond tools (*repeatedly*)
diamentowanie [dyah-men-to-**vah**-ńe] n. cutting with diamond tools
diamentowo [dyah-men-**to**-vo] adv. like diamonds (shine, etc.)
diamentowy [dyah-men-**to**-vi] adj.m. diamond (field, shine, etc.)
diamentówka [dyah-men-**toof**-kah] f. machine equipped with diamond tools for cutting
diametralnie [dyah-me-**trahl**-ńe] adv. diametrically; completely opposed
diametralny [dyah-me-**trahl**-ni] adj.m. diametrical; opposite
diapauza [dyah-**pahw**-zah] f. diapause
diapazon [dyah-**pah**-zon] m. diapazon (range of sounds); tuning-fork
diapozytyw [dyah-po-**zi**-tif] m. diapositive; transparent photographic positive; slide; transparency
diapozytywowy [dyah-po-zi-ti-**vo**-vi] adj.m. diapositive (plate, film, etc.)
diariusz [**dyah**-ryoosh] m. diary; journal; diary book
diasek [**dyah**-sek] m. little devil
co do diaska [tso do **dyahs**-kah] excl.: what's going on?!
diaskop [**dyahs**-kop] m. slide projector; projection lantern
diaspora [dyahs-**po**-rah] f. Diaspora; migration
diastaza [dyahs-**tah**-zah] f. diastasis
diastem [**dyah**-stem] m. space between sedimentary layers
diastema [dyah-**ste**-mah] f. space between teeth in a jaw
diatermia [dyah-**ter**-myah] f. diathermia; diathermy; electric heating for medical purposes
diatermiczny [dyah-ter-**meech**-ni] f. diathermic
diateza [dyah-**te**-zah] f. diathesis
diatomit [dyah-**to**-meet] m. diatomite
diatonicznie [dyah-to-**ńeech**-ńe] adv. diatonically
diatoniczny [dyah-to-**ńeech**-ni] adj.m. diatonic
diatonika [dyah-**to**-ńee-kah] f. diatonic (musical) composition
diatryba [dyah-**tri**-bah] f. diatribe; bitter and abusive speech; ironical or satirical criticism
diazotyp [dyah-**zo**-tip] m. diazotype
diazotypia [dyah-zo-**ti**-pyah] f. making of diazotypes (color pictures)
dichroizm [dee-**khro**-eezm] m. dichroism
didaskalia [dee-dah-**skah**-lyah] pl. author's notes on staging a play
diecezja [dye-**tse**-zyah] f. diocese
diecezjalny [dye-tse-**zyah**-lni] adj.m. diocesan
dielektryczny [dee-e-lek-**trich**-ni] adj.m. dielectric
dielektryk [dee-e-**le**-ktrik] m. dielectric
diereza [dye-**re**-zah] f. diaeresis (gram. and a diacritical mark)

diesel [**dee**-zel] m. diesel engine
dieselizacja [dee-ze-lee-**zah**-tsyah] f. bringing of diesel engines (to railroads, etc.)
dieslowski [deez-**lof**-skee] adj.m. diesel (engine, etc.)
dieslowy [deez-**lo**-vi] adj.m. diesel (oil, etc.)
dieta [**dye**-tah] f. diet; regimen; travelling allowance
dietetyczka [dye-te-**tich**-kah] f. (woman) dietician
dietetycznie [dye-te-**tich**-ńe] adv. dietetically
dietetyczny [dye-te-**tich**-ni] adj.m. dietetic
dietetyk [dye-**te**-tik] m. dietician
dietetyka [dye-**te**-ti-kah] f. dietetics; sitiology; sitology
dietka [**dyet**-kah] f. light diet
digitalina [dee-gee-tah-**lee**-nah] f. digitalin; steroid glycoside
digitalis [dee-gee-**tah**-lis] m. digitalis; foxglove (cardiac stimulant and a diuretic)
din don din [deen don deen] exp.: ding-dong
dinar [**dee**-nahr] m. dinar
dingi [**deen**-gee] n. dinghy
dingo [**deen**-go] m. dingo; Australian wild dog
dinozaur [dee-**no**-zahwr] m. dinosaur
dintojra [deen-**toy**-rah] f. gangland violence; Jewish rabbinical court
dioda [**dyo**-dah] f. diode
diodowy [dyo-**do**-vi] adj.m. of diode
dionizyjski [dyo-ńee-**ziy**-skee] adj.m. Dionysical; Bacchic
diopter [**dyop**-ter] m. diopter; gun sight; vane
dioptra [**dyop**-trah] f. diopter
dioptraż [**dyop**-trahsh] m. dioptric rating
dioptria [**dyop**-tryah] f. diopter
dioptryczny [dyop-**trich**-ni] adj.m. dioptric
dioptryka [**dyop**-tri-kah] f. dioptrics
diorama [dyo-**rah**-mah] f. diorama
dioramiczny [dyo-rah-**meech**-ni] adj.m. dioramic
dioryt [**dyo**-rit] m. diorite (mineral)
diorytowy [dyo-ri-**to**-vi] adj.m. dioritic
dipis [**dee**-pees] m. displaced person in Germany after World War II
diplodok [dee-**plo**-dok] m. diplodocus (dinosaur)
diploid [dee-**plo**-eet] m. diploidy
diploidalność [dee-plo-ee-**dahl**-nośhćh] f. double basic chromosome number
diploidalny [dee-plo-ee-**dahl**-ni] adj.m. diploid
diplokok [dee-**plo**-kok] m. diplococcus
diplokokowy [dee-plo-ko-**ko**-vi] adj.m. diplococcal; diplococcic
diplopia [de-**plo**-pyah] f. diplopia; double vision
dipol [**dee**-pol] m. dipole
dipolowy [dee-po-**lo**-vi] adj.m. dipolar (antenna, etc.)
direktor [dee-**rek**-tor] m. directional element in a dipolar antenna
dirhem [**deer**-khem] m. Moroccan monetary unit
dirka [**deer**-kah] f. gaff-sail line
dis [dees] n. D sharp (music)
disc jockey [deesk **dzho**-key] m. disc jockey; radio announcer of a show of popular music (Engl.)
disco [**dees**-ko] n. disco
diuk [dyook] m. duke
diukostwo [dyoo-**kos**-tfo] n. dukedom
diuna [**dyoo**-nah] f. dune
diuretyczny [dyoo-re-**tich**-ni] adj.m. diuretic; tending to increase the flow of urine
diuretyna [dyoo-re-**ti**-nah] f. diuretin
diureza [dyoo-**re**-zah] f. diuresis
diuszesa [dyoo-**she**-sah] f. variety of pear tree; pear fruit
diurnał [**dyoor**-nahw] m. diurnal
divertimento [dee-ver-tee-**men**-to] n. serenade; ballet part in an opera
diwa [**dee**-vah] f. diva; prima donna; prima ballerina; goddess
dla [dlah] prep. for; for the sake; to; towards
dla pozbycia się [dlah poz-bi-ćhah śh<u>an</u>] exp.: towards ridding oneself of; in order to get rid of
przyjemne dla oka [pshi-**yem**-ne dlah **o**-kah] exp.: pleasant to the eye
dlaboga! [dlah-**bo**-gah] excl.: my Goodness! oh dear!

dlaczego [dlah-**che**-go] prep. why; what for; why are you ...?
dlaczego to robisz? [dlah-**che**-go to **ro**-beesh] exp.: what are you doing that for?
oto dlaczego [o-to dlah-**che**-go] exp.: that's why; this is why
dlaczegoż [dlah-**che**-gosh] prep. (emphatic) why; what for
dlaczegóż [dlah-**che**-goosh] prep. (emphatic) why; what for; why on earth?; vulg.: why the devil?
dlań [dlahń] exp.: for him
dlatego [dlah-**te**-go] prep. because; this is why; and so; so
dlatego też [dlah-**te**-go tesh] exp.: therefore; so; and so; this is why; that is why
dlatego, że [dlah-**te**-go zhe] exp.: because
właśnie dlatego [**vwahśh**-ńe dlah-**te**-go] exp.: that is just why
dławiąco [dwah-**vyown**-tso] adv. chokingly
dławiący [dwah-**vyown**-tsi] adj.m. choking
dławica [dwah-**vee**-tsah] f. choky feeling; stuffing box; pressure by thyroid gland; dyspnea; shortness of breath
dławica bolesna [dwah-**vee**-tsah bo-**les**-nah] exp.: angina
dławicowy [dwah-vee-**tso**-vi] adj.m. of shortness of breath
dławić [**dwah**-veećh] v. choke; squash; throttle; strangle (*repeatedly*)
dławić się [**dwah**-veećh śhan] v. choke
dławić się chlebem [**dwah**-veećh śhan **khle**-bem] exp.: to choke on bread
dławić się śmiechem [**dwah**-veećh śhan **śhmye**-khem] exp.: to choke with laughter
dławiec [**dwah**-vyets] m. croup
dławienie [dwah-**vye**-ńe] n. the feeling of choking; choking
dławienie się [dwah-**vye**-ńe śhan] n. becoming choked; getting choked
dławik [**dwah**-veek] m. throttle; choking-coil; stuffing box
dławisz [**dwah**-veesh] m. staff-tree
dławnica [dwah-**vńee**-tsah] f. stuffing box; gland
dłoniak [**dwo**-ńahk] m. fry; carp fry; sailmaker's palm
dłoniasto [dwo-**ńah**-sto] adv. like the palm of a hand with outstretched fingers
dłoniasty [dwo-**ńah**-sti] adj.m. palm-like; palmate
dłonica [dwo-**ńee**-tsah] f. body of a check-valve
dłoniowy [dwo-**ńo**-vi] adj.m. palmar; volar
dłoń [dwoń] f. palm of the hand; hand; metacarpus; quart (in fencing)
bratnia dłoń [**braht**-ńah dwoń] exp.: helping hand
jasne jak na dłoni [**yahs**-ne yahk nah **dwo**-ńee] exp.: clear as daylight
pełna dłoń [**pew**-nah dwoń] exp.: handful; the handful
wyciągnąć dłoń [vi-**ćhowng**-nownćh dwoń] exp.: to hold out a hand (to somebody, etc.)
dłubacz [**dwoo**-bahch] m. ineffective worker; procrastinator
dłubaczka [dwoo-**bahch**-kah] f. gouge; chisel
dłubać [**dwoo**-bahćh] v. groove; gouge; hollow out (*repeatedly*)
dłubać się [**dwoo**-bahćh śhan] v. tinker; mess about; potter about; poke; pick (one's teeth, one's nose, etc.) (*repeatedly*)
dłubak [**dwoo**-bahk] m. one of well-drilling tools
dłubanie [dwoo-**bah**-ńe] n. hollowing out; poking; messing about; pottering about
dłubanina [dwoo-bah-**ńee**-nah] f. painstaking work; drudgery; pottering about; messing about
dłubanka [dwoo-**bahn**-kah] f. canoe hollowed out of a tree trunk
dług [dwoog] m. debt; obligation; indebtedness
dług wdzięczności [dwoog vdźhanch-**nośh**-ćhee] exp.: a debt of gratitude
spłacić dług [**spwah**-ćheećh dwoog] exp.: to pay off a debt
zaciągnąć dług [zah-**ćhowng**-

nownćh dwoog] exp.: to contract a debt
wpaść w długi [fpahśhćh v **dwoo**-gee] exp.: to incur debts
długachny [dwoo-**gahkh**-ni] adj.m. slang: very long
długaśny [dwoo-**gahśh**-ni] adj.m. slang: very long
długawo [dwoo-**gah**-vo] adv. rather long (time, etc.)
długawy [dwoo-**gah**-vi] adj.m. slightly too long
długi [**dwoo**-gee] adj.m. long; long drawn; sustained; pl. debts
jak długi [yahk **dwoo**-gee] exp.: at full length
przez długi czas [pshes **dwoo**-gee chahs] exp.: a long time; long; for a good while; a good while
upadł jak długi [oo-pahdw yahk **dwoo**-gee] exp: he fell down flat
długo [**dwoo**-go] adv. a long time; a long way; to a long distance; far; long before; for a long time; long-drawn; sustained; protracted
jak długo [yahk **dwoo**-go] exp.: as long as
jak długo? [yahk **dwoo**-go] exp.: how long ?
jak długo jeszcze? [yahk **dwoo**-go **yesh**-che] exp.: how much longer?
na długo [nah **dwoo**-go] exp.: for a long time; for long
długobrody [dwoo-go-**bro**-di] adj.m. long-bearded
długodystansowiec [dwoo-go-dis-tahn-**so**-vyets] m. long-distance runner
długodystansowy [dwoo-go-dis-tahn-**so**-vi] adj.m. long-distance (race, etc.)
długodzioby [dwoo-go-**dźho**-bi] adj.m. having a long beak
długofalowo [dwoo-go-fah-**lo**-vo] adv. in the long run; in long-term
długofalowość [dwoo-go-fah-**lo**-vośhćh] f. long run; long range
długofalowy [dwoo-go-fah-**lo**-vi] adj.m. long-wave; long-range (plans, prospects, etc.)
długogłowiec [dwoo-go-**gwo**-vyets] m. dolichocephal; long-headed person
długogłowość [dwoo-go-**gwo**-vośhćh] f. dolichocephaly; long-headedness
długogłowy [dwoo-go-**gwo**-vi] adj.m. dolichocephalic; long-headed
długogrający [dwoo-go-grah-**yown**-tsi] adj.m. long-play (record, etc.)
długogrzywy [dwoo-go-**gzhi**-vi] adj.m. long-maned
długoletni [dwoo-go-**let**-ńee] adj.m. of long-time; of many years; of long standing
długoletniość [dwoo-go-**let**-ńośhćh] f. seniority of many years; long standing
długometrażowy [dwoo-go-me-trah-**zho**-vi] adj.m. exp.:
film długometrażowy [feelm dwoo-go-me-trah-**zho**-vi] exp.: feature film (tape of over 600 meters length; projection of over 22 minutes duration)
długonogi [dwoo-go-**no**-gee] adj.m. long-legged; leggy
długoogniskowy [dwoo-go-og-ńees-**ko**-vi] adj.m. of great focal length
długookresowy [dwoo-go-o-kre-**so**-vi] adj.m. long-term
długopis [dwoo-**go**-pees] m. ball-point pen
długopisowy [dwoo-go-pee-**so**-vi] adj.m. (insert, etc.) of a ball-point pen
długopłetwiec [dwoo-go-**pwet**-fyets] m. humpback whale
długoręki [dwoo-go-**ran**-kee] adj.m. long-armed; with long arms
długorogi [dwoo-go-**ro**-gee] adj.m. long-horned
długoseryjny [dwoo-go-se-**riy**-ni] adj.m. made in long series
długoskrzydlaty [dwoo-go-skshi-**dlah**-ti] adj.m. long-winged
długoskrzydły [dwoo-go-**skshid**-wi] adj.m. long-winged
długoskrzydłe [dwoo-go-**skshid**-we] pl. humming-birds
długosz [**dwoo**-gosh] m. royal fern; water-fern; osmund royal
długoszowaty [dwoo-go-sho-**vah**-ti] adj.m. osmundaceous; fern-like
długoszowate [dwoo-go-sho-**vah**-te] pl. the family of

osmundaceous ferns
długoszpon [dwoo-**go**-shpon] m. jacana (Mexican) bird
długoszpony [dwoo-go-**shpo**-ni] pl. the family of jacana birds
długościowy [dwoo-gośh-**ćho**-vi] adj.m. pertaining to length
długość [**dwoo**-gośhćh] f. length; longitude; long duration; span (of life, etc.); long duration; length of time
mieć pięć metrów długości [myećh pyanćh **me**-troof dwoo-**gośh**-ćhee] exp.: to be five meters long
na długość [nah **dwoo**-gośhćh] exp.: lengthwise; lengthways; endwise; endways; longitudinally
długoterminowy [dwoo-go-ter-mee-**no**-vi] adj.m. long-term
długotrwale [dwoo-go-**trfah**-le] adv. for a long time; persistently; unendingly; durably
długotrwałość [dwoo-go-**trfah**-wośhćh] f. long duration
długotrwały [dwoo-go-**trfah**-wi] adj.m. lasting; durable; prolonged; sustained; long-lasting; long-drawn; of long standing; unending
długouchy [dwoo-go-**oo**-khi] adj.m. long-eared
długouszka [dwoo-go-**oosh**-kah] f. tamarin
długowełniasty [dwoo-go-vew-**ńah**-sti] adj.m. long-fleeced
długowełnisty [dwoo-go-vew-**ńees**-ti] adj.m. long-fleeced
długowieczność [dwoo-go-**vyech**-nośhćh] f. longevity
długowieczny [dwoo-go-**vyech**-ni] adj.m. long-lived
długowiekowy [dwoo-go-vye-**ko**-vi] adj.m. lasting many centuries
długowłosy [dwoo-go-**vwo**-si] adj.m. long-haired
długowzroczność [dwoo-go-**vzroch**-nośhćh] f. long-sightedness; long sight; presbyopia; far-sightedness; foresight; sagacity
dłutarka [dwoo-**tahr**-kah] f. (chisel) mortiser
dłutko [**dwoo**-tko] n. (small) chisel; burin; graver
dłuto [**dwoo**-to] n. chisel; burin; graver
dłutować [dwoo-**to**-vahćh] v. chisel; cut with chisel; shape with chisel (*repeatedly*)
dłutowanie [dwoo-to-**vah**-ńe] n. chiseling; shaping with chisel
dłutownica [dwoo-to-**vńee**-tsah] f. (chisel) mortiser
dłutownik [dwoo-**tov**-ńeek] m. chisel-hammer for work in stone
dłużej [**dwoo**-zhey] adv. longer than
na dłużej [nah **dwoo**-zhey] exp.: for any length of time
nie dłużej [ńe dwoo-zhey] exp.: no longer; no more; not any longer; not any more
tak dłużej być nie może [tahk **dwoo**-zhey bićh ńe **mo**-zhe] exp.: this cannot go on
dłużniczka [dwoozh-**ńeech**-kah] f. (woman) debtor; borrower; mortgager
dłużniczy [dwoozh-**ńee**-chi] adj.m. debtor's (law, etc.)
dłużnik [**dwoozh**-ńeek] m. debtor; borrower; mortgager
dłużny [**dwoozh**-ni] adj.m. owing; indebted; owing money; owing gratitude; under an obligation
być dłużnym [bićh **dwoozh**-nim] exp.: to owe; to be in debt for (money, a reply, etc.:)
jestem mu dłużny [**yes**-tem moo **dwoozh**-ni] exp.: I owe him
dłuższy [**dwoosh**-shi] adj.m. longer; sustained; protracted
na dłuższy czas [nah **dwoosh**-shi chahs] exp.: for any length of time
dłużyca [dwoo-**zhi**-tsah] f. log (cut for lumber in standard length)
toczenie dłużycy [to-**che**-ńe dwoo-**zhi**-tsi] exp.: log-rolling
dłużycowy [dwoo-zhi-**tso**-vi] adj.m. long-log (trailer, etc.)
dłużyć się [**dwoo**-zhićh śhan] v. drag on; wear on; seem interminable; pass slowly (*repeatedly*)
dłużyzna [dwoo-**zhi**-znah] f. long spell; tedious passage
dmuch [dmookh] m. air-blast; blast; wind; blow

dmuchacz [**dmoo**-khahch] m. glass-blower
dmuchać [**dmoo**-khahćh] v. blow; whiff; slang: steal (*repeatedly*)
dmuchać w trąbę [**dmoo**-khahćh f **trown**-ban] exp.: to blow a trumpet
dmuchanie [dmoo-**khah**-ńe] n. blowing
dmucharka [dmoo-**khahr**-kah] f. blower (used in coal mines)
dmuchawa [dmoo-**khah**-vah] f. blower; blast machine
dmuchawiec [dmoo-**khah**-vyets] m. blow-ball
dmuchawka [dmoo-**khah**-fkah] f. blow-pipe
dmuchawkowy [dmoo-khahf-**ko**-vi] adj.m. blow-pipe (nozzle, etc.)
dmuchnąć [**dmookh**-nownćh] v. blow; whiff
dmuchnięcie [dmookh-**ńan**-ćhe] n. puff (of wind, etc.)
dna [dnah] f. gout
dnawy [**dnah**-vi] adj.m. of the gout; gouty
dni [dńee] pl. days; festival; lifetime
dni otwarte [dńee ot-**fahr**-te] exp.: open house days; introductory school days
dnieć [dńećh] v. dawn (*repeatedly*)
dnieje [**dńe**-ye] exp.: day is dawning
kiedy dnieje [**ke**-di **dńe**-ye] exp.: at daybreak
dniówka [**dńoof**-kah] f. day's work; work by day; time work; a day's wages
dniówkarz [**dńoof**-kahsh] m. day-laborer; worker paid by the day
dniówkowy [dńoof-**ko**-vi] adj.: paid by the day
dno [dno] n. bottom; depth; rock-bottom; utterness
dnem do góry [dnem do **goo**-ri] exp.: bottom up
drugie dno [**droo**-ge dno] exp.: hidden content
odbić się od dna [**od**-beećh śhan od dnah] exp.: to rebound; to start recovering; make up for lost time; regain lost standing
wypić do dna [**vi**-peećh do dnah] exp.: to drink to the last drop
do [do] prep. to; into; in; down; up; till; until
aż do [ahsh do] exp.: pending; back to; back up to; as late as
do diabła! [do **dyah**-bwah] excl.: damn! vulg.: hell! to hell with ...!
do mnie [do mńe] exp.: to me
do nich [do ńeekh] exp.: to them
do was [do vahs] exp.: to you
do teraz [do **te**-rahs] exp.: by now; up till now
do trzech dni [do tshekh dńee] exp.: within three days
do przepaści [do pshe-**pahśh**-ćhee] exp.: down a precipice
nie do przetłumaczenia [ńe do pshe-twoo-mah-**che**-ńah] exp.: untranslatable
porównać do [po-**roov**-nahćh do] exp.: to compare with
strzelić do [**stshe**-leećh do] exp.: to shoot at
do- [do] prefix: up, additionally, extra; some more; enough; quite; so much as; under; long enough; till the end; get; acquire
dorobić się [do-**ro**-beećh śhan] v. to acquire a fortune by work
nie dojadać [ńe do-**yah**-dahćh] exp.: to hunger; to starve; to have something additional to eat
doangażować [do-ahn-gah-**zho**-vahćh] v. engage additionally; hire additionally
doba [**do**-bah] f. 24 hours; day and night; era; age
raz na dobę [rahs nah **do**-ban] exp.: once a day
w dzisiejszej dobie [v dźhee-**śhey**-shey **do**-bye] exp.: nowadays; in this day and age; at present; at the present time
całą dobę [tsah-wown **do**-ban] exp.: round the clock; day and night
dobadać [do-**bah**-dahćh] v. study thoroughly; make a thorough investigation; inquire
dobadać się [do-**bah**-dahćh śhan] v. obtain results in one's investigation
dobarwiać [do-**bahr**-vyahćh] v. add color; add dye (*repeatedly*)
dobarwić [do-**bahr**-veećh] v. add

color; add dye
doberman [do-**ber**-mahn] m. Doberman pincher
dobić [**do**-beećh] v. deal a death blow; kill off; finish off; dispatch; drive home (a point, etc.); reach (a shore); close; strike; drive; clinch
dobić swego [**do**-beećh **sfe**-go] exp.: to succeed in reaching one's goal; to impose one's will
dobić targu [**do**-beećh **tahr**-goo] exp.: to close a bargain; strike, drive, clinch a bargain; to come to terms
dobić się [**do**-beećh śhan] v. strive for; strive after; reach (a goal)
dobijać [do-**bee**-yahćh] v. deal a death blow; kill off; finish off; dispatch; drive home (a point, etc.); reach (a shore); close; strike; drive; clinch (*repeatedly*)
dobijać się [do-**bee**-yahćh śhan] v. knock (at the door); strive for; strive after; reach (a goal) (*repeatedly*)
dobiec [**do**-byets] v. run up; reach; run out; come up; be nearing; be getting on towards; be near; approach; be coming near; be giving out
dobieg [**do**-byeg] m. ending of a run; rolling to a stop after landing
dobiegać [do-**bye**-gahćh] v. run up; reach; run out; come up; be nearing; be getting on towards; be near; approach; be coming near; be giving out (*repeatedly*)
dobiegać końca [do-**bye**-gahćh **koń**-tsah] exp.: to be nearing the end; to be coming to an end; to be coming to a close; to be nearing completion; to be giving out (the rest of...)
dobiegnąć [do-**byeg**-nownćh] v. run up; come up
dobiegowy [do-bye-**go**-vi] adj.m. (trench, etc.) used for running up
dobielać [do-**bye**-lahćh] v. finish whitening; complete whitening; add cream; add milk (*repeatedly*)
dobierać [do-**bye**-rahćh] v. match; take more; select (*repeatedly*)
dobierać się [do-**bye**-rahćh śhan] v. try to get (at something) (*repeatedly*)
dobijać [do-**bee**-yahćh] v. deal a death-blow (*repeatedly*)
dobijać targu [do-**bee**-yahćh **tahr**-goo] exp.: to strike a bargain
dobijać do lądu [do-**bee**-yahćh do **lown**-doo] exp.: to reach land
dobijać się [do-**bee**-yahćh śhan] v. try to enter; contend; scramble for (*repeatedly*)
dobijać się do drzwi [do-**bee**-yahćh śhan do dzhvee] exp.: to knock at the door; to rattle at the door; to batter the door
dobijak [do-**bee**-yahk] m. nail follower; nail sinker; sand-eel; sand launce (fish)
dobijakowaty [do-bee-yah-ko-**vah**-ti] adj.m. of small (eel-like) sea fish
dobijakowate [do-bee-yah-ko-**vah**-te] pl. family of small (eel-like) sea fish; Ammodytidae
dobitek [do-**bee**-tek] m. idiomatic:
na dobitek [nah do-**bee**-tek] exp.: on top of it; on top of all that; what is worse; to make things worse; worst of all; to crown all; as a final misfortune
dobitka [do-**bee**-tkah] f. final shot scoring a goal; see: **dobitek**
na dobitkę [nah do-**beet**-kan] exp.: on top of it; on top of all that; what is worse; to make things worse
dobitnie [do-**beet**-ńe] adv. clearly; distinctly; forcibly; expressively; emphatically; perspicuously
dobitność [do-**beet**-nośhćh] f. clearness; expressiveness; emphasis; distinctness; forcibleness; perspicuity
dobitny [do-**beet**-ni] adj.m. clear; expressive; emphatic; distinct; forcible; perspicuous
dobniak [**dob**-ńahk] m. mallet
doborowość [do-bo-**ro**-vośhćh] f. choiceness; excellence; high-grade quality; high quality
doborowy [do-bo-**ro**-vi] adj.m. choice; select; picked; excellent; high-grade; of the best quality; high quality (product, etc.)
dobosz [**do**-bosh] m. drummer

dobowy [do-**bo**-vi] adj.m. of twenty-four hours; twenty-four hours'; a day and night's (work, etc.)
dobór [**do**-boor] m. selection; assortment; choice
dobór naturalny [**do**-boor nah-too-**rahl**-ni] exp.: natural selection
dobóść [**do**-boośhćh] v. finish off (kill) by piercing with the horn; worry; harass; molest; oppress
dobra [**do**-brah] pl. riches; adj.f. good; hearty; discerning; retentive (memory, etc.); nice; tasty
dobra ruchome [**do**-brah roo-**kho**-me] exp.: movable property; personal property
dobra! [**do**-brah] excl.: good!; all right!; O.K.!; okay!; agreed! splendid!;
dobra nasza! [**do**-brah **nah**-shah] excl.: righto!; hurray!; good for us! we won!
rozległe dobra [roz-**leg**-we **dob**-rah] exp.: a large (landed) estate
dobrać [**do**-brahćh] v. have some more; help oneself to some more; take additionally; select; choose; pick; fit; get at; mate
dobrać się [**do**-brahćh śhan] v. lay one's hands (on treasures, etc.); reach for; try to get at; be after (money, etc.); be well-matched; mate; fit (in a group, etc.)
dobranie [do-**brah**-ńe] n. matching; second helping; selection
dobranoc [do-**brah**-nots] indecl.: good night
całować na dobranoc [tsah-**wo**-vahćh nah do-**brah**-nots] exp.: to kiss good-night
dobranocka [do-brah-**no**-tskah] f. short television or radio program for children (at night)
dobrany [do-**brah**-ni] adj.m. matching; becoming; well-chosen; accordant; hand and glove
dobre [**do**-bre] adj.n. & f.pl. good
na dobre [nah **do**-bre] exp.: in full; for good; once and for all; for good and all; for keeps
po dobremu [po do-**bre**-moo] exp.: gently; without malice; politely
dobrnąć [**dobr**-nownćh] v. wade through; reach (at last); pull through (to the end); (manage) to reach; reach somehow
dobro [**do**-bro] n. good; right; property; well-fare-; well-being; credit (side of an account);
dla mojego dobra [dlah mo-**ye**-go **do**-brah] exp.: for my good
dobrobyt [do-**bro**-bit] m. well being; prosperity; welfare
żyć w dobrobycie [zhićh v do-bro-**bi**-ćhe] exp.: to be prosperous; to prosper; to live in comfort; be on an easy street
dobroczynnie [do-bro-**chin**-ńe] adv. beneficially; beneficently; charitably; with philanthropy; profitably
dobroczynność [do-bro-**chin**-nośhćh] f. charity; works of mercy; philanthropy
dobroczynny [do-bro-**chin**-ni] adj.m. beneficent; charitable
cele dobroczynne [**tse**-le do-bro-**chin**-ne] exp.: charities
dobroczyńca [do-bro-**chiń**-tsah] m. benefactor; philanthropist
dobroć [**do**-broćh] f. kindness; kindliness; kind heart; kind-heartedness; good quality; quality factor
po dobroci [po do-**bro**-ćhee] adv. amicably; gently; without compulsion
dobrodusznie [do-bro-**doosh**-ńe] adv. kindheartedly; with kindness; good-naturedly; with good-humor
dobroduszność [do-bro-**doosh**-nośhćh] f. kind-heartedness; good nature; geniality; good humor; kindliness
dobroduszny [do-bro-**doosh**-ni] adj.m. kindhearted; kindly; good-natured; genial
dobrodziej [do-**bro**-dźhey] m. benefactor; his reverence
dobrodziejka [do-bro-**dźhey**-kah] f. benefactress
dobrodziejstwo [do-bro-**dźhey**-stfo] n. benefaction; boon; benefit (of the law); good deed; act of kindness; blessing
dobrosąsiedzki [do-bro-sown-**śhets**-kee] adj.m. good-neighborly

dobrotliwie [do-bro-**tlee**-vye] adv. kindly; good-naturedly; with good humor; blandly; benignly; genially
dobrotliwość [do-bro-**tlee**-vośhćh] f. kindness; good nature; good humor; geniality
dobrotliwy [do-bro-**tlee**-vi] adj.m. kind; good natured; good-humored; bland; benign; genial
dobrowolnie [do-bro-**vol**-ńe] adv. of one's own free will; voluntarily; gratuitously
dobrowolność [do-bro-**vol**-nośhćh] f. voluntary nature (of an action, etc.); gratuitous character
dobrowolny [do-bro-**vol**-ni] adj.m. voluntary; gratuitous; free; of one's own accord
dobrudzać [do-**broo**-dzahćh] v. use till (something) is completely dirty (*repeatedly*)
dobrudzić [do-**broo**-dźheećh] v. use till it is completely dirty
dobry [**dob**-ri] adj.m. good; kind; right; hearty; retentive; discerning; righteous; optimistic; proper; suitable; nice; tasty; palatable; full; m. the good
a to dobre! [ah to **do**-bre] excl.: I like this!
co dobrego? [tso do-**bre**-go] exp.: what is the best news?
dobra! [**dob**-rah] excl.: all right! alright! O.K.! okay!
dobra nasza! [**dob**-rah **nah**-shah] excl.: righto! hurray! good for us!
na dobre [nah **dob**-re] adv. for good; for good and all; for keeps
nie wyjdzie z tego nic dobrego [ńe **viy**-dźhe s **te**-go ńeets do-**bre**-go] exp.: no good will come of it
przez dobre dwie godziny [pshes do-bre dvye go-**dźhee**-ni] exp.: for a good two hours
to wyjdzie na dobre [to **viy**-dźhe nah **do**-bre] exp.: this will come to good; this will take a good turn
życzyć wszystkiego dobrego [zhi-chićh vshi-**stke**-go do-**bre**-go] exp.: to give one's best wishes
dobrze [do-bzhe] adv. well; OK; rightly; properly; okay
czuję się dobrze [choo-yan śhan do-bzhe] exp.: I'm feeling well
dobrze czy źle [do-bzhe chi źhle] exp.: right or wrong
to ci dobrze zrobi [to ćhee **do**-bzhe **zro**-bee] exp.: this will do you good
dobrze ci tak! [**do**-bzhe ćhee tahk] excl.: it serves you right!; it has served you right!
dobrzeć [**do**-bzhećh] v. recover; become stronger; look healthier; become gentler (*repeatedly*)
dobrzmieć [**do**-bzhmyećh] v. still to sound (barely)
dobrzmiewać [do-**bzhmye**-vahćh] v. still to sound (barely) (*repeatedly*)
dobudowa [do-boo-**do**-vah] f. an annex; built-on; completion of a building; addition
dobudować [do-boo-**do**-vahćh] v. build an annex; build on; complete the building; add
dobudowywać [do-boo-do-**vi**-vahćh] v. build an annex; build on; complete the building; add (*repeatedly*)
dobudówka [do-boo-**doof**-kah] f. building extension
dobudzić [do-**boo**-dźheećh] v. wake up
dobudzić się [do-**boo**-dźheećh śhan] v. succeed in waking up; manage to wake up; shake (somebody, etc.) out of sleep
dobyć [**do**-bićh] v. pull out; extract; draw out; capture
dobyć się [**do**-bićh śhan] v. escape; emerge; issue
dobytek [do-**bi**-tek] m. belongings; effects; livestock; property; possessions; effects; goods and chattels
dobywać [do-**bi**-vahćh] v. pull out; extract; draw out; capture (*repeatedly*)
dobywać się [do-**bi**-vahćh śhan] v. escape; emerge; issue (*repeatedly*)
docel [**do**-tsel] m. outward flight
docelowo [do-tse-**lo**-vo] adv. with a purpose; towards approach; towards access; towards destination

docelowy [do-tse-**lo**-vi] adj.m. incoming; of approach; of access; of destination
docelówka [do-tse-**loof**-kah] f. outward flight
docencki [do-**tsen**-tskee] adj.m. of assistant professor
doceniać [do-**tse**-ńahćh] v. duly appreciate (a service rendered, etc.); value; esteem; be alive to; be sensible of (*repeatedly*)
docenić [do-**tse**-ńeećh] v. duly appreciate (a service rendered, etc.); value; esteem; be alive to; be sensible of
docenienie [do-tse-**ńe**-ńe] n. appreciation
docent [**do**-tsent] m. associate professor; lecturer
docentura [do-tsen-**too**-rah] f. associate professorship
dochładzacz [do-**khwah**-dzahch] m. device for secondary cooling
dochładzać [do-**khwah**-dzahćh] v. finish cooling (*repeatedly*)
dochładzać się [do-**khwah**-dzahćh śh<u>an</u>] v. finish cooling oneself (*repeatedly*)
dochłodzić [do-**khwo**-dźheećh] v. finish cooling
dochłodzić się [do-**khwo**-dźheećh śh<u>an</u>] v. finish cooling oneself
dochodowo [do-kho-**do**-vo] adv. profitably; lucratively
dochodowość [do-kho-**do**-vośhćh] f. good returns; profitability
dochodowy [do-kho-**do**-vi] adj.m. profitable; lucrative; profit-making; profit-yielding; of income
podatek dochodowy [po-**dah**-tek do-kho-**do**-vi] exp.: income tax
dochodzący [do-kho-**dz<u>own</u>**-tsi] adj.m. part-time (worker, etc.); out- (patient, etc.)
dochodząca do dziecka [do-kho-**dz<u>own</u>**-tsah do **dźhe**-tskah] exp.: baby-sitter
dochodzenie [do-kho-**dze**-ńe] n. investigation; inquiry; inquest; vindication (of one's rights)
dochodzeniowy [do-kho-dze-**ńo**-vi] adj.m. of an investigation; of an inquiry; of an inquest; of a vindication (of one's rights)
dochodzeniówka [do-kho-dze-**ńoof**-kah] f. police department of investigation
dochodzić [do-**kho**-dźheećh] v. draw near; investigate; reach; go down (to); come down (to); go as far as; be delivered; come; arrive; range; come up to; run up to; amount to; approximate; be nearing; near upon; close on; come by; attain; claim; vindicate (one's rights, etc.); be added; find out; inquire; investigate; ripen; mellow; stalk (game, etc.) (*repeatedly*)
dochodzi trzecia godzina [do-**kho**-dźhee **tshe**-ćhah go-**dźhee**-nah] exp.: it is getting on to three o'clock
on dochodzi siedemdziesiątki [on do-**kho**-dźhee śhe-dem-dźhe-**śh<u>own</u>**-tkee] exp.: he is getting on for seventy; he is close on seventy
rachunek dochodzi do stu dolarów [rah-**khoo**-nek do-**kho**-dźhee do stoo do-**lah**-roof] exp.: the bill amounts to $100
jak do tego doszło? [yahk do **te**-go **do**-shwo] exp.: how did it come about?
dochodzić do źródła [do-**kho**-dźheećh do **źhroo**-dwah] exp.: to get to the source; to trace to the source
dochodzik [do-**kho**-dźheek] m. a tidy income; a nice income
dochować [do-**kho**-vahćh] v. preserve; keep
dochować się [do-**kho**-vahćh śh<u>an</u>] v. manage to bring up; manage to rear (breed); have brought up; be preserved; have reared
dochowywać [do-kho-**vi**-vahćh] v. preserve; keep (*repeatedly*)
dochowywać się [do-kho-**vi**-vahćh śh<u>an</u>] v. manage to bring up; manage to rear (breed); have brought up; be preserved; have reared (*repeatedly*)
dochód [**do**-khoot] m. income; revenue; profit; returns; takings
dochówek [do-**khoo**-vek] m. colloq: young cattle (born on one's farm)

dochrapać się [do-**khrah**-pahćh śhan] v. reach with a great effort; reach with great pains; succeed in reaching; get at; obtain with difficulty; procure with a great effort

dochrapywać się [do-khrah-**pi**-vahćh śhan] v. reach with a great effort; reach with great pains; succeed in reaching; get at; obtain with difficulty; procure with a great effort (*repeatedly*)

dociąć [**do**-ćhownćh] c. sting; tease; provoke; taunt; peck at; fit by cutting off; finish cutting; adapt by cutting; bandy (words)

dociągać [do-**ćhown**-gahćh] v. pull up (to); bring; carry; draw; reach with a great effort; tighten (*repeatedly*)

dociągać do końca [do-**ćhown**-gahćh do **koń**-tsah] exp.: to reach the end; pull through till the end; to last till the end; drag oneself to the end

dociąganie [do-ćhown-**gah**-ńe] n. pulling till the end; pulling up

dociągnąć [do-**ćhown**-gnownćh] v. pull up (to); bring ; carry; draw; reach with a great effort; tighten

dociągnąć się [do-**ćhown**-gnownćh śhan] v. drag oneself (to a place, etc.); rise oneself (to a level, etc.)

dociążać [do-**ćhown**-zhahćh] v. add weight; add more work; put more pressure on (*repeatedly*)

dociążenie [do-ćhown-**zhe**-ńe] n. adding weight; virtual increase of weight of a helicopter resulting from the action of its rotor

dociążyć [do-**ćhown**-zhićh] v. add weight; add more work; put more pressure on

dociec [**do**-ćhets] v. find out; investigate; inquire into; search; study; make a study; reason out

dociekać [do-**ćhe**-kahćh] v. search; investigate; find out; reason out (*repeatedly*)

dociekanie [do-ćhe-**kah**-ńe] n. investigation; inquiry; enquiry; search; research; study

dociekliwie [do-ćhe-**klee**-vye] adv. inquisitively; searchingly

dociekliwość [do-ćhe-**klee**-vośhćh] f. inquisitiveness; inquiring disposition; inquiries

dociekliwy [do-ćhe-**klee**-vi] adj.m. inquisitive; inquiring; searching

docierać [do-**ćhe**-rahćh] v. draw near; reach; reduce friction; rub up; get at; come at; break in; fetch up to (a port); dart forward; pounce; snatch (attack by dogs) (*repeatedly*)

docierak [do-**ćhe**-rahk] m. tool for final polishing of a surface

docieranie [do-ćhe-**rah**-ńe] n. drawing near; reaching; reducing friction; rubbing up; getting at; coming at; breaking in; fetching up to (a port); darting forward; pouncing; snatching (attack by dogs)

docierarka [do-ćhe-**rahr**-kah] f. machine for final polishing of a surface

docinać [do-**ćhee**-nahćh] v. taunt; sting; tease; provoke; nettle; finish cutting; adapt by cutting (*repeatedly*)

docinanie [do-ćhee-**nah**-ńe] n. taunting; stinging; teasing; provoking; nettling; finishing cutting; adapting by cutting

docinek [do-**ćhee**-nek] m. taunt; gibe; flout; jeer; scoff; sally

docisk [**do**-ćheesk] m. pressure; vice; holdfast; clamp

dociskacz [do-**ćhee**-skahch] m. vice; holdfast; clamp

dociskać [do-**ćhee**-skahćh] v. tighten; press home; harass; worry (*repeatedly*)

dociskać się [do-**ćhee**-skahćh śhan] v. be tightened; be pressing home; elbow one's way (*repeatedly*)

dociskowy [do-ćhee-**sko**-vi] adj.m. set (screw, bolt, pin, etc.)

docisnąć [do-**ćhee**-snownćh] v. tighten; press home; harass; worry

docisnąć się [do-**ćhee**-snownćh śhan] v. force one's way through

dociułać [do-**ćhoo**-wahćh] v. save up; add to one's savings

do cna [do tsnah] adv. altogether;

utterly; completely; entirely
docucić [do-**tsoo**-ćheećh] v. succeed to bring (a man, etc.) back to consciousness
docucić się [do-**tsoo**-ćheećh śhan] v. overcome difficulties to bring (a man, etc.) back to consciousness
doczekać [do-**che**-kahćh] v. wait; live to see; wait till; reach (old age, etc.)
doczekać się [do-**che**-kahćh śhan] v. at long last live to see; reach (after a long effort); pull through till; last till
nie doczekasz się go [ńe do-**che**-kahsh śhan go] exp.: no use waiting for him
doczekać się późnej starości [do-**che**-kahćh śhan **poo**-źhney stah-**ro**-śhćhee] exp.: to live to an old age
nie mogę się doczekać... [ńe **mo**-gan śhan do-**che**-kahćh] exp.: I can't hardly wait to (know, etc.); I am impatient for
doczekanie [do-che-**kah**-ńe] n. attainment
doczekiwać [do-che-**kee**-vahćh] v. wait; live to see; wait till; reach (old age, etc.) (*repeatedly*)
doczekiwać się [do-che-**kee**-vahćh śhan] v. at long last live to see; reach (after a long effort); pull through till; last till (*repeatedly*)
doczepa [do-**che**-pah] f. trailer
doczepiać [do-**che**-pyahćh] v. fix append; attach; hitch; link; tack on; hook on; couple up; put to (*repeatedly*)
doczepiać się [do-**che**-pyahćh śhan] v. be fixed; be attached; be hitched; be linked; be tacked on; be hooked on; be coupled up; be put to (*repeatedly*)
doczepianie [do-che-**pyah**-ńe] n. linking; hitching
doczepić [do-**che**-peećh] v. fix; append; attach; hitch; link; tack on; hook on; couple up; put to
doczepić się [do-**che**-peećh śhan] v. be fixed; be attached; be hitched; be linked; be tacked on; be hooked on; be coupled up; be put to
doczepienie [do-che-**pye**-ńe] n. linking; hitching
doczepka [do-**che**-pkah] f. trailer; attachment
doczepny [do-**che**-pni] adj.m. attachable; linkable
doczesność [do-**che**-snośhćh] f. temporality; worldliness
doczesny [do-**che**-sni] adj.m. temporal; worldly; mundane
docześnie [do-**che**-śhńe] adv. temporarily; terrestrially; in a worldly way
doczłapać [do-**chwah**-pahćh] v. come clacking one's sandals; come dragging one's feet
doczłapać się [do-**chwah**-pahćh śhan] v. (finally) come clacking one's sandals; come dragging one's feet (with an effort)
doczołgać się [do-**chow**-gahćh śhan] v. crawl (to a place); drag oneself (to a spot)
doczołowy [do-cho-**wo**-vi] adj.m. oriented towards the front; frontal; foremost
do czysta [do **chis**-tah] adv. clean; completely
doczyszczać [do-**chi**-shchahćh] v. complete the cleaning; polish to a finish; clean thoroughly (*repeatedly*)
doczyszczać się [do-**chi**-shchahćh śhan] v. succeed in cleaning thoroughly (*repeatedly*)
doczyścić [do-**chi**-śhćheećh] v. complete the cleaning; polish to a finish; clean thoroughly
doczyścić się [do-chi-**śhćheećh** śhan] v. succeed in cleaning thoroughly
doczytać [do-**chi**-tahćh] v. read through; read to the end; read up to a certain place; read into a text something which is not there
doczytać się [do-**chi**-tahćh śhan] v. read into a text something which is not there; find out through reading
doczytywać [do-chi-**ti**-vahćh] v. read through; read to the end; read up to a certain place; read into a text something which is

not there (*repeatedly*)
doczytywać się [do-chi-ti-vahćh śhan] v. read into a text something which is not there; find out through reading (*repeatedly*)
dodać [do-dahćh] v. add; add up; sum up; join; affix; insert; lend; impart; reckon up; cast up
dodajna [do-dahy-nah] f. addend; a number to which an other number is added
dodajnik [do-dahy-ńeek] m. addend
dodanie [do-dah-ńe] n. addition; cast
dodatek [do-dah-tek] m. supplement; addition; fixture; extra; appendage; bonus
na dodatek [nah do-dah-tek] adv. furthermore; besides; moreover; on top of it all; too; into the bargain; to make things worse
w dodatku [v do-dah-tkoo] adv. see: **na dodatek**
a w dodatku do [a v do-dah-tkoo do] exp.: added to which
w dodatku do tego [v do-dah-tkoo do te-go] exp.: in conjunction with that
dodatkowo [do-dah-tko-vo] adv. additionally; in addition; extra; furthermore; by way of supplement; into the bargain
dodatkowy [do-dah-tko-vi] adj.m. additional; supplementary; extra
dodatni [do-dah-tńee] adj.m. positive; advantageous; active; favorable; beneficial
strona dodatnia [stro-nah do-dah-tńah] exp.: good side; advantage
dodatnio [do-dah-tńo] adv. positively; advantageously; to somebody's advantage; actively (balanced in bookkeeping); favorably; beneficially
wpływać dodatnio na [fpwi-vahćh do-dah-tńo nah] exp.: to have a good influence on
dodawać [do-dah-vahćh] v. add; add up; sum up; give in addition (*repeatedly*)
dodawać odwagi [do-dah-vahćh o-dvah-gee] exp.: to encourage
dodawanie [do-dah-vah-ńe] n. addition
znak dodawania [znahk do-dah-vah-ńah] exp.: plus sign; positive sign
dodekaedr [do-de-kah-edr] m. dodecahedron; a solid having 12 plane faces
dodekafonia [do-de-kah-fo-ńyah] f. dodecaphony
dodekafoniczny [do-de-kah-fo-ńeech-ni] adj.m. dodecaphonic
dodekafonista [do-de-kah-fo-ńee-stah] m. dodecaphonist
do dna [do dnah] adv. to the bottom; bottoms up
do dnia [do dńah] adv. at down; very early
dodruk [do-drook] m. additional printing using original setup
dodrukować [do-droo-ko-vahćh] v. complete the printing; supplement in the press; print additionally; print additional number of copies
dodrukowywać [do-droo-ko-vi-vahćh] v. complete the printing; supplement in the press; print additionally; print additional number of copies (*repeatedly*)
dodrzeć [do-dzhećh] v. wear (clothes) to tatters; wear (clothes) out of use
dodrzeć się [do-dzhećh śhan] v. become worn (clothes) to tatters; be worn (clothes) out of use
dodrzewiać [do-dzhe-vyahćh] v. plant additional trees
dodupizm [do-doo-peezm] m. vulg. uselessness; asininity
do dupy [do doo-pi] adv. vulg.: useless; no good; asinine
dodusić [do-doo-śheećh] v. strangle to death
dodzierać [do-dźhe-rahćh] v. wear (clothes) to tatters; wear (clothes) out of use (*repeatedly*)
dodzieranie [do-dźhe-rah-ńe] n. wearing (clothes) to tatters; wearing (clothes) out of use
dodzwaniać [do-dzvah-ńahćh] v. ring till the end; not to cease ringing before appointed time (*repeatedly*)
dodzwaniać się [do-dzvah-ńahćh śhan] v. get through on the

phone; get a telephone connection; ring the door bell and get an answer (*repeatedly*)
dodzwonić [do-**dzvo**-ńeećh] v. ring till the end; not to cease ringing before appointed time
dodzwonić się [do-**dzvo**-ńeećh śhan] v. get through on the phone; get a telephone connection; ring the door bell and get an answer
dodźwigać [do-**dźhvee**-gahćh] v. carry to a destination (*repeatedly*)
dodźwignąć [do-**dźhvee**-gnownćh] v. carry to a destination
dofinansować [do-fee-nahn-**so**-vahćh] v. appropriate additional funds; supply needed funds
dofinansowywać [do-fee-nahn-so-**vi**-vahćh] v. appropriate additional funds; supply needed funds (*repeatedly*)
dog [dog] m. great Dane
dogadać [do-**gah**-dahćh] v. scoff; jibe; gibe; flout; bicker; remark
dogadać się [do-**gah**-dahćh śhan] v. make oneself understood; understand one another; understand each other; come to terms; come to an agreement; communicate well; find out (in the course of a conversation)
dogadanie [do-gah-**dah**-ńe] n. scoff; jibe; gibe; flout
dogadywać [do-gah-**di**-vahćh] v. scoff; jibe; gibe; flout; bicker; remark (*repeatedly*)
dogadywać się [do-gah-**di**-vahćh śhan] v. make oneself understood; understand one another; understand each other; come to terms; come to an agreement; communicate well; find out (in the course of a conversation) (*repeatedly*)
dogadywanie [do-gah-di-**vah**-ńe] n. taunts; banter; jibes; gibes; flouts; scoffing; bickering
dogadzać [do-**gah**-dzahćh] v. please; accommodate; satisfy; pamper; humor; gratify; do oneself a bad turn (*repeatedly*) **dogadzać sobie** [do-**gah**-dzahćh **so**-bye] exp.: to indulge oneself; to indulge too freely (in); to do oneself well; to be intemperate
dogadzanie [do-gah-**dzah**-ńe] n. pampering; accommodating
dogalopować [do-gah-lo-**po**-vahćh] v. gallop till the end; gallop up (to a place, etc.)
dogalopowywać [do-gah-lo-po-**vi**-vahćh] v. gallop till the end; gallop up (to a place, etc.) (*repeatedly*)
doganiać [do-**gah**-ńahćh] v. catch up (with); overtake; be in hot pursuit; be hot on the track; follow hot upon (the enemy, etc.) (*repeatedly*)
doganianie [do-gah-**ńah**-ńe] n. catching up (with); overtaking
dogasać [do-**gah**-sahćh] v. be dying out (*repeatedly*)
dogasanie [do-gah-**sah**-ńe] n. dying out (of embers, etc.)
dogasić [do-**gah**-śheećh] v. extinguish; put out (fire)
dogasnąć [do-**gah**-snownćh] v. die out; quit burning; be burned out completely; near the end
dogaszać [do-**gah**-shahćh] v. extinguish; put out (fire) (*repeatedly*)
dogaszenie [do-gah-**she**-ńe] n. extinguishing; putting out (fire)
dogaśnięcie [do-gah-**śhńan**-ćhe] n. dying out; nearing the end
dogena [do-**ge**-nah] f. duenna; chaperon
dogęszczać [do-**gan**-shchahćh] v. increase viscosity (of a liquid, etc.); make denser (*repeatedly*)
dogęścić [do-**gan**-śhćheećh] v. increase viscosity (of a liquid, etc.); make denser
dogger [**do**-ger] m. second part within the Jurassic period
dogiąć [**do**-gyownćh] v. bend (as far as necessary)
dogięcie [do-**gyan**-ćhe] n. bending (as far as necessary)
doginać [do-**gee**-nahćh] v. bend (as far as necessary) (*repeatedly*)
dogląd [**do**-glownt] m. supervision; superintendence; inspection; care; servicing
doglądać [do-**glown**-dahćh] v.

supervise; tend; care for; nurse; look after; see to; watch; keep an eye on; oversee; service (*repeatedly*)

doglądanie [do-glown-**dah**-ńe] n. inspection; care; supervision

dogładzać [do-**gwah**-dzahćh] v. polish up; finish starving (*repeatedly*)

dogładzak [do-**gwah**-dzahk] m. super-finishing tool; super-polishing tool

dogładzarka [do-gwah-**dzahr**-kah] f. super-finisher; super-polisher

dogładzenie [do-gwah-**dze**-ńe] n. finished polishing

dogładzić [do-**gwah**-dźheećh] v. finish polishing

dogłębnie [do-**gwanb**-ńe] adv. deeply; profoundly

dogłębność [do-**gwanb**-nośhćh] f. depth; profoundness

dogłębny [do-**gwanb**-ni] adj.m. deep; profound

dogłos [**do**-gwos] m. mixing of a sound with its echo

dogmat [**do**-gmaht] m. dogma; tenet

dogmatycznie [do-gmah-**tich**-ńe] adv. dogmatically

dogmatyczność [do-gmah-**tich**-nośhćh] f. dogmaticalness; authoritativeness; dogmatism; dictatorial behavior

dogmatyczny [do-gmah-**tich**-ni] adj.m. dogmatic; authoritative; dictatorial

dogmatyk [do-**gmah**-tik] m. dogmatist

dogmatyka [do-**gmah**-ti-kah] f. dogmatics

dogmatyzacja [do-gmah-ti-**zah**-tsyah] f. dogmatization

dogmatyzm [do-**gmah**-tizm] m. dogmatism

dogmatyzować [do-gmah-ti-**zo**-vahćh] v. dogmatize (*repeatedly*)

dogmatyzowanie [do-gmah-ti-zo-**vah**-ńe] n. dogmatization

dognać [**dog**-nahćh] v. catch up (with); overtake; be in hot pursuit; be hot on the track; follow hot upon (the enemy, etc.)

dognębić [do-**gnan**-beećh] v. harass (people, etc.) to death

dogniatać [do-**gńah**-tahćh] v. finish pressing out; finish hammering out; finish rolling out (sheet metal, etc.)

dognić [**do**-gńeećh] v. rot away; reach the state of complete putrefaction

dogniwać [do-**gńee**-vahćh] v. rot away; reach the state of complete putrefaction (*repeatedly*)

dogodnie [do-**go**-dńe] adv. conveniently

dogodność [do-**go**-dnośhćh] f. convenience

dogodny [do-**go**-dni] adj.m. convenient; suitable; handy; profitable; giving easy terms
na dogodnych warunkach [nah do-**go**-dnikh vah-**roon**-kahkh] exp.: on easy terms

dogodzić [do-**go**-dźheećh] v. please; satisfy; accommodate; pamper; humor; gratify

dogonić [do-**go**-ńeećh] v. catch up; overtake; be in hot pursuit; be hot on the track

dogorywać [do-go-**ri**-vahćh] v. be in death-agony; be dying away; be expiring; be on one's death bed; be breathing one's last; be sinking; be declining (*repeatedly*)

dogorywanie [do-go-ri-**vah**-ńe] n. decline; dying breath; agony

dogorzeć [do-**go**-zhećh] v. die out

dogotować [do-go-**to**-vahćh] v. cook thoroughly; boil thoroughly; cook some more; boil some more

dogotować się [do-go-**to**-vahćh śhan] v. become cooked thoroughly; be boiled thoroughly; be cooked some more; be boiled some more; be almost ready

dogotowanie [do-go-to-**vah**-ńe] n. the finishing of cooking
na dogotowaniu [nah do-go-to-**vah**-ńoo] exp.: in a moment before the cooking is finished

dogotowywacz [do-go-to-**vi**-vahch] m. pressure cooker for keeping food hot

dogotowywać [do-go-to-**vi**-vahćh] v. cook thoroughly; boil thoroughly; cook some more; boil some more (*repeatedly*)

dogotowywać się [do-go-to-vi-vahćh śhan] v. become cooked thoroughly; be boiled thoroughly; be cooked some more; be boiled some more; be almost ready (*repeatedly*)
dograbiać [do-grah-byahćh] v. finish the raking; rake up all that is to be raked; rake up to (a spot, etc.) (*repeatedly*)
dograbić [do-grah-beećh] v. finish the raking; rake up all that is to be raked; rake up to (a spot, etc.)
dograć [do-grahćh] v. finish a game; play to the end; play off
dogrywać [do-gri-vahćh] v. finish a game; play to the end; play off (*repeatedly*)
dogrywka [do-grif-kah] f. play-off
dogryzać [do-gri-zahćh] v. vex; sting; tease; nettle; finish munching; finish gnawing; disturb; gall; molest; worry; be painful to (*repeatedly*)
dogryzanie [do-gri-zah-ńe] n. jeers; gibes; jibes
dogryźć [do-griśhćh] v. vex; sting; tease; nettle; finish munching; finish gnawing; disturb; gall; molest; worry; be painful to
dogrzać [do-gzhahćh] v. warm additionally; heat up; scorch; warm up some more
dogrzać się [do-gzhahćh śhan] v. warm oneself up
dogrzebać się [do-gzhe-bahćh śhan] v. burrow (down to); dig out; rummage up
dogrzewać [do-gzhe-vahćh] v. warm additionally; heat up; scorch; warm up some more (*repeatedly*)
słońce dogrzewa [swoń-tse do-gzhe-vah] exp.: the sun is scorching
dogrzewać się [do-gzhe-vahćh śhan] v. warm oneself up (*repeatedly*)
dogrzewanie [do-gzhe-vah-ńe] n. warming additionally
dohodować [do-kho-do-vahćh] v. bring the animal husbandry up to a certain point
dohodować się [do-kho-do-vahćh śhan] v. reap (from one's orchard, etc.)
doholować [do-kho-lo-vahćh] v. tow in (a barge, etc.); bring (a drunk, etc.) to a destination
doholowywać [do-kho-lo-vi-vahćh] v. tow in (a barge, etc.); bring (a drunk, etc.) to a destination (*repeatedly*)
doić [do-eećh] v. milk; fleece; slang: bib; suck (one's pipe, etc.) (mob jargon) (*repeatedly*)
doić się [do-eećh śhan] v. yield milk (*repeatedly*)
doigrać się [do-ee-grahćh śhan] v. bring misfortune to oneself by one's own recklessness
doigrasz się [do-ee-grahsh śhan] exp.: you will be sorry; you will regret it
doigranie się [do-ee-grah-ńe śhan] n. bringing misfortune to oneself by one's own recklessness
doinformować [do-een-for-mo-vahćh] v. give additional information
doinformować się [do-een-for-mo-vahćh śhan] v. obtain additional information
doinformowywać [do-een-for-mo-vi-vahćh] v. give additional information (*repeatedly*)
doinformowywać się [do-een-for-mo-vi-vahćh śhan] v. obtain additional information (*repeatedly*)
doinwestować [do-een-ve-sto-vahćh] v. invest additionally
doinwestowywać [do-een-ve-sto-vi-vahćh] v. invest additionally (*repeatedly*)
dojadać [do-yah-dahćh] v. eat up (the rest); finish eating; finish up (a plate, etc.); eat additionally; cause pain; disturb; molest; worry; get on (somebody's, etc.) nerves (*repeatedly*)
nie dojadać [ńe do-yah-dahćh] exp.: to hunger; to starve; not to eat enough
dojadanie [do-yah-dah-ńe] n. finishing up (a plate, etc.); eating additionally; causing pain; disturbing; molesting
dojarka [do-yahr-kah] f. milk maid;

milking machine
dojarz [**do**-yahsh] m. dairyman; operator of milking machine
dojazd [**do**-yahst] m. access; drive; approach; avenue; be coming; means of transport; journey
dojazdowy [do-yah-**zdo**-vi] adj.m. of access; of approach
dojąć [**do**-yownćh] v. cause pain; torment; pinch; gripe; sting; nettle
dojechać [do-**ye**-khahćh] v. reach; get to; arrive; approach; pull in; bang; hit; give a blow; jeer; peck
dojechanie [do-ye-**khah**-ńe] n. arrival at; pulling in; giving a blow
dojenie [do-**ye**-ńe] n. milking
dojeść [**do**-yeśhćh] v. finish eating; eat up the rest
nie dojeść [ńe **do**-yeśhćh] exp.: not to eat up one's fill
dojeżdżacz [do-**yezh**-dzhahch] m. mounted hunter
dojeżdżać [do-**yezh**-dzhahćh] v. commute; be coming; pull in; give a blow; hit; bang; jeer; molest (*repeatedly*)
dojeżdżający [do-yezh-dzhah-**yown**-tsi] adj.m. non-resident; commuting person
dojeżdżanie [do-yezh-**dzhah**-ńe] n. arrival at; commuting; jeering
dojmować [doy-**mo**-vahćh] v. torment; pinch; gripe; sting; nettle (*repeatedly*)
dojmująco [doy-moo-**yown**-tso] adv. acutely; piercingly; sharply; keenly
dojmujący [doy-moo-**yown**-tsi] adj.m. acute; piercing; sharp; keen; tormenting; stinging
dojna [**doy**-nah] f. milking cow; milking female
dojna krowa [**doy**-nah **kro**-vah] exp.: milch cow; milking cow
dojnica [doy-**ńee**-tsah] f. milk pail
dojny [**doy**-ni] adj.m. milking (machine, apparatus, etc.)
dojrzale [doy-**zhah**-le] adv. ripely; maturely
dojrzałość [doy-**zhah**-wośhćh] f. maturity; ripeness; mellowness; puberty; manhood; womanhood
egzamin dojrzałości [e-**gzah**-meen doy-zhah-**wo**-śhćhee] exp.: secondary school (leaving) final examination
świadectwo dojrzałości [śhfyah-de-tstfo doy-zhah-**wo**-śhćhee] exp.: secondary school certificate; high school diploma
dojrzały [doy-**zhah**-wi] adj.m. ripe; mellow; mature; adult
dojrzały artysta [doy-**zhah**-wi ahr-**tis**-tah] exp.: full-fledged artist; fully fledged artist
wiek dojrzały [vyek doy-**zhah**-wi] exp.: maturity; the age of understanding; years of discretion
dojrzeć [**doy**-zhećh] v. glimpse; notice; perceive; catch a glimpse; ripen; be ripe; mellow
dojrzenie [doy-**zhe**-ńe] n. a glimpse
dojrzewać [doy-**zhe**-vahćh] v. ripen; grow ripe; mature; reach the age of manhood (womanhood); notice; see despite a difficulty (*repeatedly*)
dojrzewający [doy-zhe-vah-**yown**-tsi] adj.m. pubescent
dojrzewalnia [doy-zhe-**vahl**-ńah] f. ripening chamber
dojrzewanie [doy-zhe-**vah**-ńe] n. ripening; maturation
dojście [**doy**-śhćhe] n. access; (avenue of) approach
dojść [doyśhćh] v. arrive; reach
dojść do skutku [doyśhćh do **skoot**-koo] exp.: to come off (about); to attain results
dojść do sławy [doyśhćh do **swah**-vi] exp.: to win fame
dojść do władzy [doyśhćh do **vwah**-dzi] exp.: to reach power; to arrive at a power
dojść do wniosku [doyśhćh do **vńo**-skoo] exp.: to arrive to (at) a conclusion
dojść w czymś do doskonałości [doyśhćh f chimśh do do-sko-nah-**wo**-śhćhee] exp.: to bring something to perfection
dojść do przekonania [doyśhćh do pshe-ko-**nah**-ńah] exp.: to come to believe; to come to the conviction
dojść do porozumienia [doyśhćh do po-ro-zoo-**mye**-ńah] exp.: to

establish an understanding; to reach an agreement
jak do tego doszło? [yahk do te-go do-shwo] exp.: how did this come about?
dojutrek [do-**yoo**-trek] m. slang: procrastinator; temporizer
dojutrkostwo [do-yootr-**ko**-stfo] n. procrastination; temporizing; putting off
dojutrkowość [do-yootr-**ko**-vośhćh] f. temporariness
dok [dok] m. dock
doki [**do**-kee] pl. dockyard
suchy dok [**soo**-khi dok] exp.: dry dock
wprowadzić statek do doku [fpro-**vah**-dźheećh **stah**-tek do **do**-koo] exp.: to dock a ship
dokańczać [do-**kahń**-chahćh] v. finish up; finish off; complete; conclude; end; do away with (somebody, etc.) (*repeatedly*)
dokarmiać [do-**kahr**-myahćh] v. nourish additionally; finish feeding; give enough food to eat; feed well (*repeatedly*)
dokarmiać się [do-**kahr**-myahćh śhan] v. eat additionally (*repeatedly*)
dokarmianie [do-kahr-**myah**-ńe] n. nourishing additionally
dokarmić [do-**kahr**-meećh] v. nourish additionally; finish feeding; give enough food to eat; feed well
dokarmić się [do-**kahr**-meećh śhan] v. nourish oneself additionally
dokazać [do-**kah**-zahćh] v. prove; achieve; accomplish; do the trick; get by effort
dokazać swego [do-**kah**-zahćh **sfe**-go] exp.: to accomplish one's design; to have one's way; to prove; to carry one's point
dokazywać [do-kah-**zi**-vahćh] v. frolic; gambol; romp and play; sport; skylark (*repeatedly*)
dokazywanie [do-kah-zi-**vah**-ńe] n. frolics; gambols; romps
dokąd [**do**-kownt] adv. where?; till when? whither; where to? how far? till when? how long?
dokąd to potrwa? [do-kownt to **po**-trfah] exp.: how long will this last?
dotąd, dokąd [**do**-townd **do**-kownt] exp.: as long as
dokądkolwiek [do-kownt-**kol**-vyek] pron. wherever; no matter where; as long as
dokądś [**do**-kowntśh] pron. somewhere
dokądże [**do**-kownd-zhe] pron. = emphatic form of: **dokąd**
doker [**do**-ker] m. docker; stevedore; lumper; longshoreman
dokerski [do-**ker**-skee] adj.m. of a docker; docker (crew, etc.)
dokleić [do-**kle**-eećh] v. stick on
doklejać [do-**kle**-yahćh] v. stick on (*repeatedly*)
doklejenie [do-kle-**ye**-ńe] n. sticking on; pasting on
dokładać [do-**kwah**-dahćh] v. add to; throw in; say more; give more (*repeatedly*)
dokładać do interesu [do-**kwah**-dahćh do een-te-re-soo] exp.: to have a losing business
dokładać wszelkich starań [do-**kwah**-dahćh **fshel**-keekh **stah**-rahń] exp.: to do one's best
dokładać się [do-**kwah**-dahćh śhan] v. contribute (to); take pains; show diligence
dokładanie [do-kwah-**dah**-ńe] n. addition
dokładka [do-**kwah**-tkah] f. something thrown into the bargain; an extra; makeweight
na dokładkę [nah do-**kwah**-tkan] adv. furthermore; besides; moreover; on top of it; on top of this; too; into the bargain; to make things worse
dokładnie [do-**kwah**-dńe] adv. exactly; precisely; accurately; rightly; rigorously; thoroughly; carefully; scrupulously; strictly; closely; narrowly; nicely; punctually; faithfully; correctly
dokładnie w tym momencie [do-**kwah**-dńe f tim mo-**men**-ćhe] exp.: at the precise moment; just then
dokładność [do-**kwah**-dnośhćh] f. exactitude; precision; accuracy;

care; strictness; exactness; precision; faithfulness; correctness
z dokładnością do sekundy [z do-kwah-**dno**-śhćhown do se-**koon**-di] exp.: exact to one second
dokładny [dok-**wah**-dni] adj.m. accurate; exact; precise; careful; strict; business-like; searching; punctual; correct; faithful
dokładne badanie [do-**kwah**-dne bah-**dah**-ńe] exp.: close examination
dokłosie [do-**kwo**-śhe] n. stem immediately below ear (of corn, wheat, etc.)
dokolusia [do-ko-**loo**-śhah] adv. diminutive form of: **dokoła**
dokoluśka [do-ko-**loośh**-kah] adv. diminutive form of: **dokoła**
dokolutka [do-ko-**loot**-kah] adv. diminutive form of: **dokoła**
dokoła [do-**ko**-wah] adv. round; round about; all round; right round; all around
dokoła Wojtek [do-**ko**-wah **voy**-tek] exp.: slang: once again from the start; back to square one
dokompletować [do-kom-ple-**to**-vahćh] v. complete (a set, etc.); supply the missing parts
dokompletowywać [do-kom-ple-to-**vi**-vahćh] v. complete (a set, etc.); supply the missing parts (*repeatedly*)
dokomponować [do-kom-po-**no**-vahćh] v. compose (additional parts, etc.)
dokomponować sobie [do-kom-po-**no**-vahćh **so**-bye] exp.: slang: to add (meaning, etc.)
dokomponowywać [do-kom-po-no-**vi**-vahćh] v. compose (additional parts, etc.) (*repeatedly*)
dokonać [do-**ko**-nahćh] v. achieve; accomplish; carry out; fulfil; do; make; execute; commit; bring about; perpetrate; perform
dokonać żywota [do-**ko**-nahćh zhi-**vo**-tah] exp.: to end one's days; to die
dokonać się [do-**ko**-nahćh śhan] v. take place (effect); come off (about); occur; happen; be carried out; be achieved; be brought about; be accomplished
dokonanie [do-ko-**nah**-ńe] n. achievement; fulfillment; accomplishment; execution
dokonanie się [do-ko-**nah**-ńe śhan] n. self-fulfillment
dokonaność [do-ko-**nah**-nośhćh] f. accomplishing (of an activity) (*not repeatedly*)
dokonany [do-ko-**nah**-ni] adj.m. accomplished; perfect (gram.)
fakt dokonany [fahkt do-ko-**nah**-ni] exp.: an actual event
dokonywać [do-ko-**ni**-vahćh] v. achieve; accomplish; carry out; fulfil; do; make; execute; commit; bring about; perpetrate; perform (*repeatedly*)
dokonywać się [do-ko-**ni**-vahćh śhan] v. take place (effect); come off (about); occur; happen; be carried out; be achieved; be brought about; be accomplished (*repeatedly*)
dokończać [do-**koń**-chahćh] v. finish up (off); conclude; complete; end; do away with (*repeatedly*)
dokończenie [do-koń-**che**-ńe] n. conclusion; completion; end
dokończyć [do-**koń**-chićh] v. finish up (off); conclude; complete; end; do away with
dokooptować [do-ko-o-**pto**-vahćh] v. co-opt
dokooptowanie [do-ko-o-pto-**vah**-ńe] n. co-option
dokopać [do-**ko**-pahćh] v. finish digging; dig out
dokopać się [do-**ko**-pahćh śhan] v. dig down to (ore, etc.)
dokopywać [do-ko-**pi**-vahćh] v. finish digging; dig out (*repeatedly*)
dokopywać się [do-ko-**pi**-vahćh śhan] v. dig down to (ore, etc.) (*repeatedly*)
dokować [do-**ko**-vahćh] v. dock (a ship, etc.)
dokowanie [do-ko-**vah**-ńe] n. docking (a ship, etc.)
dokrajać [do-**krah**-yahćh] v. cut some more (bread, etc.)
dokrajanie [do-krah-**yah**-ńe] n.

cutting some more (bread, etc.)
dokrasić [do-**krah**-śheećh] v. season somewhat more; add more (seasoning, fat, gravy, etc.) to a dish
dokraszenie [do-krah-**she**-ńe] n. seasoning somewhat more
dokraszać [do-**krah**-shahćh] v. season somewhat more; add more (seasoning, fat, gravy, etc.) to a dish (*repeatedly*)
dokrawać [do-**krah**-vahćh] v. cut some more (bread, etc.) (*repeatedly*)
dokrewny [do-**kre**-vni] adj.m. endocrine (gland, etc.)
dokręcać [do-**kran**-tsahćh] v. tighten; screw tight; turn off (*repeatedly*)
dokręcać się [do-**kran**-tsahćh śhan] v. self-tighten; screw (itself) tight; turn (itself) off (*repeatedly*)
dokręcić [do-**kran**-ćheećh] v. tighten; screw tight; turn off
dokręcić się [do-**kran**-ćheećh śhan] v. self-tighten; screw (itself) tight; turn (itself) off
dokręt [**do**-krant] m. final tightening during weaving
dokrętka [do-**kran**-tkah] f. nut; additional camera work in film making
dokroić [do-**kro**-eećh] v. cut some more (bread, etc.)
dokształcać [do-**kshtahw**-tsahćh] v. impart further instruction; give additional training (*repeatedly*)
dokształcać się [do-**kshtahw**-tsahćh śhan] v. acquire (receive) further instruction (*repeatedly*)
dokształcanie [do-kshtahw-**tsah**-ńe] n. additional schooling; additional training
dokształcanie się [do-kshtahw-**tsah**-ńe śhan] n. self-improvement
doktor [**do**-ktor] m. doctor; physician
doktorancki [do-kto-**rahn**-tskee] adj.m. doctoral (studies, etc.)
doktorant [do-**kto**-rahnt] m. doctoral student; postgraduate student; candidate for doctor's degree
doktorat [do-**kto**-raht] m. doctorate
zrobić doktorat [**zro**-beećh do-**kto**-raht] exp.: to obtain the doctor's degree; to obtain one's (Ph.D., Sc.D. etc.) degree
doktorka [do-**ktor**-kah] f. colloq: (female) doctor; physician
doktorostwo [do-kto-**ros**-tfo] n. doctor and his wife
doktorowa [do-kto-**ro**-vah] f. doctor's wife
doktorówna [do-kto-**roov**-nah] f. doctor's daughter
doktorski [do-**ktor**-skee] adj.m. doctor's; doctoral; Ph D's
praca doktorska [**prah**-tsah do-**ktor**-skah] exp.: doctor's thesis
doktoryzacja [do-kto-ri-**zah**-tsyah] f. the process of getting doctor's degree (Ph D dissertation)
doktoryzować [do-kto-ri-**zo**-vahćh] v. confer a doctor's degree
doktoryzować się [do-kto-ri-**zo**-vahćh śhan] v. take one's doctor's degree (*repeatedly*)
doktoryzowanie [do-kto-ri-zo-**vah**-ńe] n. graduation with doctor's degree
doktoryzowanie się [do-kto-ri-zo-**vah**-ńe śhan] n. obtaining of doctor's degree
doktór [**do**-ktoor] m. doctor; physician; see: **doktor**
doktryna [dok-**tri**-nah] f. doctrine; principles; tenet; tenets
doktrynalnie [dok-tri-**nahl**-ńe] adv. doctrinally
doktrynalny [dok-tri-**nahl**-ni] adj.m. doctrinal
doktryner [dok-**tri**-ner] m. doctrinaire
doktrynerski [dok-tri-**ner**-skee] adj.m. doctrinaire; doctrinarian
doktrynersko [dok-tri-**ner**-sko] adv. like a doctrinaire; doctrinally
doktrynerstwo [dok-tri-**ner**-stfo] n. doctrinairism; doctrinarianism
dokuczać [do-**koo**-chahćh] v. vex; annoy; nag; bully; sting; trouble; spite; worry; torment; be a nuisance; bother; pinch; be painful; prey on another's mind; pester; harass; become a bore (*repeatedly*)
dokuczanie [do-koo-**chah**-ńe] n. vexation (*repeated*)

dokuczenie [do-koo-che-ńe] n. vexation; irritation; troubling
dokuczliwie [do-koo-chlee-vye] adv. vexatiously; annoyingly; grievously; spitefully; tryingly; nastily; troublesomely; painfully
dokuczliwość [do-koo-chlee-vośhćh] f. vexatiousness; spite; spitefulness; troublesomeness
dokuczliwy [do-koo-chlee-vi] adj.m. vexing; annoying; grievous; vexatious; trying; mischievous; troublesome; aggravating; nasty; nagging; bad (headache, etc.) **rzecz dokuczliwa** [zhech do-koo-chlee-vah] exp.: nuisance
dokuczyć [do-koo-chićh] v. vex; annoy; nag; bully; sting; trouble; spite; worry; torment; be a nuisance; bother; pinch; be painful; prey on another's mind; pester; harass; become a bore
dokuć [do-koośh] v. finish hammering; finish shoeing (a horse); finish forging; forge (additional parts, etc.)
dokument [do-koo-ment] m. document; record; deed; identity card; passport; instrument; act **dokument urzędowo poświadczony** [do-koo-ment oo-zhan-do-vo po-śhfyaht-cho-ni] exp.: legalized deed (document) **dokumenty tożsamości** [do-koo-men-ti tosh-sah-mo-śhćhee] exp.: (one's) papers
dokumentacja [do-koo-men-tah-tsyah] f. records; working plans; working drawings; specifications
dokumentacyjny [do-koo-men-tah-tsiy-ni] adj.m. of the records; relative to records; documental
dokumentalista [do-koo-men-tah-lee-stah] m. documentarist
dokumentalistyka [do-koo-men-tah-lees-ti-kah] f. making of documentary films
dokumentalizm [do-koo-men-tah-leezm] m. documental value
dokumentalnie [do-koo-men-tahl-ńe] adv. documentarily
dokumentalność [do-koo-men-tahl-nośhćh] f. documental nature
dokumentalny [do-koo-men-tahl-ni] adj.m. documental
dokumentarnie [do-koo-men-tahr-ńe] adv. documentarily
dokumentarność [do-koo-men-tahr-nośhćh] f. documentary character
dokumentarny [do-koo-men-tahr-ni] adj.m. documentary
dokumentaryzm [do-koo-men-tah-rizm] m. documental value (of a flim, etc.); documentary work
dokumentarzysta [do-koo-men-tah-zhis-tah] m. documentarian; documentarist
dokumentnie [do-koo-men-tńe] adv. completely; thoroughly; utterly; in detail
dokumentny [do-koo-men-tni] adj.m. complete; thorough; utter; detailed
dokumentować [do-koo-men-to-vahćh] v. document; attest; evidence; testify to; be evidence of; justify (a claim, etc.) (*repeatedly*)
dokumentowanie [do-koo-men-to-vah-ńe] n. attestation; evidence; testification
dokumentowy [do-koo-men-to-vi] adj.m. documental
dokupić [do-koo-peećh] v. purchase more; buy more; acquire more
dokupić się [do-koo-peećh śhan] v. purchase; buy; acquire; obtain
dokupować [do-koo-po-vahćh] v. purchase more; buy more; acquire more (*repeatedly*)
dokupować się [do-koo-po-vahćh śhan] v. purchase; buy; acquire; obtain (a share) (*repeatedly*)
do kupy [do koo-pi] exp.: together
dokupywać [do-koo-pi-vahćh] v. purchase more; buy more; acquire more (*repeatedly*)
dokupywać się [do-koo-pi-vahćh śhan] v. purchase; buy; acquire; obtain (*repeatedly*)
dokuwać [do-koo-vahćh] v. finish hammering; finish shoeing (a horse); finish forging (*repeatedly*)
dokwasić [do-kfah-śheećh] v. make more acid; finish fermenting
dokwasić się [do-kfah-śheećh śhan] v. become more acid;

become fully fermented
dokwaszać [do-**kfah**-shahćh] v. make more acid; finish fermenting (*repeatedly*)
dokwaszać się [do-**kfah**-shahćh śhan] v. become more acid; become fully fermented (*repeatedly*)
dokwaterować [do-kfah-te-**ro**-vahćh] v. officially assign living quarters to a person in someone else's residence
dokwaterować się [do-kfah-te-**ro**-vahćh śhan] v. move into someone else's residence as an additional tenant (occupant)
dokwitać [do-**kfee**-tahćh] v. blossom out (*repeatedly*)
dokwitanie [do-kfee-**tah**-ńe] n. blossoming out
dokwitnąć [do-**kfeet**-nownćh] v. blossom out
dola [**do**-lah] f. fortune; lot; share; portion; destiny
w doli i niedoli [v **do**-lee ee ńe-do-lee] exp.: through thick and thin; through foul and fair; in weal and woe
dolać [**do**-lahćh] v. pour out more; replenish; refill; fill another glass
dolać oliwy do ognia [**do**-lahćh o-**lee**-vi do **o**-gńah] exp.: to add oil to fire; to fan the flame
dolanie [do-**lah**-ńe] n. pouring out more; replenishing
dolar [**do**-lahr] m. dollar; slang: green back; buck
dolarowy [do-lah-**ro**-vi] adj.m. of the dollar; dollar (note, etc.)
dolarówka [do-lah-**roof**-kah] f. dollar note; dollar bill
dolatywać [do-lah-**ti**-vahćh] v. come flying; reach by flying; be heard; be felt; hit (the ground); reach up to (*repeatedly*)
dolatuje zapach [do-lah-**too**-ye **zah**-pahkh] exp.: the smell makes itself noticeable (felt)
dolatywanie [do-lah-ti-**vah**-ńe] n. reaching (by flying)
dolce [**dol**-tse] pl. slang: dollars
dolecieć [do-**le**-ćhećh] v. come flying; reach by flying; be heard; be felt; hit (the ground); reach up to; reach as far as
doleczać [do-**le**-chahćh] v. complete curing (*repeatedly*)
doleczać się [do-**le**-chahćh śhan] v. complete one's cure (*repeatedly*)
doleczyć [do-**le**-chićh] v. complete curing
doleczyć się [do-**le**-chićh śhan] v. complete one's cure
dolegać [do-**le**-gahćh] v. pain; ail; trouble; hurt; be painful; worry; distress (*repeatedly*)
co ci dolega? [tso ćhee do-**le**-gah] exp.: what's the matter with you?; what ails you? what bothers you?
dolega mi...[do-**le**-gah mee] exp.: I am troubled with...
nic mi nie dolega [ńeets mee ńe do-**le**-gah] exp.: nothing is the matter with me; I am O.K.
doleganie [do-le-**gah**-ńe] n. pain; ache; trouble
dolegiwać [do-le-**gee**-vahćh] v. stay in bed till (late, morning, etc.] (*repeatedly*)
dolegliwie [do-le-**glee**-vye] adv. painfully; acutely
dolegliwość [do-le-**glee**-vośhćh] f. suffering; pain; ailment; disease; indisposition; complaint; disorder; trouble; distemper; malady; worry; concern; affliction; distress
dolegliwy [do-le-**glee**-vi] adj.m. painful; acute
dolepiać [do-**le**-pyahćh] v. stick on more; finish sticking on (*repeatedly*)
dolepić [do-**le**-peećh] v. stick on more; finish sticking on
doleryt [do-**le**-rit] m. dolerite
dolesiać [do-**le**-śhahćh] v. extend the afforestation (*repeatedly*)
dolesić [do-**le**-śheećh] v. extend the afforestation
dolewać [do-**le**-vahćh] v. pour additionally; pour more (*repeatedly*)
dolewać sobie herbaty [do-**le**-vahćh **so**-bye kher-**bah**-ti] exp.: to help oneself to more tea
dolewanie [do-le-**vah**-ńe] n. pouring additionally

dolewka [do-lef-kah] f. additional liquid portion (of soup, beer, etc.)
dolezienie [do-le-źhe-ńe] n. crawling up to
doleźć [do-leśhćh] v. drag oneself to; trudge up to; crawl up to
doleżeć [do-le-zhećh] v. stay in bed till (late, morning, etc.); lay down till a certain time
dolędźwiowo [do-landźh-vyo-vo] adv. into lumbar area
dolędźwiowy [do-landźh-vyo-vi] adj.m. lumbar (pain, etc.)
dolichocefal [do-lee-kho-tse-fahl] m. dolichocephalic man
dolichocefalia [do-lee-kho-tse-fah-lyah] f. dolichocephaly; dolichocephalism
dolicytować [do-lee-tsi-to-vahćh] v. push the bidding; carry on the bidding; go on bidding (to a certain figure)
dolicytować się [do-lee-tsi-to-vahćh śhan] v. push the bidding to a successful conclusion
doliczać [do-lee-chahćh] v. count up; add; charge more; reckon up to; count to (a certain figure); make an additional charge (*repeatedly*)
doliczać się [do-lee-chahćh śhan] v. find out by counting; reckon up to; count to (a certain figure) (*repeatedly*)
doliczenie [do-lee-che-ńe] n. additional charge; addition to a bill
doliczyć [do-lee-chićh] v. count up; add; charge more; reckon up to; count to (a certain figure); make an additional charge; find out by counting; reckon up to; count up to (a certain figure)
dolina [do-lee-nah] f. valley; dale; glen; coomb; mob slang: pocket
doliniarstwo [do-lee-ńahr-stfo] n. occupation of a pickpocket
doliniarz [do-lee-ńahsh] m. slang: pickpocket (mob jargon)
dolinka [do-lee-nkah] f. (small, nice) valley; dale; glen; coomb
dolinny [do-leen-ni] adj.m. of the valley; valley (vegetation, etc.)
dolinowy [do-lee-no-vi] adj.m. of the valley; valley (glacial, etc.)
dolman [dol-mahn] m. Turkish silk coat; Hungarian national costume
dolmen [dol-men] m. dolmen
dolnoniemiecki [dol-no-ńe-mye-tskee] adj.m. Low-German
dolnopłat [dol-no-pwaht] m. low-wing monoplane (or glider)
dolnopłatowiec [dol-no-pwah-to-vyets] m. low-wing monoplane
dolnoreglowy [dol-no-reg-lo-vi] adj.m. of subalpine forest; prealpine
dolnośląski [dol-no-śhlown-skee] adj.m. of Lower-Silesia; Lower-Silesian
dolnozaworowy [dol-no-zah-vo-ro-vi] adj.m. side valve (engine)
dolny [dol-ni] adj.m. lower; bottom (shelf, etc.); under (part, etc.)
dolomit [do-lo-meet] m. dolomite
dolomitowy [do-lo-mee-to-vi] adj.m. dolomitic
dolomitówka [do-lo-mee-toof-kah] f. brick made of dolomite
dolosować [do-lo-so-vahćh] v. win additionally in a lottery; draw lots additionally
dolot [do-lot] m. last stage of a flight; inflow (of water, etc.)
dolutować [do-loo-to-vahćh] v. finish soldering; solder on (a piece of pipe, etc.)
dolutowywać [do-loo-to-vi-vahćh] v. finish soldering; solder on (a piece of pipe, etc.) (*repeatedly*)
doładować [do-wah-do-vahćh] v. finish loading; supplement the loading; boost (a battery)
doładowywać [do-wah-do-vi-vahćh] v. finish loading; supplement the loading; boost (a battery) (*repeatedly*)
dołączać [do-wown-chahćh] v. add; join; enclose; affix; tack on; annex (*repeatedly*)
dołączać się [do-wown-chahćh śhan] v. join; accede; crop up; arise; supervene (*repeatedly*)
dołączenie [do-wown-che-ńe] n. addition
dołączyć [do-wown-chićh] v. add; join; enclose; affix; tack on; annex

dołączyć się [do-**wown**-chićh śhan] v. join; accede; crop up; arise; supervene
dołeczek [do-**we**-chek] m. (diminutive) dimple; pit
dołek [**do**-wek] m. dimple; pit; hollow; hole (in the ground); depression; dale; pock-mark; fossa; psychological crisis
być w dołku [bićh v **dow**-koo] exp.: to be depressed; to be in serious trouble
wyjść z dołka [viyśhćh z **dow**-kah] exp.: to recover; to get out of crisis
dołem [**do**-wem] adv. at the bottom; at the base; below; down below
dołgać [**do**-wgahćh] v. add another lie; add more lies
dołkowaty [dow-ko-**vah**-ti] adj.m. pitted
dołować [do-**wo**-vahćh] v. pit (vegetables); earth (shrubs, etc.); shoot too low (*repeatedly*)
dołowanie [do-wo-**vah**-ńe] n. pitting (of vegetables); earthing (of shrubs, etc.); shooting too low
dołowy [do-**wo**-vi] adj.m. located underground; located under deck
dołownik [do-**wo**-vńeek] m. potato planting machine
dołożyć [do-**wo**-zhićh] v. add to; throw in; say more; give more
dołożyć się [do-**wo**-zhićh śhan] v. contribute (to); take pains; show diligence
dom [dom] m. house; home; cottage; residence; living quarters; household; housekeeping; dynasty
czuć się jak u siebie w domu [chooćh śhan yahk oo **śhe**-bye v **do**-moo] exp.: to feel at home
do domu [do **do**-moo] exp.: home
poza domem [po-zah **do**-mem] exp.: abroad; away from home; out of doors
dom handlowy [dom khahn-**dlo**-vi] exp.: firm; business enterprise; business concern
w domu [v **do**-moo] exp.: at home
domacać [do-**mah**-tsahćh] v. find by touch; feel by touch
domacać się [do-**mah**-tsahćh śhan] v. find by touch; feel by touch
domaczać [do-**mah**-chahćh] v. soak to a sufficient degree (*repeatedly*)
domaciczny [do-mah-**ćhee**-chni] adj.m. intrauterine
domagać się [do-**mah**-gahćh śhan] v. demand; claim; insist; cry for; call for; stick out for (*repeatedly*)
domaganie się [do-mah-**gah**-ńe śhan] n. demand for; call for; insistence on
domalować [do-mah-**lo**-vahćh] v. finish painting; complete a painting; add to a painting
domalowywać [do-mah-lo-**vi**-vahćh] v. finish painting; complete a painting; add to a painting (*repeatedly*)
domator [do-**mah**-tor] m. stay-at-home; home-body
domatorka [do-mah-**tor**-kah] f. (female) stay-at-home; home-body
domatorski [do-mah-**tor**-skee] adj. domestic; fond of home-life
domatorstwo [do-mah-**tor**-stfo] n. domesticity; fondness of home-life; home-keeping
domawiać [do-**mah**-vyahćh] v. finish saying; break off talking; leave unsaid; scoff at; jibe at (*repeatedly*)
domawiać się [do-**mah**-vyahćh śhan] v. hint at (*repeatedly*)
domawianie się [do-mah-**vyah**-ńe śhan] v. hinting at; asking for (something)
domeykit [do-**mey**-keet] m. domeykite (mineral)
domek [**do**-mek] m. little house; cottage; maisonette
domek z kart [**do**-mek s kahrt] exp.: house of cards
domeldować [do-mel-**do**-vahćh] v. register additional (person)
domeldować się [do-mel-**do**-vahćh śhan] v. register oneself in addition to others
domeldowywać [do-mel-do-**vi**-vahćh] v. register additional (person) (*repeatedly*)
domeldowywać się [do-mel-do-**vi**-vahćh śhan] v. register oneself in addition to others (*repeatedly*)

domena [do-**me**-nah] f. domain; realm; sphere; demesne; estate
domestykacja [do-me-sti-**kah**-tsyah] f. domestication
domestykacyjny [do-mes-ti-kah-**tsiy**-ni] adj.m. of domestication
domestykalny [do-mes-ti-**kahl**-ni] adj.m. domestic (policy, etc.)
domęczać [do-**man**-chahćh] v. harass to death; get through a tedious (book; work, etc.) (*repeatedly*)
domęczyć [do-**man**-chićh] v. harass to death; get through a tedious (book; work, etc.)
domiar [**do**-myahr] m. additional assessment; surtax; surcharge; adv.: on top of it all; in addition; to make things worse
na domiar [nah **do**-myahr] adv. in addition; on top (of it, etc.)
domiarkować się [do-myahr-**ko**-vahćh śhan] v. guess; notice
domicyl [do-**mee**-tsil] m. domicile
domicylować [do-mee-tsi-**lo**-vahćh] v. domicile (a bill of exchange)
domierzać [do-**mye**-zhahćh] v. fill the measure; assess additionally; finish measuring; measure out; add more tax (*repeatedly*)
domierzanie [do-mye-**zhah**-ńe] n. assessing additionally; measuring out; adding more tax
domierzyć [do-**mye**-zhićh] v. fill the measure; assess additionally; finish measuring; measure out; add more tax
domieszać [do-**mye**-shahćh] v. admix; add (to a mixture)
domieszać się [do-**mye**-shahćh śhan] v. mix; be joined
domieszczać [do-**mye**-shchahćh] v. add (*repeatedly*)
domieszka [do-**myesh**-kah] f. admixture; addition; dash; touch; tincture
bez domieszki [bez do-**myesh**-kee] exp.: pure; unmingled; unmixed; unadulterated
domieszkać [do-**mye**-shkahćh] v. live (in a lodging till a certain date); stay in a lodging (till certain date)
domieszkowy [do-mye-**shko**-vi] adj.m. of an admixture
domieścić [do-**mye**-śhćheećh] v. add; place more
domięśniowo [do-myan-**śhńo**-vo] adv. intramuscularly
domięśniowy [do-myan-**śhńo**-vi] adj.m. intramuscular
dominacja [do-mee-**nah**-tsyah] f. domination; rule or control by superior power
dominanta [do-mee-**nahn**-tah] f. dominant recurring theme; dominant specie; dominant feature; main characteristic
dominantowy [do-mee-nahn-**to**-vi] adj.m. dominant (sound, etc.)
dominant [do-**mee**-nahnt] m. dominant rule (in Rome)
dominialny [do-mee-**ńyahl**-ni] adj.m. manorial; domanial
dominikanin [do-mee-ńee-**kah**-ńeen] m. Dominican friar
dominikanka [do-mee-ńee-**kahn**-kah] f. Dominican nun
dominikański [do-mee-ńee-**kahń**-skee] adj.m. Dominican
dominium [do-**mee**-ńyoom] n. dominion
domino [do-**mee**-no] n. domino; dominoes (pl.)
dominować [do-mee-**no**-vahćh] v. prevail; predominate; preponderate; dominate; be predominant; prevail; pervade; command (a region, etc.) (*repeatedly*)
dominowanie [do-mee-no-**vah**-ńe] n. domination; predomination
dominowy [do-mee-**no**-vi] adj.m. of domino; of dominoes
dominujący [do-mee-noo-**yown**-tsi] adj.m. dominant; predominant; prevailing
domknąć [**dom**-knownćh] v. push to slightly open (door, window, etc.); close (door, window, etc.) left ajar; see: **domykać**
domniemać się [do-**mńe**-mahćh śhan] v. guess; conjecture; supposition
domniemanie [do-mńe-**mah**-ńe] n. guess; conjecture; supposition
domniemany [do-mńe-**mah**-ni] adj.m. supposed; assumed;

alleged; presumed
domniemywać się [do-mńe-**mi**-vahćh śh<u>an</u>] v. guess; conjecture; supposition (*repeatedly*)
domoczyć [do-**mo**-chićh] v. soak to a sufficient degree
domofon [do-**mo**-fon] m. house-intercom
domokrąstwo [do-mo-**kr<u>owns</u>**-tfo] n. pedlary; the hawking of goods; the peddling of goods
domokrążca [do-mo-**kr<u>own</u>**-shtsah] m. peddlar; hawker; an itinerant dealer; cadger
domokrążny [do-mo-**kr<u>own</u>**-zhni] adj.m. peddlar's; hawker's
domordować [do-mor-**do**-vahćh] v. torture to death; kill off; finish killing
domorodny [do-mo-**ro**-dni] adj.m. home-grown; home-bred; home-made; self-taught
domorosły [do-mo-**ro**-swi] adj.m. home-grown; home-bred; home-made; self-taught
domostwo [do-**mos**-tfo] n. household; homestead; farmstead; family's home
domownik [do-**mo**-vńeek] m. inmate; household member
domownicy [do-mo-**vńee**-tsi] pl. the household
domowy [do-**mo**-vi] adj.m. domestic; homemade; home-baked; private
gospodarstwo domowe [gos-po-**dahr**-stfo do-**mo**-ve] exp.: housekeeping
po domowemu [po do-mo-**ve**-moo] adv. informally; unceremoniously
ubrany po domowemu [oo-**brah**-ni po do-mo-**ve**-moo] exp.: wearing house clothes
wojna domowa [**voy**-nah do-**mo**-vah] exp.: civil war
domówić [do-**moo**-veećh] v. finish saying; scoff; jibe at
nie domówić [ńe do-**moo**-veećh] exp.: to leave unsaid; break off (a sentence)
domówić się [do-**moo**-veećh śh<u>an</u>] v. hint at; ask indirectly
domówienie [do-moo-**vye**-ńe] n. completing (a statement, etc.)
domurować [do-moo-**ro**-vahćh] v. finish the bricklaying; add to (a house, etc.]
domurowywać [do-moo-ro-**vi**-vahćh] v. finish the bricklaying; add to (a house, etc.] (*repeatedly*)
domycie [do-**mi**-ćhe] n. washing clean
domyć [**do**-mićh] v. wash clean
domyć się [**do**-mićh śh<u>an</u>] v. wash oneself clean
domykać [do-**mi**-kahćh] v. shut; close; push to close (a door, window, etc. left ajar) (*repeatedly*)
drzwi się nie domykają [dzhvee śh<u>an</u> ńe do-mi-**kah**-y<u>own</u>] exp.: the door won't shut
domykanie [do-mi-**kah**-ńe] n. pushing to close (a door, etc.)
domysł [**do**-misw] m. guess; conjecture; speculation; surmise; guess-work; supposition
to tylko domysł [to til-ko **do**-misw] exp.: it's just a guess
domyślać [do-**mi**-śhlahćh] v. think through (*repeatedly*)
domyślać się [do-**mi**-śhlahćh śh<u>an</u>] v. conjecture; surmise; guess; assume; presume; suspect (*repeatedly*)
kazać się domyślać [**kah**-zahćh śh<u>an</u> do-**mi**-śhlahćh] exp.: to imply
domyśleć [do-**mi**-śhlećh] v. think through
domyślić [do-mi-śhleećh] v. think through
domyślić się [do-**mi**-śhleećh śh<u>an</u>] v. conjecture; surmise; guess; assume; presume; suspect
domyślnie [do-**mi**-śhlńe] adv. significantly; expressively; understandingly
domyślnik [do-mi-śhlńeek] m. implication; insinuation; hint; double meaning
domyślność [do-mi-śhlnośhćh] f. quickness to understand; quick-wittedness
domyślny [do-**mi**-śhlni] adj.m. quick to understand; quick-witted;

alleged; inferred; implied
domywać [do-mi-vahćh] v. wash clean (*repeatedly*)
domywać się [do-mi-vahćh śhan] v. wash oneself clean (*repeatedly*)
donacja [do-nah-tsyah] f. donation
do naga [do nah-gah] exp.: to the skin; nakedly
donająć [do-nah-yownćh] v. hire additionally; engage additionally
donajęcie [do-nah-yan-ćhe] n. hiring additionally; engaging additionally
donajmować [do-nahy-mo-vahćh] v. hire additionally; engage additionally (*repeatedly*)
donaszać [do-nah-shahćh] v. bring; carry; deliver; inform (against); notify; denounce; wear out clothes (*repeatedly*)
donatariusz [do-nah-tah-ryoosh] m. donatory
donator [do-nah-tor] m. donor
donękać [do-nan-kahćh] v. oppress to the utmost limit
donica [do-ńee-tsah] f. (large) plant-pot; flower-pot
donicowaty [do-ńee-tso-vah-ti] adj.m. bowl-shaped; bowl-like
donicowy [do-ńee-tso-vi] adj.m. bowl-shaped; of a bowl
doniczka [do-ńee-chkah] f. plant-pot; flower-pot
doniczkowiec [do-ńee-chko-vyets] m. Enchytraeus worm
doniczkowce [do-ńee-chko-ftse] pl. the Enchytraeidae family of worms (food of aquarium fishes)
doniczkowy [do-ńee-chko-vi] adj.m. potted (plant, culture, etc.)
do niczego [do ńee-che-go] adj. useless; no good; good for nothing; fit for nothing; adv. without anything on; with nothing on; penniless
do niedawna [do ńe-dah-vnah] adv. till recently; until recently
do niepoznaki [do ńe-po-znah-kee] adv. unrecognizably; beyond recognition
do niepoznania [do ńe-po-znah-ńah] adv. unrecognizably; beyond recognition
doniesienie [do-ńe-śhe-ńe] m. denunciation; information (against); intelligence; report; news
doniesienie się [do-ńe-śhe-ńe śhan] n. carrying of sound; reaching (somebody's ears, etc.)
donieść [do-ńeśhćh] v. communicate; report; announce; denounce; inform (against); advise; bring; carry; deliver (to a destination); deliver additional (items, etc.); reach; notify
donieść się [do-ńeśhćh śhan] v. reach (somebody's ears, etc.); be heard (at a distance, etc.)
donikąd [do-ńee-kownt] adv. nowhere
doniosłość [do-ńo-swośhćh] f. importance; weightiness; significance
doniosły [do-ńo-swi] adj.m. significant; far reaching; weighty; grave; monumental; important
doniszczać [do-ńee-shchahćh] v. complete the destruction; wear out of use (*repeatedly*)
doniszczyć [do-ńee-shchićh] v. complete the destruction; wear out of use
donkiszocki [don-kee-sho-tskee] adj.m. quixotic
donkiszot [don-kee-shot] m. quixote; knight-errant; Don Quixote
donkiszoteria [don-kee-sho-te-ryah] f. quixotry; errantry; quixotism
donkiszotowski [don-kee-sho-tof-skee] adj.m. quixotic; quixotical
donkiszotyzm [don-kee-sho-tizm] m. quixotism; quixotry
donna [don-nah] f. girl; young lady; lady-love
donos [do-nos] m. information (against somebody, etc.); denunciation
donosiciel [do-no-śhee-ćhel] m. denunciator; informer
donosicielski [do-no-śhee-ćhel-skee] adj.m. denunciatory
donosicielstwo [do-no-śhee-ćhel-stfo] n. denunciatory activities; informing against (neighbors, colleagues, etc.); spying
donosić [do-no-śheećh] v. wear out of use; carry the fetus to term; inform against; spy

donoszenie [do-no-**she**-ńe] n. wearing out of use; carrying the fetus to term; spying
donoszenie się [do-no-**she**-ńe śhan] n. reaching across distance; ranging
donośnie [do-**no**-śhńe] adv. resonantly; sonorously; loudly; audibly; out loud; in a loud voice
donośność [do-**no**-śhnośhćh] f. sonority; resonance; range
donośny [do-**no**-śhni] adj.m. resounding; ringing; loud; sonorous; resonant; stentorian
donucić [do-**noo**-ćheećh] v. hum to the end; finish humming
donudzić [do-**noo**-dźheećh] v. bore to the last; bore to the end; finish boring somebody
donżuan [don-**zhoo**-ahn] m. lady-killer (Don Juan); libertine; rake
donżuaneria [don-zhoo-ah-**ner**-yah] f. womanizing
donżuanizm [don-zhoo-**ah**-ńeezm] m. libertinism; lady-killing
donżuański [don-zhoo-**ahń**-skee] adj.m. libertine; womanizer's
doodbytniczo [do-od-bi-**tńee**-cho] adv. rectally
doodbytniczy [do-od-bi-**tńee**-chi] adj.m. rectal
dookolny [do-o-**kol**-ni] adj.m. ambient; surrounding; environmental
dookoła [do-o-**ko**-wah] adv. round; round about; all around; all around; right round
doorać [do-**o**-rahćh] v. finish ploughing; plough (to a given spot); plough (an extra furrow)
doorywać [do-o-**ri**-vahćh] v. finish ploughing; plough (to a given spot); plough (an extra furrow) (*repeatedly*)
do ostatka [do o-**stah**-tkah] exp.: to the last; to the bitter end
dootrzewnowo [do-o-tshe-**vno**-vo] adv. peritoneally
dootrzewnowy [do-o-tshe-**vno**-vi] adj.m. peritoneal
dopadać [do-**pah**-dahćh] v. get; reach; catch (suddenly); fall (more); rain (more); snow (more); snow (up to a certain place); run up; overtake; reach at a run; catch up; hunt down; seize
dopadek [do-**pah**-dek] m. an incremental event
robić dopadkami [**ro**-beećh do-paht-**kah**-mee] exp: to do by fits and starts
dopakować [do-pah-**ko**-vahćh] v. finish packing; add to a package; add to a valise (to a piece of luggage)
dopakowywać [do-pah-ko-**vi**-vahćh] v. finish packing; add to a package; add to a valise (to a piece of luggage) (*repeatedly*)
dopalacz [do-**pah**-lahch] m. after-burner
dopalać [do-**pah**-lahćh] v. after burn; finish burning; burn out; finish smoking; smoke to the end; warm sufficiently (a room, etc.); bake properly (bricks, etc.); roast properly (coffee, etc.); bake (more) (*repeatedly*)
dopalać się [do-**pah**-lahćh śhan] v. be burning out; burn down; burn to cinders (*repeatedly*)
dopalenie [do-pah-**le**-ńe] v. after burning; finishing smoking
dopalić [do-**pah**-leećh] v. after burn; finish burning; burn out; finish smoking; smoke to the end; warm sufficiently (a room, etc.); bake properly (bricks, etc.); roast properly (coffee, etc.); bake (more)
dopalić się [do-**pah**-leećh śhan] v. be burning out; burn down; burn to cinders
doparzać [do-**pah**-zhahćh] v. infuse (some more tea, etc.) (*repeatedly*)
doparzyć [do-**pah**-zhićh] v. infuse (some more tea, etc.)
dopasać [do-**pah**-sahćh] v. finish grazing; graze (more, longer, up to a certain place, etc.) (*repeatedly*)
dopasować [do-pah-**so**-vahćh] v. fit; fit together; adapt (to); adjust; match; tone (with)
dopasować się [do-pah-**so**-vahćh śhan] v. adapt oneself; conform oneself; be matched; be adapted
dopasowanie [do-pah-so-**vah**-ńe] n.

adjustment; adaptation; fitting
dopasowany [do-pah-so-**vah**-ni] adj.m. well-fitting
ciasno dopasowany [**ćhah**-sno do-pah-so-**vah**-ni] exp.: tight-fitting
dopasowywać [do-pah-so-**vi**-vahćh] v. fit; fit together; adapt (to); adjust; match; tone (with) (*repeatedly*)
dopasowywać się [do-pah-so-**vi**-vahćh śhan] v. adapt oneself; conform oneself; be matched; tone in (with); be adapted (*repeatedly*)
dopaść [**do**-pahśhćh] v. run up; overtake; reach at a run; catch up (with); hunt down (a thief); seize; grab; lay hands on; finish grazing (cattle, etc.); graze (more)
dopaść się [**do**-pahśhćh śhan] v. catch one another; meet suddenly; come together; finish grazing; graze (more, longer, somewhat longer)
dopatrywać [do-pah-**tri**-vahćh] v. watch; see; see to it; find out; keep an eye; discern; perceive; detect (*repeatedly*)
dopatrywać się [do-pah-**tri**-vahćh śhan] v. discern; perceive; detect; scent; suspect (*repeatedly*)
dopatrywanie się [do-pah-tri-**vah**-ńe śhan] n. discerning; perceiving
dopatrzyć [do-**pah**-tshićh] v. watch; see; see to it; find out; keep an eye; discern; perceive; detect
dopatrzyć się [do-**pah**-tshićh śhan] v. discern; perceive; detect; scent; suspect
dopchać [**do**-pkhahćh] v. cram (full); push home; push to a certain limit
dopchać się [**do**-pkhahćh śhan] v. push one's way; elbow one's way
dopchać się do [**do**-pkhahćh śhan do] exp.: to elbow one's way to (a given spot, etc.); to push one's way (to a place, etc.)
dopchanie [do-**pkhah**-ńe] n. cramming (full); pushing home
dopchnąć [do-pkhnownćh] v. cram (full); push home; push to a certain limit
dopchnąć się [**do**-pkhnownćh śhan] v. push one's way; elbow one's way
do pełna [do **pew**-nah] adv. brim-full; up to the brim
dopełniacz [do-**pew**-ńahch] m. gram.: genitive; passive case; biol.: complement
dopełniaczowy [do-pew-ńah-**cho**-vi] adj.m. gram.: genitival
dopełniający [do-pew-ńah-**yown**-tsi] adj.m. complementary; supplementary
dopełniać [do-**pew**-ńahćh] v. fulfil; fill up; complete; make up; complement; supplement (*repeatedly*)
dopełniać się [do-**pew**-ńahćh śhan] v. be completed; complement one another; supplement one another; be achieved; be accomplished; be effected (*repeatedly*)
dopełnić [do-**pew**-ńeećh] v. fulfil; fill up; complete; make up; complement; supplement
dopełnić zobowiązań [do-pew-ńeećh zo-bo-**vyown**-zahń] exp.: to meet one's obligations
dopełnić ślubu [do-**pew**-ńeećh **śhloo**-boo] exp.: to keep one's vow; to keep one's promise
dopełnić się [do-**pew**-ńeećh śhan] v. be completed; complement one another; supplement one another; be achieved; be accomplished; be effected
dopełnienie [do-pew-**ńe**-ńe] n. completion; fulfillment; execution; fulfillment; gram.: object
dopełnienie bliższe (dalsze) [do-pew-**ńe**-ńe **bleesh**-she (**dahl**-she)] exp.: direct (indirect) object
dopełnienie się [do-pew-**ńe**-ńe śhan] n. complementing each other; supplementing each other; be affected; be completed
dopełnieniowy [do-pew-ńe-**ńo**-vi] adj.m. objective (gram)
dopełzać [do-**pew**-zahćh] v. crawl up (to a certain spot) (*repeatedly*)
dopełzać się [do-**pew**-zahćh śhan]

v. (emphatic) crawl up (to) (*repeatedly*)
dopełzanie [do-pew-**zah**-ńe] n. crawling up (to) (*repeatedly*)
dopełznąć [do-**pew**-znownćh] v. crawl up (to a certain spot)
dopełznąć się [do-**pewz**-nownćh śhan] v. (emphatic) crawl up (to)
dopełznięcie [do-pewz-**ńan**-ćhe] n. crawling up (to a certain spot)
dopędzać [do-**pan**-dzahćh] v. catch up with; overtake; gain on; drive (cattle to...); reach at a run (*repeatedly*)
dopędzenie [do-pan-**dze**-ńe] n. catching up with; overtaking; gaining on; driving (cattle to...); reaching (home, etc.) at a run
dopędzić [do-**pan**-dźheećh] v. catch up with; overtake; gain on; drive (cattle to...); reach at a run
dopiąć [**do**-pyownćh] v. attain; buckle up; button up; finish buttoning; fasten up; obtain; get
dopiąć swego [**do**-pyownćh **sfe**-go] exp.: to gain one's end
dopiąć się [**do**-pyownćh śhan] exp.: to button up one's clothes
dopicie [do-**pee**-ćhe] n. finishing a drink; drinking up
dopić [**do**-peećh] v. finish drinking; drink up; empty one's cup
dopiec [**do**-pyets] v. finish baking; finish roasting; bake more; roast more; swelter; scorch; sting; nettle; pique
dopiec do żywego [**do**-pyets do zhi-**ve**-go] exp.: to sting (somebody) to the quick
dopieczenie [do-pye-**che**-ńe] n. finishing the baking; sting
dopiekać [do-**pye**-kahćh] v. finish baking; finish roasting; bake more; roast more; swelter; scorch; sting; nettle; pique (*repeatedly*)
dopiekanie [do-pye-**kah**-ńe] n. finishing the baking; stinging (*repeatedly*)
dopieprzać [do-**pye**-pshahćh] v. add pepper; season with pepper; mob slang: vulg.: fuck; copulate; hit hard; sting (*repeatedly*)
dopieprzyć [do-**pye**-pshićh] v. add pepper; season with pepper; mob slang: vulg.: fuck; copulate; hit hard; nettle; sting; tease
dopierać [do-**pye**-rahćh] v. finish washing; wash some more; wash clean (*repeatedly*)
dopierać się [do-**pye**-rahćh śhan] v. be washed clean; wash clean (*repeatedly*)
dopierdalać [do-pyer-**dah**-lahćh] v. slang: vulg.: fuck; copulate; hit hard; nettle; sting; tease (mob jargon) (*repeatedly*)
dopierdolić [do-pyer-**do**-leećh] v. mob slang: vulg.: fuck; copulate; hit hard; nettle; sting; tease
dopiero [do-**pye**-ro] adv. only; just; hardly; barely; scarcely; only just; not before; only when; not till
dopiero co [do-**pye**-ro tso] exp.: only just; just now
dopiero wtedy [do-**pye**-ro **fte**-di] exp.: not till then
to dopiero! [to do-**pye**-ro] excl.: well, well!; well I never!; incredible!; unbelievable!
dopieszczać [do-**pye**-shchahćh] v. finish with precision and care; show tenderness; show affection (*repeatedly*)
dopieścić [do-**pye**-śhćheećh] v. finish with precision and care; show tenderness; show affection
dopięcie [do-**pyan**-ćhe] n. buttoning up; buckling up
dopijać [do-**pee**-yahćh] v. finish drinking; drink up; empty one's cup (*repeatedly*)
dopijanie [do-pee-**yah**-ńe] n. finishing a drink; drinking up; emptying one's cup (*repeatedly*)
dopilnować [do-peel-**no**-vahćh] v. see (something) done; make sure (that); see (that); supervise; take care (of); watch (over); keep an eye (on)
nie dopilnować się [ńe do-peel-no-vahćh śhan] exp.: to be off (one's) guard
dopilnować się [do-peel-**no**-vahćh śhan] v. be on one's guard
dopilnowywać [do-peel-no-**vi**-vahćh] v. see (something) done; make sure (that); see (that);

supervise; take care (of); watch (over); keep an eye (on) (*repeatedly*)
dopilnowywać się [do-peel-no-**vi**-vahćh śh<u>an</u>] v. be on one's guard (*repeatedly*)
dopiłować [do-pee-**wo**-vahćh] v. finish sawing; saw as to adjust; saw to make fit
dopiłowywać [do-pee-wo-**vi**-vahćh] v. finish sawing; saw as to adjust; saw to make fit (*repeatedly*)
dopinać [do-**pee**-nahćh] v. attain; buckle up; button up; finish buttoning; fasten up; obtain; get (*repeatedly*)
dopinać swego [do-**pee**-nahćh **sfe**-go] exp.: to gain one's end
dopinać się [do-**pee**-nahćh śh<u>an</u>] exp.: to button up one's clothes (*repeatedly*)
dopinanie [do-pee-**nah**-ńe] n. buttoning up
doping [**do**-peeng] m. cheering; cheers (at sporting events)
dopingować [do-peen-**go**-vahćh] v. spur on; incite; stimulate; cheer on (a team, etc.); encourage; put spunk (into); urge; slang: root (for); cheer (for) (*repeatedly*)
dopingować się [do-peen-**go**-vahćh śh<u>an</u>] v. stimulate oneself (with drugs, etc.)
dopingowanie [do-peen-go-**vah**-ńe] n. cheering; cheers (at sporting events)
dopingowanie się [do-peen-go-**vah**-ńe śh<u>an</u>] n. stimulating oneself (with drugs, etc.)
dopingowy [do-peen-**go**-vi] adj.m. encouraging (cheers, etc.)
dopisać [do-**pee**-sahćh] v. write in addition; add in writing; insert (notes, remarks, etc.); annotate; add critical or explanatory notes; come up to expectations; favor; be favorable; not to fail; turn up; be as good as ever
pogoda dopisuje [po-**go**-dah do-pee-**soo**-ye] exp.: the weather is fine
szczęście mi nie dopisało [shch<u>an</u>-śhćhe mee ńe do-pee-**sah**-wo] exp.: I have failed
szczęście mu dopisało [shch<u>an</u>-śhćhe moo do-pee-**sah**-wo] exp.: he met with success; he was successful
zdrowie mi dopisuje [**zdro**-vye mee do-pee-**soo**-ye] exp.: I'm well
dopisać się [do-**pee**-sahćh śh<u>an</u>] v. add a word to a letter
dopisek [do-**pee**-sek] m. postscript; foot note; insertion
dopisywacz [do-pee-**si**-vahch] m. annotator
dopisywać [do-pee-**si**-vahćh] v. write in addition; add in writing; insert (notes, remarks, etc.); annotate; add critical or explanatory notes; come up to expectations; favor; be favorable; not to fail; turn up; be as good as ever (*repeatedly*)
dopisywać się [do-pee-**si**-vahćh śh<u>an</u>] v. add a word to a letter written by another person (*repeatedly*)
dopisywanie [do-pee-si-**vah**-ńe] n. annotating; turning up
doplątać się [do-**pl<u>own</u>**-tahćh śh<u>an</u>] v. join; get involved with (a group, etc.)
doplątywać się [do-pl<u>own</u>-**ti**-vahćh śh<u>an</u>] v. join; get involved with (a group, etc.) (*repeatedly*)
dopłacać [do-**pwah**-tsahćh] v. pay in addition; pay extra; lose (in a deal, etc.) (*repeatedly*)
dopłacanie [do-pwah-**tsah**-ńe] n. paying in addition; paying extra
dopłacić [do-**pwah**-ćheećh] v. pay in addition; pay extra; lose (in a deal, etc.)
dopłata [do-**pwah**-tah] f. extra payment; surcharge; extra fare; supplement (to be paid)
dopłynąć [do-**pwi**-n<u>own</u>ćh] v. reach swimming, sailing, floating; flow up (to a limit); make (a port by a ship); arrive (at a port)
dopłynięcie [do-pwi-**ń<u>an</u>**-ćhe] n. arrival by water
dopływ [**do**-pwif] m. tributary; confluent; feeder; influx; intake; inlet; inflow (of energy; gas, etc)
dopływać [do-**pwi**-vahćh] v. flow

in; arrive (at a port by a ship); reach swimming, sailing, floating; flow up (to a limit); make (a port by a ship); arrive (at a port) (*repeatedly*)

dopływowy [do-pwi-**vo**-vi] adj.m. inflow; intake; tributary; subsidiary

dopochwowy [do-po-**khfo**-vi] adj.m. intravaginal

dopokąd [do-**po**-kownt] adv. as long as; so long as; as far; while; until; till; see: **dopóki**

dopomagać [do-po-**mah**-gahćh] v. help; be of assistance; come to aid; see through; see through difficulties (*repeatedly*)

dopomaganie [do-po-mah-**gah**-ńe] n. help; assistance

dopominać się [do-po-**mee**-nahćh śhan] v. put in a claim (for); demand; call for; make demands (*repeatedly*)

dopominanie się [do-po-mee-**nah**-ńe śhan] n. claim; demand; call (for something); clamor (for)

dopomnieć się [do-**po**-mńećh śhan] v. put in a claim (for); demand; call for; make demands

dopomożenie [do-po-mo-**zhe**-ńe] n. help assistance

dopomóc [do-**po**-moots] v. help; be of assistance; come to aid; see through; see through difficulties

dopompować [do-pom-**po**-vahćh] v. inflate (more); pump (more); pump up (a car tire) (*repeatedly*)

nie dopompowany [ńe do-pom-po-**vah**-ni] exp.: under-inflated; insufficiently inflated

dopotąd [do-**po**-townt] adv. as long as; until; till

dopowiadać [do-po-**vyah**-dahćh] v. finish saying; add a few words; supplement (what was said) (*repeatedly*)

dopowiadanie [do-po-vyah-**dah**-ńe] n. adding a few words

dopowiedzenie [do-po-vye-**dze**-ńe] n. gram.: adherent qualifier; apposition

dopowiedzieć [do-po-**vye**-dźhećh] v. finish saying; add a few words; supplement (what was said)

dopożyczać [do-po-**zhi**-chahćh] v. borrow more; lend more (*repeatedly*)

dopożyczanie [do-po-zhi-**chah**-ńe] n. borrowing more; lending more

dopożyczyć [do-po-**zhi**-chićh] v. borrow more; lend more

dopóki [do-**poo**-kee] adv. as long as; so long as; as far; while; until; till
zaczekaj, dopóki nie przyjdę [zah-**che**-kahy do-**poo**-kee ńe **pshiy**-dan] exp.: wait until I come

dopókiż [do-**poo**-keesh] conj. = emphatic form of: **dopóki** (above)

dopóty [do-**poo**-ti] adv. till; until; so far; up to here; as long as; till the time (when)
dopóty ... dopóki [do-**poo**-ti do-**poo**-kee] exp.: as long as

do późna [do **poośh**-nah] adv. late into the night; deep into the night

dopracować [do-prah-**tso**-vahćh] v. polish up (one's style, etc.)

dopracować się [do-prah-**tso**-vahćh śhan] v. obtain by one's work

dopracowanie się [do-prah-tso-**vah**-ńe śhan] n. obtaining by one's work

dopracowywać [do-prah-tso-**vi**-vahćh] v. polish up (one's style, a literary composition, etc.) (*repeatedly*)

dopracowywać się [do-prah-tso-**vi**-vahćh śhan] v. obtain by one's work (*repeatedly*)

doprać [**do**-prahćh] v. finish washing; wash more (linen, etc.); wash clean

doprać się [**do**-prahćh śhan] v. be washed clean; wash clean

doprasować [do-prah-**so**-vahćh] v. finish ironing

doprasować się [do-prah-**so**-vahćh śhan] v. succeed in ironing properly; iron out

doprasowywać [do-prah-so-**vi**-vahćh] v. finish ironing (*repeatedly*)

doprasowywać się [do-prah-so-**vi**-vahćh śhan] v. succeed in ironing properly; iron out (*repeatedly*)

dopraszać [do-**prah**-shahćh] v.

invite additionally (*repeatedly*)
dopraszać się [do-**prah**-shahćh śhan] v. solicit; beg; entreat; insist (on); claim; demand (of, from) (*repeatedly*)
dopraszanie [do-prah-**shah**-ńe] n. entreaties; demands; claims
doprawa [do-**prah**-vah] f. seasoning; preparation (for use)
doprawdy [do-**prah**-vdi] adv. truly; indeed; really; really?; is that so?; do you mean it?
doprawiać [do-**prah**-vyahćh] v. add (to taste); season; prepare (soil); replace (broken parts, etc.) (*repeatedly*)
doprawiać się [do-**prah**-vyahćh śhan] v. get drunk (*repeatedly*)
doprawić [do-**prah**-veećh] v. add (to taste); season; prepare (soil); replace (broken parts, etc.)
doprawić się [do-**prah**-veećh śhan] v. get drunk
doprawienie [do-prah-**vye**-ńe] n. seasoning (of food)
doprażać [do-**prah**-zhahćh] v. swelter; scorch; finish roasting; roast more (*repeatedly*)
doprażyć [do-**prah**-zhićh] v. swelter; scorch; finish roasting; roast more
doprecyzować [do-pre-tsi-**zo**-vahćh] v. make more precise; finish more accurately
doprecyzowywać [do-pre-tsi-zo-**vi**-vahćh] v. make more precise; finish more accurately (*repeatedly*)
doprojektować [do-pro-ye-**kto**-vahćh] v. finish designing; make an additional design
doprojektowywać [do-pro-ye-kto-**vi**-vahćh] v. finish designing; make an additional design (*repeatedly*)
doprosić [do-**pro**-śheećh] v. invite additionally
doprosić się [do-**pro**-śheećh śhan] v. obtain by one's entreaties; get by persistent requests
doprowadzać [do-pro-**vah**-dzahćh] v. lead to; take to; bring to; bring about; cause; provoke; reduce; achieve; convey; result; bring (*repeatedly*)
doprowadzać się [do-pro-**vah**-dzahćh śhan] v. bring oneself to (a rage, etc.); work oneself up (*repeatedly*)
doprowadzalnik [do-pro-vah-**dzahl**-ńeek] m. gravitational pipeline; drainage canal
doprowadzenie [do-pro-vah-**dze**-ńe] n. reduction (to folly, etc.); hook-up (of telephone, etc.)
doprowadzić [do-pro-**vah**-dźheećh] v. lead to; take to; bring to; bring about; cause; provoke; reduce; achieve; convey; result; bring
doprowadzić do doskonałości [do-pro-**vah**-dźheećh do do-sko-nah-**wo**-śhćhee] exp.: to bring to perfection
doprowadzić do końca [do-pro-**vah**-dźheećh do **koń**-tsah] exp.: to bring to an end
doprowadzić do nędzy [do-pro-**vah**-dźheećh do **nan**-dzi] exp.: to reduce to misery
doprowadzić do porządku [do-pro-**vah**-dźheećh do po-**zhownt**-koo] exp.: to put in order
doprowadzić do rozpaczy [do-pro-**vah**-dźheećh do ros-**pah**-chi] exp.: to drive into despair
doprowadzić do skutku [do-pro-**vah**-dźheećh do **skoo**-tkoo] exp.: to carry into effect
doprowadzić do szału [do-pro-**vah**-dźheećh do **shah**-woo] exp.: to drive (somebody) mad
nie doprowadzić do niczego [ńe do-pro-**vah**-dźheećh do ńee-**che**-go] exp.: to lead nowhere; to fail completely; to prove a complete failure; to be of no avail
doprowadzić się [do-pro-**vah**-dźheećh śhan] v. bring oneself to (a rage, etc.); work oneself up
doprząc [do-pshownts] v. harness an additional horse
doprząść [**do**-pshownśhćh] v. finish weaving; weave additional (piece of cloth, etc.)
doprzęgać [do-**pshan**-gahćh] v. harness an additional horse (*repeatedly*)
doprzęganie [do-pshan-**gah**-ńe] n. harnessing additional horses

doprzęgnąć [do-**pshan**-gnownćh] v. harness an additional horse
dopukać [do-**poo**-kahćh] v. finish knocking
dopukać się [do-**poo**-kahćh śhan] v. knock (at the door, etc.) till one is heard (till somebody answers)
dopukiwać [do-poo-**kee**-vahćh] v. finish knocking (*repeatedly*)
dopukiwać się [do-poo-**kee**-vahćh śhan] v. knock (at the door, etc.) till one is heard (till somebody answers) (*repeatedly*)
dopust [**do**-poost] m. visitation; heavenly dispensation
dopust Boży [**do**-poost **bo**-zhi] exp.: calamity; scourge; act of God; decree of Providence
dopuszczać [do-**poo**-shchahćh] v. admit; receive; give entrance; allow; permit; be open; give access; be patient (*repeatedly*)
dopuszczać się [do-**poo**-shchahćh śhan] v. commit; perpetrate
dopuszczalność [do-poo-**shchahl**-nośhćh] f. admissibility; permissibility
dopuszczalny [do-poo-**shchahl**-ni] adj.m. admissible; permissible
dopuszczenie [do-poo-**shche**-ńe] n. admission; admittance; reception
dopuścić [do-**poo**-śhćheećh] v. admit; receive; give entrance; allow; permit; be open; give access; be patient
dopuścić się [do-**poo**-śhćheećh śhan] v. commit; perpetrate
dopychać [do-**pi**-khahćh] v. finish pushing; push home
dopychać się [do-**pi**-khahćh śhan] v. push one's way; elbow one's way
dopytać [do-**pi**-tahćh] v. finish questioning; find out (from)
dopytać się [do-**pi**-tahćh śhan] v. find out (from, out of); inquire; question; finish questioning; bring down (misfortune, etc. on oneself); gather information (from, about)
dopytywać [do-pi-**ti**-vahćh] v. ask (about, fore, after); inquire (about); gather information (from); question (about); finish questioning; find out (from) (*repeatedly*)
dopytywać się [do-pi-**ti**-vahćh śhan] v. find out (from, out of); inquire; question; finish questioning; bring down (misfortune, etc. on oneself); gather information (from, about) (*repeatedly*)
dorabiać [do-**rah**-byahćh] v. make additionally; replace; finish; make new (part, etc.) (*repeatedly*)
dorabiać się [do-**rah**-byahćh śhan] v. make one's way; grow more prosperous; amass by one's work; make a fortune; grow rich (*repeatedly*)
dorachować [do-rah-**kho**-vahćh] v. add (to a sum); reckon (up to); finish counting
dorachować się [do-rah-**kho**-vahćh śhan] v. make one's account square
nie móc się dorachować [ńe moots śhan do-rah-**kho**-vahćh] exp.: to find that one's account does not square up; to miss; to be ... short
dorachowywać [do-rah-kho-**vi**-vahćh] v. add (to a sum); reckon (up to); finish counting (*repeatedly*)
dorachowywać się [do-rah-kho-**vi**-vahćh śhan] v. make one's account square (*repeatedly*)
dorada [do-**rah**-dah] f. piece of advise; counsel; gilthead (fish)
doradca [do-**raht**-tsah] m. adviser; counselor; guide; consultant
doradczy [do-**raht**-chi] adj.m. advisory; consultative
doradczyni [do-raht-**chi**-ńee] f. (woman) advisor; consultant; counsellor; guide
doradzać [do-**rah**-dzahćh] v. advise; counsel; recommend (*repeatedly*)
doradzić [do-**rah**-dźheećh] v. advise (to do something); recommend; counsel
doradztwo [do-**rats**-tfo] n. consulting
dorastać [do-**rah**-stahćh] v. mature; grow; grow up; reach (certain

size; etc.); match in size; be as tall as; rise to the level of; be on the level with (*repeatedly*)
dorastający [do-rah-stah-yown-tsi] adj.m. adolescent
dorastająca młodzież [do-rah-stah-yown-tsah mwo-dźhesh] exp.: teenagers
do razu [do rah-zoo] conj. till; until
do pewnego razu [do pev-ne-go rah-zoo] exp.: until certain time
doraźnie [do-rah-źhńe] adv. (immediately) on the spot; on the spur of the occasion; in an emergency; in case of an emergency
doraźność [do-rah-źhnośhćh] f. immediacy; emergency
doraźny [do-rah-źhni] adj.m. immediate; extemporary; summary; improvised; hasty; casual; extemporaneous; off-handed; emergency- (repairs, meeting, fund, etc.)
sąd doraźny [sownd do-rah-źhni] exp.: court-martial
dordzeniowy [do-rdze-ńo-vi] adj.m. spinal (injection, etc.)
doregulować [do-re-goo-lo-vahćh] v. finish regulating; adjust (to a proper condition); set (to perfection, etc.)
do reszty [do resh-ti] exp.: completely; utterly
doręczać [do-ran-chahćh] v. deliver; transmit; hand; hand over; serve (summons, etc.) (*repeatedly*)
doręczenie [do-ran-che-ńe] n. delivery
doręczeniowy [do-ran-che-ńo-vi] adj.m. of delivery
doręczyna [do-ran-chi-nah] f. oar (between oarlock and handgrip)
doręczyciel [do-ran-chi-ćhel] m. deliverer
doręczycielka [do-ran-chi-ćhel-kah] f. (woman) deliverer
doręczyć [do-ran-chićh] v. hand in; deliver; transmit
dormitorium [dor-mee-to-ryoom] n. dormitory
dorobek [do-ro-bek] m. acquisition; rise to affluence; possessions; fortune; goods and chattels
być na dorobku [bićh nah do-rop-koo] exp.: to make one's way to well being; to be feathering one's nest; be on one's way to a fortune
dorobić [do-ro-beećh] v. replace (missing part, etc.); make additionally; replace; finish; make new (part, etc.)
dorobić się [do-ro-beećh śhan] v. make one's way; grow more prosperous; amass by one's work; make a fortune; grow rich
dorobienie [do-ro-bye-ńe] n. replacement (of a missing part, broken object, etc.)
dorobkiewicz [do-rop-ke-veech] m. upstart; parvenu; new rich
dorobkiewiczostwo [do-rop-ke-vee-chost-fo] n. eagerness to gain
dorobkiewiczowski [do-rop-ke-vee-chof-skee] adj.m. upstart's
dorobkowy [do-rop-ko-vi] adj.m. earned by work
dorocznie [do-roch-ńe] adv. yearly; annually; year in year out; year after year
doroczny [do-roch-ni] adj.m. yearly; annual; recurring yearly
dorodnie [do-ro-dńe] adv. handsomely
dorodność [do-ro-dnośhćh] f. good looks; shapeliness
dorodny [do-rod-ni] adj.m. handsome; fine-looking; shapely; good-looking
dorosłość [do-ro-swośhćh] f. maturity; adulthood
dorosły [do-ro-swi] adj.m. adult; grown up; mature; grown; full-grown; full-fledged
dorosnąć [do-ro-snownćh] v. mature; grow; grow up; reach (certain size; etc.); match in size; be as tall as; rise to the level of; be on the level with
dorośle [do-ro-śhle] adv. maturely
dorośleć [do-ro-śhlećh] v. grow up; mature (*repeatedly*)
dorośnięcie [do-ro-śhńan-ćhe] n. growing up; maturing
do rozpuku [do ros-poo-koo] exp.:
śmiać się do rozpuku

[śhmyahćh śh<u>an</u> do ros-**poo**-koo] exp.: to be bursting with laughter; to shake with laughter
dorozumiany [do-ro-zoo-**myah**-ni] adj.m. implied
dorozumieć się [do-ro-**zoo**-myećh śh<u>an</u>] v. infer; guess; suspect; understand; gather; make out; read between the lines; read into (a text, a letter, etc.); put two and two together
dorozumiewać się [do-ro-zoo-**mye**-vahćh śh<u>an</u>] v. infer; guess; suspect; understand; gather; make out; read between the lines; read into (a text, a letter, etc.); put two and two together (*repeatedly*)
dorozumiewany [do-ro-zoo-mye-**vah**-ni] adj.m. implied (*repeatedly*)
dorożka [do-**ro**-shkah] f. cab; droshky; hackney-coach
dorożkarski [do-ro-**shkahr**-skee] adj.m. cabman's
koń dorożkarski [koń do-ro-**shkahr**-skee] exp.: cab-horse
dorożkarstwo [do-rosh-**kahr**-stfo] n. cabman's occupation
dorożkarz [do-**rosh**-kahsh] m. cabman; cab-driver; cabby
doróść [**do**-roośhćh] v. mature; grow; grow up; reach (certain size; etc.); match in size; be as tall as; rise to the level of; be on the level with
dorównać [do-**roo**-vnahćh] v. match; equal; parallel; catch up with; come up to be equal; be on the level; level; make level
dorównywać [do-roo-**vni**-vahćh] v. match; equal; parallel; catch up with; come up to be equal; be on the level; level; make level (*repeatedly*)
dorsalny [dor-**sahl**-ni] adj.m. dorsal
dorsz [dorsh] m. cod (fish)
dorszowaty [dor-sho-**vah**-ti] adj.m. gadid (fish)
dorszowate [dor-sho-**vah**-te] pl. the gadid family of fishes
dorszowy [dor-**sho**-vi] adj.m. of a cod; cod (fillet, etc.)
dorwać [**dor**-vahćh] v. tear out; tear out more; pluck; pluck more
dorwać się [**dor**-vahćh śh<u>an</u>] v. grab; seize; take hold; lay hold; lay hands on
dorycki [do-**rits**-kee] adj.m. Doric; Dorian
doryć [**do**-rićh] v. finish burrowing; root up to (a spot, etc.)
doryć się [**do**-rićh śh<u>an</u>] v. burrow up (to); burrow down (to); root up (to); root down (to)
dorysować [do-ri-**so**-vahćh] v. finish drawing; add to a drawing; supplement a drawing (with)
dorysowywać [do-ri-so-**vi**-vahćh] v. finish drawing; add to a drawing; supplement a drawing (with) (*repeatedly*)
dorywać [do-**ri**-vahćh] v. tear out; tear out more; pluck; pluck more (*repeatedly*)
dorywać się [do-ri-vahćh śh<u>an</u>] v. grab; seize; take hold; lay hold; lay hands on (*repeatedly*)
dorywczo [do-**rif**-cho] adv. occasionally; irregularly; by fits and starts; at haphazard; by snatches; in snatches; hurriedly; extemporaneously; haphazardly
pracować dorywczo [prah-**tso**-vahćh do-**rif**-cho] exp.: to work part-time; to do odd jobs
dorywczość [do-**rif**-chośhćh] f. casual nature; haphazard character
dorywczy [do-**rif**-chi] adj.m. occasional; improvised; fitful; off-and-on; hit-and-run; casual; haphazard; snatchy; done by fits and starts
praca dorywcza [**prah**-tsah do-**rif**-chah] exp.: odd job; part-time work
dorywkami [do-rif-**kah**-mee] adv. occasionally; irregularly; by fits and starts; at haphazard; by snatches; in snatches; hurriedly; extemporaneously; haphazardly
dorzecze [do-**zhe**-che] n. river basin; drainage area; catchment-area
dorzecznie [do-**zhech**-ńe] adv. reasonably; sensibly; efficiently; adequately; acceptably; logically; with sense; to the point
dorzeczność [do-**zhech**-nośhćh] f.

common sense; efficiency
dorzeczny [do-**zhech**-ni] adj.m. reasonable; sensible; efficient; adequate; acceptable; logical
dorzeźbić [do-**zhe**-źhbeećh] v. finish sculpting; complete a sculpture; add to a sculpture
dorznąć [**do**-zhnownćh] v. finish cutting; finish off (an animal)
dorznąć się [**do**-zhnownćh śhan] v. ruin oneself
dorzucać [do-**zhoo**-tsahćh] v. throw in; add; throw as far as (*repeatedly*)
dorzucić [do-**zhoo**-ćheećh] v. throw in; add; throw as far as
dorzynać [do-zhi-nahćh] v. finish cutting; finish off (an animal) (*repeatedly*)
dorzynać się [do-**zhi**-nahćh śhan] v. ruin oneself (*repeatedly*)
dorżnąć [**dor**-zhnownćh] v. finish cutting; finish off (an animal)
dorżnąć się [**dor**-zhnownćh śhan] v. ruin oneself
dosadnie [do-**sahd**-ńe] adv. forcefully; expressively; crisply; pointedly; neatly; roundly; abruptly; forcibly; plainly; straight-forwardly; bluntly; in strong (language); crudely
dosadność [do-**sahd**-nośhćh] f. forcefulness; expressiveness
dosadny [do-**sahd**-ni] adj.m. forceful; expressive; crisp; pointed; neat; round; abrupt; forcible; plain; straight-forward; blunt; strong (language); crude (terms)
dosadzać [do-**sah**-dzahćh] v. finish planting; plant more (*repeatedly*)
dosadzić [do-**sah**-dźheećh] v. finish planting; plant more; place in an additional seat
dosalać [do-**sah**-lahćh] v. add some salt; finish salting (*repeatedly*)
doschnąć [**do**-skhnownćh] v. dry up; become quite dry; reach the necessary state of dryness
doschnięcie [do-**skhńan**-ćhe] n. the process of drying up to (the necessary condition, etc.)
dosercowy [do-ser-**tso**-vi] adj.m. (massage, etc.) toward the heart
dosiać [**do**-śhahćh] v. finish sowing; sow some more
dosiad [**do**-śhaht] m. pounce; swoop; way of sitting on a saddled horse
dosiadać [do-**śhah**-dahćh] v. mount (horse, etc.); bestride; cross (*repeatedly*)
dosiadać się [do-**śhah**-dahćh śhan] v. sit by; sit at; join company (at a table); walk in (a bus, etc.) (*repeatedly*)
dosiadywać [do-śhah-**di**-vahćh] v. finish hatching (eggs); finish serving (a prison term); sit out (a lecture, etc.); stand it; hold out (*repeatedly*)
dosiąc [**do**-śhownts] v. reach; attain
dosiąść [**do**-śhownśhćh] v. mount (horse, etc.); bestride; cross
dosiebny [do-**śheb**-ni] adj.m. heading towards each other
dosiec [**do**-śhets] v. finish mowing (a lawn, etc.); mow some more; mow up to a limit
dosieczna [do-**śhech**-nah] f. cosecant
dosiedzieć [do-**śhe**-dźhećh] v. finish hatching (eggs); finish serving (a prison term); sit out (a lecture, etc.); stand it; hold out
Do siego Roku! [do **śhe**-go **ro**-koo] exp.: Happy New Year!
dosiekać [do-**śhe**-kahćh] v. finish mowing (a lawn, etc.); mow some more; mow up to a limit (*repeatedly*)
dosiewać [do-**śhe**-vahćh] v. finish sowing; sow more (*repeatedly*)
dosiewanie [do-śhe-**vah**-ńe] n. additional sowing
dosiewek [do-**śhe**-vek] m. festival of the close of the sowing
dosięgać [do-**śhan**-gahćh] v. reach; attain; catch up with; hit (with a bullet, etc.); strike (*repeatedly*)
dosięgalność [do-śhan-**gahl**-nośhćh] f. attainability; accessibility
dosięgalny [do-śhan-**gahl**-ni] adj.m. attainable; accessible
dosięgnąć [do-**śhang**-nownćh] v. reach; attain; catch up with; hit

(with a bullet, etc.); strike
dosięgnięcie [do-śhang-ńan-ćhe] n. attainment
dosiężnie [do-śhanzh-ńe] adv. accessibly (sports exp.)
dosiężny [do-śhanzh-ni] adj.m. accessible; attainable (to)
doskakiwać [do-skah-kee-vahćh] v. jump up to (a spot); jump as far as; jump as high as; come bouncing up to (somebody); make a leap for; run (on a short errand) (*repeatedly*)
doskładać [do-skwah-dahćh] v. finish piling; add to a pile; finish folding (blankets, etc.); fold more
doskoczyć [do-sko-chićh] v. jump up to (a spot); jump as far as; jump as high as; come bouncing up to (somebody); make a leap for; run (on a short errand)
doskok [do-skok] m. landing (after a jump); jump (to a height or distance)
doskonale [do-sko-nah-le] adv. perfectly; to perfection; faultlessly; splendidly; excellently; exquisitely; thoroughly; excl.: good!; fine!; righto!; right you are!; splendid!
doskonalenie [do-sko-nah-le-ńe] n. improvement; betterment; advancement
doskonalenie się [do-sko-nah-le-ńe śhan] n. self-improvement
doskonalić [do-sko-nah-leećh] v. perfect; improve; cultivate; bring to perfection; accomplish (*repeatedly*)
doskonalić się [do-sko-nah-leećh śhan] v. perfect oneself; strive for perfection; improve one's knowledge; make progress (*repeatedly*)
doskonałość [do-sko-nah-wośhćh] f. perfection; excellence; exquisiteness; faultlessness
doskonały [do-sko-nah-wi] adj.m. perfect; excellent; supreme; splendid; faultless; exquisite; consummate; accomplished; tip-top
doskórnie [do-skoor-ńe] adv. intradermically
doskórny [do-skoor-ni] adj.m. intradermic
doskrobać [do-skro-bahćh] v. finish peeling; finish scratching; peel more; scrub more
doskrobać się [do-skro-bahćh śhan] v. come by; scrape together (some money)
doskwierać [do-skfye-rahćh] v. pinch; gripe; trouble; worry; beset; importune; swelter; scorch (*repeatedly*)
doskwieranie [do-skfye-rah-ńe] n. sweltering heat; scorching sun
dosłać [do-swahćh] v. send more; send on; forward; finish littering down (a horse, etc.); finish making (a bed, etc.)
dosładzać [do-swah-dzahćh] v. sweeten more; add some sugar (to); put more sugar (in); put enough sugar (in); sweeten sufficiently (*repeatedly*)
dosłodzenie [do-swo-dze-ńe] n. adding some sugar
dosłodzić [do-swo-dźheećh] v. sweeten more; add some sugar (to); put more sugar (in); put enough sugar (in); sweeten sufficiently
dosłownie [do-swov-ńe] adv. literally; to the letter; verbally; textually; verbatim; literatim
tłumaczyć dosłownie [twoo-mah-chićh do-swov-ńe] exp.: to translate word for word
dosłowność [do-swov-nośhćh] f. literalism
dosłowny [do-swov-ni] adj.m. literal; verbal; textual; verbatim
w dosłownym znaczeniu [v do-swov-nim znah-che-ńoo] exp.: literally
dosłuchać [do-swoo-khahćh] v. listen to the end; hear very well
dosłuchać się [do-swoo-khahćh śhan] v. infer; understand (from words, speech, etc.)
dosłuchiwać [do-swoo-khee-vahćh] v. listen to the end; hear very well (*repeatedly*)
dosłuchiwać się [do-swoo-khee-vahćh śhan] v. infer; understand (from words, speech, etc.)

(*repeatedly*)
dosługiwać [do-swoo-**gee**-vahćh] v. serve one's term; serve (a year, a term.etc.) (*repeatedly*)
dosługiwać się [do-swoo-gee-vahćh śhan] v. gain through service; be promoted (*repeatedly*)
dosłużyć [do-**swoo**-zhićh] v. serve one's term; serve (a year, etc.)
dosłużyć się [do-**swoo**-zhićh śhan] v. gain through service; be promoted
dosłyszalnie [do-swi-**shahl**-ńe] adv. audibly
dosłyszalność [do-swi-**shahl**-nośhćh] f. audibility
dosłyszalny [do-swi-**shahl**-ni] adj.m. audible
dosłyszeć [do-**swi**-shećh] v. hear well; catch a sound
nie dosłyszeć [ńe do-**swi**-shećh] exp.: to hear badly; to be hard of hearing
dosmakować się [do-smah-**ko**-vahćh śhan] v. know the taste (of); recognize the taste (of)
dosmażać [do-**smah**-zhahćh] v. finish frying; fry thoroughly; fry some more (*repeatedly*)
dosmażać się [do-**smah**-zhahćh śhan] v. be frying; be boiling (*repeatedly*)
dosmażyć [do-**smah**-zhićh] v. finish frying; fry thoroughly; fry some more
dosmażyć się [do-**smah**-zhićh śhan] v. be frying; be boiling
dosnuć [**do**-snooćh] v. finish spinning; spin to the end; spin some more; imagine (an end of a story, etc.)
dosnuwać [do-**snoo**-vahćh] v. finish spinning; spin to the end; spin some more; imagine (an end of a story, etc.) (*repeatedly*)
dosolić [do-**so**-leećh] v. add some salt; finish salting; see: **dosalać**
dospać [**do**-spahćh] v. sleep (till morning, etc.); sleep as long as one needs; sleep enough
dossier [do-**sye**] n. (French) personal file; document file
dostać [**do**-stahćh] v. obtain; reach; take out; get; be given; come by; gain possession of; procure; catch (cold, etc.); be wounded; be attended to; stand till the end; mellow; ripen
dostać adidasa [**do**-stahćh ah-dee-**dah**-sah] exp.: to get an Addidas shoe; slang: to be infected with AIDS (mob jargon)
dostać aidsa [**dos**-tahćh **eyt**-sah] exp.: colloq.: to be infected with AIDS (Acquired Immune Deficiency Syndrome)
dostać szczękościsku [**dos**-tahćh shchan-ko-**śhćhees**-koo] exp.: to suffer from lock-jaw; slang: to quit talking; to refuse to talk
dostać się [**do**-stahćh śhan] v. get; get at; fall to; fall under; be caught; land (in jail, etc.); find (one's way, etc.)
dostać się w czyjeś ręce [**do**-stahćh śhan f **chi**-yeśh **ran**-tse] exp.: to fall (get) into somebody's hands
dostać się do domu [**do**-stahćh śhan do **do**-moo] exp.: to get home
dostać się do niewoli [**do**-stahćh śhan do ńe-**vo**-lee] exp.: to be taken prisoner
dostać się do środka [**do**-stahćh śhan do **śhrot**-kah] exp.: to get in; to get inside
dostały [do-**stah**-wi] adj.m. ripe; mellow (wine, etc.)
dostanie [do-**stah**-ńe] n. obtainment
nie do dostania [ńe do dos-**tah**-ńah] exp.: unobtainable
dostarczać [do-**stahr**-chahćh] v. furnish; procure; provide; supply with; supply for; offer (an opportunity, etc.); purvey; deliver; afford; yield; give; bring; carry (*repeatedly*)
dostarczanie [do-stahr-**chah**-ńe] n. delivery; supply; procurement
dostarczyciel [do-stahr-**chi**-ćhel] m. caterer; purveyor; furnisher; source (of jokes, etc.)
dostarczycielka [do-stahr-chi-**ćhel**-kah] f. (female) caterer; purveyor; furnisher; source (of jokes, gossip, etc.)
dostarczyć [do-**stahr**-chićh] v.

furnish; procure; provide; supply with; supply for; offer (an opportunity, etc.); purvey; deliver; afford; yield; give; bring; carry
dostatecznie [do-stah-**tech**-ńe] adv. sufficiently; adequately; enough
dostateczny [do-stah-**tech**-ni] adj.m. sufficient; adequate; passable; satisfactory; fair; adequate
stopień dostateczny [**sto**-pyeń do-stah-**tech**-ni] exp.: passing grade; a "C" or satisfactory
dostatek [do-**stah**-tek] m. abundance; wealth; affluence; profusion; plenty
pod dostatkiem [pod do-**staht**-kem] exp.: in abundance; in plenty; more than enough; enough; in profusion
dostatni [do-**staht**-ńee] adj.m. abundant; wealthy; well-to-do; thriving; rich; ample; prosperous
dostatnio [do-**staht**-ńo] adv. abundantly; richly
dostatniość [do-**staht**-ńośhćh] f. affluence; easy circumstances
dostawa [do-**stah**-vah] f. delivery; supply; purveyance
dostawać [do-**stah**-vahćh] v. reach; receive; be attended to; (*repeatedly*) see: **dostać**
dostawca [do-**stahf**-tsah] m. supplier; provider; deliverer; furnisher; tradesman; contractor
dostawczyni [do-stahf-**chi**-ńee] f. (woman) supplier; provider; deliverer; furnisher; tradesman; contractor
dostawczy [do-**stahf**-chi] adj.m. supply (vehicle, etc.)
dostawiać [do-**stah**-vyahćh] v. supply; deliver; convoy; escort; bring under escort; add; fetch (an extra chair, etc.) (*repeatedly*)
dostawiać się [do-**stah**-vyahćh śhan] v. accost a woman; accompany a woman against her will; court (*repeatedly*)
dostawić [do-**stah**-veećh] v. supply; deliver; convoy; escort; bring under escort; add; fetch; see: **dostawiać**
dostawić się [do-**stah**-veećh śhan] v. accost a woman; accompany a woman against her will; court
dostawienie [do-stah-**vye**-ńe] n. supply; delivery
dostawka [do-**stahf**-kah] f. roll-away (bed, etc.)
dostawny [dos-**tahv**-ni] adj.m. additional; extra
dostawowy [dos-tah-**vo**-vi] adj.m. intra-articular
dostąpić [do-**stown**-peećh] v. approach; come up to; accost; attain; accede (an office, etc.)
dostąpić łaski [do-**stown**-peećh **wahs**-kee] exp.: to find favor
dostąpić zaszczytów [do-**stown**-peećh zah-**shchi**-toof] exp.: to gain (to obtain) honors
dostęp [**dos**-tanp] m. access; approach; admission; admittance; entrance
dostępnie [do-**stanp**-ńe] adv. accessibly
dostępność [do-**stanp**-nośhćh] f. accessibility
dostępny [do-**stanp**-ni] adj.m. accessible; easy of approach; popular; attainable; approachable; available; within grasp; within range; affable; get-at-able
dostępować [dos-tan-**po**-vahćh] v. approach; come up to; accost; attain; accede (an office, etc.) (*repeatedly*) see: **dostąpić**
dostojeństwo [do-sto-**yeń**-stfo] n. dignity; majesty; stateliness; lordliness; lordly bearing; high office
dostojnie [do-**stoy**-ńe] adv. with dignity; with stateliness; in lordly manner; proudly; eminently
dostojnik [do-**stoy**-ńeek] m. dignitary; notable of high rank
dostojność [dos-**toy**-nośhćh] f. dignity; stateliness; majesty; lordliness
dostojny [do-**stoy**-ni] adj.m. dignified; worthy; stately; lordly; proud; eminent
dostosować [do-sto-**so**-vahćh] v. accommodate; subordinate; fit; adapt; suit; conform; adjust; shape; square (with); regulate (by); proportion (to)
dostosować się [do-sto-**so**-vahćh

śhan] v. adapt oneself; conform
dostosowanie [do-sto-so-**vah**-ńe] n. adaptation; adjustment; conformity
dostosowany [do-sto-so-**vah**-ni] adj.m. adapted; adjusted; conformable; concordant (with)
dostosowywać [do-sto-so-**vi**-vahćh] v. accommodate; subordinate; fit; adapt; suit; conform; adjust; shape; square (with); regulate (by); proportion (to) (*repeatedly*)
dostosowywać się [do-sto-so-**vi**-vahćh śhan] v. adapt oneself; conform (*repeatedly*)
dostrajać [do-**strah**-yahćh] v. tune up; conform; adapt; finish dressing; finish trimming; finish tuning; adjust (to) (*repeatedly*) see: **dostroić**
dostrajać się [do-**strah**-yahćh śhan] v. adapt oneself (to); conform (with); come into tune (with); chime (with); be in tune (with); accord (with)
dostrajanie [do-strah-**yah**-ńe] n. tuneup; adjustment; adaptation
dostroić [do-**stro**-eećh] v. tune up; conform; adapt; finish dressing; finish trimming; finish tuning; adjust (to)
dostroić się [do-**stro**-eećh śhan] v. adapt oneself (to); conform (with); come into tune (with); chime (with); be in tune (with); accord (with)
dostrojenie [do-stro-**ye**-ńe] n. tune-up; tune-up (of an engine, etc.); adaptation; adjustment; adapting
dostrzec [do-stshets] v. notice; behold; perceive; spot; spy; see; catch a glimpse of; sight; spot; distinguish; make out; detect; notice
dostrzegać [do-**stshe**-gahćh] v. notice; behold; perceive; spot; spy; see; catch a glimpse of; sight; spot; distinguish; make out; detect; notice (*repeatedly*)
dostrzegalnia [do-stshe-**gahl**-ńah] f. watch tower (used to prevent forest fires)
dostrzegalnie [do-stshe-**gahl**-ńe] adv. perceptibly; visibly; noticeably; observably; appreciably; discernibly
dostrzegalność [do-stshe-**gahl**-nośhćh] f. perceptibility
dostrzegalny [do-stshe-**gahl**-ni] adj.m. perceptible; visible; noticeable; observable; appreciable; discernible
dostrzeganie [do-stshe-**gah**-ńe] n. perception; apprehension
dostrzelenie [do-stshe-**le**-ńe] n. shooting up to; finishing off
dostrzelić [do-**stshe**-leećh] v. shoot (up to); shoot down; finish off (a wounded animal, etc)
dostrzeżenie [do-stshe-**zhe**-ńe] n. perception; spotting; detection
dostrzeżony [do-stshe-**zho**-ni] adj.m. perceived; noticed; observed
dostudzić [do-**stoo**-dźheećh] v. cool off
dostukać się [do-**stoo**-kahćh śhan] v. knock (until somebody answers)
do sucha [do **soo**-khah] exp.: (wipe, pump, etc.) dry
dosunąć [do-**soo**-nownćh] v. shove close to; pull up to; push right up to; pull nearer
dosunąć się [do-**soo**-nownćh śhan] v. come closer; move closer
dosuszać [do-**soo**-shahćh] v. finish drying; get quite dry; dry up (*repeatedly*)
dosuszanie [do-soo-**shah**-ńe] n. additional drying
dosuszyć [do-**soo**-shićh] v. finish drying; get quite dry; dry up
dosuszyć się [do-**soo**-shićh śhan] v. dry up; get quite dry
dosuwać [do-**soo**-vahćh] v. shove close to; pull up to; push right up to; pull nearer (*repeatedly*)
dosuwać się [do-**soo**-vahćh śhan] v. come closer; move closer (*repeatedly*)
dosuwanie [do-soo-vah-ńe] v. moving closer
dosycać [do-**si**-tsahćh] v. satiate (*repeatedly*)
dosycanie [do-si-**tsah**-ńe] n. satiation
dosychać [do-**si**-khahćh] v. dry up; become quite dry (*repeatedly*)

see: **doschnąć**
dosycić [do-**si**-ćheećh] v. satiate
dosyć [**do**-sićh] adv. enough; plenty; sufficient; sufficiently; pretty; fairly; rather; tolerably; passably; excl.: enough of that!; be done with that!; none of that!; stop that!; cut it out!
dosyć tego [**do**-sićh **te**-go] exp.: enough of it; that's enough; that will do; let's call it off
dosyłać [do-**si**-wahćh] v. send; send on; send more (parcels, etc.); forward (*repeatedly*)
dosyłka [do-**siw**-kah] f. consignment
dosypać [do-**si**-pahćh] v. add; strew additionally; fill up (with)
dosypiać [do-**si**-pyahćh] v. get enough sleep; sleep as long as one needs (*repeatedly*)
dosypiać się [do-**si**-pyahćh śhan] v. get enough sleep; make up the loss of sleep (*repeatedly*)
dosypianie [do-si-**pyah**-ńe] v. getting enough sleep
dosypka [do-**sip**-kah] f. additional sprinkling (of salt, etc.); makeweight; overflow
dosypywać [do-si-**pi**-vahćh] v. add; strew additionally; fill up (with) (*repeatedly*)
dosyt [**do**-sit] m. satiation; satiety
do syta [do **si**-tah] exp.: adv. amply
najeść się do syta [nah-yeśhćh śhan do **si**-tah] exp.: to eat one's fill
doszczelniacz [do-**shchel**-ńahch] m. caulker
doszczelniać [do-**shchel**-ńahćh] v. caulk; tighten; seal hermetically (*repeatedly*)
doszczelniak [do-**shchel**-ńahk] m. caulking gun; caulking tool; caulker
doszczelnianie [do-shchel-**ńah**-ńe] n. caulking
doszczelnić [do-**shchel**-ńeećh] v. caulk; tighten; seal hermetically
doszczętnie [do-**shchant**-ńe] adv. completely; utterly; down to the ground; totally; sweepingly; root and branch
doszczętny [dosh-**chant**-ni] adj.m. complete; total; utter; radical
do szczętu [do **shchan**-too] adv. = **doszczętnie** (see: above)
doszepnąć [do-**shep**-nownćh] v. add in a whisper
doszeptać [do-**shep**-tahćh] v. add in a whisper
doszeptywać [do-shep-**ti**-vahćh] v. add in a whisper; (*repeatedly*) see: **doszeptać**
doszkalać [do-**shkah**-lahćh] v. complete somebody's education; give additional training (*repeatedly*)
doszkalać się [do-**shkah**-lahćh śhan] v. complete one's education; get additional training; improve one's knowledge (*repeatedly*)
doszkolenie [do-shko-**le**-ńe] n. supplementary education, training, schooling
doszkoleniowy [do-shko-le-**ńo**-vi] adv. of supplementary education; of supplementary training
doszkolić [do-**shko**-leećh] v. complete somebody's education; give additional training
doszkolić się [do-**shko**-leećh śhan] v. complete one's education; get additional training; improve one's knowledge
doszlifować [do-shlee-**fo**-vahćh] v. finish grinding; adjust by grinding; grind to shape; polish up
doszlifowywać [do-shlee-fo-**vi**-vahćh] v. finish grinding; adjust by grinding; grind to shape; polish up (*repeatedly*)
doszlusować [do-shloo-**so**-vahćh] v. joint (a military unit, etc.)
doszlusowywać [do-shloo-so-**vi**-vahćh] v. joint (a military unit, etc.) (*repeatedly*)
doszły [**do**-shwi] adj.m. mellow (fruit, wine, etc.)
doszorować [do-sho-**ro**-vahćh] v. finish scrubbing
doszorować się [do-sho-**ro**-vahćh śhan] v. make spick and span
doszorowywać [do-sho-ro-**vi**-vahćh] v. finish scrubbing (*repeatedly*)
doszorowywać się [do-sho-ro-**vi**-vahćh śhan] v. make spick and span (*repeatedly*)

doszperać [do-**shpe**-rahćh] v. rummage till one finds
doszperać się [do-**shpe**-rahćh śhan] v. find after much rummaging; strike upon; come upon
dosztukować [do-shtoo-**ko**-vahćh] v. piece on; eke out; sew on; add on; patch with
dosztukowywać [do-shtoo-ko-**vi**-vahćh] v. piece on; eke out; sew on; add on; patch with (*repeatedly*)
doszukać się [do-**shoo**-kahćh śhan] v. succeed in finding; detect; discern; perceive; suspect; scent; pick up a meaning in
doszukiwać się [do-shoo-**kee**-vahćh śhan] v. succeed in finding; detect; discern; perceive; suspect; scent; pick up a meaning in (*repeatedly*)
doszycie [do-**shi**-ćhe] n. sewing on
doszyć [**do**-shićh] v. sew on; finish sowing; add
doszywać [do-**shi**-vahćh] v. sew on; finish sowing; add (*repeatedly*)
doszywanie [do-shi-**vah**-ńe] n. sewing on
dościelać [do-**śhćhe**-lahćh] v. finish making a bed; make an additional bed
dościgać [do-**śhćhee**-gahćh] v. overtake; catch up with; catch; come to a level with (*repeatedly*)
dościganie [do-śhćhee-**gah**-ńe] n. overtaking; catching up with
dościgły [do-**śhćheeg**-wi] adj.m. attainable
doścignąć [do-**śhćheeg**-nownćh] v. overtake; catch up with; catch; come to a level with
dość [dośhćh] adv. enough; plenty; fairly; see: **dosyć**
dośledzać [do-**śhle**-dzahćh] v. spy out; detect (*repeatedly*)
dośledzić [do-**śhle**-dźheećh] v. spy out; detect
dośnić [**do**-śhńeećh] v. finish dreaming; dream up; dream out
dośpiew [**do**-śhpyef] m. end; epilogue
dośpiewać [do-**śhpye**-vahćh] v. finish singing; sing to the end; continue the singing; guess; imagine; to sing till
dośpiewywać [do-śhpye-**vi**-vahćh] v. finish singing; sing to the end; continue the singing; guess; imagine; to sing till (*repeatedly*)
dośrodkowa [do-śhrot-**ko**-vah] f. median (of a triangle)
dośrodkować [do-śhrot-**ko**-vahćh] v. center
dośrodkowanie [do-śhrot-ko-**vah**-ńe] n. centering
dośrodkowo [do-śhrot-**ko**-vo] adv. centripetally; concentrically
dośrodkowy [do-śhrot-**ko**-vi] adj.m. centripetal; concentric
dośrodkowywać [do-śhrot-ko-**vi**-vahćh] v. center (*repeatedly*)
dośrubować [do-śhroo-**bo**-vahćh] v. screw tight; screw home
dośrubowywać [do-śhroo-bo-**vi**-vahćh] v. screw tight; screw home (*repeatedly*)
doświadczać [do-**śhfyaht**-chahćh] v. experience; undergo; suffer; feel; sustain; go through; receive; meet with (kindness, etc.); try; try out; put to the test; afflict; scourge; visit (one's wrath upon, etc.); inflict; find; establish; ascertain; learn by experience (*repeatedly*)
doświadczać się [do-**śhfyaht**-chahćh śhan] v. put oneself to the test (*repeatedly*)
doświadczalnictwo [do-śhfyaht-chahl-**ńeets**-tfo] n. experimenting; experimentation
doświadczalnie [do-śhfyaht-**chahl**-ńe] adv. experimentally
doświadczalnik [do-śhfyaht-**chahl**-ńeek] m. experimenter
doświadczalny [do-śhfyaht-**chahl**-ni] adj.m. experimental; testing; trial (balloon, etc.)
doświadczanie [do-śhfyaht-**chah**-ńe] n. experimentation; tests
doświadczenie [do-śhfyaht-**che**-ńe] n. experience; experiment; worldly wisdom; ordeal; trial; affliction; hardship; visitation; test; experiment on (mice, etc.)
robić doświadczenie [ro-beećh

do-śhfyaht-**che**-ńe] exp.: to experiment; to make an experiment
doświadczony [do-śhfyaht-**cho**-ni] adj.m. experienced; expert; worldly-wise; veteran (golfer, etc.); versed in; severely tried
doświadczony gość [do-śhfyaht-**cho**-ni gośhćh] exp.: old hand; old stager; veteran
doświadczyć [do-**śhfyaht**-chićh] v. experience; undergo; suffer; feel; sustain; go through; receive; meet with (kindness, etc.); try; try out; put to the test; afflict; scourge; visit (one's wrath upon, etc.); inflict; find; establish; ascertain; learn by experience
doświadczyć nieszczęścia [do-**śhfyaht**-chićh ńe-**shchan**-śhćhah] exp.: to undergo a misfortune
los go ciężko doświadczył [los go ćhansh-ko do-śhfyaht-chiw] exp.: fate has severely tried him; he has been sorely afflicted
doświadczyć się [do-**śhfyaht**-chićh śhan] v. put oneself to the test
doświdrować [do-śhfee-**dro**-vahćh] v. finish drilling
doświdrować się [do-śhfee-**dro**-vahćh śhan] v. reach by drilling; reach when drilling
doświdrowywać [do-śhfee-dro-**vi**-vahćh] v. finish drilling (*repeatedly*)
doświdrowywać się [do-śhfee-dro-**vi**-vahćh śhan] v. reach by drilling; reach when drilling (*repeatedly*)
doświetlać [do-**śhfye**-tlahćh] v. give a right exposure (to a photograph) (*repeatedly*)
doświetlić [do-**śhfye**-tleećh] v. give a right exposure (to a photograph)
dotacja [do-**tah**-tsyah] f. donation; endowment; allowance; subsidy; grant-in-aid; allocation; grant; donated property
dotacyjny [do-tah-**tsiy**-ni] adj.m. of a grant-in-aid
dotaczać [do-**tah**-chahćh] v. wheel up to (a point, etc); finish turning (on a lathe, etc.); finish drawing (liquid from a barrel, etc.); fill (a barrel, etc. with an additional fluid) (*repeatedly*)
dotańczyć [do-**tahń**-chićh] v. finish dancing (a performance, etc.)
dotapiać [do-**tah**-pyahćh] v. finish melting; finish; smelting; add more (fat) to melting (*repeatedly*)
dotarcie [do-**tahr**-ćhe] n. reaching; overcoming friction; attainment (of something)
dotąd [**do**-townt] adv. up till now; here to fore; hitherto; thus far; so far; yet; by then; till then; still; not... yet; up to here; up to the present; to date; at this time; not as ... yet
dotelefonować się [do-te-le-fo-**no**-vahćh śhan] v. get the connection (on the telephone); get through to somebody on the telephone
dotętniczy [do-tant-**ńee**-chi] adj.m. intra-arterial (injection, etc.)
dotkać [**do**-tkahćh] v. finish weaving; weave additionally
dotkliwie [do-**tklee**-vye] adv. painfully; keenly; intensely; severely; badly
dotkliwość [do-**tklee**-vośhćh] f. keenness; intensity; severity
dotkliwy [do-**tklee**-vi] adj.m. painful; severe; intense; keen; galling
dotknąć [**dot**-knownćh] v. touch; handle; manipulate; finger; palpate; offend; hurt (feelings, etc.); nettle; sting; pique; cut to the quick; cut to the core; affect; afflict; aggrieve; smite; visit
dotknąć się [**dot**-knownćh śhan] v. touch (each other); touch
dotknięcie [dot-**kńan**-ćhe] n. touch; contact; feeling; stroke (of a brush, etc.)
dotknięty [dot-**kńan**-ti] adj.m. touched; offended
dotleniać [do-**tle**-ńahćh] v. add more oxygen (*repeatedly*)
dotleniać się [do-**tle**-ńahćh śhan] v. breathe more oxygen; get enough oxygen (*repeatedly*)
dotlenić [do-**tle**-ńeećh] v. add more oxygen

dotlenić się [do-**tle**-ńeećh śhan] v. breathe more oxygen; get enough oxygen
dotlewać się [do-**tle**-vahćh śhan] v. smoulder away (*repeatedly*)
dotlić się [do-tleećh śhan] v. smoulder away
dotłaczać [do-**twah**-chahćh] v. finish pressing out; shape up to final condition (*repeatedly*)
dotłoczyć [do-**two**-chićh] v. finish pressing out; shape up to final condition
dotłoczyć się [do-**two**-chićh śhan] v. elbow one's way; push one's way
dotłuc [do-twoots] v. finish crushing; finish pounding
dotłuc się [do-twoots śhan] v. finish breaking up; arrive after a harrowing trip
dotoczyć [do-**to**-chićh] v. wheel up (to a spot, etc.); finish turning on a lathe; finish drawing liquid; fill up (a cask, etc.) with additional fluid
dotopić [do-**to**-peećh] v. finish melting (a fat); finish smelting; add more (fat, etc.) to melting
dotować [do-**to**-vahćh] v. allocate grant-in-aid; subsidize; endow
dotowanie [do-to-**vah**-ńe] n. grant-in-aid; subsidy; endowment
dotrenować [do-tre-**no**-vahćh] v. give sufficient training; train properly
dotransportować [do-trahn-spor-**to**-vahćh] v. bring to a destination
dotrawiać [do-**trah**-vyahćh] v. finish digesting; finish cleaning with acid (*repeatedly*)
dotrawić [do-**trah**-veećh] v. finish digesting; finish cleaning with acid
dotrwać [do-trfahćh] v. persevere; hold out; last; survive; keep faith; be true; endure
dotrzeć [do-tshećh] v. reach; overcome friction; rub up; break in (a car, etc.)
dotrzeć się [do-tshećh śhan] v. become broken-in
dotrzeźwiać [do-**tsheźh**-vyahćh] v. bring back to consciousness; revive; sober (*repeatedly*)
dotrzeźwić [do-**tsheźh**-veećh] v. bring back to consciousness; revive; sober
dotrzeźwieć [do-**tsheźh**-vyećh] v. sober; sober up; sober down; become sober
dotrzymać [do-**tshi**-mahćh] v. keep; stick to one's commitment; adhere; redeem; hold fast; hold till the end; abide; stand (by); endure
dotrzymać słowa [do-**tshi**-mahćh **swo**-vah] exp.: to keep a promise
dotrzymać komuś kroku [do-**tshi**-mahćh **ko**-moośh **kro**-koo] exp.: to keep pace with somebody; keep up with somebody
dotrzymać komuś towarzystwa [do-**tshi**-mahćh **ko**-moośh to-vah-**zhi**-stfah] exp.: to keep somebody company
dotrzymać warunków [do-**tshi**-mahćh vah-**roon**-koof] exp.: to stand by (keep) the terms
dotrzymywać [do-tshi-**mi**-vahćh] v. keep; stick to one's commitment; adhere; redeem; hold fast; hold till the end; abide; stand (by); endure (*repeatedly*)
dotrzymanie [do-tshi-**mah**-ńe] n. adherence (to a contract, etc.)
dotuczać [do-**too**-chahćh] v. finish fattening; fatten properly; fatten more (hogs, etc.) (*repeatedly*)
dotuczać się [do-**too**-chahćh śhan] v. be fattened (*repeatedly*)
dotuczyć [do-**too**-chićh] v. finish fattening; fatten properly; fatten more (hogs, etc.)
dotuczyć się [do-**too**-chićh śhan] v. be fattened
doturlać się [do-**toor**-lahćh śhan] v. roll up to; roll as far as
dotychczas [do-**tikh**-chahs] adv. up to now; hitherto; to date; see: **dotąd**
dotychczasowo [do-tikh-chah-**so**-vo] adv. hitherto
dotychczasowość [do-tikh-chah-**so**-vośhćh] f. the present; the present state of affairs
dotychczasowy [do-tikh-chah-**so**-vi] adj.m. hitherto prevailing; hitherto

existing; past; former; previous
dotychczasowe wiadomości [do-tikh-chah-so-ve vyah-do-mośh-ćhee] exp.: the news received up to now
dotyczna [do-tich-nah] f. cotangent
dotyczący [do-ti-chown-tsi] adj.m. relative; concerning; relating
dotyczyć [do-ti-chićh] v. concern; relate; regard; affect; refer (to); deal (with); have to do (with); appertain (to); apply (to) (*repeatedly*)
to mnie nie dotyczy [to mńe ńe do-ti-chi] exp.: it is no concern of mine; it does not concern me
dotyk [do-tik] m. touch; feel; the touch; the feel
dotykać [do-ti-kahćh] v. touch; handle; manipulate; finger; palpate; offend; hurt (feelings, etc.); nettle; sting; pique; cut to the quick; cut to the core; affect; afflict; aggrieve; smite; visit (*repeatedly*)
dotykać się [do-ti-kahćh śhan] v. touch (each other); touch (*repeatedly*)
dotykalnie [do-ti-kahl-ńe] adv. tangibly; palpably
dotykalność [do-ti-kahl-nośhćh] f. tangibility; palpability
dotykalny [do-ti-kahl-ni] adj.m. tangible; palpable; touchable; self-evident; manifest
dotykowo [do-ti-ko-vo] adv. by touch; tactually
dotykowy [do-ti-ko-vi] adj.m. tactile; tactual
do tyłu [do ti-woo] exp.: adv. backwards; to the back; to the rear
douczać [do-oo-chahćh] v. coach; tutor; complete education; supplement schooling (*repeatedly*)
douczać się [do-oo-chahćh śhan] v. complete one's education; supplement one's schooling (*repeatedly*)
douczanie [do-oo-chah-ńe] n. complementary education; supplementary training
douczyć [do-oo-chićh] v. coach; tutor; complete education; supplement schooling
douczyć się [do-oo-chićh śhan] v. complete one's education; supplement one's schooling
do upadłego [do oo-pahd-we-go] exp.: till the bitter end; to complete exhaustion
doustnie [do-oost-ńe] adv. orally
doustny [do-oost-ni] adj.m. oral
dowarzać [do-vah-zhahćh] v. finish cooking; cook thoroughly; cook (some or much) more (*repeatedly*)
dowarzać się [do-vah-zhahćh śhan] v. be almost cooked (*repeatedly*)
dowarzyć [do-vah-zhićh] v. finish cooking; cook thoroughly; cook (some or much) more
dowarzyć się [do-vah-zhićh śhan] v. be almost cooked; be almost ready
doważać [do-vah-zhahćh] v. finish weighing; add (in the balance); give good weight (*repeatedly*)
doważyć [do-vah-zhićh] v. finish weighing; add (in the balance); give good weight
dowąchać się [do-vown-khahćh śhan] v. scent; find by smelling
dowcip [dof-ćheep] m. wit; joke; jest; gag; quip; sally; witticism; pleasantry; piece of waggery; yarn; salt; humor; esprit; trait of humor; ingenuity; smartness; intelligence; acumen; sagacity
dowcipas [dof-ćhee-pahs] m. clumsy joke; distasteful joke; man telling distasteful jokes
dowcipasek [dof-ćhee-pah-sek] m. stupid joke; somewhat distasteful joke; man telling stupid jokes
dowcipek [dof-ćhee-pek] m. little joke; small pleasantry
dowcipkować [dof-ćheep-ko-vahćh] v. display one's wit; joke; crack jokes; be jocose (*repeatedly*)
dowcipkowanie [dof-ćheep-ko-vah-ńe] n. jokes; jests; waggery
dowcipnie [dof-ćheep-ńe] adv. wittily; humorously; with humor; facetiously; waggishly; in jest; jokingly; jestingly; jocosely; cleverly

dowcipniś [dof-ćheep-ńeeśh] m. wit; facetious person; jester; joker; wag

dowcipny [dof-**ćheep**-ni] adj.m. witty; humorous; facetious; waggish; jocose; full of humor; funny; amusing; clever; ingenious; subtle; cute; shrewd; smart

dowcipuszek [dof-ćhee-**poo**-shek] m. joke; jest; piece of waggery

dowędrować [do-van-**dro**-vahćh] v. reach by wandering; come to (a place, etc.)

dowędrowywać [do-van-dro-**vi**-vahćh] v. reach by wandering; come to (a place, etc.) (*repeatedly*)

dowędzać [do-**van**-dzahćh] v. smoke-cure thoroughly; finish smoke-curing (*repeatedly*)

dowędzić [do-**van**-dźheećh] v. smoke-cure thoroughly; finish smoke-curing

dowiadywać się [do-vyah-**di**-vahćh śhan] v. inquire; ask about; ask for; ask after; ask questions; make inquiries (about); learn (about) (*repeatedly*)

dowiadywanie się [do-vyah-di-**vah**-ńe śhan] n. inquiry; investigation; questions asked

dowiązać [do-**vyown**-zahćh] v. finish binding; tie up; tie more

dowiązywać [do-vyown-**zi**-vahćh] v. finish binding; tie up; tie more (*repeatedly*)

do widzenia [do vee-**dze**-ńah] exp.: good bye; see you later

dowidzieć [do-**vee**-dźhećh] v. see well; not to miss seeing
niedowidzieć [ńe-do-**vee**-dźhećh] v. to be short-sighted

dowiedzieć się [do-**vye**-dźhećh śhan] v. get to know; learn (about); hear (of); find out (about); be informed of; come to know; get knowledge (of)

dowiercać [do-**vyer**-tsahćh] v. finish boring; drill more (*repeatedly*)

dowiercać się [do-**vyer**-tsahćh śhan] v. reach by boring; reach by drilling; come upon (oil, water, salt, etc.) (*repeatedly*)

dowiercić [do-**vyer**-ćheećh] v. finish boring; drill more

dowiercić się [do-**vyer**-ćheećh śhan] v. reach by boring; reach by drilling; come upon (oil, water, salt, etc.)

dowierzać [do-**vye**-zhahćh] v. trust; have confidence in (*repeatedly*)
nie dowierzać [ńe do-**vye**-zhahćh] exp.: to distrust; to mistrust

dowierzanie [do-vye-**zhah**-ńe] n. trust; confidence

dowierzchnia [do-**vyesh**-khńah] f. inclined mine corridor (often used for ventilation); riser

dowieść [**do**-vyeśhćh] v. prove; demonstrate; argue; bring (to a place); show; reveal; be a proof of; be indicative of; vindicate; testify to; bear witness to; give proof of; go to prove; reveal

dowietrzny [do-**vyetsh**-ni] adj.m. windward (side, etc.); weather (side, etc.)

dowiezienie [do-vye-**źhe**-ńe] n. bringing (by means of transportation)

dowieźć [**do**-vyeśhćh] v. supply; take (by means of transportation); drive to; drop at (a destination)

dowlec [**do**-vlets] v. drag as far as; drag to the end

dowlec się [**do**-vlets śhan] v. come dragging along; drag oneself; crawl (to a certain spot)

dowlekać [do-**vle**-kahćh] v. drag as far as; drag to the end (*repeatedly*)

dowlekać się [do-**vle**-kahćh śhan] v. come dragging along; drag oneself; crawl (to a certain spot) (*repeatedly*)

dowodnie [do-**vo**-dńe] adv. conclusively; irrefutably; undeniably

dowodny [do-**vo**-dni] adj.m. conclusive; irrefutable; undeniable

dowodowy [do-vo-**do**-vi] adj.m. evidential; demonstrative; giving proof; conclusive; probative
materiał dowodowy [mah-**te**-ryahw do-vo-**do**-vi] exp.: the evidence

dowodzenie [do-vo-**dze**-ńe] n. demonstration; proof; contention; command; generalship; leadership
dowodzić [do-**vo**-dźheećh] v. conduct; command; be in command; lead; be leader; keep proving
dowojować się [do-vo-**yo**-vahćh śhan] v. get by force of arms; bring (trouble, etc.) down on oneself
do woli [do **vo**-lee] exp.: as much as possible; as much as desired
dowolnie [do-**vol**-ńe] adv. at will; optionally; freely; at choice; as one likes
dowolność [do-**vol**-nośhćh] f. freedom; free choice; option; arbitrariness; discretion
dowolny [do-**vol**-ni] adj.m. optional; any; of one's free choice; whichever; no matter which; no matter what; facultative; discretional; discretionary; free; unrestricted
w dowolnym kierunku [v do-**vol**-nim ke-**roon**-koo] exp.: in any direction
w dowolnym kolorze [v do-**vol**-nim ko-**lo**-zhe] exp.: of any color (you choose, want, etc.)
dowołać się [do-**vo**-wahćh śhan] v. call till someone answers; succeed in calling somebody
dowozić [do-**vo**-źheećh] v. bring; supply (by means of transportation) (*repeatedly*)
dowozowy [do-vo-**zo**-vi] adj.m. supply (ramp, etc.); delivery (truck, etc.)
dowożenie [do-vo-**zhe**-ńe] v. bringing (by means of transportation)
dowód [do-voot] m. proof; evidence; testimony; record; token; mark; manifestation (of feelings, etc.); deed; document; warrant; paper; argument
dowód osobisty [**do**-voot o-so-**bee**-sti] exp.: identity card
dowód rzeczowy [**do**-voot zhe-**cho**-vi] exp.: legal proof; legal instrument
niezbity dowód [ńe-**zbee**-ti **do**-voot] exp.: irrefutable proof; irrefutable argument
dowódca [do-**voot**-tsah] m. commander; (military) officer
dowódczy [do-**voot**-chi] adj.m. leadership (talent, etc.)
dowództwo [do-**voots**-tfo] n. command; generalship; leadership; commanding staff; those in command; headquarters
objąć dowództwo [o-byownćh do-**voots**-tfo] exp.: to take command
dowóz [**do**-voos] m. supply; supplies; delivery; deliveries; transportation
doza [**do**-zah] f. dose (of medicine, etc.); degree; amount; quantity
dozator [do-**zah**-tor] m. dosage meter for fluids and granular substances
dozbrajać [do-**zbrah**-yahćh] v. rearm; supplement weapons; supply a deficiency in the military equipment; complete the armament (*repeatedly*)
dozbrajać się [do-**zbrah**-yahćh śhan] v. complete one's armaments (*repeatedly*)
dozbroić [do-**zbro**-eećh] v. rearm; supplement weapons; supply a deficiency in the military equipment; complete the armament
dozbroić się [do-**zbro**-eećh śhan] v. complete arming oneself
dozbrojenie [do-zbro-**ye**-ńe] n. rearmament; supplementary equipment
dozgonnie [do-**zgon**-ńe] adv. for life; till death
dozgonny [do-**zgon**-ni] adj.m. lifelong; lasting till death; undying (gratitude, etc.)
doziemny [do-**źhem**-ni] adj.m. reaching almost to the ground
doziębić się [do-**źhan**-beećh śhan] v. worsen one's cold
doznać [do-znahćh] v. go through; undergo; endure; feel; suffer; experience; meet with (kindness, insults, etc.); be percipient of; receive (impression, etc.); taste (poverty, etc.); have (pains, etc.)

doznać rozczarowania [**do**-znahćh ros-chah-ro-**vah**-ńah] exp.: to meet with disappointment
doznanie [do-**znah**-ńe] n. an experience; feeling; sensation
doznawać [do-**znah**-vahćh] v. go through; undergo; endure; feel; suffer; experience; meet with (kindness, insults, etc.); be percipient of; receive (impression, etc.); taste (poverty, etc.); have (pains, etc.) (*repeatedly*)
doznawanie [do-znah-**vah**-ńe] n. an experience; feeling; sensation (*repeated*)
do zobaczenia [do zo-bah-**che**-ńah] exp.: good-bye
do zobaczyska [do zo-bah-**chi**-skah] exp.: bye-bye; cheerio
dozorca [do-**zor**-tsah] m. caretaker; watchman; overseer; custodian; janitor; door-keeper
dozorcostwo [do-zor-**tso**-stfo] n. caretaker's job
dozorcówka [do-zor-**tsoof**-kah] f. caretaker's dwelling
dozorczyni [do-zor-**chi**-ńee] f. (female) caretaker; custodian; janitor; door-keeper; caretaker's wife
dozorować [do-zo-**ro**-vahćh] v. oversee; supervise; attend; see to; keep watch on; keep watch over; take care of (*repeatedly*)
dozorowanie [do-zo-ro-**vah**-ńe] n. overseeing; supervision; inspection
dozorowiec [do-zo-**ro**-vyets] m. ship on convoy duty
dozorowy [do-zo-**ro**-vi] adj.m. supervision (work, etc.)
dozorujący [do-zo-roo-**yown**-tsi] m. tender
dozować [do-**zo**-vahćh] v. doze; proportion (*repeatedly*)
dozowanie [do-zo-**vah**-ńe] n. dosage; proportioning; measurement (of a dose)
dozownik [do-**zo**-vńeek] m. feeder; dose-dispensing device (for fluids, powders, and granular materials)
dozór [**do**-zoor] m. surveillance; supervision; care; watch; attendance; inspection; supervising body or (person)
dozwalać [do-**zvah**-lahćh] v. allow to happen; let happen; permit; admit (of something) (*repeatedly*)
dozwolenie [do-zvo-**le**-ńe] n. permission
dozwolić [do-**zvo**-leećh] v. allow to happen; let happen; permit; admit (of something)
dozwolony [do-zvo-**lo**-ni] adj.m. permissible; allowed; permitted
dozwolony okres polowania [do-zvo-**lo**-ni **o**-kres po-lo-**vah**-ńah] exp.: open season
dozymetr [do-**zi**-metr] m. dosimeter
dozymetria [do-zi-**me**-tryah] f. dosimetry
dozymetryczny [do-zi-met-**rich**-ni] adj.m. dosimetric
dozymetrysta [do-zi-me-**tris**-tah] m. specialist in dosimetry
doża [**do**-zhah] m. doge (magistrate)
dożąć [**do**-zhownćh] v. finish harvesting; finish reaping (a crop)
dożeglować [do-zhe-**glo**-vahćh] v. sail up to; reach by sailing
dożerać [do-**zhe**-rahćh] v. devour to the last scrap; eat up; harass; worry (somebody, etc.) (*repeatedly*)
dożreć [**do**-zhrećh] v. devour to the last scrap; eat up; harass; worry (somebody, etc.)
dożuć [**do**-zhoooćh] v. finish chewing; finish munching
dożuwać [do-**zhoo**-vahćh] v. finish chewing; finish munching (*repeatedly*)
dożycie [do-**zhi**-ćhe] n. life-expectancy; reaching an age
dożyć [**do**-zhićh] v. live till; live to see; last till; reach (an age, etc.); live to be (eighty, etc.); live long enough
dożyć późnego wieku [**do**-zhićh pooźh-**ne**-go **vye**-koo] exp.: to live to an old age
dożyć stu lat [**do**-zhićh stoo laht] exp.: to live to be a hundred years old
dożylnie [do-**zhil**-ńe] adv. intravenously
dożylny [do-**zhil**-ni] adj.m.

intravenous
dożynać [do-**zhi**-nahćh] v. finish harvesting; finish reaping (a crop) (*repeatedly*)
dożynki [do-**zhin**-kee] pl. harvest festivities
dożynkowy [do-zhin-**ko**-vi] adj.m. harvest-home (songs, etc.)
do żywa [do **zhi**-vah] exp.: to the quick; painfully; to the raw
dożywać [do-**zhi**-vahćh] v. live till; live to see; last till; reach (an age, etc.); live to be (eighty, etc.); live long enough (*repeatedly*)
dożywalność [do-zhi-**vahl**-nośhćh] f. life expectancy based on statistical probability
do żywego [do zhi-**ve**-go] exp.: to the raw; to the quick = **do żywa**
dożywiać [do-**zhi**-vyahćh] v. give supplementary alimentation; supply necessary food (*repeatedly*)
dożywiać się [do-**zhi**-vyahćh śh<u>an</u>] v. supplement one's alimentation; find extra food (*repeatedly*)
dożywić [do-**zhi**-veećh] v. give supplementary alimentation; supply necessary food
dożywić się [do-**zhi**-veećh śh<u>an</u>] v. supplement one's alimentation; find extra food
dożywienie [do-zhi-**vye**-ńe] n. extra food; supplementary alimentation
dożywocie [do-zhi-**vo**-ćhe] n. life estate; life pension; annuity; perpetuity
dożywotni [do-zhi-**vo**-tńee] adj.m. lifelong; life (pension, etc.); held for life
kara dożywotniego więzienia [**kah**-rah do-zhi-vo-**tńe**-go vy<u>an</u>-**źhe**-ńah] exp.: imprisonment for life; life sentence
dożywotniczka [do-zhi-vo-**tńeech**-kah] f. woman living on an annuity; lifer; woman sentenced for life
dożywotnik [do-zhi-**vo**-tńeek] m. man living on an annuity; lifer; man sentenced for life
dożywotnio [do-zhi-**vo**-tńo] adv. for life; in perpetuity
dożywotność [do-zhi-**vo**-tnośhćh] f. lifelong enjoyment (of a privilege, etc.)
dój [dooy] m. milking
dójka [**dooy**-kah] f. milch cow; milker; milkmaid
dół [doow] m. pit; hole in the ground; excavation; concavity; cavity; depression; grave; bottom part; bottom; foot (of a page, etc.); the lower classes; the masses
dół rzeki [doow **zhe**-kee] exp.: the lower course of a river
dołem [**do**-wem] exp.: at the bottom; at the base; below; down below
na dole [nah **do**-le] exp.: below; down; downstairs
w dole [v **do**-le] exp.: down hill
z dołu [z **do**-woo] exp.: from below
schodzić na dół [**skho**-dźheećh nah doow] exp.: to go down (downstairs; downhill)
drab [drahp] m. tall strapping fellow; ruffian; scamp; rowdy; scoundrel
drabina [drah-**bee**-nah] f. ladder; rack (of a cart, etc.)
drabiniasty [drah-bee-**ńah**-sti] adj.m. ladderlike
wóz drabiniasty [voos drah-bee-**ńah**-sti] exp.: rack wagon
drabinka [drah-**been**-kah] f. small ladder; ladder-stitch; wall-bars
drabinkowy [drah-been-**ko**-vi] adj.m. ladder (stitch)
drabinowy [drah-bee-**no**-vi] adj.m. of a ladder
drabisko [drah-**bee**-sko] n. big strapping man; ruffian; scamp; rowdy; scoundrel
dracena [drah-**tse**-nah] f. dracena; dragon tree; dragon's blood
drachma [**drakh**-mah] f. drachma; drachm
draczny [**drahch**-ni] adj.m. slang: comical; strange; laughable; odd; silly
draczna mina [**drahch**-nah **mee**-nah] exp.: funny look
draga [**drah**-gah] f. dredge; dredge-anchor
dragoman [drah-**go**-mahn] m.

dragoman; an interpreter of Near-Eastern languages

dragon [**drah**-gon] m. dragoon; amazon; virago; fixed belt (at the back of an overcoat)

dragonia [drah-**go**-ńyah] f. Polish light cavalry (of old)

dragoński [drah-**goń**-skee] adj.m. dragoon's

po dragońsku [po drah-**goń**-skoo] exp.: cavalierly; roughly

dragować [drah-**go**-vahćh] v. dredge (*repeatedly*)

dragowanie [drah-go-**vah**-ńe] n. dredging

drajw [drahyf] m. drive (in sport)

draka [**drah**-kah] f. row; rumpus; hullabaloo

drako [**drah**-ko] f. variety of palm bush with red resin; dragon palm

drakoński [drah-**koń**-skee] v. Draconian; severe; drastic; ruthless

drałować [drah-**wo**-vahćh] v. tramp; go on foot

drałowanie [drah-wo-**vah**-ńe] n. a tramp; tramp

drama [**drah**-mah] m. melodrama of 19th century

dramat [**drah**-maht] m. drama; tragedy

dramatopisarka [drah-mah-to-pee-**sahr**-kah] m. (woman) playwright

dramatopisarski [drah-mah-to-pee-**sahr**-skee] adj.m. of a playwright

dramatopisarstwo [drah-mah-to-pee-**sahr**-stfo] n. dramaturgy

dramatopisarz [drah-mah-to-**pee**-sash] m. playwright

dramaturg [drah-**mah**-toorg] m. dramatist; playwright

dramaturgia [drah-mah-**toor**-gyah] f. dramaturgy; play writing

dramaturgicznie [drah-mah-toor-**gich**-ńe] adv. dramaturgically

dramaturgiczny [drah-mah-toor-**gich**-ni] adj.m. dramaturgic; dramaturgical

dramatycznie [drah-mah-**tich**-ńe] adv. dramatically; dramaturgically

dramatyczność [drah-mah-**tich**-nośhćh] f. dramatizing; the dramatic aspect (of a situation); horror

dramatyczny [drah-mah-**tich**-ni] adj.m. dramatic; scenic; pathetic; tragic

dramatyzacja [drah-mah-ti-**zah**-tsyah] f. dramatization

dramatyzm [drah-**mah**-tizm] m. dramatizing; the dramatic aspect (of a situation); horror

dramatyzować [drah-mah-ti-**zo**-vahćh] v. dramatize (a novel) (*repeatedly*)

dramatyzować się [drah-mah-ti-**zo**-vahćh śh<u>an</u>] v. become dramatized (*repeatedly*)

dramatyzowanie [drah-mah-ti-zo-**vah**-ńe] n. dramatization; dramatizing

dramatyzowanie się [drah-mah-ti-zo-**vah**-ńe śh<u>an</u>] n. dramatizing oneself

dranica [drah-**ńee**-tsah] f. batten; lath; piece of lathing; shingle

dranicowy [drah-ńee-**tso**-vi] adj.m. shingle (roof, etc.)

drań [drahń] m. vulg.: scoundrel; crumb; rotter; cad; dirty dog

drański [**drahń**-skee] adj.m. vulg.: mean; scurvy

draństwo [**drahń**-stfo] n. vulg.: scurvy trick; meanness; riff-raff; rabble; (human) trash

drapacz [**drah**-pahch] m. scraper; spring-tooth harrow

drapacz chmur [**drah**-pahch khmoor] exp.: skyscraper

drapaczować [drah-pah-**cho**-vahćh] v. work the soil with spring-tooth harrow (*repeatedly*)

drapać [**drah**-pahćh] v. scratch (*repeatedly*)

drapać się [**drah**-pahćh śh<u>an</u>] v. clamber; scramble; climb (up a mountain); scratch (one's head, etc.) (*repeatedly*)

drapać się w głowę [**drah**-pahćh śh<u>an</u> v **gwo**-v<u>an</u>] exp.: to scratch one's head

drapak [**drah**-pahk] m. stubby old broom

dać drapaka [dahćh drah-**pah**-kah] exp.: to bolt; to decamp; to run away; to scamper; to scoot

drapalnia [drah-**pahl**-ńah] f. gig-mill; (weaver's) raising-machine

department
drapanie [drah-**pah**-ńe] n. scraping; scratching
draparka [drah-**pahr**-kah] f. gig-mill; (weaver's) raising-machine
draperia [drah-**pe**-ryah] f. drapery; hanging; tapestry
draperiowy [drah-per-**yo**-vi] adj.m. of a drapery; of a tapestry
drapichrust [drah-**pee**-khroost] m. scamp; rogue; loafer
drapiestwo [drah-**pye**-stfo] n. plunder
drapieżca [drah-**pyesh**-tsah] m. plunderer
drapieżczy [drah-**pyesh**-chi] adj.m. predatory; rapacious; grasping
drapieżnica [drah-pyezh-**ńee**-tsah] f. plunderer; extortioner
drapieżnie [drah-**pyezh**-ńe] adv. rapaciously
drapieżnik [drah-**pyezh**-ńeek] m. beast of prey; plunderer; extortioner
drapieżność [drah-**pyezh**-nośhćh] f. rapacity; predacity
drapieżny [drah-**pyezh**-ni] adj.m. rapacious; predatory; grasping
zwierzę drapieżne [zvye-zhan drah-**pyezh**-ne] exp.: beast of prey
drapnąć [**drahp**-nownćh] v. scratch; run away; bolt; decamp; scamper; scoot
drapnięcie [drahp-**ńan**-ćhe] n. flight; bolt; scratch
drapować [drah-**po**-vahćh] v. drape (*repeatedly*)
drapować się [drah-**po**-vahćh śhan] v. drape oneself (*repeatedly*)
drapowanie [drah-po-**vah**-ńe] n. drapery
drapowanie się [drah-po-**vah**-ńe śhan] n. draping oneself
drasnąć [**drah**-snownćh] v. scratch; graze; hurt; wound slightly; brush past; inflict a slight wound
drasnąć się [**drah**-snownćh śhan] v. scratch oneself; hurt oneself
drastycznie [drah-**stich**-ńe] adv. drastically; roughly; violently; coarsely; severely; indecently; in a risky manner; piquantly
drastyczność [drah-**stich**-nośhćh] f. indecency; severity; riskiness; piquancy; spiciness; coarseness (of language)
drastyczny [drah-**stich**-ni] adj.m. drastic; rough; violent; severe; scabrous; risky; risque; slippery; spicy; coarse
draśnięcie [drah-**śhńan**-ćhe] n. slight wound; scratch
draśnięcie się [drah-**śhńan**-ćhe śhan] n. self-inflicted slight wound
dratwa [**draht**-fah] f. pitched tread; shoemaker's twine
drażetka [drah-**zhet**-kah] f. bolus; sugar plum; sugar almond; pill
drażliwie [drah-**zhlee**-vye] adv. testily; fretfully; peevishly; irritably; ticklishly
drażliwość [drah-**zhlee**-vośhćh] f. susceptibility; ticklishness
drażliwy [drah-**zhlee**-vi] adj.m. touchy; irritable; ticklish; thorny; spiny; sore; tender; testy; edgy; huffish; fretful; petulant; peevish; thin-skinned; sensitive; susceptible; delicate; confidential; scabrous; slippery; risky; risque
drażniąco [drah-**zhńown**-tso] adv. provocatively; irritably; jeeringly; gratingly; pungently; acridly; huffishly
drażniący [drah-**zhńown**-tsi] adj.m. irritating; provocative; provoking; irritant; jarring; grating; pungent; acrid
drażnić [**drah**-zhńeećh] v. vex; tease; irritate; whet; annoy; jar; provoke; stimulate; gall; excite; chafe; tease (*repeatedly*)
drażnić się [**drah**-zhńeećh śhan] v. tease (somebody, etc.)
drażnienie [drah-**zhńe**-ńe] n. irritation; stimulation; provocation; vexation; annoyance
drażnienie się [drahzh-**ńe**-ńe śhan] n. irritating one another
drąg [drowng] m. pole; bar; rod
drągal [**drown**-gahl] m. lout; lubber; clumsy big man; clumsy tall kid
drągowina [drown-go-**vee**-nah] f. trees used for pole-making
drągowy [drown-**go**-vi] adj.m. of a

rod; of pole-making
drążarka [drown-**zhahr**-kah] f. drill; dowelling-machine
drążący [drown-**zhown**-tsi] adj.m. penetrating
drążek [**drown**-zhek] m. bar; rod; shaft; spar; lever
drążki gimnastyczne [**drown**-shkee geem-nah-**stich**-ne] exp.: bars
drążenie [drown-**zhe**-ńe] n. seeding; boring
drążkarka [drownsh-**kahr**-kah] f. dowell making machine
drążkowy [drownsh-**shko**-vi] adj.m. of rod; of shaft
cyrkiel drążkowy [**tsir**-kel drown-**shko**-vi] exp.: beam compasses; trammels
boja drążkowa [bo-yah drown-**shko**-vah] exp.: spar-buoy
drążnia [**drown**-zhńah] f. Cecropia tree; mulberry tree
drążnica [drown-**zhńee**-tsah] f. variety of butterfly (with parasitic larva living in stems of tomatoes, potatoes and tobacco plants); Xanthoecia flavago
drążyć [**drown**-zhićh] v. hollow out; bore; torment; fret; gnaw; seed (berries, etc.); stone (fruit) (*repeatedly*)
drebel [**dre**-bel] m. ship built for transporting of live fish
drefić [**dre**-feećh] v. slang: be scared; be afraid; be uneasy about (something) (mob jargon)
drelich [**dre**-leekh] m. denim; jean; dungaree; denim overalls; jeans; dungarees
drelichowy [dre-lee-**kho**-vi] adj.m. of denim; of jean; of dungaree; denim (overalls, etc.); jean (trousers, etc.); dungaree
dren [dren] m. drain (pipe or tile)
drenarka [dre-**nahr**-kah] f.machine of draining boggy terrain; draining of land; installing drainage system
drenarski [dre-**nahr**-skee] adj.m. draining (system, etc.); drainage (ditch, etc.)
drenaż [**dre**-nahsh] m. drainage
drenażowy [dre-nah-**zho**-vi] adj.m. drainage (tube, pipe, etc.)
drenować [dre-**no**-vahćh] v. drain (*repeatedly*)
drenowanie [dre-no-**vah**-ńe] n. drainage
drenowy [dre-**no**-vi] adj.m. draining (system, etc.); drainage (ditch, pipe, etc.)
dreptać [**drep**-tahćh] v. walk with a tripping step; walk with a mincing step; trip-trot; toddle; totter (along); patter; come tottering; go tottering; stamp one's feet; take pains to obtain; exert oneself to obtain; give oneself a lot of trouble to obtain (something, etc.) (*repeatedly*)
dreptanie [drep-**tah**-ńe] n. mincing steps; tripping steps
dreptanina [drep-tah-**ńee**-nah] f. mincing steps; endeavors; bustle
dres [dres] m. track suit
dreszcz [dreshch] m. chill; shudder; thrill (of joy, etc.); flutter; shiver
dreszczowiec [dre-**shcho**-vyets] m. thriller (novel or movie)
dreszczowy [dre-**shcho**-vi] adj.m. thrilling
dreszczyk [**dre**-shchik] m. thrill; shudder; shiver
drewienko [dre-**vyen**-ko] n. piece of wood; stick
drewko [**dref**-ko] n. small firewood
drewniak [**drev**-ńahk] m. clog; wooden house; log cabin
drewniany [dre-**vńah**-ni] adj.m. wooden; timber (yard); timbered
drewnieć [**dre**-vńećh] v. lignify; become wooden; grow stiff; stiffen (*repeatedly*)
drewnienie [dre-**vńe**-ńe] n. lignification
drewno [**dre**-vno] n. piece of wood; timber; stick; log; xylem
drewnopochodny [drev-no-po-**kho**-dni] adj.m. made of processed wood
drewnopodobny [dre-vno-po-**do**-bni] adj.m. similar to wood
drewnowiec [dre-**vno**-vyets] m. ship built to carry lumber
drewutnia [dre-**voot**-ńah] f. wood-shed; shed for fire-wood
drezdeński [dre-**zdeń**-skee] adj.m. of Dresden; Dresden (china,

porcelain, etc.)
drezyna [dre-**zi**-nah] f. trolley
dręczący [dr_an_-**ch_own_**-tsi] adj.m. besetting; agonizing; torturing; oppressive; excruciating; racking; tantalizing
dręczenie [dr_an_-**che**-ńe] n. worry; trouble; agony; torment; torture
dręczenie się [dr_an_-**che**-ńe śh_an_] n. tormenting one another; troubling oneself
dręczony [dr_an_-**cho**-ni] adj.m. tormented; tortured; vexed
dręczyciel [dr_an_-**chi**-ćhel] m. tormentor; oppressor; torturer
dręczycielka [dr_an_-chi-**ćhel**-kah] f. (female) tormentor; oppressor; torturer
dręczyć [dr_an_-chićh] v. torment; harass; vex; oppress; tyrannize; badger; torture; distress; prey (on); agonize; tantalize; rankle (in); trouble; worry; bother (*repeatedly*)
dręczyć się [dr_an_-chićh śh_an_] v. worry; be vexed; fret; be distressed; worry to death; trouble oneself (about); be tormented (by); trouble one another; bother one another (*repeatedly*)
drętwa [dr_an_-tfah] f. electric ray; cramp-fish; numb-fish
drętwawy [dr_an_-**tfah**-vi] adj.m. somewhat numb
drętwica [dr_an_-**tfee**-tsah] f. cerebrospinal meningitis
drętwieć [**dr_an_**-tfyećh] v. grow numb; grow stiff; stiffen; be cramped; anchylose (*repeatedly*)
drętwieć ze strachu [dr_an_-tfyećh ze **strah**-khoo] exp.: to be paralyzed with fear
drętwienie [dr_an_-**tfye**-ńe] n. a cramp; cramp; numbness; anchylosis
drętwo [dr_an_-tfo] adv. torpidly; numbly; rigidly; lifelessly
drętwota [dr_an_-**tfo**-tah] f. torpidity; numbness; stiffness; lifelessness
drętwy [dr_an_-tfi] adj.m. stiff; numb; rigid; lifeless; cramped; torpid
drętwa mowa [dr_an_-tfah **mo**-vah] exp.: empty talk; hot air; speech full of platitudes
drgać [drgahćh] v. vibrate; oscillate; pulsate; throb; tremble; twitch; quiver; twinkle; flicker; quaver; wobble (*repeatedly*)
drgalnica [drgahl-**ńee**-tsah] f. oscillator
drganie [**drgah**-ńe] n. trembling; palpitation; vibration; twitch; twinkle; flicker; wobble
drganiowy [drgah-**ńo**-vi] adj.m. oscillatory; vibratory
drgawka [**drgah**-fkah] f. spasm; convulsion; jerk; twitch
drgawkowy [drgah-**fko**-vi] adj.m. clonic; convulsive
drgnąć [drgn_own_ćh] v. start; give a start; budge; stir; wince; tremble; vibrate; quiver; throb; wobble
drgnienie [**drgńe**-ńe] n. a start; tremor; flicker; twitch; wince
drgnięcie [**drgń_an_**-ćhe] n. tremor; twitch; wince; see: **drgnienie**
driada [**dryah**-dah] f. dryad; wood-nymph
driakiew [**dryah**-_k_ef] f. scabious; gypsy rose; theriac
dribler [**dri**-bler] m. dribler
dribling [**dri**-bleeng] m. = **drybling**
driblować [dri-**blo**-vahćh] v. (*repeatedly*) = **dryblować**
drifter [**dree**-fter] m. = **dryfter**
drink [dreenk] m. glass of vodka; a single drink of liquor
driopitek [dryo-**pee**-tek] m. Dryopithecus (extinct ape)
driopiteki [dryo-pee-**te**-kee] pl. the Dryopithecus ape family
drobiarka [dro-**byahr**-kah] f. poultry-breeding
drobiarski [dro-**byahr**-skee] adj.m. of poultry-breeding
drobiarstwo [dro-**byahr**-stfo] n. poultry-breeding
drobiazg [**dro**-byahzg] m. trifle; detail; trinket; small fry; knick-knack; bagatelle; triviality; trifling detail; a mere nothing; youngster; derisive slang: small beer
drobiazgowo [dro-byahz-**go**-vo] adv. pedantically; punctiliously; in detail; with circumstance; minutely; with precision; with

accuracy; scrupulously; meticulously; fussily
drobiazgowość [dro-byah-**zgo**-vośhćh] f. pedantry; punctiliousness
drobiazgowy [dro-byah-**zgo**-vi] adj.m. pedantic; punctilious; detailed; circumstantial; minute; precise; accurate; trivial; trifling; hair-splitting; scrupulous; meticulous; fussy; finical; finicking; niggling
drobiażdżek [dro-**byah**-zhdzhek] m. small detail; see: **drobiazg**
drobić [**dro**-beećh] v. crumble; mince; trip along; toddle; totter along; come tottering (*repeatedly*)
drobienie [dro-**bye**-ńe] n. tripping step; tottering walk
drobina [dro-**bee**-nah] f. particle; atom; scrap; mite; chit; dot; molecule; corpuscle
drobinka [dro-**bee**-nkah] f. tiny particle (dot) = (dim.) **drobina**
drobinowy [dro-bee-**no**-vi] adj.m. of atom; of molecule
drobiony [dro-**byo**-ni] m. quick-step dance of Tatra Mountains
drobiowy [dro-**byo**-vi] adj.m. poultry (farm, business, etc.)
drobne [**dro**-bne] pl. small change; petty cash; small coin
drobniak [**dro**-bńahk] m. small coin; smooth file
drobnica [dro-**bńee**-tsah] f. debris; small fragments; small change; petty cash; small articles of freight; parcels; packages; small fry; small pieces of lumber
drobnicowiec [dro-bńee-**tso**-vyets] m. general cargo ship
drobnicowy [dro-**bńee**-tso-vi] adj.m. parcel (delivery, etc.)
drobnieć [**dro**-bńećh] v. grow smaller; lessen (*repeatedly*)
drobnienie [dro-**bńe**-ńe] n. fragmentation; growing smaller
drobniuchny [dro-**bńookh**-ni] adj.m. dim. of **drobny** = nicely small
drobniusi [dro-**bńoo**-śhee] adj.m. dim. of **drobny** = nicely small
drobniusieńki [dro-bńoo-**śheń**-kee] adj.m. diminutive of: **drobny** = very nicely small
drobniuteńki [dro-bńoo-**teń**-kee] adj.m. diminutive of: **drobny** = very nicely small
drobniutki [dro-**bńoot**-kee] adj.m. dim. of **drobny** = nicely small
drobniutko [dro-**bńoot**-ko] adv. dim. of **drobno** = in a nicely small way; in a very small way
drobno [**dro**-bno] adv. small; tiny; fine; slight; into small bits; into tiny slices; into fine pieces
drobnoburżuazyjny [dro-bno-boor-zhoo-ah-**ziy**-ni] adj.m. of the lower middle-class; lower middle-class-
drobnochłopski [dro-bno-**khwop**-skee] adj.m. of small-holder's
drobnokapitalistyczny [dro-bno-kah-pee-tah-lee-**stich**-ni] adj.m. of small capital; small-traders'-(mentality, etc.)
drobnokrystaliczny [dro-bno-kri-stah-**leech**-ni] adj.m. fine-crystalline
drobnokwiatowy [dro-bno-kfyah-**to**-vi] adj.m. of small-flowered
drobnolistny [dro-bno-**lee**-stni] adj.m. of small-leaved
drobnomiasteczkowy [dro-bno-myah-stech-**ko**-vi] adj.m. of small town; small-town (mentality, atmosphere, etc.)
drobnomieszczanin [dro-bno-mye-**shchah**-ńeen] m. a member of the lower middle class
drobnomieszczański [dro-bno-mye-**shchahń**-skee] adj.m. of the lower middle class; smug
drobnomieszczańskość [dro-bno-mye-**shchahń**-skośhćh] f. of the lower middle class; smug
drobnomieszczaństwo [dro-bno-mye-**shchahń**-stfo] n. the lower middle class; smugness
drobnonasienny [dro-bno-nah-**śhen**-ni] adj.m. small-seed
drobnorolny [dro-bno-**rol**-ni] adj.m. small-holder's (land, etc.)
drobnostadny [dro-bno-**stah**-dni] adj.m. small-herd
drobnostka [dro-**bno**-stkah] f. trifle; small matter; trinket; matter of no importance
drobnostkowość [dro-dno-**stko**-vośhćh] f. petty-mindedness
drobnostkowo [dro-bno-**stko**-vo]

adv. punctiliously; pedantically; in a petty-minded way; unpleasantly
drobnostkowy [dro-bno-**stko**-vi] adj.m. punctilious; pedantic; petty-minded; mean
drobnoszlachecki [dro-bno-shlah-**khe**-tskee] adj.m. of the yeomanry
drobność [dro-bnośhćh] f. smallness; small size
drobnotowarowy [dro-bno-to-vah-**ro**-vi] adj.m. small-producers' (business, etc.)
drobnoustrojowy [dro-bno-oo-stro-**yo**-vi] adj.m. microbial; of microorganism; of germs
drobnoustrój [dro-bno-**oo**-strooy] m. microbe; microorganism; germ
drobnoustroje [dro-bno-oos-**tro**-ye] pl. microbes; microorganisms; germs
drobnowłościański [dro-bno-vwo-**śhćhahń**-skee] adj.m. smallholders'; small-producers'
drobnowymiarowy [dro-bno-vi-myah-**ro**-vi] adj.m. small-size (car, etc.)
drobnowzorzysty [dro-bno-vzo-**zhi**-sti] adj.m. small-pattern (design, etc.)
drobnoząbkowy [dro-bno-zown-**pko**-vi] adj.m. serrulate
drobnoziarnistość [dro-bno-źhahr-**ńee**-stośhćh] f. fine-grained size; close-grained size
drobnoziarnisty [dro-bno-źhahr-**ńee**-sti] adj.m. fine-grained; close-grained
drobnozwojowy [dro-bno-zvo-**yo**-vi] adj.m. of fine thread; of fine pitch; fine-pitch (thread, etc.)
drobny [**dro**-bni] adj.m. small; tiny; trivial; petty; slight; little; diminutive; undersized; mean; petty-minded; short; very young; insignificant; inconsiderable; minor; niggling; fine; frail; dainty; tripping; mincing; rapid; imperceptible; of small means
czy masz drobne? [chi mahsh **dro**-bne] exp.: do you have any change?; have you got any change?
drobne [**dro**-bne] pl.: small change; change; petty cash
drobne wydatki [**dro**-bne vi-**dah**-tkee] exp.: pocket expenses
drobna suma [**dro**-bnah **soo**-mah] exp.: petty sum
drobna chwila [**dro**-bnah **khfee**-lah] exp.: a little while; a short space of time
droczenie się [dro-**che**-ńe śhan] n. teasing; teasing one another; baiting; baiting one another
droczyć [**dro**-chićh] v. tease (somebody); bait (*repeatedly*)
droczyć się [**dro**-chićh śhan] v. tease; banter; rally; poke fun at (*repeatedly*)
droczyć się ze sobą [**dro**-chićh śhan ze **so**-bown] exp.: to poke fun at one another; to tease one another; to spar at one another; to rally one another; to banter one another
droga [**dro**-gah] f. road; the public road; highway; pass; track; route; pathway; tract; passage; journey; trip; voyage; way course; means; channels; adj. f. dear
być na dobrej drodze [bićh nah **do**-brey **dro**-dze] exp.: to be on the right path (or track)
droga dla pieszych [**dro**-gah dlah **pye**-shikh] exp.: footpath
drogą lądową [**dro**-gown lown-**do**-vown] exp.: by land
drogą na Warszawę [**dro**-gown nah vahr-**shah**-van] exp.: by way of Warsaw; on a road to Warsaw
droga powietrzna [**dro**-gah po-**vye**-tshnah] exp.: airway
droga wodna [**dro**-gah **vo**-dnah] exp.: waterway
drogą wodną [**dro**-gown **vo**-dnown] exp.: by water; by sea
drogą służbową [**dro**-gown swoo-**zhbo**-vown] exp.: through official channels
iść tą samą drogą [eeśhćh town **sah**-mown **dro**-gown] exp.: to go the same way
krótsza droga [**kroot**-shah **dro**-gah] exp.: short cut
na drodze [nah **dro**-dze] exp.: by way of; by means of: through
nie po drodze [ńe po **dro**-dze]

exp.: out of the way
po drodze [po **dro**-dze] exp.: on the way
pół godziny drogi [poow go-**dźhee**-ni **dro**-gee] exp.: half-an-hour's walk (drive, ride)
rozstajne drogi [ros-**stahy**-ne **dro**-gee] exp.: cross-roads; a fork in a road; turn-off; intersection
rozwidlenie drogi [roz-vee-**dle**-ńe **dro**-gee] exp.: a fork in the road
skrzyżowanie dróg [skshi-zho-**vah**-ńe droog] exp.: intersection
szczęśliwej drogi! [shchan-**śhlee**-vey **dro**-gee] exp.: good-bye!; farewell!
w drodze [v **dro**-dze] exp.: adv. under way; by; in way of (help, grace, etc.)
w drodze dedukcji [v **dro**-dze de-**doo**-ktsyee] exp.: by way of deduction
w drodze wyjątku [v **dro**-dze vi-**yown**-tkoo] exp.: by way of exception
wejść komuś w drogę [veyśhćh ko-moośh v **dro**-gan] exp.: to get in somebody's way
wolna droga [**vol**-nah **dro**-gah] exp.: the way is clear
w pół drogi [f poow **dro**-gee] exp.: half-way
wybrać się w drogę [vi-brahćh śhan v **dro**-gan] exp.: to set out on one's way (or trip)
zejść z drogi [zeyśhćh z **dro**-gee] exp.: to give way; to yield (to traffic); to leave the road; to lose the way
zjechać z drogi [**zye**-khahćh z **dro**-gee] exp.: to turn off the road
drogeria [dro-**ge**-ryah] f. drugstore; drysaltery
drogerzysta [dro-ge-**zhi**-stah] m. owner of a drugstore; druggist
drogeryjny [dro-ge-**riy**-ni] adj.m. drugstore (business, etc.)
drogi [**dro**-gee] adj.m. dear; expensive; costly; beloved; precious; close; valued; m. one dear to us; sweetheart
droga pani! [**dro**-gah **pah**-ńee] excl.: my good lady!
drogie [**dro**-ge] n. what we hold dear; what we prize most
drogi panie! [**dro**-gee **pah**-ńe] excl.: my dear man!
mój drogi [mooy **dro**-gee] excl.: old boy! old chap!
drogista [dro-**gee**-stah] m. owner of a drugstore; druggist
drogistka [dro-**gee**-stkah] f. (female) owner of a drugstore; druggist
drogistowski [dro-gee-**sto**-fskee] adj.m. of a drugstore; druggist's
drogistyczny [dro-gee-**stich**-ni] adj.m. of a drugstore; druggist's
drogman [**dro**-gmahn] m. dragoman; interpreter of Arabic, Turkish, or Persian employed in the Near East
drogo [**dro**-go] adv. dear; dearly
to za drogo [to zah **dro**-go] exp.: it's too dear; it's too expensive; it isn't worth the money
drogocenność [dro-go-**tsen**-nośhćh] f. preciousness; high value; costliness; high price
drogocenności [dro-go-tsen-**nośh**-ćhee] pl. valuables; jeweler
drogocenny [dro-go-**tsen**-ni] adj.m. precious; valuable; costly
drogomierz [dro-**go**-myesh] m. odometer; ion counter tracing ion's path
drogomistrz [dro-**go**-meestsh] m. local road inspector
drogość [**dro**-gośhćh] f. high price; costliness
drogowiec [dro-**go**-vyets] m. road worker; road builder
drogownictwo [dro-go-**vńee**-tstfo] n. road-building; road-planning
drogowskaz [dro-**go**-fskahs] m. road sign; signpost; guide-post
drogowskazowy [dro-go-fskah-**zo**-vi] adj.m. of a road sign
drogowy [dro-**go**-vi] adj.m. road
przepisy drogowe [pshe-**pee**-si dro-**go**-ve] exp.: traffic regulations
węzeł drogowy [**van**-zew dro-**go**-vi] exp.: crossroads; multiple intersection
wypadki drogowe [vi-**pah**-tkee dro-**go**-ve] exp.: traffic accidents
znaki drogowe [**znah**-kee dro-**go**-ve] exp.: road signs
drogówka [dro-**goof**-kah] f. highway patrol police-car

dromader [dro-**mah**-der] m. dromedary (camel)
dront [dront] m. dodo (bird)
drop [drop] m. bustard (a game bird); Otis
dropiaty [dro-**pyah-ti**] adj.m. spotted
drops [drops] m. hard, small bonbon
drozd [drozd] m. thrush; robin (bird)
drozofila [dro-zo-**fee**-lah] f. drosophila
droździk [**droźh**-dźheek] m. song-thrush (bird)
drożdżak [**drozh**-dzhahk] m. yeast (fungus); saccharomycete
drożdżarnia [drozh-**dzhahr**-ńah] f. yeast plant
drożdżarz [**drozh**-dzhahsh] m. yeast maker
drożdże [**drozh**-dzhe] pl. yeast
drożdżować [drozh-**dzho**-vahćh] v. add yeast (to pork feed) (*repeatedly*)
drożdżowanie [drozh-dzho-**vah**-ńe] n. adding yeast (to pork feed)
drożdżowiec [drozh-**dzho**-vyets] m. leaven dough
drożdżownia [drozh-**dzho**-vńah] f. yeast plant; yeast factory
drożdżownictwo [drozh-dzhov-**ńeets**-tfo] n. yeast production
drożdżowy [drozh-**dzho**-vi] adj.m. of yeast; leavened; raised
drożdżówka [drozh-**dzhoof**-kah] f. leaven cake; leaven roll
drożdżyca [drozh-**dzhi**-tsah] f. yeast infection of skin
drożeć [dro-zhećh] v. grow dear; rise in price; go up in price; appreciate (*repeatedly*)
drożenie [dro-**zhe**-ńe] n. (a) rise in price
drożenie się [dro-**zhe**-ńe śhan] n. getting up in price
drożność [**drozh**-nośhćh] f. permeability
drożny [**drozh**-ni] adj.m. permeable; pervious; patent; of (free) passage; passable; unobstructed
drożyć się [dro-zhićh śhan] v. charge high prices; demur; make difficulties; raise objections (*repeatedly*)
drożyna [dro-**zhi**-nah] f. cart-track; footpath; pathway
drożynka [dro-**zhin**-kah] f. small cart-track; footpath; little pathway
drożyzna [dro-**zhi**-znah] f. high cost of living; high prices
drożyźniany [dro-zhi-**źhńah**-ni] adj.m. due to rising cost of living
drób [droop] pl. poultry
dróbka [**droop**-kah] pl. giblets
dróżka [**droosh**-kah] f. path; lane
dróżniczka [droozh-**ńeech**-kah] f. (woman) lineman; railway watchman; track-walker
dróżniczy [droozh-**ńee**-chi] adj.m. lineman's; railway watchman's; track-walker's
dróżnik [**droozh**-ńeek] m. lineman; railway watchman; track-walker
druciak [**droo**-ćhahk] m. pot scourer; brad
drucianka [droo-**ćhahn**-kah] f. shoe-scraper
druciany [droo-**ćhah**-ni] adj.m. of wire; made out of wire; wire-
druciarka [droo-**ćhahr**-kah] f. wire-drawing bench
druciarnia [droo-**ćhahr**-ńah] f. wire-drawing mill; wire-works
druciarski [droo-**ćhahr**-skee] adj.m. wire-drawing (machine, etc.)
druciarstwo [droo-**ćhahr**-stfo] n. wire-drawing
druciarz [**droo**-ćhahsh] m. tinker; wire-drawer
drucidło [droo-**ćhee**-dwo] n. draw-plate for wire making
drucik [**droo**-ćheek] m. filament
druczek [**droo**-chek] m. form; leaflet; small print
druczkować [drooch-**ko**-vahćh] v. colloq: print (leaflets, etc.)
druga [droo-gah] f. two o'clock
drugi [**droo**-gee] num. second ; other; the other one; latter; next; further; the latter; m. something different; something else
co drugi [tso **droo**-gee] exp.: every other
drudzy [**droo**-dzi] exp.: other people
druga strona [**droo**-gah **stro**-nah] exp.: the other side
drugi obieg [**droo**-gee **o**-byeg] exp.: uncensored publications;

circulation of illegal publications
drugie danie [droo-ge dah-ńe] exp.: second serving; second course (of a meal)
drugie tyle [droo-ge ti-le] exp.: twice as much
jeden po drugim [ye-den po droo-geem] exp.: one after another; one after each other
jeden w drugiego [ye-den v droo-ge-go] exp.: all without exception
po drugie [po droo-ge] exp.: in the second place
po drugiej stronie [po droo-gey stro-ńe] exp.: on the other side
z drugiej strony...[z droo-gey stro-ni] exp.: on the other hand...
z drugiej ręki [z droo-gey ran-kee] exp.: second-hand
drugo- [droo-go] = second-
drugoklasista [droo-go-klah-śhee-stah] m. second-grade pupil
drugoklasowy [droo-go-klah-so-vi] adj.m. second-class; of second-class quality
drugoligowiec [droo-go-lee-go-vyets] m. junior league player
drugoligowy [droo-go-lee-go-vi] adj.m. of junior league (player, etc.); of the second division
drugoplanowo [droo-go-plah-no-vo] adv. as a matter of secondary importance
drugoplanowy [droo-go-plah-no-vi] adj.m. of secondary importance
drugoroczniak [droo-go-roch-ńahk] m. pupil repeating a class
drugoroczność [droo-go-roch-nośhćh] f. being in the second year of graduate studies
drugoroczny [droo-go-roch-ni] adj.m. of second grade; second-grade pupil
drugorzędnie [droo-go-zhand-ńe] adv. second-rate make; shabbily
drugorzędność [droo-go-zhand-nośhćh] f. secondary importance; minor importance
drugorzędny [droo-go-zhand-ni] adj.m. second-class; second-rate; secondary; subordinate; of second rank
drugorzędowy [droo-go-zhan-do-vi] adj.m. of the second stage; of the second phase
drugostronnie [droo-go-stron-ńe] adv. overleaf; at the back
drugostronny [droo-go-stron-ni] adj.m. overleaf; at the back; on the following page
druh [drookh] m. buddy; companion; friend; boy scout
druhna [drookh-nah] f. bridesmaid; girl guide
druid [droo-eet] m. Druid
druidyczny [droo-ee-dich-ni] adj.m. Druidic; Druidical
druidyzm [droo-ee-dizm] m. Druidism
druk [drook] m. print; printing; the press; type; (application, etc.) form; slip
błąd w druku [bwownt v droo-koo] exp.: misprint
druk batikowy [drook bah-tee-ko-vi] exp.: batik
druki [droo-kee] pl.exp.: printed matter; third-class mail
drobny druk [drob-ni drook] exp.: small type
omyłka w druku [o-miw-kah v droo-koo] exp.: misprint
tłusty druk [twoos-ti drook] exp.: bold type
w druku [v droo-koo] exp.: in the press
wydać drukiem [vi-dahćh droo-kem] exp.: to publish
drukarenka [droo-kah-ren-kah] f. print shop; dim.: **drukarnia**
drukarka [droo-kahr-kah] f. computer printer; hand-press
drukarnia [droo-kahr-ńah] f. printing office; printing firm; printing house; the printers
drukarniany [droo-kahr-ńah-ni] adj.m. of a printing-office; of a printing-firm
drukarski [droo-kahr-skee] adj.m. printer's; typographical
błąd drukarski [bwownd droo-kahr-skee] exp.: misprint
farba drukarska [fahr-bah droo-kahr-skah] exp.: printing ink
maszyna drukarska [mah-shi-nah droo-kahr-skah] exp.: printing machine
drukarstwo [droo-kahr-stfo] n.

printing; typography
drukarz [**droo**-kahsh] m. printer
kornik drukarz [**kor**-ńeek **droo**-kahsh] exp.: engraver beetle
drukować [droo-**ko**-vahćh] v. print; run off (*repeatedly*)
drukować się [droo-**ko**-vahćh śhan] v. be printing; be in the press (*repeatedly*)
drukowanie [droo-ko-**vah**-ńe] n. printing
drukowanie się [droo-ko-**vah**-ńe śhan] n. being published
drukowanka [droo-ko-**vahn**-kah] f. colloq: printed cloth
drukowany [droo-ko-**vah**-ni] adj.m. printed (page, etc.)
litery drukowane [lee-**te**-ri droo-ko-**vah**-ne] exp.: block letters
słowo drukowane [**swo**-vo droo-ko-**vah**-ne] exp.: print
drukowy [droo-**ko**-vi] adj.m. of print; printing (paper, etc.)
drumla [**droom**-lah] f. Jew's harp
drumlin [**droom**-leen] m. drumlin (hill)
drut [droot] m. wire; rib (of an umbrella, etc.); knitting needle; wire-edge
drut do robienia [droot do ro-**bye**-ńah] exp.: knitting needle
drut kolczasty [droot kol-**chah**-sti] exp.: barbed wire
robić na drutach [ro-beećh nah **droo**-tahkh] exp.: to knit
drutować [droo-to-vahćh] v. wire; fasten with wire (*repeatedly*)
drutowanie [droo-to-**vah**-ńe] n. wiring (broken pots, house, etc.)
drutowaty [droo-to-**vah**-ti] adj.m. wiry; like wire; lean and strong
drutowiec [droo-to-vyets] m. wire worm
drutownia [droo-**to**-vńah] f. wire-drawing mill; wire-works
drutownica [droo-to-**vńee**-tsah] f. drawplate for wire making
drutowy [droo-**to**-vi] adj.m. of wire; wire ; knitting (work, etc.)
drutówka [droo-**toof**-kah] f. steel belted tire
druz [droos] m. member of an Arabic sect (including elements of Islam, Judaism, Christianity, and earlier religions)
druza [**droo**-zah] f. druse; goede
druzgocąco [drooz-go-**tsown**-tso] adv. in a crushing way; in a shattering way
druzgocący [drooz-go-**tsown**-tsi] adj.m. crushing; shattering; smashing; overwhelming
druzgot [**drooz**-got] m. breccia
druzgotać [drooz-**go**-tahćh] v. smash; shatter; crush to pieces; pulverize; crush (*repeatedly*)
druzgotać się [drooz-**go**-tahćh śhan] v. be smashed; be shattered; be crushed; be pulverized (*repeatedly*)
druzgotanie [drooz-go-**tah**-ńe] n. smashing; pulverizing
drużak [**droo**-zhahk] m. cast (of bees); after-swarm
drużba [**droozh**-bah] m. best man; bridesman; groomsman; friendship
drużbart [**droozh**-bahrt] m. ancient card game
drużbować [droozh-**bo**-vahćh] v. be (somebody's) best man; be a bridesman; be a groomsman (*repeatedly*)
drużbowanie [droozh-bo-**vah**-ńe] n. being somebody's best man
drużka [**droosh**-kah] f. bridesmaid; girl friend
drużyna [droo-**zhi**-nah] f. team; crew; side; party; squad; gang; retinue; suite
drużyna ratownicza [droo-**zhi**-nah rah-to-**vńee**-chah] exp.: relief party; rescue squad
drużynka [droo-**zhin**-kah] f. (small) team; crew; side; party; squad
drużynowo [droo-zhi-**no**-vo] adv. as a team
drużynowy [droo-zhi-**no**-vi] m. group leader; adj.m.: of a team; of a squad; of a crew
drwa [drvah] pl. wood; firewood
drwal [drvahl] m. lumber jack; woodcutter; lumberman; logger
drwalka [**drvahl**-kah] f. woodshed
drwalnia [**drvahl**-ńah] f. woodshed
drwalnictwo [drvahl-**ńee**-tstfo] n. logging
drwalnik [**drvahl**-ńeek] m. a variety of beetle

drwiąco [drvyown-tso] adv. derisively; sneeringly; scoffingly; jeeringly
drwić [drveećh] v. mock; deride; sneer (at); scoff (at); jeer (at); jibe (at); rail (at); fleer (at); disregard (the rain, etc.) (*repeatedly*)
drwienie [**drvye**-ńe] n. derision; sneers; scoffs; jeers
drwina [**drvee**-nah] f. sneer; scoff; jeer; gibe; fleer
drwinka [**drveen**-kah] f. (minor) sneer; scoff; jeer; gibe; fleer
drwinkarz [**drveen**-kahsh] m. scoffer; giber; railer
drwinkować [drveen-**ko**-vahćh] v. jeer; banter; chaff; joke
drwinkowanie [drveen-ko-**vah**-ńe] n. jeers; banter; chaff; jokes
drwiny [**drvee**-ni] pl. mockery
drwionek [**drvyo**-nek] m. a variety of (ship's boring) beetle
drwionkowaty [drvyon-ko-**vah**-ti] adj.m. of (Lymexylon navale) beetle
drwionkowate [drvyon-ko-**vah**-te] pl. the family of Lymexylon navale beetles
dryblas [**dri**-blahs] m. colloq: tall fellow; strapping fellow; lanky man; strapper; cornstalk
drybler [**dri**-bler] m. dribbler
drybling [**dri**-bleeng] m. dribble
dryblować [dri-**blo**-vahćh] v. dribble (*repeatedly*)
dryblowanie [drib-lo-**vah**-ńe] n. dribbling
dryf [drif] m. drift; driftage; leeway
dryfkotwa [drif-**ko**-tfah] f. drift anchor; drag anchor
dryfomierz [dri-**fo**-myesh] m. drift meter
dryfować [dri-**fo**-vahćh] v. drift (*repeatedly*)
dryfowanie [dri-fo-**vah**-ńe] n. drifting
dryft [drift] m. something washed ashore (as driftwood)
dryfter [**dri**-fter] m. drifter
dryftowy [dri-**fto**-vi] adj.j. of drift; drift (wood, etc.)
dryg [drig] m. knack; flair (for)
dryga [**dri**-gah] f. fishing net
drygać [**dri**-gahćh] v. colloq: hop; skip; jump (*repeatedly*)
dryganie [dri-**gah**-ńe] n. colloq: hopping; skipping; jumping
drygnięcie [dri-**gńan**-ćhe] n. colloq: hop; skip; jump
drygawica [dri-gah-**vee**-tsah] f. (type of) fishing net
drygnąć [**dri**-gnownćh] v. hop; skip; jump
drygubica [dri-goo-**bee**-tsah] f. (type of) fishing net; see: **dryga**
dryl [dril] m. drill; training; strict military discipline
dryling [**dri**-leeng] m. three-barrelled hunting gun
drylować [dri-**lo**-vahćh] v. seed (berries); stone (fruits); sow in drills; drill
drylowanie [dri-lo-**vah**-ńe] n. seeding (berries); stoning (fruits); sowing in drills; drilling
drymba [**drim**-bah] f. a musical instrument (a kind of pipe)
drynda [**drin**-dah] f. colloq: hackney; four-wheel cab; growler
dryndula [drin-**doo**-lah] f. slang: gig
dryndziarski [drin-**dźhahr**-skee] adj.m. cabby's; cabman's
dryndziarz [**drin**-dźhahsh] m. cabby; cabman
drzazga [**dzhahz**-gah] f. splinter; sliver; chip
drzeć [dzhećh] v. tear; pull apart; rend; scratch; strip; wear out; wear down; cause shooting pains (*repeatedly*)
drzeć się [dzhećh śhan] v. wear out; scream; tear; rend; wear away; deteriorate; squabble; quarrel; climb; clamber up; shout; scream; roar; yell (*repeatedly*)
drzemać [dzhe-**mah**ćh] v. doze; nap; nod; drowse; snooze; slumber; lurk; lie dormant (*repeatedly*)
drzemanie [dzhe-**mah**-ńe] n. nap; doze; snooze
drzemka [**dzhem**-kah] f. nap; doze; snooze
uciąć drzemkę [oo-ćhownćh **dzhem**-kan] exp.: to take a nap
drzemlik [**dzhem**-leek] m. the smallest variety of hawk
drzewce [**dzhef**-tse] n. flag-staff;

spear shaft; shaft
drzewiarka [dzhe-**vyahr**-kah] f. wagon for mine supports
drzewiarz [**dzhe**-vyahsh] m. wood technologist
drzewko [**dzhef**-ko] n. little tree; Christmas tree
drzewiasto [dzhe-**vyah**-sto] adv. arborescently
drzewiasty [dzhe-**vyah**-sti] adj.m. arborescent; ligneous; dendritic; woody
drzewiej [**dzhe**-vyey] adv. formerly; at one time; in the past; formerly; see: **dawniej**
drzewiga [dzhe-**vee**-gah] f. a parasitic fly larva in beehives
drzewigowaty [dzhe-vee-go-**vah**-ti] m. of parasitic fly larva in beehives
drzewigowate [dzhe-vee-go-**vah**-te] pl. the family of parasitic fly larva in beehives; Phoridae
drzewigroszek [dzhe-vee-**gro**-shek] m. bitter vetch (Vicia Orobus)
drzewina [dzhe-**vee**-nah] f. pitiful tree; decaying tree; trees
drzewisz [**dzhe**-veesh] m. pine-beetle; pine chafer
drzewko [**dzhef**-ko] n. little tree; young tree; Christmas tree
drzewnictwo [dzhev-**ńeets**-tfo] n. arboriculture
drzewnik [**dzhev**-ńeek] m. lignin
drzewny [**dzhev**-ni] adj.m. wooden; of wood; of a tree; of timber; timber-; wood-
papier drzewny [pah-pyer **dzhev**-ni] exp.: wood-paper
spirytus drzewny [spee-ri-toos **dzhev**-ni] exp.: wood-spirit
węgiel drzewny [v<u>an</u>-<u>g</u>el **dzhev**-ni] exp.: charcoal
drzewo [**dzhe**-vo] n. tree; wood; timber; lumber
handel drzewem [khahn-del **dzhe**-vem] exp.: lumber-trade
skład drzewa [skwahd **dzhe**-vah] exp.: lumberyard
drzewojad [dzhe-**vo**-yaht] m. a variety of wood-borer (shipworm)
drzewołaz [dzhe-**vo**-wahs] m. shoe-mounted clamp (for climbing poles, trees, etc.)
drzeworyt [dzhe-**vo**-rit] m. woodcut; wood-engraving
drzeworytnia [dzhe-vo-**ri**-tńah] f. wood-engraving studio
drzeworytnictwo [dzhe-vo-ri-**tńee**-tstfo] n. wood-engraving; engraving in wood; xylography
drzeworytniczy [dzhe-vo-ri-**tńee**-chi] adj.m. wood-engraver's; woodcutter's
drzeworytnik [dzhe-vo-**ri**-tńeek] m. wood-engraver; woodcutter; xylographer
drzeworytowy [dzhe-vo-ri-**to**-vi] adj.m. of wood-engraving; of woodcutting
drzewostan [dzhe-**vo**-stahn] m. stand of trees; standing timber
drzewostanowy [dzhe-vo-stah-**no**-vi] adj.m. of standing timber
drzewozbiór [dzhe-**vo**-zbyoor] m. arboretum
drzewoznawca [dzhe-vo-**znahf**-tsah] m. dendrologist
drzewoznawczo [dzhe-vo-**znahf**-cho] adv. dendrologically
drzewoznawczy [dzhe-vo-**znahf**-chi] adj.m. dendrological
drzewoznawstwo [dzhe-vo-**znahf**-stfo] n. dendrology
drzewożerny [dzhe-vo-**zher**-ni] adj.m. wood-eating (insect, etc.)
drzwi [dzhvee] pl. door
drzwi wejściowe [dzhvee vey-**śhćho**-ve] exp.: front door
w drzwiach [v dzhvyahkh] exp.: in the doorway
za drzwi! [zah dzhvee] excl.: out! turn him out!
drzwiczki [**dzhvee**-chkee] pl. little door; fire door; soot door
drzwiowy [**dzhvyo**-vi] adj.m. of a door; door- (handle, frame, etc.)
drżąco [**drzh<u>own</u>**-tso] adv. tremblingly; shakily; tremulously
drżący [**drzh<u>own</u>**-tsi] adj.m. trembling; shaky; tremulous; shivery; quaky; quavery
drżączka [**drzh<u>own</u>**-chkah] f. shivers; shivering fit; trembles; quaking-grass
drżeć [drzhećh] v. shiver; shake; tremble; quiver; quake; palpitate; vibrate; shudder (*repeatedly*)

drżeć o kogoś [drzhećh o **ko**-gośh] exp.: to tremble for somebody
drżeć z zimna [drzhećh z **źheem**-nah] exp.: to shiver with cold
drżeć ze strachu [drzhećh ze **strah**-khoo] exp.: to tremble with fear
drżenie [**drzhe**-ńe] n. trembling; tremor; tremble; shakiness; trepidation; shivers; thrill
dual [**doo**-ahl] m. grammatical form denoting reference to two; two move checkmate
dualin [doo-**ah**-leen] m. dualin
dualis [doo-**ah**-lees] n. one of a pair
dualista [doo-ah-**lee**-stah] m. dualist
dualistyczny [doo-ah-lee-**stich**-ni] adj.m. dualistic
dualizm [doo-**ah**-leezm] m. dualism
dualny [doo-**ahl**-ni] adj.m. dual (denoting reference to two)
dubas [**doo**-bahs] m. 16th cent. large river boat with sails and oars
dubbing [**dah**-beeng] m. dubbing (in a movie)
dubbingować [dah-been-**go**-vahćh] v. dub (*repeatedly*)
dubbingowanie [dah-been-go-**vah**-ńe] n. dubbing
dubbingowy [dah-been-**go**-vi] adj.m. dubbed
dubel [**doo**-bel] m. one of a number of shots of the same movie scene
dubelt [**doo**-belt] m. double snipe
dubeltowo [doo-bel-**to**-vo] adv. doubly
dubeltowy [doo-bel-**to**-vi] adj.m. double (precision, etc.)
dubeltówka [doo-bel-**toof**-kah] f. double barrel gun; shotgun
całować z dubeltówki [tsah-**wo**-vahćh z doo-bel-**toof**-kee] exp.: to kiss with a smack on both cheeks
dubia [**doo**-byah] f. doubtful matters
dubla [**doo**-blah] f. double bet; imitation of a precious stone
dubler [**doo**-bler] m. double
dublerka [doo-**bler**-kah] f. (female) double
dublet [**doo**-blet] m. duplicate; double; counterpart; doublet
dublować [doo-**blo**-vahćh] v. double (a part); understudy (*repeatedly*)
dublowanie [doo-blo-**vah**-ńe] n. doubling
duby [**doo**-bi] pl. (only in) exp.:
duby smalone [**doo**-bi smah-**lo**-ne] exp.: nonsense; balderdash; flapdoodle; bunkum; bosh; slang: fish story
duch [dookh] m. spirit; ghost; state of mind; intendment; soul; apparition; intendment; morale; mettle; courage; life
co duch [tso dookh] exp.: with all speed
dodać ducha [**do**-dahćh **doo**-khah] exp.: to cheer up; to encourage
nie ma żywego ducha [ńe mah zhi-**ve**-go **doo**-khah] exp.: there is not a living soul
paść bez ducha [pahśhćh bes **doo**-khah] exp.: to fall lifeless
podnosić na duchu [pod-**no**-śheećh nah **doo**-khoo] exp.: to encourage; to hearten; to buck up; to uplift; to put spunk into
tracić ducha [**trah**-ćheećh **doo**-khah] exp.: to lose heart
upadać na duchu [oo-**pah**-dahćh nah **doo**-khoo] exp.: to lose heart
wyzionąć ducha [vi-**źho**-nownćh **doo**-khah] exp.: to breathe one's last; to expire
duchota [doo-**kho**-tah] f. sultry weather
duchowieństwo [doo-kho-**vyeń**-stfo] pl. clergy; priesthood
duchowny [doo-**kho**-vni] adj.m. spiritual; ecclesiastical; church-; m. priest; clergyman
stan duchowny [stahn doo-**kho**-vni] exp.: clerical state; clergyman
duchowo [doo-**kho**-vo] adv. spiritually; mentally; psychically; intellectually; inwardly
duchowość [doo-**kho**-vośhćh] f. spirituality; inwardness
duchowy [doo-**kho**-vi] adj.m. spiritual; of the spirit; intellectual; of the mind; mental; psychical;

inner; internal; moral
duchówka [doo-**khoof**-kah] f. cooking oven
ducka [**doots**-kah] f. pannier; basket carried on the back
duda [**doo**-dah] f. bagpipe; hornpipe; pipe (of a musical instrument); m. piper; fool; booby; noodle; fathead; gut
dudy [**doo**-di] pl. bagpipes; guts, bowels; offal
dudarz [**doo**-dahsh] m. piper
dudek [**doo**-dek] m. hoopoe (bird); dupe; fool; dolt; booby
wystrychnąć na dudka [vi-**strikh**-nownćh nah **doo**-tkah] exp.: to con (someone); to dope; to chide; to deceive; to (make a) fool; to pull wool over (someone's) eyes
dudka [**doo**-tkah] f. pipe; tube; quill
dudkować [doo-**tko**-vahćh] v. play bagpipes; make fun (of) (*repeatedly*)
dudkowanie [doo-tko-**vah**-ńe] n. playing bagpipes; making fun (of)
dudkowaty [doo-tko-**vah**-ti] adj.m. upupoid; of the family Upupidae
dudlić [**doo**-dleećh] v. rasp on a violin; swill; drink (*repeatedly*)
dudniący [doo-**dńown**-tsi] adj.m. rumbling; rolling; emitting hollow sounds
dudnić [doo-dńeećh] v. rumble; roll; emit hollow sounds; thump (the keys of a piano); play bagpipes (*repeatedly*)
dudnieć [doo-dńećh] v. resound; ring; echo; rumble; roll; emit hollow sounds (*repeatedly*)
dudnienie [doo-**dńe**-ńe] n. rumble; roll; hollow sounds
dudu [doo-doo] not declined: exp.: **ani dudu** [ah-ńee **doo**-doo] exp.: not a single word; hush!; tush!
duduś [doo-doośh] m. tot; chit; kiddy
dudziarz [**doo**-dźhahsh] m. piper
dudy [**doo**-di] pl. bagpipes
duet [**doo**-et] m. duet; duo
dufnie [**doof**-ńe] adv. with self-confidence; with self-assurance
dufność [**doof**-nośhćh] f. self-confidence; self-assurance
dufny [**doof**-ni] adj.m. self-confident; self-assured
duga [**doo**-gah] f. wooden bow joining the shafts of a one-horse cart or sledge
duha [**doo**-khah] f. wooden bow joining the shafts of a one-horse cart or sledge
dujawica [doo-yah-**vee**-tsah] f. snowstorm; rainstorm
dujker [**dooy**-ker] m. Cephalophus antelope
dukacik [doo-**kah**-ćheek] m. (nice) ducat
dukać [**doo**-kahćh] v. stammer; falter; falter out (one's lessons) (*repeatedly*)
dukanie [doo-**kah**-ńe] n. stammering
dukat [**doo**-kaht] m. ducat
dukatowy [doo-kah-**to**-vi] adj.m. of pure gold; of 24 carat gold
dukla [**doo**-klah] f. test hole; prospect hole
dukt [dookt] m. vista; style of printing
duktor [**doo**-ktor] m. ink-roller in printing machine
dulcynea [dool-tsi-**ne**-ah] f. mistress; sweetheart (Dulcinea del Toboso, beloved of Don Quixote)
dulcyt [**dool**-tsit] m. dulcite
dulczeć [**dool**-chećh] v. plod; drudge; slog away; boggle; pore over; be confined (out of necessity) (*repeatedly*)
dulka [**dool**-kah] f. oarlock
dulszczyzna [dool-**shchiz**-nah] f. prudery
duma [**doo**-mah] f. pride; self-respect; stateliness; loftiness; lordliness; self-conceit; haughtiness; uppishness; boast; source of pride; epic; elegy
Duma [**doo**-mah] f. Duma; Russian parliament
dumać [**doo**-mahćh] v. meditate (on); muse (upon); ponder (on); brood (over) (*repeatedly*)
dumanie [doo-**mah**-ńe] n. meditation; musings (upon); brown study; reverie
dum-dum [doom-doom] indecl.: dumdum (bullet)
dumka [**doom**-kah] f. elegiac ditty; dumka (music or poetry in

Ukrainian style)
dumnie [**doom**-ńe] adv. proudly; with stateliness; loftily; majestically; uppishly; haughtily; in stately fashion
dumny [**doom**-ni] adj.m. proud; proud-hearted; proud-spirited; stately; lofty; lordly; majestic; uppish; haughty; self-conceited
dumping [**dahm**-peeng] m. dumping (goods on foreign markets)
dumpingowy [dahm-peen-**go**-vi] adj.m. dumping (prices, etc.)
dunajski [doo-**nahy**-skee] adj.m. Danubian; of Danube River
dunder [**doon**-der] m. (only in:) **niech go dunder świśnie** [ńekh go **doon**-der **śhfeeśh**-ńe] exp.: slang: to hell with him
dunderować [doon-de-**ro**-vahćh] v. fret and fume (*repeatedly*)
dunit [doo-ńeet] m. dunite (mineral)
Dunka [**doon**-kah] f. Danish woman
Duńczyk [**dooń**-chik] m. Dane
duński [**dooń**-skee] adj.m. Danish
duodecyma [doo-o-**de**-tsi-mah] f. duodecimo; musical interval of the twelfth
duola [doo-**o**-lah] f. duole
duopol [doo-**o**-pol] m. duopoly; an oligopoly limited to two producers
dupa [**doo**-pah] f. vulg.: ass; anus; buttocks; fanny; slang: babe; fox; sexual intercourse; idiot; gawk **do dupy** [do **doo**-pi] exp.: vulg.: not worth a fart; to hell with it **dupa wołowa** [**doo**-pah vo-**wo**-vah] exp.: slang: dullard; fool **dupa z uszami** [**doo**-pah z oo-**shah**-mee] exp.: vulg.: coward **mam to w dupie** [mahm to v **doo**-pye] vulg. exp.: I ignore it; I don't give a damn about it
dupczyć [**doop**-chićh] v. vulg.: mob slang: screw; screw up; copulate; vulg.: fuck (*repeatedly*)
dupek [**doo**-pek] m. slang: dolt; duffer; muff; oaf; slacker
duperele [doo-pe-**re**-le] pl. vulg.: slang: silly jabber; nonsense
dupleks [**doo**-pleks] m. duplex; copy; duplex escapement
duplika [doo-**plee**-kah] f. (legal) surrebutter; surrejoinder
duplikat [doo-**plee**-kaht] m. duplicate; copy; counterpart; replica
dupowaty [doo-po-**vah**-ti] adj.m. vulg.: slang: helpless; awkward; clumsy; goofy (mob jargon)
dur [door] m. typhoid fever; indecl.: (music) major
dural [**doo**-rahl] m. colloq: duralumin
duralowy [doo-rah-**lo**-vi] adj.m. of duralumin (pipes, etc.)
duraluminiowy [doo-rah-loo-mee-**ńyo**-vi] adj.m. duralumin (pipe, sheet, etc.)
duraluminium [doo-rah-loo-**mee**-ńyoom] n. duralumin
dureń [**doo**-reń] m. colloq: fool; dolt; blockhead; slacker
durnieć [**door**-ńećh] v. grow stupid; become stupid; go silly (*repeatedly*)
durnienie [door-**ńe**-ńe] n. becoming stupid; becoming asinine
durność [**door**-nośhćh] f. stupidity
durnowatość [door-no-**vah**-tośhćh] f. foolishness
durnowaty [door-no-**vah**-ti] adj.m. barmy; cracked; dotty; crazy; ridiculous
durny [**door**-ni] adj.m. silly; foolish; stupid
durometr [doo-**ro**-metr] m. durometer
duroplast [doo-**ro**-plahst] m. hard, not breakable plastic (used for kitchenware, etc.)
duroplasty [doo-ro-**plahs**-ti] pl. plastics for making dishes, brackets, etc.
durowy [doo-**ro**-vi] adj.m. typhoidal; typhoid; (musical) major
durra [**door**-rah] f. sorghum
durszlak [**door**-shlahk] m. colander; strainer; piercer
duryt [**doo**-rit] m. durain (mineral)
durzenie [doo-**zhe**-ńe] n. fooling; duping
durzenie się [doo-**zhe**-ńe śhan] n. fooling oneself; becoming duped
durzyć [**doo**-zhićh] v. fool; gull; infatuate; bewilder; dupe; dizzy (*repeatedly*)
durzyć się [**doo**-zhićh śhan] v. fool oneself; be infatuated; be

enamored (of); have lost one's heart (to); be soft (on) (*repeatedly*)
duser [doo-ser] m. compliment
dusery [doo-se-ri] pl. compliments; sweet talk
dusiciel [doo-śhee-ćhel] m. strangler
boa dusiciel [bo-ah doo-śhee-ćhel] exp.: boa constrictor
dusić [doo-śheećh] v. strangle; throttle; strangulate; choke; stifle; suffocate; squeeze; press hard; crush; oppress; overtax; stew; braise; simmer; jug (*repeatedly*)
dusić się [doo-śheećh śhan] v. choke; be asphyxiated; stifle; suffocate; stew; be stewing; simmer; strangle one another; throttle one another (*repeatedly*)
dusigrosz [doo-śhee-grosh] m. colloq: penny pincher; niggard; cheapskate; miser; skinflint
dusikufel [doo-śhee-koo-fel] m. colloq: tipper; bibber; thirsty soul
dusza [doo-shah] f. soul; psyche; mind; heart; one's inner self; courage; life; the life and the soul; core; pith; heater (of a flatiron); vulg.: slang: ass; arse
ile dusz? [ee-le doosh] exp.: how many people?; how many inhabitants?
ile dusza zapragnie [ee-le doo-shah zah-prah-gńe] exp.: to one's heart content
nie mam grosza przy duszy [ńe mahm gro-shah pshi doo-shi] exp.: I am stone-broke
nie ma tu żywej duszy [ńe mah too zhi-vey doo-shi] exp.: there is not a living soul here
z całej duszy [s tsah-wey doo-shi] exp.: with all my soul
dusząco [doo-shown-tso] adv. oppressively
duszek [doo-shek] m. imp; brownie
duszenie [doo-she-ńe] n. suffocation; asphyxiation
duszenie się [doo-she-ńe śhan] n. suffocation; asphyxiation
duszka [doosh-kah] f. little soul
duszko! [doosh-ko] excl.: darling!; dearie!; honey!
duszkiem [doosh-kem] adv. at a draught; at one gulp
dusznawo [doosh-nah-vo] adv. stiflingly
dusznawy [doosh-nah-vi] adj.m. stifling; close; oppressive
dusznica [doosh-ńee-tsah] f. asthma
dusznicowy [doosh-ńee-tso-vi] adj.m. asthmatic
duszno [doosh-no] adv. sultrily; stiflingly
duszności [doosh-no-śhćhee] pl. oppression; asthma attack
duszność [doosh-nośhćh] f. sultriness; dyspnoea; difficult breathing; sultry weather; sultriness; stifling heat; languor; stuffy atmosphere; sickly scent
dusznota [doosh-no-tah] f. asthma attack; also = **duszność**
duszny [doosh-ni] adj.m. sultry; close; stifling; stuffy; fusty; frowzy; faint; sickly; oppressive; muggy
duszpasterski [doosh-pah-ster-skee] adj.m. pastoral; priestly
duszpasterstwo [doosh-pah-ster-stfo] n. pastoral office; priesthood; ministry
duszpasterz [doosh-pah-stesh] m. pastor; clergyman
duszyczka [doo-shich-kah] f. child's soul; (diminutive: **dusza**)
dutka [doo-tkah] f. quill
duumwir [doo-oom-veer] m. duumvir
duumwirat [doo-oom-vee-raht] m. duumvirate
duża [doo-zhah] adj.f. big; large; great; fair-sized; pretty large; grown up (female)
dużo [doo-zho] adv. much; many; a lot; lots
duży [doo-zhi] adj.m. big; large; great; fair-sized; pretty large; grown up (male)
dwa [dvah] num. two; 2; a couple; colloq: an "F"; failing grade
dwadzieścia [dvah-dźhe-śhćhah] num. twenty; a score; 20
dwadzieścioro [dvah-dźheśh-ćho-ro] num. twenty; a score; 20
dwaj [dvahy] num. two (men); 2
dwakroć [dvah-kroćh] num. twice; two times

dwanaście [dvah-nah-śhćhe] num. twelve; 12
dwanaścioro [dvah-nahśh-ćho-ro] num. (n.) twelve (children, etc.)
dwie [dvye] num. two (females); 2
dwieście [dvye-śhćhe] num. two hundred; 200
dwoić [dvo-eećh] v. double; split in two; set people at variance (*repeatedly*)
dwoić się [dvo-eećh śhan] v. double; stir about; have many irons in the fire (*repeatedly*)
dwoi mu się w oczach [dvo-ee moo śhan v o-chahkh] exp.: he sees double
dwoina [dvo-ee-nah] f. split (in tanning)
dwoinka [dvo-een-kah] f. diplococcus (bacteria)
dwoistość [dvo-ee-stośhćh] f. doubleness; duality; dualism
dwoisty [dvo-ee-sti] adj.m. double; dual; twofold
dwoiście [dvo-ee-śhćhe] adv. doubly; dually; twofold
dwojaczki [dvo-yah-chkee] pl. twins; double pot
dwojak [dvo-yahk] m. duplex (house); double pot; twin; twin mineral
dwojaki [dvo-yah-kee] adj.m. double; twofold
dwojako [dvo-yah-ko] adv. doubly; twofold
dwojarka [dvo-yahr-kah] f. tanning machine; fabric folding machine
dwoje [dvo-ye] num. the two; two; in two; couple; twofold; two (hands, eyes, ways, etc.); 2
jedno z dwojga [yed-no z dvoy-gah] exp.: one of two things; there is no middle course
na dwoje babka wróżyła [nah dvo-ye bahp-kah vroo-zhi-wah] exp.: there's no telling how or what the outcome will be
dwojenie [dvo-ye-ńe] n. doubling; splitting in two; setting people at variance
dwojenie się [dvo-ye-ńe śhan] n. doubling oneself; being in two different places (*repeatedly*)
dworacki [dvo-rah-tskee] adj.m. courtly; courtier's
dworacko [dvo-rah-tsko] adv. in a courtly manner; like a courtier
dworactwo [dvo-rah-tstfo] n. courtliness; courtier's life
dworak [dvo-rahk] m. courtier; colloq: farmhand
dworcowiec [dvor-tso-vyets] m. slang: homeless person; loiterer; thief stealing on a railroad station
dworcowy [dvor-tso-vi] adj.m. of the railroad station
dworcówka [dvor-tsoof-kah] f. mob slang: prostitute frequenting a railroad station; (woman) thief stealing on a railroad station
dworek [dvo-rek] m. country house; small manor house; cottage
dworka [dvor-kah] f. maid of honor (at the court); servant-maid (in a country estate)
dworkowy [dvor-ko-vi] adj.m. manorial (architecture, etc.)
dwornie [dvor-ńe] adv. in courtly fashion
dworność [dvor-nośhćh] f. courtly manners; elegance
dworny [dvor-ni] adj.m. courtly; urbane
dworować [dvo-ro-vahćh] v. make fun (of); ridicule (*repeatedly*)
dworski [dvor-skee] adj.m. courtly; manorial; of a court
dworsko [dvor-sko] adv. in courtly fashion
dworskość [dvor-skośhćh] f. courtliness; courtly manners
dworzanin [dvo-zhah-ńeen] m. courtier
dworzec [dvo-zhets] m. (railroad) station; depot
dworzec lotniczy [dvo-zhets lot-ńee-chi] exp.: airport
dwóch [dvookh] num. two (men); 2
dwóchsetlecie [dvookh-set-le-ćhe] n. two centuries; 200th anniversary; bicentennial
dwóchsetny [dvookh-set-ni] adj.m. two hundredth; 200th
dwója [dvoo-yah] f. colloq: bad mark in school
dwójczyna [dvooy-chi-nah] f. slang: measly (bad) mark in school
dwójka [dvooy-kah] f. couple; pair;

two; bad mark; the numerical symbol: 2; dyad; a two; Polish Army Intelligence Dept.; two-oar (boat for two men)
dwójkowicz [dvooy-**ko**-veech] m. colloq: failing student
dwójkowy [dvooy-**ko**-vi] adj.m. dual; binary; meant for two persons; (student, etc.) with bad marks
dwójlist [**dvooy**-leest] m. spider-orchis (plant); orchid
dwójłomność [dvooy-**wom**-nośhćh] f. birefringence; double refraction
dwójłomny [dvooy-**wom**-ni] adj.m. birefringent; of double refraction
dwójnasób [dvooy-**nah**-soop] exp.:
w dwójnasób [v dvooy-**nah**-soop] exp.: twofold; doubly
podnieść w dwójnasób [**pod**-ńeśhćh v dvooy-**nah**-soop] exp.: to double
dwójniak [**dvooy**-ńahk] m. kind of mead (honey mixed with equal volume of water)
dwójnóg [**dvooy**-noog] m. two-legged support
dwór [dvoor] m. country manor; mansion; manorial estate; courtyard; court; (royal, etc.) household
na dworze [nah **dvo**-zhe] exp.: out; outside; out-of-doors; in the open; outdoor; outdoors
idź na dwór [eedźh nah dvoor] exp.: go outside (in the open)
dwuaktowy [dvoo-ahk-**to**-vi] adj.m. two-act (play, etc.)
dwuaktówka [dvoo-ahk-**toof**-kah] f. two-act play
dwuarkuszowy [dvoo-ahr-koo-**sho**-vi] adj.m. two-sheet (pamphlet, etc.); composed of two printed sheets
dwuatomowy [dvoo-ah-to-**mo**-vi] adj.m. diatomic
dwuazowy [dvoo-ah-**zo**-vi] adj.m. diazo (compound, etc.)
dwubarwność [dvoo-**bahr**-vnośhćh] f. two-colors
dwubarwny [dvoo-**bahr**-vni] adj.m. two-colored; in two colors; of two colors; dichroic
dwubiegunowość [dvoo-bye-goo-**no**-vośhćh] f. bipolarity
dwubiegunowy [dvoo-bye-goo-**no**-vi] adj.m. bipolar
dwubocznie [dvoo-**bo**-chńe] adv. bilaterally
dwuboczność [dvoo-**bo**-chnośhćh] f. two-sidedness; bilaterality
dwuboczny [dvoo-**bo**-chni] adj.m. two-sided; bilateral
dwuboista [dvoo-bo-**ee**-stah] m. contestant in biathlon
dwubój [**dvoo**-booy] m. biathlon
dwubranżowość [dvoo-brahn-**zho**-vośhćh] f. having two specialties
dwubranżowy [dvoo-brahn-**zho**-vi] adj.m. two-specialty (store, etc.)
dwubrzeżny [dvoo-**bzhezh**-ni] adj.m. two-edged; of two coasts; on both banks (of a stream, etc.)
dwubrzuścowy [dvoo-bzhoośh-**tso**-vi] adj.m. digastric (muscle)
dwubuńczuczny [dvoo-booń-**chooch**-ni] adj.m. of two horsetails (Turkish dignitary)
dwucalowy [dvoo-tsah-**lo**-vi] adj.m. two-inch (plank, depth, etc.); two inches long; two inches wide, etc.
dwucalówka [dvoo-tsah-**loof**-kah] f. two-inch board; two-inch pipe
dwuchlorek [dvoo-**khlo**-rek] m. dichloride
dwuchodówka [dvoo-kho-**doof**-kah] f. checkmate in the first two moves by white chess
dwuchromian [dvoo-**khro**-myahn] m. bichromate
dwuchromowy [dvoo-khro-**mo**-vi] adj.m. dichromic (acid, etc.)
dwucukier [dvoo-**tsoo**-ker] m. disaccharide
dwucyfrowy [dvoo-tsi-**fro**-vi] adj.m. of two figures
dwucyjan [dvoo-**tsi**-yahn] m. cyanogen
dwucylindrowy [dvoo-tsi-leen-**dro**-vi] adj.m. two-cylinder (motor, engine, etc.)
dwuczęściowy [dvoo-chan-**śhćho**-vi] adj.m. composed of two parts; two-piece (suit, dress, etc.); binary (composition, etc.)
dwuczłonowość [dvoo-chwo-**no**-vośhćh] f. dimerism

dwuczłonowy [dvoo-chwo-**no**-vi] adj.m. compound; dimerous
dwuczub [**dvoo**-choop] m. bifurcated crest
dwuczuby [dvoo-**choo**-bi] adj.m. with a bifurcated crest
dwudaniowy [dvoo-dah-**ńo**-vi] adj.m. two-course (dinner, meal, etc.)
dwudniowy [dvoo-**dńo**-vi] adj.m. two-day (period, etc.); lasting two days; two days' (work, trip, program, etc.)
dwudrogowy [dvoo-dro-**go**-vi] adj.m. two-way
dwudrzwiowy [dvoo-**dzhvyo**-vi] adj.m. double-doored (wardrobe, etc.); (room, etc.) with two doors
dwudyszny [dvoo-**dish**-ni] adj.m. dipnoan; pulmobranchiate **dwudyszne** [dvoo-**dish**-ne] pl. Dipnoi; the lungfishes
dwudzielność [dvoo-**dźhel**-nośhćh] f. duality; dichotomy
dwudzielny [dvoo-**dźhel**-ni] adj.m. dual; bipartite; mitral; dichotomous; bicipital; two-cleft; duple
dwudziesta [dvoo-**dźhe**-stah] f. eight o'clock p.m.; 8 p.m.
dwudziestka [dvoo-**dźhe**-stkah] f. twenty; score; twenty-millimeter shotgun
dwudziestoczterogodzinny [dvoo-dźhe-sto-chte-ro-go-**dźheen**-ni] adj.m. twenty-four-hours (journey, etc.); twenty-four hour's (work, etc.); lasting twenty-four hours
dwudziestodolarówka [dvoo-dźhe-sto-do-lah-**roof**-kah] f. twenty-dollar (coin, banknote, bill, etc.)
dwudziestogroszowy [dvoo-dźhe-sto-gro-**sho**-vi] adj.m. twenty-groszy (coin, etc.); worth twenty groszy
dwudziestogroszówka [dvoo-dźhe-sto-gro-**shoof**-kah] f. twenty-groszy coin
dwudziestokilkuletni [dvoo-dźhe-sto-keel-koo-**let**-ńee] adj.m. twenty odd years old; twenty odd years of age
dwudziestokrotny [dvoo-dźhe-sto-**krot**-ni] adj.m. twentyfold; twenty times greater; repeated twenty times
dwudziestolatek [dvoo-dźhe-sto-**lah**-tek] m. young man twenty years old
dwudziestolatka [dvoo-dźhe-sto-**laht**-kah] f. young woman twenty years old
dwudziestolecie [dvoo-dźhe-sto-**le**-ćhe] n. period of twenty years; twentieth anniversary; twenty years of Poland's independence after World War I
dwudziestoletni [dvoo-dźhe-sto-**let**-ńee] adj.m. twenty years old; twenty years' (service, etc.); twenty-year (period, etc.); of twenty years duration
dwudziestomilionowy [dvoo-dźhe-sto-meel-yo-**no**-vi] adj.m. of twenty million
dwudziestopięciolecie [dvoo-dźhe-sto-pyan-ćho-**le**-ćhe] n. period of twenty-five years; twenty-fifth anniversary
dwudziestopięcioletni [dvoo-dźhe-sto-pyan-ćho-**let**-ńee] adj.m. of twenty-five years; twenty-five year (period, etc.); twenty-five years old (man, etc.)
dwudziestopiętrowy [dvoo-dźhe-sto-pyan-**tro**-vi] adj.m. of twenty stories; twenty stories high
dwudziestoprocentowy [dvoo-dźhe-sto-pro-tsen-**to**-vi] adj.m. twenty percent (profit, etc.)
dwudziestotysięczny [dvoo-dźhe-sto-ti-**śhanch**-ni] adj.m. twenty-thousandth; of twenty thousand
dwudziestowieczny [dvoo-dźhe-sto-**vyech**-ni] adj.m. of the twentieth century; twentieth-century
dwudziestowiekowy [dvoo-dźhe-sto-vye-**ko**-vi] adj.m. of twenty centuries; lasting twenty centuries
dwudziestozłotowy [dvoo-dźhe-sto-zwo-**to**-vi] adj.m. twenty-zloty (coin, banknote, bill, etc.)
dwudziestozłotówka [dvoo-dźhe-sto-zwo-**toof**-kah] f. twenty-zloty coin (or banknote, bill)
dwudziesty [dvoo-**dźhe**-sti] num. twentieth (day, etc.)

lata **dwudzieste** [lah-tah dvoo-**dźhe**-ste] exp.: the twenties; the second decade (of a century, of a person's life, etc.)
dwudźwięk [**dvoo**-dźhvyank] m. simultaneous sound of two musical notes
dwuelektrodowy [dvoo-e-le-ktro-**do**-vi] adj.m. two-electrode (tube, etc.)
dwufazowy [dvoo-fah-**zo**-vi] adj.m. two-phase (current, etc.); diphase
dwufenyl [dvoo-**fe**-nil] m. biphenyl; diphenyl (aromatic hydrocarbon)
dwufosfat [dvoo-**fo**-sfaht] m. diphosphate (mineral fertilizer)
dwufuntowy [dvoo-foon-**to**-vi] adj.m. of two pounds
dwugarbny [dvoo-**gahr**-bni] adj.m. two-humped; of two humps
dwugarmond [dvoo-**gahr**-mont] m. paragon (20 typographic points)
dwugatunkowy [dvoo-gah-toon-**ko**-vi] adj.m. two-quality (production, etc.); of two qualities
dwugłos [**dvoo**-gwos] m. dialogue; duet
dwugłoska [dwoo-**gwo**-skah] f. diphthong
dwugłoskowy [dvoo-gwos-**ko**-vi] adj.m. diphthongal
dwugłowy [dvoo-**gwo**-vi] adj.m. two-headed; double-headed; bicipital (muscle, etc.)
dwugodzinny [dvoo-go-**dźheen**-ni] adj.m. two hours'; of two hours
dwugroszówka [dvoo-gro-**shoof**-kah] f. two-groszy coin
dwuimienny [dvoo-ee-**myen**-ni] adj.m. of two names; binomial (nomenclature, etc.); having a double name; with a double name
dwuizbowość [dvoo-eez-**bo**-vośhćh] f. bicameral system
dwuizbowy [dvoo-eez-**bo**-vi] adj.m. bicameral; two-chamber
dwujądrowy [dvoo-yown-**dro**-vi] adj.m. binuclear
dwujęzyczność [dvoo-yan-**zi**-chnośhćh] f. bilingualism
dwujęzyczny [dvoo-yan-**zi**-chni] adj.m. bilingual
dwukadłubowiec [dvoo-kah-dwoo-**bo**-vyets] m. catamaran
dwukanałowy [dvoo-kah-nah-**wo**-vi] adj.m. of two channels
dwukaratowy [dvoo-kah-rah-**to**-vi] adj.m. two-carat (diamond, etc.)
dwukasetowy [dvoo-kah-se-**to**-vi] adj.m. holding two (sound, etc.) tapes
dwukierunkowy [dvoo-ke-roon-**ko**-vi] adj.m. two-way (traffic, etc.); two-directional
dwukilogramowy [dvoo-kee-lo-grah-**mo**-vi] adj.m. two-kilogram (weight, etc.)
dwukilometrowy [dvoo-kee-lo-me-**tro**-vi] adj.m. of two kilometers; two-kilometer (distance, etc.)
dwukilowy [dvoo-kee-**lo**-vi] adj.m. of two kilograms; two-kilogram (weight, etc.)
dwuklasowy [dvoo-klah-**so**-vi] adj.m. of two grades; of two classes; two-grade (course, etc.)
dwukolorowy [dvoo-ko-lo-**ro**-vi] adj.m. of two colors; two-color (flag, etc.)
dwukołowy [dvoo-ko-**wo**-vi] adj.m. two-wheeled; with two wheels
dwukomorowy [dvoo-ko-mo-**ro**-vi] adj.m. two-chamber
dwukondygnacjowy [dvoo-kon-di-gnah-**tsyo**-vi] adj.m. two-stories (high, etc.)
dwukondygnacyjny [dvoo-kon-di-gnah-**tsiy**-ni] adj.m. two-stories high
dwukonka [dvoo-**kon**-kah] f. two-horse carriage
dwukonny [dvoo-**kon**-ni] adj.m. two-horse (carriage, etc.)
dwukopytny [dvoo-ko-**pit**-ni] adj.m. cloven-hoofed; cloven-footed
dwukośny [dvoo-**kośh**-ni] adj.m. yielding two crops of hay a year
dwukółka [dvoo-**koow**-kah] f. two-wheeled vehicle; gig
dwukrok [**dvoo**-krok] m. cross-country skiing; two-step rhythm
dwukropek [dvoo-**kro**-pek] m. colon
dwukrotnie [dvoo-**krot**-ńe] adv. twice (over)
dwukrotny [dvoo-**krot**-ni] adj.m. twofold; repeated (once); twice (done, said, etc.); twice as numerous; twice as large; double

dwukwadratowy [dvoo-kfah-drah-**to**-vi] adj.m. biquadratic
dwulatek [dvoo-**lah**-tek] m. two-year-old (boy, etc.)
dwulecie [dvoo-**le**-ćhe] n. period of two years; second anniversary
dwuletni [dvoo-**let**-ńee] adj.m. two years' (work, etc.); two years old; (child) of two; two-year (period, etc.)
dwulicowiec [dvoo-lee-**tso**-vyets] m. double-faced person; double-tongued person
dwulicowość [dvoo-lee-**tso**-vośhćh] f. duplicity; double-dealing; doubleness
dwulicowy [dvoo-lee-**tso**-vi] adj.m. double-faced; hypocritical; double-dealing; double-tongued
dwulist [**dvoo**-leest] m. spider-orchis (plant); orchid
dwulistnik [dvoo-**lees**-tńeek] m. spider-orchis (plant, flower)
dwulistny [dvoo-**lees**-tni] adj.m. bifoliate; two-leaved
dwuliścienny [dvoo-lee-**śhćhen**-ni] adj.m. dicotyledonous
  dwuliścienne [dvoo-lee-**śhćhen**-ne] pl. the dicotyledons
dwułokciowy [dvoo-wo-**kćho**-vi] adj.m. measuring two ells (in length, height, width, depth, etc.)
dwułomność [dvoo-**wom**-nośhćh] f. double refraction
dwułożyskowy [dvoo-wo-zhi-**sko**-vi] adj.m. with two bearings
dwułuczny [dvoo-**wooch**-ni] adj.m. ogival
dwułuk [**dvoo**-wook] m. ogive; ogee; molding with an S-shaped profile; reversed-curve arch
dwumasztowiec [dvoo-mah-**shto**-vyets] m. two-master; two-masted ship
dwumasztowy [dvoo-mah-**shto**-vi] adj.m. two-masted (ship)
dwumetrowy [dvoo-me-**tro**-vi] adj.m. of two meters; two-meters (long, wide, high, deep, etc.)
dwumetylobenzen [dvoo-me-ti-lo-**ben**-zen] m. xylene
dwumęstwo [dvoo-**man**-stfo] n. second marriage by a married woman
dwumian [**dvoo**-myahn] m. binomial
dwumianowy [dvoo-myah-**no**-vi] adj.m. binomial (coefficient, theorem, distribution, etc.)
dwumiarowy [dvoo-myah-**ro**-vi] adj.m. two-beat (rhythm, etc.)
dwumiejscowy [dvoo-myey-**stso**-vi] adj.m. two-seat (car, etc.); with room (space) for two persons
dwumienny [dvoo-**myen**-ni] adj.m. of two algebraic terms
dwumiesięcznik [dvoo-mye-**śhanch**-ńeek] m. bimonthly (publication)
dwumiesięczny [dvoo-mye-**śhanch**-ni] adj.m. two-month (work, etc.); of two months; lasting two months; of two months' duration; bimonthly
dwuminutowy [dvoo-mee-noo-**to**-vi] adj.m. two-minutes (rest, etc.); of two minutes; lasting two minutes
dwumotorowy [dvoo-mo-to-**ro**-vi] adj.m. two-engine (plane, etc.); two-engined; twin-engined
dwunastka [dvoo-**nah**-stkah] f. twelve; (team) of twelve; the numeral twelve; twelve-caliber shotgun
dwunastkowy [dvoo-nahst-**ko**-vi] adj.m. duodecimal
dwunastnica [dvoo-nah-**stńee**-tsah] f. duodenum
  wrzód na dwunastnicy [vzhoot nah dvoo-nah-**stńee**-tsi] exp.: duodenal ulcer
  zapalenie dwunastnicy [zah-pah-**le**-ńe dvoo-nah-**stńee**-tsi] exp.: duodenitis
dwunastniczy [dvoo-nah-**stńee**-chi] adj.m. duodenal
dwunastogodzinny [dvoo-nah-sto-go-**dźheen**-ni] adj.m. twelve hours' (work, etc.); of twelve hours; lasting twelve hours; of twelve hours' duration
dwunastokrotny [dvoo-nah-sto-**krot**-ni] adj.m. twelvefold; twelve times greater
dwunastoletni [dvoo-nah-sto-**let**-ńee] adj.m. twelve years old; twelve-year-old; of twelve years; lasting twelve years
dwunastomiesięczny [dvoo-nah-sto-mye-**śhanch**-ni] adj.m. twelve

months old; twelve-month period; of twelve month
dwunastościan [dvoo-nah-**stośh**-ćhahn] m. dodecahedron
dwunastozgłoskowiec [dvoo-nah-sto-zgwo-**sko**-vyets] m. dodecasyllable; verse of twelve syllables
dwunastozgłoskowy [dvoo-nah-sto-zgwo-**sko**-vi] adj.m. of twelve syllables; dodecasyllabic
dwunasty [dvoo-nah-sti] adj.m. twelfth; 12th
dwunawowy [dvoo-nah-**vo**-vi] adj.m. cruciform
dwunocny [dvoo-**no**-tsni] adj.m. two nights' (stay, etc.); of two successive nights
dwunogi [dvoo-**no**-gee] adj.m. two-legged; bipedal
dwunożnie [dvoo-**nozh**-ńe] adv. on two legs; with two legs; on two feet; with two feet
dwunożność [dvoo-**nozh**-nośhćh] f. bipedality; being bipedal; quality of being two-footed
dwunożny [dvoo-**nozh**-ni] adj.m. two-legged; bipedal
dwunożne stworzenie [dvoo-**nozh**-ne stfo-**zhe**-ńe] exp.: biped
dwuoczny [dvoo-**och**-ni] adj.m. two-eyed; binocular
widzenie dwuoczne [vee-**dze**-ńe dvoo-**och**-ne] exp.: binocular vision
dwuogniskowy [dvoo-o-gńee-**sko**-vi] adj.m. bifocal
dwuokapowy dach [dvoo-o-kah-**po**-vi dahkh] exp.: ridge roof; gable roof; saddle roof; span roof
dwuokienny [dvoo-o-k̲**en**-ni] adj.m. two-windowed; with two windows
dwuoktawowy [dvoo-o-ktah-**vo**-vi] adj.m. two-octave (scale, etc.); of two octaves
dwuosiowy [dvoo-o-**śho**-vi] adj.m. biaxial; two-axle (vehicle, etc.)
dwuosnowowy [dvoo-os-no-**vo**-vi] adj.m. double-wrapped; two-ply (carpet, etc.)
dwuosobowy [dvoo-o-so-**bo**-vi] adj.m. for two persons; two-handed (piano playing, etc.); two-seat (car, etc.)
dwupalcowy [dvoo-pahl-**tso**-vi] adj.m. two-fingered; two-fingers' (wide, long, deep, etc.)
dwupalnikowy [dvoo-pahl-ńee-**ko**-vi] adj.m. having two burners
dwupartyjny [dvoo-pahr-**tiy**-ni] adj.m. two-party (system, etc.)
dwuparzec [dvoo-**pah**-zhets] m. diplopod
dwupasowy [dvoo-pah-**so**-vi] adj.m. two-lane (highway, etc.)
dwupiennie [dvoo-**pyen**-ńe] adv. dioeciously
dwupienność [dvoo-**pyen**-nośhćh] f. dioecism
dwupienny [dvoo-**pyen**-ni] adj.m. dioecious
dwupiętrowy [dvoo-py̲a̲n̲-**tro**-vi] adj.m. three-storied; two-tier
dwupiórowy [dvoo-pyoo-**ro**-vi] adj.m. two-feathered (paddle, etc.)
dwupióry [dvoo-**pyoo**-ri] adj.m. two-blade (oar, etc.)
dwuplanowy [dvoo-plah-**no**-vi] adj.m. double-plan (action, etc.)
dwupłaszczyznowość [dvoo-pwahsh-chiz-**no**-vośhćh] f. two-plane nature (characteristic)
dwupłaszczyznowy [dvoo-pwah-shchi-**zno**-vi] adj.m. two-plane (plot, drama, etc.)
dwupłat [**dvoo**-pwaht] m. biplane
dwupłatowiec [dvoo-pwah-**to**-vyets] m. biplane
dwupłatowy [dvoo-pwah-**to**-vi] adj.m. of a biplane
dwupłciowość [dvoo-**pwćho**-vośhćh] f. hermaphroditism; androgyny (of plants)
dwupłciowy [dvoo-**pwćho**-vi] adj.m. hermaphroditic; bisexual; androgynous
dwupokładowy [dvoo-po-kwah-**do**-vi] adj.m. double-decked
statek dwupokładowy [stah-tek dvoo-po-kwah-**do**-vi] exp.: double-decker
dwupokojowy [dvoo-po-ko-**yo**-vi] adj.m. two-room (apartment, etc.); of two rooms
dwupolowy [dvoo-po-**lo**-vi] adj.m. two-course (field rotation)

dwupolówka [dvoo-po-**loof**-kah] f. two-course rotation
dwupostaciowość [dvoo-po-stah-**ćho**-vośhćh] f. dimorphism
dwupostaciowy [dvoo-po-stah-**ćho**-vi] adj.m. dimorphic
dwupoziomowo [dvoo-po-źho-**mo**-vo] adv. on two planes; on two levels; with two planes
dwupoziomowość [dvoo-po-źho-mo-vośhćh] f. two-planes feature
dwupoziomowy [dvoo-po-źho-**mo**-vi] adj.m. having two planes; having two levels
dwuprzęsłowy [dvoo-pshan-**swo**-vi] adj.m. two-span (bridge, etc.)
dwuprzymierze [dvoo-pshi-**mye**-zhe] n. alliance of two countries; dual alliance
dwuramienny [dvoo-rah-**myen**-ni] adj.m. two-armed
dwuręcznie [dvoo-ran-chńe] adv. bimanually
dwuręczny [dvoo-ran-chni] adj.m. two-handed; bimanual
dwuręki [dvoo-ran-kee] adj.m. two-handed; bimanous
dwurękie [dvoo-ran-ke] pl. the Bimanes
dwurodzajowy [dvoo-ro-dzah-**yo**-vi] adj.m. bigeneric; (language, etc.) having two genders
dwurodzinny [dvoo-ro-**dźheen**-ni] adj.m. semidetached (cottage); duplex (house)
dwurogi [dvoo-**ro**-gee] adj.m. two-horned
dwurożny [dvoo-**rozh**-ni] adj.m. two-horned
dwurożne [dvoo-**rozh**-ne] pl. the family of two-horned animals
dwuróg [**dvoo**-roog] m. two-horned anvil
dwururka [dvoo-**roor**-kah] f. double-barrelled gun
dwurząd [**dvoo**-zhownt] m. file
dwurzędem [dvoo-**zhan**-dem] exp.: in file
dwurzędowiec [dvoo-zhan-**do**-vyets] m. Phoenician ship with two rows of oars; bireme
dwurzędowy [dvoo-zhan-**do**-vi] adj.m. double-rowed; double-breasted
dwurzędówka [dvoo-zhan-**doo**-fkah] f. double-breasted suit (coat)
dwuseryjny [dvoo-se-**riy**-ni] adj.m. (film, etc.) composed of two parts
dwusetlecie [dvoo-set-**le**-ćhe] n. bicentennial
dwusetny [dvoo-**se**-tni] adj.m. two-hundredth
dwusiarczan [dvoo-**śhahr**-chahn] m. disulfate; bisulfate
dwusiarczek [dvoo-**śhahr**-chek] m. disulfide; bisulfide
dwusieczna [dvoo-**śhe**-chnah] f. bisectrix; bisector; bisecting line
dwusieczny [dvoo-**śhe**-chni] adj.m. two-edged; double-edged
dwusiekaczowiec [dvoo-śhe-kah-**cho**-vyets] m. animal with ever-growing two incisors
dwusiekaczowce [dvoo-śhe-kah-**chof**-tse] pl. the family of animals with ever-growing two incisors
dwusilnikowy [dvoo-śheel-ńee-**ko**-vi] adj.m. two-engined; twin-engined
dwusilny [dvoo-**śheel**-ni] adj.m. two-stamen (flower, etc.)
dwuskibowiec [dvoo-skee-**bo**-vyets] m. two-furrow plow
dwuskibowy [dvoo-skee-**bo**-vi] adj.m. two-furrow (plough)
dwuskrzydłowy [dvoo-skshi-**dwo**-vi] adj.m. two-winged
dwuskrzydły [dvoo-**skshi**-dwi] adj.m. two-winged
dwuskrzydłe [dvoo-**skshi**-dwe] pl. two-winged insects; Diptera
dwusłupkowy [dvoo-swoop-**ko**-vi] adj.m. digynous (plant)
dwuspadkowy [dvoo-spah-**tko**-vi] adj.m. ridge (roof); gable (roof); saddle (roof); span (roof)
dwuspadowy [dvoo-spah-**do**-vi] adj.m. ridge (roof); gable (roof); saddle (roof); span (roof); see: **dwuokapowy**
dwuster [**dvoo**-ster] m. double steering (for two pilots)
dwustoletni [dvoo-sto-**le**-tńee] adj.m. two hundred years old
dwustopniowo [dvoo-sto-**pńo**-vo] adv. with two stages; with two degrees; with two grades

dwustopniowość [dvoo-sto-**pńo**-vośhćh] f. two-stage feature
dwustopniowy [dvoo-sto-**pńo**-vi] adj.m. two-stage; two-degree; two-grade
dwustopowy [dvoo-sto-**po**-vi] adj.m. two-foot (measure, etc.)
dwustożkowy [dvoo-sto-**shko**-vi] adj.m. double-cone
dwustronnie [dvoo-**stron**-ńe] adv. in a two-sided way; bilaterally
dwustronność [dvoo-**stron**-nośhćh] f. two-sidedness
dwustronny [dvoo-**stron**-ni] adj.m. two-sided; double-faced (material, etc.); bilateral
dwustrunny [dvoo-**stroon**-ni] adj.m. two-stringed (instrument, etc.)
dwustrzałowy [dvoo-stshah-**wo**-vi] adj.m. two-shooting; two-shot (gun)
dwustuletni [dvoo-stoo-**le**-tńee] adj.m. two-hundred years old; of two hundred years; lasting two hundred years
dwustumetrowiec [dvoo-stoo-me-**tro**-vyets] m. 200-meter racer
dwustumetrówka [dvoo-stoo-me-**troof**-kah] f. two-hundred-meter race
dwusuw [**dvoo**-soof] m. two-stroke engine; double-acting engine
dwusuwowy [dvoo-soo-**vo**-vi] adj.m. two-cycle (engine); double-acting (engine); two-stroke (engine)
dwusylabowiec [dvoo-si-lah-**bo**-vyets] m. word of two syllables
dwusylabowy [dvoo-si-lah-**bo**-vi] adj.m. two-syllable (word, etc.)
dwuszczytowy [dvoo-shchi-**to**-vi] adj.m. two-peaked (mountain, etc.)
dwuszereg [dvoo-**she**-reg] m. line (two deep)
  w dwuszeregu [v dvoo-she-**re**-goo] exp.: in line; two deep
dwuszpaltowy [dvoo-shpahl-**to**-vi] adj.m. of two columns (print, etc.); two-column (page, etc.)
dwuścian [**dvoo**-śhćhahn] m. dihedron; pinacoid (mineral)
dwuścienny [dvoo-**śhćhen**-ni] adj.m. dihedral (angle); interfacial (angle)
dwuślad [**dvoo**-śhlaht] m. vehicle with parallel wheels
dwuśladowiec [dvoo-śhlah-**do**-vyets] m. vehicle with parallel wheels
dwuśladowy [dvoo-śhlah-**do**-vi] adj.m. (vehicle, etc.) with parallel wheels
dwuśpiew [**dvoo**-śhpyef] m. duet
dwuśrednian [dvoo-**śhre**-dńahn] m. 28-point typographic font
dwuśrodowiskowy [dvoo-śhro-do-vee-**sko**-vi] adj.m. compatible with two environments (fresh and sea water, etc.)
dwuśrubowy [dvoo-śhroo-**bo**-vi] adj.m. twin-screw (ship, etc.)
dwutakt [**dvoo**-tahkt] m. two-stroke engine; double action
dwutaktowy [dvoo-tah-**kto**-vi] adj.m. of two rhythmic strokes; two-stroke (engine); double action
dwutaryfowy [dvoo-tah-ri-**fo**-vi] adj.m. two-rate (day and night taxi fare, etc.)
dwuteownik [dvoo-te-**o**-vńeek] m. I-beam; I-section; double-tee beam
dwuteowy [dvoo-te-**o**-vi] adj.m. I-(bar, section, beam, iron, etc.)
dwuteówka [dvoo-te-**oof**-kah] f. I-beam; I-section; double-tee beam
dwutlenek [dvoo-**tle**-nek] m. dioxide
dwutłokowy [dvoo-two-**ko**-vi] adj.m. two-piston (engine, etc.)
dwutomowy [dvoo-to-**mo**-vi] adj.m. two-volume; of two volumes
dwuton [**dvoo**-ton] m. bitonal chord
dwutonowy [dvoo-to-**no**-vi] adj.m. two-ton; weighing two tons; of two tons weight; bitonal (music)
dwutorowo [dvoo-to-**ro**-vo] adv. by means of double-lane (traffic, etc.); by means of two-track (research, etc.)
dwutorowość [dvoo-to-ro-vośhćh] f. double-lane (traffic, etc.); two-track (plot, script, etc.)
dwutorowy [dvoo-to-**ro**-vi] adj.m. double-track (railroad line, etc.); two-track (approach, etc.)
dwutrakt [**dvoo**-trahkt] m. two-support construction (roof, etc.)
dwutraktowy [dvoo-trah-**kto**-vi] adj.m. two-support (roof, etc.)

dwutygodnik [dvoo-ti-go-dńeek] m. biweekly; fortnightly (publication, newsletter, etc.)
dwutygodniowy [dvoo-ti-go-dńo-vi] adj.m. fortnightly; two-weeks-old; of two weeks
dwutygodniówka [dvoo-ti-go-dńoof-kah] f. two-weeks' pay
dwutysięcznik [dvoo-ti-śhan-chńeek] m. two-thousand-ton ship
dwutysięczny [dvoo-ti-śhan-chni] adj.m. two-thousandth
dwuuchy [dvoo-oo-khi] adj.m. two-eared
dwuuszny [dvoo-oosh-ni] adj.m. with both ears; two-eared
dwuwargowy [dvoo-vahr-go-vi] adj.m. bilabial; bilabiate
dwuwarstwowo [dvoo-vahr-stfo-vo] adv. in a two-ply fashion
dwuwarstwowość [dvoo-vahr-stfo-vośhćh] f. two-ply feature
dwuwarstwowy [dvoo-vahr-stfo-vi] adj.m. two-ply (structure, etc.)
dwuwartościowość [dvoo-vahr-tośh-ćho-vośhćh] f. bivalency
dwuwartościowy [dvoo-vahr-to-śhćho-vi] adj.m. two-way; bivalent; divalent
pierwiastek dwuwartościowy [pyer-vyahs-tek dvoo-vahr-to-śhćho-vi] exp.: dyad
dwuwęglan [dvoo-van-glahn] m. bicarbonate
dwuwiekowy [dvoo-vye-ko-vi] adj.m. two centuries old; of two centuries; lasting two centuries; of two centuries' duration
dwuwiersz [dvoo-vyersh] m. couplet; distich
dwuwierszowy [dvoo-vyer-sho-vi] adj.m. two-line (verse, etc.); couplet (form, etc.)
dwuwierzchołkowy [dvoo-vyesh-khow-ko-vi] adj.m. two-summit (mountain, etc.)
dwuwiosłowy [dvoo-vyo-swo-vi] adj.m. two-oar (boat, etc.)
dwuwklęsły [dvoo-fklan-swi] adj.m. biconcave; concavo-concave
dwuwładza [dvoo-vwah-dzah] f. diarchy; two centers of power in one country
dwuwładztwo [dvoo-vwahts-tfo] n. diarchy
dwuwymiarowość [dvoo-vi-myah-ro-vośhćh] f. having two dimensions
dwuwymiarowy [dvoo-vi-myah-ro-vi] adj.m. two-dimensional
dwuwypukły [dvoo-vi-poo-kwi] adj.m. biconvex; convexo-convex
dwuwyrazowy [dvoo-vi-rah-zo-vi] adj.m. two-word (name, etc.)
dwuzasadowy [dvoo-zah-sah-do-vi] adj.m. dibasic
dwuzębny [dvoo-zanb-ni] adj.m. bidentate
dwuzgłoskowiec [dvoo-zgwo-sko-vyets] m. word of two syllables
dwuzgłoskowy [dvoo-zgwo-sko-vi] adj.m. disyllabic; of two syllables
dwuziarnowy [dvoo-źhahr-no-vi] adj.m. two-grained (wheat, etc.)
dwuzłączka [dvoo-zwown-chkah] f. conduit connector
dwuzłotowy [dvoo-zwo-to-vi] adj.m. two-zloty (coin, etc.)
dwuzłotówka [dvoo-zwo-toof-kah] f. two-zloty coin
dwuzmianowość [dvoo-zmyah-no-vośhćh] f. two-shift work
dwuzmianowy [dvoo-zmyah-no-vi] adj.m. two-shift (work, etc.)
dwuznacznie [dvoo-znah-chńe] adv. equivocally; ambiguously; with double meaning; dubiously; suggestively; in an insinuating manner
dwuznacznik [dvoo-znah-chńeek] m. ambiguity; insinuation; prevarication; quibble; equivoke; pun; play on words; word with a double meaning
dwuznaczność [dvoo-znah-chnośhćh] f. ambiguity; equivocation
dwuznaczny [dvoo-znah-chni] adj.m. equivocal; ambiguous; of double meaning; dubious; suggestive; insinuating; backhanded; two-edged (joke, etc.)
dwuznak [dvoo-znahk] m. digraph
dwuzwężkowy [dvoo-zvansh-ko-vi] adj.m. two-orifice (flow, etc.)
dwuzwiązkowy [dvoo-zvyowns-ko-vi] adj.m. diadelphous (plant)

dwużeniec [dvoo-**zhe**-ńets] m. bigamist; remarried widower
dwużeństwo [dvoo-**zheń**-stfo] n. bigamy
dybać [**di**-bahćh] v. lie in wait; lurk; watch; be on the lookout; scheme (against); dog; have designs (on) (*repeatedly*)
dybanie [di-**bah**-ńe] n. lying in wait
dybel [**di**-bel] m. tie bar; coak; dowel
dyblarka [di-**blahr**-kah] f. tie bar placing machine
dyblować [di-**blo**-vahćh] v. joint with tie bars; joint with dowels (*repeatedly*)
dyblowanie [dib-lo-**vah**-ńe] n. connecting with tie bars
dybrach [di-brahkh] m. (a) pyrrhic
dybuk [**di**-book] m. evil spirit in Jewish tradition
dyby [**di**-bi] pl. (wooden) stocks (used as a punishment)
dych [dikh] m. (only in) exp.: **ani słychu, ani dychu** [ah-ńee **swi**-khoo **ah**-ńee **di**-khoo] exp.: no sign of life; no news whatever
dycha [**di**-khah] f. slang: a tenner; ten; 10 (mob jargon)
dychać [**di**-khahćh] v. breathe; pant; gasp for breath (*repeatedly*)
dychanie [di-**khah**-ńe] n. breathing; panting; gasping for breath
dychawica [di-khah-**vee**-tsah] f. asthma
dychawiczny [di-khah-**vee**-chni] adj.m. asthmatic; short-winded; pursy; broken-winded (horse); puffy; wheezy
dychawka [di-**khahf**-kah] f. trachea
dychorej [di-**kho**-rey] m. variety of Roman verse
dychotomia [di-kho-**to**-myah] f. dichotomy; division into two parts
dychotomicznie [di-kho-to-**meech**-ńe] adj.m. dichotomously
dychotomiczny [di-kho-to-**meech**-ni] adj.m. dichotomous
dydaktycznie [di-dahk-**tich**-ńe] adv. didactically; in an instructive manner
dydaktyczność [di-dahk-**tich**-nośhćh] f. didactic nature (of a book, etc.); instructive character (of a publication, etc.)
dydaktyczny [di-dahk-**tich**-ni] adj.m. didactic; instructive
dydaktyk [di-**dahk**-tik] m. didactician; teacher; educator
dydaktyka [di-**dahk**-ti-kah] f. didactics; teaching methods; teaching; instruction; moralizing
dydaktyzm [di-**dahk**-tizm] m. didacticism
dydek [**di**-dek] m. an ancient Polish coin
dydelf [**di**-delf] m. didelph; opossum; marsupial having a double uterus
dydym [**di**-dim] m. didymium
dyferencjacja [di-fe-ren-**tsyah**-tsyah] f. differentiation
dyferencjalny [di-fe-ren-**tsyahl**-ni] adj.m. differential (gear, etc.)
dyferencjał [di-fe-**ren**-tsyahw] m. differential gear
dyfrakcja [di-**frah**-ktsyah] f. diffraction
dyfrakcyjny [di-frah-**ktsiy**-ni] adj.m. diffraction (spectrum, grating, etc.)
dyfraktometr [di-frah-**kto**-metr] m. diffraction meter
dyfteria [di-**fte**-ryah] f. diphtheria; putrid sore throat
dyfteryczny [di-fte-**rich**-ni] adj.m. diphtheric
dyfteryt [di-**fte**-rit] m. diphtheria; putrid sore throat
dyftong [**dif**-tong] m. diphthong; a sound made by gliding from one vowel to another in one syllable as in "oil"
dyftongiczny [dif-ton-**geech**-ni] adj.m. diphthongal
dyftongizacja [dif-ton-gee-**zah**-tsyah] f. diphthongization
dyftongizować [dif-ton-gee-**zo**-vahćh] v. diphthongize (*repeatedly*)
dyftongizować się [dif-ton-gee-**zo**-vahćh śhan] v. be diphthongized (*repeatedly*)
dyftongizowanie [dif-ton-gee-zo-**vah**-ńe] n. diphthongization
dyftongizowanie się [dif-ton-gee-zo-**vah**-ńe śhan] n. becoming diphthongized

dyfundować [di-foon-**do**-vahćh] v. diffuse (*repeatedly*)
dyfundowanie [di-foon-do-**vah**-ńe] n. diffusion
dyfuzja [di-**foo**-zyah] f. diffusion
dyfuzjonizm [di-foo-**zyo**-ńeezm] m. diffusion of ethnic culture as a source of cultural progress
dyfuzor [di-**foo**-zor] m. diffuser
dyfuzyjnie [di-foo-**ziy**-ńe] adv. diffusively
dyfuzyjność [di-foo-**ziy**-nośhćh] f. diffusiveness
dyfuzyjny [di-foo-**ziy**-ni] adj.m. diffusive; diffusion (process, experiment, etc.)
dyg [dig] m. curtsy; bob
dygać [**di**-gahćh] v. drop a curtsy; curtsy; bob (*repeatedly*)
dyganie [di-**gah**-ńe] n. curtsy; bob
dygestorium [di-ge-**stor**-yoom] n. enclosure for handling toxic and inflammable substances
dygnąć [**di**-gnownćh] v. curtsy; drop a curtsy; bob
dygnięcie [dig-**ńan**-ćhe] n. curtsy; bob; dropping a curtsy
dygnitarski [dig-ńee-**tahr**-skee] adj.m. dignitary's; self-important
po dygnitarsku [po dig-ńee-**tahr**-skoo] exp.: with dignity
dygnitarstwo [dig-ńee-**tahr**-stfo] n. dignity; high office; haughtiness; loftiness
dygnitarz [dig-**ńee**-tahsh] m. dignitary; high-ranking man; high public officer
dygocący [di-go-**tsown**-tsi] adj.m. vibrant; vibrating; trembling; shaking; thrilling
dygot [**di**-got] m. tremble; shiver; shudder; shake; thrill; throb (of joy, etc.); flutter; palpitation; agitation; trembling; shivering
dygotać [di-**go**-tahćh] v. tremble; vibrate; shiver; shudder (with); shake; thrill; be thrilled; throb; flutter; palpitate; be vibrant (*repeatedly*)
dygotanie [di-go-**tah**-ńe] n. throbs; thrills (of joy, etc.); shivers (of cold, etc.)
dygotki [di-**go**-tkee] pl. trembling; shivering
dygotliwy [di-go-**tlee**-vi] adj.m. shivering
dygować [di-**go**-vahćh] v. drag heavy objects; carry too much weight (*repeatedly*)
dygowanie [di-go-**vah**-ńe] n. dragging heavy objects; carrying too much weight
dygresja [di-**gre**-syah] f. digression
robić dygresję od tematu [**ro**-beećh di-**gre**-syan ot te-**mah**-too] exp.: to digress (to stray, to depart) from one's subject; to wander away from one's subject
dygresyjność [di-gre-**siy**-nośhćh] f. digressiveness
dygresyjny [di-gre-**siy**-ni] adj.m. digressional; digressionary
dykasteria [di-kahs-**te**-ryah] f. branch, division, section of the Civil Service
dykcja [**dik**-tsyah] f. diction; enunciation; elocution; delivery
dykcjonarz [dik-**tsyo**-nahsh] m. dictionary
dykta [**dik**-tah] f. plywood; slang: methylated spirit; dictation in a class; pupil's bench
dyktafon [dik-**tah**-fon] m. dictaphone
dyktando [dik-**tahn**-do] n. dictation; passage taken down from dictation; dictation exercise
dyktat [**dik**-taht] m. dictation; dictate
dyktator [dik-**tah**-tor] m. dictator; absolute ruler; tyrant
dyktatorski [dik-tah-**tor**-skee] adj.m. dictatorial
po dyktatorsku [po dik-tah-**tor**-skoo] exp.: dictatorially
dyktatorstwo [dik-tah-**tor**-stfo] n. dictatorial power; dictatorial authority
dyktatura [dik-tah-**too**-rah] f. dictatorship
dykteryjka [dik-te-**riy**-kah] f. anecdote; story; yarn
dyktograf [dik-**to**-grahf] m. Dictograph
dyktować [dik-**to**-vahćh] v. dictate; tell; advise; prescribe; impose (*repeatedly*)
dyktowanie [dik-to-**vah**-ńe] n. dictation; dictate; dictating

dyl [dil] m. deal (beam); dowel; deal board; pine or fir wood; slang: escape (mob jargon)
dylatacja [di-lah-**tah**-tsyah] f. dilatation
dylatacyjny [di-lah-tah-**tsiy**-ni] adj.m. dilatational
dylatometr [di-lah-**to**-metr] m. dilatometer
dyląż [**di**-lownsh] m. a variety of beetle
dylemat [di-**le**-maht] m. dilemma; perplexity; fix
dyletancki [di-le-**tahn**-tskee] adj.m. dilettantish; amateurish; nonprofessional; unprofessional
po dyletancku [po di-le-tahn-tskoo] exp.: = **dyletancko**
dyletancko [di-le-**tahn**-tsko] adv. in a dilettante manner; amateurishly; nonprofessionally; unprofessionally
dyletanctwo [di-le-**tahn**-tstfo] n. dilettantism; amateurism; lack of professionalism; amateurishness
dyletant [di-**le**-tahnt] m. dilettante; amateur; dabbler; a nonprofessional
dyletantka [di-le-**tahn**-tkah] f. (female) dilettante; amateur; dabbler; a nonprofessional
dyletantyzm [di-le-**tahn**-tizm] m. dilettantism; amateurishness
dylina [di-**lee**-nah] f. deal floor; deal fence; fence of deal piles
dyliżans [di-**lee**-zhahns] m. stagecoach
dyliżansowy [di-lee-zhahn-**so**-vi] adj.m. of a stagecoach
dylogia [di-**lo**-gyah] f. two-part play or novel (of two separate parts)
dylować [di-**lo**-vahćh] v. board (a floor); slang: escape (*repeatedly*)
dylowanie [di-lo-**vah**-ńe] n. installing a deal floor
dylowy [di-**lo**-vi] adj.m. of deals; deal (floor, etc.)
dylu-dylu [di-loo **di**-loo] exp.: (hand movement of a violinist)
dyluwialny [di-loo-**vyahl**-ni] adj.m. diluvial
dyluwium [di-**loo**-vyoom] n. diluvium
dym [dim] m. smoke; reek; steam (of soup, etc.); fumes (of a roast, etc.); mob slang: cigarette; one puff of tobacco smoke; (an old expression:) homestead (hist.)
jak w dym [yahk v dim] exp.: without hesitation
pójść z dymem [pooyśhćh z **di**-mem] exp.: to go up in smoke
puścić z dymem [poo-śhćheećh z **di**-mem] exp.: to send up in smoke
dymać [**di**-mahćh] v. colloq: run like mad; hasten; hurry; lose on time; slang: have sex (*repeatedly*)
dymanie [di-**mah**-ńe] n. colloq: haste; vulg.: slang: having sex
dymarka [di-**mahr**-kah] f. primitive smelting furnace; primitive chimney-less hut
dymarski [di-**mahr**-skee] adj.m. of a primitive smelting furnace
dymarstwo [di-**mahr**-stfo] n. primitive smelting
dymarz [**di**-mash] m. worker in primitive smelting
dymek [**di**-mek] m. light cloud of smoke; steam; haze
dymetr [**di**-metr] m. variety of Roman verse
dymiący [di-**myown**-tsi] adj.m. smoky; reeky; fumy
dymić [di-**meećh**] v. smoke; reek; steam; emit fumes (*repeatedly*)
dymić się [di-meećh śhan] v. smoke; reek; steam; fume (*repeatedly*)
dymienica [di-mye-**ńee**-tsah] f. bubo
dymienica morowa [di-mye-**ńee**-tsah mo-**ro**-vah] exp.: bubonic plague
dymieniczy [di-mye-**ńee**-chi] adj.m. bubonic
dymienie [di-**mye**-ńe] n. smoking; reeking; emitting fumes
dymienie się [di-**mye**-ńe śhan] n. smoking; reeking; emitting fumes
dyminucja [di-mee-**noo**-tsyah] f. repetition of a musical refrain at lower rhythmic values
dymisja [di-**mee**-syah] f. dismissal; resignation
podać się do dymisji [po-dahćh śhan do di-mee-syee] exp.: to hand in one's resignation; to resign

dymisjonować [di-mee-syo-**no**-vahćh] v. dismiss (*repeatedly*)
dymisjonowany [di-mee-syo-no-**vah**-ni] adj.m. discharged
dymka [**dim**-kah] f. diaper; small onion bulb
dymnica [dim-**ńee**-tsah] f. smoke-box; fumitory (plant)
dymnicowate [dim-ńee-tso-**vah**-te] pl. the family Fumariaceae (herbs)
dymnicowy [dim-ńee-**tso**-vi] adj.m. protecting against smoke; separated from smoke
dymnik [**dim**-ńeek] m. smoke hole; squint window; skylight
okno dymnikowe [**ok**-no dim-ńee-**ko**-ve] exp.: squint window
dymnikowy [dim-ńee-**ko**-vi] adj.m. vent (hole, etc.); smoke (hole, etc.)
dymny [**dim**-ni] adj.m. smoky; reeky; smoke-filled; smoke-blackened
dymochłon [di-**mo**-khwon] m. smoke-inhibitor; smoke-consumer
dymochłonny [di-mo-**khwon**-ni] adj.m. of a smoke-inhibitor
dymomierz [di-**mo**-myesh] m. soot gauge
dymorfizm [di-**mor**-feezm] m. dimorphism
dymotwórczy [di-mo-**tfoor**-chi] adj.m. smoke-producing
dymowy [di-**mo**-vi] adj.m. smoky; reeky; smoke-filled; smoke-blackened; diaper (napkin, etc.)
dymówka [di-**moof**-kah] f. chimney swallow; barn swallow
dyn [din] m. dyne = **dyna**
dyna [**di**-nah] f. dyne
dynamicznie [di-nah-**meech**-ńe] adv. dynamically; potently; forcefully
dynamiczność [di-nah-**meech**-nośhćh] f. dynamism
dynamiczny [di-nah-**meech**-ni] adj.m. dynamic; potent; forceful
dynamika [di-**nah**-mee-kah] f. dynamics; dynamism
dynamit [di-**nah**-meet] m. dynamite; slang: W.W.II German ersatz (artificial) bread
dynamitowy [di-nah-mee-**to**-vi] adj.m. of dynamite; dynamite (bomb, charge, etc.)
dynamizacja [di-nah-mee-**zah**-tsyah] f. the imparting of dynamism (energy) (to); actuation
dynamizm [di-**nah**-meezm] m. dynamism
dynamizować [di-nah-mee-**zo**-vahćh] v. impart dynamism; impart energy; actuate (*repeatedly*)
dynamizowanie [di-nah-mee-zo-**vah**-ńe] n. imparting of dynamism
dynamo [di-**nah**-mo] n. dynamo
dynamograf [di-nah-**mo**-grahph] m. dynamograph
dynamomaszyna [di-nah-mo-mah-**shi**-nah] f. dynamo; dynamo electric machine
dynamometamorfizm [di-nah-mo-me-tah-**mor**-feezm] m. dynamic metamorphism
dynamometamorfoza [di-nah-mo-me-tah-mor-**fo**-zah] f. dynamometamorphism
dynamometr [di-nah-**mo**-metr] m. dynamometer
dynamometryczny [di-nah-mo-met-**rich**-ni] adj.m. dynamometric
dynamostarter [di-nah-mo-**stahr**-ter] m. dynamo-starter
dynar [**di**-nahr] m. dinar
dynarski [di-**nahr**-skee] adj.m. dinar (type, etc.)
dynasowy [di-nah-**so**-vi] adj.m. fireproof (bricks, ceramics, etc.)
dynasówka [di-nah-**soof**-kah] f. fireproof brick
dynasta [di-**nah**-stah] m. dynast; ruler
dynastia [di-**nah**-styah] f. dynasty
dynastyczność [di-nah-**stich**-nośhćh] f. dynastic succession
dynastyczny [di-nah-**stich**-ni] adj.m. dynastic
dynatron [di-**nah**-tron] m. dynatron (a vacuum tube)
dyndać [**din**-dahćh] v. dangle; swing; slang: hang; be hanged; dance upon nothing (*repeatedly*)
dyndać się [**din**-dahćh śh<u>an</u>] v. (emphatic:) dangle; swing (*repeatedly*)
dyndanie [din-**dah**-ńe] n. dangling; swinging
dyndanie się [din-**dah**-ńe śh<u>an</u>] n.

dangling (oneself)
dyndele [din-**de**-le] indecl.: tinkling of bells; tintinnabulation
dyndolenie [din-do-**le**-ńe] n. colloq: twiddle; fiddle; doing nothing
dyndolić [din-**do**-leećh] v. colloq: twiddle; do nothing (*repeatedly*)
dyngus [**din**-goos] m. traditional dousing of womenfolk on Easter Monday; Easter Monday
dynia [**di**-ńah] f. pumpkin; squash
dyniasty [di-**ńah**-sti] adj.m. gourdlike; bulbous; gibbous
dyniasta głowa [di-**ńah**-stah **gwo**-vah] exp.: pumpkin head
dyniowaty [di-ńo-**vah**-ti] adj.m. gourdlike; bulbous; gibbous; of the gourd family
dyniowate [di-ńo-**vah**-te] pl. the gourd family
dyniowy [di-**ńo**-vi] adj.m. pumpkin (seed, etc.)
dynoda [di-**no**-dah] f. secondary cathode
dynozaur [di-**no**-zahwr] m. dinosaur
dyon [**di**-on] m. squadron
dyplom [**di**-plom] m. diploma; certificate of proficiency; qualifying certificate; brevet
dyplomacja [di-plo-**mah**-tsyah] f. diplomacy; diplomatic service; statecraft; policy; tact
dyplomant [di-**plo**-mahnt] m. graduate of an institution of higher education
dyplomata [di-plo-**mah**-tah] m. diplomat; career man
dyplomatka [di-plo-**mah**-tkah] f. (woman) diplomat; career woman
dyplomatycznie [di-plo-mah-**tich**-ńe] adv. diplomatically; with tact
dyplomatyczny [di-plo-mah-**tich**-ni] adj.m. diplomatic; tactful; noncommittal
dyplomatyk [di-plo-**mah**-tik] m. person engaged in diplomatic research
dyplomatyka [di-plo-**mah**-ti-kah] f. diplomacy
dyplomatyzować [di-plo-mah-ti-**zo**-vahćh] v. act diplomatically; make diplomatic (move, etc.); use tact (*repeatedly*)
dyplomatyzowanie [di-plo-mah-ti-zo-**vah**-ńe] n. acting diplomatically; using tact
dyplomować [di-plo-**mo**-vahćh] v. grant a diploma (*repeatedly*)
dyplomowanie [di-plo-mo-**vah**-ńe] n. granting a diploma
dyplomowany [di-plo-mo-**vah**-ni] adj.m. certified; qualified; with a diploma
dyplomowy [di-plo-**mo**-vi] adj.m. of diploma
egzamin dyplomowy [e-**gzah**-meen di-plo-**mo**-vi] exp.: candidate's final examination
praca dyplomowa [**prah**-tsah di-plo-**mo**-vah] exp.: thesis; dissertation
dyplomówka [di-plo-**moof**-kah] f. colloq: thesis; dissertation
dypodia [di-**po**-dyah] f. dipody
dypodialny [di-po-**dyahl**-ni] adj.m. dipodic
dypsomania [dip-so-**mah**-ńyah] f. recurring alcoholism; dipsomania
dypsomaniak [dip-so-**mah**-ńyahk] m. dipsomaniac
dyptam [**dip**-tahm] m. Dictamnus herb; fraxinella; dittany
dyptotyzm [dip-**to**-tizm] m. diptote; a noun which has only two cases
dyptych [**dip**-tikh] m. diptych
dyptyk [**dip**-tik] m. diptych
dyr [dir] m. slang: school principal; the head of a school (also: **dyrcio** [**dir**-ćho], **dyrek** [**di**-rek], **dyro** [**di**-ro]
dyrdać [**dir**-dahćh] v. slang: run like mad; scurry (*repeatedly*)
dyrdanie [dir-**dah**-ńe] n. slang: running like mad
dyrdum [**dir**-doom] n. (only in) exp.: **mieć fiksum-dyrdum** [myećh **fik**-soom **dir**-doom] exp.: to be crazy
dyrdy [**dir**-di] (only in) exp.: slang: **w dyrdy** [v **dir**-di] exp.: full speed; gallop; double-quick
dyrdymała [dir-di-**mah**-wah] f. slang: nonsense; twaddle; prating
dyrdymałka [dir-di-**mahw**-kah] f. slang: nonsense; twaddle; prating
dyrekcja [di-**re**-ktsyah] f. management; headquarters; head office; board of directors; leadership (of an orchestra)

dyrekcyjny [di-re-**ktsiy**-ni] adj.m. of the management; managing; manager's; managers'
dyrektor [di-**re**-ktor] m. director; manager; managing director; principal; chief; boss
dyrektorialny [di-re-kto-**ryahl**-ni] adj.m. directorial
dyrektoriat [di-re-**ktor**-yaht] m. Directoriate
dyrektorka [di-re-**ktor**-kah] f. (woman) director; manager; managing director; principal; schoolmistress; headmistress
dyrektorowa [di-re-kto-**ro**-vah] f. the wife of (director, manager, principal, boss, chief, etc.)
dyrektorować [di-re-kto-**ro**-vahćh] v. manage an enterprise; run an institution (*repeatedly*)
dyrektorowanie [di-re-kto-ro-**vah**-ńe] n. managing an enterprise; running an institution
dyrektorski [di-re-**ktor**-skee] adj.m. director's; manager's; principal's; schoolmaster's; headmaster's; chief's; boss's
dyrektorstwo [di-re-**ktor**-stfo] n. the post of (director, manager, principal, schoolmaster, headmaster); director and his wife
dyrektywa [di-re-**kti**-vah] f. instructions; directions; orders
dyrektywność [di-re-**ktiv**-nośhćh] f. instructive character of directions or orders
dyrektywny [di-re-**ktiv**-ni] adj.m. instructive; directive; in form of an order
dyrygencki [di-ri-**gen**-tskee] adj.m. orchestra conductor's; orchestra leader's; conducting (classes, program, etc.)
dyrygent [di-**ri**-gent] m. orchestra conductor; orchestra leader
dyrygentka [di-ri-**gen**-tkah] f. (woman) orchestra conductor; orchestra leader
dyrygentura [di-ri-gen-**too**-rah] f. profession of orchestra conductor or orchestra leader
dyrygować [di-ri-**go**-vahćh] v. conduct; lead; manage; superintend (*repeatedly*)
dyrygowanie [di-ri-go-**vah**-ńe] n. conducting; leading; managing
dys- [dis] prefix: dis-
dysalteracja [di-sahl-te-**rahts**-yah] f. simultaneous variation of tone (in music)
dysażio [di-**sahzh**-yo] n. disagio; fall of exchange rate below nominal value
dyscyplina [dis-tsi-**plee**-nah] f. discipline; branch; line (of work); scourge; lash of the scourge
brak dyscypliny [brahk dis-tsi-**plee**-ni] exp.: unruliness
dyscyplinarka [dis-tsi-plee-**nahr**-kah] f. disciplinary proceedings; disciplinary actions
dyscyplinarnie [dis-tsi-plee-**nahr**-ńe] adv. disciplinarily
dyscyplinarny [dis-tsi-plee-**nahr**-ni] adj.m. disciplinary
postępowanie dyscyplinarne [po-st<u>an</u>-po-**vah**-ńe dis-tsi-plee-**nahr**-ne] exp.: disciplinary measures
dyscyplinować [dis-tsi-plee-**no**-vahćh] v. discipline; punish; control; train (*repeatedly*)
dysertacja [di-ser-**tah**-tsyah] f. dissertation; disquisition; thesis (of a candidate for a degree)
dysertacyjny [di-ser-tah-**tsiy**-ni] adj.m. of a dissertation; of a disquisition; of a thesis (of a candidate for a degree)
dysertant [di-**ser**-tahnt] m. author defending his dissertation
dysfagia [dis-**fah**-gyah] f. inability to swallow; dysphagia
dysfazja [dis-**fah**-zyah] f. temporary inability to speak
dysfunkcja [dis-**foonk**-tsyah] f. dysfunction
dysfunkcjonalny [dis-foonk-tsyo-**nahl**-ni] adj.m. dysfunctional
dysforia [dis-**fo**-ryah] f. opposite of euphoria; depression
dysgrafia [diz-**grah**-fyah] f. inability to write caused by changes in the brain
dysgrafik [diz-**grah**-feek] m. person suffering from inability to write (caused by changes in the brain)
dysharmonia [dis-khahr-**mo**-ńyah] f. disharmony; dissonance; discord;

jar; lack of harmony
dysharmoniczny [dis-khahr-mo-ńeech-ni] adj.m. disharmonic (composition, etc.); disharmonious; dissonant
dysharmonijny [dis-khahr-mo-ńeey-ni] adj.m. disharmonious; dissonant
dysharmonizować [dis-khahr-mo-ńee-zo-vahćh] v. disharmonize (*repeatedly*)
dyshonor [dis-kho-nor] m. dishonor; disgrace; discredit; disparagement
dysjunkcja [dis-yoon-ktsyah] f. disjunction; separation
dysjunkcyjny [dis-yoon-ktsiy-ni] adj.m. disjunctive
dysjunktywny [dis-yoon-ktiv-ni] adj.m. disjunctive; disjunct; discontinuous
dysk [disk] m. disk; disc; discus
dyska [dis-kah] f. colloq: ten
dyskant [dis-kahnt] m. soprano; treble; colloq: fluty voice
dyskietka [dis-ket-kah] f. floppy disk (used in computers)
dyskobol [dis-ko-bol] m. discus thrower; discobolus
dyskobolka [dis-ko-bol-kah] f. (woman) discus thrower; discobolus
dyskografia [dis-ko-grah-fyah] f. discography
dyskont [dis-kont] m. discount; discounting of bills
dyskonter [dis-kon-ter] m. discount broker
dyskonto [dis-kon-to] n. discount; discounting of bills
dyskontować [dis-kon-to-vahćh] v. discount; negotiate (a bill); turn to profit (*repeatedly*)
dyskontowanie [dis-kon-to-vah-ńe] n. discounting; negotiating (a bill); turning to profit
dyskontowy [dis-kon-to-vi] adj.m. discount; of discount
dyskopatia [dis-ko-pah-tyah] f. degeneration of discs in the spinal column
dyskordancja [dis-kor-dahn-tsyah] f. (geological) unconformity
dyskoteka [dis-ko-te-kah] f. disco; discotheque; library of recordings
dyskotekowy [dis-ko-te-ko-vi] adj.m. disco (music, etc.); of a discotheque; of a library of recordings
dyskrecja [dis-kre-tsyah] f. discretion; reserve (in speech, etc.); confidentiality; circumspection
diskrecjonalny [dis-kre-tsyo-nahl-ni] adj.m. confidential; discretionary (powers, etc.)
dyskredytacja [dis-kre-di-tah-tsyah] f. making discreditable
dyskredytować [dis-kre-di-to-vahćh] v. discredit; bring discredit (on); throw discredit (on); disparage; bring into disrepute (*repeatedly*)
dyskredytować teorię [dis-kre-di-to-vahćh te-o-ryan] exp.: refute a theory; expose a theory; disprove a theory; discredit a theory
dyskredytować się [dis-kre-di-to-vahćh śhan] v. fall into discredit; bring discredit on oneself (*repeatedly*)
dyskredytowanie [dis-kre-di-to-vah-ńe] n. discrediting
dyskredytowanie się [dis-kre-di-to-vah-ńe śhan] n. bringing discredit on oneself
dyskretnie [dis-kret-ńe] adv. discreetly; with discretion; with circumspection; imperceptibly; undiscernibly; unobtrusively; confidentially
dyskretny [dis-kret-ni] adj.m. discreet; circumspect; reticent; sober; unobtrusive
dyskryminacja [dis-kri-mee-nah-tsyah] f. discrimination
dyskryminacyjny [dis-kri-mee-nah-tsiy-ni] adj.m. discriminating; distinguishing; discerning; judicious; discriminatory
dyskryminator [dis-kri-mee-nah-tor] m. electrical modulator
dyskryminować [dis-kri-mee-no-vahćh] v. discriminate (*repeatedly*)
dyskryminowanie [dis-kri-mee-no-vah-ńe] n. discrimination
dyskurs [dis-koors] m. speech; discourse
dyskursywizm [dis-koor-si-veezm]

m. discursiveness
dyskursywnie [dis-koor-**siv**-ńe] adv. discursively; digressively
dyskursywność [dis-koor-**siv**-nośhćh] f. discursiveness
dyskursywny [dis-koor-**siv**-ni] adj.m. discursive; digressive
dyskusja [dis-**koo**-syah] f. discussion; debate; controversy
nie podlegający dyskusji [ńe po-dle-gah-yown-tsi dis-**koo**-syee] exp.: incontrovertible; beyond argument
dyskusyjność [dis-koo-**siy**-nośhćh] f. controversy; controversial character
dyskusyjny [dis-koo-**siy**-ni] adj.m. controversial; debating (society, competition, etc.)
dyskutant [dis-**koo**-tahnt] m. debater; disputant
dyskutantka [dis-koo-**tahn**-tkah] f. (woman) debater; disputant
dyskutować [dis-koo-**to**-vahćh] v. discuss; debate; thrash out; ventilate (a question, etc.) (*repeatedly*)
dyskutowanie [dis-koo-to-**vah**-ńe] n. discussion; debate
dyskwalifikacja [dis-kfah-lee-fee-**kah**-tsyah] f. disqualification; incapacitation
dyskwalifikować [dis-kfah-lee-fee-**ko**-vahćh] v. disqualify; disable; incapacitate; pronounce unfit; pronounce inadequate; condemn; disparage (*repeatedly*)
dyskwalifikowanie [dis-kfah-lee-fee-ko-**vah**-ńe] n. disqualification
dysleksja [dis-**lek**-syah] f. dyslexia
dysleksyjny [dis-lek-**siy**-ni] adj.m. dyslexic
dyslektyczny [dis-lek-**tich**-ni] adj.m. dyslexic
dyslektyk [dis-**lek**-tik] m. person suffering from dyslexia
dyslokacja [dis-lo-**kah**-tsyah] f. arrangement; order; dislocation; displacement
dyslokacyjny [dis-lo-kah-**tsiy**-ni] adj.m. of an arrangement; of an order; of a dislocation; of a displacement
dyslokować [dis-lo-**ko**-vahćh] v. arrange; order; dislocate; displace (*repeatedly*)
dysocjacja [di-sots-**yah**-tsyah] f. dissociation; multiple personality; mechanism of ego defense
dysocjować [di-sots-**yo**-vahćh] v. dissociate; decompose; disunite; disconnect (*repeatedly*)
dysocjowanie [di-so-tsyo-**vah**-ńe] n. dissociation
dysonans [di-**so**-nahns] m. dissonance; disharmony; discordance; incongruity
dysonansowo [di-so-nahn-**so**-vo] adv. dissonantly; discordantly
dysonansowość [di-so-nahn-**so**-vośhćh] f. dissonance; discordance; nonconformity
dysonansowy [di-so-nahn-**so**-vi] adj.m. dissonant; discordant
dysonować [di-so-**no**-vahćh] v. make dissonance (*repeatedly*)
dysonowanie [di-so-no-**vah**-ńe] n. dissonance; making discord
dyspalatalizacja [dis-pah-tah-lee-zah-tsyah] f. removal of palatalization
dyspanseryjny [dis-pahn-se-**riy**-ni] adj.m. of preventive medicine
dyspareunia [dis-pah-re-**oo**-ńyah] f. lack of simultaneous orgasm
dyspasza [dis-**pah**-shah] f. adjusted payment of maritime insurance
dyspaszer [dis-**pah**-sher] m. maritime insurance adjustor
dyspeczer [dis-**pe**-cher] m. dispatcher
dyspeczerski [dis-pe-**cher**-skee] adj. m. dispatcher's; of a dispatcher
dyspensa [dis-**pen**-sah] f. dispensation (from fasting, etc.)
dyspensować [dis-pen-**so**-vahćh] v. give dispensation (from fasting, etc.) (*repeatedly*)
dyspensowanie [dis-pen-so-**vah**-ńe] n. giving dispensation (from fasting, etc.)
dyspepsja [dis-**pep**-syah] f. dyspepsia; indigestion
dyspergator [dis-per-**gah**-tor] m. dispersive substance
dyspergować [dis-per-**go**-vahćh] v. prepare colloidal substances (*repeatedly*)
dyspergowanie [dis-per-go-**vah**-ńe]

n. preparation of colloidal substances
dyspersja [dis-**per**-syah] f. dispersion
dyspersyjny [dis-per-**siy**-ni] adj.m. dispersive; of dispersion; dispersion (medium, etc.)
dysplastyczny [dis-plahs-**tich**-ni] adj.m. not fitting the classification of three basic types
dysplastyk [dis-**plahs**-tik] m. individual not fitting the classification of three basic types
dysponenda [dis-po-**nen**-dah] f. list of books in publisher's warehouse
dysponent [dis-**po**-nent] m. disposer
dysponentka [dis-po-**nen**-tkah] f. (woman) disposer
dysponować [dis-po-**no**-vahćh] v. dispose; control; order; have at one's disposal; exercise control (over); administer; give instructions (to do) (*repeatedly*)
dysponowanie [dis-po-no-**vah**-ńe] n. control (over); control (of); administration (of)
dysponowany [dis-po-no-**vah**-ni] adj.m. fit; well; in good form; well disposed (to do)
dyspozycja [dis-po-**zi**-tsyah] f. instructions; directions; orders; command; disposition; disposal; plan; outline; scheme; inclination (to do); bent (for)
być do dyspozycji [bićh do dis-po-**zi**-tsyee] exp.: to be at (somebody's) disposal
dyspozycyjność [dis-po-zi-**tsiy**-nośhćh] f. having discretionary powers
dyspozycyjny [dis-po-zi-**tsiy**-ni] adj.m. discretionary (fund, etc.)
dyspozytor [dis-po-**zi**-tor] m. dispatcher; setter (miner)
dyspozytornia [dis-po-zi-**tor**-ńah] f. dispatcher's office
dyspozytorski [dis-po-zi-**tor**-skee] adj.m. dispatcher's (work, etc.)
dyspozytura [dis-po-zi-**too**-rah] f. office of chief dispatcher; dispatching center
dyspozytywnie [dis-po-zi-**tiv**-ńe] adv. in form of an order
dyspozytywny [dis-po-zi-**tiv**-ni] adj.m. disposable
dysproporcja [dis-pro-**por**-tsyah] f. disproportion; lack (want) of proportion; mismatch; disparity
dysproporcjonalnie [dis-pro-por-tsyo-**nahl**-ńe] adv. disproportionately
dysproporcjonalny [dis-pro-por-tsyo-**nahl**-ni] adj.m. disproportional; disproportionate; being out of proportion
dysproz [**dis**-pros] m. dysprosium (atomic number 66)
dysputa [dis-**poo**-tah] f. dispute; debate; controversy
dysputant [dis-**poo**-tahnt] m. debater
dysputować [dis-poo-**to**-vahćh] v. dispute; debate; hold a disputation (on) (*repeatedly*)
dystans [**dis**-tahns] m. distance
dystansować [dis-tahn-**so**-vahćh] v. outdistance; outstrip; outrace (*repeatedly*)
dystansować się [dis-tahn-**so**-vahćh śhan] v. keep one's distance; treat with cool reserve (*repeatedly*)
dystansowanie [dis-tahn-so-**vah**-ńe] n. outdistancing; outstripping; outracing
dystansowy [dis-tahn-**so**-vi] adj.m. distance (runner, etc.)
dysteleolgia [dis-te-le-o-**lo**-gyah] f. theory of chaotic development of the universe
dysten [**dis**-ten] m. cyanite mineral; kyanite mineral
dystorsja [dis-**tor**-syah] f. optical distortion
dystrakcja [dis-**trahk**-tsyah] f. distraction; amusement; the act of distracting
dystrofia [dis-**tro**-fyah] f. dystrophy; imperfect nutrition
dystroficzny [dis-tro-**feech**-ni] adj.m. dystrophic
dystrofizm [dis-**tro**-feezm] m. lack of nutrition in an aquarium
dystrybucja [dis-tri-**boo**-tsyah] f. distribution
dystrybucjonizm [dis-tri-boo-**tsyo**-ńeezm] m. distributive method of describing a language
dystrybucyjny [dis-tri-boo-**tsiy**-ni] adj.m. distributive; of distribution

dystrybuować [dis-tri-boo-**o**-vahćh] v. distribute; apportion; scatter; deliver (*repeatedly*)
dystrybutor [dis-tri-**boo**-tor] m. distributor; (gasoline) storage tank; (gasoline) pump (at a service station)
dystrybutywny [dis-tri-boo-**tiv**-ni] adj.m. distributive (function, etc.)
dystrykt [**dis**-trikt] m. district
dystych [**dis**-tikh] m. distich; couplet
dystylacja [dis-ti-**lah**-tsyah] f. colloq: distillation; see: **destylacja**
dystylarnia [dis-ti-**lahr**-ńah] f. colloq: distillery; stillroom
dystylować [dis-ti-**lo**-vahćh] v. colloq: distill (*repeatedly*)
dystylować się [dis-ti-**lo**-vahćh śhan] v. be distilled (*repeatedly*)
dystyngowanie [dis-tin-go-**vah**-ńe] adv. with distinction; with refinement; in a dignified manner
dystyngowany [dis-tin-go-**vah**-ni] adj.m. distinguished; refined; dignified
dystynkcja [di-**stink**-tsyah] f. distinction; refinement; dignity; distinguished manners **dystynkcje** [di-**stink**-tsye] pl. insignia of rank
dystynkcyjny [di-stink-**tsiy**-ni] adj.m. of insignia of rank
dystynktywny [di-stink-**tiv**-ni] adj.m. distinctive
dysydencki [di-si-**den**-tskee] adj.m. dissenting; dissenters'
dysydent [di-**si**-dent] m. dissident; dissenter; nonconformist
dysymilacja [di-si-mee-**lah**-tsyah] f. dissimilation
dysymilacyjny [di-si-mee-lah-**tsiy**-ni] adj.m. dissimilative; dissimilatory
dysza [**di**-shah] f. nozzle; blast pipe; snout; twyer; adjutage
dyszeć [**di**-shećh] v. gasp; pant; breathe hard; pant for breath; puff; puff and blow; chug; breathe forth; betoken (peace, springtime, etc.) (*repeatedly*)
dyszek [**di**-shek] m. leg (of mutton, of veal)
dyszel [**di**-shel] m. thill; shaft; pole
dyszenie [di-**she**-ńe] n. panting; puffing; gasping; chugging
dyszkancista [dish-kahn-**ćhees**-tah] m. treble singer; soprano singer
dyszkant [**dish**-kahnt] m. treble; soprano; fluty voice
dyszkantowy [dish-kahn-**to**-vi] adj.m. of treble pitch
dyszlowy [dish-**lo**-vi] adj.m. thill (horse); m. thill-horse; thiller; pole horse; shaft-horse
dyszolot [di-**sho**-lot] m. variety of aerodyne
dyszowy [di-**sho**-vi] adj.m. of a nozzle; nozzle (structure, etc.)
dytrochej [di-**tro**-khey] m. four-syllable verse
dytyramb [di-**ti**-rahmp] m. dithyramb
dytyrambiczny [di-ti-rahm-**beech**-ni] adj.m. dithyrambic
dywagacja [di-vah-**gah**-tsyah] f. swerving from a subject; irrelevant talk
dywagować [di-vah-**go**-vahćh] v. swerve from a subject; talk irrelevantly (*repeatedly*)
dywan [**di**-vahn] m. carpet; rug; tapestry; (Turkish) divan; slang: criminal investigation; director's office; oral exam (mob jargon)
dywaniarka [di-vah-**ńahr**-kah] f. woman carpet maker
dywaniarz [di-**vah**-ńahsh] m. carpet maker
dywanik [di-**vah**-ńeek] m. small rug
dywanowy [di-vah-**no**-vi] adj.m. of a carpet; for carpets **nalot dywanowy** [**nah**-lot di-vah-**no**-vi] exp.: carpet bombing
dywergencja [di-ver-**gen**-tsyah] f. divergence
dywersant [di-**ver**-sahnt] m. guerilla fighter; partisan; saboteur
dywersja [di-**ver**-syah] f. diversion; sabotage; acts of sabotage
dywersyjny [di-ver-**siy**-ni] adj.m. diversion (program, etc.); sabotage
dywetyna [di-ve-**ti**-nah] f. duvetyn; doeskin; chamois-leather imitation
dywidenda [di-vee-**den**-dah] f. dividend; bonus
dywidendowy [di-vee-den-**do**-vi] adj.m. dividend (payment, etc.); bonus (distribution, etc.)
dywiz [**di**-vees] m. dash (mark)

dywizja [di-**vee**-zyah] f. division
dywizjon [di-**vee**-zyon] m. unit; wing; command
dywizjoner [di-vee-**zyo**-ner] m. division commander; general
dywizjonista [di-vee-zyo-**ńee**-stah] m. divisionist
dywizjonistyczny [di-vee-zyo-ńees-**tich**-ni] adj.m. divisionist
dywizjonizm [di-vee-**zyo**-ńeezm] m. divisionism; pointillism
dywizjonowy [di-vee-zyo-**no**-vi] adj.m. of a unit; of a wing; command (quarters, etc.)
dywizorek [di-vee-**zo**-rek] m. copy holder
dywizyjny [di-vee-**ziy**-ni] adj.m. divisional
dyzartria [diz-**ahr**-tryah] f. disarticulation
dyzartryczny [diz-ahr-**trich**-ni] adj.m. disarticulate (speech, etc.)
dyzażio [di-**zah**-zhyo] n. drop of nominal (book) value
dyzenteria [di-zen-**te**-ryah] f. dysentery
dyzgust [**diz**-goost] m. disgust; aversion; displeasure; insult
dyzunicki [di-zoo-**ńee**-tskee] adj.m. of Russian Orthodox who refused to join the Union of Brest of 1596
dyzunita [di-zoo-**ńee**-tah] m. Russian Orthodox who refused to join the Union of Brest of 1596
dyżur [**di**-zhoor] m. duty; turn of duty; orderly duty
mieć dyżur [myećh **di**-zhoor] exp.: to be on duty; to be on call
nie być na dyżurze [ńe bićh nah di-**zhoo**-zhe] exp.: to be off duty; to be off call
dyżurka [di-**zhoor**-kah] f. duty-room; orderly-room; dispatcher's office
dyżurny [di-**zhoor**-ni] adj.m. on call; on duty; m. orderly; person on duty; dispatcher
dyżurować [di-zhoo-**ro**-vahćh] v. be on call; be on duty (*repeatedly*)
dyżurowanie [di-zhoo-ro-**vah**-ńe] n. being on call
dzban [dzbahn] m. jug; pitcher; ewer
dzbanecznik [dzbah-**nech**-ńeek] m. pitcher plant; nepenthe
dzbanecznikowaty [dzbah-nech-ńee-ko-**vah**-ti] adj.m. nepenthean
dzbanecznikowate [dzbah-nech-ńee-ko-**vah**-te] pl. the pitcher plant family
dzbanek [**dzbah**-nek] m. (little) jug
dzbanuszek [dzbah-**noo**-shek] m. very small jug; nice little jug
dzeolit [dze-**o**-leet] m. variety of silicate mineral
dziabać [**dźhah**-bahćh] v. jab; hit; strike with a sharp tool (*repeatedly*)
dziabać się [**dźhah**-bahćh śh<u>an</u>] v. cut oneself with a sharp tool (*repeatedly*)
dziabanie [dźhah-**bah**-ńe] n. jabbing; hitting; striking with a sharp tool (*repeated*)
dziabanie się [dźhah-**bah**-ńe śh<u>an</u>] n. jabbing one another; hitting oneself
dziabnąć [**dźhah**-bn<u>own</u>ćh] v. jab; hit; strike with a sharp tool
dziabnąć się [**dźhah**-bn<u>own</u>ćh śh<u>an</u>] v. cut oneself with a sharp tool
dziabnięcie [dźhah-**bń<u>an</u>**-ćhe] n. jabbing; hitting; striking with a sharp tool
dziabnięcie się [dźhah-**bń<u>an</u>**-ćhe śh<u>an</u>] n. jabbing one another; hitting oneself; striking oneself with a sharp tool
dziać [dźhahćh] v. knit (*repeatedly*)
dziać się [dźhahćh śh<u>an</u>] v. occur; happen; take place; go on; be going on (*repeatedly*)
co się tu dzieje? [tso śh<u>an</u> too **dźhe**-ye] exp.: what's going on?; what's up here?
co się z nim dzieje? [tso śh<u>an</u> z ńeem **dźhe**-ye] exp.: what's happening to him?
niech się dzieje, co chce [ńekh śh<u>an</u> **dźhe**-ye tso khtse] exp.: happen what may; come what may; sink or swim!
źle się dzieje [źhle śh<u>an</u> **dźhe**-ye] exp.: it's a bad situation; affairs are in a bad way
dziad [dźhaht] m. old man; beggar; bungler; duffer; lout

zejść na dziady [zeyśhćh nah dźhah-di] exp.: to go to the dogs; to be reduced to beggary
dziadek [**dźhah**-dek] m. grandfather
dziadek do orzechów [**dźhah**-dek do o-**zhe**-khoof] exp.: nutcracker
dziadkowy [dźhah-**tko**-vi] adj.m. of grandfather; grandfather's
dziadostwo [dźhah-**do**-stfo] n. extreme poverty; beggary; the poor; the needy; paupers; trash
dziadować [dźhah-**do**-vahćh] v. live a beggar's life; live from hand to mouth (*repeatedly*)
dziadowanie [dźhah-do-**vah**-ńe] n. poverty; beggary
dziadowina [dźhah-do-**vee**-nah] m. poor old guy; poor beggar
dziadowizna [dźhah-do-**vee**-znah] f. inheritance from grandfather
dziadowski [dźhah-**dof**-skee] adj.m. beggarly; rotten; beggar's
po dziadowsku [po dźhah-**dof**-skoo] exp.: like a beggar
dziadówka [dźhah-**doof**-kah] f. beggar woman
dziadunio [dźhah-**doo**-ńo] m. (dear) grandpa; granddad
dziadyga [dźhah-**di**-gah] m. old geezer; an eccentric old man
dziadzia [**dźhah**-dźhah] m. grandpa
dziadzieć [**dźhah**-dźhećh] v. age badly; grow old; bend under the weight of years (*repeatedly*)
dziadzienie [dźhah-**dźhe**-ńe] n. aging badly; growing old
dziadzina [dźhah-**dźhee**-ńah] m. poor old man; beggar
dziadzio [**dźhah**-dźho] m. grandpa
dziadzisko [dźhah-**dźhee**-sko] n. & m. nasty old man; nasty beggar
dziadziuś [**dźhah**-dźhoośh] m. dear grandpa
dział [dźhahw] m. section; division; part; sphere; head; heading; department; (newspaper) column; shop; divide
dział wód [dźhahw voot] exp.: watershed; divide
działacz [**dźhah**-wahch] m. activist (in politics, religion, etc.)
działaczka [dźhah-**wahch**-kah] f. (woman) activist (in politics, religion, etc.)
działać [**dźhah**-wahćh] v. act; work; be active; be effective; operate; produce; have an effect (on); influence; affect; jar (nerves); be operative; be efficacious; be in working order; function; run; behave; be in force (of law); do (wanders, etc.) (*repeatedly*)
działać cuda [**dźhah**-wahćh **tsoo**-dah] exp.: to work miracles; to do wonders
działać komuś na nerwy [**dźhah**-wahćh **ko**-moośh nah **ner**-vi] exp.: to get on somebody's nerves
zacząć działać [zah-ch<u>own</u>ćh **dźhah**-wahćh] exp.: to come into operation
działalność [dźhah-**wahl**-nośhćh] f. activity; action
działanie [dźhah-**wah**-ńe] n. activity; effect; impact; stress; influence; grip; poignancy; treatment; action; agency; efficacy; efficacity; effectiveness; work; operation; arithmetical rule
działka [**dźhahw**-kah] f. parcel; plot; degree (on a graduated scale); mob slang: dose of a narcotic
działko [**dźhahw**-ko] n. light artillery piece; light field gun
działkowicz [dźhahw-**ko**-veech] m. colloq: holder of an allotment (garden, plot, etc.)
działkowiec [dźhahw-**ko**-vyets] m. colloq: holder of an allotment (garden, plot, etc.)
działkowy [dźhahw-**ko**-vi] adj.m. allotment (garden, plot, etc.)
działo [**dźhah**-wo] n. cannon; gun
działobitnia [dźhah-wo-**beet**-ńah] f. fortified heavy gun position
działon [**dźhah**-won] m. cannon crew
działonowy [dźhah-wo-**no**-vi] m. noncommissioned officer in charge of a cannon crew
działownia [dźhah-**wov**-ńah] f. gun emplacement
działowy [dźhah-**wo**-vi] adj.m. of a cannon; of a branch; sectional; dividing (wall, etc.)
działówka [dźhah-**woof**-kah] f.

partition wall
dziamdzia [dźhahm-dźhah] m. & f. slang: sluggard; slowcoach; slouch; slacker
dziamdziać [dźhahm-dźhahćh] v. slang: mumble (*repeatedly*)
dzianet [dźhah-net] m. janet; spanish parade horse
dzianie [dźhah-ńe] n. knitting
dzianie się [dźhah-ńe śhan] n. taking place; happening
dzianina [dźhah-ńee-nah] f. knit goods; hosiery
dzianinowy [dźhah-ńee-no-vi] adj.m. knit (goods, etc.); hosiery (material, etc.)
dziany [dźhah-ni] adj.m. knitted; slang: rich (man)
wyroby dziane [vi-ro-bi dźhah-ne] exp.: knitted goods
dziarnina [dźhahr-ńee-nah] f. crystallized honey
dziarski [dźhahr-skee] adj.m. brisk; lively; sprightly; perky; swinging; rakish
dziarsko [dźhahr-sko] adv. briskly; lively; sprightly; in a perky manner; swingingly; rakishly; with dash
dziarskość [dźhahr-skośhćh] f. briskness; liveliness; sprightliness; perkiness; rakishness; dash
dziatki [dźhah-tkee] pl. children
dziatwa [dźhah-tfah] f. children; young folks
dziąsło [dźhown-swo] n. gum
dziąsłowość [dźhown-swo-vośhćh] f. alveolar feature
dziąsłowy [dźhown-swo-vi] adj.m. gingival; of the gums; alveolar (consonant, etc.)
dzicz [dźheech] f. savages; barbarians; wilderness
dziczeć [dźhee-chećh] v. become savage; grow wild; fall into savagery; run wild; become recluse; seclude oneself; become unsociable (*repeatedly*)
dziczenie [dźhee-che-ńe] n. becoming wild
dziczek [dźhee-chek] m. wilding; young boar
dziczka [dźheech-kah] f. wilding; unsociable woman
dziczy [dźhee-chi] adj.m. of a wild hog; of a boar
dziczyca [dźhee-chi-tsah] f. female (Old World) wild boar (hog)
dziczyzna [dźhee-chi-znah] f. venison; game; plants growing in a wild state
dzida [dźhee-dah] f. spear; pike
dzidzi [dźhee-dźhee] n. baby
dzidzia [dźhee-dźhah] f. baby
dzidziuś [dźhee-dźhoośh] m. baby
dzidziaczek [dźhee-dźhah-chek] m. nice kid
dzidziaczyna [dźhee-dźhah-chi-nah] m. & f. poor kid; measly kid
dzidziaczysko [dźhee-dźhah-chi-sko] m. nasty kid; measly kid
dzieci [dźhe-ćhee] pl. children
dzieciaczek [dźhe-ćhah-chek] m. sweet little baby
dzieciaczyna [dźhe-ćhah-chi-nah] f. (or m.) colloq: poor little kid
dzieciaczysko [dźhe-ćhah-chis-ko] n. colloq: nasty little kid
dzieciak [dźhe-ćhahk] m. kid; kiddy; whippersnapper; youth
dzieciarnia [dźhe-ćhahr-ńah] f. children; small fry
dzieciaty [dźhe-ćhah-ti] adj.m. (man) with children
dzieciątko [dźhe-ćhown-tko] n. little baby darling
dziecię [dźhe-ćhan] n. (small) child
dziecięco [dźhe-ćhan-tso] adv. childishly
dziecięcość [dźhe-ćhan-tsośhćh] f. childlike quality
dziecięctwo [dźhe-ćhan-tstfo] n. childhood
dziecięcy [dźhe-ćhan-tsi] adj.m. child's; children's
paraliż dziecięcy [pah-rah-leesh dźhe-ćhan-tsi] exp.: infantile paralysis; poliomyelitis; polio
dziecina [dźhe-ćhee-nah] f. baby
dziecino! [dźhe-ćhee-no] excl.: darling!; honey!
dziecinada [dźhe-ćhee-nah-dah] f. childishness; puerility
dzieciniec [dźhe-ćhee-ńets] m. kindergarten
dziecinka [dźhe-ćhee-nkah] f. baby
dziecinnie [dźhe-ćheen-ńe] adv. childishly; like a baby

dziecinnieć [dźhe-**ćheen**-ńećh] v. become childish (*repeatedly*)
dziecinność [dźhe-**ćheen**-nośhćh] f. childishness; childish behavior
dziecinny [dźhe-**ćheen**-ni] adj.m. childish; infantile; babyish; unmanly; puerile
po dziecinnemu [po dźhe-ćheen-ne-moo] exp.: like a child; childishly
dzieciństwo [dźhe-**ćheeń**-stfo] n. childhood; boyhood; infancy; babyhood
dzieciobójca [dźhe-ćho-**booy**-tsah] m. infanticide; child-murderer
dzieciobójczy [dźhe-ćho-**booy**-chi] adj.m. infanticidal
dzieciobójczyni [dźhe-ćho-booy-**chi**-ńee] f. (woman) infanticide; child-murderess
dzieciobójstwo [dźhe-ćho-**booy**-stfo] n. infanticide; child-murder
dzieciorób [dźhe-**ćho**-roop] m. slang: man who fathered too many children
dzieciska [dźhe-**ćhee**-skah] pl. the kids; the brats; the little ones
dzieciuch [**dźhe**-ćhookh] m. child; brat; kid; big baby
dziecko [**dźhe**-tsko] n. child; baby; trot; brat; youngster; kid; excl.: dear!; my dear!
dziedzic [**dźhe**-dźheets] m. heir; inheritor; successor; squire; country gentleman; lord of the manor
dziedzicowy [dźhe-dźhee-**tso**-vi] adj.m. squire's
dziedzictwo [dźhe-**dźhee**-tstfo] n. inheritance; heritage; legacy; heirloom; devotion; succession (to the throne, etc.)
dziedziczenie [dźhe-dźhee-**che**-ńe] n. inheriting
dziedziczka [dźhe-**dźhee**-chkah] f. heiress; lady of the manor
dziedzicznie [dźhe-**dźhee**-chńe] adv. hereditarily; by inheritance; by right of succession
dziedziczność [dźhe-**dźhee**-chnośhćh] f. heredity; succession (to the throne, etc.)
dziedziczny [dźhe-**dźhee**-chni] adj.m. hereditary; ancestral; inherited; patrimonial
obciążenie dziedziczne [op-ćhown-**zhe**-ńe dźhe-**dźhee**-chne] exp.: inherited taint
dziedziczyć [dźhe-**dźhee**-chićh] v. inherit (property, features); come into (money) (*repeatedly*)
dziedziczyć się [dźhe-**dźhee**-chićh śhan] v. be hereditary; be hereditable; be inherited (*repeatedly*)
dziedzina [dźhe-**dźhee**-nah] f. realm; area; sphere; domain; scope; range; province; branch; region; arena
dziedziniec [dźhe-**dźhee**-ńets] m. yard; court; courtyard
dziegciować [dźhe-**kćho**-vahćh] v. tar; smear with wood tar (*repeatedly*)
dziegciowy [dźhe-**kćho**-vi] adj.m. of wood tar; wood tar (soap, ointment, etc.)
dziegieć [**dźhe**-gećh] m. birch tar
dzieje [**dźhe**-ye] pl. history
stare dzieje [**stah**-re **dźhe**-ye] exp.: ancient history; rehash; past; past course of events
dziejopis [dźhe-**yo**-pees] m. historiographer
dziejopisarstwo [dźhe-yo-pee-**sahr**-stfo] n. historiography
dziejopisarz [dźhe-yo-**pee**-sahsh] m. historian
dziejotwórczy [dźhe-yo-**tfoor**-chi] adj.m. history-making (events, etc.)
dziejowy [dźhe-**yo**-vi] adj.m. historical; historic
dzieju [**dźhe**-yoo] (only in) exp.: **Panie dzieju!** [**pah**-ńe **dźhe**-yoo] excl.: my good Sir!
dziekan [**dźhe**-kahn] m. dean
dziekanat [dźhe-**kah**-naht] m. dean's office; deanery
dziekanowa [dźhe-kah-**no**-vah] f. dean's wife
dziekański [dźhe-**kahń**-skee] adj.m. dean's; decanal
dziekaństwo [dźhe-**kahń**-stfo] n. deanship
dzielarka [dźhe-**lahr**-kah] f. baker's dough-cutting machine
dzielenie [dźhe-**le**-ńe] n. division

znak dzielenia [znahk dźhe-le-ńah] exp.: division sign
dzielenie się [dźhe-le-ńe śhan] n. division; split; breakup; sharing (with); exchange (of views, etc.); participation (in); divisibility
dzielić [**dźhe**-leećh] v. divide; share; split; distribute; partition; break up; divide up; portion out; share out; separate; apportion; participate (in sorrow, etc.) (*repeatedly*)
dzielić skórę na niedźwiedziu [**dźhe**-leećh **skoo**-ran nah ńe-**dźhvye**-dźhoo] exp.: to make unreasonably optimistic assumptions and plans
dzielić przez [**dźhe**-leećh pshes] exp.: to divide by
dzielić się [**dźhe**-leećh śhan] v. be divided; split up; break up (into); consist (of); be composed (of parts, etc.); share (with); go shares (in something with somebody); separate oneself (from); be divisible (by) (*repeatedly*)
dzielna [**dźhel**-nah] f. dividend
dzielnica [dźhel-**ńee**-tsah] f. province; quarter; section; district; region
dzielnicowość [dźhel-ńee-**tso**-vośhćh] f. regional patriotism
dzielnicowy [dźhel-ńee-**tso**-vi] adj.m. provincial; sectional; regional; m. district constable
dzielnie [**dźhel**-ńe] adv. bravely; resourcefully; competently; efficiently; valiantly; gallantly; courageously; stalwartly
dzielnie się spisać [**dźhel**-ńe śhan **spee**-sahćh] exp.: to do very well
dzielnik [**dźhel**-ńeek] m. math.: divisor; divider; print: hyphen
dzielność [**dźhel**-nośhćh] f. resourcefulness; ingenuity; proficiency; competence; efficiency; courage; gallantry; prowess; stalwartness; pluck; bravery
dzielny [**dźhel**-ni] adj.m. brave; ingenious; proficient; resourceful; valiant; courageous; efficient; gallant; stalwart; plucky
dzielny opór [**dźhel**-ni **o**-poor] exp.: a stout resistance
dziełko [**dźhew**-ko] n. minor achievement; minor composition; opuscule
dzieło [**dźhe**-wo] n. achievement; work; composition; cause; result; outcome; doing
dziełowy [dźhe-**wo**-vi] adj.m. of printed volume
dziennica [dźhen-**ńee**-tsah] f. Hemerocallis herb; day lily
dzienniczek [dźhen-**ńee**-chek] m. (child's) diary; parent-teacher correspondence notebook
dziennie [**dźhen**-ńe] adv. daily; a day; by the day
dwa razy dziennie [dvah rah-zi **dźhen**-ńe] exp.: twice a day
dziennik [**dźhen**-ńeek] m. daily news; daily; journal; diary
dziennik lekcyjny [**dźhen**-ńeek lek-**tsiy**-ni] exp.: classbook
dziennikarka [dźhen-ńee-**kahr**-kah] f. (woman) journalist; (press) reporter; slang: journalism; school of journalism
dziennikarski [dźhen-ńee-**kahr**-skee] adj.m. journalistic
dziennikarstwo [dźhen-ńee-**kahr**-stfo] n. journalism
dziennikarz [dźhen-**ńee**-kahsh] m. reporter; journalist
dziennikarzyna [dźhen-ńee-kah-**zhi**-nah] m. miserable reporter; measly journalist
dziennikowy [dźhen-ńee-**ko**-vi] adj.m. of a journal
dzienny [**dźhen**-ni] adj.m. daily; diurnal; day's (pay, work, etc.)
światło dzienne [**śhfyah**-two **dźhen**-ne] exp.: daylight
dzień [dźheń] m. day; daylight; daytime; a day and night; 24 hours; date; pl.: **dni** [dńee] pl. festival; lifetime
co dzień [tso dźheń] exp.: every day; daily; day in and day out; commonly
cały dzień [**tsah**-wi dźheń] exp.: the whole day long
co drugi dzień [tso **droo**-gee dźheń] exp.: every other day

do dnia [do dńah] exp.: very early; at daybreak
dzień dobry [dźheń do-bri] exp.: good day; good morning; good afternoon; hi!; hi everybody!; hello!; hello everybody!
dzień po dniu [dźheń po dńoo] exp.: day by day
dzień powszedni [dźheń po-fshe-dńee] exp.: workday
któregoś dnia [ktoo-re-gośh dńah] exp.: some day; the other day; some day or other; one of these days
lada dzień [lah-dah dźheń] exp.: any day
nade dniem [nah-de dńem] exp.: before daybreak
na drugi dzień [nah droo-gee dźheń] exp.: on the next day
po dziś dzień [po dźheeśh dźheń] exp.: till this very day
raz na dzień [rahs nah dźheń] exp.: once a day
za dnia [zah dńah] exp.: by day; in the day time; during daylight
z dnia na dzień [z dńah nah dźheń] exp.: from day to day
dzieńdoberek [dźheń-do-be-rek] m. (exp.:) colloq: the top of the morning to you
dziergaczka [dźher-gah-chkah] f. ripple; iron comb for production of linen
dziergać [dźher-gahćh] v. embroider; crochet; make a border; make an edge (*repeatedly*)
dzierganie [dźher-gah-ńe] n. embroidery
dziergarka [dźher-gahr-kah] f. sewing machine for protecting the edges of fabrics
dzierlatka [dźher-lah-tkah] f. crested lark; lassie; lass; filly
dzierlica [dźher-lee-tsah] f. ripple; hackle
dzieżba [dźhezh-bah] f. shrike; woodchat
dzierżak [dźher-zhahk] m. the longer part of a flail; flail handle
dzierżawa [dźher-zhah-vah] f. lease; rental; tenancy; rent; holding; leasehold
dzierżawca [dźher-zhahf-tsah] m. tenant; leaseholder; lessee; occupant
dzierżawczość [dźher-zhahf-chośhćh] f. possessive function of pronouns (in grammar)
dzierżawczy [dźher-zhahf-chi] adj.m. possessive (case in grammar)
dzierżawczyni [dźher-zhahf-chi-ńee] f. woman leaseholder
dzierżawić [dźher-zhah-veećh] v. rent; hire; hold on lease; take on lease; hold as a lease (*repeatedly*)
dzierżawienie [dźher-zhah-vye-ńe] n. leasing (of property)
dzierżawny [dźher-zhah-vni] adj.m. lease (payment, rent, etc.)
dzierżenie [dźher-zhe-ńe] n. holding; wielding
dzierżyć [dźher-zhićh] v. wield (power); hold tight; grip (*repeatedly*)
dzierżymorda [dźher-zhi-mor-dah] m. vulg.: tyrant; oppressor
dziesiątak [dźhe-śhown-tahk] m. ten point buck (stag)
dziesiątek [dźhe-śhown-tek] m. num. ten; group of ten; series of ten; ten antlered stag (buck)
dziesiątki [dźhe-śhown-tkee] pl. scores; dozens
dziesiąta [dźhe-śhown-tah] adj.f. num. tenth; 10th (girl); f. ten (o'clock); tenth part
dziesiąta muza [dźhe-śhown-tah moo-zah] exp.: the tenth muse; film-making; cinematography
dziesiątka [dźhe-śhown-tkah] f. ten; (team of) ten; 10
dziesiątkować [dźhe-śhown-tko-vahćh] v. decimate (*repeatedly*)
dziesiątkowanie [dźhe-śhown-tko-vah-ńe] n. decimation
dziesiątkowy [dźhe-śhown-tko-vi] adj.m. decimal
dziesiąty [dźhe-śhown-ti] num. tenth; 10th
dziesięcina [dźhe-śhan-ćhee-nah] f. tithes; a Russian unit of 1.1 hectares or nearly 3 acres
dziesięcioboista [dźhe-śhan-ćho-bo-ee-stah] m. contestant in a decathlon; contestant in ten track-and-field events

dziesięciobok [dźhe-śhan-**ćho**-bok] m. decagon
dziesięciobój [dźhe-śhan-**ćho**-booy] m. decathlon; athletic contest of ten track-and-field events
dziesięciodniowy [dźhe-śhan-ćho-**dńo**-vi] adj.m. ten-day (period, etc.); ten-days' (work, etc.); lasting ten days
dziesięciodolarówka [dźhe-śhan-ćho-do-lah-**roof**-kah] f. ten dollar bill
dziesięciogodzinny [dźhe-śhan-ćho-go-**dźheen**-ni] adj.m. ten-hour (period, etc.); ten-hours' (work, etc.); lasting ten hours
dziesięciogroszowy [dźhe-śhan-ćho-gro-**sho**-vi] adj.m. of ten groszy value
dziesięciogroszówka [dźhe-śhan-ćho-gro-**shoof**-kah] f. ten groszy coin
dziesięcioklasowy [dźhe-śhan-ćho-klah-**so**-vi] adj.m. ten-grade (school, etc.)
dziesięciokrotnie [dźhe-śhan-ćho-**krot**-ńe] adv. ten times; tenfold
dziesięciokrotny [dźhe-śhan-ćho-**krot**-ni] adj.m. tenfold
dziesięciolatek [dźhe-śhan-ćho-**lah**-tek] m. boy of ten; ten-year-old (animal, plant, etc.)
dziesięciolatka [dźhe-śhan-ćho-**lah**-tkah] f. girl of ten; ten-year-old (female animal, plant, etc.)
dziesięciolecie [dźhe-śhan-ćho-**le**-ćhe] n. tenth anniversary; decade; period of ten years
dziesięcioletni [dźhe-śhan-ćho-**let**-ńee] adj.m. of ten years; ten-year (plan, etc.); ten-years' (stay, etc.); ten years old; lasting ten years; of ten years' duration
dziesięciolistny [dźhe-śhan-ćho-**leest**-ni] adj.m. decaphyllous
dziesięciomiesięczny [dźhe-śhan-ćho-mye-**śhanch**-ni] adj.m. ten-month (period); ten-months' (work, etc.); ten months old; lasting ten months
dziesięciominutowy [dźhe-śhan-ćho-mee-noo-**to**-vi] adj.m. of ten minutes; ten-minute (pause, etc.); ten-minutes' (wait, etc.); lasting ten minutes; of ten minutes' duration
dziesięcionogi [dźhe-śhan-ćho-**no**-gee] adj.m. decapodal
dziesięcionóg [dźhe-śhan-**ćho**-noog] m. decapod
dziesięciopiętrowy [dźhe-śhan-ćho-pyan-**tro**-vi] adj.m. of eleven stories; eleven-story (building, apartment house, etc.);
dziesięcioraki [dźhe-śhan-ćho-**rah**-kee] adj.m. of ten different kinds; of ten different varieties; of ten sorts
dziesięciornica [dźhe-śhan-ćhor-**ńee**-tsah] f. decapod (shrimp, lobster, crab, etc.); decapodan
dziesięciornice [dźhe-śhan-ćhor-**ńee**-tse] pl. Decapoda order of crustaceans
dziesięciorniczy [dźhe-śhan-ćhor-**ńee**-chi] adj.m. decapodal; decapodous; decapodan
dziesięcioro [dźhe-śhan-**ćho**-ro] num. ten (persons of both sexes, children, kids. commandments, doors, piglets, etc.)
w dziesięcioro [v dźhe-śhan-**ćho**-ro] exp.: tenfold
dziesięciorublówka [dźhe-śhan-ćho-roob-**loof**-kah] f. ten-ruble bill (note, coin)
dziesięciościan [dźhe-śhan-**ćho**-śhćhahn] m. decahedron
dziesięciotysięcznik [dźhe-śhan-ćho-ti-**śhanch**-ńeek] m. ship of ten thousand tons displacement
dziesięciotysięczny [dźhe-śhan-ćho-ti-**śhanch**-ni] adj.m. ten-thousands
dziesięciowiosłówka [dźhe-śhan-ćho-vyo-**swoof**-kah] f. ten-oar boat
dziesięciozgłoskowiec [dźhe-śhan-ćho-zgwos-**ko**-vyets] m. decasyllable
dziesięciozgłoskowy [dźhe-śhan-ćho-zgwo-**sko**-vi] adj.m. of ten-syllable; decasyllabic
dziesięciozłotowy [dźhe-śhan-ćho-zwo-**to**-vi] adj.m. of ten-zloty
dziesięciozłotówka [dźhe-śhan-ćho-zwo-**toof**-kah] f. ten-zloty bill; ten-zloty coin

dziesięciu [dźhe-**śh**an-ćhoo] num. ten (men); 10
dziesięć [**dźhe**-śhanćh] num. ten; 10
dziesięćkroć [dźhe-**śh**an**ćh**-kroćh] num. ten times; tenfold
dziesiętnik [dźhe-**śh**an-tńeek] m. chief of a group of ten (workers, soldiers, etc.)
dziesiętny [dźhe-**śh**an-tni] adj.m. decimal (system, etc.); denary
dzietność [**dźhet**-nośhćh] f. reproductivity of women (marriages, etc.)
dzietny [**dźhet**-ni] adj.m. having children; childish; infantile
dziewanna [dźhe-**vahn**-nah] f. mullein (plant)
dziewczątko [dźhef-**ch**own-tko] n. little girl; lassie
dziewczę [**dźhef**-chan] n. girl; maiden; young woman; slang: chick; babe; fox; looker
dziewczęta [dźhef-**ch**an-tah] pl. girls; young women
dziewczęco [dźhef-**ch**an-tso] adv. like a little girl; girlishly
dziewczęcość [dźhef-**ch**an-tsośhćh] f. girlishness
dziewczęcy [dźhef-**ch**an-tsi] adj.m. girl's; girlish; maidenly
dziewczyna [dźhef-**chi**-nah] f. girl; lass; wench; maid; slang: chick
dziewczynina [dźhef-chi-**ńee**-nah] f. (pale) girl; flapper
dziewczynisko [dźhef-chi-**ńees**-ko] n. (big, old) girl
dziewczynka [dźhef-**chin**-kah] f. (little) girl; flapper
dziewczyński [dźhef-**chiń**-skee] adj.m. girl's; girl-like
dzieweczka [dźhe-**vech**-kah] f. girl; lass; wench; maid; slang: chick
dziewiarka [dźhe-**vyahr**-kah] f. knitter; knitting-frame; knitting-machine; knitting-loom
dziewiarnia [dźhe-**vyahr**-ńah] f. knitting factory
dziewiarski [dźhe-**vyahr**-skee] adj.m. knitting (industry, etc.); hosiery (sales, etc.)
dziewiarstwo [dźhe-**vyahr**-stfo] n. knitting
dziewiarz [**dźhe**-vyahsh] m. knitter
dziewiąta [dźhe-**vy**own-tah] f. nine o'clock; the ninth (girl, etc.)
dziewiątka [dźhe-**vyownt**-kah] f. 9; nine; figure nine; group of nine
dziewiąty [dźhe-**vyown**-ti] num. ninth; 9th; the ninth (boy, etc.)
dziewica [dźhe-**vee**-tsah] f. virgin; maiden; vestal virgin (consecrated to the service of the Roman goddess Vesta)
dziewictwo [dźhe-**vee**-tstfo] n. virginity; maidenhood
dziewiczo [dźhe-**vee**-cho] adv. maidenly; maidenlike
dziewiczość [dźhe-**vee**-chośhćh] f. virginity; chastity; purity; innocence
dziewiczy [dźhe-**vee**-chi] adj.m. virginal; maidenly; virgin; chaste; pure; intact; innocent; primeval; trackless; unbroken (soil, etc.)
dziewicza gleba [dźhe-**vee**-chah **gle**-bah] exp.: virgin soil
las dziewiczy [lahs dźhe-**vee**-chi] exp.: virgin forest; primeval forest
dziewięciokrotnie [dźhe-vyan-ćho-**krot**-ńe] adv. nine times; ninefold
dziewięciokrotny [dźhe-vyan-ćho-**krot**-ni] adj.m. nine-time; ninefold
dziewięciolecie [dźhe-vyan-ćho-**le**-ćhe] n. period of nine years; ninth anniversary
dziewięcioletni [dźhe-vyan-ćho-**let**-ńee] adj.m. of nine years; nine-year (period, etc.); nine years old; nine-year-old
dziewięciomiesięczny [dźhe-vyan-ćho-mye-**śh**an**ch**-ni] adj.m. of nine months; nine-months (period, etc.); nine months old; nine-month-old
dziewięciornik [dźhe-vyan-**ćhor**-ńeek] m. grass of Parnassus
dziewięcioro [dźhe-vyan-**ćho**-ro] num. nine (persons of both sexes, children, kittens, small animals, chickens, etc.)
dziewięciozgłoskowiec [dźhe-vyan-ćho-zgwo-**sko**-vyets] m. line of nine syllables; word of nine syllables
dziewięciozgłoskowy [dźhe-vyan-ćho-zgwo-**sko**-vi] adj.m. of nine syllables

dziewięciu [dźhe-**vy**an-ćhoo] num. nine (men); 9
dziewięciuset [dźhe-vyan-**ćhoo**-set] num. nine hundred (men); 900
dziewięć [**dźhe**-vyanćh] num. nine; 9
dziewięćdziesiąt [dźhe-vyanćh-**dźhe**-śhownt] num. ninety; 90
dziewięćdziesiątka [dźhe-vyanćh-dźhe-**śhown**-tkah] f. ninety; number 90; group of ninety; ninety years of age
dziewięćdziesiąty [dźhe-vyanćh-dźhe-**śhown**-ti] num. ninetieth
dziewięćdziesięciu [dźhe-vyanćh-dźhe-**śhan**-ćhoo] num. ninety (men); 90
dziewięćdziesięcioletni [dźhe-vyanćh-dźhe-śhan-ćho-**let**-ńee] adj.m. ninety years old
dziewięćset [dźhe-**vyanćh**-set] num. nine hundred; 900
dziewięćsetny [dźhe-vyanćh-**set**-ni] num. nine hundredth; 900th
dziewięćsił [dźhe-**vyanćh**-śheew] m. carline (plant)
dziewiętnasta [dźhe-vyant-**nah**-stah] f. seven p.m.
dziewiętnastka [dźhe-vyant-**nah**-stkah] f. nineteen; the figure 19; group of nineteen; (object or person) number nineteen
dziewiętnastolatek [dźhe-vyant-nah-sto-**lah**-tek] m. young man of nineteen
dziewiętnastolatka [dźhe-vyant-nah-sto-**laht**-kah] f. young woman of nineteen
dziewiętnastolecie [dźhe-vyant-nah-sto-le-ćhe] n. period of nineteen years; nineteenth anniversary
dziewiętnastoletni [dźhe-vyant-nah-sto-let-ńee] adj.m. of nineteen years; nineteen-year (period, etc.); nineteen years old; nineteen-year-old
dziewiętnastowieczny [dźhe-vyant-nah-sto-**vyech**-ni] adj.m. of the nineteenth century; nineteenth-century (literature, etc.)
dziewiętnastu [dźhe-vyant-**nah**-stoo] num. nineteen (men); 19
dziewiętnasty [dźhe-vyant-**nah**-sti] num. nineteenth; 19th (day of the month, etc.)
dziewiętnaście [dźhe-vyant-**nah**-śhćhe] num. nineteen; 19
dziewiętnaścioro [dźhe-vyant-nah-**śhćho**-ro] num. nineteen (persons of both sexes, children, objects, etc.)
dziewka [**dźhef**-kah] f. maid; wench; strumpet; prostitute
dziewkarz [**dźhef**-kahsh] m. womanizer
dziewoja [dźhe-**vo**-yah] f. girl; lass; wench
dzieworodny [dźhe-vo-**rod**-ni] adj.m. parthenogenetic
dzieworództwo [dźhe-vo-**roots**-tfo] n. parthenogenesis; parthenogeny
dziewosłąb [dźhe-**vo**-swownp] m. marriage broker; matchmaker
dziewosłęb [dźhe-**vo**-swanp] m. marriage broker; match maker
dziewucha [dźhe-**voo**-khah] f. girl; wench; crude girl
dziewuszka [dźhe-**voo**-shkah] f. young girl; lassie
dziewuszysko [dźhe-voo-**shi**-sko] n. (augmentative:) girl; wench; crude girl; good old girl
dzieża [**dźhe**-zhah] f. kneading-trough; earthen pot; crock
dzieżka [**dźhesh**-kah] f. (small) kneading-trough; earthen pot; crock
dzięcielina [dźhan-ćhe-**lee**-nah] f. white clover
dzięcierzawa [dźhan-ćhe-**zhah**-vah] f. thorn apple
dzięcioł [**dźhan**-ćhow] m. woodpecker; slang: naive man, easily cheated; good student
dziędzierzawa [dźhan-dźhe-**zhah**-vah] f. thorn apple
dzięgiel [**dźhan**-gel] m. angelica
dzięgielowy [dźhan-ge-lo-vi] adj.m. angelica (flavor, etc.)
dzięgielówka [dźhan-ge-**loof**-kah] f. angelica-flavored vodka
dziękczynienie [dźhank-chi-**ńe**-ńe] n. thanksgiving
dziękczynnie [dźhank-**chin**-ńe] adv. thankfully
dziękczynność [dźhank-**chin**-nośhćh] f. thankfulness
dziękczynny [dźhank-**chin**-ni] adj.m.

thankful
list dziękczynny [leest dźhank-chin-ni] exp.: letter of thanks
dzięki [**dźhan**-kee] pl. thanks; (preposition:) thanks to; owing to
dziękować [dźhan-**ko**-vahćh] v. thank; give thanks (*repeatedly*)
nie ma za co dziękować [ńe mah zah tso dźhan-**ko**-vahćh] exp.: don't mention it; not at all; you are welcome
dziękowanie [dźhan-ko-**vah**-ńe] n. thanks
dzik [dźheek] m. boar; tusker; sucker (on a fruit tree)
dzikarz [**dźhee**-kahsh] m. dog trained for hunting wild boar
dzikawy [dźhee-**kah**-vi] adj.m. wildish
dziki [**dźhee**-kee] adj.m. wild; savage; feral; untamed; uncivilized; barbarous; fierce; ferocious; horrible; terrible; haggard; wildcat (speculation, etc.); uncouth; shy; strange (claims, etc.); odd; crazy; bizarre; frantic; unrestrained; uncultivated (vegetation, etc.); m. savage; barbarian
dziko [**dźhee**-ko] adv. wildly; in the wild state; horribly; terribly; strangely; frantically; without restraint
dzikość [**dźhee**-kośhćh] f. wildness; the wild state; savagery; fierceness; ferocity; uncouthness; shyness
dzikus [**dźhee**-koos] m. wild man; savage; barbarian; untamed horse
dzikuska [dźhee-**koo**-skah] f. wild woman; savage; barbarian; shy girl; coy girl; bashful girl
dziń [dźheeń] (interjection:) ding
dziobać [**dźho**-bahćh] v. peck; pick (corn, etc.); dab; goad; prod; jab; stab (*repeatedly*)
dziobacz [**dźho**-bahch] m. cetacean (whale, etc.)
dziobak [**dźho**-bahk] m. duckbill; platypus; steeve
dziobanie [dźho-**bah**-ńe] n. pecking; goading; stabbing
dziobaty [dźho-**bah**-ti] adj.m. pockmarked; pitted; with a pockmarked face; rostrated (bird)
dziobek [**dźho**-bek] m. spout; nozzle; beak; lip (of a vessel); little beak; little bill; (child's) face; cheeks; mouth; lips; nose; tapering extremity (of an object)
dziobnąć [**dźhob**-nownćh] v. peck; pick (corn, etc.); dab; goad; prod; jab; stab
dziobnięcie [dźhob-**ńan**-ćhe] n. peck; a peck; dab; a dab; job; a job
dziobnica [dźhob-**ńee**-tsah] f. stem; cutwater (part of ship's bow)
dzioborożec [dźho-bo-**ro**-zhets] m. hornbill
dziobowaty [dźho-bo-**vah**-ti] adj.m. beaklike; rostriform
dziobowy [dźho-**bo**-vi] adj.m. fore (deck, cabin, etc.)
dziobówka [dźho-**boo**-fkah] f. topgallant forecastle
dzion [dźhon] m. thatched beehive; skep
dzionek [**dźho**-nek] m. (nice, sunny, etc.) day
dziób [dźhoop] m. beak; bill; rostrum; (boat, etc.) stem; bow; bows; nose (of an airplane, etc.); pockmark; pit; slang: face; mouth
dać w dziób [dahćh v dźhoop] exp.: slang: to hit (somebody) in the face (mob jargon)
stulić dziób [**stoo**-leećh dźhoop] exp.: slang: to shut up; to stop (or make stop) talking; to be silent (mob jargon)
dzióbać [**dźhoo**-bahćh] v. peck; pick (corn, etc.); dab; goad; prod; jab; stab (*repeatedly*)
dzióbać igłą [**dźhoo**-bahćh **eeg**-wown] exp.: to stick a needle (into); to prick (skin, etc.) with a needle
dzióbaty [dźhoo-**bah**-ti] adj.m. pockmarked (face, etc.); pitted; with a pockmarked face; rostrated (bird)
dzióbek [**dźhoo**-bek] m. small beak; little bill; small bow
dzióbnąć [**dźhoob**-nownćh] v. peck; pick (corn, etc.); dab; goad; prod; jab; stab
dziryt [**dźhee**-rit] m. javelin; dart

dzisiaj [**dźhee**-śhahy] adv. today; to-day; nowadays; at the present time; m. today; the present day; the present age
do dzisiaj [do **dźhee**-śhahy] exp.: till today; to this day; to the present day
dzisiaj rano [**dźhee**-śhahy **rah**-no] exp.: this morning
dzisiaj wieczór [**dźhee**-śhahy **vye**-choor] exp.: this evening
od dzisiaj za tydzień [od **dźhee**-śhahy zah ti-dźheń] exp.: one week from today
dzisiaj się tak nie mówi [**dźhee**-śhahy śhan tahk ńe **moo**-vee] exp.: that word is no longer in current use; that expression is no longer in current use; that is now obsolete
dzisiejszość [dźhee-**śhey**-shośhćh] f. the present
dzisiejszy [dźhee-**śhey**-shi] adj.m. today's; today's; of today; present-day (rate, fashion, etc.); nowadays; contemporary; modern
po dzisiejszemu [po dźhee-śhey-**she**-moo] exp.: as it is done today; as we do it today; according to the present day (needs, requirements, etc.)
w dzisiejszych czasach [v dźhee-**śhey**-shikh **chah**-sahkh] exp.: nowadays; these days; in these latter days
dziś [dźheeśh] adv. today
dziś, jutro [dźheeśh **yoo**-tro] exp.: any day
dziś dziś [dźheeśh dźheeśh] exp.: song sound expressing joy
dziubałkowaty [dźhoo-bahw-ko-**vah**-ti] adj.m. heteropterous
dziubałkowate [dźhoo-bahw-ko-**vah**-te] pl. the order of Heteroptera
dziumdzia [**dźhoom**-dźhah] f. pedantic woman lacking energy; sluggard
dziunia [**dźhoo**-ńah] f. sexy, attractive young woman
dziupla [**dźhoo**-plah] f. (tree) hollow; (tree) cavity
dziuplak [**dźhoo**-plahk] m. bird dwelling in (tree) cavity
dziuplasty [dźhoo-**plah**-sti] adj.m. with holes scooped out in a tree
dziura [**dźhoo**-rah] f. hole; tear; rend; leak (in a vessel, etc.); gap (in a fence, etc.); puncture (in a tire); (air-) pocket; hollow; cavity; hole of a place; hovel
czarna dziura [**chahr**-nah **dźhoo**-rah] exp.: black hole; intense gravitational field that pulls in all matter and light (held to be a collapsed star)
mieć dziurę w głowie [myećh **dźhoo**-ran v **gwo**-vye] exp.: to forget everything; to remember nothing
mieć dziurę w pamięci [myećh **dźhoo**-ran f pah-**myan**-ćhee] exp.: to forget everything; to remember nothing
szukać dziury w całym [**shoo**-kahćh **dźhoo**-ri f **tsah**-wim] exp.: colloq: to be faultfinding; to pick holes; to look for trouble
szukanie dziury w całym [shoo-**kah**-ńe **dźhoo**-ri f **tsah**-wim] exp.: faultfinding
zapadła dziura [zah-**pah**-dwah **dźhoo**-rah] exp.: god-forsaken hole (locality)
dziurawcowaty [dźhoo-rahf-tso-**vah**-ti] adj.m. tutsan-like (plant); like St. John's wort
dziurawcowate [dźhoo-rahf-tso-**vah**-te] pl. the St. John's wort family of plants
dziurawić [dźhoo-**rah**-veećh] v. hole; make holes; open holes; bore holes (*repeatedly*)
dziurawiec [dźhoo-**rah**-vyets] m. tutsan (plant); St. John's wort
dziurawieć [dźhoo-**rah**-vyećh] v. wear; be worn into holes; tear (*repeatedly*)
dziurawienie [dźhoo-rah-**vye**-ńe] n. making holes
dziurawka [dźhoo-**rahf**-kah] f. ceramic cavity brick for low heat conductivity
dziurawy [dźhoo-**rah**-vi] adj.m. leaky; full of holes; worn into holes (shoes, etc.)
dziurawe ręce [dźhoo-**rah**-ve **ran**-tse] exp.: all thumbs; oaf

dziureczka [dźhoo-**rech**-kah] f. small eyelet; very little hole; very small opening
dziurka [**dźhoor**-kah] f. eyelet; little hole; little opening
dziurka od klucza [**dźhoor**-kah ot kloo-chah] exp.: keyhole
dziurka w nosie [**dźhoor**-kah v no-śhe] exp.: nostril
mieć po dziurki w nosie [myećh po **dźhoor**-kee v **no**-śhe] exp.: to be fed up (with)
dziurkacz [**dźhoor**-kahch] m. perforator; puncher; punch
dziurkarka [dźhoor-**kahr**-kah] f. punching press
dziurkować [dźhoor-**ko**-vahćh] v. perforate; punch; pink; mob slang: make tattoos (*repeatedly*)
dziurkować bilety [dźhoor-**ko**-vahćh bee-**le**-ti] exp.: to cancel tickets; to punch tickets
dziurkowanie [dźhoor-ko-**vah**-ńe] n. punching holes
dziurkowany [dźhoor-ko-**vah**-ni] adj.m. covered with perforations; perforated
dziurkowatość [dźhoor-ko-**vah**-tośhćh] f. porosity; characteristic perforations
dziurkowaty [dźhoor-ko-**vah**-ti] adj.m. porous; perforated
dziurkownik [dźhoor-**ko**-vńeek] m. punch; punching tool
dziurownica [dźhoo-ro-**vńee**-tsah] f. backup plate for punching holes
dziw [dźheef] m. wonder; strange thing
dziwa [**dźhee**-vah] f. an uncouth girl; slang: pickpocket's helper
dziwactwo [dźhee-**vah**-tstfo] n. fad; craze; (accidental) vagary; caprice; crotchet; eccentricity; whimsicality; peculiarity
dziwaczeć [dźhee-**vah**-chećh] v. become eccentric; grow queer; grow crotchety (*repeatedly*)
dziwaczek [dźhee-**vah**-chek] m. four-o'clock (flower); mirabilis; marvel-of-Peru
dziwaczenie [dźhee-vah-**che**-ńe] n. becoming eccentric; acting eccentric
dziwaczka [dźhee-**vahch**-kah] f. original; eccentric woman; crank; a character
dziwacznie [dźhee-**vahch**-ńe] adv. eccentrically; oddly; queerly; singularly; strangely; fantastically; weirdly; whimsically; freakishly
dziwaczność [dźhee-**vahch**-nośhćh] f. oddity; oddness; queerness; singularity; whimsicality; eccentricity; strangeness; weirdness
dziwaczny [dźhee-**vahch**-ni] adj.m. eccentric; odd; queer; singular; strange; bizarre; fantastic; weird; rum; whimsical; freakish
dziwaczyć [dźhee-**vah**-chićh] v. act oddly; act queerly; act eccentrically; be freakish; be maggoty (*repeatedly*)
dziwaczysko [dźhee-vah-**chi**-sko] n. & m. an old eccentric; an original; crank; a strange (odd) character
dziwadło [dźhee-**vah**-dwo] n. an oddity; a monstrosity; freak; eccentric; an original; crank; a character
dziwak [**dźhee**-vahk] m. eccentric; an original; crank; a character; colloq: queer customer
dziwerówka [dźhee-ve-**roof**-kah] f. gun made of Damascus steel
dziwić [**dźhee**-veećh] v. astonish; surprise; wonder (*repeatedly*)
dziwić się [**dźhee**-veećh śhan] v. be astonished (at); be surprised (at); wonder (at) (*repeatedly*)
nie ma się czemu dziwić [ńe mah śhan **che**-moo **dźhee**-veećh] exp.: it is no wonder
dziwienie [dźhee-**vye**-ńe] n. surprise; astonishment
dziwienie się [dźhee-**vye**-ńe śhan] n. surprise; astonishment
dziwka [**dźheef**-kah] f. vulg.: whore; prostitute; slut; slattern
chodzić na dziwki [**kho**-dźheećh nah **dźheef**-kee] exp.: vulg.: to go wenching; to womanize
dziwkarz [**dźheef**-kahsh] m. vulg.: womanizer; rake; whoremonger; john; a prostitute's client
dziwnie [**dźheev**-ńe] adv. strangely; oddly; queerly; peculiarly; singularly; in a funny way;

unaccountably
to dziwnie brzmi [to **dźheev**-ńe bzhmee] exp.: it sounds strange
dziwno [**dźheev**-no] adv. colloq: (an old word) strangely; oddly; queerly; peculiarly; singularly; in a funny way; unaccountably
dziwno mi [**dźheev**-no mee] exp.: colloq: I feel strangely; I feel in a funny way
dziwność [**dźheev**-nośhćh] f. oddity; strangeness
dziwny [**dźheev**-ni] adj.m. strange; odd; queer; peculiar; singular; funny; unaccountable; odd-looking
nic dziwnego, że... [ńeets dźheev-**ne**-go zhe] exp.: small wonder that...; no wonder that...
w dziwny sposób [v **dźheev**-ni **spo**-soop] exp.: unaccountably; in a strange way
dziwo [**dźhee**-vo] n. marvel; wonder; prodigy; strange thing
o dziwo! [o **dźhee**-vo] excl.: fancy!; imagine!
dziwojaszczur [dźhee-vo-**yahsh**-choor] m. dinosaur
dziwoląg [dźhee-**vo**-lowng] m. monster; deformed creature; monstrosity; oddity; freak; absurdity; stupidity
dziwonia [dźhee-**voń**-yah] f. purple finch; house finch
dziwota [dźhee-**vo**-tah] f. strange thing
nie dziwota [ńe dźhee-**vo**-tah] exp.: no wonder; no small wonder
dziwotwór [dźhee-**vo**-tfoor] m. freak; monster; monstrosity
dziwować się [dźhee-**vo**-vahćh śhan] v. be surprised (at); be astonished (at); marvel (at); wonder (at) (*repeatedly*)
dziwowanie się [dźhee-vo-**vah**-ńe śhan] n. surprise; astonishment
dziwowisko [dźhee-vo-**vee**-sko] n. uncommon sight; a wonder; a marvel; astonishment; wonder
dziwożona [dźhee-vo-**zho**-nah] f. ancient Slavic marshlands deity; mischievous demon; goblin
dzwon [dzvon] m. bell; chime; ringing; clang; clank; peal (of bells); bell-shaped object
bić w dzwony [beećh v **dzvo**-ni] exp.: to ring the bells
dzwoneczek [dzvo-**ne**-chek] m. very small bell; very small clang
dzwonek [**dzvo**-nek] m. small bell; ring (at the door, etc.); call
dzwoniasty [dzvo-**ńah**-sti] adj.m. bell-shaped
dzwonić [**dzvo**-ńeećh] v. ring up someone; ring (the bell); peal; tinkle; jingle; clang; clash; phone (*repeatedly*)
dzwoni mi w uszach [**dzvo**-ńee mee v **oo**-shahkh] exp.: my ears tingle; it rings in my ears
dzwonić do drzwi [**dzvo**-ńeećh do dzhvee] exp.: to ring at the door
dzwonić do kogoś [**dzvo**-ńeećh do **ko**-gośh] exp.: to ring somebody up; to call somebody up; to give somebody a call
dzwonić na alarm [**dzvo**-ńeećh nah **ah**-lahrm] exp.: to sound the alarm; to ring the alarm
dzwoniłem zębami [dzvo-**ńee**-wem zan-**bah**-mee] exp.: my teeth chattered
dzwoń do niego [dzvoń do **ńe**-go] exp.: ring him up; call him up; give him a ring; give him a call
dzwoniec [**dzvo**-ńets] m. green finch; linnet (bird)
dzwonienie [dzvo-**ńe**-ńe] n. ringing (of a bell); peal; ring; tinkle; jingle; clang; clash
dzwonienie do drzwi [dzvo-**ńe**-ńe do dzhvee] exp.: a ring (at the door)
dzwonienie w uszach [dzvo-**ńe**-ńe v **oo**-shahkh] exp.: ringing in the ears; tingle; tinnitus
dzwonko [**dzvon**-ko] n. slice (of fish)
dzwonkowaty [dzvon-ko-**vah**-ti] adj.m. bell-shaped; campanulate
dzwonkowate [dzvon-ko-**vah**-te] pl. the bellflower family of plants; Campanulaceae
dzwonkowy [dzvon-**ko**-vi] adj.m. of the nature of a bell; of diamonds (in cards)
dzwonnica [dzvon-**ńee**-tsah] f.

belfry
dzwonniczka [dzvon-ńee-chkah] f. campanile
dzwonnik [dzvon-ńeek] m. bell-ringer
dzwono [dzvo-no] n. large slice (of fish); ring; coil; hub (of a wheel)
dzwonowy [dzvo-no-vi] adj.m. bell (metal, etc.)
dzyndzyk [dzin-dzik] m. pendant
dzyń-dzyń [dziń dziń] exp.: clang-clang
dźgać [dźhgahćh] v. prod; poke; jab; stab (*repeatedly*)
dźgać się [dźhgahćh śhan] v. jab oneself; stab oneself (*repeatedly*)
dźganie [dźhgah-ńe] n. prodding; poking; jabbing; stabbing
dźganie się [dźhgah-ńe śhan] n. jabbing oneself; stabbing oneself
dźgnąć [dźhgnownhćh] v. prod; poke; jab; stab
dźgnąć w plecy [dźhgnownhćh f ple-tsi] exp.: to stab (somebody) in the back
dźgnąć się [dźhgnownćh śhan] v. jab oneself; stab oneself
dźgnięcie [dźhgńan-ćhe] n. prod; poke; jab; stab; thrust
dźgnięcie się [dźhgńan-ćhe śhan] n. stabbing oneself
dźwięczeć [dźhvyan-chećh] v. ring; sound; jingle; clang; be heard; strike the ear; clash (*repeatedly*)
dźwięczeć czysto [dźhvyan-chećh chi-sto] exp.: to ring clear
dźwięczeć fałszywie [dźhvyan-chećh fahw-shi-vye] exp.: to ring false
dźwięczenie [dźhvyan-che-ńe] n. a sound; a jingle; clangor; clash
dźwięcznie [dźhvyanch-ńe] adv. sonorously; resonantly; resoundingly; harmoniously; melodiously
dźwięczność [dźhvyanch-nośhćh] f. sonority; resonance; harmoniousness; melodiousness; tone (of a sound)
dźwięczny [dźhvyanch-ni] adj.m. sonorous; resonant; resounding; harmonious; melodious
dźwięk [dźhvyank] m. sound; speech sound; clang (of a bell, etc.); blast (of a siren, etc.); blare (of a trumpet); ring (of a coin)
dźwięk dzwonka [dźhvyank dzvon-kah] exp.: the tinkle of a bell
dźwięk dzwonu [dźhvyank dzvo-noo] exp.: the ring of a bell; the pealing (sound) of a bell
dźwięk monety [dźhvyank mo-ne-ti] exp.: the ring of a coin
dźwięk trąbki [dźhvyank trownp-kee] exp.: the blare of a trumpet
regulacja dźwięku [re-goo-lahts-yah dźhvyan-koo] exp.: tone correction
szybkość dźwięku [ship-kośhćh dźhvyan-koo] exp.: the speed of sound
dźwięknąć [dźhvyank-nownćh] v. ring; sound; jingle; clang; be heard; strike the ear; clash
dźwięknięcie [dźhvyank-ńan-ćhe] n. ring; sound
dźwiękochłonność [dźhvyan-ko-khwon-nośhćh] f. sound-absorption
dźwiękochłonny [dźhvyan-ko-khwon-ni] adj.m. sound-absorbing
dźwiękonaśladowczo [dźhvyan-ko-nah-śhlah-do-fcho] adv. onomatopoeically
dźwiękonaśladowczość [dźhvyan-ko-nah-śhlah-do-fchośhćh] f. onomatopoeia
dźwiękonaśladowczy [dźhvyan-ko-nah-śhlah-do-fchi] adj.m. onomatopoeic; imitative; echoic
dźwiękoszczelny [dźhvyan-ko-shchel-ni] adj.m. soundproof
dźwiękowiec [dźhvyan-ko-vyets] m. motion picture; talkie; sound film; phonolite (a volcanic rock)
dźwiękowiec literowy [dźhvyan-ko-vyets lee-te-ro-vi] exp.: abbreviation
dźwiękowo [dźhvyan-ko-vo] adv. by means of sound
dźwiękowy [dźhvyan-ko-vi] adj.m. of a sound; of sounds; sonic; sound (wave, film, etc.)
film dźwiękowy [feelm dźhvyan-ko-vi] exp.: sound film; talkies; motion picture

dźwig [dźhveeg] m. crane; hoist; lift; winch; crab; elevator
dźwigacz [**dźhvee**-gahch] m. levator
dźwigacz kotwiczny [**dźhvee**-gahch ko-**tfeech**-ni] exp.: cathead (ship's anchor support beam)
dźwigać [**dźhvee**-gahćh] v. lift; hoist; raise; heave; erect; carry; heave up; elevate; uplift; bear; support; sustain (*repeatedly*)
dźwigać się [**dźhvee**-gahćh śhan] v. raise; lift oneself up; move up; recover; come to oneself; pull through; be pulling through; be in process of construction; stand (tall) (*repeatedly*)
dźwiganie [dźhvee-**gah**-ńe] n. raising; lifting; elevation; erection
dźwiganie się [dźhvee-**gah**-ńe śhan] n. recovery (from an illness, etc.); rise
dźwiganie się z choroby [dźhvee-**gah**-ńe śhan s kho-**ro**-bi] exp.: recovery (from an illness)
dźwigar [**dźhvee**-gahr] m. girder; crane
dźwigarka [dźhvee-**gahr**-kah] f. windlass; hoisting jack
dźwigarowy [dźhvee-gah-**ro**-vi] adj.m. of a girder; of girders
dźwignąć [**dźhvee**-gnownćh] v. lift; hoist; raise; heave; erect; carry; heave up; elevate; uplift; bear; support; sustain
dźwignąć się [**dźhvee**-gnownćh śhan] v. raise; lift oneself up; move up; recover; come to oneself; pull through
dźwignia [**dźhvee**-gńah] f. lever; pivot; colloq: mainspring
siła dźwigni [**śhee**-wah **dźhvee**-gńee] exp.: leverage
dźwignica [dźhvee-**gńee**-tsah] f. crane
dźwignica linomostowa [dźhvee-**gńee**-tsah lee-no-mo-**sto**-vah] exp.: cableway
dźwignicowy [dźhvee-gńee-**tso**-vi] adj.m. of a lifting device
dźwignięcie [dźhvee-**gńan**-ćhe] n. a lift; a hoist; a heave; lift; hoist; heave
dźwignięcie się [dźhvee-**gńan**-ćhe śhan] n. lifting oneself; hoisting oneself
dźwignik [**dźhvee**-gńeek] m. crane; lift; hoist
dźwigniowo [dźhvee-**gńo**-vo] adv. with a lever; with leverage
dźwigniowy [dźhvee-**gńo**-vi] adj.m. of a lever; of leverage
dźwigowy [dźhvee-**go**-vi] adj.m. of a crane; of a hoist; of a jack; of an elevator; of a lift; lifting (gear, etc.); m. crane operator
mechanizm dźwigowy [me-**khah**-ńeezm dźhvee-**go**-vi] exp.: purchasing leverage; buying leverage
dżajnizm [dzhahy-ńeezm] m. atheistic philosophy of ancient India
dżaul [**dzhah**-ool] m. joule
dżaz [dzhahs] m. jazz
dżazowy [dzhah-**zo**-vi] adj.m. jazzy; of jazz; like jazz
dżdża [dzhdzhah] f. drizzle
dżdżownica [dzhdzho-**vńee**-tsah] f. rain-worm; earthworm; angleworm; worm; lug
dżdżownik [**dzhdzhov**-ńeek] m. a variety of sea gull
dżdżu [dzhdzhoo] m. colloq: very light rain; drizzle
dżdżyć [dzhdzhićh] v. rain very lightly; drizzle (*repeatedly*)
dżdżysto [**dzhdzhi**-sto] adv. wet; rainy; drizzly
było dżdżysto [bi-wo **dzhdzhi**-sto] exp.: it was drizzly; it was wet
dżdżystość [**dzhdzhi**-stośhćh] f. rainy weather; rain
dżdżysty [**dzhdzhi**-sti] adj.m. wet; rainy; drizzly (weather); rough (weather)
dżdżyście [**dzhdzhi**-śhćhe] adv. wet; rainy; drizzly
dżdżyściej [**dzhdzhi**-śhćhey] adv. more wet; more rainy; more drizzly
dżem [dzhem] m. jam; fruit jam; fruit preserve
dżemper [**dzhem**-per] m. jumper
dżentelmen [dzhen-**tel**-men] m. gentleman
dżentelmeneria [dzhen-tel-me-**ner**-yah] f. gentlemanly behavior;

good-breeding
dżentelmeński [dzhen-tel-**meń**-skee] adj.m. gentlemanly; well-bred
po dżentelmeńsku [po dzhen-tel-**meń**-skoo] exp.: like a gentleman; in a gentlemanly manner
dżentelmeńsko [dzhen-tel-**meń**-sko] adv. like a gentleman
dżersej [**dzher**-sey] m. jersey weave; close-fitting garment for the upper body; jersey dairy cattle
dżersejowy [dzher-se-**yo**-vi] adj.m. jersey (knitted fabric, garment, dairy cow, etc.)
dżet [dzhet] m. jet (black); (variety of hard) lignite coal
dżetowy [dzhe-**to**-vi] adj.m. of jet (black); of hard lignite coal; jet (jewelry, etc.)
dżez [dzhes] m. jazz
dżezbend [**dzhez**-bent] m. jazz band
dżezman [**dzhez**-mahn] m. jazzman; member of a jazz band; devotee of jazz
dżezmen [**dzhez**-men] m. jazzman; member of a jazz band; devotee of jazz
dżezować [dzhe-**zo**-vahćh] v. play jazz music; dance to jazz music; be in a jazz band (*repeatedly*)
dżezowanie [dzhe-zo-**vah**-ńe] n. playing jazz music; being in a jazz band
dżezowy [dzhe-**zo**-vi] adj.m. of jazz music; like jazz; jazz (music, concert, band, etc.)
dżig [dzheeg] m. jig
dżin [dzheen] m. gin; gin rummy
dżinizm [**dzhee**-ńeezm] m. atheistic philosophy of ancient India
dżins [dzheens] m. jean; a durable twilled cotton
dżinsowy [dzheen-**so**-vi] adj.m. of blue jeans
dżinsy [**dzheen**-si] pl. blue jeans (pants, trousers); jeans
dżip [dzheep] m. jeep; four-wheel drive, 80-inch wheelbase, half-ton capacity vehicle
dżiu-dżitsu [dzhyoo **dzheet**-soo] n. ju-jitsu; jiu-jitsu; jujutsu
dżokej [**dzho**-key] m. jockey; colloq: jock
dżokejka [dzho-**key**-kah] f. jockey cap; woman jockey
dżokejski [dzho-**key**-skee] adj.m. jockey's; jockey (cap, boots, saddle, club, etc.)
dżokejstwo [dzho-**key**-stfo] n. jockey's occupation
dżoker [**dzho**-ker] m. joker; an extra playing card
dżonka [**dzhon**-kah] f. (Chinese) junk
dżudo [**dzhoo**-do] n. judo (sport)
dżudok [**dzhoo**-dok] m. judo practitioner
dżudoka [dzhoo-**do**-kah] m. judo practitioner
dżudowiec [dzhoo-**do**-vyets] m. judo practitioner
dżudystka [dzhoo-**dis**-tkah] f. woman judo practitioner
dżul [dzhool] m. joule
dżuma [**dzhoo**-mah] f. plague; pest; pestilence
dżumowy [dzhoo-**mo**-vi] adj.m. of the plague; plague (victim, etc.)
dżungla [**dzhoon**-glah] f. jungle
prawo dżungli [**prah**-vo **dzhoon**-glee] exp.: law of the jungle; the rule of the jungle
dżunglowy [dzhoon-**glo**-vi] adj.m. jungly; jungle (law, etc.)
dżygit [**dzhi**-geet] m. Caucasian horseback rider; expert in riding
dżygitówka [dzhi-gee-**toof**-kah] f. fancy riding on horseback; trick riding on horseback
dżyn [dzhin] m. gin (alcoholic liquor of juniper berries)

E

E, e [e] the letter "e"; excl.: oh!
ebenista [e-be-**ńee**-stah] m. (artistic) cabinetmaker
ebenisteria [e-be-ńee-**ste**-ryah] f. (artistic) cabinetmaking
eblis [**e**-blees] m. Eblis; Satan
ebonit [e-**bo**-ńeet] m. ebonite; vulcanite

ebonitowy [e-bo-ńee-**to**-vi] adj.m. of ebonite; ebonite (lid, comb, hard rubber, etc.)
ebuliometr [e-boo-**lyo**-metr] m. ebulliometer; ebullioscope; boiling meter; boiling gauge
ebuliometria [e-boo-lyo-**met**-ryah] f. ebulliometry; ebullioscopy
ebuliometryczny [e-boo-lyo-me-**trich**-ni] adj.m. ebullioscopic
ebulioskop [e-boo-**lyo**-skop] m. ebullioscope
ebulioskopia [e-boo-lyo-**sko**-pyah] f. ebulliometry; ebullioscopy
ebulioskopowy [e-boo-lyo-sko-**po**-vi] adj.m. ebullioscopic
ech! [ekh] excl.: oh!; tut!; tut-tut!
echin [**e**-kheen] m. echinus
echinokok [e-khee-**no**-kok] m. echinococcus; tapeworm; hydatid
echinokokoza [e-khee-no-ko-**ko**-zah] f. echinococcosis
echinus [e-**khee**-noos] m. echinus
echo [**e**-kho] n. echo; response; a memory; memories; repercussion; repercussions; rumor; trace; vestige; result
bez echa [bes **e**-khah] exp.: echoless; vanished without trace; vanished unnoticed
być echem [bićh **e**-khem] exp.: to imitate exactly; to repeat exactly
minąć bez echa [**mee**-nownćh bes **e**-khah] exp.: to meet with no response; to make no impression; to leave no trace
odbić się echem [**od**-beećh śhan **e**-khem] exp.: to meet with a response; to call for a response
echoencefalografia [e-kho-en-tse-fah-lo-**grah**-fyah] f. ultrasound measurement of internal structures of the skull and in the diagnosis of abnormalities; echoencephalography
echoencefalograficzny [e-kho-en-tse-fah-lo-grah-**feech**-ni] adj.m. of echoencephalography
echograf [e-**kho**-grahf] m. recorder of the output of an echo sounder
echografia [e-kho-**grah**-fyah] f. ultrasonography
echogram [e-**kho**-grahm] m. record of an echo sounder
echokardiograf [e-kho-kahr-**dyo**-grahf] m. echocardiograph
echokardiografia [e-kho-kahr-dyo-**grah**-fyah] f. echocardiography
echokardiogram [e-kho-kahr-**dyo**-grahm] m. tracing made by an echocardiograph
echolalia [e-kho-**lah**-lyah] f. echolalia; repetition of what is said by other people (e.g. by children and some mentally sick people)
echolokacja [e-kho-lo-**kah**-tsyah] f. echolocation
echolokacyjny [e-kho-lo-kah-**tsiy**-ni] adj.m. of echolocation
echolokator [e-kho-lo-**kah**-tor] m. echo locator
echometr [e-**kho**-metr] m. echo sounder; sonic depth finder
echometria [e-kho-**me**-tryah] f. echo sounding
echomierz [e-**kho**-myesh] m. echo sounder; sonic depth finder
echomimia [e-kho-**mee**-myah] f. mimicry of facial expressions and gestures by the mentally sick
echopraksja [e-kho-**prah**-ksyah] f. echopraxia; automatic imitation of movements by the mentally sick
echosonda [e-kho-**son**-dah] f. echo sounder; sonic depth finder
echowy [e-**kho**-vi] adj.m. of the echo; echo (sounding, etc.)
sonda echowa [**son**-dah e-**kho**-vah] exp.: echo sounder; sonic depth finder
ecru [**e**-kroo] adj.m. beige
ecu [**e**-koo] n. European Currency Unit
ecydiospor [e-tsi-**dyo**-spor] m. aeciospore; aecidiospore
ecydium [e-**tsi**-dyoom] n. aecia; aecium
edaficznie [e-dah-**feech**-ńe] adv. edaphically
edaficzny [e-dah-**feech**-ni] adj.m. edaphic; autochthonous
edafon [e-**dah**-fon] m. edaphon; organism living in the top soil
edamski [e-**dahm**-skee] adj.m. of Edam; Edam (cheese, etc.)
eden [**e**-den] m. Eden

edeński [e-**deń**-skee] adj.m. of Eden (sight, vista, etc.)
edometr [e-**do**-metr] m. gauge for measuring soil density and resilience
edredon [e-**dre**-don] m. eider; eiderdown
edredonowy [e-dre-do-**no**-vi] adj.m. of eiderdown; eiderdown (quilt, cushion, pillow, etc.)
edukacja [e-doo-**kah**-tsyah] f. education; formal schooling; instruction; teaching
edukacjonizm [e-doo-kah-**tsyo**-ńeezm] m. belief in planned education
edukacyjny [e-doo-kah-**tsiy**-ni] adj.m. educational; of education
edukować [e-doo-**ko**-vahćh] v. educate; teach (*repeatedly*)
edukować się [e-doo-**ko**-vahćh śhan] v. educate oneself; teach oneself (*repeatedly*)
edukowanie [e-doo-ko-**vah**-ńe] n. education; teaching
edukowanie się [e-doo-ko-**vah**-ńe śhan] n. self-education; self-teaching
edycja [e-**di**-tsyah] f. edition
edycyjny [e-di-**tsiy**-ni] adj.m. of edition
edykt [**e**-dikt] m. edict
edyl [**e**-dil] m. aedile; Roman town manager
edylitet [e-di-**lee**-tet] m. aedileship; office of Roman town manager
Edyp [**e**-dip] m. Oedipus
edypowy [e-di-**po**-vi] adj.m. of Oedipus; Oedipus (complex, etc.)
edytor [e-**di**-tor] m. editor; publisher
edytorski [e-di-**tor**-skee] adj.m. editor's; publisher's; publishing (firm, house, etc.); editorial (principles, work, etc.)
edytorstwo [e-di-**tor**-stfo] n. editing; publishing; editor's work
e-e [e-e] exp.: colloq: first rate; tiptop; posh; A 1
efeb [**e**-fep] m. ephebe; ephebus; a young man in training for Athenian citizenship
efebia [e-**fe**-byah] f. Athenian academy
efedra [e-**fe**-drah] f. ephedra shrub
efedryna [e-fe-**dri**-nah] f. ephedrine (salt used in medicine)
ef-ef! [ef-ef] excl.: colloq: first-rate; tiptop; posh; A-1
efekciarski [e-fek-**ćhahr**-skee] adj.m. claptrap; showy; meant for effect
efekciarsko [e-fek-**ćhahr**-sko] adv. claptrap; showy; meant for effect
efekciarstwo [e-fek-**ćhahr**-stfo] n. claptrap; showiness
efekciarz [e-**fek**-ćhahsh] m. effect seeker; showman; man trying to impress others by easy effects
efekcik [e-**fek**-ćheek] m. small, cheap effect
efekt [**e**-fekt] m. effect; impression; result; upshot; consequence; outcome
brak efektu [brahk e-**fek**-too] exp.: lack of result; inefficiency
efekta [e-**fek**-tah] pl. movable property; stocks and bonds; movables; chattels; personal property; belongings (hist.)
efekty [e-**fek**-ti] pl. movables; chattels; personal property; belongings; effects
na efekt [nah **e**-fekt] exp.: for effect
efektor [e-**fek**-tor] m. effector (biol.)
efektownie [e-fek-**tov**-ńe] adv. with effect; strikingly; attractively; smartly; impressively; effectively; brilliantly
efektowność [e-fek-**tov**-nośhćh] f. impressiveness; effectiveness; brilliance; smartness
efektowny [e-fek-**tov**-ni] adj.m. showy; striking; attractive; smart; dainty; impressive; effective; brilliant
efektywnie [e-fek-**tiv**-ńe] adv. efficiently; effectively; actually; efficaciously; in fact; in reality
efektywność [e-fek-**tiv**-nośhćh] f. efficiency; effectiveness; efficacy; efficacity; reality; genuineness
efektywny [e-fek-**tiv**-ni] adj.m. efficient; effective; real; actual; genuine; efficacious
efemera [e-fe-**me**-rah] f. ephemeral; ephemeron
efemery [e-fe-**me**-ri] pl. ephemera
efemerycznie [e-fe-me-**rich**-ńe] adv.

transitorily; ephemerally
efemeryczność [e-fe-me-**rich**-nośhćh] f. transitoriness; evanescence; ephemerality
efemeryczny [e-fe-me-**rich**-ni] adj.m. ephemeral; transitory; short-lived; evanescent
efemeryda [e-fe-me-**ri**-dah] f. ephemeron; dayfly (lasting one day only); transitory being vanishing without a trace; ephemera
efemerydy [e-fe-me-**ri**-di] pl. ephemerides
efemerydalnie [e-fe-me-ri-**dahl**-ńe] adv. ephemerally; in a transitory way; transiently
efemerydalny [e-fe-me-ri-**dahl**-ni] adj.m. ephemeral; transitory; transient; like an ephemeron; short-lived; evanescent
efemeryzm [e-fe-**me**-rizm] m. ephemerality; transitoriness; evanescence
efendi [e-**fen**-dee] m. effendi; a man of property, education, or authority in an eastern Mediterranean country
efor [**e**-for] m. ephor; Spartan governor
eforat [e-**fo**-raht] m. ephorate
eforostwo [e-fo-**ro**-stfo] n. ephoralty
efuzja [e-**foo**-zyah] f. outflow (of lava, gas, etc.)
egalitarny [e-gah-lee-**tahr**-ni] adj.m. egalitarian; tending toward egalitarianism; marked by egalitarianism; equalitarian
egalitarystyczny [e-gah-lee-tah-ris-**tich**-ni] adj.m. egalitarian; tending toward egalitarianism; marked by egalitarianism
egalitaryzacja [e-gah-lee-tah-ri-**zah**-tsyah] f. equalization
egalitaryzm [e-gah-lee-**tah**-rizm] m. egalitarianism; belief in human equality; equalitarianism
egejski [e-**gey**-skee] adj.m. Aegean
egida [e-**gee**-dah] f. protection; auspices; protectorate; sponsorship
Egipcjanin [e-geep-**tsyah**-ńeen] m. Egyptian
Egipcjanka [e-geep-**tsyahn**-kah] f. Egyptian woman
egipski [e-**geep**-skee] adj.m. Egyptian
plaga egipska [**plah**-gah e-**geep**-skah] exp.: Egyptian plague; confounded nuisance
egiptolog [e-geep-**to**-log] m. Egyptologist
egiptologia [e-geep-to-**lo**-gyah] f. Egyptology
egiptologicznie [e-geep-to-lo-**geech**-ńe] adv. by (with) Egyptology
egiptologiczny [e-geep-to-lo-**geech**-ni] adj.m. Egyptological
ego [**e**-go] n. the self; egotism; self-esteem; the organized conscious mediator between the person and reality in perception and adaptation
egocentrycznie [e-go-tsen-**trich**-ńe] adv. selfishly; egocentrically
egocentryczny [e-go-tsen-**trich**-ni] adj.m. self-centered; egocentric; concerned with the individual rather than society
egocentryk [e-go-**tsen**-trik] m. self-centered person; an egocentric
egocentryzm [e-go-**tsen**-trizm] m. egocentrism
egoista [e-go-**ee**-stah] m. egoist; selfish person
egoistka [e-go-**ee**-stkah] f. (woman) egoist; selfish woman
egoistycznie [e-go-ee-**stich**-ńe] adv. selfishly; egoistically
egoistyczny [e-go-ee-**stich**-ni] adj.m. selfish; self-seeking; egoistic
egoizm [e-**go**-eezm] m. egoism; selfishness
egoteizm [e-go-**te**-eezm] m. belief that one is a god
egotyczny [e-go-**tich**-ni] adj.m. egotistic; conceited
egotysta [e-go-**tis**-tah] m. egotist; egotistic person (man)
egotystka [e-go-**tis**-tkah] f. (female) egotist; egotistic woman
egotyzm [e-**go**-tizm] m. egotism
egreta [e-**gre**-tah] f. aigrette; a spray (of gems, of feathers for the head decoration); osprey
egzaltacja [eg-zahl-**tah**-tsyah] f. exaltation
egzaltować [eg-zahl-**to**-vahćh] v.

exalt; impassion; enrapture; entrance (*repeatedly*)
egzaltować się [eg-zahl-**to**-vahćh śhan] v. go into ecstasies; be enraptured; be entranced (*repeatedly*)
egzaltowanie się [eg-zahl-to-**vah**-ńe śhan] n. enrapture; entrance
egzaltowany [eg-zahl-to-**vah**-ni] adj.m. excessively impressible; over-sensitive; excitable
egzamin [eg-**zah**-meen] m. examination; exam; undergoing a test; a set of questions
egzamin ustny [eg-**zah**-meen **oo**-stni] exp.: oral examination
nie zdać egzaminu [ńe zdahćh eg-zah-**mee**-noo] exp.: to fail in a test; to fail; not to make the grade; to be found wanting
zdać egzamin [zdahćh eg-**zah**-meen] exp.: to pass an examination; qualify (as a pilot, etc.); stand the test; pass muster
zdawać egzamin [**zdah**-vahćh eg-**zah**-meen] exp.: to sit for an examination
egzaminacyjny [eg-zah-mee-nah-**tsiy**-ni] adj.m. of an examination; examination (procedure, etc.)
egzaminator [eg-zah-mee-**nah**-tor] m. examiner
egzaminatorka [eg-zah-mee-nah-**tor**-kah] f. (woman) examiner
egzaminatorski [eg-zah-mee-nah-**tor**-skee] adj.m. of an examiner
egzaminować [eg-zah-mee-**no**-vahćh] v. examine; look over; ask questions (*repeatedly*)
egzaminowanie [eg-zah-mee-no-**vah**-ńe] n. examination; examinations
egzaminowy [eg-zah-mee-**no**-vi] adj.m. of an examination; of examinations; examination (results, etc.)
egzaminujący [eg-zah-mee-noo-**yown**-tsi] adj.m. examinatorial
komisja egzaminująca [ko-**mees**-yah eg-zah-mee-noo-**yown**-tsah] exp.: board of examiners
egzaracja [eg-zah-**rah**-tsyah] f. glacial (smooth) erosion of rocks
egzarcha [eg-**zahr**-khah] m. exarch
egzarchat [eg-**zahr**-khaht] m. (Byzantine) exarchate (hist.)
egzegeta [eg-ze-**ge**-tah] m. exegete
egzegetycznie [eg-ze-ge-**tich**-ńe] adv. exegetically
egzegetyczny [eg-ze-ge-**tich**-ni] adj.m. exegetical
egzegetyka [eg-ze-**ge**-ti-kah] f. explanation of the Bible
egzegeza [eg-ze-**ge**-zah] f. exegesis; explanation; exposition (of a text, etc.)
egzekucja [eg-ze-**koo**-tsyah] f. execution; distraint; seizure; infliction of corporal punishment; flogging
egzekucyjny [eg-ze-koo-**tsiy**-ni] adj.m. executive (power, etc.); of execution; of seizure
pluton egzekucyjny [**ploo**-ton eg-ze-koo-**tsiy**-ni] exp.: firing squad
egzekutor [eg-ze-**koo**-tor] m. executor (of an estate, etc.); bailiff
egzekutywa [eg-ze-koo-**ti**-vah] f. enforcement (of laws, etc.); means of enforcing (the law, etc.); executive (power, etc.)
egzekwatur [eg-ze-**kfah**-toor] (not declined:) exequatur; written official accreditation
egzekwie [eg-**ze**-kfye] pl. burial services; exequies; obsequies
egzekwować [eg-ze-**kfo**-vahćh] v. execute; exact; perform; carry into effect; enforce (laws, payments, etc.) (*repeatedly*)
egzekwowanie [eg-ze-kfo-**vah**-ńe] n. execution (of an action, etc.); performance (of a task, etc.); enforcement (of the law); exaction (of money)
egzema [eg-**ze**-mah] f. eczema
egzemplarz [eg-**zem**-plahsh] m. copy (sample); specimen
w trzech egzemplarzach [f tshekh eg-zem-**plah**-zhahkh] exp.: in triplicate; triplicated
egzemplifikacja [eg-zem-plee-fee-**kah**-tsyah] f. exemplification
egzemplifikacyjny [eg-zem-plee-fee-kah-**tsiy**-ni] adj.m. exemplifying
egzemplifikować [eg-zem-plee-fee-**ko**-vahćh] v. exemplify (*repeatedly*)

egzerga [eg-**zer**-gah] f. exergue
egzo- [**eg**-zo] prefix: exo-; ex-; outer-; outside-; out-
egzobiolog [eg-zo-**byo**-log] m. exobiologist
egzobiologia [eg-zo-byo-**lo**-gyah] f. exobiology; extraterrestrial biology
egzobiologiczny [eg-zo-byo-lo-**geech**-ni] adj.m. exobiologic; of extraterrestrial biology
egzoderma [eg-zo-**der**-mah] f. exodermis
egzogamia [eg-zo-**gah**-myah] f. exogamy; intertribal marriage
egzogamiczny [eg-zo-gah-**meech**-ni] adj.m. exgamic; exogamous
egzogeneza [eg-zo-ge-**ne**-zah] f. origin from or due to external causes
egzogenicznie [eg-zo-ge-**ńeech**-ńe] adj.m. exogenously
egzogeniczny [eg-zo-ge-**ńeech**-ni] adj.m. exogenous
egzogenny [eg-zo-**gen**-ni] adj.m. exogenous
egzorcysta [eg-zor-**tsi**-stah] m. exorcist
egzorcyzm [eg-**zor**-tsizm] m. exorcism
egzorcyzmować [eg-zor-tsi-**zmo**-vahćh] v. exorcise (*repeatedly*)
egzorcyzmowanie [eg-zor-tsi-zmo-**vah**-ńe] n. exorcism
egzorta [eg-**zor**-tah] f. homily; sermon; (funeral, etc.) oration
egzosfera [eg-zo-**sfe**-rah] f. exosphere; the outer fringe region of the atmosphere of the earth (above 600-1000 km)
egzospor [eg-**zo**-spor] m. exospore
egzot [**eg**-zot] m. an exotic plant
egzotermicznie [eg-zo-ter-**meech**-ńe] adv. exothermically
egzotermiczny [eg-zo-ter-**meech**-ni] adj.m. exothermic; exothermal
egzoteryczny [eg-zo-te-**rich**-ni] adj.m. exoteric; understandable to the general public
egzotoksyna [eg-zo-to-**ksi**-nah] f. exotoxin
egzotycznie [eg-zo-**tich**-ńe] adv. exotically
egzotyczność [eg-zo-**tich**-nośhćh] f. exoticism
egzotyczny [eg-zo-**tich**-ni] adj.m. exotic (impression, etc.)
egzotyk [eg-**zo**-tik] m. an exotic; exotic
egzotyka [eg-**zo**-ti-kah] f. exoticism; exotic nature
egzotyki [eg-**zo**-ti-kee] pl. exotica; exotic themes
egzotyzacja [eg-zo-ti-**zah**-tsyah] f. making (something) exotic
egzotyzm [eg-**zo**-tizm] m. exotism; exoticism; state of being exotic
egzystencja [eg-zi-**sten**-tsyah] f. existence; livelihood; living conditions; subsistence
środki egzystencji [**śhrot**-kee eg-zi-**sten**-tsyee] exp.: subsistence; means of subsistence; maintenance
egzystencjalista [eg-zi-sten-tsyah-**lees**-tah] m. existentialist
egzystencjalistycznie [eg-zi-sten-tsyah-lees-**tich**-ńe] adv. existentialistically
egzystencjalistyczny [eg-zi-sten-tsyah-lees-**tich**-ni] adj.m. existentialistic
egzystencjalizm [eg-zi-sten-**tsyah**-leezm] m. existentialism
egzystencjalny [eg-zi-sten-**tsyahl**-ni] adj.m. existential
egzystować [eg-zi-**sto**-vahćh] v. exist; subsist (*repeatedly*)
egzystowanie [eg-zi-sto-**vah**-ńe] n. existence
eh! [ekh] excl.: oh!
einstein [**ahyn**-shtahyn] m. einsteinium; artificial radioactive element number 99
eis [eys] n. E sharp
ej! [ey] excl.: look out!; be careful!; I warn you!; really?!; you don't say so!; careful!; no nonsense!
ejakulacja [e-yah-koo-**lah**-tsyah] f. ejaculation (of the sperm)
ejakulat [e-yah-**koo**-laht] m. ejaculated sperm
ejdetycznie [ey-de-**tich**-ńe] adv. eidetically
ejdetyczny [ey-de-**tich**-ni] adj.m. eidetic
ejdetyk [ey-**de**-tik] m. eidetic person
ejdetyzm [ey-**de**-tizm] m. eidetic

condition
ejektor [e-**ye**-ktor] m. ejector
ejektywny [e-ye-**ktiv**-ni] adj.m. ejective (consonant, etc.)
ejże! [**ey**-zhe] excl.: look out!; be careful!; I warn you!; really?!; you don't say so!; go on!; do it!
eka-pierwiastki [e-kah pyer-**vyahst**-kee] pl. elements predicted by Mendeleyev
ekierka [e-**ker**-kah] f. set square; draftsman's triangle
ekipa [e-**kee**-pah] f. team; crew; group; party; gang
ekiwok [e-**kee**-vok] m. play on identically sounding words; word of double meaning; quibble
eklektycznie [e-kle-**ktich**-ńe] adv. eclectically; selecting from various sources; by the eclectic method
eklektyczny [e-kle-**ktich**-ni] adj.m. eclectic; selecting; selected from various sources
eklektyk [e-**kle**-ktik] m. an eclectic
eklektyzm [e-**kle**-ktizm] m. eclecticism
ekler [**e**-kler] m. zipper; zip; zip fastener; (cake) eclair
eklezjasta [e-kle-**zyah**-stah] m. clergyman; priest
eklezjologia [e-kle-zyo-**lo**-gyah] f. the theology of Catholic scriptures
eklimetr [e-**klee**-metr] m. slope measuring device; inclinometer
ekliptyczny [e-klee-**ptich**-ni] adj.m. ecliptic
ekliptyka [e-**klee**-pti-kah] f. ecliptic; the great circle of the celestial sphere of the apparent solar path
ekloga [ek-**lo**-gah] f. eclogue; short pastoral poem
ekoklimat [e-ko-**klee**-maht] m. bio-climate; eco-climate
ekolog [e-**ko**-log] m. ecologist; environmentalist
ekologia [e-ko-**lo**-gyah] f. ecology; relations between living organisms and their environment
ekologicznie [e-ko-lo-**geech**-ńe] adv. ecologically
ekologiczny [e-ko-lo-**geech**-ni] adj.m. of ecology; ecological
ekonom [e-**ko**-nom] m. (land or estate) steward
ekonomajzer [e-ko-no-**mahy**-zer] m. colloq: economizer
ekonometria [e-ko-no-**me**-tryah] f. econometrics
ekonometrycznie [e-ko-no-me-**trich**-ńe] adv. econometrically
ekonometryczny [e-ko-no-me-**trich**-ni] adj.m. econometric
ekonometryk [e-ko-no-**me**-trik] m. econometrician
ekonomia [e-ko-**no**-myah] f. economics; thrift; economy; husbandry; political economy
ekonomicznie [e-ko-no-**meech**-ńe] adv. with economy; economically; thriftily; sparingly
ekonomiczność [e-ko-no-**meech**-nośhćh] f. economy; thrift
ekonomiczny [e-ko-no-**meech**-ni] adj.m. economic; economical; thrifty; sparing
ekonomika [e-ko-**no**-mee-kah] f. economics
ekonomista [e-ko-no-**mee**-stah] m. economist
ekonomistka [e-ko-no-**mee**-stkah] f. (woman) economist
ekonomizacja [e-ko-no-mee-**zah**-tsyah] f. economizing; frugality
ekonomizer [e-ko-no-**mee**-zer] m. (special) economizing carburetor
ekonomizm [e-ko-**no**-meezm] m. economic materialism
ekonomski [e-ko-**nom**-skee] adj.m. steward's (duties, etc.)
ekosfera [e-ko-**sfe**-rah] f. ecosphere; biosphere; habitable parts of the universe
ekosystem [e-ko-**si**-stem] m. ecosystem; an ecological unit in nature
ekoton [e-**ko**-ton] m. ecotone; a transition area between two adjacent ecological communities
ekotyp [e-**ko**-tip] m. ecological type
ekran [**e**-krahn] m. screen; shield; silver screen; monitor screen
ekranik [e-**krah**-ńeek] m. small (television, etc.) screen
ekranizacja [e-krah-ńee-**zah**-tsyah] f. screening (of a novel, etc.); filming
ekranizator [e-krah-ńee-**zah**-tor] m.

producer (screening a novel, etc.)
ekranizować [e-krah-ńee-**zo**-vahćh] v. screen (a novel, etc.); film (a scene, etc.) (*repeatedly*)
ekranizowanie [e-krah-ńee-zo-**vah**-ńe] n. screening (of a novel, etc.); filming
ekranopis [e-krah-**no**-pees] m. monitor; computer graphics
ekranoplan [e-krah-**no**-plahn] m. hydrofoil (ship or boat)
ekranować [e-krah-**no**-vahćh] v. shield (electrically) (*repeatedly*)
ekranowanie [e-krah-no-**vah**-ńe] n. shielding (electrically)
ekranowy [e-krah-**no**-vi] adj.m. screen (version, etc.); film (scene, plot, etc.); of the screen; of the film
ekrazyt [e-**krah**-zit] m. a type of explosive; ecrasite
ekrazytowy [e-krah-zi-**to**-vi] adj.m. of ecrasite; ecrasite (explosion)
eks- [eks] prefix: ex-
eks-dyrektor [eks di-**re**-ktor] exp.: an ex-director; former director
ekscelencja [ek-stse-**len**-tsyah] m. excellency
ekscentrycznie [ek-stsen-**trich**-ńe] adv. eccentrically; queerly; whimsically
ekscentryczność [ek-stsen-**trich**-nośhćh] f. eccentricity; queerness; whimsicality
ekscentryczny [ek-stsen-**trich**-ni] adj.m. eccentric; quaint; queer; odd
ekscentryk [ek-**stsen**-trik] m. odd person; an eccentric; queer person; whimsical person
ekscentryzm [ek-**stsen**-trizm] m. oddness; eccentricity; queerness; whimsicality
ekscepcjonalizm [eks-tsep-tsyo-**nah**-leezm] m. an outdated geological theory
ekscerpcja [eks-**tser**-ptsyah] f. excerpt; selecting quotes out of a text; extract; excerption
ekscerpcyjny [eks-tser-**ptsiy**-ni] adj.m. excerpt (quote, etc.); extract (product, etc.)
ekscerpować [eks-tser-**po**-vahćh] v. excerpt; extract; take extracts from (a book, etc.) (*repeatedly*)
ekscerpowanie [eks-tser-po-**vah**-ńe] n. excerpting; extracting
ekscerptor [eks-**tser**-ptor] m. excerpter; excerptor
eksces [**eks**-tses] m. excesses
ekscesy [ek-**stse**-si] pl. excesses; disturbance
popełniać ekscesy [po-**pew**-ńahćh ek-**stse**-si] exp.: to commit excesses; to make disturbances
ekscesywny [eks-tse-**siv**-ni] adj.m. excessive
ekscytacja [eks-tsi-**tah**-tsyah] f. excitement; stimulation; arousal
ekscytować [eks-tsi-**to**-vahćh] v. excite; stimulate; arouse (*repeatedly*)
ekscytować się [eks-tsi-**to**-vahćh śhan] v. become excited; get excited; get stimulated; become aroused (*repeatedly*)
ekscytowanie [eks-tsi-to-**vah**-ńe] n. excitement; stimulation
eksfoliacja [eks-fo-**lyah**-tsyah] f. exfoliation; splitting of rocks by temperature changes
ekshalacja [eks-khah-**lah**-tsyah] f. exhalation
ekshaustor [eks-**khahw**-stor] m. exhauster
ekshaustor powietrzny [eks-**khahw**-stor po-**vye**-tshni] adj.m. air-exhauster; suction fan
ekshibicjonista [eks-khee-bee-tsyo-**ńee**-stah] m. exhibitionist
ekshibicjonistyczny [eks-khee-bee-tsyo-ńee-**stich**-ni] adj.m. exhibitionistic; of indecent exposure
ekshibicjonizm [eks-khee-bee-**tsyo**-ńeezm] m. exhibitionism; a perversion marked by a tendency to indecent exposure
ekshumacja [ek-skhoo-**mah**-tsyah] f. exhumation
ekshumacyjny [ek-skhoo-mah-**tsiy**-ni] adj.m. of exhumation
ekshumować [ek-skhoo-**mo**-vahćh] v. exhume; disinter (*repeatedly*)
ekshumowanie [ek-skhoo-mo-**vah**-ńe] n. exhumation

ekshumowany [ek-skhoo-mo-**vah**-ni] adj.m. exhumed; disinterred
ekskawacja [eks-kah-**vah**-tsyah] f. excavation; removal of tooth-root
ekskawator [eks-kah-**vah**-tor] m. excavator; steam shovel; backhoe; dental excavator
eksklamacja [eks-klah-**mah**-tsyah] f. exclamation
eksklawa [eks-**klah**-vah] f. exclave
ekskluzywizm [ek-skloo-**zi**-veezm] m. exclusiveness; exclusivity
ekskluzywnie [ek-skloo-**ziv**-ńe] adv. exclusively; selectively
ekskluzywność [ek-skloo-**ziv**-nośhćh] f. exclusivity
ekskluzywny [ek-skloo-**ziv**-ni] adj.m. exclusive; select; clannish
ekskomunika [eks-ko-**moo**-ńee-kah] f. excommunication
ekskomunikować [eks-ko-moo-ńee-**ko**-vahćh] v. excommunicate; subject to excommunication (*repeatedly*)
ekskomunikowanie [eks-ko-moo-ńee-ko-**vah**-ńe] n. subjecting to excommunication
ekskrecja [eks-**kre**-tsyah] f. excretion
ekskrement [eks-**kre**-ment] m. excrement; waste matter excreted from the bowels
nauka o ekskrementach [nah-oo-kah o eks-kre-**men**-tahkh] exp.: scatology
ekskursja [eks-**koor**-syah] f. excursion; expedition
ekslibris [eks-**lee**-brees] m. ex libris; bookplate; ex libris; artistic property mark used in books
ekslibrys [eks-**lee**-bris] m. ex libris; bookplate; artistic property mark used in books
eksmisja [eks-**mee**-syah] f. eviction; ejection; ejectment
eksmisyjny [eks-mee-**siy**-ni] adj.m. of eviction
eksmitować [eks-mee-**to**-vahćh] v. evict; eject (*repeatedly*)
eksmitowanie [eks-mee-to-**vah**-ńe] n. eviction; ejectment
ekspander [eks-**pahn**-der] m. device for muscle exercise by stretching rubber bands or springs
ekspandować [eks-pahn-**do**-vahćh] v. expand; spread (into territory of others, etc.) (*repeatedly*)
ekspansja [eks-**pahn**-syah] f. expansion; expansionary tendency
ekspansjonista [eks-pahn-syo-**ńee**-stah] m. expansionist
ekspansjonistyczny [eks-pahn-syo-ńee-**stich**-ni] adj.m. expansionistic
ekspansjonizm [eks-pahn-**syo**-ńeezm] m. expansionism; policy of territorial expansion
ekspansyjny [eks-pahn-**siy**-ni] adj.m. expansional; expansionary; expansionist; expansionistic
ekspansywnie [eks-pahn-**siv**-ńe] adv. expansively; demonstratively; in an unrestrained manner
ekspansywność [eks-pahn-**siv**-nośhćh] f. expansiveness; demonstrativeness; expansivity
ekspansywny [eks-pahn-**siv**-ni] adj.m. expansive; demonstrative; unrestrained
ekspatriacja [eks-pah-**tryah**-tsyah] f. expatriation; banishment
ekspatriant [eks-**pah**-tryahnt] m. expatriate (living in a foreign country); expatriated person
ekspatriować [eks-pah-**tryo**-vahćh] v. expatriate; banish (*repeatedly*)
ekspatriować się [eks-pah-**tryo**-vahćh śhan] v. expatriate oneself; migrate (*repeatedly*)
ekspatriowanie [eks-pah-tryo-**vah**-ńe] n. expatriation; banishment
ekspedient [eks-**pe**-dyent] m. salesman; clerk; shop assistant
ekspedientka [eks-pe-**dyen**-tkah] f. salesgirl; clerk; saleswoman
ekspediować [eks-pe-**dyo**-vahćh] v. dispatch; send (off); forward; serve (customers, etc.); sell (*repeatedly*)
ekspediowanie [eks-pe-dyo-**vah**-ńe] n. dispatching; sending (off); forwarding; serving
ekspedite [eks-pe-**dee**-te] adv. colloq: perfectly; fluently; very well; skillfully; with ease
ekspedycja [eks-pe-**di**-tsyah] f. dispatch; expedition; service (of customers, etc.); dispatch office;

shipping department; shipment (of goods, etc.)
ekspedycja karna [eks-pe-**di**-tsyah **kahr**-nah] exp.: punitive expedition
ekspedycja naukowa [eks-pe-**di**-tsyah nah-oo-**ko**-vah] exp.: scientific expedition
ekspedycja ratunkowa [eks-pe-**di**-tsyah rah-toon-**ko**-vah] exp.: rescue expedition; rescue party
ekspedycyjny [eks-pe-di-**tsiy**-ni] adj.m. expeditionary; of shipping agency or department
ekspedytor [eks-pe-**di**-tor] m. forwarding agent; shipping clerk
ekspedytura [eks-pe-di-**too**-rah] f. dispatch; forwarding; shipping (office, etc.); shipment; service (of customers)
ekspektatywa [eks-pek-tah-**ti**-vah] f. expectancy; expectation (on a statistical basis, etc.)
ekspens [**eks**-pens] m. expense; spending; cost
eksperiencja [eks-pe-**ryen**-tsyah] f. experience; expertness
ekspert [**eks**-pert] m. expert; specialist; connoisseur
ekspertyza [eks-per-**ti**-zah] f. expert's report (inquiry, appraisement, etc.); experts' appraisement report
eksperyment [eks-pe-**ri**-ment] m. experiment; test; trial
eksperymentalista [eks-pe-ri-men-tah-**lee**-stah] m. experimentalist
eksperymentalizm [eks-pe-ri-men-**tah**-leezm] m. experimentalism; experimental verification
eksperymentalnie [eks-pe-ri-men-**tahl**-ńe] adv. experimentally; as an experiment; by way of experiment
eksperymentalny [eks-pe-ri-men-**tahl**-ni] adj.m. experimental
eksperymentator [eks-pe-ri-men-**tah**-tor] m. experimenter; scientific experimentalist
eksperymentatorski [eks-pe-ri-men-tah-**tor**-skee] adj.m. experimenter's
eksperymentatorstwo [eks-pe-ri-men-tah-**tor**-stfo] n. experimentation
eksperymentować [eks-pe-ri-men-**to**-vahćh] v. experiment (on); experiment (with); experiment (in) (*repeatedly*)
eksperymentowanie [eks-pe-ri-men-to-**vah**-ńe] n. experimentation
ekspiacja [eks-**pyah**-tsyah] f. expiation; atonement; amendment for wrongdoing or guilt
ekspiacyjny [eks-pyah-**tsiy**-ni] adj.m. expiatory
ekspiracja [eks-pee-**rah**-tsyah] f. expiration; exhalation; death
ekspiracyjny [eks-pee-rah-**tsiy**-ni] adj.m. expiratory (pronunciation, way of speaking, etc.)
eksplantacja [eks-plahn-**tah**-tsyah] f. transplantation; explantation
eksplicytny [eks-plee-**tsi**-tni] adj.m. explicit; express; specific; definite
eksplikacja [eks-plee-**kah**-tsyah] f. explication
eksplikacyjnie [eks-plee-kah-**tsiy**-ńe] adv. explanatorily; explicatively
eksplikacyjny [eks-plee-kah-**tsiy**-ni] adj.m. explanatory; explicative
eksplikatywny [eks-plee-kah-**tiv**-ni] adj.m. explicative; interpretative
eksplikować [eks-plee-**ko**-vahćh] v. explain (*repeatedly*)
eksploatacja [eks-plo-ah-**tah**-tsyah] f. exploitation; utilization; working (of a mine, etc.)
eksploatacyjny [eks-plo-ah-tah-**tsiy**-ni] adj.m. of exploitation; of utilization; working (expenses, schedule, etc.)
eksploatator [eks-plo-ah-**tah**-tor] m. exploiter
eksploatatorski [eks-plo-ah-tah-**tor**-skee] adj.m. of exploiter; exploiter (tools, etc.)
eksploatować [eks-plo-ah-**to**-vahćh] v. exploit; work (a mine, etc.); sweat (workers, etc.); utilize (machines, etc.); operate (an enterprise, etc.); make use (of) (*repeatedly*)
eksploatowanie [eks-plo-ah-to-**vah**-ńe] n. exploitation
eksplodować [eks-plo-**do**-vahćh] v. explode; blow up; cause to burst with a loud noise (*repeatedly*)

eksplodowanie [eks-plo-do-**vah**-ńe] n. explosion; blowup; burst (with a loud noise) (*repeatedly*)
eksploracja [eks-plo-**rah**-tsyah] f. exploration; systematic search
eksploracyjnie [eks-plo-rah-**tsiy**-ńe] adv. exploratively
eksploracyjny [eks-plo-rah-**tsiy**-ni] adj.m. of exploration; of systematic search; explorative; exploratory
eksplorator [eks-plo-**rah**-tor] m. explorer; systematic searcher
eksploratorski [eks-plo-rah-**tor**-skee] adj.m. exploratory; explorative; explorer's; systematic searcher's
eksplorować [eks-plo-**ro**-vahćh] v. explore; search; seek for; seek after; examine minutely; conduct a systematic search (for oil, etc.) (*repeatedly*)
eksplorowanie [eks-plo-ro-**vah**-ńe] n. exploration; systematic search
eksplozja [eks-**plo**-zyah] f. explosion; plosion (in pronunciation); the noise made by exploding (something); a noisy outburst; a sudden and widespread increase
eksplozyjnie [eks-plo-**ziy**-ńe] adv. explosively
eksplozyjność [eks-plo-**ziy**-nośhćh] f. explosive nature
eksplozyjny [eks-plo-**ziy**-ni] adj.m. explosive
eksplozywnie [eks-plo-**ziv**-ńe] adv. explosively; with explosiveness
eksplozywność [eks-plo-**ziv**-nośhćh] f. explosiveness; explosibility
eksplozywny [eks-plo-**ziv**-ni] adj.m. explosive; explosible; capable of being exploded
spółgłoska eksplozywna [spoow-**gwo**-skah eks-plo-**ziv**-nah] exp.: an explosive (consonant); a plosive (consonant)
eksponant [eks-**po**-nahnt] m. exhibitor; exponent; index
eksponat [eks-**po**-naht] m. exhibit
eksponent [eks-**po**-nent] m. exhibitor; exponent
eksponować [eks-po-**no**-vahćh] v. expose; exhibit; endanger; lay open (to danger, attack, etc.); reveal; make known (*repeatedly*)
eksponować się [eks-po-**no**-vahćh śhan] v. expose oneself; be exposed (*repeatedly*)
eksponowanie [eks-po-no-**vah**-ńe] n. exposure; frequent appearance before the public
eksponowany [eks-po-no-**vah**-ni] adj.m. responsible (position, etc.); exposed (to danger, attacks, etc.); dangerous; perilous
eksport [**eks**-port] m. export (goods, etc.); exportation; export trade
eksportacja [eks-por-**tah**-tsyah] f. funeral procession to the church for burial service
eksporter [eks-**por**-ter] m. exporter
eksportować [eks-por-**to**-vahćh] v. export; send abroad (goods, capital, etc.) (*repeatedly*)
eksportowanie [eks-por-to-**vah**-ńe] n. exportation; exporting
eksportowy [eks-por-**to**-vi] adj.m. of export; export (trade, duty, etc.)
ekspozycja [eks-po-**zi**-tsyah] f. exhibition; exposition (of a principle, etc.); setting forth (a plan, etc.); exposure (to sunshine, etc.); exposure (of a film, etc.)
ekspozycyjny [eks-po-zi-**tsiy**-ni] adj.m. of exhibition; of exposition; exhibition (hall, etc.); exposition (program, etc.)
ekspozytura [eks-po-zi-**too**-rah] f. agency; branch office; branch
ekspres [**eks**-pres] m. express (mail); express letter; special delivery letter; espresso (coffee); express train
ekspresja [eks-**pre**-syah] f. expression; manifestation of feelings; ability to express; strength of expression
pełen ekspresji [**pe**-wen eks-**pre**-syee] exp.: very expressive
ekspresjonista [eks-pre-syo-**ńee**-stah] m. expressionist
ekspresjonistycznie [eks-pre-syo-ńee-**stich**-ńe] adv. expressionistically
ekspresjonistyczny [eks-pre-syo-ńee-**stich**-ni] adj.m. expressionistic
ekspresjonizm [eks-pre-**syo**-ńeezm]

m. expressionism
ekspresowy [eks-pre-**so**-vi] adj.m. sent by special delivery; speedy; speed (train, etc.)
ekspresyjność [eks-pre-**siy**-nośhćh] f. expressiveness
ekspresyjny [eks-pre-**siy**-ni] adj.m. expressive (colors, music, etc.)
ekspresywizm [eks-pre-**si**-veezm] m. an expressive word
ekspresywnie [eks-pre-**siv**-ńe] adv. expressively
ekspresywność [eks-pre-**siv**-nośhćh] f. expressiveness
ekspresywny [eks-pre-**siv**-ni] adj.m. expressive
ekspropriacja [eks-pro-**pryah**-tsyah] f. expropriation; dispossession
ekspropriacyjny [eks-pro-pryah-**tsiy**-ni] adj.m. of expropriation; of dispossession
ekspulsja [eks-**pool**-syah] f. expulsion
ekstatycznie [eks-tah-**tich**-ńe] adv. ecstatically; with exaltation
ekstatyczność [eks-tah-**tich**-nośhćh] f. (youthful, etc.) ecstasy; rapture; swoon; intense exaltation
ekstatyczny [eks-tah-**tich**-ni] adj.m. ecstatic; rapturous; entranced
ekstatyzm [eks-**tah**-tizm] m. (youthful, etc.) ecstasy; rapture; swoon; intense exaltation
ekstaza [eks-**tah**-zah] f. ecstasy; rapture; trance; intense exaltation; swoon
ekstensja [eks-**ten**-syah] f. extensity
ekstensjonalny [eks-ten-syo-**nahl**-ni] adj.m. of extensity
ekstensyfikacja [eks-ten-si-fee-**kah**-tsyah] f. making more extensive
ekstensywnie [eks-ten-**siv**-ńe] adv. extensively
ekstensywność [eks-ten-**siv**-nośhćh] f. extensiveness
ekstensywny [eks-ten-**siv**-ni] adj.m. extensive; extensional; denotative
eksterier [eks-**ter**-yer] m. characteristic outward appearance
eksterioryzacja [eks-ter-yo-ri-**zah**-tsyah] f. exteriorization; externalization
eksterminacja [eks-ter-mee-**nah**-tsyah] f. extermination
eksterminacyjny [eks-ter-mee-nah-**tsiy**-ni] adj.m. of extermination; exterminatory
eksterminować [eks-ter-mee-**no**-vahćh] v. exterminate (*repeatedly*)
eksterminowanie [eks-ter-mee-no-**vah**-ńe] n. extermination (of people, etc.)
ekstern [**eks**-tern] m. candidate for an examination from outside a school
eksternista [eks-ter-**ńee**-stah] m. extramural student
eksternistycznie [eks-ter-ńee-**stich**-ńe] adv. as an extramural student
eksternistyczny [eks-ter-ńee-**stich**-ni] adj.m. of university extension
eksteroceptor [eks-te-ro-**tse**-ptor] m. exteroceptor; sense organ excited by exteroceptive stimuli
eksterytorialnie [eks-te-ri-to-**ryahl**-ńe] adv. by extraterritoriality; with exterritoriality
eksterytorialność [eks-te-ri-to-**ryahl**-nośhćh] f. extraterritoriality; exterritoriality
eksterytorialny [eks-te-ri-to-**ryahl**-ni] adj.m. extraterritorial; exterritorial
ekstra [**ek**-strah] adv. additionally; apart; separately; extremely; adj. extraordinary; exceptional; indecl. high-quality (choice) goods
ekstradować [eks-trah-**do**-vahćh] v. extradite; turn over to the jurisdiction of another country; obtain the extradition of (*repeatedly*)
ekstradycja [eks-trah-**di**-tsyah] f. extradition
ekstradycyjny [eks-trah-di-**tsiy**-ni] adj.m. of extradition; extraditable
ekstragalaktyczny [eks-trah-gah-lah-**ktich**-ni] adj.m. from outside of a galaxy
ekstrahować [eks-trah-**kho**-vahćh] v. extract (chemically); excerpt (*repeatedly*)
ekstrahowanie [eks-trah-kho-**vah**-ńe] n. extraction; extracting
ekstrakcja [eks-**trahk**-tsyah] f. extraction; pulling (of a tooth)
ekstrakcyjnie [eks-trahk-**tsiy**-ńe]

adv. extractively
ekstrakcyjny [eks-trah-**ktsiy**-ni] adj.m. of extraction; extractive
ekstraklasa [eks-trah-**klah**-sah] f. top teams; top sportsmen; world-class; first division
ekstrakt [**eks**-trahkt] m. extract; essence; (tanner's) leach; excerpt
ekstraktor [eks-**trah**-ktor] m. extractor (a dental tool)
ekstraktywnie [eks-trah-**ktiv**-ńe] adv. extractively
ekstraktywny [eks-trah-**ktiv**-ni] adj.m. extractive; capable of being extracted
ekstranowoczesny [eks-trah-no-vo-**che**-sni] adj.m. ultra-modern
ekstrapolacja [eks-trah-po-**lah**-tsyah] f. extrapolation; projection from known data into an area not known; prediction by projecting past experience
ekstrapolować [eks-trah-po-**lo**-vahćh] v. extrapolate; project from known data into an area not known; predict by projecting past experience (*repeatedly*)
ekstraspekcja [eks-trah-**spe**-ktsyah] f. external observation (of symptoms)
ekstrawagancja [eks-trah-vah-**gahn**-tsyah] f. extravagance; folly; eccentricity
ekstrawagancki [eks-trah-vah-**gahn**-tskee] adj.m. extravagant; wild; eccentric; immoderate; bizarre
ekstrawagancko [eks-trah-vah-**gahn**-tsko] adv. extravagantly; wildly; eccentrically; immoderately
ekstrawersja [eks-trah-**ver**-syah] f. extroversion; extraversion; directing attention outside the self
ekstrawersyjnie [eks-trah-ver-**siy**-ńe] adv. like an extrovert
ekstrawersyjny [eks-trah-ver-**siy**-ni] adj.m. extroversive
ekstrawersyjny typ [eks-trah-ver-**siy**-ni tip] exp.: an extrovert
ekstrawertyk [eks-trah-**ver**-tik] m. extrovert; extravert
ekstrem [**eks**-trem] m. intense degree; absolute necessity
ekstrema [eks-**tre**-mah] f. extremists; (political) radicals
ekstremalny [eks-tre-**mahl**-ni] adj.m. extreme; of outer limit
ekstremista [eks-tre-**mee**-stah] m. extremist; ultraist
ekstremistyczny [eks-tre-mee-**stich**-ni] adj.m. extremist
ekstremizm [eks-**tre**-meezm] m. extremism; radicalism
ekstremum [eks-**tre**-moom] n. (math.) extreme
ekstynkcja [eks-**tink**-tsyah] f. weakening of light by scattering and absorption
ekstyrpacja [eks-tir-**pah**-tsyah] f. extirpation; cutting out by surgery an entire organ
ekstyrpator [eks-tir-**pah**-tor] m. extirpator; grubber
ekstyrpować [eks-tir-**po**-vahćh] v. extripate; cut out an entire organ (*repeatedly*)
ekstyrpowany [eks-tir-po-**vah**-ni] adj.m. extirpative
eksudacja [ek-soo-**dah**-tsyah] f. exudation; oozing out; undergoing diffusion; abundant display (of charm, etc.)
eksudat [ek-**soo**-daht] m. exudate
eksukacja [ek-soo-**kah**-tsyah] f. drying and preserving of hygroscopic substances in a desiccator
eksykator [ek-si-**kah**-tor] m. exsiccator; desiccator
ektoblast [ek-**to**-blahst] m. ectoderm; ectoblast; epiblast; the outer layer of the blastoderm
ektoderma [ek-to-**der**-mah] f. ectoderm
ektogeniczny [ek-to-ge-**ńeech**-ni] adj.m. ectogenic
ektopasożyt [ek-to-pah-**so**-zhit] m. ectoparasite
ektopia [ek-**to**-pyah] f. ectopia
ektoplazma [ek-to-**plah**-zmah] f. ectoplasm
ektotoksyna [ek-to-tok-**si**-nah] f. bacterial toxin
ektotroficzny [ek-to-tro-**feech**-ni] adj.m. ectotrophic
ektropion [ek-**tro**-pyon] m. ectropion; eyelid condition resulting in drying of the eye

ekumena [e-koo-**me**-nah] f. area permanently inhabited and exploited by humans
ekumenicznie [e-koo-me-**ńeech**-ńe] adv. ecumenically
ekumeniczny [e-koo-me-**ńeech**-ni] adj.m. ecumenical
ekumenista [e-koo-me-**ńee**-stah] m. man propagating ecumenism
ekumenizm [e-koo-**me**-ńeezm] m. ecumenism
ekwadorski [ek-fah-**dor**-skee] adj.m. of Ecuador; Ecuadorian
ekwatorial [ek-fah-**tor**-yahl] m. telescope following daily movement of the sky
ekwidystanta [ek-fee-di-**stahn**-tah] f. equidistant line; parallel line
ekwilibrysta [ek-fee-lee-**bris**-tah] m. ropewalker; acrobat; equilibrist; tumbler; tightrope-acrobat
ekwilibrystyczny [ek-fee-lee-bri-**stich**-ni] adj.m. equilibratory
ekwilibrystyka [ek-fee-lee-**bri**-sti-kah] f. tightrope-walking; acrobatics; tumbling; tightrope-acrobatics
ekwinokcjum [ek-fee-**no**-ktsyoom] n. equinox (March 21, Sept. 23)
ekwipaż [ek-**fee**-pahsh] m. luxurious, light horse-drawn cart
ekwipolentny [ek-fee-po-**lent**-ni] adj.m. equipolent; the same in effect or signification
ekwipotencjalny [ek-fee-po-ten-**tsyahl**-ni] adj.m. equipotent; equipotential
ekwipować [ek-fee-**po**-vahćh] v. equip; fit out with; provide with (*repeatedly*)
ekwipować się [ek-fee-**po**-vahćh śhan] v. equip oneself; fit oneself out with; provide oneself with (*repeatedly*)
ekwipowanie [e-kfee-po-**vah**-ńe] n. equipping; outfitting
ekwipunek [e-kfee-**poo**-nek] m. equipment; outfit
ekwipunkowy [e-kfee-poon-**ko**-vi] adj.m. of equipment; of an outfit
ekwiwalencja [ek-fee-vah-**len**-tsyah] f. equivalency
ekwiwalent [ek-fee-**vah**-lent] m. equivalent
ekwiwalent pieniężny [ek-fee-**vah**-lent pye-**ńanzh**-ni] exp.: equivalent in money
ekwiwalentnie [ek-fee-vah-**lent**-ńe] adv. equivalently
ekwiwalentny [ek-fee-vah-**lent**-ni] adj.m. equivalent
ekwiwok [e-**kfee**-vok] m. play on identically sounding words; word of double meaning; quibble
ekwiwokacja [e-kfee-vo-**kah**-tsyah] f. equivocation
elaborat [e-lah-**bo**-raht] m. study; elaborate essay; dissertation; laborious document
elajoplast [e-lah-**yo**-plahst] m. elaioplast; oil-forming plant
elajosom [e-lah-**yo**-som] m. elaiosome; oil-secreting plant
elana [e-**lah**-nah] f. Polish polyester fabric
elanobawełna [e-lah-no-bah-**vew**-nah] f. polyester-cotton fabric
elanobawełniany [e-lah-no-bah-vew-**ńah**-ni] adj.m. of polyester-cotton fabric
elanolen [e-lah-**no**-len] m. polyester-flax fabric
elanolniany [e-lah-no-**lńah**-ni] adj.m. of polyester-flax fabric
elanowy [e-lah-**no**-vi] adj.m. of Polish polyester
elastik [e-**lah**-steek] m. wrinkle-resistant plastic fabric
elastil [e-**lah**-steel] m. variety of knitted artificial fabric
elastilowy [e-lah-stee-**lo**-vi] adj.m. of a variety of knitted artificial fabric
elastomer [e-lah-**sto**-mer] m. elastomer
elastomerowy [e-lah-sto-me-**ro**-vi] adj.m. elastomeric
elastooptyczny [e-lah-sto-op-**tich**-ni] adj.m. of an optical stress analysis in translucent materials
elastooptyka [e-lah-sto-**op**-ti-kah] f. optical stress analysis in translucent materials
elastoplastyczny [e-lah-sto-plahs-**tich**-ni] adj.m. undergoing plastic flow; subject to the plastic flow
elastor [e-**lah**-stor] m. variety of knitted fabric, of Polish production
elastorowy [e-lah-sto-**ro**-vi] adj.m. of

a variety of knitted fabric, of Polish production
elastycznie [e-lah-**stich**-ńe] adv. elastically; with resilience; flexibly
elastyczność [e-lah-**stich**-nośhćh] f. elasticity; resilience; flexibility; buoyancy
elastyczny [e-lah-**stich**-ni] adj.m. elastic; resilient; flexible; stretchy; springy; buoyant
elastyki [e-lah-**sti**-kee] pl. tight elastic pants or shorts
elastyl [e-**lah**-stil] m. variety of knitted artificial fabric
elastylowy [e-lah-sti-**lo**-vi] adj.m. of a variety of knitted artificial fabric
elastyna [e-lah-**sti**-nah] f. elastin
eldorado [el-do-**rah**-do] n. El Dorado; a place of fabulous wealth, abundance, or opportunity
eleacki [e-le-**ah**-tskee] adj.m. Eleatic
elear [e-**le**-ahr] m. skirmisher; free lance
eleata [e-le-**ah**-tah] m. Eleatic philosopher
eleatyzm [e-le-**ah**-tizm] m. Eleaticism
elegancik [e-le-**gahn**-ćheek] m. dandy; swell; stylish man; dude
elegancja [e-le-**gahn**-tsyah] f. elegance; fashion; style
elegancki [e-le-**gahn**-tskee] adj.m. elegant; smart; fashionable; dapper; chic; swell; dudish
elegancko [e-le-**gahn**-tsko] adv. with elegance; smartly; fashionably; with style; dudishly
elegant [e-**le**-gahnt] m. dandy; dude; man of fashion
elegantka [e-le-**gahn**-tkah]] f. smartly dressed lady; woman of fashion
elegantować się [e-le-gahn-**to**-vahćh śhan] v. smarten oneself; prank oneself out; slang: jazz oneself up (*repeatedly*)
elegia [e-**le**-gyah] f. elegy; lament
elegiacki [e-le-**gyah**-tskee] adj.m. elegiac; elegiacal
elegijność [e-le-**geey**-nośhćh] f. elegiac quality; elegiac character
elegijny [e-le-**geey**-ni] adj.m. elegiac
elekcja [e-**lek**-tsyah] f. general election in Poland (1569-1793)
elekcyjność [e-lek-**tsiy**-nośhćh] f. eligibility; electability
elekcyjny [e-lek-**tsiy**-ni] adj.m. elective
elekt [**e**-lekt] m. the elect
elektor [e-**lek**-tor] m. elector
elektoralny [e-lek-to-**rahl**-ni] adj.m. electoral
elektorat [e-lek-**to**-raht] m. power of an elector; territory ruled by an elector; dignity of an elector
elektorski [e-lek-**tor**-skee] adj.m. of elector; electoral
elektorstwo [e-lek-**tor**-stfo] n. power of an elector; territory ruled by an elector; dignity of an elector
elektro- [e-**lek**-tro] prefix: electro-
elektroakustyczny [e-lek-tro-ah-koos-**tich**-ni] adj.m. electroacoustic
elektroakustyk [e-lek-tro-ah-**koo**-stik] m. specialist in electroacoustics
elektroakustyka [e-lek-tro-ah-**koo**-sti-kah] f. electroacoustics
elektroanaliza [e-lek-tro-ah-**nah**-lee-zah] f. electroanalysis
elektrobiologia [e-lek-tro-byo-**lo**-gyah] f. electrobiology
elektrobodziec [e-lek-tro-**bo**-dźhets] m. electro-motor; electromotive force
elektrobodźczy [e-lek-tro-**boćh**-chi] adj.m. electromotive
elektrobus [e-lek-**tro**-boos] m. electro-bus; an electric streetcar
elektrochemia [e-lek-tro-**khe**-myah] f. electrochemistry
elektrochemiczny [e-lek-tro-khe-**meech**-ni] adj.m. electrochemical
elektrochirurgia [e-lek-tro-khee-**roor**-gyah] f. electrosurgery; surgery by means of diathermy
elektrociepłownia [e-lek-tro-ćhep-**wov**-ńah] f. steam plant
elektrociepłowniczy [e-lek-tro-ćhep-wov-**ńee**-chi] adj.m. of a steam plant
elektrociepłownik [e-lek-tro-ćhep-**wov**-ńeek] m. steam plant worker; steam plant specialist
elektroda [e-lek-**tro**-dah] f. electrode
elektrodiagnostyka [e-lek-tro-dyah-**gno**-sti-kah] f. diagnostics using galvanic and faradic current
elektrodializa [e-lek-tro-dyah-**lee**-zah] f. electrodialysis

elektrododatni [e-lek-tro-do-**daht**-ńee] adj.m. electropositive
elektrododatniość [e-lek-tro-do-**daht**-ńośhćh] f. electropositive state
elektrodowy [e-lek-tro-**do**-vi] adj.m. electrode-; electrode (furnace)
elektrodruk [e-le-**ktro**-drook] m. xerography
elektrodynamiczny [e-lek-tro-di-nah-**meech**-ni] adj.m. electrodynamic
elektrodynamika [e-lek-tro-di-**nah**-mee-kah] f. electrodynamics
elektrodynamometr [e-lek-tro-di-nah-**mo**-metr] m. electrodynamometer
elektroencefalograf [e-lek-tro-en-tse-fah-**lo**-grahf] m. an apparatus for detecting and recording brain waves; electroencephalograph
elektroencefalografia [e-lek-tro-en-tse-fah-lo-**grah**-fyah] f. electroencephalography
elektroencefalograficzny [e-lek-tro-en-tse-fah-lo-grah-**feech**-ni] adj.m. electroencephalographic
elektroencefalogram [e-lek-tro-en-tse-fah-**lo**-grahm] m. electroencephalogram (record of brain waves)
elektroenergetyczny [e-lek-tro-e-ner-ge-**tich**-ni] adj.m. of industrial production of electricity
elektroenergetyka [e-lek-tro-e-ner-**ge**-ti-kah] f. industrial production of electricity
elektroerozja [e-lek-tro-e-**ro**-zyah] f. electric erosion
elektroerozyjny [e-lek-tro-e-ro-**ziy**-ni] adj.m. of electric erosion
elektrofiltr [e-lek-**tro**-feeltr] m. electrical filter
elektrofizjolog [e-lek-tro-fee-**zyo**-log] m. electrophysiologist
elektrofizjologia [e-lek-tro-fee-zyo-**lo**-gyah] f. electrophysiology
elektrofizjologiczny [e-lek-tro-fee-zyo-lo-**geech**-ni] adj.m. electrophysiological; electrophysiologic
elektrofon [e-lek-**tro**-fon] m. an electric musical instrument (guitar, piano, etc.)
elektrofonia [e-lek-tro-**fo**-ńyah] f. electroacoustics
elektrofor [e-lek-**tro**-for] m. electrophorus
elektroforeza [e-lek-tro-fo-**re**-zah] f. electrophoresis
elektrofotografia [e-lek-tro-fo-to-**grah**-fyah] f. electrophotography; xerography
elektrograf [e-lek-**tro**-grahf] m. device for making of electrograms
elektrografia [e-lek-tro-**grah**-fyah] f. the making of electrograms; electrography
elektroindukcja [e-lek-tro-een-**doo**-ktsyah] f. electrical induction by a field of force
elektroiskrowy [e-lek-tro-ee-**skro**-vi] adj.m. using electric erosion for cutting of metal
elektroizolacyjny [e-lek-tro-ee-zo-lah-**tsiy**-ni] adj.m. insulating electrically; nonconducting (materials); used for insulation
elektrokardiograf [e-lek-tro-kahr-**dyo**-grahf] m. electrocardiograph
elektrokardiografia [e-lek-tro-kahr-dyo-**grah**-fyah] f. electrocardiography
elektrokardiograficzny [e-lek-tro-kahr-dyo-grah-**feech**-ni] adj.m. electrocardiographic
elektrokardiogram [e-lek-tro-kahr-**dyo**-grahm] m. electrocardiogram
elektrokaustyka [e-lek-tro-**kahw**-sti-kah] f. a type of electrosurgery
elektrokauter [e-lek-tro-**kahw**-ter] m. electrosurgical instrument
elektrokinetyczny [e-lek-tro-kee-ne-**tich**-ni] adj.m. electrokinetic (movement of electricity)
elektrokinetyka [e-lek-tro-kee-**ne**-ti-kah] f. electrokinetics (study of movement of electricity)
elektrokoagulacja [e-lek-tro-ko-ah-goo-**lah**-tsyah] f. electrical coagulation
elektrokorund [e-lek-tro-**ko**-roont] m. synthetic corundum
elektrolit [e-lek-**tro**-leet] m. electrolyte
elektrolitowy [e-lek-tro-lee-**to**-vi] adj.m. electrolytic
elektrolitycznie [e-lek-tro-lee-**tich**-ńe] adv. electrolytically
elektrolityczny [e-lek-tro-lee-**tich**-ni]

adj.m. electrolytic
elektroliza [e-lek-tro-**lee**-zah] f. electrolysis
elektrolizer [e-lek-tro-**lee**-zer] m. electrolyzer; cell
elektrolizować [e-lek-tro-lee-**zo**-vahćh] v. electrolyze (*repeatedly*)
elektrolizowanie [e-lek-tro-lee-zo-**vah**-ńe] n. electrolyzing
elektroluks [e-lek-**tro**-looks] m. vacuum cleaner; carpet-cleaner
elektroluminescencja [e-lek-tro-loo-mee-ne-**stsen**-tsyah] f. electroluminescence
elektromagnes [e-lek-tro-**mah**-gnes] m. electromagnet
elektromagnetyczny [e-lek-tro-mah-gne-**tich**-ni] adj.m. electromagnetic
elektromagnetyzm [e-lek-tro-mah-**gne**-tizm] m. electromagnetism
elektromaszynowy [e-lek-tro-mah-shi-**no**-vi] adj.m. of electrical machinery
elektromechaniczny [e-lek-tro-me-khah-**ńeech**-ni] adj.m. electromechanical
elektromechanik [e-lek-tro-me-**khah**-ńeek] m. specialist in electromechanics
elektromechanika [e-lek-tro-me-**khah**-ńee-kah] f. electromechanics
elekromedycyna [e-lek-tro-me-di-**tsi**-nah] f. the use of electric current for medical purposes
elekromedyczny [e-lek-tro-me-**dich**-ni] adj.m. of the use of electric current for medical purposes
elekrometalurgia [e-lek-tro-me-tah-**loor**-gyah] f. electrometallurgy
elektrometeor [e-lek-tro-me-**te**-or] m. electric meteor; lightning
elektrometr [e-lek-**tro**-metr] m. electrometer
elektrometria [e-lek-tro-**me**-tryah] f. electrometry
elektrometryczny [e-lek-tro-me-**trich**-ni] adj.m. electrometric
elektromiograf [e-lek-tro-**myo**-grahf] m. electromyograph
elektromiografia [e-lek-tro-myo-**grah**-fyah] f. electromyography
elektromiograficznie [e-lek-tro-myo-grah-**feech**-ńe] adv. electromyographically
elektromiograficzny [e-lek-tro-myo-grah-**feech**-ni] adj.m. electromyographic; electromyographical
elektromiogram [e-lek-tro-**myo**-grahm] m. electromyogram; electrogram of bioelectric potential of working muscles
elektromobil [e-lek-tro-**mo**-beel] m. electric car
elektromonter [e-lek-tro-**mon**-ter] m. electrician; installer
elektromonterka [e-lek-tro-mon-**ter**-kah] f. woman electrician; work of electrician; electrician's trade
elektromotor [e-lek-tro-**mo**-tor] m. electric motor
elektromotorowiec [e-lek-tro-mo-to-**ro**-vyets] m. diesel-electric ship (with engine driving a dynamo used for electric propulsion)
elektromotoryczny [e-lek-tro-mo-to-**rich**-ni] adj.m. electromotive
elektron [e-**lek**-tron] m. electron
elektronegatywność [e-lek-tro-ne-gah-**tiv**-nośhćh] f. electronegativity
elektronegatywny [e-lek-tro-ne-gah-**tiv**-ni] adj.m. electronegative
elektroneurograf [e-lek-tro-new-**ro**-grahf] m. device for graphic plotting of bioelectricity of nerves
elektronicznie [e-lek-tro-**ńeech**-ńe] adv. electronically
elektroniczny [e-lek-tro-**ńeech**-ni] adj.m. electronic
elektronik [e-lek-**tro**-ńeek] m. electronics specialist
elektronika [e-lek-**tro**-ńee-kah] f. electronics
elektronizacja [e-lek-tro-ńee-**zah**-tsyah] f. application of electronics; computerization
elektronografia [e-lek-tro-no-**grah**-fyah] f. study based on electronic diffraction
elektronoluminescencja [e-lek-tro-no-loo-mee-ne-**stsen**-tsyah] f. electroluminescence
elekronowolt [e-lek-tro-**no**-volt] m. electron-volt; eV; e.v.
elektronowy [e-lek-tro-**no**-vi] adj.m.

electronic; electron
elektronówka [e-lek-tro-**noof**-kah] f. electron tube; electron valve
elektrooptyka [e-lek-tro-**op**-ti-kah] f. electron optics
elektroosmotyczny [e-lek-tro-os-mo-**tich**-ni] adj.m. electroosmotic
elektroosmoza [e-lek-tro-os-**mo**-zah] f. electroosmosis; electroosmose
elekropetryfikacja [e-lek-tro-pe-tri-fee-**kah**-tsyah] f. use of an electric field for hardening of ground (first used in Poland)
elektrorafinacja [e-lek-tro-rah-fee-**nah**-tsyah] f. electrolytic purification of metals
elektroskalpel [e-lek-tro-**skahl**-pel] m. electrical knife used in surgery
elektroskop [e-lek-**tro**-skop] m. electroscope
elektrostal [e-lek-**tro**-stahl] f. electrosteel; electric steel
elektrostatycznie [e-lek-tro-stah-**tich**-ńe] adv. electrostatically
elektrostatyczny [e-lek-tro-stah-**tich**-ni] adj.m. electrostatic
elektrostatyka [e-lek-tro-**stah**-ti-kah] f. electrostatics
elektrostrykcja [e-lek-tro-**stri**-ktsyah] f. electrostriction
elektrotaksja [e-lek-tro-**tah**-ksyah] f. electrotaxis (of organisms in presence of electric current)
elektrotechniczny [e-lek-tro-tekh-**ńeech**-ni] adj.m. electrotechnical
słownik elektrotechniczny [**swov**-ńeek e-lek-tro-tekh-**ńeech**-ni] exp.: dictionary of electrical engineering
elektrotechnik [e-lek-tro-**tekh**-ńeek] m. electrician; electrotechnician
elektrotechnika [e-lek-tro-**tekh**-ńee-kah] f. electrical engineering
elektroterapia [e-lek-tro-te-**rah**-pyah] f. electrotherapy
elektrotermia [e-lek-tro-**ter**-myah] f. electrothermics
elektrotermiczny [e-lek-tro-ter-**meech**-ni] adj.m. electrothermic
elektrotermometria [e-lek-tro-ter-mo-**metr**-yah] f. technology of electrical thermostats
elektrotinta [e-lek-tro-**teen**-tah] f. electrical engraving
elektrotomia [e-lek-tro-**to**-myah] f. surgery with an electrical instrument
elektrotrakcja [e-lek-tro-**trahk**-tsyah] f. electric traction
elektrotyp [e-lek-**tro**-tip] m. electrotype (print)
elektrotypia [e-lek-tro-**ti**-pyah] f. the making of electrotype print
elektroujemność [e-lek-tro-oo-**yem**-nośhćh] f. electronegativity
elektroujemny [e-lek-tro-oo-**yem**-ni] adj.m. electronegative
elektrowiert [e-lek-**tro**-vyert] m. down-hole electric drill
elektrownia [e-lek-**trov**-ńah] f. power station; power plant; powerhouse; generating station
elektrowozownia [e-lek-tro-vo-**zov**-ńah] f. shed for electric locomotives
elektrowóz [e-lek-**tro**-voos] m. electric locomotive
elektrowózek [e-lek-tro-**voo**-zek] m. electric cart
elektrowstrząs [e-lek-**tro**-fstshowns] m. electric shock
elektrum [e-**lek**-troom] n. electrum (mineral)
elektrycznie [e-lek-**trich**-ńe] adv. electrically
elektryczność [e-lek-**trich**-nośhćh] f. electricity; electric power; electric current; electric light
elektryczny [e-lek-**trich**-ni] adj.m. electric (light, etc.); electrical (drainage, etc.)
elektryfikacja [e-lek-tri-fee-**kah**-tsyah] f. electrification
elektryfikacyjny [e-lek-tri-fee-kah-**tsiy**-ni] adj.m. electrification (program, etc.)
elektryfikować [e-lek-tri-fee-**ko**-vahćh] v. electrify (*repeatedly*)
elektryfikowanie [e-lek-tri-fee-ko-**vah**-ńe] n. electrification
elektryk [e-**lek**-trik] m. electrician
inżynier elektryk [een-**zhi**-ńer e-**lek**-trik] exp.: electrical engineer
elektryka [e-**lek**-tri-kah] f. electricity; electric current; electric light
elektrykarz [e-lek-**tri**-kahsh] m. mine electrician
elektryzacja [e-lek-tri-**zah**-tsyah] f.

electrification; diathermy
elektryzator [e-lek-tri-**zah**-tor] m. electric fence
elektryzować [e-lek-tri-**zo**-vahćh] v. electrify; galvanize; thrill; set on edge with interest or excitement; set agog (*repeatedly*)
elektryzować się [e-lek-tri-**zo**-vahćh śhan] v. become electrified; become galvanized; become thrilled; set oneself on edge with interest or excitement (*repeatedly*)
elektryzowanie [e-lek-tri-zo-**vah**-ńe] n. electrification; diathermy; galvanization; colloq: thrilling
elektryzowanie się [e-lek-tri-zo-**vah**-ńe śhan] n. becoming electrified
elektryzująco [e-lek-tri-zoo-**yown**-tso] adv. thrillingly
podziałać elektryzująco [po-**dźhah**-wahćh e-lek-tri-zoo-**yown**-tso] exp.: to thrill; to galvanize (an audience, etc.)
element [e-**le**-ment] m. element
elementarność [e-le-men-**tahr**-nośhćh] f. elementary character; fundamental nature (of an assertion, etc.)
elementarnie [e-le-men-**tahr**-ńe] adv. elementarily; rudimentarily
elementarny [e-le-men-**tahr**-ni] adj.m. elementary; rudimental; rudimentary; fundamental; primary
elementarne pojęcie [e-le-men-**tahr**-ne po-**yan**-ćhe] exp.: a smattering of (a subject, etc.)
elementarz [e-le-**men**-tahsh] m. primer; ABC; spelling book
elementarzowy [e-le-men-tah-**zho**-vi] adj.m. of primer; (studies, etc.) of spelling book
elemi [e-**le**-mee] indecl.: elemi; a fragrant oleoresin
elenium [e-**le**-ńyoom] n. tranquilizer (used against fear and stress)
eleometr [e-le-**o**-metr] m. oleometer; elaeometer
eleuterie [e-lew-**ter**-ye] pl. Eleutheria in honor of Zeus and Greek victory over Persia in 479 B.C.
elew [e-lef] m. student at a military academy
elewacja [e-le-**vah**-tsyah] f. elevation
elewacja frontowa [e-le-**vah**-tsyah fron-**to**-vah] exp.: front elevation; front view
elewacyjny [e-le-vah-**tsiy**-ni] adj.m. of elevation; of the front view
elewator [e-le-**vah**-tor] m. (grain) elevator; hoist; hoister
elewatorowy [e-le-vah-to-**ro**-vi] adj.m. elevator (shaft); hoist (hook, etc.); hoister; of a hoist
elewon [e-**le**-von] m. elevon
elf [elf] m. elf; elfin; sprite; a tiny, often mischievous fairy
eliksir [e-**leek**-seer] m. elixir; medieval alcoholic medicine used to prolong life indefinitely; cure-all
eliksir młodości [e-**leek**-seer mwo-**do**-śhćhee] exp.: elixir of (eternal) youth
eliksir życia [e-**leek**-seer **zhi**-ćhah] exp.: life-prolonging elixir
eliminacja [e-lee-mee-**nah**-tsyah] f. elimination; qualifying selection; test match; cup-tie; selection race
eliminacyjny [e-lee-mee-nah-**tsiy**-ni] adj.m. eliminating; eliminatory
zawody eliminacyjne [zah-**vo**-di e-lee-mee-nah-**tsiy**-ne] exp.: trial heats; test match
eliminator [e-lee-mee-**nah**-tor] m. anti-jamming radio device
eliminować [e-lee-mee-**no**-vahćh] v. eliminate; get rid of; remove; omit; excrete; leave out (*repeatedly*)
eliminowanie [e-lee-mee-no-**vah**-ńe] n. elimination
elinwar [e-**leen**-vahr] m. Elinvar (alloy)
elipsa [e-**leep**-sah] f. ellipse; ellipsis
elipsograf [e-leep-**so**-grahf] m. drafting instrument for drawing ellipses
elipsoida [e-leep-**soy**-dah] f. ellipsoid
elipsoidalny [e-leep-so-ee-**dahl**-ni] adj.m. ellipsoidal; ellipsoid
elipsowaty [e-leep-so-**vah**-ti] adj.m. elliptic
eliptycznie [e-leep-**tich**-ńe] adv. elliptically
eliptyczność [e-leep-**tich**-nośhćh] f. ellipticity

eliptyczny [e-leep-**tich**-ni] adj.m. elliptical (projection, phrase, etc.); elliptic (arch, curve, etc.)
elita [e-**lee**-tah] f. elite; the best; the most powerful; the flower (of the army, etc.); the pick (of the nation, etc.); the choice part
elitarność [e-lee-**tahr**-nośhćh] f. exclusivity; being a part of an elite
elitarny [e-lee-**tahr**-ni] adj.m. exclusive; selective; destined for the privileged
elitarysta [e-lee-tah-**ris**-tah] m. (an) elitist
elitarystyczny [e-lee-tah-ris-**tich**-ni] adj.m. elitist
elitaryzm [e-lee-**tah**-rizm] m. exclusivity; government by an elite; control by an elite
elizejski [e-lee-**zey**-skee] adj.m. Elysian
elizja [e-**lee**-zyah] f. elysion
elki [**el**-kee] pl. fur coat of skunk furs; skunk furs
Elizjum [e-**lee**-zyoom] n. Elisium
eloksalacja [e-lo-ksah-**lah**-tsyah] f. anodization
eloksalować [e-lo-ksah-**lo**-vahćh] v. anodize (*repeatedly*)
eloksalowanie [e-lo-ksah-lo-**vah**-ńe] n. anodization
elokwencja [e-lo-**kfen**-tsyah] f. eloquence; oratory
elokwentnie [e-lo-**kfent**-ńe] adv. with eloquence
elokwentny [e-lo-**kfent**-ni] adj.m. eloquent
elongacja [e-lon-**gah**-tsyah] f. elongation
elukubracja [e-loo-koo-**brah**-tsyah] f. lucubration; meditation; laborious study; pretentious expression
eluwialny [e-loo-**vyahl**-ni] adj.m. eluvial
eluwium [e-**loo**-vyoom] n. eluvium
elzewir [el-**ze**-veer] m. Elzevir font
elżbietanka [el-zhbye-**tahn**-kah] f. Elizabethan nun
elżbietański [el-zhbye-**tahń**-skee] adj.m. Elizabethan (style, etc.)
emablować [e-mah-**blo**-vahćh] v. curry favor with; pay court to; shower attentions upon (*repeatedly*)
emablowanie [e-mah-blo-**vah**-ńe] n. attentions (paid to a woman)
emalia [e-**mah**-lyah] f. enamel; glaze; enamel ware; lacquer; lacker
emalier [e-**mah**-lyer] m. enameler
emaliernia [e-mahl-**yer**-ńah] f. enameler's shop
emaliernik [e-mahl-**yer**-ńeek] m. enameler; enamelist
emalierski [e-mahl-**yer**-skee] adj.m. of an enameler
emalierstwo [e-mahl-**yer**-stfo] n. art of an enameler
emaliować [e-mah-**lyo**-vahćh] v. enamel; glaze (*repeatedly*)
emaliowanie [e-mah-lyo-**vah**-ńe] n. enamelling; glazing
emaliowy [e-mah-**lyo**-vi] adj.m. enamel (ware, etc.)
eman [**e**-mahn] m. unit of rate of radioactivity
emanacja [e-mah-**nah**-tsyah] f. emanation; efflux; effluence
emanatyzm [e-mah-**nah**-tizm] m. emanationism; creation by emanation
emancypacja [e-mahn-tsi-**pah**-tsyah] f. emancipation; manumission (of a slave); the act of emancipating; the process of emancipating
emancypacyjny [e-mahn-tsi-pah-**tsiy**-ni] adj.m. of emancipation
emancypantka [e-mahn-tsi-**pahn**-tkah] f. suffragette; new woman; advocate of women's rights
emancypować [e-mahn-tsi-**po**-vahćh] v. emancipate; manumit (a slave) (*repeatedly*)
emancypować się [e-mahn-tsi-**po**-vahćh śhan] v. free oneself from control; become independent (*repeatedly*)
emancypowanie [e-mahn-tsi-po-**vah**-ńe] n. emancipation
emancypowanie się [e-mahn-tsi-po-**vah**-ńe śhan] n. freeing oneself from control; becoming independent
emanować [e-mah-**no**-vahćh] v. emanate; emit; diffuse; radiate (*repeatedly*)
emanowanie [e-mah-no-**vah**-ńe] n.

emanation; diffusion
embargo [em-**bahr**-go] n. embargo
nałożyć embargo [nah-**wo**-zhićh em-**bahr**-go] exp.: to impose an embargo (on); to put under an embargo
emblemacik [em-ble-**mah**-ćheek] m. small emblem
emblemat [em-**ble**-maht] m. emblem; visible symbol; sign; badge
emblematycznie [em-ble-mah-**tich**-ńe] adv. emblematically
emblematyczny [em-ble-mah-**tich**-ni] adj.m. emblematic; emblematical; symbolic
embolia [em-**bo**-lyah] f. embolia
embriogenetyczny [em-bryo-ge-ne-**tich**-ni] adj.m. embryogenetic
embriogeneza [em-bryo-ge-**ne**-zah] f. embryogenesis
embriogenia [em-bryo-**ge**-ńyah] f. embryogeny; embryogenesis
embriolog [em-**bryo**-log] m. embryologist
embriologia [em-bryo-**lo**-gyah] f. embryology
embriologiczny [em-bryo-lo-**geech**-ni] adj.m. embryological
embrion [**em**-bryon] m. embryo
embrionalny [em-bryo-**nahl**-ni] adj.m. embryonic
w stanie embrionalnym [f **stah**-ńe em-bryo-**nahl**-nim] exp.: in embryo
embriotomia [em-bryo-**to**-myah] f. embryotomy
emendacja [e-men-**dah**-tsyah] f. emendation (of texts of a deceased author by the publisher)
ementaler [e-men-**tah**-ler] m. Emmenthaler cheese
ementalski [e-men-**tahl**-skee] adj.m. Emmenthaler (cheese)
emergencja [e-mer-**gen**-tsyah] f. emergent evolution (theory)
emergentny [e-mer-**gen**-tni] adj.m. of an emergent evolution (theory)
emergentyzm [e-mer-**gen**-tizm] m. emergent evolution theory
emerycki [e-me-**rits**-kee] adj.m. of a retired person; pensioner's; of a pensionary
emeryt [e-**me**-rit] m. retired person; pensioner; pensionary
on jest emerytem [on yest e-me-**ri**-tem] exp.: he has retired
emerytalny [e-me-ri-**tahl**-ni] adj.m. of (a) pension; pensions'
fundusz emerytalny [**foon**-doosh e-me-ri-**tahl**-ni] exp.: pension fund
wiek emerytalny [vyek e-me-ri-**tahl**-ni] exp.: retirement age
emerytka [e-me-**rit**-kah] f. retired woman; woman pensioner
emerytować [e-me-ri-**to**-vahćh] v. pension off; retire (an employee) (*repeatedly*)
emerytowanie [e-me-ri-to-**vah**-ńe] n. pensioning off; retiring
emerytowany [e-me-ri-to-**vah**-ni] adj.m. retired; pensioned
emerytura [e-me-ri-**too**-rah] f. retiring pension; retired pay; old age pension
przejście na emeryturę [pshey-śhćhe nah e-me-ri-**too**-ran] exp.: retirement; taking one's retirement
emetyk [e-**me**-tik] m. emetic; an agent that induces vomiting
emfatycznie [em-fah-**tich**-ńe] adv. emphatically; with emphasis
emfatyczny [em-fah-**tich**-ni] adj.m. emphatic
emfaza [em-**fah**-zah] f. emphasis; bombast; force of expression
emfiteuza [em-fee-**tew**-zah] f. emphyteusis
emigracja [e-mee-**grah**-tsyah] f. emigration; exile; emigrants
emigracyjny [e-mee-grah-**tsiy**-ni] adj.m. of emigration; emigration (office, etc.)
rząd emigracyjny [zhownt e-mee-grah-**tsiy**-ni] exp.: government in exile
emigrancki [e-mee-**grahn**-tskee] adj.m. emigrant's (tribulations, etc.)
emigrant [e-**mee**-grahnt] m. emigrant; an emigrant; an exile
emigrantka [e-mee-**grahn**-tkah] f. (woman) emigrant; an emigrant; an exile
emigrować [e-mee-**gro**-vahćh] v. emigrate (*repeatedly*)
emigrowanie [e-mee-gro-**vah**-ńe] n.

emigration
emigrus [e-**mee**-groos] m. slang: emigrant
eminencja [e-mee-**nen**-tsyah] f. eminence
szara eminencja [**shah**-rah e-mee-**nen**-tsyah] exp.: the power behind the throne
eminentny [e-mee-**nen**-tni] adj.m. eminent; conspicuous; prominent; leading; outstanding; famous
emir [**e**-meer] m. emir
emirat [e-**mee**-raht] m. emirate
emisariusz [e-mee-**sah**-ryoosh] m. emissary
emisariuszka [e-mee-sah-**ryoosh**-kah] f. (female) emissary
emisarka [e-mee-**sahr**-kah] f. emissary's mission
emisja [e-**mee**-syah] f. emission; issuing (of bank notes, etc.)
emisyjny [e-mee-**siy**-ni] adj.m. of emission; of issue
bank emisyjny [bahnk e-mee-**siy**-ni] exp.: bank of issue
kurs emisyjny [koors e-mee-**siy**-ni] exp.: issue price; rate of issue
widmo emisyjne [**veed**-mo e-mee-**siy**-ne] exp.: emission spectrum
emiter [e-**mee**-ter] m. emitting substance
emitować [e-mee-**to**-vahćh] v. emit (rays, light, heat, etc.); issue (of bank notes, etc.); broadcast (*repeatedly*)
emitowanie [e-mee-to-**vah**-ńe] n. emission
emitron [e-**mee**-tron] m. television picture tube
emocja [e-**mo**-tsyah] f. thrill; excitement; agitation; flutter; feeling
emocjonalista [e-mo-tsyo-nah-**lee**-stah] m. emotionalist
emocjonalistyczny [e-mo-tsyo-nah-lees-**tich**-ni] adj.m. emotionalistic
emocjonalizm [e-mo-tsyo-**nah**-leezm] m. emotionalism
emocjonalnie [e-mo-tsyo-**nahl**-ńe] adv. emotionally
emocjonalność [e-mo-tsyo-**nahl**-nośhćh] f. emotionality; sensibility
emocjonalny [e-mo-tsyo-**nahl**-ni] adj.m. emotional; affectionate; sensitive; intense
emocjonować [e-mo-tsyo-**no**-vahćh] v. thrill; excite; agitate; flutter (*repeatedly*)
emocjonować się [e-mo-tsyo-**no**-vahćh śhan] v. be thrilled; get excited; be agitated; flutter; be in a flutter; become excited (*repeatedly*)
emocjonowanie [e-mo-tsyo-no-**vah**-ńe] n. thrilling; excitement; agitation
emocjonowanie się [e-mo-tsyo-no-**vah**-ńe śhan] n. being thrilled; getting excited
emocjonujący [e-mo-tsyo-noo-**yown**-tsi] adj.m. thrilling; exciting; tense
nie emocjonujący [ńe e-mo-tsyo-noo-**yown**-tsi] exp.: not thrilling; unexciting
emocyjnie [e-mo-**tsiy**-ńe] adv. emotionally (indifferent words, indifferent actions, etc.)
emocyjny [e-mo-**tsiy**-ni] adj.m. emotional
emotywny [e-mo-**tiv**-ni] adj.m. emotive (use of language, etc.); appealing to emotions; expressing emotions
empatia [em-**pah**-tyah] f. empathy; sympathy
empi [em-**pee**] n. submachine gun
empire [em-**peer**] m. Empire style
empirejski [em-pee-**rey**-skee] adj.m. empyrean; empyreal
empireum [em-pee-**re**-oom] n. empyrean
empiria [em-**pee**-ryah] f. experience; knowing by senses; empiricism
empiriokrytycyzm [em-pee-ryo-kri-**ti**-tsizm] m. positivistic philosophy trying to reconcile idealism with materialism
empiriokrytyczny [em-pee-ryo-kri-**tich**-ni] adj.m. of the positivistic philosophy (trying to reconcile idealism with materialism)
empiriokrytyk [em-pee-ryo-**kri**-tik] m. follower of the positivistic philosophy (trying to reconcile idealism with materialism)
empirowy [em-pee-**ro**-vi] adj.m. Empire (style of furniture, etc.)

empirycznie [em-pee-**rich**-ńe] adv. empirically
empiryczność [em-pee-**rich**-nośhćh] f. relying on experience alone; empiricism; logical positivism
empiryczny [em-pee-**rich**-ni] adj.m. empirical
empiryk [em-**pee**-rik] m. an empiric; one who relies on practical experience; empiricist
empirysta [em-pee-**ri**-stah] m. an empiric; one who relies on practical experience; empiricist
empiryzm [em-**pee**-rizm] m. empiricism; logical positivism
emploi [ahmp-**loo**-ah] n. actor's part in which he specialized for a long time; actor's specialty
empora [em-**po**-rah] f. gallery
emporium [em-**po**-ryoom] n. emporium; mart
emporowy [em-po-**ro**-vi] adj.m. having galleries; gallery (yard, patio, etc.)
emski [**em**-skee] adj.m. of Ems
emu [e-moo] m. emu (an Australian swift-running bird)
emulacja [e-moo-**lah**-tsyah] f. rivalry; competition; imitation (hist.)
emulgator [e-mool-**gah**-tor] m. emulgent; emulsifier
emulgować [e-mool-**go**-vahćh] v. emulsify (*repeatedly*)
emulgować się [e-mool-**go**-vahćh śh<u>an</u>] v. become emulsified (*repeatedly*)
emulgowanie [e-mool-go-**vah**-ńe] n. emulsification
emulgowanie się [e-mool-go-**vah**-ńe śh<u>an</u>] n. becoming emulsified
emulsja [e-**mool**-syah] f. emulsion
emulsyjny [e-mool-**siy**-ni] adj.m. emulsive
enargit [e-**nahr**-geet] m. enargite (mineral)
encefalografia [en-tse-fah-lo-**grah**-fyah] f. encephalography
encefalograficzny [en-tse-fah-lo-grah-**eech**-ni] adj.m. encephalographic
encefalogram [en-tse-fah-**lo**-grahm] m. encephalogram; an X-ray picture of the brain made by encephalography
encefalopatia [en-tse-fah-lo-**pah**-tyah] f. encephalopathy
encykliczny [en-tsi-**kleech**-ni] adj.m. encyclical; general
encyklika [en-**tsi**-klee-kah] f. encyclical
encyklopedia [en-tsi-klo-**pe**-dyah] f. encyclopedia
chodząca encyklopedia [kho-dz<u>own</u>-tsah en-tsi-klo-**pe**-dyah] exp.: walking encyclopedia
encyklopedyczność [en-tsi-klo-pe-**dich**-nośhćh] f. encyclopedic quality (of memory, etc.); encyclopedism
encyklopedyczny [en-tsi-klo-pe-**dich**-ni] adj.m. encyclopedic
encyklopedysta [en-tsi-klo-pe-**dis**-tah] m. encyclopedist
encyklopedyści [en-tsi-klo-pe-**diśh**-ćhee] pl. (French) encyclopedists
encyklopedyzm [en-tsi-klo-**pe**-dizm] m. encyclopedism
endecja [en-**de**-tsyah] f. National Democratic Party
endecki [en-**de**-tskee] adj.m. of National Democratic Party; of the National Democrats
endek [**en**-dek] m. member of National Democratic Party; National Democrat
endemia [en-**de**-myah] f. endemicity
endemicznie [en-de-**meech**-ńe] adv. endemically
endemiczny [en-de-**meech**-ni] adj.m. endemic; native (diseases, etc.)
endemit [en-**de**-meet] m. endemic animal; endemic plant
endemity [en-de-**mee**-ti] pl. endemic character (nature)
endemizm [en-**de**-meezm] m. endemism
endo- [**en**-do-] prefix: inside-; internal-
endoderma [en-do-**der**-mah] f. endodermis; endoderm
endodermalny [en-do-der-**mahl**-ni] adj.m. endodermal
endoenergetyczny [en-do-e-ner-ge-**tich**-ni] adj.m. absorbing energy (from the environment)
endogamia [en-do-**gah**-myah] f.

endogamy (marriage within a specific group)
endogamiczny [en-do-gah-**meech**-ni] adj.m. endogamous; endogamic
endogeneza [en-do-ge-**ne**-zah] f. endogeny; growth from within; growth from a deep layer
endogeniczny [en-do-ge-**ńeech**-ni] adj.m. endogenous; endogenic
endogenny [en-do-**gen**-ni] adj.m. endogenous
endokrynolog [en-do-kri-**no**-log] m. endocrinologist
endokrynologia [en-do-kri-no-**lo**-gyah] f. endocrinology
endokrynologiczny [en-do-kri-no-lo-**geech**-ni] adj.m. endocrinologic; endocrinological
endolimfa [en-do-**leem**-fah] f. endolymph
endomitoza [en-do-mee-**to**-zah] f. endomitosis
endopasożyt [en-do-pah-**so**-zhit] m. endoparasite
endoplazma [en-do-**plahz**-mah] f. endoplasm
endoproteza [en-do-pro-**te**-zah] f. internal replacement of tissue losses after a surgery
endoreiczny [en-do-re-**eech**-ni] adj.m. draining into an inland body of water (not to the sea)
endoskop [en-**do**-skop] m. endoscope
endoskopia [en-do-**sko**-pyah] f. endoscopy
endosmotyczny [en-do-smo-**tich**-ni] adj.m. endosmotic
endosmoza [en-do-**smo**-zah] f. endosmosis
endosperm [en-**do**-sperm] m. endosperm
endospor [en-**do**-spor] m. endospore
endotermiczny [en-do-ter-**meech**-ni] adj.m. endothermic
endotoksyczny [en-do-to-**ksich**-ni] adj.m. endotoxic
endotoksyna [en-do-to-**ksi**-nah] f. endotoxin
endywia [en-**di**-vyah] f. endive; witloof
enema [e-**ne**-mah] f. enema
eneolit [e-ne-**o**-leet] m. period between neolith and the bronze age
energetycznie [e-ner-ge-**tich**-ńe] adv. energetically
energetyczny [e-ner-ge-**tich**-ni] adj.m. of power engineering
energetyk [e-ner-**ge**-tik] m. electric power engineer
energetyka [e-ner-**ge**-ti-kah] f. energetics; power industry; power engineering
energetyzm [e-ner-**ge**-tizm] m. a theory of energy
energia [e-**ner**-gyah] f. energy; vigor; drive; push; nerve; spirit; guts; pep; activity; power
bez energii [bes e-**ner**-gyee] exp.: without energy; listless; nerveless; spiritless; sluggish
energia wodna [e-**ner**-gyah **vod**-nah] exp.: water-power
energicznie [e-ner-**geech**-ńe] adv. energetically; vigorously
energiczny [e-ner-**geech**-ni] adj.m. energetic; vigorous
energiochłonność [e-ner-gyo-**khwon**-nośhćh] f. energy consumption
energiochłonny [e-ner-gyo-**khwon**-ni] adj.m. energy-consuming
energiotwórczy [e-ner-gyo-**tfoor**-chi] adj.m. energy-producing (process, etc.)
energochłonność [e-ner-go-**khwon**-nośhćh] f. energy consumption
energochłonny [e-ner-go-**khwon**-ni] adj.m. energy-consuming
energoelektryka [e-ner-go-e-**lek**-tri-kah] f. study of the use of electricity as a source of power
energooszczędny [e-ner-go-o-**shchand**-ni] adj.m. energy-saving
energotwórczy [e-ner-go-**tfoor**-chi] adj.m. energy-producing
engagement [en-**gahzh**-mah] n. (French) work contract of an actor (or opera singer, etc.)
engram [**en**-grahm] m. engram; memory trace
enharmonia [en-khahr-**mo**-ńyah] f. an enharmonic (chord, etc.)
enharmoniczny [en-khahr-mo-**ńeech**-ni] adj.m. enharmonic
enigma [e-**ńeeg**-mah] f. enigma; mystery; puzzle; inscrutable

person; an obscure speech or writing; German World War II code broken by the Polish Intelligence (the Polish solution was shared with Gr. Britain and France on July 25, 1939)
enigmatycznie [e-ńeeg-mah-**tich**-ńe] adv. enigmatically
enigmatyczność [e-ńeeg-mah-**tich**-nośhćh] f. enigmaticalness
enigmatyczny [e-ńeeg-mah-**tich**-ni] adj.m. enigmatic; enigmatical
enkausta [en-**kahw**-stah] f. antique painting technique using hot bee wax; encaustic painting
enkaustyczny [en-kahw-**stich**-ni] adj.m. encaustic
enkaustyka [en-**kahw**-sti-kah] f. antique painting technique using hot bee wax; an encaustic
enklawa [en-**klah**-vah] f. enclave
enklityczność [en-klee-**tich**-nośhćh] f. enclitic character (of a word)
enklityczny [en-klee-**tich**-ni] adj.m. enclitic
enklityka [en-**klee**-ti-kah] f. an enclitic; postposition (for inclusion in a phonetic accent)
enkliza [en-**klee**-zah] f. (linguistic) joining of an unaccented word with a preceding accented word
enologia [e-no-**lo**-gyah] f. study of wine production including wine chemistry and analysis
enotanina [e-no-tah-**ńee**-nah] f. the ingredients of dryness in wine
ensemble [ahn-**sahmbl**] m. ensemble; group performance
ensemblowy [ahn-sahm-**blo**-vi] adj.m. of an ensemble; of a group performance
entalpia [en-**tahl**-pyah] f. enthalpy; heat content
entameba [en-tah-**me**-bah] f. variety of amoeba; entameba
entameby [en-tah-**me**-bi] pl. Entamoebae
entamebioza [en-tah-me-**byo**-zah] f. entamoebiasis; entamebiasis
entaza [en-**tah**-zah] f. entasis
entelechia [en-te-**le**-khyah] f. entelechy
ententa [ahn-**tahn**-tah] f. entente; an international understanding of a common purpose; a coalition of parties to an entente; the Entente of the World War I
enteroskop [en-te-**ro**-skop] m. optical intestinal probe
enteroskopia [en-te-ro-**sko**-pyah] f. examination using an optical intestinal probe
enterotoksyna [en-te-ro-to-**ksi**-nah] f. enterotoxin
entliczek [ent-**lee**-chek] m. a word in children's number game
entoblast [en-**to**-blahst] m. entoblast; hypoblast
entoderma [en-to-**der**-mah] f. entoderm; endoderm
entodermalny [en-to-der-**mahl**-ni] adj.m. endodermal
entomofag [en-to-**mo**-fahg] m. entomophagous organism
entomofagi [en-to-mo-**fah**-gee] pl. Entomophaga
entomofauna [en-to-mo-**fahw**-nah] f. entomofauna
entomogam [en-to-**mo**-gahm] m. flower fertilized by insects
entomogamy [en-to-mo-**gah**-mi] pl. flowers fertilized by insects
entomogamia [en-to-mo-**gah**-myah] f. flower-fertilization by insects
entomolog [en-to-**mo**-log] m. entomologist
entomologia [en-to-mo-**lo**-gyah] f. study of insects; entomology
entomologicznie [en-to-mo-lo-**geech**-ńe] adv. entomologically
entomologiczny [en-to-mo-lo-**geech**-ni] adj.m. entomological
entoplazma [en-to-**plah**-zmah] f. endoplasm
entropia [en-**tro**-pyah] f. entropy; measure (of energy, of disorder in a system, of amount of information in a logarithmic message, the degradation of matter and energy in the universe leading to an ultimate state of inert uniformity)
entropowy [en-tro-**po**-vi] adj.m. of entropy
entuzjasta [en-too-**zyah**-stah] m. enthusiast; devotee; fan
entuzjastka [en-too-**zyah**-stkah] f.

(woman) enthusiast; devotee; fan
entuzjastycznie [en-too-zyah-**stich**-ńe] adv. enthusiastically; with enthusiasm
entuzjastyczny [en-too-zyah-**stich**-ni] adj.m. enthusiastic
entuzjazm [en-**too**-zyahzm] m. enthusiasm; rapture
entuzjazmować [en-too-zyah-**zmo**-vahćh] v. bring enthusiasm; excite; enthuse (about, over something) (*repeatedly*)
entuzjazmować się [en-too-zyah-**zmo**-vahćh śhan] v. be enthusiastic (over, about); be excited (over, about); be enthused (about; over something) (*repeatedly*)
entuzjazmowanie [en-too-zyah-zmo-**vah**-ńe] n. bringing excitement; causing enthusiasm
entuzjazmowanie się [en-too-zyah-zmo-**vah**-ńe śhan]] n. being enthusiastic
entymemat [en-ti-**me**-maht] m. enthymeme
enumeracja [e-noo-me-**rah**-tsyah] f. enumeration; list
enumerować [e-noo-me-**ro**-vahćh] v. enumerate; specify one after another; list; detail; tell item by item (*repeatedly*)
enuncjacja [e-noon-**tsyah**-tsyah] f. enunciation; (official) statement
enzootia [en-zo-**o**-tyah] f. an animal disease
enzootycznie [en-zo-o-**tich**-ńe] adv. in enzootic manner
enzootyczny [en-zo-o-**tich**-ni] adj.m. enzootic (animal, etc.)
enzym [**en**-zim] m. enzyme; protein-like catalyst in chemical reactions **enzymy** [en-**zi**-mi] pl. enzymes
enzymatyczny [en-zi-mah-**tich**-ni] adj.m. enzymatic
enzymolog [en-zi-**mo**-log] m. enzymologist
enzymologia [en-zi-mo-**lo**-gyah] f. enzymology
eocen [e-**o**-tsen] m. Eocene
eoceński [e-o-**tseń**-skee] adj.m. of the Eocene period
eofityczny [e-o-fee-**tich**-ni] adj.m. eophytic
eoliczny [e-o-**leech**-ni] adj.m. windblown (erosion, sediment)
eolit [e-**o**-leet] m. eolith
eolowy [e-o-**lo**-vi] adj.m. Aeolian
eolski [e-**ol**-skee] adj.m. Aeolian
eon [**e**-on] m. eon; an extremely long, indefinite period of time
eozoiczny [e-o-zo-**eech**-ni] adj.m. Eozoic (epoch, etc.); Precambrian; Proterozoic
eozoik [e-o-**zo**-eek] m. Eozoic period
eozyna [e-o-**zi**-nah] f. eosin
epakta [e-**pahk**-tah] f. epact
eparch [**e**-pahrkh] m. head of eparchy
eparchia [e-**pahr**-khyah] f. Greco-Roman province (colony); eparchy
epatować [e-pah-**to**-vahćh] v. make a great impression; astonish; surprise (with achievement, etc.) (*repeatedly*)
epejrogenetyczny [e-pey-ro-ge-ne-**tich**-ni] adj.m. of epeirogeny; epirogeny
epejrogeneza [e-pey-ro-ge-**ne**-zah] f. epeirogeny
epejrogenicznie [e-pey-ro-ge-**ńeech**-ńe] adv. epeirogenically
epejrogeniczny [e-pey-ro-ge-**ńeech**-ni] adj.m. epeirogenic
epejsodion [e-pey-**so**-dyon] m. epeisodion; episode (in Greek drama)
epentetyczny [e-pen-te-**tich**-ni] adj.m. epenthetic; of inserting of a letter in the body of a word; of developing of a sound in the body of a word
epenteza [e-pen-**te**-zah] f. epenthesis
epiblast [e-**pee**-blahst] m. epiblast
epicentralny [e-pee-tsen-**trahl**-ni] adj.m. epicentral; of epicenter
epicentrum [e-pee-**tsen**-troom] epicenter; the part of the earth's surface directly above the focus of an earthquake
epicheremat [e-pee-khe-**re**-maht] m. epicheirema
epicki [e-**pee**-tskee] adj.m. epic; epical; of or like an epic; heroic; grand; of work of art that resembles or suggests an epic
epicko [e-**pee**-tsko] adv. epically

epickość [e-**pee**-tskośhćh] f. epic character
epicykl [e-**pee**-tsikl] m. epicycle of the geocentric theory
epicykloida [e-pee-tsi-**kloy**-dah] f. epicycloid curve
epicznie [e-**peech**-ńe] adv. epically
epiczny [e-**peech**-ni] adj.m. epical; epic (see: **epicki**)
epideiktyczny [e-pee-de-eek-**tich**-ni] adj.m. epideictic (oratory, etc.)
epidemia [e-pee-**de**-myah] f. epidemic; an epidemic disease
epidemicznie [e-pee-de-**meech**-ńe] adv. epidemically
epidemiczny [e-pee-de-**meech**-ni] adj.m. epidemic
epidemiolog [e-pee-de-**myo**-lok] m. epidemiologist
epidemiologia [e-pee-de-myo-**lo**-gyah] f. epidemiology
epidemiologiczny [e-pee-de-myo-lo-**geech**-ni] adj.m. epidemiologic
epiderma [e-pee-**der**-mah] f. epidermis; the outermost layer of the skin
epidiaskop [e-pee-**dyah**-skop] m. epidiascope; projection lantern; slide projector
epidiaskopowy [e-pee-dyah-sko-**po**-vi] adj.m. epidiascopic
epidot [e-**pee**-dot] m. epidote (mineral)
epifauna [e-pee-**fahw**-nah] f. epifauna
epifenomen [e-pee-fe-**no**-men] m. epiphenomenon
epifit [e-**pee**-feet] m. epiphyte
epifity [e-pee-**fee**-ti] pl. epiphytes
epifitoza [e-pee-fee-**to**-zah] f. epiphytous fungus disease
epifitycznie [e-pee-fee-**tich**-ńe] adv. epiphytically
epifityczny [e-pee-fee-**tich**-ni] adj.m. epiphytic
epifityzm [e-pee-**fee**-tizm] m. epiphyticism
epifonem [e-pee-**fo**-nem] m. exclamatory expression
epifora [e-pee-**fo**-rah] f. epiphora
epifraza [e-pee-**frah**-zah] f. long phrase including added details
epigenetyczny [e-pee-ge-ne-**tich**-ni] adj.m. epigenetic; epigene
epigeneza [e-pee-ge-**ne**-zah] f. epigenesis
epigon [e-**pee**-gon] m. epigone; imitative follower; successor; epigonus
epigonizm [e-pee-**go**-ńeezm] m. imitative following; epigonism
epigonka [e-pee-**gon**-kah] f. (woman) epigone; imitative follower; successor
epigoński [e-pee-**goń**-skee] adj.m. of epigonus
epigraf [e-**pee**-grahf] m. epigraph; an engraved inscription; a quotation set at the beginning (of a book, etc.)
epigraficznie [e-pee-grah-**feech**-ńe] adv. epigraphically
epigraficzny [e-pee-grah-**feech**-ni] adj.m. epigraphic
epigrafika [e-pee-**grah**-fee-kah] f. epigraphy; inscriptions; deciphering of ancient inscriptions
epigram [e-**pee**-grahm] m. epigram
epigramat [e-pee-**grah**-maht] m. light, clever epigram
epigramatycznie [e-pee-grah-mah-**tich**-ńe] adv. epigrammatically
epigramatyczny [e-pee-grah-mah-**tich**-ni] adj.m. epigrammatic
epigramatyk [e-pee-grah-**mah**-tik] m. author of epigrams; epigrammatist; epigrammatizer
epigramatyka [e-pee-grah-**mah**-ti-kah] f. epigrammatism
epik [**e**-peek] m. epic writer
epika [**e**-pee-kah] f. epic poetry
epikontynentalny [e-pee-kon-ti-nen-**tahl**-ni] adj.m. epicontinental; (sea) lying upon a continent or a continental shelf
epikryza [e-pee-**kri**-zah] f. patient's disease history; second crisis in a disease
epikureizm [e-pee-koo-**re**-eezm] m. Epicureanism; the hedonistic philosophy of Epicurus
epikurejczyk [e-pee-koo-**rey**-chik] m. Epicurean; sybarite; gourmet; gourmand; glutton
epikurejski [e-pee-koo-**rey**-skee] adj.m. Epicurean
po epikurejsku [po e-pee-koo-**rey**-skoo] exp.: after the epicurean

fashion; sybaritically; in the notorious luxury of the Sybarites
epilacja [e-pee-**lah**-tsyah] f. epilation; depilation; loss of hair; removal of hair
epilacyjny [e-pee-lah-**tsiy**-ni] adj.m. depilatory; removing hair
epilepsja [e-pee-**lep**-syah] f. epilepsy
epileptyczka [e-pee-lep-**tich**-kah] f. (woman) epileptic
epileptycznie [e-pee-lep-**tich**-ńe] adv. epileptically
epileptyczny [e-pee-lep-**tich**-ni] adj.m. epileptic
epileptyk [e-pee-**lep**-tik] m. epileptic
epilit [e-**pee**-leet] m. rock-moss
epilog [e-**pee**-lok] m. epilogue
epilogowy [e-pee-lo-**go**-vi] adj.m. of epilogue
epilować [e-pee-**lo**-vahćh] v. lose hair; remove hair (*repeatedly*)
epilowanie [e-pee-lo-**vah**-ńe] n. epilation; loss of hair; removal of hair
epimer [e-**pee**-mer] m. epimer
epimery [e-pee-**me**-ri] pl. epimers
epimerowy [e-pee-me-**ro**-vi] adj.m. epimeric
epimorfoza [e-pee-mor-**fo**-zah] f. epimorphosis
epinicjon [e-pee-**ńee**-tsyon] m. triumphal song for olympic champions
epipelagial [e-pee-pe-**lah**-gyahl] m. epipelagic sea depth
epipelagialny [e-pee-pe-lah-**gyahl**-ni] adj.m. epipelagic
episkop [e-**pee**-skop] m. episcope (projector)
episkopalny [e-pee-sko-**pahl**-ni] adj.m. episcopal; of the Protestant Episcopal Church
episkopat [e-pee-**sko**-paht] m. episcopate
episkopowy [e-pee-sko-**po**-vi] adj.m. of episcope; episcope (projection, etc.)
epistemologia [e-pee-ste-mo-**lo**-gyah] f. epistemology; the study of the nature, validity, and limits of knowledge
epistemologicznie [e-pee-ste-mo-lo-**geech**-ńe] adv. epistemologically
epistemologiczny [e-pee-ste-mo-lo-**geech**-ni] adj.m. epistemological
epistolarny [e-pee-sto-**lahr**-ni] adj.m. epistolary; written in form of a series of letters
epistolograf [e-pee-sto-**lo**-grahf] m. novelist writing in form of letters
epistolografia [e-pee-sto-**lo**-grah-fyah] f. writing in form of letters
epistolograficzny [e-pee-sto-lo-grah-**feech**-ni] adj.m. of writing in form of letters
epistoła [e-pee-**sto**-wah] f. Epistle; Lesson; epistle; long, tedious letter
epistrefa [e-pee-**stre**-fah] f. upper layer of earth's crust
epistyl [e-**pee**-stil] m. epistyle; architrave
episylogizm [e-pee-si-**lo**-geezm] m. episyllogism
epitafijny [e-pee-tah-**feey**-ni] adj.m. epitaphial; epitaphic
epitafium [e-pee-**tah**-fyoom] n. epitaph; inscription on a grave
epitalamium [e-pee-tah-**lah**-myoom] n. epithalamium
epitaza [e-pee-**tah**-zah] f. epitasis
epitet [e-**pee**-tet] m. epithet; invective
epitety [e-pee-**te**-ti] pl. epithets; invectives; abuse
epitryt [e-**pee**-trit] m. epitrite
epizacja [e-pee-**zah**-tsyah] f. conversion into the style of an epic
epizod [e-**pee**-zot] m. episode; incident; a part of a series; occurrence; secondary action (of a plot, etc.)
epizodycznie [e-pee-zo-**dich**-ńe] adv. irregularly; at irregular intervals; in form of an episode; episodically
epizodyczność [e-pee-zo-**dich**-nośhćh] f. episodic character (of a personage in a play, etc.)
epizodyczny [e-pee-zo-**dich**-ni] adj.m. irregular; occasional; episodic
rola epizodyczna [**ro**-lah e-pee-zo-**dich**-nah] exp.: bit part
epizodysta [e-pee-zo-**di**-stah] m. second-rate actor
epizodzik [e-pee-**zo**-dźheek] m. (small, funny, etc.) episode

epizoiczny [e-pee-zo-**eech**-ni] adj.m. epizoic; dwelling upon the body of an animal (or plant)
epizoocja [e-pee-zo-**o**-tsyah] f. an epizootic disease
epizootia [e-pee-zo-**o**-tyah] f. an epizootic disease
epizootycznie [e-pee-zo-o-**tich**-ńe] adv. epizootically
epizootyczny [e-pee-zo-o-**tich**-ni] adj.m. epizootic (animal disease, etc.)
epizować [e-pee-**zo**-vahćh] v. convert into the style of an epic (*repeatedly*)
epoda [e-**po**-dah] f. epode; a lyric poem; third part of a Greek ode
epoka [e-**po**-kah] f. epoch; era; period; age; a period of time (in terms of memorable events, persons, etc.)
epoka brązu [e-**po**-kah **br**<u>**own**</u>-zoo] exp.: the bronze epoch
epokowo [e-po-**ko**-vo] adv. in an epoch-making fashion; epochally
epokowy [e-po-**ko**-vi] adj.m. epoch-making; epochal; momentous; unparalleled
epoksydowy [e-po-ksi-**do**-vi] adj.m. of epoxy resin
epolet [e-**po**-let] m. epaulet; epaulette
eponim [e-**po**-ńeem] m. eponym
epopeja [e-po-**pe**-yah] f. epic; epos
epos [**e**-pos] m. epos
eposowy [e-po-**so**-vi] adj.m. of an epos; epic; epical
epruwetka [e-proo-**vet**-kah] f. test tube; test-glass
epsilon [ep-**see**-lon] m. epsilon; the 5th letter of the Greek alphabet
epsomit [ep-**so**-meet] m. epsom; epsom salt
epuzer [e-**poo**-zer] m. marrying man; candidate for marriage
era [**e**-rah] f. era; epoch
eratyczny [e-rah-**tich**-ni] adj.m. erratic (rock, etc.) (geol. exp.)
eratyk [e-**rah**-tik] m. an erratic (boulder or block of rock transported by a glacial)
erb [erp] m. erbium
Ereb [e-rep] m. Erebus
erekcja [e-**rek**-tsyah] f. erection
erekcyjny [e-rek-**tsiy**-ni] adj.m. of erection; of foundation
akt erekcyjny [ahkt e-rek-**tsiy**-ni] exp.: charter of foundation
erem [**e**-rem] m. hermitage
eremita [e-re-**mee**-tah] m. hermit; eremite
erepsyna [e-re-**psi**-nah] f. erepsin
erg [erg] m. erg
ergatywny [er-gah-**tiv**-ni] adj.m. of a complex sentence structure
ergocentryczny [er-go-tsen-**trich**-ni] adj.m. concerned with a work without considering the author
ergograf [er-**go**-grahf] m. ergograph; an apparatus for measuring the work capacity of a muscle
ergograficzny [er-go-grah-**feech**-ni] adj.m. of an ergograph
ergogram [er-**go**-gram] m. ergogram
ergologia [er-go-**lo**-gyah] f. ethnologic study of material culture
ergometr [er-**go**-metr] m. ergometer; an apparatus for measuring the work performed by a group of muscles
ergometria [er-go-**me**-tryah] f. economy of movements; efficient use of human energy
ergometryczny [er-go-met-**rich**-ni] adj.m. ergometric
ergonom [er-**go**-nom] m. specialist in ergonomics
ergonomia [er-go-**no**-myah] f. ergonomics
ergonomiczność [er-go-no-**meech**-nośhćh] f. ergonomic character (nature)
ergonomiczny [er-go-no-**meech**-ni] adj.m. ergonomic
ergonomika [er-go-**no**-mee-kah] f. ergonomics
ergonomista [er-go-no-**mee**-stah] m. ergonomist
ergosterol [er-go-**ste**-rol] m. ergosterol
ergotyna [er-go-**ti**-nah] f. ergotine
eriometr [er-**yo**-metr] m. an apparatus for measuring the thickness of wool fibers
erka [**er**-kah] f. ambulance with resuscitation equipment
erkaem [er-**kah**-em] m. light

machine gun
erkaemista [er-kah-e-**mee**-stah] m. light machine gunner
ermitaż [er-**mee**-tahsh] m. hermitage
erodować [e-ro-**do**-vahćh] v. erode (by water or glacier) (*repeatedly*)
erodowanie [e-ro-do-**vah**-ńe] n. erosion; eroding
erogeniczny [e-ro-ge-**ńeech**-ni] adj.m. erotically sensitive (parts of the body, etc.)
erogenny [e-ro-**gen**-ni] adj.m. erotically sensitive (parts of the body, etc.)
eros [**e**-ros] m. eros
erotematyczny [e-ro-te-mah-**tich**-ni] adj.m. consisting of questions and answers
erotoman [e-ro-**to**-mahn] m. sex maniac; erotomaniac
erotomania [e-ro-to-**mah**-ńyah] f. erotomania; eroticomania
erotomanka [e-ro-to-**mahn**-kah] f. (woman) sex maniac; erotomaniac
erotomański [e-ro-to-**mahń**-skee] adj.m. of a sex maniac; of erotomaniac; of erotomania
erotycznie [e-ro-**tich**-ńe] adv. erotically; sexually
erotyczność [e-ro-**tich**-nośhćh] f. eroticism (of films, poetry, etc.)
erotyczny [e-ro-**tich**-ni] adj.m. erotic; sexual; amatory
erotyk [e-**ro**-tik] m. an erotic
erotyka [e-**ro**-ti-kah] f. erotica; erotic books, pictures, etc.
erotyzm [e-**ro**-tizm] m. eroticism; erotism
erozja [e-**ro**-zyah] f. erosion
erozyjny [e-ro-**ziy**-ni] adj.m. erosive
proces erozyjny [**pro**-tses e-ro-**ziy**-ni] exp.: process of erosion
errata [er-**rah**-tah] f. errata; list of errors in printing
ersted [**er**-stet] m. oersted (unit of measure of magnetic field)
erudycja [e-roo-**di**-tsyah] f. erudition; scholarship; learning acquired by reading and study
erudycyjny [e-roo-di-**tsiy**-ni] adj.m. erudite; scholarly; learned
erudyta [e-roo-**di**-tah] m. erudite; man of learning; scholar; savant
erudytka [e-roo-**di**-tkah] f. (woman) erudite; woman of learning; scholar; savant
erupcja [e-**roop**-tsyah] f. eruption
erupcyjny [e-roop-**tsiy**-ni] adj.m. eruptive
erygować [e-ri-**go**-vahćh] v. found; erect; establish (*repeatedly*)
erynia [e-**ri**-ńah] f. Erinys; avenging spirit
erystyczny [e-ri-**stich**-ni] adj.m. eristic; characterized by logical disputations and subtle and specious reasoning
erystyk [e-**ri**-stik] m. an eristic; a person devoted to logical disputations and subtle and specious reasoning
erystyka [e-**ri**-sti-kah] f. eristic
erytrejski [e-ri-**trey**-skee] adj.m. Eritrean
erytrocyt [e-ri-**tro**-tsit] m. erythrocyte; red blood cell
erytrocyty [e-ri-tro-**tsi**-ti] pl. erythrocytes; red blood cells
erytromycyna [e-ri-tro-mi-**tsi**-nah] f. erythromycin
erytrotoksyna [e-ri-tro-to-**ksi**-nah] f. toxin of red blood-cells
erzac [**er**-zahts] m. an artificial and inferior substitute; ersatz
es [es] m. the letter "s"; s-shaped curve; an ess; indecl.: E flat
esauł [e-**sah**-oow] m. officer commanding a detachment of Cossack cavalry
eschatologia [es-khah-to-**lo**-gyah] f. eschatology; theology of final events of the world and human history
eschatologicznie [es-khah-to-lo-**geech**-ńe] adv. eschatologically
eschatologiczny [es-khah-to-lo-**geech**-ni] adj.m. eschatological
escudo [es-**koo**-do] m. & n. escudo; monetary unit of Portugal
esdecja [es-**de**-tsyah] f. Social Democratic Party
esdek [**es**-dek] m. social democrat
eseista [e-se-**ee**-stah] m. essayist
eseistka [e-se-**ee**-stkah] f. (female) essayist
eseistycznie [e-se-ee-**stich**-ńe] adv. in form of an essay
eseistyczny [e-se-ee-**stich**-ni] adj.m.

of an essay
eseistyka [e-se-**ee**-sti-kah] f. essay writing
eseizować [e-se-ee-**zo**-vahćh] v. write in form of essays (*repeatedly*)
esej [**e**-sey] m. essay
esencja [e-**sen**-tsyah] f. essence; extract; infusion of tea; brewed tea; gist
esencjonalnie [e-sen-tsyo-**nahl**-ńe] adv. essentially; strongly; inherently; basically
esencjonalność [e-sen-tsyo-**nahl**-nośhćh] f. concentration
esencjonalny [e-sen-tsyo-**nahl**-ni] adj.m. essential; inherent; basic; indispensable; necessary; strong; concentrated; undiluted
eser [**e**-ser] m. social-revolutionary
eserowiec [e-se-**ro**-vyets] m. Social-Revolutionary (in Russia)
eserowski [e-se-**ro**-fskee] adj.m. of Social Revolutionary (movement, party, etc.)
esesman [e-**ses**-mahn] m. member of the German SS (shock) troops; Black-Shirt
esesmanka [e-ses-**mahn**-kah] f. (female) member of the German SS troops; black-shirt
esesmański [e-ses-**mahń**-skee] adj.m. of a member of the German SS troops (also used for extermination of undesirables)
esesowiec [e-se-**so**-vyets] m. member of the German SS (shock) troops; Black-Shirt
esesowski [e-se-**sof**-skee] adj.m. of a member of the German SS shock troops; black-shirt's
esica [e-**śhee**-tsah] f. sigmoid; S-shaped intestine; the crooked part of the colon immediately above the rectum; sigmoid colon
eskadra [es-**kah**-drah] f. squadron; aerial fleet; flight
eskalacja [es-kah-**lah**-tsyah] f. escalation
eskalacyjny [es-kah-lah-**tsiy**-ni] adj.m. escalatory
eskalator [es-kah-**lah**-tor] m. escalator; moving stairs
eskalopek [es-kah-**lo**-pek] m. flattened cutlet of meat or fish
eskapada [es-kah-**pah**-dah] f. escapade; a reckless adventure; a reckless prank
eskapista [es-kah-**pee**-stah] m. escapist
eskapistyczny [es-kah-pee-**stich**-ni] adj.m. escapist (way of thinking, writing, etc.)
eskapizm [es-**kah**-peezm] m. escapism; escape from reality (or routine)
eskimoski [es-kee-**mo**-skee] adj.m. Eskimo; Husky
eskonter [es-**kon**-ter] m. broker buying at a discount bills of exchange before their maturation
eskonto [es-**kon**-to] n. discount for paying off a loan before the due date
eskorta [es-**kor**-tah] f. escort; convoy; safeguard
eskortant [es-**kor**-tahnt] m. escort; member of a convoy
eskorter [es-**kor**-ter] m. an escort ship; a convoy ship
eskortować [es-kor-**to**-vahćh] v. escort; convoy (*repeatedly*)
eskortowanie [es-kor-to-**vah**-ńe] n. an escort; a convoy
eskortowiec [es-kor-**to**-vyets] m. an escort ship; a convoy ship
eskortowy [es-kor-**to**-vi] adj.m. escort (ship, detachment, etc.); convoy (ship, car, etc.)
eskulap [es-**koo**-lahp] m. medical doctor (an ironic term)
eskulapski [es-koo-**lahp**-skee] adj.m. of a medical doctor (an ironic term)
esowato [e-so-**vah**-to] adv. in form of esses; in the shape of an "s"; in s-shape
esowaty [e-so-**vah**-ti] adj.m. sinus; s-shaped
esownica [e-sov-**ńee**-tsah] f. ogee; cyma; molding (trim) of s-shaped profile
esówka [e-**soof**-kah] f. pantile; roofing tile of s-shaped profile
espadryla [es-pah-**dri**-lah] f. espadrille
esparceta [es-pahr-**tse**-tah] f. sainfoin (legume)

esparto [es-**pahr**-to] n. esparto (grass, paper, etc.)
esperancja [es-pe-**rahn**-tsyah] f. expected value; expected winning number in the drawing of lots based on probability calculation
esperancki [es-pe-**rahn**-tskee] adj.m. Esperanto (version of a language, etc.)
esperanto [es-pe-**rahn**-to] n. Esperanto; an artificial international language
esperantysta [es-pe-rahn-**ti**-stah] m. Esperantist
esplanada [es-plah-**nah**-dah] f. esplanade; promenade
establishment [es-**tahb**-leesh-ment] m. establishment
estakada [es-tah-**kah**-dah] f. palisade; pier; breakwater; wharf; elevated roadway
ester [**es**-ter] m. ester
esteta [es-**te**-tah] m. aesthete; esthete
estetycznie [es-te-**tich**-ńe] adv. aesthetically; with taste; beautifully
estetyczność [es-te-**tich**-nośhćh] f. (a)esthetic quality
estetyczny [es-te-**tich**-ni] adj.m. aesthetic; in good taste; beautiful
estetyk [es-**te**-tik] m. aesthete
estetyka [es-**te**-ti-kah] f. aesthetics; beauty
estetyzacja [es-te-ti-**zah**-tsyah] f. beautification
estetyzm [es-**te**-tizm] m. aestheticism
estetyzować [es-te-ti-**zo**-vahćh] v. make aesthetic; act aesthetically (*repeatedly*)
estetyzowanie [es-te-ti-zo-**vah**-ńe] n. making aesthetic; acting aesthetically
estezjologia [es-te-zyo-**lo**-gyah] f. esthesiology
estezjometr [es-tez-**zyo**-metr] m. esthesiometer
estokada [es-to-**kah**-dah] f. fencing thrust (under the arm of an opponent)
Estończyk [e-**stoń**-chik] m. Estonian
estoński [e-**stoń**-skee] adj.m. Estonian
estrada [e-**strah**-dah] f. platform; dais; bandstand
estradowiec [es-trah-**do**-vyets] m. concert-hall artist
estradowy [es-trah-**do**-vi] adj.m. concert-hall (singer, performance, etc.); platform (act, etc.)
estragon [es-**trah**-gon] m. tarragon; perennial wormwood used for flavoring
estragonowy [es-trah-go-**no**-vi] adj.m. tarragon (oil, etc.)
estrogen [es-**tro**-gen] m. estrogen; female sex hormone
estrogeny [es-tro-**ge**-ni] pl. estrogens; female sex hormones
estrogenicznie [es-tro-ge-**ńeech**-ńe] adv. estrogenically
estrogeniczny [es-tro-ge-**ńeech**-ni] adj.m. estrogenic
estrowy [es-**tro**-vi] adj.m. ester (gum, etc.); of an organic compound formed by the reaction of an acid and an alcohol
estryfikacja [es-tri-fee-**kah**-tsyah] f. esterification
estryfikować [es-tri-fee-**ko**-vahćh] v. esterify (*repeatedly*)
estryfikowanie [es-tri-fee-ko-**vah**-ńe] n. esterification
estuarium [es-too-**ahr**-yoom] n. estuary; the wide mouth of a river into which the tide flows
estyma [es-**ti**-mah] f. respect; esteem; honor
estymacja [es-ti-**mah**-tsyah] f. estimation
estymator [es-ti-**mah**-tor] m. a statistical function for estimating a (population, etc.) parameter (based on a sample); estimator
estymować [es-ti-**mo**-vahćh] v. appraise; estimate; evaluate; value; rate; assess; determine unknown parameters (*repeatedly*)
estymowanie [es-ti-mo-**vah**-ńe] n. estimation; the act of estimating
estywacja [es-ti-**vah**-tsyah] f. aestivation; passing the summer in the state of torpor
eszelon [e-**she**-lon] m. echelon; troop train
eszelonować [e-she-lo-**no**-vahćh] v. echelon (troops) (*repeatedly*)

eszeweria [e-she-**ve**-ryah] f. echeveria (tropical American orpine plant)
eszolcja [e-**shol**-tsyah] f. Eschscholtzia herb
et! [et] excl.: pshaw!
etacik [e-**tah**-ćheek] m. (nice, pleasant) permanent employment; diminutive of: **etat**
etamina [e-tah-**mee**-nah] f. cheesecloth; etamine
etaminowy [e-tah-mee-**no**-vi] adj.m. of a cheesecloth; etamine (cloth, etc.)
etan [**e**-tahn] m. ethane
etanol [e-**tah**-nol] m. ethanol; ethyl alcohol
etap [**e**-tahp] m. stage (of development); halting place
na tym etapie [nah tim e-**tah**-pye] exp.: at this stage
podróżować etapami [po-droo-**zho**-vahćh e-tah-**pah**-mee] exp.: to travel by stages
etapować [e-tah-**po**-vahćh] v. divide into stages (*repeatedly*)
etapowo [e-tah-**po**-vo] adv. by stages; gradually
etapowość [e-tah-**po**-vośhćh] f. gradualism
etapowy [e-tah-**po**-vi] adj.m. gradual
etat [**e**-taht] m. permanency; permanent post; regular job; permanent employment
być na etacie [bićh nah e-**tah**-ćhe] exp.: to hold a regular job (post, positiopn); have tenure
etatowo [e-tah-**to**-vo] adv. permanently; regularly
etatowy [e-tah-**to**-vi] adj.m. permanent (job); full-time (employee, etc.); tenured
etatysta [e-tah-**ti**-stah] m. advocate of nationalization; advocate of state socialism
etatyzacja [e-tah-ti-**zah**-tsyah] f. nationalization; state control; fixing the number of permanent posts (in an institution, etc.)
etatyzm [e-**tah**-tizm] m. state control; state management; state socialism; (centralized) statism
etażerka [e-tah-**zher**-kah] f. (book) shelf; rack; stand; whatnot; set of open shelves
eter [**e**-ter] m. ether; the ether
na falach eteru [nah **fah**-lahkh e-**te**-roo] exp.: over the ether; on the air (radio transmission, etc.)
eternit [e-**ter**-ńeet] m. tile of asbestos; asbestos tile
eternitowy [e-ter-ńee-**to**-vi] adj.m. asbestos (roof, tiles, etc.)
eteromania [e-te-ro-**mah**-ńyah] f. addiction to sniff ether; addiction to drink ether
eterowy [e-te-**ro**-vi] adj.m. of ether; ether (extract, etc.)
eterycznie [e-te-**rich**-ńe] adv. ethereally; airily; in sprightly manner; with an unusual delicacy and refinement
eteryczność [e-te-**rich**-nośhćh] f. etherealness; volatility; airiness; lightness; sprightliness
eteryczny [e-te-**rich**-ni] adj.m. ethereal; volatile; airy; light; sprightly; heavenly; marked by unusual delicacy and refinement
olejki eteryczne [o-**ley**-kee e-te-**rich**-ne] exp.: volatile oils
etiolacja [e-tyo-**lah**-tsyah] f. etiolation; bleaching and altering by exclusion of sunlight
etiologia [e-tyo-**lo**-gyah] f. etiology; aetiology; studies of causes (of diseases, etc.)
etiologicznie [e-tyo-lo-**geech**-ńe] adv. etiologically
etiologiczny [e-tyo-lo-**geech**-ni] adj.m. etiologic; etiological; assigning or seeking to assign a cause; of etiology
Etiopczyk [e-**tyop**-chik] m. Ethiopian
etiopista [e-tyo-**pee**-stah] m. student of Ethiopian culture
etiopistyczny [e-tyo-pee-**stich**-ni] adj.m. of Ethiopian culture
etiopistyka [e-tyo-**pee**-sti-kah] f. study of Ethiopian culture
etiopski [e-**tyop**-skee] adj.m. Ethiopian
etiuda [e-**tyoo**-dah] f. etude; musical study; painter's study
etnicznie [et-**ńeech**-ńe] adv. ethnically
etniczność [et-**ńeech**-nośhćh] f. ethnicity; ethnic quality or

affiliation
etniczny [et-ńeech-ni] adj.m. ethnic
etno- [et-no] prefix: ethno-; race-; people-
etnocentrycznie [et-no-tsen-trich-ńe] adv. in an ethnocentric manner
etnocentryczny [et-no-tsen-trich-ni] adj.m. ethnocentric; having race as a central interest; having the attitude that one's own group is superior
etnocentryzm [et-no-tsen-trizm] m. ethnocentrism
etnogeneza [et-no-ge-ne-zah] f. genesis of ethnicity; development of ethnicity
etnogenia [et-no-ge-ńyah] f. study of development of nations
etnograf [et-no-grahf] m. ethnographer
etnografia [et-no-grah-fyah] f. ethnography; descriptive anthropology; ethnology
etnograficznie [et-no-grah-feech-ńe] adv. ethnographically
etnograficzny [et-no-grah-feech-ni] adj.m. ethnographic; ethnographical
etnolingwistyka [et-no-leen-gvee-sti-kah] f. ethnolunguistics; the influence of language on ethnicity
etnolog [et-no-log] m. ethnologist
etnologia [et-no-lo-gyah] f. ethnology; cultural anthropology
etnologicznie [et-no-lo-geech-ńe] adv. ethnologically
etnologiczny [et-no-lo-geech-ni] adj.m. ethnologic; ethnological
etnonim [et-no-ńeem] m. name of a tribe (people, etc.)
etnonimia [et-no-ńee-myah] f. study of names (of peoples, tribes, etc.)
etnopsychologia [et-no-psi-kho-lo-gyah] f. study of the psychology of ethnicity
etnosocjologia [et-no-so-tsyo-lo-gyah] f. sociological study of ethnicity
etola [e-to-lah] f. (woman's) fur stole
etolog [e-to-log] m. ethologist
etologia [e-to-lo-gyah] f. ethology; study of character formation; study of human ethos; study of animal behavior
etos [e-tos] m. ethos; the distinguishing character, sentiment, moral nature, or guiding beliefs of a person, group, institution, etc.
etos demokratyczny [e-tos de-mo-krah-tich-ni] exp.: ethos of democracy
etranżer [e-trahn-zher] m. foreigner (rarely used)
Etrusk [e-troosk] m. Etruscan
etruski [et-roo-skee] adj.m. Etruscan
etruskolog [et-roo-sko-log] m. student of Etruscan culture
etruskologia [et-roo-sko-lo-gyah] f. study of Etruscan culture
etui [e-too-ee] indecl. a small ornamental case; etui (for glasses, etc.)
etycznie [e-tich-ńe] adv. ethically; morally
etyczny [e-tich-ni] adj.m. ethical; moral (standard, conduct, etc.)
etyk [e-tik] m. ethicist; a specialist in ethics
etyka [e-ti-kah] f. ethics; a set of moral principles, or values; moral philosophy; morals; moral science
etyka zawodowa [e-ti-kah zah-vo-do-vah] exp.: professional ethics
etykieta [e-ti-ke-tah] f. label; tag; tab; tally; etiquette; formality; ceremonial; acceptable manners
etykietalnie [e-ti-ke-tahl-ńe] adv. ceremonially; formally
etykietalny [e-ti-ke-tahl-ni] adj.m. ceremonial; formal
etykietka [e-ti-ket-kah] f. label; tab; tag; tally; (nice, funny, etc.) etiquette
etykietować [e-ti-ke-to-vahćh] v. label; tab; tag; tally (*repeatedly*)
etykietowanie [e-ti-ke-to-vah-ńe] n. labelling; tabbing; tagging; tallying
etyl [e-til] m. ethyl
etylen [e-ti-len] m. ethylene
etylenizacja [e-ti-le-ńee-zah-tsyah] f. treating of plants with ethylene
etylenowy [e-ti-le-no-vi] adj.m. of ethylene
etylina [e-ti-lee-nah] f. ethyl gasoline
etylizować [e-ti-lee-zo-vahćh] v. ethylate (*repeatedly*)

etylizowanie [e-ti-lee-zo-**vah**-ńe] n. ethylation
etyloceluloza [e-ti-lo-tse-loo-**lo**-zah] f. ethyl cellulose
etylować [e-ti-**lo**-vahćh] v. ethylate (*repeatedly*)
etylowanie [e-ti-lo-**vah**-ńe] n. ethylation
etylowy [e-ti-**lo**-vi] adj.m. of ethyl; ethyl (alcohol, etc.)
etymolog [e-ti-**mo**-log] m. etymologist
etymologia [e-ti-mo-**lo**-gyah] f. etymology; derivation (of words)
etymologicznie [e-ti-mo-lo-**geech**-ńe] adv. etymologically
etymologiczny [e-ti-mo-lo-**geech**-ni] adj.m. etymological
etymologista [e-ti-mo-lo-**gees**-tah] m. etymologist
etymologizować [e-ti-mo-lo-gee-**zo**-vahćh] v. etymologize; study, or formulate etymologies; define etymologically (*repeatedly*)
etymologizowanie [e-ti-mo-lo-gee-zo-**vah**-ńe] n. etymologizing
etymon [e-**ti**-mon] m. etymon
eucharystia [ew-khah-**rist**-yah] f. Eucharist; spiritual communion
eucharystyczny [ew-khah-ris-**tich**-ni] adj.m. Eucharistic (Congress, etc.); of spiritual communion
eudajmonia [ew-dahy-**mo**-ńyah] f. eudaemonism
eudajmonista [ew-dahy-mo-**ńee**-stah] m. eudaemonist
eudajmonistyczny [ew-dahy-mo-ńees-**tich**-ni] adj.m. eudaemonistic
eudajmonizm [ew-dahy-**mo**-ńeezm] m. eudaemonism; moral obligation based on personal well-being through a life governed by reason
eudemonizm [ew-de-**mo**-ńeezm] m. eudaemonism
eudiometr [ew-**dyo**-metr] m. eudiometer; instrument for the volumetric measurement and analysis of gases
eufemicznie [ew-fe-**meech**-ńe] adv. euphemistically
eufemiczny [ew-fe-**meech**-ni] adj.m. pleasant sounding; euphemistic; euphemistical
eufemistycznie [ew-fe-mee-**stich**-ńe] adv. euphemistically
eufemistyczny [ew-fe-mee-**stich**-ni] adj.m. euphemistic
eufemizacja [ew-fe-mee-**zah**-tsyah] f. euphemism; the use of a less offensive word or phrase for one considered offensive
eufemizm [ew-**fe**-meezm] m. euphemism; the use of a less offensive word or phrase for one considered offensive
eufonia [ew-**fo**-ńyah] f. euphony; pleasing or sweet sound
eufonicznie [ew-fo-**ńeech**-ńe] adv. euphonically
eufoniczny [ew-fo-**ńeech**-ni] adj.m. euphonic
euforbia [ew-**for**-byah] f. euphorbia; spurge
euforia [ew-**fo**-ryah] f. euphoria; elation; feeling of well-being; buoyancy; light-heartedness
euforycznie [ew-fo-**rich**-ńe] adv. euphorically
euforyczny [ew-fo-**rich**-ni] adj.m. euphoric
euforyk [ew-**fo**-rik] m. (an) euphoric
eugeniczny [ew-ge-**ńeech**-ni] adj.m. eugenic; fitted for the production of good offspring
eugenik [ew-**ge**-ńeek] m. eugenicist; student of eugenics; advocate of eugenics
eugenika [ew-**ge**-ńee-kah] f. eugenics; study of the improvement of hereditary features and qualities
euglena [e-oo-**gle**-nah] f. euglena (a type of algae)
euhemeryzm [ew-khe-**me**-rizm] m. euhemerism; interpretation of myths as traditional accounts of historical persons and events
eukaliptol [ew-kah-**leep**-tol] m. eucalyptole; cineole
eukaliptus [ew-kah-**leep**-toos] m. eucalyptus (oil)
eukaliptusowy [ew-kah-leep-too-**so**-vi] adj.m. eucalyptus (oil, gum, wood, lozenges, leaves, etc.)
euklidesowy [e-oo-klee-de-**so**-vi] adj.m. Euclidean (geometry, etc.)
eunuch [**ew**-nookh] m. eunuch

eunuchoid [ew-noo-**kho**-eet] m. eunuchoid; a sexually deficient individual; one tending toward the intersex state
eunuchoidowy [ew-noo-kho-ee-**do**-vi] adj.m. eunuchoid; of a sexually deficient individual
eunuchoidyzm [ew-noo-**khoy**-dizm] m. eunuchism
eupatryda [ew-pah-**tri**-dah] m. eupatrid; hereditary aristocrat of ancient Athens
Eurazjata [ewr-ah-**zyah**-tah] m. (a) Eurasian
eurazjatycki [ewr-ah-zyah-**ti**-tskee] adj.m. Eurasian
eurocentryczny [ew-ro-tsen-**trich**-ni] adj.m. Europocentric; centered on Europe and the Europeans
eurocentryzm [ew-ro-**tsen**-trizm] m. Europocentrism
eureka [e-oo-**re**-kah] excl.: success!; finally!; eureka!
europ [**ew**-rop] m. europium (Eu)
europeizacja [ew-ro-pe-ee-**zah**-tsyah] f. making European
europeizm [ew-ro-**pe**-eezm] m. European cultural borrowing, etc.
europeizować [ew-ro-pe-ee-**zo**-vahćh] v. turn European; make into a European; Europeanize (*repeatedly*)
europeizować się [ew-ro-pe-ee-**zo**-vahćh śh<u>an</u>] v. become European; take on European characteristics (*repeatedly*)
europeizowanie [ew-ro-pe-ee-zo-**vah**-ńe] n. Europeanization
europeizowanie się [ew-ro-pe-ee-zo-**vah**-ńe śh<u>an</u>] n. becoming a European
Europejczyk [ew-ro-**pey**-chik] m. European
europejczyk [ew-ro-**pey**-chik] m. man of European culture
Europejka [ew-ro-**pey**-kah] f. European woman
europejski [ew-ro-**pey**-skee] adj.m. European
po europejsku [po ew-ro-**pey**-skoo] exp.: like a European; in accordance with European standards
europejskość [ew-ro-**pey**-skośhćh] f. European character (of culture, etc.)
europocentryczny [ew-ro-po-tsen-**trich**-ni] adj.m. Europocentric; centered on Europe and the Europeans
europocentryzm [ew-ro-po-**tsen**-trizm] m. Europocentrism
eurorakieta [ew-ro-rah-<u>**ke**</u>-tah] f. rocket based in Europe and threatening European countries
eurorynek [ew-ro-**ri**-nek] m. European banking and exchange network
eurowizyjny [ew-ro-vee-**ziy**-ni] adj.m. of Eurovision (institution exchanging programs of the Union on European Broadcasters)
transmisja eurowizyjna [trahns-**mees**-yah ew-ro-vee-**ziy**-nah] exp.: broadcast by Eurovision
euryfag [ew-**ri**-fahg] m. an organism that feeds on a wide variety of food
euryfot [ew-**ri**-fot] m. an organism that tolerates wide range of light
euryterm [ew-**ri**-term] m. eurytherm; organism that tolerates wide range of temperatures
eurytermiczność [ew-ri-ter-**meech**-nośhćh] f. eurythermic nature
eurytermiczny [ew-ri-ter-**meech**-ni] adj.m. eurythermal; eurythermic; eurythermous; tolerating wide range of temperatures
eurytmia [ew-**rit**-myah] f. eurhythmy; eurythmy; harmonious body movement to the rhythm of spoken words; eurhythmics; art of harmonious bodily movements in response to improvised music
eurytmiczny [ew-rit-**meech**-ni] adj.m. eurhythmic (physical exercises, etc.)
eurytop [ew-**ri**-top] m. organism tolerant of wide variations in environment
eurytopiczny [ew-ri-to-**peech**-ni] adj.m. eurytopic
eurytopizm [ew-ri-**to**-peezm] m. eurytopicity
eutanazja [ew-tah-**nah**-zyah] f. euthanasia; mercy killing
eutektyczny [ew-tek-**tich**-ni] adj.m.

eutectic; having the lowest melting point possible
eutektyk [ew-**tek**-tik] m. a eutectic; eutectic alloy
eutrofia [ew-**tro**-fyah] f. eutrophy
eutroficzny [ew-tro-**feech**-ni] adj.m. eutrophic
eutrofizm [ew-**tro**-feezm] m. eutrophy; eutrophication
ewakuacja [e-vah-koo-**ah**-tsyah] f. evacuation; removal; emptying
ewakuacyjny [e-vah-koo-ah-**tsiy**-ni] adj.m. of evacuation; evacuation (hospital, etc.)
ewakuant [e-vah-**koo**-ahnt] m. evacuee; person evacuated; person self-evacuated
ewakuować [e-vah-koo-**o**-vahćh] v. evacuate (troops, a population, etc.); withdraw (*repeatedly*)
ewakuować się [e-vah-koo-**o**-vahćh śhan] v. evacuate oneself; withdraw (*repeatedly*)
ewakuowanie [e-vah-koo-o-**vah**-ńe] n. evacuation (of a city, etc.); withdrawal
ewakuowanie się [e-vah-koo-o-**vah**-ńe śhan] n. evacuation; withdrawal (of an army, etc.)
ewaluacja [e-vah-loo-**ah**-tsyah] f. evaluation; fixing of value; appraisal
ewaluować [e-vah-loo-**o**-vahćh] v. evaluate; determine the value; fix the value by careful appraisal and study; estimate the value (*repeatedly*)
ewangelia [e-vahn-**ge**-lyah] f. gospel; gospel truth
Ewangelia [e-vahn-**ge**-lyah] f. book containing the texts of the four evangelists
ewangeliarz [e-vahn-**ge**-lyahsh] m. book of daily reading of the gospel
ewangelicki [e-vahn-ge-**lee**-tskee] adj.m. Protestant; Lutheran; Evangelical; evangelic
ewangelicyzm [e-vahn-ge-**lee**-tsizm] m. Protestantism
ewangeliczka [e-vahn-ge-**leech**-kah] f. Protestant woman; Lutheran woman
ewangeliczny [e-vahn-ge-**leech**-ni] adj.m. evangelic; evangelical
ewangelijny [e-vahn-ge-**leey**-ni] adj.m. evangelic; evangelical
ewangelik [e-vahn-**ge**-leek] m. Protestant; Lutheran
ewangelista [e-vahn-ge-**lee**-stah] m. evangelist
ewangelizacja [e-vahn-ge-lee-**zah**-tsyah] f. evangelization; missionary work; propagation of the faith; preaching the gospel
ewaporacja [e-vah-po-**rah**-tsyah] f. evaporation
ewaporacyjny [e-vah-po-rah-**tsiy**-ni] adj.m. evaporative
ewaporat [e-vah-**po**-raht] m. sedimentary rock formed by evaporation; evaporite
ewaporaty [e-vah-po-**rah**-ti] pl. evaporites
ewaporometr [e-vah-po-**ro**-metr] m. evaporation gauge; instrument for measuring the evaporation of water
ewaporymetr [e-vah-po-**ri**-metr] m. evaporation gauge; instrument for measuring the evaporation of water
ewekcja [e-**vek**-tsyah] f. irregularity in the movement of the moon caused by the sun
ewenement [e-ve-**ne**-ment] m. an unusual event; a sensation
ewentualnie [e-ven-too-**ahl**-ńe] adv. possibly; if need be; if necessary; should the occasion arise; possibly; God willing; or
ewentualność [e-ven-too-ahl-**no**śhćh] f. possibility; eventuality; contingency; circumstance; case; emergency
ewentualny [e-ven-too-**ahl**-ni] adj.m. contingent; possible; likely; conceivable; imaginable; probable
ewidencja [e-vee-**den**-tsyah] f. records; lists; files; roll
biuro ewidencji [**byoo**-ro e-vee-**den**-tsyee] exp.: registry office
ewidencja ludności [e-vee-**den**-tsyah lood-**no**-śhćhee] exp.: census
mam to w ewidencji [mahm to v e-vee-**den**-tsyee] exp.: I have it on the record; I have it in the

files
prowadzić ewidencję [pro-**vah**-dźheećh e-vee-**den**-tsyan] exp.: to keep a record (of)
skreślić z ewidencji [**skre**-śhleećh z e-vee-**den**-tsyee] exp.: to strike off the record
ewidencjonować [e-vee-den-tsyo-**no**-vahćh] v. compile records; file; record (*repeatedly*)
ewidencjonowanie [e-vee-den-tsyo-no-**vah**-ńe] n. compiling records; filing; recording
ewidencjować [e-vee-den-**tsyo**-vahćh] v. compile records; file; record (*repeatedly*)
ewidencyjnie [e-vee-den-**tsiy**-ńe] adv. by information; by means of record (or index)
ewidencyjny [e-vee-den-**tsiy**-ni] adj.m. of information; of record or index (card, etc.)
arkusz ewidencyjny [ahr-koosh e-vee-den-**tsiy**-ni] exp.: index card; record
ewidentnie [e-vee-**dent**-ńe] adv. obviously; apparently; evidently; patently; distinctly; plainly; clearly to vision; clearly to understanding; manifestly
ewidentny [e-vee-**dent**-ni] adj.m. obvious; apparent; evident; patent; distinct; plain; clear to vision; clear to understanding; manifest
ewikcja [e-**veek**-tsyah] f. judicial guarantee (by a court order) of the transfer of ownership
ewinkować [e-veen-**ko**-vahćh] v. sue for the repossession of one's property sold illegally (*repeatedly*)
ewinkowanie [e-veen-ko-**vah**-ńe] n. legal action to repossess one's property sold illegally by others
ewokacja [e-vo-**kah**-tsyah] f. evocation; imaginative recreation; summoning
ewokacyjny [e-vo-kah-**tsiy**-ni] adj.m. evocative; tending to evoke; serving to evoke
ewokować [e-vo-**ko**-vahćh] v. evoke; bring to mind; bring to recollection; re-create imaginatively (*repeatedly*)
ewokowanie [e-vo-ko-**vah**-ńe] n. evoking; bringing to mind
ewolucja [e-vo-**loo**-tsyah] f. evolution; development
ewolucje [e-vo-**loo**-tsye] pl. evolutions; aerobatics
ewolucjonista [e-vo-loo-tsyo-**ńee**-stah] m. evolutionist
ewolucjonistyczny [e-vo-loo-tsyo-ńee-**stich**-ni] adj.m. evolutionist
ewolucjonizm [e-vo-loo-**tsyo**-ńeezm] m. evolutionism
ewolucyjnie [e-vo-loo-**tsiy**-ńe] adv. in an evolutionary manner; by evolution; by process of evolution
ewolucyjność [e-vo-loo-**tsiy**-nośhćh] f. evolution
ewolucyjny [e-vo-loo-**tsiy**-ni] adj.m. evolutionary; of evolution
ewoluować [e-vo-loo-**o**-vahćh] v. evolve; develop gradually; unfold; develop by evolution (*repeatedly*)
ewoluta [e-vo-**loo**-tah] f. evolute; the locus of the center of curvature; the envelope of the normals of a curvature
ewolwenta [e-vol-**ven**-tah] f. involute (a curve traced by a point departing from another curve)
eworsja [e-**vor**-syah] f. the scouring of rocks on the bottom of streams and rivers by moving gravel
eworsyjny [e-vor-**siy**-ni] adj.m. scouring (stream, etc.)
ex- [eks] prefix: see eks-
ex libris [ex **lee**-brees] m. ex libris; bookplate
exodus [e-**gzo**-doos] m. exodus; a going out; the second book of the Bible describing this
expose [eks-po-**ze**] n. (French) expose; statement
explicite [eks-**plee**-tsee-te] adv. (Latin) clearly; directly; explicitly
expres [**eks**-pres] m. special delivery (letter with a return receipt, etc.)
ezofagoskop [e-zo-fah-**go**-skop] m. esophagoscope; endoscope for examination of the throat and esophagus
ezofagoskopia [e-zo-fah-go-**sko**-pyah] f. esophagoscopy

ezopowy [e-zo-**po**-vi] adj.m. Aesopian; Aesopic; in the style of fables of Aesop; tart; to the point; witty; sharp; terse
ezopowy język [e-zo-**po**-vi **yan**-zik] exp.: the language of Aesop
morał ezopowy [**mo**-rahw e-zo-**po**-vi] exp.: Aesop's teaching; Aesop's moral
ezoteryczny [e-zo-te-**rich**-ni] adj.m. esoteric; meant for a chosen few; private; confidential; secret
ezoteryczna wiedza [e-zo-te-**rich**-nah **vye**-dzah] exp.: esoteric knowledge
ezoteryk [e-zo-**te**-rik] m. an esoteric; especially initiated man
ezoteryzm [e-zo-**te**-rizm] m. esotericism; esoteric doctrines or practices; the quality or state of being esoteric

Ę

Ę, ę [an] n. the letter "ę"
ęsi [an-śhee] excl.: child's word for impending bowel movement; child's bowel movement

F

F, f [ef] m. the letter "f"
fa [fah] (not declined:) the name of the musical "f" sound
fabianin [fahb-**yah**-ńeen] m. follower of Fabianism
fabianism [fahb-**yah**-ńeezm] m. Fabianism
faborek [fah-**bo**-rek] m. ribbon (in Cracovian regional costumes)
fabryczka [fah-**brich**-kah] f. small factory
fabrycznie [fah-**brich**-ńe] adv. by machinery
zrobiony fabrycznie [zro-**byo**-ni fah-**brich**-ńe] exp.: machine-made; manufactured
fabryczny [fah-**brich**-ni] adj.m. machine made; manufactured
fabryka [fah-**bri**-kah] f. factory; works; mill; industrial plant
fabrykacja [fah-bri-**kah**-tsyah] f. manufacture; manufacturing; production; forgery; fabrication
fabrykancki [fah-bri-**kahnts**-kee] adj.m. of factory owner; industrial plant owner's; manufacturer's
fabrykant [fah-**bri**-kahnt] m. factory owner; industrial plant owner; manufacturer; producer; maker; forger; fabricator
fabrykantka [fah-bri-**kahnt**-kah] f. (woman) factory owner; industrial plant owner; manufacturer; producer; maker; forger; fabricator
fabrykat [fah-**bri**-kaht] m. product; production; forgery; fabrication
fabrykaty [fah-bri-**kah**-ti] pl. manufactured goods
fabrykować [fah-bri-**ko**-vahćh] v. produce; manufacture; make; fabricate; forge; fake; falsify; lie; make up (a story, etc.); invent (*repeatedly*)
fabrykowanie [fah-bri-ko-**vah**-ńe] n. production; manufacture
fabulacja [fah-boo-**lahts**-yah] f. fictitious account; imaginary events
fabularnie [fah-boo-**lahr**-ńe] adv. in a manner of fiction; fictitiously; in an imaginary way
fabularność [fah-boo-**lahr**-nośhćh] f. fiction; imaginary plot
fabularny [fah-boo-**lahr**-ni] adj.m. of fiction; fabled; having the form of a fable; fabulous
film fabularny [feelm fah-boo-**lahr**-ni] exp.: feature film; photodrama
fabularyzacja [fah-boo-lah-ri-**zah**-tsyah] f. giving the form of a story (to news, chronicle, diary)
fabularyzm [fah-boo-**lah**-rizm] m. fabular character (in works of art, etc.)
fabularyzować [fah-boo-lah-ri-**zo**-vahćh] v. give the form of a story (to news, chronicle, diary, etc.) (*repeatedly*)

fabularyzowanie [fah-boo-lah-ri-zo-**vah**-ńe] n. giving the form of a story (to news, chronicle, etc.)
fabulistyczny [fah-boo-lees-**tich**-ni] adj.m. having the form of a story (in news, chronicle, diary, etc.)
fabulistyka [fah-boo-**lees**-ti-kah] f. the writing of fables; the writing of fabulists
fabuła [**fah**-boo-wah] f. plot (of a novel, etc.); fable; story
facecja [fah-**tse**-tsyah] f. anecdote; jest; facetiae; facetiousness
facecjonista [fah-tse-tsyo-**ńees**-tah] m. facetious person; anecdote teller; jester; joker; wag; wit
facecjonistycznie [fah-tse-tsyo-ńees-**tich**-ńe] adv. facetiously
facecjonistyczny [fah-tse-tsyo-ńees-**tich**-ni] adj.m. facetious; anecdotal; joking; facete; witty
facelia [fah-**tsel**-yah] f. Phacelia herb of the waterleaf family
faceliowaty [fah-tsel-yo-**vah**-ti] adj.m. of the Phacelia herb of the waterleaf family
faceliowate [fah-tsel-yo-**vah**-te] pl. the waterleaf family of the Phacelia herbs
facet [**fah**-tset] m. colloq: dude; guy; man; person; individual; somebody; character; fellow
facetka [fah-**tset**-kah] f. not a well-known woman (or girl)
fach [fahkh] m. occupation; profession; business; calling; trade; job; line (of work)
fachowiec [fah-**kho**-vyets] m. expert; specialist; connoisseur
fachowo [fah-**kho**-vo] adv. professionally; expertly; with competence; proficiently
fachowość [fah-**kho**-vośhćh] f. expertness; professional competence; knowledge of a trade
fachowy [fah-**kho**-vi] adj.m. professional; expert; competent; skilled; workmanlike
facja [**fah**-tsyah] f. facies; stage
facjata [fah-**tsyah**-tah] f. attic; garret; dormer window; slang: mug; phiz; dial
facjatka [fah-**tsyah**-tkah] f. (small, nice) attic; garret; dormer window
facsimile [fahk-see-**mee**-le] n. (Engl.) colloq: facsimile; an exact copy; transmission of graphic matter by wire and its reproduction; FAX
fading [**fah**-deeng] or [**fey**-deeng] m. fading (of radio broadcast)
faeton [fah-**e**-ton] m. touring car
fafle [**fahf**-le] pl. drooping lips of hunting dogs
fafuła [fah-**foo**-wah] f. slang: fathead; booby; slacker
fag [fahg] m. phage; bacteriophage
fagas [**fah**-gahs] m. servant; flunkey; underling; yes man; adulator
fagasostwo [fah-gah-**sos**-tfo] n. servility; flattery
fagasować [fah-gah-**so**-vahćh] v. adulate; flatter; be servile (*repeatedly*)
fagasowanie [fah-gah-so-**vah**-ńe] n. adulation; flattery; being servile; servility
fagasowski [fah-gah-**sof**-skee] adj.m. adulatory; servile
fagocista [fah-go-**ćhees**-tah] m. bassoon player; bassoonist
fagocyt [fah-**go**-tsit] m. phagocyte
fagocytarny [fah-go-tsi-**tahr**-ni] adj.m. phagocytic
fagocytoblast [fah-go-tsi-**to**-blahst] m. phagocytoblast
fagocytoza [fah-go-tsi-**to**-zah] f. phagocytosis
fagot [**fah**-got] m. bassoon
fagotowy [fah-go-**to**-vi] adj.m. of bassoon
fair [fer] adj. (Engl.) fair; just and honest; loyal; adv. fair; justly and honestly; loyally
fair-play [fer pley] exp.: (Engl.) loyal behavior; playing according to the rules; honest contest; clean fight
faja [**fah**-yah] f. large pipe (for smoking)
fajans [**fah**-yahns] m. earthenware; colloq: china; dishes; glasses; kitchen utensils
fajansowy [fah-yahn-**so**-vi] adj.m. of earthenware; earthenware (vessel, etc.)
fajczany [fahy-**chah**-ni] adj.m. of a tobacco-pipe (smoke, etc.)

fajczarz [**fahy**-chahsh] m. tobacco-pipe smoker
fajczyć [**fahy**-chićh] v. slang: smoke (pipe, cigarettes, etc.) (*repeatedly*)
fajczyć się [**fahy**-chićh śhan] v. slang: burn (*repeatedly*)
fajdać [**fahy**-dahćh] v. shit (vulg.) (*repeatedly*)
fajeczka [fah-**yech**-kah] f. (small, nice) tobacco-pipe
fajer [**fah**-yer] m. colloq: enthusiasm; zeal; fervor; eagerness; keenness; mettle
fajerant [fah-**ye**-rahnt] m. colloq: end of a day's work; rest period during work
fajerka [fah-**yer**-kah] f. cook-top unit; gas stove lid; burner
fajerwerk [fah-**yer**-verk] m. firework; firecracker
fajf [fahyf] m. afternoon get-together; afternoon tea party
fajfa [**fahy**-fah] f. slang: high mark in school
fajka [**fahy**-kah] f. pipe (for smoking); wild boar's tusk; colloq: cigarette
fajkować [fahy-**ko**-vahćh] v. check off (items on a list); put a verification mark (*repeatedly*)
fajkowanie [fahy-ko-**vah**-ńe] n. checking-off
fajkowy [fahy-**ko**-vi] adj.m. pipe (tobacco, etc.)
fajnie [**fahy**-ńe] adv. slang: fine!; good!; right you are!
fajno [**fahy**-no] adv. slang: fine!; good!; right you are!
fajny [**fahy**-ni] adj.m. slang: first-rate; tiptop; honky-dory
fajny bajer [**fahy**-ni **bah**-yer] exp.: slang: a lie; falsehood(jargon)
fajrant [**fahy**-rahnt] m. slang: end of a day's work; rest period during work
fajt! [fahyt] excl.: plump!
fajtać [**fahy**-tahćh] v. dangle (one's legs, etc.); turn somersaults (*repeatedly*)
fajtać się [**fahy**-tahćh śhan] v. swing oneself; rock oneself; dangle oneself; turn somersaults (*repeatedly*)
fajtanie [fahy-**tah**-ńe] n. dangling
fajtanie się [fahy-**tah**-ńe śhan] n. swinging oneself; rocking oneself; dangling oneself; turning somersaults
fajtłapa [fahy-**twah**-pah] m. & f. all thumbs guy (awkward, clumsy man); dangling hand; crock; mob slang: victim of a robbery
fajtłapowaty [fahy-twah-po-**vah**-ti] adj.m. awkward; clumsy; shabby
fajtnąć [**fahyt**-nownćh] v. turn somersaults; dangle
fajtnąć się [**fahyt**-nownćh śhan] v. swing oneself; rock oneself; dangle oneself; turn somersaults
fajtnięcie [fahyt-**ńan**-ćhe] n. flip; somersault
fajtnięcie się [fahyt-**ńan**-ćhe śhan] n. falling down; flipping
fakcik [**fahk**-ćheek] m. (small, not important) fact
fakir [**fah**-keer] m. fakir
fakirek [fah-**kee**-rek] m. shoe-insert for massaging feet
faksymile [fahk-si-**mee**-le] n. facsimile; an exact copy; transmission of graphic matter by wire and its reproduction; FAX
faksymilowany [fahk-si-mee-lo-**vah**-ni] adj.m. copied exactly; pictorially transmitted by wire; FAX-ed
faksymilowy [fahk-si-mee-**lo**-vi] adj.m. of facsimile; of FAX
fakt [fahkt] m. fact; matter of fact; reality
fakt dokonany [fahkt do-ko-**nah**-ni] exp.: accomplished fact
fakty [**fahk**-ti] pl. data; facts
operować faktami [o-pe-ro-vahćh fahk-**tah**-mee] exp.: to get down to facts
faktograf [fahk-**to**-grahf] m. collector and recorder of facts; fact finder
faktografia [fahk-to-**grah**-fyah] f. collection and recording of facts
faktograficzny [fahk-to-grah-**feech**-ni] adj.m. of the collection and recording of facts
faktomontaż [fahk-to-**mon**-tahsh] m. presentation of facts (in a dramatic form, literary form,

etc.); arrangement of facts
faktor [**fahk**-tor] m. broker; agent; factor (math.); intermediary
faktoria [fahk-**tor**-yah] f. trading post
faktorka [fahk-**tor**-kah] f. (woman) broker; agent; factor
faktorne [fahk-**tor**-ne] n. commission; factorage; fee
faktorować [fahk-to-**ro**-vahćh] v. act as an agent; act as a broker (*repeatedly*)
faktorowanie [fahk-to-ro-**vah**-ńe] n. brokerage; factorage
faktorski [fahk-**tor**-skee] adj.m. agent's; broker's; of a broker; of an agent
faktorstwo [fahk-**tor**-stfo] n. agency; brokerage; factorage
faktotum [fahk-**to**-toom] indecl.: handyman; do-all; factotum
faktura [fahk-**too**-rah] f. invoice; bill
fakturalny [fahk-too-**rahl**-ni] adj.m. of an invoice; of a bill
fakturować [fahk-too-**ro**-vahćh] v. submit an invoice (for, to); invoice; bill (*repeatedly*)
fakturowanie [fahk-too-ro-**vah**-ńe] n. sending invoices; invoicing; billing
fakturowy [fahk-too-**ro**-vi] adj.m. invoice (book, price, etc.)
fakturzysta [fahk-too-**zhis**-tah] m. invoice clerk
fakturzystka [fahk-too-**zhist**-kah] f. (woman) invoice clerk
faktycznie [fahk-**tich**-ńe] adv. in fact; actually; indeed; truly
faktyczność [fahk-**tich**-nośhćh] f. factuality
faktyczny [fahk-**tich**-ni] adj.m. factual; actual; real; intrinsic; true; practical
fakultatywnie [fah-kool-tah-**tiv**-ńe] adv. at will; optionally; at discretion
fakultatywność [fah-kool-tah-**tiv**-nośhćh] f. optional character; facultative nature
fakultatywny [fah-kool-tah-**tiv**-ni] adj.m. optional; facultative; not obligatory
fakultet [fah-**kool**-tet] m. faculty
fala [**fah**-lah] f. wave; tide; surge; billow; roller
drobna fala [**drob**-nah **fah**-lah] exp.: ripple
krótka fala [**kroot**-kah **fah**-lah] exp.: short wave
fala zimna [**fah**-lah **źheem**-nah] exp.: cold wave
falanga [fah-**lahn**-gah] f. Falanga; host; flock; army (of people, etc.); phalanx
falangista [fah-lahn-**gees**-tah] m. member of Spanish Phalanx; member of Polish Radical Nationalist Party (1934-1939)
falangistowski [fah-lahn-gees-**tof**-skee] adj.m. of Falanga
falanster [fah-**lahn**-ster] m. phalanstery (cooperative community)
falansteryjny [fah-lahn-ste-**riy**-ni] adj.m. of a phalanstery
falansteryzm [fah-lahn-**ste**-rizm] m. phalanstery; phalansterianism
falansterzysta [fah-lahn-ste-**zhis**-tah] m. member of a phalanstery
falbana [fahl-**bah**-nah] f. flounce; furbelow; frill
falbaneczka [fahl-bah-**nech**-kah] f. (very nice, little, etc.) flounce; furbelow; frill
falbaniasty [fahl-bah-**ńahs**-ti] adj.m. covered with flounce; full of frills
falbanka [fahl-**bahn**-kah] f. (nice, little, etc.) flounce; furbelow; frill
falc [fahlts] m. fold; slip-fold (of a book, etc.); rabbet; rebate; groove
falcować [fahl-**tso**-vahćh] v. fold; rabbet; rebate; groove; join by means of a fold (*repeatedly*)
falcowanie [fahl-tso-**vah**-ńe] n. folding; rabbeting; grooving; joining by means of a fold
falcówka [fahl-**tsoof**-kah] f. folder; folding machine
faldistorium [fahl-dees-**tor**-yoom] n. faldstool
faleń [**fah**-leń] m. mooring line
faleza [fah-**le**-zah] f. cliff
falisto [fah-**lees**-to] adv. in waves; in ripples
falistość [fah-**lees**-tośhćh] f. waviness; ripple; wave; undulations; hilliness; sinuosity
falisty [fah-**lees**-ti] adj.m. wavy;

rolling; corrugated
faliście [fah-leeśh-ćhe] adv. in waves; in ripples
falkonet [fahl-**ko**-net] m. falconet
falliczny [fahl-**leech**-ni] adj.m. phallic (worship, emblems, etc.); of penis
fallus [**fahl**-loos] m. (Greek) phallus; penis; symbol of the penis
falochron [fah-**lo**-khron] m. breakwater; pier; jetty; mole
falomierz [fah-**lo**-myesh] m. wave-meter; ondometer; ondograph
falować [fah-**lo**-vahćh] v. wave; undulate; ripple; flow; roll; corrugate (*repeatedly*)
falowanie [fah-lo-**vah**-ńe] n. wave; waving; undulation; ripple; roll (of the sea)
falowarka [fah-lo-**vahr**-kah] f. knitting machine
falownica [fah-lov-**ńee**-tsah] f. wave generator
falownik [fah-**lov**-ńeek] m. current rectifier
falowodowy [fah-lo-vo-**do**-vi] adj.m. of a conduit of electromagnetic waves
falowód [fah-**lo**-voot] m. conduit of electromagnetic waves
falowy [fah-**lo**-vi] adj.m. wavy; waving; of waves; of undulations; undulating; rolling
falrep [**fahl**-rep] m. lanyard; rope serving as a handrail
falsburta [fahls-**boor**-tah] f. bulwark
falsecik [fahl-**se**-ćheek] m. small falsetto voice
falsecista [fahl-se-**ćhees**-tah] m. man singing with the falsetto voice; falsetto singer; falsettist
falset [**fahl**-set] m. falsetto; head-voice
falsetować [fahl-se-**to**-vahćh] v. sing falsetto (*repeatedly*)
falsetowanie [fahl-se-to-**vah**-ńe] n. singing falsetto
falsetowy [fahl-se-**to**-vi] adj.m. falsetto (tone, sentiment, etc.)
falstart [**fahl**-stahrt] m. false start
falsyfikacja [fahl-si-fee-**kah**-tsyah] f. forgery; falsification; counterfeit
falsyfikat [fahl-si-**fee**-kaht] m. forgery; counterfeit; fake
falsyfikować [fahl-si-fee-**ko**-vahćh] v. forge (*repeatedly*)
falsyfikowanie [fahl-si-fee-ko-**vah**-ńe] n. forgery; counterfeit; faking
falszburta [fahlsh-**boor**-tah] f. bulwark
falszkil [**fahlsh**-keel] m. false keel
falujący [fah-loo-**y**<u>**own**</u>-tsi] adj.m. wavy; undulating; rippling
fał [fahw] m. halyard
fałat [**fah**-waht] m. colloq: piece of (bread, bacon, etc.)
fałd [fahwt] m. fold; wrinkle; ply; crease; tuck; pucker; gathering; plica; flexure
fałda [**fahw**-dah] f. crease; fold
fałdka [**fahwt**-kah] f. small crease
fałdować [fahw-**do**-vahćh] v. gather in folds; gather in pleats; crease; rumple; wrinkle; corrugate (*repeatedly*)
fałdować się [fahw-**do**-vahćh śh<u>an</u>] v. take a fold; take a ply; crease; ruckle up; crumple; pucker (*repeatedly*)
fałdowanie [fahw-do-**vah**-ńe] n. folds; pleats; creases; plies; rucks; puckers; wrinkles; corrugations
fałdowanie się [fahw-do-**vah**-ńe śh<u>an</u>] n. taking a fold; taking a ply; folding; creasing
fałdowy [fahw-**do**-vi] adj.m. folded
fałdzistka [fahw-**dźheest**-kah] f. an oily Asiatic plant
fałdzisty [fahw-**dźhees**-ti] adj.m. falling in folds; falling into creases; full (skirt, etc.); voluminous (draperies, etc.); ample (folds, etc.)
fałdziście [fahw-**dźheeśh**-ćhe] adv. in folds; loosely; voluminously; amply
fałsz [fahwsh] m. falsehood; piece of deceit; lie; falseness; deceitfulness; duplicity; falsification; counterfeit; forgery; false note; discordance; twist (of a ball); spinning motion
fałszerstwo [fahw-**sher**-stfo] n. falsification; counterfeit; forgery; fake; fakement; artifice
fałszerz [**fahw**-shesh] m. falsifier; counterfeiter; forger; fabricator
fałszować [fahw-**sho**-vahćh] v.

falsify; fake; forge; counterfeit; sing flat; sing out of tune; take false note (playing music) (*repeatedly*)
fałszowanie [fahw-sho-**vah**-ńe] n. falsification
fałszowany [fahw-sho-**vah**-ni] adj.m. falsified; loaded (dice, etc.)
fałszywie [fahw-**shi**-vye] adv. falsely; spuriously; wrong; wrongly; erroneously; artificially; deceitfully; insincerely; underhand; perfidiously; viciously; discordantly; (sing) flat
fałszywiec [fahw-**shi**-vyets] m. deceiver; dissembler; pretender
fałszywość [fahw-**shi**-vośhćh] f. falseness; spuriousness; artificiality; deceit; mendacity; perfidy; double-dealing; insincerity; shiftiness
fałszywy [fahw-**shi**-vi] adj.m. false; counterfeit; wrong; imitation (gold, etc.); forged; sham; faked; spurious; fake; pretended; feigned; erroneous; misleading; mistaken; deceitful; mendacious; perfidious; double-dealing; double-faced; insincere; shifty (look); dissembling; discordant; jarring; out of tune
fama [**fah**-mah] f. fame; rumor; reputation; mob slang: opinion
familia [fah-**meel**-yah] f. clan; kinfolk; kinfolks
familiarnie [fah-meel-**yahr**-ńe] adv. informally; unceremoniously; in a free and easy manner; familiarly
familiarność [fah-meel-**yahr**-nośhćh] f. informality; unceremonious behavior; free and easy manner; familiarity
familiarny [fah-meel-**yahr**-ni] adj.m. informal; unceremonious; free and easy; chummy; familiar
familijnie [fah-mee-**leey**-ńe] adv. by family ties
familijny [fah-mee-**leey**-ni] adj.m. informal; unceremonious; free and easy; of the family
famulus [fah-**moo**-loos] m. trusted servant
famuła [fah-**moo**-wah] f. slang: family
fan [fahn] m. colloq: fan; a person enthusiastic about a specified sport, performer, etc.
fanaberie [fah-nah-**be**-rye] pl. whims; fads; frills; ostentation
fanatyczka [fah-nah-**tich**-kah] f. (woman) fanatic; enthusiast; bigot; maniac
fanatycznie [fah-nah-**tich**-ńe] adv. fanatically; with fanaticism
fanatyczny [fah-nah-**tich**-ni] adj.m. fanatical; crazy; bigoted; enthusiastic
fanatyk [fah-**nah**-tik] m. fanatic; enthusiast; bigot; maniac
fanatyzm [fah-**nah**-tizm] m. fanaticism; craze; bigotry; mania
fanatyzować [fah-nah-ti-**zo**-vahćh] v. fanaticize; cause to become fanatic (*repeatedly*)
fandango [fahn-**dahn**-go] n. triple-time (Spanish dance) fandango
fanerofit [fah-ne-**ro**-feet] m. phanerophyte
fanerofity [fah-ne-ro-**fee**-ti] pl. phanerophytes
fanfara [fahn-**fah**-rah] f. fanfare; flourish of trumpets; trumpet; bugle
fanfaron [fahn-**fah**-ron] m. braggart; coxcomb; swaggerer
fanfaronada [fahn-fah-ro-**nah**-dah] f. brag; foppery; coxcombry; swagger; vain boasting; bluster; rant
fanfaronować [fahn-fah-ro-**no**-vahćh] v. brag; swagger; boast vainly; bluster; rant (*repeatedly*)
fanfarowy [fahn-fah-**ro**-vi] adj.m. of fanfare; of trumpet; of bugle; trumpet (sound, etc.); fanfare (music, etc.)
fanfarzysta [fahn-fah-**zhis**-tah] m. bugler; trumpeter
fanga [**fahn**-gah] f. slang: fang (in baseball); punch (in the face, etc.) (mob jargon)
fango [**fahn**-go] n. volcanic clay (used for therapy)
fant [fahnt] m. pledge; gage; (lottery) prize; forfeit
co robić z tym fantem? [tso **ro**-**beećh** s tim **fahn**-tem] exp.: what is to be done?; what to do in this

contingency?; here's a dilemma for you!
fantasmagoria [fahn-tahs-mah-**gor**-yah] f. phantasmagoria
fantasmagoryczny [fahn-tahs-mah-go-**rich**-ni] adj.m. phantasmagoric
fantasta [fahn-**tahs**-tah] m. fantast; phantast; visionary; dreamer; fantastico; eccentric
fantastka [fahn-**tahst**-kah] f. (woman) fantast; phantast; visionary; dreamer
fantastycznie [fahn-tahs-**tich**-ńe] adv. fantastically; fancifully; extravagantly; prodigiously; fabulously; extraordinarily; immensely; in a bizarre manner
fantastyczność [fahn-tahs-**tich**-nośhćh] f. fantasticalness; extravagance; fantasticality
fantastyczny [fahn-tahs-**tich**-ni] adj.m. fantastic; fanciful; visionary; imaginary; wild; wildcat (schemes, etc.); extravagant; odd; prodigious; fabulous; extraordinary; immense; stunning; bizarre
fantastyka [fahn-**tahs**-ti-kah] f. the fantastic; science fiction; the bizarre
fantazja [fahn-**tah**-zyah] f. dash; fancy; imagination; fiction; whim; daydream; notion; vagary; folly; act of folly; (musical) extravaganza
fantazjować [fahn-tah-**zyo**-vahćh] v. dream; give play to one's imagination; indulge in fiction; improvise; romance; romanticize; daydream (*repeatedly*)
fantazjowanie [fahn-tah-zyo-**vah**-ńe] n. daydreams; fiction; empty talk
fantazjujący [fahn-tah-zyoo-**yown**-tsi] adj.m. fanciful; imaginative; fancy-free
fantazmat [fahn-**tahz**-maht] m. phantasm; product of phantasy; ghost; specter; illusion; fantasy
fantazyjnie [fahn-tah-**ziy**-ńe] adv. fancifully; in daydreamlike manner
fantazyjność [fahn-tah-**ziy**-nośhćh] f. fancifulness
fantazyjny [fahn-tah-**ziy**-ni] adj.m. fanciful; fancy (dress, etc.)
fantom [**fahn**-tom] m. phantom; fantom; ghost; specter; apparition
fantowy [fahn-**to**-vi] adj.m. of lottery (with prizes excluding money)
fara [**fah**-rah] f. parish church
farad [**fah**-raht] m. farad
faradyczny [fah-rah-**dich**-ni] adj.m. faradic; faradaic
faradyzacja [fah-rah-di-**zah**-tsyah] f. application of a faradic current
faradyzm [fah-**rah**-dizm] m. faradism
faradyzować [fah-rah-di-**zo**-vahćh] v. faradize (*repeatedly*)
faradyzowanie [fah-rah-di-zo-**vah**-ńe] n. treating with faradic current
faramuszka [fah-rah-**moosh**-kah] f. trifle; bagatelle
farandola [fah-rahn-**do**-lah] f. farandole (dance)
faraon [fah-**rah**-on] m. Pharaoh; faro
farba [**fahr**-bah] f. paint; dye color; dyeing; oil color; watercolor; color; ink; distemper; slang: blood (mob jargon)
farbiarka [fahr-**byahr**-kah] f. (woman) dyer; stainer
farbiarnia [fahr-**byahr**-ńah] f. dye-works; dye-house; the dyer's
farbiarski [fahr-**byahr**-skee] adj.m. dye; dyer's; tinctorial
proces farbiarski [**pro**-tses fahr-**byahr**-skee] exp.: tinctorial process
farbiarstwo [fahr-**byahr**-stfo] n. dyeing trade
farbiarz [**fahr**-byahsh] m. dyer; stainer
farbka [**fahrp**-kah] f. washing blue; bluing; powder blue; ultramarine
farbkować [fahr-**pko**-vahćh] v. add blue to washing; treat with laundress's blue (*repeatedly*)
farbkowanie [fahr-pko-**vah**-ńe] n. adding blue to washing
farbkowy [fahr-**pko**-vi] adj.m. of the color of washing blue
farbować [fahr-**bo**-vahćh] v. dye; stain; tincture; discolor; color; mob slang: bleed (*repeatedly*)
farbować się [fahr-**bo**-vahćh śhan] v. dye; stain (*repeatedly*)
farbowanie [fahr-bo-**vah**-ńe] n.

dyeing
farbowanie się [fahr-bo-**vah**-ńe śh<u>an</u>] n. getting dyed
farbownik [fahr-**bov**-ńeek] m. bugloss
farfocel [fahr-**fo**-tsel] m. vulg.: tatter; shred (derived from a vulgar German expression related to female sex organ)
farma [**fahr**-mah] f. (specialized) farm
farmaceuta [fahr-mah-**tsew**-tah] m. chemist; druggist; pharmacist
farmaceutka [fahr-mah-**tsewt**-kah] f. (woman) chemist; druggist; pharmacist
farmaceutyczny [fahr-mah-tsew-**tich**-ni] adj.m. pharmaceutical; pharmaceutic
farmaceutyk [fahr-mah-**tsew**-tik] m. drug; medication; pharmaceutical
farmacja [fahr-**mah**-tsyah] f. pharmacy; pharmaceutics
farmakodynamicznie [fahr-mah-ko-di-nah-**meech**-ńe] adv. pharmacodynamically
farmakodynamiczny [fahr-mah-ko-di-**nah**-meech-ni] adj.m. pharmacodynamic
farmakodynamika [fahr-mah-ko-di-**nah**-mee-kah] f. pharmacodynamics
farmakognosta [fahr-mah-ko-**gnos**-tah] m. specialist in pharmacognosy
farmakognostyczny [fahr-mah-ko-gnos-**tich**-ni] adj.m. pharmacognostical; pharmacognostic
farmakognozja [fahr-mah-ko-**gno**-zyah] f. pharmacognosy
farmakolog [fahr-mah-**ko**-log] m. pharmacologist
farmakologia [fahr-mah-ko-**lo**-gyah] f. pharmacology
farmakologicznie [fahr-mah-ko-lo-**geech**-ńe] adv. pharmacologically
farmakologiczny [fahr-mah-ko-lo-**geech**-ni] adj.m. pharmacological; pharmacologic
farmakomania [fahr-mah-ko-**mah**-ńyah] f. abnormal dependency on drugs
farmakopea [fahr-mah-ko-**pe**-ah] f. pharmacopoeia; stock of drugs
farmakoterapia [fahr-mah-ko-te-**rah**-pyah] f. pharmacotherapy
farmazon [fahr-**mah**-zon] m. colloq: freemason; freethinker; cheat; liar; clown
farmazony [fahr-mah-**zo**-ni] pl. colloq: nonsense; foolishness; falsehoods
farmazonić [fahr-mah-**zo**-ńeećh] v. mob slang: lie; talk nonsense (*repeatedly*)
farmer [**fahr**-mer] m. farmer
farmerka [fahr-**mer**-kah] f. farmer's wife; woman owner of a farm
farmerski [fahr-**mer**-skee] adj.m. farmer's; farmers'
farmerstwo [fahr-**mer**-stfo] n. farming; farmer's work
farny [**fahr**-ni] adj.m. parish (church, community, etc.); parish-church (bells, etc.)
farsa [**fahr**-sah] f. farce; mockery
farsidło [fahr-**śheed**-wo] n. cheap farce; stupid mockery
farsopisarz [fahr-so-**pee**-sahsh] m. writer of farces; author of farces
farsopisarstwo [fahr-so-pee-**sahr**-stfo] n. writing of farces
farsowo [fahr-**so**-vo] adv. farcically; ludicrously; in a laughably inept manner; absurdly
farsowość [fahr-**so**-vośhćh] f. farcicality
farsowy [fahr-**so**-vi] adj.m. farcical; ludicrous; laughably inept; absurd; comedy (theater, satirical plot, improbable plot, etc.)
farsz [fahrsh] m. stuffing; forcemeat
fart [fahrt] m. good luck; slang: successful robbery (mob jargon)
fartuch [**fahr**-tookh] m. apron; raking; flashing; drift; fender; apron piece; trash shield (in water works)
fartuchowy [fahr-too-**kho**-vi] adj.m. of an apron; apron (shape, etc.)
fartuchówka [fahr-too-**khoof**-kah] f. tire with a protective extended rim
fartuszek [fahr-**too**-shek] m. small apron; pinafore; pinny
fartuszkowy [fahr-toosh-**ko**-vi] adj.m. apron (fabric, etc.)

fartuszyna [fahr-too-**shi**-nah] m. & f. shabby apron; badly worn out apron
farwater [fahr-**vah**-ter] m. fairway; channel; water pass (marked with buoys, etc.)
farwaterowy [fahr-vah-te-**ro**-vi] adj.m. of a fairway; of a channel; of a water pass
farys [**fah**-ris] m. Arabian horseman
faryzeizm [fah-ri-**ze**-eezm] m. Pharisaism; hypocrisy
faryzejski [fah-ri-**zey**-skee] adj.m. Pharisaical; hypocritical
faryzeusz [fah-ri-**ze**-oosh] m. Pharisee; hypocrite
faryzeuszostwo [fah-ri-ze-oo-**sho**-stfo] n. Pharisaism; hypocrisy
faryzeuszowski [fah-ri-ze-oo-**shof**-skee] adj.m. Pharisaical; hypocritical
fasa [**fah**-sah] f. vat; tan vat
fasada [fah-**sah**-dah] f. front elevation; outside (of a building); exterior
fasadowość [fah-sah-**do**-vośhćh] f. ostentation; ostentatiousness; showiness; window dressing
fasadowy [fah-sah-**do**-vi] adj.m. frontage (decorations, etc.); showy; ostentatious; window-dressing (statement, etc.)
fascjoloza [fahs-tsyo-**lo**-zah] f. fascioliasis
fascykuł [fahs-**tsi**-koow] m. fascicle
fascynacja [fahs-tsi-**nah**-tsyah] f. fascination
fascynować [fahs-tsi-**no**-vahćh] v. fascinate; enchant; charm; allure; bewitch (*repeatedly*)
fascynować się [fahs-tsi-**no**-vahćh śhan] v. be fascinated; be enchanted; be charmed; be allured; be bewitched (*repeatedly*)
fascynowanie [fahs-tsi-no-**vah**-ńe] n. fascination; enchanting; charming; alluring; bewitching
fascynująco [fahs-tsi-noo-**yown**-tso] adv. in a fascinating way
fascynujący [fahs-tsi-noo-**yown**-tsi] adj.m. fascinating; captivating
faseta [fah-**se**-tah] f. facet; bed molding; a fillet molding
fasetka [fah-**set**-kah] f. (small) facet; bed molding; a fillet molding
fasetować [fah-se-**to**-vahćh] v. make a facet edge by polishing (*repeatedly*)
fasetowanie [fah-se-to-**vah**-ńe] n. making of a facet edge by polishing
faska [**fahs**-kah] f. tub; wooden cask; firkin
fasola [fah-**so**-lah] f. bean; kidney bean
łodyga fasoli [wo-**di**-gah fah-**so**-lee] exp.: bean-stalk
fasolisko [fah-so-**lees**-ko] n. bean field; rows of bean-stalks
fasolka [fah-**sol**-kah] f. (small) bean; kidney bean
fasolowaty [fah-so-lo-**vah**-ti] adj.m. bean-shaped
fasolowy [fah-so-**lo**-vi] adj.m. bean (soup, dish, etc.)
fasolówka [fah-so-**loof**-kah] f. bean soup
fason [**fah**-son] m. fashion; cut; form; self-assurance; dash; manner; slang: style; manners
trzymać fason [**tshi**-mahćh **fah**-son] exp.: to keep up appearances; not to lose countenance; be unflappable; to put one's best foot forwrd
fasonować [fah-so-**no**-vahćh] v. fashion; shape; make a model; form; mold; make up (a dress, etc.); restore; make it look like new (*repeatedly*)
fasonowanie [fah-so-no-**vah**-ńe] n. fashioning; shaping
fasonowy [fah-so-**no**-vi] adj.m. fancy; fashionable; ornamental; of complicated design
fasowaczka [fah-so-**vahch**-kah] f. pharmacy worker measuring dosages of drugs
fasować [fah-**so**-vahćh] v. pack; package; strain; put through a sieve; draw (one's rations, etc.); collect (one's gear, etc.) (*repeatedly*)
fasowanie [fah-so-**vah**-ńe] n. packing; straining; drawing; collecting
fasownia [fah-**sov**-ńah] f. packing room in a pharmacy

fastryga [fahs-**tri**-gah] f. tack; basting; baste; tacks
fastrygarka [fahs-tri-**gahr**-kah] f. tacking machine; basting machine
fastrygować [fahs-tri-**go**-vahćh] v. tack; baste (*repeatedly*)
fastrygowanie [fahs-tri-go-**vah**-ńe] n. tacking; basting
fasulec [fah-**soo**-lets] m. checkrein
fasunek [fah-**soo**-nek] m. issue; drawing (of rations, etc.); collecting (one's equipment, etc)
faszerować [fah-she-**ro**-vahćh] v. stuff (fowl, veal, etc.); farce; lard; cram (with information, etc.) (*repeatedly*)
faszyna [fah-**shi**-nah] f. fascine
faszynada [fah-shi-**nah**-dah] f. fascine construction of a dike
faszynować [fah-shi-**no**-vahćh] v. line with fascine; fill with fascine (*repeatedly*)
faszynowanie [fah-shi-no-**vah**-ńe] n. reinforcing with fascine
faszynowy [fah-shi-**no**-vi] adj.m. fascine (fence, fortification, dike, etc.)
faszysta [fah-**shis**-tah] m. fascist
faszystka [fah-**shist**-kah] f. (female) fascist
faszystowski [fah-shis-**tof**-skee] adj.m. fascist (tendencies, etc.)
faszyzacja [fah-shi-**zah**-tsyah] f. fascistization
faszyzacyjny [fah-shi-zah-**tsiy**-ni] adj.m. of fascistization
faszyzm [**fah**-shizm] m. fascism
brutalny faszyzm [broo-**tahl**-ni **fah**-shizm] exp.: nazism; Hitlerism
faszyzować [fah-shi-**zo**-vahćh] v. convert to fascism; transform into a Fascista; fascistize (*repeatedly*)
faszyzować się [fah-shi-**zo**-vahćh śhan] v. be converted to fascism; transform oneself into a Fascista; fascistize oneself (*repeatedly*)
faszyzowanie [fah-shi-zo-**vah**-ńe] n. fascistization
faszyzowanie się [fah-shi-zo-**vah**-ńe śhan] n. transforming oneself into a Fascista
fatalista [fah-tah-**lees**-tah] m. fatalist
fatalistycznie [fah-tah-lees-**tich**-ńe] adv. fatalistically
fatalistyczny [fah-tah-lees-**tich**-ni] adj.m. fatalistic
fatalizm [fah-**tah**-leezm] m. fatalism; fatality (of fate, etc.); fate; doom
fatalnie [fah-**tahl**-ńe] adv. fatally; calamitously; disastrously; badly; nastily; fatefully; inescapably
czuć się fatalnie [chooćh śhan fah-**tahl**-ńe] exp.: to feel terribly bad; to feel rotten
fatalnie się zblamować [fah-**tahl**-ńe śhan zblah-**mo**-vahćh] exp.: to make an atrocious blunder
fatalność [fah-**tahl**-nośhćh] f. fatality; doom
fatalny [fah-**tahl**-ni] adj.m. fatal; ill-fated; calamitous; disastrous; awful; nasty; wretched; execrable; fateful; unescapable
fatałach [fah-**tah**-wahkh] m. fal-lal; ornament in a dress; frippery; trifle; trinket; knickknack; nicknack; fiddle-faddle
fatałaszek [fah-tah-**wah**-shek] m. (small, nice) fal-lal; ornament in a dress; frippery; trifle; trinket; knickknack; nickknack (diminutive of **fatałach**)
fatałaszki [fah-tah-**wahsh**-kee] pl. knickknacks; frippery; trinkets; fiddle-faddle
fatamorgana [fah-tah-mor-**gah**-nah] f. fata morgana; Fata Morgana; mirage; slang: nonsense
fatum [**fah**-toom] n. fate; doom; fatality; ill-fortune
fatyga [fah-**ti**-gah] f. trouble; fatigue; bother; pains
zadać sobie fatygę [zah-dahćh so-bye fah-**ti**-gan] exp.: to take trouble (to do); to take pains (to do); to go to the trouble (of doing); to bother (to do)
fatygant [fah-**ti**-gahnt] m. gallant; escort; adulator; hanger-on
fatygować [fah-ti-**go**-vahćh] v. trouble; disturb (*repeatedly*)
fatygować się [fah-ti-**go**-vahćh śhan] v. trouble; bother (*repeatedly*)
proszę się nie fatygować [**pro**-shan śhan ńe fah-ti-**go**-vahćh] exp.: don't trouble; don't bother (to do); don't take the trouble;

don't go to the trouble (to do)
fatygowanie [fah-ti-go-**vah**-ńe] n. trouble; pains; bother
fatygowanie się [fah-ti-go-**vah**-ńe śhan] n. getting tired
faul [fahwl] m. foul hit; foul blow; foul move
faulować [fahw-lo-vahćh] v. foul (*repeatedly*)
faun [fahwn] m. faun (a figure of mythology)
fauna [**fahw**-nah] f. fauna
faunicznie [fahw-**ńeech**-ńe] adv. faunally
fauniczny [fahw-**ńeech**-ni] adj.m. faun (mask, etc.); of a faun; faunal
faunista [fahw-**ńees**-tah] m. faunist
faunistycznie [fahw-**ńees**-tich-ńe] adv. faunistically
faunistyczny [fahw-ńees-**tich**-ni] adj.m. faunistic
faunistyka [fahw-**ńees**-ti-kah] f. study of fauna
faustowski [fahw-**stof**-skee] adj.m. Faustian
faustyczny [fahw-**stich**-ni] adj.m. Faustian; Faust-like
fawor [**fah**-vor] m. (ironic) grace; favor; sympathy
faworek [fah-**vo**-rek] m. twisted dry biscuit of fried paste (served with sugar)
faworyt [fah-**vo**-rit] m. favorite; pet; contestant most likely to win
faworyta [fah-vo-**ri**-tah] f. favorite
faworytka [fah-vo-**rit**-kah] f. (female) favorite
faworyzacja [fah-vo-ri-**zah**-tsyah] f. favoritism; partiality
faworyzować [fah-vo-ri-**zo**-vahćh] v. favor; play favorites; show favoritism (to); facilitate; sustain (*repeatedly*)
faworyzowanie [fah-vo-ri-zo-**vah**-ńe] n. favoritism
faza [**fah**-zah] f. phase; phasis (speech disorder); stage; aspect; bevel (of an edge); chamfer (of an edge)
fazenda [fah-**zen**-dah] f. fazenda; (coffee) hacienda
fazender [fah-**zen**-der] m. owner of a coffee plantation
fazomierz [fah-**zo**-myesh] m. electric phase meter
fazować [fah-**zo**-vahćh] v. bevel; chamfer (*repeatedly*)
fazowanie [fah-zo-**vah**-ńe] n. beveling; making a chamfer
fazowy [fah-**zo**-vi] adj.m. phasic; phase (converter, etc.)
fąfel [fown-fel] m. colloq: small kid
fąfry [fown-fri] pl. colloq: sulks; whims; caprices; vagaries; pouts; mumps; acting with a chip on one's shoulder
fe! [fe] excl.: bad!; yah!; shame!
feblik [**feb**-leek] m.colloq: sympathy; weakness (for); attraction (to)
febra [**feb**-rah] f. fever; ague; the shakes; fever with chills
febrycznie [feb-**rich**-ńe] adv. feverishly; aguishly
febryczny [feb-**rich**-ni] adj.m. feverish; aguish
fechmistrz [**fekh**-meestsh] m. master of fence; swordsman
fechtować się [fekh-**to**-vahćh śhan] v. fence; go in for fencing (*repeatedly*)
fechtowanie się [fekh-to-**vah**-ńe śhan] n. fencing; swordsmanship
fechtunek [fekh-**too**-nek] m. fence; fencing; swordsmanship; the art of attack and defence with saber, foil, or eppee
fedain [fe-**dah**-een] m. fedayeen; member of Arab commando operating against Israel
federacja [fe-de-**rah**-tsyah] f. federation
federacyjnie [fe-de-rah-**tsiy**-ńe] adv. federally
federacyjny [fe-de-rah-**tsiy**-ni] adj.m. federal; federative
federalista [fe-de-rah-**lees**-tah] m. federalist
federalistyczny [fe-de-rah-lees-**tich**-ni] adj.m. federalist
federalizacja [fe-de-rah-lee-**zah**-tsyah] f. federalization
federalizm [fe-de-**rah**-leezm] m. federalism
federalizować [fe-de-rah-lee-**zo**-vahćh] v. federalize; put under federal jurisdiction; unite in a federal system (*repeatedly*)

federalizować się [fe-de-rah-lee-**zo**-vahćh śhan] v. federate; federalize; join in an federation; unite under a federal system; bring under the jurisdiction of a federal government (*repeatedly*)
federalnie [fe-de-**rahl**-ńe] adv. federally
federalny [fe-de-**rahl**-ni] adj.m. federal
fedrować [fed-**ro**-vahćh] v. mine (coal) (*repeatedly*)
fedrowanie [fed-ro-**vah**-ńe] n. mining (of coal)
fedrunek [fed-**roo**-nek] m. mined coal
feeria [fe-**er**-yah] f. fairy-like spectacle
feerycznie [fe-e-**rich**-ńe] adv. like a fairy; enchantingly; magically
feeryczny [fe-e-**rich**-ni] adj.m. fairy-like; enchanting; magic
fekalia [fe-**kah**-lyah] pl. faeces
felc [felts] m. fold; slip-fold; rabbet; rebate; groove
felcować [fel-**tso**-vahćh] v. fold; rabbet; rebate; groove; join by means of a fold (*repeatedly*)
felcowanie [fel-tso-**vah**-ńe] n. folding; rabbeting; grooving; joining by means of a fold
felczer [**fel**-cher] m. male nurse; medical assistant; army surgeon
felczerka [fel-**cher**-kah] f. (female) nurse; hospital nurse
felczerski [fel-**cher**-skee] adj.m. nurse's (aide, assistant, etc.)
feldfebel [felt-**fe**-bel] m. sergeant
feldjeger [feld-**ye**-ger] m. rifleman
feldmarszałek [feld-mahr-**shah**-wek] m. Field Marshal
feldmarszałkowski [feld-mahr-shahw-**kof**-skee] adj.m. Field Marshal's
feler [**fe**-ler] m. defect; flaw; drawback; shortcoming
felga [**fel**-gah] f. wheel rim
felieton [fel-**ye**-ton] m. radio essay; newspaper essay; television essay; short literary composition dealing with a single subject
felietonik [fel-ye-to-ńeek] m. small essay; see: **felieton**
felietonista [fel-ye-to-**ńees**-tah] m. essayist; essayer; columnist
felietonistka [fel-ye-to-**ńeest**-kah] f. (woman) essayist; essayer; columnist
felietonowo [fel-ye-to-**no**-vo] adv. in form of an essay; in style of an essay
felietonowy [fel-ye-to-**no**-vi] adj.m. of an essay
fellach [**fel**-lahkh] m. fellah
fellogen [fel-**lo**-gen] m. phellogen
felonia [fe-**lo**-ńyah] f. felony
felzyt [**fel**-zit] m. felstone; felsite
feminista [fe-mee-**ńees**-tah] m. feminist
feministka [fe-mee-**ńeest**-kah] f. (woman) feminist
feministyczny [fe-mee-ńees-**tich**-ni] adj.m. feministic
feminizacja [fe-mee-ńee-**zah**-tsyah] f. feminization
feminizm [fe-**mee**-ńeezm] m. feminism
feminizować [fe-mee-ńee-**zo**-vahćh] v. give female characteristics; feminize (*repeatedly*)
feminizować się [fe-mee-ńee-**zo**-vahćh śhan] v. acquire female characteristics; become predominantly female (occupation, etc.); feminize oneself (*repeatedly*)
feminizowanie [fe-mee-ńee-zo-**vah**-ńe] n. making feminine
feminizowanie się [fe-mee-ńee-zo-**vah**-ńe śhan] n. acquiring female characteristics
fen [fen] m. foen (warm dry mountain wind)
fenek [**fe**-nek] m. fennec; African fox
Fenicjanin [fe-ńee-**tsyah**-ńeen] m. a Phoenician
Fenicjanka [fe-ńee-**tsyahn**-kah] f. a Phoenician woman
fenicki [fe-**ńeets**-kee] adj.m. Phoenician
fenig [**fe**-ńeeg] m. pfennig (coin)
feniks [**fe**-ńeeks] m. phoenix
fenogenetyka [fe-no-ge-**ne**-ti-kah] f. study of the influence of heredity on development of an organism
fenokopia [fe-no-**ko**-pyah] f. phenocopy

fenol [**fe**-nol] m. phenol
fenole [fe-**no**-le] pl. the phenol compounds
fenolan [fe-**no**-lahn] m. phenolate
fenoloftaleina [fe-no-lof-tah-le-**ee**-nah] f. phenolphthalein
fenolog [fe-**no**-log] m. specialist in phenology
fenologia [fe-no-**lo**-gyah] f. phenology
fenologicznie [fe-no-lo-**geech**-ńe] adv. phenologically
fenologiczny [fe-no-lo-**geech**-ni] adj.m. phenological
fenolowy [fe-no-**lo**-vi] adj.m. phenolic; of thermosetting resin
fenomen [fe-**no**-men] m. phenomenon; marvel
fenomenalista [fe-no-me-nah-**lees**-tah] m. phenomenalist
fenomenalistycznie [fe-no-me-nah-lees-**tich**-ńe] adv. phenomenalistically
fenomenalistyczny [fe-no-me-nah-lees-**tich**-ni] adj.m. phenomenalistic
fenomenalizm [fe-no-me-**nah**-leezm] m. phenomenalism
fenomenalnie [fe-no-me-**nahl**-ńe] adv. marvelously; wonderfully; superbly; phenomenally
fenomenalny [fe-no-me-**nahl**-ni] adj.m. marvelous; wonderful; superb; phenomenal; extraordinary; remarkable
fenomenolog [fe-no-me-**no**-log] m. phenomenologist
fenomenologia [fe-no-me-no-**lo**-gyah] f. phenomenology
fenomenologicznie [fe-no-me-no-lo-**geech**-ńe] adv. phenomenologically
fenomenologiczny [fe-no-me-no-lo-**geech**-ni] adj.m. phenomenological
fenoplast [fe-**no**-plahst] m. phenolic compound
fenoplasty [fe-no-**plahs**-ti] pl. phenolics; phenolic resins
fenotyp [fe-**no**-tip] m. phenotype
fenyl [**fe**-nil] m. phenyl
fenowy [fe-**no**-vi] adj.m. of foen (the warm dry mountain wind)
ferajna [fe-**rahy**-nah] f. slang: gang bunch; set; lot
cała ferajna [**tsah**-wah fe-**rahy**-nah] exp.: the whole caboodle
feralnie [fe-**rahl**-ńe] adv. unluckily; haplessly; balefully; disastrously
feralny [fe-**rahl**-ni] adj.m. unlucky; ill-fated; hapless; baleful; disastrous
feretron [fe-**re**-tron] m. feretory
ferie [**fe**-rye] pl. holidays
ferm [ferm] m. fermium (atomic number 100)
ferma [**fer**-mah] f. farm; ranch
fermata [fer-**mah**-tah] f. (musical) pause; fermata
ferment [**fer**-ment] m. ferment; intense activity; agitation; unrest; leaven; enzyme; slang: confusion
fermenty [fer-**men**-ti] pl. enzymes
fermentacja [fer-men-**tah**-tsyah] f. fermentation; zymosis
poddać fermentacji [**pod**-dahćh fer-men-**tah**-tsyee] exp.: to ferment
fermentacyjny [fer-men-tah-**tsiy**-ni] adj.m. fermentative; zymotic
kadź fermentacyjna [kahćh fer-men-tah-**tsiy**-nah] exp.: settling vat
fermentować [fer-men-**to**-vahćh] v. work up (into the state of agitation); ferment; be agitated; seethe; foment (*repeatedly*)
fermentowanie [fer-men-to-**vah**-ńe] n. fermentation; zymosis
fermentownia [fer-men-**tov**-ńah] f. fermentation plant (of tobacco, etc.)
fermer [**fer**-mer] m. farmer; rancher
fermi [**fer**-mee] m. fermi (unit of atomic length)
fermuar [fer-**moo**-ahr] m. jewelry clasp; ornamental buckle
fernambuk [fer-**nahm**-book] m. variety of Brazilian hardwood
fernambukowy [fer-nahm-boo-**ko**-vi] adj.m. of Fernambuco wood
ferniko [fer-**ńee**-ko] n. alloy of iron, nickel, and cobalt
ferować [fe-**ro**-vahćh] v. pass (a sentence); assess (a penalty) (*repeatedly*)
ferowanie [fe-ro-**vah**-ńe] n. passing (a sentence); assessing (a

penalty)
ferro- [**fer**-ro] prefix: ferro-; iron; iron and (in names of alloys); ferrous
ferrochrom [fer-**ro**-khrom] m. alloy of iron, cobalt, and chrome
ferroelektryczność [fer-ro-e-lek-**trich**-nośhćh] f. ferroelectricity
ferroelektryczny [fer-ro-e-lek-**trich**-ni] adj.m. ferroelectric
ferroelektryk [fer-ro-e-**lek**-trik] m. ferroelectric
ferrolit [fer-**ro**-leet] m. rock rich in iron, titanium, and chromium ore
ferrolity [fer-ro-**lee**-ti] pl. rocks rich in iron, titanium, and chromium ore
ferromagnetyczny [fer-ro-mahg-ne-**tich**-ni] adj.m. ferromagnetic
ferromagnetyk [fer-ro-mahg-**ne**-tik] m. ferromagnetic
ferromagnetyzm [fer-ro-mahg-**ne**-tizm] m. ferromagnetism
ferromangan [fer-ro-**mahn**-gahn] m. ferromanganese
ferrostop [fer-**ro**-stop] m. ferroalloy
ferrostopowy [fer-ro-sto-**po**-vi] adj.m. ferroalloy (components, raw materials, etc.)
ferryt [**fer**-rit] m. ferrite
ferryty [fer-**ri**-ti] pl. ferrites
ferrytowy [fer-ri-**to**-vi] adj.m. of ferrite
fertać [**fer**-tahćh] v. slang: wag; shake; jostle (*repeatedly*)
fertać się [**fer**-tahćh śh<u>an</u>] v. slang: stir about; bustle (*repeatedly*)
fertanie [fer-**tah**-ńe] n. a stir; stir
fertnąć [**fert**-n<u>own</u>ćh] v. slang: wag; shake; jostle
fertnąć się [**fert**-n<u>own</u>ćh śh<u>an</u>] v. slang: stir about; bustle
fertycznie [fer-**tich**-ńe] adv. nimbly; briskly
fertyczność [fer-**tich**-nośhćh] f. nimbleness; briskness; liveliness
fertyczny [fer-**tich**-ni] adj.m. nimble; brisk; lively; dapper; light-footed; corky
feruła [fe-**roo**-wah] f. ferula; cane; school discipline; rigor
ferwor [**fer**-vor] m. fervor; zeal; gusto
z ferworem [s fer-**vo**-rem] exp.: with gusto; zealously; earnestly
w pierwszym ferworze [f **pyerf**-shim fer-**vo**-zhe] exp.: in the heat of the moment
zawsze w ferworze [**zahf**-she f fer-**vo**-zhe] exp.: always full of vigor; slang: always full of vinegar
fes [fes] m. F flat (in music)
fest [fest] adj.m. slang: spanking; whacking; whooping; adv. slang: mightily
na fest [nah fest] exp.: slang: for good; for good and all
festiwal [fes-**tee**-vahl] m. festival; sequence of joyous events
festiwalowy [fes-tee-vah-**lo**-vi] adj.m. of festival; of (periodic) program of artistic competition
feston [**fes**-ton] m. festoon (of flowers, cobwebs, etc.); garland
festonowy [fes-to-**no**-vi] adj.m. festoon (flowers, cobwebs, etc.); of a garland
festyn [**fes**-tin] m. garden party; picnic; banquet
festynowy [fes-ti-**no**-vi] adj.m. of a garden party; picnic (table, etc.); banquet (invitation, etc.)
feta [**fe**-tah] f. celebration; banquet
fetor [**fe**-tor] m. stench; reek
fetować [fe-**to**-vahćh] v. give a rousing welcome; entertain magnificently (*repeatedly*)
fetować się [fe-**to**-vahćh śh<u>an</u>] v. give one another a rousing welcome; entertain one another magnificently (*repeatedly*)
fetowanie [fe-to-**vah**-ńe] n. rousing welcome
fetowanie się [fe-to-**vah**-ńe śh<u>an</u>] n. giving one another a rousing welcome
fetysz [**fe**-tish] m. fetish; amulet; talisman; charm
fetyszysta [fe-ti-**shis**-tah] m. fetishist
fetyszystyczny [fe-ti-shis-**tich**-ni] adj.m. fetishistic
fetyszyzacja [fe-ti-shi-**zah**-tsyah] f. making something into a fetish
fetyszyzm [fe-**ti**-shizm] m. fetishism; irrational devotion; fetichism

fetyszyzować [fe-ti-shi-**zo**-vahćh] v. treat with an irrational devotion (*repeatedly*)
feudalizacja [fe-oo-dah-lee-**zah**-tsyah] f. feudalization
feudalizm [fe-oo-**dah**-leezm] m. feudalism; feudal system; feudality
feudalizować [fe-oo-dah-lee-**zo**-vahćh] v. feudalize; put under the feudal system; make feudal (*repeatedly*)
feudalizować się [fe-oo-dah-lee-**zo**-vahćh śhan] v. become feudalized (*repeatedly*)
feudalnie [fe-oo-**dahl**-ńe] adv. feudally
feudalny [fe-oo-**dahl**-ni] adj.m. feudal; feudatory
feudał [fe-**oo**-dahw] m. feudal lord; liege lord
fez [fes] m. fez; tarboosh
fi! [fee] excl.: pooh!
fiacik [**fyah**-ćheek] m. (small, nice) Fiat car; Fiat 126
fiakier [**fyah**-ker] m. (horse drawn) cab; cabman; cabby
fiala [**fyah**-lah] f. turret
fiasko [**fyahs**-ko] n. fiasco; failure; breakdown; fizzle; flash in the pan; slang: flop
skończyć się fiaskiem [**skoń**-chićh śhan **fyahs**-kem] exp.: to prove abortive; to fall to the ground; to turn out crabs; to fizzle out; to be a washout; to fail completely
fiat [fyaht] m. Fiat car
fibra [**feeb**-rah] f. fiber; fibre; nerve
fibry ludzkiej istoty [**feeb**-ri **loots**-key ee-**sto**-ti] exp.: the fibers of our being; human fibers
fibroblast [fee-**bro**-blahst] m. fibroblast
fibroblasty [fee-bro-**blahs**-ti] pl. fibroblasts
fibroina [fee-bro-ee-nah] f. fibroin
fibrowy [fee-**bro**-vi] adj.m. of fiber
fibryl [**fee**-bril] m. root hair; fibril
fibryle [fee-**bri**-le] pl. fibrils
fibryna [fee-**bri**-nah] f. fibrin; gluten
fibrynogen [fee-bri-**no**-gen] m. fibrinogen
fibrynolityczny [fee-bri-no-lee-**tich**-ni] adj.m. fibrinolytic
fibrynoliza [fee-bri-no-**lee**-zah] f. fibrinolysis
fibrynolizyna [fee-bri-no-lee-**zi**-nah] f. fibrinolysin; plasmin
fibrynowy [fee-bri-**no**-vi] adj.m. fibrinous; glutinous
fibula [fee-**boo**-lah] f. fibula; Greek large safety pin
fideikomisowy [fee-de-ee-ko-mee-**so**-vi] adj.m. fiduciary
fideista [fee-de-**ees**-tah] m. fideist
fideistyczny [fee-de-ees-**tich**-ni] adj.m. fideistic
fideizm [fee-**de**-eezm] m. fideism; reliance on faith rather than reason
fidiaszowski [feed-yah-**shof**-skee] adj.m. of Pfidias
fidiaszowy [feed-yah-**sho**-vi] adj.m. of Pfidias
fidrygałki [feed-ri-**gahw**-kee] pl. trivialities; frivolities; fiddle-faddle; nonsense; tomfoolery
fidrygansy [feed-ri-**gahn**-si] pl. caper; gambols; pranks
field [feeld] m. highland flattened by a glacier
fiesta [**fyes**-tah] f. fiesta; festival
fifka [**feef**-kah] f. cigarette holder
figa [**fee**-gah] f. fig tree; fig; fig gesture (sign of contempt made by thrusting one's thumb between two fingers)
figę mnie to obchodzi [**fee**-gan mńe to op-**kho**-dźhee] exp.: I don't give a damn about it; I don't care a bit about it
na figę! [nah **fee**-gan] excl.: nothing doing!
figi [**fee**-gee] pl. women's panties; briefs
figiel [**fee**-gel] m. practical joke; prank; trick; ill turn
figielek [fee-**ge**-lek] m. inoffensive practical joke; prank; little trick
figlarka [feeg-**lahr**-kah] f. skittish girl; kitten; minx; giddy goast
figlarnie [feeg-**lahr**-ńe] adv. playfully; slyly; roguishly; by way of a joke; jocularly; skittishly; wantonly
figlarność [feeg-**lahr**-nośhćh] f. playfulness; frolics; skittishness;

sportiveness; roguishness; jocularity; wantonness
figlarny [feeg-**lahr**-ni] adj.m. playful; sly; roguish; arch; jocular; skittish; frolicsome; sportive; wanton
figlarski [feeg-**lahr**-skee] adj.m. playful; jocular
figlarz [**feeg**-lahsh] m. joker; jester; rogue; rascal
figle-migle [**feeg**-le **meeg**-le] pl. pranks
figlować [feeg-**lo**-vahćh] v. play pranks; lark; frolic (*repeatedly*)
figlowanie [feeg-lo-**vah**-ńe] n. playing pranks; larking; frolicking
figowiec [fee-**go**-vyets] m. fig tree
figowy [fee-**go**-vi] adj.m. fig (leaf, tree, etc.)
figówka [fee-**goof**-kah] f. sycosis (a chronic hair disorder)
figura [fee-**goo**-rah] f. figure; shape; waist; form; image; bigwig; dummy; wayside shrine; (literary) character; (chess) piece; figure (of speech, etc.); slang: individual
figuracja [fee-goo-**rah**-tsyah] f. (musical) figuration
figuracyjny [fee-goo-rah-**tsiy**-ni] adj.m. figurative
figuralnie [fee-goo-**rahl**-ńe] adv. in figural fashion; figuratively
figuralny [fee-goo-**rahl**-ni] adj.m. figural; figurate (counterpoint)
figurant [fee-**goo**-rahnt] m. figurehead; dummy; man of straw
figurantka [fee-goo-**rahnt**-kah] f. (woman) figurehead; dummy
figuratywnie [fee-goo-rah-**tiv**-ńe] adv. figuratively
figuratywność [fee-goo-rah-**tiv**-nośhćh] f. figurativeness
figuratywny [fee-goo-rah-**tiv**-ni] adj.m. figurative
figurka [fee-**goor**-kah] f. (nice, little) figure; diminutive of **figura**
figurować [fee-goo-**ro**-vahćh] v. figure (on); appear (in, on) (*repeatedly*)
figurować na liście [fee-goo-ro-vahćh nah **leeśh**-ćhe] exp.: to be on a list
figurowanie [fee-goo-ro-**vah**-ńe] n. being (on a list, etc.)
figurowiec [fee-goo-**ro**-vyets] m. figure-skater
figurowy [fee-goo-**ro**-vi] adj.m. figure (skating, etc.)
figurówki [fee-goo-**roof**-kee] pl. skates for figure skating
figurynka [fee-goo-**rin**-kah] f. statuette
figus [**fee**-goos] m. cultivated rubber plant
fik! [feek] excl.: oops!
fikać [**fee**-kahćh] v. kick; jump; hop (*repeatedly*)
fikać kozły [**fee**-kahćh **koz**-wi] exp.: turn somersaults
fikanie [fee-**kah**-ńe] n. kicking; jumping; hopping
fikcja [**feek**-tsyah] f. fiction; invention; idle notion; figment; imagination; illusion; sham; pretence; delusion
fikcja prawna [**feek**-tsyah **prahv**-nah] exp.: legal fiction
fikcjonalizm [feek-tsyo-**nah**-leezm] m. product of fictionalization; theory of fictionalization
fikcyjnie [feek-**tsiy**-ńe] adv. fictitiously; fictionally
fikcyjny [feek-**tsiy**-ni] adj.m. fictitious; imaginary; sham; fictional
fiknąć [**feek**-nownćh] v. kick; jump; hop
fikofeina [fee-ko-fe-**ee**-nah] f. phycophaein
fikołek [fee-**ko**-wek] m. flip; slang: pornographic film; alcohol diluted with water or juice (mob jargon)
fiks [feeks] m. mania; craze; fad
mieć fiksa [myećh **feek**-sah] exp.: to be crazy
fiksacja [feek-**sah**-tsyah] f. (dental) fixation
fiksatywa [feek-sah-**ti**-vah] f. fluid that preserves drawings
fiksować [feek-**so**-vahćh] v. be crazy; be mad; rave (*repeatedly*)
fiksowanie [feek-so-**vah**-ńe] n. madness; craze
fiksum [**feek**-soom] n. madness; craze
mieć fiksum dyrdum [myećh **feek**-soom **dir**-doom] exp.: to be crazy; to be cracked; to have a

tile loose
fikus [**fee**-koos] m. cultivated rubber plant
fikuśnie [fee-**koośh**-ńe] adv. in a fancy manner; in a funny way
fikuśność [fee-**koośh**-nośhćh] f. fancy manner; funny way
fikuśny [fee-**koośh**-ni] adj.m. fancy; funny; laughable; bizarre
filakteria [fee-lahk-**ter**-yah] f. phylactery; small leather box with Jewish scriptural passages; amulet
filantrop [fee-**lahn**-trop] m. philanthropist; humanitarian
filantropia [fee-lahn-**tro**-pyah] f. philanthropy; humanitarianism
filantropijność [fee-lahn-tro-**peey**-nośhćh] f. philanthropy
filantropijny [fee-lahn-tro-**peey**-ni] adj.m. philanthropic
filantropka [fee-lahn-**trop**-kah] f. (woman) philanthropist; humanitarian
filar [**fee**-lahr] m. pillar; pier; tower; mainstay; post; stop; rib
filarecki [fee-lah-**rets**-kee] adj.m. of the secret patriotic society at Wilno University (1819-1823)
filarek [fee-**lah**-rek] m. small pillar; small post
filareta [fee-lah-**re**-tah] m. member of a secret patriotic society at Wilno University (1819-1823)
filaria [fee-**lahr**-yah] f. filaria
 filarie [fee-**lahr**-ye] pl. filariae
filarioza [fee-lahr-**yo**-zah] f. filariasis
 filariozy [fee-lahr-**yo**-zi] pl. filariases
filarowanie [fee-lah-ro-**vah**-ńe] n. supporting on pillars; piling
filarowy [fee-lah-**ro**-vi] adj.m. of a pillar; of pillars; pillared
filarowiec [fee-lah-**ro**-vyets] m. miner working between pillars
filatelista [fee-lah-te-**lees**-tah] m. stamp collector; philatelist
filatelistycznie [fee-lah-te-lees-**tich**-ńe] adv. philatelically
filatelistyczny [fee-lah-te-lees-**tich**-ni] adj.m. stamp collection (club, etc.); philatelic
filatelistyka [fee-lah-te-**lees**-ti-kah] f. stamp collecting; philately
filc [feelts] m. felt
filcować [feel-**tso**-vahćh] v. felt; slang: search (*repeatedly*)
filcować się [feel-**tso**-vahćh śhan] v. become like felt; slang: search one another (*repeatedly*)
filcowanie [feel-tso-**vah**-ńe] n. covering with felt; slang: searching
filcowanie się [feel-tso-**vah**-ńe śhan] n. slang: searching each other
filcowaty [feel-tso-**vah**-ti] adj.m. like felt
filcowy [feel-**tso**-vi] adj.m. of felt; felt (hat, etc.)
fildekos [feel-**de**-kos] m. lisle (cotton) thread
 fildekosy [feel-de-**ko**-si] pl. lisle (cotton) thread stockings (hosiery)
fildekosowy [feel-de-ko-**so**-vi] adj.m. of lisle thread; lisle-thread (stockings, hosiery, etc.)
fildystor [feel-**dis**-tor] m. device with semi-conductors for intensification of electrical signals
fileciarka [fee-le-**ćhahr**-kah] f. (fish) filleting machine
filer [**fee**-ler] m. young fruit tree placed between grown trees in an orchard
filet [**fee**-let] m. fillet (of meat, fish, etc.); (bookbinding) fillet; netting
filetować [fee-le-**to**-vahćh] v. cut fillets (of meat, etc.) (*repeatedly*)
filetowanie [fee-le-to-**vah**-ńe] n. cutting fillets (of meat, fish, etc.)
filharmonia [feel-khahr-**mo**-ńyah] f. Philharmonic (Society)
filharmoniczny [feel-khahr-mo-**ńeech**-ni] adj.m. philharmonic
filharmonijny [feel-khahr-mo-**ńeey**-ni] adj.m. philharmonic
filharmonik [feel-khahr-**mo**-ńeek] m. member of philharmonic orchestra
filhellenista [feel-hel-le-**ńees**-tah] m. philhellene; philhellenist
filhellenizm [feel-**hel**-le-ńeezm] m. philhellenizm
filhelleński [feel-hel-**leń**-skee] adj.m. philhellenic; admiring Greece or Greeks; philhellene
filia [**fee**-lyah] f. branch (store);

branch-office; branch
filiacja [feel-**yah**-tsyah] f. filiation; descent
filialny [feel-**yahl**-ni] adj.m. filial; of a branch; branch (office, etc.)
filiera [feel-**ye**-rah] f. nozzle for production of artificial fibers
filierka [feel-**yer**-kah] f. small nozzle for production of artificial fibers
filigran [fee-**lee**-grahn] f. filigree; watermark
filigranować [fee-lee-grah-**no**-vahćh] v. make a filigree; watermark (*repeatedly*)
filigranowanie [fee-lee-grah-no-**vah**-ńe] n. making a filigree; making watermarks
filigranowo [fee-lee-grah-**no**-vo] adv. minutely; daintily; delicately
filigranowość [fee-lee-grah-**no**-vośhćh] f. minuteness; daintiness; filigree openwork; filigree ornamentation
filigranowy [fee-lee-grah-**no**-vi] adj.m. minute; dainty; delicate; filigree; openwork (decoration, ornamentation, etc.)
filip [**fee**-leep] m. slang: hare
wyrwać się jak filip z konopi [**vir**-vahćh śhan yahk **fee**-leep s ko-**no**-pee] exp.: to speak out of turn; to talk improperly
filipika [fee-lee-**pee**-kah] f. philippic; tirade
filipin [fee-**lee**-peen] m. member of a Catholic monastic order which does not require vows
Filipinka [fee-lee-**peen**-kah] f. Filipino (woman)
Filipińczyk [fee-lee-**peeń**-chik] m. Filipino
filipon [fee-**lee**-pon] m. member of a persecuted Russian sect
filipsyt [fee-**leep**-sit] m. phillipsite (mineral)
filister [fee-**lees**-ter] m. Philistine
filisterski [fee-lees-**ter**-skee] adj.m. smug; narrow-minded
po filistersku [po fee-lees-**ter**-skoo] exp.: smugly; narrow-mindedly
filisterstwo [fee-lees-**ter**-stfo] n. smugness; narrow-mindedness
filiżaneczka [fee-lee-zhah-**nech**-kah] f. (small, nice) cup; cupful
filiżanka [fee-lee-**zhahn**-kah] f. cup; cupful; coffee-cup
film [feelm] m. film; picture; motion picture; movies; reel; the cinema; the films; cinematography
filmik [**feel**-meek] m. small film; unimportant motion picture
filmodruk [feel-**mo**-drook] m. offset printing
filmografia [feel-mo-**grah**-fyah] f. filmography
filmologia [feel-mo-**lo**-gyah] f. history and theory of film making
filmologiczny [feel-mo-lo-**geech**-ni] adj.m. of the history and theory of film making
filmoteka [feel-mo-**te**-kah] f. film library; collection of films
filmować [feel-**mo**-vahćh] v. film; screen (a novel, etc.); shoot (a scene, etc.) (*repeatedly*)
filmowanie [feel-mo-**vah**-ńe] n. filming; screening (a novel, etc.); shooting (a scene, etc.)
filmowiec [feel-**mo**-vyets] m. film producer; film recorder; cinema operator
filmowo [feel-**mo**-vo] adv. as in a film
filmowość [feel-**mo**-vośhćh] f. suitability for filming
filmowy [feel-**mo**-vi] adj.m. of a film; of the film; film (star, etc.)
gwiazda filmowa [**gvyahz**-dah feel-**mo**-vah] exp.: film star; movie star
filmoznawczy [feel-mo-**znahf**-chi] adj.m. of the history and theory of film making
filmoznawstwo [feel-mo-**znahf**-stfo] n. the history and theory of film making
filodendron [fee-lo-**den**-dron] m. ceriman; philodendron
filofora [fee-lo-**fo**-rah] f. Phylopfora (leaf-like algae)
filofrancuski [fee-lo-frahn-**tsoo**-skee] adj.m. Francophile
filogenetyczny [fee-lo-ge-ne-**tich**-ni] adj.m. phylogenetic
filogenetyka [fee-lo-ge-ne-ti-kah] f. phylogenetic studies
filogeneza [fee-lo-ge-**ne**-zah] f.

phylogenesis
filogenia [fee-lo-**ge**-ńyah] f. phylogeny
filokaktus [fee-lo-**kahk**-toos] m. phyllocactus
filoksera [fee-lo-**kse**-rah] f. phylloxera
filolog [fee-**lo**-log] m. philologist; linguist; linguistics teacher
filologia [fee-lo-**lo**-gyah] f. philology
filologicznie [fee-lo-lo-**gee**-chńe] adv. philologically
filologiczny [fee-lo-lo-**gee**-chni] adj.m. of philology; philological
filomacki [fee-lo-**mah**-tskee] adj.m. of a secret Polish student society at Wilno University (1817-1823)
filomata [fee-lo-**mah**-tah] m. member of a secret student society at Wilno University (1817-1823)
filosemita [fee-lo-se-**mee**-tah] m. philo-Semite; philo-Jew
filować [fee-**lo**-vahćh] v. put out dirty smoke; ostentatiously scan playing cards; peep; mob slang: notice; cheat in class (*repeatedly*)
filowanie [fee-lo-**vah**-ńe] n. putting out dirty smoke; ostentatious scanning of playing cards
filozof [fee-**lo**-zof] m. philosopher
filozofia [fee-lo-**zo**-fyah] f. philosophy; wisdom; colloq: concept; notion; principles; ideas
filozoficznie [fee-lo-zo-**feech**-ńe] adv. philosophically
filozoficzny [fee-lo-zo-**feech**-ni] adj.m. philosophic; philosophical; calm in the face of trouble
filozofka [fee-lo-**zof**-kah] f. (woman) philosopher
filozofować [fee-lo-zo-**fo**-vahćh] v. philosophize; play the philosopher; reason (*repeatedly*)
filozofowanie [fee-lo-zo-fo-**vah**-ńe] n. philosophizing; playing the philosopher; reasoning
filtr [feeltr] m. filter; strainer; percolator
filtracja [feel-**trah**-tsyah] f. filtration; percolation
filtracyjny [feel-trah-**tsiy**-ni] adj.m. of filtration; filter (paper, etc.)
filtrat [**feel**-traht] m. filtrate
filtrator [feel-**trah**-tor] m. plankton filtrating animal
filtrować [feel-**tro**-vahćh] v. filter; strain; percolate (*repeatedly*)
filtrować się [feel-**tro**-vahćh śhan] v. filter; strain; percolate; undergo filtration (*repeatedly*)
filtrowanie [feel-tro-**vah**-ńe] n. filtration
filtrowy [feel-**tro**-vi] adj.m. filter (cloth, etc.)
filumenista [fee-loo-me-**ńees**-tah] m. collector of labels
filumenistyczny [fee-loo-me-ńees-**tich**-ni] adj.m. of a collection of labels
filumenistyka [fee-loo-me-**ńees**-ti-kah] f. collecting of labels
filunek [fee-**loo**-nek] m. panel
filut [**fee**-loot] m. jester; rogue; joker; fox; sly boots
filutek [fee-**loo**-tek] m. little jester; little joker
filuteria [fee-loo-**ter**-yah] f. playfulness; skittishness; slyness; roguery; cunning
filuternie [fee-loo-**ter**-ńe] adv. playfully; skittishly; roguishly; cunningly; slyly
filuterność [fee-loo-**ter**-nośhćh] f. playfulness; skittishness; slyness; roguery; cunning
filuterny [fee-loo-**ter**-ni] adj.m. playful; skittish; frolicsome; roguish; cunning; sly
filutka [fee-**loot**-kah] f. skittish girl; chick; kitten; minx; roguish girl; sly girl; cunning girl
filutowaty [fee-loo-to-**vah**-ti] adj.m. playful; skittish; frolicsome; roguish; cunning; sly
Fin [feen] m. Finn
finalik [fee-**nah**-leek] m. decoration printed at the end of a chapter
finalista [fee-nah-**lees**-tah] m. finalist; follower of the theology of finality
finalistka [fee-nah-**leest**-kah] f. (woman) finalist
finalistyczny [fee-nah-lees-**tich**-ni] adj.m. of the theology of finality
finalizacja [fee-nah-lee-**zah**-tsyah] f. finalization
finalizm [fee-**nah**-leezm] m. finalism; teleology; study of evidences of

design and purpose in nature; the use of pupose as an explanation
finalizować [fee-nah-lee-**zo**-vahćh] v. finalize; settle; conclude; bring to an end (*repeatedly*)
finalizowanie [fee-nah-lee-zo-**vah**-ńe] n. finalization; settlement; conclusion; signing (a contract, a treaty, etc.)
finalny [fee-**nahl**-ni] adj.m. final (product, etc.); end (result, etc.)
finał [**fee**-nahw] m. end; end game; close; epilogue; termination; cup-final; final heats; (musical) finale
finałowy [fee-nah-**wo**-vi] adj.m. final (scene, game, contest, etc.)
finanse [fee-**nahn**-se] pl. finances; funds; money resources
finansista [fee-nahn-**śhees**-tah] m. financier; capitalist; expert in finances
finansjera [fee-nahn-**sye**-rah] f. financiers; capitalists; financial circles; Wall Street
finansować [fee-nahn-**so**-vahćh] v. finance (an undertaking, etc.); cover the cost (of); defray the cost (of); bear the expense (*repeatedly*)
finansowanie [fee-nahn-so-**vah**-ńe] n. financing
finansowiec [fee-nahn-**so**-vyets] m. financier; capitalist; expert in finances; worker in a financial institution
finansowo [fee-nahn-**so**-vo] adv. financially
finansowość [fee-nahn-**so**-vośhćh] f. treasury science; finances
finansowy [fee-nahn-**so**-vi] adj.m. of finance; financial; pecuniary
finezja [fee-**nez**-yah] f. fineness; delicacy; nicety; niceties
finezyjnie [fee-ne-**ziy**-ńe] adv. with delicacy; with nicety; with precision
finezyjność [fee-ne-**ziy**-nośhćh] f. delicacy; nicety; subtlety; precision
finezyjny [fee-ne-**ziy**-ni] adj.m. fine; delicate; nice; subtle
fingować [feen-**go**-vahćh] v. fake; simulate; sham (*repeatedly*)
fingowanie [feen-go-**vah**-ńe] n. faking; simulation
finisz [**fee**-ńeesh] m. end (of a run); the finish; finis; the end
finiszować [fee-ńee-**sho**-vahćh] v. make the end run; be finishing; make the final spurt; spurt (*repeatedly*)
finiszowanie [fee-ńee-sho-**vah**-ńe] n. making the end run
finiszowy [fee-ńee-**sho**-vi] adj.m. of the end (of a run); of the finish; of the final spurt
finka [**feen**-kah] f. bowie knife
Finka [**feen**-kah] f. Finnish woman
finta [**feen**-tah] f. trick; deception; artifice; stratagem; feint; dodge
finwal [**feen**-vahl] m. baleen whale
fiński [**feeń**-skee] adj.m. Finnish
fiński nóż [**feeń**-skee noosh] exp.: bowie knife
fioczek [**fyo**-chek] m. (small, little) curls and toupees
fiok [fyok] m. curls and toupees; pretentious hairdo
fiokować się [fyo-**ko**-vahćh śh<u>an</u>] v. dress with gaudy finery; bedizen oneself (*repeatedly*)
fiokowanie się [fyo-ko-**vah**-ńe śh<u>an</u>] n. dressing oneself with gaudy finery; bedizening oneself
fiolet [**fyo**-let] m. the color violet; violet pigment
fioletowieć [fyo-le-**to**-vyećh] v. become violet; grow violet; turn violet; get violet; show violet; form violet patches; appear as violet patches (*repeatedly*)
fioletowienie [fyo-le-to-**vye**-ńe] n. becoming violet
fioletowo [fyo-le-**to**-vo] adv. in violet color
fioletowy [fyo-le-**to**-vi] adj.m. violet
fioletowy nos [fyo-le-**to**-vi nos] exp.: blue nose
promienie fioletowe [pro-**mye**-ńe fyo-le-**to**-ve] exp.: violet rays
fiolka [**fyol**-kah] f. flask; vial; phial
fioł [fyow] m. mania; craze; eccentricity; eccentric; crank; nuts
mieć fioła [myećh **fyo**-wah] exp.: to be crazy; to be wrong; to be barmy
fiołeczek [fyo-**we**-chek] m. nice little

violet; sweet violet
fiołek [**fyo**-wek] m. violet; sweet violet; mania; craze; eccentricity; eccentric; crank; nuts
fiołkowaty [fyow-ko-**vah**-ti] adj.m. violaceous
fiołkowate [fyow-ko-**vah**-te] pl. the violet family of flowers
fiołkowo [fyow-**ko**-vo] adv. in violet color
fiołkowy [fyow-**ko**-vi] adj.m. purple; violet; of the violet
fiord [fyort] m. fiord
fiording [**fyor**-deeng] m. fiording; small Scandinavian horse
fiordowy [fyor-**do**-vi] adj.m. of a fiord; fiord (scenery, etc.)
fiordyng [**fyor**-ding] m. fiording; small Scandinavian horse
fiorytura [fyo-ri-**too**-rah] f. (musical) fioritura
firana [fee-**rah**-nah] f. curtain; drapery
firaneczka [fee-rah-**nech**-kah] f. (small, nice) curtain; drapery
firanka [fee-**rahn**-kah] f. curtain; drapery
firanki [fee-**rahn**-kee] pl. curtains; hangings
fircyk [**feer**-tsik] m. dasher; spark; dandy; fop; gallant
fircykowatość [feer-tsi-ko-**vah**-tośhćh] f. gallantry; dandyism
fircykowaty [feer-tsi-ko-**vah**-ti] adj.m. flashy; dapper; dandyish
firet [**fee**-ret] m. printed quotation
firletka [feer-**let**-kah] f. campion (plant of the pink family); lychnis; ragged robin
firma [**feer**-mah] f. business; firm; name of a firm; style of a firm; establishment
firmament [feer-**mah**-ment] m. sky; the vault of heaven; firmament
firman [**feer**-mahn] m. firman
firmant [**feer**-mahnt] m. figurehead
firmować [feer-**mo**-vahćh] v. act as a figurehead (*repeatedly*)
firmowanie [feer-mo-**vah**-ńe] n. acting as a figurehead
firmowy [feer-**mo**-vi] adj.m. of a firm; firm's (trademark, etc.)
papier firmowy [**pah**-pyer feer-**mo**-vi] exp.: letterhead
firn [feern] m. firn
firnowy [feer-**no**-vi] adj.m. of a firn; of accumulation of granular snow
fis [fees] m. F sharp
fisharmonia [fees-hahr-**mo**-ńyah] f. reed organ (musical instrument)
fiskalizm [fees-**kah**-leezm] m. fiscal stringency
fiskalny [fees-**kahl**-ni] adj.m. fiscal
fiskus [**fees**-koos] m. fisc; fisk
fistaszek [fees-**tah**-shek] m. peanut
fistuła [fees-**too**-wah] f. fistula; high-toned organ pipe; falsetto voice
fistułowaty [fees-too-wo-**vah**-ti] adj.m. of fistula; fistuous
fisza [**fee**-shah] f. important person
gruba fisza [**groo**-bah **fee**-shah] exp.: bigwig; big gun; VIP (very important person)
fiszbin [**feezh**-been] m. whalebone; baleen
fiszbinowiec [feezh-bee-**no**-vyets] m. baleen whale
fiszbinowce [feezh-bee-**nof**-tse] pl. baleen whale family
fiszbinowy [feezh-bee-**no**-vi] adj.m. of whalebone; whalebone (stiffening, etc.)
fiszka [**feesh**-kah] f. slip of paper; card; index card; counter; token
fiś [feeśh] m. (only in exp.:)
mieć fisia [myećh **fee**-śhah] exp.: to have a screw loose; to be crazy; to be wrong in the head; to go bananas
fito- [**fee**-to] prefix: phyto-; plant-
fitobentos [fee-to-**ben**-tos] m. plants living on the bottom of water storage tanks
fitobiologia [fee-to-byo-**lo**-gyah] f. biology of plants
fitocenologia [fee-to-tse-no-lo-gyah] f. phytosociology
fitocenotyczny [fee-to-tse-no-**tich**-ni] adj.m. phytosociological
fitocenoza [fee-to-tse-**no**-zah] f. natural grouping of plants
fitochemia [fee-to-**khe**-myah] f. phytochemistry
fitocyd [fee-**to**-tsit] m. fluid or gaseous substance killing bacteria and fungi (naturally produced by plants)

fitocydy [fee-to-**tsi**-di] pl. fluid or gaseous substances killing bacteria and fungi (naturally produced by plants)
fitofag [fee-**to**-fahg] m. phytophagous
fitofagi [fee-to-**fah**-gee] pl. plant-eating animals
fitofagia [fee-to-**fah**-gyah] f. phytophagy
fitofizjologia [fee-to-feez-yo-**lo**-gyah] f. plant physiology
fitogeniczny [fee-to-ge-**ńeech**-ni] adj.m. phytogenic; of plant origin
fitogeografia [fee-to-ge-o-**grah**-fyah] f. phytogeography
fitogeograficzny [fee-to-ge-o-grah-**feech**-ni] adj.m. phytogeographic; phytogeographical
fitohormon [fee-to-**hor**-mon] m. phytohormone
fitohormony [fee-to-hor-**mo**-ni] pl. phytohormones
fitoklimat [fee-to-**klee**-maht] m. local climate influenced by vegetation
fitomelioracja [fee-to-mel-yo-**rahts**-yah] f. man-made changes in local climate
fitoncyd [feet-**no**-tsit] m. fluid or gaseous substance killing bacteria and fungi (naturally produced by plants)
fitopatolog [fee-to-pah-**to**-log] m. phytopathologist
fitopatologia [fee-to-pah-to-**lo**-gyah] f. phytopathology
fitopatologicznie [fee-to-pah-to-lo-**geech**-ńe] adv. in phytopathological manner
fitopatologiczny [fee-to-pah-to-lo-**geech**-ni] adj.m. phytopathologic; phytopathological
fitoplankton [fee-to-**plahn**-kton] m. phytoplankton
fitosocjolog [fee-to-sots-**yo**-log] m. phytosociologist
fitosocjologia [fee-to-sots-yo-**lo**-gyah] f. phytosociology
fitosocjologicznie [fee-to-sots-yo-lo-**geech**-ńe] adv. phytosociologically
fitosocjologiczny [fee-to-sots-yo-lo-**geech**-ni] adj.m. phytosociological
fitoterapia [fee-to-te-**rah**-pyah] f. phytotherapy; treatment by the use of medicinal plants
fitotoksyczność [fee-to-tok-**sich**-nośhćh] f. phytotoxicity
fitotoksyczny [fee-to-tok-**sich**-ni] adj.m. phytotoxic
fitotron [fee-**to**-tron] m. experimental chamber with controlled climate for study of plants
fityna [fee-**ti**-nah] f. phytin
fiu! [fyoo] excl.: phew!; whew!; coo!
fiu fiu w głowie [fyoo fyoo v **gwo**-vye] exp.: featherbrain
fiukać [**fyoo**-kahćh] v. whistle; tootle (on a clarinet) (*repeatedly*)
fiukanie [fyoo-**kah**-ńe] n. whistling (*repeated*)
fiuknąć [**fyook**-nownćh] v. whistle; tootle (on a clarinet)
fiuknięcie [fyook-**ńan**-ćhe] n. whistling
fiume [**fyoo**-me] n. trifle
fiut! [fyoot] excl.: gone suddenly!
fizetyna [fee-ze-**ti**-nah] f. natural flavone dye
fizis [**fee**-zees] (not declined:) physiognomy; face; countenance
fizjo- [**feez**-yo] prefix: physio-
fizjogeografia [fee-zyo-ge-o-**grah**-fyah] f. physical geography; physiography
fizjognomia [fee-zyo-**gno**-myah] f. physiognomy; face (hist.)
fizjognomika [fee-zyo-**gno**-mee-kah] f. science of physiognomy (hist.)
fizjograf [fee-**zyo**-grahf] m. physiographer
fizjografia [fee-zyo-**grah**-fyah] f. physiography
fizjograficzny [fees-yo-grah-**feech**-ni] adj.m. physiographic
fizjokrata [fee-zyo-**krah**-tah] m. Physiocrat
fizjokratyczny [fee-zyo-krah-**tich**-ni] adj.m. physiocratic
fizjokratyzm [fee-zyo-**krah**-tizm] m. physiocratic doctrine
fizjolog [fee-**zyo**-log] m. physiologist
fizjologia [fee-zyo-**lo**-gyah] f. physiology; functions of the human body
fizjologicznie [fee-zyo-lo-**geech**-ńe]

adv. physiologically
fizjologiczny [fee-zyo-lo-**geech**-ni] adj.m. physiological
fizjonomia [fee-zyo-**no**-myah] f. physiognomy; face; countenance; cast of features; external aspect
fizjonomicznie [fee-zyo-no-**meech**-ńe] adv. physiognomically
fizjonomiczny [fee-zyo-no-**meech**-ni] adj.m. physiognomical
fizjonomika [fee-zyo-**no**-mee-kah] f. the science of physiognomy
fizjonomista [feez-yo-no-**mees**-tah] m. student of physiognomy
fizjopatolog [feez-yo-pah-**to**-log] m. specialist in physiopathology
fizjopatologia [feez-yo-pah-to-**lo**-gyah] f. physiopathology
fizjopatologiczny [feez-yo-pah-to-lo-**geech**-ni] adj.m. physiopathologic; physiopathological
fizjoterapeuta [feez-yo-te-rah-**pew**-tah] m. physiotherapist
fizjoterapeutycznie [feez-yo-te-rah-pew-**tich**-ńe] adv. with physiotherapy
fizjoterapeutyczny [feez-yo-te-rah-pew-**tich**-ni] adj.m. physiotherapeutic
fizjoterapia [fees-yo-te-**rah**-pyah] f. physiotherapy
fizycznie [fee-**zich**-ńe] adv. physically
fizyczność [fee-**zich**-nośhćh] f. physical nature
fizyczny [fee-**zich**-ni] adj.m. physical (experiment, training; geography, etc.); of physics; bodily; carnal; material; manual (worker, etc.)
fizyk [**fee**-zik] m. physicist; natural philosopher
ryzyk-fizyk [ri-zik **fee**-zik] exp.: happen what may; at all hazards; sink or swim!
fizyka [**fee**-zi-kah] f. physics; natural philosophy
fizyka atomowa [**fee**-zi-kah ah-to-**mo**-vah] exp.: atomic physics
fizyka jądrowa [**fee**-zi-kah <u>yown</u>-**dro**-vah] exp.: nuclear physics
fizykalny [fee-zi-**kahl**-ni] adj.m. physical
z fizykalnego punktu widzenia [s fee-zi-kahl-**ne**-go **poon**-ktoo vee-**dze**-ńah] exp.: from the point of view of physics
fizykochemia [fee-zi-ko-**khe**-myah] f. physical chemistry
fizykochemiczny [fee-zi-ko-khe-**meech**-ni] adj.m. of physical chemistry
fizykochemik [fee-zi-ko-**khe**-meek] m. physical chemist
fizykoterapia [fee-zi-ko-te-**rah**-pyah] f. physiotherapy
fizylier [fee-**zil**-yer] m. rifleman
fizylierka [fee-zil-**yer**-kah] f. riflewoman
fizylierski [fee-zil-**yer**-skee] adj.m. of riflemen
fizys [**fee**-zis] indecl. face; dial; mug
fiżon [**fee**-zhon] m. Brazilian bean dish
flacha [**flah**-khah] f. outsize bottle; large bottle; flagon; carboy
flachcęgi [flahkh-**tsan**-gee] pl. flat pliers
flaczarz [**flah**-chahsh] m. tripe dealer; tripe man
flaczeć [**flah**-chećh] v. grow flabby; become flabby (*repeatedly*)
flaczek [**flah**-chek] m. small rag
flaczenie [flah-**che**-ńe] n. growing flabby
flaczki [**flahch**-kee] pl. tripe (cooked)
flader [**flah**-der] m. vein; streak; grain (in wood, stone, etc.); rope marking hunting area
fladrować [flahd-**ro**-vahćh] v. vein; streak; grain (wood, etc.); mark hunting area (*repeatedly*)
fladrowanie [flahd-ro-**vah**-ńe] n. streaking
fladrowy [flahd-**ro**-vi] adj.m. veined; streaked; grained (wood, etc.)
flaga [**flah**-gah] f. banner; flag; ensign; standard; signal
biała flaga [**byah**-wah **flah**-gah] exp.: white banner; flag of truce
flagelant [flah-**ge**-lahnt] m. flagellant; whipper; whip
flaglinka [flahg-**leen**-kah] f. line for raising signal flag on ship's mast
flagować [flah-**go**-vahćh] v. flag (down); make flag signals; signalize (*repeatedly*)
flagowanie [flah-go-**vah**-ńe] n. flagging

flagowiec [flah-**go**-vyets] m. colloq: flagship
flagowy [flah-**go**-vi] adj.m. flag (ship, etc.)
flagstenga [flahk-**sten**-gah] f. flagstaff
flagsztok [**flahk**-shtok] m. flagstaff
flak [flahk] m. bowel; gut; limp rag; worn-out man; weakling
flaki [**flah**-kee] pl. bowels; guts; entrails; tripe; limp rags
flakon [**flah**-kon] m. vase; bowl
flakonik [flah-**ko**-ńeek] m. (small, nice) vase; bowl
flakowacenie [flah-ko-vah-**tse**-ńe] n. becoming flabby; growing flabby
flakowacieć [flah-ko-**vah**-ćhećh] v. become flabby; grow flabby (*repeatedly*)
flakowato [flah-ko-**vah**-to] adv. flabbily; nervelessly
flakowatość [flah-ko-**vah**-tośhćh] f. flabbiness
flakowaty [flah-ko-**vah**-ti] adj.m. flabby; flaccid; nerveless
flama [**flah**-mah] f. sweetheart; ladylove; flame (of the moment)
Flamand [**flah**-mahnt] m. Fleming; painting of Flemish school
Flamandczyk [flah-**mahnt**-chik] m. Fleming; of Flanders
flamandczyzna [flah-mahnt-**chiz**-nah] f. characteristics of the Flemish school of painting
Flamandka [flah-**mahnt**-kah] f. Flemish woman
flamandzki [flah-**mahnts**-kee] adj.m. Flemish (language, etc.)
flamaster [flah-**mahs**-ter] m. marker filled with ink
flaming [**flah**-meeng] m. flamingo
flanca [**flahn**-tsah] f. set; shoot; a new growth; sprout
flancować [flahn-**tso**-vahćh] v. plant (sprouting seeds); set (new growth) (*repeatedly*)
flancowanie [flahn-tso-**vah**-ńe] n. planting; setting (new growth)
flandryjski [flahn-**driy**-skee] adj.m. of Flanders; Flanders
flanela [flah-**ne**-lah] f. flannel
flanelka [flah-**nel**-kah] f. (small, nice) flannel
flanelkowy [flah-nel-**ko**-vi] adj.m. flannel (cloth, etc.)
flanelowy [flah-ne-**lo**-vi] adj.m. flannel (cloth, etc.)
flank [flahnk] m. flank; side; lateral military force
flanka [**flahn**-kah] f. flank; side; lateral military force
flankier [**flahn**-ker] m. unit (or soldier) protecting a flank
flankować [flahn-**ko**-vahćh] v. protect a flank; attack a flank; attack from the flank; threaten a flank; fortify a flank (*repeatedly*)
flankowanie [flahn-ko-**vah**-ńe] n. flanking operations
flankowy [flahn-**ko**-vi] adj.m. flanking (artillery fire, etc.); outflanking (maneuver, etc.)
flara [**flah**-rah] f. flare (signal); illumination (of a target, etc.)
flasza [**flah**-shah] f. large bottle; outsize bottle; flagon
flaszczyna [flahsh-**chi**-nah] f. (small, measly) bottle
flaszeczka [flah-**shech**-kah] f. (small) bottle; cruet
flaszka [**flahsh**-kah] f. bottle; bottleful; slang: drink; booze
flaszkowaty [flahsh-ko-**vah**-ti] adj.m. bottle-shaped
flaszowiec [flah-**sho**-vyets] m. custard apple (tree or fruit)
flausz [flahwsh] m. pilot-cloth
flauta [**flahw**-tah] f. windless weather at sea; doldrums; calm; lull
flawina [flah-**vee**-nah] f. flavin
flawon [**flah**-von] m. flavone
flawoproteid [flah-vo-pro-**te**-eet] m. flavoprotein
flażelant [flah-**zhe**-lahnt] m. flagellant; whipper; whip
flażeolet [flah-zhe-**o**-let] m. flageolet
flażolet [flah-**zho**-let] m. flageolet
flażoletowy [flah-zho-le-**to**-vi] adj.m. of a flageolet; of organ stop
flądерka [flown-**der**-kah] f. little flounder
flądra [**flown**-drah] f. flounder; plaice; fluke; flatfish; slang: slut; slattern; sloven; draggletail; strumpet; tart (mob jargon)
flądrowaty [flown-dro-**vah**-ti] adj.m. like a flounder; slang: slatternly;

slovenly (mob jargon)
flebografia [fle-bo-**grah**-fyah] f. phlebography
flebograficzny [fle-bo-grah-**feech**-ni] adj.m. phlebographic
flebolit [fle-**bo**-leet] m. phlebolith
flecik [**fle**-ćheek] m. piccolo (flute)
flecista [fle-**ćhees**-tah] m. flutist; flute player
flecistka [fle-**ćheest**-kah] f. (woman) flutist; flute player
fleczek [**fle**-chek] m. small heel-tap
fleczer [**fle**-cher] m. temporary tooth filling
flegma [**fleg**-mah] f. phlegm; calm; coolness; cold blood; cool-headedness; stolidity; sluggishness; equanimity
flegmatyczka [fleg-mah-**tich**-kah] f. phlegmatic woman; cool-headed woman; sluggish woman; apathetic woman; not easily excited woman
flegmatycznie [fleg-mah-**tich**-ńe] adv. phlegmatically; coolly; stolidly; sluggishly
flegmatyczność [fleg-mah-**tich**-nośhćh] f. sluggishness
flegmatyczny [fleg-mah-**tich**-ni] adj.m. phlegmatic; cool; stolid
flegmatyk [fleg-**mah**-tik] m. phlegmatic; cool-headed man; sluggish man; apathetic man; not easily excited man
flegmatyzacja [fleg-mah-ti-**zah**-tsyah] f. alteration of explosives making them less sensitive to handling
flegmatyzator [fleg-mah-ti-**zah**-tor] m. additive in explosives making them less sensitive to handling
flegmisty [fleg-**mees**-ti] adj.m. pituitary; full of mucus
flegmona [fleg-**mo**-nah] f. phlegmon (ulcer); phlogistic ulcer
fleja [**fle**-yah] f. slang: shabby woman; slut; slattern; sloven
flejtuch [**fley**-tookh] m. slut; slattern; sloven
flejtuchowato [fley-too-kho-**vah**-to] adv. in a slatternly manner; in a slovenly way
flejtuchowaty [fley-too-kho-**vah**-ti] adj.m. slatternly; slovenly
flejtuszek [fley-**too**-shek] m. (little) slut; slattern; sloven
flek [flek] m. tap; heeltap; lift; slang: kick (mob jargon)
być pod flekiem [bićh pot fle-kem] exp.: slang: to be drunk
fleksja [**fleks**-yah] f. inflection; accidence (in grammar)
fleksometr [flek-**so**-metr] m. fleximeter; flexing machine
fleksor [**flek**-sor] m. flexor (muscle)
fleksura [flek-**soo**-rah] f. flexure
fleksyjnie [flek-**siy**-ńe] adv. inflectionally
fleksyjny [flek-**siy**-ni] adj.m. inflectional; inflected
flesz [flesh] m. flashlight; flash attack (in fencing)
flesza [**fle**-shah] f. fortified emplacement for a shooter
fleszować [fle-**sho**-vahćh] v. make flash attacks (*repeatedly*)
fleszowanie [fle-sho-**vah**-ńe] n. making flash attacks in fencing
flet [flet] m. flute
fletnia [**flet**-ńah] f. colloq: flute
fletnista [flet-**ńees**-tah] m. piper
fletnistka [flet-**ńeest**-kah] f. (woman) piper
fletowy [fle-**to**-vi] adj.m. of flute; flute (tones, etc.)
flibustier [flee-**boos**-tyer] m. filibuster (pirate, smuggler); obstruction of legislative action by making long speeches
flik [fleek] m. slang: shabby French cop (mob jargon)
flint [fleent] m. flint glass
flinta [**fleen**-tah] f. shotgun; musket; flintlock gun
flintowy [fleen-**to**-vi] adj.m. of flint; flint (glass, etc.); of a shotgun; of a musket
flirciarka [fleer-**ćhahr**-kah] f. flirt; flirtatious woman; coquette
flirciarski [fleer-**ćhahr**-skee] adj.m. flirt; flirtatious
flirciarz [**fleer**-ćhahsh] m. philanderer; a flirt
flircik [**fleer**-ćheek] m. a small flirt
flirt [fleert] m. flirt; flirtation; philandering; carrying-on; dalliance
flirtować [fleer-**to**-vahćh] v. flirt; trifle; philander; coquet; carry-on;

dally; toy (*repeatedly*)
flirtowanie [fleer-to-**vah**-ńe] n. flirtation; flirtations
flis [flees] m. river transport of timber; log rafting
flisacki [flee-**sahts**-kee] adj.m. rafter's; raftsman's; tracker's; bargeman's
flisactwo [flee-**sahts**-tfo] n. rafting
flisaczy [flee-**sah**-chi] adj.m. of a raftsman
flisak [**flee**-sahk] m. raftsman; rafter; tracker; bargeman
flisz [fleesh] m. (geologic) Flysch
fliszowy [flee-**sho**-vi] adj.m. Flysch (strata, deposit, etc.)
flit [fleet] m. (trade name of an) insecticide
flitować [flee-**to**-vahćh] v. spray with an insecticide (*repeatedly*)
flitowanie [flee-to-**vah**-ńe] n. spraying with an insecticide
fliz [flees] m. flagstone; printer's inking table
fliza [**flee**-zah] f. flagstone; printer's inking table
flizowy [flee-**zo**-vi] adj.m. flagstone (floor, etc.)
flobert [**flo**-bert] m. small caliber rifle
flokeny [flo-**ke**-ni] pl. snow flakes; flaky spots (in cast steel)
floks [floks] m. phlox (an herb)
flokulacja [flo-koo-**lah**-tsyah] f. flocculation; aggregation
flokulator [flo-koo-**lah**-tor] m. flocculator
flokuły [flo-**koo**-wi] pl. solar flares
flora [**flo**-rah] f. flora; gauze; crepe (mourning arm band)
florecista [flo-re-**ćhees**-tah] m. foilsman; fencer
florecistka [flo-re-**ćheest**-kah] f. (woman) fencer
floren [**flo**-ren] m. florin
florencki [flo-**rents**-kee] adj.m. Florentine
florentyńczyk [flo-ren-**tiń**-chik] m. Florentine
florentynka [flo-ren-**tin**-kah] f. Florentine (woman)
flores [**flo**-res] m. ornamental flowing curve
floresy [flo-**re**-si] pl. ornamental flowing curves; flourishes
floresowaty [flo-re-so-**vah**-ti] adj.m. in ornamental flowing curves
floret [**flo**-ret] m. foil
floretowy [flo-re-**to**-vi] adj.m. foil (tournament, etc.)
floriański [flor-**yahń**-skee] adj.m. of St. Florian
florystycznie [flo-ris-**tich**-ńe] adv. floristically
florystyczny [flo-ris-**tich**-ni] adj.m. floristic
florystyka [flo-**ris**-ti-kah] f. floristics
flota [**flo**-tah] f. fleet
flota handlowa [**flo**-tah khahnd-**lo**-vah] exp.: merchant marine
flota powietrzna [**flo**-tah po-**vyetsh**-nah] exp.: aerial fleet
flota wojenna [**flo**-tah vo-**yen**-nah] exp.: navy
flotacja [flo-**tah**-tsyah] f. flotation
flotacyjny [flo-tah-**tsiy**-ni] adj.m. flotation (process, etc.)
flotownia [flo-**tov**-ńah] f. flotation plant
flotownik [flo-**tov**-ńeek] m. flotation plant worker
flotylla [flo-**til**-lah] f. flotilla
flotylla rybacka [flo-**til**-lah ri-**bahts**-kah] exp.: fishing fleet
flower [**flo**-ver] m. small caliber rifle; fowling piece
flowerowy [flo-ve-**ro**-vi] adj.m. of a small caliber rifle
fluid [**floo**-eet] m. psychic fluid emanating from human body; aura; invisible emanation
fluidyzacja [floo-ee-di-**zah**-tsyah] f. fluidization
fluidyzator [floo-ee-di-**zah**-tor] m. fluidizer
fluksja [**flook**-syah] f. tooth infection; swelling; gumboil
fluksometr [flook-**so**-metr] m. magnetic-flux meter
fluktuacja [flook-too-**ah**-tsyah] f. fluctuation; wavering; oscillation
fluktuacyjny [flook-too-ah-**tsiy**-ni] adj.m. of fluctuation; of oscillation
flukty [**flook**-ti] pl. waves; high seas
fluor [**floo**-or] m. fluorine
fluorek [floo-**o**-rek] m. fluoride
fluorescencja [floo-o-res-**tsen**-tsyah]

f. fluorescence
fluorescencyjnie [floo-o-res-tsen-**tsiy**-ńe] adv. with fluorescence
fluorescencyjny [floo-o-res-tsen-**tsiy**-ni] adj.m. fluorescent
fluoroforta [floo-o-ro-**for**-tah] f. fluoro-etching
fluorografia [floo-o-ro-**grah**-fyah] f. fluorography
fluoroskop [floo-o-**ro**-skop] m. fluoroscope
fluoroskopia [floo-o-ro-**sko**-pyah] f. fluoroscopy
fluorować [floo-o-**ro**-vahćh] v. introduce fluoride compounds in place of hydrogen atoms (*repeatedly*)
fluorowanie [floo-o-ro-**vah**-ńe] n. introduction of fluoride compounds in place of hydrogen atoms
fluorowiec [floo-o-**ro**-vyets] m. halogen
fluorowce [floo-o-**rof**-tse] pl. halogens
fluorowodorowy [floo-o-ro-vo-do-**ro**-vi] adj.m. of hydrogen fluoride
fluorowodór [floo-o-ro-**vo**-door] m. hydrogen fluoride
fluorowy [floo-o-**ro**-vi] adj.m. of fluor
fluoryt [floo-**o**-rit] m. fluorite; fluorspar (common mineral)
fluoryzacja [floo-o-ri-**zah**-tsyah] f. fluorination of teeth
fluoryzować [floo-o-ri-**zo**-vahćh] v. fluoresce; become luminous when exposed to invisible radiation (*repeatedly*)
fluoryzowanie [floo-o-ri-zo-**vah**-ńe] n. fluorescence
fluoryzujący [floo-o-ri-zoo-**yown**-tsi] adj.m. fluorescent
fluwialny [floo-**vyahl**-ni] adj.m. fluvial; of stream action
fluwioglacjalny [floo-vyo-glah-**tsyahl**-ni] adj.m. fluvioglacial
fluwioglacjał [floo-vyo-**glah**-tsyahw] m. fluvioglacial deposits
fobia [**fo**-byah] f. phobia
fochy [**fo**-khi] pl. blues; whims; sulks; pouts; sudden fancy
foczy [**fo**-chi] adj.m. of a seal; sealskin (fur, etc.)
fok [fok] m. foresail
fok- [fok] prefix: of foremast
foka [**fo**-kah] f. seal; sealskin; sealskin fur
foki [**fo**-kee] pl. seals; sealskins; sealskin fur
fokmaszt [**fok**-mahsht] m. foremast
fokowaty [fo-ko-**vah**-ti] adj.m. seal-like; resembling a seal
fokowy [fo-**ko**-vi] adj.m. of a sealskin fur; of a seal
fokreja [fok-**re**-yah] f. foreyard
foks [foks] m. colloq: fox terrier; foxtrot
foksik [**fok**-śheek] m. (small) fox terrier
foksterier [foks-**ter**-yer] m. fox terrier
foksterierek [foks-ter-**ye**-rek] m. (small) fox terrier
fokstrot [**foks**-trot] m. foxtrot; quickstep
foksztaksel [fok-**shtahk**-sel] m. forestay sail
fokus [**fo**-koos] m. focus; slang: jugglery
fokus pokus [**fo**-koos **po**-koos] exp.: hocus-pocus (hist.)
fola [**fo**-lah] f. fishing net; slaking vessel
folarski [fo-**lahr**-skee] adj.m. fuller's (earth, etc.)
folarz [**fo**-lahsh] m. fuller
folblut [**fol**-bloot] m. thoroughbred horse; full-bred horse
folder [**fol**-der] m. folder; brochure
folga [**fol**-gah] f. relaxation; foil
folgować [fol-**go**-vahćh] v. slacken; relax; indulge; abate; lessen; decrease; subside; be lenient; give vent (to); relieve (*repeatedly*)
folgować sobie [fol-**go**-vahćh **so**-bye] exp.: to let oneself relax; be lenient with oneself; to let oneself indulge
folgowanie [fol-go-**vah**-ńe] n. leniency; indulgence
folia [**fol**-yah] f. foil
złota folia [**zwo**-tah **fol**-yah] exp.: gold leaf; gold foil
foliacja [fol-**yah**-tsyah] f. foliated texture in rocks
foliał [**fol**-yahw] m. folio book; volume

foliałowy [fol-yah-**wo**-vi] adj.m. folio (format, etc.)
foliant [**fol**-yahnt] m. folio book; volume
folidoid [fo-lee-**do**-eet] m. marly sedimentary rock (mineral)
folikulina [fo-lee-koo-**lee**-nah] f. estrone
folio [**fol**-yo] (not decline:) folio
foliować [fol-**yo**-vahćh] v. number the folios; paginate (a book); folio; cover with foil (*repeatedly*)
foliowanie [fol-yo-**vah**-ńe] n. foliation; pagination
foliowy [fol-**yo**-vi] adj.m. folio; folic (acid, etc.)
folklor [**fol**-klor] m. folklore; custom; traditions; beliefs
folkloryczny [fol-klo-**rich**-ni] adj.m. folkloric
folklorysta [fol-klo-**ris**-tah] m. folklorist
folklorystyczny [fol-klo-ris-**tich**-ni] adj.m. folkloristic
folklorystyka [fol-klo-**ris**-ti-kah] f. folklore; study of folklore
folkloryzm [fol-**klo**-rizm] m. introduction of folkloric elements into art work
folksdojcz [**folks**-doych] m. Volksdeutscher; "racial" German born outside Germany
folować [fo-**lo**-vahćh] v. full (cloth) (*repeatedly*)
folowanie [fo-lo-**vah**-ńe] n. fulling (cloth)
folusz [**fo**-loosh] m. fulling mill; fullery
folusznictwo [fo-loosh-**ńeets**-tfo] n. fulling
foluszniczy [fo-loosh-**ńee**-chi] adj.m. fuller's; fulling (trade, work, etc.)
folusznik [fo-**loosh**-ńeek] m. fuller
foluszować [fo-loo-**sho**-vahćh] v. full (cloth) (*repeatedly*)
foluszowanie [fo-loo-sho-**vah**-ńe] n. fulling (cloth)
foluszowy [fo-loo-**sho**-vi] adj.m. fulled (surface, etc.)
folwarczek [fol-**vahr**-chek] m. (small, nice) farm; grange
folwarczny [fol-**vahrch**-ni] adj.m. of a farm; of a grange; m. farm hand
folwark [**fol**-vahrk] m. farm; grange
fomoza [fo-**mo**-zah] f. a plant disease caused by a fungus
fon [fon] m. phone
fonacja [fo-**nah**-tsyah] f. phonation
fonacyjny [fo-nah-**tsiy**-ni] adj.m. phonatory
fonem [**fo**-nem] m. phoneme
fonematycznie [fo-ne-mah-**tich**-ńe] adv. phonemically
fonematyczny [fo-ne-mah-**tich**-ni] adj.m. phonemic
fonemowy [fo-ne-**mo**-vi] adj.m. phonemic
fonendoskop [fo-nen-**dos**-kop] m. phonendoscope
fonetyczka [fo-ne-**tich**-kah] f. (woman) phonetician
fonetycznie [fo-ne-**tich**-ńe] adv. phonetically
fonetyczny [fo-ne-**tich**-ni] adj.m. phonetic; of speech sounds
fonetyk [fo-**ne**-tik] m. phonetician
fonetyka [fo-**ne**-ti-kah] f. phonetics; analysis, classification of speech sounds or phones
fonetyzacja [fo-ne-ti-**zah**-tsyah] f. phonetization
fonetyzować [fo-ne-ti-**zo**-vahćh] v. phonetize (*repeatedly*)
fonetyzowanie [fo-ne-ti-zo-**vah**-ńe] n. phonetization
fonia [**fo**-ńyah] f. sound transmission; TV sound
foniatria [fo-**ńyah**-tryah] f. phoniatrics; phoniatry
foniatryczny [fo-ńyah-**trich**-ni] adj.m. phoniatric
fonicznie [fo-**ńeech**-ńe] adv. phonically
foniczny [fo-**ńeech**-ni] adj.m. phonic
fonizacja [fo-ńee-**zah**-tsyah] f. production of sounds through installed speakers
fono- [**fo**-no] prefix: phono-; sound-; voice-; speech-
fonoamator [fo-no-ah-**mah**-tor] m. hobbyist in phonics and acoustics
fonogeniczny [fo-no-ge-**ńeech**-ni] adj.m. of sound suitable for recording
fonograf [fo-**no**-grahf] m. phonograph
fonografia [fo-no-**grah**-fyah] f.

phonography
fonograficznie [fo-no-grah-**feech**-ńe] adv. phonographically
fonograficzny [fo-no-grah-**feech**-ni] adj.m. phonographic
fonogram [fo-**no**-grahm] m. phonogram
fonogramicznie [fo-no-grah-**meech**-ńe] adv. phonogramically; phonogrammically
fonogramiczny [fo-no-grah-**meech**-ni] adj.m. phonogrammic; phonogramic
fonokardiograf [fo-no-kahr-**dyo**-grahf] m. phonocardiograph
fonokardiografia [fo-no-kahr-dyo-**grah**-fyah] f. phonocardiography
fonokardiograficzny [fo-no-kahr-dyo-grah-**feech**-ni] adj.m. phonocardiographic
fonokardiogram [fo-no-kahr-**dyo**-grahm] m. phonocardiogram
fonokraniograf [fo-no-krah-**ńyo**-grahf] m. phonograph of the skull
fonolit [fo-**no**-leet] m. clingstone; phonolite
fonolog [fo-**no**-log] m. specialist in the sound of speech
fonologia [fo-no-**lo**-gyah] f. phonology; phonetics
fonologicznie [fo-no-lo-**geech**-ńe] adv. phonologically
fonologiczność [fo-no-lo-**geech**-nośhćh] f. phonology
fonologiczny [fo-no-lo-**geech**-ni] adj.m. phonological
fonometr [fo-**no**-metr] m. phonometer
fonometria [fo-no-**metr**-yah] f. phonometry
fonometryczny [fo-no-me-**trich**-ni] adj.m. phonometric
fonopulmograf [fo-no-pool-**mo**-grahf] m. phonograph of the lungs
fonotaksja [fo-no-**tah**-ksyah] f. reaction to sounds in movements of animals
fonoskop [fo-**no**-skop] m. phonoscope
fonoteka [fo-no-**te**-kah] f. record or tape library
fontanna [fon-**tahn**-nah] f. fountain; spurt of water; waterworks
fontanna z wodą do picia [fon-tahn-nah z **vo**-down do **pee**-ćhah] exp.: drinking fountain
fontaź [**fon**-tahśh] m. fancy knot (in a scarf, etc.); tassel; feather duster
football [**foot**-bol] m. football; soccer
for [for] m. colloq: advantage given in advance; handicap; start; law; odds
fory [**fo**-ri] pl. favor; good graces
fora! [**fo**-rah] excl.: out!; out you go!; get out!; beat it!
forbramsel [for-**brahm**-sel] m. fore-topgallant sail
ford [fort] m. Ford car
fordanser [for-**dahn**-ser] m. gigolo; male escort
fordanserka [for-dahn-**ser**-kah] f. professional (female) dancing partner (hist.)
fordewind [for-**de**-veent] m. leading wind
foremka [fo-**rem**-kah] f. little mold (for baking, etc.)
foremnie [fo-**rem**-ńe] adv. shapely; regularly; symmetrically; in a well-proportioned manner
foremnik [fo-**rem**-ńeek] m. shaping tool
foremność [fo-**rem**-nośhćh] f. shapeliness; handsomeness; regularity; symmetry; good proportions
foremny [fo-**rem**-ni] adj.m. shapely; handsome; regular; symmetrical; well-proportioned
forhend [**for**-hent] m. forehand stroke
forint [**fo**-reent] m. forint (Hungarian currency)
forma [**for**-mah] f. shape; mold; mould; form; formality; manners; behavior; sort; model; cut; pattern; condition; fettle; trim
formy towarzyskie [**for**-mi to-vah-**zhis**-ke] exp.: conventions
być w dobrej formie [bićh v **dob**-rey **for**-mye] exp.: to be in good form, shape, or condition
formacja [for-**mah**-tsyah] f. unit; formation; structure; system; stage of development
formak [for-**mahk**] m. block of slate

of regular shape
formaldehyd [for-mahl-**de**-khit] m. formaldehyde
formalina [for-mah-**lee**-nah] f. formalin
formalista [for-mah-**lees**-tah] m. formalist; precisian
formalistycznie [for-mah-lees-**tich**-ńe] adv. formalistically; formally
formalistyczny [for-mah-lees-**tich**-ni] adj.m. formalistic; formal; precisian; puritan
formalistyka [for-mah-**lees**-ti-kah] f. formalism; precisianism; barratry; puritanism
formalizacja [for-mah-lee-**zah**-tsyah] f. formalization
formalizm [for-**mah**-leezm] m. formalism; stiffness of manners or behavior
formalizować [for-mah-lee-**zo**-vahćh] v. formalize (*repeatedly*)
formalizowanie [for-mah-lee-zo-**vah**-ńe] n. formalism; precisianism
formalnie [for-**mahl**-ńe] adv. formally; officially; regularly; structurally; in form; in due form; in principle; positively; actually; simply; literally
formalność [for-**mahl**-nośhćh] f. external form; outer form; formality
to zwykła formalność [to **zvik**-wah for-**mahl**-nośhćh] exp.: it is a mere formality
formalny [for-**mahl**-ni] adj.m. formal; official; structural; positive; regular; literal
formant [**for**-mahnt] m. formant; a resonance band held to determine the phonetic quality of a vowel
format [**for**-maht] m. size; style
formatka [for-**maht**-kah] f. veneer sheet of standardized size
formatnik [for-**maht**-ńeek] m. device for sizing monotype
formatownik [for-mah-**tov**-ńeek] m. formatting device
formatowy [for-mah-**to**-vi] adj.m. of a format
formierczy [for-**myer**-chi] adj.m. moulder's; molding
formierka [for-**myer**-kah] f. molding machine
formiernia [for-**myer**-ńah] f. foundry
formierski [for-**myer**-skee] adj.m. moulder's; molding
formierstwo [for-**myers**-tfo] n. molding
formierz [**for**-myesh] m. moulder; founder; former
forminga [for-**meen**-gah] f. ancient Greek lyre
formista [for-**mees**-tah] m. adherent of "Polish formizm"
formistyczny [for-mees-**tich**-ni] adj.m. of the style of "formizm"
formizm [**for**-meezm] m. "formizm" (a phase of Polish art)
formować [for-**mo**-vahćh] v. shape; form; fashion; frame; create; arrange; make (*repeatedly*)
formować się [for-**mo**-vahćh śhan] v. be shaped; be formed; be fashioned; be framed; be created; come into being; spring up; form (into a line, etc.) (*repeatedly*)
formowanie [for-mo-**vah**-ńe] n. formation
formowanie się [for-mo-**vah**-ńe śhan] n. being formed
formownia [for-**mov**-ńah] f. form finishing room
formowniczy [for-mov-**ńee**-chi] adj.m. of formatting
formowy [for-**mo**-vi] adj.m. of molding
formularz [for-**moo**-lahsh] m. blank; (application) form; sheet
formularzowy [for-moo-lah-**zho**-vi] adj.m. of a blank; of an application form
formuła [for-**moo**-wah] f. formula; words; canon; expression; wording; recipe
formułka [for-**moow**-kah] f. (small, concise) formula; words; canon; expression; wording; recipe
formułkowy [for-moow-**ko**-vi] adj.m. of a (small, concise) formula; of an expression; of a wording; of a recipe
formułować [for-moo-**wo**-vahćh] v. express; put into words; formulate; shape (an idea, etc.) (*repeatedly*)
formułować się [for-moo-**wo**-vahćh śhan] v. be in a process of

formulation (*repeatedly*)
formułowanie [for-moo-wo-**vah**-ńe] n. wording (of a text, etc.); cast (of a sentence, etc.); formulation
formułowanie się [for-moo-wo-**vah**-ńe śh<u>an</u>] n. formulation (of opinion, etc.); being in a process of formulation
fornal [**for**-nahl] m. groom; stableboy; carter
fornalski [for-**nahl**-skee] adj.m. groom's; stableboy's; carter's
forniernia [for-**ńer**-ńah] f. veneer-cutting machine
fornir [**for**-ńeer] m. veneer
fornirować [for-ńee-**ro**-vahćh] v. veneer (furniture, etc.) (*repeatedly*)
fornirowanie [for-ńee-ro-**vah**-ńe] n. veneer
fornirowy [for-ńee-**ro**-vi] adj.m. of veneer; veneer (wood, etc.)
forować [fo-**ro**-vahćh] v. favor; patronize; support; help (*repeatedly*)
forowanie [fo-ro-**vah**-ńe] n. favoritism
forpik [**for**-peek] m. forepeak
forpoczta [for-**poch**-tah] f. outpost
forsa [**for**-sah] f. colloq: dough; chink; bread; tin; a pot of money
forsiasty [for-**śhahs**-ti] adj.m. slang: with moneybags; rich; oofy; padded (mob jargon)
forsować [for-**so**-vahćh] v. force; strain; urge; exhort; advocate; overcome; exert; drive; jump; run down (a game, etc.) (*repeatedly*)
forsować się [for-**so**-vahćh śh<u>an</u>] v. strain; overstrain oneself; exert oneself; labor (*repeatedly*)
forsowanie [for-so-**vah**-ńe] n. strain; exertion; push; drive
forsowanie się [for-so-**vah**-ńe śh<u>an</u>] n. overstraining oneself
forsownie [for-**sov**-ńe] adv. forcefully; forcibly; strenuously; intensively
forsowny [for-**sov**-ni] adj.m. forcible; intensive; forceful; strenuous
forsowny marsz [for-**sov**-ni mahrsh] exp.: forced march
forsycja [for-si-tsyah] f. forsythia
forszmak [**forsh**-mahk] m. appetizer made of minced herring, potatoes, butter and eggs
fort [fort] m. fort; stronghold
forta [**for**-tah] f. winning card
fortalicja [for-tah-**lee**-tsyah] f. old style wooden frontier fort
fortancerka [for-tahn-**tser**-kah] f. professional (female) dancing partner (hist.)
forte [**for**-te] indecl.: (musical) forte; loudly
forteca [for-**te**-tsah] f. fortress; citadel; stronghold
forteczka [for-**tech**-kah] f. (small) fortress; citadel; stronghold
forteczny [for-**tech**-ni] adj.m. of a fortress; fortress (walls, etc.)
mury forteczne [**moo**-ri for-**tech**-ne] exp.: ramparts; battlements
fortel [**for**-tel] m. stratagem; ruse; subterfuge; trick; device
fortepian [for-**te**-pyahn] m. piano; grand piano; stringed keyboard
fortepianowy [for-te-pyah-**no**-vi] adj.m. of a piano; of a grand piano
fortopsel [for-**top**-sel] m. fore-topsail
fortowy [for-**to**-vi] adj.m. of a fort
fortuna [for-**too**-nah] f. fortune; wealth; riches
fortunat [for-**too**-naht] m. rich man
fortunka [for-**toon**-kah] f. small fortune
fortunnie [for-**toon**-ńe] adv. luckily; happily; with luck; aptly
fortunny [for-**toon**-ni] adj.m. fortunate; lucky; happy
fortyfikacja [for-ti-fee-**kah**-tsyah] f. fortifications; defense works; defenses
fortyfikacyjny [for-ti-fee-kah-**tsiy**-ni] adj.m. of fortifications
fortyfikować [for-ti-fee-**ko**-vahćh] v. fortify; build defense works; strengthen (a town, etc.) (*repeatedly*)
fortyfikować się [for-ti-fee-**ko**-vahćh śh<u>an</u>] v. be fortified; build one's defenses; be strengthened (*repeatedly*)
fortyfikowanie [for-ti-fee-ko-**vah**-ńe] n. fortification; fortifying
fortyfikowanie się [for-ti-fee-ko-**vah**-ńe śh<u>an</u>] n. being strengthened

forum [fo-room] n. forum
na forum organizacji [nah fo-room or-gah-ńee-zah-tsyee] exp.: in the assembly
na forum publicznym [nah fo-room poo-bleech-nim] exp.: in public
forynt [fo-rint] m. (Hungarian) forint
forytować [fo-ri-to-vahćh] v. favor; show favoritism (to) (*repeatedly*)
fosa [fo-sah] f. moat; broad ditch
fosfagen [fos-fah-gen] m. phosphagen; high energy phosphoric compound in muscles
fosfageny [fos-fah-ge-ni] pl. energy reserve in muscles
fosfat [fos-faht] m. phosphate
fosfaty [fos-fah-ti] pl. phosphates
fosfatyzować [fos-fah-ti-zo-vahćh] v. phosphatize; change to phosphate (*repeatedly*)
fosfor [fos-for] m. phosphorus
fosforan [fos-fo-rahn] m. phosphate
fosforanować [fos-fo-rah-no-vahćh] v. phosphatize (*repeatedly*)
fosforanowanie [fos-fo-rah-no-vah-ńe] n. phosphatization
fosforanowy [fos-fo-rah-no-vi] adj.m. phosphatic
fosforawy [fos-fo-rah-vi] adj.m. phosphorous
fosforek [fos-fo-rek] m. phosphide
fosforescencja [fos-fo-res-tsen-tsyah] f. phosphorescence
fosforobrąz [fos-fo-ro-browns] m. phosphor bronze
fosforowodór [fos-fo-ro-vo-door] m. phosphor hydrogen
fosforowy [fos-fo-ro-vi] adj.m. phosphoric
fosforyczność [fos-fo-rich-nośhćh] f. phosphorescence
fosforyczny [fos-fo-rich-ni] adj.m. phosphoric; phosphorescent
fosforyn [fos-fo-rin] m. phosphite
fosforyny [fos-fo-ri-ni] pl. phosphites
fosforyt [fos-fo-rit] m. phosphorite; phosphate rock
fosforytowy [fos-fo-ri-to-vi] adj.m. phosphoritic
fosforyzować [fos-fo-ri-zo-vahćh] v. phosphoresce (*repeatedly*)
fosforyzowanie [fos-fo-ri-zo-vah-ńe] n. phosphorescing
fosgen [foz-gen] m. phosgene
fosgenit [foz-ge-ńeet] m. phosgenite (mineral)
fosylia [fo-si-lyah] pl. fossils
fosylizacja [fo-si-lee-zah-tsyah] f. fossilization
fot [fot] m. phot; unit of illumination; one lumen per square centimeter
fotel [fo-tel] m. armchair; theater stall; orchestra seat
fotel na kółkach [fo-tel nah koow-kahkh] exp.: colloq: wheelchair
fotelik [fo-te-leek] m. small armchair
fotelowy [fo-te-lo-vi] adj.m. of an armchair (upholstery, etc.)
fotka [fot-kah] f. (small) photo; snapshot; a casual photograph
foto- [fo-to] prefix: photo-
fotoamator [fo-to-ah-mah-tor] m. amateur photographer
fotoamatorski [fo-to-ah-mah-tor-skee] adj.m. amateur photographer's
fotochemia [fo-to-khe-myah] f. photochemistry
fotochemiczny [fo-to-khe-meech-ni] adj.m. photochemical
fotochemigrafia [fo-to-khe-mee-grah-fyah] f. photochemigraphy; a printing technique
fotochromografia [fo-to-khro-mo-grah-fyah] f. photochromography
fotocynkografia [fo-to-tsin-ko-grah-fyah] f. photozincography
fotodetektor [fo-to-de-tek-tor] m. photodetector (for detecting and measuring the intensity of radiant energy through photoelectric action)
fotodioda [fo-to-dyo-dah] f. light sensitive diode
fotoelektron [fo-to-e-lek-tron] m. photoelectron
fotoelektronowy [fo-to-e-lek-tro-no-vi] adj.m. photoelectronic
fotoelektrycznie [fo-to-e-lek-trich-ńe] adv. photoelectrically
fotoelektryczność [fo-to-e-lek-trich-nośhćh] f. photoelectricity
fotoelektryczny [fo-to-e-lek-trich-ni] adj.m. photoelectric
fotoemisja [fo-to-e-mee-syah] f.

photoemission
fotoemisyjny [fo-to-e-mee-**siy**-ni] adj.m. photoemissive
fotofon [fo-**to**-fon] m. photophone
fotogazetka [fo-to-gah-**zet**-kah] f. news in picture form
fotogenicznie [fo-to-ge-**ńeech**-ńe] adv. photogenically
fotogeniczność [fo-to-ge-**ńeech**-nośhćh] f. exterior characteristics resulting in good appearance on photographs and motion pictures
fotogeniczny [fo-to-ge-**ńeech**-ni] adj.m. photogenic
być fotogenicznym [bićh fo-to-ge-**ńeech**-nim] exp.: to photograph well
fotograf [fo-**to**-grahf] m. photographer
fotografia [fo-to-**grah**-fyah] f. photography; snapshot; picture
zrobić fotografię [**zro**-beećh fo-to-**grah**-fyan] exp.: to take a picture
fotograficzny [fo-to-grah-**feech**-ni] adj.m. photographic
aparat fotograficzny [ah-**pah**-raht fo-to-grah-**feech**-ni] exp.: camera
błona fotograficzna [**bwo**-nah fo-to-grah-**feech**-nah] exp.: film
ciemnia fotograficzna [**ćhem**-ńah fo-to-grah-**feech**-nah] exp.: darkroom
odbitka fotograficzna [od-**beet**-kah fo-to-grah-**feech**-nah] exp.: print
fotografijka [fo-to-grah-**feey**-kah] f. (small, nice) photograph; picture
fotografik [fo-to-**grah**-feek] m. artistic photographer
fotografika [fo-to-**grah**-fee-kah] f. artistic photography
fotografizm [fo-to-**grah**-feezm] m. photographic rendering in painting
fotografować [fo-to-grah-**fo**-vahćh] v. photograph; take a picture (*repeatedly*)
fotografować się [fo-to-grah-**fo**-vahćh śhan] v. have one's photograph taken; have one's picture taken (*repeatedly*)
fotografowanie [fo-to-grah-fo-**vah**-ńe] n. photography
fotografowanie się [fo-to-grah-fo-**vah**-ńe śhan] n. having one's picture taken
fotogram [fo-**to**-grahm] m. photogram
fotogrametria [fo-to-grah-**metr**-yah] f. photogrammetry
fotogrametryczny [fo-to-grah-met-**rich**-ni] adj.m. photogrammetric
fotograwiura [fo-to-grah-**vyoo**-rah] f. photoengraving; photogravure; photographic print
fotoheliograf [fo-to-khel-**yo**-grahf] m. photoheliograph
fotojądrowy [fo-to-yownd-**ro**-vi] adj.m. of reaction of a photon with a nucleus
fotojonizacja [fo-to-yo-ńee-**zah**-tsyah] f. photoionization; formation of ions by electromagnetic radiation
fotokarabin [fo-to-kah-**rah**-been] m. fighter-plane-mounted movie camera
fotokatoda [fo-to-kah-**to**-dah] f. photocathode
fotokineza [fo-to-kee-**ne**-zah] f. photokinesis
fotokomórka [fo-to-ko-**moor**-kah] f. photocell; photoelectric cell
fotokomórkowy [fo-to-ko-moor-**ko**-vi] adj.m. of a photocell
fotokopia [fo-to-**ko**-pyah] f. photocopy; photographic print
fotokopiarka [fo-to-ko-**pyahr**-kah] f. photocopier
fotolitografia [fo-to-lee-too-**grah**-fyah] f. photolithography; photolithograph
fotoliza [fo-to-**lee**-zah] f. photolysis
fotoluminescencja [fo-to-loo-mee-nes-**tsen**-tsyah] f. photoluminescence
fotoluminofor [fo-to-loo-mee-**no**-for] m. photo-luminiferous object
fotoluminofory [fo-to-loo-mee-no-**fo**-ri] pl. photo-luminiferous objects
fotoluminoforyczny [fo-to-loo-mee-no-fo-**rich**-ni] adj.m. photo-luminiferous
fotomapa [fo-to-**mah**-pah] f. aerial map
fotomechaniczny [fo-to-me-khah-**ńeech**-ni] adj.m. photomechanical

fotometeor [fo-to-me-**te**-or] m. phenomenon produced by the distortion of sunlight in the atmosphere
fotometr [fo-**to**-metr] m. photometer
fotometria [fo-to-**metr**-yah] f. photometry
fotometryczny [fo-to-met-**rich**-ni] adj.m. photometric; photometrical
fotomikrografia [fo-to-mee-kro-**grah**-fyah] f. photomicrography; photomicrograph
fotomikrograficzny [fo-to-mee-kro-grah-**feech**-ni] adj.m. photomicrographic
fotomontaż [fo-to-**mon**-tahsh] m. photographic montage; trick photography; trick photo; montage photo; composite photograph
fotomontażowy [fo-to-mon-tah-**zho**-vi] adj.m. of photographic montage
foton [**fo**-ton] m. photon
fotonowy [fo-to-**no**-vi] adj.m. of a photon
fotooffset [fo-to-**of**-set] m. photo-offset
fotooffsetowy [fo-to-of-se-**to**-vi] adj.m. of photo-offset
fotoperiodycznie [fo-to-per-yo-**dich**-ńe] adv. photoperiodically
fotoperiodyczny [fo-to-per-yo-**dich**-ni] adj.m. photoperiodic
fotoperiodyzm [fo-to-per-**yo**-dizm] m. photoperiodism
fotoplan [fo-**to**-plahn] m. aerial map; aerial photo of a site
fotoplastykon [fo-to-plahs-**ti**-kon] m. peep show (of stereoscopic pictures)
fotopowielacz [fo-to-po-**vye**-lahch] m. photomultiplier
fotoprzewodnictwo [fo-to-pshe-vod-**ńeets**-tfo] n. photoconductivity
fotopunkt [fo-**to**-poonkt] m. known point located on an aerial map
fotoreportaż [fo-to-re-**por**-tahsh] m. photo-reporting
fotoreporter [fo-to-re-**por**-ter] m. cameraman
fotoreporterka [fo-to-re-por-**ter**-kah] f. woman camera operator (for illustration of news, etc.)
fotoreporterski [fo-to-re-por-**ter**-skee] adj.m. of illustrated news; (supplies, etc.) of cameraman
fotos [**fo**-tos] m. still; a still
fotosensybilizator [fo-to-sen-si-bee-lee-**zah**-tor] m. photosensitizer
fotosensybilizatory [fo-to-sen-si-bee-lee-zah-**to**-ri] pl. photosensitive compounds
fotosetter [fo-to-**se**-ter] m. photosetter
fotosfera [fo-to-**sfe**-rah] f. photosphere
fotosferyczny [fo-to-sfe-**rich**-ni] adj.m. photospheric
fotoskład [fo-**to**-skwaht] m. prototype setting
fotoskulptura [fo-to-skoolp-**too**-rah] f. photosculpture
fotostat [fo-**to**-staht] m. photostat
fotosynteza [fo-to-sin-**te**-zah] f. photosynthesis
fotoszkic [fo-**to**-shkeets] m. preliminary fitting of aerial photographs
fototaksja [fo-to-**tahks**-yah] f. phototaxis
fototaktyzm [fo-to-**tahk**-tizm] m. phototaxis
fototapeta [fo-to-tah-**pe**-tah] f. landscape photography used as a decorative wallpaper
fototechniczny [fo-to-tekh-**ńeech**-ni] adj.m. of theory and practice of photography
fototechnik [fo-to-**tekh**-ńeek] m. specialist in theory and practice of photography
fototechnika [fo-to-**tekh**-ńee-kah] f. theory and practice of photography
fototelegraf [fo-to-te-**le**-grahf] m. phototelegraph; facsimile; FAX
fototelegrafia [fo-to-te-le-**grah**-fyah] f. phototelegraphy; facsimile; FAX
fototelegram [fo-to-te-**le**-grahm] m. phototelegram; facsimile transmission; FAX
fototeodolit [fo-to-te-o-**do**-leet] m. theodolite (transit) combined with a camera
fototopografia [fo-to-to-po-**grah**-fyah] f. photogrammetric topography

fototranzystor [fo-to-trahn-**zis**-tor] m. photoconductive transistor
fototraser [fo-to-**trah**-ser] m. device for photo-optical automatic marking of sheet metal, etc.
fototropizm [fo-to-**tro**-peezm] m. phototropism
fototyp [fo-**to**-tip] m. phototype (printing)
fototypia [fo-to-**ti**-pyah] f. phototypy; phototypography
fototypiczny [fo-to-ti-**peech**-ni] adj.m. phototypic
fototypowy [fo-to-ti-**po**-vi] adj.m. phototypic
fotyczny [fo-**tich**-ni] adj.m. of the layer of seawater penetrated by sunlight
fowista [fo-**vees**-tah] m. fauvist
fowistyczny [fo-vees-**tich**-ni] adj.m. of fauvism
fowizm [**fo**-veezm] m. fauvism
foyer [fwah-**ye**] indecl.: foyer; lobby
fracht [frahkht] m. freight; carriage; consignment; freight expense; cost of transportation; shipment; cargo; consignment note; bill of lading
frachtować [frahkh-**to**-vahćh] v. freight; consign goods; ship goods; charter (*repeatedly*)
frachtowanie [frahkh-to-**vah**-ńe] n. consigning of goods
frachtowe [frahkh-**to**-ve] n. freight expense; transportation cost
frachtowiec [frahkh-**to**-vyets] m. freight ship
frachtowy [frahkh-**to**-vi] adj.m. of freight; shipment; consignment (note, etc.)
list frachtowy [leest frahkh-**to**-vi] exp.: bill of lading; consignment note
fractocumulus [frahk-to-koo-**moo**-loos] m. broken up cumulus
fractostratus [frahk-to-**strah**-toos] m. broken up stratus
fraczek [**frah**-chek] m. (small, nice, short) dress coat
fragmencik [frahg-**men**-ćheek] m. (small, pleasant) fragment; episode; excerpt
fragment [**frahg**-ment] m. fragment; episode; excerpt; scrap (of conversation, etc.)
fragmentacja [frahg-men-**tah**-tsyah] f. fragmentation
fragmentarycznie [frahg-men-tah-**rich**-ńe] adv. fragmentarily; incompletely; in fragmentary form; by snatches; piecemeal
fragmentaryczność [frahg-men-tah-**rich**-nośhćh] f. fragmentary nature
fragmentaryczny [frahg-men-tah-**rich**-ni] adj.m. fragmentary; scrappy; piecemeal
frajda [**frahy**-dah] f. slang: delight; pleasure; glee; lark; fun
frajer [**frah**-yer] m. person easily tricked; slang: dupe; mug; gull; fool; hard-working man; citizen
za frajer [zah **frah**-yer] exp.: for nix; for free
frajerka [frah-**yer**-kah] f. woman easily tricked; gull; fool
frajerski [frah-**yer**-skee] adj.m. slang: stupid; nonsensical
frajerstwo [frah-**yer**-stfo] n. gullibility; naivete
frak [frahk] m. dress coat; full dress
weź go za frak [veźh go zah frahk] exp.: colloq: take him to task
frakcja [**frahk**-tsyah] f. faction; piece; scrap; group
frakcjonalista [frahk-tsyo-nah-**lees**-tah] m. member of a political faction
frakcjonalnie [frahk-tsyo-**nahl**-ńe] adv. factionally
frakcjonalny [frahk-tsyo-**nahl**-ni] adj.m. factional
frakcjonista [frahk-tsyo-**ńees**-tah] m. member of a (political) faction
frakcjonować [frahk-tsyo-**no**-vahćh] v. crack catalytically, thermally, etc.; fractionalize (*repeatedly*)
frakcjonowanie [frahk-tsyo-no-**vah**-ńe] n. fractionalization; cracking
frakcjonowany [frahk-tsyo-no-**vah**-ni] adj.m. fractionalized; factional
frakcyjność [frahk-**tsiy**-nośhćh] f. factionalism
frakcyjny [frahk-**tsiy**-ni] adj.m. factional; of a faction
frakowy [frah-**ko**-vi] adj.m. of a dress coat; dress (shirt, etc.)

fraktura [frahk-**too**-rah] f. gothic font; Fraktur; German type
frakturowy [frahk-too-**ro**-vi] adj.m. gothic (font, etc.); of gothic font
frambesia [frahm-**bez**-yah] f. frambesia; jaws
framuga [frah-**moo**-gah] f. recess (structure); bay; embrasure; window frame; door frame
franca [**frahn**-tsah] f. colloq: syphilis
franciszkanin [frahn-ćheesh-**kah**-ńeen] m. Franciscan Friar
franciszkanka [frahn-ćheesh-**kahn**-kah] f. Franciscan Nun
franciszkański [frahn-ćheesh-**kahń**-skee] adj.m. Franciscan
franco [**frahn**-ko] adv. postage paid; free; carriage free
francuski [frahn-**tsoo**-skee] adj.m. French; m. French language
choroba francuska [kho-**ro**-bah frahn-**tsoos**-kah] exp.: syphilis
klucz francuski [klooch frahn-**tsoos**-kee] exp.: adjustable wrench; monkey wrench
pocałunek francuski [po-tsah-**woo**-nek frahn-**tsoos**-kee] exp.: French kiss; an open-mouth kiss involving tongue-to-tongue contact
po francusku [po frahn-**tsoos**-koo] exp.: in French; after the French manner
z francuska [s frahn-**tsoos**-kah] exp.: with a French accent; after the French fashion
francuskojęzyczny [frahn-tsoos-ko-y<u>an</u>-**zich**-ni] adj.m. French speaking
francuskość [frahn-**tsoos**-kośhćh] f. French characteristics (way of thinking, customs, etc.)
francuszczyzna [frahn-tsoosh-**chiz**-nah] f. French manners; things French; French language
Francuz [**frahn**-tsoos] m. Frenchman
francuz [**frahn**-tsoos] m. adjustable wrench; teacher of French; cockroach
Francuzica [frahn-tsoo-**źhee**-tsah] f. old, ugly French woman; Frenchie
francuzieć [frahn-**tsoo**-źhećh] v. become Frenchified (*repeatedly*)
Francuzik [frahn-**tsoo**-źheek] m. Frenchie; small Frenchman
Francuzka [frahn-**tsoos**-kah] f. Frenchwoman
frank [frahnk] m. (French, Swiss) franc
frankista [frahn-**kees**-tah] m. member of Polish-Jewish sect of converts; follower of Gen. Franco
frankistowski [frahn-kees-**tof**-skee] adj.m. of the regime of General Francisco Franco of Spain
franko [**frahn**-ko] adv. postage paid; free; carriage free; postpaid
franko pokład [**frahn**-ko **po**-kwaht] exp.: free on board; f.o.b.
frankofil [frahn-**ko**-feel] m. Francophile
frankofilstwo [frahn-ko-**feel**-stfo] n. Francophile tendency
frankofob [frahn-**ko**-fop] m. Francophobe
frankofobia [frahn-ko-**fo**-byah] f. Francophobe tendency
frankować [frahn-**ko**-vahćh] v. place postage stamps on mail (*repeatedly*)
frankowanie [frahn-ko-**vah**-ńe] n. placing postage stamps on mail
frans [frahns] m. francium; virginium
franszyza [frahn-**shi**-zah] f. limit on insurance coverage
frant [frahnt] m. sly boots; knave; rogue; rascal; fox; dandy; jester
z głupia frant [z **gwoo**-pyah frahnt] exp.: acting the simpleton
frantostwo [frahn-**tos**-tfo] n. cunning; roguery; roguishness
frantowski [frahn-**tof**-skee] adj.m. cunning; roguish; dandyish
frapować [frah-**po**-vahćh] v. impress; strike; arrest (attention, etc.); make a strong impression (*repeatedly*)
frapująco [frah-poo-<u>yown</u>-tso] adv. impressively; strikingly
frapujący [frah-poo-<u>yown</u>-tsi] adj.m. impressive; striking
frapujące podobieństwo [frah-poo-<u>yown</u>-tse po-do-**byeń**-stfo] exp.: speaking likeness
frasobliwie [frah-so-**blee**-vye] adv. anxiously; with anxiety; sorrowfully
frasobliwość [frah-so-**blee**-vośhćh]

f. worry; anxiety; sadness; affliction
frasobliwy [frah-so-**blee**-vi] adj.m. worried; sorrowful; full of anxiety; afflicted
frasować się [frah-**so**-vahćh śhan] v. worry; be sorrowful (*repeatedly*)
frasunek [frah-**soo**-nek] m. worry; grief; sorrow; care; trouble
fraszka [**frahsh**-kah] f. trifle; nothing worth speaking of; epigram; facetious verse
fraszkopis [frahsh-**ko**-pees] m. writer of epigrams
fraszkopisarstwo [frahsh-ko-pee-**sahr**-stfo] n. writing of epigrams
fraternizacja [frah-ter-ńee-**zah**-tsyah] f. fraternization; fraternizing
fraternizować się [frah-ter-ńee-**zo**-vahćh śhan] v. fraternize (*repeatedly*)
fraza [**frah**-zah] f. sentence; phrase; brief expression
frazeolog [frah-ze-**o**-log] m. phraseologist
frazeologia [frah-ze-o-**lo**-gyah] f. idioms; expressions and sayings typical of a language; manner of expression; style; phraseology; choice of words; platitudes; mere verbiage
frazeologicznie [frah-ze-o-lo-**geech**-ńe] adv. phraseologically
frazeologiczny [frah-ze-o-lo-**geech**-ni] adj.m. phraseological (dictionary, etc.); of phraseology
frazeologizacja [frah-ze-o-lo-gee-**zah**-tsyah] f. joining of words into idiomatic phrases
frazeologizm [frah-ze-o-**lo**-geezm] m. established idiomatic phrase
frazes [**frah**-zes] m. platitude; commonplace remark; triteness; catchword; slogan
frazesik [frah-**ze**-śheek] m. (little, silly) platitude; commonplace remark; triteness; catchword; slogan
frazesowicz [frah-ze-**so**-veech] m. platitudinarian; verbalist; phrase-monger; slang: windbag
frazesowy [frah-ze-**so**-vi] adj.m. catchword (style, manner, etc.)
frazować [frah-**zo**-vahćh] v. phrase (in poetry and music) (*repeatedly*)
frazowanie [frah-zo-**vah**-ńe] n. phrasing (in poetry and music); dividing into melodic phrases
frazowy [frah-**zo**-vi] adj.m. of the structure of a phrase
frażetowski [frah-zhe-**tof**-skee] adj.m. of silver-plated utensils
frażetowy [frah-zhe-**to**-vi] adj.m. of silver-plated utensils
frażety [frah-**zhe**-ti] pl. silver plated utensils
freblanka [fre-**blahn**-kah] f. kindergarten teacher
freblowski [fre-**blof**-skee] adj.m. of the universal teaching system of Froebl
freblówka [fre-**bloof**-kah] f. kindergarten; infant school
fredrolog [fre-**dro**-log] m. scholar specializing in the writings of Aleksander Fredro
fregata [fre-**gah**-tah] f. frigate
frekwencja [fre-**kfen**-tsyah] f. attendance; turnout; number of spectators (at a show, game, etc.); frequency
frekwencyjnie [fre-kfen-**tsiy**-ńe] adv. by the way of frequency
frekwencyjny [fre-kfen-**tsiy**-ni] adj.m. of frequency (of word-usage, etc.); of the number of spectators; frequentative
frencz [french] m. trench coat
frenetycznie [fre-ne-**tich**-ńe] adv. franticly; frantically; rapturously
frenetyczny [fre-ne-**tich**-ni] adj.m. frantic; rapturous; wild (cry, etc.)
frenezja [fre-**ne**-zyah] f. description of frenzy; literary rendition of violence, wild excitement, etc.
frenologia [fre-no-**lo**-gyah] f. phrenology
freon [**fre**-on] m. freon (gas)
freony [fre-**o**-ni] pl. fluorinated hydrocarbons used in refrigeration
fresk [fresk] m. wall painting
pokrywać freskami [po-**kri**-vahćh fres-**kah**-mee] exp.: to fresco
freskowy [fres-**ko**-vi] adj.m. of a wall painting
fretka [**fret**-kah] f. ferret; albino skunk

freudowski [froy-**dof**-skee] adj.m. Freudian
freudysta [froy-**dis**-tah] m. Freudian
freudyzm [**froy**-dizm] m. Freudianism
frez [fres] m. milling cutter; fraise
frezarka [fre-**zahr**-kah] f. milling machine; miller
frezer [**fre**-zer] m. milling-machine operator
frezerstwo [fre-**zer**-stfo] n. milling-machine operation
frezja [**fre**-zyah] f. iridaceous flower; variety of iris
frezować [fre-**zo**-vahćh] v. mill (*repeatedly*)
frezowanie [fre-zo-**vah**-ńe] n. milling
frędzel [fran-dzel] m. fringe
frędzelek [fran-**dze**-lek] m. small fringe
frędzelka [fran-**dzel**-kah] f. (small, nice) fringe
frędzla [frandz-lah] f. fringe
frędzlasty [frandz-**lahs**-ti] adj.m. fringed; frayed
frędzlisty [frandz-**lees**-ti] adj.m. fringed; frayed
fronda [**fron**-dah] f. Fronde; malcontent party; violent political opposition
frondować [fron-**do**-vahćh] v. oppose; brawl; squabble; sow dissension (*repeatedly*)
front [front] m. front; face; fore part; facade; elevation; frontage
front chłodny [front **khwod**-ni] exp.: cold front
front ciepły [front **ćhep**-wi] exp.: warm front
frontalizm [fron-**tah**-leezm] m. frontality
frontalnie [fron-**tahl**-ńe] adv. frontally; towards front
frontalny [fron-**tahl**-ni] adj.m. frontal (attack, etc.); seen from the front
atak frontalny [ah-tahk fron-**tahl**-ni] exp.: frontal attack
zderzenie frontalne [zde-**zhe**-ńe fron-**tahl**-ne] exp.: head-on collision; frontal collision
fronton [**fron**-ton] m. fronton; frontal; pediment; facade
frontonik [fron-**to**-ńeek] m. small facade
frontonowy [fron-to-**no**-vi] adj.m. of fronton; of facade
frontowiec [fron-**to**-vyets] m. front-line soldier
frontowy [fron-**to**-vi] adj.m. frontal; front (line, man, elevation, etc.)
drzwi frontowe [dzhvee fron-**to**-ve] exp.: street door; front door
frontyspis [fron-**tis**-pees] m. frontispiece
frot [frot] m. sponge cloth
froter [**fro**-ter] m. floor polisher
froterka [fro-**ter**-kah] f. floor polisher; floor polishing
froterować [fro-te-**ro**-vahćh] v. rub; polish; wax (floors) (*repeatedly*)
froterowanie [fro-te-ro-**vah**-ńe] n. rubbing; polishing; waxing (floors)
frotowy [fro-**to**-vi] adj.m. of sponge cloth; of towel cloth
frotte [fro-**te**] indecl.: towel cloth
frr! [frr] excl.: whirr!
fru, fru [froo froo] exp.: frou-frou; airy (garment, etc.); flowing (draperies, etc.); ethereal (steps, etc.); made of very light fabric
fruktoza [frook-**to**-zah] f. fructose; levulose; fruit sugar
frunąć [**froo**-nownćh] v. fly away; fly about; fly up in the air; flee
frunięcie [froo-**ńan**-ćhe] n. flying up in the air
frustracja [froos-**trah**-tsyah] f. frustration
frustracyjnie [froos-trah-**tsiy**-ńe] adv. with frustrating influence
frustracyjny [froos-trah-**tsiy**-ni] adj.m. frustrating; of frustration
frustrat [**froos**-traht] m. frustrated individual
frustrować [froos-**tro**-vahćh] v. frustrate; cause to have no effect; prevent from achieving (*repeatedly*)
frustrować się [froos-**tro**-vahćh śhan] v. become frustrated (*repeatedly*)
frustrowanie [froos-tro-**vah**-ńe] n. frustration
frustrowanie się [froos-tro-**vah**-ńe śhan] n. becoming frustrated
fruwać [**froo**-vahćh] v. fly away; fly about; fly up in the air; flit; flit about; flit to and fro; flutter (*repeatedly*)

fruwanie [froo-**vah**-ńe] n. flight; flutter
fryc [frits] m. greenhorn; raw hand; slang: Kraut; German
frycowe [fri-**tso**-ve] n. the price of inexperience
płacić frycowe [**pwah**-ćheećh fri-**tso**-ve] exp.: to pay a high price for one's inexperience; to learn through bitter experience
fryga [**fri**-gah] f. spinning toy; humming top
frygać [**fri**-gahćh] v. throw; let fly (a rock, etc.); eat fast; run; scurry; scamper (*repeatedly*)
fryganie [fri-**gah**-ńe] n. throwing; letting fly (a rock, etc.); eating fast; running; scurrying; scampering
frygijski [fri-**geey**-skee] adj.m. Phrigian (cap, etc.)
frygnąć [**frig**-nownćh] v. throw; let fly (a rock, etc.); eat fast; run; scurry; scamper
frygnięcie [frig-**ńan**-ćhe] n. scurrying
frykać [**fri**-kahćh] v. snort; spit like a cat (*repeatedly*)
frykanie [fri-**kah**-ńe] n. snort; spit (of a cat)
fryknąć [**frik**-nownćh] v. flutter away
frykas [**fri**-kahs] m. delicacy; dainty (bit); tidbit
frykatywność [fri-kah-**tiv**-nośhćh] f. fricative nature
frykatywny [fri-kah-**tiv**-ni] adj.m. fricative; frictional (consonant)
frykcja [**frik**-tsyah] f. friction; medical chafing
frykcyjny [frik-**tsiy**-ni] adj.m. frictional; friction (clutch, etc.)
frymarczenie [fri-mahr-**che**-ńe] n. barter; trade; traffic
frymarczyć [fri-**mahr**-chićh] v. barter; trade; traffic (*repeatedly*)
frymuśnie [fri-**moośh**-ńe] adv. exquisitely
frymuśny [fri-**moośh**-ni] adj.m. exquisite
frytek [**fri**-tek] m. fried potato
frytka [**frit**-kah] f. French fried potato
frytki [**frit**-kee] pl. French fries (potatoes); potato chips; crisps
frytura [fri-**too**-rah] f. frying grease; frying fat
frywolitki [fri-vo-**leet**-kee] pl. delicate lace (napkins); tatting
frywolnie [fri-**vol**-ńe] adv. in a risque manner; frivolously; trivially
frywolność [fri-**vol**-nośhćh] f. frivolity; levity
frywolny [fri-**vol**-ni] adj.m. off-color; frivolous; trivial; silly
fryz [fris] m. frieze; framing; strip; border; Frisian cow
fryzy [**fri**-zi] pl. parquet boards
fryza [**fri**-zah] f. ruffle; ornamental border
fryzarnia [fri-**zahr**-ńah] f. plank-making section of a sawmill
fryzernia [fri-**zer**-ńah] f. plank-making section of a sawmill
fryzjer [**fri**-zyer] m. hairdresser
fryzjer damski [**fri**-zyer **dahm**-skee] exp.: hairdresser; beautician
fryzjer męski [**fri**-zyer **mans**-kee] exp.: barber; gentleman's hairdresser
fryzjerczyk [fri-**zyer**-chik] m. hairdresser's apprentice
fryzjerka [fri-**zyer**-kah] f. (woman) hairdresser; beautician; hairdressing (profession)
fryzjerski [fri-**zyer**-skee] adj.m. hairdresser's
zakład fryzjerski [**zah**-kwaht fri-**zyer**-skee] exp.: barber shop
salon fryzjerski [**sah**-lon fri-**zyer**-skee] exp.: hairdressing saloon
fryzjerstwo [fri-**zyer**-stfo] n. hairdressing
fryzka [**fris**-kah] f. (small, nice) ruffle; ornamental border
fryzować [fri-**zo**-vahćh] v. curl; wave (one's hair) (*repeatedly*)
fryzować bilans [fri-**zo**-vahćh **bee**-lahns] exp.: to stretch one's account
fryzować się [fri-**zo**-vahćh śhan] v. curl one's hair; dress one's hair (*repeatedly*)
fryzowanie [fri-zo-**vah**-ńe] n. hair curling
fryzowanie się [fri-zo-**vah**-ńe śhan] n. curling one's hair
fryzura [fri-**zoo**-rah] f. hairdo; hair

style; hair dress; coiffure; crop of hair; manner of hairdressing
fryzurka [fri-**zoor**-kah] f. (nice, little) hairdo; hair style; hair dress; coiffure
Fryzyjczyk [fri-**ziy**-chik] m. Frisian
fryzyjczyk [fri-**ziy**-chik] m. Frisian horse
Fryzyjka [fri-**ziy**-kah] f. Frisian (woman)
fryzyjski [fri-**ziy**-skee] adj.m. Frisian
ftaleina [ftah-le-**ee**-nah] f. phthalein
ftalowy [ftah-**lo**-vi] adj.m. phthalic
ftyzjatra [fti-**zyaht**-rah] m. specialist in phthisiology
ftyzjatria [fti-**zyahtr**-yah] f. phthisiology
ftyzjatryczny [fti-zyaht-**rich**-ni] adj.m. phthisic
ftyzjologia [ftiz-yo-**lo**-gyah] f. phthisiology
fu! [foo] excl.: fie!
fucha [**foo**-khah] f. slang: bungled work
fuck off [fahk of] v. (Engl.) vulg. exp.: fuck off; get lost (jargon)
fufajka [foo-**fahy**-kah] f. quilted jacket
fuga [**foo**-gah] f. rift; joint; fugue
fugas [**foo**-gahs] m. land mine made up of available explosives
fugasowy [foo-gah-**so**-vi] adj.m. of a land mine put together with available explosives
fugato [foo-**gah**-to] n. fugato (music)
fugatywność [foo-gah-**tiv**-nośhćh] f. fugacious nature; fugacity
fugatywny [foo-gah-**tiv**-ni] adj.m. fugacious
fugować [foo-**go**-vahćh] v. joint; feather-edge; point; clean brick joints; finish joints (*repeatedly*)
fugowanie [foo-go-**vah**-ńe] n. making joints
fugownik [foo-**gov**-ńeek] m. joint finishing tool
fugowy [foo-**go**-vi] adj.m. of a joint
fuj! [fooy] excl.: phew!; bad dog!
fujara [foo-**yah**-rah] m. & f. all thumbs; nincompoop; oaf; ninny; f. (musical) pipe; panpipe
fujareczka [foo-yah-**rech**-kah] f. (small, nice) (musical) pipe; panpipe
fujarka [foo-**yahr**-kah] f. (musical) pipe; panpipe
fujarkowy [foo-yahr-**ko**-vi] adj.m. of a (musical) pipe; pipe (sounds)
fukać [**foo**-kahćh] v. scold; puff; snort; chide; rate (*repeatedly*)
fukanie [foo-**kah**-ńe] n. scolding; puffing; rating
fuknąć [**fook**-nownćh] v. scold; puff; snort; chide; rate
fuknięcie [fook-**ńan**-ćhe] n. scolding; puffing; rating
fukoid [foo-**ko**-eet] m. chondrite
fukoksantyna [foo-ko-ksahn-**ti**-nah] f. phycoxanthin (pigment)
fuks [fooks] m. beginner; greenhorn; windfall; stroke of luck; fluke; dark horse; unexpected winner; nymphalid; four-footed butterfly
fuksem [**fook**-sem] adv. by chance; by good luck; by fluke; quite unexpectedly; by stroke of luck
fuksja [**foo**-ksyah] f. fuchsia
fuksyna [fook-**si**-nah] f. fuchsine; magenta
fukus [**foo**-koos] m. fucus; rockweed
ful [fool] m. full (of 3+2) in poker game
fular [**foo**-lahr] m. foulard; silk scarf; silk neckerchief
fularowy [foo-lah-**ro**-vi] adj.m. foulard (neckerchief, etc.)
fulguryt [fool-**goo**-rit] m. fulgurite
fulwokwas [fool-**vo**-kfahs] m. humus acid
fulwokwasy [fool-vo-**kfah**-si] pl. humus acids
fumarola [foo-mah-**ro**-lah] f. fumarole (chamber, vent hole)
fumarole [foo-mah-**ro**-le] pl. fumarolic gases; fumaroles
fumarowy [foo-mah-**ro**-vi] adj.m. fumarolic
fumator [foo-**mah**-tor] m. smoke screen generator
fumigacja [foo-mee-**gah**-tsyah] f. fumigation
fumigacyjny [foo-mee-gah-**tsiy**-ni] adj.m. of fumigation
fumigant [foo-**mee**-gahnt] m. fumigant
fumigator [foo-mee-**gah**-tor] m.

fumigator
fumologia [foo-mo-**lo**-gyah] f. study of the effects of tobacco smoking
fumy [**foo**-mi] pl. airs; arrogance; overbearing
stroić fumy [**stro**-eećh **foo**-mi] exp.: to give oneself airs
funda [**foon**-dah] f. a treat; treat; a round (of beer, vodka, etc.)
fundacja [foon-**dah**-tsyah] f. foundation; endowment; base
fundacyjny [foon-dah-**tsiy**-ni] adj.m. foundation (school, etc.)
fundament [foon-**dah**-ment] m. foundation; substructure groundwork; platform
fundamentalista [foon-dah-men-tah-**lees**-tah] m. fundamentalist (of Islam, etc.)
fundamentalizm [foon-dah-men-**tah**-leezm] m. fundamentalism; orthodoxy
fundamentalnie [foon-dah-men-**tahl**-ńe] adv. fundamentally; basically
fundamentalność [foon-dah-men-**tahl**-nośhćh] f. fundamentalism
fundamentalny [foon-dah-men-**tahl**-ni] adj.m. fundamental; basic
fundamentować [foon-dah-men-**to**-vahćh] v. build foundations (*repeatedly*)
fundamentowanie [foon-dah-men-to-**vah**-ńe] n. building of a foundation engineering; foundation work
fundamentowy [foon-dah-men-**to**-vi] adj.m. of foundations
fundator [foon-**dah**-tor] m. founder; one who founds; one who establishes; one who endows
fundatorka [foon-dah-**tor**-kah] f. (female) founder; foundress; one who founds; one who establishes; one who endows
fundnąć [**foond**-nownćh] v. treat; found; establish; endow
fundnięcie [foond-**ńan**-ćhe] n. treat
fundować [foon-**do**-vahćh] v. treat; found; establish; endow (*repeatedly*)
fundowanie [foon-do-**vah**-ńe] n. foundation; endowment
fundusik [foon-**doo**-śheek] m. (small, nice, little) fund; capital; money
fundusz [**foon**-doosh] m. fund; capital; money
fundusz rezerwowy [**foon**-doosh re-zer-**vo**-vi] exp.: reserve capital
fundusz wspólny [**foon**-doosh **fspool**-ni] exp.: pool
zarządzać funduszami [zah-**zhown**-dzahćh foon-doo-**shah**-mee] exp.: to hold the purse strings
fungicyd [foon-**gee**-tsit] m. fungicide
fungicydy [foon-gee-**tsi**-di] pl. fungicidal agents
fungicydowy [foon-gee-tsi-**do**-vi] adj.m. fungicidal
funkcja [**foonk**-tsyah] f. function; functions; duties
pełnić funkcję [**pew**-ńeećh **foonk**-tsyan] exp.: to perform functions (duties)
funkcjonalistyczny [foonk-tsyo-nah-lees-**tich**-ni] adj.m. functionalist; functionalistic
funkcjonalizacja [foonk-tsyo-nah-lee-**zah**-tsyah] f. making functional
funkcjonalizm [foonk-tsyo-**nah**-leezm] m. functionalism
funkcjonalnie [foonk-tsyo-**nahl**-ńe] adv. functionally
funkcjonalność [foonk-tsyo-**nahl**-nośhćh] f. functionality
funkcjonalny [foonk-tsyo-**nahl**-ni] adj.m. functional; operational
funkcjonał [foonk-**tsyo**-nahw] m. functional calculus
funkcjonariusz [foonk-tsyo-nahr-yoosh] m. functionary; official; civil servant
funkcjonować [foonk-tsyo-**no**-vahćh] v. function; perform a duty (*repeatedly*)
nie funkcjonować [ńe foonk-tsyo-**no**-vahćh] exp.: to be out of order
funkcjonowanie [foonk-tsyo-no-**vah**-ńe] n. function
funkcyjnie [foonk-**tsiy**-ńe] adv. functionally
funkcyjność [foonk-**tsiy**-nośhćh] f. functionality
funkcyjny [foonk-**tsiy**-ni] adj.m. functional; m. man assigned to keep orderly conditions

funkia [**foon**-kyah] f. plantain lily
funktor [**foonk**-tor] m. functor
funt [foont] m. pound (weight)
funtowy [foon-**to**-vi] adj.m. pound (weight, note, etc.)
fura [**foo**-rah] f. cart; wagon; tumbrel; cartload; wagonload; slang: a lot; a great deal; a great many; heaps; umpteen
furaż [**foo**-rahsh] m. animal feed
furażerka [foo-rah-**zher**-kah] f. field cap; forage cap; undress cap; fatigue cap
furażowy [foo-rah-**zho**-vi] adj.m. of animal feed; m. (soldier) supplier of horse feed
furczeć [**foor**-chećh] v. whirr; hum; rumble; buzz; flutter; flutter away (*repeatedly*)
furczenie [foor-**che**-ńe] n. buzzing; a whirr; a rumble; a buzz; a flutter
furda [**foor**-dah] f. colloq: item of no importance
furgon [**foor**-gon] m. truck; van
furgonetka [foor-go-**net**-kah] f. delivery van
furgonowy [foor-go-**no**-vi] adj.m. of a delivery van
furia [**foo**-ryah] f. fury; rage
  atak furii [ah-tahk **foo**-ryee] exp.: a fit of raving madness; fury; a fit of rage
furiacki [foor-**yahts**-kee] adj.m. mad; raving; violent; in a fury; in a rage
furiant [**foo**-ryahnt] m. a Czech dance
furiat [**foo**-ryaht] m. madman
furiatka [foo-**ryaht**-kah] f. madwoman
furieryzm [foor-**ye**-rizm] m. Fourierism
furka [**foor**-kah] f. small cart
furkacja [foor-**kah**-tsyah] f. furcation; process of branching
furkać [**foor**-kahćh] v. whirr; hum; rumble; buzz; flutter; flutter away (*repeatedly*)
furkadło [foor-**kahd**-wo] n. colloq: small hand drill
furkanie [foor-**kah**-ńe] n. buzzing
furknąć [**foork**-nownćh] v. whirr; hum; rumble; buzz; flutter
furknięcie [foork-**ńan**-ćhe] n. whirr; hum; rumble; buzz; flutter
furkot [**foor**-kot] m. flutter; whir; hum; buzz
furkotać [foor-**ko**-tahćh] v. whirr; hum; rumble; buzz; flutter; flutter away (*repeatedly*)
furkotanie [foor-ko-**tah**-ńe] n. flutter; whir; hum; buzz
furman [**foor**-mahn] m. carter; wagoner; teamster; wagon driver
furmanić [foor-**mah**-ńeećh] v. cart; be a wagon driver (*repeatedly*)
furmanienie [foor-mah-**ńe**-ńe] n. cart; wagon-driving
furmanka [foor-**mahn**-kah] f. cart; wagon; tumbrel; cartload; wagonload; wagoner's work; wagoner's job; wagon-driving
furmański [foor-**mahń**-skee] adj.m. carter's; wagoner's; teamster's; wagon driver's
furmaństwo [foor-**mahń**-stfo] n. wagoner's work; wagoner's job; wagon-driving
furora [foo-**ro**-rah] f. sensation
  zrobić furorę [**zro**-beećh foo-**ro**-ran] exp.: to create a sensation; to excite admiration; to win applause; to make a hit; to be a tremendous success; to be the rage of the town
furt [foort] adv. slang: all the time; on and on
furta [**foor**-tah] f. (old, crude) gate; door
furtian [**foor**-tyahn] m. brother gatekeeper; porter
furtianka [foor-**tyahn**-kah] f. sister (nun) gatekeeper; portress
furtka [**foort**-kah] f. gate; door
furunkuloza [foo-roon-koo-**lo**-zah] f. furunculosis
furunkularny [foo-roon-koo-**lahr**-ni] adj.m. furuncular
furunkuł [foo-**roon**-koow] m. furuncle; boil
fusowaty [foo-so-**vah**-ti] adj.m. having the appearance of coffee grounds
fusy [**foo**-si] pl. lees; dregs
  fusy z kawy [**foo**-si s **kah**-vi] exp.: coffee grounds; grounds
fuszer [**foo**-sher] m. bungler; botcher; fumbler
fuszerka [foo-**sher**-kah] f. fudge;

botch; bungle; odd job; mull; slang: foozle; bungled job; botched job; botched piece of work
fuszerować [foo-she-**ro**-vahćh] v. bungle; botch; scamp; make a mess; slobber; make a mull; slang: foozle (*repeatedly*)
fuszerowanie [foo-she-ro-**vah**-ńe] n. bungling; botching
fuszerski [foo-**sher**-skee] adj.m. bungled; botched; scamped; made into a mess; slobbered
po fuszersku [po foo-**sher**-skoo] exp.: like a bungler
fuszerstwo [foo-**sher**-stfo] n. bungling; botching; fudge; botch; bungle; odd job; mull; slang: foozle; bungled job; scamped job; botched-up piece of work
futbol [**foot**-bol] m. soccer (football)
futbolista [foot-bo-**lees**-tah] m. soccer (football) player; footballer
futbolowy [foot-bo-**lo**-vi] adj.m. soccer (field, game, match, etc.); football (field, game, match, etc.)
futbolówka [foot-bo-**loof**-kah] f. ball (used in soccer or football)
futeralik [foo-te-**rah**-leek] m. (small gun) case; holster; sheath; box
futerał [foo-**te**-rahw] m. (gun) case; holster; sheath; box; container; carton
futerko [foo-**ter**-ko] n. (pretty, nice) fur (skin, coat); animal's hair; animal's coat; animal's fur; pelage; fur-lined coat
futerkowy [foo-ter-**ko**-vi] adj.m. of fur; fur (coat, collar, cap, animal, etc.)
futor [**foo**-tor] m. isolated farm on the eastern borderlands of Poland
futro [**foo**-tro] n. fur (skin, coat); animal's hair; animal's coat; animal's fur; pelage; fur-lined coat
futropodobny [foo-tro-po-**dob**-ni] adj.m. of artificial fur; similar to a fur
futrować [foo-**tro**-vahćh] v. eat; feed; stoke; grub; plaster; coat; line; board; timber (*repeatedly*)
futrówka [foo-**troof**-kah] f. lining (of a shoe, etc.); feed; lagging (of a boiler, etc.); furring (of a ship)
futryna [foo-**tri**-nah] f. doorframe; window frame; opening frame
futrynowy [foo-tri-**no**-vi] adj.m. doorframe (boards, etc.)
futrzak [**foot**-shahk] m. fur-quilt rug
futrzany [foot-**shah**-ni] adj.m. fur (collar, coat)
futrzarski [foot-**shahr**-skee] adj.m. furrier's
futrzarstwo [foot-**shahr**-stfo] n. furriery
futrzarz [**foot**-shahsh] m. furrier
futura [foo-**too**-rah] f. grotesque font
futurolog [foo-too-**ro**-log] m. future forecaster
futurologia [foo-too-ro-**lo**-gyah] f. futurology
futurologiczny [foo-too-ro-lo-**geech**-ni] adj.m. futurologic
futurum [foo-**too**-room] n. future tense
futurysta [foo-too-**ris**-tah] m. futurist
futurystycznie [foo-too-ris-**tich**-ńe] adv. futuristically
futurystyczny [foo-too-ris-**tich**-ni] adj.m. futuristic
futuryzm [foo-**too**-rizm] m. futurism
fuzarioza [foo-zahr-**yo**-zah] f. variety of plant diseases caused by fungus
fuzariozy [foo-zahr-**yo**-zi] pl. plant diseases caused by fungus
fuzel [**foo**-zel] m. fusel oil; faints
fuzja [**foo**-zyah] f. fusion; merger; blending; amalgamation; shotgun; rifle
fuzlowy [fooz-**lo**-vi] adj.m. of fusel oil; fusel oil (odors, etc.)
fuzulina [foo-zoo-**lee**-nah] f. Fusulina
fuzulinowy [foo-zoo-lee-**no**-vi] adj.m. of Fusulina
fuzyjka [foo-**ziy**-kah] f. small shotgun; small rifle
fuzynit [foo-**zi**-ńeet] m. fusinite (mineral)
fuzyt [**foo**-zit] m. fusain (mineral)
fyrkać [**fir**-kahćh] v. colloq: snort; spit (by a cat) (*repeatedly*)
fyrkanie [fir-**kah**-ńe] n. colloq: snorting
fyrknąć [**fir**-knownćh] v. colloq: flutter away

G

G, g [ge] the letter "**g**," always pronounced like in the word "get"
gabardyna [gah-bahr-**di**-nah] f. gabardine; twilled cloth
gabardynowy [gah-bahr-di-**no**-vi] adj.m. of gabardine; of twilled cloth; gabardine (coat, etc.)
gabaryt [gah-**bah**-rit] m. gabarit; overall measurements; gauge for measuring distance between rails
gabarytowy [gah-bah-ri-**to**-vi] adj.m. gabarit (lamp, light, etc.)
gabarytówka [gah-bah-ri-**toof**-kah] f. gabarit lamp
gabinecik [gah-bee-**ne**-ćheek] m. small set of furniture; small study
gabinet [gah-**bee**-net] m. study; (ruling) cabinet; office; consulting room
gabinetowy [gah-bee-ne-**to**-vi] adj.m. of a study; of a (ruling) cabinet; of an office; of a consulting room
gable [**gahb**-le] pl. pitchfork with spherically shaped tips
gablota [gahb-**lo**-tah] f. showcase; glass case; cabinet; colloq: passenger car; car
gablotka [gahb-**lot**-kah] f. (small) showcase; glass case; cabinet
gabro [**gahb**-ro] n. gabbro (a dark green rock)
gacek [**gah**-tsek] m. bat (a flying mammal)
gacenie [gah-**tse**-ńe] n. weatherstripping
gach [gahkh] m. colloq: lover; seducer (of someone else's wife)
gacić [**gah**-ćheećh] v. weatherstrip; fascine (a dam, etc.) (*repeatedly*)
gacie [**gah**-ćhe] pl. colloq: shorts; drawers; pants; trousers
gać [gahćh] f. fascine
gad [gaht] m. reptile; colloq: mean guy; unconscionable man
gady [**gah**-di] pl. reptiles
gadać [**gah**-dahćh] v. colloq: talk; yak; prattle; talk nonsense; chat (*repeatedly*)
co tu dużo gadać [tso too **doo**-zho **gah**-dahćh] exp.: colloq: it's no use talking
gadać do rzeczy [**gah**-dahćh do **zhe**-chi] exp.: to talk sense
gadać od rzeczy [**gah**-dahćh od **zhe**-chi] exp.: to talk nonsense
przestań gadać [**pshes**-tahń **gah**-dahćh] exp.: colloq: hold your tongue; shut up
gadaj! [**gah**-dahy] excl.: colloq: say it!; fire away!; shoot!; slang: spit it out!; out with it!
szkoda gadać [**shko**-dah **gah**-dahćh] exp.: colloq: nothing doing!
gadane [gah-**dah**-ne] n. colloq: debating skill; knack for talking
gadanie [gah-**dah**-ńe] n. colloq: talk; chattering; tattle; gab; colloq: rubbish
głupie gadanie [**gwoo**-pye gah-**dah**-ńe] exp.: nonsense
mieć coś do gadania [myećh tsośh do gah-**dah**-ńah] exp.: to have one's say in the matter
nie masz tu nic do gadania [ńe mash too ńeets do gah-**dah**-ńah] exp.: it's no business of yours
bez gadania! [bez gah-**dah**-ńah] exp.: silence!; enough said!
gadanina [gah-dah-**ńee**-nah] f. colloq: talk; idle talk; prattle; gab
gadatliwie [gah-dah-**tlee**-vye] adv. wordily; diffusely; long-windedly
gadatliwość [gah-dah-**tlee**-vośhćh] f. talkativeness; long-windedness; loquacity; rattle; prate; verbiage; wordiness
gadatliwy [gah-dah-**tlee**-vi] adj.m. talkative; garrulous; windy
człowiek gadatliwy [**chwo**-vyek gah-dah-**tlee**-vi] exp.: talker; rattle
gadget [**gah**-dzhet] m. gadget
gadka [**gaht**-kah] f. colloq: chat; chatting; story; piece of gossip
gadolin [gah-**do**-leen] m. gadolinium (atomic number 64)
gadoptak [gah-**do**-ptahk] m. ancestral bird; bird reptile
gadożer [gah-**do**-zher] m. snake-

eating hawk
gadu-gadu [**gah**-doo **gah**-doo] exp.: colloq: talk; chatting
gadulski [gah-**dool**-skee] adj.m. colloq: talkative; garrulous; windy
gadulstwo [gah-**dool**-stfo] n. talkativeness; long-windedness; loquacity; rattle; prate; verbiage; wordiness
gaduła [gah-**doo**-wah] m. & f. rattle; chatterer; prater; talker; windbag
gadzi [**gah**-dźhee] adj.m. reptilian; reptile's; of reptiles
gadzina [gah-**dźhee**-nah] f. reptiles; amphibians; cattle; poultry; vermin; livestock
gadzinowaty [gah-dźhee-no-**vah**-ti] adj.m. reptilian
gadzinowy [gah-dźhee-**no**-vi] adj.m. reptilian; reptile; creeping; colloq: mean; grovelling
fundusz gadzinowy [**foon**-doosh gah-dźhee-**no**-vi] exp.: funds allotted to bribery
gadzinówka [gah-dźhee-**noof**-kah] f. colloq: reptile paper
gadżet [**gah**-dzhet] m. gadget
gaf [gahf] m. gaff topsail
gafa [**gah**-fah] f. blunder; slip-up; bloomer
popełnić gafę [po-**pew**-ńeećh **gah**-fan] exp.: to make a blunder
gafel [**gah**-fel] m. gaff
gaflowy [gah-**flo**-vi] adj.m. of gaff topsail
gaftopsel [gahf-**top**-sel] m. gaff topsail
gag [gahg] m. situation comedy joke
gagat [**gah**-gaht] m. jet
gagatek [gah-**gah**-tek] m. colloq: spoiled favorite; mother's darling; blighter; rascal; rogue
gagman [**gahg**-men] m. writer of jokes for film scripts
gagowy [gah-**go**-vi] adj.m. of a situation comedy joke
gaić [**gah**-eećh] v. adorn with verdure; deck with verdure (hist.) (*repeatedly*)
gaić się [**gah**-eećh śhan] v. grow green (hist.) (*repeatedly*)
gaik [**gah**-eek] m. small grove; bosk; bosket; coppice; country folks' spring festival
gaj [gahy] m. grove
gaja [**gah**-yah] f. ship's crane operating line
gajda [**gahy**-dah] f. dudeen; variety of bagpipes
gajenie [gah-**ye**-ńe] n. adorning with verdure; decking with verdure
gajowiec [gah-**yo**-vyets] m. weasel snout
gajowy [gah-**yo**-vi] m. gamekeeper; adj.m. of a grove
gajówka [gah-**yoof**-kah] f. gamekeeper's cottage (lodge); warbler; blackcap; whitethroat
gal [gahl] m. gallium (atomic number 31)
gala [**gah**-lah] f. gala; festivity; banquet; gala dress; colloq: in full fig; in one's Sunday best; festive decoration
galabija [gah-lah-**bee**-yah] f. outer garment of the Arabs
galabijka [gah-lah-**beey**-kyah] f. outer garment of the Arabs
galago [gah-**lah**-go] n. galago
galaktaza [gah-lahk-**tah**-zah] f. galactase (enzyme)
galaktolipid [gah-lahk-to-**lee**-peet] m. galactolipid
galaktometr [gah-lahk-**to**-metr] m. galactometer
galaktoza [gah-lahk-**to**-zah] f. galactose
galaktyczny [gah-**lahk**-tich-ni] adj.m. of a galaxy; galactic
galaktyka [gah-**lah**-kti-kah] f. galaxy
galalit [gah-**lah**-leet] m. galalith; artificial horn
galalitowy [gah-lah-lee-**to**-vi] adj.m. of artificial horn
galant [**gah**-lahnt] m. gallant; man of fashion
galanteria [gah-lahn-**ter**-yah] f. gallantry; haberdashery
galanteryjny [gah-lahn-te-**riy**-ni] adj.m. of haberdashery; of fancy goods; of fancy articles
galantyna [gah-lahn-**ti**-nah] f. galantine (dish)
galar [**gah**-lahr] m. flat-bottomed river ship (for grain transport)
galareta [gah-lah-**re**-tah] f. jelly
galaretka [gah-lah-**ret**-kah] f. jelly
galaretnica [gah-lah-ret-**ńee**-tsah] f.

star jelly
galaretowacenie [gah-lah-re-to-vah-**tse**-ńe] n. becoming jelly-like
galaretowacieć [gah-lah-re-to-**vah**-ćhećh] v. become jelly-like (*repeatedly*)
galaretować [gah-lah-re-**to**-vahćh] v. make jelly (*repeatedly*)
galaretowanie [gah-lah-re-to-**vah**-ńe] n. making jelly
galaretowato [gah-lah-re-to-**vah**-to] adv. like jelly
galaretowatość [gah-lah-re-to-**vah**-tośhćh] f. jelly-like quality
galaretowaty [gah-lah-re-to-**vah**-ti] adj.m. jelly-like; gelatinous
galaretowy [gah-lah-re-**to**-vi] adj.m. of jelly; of gelatine
galaretówka [gah-lah-re-**toof**-kah] f. variety of algae
galarowy [gah-lah-**ro**-vi] adj.m. of flat-bottomed river ship
galas [**gah**-lahs] m. gall; gallnut; oak apple
galasowy [gah-lah-**so**-vi] adj.m. gall (nut, acid, etc.); of gallnut
kwas galasowy [kfahs gah-lah-**so**-vi] exp.: gallic acid
galasówka [gah-lah-**soof**-kah] f. gallfly; gallnut; oak apple
galasówki [gah-lah-**soof**-kee] pl. galls; gallnuts; oak apples
galbanum [gahl-**bah**-noom] n. galbanum
galeas [gah-**le**-ahs] m. galleass
galena [gah-**le**-nah] f. galena; lead sulfide
galenit [gah-**le**-ńeet] m. galena; lead sulfide
galenowy [gah-le-**no**-vi] adj.m. of galena; galenic; of lead sulfide
galeon [gah-**le**-on] m. galleon; figure-head
galeota [gah-le-**o**-tah] f. small galley
galera [gah-**le**-rah] f. galley; galleys
galeria [gah-**le**-ryah] f. gallery; art gallery; picture gallery
galeriowiec [gah-le-**ryo**-vyets] m. gallery-access apartment
galeriowy [gah-le-**ryo**-vi] adj.m. of a gallery; galley (ship); of galleries
galerniczy [gah-ler-**ńee**-chi] adj.m. of a galley slave
galernik [gah-**ler**-ńeek] m. galley slave
galerowy [gah-le-**ro**-vi] adj.m. of a galley; galley (slave, etc.)
galeryjka [gah-le-**riy**-kah] f. small gallery; arcade; balustrade
galeryjny [gah-le-**riy**-ni] adj.m. of an art gallery; of theater gallery
Galicjanin [gah-lee-**tsyah**-ńeen] m. Galician
galicyjski [gah-lee-**tsiy**-skee] adj.m. of Galicia; Galician
galicyzm [gah-**lee**-tsizm] m. a borrowing from the French language; Galician expression
galijski [gah-**leey**-skee] adj.m. Gallic
Galilejczyk [gah-lee-**ley**-chik] m. Galilean
galimatias [gah-lee-**mah**-tyahs] m. gibberish; hotchpotch; mess; muddle; mull; jumble; welter
narobić galimatiasu [nah-**ro**-beećh gah-lee-mah-**tyah**-soo] exp.: to make a mess
galion [**gahl**-yon] m. galleon
galiota [gahl-**yo**-tah] f. galliot (hist.)
galipot [gah-**lee**-pot] m. galipot resin
gallikanin [gahl-lee-**kah**-ńeen] m. follower of Gallicanism
gallikanizm [gahl-lee-**kah**-ńeezm] m. Gallicanism (opposition to the pope)
gallikański [gahl-lee-**kahń**-skee] adj.m. Gallican
galman [**gahl**-mahn] m. calamine (mineral); tin ore
gallomania [gahl-lo-**mah**-ńyah] f. Gallomania
galmanowy [gahl-mah-**no**-vi] adj.m. of calamine; calamine (ore, etc.)
galon [**gah**-lon] m. gallon (English gallon = 4.546 liter, American gallon = 3.785 liter); braid; galloon
galonik [gah-**lo**-ńeek] m. small galloon
galonować [gah-lo-**no**-vahćh] v. braid (*repeatedly*)
galonowy [gah-lo-**no**-vi] adj.m. braided; m. lackey
galop [**gah**-lop] m. gallop; run
krótki galop [**kroot**-kee **gah**-lop] exp.: canter; hand-gallop
weź go do galopu [veźh go do gah-**lo**-poo] exp.: put his nose to

the grindstone
galopada [gah-lo-**pah**-dah] f. gallopade (dance); whirl
galopant [gah-**lo**-pahnt] m. colloq: suitor; gallant
galopem [gah-**lo**-pem] adv. at full gallop; at full speed; in full career; posthaste; like a shot; in double-quick time
galopka [gah-**lop**-kah] f. quick polka (dance)
galopować [gah-lo-**po**-vahćh] v. gallop; ride full gallop; dance a gallopade (*repeatedly*)
galopowanie [gah-lo-po-**vah**-ńe] n. galloping; riding full gallop; dancing a gallopade
galopowy [gah-lo-**po**-vi] adj.m. of a gallop; gallop (gate, etc.)
galoty [gah-**lo**-ti] pl. loose pants
galowo [gah-**lo**-vo] adv. in gala dress; colloq: in full fig
galowy [gah-**lo**-vi] adj.m. gala (uniform, day, etc.)
galówka [gah-**loof**-kah] f. gala day; gala performance; gale event
galusowy [gah-loo-**so**-vi] adj.m. gallic (acid, etc.)
galwanicznie [gahl-vah-**ńeech**-ńe] adv. galvanically
galwaniczny [gahl-vah-**ńeech**-ni] adj.m. galvanic; volcanic
galwanizacja [gahl-vah-ńee-**zah**-tsyah] f. galvanization; plating
galwanizacyjny [gahl-vah-ńee-zah-**tsiy**-ni] adj.m. galvanization (plant, works, etc.)
galwanizator [gahl-vah-ńee-**zah**-tor] m. galvanizer
galwanizer [gahl-vah-**ńee**-zer] m. galvanizer
galwanizernia [gahl-vah-ńee-**zer**-ńah] f. galvanizing shop
galwanizerski [gahl-vah-ńee-**zer**-skee] adj.m. of galvanizing; of galvanizer
galwanizerstwo [gahl-vah-ńee-**zer**-stfo] n. galvanization; galvanizer's trade
galwanizm [gahl-**vah**-ńeezm] m. galvanism
galwanizować [gahl-vah-ńee-**zo**-vahćh] v. galvanize; electroplate (*repeatedly*)
galwanizowanie [gahl-vah-ńee-zo-**vah**-ńe] n. galvanizing; electroplating
galwano [gahl-**vah**-no] n. electrotyped plate
galwanochromia [gahl-vah-no-**khro**-myah] f. electrolytic coloring of metals; galvanic coloring
galwanokaustyka [gahl-vah-no-**kahws**-ti-kah] f. galvanocautery
galwanokauter [gahl-vah-no-**kahw**-ter] m. tool for galvanocautery
galwanomagnetyczny [gah-vah-no-mahg-ne-**tich**-ni] adj.m. galvanomagnetic
galwanometr [gahl-vah-**no**-metr] m. galvanometer
galwanoplastycznie [gahl-vah-no-plahs-**tich**-ńe] adv. by means of electrolytic coating
galwanoplastyczny [gahl-vah-no-plahs-**tich**-ni] adj.m. of electrolytic coating
galwanoplastyka [gahl-vah-no-**plahs**-ti-kah] f. electrolytic coating
galwanoskop [gahl-vah-**no**-skop] m. galvanoscope
galwanostegia [gahl-vah-no-**ste**-gyah] f. electrolytic coating by different metals
galwanotaksja [gah-vah-no-**tahks**-yah] f. galvanotaxis
galwanotechnicznie [gahl-vah-no-tekh-**ńeech**-ńe] adv. by means of electroplating
galwanotechniczny [gahl-vah-no-tekh-**ńeech**-ni] adj.m. of electroplating
galwanotechnik [gahl-vah-no-**tekh**-ńeek] m. specialist in electroplating
galwanotechnika [gahl-vah-no-**tekh**-ńee-kah] f. electroplating
galwanoterapia [gahl-vah-no-te-**rah**-pyah] f. therapeutic application of electric current
galwanotropizm [gahl-vah-no-**tro**-peezm] m. galvanotropism
galwanotyp [gahl-vah-**no**-tip] m. electrotype
galwanotypia [gahl-vah-no-**ti**-pyah] f. electrotypy
gała [**gah**-wah] f. large sphere; large ball; slang: vulg.: eyeball; fist;

failing grade
gałązeczka [gah-wown-**zech**-kah] f. very small branch
gałązka [gah-**wowns**-kah] f. small branch
gałązkowy [gah-wowns-**ko**-vi] adj.m. of a small branch
gałąź [**gah**-wownśh] f. branch
gałeczka [gah-**wech**-kah] f. (small) knob; ball; sphere
gałgan [**gahw**-gahn] m. rag; rascal; good-for-nothing; scamp
gałganiarz [gahw-**gah**-ńahsh] m. ragman; rag dealer
gałęzatka [gah-wan-**zaht**-kah] f. variety of seaweed
gałęziak [gah-**wan**-źhahk] m. cladode; cladophyll
gałęziaki [gah-wan-**źhah**-kee] pl. the cladode family of plants; the cladophyll family of plants
gałęzianka [gah-wan-**źhahn**-kah] f. foliation
gałęziasty [gah-wan-**źhahs**-ti] adj.m. branchy; branch-like
gałęziowy [gah-wan-**źho**-vi] adj.m. of a branch
gałęzistość [gah-wan-**źhees**-tośhćh] f. abundance of tree's branches; thicket of tree's branches
gałęzisty [gah-wan-**źhees**-ti] adj.m. branchy; having many branches
gałgan [**gahw**-gahn] m. rag; clout; good-for-nothing; scamp; scoundrel; rascal; rogue; sun of a gun
gałganek [gahw-**gah**-nek] m. rag; piece of cloth
gałganki [gahw-**gahn**-kee] pl. finery; dresses
gałganeria [gahw-gah-**ner**-yah] f. gang of rascals
gałganiany [gahw-gah-**ńah**-ni] adj.m. rag (doll, etc.)
gałganiarka [gahw-gah-**ńahr**-kah] f. woman ragpicker
gałganiarz [gahw-**gah**-ńahsh] m. rag-and-bone man; ragpicker; ragman; ragamuffin
gałganica [gahw-gah-**ńee**-tsah] f. hussy; strumpet; slut
gałgankowy [gahw-gahn-**ko**-vi] adj.m. rag (doll, etc.)
gałgański [gahw-**gahń**-skee] adj.m. roguish; mean; scampish; scoundrelly; shabby; scurvy
po gałgańsku [po gahw-**gahń**-skoo] exp.: adv. meanly; shabbily; scurvily
gałgaństwo [gahw-**gahń**-stfo] n. roguery; mean trick; band of rascals; riffraff; ragtag; odds and ends; rags
gałka [**gahw**-kah] f. knob; ball
gałka muszkatołowa [**gahw**-kah moosh-kah-to-**wo**-vah] exp.: nutmeg
gałka oczna [**gahw**-kah **och**-nah] exp.: eyeball
gałkowaty [gahw-ko-**vah**-ti] adj.m. spherical; sphere-like
gałkowy [gahw-**ko**-vi] adj.m. of an eyeball
gałuszka [gah-**woosh**-kah] f. pillwort
gama [**gah**-mah] f. scale
gamajda [gah-**mahy**-dah] m. & f. yokel; simpleton; numskull; dunce; noodle; bumpkin
gamba [**gahm**-bah] f. gamba; viola da gamba
gambir [**gahm**-beer] m. gambier
gambit [**gahm**-beet] m. gambit (in chess)
gambo [**gahm**-bo] n. natural fiber; jute
gambuzja [gahm-**booz**-yah] f. gambusia
gameta [gah-**me**-tah] f. gamete
gamety [gah-**me**-ti] pl. gamete germinal (sex) cells
gametangium [gah-me-**tahng**-yoom] n. gametangium
gametofit [gah-me-**to**-feet] m. gametophyte
gametycznie [gah-me-**tich**-ńe] adv. gametically
gametyczny [gah-me-**tich**-ni] adj.m. gametic
gamma [**gahm**-mah] f. gamma
promienie gamma [pro-**mye**-ńe **gahm**-mah] exp.: gamma rays
gamma-globulina [**gahm**-mah glo-boo-**lee**-nah] f. gamma globulin
gamoniowaty [gah-mo-ńo-**vah**-ti] adj.m. gawky; half-witted; half-baked
gamoń [**gah**-moń] m. lout; oaf

ganasze [gah-**nah**-she] pl. horse's mandibles
ganaszować [gah-nah-**sho**-vahćh] v. tighten the reins (*repeatedly*)
ganaszowanie [gah-nah-sho-**vah**-ńe] n. precision (show) riding
gandysta [gahn-**dis**-tah] m. follower of M.K. Gandhi (1869-1948)
gandystowski [gahn-dis-**tof**-skee] adj.m. Gandhian
gandyzm [**gahn**-dizm] m. Gandhian principle of nonviolence and program
ganeczek [gah-**ne**-chek] m. (small, nice) porch; balcony
ganek [**gah**-nek] m. porch; balcony
gang [gahng] m. slang: gang of thieves (mob jargon)
ganglion [**gahn**-glyon] m. ganglion
gangrena [gahn-**gre**-nah] f. gangrene; depravity; corruption; decay of tissue
gangrenować [gahn-gre-**no**-vahćh] v. gangrene; corrupt (*repeatedly*)
gangrenować się [gahn-gre-**no**-vahćh śhan] v. become corrupt; become polluted; decay (*repeatedly*)
gangrenowaty [gahn-gre-no-**vah**-ti] adj.m. gangrenous
gangrenowy [gahn-gre-**no**-vi] adj.m. of gangrene; gangrenous
gangster [**gahnk**-ster] m. gangster; bandit; rowdy; racketeer; ruffian; tough
gangsterski [gahnk-**ster**-skee] adj.m. gangster's; bandit's; ruffianly
gangsterstwo [gahnk-**ster**-stfo] n. gangsterism; banditism; racketeering
ganiać [**gah**-ńahćh] v. run about; run after; chase; urge on; rush about; pursue; press on; drive on; goad (*repeatedly*)
ganiać się [**gah**-ńahćh śhan] v. chase one another (*repeatedly*)
ganianie [gah-**ńah**-ńe] n. running (around)
ganianie się [gah-**ńah**-ńe śhan] n. chasing one another
ganić [gah-ńeećh] v. blame; criticize; rebuke; upbraid; censure; find fault with; pick holes in; condemn; blame; reprehend (*repeatedly*)
ganienie [gah-**ńe**-ńe] n. criticism; censure; condemnation
gankowy [gahn-**ko**-vi] adj.m. of a porch; of a gallery; of a balcony
ganoid [gah-**no**-eet] m. ganoid
ganoidy [gah-no-**ee**-di] pl. ganoids
gaolan [gah-**o**-lahn] m. sorghum; sorgo
gap [gahp] m. gaping spectator; gaping passer-by; staring saunterer; gaper; oaf; stowaway; free rider; booby; lout; giddy head
gapa [**gah**-pah] m. & f. oaf; free rider; stowaway; giddy head; lout
gapić się [**gah**-peećh śhan] v. gape; stargaze; stare (*repeatedly*)
gapienie [gah-**pye**-ńe] n. a stare; stare
gapienie się [gah-**pye**-ńe śhan] n. gape; stargaze; stare (*repeated*)
gapiostwo [gah-**pyo**-stfo] n. carelessness; woolgathering
gapiowato [gah-pyo-**vah**-to] adv. carelessly; stupidly; with a stare; absent-mindedly
gapiowatość [gah-pyo-**vah**-tośhćh] f. colloq: stupidity; absent-mindedness
gapiowaty [gah-pyo-**vah**-ti] adj.m. careless; stupid; scatterbrained; empty-headed
gapiowski [gah-**pyof**-skee] adj.m. staring; gaping
po gapiowsku [po gah-**pyof**-skoo] exp.: adv. in a gaping way; with a stare; absent-mindedly
gapowaty [gah-po-**vah**-ti] adj.m. empty-headed; feeble-minded; slow in the uptake
gapowe [gah-**po**-ve] n. loss due to absent-mindedness
gapowicz [gah-**po**-veech] m. stowaway; lout
gar [gahr] m. large pot; large jug; well
gara [**gah**-rah] f. brace
garaż [**gah**-rahsh] m. garage
garażować [gah-rah-**zho**-vahćh] v. garage (*repeatedly*)
garażowy [gah-rah-**zho**-vi] adj.m. of a garage
garażowanie [gah-rah-zho-**vah**-ńe] n. garaging

garb [gahrp] m. hunch; hump; hummock; projection
garbacieć [gahr-**bah**-ćhećh] v. hump; hunch one's back (*repeatedly*)
garbarnia [gahr-**bahr**-ńah] f. tannery; tan-yard
garbarski [gahr-**bahr**-skee] adj.m. tanner's; tan (pit, etc.); tanning (bark, etc.)
garbarstwo [gahr-**bahr**-stfo] n. tanning; the tanning industry
garbarz [**gahr**-bahsh] m. tanner
garbatka [gahr-**baht**-kah] f. variety of moth
garbatki [gahr-**baht**-kee] pl. the family of Notodontidae (night) moths
garbato [gahr-**bah**-to] adv. at a slope; crookedly
garbaty [gahr-**bah**-ti] adj.m. crook-backed; humpbacked; with a hump; hunchbacked; with a high bridge (nose); humpy; uneven; hilly; m. hunchback; humpback
garbek [**gahr**-bek] m. bump; knoll
garbić [**gahr**-beećh] v. stoop; bend; arch; hunch (*repeatedly*)
garbić się [**gahr**-beećh śh<u>an</u>] v. stoop; hunch one's back; be distorted; crook; curve (*repeatedly*)
garbienie [gahr-**bye**-ńe] n. hunching; arching
garbienie się [gahr-**bye**-ńe śh<u>an</u>] n. stooping; hunching one's back
garbnica [gahrb-**ńee**-tsah] f. tanning extract; tan liquor; tan ooze; tan pickle
garbnik [**gahrb**-ńeek] m. tan; tannin
garbnikodajny [gahrb-ńee-ko-**dahy**-ni] adj.m. tanniferous
garbnikować [gahrb-ńee-**ko**-vahćh] v. tan; steep in tan (*repeatedly*)
garbnikowy [gahrb-ńee-**ko**-vi] adj.m. tannic (acid, etc.)
garbonosy [gahr-bo-**no**-si] adj.m. Roman-nosed
garbować [gahr-**bo**-vahćh] v. tan; dress hides (*repeatedly*)
garbować mu skórę [gahr-**bo**-vahćh moo **skoo**-r<u>an</u>] exp.: to give him a hiding
garbowanie [gahr-bo-**vah**-ńe] n. tanning; tannage
garbowiny [gahr-bo-**vee**-ni] pl. used tanbark
garbunek [gahr-**boo**-nek] m. tannin; tan
garbus [**gahr**-boos] m. humpback; hunchback; Volkswagen Beetle
garbusek [gahr-**boo**-sek] m. small humpback; little hunchback
garbuska [gahr-**boo**-skah] f. (female) humpback; hunchback
garcowy [gahr-**tso**-vi] adj.m. of gallon-size; of half a peck
garcynia [gahr-**tsi**-ńah] f. garcinia
garczek [**gahr**-chek] m. small pot; little jug; goblet; little mug
garda [**gahr**-dah] f. hilt-guard; shell; guard (in a ball game, etc.)
garden party [**gahr**-den **pahr**-ti] exp.: garden party
gardenia [gahr-**de**-ńyah] f. gardenia
garderoba [gahr-de-**ro**-bah] f. wardrobe; dressing room
garderobiana [gahr-de-ro-**byah**-nah] f. dresser
garderobiany [gahr-de-ro-**byah**-ni] m. dresser; adj.m. of a wardrobe; of a dressing room
gardlany [gahr-**dlah**-ni] adj.m. of the throat; throat (wash, etc.); guttural; throaty
gardłacz [**gahr**-dwahch] m. pouter (pigeon); blunderbuss (musket)
gardło [**gahr**-dwo] n. throat; pharynx; fauces; gullet; colloq: capital punishment
pod gardłem [pot **gahr**-dwem] exp.: under penalty of death
gardłować [gahr-**dwo**-vahćh] v. talk big; clamor; cry for (*repeatedly*)
gardłowanie [gahr-dwo-**vah**-ńe] n. talking big; clamoring
gardłowo [gahr-**dwo**-vo] adv. gutturally
gardłowy [gahr-**dwo**-vi] adj.m. guttural; punishable by death
gardzenie [gahr-**dze**-ńe] n. contempt; scorn
gardzić [**gahr**-dźheećh] v. despise; scorn; have in contempt; hold in contempt (*repeatedly*)
gardziel [**gahr**-dźhel] f. throat; pharynx; fauces; gullet; choke; gorge; defile; gut; jaws

gardzielowy [gahr-dźhe-**lo**-vi] adj.m. pharyngeal; of fauces; of a gullet; of a choke; of a gorge
gardziołek [gahr-**dźho**-wek] m. small throat; colloq: bottleneck
gardziołko [gahr-**dźhow**-ko] n. small throat
gargantuiczny [gahr-gahn-too-**eech**-ni] adj.m. gargantuan; gigantic; colossal; huge; gruff; ribald
gargantuizm [gahr-gahn-**too**-eezm] m. gluttony; drunkenness
gargulec [gahr-**goo**-lets] m. gargoyle
garkotłuk [gahr-**ko**-twook] m. colloq: awkward cook; kitchen wench
garkuchnia [gahr-**kookh**-ńah] f. chop-shop; cookshop
garłacz [**gahr**-wahch] m. pouter (pigeon); blunderbuss (musket)
garmażer [gahr-**mah**-zher] m. owner of delicatessen; producer of ready-to-eat food
garmażeria [gahr-mah-**zher**-yah] f. delicatessen; shop selling ready-to-eat food
garmażerka [gahr-mah-**zher**-kah] f. (woman) owner of delicatessen; producer of ready-to-eat food
garmażernia [gahr-mah-**zher**-ńah] f. delicatessen; shop selling ready-to-eat food
garmażeryjny [gahr-mah-zhe-**riy**-ni] adj.m. of delicatessen; of ready-to-eat food
garmond [**gahr**-mont] m. garamond (font)
garmondowy [gahr-mon-**do**-vi] adj.m. garamond (font)
garna [**gahr**-nah] f. Indian antelope
garnąć [**gahr**-nownćh] v. gather; cuddle; cling; hug; assemble; give refuge (*repeatedly*)
garnąć się [**gahr**-nownćh śhan] v. cuddle up to; feel attracted; cling to; crave for; be eager for (*repeatedly*)
garncarczyk [gahrn-**tsahr**-chik] m. potter's apprentice
garncarka [gahrn-**tsahr**-kah] f. (woman) potter
garncarnia [gahrn-**tsahr**-ńah] f. potter's workshop
garncarski [gahrn-**tsahr**-skee] adj.m. of pottery; potter's
garncarstwo [gahrn-**tsahr**-stfo] n. pottery
garncarz [**gahrn**-tsahsh] m. potter
garncowy [gahrn-**tso**-vi] adj.m. of gallon-size; of half a peck
garnczek [**gahrn**-chek] m. (small) pot; jug; crock; potful
garnek [**gahr**-nek] m. pot; jug; crock; potful
zaglądać w cudze garnki [zah-glown-dahćh f **tsoo**-dze **gahr**-nkee] exp.: to poke one's nose into other people's business
garnela [gahr-**ne**-lah] f. variety of sea crab
garniec [**gahr**-ńets] m. four-quarts measure; gallon; half a peck; large pot; large jug
garnieryt [gahr-**ńe**-rit] m. gernierite (mineral)
garnięcie [gahr-**ńan**-ćhe] n. hug; cuddle; gathering
garnięcie się [gahr-**ńan**-ćhe śhan] n. cuddling up (to); clinging (to)
garnirować [gahr-ńee-**ro**-vahćh] v. garnish; trim (a dress, etc.) (*repeatedly*)
garnirowanie [gahr-ńee-ro-**vah**-ńe] n. garnishing; fixing (a dish, etc.)
garnirunek [gahr-ńee-**roo**-nek] m. garnish; trimmings
garnitur [gahr-**ńee**-toor] m. suit; set; assortment; trimmings
garniturek [gahr-ńee-**too**-rek] m. school uniform; set of toy furniture
garniturowy [gahr-ńee-too-**ro**-vi] adj.m. of a suit; of a set
garnizon [gahr-**ńee**-zon] m. garrison; stationed troops
garnizonowy [gahr-ńee-zo-**no**-vi] adj.m. of a garrison; of stationed troops
garnkotłuk [gahrn-**ko**-twook] m. colloq: awkward servant-girl; kitchen wench
garnuszeczek [gahr-noo-**she**-chek] m. little cup; very little mug
garnuszek [gahr-**noo**-shek] m. cup; little mug; goblet; mug-full; potfull; jugfull
być na garnuszku [bićh nah gahr-**noosh**-koo] exp.: colloq: to eat somebody else's bread and salt;

to live on somebody else's keep
garować [gah-ro-vahćh] v. ferment dough (*repeatedly*)
garowanie [gah-ro-vah-ńe] n. fermenting dough
garownia [gah-rov-ńah] f. dough fermentation room
garson [gahr-son] m. colloq: waiter; messenger boy
garsonada [gahr-so-nah-dah] f. cheek; audacity; boisterousness
garsoniera [gahr-so-ńe-rah] f. bachelor's apartment
garsonka [gahr-son-kah] f. tailor-made dress; outfit; woman's hairdo styled like a man
garsteczka [gahr-stech-kah] f. little bit; pinch; sprinkling; scattering; colloq: very few
garstka [gahrst-kah] f. small handful; colloq: a few
garść [gahrśhćh] f. handful; hand; the hollow of the hand; colloq: batch; bunch; a scattering
pełną garścią [pew-nown gahrśh-ćhown] exp.: adv. abundantly; unstintingly; without stint
wziąć się w garść [vźhownćh śhan v gahrśhćh] exp.: control oneself; to pull oneself together
garus [gah-roos] m. a dish of cooked fruit; colloq: mess; chyme; lazybones; a topsy-turvy
gasić [gah-śheećh] v. expire; go out; die down; extinguish; quench; put out; eclipse; black out; damp; dash; disconcert; do away with; do in (*repeatedly*)
gasić motor [gah-śheećh mo-tor] exp.: to switch off an engine
gasić papierosa [gah-śheećh pah-pye-ro-sah] exp.: to stub out a cigarette
gasidło [gah-śheed-wo] n. candle extinguisher; colloq: big nose
gasik [gah-śheek] m. electrical spark-proof connection
gasiwo [gah-śhee-vo] n. (electrical) spark-killer
gasnąć [gahs-nownćh] v. go out; die down; expire; wane; be on the wane; fade; shrink; dwarf; be disconcerted; lose countenance; be dying away; be at a low ebb (*repeatedly*)
gastarbeiter [gahst-ahr-bahy-ter] m. foreign worker in Germany
gastro- [gahs-tro] prefix: gastro-; stomach-
gastrolog [gahs-tro-log] m. gastrologist
gastrologia [gahs-tro-lo-gyah] f. gastrology
gastrologiczny [gahs-tro-lo-geech-ni] adj.m. of gastrology
gastronom [gahs-tro-nom] m. gastronome; gastronomist; gourmet; epicure
gastronomia [gahs-tro-no-myah] f. the art of cooking; good cooking; the catering business
gastronomiczny [gahs-tro-no-meech-ni] adj.m. gastronomic; of good cooking
gastronomik [gahs-tro-no-meek] m. gastronome; gastronomist
gastroskop [gahs-tro-skop] m. gastroscope
gastroskopia [gahs-tro-sko-pyah] f. gastroscopy
gastrostomia [gahs-tro-sto-myah] f. gastrostomy
gastrula [gahs-troo-lah] f. gastrula
gastrulacja [gahs-troo-lah-tsyah] f. gastrulation
gastryczny [gahs-trich-ni] adj.m. gastric; in or near the stomach
gastryk [gahs-trik] m. gastric patient; man suffering from gastritis
gastryna [gahs-tri-nah] f. gastrin
gaszek [gah-shek] m. colloq: small-time seducer
gaszenie [gah-she-ńe] n. extinction; quenching
gaszenie świateł [gah-she-ńe śhfyah-tew] exp.: curfew
gaśnica [gaśh-ńee-tsah] f. fire extinguisher
gaśniczy [gahśh-ńee-chi] adj.m. of extinguishing
gaśnięcie [gahśh-ńan-ćhe] n. dying out; waning
gatki [gaht-kee] pl. colloq: underpants
gatunek [gah-too-nek] m. kind; quality; sort; class; species

gatunek jabłek [gah-**too**-nek **yahb**-wek] exp.: variety of apples
gatunek piwa [gah-**too**-nek **pee**-vah] exp.: brew of beer
rzeczy tego gatunku [zhe-chi **te**-go gah-**toon**-koo] exp.: things of that kind
ten gatunek ludzi [ten gah-**too**-nek loo-dźhee] exp.: that type of people
wszelkiego gatunku [fshel-ke-go gah-**toon**-koo] exp.: of all kinds
gatunkotwórczy [gah-toon-ko-**tfoor**-chi] adj.m. species-forming (evolution, etc.)
gatunkować [gah-toon-**ko**-vahćh] v. sort; classify (*repeatedly*)
gatunkowanie [gah-toon-ko-**vah**-ńe] n. classification
gatunkowo [gah-toon-**ko**-vo] adv. qualitatively; in respect of quality; typically; specifically
gatunkowy [gah-toon-**ko**-vi] adj.m. typical; type (species, etc.); specific; of high quality; high-grade (article, etc.)
gaucho [**gahw**-cho] m. gaucho
gauczo [**gahw**-cho] m. gaucho
gaullizm [**go**-leezm] m. Gaullism; political movement led by General Charles de Gaulle
gaur [gahwr] m. gaur
gaus [gahws] m. gauss
gawęda [gah-**van**-dah] f. chat; tale; piece of gossip; gossip
gawędka [gah-**vant**-kah] f. (little) chat; tale; piece of gossip; gossip
gawędowy [gah-van-**do**-vi] adj.m. of a chat; of a tale
gawędzenie [gah-van-**dze**-ńe] n. storytelling; chat; chatting
gawędziarski [gah-van-**dźhahr**-skee] adj.m. narrative; chatty
gawędziarsko [gah-van-**dźhahr**-sko] adv. in a chatty manner
gawędziarstwo [gah-van-**dźhahr**-stfo] n. chatty style; conversational powers; prattling
gawędziarz [gah-**van**-dźhahsh] m. storyteller; talker; narrator; story-writer
gawędzić [gah-**van**-dźheećh] v. chat; tattle (*repeatedly*)
gawial [**gah**-vyahl] m. gavial (crocodile in India)
gawiale [gah-**vyah**-le] pl. the gavial family of Indian crocodiles
gawiedź [**gah**-vyećh] f. mob; rabble; populace; gaping crowd; the common people
gaworzenie [gah-vo-**zhe**-ńe] n. babble; cooing (by a baby); chat; twitter; warble; chirping (by a bird, etc.)
gaworzyć [gah-**vo**-zhićh] v. babble; coo; chat; twitter; warble; chirp (*repeatedly*)
gawot [**gah**-vot] m. gavotte
gawra [**gahv**-rah] f. bear's hibernation den
gawron [**gah**-vron] m. rook (a bird); gawk; colloq: gaper (man)
gawroni [gah-**vro**-ńee] adj.m. rook's (nest); gawkish
gawronić się [gah-**vro**-ńeećh śhan] v. gape; stand gaping; look on open-mouthed (*repeatedly*)
gawronię [gah-**vro**-ńan] n. young rook; young raven
gawrosz [**gahv**-rosh] m. street kid; street arab
gawroszka [gahv-**rosh**-kah] f. scarf
gawrować [gahv-**ro**-vahćh] v. hibernate in a lair; winter (*repeatedly*)
gawrowanie [gahv-ro-**vah**-ńe] n. bear's hibernation
gaz [gahs] m. gas; slang: liquor; alcoholic beverages; drinking spree (mob jargon)
gaz do dechy [gahs do **de**-khi] exp.: to floor the (gas) pedal
gaz generatorowy [gahs ge-ne-rah-to-ro-vi] exp.: generator gas
gaz ziemny [gahz **źhem**-ni] exp.: natural gas
gazy spalinowe [**gah**-zi spah-lee-**no**-ve] exp.: combustion gases
gaza [**gah**-zah] f. gauze; antiseptic gauze
gazda [**gahz**-dah] m. farmer; sheep-breeder
gazdostwo [gahz-**do**-stfo] n. (Carpathian mountaineer's) farm
gazdować [gahz-**do**-vahćh] v. run a mountain farm (in southern Poland) (*repeatedly*)
gazdowanie [gahz-do-**vah**-ńe] n.

runnig a farm (in the Carpathian mountains)
gazdowski [gahz-**dof**-skee] adj.m. farmer's; sheep breeder's
gazdówka [gahz-**doof**-kah] f. sheep farming; sheep farm
gazeciarka [gah-ze-**ćhahr**-kah] f. woman newsvendor
gazeciarski [gah-ze-**ćhahr**-skee] adj.m. journalistic; newspaper (style, etc.)
język gazeciarski [yan-zik gah-ze-**ćhahr**-skee] exp.: journalese
gazeciarstwo [gah-ze-**ćhahr**-stfo] n. news-vending
gazeciarz [gah-**ze**-ćhahsh] m. paperboy; newsboy; newsvendor; owner of a newsstand; colloq.: editor of a newspaper
gazela [gah-**ze**-lah] f. gazelle
gazeta [gah-**ze**-tah] f. paper; newspaper; daily
gazetka [gah-**zet**-kah] f. news-sheet; school paper
gazetowy [gah-ze-**to**-vi] adj.m. of a newspaper; newspaper (columns, etc.)
gaziarz [**gah**-źhahsh] m. collector for gas utility; worker in gas utility works
gazik [**gah**-źheek] m. small jeep; piece of gauze
gazobeton [gah-zo-**be**-ton] m. gas-entrained concrete
gazobetonownia [gah-zo-be-to-**nov**-ńah] f. plant producing gas-entrained concrete
gazobetonowy [gah-zo-be-to-**no**-vi] adj.m. of gas-entrained concrete
gazociąg [gah-**zo**-ćhowng] m. gas pipeline
gazociągowy [gah-zo-ćhown-**go**-vi] adj.m. of gas pipeline
gazodynamiczny [gah-zo-di-nah-**meech**-ni] adj.m. of gas dynamics
gazodynamika [gah-zo-di-**nah**-mee-kah] f. aerodynamics; dynamics of gases
gazogenerator [gah-zo-ge-ne-**rah**-tor] m. gas generator
gazogeneratorowy [gah-zo-ge-ne-rah-to-**ro**-vi] adj.m. of gas generator; gas generator (fuel, etc.)
gazogips [gah-**zo**-geeps] m. gas-entrained gypsum
gazogipsowy [gah-zo-geep-**so**-vi] adj.m. of gas-entrained gypsum
gazol [**gah**-zol] m. liquid gas
gazolina [gah-zo-**lee**-nah] f. gasoline; gasolene; petrol
gazoliniarnia [gah-zo-lee-**ńahr**-ńah] f. gasoline-producing plant
gazometr [gah-**zo**-metr] m. gasometer; gasholder; gas burette
gazomierz [gah-**zo**-myesh] m. gas meter; gas gauge
gazon [**gah**-zon] m. lawn
gazonik [gah-**zo**-ńeek] m. small lawn
gazonośny [gah-zo-**nośh**-ni] adj.m. gas-rich; gas-carrying; gas-containing
gazoskop [gah-**zo**-skop] m. gas detector
gazoszczelny [gah-zo-**shchel**-ni] adj.m. gastight; airtight
gazotron [gah-**zo**-tron] m. mercury-vapor lamp
gazować [gah-**zo**-vahćh] v. gas; treat with gas; aerate; impregnate (water) with carbon dioxide; colloq: rush; tear along; drink vodka (*repeatedly*)
gazowanie [gah-zo-**vah**-ńe] n. gassing; aerating
gazowany [gah-zo-**vah**-ni] adj.m. aerated; charged with carbon dioxide; sparkling; fizzy; effervescent
woda gazowana [**vo**-dah gah-zo-**vah**-nah] exp.: soda water
gazownia [gah-**zov**-ńah] f. gas plant; gas works
gazownictwo [gah-zov-**ńee**-tstfo] n. the gas industry
gazowniczy [gah-zov-**ńee**-chi] adj.m. gas-producing (coal, etc.)
gazownik [gah-**zov**-ńeek] m. gas fitter; gas generator; slang: drunk
gazowociekły [gah-zo-vo-**ćhek**-wi] adj.m. liquefying gas
gazowy [gah-**zo**-vi] adj.m. gassy; gaseous; gasiform; of gauze; gauzy; gauze
komora gazowa [ko-**mo**-rah gah-**zo**-vah] exp.: gas chamber
maska gazowa [**mahs**-kah gah-**zo**-

vah] exp.: gas mask
kuchenka gazowa [koo-**khen**-kah gah-**zo**-vah] exp.: gas cooker
gazówka [gah-**zoof**-kah] f. scarf of very thin fabric
gazyfikacja [gah-zi-fee-**kah**-tsyah] f. gasification
gazyfikacyjny [gah-zi-fee-kah-**tsiy**-ni] adj.m. of gasification
gazyfikować [gah-zi-fee-**ko**-vahćh] v. convert into gas; gasify (*repeatedly*)
gazyfikować się [gah-zi-fee-**ko**-vahćh śhan] v. become gaseous (*repeatedly*)
gazyfikowanie [gah-zi-fee-ko-**vah**-ńe] n. gasification
gazyfikowanie się [gah-zi-fee-ko-**vah**-ńe śhan] n. becoming gaseous
gaździna [gahźh-**dźhee**-nah] f. wife of Carpathian mountain farmer
gaździnka [gahźh-**dźheen**-kah] f. (nice, little) wife of Carpathian mountain farmer
gaźnik [**gahźh**-ńeek] m. carburetor (for mixing gasoline with air)
gaźnikowy [gahźh-ńee-**ko**-vi] adj.m. of a carburetor
gaża [gah-zhah] f. wage; salary
gąbczasto [gownp-**chah**-sto] adv. spongily; with spongy quality
gąbczasty [gownp-**chah**-sti] adj.m. spongy; squashy; mushy
gąbka [**gownp**-kah] f. sponge
gąbkowaty [gownp-ko-**vah**-ti] adj.m. sponge-like; porous; mushy; squashy
gąbkowy [gownp-**ko**-vi] adj.m. spongy; of a sponge
gądziel [**gown**-dźhel] f. bugle (plant)
gągoł [**gown**-gow] m. goldeneye (a duck)
gąseczka [gown-**sech**-kah] f. little goose
gąsiątko [gown-**śhownt**-ko] n. little goose; gosling
gąsienica [gown-śhe-**ńee**-tsah] f. grub; caterpillar; band; track
gąsienicowaty [gown-śhe-ńee-tso-**vah**-ti] adj.m. caterpillar-like
gąsienicowy [gown-śhe-ńee-**tso**-vi] adj.m. of a caterpillar; caterpillar (traction, chain, etc.)
gąsieniczka [gown-śhe-**ńeech**-kah] f. small caterpillar
gąsienicznik [gown-śhe-**ńeech**-ńeek] m. ichneumon (insect)
gąsieniczniki [gown-śhe-ńeech-**ńee**-kee] pl. the Ichneumonidae (insect) family
gąsię [**gown**-śhan] n. goose chick
gąsior [**gown**-śhor] m. gander; jar; demijohn; ridge tile
gąsiorek [gown-**śho**-rek] m. red-backed shrike; (small) gander; jar; demijohn; ridge tile
gąsiorowaty [gown-śho-ro-**vah**-ti] adj.m. gander-like
gąska [**gowns**-kah] f. little goose; agaric; trichoma; colloq: silly girl; young goose; chit
gąszcz [gownshch] m. thicket; brushwood; congestion of plants; mushy liquid
gązewnik [gown-**zev**-ńeek] m. loranthus (bush)
gązewnikowaty [gown-zev-ńee-ko-**vah**-ti] adj.m. loranthaceous; of the mistletoe family
gązewnikowate [gown-zev-ńee-ko-**vah**-te] pl. the mistletoe family
gązwa [**gownz**-vah] f. flail-strap
gbur [gboor] m. rude; boor; yokel; churl; bumpkin; lout; clodhopper; rustic
gburliwie [gboor-**lee**-vye] adv. ruddily; boorishly
gburliwy [gboor-**lee**-vi] adj.m. rude; boorish
gburowacieć [gboo-ro-**vah**-ćhećh] v. become boorish; become rude (*repeatedly*)
gburowato [gboo-ro-**vah**-to] adv. boorishly; rudely; churlishly; surly; gruffly; loutishly
gburowatość [gboo-ro-**vah**-tośhćh] f. boorishness; rudeness; churlishness; surliness; gruffness; loutishness
gburowaty [gboo-ro-**vah**-ti] adj.m. boorish; rude; churlish; surly; gruff; loutish
gburzysko [gboo-**zhis**-ko] n. & m. nasty boor; big lout
gdakać [**gdah**-kahćh] v. cackle; yak; sound like a hen (*repeatedly*)
gdakanie [gdah-**kah**-ńe] n. cackle; a

cackle
gdaknąć [gdahk-nownćh] v. cackle; yak; sound like a hen
gdaknięcie [gdahk-ńan-ćhe] n. a cackle
gdańska [gdahń-skah] f. slang: heroine of Gdańsk; lquid mixture of opium; morphine and heroine used intravenously (mob jargon)
gdański [gdahń-skee] adj.m. of Gdańsk
gdańska wódka [gdahń-skah voot-kah] exp.: Gdańsk vodka
gdańszczanin [gdahń-shchah-ńeen] m. inhabitant of Gdańsk
gderacz [gde-rahch] m. colloq: grumbler; croaker; grouch
gderać [gde-rahćh] v. colloq: grumble; grouch; nag (at) (*repeatedly*)
gderanie [gde-rah-ńe] n. colloq: grumbling; nagging
gderanina [gde-rah-ńee-nah] f. grumbling; nagging
gderliwie [gder-lee-vye] adv. grumpily
gderliwość [gder-lee-vośhćh] f. bad temper; cross-grained disposition; grumpiness
gderliwy [gder-lee-vi] adj.m. bad tempered; cross-grained; disgruntled; grumpy
gdy [gdi] conj. when; while; as; that; after
podczas gdy [pot-chahs gdi] exp.: while; as
gdyby [gdi-bi] conj. if
gdyby nawet [gdi-bi nah-vet] exp.: even though
gdyby nie [gdi-bi ńe] exp.: but for
gdyby tylko [gdi-bi til-ko] exp.: if only
gdybym wiedział [gdi-bim vye-dźhahw] exp.: if I knew
gdybym był wiedział [gdi-bim biw vye-dźhahw] exp.: if I had known; had I known
jak gdyby [yahk gdi-bi] exp.: as if; so to say
gdybyż [gdi-bish] conj. if (emphatic: **gdyby**)
gdyż [gdish] conj. for; because; since; inasmuch as
gdzie [gdźhe] adv. & conj. where; where to?
byle gdzie [bi-le gdźhe] exp.: anywhere; wherever you like; no matter where
gdzie bądź [gdźhe bownćh] exp.: adv. anywhere; wherever; no matter where
gdzie indziej [gdźhe een-dźhey] exp.: elsewhere; somewhere else
gdzie mi do tego! [gdźhe mee do te-go] exp.: colloq: it's more than I can handle!; it's over my head!
gdzie tam! [gdźhe tahm] exp.: nothing of the kind!; far from it!; not by a long shot!; nonsense!
gdziekolwiek [gdźhe-kol-vyek] adv. anywhere; wherever; no matter where
gdzieniegdzie [gdźhe-ńe-gdźhe] adv. here and there; in places; at intervals
gdzieś [gdźheśh] adv. somewhere; slang: vulg. exp.: up my ass
gdzież [gdźhesh] adv. where (emphatic: **gdzie**)
gedanit [ge-dah-ńeet] m. variety of amber from Gdańsk region
gees [ge-es] m. rural cooperative
geesowski [ge-e-sof-skee] adj.m. of rural cooperative
gehenna [ge-khen-nah] f. Gehenna
gejsza [gey-shah] f. geisha
gejtaw [gey-tahf] m. clew; brail; guy-rope
gejzer [gey-zer] m. geyser
gejzeryt [gey-ze-rit] m. geyserit
gekon [ge-kon] m. gecko (lizard)
gekony [ge-ko-ni] pl. the family Gekkonidae (of gecko lizards)
gem [gem] m. (tennis) game
gemeliologia [ge-mel-yo-lo-gyah] f. genetic study of twins
geminacja [ge-mee-nah-tsyah] f. gemination; doubling
geminata [ge-mee-nah-tah] f. double consonant (each pronounced)
gemma [gem-mah] f. gem; jewel
gemmologia [gem-mo-lo-gyah] f. gemology
gemowy [ge-mo-vi] adj.m. of a (tennis) game
gemula [ge-moo-lah] f. freshwater sponge
gemule [ge-moo-le] pl. family of

freshwater sponges
gen [gen] m. gene
gencjana [gen-**tsyah**-nah] f. gentian (herb)
gencjanowy [gen-tsyah-**no**-vi] adj.m. of the gentian (herb)
genealog [ge-ne-**ah**-log] m. genealogist
genealogia [ge-ne-ah-**lo**-gyah] f. genealogy; origin; pedigree
genealogicznie [ge-ne-ah-lo-**geech**-ńe] adv. genealogically
genealogiczny [ge-ne-ah-lo-**geech**-ni] adj.m. genealogical; of the origin; of pedigree
generacja [ge-ne-**rah**-tsyah] f. generation; production
generacyjny [ge-ne-rah-**tsiy**-ni] adj.m. generational
generalia [ge-ne-**rah**-lyah] pl. general expenses; overall costs; personal data; particulars (of a person)
generalicja [ge-ne-rah-**lee**-tsyah] f. staff of generals; body of generals
generalissimus [ge-ne-rah-lees-**see**-moos] m. generalissimo
generalizacja [ge-ne-rah-lee-**zah**-tsyah] f. generalization
generalizator [ge-ne-rah-lee-**zah**-tor] m. generalizer
generalizować [ge-ne-rah-lee-**zo**-vahćh] v. generalize; make a sweeping statement (*repeatedly*)
generalizowanie [ge-ne-rah-lee-zo-**vah**-ńe] n. generalization
generalizujący [ge-ne-rah-lee-zoo-**yown**-tsi] adj.m. sweeping; making sweeping generalizations
generalnie [ge-ne-**rahl**-ńe] adv. generally; in general; universally
generalny [ge-ne-**rahl**-ni] adj.m. general; widespread; full-scale
generalski [ge-ne-**rahl**-skee] adj.m. general's (function, etc.)
generalstwo [ge-ne-**rahl**-stfo] n. generalship
generał [ge-**ne**-rahw] m. general
generałbas [ge-ne-**rahw**-bahs] m. thoroughbass; continuo
generałostwo [ge-ne-rah-**wos**-tfo] n. general and his wife
generałowa [ge-ne-rah-**wo**-vah] f. general's wife
generałówna [ge-ne-rah-**woov**-nah] f. general's daughter
generator [ge-ne-**rah**-tor] m. generator; alternator
generator gazowy [ge-ne-**rah**-tor gah-**zo**-vi] exp.: gas generator
generator pomocniczy [ge-ne-**rah**-tor po-mots-**ńee**-chi] exp.: booster
generatorowy [ge-ne-rah-to-**ro**-vi] adj.m. of a generator
generatywista [ge-ne-rah-ti-**vees**-tah] m. linguist using the theory of language (being an endless accumulation of sentences and expressions)
generatywizm [ge-ne-rah-**ti**-veezm] m. theory of language as endless accumulation of sentences and expressions
generatywnie [ge-ne-rah-**tiv**-ńe] adv. generatively
generatywność [ge-ne-rah-**tiv**-nośhćh] f. generativeness
generatywny [ge-ne-rah-**tiv**-ni] adj.m. generative
komórka generatywna [ko-**moor**-kah ge-ne-rah-**tiv**-nah] exp.: generative cell
generować [ge-ne-**ro**-vahćh] v. generate (energy, etc.) (*repeatedly*)
generowanie [ge-ne-ro-**vah**-ńe] n. generation (of energy, etc.)
genetivus [ge-ne-**tee**-voos] m. genitive; possessive
genetycznie [ge-ne-**tich**-ńe] adv. genetically
genetyczny [ge-ne-**tich**-ni] adj.m. genetic
genetyk [ge-**ne**-tik] m. geneticist
genetyka [ge-**ne**-ti-kah] f. genetics
genetyzm [ge-**ne**-tizm] m. genetic explanation
geneza [ge-**ne**-zah] f. origin; genesis; birth; the beginning (of something)
genialnie [ge-**ńyahl**-ńe] adv. splendidly; brilliantly; magnificently
genialność [ge-**ńyahl**-nośhćh] f. brilliance; genius; greatness
genialny [ge-**ńyahl**-ni] adj.m. splendid; brilliant; genial; great

genina [ge-ńee-nah] f. aglucon
genitalia [ge-ńee-tah-lyah] pl. genitals; privy parts; external sexual organs
geniusz [ge-ńyoosh] m. genius; extraordinary creative intellectual or artistic talent
genologia [ge-no-lo-gyah] f. theory of literature
genom [ge-nom] m. genome
genomowy [ge-no-mo-vi] adj.m. genomic
gerundium [ge-roon-dyoom] n. gerund
genotyp [ge-no-tip] m. genotype
genotypowo [ge-no-ti-po-vo] adv. genotypically
genotypowy [ge-no-ti-po-vi] adj.m. genotypical; genotypic
genowy [ge-no-vi] adj.m. genic; gene (groups, etc.)
genre [zhahnr] m. indecl.: (French) genre; style; genre-painting
gentleman [dzhen-tel-men] m. (Engl.) gentleman
genua [ge-noo-ah] f. triangular Genoa sail; genoese jib
genueńczyk [ge-noo-eń-chik] m. (a) Genoese
genueński [ge-noo-eń-skee] adj.m. Genoese
geo- [ge-o] prefix: earth-; ground-; soil-
geoakustyka [ge-o-ah-koos-ti-kah] f. application of acoustics to geology
geoantyklina [ge-o-ahn-ti-klee-nah] f. mountain range generated by folding
geobiont [ge-o-byont] m. soil insect; mole
geobionty [ge-o-byon-ti] pl. soil organisms
geobotanicznie [ge-o-bo-tah-ńeech-ńe] adv. geobotanically
geobotaniczny [ge-o-bo-tah-ńeech-ni] adj.m. geobotanical; geobotanic
geobotanika [ge-o-bo-tah-ńee-kah] f. geobotany; phytogeography
geocentrycznie [ge-o-tsen-trich-ńe] adv. geocentrically
geocentryczny [ge-o-tsen-trich-ni] adj.m. geocentric
geocentryzm [ge-o-tsen-trizm] m. geocentric theory
geochemia [ge-o-khe-myah] f. geochemistry
geochemicznie [ge-o-khe-meech-ńe] adv. geochemically
geochemiczny [ge-o-khe-meech-ni] adj.m. geochemical
geochemik [ge-o-khe-meek] m. geochemist
geochronolog [ge-o-khro-no-log] m. geochronologist
geochronologia [ge-o-khro-no-lo-gyah] f. geochronology
geochronologicznie [ge-o-khro-no-lo-geech-ńe] adv. geochronologically
geochronologiczny [ge-o-khro-no-lo-geech-ni] adj.m. geochronological; geochronologic
geoda [ge-o-dah] f. geode
geodeta [ge-o-de-tah] m. geodesist
geodetycznie [ge-o-de-tich-ńe] adv. geodetically
geodetyczny [ge-o-de-tich-ni] adj.m. geodetical
geodetyka [ge-o-de-ti-kah] f. geodetical line
geodezja [ge-o-de-zyah] f. geodesy (grid of polygons); land-surveying
geodezyjnie [ge-o-de-ziy-ńe] adv. geodetically
geodezyjny [ge-o-de-ziy-ni] adj.m. geodetic; geodetical
geodimetr [ge-o-dee-metr] m. Geodimeter
geoenergetyczny [ge-o-e-ner-ge-tich-ni] adj.m. of the use of the thermal energy of the earth for power and heating
geoenergetyka [ge-o-e-ner-ge-ti-kah] f. the use of the thermal energy of the earth for power and heating
geofil [ge-o-feel] m. any of the animals and insects dwelling in the soil
geofile [ge-o-fee-le] pl. organisms dwelling in the soil
geofit [ge-o-feet] m. geophyte
geofity [ge-o-fee-ti] pl. geophyte perennial plant family
geofizycznie [ge-o-fee-zich-ńe] adv. geophysically
geofizyczny [ge-o-fee-zich-ni] adj.m.

geophysical
geofizyk [ge-o-**fee**-zik] m. geophysicist
geofizyka [ge-o-**fee**-zi-kah] f. geophysics
geofon [ge-**o**-fon] m. geophone
geograf [ge-**o**-grahf] m. geographer
geografia [ge-o-**grah**-fyah] f. geography; the physical traits
geograficznie [ge-o-grah-**feech**-ńe] adv. geographically
geograficzny [ge-o-grah-**feech**-ni] adj.m. geographic
geoida [ge-**oy**-dah] f. geoid
geolog [ge-**o**-log] m. geologist
geologia [ge-o-**lo**-gyah] f. geology
geologicznie [ge-o-lo-**geech**-ńe] adv. geologically
geologiczny [ge-o-lo-**geech**-ni] adj.m. geologic; geological
geomagnetycznie [ge-o-mahg-ne-**tich**-ńe] adv. geomagnetically
geomagnetyczny [ge-o-mahg-ne-**tich**-ni] adj.m. geomagnetic
geomagnetyzm [ge-o-mahg-**ne**-tizm] m. geomagnetism; terrestrial magnetism
geometra [ge-o-**met**-rah] m. surveyor; land surveyor
geometria [ge-o-**met**-ryah] f. geometry (of points, lines, etc.)
geometrycznie [ge-o-met-**rich**-ńe] adv. geometrically
geometryczność [ge-o-met-**rich**-nośhćh] f. geometric quality of shapes
geometryczny [ge-o-met-**rich**-ni] adj.m. geometric; geometrical
figura geometryczna [fee-**goo**-rah ge-o-met-**rich**-nah] exp.: geometrical figure
postęp geometryczny [**po**-stanp ge-o-met-**rich**-ni] exp.: geometric progression
geometryzacja [ge-o-me-tri-**zah**-tsyah] f. geometrizing
geometryzować [ge-o-me-tri-**zo**-vahćh] v. geometrize (*repeatedly*)
geometryzowanie [ge-o-me-tri-zo-**vah**-ńe] n. geometrizing
geomorfolog [ge-o-mor-**fo**-log] m. geomorphologist
geomorfologia [ge-o-mor-fo-**lo**-gyah] f. geomorphology
geomorfologicznie [ge-o-mor-fo-lo-**geech**-ńe] adv. geomorphologically
geomorfologiczny [ge-o-mor-fo-lo-**geech**-ni] adj.m. geomorphological
geonim [ge-**o**-ńeem] m. pseudonym derived from geographic name
geoplastycznie [ge-o-plahs-**tich**-ńe] adv. by means of a relief map
geoplastyczny [ge-o-plahs-**tich**-ni] adj.m. of a relief map
geoplastyk [ge-o-**plahs**-tik] m. maker of relief maps
geoplastyka [ge-o-**plahs**-ti-kah] f. making of relief maps
geopolitycznie [ge-o-po-lee-**tich**-ńe] adv. geopolitically
geopolityczny [ge-o-po-lee-**tich**-ni] adj.m. geopolitical
geopolityk [ge-o-po-**lee**-tik] m. geopolitician
geopolityka [ge-o-po-**lee**-ti-kah] f. geopolitics
geopotencjał [ge-o-po-**ten**-tsyahw] m. potential energy of air mass at a particular elevation
georgika [ge-**or**-gee-kah] f. georgics (poetry)
georginia [ge-or-**gee**-ńyah] f. dahlia
geosfera [ge-o-**sfe**-rah] f. one of the concentric spheres of the earth (atmosphere, etc.)
geosfery [ge-o-**sfe**-ri] pl. concentric spheres of the earth (atmosphere, etc.)
geosynklina [ge-o-sin-**klee**-nah] f. geosyncline
geosynklinalny [ge-o-sin-klee-**nahl**-ni] adj.m. geosynclinal
geotechniczny [ge-o-tekh-**ńeech**-ni] adj.m. of geology, mining, and geochemistry
geotechnologia [ge-o-tekh-no-**lo**-gyah] f. combined geology, mining, and geochemistry
geotermicznie [ge-o-ter-**meech**-ńe] adv. geothermally
geotermiczny [ge-o-ter-**meech**-ni] adj.m. geothermal; geothermic
geotropicznie [ge-o-tro-**peech**-ńe] adv. geotropically
geotropiczny [ge-o-tro-**peech**-ni] adj.m. geotropic
geotropizm [ge-o-**tro**-peezm] m.

geotropism
geotyp [go-**o**-tip] m. geographic variation of the same species
gepard [**ge**-pahrt] m. cheetah
geraniol [ge-**rah**-ńyol] m. geraniol
geraniowy [ge-rahń-**yo**-vi] adj.m. geraniol (fragrant unsaturated alcohol, perfume, soap, etc.)
geranium [ge-**rah**-ńyoom] n. geranium
gerbera [ger-**be**-rah] f. gerbera
gereza [ge-**re**-zah] f. variety of monkey (of Somali)
geriatra [ger-**yaht**-rah] m. geriatrician; geriatrist
geriatria [ger-**yah**-tryah] f. geriatrics
geriatryczny [ger-yaht-**rich**-ni] adj.m. geriatric
german [**ger**-mahn] m. germanium (atomic number 32)
germanista [ger-mah-**ńees**-tah] m. Germanist
germanistka [ger-mah-**ńeest**-kah] f. (woman) Germanist
germanistyczny [ger-mah-ńees-**tich**-ni] adj.m. of German philology
germanistyka [ger-mah-**ńees**-ti-kah] f. German philology
germanizacja [ger-mah-ńee-**zah**-tsyah] f. germanization
germanizacyjny [ger-mah-ńee-zah-**tsiy**-ni] adj.m. of germanization; germanizing (policy, etc.)
germanizator [ger-mah-ńee-**zah**-tor] m. germanizer
germanizatorski [ger-mah-ńee-zah-**tor**-skee] adj.m. germanizing (policy, etc.)
germanizm [ger-**mah**-ńeezm] m. Germanizm
germanizować [ger-mah-ńee-**zo**-vahćh] v. germanize (*repeatedly*)
germanizować się [ger-mah-ńee-**zo**-vahćh śhan] v. become germanized (*repeatedly*)
germanizowanie [ger-mah-ńee-zo-**vah**-ńe] n. germanizing
germanizowanie się [ger-mah-ńee-zo-**vah**-ńe śhan] n. becoming germanized
germanofil [ger-mah-**no**-feel] m. Germanophile
germanofilski [ger-mah-no-**feel**-skee] adj.m. Germanophile (tendency, etc.)
germanofilstwo [ger-mah-no-**feel**-stfo] n. Germanomania
germanofobia [ger-mah-no-**fo**-byah] f. Germanophobia
germanomania [ger-mah-no-**mah**-ńyah] f. Germanomania
germanowy [ger-mah-**no**-vi] adj.m. germanium (oxide, etc.)
germański [ger-**mahń**-skee] adj.m. Germanic (languages)
geront [**ge**-ront] m. gerontocrat
gerontofilia [ge-ron-to-**fee**-lyah] f. sexual attraction to older people; gerontophilia
gerontolog [ge-ron-**to**-log] m. gerontologist
gerontologia [ge-ron-to-**lo**-gyah] f. gerontology
gerontologiczny [ge-ron-to-lo-**geech**-ni] adj.m. gerontologic; gerontological
geruzja [ge-**roo**-zyah] f. gerusia
gerylas [ge-**ri**-lahs] m. Spanish guerrilla fighter
gerylasówka [ge-ri-lah-**soof**-kah] f. guerrilla war
ges [ges] m. G flat (in music)
gest [gest] m. gesture; motion; action; gesticulation
mieć gest [myećh gest] exp.: to do the handsome thing
gestaltyzm [ge-**stahl**-tizm] m. Gestalt psychology
gestapo [ge-**stah**-po] n. Gestapo
gestapowiec [ge-stah-**po**-vyets] m. Gestapo agent
gestapowski [ge-stah-**pof**-skee] adj.m. of the Gestapo
gestia [**gest**-yah] f. gestion; management; conduct
gestor [**ges**-tor] m. manager
gestykulacja [ges-ti-koo-**lah**-tsyah] f. gesticulation
gestykulować [ges-ti-koo-**lo**-vahćh] v. gesticulate (*repeatedly*)
gestykulowanie [ges-ti-koo-lo-**vah**-ńe] n. gesticulation
geszefciarski [ge-shef-**ćhahr**-skee] adj.m. speculating; profiteering; shady (deal, etc.)
geszefciarstwo [ge-shef-**ćhahr**-stfo] n. speculating; speculations; profiteering; shady dealings

geszefciarz [ge-**shef**-ćhahsh] m. spiv; profiteer; speculator; shady jobber; duffer
geszeft [**ge**-sheft] m. speculation; shady deal; business
geścik [**geśh**-ćheek] m. (nice, little) gesture
getr [getr] m. gaiter; spat
w getrach [v **get**-rahkh] exp.: gaitered
getto [**get**-to] n. ghetto
getyt [**ge**-tit] m. xanthosiderite
geza [**ge**-zah] f. porous sedimentary rock used for electrical and thermal insulation
gę, gę [gan gan] (sound imitating gaggle)
gęba [**gan**-bah] f. mug; mouth; puss; snout; muzzle; face; gob
gębować [gan-**bo**-vahćh] v. swear at; be saucy; bawl (*repeatedly*)
gębowanie [gan-bo-**vah**-ńe] n. swearing; being saucy; bawling
gębowy [gan-**bo**-vi] adj.m. of mouth
gębula [gan-**boo**-lah] f. (litte) mouth; face (diminutive: **gęba**)
gębusia [gan-**boo**-śhah] f. (very small) face (diminutive: **gęba**)
gęg [gang] m. gaggle
gęgać [**gan**-gahćh] v. cackle; gaggle (of geese); gabble (of men) (*repeatedly*)
gęgała [gan-**gah**-wah] m. mumbler
gęganie [gan-**gah**-ńe] n. (a) gaggle
gęgawa [gan-**gah**-vah] f. variety of goose
gęgnąć [**gang**-nownćh] v. cackle; gaggle (of geese); gabble (of men)
gęgnięcie [gang-**ńan**-ćhe] n. (a) cackle; (a) gaggle
gęgot [**gan**-got] m. cackle; gaggle (of geese)
gęsi [**gan**-śhee] adj.m. of a goose; of geese; goose's (grease, etc.)
gęsiarek [gan-**śhah**-rek] m. gooseherd
gęsiarka [gan-**śhahr**-kah] f. (girl) gooseherd
gęsina [gan-**śhee**-nah] f. goose meat
gęsior [**gan**-śhor] m. gander; demijohn (bottle)
gęsiorek [gan-**śho**-rek] m. demijohn (bottle); carboy
gęsiówka [gan-**śhoof**-kah] f. wall cress
gęstawo [gan-**stah**-vo] adv. in a rather thick way
gęstawy [gan-**stah**-vi] adj.m. thickish; rather thick
gęstnąć [**ganst**-nownćh] v. thicken; become thick; become dense (*repeatedly*)
gęstnieć [**ganst**-ńećh] v. thicken; become thick; become dense (*repeatedly*)
gęstnienie [ganst-**ńe**-ńe] n. thickening
gęsto [**gan**-sto] adv. thick; thickly; compactly; densely
gęstopłynny [gan-sto-**pwin**-ni] adj.m. thick; viscous
gęstościomierz [gan-stośh-**ćho**-myesh] m. densimeter; aerometer; hydrometer
gęstość [**gan**-stośhćh] f. density; thickness; closeness
gęstowłosy [gan-sto-**vwo**-si] adj.m. thick-haired
gęstwa [**ganst**-fah] f. thicket; array; accumulation
gęstwina [ganst-**fee**-nah] f. thicket; array; accumulation
gęsty [**gan**-sti] adj.m. thick; close; compact; viscid; dense
gęsta mina [**gan**-stah **mee**-nah] exp.: self-confident air; rakish air
gęś [ganśh] f. goose
dzika gęś [**dźhee**-kah ganśh] exp.: wild goose
szara gęś [**shah**-rah ganśh] exp.: graylag
gęślarz [**ganśh**-lahsh] m. wandering singer playing on a primitive fiddle
gęśle [**ganśh**-le] pl. primitive fiddle (hist.)
gęśnik [**ganśh**-ńeek] m. goose shed
giaur [gyahwr] m. giaour; infidel
giąć [gyownćh] v. bow; bend; curve; incline (*repeatedly*)
giąć się [gyownćh śhan] v. bow; bend; be curved; incline; be bent (*repeatedly*)
giberelina [gee-be-re-**lee**-nah] f. gibberellin; plant-growth regulator

gibereliny [gee-be-re-lee-ni] pl. gibberellin fungi; plant-growth regulators
giberelinowy [gee-be-re-lee-no-vi] adj.m. gibberellic (acid, etc.)
gibki [gee-pkee] adj.m. pliant; flexible; limber; supple; nimble
gibko [gee-pko] adv. flexibly; nimbly; supply
gibkość [gee-pkośhćh] f. flexibility; litheness; nimbleness; suppleness
gibon [gee-bon] m. gibbon
gibony [gee-bo-ni] pl. the family of gibbons (tailless apes)
gibonowate [gee-bo-no-vah-te] pl. the family of gibbons
gicz [geech] m. part of the shank of a steer
giczoł [gee-chow] m. colloq: shank; pin; trotter; stump; trilby (soft felt hat); leg
gid [geet] m. escorting guide; scout
gidia [gee-dyah] f. colloq: weed; lanky and weakly person
gidran [gee-drahn] m. half-blood Anglo-Arabian horse
giełda [gew-dah] f. stock exchange; money market
giełdowy [gew-do-vi] adj.m. of stock exchange; of money market
agent giełdowy [ah-gent gew-do-vi] exp.: stockbroker
spekulant giełdowy [spe-koo-lahnt gew-do-vi] exp.: stockjobber
giełdziarski [gew-dźhahr-skee] adj.m. of stock exchange; of money market
giełdziarz [gew-dźhash] m. stock exchange speculator; stock market trader
giemza [gem-zah] f. chamois; chamois leather
giemzowy [gem-zo-vi] adj.m. of chamois; of chammy leather
gierka [ger-kah] f. small game; little sham; little play
gierlsa [gerl-sah] f. slang: chorus girl
giermek [ger-mek] m. henchman; bishop (in chess)
giez [ges] m. gadfly; breeze
giezło [gez-wo] n. woman's long shirt (also used as a shroud)
gięcie [gan-ćhe] n. flexing; bending
gięcie się [gan-ćhe śhan] n. bowing; being bent
giętarka [gan-tahr-kah] f. bending machine
giętki [gant-kee] adj.m. flexible; nimble; elastic; adaptable
giętko [gant-ko] adv. flexibly; nimbly; elastically; supply
giętkość [gant-kośhćh] f. flexibility; nimbleness; elasticity; pliability; docility; ductility; adaptability; versatility
gig [geeg] m. gig (boat); gig (one-horse carriage)
giga [gee-gah] f. jig (early violin, quick dance, dance music)
giga- [gee-gah] prefix: billion-; 1,000,000,000
gigabajt [gee-gah-bahyt] m. gigabyte; 1,000,000,000 bytes
gigabit [gee-gah-beet] m. gigabit; a unit of information of 1,000,000,000 bits
gigaherc [gee-gah-herts] m. gigahertz; 1,000,000,000 hertz
gigakaloria [gee-gah-kah-lo-ryah] f. 1,000,000,000 calories
gigametr [gee-gah-metr] m. 1,000,000,000 meters
gigant [gee-gahnt] m. giant
gigantofon [gee-ghan-to-fon] m. giant loudspeaker
gigantomachia [gee-gahn-to-mahkh-yah] f. gigantomachia; straggle of giants with Greek gods
gigantomania [gee-gahn-to-mah-ńyah] f. mania to build gigantesque projects (especially in the Communists countries)
gigantomański [gee-gahn-to-mahń-skee] adj.m. of a mania to build gigantesque projects
gigantopitek [gee-gahn-to-pee-tek] m. gigantopithecus
gigantostrak [gee-gahn-to-strahk] m. gigantostarcan
gigantozaur [gee-gahn-to-zahwr] m. gigantosaurus
gigantycznie [gee-gahn-tich-ńe] adv. gigantically
gigantyczność [gee-gahn-tich-nośhćh] f. gigantism
gigantyczny [gee-gahn-tich-ni] adj.m. gigantic; huge

gigantyzm [gee-**gahn**-tizm] m. gigantism; giantism
gigawat [**gee**-gah-vaht] m. gigawatt; 1,000,000,000 watts
gigolo [**zhee**-go-lo] m. gigolo; man supported by a woman; male escort; professional dancing partner; fancy man
gik [geek] m. boom
gil [geel] m. bullfinch
gilbert [**geel**-bert] m. gilbert; unit of magnetomotive force
gildia [**geel**-dyah] f. guild; gild
gildyjny [geel-**diy**-ni] adj.m. guild (certificate, etc.)
gilosz [**gee**-losh] m. checkering tool; pattern of lines on banknotes (used to impede forgery); guilloche
giloszować [gee-lo-**sho**-vahćh] v. adorn with guilloches (*repeatedly*)
giloszowanie [gee-lo-sho-**vah**-ńe] n. decorating with guilloches
gilotyna [gee-lo-**ti**-nah] f. guillotine
gilotyniarz [gee-lo-**ti**-ńahsh] m. worker operating an industrial guillotine (cutting machine)
gilotynka [gee-lo-**tin**-kah] f. small guillotine; printer's guillotine; cigar-cutter
gilotynować [gee-lo-ti-**no**-vahćh] v. behead; cut off (*repeatedly*)
gilotynowanie [gee-lo-ti-no-**vah**-ńe] n. beheading; cutting off
gilotynowy [gee-lo-ti-**no**-vi] adj.m. of a guillotine; guillotine (knife, execution, etc.)
gilowy [gee-**lo**-vi] adj.m. of a bullfinch
gilza [**geel**-zah] f. (cartridge) case; cartridge shell; cigarette tube
gimnasta [geem-**nahs**-tah] m. ancient judge of athletic events
gimnastyczka [geem-nah-**stich**-kah] f. woman gymnast; athlete
gimnastyczny [geem-nah-**stich**-ni] adj.m. gymnastic; athletic
gimnastyk [geem-**nahs**-tik] m. gymnast
gimnastyka [geem-nahs-**ti**-kah] f. gymnastics; athletics
gimnastykować [geem-nahs-ti-**ko**-vahćh] v. exercise; train; drill (*repeatedly*)
gimnastykować się [geem-nahs-ti-**ko**-vahćh śhan] v. take exercise; train (*repeatedly*)
gimnastykowanie [geem-nahs-ti-ko-**vah**-ńe] n. exercising; training; drilling
gimnastykowanie się [geem-nahs-ti-ko-**vah**-ńe śhan] n. making physical exercises
gimnazjalista [geem-nah-zyah-**lees**-tah] m. high-school student
gimnazjalistka [geem-nah-zyah-**leest**-kah] f. (girl) high-school student
gimnazjalny [geem-nah-**zyahl**-ni] adj.m. high-school (diploma, curriculum, etc.)
gimnazjon [geem-**nah**-zyon] m. gymnasium; gym (in old Greece)
gimnazjum [geem-**nah**-zyoom] n. high school; middle school
gimniczny [geem-**ńeech**-ni] adj.m. of Greek track-and-field events
gin [dzheen] m. gin
ginąć [**gee**-nownćh] v. perish; die; fall; die out; vanish; fade out of sight; disappear; die away; be lost; go astray (*repeatedly*)
  ginąć powoli [**gee**-nownćh po-**vo**-lee] exp.: to waste away
  ginąć w oczach [**gee**-nownćh v o-chahkh] exp.: to be sinking fast
gineceum [gee-ne-**tse**-oom] n. women's quarters in ancient Greece; gynaeceum
ginekolog [gee-ne-**ko**-lok] m. gynecologist
ginekologia [gee-ne-ko-**lo**-gyah] f. gynecology
ginekologiczny [gee-ne-ko-lo-**gee**-chni] adj.m. gynecological
ginięcie [gee-**ńan**-ćhe] n. perishing; dying; falling; dying out; vanishing; fading out of sight; disappearing
gipiura [gee-**pyoo**-rah] f. guipure
gips [geeps] m. gypsum; plaster; plaster cast; plaster figure
gipsatura [geep-sah-**too**-rah] f. plaster decorations
gipsaturowy [geep-sah-too-**ro**-vi] adj.m. of plaster decorations
gipsobeton [geep-so-**be**-ton] m. cement-gipsum concrete
gipsoryt [geep-**so**-rit] m. engraving

made using gipsum plates
gipsoteka [geep-so-**te**-kah] f. collection of plaster reproductions of antique sculptures
gipsiarz [**geep**-śhahsh] m. plasterer
gipsować [gee-**pso**-vahćh] v. plaster (*repeatedly*)
gipsowanie [gee-pso-**vah**-ńe] n. plastering
gipsowy [gee-**pso**-vi] adj.m. of plaster; of gypsum; plaster
gira [**gee**-rah] f. vulg.: leg
girl [gerl] f. (Engl.) slang: girl; girl from demimonde (mob jargon)
girlanda [geer-**lahn**-dah] f. garland; festoon wreath
girlaska [ger-**lahs**-kah] f. chorus girl
girlsa [**gerl**-sah] f. chorus girl
giro- [**zhi**-ro] prefix: gyro-
girobus [zhi-**ro**-boos] m. bus operated with a fly-wheel engine
girobusola [zhi-ro-boo-**so**-lah] f. gyrocompass
giroklinometr [zhi-ro-klee-**no**-metr] m. gyro-clinometer
girokompas [zhi-ro-**kom**-pahs] m. gyrocompass
giroskop [zhi-**ro**-skop] m. gyroscope
giroskopowo [zhi-ro-sko-**po**-vo] adv. gyroscopically
giroskopowy [zhi-ro-sko-**po**-vi] adj.m. gyroscopic
girostat [zhi-**ro**-staht] m. gyrostat; gyrostabilizer
girotron [zhi-**ro**-tron] m. device for measuring angular velocity
gis [gees] m. G sharp (in music)
giser [**gee**-ser] m. molder; foundry worker; foundry specialist
gisernia [gee-**ser**-ńah] f. foundry
giserski [gee-**ser**-skee] adj.m. of foundry; foundry
giserstwo [gee-**ser**-stfo] n. molders work; foundry work
git [geet] adj.m. slang: okay; good
gitana [gee-**tah**-nah] f. Gitana (Spanish dance)
gitara [gee-**tah**-rah] f. guitar
zawracać gitarę [zah-**vrah**-tsahćh gee-**tah**-ran] exp.: slang: to brag; to bore; to bother; to make nuisance of oneself
gitarowy [gee-tah-**ro**-vi] adj.m. of guitar; of guitars; guitarist's
gitarzysta [gee-tah-**zhis**-tah] m. guitarist
gitarzystka [gee-tah-**zhist**-kah] f. (woman) guitarist
gitowiec [gee-**to**-vyets] m. colloq: member of gang subculture
glaca [**glah**-tsah] f. slang: head; skull; baldheaded man
glacjalny [glah-**tsyahl**-ni] adj.m. glacial
glacjał [**glah**-tsyahw] m. glacial period
glacjolog [glah-**tsyo**-log] m. glaciologist
glacjologia [glah-tsyo-**lo**-gyah] f. glaciology
glacjologiczny [glah-tsyo-lo-**geech**-ni] adj.m. glaciologic; glaciological
gladiator [glah-**dyah**-tor] m. gladiator; prizefighter
gladiatorski [glah-dyah-**tor**-skee] adj.m. gladiatorial
gladiolus [glahd-**yo**-loos] m. gladiolus
glancować [glahn-**tso**-vahćh] v. colloq: polish; gloss; shine (brass, shoes, etc.); luster (*repeatedly*)
na glanc [nah glahnts] exp.: polished (shoes, etc.)
glancowanie [glahn-tso-**vah**-ńe] n. polishing; shining
glanek [**glah**-nek] m. rand (strip)
glans [glahns] m. shine; luster
glansować [glahn-**so**-vahćh] v. polish; gloss; shine (*repeatedly*)
glansowanie [glahn-so-**vah**-ńe] n. polishing; shining
glansowany [glahn-so-**vah**-ni] adj.m. glossy; shiny; glace
glaspapier [glahs-**pah**-pyer] m. glass-paper
glauberski [glahw-**ber**-skee] adj.m. Glauber's (salt, etc.)
glauberyt [glahw-**be**-rit] m. Glauber's compound
glaukofan [glahw-**ko**-fahn] m. Silesian amphibole (mineral)
glaukoma [glahw-**ko**-mah] f. glaucoma
glaukonit [glahw-**ko**-ńeet] m. glauconite
glaukonitowy [glahw-ko-ńee-**to**-vi] adj.m. glauconitic
glaukonityt [glahw-ko-**ńee**-tit] m.

glauconitic rock
glazgal [**glahz**-gahl] m. sandiver; glass gall
glazura [glah-**zoo**-rah] f. glaze; glazing; varnish; icing; frosting
glazurnik [glah-**zoor**-ńeek] m. glazed tile installer
glazurować [glah-zoo-**ro**-vahćh] v. glaze; varnish; enamel; ice; frost (*repeatedly*)
glazurowanie [glah-zoo-ro-**vah**-ńe] n. glazing; varnishing; enameling; icing; frosting
gleba [**gle**-bah] f. soil
glebogryzarka [gle-bo-gri-**zahr**-kah] f. combined plow, cultivator and harrow
glebostan [gle-**bo**-stahn] m. natural features of the soil
glebotwórczy [gle-bo-**tfoor**-chi] adj.m. top soil producing (process, etc.)
glebowy [gle-**bo**-vi] adj.m. soil (specialist, etc.)
gleboznawca [gle-bo-**znahf**-tsah] m. soil specialist
gleboznawczy [gle-bo-**znahf**-chi] adj.m. soil-science (program, etc.)
gleboznawstwo [gle-bo-**znahf**-stfo] n. science of the soil
gleczer [**gle**-cher] m. glacial
glediczia [gle-**dee**-chyah] f. honey locust
glej [gley] m. gley (clay); neuron base
glejak [**gle**-yahk] m. variety of brain tumor
glejowy [gle-**yo**-vi] adj.m. gley (strata of the ground, etc.)
glejt [gleyt] m. safe-conduct; mob slang: money; currency; cash
glejta [**gley**-tah] f. litharge (lead oxide)
ględa [**gl<u>an</u>**-dah] f. colloq: bore; tiresome fellow
ględy [**gl<u>an</u>**-di] pl. colloq: bosh; twaddle
ględzenie [gl<u>an</u>-**dze**-ńe] n. talking through one's hat; talking nonsense; twaddling
ględzić [**gl<u>an</u>**-dźheećh] v. talk through one's hat; talk nonsense; twaddle; blather; prate (*repeatedly*)

glicerofosfat [glee-tse-ro-**fos**-faht] m. glycerophosphate
glicerol [glee-**tse**-rol] m. glycerol; glycerin
gliceryd [glee-**tse**-rit] m. glyceride
glicerydy [glee-tse-**ri**-di] pl. glicerides; main components of natural fats
gliceryna [glee-tse-**ri**-nah] f. glycerin; glycerine
glicerynować [glee-tse-ri-**no**-vahćh] v. glycerinate (*repeatedly*)
glicerynowanie [glee-tse-ri-no-**vah**-ńe] n. glycerination
glicerynowy [glee-tse-ri-**no**-vi] adj.m. glyceric (acid, etc.); glyceridic
glicyna [glee-**tsi**-nah] f. glycine
glicynia [glee-**tsi**-ńah] f. Wisteria; Wistaria (plant)
glif [gleef] m. splay; reveal; embrasure
glikogen [glee-**ko**-gen] m. glycogen
glikogenowy [glee-ko-ge-**no**-vi] adj.m. glycogenetic
glikol [**glee**-kol] m. glycol
glikoproteid [glee-ko-pro-**te**-eet] m. glycoprotein
glikoproteidy [glee-ko-pro-te-**ee**-di] pl. glycoproteins
glikoza [glee-**ko**-zah] f. glucose; dextrose; grape sugar
glikozyd [glee-**ko**-zit] m. glycoside
glikozydowo [glee-ko-zi-**do**-vo] adv. glycosidically
glikozydowy [glee-ko-zi-**do**-vi] adj.m. glycosidic
glin [gleen] m. aluminum
glina [**glee**-nah] f. clay; loam; slang: vulg.: shit; cop (mob jargon)
glina garncarska [**glee**-nah gahrn-**tsahr**-skah] exp.: argil; potter's clay
glina ogniotrwała [**glee**-nah o-gńo-**trfah**-wah] exp.: fire clay
kopać glinę [**ko**-pahćh **glee**-n<u>an</u>] exp.: vulg. mob slang: to have homosexual (anal) intercourse
gliniak [**glee**-ńahk] m. pot of earthenware
glinian [**glee**-ńahn] m. aluminate
gliniany [glee-**ńah**-ni] pl. aluminate compounds
glinianka [glee-**ńahn**-kah] f. clay pit; piece of earthenware

gliniankowy [glee-ńahn-**ko**-vi] adj.m. of clay pit
gliniany [glee-**ńah**-ni] adj.m. of clay; of earthenware; clay (pipe, etc.)
gliniarz [**glee**-ńahsh] m. mob slang: cop; policeman; gay; homosexual
gliniasty [glee-**ńahs**-ti] adj.m. clayey; argillaceous; loamy
gliniec [**glee**-ńets] m. gravelite; lightweight concrete aggregate
glinka [**gleen**-kah] f. clay; white bole; alumina
glinkarz [**gleen**-kahsh] m. clay digger; potter
glinkowaty [gleen-ko-**vah**-ti] adj.m. argillaceous
glinokrzemian [glee-no-**kshe**-myahn] m. aluminosilicate; pimelite
glinokrzemiany [glee-no-kshe-**myah**-ni] pl. aluminosilicates; pimelites
glinować [glee-**no**-vahćh] v. cover with aluminum (*repeatedly*)
glinowanie [glee-no-**vah**-ńe] n. covering with aluminum
glinowiec [glee-**no**-vyets] m. one of the elements of boron group
glinowce [glee-**nof**-tse] pl. boron group elements
glinowy [glee-**no**-vi] adj.m. aluminum (earth, etc.)
glipoteka [glee-po-**te**-kah] f. collection of gems and works of sculpture
gliptal [**gleep**-tahl] m. variety of polyester resin
gliptalowy [gleep-tah-**lo**-vi] adj.m. of polyester resin
gliptodont [gleep-**to**-dont] m. glypodont (extinct mammal)
gliptoteka [gleep-to-**te**-kah] f. collection of cut gems
gliptyka [**gleep**-ti-kah] f. glyptic art; art of engraving gems
glissando [glees-**sahn**-do] n. glissando; glide; slur
glissandowy [glees-sahn-**do**-vi] adj.m. of glissando; gliding; slurry
glista [**glees**-tah] f. earthworm; worm; ascaris; nematode
glistnica [gleest-**ńee**-tsah] f. ascaridiasis; nematodiasis
glistnik [**glist**-ńeek] m. celandine
gliwieć [**glee**-vyećh] v. go moldy; mildew; ferment (*repeatedly*)
gliwienie [glee-**vye**-ńe] n. mildewing; becoming mildewed
glob [glop] m. globe; sphere
globalnie [glo-**bahl**-ńe] adv. totally; globally; in the aggregate; in bulk; in the lump
globalny [glo-**bahl**-ni] adj.m. total; global; aggregate
globigeryna [glo-bee-ge-**ri**-nah] f. Globigerina
globigerynowy [glo-bee-ge-ri-**no**-vi] adj.m. globigerine (ooze, etc.)
globina [glo-**bee**-nah] f. globin
globtroter [glop-**tro**-ter] m. globetrotter
globtroterski [glop-tro-**ter**-skee] adj.m. globetrotter's
globtroterstwo [glop-tro-**ter**-stfo] n. globetrotting
globula [glo-**boo**-lah] f. globule
globularnie [glo-boo-**lahr**-ńe] adv. globularly
globularność [glo-boo-**lahr**-nośhćh] f. globularness
globularny [glo-boo-**lahr**-ni] adj.m. globular
globulina [glo-boo-**lee**-nah] f. globulin (simple protein)
globuliny [glo-boo-**lee**-ni] pl. globulins (myosins, etc.)
globulka [glo-**bool**-kah] f. globule
globus [**glo**-boos] m. globe; sphere; slang: head; skull (mob jargon)
globusik [glo-**boo**-śheek] m. small globe; model of the earth
glogierówka [glo-g̲e-**roof**-kah] f. variety of apple
gloksynia [glo-**ksi**-ńah] f. gloxinia
glon [glon] m. alga; colloq: chunk; slice (of bread, etc.)
glony [**glo**-ni] pl. algae
glonowiec [glo-**no**-vyets] m. Phycomycete fungus
glonowce [glo-**nof**-tse] pl. Phycomycetes
glonowy [glo-**no**-vi] adj.m. algal; algoid
gloria [**glo**-ryah] f. glory; aureola; nimbus
glorieta [glo-**rye**-tah] f. gloriette; pavilion
gloryfikacja [glo-ri-fee-**kah**-tsyah] f. glorification

gloryfikacyjny [glo-ri-fee-kah-**tsiy**-ni] adj.m. of glorification
gloryfikator [glo-ri-fee-**kah**-tor] m. glorifier
gloryfikatorka [glo-ri-fee-kah-**tor**-kah] f. (woman) glorifier
gloryfikować [glo-ri-fee-**ko**-vahćh] v. glorify (*repeatedly*)
gloryfikowanie [glo-ri-fee-ko-**vah**-ńe] n. glorification
glosa [**glo**-sah] f. gloss
glosarium [glo-**sahr**-yoom] n. glossary
glosariusz [glo-**sahr**-yoosh] m. glossary; dictionary
glosator [glo-**sah**-tor] m. glossator; glossarist
glosatorka [glo-sah-**tor**-kah] f. (woman) glossator; glossarist
glosograf [glo-**so**-grahf] m. glossographer; glossarist
glosografia [glo-so-**grah**-fyah] f. glossography
glosolalia [glo-so-**lah**-lyah] f. glossolalia; unintelligible utterance
glosować [glo-**so**-vahćh] v. gloss (*repeatedly*)
glossematyka [glos-se-**mah**-ti-kah] f. theory of language (sound and meaning)
glottogeneza [glot-to-ge-**ne**-zah] f. theory of the origin of speech
glottogonia [glot-to-**go**-ńyah] f. theory of the origin of speech
glukoza [gloo-**ko**-zah] f. glucose; dextrose; grape sugar
glukozyd [gloo-**ko**-zit] m. glycoside
glukozydowo [gloo-ko-zi-**do**-vo] adv. glycosidically
glukozydowy [gloo-ko-zi-**do**-vi] adj.m. glycosidic
glut [gloot] m. snot; nasal mucus; muck from the nose
glutamina [gloo-tah-**mee**-nah] f. glutamine
glutaminian [gloo-tah-**mee**-ńyahn] m. monosodium glutamate
glutaminizacja [gloo-tah-mee-ńee-**zah**-tsyah] f. flavor stabilization with glutamine
glutaminowy [gloo-tah-mee-**no**-vi] adj.m. glutamic (acid, etc.); glutaminic
gluten [**gloo**-ten] m. gluten
glutenowy [gloo-te-**no**-vi] adj.m. glutenous; gluten (bread, etc.)
glutyna [gloo-**ti**-nah] f. gluten; glue
glyptodont [glip-**to**-dont] m. glyptodont
gładki [**gwaht**-kee] adj.m. plain; smooth; sleek; even; level; glib; straight; lank; fluent
gładko [**gwaht**-ko] adv. smoothly; evenly; level; fluently; glibly
gładkość [**gwaht**-kośhćh] f. smoothness; evenness; level surface; sleekness; polish
gładkowłosy [gwaht-ko-**vwo**-si] adj.m. smooth-haired (dog, etc.)
gładszy [**gwaht**-shi] adj.m. smoother; sleeker; straighter
gładysz [**gwah**-dish] m. dude
gładzak [**gwah**-dzahk] m. reaming tool
gładzarka [gwah-**dzahr**-kah] f. drilled hole polishing machine
gładzenie [gwah-**dze**-ńe] n. polishing
gładzenie się [gwah-**dze**-ńe śhan] n. polishing oneself
gładziarka [gwah-**dźhahr**-kah] f. reaming machine
gładzica [gwah-**dźhee**-tsah] f. large smooth-skin flounder; scraper (tool)
gładzić [**gwah**-dźheećh] v. level; smooth; sleek; put to death; mangle; stroke; press (*repeatedly*)
gładzić się [**gwah**-dźheećh śhan] v. stroke oneself; smooth one's hair (*repeatedly*)
gładzik [**gwah**-dźheek] m. calender; polisher; smooth file; smoothing-plane
gładziuteńki [gwah-dźhoo-**teń**-kee] adj.m. very nice and smooth
gładziuteńko [gwah-dźhoo-**teń**-ko] adv. very nicely and smoothly
gładziutki [gwah-**dźhoot**-kee] adj.m. nice and smooth
gładziutko [gwah-**dźhoot**-ko] adv. nicely and smoothly
gładzizna [gwah-**dźheez**-nah] f. smooth surface; sliding surface
gładź [gwahćh] f. smooth surface; sliding surface; finishing coat; setting coat (of plaster)
głagolica [gwah-go-**lee**-tsah] f.

Glagolitsa; Glagolic (Slavic) alphabet (of St. Cyril)
głagolicki [gwah-go-**leets**-kee] adj.m. Glagolitic; Glagolic
głaskać [**gwahs**-kahćh] v. caress; fondle; stroke; pet; tickle (*repeatedly*)
głaskać się [**gwahs**-kahćh śhan] v. stroke (one's cheek, etc.) (*repeatedly*)
głaskanie [gwahs-**kah**-ńe] n. caressing; fondling
głaskanie się [gwahs-**kah**-ńe śhan] n. caressing oneself
głasnąć [**gwahs**-nownćh] v. caress; fondle; stroke; pet; tickle
głasnąć się [**gwahs**-nownćh śhan] v. stroke (one's cheek, etc.)
głaszczka [**gwahshch**-kah] f. palpus; palp
głaśnięcie [gwahśh-**ńan**-ćhe] n. caressing; fondling
głaśnięcie się [gwahśh-**ńan**-ćhe śhan] n. caressing oneself
głaz [gwahs] m. boulder; rock
głąb [gwownp] f. depth; abyss
w głąb czegoś [v gwownp **che**-gośh] exp.: deep into something
w głąb sceny [v gwownp **stse**-ni] exp.: upstage
w głąb kraju [v gwownp **krah**-yoo] exp.: upcountry
głąb [gwownp] m. stump; stalk; colloq: fool; bad student
głąbiasty [gwown-**byahs**-ti] adj.m. having large stump (stalk)
głąbik [**gwown**-beek] m. scape; variety of lettuce
głębia [**gwan**-byah] f. depth; deep; interior; intensity; keenness; profundity
głębić [**gwan**-beećh] v. dig; sink (a shaft, etc.) (*repeatedly*)
głębiel [**gwan**-byel] f. vendace (a white fish)
głębienie [gwan-**bye**-ńe] n. digging; sinking (a shaft, etc.)
głębina [gwan-**bee**-nah] f. depth; abyss
głębinowy [gwan-bee-**no**-vi] adj.m. deepwater (navigation, etc.); deep-sea (fishing, fish, etc.)
głęboki [gwan-**bo**-kee] adj.m. deep; distant; remote; intense
głęboko [gwan-**bo**-ko] adv. deep; deep down; deep into; deep inside; profoundly; deeply; intensely
głęboko odetchnąć [gwan-**bo**-ko o-**de**-tkhnownćh] exp.: to breathe deep
głęboko spać [gwan-**bo**-ko spahćh] exp.: to sleep soundly
głębokomorski [gwan-bo-ko-**mor**-skee] adj.m. deep-sea (fishing, etc.)
głębokościomierz [gwan-bo-ko-**śhćho**-myesh] m. depth gauge
głębokość [gwan-**bo**-kośhćh] f. depth; profundity; keenness
na głębokość [nah gwan-**bo**-kośhćh] exp.: in depth
do głębokości [do gwan-bo-**ko**-śhćhee] exp.: to a depth
głębokowodny [gwan-bo-ko-**vod**-ni] adj.m. deepwater (fish, etc.)
głębszy [**gwanp**-shi] adj.m. deeper; m. colloq: large glass of liquor; double shot of vodka
głodek [**gwo**-dek] m. slight feeling of hunger; whitlow grass
głodnieć [**gwod**-ńećh] v. get hungry; begin feeling the pangs of hunger (*repeatedly*)
głodnienie [gwod-**ńe**-ńe] n. getting hungry
głodno [**gwod**-no] adv. without (enough) food; with an empty stomach; hungrily
na głodno [nah **gwod**-no] exp.: without having had a bite to eat; on an empty stomach
głodny [**gwod**-ni] adj.m. hungry; starving; avid; greedy; meager; m. hungry person
na głodnego [nah gwod-**ne**-go] exp.: without having had a bite to eat; on an empty stomach
głodomorek [gwo-do-**mo**-rek] m. little starveling
głodomór [gwo-**do**-moor] m. starveling
głodować [gwo-**do**-vahćh] v. starve; hunger; lay off food; famish (*repeatedly*)
głodowanie [gwo-do-**vah**-ńe] n. starvation; hunger; famine
głodowy [gwo-**do**-vi] adj.m. of

starvation; of hunger; of famine; starvation (diet, etc.); beggarly (wage, etc.); hunger (years, rations, etc.)
strajk głodowy [strahyk gwo-**do**-vi] exp.: hunger strike
głodówka [gwo-**doof**-kah] f. hunger strike; hungry days; hungry years; starvation diet; hunger-cure
głodzenie [gwo-**dze**-ńe] n. starvation; malnutrition
głodzenie się [gwo-**dze**-ńe śhan] n. starving oneself
głodzić [**gwo**-dźheećh] v. deprive (of food); starve (someone); underfeed (*repeatedly*)
głodzić się [**gwo**-dźheećh śhan] v. deprive oneself of food; starve oneself; underfeed oneself (*repeatedly*)
głogowiec [gwo-**go**-vyets] m. black-veined white
głogowy [gwo-**go**-vi] adj.m. of hawthorn; hawthorn (wine, etc.)
głos [gwos] m. voice; sound; tone; toot; vote; opinion; comment; utterance; part (singing); musical strains
głos sprzeciwu [gwos spshe-**ćhee**-voo] exp.: dissenting voice
szybkość głosu [**ship**-kośhćh **gwo**-soo] exp.: speed of sound (340 meters per second)
udzielić komuś głosu [oo-**dźhe**-leećh **ko**-moośh **gwo**-soo] exp.: to allow somebody to speak
zabrać głos [zah-brahćh gwos] exp.: to rise to speak
wstrzymać się od głosu [fstshi-mahćh śhan od **gwo**-soo] exp.: to abstain
głosiciel [gwo-**śhee**-ćhel] m. spokesman; champion; advocate; protagonist
głosicielka [gwo-śhee-**ćhel**-kah] f. spokeswoman; (woman) champion; advocate; protagonist
głosić [**gwo**-śheećh] v. proclaim; announce; make known; spread abroad; propagate; preach (*repeatedly*)
głosik [**gwo**-śheek] m. (nice, little) voice
głoska [**gwos**-kah] f. speech sound; phone; letter; character
głoskowiec [gwos-**ko**-vyets] m. abbreviation; shortening
głoskowy [gwos-**ko**-vi] adj.m. of speech sound; of a letter
głosować [gwo-**so**-vahćh] v. vote (for, against); cast one's vote; go to the polls (*repeatedly*)
głosowanie [gwo-so-**vah**-ńe] n. voting (on, in); election; vote
głosownia [gwo-**sov**-ńah] f. phonetics; phonology; pronunciation
głosowo [gwo-**so**-vo] adv. vocally
głosowy [gwo-**so**-vi] adj.m. vocal; voice (chord, fold, etc.); phonic
głosujący [gwo-soo-**yown**-tsi] m. voter
głoszenie [gwo-**she**-ńe] n. proclamation; propagation
głośnia [**gwośh**-ńah] f. glottis
głośnik [**gwośh**-ńeek] m. loudspeaker; public-address system; speaking trumpet
głośnikowy [gwośh-ńee-**ko**-vi] adj.m. of a loudspeaker
głośniowy [gwośh-**ńo**-vi] adj.m. of the glottis; glottal
głośno [**gwośh**-no] adv. out loud; loud; loudly; aloud; noisily; openly; vocally; orally
głośność [**gwośh**-nośhćh] f. loudness; audibility; volume; fullness of tone
głośny [**gwośh**-ni] adj.m. loud; audible; noisy; open; well-known; famous; prominent; celebrated; far-famed; vocal; oral; spoken out loud; sounding; resounding; conspicuous; notorious
głowa [**gwo**-vah] f. head; chief
ból głowy [bool **gwo**-vi] exp.: headache
głowa mnie boli [**gwo**-vah mńe **bo**-lee] exp.: I have a headache
mieć głowę na karku [myećh **gwo**-van nah **kahr**-koo] exp.: to have one's head screwed on the right way
niech cię o to głowa nie boli [ńekh ćhan o to **gwo**-vah ńe **bo**-lee] exp.: don't bother your head about that
od przybytku głowa nie boli [ot

pshi-**bit**-koo **gwo**-vah ńe **bo**-lee] exp.: there is never too much of a good thing
głowacica [gwo-vah-**ćhee**-tsah] f. huchen (salmonoid fish)
głowacz [**gwo**-vahch] m. pistillate flower of hemp; miller's thumb; variety of freshwater fish; colloq: brainy guy; wise guy; egghead
głowaczowaty [gwo-vah-cho-**vah**-ti] adj.m. of variety of freshwater fish
głowaczowate [gwo-vah-cho-**vah**-te] pl. the Cottidae family of spiny-finned freshwater fishes
głowiasty [gwo-**vyahs**-ti] adj.m. shaped like a head; spherical; headed (cabbage, lettuce, etc.)
głowica [gwo-**vee**-tsah] f. capital; cap; head (of a lathe, etc.); knob; tip; top; pommel; ball and socket joint; warhead; handle of a sword
głowić się [**gwo**-veećh śhan] v. beat one's brains out (about); puzzle (over, about); rack one's brains (for); set one's wits (to) (*repeatedly*)
głowienie się [gwo-**vye**-ńe śhan] n. beating one's brains out (about); puzzling (over, about); racking one's brains (for); setting one's wits (to)
głowienka [gwo-**vyen**-kah] f. (small)(fire-)brand; pommel; smut; prunella; self-heal
głowina [gwo-**vee**-nah] f. (poor, little) head
głowizna [gwo-**veez**-nah] f. potted head; brawn; headcheese; colloq: head; chump
głownia [**gwov**-ńah] f. (fire-)brand; pommel; smut
głowniowaty [gwov-ńo-**vah**-ti] adj.m. ustilaginaceous; of the family of smuts
głowniowate [gwov-ńo-**vah**-te] pl. the family of smuts
głowniowy [gwov-**ńo**-vi] adj.m. of variety of parasitic fungus
głowniowe [gwov-**ńo**-ve] pl. the stilaginales
głowonóg [gwo-**vo**-noog] m. cephalopod; mollusk
głowonogi [gwo-vo-**no**-gee] pl. the cephalopoda
głowotułów [gwo-vo-**too**-woof] m. cephalothorax
głowowy [gwo-**vo**-vi] adj.m. of the head; head (louse, etc.); cephalic (vein, etc.)
głód [gwoot] m. hunger; famine; starvation; shortage; bulimia; thirst (for, after); scarcity; dearth
cierpieć głód [**ćher**-pyećh gwoot] exp.: to hunger; to go hungry; to be pinched with hunger; to feel pangs of hunger (for knowledge)
głód mieszkaniowy [gwood myesh-kah-**ńo**-vi] exp.: housing shortage
morzyć kogoś głodem [**mo**-zhićh **ko**-gośh **gwo**-dem] exp.: to famish somebody; to starve somebody
przymierać głodem [pshi-**mye**-rahćh **gwo**-dem] exp.: to be starving
umrzeć z głodu [oom-zhećh z **gwo**-doo] exp.: to die of starvation
o głodzie [o **gwo**-dźhe] exp.: on an empty stomach
głóg [gwoog] m. hawthorn; hip (of a wild rose)
główczyzna [gwoof-**chiz**-nah] f. fine paid in medieval Poland for committing slaughter
główeczka [gwoo-**vech**-kah] f. (small, nice) head; pinhead; knob; tip; top; boss
główka [**gwoof**-kah] f. pinhead; knob; tip; top; boss; heading (in a ball game)
główkować [gwoof-**ko**-vahćh] v. to hit the ball with one's head in a ball game (*repeatedly*)
główkowanie [gwoof-ko-**vah**-ńe] n. hitting the ball with one's head in a ball game
główkowaty [gwoof-ko-**vah**-ti] adj.m. spherical; bulbiform; capitate; capitular
główkowy [gwoof-**ko**-vi] adj.m. of hitting the ball with one's head in a ball game; of head-first position at birth
głównie [**gwoov**-ńe] adv. principally; chiefly; mainly; primarily; most of

all; mostly; in the main; for the most part; above all; especially; first and foremost

głównodowodzący [gwoov-no-do-vo-**dzown**-tsi] m. commander in chief (of an army)

główny [**gwoov**-ni] adj.m. main; predominant; predominating; paramount; dominant; foremost; chief

liczebnik główny [lee-**cheb**-ńeek **gwoov**-ni] exp.: cardinal number

tętnica główna [tant-**ńee**-tsah **gwoov**-nah] exp.: aorta

zdanie główne [**zdah**-ńe **gwoov**-ne] exp.: the main clause; the principal clause

w głównej mierze [v **gwoov**-ney **mye**-zhe] exp.: principally; chiefly; mainly; primarily; most of all; mostly; in the main; for the most part; above all; especially; first and foremost

głuchawy [gwoo-**khah**-vi] adj.m. hard of hearing; dullish; muffled

głuchnąć [**gwookh**-nownćh] v. grow deaf; become deaf; die down; die away (*repeatedly*)

głuchnięcie [gwookh-**ńan**-ćhe] n. the loss of one's sense of hearing

głucho [**gwoo**-kho] adv. dully; noiselessly; with a dull sound; with a hollow sound; with a thud; silently

brzmieć głucho [bzhmyećh **gwoo**-kho] exp.: to sound hollow

głuchoniemota [gwoo-kho-ńe-**mo**-tah] f. deaf-mutism; deaf-dumbness

głuchoniemy [gwoo-kho-**ńe**-mi] adj.m. deaf-and-dumb; deaf mute; m. deaf-and-dumb person; deaf-mute

alfabet głuchoniemych [ahl-**fah**-bet gwoo-kho-**ńe**-mikh] exp.: deaf-and-dumb alphabet

głuchoniewidomy [gwoo-kho-ńe-vee-**do**-mi] adj.m. deaf-blind; m. deaf-blind person

głuchota [gwoo-**kho**-tah] f. deafness; imperviousness

głuchy [**gwoo**-khi] adj.m. deaf; irresponsive; dull; hollow; silent; dead; muffled; smothered; hollow- sounding; noiseless; blank

głuchy jak pień [**gwoo**-khi yahk pyeń] exp.: deaf as a post

wydawać głuchy dźwięk [vi-**dah**-vahćh **gwoo**-khi dźhvyank] exp.: to sound hollow

w głuchą noc [**v gwoo**-khown nots] exp.: at dead of night

głupawo [gwoo-**pah**-vo] adv. weak-mindedly; fatuously; idiotically

głupawość [gwoo-**pah**-vośhćh] f. weak-mindedness

głupawy [gwoo-**pah**-vi] adj.m. weak-minded; fatuous; idiotic; insipid; silly; vacant (look); slang: spoony

głupek [**gwoo**-pek] m. colloq: dolt; booby; dullard; zany

głupia [**gwoo**-pyah] adj.f. silly (woman); stupid; foolish; asinine; naive (girl)

głupi [**gwoo**-pee] adj.m. silly; stupid; foolish; asinine; naive

głupi uśmiech [**gwoo**-pee **oo**-śhmyekh] exp.: insipid smile

on nie jest taki głupi, na jakiego wygląda [on ńe yest **tah**-kee **gwoo**-pee nah yah-**ke**-go vig-**lown**-dah] exp.: colloq: he is not such a fool as he looks

nadzieja jest matką głupich [nah-**dźhe**-yah yest **maht**-kown **gwoo**-peekh] exp.: hope is the mother of fools; hope often disappoints

głupiec [**gwoo**-pyets] m. addle-brain; fool; idiot; loony; goof; numskull; booby

robić z siebie głupca [ro-beećh s **śhe**-bye **gwoop**-tsah] exp.: to play the fool

głupieć [**gwoo**-pyećh] v. lose one's head; go daft; grow stupid; colloq: go off one's head (*repeatedly*)

głupio [**gwoo**-pyo] adv. stupidly; idiotically; foolishly; awkwardly

głupio mówić [**gwoo**-pyo **moo**-veećh] exp.: to talk nonsense

głupio zrobiłeś [**gwoo**-pyo zro-**bee**-weśh] exp.: that was stupid of you

czuć się głupio [choośh śhan **gwoo**-pyo] exp.: to feel awkward; to feel like a fool; to be at one's wits ends

głupiutki [gwoo-**pyoot**-kee] adj.m. silly; stupid; foolish; asinine; naive
głupkowato [gwoop-ko-**vah**-to] adv. weak-mindedly; doltishly; inanely
głupkowatość [gwoop-ko-**vah**-tośhćh] f. weak-mindedness; doltishness; inanity
głupkowaty [gwoop-ko-**vah**-ti] adj.m. weak-minded; doltish; inane; soft-headed; simple; silly; goofy; colloq: not all there; slang: loony
głupol [**gwoo**-pol] m. colloq: blockhead; slang: insane
głupota [gwoo-**po**-tah] f. stupidity; imbecility; foolishness; inanity
co za głupota! [tso zah gwoo-**po**-tah] excl.: how stupid!; what nonsense!
głupowatość [gwoo-po-**vah**-tośhćh] f. weak-mindedness; doltishness; inanity
głupowaty [gwoo-po-**vah**-ti] adj.m. weak-minded; doltish; inane; soft-headed; simple; silly; goofy; colloq: not all there; slang: loony
głupstewko [gwoop-**stef**-ko] n. (silly) nonsense; trifle; blunder; mistake
głupstwo [**gwoop**-stfo] n. nonsense; trifle; blunder; mistake
palnąć głupstwo [**pahl**-nownćh **gwoop**-stfo] exp.: to say something silly
zrobić głupstwo [**zro**-beećh **gwoop**-stfo] exp.: to make a mistake
pleść głupstwa [pleśhćh **gwoop**-stfah] exp.: to talk nonsense
głuptak [**gwoop**-tahk] m. imbecile; idiot; gannet (bird)
głuptas [**gwoop**-tahs] m. simpleton
ty głuptasie! [ti gwoop-**tah**-śhe] excl.: you silly; you little stupid!; silly boy!
głuptasek [gwoop-**tah**-sek] m. little simpleton
głusza [**gwoo**-shah] f. dead silence; deathlike stillness; lifelessness; solitude; wilderness
głuszcowy [gwoosh-**tso**-vi] adj.m. of the wood grouse; of the heath cock; of the capercailzie
głuszec [**gwoo**-shets] m. grouse
głuszenie [gwoo-**she**-ńe] n. muffling; damping
głuszenie się [gwoo-**she**-ńe śhan] n. muffling oneself
głuszka [**gwoosh**-kah] f. greyhen (female wood grouse)
głuszyca [gwoo-**shi**-tsah] f. greyhen (female wood grouse)
głuszyć [**gwoo**-shićh] v. deaden (sounds); dampen; muffle; smother; stifle; choke; finish off (a wounded game animal) (*repeatedly*)
głuszyć się [**gwoo**-shićh śhan] v. deaden (sounds); dampen each other; smother each other (*repeatedly*)
gmach [gmahkh] m. large building
gmachówka [gmah-**khoof**-kah] f. large wood-eating ant
gmaszysko [gmah-**shis**-ko] n. (nasty, old) large building
gmatwać [**gmaht**-fahćh] v. mix up; tangle; embroil; complicate; muddle; jumble; confuse; complicate (*repeatedly*)
gmatwać się [**gmaht**-fahćh śhan] v. get mixed up; get entangled; get embroiled; become complicated; be confused (*repeatedly*)
gmatwanie [gmaht-**fah**-ńe] n. entangling; confusion
gmatwanie się [gmaht-**fah**-ńe śhan] n. entangling oneself; getting confused
gmatwanina [gmaht-fah-**ńee**-nah] f. tangle; muddle; confusion; complexity; mix-up; involvement; intricacy; embroilment
gmeracz [gme-**rahch**] m. prober; seeker; searcher; fumbler; duffer; dawdler
gmerać [**gme**-rahćh] v. rummage; search; pry; poke (about) (*repeatedly*)
gmerać się [**gme**-rahćh śhan] v. fumble (for, after); potter (about); dawdle (*repeatedly*)
gmeranie [gme-**rah**-ńe] n. searching; poking (about)
gmerk [gmerk] m. crest of burger's family; medieval trademark

gmin [gmeen] m. populace; the vulgar herd; the rabble
gmina [**gmee**-nah] f. county; parish; community; commune
gminnie [**gmeen**-ńe] adv. vulgarly
gminność [**gmeen**-nośhćh] f. vulgarity
gminny [**gmeen**-ni] adj.m. of a commune; communal; of a community; of a parish; vulgar
gminne wyrażenie [**gmeen**-ne vi-rah-**zhe**-ńe] exp.: vulgarism
gnać [gnahćh] v. speed; career; chase; rush along; scuttle along; spank ahead; bowl along; rip; drive (a worker, etc.) (*repeatedly*)
gnanie [**gnah**-ńe] n. chase; rushing along; driving (somebody)
gnat [gnaht] m. colloq: bone; slang: pistol; gun (mob jargon)
gnatarz [**gnah**-tahsh] m. turnip sawfly
gnatki [**gnaht**-kee] pl. (sledge) runners; colloq: sledge
gnejs [gneys] m. gneiss; bastard granite
gnejsowy [gney-**so**-vi] adj.m. of gneiss; gneiss (rock, etc.)
gnet [gnet] m. gnetum
gnetowy [gne-**to**-vi] adj.m. gnetaceous; of the fir family
gnębiąco [gnan-**byown**-tso] adv. oppressively
gnębiciel [gnan-**bee**-ćhel] m. oppressor; taskmaster
gnębicielka [gnan-bee-**ćhel**-kah] f. (woman) oppressor; taskmaster
gnębicielski [gnan-bee-**ćhel**-skee] adj.m. of oppression; oppressive
gnębić [**gnan**-beećh] v. oppress; tread down; worry; harass (*repeatedly*)
co cię gnębi? [tso ćhan **gnan**-bee] exp.: what is on your mind?
gnębić się [**gnan**-beećh śhan] v. worry oneself; get depressed (*repeatedly*)
gnębienie [gnan-**bye**-ńe] n. oppression; worry; worries
gnębienie się [gnan-**bye**-ńe śhan] n. worrying oneself; getting depressed
gniadosz [**gńah**-dosh] m. bay (horse); dark brown horse
gniada [**gńah**-dah] adj.f. bay (mare); f. dark brown mare
gniady [**gńah**-di] adj.m. bay (horse); m. dark brown horse
gniazdeczko [gńahz-**dech**-ko] n. (nice, little) nest
gniazdko [**gńahst**-ko] n. nest; hearth; snuggery; socket; seat; mortise; group; nidus; cluster; pocket; female connector
gniazdkowy [gńahst-**ko**-vi] adj.m. socket (wrench, etc.)
gniazdo [**gńahz**-do] n. nest; home; hearth; hotbed (of vice, etc.); socket; seat; mortise; group; nidus; cluster; pocket
gniazdosz [**gńahz**-dosh] m. variety of forest flower
gniazdować [gńahz-**do**-vahćh] v. nest; group (words) (*repeatedly*)
gniazdowanie [gńahz-do-**vah**-ńe] n. nesting
gniazdowisko [gńahz-do-**vees**-ko] n. nestage
gniazdownik [gńahz-**dov**-ńeek] m. nestling; fledgling; eyas
gniazdowy [gńahz-**do**-vi] adj.m. of a nest; of nests
gniazdówka [gńahz-**doof**-kah] f. anisomyariam mollusk
gnicie [**gńee**-ćhe] n. decay; putrefaction; putridity; rot
gnić [gńeećh] v. rot; decay; molder; fester; rankle; ret (hay) (*repeatedly*)
gnida [**gńee**-dah] f. nit
gnidosz [**gńee**-dosh] m. lousewort; red rattle
gniecenie [gńe-**tse**-ńe] n. pressure; squeeze
gniecenie w żołądku [gńe-**tse**-ńe v zho-**wownt**-koo] exp.: heaviness in the stomach
gniecenie się [gńe-**tse**-ńe śhan] n. getting crowded; getting squeezed
gnieciuch [**gńe**-ćhookh] m. half-baked bread; kind of cake
gnieść [gńeśhćh] v. squeeze; press; crush; squash; mash; knead; oppress; wrinkle (one's clothes); be tight (*repeatedly*)
gnieść się [gńeśhćh śhan] v. be squeezed together; huddle

together; be crowded; be cooped up; be (get) wrinkled (*repeatedly*)
gniew [gńef] m. anger; wrath; irritation; temper; exasperation; colloq: dander
gniewać [gńe-vahćh] v. irritate; exasperate; infuriate; anger; make angry (*repeatedly*)
gniewać się [**gńe**-vahćh śhan] v. be angry (with, about); be in temper (with); be irritated (by); be cross with; be on bad terms (with); quarrel (with) (*repeatedly*)
gniewanie [gńe-**vah**-ńe] n. exasperating; irritating
gniewanie się [gńe-**vah**-ńe śhan] n. being cross with each other
gniewliwie [gńev-**lee**-vye] adv. irritably; testily
gniewliwość [gńev-**lee**-vośhćh] f. irritability; testiness; irascibility; quick temper; ill temper
gniewliwy [gńev-**lee**-vi] adj.m. irritable; testy; irascible; quick-tempered; ill-tempered
gniewnie [**gńev**-ńe] adv. angrily; in anger
spojrzeć gniewnie [**spoy**-zhećh **gńev**-ńe] exp.: to scowl; to frown with ill-temper
gniewny [**gńev**-ni] adj.m. angry; bitter; exasperated; cross; scowling
gniewosz [**gńe**-vosh] m. smooth snake; copperhead; touch-me-not
gnieździć się [**gńeźh**-dźheećh śhan] v. nestle; cluster; assemble; collect; be cooped up (*repeatedly*)
gnieźnik [**gńeźh**-ńeek] m. variety of forest flower
gnieżdżenie się [gńezh-**dzhe**-ńe śhan] n. nestling
gnilcowy [gńeel-**tso**-vi] adj.m. scorbutic
gnilec [**gńee**-lets] m. scurvy; foulbrood (of insects)
gnilny [**gńeel**-ni] adj.m. putrid; of rot; septic; putrefactive
gniłek [**gńee**-wek] m. aethalium fungus
gniot [gńot] m. colloq: half-baked cake; long, dull work of literature or film
gniotowiec [gńo-**to**-vyets] m. variety of Gnetinae plant
gniotowce [gńo-**tof**-tse] pl. the Gnetinae plant family
gniotownik [gńo-**tov**-ńeek] m. stone-crusher; mill
gnoić [**gno**-eećh] v. putrefy; rot; decompose; manure; foul; soil; dirty; dung; mob slang: prosecute; vandalize (*repeatedly*)
gnoić się [**gno**-eećh śhan] v. fester; putrefy; rot; decay (*repeatedly*)
gnoisko [gno-**ees**-ko] n. dunghill; manure pit; sink of iniquity
gnojak [**gno**-yahk] m. dung-bug
gnojarnia [gno-**yahr**-ńah] f. dunghill; manure pit; laystall; muck heap
gnojarz [**gno**-yahsh] m. colloq: lout; clodhopper
gnojek [**gno**-yek] m. stinkard; stinker
gnojenie [gno-**ye**-ńe] n. putrefaction; rot; decomposition
gnojenie się [gno-**ye**-ńe śhan] n. undergoing decomposition
gnojka [**gnoy**-kah] f. drone fly
gnojnica [gnoy-**ńee**-tsah] f. dung-cart; side plank of a dung-cart
gnojnik [**gnoy**-ńeek] m. a species of agaric
gnojowica [gno-yo-**vee**-tsah] f. liquid dung fertilizer; manure fertilizer
gnojowiec [gno-**yo**-veets] m. Coprinae beetle
gnojowce [gno-**yof**-tse] pl. the family of Coprinae beetles
gnojowisko [gno-yo-**vees**-ko] n. dunghill; manure pit; sink of iniquity
gnojownia [gno-**yov**-ńah] f. dunghill; manure pit; laystall; muck heap
gnojownica [gno-yov-**ńee**-tsah] f. dung fertilizer liquid; manure fertilizer
gnojowy [gno-**yo**-vi] adj.m. of dung; of manure; dung (pile, etc.); manure (cart, etc.)
gnojówka [gno-**yoof**-kah] f. liquid manure; manure pit; dunghill
gnom [gnom] m. gnome; maxim; aphorism
gnoma [**gno**-mah] f. gnome; maxim;

aphorism
gnomiczny [gno-**meech**-ni] adj.m. gnomic (verse, etc.)
gnomolog [gno-**mo**-log] m. sundial specialist
gnomon [**gno**-mon] m. gnomon
gnomoniczny [gno-mo-**ńeech**-ni] adj.m. of sundials
gnomonika [gno-**mo**-ńee-kah] f. art of making sundials; gnomonics; horography
gnomonologia [gno-mo-no-**lo**-gyah] f. gnomonology
gnomonologicznie [gno-mo-no-lo-**geech**-ńe] adv. gnomonologically
gnomonologiczny [gno-mo-no-lo-**geech**-ni] adj.m. gnomonological
gnoseologia [gno-se-o-**lo**-gyah] f. gnosiology; study of the validity of knowledge
gnoseologiczny [gno-se-o-lo-**geech**-ni] adj.m. gnosiological
gnostycyzm [gno-**sti**-tsizm] m. Gnosticism
gnostyczny [gno-**stich**-ni] adj.m. Gnostic
gnostyk [**gnos**-tik] m. Gnostic
gnoza [**gno**-zah] f. gnosis
gnozeologia [gno-ze-o-**lo**-gyah] f. gnosiology
gnozeologiczny [gno-ze-o-lo-**geech**-ni] adj.m. gnosiological
gnój [gnooy] m. manure; dung; filth; muck; sluggard; stinker (vulg.); lousy bum
gnój pod bydłem [gnooy pod **bid**-wem] exp.: litter
gnójka [**gnooy**-kah] f. drone fly
gnu [gnoo] f. gnu; wildebeest
gnuśnie [**gnoośh**-ńe] adv. sluggishly; lazily; indolently; languidly; idly; listlessly
gnuśnieć [gnoośh-**ńećh**] v. lose one's energy; become listless, sluggish, languid (*repeatedly*)
gnuśnienie [gnoośh-**ńe**-ńe] n. listlessness; laziness
gnuśność [**gnoośh**-nośhćh] f. laziness; sloth; idleness; indolence; languidness; sluggishness; listlessness
gnuśny [**gnoośh**-ni] adj.m. sluggish; lazy; idle; listless
gnyk [gnik] m. hyoid (bone); tongue-bone
gnykować [gni-**ko**-vahćh] v. pith (*repeatedly*)
gnykowy [gni-**ko**-vi] adj.m. hyoid
gobelin [go-**be**-leen] m. Gobelin (tapestry); arras
gobeliniarski [go-be-lee-**ńahr**-skee] adj.m. Gobelin (tapestry, stitch, etc.)
gobeliniarstwo [go-be-lee-**ńahr**-stfo] n. art of Gobelin making
gobelinowy [go-be-lee-**no**-vi] adj.m. Gobelin (tapestry, stitch, etc.)
gocki [**gots**-kee] adj.m. Gothic (language, etc.)
godecja [go-**de**-tsyah] f. godetia (plant)
godet [**go**-det] m. godet; gore
godło [**god**-wo] n. emblem; badge; motto; trademark; sign; heraldic device
godnie [**god**-ńe] adv. worthily; suitably; appropriately; adequately; with dignity; in a dignified manner; with due decorum; proudly
godnościowy [god-nośh-**ćho**-vi] adj.m. of self-respect
godność [**god**-nośhćh] f. dignity; name; pride; self-esteem; self-respect; post; high rank
bez godności [bez god-**no**-śhćhee] exp.: undignified
jak godność? [yahk **god**-nośhćh] exp.: your name, please?
nadać komuś godność [nah-dahćh **ko**-moośh **god**-nośhćh] exp.: to confer a distinction on somebody
godny [**god**-ni] adj.m. worthy; deserving; suitable; proper; adequate; dignified; proud
godny pochwały [**go**-dni po-**khfah**-wi] exp.: praiseworthy
godny pogardy [**go**-dni po-**gahr**-di] exp.: despicable
godny pożałowania [**go**-dni po-zhah-wo-**vah**-ńah] exp.: lamentable
godny uwagi [**go**-dni oo-**vah**-gee] exp.: worthy of notice
godny zapamiętania [**go**-dni zah-pah-myan-**tah**-ńah] exp.: worthy of remembrance

godowy [go-**do**-vi] adj.m. nuptial; festive
gody [**go**-di] pl. nuptials; mating; festivities
godzenie [go-**dze**-ńe] n. reconciliation
godzenie się [go-**dze**-ńe śhan] n. reconciling oneself
godzić [**go**-dźheećh] v. reconcile; hire; square; engage; aim; hit; strike a blow; menace; threaten (*repeatedly*)
godzić strony [**go**-dźheećh **stro**-ni] exp.: to arrange a dispute
godzić w czyjeś uczucia [**go**-dźheećh f **chi**-yeśh oo-**choo**-ćhah] exp.: to hurt somebody's feelings
godzić się [**go**-dźheećh śhan] v. become reconciled; be reconciled; agree; consent (to); resign oneself; put up with (a fact, etc.); be reconcilable; hire oneself out; negotiate (*repeatedly*)
godzi się [**go**-dźhee śhan] exp.: it is proper (to do); one should
godzić się z faktem [**go**-dźheećh śhan s **fahk**-tem] exp.: to accept a fact; to put up with a fact
godzien [**go**-dźhen] adj.m. deserving; worth; worthy
godzina [go-**dźhee**-nah] f. hour; time; moment; lesson; class; lecture
godzinami [go-dźhee-**nah**-mee] exp.: for hours
godziny przyjęć [go-**dźhee**-ni **pshi**-yanćh] exp.: consulting-hours
godziny urzędowe [go-**dźhee**-ni oo-zhan-**do**-ve] exp.: office hours
która godzina? [**ktoo**-rah go-**dźhee**-nah] exp.: what time is it?
godzina policyjna [go-**dźhee**-nah po-lee-**tsiy**-nah] exp.: curfew
godzinka [go-**dźheen**-kah] f. about one hour; an hour at most; canonical hour
godzinny [go-**dźheen**-ni] adj.m. of one hour; an hour's (rest, etc.); short-lived
godzinowo [go-dźhee-**no**-vo] adv. per hour
godzinowy [go-dźhee-**no**-vi] adj.m. hourly; of an hour; one-hour (period, etc.)
godziwie [go-**dźhee**-vye] adv. properly; suitably; justly; fairly
godziwość [go-**dźhee**-vośhćh] f. proper behavior; justice; fairness; equity
godziwy [go-**dźhee**-vi] adj.m. proper; suitable; just; fair
gofr [gofr] m. variety of hot waffle
gofrować [go-**fro**-vahćh] v. corrugate; emboss (*repeatedly*)
gofrowanie [go-fro-**vah**-ńe] n. corrugation
gofrykra [go-**frir**-kah] f. embosser; embossing press
gogle [**gog**-le] pl. goggles
gogusiowaty [go-goo-śho-**vah**-ti] adj.m. foppish; dandyish
goguś [**go**-goośh] m. fop; dandy; dude
goić [**go**-eećh] v. heal; cure (*repeatedly*)
goić się [**go**-eećh śhan] v. heal; cure; cicatrize; skin over (*repeatedly*)
goj [goy] m. goi; goy; non-Jew; gentile; (often a term with negative connotations)
gojenie [go-**ye**-ńe] n. healing; cicatrization (of a wound)
gojenie się [go-**ye**-ńe śhan] n. healing (oneself, itself)
gojnik [**goy**-ńeek] m. ironwort (mint)
gokart [**go**-kahrt] m. go-cart
gokartowy [go-kahr-**to**-vi] adj.m. go-cart (race, etc.)
gol [gol] m. goal
zdobyć gola [**zdo**-bićh **go**-lah] exp.: to score a goal
golarka [go-**lahr**-kah] f. electric shaver
golarz [**go**-lahsh] m. barber; shaver
golas [**go**-lahs] m. naked man; unclothed man; nude
golasek [go-**lah**-sek] m. naked baby; naked kid
golec [**go**-lets] m. naked man; unclothed man; nude; unhaired hide; colloq: poor beggar
golem [**go**-lem] m. golem; blockhead
golenie [go-**le**-ńe] n. shaving; a shave; shave
golenie się [go-**le**-ńe śhan] n.

shaving oneself
goleniowy [go-le-ńo-vi] adj.m. tibial
goleń [go-leń] f. shinbone; shank; tibia; cannon bone (of a horse)
golenie [go-le-ńe] pl. shinbones
golf [golf] m. golf; turtle-necked pullover
golfowy [gol-fo-vi] adj.m. of golf (game, etc.); golf (club, etc.)
golgota [gol-go-tah] f. suffering
Golgota [gol-go-tah] f. Golgotha
goliard [gol-yahrt] m. medieval entertainer (actor, singer)
Goliat [gol-yaht] m. Goliath; giant
golibroda [go-lee-bro-dah] m. barber
golić [go-leećh] v. shave; colloq: soak; booze; drink; fleece; slang: steal (mob jargon) (*repeatedly*)
golić się [go-leećh śhan] v. shave; shave oneself; have a shave (*repeatedly*)
golizna [go-leez-nah] f. nakedness; bareness; poverty; indigence; destitution; bare spot; gall
golnąć [gol-nownćh] v. colloq: have a drink; gulp down (a drink)
golnięcie [gol-ńan-ćhe] n. a gulp
golonka [go-lon-kah] f. pig's feet dish; ham below the knee
golusieńki [go-loo-śheń-kee] adj.m. (very much) naked
goluśki [go-loośh-kee] adj.m. (very) naked
goluteńki [go-loo-teń-kee] adj.m. (nicely) naked (baby); colloq: completely empty; with no money; broke; penniless
golutki [go-loot-kee] adj.m. naked
gołąb [go-wownp] m. pigeon
gołąbeczek [go-wown-be-chek] m. (nice, little) pigeon; honey; darling
gołąbeczka [go-wown-bech-kah] f. (nice, little) pigeon; honey; darling
gołąbek [go-wown-bek] m. young pigeon; stuffed cabbage leaf; russula fungus
gołąbka [go-wownp-kah] f. dove
gołda [gow-dah] f. colloq: cheap booze
gołek [go-wek] m. gymnadenia (a terrestrial orchid)
gołębi [go-wan-bee] adj.m. of a pigeon; pigeon's; pigeon; dovelike
gołębiarka [go-wan-byahr-kah] f. (woman) pigeon-fancier; pigeon-breeder
gołębiarski [go-wan-byahr-skee] adj.m. of pigeon-fanciers; of pigeon-breeders
gołębiarstwo [go-wan-byahr-stfo] n. pigeon-fancying; pigeon-breeding
gołębiarz [go-wan-byahsh] m. pigeon-fancier; pigeon-breeder; colloq: sniper (in guerrilla movement in Poland, 1939-1945)
gołębiątko [go-wan-byownt-ko] n. young pigeon; squab
gołębica [go-wan-bee-tsah] f. dove
gołębię [go-wan-byan] n. young pigeon; squab
gołębiowaty [go-wan-byo-vah-ti] adj.m. pigeon-like
gołębiowate [go-wan-byo-vah-te] pl. the Columbidae family of birds
gołębnik [go-wan-bńeek] m. dovecote; pigeon-house
gołka [gow-kah] f. a variety of wheat
goło [go-wo] adv. with no cloth on; without covering
gołoborze [go-wo-bo-zhe] n. treeless region
gołoledź [go-wo-lećh] f. glazed frost; frozen dew; sleet; glaze
gołomianka [go-wo-myahn-kah] f. a variety of deepwater fish
gołosłownie [go-wo-swov-ńe] adv. without proof; groundlessly; vainly
gołosłowność [go-wo-swov-nośhćh] f. groundlessness
gołosłowny [go-wo-swov-ni] adj.m. unfounded; proofless; vain
gołowąs [go-wo-vowns] m. young shaver; raw lad; whippersnapper; cub
gołoziarnisty [go-wo-źhahr-ńees-ti] adj.m. having exposed grain
pszenica gołoziarnista [pshe-ńee-tsah go-wo-źhahr-ńees-tah] exp.: a variety of wheat
gołożer [go-wo-zher] m. complete defoliation by insects
goły [go-wi] adj.m. naked; bare; nude; stripped; slang: penniless; poor; stone-broke
pod gołym niebem [pod go-wim ńe-bem] exp.: in the open air;

under the open sky
z gołymi nogami [z go-**wi**-mee no-gah-mee] exp.: barefoot
z gołymi rękami [z go-**wi**-mee ran-kah-mee] exp.: with bare hands
Gomora [go-**mo**-rah] f. Gomorrah
sodoma i gomora [so-**do**-mah ee go-**mo**-rah] exp.: utter confusion; debauch; debauchery
gomóła [go-**moo**-wah] f. large lump; deer without antlers; bull without horns
gomółka [go-**moow**-kah] f. lump; homemade round cheese
gomółkowy [go-moow-**ko**-vi] adj.m. lumpy
gon [gon] m. chase
gonada [go-**nah**-dah] f. gonad
gonady [go-**nah**-di] pl. gonads
gonadotropina [go-nah-do-tro-**pee**-nah] f. gonadotrophin (hormone); gonadotropin
gonadotropiny [go-nah-do-tro-**pee**-ni] pl. gonadotrophins
gonadotropowy [go-nah-do-tro-**po**-vi] adj.m. gonadotrophic (hormone, etc.)
gonciany [gon-**ćhah**-ni] adj.m. of shingles; shingle (roof, etc.)
gonciarz [**gon**-ćhahsh] m. shingler
gondola [gon-**do**-lah] f. gondola
gondolier [gon-**dol**-yer] m. gondolier
gondoliera [gon-dol-**ye**-rah] f. gondolier's song
gondolowy [gon-do-**lo**-vi] adj.m. of gondola
gong [gong] m. gong
gongoryzm [gon-**go**-rizm] m. Gongorism
goniatyty [go-ńah-**ti**-ti] pl. Goniatites (ammonoids)
gonić [**go**-ńeećh] v. chase; hunt; pursue; track; run after; urge; goad; harass; drive hard; roam; race; roll (*repeatedly*)
goniony pies [go-**ńo**-ni pyes] exp.: chased dog
gonić się [**go**-ńeećh śhan] v. chase one another; race; be in heat; rut (*repeatedly*)
gonidium [go-**ńee**-dyoom] n. gonidial algae; gonidium
gonidia [go-**ńee**-dyah] pl. gonidia
goniec [**go**-ńets] m. messenger; office boy; errand-boy
gonienie [go-**ńe**-ńe] n. chase; pursuit; search (for)
gonienie się [go-**ńe**-ńe śhan] n. chasing one another
goniometr [go-**ńo**-metr] m. goniometer; radio-goniometer
goniometria [go-ńo-**metr**-yah] f. goniometry
goniometryczny [go-ńo-met-**rich**-ni] adj.m. goniometric
goniony [go-**ńo**-ni] adj.m. chased
gonitwa [go-**ńeet**-fah] f. chase; race
gonność [**gon**-nośhćh] f. tallness and slimness (tree, etc.)
gonny [**gon**-ni] adj.m. tall and slim (tree, etc.)
gonocyt [go-**no**-tsit] m. gonocyte
gonochoryzm [go-no-**kho**-rizm] m. gonochorism; separation of sex; sexual distinction
gonokok [go-**no**-kok] m. gonococcus
gonokoki [go-no-**ko**-kee] pl. gonococci
gonokokowy [go-no-ko-**ko**-vi] adj.m. gonococcal
gonorea [go-no-**re**-ah] f. gonorrhea
gont [gont] m. shingle
gontowy [gon-**to**-vi] adj.m. of shingles; shingled (roof)
gontyna [gon-**ti**-nah] f. pagan temple of ancient Slavs
gończak [**goń**-chahk] m. hunting dog; hound
gończy [**goń**-chi] adj.m. of chase; m. warrant for arrest; hound
goplana [gop-**lah**-nah] f. water nymph; a mollusk
goprowiec [go-**pro**-vyets] m. mountain rescue team member
goprowski [go-**prof**-skee] adj.m. of the mountain rescue operation
gorąc [**go**-rownts] m. heat; hot weather
gorące [go-**rown**-tse] n. hot food; hot drink
gorąco [go-**rown**-tso] n. heat; hot; adv. warmly; heartily; keenly; fervently; hotly; riskily
gorąco dziękować [go-**rown**-tso dźhan-**ko**-vahćh] exp.: to thank warmly
gorąco czegoś pragnąć [go-**rown**-tso **che**-gośh **prahg**-

nownćh] exp.: to wish for something keenly
gorąco się modlić [go-**rown**-tso śhan **mo**-dleećh] exp.: to pray fervently
gorącokrwisty [go-rown-tso-**krfees**-ti] adj.m. hot-blooded
gorący [go-**rown**-tsi] adj.m. hot; sultry; warm; hearty; lively
gorączka [go-**rownch**-kah] f. fever; shakes; excitement; heat; temperature; passion
biała gorączka [**byah**-wah go-**rownch**-kah] exp.: delirium
zmierzyć komuś gorączkę [zmye-zhićh **ko**-moośh go-**rownch**-kan] exp.: to take somebody's temperature
gorączkotwórczy [go-rownch-ko-**tfoor**-chi] adj.m. febrific; pyretic
gorączkować [go-rownch-**ko**-vahćh] v. have a fever (*repeatedly*)
gorączkować się [go-rown-**chko**-vahćh śhan] v. be feverish; be excited (*repeatedly*)
gorączkowanie [go-rownch-ko-**vah**-ńe] n. feverish state; excitement
gorączkowanie się [go-rownch-ko-**vah**-ńe śhan] n. becoming feverish; getting excited
gorączkowo [go-rownch-**ko**-vo] adv. feverishly; hectically
gorączkowość [go-rownch-**ko**-vośhćh] f. feverishness
gorączkowy [go-rownch-**ko**-vi] adj.m. of fever; febrile
gorbusza [gor-**boo**-shah] f. a variety of salmon
gorczyca [gor-**chi**-tsah] f. white mustard; charlock
gorczycowy [gor-chi-**tso**-vi] adj.m. of white mustard; of charlock; mustard (seed, oil, etc.)
gorczycznik [gor-**chich**-ńeek] m. winter cress; erysimum; mustard plaster; a variety of butterfly
gorczyczny [gor-**chich**-ni] adj.m. mustard (plaster, poultice, etc.)
gording [**gor**-deeng] m. earing (line)
gordon [**gor**-don] m. Gordon setter
gordonia [gor-**do**-ńyah] f. gordonia; mountain bay
gordyjski [gor-**diy**-skee] adj.m. Gordian (knot, etc.)
goreć [**go**-rećh] v. burn; blaze; be ablaze; glow; flare; be aglow; flush; be flushed (*repeatedly*)
gore! [**go**-re] excl.: fire!
gorejący [go-re-**yown**-tsi] adj.m. ardent; fiery
gorętszy [go-**rant**-shi] adj.m. hotter; more fervent; more intense
gorg [gorg] m. a kind of coloratura
gorgona [gor-**go**-nah] f. Gorgon
gorliwie [gor-**lee**-vye] adv. zealously; keenly; fervently; eagerly; devoutly; with zeal; ardently
gorliwiec [gor-**lee**-vyets] m. zealot; ardent supporter; ardent worker
gorliwość [gor-**lee**-vośhćh] f. zeal; keenness; fervor; devotion
gorliwy [gor-**lee**-vi] adj.m. zealous; keen; eager; devout; fervent; earnest; colloq: gung ho
gors [gors] m. chest; breast; bosom; bust; shirt front; neckline (of a dress)
gorseciarka [gor-se-**ćhahr**-kah] f. stay-maker; corset-maker
gorseciarski [gor-se-**ćhahr**-skee] adj.m. stay-maker's; corset-maker's
gorseciarstwo [gor-se-**ćhahr**-stfo] n. stay-making; corset-making
gorsecik [gor-**se**-ćheek] m. (small, nice) girdle
gorset [**gor**-set] m. girdle; corset; stays
gorsetowy [gor-se-**to**-vi] adj.m. of a girdle; corset (lace, etc.)
gorsząco [gor-**shown**-tso] adv. scandalously; shockingly; shamefully; in a scandalizing manner; disgracefully
gorszący [gor-**shown**-tsi] adj.m. scandalous; shocking; disgraceful; out of place; offensive to propriety; offensive to morality
gorszenie [gor-**she**-ńe] n. corruption; demoralization
gorszenie się [gor-**she**-ńe śhan] n. becoming scandalized
gorszy [**gor**-shi] adj.m. worse
co gorsze ... [tso **gor**-she] exp.: what worse ...
gorsza jakość [**gor**-shah **yah**-kośhćh] exp.: second quality
coraz gorszy [**tso**-rahz **gor**-shi]

exp.: worse and worse
gorsze [gor-she] exp.: something worse; worse things
zmiana na gorsze [zmyah-nah nah gor-she] exp.: a change for the worse
gorszyciel [gor-shi-ćhel] m. scandalizer; depraver
gorszycielka [gor-shi-ćhel-kah] f. (woman) scandalizer; depraver
gorszyć [gor-shićh] v. demoralize; scandalize; shock; deprave; make improper; corrupt (*repeatedly*)
gorszyć się [gor-shićh śhan] v. be scandalized; be shocked (at, by) (*repeatedly*)
gorycz [go-rich] f. bitterness; bitter taste; gall; acrimony
goryczak [go-ri-chahk] m. boletus fungus
goryczel [go-ri-chel] m. oxtongue (a herb)
goryczka [go-rich-kah] f. gentian; slightly bitter taste; bitterish taste
goryczkowaty [go-rich-ko-vah-ti] adj.m. gentianaceous
goryczkowate [go-rich-ko-vah-te] pl. the Gentianaceae family of bitter herbs
goryczkowy [go-rich-ko-vi] adj.m. bitterish; gentianaceous
gorycznik [go-rich-ńeek] m. winter cress; erysimum (herb of mustard family)
goryl [go-ril] m. gorilla; slang: bodyguard (mob jargon)
gorylica [go-ri-lee-tsah] f. female gorilla
gorysz [go-rish] f. sulfur-wort; sulfur-weed; brimstone-wort; masterwort; milkweed
gorzała [go-zhah-wah] f. brandy; spirits; booze; spirit
gorzałka [go-zhahw-kah] f. brandy; spirits; booze; spirit; tangle-foot
gorzeć [go-zhećh] v. be ablaze; burn; glow; blaze; flush; be flushed (*repeatedly*)
gorzej [go-zhey] adv. worse
czuć się gorzej [chooć śhan go-zhey] exp.: to feel worse
tym gorzej [tim go-zhey] exp.: all the worse; so much the worse
gorzelany [go-zhe-lah-ni] adj.m. alcohol-distilling (trade, etc.)
gorzelnia [go-zhel-ńah] f. distillery; still; colloq: smell of booze
gorzelniany [go-zhel-ńah-ni] adj.m. alcohol-distilling (trade, etc.)
gorzelnictwo [go-zhel-ńeets-tfo] n. distilling of alcohol
gorzelniczy [go-zhel-ńee-chi] adj.m. alcohol-distilling (trade, etc.)
gorzelnik [go-zhel-ńeek] m. alcohol-distiller
gorzka [gosh-kah] f. bitter vodka
gorzkawo [gosh-kah-vo] adv. with a bitterish taste; with pungent smell
gorzkawosłonawy [gosh-kah-vo-swo-nah-vi] adj.m. salty-bitterish
gorzkawy [gosh-kah-vi] adj.m. bitterish
gorzki [gosh-kee] adj.m. bitter; pungent; painful
gorzknąć [gosh-knownćh] v. grow bitter; acquire a bitter taste; grow embittered (*repeatedly*)
gorzknia [gosh-kńah] f. quassia (shrub)
gorzknieć [gosh-kńećh] v. grow bitter; acquire a bitter taste; grow embittered (*repeatedly*)
gorzknienie [gosh-kńe-ńe] n. embitterment
gorzknięcie [gosh-kńan-ćhe] n. growing bitter
gorzknik [goshk-ńeek] m. hydrastis; golden seal
gorzko [gosh-ko] adv. bitterly
gorzko płakać [gosh-ko pwah-kahćh] exp.: to cry bitter tears
gorzko mi w ustach [gosh-ko mee v oos-tahkh] exp.: I have a bitter taste in the mouth
gorzkokwaśny [gosh-ko-kfahśh-ni] adj.m. acid-bitter
gorzkosłony [gosh-ko-swo-ni] adj.m. salty-bitter
gorzkość [gosh-kośhćh] f. bitter taste; bitterness
gospocha [gos-po-khah] f. colloq: good housekeeper
gospoda [gos-po-dah] f. inn; eating house; restaurant
gospodarczo [gos-po-dahr-cho] adv. economically
gospodarczy [gos-po-dahr-chi] adj.m. economic; farm; charring

artykuły gospodarcze [ahr-ti-**koo**-wi gos-po-**dahr**-che] exp.: household goods
prace gospodarcze [**prah**-tse gos-po-**dahr**-che] exp.: chars
gospodarka [gos-po-**dahr**-kah] f. economy; housekeeping; farming; husbandry; management
gospodarka narodowa [gos-po-**dahr**-kah nah-ro-**do**-vah] exp.: national economy
gospodarka prywatna [gos-po-**dahr**-kah pri-**vaht**-nah] exp.: private enterprise
gospodarka uspołeczniona [gos-po-**dahr**-kah oo-spo-wech-**ńo**-nah] exp.: state-controlled economy
gospodarnie [gos-po-**dahr**-ńe] adv. economically; thriftily
gospodarność [gos-po-**dahr**-nośhćh] f. thrift
gospodarny [gos-po-**dahr**-ni] adj.m. economical; thrifty
gospodarować [gos-po-dah-**ro**-vahćh] v. run a farm; keep house; manage (*repeatedly*)
gospodarowanie [gos-po-dah-ro-**vah**-ńe] n. running a farm; keeping house; managing
gospodarski [gos-po-**dahr**-skee] adj.m. of a farm; farm (building, etc.); rural; proprietor's; agricultural
po gospodarsku [po gos-po-**dahr**-skoo] exp.: as farmers do; as farmers will
gospodarstwo [gos-po-**dahr**-stfo] n. household; farm; property; possession; holding
gospodarstwo hodowlane [gos-po-**dahr**-stfo kho-do-**vlah**-ne] exp.: stockfarm
prowadzić gospodarstwo [pro-**vah**-dźheećh gos-po-**dahr**-stfo] exp.: to run a farm
gospodarz [gos-**po**-dahsh] m. landlord; landholder; host; farmer; manager; home-steward
gospodarzenie [gos-po-dah-**zhe**-ńe] n. running a farm; keeping house; managing; housekeeping
gospodarzenie się [gos-po-dah-**zhe**-ńe śhan] n. running one's house
gospodarzyć [gos-po-**dah**-zhićh] v. run a farm; keep house; manage (*repeatedly*)
gospodarzyć się [gos-po-**dah**-zhićh śhan] v. run one's own house (*repeatedly*)
gospodyni [gos-po-**di**-ńee] f. landlady; hostess; manageress; housewife
gosposia [gos-**po**-śhah] f. housekeeper; maid; servant
goszczenie [gosh-**che**-ńe] n. a stay (as a guest, etc.)
gościć [**gośh**-ćheećh] v. receive; entertain; treat; stay at; to enjoy hospitality; be a guest; be received (by) (*repeatedly*)
gościec [**gośh**-ćhets] m. rheumatism; gout; arthritis
gościna [gośh-**ćhee**-nah] f. visit; stay at somebody's house; sojourn
gościniec [gośh-**ćhee**-ńets] m. road; highway; present
gościnnie [gośh-**ćheen**-ńe] adv. hospitably
gościnność [gośh-**ćheen**-nośhćh] f. hospitality
gościnny [gośh-**ćheen**-ni] adj.m. hospitable; hearty
gość [gośhćh] m. guest; caller; visitor; colloq: customer; inmate; boarder; colloq: dude; fellow; guy; man; bloke; beggar
nieproszony gość [ńe-pro-**sho**-ni gośhćh] exp.: uninvited guest; intruder
stały gość [**stah**-wi gośhćh] exp.: regular customer; patron
gośćcowy [gośhćh-**tso**-vi] adj.m. rheumatic
Got [got] m. Goth
gotować [go-**to**-vahćh] v. cook; boil; get ready; prepare; make; stew (*repeatedly*)
gotować na parze [go-**to**-vahćh nah **pah**-zhe] exp.: to steam
gotować na wolnym ogniu [go-**to**-vahćh nah **vol**-nim **og**-ńoo] exp.: to simmer
gotować się [go-**to**-vahćh śhan] v. boil; seethe; get ready; prepare; stew; be brewing; threaten (*repeatedly*)
gotowalnia [go-to-**vahl**-ńah] f.

dressing room
gotowanie [go-to-**vah**-ńe] n. cooking; boiling; preparation
gotowanie się [go-to-**vah**-ńe śhan] n. boiling; being cooked
gotowiuśki [go-to-**vyoośh**-kee] adj.m. (nice and) ready; completely ready; very much ready
gotowiutki [go-to-**vyoot**-kee] adj.m. (just) ready; quite ready
gotowość [go-**to**-vośhćh] f. readiness; willingness; being ready; stand-by; eagerness for; preparedness; alacrity
gotowy [go-**to**-vi] adj.m. ready; done; complete; ripe; willing; done for; cooked
gotów [**go**-toof] adj.m. ready; done; complete; ripe; willing; done for; cooked; prepared
gotówka [go-**toof**-kah] f. cash; ready money; slang: (school) crib
mieć gotówkę [myećh go-**toof**-kan] exp.: to be in cash
nie mieć gotówki [ńe myećh go-**toof**-kee] exp.: to be out of cash
płacić gotówką [**pwah**-ćheećh go-**toof**-kown] exp.: to pay in cash
gotówkowy [go-toof-**ko**-vi] adj.m. cash (transaction, payment, etc.)
gotycki [go-**tits**-kee] adj.m. Gothic; Gothic font
gotycyzm [go-**ti**-tsizm] m. Gothicism
gotyk [**go**-tik] m. Gothic
goździanka [gośh-**dźhahn**-kah] f. illecebrum; calvaria; coral fungus
goździeniec [gośh-**dźhe**-ńets] m. illecebrum; calvaria; coral fungus
goździeńcowaty [gośh-dźheń-tso-**vah**-ti] adj.m. calvariaceous; of the family of club and coral fungus
goździeńcowate [gośh-dźheń-tso-**vah**-te] pl. the family of club and coral fungi
goździk [**gośh**-dźheek] m. carnation; clove pink
goździkowaty [gośh-dźhee-ko-**vah**-ti] adj.m. of the pink family; caryophyllaceous
goździkowate [gośh-dźhee-ko-**vah**-te] pl. the pink family; the caryophyllaceous family
goździkowiec [gośh-dźhee-**ko**-vyets] m. Eugenia shrub or tree
goździkowy [gośh-dźhee-**ko**-vi] adj.m. clove (bud, etc.)
goździkówka [gośh-dźhee-**koof**-kah] f. clove-flavored vodka
gółka [**goow**-kah] f. variety of wheat
góra [**goo**-rah] f. mountain; hill; pile; top; upper part; slang: prison management (mob jargon)
do góry [do **goo**-ri] exp.: upwards
do samej góry [do **sah**-mey **goo**-ri] exp.: all the way up
do góry nogami [do **goo**-ri no-**gah**-mee] exp.: upside down
na górę [nah **goo**-ran] exp.: to the top; at the top; upstairs
na górze [nah **goo**-zhe] exp.: to the top; at the top; upstairs
pod górę [pod **goo**-ran] exp.: uphill
w górze [v **goo**-zhe] exp.: upstairs; high up; in the air
schodzić z góry [**skho**-dźheećh z **goo**-ri] exp.: to go downstairs; from above; downhill
z górą [z **goo**-rown] exp.: upwards of (five years, etc.)
górą [**goo**-rown] exp.: up above
górą nasi [**goo**-rown **nah**-śhee] exp.: excl.: good for us!
góral [**goo**-rahl] m. mountaineer; colloq: 500-zloty wartime bill
góralczyk [goo-**rahl**-chik] m. young mountaineer
góraleczka [goo-rah-**lech**-kah] f. mountaineer girl; young mountaineer woman
góralek [goo-**rah**-lek] m. hyrax (Hyracoidea)
góralki [goo-**rahl**-kee] pl. hyraxes; hyraces
góralka [goo-**rahl**-kah] f. mountaineer girl; mountaineer woman
góralski [goo-**rahl**-skee] adj.m. mountaineer's; mountaineers'
góralszczyzna [goo-rahlsh-**chiz**-nah] f. the mountaineers' way of life; folklore of the Carpathian mountaineers; Carpathian uplands
góreczka [goo-**rech**-kah] f. (small)

elevation
z góreczką [z goo-**rech**-kown] exp.: colloq: with a little addition; with something into the bargain
górka [**goor**-kah] f. hill; hillock; top floor; attic
górkowaty [goor-ko-**vah**-ti] adj.m. hillocky
górmistrz [**goor**-meestsh] m. mine foreman
górnica [goor-**ńee**-tsah] f. upper cut of meat
górnictwo [goor-**ńeets**-tfo] n. mining; mining industry
górniczka [goor-**ńeech**-kah] f. miner's wife
górniczo [goor-**ńee**-cho] adv. by means of mining
górniczy [goor-**ńee**-chi] adj.m. mining (engineer, village, etc.); miner's; miners' (work, etc.)
górnie [**goor**-ńe] adv. loftily
górnik [**goor**-ńeek] m. miner; collier; coal miner; pitman; digger
górnobrzmiący [goor-no-**bzhmyown**-tsi] adj.m. high-sounding
górnolotnie [goor-no-**lot**-ńe] adv. with big words; with bombast; with high-flown speech; in grandiloquent terms; in sonorous terms
górnolotność [goor-no-**lot**-nośhćh] f. big words; bombast; high-flown speech
górnolotny [goor-no-**lot**-ni] adj.m. of big words; bombastic; grandiloquent; high-flown; rotund; sonorous; fustian; gaudy; lofty; soaring
górnoniemiecki [goor-no-ńe-**myets**-kee] adj.m. High German
górnopłat [goor-**no**-pwaht] m. high-wing monoplane
górność [**goor**-nośhćh] f. exalted style; pathos
górnozaworowy [goor-no-zah-vo-**ro**-vi] adj.m. having valves at the top of engine block
górny [**goor**-ni] adj.m. upper; higher; top; upper limit; of big words; bombastic; grandiloquent; high-flown; rotund; sonorous; fustian; gaudy; lofty; soaring
górna granica [**goor**-nah grah-**ńee**-tsah] exp.: upper limit; top ceiling
górne światło [**goor**-ne **śhfyaht**-wo] exp.: overhead light; skylight
górny bieg [**goor**-ni byeg] exp.: the upper course; headwaters (of a river)
górotwór [goo-**ro**-tfoor] m. geological formation; orogeny (folding of earth crust)
górotwórczość [goo-ro-**tfoor**-chośhćh] f. tectonics; mountain-forming; orogeny; orogenesis
górotwórczy [goo-ro-**tfoor**-chi] adj.m. tectonic; mountain-forming; orogenic
górować [goo-**ro**-vahćh] v. prevail; excel; dominate; rise; predominate (*repeatedly*)
górowanie [goo-ro-**vah**-ńe] n. preeminence; domination
górowaty [goo-ro-**vah**-ti] adj.m. hilly; hillocky
górski [**goor**-skee] adj.m. mountainous; mountain (climate, resort, railway)
łańcuch górski [**wahń**-tsookh **goor**-skee] exp.: mountain range
okolice górskie [o-ko-**lee**-tse **goor**-ske] exp.: uplands
pasmo górskie [**pahs**-mo **goor**-ske] exp.: mountain range
górujący [goo-roo-**yown**-tsi] adj.m. dominant; predominant; preeminent; preponderant
górzystość [goo-**zhis**-tośhćh] f. mountainous character (of a region, etc.)
górzysty [goo-**zhis**-ti] adj.m. hilly; mountainous
gówniarz [**goov**-ńahsh] m. (vulg.) shit-ass; hipster; squirt; shit-head; inexperienced criminal
gówno [**goov**-no] n. (vulg.) shit; nothing; refuse; trash
gra [grah] f. game; sham; manner of playing; acting; pretence; gambling; gaming; play; a gamble
gra na giełdzie [grah nah **gew**-dźhe] exp.: speculating on stock market
gra w karty [grah f **kahr**-ti] exp.: card game
gra słów [grah swoof] exp.: pun; play on words; quibble

gra wojenna [grah vo-**yen**-nah] exp.: war game; sham fight
uczciwa gra [ooch-**ćhee**-vah grah] exp.: fair play
wchodzić w grę [fkho-dźheećh v gran] exp.: to be involved; to be concerned; to come into play
plac gier i zabaw [plahts ger ee zah-bahf] exp.: playground
grab [grahp] m. hornbeam tree; hardbeam tree
graba [**grah**-bah] f. fireplace; grate; mob slang: man's paw; flapper
grabarka [grah-**bahr**-kah] f. grave-digging; gravedigger's wife
grabarski [grah-**bahr**-skee] adj.m. gravedigger's; grave-digging (work, etc.)
grabarstwo [grah-**bahr**-stfo] n. grave-digging
grabarz [**grah**-bahsh] m. sexton; gravedigger; burying beetle
grabczak [**grahp**-chahk] m. young hornbeam
grabiarka [grah-**byahr**-kah] f. hay-raking machine; dump rake; woman haymaker
grabić [**grah**-beećh] v. rake; plunder; rob; sack (a town, etc.); rake up (*repeatedly*)
grabie [**grah**-bye] pl. rake
grabieć [**grah**-byećh] v. grow numb (*repeatedly*)
grabienie [grah-**bye**-ńe] n. growing numb
grabież [**grah**-byesh] f. plunder; robbery; loot
grabieżca [grah-**byesh**-tsah] m. plunderer; robber; looter
grabieżczy [grah-**byesh**-chi] adj.m. plundering (raid, etc.); predatory
grabieżyć [grah-**bye**-zhićh] v. plunder; loot; grab (*repeatedly*)
grabina [grah-**bee**-nah] f. hornbeam wood; hornbeam grove
grabinka [grah-**been**-kah] f. hornbeam forest
grabisko [grah-**bees**-ko] n. rake handle
grabka [**grahp**-kah] f. slang: hand
grabki [**grahp**-kee] pl. little rake
grabniak [**grahb**-ńahk] m. hornbeam tree stand
grabołusk [grah-**bo**-woosk] m. hawfinch
grabowy [grah-**bo**-vi] adj.m. of hornbeam; hornbeam (hard white wood, etc.)
grabula [grah-**boo**-lah] f. fireplace; grate; slang: man's paw; flapper
graca [**grah**-tsah] f. rabbler; hoe; larry
graciarnia [grah-**ćhahr**-ńah] f. lumber-room; untidy room; messy room
gracja [**grah**-tsyah] f. grace; graceful woman; charm
gracka [**grahts**-kah] f. (small) rabbler; hoe; larry
gracki [**grahts**-kee] adj.m. plucky; brave; dashing; gallant; clever; deft; skillful
gracko [**grahts**-ko] adv. pluckily; bravely; with dash; gallantly; with gallantry; deftly; skillfully
gracować [grah-**tso**-vahćh] v. scrape; rake; mix mortar; hoe (*repeatedly*)
gracowanie [grah-tso-**vah**-ńe] n. scraping; raking; mixing mortar; hoeing
gracz [grahch] m. player; gambler; crafty double-dealer; sly fox
grać [grahćh] v. play (football, tennis, cards, piano, violin); act; gamble; pretend; pulsate (*repeatedly*)
grać dla tłumu [grahćh dlah **twoo**-moo] exp.: to play down to the crowd
grać na giełdzie [grahćh nah gew-dźhe] exp.: to speculate on the stock market
grać na nerwach [grahćh nah **ner**-vahkh] exp.: get on (somebody's) nerves; to irritate (somebody); to aggravate
grad [graht] m. hail; volley; degree of a horizontal angle
pada grad [**pah**-dah graht] exp.: it hails; it is hailing
gradacja [grah-**dah**-tsyah] f. gradation; stages
gradient [**grahd**-yent] m. gradient
gradientowy [grahd-yen-to-vi] adj.m. gradient (measurements, etc.)
gradiernia [grahd-**yer**-ńah] f. gradation works

gradobicie [grah-do-**bee**-ćhe] n. hailstorm; the hail
gradonośny [grah-do-**nośh**-ni] adj.m. hail-carrying (cloud, etc.)
gradowy [grah-**do**-vi] adj.m. of hail
burza gradowa [**boo**-zhah grah-**do**-vah] exp.: hailstorm
chmura gradowa [**khmoo**-rah grah-**do**-vah] exp.: thundercloud
gradówka [grah-**doof**-kah] f. blepharo-conjunctivitis
gradualny [grah-doo-**ahl**-ni] adj.m. gradual (psalm)
graduał [grah-**doo**-ahw] m. gradual (a book of the choral part of the Mass)
gradus [**grah**-doos] m. grade
gradzina [grah-**dźhee**-nah] f. hailstone
gradzinka [grah-**dźheen**-kah] f. (small) hailstone
gradzinować [grah-dźhee-**no**-vahćh] v. leave parallel chisel marks on cut stone (*repeatedly*)
gradzinowanie [grah-dźhee-no-**vah**-ńe] n. leaving parallel chisel marks on cut stone
graf [grahf] m. count; grid
graffiti [grah-**fee**-tee] pl. indecl. drawings and writings on walls; graffito writings and grawings
graficznie [grah-**feech**-ńe] adv. graphically
graficzny [grah-**feech**-ni] adj.m. graphic; of engraving
grafik [**grah**-feek] m. graphic artist; engraver
grafika [**grah**-fee-kah] f. graphics; arts; art of writing; engraving
grafikon [**grah**-fee-kon] m. drawing pen; ruling pen
grafion [**grah**-fyon] m. drafting pen
grafit [**grah**-feet] m. graphite
grafitować [grah-fee-**to**-vahćh] v. cover with graphite (*repeatedly*)
grafitowanie [grah-fee-to-**vah**-ńe] n. covering with graphite
grafitowy [grah-fee-**to**-vi] adj.m. of graphite; graphite (lubrication, etc.)
grafityzacja [grah-fee-ti-**zah**-tsyah] f. graphitization
grafolog [grah-**fo**-log] m. graphologist; handwriting expert
grafologia [grah-fo-**lo**-gyah] f. graphology; the study of handwriting
grafologiczny [grah-fo-lo-**geech**-ni] adj.m. graphological; of the study of handwriting
grafoman [grah-**fo**-mahn] m. graphomaniac; scribbler
grafomania [grah-fo-**mah**-ńyah] f. graphomania; mania of writing; scribbling
grafomanka [grah-fo-**mahn**-kah] f. (woman) graphomaniac; scribbler
grafomański [grah-fo-**mahń**-skee] adj.m. of graphomania; of mania of writing; of scribbling
grafomaństwo [grah-fo-**mahń**-stfo] n. graphomania; mania of writing; scribbling
grafometr [grah-**fo**-metr] m. graphometer
grafometria [grah-fo-**metr**-yah] f. graphometry
grafometryczny [grah-fo-met-**rich**-ni] adj.m. of graphometry
grafoskop [grah-**fo**-skop] m. graphoscope (projector)
grafowski [grah-**fof**-skee] adj.m. of a count
graham [**grah**-khahm] m. graham bread; bread of entire wheat-flour
grahamka [grah-**khahm**-kah] f. dietetic roll
grajcar [**grahy**-tsahr] m. kreutzer; farthing; cartridge-extractor; corkscrew; mob slang: money
grajcarek [grahy-**tsah**-rek] m. (little) kreutzer; farthing; a curl
grajdoł [**grahy**-dow] m. slang: closet
grajdołek [grahy-**do**-wek] m. colloq: forlorn country place; godforsaken spot; outlandish spot
grajek [**grah**-yek] m. homebred musician
grajszafa [grahy-**shah**-fah] f. music box; (coin operated) jukebox
gram [grahm] m. gram
gramatura [grah-mah-**too**-rah] f. sheet weight (grams per square meter)
gramatyczka [grah-mah-**tich**-kah] f. (woman) grammarian
gramatycznie [grah-mah-**tich**-ńe] adv. grammatically

pisać gramatycznie [pee-sahćh grah-mah-**tich**-ńe] exp.: to spell correctly
poprawny gramatycznie [po-**prahv**-ni grah-mah-**tich**-ńe] exp.: grammatical
gramatyczność [grah-mah-**tich**-**nośhćh**] f. good grammar (of a sentence); grammaticality
gramatyczny [grah-mah-**tich**-ni] adj.m. grammatical; correct
gramatyk [grah-**mah**-tik] m. grammarian
gramatyka [grah-**mah**-ti-kah] f. grammar
gramatykalizm [grah-mah-ti-**kah**-leezm] m. grammaticalness
gramoatom [grah-mo-**ah**-tom] m. gram atom; gram-atomic weight
gramocząsteczka [grah-mo-chown-**stech**-kah] f. gram molecule; gram-molecular weight
gramocząsteczkowy [grah-mo-chown-stech-**ko**-vi] adj.m. of gram molecule; gram molecular (weight, etc.)
gramodrobina [grah-mo-dro-**bee**-nah] f. gram molecule; gram-molecular weight
gramodrobinowy [grah-mo-dro-bee-**no**-vi] adj.m. of gram molecule; gram-molecular (weight, etc.)
gramofon [grah-**mo**-fon] m. record player (turntable); phonograph; gramophone
gramofonowy [grah-mo-fo-**no**-vi] adj.m. of a record player; of a phonograph; of a gramophone
gramojon [grah-**mo**-yon] m. gram ion
gramolić się [grah-**mo**-leećh śhan] v. clamber up; climb; scramble; tumble along (*repeatedly*)
gramorównoważnik [grah-mo-roov-no-**vahzh**-ńeek] m. equivalent weight; gram equivalent
gramota [grah-**mo**-tah] f. written document of early Lithuania and Ruthenia
gramoty [grah-**mo**-ti] pl. written documents of early Lithuania and Ruthenia
gramowid [grah-**mo**-veet] m. device for projection of recorded moving color pictures and sound from a disc (playback of optical disc)
gramowy [grah-**mo**-vi] adj.m. of one gram; one-gram (weight, etc.)
kaloria gramowa [kah-**lor**-yah grah-**mo**-vah] exp.: gram calorie
gran [grahn] m. grain
granacik [grah-**nah**-ćheek] m. garnet ring; small caliber shell; small grenade
granat [**grah**-naht] m. grenade; pomegranate; navy blue color; navy blue cloth; garnet
granat ręczny [**grah**-naht **ranch**-ni] exp.: hand grenade
granatek [grah-**nah**-tek] m. small grenade; plant of the mint family; a beetle
granatnik [grah-**naht**-ńeek] m. (muzzle-loaded) mortar
granatowcowaty [grah-nah-tof-tso-**vah**-ti] adj.m. of punicaceous family of shrubs
granatowcowate [grah-nah-tof-tso-**vah**-te] pl. the punicaceous family of shrubs
granatowiec [grah-nah-**to**-vyets] m. pomegranate
granatowieć [grah-nah-**to**-vyećh] v. show blue colors; appear as a blue patch (*repeatedly*)
granatowo [grah-nah-**to**-vo] adv. in navy blue
granatowo- [grah-nah-**to**-vo] prefix: blue-; navy-(blue color)
granatowy [grah-nah-**to**-vi] adj.m. navy blue; of grenades; of hand grenades; of pomegranates
granatowa policja [grah-nah-**to**-va po-**lee**-tsyah] exp.: pre-war Polish police force
grand [grahnt] m. (Spanish) grandee
granda [**grahn**-dah] f. swindle; rumpus; gang; ruction; uproar; disturbance; racket; slang: holdup; robbery (mob jargon)
grandezza [grahn-**dez**-zah] f. (Spanish) great lady; dignity; proud bearing
grandilokwencja [grahn-dee-lok-**fen**-tsyah] f. grandiloquence
grandilokwentnie [grahn-dee-lok-**fent**-ńe] adv. grandiloquently
grandilokwentny [grahn-dee-lok-**fent**-

ni] adj.m. grandiloquent
grand prix [grahn pree] (French) exp.: grand prix
grandziarz [**grahn**-dźhahsh] m. shyster; racketeer; a rough; a rowdy; a tough
grandzić [**grahn**-dźheećh] v. slang: pinch; bone; steal (*repeatedly*)
graniak [**grah**-ńahk] m. wind-polished piece of angular rock
graniastosłup [grah-ńah-**sto**-swoop] m. prism (regular, right, etc.)
graniastosłupowy [grah-ńah-sto-swoo-**po**-vi] adj.m. of a prism
graniasty [grah-**ńahs**-ti] adj.m. angular; roan (color)
granica [grah-**ńee**-tsah] f. border; boundary; limit; frontier; range; reach; confines; bounds
granica celna [grah-**ńee**-tsah **tsel**-nah] exp.: frontier customs
przejść zieloną granicę [psheyśhćh źhe-**lo**-nown grah-ńee-tsan] exp.: to cross the border illegally
za granicą [zah grah-**ńee**-tsown] exp.: abroad
bez granicy [bez grah-**ńee**-tsi] exp.: unlimited; boundless; endless; without limit
do jakich granic? [do **yah**-keekh **grah**-ńeets] exp.: to what extent?
graniczący [grah-ńee-**chown**-tsi] adj.m. adjacent; limitrophe; situated on a border
graniczenie [grah-ńee-**che**-ńe] n. adjacency (to); neighborhood (of)
graniczny [grah-**ńeech**-ni] adj.m. terminal; limitary; of a frontier
graniczyć [grah-**ńee**-chićh] v. adjoin; be contiguous; border (on); abut; verge (on); fringe (upon); be little short of (swindle, etc.) (*repeatedly*)
granie [**grah**-ńe] n. playing; gambling; acting; pretending
graniowy [grah-**ńo**-vi] adj.m. of mountain ridge; of a crest
granit [**grah**-ńeet] m. granite
granitol [grah-**ńee**-tol] m. a leather substitute
granitowy [grah-ńee-**to**-vi] adj.m. of granite; granite (rock, slab, etc.)
granityzacja [grah-ńee-ti-**zah**-tsyah] f. granite forming; making granite-like
grankulka [grahn-**kool**-kah] f. shot
granula [grah-**noo**-lah] f. granule
granulacja [grah-noo-**lah**-tsyah] f. granulation; granularity
granulacyjnie [grah-noo-lah-**tsiy**-ńe] adv. granularly
granulacyjny [grah-noo-lah-**tsiy**-ni] adj.m. granular; granulative
granulat [grah-**noo**-laht] m. product of granulation
granulator [grah-noo-**lah**-tor] m. granulator
granulit [grah-**noo**-leet] m. granulite
granulka [grah-**nool**-kah] f. (small) granule
granulocyt [grah-noo-**lo**-tsit] m. granulocyte
granulocyty [grah-noo-lo-**tsi**-ti] pl. granulocytes
granuloma [grah-noo-**lo**-mah] f. granuloma
granulometria [grah-noo-lo-**metr**-yah] f. measuring of granularity in photographs
granulować [grah-noo-**lo**-vahćh] v. granulate (form into grains) (*repeatedly*)
granulowanie [grah-noo-lo-**vah**-ńe] n. granulation
granulowany [grah-noo-lo-**vah**-ni] adj.m. granulated
granuloza [grah-noo-**lo**-zah] f. granulose
grań [grahń] f. mountain ridge; crest; edge; razor's edge
grapefruit [**greyp**-froot] m. grapefruit
grapefruitowy [greyp-froo-**to**-vi] adj.m. of grapefruit; grapefruit (juice, etc.)
graptolit [grahp-**to**-leet] m. graptolite
graptolitowy [grahp-to-lee-**to**-vi] adj.m. graptolitic (extinct colonial Paleozoic animals, fossils, etc.)
grasejować [grah-se-**yo**-vahćh] v. roll the consonant "r" with vibration of the tongue; pronounce "r" as an uvular consonant (*repeatedly*)
grasejowanie [grah-se-yo-**vah**-ńe] n. rolling the consonant "r" with vibration of the tongue
grasica [grah-**śhee**-tsah] f. thymus

gland
grasować [grah-**so**-vahćh] v. ravage; roam about; prowl; maraud; overrun; rove; scour; be at large; be rampant; prevail; stalk (*repeatedly*)
grasowanie [grah-so-**vah**-ńe] n. ravaging; roaming
grat [graht] m. run-down furniture (or man); crock; old geezer; trash
gratis [**grah**-tees] adv. free of charge; giving something free; giving free copy of a book
gratisowo [grah-tee-**so**-vo] adv. free of charge
gratisowy [grah-tee-**so**-vi] adj.m. given free of charge
gratka [**graht**-kah] f. windfall
gratulacje [grah-too-**lah**-tsye] pl. congratulations; felicitations; compliments
gratulacyjnie [grah-too-lah-**tsiy**-ńe] adv. felicitously
gratulacyjny [grah-too-lah-**tsiy**-ni] adj.m. congratulatory; felicitous
gratulant [grah-**too**-lahnt] m. colloq: person expressing congratulations
gratulować [grah-too-**lo**-vahćh] v. congratulate; compliment (*repeatedly*)
gratyfikacja [grah-ti-fee-**kah**-tsyah] f. bonus; extra pay; tip; gratuity
gratyfikacyjny [grah-ti-fee-kah-**tsiy**-ni] adj.m. of a bonus; of extra pay; of a tip; gratuitous
grawamin [grah-**vah**-meen] m. gravamen
grawer [**grah**-ver] m. engraver
grawerka [grah-**ver**-kah] f. engraver's trade; engraving
grawerować [grah-ve-**ro**-vahćh] v. engrave (*repeatedly*)
grawerowanie [grah-ve-ro-**vah**-ńe] n. engraving
grawerski [grah-**ver**-skee] adj.m. engraver's
grawerstwo [grah-**ver**-stfo] n. engraver's trade; engraving
grawerunek [grah-ve-**roo**-nek] m. an engraving
grawigrad [grah-**vee**-graht] m. gravigrade
grawimetr [grah-**vee**-metr] m. gravimeter
grawimetria [grah-vee-**metr**-yah] f. gravimetry
grawimetryczny [grah-vee-met-**rich**-ni] adj.m. gravimetric
grawitacja [grah-vee-**tah**-tsyah] f. gravitation; pull of gravity; gravitational pull
grawitacyjnie [grah-vee-tah-**tsiy**-ńe] adv. gravitationally
grawitacyjny [grah-vee-tah-**tsiy**-ni] adj.m. of gravitation; gravitational; gravitation (constant, etc.)
grawitować [grah-vee-**to**-vahćh] v. gravitate; have a leaning towards; lean (*repeatedly*)
grawitowanie [grah-vee-to-**vah**-ńe] n. gravitation; leaning towards
grawiura [grah-**vyoo**-rah] f. engraving
skład grawiury [skwaht grah-**vyoo**-ri] exp.: print shop
grawiurowy [grah-vyoo-**ro**-vi] adj.m. of engraving
grażdanka [grahzh-**dahn**-kah] f. the Russian alphabet; modern Cyrillic
grąd [gr<u>own</u>t] m. forest growing on dry land
grądowy [gr<u>own</u>-**do**-vi] adj.m. of a forest growing on dry land
grążel [gr<u>own</u>-zhel] m. water lily; nuphar
grążyca [gr<u>own</u>-**zhi**-tsah] f. duck feeding under water
grążyce [gr<u>own</u>-**zhi**-tse] pl. the family of ducks feeding under water
grążyć [gr<u>own</u>-zhićh] v. plunge (hist.) (*repeatedly*)
grążyć się [gr<u>own</u>-zhićh śh<u>an</u>] v. sink (hist.) (*repeatedly*)
grdać [grdahćh] v. (corncrake) call (*repeatedly*)
grdanie [**grdah**-ńe] n. corncrake call; land rail call
grdyka [**grdi**-kah] f. Adam's apple
grecki [**grets**-kee] adj.m. Greek; Grecian
grecki krzyż [**grets**-kee kshish] exp.: Greek Cross
po grecku [po **grets**-koo] exp.: in Greek
greckokatolicki [grets-ko-kah-to-**leets**-kee] adj.m. Greek Catholic;

Uniat
grecysta [gre-**tsis**-tah] m. Greekist; Greek scholar; Grecian; Greek student
grecystyczny [gre-tsis-**tich**-ni] adj.m. of Greek studies
grecyzacja [gre-tsi-**zah**-tsyah] f. giving Greek character
grecyzm [**gre**-tsizm] m. Grecism
greczany [gre-**chah**-ni] adj.m. of buckwheat; buckwheat (kasha, porridge, etc.)
Greczynka [gre-**chin**-kah] f. Greek woman; gown in Greek style
greczyzna [gre-**chiz**-nah] f. Greek language; Greek studies; Greek
gregaryna [gre-gah-**ri**-nah] f. gregarine
gregoriański [gre-gor-**yahń**-skee] adj.m. gregorian (music, chant, calendar, etc.)
grejpfrut [**greyp**-froot] m. grapefruit
grejpfrutowy [greyp-froo-**to**-vi] adj.m. of grapefruit; grapefruit (juice, etc.)
grejzen [**grey**-zen] m. greisen (rock)
Grek [grek] m. Greek
greka [**gre**-kah] f. Greek language; Greek studies; Greek
grekofil [gre-**ko**-feel] m. Grecophile
grekokatolik [gre-ko-kah-**to**-leek] m. Greek Catholic
grekolatinizm [gre-ko-lah-**ti**-ńeezm] m. Greco-Romanism
gremialnie [gre-**myahl**-ńe] adv. in a mass; collectively; altogether; in a group; one and all
gremialny [gre-**myahl**-ni] adj.m. general; corporate; collective
gremiał [**gre**-myahw] m. gremial (episcopal)
gremium [**gre**-myoom] n. body (of persons); group
grena [**gre**-nah] f. fertilized eggs of silk butterfly
grenadier [gre-**nah**-dyer] m. grenadier
grenadierski [gre-nah-**dyer**-skee] adj.m. of a grenadier; of grenadiers
grenadyna [gre-nah-**di**-nah] f. grenadine (cloth, drink)
grenarstwo [gre-**nahr**-stfo] n. natural silk production
Grenlandczyk [gren-**lahnt**-chik] m. Greenlander
grenlandzki [gren-**lahnts**-kee] adj.m. Greenlandic
Grenlandka [gren-**lahnt**-kah] f. (woman) Greenlander
greps [greps] m. trick-word or ploy in a situation comedy
greża [**gre**-zhah] f. raw silk
gręplel [**gran**-pel] m. card
gręplа [**gran**-plah] f. carding tool
gręplarka [gran-**plahr**-kah] f. carding machine
gręplarnia [gran-**plahr**-ńah] f. carding shop
gręplarski [gran-**plahr**-skee] adj.m. of carding; of a carder
gręplarz [**gran**-plahsh] m. carder
gręplować [gran-**plo**-vahćh] v. card (wool, cotton) (*repeatedly*)
gręplowanie [gran-plo-**vah**-ńe] n. carding (of wool, cotton)
gręplownia [gran-**plov**-ńah] f. carding shop
gręplowy [gran-**plo**-vi] adj.m. of carding tool; of carding
gręplo [**gran**-pwo] n. thread made out of rope
grill [greel] m. grill
grindwal [**greend**-vahl] m. variety of dolphin
gringo [**green**-go] m. gringo
grizzly [**greez**-lee] m. grizzly (bear)
grobek [**gro**-bek] m. child's grave
grobelka [gro-**bel**-kah] f. (small) dike; dam
grobelny [gro-**bel**-ni] adj.m. of a dike; of a dam
grobla [**grob**-lah] f. dike; dam
grobowcowy [gro-bof-**tso**-vi] adj.m. tomb; sepulchral; of a family vault
grobowiec [gro-**bo**-vyets] m. tomb; sepulcher; family vault
grobowo [gro-**bo**-vo] adv. sepulchrally; gravely; gloomily; dismally
grobowy [gro-**bo**-vi] adj.m. grave; deathly; gloomy; dismal
groch [grokh] m. pea; pea plant; dot
grochodrzew [gro-**kho**-dzhef] m. robinia (tree or shrub)
grochowianka [gro-kho-**vyahn**-kah] f. pea aphid

grochowina [gro-kho-**vee**-nah] f. thrashed pea plants; haulm
grochowisko [gro-kho-**vees**-ko] n. pea field
grochowy [gro-**kho**-vi] adj.m. of peas; of the pea plant; pea (soup, etc.)
grochówka [gro-**khoof**-kah] f. pea soup
grodka [**grot**-kah] f. (small) pen; cage; cofferdam
grododzierżca [gro-do-**dźhersh**-tsah] m. castellan (hist.)
grodowy [gro-**do**-vi] adj.m. castle (fortifications, etc.)
grodza [**gro**-dzah] f. box in a stable; cofferdam
grodzenie [gro-**dze**-ńe] n. fencing (of a property, etc.)
grodzić [**gro**-dźheećh] v. fence; fence off; wall; enclose with a fence (wall) (*repeatedly*)
grodziec [**gro**-dźhets] m. castle; stronghold; medieval city
grodzisko [gro-**dźhees**-ko] n. powerful castle; stronghold; ruins of a medieval castle
grodziszcze [gro-**dźheesh**-che] n. powerful castle; stronghold; ruins of a medieval castle
grodzki [**grots**-kee] adj.m. of a town; of a city; town; city (management, hall, etc.)
sąd grodzki [sownt **grots**-kee] exp.: court of the first instance
grog [grog] m. grog; toddy
grom [grom] m. thunderclap; thunder
spaść jak grom [spahśhćh yahk grom] exp.: to come like a thunderclap
gromada [gro-mah-dah] f. crowd; throng; community; team
gromadka [gro-**maht**-kah] f. (small) crowd; throng; community; team
gromadnie [gro-**mahd**-ńe] adv. in a group; in a mass; together; in clusters
gromadnik [gro-**mahd**-ńeek] m. capelin (marine fish)
gromadny [gro-**mah**-dni] adj.m. collective; sociable; social; corporate; joint; united; gregarious; common; numerous
gromadzenie [gro-mah-**dze**-ńe] n. amassing; hoarding; accumulating
gromadzenie się [gro-mah-**dze**-ńe śhan] n. assembling; gathering
gromadzić [gro-**mah**-dźheećh] v. amass; hoard; gather; attract; accumulate; collect; store; cluster (*repeatedly*)
gromadzić się [gro-**mah**-dźheećh śhan] v. assemble; gather; collect; meet; get together; flock together; cluster; muster; accumulate (dust, etc.); heap up; drift (together); blank up; lour (clouds, etc.); lower (clouds) (*repeatedly*)
gromadzki [gro-**mahts**-kee] adj.m. of a district; district (council, etc.)
gromić [**gro**-meećh] v. storm; rout; reprimand; defeat (*repeatedly*)
gromienie [gro-**mye**-ńe] n. reprimand; defeat; a defeat
gromki [**grom**-kee] adj.m. loud; resounding; ringing; rousing; sonorous; stormy
gromko [**grom**-ko] adv. loudly; resoundingly; stormily; in a rousing manner
gromnica [grom-**ńee**-tsah] f. blessed candle
gromniczny [grom-**ńeech**-ni] adj.m. Candlemas (day)
gromowładca [gro-mo-**vwaht**-tsah] m. the Thunderer
gromowładny [gro-mo-**vwahd**-ni] adj.m. thundering
gromowy [gro-**mo**-vi] adj.m. thundering
groniasty [gro-**ńahs**-ti] adj.m. racemose
gronik [**gro**-ńeek] m. botrytis
gronko [**gron**-ko] n. (small) bunch of grapes; cluster
gronkowaty [gron-ko-**vah**-ti] adj.m. shaped like a bunch of grapes
gronkowcowy [gron-kof-**tso**-vi] adj.m. staphylococcus (infection, etc.)
gronkowiec [gron-**ko**-vyets] m. staphylococcus
gronkowce [gron-**kof**-tse] pl. the genus Staphylococci
grono [**gro**-no] n. bunch of grapes; cluster; group; body of people;

company; circle
gronodrzew [gro-**no**-dzhef] m. sea grape
gronorost [gro-**no**-rost] m. sargasso weed; gulfweed
gronostaj [gro-**no**-stahy] m. ermine
gronostajowy [gro-no-stah-**yo**-vi] adj.m. ermine (coat, etc.); of ermine
gronowy [gro-**no**-vi] adj.m. of grapes; grape (wine, etc.); racemic
cukier gronowy [tsoo-ker gro-no-vi] exp.: grape sugar; glucose
groom [groom] m. groom; tiger
gros [gro] indecl.: m. gross; twelve dozen; n. main part; majority
grosik [**gro**-śheek] m. small penny
grosista [gro-**śhees**-tah] m. wholesale dealer; wholesaler
grosiwo [gro-**śhee**-vo] n. money; cash; slang: funds; brass
grosular [gro-**soo**-lahr] m. grossular; grossularite
grosz [grosh] m. grosz; penny; one-hundredth of a zloty; money; funds
groszak [gro-shahk] m. a copper; a brass farthing; a red cent
groszek [**gro**-shek] m. green pea; spotted pattern; grainy surface; (sweet) pea
groszkować [grosh-**ko**-vahćh] v. grain (leather); cover with spots (*repeatedly*)
groszkowanie [grosh-ko-**vah**-ńe] n. spots
groszkowany [grosh-ko-**vah**-ni] adj.m. spotted; covered with spots
groszkowaty [grosh-ko-**vah**-ti] adj.m. grained (paper)
groszkownica [grosh-kov-**ńee**-tsah] f. leather graining machine
groszkownik [grosh-**kov**-ńeek] m. chipping hammer
groszkowy [grosh-**ko**-vi] adj.m. grained (leather)
groszkówka [grosh-**koof**-kah] f. pisidium
groszorób [gro-**sho**-roop] m. money-grabber
groszoróbstwo [gro-sho-**roop**-stfo] n. money-grabbing
groszowy [gro-**sho**-vi] adj.m. bought for a penny; sold for a penny; made for a penny; cheap; inexpensive
groszówka [gro-**shoof**-kah] f. one-grosz coin
grot [grot] m. dart; pike; arrow; javelin; arrow-head; spear-head; fluke; mainmast; mainsail
grot- [grot] prefix: main-(sail, etc.)
grota [**gro**-tah] f. grotto; cave
grotesk [**gro**-tesk] m. bold-faced font (type); text printed in bold letters
groteska [gro-**tes**-kah] f. burlesque; grotesque
groteskowo [gro-tes-**ko**-vo] adv. grotesquely; farcically; ludicrously
groteskowość [gro-tes-**ko**-vośhćh] f. grotesqueness; farcicality
groteskowy [gro-tes-**ko**-vi] adj.m. grotesque; farcical; ludicrous
grotmarsel [grot-**mahr**-sel] m. second lowest sail on the mainmast
grotmaszt [**grot**-mahsht] m. mainmast
grotołaz [gro-**to**-wahs] m. cave climber
grotować [gro-**to**-vahćh] v. shape stone surface with a chisel (*repeatedly*)
grotowanie [gro-to-**vah**-ńe] n. shaping stone surface with a chisel
grotreja [grot-**re**-yah] f. bottom boom on mainmast
grottopsel [grot-**top**-sel] m. topsail
grotżagiel [grot-**zhah**-gel] m. mainsail
groza [**gro**-zah] f. dread; horror; grimness; danger; threat; menace; awe; terror
grozić [**gro**-źheećh] v. threaten; menace; impend; be imminent; hang over (*repeatedly*)
nic ci nie grozi [ńeets ćhee ńe gro-źhee] exp.: you are quite safe; you are out of danger
groźba [**groźh**-bah] f. threat; danger; menace; imminence; liability (to fines; penalty, etc.)
groźnie [**groźh**-ńe] adv. menacingly; threateningly; grimly;

ominously; formidably
groźny [grożh-ni] adj.m. threatening; menacing; grim; ominous; imminent; dangerous; formidable; forbidding; pressing; grave; ugly; nasty; glaring; scowling
grożenie [gro-zhe-ńe] n. threatening
grób [groop] m. grave; tomb; Sepulcher
gród [groot] m. (fortified) town; castle; stronghold; medieval city
gródek [groo-dek] m. (small) castle; stronghold
gródź [grooćh] f. watertight bulkhead
gruba [groo-bah] f. stove; hearth; mine; quarry
grubachny [groo-bahkh-ni] adj.m. very fat; very thick
grubas [groo-bahs] m. fatty man; corpulent person
grubasek [groo-bah-sek] m. (nice, small) fatty man; corpulent boy
grubaska [groo-bahs-kah] f. (nice, small) fatty girl; corpulent woman (girl); stout woman
grubaśny [groo-baśh-ni] adj.m. very fat; very thick
grubawo [groo-bah-vo] adv. pretty fat; pretty stout; pretty thick
grubawy [groo-bah-vi] adj.m. fattish; stoutish; thickish
gruber [groo-ber] m. grubber
gruberować [groo-be-ro-vahćh] v. grub (*repeatedly*)
gruberowanie [groo-be-ro-vah-ńe] n. grubbing
grubianin [groo-byah-ńeen] m. yokel; boor; lout
grubianka [groo-byahn-kah] f. (woman) yokel; boor; lout
grubiański [groo-byahń-skee] adj.m. rude; coarse; obscene; rough; brutal; unmannerly; obscene; ribald; scurrilous; churlish; uncivil; ill-mannered; uncouth; rough-hewn
po grubiańsku [po groo-byahń-skoo] exp.: in an ill-mannered way; rudely; roughly; brutally; coarsely; grossly; churlishly; uncivilly; in an unmannerly fashion
grubiańsko [groo-byahń-sko] adv. rudely; roughly; brutally; coarsely; grossly; churlishly; uncivilly; in an unmannerly fashion
grubiańskość [groo-byahń-skośhćh] f. rudeness; bad manners
grubiaństwo [groo-byahń-stfo] n. rudeness; coarseness; roughness; bad manners; grossness; bad language; swearing; foul word; coarse expression
grubiarka [groo-byahr-kah] f. planing machine
grubieć [groo-byećh] v. grow stouter; put on flesh; grow bigger; thicken; coarsen; roughen; become low-pitched (*repeatedly*)
grubienie [groo-bye-ńe] n. growing stouter (thicker)
grubizna [groo-beez-nah] f. big timber (minimum three inches thick)
grubo [groo-bo] adv. thick; thickly; in a low voice; coarsely; crudely
chleb grubo krajany [khleb groo-bo krah-yah-ni] exp.: bread cut thick
grubo po godzinie [groo-bo po go-dźhee-ńe] exp.: long past the hour
grubo więcej [groo-bo vyan-tsey] exp.: a lot more
grubodzioby [groo-bo-dźho-bi] adj.m. grosbeak (nest, etc.)
grubodziób [groo-bo-dźhoop] m. hawfinch; grosbeak
grubokościsty [groo-bo-kośh-ćhees-ti] adj.m. heavy-boned
grubokroplisty [groo-bo-krop-lees-ti] adj.m. appearing in large drops
grubokrystaliczny [groo-bo-kris-tah-leech-ni] adj.m. coarse-crystalline
grubomierz [groo-bo-myesh] m. thickness gauge
grubonasienny [groo-bo-nah-śhen-ni] adj.m. coarse-grained
gruboskórnie [groo-bo-skoor-ńe] adv. callously; coarsely; rudely
gruboskórność [groo-bo-skoor-nośhćh] f. callosity; callousness; coarseness; thick skin
gruboskórny [groo-bo-skoor-ni] adj.m. callous; coarse; rude;

rough; crude
gruboskóry [groo-bo-**skoo**-ri] adj.m. thick-skinned; pachydermatous
grubosz [**groo**-bosh] m. crassula (herb)
gruboszowaty [groo-bo-sho-**vah**-ti] adj.m. crassulaceous
gruboszowate [groo-bo-sho-**vah**-te] pl. the family Crassulaceae of herbs
grubościenny [groo-bo-**śhćhen**-ni] adj.m. thick-walled
grubościomierz [groo-bośh-**ćho**-myesh] m. thickness gauge
grubość [**groo**-bośhćh] f. thickness; girth; size; volume; grist; coarseness; roughness; stoutness; bulk; portliness; crudeness
grubowełnisty [groo-bo-vew-**ńees**-ti] adj.m. thick-wooled
gruboziarnistość [groo-bo-źhahr-**ńees**-tośhćh] f. coarse grain
gruboziarnisty [groo-bo-źhahr-**ńees**-ti] adj.m. coarse-grained
gruby [**groo**-bi] adj.m. thick; fat; big; stout; large; low-pitched
z grubsza [z **groop**-shah] exp.: roughly; roughly speaking
gruch [grookh] m. coo; cooing; warble; gurgle; excl.: crash!; bang!
gruchacz [**groo**-khahch] m. a variety of tropical bird
gruchać [**groo**-khahćh] v. coo; warble; speak in a warble; sing in a warble; gurgle; bill and coo (*repeatedly*)
gruchanie [groo-**khah**-ńe] n. cooing; warbling; speaking in a warble; singing in a warble; gurgling; billing and cooing
gruchawka [groo-**khahf**-kah] f. coo; cooing; warble; gurgle; turtle dove; rattle; a primitive percussion instrument
gruchnąć [**grookh**-nownćh] v. crash; resound; shoot; bash; whack; run; fall with a crash; burst on the ear; come like a bombshell; hit; knock; smash; fall to; tumble down; rattle down; collapse
gruchnięcie [grookh-**ńan**-ćhe] n. crash; shot; knock; whack; fall; rattle; collapse
gruchnięcie się [grookh-ńan-ćhe śhan] n. having a fall; knocking oneself
gruchot [**groo**-khot] m. crash; rattle; dilapidated object; worn-out object; rattletrap; shandrydan; jalopy; old crook
gruchotać [groo-**kho**-tahćh] v. shatter; batter; rattle; crash; smash; resound; ring (*repeatedly*)
gruchotanie [groo-kho-**tah**-ńe] n. shattering; battering; rattling; crashing; smashing; resounding; ringing
gruczolak [groo-**cho**-lahk] m. adenoma
gruczoł [**groo**-chow] m. gland
gruczołek [groo-**cho**-wek] m. glandule; a small (nectar) gland; nectary
gruczołowaty [groo-cho-wo-**vah**-ti] adj.m. glandular; glandiform; glandlike
gruczołowy [groo-cho-**wo**-vi] adj.m. of a gland; of glands; glandular
gruda [**groo**-dah] f. lump (of earth); clod; frozen ground; (horse's) grapes; sallenders (eczematous eruption on horse's hind leg)
grudka [**groot**-kah] f. lump (of earth); clot (of blood, etc.); nodule; papule; papula
grudkować [groot-**ko**-vahćh] v. make nodular (*repeatedly*)
grudkować się [groot-**ko**-vahćh śhan] v. clot (*repeatedly*)
grudkowanie [groot-ko-**vah**-ńe] n. clotting
grudkowanie się [groot-ko-**vah**-ńe śhan] n. getting clotted
grudkowatość [groot-ko-vah-tośhćh] f. cloddishness; lumpiness
grudkowaty [groot-ko-**vah**-ti] adj.m. cloddy; cloddish; clotty; lumpy; nodular
grudkownia [groot-**kov**-ńah] f. (ore, etc.) pelletizing plant
grudkowy [groot-**ko**-vi] adj.m. in form of nodules; containing lumps
grudniowiec [grood-**ńo**-vyets] m. decembrist

grudniowy [grood-ńo-vi] adj.m. of December; December (day, etc.)
grudowaty [groo-do-**vah**-ti] adj.m. cloddish
grudzić [**groo**-dźheećh] v. freeze into clods (*repeatedly*)
grudzień [**groo**-dźheń] m. (the month of) December
grujer [**groo**-yer] m. gruyere (cheese)
grula [**groo**-lah] f. colloq: potato; tater
grum [groom] m. groom
grumot [**groo**-mot] m. reinforced edge of a hole in a sail; reinforced ring made of rope or wire
grundwaga [groond-**vah**-gah] f. (mason's) plumb line
grunt [groont] m. ground; soil; earth; land; grounds; bottom; base; basis; ground color; undercoat (of paint)
do gruntu [do **groon**-too] exp.: thoroughly; radically; to the core
to grunt [to groont] exp.: that is the main thing
trafić na podatny grunt [trah-feećh nah po-**daht**-ni groont] exp.: to find favorable conditions
w gruncie rzeczy [v **groon**-ćhe **zhe**-chi] exp.: in fact; as a matter of fact
z gruntu [z **groon**-too] exp.: thoroughly; from the very foundations; basically; fundamentally
znaleźć grunt pod nogami [znah-leśhćh groont pod no-**gah**-mee] exp.: to find bottom
gruntogryzarka [groon-to-gri-**zahr**-kah] f. road-building machine (mixing soil with cement)
gruntoszpachlówka [groon-to-shpahkh-**loof**-kah] f. filler-paint
gruntować [groon-**to**-vahćh] v. ground; base; to touch bottom; stand on firm ground; run ashore (*repeatedly*)
gruntować się [groon-**to**-vahćh śh<u>an</u>] v. base oneself (*repeatedly*)
gruntowanie [groon-to-**vah**-ńe] n. grounding; running ashore; touching bottom
gruntownie [groon-**tov**-ńe] adv. thoroughly; radically; completely; altogether; downright; to the backbone
gruntowność [groon-**tov**-nośhćh] f. thoroughness; completeness
gruntowny [groon-**tov**-ni] adj.m. radical; profound; mature; serious; deep; complete; downright; close; searching; intimate
gruntowy [groon-**to**-vi] adj.m. of the land; (tax, value, etc.); of the ground landlord; ground (color, rent, etc.); dirt (road, etc.)
gruntoznawstwo [groon-to-**znahf**-stfo] n. soil mechanics; foundation engineering
gruntówka [groon-**toof**-kah] f. ground-angling line; ground color (coat in a painting)
grupa [**groo**-pah] f. group; class; division; party; cluster; clump; nucleus; body; set; series; squad
grupet [**groo**-pet] m. (musical) turn
grupka [**groop**-kah] f. (small) group; class; division; party; cluster; clump; nucleus; body; set; series; squad
grupowa [groo-**po**-vah] f. woman in charge of a group
grupować [groo-**po**-vahćh] v. assemble; bring together; group; classify (*repeatedly*)
grupować się [groo-**po**-vahćh śh<u>an</u>] v. assemble; come together; cluster; form a nucleus (*repeatedly*)
grupowanie [groo-po-**vah**-ńe] n. grouping; clustering
grupowanie się [groo-po-**vah**-ńe śh<u>an</u>] n. assembling; coming together; clustering; forming a nucleus
grupowo [groo-**po**-vo] adv. in groups; in clusters
grupowy [groo-**po**-vi] adj.m. of a group; of a class; group (solidarity, etc.); joint; collective; common; m. man in charge of a group
grusza [**groo**-shah] f. pear tree
gruszczanka [groosh-**chahn**-kah] f. pear soup
gruszecznik [groo-**shech**-ńeek] m.

pear-juice drink
gruszka [**groosh**-kah] f. pear; pear tree; pear-shaped object; bulb; punching ball; colloq: punch on the head
gruszkowaty [groosh-ko-**vah**-ti] adj.m. pear-shaped
gruszkownik [groosh-**kov**-ńeek] m. pear-juice drink
gruszowy [groo-**sho**-vi] adj.m. pear-tree (trunk, etc.)
gruszyczka [groo-**shich**-kah] f. wintergreen; pyrola herb
gruszyczkowaty [groo-shich-ko-**vah**-ti] adj.m. pyrolaceous
gruszyczkowate [groo-shich-ko-**vah**-te] pl. the pyrolaceous family of plants
gruz [groos] m. rubble; ruins
gruzy [**groo**-zi] pl. debris; ruins; wreckage
leżeć w gruzach [le-zhećh v **groo**-zahkh] exp.: to lie in ruin
odgarniać gruzy [od-**gahr**-ńahćh **groo**-zi] exp.: to clear debris; to remove wreckage (of structures)
rozpadać się w gruzy [ros-**pah**-dahćh śhan v **groo**-zi] exp.: to fall into ruin; to go to pieces
gruzeł [**groo**-zew] m. clod; lump (of earth, etc.); clot; excrescence
gruzełek [groo-**ze**-wek] m. (small) clod; lump (of earth, etc.); clot; excrescence; tubercle
gruzełkowatość [groo-zew-ko-**vah**-tośhćh] f. lumpy nature
gruzełkowaty [groo-zew-ko-**vah**-ti] adj.m. cloddish; lumpy
gruzełkowate [groo-zew-ko-**vah**-te] pl. the sac fungi
gruzełkowy [groo-zew-**ko**-vi] adj.m. lumpy
Gruzin [**groo**-źheen] m. Georgian man
Gruzinka [groo-**źheen**-kah] f. Georgian woman
gruziński [groo-**źheeń**-skee] adj.m. Georgian
gruzłek [**grooz**-wek] m. nectria (a sac fungus)
gruzłowaty [grooz-wo-**vah**-ti] adj.m. cloddish; lumpy
gruzobeton [groo-zo-**be**-ton] m. concrete made of crushed bricks and stones
gruzowisko [groo-zo-**vees**-ko] n. rubble heap; ruins
gruzowy [groo-**zo**-vi] adj.m. of rubble; of debris; of wreckage
gruzy [**groo**-zi] pl. debris; ruins; wreckage
gruźlica [grooźh-**lee**-tsah] f. tuberculosis; consumption
gruźliczak [grooźh-**lee**-chahk] m. tuberculous tumor
gruźliczka [grooźh-**leech**-kah] f. (female) consumptive
gruźliczy [grooźh-**lee**-chi] adj.m. tuberculous; consumptive
gruźlik [**grooźh**-leek] m. consumptive (man)
gryczanka [gri-**chahn**-kah] f. buckwheat straw
gryczany [gri-**chah**-ni] adj.m. of buckwheat; buckwheat (porridge, kasha, etc.)
gryf [grif] m. griffon; griffin; griffonne; neck (of a violin); calk (of a horseshoe)
gryfon [**gri**-fon] m. griffon; griffonne (hunting dog)
gryka [**gri**-kah] f. buckwheat
grylaż [**gri**-lahsh] m. kind of sweetmeat
grylażowy [gri-lah-**zho**-vi] adj.m. sweetmeat (candy, etc.)
grymas [**gri**-mahs] m. grimace; grin; wry face
grymasić [gri-**mah**-śheećh] v. be fussy; grizzle; whimper; be choosy; be fastidious; be fretful; be particular; colloq: pick and choose (*repeatedly*)
grymaszenie [gri-mah-**she**-ńe] n. fussing; fuss
grymaśnica [gri-mahśh-**ńee**-tsah] f. fussy woman (girl); fastidious; exacting woman; pernickety woman; woman given to whims
grymaśnie [gri-**mahśh**-ńe] adv. with a wry face; with a grimace; fussily; fastidiously
grymaśnik [gri-**mahśh**-ńeek] m. fussy man (boy); colloq: pernickety man; man given to whims
grymaśny [gri-**mahśh**-ni] adj.m. fussy; fastidious; colloq:

pernickety; given to whims
grynderstwo [grin-**der**-stfo] n. launching of a business enterprise
grynszpan [**grin**-shpahn] m. verdigris; green rust (of copper); copper rust
grynszpanowy [grin-shpah-**no**-vi] adj.m. aeruginous; verdigris
kolor grynszpanowy [**ko**-lor grin-shpah-**no**-vi] exp.: verdigris green
grypa [**gri**-pah] f. flu; influenza; flue; grippe
grypka [**grip**-kah] f. touch of flu; influenza; flue; grippe
grypowicz [gri-**po**-veech] m. colloq: man sick with the flu
grypowy [gri-**po**-vi] adj.m. of the flu; of influenza; of grippe
gryps [grips] m. colloq: message smuggled through, to or from a prison
grypser [**grip**-ser] m. mob slang: man speaking in prison slang
grypsera [grip-**se**-rah] f. slang: prison slang (mob jargon)
grypsować [grip-**so**-vahćh] v. slang: smuggle messages through, to or from a prison (*repeatedly*)
grys [gris] m. clippings; crushed gravel; grits; whole meal
grysik [**gri**-śheek] m. manna-croup; semolina; cream of wheat; granulated sugar; sorted small chunks of coal; crushed gravel
grysikowy [gri-śhee-**ko**-vi] adj.m. of manna-croup
grysowy [gri-**so**-vi] adj.m. crushed-gravel (concrete, road, etc.)
grywać [**gri**-vahćh] v. play occasionally; play now and then; play from time to time; play now and again; be accustomed to play (*repeatedly*)
grywanie [gri-**vah**-ńe] n. frequent playing; occasional playing; the custom of playing
gryz [gris] m. drilling bit
gryzak [**gri**-zahk] m. pacifier; baby's toy suitable for biting while teething; drilling roller bit
gryzący [gri-**zown**-tsi] adj.m. pungent; acrid; corrosive; scratchy
gryzetka [gri-**zet**-kah] f. grisette
gryzienie [gri-**źhe**-ńe] n. biting; gnawing
gryzienie się [gri-**źhe**-ńe śhan] n. biting (one's lips, etc.); worry; fretting; being at loggerheads
gryzipiórek [gri-źhee-**pyoo**-rek] m. colloq: scribbler; quill-driller; pen pusher; second-class writer; slang: official
gryzki [**gris**-kee] pl. an order of insects (book lice, etc.)
gryzmolenie [griz-mo-**le**-ńe] n. scrawls; scribbles
gryzmolić [griz-**mo**-leećh] v. scrawl; scribble (*repeatedly*)
gryzmoła [griz-**mo**-wah] m. & f. colloq: scribbler; quill-driller; pen pusher; second-class writer
gryzoniobójczy [gri-zo-ńo-**booy**-chi] adj.m. rodent-killing
gryzoń [**gri**-zoń] m. rodent
gryzonie [gri-**zo**-ńe] pl. rodents
gryzowy [gri-**zo**-vi] adj.m. of a drilling bit
gryźć [griśhćh] v. bite; gnaw; chew; prick; torment; worry; fret (*repeatedly*)
gryźć się [griśhćh śhan] v. bite (one's lips, tongue, etc.); bite one another; be at loggerheads; torment oneself; jar; worry; eat one's heart out (*repeatedly*)
grzać [gzhahćh] v. warm; fire; warm up; get warm; get hot; keep warm; batter; beat; shoot like blazes; thrash; give out heat; be hot (*repeatedly*)
grzać się [gzhahćh śhan] v. warm oneself; get warm; be getting warm; sweat; be in heat; colloq: batter one another (*repeatedly*)
grzać się w słońcu [gzhahćh śhan f **swoń**-tsoo] exp.: to bask in the sun
woda się grzeje [**vo**-dah śhan **gzhe**-ye] exp.: I am getting some water hot; the water is on
grzałka [**gzhahw**-kah] f. warmer; heater
grzaneczka [gzhah-**nech**-kah] f. (nice, little) toast; French toast; sop; sippet; mulled mead (soup)
grzanie [**gzhah**-ńe] n. warming (up)
grzanie się [**gzhah**-ńe śhan] n.

warming oneself up
grzanka [**gzhahn**-kah] f. toast; French toast
grzanki do zupy [**gzhahn**-kee do **zoo**-pi] exp.: croutons
grządka [**gzhownt**-kah] f. flower bed; patch; (hen-) roost
grządziel [**gzhown**-dźhel] m. & f. plow-beam
grząski [**gzhowns**-kee] adj.m. slimy; miry; quaggy; slushy
grząsko [**gzhowns**-ko] adv. exp.: it is (the road is) slimy; it is miry; it is quaggy; it is slushy
grząść [gzhownśhćh] v. wade; proceed with difficulty; flounder; get stuck (*repeatedly*)
grzbiecik [**gzhbye**-ćheek] m. (small) back; spine; ridge; butt; edge; rib
grzbiecisty [gzhbye-**ćhees**-ti] adj.m. with a strong back
grzbiet [gzhbyet] m. back; spine; ridge; butt; edge; rib
nadstawiać grzbietu [naht-**stah**-vyahćh **gzhbye**-too] exp.: to run great risks
z nagim grzbietem [z **nah**-geem **gzhbye**-tem] exp.: bare-backed
ostry grzbiet [os-tri gzhbyet] exp.: razor-edge
grzbietnica [gzhbyet-**ńee**-tsah] f. handsaw with stiffened back edge of the cutting blade; backsaw
grzbietopłat [gzhbye-**to**-pwaht] m. high-wing monoplane
grzbietopławek [gzhbye-to-**pwah**-vek] m. water boatman (bug)
grzbietoród [gzhbye-**to**-root] m. tailless reptile
grzbietowy [gzhbye-**to**-vi] adj.m. dorsal (fin, etc.); tergal; of tergum
styl grzbietowy [stil gzhbye-**to**-vi] exp.: backstroke
grzbietówka [gzhbye-**toof**-kah] f. book-spine (reinforcing) strip
grzdykać [**gzhdi**-kahćh] v. gobble; gulp noisily (*repeatedly*)
grzdyknąć [**gzhdik**-nownćh] v. gobble; gulp noisily
grzdykanie [gzhdi-**kah**-ńe] n. gobbling; noisy gulps
grzdyl [gzhdil] m. colloq: stripling; callow youth; raw lad
grzebacz [**gzhe**-bahch] m. digger wasp
grzebacze [gzhe-**bah**-che] pl. the family Sphecidae of diger wasps
grzebaczkowaty [gzhe-bahch-ko-**vah**-ti] adj.m. of the digger-wasps family; sphecid
grzebać [**gzhe**-bahćh] v. bury; rummage; dig (in books); search; rake up; fumble (*repeatedly*)
grzebać się [**gzhe**-bahćh śhan] v. be buried; dawdle; potter (at, with); boggle (over); plod along (*repeatedly*)
grzebak [**gzhe**-bahk] m. poker; rake
grzebalisko [gzhe-bah-**lees**-ko] n. chicken digging sand-pad
grzebalny [gzhe-**bahl**-ni] adj.m. of burial; burial (service, etc.); burying (ground, etc.)
grzebała [gzhe-**bah**-wah] m. & f. colloq: fumbler; potterer; slacker
grzebuła [gzhe-**boo**-wah] m. & f. colloq: fumbler; potterer; slacker
grzebanie [gzhe-**bah**-ńe] n. burial
grzebanie się [gzhe-**bah**-ńe śhan] n. fumble
grzebanina [gzhe-bah-**ńee**-nah] f. fumbling; pottering
grzebiący [gzhe-**byown**-tsi] adj.m. gallinaceous; of a bird of terrestrial habits; of domestic fowl
grzebiące [gzhe-**byown**-tse] adj.m. birds of terrestrial habits
grzebielucha [gzhe-bye-**loo**-khah] f. sand martin; bank swallow
grzebieniarstwo [gzhe-bye-**ńahr**-stfo] n. comb making
grzebieniarz [gzhe-**bye**-ńahsh] m. comb maker
grzebieniasty [gzhe-bye-**ńahs**-ti] adj.m. comb-shaped; pectinate; pectinated; crested; catenoid
grzebienica [gzhe-bye-**ńee**-tsah] f. dog's-tail (grass)
grzebieniowaty [gzhe-bye-ńo-**vah**-ti] adj.m. comb-like
grzebieniowiec [gzhe-bye-**ńo**-vyets] m. of the Carinatae class of birds
grzebieniowce [gzhe-bye-**ńof**-tse] pl. the Carinatae class of birds
grzebieniowy [gzhe-bye-**ńo**-vi] adj.m. of a comb; of the Carinate

class of birds
grzebień [**gzhe**-byeń] m. comb; crest of a wave; teaser
grzebionatka [gzhe-byo-**naht**-kah] f. cockscomb (shrub)
grzebiuszka [gzhe-**byoosh**-kah] f. pelobatid arciferous amphibian (spadefoot toad, etc.)
grzebnąć [**gzheb**-nownćh] v. bury; rummage; dig; rake up; search
grzebnięcie [gzheb-**ńan**-ćhe] n. dig; raking up
grzebowisko [gzhe-bo-**vees**-ko] n. terrain designated for burial of animals
grzebyczek [gzhe-**bi**-chek] m. very small comb
grzebyk [**gzhe**-bik] m. small comb; side comb
grzebykowaty [gzhe-bi-ko-**vah**-ti] adj.m. comb-shaped
grzech [gzhekh] m. sin; fault
grzech: pierworodny, powszedni, śmiertelny [gzhekh pyer-vo-**rod**-ni, po-**fshed**-ńee, śhmyer-**tel**-ni] exp.: sin: original, venial, mortal
bez grzechu [bez **gzhe**-khoo] exp.: sinless; innocent
popełnić grzech [po-**pew**-ńeećh gzhekh] exp.: to sin; to commit a sin
mieć grzechy na sumieniu [myećh **gzhe**-khi nah soo-**mye**-ńoo] exp.: to have a guilty conscience
grzechot [**gzhe**-khot] m. rattle; din
grzechotać [gzhe-**kho**-tahćh] v. rattle; croak (*repeatedly*)
grzechotanie [gzhe-kho-**tah**-ńe] n. rattle; croak
grzechotka [gzhe-**khot**-kah] f. rattle-box; flapper; clapper; colloq: chatterbox (woman)
grzechotliwy [gzhe-khot-**lee**-vi] adj.m. rattling
grzechotnik [gzhe-**khot**-ńeek] m. rattlesnake
grzecznie [**gzhech**-ńe] adv. kindly; politely; nicely; with courtesy; urbanely; civilly
zachowuj się grzecznie [zah-**kho**-vooy śhan **gzhech**-ńe] exp.: behave yourself; be good; be a good boy; be a good girl
grzeczniś [**gzhech**-ńeeśh] m. obsequious person; subservient person
grzeczniutki [gzhech-**ńoot**-kee] adj.m. extremely polite; very courteous; well-behaved
grzeczniutko [gzhech-**ńoot**-ko] adv. very politely; with great courtesy; with extreme politeness
grzecznostka [gzhech-**nost**-kah] f. kind word; compliment; favor; service; little deed of kindness
grzecznościowy [gzhech-nośh-**ćho**-vi] adj.m. polite; honorific; complimentary; out of courtesy
grzeczność [**gzhech**-nośhćh] f. politeness; favor; attentions; courteousness; mannerliness; good behavior; favor; kindness
zrobić komuś grzeczność [**zro**-beećh **ko**-moośh **gzhech**-nośhćh] exp.: to do somebody a favor (a kindness)
przez czyjąś grzechność [pshes **chi**-yownśh **gzhech**-nośhćh] exp.: by favor of somebody
grzeczny [**gzhech**-ni] adj.m. polite; courteous; mannerly; well-behaved; kind; obliging; urbane; civil; well-bred; affable; considerable
grzejka [**gzhey**-kah] f. hot water bottle
grzejnictwo [gzhey-**ńeets**-tfo] n. calorific studies
grzejnik [**gzhey**-ńeek] m. radiator; heater; warming device
grzejnikowy [gzhey-ńee-**ko**-vi] adj.m. of a radiator; of a heater; of a warming device
grzejny [**gzhey**-ni] adj.m. heating (surface, etc.)
grzeszek [**gzhe**-shek] m. minor sin; peccadillo
grzeszenie [gzhe-**she**-ńe] n. sins
grzesznica [gzhesh-**ńee**-tsah] f. (woman) sinner; transgressor; offender; wrongdoer
grzesznie [**gzhesh**-ńe] adv. sinfully; wickedly
grzesznik [**gzhesh**-ńeek] m. sinner; offender; transgressor; wrongdoer; reprobate; scamp
grzeszność [**gzhesh**-nośhćh] f.

sinfulness; wickedness; peccancy; iniquity
grzeszny [**gzhesh**-ni] adj.m. sinful; guilty; immoral; unholy; ungodly; iniquitous; wrong; peccant
grzeszyć [**gzhe**-shićh] v. sin; commit a sin; do wrong; trespass; err; transgress; offend (against) (*repeatedly*)
grzewczy [**gzhef**-chi] adj.m. heating (installation, etc.)
grzęda [**gzhan**-dah] f. patch; roost; hen-roost; perch
siedzieć na grzędzie [**śhe**-dźhećh nah **gzhan**-dźhe] exp.: to roost; to perch
grzędowy [gzhan-**do**-vi] adj.m. patchy (structure, etc.)
grzędziel [**gzhan**-dźhel] m. plow-beam
grzęzawisko [gzhan-zah-**vees**-ko] n. quag; shaky quagmire; morass
grzęznąć [**gzhanz**-nownćh] v. get stuck; wade; flounder; sink in (a quagmire, mud) (*repeatedly*)
grzęzy [**gzhan**-zi] pl. udders
grzęźnięcie [gzhanz-**ńan**-ćhe] n. getting stuck; wading; floundering
grzęzy [**gzhan**-zi] pl. fallow-deer nipple; weights on a net
grzmiąco [**gzhmyown**-tso] adv. thunderously
grzmiący [**gzhmyown**-tsi] adj.m. thundering; thunderous; booming; fulminatory
grzmieć [gzhmyećh] v. thunder; peal; boom; rumble; roar; roll; ring; blare (*repeatedly*)
grzmi [gzhmee] exp.: it is thundering
grzmienie [**gzhmye**-ńe] n. peals of thunder
grzmocenie [gzhmo-**tse**-ńe] n. blows
grzmocenie się [gzhmo-**tse**-ńe śhan] n. exchanging blows
grzmocić [**gzhmo**-ćheećh] v. bang; whack; slog; pelt; slang: plug (mob jargon) (*repeatedly*)
grzmocić w ping-ponga [**gzhmo**-ćheećh f peeng-**pon**-gah] exp.: colloq: to bang away at Ping-Pong; to slog at Ping-Pong
grzmocić się [**gzhmo**-ćheećh śhan] v. batter one another; whack one another (*repeatedly*)
grzmot [gzhmot] m. thunder; roar; boom; rumble; crash
grzmotnąć [**gzhmot**-nownćh] v. bang; whack; slog; pelt; hurl down; fling down; crash; boom; roar
grzmotnąć się [**gzhmot**-nownćh śhan] v. bang (one's head, elbow, etc.) against; tumble down; pitch; slang: come a cropper
grzmotnięcie [gzhmot-**ńan**-ćhe] n. blow; knock; smash; whack; downfall; thump; tumble; cropper
grzmotnięcie się [gzhmot-**ńan**-ćhe śhan] n. self-inflicted injury
grzyb [gzhip] m. mushroom; fungus; snuff; dry rot
nauka o grzybach [nah-oo-kah o **gzhi**-bahkh] exp.: mycology
zatrucie grzybami [zah-**troo**-ćhe gzhi-**bah**-mee] exp.: mushroom poisoning
grzybek [**gzhi**-bek] m. (small) fungus; mushroom
grzybek drożdżowy [**gzhi**-bek drozh-**dzho**-vi] exp.: torula
grzybiarz [**gzhi**-byahsh] m. person fond of mushrooms
grzybiasty [gzhi-**byahs**-ti] adj.m. mushroom-shaped
grzybica [gzhi-**bee**-tsah] f. mycosis; tetter
grzybicowy [gzhi-bee-**tso**-vi] adj.m. mycotic
grzybiczy [gzhi-**bee**-chi] adj. mycotic
grzybieć [**gzhi**-byećh] v. shrivel up (*repeatedly*)
grzybieniowaty [gzhi-bye-ńo-**vah**-ti] adj.m. of the family of water lilies; nymphaeaceous
grzybieniowate [gzhi-bye-ńo-**vah**-te] pl. the family of water lilies
grzybień [**gzhi**-byeń] m. water-lily
grzybkowaty [gzhi-pko-**vah**-ti] adj.m. mushroom-shaped
grzybkowy [gzhi-**pko**-vi] adj.m. mushroom-shaped; mycotic
grzybnia [**gzhib**-ńah] f. spawn of fungi; mushroom spawn
grzybniowy [gzhib-**ńo**-vi] adj.m. of mushroom spawn; of mycelium; mycelial

grzybny [**gzhib**-ni] adj.m. abounding in mushrooms
grzybobójczy [gzhi-bo-**booy**-chi] adj.m. fungicidal
grzybobranie [gzhi-bo-**brah**-ńe] n. mushrooming party
grzybodajny [gzhi-bo-**dahy**-ni] adj.m. mushroom-rich
grzybolubka [gzhi-bo-**loop**-kah] f. dipterous larva feeding on mushrooms
grzybowaty [gzhi-bo-**vah**-ti] adj.m. mushroom-shaped
grzybowisko [gzhi-bo-**vees**-ko] n. place abounding in mushrooms
grzybowy [gzhi-**bo**-vi] adj.m. of a mushroom
grzybożywność [gzhi-bo-**zhiv**-nośhćh] f. mycorhiza; mycorrhiza
grzybożywny [gzhi-bo-**zhiv**-ni] adj.m. mycorhizal; mycorrhizal
grzywa [**gzhi**-vah] f. mane; foretop; crest of a wave; comb of a wave; huge head of hair
grzywacz [**gzhi**-vahch] m. ring dove; ring-pigeon; comber; breaking wave
grzyweczka [gzhi-**vech**-kah] f. child's forelock
grzywiasty [gzhi-**vyahs**-ti] adj.m. having large mane
grzywka [**gzhif**-kah] f. forelock; fringe; bang; front toupee; frisette
grzywna [**gzhiv**-nah] f. fine; penalty; forfeit; mulct; ancient monetary unit
guanako [gwah-**nah**-ko] m. guanaco (lama)
guanidyna [gwah-ńee-**di**-nah] f. guanidine
guanina [gwah-**ńee**-nah] f. guanine
guano [**gwah**-no] n. guano
guarana [gwah-**rah**-nah] f. Paullinia woody vine; guarana
guasz [gwahsh] m. gouache (paint and painting technique)
gubernator [goo-ber-**nah**-tor] m. governor (general)
gubernatorowa [goo-ber-nah-to-**ro**-vah] f. governor's wife
gubernatorówna [goo-ber-nah-to-**roov**-nah] f. governor's daughter
gubernatorski [goo-ber-nah-**tor**-skee] adj.m. governor's; gubernatorial
gubernatorstwo [goo-ber-nah-**tor**-stfo] n. province; governor's headquarters
gubernia [goo-**ber**-ńah] f. province; governor's headquarters
Generalna Gubernia [ge-ne-**rahl**-nah goo-**ber**-ńah] exp.: colloq: German-occupied and German-run Poland (without any Polish puppet regime, 1939-1945)
gubernialny [goo-ber-**ńahl**-ni] adj.m. of a province
gubernium [goo-**ber**-ńoom] n. administration of Austro-Hungarian province
gubić [**goo**-beećh] v. loose; mislay; ruin; bring to ruin (*repeatedly*)
gubić się [**goo**-beećh śh<u>an</u>] v. bring about one's ruin; lose one another; get lost; go astray; vanish; get confused; lose one's way; lose oneself (*repeatedly*)
gubić się w domysłach [**goo**-beećh śh<u>an</u> v do-mis-wahkh] exp.: to be lost in conjecture; to speculate; to wonder (why, who, etc.); to be preoccupied with a problem (a question)
gubienie [goo-**bye**-ńe] n. loosing; mislaying; ruining; bringing to ruin
gubienie się [goo-**bye**-ńe śh<u>an</u>] n. getting lost
gudłaj [**good**-wahy] m. slang: vulg.: Yid (mob jargon)
gudron [**good**-ron] m. soft asphalt
guignol [**geen**-yol] m. French puppet doll; marionette
gujot [**goo**-yot] m. underwater volcanic mountain
gul [gool] m. ghoul
gula [**goo**-lah] f. knob; bump; protuberance
gulardowy [goo-lahr-**do**-vi] adj.m. of Goulard's medicine
gulasz [**goo**-lahsh] m. meat soup; stew
gulden [**gool**-den] m. guilder; gulden
gulgot [**gool**-got] m. gurgle; bubbling sound; gobble
gulgotać [gool-**go**-tahćh] v. gurgle; bubble; mumble; gobble (*repeatedly*)
gulgotanie [gool-go-**tah**-ńe] n. bubbling; gurgling

gul-gul [gool gool] indecl.: bubble; gurgle; gobble; gurgling sound
gulka [**gool**-kah] f. (small) knob; bump; protuberance
guła [**goo**-wah] m. & f. bump; mob slang: retard; slow learner
gułag [**goo**-wahg] m. gulag; system of slave-labor camps in the Soviet Union
guma [**goo**-mah] f. rubber; gum; caoutchouc
gumiak [**goo**-myahk] m. rubber boot; cart on rubber tires
gumiguta [goo-mee-**goo**-tah] f. gamboge
gumilaka [goo-mee-**lah**-kah] f. shellac
gumka [**goom**-kah] f. (small) rubber; elastic; eraser; condom
gumno [**goom**-no] n. barn; threshing floor; barn yard
gumodajny [goo-mo-**dahy**-ni] adj.m. guttiferous
gumoleum [goo-mo-**le**-oom] n. linoleum with rubber surface
gumolit [goo-**mo**-leet] m. floor-cover made of rubber
gumolitowy [goo-mo-lee-**to**-vi] adj.m. rubber (floor-cover, etc.)
gumować [goo-**mo**-vahćh] v. gum; rubber; waterproof (*repeatedly*)
gumowanie [goo-mo-**vah**-ńe] n. covering with rubber; waterproofing
gumowaty [goo-mo-**vah**-ti] adj.m. gummy; viscid
gumowiec [goo-**mo**-vyets] m. rubber boot; cart on rubber tires
gumowy [goo-**mo**-vi] adj.m. of gum; of rubber; elastic; gum (boots, etc.); rubber (ball, tube, coat, etc.); guttiferous
gumowe nogi [goo-**mo**-ve **no**-gee] exp.: condition under the influence of narcotics
gumoza [goo-**mo**-zah] f. gummosis (tree disease)
gumożywica [goo-mo-zhi-**vee**-tsah] f. gum resin
gumówka [goo-**moof**-kah] f. elastic-propelled model of an airplane
gunia [**goo**-ńah] f. overcoat in the national costume of Carpathian mountaineers
guniak [**goo**-ńahk] m. Amphimallon beetle
guńka [**gooń**-kah] f. overcoat in the national costume of Carpathian mountaineers
gupik [**goo**-peek] m. a small aquarium fish
gur [goor] m. homespun cloth
gurami [goo-**rah**-mee] indecl.: a small aquarium fish
gurda [**goor**-dah] f. gourd
gurowy [goo-**ro**-vi] adj.m. cotton (cloth)
gurówka [goo-**roof**-kah] f. homespun cotton cloth; skirt of home-spun cotton cloth
gurt [goort] m. buttress; petersham; strap; girth
guru [**goo**-roo] m. guru; slang: whorehouse madam (mob jargon)
gusła [**goos**-wah] pl. wizardry; witchcraft; sorcery
gust [goost] m. taste; palate; liking (for); kind; sort; style
to nie w moim guście [to ńe v mo-eem **goośh**-ćhe] exp.: it is not to my taste
w dobrym guście [v **do**-brim **goośh**-ćhe] exp.: in good taste; tasteful; elegant; correct
w złym guście [v zwim **goośh**-ćhe] exp.: tasteless; inelegant; indecorous; cheap
wybredny gust [vi-**bred**-ni goost] exp.: delicate palate
gustować [goos-**to**-vahćh] v. like; enjoy; relish; have a taste (for) (*repeatedly*)
gustowanie [goos-to-**vah**-ńe] n. tasting
gustownie [goos-**tov**-ńe] adv. with taste; tastefully; with elegance; in good taste
gustowność [goos-**tov**-nośhćh] f. good taste; elegance; neatness
gustowny [goos-**tov**-ni] adj.m. in good taste; tasteful; elegant; dainty; neat; stylish
guścik [**goośh**-ćheek] m. (nice) taste; palate; liking (for); kind; sort; style
guślarka [goośh-**lahr**-kah] f. sorceress; witch
guślarski [goośh-**lahr**-skee] adj.m.

sorcerer's; witch's; wizard's
guślarstwo [goośh-**lahrs**-tfo] n. sorcery; witchcraft; wizardry
guślarz [**goośh**-lahsh] m. sorcerer; witch doctor; wizard
gut [goot] adj.m. slang: good
gutacja [goo-**tah**-tsyah] f. secretion of water droplets by plant leaves
gutaperczany [goo-tah-per-**chah**-ni] adj.m. of gutta-percha
gutaperka [goo-tah-**per**-kah] f. gutta-percha
gutaperkowy [goo-tah-per-**ko**-vi] adj.m. of gutta-percha
guturalny [goo-too-**rahl**-ni] adj.m. guttural (consonant, etc.); velar
guwernantka [goo-ver-**nahnt**-kah] f. governess
guwerner [goo-**ver**-ner] m. private tutor
guwernerski [goo-ver-**ner**-skee] adj.m. tutorial; tutor's
guz [goos] m. button; bump; tumor; nodosity; lump; swelling; nodule; umbo; protuberance; bruise; tuber
guzdracz [**gooz**-drahch] m. dawdler; potter; loiter
guzdrać się [**gooz**-drahćh śhan] v. dawdle; dally; waste time in trifling; trifle; delay; lag (*repeatedly*)
guzdralska [gooz-**drahl**-skah] adj.f. colloq: sluggish (woman); tardy; slack; slow; time-wasting
guzdralski [gooz-**drahl**-skee] adj.m. colloq: sluggish; tardy; slack; slow; time-wasting
guzdralstwo [gooz-**drahl**-stfo] n. colloq: dawdling; dallying; sluggishness; tardiness
guzdrała [gooz-**drah**-wah] m. & f. dawdler; potter; loiter; slacker
guzdranie się [gooz-**drah**-ńe śhan] n. colloq: dawdling; dallying; sluggishness; tardiness
guzek [**goo**-zek] m. bump; boss; knob; nodule
guziczek [goo-**źhee**-chek] m. (tiny) button; knob
guziczkowy [goo-źheech-**ko**-vi] adj.m. button (shape, etc.)
guziec [goo-źhets] m. warthog
guzik [goo-źheek] m. button; knob; colloq: nothing
guzikarka [goo-źhee-**kahr**-kah] f. (woman) button maker
guzikarski [goo-źhee-**kahr**-skee] adj.m. button-maker's
guzikarstwo [goo-źhee-**kahr**-stfo] n. button making
guzikarz [goo-**źhee**-kahsh] m. button maker
guzikowaty [goo-źhee-ko-**vah**-ti] adj.m. button-shaped
guzikowy [goo-źhee-**ko**-vi] adj.m. of button; of buttons
guzkowatość [goos-ko-**vah**-tośhćh] f. nodosity; tuberosity; protuberance
guzkowaty [goos-ko-**vah**-ti] adj.m. nodulous
guzowaty [goo-zo-**vah**-ti] adj.m. knobby; nodular; nodulous; bossy
gwajak [**gvah**-yahk] m. guaiacum; lignum vitae
gwajakol [gvah-**yah**-kol] m. guaiacol
gwajakowiec [gvah-yah-**ko**-vyets] m. Guaiacum (tropical) tree
gwajakowy [gvah-yah-**ko**-vi] adj.m. guaiac (gum, resin, etc.)
gwajawa [gvah-**yah**-vah] f. guava (shrub, fruit)
gwałcenie [gvahw-**tse**-ńe] n. violation; rape; compulsion; constraint; coercion; infringement
gwałciciel [gvahw-**ćhee**-ćhel] m. rapist; violator; ravisher; lawbreaker; transgressor
gwałcić [**gvahw**-ćheećh] v. rape; violate; dishonor; ravish; compel; coerce; force; outrage; transgress; infringe (*repeatedly*)
gwałt [gvahwt] m. rape; outrage; force; compulsion; violation; constraint; lawlessness; wrong; wrongdoing; confusion; tumult; turmoil; pandemonium; hubbub; uproar; hullabaloo; hurry; haste
gwałtem [**gvahw**-tem] adv. exp.: forcibly; by force; at once; immediately; without delay
na gwałt [nah gvahwt] exp.: in all haste; at once; instantly; urgently; at all costs
gwałtu! [**gvahw**-too] excl.: help!; good heavens!; goodness alive!
gwałtować [gvahw-**to**-vahćh] v. make a fuss (about); clamor (for);

urge; importune; beset; make a noise; harass; assail; annoy; trouble; colloq: kick up a stink (*repeatedly*)

gwałtowanie [gvahw-to-**vah**-ńe] n. fuss; clamor

gwałtownie [gvahw-**tov**-ńe] adv. impetuously; violently; passionately; rapidly; vehemently; with vehemence; fiercely; boisterously; suddenly; instantly

gwałtowność [gvahw-**tov**-nośhćh] f. impetuosity; vehemence; violence; fury (of a storm); acuteness (of a pain); suddenness; rapidity; hotheadedness; fierceness; urgency (of a need)

gwałtowny [gvahw-**tov**-ni] adj.m. outrageous; urgent (need); pressing (need); violent; passionate; volcanic; vehement; fierce; furious; sharp; sudden; rapid; instant; instantaneous; impetuous; hotheaded; rampageous; tear-away; towering (rage); boisterous; gusty (wind); acute (pain)

gwar [gvahr] m. hum; noise; buzz; loud talk; clatter; hubbub; uproar; murmur of voices; din; chirping (of birds)

gwara [**gvah**-rah] f. dialect; slang; jargon; cant; patter jargon; lingo; cant; colloquial regional language

gwarancja [gvah-**rahn**-tsyah] f. warranty; guarantee; bail; pledge; safeguard; security; guaranty

gwarancyjny [gvah-rahn-**tsiy**-ni] adj.m. of warranty; of guarantee

gwarant [**gvah**-rahnt] m. guarantor; warranter; bailsman; warrantor; security; underwriter

gwarantka [gvah-**rahnt**-kah] f. (woman) guarantor; warranter; warrantor; security; underwriter

gwarantować [gvah-rahn-**to**-vahćh] v. warrant; vouch (for); assure; ensure; safeguard; guarantee (*repeatedly*)

gwarantowanie [gvah-rahn-to-**vah**-ńe] n. warranty; vouching (for); assurance; insurance; safeguarding (*repeated*)

gwarantowany [gvah-rahn-to-**vah**-ni] adj.m. warranted

gwardia [**gvahr**-dyah] f. guard

gwardian [**gvahr**-dyahn] m. guardian; superior of a religious community

gwardiański [gvahr-**dyahń**-skee] adj.m. of a guardian

gwardyjski [gvahr-**diy**-skee] adj.m. guard (uniform, etc.)

gwardzista [gvahr-**dźhees**-tah] m. guardsman

gwardzistka [gvahr-**dźheest**-kah] f. member of a women-volunteer corps

gwarectwo [gvah-**rets**-tfo] n. miner's guild; mining; mining company

gwarek [**gvah**-rek] m. sound of (children) voices

gwarliwy [gvahr-**lee**-vi] adj.m. noisy; loud; full of the murmur of voices; buzzing with voices

gwarno [**gvahr**-no] adv. noisily; loudly; loud

gwarny [**gvahr**-ni] adj.m. noisy; loud; full of the murmur of voices; buzzing with voices; humming with voices

gwarowo [gvah-**ro**-vo] adv. in dialect; in slang

gwarowość [gvah-**ro**-vośhćh] f. colloquial character

gwarowy [gvah-**ro**-vi] adj.m. dialectal; slang

gwaroznawca [gvah-ro-**znahf**-tsah] m. dialectologist

gwaroznawczy [gvah-ro-**znahf**-chi] adj.m. dialectologic

gwaroznawstwo [gvah-ro-**znahf**-stfo] n. dialectology

gwarzenie [gvah-**zhe**-ńe] n. chatting; telling things

gwarzyć [**gvah**-zhićh] v. chat; talk; tell things (*repeatedly*)

gwasz [gvahsh] m. gouache (paint, painting, technique, etc.)

gwaszować [gvah-**sho**-vahćh] v. paint in gouache (*repeatedly*)

gwaszowy [gvah-**sho**-vi] adj.m. of gouache

gwiazda [**gvyahz**-dah] f. star

gwiazdeczka [gvyahz-**dech**-kah] f. (nice, little) star

gwiazdka [gvyahst-kah] f. starlet; star; asterisk; blaze; Christmas Eve
gwiazdkowaty [gvyahst-ko-vah-ti] adj.m. star-shaped; starlike
gwiazdkowy [gvyahst-ko-vi] adj.m. Christmas (gift, etc.)
gwiazdnica [gvyahzd-ńee-tsah] f. chickweed; stitchwort
gwiazdnik [gvyahzd-ńeek] m. scabious (herb)
gwiazdor [gvyahz-dor] m. (film) star (male); celebrity
gwiazdorski [gvyahz-dor-skee] adj.m. (film) star's
gwiazdorstwo [gvyahz-dor-stfo] n. being a celebrity; trying to be a celebrity
gwiazdowaty [gvyahz-do-vah-ti] adj.m. star-shaped; starlike
gwiazdowy [gvyahz-do-vi] adj.m. star; astral; stellar
gwiazdozbiór [gvyahz-do-zbyoor] m. constellation
gwiaździsty [gvyahźh-dźhees-ti] adj.m. starry; starlit; radiant; starlike; radial; asteroid
gwiaździście [gvyahźh-dźheeśh-ćhe] adv. starlike; in the shape of a star
gwicht [gveekht] m. (scale) weight
gwiezdny [gvyezd-ni] adj.m. of a star; of the stars; star (system, etc.); sidereal; stellar; starry; starlit (night, etc.); star-shaped; radial; asteroid
gwieździsty [gvyeźh-dźhees-ti] adj.m. starry; starlit; radiant; starlike; radial; asteroid
gwinciarka [gveen-ćhahr-kah] f. threading machine; screw-cutter
gwinea [gvee-ne-ah] f. guinea
gwint [gveent] m. screw thread; rifle-bore; screw
gwintować [gveen-to-vahćh] v. cut thread; tap; rifle (*repeatedly*)
gwintowanie [gveen-to-vah-ńe] n. rifling
gwintownica [gveen-tov-ńee-tsah] f. screw stock; screw-cutter; threader
gwintownik [gveen-tov-ńeek] m. screw-tap; die; threading tool
gwintowy [gveen-to-vi] adj.m. screw (coupling, joint, etc.)
gwintówka [gveen-toof-kah] f. rifle
gwizd [gveest] m. whistle
gwizdać [gveez-dahćh] v. whistle; blow a whistle; hoot; hiss; boo; catcall; whiz; whizz; scorn; despise; snap at (*repeatedly*)
gwizdanie [gveez-dah-ńe] n. whistling
gwizdawka [gveez-dahf-kah] f. whistle
gwizdek [gveez-dek] m. buzzer; whistle; the sound of a whistle; hoot; toot
gwizdnąć [gveezd-nownćh] v. whistle; blow a whistle; hoot; slang: steal; pinch; bone; make away with; sneak; knock; bang
gwizdnięcie [gveezd-ńan-ćhe] n. a whistle; the blast of a steam whistle
gwizocja [gvee-zots-yah] f. Guizotia plant
gwoli [gvo-lee] conj. for the sake of; because of; in order to; due to; on account of; owing to; for
gwoździak [gvoźh-dźhahk] m. hand drill
gwoździarka [gvoźh-dźhahr-kah] f. (woman) nailer; nail-maker; nail-making machine
gwoździarnia [gvoźh-dźhahr-ńah] f. nailery; nail factory; nail-works
gwoździarstwo [gvoźh-dźhahr-stfo] n. nail-making
gwoździarz [gvoźh-dźhahsh] m. nailer; nail-maker; nail-smith; nail-dealer
gwoździć [gvoźh-dźheećh] v. spike (a gun) (*repeatedly*)
gwoździk [gvoźh-dźheek] m. small nail; highlight; clou; carnation
gwoździkować [gvoźh-dźhee-ko-vahćh] v. pin (a bone); insert a rod (into a bone) (*repeatedly*)
gwoździkowanie [gvoźh-dźhee-ko-vah-ńe] n. pinning (of a bone); rod inserting (into a bone); internal fixation (of a bone)
gwoździkowy [gvoźh-dźhee-ko-vi] adj.m. of a carnation; of a pink; of carnations; of cloves
gwoździować [gvoźh-dźho-vahćh] v. pin broken bones (*repeatedly*)

gwoździowanie [gvoźh-dźho-**vah**-ńe] n. pinning broken bones
gwoździownica [gvoźh-dźhov-**ńee**-tsah] f. nail-making machine; plate with holes for making of nails; blacksmith's device for making of nails
gwożdżenie [gvozh-**dzhe**-ńe] n. spiking (a gun, etc.)
gwóźdź [gvoośhćh] m. nail; clou; highlight; high spot
gytia [**gi**-tyah] f. lake-bottom organic mud
gymkhana [gim-**kkhah**-nah] f. gymkhana (sport)
gza [gzah] f. sex-frenzy; oestrus
gzić się [gźheećh śhan] v. run wild; be in (sexual) heat; run amuck (*repeatedly*)
gzik [gźheek] m. gastric parasite (in horses, etc.)
gziki [**gźhee**-kee] pl. gastric parasites (in horses, etc.)
gzowy [**gzo**-vi] adj.m. of the gadfly; of the botfly; of the breeze
gzygzak [**gzig**-zahk] m. zigzag (line)
gzyms [gzims] m. molding; mould; shelf; cornice; ledge
gzymsik [**gzim**-śheek] m. (small) molding; mould; shelf; cornice; ledge
gzymsowanie [gzim-so-**vah**-ńe] n. cornice decoration
gzymsowy [gzim-**so**-vi] adj.m. cornice (decoration, etc.)
gzymsówka [gzim-**soof**-kah] f. cornice brick (or tile)
gżegżółka [gzheg-**zhoow**-kah] f. slang: cuckoo bird
gżenie się [**gzhe**-ńe śhan] n. sex-frenzy; oestrus; see: **gza**

H

H, h [khah] letter "h" also written as "ch"; both sound: [kh]
ha! [khah] excl.: ha!
ha! ha! [khah khah] excl.: haw! haw!
habanera [khah-bah-**ne**-rah] f. habanera
habanina [khah-bah-**ńe**-nah] f. horse meat
habenda [kah-**ben**-dah] f. small manorial estate (of old)
habilitacja [khah-bee-lee-**tah**-tsyah] f. oral examination on a thesis presented to qualify as assistant professor
habilitacyjny [khah-bee-lee-tah-**tsiy**-ni] adj.m. qualifying for assistant-professorship
habilitant [khah-bee-**lee**-tahnt] m. assistant professor (candidate)
habilitować [khah-bee-lee-**to**-vahćh] v. qualify as assistant professor (*repeatedly*)
habilitować się [khah-bee-lee-**to**-vahćh śhan] v. qualify oneself as assistant professor (*repeatedly*)
habilitowanie [khah-bee-lee-to-**vah**-ńe] n. qualifying for assistant-professorship
habilitowanie się [khah-bee-lee-to-**vah**-ńe śhan] n. qualifying oneself for assistant-professorship
habilitowany [khah-bee-lee-to-**vah**-ni] adj.m. qualified as assistant professor
habit [**khah**-beet] m. monk's frock; habit; nun's frock
habitat [khah-**bee**-taht] m. habitat
habituacja [khah-bee-too-**ahts**-yah] f. habituation
habitus [khah-**bee**-toos] m. habitus
hacel [**khah**-tsel] m. toe of a horse; spike; calk
hacjenda [khah-**tsyen**-dah] f. hacienda; mob slang: warehouse; stolen objects; dwelling
haczyć [**khah**-chićh] v. hoot; colloq: take to task (*repeatedly*)
haczyk [**khah**-chik] m. small hook; barb; snag; catch
haczykowato [khah-chi-ko-**vah**-to] adv. in the shape of a hook
haczykowaty [khah-chi-ko-**vah**-ti] adj.m. hooked; barbed; unciform; uncinate
haczystodzielny [khah-chis-to-**dźhel**-ni] adj.m. runcinate (leaf)
Hades [**khah**-des] m. Hades
hafciarka [khahf-**ćhahr**-kah] f. embroidering machine; (woman)

embroideress
hafciarnia [khahf-**ćhahr**-ńah] f. embroidery workshop
hafciarski [khahf-**ćhahr**-skee] adj.m. of embroidery; embroidering (machine, etc.); embroidery (frame, etc.)
hafciarstwo [khahf-**ćhahr**-stfo] n. embroidery; embroidering
hafciarz [**khaf**-ćhahsh] m. embroiderer
hafcik [**khahf**-ćheek] m. (small, nice) embroidery
hafn [khahfn] m. hafnium (atomic number 72)
haft [khahft] m. embroidery; embroidering
haftka [**khahft**-kah] f. hook and eye; clasp
haftować [khahf-**to**-vahćh] v. embroider; slang: vomit; spew; upchuck (mob jargon) (*repeatedly*)
haftowanie [khahf-to-**vah**-ńe] n. embroidering
hagada [khah-**gah**-dah] f. haggada; haggadah
hagiograf [khah-**gyo**-grahf] m. hagiographer
hagiografia [khah-gyo-**grah**-fyah] f. hagiography
hagiograficznie [khah-gyo-grah-**feech**-ńe] adv. in hagiographic style
hagiograficzny [khah-gyo-grah-**feech**-ni] adj.m. hagiographic
haik [khahyk] m. oriental robe spirally draped
haiku [**khahy**-koo] n. haiku; form of Japanese poetry
haj [khahy] m. slang: noise; brawl; unpleasantness (mob jargon)
być na haju [bićh nah **khah**-yoo] exp.: mob slang: to be under the influence of narcotics (jargon)
mieć haj [myećh khahy] exp.: slang: to be under the influence of narcotics (mob jargon)
hajda [**khahy**-dah] excl.: forwards!; move on!; off you go!; get going!; get out (of here)
hajdamacczyzna [khahy-dah-mahts-**chiz**-nah] f. 18th century Cossack rebellion
hajdamacki [khahy-dah-**mahts**-kee] adj.m. ruffianly
hajdamak [khahy-**dah**-mahk] m. 18th century Cossack rebel; colloq: ruffian; robber; bandit
hajdamaka [khahy-dah-**mah**-kah] m. 18th century Cossack rebel; colloq: ruffian; robber; bandit
hajdawery [khahy-dah-**ve**-ri] pl. galligaskins; very loose trousers; slang: pants
hajducki [khahy-**doots**-kee] adj.m. of a Haiduk; of Haiduks
hajduczek [khahy-**doo**-chek] m. (small, nice) Haiduk
hajduczy [khahy-**doo**-chi] adj.m. of a Haiduk; of Haiduks
hajduk [**khahy**-dook] m. 16th century Hungarian foot soldier in the Polish army; Haiduk (man, dance)
hajstra [**khahy**-strah] f. black stork
hajtać się [**khahy**-tahćh śhan] v. slang: get married; hurt oneself badly (mob jargon) (*repeatedly*)
hajtanie się [khahy-**tah**-ńe śhan] n. slang: getting married; wounding oneself badly (mob jargon)
hajże [**khahy**-zhe] excl.: forwards!; move on!; off you go!; get going!; get out (of here)
hak [khahk] m. hook; clamp; clasp; grapnel; uppercut (box)
hak rzeźnicki [khahk zheźh-**ńeets**-kee] exp.: cambrel
hakata [khah-**kah**-tah] f. German chauvinistic organization formed in 1894 for the purpose of eradicating Polish elements in the Poznań province
hakatysta [khah-kah-**tis**-tah] m. German, sworn enemy of Poles
hakatystyczny [khah-kah-tis-**tich**-ni] adj.m. marked by deadly hatred of Poles
hakatyzm [khah-**kah**-tizm] m. deadly hatred of Poles
hakonóg [khah-**ko**-noog] m. talipes
hakowato [khah-ko-**vah**-to] adv. in the shape of a hook
hakowaty [khah-ko-**vah**-ti] adj.m. hooked; crooked; bent; curved
hakownica [khah-kov-**ńee**-tsah] f. harquebus
hakowy [khah-**ko**-vi] adj.m. of a

hook; shaped like a hook
hala [**khah**-lah] f. (sports) hall; mountain pasture; alp; coom; coomb
halabarda [khah-lah-**bahr**-dah] f. halberd; bill; poleaxe
halabardnik [khah-lah-**bahrd**-ńeek] m. halberdier; Beefeater
halabardzista [khah-lah-bahr-**dźhees**-tah] m. halberdier
haleczka [khah-**lech**-kah] f. (nice, pretty) underskirt; slip
halerczyk [khah-**ler**-chik] m. soldier of General J. Haller (1918)
halerz [**khah**-lesh] m. Austrian coin; heller
halfa [**khahl**-fah] f. esparto grass
halfwind [**khahlf**-veent] m. wind perpendicular to a ship; ship's course perpendicular to the wind
halibut [khah-**lee**-boot] m. halibut
halifaksy [khah-lee-**fahk**-si] pl. Canadian style of skates for figure skating
halimetr [khah-**lee**-metr] m. salinometer
halit [**khah**-leet] m. halite; rock salt
halityt [khah-**lee**-tit] m. rock of evaporated shallow water sediments rich in sodium and chlorine
halizna [khah-**leez**-nah] f. glade; clearing
halka [**khahl**-kah] f. underskirt; slip
hall [hol] m. hall; lounge; lobby; foyer; large room
hallo [**khah**-lo] excl.: hallo!; hi!; say!
hallotron [khah-**lo**-tron] m. electronic device for measuring the magnetic field and power supply in computers
hallotronowy [khah-lo-tro-**no**-vi] adj.m. of electronic device for measuring the magnetic field and power supply in computers
halma [**khahl**-mah] f. halma
halniak [**khahl**-ńahk] m. Tatra wind (foehn)
halny [**khahl**-ni] adj.m. mountain (pasture, etc.); alpine
halny wiatr [**khahl**-ni vyahtr] exp.: Tatra wind (foehn)
halo [**khah**-lo] excl.: hallo!; hi!; say!; n. halo; halation
halobiont [khah-**lo**-byont] m. halobiont; halophile
halobionty [khah-lo-**byon**-ti] pl. salt water and salty soil plants and organisms
halofil [khah-**lo**-feel] m. halophile
halofile [khah-lo-**fee**-le] pl. salt water and salty soil plants and organisms
halofilny [khah-lo-**feel**-ni] adj.m. halophilic; halophilous
halofit [khah-**lo**-feet] m. halophyte
halofity [khah-lo-**fee**-ti] pl. salty soil plants and organisms
halofitowy [khah-lo-fee-**to**-vi] adj.m. halophytic
halogen [khah-**lo**-gen] m. halogen
halogenek [khah-lo-**ge**-nek] m. halogenous compound
halogenki [khah-lo-**gen**-kee] pl. halogenous compounds
halogenowy [khah-lo-ge-**no**-vi] adj.m. halogenous
halon [**khah**-lon] m. variety of fire-extinguishing gas
halonowy [khah-lo-**no**-vi] adj.m. of fire-extinguishing gas
halowy [khah-**lo**-vi] adj.m. indoor (sport, game, event, etc.)
hals [khahls] m. tack; tackle
halslina [khahls-**lee**-nah] f. tackle
halsować [khahl-**so**-vahćh] v. tack (about); follow a zigzag course (*repeatedly*)
halsowanie [khahl-so-**vah**-ńe] n. tacking (about); following a zigzag course
halsowy [khahl-**so**-vi] adj.m. of bottom-front corner of a sail
halsztacki [khahl-**shtahts**-kee] adj.m. of Hallstatt (culture, etc.)
halsztuk [**khahl**-shtook] m. wide (man's) tie
halucynacja [khah-loo-tsi-**nah**-tsyah] f. hallucination; colloq: seeing things
halucynacyjny [khah-loo-tsi-nah-**tsiy**-ni] adj.m. hallucinatory
halucynogen [khah-loo-tsi-**no**-gen] m. hallucinogen
halucynogenny [khah-loo-tsi-no-**gen**-ni] adj.m. hallucinogenic
halucynoza [khah-loo-tsi-**no**-zah] f. hallucinosis

halurgia [khah-**loor**-gyah] f. salt working mine
haɫaburda [khah-wah-**boor**-dah] m. blusterer; swaggerer; brawler; fire-eater; brawl
haɫas [**khah**-wahs] m. noise; fuss; ado; racket; row; din; hubbub; clamor; bang; clatter; pother; commotion; boisterousness; colloq.: shindy
narobić haɫasu [nah-**ro**-beećh khah-**wah**-soo] exp.: colloq: to kick up a row; to rise Cain; to make a racket; to make a noise in the world
z haɫasem [s khah-**wah**-sem] exp.: noisily; with a bang
haɫasować [khah-wah-**so**-vahćh] v. make noise; make racket; be noisy (*repeatedly*)
haɫasowanie [khah-wah-so-**vah**-ńe] n. making noise; making a racket; being noisy
haɫastra [khah-**wahst**-rah] f. mob; rabble; riffraff; ragtag
haɫaśliwie [khah-wah-**śhlee**-vye] adv. noisily; loudly; loud; rowdily; boisterously; riotously
haɫaśliwość [khah-wah-**śhlee**-vośhćh] f. noisiness; loudness; rowdiness; boisterousness; riotousness; clamorousness; uproariousness
haɫaśliwy [khah-wah-**śhlee**-vi] adj. m. noisy; loud; rackety; rowdy; boisterous; vociferous; clamorous
haɫda [**khahw**-dah] f. (waste-)heap; (waste-)dump
haɫdować [khahw-**do**-vahćh] v. make (waste-)heap; make (waste-) dump (*repeatedly*)
haɫɫa [**khahw**-wah] excl.: Tartars' and Turks' war cry; Allah!
hamada [khah-**mah**-dah] f. rocky desert
hamadriada [khah-mah-**dryah**-dah] f. hamadryad
hamak [**khah**-mahk] m. hammock
haman [**khah**-mahn] m. giant; bulky creature
hamanować [kah-mah-**no**-vahćh] v. slang: brutally mistreat (*repeatedly*)
hamburger [khahm-**boor**-ger] m. hamburger; patty of ground beef
hamburka [khahm-**boor**-kah] f. two-oar rowboat
hamburski [khahm-**boor**-skee] adj.m. of Hamburg
hamletowski [khahm-le-**tof**-skee] adj.m. like Hamlet
hamletyczny [khahm-le-**tich**-ni] adj.m. like Hamlet
hamletyzm [khahm-**le**-tizm] m. attitude of Hamlet
hamletyzować [khahm-le-ti-**zo**-vahćh] v. feel (act) like Hamlet; philosophize (*repeatedly*)
hamletyzowanie [khahm-le-ti-zo-**vah**-ńe] n. feeling (acting) like Hamlet
hamować [khah-**mo**-vahćh] v. apply brakes; restrain; hamper; curb; cramp; delay; retard; moderate; hold in; control; deter (*repeatedly*)
hamować się [khah-**mo**-vahćh śhan] v. restrain oneself; control oneself (*repeatedly*)
nie hamować się [ńe khah-**mo**-vahćh śhan] exp.: to let oneself go
hamowanie [khah-mo-**vah**-ńe] n. applying of the brakes; check; impediment; restraint; repression
światɫo hamowania [**śhfyaht**-wo khah-mo-**vah**-ńah] exp.: stoplight
hamowanie się [khah-mo-**vah**-ńe śhan] n. restraining oneself; controlling oneself; restraint
hamownia [khah-**mov**-ńah] f. engine test house; engine test bed; engine test bench
hamująco [khah-moo-**yown**-tso] adv. with restraining effect
hamujący [khah-moo-**yown**-tsi] adj.m. inhibitory; retardant
czynnik hamujący [**chin**-ńeek khah-moo-**yown**-tsi] exp.: inhibitor; retardant
środek hamujący [**śhro**-dek khah-moo-**yown**-tsi] exp.: depressant
hamulcowy [khah-mool-**tso**-vi] adj.m. of a brake; of the brake; brake (drum, etc.); m. brakeman; brake operator
hamulec [khah-**moo**-lets] m. brake; check; curb; restrain; inhibition
bez hamulców [bes khah-**mool**-tsoof] exp.: adv. unrestrainedly

brak hamulców [brahk khah-**mool**-tsoof] exp.: to (show) lack of restraint; to (do) with abandon
hamulec bębnowy [khah-**moo**-lets banb-no-vi] exp.: drum brake
hamulec klockowy [khah-**moo**-lets klots-**ko**-vi] exp.: shoe brake; drag
hamulec pneumatyczny [khah-**moo**-lets pnew-mah-**tich**-ni] exp.: air brake
hamulec ręczny [khah-**moo**-lets **ranch**-ni] exp.: hand brake
hamulec tarczowy [khah-**moo**-lets tahr-**cho**-vi] exp.: disk brake
hamulec taśmowy [khah-**moo**-lets tahśh-**mo**-vi] exp.: band brake

han [khahn] m. khan; see: **chan**
handel [**khahn**-del] m. commerce; trade; business; shop
handel detaliczny [**khahn**-del de-tah-**leech**-ni] exp.: retail trade
handel hurtowy [**khahn**-del khoor-**to**-vi] exp.: wholesale trade
handel wewnętrzny [**khahn**-del ve-**vnan**-tshni] exp.: domestic trade
handel zagraniczny [**khahn**-del zah-grah-**ńeech**-ni] exp.: foreign trade

handelek [khahn-**de**-lek] m. business in a small way; small restaurant
handełes [khahn-**de**-wes] m. Yiddish colloq: old-clothes man; shabby trader
handicap [**khahn**-dee-kahp] m. handicap
handicapować [khahn-dee-kah-**po**-vahćh] v. handicap (*repeatedly*)
handlara [khahn-**dlah**-rah] f. (crude, etc.) (woman) merchant; shopkeeper; peddler; huckster
handlarka [khahn-**dlahr**-kah] f. (woman) merchant; shopkeeper; peddler
handlarski [khahn-**dlahr**-skee] adj.m. trading (people, etc.)
handlarstwo [khahn-**dlahr**-stfo] n. trade
handlarz [**khahn**-dlahsh] m. merchant; shopkeeper; peddler
handlować [khahn-**dlo**-vahćh] v. trade; deal; be in business; run a shop (*repeatedly*)
handlowanie [khahn-dlo-**vah**-ńe] n. trading; dealing
handlowiec [khahn-**dlo**-vyets] m. businessman; merchant; trader; dealer; shopkeeper; merchant ship
handlowo [khahn-**dlo**-vo] adv. commercially
handlowy [khahn-**dlo**-vi] adj.m. commercial; of commerce; of trade
centrum handlowe [**tsen**-troom khahn-**dlo**-ve] exp.: shopping center
handlowego wyznania [khahn-dlo-**ve**-go viz-**nah**-ńah] exp.: slang: of Jewish creed (mob jargon)
Izba Handlowa [**eez**-bah khahn-**dlo**-vah] exp.: Chamber of Commerce
marynarka handlowa [mah-ri-**nahr**-kah khahn-**dlo**-vah] exp.: merchant marine
obrót handlowy [**ob**-root khahn-**dlo**-vi] exp.: turnover
spółka handlowa [**spoow**-kah khahn-**dlo**-vah] exp.: trading company
szlak handlowy [shlahk khahn-**dlo**-vi] exp.: trade route

handlówka [khahn-**dloof**-kah] f. colloq: commercial school
handryczenie się [khahn-dri-**che**-ńe śhan] n. quarrel; quarrels; dispute; disputes; squabble; squabbles
handryczyć się [khahn-**dri**-chićh śhan] v. quarrel; dispute; bicker; squabble (*repeatedly*)
handżar [**khahn**-dzhahr] m. khanjar
hangar [**khahn**-gahr] m. hangar
hangarować [khahn-gah-**ro**-vahćh] v. place in a hangar (*repeatedly*)
haniebnie [khah-**ńeb**-ńe] adv. disgracefully; shamefully; scandalously; infamously; ignominiously; horribly; dreadfully; terribly; ingloriously
haniebność [khah-**ńeb**-nośhćh] f. shame; infamy; ignominy
haniebny [khah-**ńeb**-ni] adj.m. disgraceful; dirty; foul; vile
hantle [**khahn**-tle] pl. dumbbells
hanza [**khahn**-zah] f. Hanse
hanzeata [khahn-ze-**ah**-tah] m. member of the Hanse

hanzeatycki [khahn-ze-ah-**tits**-kee] adj.m. Hanseatic
hań [khahń] adv. (over) there
hańba [**khahń**-bah] f. disgrace; shame; infamy; ignominy; opprobrium
hańbiący [khahń-**by**own-tsi] adj.m. shameful; disgraceful; dishonorable; degrading
hańbić [**khahń**-beećh] v. disgrace; bring shame; dishonor (*repeatedly*)
hańbić się [**khahń**-beećh śhan] v. disgrace oneself; bring shame on oneself; dishonor oneself (*repeatedly*)
hańbienie [khahń-**bye**-ńe] n. shame; disgrace; dishonor; defilement; disgracing; shaming
hańbienie się [khahń-**bye**-ńe śhan] n. disgracing oneself; dishonoring oneself
hapening [**khah**-pe-ńeeng] m. slang: taking narcotics (mob jargon)
haplografia [khahp-lo-**grah**-fyah] f. omitting in writing one of two similar letters, words, passages, pages, etc.
haplologia [khahp-lo-**lo**-gyah] f. abbreviating of words by removal of one of two similar syllables
happening [**khah**-pe-ńeeng] m. (Engl.) happening; show
happeningowy [khah-pe-ńeen-**go**-vi] adj.m. of a happening; of a show
happy end [**khe**-pee end] m. (Engl.) happy end
haracz [**khah**-rahch] m. tribute; extortion; squeeze; slang: fine
harakiri [khah-rah-**kee**-ree] n. (Jap.) hara-kiri; happy dispatch
harap [**khah**-rahp] m. riding-whip; hunting-crop
haratać [khah-**rah**-tahćh] v. strike; knock; hit; bash; batter (*repeatedly*)
haratać się [khah-**rah**-tahćh śhan] v. strike oneself; knock oneself; hit oneself (*repeatedly*)
haratanie [khah-rah-**tah**-ńe] n. hitting; battering
haratanie się [khah-rah-**tah**-ńe śhan] n. hitting one another; battering each other
haratanina [khah-rah-tah-**ńee**-nah] f. fight; scrap; scuffle
haratnąć [khah-**raht**-nownćh] v. strike; knock; hit; bash; batter
haratnąć się [khah-**raht**-nownćh śhan] v. bash oneself; inflict a wound on oneself
harc [khahrts] m. single combat
harce [**khahr**-tse] pl. slang: youth event; youth concert
harcap [**khahr**-tsahp] m. pigtail; bob-wig
harcerka [khahr-**tser**-kah] f. girl scout
harcerski [khahr-**tser**-skee] adj.m. of Boy Scouts; of Girl Scouts
harcerstwo [khahr-**tser**-stfo] n. scouting; Boy Scouts
harcerz [**khahr**-tsesh] m. boy scout
harcerzyk [khahr-**tse**-zhik] m. small boy scout
harcmistrz [**khahrts**-meestsh] m. scoutmaster
harcować [khahr-**tso**-vahćh] v. gambol; caper; frisk; prance; caracole (*repeatedly*)
harcowanie [khahr-tso-**vah**-ńe] n. gambol; caper; frisk; prancing
harcownik [khahr-**tsov**-ńeek] m. skirmisher
harcówka [khahr-**tsoof**-kah] f. boy scouts hall
hardo [**khahr**-do] adv. haughtily; proudly; with arrogance; impudently; cheekily
hardość [**khahr**-dośhćh] f. haughtiness; pride; loftiness; arrogance; bumptiousness; obtrusiveness
hardy [**khahr**-di] adj.m. haughty; proud; overbearing; arrogant
hardware [**khahr**-dwer] m. (Engl.) computer hardware
hardzieć [**khahr**-dźhećh] v. become haughty; became arrogant (*repeatedly*)
harem [**khah**-rem] m. harem
haremowy [khah-re-**mo**-vi] adj.m. of a harem
harfa [**khahr**-fah] f. harp
harfiany [khahr-**fyah**-ni] adj.m. of a harp
harfiarka [khahr-**fyahr**-kah] f. harper; harpist (woman)

harfiarz [khahr-fyahsh] m. harper; harpist
harfista [khahr-**fees**-tah] m. harper; harpist
harfistka [khahr-**feest**-kah] f. (woman) harper; harpist
harfowy [khahr-**fo**-vi] adj.m. harp's
harmatan [khahr-**mah**-tahn] m. harmattan (wind)
harmider [khahr-**mee**-der] m. uproar; hullabaloo; clatter; din; row; colloq: shindy
harmonia [khahr-**mo**-ńyah] f. harmony; accordion; harmonics; concord; chord
harmonicznie [khahr-mo-**ńeech**-ńe] adv. harmoniously; melodiously; musically
harmoniczność [khahr-mo-**ńeech**-nośhćh] f. harmony; melodiousness
harmoniczny [khahr-mo-**ńeech**-ni] adj.m. harmonic; harmonious; melodious; musical
harmonijka [khahr-mo-**ńeey**-kah] f. harmonica; mouth organ; panpipe
harmonijnie [khahr-mo-**ńeey**-ńe] adv. harmoniously
harmonijność [khahr-mo-**ńeey**-nośhćh] f. harmony; concord
harmonijny [khahr-mo-**ńeey**-ni] adj.m. harmonious; melodious; musical
harmonika [khahr-**mo**-ńee-kah] f. harmonica; mouth organ; panpipe
harmonista [khahr-mo-**ńees**-tah] m. accordionist; harmonist; harmonizer
harmonium [khahr-**mo**-ńyoom] n. harmonium
harmonizować [khahr-mo-ńee-**zo**-vahćh] v. harmonize; concord; chime; keep in tune (*repeatedly*)
harmonizować się [khahr-mo-ńee-**zo**-vahćh śhan] v. be in tune; be in harmony (*repeatedly*)
nie harmonizować się [ńe khahr-mo-ńee-**zo**-vahćh śhan] exp.: to be out of tune; to be out of keeping; to clash
harmonizowanie [khahr-mo-ńee-zo-**vah**-ńe] n. harmonizing; keeping in tune
harmonogram [khahr-mo-**no**-grahm] m. schedule; plan of procedure
harmonogramowy [khahr-mo-no-grah-**mo**-vi] adj.m. of a schedule; pertaining to a plan of procedure
harmoszka [khahr-**mosh**-kah] f. colloq: harmony; accordion; harmonics; concord; chord
harnaś [**khahr**-nahśh] m. ring leader of a band of robbers in the Tatra mountains
harować [khah-**ro**-vahćh] v. toil; sweat; grind; slave (*repeatedly*)
harowanie [khah-ro-**vah**-ńe] n. toiling; sweating; grinding; slaving
harówa [khah-**roo**-vah] f. colloq: very hard work; toil; grind; drudgery; slavery
harówka [khah-**roof**-kah] f. colloq: hard work; toil; grind; drudgery; slavery
harpagon [khahr-**pah**-gon] m. miser; niggard; skinflint
harpia [**khahr**-pyah] f. harpy eagle; harpy
harpun [**khahr**-poon] m. harpoon
harpunniczy [khahr-poon-**ńee**-chi] adj.m. of a harpoon
harpunnik [khahr-**poon**-ńeek] m. harpooner
harpunowy [khahr-poo-**no**-vi] adj.m. harpoon (canon, etc.)
harry [**khahr**-ri] m. slang: heroin
hart [khahrt] m. fortitude; hardness; sternness; temper; endurance; inflexibility; grit
hart ducha [khahrt **doo**-khah] exp.: fortitude
hartowacz [khahr-**to**-vahch] m. quencher
hartować [khahr-**to**-vahćh] v. temper; harden; anneal; season; inure; quench; toughen (*repeatedly*)
hartować się [khahr-**to**-vahćh śhan] v. harden oneself; toughen oneself (*repeatedly*)
hartowanie [khahr-to-**vah**-ńe] n. tempering; hardening; annealing
hartowanie się [khahr-to-**vah**-ńe śhan] n. hardening oneself; toughening oneself
hartownia [khahr-**tov**-ńah] f. annealing shop; quenching shop
hartowniczy [khahr-tov-**ńee**-chi]

adj.m. of quenching
hartownik [khahr-**tov**-ńeek] m. quencher
hartowność [khahr-**tov**-nośhćh] f. temper (of steel, etc.)
hartowny [khahr-**tov**-ni] adj.m. tempered; hardened
hasać [**khah**-sahćh] v. frisk; frolic; romp; gambol; dance; caper (*repeatedly*)
hasanie [khah-**sah**-ńe] n. gambols; frolics; capers
haski [**khahs**-kee] adj.m. of the Hague
hasełko [khah-**sew**-ko] n. (silly) password; motto; slogan
hasło [**khahs**-wo] n. password; motto; slogan; (dictionary) entry; catchword; article; war cry; battle cry
hasłowy [khahs-**wo**-vi] adj.m. of a password; of a slogan
hasz [khahsh] m. slang: hashish
haszysz [**khah**-shish] m. hashish
haszyszowy [khah-shi-**sho**-vi] adj.m. of hashish
haszyszyzm [khah-**shi**-shizm] m. habit of smoking hashish
hatha-joga [**khah**-tah **yo**-gah] f. (Sanskrit) hatha yoga
hatteria [khaht-**ter**-yah] f. sphenodon; tuatara reptile
hau hau [khahw khahw] interj. (dog's bark) woof-woof; bowwow
haubica [khahw-**bee**-tsah] f. howitzer (a short cannon)
haubiczny [khahw-**beech**-ni] adj.m. of a howitzer
haust [khahwst] m. gulp; swing
jednym haustem [**yed**-nim **khahws**-tem] exp.: at one gulp; at a draught
hawajski [khah-**vahy**-skee] adj.m. Hawaiian; of Hawaii
hawana [khah-**vah**-nah] f. colloq: Havana cigar
hawański [khah-**vahń**-skee] adj.m. of Havana
hawelok [khah-**ve**-lok] m. Havelock coat
hazard [**khah**-zahrt] m. risk; hazard; gambling; recklessness; a gamble
uprawiać hazard [oo-**prah**-vyahćh khah-zahrt] exp.: to gamble
hazardować się [khah-zahr-**do**-vahćh śhan] v. gamble; feel the thrill of the chase (*repeatedly*)
hazardowanie się [khah-zahr-do-**vah**-ńe śhan] n. gambling
hazardowo [khah-zahr-**do**-vo] adv. recklessly
hazardowy [khah-zahr-**do**-vi] adj.m. risky; hazardous; m. reckless gambler; mob slang: plunger
hazardzista [khah-zahr-**dźhee**-stah] m. gambler; colloq: plunger
hazena [khah-**ze**-nah] f. women's handball game
he [khe] exp.: well?; what?; hm!; well, well!; haw, haw!
heban [**khe**-bahn] m. ebony
hebankowaty [khe-bahn-ko-**vah**-ti] adj.m. like ebony
hebankowate [khe-bahn-ko-**vah**-te] pl. the ebony family of trees
hebanowy [khe-bah-**no**-vi] adj.m. of ebony; ebony black; ebonaceous
hebel [**khe**-bel] m. plane (tool)
hebelek [khe-**be**-lek] m. (small) plane (tool)
hebes [**khe**-bes] m. dullard; dunce; never-do-well; good-for-nothing
heblarka [khe-**blahr**-kah] f. planing machine
heblarnia [khe-**blahr**-ńah] f. planing mill
heblować [khe-**blo**-vahćh] v. plane; shave; try up (*repeatedly*)
heblowanie [khe-blo-**vah**-ńe] n. planing; shaving
heblowiny [khe-blo-**vee**-ni] pl. (wood) shavings
hebraista [khe-brah-**ees**-tah] m. hebraist
hebraistyka [khe-brah-**ees**-ti-kah] f. study of Hebrew language and literature
hebraizm [khe-**brah**-eezm] m. Hebraism; Hebrew idiom
hebrajski [khe-**brahy**-skee] adj. m. Hebrew (language); Hebraic
po hebrajsku [po khe-**brahy**-skoo] exp.: in Hebrew
hebrajszczyzna [khe-brahy-**shchiz**-nah] f. Hebrew language; Hebraism
heca [**khe**-tsah] f. fun; fuss; affair
hecny [**khets**-ni] adj.m. colloq:

funny; amusing
hecować [khe-**tso**-vahćh] v. frolic; play pranks; sport (*repeatedly*)
hedonista [khe-do-**ńees**-tah] m. hedonist
hedonistyczny [khe-do-ńees-**tich**-ni] adj.m. hedonistic
hedonizm [khe-**do**-ńeezm] m. hedonism
hedżra [**khedzh**-rah] f. hegira
hegelianizm [khe-gel-**yah**-ńeezm] m. Hegelianism
hegemon [khe-**ge**-mon] m. leader
hegemonia [khe-ge-**mo**-ńyah] f. hegemony; dominance
hegemoniczny [khe-ge-mo-**ńeech**-ni] adj.m. hegemonic; dominant
hegemonistyczny [khe-ge-mo-ńees-**tich**-ni] adj.m. hegemonic
hegira [khe-**gee**-rah] f. hegira
heglista [kheg-**lees**-tah] m. (a) Hegelian
heglizm [**kheg**-leezm] m. Hegelianism
heglowski [heg-**lof**-skee] adj.m. Hegelian
hej [khey] excl.: hey!; ho!; there!; hi!; heigh-ho!
hejnalista [khey-nah-**lees**-tah] m. trumpeter of the reveille
hejnał [**khey**-nahw] m. trumpet call; bugle-call; reveille
hejnałowy [khey-nah-**wo**-vi] adj.m. of trumpet call; of bugle-call; of a reveille
hejt! [kheyt] excl.: hup!; gee!
hejta! [**khey**-tah] excl.: hup!; gee!
hejże! [**khey**-zhe] excl.: heigh ho!; on!; forward!
hekatomba [khe-kah-**tom**-bah] f. hecatomb
heksachord [khek-**sah**-kort] m. hexachord
heksaedr [khek-**sah**-edr] m. cube
heksagon [khek-**sah**-gon] m. hexagon
heksagonalny [khek-sah-go-**nahl**-ni] adj.m. hexagonal
heksametr [khek-**sah**-metr] m. hexameter
heksametrowy [khek-sah-met-**ro**-vi] adj.m. of hexameter
heksametryczny [khek-sah-met-**rich**-ni] adj.m. of hexameter
heksan [**khek**-sahn] m. hexane
heksastyl [khek-**sahs**-til] m. hexastyle; a building having six columns in front elevation
heksoda [khek-**so**-dah] f. six-electrode lamp
heksoza [khek-**so**-zah] f. hexose
hektar [**khek**-tahr] m. hectare
hektarowy [khek-tah-**ro**-vi] adj.m. of an area of one hectare
hekto- [**khek**-to] prefix: hecto-; hundred-
hektograf [khek-**to**-grahf] m. hectograph
hektografia [khek-to-**grah**-fyah] f. hectography
hektograficzny [khek-to-grah-**feech**-ni] adj.m. hectographic
hektografować [khek-to-grah-**fo**-vahćh] v. hectograph; making a hectograph (*repeatedly*)
hektogram [khek-**to**-grahm] m. hectogram
hektolitr [khek-**to**-leetr] m. hectoliter
hektometr [khek-**to**-metr] m. hectometer
hektopaskal [khek-to-**pahs**-kahl] m. 100 pascals (hPa) of atmospheric pressure
hektyczny [khek-**tich**-ni] adj.m. hectic
hel [khel] m. helium (atomic number 2); helium gas
helanco [khe-**lahn**-ko] n. variety of artificial fiber
helanko [khe-**lahn**-ko] n. variety of artificial fiber
helankowy [khe-lahn-**ko**-vi] adj.m. of (a variety of) artificial fiber
heliakalnie [khel-yah-**kahl**-ńe] adv. heliacally
heliakalny [khel-yah-**kahl**-ni] adj.m. heliacal
helikoida [khe-lee-**koy**-dah] f. helicoid
helikon [khe-**lee**-kon] m. helicon
helikopter [khe-lee-**kop**-ter] m. helicopter
helikopterowy [khe-lee-kop-te-**ro**-vi] adj.m. of a helicopter
heling [**khe**-leeng] m. support frame for building yachts, gliders, and small planes
heliocentryczny [khel-yo-tsen-**trich**-

ni] adj.m. heliocentric
heliocentryzm [khel-yo-**tsen**-trizm] m. heliocentrism
heliodor [khel-**yo**-dor] m. heliodor
helioelektrownia [khel-yo-e-lek-**trov**-ńah] f. electric plant using solar energy
helioenergetyczny [khel-yo-e-ner-ge-**tich**-ni] adj.m. of solar energy
helioenergetyka [khel-yo-e-ner-**ge**-ti-kah] f. science of solar energy
heliofil [khel-**yo**-feel] m. plant thriving in sunshine
heliofile [khel-yo-**fee**-le] pl. plants thriving in sunshine
heliofit [khel-**yo**-feet] m. heliophyte
heliofity [khel-yo-**fee**-ti] pl. heliophyte plants
heliofizyczny [khel-yo-fee-**zich**-ni] adj.m. of physics of the Sun
heliofizyk [khel-yo-**fee**-zik] m. physicist studying the Sun
heliofizyka [khel-yo-**fee**-zi-kah] f. physics of the Sun
heliograf [khel-**yo**-grahf] m. heliograph
heliografia [khel-yo-**grah**-fyah] f. heliography
heliograwiura [khel-yo-grah-**vyoo**-rah] f. heliogravure; heliography; photogravure
heliograwiurowy [khel-yo-grah-vyoo-**ro**-vi] adj.m. of heliogravure; of heliography; of photogravure
heliolatria [khel-yo-**lahtr**-yah] f. sun worship; heliolatry
heliometr [khel-**yo**-metr] m. heliometer
helioskop [khel-**yo**-skop] m. helioscope
heliostat [khel-**yo**-staht] m. heliostat
heliotechniczny [khel-yo-tekh-**ńeech**-ni] adj.m. of the technology of the use of solar energy
heliotechnika [khel-yo-**tekh**-ńee-kah] f. technology of the use of solar energy
helioterapia [khel-yo-te-**rah**-pyah] f. heliotherapy
heliotrop [khel-**yo**-trop] m. heliotrope; turnsole; bloodstone
heliotropiczny [khel-yo-tro-**peech**-ni] adj.m. heliotropic
heliotropizm [khel-yo-**tro**-peezm] m. heliotropism
heliotropowy [khel-yo-tro-**po**-vi] adj.m. of the heliotrope (gray, etc.)
hellenista [khel-le-**ńees**-tah] m. Hellenist
hellenistyczny [khel-le-ńees-**tich**-ni] adj.m. Hellenistic
hellenistyka [khel-le-**ńees**-ti-kah] f. Hellenistic studies
hellenizacja [khel-le-ńee-**zah**-tsyah] f. Hellenization
hellenizm [khel-**le**-ńeezm] m. Hellenism
hellenizować [khel-le-ńee-**zo**-vahćh] v. Hellenize (*repeatedly*)
hellenizowanie [khel-le-ńee-zo-**vah**-ńe] n. Hellenization
hellenofil [khel-le-**no**-feel] m. Hellenophile
helleński [khel-**leń**-skee] adj.m. Hellenic
helmintolog [khel-meen-**to**-log] m. helminthology specialist
helmintologia [khel-meen-to-**lo**-gyah] f. helminthology; study of parasitic worms
helmintologiczny [khel-meen-to-lo-**geech**-ni] adj.m. of helminthology; helminthological
helmintoza [khel-meen-**to**-zah] f. helminthiasis
helmintozy [khel-meen-**to**-zi] pl. diseases caused by parasitic worms
helo, helo [**khe**-lo **khe**-lo] excl.: hello! hello!
heloderma [khe-lo-**der**-mah] f. poisonous Mexican lizard 60 cm long
helofit [khe-**lo**-feet] m. marshlands plant
helofity [khe-lo-**fee**-ti] pl. marshlands vegetation
helokać [khe-**lo**-kahćh] v. colloq: a mountaineers call, see: **helo, helo** (*repeatedly*)
helokanie [khe-lo-**kah**-ńe] n. shouting: **helo, helo**
helota [khe-**lo**-tah] m. helot
helotyzm [khe-**lo**-tizm] m. helotism; helotry; serfdom
helowiec [khe-**lo**-vyets] m. inert gas
helowce [khe-**lof**-tse] pl. inert

gases
helowy [khe-**lo**-vi] adj.m. helium (ions, group, etc.)
helwecki [khel-**vets**-kee] adj.m. Helvetian; Swiss
helweta [khel-**ve**-tah] m. Helvetian
hełm [khewm] m. helmet; dome; headpiece; cupola; slang: tin hat
hełmiasty [khew-**myahs**-ti] adj.m. dome-shaped
hełmofon [khew-**mo**-fon] m. headphone built into a helmet
hełmowy [khew-**mo**-vi] adj.m. of a helmet; of a dome
hem [khem] m. heme
hemant [**khe**-mahnt] m. Haemantus herb
hemantus [khe-**mahn**-toos] m. Haemantus herb
hemato- [khe-**mah**-to] prefix: hemat-; haemat-
hematoblast [khe-mah-**to**-blahst] m. hematoblast
hematochrom [khe-mah-**to**-khrom] m. hematochrome
hematofag [khe-mah-**to**-fahg] m. hematophagous animal or insect
hematofagi [khe-mah-to-**fah**-gee] pl. hematophagous animals or insects
hematogen [khe-mah-**to**-gen] m. hematogen
hematolog [khe-mah-**to**-log] m. hematologist
hematologia [khe-mah-to-**lo**-gyah] f. hematology
hematologiczny [khe-mah-to-lo-**geech**-ni] adj.m. hematologic
hematuria [khe-mah-**toor**-yah] f. hematuria; urine in blood
hematyna [khe-mah-**ti**-nah] f. hematin
hematyt [khe-**mah**-tit] m. hematite; iron glance; specular iron
hematytowy [khe-mah-ti-**to**-vi] adj.m. hematite (red, etc.); hematitic
hemeralopia [khe-me-rah-**lo**-pyah] f. hemeralopia; night blindness
hemeralopiczny [khe-me-rah-lo-**peech**-ni] adj.m. hemeralopic; of night blindness
hemi- [**khe**-mee] prefix: hemi-; semi-; half-
hemiceluloza [khe-mee-tse-loo-**lo**-zah] f. hemicellulose
hemicelulozy [khe-mee-tse-loo-**lo**-zi] pl. hemicellulose plants
hemicykl [khe-**mee**-tsikl] m. hemicycle; half-circle; half-moon
hemikryptofit [khe-mee-krip-**to**-feet] m. plant protected against freezing in the soil
hemikryptofity [khe-mee-krip-to-**fee**-ti] pl. plants protected against freezing in the soil
hemimetabolia [khe-mee-me-tah-**bol**-yah] f. hemimetabolism
hemimetaboliczny [khe-mee-me-tah-bo-**leech**-ni] adj.m. hemimetabolic; hemimetabolous
hemimetamorficzny [khe-mee-me-tah-mor-**feech**-ni] adj.m. hemimetabolic
hemimetamorfoza [khe-mee-me-tah-mor-**fo**-zah] f. hemimetabolism
hemimorfit [khe-mee-**mor**-feet] m. hemimorphite
hemina [khe-**mee**-nah] f. hemin; hematin chloride
hemiola [khe-**myo**-lah] f. hemiola
hemipelagiczny [khe-mee-pe-lah-**geech**-ni] adj.m. of the limit of coastal waters
hemisfera [khe-mee-**sfe**-rah] f. hemisphere
hemistych [khe-**mee**-stikh] m. hemistich
hemitropowy [khe-mee-tro-**po**-vi] adj.m. hemitropous
hemo- [**khe**-mo] prefix: hemo-
hemodializa [khe-mo-dyah-**lee**-zah] f. hemodialysis; purification of blood
hemodynamiczny [khe-mo-di-nah-**meech**-ni] adj.m. hemodynamic
hemodynamika [khe-mo-di-**nah**-mee-kah] f. hemodynamics
hemofilia [khe-mo-**feel**-yah] f. hemophilia
hemofiliak [khe-mo-**feel**-yahk] m. hemophiliac
hemofilik [khe-mo-**fee**-leek] m. hemophiliac
hemofilityk [khe-mo-fee-**lee**-tik] m. hemophiliac
hemoglobina [khe-mo-glo-**bee**-nah] f. hemoglobin
hemoglobinemia [khe-mo-glo-bee-**ne**-

myah] f. hemoglobinemia
hemoglobinometr [khe-mo-glo-bee-no-metr] m. hemoglobin counter
hemoglobinuria [khe-mo-glo-bee-noor-yah] f. hemoglobinuria
hemoglobinuryczny [khe-mo-glo-bee-noo-**rich**-ni] adj.m. hemoglobinuric
hemolimfa [khe-mo-**leem**-fah] f. hemolymph
hemolitycznie [khe-mo-lee-**tich**-ńe] adv. by the way of hemolysis
hemolityczny [khe-mo-lee-**tich**-ni] adj.m. hemolytic
hemoliza [khe-mo-**lee**-zah] f. hemolysis
hemolizować [khe-mo-lee-**zo**-vahćh] v. hemolyze (*repeatedly*)
hemolizowanie [khe-mo-lee-zo-**vah**-ńe] n. causing hemolysis
hemolizyna [khe-mo-lee-**zi**-nah] f. hemolysin
hemolizyny [khe-mo-lee-**zi**-ni] pl. substances dissolving red blood cells
hemometr [khe-**mo**-metr] m. hemoglobin counter
hemoproteid [khe-mo-pro-**te**-eet] m. hemoprotein
hemoproteidy [khe-mo-pro-te-**ee**-di] pl. conjugated proteins
hemoproteidalny [khe-mo-pro-te-ee-**dahl**-ni] adj.m. of hemoprotein
hemoroidalny [khe-mo-ro-ee-**dahl**-ni] adj.m. hemorrhoidal
hemoroidy [khe-mo-**roy**-di] pl. piles; hemorrhoids
hemoterapia [khe-mo-te-**rah**-pyah] f. hemotherapy; therapy based on the injection of one's blood into one's muscles
hemotoksyna [khe-mo-to-**ksi**-nah] f. hemotoxin
hen [khen] adv. far; away; high up; way up
heneken [khe-**ne**-ken] m. henequen (fiber)
henna [**khen**-nah] f. henna (shrub, dye)
henoteistyczny [khe-no-te-ees-**tich**-ni] adj.m. henotheistic
hennowy [khen-**no**-vi] adj.m. henna (shrub, dye, etc.)
henoteizm [khe-no-**te**-eezm] m. henotheism
henr [khenr] m. henry (meter-kilogram-second unit)
heparyna [khe-pah-**ri**-nah] f. heparin
hepatologia [khe-pah-to-**lo**-gyah] f. study and treatment of liver diseases
hepatologiczny [khe-pah-to-lo-**geech**-ni] adj.m. of the study and treatment of liver diseases
heptametr [khep-**tah**-metr] m. heptameter
heptan [**khep**-tahn] m. heptane
heptatonika [khep-tah-**to**-ńee-kah] f. scale of seven sounds
heptoda [khep-**to**-dah] f. electronic tube of seven electrodes
heptoza [khep-**to**-zah] f. heptose
hera [**khe**-rah] f. colloq: heroin
heraklejski [khe-rah-**kley**-skee] adj.m. Heraclean
heraklitejski [khe-rah-klee-**tey**-skee] adj.m. Heraclitean (philosophy)
heraklitowy [khe-rah-klee-**to**-vi] adj.m. Heraclitean (philosophy)
heraklityzm [khe-rah-**klee**-tizm] m. Heracliteanism
heraldyczny [khe-rahl-**dich**-ni] adj.m. heraldic; of heraldry
heraldyk [khe-**rahl**-dik] m. heraldist
heraldyka [khe-**rahl**-di-kah] f. heraldry; insignia; pageantry; blazonry
herb [kherp] m. coat of arms
herbaciany [kher-bah-**ćhah**-ni] adj.m. of tea; of the tea-plant; tea (leaves, etc.)
herbaciarnia [kher-bah-**ćhahr**-ńah] f. teahouse; tearoom
herbarium [kher-**bahr**-yoom] n. herbarium
herbarz [**kher**-bahsh] m. book of heraldry; baronage; armorial
herbaciarka [kher-bah-**ćhahr**-kah] f. woman brewing tea
herbata [kher-**bah**-tah] f. tea; tea-plant; tea party
herbatka [kher-**baht**-kah] f. (small, nice) tea; tea-plant; tea party
herbatni [kher-**baht**-ńee] adj.m. of tea; of the tea-plant
herbatnik [kher-**baht**-ńeek] m. biscuit; small dry cake
herbicyd [kher-**bee**-tsit] m. herbicide; weed-killer

herbicydy [kher-bee-**tsi**-di] pl. weed-killers
herbicydowy [kher-bee-tsi-**do**-vi] adj.m. of herbicide; weed-killer (spray, fluid, etc.)
herboryzacja [kher-bo-ri-**zah**-tsyah] f. collection of herbs for scientific purposes; herborization
herboryzować [kher-bo-ri-**zo**-vahćh] v. collect herbs (*repeatedly*)
herboryzowanie [kher-bo-ri-zo-**vah**-ńe] n. collecting herbs for scientific purposes
herbowy [kher-**bo**-vi] adj.m. heraldic; armorial; nobleman's; of the nobility
herc [kherts] m. hertz; one cycle per second
hercynidy [kher-tsi-**ńee**-di] pl. Hartz-type mountains
hercyński [kher-**tsiń**-skee] adj.m. of Hartz-like mountain forming
heretycki [khe-re-**tits**-kee] adj.m. heretic; heretical; infidel's
heretyczka [khe-re-**tich**-kah] f. (woman) heretic; misbeliever
heretycznie [khe-re-**tich**-ńe] adv. heretically
heretyczność [khe-re-**tich**-nośhćh] f. hereticalness
heretyk [khe-**re**-tik] m. heretic; misbeliever
herezja [khe-**re**-zyah] f. heresy
herezjarcha [khe-rez-**yahr**-khah] m. founder of a heresy; heresiarch
herkules [kher-**koo**-les] m. man of Herculean power
Herkules [kher-**koo**-les] m. Hercules
herkulesowy [kher-koo-le-**so**-vi] adj.m. Herculean
herma [**kher**-mah] f. herma
hermafrodyta [kher-mah-fro-**di**-tah] m. hermaphrodite; epicene
hermafrodytyczny [kher-mah-fro-di-**tich**-ni] adj.m. hermaphroditic
hermafrodytyzm [kher-mah-fro-**di**-tizm] m. hermaphroditism; androgyny
hermeneutyczny [kher-me-new-**tich**-ni] adj.m. hermeneutic; of interpretation
hermeneutyka [kher-me-**new**-ti-kah] f. hermeneutics; interpretation
hermetycznie [kher-me-**tich**-ńe] adv. tight; hermetically
hermetyczność [kher-me-**tich**-nośhćh] f. airtightness
hermetyczny [kher-me-**tich**-ni] adj.m. airtight; hermetic
hermetyzacja [kher-me-ti-**zah**-tsyah] f. hermetic sealing; airtight sealing
hermetyzm [kher-**me**-tizm] m. hermetic nature
hermetyzować [kher-me-ti-**zo**-vahćh] v. make (something) hermetic (*repeatedly*)
hermetyzowanie [kher-me-ti-zo-**vah**-ńe] n. making (something) hermetic
hermowy [kher-**mo**-vi] adj.m. of herma
herod [**khe**-rot] m. Herod's play
herod-baba [**khe**-rod **bah**-bah] f. virago; termagant
herodowy [khe-ro-**do**-vi] adj.m. like Herod; despotic; merciless
heroicznie [khe-ro-**eech**-ńe] adv. heroically; with heroism
heroiczność [khe-ro-**eech**-nośhćh] f. heroism; heroic deeds
heroiczny [khe-ro-**eech**-ni] adj.m. heroic; daring and risky
heroika [khe-**ro**-ee-kah] f. heroic poetry; epic poetry
heroikomiczny [khe-ro-ee-ko-**meech**-ni] adj.m. heroic-comic; mock-heroic; Hudibrastic
heroikomika [khe-ro-ee-**ko**-mee-kah] f. heroic comedy
heroina [khe-ro-**ee**-nah] f. heroine; heroin
  Gdańska heroina [**gdahń**-skah khe-ro-**ee**-nah] exp.: Gdańsk-heroine; liquid mixture of opium, morphine, and heroin (used intravenously)
heroinizm [khe-ro-**ee**-ńeezm] m. heroin addiction; heroinism
heroinomania [khe-ro-ee-no-**mah**-ńyah] f. heroin addiction
heroinowy [khe-ro-ee-**no**-vi] adj.m. of heroin
heroistyczny [khe-ro-ees-**tich**-ni] adj.m. treated as heroic
heroizacja [khe-ro-ee-**zah**-tsyah] f. making appear heroic
heroizm [khe-**ro**-eezm] m. heroism

heroizować [khe-ro-ee-**zo**-vahćh] v. make (someone) appear (to be) heroic (*repeatedly*)
heroizowanie [khe-ro-ee-zo-**vah**-ńe] n. making appear heroic
herold [**khe**-rold] m. herald; harbinger
heroldia [khe-**rol**-dyah] f. equivalent of the Herald's College in the Russian sector of partitioned Poland (1831-1861)
heroldowski [khe-rol-**dof**-skee] adj.m. of herald; of harbinger
heros [**khe**-ros] m. hero; demigod
herostratesowy [khe-ros-trah-te-**so**-vi] adj.m. eager for fame at any cost; like Herostrates
herostratowy [khe-ros-trah-**to**-vi] adj.m. eager for fame at any cost; like Herostrates
herpetolog [kher-pe-**to**-log] m. herpetologist
herpetologia [kher-pe-to-**lo**-gyah] f. herpetology; study of reptiles and amphibians
herpetologicznie [kher-pe-to-lo-**geech**-ńe] adv. herpetologically
herpetologiczny [kher-pe-to-lo-**geech**-ni] adj.m. herpetologic
herszt [khersht] m. ringleader; chieftain; bellwether
heski [**khes**-kee] adj.m. Hessian
hesperydowy [khes-pe-ri-**do**-vi] adj.m. of Hesperides
hesperyjski [khes-pe-**riy**-skee] adj.m. of Hesperides
hester [**khes**-ter] m. heavy horse of Swedish breed
het [khet] adv. far; away; long (ago); colloq: excl.: hup!; gee!
hetera [khe-**te**-rah] f. hetaera; courtesan; shrew
hetero- [khe-**te**-ro] prefix: hetero-
heterochromosom [khe-te-ro-khro-**mo**-som] m. heterochromosome
heterochromosomy [khe-te-ro-khro-mo-**so**-mi] pl. sex chromosomes
heterocykliczny [khe-te-ro-tsik-**leech**-ni] adj.m. heterocyclic
heterodoksalność [khe-te-ro-dok-**sahl**-nośhćh] f. heterodoxy
heterodoksja [khe-te-ro-**doks**-yah] f. heterodoxy
heterodoksyjny [khe-te-ro-dok-**siy**-ni] adj.m. heterodox
heterodyna [khe-te-ro-**di**-nah] f. heterodyne
heterodynować [khe-te-ro-di-**no**-vahćh] v. heterodyne (*repeatedly*)
heterodynowanie [khe-te-ro-di-no-**vah**-ńe] n. heterodyning
heterofilia [khe-te-ro-**feel**-yah] f. heterophile condition
heterofonia [khe-te-ro-**fo**-ńyah] f. heterophony
heterogameta [khe-te-ro-gah-**me**-tah] f. heterogamete
heterogamety [khe-te-ro-gah-**me**-ti] pl. heterogametes (male and female)
heterogamia [khe-te-ro-**gah**-myah] f. heterogamy
heterogenetyczny [khe-te-ro-ge-ne-**tich**-ni] adj.m. heterogenetic; heterogenic
heterogeneza [khe-te-ro-ge-**ne**-zah] f. heterogenesis; heterogeny
heterogenia [khe-te-ro-**ge**-ńyah] f. heterogeny
heterogeniczność [khe-te-ro-ge-**ńeech**-nośhćh] f. heterogeny
heterogeniczny [khe-te-ro-ge-**ńeech**-ni] adj.m. heterogeneous
heterogonia [khe-te-ro-**go**-ńyah] f. heterogony
heteromorfizm [khe-te-ro-**mor**-feezm] m. heteromorphism
heteromorfoza [khe-te-ro-mor-**fo**-zah] f. heteromorphosis
heteronomia [khe-te-ro-**nom**-yah] f. heteronomy
heteronomicznie [khe-te-ro-no-**meech**-ńe] adv. heteronomously
heteronomiczny [khe-te-ro-no-**meech**-ni] adj.m. heteronomous
heteropolarny [khe-te-ro-po-**lahr**-ni] adj.m. heteropolar
heteroseksualizm [khe-te-ro-sek-soo-**ah**-leezm] m. heterosexuality
heteroseksualny [khe-te-ro-sek-soo-**ahl**-ni] adj.m. heterosexual
heterosemantyczny [khe-te-ro-se-mahn-**tich**-ni] adj.m. hetero-semantic
heterosfera [khe-te-ro-**sfe**-rah] f. a part of upper atmosphere
heterospermia [khe-te-ro-**sper**-myah]

f. fertilization of one egg by the sperm of two or more males
heterospermiczny [khe-te-ro-sper-**meech**-ni] adj.m. of fertilization of one egg by the sperm of two or more males
heterosporia [khe-te-ro-**spor**-yah] f. heterospory
heterosporyczny [khe-te-ro-spo-**rich**-ni] adj.m. heterosporous
heterosylabiczny [khe-te-ro-si-lah-**beech**-ni] adj.m. heterosyllabic
heterotransplantacja [khe-te-ro-trahns-plahn-**tah**-tsyah] f. inter-species transplantation (of organs, tissues, etc.)
heterotrof [khe-te-**ro**-trof] m. heterotroph
heterotrofia [khe-te-ro-**tro**-fyah] f. heterotrophy
heterotroficznie [khe-te-ro-tro-**feech**-ńe] adv. heterotrophically
heterotroficzny [khe-te-ro-tro-**feech**-ni] adj.m. heterotrophic
heterotrofizm [khe-te-ro-**tro**-feezm] m. heterotrophy
heterotropiczny [khe-te-ro-tro-**peech**-ni] adj.m. heterotropic
heterozja [khe-te-**ro**-zyah] f. heterosis
heterozygota [khe-te-ro-zi-**go**-tah] f. heterozygote
heterozygotyczny [khe-te-ro-zi-go-**tich**-ni] adj.m. heterozygous
heterozyjny [khe-te-ro-**ziy**-ni] adj.m. heterotic
hetka [**khet**-kah] f. a type of yacht; insignificant person
być hetką-pentelką [bich **khet**-kown pen-**tel**-kown] exp.: colloq: to be held in disrespect; to be looked down upon
hetman [**khet**-mahn] m. commander in chief (Polish, Ukrainian); (chess) queen
hetmanić [khet-**mah**-ńeech] v. command (troops, etc.); be at the head (of a movement, etc.) (*repeatedly*)
hetmański [khet-**mahń**-skee] adj.m. of commander in chief; of (chess) queen
hetmaństwo [khet-**mahń**-stfo] n. hetmanship; command
hetta! [**khet**-tah] excl.: hup!; gee!
hetytolog [khe-ti-**to**-log] m. Hittologist; Hittitologist
hetytologia [khe-ti-to-**lo**-gyah] f. Hittology; Hittitics; Hittitology; study of the Hittites
heureka! [khew-**re**-kah] excl.: eureka!; I found it!
heureza [khew-**re**-zah] f. heuristics
heurystycznie [khew-ris-**tich**-ńe] adv. heuristically; by the heuristic method
heurystyczny [khew-ris-**tich**-ni] adj.m. heuristic; of the heuristic method
heurystyka [khew-**ris**-ti-kah] f. heuristics
hewea [khe-**ve**-ah] f. a variety of rubber tree
hę [khan] exp.: what?; eh?
he! he! [khee khee] excl.: ha! ha!
hi! he! [khee khee] excl.: ha! ha!
hiacynt [**khyah**-tsint] m. hyacinth
hiacyntowy [khyah-tsin-**to**-vi] adj.m. hyacinthine
hialit [**khyah**-leet] m. hyalite
hialuronianowy [khyah-loo-ro-ńyah-**no**-vi] adj.m. hyaluronidase (enzyme, etc.)
hialuronidaza [khyah-loo-ro-ńee-**dah**-zah] f. hyaluronidase
hialuronowy [khyah-loo-ro-**no**-vi] adj.m. hyaluronic (acid, etc.)
hiat [khyaht] m. occurrence of two vowel sounds without pause
hiatus [**khyah**-toos] m. hiatus; gad
hiberna [khee-**ber**-nah] f. land tax for wintering of troops
hibernacja [khee-ber-**nah**-tsyah] f. hibernation
hibernacyjny [khee-ber-nah-**tsiy**-ni] adj.m. of hibernation
hibiskus [khee-**bees**-koos] m. hibiscus
hidalgo [khee-**dahl**-go] m. hidalgo
hidumin [khee-**do**-meen] m. high strength aluminum alloy
hiduminium [khee-do-**mee**-ńyoom] n. high strength aluminum alloy
hidżra [**kheedzh**-rah] f. hegira; exodus; flight of Mahomet from Mecca to Medina in A.D. 622
hiemalny [khe-**mahl**-ni] adj.m. of plants and organisms living in the

hiena [khe-nah] f. hyena; slang: robber of graves (mob jargon)
hieni [khe-ńee] adj.m. hyenic; hyenoid
hierarcha [khe-**rahr**-khah] m. hierarch
hierarchia [khe-**rahr**-khyah] f. hierarchy; order of ranks
hierarchicznie [khe-rahr-**kheech**-ńe] adv. hierarchically; in respect of hierarchy
hierarchiczność [khe-rahr-**kheech**-nośhćh] f. hierarchic character
hierarchiczny [khe-rahr-**kheech**-ni] adj.m. hierarchic; hierarchical
hierarchizacja [khe-rahr-khee-**zah**-tsyah] f. placing in a hierarchic order
hierarchizować [khe-rahr-khee-**zo**-vahćh] v. place in a hierarchic order (*repeatedly*)
hierarchizowanie [khe-rahr-khee-zo-**vah**-ńe] n. placing in a hierarchic order
hieratycznie [khe-rah-**tich**-ńe] adv. hieratically
hieratyczność [khe-rah-**tich**-nośhćh] f. hieratic nature; monumentality
hieratyczny [khe-rah-**tich**-ni] adj.m. hieratic (script, etc.)
hieratyka [khe-**rah**-ti-kah] f. study of monumentality
hieratyzm [khe-**rah**-tizm] m. monumentality
hieratyzować [khe-rah-ti-**zo**-vahćh] v. monumentalize (*repeatedly*)
hieratyzować się [khe-rah-ti-**zo**-vahćh śhan] v. monumentalize oneself (*repeatedly*)
hieratyzowanie [khe-rah-ti-zo-**vah**-ńe] n. monumentalizing
hieratyzowanie się [khe-rah-ti-zo-**vah**-ńe śhan] n. monumentalizing oneself
hierofant [khe-**ro**-fahnt] m. hierophant
hieroglif [khe-**ro**-gleef] m. hieroglyph; illegible writing
hieroglificznie [khe-ro-glee-**feech**-ńe] adv. hieroglyphically
hieroglificzny [khe-ro-glee-**feech**-ni] adj.m. hieroglyphic
hieroglifika [khe-ro-**glee**-fee-kah] f. the art of reading hieroglyphs
hieroglifowy [khe-ro-glee-**fo**-vi] adj.m. hieroglyphic
hierokracja [khe-ro-**krah**-tsyah] f. government by priests; priestly rule
hierokratyczny [khe-ro-krah-**tich**-ni] adj.m. of a government by priests; of priestly rule
hieromancja [khe-ro-**mahn**-tsyah] f. fortunetelling by inspection of intestines of sacrificial animals
hi-fi [khahy-fee] exp.: high fidelity
high life [khahy-lahyf] exp.: high life
higiena [khee-**ge**-nah] f. hygiene; sanitation; hygienics
higienicznie [khee-ge-**ńeech**-ńe] adv. hygienically; healthily; sanitarily
higieniczny [khee-ge-**ńee**-chni] adj.m. hygienic; healthy; sanitary
higienista [khee-ge-**ńees**-tah] m. hygienist; sanitarian
higienistka [khee-ge-**ńeest**-kah] f. (female) hygienist; sanitarian
higienizacja [khee-ge-ńee-**zah**-tsyah] f. enforcing hygiene; introducing sanitary conditions
higienizacyjny [khee-ge-ńee-zah-**tsiy**-ni] adj.m. of enforcing hygiene; of introduction of sanitary conditions
higro- [**khee**-gro] prefix: hygro-; wet-; moist-
higrofil [khee-**gro**-feel] m. hygrophilous organism
higrofile [khee-gro-**fee**-le] pl. hygrophilous organisms
higrofilny [khee-gro-**feel**-ni] adj.m. hygrophilous; living or growing in moist places
higrofit [khee-**gro**-feet] m. hygrophyte; hydrophyte
higrofity [khee-gro-**fee**-ti] pl. aquatic plants
higrofitowy [khee-gro-fee-**to**-vi] adj.m. hygrophytic
higrofobia [khee-gro-**fo**-byah] f. hygro-phobia
higrograf [khee-**gro**-grahf] m. hygrograph
higrometr [khee-**gro**-metr] m. hygrometer
higrometria [khee-gro-**metr**-yah] f.

hygrometry
higromorficzny [khee-gro-mor-**feech**-ni] adj.m. adapted to living or growing in moist places
higromorfizm [khee-gro-**mor**-feezm] m. characteristic of plants adapted to living or growing in moist places
higronastia [khee-gro-**nahs**-tyah] f. movement of plants according to changes in moisture
higroskop [khee-**gro**-skop] m. hygroscope
higroskopiczny [khee-gro-sko-**peech**-ni] adj.m. hygroscopic
higroskopijnie [khee-gro-sko-**peey**-ńe] adv. hygroscopically
higroskopijność [khee-gro-sko-**peey**-nośhćh] f. hygroscopicity
higroskopijny [khee-gro-sko-**peey**-ni] adj.m. hygroscopic (water, etc.)
higroskopowy [khee-gro-sko-**po**-vi] adj.m. hygroscopic
higrostat [khee-**gro**-staht] m. humidistat
hikora [khee-**ko**-rah] f. hickory
hikorowy [khee-ko-**ro**-vi] adj.m. of hickory; hickory (skis, etc.)
hilemorfizm [khee-le-**mor**-pheezm] m. Aristotelian theory of form and matter
hilobiologia [khee-lo-byo-**lo**-gyah] f. biology of forests
hilobiont [khee-**lo**-byont] m. organism living exclusively in forests
hilobionty [khee-lo-**byon**-ti] pl. organisms living exclusively in forests
hilofil [khee-**lo**-feel] m. organism adapted and thriving in forests
hilofile [khee-lo-**fee**-le] pl. organisms adapted and thriving in forests
hiloteizm [khee-lo-**te**-eezm] m. doctrine of matter being identical with God
hilozoizm [khee-lo-**zo**-eezm] m. hylozoism
himalaista [khee-mah-lah-**ees**-tah] m. Himalayan mountain climber
himalaizm [khee-mah-**lah**-eezm] m. Himalayan mountain climbing
himalajski [khee-mah-**lahy**-skee] adj.m. Himalayan
himation [khee-**maht**-yon] m. himation
hindi [**kheen**-dee] n. official language of India
hinduista [kheen-doo-**ees**-tah] m. student of Hinduism; follower of Hinduism
hinduistyczny [kheen-doo-ees-**tich**-ni] adj.m. of Hinduism; Hindu; Hindoo
hinduistyka [kheen-doo-**ees**-ti-kah] f. study of Hinduism
hinduizm [kheen-**doo**-eezm] m. Hinduism
Hindus [**kheen**-doos] m. Hindu; Hindoo
Hinduska [kheen-**doos**-kah] f. (female) Hindu; Hindoo
hinduski [kheen-**doos**-kee] adj.m. Hindu (language, etc.)
hindustani [kheen-doo-**stah**-ńee] m. Hindustani; Hindostani
hindustański [kheen-doo-**stahń**-skee] adj.m. Hindustani; Hindostani
hiobowy [khyo-**bo**-vi] adj.m. distressing; woeful (news, etc.)
hiobowe wieści [khyo-**bo**-ve **vyeśh**-ćhee] exp.: distressing news; Job's news
hiparion [khee-**pahr**-yon] m. hipparion
hiper- [**khee**-per] prefix: hyper-; above-; beyond-; super-
hiperatom [khee-per-**ah**-tom] m. atom with one unstable negative particle replacing an electron
hiperbola [khee-per-**bo**-lah] f. hyperbole; hyperbola
hiperbolicznie [khee-per-bo-**leech**-ńe] adv. hyperbolically
hiperboliczność [khee-per-bo-**leech**-nośhćh] f. hyperbolic character
hiperboliczny [khee-per-bo-**leech**-ni] adj.m. hyperbolic; hyperbolical
hiperbolizacja [khee-per-bo-lee-**zah**-tsyah] f. hyperbolizing
hiperbolizm [khee-per-**bo**-leezm] m. use of hyperbolic expressions
hiperbolizować [khee-per-bo-lee-**zo**-vahćh] v. hyperbolize (*repeatedly*)
hiperbolizowanie [khee-per-bo-lee-zo-**vah**-ńe] n. hyperbolizing

hiperboloida [khee-per-bo-**loy**-dah] f. hyperboloid
hiperboloidalny [khee-per-bo-lo-ee-**dahl**-ni] adj.m. hyperboloidal
Hiperborejczyk [khee-per-bo-**rey**-chik] m. Hyperborean
hiperborejski [khee-per-bo-**rey**-skee] adj.m. hyperborean
hiperdźwięk [khee-**per**-dźhvyank] m. acoustic wave of more than one billion (1,000,000,000) hertz frequency
hiperesteta [khee-per-es-**te**-tah] m. hyperesthetic person
hiperestezja [khee-per-es-**te**-zyah] f. hyperesthesia
hiperfragment [khee-per-**frahg**-ment] m. atomic nucleus containing at least one unstable negative particle replacing one electron
hipergeniczny [khee-per-ge-**ńeech**-ni] adj.m. related to natural process of weathering etc.
hiperglikemia [khee-per-glee-**ke**-myah] f. hyperglycemia
hiperglikemiczny [khee-per-glee-ke-**meech**-ni] adj.m. hyperglycemic
hipergol [khee-**per**-gol] m. hypergol
hiperinflacja [khee-per-een-**flah**-tsyah] f. hyperinflation
hiperjądro [khee-per-**yown**-dro] n. atomic nucleus containing at least one unstable negative particle (hyperon) replacing one electron
hiperjądrowy [khee-per-yown-**dro**-vi] adj.m. of atomic nucleus containing at least one negative unstable particle (hyperon) replacing one electron
hiperkataleksa [khee-per-kah-tah-**le**-ksah] f. hypercatalexis
hiperkatalektyczny [khee-per-kah-tah-lek-**tich**-ni] adj.m. hypercatalectic
hiperkrytycyzm [khee-per-kri-**ti**-tsizm] m. hypercriticism
hiperkrytycznie [khee-per-kri-**tich**-ńe] adv. hypercritically
hiperkrytyczny [khee-per-kri-**tich**-ni] adj.m. hypercritical; over-critical
hiperkrytyk [khee-per-**kri**-tik] m. hypercritic
hipermetria [khee-per-**metr**-yah] f. hypermetric nature
hipermetryczny [khee-per-met-**rich**-ni] adj.m. hypermetric; hypermetrical
hipernik [khee-**per**-ńeek] m. alloy of half iron and half nickel
hiperon [khee-**pe**-ron] m. hyperon
hiperpoprawność [khee-per-po-**prahv**-nośhćh] f. hypercorrectness; over-correctness
hiperpoprawny [khee-per-po-**prahv**-ni] adj.m. hypercorrect; over-correct; excessively proper
hiperprodukcja [khee-per-pro-**dook**-tsyah] f. overproduction
hipersonicznie [khee-per-so-**ńeech**-ńe] adv. hypersonically
hipersoniczny [khee-per-so-**ńeech**-ni] adj.m. hypersonic
hiperstatyczny [khee-per-stah-**tich**-ni] adj.m. statically indeterminate (not calculable without consideration of deflections)
hipersten [khee-**per**-sten] m. hypersthene
hiperssteniczny [khee-per-ste-**ńeech**-ni] adj.m. hypersthenic
hipertensja [khee-per-**ten**-syah] f. hypertension
hipertensyjny [khee-per-ten-**siy**-ni] adj.m. hypertensive
hipertermia [khee-per-**ter**-myah] f. hyperthermia
hipertonia [khee-per-**to**-ńyah] f. hypertonicity
hipertoniczny [khee-per-to-**ńeech**-ni] adj.m. hypertonic
hipertrofia [khee-per-**tro**-fyah] f. hypertrophy
hipertroficznie [khee-per-tro-**feech**-ńe] adv. in a hypertrophic manner
hipertroficzny [khee-per-tro-**feech**-ni] adj.m. hypertrophic
hiperwitaminoza [khee-per-vee-tah-mee-**no**-zah] f. hypervitaminosis
hipiczny [khee-**peech**-ni] adj.m. equestrian; of horse-riding; of horsemanship
hipika [**khee**-pee-kah] f. horse-riding; horsemanship
hipis [**khee**-pees] m. hippy; hippie
hipiska [khee-**pees**-kah] f. colloq: (female) hippy; hippie
hipisowski [khee-pee-**sof**-skee]

adj.m. colloq: of hippy; of hippie; of hippies
hipisowstwo [khee-pee-**sof**-stfo] n. colloq: hippiedom; hippiehood
hipnologia [kheep-no-**lo**-gyah] f. hypnotism
hipnologiczny [kheep-no-lo-**geech**-ni] adj.m. of study of hypnotism
hipnopedia [kheep-no-**pe**-dyah] f. teaching during sleep
hipnopedyczny [kheep-no-pe-**dich**-ni] adj.m. of teaching during sleep
hipnoterapia [kheep-no-te-**rah**-pyah] f. hypnotherapy
hipnotycznie [kheep-no-**tich**-ńe] adv. hypnotically; mesmerically
hipnotyczny [kheep-no-**tich**-ni] adj.m. hypnotic; mesmeric
hipnotyzacja [kheep-no-ti-**zah**-tsyah] f. hypnotization; fascination; bewitching; bringing oneself into a state of trance
hipnotyzer [kheep-no-**ti**-zer] m. hypnotizer; hypnotist
hipnotyzerka [kheep-no-ti-**zer**-kah] f. (female) hypnotizer
hipnotyzerski [kheep-no-ti-**zer**-skee] adj.m. of a hypnotizer; hypnotizer's
hipnotyzować [kheep-no-ti-**zo**-vahćh] v. hypnotize; fascinate; bewitch (*repeatedly*)
hipnotyzować się [kheep-no-ti-**zo**-vahćh śhan] v. hypnotize oneself; bring oneself into a state of trance (*repeatedly*)
hipnotyzowanie [khee-pno-ti-zo-**vah**-ńe] n. hypnotization
hipnoza [kheep-**no**-zah] f. hypnosis
hipo- [**khee**-po] prefix: hypo-
hipocentrum [khee-po-**tsen**-troom] n. hypocenter
hipocentryczny [khee-po-tsent-**rich**-ni] adj.m. hypocentral
hipochondria [khee-po-**khon**-dryah] f. hypochondria; hypochondriasis
hipochondryczka [khee-po-khon-**drich**-kah] f. (female) hypochondriac
hipochondrycznie [khee-po-khon-**drich**-ńe] adv. hypochondriacally
hipochondryczny [khee-po-khon-**drich**-ni] adj.m. hypochondriac; hypochondriacal
hipochondryk [khee-po-**khon**-drik] m. hypochondriac
hipocykloida [khee-po-tsik-**loy**-dah] f. hypocycloid
hipoderma [khee-po-**der**-mah] f. hypoderm; hypodermis
hipodermicznie [khee-po-der-**meech**-ńe] adv. hypodermically
hipodermiczny [khee-po-der-**meech**-ni] adj.m. hypodermic (injection, etc.); hypodermal
hipodrom [khee-**po**-drom] m. horse-race track; hippodrome
hipoglikemia [khee-po-glee-**ke**-myah] f. hypoglycemia
hipoglikemiczny [khee-po-glee-ke-**meech**-ni] adj.m. hypoglycemic
hipogryf [khee-**po**-grif] m. winged horse
hipokorystycznie [khee-po-ko-ris-**tich**-ńe] adv. hypocoristically
hipokorystyczny [khee-po-ko-ris-**tich**-ni] adj.m. hypocoristic; hypocoristical
hipokorystyk [khee-po-ko-**ris**-tik] m. hypocorism; term of endearment; pet name
hipokorystykum [khee-po-ko-ris-**ti**-koom] n. hypocorism; term of endearment; pet name
hipokryta [khee-po-**kri**-tah] m. hypocrite; one who pretends or dissembles; dissembler
hipokrytka [khee-po-**krit**-kah] f. (female) hypocrite; one who pretends or dissembles; dissembler
hipokryzja [khee-po-**kri**-zyah] f. hypocrisy; falseness; pretense; cant; double-dealing
hipolimnion [khee-po-**leem**-ńon] m. hypolimnion
hipolog [khee-**po**-log] m. horse specialist
hipologia [khee-po-**lo**-gyah] f. hippology; study of horses
hipomania [khee-po-**mah**-ńyah] f. excessive attachment to horses
hipopotam [khee-po-**po**-tahm] m. hippopotamus; hippo
hipopotamowy [khee-po-po-tah-**mo**-vi] adj.m. of hippopotamus; hippo's
hipostaza [khee-po-**stah**-zah] f.

hypostasis
hipostazować [khee-po-stah-**zo**-vahćh] v. hypostatize; reify (*repeatedly*)
hipostazowanie [khee-po-stah-zo-**vah**-ńe] n. hypostatization
hipostyl [khee-**po**-stil] m. hipostyle
hipotaksa [khee-po-**tahk**-sah] f. hypotaxis
hipotaktyczny [khee-po-tahk-**tich**-ni] adj.m. hypotactic
hipotecznie [khee-po-**tech**-ńe] adv. by a mortgage
hipoteczny [khee-po-**tech**-ni] adj.m. of a mortgage; hypothecary; mortgage (debt, etc.)
weksel hipoteczny [**vek**-sel khee-po-**tech**-ni] exp.: mortgage note
hipoteka [khee-po-**te**-kah] f. title; mortgage; records office
hipotekować [khee-po-te-**ko**-vahćh] v. enter a mortgage into official records (*repeatedly*)
hipotekowanie [khee-po-te-ko-**vah**-ńe] n. entering a mortgage into official records
hipotensja [khee-po-**ten**-syah] f. hypotension; abnormally low blood pressure
hipotensyjny [khee-po-ten-**siy**-ni] adj.m. hypotensive; due to abnormally low blood pressure
hipotermia [khee-po-**ter**-myah] f. hypothermia
hipotermiczny [khee-po-ter-**meech**-ni] adj.m. hypothermal
hipotetycznie [khee-po-te-**tich**-ńe] adv. hypothetically; supposedly
hipotetyczność [khee-po-te-**tich**-nośhćh] f. hypothetical nature
hipotetyczny [khee-po-te-**tich**-ni] adj.m. hypothetical; assumed; assumptive; supposed
hipoteza [khee-po-**te**-zah] f. hypothesis; assumption; theory
hipotonia [khee-po-**to**-ńyah] f. hypotonicity
hipotonicznie [khee-po-to-**ńeech**-ńe] adv. hypotonically
hipotoniczny [khee-po-to-**ńeech**-ni] adj.m. hypotonic
hipotrochoida [khee-po-tro-**khoy**-dah] f. a mathematical curve
hipowitaminoza [khee-po-vee-tah-mee-**no**-zah] f. hypovitaminosis
hipparion [kheep-**pahr**-yon] m. hipparion
hippiczny [kheep-**peech**-ni] adj.m. of horse-riding; of horsemanship; equestrian
hippika [kheep-**pee**-kah] f. horse-riding; horsemanship
hippis [**khee**-pees] m. hippie; hippy
hipsografia [kheep-so-**grah**-fyah] f. hypsography
hipsograficzny [kheep-so-grah-**feech**-ni] adj.m. of hypsography
hipsometria [kheep-so-**metr**-yah] f. hypsometry
hipsometryczny [kheep-so-met-**rich**-ni] adj.m. hypsometric
hipsotermometr [kheep-so-ter-**mo**-metr] m. hypsometer (measuring elevation by the boiling point)
hipuryt [khee-**poo**-rit] m. hippurate
hipurytowy [khee-poo-ri-**to**-vi] adj.m. of hippurate
hirudyna [khee-roo-**di**-nah] f. hirudin
his [khees] m. his (sound)
hislina [khees-**lee**-nah] f. one of sail rigging lines
hisować [khee-**so**-vahćh] v. pull up a sail with the line passing through a pulley (*repeatedly*)
hisowanie [khee-so-**vah**-ńe] n. pulling up a sail with the line passing through a pulley
hispanistyka [khees-pah-**ńees**-ti-kah] f. Spanish studies
histamina [khees-tah-**mee**-nah] f. histamine
histaminowy [khees-tah-mee-**no**-vi] adj.m. histaminic
histereza [khees-te-**re**-zah] f. hysteresis
histerezowy [khees-te-re-**zo**-vi] adj.m. hysteretic
histeria [khee-**ster**-yah] f. hysteria; hysterics; unmanageable fear or emotional excess
paroksyzm histerii [pah-**rok**-sizm khee-**ster**-yee] exp.: outbreak of a hysterical fit
histerologia [khees-te-ro-**lo**-gyah] f. erroneous reversal of natural chronological order
histeryczka [khee-ste-**rich**-kah] f. hysterical woman

histerycznie [khee-ste-**rich**-ńe] adv. hysterically
histeryczny [khee-ste-**rich**-ni] adj.m. hysterical; having a fit of nerves; gone into hysterics
histeryk [khee-**ste**-rik] m. hysterical man
histeryzować [khee-ste-ri-**zo**-vahćh] v. be hysterical (*repeatedly*)
histeryzowanie [khee-ste-ri-zo-**vah**-ńe] n. being hysterical
histiocyt [khees-**tyo**-tsit] m. histiocyte; clasmatocyte
histo- [**khees**-to] prefix: histo-
histochemia [khees-to-**khe**-myah] f. histochemistry
histochemicznie [khees-to-khe-**meech**-ńe] adv. histochemically
histochemiczny [khees-to-khe-**meech**-ni] adj.m. histochemical
histogeneza [khees-to-ge-**ne**-zah] f. histogenesis
histogenetycznie [khees-to-ge-ne-**tich**-ńe] adv. histogenetically
histogenetyczny [khees-to-ge-ne-**tich**-ni] adj.m. histogenetic
histogram [khees-**to**-grahm] m. histogram
histolog [khees-**to**-log] m. histologist
histologia [khees-to-**lo**-gyah] f. histology
histologicznie [khees-to-lo-**geech**-ńe] adv. histologically
histologiczny [khees-to-lo-**geech**-ni] adj.m. histological
histopatolog [khees-to-pah-**to**-log] m. histopathologist
histopatologia [khees-to-pah-to-**lo**-gyah] f. histopathology
histopatologicznie [khees-to-pah-to-lo-**geech**-ńe] adv. histopathologically
histopatologiczny [khees-to-pah-to-lo-**geech**-ni] adj.m. histopathological
historia [khee-**stor**-yah] f. story; history; history lesson; history class; history department; affair; business; show; fuss; palaver
historie [khee-**stor**-ye] pl. extraordinary things; goodness knows what; all sorts of things
dziwna historia! [**dźheev**-nah khee-**stor**-yah] exp.: strange going-on; a queer show
historia choroby [khee-**stor**-yah kho-**ro**-bi] exp.: case history; (patient's) hospital record
ładna historia! [**wahd**-nah khee-**stor**-yah] exp.: nasty surprise!; what a surprise!
przejść do historii [psheyśhćh do khee-**stor**-yee] exp.: to make history
robić historie [**ro**-beećh khee-**stor**-ye] exp.: to make fuss; to be fussy
to stara historia [to **stah**-rah khee-**stor**-yah] exp.: that's old stuff; it's as old as the hills
wciąż ta sama historia [fćhownsh tah **sah**-mah khee-**stor**-yah] exp.: the same old tune
historiograf [khee-stor-**yo**-grahf] m. historiographer
historiografia [khee-stor-yo-**grahf**-yah] f. historiography; the writing of history
historiograficznie [khee-stor-yo-grah-**feech**-ńe] adv. historiographically
historiograficzny [khee-stor-yo-grah-**feech**-ni] adj.m. historiographical; historiographic
historiotwórczy [khee-stor-yo-**tfoor**-chi] adj.m. history-making
historiozof [khee-stor-**yo**-zof] m. specialist in the philosophy of history
historiozofia [khee-stor-yo-**zof**-yah] f. philosophy of history
historiozoficzny [khee-stor-yo-zo-**feech**-ni] adj.m. of philosophy of history
historycyzm [hkee-sto-**ri**-tsizm] m. historical perspective
historyczka [khee-sto-**rich**-kah] f. (woman) historian
historycznie [khee-sto-**rich**-ńe] adv. historically
historycznojęzykowy [khee-sto-rich-no-yan-zi-**ko**-vi] adj.m. historic-linguistic; pertaining to the history of a language
historycznoliteracki [khee-sto-rich-no-lee-te-**rahts**-kee] adj.m. historic-literary; pertaining to the history of literature
historyczno-literacki [khee-sto-**rich**-

no lee-te-**rahts**-kee] adj.m. pertaining to the history and to the literature
historyczność [khee-sto-**rich**-nośhćh] f. historicity; historical actuality; fact
historyczny [khee-sto-**rich**-ni] adj.m. historic (day, event, speech); historical (evidence, truth, novel, year); history-making (event, person, etc.)
historyjka [khee-sto-**riy**-kah] f. (a little) story; tale; anecdote; affair
historyk [khee-**sto**-rik] m. historian
historyka [khee-**sto**-ri-kah] f. theory and methodology of historical research
historyzm [khee-**sto**-rizm] m. historical perspective; art-style at the end of 19th century
histrion [**khees**-tryon] m. histrion; an actor
histydyna [khees-ti-**di**-nah] f. histidine
Hiszpan [**kheesh**-pahn] m. Spaniard
Hiszpanka [kheesh-**pahn**-kah] f. Spanish woman
hiszpanka [kheesh-**pahn**-kah] f. (Spanish) pointed beard; influenza
hiszpański [kheesh-**pahń**-skee] adj.m. Spanish (language, etc.); of Spain
po hiszpańsku [po kheesh-**pahń**-skoo] exp.: in Spanish
hiszpańskojęzyczny [kheesh-pahń-sko-y<u>an</u>-**zich**-ni] adj.m. Spanish-speaking
hiszpańszczyzna [kheesh-pahń-**shchiz**-nah] f. Spanish language; things Spanish
hit [kheet] m. (a) hit (song, etc.); mob slang: a strong narcotic
hitlerowiec [khee-tle-**ro**-vyets] m. hitlerite; German Nazi
hitlerowski [khee-tle-**rof**-skee] adj.m. hitlerite; German Nazi; Hitler's
hitleryzm [khee-**tle**-rizm] m. Hitlerism; Nazism
HIV [kheef] m. HIV virus; Human Immunodeficiency Virus; AIDS virus
hiw [kheef] m. lift; the act of heaving
hizop [**khee**-zop] m. hyssop; hyssop oil
hładysza [khwah-**di**-shah] f. (Ukr.) pot of earthenware
hm [khm] exp.: humph!; umph!
ho! ho! [kho] excl.: gee!; well, well!
hoacyn [kho-**ah**-tsin] m. hoatzin (bird)
hobbista [khob-**bees**-tah] m. hobbyist
hobbistka [khob-**beest**-kah] f. (woman) hobbyist
hobbistowski [khob-bees-**tof**-skee] adj.m. of a hobby; of a hobbyist
hobbistyczny [khob-bees-**tich**-ni] adj.m. of a hobby; of hobbies
hobby [**khob**-bi] n. (Engl.) hobby
hoc, hoc! [khots khots] exp.: an exclamation expressing good humor
hochsztapler [khokh-**shtahp**-ler] m. impostor; fraud; humbug; crook; swindler; confidence man
hochsztaplerka [khokh-shtahp-**ler**-kah] f. (female) impostor; fraud; humbug; crook; swindler
hochsztaplerski [khokh-shtahp-**ler**-skee] adj.m. impostor's; fraudulent; crook's; swindler's
hochsztaplerstwo [khokh-shtahp-**ler**-stfo] n. fraud; deception; swindle; humbug; sham; the confidence men
hocki-klocki [**khots**-kee **klots**-kee] exp.: pranks; antics; monkey tricks; skylarking
hodograf [kho-**do**-grahf] m. hydrograph (a plotted curve)
hodoskop [kho-**do**-skop] m. hodoscope
hodować [kho-**do**-vahćh] v. rear; breed; raise; keep; nurse (*repeatedly*)
hodować się [kho-**do**-vahćh śh<u>an</u>] v. grow; develop oneself (*repeatedly*)
hodowanie [kho-do-**vah**-ńe] n. rearing; bringing up
hodowca [kho-**dof**-tsah] m. breeder (of cattle, pigs, horses, etc.); farmer; raiser; grower; cultivator
hodowczyni [kho-dof-**chi**-ńee] f. (female) breeder; farmer; raiser; cultivator; grower
hodowla [kho-**do**-vlah] f. animal

husbandry; raising; breeding
hodowla drobiu [kho-**do**-vlah **dro**-byoo] exp.: chicken-farming
hodowla koni [kho-**do**-vlah **ko**-ńee] exp.: stud-farm
hodowla pszczół [kho-**do**-vlah pshchoow] exp.: beekeeping
hodowlany [kho-do-**vlah**-ni] adj.m. of cultivation; of raising
hodża [**kho**-dzhah] m. Muslim clergyman
hoja [**kho**-yah] f. Hoya (plant)
hojer [**kho**-yer] m. hauler boat built for transport of live fish
hojnie [**khoy**-ńe] adv. generously; lavishly; freely; with liberality; amply; profusely; largely; without stint
hojność [**khoy**-nośhćh] f. generosity; lavishness; liberality; bounty; munificence
hojny [**khoy**-ni] adj.m. generous; lavish; liberal; profuse; ample
hokeista [kho-ke-**ees**-tah] m. hockey player
hokej [**kho**-key] m. (ice) hockey
hokejka [kho-**key**-kah] f. hockey skate
hokejki [kho-**key**-kee] pl. hockey skates
hokejówka [kho-ke-**yoof**-kah] f. hockey skate
hokejówki [kho-ke-**yoof**-kee] pl. hockey skates
hokus-pokus [**kho**-koos **po**-koos] exp.: hocus-pocus; sleight of hand; nonsense; sham to cloak a deception
hol [khol] m. towline; haul (of fish net); (waiting) hall; (hotel) lounge
hola! [**kho**-lah] excl.: here!; you, there!; stop!; stay!; wait!
holding [**khol**-deeng] m. holding company
holdingowy [khol-deen-**go**-vi] adj.m. of a holding company
holender [kho-**len**-der] m. Dutch figure in figure skating; Dutch windmill; colloq: Dutch bull; slang: damn it!
latający Holender [lah-tah-<u>yown</u>-tsi kho-**len**-der] exp.: flying Dutchman; hustler; bustler
holenderka [kho-len-**der**-kah] f. Holstein-Friesian cow; Dutch skate; Dutch roof-tile
holendernia [kho-len-**der**-ńah] f. Dutch settlement; cow-house; byre
holenderski [kho-len-**der**-skee] adj.m. Dutch; of Holland; m. Dutch language
po holendersku [po kho-len-**der**-skoo] exp.: in Dutch (language)
holendrować [kho-len-**dro**-vahćh] v. make rocking-turns (on skates) (*repeatedly*)
holendrowanie [kho-len-dro-**vah**-ńe] n. making rocking-turns (on skates)
holendrowy [kho-len-**dro**-vi] adj.m. of Dutch-style paper-making device; Dutch beater
holik [**kho**-leek] m. (small, nice) entry hall
holistyczny [kho-lees-**tich**-ni] adj.m. holistic
holizm [**kho**-leezm] m. holism
hollina [khol-**lee**-nah] f. towline
holm [kholm] m. holmium (a metal) (atomic number 67)
holo- [**kho**-lo] prefix: holo-; total-
holocaust [kho-**lo**-kahwst] m. holocaust
holocen [kho-**lo**-tsen] m. Holocene
holoceński [kho-lo-**tseń**-skee] adj.m. Holocene (epoch, etc.)
holograf [kho-**lo**-grahf] m. holograph
holografia [kho-lo-**grah**-fyah] f. holography
holograficznie [kho-lo-grah-**feech**-ńe] adv. holographically
holograficzny [kho-lo-grah-**feech**-ni] adj.m. holographic
holografować [kho-lo-grah-**fo**-vahćh] v. make holograms (*repeatedly*)
holografowanie [kho-lo-grah-fo-**vah**-ńe] n. making holograms
hologram [kho-**lo**-grahm] m. hologram
hologramowy [kho-lo-grah-**mo**-vi] adj.m. of a hologram
holometabolia [kho-lo-me-tah-**bol**-yah] f. holometabolism
holometaboliczny [kho-lo-me-tah-bo-**leech**-ni] adj.m. holometabolous
holometamorfoza [kho-lo-me-tah-

mor-**fo**-zah] f. holometabolism
holotyp [kho-**lo**-tip] m. holotype
holować [kho-**lo**-vahćh] v. tow; haul; drag; tug; track; truck (*repeatedly*)
holowanie [kho-lo-**vah**-ńe] n. towage; haulage; trackage; truckage
holowniczy [kho-lov-**ńee**-chi] adj.m. tow (boat, line, etc.); towing (line, path, etc.)
holownik [kho-**lov**-ńeek] m. tug; tugboat
holweg [**khol**-vek] m. ski path
hołd [khowd] m. tribute; homage; oath of allegiance
hołdować [khow-**do**-vahćh] v. advocate; be in favor; profess (certain principles, etc.); be an admirer (of); be an adherent (of); pay homage; render homage; swear allegiance; subject; subdue (*repeatedly*)
hołdowanie [khow-do-**vah**-ńe] n. swearing allegiance; paying homage
hołdownictwo [khow-dov-**ńeets**-tfo] n. allegiance; vassalage
hołdowniczy [khow-dov-**ńee**-chi] adj.m. vassal's; tributary
hołdownik [khow-**dov**-ńeek] m. vassal; (a) tributary; homager
hołobelny [kho-wo-**bel**-ni] adj.m. of shaft; of thill; of shafts
hołobla [kho-**wob**-lah] f. two-shaft; two-thill (of a cart, of a carriage)
hołoblowy [kho-wob-**lo**-vi] adj.m. two-shaft; two-thill (cart, carriage, gear, harness, etc.)
hołota [kho-**wo**-tah] f. riffraff; rabble; bunch of rascals; distress; colloq: starveling
hołubić [kho-**woo**-beećh] v. snuggle; cuddle; fondle; endear to oneself (*repeatedly*)
hołubiec [kho-**woo**-byets] m. Ukrainian dance figure; jump accompanied by clicking of the heels
hołubienie [kho-woo-**bye**-ńe] n. snuggling; cuddling; fondling; endearing to oneself
hołysz [**kho**-wish] m. starveling
homagialny [kho-mah-**gyahl**-ni] adj.m. of homage
homagium [kho-**mah**-gyoom] n. homage
homal [**kho**-mahl] m. microphotographic lens
homar [**kho**-mahr] m. lobster
homarzec [kho-**mah**-zhets] m. Norway lobster
homeomorfia [kho-me-o-**mor**-fyah] f. homeomorphism
homeomorficzny [kho-me-o-mor-**feech**-ni] adj.m. homeomorphic
homeomorfizm [kho-me-o-**mor**-feezm] m. homeomorphism
homeopata [kho-me-o-**pah**-tah] m. homeopath
homeopatia [kho-me-o-**pah**-tyah] f. homeopathy
homeopatycznie [kho-me-o-pah-**tich**-ńe] adv. homeopathically
homeopatyczny [kho-me-o-pah-**tich**-ni] adj.m. homeopathic
homeostat [kho-me-**o**-staht] m. homeostatic regulator
homeostatyczy [kho-me-o-stah-**tich**-ni] adj.m. homeostatic
homeostaza [kho-me-o-**stah**-zah] f. homeostasis
homerolog [kho-me-**ro**-log] m. specialist in Homer's poetry
homerowy [kho-me-**ro**-vi] adj.m. Homer's; homeric
homerycki [kho-me-**rits**-kee] adj.m. Homeric (age, epic, etc.)
homerycznie [kho-me-**rich**-ńe] adv. Homerically; gigantically
homeryczny [kho-me-**rich**-ni] adj.m. Homeric; gigantic; homeric; Homer's
homeryda [kho-me-**ri**-dah] m. Homerid; Homeric rhapsodist
homiletycznie [kho-mee-le-**tich**-ńe] adv. homiletically
homiletyczny [kho-mee-le-**tich**-ni] adj.m. homiletic
homiletyk [kho-mee-**le**-tik] m. student of homiletics
homiletyka [kho-mee-**le**-ti-kah] f. homiletics
homilia [kho-**meel**-yah] f. homily
homiliarz [kho-**meel**-yahsh] m. book of homilies
hominidy [kho-mee-**ńee**-di] pl. Hominidae

homo- [**kho**-mo] prefix: homo-
homocentryczny [kho-mo-tsent-**rich**-ni] adj.m. homocentric
homochroniczny [kho-mo-khro-**ńeech**-ni] adj.m. simultaneous; simultaneously created
homofon [kho-**mo**-fon] m. homophone
homofonia [kho-mo-**fo**-ńyah] f. homophony
homofoniczny [kho-mo-fo-ńeech-ni] adj.m. homophonic; homophonous
homogamia [kho-mo-**gah**-myah] f. homogamy
homogamiczny [kho-mo-gah-**meech**-ni] adj.m. homogamic; homogamous
homogen [kho-**mo**-gen] m. homogenous thing; homogenous being
homogenia [kho-mo-**ge**-ńyah] f. homogeny
homogeniczność [kho-mo-ge-**ńeech**-nośhćh] f. homogeneity; homogeneousness
homogenicznie [kho-mo-ge-**ńeech**-ńe] adv. homogeneously
homogeniczny [kho-mo-ge-**ńeech**-ni] adj.m. homogeneous; homogenous
homogenizacja [kho-mo-ge-ńee-**zah**-tsyah] f. homogenization
homogenizator [kho-mo-ge-ńee-**zah**-tor] m. homogenizer
homogenizować [kho-mo-ge-ńee-**zo**-vahćh] v. homogenize (*repeatedly*)
homografia [kho-mo-**grah**-fyah] f. one of collinear geometric operations
homograficzny [kho-mo-grah-**feech**-ni] adj.m. of one of collinear geometric operations; homographic
homogram [kho-**mo**-grahm] m. homograph
homojotermia [kho-mo-yo-**ter**-myah] f. homoiothermic condition
homojotermiczny [kho-mo-yo-ter-**meech**-ni] adj.m. homoiothermic; homoiothermal; warm-blooded
homolog [kho-**mo**-log] m. homolog; homologue; homologous compound
homologi [kho-mo-**lo**-gee] pl. homologous compounds
homologacja [kho-mo-lo-**gah**-tsyah] f. homologation
homologacyjnie [kho-mo-lo-gah-**tsiy**-ńe] adv. by homologation
homologacyjny [kho-mo-lo-gah-**tsiy**-ni] adj.m. of homologation
homologia [kho-mo-**lo**-gyah] f. homology
homologiczny [kho-mo-lo-**geech**-ni] adj.m. of homology; homologous
homologować [kho-mo-lo-**go**-vahćh] v. homologize (*repeatedly*)
homolograficzny [kho-mo-lo-grah-**feech**-ni] adj.m. homolographic
homomorficzny [kho-mo-mor-**feech**-ni] adj.m. homomorphic
homomorfizm [kho-mo-**mor**-feezm] m. homomorphism
homonim [kho-**mo**-ńeem] m. homonym
homonimia [kho-mo-**ńee**-myah] f. homonymy
homonimiczność [kho-mo-ńee-**meech**-nośhćh] f. homonymy
homonimicznie [kho-mo-ńee-**meech**-ńe] adv. homonymously
homonimiczny [kho-mo-ńee-**meech**-ni] adj.m. homonymous; honomymic
homonimika [kho-mo-**ńee**-mee-kah] f. homonyms of a given language
homosejsta [kho-mo-**seys**-tah] f. line on a map showing an earthquake
homoseksualista [kho-mo-sek-soo-ah-**lees**-tah] m. homosexual; slang: homo (jargon)
homoseksualizm [kho-mo-sek-soo-**ah**-leezm] m. homosexuality; homoerotism
homoseksualnie [kho-mo-sek-soo-**ahl**-ńe] adv. homosexually
homoseksualny [kho-mo-sek-soo-**ahl**-ni] adj.m. homosexual; homoerotic
homosfera [kho-mo-**sfe**-rah] f. homosphere (strata in which specific gravity of air remains constant) (located above 90 km)
homotermia [kho-mo-**ter**-myah] f. equalization of temperature in bodies of water at 4 degree C

twice yearly (in spring and fall)
homotetia [kho-mo-**tet**-yah] f. homothety; like placement
homotetyczny [kho-mo-te-**tich**-ni] adj.m. homothetic (figures, etc.)
homozygota [kho-mo-zi-**go**-tah] f. homozygote
homozygotycznie [kho-mo-zi-go-**tich**-ńe] adv. homozygously
homozygotyczność [kho-mo-zi-go-**tich**-nośhćh] f. homozygosity
homozygotyczny [kho-mo-zi-go-**tich**-ni] adj.m. homozygous; homozygotic
homozygoza [kho-mo-zi-**go**-zah] f. homozygosis
homunkulus [kho-moon-**koo**-loos] m. homunculus; manikin
homuś [**kho**-moośh] m. slang: homo; gay (mob jargon)
honingować [kho-ńeen-**go**-vahćh] v. hone (*repeatedly*)
honor [**kho**-nor] m. honor; distinctions
odbierać honory [od-**bye**-rahćh kho-**no**-ri] exp.: to take the salute
oddać komuś ostatnie honory [od-dahćh **ko**-moośh o-**staht**-ńe kho-**no**-ri] exp.: to pay somebody the last honors
poczucie honoru [po-**choo**-ćhe kho-**no**-roo] exp.: sense of honor
honorarium [kho-no-**rahr**-yoom] n. fee; honorarium; charge
honorować [kho-no-**ro**-vahćh] v. honor; show marks of respect; acknowledge (*repeatedly*)
honorowanie [kho-no-ro-**vah**-ńe] n. honoring; marks of respect; acknowledgment; paying royalties; paying fees
honorowo [kho-no-**ro**-vo] adv. honorably; like a gentleman; with credit; gratuitously
honorowość [kho-no-**ro**-vośhćh] f. self-respect; pride
honorowy [kho-no-**ro**-vi] adj.m. gentlemanly; honorable; respectable; of honor; voluntary; unpaid; honorary
dług honorowy [dwook kho-no-**ro**-vi] exp.: debt of honor
gość honorowy [gośhćh kho-no-**ro**-vi] exp.: guest of honor
hop! [khop] excl.: jump!
hopak [**kho**-pahk] m. lively Ukrainian dance
hopki [**khop**-kee] pl. gambols; capers; frolics
hopla! [**khop**-lah] excl.: jump!
hoplita [khop-**lee**-tah] m. hoplite
hops! [khops] excl.: jump!
hopsa! [**khop**-sah] excl.: jump!
hopsasa! [khop-**sah**-sah] excl.: jump!
hora [**kho**-rah] f. Romanian folk dance
horacjanin [kho-rah-**tsyah**-ńeen] m. admirer of Horace
horacjański [kho-rah-**tsyahń**-skee] adj.m. Horacian
horda [**khor**-dah] f. horde; throng; swarm
hordeina [khor-de-**ee**-nah] f. hordein
hordowina [khor-do-**vee**-nah] f. wayfaring tree
hordynka [khor-**din**-kah] f. Tartar sword
hormon [**khor**-mon] m. hormone
hormonalnie [khor-mo-**nahl**-ńe] adv. hormonally
hormonalny [khor-mo-**nahl**-ni] adj.m. hormonal; hormone-like
hormonizacja [khor-mo-ńee-**zah**-tsyah] f. use of hormone-like substances for regulation of growth
hormonizować [khor-mo-ńee-**zo**-vahćh] v. use hormone-like substances for regulation of growth (*repeatedly*)
hormonizowanie [khor-mo-ńee-zo-**vah**-ńe] n. using hormone-like substances for regulation of growth
hormonoterapia [khor-mo-no-te-**rah**-pyah] f. hormonal therapy
hormonowy [khor-mo-**no**-vi] adj.m. hormonal; hormone-like
hornblenda [khorn-**blen**-dah] f. hornblende (mineral)
horoskop [kho-**ro**-skop] m. horoscope; prospect
horoskopowy [kho-ros-ko-**po**-vi] adj.m. of horoscope; prospective
horrendalnie [kho-ren-**dahl**-ńe] adv. awfully; horribly
horrendalny [kho-ren-**dahl**-ni] adj.m. awful; horrible; exorbitant; horror

(story, etc.)
horrendum [kho-**ren**-doom] n. monstrosity; something outrageous
horror [**khor**-ror] m. horror
hortensja [khor-**ten**-syah] f. hydrangea
horyzont [kho-**ri**-zont] m. horizon; vistas; prospect; possibilities; (artistic, etc.) environment
horyzontalizm [kho-ri-zon-**tah**-leezm] m. horizontal composition
horyzontalnie [kho-ri-zon-**tahl**-ńe] adv. horizontally
horyzontalność [kho-ri-zon-**tahl**-nośhćh] f. horizontal position
horyzontalny [kho-ri-zon-**tahl**-ni] adj.m. horizontal
hosanna [kho-**sahn**-nah] f. hosanna
hospicjum [khos-**peets**-yoom] n. hospice
hospitacja [khos-pee-**tah**-tsyah] f. mutual attending of classes by pupils and teachers for improving of schooling
hospitacyjny [khos-pee-tah-**tsiy**-ni] adj.m. of mutual attending of classes (by pupils and teachers for improving of schooling)
hospitalizacja [khos-pee-tah-lee-**zah**-tsyah] f. hospitalization
hospitalizacyjny [khos-pee-tah-lee-zah-**tsiy**-ni] adj.m. of hospitalization
hospitalizować [khos-pee-tah-lee-**zo**-vahćh] v. hospitalize (*repeatedly*)
hospitalizowanie [khos-pee-tah-lee-zo-**vah**-ńe] n. hospitalization
hospitant [khos-**pee**-tahnt] m. pupil-teacher
hospitantka [khos-pee-**tahnt**-kah] f. (female) pupil-teacher
hospitować [khos-pee-**to**-vahćh] v. attend the lessons of a fellow pupil-teacher (*repeatedly*)
hospitowanie [khos-pee-to-**vah**-ńe] n. attendance of lessons for evaluation and improvement purposes (by faculty) (*repeated*)
hospodar [khos-**po**-dahr] m. Moldovan prince
hospodyn [khos-**po**-din] m. Ukrainian ruler (lord)
hossa [**khos**-sah] f. boom; rise (of prices)
hostessa [khos-**tes**-sah] f. hostess
hostia [**khos**-tyah] f. (Catholic) host
hot dog [khot dog] m. (Engl.) hot dog (sandwich)
hotel [**kho**-tel] m. hotel
hotelarka [kho-te-**lahr**-kah] f. (female) hotelkeeper; manager of a hotel
hotelarski [kho-te-**lahr**-skee] adj.m. of hotel management
hotelarstwo [kho-te-**lahr**-stfo] n. hotel trade; hotel management
hotelarz [kho-**te**-lahsh] m. hotelkeeper; manager of a hotel
hotelik [kho-**te**-leek] m. (small, nice) hotel
hotelowy [kho-te-**lo**-vi] adj.m. of a hotel; hotel (management, room, etc.)
hotentocki [kho-ten-**tots**-kee] adj.m. Hottentotic
hotentot [kho-**ten**-tot] m. Hottentot; savage
hożo [**kho**-zho] adv. briskly; handsomely; prettily; comely; seemly; freshly
hoży [**kho**-zhi] adj.m. brisk; handsome; comely; fresh
hrabia [**khrah**-byah] m. count; earl
hrabianka [khrah-**byahn**-kah] f. countess (miss)
hrabiątko [khrah-**byownt**-ko] n. young count; colloq: pesky count; petty count
hrabicz [**khrah**-beech] m. count's son
hrabina [khrah-**bee**-nah] f. countess
hrabiostwo [khrah-**byos**-tfo] n. countship; count and countess
hrabiowski [khrah-**byo**-skee] adj.m. of a count; count's
hrabstwo [**khrahp**-stfo] n. county
hreczka [**khrech**-kah] f. buckwheat
hreczkosiej [khrech-**ko**-śhey] m. country bumpkin; clod-breaker
hu! [khoo] excl.: gee! (also sound imitating some birds)
huba [**khoo**-bah] f. polypore; pore fungus; bracket fungus
hubka [**khoop**-kah] f. tinder; punk; polypore; pore fungus
hubalczyk [khoo-**bahl**-chik] m. soldier in major Hubal's (Henryk

Dobrzański's) unit in 1939-1940
hucba [**khoots**-bah] f. colloq: hutzpah; hutzpa; chutzpah; swindle; whooping lie; nerve; cheek
hucpa [**khoots**-pah] f. colloq: hutzpah; hutzpa; chutzpah; swindle; whooping lie; nerve; cheek; gall
hucpiarski [khoots-**pyahr**-skee] adj.m. shameless; brazen
hucpiarz [**khoots**-pyahsh] m. colloq: shyster; cheat; swindler; brazen man
huculski [khoo-**tsool**-skee] adj.m. of East Carpathian mountaineers
huculszczyzna [khoo-tsoolsh-**chiz**-nah] f. land and culture of East Carpathian mountaineers
Hucuł [**khoo**-tsoow] m. East Carpathian mountaineer; horse of East Carpathian mountaineers
huczeć [**khoo**-chećh] v. roar; ring; resound; echo; rumble; bellow; bawl; trounce; blow up (*repeatedly*)
huczek [**khoo**-chek] m. (small) noise; stir; commotion; excitement
huczenie [khoo-**che**-ńe] n. roaring; ringing; resounding; echo; rumble; bellowing
huczka [**khooch**-kah] f. heat of swine
hucznie [**khooch**-ńe] adv. ostentatiously; pompously; in style; noisily; clamorously
huczny [**khooch**-ni] adj.m. ostentatious; pompous; noisy; clamorous; blatant; uproarious; pompous; deafening (applause, noise, etc.); ringing (cheers, sound, etc.)
hufcowa [khoof-**tso**-vah] f. (female) chief of a scout troop
hufcowy [khoof-**tso**-vi] adj.m. of detachment; of troops; m. chief of scout troop
hufiec [**khoo**-fyets] m. detachment; troops
hufiec harcerski [**khoo**-fyets khahr-**tser**-ksee] exp.: scout troop
hufnal [**khoof**-nahl] m. horseshoe nail; horseshoe fastener
hugenocki [khoo-ge-**nots**-kee] adj.m. of the Huguenots; Huguenot (synod, etc.)
hugenot [khoo-**ge**-not] m. Huguenot
hugonocki [khoo-go-**no**-tskee] adj.m. of the Huguenots; Huguenot (synod, etc.) (hist.)
hugonot [khoo-**go**-not] m. Huguenot
hu-ha! [khoo khah] excl.: (expressing gaiety or joy)
huj [khooy] m. vulg.: man's sex organ; prick; penis; slang: man; clumsy man; slacker; see: **chuj**
huje [**khoo**-ye] pl. vulg.: men's sex organs; pricks; penises; penes; vulg.: mob slang: men
huk [khook] m. bang; roar; rumble; crash; explosion; reverberation; whack; adv. colloq: a lot; very many; very much
hukać [**khoo**-kahćh] v. roar; ring; resound; echo; rumble; bellow; bawl; trounce; blow up (*repeatedly*)
hukać się [**khoo**-kahćh śhan] v. (swine) be in heat (*repeatedly*)
hukanie [khoo-**kah**-ńe] n. roaring; ringing; resounding; echo; rumble; bellowing
huknąć [**khook**-nownćh] v. knock; thump; punch; whack; roar; ring; resound; echo; rumble; bellow; bawl; trounce; blow up
huknąć się [**khook**-nownćh śhan] v. colloq: knock oneself
huknięcie [khook-**ńan**-ćhe] n. rumble; boom; clap
huknięcie się [khook-**ńan**-ćhe śhan] n. knocking oneself
hula [**khoo**-lah] f. Hawaiian dance
hulać [**khoo**-lahćh] v. carouse; riot; make merry; run wild; revel; rollick; dissipate; be on the spree; gambol; frolic; romp; run riot; rage; indulge oneself; have a fling; loot; pillage; buccaneer (*repeatedly*)
hula-hoop [**khoo**-lah khoop] exp.: hula hoop
hulajdusza [khoo-lahy-**doo**-shah] m. rioter
hulajnoga [khoo-lahy-**no**-gah] f. scooter (without motor)
hulaka [khoo-**lah**-kah] m. carouser; debaucher; rioter; rake

hulanie [khoo-lah-ńe] n. carousing; rioting
hulanka [khoo-lahn-kah] f. riot; debauch; junket; carouse
hulaszczo [khoo-lah-shcho] adv. rakishly
hulaszczość [khoo-lah-shchośhćh] f. rakishness; dissipation; rakish life
hulaszczy [khoo-lah-shchi] adj.m. rakish; roistering; rackety; rollicking; dissipated
hulatyka [khoo-lah-ti-kah] f. riot; debauch; junket; carouse
hulk [khoolk] m. hulk; body of a ship
hultaj [khool-tahy] m. libertine; rascal; good-for-nothing
hultajka [khool-tahy-kah] f. roguish girl; minx; libertine; good-for-nothing
hultajski [khool-tahy-skee] adj.m. rascally; roguish; scampish; good-for-nothing
hultajstwo [khool-tahy-stfo] n. roguishness
hułan [khoo-wahn] m. uhlan (hist.)
hum [khoom] exp.: humph
humaniora [khoo-mah-ńo-rah] pl. humanities
humanista [khoo-mah-ńees-tah] m. humanist; classical scholar
humanistka [khoo-mah-ńeest-kah] f. humanist; classical scholar
humanistycznie [khoo-mah-ńees-tich-ńe] adv. humanistically; having classical education; having studied the humanities
humanistyczny [khoo-mah-ńees-tich-ni] adj.m. humanistic; of classical education; humane
humanistyka [khoo-mah-ńees-ti-kah] f. the Arts; the humanities; colloq: Faculty of Arts
humanitarnie [khoo-mah-ńee-tahr-ńe] adv. humanely
humanitarność [khoo-mah-ńee-tahr-nośhćh] f. humaneness; humane attitude
humanitarny [khoo-mah-ńee-tahr-ni] adj.m. humane; humanitarian
humanitarysta [khoo-mah-ńee-tah-ris-tah] m. humanitarian
humanitaryzacja [khoo-mah-ńee-tah-ri-zah-tsyah] f. making (something, somebody) humanitarian
humanitaryzm [khoo-mah-ńee-tah-rizm] m. humanitarianism
humanizacja [khoo-mah-ńee-zah-tsyah] f. humanization
humanizacyjny [khoo-mah-ńee-zah-tsiy-ni] adj.m. humanizing
humanizm [khoo-mah-ńeezm] m. humanism
humanizować [khoo-mah-ńee-zo-vahćh] v. humanize (*repeatedly*)
humanizowanie [khoo-mah-ńee-zo-vah-ńe] n. humanization
humbug [khoom-boog] m. humbug; nonsense; drivel
humerał [khoo-me-rahw] m. humeral
humidostat [khoo-mee-do-staht] m. humidistat
humifikacja [khoo-mee-fee-kah-tsyah] f. humus formation; humification
humina [khoo-mee-nah] f. humus compound in coal
huminy [khoo-mee-ni] pl. humus compounds in coal
huminowy [khoo-mee-no-vi] adj.m. of humus compound in coal
humolit [khoo-mo-leet] m. fertile limy soil
humor [khoo-mor] m. humor; whims; caprices; moods; mood; temper
poczucie humoru [po-choo-ćhe khoo-mo-roo] exp.: sense of humor
być w dobrym humorze [bićh v do-brim khoo-mo-zhe] exp.: be in a good mood
humoralny [khoo-mo-rahl-ni] adj.m. humoral (pathology, etc.)
humorek [khoo-mo-rek] m. little whim
humoreska [khoo-mo-res-kah] f. humorous sketch; humorous story; humoresque
humorysta [khoo-mo-ris-tah] m. humorist
humorystka [khoo-mo-rist-kah] f. (woman) humorist
humorystycznie [khoo-mo-ris-tich-ńe] adv. comically; facetiously; with humor

humorystyczny [khoo-mo-ris-**tich**-ni] adj.m. humoristic; funny; comical
humorystyka [khoo-mo-**ris**-ti-kah] f. humoristic literature; humoristic writing
humorzasty [khoo-mo-**zhahs**-ti] adj.m. facetious; capricious; moody
humus [**khoo**-moos] m. humus
humusowy [khoo-moo-**so**-vi] adj.m. of humus
Hun [khoon] m. Hun
huncwot [**khoon**-tsfot] m. colloq: scamp; rascal; rogue
hungarysta [khoon-gah-**ris**-tah] m. student of Hungarian language and culture
hungarystyka [khoon-gah-**ris**-ti-kah] f. study of Hungarian language and culture
hungaryzm [khoon-**gah**-rizm] m. borrowing from Hungarian language
hunhuz [**khoon**-khoos] m. member of Chinese mafia
hunter [**khoon**-ter] m. hunter (horse)
hura! [khoo-**rah**] excl.: hurrah!; cheers!; long live!; hurray!
hura- [**khoo**-rah] prefix: hurrah
huragan [khoo-**rah**-gahn] m. hurricane; cyclone; storm
huraganowo [khoo-rah-gah-**no**-vo] adv. like a hurricane; stormily
huraganowy [khoo-rah-gah-**no**-vi] adj.m. of a hurricane; stormy
huraoptymistyczny [khoo-rah-op-ti-mees-**tich**-ni] adj.m. uncritically optimistic; excessively optimistic
huraoptymizm [khoo-rah-op-**ti**-meezm] m. uncritical optimism; excessive optimism
hurapatriota [khoo-rah-paht-**ryo**-tah] m. Colonel Blimp; man flaunting his own patriotism; patriotic demagogue; colloq: blimp
hurapatriotyczny [khoo-rah-paht-ryo-**tich**-ni] adj.m. of flaunting patriotism
hurapatriotyzm [khoo-rah-paht-**ryo**-tizm] m. noisily flaunted patriotism
hurgot [**khoor**-got] m. slang: quarrel; din; rumble; crash; clatter
hurkot [**khoor**-kot] m. din; rumble; crash; clatter
hurkotać [khoor-**ko**-tahćh] v. rumble; crash; clatter (down) (*repeatedly*)
hurkotanie [khoor-ko-**tah**-ńe] n. rumble; crash; clatter
hurma [**khoor**-mah] f. multitude; swarm; host
hurmą [**khoor**-mown] adv. in swarms; in a mass; altogether; in a crowd; in a body
hurmem [**khoor**-mem] adv. in swarms; in a mass; altogether; in a crowd; in a body
huron [**khoo**-ron] m. Huronian rock
huroński [khoo-**roń**-skee] adj.m. Huronian
hurra! [khoor-**rah**] excl.: hurrah! cheers!; long live! hurray
hurraoptymistyczny [khoor-rah-op-ti-mees-**tich**-ni] adj.m. uncritically optimistic; excessively optimistic
hurraoptymizm [khoor-rah-op-**ti**-meezm] m. uncritical optimism; excessive optimism
hurrapatriota [khoor-rah-paht-**ryo**-tah] m. Colonel Blimp; person flaunting his/hers own patriotism; patriotic demagogue
hurrapatriotyczny [khoor-rah-paht-ryo-**tich**-ni] adj.m. of flaunting patriotism
hurrapatriotyzm [khoor-rah-paht-**ryo**-tizm] m. noisily flaunted patriotism
hurt [khoort] m. wholesale trade
hurtem [**khoor**-tem] adv. colloq: wholesale; in the lump; in the mass; in bulk; as a whole; in great numbers
hurtownia [khoor-**tov**-ńah] f. wholesale firm; wholesale company
hurtownik [khoor-**tov**-ńeek] m. wholesale dealer; wholesaler; merchant
hurtowny [khoor-**tov**-ni] adj.m. wholesale (dealer, trade, etc.); mass (production, trade, etc.)
hurtowo [khoor-**to**-vo] adv. wholesale; in the lump; in the mass; in bulk; as a whole; in great numbers
hurtowy [khoor-**to**-vi] adj.m.

wholesale (dealer, trade, etc.); mass (production, trade, etc.)
huru-buru [khoo-roo boo-roo] exp.: nagging; complaints
hurysa [khoo-ri-sah] f. houri; voluptuous beauty
huryska [khoo-ris-kah] f. houri; voluptuous beauty
husar [khoo-sahr] m. domestic in Hungarian costume
husaria [khoo-sahr-yah] f. Polish winged-armor cavalry (hist.)
husarski [khoo-sahr-skee] adj.m. of Polish winged-armor cavalry (hist.)
husarstwo [khoo-sahr-stfo] n. soldiers of Polish winged-armor cavalry (hist.)
husarz [khoo-sahsh] m. Polish winged-armor cavalryman; light cavalryman (hist. of Serbian and Hungarian origin)
husky [khahs-ki] m. Siberian husky
husycki [khoo-sits-kee] adj.m. Hussite (movement, heresy, etc.); Hussites'; of Hussitism
husyta [khoo-si-tah] m. Hussite; follower of Czech religious reformer Jan Huss (1374-1415)
husytyzm [khoo-si-tizm] m. Hussitism
huśtać [khoośh-tahćh] v. swing; rock; dandle; toss up and down; seesaw; sway (*repeatedly*)
huśtać się [khoo-śhtahćh śhan] v. balance; rock oneself; seesaw; sway; be tossed; dangle (*repeatedly*)
huśtanie [khoośh-tah-ńe] n. swinging motion; rocking motion
huśtanie się [khoośh-tah-ńe śhan] n. swinging oneself; rocking oneself
huśtawka [khoośh-tahf-kah] f. swing; seesaw; swing boat
huśtawka cen [khoośh-tahf-kah tsen] exp.: swinging prices; fluctuations
huśtawkowy [khoośh-tahf-ko-vi] adj.m. of a swing; of the swinging; of the swing-boats; swinging; rocking; balancing; seesaw; up-and-down (motion, etc.)
huta [khoo-tah] f. metal or glass mill; smelting works
hutnicki [khoot-ńeets-kee] adj.m. of a metallurgist (hist.)
hutnictwo [khoot-ńeets-tfo] n. metallurgy
hutniczy [khoot-ńee-chi] adj.m. metallurgic; metallurgist's
piec hutniczy [pyets khoot-ńee-chi] exp.: blast furnace
hutnik [khoot-ńeek] m. metal or glass (man) worker; iron master; metallurgist
huzar [khoo-zahr] m. hussar; colloq.: dragon
huzarski [khoo-zahr-skee] adj.m. hussar's
huzia! [khoo-źhah] excl.: hoiks!; yoicks!; hyke! (a call used to incite the hounds, a call to urge)
huzia na niego! [khoo-źhah nah ńe-go] excl.: sick him!
huź! [khoośh] excl.: hoiks!
hybryd [khi-brit] m. hybrid
hybryda [khi-bri-dah] f. hybrid word; word made up of two languages
hybrydowy [khi-bri-do-vi] adj.m. hybrid (variety, etc.)
hybrydyczny [khi-bri-dich-ni] adj.m. hybrid (variety, etc.)
hybrydyzacja [khi-bri-di-zah-tsyah] f. hybridization
hybrydyzm [khi-bri-dizm] m. hybridism; hybridization
hybrydyzować [khi-bri-di-zo-vahćh] v. hybridize (*repeatedly*)
hybrydyzowanie [khi-bri-di-zo-vah-ńe] n. hybridization
hyc! [khits] excl.: jump!
hycać [khi-tsahćh] v. jump; jump up (*repeatedly*)
hycanie [khi-tsah-ńe] n. jumping; jump
hycel [khi-tsel] m. dogcatcher; colloq.: rascal; good-for-nothing
hyclowski [khits-lof-skee] adj.m. dogcatcher's
hycnąć [khits-nownćh] v. jump; jump up
hycnięcie [khits-ńan-ćhe] n. jumping; jump
hydatoda [khi-dah-to-dah] f. hydathode; water pore
hydra [khid-rah] f. hydra

hydrant [**khid**-rahnt] m. hydrant
hydrat [**khid**-raht] m. hydrate; hydroxide; calcium hydrate
hydratacja [khid-rah-**tah**-tsyah] f. hydration
hydratyzacja [khid-rah-ti-**zah**-tsyah] f. saturation with water
hydratyzować [khid-rah-ti-**zo**-vahćh] v. hydrate; saturate with water (*repeatedly*)
hydraulicznie [khid-rahw-**leech**-ńe] adv. hydraulically
hydrauliczny [khid-rahw-**leech**-ni] adj.m. hydraulic
hydraulik [khid-**rahw**-leek] m. plumber
hydraulika [khid-rahw-**lee**-kah] f. hydraulics; plumbing
hydrazyd [khid-**rah**-zit] m. hydrazide
hydrazydy [khid-rah-**zi**-di] pl. hydrazide compounds
hydrazyna [khid-rah-**zi**-nah] f. hydrazine
hydria [**khidr**-yah] f. antique water container
hydro- [**khid**-ro] prefix: hydro-; water-
hydroakustyk [khid-ro-ah-**koos**-tik] m. specialist in underwater acoustics
hydroakustyka [khid-ro-ah-**koos**-ti-kah] f. underwater acoustics
hydrobiolog [khid-ro-**byo**-log] m. hydrobiologist
hydrobiologia [khid-ro-byo-**lo**-gyah] f. hydrobiology
hydrobiologiczny [khid-ro-byo-lo-**geech**-ni] adj.m. hydrobiological
hydrobiont [khid-**ro**-byont] m. animal and plant living in water environment
hydrobionty [khid-ro-**byon**-ti] pl. animals and plants living in water environment
hydrobudowa [khid-ro-boo-**do**-vah] f. dam construction; dike construction; waterfront construction
hydrobus [khid-**ro**-boos] m. commuter-boat
hydrocefalia [khid-ro-tse-**fahl**-yah] f. hydrocephaly; hydrocephalus
hydrocefaliczny [khid-ro-tse-fah-**leech**-ni] adj.m. hydrocephalic
hydrochemia [khid-ro-**khe**-myah] f. chemistry of water
hydrochemiczny [khid-ro-khe-**meech**-ni] adj.m. hydrochemic
hydrochinon [khid-ro-**khee**-non] m. hydroquinone
hydrochoria [khid-ro-**khor**-yah] f. sowing by means of water
hydrodynamiczny [khid-ro-di-nah-**meech**-ni] adj.m. hydrodynamic
hydrodynamika [khid-ro-di-**nah**-mee-kah] f. hydrodynamics
hydroelektrometalurgia [khid-ro-e-lek-tro-me-tah-**loor**-gyah] f. electrolytic metallurgy
hydroelektrometalurgiczny [khid-ro-e-lek-tro-me-tah-loor-**geech**-ni] adj.m. of electrolytic metallurgy
hydroelektrownia [khid-ro-e-lek-**trov**-ńah] f. hydroelectric generating plant; hydroelectric power plant
hydroelektryczny [khid-ro-e-lek-**trich**-ni] adj.m. hydroelectric
hydroelektryk [khid-ro-e-**lek**-trik] m. water-power specialist; water-power engineer
hydroelektryka [khid-ro-e-**lek**-tri-kah] f. water-power engineering
hydroelewator [khid-ro-e-le-**vah**-tor] m. pump for raising of water level (behind a dam, etc.)
hydroenergetyczny [khid-ro-e-ner-ge-**tich**-ni] adj.m. of hydro-energy
hydroenergetyk [khid-ro-e-ner-**ge**-tik] m. water-power engineer
hydroenergetyka [khid-ro-e-ner-**ge**-ti-kah] f. water-power engineering
hydroenergia [khid-ro-e-**ner**-gyah] f. water power
hydrofil [khid-**ro**-feel] m. hydrophile; hydrophyte
hydrofile [khid-ro-**fee**-le] pl. aquatic plants
hydrofilia [khid-ro-**feel**-yah] f. hydrophilicity
hydrofilny [khid-ro-**feel**-ni] adj.m. hydrophilous; hydrophilic; hydrophile
hydrofilowy [khid-ro-fee-**lo**-vi] adj.m. hydrophilous
hydrofit [khid-**ro**-feet] m. hydrophyte
hydrofity [khid-ro-**fee**-ti] pl. perennial vascular aquatic plants
hydrofitowy [khid-ro-fee-**to**-vi]

adj.m. hydrophytic
hydrofob [khid-**ro**-fob] m. hydrophobic person; hydrophobic particle
hydrofobia [khid-ro-**fo**-byah] f. hydrophobia; hydrophobicity
hydrofobowy [khid-ro-fo-**bo**-vi] adj.m. hydrophobic
hydrofon [khid-**ro**-fon] m. hydrophone
hydrofor [khid-**ro**-for] m. (private building) water-supply system
hydrofornia [khid-ro-**for**-ńah] f. enclosure for (private) water-supply system equipment
hydroforowy [khid-ro-fo-**ro**-vi] adj.m. of (private) water-supply system
hydrogenerator [khid-ro-ge-ne-**rah**-tor] m. water-power generation equipment
hydrogenizacja [khid-ro-ge-ńee-**zah**-tsyah] f. hydrogenation
hydrogenizować [khid-ro-ge-ńee-**zo**-vahćh] v. hydrogenate (*repeatedly*)
hydrogenizowanie [khid-ro-ge-ńee-zo-**vah**-ńe] n. hydrogenation
hydrogeolog [khid-ro-ge-**o**-log] m. geologist of waters
hydrogeologia [khid-ro-ge-o-**lo**-gyah] f. geology of waters
hydrogeologiczny [khid-ro-ge-o-lo-**geech**-ni] adj.m. of geological aspects of water
hydrognomonia [khid-ro-gno-**mo**-ńyah] f. dowsing
hydrograf [khid-**ro**-grahf] m. hydrographer
hydrografia [khid-ro-**grah**-fyah] f. hydrography
hydrograficznie [khid-ro-grah-**feech**-ńe] adv. hydrographically
hydrograficzny [khid-ro-grah-**feech**-ni] adj.m. hydrographic
hydroizobata [khid-ro-ee-zo-**bah**-tah] f. line on a map showing points of equal elevation of water table
hydroizohipsa [khid-ro-ee-zo-**kheep**-sah] f. line on a map showing points of equal elevation of water table above sea level
hydrokinetyczny [khid-ro-kee-ne-**tich**-ni] adj.m. hydrokinetic
hydrokinetyka [khid-ro-kee-**ne**-ti-kah] f. hydrokinetics
hydroksybenzen [khi-dro-ksi-**ben**-zen] m. phenol
hydroksywas [khi-dro-**ksi**-kfahs] m. carboxylic acid
hydroksywasy [khi-dro-ksi-**kfah**-si] pl. carboxylic acids
hydroksyl [khid-**ro**-ksil] m. hydroxyl
hydroksylować [khid-ro-ksi-**lo**-vahćh] v. hydroxylate (*repeatedly*)
hydroksylowanie [khid-ro-ksi-lo-**vah**-ńe] n. hydroxylation
hydroksylowy [khid-ro-ksi-**lo**-vi] adj.m. of hydroxyl
hydrokwas [khid-**ro**-kfahs] m. oxygen-free acid
hydrokwasy [khid-ro-**kfah**-si] pl. oxygen-free acids
hydrolaza [khid-ro-**lah**-zah] f. hydrolase
hydrolazy [khid-ro-**lah**-zi] pl. hydrolytic enzymes
hydrolitycznie [khid-ro-lee-**tich**-ńe] adv. hydrolytically
hydrolityczny [khid-ro-lee-**tich**-ni] adj.m. hydrolytic
hydroliza [khid-ro-**lee**-zah] f. hydrolysis; saponification
hydrolizat [khid-ro-**lee**-zaht] m. hydrolysate
hydrolizować [khid-ro-lee-**zo**-vahćh] v. hydrolyze (*repeatedly*)
hydrolizowanie [khid-ro-lee-zo-**vah**-ńe] n. hydrolysis
hydrolog [khid-**ro**-log] m. hydrologist
hydrologia [khid-ro-**lo**-gyah] f. hydrology
hydrologicznie [khid-ro-lo-**geech**-ńe] adv. hydrologically
hydrologiczny [khid-ro-lo-**geech**-ni] adj.m. hydrologic; hydrological
hydrolokacja [khid-ro-lo-**kahts**-yah] f. finding of objects under water surface
hydrolokacyjny [khid-ro-lo-kah-**tsiy**-ni] adj.m. of finding of objects under water
hydrolokator [khid-ro-lo-**kah**-tor] m. device for finding of objects under water
hydromagnetyka [khid-ro-mahg-**ne**-ti-kah] f. hydromagnetic studies

hydromechaniczny [khid-ro-me-khah-**ńeech**-ni] adj.m. hydromechanical
hydromechanik [khid-ro-me-**khah**-ńeek] m. specialist in hydromechanics
hydromechanika [khid-ro-me-**khah**-ńee-kah] f. hydromechanics
hydromechanizacja [khid-ro-me-khah-ńee-**zah**-tsyah] f. hydraulic mining
hydrometalurgia [khid-ro-me-tah-**loor**-gyah] f. hydrometallurgy
hydrometalurgiczny [khid-ro-me-tah-loor-**geech**-ni] adj.m. hydrometallurgical
hydrometeor [khid-ro-me-**te**-or] m. hydrometeor
hydrometeory [khid-ro-me-te-**o**-ri] pl. products of condensation of atmospheric water
hydrometeorolog [khid-ro-me-te-o-**ro**-log] m. hydrometeorologist
hydrometeorologia [khid-ro-me-te-o-ro-**lo**-gyah] f. hydrometeorology
hydrometeorologiczny [khid-ro-me-te-o-ro-lo-**geech**-ni] adj.m. hydrometeorological
hydrometr [khid-**ro**-metr] m. hydrometer
hydrometria [khid-ro-**metr**-yah] f. hydrometry
hydrometryczny [khid-ro-me-**trich**-ni] adj.m. hydrometrical; hydromeric
hydromonitor [khid-ro-mo-**ńee**-tor] m. monitor; hydraulic giant (pump)
hydromotor [khid-ro-**mo**-tor] m. hydromotor
hydronal [khid-**ro**-nahl] m. aluminum alloy resistant to sea corrosion
hydronetka [khid-ro-**net**-kah] f. small fire extinguisher
hydronim [khid-**ro**-ńeem] m. name of a body of water (river, lake)
hydronimia [khid-ro-**ńee**-myah] f. study of names of bodies of water (rivers, lakes, etc.)
hydronimiczny [khid-ro-ńee-**meech**-ni] adj.m. of the study of names of bodies of water (rivers, lakes, streams, etc.)
hydronimik [khid-ro-**ńee**-meek] m. student of names of bodies of water (rivers, lakes, etc.)
hydronomia [khid-ro-**no**-myah] f. hydrology of the hydrosphere
hydropata [khid-ro-**pah**-tah] m. specialist in hydropathy
hydropatia [khid-ro-**pah**-tyah] f. hydropathy
hydropatycznie [khid-ro-pah-**tich**-ńe] adv. hydropathically
hydropatyczny [khid-ro-pah-**tich**-ni] adj.m. hydropathic
hydroplan [khid-**ro**-plahn] m. seaplane; hydroplane
hydroplankton [khid-ro-**plahnk**-ton] m. plankton
hydroponicznie [khid-ro-po-**ńeech**-ńe] adv. hydroponically
hydroponiczny [khid-ro-po-**ńeech**-ni] adj.m. hydroponic
hydroponika [khid-ro-**po**-ńee-kah] f. hydroponics
hydrorafinacja [khid-ro-rah-fee-**nah**-tsyah] f. cathodic refining of liquid hydrocarbons
hydrosfera [khid-ro-**sfe**-rah] f. hydrosphere
hydrosferyczny [khid-ro-sfe-**rich**-ni] adj.m. hydrospheric
hydrostatycznie [khid-ro-stah-**tich**-ńe] adv. hydrostatically
hydrostatyczny [khid-ro-stah-**tich**-ni] adj.m. hydrostatic
hydrostatyka [khid-ro-**stah**-ti-kah] f. hydrostatics
hydrotechniczny [khid-ro-tekh-**ńeech**-ni] adj.m. of hydraulic engineering
hydrotechnik [khid-ro-**tekh**-ńeek] m. hydraulic engineer
hydrotechnika [khid-ro-**tekh**-ńee-kah] f. hydraulic engineering
hydroterapia [khid-ro-te-**rah**-pyah] f. hydrotherapy
hydrotermalnie [khid-ro-ter-**mahl**-ńe] adv. hydrothermally
hydrotermalny [khid-ro-ter-**mahl**-ni] adj.m. hydrothermal
hydrotermiczny [khid-ro-ter-**meech**-ni] adj.m. of moist air treating of wood
hydrotorf [khid-**ro**-torf] m. hydropeat; peat
hydrotransport [khid-ro-**trahns**-port] m. transport of solids in water
hydrotropizm [khid-ro-**tro**-peezm] m.

hydrotropism
hydrowęzeł [khid-ro-w<u>an</u>-zew] m. water engineering system
hydrozespół [khid-ro-**zes**-poow] m. combination of water turbine and an electric generator
hydrozol [khid-**ro**-zol] m. hydrosol
hydrożel [khid-**ro**-zhel] m. hydrogel
hylemorfizm [khi-le-**mor**-feezm] m. Greek theory that all substances are composed of matter and form
hylobiologia [khi-lo-byo-**lo**-gyah] f. biology of forests
hylobiont [khi-**lo**-byont] m. organism living exclusively in forests
hylofil [khi-**lo**-feel] m. organism adapted and thriving in forests
hyloteizm [khi-lo-**te**-eezm] m. doctrine of matter being identical with God
hylozoistyczny [khi-lo-zo-ees-**tich**-ni] adj.m. hylozoistic
hylozoizm [khi-lo-**zo**-eezm] m. hylozoism
hymen [**khi**-men] m. hymen; vaginal (virginal) membrane; maidenhead
hymeniczny [khi-me-**ńeech**-ni] adj.m. hymenal
hymenofor [khi-me-**no**-for] m. part of fructification (of a fungus)
hymn [khimn] m. anthem; hymn
hymniczny [khim-**ńeech**-ni] adj.m. solemn; hymn-like
hymnografia [khim-no-**grah**-fyah] f. literature of hymns
hymnolog [khim-**no**-log] f. specialist in hymnology
hymnologia [khim-no-**lo**-gyah] f. hymnology
hyslina [khis-**lee**-nah] f. halyard (one of sail rigging lines)
hysować [khi-**so**-vahćh] v. pull up a sail with line passing through a pulley (*repeatedly*)
hysowanie [khi-so-**vah**-ńe] n. pulling up a sail
hysówka [khi-**soof**-kah] f. halyard; hoist-rope
hyś [khiśh] m. see: **hyź**
hyzop [**khi**-zop] m. hyssop
hyź [khiśh] m. craze
mieć hyzia [myećh **khi**-źhah] exp.: to be crazy; to be wrong in the head; to have a screw loose
on ma lekkiego hyzia [on mah lek-<u>k</u>e-go **khi**-źhah] exp.: he is not all there

I

I, i [ee] the letter "i", the sound [ee] or a softener. For example, in "nie" it softens the letter "n," and the pronunciation is "ńe" (please, see the phonetic notation); conj.: and; also; too; likewise; as well
i owszem [ee **of**-shem] exp.: why yes; by all means
i tak [ee tahk] exp.: in any case; anyway; as it is
i to nie pomoże [ee to ńe po-**mo**-zhe] exp.: even that will not help
i tu i tam [ee too ee tahm] exp.: both here and there
i tyle [ee **ti**-le] exp.: and that's all; and there is an end
postawić kropkę nad i [po-**stah**-veećh **krop**-k<u>an</u> nahd ee] exp.: colloq: to make things perfectly clear; to leave no room for doubt
i! [ee] excl.: (slight or impatience) fiddle-de-dee
i-cha-cha [ee khah khah] not declined: mob slang: horse meat
ii! [ee] excl.: (disregard, etc.)
iberoamerykański [ee-be-ro-ah-me-ri-**kahń**-skee] adj.m. Latin American
iberyjski [ee-be-**riy**-skee] adj.m. Iberian
iberystyka [ee-be-**ris**-ti-kah] f. Iberian studies
ibis [**ee**-bees] m. ibis (bird); the Sacred Ibis (of Egypt)
ibisy [ee-**bee**-si] pl. the Ibididae
ibiszek [ee-**bee**-shek] m. hibiscus (tropical flowering shrub)
ibsenizm [eep-**se**-ńeezm] m. Ibsenism
ich [eekh] pron.: their
ichmościanki [eekh-mośh-**ćhahn**-kee] pl. young ladies
ichmoście [eekh-**mośh**-ćhe] pl. the Honorable Gentlemen; Mesdames
ichmościowie [eekh-mośh-**ćho**-vye]

pl. the Honorable Gentlemen; Mesdames
ichneumon [eekh-**new**-mon] m. ichneumon; mongoose
ichni [**eekh**-ńee] pron.: theirs; belonging to them
ichnologia [eekh-no-**lo**-gyah] f. ichnology
ichtiobiologia [eekh-tyo-byo-**lo**-gyah] f. the biology of fishes
ichtiofauna [eekh-tyo-**fahw**-nah] f. the fishes in a given body of water
ichtiofag [eekh-**tyo**-fahg] m. ichthyophagist; fish eater
ichtiofagowy [eekh-tyo-fah-**go**-vi] adj.m. ichthyophagous
ichtiol [**eekht**-yol] m. ichthyol
ichtiolog [eekh-**tyo**-log] m. ichthyologist
ichtiologia [eekh-tyo-**lo**-gyah] f. ichthyology; zoology of fish
ichtiologicznie [eekh-tyo-lo-**geech**-ńe] adv. ichthyologically
ichtiologiczny [eekh-tyo-lo-**geech**-ni] adj.m. ichthyological; ichthyologic
ichtiolowy [eekh-tyo-**lo**-vi] adj.m. ichthyol (ointment, soap, etc.)
ichtioskop [eekh-**tyo**-skop] m. an electronic device for finding schools of fish
ichtiotoksyna [eekh-tyo-tok-**si**-nah] f. ichthyotoxin
ichtioza [eekh-**tyo**-zah] f. ichthyosis; excessive scaling of skin
ichtiozaur [eekh-**tyo**-zahwr] m. ichthyosaurus
id [eed] n. (not declined) id (one of the three divisions of the psyche in psychoanalytic theory that is completely unconscious)
idea [ee-**de**-ah] f. idea; aim; notion; conception; cause; object; end
idealista [ee-de-ah-**lees**-tah] m. idealist; dreamer; visionary
idealistka [ee-de-ah-**lees**-tkah] f. (woman) idealist; dreamer; visionary
idealistycznie [ee-de-ah-lees-**tich**-ńe] adv. idealistically
idealistyczny [ee-de-ah-lees-**tich**-ni] adj.m. idealistic
idealizacja [ee-de-ah-lee-**zah**-tsyah] f. idealization
idealizm [ee-de-**ah**-leezm] m. idealism
idealizować [ee-de-ah-lee-**zo**-vahćh] v. idealize; sublime (*repeatedly*)
idealizowanie [ee-de-ah-lee-zo-**vah**-ńe] n. idealization; sublimation
idealnie [ee-de-**ahl**-ńe] adv. ideally; perfectly; sublimely
idealny [ee-de-**ahl**-ni] adj.m. ideal; perfect; visionary; sublime
ideał [ee-**de**-ahw] m. ideal; dream boy (girl); perfection; perfect specimen
idejka [ee-**dey**-kah] f. (provincial, narrow-minded, small) idea
identycznie [ee-den-**tich**-ńe] adv. identically; in the same fashion; in the same way
identyczność [ee-den-**tich**-nośhćh] f. identity; sameness
identyczny [ee-den-**tich**-ni] adj.m. identical; similar
identyfikacja [ee-den-ti-fee-**kah**-tsyah] f. identification
identyfikator [ee-den-ti-fee-**kah**-tor] m. identifier; identification symbol
identyfikować [ee-den-ti-fee-**ko**-vahćh] v. identify (*repeatedly*)
indentyfikować kogoś [ee-den-ti-fee-**ko**-vahćh **ko**-gośh] exp.: to establish somebody's identity
identyfikować się [ee-den-ti-fee-**ko**-vahćh śhan] v. identify oneself (with, as) (*repeatedly*)
identyfikowanie [ee-den-ti-fee-ko-**vah**-ńe] n. identifying; identification
ideografia [ee-de-o-**grah**-fyah] f. ideography
ideograficznie [ee-de-o-grah-**feech**-ńe] adv. ideographically
ideograficzny [ee-de-o-grah-**feech**-ni] adj.m. ideographical; ideographic
ideogram [ee-de-**o**-grahm] m. ideogram; ideograph
ideolog [ee-de-**o**-log] m. ideologist; champion; advocate
ideologia [ee-de-o-**lo**-gyah] f. ideology; doctrines; opinions
ideologicznie [ee-de-o-lo-**geech**-ńe] adv. ideologically
ideologiczny [ee-de-o-lo-**geech**-ni] adj.m. ideological
ideologizacja [ee-de-o-lo-gee-**zah**-

tsyah] f. spreading the influence of an ideology
ideologizować [ee-de-o-lo-gee-**zo**-vahćh] v. present in light of an ideology; idealize (history, etc.) (*repeatedly*)
ideologizowanie [ee-de-o-lo-gee-zo-**vah**-ńe] n. idealization (of history, etc.)
ideomotoryczny [ee-de-o-mo-to-**rich**-ni] adj.m. ideomotor (movement)
ideoplastyczny [ee-de-o-plahs-**tich**-ni] adj.m. ideoplastic
ideowiec [ee-de-**o**-vyets] m. devoted adherent of an ideology
ideowo [ee-de-**o**-vo] adv. ideologically; wholeheartedly
ideowość [ee-de-**o**-vośhćh] f. (materially disinterested) support of an ideology; espousal of an ideology
ideowy [ee-de-**o**-vi] adj.m. ideological; disinterested; devoted; (sketch) showing the general idea
ideowo-wychowawczy [ee-de-**o**-vo vi-kho-**vahf**-chi] exp.: concerning an ideology and upbringing
idio- [**ee**-dyo] prefix: idio-
idiocenie [ee-dyo-**tse**-ńe] n. loss of one's reason
idiochromatyczny [ee-dyo-khro-mah-**tich**-ni] adj.m. idiochromatic
idiochromatyzm [ee-dyo-khro-**mah**-tizm] m. idiochromatic nature
idiocieć [ee-**dyo**-ćhećh] v. lose one's wits; become idiotic; grow idiotic (*repeatedly*)
idioctwo [ee-**dyo**-tstfo] n. idiocy
idiofon [ee-**dyo**-fon] m. idiophone (a percussive musical instrument)
idiograficzny [ee-dyo-grah-**feech**-ni] adj.m. idiographic; idiographical
idiografizm [ee-dyo-**grah**-feezm] m. idiographic interpretation of history
idiolatria [ee-dyo-**lahtr**-yah] f. idiolatry; self-worship
idiom [**ee**-dyom] m. idiom
idiomat [ee-**dyo**-maht] m. idiomatic expression
idiomatycznie [ee-dyo-mah-**tich**-ńe] adv. idiomatically
idiomatyczny [ee-dyo-mah-**tich**-ni] adj.m. idiomatic
idiomatyka [ee-dyo-**mah**-ti-kah] f. the study of idiom; collection of idioms
idiomatyzm [ee-dyo-**mah**-tizm] m. idiom; idiomatic expression
idiomorfizm [ee-dyo-**mor**-feezm] m. idiomorphism
idiosynkratycznie [ee-dyo-sin-krah-**tich**-ńe] adv. idiosyncratically
idiosynkratyczny [ee-dyo-sin-krah-**tich**-ni] adj.m. idiosyncratic; idiosyncratical
idiosynkrazja [ee-dyo-sin-**krah**-zyah] f. idiosyncrasy; mannerism; allergy; dislike (to, of); sensitiveness (to)
idiota [ee-**dyo**-tah] m. idiot; colloq: imbecile; fool; silly ass; damfool
idiotka [ee-**dyo**-tkah] f. (female) idiot
idiotowaty [ee-dyo-to-**vah**-ti] adj.m. like an idiot
idiotycznie [ee-dyo-**tich**-ńe] adv. idiotically; stupidly; like a fool
idiotyczność [ee-dyo-**tich**-nośhćh] f. idiocy
idiotyczny [ee-dyo-**tich**-ni] adj.m. idiotic; stupid; senseless; inane; asinine
idiotyzm [ee-**dyo**-tizm] m. idiocy; stupidity; nonsense; absurdity; imbecility
idiotyzować [ee-dyo-ti-**zo**-vahćh] v. colloq: make senseless; fool (*repeatedly*)
ido [**ee**-do] n. Ido; variety of the Esperanto language
idol [**ee**-dol] m. idol; false god
idolatria [ee-do-**lahtr**-yah] f. idolatry
idololatria [ee-do-lo-**lahtr**-yah] f. idolatry
idy [**ee**-di] pl. Ides (of the Roman calendar)
idylla [ee-**dil**-lah] f. idyll; pastoral
idyllicznie [ee-dil-**leech**-ńe] adv. idyllically
idylliczność [ee-dil-**leech**-nośhćh] f. idyllic condition
idylliczny [ee-dil-**leech**-ni] adj.m. idyllical; idyllic; bucolic; pastoral
idyllik [ee-**dil**-leek] m. idyllist
idyllista [ee-dil-**lees**-tah] m. idyllist
igelit [ee-**ge**-leet] m. igelite (plastic)

igelitowy [ee-ge-lee-**to**-vi] adj.m. of igelite; igelite (insulation, etc.)
igielnica [ee-gel-**ńee**-tsah] f. needle holder in a sawing machine
igielnik [ee-**gel**-ńeek] m. needle-case
igielny [ee-**gel**-ni] adj.m. of a needle
igiełka [ee-**gew**-kah] f. small needle
igiełkowaty [ee-gew-ko-**vah**-ti] adj.m. needle-shaped; acerose
igiełkowy [ee-gew-**ko**-vi] adj.m. needle-shaped; having needles
iglak [**eeg**-lahk] m. evergreen tree; pointed round file; needle-shaped small file
iglarka [eeg-**lahr**-kah] f. (woman) needle-maker; gill-box; wool-combing machine
iglarz [**eeg**-lahsh] m. needle-maker
iglasty [eeg-**lahs**-ti] adj.m. coniferous; cone-bearing; slim; slender; tapering
drzewo iglaste [**dzhe**-vo eeg-**lahs**-te] exp.: coniferous tree
iglica [eeg-**lee**-tsah] f. spire; peak; jag; aiguille; pin; point; switch-point; point-rail; tongue-rail; needle; firing-pin; hammer; netting-needle; pin-clover; alfilaria (plant); pin-grass
iglicowy [eeg-lee-**tso**-vi] adj.m. needle-shaped; needle (file, valve, etc.)
iglicówka [eeg-lee-**tsoof**-kah] f. variety of rifle
igliczka [eeg-**leech**-kah] f. (small) spire; peak; jag; aiguille; pin; point; switch-point; point-rail; tongue-rail; needle; firing-pin; hammer; netting-needle; pin-clover; alfilaria; pin-grass
igliczkowy [eeg-leech-**ko**-vi] adj.m. needle-shaped; small-needle (file, etc.); made with a small needle
iglicznia [eeg-**leech**-ńah] f. honey locust (tree); pipefish
igliczniowaty [eeg-leech-ńo-**vah**-ti] adj.m. of pipefish family
igliczniowate [eeg-leech-ńo-**vah**-te] pl. the pipefish family
igliczny [eeg-**leech**-ni] adj.m. needle-shaped; needle (spire, peak, etc.)
igliwie [eeg-**lee**-vye] n. litter of conifer needles
igloo [**eeg**-loo] n. igloo; dome-shaped Eskimo hut; igloo-like shed
igła [**eeg**-wah] f. needle
prosto z igły [**pros**-to z **eeg**-wi] exp.: brand-new; spick-and-span
igława [eeg-**wah**-vah] f. araucaria (tree)
igłofiltr [eeg-**wo**-feeltr] f. suction-pump intake-pipe (small-diameter) with screen-filter; wellpoint
igłować [eeg-**wo**-vahćh] v. process felt in a machine equipped with multidirectional needles (*repeatedly*)
igłowanie [eeg-wo-**vah**-ńe] n. processing felt in a machine equipped with multidirectional needles
igłowaty [eeg-wo-**vah**-ti] adj.m. needle-shaped
igłowiec [eeg-**wo**-vyets] m. fibrous material processed in a machine equipped with multi-directional needles; carpet padding
igłowy [eeg-**wo**-vi] adj.m. needle-shaped; made with a needle
ignam [**eeg**-nahm] m. yam
ignipunktura [eeg-ńee-poonk-**too**-rah] f. ignipuncture; minor skin surgery with an electrical knife
ignitron [eeg-**ńee**-tron] m. ignitron (an electronic steering device)
ignitronowy [eeg-ńee-tro-**no**-vi] adj.m. of an electronic steering device
ignorancja [eeg-no-**rahn**-tsyah] f. ignorance; lack of knowledge
ignorancki [eeg-no-**rahn**-tskee] adj.m. ignorant
ignorant [eeg-**no**-rahnt] m. ignorant man; ignoramus
ignorantka [eeg-no-**rahnt**-kah] f. ignorant woman; ignoramus
ignorować [eeg-no-**ro**-vahćh] v. ignore; disregard; cut (somebody) (*repeatedly*)
ignorować się [eeg-no-**ro**-vahćh śhan] v. ignore one another; disregard one another (*repeatedly*)
ignorowanie [eeg-no-ro-**vah**-ńe] n. disregard (of); ignoring; disregarding
igra [**eeg**-rah] f. play; contest
igrać [**eeg**-rahćh] v. play fast and

loose (with somebody's affections, etc.); trifle (with); dally (with); sport (with); play; flicker; glimmer; twinkle (*repeatedly*)
igranie [eeg-**rah**-ńe] n. playing; twinkling
igraszka [ee-**grah**-shkah] f. toy; plaything; trifle
trwonić czas na igraszki [trfo-**neećh** chahs nah ee-**grah**-shkhee] exp.: to trifle away one's time
igrce [**eegr**-tse] pl. strolling players
igrek [**eeg**-rek] m. the letter "y"; the quantity "y"
igrzec [**eeg**-zhets] m. strolling player
igrzysko [eeg-**zhis**-ko] n. spectacle (games); athletic contest; tooting grounds of grouse
iguana [eeg-**wah**-nah] f. iguana
iguanodon [eeg-wah-**no**-don] m. iguanodon
igumen [ee-**goo**-men] m. head of an Orthodox monastery
ihumen [ee-**khoo**-men] m. head of an Orthodox monastery
ikarowy [ee-kah-**ro**-vi] adj.m. of Icarus; Icarus's; Icarian (flight)
ikebana [ee-ke-**bah**-nah] f. art of arranging flowers; container for cut flowers
ikona [ee-**ko**-nah] f. icon
ikoniczny [ee-ko-**ńeech**-ni] adj.m. iconic; iconical
ikono [ee-**ko**-no] prefix: icono-; image-
ikonoburca [ee-ko-no-**boor**-tsah] m. iconoclast
ikonografia [ee-ko-no-**grah**-fyah] f. iconography
ikonograficzny [ee-ko-no-grah-**feech**-ni] adj.m. iconographic
ikonoklasta [ee-ko-no-**klahs**-tah] m. iconoclast
ikonoklazm [ee-ko-**no**-klahzm] m. iconoclasm
ikonolatria [ee-ko-no-**lahtr**-yah] f. iconolatry
ikonolog [ee-ko-**no**-log] m. iconologist
ikonologia [ee-ko-no-**lo**-gyah] f. iconology
ikonologiczny [ee-ko-no-lo-**geech**-ni] adj.m. iconological
ikonometr [ee-ko-**no**-metr] m. iconometer
ikonometria [ee-ko-no-**metr**-yah] f. iconometry
ikonometrycznie [ee-ko-no-met-**rich**-ńe] adv. iconometrically
ikonometryczny [ee-ko-no-met-**rich**-ni] adj.m. iconometrical; iconometric
ikonoskop [ee-ko-**no**-skop] m. iconoscope
ikonostas [ee-ko-**no**-stahs] m. iconostas; iconostasion
ikonowy [ee-ko-**no**-vi] adj.m. iconic
ikra [**eek**-rah] f. spawn; hard roe; colloq: spirit; slang: pep
mieć ikrę [myećh **eek**-ran] exp.: to be full of pep
ikrowiec [ee-**kro**-vyets] m. roe-stone; egg stone; oolite (mineral)
ikrzak [**eek**-shahk] m. fish with spawn ready for insemination; spawner
ikrzenie się [eek-**she**-ńe śhan] n. (fish) being ready for insemination
ikrzyca [eek-**shi**-tsah] f. fish with spawn ready for insemination; spawner
ikrzyć się [**eek**-shićh śhan] v. (fish) be ready for insemination (*repeatedly*)
ikrzysko [eek-**shis**-ko] n. spawning site
iks [eeks] m. letter "x"; unknown quantity; colloq: somebody; John Doe; So-and-so; slang: a lot (of)
iks razy [eeks **rah**-zi] exp.: endlessly; many times
nogi w iks [**no**-gee v eeks] exp.: knock-knees
iksińska [eek-**śheeń**-skah] f. unknown woman; colloq: somebody; So-and-so
iksiński [eek-**śheeń**-skee] m. unknown man; colloq: somebody; John Doe; So-and-so
iksowaty [eek-so-**vah**-ti] adj.m. x-shaped
iksty [**eeks**-ti] adj.m. colloq:
po raz iksty [po rahs **eeks**-ti] exp.: God knows which time; again after many times
il- [eel] prefix: il-; or an equivalent prefix: in-; un-; im-; ir-; not

ilasty [ee-**lahs**-ti] adj.m. loamy
ile [**ee**-le] pron. how much; how many; how far; as much; if; colloq: how awfully
ile jest stąd do Krakowa? [ee-le yest stownt do Krah-**ko**-vah] exp.: how far is it from here to Cracow?
ile masz lat? [**ee**-le mash laht] exp.: how old are you?
ile możności [ee-le mozh-**nośh**-ćhee] exp.: as far as possible; if at all possible
ile sił! [ee-le śheew] excl.: as hard as you can!; with all your might!; with might and main!; colloq: for all you are worth!
ile tego! [ee-le **te**-go] excl.: what a lot!
ile tego jest? [ee-le **te**-go yest] exp.: colloq: what amount is there?; how many are there?
ile to kosztuje? [ee-le to kosh-**too**-ye] exp.: how much is it?; how much is this?
ile wlezie [ee-le **vle**-źhe] exp.: colloq: devilishly; with a vengeance
ilu ludzi? [**ee**-loo **loo**-dźhee] exp.: how many people?
o ile nie [o **ee**-le ńe] exp.: if not; unless
o ile wiem [o **ee**-le vyem] exp.: as far as I know
o tyle o ile [o ti-le o **ee**-le] exp.: inasmuch as; in so far as
po ile są te owoce? [po ee-le sown te o-**vo**-tse] exp.: how much are these fruits?
weź ile chcesz [veźh **ee**-le khtsesh] exp.: take as much as you like; take as many as you like
z iloma ludźmi? [z ee-**lo**-mah **loodźh**-mee] exp.: with how many people?
ilekolwiek [ee-le-**kol**-vyek] pron. any number; any amount; any quantity
ilekroć [ee-**le**-kroćh] adv. every time; whenever; when
ileś [**ee**-leśh] pron. any number; any amount; any quantity
ileż [**ee**-lesh] pron. = emphatic: **ile**
illit [**eel**-leet] m. a mineral used in ceramics
ilmenit [eel-**me**-ńeet] m. ilmenite (mineral)
ilmenitowy [eel-me-ńee-**to**-vi] adj.m. of ilmenite
iloczas [ee-**lo**-chahs] m. quantity (of a vowel or syllable)
iloczasowo [ee-lo-chah-**so**-vo] adv. as related to the quantity (of a vowel or syllable)
iloczasowy [ee-lo-chah-**so**-vi] adj.m. of quantity; quantity (sign, etc.); quantitative
iloczyn [ee-**lo**-chin] m. (multiplication) product; ratio
iloletni [ee-lo-**let**-ńee] adj.m. of so many years (old, lasting, etc.); of how many years?
ilometrowy [ee-lo-met-**ro**-vi] adj.m. of so many meters; how long?; of how many meters?
iloprocentowy [ee-lo-pro-tsen-**to**-vi] adj.m. of so many percents (loan, etc.); of what percentage?
iloraki [ee-lo-**rah**-kee] adj.m. of how many kinds; of how many sorts
iloraz [ee-**lo**-rahs] m. (division) quotient
ilorazowy [ee-lo-rah-**zo**-vi] adj.m. of a (division) quotient; of how many times
ilostopniowy [ee-lo-stop-**ńo**-vi] adj.m. of so many degrees; of how many degrees?
ilościowo [ee-lośh-**ćho**-vo] adv. quantitatively; numerically
ilościowy [ee-lośh-**ćho**-vi] adj.m. quantitative (analysis, etc.); numerical (ratio, etc.)
ilość [**ee**-lośhćh] f. quantity; amount; number; volume; colloq: a lot; a great deal; tons
ilu [**ee**-loo] pron.: how many; see: **ile**
ilukolwiek [ee-loo-**kol**-vyek] pron. any number (of men)
ilumetrowy [ee-loo-met-**ro**-vi] adj.m. of so many meters (of length, etc.); of how many meters?
iluminacja [ee-loo-mee-**nah**-tsyah] f. illumination; floodlight; floodlighting
iluminator [ee-loo-mee-**nah**-tor] m. (artist) illuminator; (ship's)

porthole
iluminatorski [ee-loo-mee-nah-**tor**-skee] adj.m. of an (artist) illuminator (of books)
iluminizm [ee-loo-**mee**-ńeezm] m. Illuminism
iluminować [ee-loo-mee-**no**-vahćh] v. illuminate; light up (*repeatedly*)
iluminowanie [ee-loo-mee-no-**vah**-ńe] n. illumination; floodlighting
iluprocentowy [ee-loo-pro-tsen-**to**-vi] adj.m. of so many percents (loan, etc.); of what percentage?
ilustopniowy [ee-loo-stop-**ńo**-vi] adj.m. of so many degrees of; how many degrees?
ilustracja [ee-loo-**strah**-tsyah] f. illustration; figure; picture; example; illustrated magazine
ilustracyjnie [ee-loo-strah-**tsiy**-ńe] adv. by way of illustration
ilustracyjność [ee-loo-strah-**tsiy**-nośhćh] f. illustrative quality; pictorial character
ilustracyjny [ee-loo-strah-**tsiy**-ni] adj.m. of illustrations; pictorial; illustrative
illustrator [ee-loo-**strah**-tor] m. illustrator
ilustratorka [ee-loo-strah-**tor**-kah] f. (woman) illustrator
ilustratorski [ee-loo-strah-**tor**-skee] adj.m. illustrator's
ilustratorstwo [ee-loo-strah-**tor**-stfo] n. the art and technique of illustrating printed texts
ilustratywność [ee-loo-strah-**tiv**-nośhćh] f. illustrative quality
ilustratywny [ee-loo-strah-**tiv**-ni] adj.m. illustrative; illustratory
ilustrować [ee-loo-**stro**-vahćh] v. illustrate (text, etc.); be illustrative (of) (*repeatedly*)
ilustrowanie [ee-loo-stro-**vah**-ńe] n. making of illustrations
iluwialny [ee-loo-**vyahl**-ni] adj.m. of flood-deposited soil
iluwium [ee-**loo**-vyoom] n. soil deposited by flooding
iluzja [ee-**loo**-zyah] f. illusion; unreality
iluzjon [ee-**loo**-zyon] m. soundless film; soundless movie
iluzjonista [ee-loo-zyo-**ńee**-stah] m. illusionist; visionary; dreamer; conjurer
iluzjonistka [ee-loo-zyo-**ńee**-stkah] f. (woman) illusionist; visionary; dreamer; conjurer
iluzjonistyczny [ee-loo-zyo-ńee-**stich**-ni] adj.m. illusionistic
iluzjonizm [ee-loo-**zyo**-ńeezm] m. illusionism
iluzorycznie [ee-loo-zo-**rich**-ńe] adv. illusively; illusorily; deceptively
iluzoryczność [ee-loo-zo-**rich**-nośhćh] f. illusiveness; delusion; deceptiveness; unreality; fiction
iluzoryczny [ee-loo-zo-**rich**-ni] adj.m. illusive; illusory; deceptive; unreal; fictitious
iluzyjnie [ee-loo-**ziy**-ńe] adv. illusively; illusorily; fictitiously
iluzyjność [ee-loo-**ziy**-nośhćh] f. fictitiousness; illusiveness; delusion; deceptiveness
iluzyjny [ee-loo-**ziy**-ni] adj.m. illusive; illusory; deceptive; fictitious; imaginary
iluż [**ee**-loosh] pron. how many (men, etc.) = emphatic: **ilu**
ił [eew] m. loam; rich soil
iłołupek [ee-wo-**woo**-pek] m. shale
iłowacieć [ee-wo-**vah**-ćhećh] v. become loamy (*repeatedly*)
iłować [ee-**wo**-vahćh] v. waterproof with loam (in coal mines) (*repeatedly*)
iłowaty [ee-wo-**vah**-ti] adj.m. loamy
im [eem] conj.: the more...; pron.: for them
dać im [dahćh eem] exp.: to give them
im wcześniej tym lepiej [eem fcheśh-ńey tim **le**-pyey] exp.: the sooner, the better
imać [**ee**-mahćh] v. seize upon; take; catch; slang: steal (mob jargon) (*repeatedly*)
imać się [**ee**-mahćh śhan] v. take hold (of); catch hold (of); undertake; turn one's hand (to) (*repeatedly*)
imadełko [ee-mah-**dew**-ko] n. (small) (shop) vise; chuck; holder; vise for small items
imadło [ee-**mah**-dwo] n. (shop) vise; chuck; holder; vise

image [ee-**mahzh**] m. image; impression; mental picture
imaginacja [ee-mah-gee-**nah**-tsyah] f. imagination; empty fancy
imaginacyjny [ee-mah-gee-nah-**tsiy**-ni] adj.m. imaginary
imaginatywnie [ee-mah-gee-nah-**tiv**-ńe] adv. imaginatively
imaginatywny [ee-mah-gee-nah-**tiv**-ni] adj.m. imaginative
imaginista [ee-mah-gee-**ńee**-stah] m. imaginist; imagist
imaginistyczny [ee-mah-gee-ńee-**stich**-ni] adj.m. imagistic
imaginizm [ee-mah-**gee**-ńeezm] m. imagist movement in poetry; imagism
imaginować [ee-mah-gee-**no**-vahćh] v. imagine; make up; fantasize (*repeatedly*)
imagista [ee-mah-**gees**-tah] m. imagist
imagizm [ee-**mah**-geezm] m. imagist movement in poetry; imagism
imago [ee-**mah**-go] n. imago; adult stage of development of an insect
imak [**ee**-mahk] m. jaws; gripper; grasp
imam [**ee**-mahm] m. imam; iman
iman [**ee**-mahn] m. imam; iman
imanie się [ee-**mah**-ńe śhan] n. taking hold (of); catching hold (of); undertaking; turning one's hand (to)
imażynista [ee-mah-zhi-**ńees**-tah] m. Russian follower of (Anglo-American) imagism
imażynizm [ee-mah-**zhi**-ńeezm] m. Russian version of (Anglo-American) imagism
imbecyl [eem-**be**-tsil] m. imbecile; feeble-minded person; half-witted person; idiot
imbecylizm [eem-be-**tsi**-leezm] m. imbecility; mental deficiency
imbecylnie [eem-be-**tsil**-ńe] adv. imbecilely
imbecylny [eem-be-**tsil**-ni] adj.m. imbecile; feeble-minded; half-witted
imbecylowaty [eem-be-tsi-lo-**vah**-ti] adj.m. like an imbecile
imbibicja [eem-bee-**bee**-tsyah] f. imbibition
imbir [**eem**-beer] m. ginger; ginger seasoning
imbirowaty [eem-bee-ro-**vah**-ti] adj.m. of ginger plant family; ginger like
imbirowy [eem-bee-**ro**-vi] adj.m. of ginger; ginger (wine, extract, etc.)
imbryczek [eem-**bri**-chek] m. small teapot
imbryk [**eem**-brik] m. teapot
imć [eemćh] m. gentleman (of old)
imćpan [**eemćh**-pahn] m. gentleman; stranger; chap; Reverend Father
iment [**ee**-ment] (only in) exp.:
do imentu [do ee-**men**-too] exp.: altogether; completely
imersja [ee-**mer**-syah] f. immersion
imieninowy [ee-mye-ńee-**no**-vi] adj.m. of name day; of name-day party
imieniny [ee-mye-**ńee**-ni] pl. name day; name-day party
imiennictwo [ee-myen-**nee**-tstfo] n. collection of names; study of names and place names; onomasticon; onomastics
imienniczka [ee-myen-**ńeech**-kah] f. (woman) namesake
imienniczy [ee-myen-**ńee**-chi] adj.m. onomastic
imiennie [ee-**myen**-ńe] adv. by name; personally; individually
imiennik [ee-**myen**-ńeek] m. namesake
imienność [ee-**myen**-nośhćh] f. having a name
imienny [ee-**myen**-ni] adj.m. personal; individual; nominal
imiesłowowy [ee-mye-swo-**vo**-vi] adj.m. participial
imiesłów [ee-**mye**-swoof] m. participle
imiesłów bierny [ee-**mye**-swoof **byer**-ni] exp.: past participle
imiesłów uprzedni [ee-**mye**-swoov oo-**pshed**-ńee] exp.: perfect participle
imiesłów współczesny [ee-**mye**-swoof fspoow-**ches**-ni] exp.: present participle
imię [**ee**-myan] n. name (given); first name; Christian name; forename;

fame; good name; reputation; noun
w czyim imieniu pan występuje [f chi-eem ee-**mye**-ńoo pahn vi-stan-**poo**-ye] exp.: whom do you represent?
w imię zdrowego rozsądku [v ee-myan zdro-**ve**-go ros-**sown**-tkoo] exp.: in the name of common sense
zdobyć imię [**zdo**-bićh **ee**-myan] exp.: to become famous; achieve reputation
imigracja [ee-mee-**grah**-tsyah] f. immigration; the immigrants
imigracyjny [ee-mee-grah-**tsiy**-ni] adj.m. of immigration
imigrant [ee-**mee**-grahnt] m. immigrant; foreign settler
imigrantka [ee-mee-**grahnt**-kah] f. (female) immigrant; foreign settler; incomer
imigrować [ee-mee-**gro**-vahćh] v. immigrate; settle in a new land; come into a new land (*repeatedly*)
imigrowanie [ee-mee-gro-**vah**-ńe] n. immigration
imitacja [ee-mee-**tah**-tsyah] f. imitation; counterfeit; fake; imitation skill
imitacyjny [ee-mee-tah-**tsiy**-ni] adj.m. imitative
imitator [ee-mee-**tah**-tor] m. imitator; mimic
imitatorski [ee-mee-tah-**tor**-skee] adj.m. imitator's; of imitation; of mimicry
imitatorstwo [ee-mee-tah-**tor**-stfo] n. imitative art
imitować [ee-mee-**to**-vahćh] v. imitate; mimic; simulate (*repeatedly*)
imitowanie [ee-mee-to-**vah**-ńe] n. imitation; mimicry; simulation
immanencja [eem-mah-**nen**-tsyah] f. immanency
immanentnie [eem-mah-**nent**-ńe] adv. immanently
immanentność [eem-mah-**nent**-nośhćh] f. immanence; immanency
immanentny [ee-mah-**nen**-tni] adj.m. immanent
immanentyzm [eem-mah-**nen**-tizm] m. immanentism
immaterializm [eem-mah-ter-**yah**-leezm] m. theory that matter does not exist; immaterlialism
immatrykulacja [eem-mah-tri-koo-**lah**-tsyah] f. matriculation
immatrykulacyjny [eem-mah-tri-koo-lah-**tsiy**-ni] adj.m. of matriculation
immatrykulować [eem-mah-tri-koo-**lo**-vahćh] v. matriculate (*repeatedly*)
immatrykulować się [eem-mah-tri-koo-**lo**-vahćh śhan] v. matriculate (oneself) (*repeatedly*)
immatrykulowanie [eem-mah-tri-koo-lo-**vah**-ńe] n. matriculation
immelman [eem-**mel**-mahn] m. Immelman turn
immersja [eem-**mer**-syah] f. immersion
immersyjny [eem-mer-**siy**-ni] adj.m. of immersion; immersion (lens, etc.)
immobilizacja [eem-mo-bee-lee-**zah**-tsyah] f. immobilization
immobilizm [eem-mo-**bee**-leezm] m. immobility
immoralizm [eem-mo-**rah**-leezm] m. immoralism
immunitet [eem-moo-**ńee**-tet] m. immunity; privilege
immunitetowy [eem-moo-ńee-te-**to**-vi] adj.m. of immunity; of privilege
immunizacja [eem-moo-ńee-**zah**-tsyah] f. immunization
immunizacyjny [eem-moo-ńee-zah-**tsiy**-ni] adj.m. of immunization
immunizator [eem-moo-ńee-**zah**-tor] m. immunization agent
immunizować [eem-moo-ńee-**zo**-vahćh] v. immunize (*repeatedly*)
immuno- [eem-**moo**-no] prefix: immuno-
immunochemia [eem-moo-no-**khem**-yah] f. immunochemistry
immunodepresja [eem-moo-no-de-**pres**-yah] f. lowering of immunity
immunogenetyka [eem-moo-no-ge-**ne**-ti-kah] f. immunogenetics
immunoglobulina [eem-moo-no-glo-**boo**-**lee**-nah] f. immunoglobulin
immunolog [eem-moo-**no**-log] m. immunologist

immunologia [eem-moo-no-**lo**-gyah] f. immunology
immunologicznie [eem-moo-no-lo-**geech**-ńe] adv. immunologically
immunologiczny [eem-moo-no-lo-**geech**-ni] adj.m. immunological
immunopatologia [eem-moo-no-pah-to-**lo**-gyah] f. immunopathology
immunosupresja [eem-moo-no-soo-**pres**-yah] f. suppression of immunity; immunosuppression
immunosupresyjny [eem-moo-no-soo-pre-**siy**-ni] adj.m. immunosuppressive; immunosuppressant
immunoterapia [eem-moo-no-te-**rahp**-yah] f. immunotherapy
impas [**eem**-pahs] m. impasse; deadlock; blind alley; stagnation **w impasie** [v eem-**pah**-śhe] exp.: at a deadlock; in a tight corner; at a nonplus; colloq: up a creek without a paddle; up a tree
impasować [eem-pah-**so**-vahćh] v. finesse (in a card game) (*repeatedly*)
impasowy [eem-pah-**so**-vi] adj.m. of impasse; of deadlock; causing stagnation
impast [**eem**-pahst] m. impasto; impasto pigment, ceramic, etc.
impastować [eem-pahs-**to**-vahćh] v. impaste (*repeatedly*)
impastowy [eem-pahs-**to**-vi] adj.m. impasto (painting, etc.); impastoed
imperatiwus [eem-pe-rah-**tee**-voos] m. imperative mood
imperator [eem-pe-**rah**-tor] m. emperor
imperatorowa [eem-pe-rah-to-**ro**-vah] f. empress
imperatorski [eem-pe-rah-**tor**-skee] adj.m. imperatorial
imperatyw [eem-pe-**rah**-tif] m. (an) imperative
imperatywnie [eem-pe-rah-**tiv**-ńe] adv. imperatively
imperatywność [eem-pe-rah-**tiv**-nośhćh] f. imperativeness
imperatywny [eem-pe-rah-**tiv**-ni] adj.m. imperative; imperious
imperfektum [eem-per-**fek**-toom] n. imperfect tense
imperialista [eem-per-yah-**lees**-tah] m. imperialist; empire builder
imperialistyczny [eem-per-yah-lees-**tich**-ni] adj.m. imperialistic; imperialist
imperializm [eem-per-**yah**-leezm] m. imperialism
imperialny [eem-per-**yahl**-ni] adj.m. imperial
imperiał [eem-**per**-yahw] m. Russian imperial golden coin; an imperial
imperium [eem-**per**-yoom] n. empire; countries under one ruler
impersonalny [eem-per-so-**nahl**-ni] adj.m. impersonal
impertynencja [eem-per-ti-**nen**-tsyah] f. impertinence; cheek; forwardness; impudence
impertynencki [eem-per-ti-**nen**-tskee] adj.m. impertinent; cheeky; forward; impudent
impertynencko [eem-per-ti-**nen**-tsko] adv. with impertinence; cheekily; impudently
impertynent [eem-per-**ti**-nent] m. an arrogant man; pert, impertinent, saucy, cheeky man
impertynentka [eem-per-ti-**nent**-kah] f. an arrogant woman; pert, impertinent, saucy, cheeky woman
impet [**eem**-pet] m. impetus; impulse; violence; vehemence **z impetem** [z eem-**pe**-tem] exp.: violently; with violence; with vehemence; vehemently
impetycja [eem-pe-**ti**-tsyah] f. impetition; charge; accusation
impetyk [eem-**pe**-tik] m. impetuous person
implantacja [eem-plahn-**tah**-tsyah] f. implantation
implantować [eem-plahn-**to**-vahćh] v. implant (*repeatedly*)
implantowanie [eem-plahn-to-**vah**-ńe] n. implantation
implicite [eem-plee-**tsee**-te] adv. implicitly; inclusively; potentially
implikacja [eem-plee-**kah**-tsyah] f. implication
implikacyjnie [eem-plee-kah-**tsiy**-ńe] adv. implicatively
implikacyjny [eem-plee-kah-**tsiy**-ni] adj.m. implicative

implikować [eem-plee-**ko**-vahćh] v. imply; hint; intimate; ascribe; implicate (*repeatedly*)
implikować się [eem-plee-**ko**-vahćh śhan] v. implicate oneself; be mutually implied (*repeatedly*)
implikowanie [eem-plee-ko-**vah**-ńe] n. implication
implodować [eem-plo-**do**-vahćh] v. implode (*repeatedly*)
implozja [eem-**plo**-zyah] f. implosion
impluwium [eem-**ploo**-vyoom] n. rain water collection basin
imponderabilia [eem-pon-de-rah-**bee**-lyah] pl. imponderable matters
imponować [eem-po-**no**-vahćh] v. impress; impose (on somebody); inspire respect; dazzle (*repeatedly*)
to mi imponuje [to mee eem-po-noo-ye] exp.: I am impressed by it; I am deeply affected by it; I find it impressive
imponowanie [eem-po-no-**vah**-ńe] n. making an impression; dazzling
imponująco [eem-po-noo-**yown**-tso] adv. impressively; magnificently; dazzlingly
imponujący [eem-po-noo-**yown**-tsi] adj.m. impressive; commanding; magnificent
import [**eem**-port] m. import; importation; imported goods; imports
importer [eem-**por**-ter] m. importer
importochłonność [eem-por-to-**khwon**-nośhćh] f. use of large quantity of imported items
importochłonny [eem-por-to-**khwon**-ni] adj.m. using a large quantity of imported items
importować [eem-por-**to**-vahćh] v. import (*repeatedly*)
importowanie [eem-por-to-**vah**-ńe] n. importation
importowy [eem-por-**to**-vi] adj.m. import (agency, credit, certificate, duty, etc.)
impost [**eem**-post] m. impost (arch base)
impotencja [eem-po-**ten**-tsyah] f. impotence
impotent [eem-**po**-tent] m. impotent
impregnacja [eem-pre-**gnah**-tsyah] f. impregnation
impregnacyjny [eem-pre-gnah-**tsiy**-ni] adj.m. impregnatory
impregnarka [eem-pre-**gnahr**-kah] f. impregnation device
impregnat [eem-**preg**-naht] m. impregnant
impregnator [eem-preg-**nah**-tor] m. impregnator
impregnować [eem-preg-**no**-vahćh] v. impregnate; make waterproof; saturate; soak; steep (*repeatedly*)
impregnowanie [eem-preg-no-**vah**-ńe] n. waterproofing
impresariat [eem-pre-**sahr**-yaht] m. office of an impresario; sponsoring and managing artistic events
impresario [eem-pre-**sahr**-yo] m. impresario; (somebody's) producer
impresja [eem-**pre**-syah] f. impression
impresjonista [eem-pre-syo-**ńees**-tah] m. impressionist
impresjonistycznie [eem-pre-syo-ńees-**tich**-ńe] adv. impressionistically
impresjonistyczny [eem-pre-syo-ńees-**tich**-ni] adj.m. impressionistic
impresjonizm [eem-pre-**syo**-ńeezm] m. impressionism
impresyjnie [eem-pre-**siy**-ńe] adv. impressionally
impresyjność [eem-pre-**siy**-nośhćh] f. impressive character
impresyjny [eem-pre-**siy**-ni] adj.m. impressional
impreza [eem-**pre**-zah] f. entertainment; spectacle; show; stunt; meet; venture
imprezowy [eem-pre-**zo**-vi] adj.m. of entertainment; of spectacle; of show; of venture; entertainment (industry, etc.)
imprimatur [eem-pree-**mah**-toor] (not declined:) imprimatur; sanction; approval; printing license
impromptu [an-**prownp**-too] (not declined:) impromptu
improwizacja [eem-pro-vee-**zah**-tsyah] f. improvisation; extemporizing

improwizacyjny [eem-pro-vee-zah-**tsiy**-ni] adj.m. improvisatorial
improwizator [eem-pro-vee-**zah**-tor] m. improviser; improvisatore
improwizatorka [eem-pro-vee-zah-**tor**-kah] f. (woman) improviser; improvisatrice
improwizatorski [eem-pro-vee-zah-**tor**-skee] adj.m. improvisatorial
improwizować [eem-pro-vee-**zo**-vahćh] v. improvise; extemporize; arrange on the spot (*repeatedly*)
improwizowanie [eem-pro-vee-zo-**vah**-ńe] n. improvisation; extemporizing; arranging on the spot
impuls [**eem**-pools] m. impulse; impetus; incentive; stimulus; urge; pulse
impulsator [eem-pool-**sah**-tor] m. impulse generator
impulsować [eem-pool-**so**-vahćh] v. impulse; give an impulse (*repeatedly*)
impulsowy [eem-pool-**so**-vi] adj.m. of impulse; generated by an impulse
impulsywnie [eem-pool-**siv**-ńe] adv. impulsively; impetuously
impulsywność [eem-pool-**siv**-nośhćh] f. impulsiveness
impulsywny [eem-pool-**siv**-ni] adj.m. impulsive; impetuous
imputować [eem-poo-**to**-vahćh] v. impute (to); ascribe (to); attribute (to) (*repeatedly*)
imputowanie [eem-poo-to-**vah**-ńe] n. imputation; accusation; attribution; insinuation
imputowany [eem-poo-to-**vah**-ni] adj.m. imputive
in- [een] prefix: in-; non-; not; in; within; into
inaczej [ee-**nah**-chey] adv. otherwise; differently; unlike; (or) else
bo inaczej [bo ee-**nah**-chey] exp.: otherwise; (or) else
czyli inaczej [chi-lee ee-**nah**-chey] exp.: also termed; in other words
ja myślę inaczej [yah mi-śhlan ee-**nah**-chey] exp.: I think otherwise; I am of a different opinion
jakże inaczej? [**yahg**-zhe ee-**nah**-chey] exp.: how else?
nie inaczej [ńe ee-**nah**-chey] exp.: for sure; unmistakably; no two ways about it
tak czy inaczej [tahk chi ee-**nah**-chey] exp.: this way or otherwise; anyway; in any case
inadekwatnie [een-ah-de-**kfaht**-ńe] adv. inadequately
inadekwatność [een-ah-de-**kfaht**-nośhćh] f. inadequateness
inadekwatny [een-ah-de-**kfaht**-ni] adj.m. inadequate
inaktywacja [een-ahk-ti-**vah**-tsyah] f. inactivation; inactivity
inaktywator [een-ahk-ti-**vah**-tor] m. inhibitor
inaktywować [een-ahk-ti-**vo**-vahćh] v. inactivate; make inactive (*repeatedly*)
inauguracja [ee-nahw-goo-**rah**-tsyah] f. inauguration; opening ceremony
inauguracyjny [ee-nahw-goo-rah-**tsiy**-ni] adj.m. inaugural; opening (ceremony, etc.); inaugurate; inaugurative; inauguratory
inaugurować [ee-nahw-goo-**ro**-vahćh] v. inaugurate; auspicate; initiate (*repeatedly*)
inaugurowanie [ee-nahw-goo-ro-**vah**-ńe] n. inauguration
in blanco [een **blahn**-ko] adv. in blank; blank check, document
inbred [**een**-bred] m. inbreeding
inchoatiwum [een-kho-ah-**tee**-voom] n. verb indicating the beginning of activity, process, or condition
inchoatywność [een-kho-ah-**tiv**-nośhćh] f. indication of the beginning of activity, process, or condition
inchoatywny [een-kho-ah-**tiv**-ni] adj.m. indicating the beginning of activity, process, or condition
incognito [een-ko-**gńee**-to] adv. incognito; anonymous; n. hiding of one's identity; anonymity; incognito
incompatibilia [een-kom-pah-tee-**beel**-yah] pl. incompatible items; incompatibles
incydencik [een-tsi-**den**-ćheek] m. (small, unimportant) incident;

happening; event
incydencja [een-tsi-**den**-tsyah] f. incidence
incydent [een-**tsi**-dent] m. incident; happening; event
incydentalnie [een-tsi-den-**tahl**-ńe] adv. incidentally
incydentalność [een-tsi-den-**tahl**-nośhćh] f. incidental nature
incydentalny [een-tsi-den-**tahl**-ni] adj.m. incidental; incident
ind [eent] m. indium (atomic number 49)
indagacja [een-dah-**gah**-tsyah] f. indagation; investigation; questioning; interrogatory
indagacyjny [een-dah-gah-**tsiy**-ni] adj.m. indagative; investigative; questioning; interrogatory
indagować [een-dah-**go**-vahćh] v. ask questions; interrogate; indagate (*repeatedly*)
indagowanie [een-dah-go-**vah**-ńe] n. asking questions; interrogation; indagation
indeks [**een**-deks] m. index; (univ.) student's book of registration of courses and grades
indeksacja [een-dek-**sah**-tsyah] f. indexing (of payments, prices, rents, etc.)
indeksowy [een-dek-**so**-vi] adj.m. of an index; indexed
indemnizacja [een-dem-ńee-**zah**-tsyah] f. indemnity (for a loss)
inden [**een**-den] m. indene
indenowy [een-de-**no**-vi] adj.m. of indene; indene (resin, etc.)
independent [een-de-**pen**-dent] m. member of Protestant Calvinist-independent Church
independentyzm [een-de-pen-**den**-tizm] m. theology of Protestant Calvinist-independent Church; pursuit of independence
indeterminista [een-de-ter-mee-**ńee**-stah] m. indeterminist
indeterministyczny [een-de-ter-mee-ńee-**stich**-ni] adj.m. indeterminist; indeterministic
indeterminizm [een-de-ter-**mee**-ńeezm] m. indeterminism
Indianin [een-**dyah**-ńeen] m. Indian
indianista [een-dyah-**ńee**-stah] m. student of the culture of India
indianistyka [een-dyah-**ńee**-sti-kah] f. study of the culture of India
indiański [een-**dyahń**-skee] adj.m. Indian
indikativus [een-dee-kah-**tee**-voos] m. indicative mood
indoaryjski [een-do-ah-**riy**-skee] adj.m. Indo-Aryan
indochiński [een-do-**kheeń**-skee] adj.m. Indo-Chinese
indoeuropeista [een-do-ew-ro-pe-**ees**-tah] m. student of Indo-European languages
indoeuropeistyczny [een-do-ew-ro-pe-ees-**tich**-ni] adj.m. of Indo-European studies
indoeuropeistyka [een-do-ew-oo-ro-pe-**ees**-ti-kah] f. Indo-European studies
indoeuropejski [een-do-ew-ro-**pey**-skee] adj.m. Indo-European
indogermański [een-do-ger-**mahń**-skee] adj.m. Indo-Germanic
indoirański [een-do-ee-**rahń**-skee] adj.m. Indo-Iranian
indoktrynacja [een-dok-tri-**nah**-tsyah] f. indoctrination
indoktrynować [een-dok-tri-**no**-vahćh] v. indoctrinate; indoctrine; indoctrinize (*repeatedly*)
indoktrynowanie [een-dok-tri-no-**vah**-ńe] n. indoctrination; indoctrinization
indol [**een**-dol] m. indole
idolencja [een-do-**len**-tsyah] f. indolence
idolentnie [een-do-**lent**-ńe] adv. indolently
idolentny [een-do-**lent**-ni] adj.m. indolent; slothful; sluggish; listless; inert
indolog [een-**do**-log] m. student of languages and culture of India
indologia [een-do-**lo**-gyah] f. study of languages and culture of India
indonezyjski [een-do-ne-**ziy**-skee] adj.m. Indonesian
indor [**een**-dor] m. turkey cock
indos [**een**-dos] m. endorsement (of a check to be cashed by another person)
indosant [een-**do**-sahnt] m. endorser (drawer) of a check to be cashed

by another person
indosat [een-**do**-saht] m. payee of a check endorsed by another person
indosatariusz [een-do-sah-**tahr**-yoosh] m. endorsee (payee of a check endorsed by another person)
indosować [een-do-**so**-vahćh] v. endorse (a check to be cashed by another person) (*repeatedly*)
indosowanie [een-do-so-**vah**-ńe] n. endorsement (of a check to be cashed by another person)
indukcja [een-**dook**-tsyah] f. induction; reasoning leading to a general conclusion
indukcjonizm [een-dook-**tsyo**-ńeezm] m. reasoning leading to a general conclusion
indukcyjnie [een-dook-**tsiy**-ńe] adv. inductively
indukcyjność [een-dook-**tsiy**-nośhćh] f. inductiveness; inductance
indukcyjny [een-dook-**tsiy**-ni] adj.m. inductive; inferential; induction
cewka indukcyjna [**tsef**-kah een-dook-**tsiy**-nah] exp.: induction coil
indukować [een-doo-**ko**-vahćh] v. induce; infer (*repeatedly*)
indukowanie [een-doo-ko-**vah**-ńe] n. induction
induktor [een-**doo**-ktor] m. inductor
indulina [een-doo-**lee**-nah] f. induline
indult [**een**-doolt] m. indult
industrializacja [een-doo-stryah-lee-**zah**-tsyah] f. industrialization
industrializacyjny [een-doo-stryah-lee-zah-**tsiy**-ni] adj.m. of industrialization
industrializm [een-doo-**stryah**-leezm] m. industrialism
industrializować [een-doo-stryah-lee-**zo**-vahćh] v. industrialize (*repeatedly*)
industrializować się [een-doo-stryah-lee-**zo**-vahćh śhan] v. become industrialized (*repeatedly*)
industrializowanie [een-doo-stryah-lee-zo-**vah**-ńe] n. industrialization
industrialny [een-doos-**tryahl**-ni] adj.m. industrial
indyczę [een-**di**-chan] n. turkey-poult
indyczka [een-**dich**-kah] f. turkey-hen; dish of turkey-hen
indycznik [een-**dich**-ńeek] m. turkey-pen
indyczy [een-**di**-chi] adj.m. of a turkey; turkey's
indyczyć się [een-**di**-chićh śhan] v. colloq: bristle up; flare up; get angry (*repeatedly*)
indyferencja [een-di-fe-**ren**-tsyah] f. indifference
indyferentnie [een-di-fe-**rent**-ńe] adv. indifferently
indyferentność [een-di-fe-**rent**-nośhćh] f. indifference
indyferentny [een-di-fe-**rent**-ni] adj.m. indifferent
indyferentyzm [een-di-fe-**ren**-tizm] m. indifferentism
indygena [een-di-**ge**-nah] m. naturalized and ennobled immigrant to pre-partitioned Poland
indygenat [een-di-**ge**-naht] m. statute on the naturalization and ennoblement of an immigrant to pre-partitioned Poland
indygo [een-**di**-go] n. indigo-plant; anil; indigo
indygowiec [een-di-**go**-vyets] m. indigo-plant; anil; indigo
indygowy [een-di-**go**-vi] adj.m. indigo (blue, etc.)
indyjski [een-**diy**-skee] adj.m. Indian; of India; India (tea, etc.)
indyk [**een**-dik] m. turkey; turkey cock
indykator [een-di-**kah**-tor] m. indicator
indykatrysa [een-di-kaht-**ri**-sah] f. indicatrix
indykatywnie [een-di-kah-**tiv**-ńe] adv. indicatively
indykatywny [een-di-kah-**tiv**-ni] adj.m. indicative
indykcja [een-**dik**-tsyah] f. indiction
indykować [een-di-**ko**-vahćh] v. indicate (*repeatedly*)
indykowanie [een-di-ko-**vah**-ńe] n. indication
indywidualista [een-di-vee-doo-ah-**lee**-stah] m. individualist
indywidualistycznie [een-di-vee-doo-

ah-lees-**tich**-ńe] adv. individualistically
indywidualistyczny [een-di-vee-doo-ah-lees-**tich**-ni] adj.m. individualistic; individualist
indywidualizacja [een-di-vee-doo-ah-lee-**zah**-tsyah] f. individualization
indywidualizować [een-di-vee-doo-ah-lee-**zo**-vahćh] v. individualize; particularize; discriminate; differentiate (*repeatedly*)
indywidualizować się [een-di-vee-doo-ah-lee-**zo**-vahćh śhan] v. become individualized; particularize oneself (*repeatedly*)
indywidualizowanie [een-di-vee-doo-ah-lee-zo-**vah**-ńe] n. individualization
indywidualnie [een-di-vee-doo-**ahl**-ńe] adv. individually; singly; separately
indywidualność [een-di-vee-doo-**ahl**-nośhćh] f. individuality; personality
indywidualny [een-di-vee-doo-**ahl**-ni] adj.m. individual; singular; separate; peculiar; personal
indywiduum [een-di-vee-**doo**-oom] n. individual; colloq: peculiar individual; undesirable creature; objectionable person
indziej [een-dźhey] adv. exp.:
gdzie indziej [gdźhe **een**-dźhey] exp.: elsewhere; somewhere else
nigdzie indziej [ńee-gdźhe **een**-dźhey] exp.: nowhere else
kiedy indziej [ke-di **een**-dźhey] exp.: some other time
inedita [een-e-**dee**-tah] pl. unpublished works of a deceased writer
inekspyrmable [een-eks-pri-**mah**-ble] pl. unmentionables; underwear
inercja [ee-**ner**-tsyah] f. inertia; inaction; inertness
inercyjnie [ee-ner-**tsiy**-ńe] adv. inertly
inercyjny [ee-ner-**tsiy**-ni] adj.m. inert; inactive
infamia [een-**fah**-myah] f. infamy; outlawry; loss of citizen's rights
infamis [een-**fah**-mees] m. man sentenced to infamy; outlaw
infant [een-fahnt] m. infant; first-born
infantka [een-**fahnt**-kah] f. (female) infant; first-born
infantylizacja [een-fahn-ti-lee-**zah**-tsyah] f. making somebody childish
infantylizm [een-fahn-**ti**-leezm] m. infantilism
infantylizować [een-fahn-ti-lee-**zo**-vahćh] v. make somebody childish (*repeatedly*)
infantylizować się [een-fahn-ti-lee-**zo**-vahćh śhan] v. make oneself childish (*repeatedly*)
infantylnie [een-fahn-**til**-ńe] adv. childishly
infantylnieć [een-fahn-**til**-ńećh] v. become childish (*repeatedly*)
infantylność [een-fahn-**til**-nośhćh] f. infantile character; childish characteristics
infantylny [een-fahn-**til**-ni] adj.m. infantile; childish
infekcja [een-**fek**-tsyah] f. infection; contamination
infekcyjny [een-fe-**ktsiy**-ni] adj.m. infectious
infekować [een-fe-**ko**-vahćh] v. infect (*repeatedly*)
inferencja [een-fe-**rents**-yah] f. inference
inferencyjnie [een-fe-ren-**tsiy**-ńe] adv. inferentially
inferencyjny [een-fe-ren-**tsiy**-ni] adj.m. inferential
infernalnie [een-fer-**nahl**-ńe] adv. infernally; hellishly; diabolically
infernalny [een-fer-**nahl**-ni] adj.m. infernal; hellish; diabolical; damnable
infeudacja [een-fe-oo-**dah**-tsyah] f. letting out land to a vassal; making a fief
infiks [**een**-feeks] m. (phonetic) infix
infiltracja [een-feel-**trah**-tsyah] f. infiltration; penetration
infiltrować [een-feel-**tro**-vahćh] v. infiltrate; penetrate (*repeatedly*)
infiltrowanie [een-feel-tro-**vah**-ńe] n. infiltration; penetration
infinitivus [een-fee-ńee-**ti**-voos] m. infinitive case
infirmeria [een-feer-**mer**-yah] f. infirmary (in Russian schools,

monasteries, etc.)
inflacja [een-**flah**-tsyah] f. inflation
inflacyjny [een-flah-**tsiy**-ni] adj.m. inflationary
influenca [een-floo-**en**-tsah] f. influenza; flu; grippe
influencja [een-floo-**en**-tsyah] f. induction (electrostatic, etc.)
influenza [een-floo-**en**-zah] f. influenza; flu; grippe
informacja [een-for-**mah**-tsyah] f. information; intelligence; news; inquiry office
udzielić komuś informacji [oo-**dźhe**-leećh **ko**-moośh een-for-**mah**-tsyee] exp.: to give somebody information; to inform somebody
według moich informacji [**ve**-dwoog **mo**-eekh een-for-**mah**-tsyee] exp.: as far as I know; to my knowledge
zła informacja [zwah een-for-**mah**-tsyah] exp.: misinformation; misguidance
informacyjnie [een-for-mah-**tsiy**-ńe] adv. for information; as information
informacyjny [een-for-mah-**tsiy**-ni] adj.m. information (office)
informator [een-for-**mah**-tor] m. informant; informer; directory; guidebook; register
informatorka [een-for-mah-**tor**-kah] f. (female) informant; informer
informatorski [een-for-mah-**tor**-skee] adj.m. of information
informatyczny [een-for-mah-**tich**-ni] adj.m. of information science; of informatics
informatyczka [een-for-mah-**tich**-kah] f. (female) specialist in information science; specialist in informatics
informatyk [een-for-**mah**-tik] m. specialist in information science; specialist in informatics; slang: stool pigeon; tatoo (mob jargon)
informatyka [een-for-**mah**-ti-kah] f. information science; informatics; computer applications
informatyzacja [een-for-mah-ti-**zah**-tsyah] f. application of informatics (to economy, technology, transport, etc.)
informel [een-**for**-mel] m. informal art introduced in France and in the U.S.A. in 1950
informować [een-for-**mo**-vahćh] v. inform; instruct; post up; give information (*repeatedly*)
źle informować [źhle een-for-**mo**-vahćh] exp.: to misinform; to give wrong information
informować się [een-for-**mo**-vahćh śhan] v. inquire about (after, for) somebody, something; find out from somebody about something; consult (*repeatedly*)
informowanie [een-for-mo-**vah**-ńe] n. giving information
informujący [een-for-moo-**yown**-tsi] adj.m. informing; m. informant; informer
informujący się [een-for-moo-**yown**-tsi śhan] m. inquirer
infraczerwień [een-frah-**cher**-vyeń] f. infrared rays
infraczerwony [een-frah-cher-**vo**-ni] adj.m. infrared
infradźwięk [een-**frah**-dźhvyank] m. sound of frequency smaller than 16 hertz
infradźwiękowy [een-frah-dźhvyan-**ko**-vi] adj.m. of sound of frequency smaller than 16 hertz; infrasonic
infrastruktura [een-frah-strook-**too**-rah] f. infrastructure; basic framework
infrastrukturalny [een-frah-strook-too-**rahl**-ni] adj.m. of infrastructure; of basic framework
infuła [een-**foo**-wah] f. mitre
infułat [een-**foo**-waht] m. mitred prelate
infuzja [een-**foo**-zyah] f. infusion
infuzyjny [een-foo-**ziy**-ni] adj.m. of infusion; infusible
ingerencja [een-ge-**ren**-tsyah] f. interference; meddling
ingerować [een-ge-**ro**-vahćh] v. interfere (*repeatedly*)
ingerowanie [een-ge-ro-**vah**-ńe] n. interference
ingrediencja [een-gre-**dyen**-tsyah] pl. ingredients; constituents
ingredient [een-**gre**-dyent] m.

ingredient; constituent
ingres [**een**-gres] m. ingress; entry
ingresja [enn-**gre**-syah] f. encroachment (of the sea)
ingresywny [enn-gre-**siv**-ni] adj.m. of ingress
inhalacja [een-khah-**lah**-tsyah] f. inhalation; breathing in
inhalacyjny [een-khah-lah-**tsiy**-ni] adj.m. of inhalation; inhaling (apparatus, etc.)
środek inhalacyjny [**śhro**-dek een-khah-lah-**tsiy**-ni] exp.: inhalant
inhalator [een-khah-**lah**-tor] m. inhaler; inhalator
inhalatorium [een-khah-lah-**tor**-yoom] n. inhalation chamber
inhalować [een-khah-**lo**-vahćh] v. inhale (*repeatedly*)
inherencja [een-khe-**ren**-tsyah] f. inherence
inhibicja [een-khee-**bee**-tsyah] f. inhibition
inhibicyjny [een-khee-bee-**tsiy**-ni] adj.m. inhibitive; inhibitory
inhibitor [een-khee-**bee**-tor] m. inhibitor
inicjacja [ee-ńee-**tsyah**-tsyah] f. initiation
inicjacyjność [ee-ńee-tsyah-**tsiy**-nośhćh] f. initial character (of Czech accent, etc.)
inicjacyjny [ee-ńee-tsyah-**tsiy**-ni] adj.m. of initiation
inicjalny [ee-ńeets-**yahl**-ni] adj.m. initial
inicjał [ee-**ńee**-tsyahw] m. initial (letter); ornate letter
inicjałowy [ee-ńee-tsyah-**wo**-vi] adj.m. of an initial (letter); of an ornate letter
inicjator [ee-ńee-**tsyah**-tor] m. originator; mover; founder
inicjatorka [ee-ńee-tsyah-**tor**-kah] f. (woman) originator; mover; founder
inicjatywa [ee-ńee-tsyah-**ti**-vah] f. initiative; enterprise; lead; push; suggestion; activity
mieć inicjatywę [myećh ee-ńee-tsyah-**ti**-van] exp.: have initiative; be enterprising
prywatna inicjatywa [pri-**vaht**-nah ee-ńee-tsyah-**ti**-vah] exp.: private enterprise
przejąć inicjatywę [pshe-yownćh ee-ńee-tsyah-**ti**-van] exp.: to take the initiative; to take the lead
inicjować [ee-ńee-**tsyo**-vahćh] v. think out; devise; initiate (*repeatedly*)
inicjowanie [ee-ńee-tsyo-**vah**-ńe] n. thinking out; devising; initiating
iniekcja [eeń-**yek**-tsyah] f. injection; shot (of cocaine, etc.)
iniekcyjny [eeń-yek-**tsiy**-ni] adj.m. of injection
iniektor [eeń-**yek**-tor] m. injector
iniektorowy [eeń-yek-to-**ro**-vi] adj.m. of an injector
inkantacja [een-kahn-**tah**-tsyah] f. incantation; use of spells or verbal charms (as a part of ritual magic)
inkarnacja [een-kahr-**nah**-tsyah] f. incarnation
inkarnatka [een-kahr-**nah**-tkah] f. crimson clover
inkasencki [een-kah-**sen**-tskee] adj.m. of a bill collector
inkasent [een-**kah**-sent] m. collector (of bills)
inkaso [een-**kah**-so] n. collection (of payments, etc.)
inkasować [een-kah-**so**-vahćh] v. collect (money); colloq: get a blow; take a blow (*repeatedly*)
inkasować czeki [een-kah-**so**-vahćh **che**-kee] exp.: to cash checks; to collect money
inkasowanie [een-kah-so-**vah**-ńe] n. collection (of payments, etc.)
inkasowy [een-kah-**so**-vi] adj.m. collection (charges, etc.); collecting (expenses, etc.)
inkaust [**een**-kahwst] m. ink
inklinacja [een-klee-**nah**-tsyah] f. inclination; liking (for); bias (towards); magnetic dip
inklinacyjny [een-klee-nah-**tsiy**-ni] adj.m. inclinational; of inclination
igła inklinacyjna [**eeg**-wah een-klee-nah-**tsiy**-nah] exp.: dipping needle
inklinator [een-klee-**nah**-tor] m. inclination compass
inklinometr [een-klee-**no**-metr] m. inclinometer

inklinować [een-klee-**no**-vahćh] v. be inclined (to); submit easily (to) (*repeatedly*)
inkluzja [een-**kloo**-zyah] f. inclusion
inkluzyjnie [een-kloo-**ziy**-ńe] adv. inclusively
inkluzyjność [een-kloo-**ziy**-nośhćh] f. inclusiveness
inkluzyjny [een-kloo-**ziy**-ni] adj.m. inclusive
inkoherencja [een-ko-khe-**ren**-tsyah] f. incoherence
inkompatibilia [een-kom-pah-ti-**beel**-yah] pl. things incompatible; items of conflict of interest
inkompetencja [een-kom-pe-**ten**-tsyah] f. lack of jurisdiction
inkompetentny [een-kom-pe-**tent**-ni] adj.m. lacking legal authority; legally incompetent
inkongruencja [een-kon-groo-**en**-tsyah] f. incongruence; incongruity
inkorporacja [een-kor-po-**rah**-tsyah] f. incorporation
inkorporacyjny [een-kor-po-rah-**tsiy**-ni] adj.m. incorporative (acts, languages, etc.)
inkorporować [een-kor-po-**ro**-vahćh] v. incorporate (*repeatedly*)
inkrustacja [een-kroos-**tah**-tsyah] f. encrustation; incrustation; inlay; overlay
inkrustować [een-kroos-**to**-vahćh] v. encrust; incrust; cover with crust; form a crust (*repeatedly*)
inkrustowanie [een-kroos-to-**vah**-ńe] n. encrustation; incrustation
inkryminacja [een-kri-mee-**nah**-tsyah] f. incrimination; blame; accusation
inkryminować [een-kri-mee-**no**-vahćh] v. incriminate; blame (with); accuse (of) (*repeatedly*)
inkryminowanie [een-kri-mee-no-**vah**-ńe] n. incrimination; blaming
inkub [**een**-koop] m. incubus (nightmare)
inkubacja [een-koo-**bah**-tsyah] f. incubation (of eggs, bacteria, etc.)
inkubacyjny [een-koo-bah-**tsiy**-ni] adj.m. incubatory; incubative
inkubator [een-koo-**bah**-tor] m. incubator
inkubatornia [een-koo-bah-**tor**-ńah] f. poultry incubator
inkunabulistyka [een-koo-nah-boo-**lees**-ti-kah] f. study of early books and art produced before 1501; study of incunabula
inkunabuł [een-koo-**nah**-boow] m. incunable; incunabulum
inkwizycja [een-kfee-**zi**-tsyah] f. inquisition; investigation
inkwizycyjny [een-kfee-zi-**tsiy**-ni] adj.m. of inquisition; of investigation; inquisitive
inkwizytor [een-kfee-**zi**-tor] m. inquisitor
inkwizytorski [een-kfee-zi-**tor**-skee] adj.m. inquisitor's; inquisitorial
inlet [**een**-let] m. ticking (textile)
inna [**een**-nah] pronoun: other (female); different (from); another (one); the other; a further; else; unlike; new; f. somebody else; anybody else
innerwacja [een-ner-**vah**-tsyah] f. innervation
innerwacyjny [een-ner-vah-**tsiy**-ni] adj.m. innervational
innogatunkowy [een-no-gah-toon-**ko**-vi] adj.m. heterogenous; of a different kind; of another species
innojęzyczny [een-no-yan-**zich**-ni] adj.m. of another language; in a different language; in foreign language
innoplemieniec [een-no-ple-**mye**-ńets] m. member of another tribe
innoplemienny [een-no-ple-**myen**-ni] adj.m. of another tribe; characteristic of a different tribe
innorodzajowy [een-no-ro-dzah-**yo**-vi] adj.m. of another specie; of a different kind
inność [**een**-nośhćh] f. difference; different character (nature)
innowacja [een-no-**vah**-tsyah] f. innovation; novelty
wprowadzać innowacje [fpro-**vah**-dzahćh een-no-**vah**-tsye] exp.: to innovate; to make changes
innowacyjny [een-no-vah-**tsiy**-ni] adj.m. innovative; innovatory
innowator [een-no-**vah**-tor] m. innovator

innowierca [een-no-**vyer**-tsah] m. dissenter; heretic
innowierczy [een-no-**vyer**-chi] adj.m. of a dissenter; heretical
innowierstwo [een-no-**vyer**-stfo] n. heresy; heterodoxy
inny [**een**-ni] pron. other; different (from); another (one); the other; a further; else; unlike; new; m. somebody else; anybody else
być innego zdania [bićh een-**ne**-go **zdah**-ńah] exp.: to have a different opinion
innym razem [**een**-nim **rah**-zem] exp.: some other time
to co innego [to tso een-**ne**-go] exp.: that's a different thing; that's quite a different matter
w taki czy inny sposób [f **tah**-kee chi **een**-ni **spo**-soop] exp.: one way or another
wszyscy inni [**fshis**-tsi **een**-ńee] exp.: the others; the rest; the remainder; all others
ino [**ee**-no] adv. colloq: only; just; merely
inoceram [ee-no-**tse**-rahm] m. inoceramus
inochód [ee-**no**-khoot] m. amble (of a horse, camel, etc.)
inozyt [ee-**no**-zit] m. inosite; inositol
inozytol [ee-no-**zi**-tol] m. inositol
inscenizacja [een-stse-ńee-**zah**-tsyah] f. putting on stage; staging; production
inscenizacyjnie [een-stse-ńee-zah-**tsiy**-ńe] adv. by way of staging
inscenizacyjność [een-stse-ńee-zah-**tsiy**-nośhćh] f. suitability for staging
inscenizacyjny [een-stse-ńee-zah-**tsiy**-ni] adj.m. producer's; stage manager's (talent, etc.)
inscenizator [een-stse-ńee-**zah**-tor] m. producer; stage manager
inscenizatorka [een-stse-ńee-zah-**tor**-kah] f. (woman) producer; stage manager
inscenizatorski [een-stse-ńee-zah-**tor**-skee] adj.m. producer's; stage-manager's
inscenizować [een-stse-ńee-**zo**-vahćh] v. produce; stage (*repeatedly*)
inscenizowanie [een-stse-ńee-zo-**vah**-ńe] n. producing; staging
insekt [**een**-sekt] m. insect; colloq: vermin
insektarium [een-sek-**tahr**-yoom] n. insectarium
insektobójczo [een-sek-to-**booy**-cho] adv. insecticidally
insektobójczy [een-sek-to-**booy**-chi] adj.m. insecticidal
insektofungicyd [een-sek-to-foon-**gee**-tsit] m. insecticide and fungicide
inseminacja [een-se-mee-**nah**-tsyah] f. artificial insemination
inseminacyjny [een-se-mee-nah-**tsiy**-ni] adj.m. of artificial insemination
inseminator [een-se-mee-**nah**-tor] m. specialist in artificial insemination
inseminować [een-se-mee-**no**-vahćh] v. artificially inseminate (*repeatedly*)
inserat [een-**se**-raht] m. printed advertisement; colloq: (newspaper) ad
inskrypcja [een-**skrip**-tsyah] f. inscription
inskrypcyjny [een-skrip-**tsiy**-ni] adj.m. inscriptional; inscriptive
insolacja [een-so-**lah**-tsyah] f. insolation
insolacyjny [een-so-lah-**tsiy**-ni] adj.m. of insolation
inspekcja [een-**spek**-tsyah] f. inspection; review; visitation; survey; tour of inspection; examination; parade; inspectorate
przeprowadzić inspekcję [pshe-pro-**vah**-dźheećh een-**spek**-tsyan] exp.: to superintend; to survey; to examine
inspekcyjny [eens-pek-**tsiy**-ni] adj.m. superintending
inspekt [**eens**-pekt] m. (garden) hotbed
inspektor [eens-**pek**-tor] m. inspector; superintendent; examiner; visitor; inspector general; supervisor
inspektorat [eens-pek-**to**-raht] m. inspectorate
inspektorka [eens-pek-**tor**-kah] f. (woman) inspector; superintendent; examiner; visitor;

inspector general; supervisor
inspektorski [een-spek-**tor**-skee] adj.m. of an inspector; inspector's; inspectorial
inspektorstwo [een-spek-**tor**-stfo] n. inspectorship
inspektowy [een-spek-**to**-vi] adj.m. of a garden frame; of a hotbed
inspekty [een-**spek**-ti] pl. hotbeds; glass covered frames
inspicjencki [eens-peets-**yen**-tskee] adj.m. backstage technician's
inspicjent [eens-**peets**-yent] m. backstage technician
inspicjentura [eens-peets-yen-**too**-rah] f. backtstage managing
inspiracja [een-spee-**rah**-tsyah] f. inspiration; breathing in
inspiracyjny [een-spee-rah-**tsiy**-ni] adj.m. inspirational
inspirator [een-spee-**rah**-tor] m. inspirer; animator; impeller
inspiratorka [een-spee-rah-**tor**-kah] f. (woman) inspirer; animator; impeller
inspirować [een-spee-**ro**-vahćh] v. inspire; animate; initiate; provoke (*repeatedly*)
inspirować się [een-spee-**ro**-vahćh śhan] v. inspire oneself; get animated (*repeatedly*)
inspirowanie [een-spee-ro-**vah**-ńe] n. inspiration
inspirująco [een-spee-roo-**yown**-tso] adv. in an inspiring manner; in an exciting manner
instalacja [een-stah-**lah**-tsyah] f. installation; plant; fittings; installation of gas, electricity, water; the laying on; induction
instalacyjny [een-stah-lah-**tsiy**-ni] adj.m. of an installation
instalator [een-stah-**lah**-tor] m. plumber; fitter; electrician
instalatorski [een-stah-lah-**tor**-skee] adj.m. plumber's; fitter's; electrician's
instalatorstwo [een-stah-lah-**tor**-stfo] n. plumber's trade; fitter's trade; electrician's trade
instalować [een-stah-**lo**-vahćh] v. install; lay on (*repeatedly*)
instalować się [een-stah-**lo**-vahćh śhan] v. install oneself; settle in; establish oneself (*repeatedly*)
instalowanie [een-stah-lo-**vah**-ńe] n. installation
instancja [een-**stahn**-tsyah] f. a level in state organization
instancyjny [een-stahn-**tsiy**-ni] adj.m. of one level in state organization
instant [**eens**-tahnt] m. prepared, premixed, or precooked food (for easy preparation)
instantyzacja [een-stahn-ti-**zah**-tsyah] f. making instant (effect, coffee, etc.)
instantyzować [een-stan-ti-**zo**-vahćh] v. make instant (effect, coffee, etc.) (*repeatedly*)
instrukcja [een-**strook**-tsyah] f. instruction; directions; order; training
instrukcyjny [een-strook-**tsiy**-ni] adj.m. instructional; of training
instruktarz [een-**strook**-tahsh] m. instruction handbook
instruktaż [een-**strook**-tahsh] m. instruction program; teaching
instruktor [een-**strook**-tor] m. instructor; trainer
instruktorka [een-strook-**tor**-kah] f. (woman) instructor; trainer
instruktorski [een-strook-**tor**-skee] adj.m. instructor's; trainer's (work, etc.)
instruktywnie [een-strook-**tiv**-ńe] adv. instructively
instruktywny [een-strook-**tiv**-ni] adj.m. instructive; illuminating
instrumencik [een-stroo-**men**-ćheek] m. (small, nice) (musical) instrument; tool; deed; legal instrument; appliance
instrument [een-**stroo**-ment] m. instrument; musical instrument; tool; deed; legal instrument; appliance; implement
instrumentacja [een-stroo-men-**tah**-tsyah] f. instrumentation; orchestration; equipping with instruments
instrumentacyjny [een-stroo-men-tah-**tsiy**-ni] adj.m. of instrumentation (techniques, etc.)
instrumentalista [een-stroo-men-tah-**lees**-tah] m. instrumentalist;

musician; follower of instrumentalism
instrumentalizacja [een-stroo-men-tah-lee-**zah**-tsyah] f. instrumentalism
instrumentalizm [een-stroo-men-**tah**-leezm] m. instrumentalism (version of pragmatism)
instrumentalnie [een-stroo-men-**tahl**-ńe] adv. instrumentally
instrumentalny [een-stroo-men-**tahl**-ni] adj.m. instrumental (music, band, investigations, analytical method, psychological reaction, help, etc.)
instrumentarium [een-stroo-men-**tahr**-yoom] n. set of instruments (musical, surgical, special, etc.)
instrumentariusz [een-stroo-men-**tahr**-yoosh] m. (male) scrub nurse
instrumentariuszka [een-stroo-men-tahr-**yoosh**-kah] f. (female) scrub nurse
instrumentologia [een-stroo-men-to-**lo**-gyah] f. study of (musical) instruments
instrumentologiczny [een-stroo-men-to-lo-**geech**-ni] adj.m. of study of musical instruments
instrumentować [een-stroo-men-**to**-vahćh] v. orchestrate (a musical composition); instrument (music); serve as scrub nurse; fish (in drill-hole of an oil well) (*repeatedly*)
instrumentowanie [een-stroo-men-to-**vah**-ńe] n. instrumentation; orchestration (of a musical composition); instrumenting (music); serving as scrub nurse; fishing (in drill-hole of an oil well)
instrumentowy [een-stroo-men-**to**-vi] adj.m. instrument (panel, landing, flying, etc.)
instrumentoznawczy [een-stroo-men-to-**znahf**-chi] adj.m. of study of instruments
instrumentoznawstwo [een-stroo-men-to-**znahf**-stfo] n. study of instruments
instruować [een-stroo-**o**-vahćh] v. instruct; teach; explain (*repeatedly*)
instruować się [een-stroo-**o**-vahćh śhan] v. get instruction; teach oneself; explain to each other (*repeatedly*)
instruowanie się [een-stroo-o-**vah**-ńe śhan] n. getting instruction; teaching oneself; explaining to each other
instynkt [**een**-stinkt] m. instinct; inborn aptitude (for); knack (for)
instynktownie [een-stink-**tov**-ńe] adv. instinctively; by instinct; spontaneously
instynktowny [een-stink-**tov**-ni] adj.m. instinctive; spontaneous; instinct (reaction, etc.)
instynktowność [een-stink-**tov**-nośhćh] f. instinctive impulses
instynktowo [een-stink-**to**-vo] adv. instinctively; by instinct; spontaneously
instynktowość [een-stink-**to**-vośhćh] f. instinctive impulses
instynktowy [een-stink-**to**-vi] adj.m. of instinct; instinctive
instytucja [een-sti-**too**-tsyah] f. institution; institutional rules; institution's charter; establishment
instytucjonalizacja [een-sti-too-tsyo-nah-lee-**zah**-tsyah] f. institutionalization
instytucjonalizm [een-sti-too-tsyo-**nah**-leezm] m. institutionalism
instytucjonalizować [een-sti-too-tsyo-nah-lee-**zo**-vahćh] v. institutionalize (*repeatedly*)
instytucjonalizować się [een-sti-too-tsyo-nah-lee-**zo**-vahćh śhan] v. institutionalize oneself; acquire character of an institution (*repeatedly*)
instytucjonalnie [een-sti-too-tsyo-**nahl**-ńe] adv. institutionally
instytucjonalny [een-sti-too-tsyo-**nahl**-ni] adj.m. institutional
instytucki [een-sti-**toots**-kee] adj.m. of an institute; institute's (property, etc.)
instytut [een-**sti**-toot] m. institute
instytutowy [een-sti-too-**to**-vi] adj.m. of an institute; institute's (property, etc.)
insulina [een-soo-**lee**-nah] f. insulin
insulinowy [een-soo-lee-**no**-vi] adj.m. of insulin; insulin (treatment, etc.)

insulit [een-**soo**-leet] m. wood-fiber slab
insurekcja [een-soo-**rek**-tsyah] f. insurrection; uprising
insygnia [een-**syg**-ńah] pl. insignia; emblems; regalia
insygnium [een-**sig**-ńoom] n. symbol; emblem
insynuacja [een-si-noo-**ah**-tsyah] f. insinuation; innuendo; derogatory utterance; hint
insynuować [een-si-noo-**o**-vahćh] v. insinuate; hint or suggest indirectly; utter derogatory remarks; suggest artfully (*repeatedly*)
insza [**een**-shah] pron. see: **inna**
inszość [**een**-shośhćh] f. see: **inność**
inszy [**een**-shi] pron. see: **inny**
intabulacja [een-tah-boo-**lah**-tsyah] f. entry into property court records
intabulować [een-tah-boo-**lo**-vahćh] v. register (into property court records) (*repeatedly*)
intaglio [een-**tahl**-yo] n. intaglio
intarsja [een-**tahr**-syah] f. inlay; inlaid work; marquetry; marqueterie
intarsjować [een-tahr-**syo**-vahćh] v. inlay (*repeatedly*)
intarsjowanie [een-tahr-syo-**vah**-ńe] n. inlaying; inlaid work
integracja [een-te-**grah**-tsyah] f. integration
integracyjny [een-te-grah-**tsiy**-ni] adj.m. of integration; integrative; integrationist
integraf [een-**te**-grahf] m. integraph
integralizm [een-te-**grah**-leezm] m. tendency to integrate
integralnie [een-te-**grahl**-ńe] adv. integrally; wholly; in its entirety
integralność [een-te-**grahl**-nośhćh] f. integrality; wholeness; entirety; entireness
integralny [een-te-**grahl**-ni] adj.m. integral; whole; entire; complete
integrator [een-te-**grah**-tor] m. integrator
integrometr [een-te-**gro**-metr] m. mechanical integrator
integrować [een-te-**gro**-vahćh] v. integrate (*repeatedly*)
integrować się [een-te-**gro**-vahćh śh<u>an</u>] v. integrate oneself (*repeatedly*)
integrowanie [een-te-gro-**vah**-ńe] n. integration
integrysta [een-te-**gri**-stah] m. integrationist
integrystyczny [een-te-gri-**stich**-ni] adj.m. integrationist
integryzm [een-**teg**-rizm] m. integrationist tendency
intelekt [een-**te**-lekt] m. intellect; (high) intelligence; mind
intelektualista [een-te-lek-too-ah-**lees**-tah] m. intellectual; intellectualist
intelektualistka [een-te-lek-too-ah-**lees**-tkah] f. (woman) intellectual; intellectualist
intelektualistyczny [een-te-lek-too-ah-lee-**stich**-ni] adj.m. intellectualistic
intelektualizacja [een-te-lek-too-ah-lee-**zah**-tsyah] f. intellectualization
intelektualizm [een-te-lek-too-**ah**-leezm] m. intellectualism
intelektualizować [een-te-lek-too-ah-lee-**zo**-vahćh] v. intellectualize; give rational form or content (to) (*repeatedly*)
intelektualizować się [een-te-lek-too-ah-lee-**zo**-vahćh śh<u>an</u>] v. intellectualize oneself (*repeatedly*)
intelektualizowanie [een-te-lek-too-ah-lee-zo-**vah**-ńe] n. intellectualization
intelektualnie [een-te-lek-too-**ahl**-ńe] adv. intellectually
intelektualny [een-te-lek-too-**ahl**-ni] adj.m. intellectual; studious
inteligencik [een-te-lee-**gen**-ćheek] m. colloq: not quite an intellectual; egghead
inteligencja [een-te-lee-**gen**-tsyah] f. intelligentsia; intelligence; ability to learn, grasp, cope; understanding; quickness of understanding; intelligentzia; white-collar workers
inteligencki [een-te-lee-**gen**-tskee] adj.m. intellectual; belonging to the intellectuals; typical of an intellectual; colloq: highbrow
inteligent [een-te-**lee**-gent] m.

intellectual; educated man
inteligentka [een-te-lee-**gent**-kah] f. (woman) intellectual; educated woman
inteligentnie [een-te-lee-**gent**-ńe] adv. intelligently; sensibly; cleverly; brightly; judiciously; with quickness of understanding
inteligentny [een-te-lee-**gent**-ni] adj.m. intelligent; clever; wise; sharp; sensible; judicious
intencja [een-**ten**-tsyah] f. intention; purpose; anything intended; determination to act
na intencję czegoś [nah een-**ten**-tsyan **che**-gośh] exp.: for the intention of something; for the benefit of something
nie było w tym złej intencji [ńe **bi**-wo f tim zwey een-**ten**-tsyee] exp.: no harm was meant
zrobić coś w najlepszej intencji [**zro**-beećh tsośh v nahy-**le**-pshey een-**ten**-tsyee] exp.: to do something with the best intention
intencjonalizm [een-ten-tsyo-**nah**-leezm] m. intentionality; act psychology
intencjonalny [een-ten-tsyo-**nahl**-ni] adj.m. intentional
intendencki [een-ten-**den**-tskee] adj.m. steward's; manciple's; commissary's
intendent [een-**ten**-dent] m. steward; manciple; commissary
intendentura [een-ten-den-**too**-rah] f. stewardship; commissariat
intensjonalnie [een-ten-syo-**nahl**-ńe] adv. with an intensional logic; intensionally
intensjonalny [een-ten-syo-**nahl**-ni] adj.m. intensional (logic, etc.)
intensyfikacja [een-ten-si-fee-**kah**-tsyah] f. intensification
intensyfikować [een-ten-si-fee-**ko**-vahćh] v. intensify (*repeatedly*)
intensyfikować się [een-ten-si-fee-**ko**-vahćh śhan] v. become intensified; increase (*repeatedly*)
intensyfikowanie [een-ten-si-fee-ko-**vah**-ńe] n. intensification
intensywnie [een-ten-**siv**-ńe] adv. intensively; intensely; deeply; profoundly
intensywnieć [een-ten-**siv**-ńećh] v. become intensive (*repeatedly*)
intensywność [een-ten-**siv**-nośhćh] f. intensity; intenseness; degree; strength
intensywny [een-ten-**siv**-ni] adj.m. intensive; strenuous; deep; profound; high; hard
inter- [**een**-ter] prefix: inter-; between; among; within
interakcja [een-ter-**ahk**-tsyah] f. interaction; mutual action; reciprocal influence
interakcjonista [een-ter-ahk-tsyo-**ńees**-tah] m. interactionist; interactant
interakcjonizm [een-ter-ahk-**tsyo**-ńeezm] m. interactionism
intercepcja [een-ter-**tsep**-tsyah] f. interception
intercesja [een-ter-**tses**-yah] f. intercession
intercyza [een-ter-**tsi**-zah] f. marriage articles
interdykt [een-**ter**-dikt] m. interdict; ban
interdyscyplinarność [een-ter-dis-tsip-lee-**nahr**-nośhćh] f. interdisciplinary character
interdyscyplinarny [een-ter-dis-tsip-lee-**nahr**-ni] adj.m. interdisciplinary
interes [een-**te**-res] m. interest; business; errand; matter; affair; transaction; deal; bargain; shop; venture; self-interest; colloq: store; workshop; slang: penis
interesy państwowe [een-te-**re**-si pahń-**stfo**-ve] exp.: affairs of State
mam do pana interes [mahm do **pah**-nah een-**te**-res] exp.: I have some business with you
podejrzany interes [po-dey-**zhah**-ni een-**te**-res] exp.: shady deal
ruch w interesie [rookh v een-te-**re**-śhe] exp.: booming business; colloq: hectic time
to nie twój interes [to ńe tfooy een-**te**-res] exp.: it is no business of yours; it is none of your business
interesant [een-te-**re**-sahnt] m. client; man who has come on business

interesantka [een-te-re-**sahnt**-kah] f. (woman) client; woman who has come on business
interesik [een-te-**re**-śheek] m. (nice, little) interest; business; errand; matter; affair; transaction; deal; bargain; venture
interesować [een-te-re-**so**-vahćh] v. interest (*repeatedly*)
te sprawy mnie interesują [te sprah-vi mńe een-te-re-**soo**-yown] exp.: I am interested in such things; I find such things interesting
nie interesuję się tym [ńe een-te-re-**soo**-yan śhan tim] exp.: I am not interested in that; I have no interest for that
interesować się [een-te-re-**so**-vahćh śhan] v. be interested (in); take an interest (in); interest oneself (in); concern oneself (with, about) (*repeatedly*)
interesowanie się [een-te-re-so-**vah**-ńe śhan] n. interest
interesownie [een-te-re-**sov**-ńe] adv. selfishly; with self-interest
interesowność [een-te-re-**sov**-nośhćh] f. selfishness; self-interest
interesowny [een-te-re-**sov**-ni] adj.m. selfish; greedy; not disinterested; self-seeking; mercenary
interesująco [een-te-re-soo-**yown**-tso] adv. in an interesting manner; in a captivating manner; in an entertaining manner
interesujący [een-te-re-soo-**yown**-tsi] adj.m. interesting; captivating; absorbing; fascinating; thrilling; sapid; of unusual interest
interfaza [een-ter-**fah**-zah] f. interphase
interfejs [een-**ter**-feys] m. interface; connection of a computer to a machine (printer, etc.)
interferencja [een-ter-fe-**ren**-tsyah] f. interference
interferencyjny [een-ter-fe-ren-**tsiy**-ni] adj.m. interferential
interferometr [een-ter-fe-**ro**-metr] m. interferometer
interferometria [een-ter-fe-ro-**metr**-yah] f. interferometry
interferometrycznie [een-ter-fe-ro-met-**rich**-ńe] adv. interferometrically
interferometryczny [een-ter-fe-ro-met-**rich**-ni] adj.m. interferometric
interferon [een-ter-**fe**-ron] m. interferon; antiviral protein
interferonowy [een-ter-fe-ro-**no**-vi] adj.m. of interferon
interferować [een-ter-fe-**ro**-vahćh] v interfere; meddle (*repeatedly*)
interfoliować [een-ter-fol-**yo**-vahćh] v. insert a blank page into a book (*repeatedly*)
interfoliowanie [een-ter-fol-yo-**vah**-ńe] n. inserting a blank page into a book (*repeated*)
interglacjalny [een-ter-glahts-**yahl**-ni] adj.m. interglacial (epoch, etc.)
interglacjał [een-ter-**glah**-tsyahw] m. interglacial period
interiekcja [een-ter-**yek**-tsyah] f. exclamatory part of pronunciation; interjection
interier [een-**ter**-yer] m. individual characteristics of internal organs of a species or race
interior [een-**ter**-yor] m. interior (of a country)
interioryzacja [een-ter-yo-ri-**zah**-tsyah] f. interiorization
interkineza [een-ter-kee-**ne**-zah] f. interkinesis
interkolumnium [een-ter-ko-loo-**mee**-ńyoom] n. intercolumniation
interkomunikacja [een-ter-ko-moo-ńee-**kah**-tsyah] f. intercommunication
interkontynentalny [een-ter-kon-ti-nen-**tahl**-ni] adj.m. intercontinental
interliga [een-ter-**lee**-gah] f. international soccer league
interlineacja [enn-ter-lee-ne-**ah**-tsyah] f. printing every second line
interlinearny [enn-ter-lee-ne-**ahr**-ni] adj.m. placed between lines
interlinia [enn-ter-**lee**-ńyah] f. lead; space (in printing or typing)
interliniować [een-ter-lee-**ńyo**-vahćh] v. space (*repeatedly*)
interlokutor [een-ter-lo-**koo**-tor] m. interlocutor
interlokutorka [een-ter-lo-koo-**tor**-

kah] f. (woman) interlocutor
interludium [een-ter-**lood**-yoom] n. interlude
intermedialny [een-ter-med-**yahl**-ni] adj.m. of interlude
intermediowy [een-ter-med-**yo**-vi] adj.m. of interlude; within interlude
intermedium [een-ter-**med**-yoom] n. interlude
intermezzo [een-ter-**medz**-dzo] n. intermezzo
intern [**een**-tern] m. boarder (pupil)
interna [een-**ter**-nah] f. colloq: internal medicine; department of internal diseases
internacjonalista [een-ter-nah-tsyo-nah-**lee**-stah] m. internationalist
internacjonalistyczny [een-ter-nah-tsyo-nah-lees-**tich**-ni] adj.m. internationalist
internacjonalizacja [een-ter-nah-tsyo-nah-lee-**zah**-tsyah] f. internationalization
internacjonalizm [een-ter-nah-tsyo-**nah**-leezm] m. internationalism
internacjonalny [een-ter-nah-tsyo-**nahl**-ni] adj.m. international
internacjonał [een-ter-nah-**tsyo**-nahw] m. first International
internalizacja [een-ter-nah-lee-**zah**-tsyah] f. internalization
internat [een-**ter**-naht] m. boarding school (for boys or for girls); colloq: place of internment; slang: prison (mob jargon)
internatowy [een-ter-nah-**to**-vi] adj.m. boarding school (life, program, etc.)
internista [een-ter-**ńee**-stah] m. internist; specialist in internal medicine
internistka [een-ter-**ńeest**-kah] f. (woman) internist; specialist in internal medicine
internistyczny [een-ter-ńees-**tich**-ni] adj.m. of internal medicine
internować [een-ter-**no**-vahćh] v. intern; confine in an internment camp (*repeatedly*)
internowanie [een-ter-no-**vah**-ńe] n. internment
internowany [een-ter-no-**vah**-ni] m. internee
internuncjusz [een-ter-**noon**-tsyoosh] m. internuncio
interoreceptor [een-te-ro-re-**tsep**-tor] m. receptor sensitive to internal changes inside the body
interpelacja [een-ter-pe-**lah**-tsyah] f. interpellation; question
interpelacyjny [een-ter-pe-lah-**tsiy**-ni] adj.m. of interpellation; of a question
interpelant [een-ter-**pe**-lahnt] m. interpellator; questioner
interpelator [een-ter-pe-**lah**-tor] m. interpellator
interpelować [een-ter-pe-**lo**-vahćh] v. interpellate; ask a question (*repeatedly*)
interpelowanie [een-ter-pe-lo-**vah**-ńe] n. interpellation
interpersonalnie [een-ter-per-so-**nahl**-ńe] adv. interpersonally
interpersonalny [een-ter-per-so-**nahl**-ni] adj.m. interpersonal
interpolacja [een-ter-po-**lah**-tsyah] f. interpolation
interpolacyjny [een-ter-po-lah-**tsiy**-ni] adj.m. interpolative
interpolować [een-ter-po-**lo**-vahćh] v. interpolate (*repeatedly*)
interpretacja [een-ter-pre-**tah**-tsyah] f. interpretation; explanation; rendition; rendering
interpretacyjnie [een-ter-pre-tah-**tsiy**-ńe] adv. interpretatively
interpretacyjny [een-ter-pre-tah-**tsiy**-ni] adj.m. interpretative; explanatory; of rendition; of rendering
interpretator [een-ter-pre-**tah**-tor] m. interpreter; concert musician; colloq: spin doctor
interpretatorka [een-ter-pre-tah-**tor**-kah] f. (woman) interpreter; concert musician; colloq: spin doctor
interpretatorski [een-ter-pre-tah-**tor**-skee] adj.m. interpretative
interpretować [een-ter-pre-**to**-vahćh] v. interpret (*repeatedly*)
błędnie coś interpretować [**bwand**-ńe tsośh een-ter-pre-**to**-vahćh] exp.: to misinterpret something
interpretowanie [een-ter-pre-to-**vah**-

ńe] n. interpretation; rendering
interpunkcja [een-ter-**poonk**-tsyah] f. punctuation
interpunkcyjny [een-ter-poonk-**tsiy**-ni] adj.m. of punctuation
interregnum [een-ter-**reg**-noom] n. interregnum
interreks [een-**ter**-reks] m. interrex
intersekcja [een-ter-**sek**-tsyah] f. intersection
interseks [een-**ter**-seks] m. intersex
interseksualizm [een-ter-sek-soo-**ah**-leezm] m. intersexualism
interseksualny [een-ter-sek-soo-**ahl**-ni] adj.m. intersexual
interstadialny [een-ter-stahd-**yahl**-ni] adj.m. interstadial
interstadiał [een-ter-**stahd**-yahw] m. interstadial period
intersubiektywizm [een-ter-soo-byek-ti-**vee**zm] m. intersubjectivity
intersubiektywnie [een-ter-soo-byek-**tiv**-ńe] adv. intersubjectively
intersubiektywność [een-ter-soo-byek-**tiv**-nośhćh] f. intersubjectivity
intersubiektywny [een-ter-soo-byek-**tiv**-ni] adj.m. intersubjective
intertyp [een-**ter**-tip] m. intertype (in printing)
intertypowy [een-ter-ti-**po**-vi] adj.m. of intertype
interwał [een-**ter**-vahw] m. interval
interwencja [een-ter-**ven**-tsyah] f. intervention; interference
interwencjonistyczny [een-ter-ven-tsyo-ńees-**tich**-ni] adj.m. interventionist
interwencjonizm [een-ter-ven-**tsyo**-ńeezm] m. interventionism (political, etc.)
interwencyjnie [een-ter-ven-**tsiy**-ńe] adv. by intervention; in an interventionist way
interwencyjny [een-ter-ven-**tsiy**-ni] adj.m. of intervention; interventionist
interwenient [een-ter-**ve**-ńyent] m. intervening party; intervener
interwenientka [een-ter-ve-**ńyent**-kah] f. intervening woman
interweniować [een-ter-ve-**ńyo**-vahćh] v. interfere; intercede; mediate (*repeatedly*)
interweniowanie [een-ter-ve-ńyo-**vah**-ńe] n. interference; intercession; mediation
interwent [een-**ter**-vent] m. intervening party; intervener
interwiew [een-ter-**vyoo**] m. colloq: interview
interwizyjny [een-ter-vee-**ziy**-ni] adj.m. of Intervision (television of Eastern Europe)
interwokalistyczny [een-ter-vo-kah-lees-**tich**-ni] adj.m. intervocalic
intestat [een-**te**-staht] m. intestate
intoksykacja [een-to-ksi-**kah**-tsyah] f. intoxication
intonacja [een-to-**nah**-tsyah] f. intonation
intonacyjny [een-to-nah-**tsiy**-ni] adj.m. of intonation; intonation (group, etc.)
intonować [een-to-**no**-vahćh] v. intone; chant (*repeatedly*)
intonowanie [een-to-no-**vah**-ńe] n. intonation; chanting
intrada [een-**trah**-dah] f. intrada
intrakauzalizm [een-trah-kahw-**zah**-leezm] m. a version of the theory of evolution
intrakauzalny [een-trah-kahw-**zahl**-ni] adj.m. of a version of the theory of evolution
intramolekularny [een-trah-mo-le-koo-**lahr**-ni] adj.m. intramolecular
intranzytywnie [een-trahn-zi-**tiv**-ńe] adv. intransitively
intranzytywny [een-trahn-zi-**tiv**-ni] adj.m. intransitive; not transitive
intrata [een-**trah**-tah] f. income; profit
intratnie [een-**traht**-ńe] adv. profitably; lucratively
intratność [een-**traht**-nośhćh] f. profit; gain; remunerativeness
intratny [een-**traht**-ni] adj.m. lucrative; profitable; paying
intro- [**een**-tro] prefix: intro-; in-; into; inward-; within-
introdukcja [een-tro-**dook**-tsyah] f. introduction
introligator [een-tro-lee-**gah**-tor] m. bookbinder; bookbinder's shop
introligatorka [een-tro-lee-gah-**tor**-kah] f. (woman) bookbinder; bookbinder's trade

introligatornia [een-tro-lee-gah-**tor**-ńah] f. bindery; bookbinder's workshop
introligatorski [een-tro-lee-gah-**tor**-skee] adj.m. bookbinder's (trade, etc.)
introligatorstwo [een-tro-lee-gah-**tor**-stfo] n. bookbinder's trade
intronizacja [een-tro-ńee-**zah**-tsyah] f. enthronement; inauguration
intronizować [een-tro-ńee-**zo**-vahćh] v. enthrone; inaugurate (*repeatedly*)
intronizowanie [een-tro-ńee-zo-**vah**-ńe] n. enthronement; inauguration
introspekcja [een-tro-**spek**-tsyah] f. introspection; self-examination
introspekcjonista [een-tro-spek-tsyo-**ńees**-tah] m. introspectionist
introspekcjonizm [een-tro-spek-**tsyo**-ńeezm] m. introspectionism
introspekcyjnie [een-tro-spek-**tsiy**-ńe] adv. introspectively
introspekcyjny [een-tro-spek-**tsiy**-ni] adj.m. introspective
introspektywizm [een-tro-spek-ti-veezm] m. introspectiveness
introspektywny [een-tro-spek-**tiv**-ni] adj.m. introspective
introwersja [een-tro-**ver**-syah] f. introversion
introwersyjny [een-tro-ver-**siy**-ni] adj.m. introversive
introwertyczka [een-tro-ver-**tich**-kah] f. (woman) introvert
introwertyk [een-tro-**ver**-tik] m. introvert
introwertyzm [een-tro-**ver**-tizm] m. introversion
intruz [een-troos] m. intruder
intruzja [een-**troo**-zyah] f. intrusion
intruzyjnie [een-troo-**ziy**-ńe] adv. intrusively
intruzyjność [een-troo-**ziy**-nośhćh] f. intrusiveness
intruzyjny [een-troo-**ziy**-ni] adj.m. intrusive
intryga [een-**tri**-gah] f. plot; intrigue; machination
intrygancki [een-tri-**gahn**-tskee] adj.m. intriguing; scheming; mischief making
intryganctwo [een-tri-**gahn**-tsfo] n. intriguing; intrigues; machinations
intrygant [een-**tri**-gahnt] m. intriguer; schemer
intrygantka [een-tri-**gahnt**-kah] f. (woman) intriguer; schemer
intrygować [een-tri-**go**-vahćh] v. intrigue; scheme; plot; machinate; make mischief; puzzle; arouse interest (in) (*repeatedly*)
intrygowanie [een-tri-go-**vah**-ńe] n. intriguing; plotting; intrigues
intrygujący [een-tri-goo-**yown**-tsi] adj.m. intriguing
intryżka [een-**tri**-shkah] f. (small, unimportant) plot; intrigue; machination
intubacja [een-too-**bah**-tsyah] f. intubation
intuicja [een-too-**ee**-tsyah] f. intuition; insight; feeling
intuicjonista [een-too-ee-tsyo-**ńees**-tah] m. intuitionist
intuicjonistka [een-too-ee-tsyo-**ńees**-tkah] f. (woman) intuitionist
intuicjonistyczny [een-too-ee-tsyo-ńees-**tich**-ni] adj.m. intuitionist; intuitionistic
intuicjonizm [een-too-eets-**yo**-ńeezm] m. intuitionism
intuicyjnie [een-too-ee-**tsiy**-ńe] adv. by intuition; intuitively
intuicyjny [een-too-ee-**tsiy**-ni] adj.m. intuitive; subconscious
intymnie [een-**ti**-mńe] adv. privately; in homely fashion; confidentially; informally; intimately; secretly; closely
intymność [een-**ti**-mnośhćh] f. intimacy; familiarity; intimateness
intymny [een-**ti**-mni] adj.m. private; informal; intimate; confidential; close; intrinsic; essential
najbardziej intymny [nahy-**bahr**-dźhey een-**tim**-ni] exp.: inmost; innermost; very intimate; very close
inwalida [een-vah-**lee**-dah] m. invalid; disabled (soldier); cripple
inwalidka [een-vah-**leet**-kah] f. (woman) invalid; disabled (woman); cripple
inwalidzki [een-vah-**lee**-tskee] adj.m. disability (rent, compensation)
krzesło inwalidzkie [kshes-wo

een-vah-lee-tske] exp.: wheelchair
renta inwalidzka [ren-tah een-vah-lee-tskah] exp.: disability benefit; disability payment
inwalidztwo [een-vah-leets-tfo] n. disability
inwar [een-vahr] m. invar (type of nickel steel)
inwazja [een-vah-zyah] f. invasion; inroad
dokonać inwazji na kraj [do-ko-nahćh een-vah-zyee nah krahy] exp.: to invade a country
inwazyjność [een-vah-ziy-nośhćh] f. invasive propensity
inwazyjny [een-vah-ziy-ni] adj.m. of invasion
inwektywa [een-vek-ti-vah] f. invective
inwektywy [een-vek-ti-vi] pl. abuse
obrzucać inwektywami [ob-zhoo-tsahćh een-vek-ti-vah-mee] exp.: to revile; to vituperate
inwencja [een-ven-tsyah] f. inventiveness; invention; ingeniousness
inwentarialnie [een-ven-tahr-yahl-ńe] adv. inventorially
inwentarialny [een-ven-tahr-yahl-ni] adj.m. liable to be inventoried; inventorial
inwentarski [een-ven-tahr-skee] adj.m. of inventory; inventoried
inwentaryzacja [een-ven-tah-ri-zah-tsyah] f. listing; stocktaking; cataloguing
inwentaryzator [een-ven-tah-ri-zah-tor] m. cataloguer
inwentaryzować [een-ven-tah-ri-zo-vahćh] v. catalogue; list; take stock (of) (*repeatedly*)
inwentaryzowanie [een-ven-tah-ri-zo-vah-ńe] n. cataloguing; listing; taking stock (of)
inwentarz [een-ven-tahsh] m. inventory; stock; list
inwentarzowy [een-ven-tah-zho-vi] adj.m. of the inventory; of an inventory
inwersja [een-ver-syah] f. inversion; reversal
inwersor [een-ver-sor] m. variety of drafting device
inwersyjnie [een-ver-siy-ńe] adv. inversely
inwersyjny [een-ver-siy-ni] adj.m. inverse
inwertor [een-ver-tor] m. invertor
inwestor [een-ve-stor] m. investor
inwestorski [een-ves-tor-skee] adj.m. of investor; investor's
inwestować [een-ves-to-vahćh] v. invest in capital expenditure (*repeatedly*)
inwestowanie [een-ves-to-vah-ńe] n. making investments
inwestycja [een-ves-ti-tsyah] f.investment; capital outlay
inwestycyjny [een-ves-ti-tsiy-ni] adj.m. of capital expenditure; investment (money, etc.)
inwestytura [een-ves-ti-too-rah] f. assignment of a fief to a vassal; formal investing of a Protestant pastor; investiture
inwigilacja [een-vee-gee-lah-tsyah] f. surveillance
inwigilować [een-vee-gee-lo-vahćh] v. watch; shadow; keep under surveillance; have under surveillance (*repeatedly*)
inwigilowany [een-vee-gee-lo-vah-ni] adj.m. shadowed (man, etc.); m. person under surveillance
inwit [een-veet] m. invitation (in card game)
inwitować [een-vee-to-vahćh] v. invite (an old expression) (*repeatedly*)
inwokacja [een-vo-kah-tsyah] f. invocation; supplication; incantation
inwokacyjny [een-vo-kah-tsiy-ni] adj.m. invocational; invocatory
inwolucja [een-vo-loo-tsyah] f. involution; complexity; intricacy; involvement
inwolucyjny [een-vo-loo-tsiy-ni] adj.m. involutional; involutionary
inżektor [een-zhek-tor] m. injector
inżynier [een-zhi-ńer] m. engineer; graduate engineer
inżynier budowlany [een-zhi-ńer boo-dov-lah-ni] exp.: structural engineer
inżynier chemik [een-zhi-ńer khe-meek] exp.: chemical engineer;

Chem.E.
inżynier elektryk [een-**zhi**-ńer e-**lek**-trik] exp.: electrical engineer E.E.
inżynier górnik [een-**zhi**-ńer **goor**-ńeek] exp.: mining engineer; E.M.
inżynier lądowy [een-**zhi**-ńer lown-**do**-vi] exp.: civil engineer; C.E.
inżynier mechanik [een-**zhi**-ńer me-**khah**-ńeek] exp.: mechanical engineer; M.E.
inżynier rolnictwa [een-**zhi**-ńer rol-**ńeets**-tfah] exp.: agricultural engineer; A.E.

inżynieria [een-zhi-**ńer**-yah] f. engineering (science)
inżynierka [een-zhi-**ńer**-kah] f. colloq: engineering work; slang: prostitute (mob jargon)
inżynierostwo [een-zhi-ńe-**ros**-tfo] n. engineer and his wife
inżynierowa [een-zhi-ńe-**ro**-vah] f. engineer's wife
inżynierski [een-zhi-**ńer**-skee] adj.m. engineer's; of engineering; engineering (office, enterprise, etc.)
inżynieryjny [een-zhi-ńe-**riy**-ni] adj.m. engineer's; of engineering; engineering (office, enterprise, etc.)
ipekakuana [ee-pe-kah-**kwah**-nah] f. ipecacuanha (shrub)
iperyt [ee-**pe**-rit] m. iperite; mustard gas
iperytowy [ee-pe-ri-**to**-vi] adj.m. of iperite; of mustard gas; iperite (poisoning, etc.)
ippon [**eep**-pon] m. win; winning (in judo and karate)
ipsacja [eep-**sah**-tsyah] f. masturbation
ipsofon [eep-**so**-fon] m. telephone answering machine
ipsotermostat [eep-so-ter-**mo**-staht] m. thermostat protecting electric motor
ipsylon [**eep**-si-lon] m. the letter "y"; ypsilon
kształt ipsylonu [kshtahwt eep-si-**lo**-noo] exp.: ypsiliform; y-shape
iracki [ee-**rah**-tskee] adj.m. of Iraq; Iraqi
Irańczyk [ee-**rahń**-chik] m. Iranian
Iranka [ee-**rahn**-kah] f. Iranian woman
irański [ee-**rahń**-skee] adj.m. Iranian
irbis [**eer**-bees] m. ounce; snow leopard
ircha [**eer**-khah] f. suede-leather; chamois-leather; suede; wash-leather
irchowy [eer-**kho**-vi] adj.m. suede-leather (coat, etc.); chamois-leather (gloves, etc,); suede (coat, etc.); wash-leather (gloves)
irga [**eer**-gah] f. cotoneaster (bush)
iron [**ee**-ron] m. irone
irlandzki [eer-**lahnts**-kee] adj.m. Irish (language, etc.)
irys [**ee**-ris] m. iris
ironia [ee-**ro**-ńyah] f. irony
jak na ironię [yahk nah ee-**ro**-ńyan] exp.: to make things worse
ironią losu [ee-**roń**-yown **lo**-soo] exp.: by an irony of fate

ironicznie [ee-ro-**ńeech**-ńe] adv. ironically; derisively
ironiczny [ee-ro-**ńeech**-ni] adj.m. ironical; derisive
ironista [ee-ro-**ńee**-stah] m. ironist
ironizować [ee-ro-ńee-**zo**-vahćh] v. deride; speak ironically; to make ironical remarks (*repeatedly*)
ironizowanie [ee-ro-ńee-zo-**vah**-ńe] n. deriding; speaking ironically
irracjonalistycznie [eer-rah-tsyo-nah-lee-**stich**-ńe] adv. irrationally
irracjonalistyczny [eer-rah-tsyo-nah-lee-**stich**-ni] adj.m. irrational; contrary to reason; absurd
irracjonalizm [eer-rah-tsyo-**nah**-leezm] m. irrationalism
irracjonalnie [eer-rah-tsyo-**nahl**-ńe] adv. irrationally
irracjonalność [eer-rah-tsyo-**nahl**-nośhćh] f. irrationality
irracjonalny [eer-rah-tsyo-**nahl**-ni] adj.m. irrational
irradiacja [eer-rahd-**yah**-tsyah] f. irradiation
irrealizm [eer-re-**ah**-leezm] m. irreality; unreality
irrealny [eer-re-**ahl**-ni] adj.m. unreal
irredenta [eer-re-**den**-tah] f. irredentism
irredentysta [eer-re-den-**tis**-tah] m.

irredentist
irredentystyczny [eer-re-den-tis-**tich**-ni] adj.m. irredentist
irrelewantnie [eer-re-le-**vahnt**-ńe] adv. irrelevantly
irrelewantny [eer-re-le-**vahnt**-ni] adj.m. irrelevant; inapplicable
iryd [**ee**-rit] m. iridium (atomic number 77)
irygacja [ee-ri-**gah**-tsyah] f. irrigation; watering
irygacyjny [ee-ri-gah-**tsiy**-ni] adj.m. of irrigation; of watering; irrigation (engineering, etc.)
irygator [ee-ri-**gah**-tor] m. irrigator
irygować [ee-ri-**go**-vahćh] v. irrigate (*repeatedly*)
irygowanie [ee-ri-go-**vah**-ńe] n. irrigation
irys [**ee**-ris] m. iris; fleur-de-lis; toffee; taffy
irysowy [ee-ri-**so**-vi] adj.m. iris (family, etc.)
irytacja [ee-ri-**tah**-tsyah] f. irritation, exasperation; soreness; fret; vexation; chafe; annoyance
irytować [ee-ri-**to**-vahćh] v. irritate; annoy; exasperate; vex; nettle; gall; colloq: get in somebody's hair (*repeatedly*)
on mnie irytuje [on mńe ee-ri-**too**-ye] exp.: I have no patience with him; he gets on my nerves
irytować się [ee-ri-**to**-vahćh śhan] v. be irritated; be annoyed; be exasperated; be sore; be vexed; be nettled; be in a temper; be put out; be put on; chafe (at); fret (at) (*repeatedly*)
irytujący [ee-ri-too-**yown**-tsi] adj.m. irritating; annoying; trying; exasperating; provoking; aggravating
iryzacja [ee-ri-**zah**-tsyah] f. iridescence
iryzować [ee-ri-**zo**-vahćh] v. be iridescent (*repeatedly*)
iryzowanie [ee-ri-zo-**vah**-ńe] n. being iridescent
isagoga [ee-sah-**go**-gah] f. isagoge; introduction (to research, etc.)
isagogika [ee-sah-**go**-gee-kah] f. isagogics; introductory study
ischias [**eesh**-yahs] m. sciatica
ischiasowy [eesh-yah-**so**-vi] adj.m. sciatic
iskać [**ees**-kahćh] v. seek lice; cleanse of vermin; delouse; slang: search; steal; pick pocket (mob jargon) (*repeatedly*)
iskać się [**ees**-kahćh śhan] v. seek one's lice; cleanse oneself of vermin; delouse oneself (*repeatedly*)
iskiereczka [ees-ke-**rech**-kah] f. (very nice, little) spark; flash; glint; gleam; sparkle
iskierka [ees-**ker**-kah] f. (nice, little) spark; flash; glint; gleam; sparkle
iskierka nadziei [ees-**ker**-kah nah-**dźhe**-ee] exp.: a flicker of hope
iskiernik [ees-**ker**-ńeek] m. spark gap
iskra [**ees**-krah] f. spark; flash; glint; gleam; colloq: sprightly person
dawać iskrę [dah-vahćh **ees**-kran] exp.: to spark
iskra boża [**ees**-krah **bo**-zhah] exp.: divine spark
iskrochron [ees-**kro**-khron] m. anti-spark screen; spark arrester
iskrownik [ees-**krov**-ńeek] m. sparkplug
iskrownikowy [ees-krov-ńee-**ko**-vi] adj.m. sparkplug (gap, etc.)
iskrowy [ees-**kro**-vi] adj.m. spark (discharge, condenser, frequency, etc.)
zgrzewanie iskrowe [zgzhe-**vah**-ńe ees-**kro**-ve] exp.: flash-welding
iskrówka [ees-**kroof**-kah] f. portable radio station; radiogram; radiotelegram
iskrzasty [ees-**kshahs**-ti] adj.m. sparkling
iskrzenie [eesk-**she**-ńe] n. sparkle; scintillation; twinkle
iskrzyć [**ees**-kshićh] v. sparkle; glint; glitter; twinkle; scintillate; coruscate (*repeatedly*)
iskrzyć się [**ees**-kshićh śhan] v. sparkle; glint; glitter; twinkle; scintillate; coruscate (*repeatedly*)
islam [**ees**-lahm] m. Islam
islamiczny [ees-lah-**meech**-ni] adj.m. Islamist
islamista [ees-lah-**mees**-tah] m. Islamist

islamistyczny [ees-lah-mees-**tich**-ni] adj.m. Islamic; Islamitic
islamizacja [ee-slah-mee-**zah**-tsyah] f. Islamization
islamizować [ee-slah-mee-**zo**-vahćh] v. Islamize (*repeatedly*)
islamski [ee-**slahm**-skee] adj. Islamic
Islandczyk [ees-**lahnt**-chik] m. Icelander
Islandka [ees-**lahnt**-kah] f. (woman) Icelander
islandzki [ees-**lahn**-tskee] adj.m. Icelandic
istnieć [**eest**-ńećh] v. exist; subsist; be in existence; be; live (*repeatedly*)
istniejący [eest-ńe-yown-tsi] adj.m. existing; in being; living; in existence; extant
istnienie [eest-**ńe**-ńe] n. existence; being; entity; subsistence
istność [**eest**-nośhćh] f. being; existence; entity; subsistence
istny [**eest**-ni] adj.m. real; veritable; downright; sheer
istota [ees-**to**-tah] f. creature; being; essence; gist; sum; entity; living thing; soul; man's nature; marrow; the heart of the matter
istota ludzka [ee-**sto**-tah **loots**-kah] exp.: human being
istota rzeczy [ee-**sto**-tah **zhe**-chi] exp.: the essence of the matter
w istocie [v ee-**sto**-ćhe] exp.: in reality; in fact; in effect; as a matter of fact; to all intents and purposes
istotka [ees-**tot**-kah] f. (small, nice) creature; being
istotnie [ee-**stot**-ńe] adv. indeed; in reality; veritably; really; in fact; as a matter of fact; actually; essentially; radically; fundamentally; substantially; vitally; considerably; to a considerable extent; colloq: sure enough
istotny [ees-**tot**-ni] adj.m. essential; substantial; vital; radical; actual; real; true; important; critical; crucial; material; intrinsic; veritable; big; outstanding
iszjas [**eesh**-yahs] m. sciatica
iszjasowy [eesh-yah-**so**-vi] adj.m. sciatic
iście [**eeśh**-ćhe] adv. indeed; truly; really; in truth
iść [eeśhćh] v. go; go along; walk; move on; march; come; approach; head for; make for; make progress; run; sail; fly; flow; spread; get along; succeed; prosper; be bound for; attack; assault; be going; be on its way; be destined for; reach; extend; sell well; have a long run (in a theater, etc.); come off well; enter; rush (*repeatedly*)
idzie o życie [**ee**-dźhe o **zhi**-ćhe] exp.: it is a question of life and death
idźcie! [**ee**ćh-ćhe] excl.: go away!; get away; get out!; leave the room!
idźże! [**eedźh**-zhe] excl.: go on!; liar!; impossible!; it's a lie!
iść dalej [eeśhćh **dah**-ley] exp.: to move on
iść do pudła [eeśhćh do **pood**-wah] exp.: slang: to be arrested; to be imprisoned (mob jargon)
interesy mu idą [een-te-**re**-si moo **ee**-down] exp.: he is doing well; his business is prospering; his affairs are shaping well
iść na bok [eeśhćh nah bok] exp.: to step aside; to be of secondary importance
iść na dno [eeśhćh nah dno] exp.: to sink; to go to the bottom
iść na jagody [eeśhćh nah yah-**go**-di] exp.: to go berry-picking
iść na kompromis [eeśhćh nah kom-**pro**-mees] exp.: to compromise
iść na polowanie [eeśhćh nah po-lo-**vah**-ńe] exp.: to go hunting
iść naprzód [eeśhćh **nah**-pshoot] exp.: to go on; to go ahead; to advance
iść na ryby [eeśhćh nah **ri**-bi] exp.: to go fishing
iść o lasce [eeśhćh o **lahs**-tse] exp.: to walk with a cane
iść o kulach [eeśhćh o **koo**-lahkh] exp.: to walk on crutches
iść o zakład [eeśhćh o **zahk**-waht] exp.: to bet; to wager

iść pełną parą [eeśhćh pew-nown pah-rown] exp.: to be in full swing; to be going full blast
iść piechotą [eeśhćh pye-kho-town] exp.: to go on foot; to walk; to make it on foot
jak ci idzie? [yahk ćhee ee-dźhe] exp.: How are you doing?
jeśli o to idzie [yeśh-lee o to ee-dźhe] exp.: as far as that goes; for that matter; as for that; if you come to that
mój zegarek nie idzie [mooy ze-gah-rek ńe ee-dźhe] exp.: colloq: my watch has stopped
ta książka nie idzie [tah kśhownsh-kah ńe ee-dźhe] exp.: this book does not sell well
ten, o którego idzie [ten o ktoo-re-go ee-dźhe] exp.: the one concerned; the one in question
to, o co idzie [to o tso ee-dźhe] exp.: what one is after; what one is aiming at; what one is trying to do; what one is trying to attain
itacyzm [ee-tah-tsizm] m. itacism; pronunciation of the Greek letter "eta"
Italczyk [ee-tahl-chik] m. (an) Italian (hist.)
italianizm [ee-tahl-yah-ńeezm] m. borrowing from the Italian language; italianism
italik [ee-tah-leek] m. italic font
italika [ee-tah-lee-kah] pl. printing in italic font; Italian literature
italski [ee-tahl-skee] adj.m. Italian
iteracja [ee-te-rah-tsyah] f. iteration; repetition (used in music and mathematics)
iteratiwum [ee-te-rah-tee-voom] n. iterative verb
iteratywny [ee-te-rah-tiv-ni] adj.m. iterative
iterb [ee-terp] m. ytterbium (atomic number 70)
itinerarium [ee-tee-ne-rahr-yoom] n. itinerary
itr [eetr] m. yttrium (atomic number 39)
iwa [ee-vah] f. sallow
iwanić [ee-vah-ńeećh] v. slang: hit; strike; steal (mob jargon)
izabelin [ee-zah-be-leen] m. an alloy
izalobary [ee-zah-lo-bah-ri] pl. isallobars
izaloterma [ee-zah-lo-ter-mah] f. isollotherm; line of equal temperature
izanomala [ee-zah-no-mah-lah] f. line of equal anomalies of weather
izarytma [ee-zah-rit-mah] f. isorithm
izatyna [ee-zah-ti-nah] f. isatin
izba [eez-bah] f. room; chamber; apartment
izba chorych [eez-bah kho-rikh] exp.: infirmary; sick-quarters
izba egzekucyjna [eez-bah eg-ze-koo-tsiy-nah] exp.: death chamber
izba handlowa [eez-bah khahn-dlo-vah] exp.: Chamber of Commerce
izba mieszkalna [eez-bah myesh-kahl-nah] exp.: habitation; dwelling room
izba porodowa [eez-bah po-ro-do-vah] exp.: delivery room
izba przyjęć [eez-bah pshi-yanćh] exp.: reception room
izba wytrzeźwień [eez-bah vi-tsheźh-vyeń] exp.: sobering chamber
izbica [eez-bee-tsah] f. large room; ice apron; icebreaker; starling
izbowy [eez-bo-vi] adj.m. of a room; of rooms; of living quarters; housing (problem, etc.)
izdebka [eez-dep-kah] f. little room; cubby
izgrzyca [eez-gzhi-tsah] f. sieglingia
izm [eezm] m. ism; a distinctive doctrine, cause or a theory
-izm [eezm] suffix: -ism
izmailita [eez-mah-ee-lee-tah] m. Muslim
izmailizm [eez-mah-ee-leezm] m. one of Islamic doctrines
izo- [ee-zo] prefix: iso-
izoamplituda [ee-zo-ahmp-lee-too-dah] f. line connecting points of equal amplitudes of temperature
izobar [ee-zo-bahr] m. isobar
izobara [ee-zo-bah-rah] f. isobar
izobaryczny [ee-zo-bah-rich-ni] adj.m. isobaric
izobata [ee-zo-bah-tah] f. isobath; having constant depth
izobutan [ee-zo-boo-tahn] m.

isobutane
izobutylen [ee-zo-boo-**ti**-len] m. isobutylene
izochora [ee-zo-**kho**-rah] f. isochor; isochore
izochoryczny [ee-zo-kho-**rich**-ni] adj.m. isochoric
izochromatyczny [ee-zo-khro-mah-**tich**-ni] adj.m. isochromatic
izochrona [ee-zo-**khro**-nah] f. isochrone
izochroniczny [ee-zo-khro-**ńeech**-ni] adj.m. isochronic; isochronal; isochronous
izochronizm [ee-zo-**khro**-ńeezm] m. isochronism
izocyjanek [ee-zo-tsi-**yah**-nek] m. isocyanide
izodynamy [ee-zo-di-**nah**-mi] pl. isodynamic lines
izofen [ee-**zo**-fen] m. isophane; isophene
izofona [ee-zo-**fo**-nah] f. line showing the limits of a phonetic phenomenon
izofoniczny [ee-zo-fo-**ńeech**-ni] adj.m. of line showing the limits of a phonetic phenomenon
izogameta [ee-zo-gah-**me**-tah] f. isogamete
izogamia [ee-zo-**gah**-myah] f. isogamy
izoglosa [ee-zo-**glo**-sah] f. isogloss; territorial extent of a language characteristic (shown on a map)
izogona [ee-zo-**go**-nah] f. isogony
izohalina [ee-zo-khah-**lee**-nah] f. isohalsine; isohaline
izohieta [ee-zo-<u>**khe**</u>-tah] f. isohyet; line of equal rain fall
izohipsa [ee-zo-**kheep**-sah] f. line of equal elevation
izokefalia [ee-zo-ke-**fahl**-yah] f. isocephaly (an ancient painting style)
izokefaliczny [ee-zo-ke-fah-**leech**-ni] adj.m. isocephalic
izokefalizm [ee-zo-ke-**fah**-leezm] m. isocephalism
izoklina [ee-zo-**klee**-nah] f. isocline
izoklinalny [ee-zo-klee-**nahl**-ni] adj.m. isoclinal
izolacja [ee-zo-**lah**-tsyah] f. isolation; insulation; seal; seclusion; insulator; insulating substance; insulating tape; lag; lagging
izolacjonista [ee-zo-lah-tsyo-**ńees**-tah] m. isolationist
izolacjonistyczny [ee-zo-lah-tsyo-ńees-**tich**-ni] adj.m. isolationist
izolacjonizm [ee-zo-lah-**tsyo**-ńeezm] m. isolationism
izolacyjność [ee-zo-lah-**tsiy**-nośhćh] f. isolationist tendency
izolacyjny [ee-zo-lah-**tsiy**-ni] adj.m. isolating; insulating
izolata [ee-so-**lah**-tah] f. slang: isolation ward; separate cell; solitary confinement (mob jargon)
izolatka [ee-so-**laht**-kah] f. slang: isolation ward; separate cell; solitary confinement (mob jargon)
izolator [ee-zo-**lah**-tor] m. insulator; non-conductor; insulating substance
izolatorium [ee-zo-lah-**tor**-yoom] n. isolation hospital
izoleksa [ee-zo-**lek**-sah] f. line on a map showing a lexical phenomenon
izolować [ee-zo-**lo**-vahćh] v. isolate; seclude; sequester; insulate; waterproof; dampproof; sound-proof (*repeatedly*)
izolować się [ee-zo-**lo**-vahćh śh<u>an</u>] v. seclude oneself; live in seclusion (*repeatedly*)
izolowanie [ee-zo-lo-**vah**-ńe] n. insulating
izomer [ee-**zo**-mer] m. isomer
izomerazy [ee-zo-me-**rah**-zi] pl. a group of catalatic enzymes
izomeria [ee-zo-**mer**-yah] f. isomery; isomerism
izomeryczny [ee-zo-me-**rich**-ni] adj.m. isomeric
izomeryzacja [ee-zo-me-ri-**zah**-tsyah] f. isomerization
izomeryzm [ee-zo-**me**-rizm] m. isomerism
izomeryzować [ee-zo-me-ri-**zo**-vahćh] v. isomerize (*repeatedly*)
izometria [ee-zo-**metr**-yah] f. isometry
izometrycznie [ee-zo-met-**rich**-ńe] adv. isometrically
izometryczny [ee-zo-met-**rich**-ni] adj.m. isometric (drawing, line,

projection, etc.); isometrical
izomorfa [ee-zo-**mor**-fah] f. line on a map showing distribution of an isomorphic characteristic of a language
izomorficznie [ee-zo-mor-**feech**-ńe] adv. isomorphically
izomorficzny [ee-zo-mor-**feech**-ni] adj.m. isomorphic; isomorphous
izomorfizm [ee-zo-**mor**-feezm] m. isomorphism
izonitryl [ee-zo-**ńee**-tril] m. isonitril; isonitrile
izonomia [ee-zo-**nom**-yah] f. isonomy
izooktan [ee-zo-**ok**-tahn] m. isooctane
izopleta [ee-zo-**ple**-tah] f. isopleth
izopern [ee-**zo**-pern] m. isoperne
izosejsta [ee-zo-**sey**-stah] f. isoseismal line
izostatycznie [ee-zo-stah-**tich**-ńe] adv. isostatically
izostatyczny [ee-zo-stah-**tich**-ni] adj.m. isostatic
izostazja [ee-zo-**stah**-zyah] f. isostasy
izostrukturalność [ee-zo-strook-too-**rahl**-nośhćh] f. occurrence of the same crystalline structure in different substances
izosylabiczny [ee-zo-si-lah-**beech**-ni] adj.m. of the same number of syllables in each line
izosylabizm [ee-zo-si-**lah**-beezm] m. the same number of syllables in each line
izoterma [ee-zo-**ter**-mah] f. isotherm; line plotted to show an equal temperature
izotermia [ee-zo-**ter**-myah] f. equality of temperature; isothermal region
izotermicznie [ee-zo-ter-**meech**-ńe] adv. isothermally
izotermiczny [ee-zo-ter-**meech**-ni] adj.m. isothermic; isothermal
izotonicznie [ee-zo-to-**ńeech**-ńe] adv. isotonically
izotoniczność [ee-zo-to-**ńeech**-nośhćh] f. isotonicity
izotoniczny [ee-zo-to-**ńeech**-ni] adj.m. isotonic
izotop [ee-**zo**-top] m. isotope
izotopia [ee-zo-**to**-pyah] f. isotopy
izotopowo [ee-zo-to-**po**-vo] adv. isotopically
izotopowy [ee-zo-to-**po**-vi] adj.m. isotopic
izotropia [ee-zo-**tro**-pyah] f. isotropy
izotropowy [ee-zo-tro-**po**-vi] adj.m. isotropic
izotypia [ee-zo-**ti**-pyah] f. occurrence of the same crystalline structure in different substances
Izraelczyk [eez-rah-**el**-chik] m Israelite
izraelicki [eez-rah-e-**lee**-tskee] adj.m. Israeli; of Israel
Izraelita [eez-rah-e-**lee**-tah] m. Israelite; citizen of Israel
iż [eesh] conj.: that (literary exp.)
iżby [**eezh**-bi] conj. in order that; in order to; lest; so that
iżby wiedział [**eezh**-bi **vye**-dźhahw] exp.: so that he might know; so that he would know
iżby to zrobił [**eezh**-bi to **zro**-beew] exp.: so that he might do it; so that he would do it

J

J, j [y] the letter "jot" [yot]
ja [yah] pron.: I; myself; n. (not declined) self
to ja [to yah] exp.: it's me
świadomość swego ja [śhfyah-**do**-mośhćh **sfe**-go yah] exp.: the consciousness of self
jabcok [**yahp**-tsok] m. colloq: apple cider; colloq: cheap wine
jabłczak [**yahp**-chahk] m. pome (fruit); apple
jabłczanka [yahp-**chahn**-kah] f. apple soup
jabłczany [yahp-**chah**-ni] adj.m. of apples; apple (pie, etc.)
jabłecznik [yahb-**wech**-ńeek] m. apple cider; apple pie
jabłeczny [yahb-**wech**-ni] adj.m. of apples; apple (pie, etc.)
jabłko [**yahp**-ko] n. apple; globe; (king's) orb; masthead; colloq:

kneecap
dzikie jabłko [**dźhee**-ke **yahp**-ko] exp.: crab; crab apple
jabłko Adama [**yahp**-ko ah-**dah**-mah] exp.: Adam's apple
jabłkowaty [yahp-ko-**vah**-ti] adj.m. apple-shaped
jabłkowiec [yahp-**ko**-vyets] m. apple-blossom weevil
jabłkowity [yahp-ko-**vee**-ti] adj.m. dapple-gray (horse)
jabłkowy [yahp-**ko**-vi] adj.m. of an apple; of apples; apple (blossom, etc.)
jabłkowe [yahp-**ko**-ve] pl. the Pomoideae family of plants
kwieciak jabłkowy [**kfye**-ćhahk yahp-**ko**-vi] exp.: apple-blossom weevil
jabłkóweczka [yahp-koo-**vech**-kah] f. a butterfly whose larva feeds on apple trees and pear trees
jabłkówka [yahp-**koof**-kah] f. a moth; colloq: kind of apple-cake
jabłoneczka [yahb-wo-**nech**-kah] f. (small, nice) apple tree
jabłoniowy [yahb-wo-**ńo**-vi] adj.m. of an apple tree; of apple trees; apple (blossom, etc.)
jabłonka [yahb-**won**-kah] f. (young) apple tree
jabłonkowy [yahb-won-**ko**-vi] adj.m. of an apple tree; of apple trees; apple (blossom, orchard, etc.)
jabłoń [**yahb**-woń] f. apple tree
dzika jabłoń [**dźhee**-kah **yahb**-woń] exp.: crab; crab tree
rajska jabłoń [**rahys**-kah **yahb**-woń] exp.: shrubby form of common apple
jabłuszko [yahb-**woosh**-ko] n. (small, nice) apple
rajskie jabłuszko [**rahys**-ke yahb-**woosh**-ko] exp.: apple-john
jachcik [**yahkh**-ćheek] m. (small) yacht
jacht [yahkht] m. yacht
pływać na jachcie [**pwi**-vahćh nah **yahkh**-ćhe] exp.: to yacht
żeglować na jachcie [zheg-**lo**-vahćh nah **yahkh**-ćhe] exp.: to yacht; to sail a yacht
jachting [**yahkh**-teenk] m. yachting
jachtingowy [yahkh-teen-**go**-vi] adj.m. yachting (cruise, etc.)
jachtklub [**yahkht**-kloop] m. yacht club (for cruises, racing, etc.)
jachtowy [yahkh-**to**-vi] adj.m. yachting (sport, etc.)
jaczka [**yahch**-kah] f. (small) jacket
jaczy [**yah**-chi] adj.m. yak's (hide, etc.)
jad [yaht] m. venom; poison
jad chorobowy [yaht kho-ro-**bo**-vi] exp.: virus
jadaczka [yah-**dahch**-kah] f. vulg.: potato-trap; mouth
zamknij jadaczkę [**zahmk**-ńeey yah-**dahch**-kan] exp.: vulg.: Shut up!; Stop talking!
jadać [**yah**-dahćh] v. eat (regularly); have something to eat (*repeatedly*)
jadalnia [yah-**dahl**-ńah] f. dining room; mess; mess hall
jadalniany [yah-dahl-**ńah**-ni] adj.m. of dining room; of mess; of mess hall
jadalniowy [yah-dahl-**ńo**-vi] adj.m. of dining room; of mess; of mess hall
jadalny [yah-**dahl**-ni] adj.m. eatable; edible; cooking (oil, etc.); dining (room)
pokój jadalny [**po**-kooy yah-**dahl**-ni] exp.: dining room; mess room
jadanie [yah-**dah**-ńe] n. the custom of eating; the habit of eating
jadeit [yah-**de**-eet] m. jadeite (mineral)
jadeitowy [yah-de-ee-**to**-vi] adj.m. jadeitic
jadło [**yah**-dwo] n. food; edibles; eatables; fare; foodstuff
jadłodajnia [yah-dwo-**dahy**-ńah] f. restaurant; eating house; chophouse; cookshop
jadłospis [yah-**dwo**-spees] m. menu; bill of fare
jadłospisowy [yah-dwo-spee-**so**-vi] adj.m. of a menu; of bill of fare; menu (item, etc.)
jadłowstręt [yah-**dwo**-fstrant] m. anorexia
jadłowstrętowy [yah-dwo-fstran-**to**-vi] adj.m. anoretic; of anorexia nervosa
jadowicie [yah-do-**vee**-ćhe] adv.

venomously; virulently; scathingly
jadowitość [yah-do-**vee**-tośhćh] f. venomousness; virulence; vitriol
jadowity [yah-do-**vee**-ti] adj.m. poisonous; venomous; toxic; scathing; viperine
jadowy [yah-**do**-vi] adj.m. poison-bearing; poisonous; venomous
gruczoł jadowy [**groo**-chow yah-**do**-vi] exp.: poison-gland
jadzica [yah-**dźhee**-tsah] f. toxemia
jafetycki [yah-fe-**tits**-kee] adj.m. Japhetic
jaga [**yah**-gah] f. kind of fur coat
baba-jaga [**bah**-bah **yah**-gah] exp.: witch
jagielloński [yah-ge-**loń**-skee] adj.m. Jagellonian
jagielnik [yah-**gel**-ńeek] m. millet-making device
jagiełka [yah-**gew**-kah] f. (nice, small) millet
jaglany [yah-**glah**-ni] adj.m. of millet; millet (pap, porridge, etc.)
kasza jaglana [**kah**-shah yah-**glah**-nah] exp.: millet-groat (porridge)
jaglica [yah-**glee**-tsah] f. trachoma; (chronic contagious) viral eye infection
jagliczy [yah-**glee**-chi] adj.m. trachomatous
jagła [**yah**-gwah] f. millet; trachomatous granulation
jagniątko [yahg-**ńownt**-ko] n. little lamb
jagnić się [**yahg**-ńeećh śhan] v. give birth to a lamb (*repeatedly*)
jagnię [**yahg**-ńan] n. lamb; lambskin
jagnięcy [yahg-**ńan**-tsi] adj.m. of a lamb; lamb's; lamb-like; lamb (fur, etc.)
jagoda [yah-**go**-dah] f. berry; colloq: cheek
czarna jagoda [**chahr**-nah yah-**go**-dah] exp.: blueberry
jagodnica [yah-god-**ńee**-tsah] f. a spirochetotic tropical disease
jagodnik [yah-**god**-ńeek] m. blueberry patch; berry patch; blueberry syrup; blueberry wine
jagododajny [yah-go-do-**dahy**-ni] adj.m. berry-bearing; bacciferous
jagodowisko [yah-go-do-**vees**-ko] n. blueberry patch; berry patch; berry thicket
jagodowy [yah-go-**do**-vi] adj.m. of a berry; of berries; berry-bearing; bacciferous
zupa jagodowa [**zoo**-pah yah-go-**do**-vah] exp.: berry soup
jagodówka [yah-go-**doof**-kah] f. berry vodka; uvea (of the iris)
jagodówkowy [yah-go-doof-**ko**-vi] adj.m. of berry vodka; uveal
jaguar [yah-**goo**-ahr] m. jaguar; American leopard; Jaguar car
jajczarski [yahy-**chahr**-skee] adj.m. egg-producing; egg-dealing
ferma jajczarska [**fer**-mah yahy-**chahr**-skah] exp.: egg farm
jajczarstwo [yahy-**chahr**-stfo] n. egg-production; egg-dealing
jaje [**yah**-ye] n. colloq: egg
jajeczko [yah-**yech**-ko] n. small egg
jajeczkowanie [yah-yech-ko-**vah**-ńe] n. ovulation
jajecznica [yah-yech-**ńee**-tsah] f. scrambled eggs
jajecznik [yah-**yech**-ńeek] m. eggnog
jajeczny [yah-**yech**-ni] adj.m. of eggs; egg (powder, yolk, etc.)
jajko [**yahy**-ko] n. egg (small)
jajko na twardo [**yahy**-ko nah **tfahr**-do] exp.: hard-boiled egg
jajko na miękko [**yahy**-ko nah **myank**-ko] exp.: soft-boiled egg
jajkowaty [yahy-ko-**vah**-ti] adj.m. egg-shaped; oval
jajnik [**yahy**-ńeek] m. ovary
usunąć jajniki samicy [oo-**soo**-nownćh yahy-**ńee**-kee sah-**mee**-tsi] exp.: to spay an animal
jajnikowy [yahy-ńee-**ko**-vi] adj.m. ovarian
jajo [**yah**-yo] n. egg; ovum; egg-shaped object
bezpłodne jajo [bes-**pwod**-ne **yah**-yo] exp.: wind-egg
jaja mięczaków [**yah**-yah myan-**chah**-koof] exp.: spat
jaja ryb [**yah**-yah rip] exp.: spawn
jaja w proszku [**yah**-yah f **prosh**-koo] exp.: dried eggs; dehydrated eggs; desiccated eggs; powdered eggs
kukułcze jajo [koo-**koow**-che **yah**-yo] exp.: foundling; cuckoo's egg

musze jajo [moo-she **yah**-yo] exp.: blow; flyblow
składać jaja [**skwah**-dahćh **yah**-yah] exp.: to spat (shellfish); to spawn (fish); to blow (flies)
świeże jajo [**śhfye**-zhe **yah**-yo] exp.: new-laid egg; fresh egg
wysiadywać jaja [vi-śhah-**di**-vahćh **yah**-yah] exp.: to brood; to hatch eggs; to be hatching
zepsute jajo [zep-**soo**-te **yah**-yo] exp.: rotten egg; bad egg

jajobójczy [yah-yo-**booy**-chi] adj.m. egg-killing (compound, etc.)

jajogłowy [yah-yo-**gwo**-vi] adj.m. egg-headed; having characteristics of an egghead; m. colloq: egghead; intellectual; highbrow

jajonośny [yah-yo-**nośh**-ni] adj.m. egg-laying
kura jajonośna [**koo**-rah yah-yo-**nośh**-nah] exp.: colloq: layer

jajorodność [yah-yo-**rod**-nośhćh] f. oviparity; oviparousness

jajorodny [yah-yo-**rod**-ni] adj.m. oviparous

jajowato [yah-yo-**vah**-to] adv. in shape of an oval; elliptically

jajowaty [yah-yo-**vah**-ti] adj.m. egg-shaped; ovate; oval; elliptical; ovoid

jajownik [yah-**yov**-ńeek] m. egg-shaped ornament; ovum; egg-and-dart ornament

jajownikowy [yah-yov-ńee-**ko**-vi] adj.m. of egg-shaped ornament; of ovum; of egg-and-dart ornament

jajowodowy [yah-yo-vo-**do**-vi] adj.m. tubal

jajowód [yah-**yo**-voot] m. Fallopian tube; oviduct

jajowy [yah-**yo**-vi] adj.m. of an egg; egg (membrane, albumen, etc.)

jajożyworodność [yah-yo-zhi-vo-**rod**-nośhćh] f. full development of a reptile inside its egg

jajożyworodny [yah-yo-zhi-vo-**rod**-ni] adj.m. of reptile fully developed inside its egg

jak [yahk] adv. how; as; if; than; m. yak
jak gdyby [yahk **gdi**-bi] adv. as if; seemingly; sort of; so to say; as much as to say; as though; as it were
jak najlepiej [yahk nahy-**le**-pyey] exp.: with the greatest diligence
jak to? [yahk to] exp.: how so?; how's that?; what do you mean?; is it possible?
jak zwykle [yahk **zvik**-le] exp.: as usually

jaka [**yah**-kah] pronoun f. what; which; f. jacket

jakby [**yahk**-bi] adv. as if; if; conj.: if; seemingly; colloq: sort of
tak jakby [tahk **yahk**-bi] exp.: almost; all but; practically; as good as

jaki [**yah**-kee] pronoun m. what; which one?; that; what a (genius, etc.); some; of some kind; like
byle jaki [**bi**-le **yah**-kee] exp.: any one; no matter which; paltry; shabby
jaki bądź [**yah**-kee bownćh] exp.: paltry; shabby; no mean...
jaki on jest? [**yah**-kee on yest] exp.: what is he like?
jakich mało [**yah**-keekh **mah**-wo] exp.: rare; exceptionally good
jaki taki [**yah**-kee **tah**-kee] exp.: tolerable; so-so; not too bad; passable; barely good enough
jakie dwie godziny [**yah**-ke dvye go-**dźhee**-ni] exp.: two hours or so; about two hours; somewhere round two hours
po jaką cholerę? [po **yah**-kown kho-**le**-ran] exp.: vulg.: what the devil for?; what the hell for?
po jakiemu? [po yah-**ke**-moo] exp.: in what manner?; which way?; in what language?

jakie [**yah**-ke] pron. n. what; which = **jaki** (feminine & neuter)

jakikolwiek [yah-kee-**kol**-vyek] pron. whichever one; no matter which; any; whichever; whatsoever

jakiś [**yah**-keeśh] pron. some; unknown; strange; a certain

jakiśkolwiek [yah-keeśh-**kol**-vyek] pron. someone; no matter which; any one; whichever; whatsoever

jakiż [yah-keesh] pronoun = (emphatic) **jaki**

jakkolwiek [yahk-**kol**-vyek] conj.: though; pronoun: somehow; anyhow; whichever; however; adv.: somehow; anyhow; as you like; however; no matter how; as you please; as you choose
jako [**yah**-ko] adv. as; by way of
jako tako [**yah**-ko **tah**-ko] exp.: so-so; tolerably well; not too badly; to a certain degree; as much as one can
jako żywo! [**yah**-ko **zhi**-vo] excl.: as I live!
jakobin [yah-**ko**-been] m. Jacobin
jakobinizm [yah-ko-**bee**-ńeezm] m. Jacobinism
jakobinka [yah-ko-**been**-kah] f. zinnia (plant)
jakobiński [yah-ko-**beeń**-skee] adj.m. Jacobinic; Jacobinical
jakoby [yah-**ko**-bi] conj. that; adv. supposedly; by all accounts; like; as if
jakoś [**yah**-kośh] adv. somehow (or other); one way or another
jakoś to będzie [**yah**-kośh to **ban**-dźhe] exp.: it'll turn out all right; let's hope for the best
jakościować [yah-kośh-**ćho**-vahćh] v. grade; segregate according to quality (*repeatedly*)
jakościowanie [yah-kośh-ćho-**vah**-ńe] n. grading; segregation according to quality
jakościowo [yah-kośh-**ćho**-vo] adv. qualitatively; as regards a quality
jakościowy [yah-kośh-**ćho**-vi] adj.m. of quality; qualitative; in quality; quality (merchandise)
jakość [**yah**-kośhćh] f. quality; standard; kind
kiepska jakość [**kep**-skah **yah**-kośhćh] exp.: poor quality; low standard
jakowyś [yah-**ko**-viśh] pron. = **jakiś**
jakoż [yah-kosh] conj. and so; therefore
jaksztag [**yahk**-shtahg] m. mast reinforcing tension line
jakubka [yah-**koop**-kah] f. knotted access line (from boat to ship)
jakubówka [yah-koo-**boof**-kah] f. (common) pear (fruit or tree)
Jakut [**yah**-koot] m. Yakut
jakże [**yahg**-zhe] pron. how on earth = (emphatic) **jak**
a jakże! [ah **yahg**-zhe] exp.: yes indeed!; oh yes!; of course!; certainly!; by all means!; colloq: sure!; sure thing!; naturally!
jakżeby [**yahg**-zhe-bi] pron. = (conditional) **jakże**
jakżesz [**yahg**-zhesh] pron. = (emphatic) **jakże**
jalapa [yah-**lah**-pah] f. jalap (plant)
jałmużna [yahw-**moozh**-nah] f. an alms; alms; charity; endowment
żyć z jałmużny [zhićh z yahw-**moozh**-ni] exp.: to live on charity
jałmużnictwo [yahw-moozh-**ńeets**-tfo] n. giving charity; receiving charity; acting as an almoner
jałmużniczy [yahw-moozh-**ńee**-chi] adj.m. charitable
jałmużnik [yahw-**moozh**-ńeek] f. almoner
jałoszka [yah-**wosh**-kah] f. colloq: heifer
jałowcowy [yah-wof-**tso**-vi] adj.m. of juniper; juniper (berry, tree, etc.)
jałowcówka [yah-wof-**tsoof**-kah] f. juniper-flavored vodka
jałowica [yah-wo-**vee**-tsah] f. colloq: heifer
jałowić [yah-**wo**-veećh] v. reduce to barrenness; render sterile (*repeatedly*)
jałowiec [yah-**wo**-vyets] m. juniper; juniper tree (Juniperus)
jałowieć [yah-**wo**-vyećh] v. grow sterile; grow unproductive; become barren (*repeatedly*)
jałowienie [yah-wo-**vye**-ńe] n. becoming sterile
jałowizna [yah-wo-**veez**-nah] f. young cattle; barren land
jałownik [yah-**wov**-ńeek] m. young cattle; barn for young cattle
jałowo [yah-**wo**-vo] adv. barrenly; unfruitfully; fruitlessly; vapidly; insipidly; dryly; meagerly (food, etc.); slang: badly; poorly
jałowość [yah-**wo**-vośhćh] f. barrenness; sterility; dryness; vapidity; insipidity; insipidness; unprofitableness

jałowy [yah-**wo**-vi] adj.m. barren; sterile; arid; aseptic; dry; plain; unseasoned; tasteless; watery
jałóweczka [yah-woo-**vech**-kah] f. (small, young) heifer
jałówka [yah-**woof**-kah] f. heifer
jam [dzhem] m. colloq: (fruit) jam
jam session [dzhem **se**-shin] exp.: jam session; jazz session
jama [**yah**-mah] f. pit; hole; den; cavity; cave; burrow; hollow; cavern; fossa
jama ustna [**yah**-mah **oost**-nah] exp.: oral cavity
jamajka [yah-**mahy**-kah] f. Jamaica rum
jamb [yahmp] m. iamb
jambiczny [yahm-**beech**-ni] adj.m. iambic
jamboree [**dzhem**-bo-ree] n. jamboree
jamistość [yah-**mees**-tośhćh] f. being covered with holes; cave-shape
jamisty [yah-**mees**-ti] adj.m. covered with holes; cave-shaped; forming a cavity
jamka [**yahm**-kah] f. (small) pit; hole; den; cavity; cave; burrow; hollow; cavern; fossa
jamniczek [yahm-**ńee**-chek] m. (small, nice) dachshund (male)
jamniczka [yahm-**ńeech**-kah] f. (small, nice) dachshund (female)
jamnik [**yahm**-ńeek] m. dachshund
jamnikowaty [yahm-ńee-ko-**vah**-ti] adj.m. looking like a dachshund
jamochłon [yah-**mo**-khwon] m. coelenterate
jamochłonny [yah-mo-**khwon**-ni] adj.m. coelenterate
jamochłony [yah-mo-**khwo**-ni] pl. the phylum Coelenterata; the Coelenterates
jamowy [yah-**mo**-vi] adj.m. of caves; of pits
janczar [**yahn**-chahr] m. janizary; janissary
janczarka [yahn-**chahr**-kah] f. janizary's (long barrel) gun
janczarski [yahn-**chahr**-skee] adj.m. of janizaries; janizarian; janissary (music, etc.)
jankes [**yahn**-kes] m. Yankee; slang: Yank
jankeski [yahn-**kes**-kee] adj.m. of Yankees; Yankee (manners, etc.)
janowiec [yah-**no**-vyets] m. genista; furze; broom; dyer's weed; greenweed
jansenista [yahn-se-**ńees**-tah] m. Jansenist
jansenistyczny [yahn-se-ńees-**tich**-ni] adj.m. Jansenistic
jansenizm [yahn-**se**-ńeezm] m. Jansenism; doctrinal system of C. Jansen (1585-1639)
jantar [**yahn**-tahr] m. amber
jantarowy [yahn-tah-**ro**-vi] adj.m. of amber; amber (beads, color, etc.); see: **bursztyn**
janusowy [yah-noo-**so**-vi] adj.m. Janus-faced
japa [**yah**-pah] f. colloq: mouth; face; muzzle; slang: mug; phiz
japać [**yah**-pahćh] v. slang: smoke cigarettes (jargon) (*repeatedly*)
japonista [yah-po-**ńees**-tah] m. student of Japanese philology
japonistyczny [yah-po-ńees-**tich**-ni] adj.m. of Japanese philology; of Japanese studies
japonistyka [yah-po-ńees-**ti**-kah] f. Japanese philology; Japanese studies
japonizm [yah-**po**-ńeezm] m. Japanism
Japonka [yah-**pon**-kah] f. Japanese woman; Japanese wheelbarrow
japonolog [yah-po-**no**-log] m. student of Japanese philology and culture
japonologia [yah-po-no-**lo**-gyah] f. Japanese philology and culture
Japończyk [yah-**poń**-chik] m. Japanese; of Japan; slang: Jap
Japończycy [yah-poń-**chi**-tsi] pl. the Japanese; slang: the Japs
japoński [yah-**poń**-skee] adj.m. Japanese; of Japan; Nipponian
po japońsku [po yah-**poń**-skoo] exp.: in Japanese
japońskość [yah-**pońs**-kośhćh] f. Japanese character
japońszczyzna [yah-pońsh-**chiz**-nah] f. Japanese language, culture, art; Japanese curios; things Japanese

jar [yahr] m. canyon; ravine; gully; gorge
jarać [**yah**-rahćh] v. slang: smoke cigarettes (jargon) (*repeatedly*)
jaranie [yah-**rah**-ńe] n. slang: smoking cigarettes (mob jargon)
jard [yahrd] m. yard
jarka [**yahr**-kah] f. spring crop; young ewe
jarl [yahrl] m. earl (Scandinavian)
jarlica [yahr-**lee**-tsah] f. spring crop; young ewe
jarliczka [yahr-**leech**-kah] f. (small) spring crop; young ewe
jarmarczność [yahr-**mahrch**-nośhćh] f. character of a fair; shoddiness; trashy character; showiness; vulgarity
jarmarczny [yahr-**mahrch**-ni] adj.m. of a fair; fair-time (purchase, etc.) shoddy; trashy; tawdry; showy; vulgar
jarmark [**yahr**-mahrk] m. fair
jarmarkowy [yahr-mahr-**ko**-vi] adj.m. fair (day, etc.)
jarmułka [yahr-**moow**-kah] f. skullcap
jarmuż [**yahr**-moosh] m. kale; variety of cabbage
jarosz [**yah**-rosh] m. vegetarian
jarować [yah-**ro**-vahćh] v. vernalize (*repeatedly*)
jarowanie [yah-ro-**vah**-ńe] n. vernalization
jarowizacja [yah-ro-vee-**zah**-tsyah] f. vernalization
jarowizacyjny [yah-ro-vee-zah-**tsiy**-ni] adj.m. of vernalization
jarowizować [yah-ro-vee-**zo**-vahćh] v. vernalize (*repeatedly*)
jarowizowanie [yah-ro-vee-zo-**vah**-ńe] n. vernalization
jarski [**yahr**-skee] adj.m. vegetarian; meatless
jary [**yah**-ri] adj.m. robust; vigorous; hale; spring (wheat, rye, etc.)
jaryzacja [yah-ri-**zah**-tsyah] f. vernalization
jarząb [**yah**-zhownp] m. sorb; servicetree
jarząb mączny [**yah**-zhownp **mownch**-ni] exp.: whitebeam
jarząbek [yah-**zhown**-bek] m. hazel grouse; hazel hen
jarząbkowy [yah-zhownb-**ko**-vi] adj.m. hazel-grouse (nest, etc.); hazel-hen (food, etc.)
jarząco [yah-**zhown**-tso] adv. in a glow; glowingly
jarzący [yah-**zhown**-tsi] adj.m. glowing
jarzec [**yah**-zhets] m. colloq: spring barley
jarzenie się [yah-**zhe**-ńe śhan] n. glow; luminescence
jarzeniowy [yah-zhe-**ńo**-vi] adj.m. glow (lamp, etc.)
jarzeniówka [yah-zhe-**ńoof**-kah] f. glow lamp
jarzębaty [yah-zhan-**bah**-ti] adj.m. dappled
jarzębiak [yah-**zhanb**-yahk] m. vodka flavored with rowan-berries; sorb brandy; rowan-berry vodka
jarzębiaty [yah-zhan-**byah**-ti] adj.m. dappled
jarzębina [yah-zhan-**bee**-nah] f. mountain ash; rowan; rowan-berry
jarzębinka [yah-zhan-**been**-kah] f. (small, nice) mountain ash; rowan; rowan-berry
jarzębinowaty [yah-zhan-bee-no-**vah**-ti] adj.m. like mountain ash; like a rowan
jarzębinowy [yah-zhan-bee-**no**-vi] adj.m. of the mountain ash; rowan (tree, etc.)
jarzębinówka [yah-zhan-bee-**noof**-kah] f. vodka flavored with rowan-berries; sorb brandy; rowan-berry vodka
jarzębolistny [yah-zhan-bo-**leest**-ni] adj.m. having rowanlike leaves
jarzmo [**yahzh**-mo] n. yoke; shackles; thraldom; shackle; trestle; bondage
jarzmowy [yahzh-**mo**-vi] adj.m. of a yoke; of shackles; of bondage; yoke (bone, etc.); zygomatic
jarzyć [**yah**-zhićh] v. sparkle; glitter; glow; shimmer (*repeatedly*)
jarzyć się [**yah**-zhićh śhan] v. sparkle; glitter; glow; shimmer; be glowing with colors; be sparkling (*repeatedly*)
jarzyna [yah-**zhi**-nah] f. vegetable;

dish of vegetables
jarzyniak [yah-**zhi**-ńahk] m. knife for peeling vegetables
jarzyniarka [yah-zhi-**ńahr**-kah] f. (woman) greengrocer; device for peeling vegetables; vegetable peeler
jarzyniarnia [yah-zhi-**ńahr**-ńah] f. greengrocer's store
jarzyniarski [yah-zhi-**ńahr**-skee] adj.m. greengrocer's; greengrocers'
jarzyniarstwo [yah-zhi-**ńahr**-stfo] n. greengrocer's business; storage of green groceries
jarzyniarz [yah-**zhi**-ńahsh] m. greengrocer
jarzynka [yah-**zhin**-kah] f. young vegetable; dish of vegetables
jarzynowy [yah-zhi-**no**-vi] adj.m. of vegetables; vegetable (soup, dish, etc.)
jarzynówka [yah-zhi-**noof**-kah] f. a noctuid moth
jasełka [yah-**sew**-kah] pl. crib; Nativity play; creche
jasełkowość [yah-sew-**ko**-vośhćh] f. atmosphere of Nativity play; nature of Nativity-play
jasełkowy [yah-sew-**ko**-vi] adj.m. of Nativity play; Nativity-play (characters, etc.)
jasiek [**yah**-śhek] m. little pillow; bean; beans; bean dish
jasieniec [yah-**śhe**-ńets] m. sheep's-bit (plat)
jaskier [**yahs**-ker] m. buttercup; crowfoot; goldilocks; spearwort
jaskinia [yahs-**kee**-ńah] f. cave; grotto
jaskiniowiec [yah-skee-**ńo**-vyets] m. cave dweller; cave man
jaskiniowy [yah-skee-**ńo**-vi] adj.m. of caves; cave (drawing, man, dweller, etc.)
jaskinioznawstwo [yah-skee-ńo-**znahf**-stfo] n. speleology
jaskółczę [yahs-**koow**-chan] n. swallow's fledgling
jaskółczy [yahs-**koow**-chi] adj.m. swallow's (flight, nest, etc.)
jaskółczy ogon [yahs-**koow**-chi **o**-gon] exp.: dovetail (joint)
jaskółeczka [yahs-koo-**wech**-kah] f. (small, nice) swallow
jaskółka [yahs-**koow**-kah] f. swallow; martin; harbinger; theater gallery; trial balloon; test review; a figure in figure skating; swallow dive; swan dive
jaskra [**yahsk**-rah] f. glaucoma
jaskrawić się [yahs-**krah**-veećh śhan] v. glow vividly; glow brightly; glow with colors (*repeatedly*)
jaskrawieć [yahs-**krah**-vyećh] v. become bright; glow vividly; glow brightly; glow with colors (*repeatedly*)
jaskrawienie [yahs-krah-**vye**-ńe] n. becoming bright; glowing vividly; glowing brightly
jaskrawo [yahs-**krah**-vo] adv. vividly; brightly; glaringly; glowingly; brilliantly; gaudily; garishly; strikingly
jaskrawoczerwony [yahs-**krah**-vo-cher-**vo**-ni] adj.m. bright-red (color); intensely red; vivid red
jaskrawościomierz [yahs-krah-vośh-**ćho**-myesh] m. light meter; brightness gauge
jaskrawość [yahs-**krah**-vośhćh] f. vividness; brightness; dazzling brightness; gaudiness
jaskrawozielony [yahs-krah-vo-źhe-**lo**-ni] adj.m. bright green (color); vivid green; intensely green
jaskrawożółty [yahs-krah-vo-**zhoow**-ti] adj.m. bright yellow (color); vivid yellow; intensely yellow
jaskrawy [yahs-**krah**-vi] adj.m. glowing; showy; vivid; bright (with colors); striking; glaring; extreme (views, etc.); flagrant; gaudy; garish; merry; dazzling; flaming; flash
jaskrowaty [yahs-kro-**vah**-ti] adj.m. ranunculaceous (plant)
jaskrowate [yahs-kro-**vah**-te] pl. Ranunculaceae plant family; the crowfoot family
jaskrowy [yahs-**kro**-vi] adj.m. glaucomatous
jasło [**yahs**-wo] n. feeding (two-sided) trough; manger
jasmon [**yahs**-mon] m. ketone of jasmine

jasno [**yahs**-no] adv. clearly; brightly; brilliantly; glaringly; intensely; serenely; placidly; lucidly; perspicuously; cheerfully; plainly; explicitly; unequivocally; definitely
jasno się wyrażać [**yahs**-no śhan vi-**rah**-zhahćh] exp.: to make oneself clear
jasnoblond [**yahs**-no-blont] adj.m. fair; fair-haired; blond; flaxen
jasnobłękitny [**yahs**-no-bwan-**keet**-ni] adj.m. light-blue; pale-blue
jasnobrązowy [**yahs**-no-brown-**zo**-vi] adj.m. light-brown; biscuit; ecru
jasnoczerwony [**yahs**-no-cher-**vo**-ni] adj.m. light-red; pale-red
jasnogłowy [**yahs**-no-**gwo**-vi] adj.m. fair-haired; blond; flaxen-haired
jasnokawowy [**yahs**-no-kah-**vo**-vi] adj.m. of a light-creme color; light-brown; biscuit; ecru
jasnolicy [**yahs**-no-lee-tsi] adj.m. fair-complexioned
jasnoniebieski [**yahs**-no-ńeb-**yes**-kee] adj.m. light-blue; pale-blue
jasnooki [**yahs**-no-**o**-kee] adj.m. clear-eyed
jasnopłowy [**yahs**-no-**pwo**-vi] adj.m. flaxen
jasnopopielaty [**yahs**-no-po-pye-**lah**-ti] adj.m. light-gray; pale-gray
jasnoróżowy [**yahs**-no-roo-**zho**-vi] adj.m. of a pale pink (color)
jasnoskóry [**yahs**-no-**skoo**-ri] adj.m. fair-skinned
jasnoszary [**yahs**-no-**shah**-ri] adj.m. light-gray; pale-gray
jasność [**yahs**-nośhćh] f. light; brilliance; glow; clarity; sheen; radiance; intensity of light; vividness; luminosity; whiteness; paleness (of color); clearness; lucidity; distinctness; perspicuity; precision
jasnota [yahs-**no**-tah] f. dead-nettle (plant)
jasnowidz [yahs-**no**-veets] m. clairvoyant person; crystal gazer; seer (of future events)
jasnowidząco [yahs-no-vee-**dzown**-tso] adv. clairvoyantly; prophetically
jasnowidzący [yahs-no-vee-**dzown**-tsi] adj.m. clairvoyant; prophetic; m. clairvoyant person; crystal gazer; seer (of future events)
jasnowidzenie [yahs-no-vee-**dze**-ńe] n. clairvoyance; second sight; crystal gazing
jasnowidztwo [yahs-no-**veets**-tfo] n. clairvoyance; second sight; crystal gazing
jasnowłosy [**yahs**-no-**vwo**-si] adj.m. fair-haired; flaxen-haired; blond
jasnowłosa [**yahs**-no-**vwo**-sah] adj.f. fair-haired (woman); flaxen-haired; blond-haired
jasnozielony [**yahs**-no-źhe-**lo**-ni] adj.m. light-green; pale-green; sap-green
jasnozłocisty [**yahs**-no-zwo-**ćhees**-ti] adj.m. gold-yellow; golden (hair, etc.)
jasnozłoty [**yahs**-no-**zwo**-ti] adj.m. gold-yellow; golden (hair, etc.); golden-haired (person, etc.)
jasnożółty [**yahs**-no-**zhoow**-ti] adj.m. light-yellow; pale-yellow
jasny [**yahs**-ni] adj.m. clear; bright; light; shining; noble; luminous; glaring; with plenty of light; sunny; pale; intense; resplendent; brilliant; dazzling; sunny; cloudless; serene; cheerful; placid; carefree; propitious; pale; fair; blond; bright-colored; lucid; perspicuous; plane; obvious; evident; distinct; explicit; unequivocal; definite; straightforwad (man, etc.)
jasne [**yahs**-ne] adj.n. clear; n. clear beer; colloq: understood; of course; naturally; evidently; colloq: light beer
jaspis [**yahs**-pees] m. jasper
jaspisowy [yahs-pee-**so**-vi] adj.m. of jasper; jasper (ware, green, etc.)
jastrun [**yahs**-troon] m. chrysanthemum
jastrych [**yahs**-trikh] m. gypsum floor without joints
jastrychowy [yahs-tri-**kho**-vi] adj.m. of gypsum floor without joints
jastrząb [**yahs**-tshownp] m. falcon; hawk; goshawk
jastrząbek [yahs-**tshown**-bek] m. (young, small) falcon; hawk;

goshawk; sparrow hawk
jastrzębi [yahs-**tshan**-bee] adj.m. falcon's; hawk's; accipitral; like a hawk
jastrzębiec [yahs-tshan-byets] m. hawkweed (Hieratium)
jasyr [**yah**-sir] m. Tatar captivity; Turkish captivity; captives taken by the Tartars (or Turks)
jaszcz [yahshch] m. armored container for ammunition
jaszcz amunicyjny [yahshch ah-moo-ńee-**tsiy**-ni] exp.: ammunition trailer
jaszcz artyleryjski [yahshch ahr-ti-le-**riy**-skee] exp.: artillery caisson
jaszczur [**yahsh**-choor] m. salamander; saurian; shagreen (leather)
jaszczurczy [yahsh-**choor**-chi] adj.m. lizard's; lizardlike; reptile; colloq: mean; grovelling
jaszczureczka [yahsh-choo-**rech**-kah] f. (small, little) lizard; reptile
jaszczurka [yahsh-**choor**-kah] f. lizard; reptile
jaszczurki [yahsh-**choor**-kee] pl. lizards; reptiles; Sauria; Lacertilia; colloq: molding tools
jaszczurowy [yahsh-choo-**ro**-vi] adj.m. of shagreen; shagreened
jaszczyk [**yahsh**-chik] m. (small) munitions box; ammunition trailer
jaszmak [**yahsh**-mahk] m. yashmak (veil)
jaślinek [yahśh-**lee**-nek] m. mountain bindweed; soldanella
jaśmin [**yahśh**-meen] m. jasmine
jaśminowiec [yah-śhmee-**no**-vyets] m. jasmine shrub
jaśminowy [yah-śhmee-**no**-vi] adj.m. of the jasmine; jasmine (oil, etc.)
jaśnia [**yahśh**-ńah] f. = **jasność**
jaśnie [**yahśh**-ńe] adv. in exp.:
jaśnie wielmożny [**yahśh**-ńe vyel-**mozh**-ni] exp.: the Honorable
jaśnie oświecony [**yahśh**-ńe ośh-fye-**tso**-ni] exp.: His Grace
jaśnie pan [**yahśh**-ńe pahn] exp.: His Lordship
jaśnie pani [**yahśh**-ńe **pah**-ńee] exp.: Her Ladyship
jaśnieć [**yahśh**-ńećh] v. shine; sparkle; radiate; gleam; glimmer; glitter; pale; fade (*repeatedly*)
jaśniejący [yahśh-ńe-**yown**-tsi] adj.m. bright; brilliant; sheeny; refulgent
jaśnienie [yaśh-**ńe**-ńe] n. shining; fading
jaśniepanowie [yaśh-ńe-pah-**no**-vye] pl. Their Lordships; colloq: pretentious characters
jaśniepański [yaśh-ńe-**pahń**-skee] adj.m. lordly; superior; condescending; cavalier
jaśniepaństwo [yaśh-ńe-**pahń**-stfo] n. lordly manner; domineering; cavalier manner; upper ten thousand; aristocracy; nobility
jaśniutki [yahśh-**ńoot**-kee] adj.m. diminutive of: **jasny**
jata [**yah**-tah] f. slang: shed; shanty
jatagan [yah-**tah**-gahn] m. Yatagan; yataghan (Muslim short saber)
jatka [**yaht**-kah] f. butcher's stall
jatki [**yaht**-kee] pl. massacre; shambles; wholesale slaughter; scene of carnage
jatrochemia [yah-tro-**khem**-yah] f. iatrochemistry
jatrogenicznie [yah-tro-ge-**ńeech**-ńe] adv. iatrogenically
jatrogeniczny [yah-tro-ge-**ńeech**-ni] adj.m. iatrogenic
jatrogenny [yah-tro-**gen**-ni] adj.m. iatrogenic
jaw [yahf] m. consciousness; (one's) conscious state; reality
wydobyć na jaw [vi-**do**-bićh nah yahf] exp.: to unearth; to expose; to lay open to view
wyjść na jaw [viyśhćh nah yahf] exp.: to show itself; to become evident; to appear; to come out; to leak out; to transpire; to trickle out
jawa [**yah**-vah] f. consciousness; (one's) conscious state; reality
sen na jawie [sen nah **yah**-vye] exp.: walking dream
śnić na jawie [śhńeećh nah **yah**-vye] exp.: to daydream; to indulge in daydreams
Jawajczyk [yah-**vahy**-chik] m. Javanese
Jawajka [yah-**vahy**-kah] f. Javanese

woman; puppet doll
jawajski [yah-**vahy**-skee] adj.m. Javanese
Jawańczyk [yah-**vahń**-chik] m. Javanese
jawić [**yah**-veećh] v. appear; show; make public; disclose (*repeatedly*)
jawić się [**yah**-veećh śhan] v. appear; show oneself (*repeatedly*)
jawienie [yah-**vye**-ńe] n. disclosure
jawnie [**yahv**-ńe] adv. publicly; in public; openly; overtly; manifestly; evidently; patently; flagrantly; notoriously; avowedly; professedly; confessedly; admittedly
jawnogrzesznica [yahv-no-gzhesh-**ńee**-tsah] f. harlot
jawnopączkowy [yahv-no-pownch-**ko**-vi] adj.m. phanerogamous
jawność [**yahv**-nośhćh] f. public character (of a scandal, etc.); publicity; patency; notoriousness; flagrancy
jawny [**yahv**-ni] adj.m. evident; public; open; notorious; sheer; overt; manifest; apparent; declared (enemy, etc.); avowed; professed; admitted (adherent, etc.); downright (falsehood, etc.)
jawor [**yah**-vor] m. plane tree; maple tree; sycamore tree; sycamore wood (lumber)
jaworowy [yah-vo-**ro**-vi] adj.m. of plane tree; of maple tree; of sycamore tree; of sycamore wood; sycamore (lumber, etc.)
jaz [yahz] m. weir; milldam; dam; wear
jazda [**yahz**-dah] f. ride; driving; cavalry
jazda! [**yahz**-dah] exp.: off you go!; clear out!; come along!; go ahead!; here we go!; let's go!; let's get going!; let's start
jazda autem [**yahz**-dah **ahw**-tem] exp.: car ride; ride in a car
jazda figurowa [**yahz**-dah fee-goo-**ro**-vah] exp.: figure skating
jazda na łyżwach [**yahz**-dah nah **wizh**-vahkh] exp.: skating
jazda na nartach [**yahz**-dah nah **nahr**-tahkh] exp.: skiing
jazda na rowerze [**yahz**-dah nah ro-**ve**-zhe] exp.: riding a bicycle
konna jazda [**kon**-nah **yahz**-dah] exp.: horse-riding; riding on horseback
lekka jazda [lek-kah **yahz**-dah] exp.: light horse; light cavalry
prawo jazdy [**prah**-vo **yahz**-di] exp.: driver's license
rozkład jazdy [**ros**-kwaht **yahz**-di] exp.: flight schedule; train schedule; timetable
szkoła konnej jazdy [**shko**-wah **kon**-ney **yahz**-di] exp.: riding school; manege
jazgarnik [yahz-**gahr**-ńeek] m. ruff-net; pope-net
jazgarz [**yahz**-gahsh] m. ruff; pope (fish)
jazgot [**yahz**-got] m. hum; murmur of voices; clamor; vociferations; yelling; yells; hullabaloo; gibberish; clatter; rattle
jazgotać [yahz-**go**-tahćh] v. clamor; yell; vociferate; clatter; rattle (*repeatedly*)
jazgotanie [yahz-go-**tah**-ńe] n. hum; murmur of voices; clamor; vociferations; yelling; yells; hullabaloo; gibberish; clatter; rattle
jazgotliwie [yahz-go-**tlee**-vye] adv. vociferously; clamorously; shrilly
jazgotliwy [yahz-go-**tlee**-vi] adj.m. vociferous; clamorous; shrill
jazowy [yah-**zo**-vi] adj.m. of a dam; of a weir; of a milldam; dam (spillway, etc.); weir (flow, etc.)
jazz [dzhez] m. jazz; jazz music; jazz band
jazzband [**dzhez**-bent] m. jazz band
jazz jamboree [dzhez dzhem-**bo**-ree] n. jazz jamboree
jazzman [**dzhez**-mahn] m. jazzman
jazzować [dzhe-**zo**-vahćh] v. jazz; play in the manner of jazz; play jazz; dance jazz (*repeatedly*)
jazzowy [dzhe-**zo**-vi] adj.m. of jazz; of jazz music; of a jazz band; jazz (band, etc.)
jaź [yahźh] f. ide (fish)
jaźń [yahźhń] f. ego; self; the I; the inner man; psyche
jaźwiec [**yahźh**-vyets] m. badger
ją [yown] pron.: her

jąć [yownćh] v. seize; grasp; begin; commence; start (doing, to do)
jąć się [yownćh śhan] v. take up; turn one's hand (to); take to (writing, etc.)
jąderko [yown-**der**-ko] n. molecule
jąderkowy [yown-der-**ko**-vi] adj.m. molecular
jądro [**yown**-dro] n. nucleus; testicle; kernel; core; gist of a matter; heart of a matter; testis
jądrowy [yown-**dro**-vi] adj.m. nuclear
błona jądrowa [**bwo**-nah yown-**dro**-vah] exp.: nuclear membrane
energia jądrowa [e-**nerg**-yah yown-**dro**-vah] exp.: nuclear energy
jądrzak [**yown**-dzhahk] m. pyrenomycete
jądrzaki [yown-**dzhah**-kee] pl. the Pyrenomycetes
jądrzasty [yown-**dzhahs**-ti] adj.m. nuclear; nucleary (Brit.); nucleiform
jąkać [**yown**-kahćh] v. stutter out; stammer out (*repeatedly*)
jąkać się [**yown**-kahćh śhan] v. stutter; stammer; stumble in one's speech (*repeatedly*)
jąkała [yown-**kah**-wah] m. stutterer; stammerer
jąkanie [yown-**kah**-ńe] n. stuttering out; stammering
jąkliwie [yownk-**lee**-vye] adv. stutteringly; stammeringly
jąkliwy [yownk-**lee**-vi] adj.m. stuttering; stammering; prone to stutter; prone to stammer
jątrzenie [yown-**tshe**-ńe] n. irritation; festering; vexing; embittering; inflaming
jątrzyć [**yown**-tshićh] v. irritate; fester; vex; embitter; inflame (*repeatedly*)
jątrzyć się [**yown**-tshićh śhan] v. rankle; fester; be vexed; be embittered; be exasperated; become envenomed (*repeatedly*)
jeans [dzheens] m. jeans; denim trousers
jechać [**ye**-khahćh] v. ride; drive; travel; voyage; sail; be on a journey; be on one's way; push on; go on; motor (to); cycle; leave (for a place); run (at a speed of); advance; move forward; stem; be bound (for a place) (*repeatedly*)
jechać do Rygi [**ye**-khahćh do ri-gee] exp.: colloq: to vomit
jechać do Warszawy [**ye**-khahćh do vahr-**shah**-vi] exp.: to leave for Warsaw; to travel to Warsaw
jechać konno [**ye**-khahćh **kon**-no] exp.: to ride on horseback
jechać lewą stroną [**ye**-khahćh le-vown **stro**-nown] exp.: to keep to the left
jechać na łyżwach [**ye**-khahćh nah **wizh**-vahkh] exp.: to skate
jechać na lewo [**ye**-khahćh nah le-vo] exp.: to drive to the left
jechać na nartach [**ye**-khahćh nah **nahr**-tahkh] exp.: to ski
jechać na rowerze [**ye**-khahćh nah ro-**ve**-zhe] exp.: to ride a bicycle; to cycle
jechać prawą stroną [**ye**-khahćh **prah**-vown **stro**-nown] exp.: to keep to the right
jechać przez morze [**ye**-khahćh pshes **mo**-zhe] exp.: to cross the sea
jechać z szybkością ... [**ye**-khahćh s ship-**kośh**-ćhown] exp.: to run at a speed ...; to ride at a speed ...
jechanie [ye-**khah**-ńe] n. riding; driving; travelling
jeden [**ye**-den] num. one; some
jeden drugiego [**ye**-den droo-**ge**-go] exp.: one another; each other
jeden po drugim [**ye**-den po **droo**-geem] exp.: one after the other; in turn; by turns
jeden przez drugiego [**ye**-den pshes droo-**ge**-go] exp.: in rivalry; by scrambling
jednym słowem [**yed**-nim **swo**-vem] exp.: in one word
jedenastka [ye-de-**nahst**-kah] f. number eleven; eleven persons; eleven objects; penalty shot (in soccer); no.: 11
jedenastodniowy [ye-de-nah-sto-**dńo**-vi] adj.m. eleven-days-old; of

eleven days; of eleven days' duration; eleven-day (period, etc.)
jedenastokondygnacyjny [ye-de-nah-sto-kon-dig-nah-**tsiy**-ni] adj.m. eleven-story (building, etc.)
jedenastolatek [ye-de-nahs-to-**lah**-tek] m. a boy of eleven; a boy eleven years old; an eleven-year-old
jedenastolatka [ye-de-nahs-to-**laht**-kah] f. a girl of eleven; a girl eleven years old; an eleven-year-old (female animal)
jedenastoletni [ye-de-nahs-to-**let**-ńee] adj.m. (a boy) of eleven; eleven years old; of eleven years; of eleven years' duration; eleven-years (period, etc.); lasting eleven years
jedenastozgłoskowiec [ye-de-nahs-to-zgwos-**ko**-vyets] m. verse of eleven syllables
jedenastozgłoskowy [ye-de-nahs-to-zgwos-**ko**-vi] adj.m. of eleven syllables
jedenasty [ye-de-**nahs**-ti] num. eleventh; m. eleventh day of the month
jedenasta [ye-de-**nahs**-tah] exp.: eleventh hour; eleven o'clock
o jedenastej [o ye-de-**nahs**-tey] exp.: at the eleventh hour; at eleven o'clock
jedenaście [ye-de-**nahśh**-ćhe] num. eleven; 11
jedenaścioro [ye-de-nahśh-**ćho**-ro] num. eleven (persons, children, objects)
jedlica [yed-**lee**-tsah] f. fir (tree)
jedlina [yed-**lee**-nah] f. fir grove; fir and spruce branches; fir-wood
jedlinka [yed-**leen**-kah] f. (young, nice) fir grove; fir and spruce branches
jedlinowy [yed-lee-**no**-vi] adj.m. of fir; of spruce; fir-(wood, cones, needles, etc.)
jednać [**yed**-nahćh] v. conciliate; win over; gain over; reconcile (*repeatedly*)
jednać się [**yed**-nahćh śhan] v. become reconciled; patch matters up (*repeatedly*)
jednak [**yed**-nahk] conj. however; yet; still; but; after all; though; nevertheless
jednaki [yed-**nah**-kee] adj.m. identical; similar; equal; alike
jednako [yed-**nah**-ko] adv. similarly; identically; the same way; equally; evenly
jednakowiusieńki [yed-nah-ko-vyoo-**śheń**-kee] adj.m. exactly the same
jednakowiuśki [yed-nah-ko-**vyoośh**-kee] adj.m. exactly the same
jednakowiuteńki [yed-nah-ko-vyoo-**teń**-kee] adj.m. exactly the same
jednakowiutki [yed-nah-ko-**vyoot**-kee] adj.m. exactly the same
jednakowo [yed-nah-**ko**-vo] adv. similarly; identically; the same way; equally; evenly
jednakowość [yed-nah-**ko**-vośhćh] f. similarity; identicalness
jednakowoż [yed-nah-**ko**-vosh] conj. however; yet; still; but; after all; though; nevertheless
jednakowy [yed-nah-**ko**-vi] adj.m. identical; similar; the same; equal; alike
jednakże [yed-**nahk**-zhe] conj. however; yet; still; but; after all; though; nevertheless
jednanie [yed-**nah**-ńe] n. conciliation; winning over; reconciliation
jednia [**yed**-ńah] f. entity; unity; union; bond; link; tie
jedno [**yed**-no] num. n. one; 1
jedno- [**yed**-no] prefix: one-; uni-; single-
jednoaktowy [yed-no-ahk-**to**-vi] adj.m. one-act (play, etc.)
jednoaktówka [yed-no-ahk-**toof**-kah] f. one-act play
jednoarkuszowy [yed-no-ahr-koo-**sho**-vi] adj.m. one-sheet (publication, etc.)
jednobarwny [yed-no-**bahrv**-ni] adj.m. one-colored; unicolored; monochromatic
jednobiegowy [yed-no-bye-**go**-vi] adj.m. one-way; straight-flight (stairs)
jednobiegunowy [yed-no-bye-goo-**no**-vi] adj.m. unipolar
jednobrzmiący [yed-no-**bzhmyown**-

tsi] adj.m. sounding alik; sounding (pronounced) identically
jednochodziec [yed-no-**kho**-dźhets] m. ambler; ambling horse
jednocukier [yed-no-**tsoo**-ker] m. monosaccharide
jednocylindrowy [yed-no-tsi-leend-**ro**-vi] adj.m. one-cylinder (motor, etc.); single-cylinder (motor, etc.)
jednoczenie [yed-no-**che**-ńe] n. union; unification
jednoczesność [yed-no-**ches**-nośhćh] f. simultaneousness; simultaneity; synchronism; synchrony; contemporaneousness; contemporaneity
jednoczesny [yed-no-**ches**-ni] adj.m. simultaneous; synchronous; contemporaneous; contemporary
jednocześnie [yed-no-**cheśh**-ńe] adv. simultaneously; contemporaneously; also; at the same time
jednoczłonowy [yed-no-chwo-**no**-vi] adj.m. of one segment
jednoczyć [yed-**no**-chićh] v. unify; merge; join; unite; bring together (*repeatedly*)
jednoczyć się [yed-**no**-chićh śhan] v. unify; merge; join (together); unite; come together (*repeatedly*)
jednodaniowy [yed-no-dah-**ńo**-vi] adj.m. one-course (meal, etc.)
jednodniowy [yed-no-**dńo**-vi] adj.m. one-day (periods, etc.); of one day; one day's (journey, etc.); lasting one day; transient; fleeting; ephemeral
jednodniówka [yed-no-**dńoof**-kah] f. leaflet for one day; special number (of a newspaper, etc.); special performance; dayfly; ephemerida
jednodzielny [yed-no-**dźhel**-ni] adj.m. of a single panel
jednoetapowy [yed-no-e-tah-**po**-vi] adj.m. single-stage (rocket, etc.)
jednofazowy [yed-no-fah-**zo**-vi] adj.m. single-phase (current); mono-phase (current)
jednofrakcjowy [yed-no-frahk-**tsyo**-vi] adj.m. one-size (sand, gravel, etc.)
jednogarbny [yed-no-**gahrb**-ni] adj.m. one-humped (camel, etc.)
jednogarnkowy [yed-no-gahrn-**ko**-vi] adj.m. one-dish (meal)
jednogatunkowy [yed-no-gah-toon-**ko**-vi] adj.m. congeneric
jednogłosowo [yed-no-gwo-**so**-vo] adv. monodically
jednogłosowość [yed-no-gwo-**so**-vośhćh] f. monody
jednogłosowy [yed-no-gwo-**so**-vi] adj.m. monodic; monodical
jednogłośnie [yed-no-**gwośh**-ńe] adv. unanimously; in a chorus; with one voice; with one assent
jednogłośny [yed-no-**gwośh**-ni] adj.m. unanimous
jednogłowy [yed-no-**gwo**-vi] adj.m. single-headed (heraldic eagle, etc.)
jednogodzinny [yed-no-go-**dźheen**-ni] adj.m. of one hour; one hour's (journey, etc.); one-hour (periods, etc.); lasting an hour
jednoimiennie [yed-no-ee-**myen**-ńe] adv. with one name; with one initial; with monomial
jednoimienny [yed-no-ee-**myen**-ni] adj.m. having one name; having one initial; monomial
jednoizbowy [yed-no-eez-**bo**-vi] adj.m. single-chamber; unicameral; one-room (apartment, etc.)
jednojajowy [yed-no-yah-**yo**-vi] adj.m. identical (twin); conceived in one egg
jednojęzyczny [yed-no-yan-**zich**-ni] adj.m. monolingual; using only one language
jednokadłubowiec [yed-no-kahd-woo-**bo**-vyets] m. colloq: ship with one hull
jednokadłubowy [yed-no-kahd-woo-**bo**-vi] adj.m. having one hull
jednokierunkowo [yed-no-ke-roon-**ko**-vo] adv. by one-way (traffic, etc.); unidirectionally (transmitted current); with check (valve); by non-return (valve); in one-sided manner
jednokierunkowość [yed-no-ke-roon-**ko**-vośhćh] f. unidirectional character

jednokierunkowy [yed-no-<u>k</u>e-roon-**ko**-vi] adj.m. one-way (traffic, etc.); unidirectional (current); check (valve); non-return (valve); one-sided

jednoklasowy [yed-no-klah-**so**-vi] adj.m. of one class

jednoklasówka [yed-no-klah-**soof**-kah] f. one-class school; one-year school; one-standard

jednokładność [yed-no-**kwahd**-nośhćh] f. homothety; like placement

jednokładny [yed-no-**kwahd**-ni] adj.m. homothetic; similar and similarly placed

jednokolorowy [yed-no-ko-lo-**ro**-vi] adj.m. one-colored; unicolored; monochromatic

jednokołowy [yed-no-ko-**wo**-vi] adj.m. one-wheel (cart, etc.)

jednokomorowy [yed-no-ko-mo-**ro**-vi] adj.m. of a single chamber; single-chamber (stomach, etc.)

jednokomórkowiec [yed-no-ko-moor-**ko**-vyets] m. protozoon; a protozoan

jednokomórkowy [yed-no-ko-moor-**ko**-vi] adj.m. unicellular

jednokonka [yed-no-**kon**-kah] f. one-horse vehicle

jednokonny [yed-no-**kon**-ni] adj.m. one-horse (vehicle, etc.); one-horsepower (motor, etc.)

jednokopytny [yed-no-ko-**pit**-ni] adj.m. solid-hoofed; solidungular; solidungulate
jednokopytne [yed-no-ko-**pit**-ne] pl. the solidungulates (Solidungula)

jednokreślność [yed-no-**kreśhl**-nośhćh] f. homography

jednokrok [yed-**no**-krok] m. skiing step with both hands pushing at each step

jednokrotnie [yed-no-**krot**-ńe] adv. one time; (only) once

jednokrotność [yed-no-**krot**-nośhćh] f. momentaneous character

jednokrotny [yed-no-**krot**-ni] adj.m. single; happening only once; done but once; unreiterated; of one time; momentaneous

jednokwiatowy [yed-no-kfyah-**to**-vi] adj.m. uniflorous; monochlamydeous (plant)

jednolampowy [yed-no-lahm-**po**-vi] adj.m. one-tube (radio set)

jednolatek [yed-no-**lah**-tek] m. one-year-old

jednolatka [yed-no-**laht**-kah] f. one-year-old (female)

jednoletni [yed-no-**let**-ńee] adj.m. one-year-old; of one year (duration, etc.)

jednolicenie [yed-no-lee-**tse**-ńe] n. assimilation; unification

jednolicić [yed-no-**lee**-ćheećh] v. unify; homogenize (*repeatedly*)

jednolicić się [yed-no-**lee**-ćheećh śh<u>an</u>] v. become unified; become homogenized (*repeatedly*)

jednolicie [yed-no-**lee**-ćhe] adv. uniformly; evenly; equally; homogeneously; indiscriminately

jednoliścienny [yed-no-leeśh-**ćhen**-ni] adj.m. monocotyledonous (plant, etc.)
jednoliścienne [yed-no-leeśh-**ćhen**-ne] pl. Monocotyledonae plants

jednolitość [yed-no-**lee**-tośhćh] f. uniformity; homogeneity; equality
jednolitość poglądów [yed-no-lee-tośhćh po-**gl<u>own</u>**-doof] exp.: unity of opinion

jednolity [yed-no-**lee**-ti] adj.m. uniform; equal; indiscriminate; all of a piece

jednołamowy [yed-no-wah-**mo**-vi] adj.m. of one column; one-column (article, etc.)

jednołukowy [yed-no-woo-**ko**-vi] adj.m. one-arched

jednomandatowy [yed-no-mahn-dah-**to**-vi] adj.m. of one mandate

jednomasztowiec [yed-no-mahsh-**to**-vyets] m. single-masted boat

jednomasztowy [yed-no-mahsh-**to**-vi] adj.m. single-masted

jednomian [yed-**no**-myahn] m. monomial

jednomiarowy [yed-no-myah-**ro**-vi] adj.m. monometric (music)

jednomiejscowy [yed-no-myeys-**tso**-vi] adj.m. one-seater (plane, etc.); one-person (cabin, etc.)

jednomiesięczny [yed-no-mye-**śhanch**-ni] adj.m. of one month; one-month's (notice, etc.); one-month (periods, etc.); lasting one month
jednominutowy [yed-no-mee-noo-**to**-vi] adj.m. of one minute; one-minute's (notice, etc.); one-minute (periods, etc.); lasting one minute
jednomorgowy [yed-no-mor-**go**-vi] adj.m. of approximately one and a half acres; owning approximately one and a half acres
jednomotorowiec [yed-no-mo-to-**ro**-vyets] m. one-engine boat; one-engine plane
jednomotorowy [yed-no-mo-to-**ro**-vi] adj.m. one-engine (boat, plane)
jednomyślnie [yed-no-**miśhl**-ńe] adv. unanimously
jednomyślność [yed-no-**miśhl**-nośhćh] f. unanimity
jednomyślny [yed-no-**miśhl**-ni] adj.m. unanimous; agreeing; having the agreement and consent of all
jednonarodowościowy [yed-no-nah-ro-do-vośh-**ćho**-vi] adj.m. of a single ethnic group; of one nationality
jednonasienny [yed-no-nah-**śhen**-ni] adj.m. having one seed
jednonawowy [yed-no-nah-**vo**-vi] adj.m. of one aisle; one-aisle (church, etc.); one-nave (chapel, etc.)
jednonogi [yed-no-**no**-gee] adj.m. one-legged; one-footed
jednonożny [yed-no-**nozh**-ni] adj.m. one legged; kicking with one foot
jednonóż [yed-**no**-noosh] m. adv. (kick, etc.) with one leg
jednoocze [yed-no-**o**-che] n. seeing with one eye
jednoocznie [yed-no-**och**-ńe] adv. monocularly
jednooczność [yed-no-**och**-nośhćh] f. monocular condition
jednooczny [yed-no-**och**-ni] adj.m. one-eyed; monocular; for use with only one eye
jednooki [yed-no-**o**-kee] adj.m. one-eyed; m. one-eyed man
jednookienny [yed-no-o-**ken**-ni] adj.m. one-windowed
jednoosiowy [yed-no-o-**śho**-vi] adj.m. uniaxial
jednoosobowo [yed-no-o-so-**bo**-vo] adv. as one person; by one person
jednoosobowy [yed-no-o-so-**bo**-vi] adj.m. one-man (management, etc.); individual; single; single-sitter
jednopalcowy [yed-no-pahl-**tso**-vi] adj.m. with one finger; monodactylous
jednopalczasty [yed-no-pahl-**chahs**-ti] adj.m. with one finger; monodactylous
jednopartyjny [yed-no-pahr-**tiy**-ni] adj.m. one-party (system, etc.)
jednopienność [yed-no-**pyen**-nośhćh] f. monoaecism
jednopienny [yed-no-**pyen**-ni] adj.m. monoaecious (plant)
jednopienne [yed-no-**pyen**-ne] pl. the monoaecian plants
jednopiętrowy [yed-no-pyan-**tro**-vi] adj.m. two-storied; of two stories; of two floor levels
jednoplanowy [yed-no-plah-**no**-vi] adj.m. based on one plan; located in one setting
jednoplemienny [yed-no-ple-**myen**-ni] adj.m. tribal; of individual tribes
jednopłaszczyznowość [yed-no-pwahsh-chiz-**no**-vośhćh] f. condition of lying in a specified plane; being in one plane
jednopłaszczyznowy [yed-no-pwahsh-chiz-**no**-vi] adj.m. uniplanar; planar; lying in one plane
jednopłat [yed-**no**-pwaht] m. monoplane
jednopłatkowy [yed-no-pwaht-**ko**-vi] adj.m. unipetalous (flower)
jednopłatowiec [yed-no-pwah-**to**-vyets] m. monoplane
jednopłatowy [yed-no-pwah-**to**-vi] adj.m. monoplane (flight, etc.)
jednopłciowość [yed-no-**pwćho**-vośhćh] f. unisexuality; phanerogamia
jednopłciowy [yed-no-**pwćho**-vi] adj.m. unisexual; phanerogamous

jednopokładowiec [yed-no-po-kwah-do-vyets] m. single-deck boat
jednopokładowy [yed-no-po-kwah-do-vi] adj.m. single-deck (boat, etc.)
jednopokojowy [yed-no-po-ko-yo-vi] adj.m. one-room (apartment, office, etc.)
jednopolowy [yed-no-po-lo-vi] adj.m. of one-crop system
jednopolówka [yed-no-po-loof-kah] f. one-crop system
jednopostaciowość [yed-no-po-stah-ćho-vośhćh] f. isomorphism
jednopostaciowy [yed-no-po-stah-ćho-vi] adj.m. isomorphic
jednopręcikowy [yed-no-pran-ćhee-ko-vi] adj.m. monandrous
jednoprocentowy [yed-no-pro-tsen-to-vi] adj.m. one percent (increase, etc.)
jednoprzestrzenny [yed-no-pshes-tshen-ni] adj.m. of single space
jednoprzewodnikowy [yed-no-pshe-vod-ńee-ko-vi] adj.m. of a single conductor
jednoprzęsłowy [yed-no-pshan-swo-vi] adj.m. of a single span; single-span (bridge, etc.)
jednorako [yed-no-rah-ko] adv. equally; in one way; simply
jednoraki [yed-no-rah-kee] adj.m. of one kind; simple; uncomplicated
jednoramienny [yed-no-rah-myen-ni] adj.m. single-armed (lever, etc.); one-arm (bandit, etc.)
jednorazowo [yed-no-rah-zo-vo] adv. (only) once
jednorazowość [yed-no-rah-zo-vośhćh] f. condition of happening (only) once
jednorazowy [yed-no-rah-zo-vi] adj.m. single; happening only once; done but once; unreiterated; of one time; momentaneous; uninterrupted (rule, etc.); continuous (reign)
jednorazówka [yed-no-rah-zoof-kah] f. (an item) for use only once (hypodermic syringe, etc.)
jednorącz [yed-no-rownch] adv. with one hand
jednoręczność [yed-no-ranch-nośhćh] f. one-handedness; having only one hand
jednoręczny [yed-no-ranch-ni] adj.m. one-handed
jednoręki [yed-no-ran-kee] adj.m. one-handed
jednoroczniak [yed-no-roch-ńahk] m. one-year-old child; one-year-old animal; yearling
jednoroczny [yed-no-roch-ni] adj.m. one-year-old; of one year; of one-year's duration; one-year's (service, etc.)
jednorodność [yed-no-rod-nośhćh] f. homogeneity; similarity; likeness
jednorodny [yed-no-rod-ni] adj.m. homogenous; congeneric; similar; alike
jednorodzinny [yed-no-ro-dźheen-ni] adj.m. one-family (house, etc.)
jednorożec [yed-no-ro-zhets] m. unicorn; narwhal
Jednorożec [yed-no-ro-zhets] m. Unicorn; Monoceros
jednorundowy [yed-no-roon-do-vi] adj.m. of one round; one-round (fight, etc.)
jednorurka [yed-no-roor-kah] f. single-barrelled gun
jednorzędowy [yed-no-zhan-do-vi] adj.m. arranged in a single row; single-breasted
jednorzędówka [yed-no-zhan-doof-kah] f. single-breasted jacket; single-breasted coat
jednosieczny [yed-no-śhech-ni] adj.m. with (only) one cutting edge
jednosilnikowy [yed-no-śheel-ńee-ko-vi] adj.m. one-engine (boat, plane)
jednoskibowy [yed-no-skee-bo-vi] adj.m. one-furrow (plow)
jednoskośny [yed-no-skośh-ni] adj.m. monoclinic; of monoclinal geologic fold
jednoskrzydłowy [yed-no-skshid-wo-vi] adj.m. single-flap (door); one-winged (building, etc.)
jednosłupkowy [yed-no-swoop-ko-vi] adj.m. monogynous
jednospadowy [yed-no-spah-do-vi] adj.m. one-way sloped (roof, ramp, etc.)

jednostajnie [yed-no-**stahy**-ńe] adv. uniformly; unvaryingly; changelessly; monotonously; dully; flatly; uneventfully; in a humdrum manner
jednostajność [yed-no-**stahy**-nośhćh] f. uniformity; sameness; absence of variety; monotony; evenness; regularity; steadiness; dullness; drabness; humdrumness
jednostajny [yed-no-**stahy**-ni] adj.m. uniform; unvarying; changeless; monotonous; regular; steady; dull; flat; uneventful; unexciting; humdrum; jogtrot
jednostka [yed-**nost**-kah] f. unit; individual; entity; measure; digit; specimen; denomination
jednostka masy atomowej [yed-**nost**-kah **mah**-si ah-to-**mo**-vey] exp.: atomic mass unit; atomic weight
jednostka metryczna [yed-**nost**-kah met-**rich**-nah] exp.: metric unit
jednostka miary [yed-**nost**-kah **myah**-ri] exp.: unit of measure
jednostki [yed-**nost**-kee] pl. digits (1 to 9)
jednostkowo [yed-nost-**ko**-vo] adv. one unit at a time; one by one
jednostkowość [yed-nost-**ko**-vośhćh] f. individuality; oneness; singularity
jednostkowy [yed-nost-**ko**-vi] adj.m. of a unit; unit (cost, price, etc.); individual; singular; separate; single; unitary; of one entity
ładunek jednostkowy [wah-**doo**-nek yed-nost-**ko**-vi] exp.: unit charge; unit load
nazwa jednostkowa [**nahz**-vah yed-nost-**ko**-vah] exp.: singular term
rzeczownik jednostkowy [zhe-**chov**-ńeek yed-nost-**ko**-vi] exp.: singular noun
sąd jednostkowy [sownt yed-nost-**ko**-vi] exp.: singular judgment; singular proposition
jednostopniowy [yed-no-stop-**ńo**-vi] adj.m. one-stage (rocket, etc.); direct (elections, etc.)
jednostronnie [yed-no-**stron**-ńe] adv. in one-sided way; unilaterally; ex parte (legal proceedings)
jednostronność [yed-no-**stron**-nośhćh] f. one-sidedness
jednostronny [yed-no-**stron**-ni] adj.m. one-sided; one-way (traffic, etc.); unilateral; secund (flower); ex parte (legal proceedings); narrow (minded, etc.); single-track (mind)
jednostrunny [yed-no-**stroon**-ni] adj.m. single-string (instrument, etc.)
jednostrzałowy [yed-no-stshah-**wo**-vi] adj.m. single-loader (rifle, canon, etc.); one-barrelled (shotgun, etc.)
broń jednostrzałowa [broń yed-no-stshah-**wo**-vah] exp.: single-loader
jednosylabowiec [yed-no-si-lah-**bo**-vyets] m. monosyllabic verse
jednosylabowy [yed-no-si-lah-**bo**-vi] adj.m. monosyllabic
jednosymetryczny [yed-no-si-met-**rich**-ni] adj.m. monosymmetric; monoclinic
jednoszczeblowy [yed-no-shcheb-**lo**-vi] adj.m. one-stage (process, etc.); one-level (house, etc.)
jednoszeregowy [yed-no-she-re-**go**-vi] adj.m. one-row (alignment)
jednoszpaltowy [yed-no-shpahl-**to**-vi] adj.m. of one column; one-column (article, etc.)
jednoszynowy [yed-no-shi-**no**-vi] adj.m. monorail (ski lift, etc.)
jednościan [yed-**no**-śhćhahn] m. one of the crystalline forms; pedion
jedność [**yed**-nośhćh] f. unity; entity; union; oneness; concord; harmony; unanimity
jedności [yed-**nośh**-ćhee] pl. units; digits (1 to 9)
jedność czasu, miejsca i akcji [**yed**-nośhćh **chah**-soo **myeys**-tsah ee ahkts-**yee**] exp.: the dramatic unities of time, place, and action
poczucie jedności [po-**choo**-ćhe yed-**nośh**-ćhee] exp.: good fellowship; the feeling of belonging

stanowić jedność [stah-no-veećh **yed**-nośhćh] exp.: to be one

jednoślad [yed-**no**-śhlaht] m. colloq: single-trace vehicle; bicycle; motorcycle

jednośladowiec [yed-no-śhlah-**do**-vyets] m. colloq: single-trace vehicle; bicycle; motorcycle

jednośladowy [yed-no-śhlah-**do**-vi] adj.m. colloq: of a single-trace vehicle; bicycle (wheel, etc.); motorcycle (tires, etc.)

jednośrodowy [yed-no-śhro-**do**-vi] adj.m. homocentric

jednośrubowy [yed-no-śhroo-**bo**-vi] adj.m. single-propeller (boat, etc.); single-screw (ship, etc.)

jednotarczowiec [yed-no-tahr-**cho**-vyets] m. variety of maritime shellfish

jednotomowy [yed-no-to-**mo**-vi] adj.m. of one volume; one-volume (publication, etc.)

jednotonowy [yed-no-to-**no**-vi] adj.m. one-ton (load, truck, etc.) monotonic (music); monotonical

jednotorebkowy [yed-no-to-rep-**ko**-vi] adj.m. unicapsular (plant)

jednotorowo [yed-no-to-**ro**-vo] adv. by one-track; by single-track (thinking, etc.)

jednotorowość [yed-no-to-**ro**-vośhćh] f. one-track system; single-track mind

jednotorowy [yed-no-to-**ro**-vi] adj.m. one-track (mind, etc.); single-track (railroad, etc.)

jednotraktowy [yed-no-trahk-**to**-vi] adj.m. of single row housing

jednotygodniowy [yed-no-ti-god-**ńo**-vi] adj.m. week-old; of one week; one-week's (time, etc.); one-week (periods, etc.); of one week's duration; lasting one week

jednouchy [yed-no-**oo**-khi] adj.m. having one ear; with one ear

jednowarstwowy [yed-no-vahrst-**fo**-vi] adj.m. one-ply (thickness, etc.)

jednowartościowy [yed-no-vahr-tośh-**ćho**-vi] adj.m. univalent; monovalent; monad; explicit (function); single-valued

jednowątkowy [yed-no-vownt-**ko**-vi] adj.m. single-threaded (story, etc.)

jednowiązkowy [yed-no-vyowns-**ko**-vi] adj.m. monadelphous (plant); of one-sheaf; of one bundle

jednowieczorowy [yed-no-vye-cho-**ro**-vi] adj.m. one-night (stand, show, etc.); of one evening; one-evening's (amusement, etc.)

jednowiekowy [yed-no-vye-**ko**-vi] adj.m. century-old; of one century; one-century's (experience, etc.); one-century's (periods, etc.); of one century duration; lasting one century; of the same age

jednowierszowy [yed-no-vyer-**sho**-vi] adj.m. of one line; one-line-

jednowiosłowy [yed-no-vyos-**wo**-vi] adj.m. one-oar (rowing, etc.)

jednowymiarowy [yed-no-vi-myah-**ro**-vi] adj.m. one-dimensional

jednowyrazowy [yed-no-vi-rah-**zo**-vi] adj.m. one-word (answer, etc.)

jednozalążkowy [yed-no-zah-lownsh-**ko**-vi] adj.m. uniovular (plant)

jednozasadowy [yed-no-zah-sah-**do**-vi] adj.m. monobasic (compound, etc.)

jednozdaniowy [yed-no-zdah-**ńo**-vi] adj.m. of one sentence; one-sentence (note, etc.)

jednozębny [yed-no-**zanb**-ni] adj.m. having one tooth; one-tooth (hook, etc.)

jednozęby [yed-no-**zan**-bi] adj.m. having one tooth; one-tooth (hook, etc.)

jednozgłoska [yed-no-**zgwos**-kah] f. monosyllable

jednozgłoskowo [yed-no-zgwos-**ko**-vo] adv. monosyllabically

jednozgłoskowość [yed-no-zgwos-**ko**-vośhćh] f. monosyllabism

jednozgłoskowy [yed-no-zgwos-**ko**-vi] adj.m. monosyllabic; of one syllable; one-syllable (verse, word, etc.)

jednozgodnie [yed-no-**zgod**-ńe] adv. unanimously

jednozgodność [yed-no-**zgod**-nośhćh] f. unanimity

jednozgodny [yed-no-**zgod**-ni] adj.m.

unanimous; agreeing; having the agreement and consent of all
jednozłotowy [yed-no-zwo-**to**-vi] adj.m. of one zloty; one-zloty (coin, etc.)
jednozmianowy [yed-no-zmyah-**no**-vi] adj.m. of one shift; one-shift (production, etc.)
jednoznacznie [yed-no-**znahch**-ńe] adv. unmistakably; univocally; unequivocally; explicitly
jednoznacznik [yed-no-**znahch**-ńeek] m. synonym; (a) univocal
jednoznaczność [yed-no-**znahch**-nośhćh] f. univocal character (of a word, etc.); synonymity
jednoznaczny [yed-no-**znahch**-ni] adj.m. univocal; unmistakable; synonymous; interchangeable; explicit; unequivocal
jednozwojny [yed-no-**zvoy**-ni] adj.m. single-thread (screw, etc.)
gwint jednozwojny [gveent yed-no-**zvoy**-ni] exp.: single-thread
jednozwojowy [yed-no-zvo-**yo**-vi] adj.m. single-thread (screw, etc.)
jednozwrotkowy [yed-no-zvrot-**ko**-vi] adj.m. of one verse; of one stanza
jednożaglowy [yed-no-zhahg-**lo**-vi] adj.m. single-sail (boat, etc.)
jednożeństwo [yed-no-**zheń**-stfo] n. monogamy
jednożerność [yed-no-**zher**-nośhćh] f. monophagy
jednożyłowy [yed-no-zhi-**wo**-vi] adj.m. one wire (cable, etc.)
jedwab [**yed**-vahp] m. silk
jedwabik [yed-**vah**-beek] m. floss silk; second-rate silk
jedwabiopodobny [yed-vah-byo-po-**dob**-ni] adj.m. silk-like; of silk imitation; silk-imitation (cloth)
jedwabisto [yed-vah-**bees**-to] adv. with the luster of silk; with the softness of silk; silkily
jedwabistość [yed-vah-**bees**-tośhćh] f. silkiness
jedwabisty [yed-vah-**bees**-ti] adj.m. silken; silky; flossy; sericeous; of silk; silk (gown, ribbon, etc.)
jedwabiście [yed-vah-**beeśh**-ćhe] adv. with the luster of silk; with the softness of silk
jedwabnictwo [yed-vahb-**ńeets**-tfo] n. the silk industry; the silk trade; sericulture (of raw silk)
jedwabniczy [yed-vahb-**ńee**-chi] adj.m. silk (trade, etc.)
klej jedwabniczy [kley yed-vahb-**ńee**-chi] exp.: silk glue; sericin
jedwabnie [yed-**vahb**-ńe] adv. with the luster of silk; silkily; with the softness of silk; in luxury
jedwabnik [yed-**vahb**-ńeek] m. silkworm
jedwabny [yed-**vahb**-ni] adj.m. silky; of silk
jedynaczek [ye-di-**nah**-chek] m. an only (little) son; only child
jedynaczka [ye-di-**nahch**-kah] f. an only (little) daughter; only child
jedynak [ye-**di**-nahk] m. (an) only son; only child; the only male (in the company); the only (male) representative
jedynie [ye-**di**-ńe] adv. only; merely; solely; nothing but (fear, etc.); nothing short of (a miracle, brute force, etc.)
jedyne [ye-**di**-ne] adj.n. & pl.f. the only (baby, etc.); the sole; unique; dearest (baby, girls, etc.); matchless
jedynka [ye-**din**-kah] f. the figure one; ace; bus number one; class room number one; skiff; colloq: bad mark in school
jedynobóstwo [ye-di-no-**boos**-tfo] n. monotheism
jedyność [ye-**di**-nośhćh] f. uniqueness; exclusivity
jedynowładca [ye-di-no-**vwaht**-tsah] m. autocrat
jedynowładczy [ye-di-no-**vwaht**-chi] adj.m. autocratic
jedynowładztwo [ye-di-no-**vwahts**-tfo] n. autocracy
jedyny [ye-**di**-ni] adj.m. the only one; the sole; unique; matchless; peerless; dearest
jeden jedyny [**ye**-den ye-**di**-ni] exp.: the one and only
jedzenie [ye-**dze**-ńe] n. meal; food; victuals; fare; colloq: feed; eats; slang: grub; chuck (jargon)
nie do jedzenia [ńe do ye-**dze**-ńah] exp.: not fit to eat

jedzeniowy [ye-dze-ńo-vi] adj.m. mealtime (customs, etc.)
jedzonko [ye-**dzon**-ko] n. (tasty, etc.) meal; food; victuals
jeep [dzheep] m. jeep (car)
jegier [**ye**-ger] m. yager; jaeger; hunter
jegierowski [ye-ge-**rof**-skee] adj.m. Jaeger (underwear, etc.)
jegiery [ye-**ge**-ri] pl. colloq: Jaeger drawers
jego [**ye**-go] pron. his; him
jegomość [ye-**go**-mośhćh] m. colloq: gentleman; stranger; chap; fellow; Reverend; the Honorable Gentleman; slang: party; customer; queer card; dude
Jehowa [ye-**kho**-vah] m. Jehovah
jehowa [ye-**kho**-vah] m. colloq: Jehovah's Witness
jehowita [ye-kho-**vee**-tah] m. Jehovah's Witness
jej [yey] pron. her; hers; excl.: my!
jejku! [**yey**-koo] excl.: my!
jejmość [**yey**-mośhćh] f. colloq: woman; female; matron; the Honorable Lady
jelec [**ye**-lets] m. (hilt) guard; dace (fish)
jeleni [ye-**le**-ńee] adj.m. stag's; cervine
  jelenie rogi [ye-**le**-ńe **ro**-gee] exp.: antlers
jeleniak [ye-**le**-ńahk] m. elaphomyces (a truffle-like fungus)
jelenię [ye-**le**-ńan] n. fawn
jelenina [ye-le-**ńee**-nah] f. venison
jeleniowaty [ye-le-ńo-**vah**-ti] adj.m. cervoid; of the deer family
  jeleniowate [ye-le-ńo-**vah**-te] pl. Cervidae; the deer family
jeleń [**ye**-leń] m. stag; hart; deer; colloq: naive man; crock
jeliciarstwo [ye-lee-**ćhahr**-stfo] n. sausage-casing manufacture (trade)
jelito [ye-**lee**-to] n. intestine
  jelita [ye-**lee**-tah] pl. intestines; entrails; bowels; viscera; guts
jelitodyszec [ye-lee-to-**di**-shets] m. enteropneust (worm)
  jelitodyszce [ye-lee-to-**dish**-tse] pl. the Enteropneusta hemichordate worms
jelitodyszny [ye-lee-to-**dish**-ni] adj.m. enteropneustan
  jelitodyszne [ye-lee-to-**dish**-ne] pl. the Enteropneusta class of worms
jelitowy [ye-lee-**to**-vi] adj.m. intestinal; enteric; visceral
jelonek [ye-**lo**-nek] m. young stag; fawn; stag beetle
  jelonki [ye-**lon**-kee] pl. young stags; stag beetles; the Lucanidae
jelonkowy [ye-lon-**ko**-vi] adj.m. fawn's; fawn (skin, etc.)
  rękawiczki jelonkowe [ran-kah-**veech**-kee ye-lon-**ko**-ve] exp.: kid gloves
jełczeć [**yew**-chećh] v. become rancid; grow rancid (*repeatedly*)
jełczenie [yew-**che**-ńe] n. becoming rancid; growing rancid
jełki [**yew**-kee] adj.m. rancid
jełop [**ye**-wop] m. colloq: blockhead; dolt; fathead; gawk; see: **jołopa**
jełopa [ye-**wo**-pah] m. colloq: blockhead; fathead; dolt; gawk
jemioła [ye-**myo**-wah] f. mistletoe
  amerykańska jemioła [ah-me-ri-**kahń**-skah ye-**myo**-wah] exp.: cedar bird; waxwing
jemiołucha [ye-myo-**woo**-khah] f. waxwing
jemiołuszka [ye-myo-**woosh**-kah] f. waxwing (bird)
jen [yen] m. yen (Japanese currency)
jena [**ye**-nah] f. Jena glass
jenajski [ye-**nahy**-skee] adj.m. of Jena
  szkło jenajskie [shkwo ye-**nahy**-ske] exp.: Jena (glass)
jenerał [ye-**ne**-rahw] m. colloq: general
jeniec [**ye**-ńets] m. captive; prisoner of war; P.O.W.
jeniecki [ye-**ńets**-kee] adj.m. of prisoners of war; for prisoners of war; prisoner-of-war (camp, etc.); P.O.W. (camp, etc.)
jeniectwo [ye-**ńets**-tfo] n. captivity of prisoners of war
jeno [**ye**-no] adv. colloq: only; merely; solely; nothing but (fear, etc.); nothing short of (a miracle, brute force, etc.)

jenot [**ye**-not] m. wild Asiatic dog with valuable fur
jer [yer] m. chaffinch (bird); type of early Slavic sound from which modern syllabic sounds originated
jeografia [ye-o-**grahf**-yah] f. colloq: geography
jeometria [ye-o-**metr**-yah] f. colloq: geometry
jeremiada [ye-re-**myah**-dah] f. jeremiad; lament (in literary usage)
jersey [**dzher**-sey] m. Jersey fabric; Jersey dairy cattle
jerseyowy [dzher-se-**yo**-vi] adj.m. of Jersey fabric; of Jersey dairy cattle
jerychoński [ye-ri-**khoń**-skee] adj.m. of Jericho; Jericho (rose, etc.)
jerzyk [**ye**-zhik] m. martlet; martin; swift (bird)
jerzyna [ye-**zhi**-nah] f. blackberry
jesiennie [ye-**śhen**-ńe] adv. autumnally; as in autumn; in autumnal garb; with autumnal coloring
jesiennieć [ye-**śhen**-ńećh] v. become like autumn; appear like autumn (*repeatedly*)
jesienny [ye-**śhen**-ni] adj.m. autumnal; of autumn
jesień [**ye**-śheń] f. autumn; fall; the fall of (one's) life
jesion [**ye**-śhon] m. ash tree
jesionczyna [ye-śhon-**chi**-nah] f. colloq: shabby fall overcoat; worn-out light overcoat
jesionek [ye-**śho**-nek] m. young ash tree
jesionka [ye-**śhon**-kah] f. fall overcoat; light overcoat
jesionolistny [ye-śho-no-**leest**-ni] adj.m. with leaves shaped like leaves of the ash tree
jesionowy [ye-śho-**no**-vi] adj.m. of the ash tree; of ash wood; ash (wood, boards, leaf, poles, etc.)
jesiotr [**ye**-śhotr] m. sturgeon (fish)
jesiotrowaty [ye-śhot-ro-**vah**-ti] adj.m. like a sturgeon; of sturgeon family; acipenserid; acipenserine
jesiotrowate [ye-śhot-ro-**vah**-te] pl. the sturgeon family; Acipenseridae; the Acipenserine family of fishes
jesiotrowy [ye-śhot-**ro**-vi] adj.m. of a sturgeon; sturgeon's; sturgeon (caviar, etc.)
jest [yest] v. (he, she, it) is
jestem [**yes**-tem] v. (I) am
jestestwo [yes-**tes**-tfo] n. being; nature; creature; existence
jeszcze [**yesh**-che] adv. still; besides; more; yet; way back; already; as early as; as far back as; another; else; even
co jeszcze? [tso **yesh**-che] exp.: what else?; what next?; what more?
jeszcze by tego brakowało [**yesh**-che bi **te**-go brah-ko-**vah**-wo] exp.: that would be the limit
jeszcze coś [**yesh**-che tsośh] exp.: something else
jeszcze dużo [**yesh**-che **doo**-zho] exp.: much more; a lot more; many more
jeszcze jak! [**yesh**-che yahk] excl.: I should say so!; sure thing!
jeszcze jest czas [**yesh**-che yest chahs] exp.: there is yet time
jeszcze kilka [**yesh**-che **keel**-kah] exp.: a few more; some more
jeszcze pięć minut [**yesh**-che pyanćh **mee**-noot] exp.: another five minutes; five minutes more
jeszcze trochę [**yesh**-che **tro**-khan] exp.: a little more
kto jeszcze? [kto **yesh**-che] exp.: who else?; who is next?
jesziba [ye-**shee**-bah] f. yeshiva; talmudic school; rabbinical seminary
jesziwa [ye-**shee**-vah] f. yeshivah; talmudic school; rabbinical seminary
jeszybot [ye-**shi**-bot] m. yeshivoth; talmudic school; rabbinical seminary
jeść [yeśhćh] v. eat; have a meal; feed (on); worry; attack; corrode; colloq: m. something to eat; food (*repeatedly*)
co jadłeś na obiad? [tso **yahd**-weśh nah **ob**-yaht] exp.: what did you have for dinner
dużo jeść [**doo**-zho yeśhćh]

exp.: to be a great eater
jeść chciwie [yeśhćh khćhee-vye] exp.: gobble; guzzle
komary go jadły [ko-mah-ri go yahd-wi] exp.: mosquitos were stinging him; he was bitten by mosquitos
jeśli [yeśh-lee] conj. if
a jeśli [ah yeśh-lee] exp.: what if; supposing
jeśli nie [yeśh-lee ńe] exp.: if not; unless
jeśli się nie mylę [yeśh-lee śhan ńe mi-lan] exp.: if I am not mistaken; unless I am mistaken
kto wie jeśli [kto vye yeśh-lee] exp.: who knows if...
jeśliby [yeśh-lee-bi] conj. if; should
jeśliby to dał [yeśh-lee-bi to dahw] exp.: should he give it; if he should give it
jezdnia [yezd-ńah] f. roadway; street
przechodzić (przez) jezdnię [pshe-kho-dźheećh pshez yezd-ńan] exp.: to cross the street; to cross the pavement (the roadway)
jezdny [yezd-ni] adj.m. carriageable; of cavalry; cavalry (charge, etc.); m. cavalryman; rider; driver
jezierza [ye-źhe-zhah] f. naiad (waterweed)
jezierzowaty [ye-źhe-zho-vah-ti] adj.m. like naiad (waterweed); naiadaceous
jezierzowate [ye-źhe-zho-vah-te] pl. the Naiadaceae family of waterweeds
jeziorko [ye-źhor-ko] n. small lake; lakelet
jeziorność [ye-źhor-nośhćh] f. the nature of lake land
jeziorny [ye-źhor-ni] adj.m. of a lake; lake (water, shore, etc.)
jezioro [ye-źho-ro] n. lake; loch (in Scotland)
brzeg jeziora [bzhek ye-źho-rah] exp.: lakeside; lakeshore
kraina jezior [krah-ee-nah ye-źhor] exp.: lake land
jeziorowy [ye-źho-ro-vi] adj.m. of a lake; lake (water, trout, etc.)
jeziorzysko [ye-źho-zhis-ko] n. (big, muddy) lake
jeziorzysty [ye-źho-zhis-ti] adj.m. abounding in lakes
jezuicki [ye-zoo-eets-kee] adj.m. Jesuit's; Jesuits'; of the Jesuits; Jesuitical; Jesuit (style, etc.); Jesuitic; colloq: crafty; hypocritical
po jezuicku [po ye-zoo-eets-koo] exp.: Jesuitically; colloq: craftily; hypocritically
jezuita [ye-zoo-ee-tah] m. Jesuit; member of Jesuit Order; colloq: hypocrite; dissembler; intriguer
jezuitka [ye-zoo-eet-kah] f. (woman) Jesuit; Daughter of Society of Jesus; colloq: m. & f. hypocrite; dissembler; intriguer
jezuityzm [ye-zoo-ee-tizm] m. Jesuitism; colloq: craftiness; hypocrisy
jezusowy [ye-zoo-so-vi] adj.m. of Jesus; Jesus'; Christlike
jezusowe lata [ye-zoo-so-ve lah-tah] exp.: 33 years of age
jeździć [yeźh-dźheećh] v. drive; ride; travel; be accustomed to drive (ride, travel); know how to drive (*repeatedly*)
jeździć komuś po głowie [yeźh-dźheećh ko-moośh po gwo-vye] exp.: to haunt somebody
jeździec [yeźh-dźhets] m. horseman; rider; equestrian; cavalier
jeździecki [yeźh-dźhets-kee] adj.m. of horsemanship; of horse-riding; of a rider; equestrian; of a cavalier
jeździectwo [yeźh-dźhets-tfo] n. horse-riding; horsemanship; horsemen; equestrians
jeż [yesh] m. hedgehog; porcupine; barbed-wire entanglement
jeżarka [ye-zhahr-kah] f. napper; teaseler; teazler; nap-making machine
jeżasty [ye-zhahs-ti] adj.m. bristly; like a porcupine
jeżatka [ye-zhaht-tkah] f. porcupine
jeżątko [ye-zhownt-ko] n. young hedgehog
jeżdżenie [yezh-dzhe-ńe] n. riding; driving; tyrannizing
jeżdżony [yezh-dzho-ni] adj.m.

ridden; mounted; used (road, car, etc.)
jeżeli [ye-**zhe**-lee] conj. if
jeżeliby [ye-zhe-**lee**-bi] conj. if; should
jeżenie [ye-**zhe**-ńe] n. bristling
jeżogłówka [ye-zho-**gwoof**-kah] f. sparganium (plant)
jeżogłówkowaty [ye-zho-gwoof-ko-**vah**-ti] adj.m. like sparganum; of sparganum family; of the bur reeds
jeżogłówkowate [ye-zho-gwoof-ko-**vah**-te] pl. the sparganum family of flowers
jeżowaty [ye-zho-**vah**-ti] adj.m. bristly; like a porcupine; stiff (attitude, etc.)
jeżowate [ye-zho-**vah**-te] pl. the porcupines; the Erinaceidae family
jeżowiec [ye-**zho**-vyets] m. sea urchin; echinus
jeżowy [ye-**zho**-vi] adj.m. hedgehog's; hedgehogs'
jeżozwierz [ye-**zho**-zvyesh] m. porcupine
jeżówka [ye-**zhoof**-kah] f. porcupine fish
jeżyć [**ye**-zhićh] v. bristle; stand on end; rough up; ruffle (*repeatedly*)
jeżyć się [**ye**-zhićh śhan] v. bristle up; stand on end; set up bristles; show one's bristles; colloq: show apprehension (*repeatedly*)
jeżyk [**ye**-zhik] m. young hedgehog
jeżyna [ye-**zhi**-nah] f. blackberry; blackberry bush; bramble
jeżynowy [ye-zhi-**no**-vi] adj.m. of the blackberry; of blackberry bush; of bramble; blackberry (jam, etc.)
jęcie się [**yan**-ćhe śhan] n. taking; grasping; seizing
jęcząco [yan-**chown**-tso] adv. moanfully; groaningly; wailingly; plaintively
jęczący [yan-**chown**-tsi] adj.m. mournful; tearful; moaning; groaning; wailing; plaintive
jęczeć [**yan**-chećh] v. moan; groan; wail; whine; complain; grumble; lament; slang: bellyache; grouch (*repeatedly*)
jęczenie [yan-**che**-ńe] n. moans; groans; wails; whines; complaints; grumbling; lament; slang: bellyaching; grouching
jęczmianka [yanch-**myahn**-kah] f. barley straw
jęczmienisko [yanch-mye-**ńees**-ko] n. barley stubble
jęczmienny [yanch-**myen**-ni] adj.m. barley (straw, porridge, corn, etc.)
jęczmień [**yanch**-myeń] m. barley; a cereal grass
jęczmionka [yanch-**myon**-kah] f. barley straw
jęczmyk [**yanch**-mik] m. colloq: barley; a cereal grass
jędrnie [**yandr**-ńe] adv. firmly; robustly; strongly; tersely; compactly; solidly; pithily
czuć się jędrnie [chooćh śhan yandr-ńe] exp.: to feel robust; to feel full of pep
jędrnieć [**yandr**-ńećh] v. become firm; become compact (*repeatedly*)
jędrnienie [yandr-**ńe**-ńe] n. becoming firm; firming up
jędrność [**yandr**-nośhćh] f. firmness; robustness; strength; haleness; terseness; pithiness; solidity; compactness
jędrny [**yandr**-ni] adj.m. firm; robust; strong; terse; pithy
jędza [**yan**-dzah] f. witch; shrew; termagant; scold; vixen; virago; fury
jędzon [**yan**-dzon] m. evil spirit
jędzowatość [yan-dzo-**vah**-tośhćh] f. shrewish nature (character)
jędzowaty [yan-dzo-**vah**-ti] adj.m. shrewish; scolding; cattish; vixenish; scratchy
jęk [**yank**] m. groan; moan; wail; whine; howl; moaning; wailing; whining; howling
jękliwie [yan-**klee**-vye] adv. groaningly; moanfully; whiningly; plaintively
jękliwy [yan-**klee**-vi] adj.m. groaning; moanful; whining
jęknąć [**yank**-nownćh] v. complain; moan; groan; whine; grumble; wail; utter a groan; slang:

bellyache
jęknięcie [yank-ńan-ćhe] n. moan; groan
jęta [yan-tah] f. top beam; roof tie; span piece; May fly; ephemerid
jętka [yant-kah] f. top beam; roof tie; span piece; May fly; mayfly; ephemerid
jętki [yant-kee] pl. the May flies; Ephemerida
jętkowy [yant-ko-vi] adj.m. of top a beam; of a roof tie; of a span piece
jęzor [yan-zor] m. tongue (of a glacier, etc.)
języczek [yan-zi-chek] m. tonguelet; uvula; ligule (plant); strap (plant); lingua (of an insect); reed (of a clarinet); pointer; index hand; (shoe) tab
języczkowaty [yan-zich-ko-vah-ti] adj.m. ligulate (flower)
języczkowy [yan-zich-ko-vi] adj.m. uvular
języcznik [yan-zich-ńeek] m. hart's-tongue; adder's-tongue
język [yan-zik] m. tongue; speech; parlance; vocabulary; language
język potoczny [yan-zik po-toch-ni] exp.: colloquial language
język spustowy [yan-zik spoos-to-vi] exp.: trigger
mówić łamanym językiem [moo-veećh wah-mah-nim yan-zi-kem] exp.: to speak broken (English, Polish, etc.) (language)
mówić obcym językiem [moo-veećh op-tsim yan-zi-kem] exp.: to speak a foreign language
trzymać język za zębami [tshi-mahćh yan-zik zah zan-bah-mee] exp.: to keep silent; to hold one's tongue
znaleźć z kimś wspólny język [znah-leśhćh s keemśh fspool-ni yan-zik] exp.: to understand one another
językowaty [yan-zi-ko-vah-ti] adj.m. tongue-shaped
językowo [yan-zi-ko-vo] adv. in respect of language; in respect of vocabulary; in respect of word usage; linguistically; as regards linguists
językowy [yan-zi-ko-vi] adj.m. of the tongue; lingual; of language; of speech; of the vocabulary; linguistic
językoznawca [yan-zi-ko-znahf-tsah] m. linguist
językoznawczo [yan-zi-ko-znahf-cho] adv. linguistically
językoznawczy [yan-zi-ko-znahf-chi] adj.m. linguistic
językoznawstwo [yan-zi-ko-znahf-stfo] n. linguistics; linguistic science
jidysz [yee-dish] m. Yiddish (language)
jidyszowy [yee-di-sho-vi] adj.m. Yiddish (language, etc.)
jidyszyzm [yee-di-shizm] m. Yiddishism; Yiddish borrowing, etc.
joanita [yo-ah-ńee-tah] m. Knight of St. John of Jerusalem
jod [yot] m. iodine (atomic number 53)
jodan [yo-dahn] m. iodate
jodek [yo-dek] m. iodide
jodel [yo-del] m. iodel
jodełka [yo-dew-kah] f. young fir tree; young spruce
jodełkowy [yo-dew-ko-vi] adj.m. herring-boned; texture in herring-bone pattern
jodlować [yod-lo-vahćh] v. yodel (*repeatedly*)
jodlowanie [yod-lo-vahńe] n. yodel
jodła [yod-wah] f. fir tree; spruce
jodłować [yod-wo-vahćh] v. yodel (*repeatedly*)
jodłowaty [yod-wo-vah-ti] adj.m. abietineous; of the pine family
jodłowate [yod-wo-vah-te] pl. Abietineae; a tribe in the pine family
jodłowiec [yod-wo-vyets] m. a beetle of the family Ipidae
jodłowy [yod-wo-vi] adj.m. of the fir tree; fir (needles, wood, etc.)
jodoform [yo-do-form] m. iodoform
jodol [yo-dol] m. iodol (crystalline)
jodometria [yo-do-metr-yah] f. iodometry (measuring of idine)
jodować [yo-do-vahćh] v. iodize (*repeatedly*)
jodowanie [yo-do-vah-ńe] n. iodizing

jodowodór [yo-do-**vo**-door] m. hydrogen iodide
jodowy [yo-**do**-vi] adj.m. iodic
jodyna [yo-**di**-nah] f. tincture of iodine (antiseptic); iodine
jodynować [yo-di-**no**-vahćh] v. paint (cover) with iodine (*repeatedly*)
jodynowanie [yo-di-no-**vah**-ńe] n. treating with iodine
jodzica [yo-**dźhee**-tsah] f. iodism
jog [yok] m. yogi
joga [**yo**-gah] f. yoga
jogaczar [yo-**gah**-chahr] m. follower of yoga philosophy and practices
jogging [**dzho**-geeng] m. jogging
jogin [**yo**-geen] m. yogi; yogin
jogizm [**yo**-geezm] m. yoga philosophy and practices
jogurt [**yo**-goort] m. yogurt; yoghurt
joint venture [dzhoynt **ven**-cher] (Engl.) exp.: joint venture
jojczyć [**yoy**-chićh] v. whimper; whine; squeal (slang) (*repeatedly*)
jo-jo [yo yo] n. yo-yo
joker [**dzho**-ker] m. joker
jol [yol] m. yawl
jola [**yo**-lah] f. jolly boat; yawl; jigger
jolbot [**yol**-bot] m. jolly boat
jolka [**yol**-kah] f. jolly boat; yawl; jigger
jołop [**yo**-wop] m. colloq: blockhead; fathead; dolt; gawk (men only)
jołopa [yo-**wo**-pah] m. & f. colloq: blockhead; fathead; dolt; gawk (men or women)
jołopowaty [yo-wo-po-**vah**-ti] adj.m. colloq: thickheaded; thick-skulled; mutton-headed
jon [yon] m. ion
jon dodatni [yon do-**daht**-ni] exp.: cation
jon ujemny [yon oo-**yem**-ni] exp.: anion
jonatan [yo-**nah**-tahn] m. Jonathan (apple)
joniczny [yo-**ńech**-ni] adj.m. Ionic
jonik [**yo**-ńeek] m. (an) Ionic
jonit [**yo**-ńeet] m. ion exchanger
jonizacja [yo-ńee-**zah**-tsyah] f. ionization
jonizacyjny [yo-ńee-zah-**tsiy**-ni] adj.m. ionizing (current, etc.)
jonizator [yo-ńee-**zah**-tor] m. ionizer
jonizować [yo-ńee-**zo**-vahćh] v. ionize (*repeatedly*)
jonizowanie [yo-ńee-zo-**vah**-ńe] n. ionization
jonogram [yo-**no**-grahm] m. record of radio-sonde of the ionosphere
jonosfera [yo-no-**sfe**-rah] f. ionosphere; Heaviside layer
jonosferycznie [yo-no-sfe-**rich**-ńe] adv. ionospherically
jonosferyczny [yo-no-sfe-**rich**-ni] adj.m. ionospheric
jonosonda [yo-no-**son**-dah] f. radiosonde of the ionosphere
jonowy [yo-**no**-vi] adj.m. ionic
jontoforeza [yon-to-fo-**re**-zah] f. ionic medication; iontophoresis
joński [**yoń**-skee] adj.m. Ionic (order, etc.); Ionian (mode, etc.)
jordanka [yor-**dahn**-kah] f. variety of girls' ball game
jordanowski [yor-dah-**nof**-skee] adj.m. of Jordan; Jordanian
ogródek jordanowski [og-**roo**-dek yor-dah-**nof**-skee] exp.: open-air (Jordan's) kindergarten
jot [yot] m. the letter: "j"
jota [**yo**-tah] f. the letter: "j"; Greek iota; Spanish dance "jota"
ani na jotę [ah-ńee nah **yo**-tan] exp.: not in the least; not a bit
co do joty [tso do **yo**-ti] exp.: to the letter; to a "T"
jota w jotę [**yo**-tah v **yo**-tan] exp.: identical; identically; exactly the same
zgadzać się co do joty [zgah-dzahćh śhan tso do **yo**-ti] exp.: to agree perfectly; to agree to the letter; to agree to a "T"; to tally; to fit like a glove
jotacja [yo-**tah**-tsyah] f. iotization
jotacyzm [yo-**tah**-tsism] m. iotacism
jotowy [yo-**to**-vi] adj.m. of the letter "j"
jowialnie [yo-**vyahl**-ńe] adv. jovially; jocosely; in debonair fashion; genially; with bonhomie
jowialność [yo-**vyahl**-nośhćh] f. joviality; jocoseness; geniality; bonhomie; breeziness
jowialny [yo-**vyahl**-ni] adj.m. jovial; debonair; genial

jowialszczyzna [yov-yahlsh-**chiz**-nah] f. carefree pleasure-seeking smug circles of society
jowiszowy [yo-vee-**sho**-vi] adj.m. Jovian
joystick [**dzhoy**-steek] m. joystick (for computer games, etc.)
józefinka [yoo-ze-**feen**-kah] f. variety of pear tree; variety of pear
juan [**yoo**-ahn] m. yuan; unit of Chinese money (100 fens)
jubel [**yoo**-bel] m. rejoicing; joy; merry-making
jubilacja [yoo-bee-**lah**-tsyah] f. jubilus (music)
jubilat [yoo-**bee**-laht] m. celebrator of a jubilee
jubilatka [yoo-bee-**laht**-kah] f. (woman) celebrator of a jubilee
jubiler [yoo-**bee**-ler] m. jeweler (store or profession)
jubilerka [yoo-bee-**ler**-kah] f. jeweler's work; jeweler's craft; jeweler's trade; (woman) jeweler
jubilerski [yoo-bee-**ler**-skee] adj.m. jeweler's (work, art, etc.)
jubilerstwo [yoo-bee-**ler**-stfo] n. jeweler's work; jeweler's craft; jeweler's trade
jubileusz [yoo-bee-**le**-oosh] m. jubilee; anniversary
jubileuszowy [yoo-bee-le-oo-**sho**-vi] adj.m. of a jubilee; of an anniversary; jubilee (celebrations, year, etc.)
jubka [**yoop**-kah] f. woman's tunic
jucha [**yoo**-khah] f. animal blood; vulg.: human blood; slang: rogue; rascal; scoundrel; scamp; jade; sauce
psia jucha! [pśhah **yoo**-khah] exp.: damn it!; be damned!
jucht [yookht] m. Russian leather; waterproof leather; yuft
juchtowy [yookh-**to**-vi] adj.m. of Russian leather; Russian-leather (boots, etc.)
juczenie [yoo-**che**-ńe] n. putting saddlebags on a horse (on a mule, etc.); burdening with saddlebags; burdening with panniers
jucznie [**yooch**-ńe] adv. (to convey, etc.) by packhorses; on horseback; in saddlebags; in panniers
juczność [**yooch**-nośhćh] f. pack-carrying capacity
juczny [**yooch**-ni] adj.m. pack (animal, horse, mule, etc.)
juczny koń [**yooch**-ni koń] exp.: packhorse; horse carrying saddlebags
zwierzę juczne [**zvye**-zhan **yooch**-ne] exp.: pack-animal; beast of burden carrying saddlebags
juczyć [**yoo**-chićh] v. put saddlebags on a horse (on a mule, on a camel, etc.); burden with saddlebags; burden with panniers (*repeatedly*)
judaica [yoo-dah-**ee**-kah] pl. Judaica
judaika [yoo-dah-**ee**-kah] pl. Judaica
judaista [yoo-dah-**ees**-tah] m. Judaist; student of Judaism; follower of Judaism
judaistyczny [yoo-dah-ees-**tich**-ni] adj.m. Judaic; Judaistic
judaizacja [yoo-dah-ee-**zah**-tsyah] f. Judaization
judaizator [yoo-dah-ee-**zah**-tor] m. Judaizer
judaizm [yoo-**dah**-eezm] m. Judaism; yiddishism
judaizować [yoo-dah-ee-**zo**-vahćh] v. Judaize; make Jewish (*repeatedly*)
judasz [**yoo**-dahsh] m. deceiver; Judas; traitor; peephole (in a prison-cell door, etc.); judas-hole; judas
judaszowski [yoo-dah-**shof**-skee] adj.m. false; deceitful; perfidious; treacherous; double-dealing
po judaszowsku [po yoo-dah-**shof**-skoo] exp.: adv. falsely; deceitfully; perfidiously; treacherously; in a double-dealing manner
judaszowy [yoo-dah-**sho**-vi] adj.m. of Judas; Judas (kiss, tree, etc.)
judo [**dzhoo**-do] n. judo
judoka [dzhoo-**do**-kah] m. judoist
judowiec [dzhoo-**do**-vyets] m. judoist
judykacyjny [yoo-di-kah-**tsiy**-ni] adj.m. judicatory
judykatura [yoo-di-kah-**too**-rah] f.

judicature
judzenie [yoo-**dze**-ńe] n. incitement; instigation; provocation
judziciel [yoo-**dźhee**-ćhel] m. instigator
judzić [**yoo**-dźheećh] v. instigate; incite; provoke; set on (*repeatedly*)
jufer [**yoo**-fer] m. deadeye; padeye
jufers [**yoo**-fers] m. deadeye; padeye
Jugosłowianin [yoo-go-swo-**vyah**-ńeen] m. Yugoslav; Jugoslav
jugosłowiański [yoo-go-swo-**vyahń**-skee] adj.m. Yugoslav; Jugoslav
juhas [**yoo**-khahs] m. young shepherd (male) in the Tatra mountains
juhasić [yoo-**khah**-śheećh] v. tend sheep (*repeatedly*)
juhaska [yoo-**khahs**-kah] f. young (girl) shepherd in the Tatra mountains
juhaski [yoo-**khahs**-kee] adj.m. young shepherd's (work, etc.) in the Tatra mountains
juhasować [yoo-khah-**so**-vahćh] v. tend sheep (*repeatedly*)
juhasowanie [yoo-khah-so-**vah**-ńe] n. tending of sheep
jujitsu [dzhoo-**dzheet**-soo] n. jujitsu; jujutsu
jujuba [yoo-**yoo**-bah] f. jujube (bush, tree)
juk [yook] m. pack; load; burden
juki [**yoo**-kee] pl. packsaddle; saddlebags; panniers; packs
juka [**yoo**-kah] f. yucca (plant)
juliański [yool-**yahń**-skee] adj.m. Julian (calendar, etc.)
jumper [**dzhahm**-per] m. jumper pulley (for bringing nets on deck)
jumping [**dzhahm**-peeng] m. jumping (sport)
jumpsaling [dzhamp-**sah**-leeng] m. stay spreader; jumper; bracket on mast for tension reinforcing
jumpszrag [**dzhahmp**-shtahk] m. line connected to mast for tension reinforcing; jumper stay
junacki [yoo-**nahts**-kee] adj.m. plucky; rash; reckless; blustering; swaggering; of the labor brigade (of young men)
po junacku [po yoo-**nahts**-koo] exp.: pluckily; with bluster; swaggeringly
junacko [yoo-**nahts**-ko] adv. pluckily; with bluster; swaggeringly
junactwo [yoo-**nahts**-tfo] n. pluck; rashness; recklessness; bluster; swagger; bravado; labor brigades of young men
junaczek [yoo-**nah**-chek] m. plucky boy
junaczka [yoo-**nahch**-kah] f. plucky girl; member of a young women's labor brigade
junaczy [yoo-**nah**-chi] adj.m. plucky; rash; reckless; blustering; swaggering; of the labor brigade (of young men)
junaczyć się [yoo-**nah**-chićh śhan] v. be rash; be reckless; act with dash; show pluck; brave danger; bluster; swagger (*repeatedly*)
junak [**yoo**-nahk] m. plucky young man; swaggerer; dashing guy; reckless man; member of a young men's labor brigade
junakieria [yoo-nah-**ker**-yah] f. pluck; rashness; recklessness; bluster; swagger; bravado; labor brigades of young men
junakować [yoo-nah-**ko**-vahćh] v. be rash; be reckless; act with dash; show pluck; brave danger; bluster; swagger (*repeatedly*)
junakowanie [yoo-nah-ko-**vah**-ńe] n. dash; bluster; swagger
junior [**yoo**-ńor] m. junior
juniorek [yoo-**ńo**-rek] m. child's orthopedic shoe
juniorka [yoo-**ńor**-kah] f. (female) junior
junkier [**yoon**-ker] m. junker; cadet (in tsarist military college)
junkierski [yoon-**ker**-skee] adj.m. junker's; junkers'; cadet (school, etc.)
junkierstwo [yoon-**ker**-stfo] n. junkerdom
junkierszczyzna [yoon-ker-**shchiz**-nah] f. colloq: junkerdom
junta [**khoon**-tah] f. (Spanish) junta
jupiter [yoo-**pee**-ter] m. stage light; film sun lamp; sun arc; sun spot

jupka [**yoop**-kah] f. woman's tonic
jura [**yoo**-rah] f. Jura; Jurassic period; Jurassic rocks
jurajski [yoo-**rahy**-skee] adj.m. Jurassic
jurgielt [**yoor**-gelt] m. mercernary's pay
jurgieltnik [yoor-**gelt**-ńeek] m. mercernary; hired soldier
jurgieltowy [yoor-gel-**to**-vi] adj.m. mercernary; venal
jurnie [**yoor**-ńe] adv. lewdly; lustfully; lasciviously
jurność [**yoor**-nośhćh] f. lewdness; lust; lasciviousness
jurny [**yoor**-ni] adj.m. lewd; lustful; lascivious
juror [**yoo**-ror] m. juror; member of the jury; juryman
główny juror [**gwoov**-ni **yoo**-ror] exp.: foreman of the jury
jurorzy [yoo-**ro**-zhi] pl. the jury; jurors; members of the jury; jurymen
jurorka [yoo-**ror**-kah] f. (woman) juror; member of the jury; jurywoman
jurta [**yoor**-tah] f. yurt; yurta; reindeer-skin tent
jury [**zhoo**-ri] n. jury; committee of judges of sport events
jurydycznie [yoo-ri-**dich**-ńe] adv. juridically
jurydyczny [yoo-ri-**dich**-ni] adj.m. juridical; legal
jurydyka [yoo-**ri**-di-kah] f. autonomous jurisdiction of suburbia and suburban guilds (17th cent. Poland)
jurysdykcja [yoo-ris-**dik**-tsyah] f. jurisdiction; legal authority
jurysdykcyjnie [yoo-ris-dik-**tsiy**-ńe] adv. jurisdictionally; by legal authority; jurisprudentially
jurysdykcyjny [yoo-ris-dik-**tsiy**-ni] adj.m. jurisdictional; of legal authority; jurisprudntial
juryskonsult [yoo-ris-**kon**-soolt] m. jurisconsult
jurysprudencja [yoo-ris-proo-**den**-tsyah] f. jurisdiction; legal authority; jurisprudence
jurysta [yoo-**ris**-tah] m. jurist
jurystka [yoo-**rist**-kah] f. (female) jurist
jurystycznie [yoo-ris-**tich**-ńe] adv. juristically
jurystyczny [yoo-ris-**tich**-ni] adj.m. juristic
justować [yoos-**to**-vahćh] v. justify (printed edge); register; adjust (spacing of print); standardize (print) (*repeatedly*)
justowanie [yoos-to-**vah**-ńe] n. justification (of a printed edge); registration; adjustment; standardization
justunek [yoos-**too**-nek] m. print spacing
justunkowy [yoos-toon-**ko**-vi] adj.m. print-spacing (material, size, etc.)
jut [yoot] m. rear end of upper deck of a ship
juta [**yoo**-tah] f. jute; jute plant
jutowy [yoo-**to**-vi] adj.m. of jute; jute (rope, weave, fiber, etc.)
materiał jutowy [mah-**ter**-yahw yoo-**to**-vi] exp.: burlap; gunny
jutro [**yoot**-ro] n. & adv. tomorrow; the next day; the following day; on the morrow; n. the future
do jutra [do **yoot**-rah] exp.: till tomorrow; see you tomorrow; good-bye till tomorrow; so long
bez jutra [bes **yoot**-rah] exp.: without a tomorrow
dziś tu a jutro tam [dźheeśh too ah **yoot**-ro tahm] exp.: here one day, elsewhere the next
jutro po południu [**yoot**-ro po po-**wood**-ńoo] exp.: tomorrow afternoon
jutro rano [**yoot**-ro **rah**-no] exp.: tomorrow morning
jutro wieczorem [**yoot**-ro vye-**cho**-rem] exp.: tomorrow night; tomorrow evening
jutro wieczór [**yoot**-ro **vye**-choor] exp.: tomorrow night; tomorrow evening
jutro w nocy [**yoot**-ro v **no**-tsi] exp.: tomorrow night; tomorrow during the night
nie dziś to jutro [ńe dźheeśh to **yoot**-ro] exp.: tomorrow
nikt nie jest pewny jutra [ńeekt ńe yest **pev**-ni **yoot**-rah] exp.: no one is sure of the future; nobody

knows what the future has in store for him
od jutra [od **yoot**-rah] exp.: from tomorrow on; beginning tomorrow; starting tomorrow
od jutra za tydzień [od **yoot**-rah zah **ti**-dźheń] exp.: tomorrow week; a week from tomorrow
jutrzejszy [yoo-**tshey**-shi] adj.m. tomorrow's; future
dzień jutrzejszy [dźheń yoo-**tshey**-shi] adj.m. tomorrow; future
jutrzenka [yoo-**tshen**-kah] f. dawn; daybreak; morning star; aurora
jutrznia [**yootsh**-ńah] f. daybreak prayer; daybreak; morning star; dawn; aurora
juwenalia [yoo-ve-**nahl**-yah] pl. yearly traditional rejoicing of university students
juwenilia [yoo-ve-**ńeehl**-yah] pl. juvenilia
juwenilny [yoo-ve-**ńeehl**-ni] adj.m. juvenile (water, etc.)
juz [yoos] m. early, primitive device for sending telegrams
juzing [**yoo**-zeeng] m. oozy line (used on ships)
już [yoosh] conj. already; as early as; at any moment; by now; no more; yet; before now
i już [ee yoosh] exp.: and that's all; and that's that; and there's an end
już? [yoosh] exp.: ready?; O.K.?
już! [yoosh] excl.: coming!; O.K.!; hurry up!; be quick!; now!
już dawno [yoosh **dahv**-no] exp.: long ago
już dawno go nie widziałem [yoosh **dahv**-no go ńe vee-**dźhah**-wem] exp.: it's a long time since I saw him; I haven't seen him for ages
już, już [yoosh yoosh] exp.: any moment; at any moment; nearer and nearer; closer and closer
już ... już [yoosh yoosh] exp.: either ... or; now ...now again
już nic nie ma [yoosh ńeets ńe mah] exp.: there is no more; there is nothing left
już nie [yoosh ńe] exp.: no more; not any more; no longer; not any longer
już niedługo [yoosh ńe-**dwoo**-go] exp.: shortly; before long
już nigdy [yoosh **ńeeg**-di] exp.: never again
już po nim [yoosh po ńeem] exp.: he is done for; he's a dead man
już po tym [yoosh po tim] exp.: it's all over; it's finished
już wkrótce [yoosh **fkroot**-tse] exp.: shortly; before long
już wczoraj [yoosh **fcho**-rahy] exp.: as early as yesterday
już wiem o tym [yoosh vyem o tim] exp.: I knew it before now
już wtedy [yoosh **fte**-di] exp.: by then; before then; already then; colloq: way back
jużci [**yoośh**-ćhee] conj.: of course!; certainly!; naturally!; rather!; sure thing!
jużcić [**yoośh**-ćheećh] adv. = emphatic: **już**
jużeż [**yoo**-zhesh] adv. = emphatic **już**
jużże [**yoozh**-zhe] adv. = emphatic **już**

K

K, k [kah] the letter "k"; the sound "k"; adv. colloq: to; towards; in the direction; about; for
kabacik [kah-**bah**-ćheek] m. (small, nice) sleeved vest; undercoat; spencer
kabaczek [kah-**bah**-chek] m. cucurbit; pumpkin; summer squash
kabalarka [kah-bah-**lahr**-kah] f. (woman) fortuneteller (by looking at cards)
kabalista [kah-bah-**lees**-tah] m. cabalist; fortuneteller (by looking at cards)
kabalistycznie [kah-bah-lees-**tich**-ńe]

adv. cabalistically
kabalistyczny [kah-bah-lees-**tich**-ni] adj.m. cabalistic (signs, etc.)
kabalistyka [kah-bah-**lees**-ti-kah] f. cabala
kabała [kah-**bah**-wah] f. cabala; fortunetelling; book on rules in fortunetelling; quandary; predicament; scrape; sorry pickle
stawianie kabały [stah-**vyah**-ńe kah-**bah**-wi] exp.: fortunetelling
wpakować się w kabałę [fpah-**ko**-vahćh śhan f kah-**bah**-wan] exp.: to get into trouble; get into a scrape; get into a mess; get into hot water
kaban [**kah**-bahn] m. boar; tusker; pig; swine; hog
kabanos [kah-**bah**-nos] m. thin dry smoked pork sausage
kabareciarz [kah-bah-**re**-ćhahsh] m. cabaret performer; cabaret producer
kabarecik [kah-bah-**re**-ćheek] m. students' cabaret; television cabaret
kabarecista [kah-bah-re-**ćhees**-tah] m. cabaret performer; cabaret producer
kabaret [kah-**bah**-ret] m. cabaret; slang: gaff (cheap theater); cafe chantant
kabaretki [kah-bah-**ret**-kee] pl. a kind of transparent stockings
kabaretowy [kah-bah-re-**to**-vi] adj.m. cabaret (performer, etc.)
kabat [**kah**-baht] m. sleeved vest; undercoat; spencer
kabe [kah-be] m. rifle; see: **karabin**
kabel [**kah**-bel] m. cable; wire rope
kabelak [kah-**be**-lahk] m. slang: electrician
kabelek [kah-**be**-lek] m. (small, thin) cable; wire rope
kabelgat [kah-**bel**-gaht] m. cable tier; storage closet for ropes and cables on a ship
kabeltaw [kah-**bel**-tahf] m. hawser
kabestan [kah-**bes**-tahn] m. capstan; winch; windlass
kabina [kah-**bee**-nah] f. cabin; cubicle; locker; call box; telephone booth
kabinet [kah-**bee**-net] m. secretary (17th cent. desk design)
kabinka [kah-**been**-kah] f. (small) cabin; cubicle; locker; call box; telephone booth
kabinowy [kah-bee-**no**-vi] adj.m. of a cabin; of a cubicle; of a locker
kablobeton [kahb-lo-**be**-ton] m. post-tensioned prestressed concrete
kablobetonowy [kahb-lo-be-to-**no**-vi] adj.m. of post-tensioned prestressed concrete
kablogram [kahb-**lo**-grahm] m. cablegram; cable
kablować [kahb-**lo**-vahćh] v. cable; send a cablegram; colloq: inform on somebody; slang: vulg.: have oral sex (mob jargon) (*repeatedly*)
kablowiec [kahb-**lo**-vyets] m. cable-layer; cable ship; slang: informer; traitor (mob jargon)
kablowy [kahb-**lo**-vi] adj.m. cable (layer, traction, railway, etc.); of a cable; for cables; m. slang: informer; traitor (mob jargon)
depesza kablowa [de-**pe**-shah kahb-**lo**-vah] exp.: cablegram; cable
kabłączasty [kahb-wown-**chahs**-ti] adj.m. like a bow; bow-shaped; arched; curved; arcuate
kabłączek [kahb-**wown**-chek] m. (small) bow; hoop; bail; trigger-guard
kabłąk [**kahb**-wownk] m. bow; hoop; bail; trigger-guard
kabłąkowato [kahb-wown-ko-**vah**-to] adv. like a bow; in bow-shaped manner; like an arch
kabłąkowatość [kahb-wown-ko-**vah**-tośhćh] f. the shape of a bow; bow-shape; arch; arcuation
kabłąkowaty [kahb-wown-ko-**vah**-ti] adj.m. like a bow; bow-shaped; arched; curved; arcuate
kabłąkowy [kahb-wown-**ko**-vi] adj.m. bow-shaped
kaboszon [kah-**bo**-shon] m. cabochon; tallow-drop stone (emerald, etc.); stone cut "en cabochon"
kabotaż [kah-**bo**-tahsh] m. cabotage; coastal trade
wielki kabotaż [**vyel**-kee kah-**bo**-tahsh] exp.: offshore coastal

trade
kabotażnik [kah-bo-**tahzh**-ńeek] m. coastal vessel; coastal ship
kabotażowiec [kah-bo-tah-**zho**-vyets] m. coastal vessel; coastal ship
kabotażowy [kah-bo-tah-**zho**-vi] adj.m. coastal (vessel, ship, steamer, etc.)
kabotyn [kah-**bo**-tin] m. poser; buffoon; second-rate actor
kabotynizm [kah-bo-**ti**-ńeezm] m. overacting; buffoonery; second-rate acting; playing a fool
kabotynka [kah-bo-**tin**-kah] f. (female) poser; buffoon; second-rate actor
kabotyński [kah-bo-**tiń**-skee] adj.m. of a poser; buffoonish; second-rate actor's; comedian's
kabotyńsko [kah-bo-**tiń**-sko] adv. like a poser; like a buffoon; like a second-rate actor; like a comedian
kabotyństwo [kah-bo-**tiń**-stfo] n. overacting; buffoonery; second-rate acting; playing a fool
kabriolecik [kah-bryo-**le**-ćheek] m. (small, nice) convertible car; gig
kabriolet [kah-**bryo**-let] m. convertible car; gig; cabriolet
kabriolimuzyna [kah-bryo-lee-moo-**zi**-nah] f. convertible car with windows in fixed frames; gig
kabul [kah-**bool**] m. piquant sauce
kabura [kah-**boo**-rah] f. gun holster
Kabyl [**kah**-bil] m. Kabyle
Kabylka [kah-**bil**-kah] f. Kabyle (female)
kabza [**kahb**-zah] f. purse; moneybag; slang: pocket; money in the pocket; billfold
nabić kabzę [nah-beećh **kahb**-zan] exp.: colloq: to make a bundle; to get rich; to make money
kac [kahts] m. hangover
mieć kaca [myećh **kah**-tsah] exp.: to suffer from a hangover; to have a hangover; to be chippy; to have a bad head
kacabaja [kah-tsah-**bah**-yah] f. colloq: quilted vest
kacabajka [kah-tsah-**bahy**-kah] f. colloq: (small) quilted vest
kacap [**kah**-tsahp] m. slang: Russian; Russian language class
kaceciarz [kah-**tse**-ćhahsh] m. colloq: inmate of one of Nazi-German concentration camps
kacenjamer [kah-tsen-**yah**-mer] m. katzenjammer; hangover; distress; depression; a discordant clamor
kacerski [kah-**tser**-skee] adj.m. heretical
kacerstwo [kah-**tser**-stfo] n. heresy; heretics
kacerz [**kah**-tsesh] m. heretic; landing net
kacet [**kah**-tset] m. colloq: Nazi-German concentration camp; slang: isolation prison cell
kacetowiec [kah-tse-**to**-vyets] m. colloq: inmate of Nazi-German concentration camp
kacheksja [kah-**kheks**-yah] f. cachexy; cachexia
kaci [kah-ćhee] adj.m. of an executioner; executioner's
kacyk [**kah**-tsik] m. cacique; oriole; colloq: domineering official; despotic official
kacykostwo [kah-tsi-**kos**-tfo] n. cacique's rule; abuse of authority; despotic conduct
kacykowski [kah-tsi-**kof**-skee] adj.m. of cacique; of the abuse of authority; despotic; tyrannical
kacykowy [kah-tsi-**ko**-vi] adj.m. of cacique; of the abuse of authority; despotic; tyrannical
kaczan [kah-chahn] m. cob; corncob; cabbage stump
kaczątko [kah-**chownt**-ko] n. duckling; duck's poult
dzikie kaczątko [**dźhee**-ke kah-**chownt**-ko] exp.: flapper
kaczenica [kah-che-**ńee**-tsah] f. variety of saltwater shellfish
kaczeniec [kah-**che**-ńets] m. marsh marigold; kingcup; cowslip
kaczeńcowy [kah-cheń-**tso**-vi] adj.m. of the marsh-marigold; marsh-marigold (leaves, etc.)
kaczę [**kah**-chan] n. duckling; duck's poult
dzikie kaczę [**dźhee**-ke **kah**-chan] exp.: flapper

kaczka [**kahch**-kah] f. duck; fabricated report; canard; hoax; false report; grapevine; colloq: (invalid's) urinal; slang: death sentence; short woman (jargon)
dzika kaczka [**dźhee**-kah **kahch**-kah] exp.: mallard
kaczka morska [**kahch**-kah **mors**-kah] exp.: garrot
kaczki [**kahch**-kee] pl. ducks; the family Anatidae of birds
puszczać kaczki [**poosh**-chahćh **kahch**-kee] exp.: to play ducks and drakes; to spread fabricated reports (canards; hoaxes; false reports; grape-wine)
kaczkowato [kahch-ko-**vah**-to] adv. like a duck; waddlingly
kaczkowaty [kahch-ko-**vah**-ti] adj.m. like a duck; waddling
kaczkowate [kahch-ko-**vah**-te] pl. the family Anatidae
kaczkowaty chód [kahch-ko-**vah**-ti khoot] exp.: walking like a duck; waddle
kacznik [**kahch**-ńeek] m. duck pen
kaczodzioby [kah-cho-**dźho**-bi] adj.m. having a duck-like beak
kaczor [**kah**-chor] m. drake
kaczorek [kah-**cho**-rek] m. young drake
kaczuchna [kah-**chookh**-nah] f. (nice, little) duckling
kaczucza [kah-**choo**-chah] f. cachucha (Spanish dance)
kaczusia [kah-**choo**-śhah] f. (nice, little) duckling
kaczuszka [kah-**choosh**-kah] f. (nice, little) duckling
kaczy [**kah**-chi] adj.m. duck's; duck (pond, etc.); like a duck
kaczy kuper [**kah**-chi **koo**-per] exp.: duck's rump; duck's rear end; duck's bottom; duck's behind
strzelać jak w kaczy kuper [**stshe**-lahćh yahk f **kah**-chi **koo**-per] exp.: to shoot point-blank
kaczyniec [kah-**chi**-ńets] m. marsh marigold; kingcup; cowslip
kadaweryna [kah-dah-ve-**ri**-nah] f. cadaverine
kadecki [kah-**dets**-kee] adj.m. cadet's; cadets'
szkoła kadecka [**shko**-wah kah-**dets**-kah] exp.: military academy; military college
kadencja [kah-**den**-tsyah] f. term of office; cadence; cadency
kadencja sędziego [kah-**den**-tsyah s<u>an</u>-**dźhe**-go] exp.: judge's term of office; judicature
odbyć kadencję [**od**-bićh kah-**den**-tsy<u>an</u>] exp.: to serve one's term of office
w czasie kadencji [f **chah**-śhe kah-**dents**-yee] exp.: during a term of office
kadencyjny [kah-den-**tsiy**-ni] adj.m. of the term of office; cadenced (music); cadential (structure, term, etc.)
kadet [**kah**-det] m. cadet; Constitutional-Democrat; slang: reformatory; correctional institution (mob jargon)
kadi [**kah**-dee] m. Cadi; Muslim judge
kadilak [kah-**dee**-lahk] m. slang: foreign car (mob jargon)
kadisz [**kah**-deesh] m. kaddish; Jewish mourning prayer and ritual
kadka [**kaht**-kah] f. small vat
kadłub [**kahd**-woop] m. trunk; (ship) hull; (airplane) fuselage; body; torso; framework; casing; mounting; pedestal (of a pump, etc.); (voice) inflection
kadłub zwierzęcia [**kahd**-woop zvye-**zh<u>an</u>**-ćhah] exp.: carcass
kadłubek [kahd-**woo**-bek] m. (small human, animal) trunk
kadłubowaty [kahd-woo-bo-**vah**-ti] adj.m. like a trunk
kadłubownia [kahd-woo-**bo**-vńah] f. hull-building department in a shipyard
kadłubowy [kahd-woo-**bo**-vi] adj.m. truncated; incomplete; rump; of a fragment remaining after the separation of the larger part of a group or an area
kadm [kahdm] m. cadmium (atomic number 48)
kadmować [kahd-**mo**-vahćh] v. coat (a metal) with cadmium (by electrolysis) (*repeatedly*)
kadmowanie [kahd-mo-**vah**-ńe] n.

coating (a metal) with cadmium (by electrolysis)
kadmowy [kahd-**mo**-vi] adj.m. of cadmium; cadmic; cadmium (yellow, etc.)
kadr [kahdr] m. frame (of a film)
kadra [**kah**-drah] f. staff; cadre (of a skeleton unit); personnel; depot
kadrować [kah-**dro**-vahćh] v. edit a film (*repeatedly*)
kadrowanie [kahd-ro-**vah**-ńe] n. editing of a film
kadrowicz [kahd-**ro**-veech] m. member of representative sport's team
kadrowiczka [kahd-ro-**veech**-kah] f. (female) member of representative sport's team
kadrowiec [kahd-**ro**-vyets] m. worker in the personnel department; specialist of human resources; slang: correctional institution (mob jargon)
kadrowy [kahd-**ro**-vi] adj.m. personnel (reserves, etc.); staff (work, etc.); cadre (of officers, etc.); m. colloq: personnel manager
kadrówka [kahd-**roof**-kah] f. cadre company of Pilsudski's legions (in 1914)
kadryl [**kahd**-ril] m. square dance; second-rate blood sausage; quadrille (music)
kaduceusz [kah-doo-**tse**-oosh] m. caduceus; herald's staff of office
kaduczny [kah-**dooch**-ni] adj.m. devilish
kaduk [**kah**-dook] m. escheat; stray; right of inheritance; devil; epilepsy
prawem kaduka [**prah**-vem kah-**doo**-kah] exp.: illegally
kadukowy [kah-doo-**ko**-vi] adj.m. of escheat
majątek kadukowy [mah-**yown**-tek kah-doo-**ko**-vi] exp.: stray (inheritance)
prawo kadukowe [**prah**-vo kah-doo-**ko**-ve] exp.: right of escheat
kady [**kah**-di] m. Cady (Muslim judge)
kadysz [**kah**-dish] m. kaddish; Jewish mourning prayer and ritual
kadzenie [kah-**dze**-ńe] n. base flattery; adulation; fulsome praise
kadzić [**kah**-dźheećh] v. incense; flatter; butter up; blarney; adulate; vulg.: fart; have sex (*repeatedly*)
kadzidlany [kah-dźheed-**lah**-ni] adj.m. of incense
kadzidło [kah-**dźhee**-dwo] n. incense (at an altar); frankincense; fragrance
kadzidłowy [kah-dźhee-**dwo**-vi] adj.m. incense (smoke, etc.)
kadzielnica [kah-dźhel-**ńee**-tsah] f. censer; thurikle
kadzielniczka [kah-dźhel-**ńeech**-kah] f. cassolette
kadziować [kah-**dźho**-vahćh] v. dissolve vat dyes (*repeatedly*)
kadziowanie [kah-dźho-**vah**-ńe] n. dissolving vat dyes in water
kadziowy [kah-**dźho**-vi] adj.m. of a vat; vat (dyes, etc.)
kadziówka [kah-**dźhoof**-kah] f. fireproof brick for foundry vats
kadź [kahdźh] f. tub; tubful; tun; gyle; vat
kaem [**kah**-em] m. machinegun
kaemista [kah-e-**mees**-tah] m. machinegunner
kaes [**kah**-es] m. slang: death sentence (mob jargon)
kaesa [kah-**e**-sah] f. slang: death sentence (mob jargon)
kafar [**kah**-fahr] m. pile driver; drop hammer; ram; rammer; slang: village man; backwoodsman; fist; punch (mob jargon)
bić kafarem [beećh kah-**fah**-rem] exp.: to ram
kafarowy [kah-fah-**ro**-vi] adj.m. of a pile driver; drop-hammer (rig, etc.); ram (frame, etc.); rammer (drop); m. drop-hammer operator
kafejka [kah-**fey**-kah] f. small coffee shop
kafejkarz [kah-**fey**-kahsh] m. owner of a small coffee shop
kafel [**kah**-fel] m. tile (ceramic); slang: face; ear (mob jargon)
wykładać kaflami [vi-**kwah**-dahćh kah-**flah**-mee] exp.: to tile
kafelek [kah-**fe**-lek] m. (small, nice) tile (ceramic)

kafelkowy [kah-fel-**ko**-vi] adj.m. tiled
kafeteria [kah-fe-**ter**-yah] f. cafeteria
kafla [**kahf**-lah] f. tile (ceramic)
kaflany [kahf-**lah**-ni] adj.m. tiled
kaflarnia [kahf-**lahr**-ńah] f. tilery
kaflarski [kahf-**lahr**-skee] adj.m. tiler's; of tiling
piec kaflarski [pyets kahf-**lahr**-skee] exp.: tile kiln
robota kaflarska [ro-**bo**-tah kahf-**lahr**-skah] exp.: tiling
kaflarstwo [kahf-**lahr**-stfo] n. tile-making
kaflarz [**kahf**-lahsh] m. tiler
kaflowy [kahf-**lo**-vi] adj.m. of tiles
piec kaflowy [pyets kahf-**lo**-vi] exp.: tile kiln; tile stove
kaftan [**kahf**-tahn] m. jacket
kaftan bezpieczeństwa [**kahf**-tahn bez-pye-**cheń**-stfah] exp.: straight jacket; "waistcoat"
kaftaniczek [kahf-tah-**ńee**-chek] m. (very nice, small) bodice; vest; (baby's) jacket; caftan
kaftanik [kahf-**tah**-ńeek] m. bodice; vest; (baby's) jacket; caftan
kaganek [kah-**gah**-nek] m. (small) oil lamp; cresset; torch of learning
kaganiec [kah-**gah**-ńets] m. muzzle; gag; oil lamp; cresset; slang: brassiere; bra (mob jargon)
nakładać kaganiec [nah-**kwah**-dahćh kah-**gah**-ńets] exp.: to muzzle (a dog); to gag (the press, etc.)
kaganiec oświaty [kah-**gah**-ńets ośh-**fyah**-ti] exp.: torch of learning
kagańcowy [kah-gahń-**tso**-vi] adj.m. of a muzzle; of a gag; gag (law, etc.)
kagańczyk [kah-**gahń**-chik] m. (small) muzzle; gag
kahalnik [kah-**khahl**-ńeek] m. a member of a kehilla
kahał [**kah**-khahw] m. the governing council of a (Jewish) kehilla
kaik [**kah**-eek] m. caique (boat)
kainit [kah-**ee**-ńeet] m. kainite
kainowy [kah-ee-**no**-vi] adj.m. Cain's; fratricidal
kajaczek [kah-**yah**-chek] m. (small, nice) canoe; kayak
kajać się [**kah**-yahćh śh<u>an</u>] v. repent; confess with contrition (*repeatedly*)
kajak [**kah**-yahk] m. kayak; canoe
kajakarka [kah-yah-**kahr**-kah] f. (female) canoeist
kajakarstwo [kah-yah-**kahr**-stfo] n. canoeing
kajakarz [kah-**yah**-kahsh] m. canoeist
kajakować [kah-yah-**ko**-vahćh] v. canoe; paddle a canoe (*repeatedly*)
kajakowiec [kah-yah-**ko**-vyets] m. canoeist
kajakowy [kah-yah-**ko**-vi] adj.m. of a canoe; canoe (paddle, etc.); canoeing (trip, etc.)
kajanie się [kah-**yah**-ńe śh<u>an</u>] n. repentance; contrition
kajdaniarski [kahy-dah-**ńahr**-skee] adj.m. convict's; convicts'; prison (life, etc.)
kajdaniarstwo [kahy-dah-**ńahr**-stfo] n. dirty trick
kajdaniarz [kahy-**dah**-ńahsh] m. convict; jailbird; goalbird; gallows bird; slang: married man (jargon)
kajdanki [kahy-**dahn**-kee] pl. handcuffs; manacles
kajdanowy [kahy-dah-**no**-vi] adj.m. of handcuffs; for shackles; of manacles; for manacles
kajdany [kahy-**dah**-ni] pl. handcuffs; manacles; shackles; chains; bond; fetters; slang: German prison shoes with wooden soles (jargon)
kajeputowy [kah-ye-poo-**to**-vi] adj.m. of one of Malayan trees (ether oil, etc.)
kajet [**kah**-yet] m. copybook; exercise-book; notebook
Kajfasz [**kahy**-fahsh] m. Caiaphas; mob slang: traitor; informer
grób Kajfasza [groop kahy-**fah**-shah] exp.: the grave of Caiaphas (with a Greek rather than Hebrew inscription)
kajmak [**kahy**-mahk] m. pastry filling of milk, sugar, chocolate, and coffee
kajmakan [kahy-**mah**-kahn] m. county chief; Turkish lieu. colonel
kajman [**kahy**-mahn] m. cayman; caiman (crocodilian)

kajper [**kahy**-per] m. red marl; Keuper
kajprowy [kahy-**pro**-vi] adj.m. of red marl
kajtek [**kahy**-tek] m. colloq: kid
kajtonia [kahy-**to**-ńyah] f. variety of fern (plant)
kajtonie [kahy-**to**-ńye] pl. Caytoniales fern family
kajuta [kah-**yoo**-tah] f. ship-cabin; slang: room; prison cell; school administration room
kajuta na dziobie [kah-**yoo**-tah nah **dźho**-bye] exp.: fore-cabin
kajuta na rufie [kah-**yoo**-tah nah **roof**-ye] exp.: after-cabin
kajutka [kah-**yoot**-kah] f. small cabin
kajutowy [kah-yoo-**to**-vi] adj.m. cabin (deck, etc.)
kajzer [**kahy**-zer] m. kaiser; colloq: German emperor
kajzerka [kahy-**zer**-kah] f. fancy roll of bread; kaiser roll; mob slang: woman's breast; sneak; telltale
kakać [**kah**-kahćh] v. go potty (baby talk) (*repeatedly*)
kakadu [kah-**kah**-doo] f. indecl.: cockatoo; variety of kaka parrot
kakanie [kah-**kah**-ńe] n. vulg.: shitting; defecation
kakao [kah-**kah**-o] n. cocoa bean; cocoa powder (drink); mob slang: rectum; homosexual intercourse
kakaowiec [kah-kah-**o**-vyets] m. cocoa-tree; theobroma
kakaowy [kah-kah-**o**-vi] adj.m. of cocoa; cocoa (tree, butter, oil, etc.); m. mob slang: homosexual
kakemon [kah-**ke**-mon] m. (Japanese) kakemono
kakemono [kah-ke-**mo**-no] n. (Japanese) kakemono
kakodyl [kah-**ko**-dil] m. cacodyl
kakodylowy [kah-ko-di-**lo**-vi] adj.m. cacodyl (oxide, etc.); cacodylic (acid, etc.)
kakofonia [kah-ko-**fo**-ńyah] f. cacophony; dissonance
kakografia [kah-ko-**grah**-fyah] f. cacography; bad writing
kaktus [**kahk**-toos] m. cactus; slang: head; unshaven man
kaktusowaty [kahk-too-so-**vah**-ti] adj.m. cactiform
kaktusowate [kahk-too-so-**vah**-te] pl. cactus (Cactaceae) family of plants
kaktusowy [kahk-too-**so**-vi] adj.m. cactus (spines, flowers, etc.)
kaku [**kah**-koo] n. poop (excrement)
robić kaku [**ro**-beećh **kah**-koo] exp.: to go potty (baby talk)
kalabasa [kah-lah-**bah**-sah] f. calabash (fruit, utensil)
kalać [**kah**-lahćh] v. pollute; foul up; stain; sully; befoul (*repeatedly*)
kalać się [**kah**-lahćh śhan] v. soil (oneself) (*repeatedly*)
kalafior [kah-**lah**-fyor] m. cauliflower (a vegetable); slang: radiator; nose; indifference (to school)
kalafiorek [kah-lah-**fyo**-rek] m. (small, nice) cauliflower
kalafiorowy [kah-lah-fyo-**ro**-vi] adj.m. cauliflower (soup, etc.)
kalafonia [kah-lah-**fo**-ńyah] f. rosin; colophony; colloq: liquor
kalafoniowy [kah-lah-fo-**ńyo**-vi] adj.m. rosin (paint, etc.)
kalamaria [kah-lah-**mahr**-yah] f. calamite
kalambur [kah-**lahm**-boor] m. pun; quibble; play on words
robić kalambury [**ro**-beećh kah-lahm-**boo**-ri] exp.: to quibble; to play on words
kalamburzysta [kah-lahm-boo-**zhis**-tah] m. punster
kalamburzystka [kah-lahm-boo-**zhist**-kah] f. (female) punster
kalamin [kah-**lah**-meen] m. calamine
kalamit [kah-**lah**-meet] m. calamite
kalamity [kah-lah-**mee**-ti] pl. the Calamite family of plants
kalander [kah-**lahn**-der] m. calender; mangle
kalandra [kah-**lahn**-drah] f. calandra (bird)
kalandrować [kah-lahn-**dro**-vahćh] v. calender; mangle (*repeatedly*)
kalandrowanie [kah-lahn-dro-**vah**-ńe] n. calendering; mangling
kalandrowy [kah-lahn-**dro**-vi] adj.m. calendering (machine, etc.); m. calenderer
kalanie [kah-**lah**-ńe] n. soiling
kalarepa [kah-lah-**re**-pah] f. turnip-

cabbage; kohlrabi
kalarepka [kah-lah-**rep**-kah] f. (small) turnip-cabbage; kohlrabi
kalceolaria [kahl-tse-o-**lahr**-yah] f. calceolaria (plant)
kalcyfil [kahl-**tsi**-feel] m. calciphile
kalcyfile [kahl-tsi-**fee**-le] pl. the family of calciphilic organisms
kalcyfilowy [kahl-tsi-fee-**lo**-vi] adj.m. calciphilic
kalcyfit [kahl-**tsi**-fit] m. organism avoiding acidic environment
kalcyfitowy [kahl-tsi-fee-**to**-vi] adj.m. calcareous
kalcynacja [kahl-tsi-**nah**-tsyah] f. calcination (act or process)
kalcynacyjny [kahl-tsi-nah-**tsiy**-ni] adj.m. calcinatory (process)
piec kalcynacyjny [pyets kahl-tsi-nah-**tsiy**-ni] exp.: calciner
kalcynować [kahl-tsi-**no**-vahćh] v. calcine (*repeatedly*)
kalcynować się [kahl-tsi-**no**-vahćh śhan] v. undergo calcination (*repeatedly*)
kalcynowanie [kahl-tsi-no-**vah**-ńe] n. calcination (act or process)
kalcyt [**kahl**-tsit] m. calcite
kaldera [kahl-**de**-rah] f. caldera
kalebasa [kah-le-**bah**-sah] f. a species of pear
kalectwo [kah-**le**-tstfo] n. disability; lameness; invalidism; crippleness
kaleczyć [kah-**le**-chićh] v. cut; wound; mutilate; hurt; injure; lacerate; cripple; mangle; murder (a language); maul; deface (*repeatedly*)
kaleczyć się [kah-**le**-chićh śhan] v. cut oneself; wound oneself; hurt oneself; injure oneself; prick one's finger (*repeatedly*)
kaledonidy [kah-le-do-**ńee**-di] pl. Caledonian Mountains
kaledoński [kah-le-**doń**-skee] adj.m. Caledonian (Mountains, etc.)
kalefaktor [kah-le-**fahk**-tor] m. poor pupil in a religious school performing menial services
kalejdofon [kah-ley-**do**-fon] m. device for producing visual effects to represent sound waves
kalejdoskop [kah-ley-**do**-skop] m. kaleidoscope; medley; miscellany; riot (of colors)
kalejdoskopowo [kah-ley-do-sko-**po**-vo] adv. kaleidoscopically
kalejdoskopowy [kah-ley-do-sko-**po**-vi] adj.m. kaleidoscopic; kaleidoscopical
kaleka [kah-**le**-kah] m. & f. cripple; invalid; disabled person
kaleki [kah-**le**-kee] adj.m. crippled; lame
kalema [kah-**le**-mah] f. sea wave resulting from underwater cliff
kalendarium [kah-len-**dahr**-yoom] n. chronological register of important dates; slang: death of a junkie; death of an addict (mob jargon)
kalendarz [kah-**len**-dahsh] m. calendar; almanac
kalendarzować [kah-len-dah-**zho**-vahćh] v. mob slang: serve a sentence in prison (*repeatedly*)
kalendarzowy [kah-len-dah-**zho**-vi] adj.m. calendar (month, year, etc.)
kalendarzyk [kah-len-**dah**-zhik] m. (small, pocket) calendar
kalendy [kah-**len**-di] pl. calends
kalenica [kah-le-**ńee**-tsah] f. ridge of a roof; crest of a roof
kalenicowy [kah-le-ńee-**tso**-vi] adj.m. of a ridge of a roof; of a crest of a roof (alinement, etc.)
kalesony [kah-le-**so**-ni] pl. underwear; drawers; shorts; underpants; trunk drawers
kaleta [kah-**le**-tah] f. purse carried on a belt
kaletka [kah-**let**-kah] f. leather purse (carried on a belt, bicycle, etc.); wallet; satchel; bursa; sac-like cavity
kaletnictwo [kah-let-**ńeets**-tfo] n. purse making
kaletniczka [kah-let-**ńeech**-kah] f. (woman) purse maker
kaletniczy [kah-let-**ńee**-chi] adj.m. purse-making (shop, etc.)
kaletnik [kah-**let**-ńeek] m. purse maker
kalfataż [kahl-**fah**-tahsh] m. caulking (of a ship, etc.)
kalia [**kahl**-yah] f. calla (lily); arum lily
kalian [**kahl**-yahn] m. (Persian) kalian

kaliber [kah-**lee**-ber] m. caliber; gauge; size; bore (size); calipers; slang: kasha; grits (mob jargon)
kalibrator [kah-lee-**brah**-tor] m. calibrator
kalibromierz [kah-lee-**bro**-myesh] m. gun-barrel gauge
kalibrować [kah-lee-**bro**-vahćh] v. calibrate; gauge; graduate (*repeatedly*)
kalibrowanie [kah-lee-bro-**vah**-ńe] n. calibration; graduation
kalibrownica [kah-lee-bro-**vńee**-tsah] f. calibration gauge; special finishing lathe
kalibrowy [kah-lee-**bro**-vi] adj.m. calibrated
kalichloricum [kah-lee-khlo-**ree**-koom] n. potassium chlorate
kalif [**kah**-leef] m. caliph
kalifaktor [kah-lee-**fahk**-tor] m. poor pupil in a religious school performing menial services; school slang: dumb pupil; telltale
kalifat [kah-**lee**-faht] m. caliphate
kaliforn [kah-**lee**-forn] m. californium (atomic number 98)
kaligraf [kah-**lee**-grahf] m. penman; calligrapher; calligraphist
kaligrafia [kah-lee-**grah**-fyah] f. calligraphy; lettering; beautiful handwriting
kaligraficznie [kah-lee-grah-**feech**-ńe] adv. in beautiful handwriting
kaligraficzny [kah-lee-grah-**feech**-ni] adj.m. calligraphic
kaligrafować [kah-lee-grah-**fo**-vahćh] v. write calligraphically (*repeatedly*)
kaligrafowanie [kah-lee-grah-fo-**vah**-ńe] n. writing calligraphically
kalikant [kah-**lee**-kahnt] m. organ blower
kaliko [kah-**lee**-ko] n. book cloth
kalikować [kah-lee-**ko**-vahćh] v. pump air into (antique) organs (*repeatedly*)
kalikowanie [kah-lee-ko-**vah**-ńe] n. pumping air into (antique) organs
kalikstyn [kah-**leek**-stin] m. moderate (Czech) Husite Church reformer
kalimagnezja [kah-lee-mahg-**nez**-yah] f. a potassium fertilizer; sulfate of potash
kalina [kah-**lee**-nah] f. guelder-rose; cranberry shrub (tree); slang: high denomination bill (mob jargon)
kalinka [kah-**leen**-kah] f. (small, nice) guelder-rose; cranberry shrub (tree)
kalinowy [kah-lee-**no**-vi] adj.m. of the cranberry shrub; cranberry (tree, etc.)
kalipso [kah-**leep**-so] n. calypso (ballad, nymph, flower)
kalit [**kah**-leet] m. Calite
kalium [**kahl**-yoom] n. potassium (atomic number 19)
kalka [**kahl**-kah] f. carbon paper; tracing paper; tracing cloth; servile copy; calque; loan translation; slang: tattoo; fingerprint (mob jargon)
kalkomania [kahl-ko-**mah**-ńyah] f. decalcomania; transfer; decal
kalkować [kahl-**ko**-vahćh] v. calk; trace (over); make a tracing; mob slang: make a tattoo (*repeatedly*)
kalkowanie [kahl-ko-**vah**-ńe] n. calking; tracing (over); making a tracing
kalkowy [kahl-**ko**-vi] adj.m. carbon (paper, etc.)
kalkulacja [kahl-koo-**lah**-tsyah] f. calculation; computation; price calculation; working out prices; reckoning
wytrzymać kalkulację [vi-**tshi**-mahćh kahl-koo-**lah**-tsy<u>an</u>] exp.: to show profit; to yield profit; to leave a margin of profit
kalkulacyjny [kahl-koo-lah-**tsiy**-ni] adj.m. of calculation; computing (scale, etc.)
kalkulator [kahl-koo-**lah**-tor] m. calculator; reckoner; computer
kalkulatorka [kahl-koo-lah-**tor**-kah] f. (woman) calculator
kalkulatorski [kahl-koo-lah-**tor**-skee] adj.m. calculator's
kalkulograf [kahl-koo-**lo**-grahf] m. recorder of time of long-distance telephone calls
kalkulować [kahl-koo-**lo**-vahćh] v. calculate; compute; work out (a price, etc.) (*repeatedly*)
kalkulować się [kahl-koo-**lo**-vahćh

śhan] v. show profit; yield profit; leave a margin of profit; work out (at a price) (*repeatedly*)
kalkulowanie [kahl-koo-lo-**vah**-ńe] n. calculating; computing
kalla [**kahl**-lah] f. calla (lily); arum lily
kalmar [**kahl**-mahr] m. calamary squid
kalmary [kahl-**mah**-ri] pl. calamary squids; the Teuthoidea family
kalo [**kah**-lo] n. loss of weight in transport or in a warehouse (due to drying, etc.)
kalomel [kah-**lo**-mel] m. calomel
kalong [**kah**-lonk] m. kalong (a large bat); flying fox
kaloria [kah-**lo**-ryah] f. calorie; slang: cake (mob jargon)
kalorycznie [kah-lo-**rich**-ńe] adv. calorically
kaloryczność [kah-lo-**rich**-nośhćh] f. calorie content; caloricity
kaloryczny [kah-lo-**rich**-ni] adj.m. caloric; calorific
kaloryfer [kah-lo-**ri**-fer] m. radiator; steam heater; (water) heater
kaloryferowy [kah-lo-ri-fe-**ro**-vi] adj.m. of a radiator; of a steam heater; radiator (pipes, etc.)
kalorymetr [kah-lo-**ri**-metr] m. calorimeter
kalorymetria [kah-lo-ri-**metr**-yah] f. calorimetry
kalorymetrycznie [kah-lo-ri-met-**rich**-ńe] adv. calorimetrically
kalorymetryczny [kah-lo-ri-met-**rich**-ni] adj.m. calorimetric
kaloryzacja [kah-lo-ri-**zah**-tsyah] f. calorization (of metal surfaces)
kaloryzator [kah-lo-ri-**zah**-tor] m. calorisator; calorizer
kaloryzować [kah-lo-ri-**zo**-vahćh] v. calorize (*repeatedly*)
kaloryzowanie [kah-lo-ri-zo-**vah**-ńe] n. calorization
kalosz [**kah**-losh] m. rubber overshoe; galosh; rubber boot; school slang: failing mark
sędzia kalosz [san-dźhah **kah**-losh] exp.: colloq: no good referee
kaloszowy [kah-lo-**sho**-vi] adj.m. of rubber overshoe; of galosh; of rubber boot
kalotka [kah-**lot**-kah] f. calotte
kalota [kah-**lo**-tah] f. calotte
kalotypia [kah-lo-**tip**-yah] f. the use of paper-negative in photography
kalumet [kah-**loo**-met] m. calumet; ceremonial pipe; peace pipe
kalumnia [kah-**loom**-ńah] f. calumny; slander; aspersion
kalus [**kah**-loos] m. callus
kalwaria [kahl-**vahr**-yah] f. Calvary; the Way of the Cross
kalwaryjski [kahl-vah-**riy**-skee] adj.m. of Calvary
dziad kalwaryjski [dźhaht kahl-vah-**riy**-skee] exp.: beggar
kalwin [**kahl**-veen] m. Calvinist
kalwinista [kahl-vee-**ńees**-tah] m. Calvinist
kalwinka [kahl-**veen**-kah] f. (woman) Calvinist
kalwinizm [kahl-**vee**-ńeezm] m. Calvinism
kalwiński [kahl-**veeń**-skee] adj.m. Calvinist
kał [kahw] m. excrement; stool; feces; dung; colloq: filth; slang: falsified document; failing grade
kałakucki [kah-wah-**koots**-kee] adj.m. of a cock of an Indian breed
kałakut [kah-**wah**-koot] m. cock of an Indian breed
kałamarnica [kah-wah-mahr-**ńee**-tsah] f. calamary squid
kałamarnice [kah-wah-mahr-**ńee**-tse] pl. calamary squids; the Teuthoidea family of squids
kałamarz [kah-**wah**-mahsh] m. inkstand; ink pot; inkwell; slang: judge (mob jargon)
kałamarzyk [kah-wah-**mah**-zhik] m. (small, nice) inkstand; ink pot; inkwell
kałamaszka [kah-wah-**mahsh**-kah] f. small four-wheel carriage
kałamutek [kah-wah-**moo**-tek] m. wooden kelly used in impact drilling of wells
kałan [**kah**-wahn] m. Russian otter
kałanek [kah-**wah**-nek] m. variety of ermine; ermine fur
kałat [**kah**-waht] m. slang: rubber hammer (mob jargon)

kałdun [**kahw**-doon] m. slang: belly; paunch; stomach (mob jargon)
kałduniasty [kahw-doo-**ńahs**-ti] adj.m. slang: big-bellied; potbellied; paunchy (jargon)
kałkan [**kahw**-kahn] m. decorative Oriental shield
kałmucki [kahw-**moots**-kee] adj.m. Kalmuck (features, etc.)
Kałmuk [**kahw**-mook] m. Kalmuck
kałmuk [**kahw**-mook] m. horse of Kalmuck breed
kałowy [kah-**wo**-vi] adj.m. excremental; faecal; stercoral; stercoraceous
kałożerny [kah-wo-**zher**-ni] adj.m. scatophagous
kałożerstwo [kah-wo-**zher**-stfo] n. coprophagy
kaługa [kah-**woo**-gah] f. Siberian sturgeon
kałuża [kah-**woo**-zhah] f. puddle; pool; plash
kałuża krwi [kah-**woo**-zhah krvee] exp.: pool of blood
kałużka [kah-**woosh**-kah] f. (small) puddle; pool; plash
kałużnica [kah-woozh-**ńee**-tsah] f. hydrophilid
kałużysty [kah-woo-**zhis**-ti] adj.m. puddly (creek, etc.); splashy
kama [**kah**-mah] f. alcelaphine antelope
kamacyt [kah-**mah**-tsit] m. meteorite with iron content
kamamber [kah-**mahm**-ber] m. Camembert cheese
kamaryla [kah-mah-**ri**-lah] f. camarilla; cabal; clique; junto; faction (of secret and scheming advisors)
kamasz [**kah**-mahsh] m. elastic-side boot; an elastic-sides
kamasze [kah-**mah**-she] pl. gaiters; spats; uppers
w kamaszach [f kah-**mah**-shahkh] exp.: gaitered
kamaszek [kah-**mah**-shek] m. (small) elastic-side boot; an elastic-sides
kamasznictwo [kah-mahsh-**ńeets**-tfo] n. leather-stitching
kamaszniczka [kah-mahsh-**ńeech**-kah] f. (woman) leather-stitcher
kamasznik [kah-**mahsh**-ńeek] m. leather-stitcher
kambar [**kahm**-bahr] m. brown Persian lamb; brown astrakhan fur; brown caracul
kambialny [kahm-**byahl**-ni] adj.m. cambial
kambium [**kahm**-byoom] n. cambium
kambr [kahmbr] n. the Cambrian period
kambryjski [kahm-**briy**-skee] adj.m. Cambrian
kambuz [**kahm**-boos] m. caboose
kambuza [kahm-**boo**-zah] f. caboose
kamea [kah-**me**-ah] f. cameo
kamedulski [kah-me-**dool**-skee] adj.m. Cameldolite (order, etc.)
kameduła [kah-me-**doo**-wah] m. a Cameldolite monk; slang: stolen object; boot; priest (mob jargon)
kamelarowy [kah-me-lah-**ro**-vi] adj.m. of camel-yarn; of camel's hair; of camelhair; camel's-hair (fabric, ribbon, etc.)
kameleon [kah-me-**le**-on] m. chameleon (lizard); colloq: fickle person
kameleony [kah-me-le-**o**-ni] pl. the chameleon family of lizards; Chamaeleonide family of tree lizards
kameleonowy [kah-me-le-o-**no**-vi] adj.m. chameleon's; chameleonic; chameleon-like; colloq: fickle; changeable (person)
kamelia [kah-**mel**-yah] f. camellia
kameliowy [kah-mel-**yo**-vi] adj.m. of a camellia; camellia (flower, white, red, etc.)
kamelor [kah-**me**-lor] m. camel's-hair; camelhair; camel-yarn
kamelorowy [kah-me-lo-**ro**-vi] adj.m. of camel-yarn (Brit.); of camel-yarn; of camelhair; camel's-hair (fabric, ribbon, etc.)
kamena [kah-**me**-nah] f. Roman nymph of spring water; Camena
kameny [kah-**me**-ni] pl. Roman nymphs of spring water; Camenae
kameowy [kah-me-**o**-vi] adj.m. cameo (carving, etc.)
kamera [kah-**me**-rah] f. chamber; camera; motion-picture camera; television camera; Treasury

department; slang: room; dwelling; prison cell; hideout; filmed robbery (mob jargon)
język do kamery [yan-zik do kah-me-ri] exp.: language used before a live televising camera; language used on camera
kameralista [kah-me-rah-lees-tah] m. performer of chamber music; member of chamber orchestra
kameralistka [kah-me-rah-leest-kah] f. (woman) performer of chamber music; member of chamber orchestra
kameralistyka [kah-me-rah-lees-ti-kah] f. chamber music; cameralistics; the science of public finance
kameralizacja [kah-me-rah-lee-zah-tsyah] f. acquiring character of chamber music (style of acting, etc.)
kameralizm [kah-me-rah-leezm] m. cameralism
kameralizować [kah-me-rah-lee-zo-vahćh] v. make private; make cozy; make cameral (*repeatedly*)
kameralizowanie [kah-me-rah-lee-zo-vah-ńe] n. acquiring (giving) cameral character (to music, style of acting, etc.)
kameralnie [kah-me-rahl-ńe] adv. cozily; snugly
kameralność [kah-me-rahl-nośhćh] f. cameral character; coziness; private character
kameralny [kah-me-rahl-ni] adj.m. private; small-audience (hall, etc.); snug; cozy; cameral
muzyka kameralna [moo-zi-kah kah-me-rahl-nah] exp.: chamber music
kamerdyner [kah-mer-di-ner] m. butler; valet (de chambre)
kamerdynerski [kah-mer-di-ner-skee] adj.m. of a butler; valet's
kamerdynerstwo [kah-mer-di-ner-stfo] n. butler's occupation; valet's occupation; the butlers
kamerjunkier [kah-mer-yoon-ker] m. Gentleman of the Bedchamber
kamerlokaj [kah-mer-lo-kahy] m. court valet
kamerownia [kah-me-rov-ńah] f. storage of television cameras; storage of motion-picture cameras
kamerowy [kah-me-ro-vi] adj.m. of camera; camera (frame, etc.)
ujęcie kamerowe [oo-yan-ćhe kah-me-ro-ve] exp.: camera frame
kamerton [kah-mer-ton] m. tuning fork ("U" shaped); pitch pipe
kamertonowy [kah-mer-to-no-vi] adj.m. of a tuning fork; of a pitch pipe
kameryzacja [kah-me-ri-zah-tsyah] f. ornamental technique of setting precious stones in gold and in weapons
kameryzować [kah-me-ri-zo-vahćh] v. set (something) with precious stones (*repeatedly*)
kameryzowanie [kah-me-ri-zo-vah-ńe] n. setting (something) with precious stones
kamerzysta [kah-me-zhis-tah] m. television-camera operator; movie-camera operator; camera man; slang: apartment thief; informer; danger (mob jargon)
kamfen [kahm-fen] m. camphene
kamfora [kahm-fo-rah] f. camphor
ulotnić się jak kamfora [oo-lot-ńeećh śhan yahk kahm-fo-rah] exp.: to vanish into thin air
kamforowiec [kahm-fo-ro-vyets] m. camphor tree
kamforowy [kahm-fo-ro-vi] adj.m. camphor (ball, etc.); camphoric (acid, oil, etc.)
kamgarn [kahm-gahrn] m. worsted
kamgarnowy [kahm-gahr-no-vi] adj.m. worsted
kamica [kah-mee-tsah] f. stone (disease); lithiasis
kamica moczowa [kah-mee-tsah mo-cho-vah] exp.: urinary stones; urolithiasis; calculi
kamica nerkowa [kah-mee-tsah ner-ko-vah] exp.: renal stones; renal calculi; nephrolithiasis
kamica żółciowa [kah-mee-tsah zhoow-ćho-vah] exp.: gall stones; cholelithiasis
kamicowy [kah-mee-tso-vi] adj.m. stone-disease (symptoms, etc.); of lithiasis
kamieniarka [kah-mye-ńahr-kah] f.

masonry; stonework; stonemasonry; stonecutter's trade
kamieniarski [kah-mye-**ńahr**-skee] adj.m. mason's; of stonework; of stonemasonry; of stonecutter's trade
kamieniarstwo [kah-mye-**ńahr**-stfo] n. masonry; stonework; stonemasonry; stonecutter's trade
kamieniarszczyzna [kah-mye-ńahrsh-**chiz**-nah] f. masonry; stonework; stonemasonry; stonecutter's trade
kamieniarz [kah-**mye**-ńahsh] m. mason; stonecutter
kamienica [kah-mye-**ńee**-tsah] f. apartment house; tenants
kamieniczka [kah-mye-**ńeech**-kah] f. (small, nice) apartment house; tenants
kamieniczniczka [kah-mye-ńeech-**ńeech**-kah] f. (woman) owner of an apartment house (houses); owner of urban real estate
kamienicznik [kah-mye-**ńeech**-ńeek] m. (man) owner of an apartment house (houses)
kamieniczny [kah-mye-**ńeech**-ni] adj.m. of an apartment house; of apartment houses
brama kamieniczna [**brah**-mah kah-mye-**ńeech**-nah] exp.: gateway
kamieniec [kah-**mye**-ńets] m. area covered with stones and gravel; rocky area
kamienieć [kah-**mye**-ńećh] v. petrify; be petrified (with fear, etc.); turn into stone; become as hard as stone; become stony-hearted; grow stony-hearted; become pitiless (*repeatedly*)
kamienienie [kah-mye-**ńe**-ńe] n. petrification
kamieniodruk [kah-mye-**ńo**-drook] m. lithography; planography
kamieniołom [kah-mye-**ńo**-wom] m. quarry; stone pit
kamienioryt [kah-mye-**ńo**-rit] m. lithography; planography
kamieniotłuk [kah-mye-**ńo**-twook] m. colloq: knapper
kamienisko [kah-mye-**ńees**-ko] n. huge stone; area covered with stones; rocky area; area covered with rubble
kamienistość [kah-mye-**ńees**-tośhćh] f. stoniness
kamienisty [kah-mye-**ńees**-ti] adj.m. stony; covered with stones; rocky
kamiennictwo [kah-myen-**ńee**-tstfo] n. science of cut stone mining and usage
kamienniczy [kah-myen-**ńee**-chi] adj.m. mason's; stonecutter's
kamiennie [kah-**myen**-ńe] adv. like stone
kamiennie twardy [kah-**myen**-ńe **tfahr**-di] exp.: as hard as stone
kamiennik [kah-**myen**-ńeek] m. stone-mason; stone-cutter
kamienność [kah-**myen**-nośhćh] f. colloq: immobility; severity (of expression, etc.)
kamienny [kah-**myen**-ni] adj.m. of stone; stony; rocky; stone (floor, slab, etc.); flinty; as hard as stone; pitiless; stolid; stony-hearted; dead
epoka kamienna [e-**po**-kah kah-**myen**-nah] exp.: Stone Age
kamienne oblicze [kah-**myen**-ne ob-**lee**-che] exp.: impassive countenance; stony face
kamienne serce [kah-**myen**-ne **ser**-tse] exp.: heart of stone; heart of flint
kamienny wyraz twarzy [kah-**myen**-ni **vi**-rahs **tfah**-zhi] exp.: impassiveness
pył kamienny [piw kah-**myen**-ni] exp.: stone
sól kamienna [sool kah-**myen**-nah] exp.: rock salt
węgiel kamienny [**v<u>an</u>**-<u>g</u>el kah-**myen**-ni] exp.: mineral coal
złom kamienny [zwom kah-**myen**-ni] exp.: rock; rock debris; block of stone
kamienować [kah-mye-**no**-vahćh] v. stone to death; lapidate; hurl; abuse (*repeatedly*)
kamienowanie [kah-mye-no-**vah**-ńe] n. lapidation
kamień [**kah**-myeń] m. stone; rock; precious stone; jewel; fur; scale; incrustation; pawn; playing piece; stone weight; calculus; concretion; tartar

kamikadze [kah-mee-**kah**-dze] m. kamikaze; mob slang: hospital; clinic; psychiatric treatment; drug-rehabilitation; drug-rehab (jargon)
kamikaze [kah-mee-**kah**-ze] m. kamikaze
kamionetka [kah-myo-**net**-kah] f. pickup truck; light truck
kamionka [kah-**myon**-kah] f. stoneware; stone pile; stone bramble; stone marten (mammal)
kamionkowy [kah-myon-**ko**-vi] adj.m. of stoneware; stoneware (jar, pipe, etc.)
kamizard [kah-**mee**-zahrt] m. 18th c. Huguenot rebel (French peasant)
kamizela [kah-mee-**ze**-lah] f. a long overcoat
kamizelka [kah-mee-**zel**-kah] f. waistcoat; vest; camisole
kamizelka ratunkowa [kah-mee-**zel**-kah rah-toon-**ko**-vah] exp.: life jacket; air jacket
kamizelkarz [kah-mee-**zel**-kahsh] m. waistcoat maker; vest maker
kamizelkowy [kah-mee-zel-**ko**-vi] adj.m. waistcoat (style); of a vest
kamlot [**kahm**-lot] m. camlet; camel's-hair fabric
kamlotowy [kahm-lo-**to**-vi] adj.m. camlet (garment, etc.); of camel's-hair fabric
kamora [kah-**mo**-rah] f. Camorra
kamorra [kah-**mor**-rah] f. Camorra
kamorysta [kah-mo-**ris**-tah] m. member of Camorra (secret criminal organization in 19th cent. Italy); camorrista
kampament [kahm-**pah**-ment] m. boot camp; maneuvers; an armed forces training exercise
kampania [kahm-**pah**-ńyah] f. campaign; drive (promotional)
kampania wyborcza [kahm-**pah**-ńyah vi-**bor**-chah] exp.: electoral campaign
kampanijny [kahm-pah-**ńeey**-ni] adj.m. campaign (promises, etc.)
kampanila [kahm-pah-**ńee**-lah] f. bell tower (freestanding); campanile
kampanula [kahm-pah-**noo**-lah] f. bell flower; campanula
kampesz [**kahm**-pesh] m. logwood (tree); (Campeachy) kampuchea wood
kampeszowy [kahm-pe-**sho**-vi] adj.m. logwood (tree, blue, etc.)
kampus [**kahm**-poos] m. (university) campus
kampusowy [kahm-poo-**so**-vi] adj.m. of a (university) campus; campus (activities, etc.)
kamracki [kahm-**rah**-tskee] adj.m. of a pal; of a chum; of pals; of a comrade; of buddies
kamrat [**kahm**-raht] m. companion; comrade; mate; chum; pal; buddy
kamuflaż [kah-**moo**-flahsh] m. camouflage; screen
kamuflażowy [kah-moo-flah-**zho**-vi] adj.m. of camouflage; of a screen
kamuflet [kah-**moo**-flet] m. camouflet (a special mine)
kamuflować [kah-moo-**flo**-vahćh] v. mask; disguise; conceal; cover up (*repeatedly*)
kamuflowanie [kah-moo-flo-**vah**-ńe] n. masking; disguise; concealment; cover up
kamuszek [kah-**moo**-shek] m. small pebble; tiny rock
kamusznik [kah-**moosh**-ńeek] m. turnstone (bird)
kamyczek [kah-**mi**-chek] m. small pebble; tiny rock
kamyczkowy [kah-mich-**ko**-vi] adj.m. of a small pebble; of a tiny rock
kamyk [**kah**-mik] m. pebble; little stone; shingle; flint; colloq: jewel
Kanada [kah-**nah**-dah] f. Canada
kanada [kah-**nah**-dah] f. colloq: abundance; riches; slang: successful robbery (mob jargon)
Kanadyjczyk [kah-nah-**diy**-chik] m. Canadian; slang: a Jew
Kanadyjka [kah-nah-**diy**-kah] f. (female) Canadian
kanadyjka [kah-nah-**diy**-kah] f. Canadian jacket; Canadian canoe
kanadyjkarski [kah-nah-diy-**kahr**-skee] adj.m. of Canadian water sports
kanadyjkarstwo [kah-nah-diy-**kahr**-stfo] n. Canadian water sports
kanadyjkarz [kah-nah-**diy**-kahsh] m. Canadian canoeist
kanadyjski [kah-nah-**diy**-skee] adj.m. Canadian; of Canada

kanafas [kah-**nah**-fahs] m. fine canvas used for bookbinding
kanak [**kah**-nahk] m. pearl necklace; diadem
kanalarz [kah-**nah**-lahsh] m. sewerman; mob slang: addict taking narcotics intravenously
kanalia [kah-**nah**-lyah] f. & m. the rabble; scoundrel; rascal; wretch; blackguard; rapscallion; riffraff
kanalik [kah-**nah**-leek] m. channel; watercourse; small ditch; duct; conduit; lead; canaliculus; tubule; (sweat-)duct; mob slang: plumber
kanalikowy [kah-nah-lee-**ko**-vi] adj.m. canal (rays, etc.)
kanalizacja [kah-nah-lee-**zah**-tsyah] f. sewers; sewage system; sewerage; sanitation; drainage; system of drains; canalization (of rivers)
kanalizacyjny [kah-nah-lee-zah-**tsiy**-ni] adj.m. sewage (pipe, system, flow, etc.)
kanalizator [kah-nah-lee-**zah**-tor] m. sewer builder; slang: plumber
kanalizować [kah-nah-lee-**zo**-vahćh] v. canalize (a river); provide with a sewage system (*repeatedly*)
kanalizowanie [kah-nah-lee-zo-**vah**-ńe] n. canalization
kanał [**kah**-nahw] m. channel; dike; (storm) sewer; duct; ditch; conduit; lead; race; tube; gully; gutter; canal; watercourse
kanał burzowy [**kah**-nahw boo-**zho**-vi] exp.: storm sewer
kanał dopływowy [**kah**-nahw do-pwi-**vo**-vi] exp.: headrace
kanał doświadczalny [**kah**-nahw dośh-fyaht-**chahl**-ni] exp.: test hole (in a reactor)
kanał dymowy [**kah**-nahw di-**mo**-vi] exp.: flue
kanał falowy [**kah**-nahw fah-**lo**-vi] exp.: wave duct
kanał filmowy [**kah**-nahw feel-**mo**-vi] exp.: film channel; film projection gate
kanał inspekcyjny [**kah**-nahw eens-pek-**tsiy**-ni] exp.: inspection pit
kanał kominowy [**kah**-nahw ko-mee-**no**-vi] exp.: breech; breeching
kanał łzowy [**kah**-nahw **wzo**-vi] exp.: lachrymal canal
kanał morski [**kah**-nahw **mor**-skee] exp.: ship canal; ship channel
kanał powietrzny [**kah**-nahw po-**vyetsh**-ni] exp.: air-duct
kanał wentylacyjny [**kah**-nahw ven-ti-lah-**tsiy**-ni] exp.: vent; ventilation duct; air trunk
kanał zapisu dźwięku [**kah**-nahw zah-**pee**-soo **dźhvyan**-koo] exp.: recording channel
kanałek [kah-**nah**-wek] m. small canal; small duct
kanałowiec [kah-nah-**wo**-vyets] m. slang: beggar; vagrant (jargon)
kanałowy [kah-nah-**wo**-vi] adj.m. canal (craft, etc.); sewer (pipe, drainpipe, system, etc.)
kanałówka [kah-nah-**woof**-kah] f. canal barge; slang: prostitute
kanangowy [kah-nahn-**go**-vi] adj.m. of one of perfume oils
kanapa [kah-**nah**-pah] f. sofa; couch; settee
kanapka [kah-**nahp**-kah] f. sandwich; small-size sofa; love seat
kanapkowy [kah-nahp-**ko**-vi] adj.m. sandwich (bread, etc.)
kanapowy [kah-nah-**po**-vi] adj.m. couch (upholstery, etc.)
kanar [**kah**-nahr] m. canary seed; Canary wine; cane sugar; slang: military policeman; controller
kanarecznik [kah-nah-**rech**-ńeek] m. Canarium tree
kanarek [kah-**nah**-rek] m. canary; colloq: soldier of the military police; scamp; rogue
kanarkowy [kah-nahr-**ko**-vi] adj.m. canary's; bright yellow
kanarowy [kah-nah-**ro**-vi] adj.m. canary (seed, etc.)
kanaryjski [kah-nah-**riy**-skee] adj.m. canary (seed, etc.)
kanarzyca [kah-nah-**zhi**-tsah] f. female canary
kanasta [kah-**nahs**-tah] f. canasta
kancelaria [kahn-tse-**lah**-ryah] f. office; chancellery; archives
kancelaryjka [kahn-tse-lah-**riy**-kah] f. (small) office; chancellery;

archives
kancelaryjność [kahn-tse-lah-**riy**-nośhćh] f. office style
kancelaryjny [kahn-tse-lah-**riy**-ni] adj.m. office (work, etc.)
kancelaryzm [kahn-tse-**lah**-rizm] m. office expression; colloq: office jargon
kancelista [kahn-tse-**lees**-tah] m. clerk
kancelistka [kahn-tse-**leest**-kah] f. (female) clerk
kancera [kahn-**tse**-rah] f. damaged postal stamp
kancerek [kahn-**tse**-rek] m. crayfish net
kancerka [kahn-**tser**-kah] f. damaged postal stamp
kancerofobia [kahn-tse-ro-**fo**-byah] f. exaggerated fear of cancer
kancerogenny [kahn-tse-ro-**gen**-ni] adj.m. cancerigenic
kancerować [kahn-tse-**ro**-vahćh] v. damage; mangle; lacerate; hack; tear jaggedly (roughly) (*repeatedly*)
kancerować się [kahn-tse-**ro**-vahćh śh<u>an</u>] v. damage oneself; mangle oneself; lacerate oneself (*repeatedly*)
kancerowanie [kahn-tse-ro-**vah**-ńe] n. damaging; mangling; lacerating
kancerowaty [kahn-tse-ro-**vah**-ti] adj.m. damaged
kanciarstwo [kahn-**ćhahr**-stfo] n. colloq: racketeering; swindle; spoofing
kanciarz [**kahn**-ćhahsh] m. colloq: swindler; trickster; con man; crook; twister; telltale
kanciasto [kahn-**ćhah**-sto] adv. angularly; with sharp edges; with sharp corners; awkwardly; stiffly
kanciastość [kahn-**ćhah**-stośhćh] f. angularity; sharp edges; sharp corners; awkwardness; stiffness
kanciasty [kahn-**ćhah**-sti] adj.m. angular; sharp-edged; sharp-cornered; square-edged; square-cornered; awkward; stiff
kancić [**kahn**-ćheećh] v. slang: steal; swindle (*repeatedly*)
kancik [**kahn**-ćheek] m. (small) swindle; small sharp-edged object
kancjonał [kahn-**tsyo**-nahw] m. psalmbook; hymn book
kanclerski [kahn-**tsler**-skee] adj.m. chancellor's
kanclerstwo [kahn-**tsler**-stfo] n. chancellorship
kanclerz [**kahn**-tslesh] m. chancellor; vicar general
kanclerzyna [kahn-tsle-**zhi**-nah] f. chancellor's wife; measly chancellor
kancona [kahn-**tso**-nah] f. canzone
kanconeta [kahn-tso-**ne**-tah] f. canzone; canzonet
kand [kahnt] m. sugar-honey mixture for feeding bees
kandahar [kahn-**dah**-khahr] m. metal ski binding
kandahary [kahn-dah-**khah**-ri] pl. metal ski bindings
kandela [kahn-**de**-lah] f. new candle; candlepower; candela
kandelabr [kahn-**de**-lahbr] m. chandelier; street lamp
kandydacki [kahn-di-**dahts**-kee] adj.m. candidate's; applicant's; aspirant's
praca kandydacka [**prah**-tsah kahn-di-**dahts**-kah] exp.: thesis
kandydat [kahn-**di**-daht] m. candidate; applicant; aspirant; holder of a university degree
kandydatka [kahn-di-**daht**-kah] f. (female) candidate; applicant; aspirant; holder of a university degree
kandydatura [kahn-di-dah-**too**-rah] f. candidature; candidacy
kandydować [kahn-di-**do**-vahćh] v. candidate; compete; run (for a post, in an election, etc.) (*repeatedly*)
kandydowanie [kahn-di-do-**vah**-ńe] n. candidature
kandyz [**kahn**-dis] m. crystallized sugar; candy
kandyzować [kahn-di-**zo**-vahćh] v. crystallize; candy (*repeatedly*)
kandyzowanie [kahn-di-zo-**vah**-ńe] n. crystallization
kandyzowany [kahn-di-zo-**vah**-ni] adj.m. crystallized fruit; candied fruit; iced fruit; sugared fruit
kanefora [kah-ne-**fo**-rah] f.

canephoros; canephora; canephore; canephorous cool
kanele [kah-**ne**-le] pl. grooves in a column; fluting of a column; flutes
kanelować [kah-ne-**lo**-vahćh] v. flute (a column) (*repeatedly*)
kanelowanie [kah-ne-lo-**vah**-ńe] n. fluting of a column
kanelury [kah-ne-**loo**-ri] pl. grooves in a column; fluting of a column; flutes
kanga [**kahn**-gah] f. cangue; Chinese shackles
kangur [**kahn**-goor] m. kangaroo; wallaroo; euro; slang: shoplifting; old woman (mob jargon)
kangurek [kahn-**goo**-rek] m. young kangaroo
kangurowy [kahn-goo-**ro**-vi] adj.m. of a kangaroo; of a wallaroo
kangurzątko [kahn-goo-**zhownt**-ko] n. young kangaroo
kangurzyca [kahn-goo-**zhi**-tsah] f. (female) kangaroo
kani [**kah**-ńee] adj.m. kite's (feather, etc.)
kania [**kah**-ńah] f. kite (bird); Lepiota; parasol mushroom
kanianka [kah-**ńahn**-kah] f. dodder; devil's-guts (plant)
kaniankowaty [kah-ńahn-ko-**vah**-ti] adj.m. cuscutaceous
kaniankowate [kah-ńahn-ko-**vah**-te] pl. the Cuscutaceae family of plants; the dodder family
kanibal [kah-**ńee**-bahl] m. cannibal
kanibalistyczny [kah-ńee-bah-lees-**tich**-ni] adj.m. cannibalistic; cannibal
kanibalizm [kah-ńee-**bah**-leezm] m. cannibalism
kanibalski [kah-ńee-**bahl**-skee] adj.m. cannibalistic; cannibal's
kanię [**kah**-ńan] n. kite's fledgling
kanikuła [kah-ńee-**koo**-wah] f. dog days; swelter; heat; sexual heat
kanikułowy [kah-ńee-koo-**wo**-vi] adj.m. canicular; of (hot and sultry) dog days; of stagnation
kanion [**kah**-ńyon] m. canyon
kanister [kah-**ńees**-ter] m. (gas, petroleum) can
kaniuk [**kah**-ńook] m. variety of hawk
kaniula [kah-**ńoo**-lah] f. large syringe needle
kanka [**kahn**-kah] f. canula; nozzle; colloq: small tin can
kankan [**kahn**-kahn] m. cancan
kankanowy [kahn-kah-**no**-vi] adj.m. cancan (step, dance, etc.)
kanna [**kahn**-nah] f. canna (plant)
kanoe [kah-**noo**] n. canoe; slang: female external sex organ; vulva
kanon [**kah**-non] m. canon (priest)
kanonada [kah-no-**nah**-dah] f. cannonade; gunfire
kanonia [kah-**noń**-yah] f. canonry; cononicate
kanonicki [kah-no-**ńeets**-kee] adj.m. canon's
kanoniczka [kah-no-**ńeech**-kah] f. cononess
kanonicznie [kah-no-**ńeech**-ńe] adv. canonically
kanoniczny [kah-no-**ńeech**-ni] adj.m. canonical
prawo kanoniczne [**prah**-vo kah-no-**ńeech**-ne] exp.: canon law
kanonier [kah-**no**-ńer] m. gunner; artilleryman
kanonierka [kah-no-**ńer**-kah] f. gunboat; patrol boat
kanonierski [kah-no-**ńer**-skee] adj.m. gunner's; artilleryman's
łódź kanonierska [woo<u></u>ćh kah-no-**ńer**-skah] exp.: gunboat; patrol boat
kanonik [kah-**no**-ńeek] m. canon (priest); monsignor; prelate; slang: member of a jury (mob jargon)
kanonikat [kah-no-**ńee**-kaht] m. canonry; canonicate
kanonista [kah-no-**ńees**-tah] m. canon law practitioner
kanonistyczny [kah-no-ńees-**tich**-ni] adj.m. canonistic
kanonistyka [kah-no-**ńees**-ti-kah] f. the science of canon law
kanonizacja [kah-no-ńee-**zah**-tsyah] f. canonization
kanonizacyjny [kah-no-ńee-zah-**tsiy**-ni] adj.m. of canonization
kanonizować [kah-no-ńee-**zo**-vahćh] v. canonize; glorify; saint (*repeatedly*)
kanonizowanie [kah-no-ńee-zo-**vah**-

ńe] n. canonization
kanopa [kah-**no**-pah] f. Canopic jar; Canopic vase
kanotier [kah-**no**-tyer] m. small straw hat
kant [kahnt] m. edge; crease; swindle; trick; racket; chant
kantak [**kahn**-tahk] m. cant hook
kantal [**kahn**-tahl] m. a fire-resistant alloy
kantalup [kahn-**tah**-loop] m. cantaloupe; muskmelon
kantar [**kahn**-tahr] m. halter
kantaryda [kahn-tah-**ri**-dah] f. Spanish fly; cantharis
kantarydyna [kahn-tah-ri-**di**-nah] f. cantharidin
kantata [kahn-**tah**-tah] f. cantata
kantatowy [kahn-tah-**to**-vi] adj.m. cantata (composition, etc.)
kantele [kahn-**te**-le] pl. Finish string instrument
kanton [**kahn**-ton] m. canton
kantonalny [kahn-to-**nahl**-ni] adj.m. cantonal
kantoniera [kahn-to-**ńe**-rah] f. set of curtains including a head strip
kantor [**kahn**-tor] m. exchange office; counter; cantor (singer)
kantorek [kahn-**to**-rek] m. small exchange office; small office; slang: basement room
kantorowy [kahn-to-**ro**-vi] adj.m. of an exchange office; of an office
kantorski [kahn-**tor**-skee] adj.m. of a singer; of a cantor
kantować [kahn-**to**-vahćh] v. give a rectangular edge (to); turn over the square edge; square (timber); colloq: cheat; swindle; trick; humbug; slang: spoof; string (mob jargon) (*repeatedly*)
kantowanie [kahn-to-**vah**-ńe] n. giving a rectangular edge (to); turning over the square edge; squaring (timber); colloq: cheating; swindling
kantowaty [kahn-to-**vah**-ti] adj.m. square-edged
kantowizna [kahn-to-**veez**-nah] f. squared timber
kantownik [kahn-**tov**-ńeek] m. worker placing brick on edge for drying; steel plate flipping device
kantowski [kahn-**tof**-skee] adj.m. Kantian (philosophy, etc.)
kantowy [kahn-**to**-vi] adj.m. of squared timber
kantówka [kahn-**toof**-kah] f. square ruler; scantling; a variety of apple
kantyczka [kahn-**tich**-kah] f. canticle; hymn; psalm; book of canticles; hymn book
kantyczkowy [kahn-tich-**ko**-vi] adj.m. canticle (songs, etc.)
kantyk [**kahn**-tik] m. hymn; psalm
kantyka [kahn-**ti**-kah] f. hymn; psalm
kantylena [kahn-ti-**le**-nah] f. cantilene; cantilena (music)
kantylenowy [kahn-ti-le-**no**-vi] adj.m. cantilene (music, etc.)
kantyna [kahn-**ti**-nah] f. canteen; messroom; Post Exchange
kantyniarka [kahn-ti-**ńahr**-kah] f. canteen manageress
kantyniarz [kahn-**ti**-ńahsh] m. canteen manager
kantysta [kahn-**tis**-tah] m. Kantian (philosopher)
kantyzm [**kahn**-tizm] m. Kantism
kanu [kah-**noo**] n. canoe
kanwa [**kahn**-vah] f. canvas; groundwork; skeleton map
kanwowy [kahn-**vo**-vi] adj.m. of canvas; canvas (work, etc.)
kanzona [kahn-**zo**-nah] f. canzone
kanzonetta [kahn-zo-**net**-tah] f. canzonet
kańczug [**kahń**-chook] m. whip; lash; whiplash
kańczuk [**kahń**-chook] m. whip; lash; whiplash
kaodaista [kah-o-dah-**ees**-tah] m. follower of Vietnamese belief in Kao-dai (supreme being)
kaodaizm [kah-o-**dah**-eezm] m. Vietnamese belief in Kao-dai
kaolian [kah-**ol**-yahn] m. Japanese sorghum (plant)
kaolin [kah-**o**-leen] m. kaolin; porcelain clay; china clay
kaolinit [kah-o-**lee**-ńeet] m. kaolinite (mineral)
kaolinizacja [kah-o-lee-ńee-**zah**-tsyah] f. kaolinization
kaolinowy [kah-o-lee-**no**-vi] adj.m. kaolinic

kaowiec [kah-**o**-vyets] m. organizer of cultural events in community centers
kap, kap [kahp kahp] exp.: drip, drip
kapa [**kah**-pah] f. bedspread; cover; horse-blanket; horsecloth; capa (in bullfight); hood; cowl; bonnet; (shoe) toecap; (mine) roof-timber; (ship's) companionway; mantle
kapać [**kah**-pahćh] v. dribble; drip; trickle; spatter; fall drop by drop; pay by driblets; pay small sums of money; slang: denounce; accuse (mob jargon) (*repeatedly*)
kapalin [kah-**pah**-leen] m. hat-like helmet
kapanie [kah-**pah**-ńe] n. drip-drop; dribble; trickle; spatter
kapanina [kah-pah-**ńee**-nah] f. (paying) by driblets; monotonous drizzle
kapar [**kah**-pahr] m. a tropical plant used for seasoning; capparis spinosa; caper; half-liter jar
kaparek [kah-**pah**-rek] m. capparis spinosa (a tropical seasoning); caper
kaparowaty [kah-pah-ro-**vah**-ti] adj.m. capparidaceous
kaparowate [kah-pah-ro-**vah**-te] pl. the Capparidaceae family of plants
kaparowy [kah-pah-**ro**-vi] adj.m. of the caper; of capers; caper (sauce, etc.)
kapcan [**kahp**-tsahn] m. colloq: crock; gawk; milksop; nincompoop
kapcanieć [kahp-**tsah**-ńećh] v. grow stupid; grow inefficient; have no energy left (*repeatedly*)
kapciuch [**kahp**-ćhookh] m. tobacco pouch
kapeador [kah-pe-**ah**-dor] m. capeador (bullfighter)
kapec [**kah**-pets] m. carpet slipper
kapeczka [kah-**pech**-kah] f. small drop; just a little; a whit; a scanting; a shade
kapeć [**kah**-pećh] m. slipper; old worn-out shoe
kapela [kah-**pe**-lah] f. band (of musicians); (church) choir
kapelan [kah-**pe**-lahn] m. chaplain (in armed forces, hospital); capelin (fish); mob slang: thief specialized in robbing churches
kapelański [kah-pe-**lahń**-skee] adj.m. chaplain's
kapelaństwo [kah-pe-**lahń**-stfo] n. chaplaincy
kapelmistrz [kah-**pel**-meestsh] m. conductor; bandmaster; choirmaster
kapelmistrzostwo [kah-pel-meest-**shos**-tfo] n. conductor's work
kapelmistrzować [kah-pel-meest-**sho**-vahćh] v. conduct (an orchestra, a choir, etc.) (*repeatedly*)
kapelmistrzowanie [kah-pel-meest-sho-**vah**-ńe] n. conducting (an orchestra, a choir, etc.)
kapelmistrzowski [kah-pel-meest-**shof**-skee] adj.m. conductor's; choirmaster's; bandmaster's
kapeluch [kah-**pe**-lookh] m. (big, old) hat
kapelusik [kah-pe-**loo**-śheek] m. (small, nice) hat
kapelusz [kah-**pe**-loosh] m. hat; slang: death penalty (mob jargon)
kapelusznictwo [kah-pe-loosh-**ńeets**-tfo] n. hat-making; hatter's trade; hat manufacture
kapeluszniczka [kah-pe-loosh-**ńeech**-kah] f. (female) hat-maker
kapeluszniczy [kah-pe-loosh-**ńee**-chi] adj.m. of hat-making
kapelusznik [kah-pe-**loosh**-ńeek] m. hat-maker
kapeluszowy [kah-pe-loo-**sho**-vi] adj.m. of a hat; hat (box, brim, rack, etc.)
kapeńka [kah-**peń**-kah] f. small drop; just a little; a whit; a scanting; a shade
kapepowiec [kah-pe-**po**-vyets] m. member of Polish Communist Party
kaper [**kah**-per] m. privateer; slang: telltale (mob jargon)
kaperka [kah-**per**-kah] f. privateering
kapernictwo [kah-per-**ńeets**-tfo] n. bribing of sport contestants
kaperować [kah-pe-**ro**-vahćh] v. carry on privateering; colloq: bribe sport contestants (*repeatedly*)

kaperski [kah-**per**-skee] adj.m. privateer's (ship, etc.)
kaperstwo [kah-**per**-stfo] n. privateering
kaperunek [kah-pe-**roo**-nek] m . bribing of sport contestants
kapiący [kah-**pyown**-tsi] adj.m. dripping (of blood, etc.)
kapibara [kah-pee-**bah**-rah] f. capybara (rodent)
kapilara [kah-pee-**lah**-rah] f. capillary (tube); capillary
kapilary [kah-pee-**lah**-ri] pl. capillaries
kapilarność [kah-pee-**lahr**-nośhćh] f. capillarity
kapilarny [kah-pee-**lahr**-ni] adj.m. capillary (attraction, etc.); of capillary tube
kapilaroskopia [kah-pee-lah-ros-**kop**-yah] f. microscopic study of skin capillaries; capillaroscopy
kapinka [kah-**peen**-kah] f. small drop; just a little; a whit; a scanting; a shade
kapinos [kah-**pee**-nos] m. drip (cap); gorge; throat; throating; beak (molding)
kapista [kah-**pees**-tah] m. Polish artist painting the "kapist" style
kapistowski [kah-pees-**tof**-skee] adj.m. of Polish art style started in 1923
kapistyczny [kah-pees-**tich**-ni] adj.m. of Polish art style started in 1923
kapiszon [kah-**pee**-shon] m. hood; cowl; percussion cap; firing cap; detonator
kapiszonowiec [kah-pee-sho-**no**-vyets] m. musket equipped with a matchlock
kapiszonowy [kah-pee-sho-**no**-vi] adj.m. of a matchlock
kapiszonówka [kah-pee-sho-**noof**-kah] f. matchlock; musket equipped with a matchlock
kapitalik [kah-pee-**tah**-leek] m. small capital; modest capital; small size capital letter
kapitalista [kah-pee-tah-**lees**-tah] m. capitalist; wealthy man
kapitalistka [kah-pee-tah-**leest**-kah] f. (female) capitalist; wealthy woman
kapitalistycznie [kah-pee-tah-lees-**tich**-ńe] adv. capitalistically; in capitalistic terms
kapitalistyczny [kah-pee-tah-lees-**tich**-ni] adj.m. capitalistic (system, enterprise, etc.); capitalist (society, etc.);
kapitalizacja [kah-pee-tah-lee-**zah**-tsyah] f. capitalization
kapitalizm [kah-pee-**tah**-leezm] m. capitalism (private or state)
kapitalizować [kah-pee-tah-lee-**zo**-vahćh] v. capitalize (*repeatedly*)
kapitalizować się [kah-pee-tah-lee-**zo**-vahćh śhan] v. be capitalized (*repeatedly*)
kapitalizowanie [kah-pee-tah-lee-zo-**vah**-ńe] n. capitalization
kapitalnie [kah-pee-**tahl**-ńe] adv. splendidly; admirably; wonderfully; perfectly; brilliantly; exquisitely
kapitalny [kah-pee-**tahl**-ni] adj.m. fundamental; essential; vital; chief; principal; capital; splendid; admirable; wonderful; perfect; brilliant; exquisite; colloq: first rate; great; slang: topping; smashing; stunning; swell
kapitalny facet [kah-pee-**tahl**-ni **fah**-tset] exp.: colloq: darn good Joe; regular guy; good dude
kapitalny pomysł [kah-pee--**tahl**-ni **po**-misw] exp.: bright idea
remont kapitalny [**re**-mont kah-pee-**tahl**-ni] exp.: capital repairs
kapitał [kah-**pee**-tahw] m. capital; the principal; colloq: funds; means; pecuniary resources; the capitalists; the money people; big business
kapitał akcyjny [kah-**pee**-tahw ah-**ktsiy**-ni] exp: stock; capital stock
kapitał obrotowy [kah-**pee**-tahw o-**bro**-to-vi] exp.: working capital
kapitała [kah-pee-**tah**-wah] f. capitals; capital letters
kapitałka [kah-pee-**tahw**-kah] f. (book's) headband
kapitałochłonność [kah-pee-tah-wo-**khwon**-nośhćh] f. the ratio of capital used up in production to the value of produced items
kapitałochłonny [kah-pee-tah-wo-

khwon-ni] adj.m. wasteful of capital
kapitałooszczędny [kah-pee-tah-wo-osh-chand-ni] adj.m. using capital efficiently
kapitałowy [kah-pee-tah-**wo**-vi] adj.m. of capital; capital (stock, market, etc.); of capital letters
kapitan [kah-**pee**-tahn] m. captain; sea captain; leader of a team
kapitan portu [kah-**pee**-tahn **por**-too] exp.: harbor master
kapitan statku [kah-**pee**-tahn **staht**-koo] exp.: shipmaster; sea captain; skipper
kapitana [kah-pee-**tah**-nah] f. admiral's ship; capitana
kapitanat [kah-pee-**tah**-naht] m. port authorities
kapitanka [kah-pee-**tahn**-kah] f. (female) leader of a team
kapitanostwo [kah-pee-tah-**nos**-tfo] n. the captain and his wife
kapitanowa [kah-pee-tah-**no**-vah] f. captain's wife
kapitanować [kah-pee-tah-**no**-vahćh] v. perform captain's duties (*repeatedly*)
kapitanowanie [kah-pee-tah-no-**vah**-ńe] n. performance of captain's duties
kapitanówna [kah-pee-tah-**noov**-nah] f. captain's daughter
kapitański [kah-pee-**tahń**-skee] adj.m. captain's
kapitaństwo [kah-pee-**tahń**-stfo] n. captaincy; the captain and his wife
kapitel [kah-**pee**-tel] m. capital; cap of a column
kapitoliński [kah-pee-to-**leeń**-skee] adj.m. Capitoline; of Capitol
kapitulacja [kah-pee-too-**lah**-tsyah] f. surrender; capitulation; giving up to an enemy
kapitulacyjny [kah-pee-too-lah-**tsiy**-ni] adj.m. of surrender; of capitulation; surrender (terms, date, etc.)
kapitulancki [kah-pee-too-**lahnts**-kee] adj.m. defeatist
kapitulanctwo [kah-pee-too-**lahnts**-tfo] n. defeatism
kapitulant [kah-pee-**too**-lahnt] m. capitulator; defeatist
kapitularny [kah-pee-too-**lahr**-ni] adj.m. capitular; capitulary
kapitularz [kah-pee-**too**-lahsh] m. chapter house; capitulary
kapitulny [kah-pee-**tool**-ni] adj.m. capitular; capitulary
sala kapitulna [**sah**-lah kah-pee-**tool**-nah] exp.: chapter house
kapitulować [kah-pee-too-**lo**-vahćh] v. surrender; give up; capitulate; colloq: throw up the sponge (*repeatedly*)
kapitulowanie [kah-pee-too-lo-**vah**-ńe] n. surrender; capitulation; giving up to an enemy
kapitulum [kah-pee-**too**-loom] n. chapter
kapituła [kah-pee-**too**-wah] f. chapter
kapizm [**kah**-peezm] m. post-impressionistic phase of Polish art
kapka [**kahp**-kah] f. small drop; just a little; a whit; a scanting; a shade; small covering; bonnet; toecap; vamp
kapkę [**kahp**-kan] exp.: adv. just a little bit; small drop; just a little; a whit; a scanting; a shade
kaplica [kah-**plee**-tsah] f. chapel; oratory
kaplicowy [kah-plee-**tso**-vi] adj.m. of a chapel; of an oratory
kapliczka [kah-**pleech**-kah] f. shrine (in a church); wayside shrine
kapliczkowy [kah-pleech-**ko**-vi] adj.m. of a shrine (in a church); of a wayside shrine
kaplin [**kahp**-leen] m. felt cone for making a hat
kapłan [**kahp**-wahn] m. priest
kapłanka [kahp-**wahn**-kah] f. priestess
kapłański [kahp-**wahń**-skee] adj.m. priestly; sacerdotal; hieratic; of the priests
kapłaństwo [kahp-**wahń**-stfo] n. priesthood; ministry
kapłon [**kah**-pwon] m. capon; castrated male chicken
kapłoni [kahp-**wo**-ńee] adj.m. capon's
kapłonić [kahp-**wo**-ńeećh] v. caponize (*repeatedly*)

kapłonienie [kahp-wo-ńe-ńe] n. castration of male chicken
kapnąć [kahp-nownćh] v. dribble; drip; trickle; spatter; fall drop by drop; pay by driblets; pay small sums of money
kapnąć się [kahp-nownćh śhan] v. colloq: understand; get on to; get wise to; twig; tumble to; watch; spy
kapnięcie [kahp-ńan-ćhe] n. dribble; drip; trickle; spatter; falling drop by drop; payment by a driblet; payment of a small sum of money
kapnięcie się [kahp-ńan-ćhe śhan] n. colloq: understanding; getting wise to; watching; spying
kapnik [kahp-ńeek] m. drip (part of a cornice); eaves
kapo [kah-po] m. prisoner foreman (in German-Nazi camps)
kapocina [kah-po-ćhee-nah] f. worn-out long coat
kapok [kah-pok] m. kapok; life jacket with kapok filling
kapoman [kah-po-mahn] m. prisoner foreman (in German-Nazi camps)
kaponiera [kah-po-ńe-rah] f. caponier; fortified bunker
kapot [kah-pot] m. hood; bonnet
kapota [kah-po-tah] f. colloq: long coat; cloak; slang: foozle; fiasco; breakdown (mob jargon)
kapotaż [kah-po-tahsh] m. turnover; upsetting; nose-over (of a plane)
kapotować [kah-po-to-vahćh] v. overturn; upset; nose-over (a plane) (*repeatedly*)
kapować [kah-po-vahćh] v. colloq: twig; tumble; understand; watch; spy; slang: denounce; accuse; testify (against); betray; telltale (mob jargon) (*repeatedly*)
kapować się [kah-po-vahćh śhan] v. colloq: twig; tumble; understand (*repeatedly*)
kapowanie [kah-po-vah-ńe] n. colloq: understanding; getting wise to; watching; spying
kapral [kah-prahl] m. corporal
kapralski [kah-prahl-skee] adj.m. corporal's
kapralstwo [kah-prahl-stfo] n. corporal's rank
kaprawiec [kah-prah-vyets] m. blear-eyed fellow
kaprawieć [kah-prah-vyećh] v. become blear; grow blear (*repeatedly*)
kaprawo [kah-prah-vo] adv. blearily; dimly
kaprawość [kah-prah-vośhćh] f. bleariness
kaprawy [kah-prah-vi] adj.m. blear; blear-eyed; bleary-eyed; dim; blur
kaprolaktam [kahp-ro-lahk-tahm] m. raw material for caproic fibers
kapron [kahp-ron] m. caproic fiber
kapronowy [kahp-ro-no-vi] adj.m. caproic
kapryfolium [kahp-ri-fol-yoom] n. honeysuckle
kaprynowy [kahp-ri-no-vi] adj.m. capric (acid)
kaprys [kahp-ris] m. caprice; fad; whim; fancy; freak; vagary; capriccio (music)
kaprysić [kah-pri-śheećh] v. be capricious; be wayward; be out of humor; sulk; be fastidious; fuss; pick and choose (*repeatedly*)
kaprysik [kah-pri-śheek] m. (small) caprice; fad; whim; fancy; freak; vagary
kapryszenie [kah-pri-she-ńe] n. whims; caprices; vagaries
kapryśnica [kah-pri-śhńee-tsah] f. skittish female; flighty female; fanciful female; erratic female; freakish female; fussy female; fastidious female; colloq: pernickety female
kapryśnie [kah-priśh-ńe] adv. erratically; freakishly; waywardly
kapryśnik [kah-priśh-ńeek] m. man of erratic behavior; colloq: cranky guy; fussy character; flighty guy; fretful guy; skittish guy; slang: choosy (fussy) thief (mob jargon)
kapryśność [kah-priśh-nośhćh] f. erratic behavior; humorsome disposition; cranky behavior; fussiness; fastidiousness
kapryśny [kah-priśh-ni] adj.m. erratic (behavior, etc.); humorsome (disposition, etc.); cranky; fussy; flighty; fitful; skittish; wanton; freakish;

wayward; colloq: pernickety
kapsel [**kahp**-sel] m. cap; metallic capsule (of a bottle); seal; percussion cap; firing cap
kapsiplast [kahp-**see**-plahst] m. band-aid with medication
kapsla [**kahps**-lah] f. cap; metallic capsule (of a bottle); seal; percussion cap; firing cap
kapslarz [**kahps**-lash] m. capsuler
kapslować [kahps-**lo**-vahćh] v. cap (bottles, etc.) (*repeatedly*)
kapslowanie [kahps-lo-**vah**-ńe] n. capping (of bottles, etc.)
kapslownia [kahps-**lov**-ńah] f. capping plant
kapslownica [kahps-lov-**ńee**-tsah] f. capping machine
kapsuła [kahp-**soo**-wah] f. space capsule; spacecraft
kapsułka [kahp-**soow**-kah] f. capsule; cachet
kapsułkować [kahp-soow-**ko**-vahćh] v. capsulize; capsule (*repeatedly*)
kapsułkowanie [kahp-soow-ko-**vah**-ńe] n. capsulizing
kapsułkowany [kahp-soow-ko-**vah**-ni] adj.m. capsulate; capsulated
kaptaż [**kahp**-tahsh] m. a type of erosion by one river infringing on another; water catchment
kaptować [kahp-**to**-vahćh] v. win over (supporters, voters, etc.); bring over; conciliate to one's side; tout (for customers); canvass (clients, voters, etc.); solicit (clients, voters, etc.); electioneer (*repeatedly*)
kaptowanie [kahp-to-**vah**-ńe] n. winning over; bringing over; touting (for customers); canvass; electioneering
kaptur [**kahp**-toor] m. hood; cowl; cap; court by vigilantes
kapturek [kahp-**too**-rek] m. candle extinguisher; little hood; child's coat with a hood
kapturnica [kahp-toor-**ńee**-tsah] f. sidesaddle flower; pitcher plant
kapturnicowaty [kahp-toor-ńee-tso-**vah**-ti] adj.m. of pitcher plant family
kapturnicowate [kahp-toor-ńee-tso-**vah**-te] pl. the pitcher plant family
kapturnik [kahp-**toor**-ńeek] m. gray seal
kapturnikowaty [kahp-toor-ńee-**ko**-vah-ti] adj.m. conifer tree beetle
kapturnikowate [kahp-toor-ńee-**ko**-vah-te] pl. the family of Bostrychidae beetles
kapturowy [kahp-too-**ro**-vi] adj.m. hooded
kapturowy sąd [kahp-too-**ro**-vi sownt] exp.: kangaroo court
kapturzasty [kahp-too-**zhahs**-ti] adj.m. hooded
kapturzyć [kahp-**too**-zhićh] v. cover with a hood; hood (a hawk, etc.) (*repeatedly*)
kapucyn [kah-**poo**-tsin] m. Capuchin monk; capuchin pigeon; colloq: black coffee with a spot of cream
kapucynka [kah-poo-**tsin**-kah] f. Capuchin nun; capuchin monkey
kapucyński [kah-poo-**tsiń**-skee] adj.m. Capuchin's; Capuchin (convent, etc.)
kapusta [kah-**poos**-tah] f. cabbage; a dish of cabbage; slang: head; money; informer (mob jargon)
groch z kapustą [grokh s kah-**poos**-town] exp.: mishmash; topsy-turvy; mess
kapusta brukselska [kah-**poos**-tah brook-**sel**-skah] exp.: Brussels sprouts
kiszona kapusta [kee-**sho**-nah kah-**poos**-tah] exp.: sauerkraut; cabbage cut fine and fermented
kapustka [kah-**poost**-kah] f. young cabbage
kapustnica [kah-poost-**ńee**-tsah] f. variety of cabbage-eating larvae
kapustnik [kah-**poost**-ńeek] m. cabbage field; cabbage butterfly
kapustny [kah-**poost**-ni] adj.m. of the cabbage; cabbage (plant, dish, etc.)
kapuś [**kah**-poośh] m. stool pigeon; informer; police spy
kapuściany [kah-poośh-**ćhah**-ni] adj.m. of the cabbage; cabbage (plant, etc.); slang: foolish; stupid
kapuściana głowa [kah-poośh-**ćhah**-nah **gwo**-vah] exp.: stupe
kapuścisko [kah-poośh-**ćhees**-ko]

n. cabbage field
kapuśniaczek [kah-poośh-ńah-chek] m. fine rain; cabbage soup
kapuśniak [kah-**poośh**-ńahk] m. cabbage soup; drizzle; mizzle; fine rain; mist; mob slang: denunciator
kapuśnisko [kah-poośh-**ńees**-ko] n. cabbage field
kaput [**kah**-poot] m. kaput
kapuza [kah-**poo**-zah] f. hood; howl
kar [kahr] m. glacial cirque
kara [**kah**-rah] f. penalty; fine; punishment; correction; chastisement; retribution; requital; a judgment; nuisance; pest; a square military formation
kara cielesna [**kah**-rah ćhe-**les**-nah] exp.: corporal punishment
kara pieniężna [**kah**-rah pye-ńanzh-nah] exp.: fine; monetary fine
kara śmierci [**kah**-rah **śhmyer**-ćhee] exp.: death penalty; capital punishment
mieć karę za coś [myećh **kah**-ran zah tsośh] exp.: to be punished for something
karabela [kah-rah-**be**-lah] f. light, curved sword (used by Polish nobility)
karabin [kah-**rah**-been] m. rifle
karabinek [kah-rah-**bee**-nek] m. (small) rifle; snap-hook
karabinier [kah-rah-**bee**-ńer] m. carabiniere; carabineer; carbineer
karabinowy [kah-rah-bee-**no**-vi] adj.m. of a rifle; rifle (fire, etc.)
karabińczyk [kah-rah-**beeń**-chik] m. snap-hook
karacena [kah-rah-**tse**-nah] f. scale-armor; coat of mail
karacenowy [kah-rah-tse-**no**-vi] adj.m. of scale armor; of the coat of mail
zbroja karacenowa [**zbro**-yah kah-rah-tse-**no**-vah] exp.: scale-armor
karaceński [kah-rah-**tseń**-skee] adj.m. of scale armor; of the coat of mail
karaczan [kah-**rah**-chahn] m. member of cockroach family of insects
karaczany [kah-rah-**chah**-ni] pl. the cockroach family of insects
karać [**kah**-rahćh] v. punish; penalize; chastise; castigate; correct; discipline (*repeatedly*)
karać się [**kah**-rahćh śhan] v. punish oneself; penalize oneself; chastise oneself (*repeatedly*)
karafeczka [kah-rah-**fech**-kah] f. (small, nice) carafe; serving-bottle; (glass or metal) bottle; flagon; decanter
karafka [kah-**rahf**-kah] f. carafe; serving-bottle; (glass or metal) bottle; flagon; decanter
karafułka [kah-rah-**foow**-kah] f. frog of a violin bow
karagana [kah-rah-**gah**-nah] f. caragana (shrub)
karaibski [kah-rah-**eep**-skee] adj.m. Caribbean (sea, etc.)
Karaim [kah-**rah**-eem] m. Karaite
Karaimka [kah-rah-**eem**-kah] f. Karaite female
karaimski [kah-rah-**eem**-skee] adj.m. Karaite (Jewish sect, etc.)
Karaita [kah-rah-**ee**-tah] m. Karaite
karaizm [kah-**rah**-eezm] m. Karaism; doctrine rejecting rabbinism and talmudism and basing itself on scripture alone
karakal [kah-**rah**-kahl] m. lynx caracal
karakan [kah-**rah**-kahn] m. cockroach; black beetle; slang: paltry thief (mob jargon)
karakol [kah-**rah**-kol] m. caracole; salvo by the first row of cavalry followed by moving to the back of the formation for reloading
karakolować [kah-rah-ko-**lo**-vahćh] v. caracole (*repeatedly*)
karakon [kah-**rah**-kon] m. cockroach; black beetle
karakuł [kah-**rah**-koow] m. Persian lamb; karakul
karakuły [kah-rah-**koo**-wi] pl. astrakhan fur; caracul fur
karakułowy [kah-rah-koo-**wo**-vi] adj.m. astrakhan (sheep, etc.); caracul (fur, pelt, etc.)
karakurt [kah-**rah**-koort] m. variety of poisonous spider (12 cm long)
karalność [kah-**rahl**-nośhćh] f. penalization record; amenability to punishment

karalny [kah-**rahl**-ni] adj.m. punishable
karaluch [kah-**rah**-lookh] m. cockroach; black beetle; slang: hotel thief (mob jargon)
karambol [kah-**rahm**-bol] m. collision; cannon; carom
karambolować [kah-rahm-bo-**lo**-vahćh] v. collide; come into collision; cannon (*repeatedly*)
karambolowanie [kah-rahm-bo-lo-**vah**-ńe] n. colliding (of billiard balls, etc.)
karambolowy [kah-rahm-bo-**lo**-vi] adj.m. collision (billiard, etc.); of collision
karanie [kah-**rah**-ńe] n. punishment
karany [kah-**rah**-ni] adj.m. previously convicted
nie karany [ńe kah-**rah**-ni] exp.: with a clean record; unpunished
karar [**kah**-rahr] m. Carrara marble
karara [kah-**rah**-rah] f. Carrara marble
kararyjski [kah-rah-**riy**-skee] adj.m. of Carrara marble
karasek [kah-**rah**-sek] m. young crucian carp
karasiowy [kah-rah-**śho**-vi] adj.m. of a crucian carp
karaś [**kah**-rahśh] m. crucian carp
karat [**kah**-raht] m. carat; slang: karate punch (mob jargon)
karate [kah-**rah**-te] n. karate
karateka [kah-rah-**te**-kah] m. karateist
karatowy [kah-rah-**to**-vi] adj.m. (24, etc.)-carat
karawaka [kah-rah-**vah**-kah] f. Caravaca cross
karawan [kah-**rah**-vahn] m. hearse; catafalque
karawana [kah-rah-**vah**-nah] f. caravan
karawaniarski [kah-rah-vah-**ńahr**-skee] adj.m. undertaker's (hearse, etc.); funeral (procession, observances, etc.); of a funeral; dismal (atmosphere, etc.)
karawaniarz [kah-rah-**vah**-ńahsh] m. undertaker; coffin bearer; slang: an oldster (mob jargon)
karawaning [kah-rah-**vah**-ńeenk] m. (Engl.) van transformed into a recreational vehicle (camper)
karawaningowy [kah-rah-vah-ńeen-**go**-vi] adj.m. (Engl.) of vans transformed into recreational vehicles (campers)
karawanowy [kah-rah-vah-**no**-vi] adj.m. caravan (route, etc.); hearse (procession, etc.)
karawanseraj [kah-rah-vahn-**se**-rahy] m. caravanserai; caravansary
karawela [kah-rah-**ve**-lah] f. caravel
karawelowy [kah-rah-ve-**lo**-vi] adj.m. caravel (staves, etc.)
karb [kahrb] m. notch; score; crease; fold; nick; indentation; tally; curl; wave (of hair)
karbamid [kahr-**bah**-meed] m. urea
karbazol [kahr-**bah**-zol] m. carbazole
karbid [**kahr**-beed] m. carbide
karbidownia [kahr-bee-**dov**-ńah] f. carbide-producing plant
karbidowy [kahr-bee-**do**-vi] adj.m. carbide (lamp, etc.)
karbidówka [kahr-bee-**doof**-kah] f. carbide lamp
karbieniec [kahr-**bye**-ńets] m. lycopus; bugle weed
karbik [**kahr**-beek] m. (small) notch; score; crease; fold; nick; indentation; tally; curl; wave (of hair)
karbikomierz [kahr-bee-**ko**-myesh] m. curl-measuring device
karbikować [kahr-bee-**ko**-vahćh] v. curl; crease; fold (*repeatedly*)
karbikowatość [kahr-bee-ko-**vah**-tośhćh] f. waviness (of wool, etc.)
karbikowaty [kahr-bee-ko-**vah**-ti] adj.m. wavy
karbinkomierz [kahr-been-**ko**-myesh] m. curl-measuring device
karbochemia [kahr-bo-**khem**-yah] f. chemistry of coke
karbocykliczny [kahr-bo-tsik-**leech**-ni] adj.m. carbocyclic
karboksyl [kahr-**bo**-ksil] m. carboxyl
karboksylowy [kahr-bo-ksi-**lo**-vi] adj.m. of carboxyl
karbol [**kahr**-bol] m. carbolic acid; phenol; (diluted) an antiseptic
karbolina [kahr-bo-**lee**-nah] f. tar distillate wash; winter wash
karbolineum [kahr-bo-lee-**ne**-oom] n.

Carbolineum
karbolować [kahr-bo-**lo**-vahćh] v. carbolize (*repeatedly*)
karbolowanie [kahr-bo-lo-**vah**-ńe] n. carbolizing
karbolowy [kahr-bo-**lo**-vi] adj.m. carbolic
karbon [**kahr**-bon] m. carbon diamond; the Carboniferous period
karbonado [kahr-bo-**nah**-do] n. industrial diamond
karbonar [kahr-**bo**-nahr] m. Carbonarist; one of Crabonari
karbonariusz [kahr-bo-**nahr**-yoosh] m. Carbonarist
karbonarski [kahr-bo-**nahr**-skee] adj.m. carbonarist
karbonaryzm [kahr-bo-**nah**-rizm] m. Carbonarism
karbonit [kahr-**bo**-ńeet] m. an explosive used in coal mines
karbonizacja [kahr-bo-ńee-**zah**-tsyah] f. carbonization (process)
karbonizacyjny [kahr-bo-ńee-zah-**tsiy**-ni] adj.m. carbonizing (stove, etc.)
karbonizator [kahr-bo-ńee-**zah**-tor] m. carbonizer
karbonizować [kahr-bo-ńee-**zo**-vahćh] v. carbonize (*repeatedly*)
karbonizowanie [kahr-bo-ńee-zo-**vah**-ńe] n. carbonization
karbonowy [kahr-bo-**no**-vi] adj.m. carbonic
karbonylek [kahr-bo-**ni**-lek] m. carbonyl
karbonylowy [kahr-bo-ni-**lo**-vi] adj.m. carbonylic
karboński [kahr-**boń**-skee] adj.m. Carboniferous (period, rocks, etc.)
karborund [kahr-**bo**-roont] m. carborundum; silicon carbide
karborundowy [kahr-bo-roon-**do**-vi] adj.m. of carborundum; of silicon carbide; carborundum (cloth, paper, etc.)
karbować [kahr-**bo**-vahćh] v. notch; curl; tally; crimp; fold; corrugate (sheet metal, etc.); goffer; crease; indent (*repeatedly*)
karbowanie [kahr-bo-**vah**-ńe] n. notching; curling; milling (the edges of coins, etc.)
karbowaniec [kahr-bo-**vah**-ńets] m. Ukrainian ruble
karbownica [kahr-bov-**ńee**-tsah] f. tally
karbownik [kahr-**bov**-ńeek] m. chiseling hammer; overseer of farm laborers
karbowy [kahr-**bo**-vi] m. overseer of farm laborers
karbówka [kahr-**boof**-kah] f. curling iron
karbunkuł [kahr-**boon**-koow] m. ulcer (under skin); carbuncle; ruby
karbunkułowy [kahr-boon-koo-**wo**-vi] adj.m. of an ulcer; of a carbuncle
karburacja [kahr-boo-**rah**-tsyah] f. carburetting; carburation
karburator [kahr-boo-**rah**-tor] m. carburetor (fuel-mixing device)
karburować [kahr-boo-**ro**-vahćh] v. carburet (*repeatedly*)
karburyzacja [kahr-boo-ri-**zah**-tsyah] f. carburizing; carburization
karburyzator [kahr-boo-ri-**zah**-tor] m. steel-carburizing agent
karburyzować [kahr-boo-ri-**zo**-vahćh] v. carburize (*repeatedly*)
karburyzowanie [kahr-boo-ri-zo-**vah**-ńe] n. carburizing
karcąco [kahr-**tsown**-tso] adv. with a reproach; with a rebuke; with a reproof; with a reprimand
karcący [kahr-**tsown**-tsi] adj.m. upbraiding; scolding
karcenie [kahr-**tse**-ńe] n. reproach; reproaches; rebuke; censure; reprimands
karcenie się [kahr-**tse**-ńe śhan] n. reproaching each other
karcer [**kahr**-tser] m. prison; dark cell; detention (in a school)
karcerowy [kahr-tse-**ro**-vi] adj.m. of a prison; prison (dark cell, etc.)
karciany [kahr-**ćhah**-ni] adj.m. of cards; of gambling; card (player, game, etc.)
karciarka [kahr-**ćhahr**-kah] f. (woman) card player; card fiend
karciarnia [kahr-**ćhahr**-ńah] f. gaming house
karciarski [kahr-**ćhahr**-skee] adj.m. of cardplayers; gambling (set, etc.)
karciarstwo [kahr-**ćhahr**-stfo] n.

card-playing; gambling; gaming
karciarz [**kahr**-ćhahsh] m. cardplayer; gambler; gamester
karcić [**kahr**-ćheećh] v. reproof; admonish; scold; castigate; reprimand; rebuke; reprehend; upbraid; rate; censure; correct (*repeatedly*)
karcić się [**kahr**-ćheećh śhan] v. reproof oneself; admonish one another (*repeatedly*)
karcięta [kahr-**ćhan**-tah] pl. colloq: playing cards; card-playing
karcinotron [kahr-tsee-**no**-tron] m. microwave generator
karcynologia [kahr-tsi-no-**lo**-gyah] f. carcinology; study of crabs
karcz [kahrch] m. stub; tree stump
karczek [**kahr**-chek] m. (small) neck; (dress) neck; yoke
karczemnie [kahr-**chem**-ńe] adv. in ribald terms; rudely; vulgarly; coarsely
karczemny [kahr-**chem**-ni] adj.m. rude; vulgar; coarse
karczma [**kahrch**-mah] f. tavern
karczmareczka [kahrch-mah-**rech**-kah] f. (young, pretty) innkeeper's wife; ale-wife (Brit.)
karczmarka [kahrch-**mahr**-kah] f. innkeeper's wife; alewife (Brit.)
karczmarz [**kahrch**-mahsh] m. innkeeper; publican (Brit.)
karczmarzyć [kahrch-**mah**-zhićh] v. keep an inn; run an inn (*repeatedly*)
karczoch [**kahr**-chokh] m. artichoke (thistle-like plant)
karczować [kahr-**cho**-vahćh] v. dig up (stumps); grub up; clear land (*repeatedly*)
karczowanie [kahr-cho-**vah**-ńe] n. digging up (stumps); grubbing up; clearing land
karczowisko [kahr-cho-**vees**-ko] n. clearing (in a forest)
karczownica [kahr-chov-**ńee**-tsah] f. (mechanical) grubber; tree dozer
karczownik [kahr-**chov**-ńeek] m. grubber; tree dozer
karczunek [kahr-**choo**-nek] m. grubbing of land; clearing of land; forest clearing
karczunkowy [kahr-choon-**ko**-vi] adj.m. of the grubbing of land; of clearing of land; of forest clearing
kard [kahrt] m. cardoon (plant)
karda [**kahr**-dah] f. carduus; thistle
kardacz [**kahr**-dahch] m. horse-brush; currycomb
kardamon [kahr-**dah**-mon] m. cardamom; cardamon
kardamonowy [kahr-dah-mo-**no**-vi] adj.m. of cardamom; of cardamon
kardan [**kahr**-dahn] m. Cardan joint; gimbals
kardanowy [kahr-dah-**no**-vi] adj.m. Cardan (shaft, joint, etc.)
kardigan [kahr-**dee**-gahn] m. cardigan; collarless sweater or jacket
kardio- [**kahr**-dyo] prefix: cardio-; heart-
kardiochirurg [kahr-dyo-**khee**-roork] m. thoracic surgeon; heart-surgeon
kardiochirurgia [kahr-dyo-khee-**roor**-gyah] f. heart-surgery
kardiochirurgiczny [kahr-dyo-khee-roor-**geech**-ni] adj.m. of heart-surgery
kardiograf [kahr-**dyo**-grahf] m. (electro-) cardiographer
kardiografia [kahr-dyo-**grah**-fyah] f. (electro-) cardiography
kardiogram [kahr-**dyo**-grahm] m. cardiogram
kardioida [kahr-dyo-**ee**-dah] f. cardioid
kardiolog [kahr-**dyo**-log] m. cardiologist; heart specialist
kardiologia [kahr-dyo-**lo**-gyah] f. cardiology
kardiologiczny [kahr-dyo-lo-**geech**-ni] adj.m. cardiological
kardiomonitor [kahr-dyo-mo-**ńee**-tor] m. monitor of the heart
kardiostymulator [kahr-dyo-sti-moo-**lah**-tor] m. stimulator of the heart; pacemaker
kardiotachometr [kahr-dyo-tah-**kho**-metr] m. cardiograph
kardiowersja [kahr-dyo-**ver**-syah] f. (electrical) pacemaking
kardynalnie [kahr-di-**nahl**-ńe] adv. fundamentally; essentially; cardinally
kardynalny [kahr-di-**nahl**-ni] adj.m.

fundamental; essential; cardinal
błąd kardynalny [bwownt kahr-di-nahl-ni] exp.: blunder; gross error; glaring error
kardynalski [kahr-di-nahl-skee] adj.m. cardinal's (hat, etc.)
kardynalstwo [kahr-di-nahl-stfo] n. cardinalate
kardynał [kahr-di-nahw] m. cardinal (elector of the pope); prince of the Catholic Church; grosbeak
kardynałek [kahr-di-nah-wek] m. variety of carp (fish)
kardynałka [kahr-di-nahw-kah] f. cardinal cloak
kareciany [kah-re-ćhah-ni] adj.m. of a carriage; carriage (horses, etc.)
karelski [kah-rel-skee] adj.m. of Karelia; Karelian (language, etc.)
karenaż [kah-re-nahsh] m. tilting of ships in order to clean below water line
karencja [kah-ren-tsyah] f. (legal, etc.) postponement
karencyjny [kah-ren-tsiy-ni] adj.m. of (legal, etc.) postponement
kares [kah-res] m. caress; blandishment; slang: exploit; flirtation (mob jargon)
karesy [kah-re-si] pl. cajolery; coaxing
kareta [kah-re-tah] f. carriage; coach; colloq: a four in a card game; mob slang: an old couple
karetka [kah-ret-kah] f. chaise; slang: police patrol car (with a radio) (mob jargon)
karetka pogotowia [kah-ret-kah po-go-to-vyah] exp.: ambulance
karetka pocztowa [kah-ret-kah poch-to-vah] exp.: mail-cart; mail-coach; mail-truck
karetka więzienna [kah-ret-kah vyan-źhen-nah] exp.: prison van
karetta [kah-ret-tah] f. sea turtle
kargowiec [kahr-go-vyets] m. cargo ship; freighter
kariatyda [kahr-yah-ti-dah] f. caryatid (support-statue)
kariatydowy [kahr-yah-ti-do-vi] adj.m. caryatidal; caryatidean; caryatidic
karibu [kah-ree-boo] n. & m. caribou
karier [kahr-yer] m. careering; full gallop
kariera [kah-rye-rah] f. career; profession
zrobić karierę [zro-beećh kah-rye-ran] exp.: to make a career; to succeed; be a success
karierowicz [kahr-ye-ro-veech] m. careerist; pusher; hustler; climber
karierowiczka [kahr-ye-ro-veech-kah] f. (woman) careerist; pusher; hustler; climber
karierowiczostwo [kahr-ye-ro-vee-cho-stfo] n. ambition to make a career at any price
karierowiczowski [kahr-ye-ro-vee-chof-skee] adj.m. careerist's; pusher's; hustler's
kariogamia [kahr-yo-gah-myah] f. karyogamy
kariokinetyczny [kahr-yo-kee-ne-tich-ni] adj.m. karyokinetic
kariokineza [kahr-yo-kee-ne-zah] f. karyokinesis
kariolimfa [kahr-yo-leem-fah] f. karyolymph
kariolka [kahr-yol-kah] f. carricle; carriole (one-horse carriage); two-horse, two wheel chaise; dog-drawn toboggan
kariologia [kahr-yo-lo-gyah] f. karyology
kariologiczny [kahr-yo-lo-geech-ni] adj.m. karyologic; karyological
kariomitoza [kahr-yo-mee-to-zah] f. karyomitosis
karioplazma [kahr-yo-plahz-mah] f. karyoplasm
kark [kahrk] m. the back of the neck; the scruff of the neck; nape
skręcić kark [skran-ćheećh kahrk] exp.: to break one's neck
karkas [kahr-kahs] m. frame (of a lampshade, etc.); body (of an electric coil, etc.)
karkołomnie [kahr-ko-wom-ńe] adv. headlong; at breakneck speed
karkołomność [kahr-ko-wom-nośhćh] f. life-threatening condition
karkołomny [kahr-ko-wom-ni] adj.m. breakneck; neck-breaking; life-threatening
karkowy [kahr-ko-vi] adj.m. cervical
karkówka [kahr-koof-kah] f. fresh

meat of pork's neck
karleć [**kahr**-lećh] v. become dwarfed; become stunted; lessen; diminish; dwindle; decrease; appear smaller; become smaller (*repeatedly*)
karlenie [kahr-**le**-ńe] n. becoming dwarfed; becoming stunted; being diminished; dwindling; decreasing
karlę [**kahr**-lan] n. dwarf
karli [**kahr**-lee] adj.m. dwarf; dwarfish
karlica [kahr-**lee**-tsah] f. (female) dwarf; midget; pygmy
karliczka [kahr-**leech**-kah] f. (young female) dwarf; midget; pygmy
karlik [**kahr**-leek] m. dwarf; colloq: variety of cauliflower
karlista [kahr-**lees**-tah] m. Carlist
karlsbadzki [kahrls-**bahts**-kee] adj.m. of Carlsbad
sól karlsbadzka [sool kahrls-**bahts**-kah] exp.: Carlsbad salt
karłatka [kahr-**waht**-kah] f. dwarf palm; fan palm
karło [**kahr**-wo] n. armchair supported by crossed s-shaped legs
karłowacenie [kahr-wo-vah-**tse**-ńe] n. becoming dwarfed
karłowacieć [kahr-wo-**vah**-ćhećh] v. become dwarfed; become stunted; lessen; diminish; dwindle; decrease (*repeatedly*)
karłowatość [kahr-wo-**vah**-tośhćh] f. dwarfness; dwarfishness; nanism
karłowaty [kahr-wo-**vah**-ti] adj.m. dwarfish; undersized
karłowy [kahr-**wo**-vi] adj.m. dwarfish; undersized
karm [kahrm] m. fodder; cattle feed; provender
karma [**kahr**-mah] f. fodder; cattle feed; provender; karma (as in Hinduism); mob slang: pocket
karman [**kahr**-mahn] m. the sum of human actions decisive for the form of the next incarnation; slang: pocket; pickpocket
karmaniola [kahr-mah-**ńyo**-lah] f. carmagnole (tune)
karmazyn [kahr-**mah**-zin] m. crimson; costly crimson fabric; Norway haddock (fish); Polish nobleman of ancient stock
karmazynek [kahr-mah-**zi**-nek] m. purple finch (cock)
karmazynka [kahr-mah-**zin**-kah] f. hen of a particular breed
karmazynowy [kahr-mah-zi-**no**-vi] adj.m. of crimson; of costly crimson fabric; colloq: of Polish nobleman of ancient stock
karmel [**kahr**-mel] m. caramel; burnt sugar
karmelarski [kahr-me-**lahr**-skee] adj.m. of burnt sugar; of caramel maker
karmelarstwo [kahr-me-**lahr**-stfo] n. caramel making
karmelarz [kahr-**me**-lahsh] m. caramel maker
karmelek [kahr-**me**-lek] m. caramel; toffee
karmelicki [kahr-me-**leets**-kee] adj.m. Carmelite
karmelita [kahr-me-**lee**-tah] m. Carmelite monk
karmelitanka [kahr-me-lee-**tahn**-kah] f. Carmelite nun
karmelitański [kahr-me-lee-**tahń**-skee] adj.m. Carmelite
karmelitka [kahr-me-**leet**-kah] f. Carmelite nun
karmelizacja [kahr-me-lee-**zah**-tsyah] f. browning of sugar
karmelizować [kahr-me-lee-**zo**-vahćh] v. brown sugar; bake sugar (*repeatedly*)
karmelizowanie [kahr-me-lee-zo-**vah**-ńe] n. browning of sugar
karmelkowaty [kahr-mel-ko-**vah**-ti] adj.m. sugary; treacly; mawkish
karmelkowy [kahr-mel-**ko**-vi] adj.m. sugary; treacly; mawkish
karmiak [**kahr**-myahk] m. (horses) nose bag
karmiciel [kahr-**mee**-ćhel] m. feeder; nourisher; breadwinner
karmicielka [kahr-mee-**ćhel**-kah] f. feeder; nourisher; foster mother; nurse; breadwinner
karmić [**kahr**-meećh] v. feed; nourish; nurse; give suck (to a child); suckle; nurture (*repeatedly*)
karmić się [**kahr**-meećh śhan] v. feed oneself; cherish (hopes, etc.)

(*repeatedly*)
karmidełko [kahr-mee-**dew**-ko] n. floating fish-feeder in aquarium
karmidło [kahr-**meed**-wo] n. automatic cattle feeder
karmienie [kahr-**mye**-ńe] n. feeding; nourishing; nursing
karmik [**kahr**-meek] m. feeding trough; hog in process of fattening (for slaughter); feeding tray; nose bag (for horses); slang: glutton; prisoner on hunger strike
karmin [**kahr**-meen] m. carmine (lake, color)
karminować [kahr-mee-**no**-vahćh] v. carmine; paint with carmine; color with carmine (*repeatedly*)
karminowanie [kahr-mee-no-**vah**-ńe] n. painting with carmine
karminowo [kahr-mee-**no**-vo] adv. in the color of carmine
karminowoczerwony [kahr-mee-no-vo-cher-**vo**-ni] adj.m. carmine red
karminowy [kahr-mee-**no**-vi] adj.m. carmine
karmiony [kahr-**myo**-ni] adj.m. fed
karmnik [**kahrm**-ńeek] m. feeding trough; hog in process of fattening; feeding tray; nose bag (of a horse)
karmnikowy [kahrm-ńee-**ko**-vi] adj.m. of feeding-through
karmny [**kahrm**-ni] adj.m. fattened; in process of fattening
karmowy [kahr-**mo**-vi] adj.m. food (material, etc.); nutritive (value, etc.)
karmuazować [kahr-moo-ah-**zo**-vahćh] v. surround larger diamond with smaller diamonds on a piece of jewelry (*repeatedly*)
karmuazowanie [kahr-moo-ah-zo-**vah**-ńe] n. surrounding larger diamond with smaller diamonds on a piece of jewelry
karnacja [kahr-**nah**-tsyah] f. complexion; flesh tints; rendering of flesh color
karnalit [kahr-**nah**-leet] m. carnallite (mineral)
karnalitowy [kahr-nah-lee-**to**-vi] adj.m. carnallite (strata, etc.)
karnat [**kahr**-naht] m. stay
karnawał [kahr-**nah**-vahw] m. carnival; period of feasting
karnawałowo [kahr-nah-vah-**wo**-vo] adv. in the spirit of carnival
karnawałowy [kahr-nah-vah-**wo**-vi] adj.m. of the carnival; carnival (feasting season, etc.)
karnecik [kahr-**ne**-ćheek] m. (small, nice) coupon-book; dance card; program card
karneol [kahr-**ne**-ol] m. carnelian (mineral)
karnet [**kahr**-net] m. coupon-book; dance card; program card
karniak [**kahr**-ńahk] m. colloq: an item of punishment; isolation cell; prison
karnie [**kahr**-ńe] adv. penally; in perfect order (discipline); in disciplinary fashion
karnik [**kahr**-ńeek] m. colloq: criminal lawyer
karnisz [**kahr**-ńeesh] m. cornice
karność [**kahr**-nośhćh] f. discipline; orderly conduct
karnotyt [kahr-**no**-tit] m. carnotite (mineral)
karnówka [kahr-**noof**-kah] f. wooly Polish sheep
karny [**kahr**-ni] adj.m. disciplined; law abiding; penal (code, colony); punitive
rzut karny [zhoot **kahr**-ni] exp.: penalty shot (in a ball game)
sąd karny [sownt **kahr**-ni] exp.: criminal court
więzienie karne [vyan-**źhe**-ńe **kahr**-ne] exp.: penitentiary
karo [**kah**-ro] n. diamonds (in cards); square cut (bodice)
karoca [kah-**ro**-tsah] f. carriage suspended on leather bands
karogniady [kah-ro-**gńah**-di] adj.m. dark-reddish chestnut (horse)
karolek [kah-**ro**-lek] m. caraway
karosaż [kah-**ro**-sahsh] m. rake (of the axle-pin)
karoseria [kah-ro-**se**-ryah] f. car (truck) body; enclosing frame
karoseryjny [kah-ro-se-**riy**-ni] adj.m. of car (truck) body; of an enclosing frame
karosz [**kah**-rosh] m. colloq: black (horse)
karota [kah-**ro**-tah] f. early variety of

carrot
karoten [kah-**ro**-ten] m. carotene; carotin
karoteny [kah-ro-**te**-ni] pl. carotenes
karotenaza [kah-ro-te-**nah**-zah] f. carotenase
karotenoid [kah-ro-te-**no**-eed] m. carotenoid; carotinoid
karotenoidowy [kah-ro-te-no-ee-**do**-vi] adj.m. carotenoid
karotka [kah-**rot**-kah] f. early variety of carrot
karotyna [kah-ro-**ti**-nah] f. carotene; carotin
karowy [kah-**ro**-vi] adj.m. of diamonds (in cards); of a square cut (bodice)
karp [kahrp] m. carp (fish)
karpa [**kahr**-pah] f. snag; rhizome; rootstock
karpacki [kahr-**pah**-tskee] adj.m. Carpathian
karpi [**kahr**-pee] adj.m. carp's (scales, etc.)
karpiel [**kahr**-pyel] m. rutabaga (a variety of turnip)
karpieńcokształtny [kahr-pyeń-tso-**kshtahwt**-ni] adj.m. shaped like Cyprinodontiform (gold) fish
karpieńcokształtne [kahr-pyeń-tso-**kshtahwt**-ne] pl. the family of Cyprinodontiformes (gold) fishes
karpina [kahr-**pee**-nah] f. roots and stumps of trees (used as veneer material, etc.)
karpiokaraś [kahr-pyo-**kah**-rahśh] m. a fish of the family Cyprinidae
karpiokształtny [kahr-pyo-**kshtahwt**-ni] adj.m. of the carp family of fishes; of Cypriniformes
karpiokształtne [kahr-pyo-**kshtahwt**-ne] pl. the carp family of fishes; the family Cypriniformes
karpiowaty [kahr-pyo-**vah**-ti] adj.m. of the carp family of fishes; cyprinid
karpiowate [kahr-pyo-**vah**-te] pl. the carp family of fishes; the family Cyprinidae
karpiowy [kahr-**pyo**-vi] adj.m. carp (pond, etc.)
karpiówka [kahr-**pyoof**-kah] f. flat scale-like tile
karple [**kahrp**-le] pl. snowshoes
karpologia [kahr-po-**lo**-gyah] f. carpology
karpowina [kahr-po-**vee**-nah] f. roots and stumps of trees (used as veneer material, etc.)
karruka [kahr-**roo**-kah] f. Roman ornamental wagon
kart [kahrt] m. go-cart
karta [**kahr**-tah] f. card; page; note; sheet; leaf; ticket; charter; playing card; (temperature, etc.) chart; map
grać w karty [grahćh f **kahr**-ti] exp.: to play cards
kartacz [**kahr**-tahch] m. grape shot; case shot
kartaczownica [kahr-tah-chov-**ńee**-tsah] f. mitrailleuse
kartaczowy [kahr-tah-**cho**-vi] adj.m. grapeshot (fire, etc.)
Kartagińczyk [kahr-tah-**geeń**-chik] m. Carthaginian
kartagiński [kahr-tah-**geeń**-skee] adj.m. Carthaginian; Punic
kartan [**kahr**-tahn] m. muzzle-loader
kartaun [**kahr**-tahwn] m. muzzle-loader
kartauna [kahr-**tahw**-nah] f. muzzle-loaded cannon
karteczka [kahr-**tech**-kah] f. (small, nice) card; slip of paper; sheet of paper; note
kartel [**kahr**-tel] m. (industrial) trust; cartel; combine; pool
kartelizacja [kahr-te-lee-**zah**-tsyah] f. cartelization
karteluszek [kahr-te-**loo**-shek] m. note; chit; slip of paper
karter [**kahr**-ter] m. crankcase; casing; chain case
kartezjanizm [kahr-tez-**yah**-ńeezm] m. Cartesianism
kartezjański [kahr-tez-**yahń**-skee] adj.m. Cartesian
karting [**kahr**-teeng] m. go-cart race
kartingowy [kahr-teen-**go**-vi] adj.m. of go-cart racing
kartka [**kahr**-tkah] f. card; slip of paper; sheet of paper; note; chit; tag; page (of history, etc.); leaf
kartkować [karht-**ko**-vahćh] v. turn over the leaves; glance (through a

book); browse; skim (through a book) (*repeatedly*)
kartkowanie [karht-ko-**vah**-ńe] n. turning over the leaves; glancing (through a book); browsing
kartkowy [karht-**ko**-vi] adj.m. card (index, etc.); coupon (system, etc.)
kartkówka [karht-**koof**-kah] f. quiz in class written on single sheets
kartodiagram [kahr-to-**dyah**-grahm] m. combination of a map and diagrams
kartofel [kahr-**to**-fel] m. potato; mob slang: nose; stupid person
kartofelek [kahr-to-**fe**-lek] m. (small) potato
kartofelkowaty [kahr-to-fel-ko-**vah**-ti] adj.m. shaped like a potato
kartoflanka [kahr-to-**flahn**-kah] f. potato soup; type of onion
kartoflany [kahr-to-**flah**-ni] adj.m. potato (field, cake, chips, etc.)
mączka kartoflana [mownch-kah kahr-to-**flah**-nah] exp.: potato flour
kartoflarnia [kahr-to-**flahr**-ńah] f. potato storage shed (room)
kartoflisko [kahr-to-**flees**-ko] n. potato field; (big, ugly) potato
kartoflowaty [kahr-to-flo-**vah**-ti] adj.m. shaped like a potato; bulbous
kartoflowy [kahr-to-**flo**-vi] adj.m. potato (field, cake, chips, etc.)
kartograf [kahr-**to**-grahf] m. cartographer; map maker
kartografia [kahr-to-**grah**-fyah] f. the science of cartography; map-drawing; map making
kartograficznie [kahr-to-grah-**feech**-ńe] adv. using cartographic means; by means of maps (charts)
opracować kartograficznie [o-prah-**tso**-vahćh kahr-to-grah-**feech**-ńe] exp.: to survey
kartograficzny [kahr-to-grah-**feech**-ni] adj.m. cartographic; cartographical
kartografika [kahr-to-**grah**-fee-kah] f. cartography; map-drawing; map making
kartograjstwo [kahr-to-**grahy**-stfo] n. card-playing
kartogram [kahr-**to**-grahm] m. cartogram
kartometr [kahr-**to**-metr] m. device for measuring the length of lines on maps
kartomierz [kahr-**to**-myesh] m. device for measuring the length of lines on maps
kartometria [kahr-to-**metr**-yah] f. methods for measuring the lengths, surfaces, and volumes of geographic objects
kartometryczny [kahr-to-met-**rich**-ni] adj.m. pertaining to methods for measuring the lengths, surfaces, and volumes of geographic objects
karton [**kahr**-ton] m. cardboard; box; package; design on a cardboard; box (of cakes, etc.)
kartonaż [kahr-**to**-nahsh] m. cardboard products
kartoniarka [kahr-to-**ńahr**-kah] f. cardboard-making machine; board-machine
kartonik [kahr-**to**-ńeek] m. small piece of cardboard; small cardboard box; boxful
kartonować [kahr-to-**no**-vahćh] v. use cardboard in bookbinding; bind books in boards (*repeatedly*)
kartonowy [kahr-to-**no**-vi] adj.m. of cardboard; of pasteboard; cardboard (box, etc.)
kartoteka [kahr-to-**te**-kah] f. card index; file
kartotekowy [kahr-to-te-**ko**-vi] adj.m. card-index (system, etc.)
kartować [kahr-**to**-vahćh] v. chart; plot (*repeatedly*)
kartowanie [kahr-to-**vah**-ńe] n. charts; plotting
kartoznawstwo [kahr-to-**znahf**-stfo] n. science of map-making
kartusz [**kahr**-toosh] m. cartouche; cartridge belt
kartuszowy [kah-too-**sho**-vi] adj.m. cartouche (decorations, etc.)
kartuz [**kahr**-toos] m. Carthusian monk
kartuzek [karh-**too**-zek] m. a variety of pink
kartuzja [karh-**too**-zyah] f.

Carthusian monastery
kartuzjański [karh-too-**zyahń**-skee] adj.m. Carthusian (rule, etc.)
karuk [**kah**-rook] m. fish-glue
karuzel [kah-**roo**-zel] m. tournament show
karuzela [kah-roo-**ze**-lah] f. merry-go-round; carousel; slang: life sentence (mob jargon)
karuzelarz [kah-roo-**ze**-lahsh] m. owner of a merry-go-round
karuzelowy [kah-roo-ze-**lo**-vi] adj.m. carousel (lathe, horses, etc.)
karuzelówka [kah-roo-ze-**loof**-kah] f. carousel lathe
karwasz [**kahr**-vahsh] m. elbow armor cover; lapel; facing
kary [**kah**-ri] adj.m. black (horse)
kara [**kah**-rah] adj.f. black (mare)
kary koń [**kah**-ri koń] adj.m. black horse
karygodnie [kah-ri-**god**-ńe] adv. culpably; guiltily; criminally; unpardonably
karygodność [kah-ri-**god**-nośhćh] f. guilt; culpability; grossness
karygodny [kah-ri-**god**-ni] adj.m. unpardonable; guilty; gross; reprehensible; blameworthy; crass
karykatura [kah-ri-kah-**too**-rah] f. cartoon; caricature; parody; distortion; travesty
karykaturalnie [kah-ri-kah-too-**rahl**-ńe] adv. in caricature; grotesquely; in a distorted fashion; ludicrously; in burlesque fashion; farcically
karykaturalność [kah-ri-kah-too-**rahl**-nośhćh] f. grotesqueness; distortion
karykaturalny [kah-ri-kah-too-**rahl**-ni] adj.m. grotesque; farcical; distorted; ludicrous
karykaturować [kah-ri-kah-too-**ro**-vahćh] v. caricature; parody; travesty (*repeatedly*)
karykaturowanie [kah-ri-kah-too-ro-**vah**-ńe] n. caricature; parody; travesty
karykaturzysta [kah-ri-kah-too-**zhis**-tah] m. cartoonist; caricaturist
karykaturzystka [kah-ri-kah-too-**zhist**-kah] f. (woman) cartoonist; caricaturist

karykiel [kah-**ri**-kel] m. gig
karylion [kah-**ril**-yon] m. carillon; chime
karyntyjski [kah-rin-**tiy**-skee] adj.m. Carinthian
karzący [kah-**zhown**-tsi] adj.m. avenging; vindicatory; castigatory; retributory
karzeł [**kah**-zhew] m. dwarf; midget; gnome; goblin; manikin; homuncule; brownie; dwarf tree; starlet (small star); type of armchair
karzełek [kah-**zhe**-wek] m. small dwarf; midget; hobgoblin; imp; sprite; elfin; dwarf chicken
karzełkowaty [kah-zhew-ko-**vah**-ti] adj.m. dwarfish
kasa [**kah**-sah] f. cashier's desk; cash register; ticket office; cash box; safe; receipts; pay-desk; box office; booking office; pay-office; bank; fund; exp.: "pay here"
kasa emerytalna [**kah**-sah e-me-ri-**tahl**-nah] exp.: old-age pension fund; retirement fund
kasa pośmiertna [**kah**-sah pośh-**myert**-nah] exp.: burial fund
kasa zapomogowa [**kah**-sah zah-po-mo-**go**-vah] exp.: provident fund
płacić przy kasie [**pwah**-ćheećh pshi **kah**-śhe] exp.: to pay over the counter; to pay at the desk
robić kasę [**ro**-beećh **kah**-san] exp.: to make money
stan kasy [stahn **kah**-si] exp.: cash balance
zamknąć kasę [**zahmk**-nownćh **kah**-san] exp.: to balance the accounts
kasacja [kah-**sah**-tsyah] f. annulment; cassation; slang: aggravated assault (mob jargon)
kasacyjny [kah-sah-**tsiy**-ni] adj.m. annulment (decision, etc.); cassation (sentence, etc.)
Sąd Kasacyjny [sownt kah-sah-**tsiy**-ni] exp.: Court of Appeal; Court of Cassation
kasak [**kah**-sahk] m. vest; long blouse; jockey's jacket
kasakowy [kah-sah-**ko**-vi] adj.m. of a vest; of a long blouse; of a

jockey's jacket
kasandryczny [kah-sahn-**drich**-ni] adj.m. Cassandra-like (notions, visions, futile prophesies, etc.)
Kasanowa [kah-sah-**no**-vah] m. Casanova; lover; promiscuous and unscrupulous lover; mob slang: blusterer; an enterprising man
kasar [**kah**-sahr] m. landing net
kasarek [kah-**sah**-rek] m. (small) landing net
kasarnia [kah-**sahr**-ńah] f. military barrack
kasata [kah-**sah**-tah] f. annulment; reversing
kaseta [kah-**se**-tah] f. casket; jewel case; film-case; cassette; (working) box
kasetka [kah-**set**-kah] f. (small) casket; jewel case; cassette; desk
kasetkowy [kah-set-**ko**-vi] adj.m. desk (pen holder, etc.); of a (working) box; of a jewel-case
kasetofon [kah-se-**to**-fon] m. tape player
kaseton [kah-**se**-ton] m. coffer; caisson
kasetonować [kah-se-to-**no**-vahćh] v. panel with ornamental sculptured plates (*repeatedly*)
kasetonowy [kah-se-to-**no**-vi] adj.m. paneled with ornamental sculptured plates; coffered (ceiling, etc.); lacunar
kasetowy [kah-se-**to**-vi] adj.m. of a casket; of a jewelcase; of a film-case; of a cassette
kasiarz [**kah**-śhahsh] m. safe-breaker; safecracker; slang: yegg; robber
kasja [**kahs**-yah] f. cassia (tree, shrub)
kasjer [**kahs**-yer] m. cashier; purser; (bank) teller
kasjerka [kahs-**yer**-kah] f. woman cashier; (bank) teller
kasjerstwo [kahs-**yer**-stfo] n. post of a cashier; post of a (bank) teller; post of booking clerk; post of a purser
kasjop [**kahs**-yop] m. lutecium (atomic number 71) (silver-white metal)
kask [kahsk] m. helmet; tin hat
kaskada [kahs-**kah**-dah] f. cascade; waterfall
kaskader [kahs-**kah**-der] m. stunt man (in movies or in circus)
kaskadowo [kahs-kah-**do**-vo] adv. in cascades
spadać kaskadowo [**spah**-dahćh kahs-kah-**do**-vo] exp.: to cascade
kaskadowy [kahs-kah-**do**-vi] adj.m. cascade (electrical connection, amplification, etc.)
kasłać [**kahs**-wahćh] v. cough (*repeatedly*)
kasłanie [kahs-**wah**-ńe] n. a cough
kasoleta [kah-so-**le**-tah] f. cassolette; incense burner
kasować [kah-**so**-vahćh] v. cancel; annul; recall; abrogate (a law, etc.); obliterate; countermand (an order, etc.); abolish (a government, etc.); do away (with a custom, etc.); cross out; strike off; take off; dissolve (an institution, etc.) (*repeatedly*)
kasować się [kah-**so**-vahćh śhan] v. be countermanded; eliminate each other (*repeatedly*)
kasowanie [kah-so-**vah**-ńe] n. cancellation; annulment; recall; abrogation (of a law, etc.); obliteration (of a stamp, etc.); countermand (of an order, etc.); abolition (of a government, etc.); erasure (of a word, etc.); doing away (with a custom, etc.); crossing out; striking off; taking off; dissolution (of an institution, etc.); deletion
kasownik [kah-**sov**-ńeek] m. a natural (in music); "delete" (sign); postmark; dater
kasowość [kah-**so**-vośhćh] f. profitability; cash records; cash control
kasowy [kah-**so**-vi] adj.m. counting-house (office, etc.); cash (payment, desk, etc.); lucrative; remunerative; profitable; paying
godziny kasowe [go-**dźhee**-ni kah-**so**-ve] exp.: business hours
księga kasowa [**kśhan**-gah kah-**so**-vah] exp.: cashbook
kwit kasowy [kfeet kah-**so**-vi] exp.: receipt; voucher

nadużycie kasowe [nahd-oo-**zhi**-ćhe kah-**so**-ve] exp.: embezzlement; peculation
sztuka kasowa [**shtoo**-kah kah-**so**-vah] exp.: box-office draw; a hit
kaspijski [kahs-**peey**-skee] adj.m. Caspian
kassata [kahs-**sah**-tah] f. serving of a variety of Italian ice cream
kasta [**kahs**-tah] f. caste
kastanietowy [kahs-tah-ńe-**to**-vi] adj.m. of the castanets
kastaniety [kahs-tah-**ńe**-ti] pl. castanets
kastet [**kahs**-tet] m. knuckle-duster; war-club; loaded stick (skull breaker)
kastor [**kahs**-tor] m. beaver-cloth; beaver hat; beaver
kastorowy [kahs-to-**ro**-vi] adj.m. beaver (cloth, hat, etc.)
kastowość [kahs-**to**-vośhćh] f. caste system
kastowy [kahs-**to**-vi] adj.m. caste (system, division, etc.)
kastra [**kahst**-rah] f. mortar through
kastracja [kahst-**rah**-tsyah] f. castration; gelding; sterilization
kastracyjny [kahst-rah-**tsiy**-ni] adj.m. of castration
kastrat [**kahst**-raht] m. castrate; castrated man; eunuch; gelding (horse, etc.); castrato (singer)
kastrator [kahst-**rah**-tor] m. castrator
kastrować [kahst-**ro**-vahćh] v. castrate; emasculate; geld; spay (a female dog, etc.); expurgate (*repeatedly*)
kastrowanie [kahst-ro-**vah**-ńe] n. castration; gelding; sterilization
kasyda [kah-**si**-dah] f. casida; type of verse in Arab poetry
kasyno [kah-**si**-no] n. casino; club; mess hall; messroom
kasynowy [kah-si-**no**-vi] adj.m. of a messroom; mess (hall, etc.)
kasyteryt [kah-si-**te**-rit] m. cassiterite; tinstone (mineral)
kasza [**kah**-shah] f. grits; groats; cereals; gruel; porridge; mush; frumenty (dish); grit; slang: mess; stolen small items (mob jargon)
wleźć w kaszę [vleśhćh f **kah**-shan] exp.: to get into a scrape
kaszak [**kah**-shahk] m. atheroma
kaszalot [kah-**shah**-lot] m. cachalot; sperm whale; whale of the Physeteridae superfamily
kaszaloty [kah-shah-**lo**-ti] pl. cachalots; sperm whales; whales of the Physeteridae superfamily
kaszanka [kah-**shahn**-kah] f. black pudding
kaszany [kah-**shah**-ni] adj.m. of black pudding
kiszka kaszana [**keesh**-kah kah-**shah**-nah] exp.: black pudding
kaszarnia [kah-**shahr**-ńah] f. grits mill
kaszarnictwo [kah-shahr-**ńeets**-tfo] n. cereals industry
kaszarstwo [kah-**shahr**-stfo] n. cereals industry
kaszel [**kah**-shel] m. cough; tussis
kaszelek [kah-**she**-lek] m. light cough
kaszerować [kah-she-**ro**-vahćh] v. make hard covers for books (*repeatedly*)
kaszerowanie [kah-she-ro-**vah**-ńe] n. making hard covers for books
kaszetka [kah-**shet**-kah] f. wafer used for pharmaceuticals
kaszetować [kah-she-**to**-vahćh] v. convert a panoramic film for projection on television and in regular movie houses (*repeatedly*)
kaszetowanie [kah-she-to-**vah**-ńe] n. conversion of a panoramic film for projection on television and in regular movie houses
kaszka [**kahsh**-kah] f. (small, nice) grits; groats; cereals; gruel; porridge; mush; frumenty; furmity; grit; mess
kaszkiecik [kahsh-ke-**ćheek**] m. (small, nice) cap
kaszkiecina [kahsh-ke-**ćhee**-nah] f. (shabby, worn-out) cap
kaszkiet [**kahsh**-ket] m. cap
kaszkowaty [kahsh-ko-**vah**-ti] adj.m. gritty (snow, etc.); grit-like
kaszkowy [kahsh-**ko**-vi] adj.m. of grit; of cereals
kaszlać [**kahsh**-lahćh] v. cough (*repeatedly*)
kaszlanie [kahsh-**lah**-ńe] n. cough
kaszlarka [kahsh-**lahr**-kah] f. device

for removal of fat from intestines of animals
kaszleć [**kahsh**-lećh] v. cough (*repeatedly*)
kaszlnąć [**kahshl**-nownćh] v. cough
kaszlnięcie [kahshl-ńan-ćhe] n. a cough
kaszlować [kahsh-**lo**-vahćh] v. remove fat from intestines of animals (*repeatedly*)
kaszlowanie [kahsh-lo-**vah**-ńe] n. removal of fat from intestines of animals
kaszlowy [kahsh-**lo**-vi] adj.m. of a cough; tussive
kaszmir [**kahsh**-meer] m. cashmere
kaszmirowy [kahsh-mee-**ro**-vi] adj.m. of cashmere; cashmere (texture, etc.)
kaszmirski [kahsh-**meer**-skee] adj.m. Kashmirian
kaszowacieć [kah-sho-**vah**-ćhećh] v. become mushy (*repeatedly*)
kaszowaty [kah-sho-**vah**-ti] adj.m. mushy
kaszt [kahsht] m. crib; cog; chock
kaszta [**kahsh**-tah] f. case (font)
kasztan [**kahsh**-tahn] m. chestnut; chestnut tree; chestnut horse; sorrel; castor; lambskin; slang: poor student
kasztany [kahsh-**tah**-ni] pl. chestnuts; horny growth on horse's legs
kasztanek [kahsh-**tah**-nek] m. (young, new) chestnut; chestnut tree; chestnut horse; sorrel
kasztanka [kahsh-**tahn**-kah] f. chestnut mare
kasztanowaty [kahsh-tah-no-**vah**-ti] adj.m. chestnut-colored; brown; maroon
kasztanowcowaty [kahsh-tah-nof-tso-**vah**-ti] adj.m. of horse chestnut; hippocastanaceous; Aesculaneous
kasztanowcowate [kahsh-tah-nof-tso-**vah**-te] pl. the Hippocastanaceae family of plants
kasztanowiec [kahsh-tah-**no**-vyets] m. horse-chestnut (tree, shrub); Aesculus
kasztanowłosy [kahsh-tah-no-**vwo**-si] adj.m. auburn-haired
kasztanowy [kahsh-tah-**no**-vi] adj.m. of the chestnut; of chestnuts; chestnut (tree, etc.); auburn; brown; chestnut-colored
kasztel [**kahsh**-tel] m. castle
kasztelan [kahsh-**te**-lahn] m. castellan; governor of a castle
kasztelania [kahsh-te-**lah**-ńyah] f. castellany; office of a castellan
kasztelanic [kahsh-te-**lah**-ńeets] m. castellan's son
kasztelanka [kahsh-te-**lahn**-kah] f. castellan's daughter
kasztelanowa [kahsh-te-lah-**no**-vah] f. castellan's wife
kasztelański [kahsh-te-**lahń**-skee] adj.m. castellan's; of a castle
kasztelaństwo [kahsh-te-**lahń**-stfo] n. castellan's office; colloq: castellan and his wife
kasztelowy [kahsh-te-**lo**-vi] adj.m. castle (architecture, etc.)
Kaszub [**kah**-shoop] m. Kashubian; Kashube
kaszubić [kah-**shoo**-beećh] v. speak with the Kashubian accent; mispronounce the soft (palatal) Polish consonants (*repeatedly*)
kaszubienie [kah-shoo-**bye**-ńe] n. speaking with the Kashubian accent; mispronouncing the soft (palatal) Polish consonants
kaszubizm [kah-**shoo**-beezm] m. Kashubian phonetic characteristics
kaszubizować [kah-shoo-bee-**zo**-vahćh] v. pronounce in the Kashubian fashion (*repeatedly*)
kaszubski [kah-**shoop**-skee] adj.m. Kashubian
język kaszubski [yan-zik kah-**shoop**-skee] exp.: Kashubian language; Kashoubish
kaszubszczyzna [kah-shoop-**shchiz**-nah] f. Kashubian speech; Kashubian language
kaszyca [kah-**shi**-tsah] f. crib(work)
kat [kaht] m. executioner; hangman; colloq: torturer; oppressor; butcher; tormentor
katabas [kah-**tah**-bahs] m. slang: sky pilot; priest (mob jargon)
katabatyczny [kah-tah-bah-**tich**-ni] adj.m. catabatic (stage of decline

of a disease, etc.)
katabolicznie [kah-tah-bo-**leech**-ńe] adv. catabolically
kataboliczny [kah-tah-bo-**leech**-ni] adj.m. catabolic
katabolizm [kah-tah-**bo**-leezm] m. catabolism; destructive metabolism
katachreza [kah-tah-**khre**-zah] f. catachresis
katadioptryczny [kah-tah-dyop-**trich**-ni] adj.m. catadioptric
katadromiczny [kah-tah-dro-**meech**-ni] adj.m. catadromous (fish, etc.)
katafalk [kah-**tah**-fahlk] m. bier
katafalkowy [kah-tah-fahl-**ko**-vi] adj.m. of a bier
kataforeza [kah-tah-fo-**re**-zah] f. cataphoresis; electrophoresis
katageneza [kah-tah-ge-**ne**-zah] f. catagenesis
katakaustyka [kah-tah-**kahws**-ti-kah] f. catacaustic surface
kataklizm [kah-**tah**-kleezm] m. cataclysm; disaster; calamity
kataklizmowy [kah-tah-kleez-**mo**-vi] adj.m. cataclysmic; disastrous; calamitous
katakumba [kah-tah-**koom**-bah] f. catacomb
katakumby [kah-tah-**koom**-bi] pl. catacombs
katakumbowy [kah-tah-koom-**bo**-vi] adj.m. of a catacomb; of catacombs
katalaza [kah-tah-**lah**-zah] f. catalase
kataleksa [kah-tah-**lek**-sah] f. catalexis
kataleksja [kah-tah-**lek**-syah] f. catalexis
katalektyczny [kah-tah-lek-**tich**-ni] adj.m. catalectic; incomplete
katalepsja [kah-tah-**lep**-syah] f. catalepsy
kataleptyczny [kah-tah-lep-**tich**-ni] adj.m. cataleptic; cataleptiform
kataleptyk [kah-tah-**lep**-tik] m. cataleptic
kataleptyzować [kah-tah-lep-ti-**zo**-vahćh] v. render cataleptic (*repeatedly*)
katalitycznie [kah-tah-lee-**tich**-ńe] adv. catalytically
katalityczny [kah-tah-lee-**tich**-ni] adj.m. catalytic
kataliza [kah-tah-**lee**-zah] f. catalysis
katalizator [kah-tah-lee-**zah**-tor] m. catalyst; agent of catalysis
katalizować [kah-tah-lee-**zo**-vahćh] v. catalyze (*repeatedly*)
katalizowanie [kah-tah-lee-zo-**vah**-ńe] n. catalysis
katalog [kah-**tah**-log] m. catalog; notebook; roll; list; register
katalogować [kah-tah-lo-**go**-vahćh] v. list (books, etc.); catalog; catalogue (*repeatedly*)
katalogowanie [kah-tah-lo-go-**vah**-ńe] n. making lists (of books, etc.); cataloging; cataloguing
katalogowo [kah-tah-lo-**go**-vo] adv. in catalog fashion
katalogowy [kah-tah-lo-**go**-vi] adj.m. of a catalog; catalogue (price, item, etc.)
Katalończyk [kah-tah-**loń**-chik] m. Catalan
kataloński [kah-tah-**loń**-skee] adj.m. Catalan
katamaran [kah-tah-**mah**-rahn] m. catamaran; boat with twin hulls
katana [kah-**tah**-nah] f. jacket (in national or military dress) (hist.); samurai sabre
katanka [kah-**tahn**-kah] f. jacket (in national or military dress) (hist.)
kataplazm [kah-**tah**-plahzm] m. cataplasm; poultice
kataplazmować [kah-tah-plahz-**mo**-vahćh] v. poultice; apply a poultice (to) (*repeatedly*)
kataplazmowanie [kah-tah-plahz-mo-**vah**-ńe] n. the application of a poultice; the application of poultices
katapulta [kah-tah-**pool**-tah] f. catapult
katapultować [kah-tah-pool-**to**-vahćh] v. catapult (*repeatedly*)
katapultować się [kah-tah-pool-**to**-vahćh śhan] v. catapult oneself (from an airplane, etc.); become catapulted (*repeatedly*)
katapultowanie [kah-tah-pool-to-**vah**-ńe] n. launching with a catapult
katapultowy [kah-tah-pool-**to**-vi] adj.m. catapult (equipment, etc.)
katar [**kah**-tahr] m. head cold;

running nose; catarrh; Catharist
katar kiszek [**kah**-tahr **kee**-shek] exp.: enteritis
katar nosa [**kah**-tahr **no**-sah] exp.: coryza; common cold
katar oskrzeli [**kah**-tahr os-**kshe**-lee] exp.: bronchitis
katar żołądka [**kah**-tahr zho-**wownt**-kah] exp.: gastritis
nabawić się kataru [nah-**bah**-veećh śhan kah-**tah**-roo] exp.: to catch a cold
katarakta [kah-tah-**rahk**-tah] f. cataract; opaque eye lens
kataraktowy [kah-tah-rahk-**to**-vi] adj.m. cataractal; cataractine; cataractous
kataralny [kah-tah-**rahl**-ni] adj.m. catarrhal (fever, etc.)
schorzenie kataralne [skho-**zhe**-ńe kah-tah-**rahl**-ne] exp.: catarrh; a cold
katarob [kah-**tah**-rop] m. organism living in clean and cool water
katarobiont [kah-tah-**rob**-yont] m. one of the family of organisms living in clean and cool water
kataryniarz [kah-tah-**ri**-ńahsh] m. (street) organ grinder
katarynka [kah-tah-**rin**-kah] f. barrel organ; street organ
powtarzać jak katarynka [pof-**tah**-zhahćh yahk kah-tah-**rin**-kah] exp.: to say over and over again; to parrot
katarynkowy [kah-tah-rin-**ko**-vi] adj.m. of barrel organ; street organ (melodies, etc.)
katarzynka [kah-tah-**zhin**-kah] f. honey-cake; Catherine pear; nun of the order of St. Catherine
katastaza [kah-tahs-**tah**-zah] f. catastasis
kataster [kah-**tahs**-ter] m. cadastre (of real estate)
katastralny [kah-tahs-**trahl**-ni] adj.m. cadastral (books, etc.)
katastrefa [kah-tah-**stre**-fah] f. the deepest stratum of earth crust (above 500 degrees Celsius)
katastrofa [kah-tah-**stro**-fah] f. catastrophe; disaster; calamity; cataclysm; crash; shipwreck
katastrofalnie [kah-tah-stro-**fahl**-ńe] adv. catastrophically; disastrously; woefully
katastrofalny [kah-tah-stro-**fahl**-ni] adj.m. catastrophic; disastrous; woeful
katastroficzny [kah-tah-stro-**feech**-ni] adj.m. of catastrophism
katastrofista [kah-tah-stro-**fees**-tah] m. catastrophist
katastrofistka [kah-tah-stro-**fees**-tkah] f. (female) catastrophist
katastrofizm [kah-tah-**stro**-feezm] m. catastrophism
katastrować [kah-tah-**stro**-vahćh] v. make a cadastre; record real estate (*repeatedly*)
katatonia [kah-tah-**to**-ńyah] f. catatonia
katatoniczny [kah-tah-to-**ńeech**-ni] adj.m. catatonic
katatonik [kah-tah-**to**-ńeek] m. catatonic
katatymia [kah-tah-**ti**-myah] f. catathymic complex
katecheta [kah-te-**khe**-tah] m. teacher of catechism; catechist
katechetka [kah-te-**khet**-kah] f. (woman) teacher of catechism
katechetycznie [kah-te-khe-**tich**-ńe] adv. catechetically
katechetyczny [kah-te-khe-**tich**-ni] adj.m. catechetical; catechetic
katechetyka [kah-te-**khe**-ti-kah] f. catechesis; religious instruction
katecheza [kah-te-**khe**-zah] f. catechesis; catechetical discourse
katechina [kah-te-**khee**-nah] f. catechin; catechol; pyrocatechol
katechizacja [kah-te-khee-**zah**-tsyah] f. catechization
katechizm [kah-**te**-kheezm] m. catechism; the basics; the ABC's
katechizmowy [kah-te-kheez-**mo**-vi] adj.m. catechismal
katechizować [kah-te-khee-**zo**-vahćh] v. catechize (*repeatedly*)
katechizowanie [kah-te-khee-zo-**vah**-ńe] n. catechization
katechu [kah-**te**-khoo] n. extract of Indian acacia tree; catechu; cashoo
katechumen [kah-te-**khoo**-men] m. catechumen
katechumenat [kah-te-khoo-**me**-

naht] m. catechumenate
katechumenka [kah-te-khoo-**men**-kah] f. (woman) catechumen
katechumeństwo [kah-te-khoo-**meń**-stfo] n. catechumenate
katedra [kah-**te**-drah] f. pulpit; university department; univeristy chair; cathedral
katedra filologii angielskiej [kah-**te**-drah fee-lo-**log**-yee ahn-gel-skey] exp.: English (Philology) Department
katedralny [kah-te-**drahl**-ni] adj.m. cathedral (church, etc.)
kategoremat [kah-te-go-**re**-maht] m. categorem
kategoria [kah-te-**go**-ryah] f. category; division; class; classification
kategorialny [kah-te-gor-**yahl**-ni] adj.m. of a category; of an idea
kategorycznie [kah-te-go-**rich**-ńe] adv. categorically; positively; definitely; decidedly; explicitly
zaprzeczyć kategorycznie [zah-**pshe**-chićh kah-te-go-**rich**-ńe] exp.: to deny flatly
kategoryczność [kah-te-go-**rich**-nośhćh] f. categorical character; explicitness; positiveness
kategoryczny [kah-te-go-**rich**-ni] adj.m. absolute; categorical; explicit; decided; flat; stiff; downright; express (rule, etc.)
kategoryzacja [kah-te-go-ri-**zah**-tsyah] f. categorization; classification
kategoryzować [kah-te-go-ri-**zo**-vahćh] v. categorize; classify (*repeatedly*)
kategoryzowanie [kah-te-go-ri-zo-**vah**-ńe] n. categorization; classification
katenoida [kah-te-**noy**-dah] f. catenoid
katergol [kah-**ter**-gol] m. rocket fuel activated by catalysis
kateszowy [kah-te-**sho**-vi] adj.m. of catechu palm
kateter [kah-**te**-ter] m. catheter
kateteryzacja [kah-te-te-ri-**zah**-tsyah] f. catheterization
kateteryzować [kah-te-te-ri-**zo**-vahćh] v. catheterize (*repeatedly*)
kateteryzowanie [kah-te-te-ri-zo-**vah**-ńe] n. catheterization
katetometr [kah-te-**to**-metr] m. cathetometer; kathetometer
katetometryczny [kah-te-to-met-**rich**-ni] adj.m. cathetometric
katgut [**kaht**-goot] m. catgut (surgery thread)
katgutowy [kaht-goo-**to**-vi] adj.m. catgut (sutures, etc.)
katharisis [kah-**tahr**-zees] indecl.: catharsis
kation [**kaht**-yon] m. cation; positive ion
kationit [kaht-**yo**-ńeet] m. cation exchanger
kationowy [kaht-yo-**no**-vi] adj.m. of a cation; of positive ion
katiusza [kaht-**yoo**-shah] f. katyusha (Soviet rocket launcher)
katleja [kaht-**le**-yah] f. Cattley's orchid
katoda [kah-**to**-dah] f. cathode; negative electrode
katodoluminofor [kah-to-do-loo-mee-**no**-for] m. luminiferous cathode (cover for oscilloscopic screens)
katodowy [kah-to-**do**-vi] adj.m. cathodic; of a negative electrode; cathode (rays, etc.)
katolicki [kah-to-**leets**-kee] adj.m. (Roman) Catholic
po katolicku [po kah-to-**leets**-koo] exp.: like a Catholic; according to the Catholic rite
katolicyzm [kah-to-**lee**-tsizm] m. Catholicism; the Roman Catholic Church
katoliczka [kah-to-**leech**-kah] f. (a Roman) Catholic (female)
katolik [kah-**to**-leek] m. (a Roman) Catholic
katolikos [kah-to-**lee**-kos] m. catholicos; katholicos
katon [**kah**-ton] m. (a) Catonian
katoński [kah-**toń**-skee] adj.m. Catonian
katoptryka [kah-**top**-tri-kah] f. study of reflected light; catoptrics
katoptrycznie [kah-top-**trich**-ńe] adv. catoptrically
katoptryczny [kah-top-**trich**-ni] adj.m. catoptric; produced by reflected light

katorga [kah-**tor**-gah] f. slavery; galleys; penal colony; deportation with hard labor; convicts; colloq: slaving; drudgery; mob slang: correctional institution; rehabilitation of a drug addict

katorżniczy [kah-torzh-**ńee**-chi] adj.m. convict's; galley-slave's

katorżnik [kah-**torzh**-ńeek] m. convict sentenced to hard labor

katorżny [kah-**torzh**-ni] adj.m. convict's; galley-slave's; convicts' (transport, etc.)

zsyłka katorżna [**ssiw**-kah kah-**torzh**-nah] exp.: deportation for hard labor

katostwo [kah-**to**-stfo] n. executioner's work; butchery; barbarous treatment; cruelty; brutality; inhuman treatment; tormenting

katować [kah-**to**-vahćh] v. torture; beat cruelly; hack; mangle; torture (*repeatedly*)

katowanie [kah-to-**vah**-ńe] n. torture; cruel beating; atrocious treatment

katownia [kah-**tov**-ńah] f. place of torture

katowski [kah-**tof**-skee] adj.m. executioner's; hangman's

po katowsku [po kah-**tof**-skoo] exp.: barbarously; cruelly; atrociously

katrupić [kah-**troo**-peećh] v. colloq: do away (with); bump off (*repeatedly*)

katta [**kaht**-tah] f. variety of Lemur monkey

katulać [kah-**too**-lahćh] v. colloq: roll (a barrel, a ball, etc.); slang: go; walk (mob jargon) (*repeatedly*)

katulać się [kah-**too**-lahćh śhan] v. colloq: roll; be rolling (downhill, etc.) (*repeatedly*)

katusza [kah-**too**-shah] f. torture; torment; agony

katzenjamer [kah-tsen-**yah**-mer] m. colloq: hangover; hot coppers; distress; depression; a discordant clamor; crapulence

kaucja [**kahw**-tsyah] f. bail; deposit; security; recognizance; surety

kaucyjny [kahw-**tsiy**-ni] adj.m. of a deposit; of a bail; of a surety

kauczuk [**kahw**-chook] m. natural or synthetic rubber; caoutchouc

kauczukodajny [kahw-choo-ko-**dahy**-ni] adj.m. rubber yielding (tree, etc.)

kauczukonośny [kahw-choo-ko-**nośh**-ni] adj.m. rubber yielding (tree, etc.)

kauczukowiec [kahw-choo-**ko**-vyets] m. hevea; rubber tree; gum tree

kauczukowy [kahw-choo-**ko**-vi] adj.m. rubber (tree, plant, cloth, etc.)

kaudyński [kahw-**diń**-skee] adj.m. Caudine (Forks, etc.)

kaukaski [kahw-**kahs**-kee] adj.m. Caucasian; of Caucasus

kauliflora [kahw-lee-**flo**-ryah] f. flowering of tree trunks and bushes

kaustobiolit [kahw-sto-**byo**-leet] m. sedimentary rock of organic origin (coal, etc.)

kaustycznie [kahw-**stich**-ńe] adv. caustically; satirically; bitingly

kaustyczność [kahw-**stich**-nośhćh] f. causticity

kaustyczny [kahw-**stich**-ni] adj.m. caustic; satirical; biting

soda kaustyczna [**so**-dah kahw-**stich**-nah] exp.: caustic soda

kaustyka [**kahw**-sti-kah] f. caustic (curved) surface of reflection or refraction

kaustyzacja [kahw-sti-**zah**-tsyah] f. causticization

kausza [**kahw**-shah] f. (rope) thimble; cord-eye; gutter ring

kauter [**kahw**-ter] m. cautery; electric cauter

kauteryzacja [kahw-te-ri-**zah**-tsyah] f. cautery; cauterization

kauteryzować [kahw-te-ri-**zo**-vahćh] v. cauterize (*repeatedly*)

kauteryzowanie [kahw-te-ri-zo-**vah**-ńe] n. cautery; cauterization

kauzalista [kahw-zah-**lees**-tah] m. follower of the deterministic theory of causality

kauzalistyczny [kahw-zah-lees-**tich**-ni] adj.m. of the deterministic theory of causality

kauzalizm [kahw-**zah**-leezm] m. the deterministic theory of causality
kauzalność [kahw-**zahl**-nośhćh] f. causality
kauzalny [kahw-**zahl**-ni] adj.m. of causality; relating to a cause
kauzatywny [kahw-zah-**tiv**-ni] adj.m. causative (verb, etc.)
kauzyperda [kahw-zi-**per**-dah] m. pettifogger; shyster; shabby lawyer
kawa [**kah**-vah] f. coffee; coffee plant (tree, shrub, etc.); coffee party
biała kawa [**byah**-wah **kah**-vah] exp.: coffee with cream; coffee with milk; colloq: white coffee
czarna kawa [**chahr**-nah **kah**-vah] exp.: black coffee; social party
dwie kawy [dvye **kah**-vi] exp.: two coffees
filiżanka do kawy [fee-lee-**zhahn**-kah do **kah**-vi] exp.: coffee cup
kawa mielona [kah-vah mye-**lo**-nah] exp.: ground coffee
kawa na ławę [kah-vah nah **wah**-van] exp.: (to talk, etc.) bluntly, in plain words, without mincing matters
kawa palona [**kah**-vah pah-**lo**-nah] exp.: roasted coffee
kawa po turecku [**kah**-vah po too-**rets**-koo] exp.: Turkish coffee
maszynka do kawy [mah-**shin**-kah do **kah**-vi] exp.: coffee pot
młynek do kawy [**mwi**-nek do **kah**-vi] exp.: coffee mill; coffee grinder
kawacja [kah-**vah**-tsyah] f. a hit with a foil in fencing
kawalarka [kah-vah-**lahr**-kah] f. (female) joker; wag; jester
kawalarstwo [kah-vah-**lahr**-stfo] n. jokes; waggishness; jesting; jests; spinning of yarns
kawalarz [kah-**vah**-lahsh] m. joker; wag; jester; spinner of yarns
kawaląteczek [kah-vah-lown-**te**-chek] m. tiny little bit
kawalątek [kah-vah-**lown**-tek] m. little bit; little piece; just a little
kawalątko [kah-vah-**lownt**-ko] n. little bit; little piece; just a little
kawaler [kah-**vah**-ler] m. bachelor; suitor; beau; cavalier; gallant; lady's man; dancing partner; man decorated (with an order, etc.); knight; (slang: syphilis (mob jargon)
kawaleria [kah-vah-**le**-ryah] f. cavalry; colloq: young folks
lekka kawaleria [**lek**-kah kah-vah-**le**-ryah] exp.: light horse
kawalerka [kah-vah-**ler**-kah] f. bachelor flat; bachelor's rooms; bachelorhood; colloq: young folks; slang: isolation cell; grave
kawalerski [kah-vah-**ler**-skee] adj.m. bachelor's; single
choroba kawalerska [kho-**ro**-bah kah-vah-**ler**-skah] exp.: colloq: venereal disease
jazda kawalerska [**yahz**-dah kah-vah-**ler**-skah] exp.: reckless driving; speeding; reckless riding
po kawalersku [po kah-vah-**ler**-skoo] exp.: bachelor fashion; chivalrously
stan kawalerski [stahn kah-vah-**ler**-skee] exp.: bachelorhood; single state
wieczór kawalerski [**vye**-choor kah-vah-**ler**-skee] exp.: stag party
kawalerskość [kah-vah-**ler**-skośhćh] f. chivalry
kawalerstwo [kah-vah-**lers**-tfo] n. bachelorhood; knighthood; chivalry
kawaleryjski [kah-vah-le-**riy**-skee] adj.m. cavalryman's; horse-soldier's; of cavalry; cavalry (officer, charge, etc.)
koń kawaleryjski [koń kah-vah-le-**riy**-skee] exp.: trooper (horse)
koszary kawaleryjskie [ko-**shah**-ri kah-vah-le-**riy**-ske] exp.: horse-barracks
pułk kawaleryjski [poowk kah-vah-le-**riy**-skee] exp.: cavalry regiment; regiment of horse
kawalerzysta [kah-vah-le-**zhis**-tah] m. cavalryman; horseman; trooper
kawalkada [kah-vahl-**kah**-dah] f. cavalcade (procession)
kawalkata [kah-vahl-**kah**-tah] f. cavalcade (procession)
kawał [**kah**-vahw] m. (large) piece;

lump; hunk; colloq: joke; cheat; funny business; piece of waggery; anecdote; story; practical joke; leg-pull
gruby kawał [**groo**-bi **kah**-vahw] exp.: spicy anecdote
kawał chleba [**kah**-vahw **khle**-bah] exp.: a living
kawał czasu [**kah**-vahw **chah**-soo] exp.: a long time; ages
kawał drania [**kah**-vahw **drah**-ńah] exp.: notorious rascal; scamp
kawał grosza [**kah**-vahw **gro**-shah] exp.: a pretty penny; a tidy sum; a bundle
paskudny kawał [pahs-**kood**-ni **kah**-vahw] exp.: dirty trick; nasty trick
wziąć się na kawał [vźh<u>own</u>ćh śh<u>an</u> nah **kah**-vahw] exp.: to let oneself be taken in; to let oneself be cheated
kawałeczek [kah-vah-**we**-chek] m. (very small) bit; morsel; scrap; chunk
kawałek [kah-**vah**-wek] m. bit; morsel; scrap; slice (of bread, etc.); cake (of soap, etc.); colloq: chunk (of wood, etc.); piece (of music, etc.); a thousand zlotys
po kawałku [po kah-**vahw**-koo] exp.: piece by piece; bit by bit; piecemeal
kawałkować [kah-vahw-**ko**-vahćh] v. break up; split up; cut up; take to pieces; dismember (*repeatedly*)
kawałkowanie [kah-vahw-ko-**vah**-ńe] n. breaking up; splitting up; dismembering
kawas [**kah**-vahs] m. kavass; Turkish policeman
kawatyna [kah-vah-**ti**-nah] f. cavatina; melodious composition
kawcia [**kahf**-ćhah] f. (very nice) cup of coffee
kawczy [**kahf**-chi] adj.m. jackdaw's
kawecan [kah-**ve**-tsahn] m. bridle with a very severe Italian bit
kawerna [kah-**ver**-nah] f. cave; cavity (in lungs, etc.)
kawęczeć [kah-**v<u>an</u>**-chećh] v. be sickly; droop; flag; pine; waste away (*repeatedly*)
kawęczenie [kah-v<u>an</u>-**che**-ńe] n. being sickly; wasting away
kawiarenka [kah-vyah-**ren**-kah] f. (modest) little cafe
kawiarka [kah-**vyahr**-kah] f. woman fond of coffee
kawiarnia [kah-**vyahr**-ńah] f. cafe
kawiarniany [kah-vyahr-**ńah**-ni] adj.m. of a cafe; cafe (rooms, etc.)
kawiarz [**kah**-vyahsh] m. man fond of coffee
kawila [kah-**vee**-lah] f. Caville apple
kawior [**kah**-vyor] m. caviar
kawitacja [kah-vee-**tah**-tsyah] f. cavitation
kawitator [kah-vee-**tah**-tor] m. sewer aerator; device for air-entraining
kawka [**kahf**-kah] f. jackdaw; colloq: little, nice coffee; slang: nun; informer (mob jargon)
kawkać [**kahf**-kahćh] v. mob slang: accuse; denounce (*repeatedly*)
kawon [**kah**-von] m. watermelon
kawowiec [kah-**vo**-vyets] m. coffee shrub
kawowy [kah-**vo**-vi] adj.m. (of) coffee; coffee (plantation, color, taste, etc.)
kawunia [kah-**voo**-ńah] f. (very nice) cup of coffee
kawusia [kah-**voo**-śhah] f. (nice, little) cup of coffee
kazać [**kah**-zahćh] v. order; tell; make (somebody) do (something); cause to be done; command; preach; deliver sermons (*repeatedly*)
kazać nie ... [**kah**-zahćh ńe] exp.: to order not to ...; to prohibit; to forbid; to disallow
kazalnica [kah-zahl-**ńee**-tsah] f. pulpit
kazamata [kah-zahl-**mah**-tah] f. casemate; underground prison cell; slang: correctional institution; isolation cell (mob jargon)
kazamatowy [kah-zah-mah-**to**-vi] adj.m. casemate (structure, etc.); of an underground prison cell
kazanie [kah-**zah**-ńe] n. sermon; colloq: peroration
wygłaszać kazanie [vi-**gwah**-

shahćh kah-**zah**-ńe] exp.: to preach
kazanko [kah-**zahn**-ko] n. light, little sermon
kazarka [kah-**zahr**-kah] f. Mediterranean variety of wild duck
kazeina [kah-ze-**ee**-nah] f. casein
kazeinowy [kah-ze-ee-**no**-vi] adj.m. casein (glue, paint, plastic, etc.)
kazetemowiec [kah-ze-te-**mo**-vyets] m. member of the Communist Youth Association
kazić [**kah**-źheećh] v. pollute; corrupt; blemish; contaminate (*repeatedly*)
kazionny [kah-**źhon**-ni] adj.m. government (issue, etc.); state's; of the treasury department; slang: issue (boots, shirts, etc.); rationed (bred, etc.) (mob jargon)
kazirodca [kah-źhee-**rot**-tsah] m. incestuous person; person guilty of incest
kazirodczo [kah-źhee-**rot**-cho] adv. incestuously
kazirodczy [kah-źhee-**rot**-chi] adj.m. incestuous
kazirodztwo [kah-źhee-**rots**-tfo] n. incest
kaznodzieja [kah-zno-**dźhe**-yah] m. preacher; evangelist
kaznodziejski [kah-zno-**dźhey**-skee] adj.m. preacher's; pulpit (eloquence, etc.); sermonizing
po kaznodziejsku [po kah-zno-dźhey-skoo] exp.: like a preacher
kaznodziejstwo [kah-zno-**dźhey**-stfo] n. preaching; moralizing; homilies
kazualizm [kah-zoo-**ah**-leezm] m. casualism; rule of chance
kazualnie [kah-zoo-**ahl**-ńe] adv. factitively
kazualny [kah-zoo-**ahl**-ni] adj.m. factitive
kazuar [kah-**zoo**-ahr] m. cassowary (bird)
kazuary [kah-zoo-**ah**-ri] pl. the Casuariidae family of birds; cassowaries
kazuaryna [kah-zoo-ah-**ri**-nah] f. casuarina (a Malay tree); casuarina wood
kazuista [kah-zoo-**ees**-tah] m. casuist
kazuistyczny [kah-zoo-ees-**tich**-ni] adj.m. casuistic; casuistical
kazuistyka [kah-zoo-**ees**-ti-kah] f. casuistry
kazus [**kah**-zoos] m. case
kaźń [kahźhń] f. torture; torment; execution; high-security prison
każdodzienny [kahzh-do-**dźhen**-ni] adj.m. daily; everyday; each day
każdorazowo [kahzh-do-rah-**zo**-vo] adv. every time; each time
każdorazowy [kahzh-do-rah-**zo**-vi] adj.m. every; each; every single (time)
każdoroczny [kahzh-do-**roch**-ni] adj.m. yearly
każdy [**kahzh**-di] pron. every; each; respective; any; all; everyone; everybody; every man; anybody
każdy ci powie [**kahzh**-di ćhee **po**-vye] exp.: anybody will tell you; anyone will tell you
każdy, kto [**kahzh**-di kto] exp.: whoever
każdy, kto się zgłosi [**kahzh**-di kto śhan **zgwo**-śhee] exp.: whoever applies; all comers
każdy, kto wie o tym [**kahzh**-di kto vye o tim] exp.: whoever knows of this
na każdym kroku [nah **kahzh**-dim **kro**-koo] exp.: at every step; wherever you turn
o każdej porze [o **kahzh**-dey **po**-zhe] exp.: at any hour of the day
z każdą godziną [s **kahzh**-down go-**dźhee**-nown] exp.: hourly
z każdym dniem [s **kahzh**-dim dńem] exp.: daily
za każdym razem [zah **kahzh**-dim razem] exp.: every time
każdziusieńki [kahzh-dźhoo-**śheń**-kee] pron. every single one
każdziutki [kahzh-**dźhoot**-kee] pron. every single one
kącik [**kown**-ćheek] m. nook; corner; niche; cubby; cubicle; recess; column (in a newspaper); slang: toilet
kącik oka [**kown**-ćheek o-kah] exp.: corner of the eye
kącik ust [**kown**-ćheek oost] exp.: angulus oris

kądziel [kown-dźhel] f. distaff
po kądzieli [po kown-**dźhe**-lee] exp.: on the distaff side
kądzielnik [kown-**dźhel**-ńeek] m. silk producing gland
kądziołek [kown-**dźho**-wek] m. spinner; spinneret; spinerette; spinning mamilla (gland)
kąkol [**kown**-kol] m. cockle; corn cockle (in a grainfield)
kąkolowy [kown-ko-**lo**-vi] adj.m. of a cockle; of corn cockle (in a grainfield)
kąpać [**kown**-pahćh] v. bathe; bath; bask; soak; steep (*repeatedly*)
kąpać się [**kown**-pahćh śhan] v. bathe; take a bath; bask (in the sun, etc.); colloq: have a dip; wallow (in blood, etc.) (*repeatedly*)
kąpanie [kown-**pah**-ńe] n. bathing
kąpanie się [kown-**pah**-ńe śhan] n. bathing oneself
kąpiel [**kown**-pyel] f. bath; tub; bath-water; solution; soaking
kąpiele [kown-**pye**-le] pl. baths; bathing establishment
kąpielisko [kown-pye-**lees**-ko] n. resort; spa; public bath; watering place; seaside resort
kąpieliskowy [kown-pye-lees-**ko**-vi] adj.m. of a watering-place; of a spa; of a resort
kąpielowicz [kown-pye-**lo**-veech] m. bather
kąpielowy [kown-pye-**lo**-vi] adj.m. bath (towel, slippers, etc.); bathing (costume, drawers, etc.)
kąpielówki [kown-pye-**loof**-kee] pl. bathing drawers; slips
kąsacz [**kown**-sahch] m. variety of voracious freshwater fish
kąsacze [kown-**sah**-che] pl. the Characinidae family of voracious fishes; variety of fresh-water (African, American) fish
kąsać [**kown**-sahćh] v. bite; sting; nip; colloq: annoy; nettle; gall (*repeatedly*)
kąsać się [**kown**-sahćh śhan] v. bite oneself; sting oneself (*repeatedly*)
kąsanie [kown-**sah**-ńe] n. biting; stinging
kąsawiec [kown-**sah**-vyets] m. rove beetle; cocktail
kąsek [**kown**-sek] m. bit; nip; a bit (to eat, etc.); morsel; mouthful; a little
kąśliwie [kown-**śhlee**-vye] adv. sharply; acutely; bitingly; painfully; nippingly
kąśliwość [kown-**śhlee**-vośhćh] f. sharpness; acuteness
kąśliwy [kown-**śhlee**-vi] adj.m. sharp; acute; biting; trenchant
kąt [kownt] m. corner; angle; a place to live in; recess; quoin; lodging; a home of one's own; nook; secluded spot; remote rustic spot; out-of-the-way place
kąt do spania [kownt do **spah**-ńah] exp.: night's lodging
kąt ostry [kownt **ost**-ri] exp.: acute angle
kąt prosty [kownt **pros**-ti] exp.: right angle
kąt przyległy [kownt pshi-**leg**-wi] exp.: adjacent (contiguous) angle
kąt rozwarty [kownt roz-**vahr**-ti] exp.: obtuse angle
kąt widzenia [kownt vee-**dze**-ńah] exp.: visual angle; point of view
pod kątem [pot **kown**-tem] exp.: at an angle
pod kątem prostym [pot **kown**-tem **pros**-tim] exp.: at right angle; perpendicularly
zapadły kąt [zah-**pahd**-wi kownt] exp.: a place at the back of beyond; God forsaken place
kątek [**kown**-tek] m. (nice, pleasant) place to live in; recess; quoin; lodging; a home of one's own; nook; secluded spot
kątnica [kownt-**ńee**-tsah] f. cecum; caecum; blind gut; thwart knee
kątnik [**kownt**-ńeek] m. bevel cutter; angle plane; (printer's) composing stick
kątomierz [kown-**to**-myesh] m. protractor; dial-sight; angle gauge
kątownica [kown-tov-**ńee**-tsah] f. angle alignment device
kątownik [kown-**tov**-ńeek] m. square; protractor; dial-sight; angle gauge

kątownikowy [kown-tov-ńee-**ko**-vi] adj.m. of a (carpenter's) square; of a protractor; of dial-sight; of angle gauge
kątowy [kown-**to**-vi] adj.m. angle (bar, meter, plate, etc.)
prędkość kątowa [prant-kośhćh kown-**to**-vah] exp.: angular velocity
stopień kątowy [**sto**-pyeń kown-**to**-vi] exp.: angular degree
żelazo kątowe [zhe-**lah**-zo kown-**to**-ve] exp.: angle iron
kciuk [kćhook] m. thumb; pollex
kebab [**ke**-bahp] m. lamb roast with eggs, onions, and spices
kebraczo [keb-**rah**-cho] n. quebracho (hard wood, tree, etc.)
kecz [kech] m. ketch (boat)
keczup [**ke**-choop] m. catchup; ketchup; catsup; a seasoned tomato puree
kedyw [**ke**-dif] m. Khedive (ruler of Egypt); AK Diversion Department
kefalina [ke-fah-**lee**-nah] f. cephalin
kefalizacja [ke-fah-lee-**zah**-tsyah] f. cephalization
kefalometria [ke-fah-lo-**metr**-yah] f. cephalometry
kefalometryczny [ke-fah-lo-met-**rich**-ni] adj.m. cephalometric
keffekilit [kef-fe-**kee**-leet] m. variety of fine clay (mineral used for production of small objects)
kefir [**ke**-feer] m. kefir; bottle of kefir
kefirowy [ke-fee-**ro**-vi] adj.m. of kefir; kefir (bottle, etc.)
kegel [**ke**-gel] m. font size; type size; shank of a letter
keja [**ke**-yah] f. mooring area
keks [keks] m. teacake; biscuit
keksy [**kek**-si] pl. teacakes; biscuits; cakes
kelner [**kel**-ner] m. waiter
kelnerka [kel-**ner**-kah] f. waitress; barmaid; woman waiter
kelnerować [kel-ne-**ro**-vahćh] v. wait (on tables); work as a waiter (*repeatedly*)
kelnerski [kel-**ner**-skee] adj.m. waiter's
kelnerstwo [kel-**ner**-stfo] n. waiter's occupation
Kelvin [**kel**-veen] m. Kelvin scale
kem [kem] m. gravel pile deposited by a thawing glacier
kemalizm [ke-**mah**-leezm] m. Turkish movement of Kemal Ataturk (1881-1938)
kemping [**kem**-peeng] m. camping; camp; camping-site; camping-ground
kempingować [kem-peen-**go**-vahćh] v. go camping; camp (*repeatedly*)
kempingowanie [kem-peen-go-**vah**-ńe] n. camping
kempingowiec [kem-peen-**go**-vyets] m. camper; one that camps
kempingowy [kem-peen-**go**-vi] adj.m. camping (equipment, hut, etc.)
kenaf [**ke**-nahf] m. variety of hibiscus (plant)
kencja [**ken**-tsyah] f. variety of small ornamental palm
kendo [**ken**-do] n. Japanese fencing with bamboo staves using both hands; kendo
kenel [**ke**-nel] m. cannel coal
kenelski [ke-**nel**-skee] adj.m. of cannel coal
kenetron [ke-**ne**-tron] m. Kenetron; rectifier tube; vacuum tube
kenezoiczny [ke-ne-zo-**eech**-ni] adj.m. cenozoic (period, fossils, etc.)
kenozoik [ke-no-**zo**-eek] m. Cenozoic period
kenozoikum [ke-no-zo-**ee**-koom] n. Cenozoic period
kent [kent] m. Kent sheep
kentum [**ken**-toom] n. centum languages; western Indo-European languages; (compare: **satem**)
kentumowy [ken-too-**mo**-vi] adj.m. of centum languages; of western Indo-European languages
kenzan [**ken**-zahn] m. cut flower positioning (brush-like) device
kepi [**ke**-pee] n. French military cap; kepi
ker [ker] m. Polish synthetic caoutchouc (rubber)
keramzyt [ke-**rahm**-zit] m. artificial light-weight concrete aggregate
keramzytowy [ke-rahm-zi-**to**-vi] adj.m. of the artificial light-weight

concrete aggregate
kerargiryt [ke-rahr-**gee**-rit] m. cerargyrite; horn silver; silver chloride (mineral)
keratoplastyka [ke-rah-to-**plahs**-ti-kah] f. transplant of cornea
keratyna [ke-rah-**ti**-nah] f. keratin
keratynizacja [ke-rah-ti-ńee-**zah**-tsyah] f. keratosis; keratinization
keratynowy [ke-rah-ti-**no**-vi] adj.m. keratinous; keratotic
kergulena [ker-goo-**le**-nah] f. variety of Indian Ocean fish similar to herring; slang: prostitute infected with a venereal disease (jargon)
kermes [**ker**-mes] m. natural red dyestuff; kermes
keroplastyka [ke-ro-plahs-**ti**-kah] f. ceroplastics; art of modeling in wax
kerykejon [ke-ri-**ke**-yon] m. an ornamental Greek cane
keson [**ke**-son] m. caisson
kesonowy [ke-so-**no**-vi] adj.m. caisson (disease, construction, etc.)
ket [ket] m. cat (boat)
keta [**ke**-tah] f. variety of Pacific salmon; slang: small chain
ketchup [**kech**-oop] m. catchup; ketchup; catsup; a seasoned tomato puree
keten [**ke**-ten] m. ketene
ketgut [**ket**-goot] m. catgut (thread)
ketmia [**ket**-myah] f. a tropical shrub or tree of the genus Hibiscus
keton [**ke**-ton] m. ketone
ketonokwas [ke-to-**no**-kfahs] m. ketone body; acetoacetic acid
ketonokwasy [ke-to-no-**kfah**-si] pl. ketone compounds; acetoacetic acid compounds
ketonowy [ke-to-**no**-vi] adj.m. ketonic
ketoza [ke-**to**-zah] f. ketose (fructose, etc.)
kędy [**k<u>an</u>**-di] pron.: where (to); whither; where; which way
kędyś [**k<u>an</u>**-diśh] pron.: somewhere
kędyż [**k<u>an</u>**-dish] pron.: where (to); whither; where; which way; (emphatic: **kędy**)
kędzierzawiarka [k<u>an</u>-dźhe-zhah-**vyahr**-kah] f. curling machine; friezing-machine
kędzierzawić [k<u>an</u>-dźhe-**zhah**-veećh] v. curl (hair); frieze (cloth) (*repeatedly*)
kędzierzawić się [k<u>an</u>-dźhe-**zhah**-veećh śh<u>an</u>] v. curl (hair); be rank; be luxuriant; be prolific; wave (the sea, etc.) (*repeatedly*)
kędzierzawieć [k<u>an</u>-dźhe-**zhah**-vyećh] v. curl (hair); fuzz (*repeatedly*)
kędzierzawienie [k<u>an</u>-dźhe-zhah-**vye**-ńe] n. curling (hair); frizzing (cloth)
kędzierzawka [k<u>an</u>-dźhe-**zhahf**-kah] f. leaf curling
kędzierzawo [k<u>an</u>-dźhe-**zhah**-vo] adv. in curls
kędzierzawość [k<u>an</u>-dźhe-**zhah**-vośhćh] f. curliness; fuzziness
kędzierzawy [k<u>an</u>-dźhe-**zhah**-vi] adj.m. curly; curled (leaf, etc.); fuzzy; frizzy; crisp; fleecy
kędzior [**k<u>an</u>**-dźhor] m. curl; lock (of hair); ringlet
kędziorek [k<u>an</u>-**dźho**-rek] m. (small, nice) curl; lock (of hair); ringlet
kępa [**k<u>an</u>**-pah] f. cluster; holm (small island); hurst; clump (of trees); tuft (of hair, etc.); hillock; ait (little island)
kępiasty [k<u>an</u>-**pyahs**-ti] adj.m. tufty; tufted; abounding in tufts; growing in clusters
kępina [k<u>an</u>-**pee**-nah] f. cluster; holm; hurst; clump (of trees); tuft (of hair, etc.); hillock; ait
kępka [**k<u>an</u>p**-kah] f. (small, nice) cluster; clump (of trees); tuft (of hair, etc.)
kępkowaty [k<u>an</u>p-ko-**vah**-ti] adj.m. planted in clumps; full of clusters
kępkowy [k<u>an</u>p-**ko**-vi] adj.m. tufty
kępowy [k<u>an</u>-**po**-vi] adj.m. growing in clumps
kęs [k<u>an</u>s] m. mouthful; hunk; bit; morsel; hunch; a little; some; billet (of steel)
kęsek [**k<u>an</u>**-sek] m. (small) bit; mouthful; hunk; morsel; hunch; a little
kęsisko [k<u>an</u>-**śhees**-ko] f. (big, clumsy) mouthful; hunk; morsel; hunch

kętnar [kant-nahr] m. stilling (of a barrel); stillion; scantling; gantry; gauntry
khaki [khah-kee] indecl.: khaki (color)
ki [kee] pron. which
ki diabeł!? [kee **dyah**-bew] excl.: colloq: what the deuce!?
po kiego diabła!? [po ke-go **dyahb**-wah] exp.: colloq: what the hell for?; what the devil for?; what on earth for?
kibel [**kee**-bel] m. prison toilet bucket; kibble; mob slang: jug; jail
kibic [**kee**-beets] m. kibitz; kibitzer; onlooker; fan; colloq: rooter
kibicować [kee-bee-**tso**-vahćh] v. look on; colloq: root for (*repeatedly*)
kibicowanie [kee-bee-tso-**vah**-ńe] n. looking on; colloq: rooting for
kibić [**kee**-beećh] f. figure of a person; waist; middle
kibitka [kee-**beet**-kah] f. kibitka (Russian vehicle)
kibitnik [kee-**beet**-ńeek] m. variety of brown butterfly
kiblować [kee-**blo**-vahćh] v. vulg.: sit on a toilet; shit; colloq: be in prison; stay a second year in the same grade in school (*repeatedly*)
kiblowanie [kee-blo-**vah**-ńe] n. vulg.: sitting on a toilet; shitting; being in prison; staying a second year in the same grade in school
kibuc [**kee**-boots] m. kibbutz; collective farm in Israel
kibucnik [kee-**boots**-ńeek] m. colloq: kibbutznik; collective farmer in Israel
kic [keets] indecl.: hop
kicać [**kee**-tsahćh] v. hop; leap; skip; jump (*repeatedly*)
kicanie [kee-**tsah**-ńe] n. hopping; leaping; skipping; jumping
kicha [**kee**-khah] f. (large) intestine; bowel; gut; black pudding; hose; (car) inner tube; slang: billy club
kicha mi nawaliła [**kee**-khah mee nah-vah-**lee**-wah] exp.: I have a flat tire
kichać [**kee**-khahćh] v. sneeze; colloq: not to care a hang about; not to give a damn about; make light of (something) (*repeatedly*)
kichanie [kee-**khah**-ńe] n. sneezing; sternutation
kichawiec [kee-**khah**-vyets] m. sneezewort (herb)
kichnąć [**keekh**-nownćh] v. sneeze
kichnięcie [keekh-**ńan**-ćhe] n. a sneeze; sternutation
kici [**kee**-ćhee] adj.m. of a kitten
kici!, kici! [**kee**-ćhee **kee**-chee] excl.: pussy, pussy!
kicia [**kee**-ćhah] f. pussy; kitten; mob slang: girl; woman; lover
kiciasty [kee-**ćhahs**-ti] adj.m. tufted
kiciunia [kee-**ćhoo**-ńah] f. (nice, little) pussy; kitten; kitty
kiciuś [**kee**-ćhoośh] m. (nice, little) pussy cat; kitten; kitty
kicnąć [**keets**-nownćh] v. hop; leap; skip; jump
kicnięcie [keets-**ńan**-ćhe] n. hop; leap; skip; jump
kicz [keech] m. daub; (literary) trash
kiczka [**keech**-kah] f. the peg used in the tipcat game
kiczki [**keech**-kee] pl. the tipcat game
kiczowato [kee-cho-**vah**-to] adv. in a trashy manner; worthlessly
kiczowaty [kee-cho-**vah**-ti] adj.m. trashy; worthless
kić [keećh] m. mob slang: clink; jail
kidnaper [keed-**nah**-per] m. kidnapper; kidnaper
kidnaperka [keed-nah-**per**-kah] f. (woman) kidnapper; kidnaper
kidnaperstwo [keed-nah-**per**-stfo] n. kidnapping; kidnaping
kidnaping [keed-**nah**-peenk] m. kidnapping; kidnaping
kiecka [kets-kah] f. frock; skirt; petticoat (inelegant)
kiedy [ke-di] conj. when; as; ever; how soon?; while; since
kiedy bądź [ke-di bownćh] exp.: any time; whenever you like
kiedy indziej [ke-di **een**-dźhey] exp.: some other time
kiedy niekiedy [ke-di ńe-ke-di] exp.: now and then; occasionally; from time to time
kiedy tylko [ke-di til-ko] exp.: as soon as; colloq: the moment; directly

mało kiedy [mah-wo ke-di] exp.: hardly ever; rarely; seldom
rzadko kiedy [zhaht-ko ke-di] exp.: hardly ever; rarely; seldom
kiedykolwiek [ke-di-**kol**-vyek] adv. whenever; at any time
kiedyś [**ke**-diśh] adv. someday; in the past; once; one day; some time (or other); when the time comes
kiedyż? [**ke**-dish] adv. when then?; when on earth?
kielich [**ke**-leekh] m. goblet; chalice; cup; cupful; glassful
kielichowato [ke-lee-kho-**vah**-to] adv. like a cup
kielichowaty [ke-lee-kho-**vah**-ti] adj.m. cup-shaped
kielichowiec [ke-lee-**kho**-vyets] m. calycanthus (shrub)
kielichowy [ke-lee-**kho**-vi] adj.m. cup-shaped
kieliszeczek [ke-lee-**she**-chek] m. (nice, little) liquor-glass
kieliszek [ke-**lee**-shek] m. liquor-glass; calyx; slang: alcoholic; drunk (mob jargon)
pójść na kieliszek [**pooy**-śhćh nah ke-**lee**-shek] exp.: to go and have a drink
kieliszkowaty [ke-leesh-ko-**vah**-ti] adj.m. shaped like a liquor-glass
kieliszkowy [ke-leesh-**ko**-vi] adj.m. of a liquor-glass
kielisznik [ke-**leesh**-ńeek] m. hedge bindweed
kielnia [**kel**-ńah] f. trowel; colloq: beaver's tail
kielować [ke-**lo**-vahćh] v. chamfer; bevel (*repeatedly*)
kielowanie [ke-lo-**vah**-ńe] n. chamfering; bevelling
kieł [kew] m. tusk; fang; canine tooth; cutting bit; lathe center
kiełb [kewp] m. gudgeon (fish)
mieć kiełbie we łbie [myećh **kew**-be ve wbye] exp.: not to be quite right in the head
kiełbasa [kew-**bah**-sah] f. sausage
nie dla psa kiełbasa [ńe dlah psah kew-**bah**-sah] exp.: it's too good for you
kiełbasiany [kew-bah-**śhah**-ni] adj.m. of sausage; sausage (meat, etc.)
jad kiełbasiany [yaht kew-bah-**śhah**-ni] exp.: botulinum; botulismus toxin
zatrucie jadem kiełbasianym [zah-**troo**-ćhe **yah**-dem kew-bah-**śhah**-nim] exp.: botulism; sausage poisoning
kiełbasić się [kew-**bah**-śheećh śhan] v. get tangled; get meddled; get confused (*repeatedly*)
kiełbaska [kew-**bahs**-kah] f. small (dry) sausage; polony; saveloy
kiełbaśnica [kew-bahśh-**ńee**-tsah] f. sausage casing
kiełek [**ke**-wek] m. sprout; sucker; germ
kiełkować [kew-**ko**-vahćh] v. sprout; germinate; shoot; spring up; pullulate (*repeatedly*)
kiełkowanie [kew-ko-**vah**-ńe] n. germination; pullulation
energia kiełkowania [e-**ner**-gyah kew-ko-**vah**-ńah] exp.: germinative energy
kiełkownik [kew-**kov**-ńeek] m. germinating field
kiełkowy [kew-**ko**-vi] adj.m. of a sprout; sucker; of a germ; of a shoot; sprout (cell, etc.); germ (nucleus, etc.)
kiełkujący [kew-koo-**yown**-tsi] adj.m. germinant; colloq: budding; young
kiełzać [**kew**-zahćh] v. colloq: bridle (a horse) (*repeatedly*)
kiełznać [**kewz**-nahćh] v. bridle (a horse); restrain; check; curb; control (*repeatedly*)
kiełznanie [kewz-**nah**-ńe] n. bridling; restraint; check; curb
kiełzno [**kewz**-no] n. mouthpiece of horse's bit
kiełż [kewsh] m. gammarus (shell fish)
kiełże [**kew**-zhe] pl. the Gammaridea family of shellfish
kiep [kep] m. colloq: oaf; fool; gull; simpleton; slang: head; cigarette; failing grade
kiepskawo [kep-**skah**-vo] adv. colloq: pretty badly; pretty bad
kiepskawy [kep-**skah**-vi] adj.m.

colloq: baddish; somewhat bad; pretty bad; rather bad; none too good
kiepski [kep-skee] adj.m. colloq: mean; bad; poor; second-rate; weak; deficient; paltry; nasty; ill; feeble; colloq: rotten; lame; shabby; thin (excuse, etc.); threadbare (pants, etc.)
kiepsko [kep-sko] adv. colloq: badly; poorly
czuć się kiepsko [chooćh śhan kep-sko] exp.: to be ill; to be weak; to be under the weather
kier [ker] m. (cards) hearts; slang: sharper; cards cheat (mob jargon)
kierat [ke-raht] m. thrasher; treadmill
kieratowy [ke-rah-to-vi] adj.m. of a treadmill; treadmill (wheel, etc.)
kierdel [ker-del] m. flock (of sheep, goats, etc.); herd
kiereja [ke-re-yah] f. heavy (old style) overcoat
kiereszować [ke-re-sho-vahćh] v. slash; gash; scar; hack (*repeatedly*)
kiereszowanie [ke-re-sho-vah-ńe] n. slashing; gashing; scarring; hacking
kierezja [ker-re-zyah] f. variety of regional coat (of Cracow)
kierkut [ker-koot] m. Jewish cemetery
kiermasz [ker-mahsh] m. fair; village fair
kiermasz książki [ker-mahsh kśhownsh-kee] exp.: book fair
kiermaszowy [ker-mah-sho-vi] adj.m. fair (stand, trade, etc.)
kiernoz [ker-nos] m. boar; male pig
kierować [ke-ro-vahćh] v. steer; manage; run (a business); show the way; tell the way; guide; lead; aim; level; drive (a car, etc.); control; manage (affairs, an institution); administer; operate (a motor, a car, a business, etc.); supervise; superintend; rule; govern (*repeatedly*)
kierować się [ke-ro-vahćh śhan] v. go towards; drive towards; run towards; ride towards; fly towards; swim towards; sail towards; be guided (by); be moved (by); be led (by); be prompted (by); be influenced (by); follow (an advice, etc.) (*repeatedly*)
kierowalność [ke-ro-vahl-nośhćh] f. ease to drive; suitability to drive
kierowanie [ke-ro-vah-ńe] n. driving (a car, etc.)
kierowanie się [ke-ro-vah-ńe śhan] n. following (advice, etc.); being led (by); going (towards)
kierowany [ke-ro-vah-ni] adj.m. steered
zdalnie kierowany [zdahl-ńe ke-ro-vah-ni] exp.: steered by remote control
kierowca [ke-rof-tsah] m. driver; chauffeur; truck driver; motorist
kierownica [ke-rov-ńee-tsah] f. steering gear; steering wheel; directrix; handlebar
kierownictwo [ke-rov-ńee-tstfo] n. management; administration; control; direction; leadership; supervision; conduct; guidance; rule; sway
złe kierownictwo [zwe ke-rov-ńee-tstfo] exp.: mismanagement; misconduct (of an enterprise, etc.)
kierowniczka [ke-rov-ńeech-kah] f. (woman) manager; director; supervisor
kierowniczy [ke-rov-ńee-chi] adj.m. control; controlling; directing; managing; leading; head (clerk, agent, etc.)
kierownicze stanowisko [ke-rov-ńee-che stah-no-vees-ko] exp.: post of authority; executive post; position of command
kierownik [ke-rov-ńeek] m. manager; director; supervisor; (bicycle) handle-bar
kierowy [ke-ro-vi] adj.m. of hearts (card)
kierpec [ker-pets] m. moccasin (of Tatra mountaineers)
kierunek [ke-roo-nek] m. direction; course; trend; line; set (of a current, etc.); phase (in painting, etc.); specialization; studies

w kierunku czegoś [f ke-**roon**-koo che-gośh] exp.: in the directon of something; towards something
w obu kierunkach [v o-boo ke-roon-kahkh] exp.: both ways; two-way (traffic, etc.)
w przeciwnym kierunku [f pshe-ćheev-nim ke-**roon**-koo] exp.: the other way; in opposite directions
zmienić kierunek [zmye-ńeećh ke-**roo**-nek] exp.: to change direction; to veer; to turn
kierunkowo [ke-roon-**ko**-vo] adv. in a direction
kierunkowość [ke-roon-**ko**-vośhćh] f. directive tendency
kierunkowskaz [ke-roon-**ko**-fskahs] m. signpost; traffic indicator
kierunkowskaz świetlny [ke-roon-ko-fskahs **śhfyetl**-ni] exp.: flashing turn indicator
kierunkowy [ke-roon-**ko**-vi] adj.m. direction (angle, etc.); directional; beam (antenna, etc.); guiding (principle, etc.)
kierznia [**kezh**-ńah] f. (large) churn
kierzanka [ke-**zhahn**-kah] f. churn
kiesa [**ke**-sah] f. purse
kieska [**kes**-kah] f. small purse
kieszeniasty [ke-she-**ńahs**-ti] adj.m. pocket-like
kieszeniowy [ke-she-**ńo**-vi] adj.m. of a pocket; of the purse
kieszeniówka [ke-she-**ńoof**-kah] f. pocketing
kieszeń [**ke**-sheń] f. pocket; colloq: purse; means; funds
kieszoneczka [ke-sho-**nech**-kah] f. (nice, small) pouch; fob; watch pocket; placket
kieszonka [ke-**shon**-kah] f. pouch; fob; watch pocket; placket
kieszonkowiec [ke-shon-**ko**-vyets] m. pickpocket; small, cheap paperback book
kieszonkowy [ke-shon-**ko**-vi] adj.m. pocket (dictionary, watch, pistol)
kieszonkowe pieniądze [ke-shon-**ko**-ve pye-**ńown**-dze] exp.: pocket money; spending money
kifoskolioza [kee-fo-skol-**yo**-zah] f. kyphoscoliosis
kifoza [kee-**fo**-zah] f. kyphosis
kij [keey] m. stick; cane; staff
kij bilardowy [keey bee-lahr-**do**-vi] exp.: billiard cue
kij do golfa [keey do **gol**-fah] exp.: golf club
kije [**kee**-ye] pl. cudgelling; beating
kijanka [kee-**yahn**-kah] f. tadpole; polliwog; battledore (used in washing clothes)
kijarka [kee-**yahr**-kah] m. device for making penholders, etc.
kijek [**kee**-yek] m. (small, nice) stick; cane; staff
kikiryki [kee-kee-**ri**-kee] exp.: cock-a-doodle-doo
kiks [keeks] m. miss; muff; miscue; squeak; squawk; false note
kiksować [keek-**so**-vahćh] v. make a miss; muff; squeak (*repeatedly*)
kiksowanie [keek-so-**vah**-ńe] n. making a miss; muffing; squeaking
kikut [**kee**-koot] m. stump (of amputated limb); stub
kikutnica [kee-koot-**ńee**-tsah] f. sea spider; pycnogonid
kikutnice [kee-koot-**ńee**-tse] pl. sea spiders; the class Pycnogonid; Pantopoda
kil [keel] m. keel
kilak [**kee**-lahk] m. syphilitic tumor; gumma
kilblok [**keel**-blok] m. keel support block in a shipyard
kilbloki [keel-**blo**-kee] pl. keel support blocks in a shipyard
kilim [**kee**-leem] m. rug; carpet; tapestry
kilimek [kee-**lee**-mek] m. (small, nice) rug; carpet; tapestry
kilimiarka [kee-lee-**myahr**-kah] f. (female) kilim weaver; carpet weaver; tapestry weaver
kilimiarnia [kee-lee-**myahr**-ńah] f. kilim production shop
kilimiarski [kee-lee-**myahr**-skee] adj.m. kilim (weaver, etc.); carpet (weaver, etc.); tapestry (maker, etc.)
kilimiarstwo [kee-lee-**myahr**-stfo] n. kilim weaving; carpet weaving; tapestry weaving
kilimiarz [kee-**lee**-myahsh] m. (male) kilim weaver; carpet weaver;

tapestry weaver
kilimkarnia [kee-leem-**kahr**-ńah] f. kilim production shop
kilimkarski [kee-leem-**kahr**-skee] adj.m. kilim (weaver, etc.); carpet (maker, etc.); of tapestry
kilimkarstwo [kee-leem-**kahr**-stfo] n. kilim weaving; carpet weaving; tapestry weaving
kilimkowy [kee-leem-**ko**-vi] adj.m. kilim (weaver, etc.)
kilimowy [kee-lee-**mo**-vi] adj.m. kilim (design, etc.)
kilka [**keel**-kah] num. a few; some; one or two; a number (of people, things); f. sprat (fish); Clupeonella
dwadzieścia kilka [dvah-**dźheśh**-ćhah **keel**-kah] exp.: twenty odd
kilkadziesiąt [keel-kah-**dźhe**-śhownt] num. tens; dozens; scores (of people, times, etc.); several dozen (men, etc.)
kilkakroć [keel-**kah**-kroćh] adv. repeatedly; again and again
kilkakrotnie [keel-kah-**krot**-ńe] adv. repeatedly; several times; more than once; a number of times; again and again
kilkakrotny [keel-kah-**krot**-ni] adj.m. repeated; recurring
kilkanaście [keel-kah-**nahśh**-ćhe] num. anywhere from ten to twenty; a dozen or so
kilkanaścioro [keel-kah-nahśh-**ćho**-ro] num. anywhere from ten to twenty; a dozen or so
kilkaset [keel-**kah**-set] num. several hundred
kilko- [**keel**-ko] prefix: several = **kilku-**
kilkoaktowy [keel-ko-ahk-**to**-vi] adj.m. (play) of several acts
kilkoarkuszowy [keel-ko-ahr-koo-**sho**-vi] adj.m. of several pages; of several printed sheets
kilkodniowy [keel-ko-**dńo**-vi] adj.m. of several days; several days'
kilkodziesięcio- [keel-ko-dźhe-**śhan**-ćho] prefix: of several score (years, people, etc.)
kilkodziesięciokrotny [keel-ko-dźhe-śhan-ćho-**krot**-ni] adj.m. repeated dozens of times
kilkodziesięcioletni [keel-ko-dźhe-śhan-ćho-**let**-ńee] adj.m. of several score years
kilkofazowy [keel-ko-fah-**zo**-vi] adj.m. of several phases
kilkogłosowy [keel-ko-gwo-**so**-vi] adj.m. of several voices; in parts
kilkogodzinny [keel-ko-go-**dźheen**-ni] adj.m. of several hours; several hours' (journey, etc.)
kilkogroszowy [keel-ko-gro-**sho**-vi] adj.m. of several groszy; costing several groszy
kilkokilometrowy [keel-ko-kee-lo-me-**tro**-vi] adj.m. of several kilometers
kilkoletni [keel-ko-**let**-ńee] adj.m. of several years; several years' (service, etc.); several years old
kilkometrowy [keel-ko-met-**ro**-vi] adj.m. of several meters; several meters' length; several meters long
kilkomiesięczny [keel-ko-mye-**śhanch**-ni] adj.m. of several months; several months' (work, etc.); several months old
kilkomilowy [keel-ko-mee-**lo**-vi] adj.m. of several miles
kilkominutowy [keel-ko-mee-noo-**to**-vi] adj.m. of several minutes; several minutes' (interval, etc.)
kilkomorgowy [keel-ko-mor-**go**-vi] adj.m. of several acres
kilkonastodniowy [keel-ko-nahs-to-**dńo**-vi] adj.m. of a dozen days or so
kilkonastogodzinny [keel-ko-nah-sto-go-**dźheen**-ni] adj.m. of more than ten hours
kilkonastolatek [keel-ko-nah-sto-**lah**-tek] m. teenager
kilkonastoletni [keel-ko-nah-sto-**let**-ńee] adj.m. of more than ten years
kilkonastostopniowy [keel-ko-nah-sto-stop-**ńo**-vi] adj.m. of more than ten degrees
kilkonastostronicowy [keel-ko-nah-sto-stro-ńee-**tso**-vi] adj.m. of more than ten pages; of over a dozen pages
kilkonastotysięczny [keel-ko-nah-sto-ti-**śhanch**-ni] adj.m. of more than ten thousand
kilkonastowierszowy [keel-ko-nah-

sto-vyer-**sho**-vi] adj.m. of more than ten lines; of over a dozen lines

kilkoosobowy [keel-ko-o-so-**bo**-vi] adj.m. of several persons

kilkopiętrowy [keel-ko-pyant-**ro**-vi] adj.m. of several stories high; of several stories

kilkoramienny [keel-ko-rah-**myen**-ni] adj.m. (many)branched-(candlestick, etc.)

kilkoro [keel-**ko**-ro] num. some; several; one or two; a number

kilkorodzinny [keel-ko-ro-**dźheen**-ni] adj.m. of several families

kilkosetletni [keel-ko-set-**let**-ńee] adj.m. of several hundred years; several hundred years old

kilkosetmetrowy [keel-ko-set-met-**ro**-vi] adj.m. of several hundred meters; several hundred meters long (high)

kilkosetny [keel-ko-**set**-ni] adj.m. several-hundredth (time, recurrence, etc.)

kilkosetosobowy [keel-ko-set-o-so-**bo**-vi] adj.m. of several hundred persons (people)

kilkosetstronicowy [keel-ko-set-stro-ńee-**tso**-vi] adj.m. of several hundred pages

kilkostopniowy [keel-ko-stop-**ńo**-vi] adj.m. of several degrees; of several steps (ladder, etc.); of several stages

kilkotomowy [keel-ko-to-**mo**-vi] adj.m. of several volumes

kilkotygodniowy [keel-ko-ti-god-**ńo**-vi] adj.m. of several weeks; several weeks' (rest, etc.); several weeks old

kilkotysięczny [keel-ko-ti-**śhanch**-ni] adj.m. of several thousand; several thousand in number

kilkowyrazowy [keel-ko-vi-rah-**zo**-vi] adj.m. of several words

kilku- [**keel**-koo] prefix: several

kilkuaktowy [keel-koo-ahk-**to**-vi] adj.m. (play) of several acts

kilkuarkuszowy [keel-koo-ahr-koo-**sho**-vi] adj.m. of several pages; of several printed sheets

kilkudniowy [keel-koo-**dńo**-vi] adj.m. of several days; several days'

kilkudziesięcio- [keel-koo-dźhe-**śhan**-ćho] prefix: of several score (years, people, etc.)

kilkudziesięciokrotny [keel-koo-dźhe-**śhan**-ćho-krot-ni] adj.m. repeated dozens of times

kilkudziesięcioletni [keel-koo-dźhe-śhan-ćho-**let**-ńee] adj.m. of several score years

kilkufazowy [keel-koo-fah-**zo**-vi] adj.m. of several phases

kilkugłosowy [keel-koo-gwo-**so**-vi] adj.m. of several voices; in parts

kilkugodzinny [keel-koo-go-**dźheen**-ni] adj.m. of several hours; several hours' (journey, etc.)

kilkugroszowy [keel-koo-gro-**sho**-vi] adj.m. of several groszy; costing several groszy

kilkukilometrowy [keel-koo-kee-lo-me-**tro**-vi] adj.m. of several kilometers

kilkuletni [keel-koo-**let**-ńee] adj.m. of several years; several years' (service, etc.); several years old

kilkumetrowy [keel-koo-met-**ro**-vi] adj.m. of several meters; several meters' length; several meters long

kilkumiesięczny [keel-koo-mye-**śhanch**-ni] adj.m. of several months; several months' (work, etc.); several months old

kilkumilowy [keel-koo-mee-**lo**-vi] adj.m. of several miles

kilkuminutowy [keel-koo-mee-noo-**to**-vi] adj.m. of several minutes; several minutes' (interval, etc.)

kilkumorgowy [keel-koo-mor-**go**-vi] adj.m. of several acres

kilkunastodniowy [keel-koo-nahs-to-**dńo**-vi] adj.m. of a dozen days or so

kilkunastogodzinny [keel-koo-nah-sto-go-**dźheen**-ni] adj.m. of more than ten hours

kilkunastolatek [keel-koo-nah-sto-**lah**-tek] m. teenager

kilkunastoletni [keel-koo-nah-sto-**let**-ńee] adj.m. of more than ten years

kilkunastostopniowy [keel-koo-nah-sto-stop-**ńo**-vi] adj.m. of more than ten degrees

kilkunastostronicowy [keel-koo-nah-sto-stro-ńee-**tso**-vi] adj.m. of more than ten pages; of over a dozen pages
kilkunastotysięczny [keel-koo-nah-sto-ti-**śh**an**ch**-ni] adj.m. of more than ten thousand
kilkunastowierszowy [keel-koo-nah-sto-vyer-**sho**-vi] adj.m. of more than ten lines; of over a dozen lines
kilkuosobowy [keel-koo-o-so-**bo**-vi] adj.m. of several persons
kilkupiętrowy [keel-koo-pyant-**ro**-vi] adj.m. of several stories high; of several stories
kilkuramienny [keel-koo-rah-**myen**-ni] adj.m. (many)branched-(candlestick, etc.)
kilkurodzinny [keel-koo-ro-**dźheen**-ni] adj.m. of several families
kilkusetletni [keel-koo-set-**let**-ńee] adj.m. of several hundred years; several hundred years old
kilkusetmetrowy [keel-koo-set-met-**ro**-vi] adj.m. of several hundred meters; several hundred meters long (high)
kilkusetny [keel-koo-**set**-ni] adj.m. several-hundredth (time, recurrence, etc.)
kilkusetosobowy [keel-koo-set-o-so-**bo**-vi] adj.m. of several hundred persons (people)
kilkusetstronicowy [keel-koo-set-stro-ńee-**tso**-vi] adj.m. of several hundred pages
kilkustopniowy [keel-koo-stop-**ńo**-vi] adj.m. of several degrees; of several steps (ladder, etc.); of several stages
kilkutomowy [keel-koo-to-**mo**-vi] adj.m. of several volumes
kilkutygodniowy [keel-koo-ti-god-**ńo**-vi] adj.m. of several weeks; several weeks' (rest, etc.); several weeks old
kilkutysięczny [keel-koo-ti-**śhanch**-ni] adj.m. of several thousand; several thousand in number
kilkuwyrazowy [keel-koo-vi-rah-**zo**-vi] adj.m. of several words
kilo [**kee**-lo] n. kilogram = 1000 grams = 2.2 pounds
kilocykl [kee-**lo**-tsikl] m. kilocycle
kilodyna [kee-lo-**di**-nah] f. kilodyne
kilof [**kee**-lof] m. pick; hack
kilogram [kee-**lo**-grahm] m. kilogram = 1000 grams = 2.2 pounds
kilogramometr [kee-lo-grah-**mo**-metr] m. kilogram-meter; mks unit of work or energy (about 7.235 ft-pounds, 9.80665 joules) (m-kgf)
kilogramowy [kee-lo-grah-**mo**-vi] adj.m. of one kilogram
kilogram-siła [kee-lo-grahm-**śhee**-wah] f. unit of force = kilogram-mass (kgf) (where earth gravity is 32.2 feet per second square = 9.80665 meters per second sq.)
kiloherc [kee-**lo**-herts] m. kilocycle
kilokaloria [kee-lo-kah-**lo**-ryah] f. kilocalorie; kilogram-calorie; great calorie; large calorie = 1000 calories
kilolitr [kee-**lo**-leetr] m. kiloliter = 1000 liters
kilometr [kee-**lo**-metr] m. kilometer = 1000 meters = 3,280.8 feet
kilometraż [kee-lo-**met**-rash] m. length in kilometers; milage (expressed in kilometers)
kilometrowy [kee-lo-met-**ro**-vi] adj.m. of one kilometer; kilometer (sign, etc.); colloq: endless
kilopond [kee-**lo**-pont] m. unit of force = kilogram-mass (kgf) (where earth gravity is 32.2 feet per second square = 9.80665 meters per second sq.)
kilopondometr [kee-lo-pon-**do**-metr] m. kilogram-meter; mks unit of work or energy (about 7.235 ft-pounds, 9.80665 joules) (m-kgf)
kilowat [kee-**lo**-vaht] m. kilowatt; 1000 watts
kilowatogodzina [kee-lo-vah-to-go-**dźhee**-nah] f. kilowatt-hour
kilowiec [kee-**lo**-vyets] m. keelboat
kilowolt [kee-**lo**-volt] m. kilovolt; 1000 volts
kilowy [kee-**lo**-vi] adj.m. of one kilogram; (boat, etc.) with a keel
kilówka [kee-**loof**-kah] f. keelboat
kilson [**keel**-son] m. keelson (fastened to the keel)
kilt [keelt] m. (Scottish) kilt
kilwater [keel-**vah**-ter] m. wake (of a

ship); dead water
kiła [**kee**-wah] f. syphilis
kiła kapuściana [**kee**-wah kah-poośh-**ćhah**-nah] exp.: clubroot
kiła końska [**kee**-wah **koń**-skah] exp.: anbury (in horses)
kiłowy [kee-**wo**-vi] adj.m. of syphilis; syphilitic; luetic
kimać [**kee**-mahćh] v. slang: doze; sleep; kip; slang: serve a prison term (mob jargon) (*repeatedly*)
kimation [kee-**maht**-yon] m. cymatium; cymation (ornament)
kimberlit [keem-**ber**-leet] m. kimberlite
kimberlitowy [keem-ber-lee-**to**-vi] adj.m. of kimberlite
kimnąć [**keem**-nownćh] v. slang: doze; sleep; kip; get some sleep
kimograf [kee-**mo**-grahf] m. kymograph
kimografia [kee-mo-**grah**-fyah] f. kymographic method; kymography
kimograficzny [kee-mo-grah-**feech**-ni] adj.m. kymographic
kimono [kee-**mo**-no] n. kimono; slang: sleep; bed
uderzyć w kimono [oo-**de**-zhićh f kee-**mo**-no] exp.: slang: to go to sleep; to go to bed
kimonowy [kee-mo-**no**-vi] adj.m. kimono (sleeve, etc.)
kinderbal [**keen**-der-bahl] m. children's party
kindersztuba [**keen**-der-**shtoo**-bah] f. (good) manners learned at home
kindżał [**keen**-dzhahw] m. (double-edged) dagger
kinematograf [kee-ne-mah-**to**-grahf] m. cinematograph
kinematografia [kee-ne-mah-to-**grah**-fyah] f. cinematography
kinematograficznie [kee-ne-mah-to-grah-**feech**-ńe] adv. cinematographically
kinematograficzny [kee-ne-mah-to-grah-**feech**-ni] adj.m. cinematographic
kinematycznie [kee-ne-mah-**tich**-ńe] adv. kinematically
kinematyczny [kee-ne-mah-**tich**-ni] adj.m. kinematical; kinematic
kinematyka [kee-ne-**mah**-ti-kah] f. kinematics
kineskop [kee-**nes**-kop] m. kinescope; picture tube
kineskopowy [kee-nes-ko-**po**-vi] adj.m. kinescope (screen, etc.)
kinestetycznie [kee-nes-te-**tich**-ńe] adv. kinesthetically
kinestetyczny [kee-nes-te-**tich**-ni] adj.m. kinesthetic
kinestezja [kee-nes-**te**-zyah] f. kinesthesia
kinetograf [kee-ne-**to**-grahf] m. prototype of moving-picture camera
kinetoskop [kee-ne-**to**-skop] m. kinetoscope
kinetostatyka [kee-ne-to-**stah**-ti-kah] f. the use of free-body analysis to calculate forces and moments
kinetoterapia [kee-ne-to-te-**rah**-pyah] f. the use of physical exercises for therapeutic purposes
kinetoza [kee-ne-**to**-zah] f. motion sickness
kinetyczność [kee-ne-**tich**-nośhćh] f. kinematics; kinetic nature
kinetyczny [kee-ne-**tich**-ni] adj.m. kinetic (theory, etc.)
kinetyka [kee-**ne**-ti-kah] f. kinetics; kinematics; science of motion
kineza [kee-**ne**-zah] f. kinesis
kinezjoterapia [kee-ne-zyo-te-**rah**-pyah] f. the use of physical exercises for therapeutic purposes
king [keeng] m. variety of woolen fabric (used for men's clothes)
kingston [**kink**-ston] m. Kingston valve (in a sea inlet)
kiniarz [**kee**-ńahsh] m. colloq: movie-fan
kinina [kee-**ńee**-nah] f. kinin (hormone)
kininy [kee-**ńee**-ni] pl. kinin hormones
kinkiecik [keen-**ke**-ćheek] m. (small, nice) lamp bracket; candlestick; sconce; theater footlight
kinkiet [**keen**-ket] m. lamp bracket; candlestick; sconce; theater footlight
ujrzeć światła kinkietów [ooy-zhećh **śhfyaht**-wah keen-**ke**-toof] exp.: to come before the footlights; to be on stage

kinkietowy [keen-k̲e-**to**-vi] adj.m. lamp bracket (light, etc.); sconce (light, etc.); of the footlights
kino [**kee**-no] n. cinema; movies; movie theater; picture palace; cinematography; the film; colloq: fun; flicker; picture show; show
amator kina [ah-**mah**-tor **kee**-nah] exp.: film-fan; movie-fan
kinobus [kee-**no**-boos] m. bus used for operators and equipment of mobile cinema
kinofikacja [kee-no-fee-**kah**-tsyah] f. extension of the network of movie-theaters
kinokamera [kee-no-kah-**me**-rah] f. movie camera
kinol [**kee**-nol] m. slang: snout; big nose (mob jargon)
kinoman [kee-**no**-mahn] m. movie-fan
kinomania [kee-no-**mah**-ńyah] f. a mania for movies
kinomechanik [kee-no-me-**khah**-ńeek] m. film-specialist; camera-mechanic
kinooperator [kee-no-o-pe-**rah**-tor] m. operator of movie-projection equipment
kinopanorama [kee-no-pah-no-**rah**-mah] f. panoramic movie projection (using three cameras)
kinoteatr [kee-no-**te**-ahtr] m. movie theater
kinotechniczny [kee-no-tekh-**ńeech**-ni] adj.m. of movie equipment
kinotechnik [kee-no-**tekh**-ńeek] m. movie technician
kinowy [kee-**no**-vi] adj.m. of the cinema; of the movies; movie (theater, etc.)
kiosk [kyosk] m. kiosk; booth
kioskarka [kyosk-**kahr**-kah] f. (woman) kiosk keeper; newsstand keeper; news-stall keeper; booth owner
kioskarz [**kyos**-kahsh] m. kiosk keeper; newsstand keeper; news-stall keeper; booth owner
kioskowy [kyos-**ko**-vi] adj.m. kiosk (sales, etc.)
kipa [**kee**-pah] f. dyeing vat; slang: cigarette stub
kiper [**kee**-per] m. taster; wine-taster; herring fillet
kiperski [kee-**per**-skee] adj.m. of wine-tasting
kiperstwo [kee-**per**-stfo] n. wine-tasting profession
kipieć [**kee**-pyećh] v. boil; seethe; surge; churn; colloq: scurry; scamper (*repeatedly*)
kipieć z radości [**kee**-pyećh z rah-**dośh**-ćhee] exp.: to boil over with joy; to bubble over with joy; to effervesce with joy
kipieć ze złości [**kee**-pyećh ze **zwośh**-ćhee] exp.: to boil over with rage
kipiel [**kee**-pyel] f. surf; welter of waves; surge; gurgitation
kipienie [kee-**pye**-ńe] n. ebullience; ebullition
kipi-kasza [**kee**-pee **kah**-shah] f. an old-style ball game
kipnąć [**keep**-n̲o̲w̲n̲ćh] v. colloq: kick the bucket; peg out
kipnięcie [keep-**ńan**-ćhe] n. colloq: death; kicking the bucket
kiprostwo [keep-**ro**-stfo] n. wine-tasting profession
kiprować [keep-**ro**-vahćh] v. twill (weave) (*repeatedly*)
kir [keer] m. pall
kirasjer [kee-**rahs**-yer] m. cuirassier
kirasjerski [kee-rahs-**yer**-skee] adj.m. of a cuirassier
kircha [**keer**-khah] f. colloq: Protestant Church
kirgiski [keer-**gees**-kee] adj.m. Khirgiz (language, dance, etc.)
Kirgiz [**keer**-gees] m. Khirgiz
kirkut [**keer**-koot] m. Jewish cemetery
kirowy [kee-**ro**-vi] adj.m. pall (cloth, etc.)
kirylica [kee-ri-**lee**-tsah] f. Cyrillic alphabet = **cyrylica**
kirys [**kee**-ris] m. cuirass
kisić [**kee**-śheećh] v. ferment; sour; pickle (cabbage, etc.); turn sour; silage (fodder, etc.) (*repeatedly*)
kisić się [**kee**-śheećh śh̲a̲n̲] v. ferment; sour; pickle; turn sour (*repeatedly*)
kisiel [**kee**-śhel] m. kind of jelly
dziesiąta woda po kisielu [dźhe-

śhown-tah vo-dah po kee-śhe-loo] exp.: very distant relative
kisielek [kee-**śhe**-lek] m. (nice) jelly
kismet [**kees**-met] m. destiny (of a Muslim)
kisnąć [**kees**-nownćh] v. turn sour; ferment; pickle; frowst; turn musty; colloq: stagnate; lie sunk in dullness; hang about; be on the shelf (unmarried, etc.) (*repeatedly*)
kistka [**keest**-kah] f. spray
kiszarnia [kee-**shahr**-ńah] f. fermentation shop
kiszeczka [kee-**shech**-kah] f. (small) intestine; bowel; gut
kiszeniak [kee-**she**-ńahk] m. cucumber suitable for pickling
kiszenie [kee-**she**-ńe] n. pickling
kiszka [**keesh**-kah] f. intestine; bowel; gut; inner tube; blood sausage; patty sausage; slang: billy club (mob jargon)
kiszkowaty [keesh-ko-**vah**-ti] adj.m. long and narrow
kiszkowiec [keesh-**ko**-vyets] m. botulinum
kiszkowy [keesh-**ko**-vi] adj.m. of the intestines; intestinal; enteric
kiszonka [kee-**shon**-kah] f. silage
kiszonkarstwo [kee-shon-**kahr**-stfo] n. fodder production business
kiszonkowy [kee-shon-**ko**-vi] adj.m. of fodder production business; of silage
kiszony [kee-**sho**-ni] adj.m. pickled
kiszona kapusta [kee-**sho**-nah kah-**poos**-tah] exp.: sauerkraut
kiściasty [keeśh-**ćhahs**-ti] adj.m. racemose
kiściec [**keeśh**-ćhets] m. variety of (Himalayan) pheasant
kiścień [**keeśh**-ćheń] m. Tartar whip with lead inserts
kiść [**keeśhćh**] f. bunch; wrist; spray; raceme; cluster; tuft; (flower) bud
kiśnieć [**keeśh**-ńećh] v. turn sour; ferment; pickle; colloq: stagnate; lie sunk in dullness; hang about; be on the shelf (unmarried, etc.) (*repeatedly*)
kiśnienie [keeśh-**ńe**-ńe] n. turning sour; fermentation
kiśnięcie [keeśh-**ńan**-ćhe] n. turning sour; fermentation
kit [keet] m. putty; mastic; lute
do kitu [do **kee**-too] exp.: good for nothing
kita [**kee**-tah] f. tuft (of feathers); crest; aigrette; panache; tassel; brush; spray; raceme
odwalić kitę [od-**vah**-leećh **kee**-tan] exp.: slang: to kick the bucket; to snuff out (mob jargon)
kitara [kee-**tah**-rah] f. cittern; cither
kitarzysta [kee-tah-**zhis**-tah] m. cither player
kitel [**kee**-tel] m. smock; frock (doctor's coat); overall; colloq: lab-coat
kitelek [kee-**te**-lek] m. (small, nice) smock; frock (doctor's coat); overall; colloq: lab-coat
kitka [**keet**-kah] f. (small, nice) tuft (of feathers); crest; aigrette; panache; tassel; brush; spray; raceme
kitla [**keet**-lah] f. traditional festive suit of Polish miners
kitować [kee-**to**-vahćh] v. putty; lute; cement; slang: die; beat; lie; have sex; shit; cheat (*repeatedly*)
kitowanie [kee-to-**vah**-ńe] n. caulking; cementation
kituś [**kee**-toośh] m. colloq: darling
kitwasić się [keet-**fah**-śheećh śhan] v. colloq: crowd in a small stuffy room; ferment; sour; pickle; turn sour (*repeatedly*)
kiur [kyoor] m. curie; curium (atomic number 96)
kiurowiec [kyoo-**ro**-vyets] m. one of the eight heaviest elements
kiurowce [kyoo-**rof**-tse] pl. the eight heaviest elements
kiwacz [**kee**-vahch] m. slang: cheat; swindler (mob jargon)
kiwać [**kee**-vahćh] v. rock; nod; wag (tail, etc.); dangle; fool; dodge; sway; swing (to and fro); motion (to); colloq: cheat; fool; jink (*repeatedly*)
kiwać się [**kee**-vahćh śhan] v. rock to and fro; shake; be shaky; be rickety; totter (*repeatedly*)
kiwający się [kee-vah-**yown**-tsi śhan] adj.m. shaky; rickety

(chair, etc.)
kiwanie [kee-**vah**-ńe] n. colloq: dodging; fooling; cheating
kiwi [**kee**-vee] n. kiwi (bird, fruit)
kiwnąć [**keev**-nownćh] v. rock; nod; wag (tail, etc.); dangle; fool; dodge; sway; swing (to and fro); motion (to); colloq: cheat; fool; jink
palcem nie kiwnąć [**pahl**-tsem ńe **keev**-nownćh] exp.: not to raise a finger
kiwnąć się [**keev**-nownćh śhan] v. rock to and fro; shake; be shaky; be rickety; totter
kiwnięcie [keev-**ńan**-ćhe] n. sign; motion; beck
kiwnięcie głową [keev-**ńan**-ćhe **gwo**-vown] exp.: a nod
kizeryt [kee-**ze**-rit] m. manganese sulfate (mineral)
kizia [**kee**-źhah] f. pussy cat
klacz [klahch] f. mare
kladofora [klah-do-**fo**-rah] f. variety of waterweed; Cladophora
kladogenetycznie [klah-do-ge-ne-**tich**-ńe] adv. cladogenetically
kladogenetyczny [klah-do-ge-ne-**tich**-ni] adj.m. cladogenetic
kladogeneza [klah-do-ge-**ne**-zah] f. cladogenesis
klag [klahk] m. a cheese additive
klajdesdal [klahy-**des**-dahl] m. variety of heavy draw-horse
klajster [**klahy**-ster] m. glue; paste; water base glue; size
klajstrować [klahy-**stro**-vahćh] v. glue; paste; slang: patch up (*repeatedly*)
klajstrowanie [klahy-stro-**vah**-ńe] n. gluing; pasting; slang: patching up
klajstrowaty [klahy-stro-**vah**-ti] adj.m. gluey; pasty; of water base glue; sticky
klaka [**klah**-kah] f. claque; hired applauders
klakier [**klah**-ker] m. claqueur; hired applauder
klakson [**klahk**-son] m. car horn
klaksonować [klahk-so-**no**-vahćh] v. colloq: blow car horn; honk; horn (*repeatedly*)
klamerka [klah-**mer**-kah] f. clip; buckle; clasp; hasp; bracket; brace
klamka [**klahm**-kah] f. doorknob; door handle; latch; hasp
klamot [**klah**-mot] m. slang: old junk; stolen item (mob jargon)
klamoty [klah-**mo**-ti] pl. colloq: belongings; chattels; slang: thief's tools (mob jargon)
klamp [klahmp] m. (artery-)clip
klamra [**klahm**-rah] f. buckle; clasp; bracket; fastener; staple
klamrować [klahm-**ro**-vahćh] v. clamp; cramp; buckle; clasp; bracket; fasten with iron clamps; staple (*repeatedly*)
klamrowanie [klahm-ro-**vah**-ńe] n. clamping; fastening
klamrowato [klahm-ro-**vah**-to] adv. in the shape of brackets
klamrowaty [klahm-ro-**vah**-ti] adj.m. clamp-like; bracket-shaped
klamrowy [klahm-**ro**-vi] adj.m. fastened with a clamp; enclosed in brackets
klan [klahn] m. clan
klang [klahng] m. (single) clang
klangor [**klahn**-gor] m. clangor
klanik [**klah**-ńeek] m. small clan
klanowość [klah-**no**-vośhćh] f. clan system; clannish character
klanowy [klah-**no**-vi] adj.m. of a clan; clan (system, etc.); colloq: clannish
klap [klahp] m. bang; tap
klapa [**klah**-pah] f. lapel; valve; trap door; hatch; gate; flap; clack; door; piston (of a trumpet, etc.); earflap; colloq: washout; flop; foozzle; defeat
klapa bezpieczeństwa [**klah**-pah bes-pye-**cheń**-stfah] exp.: safety valve; escape valve; escape door
zrobić klapę [**zro**-beećh **klah**-pan] exp.: to fall flat; go bankrupt; to give out; to be exhausted; slang: to go phut (Brit.)
klapać [**klah**-pahćh] v. tap; patter; smack; slap; chatter; clatter; slang: walk; go (*repeatedly*)
klapak [**klah**-pahk] m. duck fledgling
klapanie [klah-**pah**-ńe] n. tap; patter; clatter
klapeczka [klah-**pech**-kah] f. (very

small) lapel; valve; trap door; hatch; gate; flap; fly-flap
klapek [**klah**-pek] m. open slipper (clapping while walking)
klapiasty [klah-**pyahs**-ti] adj.m. loppy; hanging loose; limp
klapka [**klahp**-kah] f. (small) lapel; valve; trap door; hatch; gate; flap
klapnąć [**klahp**-nownćh] v. flop down; come down with a flop; turn out a washout; flash in a pan; fall flat; blurt out
klapnięcie [klahp-ńan-ćhe] n. flopping down; coming down with a flop; turning out a washout; a flash in a pan; falling flat; blurting out
klapnięty [klahp-ńan-ti] adj.m. collapsed; delated; slang: sad
klapować [klah-**po**-vahćh] v. colloq: fit together; tally; be O.K. (*repeatedly*)
klapowany [klah-po-**vah**-ni] adj.m. grooved (leaf, etc.); lobate; lobed
klapowato [klah-po-**vah**-to] adv. with grooves; with lobes
klapowaty [klah-po-**vah**-ti] adj.m. grooved (leaf, etc.); lobate
klapowy [klah-**po**-vi] adj.m. flap (valve, etc.)
zawór klapowy [**zah**-voor klah-**po**-vi] exp.: plate valve; check valve
klaps [klahps] m. spank; smack; slap; clout; slate (in movie-making)
dostać klapsa [do-stahćh **klah**-psah] exp.: to get spanked
klapser [**klahp**-ser] m. recorder of scenes taken by a movie camera
klapsnąć [**klahps**-nownćh] v. spank; box (somebody's) ears; flop down; come down with a flop; turn out a washout; flash in a pan; fall flat; blurt out
klar [klahr] m. syrup; clearing
klark [klahrk] m. recorder of unloaded ship's cargo
klarnecik [klahr-**ne**-ćheek] m. small clarinet
klarnecista [klahr-ne-**ćhees**-tah] m. clarinet player; clarinettist; clarinetist
klarnet [**klahr**-net] m. clarinet; colloq: bumpkin; clod; lubber; muff
klarnetowy [klahr-ne-**to**-vi] adj.m. of a clarinet
klarowacz [klah-**ro**-vahch] m. clarifier
klarować [klah-**ro**-vahćh] v. clarify; filter; clear; purify; colloq: explain (*repeatedly*)
klarować się [klah-**ro**-vahćh śhan] v. become clear; clarify; purify; colloq: take form; take shape; become distinct; become plain (*repeatedly*)
klarowanie [klah-ro-**vah**-ńe] n. clarification; purification; giving explanation; clearage; clearance
klarownica [klah-rov-**ńee**-tsah] f. clarifier; purifier; clarifying tank
klarownie [klah-**rov**-ńe] adv. lucidly; limpidly
klarownik [klah-**rov**-ńeek] m. system of shallow ponds used for clarifying
klarowność [klah-**rov**-nośhćh] f. clarity; lucidity; limpidness; purity
klarowny [klah-**rov**-ni] adj.m. clear; lucid; limpid; pure
klarówka [klah-**roof**-kah] f. sugar solution during refining
klaryska [klah-**ris**-kah] f. nun of the order of St. Clare; clarist; Poor Clare
klaryt [**klah**-rit] m. glance coal
klasa [**klah**-sah] f. class; classroom; rank; order; division; category; standard; grade
pierwsza klasa [**pyerf**-shah **klah**-sah] exp.: first rate; A1; first-class; tiptop
wielka klasa [**vyel**-kah **klah**-sah] exp.: high standard
wysoka klasa [vi-**so**-kah **klah**-sah] exp.: high quality
klaser [**klah**-ser] m. stamp-album
klask [klahsk] m. clap; clapping; slap; slapping
klaskać [**klahs**-kahćh] v. clap; applaud; smack; trill (*repeatedly*)
klaskanie [klahs-**kah**-ńe] n. applause; trills
klaskany [klahs-**kah**-ni] adj.m. (made, danced) with clapping
klasnąć [**klahs**-nownćh] v. clap; applaud; smack; trill

klasowo [klah-**so**-vo] adv. as regards class; as regards class distinction (divisions, character, spirit, etc.)
klasowość [klah-**so**-vośhćh] f. class divisions; class character; class spirit
klasowy [klah-**so**-vi] adj.m. of a class; of classes; class (distinction, etc.)
klasówka [klah-**soof**-kah] f. class test; written class-exercise
klaster [**klahs**-ter] m. musical composition for simultaneous play on number of instruments
klastyczny [klahs-**tich**-ni] adj.m. of eroded rocks; clastic
klasycysta [klah-si-**tsis**-tah] m. classicist; classical scholar
klasycystyczny [klah-si-tsis-**tich**-ni] adj.m. classicistic
klasycyzm [klah-**si**-tsizm] m. classicism (in art)
klasycyzować [klah-si-tsi-**zo**-vahćh] v. classicize; make classic (*repeatedly*)
klasycyzowanie [klah-si-tsi-zo-**vah**-ńe] n. making classicistic
klasycznie [klah-**sich**-ńe] adv. classically; typically
klasyczność [klah-**sich**-nośhćh] f. classical character; classical features (of work, of art, etc.)
klasyczny [klah-**sich**-ni] adj.m. classical; typical; classic; standard; classicistic; conventional
klasyczny przykład [klah-**sich**-ni **pshi**-kwaht] exp.: typical example
styl klasyczny [stil klah-**sich**-ni] exp.: breast stroke (in swimming)
klasyfikacja [klah-si-fi-**kah**-tsyah] f. classification; sorting; ordination
klasyfikacyjny [klah-si-fi-kah-**tsiy**-ni] adj.m. of classification; of sorting; classificatory
klasyfikator [klah-si-fee-**kah**-tor] m. classifier; sorter; stapler; seizer; sizing apparatus; file
klasyfikować [klah-si-fee-**ko**-vahćh] v. classify; sort; grade; categorize; give marks (to students) (*repeatedly*)
klasyfikowanie [klah-si-fee-ko-**vah**-ńe] n. classification; sorting; ordination
klasyk [**klah**-sik] m. classic; classicist
klasyka [**klah**-si-kah] f. classical works
klasztor [**klahsh**-tor] m. monastery; convent; cloister
klasztornie [klahsh-**tor**-ńe] adv. like in a monastery
klasztorny [klahsh-**tor**-ni] adj.m. monastery (building, etc.); convent (rules, etc.)
klaśnięcie [klahśh-**ńan**-ćhe] n. applause; clapping one's hands
klateczka [klah-**tech**-kah] f. (small) cage; crate
klatka [**klaht**-kah] f. cage; crate
klatka piersiowa [**klaht**-kah pyer-**śho**-vah] exp.: chest
klatka schodowa [**klaht**-kah skho-**do**-vah] exp.: staircase; stairway
zamknąć do klatki [**zahm**-knownćh do **klaht**-kee] exp.: to cage (a bird, etc.)
klatkowaty [klaht-ko-**vah**-ti] adj.m. cellular; checkered
klatkowiec [klaht-**ko**-vyets] m. apartment building (built around its staircase)
klatkowy [klaht-**ko**-vi] adj.m. caged; cellular; checkered
klaun [klahwn] m. clown; bozo
klaunada [klahw-**nah**-dah] f. clownade; clowning; buffoonery
klaunowski [klahw-**nof**-skee] adj.m. clown's; of a clown
klaustrofobia [klahws-tro-**fo**-byah] f. claustrophobia
klauzula [klahw-**zoo**-lah] f. clause; proviso; reservation; provision
klauzula dodatkowa [klahw-**zoo**-lah do-daht-**ko**-vah] exp.: rider
klauzulowy [klahw-zoo-**lo**-vi] adj.m. of a clause; of a proviso; of a reservation; of a provision
klauzura [klahw-**zoo**-rah] f. enclosure
klauzurowy [klahw-zoo-**ro**-vi] adj.m. enclosed (religious order); invigilated (examination paper)
klawesyn [klah-**ves**-in] m. clavecin; harpsichord
klawesynista [klah-ve-si-**ńees**-tah]

m. clavecinist; harpsichordist
klawesynistka [klah-ve-si-ńeest-kah] f. (woman) clavecinist; harpsichordist
klawiatura [klah-vyah-too-rah] f. keys; keyboard; computer keyboard; (organ) bank; manual
klawiaturowy [klah-vyah-too-ro-vi] adj.m. keyboard (microprocessor, instrument, etc.)
klawicymbał [klah-vee-tsim-bahw] m. clavecin; harpsichord
klawikord [klah-vee-kort] m. clavichord
klawikordzista [klah-vee-kor-dźhees-tah] m. clavichordist
klawikordzistka [klah-vee-kor-dźheest-kah] f. (woman) clavichordist
klawisz [klah-veesh] m. (piano) key; pushbutton (of a switch); colloq: stool pigeon; jailer; picklock
klawisznik [klah-veesh-ńeek] m. colloq: stool pigeon; jailer; picklock; safe-cracker; safe-breaker
klawiszowy [klah-vee-sho-vi] adj.m. keyboard (instrument, etc.)
klawo [klah-vo] adv. colloq: in fine style; on the up and up; O.K.; righto; fine
na klawo [nah klah-vo] exp.: colloq: for good
klawy [klah-vi] adj.m. colloq: first-rate; scrumptious; bang-up; plummy; swell; hunky-dory; slang: rich; reliable
kląć [klownćh] v. curse; swear; utter curses; execrate (*repeatedly*)
kląć się [klownćh śhan] v. curse (at); swear (by) (*repeatedly*)
kląskać [klowns-kahćh] v. trill; slog; tramp; smack one's tongue; smack one's lips (*repeatedly*)
kląskanie [klowns-kah-ńe] n. trilling (like a bird)
kląskawka [klowns-kahf-kah] f. thrush (bird); Saxicola torquata
klątwa [klown-tfah] f. curse; ban; excommunication; anathema
klecenie [kle-tse-ńe] n. botching; bungling up
klecha [kle-khah] m. colloq: sky pilot; slang: priest
klechda [klekh-dah] f. folk-story; ancient tale
klechdowy [klekh-do-vi] adj.m. of a folk-story; of an ancient tale
klecić [kle-ćheećh] v. botch; bungle; fudge; bring together; colloq: get up; concoct (*repeatedly*)
klecić się [kle-ćheećh śhan] v. crop forth; take shape (*repeatedly*)
nie klecić się [ńe kle-ćheećh śhan] exp.: to prove a failure
kleć [klećh] f. hutch; cabin
kleiczek [kle-ee-chek] m. (nice, little) gruel; mash; pap
kleić [kle-eećh] v. glue; stick together; paste; cement; slang: inhale narcotic vapors (*repeatedly*)
kleić się [kle-eećh śhan] v. stick together; be sticky; be gluey; slang: cling to (somebody) (mob jargon) (*repeatedly*)
nie kleić się [ńe kle-eećh śhan] exp.: to falter; to flag; to limp; to make no progress
kleidło [kle-eed-wo] n. glue; gum; paste
kleik [kle-eek] m. gruel; mash; pap
kleina [kle-ee-nah] f. collodium; collodion
kleinowski [klahy-nof-skee] adj.m. of flat ceiling construction; of Klein system
kleistość [kle-ees-tośhćh] f. stickiness; viscosity
kleisty [kle-ees-ti] adj.m. sticky; viscous; adhesive
kleiście [kle-eeśh-ćhe] adv. in a sticky manner; with viscosity; stickily; gluily
klej [kley] m. glue; cement; gum; seize
klejarka [kle-yahr-kah] f. (woman) glue applicator; cementer; glue spreader; moistener
klejarnia [kle-yahr-ńah] f. glue applicator's shop; cementation shop
klejarski [kle-yahr-skee] adj.m. glue applicator's; cementer's; of gluing
klejarz [kle-yahsh] m. glue applicator; cementer; glue spreader; moistener

klejce [**kley**-tse] pl. carpenter's clamp
klejenie [kle-**ye**-ńe] n. gluing; cementing; slang: inhaling narcotic vapors (mob jargon)
klejki [**kley**-kee] adj.m. sticky; gluey
klejnocik [kley-**no**-ćheek] m. (nice, little) jewel
klejnot [**kley**-not] m. jewel; gem; precious stone; coat of arms; crest; (armorial) bearing
klejnoty koronne [kley-**no**-ti ko-**ron**-ne] exp.: pl. Crown Jewels
klejnoty rodzinne [kley-**no**-ti ro-**dźheen**-ne] exp.: slang: testicles
klejnotka [kley-**not**-kah] f. Euglena
klejodajny [kle-yo-**dahy**-ni] adj.m. gummy; rich in collodion
klejonka [kle-**yon**-kah] f. plywood; buckram; plywood ski; colloq: medley; patchwork
klejorodny [kle-yo-**rod**-ni] adj.m. gummy; rich in collodion
klejowaty [kle-yo-**vah**-ti] adj.m. sticky; viscous; adhesive
klejownia [kle-**yov**-ńah] f. glue applicator's shop; cementation shop
klejowo [kle-**yo**-vo] adv. by means of glue
klejowy [kle-**yo**-vi] adj.m. glue (color, viscosity, paint, etc.)
klejówka [kle-**yoof**-kah] f. leather scrap used to make leather glue; variety of edible mushroom
klejstogamia [kleys-to-**gah**-myah] f. autogamy; self-fertilization
klejstogamiczny [kleys-to-gah-**meech**-ni] adj.m. autogamous; self-fertile
klekot [**kle**-kot] m. clattering; rattle; dilapidated object; rattletrap; rickety car
klekotać [kle-**ko**-tahćh] v. clatter; rattle; colloq: chatter; prate (*repeatedly*)
klekotanie [kle-ko-**tah**-ńe] n. rattle
klekotka [kle-**kot**-kah] f. rattle; colloq: chatterbox
klekotliwy [kle-kot-**lee**-vi] adj.m. rattling; clattering
kleks [kleks] m. blot; ink-spot; colloq: splash of color
kleksik [**klek**-śheek] (small) m. blot; ink-spot
klematis [kle-**mah**-tees] m. clematis
kleniec [**kle**-ńets] m. chub (fish)
kleń [kleń] m. chub (fish)
klepacz [**kle**-pahch] m. false coin; tilt hammer; hackle; flax-comb; scutch
klepaczka [kle-**pach**-kah] f. hackle; flax-comb; scutch
klepać [**kle**-pahćh] v. hammer; flatten; dress (metal); prattle; pat; blab; clap; slap; chatter; rattle off; gabble off (*repeatedly*)
klepać się [**kle**-pahćh śhan] v. slap (one's thighs, each other, etc.) (*repeatedly*)
klepadło [kle-**pahd**-wo] n. small (sheet-metal) anvil
klepak [**kle**-pahk] m. mallet; (plummer's) dresser; (tinsmith's) chasing hammer; colloq: chatterer; babbler
klepalność [kle-**pahl**-nośhćh] f. malleability; malleableness
klepalny [kle-**pahl**-ni] adj.m. malleable
klepanie [kle-**pah**-ńe] n. clapping; slapping
klepaniec [kle-**pah**-ńets] m. false coin
kleparka [kle-**pahr**-kah] f. scutcher; scutching machine; willow; mallet; (plummer's) dresser; (tinsmith's) chasing hammer
klepisko [kle-**pees**-ko] n. threshing floor; barn floor
klepisko młocarni [kle-**pees**-ko mwo-**tsahr**-ńee] exp.: concave of a thresher
klepiskowy [kle-pees-**ko**-vi] adj.m. of a threshing floor
klepka [**klep**-kah] f. stave; parquet-flooring board
bez piątej klepki [bes **pyown**-tey **klep**-kee] exp.: colloq: off his mind; loony; crackbrained
majster klepka [**mahy**-ster **klep**-kah] exp.: tinkerer; handyman
klepkarka [klep-**kahr**-kah] f. device for fabrication of staves
klepkować [klep-**ko**-vahćh] v. cover with staves; cover with thin boards (*repeatedly*)
klepkowanie [klep-ko-**vah**-ńe] n.

covering with staves
klepkowy [klep-**ko**-vi] adj.m. covered with staves; built with staves
klepnąć [**klep**-nownćh] v. hit; flatten; clap; slap
klepnięcie [klep-ńan-ćhe] n. tap; clap; slap
klepnięty [klep-ńan-ti] adj.m. slang: insane; mad; crazy
klepsydra [klep-**sid**-rah] f. hourglass; sandglass; obituary notice
klepsydra wodna [klep-**sid**-rah **vod**-nah] exp.: water-glass (for measuring time)
klepsydrowy [klep-sid-**ro**-vi] adj.m. of an hourglass; of a sandglass; of an obituary notice
kleptoman [klep-**to**-mahn] m. kleptomaniac
kleptomania [klep-to-**mah**-ńyah] f. kleptomania; impulse to steal
klepu-klepu [**kle**-poo **kle**-poo] exp.: tap-tap; knock-knock
kler [kler] m. clergy; priesthood
klerk [klerk] m. man of ivory tower; detached intellectual; wandering (medieval) student
klerkizm [**kler**-keezm] m. detachment from the society and politics
klerodendron [kle-ro-**den**-dron] m. glory bower; Clerodendron (Volcameria)
klerycki [kle-**rits**-kee] adj.m. seminarist's; seminarian's
kleryk [**kle**-rik] m. seminarist; seminarian
klerykalista [kle-ri-kah-**lees**-tah] m. advocate of clericalism
klerykalizacja [kle-ri-kah-lee-**zah**-tsyah] f. clericalism
klerykalizm [kle-ri-**kah**-leezm] m. clericalism
klerykalizować [kle-ri-kah-lee-**zo**-vahćh] v. submit to the influence of the clergy (*repeatedly*)
klerykalizowanie [kle-ri-kah-lee-zo-**vah**-ńe] n. submission to the influence of the clergy
klerykalny [kle-ri-**kahl**-ni] adj.m. clerical
klerykał [kle-**ri**-kahw] m. advocate of clericalism
kleszcz [kleshch] m. tick
kleszcze [**klesh**-che] pl. pliers; tongs; claws; pincers; nippers; ticks
kleszczenie [klesh-**che**-ńe] n. clamping; holding with pliers
kleszczka [**kleshch**-kah] f. nettling-needle
kleszczojad [klesh-**cho**-yaht] m. ani; Crotophaga; black cuckoo bird
kleszczotek [klesh-**cho**-tek] m. book scorpion; false-scorpion
kleszczowina [klesh-cho-**vee**-nah] f. the castor-oil plant
kleszczowo [klesh-**cho**-vo] adv. using forceps
kleszczowy [klesh-**cho**-vi] adj.m. of forceps; by forceps
kleszczyć [**klesh**-chićh] v. castrate (an animal); geld (*repeatedly*)
kleszczyki [klesh-**chi**-kee] pl. (small) pliers; tongs; claws; pincers; nippers; tweezers
kleszy [**kle**-shi] adj.m. colloq: of a sky pilot; slang: priest's
kleterki [kle-**ter**-kee] pl. mountain-climbing boots
klezmer [**klez**-mer] m. second-rate musician
klęcie [**klan**-ćhe] n. cursing; uttering curses; swearing
klęcząco [klan-**chown**-tso] adv. on one's knees; on bent knees
klęczeć [**klan**-chećh] v. kneel (*repeatedly*)
klęczenie [klan-**che**-ńe] n. kneeling
klęczki [**klanch**-kee] pl. kneeling position
paść na klęczki [pahśhćh nah **klanch**-kee] exp.: to fall on one's knees
klęcznik [**klanch**-ńeek] m. kneeling-chair; praying-desk
klęczny [**klanch**-ni] adj.m. of kneeling position
klękać [**klan**-kahćh] v. kneel down; bend the knee; kneel (*repeatedly*)
klękanie [klan-**kah**-ńe] n. kneeling down
klęknąć [**klank**-nownćh] v. kneel down; bend the knee; kneel
klęknięcie [klank-ńan-ćhe] n. kneeling down; bending the knee; kneeling

klępa [klan-pah] f. female elk; mare; cow; mob slang: woman; slut

klęska [klans-kah] f. defeat; disaster; calamity; repulse

klęska żywiołowa [klans-kah zhi-vyo-**wo**-vah] exp.: natural disaster; natural calamity

ponieść klęskę [**po**-ńeśhćh **klans**-kan] exp.: to suffer a defeat; to meet with a repulse

zadać klęskę [zah-dahćh **klans**-kan] exp.: to inflict a defeat; to inflict a repulse (on somebody)

klęskowy [klans-**ko**-vi] adj.m. of a defeat; disastrous; calamitous

klęsnąć [klans-nownćh] v. shrink; subside; go down; cave in; sink (*repeatedly*)

klęśnięcie [klanśh-ńan-ćhe] n. shrinking; subsidence

kliczka [**kleech**-kah] f. (small) clique

klient [**klee**-yent] m. customer; buyer; purchaser; shopper; guest (in a restaurant, etc.); client (of a lawyer, etc.); pick-up (in a taxi)

stały klient [**stah**-wi **klee**-yent] exp.: patron; habitual guest; client

klientela [klee-yen-**te**-lah] f. clientele; shoppers; buyers; customers; purchasers; the trade constituency

klientka [klee-**yent**-kah] f. (female) customer

klientowski [klee-yen-**tof**-skee] adj.m. of a client

klif [kleef] m. cliff

klifowy [klee-**fo**-vi] adj.m. of a cliff

klika [**klee**-kah] f. clique

klikowość [klee-ko-vośhćh] f. nature of a clique

klikowy [klee-**ko**-vi] adj.m. of a clique

klimacik [klee-**mah**-ćheek] m. (nice, little) climate

klimakterium [klee-mahk-**te**-ryoom] n. climacteric

klimakteryczny [klee-mahk-te-**rich**-ni] adj.m. climacteric; critical; crucial

klimat [**klee**-maht] m. climate

klimatolog [klee-mah-**to**-log] m. climatologist

klimatologia [klee-mah-to-**lo**-gyah] f. climatology

klimatologicznie [klee-mah-to-lo-**geech**-ńe] adv. climatologically

klimatologiczny [klee-mah-to-lo-**geech**-ni] adj.m. climatological

klimatoterapia [klee-mah-to-te-**rah**-pyah] f. climatic therapy

klimatycznie [klee-mah-**tich**-ńe] adv. climatically; in respect of the climate

klimatyczny [klee-mah-**tich**-ni] adj.m. climatic

klimatyp [klee-**mah**-tip] m. ecological type

klimatyzacja [klee-mah-ti-**zah**-tsyah] f. air conditioning

klimatyzacyjny [klee-mah-ti-zah-**tsiy**-ni] adj.m. air-conditioning (process, etc.)

klimatyzator [klee-mah-ti-**zah**-tor] m. air conditioner

klimatyzować [klee-mah-ti-**zo**-vahćh] v. air-condition (*repeatedly*)

klimatyzowanie [klee-mah-ti-zo-**vah**-ńe] n. air-conditioning

klimenia [klee-**me**-ńyah] f. Clymenia; Cephalopoda

klimeniowy [klee-me-**ńyo**-vi] adj.m. Clymenia (layer, stratum, etc.)

klin [kleen] m. wedge; cotter; chock; quoin; cleat; cuneus; gusset; gore

klincz [kleench] m. clinch (in sport)

klinczować [kleen-**cho**-vahćh] v. clinch (in sport) (*repeatedly*)

klinczowanie [kleen-cho-**vah**-ńe] n. clinching

klinga [**kleen**-gah] f. (sword) blade; saber-blade

klingeryt [kleen-**ge**-rit] m. gasket material of rubberized asbestos

kliniak [**klee**-ńahk] m. light pneumatic hammer

kliniasty [klee-**ńahs**-ti] adj.m. wedge-shaped

klinicysta [klee-ńee-**tsis**-tah] m. clinician

klinicznie [klee-**ńeech**-ńe] adv. clinically

kliniczny [klee-**ńeech**-ni] adj.m. clinical; clinic (hours, etc.)

kliniec [**klee**-ńets] m. keystone; gravel for grouting pavements

klinik [**klee**-ńeek] m. small wedge

klinika [klee-ńee-kah] f. clinic
klinkier [kleen-k̲er] m. clinker
klinkiernia [kleen-k̲er-ńah] f. clinker works
klinkierowy [kleen-k̲e-ro-vi] adj.m. of clinker; clinker (brick, slag, etc.)
klinkierówka [kleen-k̲e-roof-kah] f. clinker brick; clinker-built boat
klinkieryt [kleen-k̲e-rit] m. gasket material of rubberized asbestos
klinokineza [klee-no-kee-ne-zah] f. reaction of animal movements due to climatic changes (in temperature, humidity, etc.)
klinolist [klee-no-leest] m. archaic plant with wedge-shaped leaves
klinometr [klee-no-metr] m. clinometer; slope level (measuring angles of inclination)
klinometria [klee-no-metr-yah] f. clinometry
klinometryczny [klee-no-met-rich-ni] adj.m. clinometric
klinować [klee-no-vahćh] v. wedge; chock; quoin (*repeatedly*)
klinować koło [klee-no-vahćh ko-wo] exp.: to skid a wheel
klinowanie [klee-no-vah-ńe] n. wedging; chocking
klinowato [klee-no-vah-to] adv. in the shape of a wedge
klinowatość [klee-no-vah-tośhćh] f. wedge-shape; wedge-shaped characteristic
klinowaty [klee-no-vah-ti] adj.m. wedge-shaped; arrow-headed; cuneate; cuneiform
klinowo [klee-no-vo] adv. in the shape of a wedge
klinowy [klee-no-vi] adj.m. wedge-shaped; arrow-headed; cuneate; cuneiform
kość klinowa [kośhćh klee-no-vah] exp.: sphenoid bone
pismo klinowe [pees-mo klee-no-ve] exp.: cuneiform writing
klipa [klee-pah] f. tipcat (game); piggy
kliper [klee-per] m. clipper (ship)
kliprowy [klee-pro-vi] adj.m. of a clipper
klips [kleeps] m. clip
kliring [klee-ring] m. clearing
kliringowy [klee-rin-go-vi] adj.m. of a clearing
klistron [klee-stron] m. amplifier tube (in a television set, etc.)
klistronowy [klee-stro-no-vi] adj.m. of an amplifier tube
klisza [klee-shah] f. (photo) plate; printing plate; woodcut; cliche
kliszarnia [klee-shahr-ńah] f. printing plates' shop
kliszka [kleesh-kah] f. (small) printing plate
kliszograf [klee-sho-grahf] m. printing plate engraving machine
kliszogram [klee-sho-grahm] m. engraved printing plate
kliszować [klee-sho-vahćh] v. make printing blocks; make woodcuts; make cliches (*repeatedly*)
kliszowanie [klee-sho-vah-ńe] n. making printing blocks; making woodcuts; making cliches
kliszowy [klee-sho-vi] adj.m. plate (camera, etc.)
klitka [kleet-kah] f. colloq: cubicle; cell; slang: small room
klituś-bajduś [klee-toośh bahy-doośh] indecl. colloq: balderdash; fiddle-faddle; nonsense
kliważ [klee-vahsh] m. cleavage
kliwer [klee-ver] m. jib; fore-mast staysail
kliwerbom [klee-ver-bom] m. staysail boom
kliwerfał [klee-ver-fahw] m. staysail line; jib halyard
kliwia [klee-vyah] f. Clivia (herb)
klizymetr [klee-zi-metr] m. clinometer; slope level (measuring angles of inclination)
kloaczny [klo-ahch-ni] adj.m. cloacal
dół kloaczny [doow klo-ahch-ni] exp.: cesspool; latrine
kloaka [klo-ah-kah] f. latrine; cesspool; sink; sump; cloaca
kloakowy [klo-ah-ko-vi] adj.m. cloacal
kloc [klots] m. log; block; chunk; colloq: lout
klocek [klo-tsek] m. (small) log; block; chunk; building block
klocek hamulcowy [klo-tsek khah-mool-tso-vi] exp.: brake shoe
klockowy [klots-ko-vi] adj.m. of a small block

hamulec **klockowy** [khah-**moo**-lets klots-**ko**-vi] exp.: shoe brake; block brake
klocować [klo-**tso**-vahćh] v. prop mine corridors with logs (*repeatedly*)
klocowanie [klo-tso-**vah**-ńe] n. propping of a mine corridor with logs
klocowatość [klo-tso-**vah**-tośhćh] f. loutish character
klocowaty [klo-tso-**vah**-ti] adj.m. colloq: loutish (man, etc.)
klocowy [klo-**tso**-vi] adj.m. of a log; of logs
klocówka [klo-**tsoof**-kah] f. fire wall built of logs
klomb [klomp] m. flower bed
klombik [**klom**-beek] m. (small, nice) flower bed
klombowy [klom-**bo**-vi] adj.m. of a flower bed
klon [klon] m. maple (tree); clone; slang: child (mob jargon)
klonek [**klo**-nek] m. chub (fish); young maple tree
kloniczny [klo-**ńeech**-ni] adj.m. clonic (cramps, etc.)
klonik [klo-ńeek] m. young maple tree
klonina [klo-**ńee**-nah] m. maple wood
klonowaty [klo-no-**vah**-ti] adj.m. aceraceous; like a maple tree **klonowate** [klo-no-**vah-te**] pl. the Aceraceae family of (maple) trees
klonowy [klo-**no**-vi] adj.m. of a maple tree; maple (syrup, etc.)
klops [klops] m. meat loaf; colloq: flop; foozle; washout; slang: misfortune; a hopeless situation; loss in a card game; failing grade
klopsik [**klop**-śheek] m. (small, nice) meat loaf
klosterium [klos-**ter**-yoom] n. Closterium (alga)
klosz [klosh] m. glass cover; dish cover; lampshade; (skirt) flare
kloszard [**klo**-shahrt] m. homeless beggar; tramp
kloszowaty [kol-sho-**vah**-ti] adj.m. bell-like
kloszowo [kol-**sho**-vo] adv. in bell-shaped fashion
poszerzyć się kloszowo [po-**she**-zhićh śh<u>an</u> klo-**sho**-vo] exp.: to flare (out)
kloszowy [klo-**sho**-vi] adj.m. bell-shaped; flaring
kloszyk [**klo**-shik] m. (small) glass cover; lampshade; dish cover; flare (of a skirt)
klot [klot] m. cotton lining
klotoida [klo-**toy**-dah] f. flat curve used in the study of diffraction of light
klown [klahwn] m. clown
klownada [klahw-**nah**-dah] f. clowning; clownery; buffoonery
klownowski [klahw-**nof**-skee] adj.m. clownish; of a clown; of clowns
klozet [**klo**-zet] m. toilet
klozetowy [klo-ze-**to**-vi] adj.m. toilet (bowl, paper, etc.)
klub [kloop] m. club; union
kluba [**kloo**-bah] f. an instrument of torture; colloq: restraint; vice; pulley
klubik [**kloo**-beek] m. (small) club; union
klubista [kloo-**bees**-tah] m. member of a political club
klub-kawiarnia [kloop kah-**vyahr**-ńah] exp.: coffee shop in a club
klubokawiarnia [kloo-bo-kah-**vyahr**-ńah] f. coffee shop in a club
klubowicz [kloo-**bo**-veech] m. colloq: club-man; member of a club; slang: nose; man with a large nose (mob jargon)
klubowiec [kloo-**bo**-vyets] m. clubman; easy chair
klubowy [kloo-**bo**-vi] adj.m. of a club; club (member, etc.) **fotel klubowy** [**fo**-tel kloo-**bo**-vi] exp.: easy chair
kluch [klookh] m. ill-baked bread; clammy cake
klucha [**kloo**-khah] f. ill-baked bread; clammy cake; slang: fat woman; nose (mob jargon)
kluchowaty [kloo-kho-**vah**-ti] adj.m. clammy; ill-baked
klucie się [**kloo**-ćhe śh<u>an</u>] n. hatching; sprouting
klucz [klooch] m. key; wrench; passport; clue (to a riddle, etc.); code; glossary; crib; flock; flight

formation; keystone; headstone; landed estate
kluczenie [kloo-**che**-ńe] n. dodging
kluczka [**klooch**-kah] f. noose; loop; hitch; colloq: dodging
klucznica [klooch-**ńee**-tsah] f. housekeeper (in a manor)
klucznictwo [klooch-**ńee**-tstfo] n. management of landed property
klucznik [**klooch**-ńeek] m. stewart; slang: prison warden (mob jargon)
kluczować [kloo-**cho**-vahćh] v. send coded signals; classify according to a system (*repeatedly*)
kluczowanie [kloo-cho-**vah**-ńe] n. sending of coded signals; classifying (according to a system)
kluczowy [kloo-**cho**-vi] adj.m. pivotal; key (industry, etc.)
kluczyć [**kloo**-chićh] v. dodge; make a circuit; weave; take a roundabout way; colloq: be evasive; hedge (*repeatedly*)
kluczyk [**kloo**-chik] m. small key; primrose
kluć się [kloo**ć**h śhan] v. hatch; sprout (*repeatedly*)
klujnik [**klooy**-ńeek] m. hatching drawer; hatching box
klukać [**kloo**-kahćh] v. colloq: rumble; gurgle; cackle (*repeatedly*)
klupa [**kloo**-pah] f. diameter gauge (for logs)
klupować [kloo-**po**-vahćh] v. gauge diameters of logs (*repeatedly*)
klupowanie [kloo-po-**vah**-ńe] n. gauging of diameters of logs
kluseczek [kloo-**se**-chek] m. small dumpling
kluseczka [kloo-**sech**-kah] f. small dumpling
klusek [**kloo**-sek] m. boiled dough strip; dumpling; lump; noodle
kluska [**kloos**-kah] f. boiled dough strip; dumpling; lump; noodle
kluskowaty [kloos-ko-**vah**-ti] adj.m. clammy; ill-baked
kluskowy [kloos-**ko**-vi] adj.m. of boiled dough strip; of a dumpling; of a lump; of a noodle
kluszczanka [kloosh-**chahn**-kah] f. water in which noodles were boiled (used as food for swine, etc.)
kluza [**kloo**-zah] f. hawsehole; mooring pipe
kluzak [**kloo**-zahk] m. hawse bag
kluzja [**kloo**-zyah] f. Clusia (aromatic shrub or tree)
kłaczasty [kwah-**chahs**-ti] adj.m. fluffy; bushy (hair, etc.)
kłaczek [**kwah**-chek] m. flake; cluster; floccule; flocculus
kłaczkowaty [kwahch-ko-**vah**-ti] adj.m. flocculent; flaky; flocky
kład [kwaht] m. rabattment
kładka [**kwaht**-kah] f. foot-bridge; gangway; gangplank; brow
kładzenie [kwah-**dze**-ńe] n. laying down; setting; building (foundations, etc.)
kłak [kwahk] m. lock (of wool, etc.); shred; tuft; tag; wisp (of hair, etc.)
kłaki [**kwah**-kee] pl. oakum; cardings (of wool, hemp, etc.); colloq: shaggy hair; matted hair
kłam [kwahm] m. lie; falsehood
zadać kłam [zah-dahćh kwahm] exp.: to give the lie (to something, somebody)
kłamać [**kwah**-mahćh] v. lie; tell lies (*repeatedly*)
kłamanie [kwah-**mah**-ńe] n. lies
kłamca [**kwahm**-tsah] m. liar
kłamczuch [**kwahm**-chookh] m. colloq: liar; fibber; fibster; (false) storyteller; fabricator
kłamczucha [kwahm-**choo**-khah] f. colloq: (female) liar; fibber; fibster; (false) storyteller
kłamliwie [kwahm-**lee**-vye] adv. falsely; untruthfully; deceitfully; mendaciously
kłamliwość [kwahm-**lee**-vośhćh] f. falseness; deceitfulness; mendaciousness; mendacity
kłamliwy [kwahm-**lee**-vi] adj.m. deceitful; mendacious; lying; false; untruthful
kłamstewko [kwahm-**stef**-ko] n. fib; white lie; taradiddle; minor falsehood
kłamstwo [**kwahm**-stfo] n. lie; falsehood; untruth

stek kłamstw [stek kwahmstf] exp.: a pack of lies
kłaniać się [**kwah**-ńahćh śhan] v. salute; bow; greet; worship; nod (*repeatedly*)
kłaniam się [**kwah**-ńahm śhan] exp.: my greetings (to you); good morning; good afternoon; good evening; good-bye
kłańce [**kwahń**-tse] pl. wolf's teeth
kłap, kłap [kwahp kwahp] exp.: snap, snap (by animals)
kłapać [**kwah**-pahćh] v. snap; snap its teeth; rattle; clatter; slang: rattle away; talk; walk; eat; slap (mob jargon) (*repeatedly*)
kłapanie [kwah-**pah**-ńe] n. rattle; clatter; slang: speech of a defense lawyer (mob jargon)
kłapciasty [kwahp-**ćhahs**-ti] adj.m. loppy; drooping (ears, etc.)
kłapciaty [kwahp-**ćhah**-ti] adj.m. loppy; drooping (ears, etc.)
kłapczasty [kwahp-**chahs**-ti] adj.m. loppy; drooping (ears, etc.)
kłapiasty [kwahp-**yahs**-ti] adj.m. loppy; drooping (ears, etc.)
kłapiaty [kwahp-**yah**-ti] adj.m. loppy; drooping (ears, etc.)
kłapeć [**kwah**-pećh] m. shred
kłapnąć [**kwahp**-nownćh] v. snap; snap its teeth; rattle; clatter; slang: rattle away
kłapnięcie [kwahp-**ńan**-ćhe] n. a snap; snap
kłapouch [kwah-**po**-ookh] m. lop-eared donkey; lop-eared horse; lop-eared rabbit; slang: accuser; informer (mob jargon)
kłapouchy [kwah-po-**oo**-khi] adj.m. lop-eared; pl. lop-eared animals
kłaść [kwahśhćh] v. lay; put down; place; set; deposit; knock down; bend over; incline; go to bed; turn in; build (foundations, etc.); knock down; lay low; overturn; bring down; put on (clothes, etc.) (*repeatedly*)
kłaść się [kwahśhćh śhan] v. lay down; bend over; incline; go to bed; turn in; colloq: tumble in; slang: surrender; be arrested (mob jargon) (*repeatedly*)
kłaść się do grobu [kwahśhćh śhan do **gro**-boo] exp.: to go down to one's grave
kłąb [kwownp] m. clew; ball; skein (of yarn, etc.); puff (of smoke, etc.); hip; buttocks; rump; excrescence (on a tree, etc.)
kłącze [**kwown**-che] n. rootstock; rhizome
kłączowy [kwown-**cho**-vi] adj.m. rhizomic
kłębek [**kwan**-bek] m. ball (of thread); hunk of yarn; glomus
kłębiasty [kwan-**byahs**-ti] adj.m. whirling; swirling; cumulous
kłębić [**kwan**-beećh] v. whirl; swirl (*repeatedly*)
kłębić się [**kwan**-beećh śhan] v. whirl; swirl; surge; billow; roll (*repeatedly*)
kłębienie [kwan-**bye**-ńe] n. whirl
kłębienie się [kwan-**bye**-ńe śhan] n. whirling
kłębowisko [kwan-bo-**vees**-ko] n. whirl; swirl; vortex; whirling masses; eddying masses
kłębuszek [kwan-**boo**-shek] m. (small) clew; ball; skein (of yarn, etc.); puff (of smoke, etc.); glomerule; glomerulus
kłobuczka [kwo-**booch**-kah] f. herb of the genus Torilis
kłobuk [**kwo**-book] m. headgear; bud
kłoć [kwoćh] f. straw; twig rush
kłoda [**kwo**-dah] f. log; clog
kłodowisko [kwo-do-**vees**-ko] n. log storage
kłodowy [kwo-**do**-vi] adj.m. log (storage, cabin, etc.)
kłodzina [kwo-**dźhee**-nah] f. branchless trunk (of a palm, etc.)
kłokoczka [kwo-**koch**-kah] f. bladdernut (shrub)
kłokoczkowaty [kwo-koch-ko-**vah**-ti] adj.m. of the bladdernut family
kłokoczkowate [kwo-koch-ko-**vah**-te] pl. the bladdernut family
kłomia [**kwo**-myah] f. triangular net
kłomla [**kwom**-lah] f. triangular net
kłonica [kwo-**ńee**-tsah] f. stanchion; stake
kłonicowy [kwo-ńee-**tso**-vi] adj.m. of stanchion (connection)
kłonić [**kwo**-ńeećh] v. bend

(*repeatedly*)
kłonić się [**kwo**-ńeećh śhan] v. bend; take a bow; incline (*repeatedly*)
kłonienie [kwo-**ńe**-ńe] n. bending
kłonienie się [kwo-**ńe**-ńe śhan] n. paying tribute
kłopot [**kwo**-pot] m. trouble; bother; nuisance; inconvenience; a fix; difficulty; quandary; predicament
kłopoty [kwo-**po**-ti] pl. difficulties; straits; involved circumstances; a bad plight
być w kłopocie [bićh f kwo-**po**-ćhe] exp.: to be in trouble
sprawić komuś kłopot [**sprah**-veećh ko-moośh **kwo**-pot] exp.: to inconvenience somebody; to put somebody to trouble
kłopotać [kwo-**po**-tahćh] v. trouble; disturb; worry (*repeatedly*)
kłopotać się [kwo-**po**-tahćh śhan] v. worry (about); concern oneself (about) (*repeatedly*)
kłopotanie [kwo-po-**tah**-ńe] n. troubling
kłopotanie się [kwo-po-**tah**-ńe śhan] n. troubling oneself
kłopotliwie [kwo-pot-**lee**-vye] adv. troublesomely; vexatiously; bafflingly; inconveniently; perplexedly; incommodiously
kłopotliwy [kwo-pot-**lee**-vi] adj.m. troublesome; baffling; inconvenient; perplexing; vexatious
kłopotliwe pytanie [kwo-pot-**lee**-ve pi-**tah**-ńe] exp.: teaser; twister; an embarrassing question
kłos [kwos] m. (corn) ear
kłosarka [kwo-**sahr**-kah] f. gleaner
kłosek [**kwo**-sek] m. spicule; spikelet
kłosić się [**kwo**-śheećh śhan] v. ear; form ears; head (*repeatedly*)
kłosie [**kwo**-śhe] n. ears (of corn)
kłosisty [kwo-**śhees**-ti] adj.m. full-eared
kłosiście [kwo-**śheeśh**-ćhe] adv. with full ears
kłosokształtny [kwo-so-**kshtahwt**-ni] adj.m. ear-shaped; spiky; spikelike; spicular; resembling a spike
kłosować [kwo-**so**-vahćh] v. ear; form ears (*repeatedly*)
kłosować się [kwo-**so**-vahćh śhan] v. ear; form ears; head (*repeatedly*)
kłosowanie [kwo-so-**vah**-ńe] n. forming ears (of corn, etc.)
kłosowanie się [kwo-so-**vah**-ńe śhan] n. forming ears (of corn, etc.)
kłosowaty [kwo-so-**vah**-ti] adj.m. ear-shaped; spiky; spikelike; spicular
kłosownica [kwo-sov-**ńee**-tsah] f. false bromegrass
kłosownik [kwo-**sov**-ńeek] m. husking tool
kłosowy [kwo-**so**-vi] adj.m. ear forming (plants, etc.)
kłosówka [kwo-**soof**-kah] f. soft grass; velvet grass
kłoszenie się [kwo-**she**-ńe śhan] n. forming ears
kłośny [**kwośh**-ni] adj.m. full-eared
kłowy [**kwo**-vi] adj.m. of tusk; of fang
kłócenie [kwoo-**tse**-ńe] n. making a quarrel; fomenting a quarrel
kłócenie się [kwoo-**tse**-ńe śhan] n. quarreling; colloq: having words
kłócić [**kwoo**-ćheećh] v. stir; agitate; mix; disturb; shake; stir up; colloq: set at loggerheads; disturb (*repeatedly*)
kłócić się [**kwoo**-ćheećh śhan] v. quarrel; altercate; clash; jar; be out of accord; be at variance; colloq: have words (*repeatedly*)
kłódeczka [kwoo-**dech**-kah] f. small padlock
kłódka [**kwoot**-kah] f. padlock
kłódkarz [**kwoot**-kahsh] m. padlock maker
kłótliwie [kwoot-**lee**-vye] adv. quarrelsomely; cantankerously
kłótliwość [kwoot-**lee**-vośhćh] f. quarrelsomeness; cantankerousness; quarrelsome disposition; wrangling disposition
kłótliwy [kwoot-**lee**-vi] adj.m. quarrelsome; cantankerous
kłótnia [**kwoot**-ńah] f. quarrel; brawl; wrangle; bicker; row; altercation; squabble

kłótnica [kwoot-ńee-tsah] f. (female) quarreller; brawler; wrangler; squabbler
kłótnik [**kwoot**-ńeek] m. quarreller; brawler; wrangler; squabbler
kłucie [**kwoo**-će] n. stings; sting; shooting pain; piercing pain
kłucie się [**kwoo**-će śhan] n. stinging oneself
kłuć [kwooćh] v. stab; prick; sting; spear; prod; jab; poke; bite; give shooting pains; be an eyesore; slang: tattoo; inject narcotics (mob jargon) (*repeatedly*)
kłuć się [kwooćh śhan] v. prick (one's finger, etc.); stab each other (*repeatedly*)
kłujący [kwoo-yown-tsi] adj.m. prickly; shooting; piercing; stinging
kłujka [**kwooy**-kah] f. (insect's) proboscis
kłus [kwoos] m. trot; jog trot
jechać kłusem [ye-khahćh **kwoo**-sem] exp.: to trot (along)
jechać wolnym kłusem [ye-khahćh **vol**-nim **kwoo**-sem] exp.: to jog along
kłusem [**kwoo**-sem] exp.: at a trot
wolny kłus [**vol**-ni kwoos] exp.: gentle trot
wyciągnięty kłus [vi-ćhowng-ńan-ti kwoos] exp.: fast trot
kłusak [**kwoo**-sahk] m. trotter
kłusik [**kwoo**-śheek] m. gentle trot
kłusować [kwoo-**so**-vahćh] v. trot; poach (*repeatedly*)
kłusowanie [kwoo-so-**vah**-ńe] n. trot; poaching
kłusownictwo [kwoo-sov-**ńeets**-tfo] n. poaching
kłusowniczy [kwoo-sov-**ńee**-chi] adj.m. poacher's
kłusownik [kwoo-**sov**-ńeek] m. poacher; trespassing hunter
kłuty [**kwoo**-ti] adj.m. stab (wound, etc.); punctured (wound, etc.)
kłykcina [kwik-**ćhee**-nah] f. condyloma; warty growth on the skin (near the anus and genital organs)
kłykciny [kwik-**ćhee**-ni] pl. skin warts
kłykciowy [kwik-**ćho**-vi] adj.m. condyloid
kłykieć [**kwi**-kećh] m. condyle
kmiecy [**kmye**-tsi] adj.m. peasant's; serf's; peasants'; colloq: yokel's
kmieć [kmyećh] m. peasant; serf; colloq: yokel
kmin [kmeen] m. cumin plant; cumin; caraway seeds
kminek [**kmee**-nek] m. cumin; caraway (plant)
kminkowy [kmeen-**ko**-vi] adj.m. caraway (seed, oil, etc.)
kminkówka [kmeen-**koof**-kah] f. cumin-flavored vodka; caraway seed flavored liqueur
kmiotek [**kmyo**-tek] m. colloq: yokel
kmotr [kmotr] m. godfather; colloq: chum; crony
knaga [**knah**-gah] f. cleat; belaying deck; colloq: large bone
knajacki [knah-**yahts**-kee] adj.m. colloq: of a tramp; of a vagrant; of a street-smart guy
knajak [**knah**-yahk] m. colloq: tramp; vagrant; street-smart guy
knajpa [**knahy**-pah] f. colloq: taproom; drinking den; dive; tavern; pub; saloon
knajpiany [knahy-**pyah**-ni] adj.m. saloon (brawl, manners, etc.)
knajpiarski [knahy-**pyahr**-skee] adj.m. saloon (manners, etc.)
knajpiarz [**knahy**-pyahsh] m. saloon owner; taproom owner; saloon customer
knajpka [**knahyp**-kah] f. colloq: (small) taproom; drinking den; dive; tavern; pub; saloon
knajpować [knahy-**po**-vahćh] v. spend time in a drinking den (*repeatedly*)
knajpowy [knahy-**po**-vi] adj.m. saloon (brawl, manners, etc.)
knaster [**knah**-ster] m. canaster (tobacco)
knebel [**kne**-bel] m. gag
kneblować [kne-**blo**-vahćh] v. gag (*repeatedly*)
kneblowanie [kne-blo-**vah**-ńe] n. gagging
knecht [knekht] m. lansquenet; bollard; mooring post
knedel [**kne**-del] m. a kind of dumpling

knel [knel] m. meatball
kniahini [kńah-**khee**-ńee] f. Ukrainian princess
kniazić [**kńah**-źheećh] v. scream with fear and pain (of a hare) (*repeatedly*)
kniazienie [kńah-**źhe**-ńe] n. scream with fear and pain (of a hare)
kniaziówna [kńah-**źhoov**-nah] f. princess (Ukrainian, Lithuanian)
kniaź [kńahśh] m. prince (Ukrainian, Lithuanian); the sound of scream with fear and pain (of a hare)
knidoblast [kńee-**do**-blahst] m. cnidoblast; ectodermal cell of sponges
knidoblasty [knee-do-**blahs**-ti] pl. ectodermal cells of sponges
knieć [kńećh] m. marsh marigold
knieja [**kńe**-yah] f. forest; woods; dragnet
kniejowy [kńe-**yo**-vi] adj.m. of a forest; of woods
kniejówka [kńe-**yoof**-kah] f. shotgun-rifle combination; hunting trumpet
knocenie [kno-**tse**-ńe] n. bungling; botching
knocić [**kno**-ćheećh] v. bungle; botch (*repeatedly*)
knock-down [**nok**-dahwn] m. (Engl.) knockdown
knock-out [**nok**-ahwt] m. knockout
knot [knot] m. (candle) wick; snuff; colloq: fuse; kid; bad grade; bungle; a botch
dostać knoty [**dos**-tahćh **kno**-ti] exp.: to get a thrashing; to get licked
knotowy [kno-**to**-vi] adj.m. of (candle) wick
knować [**kno**-vahćh] v. plot; scheme; devise; conspire; machinate; intrigue (*repeatedly*)
knowanie [kno-**vah**-ńe] n. plotting; scheming; devising; conspiring; machinating; intriguing
knowie [**kno**-vye] n. bottom of a sheaf; sheaf base
knucie [**knoo**-ćhe] n. plotting; scheming; devising; conspiring; machinating; intriguing
knuć [knooćh] v. plot; scheme; devise; conspire; machinate; intrigue (*repeatedly*)
knur [knoor] m. boar (male of a domesticated swine)
knurek [**knoo**-rek] m. young boar (male of a domesticated swine)
knurowaty [knoo-ro-**vah**-ti] adj.m. boarish
knut [knoot] m. knout; whip
knykieć [**kni**-k̲ećh] m. knuckle
knyp [knip] m. shoemaker's paring knife
knypel [**kni**-pel] m. mallet
ko- [ko] prefix: co-; with; together; joint; jointly; relating to
koacerwat [ko-ah-**tser**-vaht] m. coacervate
koacerwaty [ko-ah-tser-**vah**-ti] pl. coacervate drops
koadiutor [ko-ah-**dyoo**-tor] m. coadjutor
koadiutoria [ko-ah-dyoo-**tor**-yah] f. the office of coadjutor
koadiutorka [ko-ah-dyoo-**tor**-kah] f. nun-coadjutor; coadjutrix
koadiutura [ko-ah-dyoo-**too**-rah] f. the office of coadjutor
koadiuturka [ko-ah-dyoo-**toor**-kah] f. nun-coadjutor; coadjutrix
koafiura [ko-ah-**fyoo**-rah] f. hairdo; coiffure
koagulacja [ko-ah-goo-**lah**-tsyah] f. coagulation
koagulant [ko-ah-**goo**-lahnt] m. coagulant
koagulat [ko-ah-**goo**-laht] m. coagulum; gel formed during coagulation
koagulator [ko-ah-goo-**lah**-tor] m. coagulant
koagulować [ko-ah-goo-**lo**-vahćh] v. coagulate (*repeatedly*)
koagulować się [ko-ah-goo-**lo**-vahćh śh̲a̲n̲] v. coagulate (*repeatedly*)
koagulowanie [ko-ah-goo-lo-**vah**-ńe] n. coagulation
koaksjalnie [ko-ahks-**yahl**-ńe] adv. coaxially
koaksjalny [ko-ahks-**yahl**-ni] adj.m. coaxial
koala [ko-**ah**-lah] f. koala bear
koalicja [ko-ah-**lee**-tsyah] f. coalition; temporary union

(alliance)
koalicyjka [ko-ah-lee-**tsiy**-kah] f. coalition belt (with a strap over the left shoulder)
koalicyjny [ko-ah-lee-**tsiy**-ni] adj.m. coalition (cabinet, etc.)
koartykulacja [ko-ahr-ti-koo-**lah**-tsyah] f. coarticulation (in speech)
kobalamina [ko-bah-lah-**me**-nah] f. cobalamin; cobalamine
kobalt [**ko**-bahlt] m. cobalt (atomic number 27)
kobaltawy [ko-bahl-**tah**-vi] adj.m. cobaltous
kobaltować [ko-bahl-**to**-vahćh] v. coat with cobalt (*repeatedly*)
kobaltowanie [ko-bahl-to-**vah**-ńe] n. coating with cobalt
kobaltowy [ko-bahl-**to**-vi] adj.m. cobaltic (compound, etc.); cobalt (bomb, blue, etc.)
kobaltron [ko-**bahl**-tron] m. cobalt bomb
kobaltyn [ko-**bahl**-tin] m. cobaltite
kobczyk [**kop**-chik] m. red-legged falcon
kobiałka [ko-**byahw**-kah] f. wicker-basket; chip basket; pottle
kobieciarstwo [ko-bye-**ćhahr**-stfo] n. gallivanting; dangling after women; philandering
kobieciarz [ko-**bye**-ćhahsh] m. lady chaser; lady's man
kobieciątko [ko-bye-**ćh**<u>own</u>**t**-ko] n. (silly) woman
kobiecina [ko-bye-**ćhee**-nah] f. (poor) woman
kobiecinka [ko-bye-**ćheen**-kah] f. (old, poor) woman
kobieco [ko-**bye**-tso] adv. like a woman; womanishly
kobiecość [ko-**bye**-tsośhćh] f. womanhood; womanliness; femininity; feminineness
kobiecy [ko-**bye**-tsi] adj.m. female; womanish; feminine; womanlike; womanly; woman's; women's
po kobiecemu [po ko-bye-**tse**-moo] exp.: after the manner of women; like a woman
kobiercowy [ko-byer-**tso**-vi] adj.m. carpet (factory, etc.)
kobiernictwo [ko-byer-**ńee**-tstfo] n. carpet-weaving
kobierzec [ko-**bye**-zhets] m. carpet; anything like a carpet
kobieta [ko-**bye**-tah] f. woman; female
kobieta lekkich obyczajów [ko-**bye**-tah **lek**-keekh o-bi-**chah**-yoof] exp.: prostitute
kobieta ulicy [ko-**bye**-tah oo-**lee**-tsi] exp.: streetwalker; prostitute
kobiety [ko-**bye**-ti] pl. women; the womenfolk
równouprawnienie kobiet [roov-no-oo-prahv-**ńe**-ńe **ko**-byet] exp.: woman's (equal) rights
kobietka [ko-**byet**-kah] f. (energetic, clever, good looking) woman; female
kobold [**ko**-bolt] m. kobold (of German folklore)
kobra [**kob**-rah] f. cobra (snake)
kobuz [**ko**-boos] m. English hobby (hawk)
kobylak [ko-**bi**-lahk] m. sorrel (plant)
kobylarz [ko-**bi**-lahsh] m. knacker; harness maker; saddle maker
kobylasty [ko-bi-**lahs**-ti] adj.m. like a clumsy old mare; misshapen
kobyli [ko-**bi**-lee] adj.m. of a mare; mare's (milk, etc.)
kobyła [ko-**bi**-wah] f. mare; slang: fat woman; old, disliked teacher
kobyłka [ko-**biw**-kah] f. (small) mare
kobza [**kob**-zah] f. bagpipe
kobziarz [**kob**-źhahsh] m. bagpipe-player
koc [kots] m. blanket; coverlet
kocanka [ko-**tsahn**-kah] f. catkin; lamb's tail (flower)
kocenie się [ko-**tse**-ńe śh<u>an</u>] n. giving birth (to kittens, hares, goats, sheep, etc.); throwing (kittens, hares, goats, sheep, etc.)
kochać [**ko**-khahćh] v. love; cherish; hold dear; have an affection (for); be in love (with); be soft on (somebody); be extremely fond (of); colloq: love (to dance, eat, etc.) (*repeatedly*)
kochać się [**ko**-khahćh śh<u>an</u>] v. be in love; love each other; cherish one another; have sex (*repeatedly*)
kochający [ko-khah-**y**<u>own</u>-tsi] adj.m.

loving; affectionate; fond; (in letters:) yours affectionate
kochaneczek [ko-khah-**ne**-chek] m. (sweet) lover; paramour; love
kochaneczka [ko-khah-**nech**-kah] f. (sweet) lover; paramour; love
kochanek [ko-**khah**-nek] m. lover; paramour; my dear; my love
kochanie [ko-**khah**-ńe] n. love; darling; sweetheart; affection; fondness; colloq: honey; my sweet; dearest; my love; darling
kochanie się [ko-**khah**-ńe śhan] n. being in love; loving each other
kochanka [ko-**khan**-kah] f. mistress
kochana [ko-**khah**-nah] adj.f. beloved; loving; affectionate; f. the woman (somebody) loves; (one's) love; (one's) beloved
kochany [ko-**khah**-ni] adj.m. beloved; loving; affectionate; m. the man (or boy) (somebody) loves; (one's) love; dear (friend)
kochaś [ko-khahśh] m. colloq: dear boy; dear fellow
kocher [**ko**-kher] m. cooker; Mayo Oschner's forceps
kochinchina [ko-kheen-**khee**-nah] f. Cochin hen
kochliwość [kokh-**lee**-vośhćh] f. amorousness; amorous disposition
kochliwy [kokh-**lee**-vi] adj.m. amorous; (the one) easily falling in love; easily in love
koci [**ko**-ćhee] adj.m. cat's; catlike; cattish; velvety (step, etc.); feline
kocia muzyka [**ko**-ćhah moo-**zi**-kah] exp.: catcall; caterwaul; harsh cry
kocie łby [**ko**-ćhe wbi] exp.: cobblestones
kociak [**ko**-ćhahk] m. kitty-cat; colloq: lassie; lass(Brit.); pinup girl; peach; smasher
kociara [ko-**ćhah**-rah] f. (woman) cat-lover
kociarnia [ko-**ćhahr**-ńah] f. cat-breeding and rearing place; multitude of cats
kociarz [**ko**-ćhahsh] m. cat-lover; cat-breeder
kociątko [ko-**ćhownt**-ko] n. kitten; kitty-cat
kocica [ko-**ćhee**-tsah] f. she-cat; (female) cat; (female) hare
kocić się [**ko**-ćheećh śhan] v. kitten; bring forth kittens (hares, goats, sheep, etc.) (*repeatedly*)
kocielić [ko-**ćhe**-leećh] v. call (by red grouse) (*repeatedly*)
kocię [**ko**-ćhan] n. kitten; kitty-cat
kocięta [ko-**ćhan**-tah] pl. litter
kocimięta [ko-ćhee-**myan**-tah] f. catmint; catnip
kocimiętka [ko-ćhee-**myant**-kah] f. catmint; catnip
kocina [ko-**ćhee**-nah] m. & f. colloq: pussy cat
kocio [**ko**-ćho] adv. catlike
kociokwik [ko-**ćho**-kfeek] m. colloq: katzenjammer; hangover; depression; a discordant clamor
kocioł [**ko**-ćhow] m. kettle; boiler; pot; cauldron; kettledrum; geological sink (pothole); encirclement; (police) trap
kociołek [ko-**ćho**-wek] m. (small) kettle; boiler; pot
kociołkowaty [ko-ćhow-ko-**vah**-ti] adj.m. cauldron-shaped
kociołkowy [ko-ćhoow-**ko**-vi] adj.m. of a kettle; of kettles
kocisko [ko-**ćhees**-ko] n. Tomcat
kociuba [ko-**ćhoo**-bah] f. fire-rake; stirrer; poker
kocmołuch [kots-**mo**-wookh] m. sloven; sloppy (person); slut; slattern (female); shut
kocować [ko-**tso**-vahćh] v. pack (a patient with blankets) (*repeatedly*)
kocowanie [ko-tso-**vah**-ńe] n. packing (a patient with blankets)
kocówa [ko-**tsoo**-vah] f. beating of a man wrapped in a blanket and unable to see who is hitting him
kocur [**ko**-tsoor] m. Tomcat; colloq: male feline (lynx, wildcat, etc.)
kocyk [**ko**-tsik] m. (small, nice) blanket; coverlet
kocz [koch] m. carriage
koczek [**ko**-chek] m. (small) bun; bob; chignon; topknot
koczkodan [koch-**ko**-dahn] m. talapoin (monkey); vervet (monkey); colloq: dowdy; frump; fright; scarecrow
koczować [ko-**cho**-vahćh] v. lead nomadic life; become nomadic;

wander about; be encamped; bivouac; inhabit (animals in a forest, etc.) (*repeatedly*)
koczowanie [ko-cho-**vah**-ńe] n. migrations; wanderings; nomadism
koczowisko [ko-cho-**vees**-ko] n. camping-place; bivouac; lair (of a deer, etc.)
koczownictwo [ko-chov-**ńeets**-tfo] n. nomadism
koczowniczo [ko-chov-**ńee**-cho] adv. like a nomad; like nomads
koczowniczy [ko-chov-**ńee**-chi] adj.m. migratory; wandering; nomadic; roving
koczownik [ko-**chov**-ńeek] m. nomad; wanderer; vagrant
koczyk [**ko**-chik] m. small carriage
kod [kot] m. code
koda [ko-dah] f. coda (music)
kodak [**ko**-dahk] m. kodak (camera)
kodeina [ko-de-**ee**-nah] f. codeine
kodeks [**ko**-deks] m. (legal) code
kodeksowy [ko-dek-**so**-vi] adj.m. of a (legal) code
koder [**ko**-der] m. encoding machine
kodopis [ko-**do**-pees] m. code-printer; card perforating machine
kodować [ko-**do**-vahćh] v. encode; code (*repeatedly*)
kodowanie [ko-do-**vah**-ńe] n. encoding; coding
kodowy [ko-**do**-vi] adj.m. of a code; code (number, etc.)
kodycyl [ko-**di**-tsil] m. codicil
kodycylowy [ko-di-tsi-**lo**-vi] adj.m. codicillary; supplementary
kodyfikacja [ko-di-fee-**kah**-tsyah] f. codification
kodyfikacyjny [ko-di-fee-kah-**tsiy**-ni] adj.m. of codification; codifying (committee, etc.)
kodyfikator [ko-di-fee-**kah**-tor] m. codifier
kodyfikatorka [ko-di-fee-kah-**tor**-kah] f. (woman) codifier
kodyfikatorski [ko-di-fee-kah-**tor**-skee] adj.m. codifier's; codifying
kodyfikować [ko-di-fee-**ko**-vahćh] v. codify; encode (*repeatedly*)
kodyfikowanie [ko-di-fee-ko-**vah**-ńe] n. codification
koedukacja [ko-e-doo-**kah**-tsyah] f. coeducation (of both sexes)
koedukacyjny [ko-e-doo-kah-**tsiy**-ni] adj.m. coeducational
koedycja [ko-e-**di**-tsyah] f. joint publication
koedycyjny [ko-e-di-**tsiy**-ni] adj.m. of joint publication
koedytor [ko-e-**di**-tor] m. one in a group of joint publishers
koegzystencja [ko-eg-zis-**ten**-tsyah] f. coexistence
koegzystencjalny [ko-eg-zis-ten-**tsyahl**-ni] adj.m. of coexistence
koegzystencyjnie [ko-eg-zis-ten-**tsiy**-ńe] adv. coexistensively
koegzystencyjny [ko-eg-zis-ten-**tsiy**-ni] adj.m. of coexistence; coexistensive
koegzystować [ko-eg-zis-**to**-vahćh] v. coexist (*repeatedly*)
koegzystowanie [ko-eg-zis-to-**vah**-ńe] n. coexistence
koel [**ko**-el] m. variety of cuckoo bird
koendu [ko-**en**-doo] n. Coendou porcupine
koenzym [ko-**en**-zim] m. coenzyme
koenzymy [ko-en-**zi**-mi] pl. coenzymes
koercja [ko-**er**-tsyah] f. coercion; coercive force
kofeina [ko-fe-**ee**-nah] f. caffeine; alkaloid in coffee
koga [**ko**-gah] f. (medieval Baltic) sailing ship
kogel-mogel [**ko**-gel **mo**-gel] m. colloq: egg yolk stirred with sugar
kognacja [kog-**nah**-tsyah] f. kinship on father's (or mother's) side
kognat [**kog**-naht] m. blood relative
kognicja [kog-**ńee**-tsyah] f. cognition; study (of a legal matter)
kognitywny [kog-ńee-**tiv**-ni] adj.m. cognitive (psychology, dissonance, etc.)
koguci [ko-**goo**-ćhee] adj.m. cock's; rooster's; colloq: small; diminutive; pertly combative; saucy
waga kogucia [**vah**-gah ko-**goo**-ćhah] exp.: bantam weight
kogucik [ko-**goo**-ćheek] m. weathercock; vane; cowlick;

(name of a) headache powder
kogucio [ko-goo-ćho] adv. like a cock; like a rooster
kogucisko [ko-goo-ćhees-ko] n. an old cock; nasty rooster
kogut [ko-goot] m. cock; rooster
kogutek [ko-goo-tek] m. weathercock; vane; cowlick; (name of a) headache powder
koherencja [ko-khe-ren-tsyah] f. coherence
brak koherencji [brahk ko-khe-ren-tsyee] exp.: incoherence
koherencyjny [ko-khe-ren-tsiy-ni] adj.m. of coherence
koherentność [ko-khe-rent-nośhćh] f. coherence; coherency
koherentnie [ko-khe-rent-ńe] adv. coherently
koherentny [ko-khe-rent-ni] adj.m. coherent
kohezja [ko-khe-zyah] f. cohesion
kohleria [ko-ler-yah] f. Kohler's (flower)
kohorta [ko-khor-tah] f. cohort
koiciel [ko-ee-ćhel] m. soother
koić [ko-eećh] v. soothe; calm; comfort; ease (pain); relieve (pain); bring peace (*repeatedly*)
koincydencja [ko-een-tsi-den-tsyah] f. coincidence
koincydencyjnie [ko-een-tsi-den-tsiy-ńe] adv. coincidentally
koincydencyjny [ko-een-tsi-den-tsiy-ni] adj.m. coincidental
koine [koy-ne] n. koine (Greek lingua franca of the Hellenic and Roman period)
koja [ko-yah] f. bunk bed
kojarzenie [ko-yah-zhe-ńe] n. matching; association (of ideas, etc.); union; coordination (of movements, etc.); linking
kojarzenie się [ko-yah-zhe-ńe śhan] n. matching with one another; forming an association
kojarzeniowy [ko-yah-zhe-ńo-vi] adj.m. associative
kojarzyć [ko-yah-zhićh] v. unite; bind; join; link; connect; put together; associate (ideas, etc.) (*repeatedly*)
kojarzyć się [ko-yah-zhićh śhan] v. unite; bind; join; link; connect; go together; associate (ideas, etc.); bring to one's mind (*repeatedly*)
kojąco [ko-yown-tso] adv. restfully; soothingly; balmily
kojący [ko-yown-tsi] adj.m. soothing; comforting; balmy
kojczyk [koy-chik] m. (small) coop; (chicken) pen
kojec [ko-yets] m. coop; pen
kojenie [ko-ye-ńe] n. alleviation; relief (from pain)
kojfnąć [koyf-nownćh] v. slang: kick the bucket; die (mob jargon)
kojot [ko-yot] m. coyote
kok [kok] m. bob; bun; chignon; topknot; variety of pigeon; colloq: ship's cook
koka [ko-kah] f. coca; slang: cocaine (mob jargon)
kokać [ko-kahćh] v. cackle (*repeatedly*)
kokaina [ko-kah-ee-nah] f. cocaine; an alkaloid addicting drug
kokainista [ko-kah-ee-ńees-tah] m. cocaine addict; cocainist
kokainistka [ko-kah-ee-ńeest-kah] f. (female) cocaine addict; cocainist
kokainistyczny [ko-kah-ee-ńees-tich-ni] adj.m. of cocaine; cocainist's
kokainizm [ko-kah-ee-ńeezm] m. cocainism; addiction to cocaine
kokainizować [ko-kah-ee-ńee-zo-vahćh] v. cocainize (*repeatedly*)
kokainizowanie [ko-kah-ee-ńee-zo-vah-ńe] n. cocainization; addiction to cocaine
kakainowy [ko-kah-ee-no-vi] adj.m. of cocaine
kokarda [ko-kahr-dah] f. rosette; bow; slipknot; truelove knot
kokardka [ko-kahrt-kah] f. (small, nice) rosette; bow; slipknot; truelove knot
kokcielić [kok-ćhe-leećh] v. call (by a grouse) (*repeatedly*)
kokcydioza [kok-tsi-dyo-zah] f. coccidiosis (infestation)
koker [ko-ker] m. cocker spaniel
kokieta [ko-ke-tah] f. flirt; coquette
kokieteria [ko-ke-ter-yah] f. coquetry; skittishness
kokieteryjnie [ko-ke-te-riy-ńe] adv. with coquetry; flirtatiously; skittishly; saucily

kokieteryjny [ko-k̲e-te-**riy**-ni] adj.m. coquettish; flirtatious
kokietka [ko-**k̲et**-kah] f. flirt; coquette
kokietliwy [ko-k̲et-**lee**-vi] adj.m. coquettish; flirtatious
kokietować [ko-k̲e-**to**-vahćh] v. flirt; court; woo; coquet (*repeatedly*)
kokietowanie [ko-k̲e-to-**vah**-ńe] n. flirting; courting; wooing
kokila [ko-**kee**-lah] f. metal mold; gravity die
kokilarka [ko-kee-**lahr**-kah] f. foundry equipment for filling the gravity dies
kokilarz [ko-**kee**-lahsh] m. worker with foundry equipment for filling the gravity dies
kokilia [ko-**keel**-yah] f. ornament made out of sea shells
kokilka [ko-**keel**-kah] f. plate made out of sea shells
kokilownia [ko-kee-**lov**-ńah] f. housing of foundry equipment for filling the gravity dies
kokilowy [ko-kee-**lo**-vi] adj.m. of foundry equipment for filling the gravity dies
koklusz [**kok**-loosh] m. whooping cough; pertussis
kokluszowy [kok-loo-**sho**-vi] adj.m. of whooping cough; pertussal
ko-ko-ko [ko-ko-ko] exp.: cackle
kokolit [ko-**ko**-leet] m. coccolith
kokolity [ko-ko-**lee**-ti] pl. coccoliths (microscopic calcareous body found in chalk)
kokon [**ko**-kon] m. cocoon; follicle
kokon jedwabnika [**ko**-kon yed-vahb-**ńee**-kah] exp.: pod
kokonizacja [ko-ko-ńee-**zah**-tsyah] f. cocooning; wrapping tightly
kokornak [ko-**kor**-nahk] m. birthwort (plant)
kokornakowaty [ko-kor-nah-ko-**vah**-ti] adj.m. aristolochiaceous
kokornakowate [ko-kor-nah-ko-**vah**-te] pl. aristolochiaceae
kokorycz [ko-**ko**-rich] f. corydalis
kokoryczka [ko-ko-**rich**-kah] f. Solomon's seal; pearlweed; sealwort; lily of the mountain
kokos [**ko**-kos] m. coconut; coco; coker (Brit.); coconut tree; coco-tree; colloq: good business; a grand thing; slang: fist; bump on a forehead (mob jargon)
kokosić się [ko-**ko**-śheećh śh<u>an</u>] v. colloq: fidget (*repeatedly*)
kokosowiec [ko-ko-**so**-vyets] m. coconut; coco; coker; coconut-tree; coco-tree
kokosowy [ko-ko-**so**-vi] adj.m. coconut (milk, matting, etc.); coconut (tree)
kokosowy interes [ko-ko-**so**-vi een-**te**-res] exp.: colloq: golden opportunity (in business)
orzech kokosowy [**o**-zhekh ko-ko-**so**-vi] exp.: coconut
włókno kokosowe [**vwook**-no ko-ko-**so**-ve] exp.: coir (fiber)
kokosz [**ko**-kosh] f. brood hen; laying hen; gallinule; waterhen; moorhen
kokosza wojna [ko-**ko**-shah **voy**-nah] exp.: nobles' rebellion in Poland (1537)
kokoszenie się [ko-ko-**she**-ńe śh<u>an</u>] n. colloq: being fidgety
kokoszka [ko-**kosh**-kah] f. brood hen; laying hen; gallinule; water hen; moorhen
kokoszyć się [ko-**ko**-shićh śh<u>an</u>] v. colloq: fidget
kokota [ko-**ko**-tah] f. cocotte; courtesan; slang: tart; prostitute
kokpit [**kok**-peet] m. (airplane's, yacht's) cockpit
koks [koks] m. coke; gas coke; mob slang: rye bread; cocaine
być na koksie [bićh nah **kok**-śhe] exp.: slang: to be on dope; to get high (mob jargon)
koks gazowniczy [koks gah-zov-**ńee**-chi] exp.: gas coke
koks hutniczy [koks khoot-**ńee**-chi] exp.: metallurgical coke
koks naftowy [koks nahf-**to**-vi] exp.: petroleum coke
koks odlewniczy [koks od-lev-**ńee**-chi] exp.: foundry coke
koks opałowy [koks o-pah-**wo**-vi] exp.: domestic coke
koks pakowy [koks pah-**ko**-vi] exp.: pitch coke
koksa [**kok**-sah] f. a variety of

rennet apple
koksagiz [kok-**sah**-gees] m. a caoutchouc-yielding plant
koksiak [**kok**-śhahk] m. colloq: coke stove; fire-basket; brazier; salamander; slang: rye bread
koksiarnia [kok-**śhahr**-ńah] f. coking plant; cokery
koksiarz [**kok**-śhahsh] m. coke-maker; cokeman; slang: drug addict (mob jargon)
koksik [**kok**-śheek] m. (coke) breeze; fly ash; quick coke
koksochemia [kok-so-**khe**-myah] f. chemistry of coke
koksochemiczny [kok-so-khe-**meech**-ni] adj.m. of the chemistry of coke
koksochemik [kok-so-**khe**-meek] m. specialist in the chemistry of coke
koksopochodny [kok-so-po-**khod**-ni] adj.m. derived from coke
koksować [kok-**so**-vahćh] v. coke (*repeatedly*)
koksowanie [kok-so-**vah**-ńe] n. (high temperature) carbonization; slang: taking drugs (mob jargon)
koksownia [kok-**sov**-ńah] f. coking plant; cokery
koksowniany [kok-sov-**ńah**-ni] adj.m. of coke engineering
koksownictwo [kok-sov-**ńee**-tstfo] n. coke engineering
koksowniczy [kok-sov-**ńee**-chi] adj.m. of coke engineering
gaz koksowniczy [gahs kok-sov-ńee-chi] exp.: coal gas
koksownik [kok-**sov**-ńeek] m. coking coal worker; coking coal stove
koksowy [kok-**so**-vi] adj.m. coke (stove, etc.)
koktajl [**kok**-tahyl] m. cocktail
koktajlbar [**kok**-tahyl-bahr] m. cocktail lounge; cocktail bar
koktajlowy [kok-tahy-**lo**-vi] adj.m. cocktail (lounge, bar, etc.); of a cocktail
kola [**ko**-lah] f. cola; cola-seed
kolaboracja [ko-lah-bo-**rah**-tsyah] f. collaboration; collaborators; quislingism
kolaboracjonista [ko-lah-bo-rah-tsyo-**ńees**-tah] m. collaborator; collaborationist; quisling; traitor who collaborates with the invaders
kolaboracjonistka [ko-lah-bo-rah-tsyo-**ńeest**-kah] f. (female) collaborator; collaborationist; quisling; traitor who collaborates with the invaders
kolaboracjonistyczny [ko-lah-bo-rah-tsyo-ńees-**tich**-ni] adj.m. collaborationist
kolaboracyjny [ko-lah-bo-rah-**tsiy**-ni] adj.m. of collaboration
kolaborancki [ko-lah-bo-**rahnts**-kee] adj.m. collaborationist
kolaborant [ko-lah-**bo**-rahnt] m. collaborator; collaborationist; quisling; traitor who collaborates with the invaders
kolaborantka [ko-lah-bo-**rahnt**-kah] f. (female) collaborator; collaborationist; quisling; traitor who collaborates with the invaders
kolaborować [ko-lah-bo-**ro**-vahćh] v. collaborate (*repeatedly*)
kolaborowanie [ko-lah-bo-ro-**vah**-ńe] n. collaboration
kolacja [ko-**lah**-tsyah] f. supper; collation
kolacjonować [ko-lah-tsyo-**no**-vahćh] v. collate (a copy with the text, etc.); check (against an oreiginal text) (*repeatedly*)
kolacjonowanie [ko-lah-tsyo-no-**vah**-ńe] n. collation
kolacyjka [ko-lah-**tsiy**-kah] f. (nice, little) supper
kolacyjny [ko-lah-**tsiy**-ni] adj.m. supper (invitation, etc.)
kolagen [ko-**lah**-gen] m. collagen
kolagenowy [ko-lah-ge-**no**-vi] adj.m. collagenic; collagenous
kolagenoza [ko-lah-ge-**no**-zah] f. collagenic disease
kolagenozy [ko-lah-ge-**no**-zi] pl. collagenic diseases
kolamina [ko-lah-**mee**-nah] f. body's emulsifying fluid
kolanisko [ko-lah-**ńees**-ko] n. (big, dirty, etc.) knee
kolanko [ko-**lahn**-ko] n. (nice, little) knee; knee-piece; ell; elbow (connection); node; nodus; knot

kolankowato [ko-lahn-ko-**vah**-to] adv. like a knee
kolankowaty [ko-lahn-ko-**vah**-ti] adj.m. kneed; nodal; geniculate
kolankowy [ko-lahn-**ko**-vi] adj.m. kneed; elbowed
kolano [ko-**lah**-no] n. knee; bend; turn; elbow; twist; loop; wimple; slang: bald head (mob jargon)
kolanowy [ko-lah-**no**-vi] adj.m. of the knee; genual; bent
odruch kolanowy [od-rookh ko-lah-**no**-vi] exp.: knee-reflex; patellar reflex; knee jerk
staw kolanowy [stahf ko-lah-**no**-vi] exp.: knee-joint
kolanówka [ko-lah-**noof**-kah] f. lining at the knees in trouser-legs; knee-stoking
kolargol [ko-**lahr**-gol] m. germicide protein solution of silver
kolarski [ko-**lahr**-skee] adj.m. cyclist's; cycling (track, etc.)
kolarstwo [ko-**lahr**-stfo] n. cycling; bicycle sport
kolarz [**ko**-lahsh] m. cyclist
kolasa [ko-**lah**-sah] f. covered carriage
kolaska [ko-**lahs**-kah] f. covered carriage (suspended on leather belts)
kolator [ko-**lah**-tor] m. patron; presenter; collator
kolaudacja [ko-lahw-**dah**-tsyah] f. verification of compliance with building plans; terminal building inspection
kolaudacyjny [ko-lahw-dah-**tsiy**-ni] adj.m. of the terminal building inspection
kolaż [**ko**-lahsh] m. collage
kolażowy [ko-lah-**zho**-vi] adj.m. collage (composition, etc.)
kolący [ko-**lown**-tsi] adj.m. prickly; thorny; spiked
kolba [**kol**-bah] f. spadix; corncob; flask; butt(-end) (of rifle)
kolba lutownicza [**kol**-bah loo-tov-ńee-chah] exp.: soldering gun; soldering tool; copper bit
kolbiasty [kol-**byahs**-ti] adj.m. spadiceous; spadicose
kolbka [**kolp**-kah] f. small flask; bulb
kolbokwiatowiec [kol-bo-kfyah-**to**-vyets] m. spadiceous plant; spadicifloral plant; spadiciflorous plant
kolbokwiatowce [kol-bo-kfyah-**tof**-tse] pl. spadiceous plants
kolbokwiatowy [kol-bo-kfyah-**to**-vi] adj.m. spadiceous; spadicifloral; spadiciflorous
kolbowaty [kol-bo-**vah**-ti] adj.m. shaped like a corncob
kolbuszowski [kol-boo-**shof**-skee] adj.m. of Kolbuszów (richly inlaid furniture, etc.)
kolchicyna [kol-khee-**tsi**-nah] f. colchicine
kolcobrzuch [kol-**tso**-bzhookh] m. porcupine fish
kolcogłów [kol-**tso**-gwoof] m. acanthocephalon (intestinal worm)
kolcogłowy [kol-tso-**gwo**-vi] pl. acanthocephala (intestinal worms)
kolcolist [kol-**tso**-leest] m. gorse; furze; whin
kolcorośl [kol-**tso**-rośhl] m. variety of thorny lily plant
kolcować [kol-**tso**-vahćh] v. spike (car tires, etc.) (*repeatedly*)
kolcowanie [kol-tso-**vah**-ńe] n. spiking (of car tires, etc.)
kolcowój [kol-**tso**-vooy] m. boxthorn
kolcowy [kol-**tso**-vi] adj.m. spiked
kolczak [**kol**-chahk] m. tooth fungus
kolczaki [kol-**chah**-kee] pl. tooth fungi
kolczakowaty [kol-chah-ko-**vah**-ti] adj.m. hydnaceous; of the tooth fungus family
kolczakowate [kol-chah-ko-**vah**-te] pl. hydnaceae
kolczasto [kol-**chahs**-to] adv. with barbs; with thorns
kolczasty [kol-**chahs**-ti] adj.m. barbed; thorny; spiny
kolczatka [kol-**chaht**-kah] f. rotary harrow; track shoe; spiked shoe; echidna; porcupine anteater; slang: knuckle-duster; loaded stick (mob jargon)
kolczaty [kol-**chah**-ti] adj.m. barbed; thorny; spiny
kolczoch [**kol**-chokh] m. chayote (squash)
kolczuga [kol-**choo**-gah] f. coat of mail; chain armor; ring armor;

chain mail; ring-mail; hauberk; mob slang: a wrapped crowbar
kolczyk [**kol**-chik] m. earring; earmark; ear tag; eardrop
kolczykować [kol-chi-**ko**-vahćh] v. earmark (*repeatedly*)
kolczykowanie [kol-chi-ko-**vah**-ńe] n. earmarking
kolczykownica [kol-chi-kov-**ńee**-tsah] f. earmarking pliers
koleba [ko-**le**-bah] f. shepherd's hut; shepherd's shanty; refuge in mountain rocks; rocker car; tip wagon; cradle car; cradle
kolebać [ko-**le**-bahćh] v. swing; sway; toss to and fro; rock (*repeatedly*)
kolebać się [ko-**le**-bahćh śhan] v. swing; pitch and toss; toss to and fro; rock oneself; sway (*repeatedly*)
kolebanie [ko-le-**bah**-ńe] n. swing; sway; waddle; roll
kolebanie się [ko-le-**bah**-ńe śhan] n. swinging; swaying
kolebka [ko-**lep**-kah] f. cradle
kolebkowaty [ko-lep-ko-**vah**-ti] adj.m. arched (ceiling, etc.)
kolebkowo [ko-lep-**ko**-vo] adv. like a cradle; like an arch
kolebkowy [ko-lep-**ko**-vi] adj.m. of a cradle; arching (ceiling, etc.)
kolec [**ko**-lets] m. thorn; prick; spine; spike; barb; prong; goad; pricket; stimulus; quill
kolce [**kol**-tse] pl. track shoes; spiked shoes
kolega [ko-**le**-gah] m. colleague; fellow worker; companion; colloq: mate; pal; chum; buddy
kolegiacki [ko-le-**gyah**-tskee] adj.m. of a collegiate church
kolegialnie [ko-le-**gyahl**-ńe] adv. jointly; collectively; collegiately
kolegialność [ko-leg-**yahl**-nośhćh] f. joint action
kolegialny [ko-le-**gyahl**-ni] adj.m. joint; collective; collegiate
kolegiata [ko-le-**gyah**-tah] f. collegiate church
kolegium [ko-**le**-gyoom] n. council; governing body; administrative body; college
kolegować [ko-le-**go**-vahćh] v. be a colleague with somebody; be a companion of somebody (*repeatedly*)
kolegować się [ko-le-**go**-vahćh śhan] v. be a colleague with somebody; be a companion of somebody (*repeatedly*)
kolegowanie [ko-le-go-**vah**-ńe] n. being (somebody's) colleague
kolegowanie się [ko-le-go-**vah**-ńe śhan] n. being a colleague with somebody
koleina [ko-le-**ee**-nah] f. truck rut; wheel groove; wheel trace
koleinowy [ko-le-ee-**no**-vi] adj.m. of wheel trace(s)
kolej [**ko**-ley] f. railroad; railway (Brit.); track; train; turn; vicissitude; change (of life, fortune, etc.)
kolej podziemna [**ko**-ley pod-**żhem**-nah] exp.: subway; the underground; the tube (Brit.)
na kogo kolej? [nah **ko**-go **ko**-ley] exp.: whose turn is it?
na mnie kolej [nah mńe **ko**-ley] exp.: it is my turn
po kolei [po ko-**le**-ee] exp.: by turns; in succession
poza koleją [**po**-zah ko-**le**-yown] exp.: out of turn
z kolei [s ko-**le**-ee] exp.: next; then; afterwards; subsequently; whereupon; whereafter
z kolei rzeczy [s ko-**le**-ee **zhe**-chi] exp.: in the course of nature; in the ordinary course of events
zmienne koleje losu [**zmyen**-ne ko-**le**-ye **lo**-soo] exp.: the changes of fortune; the ups and downs; the vicissitudes of life
kolejarka [ko-le-**yahr**-kah] f. woman railroad employee
kolejarski [ko-le-**yahr**-skee] adj.m. railroad (uniform, etc.)
kolejarz [ko-**le**-yahsh] m. railwayman; railroad man
kolejka [ko-**ley**-kah] f. (waiting) line; queue; narrow-gauge railroad; colloq: turn; round (of drinks)
kolejkowicz [ko-ley-**ko**-veech] m. colloq: man in a waiting line
kolejkowy [ko-ley-**ko**-vi] adj.m. of narrow-gauge railroad

kolejnictwo [ko-ley-**ńeets**-tfo] n. railroad industry; railway transportation
kolejno [ko-**ley**-no] adv. by turns; one after the other; in turns; in succession
kolejność [ko-**ley**-nośhćh] f. order; sequence; succession
w kolejności [f ko-ley-**nośh**-ćhee] exp.: successively
w kolejności alfabetycznej [f ko-ley-**nośh**-ćhee ahl-fah-be-**tich**-ney] exp.: in alphabetical order
kolejny [ko-**ley**-ni] adj.m. next; successive; following; consecutive; succeeding; subsequent
kolejowy [ko-le-**yo**-vi] adj.m. railroad (ticket, service, etc.); (Brit.) railway (tracks, etc.)
kolekcja [ko-**lek**-tsyah] f. collection; things collected
kolekcjoner [ko-lek-**tsyo**-ner] m. collector
kolekcjonerka [ko-lek-tsyo-**ner**-kah] f. (female) collector; collector's hobby
kolekcjonerski [ko-lek-tsyo-**ner**-skee] adj.m. collector's
kolekcjonerstwo [ko-lek-tsyo-**ner**-stfo] n. collectorship; practice of collecting
kolekcjonować [ko-lek-tsyo-**no**-vahćh] v. collect (stamps, etc.) (*repeatedly*)
kolekcjonowanie [ko-lek-tsyo-no-**vah**-ńe] n. collection
kolekcyjka [ko-lek-**tsiy**-kah] f. (small, nice) collection
kolekta [ko-**lek**-tah] f. collection; prayer upon assembly; collect
kolektanea [ko-lek-tah-**ne**-ah] pl. collection of excerpts (manuscripts, etc.)
kolektiwum [ko-**lek**-tee-voom] n. plurality; number (of persons, objects, etc.) (hist.)
kolektor [ko-**lek**-tor] m. lottery office keeper; commutator; collector; main drain; interceptor; intercepting sewer; collecting pipe
kolektorka [ko-lek-**tor**-kah] f. (female) lottery office keeper
kolektorowy [ko-lek-to-**ro**-vi] adj.m. of intercepting sewer; of collecting pipe
kolektorski [ko-lek-**tor**-skee] adj.m. of lottery office keeper
kolektura [ko-lek-**too**-rah] f. lottery office
kolektyw [ko-**lek**-tif] m. (collective) body; aggregate; group; membership
kolektywista [ko-lek-ti-**vees**-tah] m. collectivist
kolektywistycznie [ko-lek-ti-vees-**tich**-ńe] adv. collectivistically
kolektywistyczny [ko-lek-ti-vees-**tich**-ni] adj.m. collectivistic
kolektywizacja [ko-lek-ti-vee-**zah**-tsyah] f. collectivization
kolektywizm [ko-lek-**ti**-veezm] m. collectivism
kolektywizować [ko-lek-ti-vee-**zo**-vahćh] v. collectivize (*repeatedly*)
kolektywizowanie [ko-lek-ti-vee-zo-**vah**-ńe] n. collectivization
kolektywnie [ko-lek-**tiv**-ńe] adv. collectively
kolektywność [ko-lek-**tiv**-nośhćh] f. collectivity
kolektywny [ko-lek-**tiv**-ni] adj.m. collective; corporate; joint; common
kolender [ko-**len**-der] m. coriander; coriander seeds
kolendra [ko-**lend**-rah] f. coriander; coriander seeds
kolendrowy [ko-lend-**ro**-vi] adj.m. coriander (oil, etc.)
koleń [**ko**-leń] m. dogfish (a shark of the family Spinacidae)
koleopter [kah-le-**op**-ter] m. airplane with torus-shaped wing
koleś [**ko**-leśh] m. colloq: comrade; mate; pal; chum; buddy
koleśnica [ko-leśh-**ńee**-tsah] f. wheels of a plow
koleśny [ko-**leśh**-ni] adj.m. wheel-mounted (plow, etc.)
kolet [**ko**-let] m. jacket (Polish army 18th and 19th cent.); collar
koleus [ko-**le**-oos] m. coleus (herb of the mint family)
koleżanka [ko-le-**zhahn**-kah] f. (female) colleague; comrade; fellow worker; companion; colloq: mate; pal; chum; buddy

koleżeński [ko-le-**zheń**-skee] adj.m. friendly; amicable; sporting; comradely; obliging; colloq: chummy; matey (Brit.)
po koleżeńsku [po ko-le-**zheń**-skoo] exp.: in a friendly manner; in good comradeship; amicably
koleżeńsko [ko-le-**zheń**-sko] adv. in a friendly manner
koleżeńskość [ko-le-**zheń**-skośhćh] f. good-fellowship; comradeship; camaraderie
koleżeństwo [ko-le-**zheń**-stfo] n. fellowship; comradeship; comrades; camaraderie
dobre koleżeństwo [**dob**-re ko-le-**zheń**-stfo] exp.: good-fellowship among comrades
koleżka [ko-**lesh**-kah] m. colloq: comrade; mate; pal; chum; buddy
kolęda [ko-**lan**-dah] f. Christmas carol; song of joy or praise; slang: apartment robbery (mob jargon)
kolędniczy [ko-land-**ńee**-chi] adj.m. of a caroller
kolędnik [ko-**land**-ńeek] m. caroller
kolędować [ko-lan-**do**-vahćh] v. carol; go carolling; sing carols; colloq: wait for a long time; kick one's heels (*repeatedly*)
kolędowanie [ko-lan-do-**vah**-ńe] n. singing carols; colloq: waiting for a long time
kolędowy [ko-lan-**do**-vi] adj.m. carol (music, etc.)
kolia [**ko**-lyah] f. necklace
koliba [ko-**lee**-bah] f. shepherd's hut; shepherd's shanty; refuge in mountain rocks; rocker car; tip wagon; cradle car; cradle
koliber [ko-**lee**-ber] m. humming-bird of Trochilidae family
koliberek [ko-lee-**be**-rek] m. (little, nice) humming-bird
kolidar [ko-**lee**-dahr] m. range-finder using laser
kolidować [ko-lee-**do**-vahćh] v. collide; interfere; clash; stand in the way (of); be in collision; be in conflict; run counter (to) (*repeatedly*)
kolidowanie [ko-lee-do-**vah**-ńe] n. collision; interference; clashing
koligacenie [ko-lee-gah-**tse**-ńe] n. relating by marriage
koligacenie się [ko-lee-gah-**tse**-ńe śhan] n. getting related by marriage
koligacić [ko-lee-**gah**-ćheećh] v. relate by marriage; connect by marriage (*repeatedly*)
koligacić się [ko-lee-**gah**-ćheećh śhan] v. become related by marriage; become connected by marriage (*repeatedly*)
koligacja [ko-lee-**gah**-tsyah] f. (family) relationship by marriage; affinity
kolimacja [ko-lee-**mah**-tsyah] f. collimation
kolimacyjny [ko-lee-mah-**tsiy**-ni] adj.m. collimation (error, axis, etc.)
kolimator [ko-lee-**mah**-tor] m. collimator
kolinearny [ko-lee-ne-**ahr**-ni] adj.m. collinear
kolisko [ko-**lees**-ko] n. (big) circle
kolisto [ko-**lees**-to] adv. circularly; in a circle; round
kolistość [ko-**lees**-tośhćh] f. circularity; roundness
kolisty [ko-**lees**-ti] adj.m. circular; round
koliszek [ko-**lee**-shek] m. psyllid louse
koliszki [ko-**leesh**-kee] pl. Psyllidae
koliście [ko-**leeśh**-ćhe] adv. in a circle
kolizja [ko-**lee**-zyah] f. collision; clash; interference; conflict
kolizja z prawem [ko-**lee**-zyah s **prah**-vem] exp.: infringement of the law
kolizyjność [ko-lee-**ziy**-nośhćh] f. likelihood of collision
kolizyjny [ko-lee-**ziy**-ni] adj.m. collision (course, etc.)
kolka [**kol**-kah] f. colic; prickle; pains; bellyache; grips; griping; three-spined stickleback (fish)
kolkotar [kol-**ko**-tahr] m. colcothar; red iron oxide
kolkowy [kol-**ko**-vi] adj.m. colicky; colic (pains, etc.)
kollomia [kol-**lo**-myah] f. Collomia (herb and flower)
kolmatacja [kol-mah-**tah**-tsyah] f.

silting
kolnąć [**kol**-nownćh] v. stab; spear; prod; jab; poke; prick; sting; bite
kolnięcie [kol-ńan-ćhe] n. stab; spear; prod; jab; poke; prick; sting; bite
kolodion [ko-**lod**-yon] m. collodion
kolodionowy [ko-lod-yo-**no**-vi] adj.m. collodion (cotton, process, etc.)
kolodium [ko-**lod**-yoom] n. collodion
kolofon [ko-**lo**-fon] m. colophon
kologarytm [ko-lo-**gah**-ritm] m. cologarithm; negative logarithm
koloid [ko-**lo**-eet] m. colloid
koloidy [ko-lo-**ee**-di] pl. colloids
koloidalny [ko-lo-ee-**dahl**-ni] adj.m. colloidal (fuel, etc.)
koloidowy [ko-lo-ee-**do**-vi] adj.m. colloidal (fuel, etc.)
chemia koloidowa [**khe**-myah ko-lo-ee-**do**-vah] exp.: colloidal chemistry
kolokacja [ko-lo-**kah**-tsyah] f. collocation (of village properties, sequence of payments after bankruptcy, etc.)
kolokacyjny [ko-lo-kah-**tsiy**-ni] adj.m. collocational
kolokazja [ko-lo-**kahz**-yah] f. Colocasia (Egyptian plant)
kolokować [ko-lo-**ko**-vahćh] v. collocate (*repeatedly*)
kolokowanie [ko-lo-ko-**vah**-ńe] n. collocation
koloksylina [ko-lo-ksi-**lee**-nah] f. colloxylin; Pyroxylin
kolokwializm [ko-lo-**kfyah**-leezm] m. colloquialism
kolokwialnie [ko-lo-**kfyahl**-ńe] adv. colloquially
kolokwialność [ko-lo-**kfyahl**-nośhćh] f. colloquialness
kolokwialny [ko-lo-**kfyahl**-ni] adj.m. colloquial; of oral examination
kolokwinta [ko-lo-**kfeen**-tah] f. colocynth; bitter apple
kolokwium [ko-**lo**-kfyoom] n. oral examination; test; viva voce
kolombina [ko-lom-**bee**-nah] f. Columbine
kolon [**ko**-lon] m. colonus (Roman serf or tenant farmer)
kolonat [ko-**lo**-naht] m. colonate (being colonus)
kolonel [ko-**lo**-nel] m. minion (font)
kolonia [ko-**lo**-ńyah] f. colony; settlement; summer camp
kolonialista [ko-lo-ńyah-**lees**-tah] m. colonialist
kolonialka [ko-lo-**ńyahl**-kah] f. slang: grocery store
kolonializm [ko-lo-**ńyah**-leezm] m. colonialism
kolonialnie [ko-lo-**ńyahl**-ńe] adv. colonially
kolonialny [ko-lo-**ńyahl**-ni] adj.m. colonial
kolonijka [ko-lo-**ńeey**-kah] f. (small, nice) colony; settlement; summer camp
kolonijny [ko-lo-**ńeey**-ni] adj.m. of a colony; of a settlement
kolonista [ko-lo-**ńees**-tah] m. settler; colonist; colonial
kolonizacja [ko-lo-ńee-**zah**-tsyah] f. colonization; settlement (of people or of a region)
kolonizacyjny [ko-lo-ńee-zah-**tsiy**-ni] adj.m. colonization (policy, etc.)
kolonizator [ko-lo-ńee-**zah**-tor] m. colonizer
kolonizatorski [ko-lo-ńee-zah-**tor**-skee] adj.m. colonizer's
kolonizatorstwo [ko-lo-ńee-zah-**tor**-stfo] n. colonization
kolonizować [ko-lo-ńee-**zo**-vahćh] v. colonize; settle (*repeatedly*)
kolonizowanie [ko-lo-ńee-zo-**vah**-ńe] n. colonization
koloński [ko-**loń**-skee] adj.m. of Cologne
woda kolońska [**vo**-dah ko-**loń**-skah] exp.: Cologne water
kolor [**ko**-lor] m. color; tint; hue
dobór kolorów [**do**-boor ko-**lo**-roof] exp.: color scheme; tonality
kolory [ko-**lo**-ri] pl. colors (regimental, etc.); rosy complexion; suit (of cards)
kolorado [ko-lo-**rah**-do] n. Colorado (potato) beetle
koloratka [ko-lo-**raht**-kah] f. clerical collar; colloq: dog collar
koloratura [ko-lo-rah-**too**-rah] f. coloratura
koloraturowy [ko-lo-rah-too-**ro**-vi] adj.m. coloratura (soprano, etc.)
kolorek [ko-**lo**-rek] m. (light, nice)

color; tint; hue; slang: tattoo ink; play cards (mob jargon)
kolorować [ko-lo-**ro**-vahćh] v. color; paint; stain (*repeatedly*)
kolorować się [ko-lo-**ro**-vahćh śhan] v. color (oneself) (*repeatedly*)
kolorowanie [ko-lo-ro-**vah**-ńe] n. coloring
kolorowo [ko-lo-**ro**-vo] adv. in (various, different) colors
kolorowy [ko-lo-**ro**-vi] adj.m. colorful; colored; bright with colors; m. colored person; slang: man with red moustache
kolorówka [ko-lo-**roof**-kah] f. color film; paper-staining machine
kolorymetr [ko-lo-**ri**-metr] m. colorimeter
kolorymetria [ko-lo-ri-**metr**-yah] f. colorimetry
kolorymetrycznie [ko-lo-ri-met-**rich**-ńe] adv. colorimetrically
kolorymetryczny [ko-lo-ri-met-**rich**-ni] adj.m. colorimetric (analysis, etc.)
kolorysta [ko-lo-**ris**-tah] m. colorist; printer of textiles; colloq: humbug
kolorystycznie [ko-lo-ris-**tich**-ńe] adv. in respect of colors
kolorystyczny [ko-lo-ris-**tich**-ni] adj.m. coloristic
kolorystyka [ko-lo-**ris**-ti-kah] f. coloring; color of musical tone
koloryt [ko-**lo**-rit] m. coloring
kolorytowy [ko-lo-ri-**to**-vi] adj.m. of coloring; coloristic
koloryzacja [ko-lo-ri-**zah**-tsyah] f. overdrawing; excessive coloring; exaggeration
koloryzator [ko-lo-ri-**zah**-tor] m. colorist; printer of textiles; colloq: humbug
koloryzm [ko-**lo**-rizm] m. emphasis on color in painting
koloryzować [ko-lo-ri-**zo**-vahćh] v. overdraw; exaggerate (*repeatedly*)
koloryzowanie [ko-lo-ri-zo-**vah**-ńe] n. exaggeration
kolos [**ko**-los] m. colossus; colloq: giant; thumper (Brit.); slang: failing grade (school jargon)
kolosalnie [ko-lo-**sahl**-ńe] adv. colossally; vastly; tremendously; gigantically; enormously
kolosalność [ko-lo-**sahl**-nośhćh] f. vastness; gigantic nature; enormity
kolosalny [ko-lo-**sahl**-ni] adj.m. colossal; vast; tremendous; gigantic; enormous
kolportaż [kol-**por**-tahsh] m. distribution (of newspapers, books, etc.)
kolportażowy [kol-por-tah-**zho**-vi] adj.m. of (newspapers, books, etc.) distribution
kolporter [kol-**por**-ter] m. newspaper carrier; newsstand operator; colloq: paper boy
kolporterka [kol-por-**ter**-kah] f. (female) newspaper carrier; newsstand operator; distribution (of newspapers, books, etc.)
kolporterski [kol-por-**ter**-skee] adj.m. newspaper carrier's; news-stand operator's; of distribution (of newspapers, books, etc.)
kolporterstwo [kol-por-**ters**-tfo] n. distribution (of newspapers, books, etc.)
kolportować [kol-por-**to**-vahćh] v. distribute; sell; colloq: spread (rumors, etc.) (*repeatedly*)
kolportowanie [kol-por-to-**vah**-ńe] n. distribution (of newspapers, books, etc.)
kolt [kolt] m. Colt revolver
kolubryna [ko-loo-**bri**-nah] f. culverin; colloq: something huge, enormous, lengthy, voluminous, etc.
kolubryniasty [ko-loob-ri-**ńahs**-ti] adj.m. enormous
kolumbarium [ko-loom-**bahr**-yoom] n. columbarium; recess
kolumbit [ko-**loom**-beet] m. columbite (mineral)
kolumienka [ko-loo-**myen**-kah] f. (small) column
kolumna [ko-**loom**-nah] f. column; pillar; convoy; unit
kolumna rektyfikacyjna [ko-**loom**-nah rek-ti-fee-kah-**tsiy**-nah] exp.: still; rectifying column
kolumnada [ko-loom-**nah**-dah] f. colonnade
kolumnadowy [ko-loom-nah-**do**-vi] adj.m. colonnaded

kolumnowy [ko-loom-**no**-vi] adj.m. columnar; columned; pillared
kolur [**ko**-loor] m. colure; circle of the celestial sphere
koluria [ko-**loor**-yah] f. Siberian wild rose
kołacz [**ko**-wahch] m. cake; wedding cake; oil cake
kołat [**ko**-waht] m. noise; din; thud; bang
kołatać [ko-**wah**-tahćh] v. knock (at); rattle (at); beg (for); request (for); importune (for); appeal (for); solicit; throb; bang; beat palpitate; pant (*repeatedly*)
kołatać się [ko-**wah**-tahćh śhan] v. din; rattle; rumble; rumble along; drag on; endure; throb; bang; beat; palpitate; pant; go pit-pat (*repeatedly*)
kołatanie [ko-wah-**tah**-ńe] n. palpitation; requests; solicitation
kołatanie się [ko-wah-**tah**-ńe śhan] n. traveling inconveniently; enduring rumble
kołatanina [ko-wah-tah-**ńee**-nah] f. (lengthy) requests; solicitation
kołatek [ko-**wah**-tek] m. deathwatch (cockchafer beetle)
kołatki [ko-**waht**-kee] pl. the family Anobiidae of beetles
kołatka [ko-**waht**-kah] f. rattle; clapper; flapper; door-knocker
kołatnąć [ko-**waht**-nownćh] v. give a rap (at the door, etc.)
kołatnięcie [ko-waht-**ńan**-ćhe] n. a rap (at the door, etc.); a bang
kołchoz [**kow**-khos] m. kolkhoz; mob slang: common meal in a prison cell; workshop in prison
kołchozowy [kow-kho-**zo**-vi] adj.m. of a kolkhoz
kołchoźnica [kow-khoźh-**ńee**-tsah] f. (female) member of a kolkhoz
kołchoźniczy [kow-khoźh-**ńee**-chi] adj.m. of a kolkhoz
kołchoźnik [kow-**khoźh**-ńeek] m. member of a kolkhoz; slang: thieves' hideout (mob jargon)
kołczan [**kow**-chahn] m. quiver
kołderka [kow-**der**-kah] f. (small, nice) quilter-cover; quilt; coverlet; eiderdown; counterpane
kołdra [**kow**-drah] f. quilter-cover; quilt; coverlet; eiderdown
kołdrowy [kow-**dro**-vi] adj.m. of quilt; counterpane (material, etc.); quilt (size, etc.)
kołdrzarka [kowd-**zhahr**-kah] f. (woman) quilt-maker
kołdrzyna [kowd-**zhi**-nah] f. (old, worn out) quilter-cover; quilt; coverlet; eiderdown
kołdun [**kow**-doon] m. Lithuanian dumpling stuffed with meat
kołeczek [ko-**we**-chek] m. (small) peg; stake; picket; dowel; hanger
kołek [**ko**-wek] m. peg; stake; picket; dowel; hanger; tuning-peg; tuning-pin; slang: country bumpkin (mob jargon)
siedzieć kołkiem w domu [**śhe**-dźhećh **kow**-kem v **do**-moo] exp.: never to stir out of the house; not to move out of the house; never to go out of the house; always to stay at home
kołki [**kow**-kee] pl. pegs; stakes; pickets; dowels; hangers; slang: poor quality cigarettes; pupils
kołkować [kow-ko-vahćh] v. peg; picket; stake; dowel; bark (a tree) (*repeatedly*)
kołkowanie [kow-ko-**vah**-ńe] n. pegging; picketing; staking; dowelling; taking off the bark (of a tree, etc.)
kołkowaty [kow-ko-**vah**-ti] adj.m. like a peg; stiff; awkward
kołkownica [kow-kov-**ńee**-tsah] f. fife rail
kołkowy [kow-**ko**-vi] adj.m. pegged (shoe, etc.)
kołnierz [**kow**-ńesh] m. collar
kołnierzasty [kow-ńe-**zhahs**-ti] adj.m. collared; torquate; having a ring around the neck
kołnierzowy [kow-ńe-**zho**-vi] adj.m. of a collar
kołnierzyczek [kow-ńe-**zhi**-chek] m. (small, nice) collar
kołnierzyk [kow-**ńe**-zhik] m. (small, nice, soft, etc.) collar
koło [**ko**-wo] n. wheel; circle; ring; hoop; (torture) rack
błędne koło [**bwand**-ne **ko**-wo] exp.: vicious circle
kołem [**ko**-wem] exp.: in a circle

koło podbiegunowe [**ko**-wo pod-bye-goo-**no**-ve] exp.: polar circle
koło ratunkowe [**ko**-wo rah-toon-**ko**-ve] exp: life belt
koło sterowe [**ko**-wo ste-**ro**-ve] exp.: steering wheel
koło zamachowe [**ko**-wo zah-mah-**kho**-ve] exp.: flywheel
koło z zapadką [**ko**-wo z zah-**paht**-kown] exp.: ratchet; catch-wheel
w koło [f **ko**-wo] exp.: in a circle; repeatedly; encircling; over and over again
koło [**ko**-wo] prep.: around; near; about; by; close to; in the neighborhood; in the vicinity; not far from; somewhere around; (tinker, etc.) at; with
kołobieg [ko-**wo**-byek] m. giant's-stride
kołobrulion [ko-wo-**brool**-yon] m. loose-leaf notebook
kołodziej [ko-**wo**-dźhey] m. wheelwright; wheeler
kołodziejski [ko-wo-**dźhey**-skee] adj.m. wheelwright's; wheeler's
kołodziejstwo [ko-wo-**dźhey**-stfo] n. wheelwright's work
kołogniot [ko-**wo**-gńot] m. mill; crusher; stone-breaker
kołomyja [ko-wo-**mi**-yah] f. round dance
kołomyjka [ko-wo-**miy**-kah] f. round dance
kołonotatnik [ko-wo-no-**taht**-ńeek] m. loose-leaf notebook
kołonotes [ko-wo-**no**-tes] m. loose-leaf notebook
kołotocznik [ko-wo-**toch**-ńeek] m. Buphtalmum; oxeye (daisy, herb)
kołotok [ko-**wo**-tok] m. mill; crusher; stone-breaker
kołowacenie [ko-wo-vah-**tse**-ńe] n. disorientation
kołowacieć [ko-wo-**vah**-ćhećh] v. be affected with gid (sheep disease); stiffen; colloq: grow dazed; become bewildered; grow distracted; get dizzy; go silly; become perplexed (*repeatedly*)
kołowacizna [ko-wo-vah-**ćheez**-nah] f. gid (of sheep); staggers; dizziness; confusion; bewilderment
kołować [ko-**wo**-vahćh] v. go in circles; fly in circles; take roundabout course; stray; revolve; confuse; circle; whirl; be in a whirl; prevaricate; slang: strive (for); scheme; be interested (in); cheat; swindle; make up (stories, etc.); flirt with a coed in one's class (*repeatedly*)
kołować się [ko-**wo**-vahćh śhan] v. = emphatic: **kołować** (*repeatedly*)
kołowanie [ko-wo-**vah**-ńe] n. going in circles; flying in circles; taking roundabout course; straying; slang: (a) lie; (a) swindle
kołowanie się [ko-wo-**vah**-ńe śhan] n. getting confused
kołowato [ko-wo-**vah**-to] adv. in a circle; in circles
kołowatość [ko-wo-**vah**-tośhćh] f. circularity
kołowaty [ko-wo-**vah**-ti] adj.m. circular; affected with gid; colloq: dazed; bewildered; stiff; mob slang: insane; drunk; narcotized
kołowiec [ko-**wo**-vyets] m. paddle-wheel ship; paddle-steamship
kołowrotek [ko-wo-**vro**-tek] m. spinning wheel; reel; winch
kołowrotkowy [ko-wo-vrot-**ko**-vi] adj.m. windlass (hoisting, etc.)
kołowrotowy [ko-wo-vro-**to**-vi] adj.m. of a large reel
kołowrót [ko-**wo**-vroot] m. gin; windlass; hoist; whip; turnpike; turnstile; large reel; spinning wheel; colloq: confusion; spinning around; slang: country bumpkin
kołowy [ko-**wo**-vi] adj.m. circular; wheeled; vehicular (traffic)
ruch kołowy [rookh ko-**wo**-vi] exp.: vehicular traffic; traffic
kołpak [**kow**-pahk] m. pointed fur cap; calpack; calpac
kołtryna [kow-**tri**-nah] f. paper hanging
kołtun [**kow**-toon] m. hair snarl; plica; tuft of twisted hair; matted hair; colloq: mop head; tangle; bigot; moron; Philistine; gigman; obscurant; smug man; slang: hillbilly; country bumpkin

kołtuneria [kow-too-**ner**-yah] f. smugness; priggishness; Philistinism; obscurantism; prigs; Philistines; obscurants; gigmanity
kołtuniasty [kow-too-**ńahs**-ti] adj.m. tangled; matted
kołtunić [kow-**too**-ńeećh] v. tangle (*repeatedly*)
kołtunić się [kow-**too**-ńeećh śhan] v. get tangled; get matted; slang: get married (jargon) (*repeatedly*)
kołtunieć [kow-**too**-ńećh] v. get tangled; get matted; grow smug; become smug (*repeatedly*)
kołtunienie [kow-too-**ńe**-ńe] n. getting tangled; getting matted; growing smug; becoming smug
kołtunienie się [kow-too-**ńe**-ńe śhan] n. making oneself smug
kołtunka [kow-**toon**-kah] f. (female) bigot; moron; Philistine; gigman; obscurant; smug woman
kołtunowaty [kow-too-no-**vah**-ti] adj.m. tangled; matted; priggish
kołtuński [kow-**tooń**-skee] adj.m. smug; Philistine
kołtuńsko [kow-**tooń**-sko] adv. smugly; like a Philistine
kołtuństwo [kow-**tooń**-stfo] n. smugness; priggishness; Philistinism; obscurantism; prigs; Philistines; obscurants; gigmanity
kołysać [ko-**wi**-sahćh] v. rock; sway; toss to and fro; roll; swing; waddle (*repeatedly*)
kołysać się [ko-**wi**-sahćh śhan] v. rock; sway; be tossed to and fro; roll; swing; waddle (*repeatedly*)
kołysanie [ko-wi-**sah**-ńe] n. rocking
kołysanie się [ko-wi-**sah**-ńe śhan] n. waddle; swing; sway
kołysanka [ko-wi-**sahn**-kah] f. lullaby; cradlesong; berceuse
kołysankowy [ko-wi-sahn-**ko**-vi] adj.m. of a cradle
kołyseczka [ko-wi-**sech**-kah] f. (small, nice) cradle
kołyska [ko-**wis**-kah] f. cradle
kołyskowy [ko-wis-**ko**-vi] adj.m. cradle (cart, etc.)
kołyszący [ko-wi-**shown**-tsi] adj.m. up-and-down (movement); rolling (gait, etc.); waddling
koma [**ko**-mah] f. (decimal) point; coma
komando [ko-**mahn**-do] n. work detail in German concentration camp
komandor [ko-**mahn**-dor] m. commander; commodore
komandoria [ko-mahn-**dor**-yah] f. commandery (orders, decorations)
komandorski [ko-mahn-**dor**-skee] adj.m. commander's; commodore's
komandorstwo [ko-mahn-**dors**-tfo] n. commander's rank; commodore's rank
komandos [ko-**mahn**-dos] m. commando; ranger
komandytariusz [ko-mahn-di-**tahr**-yoosh] m. sleeping (business) partner
komar [**ko**-mahr] m. mosquito; gnat; midge
komary [ko-**mah**-ri] pl. the mosquitoes
komarnica [ko-mahr-**ńee**-tsah] f. crane fly; daddy-longlegs
komarowy [ko-mah-**ro**-vi] adj.m. mosquito (bite, etc.); of a gnat; of a midge
komarówka [ko-mah-**rooof**-kah] f. slang: moonshine (mob jargon)
komarzy [ko-**mah**-zhi] adj.m. mosquito (bite, leg, etc.)
komarzyca [ko-mah-**zhi**-tsah] f. female mosquito
komasacja [ko-mah-**sah**-tsyah] f. integration (of parts) into a whole
komasacyjny [ko-mah-sah-**tsiy**-ni] adj.m. of integration (of parts) into a whole
komasować [ko-mah-**so**-vahćh] v. integrate into a whole; combine into a whole (*repeatedly*)
komasowanie [ko-mah-so-**vah**-ńe] n. integration (of parts) into a whole
komat [**ko**-maht] m. coma
komatyczny [ko-mah-**tich**-ni] adj.m. comatose
kombajn [**kom**-bahyn] m. combine harvester; coal combine
kombajner [kom-**bahy**-ner] m. combine-driver
kombajnista [kom-bahy-**ńees**-tah] m. cutter-loader; loaderman (miner)
kombajnowy [kom-bahy-**no**-vi]

adj.m. of a combine
kombatancki [kom-bah-**tahn**-tskee] adj.m. combatant's; combatants'
kombatanctwo [kom-bah-**tahn**-tstfo] n. being a combatant
kombatant [kom-**bah**-tahnt] m. combatant
kombi [**kom**-bee] n. station wagon
kombinacja [kom-bee-**nah**-tsyah] f. combination; union; scheme; arrangement; grouping; (sport) contest; (sport) event; contrivance; jugglery; colloq: (woman's) slip; slang: fraud
kombinacyjny [kom-bee-nah-**tsiy**-ni] adj.m. combinative
kombinat [kom-**bee**-naht] m. works; factory; plant
kombinator [kom-bee-**nah**-tor] m. contriver; schemer; combiner; swindler; impostor; slang: experienced thief (mob jargon)
kombinatorka [kom-bee-nah-**tor**-kah] f. (female) contriver; schemer; combiner; swindler; impostor
kombinatorski [kom-bee-nah-**tor**-skee] adj.m. contriver's; schemer's; combiner's; swindler's; impostor's
kombinatorstwo [kom-bee-nah-**tor**-stfo] n. scheming; spoofing
kombinatoryczny [kom-bee-nah-to-**rich**-ni] adj.m. of the theory of combinations
kombinatoryka [kom-bee-nah-**to**-ri-kah] f. theory of combinations
kombinatowy [kom-bee-nah-**to**-vi] adj.m. of works; of a factory; of a plant
kombinerki [kom-bee-**ner**-kee] pl. pliers
kombinezon [kom-bee-**ne**-zon] m. overalls; coveralls
kombinować [kom-bee-**no**-vahćh] v. combine; join; group; compound; speculate; arrange; think; contrive; have perception; apprehend; colloq: live by one's wits; put two and two together; slang: steal; cheat; swindle (mob jargon) (*repeatedly*)
kombinowanie [kom-bee-no-**vah**-ńe] n. schemes; jugglery
kombinówka [kom-bee-**noof**-kah] f. moonshine
komedia [ko-**me**-dyah] f. comedy; amusing situation; sham; pretence; piece of acting
komedia obyczajowa [ko-**me**-dyah o-bi-chah-**yo**-vah] exp.: comedy of manners
komediancki [ko-me-**dyahn**-tskee] adj.m. faked; feigned; pretended
komediancko [ko-me-**dyahn**-tsko] adv. pretendedly
komedianctwo [ko-me-**dyahn**-tstfo] n. pretence; sham; histrionics
komediant [ko-**me**-dyahnt] m. deceiver; pretender; shammer
komediantka [ko-me-**dyahnt**-kah] f. (female) deceiver; pretender; shammer
komediofarsa [ko-med-yo-**fahr**-sah] f. farcical comedy (on stage, film, etc.)
komedioopera [ko-med-yo-**o**-pe-rah] f. vaudeville
komediooperowy [ko-med-yo-o-pe-**ro**-vi] adj.m. of vaudeville
komediopisarka [ko-med-yo-pee-**sahr**-kah] f. (woman) writer of comedies; comedian
komediopisarski [ko-med-yo-pee-**sahr**-skee] adj.m. comedian's
komediopisarstwo [ko-med-yo-pee-**sahr**-stfo] n. writing of comedies
komediopisarz [ko-med-yo-**pee**-sahsh] m. writer of comedies; comedian
komediowość [ko-med-**yo**-vośhćh] f. character of comedy
komediowy [ko-med-**yo**-vi] adj.m. comedy (actor, etc.)
komedyjka [ko-me-**diy**-kah] f. (light) comedy
komenda [ko-**men**-dah] f. word of command; command; headquarters; an order
jak na komendę [yahk nah ko-**men**-dan] exp.: in unison
sprawować komendę [sprah-**vo**-vahćh ko-**men**-dan] exp.: to be in command
komendant [ko-**men**-dahnt] m. commander; commanding officer
komendant portu [ko-**men**-dahnt **por**-too] exp.: dockmaster
komendantka [ko-men-**dahnt**-kah] f.

(female) commander; commanding officer
komendantura [ko-men-dahn-**too**-rah] f. headquarters
komenderować [ko-men-de-**ro**-vahćh] v. give an order; give orders; give command; give commands; command; issue orders; order people around (*repeatedly*)
komenderowanie [ko-men-de-ro-**vah**-ńe] n. commands
komensal [ko-**men**-sahl] m. commensal
komensaliczny [ko-men-sah-**leech**-ni] adj.m. commensal
komensalizm [ko-men-**sah**-leezm] m. commensalism
komentarz [ko-**men**-tahsh] m. commentary; glossary; remark; comment
bez komentarzy! [bes ko-men-**tah**-zhi] exp.: no comments, please!; no remarks, please!
komentarzowy [ko-men-tah-**zho**-vi] adj.m. of a commentary; of a glossary
komentator [ko-men-**tah**-tor] m. commentator; annotator; glossator
komentatorski [ko-men-tah-**tor**-skee] adj.m. commentator's; annotator's
praca komentatorska [**prah**-tsah ko-men-tah-**tor**-skah] exp.: commentation; annotation
komentować [ko-men-**to**-vahćh] v. comment (upon a text, etc.); annotate (a book, etc.); gloss; remark (upon); make remarks (upon) (*repeatedly*)
komentowanie [ko-men-to-**vah**-ńe] n. annotations
komeraż [ko-**me**-rahsh] m. gossip; tittle-tattle
komeraże [ko-me-**rah**-zhe] pl. gossips; intrigues; entanglements; misunderstandings
komercjalizacja [ko-mer-tsyah-lee-**zah**-tsyah] f. commercialization
komercjalizm [ko-mer-**tsyah**-leezm] m. commercialism
komercjalizować [ko-mer-tsyah-lee-**zo**-vahćh] v. commercialize (*repeatedly*)
komercjalizować się [ko-mer-tsyah-lee-**zo**-vahćh śhan] v. become commercialized; become profitable at the expense of quality (*repeatedly*)
komercjalizowanie [ko-mer-tsyah-lee-zo-**vah**-ńe] n. commercialization
komercjalizowanie się [ko-mer-tsyah-lee-zo-**vah**-ńe śhan] n. becoming commercialized
komercjalnie [ko-mer-**tsyahl**-ńe] adv. commercially
komercjalny [ko-mer-**tsyahl**-ni] adj.m. commercial
komercyjny [ko-mer-**tsiy**-ni] adj.m. profitable
komers [**ko**-mers] m. gaudy; reunion
komes [**ko**-mes] m. comes
komesostwo [ko-me-**sos**-tfo] n. the office of comes
kometa [ko-**me**-tah] f. comet
kometka [ko-**met**-kah] f. (small) comet; badmintion (game)
komeżka [ko-**mesh**-kah] f. (small) surplice
komfort [**kom**-fort] m. comfort; coziness; snugness; all modern conveniences
komfortowo [kom-for-**to**-vo] adv. comfortably; cozily; snugly; in well-appointed fashion
komfortowy [kom-for-**to**-vi] adj.m. comfortable; cozy; snug; well-appointed
mieszkanie komfortowe [myesh-**kah**-ńe kom-for-**to**-ve] exp.: apartment with all modern conveniences; well-appointed apartment
komicje [ko-**mee**-tsye] pl. comitia
komicjowy [ko-mee-**tsyo**-vi] adj.m. comitial
komicznie [ko-**meech**-ńe] adv. comically; in a funny manner
komiczność [ko-**meech**-nośhćh] f. comicality; a funny manner; laughableness; drollness
komiczny [ko-**meech**-ni] adj.m. comic; amusing; funny; droll
komięga [ko-**myan**-gah] f. river barge for grain transport
komik [**ko**-meek] m. comediant;

comic; comedian; wag; entertainer; funny man; clown; slang: homosexual (mob jargon)

komika [ko-me-kah] f. comicality

komiks [ko-meeks] m. comic strip; comic book

komiksowo [ko-meek-so-vo] adv. like a comic strip

komiksowy [ko-meek-so-vi] adj.m. of the comic strip

komiksy [ko-meek-si] pl. comics; comic strip

komiliton [ko-mee-lee-ton] m. colloq: companion; combatant

komin [ko-meen] m. chimney; (smoke-)stack; chimney-stack; chimney-top; kitchen range; vent (of a volcano); colloq: salary much higher than average

kominek [ko-mee-nek] m. fireplace; hearth; open fire

kominiarczyk [ko-mee-ńahr-chik] m. chimney sweep's apprentice

kominiarka [ko-mee-ńahr-kah] f. woolen cap; flying helmet

kominiarski [ko-mee-ńahr-skee] adj.m. chimney sweep's

kominiarstwo [ko-mee-ńahr-stfo] n. chimney sweep's work; chimney sweeping

kominiarz [ko-mee-ńahsh] m. chimney sweep

kominkowy [ko-meen-ko-vi] adj.m. of a fireplace; of an open hearth; of a hearth

kominowe [ko-mee-no-ve] n. chimney tax; fee for cleaning of a chimney

kominowy [ko-mee-no-vi] adj.m. of a chimney; chimney (outlet, etc.); of a flue

kominówka [ko-mee-noof-kah] f. chimney liner; flue liner; slang: moonshine (mob jargon)

komis [ko-mees] m. (on) commission sale; commission shop; commission agent

komisant [ko-mee-sahnt] m. broker

komisantka [ko-mee-sahnt-kah] f. (woman) broker

komisariat [ko-mee-sahr-yaht] m. police station; commissariat

komisarski [ko-mee-sahr-skee] adj.m. of a commissioner; of a commissar

komisarycznie [ko-mee-sah-rich-ńe] adv. by appointment

komisaryczny [ko-mee-sah-rich-ni] adj.m. chosen by appointment

komisarz [ko-mee-sahsh] m. police officer; commissioner; commissar

komisja [ko-mee-syah] f. commission; board (of inquiry) (standing) committee

komisja budżetowa [ko-mee-syah boo-dzhe-to-vah] exp.: budget committee

komisja lekarska [ko-mee-syah le-kahr-skah] exp.: medical board

komisjoner [ko-mees-yo-ner] m. commissioner; broker

komisowe [ko-mee-so-ve] n. fee; commission

komisowy [ko-mee-so-vi] adj.m. commission (sale, agent, etc.)

komisyjka [ko-mee-siy-kah] f. (small, nice) brokerage fee; commission

komisyjnie [ko-mee-siy-ńe] adv. corporately; collectively; in the presence of a committee; by a committee

komisyjny [ko-mee-siy-ni] adj.m. corporate; collective

komiśniak [ko-meeśh-ńahk] m. dark rye bread (in military rations)

komiśny [ko-meeśh-ni] adj.m. rationed (to soldiers); soldier's

komitent [ko-mee-tent] m. owner of an item placed for sale on commission

komitet [ko-mee-tet] m. committee; board

być w komitecie [bićh f ko-mee-te-ćhe] exp.: to be on a committee

komitetowa [ko-mee-te-to-vah] f. (female) member of a committee; committeewoman

komitetowy [ko-mee-te-to-vi] adj.m. committee (work, etc.); m. member of a committee; committeeman

komitywa [ko-mee-ti-vah] f. intimacy; good friendly terms

wejść w komitywę [veyśhćh f ko-mee-ti-van] exp.: to make friends (with somebody)

komiwojażer [ko-mee-vo-yah-zher]

m. travelling salesman
komiwojażerka [ko-mee-vo-yah-**zher**-kah] f. travelling saleswoman
komiwojażerski [ko-mee-vo-yah-**zher**-skee] adj.m. of a travelling salesman
komiwojażerstwo [ko-mee-vo-yah-**zher**-stfo] n. travelling salesmanship
komizm [**ko**-meezm] m. comism; comicality
komnata [kom-**nah**-tah] f. chamber
komnatka [kom-**naht**-kah] f. small chamber
komnatowy [kom-nah-**to**-vi] adj.m. of a chamber
komoda [ko-**mo**-dah] f. chest of drawers; lowboy; commode
komodor [ko-**mo**-dor] m. commodore
komondor [ko-**mon**-dor] m. Hungarian sheepdog
komonica [ko-mo-**ńee**-tsah] f. bird's foot trefoil; shoes and stockings
komora [ko-**mo**-rah] f. chamber; room; recess; bed-chamber; hall; ventricle; utricle; stall; (navigation) lock; cave
komora celna [ko-**mo**-rah **tsel**-nah] exp.: customs office; custom house (where duties are paid)
komora gazowa [ko-**mo**-rah gah-**zo**-vah] exp.: gas chamber
komora ogniowa paleniska [ko-**mo**-rah og-**ńo**-vah pah-le-**ńee**-skah] exp.: firebox
komora powietrzna [ko-**mo**-rah po-**vyetsh**-nah] exp.: air chamber
komorne [ko-**mor**-ne] n. (apartment) rent; rental
komorniany [ko-mor-**ńah**-ni] adj.m. rental; of a rent
komornica [ko-mor-**ńee**-tsah] f. (female) tenant farmer
komornictwo [ko-mor-**ńeets**-tfo] n. tenant farming
komorniczy [ko-mor-**ńee**-chi] adj.m. of a tenant farmer; of a sheriff's office; of a bailiff
komornik [ko-**mor**-ńeek] m. sheriff's officer; bailiff; tenant farmer; courtier
komorny [ko-**mor**-ni] adj.m. of a courtier; m. courtier
komorować [ko-mo-**ro**-vahćh] v. mine (for coal, etc.) using a system of chambers (*repeatedly*)
komorowanie [ko-mo-ro-**vah**-ńe] n. mining system of chambers
komorowy [ko-mo-**ro**-vi] adj.m. chamber (mining system, etc.)
komorzy [ko-**mo**-zhi] m. chamberlain
komosa [ko-**mo**-sah] f. goosefoot; blite (herb); pigweed
komosowaty [ko-mo-so-**vah**-ti] adj.m. chenopodiaceous; of the goosefoot family of herbs
komosowate [ko-mo-so-**vah**-te] pl. the family chenopodiaceae
komódka [ko-**moot**-kah] f. (small) chest of drawers; lowboy; commode
komórczak [ko-**moor**-chahk] m. cenocite; coenosite (mineral)
komóreczka [ko-moo-**rech**-kah] f. (small) cell; receptacle; alcove
komórka [ko-**moor**-kah] f. cell; receptacle; alcove; niche; alveary cell (with honey); division; section; service; cellule; loculus
komórka fotoelektryczna [ko-**moor**-kah fo-to-e-lek-**trich**-nah] exp.: photoelectric cell
komórkowaty [ko-moor-ko-**vah**-ti] adj.m. cell-like; celliform; cytoid; locular
komórkowy [ko-moor-**ko**-vi] adj.m. cellular; locular; of a cell
jądro komórkowe [y<u>own</u>-dro ko-moor-**ko**-ve] exp.: cytoblast
kompakcja [kom-**pahk**-tsyah] f. geological compaction
kompakt [**kom**-pahkt] m. compact (radio, record player, etc.)
kompaktowy [kom-pahk-**to**-vi] adj.m. of a compact (radio, record player, disk, etc.)
kompan [**kom**-pahn] m. chum; pal; comrade
kompander [kom-**pahn**-der] m. compounder of television signal
kompandor [kom-**pahn**-dor] m. compounder of television signal
kompania [kom-**pah**-ńyah] f. company; (stock, military) society; pilgrimage; slang: friendship; harmony (mob jargon)
dotrzymać komuś kompanii [do-

tshi-mahćh **ko**-moośh kom-**pah**-ńyee] exp.: to keep somebody company; to keep pace with the company

kompanić się [kom-**pah**-ńeećh śh<u>an</u>] v. slang: make friends (mob jargon) (*repeatedly*)

kompanijka [kom-pah-**ńeey**-kah] f. colloq: (small, unimportant) company; (stock, military) company; society; pilgrimage; colloq: gang; spree; binge

kompanijny [kom-pah-**ńeey**-ni] adj.m. belonging to a company; company (orchestra, cook, etc.)

kompanka [kom-**pahn**-kah] f. (female) chum; pal; comrade

komparator [kom-pah-**rah**-tor] m. comparator (of length, of computer memory)

komparatysta [kom-pah-rah-**tis**-tah] m. specialist in comparative literature; specialist of comparative linguistics

komparatystycznie [kom-pah-rah-tis-**tich**-ńe] adv. using a comparative method

komparatystyczny [kom-pah-rah-tis-**tich**-ni] adj.m. comparatival; comparativist

komparatystyka [kom-pah-rah-**tis**-ti-kah] f. comparative literature; comparative linguistics

komparatywizm [kom-pah-rah-**ti**-veezm] m. comparative method

komparatywny [kom-pah-rah-**tiv**-ni] adj.m. comparative

komparatyzm [kom-pah-**rah**-tizm] m. comparative method

kompars [**kom**-pahrs] m. supernumerary; colloq: super; dummy

kompas [**kom**-pahs] m. compass

kompasowy [kom-pah-**so**-vi] adj.m. compass (needle, etc.)

kompatybilny [kom-pah-ti-**beel**-ni] adj.m. compatible (computer, software, etc.)

kompaund [**kom**-pahwnt] m. compound (engine)

kompendialnie [kom-pen-**dyahl**-ńe] adv. compendiously

kompendialny [kom-pen-**dyahl**-ni] adj.m. compendious

kompendium [kom-**pend**-yoom] n. compendium; compend; abstract; synopsis; syllabus; brief; digest; abridgment; epitome

kompensacja [kom-pen-**sah**-tsyah] f. compensation (in biology and technology); indemnity

kompensacyjnie [kom-pen-sah-**tsiy**-ńe] adv. as a compensation

kompensacyjny [kom-pen-sah-**tsiy**-ni] adj.m. compensation (balance, bar, law, etc.); compensatory; compensative

kompensata [kom-pen-**sah**-tah] f. compensation; indemnity

kompensator [kom-pen-**sah**-tor] m. compensator; compensation balance

kompensować [kom-pen-**so**-vahćh] v. compensate; counterbalance; offset (*repeatedly*)
kompensować stratę [kom-pen-**so**-vahćh **strah**-t<u>an</u>] exp.: to make up for a loss; to pay indemnity; to recompense

kompensować się [kom-pen-**so**-vahćh śh<u>an</u>] v. offset each other; be compensated (by) (*repeatedly*)

kompensowanie [kom-pen-so-**vah**-ńe] n. compensation; paying indemnity

kompensowanie się [kom-pen-so-**vah**-ńe śh<u>an</u>] n. offsetting each other

kompetencja [kom-pe-**ten**-tsyah] f. competence; competency; authority; jurisdiction; powers; ability; qualifications; cognizance; colloq: sphere; scope; province
nie mam odpowiednich kompetencji [ńe mahm ot-po-**vyed**-ńeekh kom-pe-**ten**-tsyee] exp.: I have no authority; I have no adequate qualification
posiadać kompetencje [po-**śhah**-dahćh kom-pe-**ten**-tsye] exp.: to be competent (to do ...); to be qualified (to do ...)

kompetencyjnie [kom-pe-ten-**tsiy**-ńe] adv. by competence

kompetencyjność [kom-pe-ten-**tsiy**-nośhćh] f. competence; competency

kompetencyjny [kom-pe-ten-**tsiy**-ni] adj.m. pertaining to competence
kompetentnie [kom-pe-**ten**-tńe] adv. competently; with competence
kompetentność [kom-pe-**ten**-tnośhćh] f. competence; competency
kompetentny [kom-pe-**ten**-tni] adj.m. competent; qualified; cognizant
kompilacja [kom-pee-**lah**-tsyah] f. compilation; colloq: patchwork
kompilacyjny [kom-pee-lah-**tsiy**-ni] adj.m. of compilation
kompilator [kom-pee-**lah**-tor] m. compiler
kompilatorka [kom-pee-lah-**tor**-kah] f. (female) compiler
kompilatorski [kom-pee-lah-**tor**-skee] adj.m. compilation (ability, style of writing, etc.); compiler's
kompilatorstwo [kom-pee-lah-**tor**-stfo] n. compilatory work; compiler's work
kompilować [kom-pee-**lo**-vahćh] v. compile (*repeatedly*)
kompilowanie [kom-pee-lo-**vah**-ńe] n. compilation
komplanarny [kom-plah-**nahr**-ni] adj.m. expressing grief
komplecik [kom-**ple**-ćheek] m. (small) complete set; complete (full) group; full assembly; study group; class; complete suit (of furniture)
kompleks [**kom**-pleks] m. complex (of buildings); group; (inferiority) complex; whole
kompleksy [kom-**plek**-si] pl. complex (chemical) compounds
kompleksja [kom-**pleks**-yah] f. makeup of the body, disposition, temperament, etc.
kompleksometria [kom-plek-so-**metr**-yah] f. complexometry
kompleksometryczny [kom-plek-so-met-**rich**-ni] adj.m. complexometric
kompleksom [kom-**plek**-son] m. complexion; chelating agent
kompleksony [kom-plek-**so**-ni] pl. complexions; chelating agents (for identifying metallic cations)
kompleksowo [kom-ple-**kso**-vo] adv. as a composite unity
kompleksowość [kom-ple-**kso**-vośhćh] f. complexity; complex nature
kompleksowy [kom-ple-**kso**-vi] adj.m. complex; composite
komplemenciarski [kom-ple-men-**ćhahr**-skee] adj.m. complimentary
komplemenciarz [kom-ple-**men**-ćhahsh] m. man of compliments; flatterer
komplemencik [kom-ple-**men**-ćheek] m. (small, nice) compliment; (a) flattering remark
komplemencista [kom-ple-men-**ćhees**-tah] m. man of compliments; flatterer
komplement [kom-**ple**-ment] m. compliment; (a) flattering remark
prawić komplementy [**prah**-veećh kom-ple-**men**-ti] exp.: to pay compliments
komplementarność [kom-ple-men-**tahr**-nośhćh] f. complementarism
komplementarny [kom-ple-men-**tahr**-ni] adj.m. complementary
komplementować [kom-ple-men-**to**-vahćh] v. pay compliments; present with a token of of esteem (*repeatedly*)
komplementować się [kom-ple-men-**to**-vahćh śhan] v. pay compliments to each other (*repeatedly*)
komplementowanie [kom-ple-men-to-**vah**-ńe] n. paying compliments
komplementowanie się [kom-ple-men-to-**vah**-ńe śhan] n. paying compliments to each other
komplet [**kom**-plet] m. complete set; complete (full) group; full assembly; study group; class; complete suit (of furniture); kit (of tools); slang: bunch of thieves
kompleta [kom-**ple**-tah] f. complin; compline
kompletnie [kom-**plet**-ńe] adv. completely; utterly; wholly; entirely; altogether; colloq: regularly
kompletność [kom-**plet**-nośhćh] f. completeness
kompletny [kom-**plet**-ni] adj.m. complete; entire; utter; thorough; downright

kompletne fiasko [kom-**plet**-ne **fyahs**-ko] exp.: dead failure
kompletne zero [kom-**plet**-ne **ze**-ro] exp.: a nobody; a nonentity
kompletny nonsens [kom-**plet**-ni **non**-sens] exp.: utter nonsense; sheer nonsense
kompletować [kom-ple-**to**-vahćh] v. complete; make up (a set, etc.); complement (*repeatedly*)
kompletować się [kom-ple-**to**-vahćh śhan] v. become completed; be completed (*repeatedly*)
kompletowanie [kom-ple-to-**vah**-ńe] n. completion
kompletownia [kom-ple-**tov**-ńah] f. assembling section in a plant
kompletywnie [kom-ple-**tiv**-ńe] adv. completively
kompletywny [kom-ple-**tiv**-ni] adj.m. completive
komplikacja [kom-plee-**kah**-tsyah] f. complication; entanglement; difficulty; hitch
komplikować [kom-plee-**ko**-vahćh] v. complicate; tangle (*repeatedly*)
komplikować problem [kom-plee-**ko**-vahćh **prob**-lem] exp.: to complicate a problem; to confuse an issue
komplikować się [kom-plee-**ko**-vahćh śhan] v. become complicated; become entangled; become involved; become intricate (*repeatedly*)
komplikowanie [kom-plee-ko-**vah**-ńe] n. complication
komplikowanie się [kom-plee-ko-**vah**-ńe śhan] n. getting complicated
kompociarz [kom-**po**-ćhahsh] m. addict using the brew of poppy stems (intravenously)
kompocik [kom-**po**-ćheek] m. (nice, little) compote; fruit stew
komponent [kom-**po**-nent] m. component; constituent; component part
komponować [kom-po-**no**-vahćh] v. compose; invent (*repeatedly*)
komponowanie [kom-po-no-**vah**-ńe] n. composition
kompost [**kom**-post] m. compost; leaf mold
komposter [kom-**pos**-ter] m. device for marking tickets and documents
kompostować [kom-po-**sto**-vahćh] v. compost; treat with compost (*repeatedly*)
kompostowanie [kom-po-sto-**vah**-ńe] n. compost manuring
kompostownia [kom-po-**stov**-ńah] f. compost preparation shed and tanks
kompostowy [kom-po-**sto**-vi] adj.m. compost (mixture, etc.)
stos kompostowy [stos kom-po-**sto**-vi] exp.: compost heap
kompot [**kom**-pot] m. compote; stewed fruit; colloq: brew of poppy stems used intravenously by drug addicts
podbijacz z kompotem [pod-**bee**-yahch s kom-**po**-tem] exp.: poosher of brew of poppy stems (for intravenous use)
kompotiera [kom-po-**tye**-rah] f. (large) compote-dish
kompotierka [kom-po-**tyer**-kah] f. compote-dish
kompotowy [kom-po-**to**-vi] adj.m. suitable for stewing
kompozycja [kom-po-**zi**-tsyah] f. composition (of a piece of music, of a literary work); mixture; alloy; invention
kompozycyjnie [kom-po-zi-**tsiy**-ńe] adv. compositionally; in respect of composition; as regards composition
kompozycyjny [kom-po-zi-**tsiy**-ni] adj.m. of composition; compositional; composition (class, etc.)
kompozytor [kom-po-**zi**-tor] m. composer (of music)
kompozytorka [kom-po-zi-**tor**-kah] f. (female) composer (of music)
kompozytorski [kom-po-zi-**tor**-skee] adj.m. composer's; composers' (art, etc.)
kompozytorstwo [kom-po-zi-**tor**-stfo] n. composer's work
komprador [kom-**prah**-dor] m. comprador; compradore
kompradorski [kom-prah-**dor**-skee] adj.m. comprador's; compradore's

kompres [**kom**-pres] m. compress; poultice
kompresik [kom-**pre**-śheek] m. (small) compress
kompresja [kom-**pre**-syah] f. compression
kompresor [kom-**pre**-sor] m. compressor (of gas, of air, etc.)
kompresornia [kom-pre-**sor**-ńah] f. compressor shed
kompresorownia [kom-pre-so-**rov**-ńah] f. compressor shed
kompresorowy [kom-pre-so-**ro**-vi] adj.m. compressor (shed, etc.)
kompresować [kom-pre-**so**-vahćh] v. compress (air, etc.) (*repeatedly*)
kompresowanie [kom-pre-so-**vah**-ńe] n. compression
kompromis [kom-**pro**-mees] m. compromise; accommodation; settlement; mid course
pójść na kompromis [pooyśhćh nah kom-**pro**-mees] exp.: to compromise; to take the middle course; to split the difference
kompromisowo [kom-pro-mee-**so**-vo] adv. by way of compromise; by compromise
kompromisowość [kom-pro-mee-**so**-vośhćh] f. readiness to compromise
kompromisowy [kom-pro-mee-**so**-vi] adj.m. compromising
kompromitacja [kom-pro-mee-**tah**-tsyah] f. disgrace; loss of face; shame; humiliation; discredit
kompromitować [kom-pro-mee-**to**-vahćh] v. compromise; humiliate; bring discredit; bring shame; make (somebody) look silly; betray somebody (*repeatedly*)
kompromitować się [kom-pro-mee-**to**-vahćh śh<u>an</u>] v. compromise oneself; lose face; discredit oneself; bring shame upon oneself; disgrace oneself; betray each other (*repeatedly*)
kompromitowanie [kom-pro-mee-to-**vah**-ńe] n. humiliation; bringing discredit; loss of face
kompromitowanie się [kom-pro-mee-to-**vah**-ńe śh<u>an</u>] n. discrediting oneself
komprymować [kom-pri-**mo**-vahćh] v. compress (*repeatedly*)
komprymowanie [kom-pri-mo-**vah**-ńe] n. compression
komput [**kom**-poot] m. number (of troops, etc)
komputer [kom-**poo**-ter] m. computer; mob slang: old thief
komputernik [kom-poo-**ter**-ńeek] m. slang: computernik; computer user; mob slang: gang leader
komputerowiec [kom-poo-te-**ro**-vyets] m. computernik; computer user; mob slang: gang leader
komputerowy [kom-poo-te-**ro**-vi] adj.m. computer (program, etc.); computerlike; m. slang: old thief
komputeryzacja [kom-poo-te-ri-**zah**-tsyah] f. computerization
komputeryzować [kom-poo-te-ri-**zo**-vahćh] v. computerize; control by computer; equip with computers (*repeatedly*)
komsomolec [kom-so-**mo**-lets] m. member of the Comsomol
komsomolski [kom-so-**mol**-skee] adj.m. of the Comsomol
komsomoł [kom-**so**-mow] m. Comsomol; Communist Union of Youth (in the former USSR)
komtur [**kom**-toor] m. Commander of Teutonic Brethren (Knights)
komturia [kom-**toor**-yah] f. district governed by the Commander of Teutonic Brethren (Knights)
komturostwo [kom-too-**ros**-tfo] n. the office of the Commander of Teutonic Brethren (Knights)
komturstwo [kom-**toor**-stfo] n. the office of the Commander of Teutonic Brethren (Knights)
komuch [**ko**-mookh] m. colloq: (shabby, etc.) communist
komuna [ko-**moo**-nah] f. commune; commonalty; colloq: communist system; slang: commune of thieves (mob jargon)
komunalizacja [ko-moo-nah-lee-**zah**-tsyah] f. communalization
komunalizm [ko-moo-**nah**-leezm] m. communalism
komunalny [ko-moo-**nahl**-ni] adj.m. communal; municipal
komunał [ko-**moo**-nahw] m.

platitude; banality; trite remark; commonplace
komunard [ko-**moo**-nahrt] m. Communard
komunia [ko-**moo**-ńyah] f. Communion (in Catholic church); slang: rehabilitation of drug addicts; rehab of alcoholics
komunik [ko-**moo**-ńeek] m. old style light cavalry detachment
komunikacja [ko-moo-ńee-**kah**-tsyah] f. communication; contact
komunikacyjnie [ko-moo-ńee-kah-**tsiy**-ńe] adv. in respect of communication; as regards communication
komunikacyjny [ko-moo-ńee-kah-**tsiy**-ni] adj.m. (means, lines, etc.) of communication
komunikant [ko-moo-**ńee**-kahnt] m. communicant
komunikat [ko-moo-**ńee**-kaht] m. bulletin; report; communique
komunikat meteorologiczny [ko-moo-**ńee**-kaht me-te-o-ro-lo-**geech**-ni] exp.: weather forecast; weather report
komunikatywnie [ko-moo-ńee-kah-**tiv**-ńe] adv. communicatively talkatively
komunikatywność [ko-moo-ńee-kah-**tiv**-nośhćh] f. communicativeness; talkativeness
komunikatywny [ko-moo-ńee-kah-**tiv**-ni] adj.m. communicative; talkative; communicatory
komunikować [ko-moo-ńee-**ko**-vahćh] v. impart news; convey news; transmit news; inform; give news; report (*repeatedly*)
komunikować się [ko-moo-ńee-**ko**-vahćh śhan] v. communicate; be in communication; hold spiritual intercourse; be sociable; communicate; receive Holy Communion; be in contact (*repeatedly*)
komunikowalnie [ko-moo-ńee-ko-**vahl**-ńe] adv. communicably
komunikowalność [ko-moo-ńee-ko-**vahl**-nośhćh] f. communicability
komunikowalny [ko-moo-ńee-ko-**vahl**-ni] adj.m. communicable
komunikowanie [ko-moo-ńee-ko-**vah**-ńe] n. (inter)communication
komunikowanie się [ko-moo-ńee-ko-**vah**-ńe śhan] n. communicating with each other
komunista [ko-moo-**ńees**-tah] m. communist (party member); slang: pupil receiving the first Communion
komunistka [ko-moo-**ńeest**-kah] f. (woman) communist (party member)
komunistycznie [ko-moo-ńees-**tich**-ńe] adv. communistically; in terms of Communism
komunistyczny [ko-moo-ńees-**tich**-ni] adj.m. communist (party, etc.); communistic (tendencies, etc.)
komunizm [ko-**moo**-ńeezm] m. communism; community
komunizować [ko-moo-ńee-**zo**-vahćh] v. communize; tend towards communism (*repeatedly*)
komunizować się [ko-moo-ńee-**zo**-vahćh śhan] v. become communist; go communist (*repeatedly*)
komunizowanie [ko-moo-ńee-zo-**vah**-ńe] n. communist tendencies
komunizowanie się [ko-moo-ńee-zo-**vah**-ńe śhan] n. going communist; becoming communist
komunizujący [ko-moo-ńee-zoo-**yown**-tsi] adj.m. tending towards communism
człowiek komunizujący [**chwo**-vyek ko-moo-ńee-zoo-**yown**-tsi] exp.: fellow-traveller
komutacja [ko-moo-**tah**-tsyah] f. commutation
komutator [ko-moo-**tah**-tor] m. commutator
komutatorowy [ko-moo-tah-to-**ro**-vi] adj.m. commutator (motor, etc.)
komutatywność [ko-moo-tah-**tiv**-nośhćh] f. commutativity
komutatywny [ko-moo-tah-**tiv**-ni] adj.m. commutative
komutować [ko-moo-**to**-vahćh] v. commute; exchange; commutate (*repeatedly*)
komutowanie [ko-moo-to-**vah**-ńe] n. commuting
komysz [**ko**-mish] m. thicket; rushes

(in the marshes)
komża [**kom**-zhah] f. surplice
konać [**ko**-nahćh] v. agonize; expire; be dying; die (with greed, with laughter, etc.) (*repeatedly*)
konający [ko-nah-**yown**-tsi] adj.m. dying; in the throes of death; moribund; pl. the dying
konanie [ko-**nah**-ńe] n. the throes of death; agony; one's last gasp
konar [**ko**-nahr] m. limb; branch
konarzysty [ko-nah-**zhis**-ti] adj.m. branched; branchy; ramified
koncelebracja [kon-tse-leb-**rah**-tsyah] f. concelebration
koncentracja [kon-tsen-**trah**-tsyah] f. concentration; accumulation
koncentracyjny [kon-tsen-trah-**tsiy**-ni] adj.m. of concentration; concentration (camp, etc.)
koncentrat [kon-**tsen**-traht] m. extract; concentrate; concentration
koncentrować [kon-tsen-**tro**-vahćh] v. concentrate; accumulate (*repeatedly*)
koncentrować uwagę [kon-tsen-**tro**-vahćh oo-**vah**-gan] exp.: to fix attention (on something)
koncentrować się [kon-tsen-**tro**-vahćh śhan] v. concentrate (on); accumulate (*repeatedly*)
koncentrowanie [kon-tsen-tro-**vah**-ńe] n. concentration
koncentrowanie się [kon-tsen-tro-**vah**-ńe śhan] n. undergoing concentration; concentrating
koncentrycznie [kon-tsen-**trich**-ńe] adv. concentrically
koncentryczny [kon-tsen-**trich**-ni] adj.m. concentric; converging; convergent
koncepcik [kon-**tsep**-ćheek] m. (nice, little) idea
koncepcja [kon-**tsep**-tsyah] f. idea; conception; general outline
koncepcyjka [kon-tsep-**tsiy**-kah] f. nice little idea
koncepcyjnie [kon-tsep-**tsiy**-ńe] adv. conceptually
koncepcyjny [kon-tsep-**tsiy**-ni] adj.m. conceptional
koncept [**kon**-tsept] m. concept; idea; joke; plan; draft of a plan; scheme; acumen; keen discernment; brain wave
konceptualista [kon-tsep-too-ah-**lees**-tah] m. conceptualist
konceptualistyczny [kon-tsep-too-ah-lees-**tich**-ni] adj.m. conceptualistic
konceptualizm [kon-tsep-too-**ah**-leezm] m. conceptualism
konceptualny [kon-tsep-too-**ahl**-ni] adj.m. conceptual; conceptualistic
konceptysta [kon-tsep-**tis**-tah] m. poet writing in flowery style
konceptyzm [kon-**tsep**-tizm] m. Spanish writing in a very flowery style (17th cent.)
koncercik [kon-**tser**-ćheek] m. (small, nice) concert
koncern [**kon**-tsern] m. syndicate; consortium; colloq: horizontal combine
koncert [**kon**-tsert] m. concert
koncertant [kon-**tser**-tahnt] m. concertist; performer
koncertantka [kon-tser-**tahnt**-kah] f. (female) concertist; performer
koncertmistrz [kon-**tsert**-meestsh] m. concertmaster; leader of the strings
koncertować [kon-tser-**to**-vahćh] v. give a concert; perform (*repeatedly*)
koncertowanie [kon-tser-to-**vah**-ńe] n. giving a concert; performing
koncertowo [kon-tser-**to**-vo] adv. like a virtuoso; admirably; magnificently; in a masterly manner
koncertowy [kon-tser-**to**-vi] adj.m. concert (music, etc.); admirable; magnificent
koncertyna [kon-tser-**ti**-nah] f. concertina
koncerz [**kon**-tsesh] m. sword (long, straight)
koncesja [kon-**tse**-syah] f. concession; conceding; right to sell; license; license to do...
koncesjonariusz [kon-tse-syo-**nahr**-yoosh] m. licensee; concessionaire
koncesjonować [kon-tse-syo-**no**-vahćh] v. license; licence (*repeatedly*)
koncesjonowanie [kon-tse-syo-no-

vah-ńe] n. giving licenses; issuing licenses
koncesjonowany [kon-tse-syo-no-**vah**-ni] adj.m. licensed; licenced
koncesyjka [kon-tse-**siy**-kah] f. (small, nice) concession; conceding; right to sell; license; license to do...
koncesyjny [kon-tse-**siy**-ni] adj.m. concession (stand, etc.); of the right to sell; of a license (to do)
koncha [**kon**-khah] f. conch; concha; counter
koncha uszna [**kon**-khah **oosh**-nah] exp.: concha; external ear
konchina [kon-**khee**-nah] f. conchiolin (mother of pearl)
konchiolina [kon-khyo-**lee**-nah] f. conchiolin
konchiolinowy [kon-khyo-lee-**no**-vi] adj.m. of conchiolin
konchiolog [kon-**khyo**-lok] m. conchologist
konchiologia [kon-khyo-**log**-yah] f. conchology
konchiologicznie [kon-khyo-lo-**geech**-ńe] adv. conchologically
konchiologiczny [kon-khyo-lo-**geech**-ni] adj.m. conchological
konchoida [kon-**khoy**-dah] f. conchoid
konchoidograf [kon-kho-ee-**do**-grahf] m. device for drawing a conchoid
konchowo [kon-**kho**-vo] adv. conchoidally
konchowy [kon-**kho**-vi] adj.m. conchoidal; conchal; conchiform; shell-like
koncyliacja [kon-tsil-**yah**-tsyah] f. (legal) conciliation
koncyliacyjny [kon-tsil-yah-**tsiy**-ni] adj.m. conciliation (court, etc.); of (legal) conciliation
koncyliarysta [kon-tsil-yah-**ris**-tah] m. conciliator
koncyliaryzm [kon-tsil-**yah**-rizm] m. conciliatory theory of the 15th cent.
koncylium [kon-**tsil**-yoom] n. council
koncypient [kon-**tsi**-pyent] m. office clerk
koncypować [kon-tsi-**po**-vahćh] v. devise; compose (a text, etc.); draw up (a plan, etc.); word (a document, etc.) (*repeatedly*)
kondemnacja [kon-dem-**nah**-tsyah] f. condemnation
kondemnata [kon-dem-**nah**-tah] f. condemnation by a court in absentia
kondensacja [kon-den-**sah**-tsyah] f. condensation; compression
kondensacyjny [kon-den-sah-**tsiy**-ni] adj.m. condensation (water, etc.)
kondensat [kon-**den**-saht] m. condensate; condensation water; product of condensation
kondensator [kon-den-**sah**-tor] m. condenser; capacitor
kondensatorek [kon-den-sah-**to**-rek] m. (small) condenser; capacitor
kondensatorowy [kon-den-sah-to-**ro**-vi] adj.m. condenser (antenna, microphone, etc.)
kondensor [kon-**den**-sor] m. condenser; condensing lens
kondensować [kon-den-**so**-vahćh] v. condense; compress (*repeatedly*)
kondensować się [kon-den-**so**-vahćh śhan] v. to be condensed (*repeatedly*)
kondensowanie [kon-den-so-**vah**-ńe] n. condensation
kondensowanie się [kon-den-so-**vah**-ńe śhan] n. getting condensed; becoming condensed
kondolencja [kon-do-**len**-tsyah] f. condolence; words of sympathy; slang: failing grade
kondolencyjny [kon-do-len-**tsiy**-ni] adj.m. condolatory
kondom [**kon**-dom] m. condom
kondominium [kon-do-**meeń**-yoom] n. (political) condominium
kondor [**kon**-dor] m. condor
kondotier [kon-**do**-tyer] m. condottiere
kondotierski [kon-do-**tyer**-skee] adj.m. of a condottiere; mercenary's
kondotierstwo [kon-do-**tyer**-stfo] n. condottiere service; mercenary work
konduita [kon-doo-**ee**-tah] f. colloq: manners; behavior
kondukt [**kon**-dookt] m. funeral procession

konduktometria [kon-dook-to-**metr**-yah] f. conductomeric analysis
konduktometryczny [kon-dook-to-met-**rich**-ni] adj.m. conductomeric
konduktor [kon-**dook**-tor] m. conductor (lightning, electric, train, etc.); bus driver
konduktorka [kon-**dook**-tor-kah] f. (female) conductor; conductress
konduktorski [kon-dook-**tor**-skee] adj.m. conductor's
kondycja [kon-**di**-tsyah] f. form; social position; status; tutorship
być w dobrej kondycji [bićh v **do**-brey kon-**di**-tsyee] exp.: to be in form; to be fit
kondycjonalizm [kon-di-tsyo-**nah**-leezm] m. theory of conditionality
kondycjonalnie [kon-di-tsyo-**nahl**-ńe] adv. conditionally
kondycjonalny [kon-di-tsyo-**nahl**-ni] adj.m. conditional
kondycjoner [kon-di-**tsyo**-ner] m. grain conditioner
kondycjonować [kon-di-tsyo-**no**-vahćh] v. condition (wheat, textile, etc.) (*repeatedly*)
kondycjonowanie [kon-di-tsyo-no-**vah**-ńe] n. conditioning
kondycyjnie [kon-di-**tsiy**-ńe] adv. in respect of (athletic) condition
kondycyjny [kon-di-**tsiy**-ni] adj.m. of (athletic) condition
kondygnacja [kon-dig-**nah**-tsyah] f. storey; story; tier
kondygnacyjny [kon-dig-nah-**tsiy**-ni] adj.m. of a storey; of a story; of a tier
koneksja [ko-**nek**-syah] f. connection; relation
koneser [ko-**ne**-ser] m. expert; connoisseur
koneserka [ko-ne-**ser**-kah] f. (female) expert; connoisseur
koneserski [ko-ne-**ser**-skee] adj.m. of an expert; of a connoisseur
po konesersku [po ko-ne-**ser**-skoo] exp.: as an expert; as a connoisseur
koneserstwo [ko-ne-**ser**-stfo] n. connoisseurship
konew [**ko**-nef] f. pot; jug; (watering) can; pewter; jugful; potful; canful
koneweczka [ko-ne-**vech**-kah] f. (small, nice) pot; jug; (watering) can; pewter; jugful; potful; canful
konewka [ko-**nef**-kah] f. pot; jug; (watering) can; pewter; jugful; potful; canful; slang: machine gun
konfabulacja [kon-fah-boo-**lah**-tsyah] f. fabrication; fiction; invention; confabulation
konfabulować [kon-fah-boo-**lo**-vahćh] v. fabricate; invent; fake up (a story); give play to one's imagination (*repeatedly*)
konfederacja [kon-fe-de-**rah**-tsyah] f. confederation; confederacy
konfederacki [kon-fe-de-**rahts**-kee] adj.m. of the confederation; of the confederacy; confederate (troops, camp, etc.)
konfederacyjny [kon-fe-de-rah-**tsiy**-ni] adj.m. confederate (flag, etc.)
konfederat [kon-fe-**de**-raht] m. a confederate
konfederatka [kon-fe-de-**raht**-kah] f. square-topped cap
konfederować [kon-fe-de-**ro**-vahćh] v. confederate (*repeatedly*)
konfederować się [kon-fe-de-**ro**-vahćh śhan] v. confederate (*repeatedly*)
konfederowanie [kon-fe-de-ro-**vah**-ńe] n. confederation
konfekcja [kon-**fek**-tsyah] f. clothing manufacture; ready-made clothing; colloq: clothing store; slopshop; slops
konfekcjoner [kon-fek-**tsyo**-ner] m. manufacturer of ready-made clothes
konfekcjonować [kon-fek-tsyo-**no**-vahćh] v. manufacture (ready-made clothes) (*repeatedly*)
konfekcjonowanie [kon-fek-tsyo-no-**vah**-ńe] n. manufacture of ready-made clothes
konfekcyjny [kon-fek-**tsiy**-ni] adj.m. ready-made (clothes, etc.)
konferansjer [kon-fe-**rahns**-yer] m. master of ceremony; narrator
konferansjerka [kon-fe-rahns-**yer**-kah] f. the work of a master of ceremony; (woman) master of ceremony
konferansjerski [kon-fe-rahns-**yer**-

skee] adj.m. of a master of ceremony
konferansjerstwo [kon-fe-rahns-**yer**-stfo] n. the work of a master of ceremony
konferencja [kon-fe-**ren**-tsyah] f. conference; meeting; symposium
konferencyjka [kon-fe-ren-**tsiy**-kah] f. (small) conference; meeting; symposium
konferencyjny [kon-fe-ren-**tsiy**-ni] adj.m. conference (room, etc.)
konferować [kon-fe-**ro**-vahćh] v. have a conference; be in a meeting; hold a symposium (*repeatedly*)
konferowanie [kon-fe-ro-**vah**-ńe] n. holding of a conference
konfesja [kon-**fes**-yah] f. confession (shrine with saint's relics)
konfesjonał [kon-fes-**yo**-nahw] m. confessional; slang: debriefing room; cross-examination room
konfetti [kon-**fet**-tee] n. confetti
konfidencja [ko-fee-**den**-tsyah] f. intimacy; familiarity
konfidencjonalnie [ko-fee-den-tsyo-**nahl**-ńe] adv. familiarly; in confidence; privately; secretly; confidentially
konfidencjonalność [ko-fee-den-tsyo-**nahl**-nośhćh] f. intimacy; familiarity; confidentiality; privacy
konfidencjonalny [ko-fee-den-tsyo-**nahl**-ni] adj.m. intimate; familiar; confidential; private; said confidentially
konfident [kon-**fee**-dent] m. (common) informer; confidant; bosom friend
konfidentka [kon-fee-**dent**-kah] f. (female common) informer; confidant; bosom friend
konfiguracja [kon-fee-goo-**rah**-tsyah] f. configuration
konfiguracja terenu [kon-fee-goo-**rah**-tsyah te-**re**-noo] exp.: lay of the land
konfiguracjonizm [kon-fee-goo-rah-**tsyo**-ńeezm] m. configurationism
konfirmacja [kon-feer-**mah**-tsyah] f. confirmation; assent; sanction
konfirmacyjnie [kon-feer-mah-**tsiy**-ńe] adv. confirmatively
konfirmacyjny [kon-feer-mah-**tsiy**-ni] adj.m. confirmative; confirmatory
konfirmant [kon-**feer**-mahnt] m. man receiving confirmation
konfirmantka [kon-feer-**mahnt**-kah] f. woman receiving confirmation
konfirmować [kon-feer-**mo**-vahćh] v. confirm; administer confirmation (*repeatedly*)
konfirmowanie [kon-feer-mo-**vah**-ńe] n. confirming; administration of confirmation
konfiskata [kon-fees-**kah**-tah] f. confiscation; seizure; slang: illegal sale (mob jargon)
konfiskować [kon-fees-**ko**-vahćh] v. confiscate; sequester; seize; sequestrate (*repeatedly*)
konfiskowanie [kon-fees-ko-**vah**-ńe] n. confiscation
konfitura [kon-fee-**too**-rah] f. jam; preserve
konfitury [kon-fee-**too**-ri] pl. jams; preserves; candied fruits
konfiturowy [kon-fee-too-**ro**-vi] adj.m. of a jam; of preserves
konflikt [**kon**-fleekt] m. conflict; clash
konflikt interesu [**kon**-fleekt een-te-**re**-soo] exp.: conflict of interest
wejść w konflikt z prawem [veyśhćh f **kon**-fleekt s **prah**-vem] exp.: to infringe the law
konfliktowo [kon-fleek-**to**-vo] adv. conflictingly
konfliktowość [kon-fleek-**to**-vośhćh] f. confliction
konfliktowy [kon-fleek-**to**-vi] adj.m. conflicting; conflictive
konfluencja [kon-floo-**en**-tsyah] f. confluence
konfokalny [kon-fo-**kahl**-ni] adj.m. of common focus
konforemny [kon-fo-**rem**-ni] adj.m. of the same shape
konformista [kon-for-**mees**-tah] m. conformist
konformistycznie [kon-for-mees-**tich**-ńe] adv. conformably (to)
konformistyczny [kon-for-mees-**tich**-ni] adj.m. conformable (to)
konformizm [kon-**for**-meezm] m. conformism

konfrater [kon-**frah**-ter] m. member of a confraternity
konfraternia [kon-frah-**ter**-ńah] f. confraternity; brotherhood
konfrontacja [ko-fron-**tah**-tsyah] f. confrontation; collation; comparison
konfrontacyjny [ko-fron-tah-**tsiy**-ni] adj.m. confrontational
konfrontować [kon-fron-**to**-vahćh] v. confront; collate; bring face to face (*repeatedly*)
konfrontowanie [kon-fron-to-**vah**-ńe] n. confrontation
konfucjanista [kon-foots-yah-**ńees**-tah] m. Confucian
konfucjanizm [kon-foots-**yah**-ńeezm] m. Confucianism
konfucjański [kon-foots-**yahń**-skee] adj.m. Confucian
konfundować [kon-foon-**do**-vahćh] v. confound; confuse; perplex; abash (*repeatedly*)
konfundować się [kon-foon-**do**-vahćh śhan] v. be confounded; be confused; be perplexed; be abashed (*repeatedly*)
konfuzja [kon-**foo**-zyah] f. confusion
konfuzor [kon-**foo**-zor] m. orifice
kongelacja [kon-ge-**lah**-tsyah] f. icicle
kongelator [kon-ge-**lah**-tor] m. refrigerator; freezing machine
kongenialnie [kon-geń-**yahl**-ńe] adv. congenially; masterly
kongenialność [kon-geń-**yahl**-nośhćh] f. congeniality
kongenialny [kon-geń-**yahl**-ni] adj.m. congenial; masterly
konglomeracja [kon-glo-me-**rah**-tsyah] f. conglomeration
konglomerat [kon-glo-**me**-raht] m. conglomeration; conglomerate; hardpan (rock)
kongregacja [kon-gre-**gah**-tsyah] f. congregation; guild; association
kongregacjonalista [kon-gre-gah-tsyo-nah-**lees**-tah] m. congregationalist
kongregacjonalizm [kon-gre-gah-tsyo-**nah**-leezm] m. congregationalism
kongres [**kon**-gres] m. congress
Kongres [**kon**-gres] m. (U.S.) Congress
kongresman [kon-**gres**-men] m. congressman
kongresowiak [kon-gre-**so**-vyahk] m. inhabitant of the Congress Kingdom of Poland
kongresowy [kon-gre-**so**-vi] adj.m. of a congress
Kongresówka [kon-gre-**soof**-kah] f. The Congress Kingdom of Poland
kongruencja [kon-groo-**ents**-yah] f. congruence
kongruentnie [kon-groo-**ent**-ńe] adv. congruently
kongruentny [kon-groo-**ent**-ni] adj.m. congruent
koniaczek [ko-**ńah**-chek] m. (nice, little) cognac
koniak [**ko**-ńahk] m. cognac
koniarz [**ko**-ńahsh] m. horse lover; horse breeder; horse-dealer; horse-coper; slang: prison doctor
koniczek [ko-**ńee**-chek] m. (small) horse
koniczyna [ko-ńee-**chi**-nah] f. clover; trefoil
koniczynisko [ko-ńee-chi-**ńees**-ko] f. mown clover-field
koniczynka [ko-ńee-**chin**-kah] f. (small, nice) clover; trefoil
koniczynowy [ko-ńee-chi-**no**-vi] adj.m. clover (fodder, etc.)
konidialny [ko-ńee-**dyahl**-ni] adj.m. conidial
konidiofor [ko-ńee-**dyo**-for] m. conidiophore
konidiospory [ko-ńee-dyo-**spo**-ri] pl. conidiospores; conidia
konidium [ko-**ńeed**-yoom] n. conidium
  konidia [ko-**ńeed**-yah] pl. conidia
koniec [**ko**-ńets] m. end; finish; termination; close; extremity
  bez końca [bes **koń**-tsah] exp.: without end; interminable; unending; ceaseless; on and on; unendingly; interminably; indefinitely; ceaselessly; no end; continuing without cease
  do końca [do **koń**-tsah] exp.: to the end; to a finish; till the end;
  na koniec [nah **ko**-ńets] exp.: finally; to end with; last of all; to wind up

na końcu [nah **koń**-tsoo] exp.: lastly; at the end
na samym końcu [nah **sah**-mim **koń**-tsoo] exp.: at the very end; last of all; eventually
od końca [ot **koń**-tsah] exp.: from the end; beginning at the end; since the end
pod koniec [pot **ko**-ńets] exp.: latterly; in the latter part
w końcu [f **koń**-tsoo] exp.: at length; at last; lastly; ultimately; in conclusion; in the long run; eventually
z końcem [s **koń**-tsem] exp.: towards the end
koniecznie [ko-**ńech**-ńe] adv. absolutely; necessarily; indispensably; without fail
konieczność [ko-**ńech**-nośhćh] f. necessity; compulsion; unavoidableness; inevitability
konieczny [ko-**ńech**-ni] adj.m. necessary; needful; unavoidable; vital; requisite; indispensable
koniektura [ko-ńek-**too**-rah] f. conjecture
konietlica [ko-ńet-**lee**-tsah] f. trisetum (a forage grass)
koniina [ko-ńee-**ee**-nah] f. coniine
konik [**ko**-ńeek] m. pony; nag; cob; hobby-horse; hobby-fad; craze; (chess) knight; (crochet) hook; marker; upright support; poppet, poppethead (Brit.); colloq: scalper
konikowy [ko-ńee-**ko**-vi] adj.m. of a pony; of the chess knight
konimetr [ko-**ńee**-metr] m. gauge for measuring fluid content in the air
konina [ko-**ńee**-nah] f. horseflesh; horse meat
koniogodzina [ko-ńo-go-**dźhee**-nah] f. horsepower-hour
koniokrad [ko-**ńo**-kraht] m. horse thief; horse stealer; rustler
koniokradztwo [ko-ńo-**krahts**-tfo] n. horse stealing; cattle-lifting
koniopłoch [ko-**ńo**-pwokh] m. meadow saxifrage (herb); pepper saxifrage
koniował [ko-**ńo**-vahw] m. slang: masturbator (mob jargon)
koniowaty [ko-ńo-**vah**-ti] adj.m. equine
koniowate [ko-ńo-**vah**-te] pl. the equine family; the Equidae family
konisko [ko-**ńees**-ko] n. jade
koniś [**ko**-ńeeśh] m. (dear, good) horse
konitrut [ko-**ńee**-troot] m. hedge hyssop
koniuch [**ko**-ńookh] m. stable boy
koniugacja [ko-ńoo-**gah**-tsyah] f. conjugation
koniugacyjny [ko-ńoo-gah-**tsiy**-ni] adj.m. conjugational
koniugować [ko-ńoo-**go**-vahćh] v. conjugate (*repeatedly*)
koniugowanie [ko-ńoo-go-**vah**-ńe] n. conjugation
koniunkcja [ko-**ńoonk**-tsyah] f. (astrol. and math.) conjunction
koniunktiwus [ko-ńoonk-**tee**-voos] m. conjunctive mood
koniunktor [ko-**ńoonk**-tor] m. an electronic circuit for performing the operation (of the binary system) denoted by logical conjunction "and"; conjunctor
koniunktura [ko-ńoon-**ktoo**-rah] f. situation; circumstances; economic situation; business outlook; prosperity; state of affairs; situation of the market
dobra koniunktura [**dob**-rah ko-ńoon-**ktoo**-rah] exp.: boom; prosperity
zła koniunktura [zwah ko-ńoon-**ktoo**-rah] exp.: slump; recess; bear market
koniunkturalista [ko-ńoon-ktoo-rah-**lees**-tah] m. opportunist; temporizer; timeserver
koniunkturalizm [ko-ńoon-ktoo-**rah**-leezm] m. opportunistic behavior
koniunkturalnie [ko-ńoon-ktoo-**rahl**-ńe] adv. owing to the existing state of affairs; due to the existing situation
koniunkturalność [ko-ńoon-ktoo-**rahl**-nośhćh] f. the nature of the existing state of affairs
koniunkturalny [ko-ńoon-ktoo-**rahl**-ni] adj.m. resulting from the existing state of affairs; directed by (arising from, due to) the existing situation; transitory;

passing
cena koniunkturalna [**tse**-nah ko-ńoon-ktoo-**rahl**-nah] exp.: fancy price

koniunkturowy [ko-ńoon-ktoo-**ro**-vi] adj.m. of the existing state of affairs

koniunktyw [ko-**ńoonk**-tif] m. conjunctive mood

koniunktywny [ko-ńoonk-**tiv**-ni] adj.m. conjunctive (mood, etc.)

koniuszczek [ko-**ńoosh**-chek] m. the very tip (of a finger, etc.)

koniuszek [ko-**ńoo**-shek] m. tip (of the tongue, nose, finger, etc.); small extremity; end; rag-end (of a rope, etc.)

koniuszkowy [ko-ńoosh-**ko**-vi] adj.m. of the tip (of the tongue, nose, finger, etc.); of small extremity; of the end; of the rag-end (of a rope, etc.)
uderzenie koniuszkowe [oo-de-**zhe**-ńe ko-ńoosh-**ko**-ve] exp.: apex beat (of the heart)

koniuszy [ko-**ńoo**-shi] m. equerry; Master of the Horse (in charge of the stud of horses)

konkatenacja [kon-kah-te-**nah**-tsyah] f. concatenation

konkatenować [kon-kah-te-**no**-vahćh] v. concatenate; link (verses) together in series or chain (*repeatedly*)

konkieta [kon-**ke**-tah] f. conquest (of person's heart, etc.)

konklawe [kon-**klah**-ve] n. conclave

konklawista [kon-klah-**vees**-tah] m. conclavist

konkludować [kon-kloo-**do**-vahćh] v. conclude (a speech, etc.); infer; draw a conclusion (*repeatedly*)

konkludowanie [kon-kloo-do-**vah**-ńe] n. conclusion; inference

konkluzja [kon-**kloo**-zyah] f. conclusion; inference
w konkluzji [f kon-**kloo**-zyee] exp.: in conclusion
wyciągać konkluzję [vi-**ćhown**-gahćh kon-**kloo**-zyan] exp.: to draw a conclusion; to infer

konkordancja [kon-kor-**dahn**-tsyah] f. concordance

konkordans [kon-**kor**-dahns] m. 36 point font; variety of printing justification

konkordat [kon-**kor**-daht] m. concordat

konkrecja [kon-**kre**-tsyah] f. (geological) concretion

konkrecyjnie [kon-kre-**tsiy**-ńe] adv. by means of concretion

konkrecyjny [kon-kre-**tsiy**-ni] adj.m. concretive; of (geological) concretion; concretional; concretionary

konkret [**kon**-kret] m. (a, the) concrete
konkrety [kon-**kre**-ti] pl. hard facts; figures
przejść do konkretów [psheyśhćh do kon-**kre**-toof] exp.: to become specific; to give hard facts; slang: to come to brass tacks

konkretnie [kon-**kret**-ńe] adv. concretely; specifically; in concrete form

konkretność [kon-**kret**-nośhćh] f. concreteness; concrete nature (of a statement, etc.)

konkretny [kon-**kret**-ni] adj.m. concrete; definite; real; substantial; specific; actual; clear-cut; cut-and-dried
konkretny fakt [kon-**kret**-ni fahkt] exp.: a fact; a reality

konkretyzacja [kon-kre-ti-**zah**-tsyah] f. substantiation; realization; materialization; making specific; making definite

konkretyzm [kon-**kre**-tizm] m. concretism; representation of things as concrete; concretive philosophy of T. Kotarbiński

konkretyzować [kon-kre-ti-**zo**-vahćh] v. substantiate; realize; concretize; specify (*repeatedly*)

konkretyzować się [kon-kre-ti-**zo**-vahćh śhan] v. materialize; become realized; come off; become concrete (*repeatedly*)

konkretyzowanie [kon-kre-ti-zo-**vah**-ńe] n. substantiation; realization; materialization; making definite; making specific; making concrete

konkretyzowanie się [kon-kre-ti-zo-

vah-ńe śhan] n. self-realization; becoming materialized
konkubina [kon-koo-**bee**-nah] f. concubine
konkubinat [kon-koo-**bee**-naht] m. concubinage
konkurencja [kon-koo-**ren**-tsyah] f. competition; rivalry; contest; colloq: competitor; competitors; (sport) contest; colloq: rivalry
bez konkurencji [bes kon-koo-**ren**-tsyee] exp.: matchless; unrivalled
brudna konkurencja [**brood**-nah kon-koo-**ren**-tsyah] exp.: unfair competition
robić konkurencję [**ro**-beećh kon-koo-**ren**-tsyan] exp.: to compete (with); to spoil (somebody's) trade
wytrzymać konkurencję [vi-**tshi**-mahćh kon-koo-**ren**-tsyan] exp.: to withstand competition; to compete (successfully)
konkurencyjnie [kon-koo-ren-**tsiy**-ńe] adv. competitively
konkurencyjność [kon-koo-ren-**tsiy**-nośhćh] f. competitiveness
konkurencyjny [kon-koo-ren-**tsiy**-ni] adj.m. competitive
konkurent [kon-**koo**-rent] m. competitor; suitor; wooer
konkurentka [kon-koo-**rent**-kah] f. (female) competitor; rival
konkurować [kon-koo-**ro**-vahćh] v. rival; compete (for); vie; sue for a woman's hand (*repeatedly*)
konkurować ze sobą [kon-koo-**ro**-vahćh ze **so**-bown] exp.: to rival one another; to match one another; to contend with each other
konkurowanie [kon-koo-ro-**vah**-ńe] n. rivalry; competition
konkurs [**kon**-koors] m. contest; competition; trials; bankruptcy; insolvency
drogą konkursu [**dro**-gown kon-**koor**-soo] exp.: by open competition
ogłosić konkurs [o-**gwo**-śheećh **kon**-koors] exp.: to open to competition; to invite bids; to invite tenders
stanąć do konkursu [**stah**-nownćh do kon-**koor**-soo] exp.: to compete (for); to contest; to make a bid; to put a tender for a piece of work; to go in for a competition
konkursant [kon-**koor**-sahnt] m. contestant
konkursantka [kon-koor-**sahnt**-kah] f. (female) contestant
konkursista [kon-koor-**śhees**-tah] m. contestant
konkursistka [kon-koor-**śheest**-kah] f. (female) contestant
konkursowicz [kon-koor-**so**-veech] m. contestant
konkursowy [kon-koor-**so**-vi] adj.m. competitive; competitory
egzamin konkursowy [eg-**zah**-meen kon-koor-**so**-vi] exp.: competitive examination
masa konkursowa [**mah**-sah kon-koor-**so**-vah] exp.: bankrupt's assets
sąd konkursowy [sownt kon-koor-**so**-vi] exp.: jury
konkury [kon-**koo**-ri] pl. (love-)suit
konkwista [kon-**kfees**-tah] f. Spanish conquest in America
konkwistador [kon-kfees-**tah**-dor] m. Spanish conquistador
konkwistadorzy [kon-kfees-tah-**do**-zhi] pl. conquistadores; conquistadors
konnica [kon-**ńee**-tsah] f. cavalry; horse
oddział konnicy [**od**-dźhahw kon-**ńee**-tsi] exp.: cavalry unit; detachment of horse
konno [**kon**-no] adv. on horseback; (sit) astraddle; mounted
konny [**kon**-ni] adj.m. mounted; equestrian (statue, etc.); horsedrawn (carriage, etc.); m. mounted; man on horseback
dorożka konna [do-**rosh**-kah **kon**-nah] exp.: horse-drawn cab; four-wheeler (Brit.)
jazda konna [**yahz**-dah **kon**-nah] exp.: horsemanship; equitation
wyścigi konne [viśh-**ćhee**-gee **kon**-ne] exp.: horse-race; horse-races; horse racing
konoida [ko-**noy**-dah] f. conoid
konoidalny [ko-no-ee-**dahl**-ni] adj.m.

conoidal
konometr [ko-**no**-metr] m. device for measuring the angle between axes of a crystal
konopacić [ko-no-**pah**-ćheećh] v. caulk (*repeatedly*)
konopiany [ko-no-**pyah**-ni] adj.m. hemp (cord, etc.)
konopiasty [ko-no-**pyahs**-ti] adj.m. towy; of hackled flax
konopie [ko-**no**-pye] pl. hemp
konopiowaty [ko-no-pyo-**vah**-ti] adj.m. cannabinaceous; of the hop and hemp family
konopiowate [ko-no-pyo-**vah**-te] pl. the hop and hemp family
konopny [ko-**nop**-ni] adj.m. hemp (cord, etc.); hempen; towy
konosament [ko-no-**sah**-ment] m. bill of lading
konotacja [ko-no-**tah**-tsyah] f. connotation
konotacyjnie [ko-no-tah-**tsiy**-ńe] adv. connotatively; connotively
konotacyjny [ko-no-tah-**tsiy**-ni] adj.m. connotative; connotive
konotować [ko-no-**to**-vahćh] v. connote; make connotations; connotate (*repeatedly*)
konotowanie [ko-no-to-**vah**-ńe] n. connotation
konował [ko-**no**-vahw] m. farrier; horse-doctor; colloq: quack doctor; sawbones; medicaster (Brit.); slang: prison doctor
konradysta [kon-rah-**dis**-tah] m. student of writings of Joseph Conrad (Korzeniowski)
konsekracja [kon-sek-**rah**-tsyah] f. consecration
konsekrator [kon-sek-**rah**-tor] m. consecrator
konsekrować [kon-sek-**ro**-vahćh] v. consecrate (*repeatedly*)
konsekrowanie [kon-sek-ro-**vah**-ńe] n. consecration
konsekutywnie [kon-se-koo-**tiv**-ńe] adv. consecutively
konsekutywność [kon-se-koo-**tiv**-nośhćh] f. consecutiveness
konsekutywny [kon-se-koo-**tiv**-ni] adj.m. consecutive; successive
konsekwencja [kon-sek-**fen**-tsyah] f. consequence; effect; result; outcome; consistency (of conduct)
konsekwentnie [kon-sek-**fent**-ńe] adv. consistently; constantly
konsekwentny [kon-sek-**fent**-ni] adj.m. consistent; constant
konsens [**kon**-sens] m. consensus; agreement; permission
konsensowo [kon-sen-**so**-vo] adv. by agreement; by permission
konsensowy [kon-sen-**so**-vi] adj.m. of agreement; of permission
konsensualnie [kon-sen-soo-**ahl**-ńe] adv. consensually
konsensualny [kon-sen-soo-**ahl**-ni] adj.m. consensual
konserwa [kon-**ser**-vah] f. preserve; canned food; can of preserved food; colloq: conservatives
konserwacja [kon-ser-**vah**-tsyah] f. preservation; maintenance; upkeep
konserwacyjny [kon-ser-vah-**tsiy**-ni] adj.m. of preservation; maintenance (costs, etc.); upkeep (chores, etc.)
konserwant [kon-**ser**-vahnt] m. (a) preservative
konserwator [kon-ser-**vah**-tor] m. conservator; tender; keeper
konserwatorium [kon-ser-vah-**tor**-yoom] n. conservatory
konserwatornia [kon-ser-vah-**tor**-ńah] f. (artwork, etc.) restauration and preservation room
konserwatorski [kon-ser-vah-**tor**-skee] adj.m. conservator's; of preservation
konserwatorstwo [kon-ser-vah-**tor**-stfo] n. preservation of historical monuments, etc.
konserwatoryjny [kon-ser-vah-to-**riy**-ni] adj.m. of conservatory
konserwatysta [kon-ser-vah-**tis**-tah] m. conservatist
konserwatystka [kon-ser-vah-**tist**-kah] f. (female) conservatist
konserwatywnie [kon-ser-vah-**tiv**-ńe] adv. conservatively
konserwatywność [kon-ser-vah-**tiv**-nośhćh] f. conservative character; conservativeness
konserwatywny [kon-ser-vah-**tiv**-ni]

adj.m. conservative
konserwatyzm [kon-ser-**vah**-tizm] m. conservatism
konserwiarnia [kon-ser-**vyahr**-ńah] f. cannery
konserwować [kon-ser-**vo**-vahćh] v. conserve; preserve; cure; pack; can (*repeatedly*)
konserwować się [kon-ser-**vo**-vahćh śhan] v. be in shape; keep in good health; keep (*repeatedly*)
konserwowanie [kon-ser-vo-**vah**-ńe] n. preservation
konserwowanie się [kon-ser-vo-**vah**-ńe śhan] n. keeping in shape
konserwowy [kon-ser-**vo**-vi] adj.m. canned; pickled; tinned; potted
przemysł konserwowy [**pshe**-misw kon-ser-**vo**-vi] exp.: canning industry; packing trade
konserwująco [kon-ser-voo-**yown**-tso] adv. preserving; keeping in good condition; protecting
konsjerżka [kon-**syersh**-kah] f. (female) caretaker; janitor; doorkeeper (in France)
konskrypcja [kon-**skrip**-tsyah] f. conscription; draft
konsola [kon-**so**-lah] f. console; bracket; console table; pier table; corbel
konsole [kon-**so**-le] pl. consoles
konsolacja [kon-so-**lah**-tsyah] f. consolation; comfort
konsolacyjny [kon-so-lah-**tsiy**-ni] adj.m. consolatory; comforting
konsoleta [kon-so-**le**-tah] f. disk-jockey's desk; TV speaker's desk
konsolidacja [kon-so-lee-**dah**-tsyah] f. consolidation
konsolidacyjny [kon-so-lee-dah-**tsiy**-ni] adj.m. of consolidation
konsolidować [kon-so-lee-**do**-vahćh] v. consolidate; fund (*repeatedly*)
konsolidować się [kon-so-lee-**do**-vahćh śhan] v. become consolidated (*repeatedly*)
konsolidowanie [kon-so-lee-do-**vah**-ńe] n. consolidation
konsolidowanie się [kon-so-lee-do-**vah**-ńe śhan] n. becoming consolidated
konsolka [kon-**sol**-kah] f. (small. nice) console; bracket; console-table
konsonans [kon-**so**-nahns] m. consonance (musical)
konsonansowy [kon-so-nahn-**so**-vi] adj.m. consonant (musical)
konsonant [kon-**so**-nahnt] m. consonant
konsonantyczny [kon-so-nahn-**tich**-ni] adj.m. consonantal; sounding like a consonant
konsonantyzacja [kon-so-nahn-ti-**zah**-tsyah] f. turning into a consonant
konsonantyzm [kon-so-**nahn**-tizm] m. the consonants of a (given) language
konsonantyzować się [kon-so-nahn-ti-**zo**-vahćh śhan] v. become a consonant (*repeatedly*)
konsonantyzowanie się [kon-so-nahn-ti-zo-**vah**-ńe śhan] n. becoming a consonant
konsonować [kon-so-**no**-vahćh] v. sound together (*repeatedly*)
konsonowanie [kon-so-no-**vah**-ńe] n. sounding together
konsorcjum [kon-**sor**-tsyoom] n. consortium; association (of firms, etc.); syndicate
konspekt [**kons**-pekt] m. draft; summary; synopsis; conspectus; outline; abridgment
konspektować [kons-pek-**to**-vahćh] v. draft; summarize; prepare a synopsis; make a conspectus (*repeatedly*)
konspektowanie [kons-pek-to-**vah**-ńe] n. drafting; summarizing; preparing a synopsis; making a conspectus
konspiracja [kon-spee-**rah**-tsyah] f. conspiracy
konspiracyjnie [kon-spee-rah-**tsiy**-ńe] adv. conspiratorially; secretly; in conspiracy; mysteriously
konspiracyjność [kon-spee-rah-**tsiy**-nośhćh] f. conspiratorial character; secrecy
konspiracyjny [kon-spee-rah-**tsiy**-ni] adj.m. conspiratorial; secret; underground (movement, etc.)
konspirator [kon-spee-**rah**-tor] m. conspirator
konspiratorka [kon-spee-rah-**tor**-kah]

f. woman conspirator
konspiratorski [kon-spee-rah-**tor**-skee] adj.m. conspiratorial; conspirator's; conspirators'
konspiratorstwo [kon-spee-rah-**tor**-stfo] n. conspiracy
konspirować [kon-spee-**ro**-vahćh] v. plot; conspire; keep secret; hide (*repeatedly*)
konspirować się [kon-spee-**ro**-vahćh śhan] v. hide oneself; conceal oneself; wrap oneself in mystery; dissemble; put on a mask (*repeatedly*)
konspirowanie [kon-spee-ro-**vah**-ńe] n. plotting; conspiring
konspirowanie się [kon-spee-ro-**vah**-ńe śhan] n. concealing oneself
konstabl [**kon**-stahbl] m. constable
konstanta [kon-**stahn**-tah] f. (a) constant
konstantan [kon-**stahn**-tahn] m. constantan (alloy); advance
konstatacja [kon-stah-**tah**-tsyah] f. statement; determination (of a fact); ascertainment
konstatować [kon-stah-**to**-vahćh] v. state; ascertain; find out (that ...) (*repeatedly*)
konstatowanie [kon-stah-to-**vah**-ńe] n. ascertainment
konstelacja [kon-ste-**lah**-tsyah] f. constellation; situation; state of affairs
konsternacja [kon-ster-**nah**-tsyah] f. consternation; dismay; shock
konsternować [kon-ster-**no**-vahćh] v. fill with consternation; dismay (*repeatedly*)
konsternować się [kon-ster-**no**-vahćh śhan] v. be filled with consternation; be dismayed (*repeatedly*)
konsternowanie [kon-ster-no-**vah**-ńe] n. consternation
konsternowanie się [kon-ster-no-**vah**-ńe śhan] n. being dismayed
konstrukcja [kon-**strook**-tsyah] f. construction; design; plan; frame; structure; composition; arrangement
konstrukcja drewniana [kon-**strook**-tsyah drev-**ńah**-nah] exp.: timberwork; wooden structure
konstrukcja stalowa [kon-**strook**-tsyah stah-**lo**-vah] exp.: steelwork; steel structure
konstrukcyjnie [kon-strook-**tsiy**-ńe] adv. constructionally; structurally; in design
konstrukcyjny [kon-strook-**tsiy**-ni] adj.m. constructional; structural; tectonic
konstruktor [kon-**strook**-tor] m. constructor; builder; designer
konstruktorka [kon-strook-**tor**-kah] f. (female) constructor; builder; designer
konstruktorski [kon-strook-**tor**-skee] adj.m. constructor's; builder's; designer's
konstruktywista [kon-strook-ti-**vees**-tah] m. constructivist
konstruktywistyczny [kon-strook-ti-vees-**tich**-ni] adj.m. constructivist
konstruktywizm [kon-strook-**ti**-veezm] m. constructivism
konstruktywnie [kon-strook-**tiv**-ńe] adv. constructively
konstruktywność [kon-strook-**tiv**-nośhćh] f. constructiveness
konstruktywny [kon-strook-**tiv**-ni] adj.m. constructive
konstruować [kon-stroo-**o**-vahćh] v. construct; build; put together; combine grammatically (*repeatedly*)
konstruowanie [kon-stroo-o-**vah**-ńe] n. construction; building
konstytuanta [kon-sti-too-**ahn**-tah] f. Constituent Assembly
konstytucja [kon-sti-**too**-tsyah] f. constitution; enactment; physique; constitution (of a person, etc.); slang: billy club; policeman's club (mob jargon)
niezgodny z konstytucją [ńe-**zgod**-ni s kon-sti-**too**-tsyown] exp.: unconstitutional
konstytucjonalista [kon-sti-too-tsyo-nah-**lees**-tah] m. constitutionalist
konstytucjonalizm [kon-sti-too-tsyo-**nah**-leezm] m. constitutionalism
konstytucjonalny [kon-sti-too-tsyo-**nahl**-ni] adj.m. constitutional
konstytucyjnie [kon-sti-too-**tsiy**-ńe] adv. constitutionally
konstytucyjność [kon-sti-too-**tsiy**-

nośhćh] f. adherence to the constitution
konstytucyjny [kon-sti-too-**tsiy**-ni] adj.m. constitutional (law, etc.); pertaining to parts of the body
konstytuować [kon-sti-too-**o**-vahćh] v. constitute; form; set up (a committee, etc.) (*repeatedly*)
konstytuować się [kon-sti-too-**o**-vahćh śhan] v. be formed; be set up (*repeatedly*)
konstytuowanie [kon-sti-too-o-**vah**-ńe] n. constitution; formation
konstytuowanie się [kon-sti-too-o-**vah**-ńe śhan] n. being formed
konstytutywny [kon-sti-too-**tiv**-ni] adj.m. constitutive; essential
konsul [**kon**-sool] m. consul
konsularny [kon-soo-**lahr**-ni] adj.m. consular
konsulat [kon-**soo**-laht] m. consulate (office of a consul)
konsulowa [kon-soo-**lo**-vah] f. consul's wife
konsulostwo [kon-soo-**los**-tfo] n. consul and his wife
konsulowski [kon-soo-**lof**-skee] adj.m. consul's (office, etc.)
konsultacja [kon-sool-**tah**-tsyah] f. consultation; medical examination
konsultacyjny [kon-sool-tah-**tsiy**-ni] adj.m. consultative; advisory
konsultant [kon-**sool**-tahnt] m. consultant; consulting physician; consulting engineer
konsultatywny [kon-sool-tah-**tiv**-ni] adj.m. consultative; advisory
konsulting [kon-**sool**-teeng] m. consulting
konsultingowy [kon-sool-teen-**go**-vi] adj.m. consultative; advisory; of consulting; consultive
konsultować [kon-sool-**to**-vahćh] v. consult; give professional advice (*repeatedly*)
konsultować się [kon-sool-**to**-vahćh śhan] v. consult together; hold council; consult; seek (somebody's) advice (*repeatedly*)
konsultowanie [kon-sool-to-**vah**-ńe] n. consultation
konsultowanie się [kon-sool-to-**vah**-ńe śhan] n. seeking advice
konsum [**kon**-soom] m. cooperative store; colloq: co-op
konsumencki [kon-soo-**men**-tskee] adj.m. consumer's; consumers'
konsument [kon-**soo**-ment] m. consumer
konsumenci [kon-soo-**men**-ćhee] pl. consumers
konsumować [kon-soo-**mo**-vahćh] v. consume; eat up; drink up; use up; waste (fuel) (*repeatedly*)
konsumowanie [kon-soo-mo-**vah**-ńe] n. consumption
konsumpcja [kon-**soomp**-tsyah] f. consumption; use
konsumpcjonizm [kon-soomp-**tsyo**-ńeezm] m. consumerism; consumerist attitude
konsumpcyjny [kon-soomp-**tsiy**-ni] adj.m. consumer (goods, etc.); consumable
konsygnacja [kon-sig-**nah**-tsyah] f. consignment note; consignment; consignation
konsygnacyjny [kon-sig-nah-**tsiy**-ni] adj.m. consignment (note, shipment, terms, etc.)
skład konsygnacyjny [skwaht kon-sig-nah-**tsiy**-ni] exp.: consignment warehouse
konsygnant [kon-**sig**-nahnt] m. consignor; owner of consigned goods (who can make a transfer to a consignee)
konsygnatariusz [kon-sig-nah-**tahr**-yoosh] m. intermediary; consignor; one who signs together with others
konsygnować [kon-sig-**no**-vahćh] v. consign (*repeatedly*)
konsygnowanie [kon-sig-no-**vah**-ńe] n. consignation
konsyliarz [kon-**sil**-yahsh] m. colloq: doctor
konsylium [kon-**sil**-yoom] n. consultation (usually medical)
konsystencja [kon-sis-**ten**-tsyah] f. consistency
konsystorski [kon-sis-**tor**-skee] adj.m. consistorial
konsystorz [kon-**sis**-tosh] m. consistory
konszachciki [kon-shahkh-**ćhee**-kee] pl. (minor) collusion; (underhand) scheming

konszachtować [kon-shahkh-**to**-vahćh] v. collude; scheme (*repeatedly*)
konszachtowanie [kon-shahkh-to-**vah**-ńe] n. collusion
konszachty [kon-**shahkh**-ti] pl. collusion; (underhand) dealing; scheming
konszowanie [kon-sho-**vah**-ńe] n. hot mixing of chocolate (during production)
kontakt [**kon**-tahkt] m. contact; touch; communication; relation; connection; (wall) plug; a type of catalyzer; slang: police informer
kontakty [kon-**tahk**-ti] pl. contacts; communications; relations; connections; connexions
być w kontakcie z kimś [bićh f kon-**tahk**-ćhe s keemśh] exp.: to be in contact (in touch, in communication) with somebody
nawiązać kontakt [nah-**vyown**-zahćh **kon**-tahkt] exp.: to get in touch (with)
włączyć kontakt [**vwown**-chićh **kon**-tahkt] exp.: to switch on (the current)
kontaktować [kon-tahk-**to**-vahćh] v. be in contact; touch; contact; communicate; bring in contact; (*repeatedly*)
kontaktować się [kon-tahk-**to**-vahćh śhan] v. be in contact; be in touch; communicate (with); have relations (with) (*repeatedly*)
kontaktowanie [kon-tahk-to-**vah**-ńe] n. contacts
kontaktowanie się [kon-tahk-to-**vah**-ńe śhan] n. getting in touch
kontaktowo [kon-tahk-**to**-vo] adv. by means of contact
kontaktowy [kon-tahk-**to**-vi] adj.m. contact (agent, action, process, lens, etc.)
kontaminacja [kon-tah-mee-**nah**-tsyah] f. blending; contamination (of words, phrases, language)
kontaminacyjny [kon-tah-mee-nah-**tsiy**-ni] adj.m. of contamination; contaminative
kontaminować [kon-tah-mee-**no**-vahćh] v. contaminate (a language); blend (*repeatedly*)
kontaminowanie [kon-tah-mee-no-**vah**-ńe] n. contamination (of a language
kontekst [**kon**-tekst] m. context
kontekstowy [kon-teks-**to**-vi] adj.m. contextual
kontemplacja [kon-tem-**plah**-tsyah] f. contemplation; intention; expectation
kontemplacyjnie [kon-tem-plah-**tsiy**-ńe] adv. contemplatively
kontemplacyjność [kon-tem-plah-**tsiy**-nośhćh] f. contemplative character; contemplativeness
kontemplacyjny [kon-tem-plah-**tsiy**-ni] adj.m. contemplative
kontemplator [kon-tem-**plah**-tor] m. contemplator
kontemplować [kon-tem-**plo**-vahćh] v. contemplate (*repeatedly*)
kontemplowanie [kon-tem-plo-**vah**-ńe] n. contemplation
kontenans [kon-**te**-nahns] m. countenance
stracić kontenans [**strah**-ćheećh kon-**te**-nahns] exp.: to be put out of countenance
zachować kontenans [zah-**kho**-vahćh kon-**te**-nahns] exp.: to keep oneself in the countenance
kontener [kon-**te**-ner] m. container
kontenerować [kon-te-ne-**ro**-vahćh] v. containerize (*repeatedly*)
kontenerowanie [kon-te-ne-ro-**vah**-ńe] n. containerization
kontenerowiec [kon-te-ne-**ro**-vyets] m. containership
kontenerowo [kon-te-ne-**ro**-vo] adv. by means of containerization
kontenerowy [kon-te-ne-**ro**-vi] adj.m. container (ship, board, etc.)
konteneryzacja [kon-te-ne-ri-**zah**-tsyah] f. containerization
kontent [**kon**-tent] adj.m. pleased; satisfied; content
kontentować się [kon-ten-to-va śhan] v. be pleased; be sati be content (*repeatedly*)
konterfekt [kon-**ter**-fekt] m. portrait
kontestacja [kon-tes-**tah**-ts contestation; controver
kontestacyjnie [kon-tes-t

adv. by contestation; controversially
kontestacyjność [kon-tes-tah-**tsiy**-nośhćh] f. contestation; controversialism; controversial nature
kontestacyjny [kon-tes-tah-**tsiy**-ni] adj.m. of contestation; controversial
kontestator [kon-tes-**tah**-tor] m. contestant; contester; controversialist
kontestować [kon-tes-**to**-vahćh] v. contest; dispute; challenge; protest; demonstrate against (*repeatedly*)
kontestowanie [kon-tes-to-**vah**-ńe] n. contestation; dispute; challenge; protest; demonstration against; controversy; quarrel; strife
kontinuum [kon-tee-**noo**-oom] n. continuum; continuity
konto [**kon**-to] n. account
kontorsjonista [kon-tor-syo-**ńees**-tah] m. contortionist
kontorsjonistka [kon-tor-syo-**ńees**-tkah] f. (female) contortionist
kontorsjonistyczny [kon-tor-syo-ńees-**tich**-ni] adj.m. contortionistic
kontorsjonistyka [kon-tor-syo-**ńees**-ti-kah] f. contortive acrobatics
kontoteka [kon-to-**te**-kah] f. box with loose-leaf bookkeeping records
kontować [kon-**to**-vahćh] v. keep books; make a balance sheet (*repeatedly*)
kontowanie [kon-to-**vah**-ńe] n. keeping books; making a balance sheet (*repeated*)
kontr- [kontr] prefix: contra-; anti-; against; opposite; contrary
kontra [**kon**-trah] f. printer's negative; counter play (double) in cards; contraoctave; counterpunch; backing of oars; prep.: against; opposite; versus
ontra- [**kon**-trah] prefix: contra-; anti-; against; opposite; contrary
trabanda [kon-trah-**bahn**-dah] f. nuggled goods; contraband
abandzista [kon-trah-bahn-**ees**-tah] m. contrabandist

kontrabas [kon-**trah**-bahs] m. contrabass; double bass
kontrabasista [kon-trah-bah-**śhees**-tah] m. contrabassist
kontrabasowy [kon-trah-bah-**so**-vi] adj.m. contrabass (tuba, etc.)
kontrademonstracja [kont-rah-de-mon-**strah**-tsyah] f. counterdemonstration
kontradmiralstwo [kontr-ahd-mee-**rahl**-stfo] n. rear admiral's rank
kontradmirał [kontr-ahd-**mee**-rahw] m. rear admiral
kontradyktoryjnie [kon-trah-dik-to-**riy**-ńe] adv. contradictorily
kontradyktoryjny [kon-trah-dik-to-**riy**-ni] adj.m. contradictory; contradictable
kontrafagot [kon-trah-**fah**-got] m. contrabassoon; double bassoon
kontrafaktura [kon-trah-fahk-**too**-rah] f. substitution of lay lyrics in a religious song
kontrafał [kon-**trah**-fahw] m. line for lowering a sail; downhaul
kontrafałda [kon-trah-**fahw**-dah] f. box pleat; double fold
nie zawracaj kontrafałdy [ńe zah-**vrah**-tsahy kon-trah-**fahw**-di] exp.: colloq: don't talk nonsense; stop bothering (me, etc.)
kontragitacja [kontr-ah-gee-**tah**-tsyah] f. counteragitation
kontrahent [kon-**trah**-khent] m. one of contracting parties
kontrahentka [kon-trah-**khent**-kah] f. (woman) one of contracting parties
kontrahować [kon-trah-**kho**-vahćh] v. sign a contract; make a business deal (*repeatedly*)
kontrakcik [kon-**trahk**-ćheek] m. (small, advantageous) contract (enforceable by law)
kontrakcja [kon-**trahk**-tsyah] f. shortening (of a word, syllable, etc.) by omission of a sound or a letter; contraction (of the earth, of the volume of mixed fluids, etc.); counteraction
kontrakcyjny [kon-trahk-**tsiy**-ni] adj.m. contractive; contractional (theory, etc.)
kontrakt [**kon**-trahkt] m. contract

(enforceable by law)
kontraktacja [kon-trahk-**tah**-tsyah] f. contract buying
kontraktacyjnie [kon-trahk-tah-**tsiy**-ńe] adv. contractually
kontraktacyjny [kon-trahk-tah-**tsiy**-ni] adj.m. contract (buying, etc.); contractual
kontraktować [kon-trahk-**to**-vahćh] v. contract (to supply); hire; engage (an employee) (*repeatedly*)
kontraktowanie [kon-trahk-to-**vah**-ńe] n. contracting (to supply); hiring; engaging (an employee)
kontraktowo [kon-trahk-**to**-vo] adv. according to a contract; contractually
kontraktowy [kon-trahk-**to**-vi] adj.m. contract (terms, etc.); contracted; stipulated by contract; contractual
robotnik kontraktowy [ro-**bot**-ńeek kon-trahk-**to**-vi] exp.: temporary worker
kontralt [**kontr**-ahlt] m. contralto
kontraltowy [kontr-ahl-**to**-vi] adj.m. contralt (part, etc.)
kontramarka [kon-trah-**mahr**-kah] f. countermark (mark on coin)
kontraoktawa [kon-trah-ok-**tah**-vah] f. contraoctave
kontrapost [**kon**-trah-post] m. contrapposto (in art)
kontrapozycja [kon-trah-po-**zi**-tsyah] f. contraposition
kontrapunkcista [kon-trah-poonk-**ćhees**-tah] m. contrapuntist
kontrapunkt [kon-**trah**-poonkt] m. counterpoint
kontrapunktować [kon-trah-poonk-**to**-vahćh] v. counterpoint (*repeatedly*)
kontrapunktowanie [kon-trah-poonk-to-**vah**-ńe] n. composing in counterpoint
kontrapunktowy [kon-trah-poonk-**to**-vi] adj.m. contrapuntal
kontrapunktycznie [kon-trah-poonk-**tich**-ńe] adv. contrapuntally
kontrapunktyczny [kon-trah-poonk-**tich**-ni] adj.m. contrapuntal
kontrargument [kontr-ahr-**goo**-ment] m. counterargument
kontrargumentacja [kontr-ahr-goo-men-**tah**-tsyah] f. counterarguments
kontrargumentować [kontr-ahr-goo-men-**to**-vahćh] v. counterargue (*repeatedly*)
kontrargumentowanie [kontr-ahr-goo-men-to-**vah**-ńe] n. counterarguing
kontrasekurować [kontr-ah-se-koo-**ro**-vahćh] v. use countersecurity (*repeatedly*)
kontrast [**kon**-trahst] m. contrast (pointing the differences)
kontraster [kon-**trahs**-ter] m. counter-steering mechanism for improving the operation of ship's propeller
kontrastować [kon-trahs-**to**-vahćh] v. contrast (with); stand in contrast (with); form a contrast (to); stand out (against) (*repeatedly*)
kontrastowanie [kon-trahs-to-**vah**-ńe] n. standing in contrast (with); forming a contrast (to)
kontrastowo [kon-trah-**sto**-vo] adv. in contrast; by contrast
kontrastowość [kon-trah-**sto**-vośhćh] f. contrastive effect
kontrastowy [kon-trah-**sto**-vi] adj.m. contrastive; contrasting; contrasty (photography)
kontrastujący [kon-trah-stoo-**yown**-tsi] adj.m. contrastive; contrasting
kontrasygnata [kontr-ah-sig-**nah**-tah] f. countersignature
kontrasygnować [kontr-ah-sig-**no**-vahćh] v. countersign (*repeatedly*)
kontrasygnowanie [kontr-ah-sig-no-**vah**-ńe] n. countersigning
kontraszot [**kon**-trah-shot] m. boom stabilizing line
kontraśruba [kon-trah-**śhroo**-bah] f. flow stabilizer near a propeller
kontratak [kontr-**ah**-tahk] m. counterattack (opposing an attack)
kontratakować [kontr-ah-tah-**ko**-vahćh] v. counterattack (*repeatedly*)
kontratakowanie [kontr-ah-tah-ko-**vah**-ńe] n. counterattack

kontratyp [kon-**trah**-tip] m. film copy made out of secondary negative
kontrchwyt [**kontr**-khfit] m. counterhold (in wrestling)
kontredans [kon-**tre**-dahns] m. contredance; contradance; quadrille
kontredansowy [kon-tre-dahn-**so**-vi] adj.m. of contredance
kontrdemonstracja [kontr-de-mon-**strah**-tsyah] f. counterdemonstration
kontrfał [**kontr**-fahw] m. downhaul; rope to haul down a sail
kontrgambit [kontr-**gahm**-beet] m. counter-gambit (in chess)
kontrkandydat [kontr-kahn-**di**-daht] m. opponent
kontrmanewr [kontr-**mah**-nevr] m. counter-maneuvre
kontrmarsz [**kontr**-mahrsh] m. countermarch
kontrmina [kontr-**mee**-nah] f. countermine
kontrnatarcie [kontr-nah-**tahr**-ćhe] n. counteroffensive
kontrnegatyw [kontr-ne-**gah**-tif] m. secondary negative
kontrofensywa [kontr-o-fen-**si**-vah] f. counteroffensive
kontroferta [kontr-o-**fer**-tah] f. counteroffer
kontroktawa [kontr-ok-**tah**-vah] f. counteroctave
kontrola [kon-**tro**-lah] f. control; checking; checkup; inspection; colloq: inspectorate; supervisor(s); inspector(s)
kontrola ruchu [kon-**tro**-lah **roo**-khoo] exp.: traffic control
przeprowadzać kontrolę [pshe-pro-**vah**-dzahćh kon-**tro**-lan] exp.: to inspect; to verify; to supervise
kontroler [kon-**tro**-ler] m. inspector; supervisor; superintendent; auditor
kontrolerka [kon-tro-**ler**-kah] f. (female) inspector; supervisor; superintendent; auditor
kontrolerski [kon-tro-**ler**-skee] adj.m. of inspector; of supervisor
kontrolka [kon-**trol**-kah] f. check list; notebook; check ticket
kontrolnie [kon-**trol**-ńe] adv. by means of inspection
kontrolny [kon-**trol**-ni] adj.m. of inspection; of supervision
karta kontrolna [**kahr**-tah kon-**trol**-nah] exp.: timecard
znak kontrolny [znahk kon-**trol**-ni] exp.: check; countermark
kontrolować [kon-tro-**lo**-vahćh] v. control; check; check up; verify; inspect; supervise; superintend (*repeatedly*)
kontrolować rachunki [kon-tro-**lo**-vahćh rah-**khoon**-kee] exp.: to audit accounts
kontrolować się [kon-tro-**lo**-vahćh śhan] v. control one's nerves; control oneself (*repeatedly*)
kontrolowanie [kon-tro-lo-**vah**-ńe] n. inspection; supervision
kontrolowanie się [kon-tro-lo-**vah**-ńe śhan] n. controlling oneself
kontroskarżenie [kontr-os-kahr-**zhe**-ńe] n. counteraccusation
kontrować [kon-**tro**-vahćh] v. double (in a card game); counter a blow; back oars; back water; counter; oppose (*repeatedly*)
kontrowanie [kon-tro-**vah**-ńe] n. doubling (in a card game); countering (a blow, etc.); backing oars; backing water; opposing
kontrowersja [kon-tro-**ver**-syah] f. controversy; dispute
kontrowersyjnie [kon-tro-ver-**siy**-ńe] adv. controversially
kontrowersyjność [kon-tro-ver-**siy**-nośhćh] f. controversial nature; controversialism
kontrowersyjny [kon-tro-ver-**siy**-ni] adj.m. controversial
kontrpara [kontr-**pah**-rah] f. reversed steam
kontrpartner [kontr-**pahrt**-ner] m. opponent; rival; controversialist
kontrpropaganda [kontr-pro-pah-**gahn**-dah] f. counterpropaganda
kontrpropozycja [kontr-pro-po-**zi**-tsyah] f. counterproposal
kontrreformacja [kontr-re-for-**mah**-tsyah] f. counterreformation
kontrreformacyjny [kontr-re-for-mah-**tsiy**-ni] adj.m. of counterreformation
kontrrewolucja [kontr-re-vo-**loo**-

tsyah] f. counterrevolution
kontrrewolucjonista [kontr-re-vo-loo-tsyo-**ńees**-tah] m. counterrevolutionist
kontrrewolucjonistka [kontr-re-vo-loo-tsyo-**ńeest**-kah] f. (female) counterrevolutionist
kontrrewolucyjny [kontr-re-vo-loo-**tsiy**-ni] adj.m. counterrevolutionary
kontrtorpedowiec [kontr-tor-pe-**do**-vyets] m. (torpedo-boat) destroyer
kontrtytuł [kontr-**ti**-toow] m. counter-title
kontruderzenie [kontr-oo-de-**zhe**-ńe] n. counteroffensive; counterblow
kontrwywiad [kontr-**vi**-vyaht] m. counterintelligence (used to block enemy spying, sabotage, etc.)
kontrwywiadowca [kontr-vi-vyah-**dof**-tsah] m. counterintelligence agent
kontrwywiadowczy [kontr-vi-vyah-**dof**-chi] adj.m. counterintelligence (agent, etc.)
kontrybucja [kon-tri-**boo**-tsyah] f. contribution
ściągnąć kontrybucję [śhćh<u>owng</u>-n<u>own</u>ćh kon-tri-**boo**-tsy<u>an</u>] exp.: to levy a contribution
kontrybucyjnie [kon-tri-boo-**tsiy**-ńe] adv. contributively
kontrybucyjny [kon-tri-boo-**tsiy**-ni] adj.m. contributive; contributory
kontuar [kon-**too**-ahr] m. counter
kontur [**kon**-toor] m. outline
konturować [kon-too-**ro**-vahćh] v. outline (*repeatedly*)
konturowanie [kon-too-ro-**vah**-ńe] n. outlining
konturowy [kon-too-**ro**-vi] adj.m. contour (line, etc.)
konturówka [kon-too-**roof**-kah] f. variety of make-up pencil; pencil for maquillage
kontusz [**kon**-toosh] m. split-sleeve Polish overcoat (of old)
kontuszowy [kon-too-**sho**-vi] adj.m. of split-sleeve Polish overcoat (of old)
kontuzja [kon-**too**-zyah] f. shock; contusion; shell shock; bruise
kontuzjować [kon-too-**zyo**-vahćh] v. shock; contuse; bruise (*repeatedly*)
kontuzjowanie [kon-too-zyo-**vah**-ńe] n. contusion; shell shock
kontyna [kon-**ti**-nah] f. pagan temple of ancient Slavs
kontynent [kon-**ti**-nent] m. continent; mainland; any mainland area of the earth
kontynentalnie [kon-ti-nen-**tahl**-ńe] adv. continentally
kontynentalny [kon-ti-nen-**tahl**-ni] adj.m. continental
kontyngent [kon-**tin**-gent] m. quota (of persons, of imported goods, etc.); levy; contingent
kontyngentowy [kon-tin-gen-**to**-vi] adj.m. imposed (quota, levy, etc.); (being) levied
kontyngentyzm [kon-tin-**gen**-tizm] m. theory of contingency
kontynuacja [kon-ti-noo-**ah**-tsyah] f. continuation
kontynuacyjny [kon-ti-noo-ah-**tsiy**-ni] adj.m. continuative
kontynuant [kon-ti-**noo**-ahnt] m. continuant
kontynuantowy [kon-ti-noo-ahn-**to**-vi] adj.m. continuant
kontynuator [kon-ti-noo-**ah**-tor] m. continuator
kontynuatorka [kon-ti-noo-ah-**tor**-kah] f. (female) continuator
kontynuować [kon-ti-noo-**o**-vahćh] v. continue; carry on; go on; pursue (*repeatedly*)
kontynuowanie [kon-ti-noo-o-**vah**-ńe] n. continuation
kontysta [kon-**tis**-tah] m. account keeper; account executive
kontystka [kon-**tist**-kah] f. (female) account keeper; account executive
konularia [ko-noo-**lah**-ryah] f. Conularia (shell)
konularie [ko-noo-**lah**-rye] pl. Conularia
konurbacja [ko-noor-**bah**-tsyah] f. conurbation
konus [**ko**-noos] m. cone; colloq: shorty; shortie; short man; slang: young thief; kid (mob jargon)
konusować [ko-noo-**so**-vahćh] v. make a cone; cone (*repeatedly*)

konwalescencja [kon-vah-les-**tsen**-tsyah] f. convalescence
konwalia [kon-**vah**-lyah] f. lily of the valley; Convallaria
konwalidacja [kon-vah-lee-**dah**-tsyah] f. a change in legal power
konwalijka [kon-vah-**leey**-kah] f. Maianthemum (herb)
konwaliowy [kon-vahl-**yo**-vi] adj.m. of lily of the valley
konwejer [kon-**ve**-yer] m. conveyor; conveyer
konwekcja [kon-**vek**-tsyah] f. convection
konwekcyjnie [kon-vek-**tsiy**-ńe] adv. by convection
konwekcyjny [kon-vek-**tsiy**-ni] adj.m. convectional; convective
konwektor [kon-**vek**-tor] m. convector
konwenans [kon-**ve**-nahns] m. convention; etiquette; formalities; good forms
konwenansowo [kon-ve-nahn-**so**-vo] adv. conventionally; ceremonially
konwenansowy [kon-ve-nahn-**so**-vi] adj.m. conventional (decorum, etc.); ceremonial
konwencja [kon-**ven**-tsyah] f. convention; compact; conventionality; conventionalities; social conventions; good forms
konwencjonalista [kon-ven-tsyo-nah-**lees**-tah] m. conventionalist
konwencjonalistka [kon-ven-tsyo-nah-**leest**-kah] f. (woman) conventionalist
konwencjonalistyczny [kon-ven-tsyo-nah-lees-**tich**-ni] adj.m. conventionalist
konwencjonalizacja [kon-ven-tsyo-nah-lee-**zah**-tsyah] f. conventionalization
konwencjonalizm [kon-ven-tsyo-nah-leezm] m. conventionalism
konwencjonalizować [kon-ven-tsyo-nah-lee-**zo**-vahćh] v. conventionalize (*repeatedly*)
konwencjonalizowanie [kon-ven-tsyo-nah-lee-zo-**vah**-ńe] n. conventionalization
konwencjonalnie [kon-ven-tsyo-**nahl**-ńe] adv. conventionally
konwencjonalność [kon-ven-tsyo-**nahl**-nośhćh] f. conventionality
konwencjonalny [kon-ven-tsyo-**nahl**-ni] adj.m. conventional
konwencyjny [kon-ven-**tsiy**-ni] adj.m. conventional
konweniować [kon-veń-**yo**-vahćh] v. be convenient (to); be agreeable; suit (*repeatedly*)
konwent [**kon**-vent] m. convent; monastery
konwentowy [kon-ven-**to**-vi] adj.m. convent (rules, etc.)
konwentualny [kon-ven-too-**ahl**-ni] adj.m. conventual
konwentykiel [con-ven-**ti**-kel] m. conventicle
konwergencja [kon-ver-**gen**-tsyah] f. convergence
konwers [**kon**-vers] m. permanent resident of a monastery used for various services
konwersacja [kon-ver-**sah**-tsyah] f. conversation
konwersacyjnie [kon-ver-sah-**tsiy**-ńe] adv. conversationally
konwersacyjny [kon-ver-sah-**tsiy**-ni] adj.m. conversational
konwersatorium [kon-ver-sah-**tor**-yoom] n. conversation during a seminar
konwersatoryjny [kon-ver-sah-to-**riy**-ni] adj.m. of conversation during a seminar
konwersja [kon-**ver**-syah] f. conversion
konwersować [kon-ver-**so**-vahćh] v. carry on a conversation (*repeatedly*)
konwersowanie [kon-ver-so-**vah**-ńe] n. conversation
konwersyjny [kon-ver-**siy**-ni] adj.m. conversional; conversion (cost)
konwerter [kon-**ver**-ter] m. converter (of computer language, etc.)
konwertor [kon-**ver**-tor] m. converter (of electrical energy, etc.); (steel) converter
konwertorownia [kon-ver-to-**ro**-vńah] f. converter shed; converter area (in a steel mill)
konwertorowy [kon-ver-to-**ro**-vi] adj.m. converter (process, etc.)
konwertować [kon-ver-**to**-vahćh] v. convert; transform (*repeatedly*)

konwertowanie [kon-ver-to-**vah**-ńe] n. conversion; transformation
konwertyta [kon-ver-**ti**-tah] m. convert
konwikt [**kon**-veekt] m. boarding school (for boys or girls)
konwiktor [kon-**veek**-tor] m. boarding school pupil
konwiktorski [kon-veek-**tor**-skee] adj.m. of a boarding school
konwisarski [kon-vee-**sahr**-skee] adj.m. of a tinsmith; of a bell-maker
konwisarstwo [kon-vee-**sahr**-stfo] n. tinsmith's trade; bell-making
konwisarz [kon-**vee**-sahsh] m. tinsmith; bell-maker
konwojent [kon-**vo**-yent] m. escort; guard
konwojować [kon-vo-**yo**-vahćh] v. escort; convoy (*repeatedly*)
konwojowanie [kon-vo-yo-**vah**-ńe] n. escorting
konwojowiec [kon-vo-**yo**-vyets] m. escort ship
konwojowy [kon-vo-**yo**-vi] adj.m. escort (schedule, etc.); convoy (route, etc.)
konwokacja [kon-vo-**kah**-tsyah] f. convocation
konwokacyjny [kon-vo-kah-**tsiy**-ni] adj.m. convocational
konwój [**kon**-vooy] m. convoy; escort
pod konwojem [pot kon-**vo**-yem] exp.: under escort
konwulsja [kon-**vool**-syah] f. convulsion; a fit; a spasm
konwulsyjnie [kon-vool-**siy**-ńe] adv. convulsively
konwulsyjny [kon-vool-**siy**-ni] adj.m. convulsive; convulsionary
koń [koń] m. horse; steed
koń mechaniczny [koń me-khah-**ńeech**-ni] exp.: mechanical horsepower; horsepower
koń pod wierzch [koń pot vyeshkh] exp.: saddle horse
na koniu [nah **ko**-ńoo] exp.: on horseback; mounted
końcowy [koń-**tso**-vi] adj.m. final; terminal; last; late; finishing; rearmost; closing; concluding; ultimate; eventual
końcówka [koń-**tsoof**-kah] f. ending; remainder; tailpiece; desinence; termination
końcówkowy [koń-tsoof-**ko**-vi] adj.m. of an ending; of a tailpiece
kończasty [koń-**chah**-sti] adj.m. pointed
kończenie [koń-**che**-ńe] n. ending; finishing
kończenie się [koń-**che**-ńe śhan] n. dying; passing away
kończyć [**koń**-chićh] v. end; finish; quit; be dying; stop; put an end (to); bring to an end; get done; get finished; be through (with); make an end (of); cease; be dying; be passing away; discontinue (*repeatedly*)
kończyć się [**koń**-chićh śhan] v. end (in a marriage, etc.); finish; run out; give out; spend itself; be almost complete; be almost ready; be emptied; mob slang: die; kick the bucket (*repeatedly*)
kończyna [koń-**chi**-nah] f. extremity; limb; member; leg
kończyny [koń-**chi**-ni] pl. extremities; limbs
kończynowy [koń-chi-**no**-vi] adj.m. pertaining to limbs
koński [**koń**-skee] adj.m. horse's; horses'; equine
końskie zdrowie [**koń**-ske **zdro**-vye] exp.: colloq: an iron constitution; a constitution of iron
końskostopie [koń-sko-**sto**-pye] n. horse's foot deformation (in humans); pes equinus
kooperacja [ko-o-pe-**rah**-tsyah] f. cooperation; acting together; common effort
kooperacyjnie [ko-o-pe-rah-**tsiy**-ńe] adv. cooperatively
kooperacyjny [ko-o-pe-rah-**tsiy**-ni] adj.m. cooperative
kooperant [ko-o-**pe**-rahnt] m. cooperator
kooperatywa [ko-o-pe-rah-**ti**-vah] f. cooperative
kooperatywnie [ko-o-pe-rah-**tiv**-ńe] adv. cooperatively
kooperatywny [ko-o-pe-rah-**tiv**-ni] adj.m. cooperative
kooperatyzm [ko-o-pe-**rah**-tizm] m.

theory of cooperative integration
kooperować [ko-o-pe-**ro**-vahćh] v. cooperate (*repeatedly*)
kooperowanie [ko-o-pe-ro-**vah**-ńe] n. cooperation
kooptacja [ko-op-**tah**-tsyah] f. co-option; co-optation
kooptować [ko-op-**to**-vahćh] v. co-opt (*repeatedly*)
kooptowanie [ko-op-to-**vah**-ńe] n. co-option; co-optation
kooptowany [ko-op-to-**vah**-ni] adj.m. co-optive; co-optative
koordynacja [ko-or-di-**nah**-tsyah] f. coordination (mental & phys.)
koordynacyjny [ko-or-di-nah-**tsiy**-ni] adj.m. coordinative
koordynatograf [ko-or-di-nah-**to**-grahf] m. mapping device for points of known coordinates
koordynator [ko-or-di-**nah**-tor] m. coordinator
koordynować [ko-or-di-**no**-vahćh] v. coordinate; harmonize; (*repeatedly*)
koordynowanie [ko-or-di-no-**vah**-ńe] n. coordination
kop [kop] m. vulg. slang: kick; a kick (mob jargon)
dać kopa [dahćh **ko**-pah] exp.: to kick (somebody)
kopa [**ko**-pah] f. threescore (60); pile; dozens; stack
kopa siana [**ko**-pah **śhah**-nah] exp.: haystack; hayrick
kopacz [**ko**-pahch] m. navvy (Brit.); digger; potato-lifter; coal-cutter; undercutter; hewer; grave digger
kopaczka [ko-**pahch**-kah] f. steam shovel; hoe
kopać [**ko**-pahćh] v. kick; dig; fling out; recoil; pick; spade; mine (coal, etc.) (*repeatedly*)
kopać glinę [**ko**-pahćh **glee**-nan] exp.: to dig clay; to commit sodomy; to have homosexual relations
kopać się [**ko**-pahćh śhan] v. kick each other; work one's way (through); push one's way (through) (*repeatedly*)
kopaiwa [ko-**pahy**-vah] f. copaiba (tree)
kopal [**ko**-pahl] m. copal
kopalina [ko-pah-**lee**-nah] f. mineral
kopalnia [ko-**pahl**-ńah] f. mine
kopalnia węgla [ko-**pahl**-ńah **vang**-lah] exp.: coal mine; coal pit
kopalniak [ko-**pahl**-ńahk] m. pit-prop; mine-prop
kopalniakowy [ko-pahl-ńah-**ko**-vi] adj.m. pit-prop (timber); mine-prop (timber, etc.)
kopalniany [ko-pahl-**ńah**-ni] adj.m. mine (shaft, hoist, etc.)
kopalnictwo [ko-pahl-**ńeets**-tfo] n. the mining industry; mining
kopalny [ko-**pahl**-ni] adj.m. mineral; fossil; fossilized
kopalowy [ko-pah-**lo**-vi] adj.m. copal (ether, etc.)
kopanie [ko-**pah**-ńe] n. kicks; excavation
kopanie gliny [ko-**pah**-ńe **glee**-ni] exp.: clay-mining; vulg.: slang: sodomy; homosexual (anal) intercourse (mob jargon)
kopanie węgla [ko-**pah**-ńe **vang**-lah] exp.: coalmining
kopanie się [ko-**pah**-ńe śhan] n. kicking oneself; kicking each other
kopanina [ko-pah-**ńee**-nah] f. digging; kicking about; dug up ground; clearing
koparka [ko-**pahr**-kah] f. excavator; mechanical shovel; stripper
kopcący [kop-**tsown**-tsi] adj.m. smoky (oil lamp, stove, etc.)
kopcenie [kop-**tse**-ńe] n. smoking; blackening with smoke
kopcenie się [kop-**tse**-ńe śhan] n. blackening with smoke (by a candle, etc.)
kopcić [**kop**-ćheećh] v. soot; smoke; blacken with smoke; colloq: puff (cigarettes); smoke cigarettes, etc.) (*repeatedly*)
kopcić się [**kop**-ćheećh śhan] v. smoke; blacken with smoke (*repeatedly*)
kopciuch [**kop**-ćhookh] m. sloven; slattern; slut
kopciuszek [kop-**ćhoo**-shek] m. Cinderella; drudge; maid of all work
kopcować [kop-**tso**-vahćh] v. clamp; pit (vegetables, etc.)

(*repeatedly*)
kopcowanie [kop-tso-**vah**-ńe] n. clamping; pitting (vegetables, etc.)
kopcowaty [kop-tso-**vah**-ti] adj.m. hillcocky; tumular; like a barrow
kopcowy [kop-**tso**-vi] adj.m. of a mound; heap (shape, etc.)
kopczyk [**kop**-chik] m. small pile of earth; hillock; mound
kopczykować [kop-chi-**ko**-vahćh] v. mound; form into a mound (*repeatedly*)
kopczykowanie [kop-chi-ko-**vah**-ńe] n. mounding; forming into a mound
kopeć [**ko**-pećh] m. soot
koper [**ko**-per] m. dill; fennel
koperczaki [ko-per-**chah**-kee] pl. courtship (hist.)
uderzać w koperczaki [oo-**de**-zhahćh f ko-per-**chah**-kee] exp.: to woo; to court a woman
koperek [ko-**pe**-rek] m. dill leaves (a condiment)
koperkowy [ko-per-**ko**-vi] adj.m. dill-leaves (condiment, soup, etc.); fennel (oil, etc.)
kopernikana [ko-per-ńee-**kah**-nah] pl. Copernican studies
kopernikański [ko-per-ńee-**kahń**-skee] adj.m. Copernican
kopernikolog [ko-per-ńee-**ko**-log] m. Copernican specialist
kopernikologia [ko-per-ńee-ko-**lo**-gyah] f. Copernican studies
kopernikowski [ko-per-ńee-**kof**-skee] adj.m. Copernican
kopernikowy [ko-per-ńee-**ko**-vi] adj.m. Copernican
kopersztych [ko-**per**-shtikh] m. copper (plate) engraving
koperta [ko-**per**-tah] f. envelope; quilt-case; watchcase; linen case enclosing a quilt; lady's (small) purse; pocketbook
kopertka [ko-**pert**-kah] f. (small, nice) envelope; quilt-case; watchcase
kopertować [ko-per-**to**-vahćh] v. put in an envelope; seal (an envelope) (*repeatedly*)
kopertowanie [ko-per-to-**vah**-ńe] n. putting in an envelope; sealing (an envelope)
kopertowo [ko-per-**to**-vo] adv. by means of an envelope
kopertowy [ko-per-**to**-vi] adj.m. envelope (paper, etc.)
koperwas [ko-**per**-vahs] m. copperas
kopia [**ko**-pyah] f. copy; duplicate; replica; reproduction; print; spear; knight with a spear
kopia listu [**ko**-pyah **lees**-too] exp.: copy of a letter
nacierać kopią [nah-**ćhe**-rahćh **ko**-pyown] exp.: to tilt (at); to attack with a spear
kopiał [**ko**-pyahw] m. letter book
kopiarka [ko-**pyahr**-kah] f. copying machine; printing frame; copier
kopiarnia [ko-**pyahr**-ńah] f. printing room; copying frame
kopiarz [**ko**-pyahsh] m. duplicator; duplicating machine; copier
kopiasto [ko-**pyahs**-to] adv. heaped; in a heap; in heaps
kopiasty [ko-**pyahs**-ti] adj.m. piled up; heaped (plate); lying in a heap
kopiato [ko-**pyah**-to] adv. heaped; in a heap; in heaps
kopiaty [ko-**pyah**-ti] adj.m. piled up; heaped (plate); lying in a heap
kopica [ko-**pee**-tsah] f. cock (of hay); shock (of corn-sheaves); heap
kopić [**ko**-peećh] v. cock (hay); shock (corn-sheaves) (*repeatedly*)
kopiec [**ko**-pyets] m. mound; pile of earth; barrow; heap; knoll; clamp
kopiejka [kop-**yey**-kah] f. copeck; kopeck
kopiejkowy [kop-yey-**ko**-vi] adj.m. of one kopeck
kopieniacki [ko-pye-**ńahts**-kee] adj.m. of primitive agriculture
kopieniactwo [ko-pye-**ńahts**-tfo] n. primitive agriculture
kopieniaczy [ko-pye-**ńah**-chi] adj.m. of primitive agriculture
kopienie [ko-**pye**-ńe] n. cocking (hay); shocking (corn-sheaves)
kopijniczy [ko-peey-**ńee**-chi] adj.m. of a spearman
kopijnik [ko-**peey**-ńeek] m. spearman
kopiorama [ko-pyo-**rah**-mah] f. printing-frame

kopioramka [ko-pyo-**rahm**-kah] f. offset copier's frame
kopiować [ko-**pyo**-vahćh] v. copy; reproduce; imitate; transcribe; make a reprodction; print; make a print (*repeatedly*)
kopiowanie [ko-pyo-**vah**-ńe] n. copying; reproduction; imitation
kopiowy [ko-**pyo**-vi] adj.m. copying (ink, press, ribbon, etc.)
ołówek kopiowy [o-**woo**-vek ko-**pyo**-vi] exp.: indelible pencil
kopista [ko-**pees**-tah] m. copyist; soldier of the frontier guard
kopistka [ko-**peest**-kah] f. (woman) copyist
kopka [**kop**-kah] f. (small) pile; dozens; stack
kopnąć [**kop**-nownćh] v. kick; give a kick
kopnąć się [**kop**-nownćh śhan] v. colloq: run quickly (home, etc.)
kopniak [**kop**-ńahk] m. kick; a kick
kopnięcie [kop-**ńan**-ćhe] n. kick; a kick
kopnięcie się [kop-**ńan**-ćhe śhan] n. kicking oneself
kopnięty [kop-**ńan**-ti] adj.m. colloq: cracked; slang: barmy; slightly crazy; daft (Brit.); wacky; slang: insane (mob jargon)
kopny [**kop**-ni] adj.m. hindering; obstructive; encumbered (road, etc.); blocked (with snow, etc.)
kopra [**kop**-rah] f. copra
koproducent [ko-pro-**doo**-tsent] m. joint producer
koprodukcja [ko-pro-**dook**-tsyah] f. joint production
koprodukcyjny [ko-pro-dook-**tsiy**-ni] adj.m. of a joint production
koprofag [ko-**pro**-fahk] m. coprophagous
koprofagia [ko-pro-**fah**-gyah] f. coprophagy
koprolalia [ko-pro-**lah**-lyah] f. coprolalia
koprolit [ko-**pro**-leet] m. coprolith
koprolity [ko-pro-**lee**-ti] pl. coproliths
koprowy [ko-**pro**-vi] adj.m. dill (seed, etc.); fennel (water, etc.)
kopsać [**kop**-sahćh] v. colloq: kick (*repeatedly*)
kopsnąć [**kop**-snownćh] v. colloq: kick (a ball, etc.)
Kopt [kopt] m. Copt
koptyjski [kop-**tiy**-skee] adj.m. Coptic
kopula [ko-**poo**-lah] f. linking word; copula; copulative word
kopulacja [ko-poo-**lah**-tsyah] f. copulation
kopulacyjnie [ko-poo-lah-**tsiy**-ńe] adv. copulatively
kopulacyjny [ko-poo-lah-**tsiy**-ni] adj.m. copulative
kopulak [ko-**poo**-lahk] m. cupola-furnace; dome-kiln
kopulasto [ko-poo-**lahs**-to] adv. in semispheroidal fashion; in a semisphere; in a hemisphere
kopulasty [ko-poo-**lahs**-ti] adj.m. cupola-shaped; semispheroidal; arched; domed
kopulizacja [ko-poo-lee-**zah**-tsyah] f. grafting (plants)
kopulizować [ko-poo-lee-**zo**-vahćh] v. graft (plants) (*repeatedly*)
kopulizowanie [ko-poo-lee-zo-**vah**-ńe] n. grafting (plants)
kopulować [ko-poo-**lo**-vahćh] v. copulate (*repeatedly*)
kopulowanie [ko-poo-lo-**vah**-ńe] n. copulation
kopuła [ko-**poo**-wah] f. dome; cupola; slang: skull; ceiling
kopułka [ko-**poow**-kah] f. (small) dome; cupola; meniscus
kopułkowato [ko-poow-ko-**vah**-to] adv. like a meniscus; like a semisphere
kopułkowaty [ko-poow-ko-**vah**-ti] adj.m. meniscus; hemispherical
kopułowato [ko-poo-wo-**vah**-to] adv. in hemispheric form; in a semisphere
kopułowaty [ko-poo-wo-**vah**-ti] adj.m. cupola-shaped; hemispherical; arched; domed
kopułowy [ko-poo-**wo**-vi] adj.m. cupola-shaped; hemispherical; arched; domed
kopystka [ko-**pist**-kah] f. ladle
kopyść [**ko**-piśhćh] f. ladle
kopytko [ko-**pit**-ko] n. (small) hoof; hoof-shaped dumpling; cobbler's form

kopytkowaty [ko-pit-ko-**vah**-ti] adj.m. hoof-shaped
kopytkowe [ko-pit-**ko**-ve] pl. cattle tax
kopytkowy [ko-pit-**ko**-vi] adj.m. hoof (oil, grease, etc.)
kopytnik [ko-**pit**-ńeek] m. (farrier's) paring-knife; asarum plant
kopytny [ko-**pit**-ni] adj.m. hoofed; ungulate (hoofed mammal)
kopytne [ko-**pit**-ne] pl. the Ungulata group
kopyto [ko-**pi**-to] n. hoof; cobbler's last (shaped like human foot); slang: leg; foot; handgun; fist; heavy blow (mob jargon)
kopyta [ko-**pi**-tah] pl. hooves
wyciągnąć kopyta [vi-**ćhowng**-nownćh ko-**pi**-tah] exp.: to kick the bucket; to die
kopytowaty [ko-pi-to-**vah**-ti] adj.m. hoof-shaped
kopytowiec [ko-pi-**to**-vyets] m. hoofed mammal; ungulate
kopytowy [ko-pi-**to**-vi] adj.m. hoofed; ungulate
kora [**ko**-rah] f. bark; cortex; (earth's) crust
korab [**ko**-rahp] m. colloq: ship
koral [**ko**-rahl] m. coral (red)
korale [ko-**rah**-le] pl. bead necklace; coral beads; gills
koraliczek [ko-rah-**lee**-chek] m. (small, very nice) coral bead
koralik [ko-**rah**-leek] m. (small, nice) coral bead; mob slang: tooth
koralikowy [ko-rah-lee-**ko**-vi] adj.m. coral (beads, etc.)
koralina [ko-rah-**lee**-nah] f. nightshade (herb)
koralka [ko-**rahl**-kah] f. Corallina (red algae)
koralowaty [ko-rah-lo-**vah**-ti] adj.m. like a coral
koralowiec [ko-rah-**lo**-vyets] m. (sea) coral; anthozoon
koralowce [ko-rah-**lof**-tse] pl. the Anthozoa class
koralowina [ko-rah-lo-**vee**-nah] f. coral skeleton of coral reef
koralowo [ko-rah-**lo**-vo] adv. in coral-red color
koralowy [ko-rah-**lo**-vi] adj.m. coral (reef, etc.); coral-red
kalina koralowa [kah-**lee**-nah ko-rah-**lo**-vah] exp.: cranberry
koramina [ko-rah-**mee**-nah] f. coramin
koran [**ko**-rahn] m. Koran; Alcoran; slang: penal code (mob jargon)
koraniczny [ko-rah-**ńeech**-ni] adj.m. Koranic; Alcoranic
koranowy [ko-rah-**no**-vi] adj.m. Koranic; Alcoranic
korazja [ko-**rah**-zyah] f. wind erosion
korba [**kor**-bah] f. crank; winch
korbka [**korp**-kah] f. (small) crank; winch; handle; winding-key; window raiser
korbkowy [korp-**ko**-vi] adj.m. cranked
korbował [kor-**bo**-vahw] m. crank axle; crankshaft
korbowodowy [kor-bo-vo-**do**-vi] adj.m. of connecting rods
korbowód [kor-**bo**-voot] m. connecting rod
korbowy [kor-**bo**-vi] adj.m. crank (axle, pin, etc.)
korcenie [kor-**tse**-ńe] n. tempting; haunting
korcić [**kor**-ćheećh] v. tempt; haunt (*repeatedly*)
korcowy [kor-**tso**-vi] adj.m. bushel (measure, etc.)
korczyk [**kor**-chik] m. (small) bushel
kord [kort] m. cutlass; sword
kordait [kor-**dah**-eet] m. cordaite (tree)
kordaity [kor-dah-**ee**-ti] pl. the cordaite family of (petrified) trees; Cordaitinae
kordegarda [kor-de-**gahr**-dah] f. guardhouse; guardroom
kordelas [kor-**de**-lahs] m. hunting knife; pigsticker; cutlass
kordelier [kor-**del**-yer] m. (French) Cordelier
kordialnie [kor-**dyahl**-ńe] adv. cordially; vitally
kordialność [kor-**dyahl**-nośhćh] f. cordiality; heartiness
kordialny [kor-**dyahl**-ni] adj.m. cordial; hearty; vital
kordiał [**kor**-dyahw] m. (a) cordial
kordieryt [kor-**dye**-rit] m. cordierite (mineral)
kordon [**kor**-don] m. cordon; border

kordonek [kor-**do**-nek] m. (silk, cotton, etc.) twist; purl; chenille; gimp; gymp
kordonkowy [kor-don-**ko**-vi] adj.m. of (silk, cotton, etc.) twist
kordonowy [kor-do-**no**-vi] adj.m. border (crossing, etc.)
kordowy [kor-**do**-vi] adj.m. of cutlass; sword (blade, etc.)
kordylina [kor-di-**lee**-nah] f. Dracaena (shrub); dragon tree
kordyt [**kor**-dit] m. cordite
kordzik [**kor**-dźheek] m. (small) cutlass; sword
korealny [ko-re-**ahl**-ni] adj.m. jointly binding (contract, etc.)
Koreańczyk [ko-re-**ahń**-chik] m. Korean
Koreanka [ko-re-**ahn**-kah] f. Korean (woman)
koreański [ko-re-**ahń**-skee] adj.m. Korean
koreczek [ko-**re**-chek] m. (small) cork; fuse; stopper; traffic jam; tie-up
koreferat [ko-re-**fe**-raht] m. joint report; co-report
koreferent [ko-re-**fe**-rent] m. joint reporter; co-reporter
koregencja [ko-re-**gen**-tsyah] f. joint regency
koregencyjny [ko-re-gen-**tsiy**-ni] adj.m. of joint regency
koregent [ko-**re**-gent] m. joint regent
koregentka [ko-re-**gent**-kah] f. (woman) joint regent
korek [**ko**-rek] m. cork; fuse; stopper; traffic-jam; tie-up; stoppage; plug; mob slang: forced congestion during robbery; penis
korki [**kor**-kee] pl. (cork) heels; cork-soled shoes; (electric) fuses
korekcja [ko-**rek**-tsyah] f. (technical) correction
korekcyjnie [ko-rek-**tsiy**-ńe] adv. correctively
korekcyjny [ko-rek-**tsiy**-ni] adj.m. corrective; correctional
korekta [ko-**rek**-tah] f. correction; proofreading; proof; proof sheet; proofroom
korektor [ko-**rek**-tor] m. proofreader; tuner
korektorka [ko-rek-**tor**-kah] f. (female) proofreader
korektornia [ko-rek-**tor**-ńah] f. proofroom
korektorski [ko-rek-**tor**-skee] adj.m. proofreader's (work, etc.)
korektorstwo [ko-rek-**tor**-stfo] n. proofreading
korektowy [ko-rek-**to**-vi] adj.m. correction (print, etc.)
korektura [ko-rek-**too**-rah] f. correction; rectification
po korekturze [po ko-rek-**too**-zhe] exp.: after amendments
korektywa [ko-rek-**ti**-vah] f. correction
korelacja [ko-re-**lah**-tsyah] f. correlation
korelacyjny [ko-re-lah-**tsiy**-ni] adj.m. correlational; correlation (coefficient, ratio, etc.)
korelat [ko-**re**-laht] m. correlate; correlative
korelatywnie [ko-re-lah-**tiv**-ńe] adv. correlatively
korelatywny [ko-re-lah-**tiv**-ni] adj.m. correlatable; correlative
korelować [ko-re-**lo**-vahćh] v. correlate; be correlated (*repeatedly*)
korelowanie [ko-re-lo-**vah**-ńe] n. correlation
korepetycja [ko-re-pe-**ti**-tsyah] f. tutoring; private lesson; rehearsal
korepetycyjny [ko-re-pe-ti-**tsiy**-ni] adj.m. tutorial
korepetytor [ko-re-pe-**ti**-tor] m. private tutor; coach
korepetytorka [ko-re-pe-ti-**tor**-kah] f. (female) private tutor; coach
korepetytorski [ko-re-pe-ti-**tor**-skee] adj.m. tutor's; tutorial
korepetytorstwo [ko-re-pe-ti-**tor**-stfo] n. coaching; tutorage; tutorship
korespondencja [ko-res-pon-**den**-tsyah] f. correspondence; letters; mail; post; letter to the editor
korespondencki [ko-res-pon-**den**-tskee] adj.m. of correspondence
korespondencyjnie [ko-res-pon-den-**tsiy**-ńe] adv. by correspondence; by letters; by mail
korespondencyjny [ko-res-pon-den-**tsiy**-ni] adj.m. correspondence (school, etc.); mail (order, etc.)

korespondent [ko-res-**pon**-dent] m. correspondent
korespondent wojenny [ko-res-**pon**-dent vo-**yen**-ni] exp.: war correspondent; war reporter
korespondentka [ko-res-pon-**dent**-kah] f. (female) correspondent; postcard; postal card
korespondować [ko-res-pon-**do**-vahćh] v. correspond (*repeatedly*)
korespondowanie [ko-res-pon-do-**vah**-ńe] n. correspondence
korkociąg [kor-**ko**-ćhownk] m. corkscrew; tailspin; twist (dive); spinning dive
korkodąb [kor-**ko**-downp] m. cork oak
korkorodny [kor-ko-**rod**-ni] adj.m. cork-forming
korkotwórczy [kor-ko-**tfoor**-chi] adj.m. cork-forming
korkowacenie [kor-ko-vah-**tse**-ńe] n. suberization
korkowacieć [kor-ko-**vah**-ćhećh] v. become suberized (*repeatedly*)
korkować [kor-**ko**-vahćh] v. cork up; lock (the traffic, etc.); obstruct; choke; mob slang: have (anal) homosexual intercourse; make an artificial congestion (to facilitate robbery) (*repeatedly*)
korkowanie [kor-ko-**vah**-ńe] n. obstruction
korkowiec [kor-**ko**-vyets] m. alcyon (tree); Amur cork (tree); cork pistol
korkowina [kor-ko-**vee**-nah] f. cork; corky texture
korkownica [kor-kov-**ńee**-tsah] f. bottle-corking machine; corker; graining machine
korkowy [kor-**ko**-vi] adj.m. cork (sole, jacket, carpet, etc.)
kwas korkowy [kfahs kor-**ko**-vi] exp.: suberic acid
kormofit [kor-**mo**-feet] m. variety of fern; cormophyte
kormofity [kor-mo-**fee**-ti] pl. the Cormophyta
kormoran [kor-**mo**-rahn] m. cormorant; slang: victim of a crime (mob jargon)
kornak [**kor**-nahk] m. elephant driver
kornecik [kor-**ne**-ćheek] m. (small) cornet
kornecista [kor-ne-**ćhees**-tah] m. cornetist; cornet player
kornel [**kor**-nel] m. cornel; dogwood
korner [**kor**-ner] m. corner of price manipulation; corner kick
kornet [**kor**-net] m. cornet; nun's head cover
kornie [**kor**-ńe] adv. humbly
kornik [**kor**-ńeek] m. bark beetle; borer
korniki [kor-**ńee**-kee] pl. Scolytidae family of beetles
kornikowy [kor-ńee-**ko**-vi] adj.m. bark beetles'; borer's
korniszon [kor-**ńee**-shon] m. pickled cucumber; gherkin; slang: excrement; old man (mob jargon)
korniszonowy [kor-ńee-sho-**no**-vi] adj.m. of pickled cucumber; gherkin (dish, etc.)
kornwalijski [korn-vah-**leey**-skee] adj.m. Cornish
korny [**kor**-ni] adj.m. humble
korodować [ko-ro-**do**-vahćh] v. corrode (*repeatedly*)
korodowanie [ko-ro-do-**vah**-ńe] n. corrosion
koromysło [ko-ro-**mis**-wo] n. shoulder bar for carrying two buckets (of water, etc.)
korona [ko-**ro**-nah] f. crown; coronet; aureole; climax; culmination; acme; corona; treetop; head; (Austrian) krone; (dental) cap; coping; kingdom; head of antlers; (drill) bit; tonsure; mob slang: passive homosexual
Korona [ko-**ro**-nah] f. the Kingdom of Poland
koronacja [ko-ro-**nah**-tsyah] f. coronation; crowning
koronacyjny [ko-ro-nah-**tsiy**-ni] adj.m. coronation (ceremony, etc.)
koronarografia [ko-ro-nah-ro-**grah**-fyah] f. coronary radiological examination
koronarograficzny [ko-ro-nah-ro-grah-**feech**-ni] adj.m. of coronary radiological examination
koronczarka [ko-ron-**chahr**-kah] f. lace-maker
koronczarstwo [ko-ron-**chahr**-stfo] n.

lacemaking
koroneczka [ko-ro-**nech**-kah] f. (nice, little) lace; openwork; tracery; dental cap; crown of a tooth; (small drill) bit; rosary; chaplet; beads
koroniasty [ko-ro-**ńahs**-ti] adj.m. (animal) with crown-like head-top
koroniec [ko-**ro**-ńets] m. Goura pigeon
koronium [ko-**ro**-ńyoom] n. coronium (hypothetical element)
koronka [ko-**ron**-kah] f. lace; openwork; tracery; dental cap; crown of a tooth; (drill) bit; rosary; chaplet; beads; slang: criminal investigation (mob jargon)
koronkarka [ko-ron-**kahr**-kah] f. lace-maker
koronkarnia [ko-ron-**kahr**-ńah] f. lace factory
koronkarski [ko-ron-**kahr**-skee] adj.m. lace-maker's (work, etc.); lacemaking (industry, etc.)
warsztat koronkarski [**vahrsh**-taht ko-ron-**kahr**-skee] exp.: lace frame
koronkarstwo [ko-ron-**kahr**-stfo] n. lacemaking
koronkarz [ko-**ron**-kahsh] m. lacemaker
koronkowo [ko-ron-**ko**-vo] adv. like a lace; in lacelike fashion; subtly; delicately; exquisitely
koronkowość [ko-ron-**ko**-vośhćh] f. lace quality; lacelike nature; delicateness; exquisiteness
koronkowy [ko-ron-**ko**-vi] adj.m. lace (ornament, etc.); lacy; lacelike; fine; delicate; exquisite
koronkowa robota [ko-ron-**ko**-vah ro-**bo**-tah] exp.: fine-drawn work; delicate work; exquisite work
koronny [ko-**ron**-ni] adj.m. royal (lands, etc.); Polish (forces, etc.); of Poland
szkło koronne [shkwo ko-**ron**-ne] exp.: crown glass; optical glass
złoto koronne [**zwo**-to ko-**ron**-ne] exp.: 18-carat gold
koronograf [ko-ro-**no**-grahf] m. special camera for taking pictures of the Sun
koronować [ko-ro-**no**-vahćh] v. crown (*repeatedly*)
koronować się [ko-ro-**no**-vahćh śhan] v. be crowned; assume the crown (*repeatedly*)
koronowanie [ko-ro-no-**vah**-ńe] n. crowning; coronation
koronowanie się [ko-ro-no-**vah**-ńe śhan] n. crowning oneself
koronowany [ko-ro-no-**vah**-ni] adj.m. crowned
koronowane głowy [ko-ro-no-**vah**-ne **gwo**-vi] pl. royalty
koronowy [ko-ro-**no**-vi] adj.m. crown-like (threaded nut, etc.); castellated (nut); corolla (tube, etc.)
koroplastyka [ko-ro-**plahs**-ti-kah] f. Etrurian art form
korowacz [ko-**ro**-vahch] m. peeler; decorticator
korowaczka [ko-ro-**vahch**-kah] f. wood barker; barking machine
korować [ko-**ro**-vahćh] v. peel; decorticate (*repeatedly*)
korować się [ko-**ro**-vahćh śhan] v. be peeled; be decorticated (*repeatedly*)
korowaj [ko-**ro**-vahy] m. Ukrainian wedding cake
korowalnia [ko-ro-**vahl**-ńah] f. decortication plant
korowanie [ko-ro-**vah**-ńe] n. wood barking; decortication
korowanie się [ko-ro-**vah**-ńe śhan] n. getting decorticated
korowarka [ko-ro-**vahr**-kah] f. wood barker; barking machine
korowiec [ko-**ro**-vyets] m. an insect of the suborder Heteroptera
korowina [ko-ro-**vee**-nah] f. cork
korownik [ko-**rov**-ńeek] m. decortication tool
korowodowy [ko-ro-vo-**do**-vi] adj.m. of a pageant; ceremonial
korowód [ko-**ro**-voot] m. file; procession; pageant; train; series (of misfortunes, etc.); slang: prison recreation room (jargon)
korowody [ko-ro-**vo**-di] pl. difficulties; exertions; petty formalities; endeavors; pains; ceremony
korowódka [ko-ro-**voo**-tkah] f. variety of poisonous night moth of the family of Thaumetopoeidae

korowy [ko-**ro**-vi] adj.m. bark (pith, etc.)
korozja [ko-**ro**-zyah] f. corrosion
ulegać korozji [oo-**le**-gahćh ko-**ro**-zyee] exp.: to corrode; to undergo corrosion
korozyjny [ko-ro-**ziy**-ni] adj.m. corrosive
proces korozyjny [**pro**-tses ko-ro-**ziy**-ni] exp.: corrosion
korówka [ko-**roof**-kah] f. wooly aphid
korówkowy [ko-roof-**ko**-vi] adj.m. of wooly aphid
korporacja [kor-po-**rah**-tsyah] f. corporation; association; guild; students' association; fraternity
korporacjonizm [kor-po-rah-**tsyo**-ńeezm] m. corporateness; corporative system
korporacyjnie [kor-po-rah-**tsiy**-ńe] adv. corporately
korporacyjny [kor-po-rah-**tsiy**-ni] adj.m. corporate; corporative
korporał [kor-**po**-rahw] m. corporal (napkin)
korporancki [kor-po-**ran**-tskee] adj.m. of a fraternity; of students' corporation
korporant [kor-**po**-rahnt] m. member of (students') corporation
korpulentny [kor-poo-**lent**-ni] adj.m. fat; corpulent; obese; stout; portly
korpus [**kor**-poos] m. trunk; body; carcass (of a building); staff; (army) corps; all army officers
korpus dyplomatyczny [**kor**-poos di-plo-mah-**tich**-ni] exp.: diplomatic corps
korpuskularny [kor-poos-koo-**lahr**-ni] adj.m. corpuscular
korpusowy [kor-poo-**so**-vi] adj.m. of a corpus; corpus (of a building, etc.)
korral [**kor**-rahl] m. corral
korrida [kor-**ree**-dah] f. corrida; bullfight
korsak [**kor**-sahk] m. variety of fox
korsarka [kor-**sahr**-kah] f. piracy; privateering
korsarski [kor-**sahr**-skee] adj.m. piratic; piratical
korsarstwo [kor-**sahr**-stfo] n. piracy; privateering
korsarz [**kor**-sahsh] m. pirate; corsair; freebooter; buccaneer; privateer
korso [**kor**-so] n. (Italian) corso
Korsykanin [kor-si-**kah**-ńeen] m. (a) Corsican
Korsykanka [kor-si-**kahn**-kah] f. (a) Corsican (female)
korsykański [kor-si-**kahń**-skee] adj.m. Corsican
kort [kort] m. court; cord (fabric)
kort tenisowy [kort te-ńee-**so**-vi] exp.: tennis court
kortezy [kor-**te**-zi] pl. (Spanish) representation of estates
kortowy [kor-**to**-vi] adj.m. court (condition, etc.); of cord fabric
kortyna [kor-**ti**-nah] f. cortin
kortyzon [kor-**ti**-zon] m. cortisone
korumpować [ko-room-**po**-vahćh] v. corrupt; deprave; bribe; debase (*repeatedly*)
korumpowanie [ko-room-po-**vah**-ńe] n. corruption; depravation; bribery
korund [**ko**-roont] m. corundum (mineral)
korundowy [ko-roon-**do**-vi] adj.m. of corundum
korupcja [ko-**roop**-tsyah] f. corruption; venality; bribery
korupcyjnie [ko-roop-**tsiy**-ńe] adv. corruptly
korupcyjny [ko-roop-**tsiy**-ni] adj.m. corrupt
korweta [kor-**ve**-tah] f. corvette; sloop of war
korybant [ko-**ri**-bahnt] m. colloq: rake; carouser; frolicker; rip
koryfeusz [ko-ri-**fe**-oosh] m. leader; personality; coryphaeus; leader of a choir (chorus)
korygować [ko-ri-**go**-vahćh] v. correct; rectify; put right; revise (*repeatedly*)
korygowanie [ko-ri-go-**vah**-ńe] n. correcting; revising
koryncki [ko-**rin**-tskee] adj.m. Corinthian
koryntianka [ko-rin-**tyahn**-kah] f. harlot; prostitute
koryntka [ko-**rin**-tkah] f. dark raisin
koryntki [ko-**rin**-tkee] pl. corinths
koryntówna [ko-rin-**toov**-nah] f.

harlot; prostitute (hist.)
korytarz [ko-**ri**-tahsh] m. corridor; passageway; lobby; tunnel
korytarzowiec [ko-ri-tah-**zho**-vyets] m. apartment building with long corridors
korytarzowy [ko-ri-tah-**zho**-vi] adj.m. corridored; of a corridor
korytarzyk [ko-ri-**tah**-zhik] m. (small, nice) corridor
korytko [ko-**rit**-ko] n. (small) trough
korytkowy [ko-rit-**ko**-vi] adj.m. of a (small) trough; channel (section, etc.)
żelazo korytkowe [zhe-**lah**-zo ko-rit-**ko**-ve] exp.: channel iron
korytkówka [ko-rit-**koof**-kah] f. variety of tile
koryto [ko-**ri**-to] n. trough; riverbed; channel; chute; roadbed; mob slang: food; kitchen; plate; bowl
korytowaty [ko-ri-to-**vah**-ti] adj.m. channelled
korytownik [ko-ri-**tov**-ńeek] m. channel iron; U-iron
korytowy [ko-ri-**to**-vi] adj.m. of a riverbed; of a trough; of a channel
korzec [**ko**-zhets] m. bushel
korzeniasty [ko-zhe-**ńahs**-ti] adj.m. rooty
korzenić się [ko-**zhe**-ńeećh śh<u>an</u>] v. take root; root; colloq: become established (*repeatedly*)
korzenie się [ko-**zhe**-ńe śh<u>an</u>] n. humbling oneself
korzenienie się [ko-zhe-**ńe**-ńe śh<u>an</u>] n. taking roots; becoming established
korzenioczepny [ko-zhe-ńo-**chep**-ni] adj.m. radicant; rooting (from the stem)
korzenionóżka [ko-zhe-ńo-**noosh**-kah] f. rhizopod
korzenionóżki [ko-zhe-ńo-**noosh**-kee] pl. Rhizopoda
korzenioplastyka [ko-zhe-ńo-**plahs**-ti-kah] f. root-sculpture
korzeniowy [ko-zhe-**ńo**-vi] adj.m. root (beer, etc.)
korzeniówka [ko-zhe-**ńoof**-kah] f. root-vodka; spice-flavored vodka; Indian pipe (herb)
korzenisty [ko-zhe-**ńees**-ti] adj.m. rooty
korzennie [ko-**zhen**-ńe] adv. spicily
korzenny [ko-**zhen**-ni] adj.m. spicy; grocer's
korzeń [**ko**-zheń] m. root; spice
korzenie [ko-**zhe**-ńe] pl. roots; spices; spice; spicery
korzonek [ko-**zho**-nek] m. rootlet; radicle
korzonkowy [ko-zhon-**ko**-vi] adj.m. radical; radicular
korzyć [**ko**-zhićh] v. humble; humiliate; prostrate; mortify (*repeatedly*)
korzyć się [**ko**-zhićh śh<u>an</u>] v. humble oneself; humiliate oneself; prostrate oneself; mortify oneself (*repeatedly*)
korzystać [ko-**zhis**-tahćh] v. profit; gain; enjoy a right; benefit (by); stand to win; use to one's advantage; avail oneself (of); use; exercise (a right); enjoy (a right, etc.) (*repeatedly*)
korzystanie [ko-zhis-**tah**-ńe] n. enjoyment (of a right or privilege, etc.); exercise (of a right or privilege, etc.)
korzystnie [ko-**zhist**-ńe] adv. profitably; advantageously; favorably; with profit; beneficially
korzystny [ko-**zhist**-ni] adj.m. profitable; favorable; expedient; lucrative; beneficial; remunerative; advisable
korzyść [**ko**-zhiśhćh] f. profit; advantage; benefit; interest; gain; good; expedience
kos [kos] m. blackbird
kosa [**ko**-sah] f. scythe; knife; tress; sandbank; sand bar; slang: knife; pocket knife; dagger; homicide
kosaciec [ko-**sah**-ćhets] m. iris (herb); (rhizome) orris
kosaćcowaty [ko-sahćh-tso-**vah**-ti] adj.m. iridaceous; of the iris family
kosaćcowate [ko-sahćh-tso-**vah**-te] pl. the iris family
kosaćcowy [ko-sahćh-**tso**-vi] adj.m. iris (root, etc.); of the iris
kosarz [**ko**-sahsh] m. daddy longlegs (crane fly, harvestman)
kosatka [ko-**saht**-kah] f. Tofieldia

(herb)
kosekans [ko-**se**-kahns] m. the reciprocal of sine; cosecant
koser [**ko**-ser] m. grafting knife
kosiarka [ko-**śhahr**-kah] f. mower; mowing machine (time); (woman) haymaker; colloq: hay making
kosiarski [ko-**śhahr**-skee] adj.m. haymaker's
kosiarz [**ko**-śhahsh] m. haymaker; slang: strict teacher; thief; murderer; partner in crime; knife; dagger (mob jargon)
kosić [**ko**-śheećh] v. mow; scythe; rake; sweep; slang: steal; cut (mob jargon) (*repeatedly*)
kosinus [ko-**see**-noos] m. cosine
kosinusoida [ko-see-noo-**soy**-dah] f. cosine graph
kosisko [ko-**śhees**-ko] n. snath; snead; scythe handle; big scythe
kosmacenie [kos-mah-**tse**-ńe] n. making (something) shaggy
kosmacić [kos-**mah**-ćheećh] v. make (something) shaggy (*repeatedly*)
kosmaczek [kos-**mah**-chek] m. a plant with leafless stem
kosmarium [kos-**mahr**-yoom] n. a freshwater alga
kosmatka [kos-**maht**-kah] f. wood-rush
kosmato [kos-**mah**-to] adv. shaggily; with hairs
kosmatość [kos-**mah**-tośhćh] f. shagginess; hairiness
kosmaty [kos-**mah**-ti] adj.m. shaggy; hairy; fleecy
kosmea [kos-**me**-ah] f. cosmos (plant)
kosmek [**kos**-mek] m. wisp of hair; flock of hair; villus
kosmetolog [kos-me-**to**-log] m. cosmetologist
kosmetologia [kos-me-to-**lo**-gyah] f. cosmetology
kosmetyczka [kos-me-**tich**-kah] f. vanity bag; beautician
kosmetycznie [kos-me-**tich**-ńe] adv. cosmetically
kosmetyczny [kos-me-**tich**-ni] adj.m. cosmetic; cosmetical
chirurgia kosmetyczna [khee-**roor**-gyah kos-me-**tich**-nah] exp.: plastic surgery
kosmetyk [kos-**me**-tik] m. cosmetic; makeup (skin and hair); cosmetic preparation; slang: cheat; swindler (mob jargon)
kosmetyka [kos-**me**-ti-kah] f. cosmetics; cosmetology; slang: woman's face (mob jargon)
kosmicznie [kos-**meech**-ńe] adv. cosmically
kosmiczny [kos-**meech**-ni] adj.m. cosmic; from outer space; vast
kosmita [kos-**mee**-tah] m. creature from outer space
kosmo- [kos-mo] prefix: cosmo- (of the universe, of cosmos)
kosmobiolog [kos-mo-**byo**-log] m. cosmic biologist
kosmobiologia [kos-mo-byo-**lo**-gyah] f. cosmic biology
kosmodrom [kos-**mo**-drom] m. base for cosmic flights
kosmofizyk [kos-mo-**fee**-zik] m. cosmo-physicist
kosmofizyka [kos-mo-**fee**-zi-kah] f. cosmo-physics
kosmogonia [kos-mo-**go**-ńyah] f. cosmogony
kosmogoniczny [kos-mo-go-**ńeech**-ni] adj.m. cosmogonic; cosmogonical
kosmograf [kos-**mo**-grahf] m. cosmographer
kosmografia [kos-mo-**grah**-fyah] f. cosmography
kosmograficznie [kos-mo-grah-**feech**-ńe] adv. cosmographically
kosmograficzny [kos-mo-grah-**feech**-ni] adj.m. cosmographical; cosmographic
kosmolog [kos-**mo**-log] m. cosmologist
kosmologia [kos-mo-**lo**-gyah] f. cosmology
kosmologicznie [kos-mo-lo-**geech**-ńe] adv. cosmologically
kosmologiczny [kos-mo-lo-**geech**-ni] adj.m. cosmological; cosmologic
kosmonauta [kos-mo-**nahw**-tah] m. cosmonaut; spaceman; astronaut
kosmonautka [kos-mo-**nahwt**-kah] f. (woman) cosmonaut; spacewoman; astronaut
kosmonautyczny [kos-mo-nahw-**tich**-

ni] adj.m. of space travel; of spacemen
kosmonautyka [kos-mo-**nahw**-ti-kah] f. space travel; space navigation; cosmonautics; astronautics
kosmopolita [kos-mo-po-**lee**-tah] m. cosmopolite; cosmopolitan
kosmopolityczny [kos-mo-po-lee-**tich**-ni] adj.m. cosmopolitan
kosmopolityzacja [kos-mo-po-lee-ti-**zah**-tsyah] f. spreading of cosmopolitism
kosmopolityzm [kos-mo-po-**lee**-tizm] m. cosmopolitism
kosmos [**kos**-mos] m. cosmos; universe; outer space
kosmotron [kos-**mo**-tron] m. particle accelerator; cosmotron
kosmowizja [kos-mo-**vee**-zyah] f. televised view from the cosmos
kosmozofia [kos-mo-**zo**-fyah] f. science of cosmos; cosmosophy
kosmówczak [kos-**moof**-chahk] m. chorion adenoma (carcinoma)
kosmówka [kos-**moof**-kah] f. chorion
kosmówkowy [kos-moof-**ko**-vi] adj.m. chorionic
kosmyczek [kos-**mi**-chek] m. (small) wisp; strand; tuft; flock (of hair)
kosmyk [**kos**-mik] m. wisp; strand; tuft; flock (of hair)
koso [**ko**-so] adv. with a slant; with a squint
kosodrzew [ko-**so**-dzhef] m. dwarf mountain pine
kosodrzewina [ko-so-dzhe-**vee**-nah] f. dwarf mountain pine
kosodrzewinowy [ko-so-dzhe-vee-**no**-vi] adj.m. of dwarf mountain pine
kosoń [ko-soń] m. variety of ichneumon (mongoose)
kosooki [ko-so-**o**-kee] adj.m. with slanting eyes; with scowling eyes; cross-eyed
kosówka [ko-**soof**-kah] f. dwarf mountain pine
kosówkowy [ko-soof-**ko**-vi] adj.m. of dwarf mountain pine
kosteczka [kos-**tech**-kah] f. ossicle
kostera [kos-**te**-rah] m. trunkfish; dicer; dice gambler; surly person
kostium [**kos**-tyoom] m. suit; dress; garb; tailor-made suit; fancy dress
kostiumer [kos-**tyoo**-mer] m. costumer; wardrobe keeper
kostiumeria [kos-tyoo-**me**-ryah] f. (theater) wardrobe
kostiumik [kos-**tyoo**-meek] m. (small, nice) child's suit; dress; garb; fancy dress
kostiumolog [kos-tyoo-**mo**-log] m. costumist
kostiumologia [kos-tyoo-mo-**lo**-gyah] f. costumery
kostiumologiczny [kos-tyoo-mo-lo-**geech**-ni] adj.m. of costumery
kostiumowo [kos-tyoo-**mo**-vo] adv. by means of costumery
kostiumowość [kos-tyoo-**mo**-vośhćh] f. costumery
kostiumowy [kos-tyoo-**mo**-vi] adj.m. costumic
kostka [**kost**-kah] f. small bone; ankle; knuckle; malleolus; die; dice; lump (of sugar, etc.); cube; cake (of butter, etc.); cobbles; plectrum; pavement made of shaped rocks
kostkarka [kost-**kahr**-kah] f. rock-shaping machine
kostkarz [**kost**-kahsh] m. paver (with shaped rocks)
kostkować [kost-**ko**-vahćh] v. pave with shaped rocks (*repeatedly*)
kostkowanie [kost-ko-**vah**-ńe] n. paving with shaped rocks; making checkerboard on a metal surface
kostkowy [kost-**ko**-vi] adj.m. of little cubes; lump (sugar, etc.)
kostkówki [kost-**koof**-kee] pl. bobby-sox
kostnawy [kost-**nah**-vi] adj.m. of bone tissue without calcium
kostnica [kost-**ńee**-tsah] f. morgue; mortuary; dead house; charnel house; ossuary
kostnieć [**kost**-ńećh] v. grow stiff grow numb; ossify; fossilize; colloq: freeze; perish with cold (*repeatedly*)
kostnienie [kost-**ńe**-ńe] n. ossification
kostnina [kost-**ńee**-nah] f. callus
kostniwo [kost-**ńee**-vo] n. bone tissue at tooth-root
kostnołuski [kost-no-**woos**-kee]

adj.m. ganoid (fish)
kostnoszkieletowy [kost-no-shke-le-to-vi] adj.m. teleostean; osseous (fish, etc.)
kostnoszkieletowe [kost-no-shke-le-to-ve] pl. the Teleostei (fishes)
kostny [kost-ni] adj.m. osseous; bony
guzek kostny [goo-zek kost-ni] exp.: node
mączka kostna [mownch-kah kost-nah] exp.: bone meal; bone dust
kostolice [kos-to-lee-tse] pl. the Scleroparei group of fish
kostołuski [kos-to-woos-kee] adj.m. ganoid
kostołuskie [kos-to-woos-ke] pl. Ganoidei
kostotom [kos-to-tom] m. surgical scissors
kostotomia [kos-to-to-myah] f. surgical removal of a rib
kostromski [kos-trom-skee] adj.m. of one of Russian races of cattle
kostropaty [kos-tro-pah-ti] adj.m. rough; rugged; uneven; slang: sloppy; uncouth (mob jargon)
kostrzewa [kos-tshe-vah] f. fescue (grass)
kostrzewiasty [kos-tshe-vyah-sti] adj.m. shaggy
kostucha [kos-too-khah] f. colloq: Death; slang: methylated spirit; death sentence; grandmother
kostur [kos-toor] m. stick; poker; a fish of the Cyprinidae family
kosturek [kos-too-rek] m. (small) stick; poker; a fish of the Cyprinidae family
kostusia [kos-too-śhah] f. colloq: Death
kostycznie [kos-tich-ńe] adv. bitingly; caustically; sarcastically; colloq: roughly; bluntly
kostyczność [kos-tich-nośhćh] f. causticity; sarcasm; colloq: roughness; bluntness
kostyczny [kos-tich-ni] adj.m. biting; caustic; cutting; sarcastic; colloq: rough; blunt; dry
kosy [ko-si] adj.m. slanting; cross-eyed; scowling
kosynier [ko-si-ńer] m. scythe-bearer; scythe user
kosynierski [ko-si-ńer-skee] adj.m. of a scythe user; scythe-bearer's
kosz [kosh] m. basket; pannier; clothes-basket; hamper; wastebasket; work-basket; grabbag; snore-piece (of a pump); strand chair (at the beach); (motorcycle sidecar); gondola (of a balloon); (basketball) basket; Tartar military camp; Tartar or Cossack detachment
dać kosza [dahćh ko-shah] exp.: to turn down; to snub; to rebuff (somebody)
dostać kosza [dos-tahćh ko-shah] exp.: to be turned down; to be snubbed; to be rebuffed
koszałka [ko-shahw-kah] f. hamper
koszałki-opałki [ko-shahw-kee o-pahw-kee] pl. exp.: fiddle-faddle; nonsense
koszar [ko-shahr] m. pen; enclosure (for sheep, etc.)
koszara [ko-shah-rah] f. barrack
koszarka [ko-shahr-kah] f. floating workers' quarters
koszarniak [ko-shahr-ńahk] m. confinement to barracks
koszarować [ko-shah-ro-vahćh] v. place in military barracks (*repeatedly*)
koszarowanie [ko-shah-ro-vah-ńe] n. placing in military barracks
koszarowy [ko-shah-ro-vi] adj.m. of barracks
koszary [ko-shah-ri] pl. barracks; (military); caserns
koszarzenie [ko-shah-zhe-ńe] n. penning; placing cattle in a barn
koszarzyć [ko-shah-zhićh] v. place cattle in barns (*repeatedly*)
koszatka [ko-shaht-kah] f. dormouse
koszenie [ko-she-ńe] n. mowing; hay-making; slang: homosexual (anal) sex (mob jargon)
koszenila [ko-she-ńee-lah] f. cochineal insect; cochineal dye
koszenilina [ko-she-ńee-lee-nah] f. Dactylopius coccus insect
koszenilinowy [ko-she-ńee-lee-no-vi] adj.m. cochineal (red, etc.)
koszenilowy [ko-she-ńee-lo-vi] adj.m. cochineal (insect, dye,

etc.)
koszer [**ko**-sher] m. kosher; kasher
koszerny [ko-**sher**-ni] adj.m. kosher (clean or fit to eat)
koszerować [ko-she-**ro**-vahćh] v. prepare kosher food; clean thoroughly (*repeatedly*)
koszka [**kosh**-kah] f. straw beehive
koszmar [**kosh**-mahr] m. nightmare; frightening experience (dream)
koszmarek [kosh-**mah**-rek] m. minor nightmare; somewhat frightening experience (dream)
koszmarnie [kosh-**mahr**-ńe] adv. like a nightmare; in a ghastly manner
koszmarny [kosh-**mahr**-ni] adj.m. nightmarish; ghastly; frightening (experience, dream, etc.)
koszowy [ko-**sho**-vi] m. Tartar camp commander
łuk koszowy [wook ko-**sho**-vi] exp.: drop arch; compound curve; crooked curve
koszówka [ko-**shoof**-kah] f. psyche (butterfly)
koszówki [ko-**shoof**-kee] pl. the Psychidae family of butterflies
koszt [kosht] m. cost; price; expense; charge; economic costs; production cost, etc.
kosztela [kosh-**te**-lah] f. a variety of apple; a variety of apple tree
kosztorys [kosh-**to**-ris] m. estimate; cost calculation
kosztorysant [kosh-to-**ri**-sahnt] m. colloq: cost accountant; estimator
kosztorysować [kosh-to-ri-**so**-vahćh] v. estimate the cost (*repeatedly*)
kosztorysiarz [kosh-to-**ri**-śhahsh] m. colloq: cost accountant; estimator
kosztorysowiec [kosh-to-ri-**so**-vyets] m. colloq: cost accountant; estimator
kosztorysowy [kosh-to-ri-**so**-vi] adj.m. colloq: of cost accounting; of estimating
kosztować [kosh-**to**-vahćh] v. cost; require expenditure; require effort; be expensive; have a price; taste; try (a dish, etc.) (*repeatedly*)
kosztowanie [kosh-to-**vah**-ńe] n. tasting; trying; being expensive
kosztowiec [kosh-**to**-vyets] m. cost accountant
kosztownie [kosh-**tov**-ńe] adv. expensively; richly
kosztowność [kosh-**tov**-nośhćh] f. value; valuable piece of jewelry
kosztowny [kosh-**tov**-ni] adj.m. expensive; costly; precious
kosztur [**ko**-shtoor] m. stick; poker
koszula [ko-**shoo**-lah] f. shirt
koszularka [ko-shoo-**lahr**-kah] f. (female) shirtmaker
koszularz [ko-**shoo**-lahsh] m. shirtmaker
koszuleczka [ko-shoo-**lech**-kah] f. (nice, small) shirt
koszulina [ko-shoo-**lee**-nah] f. (small, simple) shirt
koszulinka [ko-shoo-**leen**-kah] f. (very small, simple) shirt
koszulka [ko-**shool**-kah] f. shimmy; cover; jacket (of a book, etc.); wrapper; cocoon
jaja w koszulkach [**yah**-yah f ko-**shool**-kahkh] exp.: poached eggs
koszulowy [ko-shoo-**lo**-vi] adj.m. shirt (sleeve, etc.)
koszyczek [ko-**shi**-chek] m. very small basket
koszyczkowy [ko-shich-**ko**-vi] adj.m. capitular (inflorescence, etc.)
koszyk [**ko**-shik] m. small basket; grab bag; hilt guard; basketful
koszykarka [ko-shi-**kahr**-kah] f. (female) basketball player; basket maker; colloq: basket osier
koszykarnia [ko-shi-**kahr**-ńah] f. basketry workshop
koszykarski [ko-shi-**kahr**-skee] adj.m. of a basketry workshop; of a basket maker
koszykarstwo [ko-shi-**kahr**-stfo] n. basketry; basketwork; wickerwork
koszykarz [ko-**shi**-kahsh] m. basketball player; basket maker; colloq: basket-baller
koszykowy [ko-shi-**ko**-vi] adj.m. basketwork (articles, etc.); wicker (chair, etc.); basket (osier, etc.)
koszykówka [ko-shi-**koof**-kah] f. basketball
kośba [**koźh**-bah] f. mowing; colloq: raking fire; (artillery) sweep

kościany [kośh-ćhah-ni] adj.m. bone (handle etc.); osseous
kościec [**kośh**-ćhets] m. skeleton; colloq: framework; frame
kościelny [kośh-**ćhel**-ni] adj.m. of church; ecclesiastical; sacred (music, etc.); m. sexton; sacristan
kościogubny [kośh-ćho-**goob**-ni] adj.m. ossivorous; bone-destroying
kościołek [kośh-**ćho**-wek] m. small church
kościotrup [kośh-**ćho**-troop] m. skeleton; slang: thin man (vulg.)
kościotrupi [kośh-ćho-**troo**-pee] adj.m. skeletal
kościotwórczy [kośh-ćho-**tfoor**-chi] adj.m. ossific; bone-forming; osteoblastic
kościozrost [kośh-**ćho**-zrost] m. fusion of a joint
kościół [**kośh**-ćhoow] m. church; church organization; slang: court; correctional institution; police headquarters (mob jargon)
kościółek [kośh-**ćhoo**-wek] m. (small) church
kościsko [kośh-**ćhees**-ko] n. (big, old) bone
kościstość [kośh-**ćhees**-tośhćh] f. boniness; gauntness
kościsty [kośh-**ćhees**-ti] adj.m. bony; angular; rawboned; teleostean (fish); osseous
kościste [kośh-**ćhees**-te] pl. the Teleostei group of fishes
kościuszkowiec [koś-ćhoosh-**ko**-vyets] m. Kościuszko (follower, soldier, etc.)
kościuszkowski [koś-ćhoosh-**kof**-skee] adj.m. Kościuszko (division, insurrection, foundation, etc.)
kość [kośhćh] f. bone; dice
kości [**kośh**-ćhee] pl. bones; mortal remains; dice; dicing
kość słoniowa [kośhćh swo-**ńo**-vah] exp.: ivory
zapalenie kości [zah-pah-**le**-ńe **kośh**-ćhee] exp.: osteitis; inflammation of bone
kośćcowy [kośhćh-**tso**-vi] adj.m. skeletal
koślaczek [kośh-**lah**-chek] m. an orchidaceous plant; Anacamptis
koślawić [ko-**śhlah**-veećh] v. deform; crook; distort; put out of shape (*repeatedly*)
koślawić się [ko-**śhlah**-veećh śh<u>an</u>] v. become deformed; be crooked; be distorted; get out of shape (*repeatedly*)
koślawiec [ko-**śhlah**-vyets] m. crooked being; misshapen being; vagus
koślawieć [ko-**śhlah**-vyećh] v. become deformed; be crooked; be distorted; get out of shape (*repeatedly*)
koślawienie [ko-śhlah-**vye**-ńe] n. distortion
koślawienie się [kośh-lah-**vye**-ńe śh<u>an</u>] n. becoming distorted
koślawo [ko-**śhlah**-vo] adv. out of shape; crookedly; lopsidedly
koślawość [ko-**śhlah**-vośhćh] f. crookedness; lopsidedness; being out of shape; knock-kneed condition
koślawy [ko-**śhlah**-vi] adj.m. crooked; lame; lopsided; rickety; out of shape; misshapen; knock-kneed; bow-legged
kośnik [**kośh**-ńeek] m. haymaker
kośny [**kośh**-ni] adj.m. hay-growing
kot [kot] m. cat; colloq: pussy cat; puss; a felid; tiger cat; hare; grapnel; slang: thief; pimp; Jew; prosecutor; wine (mob jargon)
koty [**ko**-ti] pl. cats; the felids; the cat family; colloq: cat skin fur
kot w worku [kot v **vor**-koo] exp.: a pig in a poke
wykręcać kota ogonem [vi-**kr<u>an</u>**-tsahćh **ko**-tah o-**go**-nem] exp.: to quibble; to evade the issue
kota [**ko**-tah] f. coordinate of height (on a map); benchmark of height
kotangens [ko-**tahn**-gens] m. cotangent
kotangensoida [ko-tahn-gen-**soy**-dah] f. cotangent curve
kotara [ko-**tah**-rah] f. curtain; door curtain; backdrop; veil (of mist, etc.)
kotawiec [ko-**tah**-vyets] m. long-tailed monkey
kotbelka [kot-**bel**-kah] f. cat head
koteczek [ko-**te**-chek] m. kitty

koteczka [ko-**tech**-kah] f. kitty
kotek [**ko**-tek] m. kitten; pussy cat; puss; sail protector on wire rope
kotelnia [ko-**tel**-ńah] f. mating of sheep; pairing of sheep
koteria [ko-**te**-ryah] f. coterie; clique; cabal
koteryjka [ko-te-**riy**-kah] f. (small-town) coterie; clique; cabal
koteryjność [ko-te-**riy**-nośhćh] f. cliquishness
koteryjny [ko-te-**riy**-ni] adj.m. cliquish
kotew [**ko**-tef] f. anchor; tie; anchor tie; anchor bolt; tie rod
kotewka [ko-**tef**-kah] f. caltrop; water caltrop
kotik [**ko**-teek] m. sea-bear
kotka [**kot**-kah] f. (female) cat; she-cat; catkin; lamb's tail; variety of clover
kotkowy [kot-**ko**-vi] adj.m. amentaceous (plant)
kotlarnia [kot-**lahr**-ńah] f. boiler works; boiler forge
kotlarski [kot-**lahr**-skee] adj.m. boilermaker's; boiler-smith's
kotlarstwo [kot-**lahr**-stfo] n. boiler-making; copper-smithing
kotlarz [**kot**-lahsh] m. boilermaker; boiler-smith; coppersmith; brazier; tinker
kotlecik [kot-**le**-ćheek] m. (small, nice) cutlet
kotlet [**kot**-let] m. cutlet
kotlina [kot-**lee**-nah] f. dale; slang: gang of thieves (mob jargon)
kotlinka [kot-**leen**-kah] f. (small, nice) dale
kotlinny [kot-**leen**-ni] adj.m. of a dale; located in a dale
kotlinowaty [kot-lee-no-**vah**-ti] adj.m. shaped like a dale
kotlista [kot-**lees**-tah] m. kettledrummer
kotłować [kot-**wo**-vahćh] v. whirl; seethe; surge; drive crazy; bother; worry (*repeatedly*)
kotłować się [kot-**wo**-vahćh śhan] v. boil; eddy; swirl; welter; whirl; seethe; surge; be agitated; be in an uproar (*repeatedly*)
kotłowanie [kot-wo-**vah**-ńe] n. confusion; agitation
kotłowanie się [kot-wo-**vah**-ńe śhan] n. participating in an uproar
kotłowanina [kot-wo-vah-**ńee**-nah] f. confusion; agitation; turmoil; uproar
kotłowiec [kot-**wo**-vyets] m. boiler scale; furring; incrustation
kotłowisko [kot-wo-**vees**-ko] n. whirl; swirl; eddying
kotłowisko prądów [kot-wo-**vees**-ko **prown**-doof] exp.: tidal races
kotłownia [kot-**wov**-ńah] f. boiler room; boiler house; fire room
kotłowy [kot-**wo**-vi] adj.m. boiler (scale, etc.); m. boiler-man
kotna [**kot**-nah] adj.f. (pregnant female) (big, heavy) with young; with kitten; in kitten; with lamb
kotnik [**kot**-ńeek] m. snug corner of female cat with kittens
kotoniarz [ko-**to**-ńahsh] m. man working with cottonized flax fiber
kotonina [ko-to-**ńee**-nah] f. cottonized (flax) fiber
kotonizacja [ko-to-ńee-**zah**-tsyah] f. cottonization
kotonizator [ko-to-ńee-**zah**-tor] m. cottonization machine
kotonizować [ko-to-ńee-**zo**-vahćh] v. cottonize; make flax like cotton (*repeatedly*)
kotonizowanie [ko-to-ńee-zo-**vah**-ńe] n. cottonization; making flax like cotton
kotować [ko-**to**-vahćh] v. quote (prices, etc.); mark (dimensions on drawings, etc.) (*repeatedly*)
kotowanie [ko-to-**vah**-ńe] n. quoting (prices, etc.); marking (dimensions on drawings, etc.)
kotuchna [ko-**too**-khnah] f. kitty; pussy cat
koturn [**ko**-toorn] m. cothurnus; buskin; wedge heel
koturny [ko-**toor**-ni] pl. wedge-heeled shoes
koturnowość [ko-toor-**no**-vośhćh] f. stiltedness; bombast
koturnowy [ko-toor-**no**-vi] adj.m. buskined; colloq: stilted; bombastic
kotuś [**ko**-toośh] m. kitty; colloq: darling; honey; popsy-wopsy

(Brit.)
kotwa [**kot**-fah] f. anchor; tie; anchor tie; anchor bolt; tie rod
kotwica [kot-**fee**-tsah] f. anchor; armature; keeper; anchor escapement (in a clock)
zarzucić kotwicę [zah-**zhoo**-ćheećh kot-**fee**-tsan] exp.: to cast anchor
kotwicowisko [kot-fee-tso-**vees**-ko] n. anchorage; moorings
kotwicowy [kot-fee-**tso**-vi] adj.m. anchor (stock, fluke, etc.)
kotwiczenie [kot-fee-**che**-ńe] n. anchoring
kotwiczka [kot-**feech**-kah] f. (small) anchor
kotwiczne [kot-**feech**-ne] n. anchorage (duties, etc.); groundage
kotwiczny [kot-**feech**-ni] adj.m. anchor (buoy, lining, etc.)
kotwiczyć [kot-**fee**-chićh] v. anchor; lie at anchor (*repeatedly*)
kotwić [**kot**-feećh] v. anchor; brace (*repeatedly*)
kotwienie [kot-**fye**-ńe] n. anchoring; bracing
kotwowy [kot-**fo**-vi] adj.m. of an anchor; of a tie rod
koty [**ko**-ti] pl. colloq: fuzz
kotylion [ko-**til**-yon] m. cotillion; favor (with a partner in cotillion)
kotylionowy [ko-til-yo-**no**-vi] adj.m. cotillion (waltz, etc.)
kotylozaur [ko-ti-**lo**-zahwr] m. cotylosaur
kotylozaury [ko-ti-lo-**zahw**-ri] pl. the order Cotylosauria
kotyzacja [ko-ti-**zah**-tsyah] f. quotation (of stock prices)
kowadełko [ko-vah-**dew**-ko] n. small anvil; (tinsmith's) stake; incus; measuring anvil (in micrometer)
kowadełkowy [ko-vah-dew-**ko**-vi] adj.m. of a small anvil; of a (tinsmith's) stake; of the incus
kowadło [ko-**vah**-dwo] n. anvil
między młotem a kowadłem [myan-dzi **mwo**-tem ah ko-**vahd**-wem] exp.: between the devil and the deep blue sea
kowal [**ko**-vahl] m. blacksmith; hammerman; farrier; red bug
kowalencyjność [ko-vah-len-**tsiy**-nośhćh] f. covalence
kowalentność [ko-vah-**lent**-nośhćh] f. covalence
kowalik [ko-**vah**-leek] m. nuthatch (bird)
kowalka [ko-**vahl**-kah] f. blacksmith's wife; smithing
kowalność [ko-**vahl**-nośhćh] f. malleability; ductility; forgeability; malleable tenacity
kowalny [ko-**vahl**-ni] adj.m. malleable; ductile; forgeable
kowalski [ko-**vahl**-skee] adj.m. (black)smith's (apprentice, etc.)
miech kowalski [myekh ko-**vahl**-skee] exp.: smith's bellows
młot kowalski [mwot ko-**vahl**-skee] exp.: sledge hammer; smith's hammer
kowalstwo [ko-**vahl**-stfo] n. smithing; smithery; forging
kowar [**ko**-vahr] m. iron, nickel, cobalt, manganese alloy
kowarka [ko-**vahr**-kah] f. hammering device
kowarowy [ko-vah-**ro**-vi] adj.m. of iron, nickel, cobalt, manganese alloy (wire, etc.)
kowboj [**kov**-boy] m. cowboy; slang: an American; undercover police agent (mob jargon)
kowbojski [kov-**boy**-skee] adj.m. cowboy's (life, boots, film, etc.)
kowerkot [ko-**ver**-kot] m. cover-coat weave
koza [**ko**-zah] f. goat; she-goat; bagpipe; spined loach (fish); colloq: nanny goat; hoyden; filly; jug; clink; lock-up; jail; detention (after school); hod (for carrying bricks); iron stove; slang; motorcycle; motorscooters; bicycle; lively girl
kozacki [ko-**zah**-tskee] adj.m. Cossack's; Cossacks'; Cossack (stanitsa, post, etc.)
po kozacku [po ko-**zah**-tskoo] exp.: Cossack-fashion
kozactwo [ko-**zah**-tstfo] n. the Cossacks
kozaczek [ko-**zah**-chek] m. small Cossack; single game of bridge
kozaczki [ko-**zah**-chkee] pl. fur-

topped half-length boots
Kozaczka [ko-**zah**-chkah] f. Cossack woman (girl)
kozaczy [ko-**zah**-chi] adj.m. Cossack's; Cossacks'; Cossack (stanitsa, post, etc.)
kozaczyzna [ko-zah-**chiz**-nah] f. Cossack population; Cossack region; Cossack territory
Kozak [**ko**-zahk] m. Cossack
kozak [**ko**-zahk] m. Cossack; colloq: plucky guy; hoyden; tomboy; a lively dance; livery servant; slang: professional thief; soldier of fortune (mob jargon)
kozakować [ko-zah-**ko**-vahćh] v. slang: show courage; display bravado; show daring; quarrel; fuss; wrangle; storm (*repeatedly*)
kozakowanie [ko-zah-ko-**vah**-ńe] n. slang: courage; bravado; daring; quarrel; fuss
kozakówka [ko-zah-**koof**-kah] f. slang: moonshine (mob jargon)
kozera [ko-**ze**-rah] f. trumps
nie bez kozery [ńe bes ko-**ze**-ri] exp.: not without reason
kozetka [ko-**zet**-kah] f. love seat; settee; a sociable
kozi [**ko**-źhee] adj.m. goat's (milk, etc.); goat-like; hircine (in smell); caprine
zapędzić w kozi róg [zah-pan-dźheećh f **ko**-źhee rook] exp.: to overwhelm (somebody); to corner (somebody)
koziarnia [ko-**źhahr**-ńah] f. goat shed
koziarz [**ko**-źhahsh] m. goatherd; bagpiper
kozibród [ko-**źhee**-broot] m. goatbeard; salsify (plant with edible root)
kozica [ko-**źhee**-tsah] f. chamois; bagpipe; colloq: filly; hoyden; slang: shoplifting (mob jargon)
kozieradka [ko-źhe-**raht**-kah] f. fenugreek (plant)
kozik [**ko**-źheek] m. clasp knife; penknife
kozina [ko-**źhee**-nah] f. goat's meat
koziniec [ko-**źhee**-ńets] m. goat-like deformation of horse's foot
kozioł [**ko**-źhow] m. buck; gambol; somersault; trestle; stack (of arms); coach box; dickey seat; sawyer's jack; roebuck; tumbler (pigeon); colloq: iron stove; hod (for carrying bricks); rebound (of a ball); dribble (of a ball); slang: drunk; victim of crime; homosexual (mob jargon)
kozioł ofiarny [**ko**-źhow o-**fyahr**-ni] exp.: scapegoat
koziołeczek [ko-źho-**we**-chek] m. (small, nice) buck; gambol
koziołek [ko-**źho**-wek] m. (small, nice) buck; gambol; bounce
koziołkować [ko-źhow-**ko**-vahćh] v. somersault; turn a somersault; roll (over); tumble over; rebound a ball; dribble a ball; overturn; bounce; upset; slang: drink alcohol (mob jargon) (*repeatedly*)
koziołkowanie [ko-źhow-ko-**vah**-ńe] n. turning a somersault; rolling (over); tumbling over; rebounding a ball; dribbling a ball; bouncing
koziołkowy [ko-źhow-**ko**-vi] adj.m. of a roebuck; of a gambol; of a somersault; of a rebounding ball; of a bouncing ball
koziołkujący [ko-źhow-koo-**yown**-tsi] adj.m. tumbling (pigeon, etc.)
kozionogi [ko-źho-**no**-gee] adj.m. goat-hoofed
koziorożec [ko-źho-**ro**-zhets] m. ibex; Capricorn
zwrotnik Koziorożca [**zwrot**-ńeek Ko-źho-**rosh**-tsah] exp.: the tropic of Capricorn
kozioróg [ko-**źho**-rook] m. longicorn (a beetle)
kozłek [**ko**-zwek] m. valeriana herb
kozłkowaty [ko-zwko-**vah**-ti] adj.m. valerianaceous; of the valerian family; of the setwall family
kozłkowate [ko-zwko-**vah**-te] pl. the Valerianaceae family
kozłonogi [ko-zwo-**no**-gee] adj.m. goat-hoofed
kozłować [ko-**zwo**-vahćh] v. slang: drink alcohol; take narcotics (mob jargon) (*repeatedly*)
kozłowiec [ko-**zwo**-vyets] m. leopard's-bane
kozłowy [ko-**zwo**-vi] adj.m. goat's; capric

skóra kozłowa [skoo-rah ko-zwo-vah] exp.: goatskin; buckskin
kozodój [ko-zo-dooy] m. goatsucker
kozodoje [ko-zo-do-ye] pl. the nightjar (Caprimulidae) birds
kozub [ko-zoop] m. vaulting cell
kozuba [ko-zoo-bah] f. vaulting cell
kozunia [ko-zoo-ńah] f. (nice, little) goat
koźlak [koźh-lahk] m. kid; yeanling; lamb kid; goatling; young deer; edible fungus
koźlarz [koźh-lahsh] m. edible fungus; brick carrier
koźlątko [koźh-lownt-ko] n. small kid; goatling
koźlę [koźh-lan] n. kid; goatling
koźlęcy [koźh-lan-tsi] adj.m. kid's; goatling's
koźli [koźh-lee] adj.m. goat's; capric
koźlina [koźh-lee-nah] f. goat's meat; basket-willow
koźlonogi [koźh-lo-no-gee] adj.m. goat-hoofed
kożuch [ko-zhookh] m. sheepskin (coat); fur coat; coating on hot milk; film; hide
kożuchować [ko-zhoo-kho-vahćh] v. graft fruit trees (*repeatedly*)
kożuchowanie [ko-zhoo-kho-vah-ńe] n. grafting of fruit trees
kożuchowy [ko-zhoo-kho-vi] adj.m. sheepskin (coat, etc.)
kożuchówka [ko-zhoo-khoof-kah] f. grafting of fruit trees
kożuszek [ko-zhoo-shek] m. small sheepskin fur coat; (nice) coating on hot milk
kożuszkarz [ko-zhoosh-kahsh] m. furrier
kożusznictwo [ko-zhoosh-ńee-tstfo] n. furriery
kożusznik [ko-zhoosh-ńeek] m. furrier
kożuszyna [ko-zhoo-shi-nah] f. shabby sheepskin coat
kożuszysko [ko-zhoo-shi-sko] n. old, shabby sheepskin coat
kół [koow] m. stake; post
stać jak kół [stahćh yahk koow] exp.: to stand as stiff as a poker
kółeczko [koo-wech-ko] n. (small, nice) wheel; ringlet
kółko [koow-ko] n. small wheel; small circle; (social) circle
kółko na klucze [koow-ko nah kloo-che] exp.: key ring
kółko u mebla [koow-ko oo meb-lah] exp.: castor
w kółko [f koow-ko] exp.: round and round; in circles; invariably
kółkować [koow-ko-vahćh] v. put a nose ring (on a bull, etc.) (*repeatedly*)
kółkowanie [koow-ko-vah-ńe] n. putting a nose ring (on a bull, etc.)
kółkowicz [koow-ko-veech] m. member of a circle
kółkowiec [koow-ko-vyets] m. member of a circle
kółkowy [koow-ko-vi] adj.m. circular; rotate (flower, etc.)
kózka [koos-kah] f. small goat; (cerambycid) beetle; mob slang: john; a prostitute's client
kózki [koos-kee] pl. the cerambycid family of beetles
kózkowaty [koos-ko-vah-ti] adj.m. like a cerambycid beetle
kózkowate [koos-ko-vah-te] pl. the cerambycid family of beetles
kpiarski [kpyahr-skee] adj.m. derisive; derisory; scoffing
kpiarstwo [kpyahr-stfo] n. derision; mockery; scoffing
kpiarz [kpyahsh] m. scoffer; giber
kpiąco [kpyown-tso] adv. derisively; scoffingly; mockingly
kpić [kpeećh] v. jeer; sneer; mock; scoff; gibe; flout (at); make light (of); laugh somebody off (*repeatedly*)
kpienie [kpye-ńe] n. mocking; jeering; sneering; scoffing; gibing; flouting (at); making light (of); laughing somebody off
kpina [kpee-nah] f. mockery; scoffing; raillery
kpiny! [kpee-ni] pl. excl.: mockery!; this is preposterous!
kpinka [kpeen-kah] f. (minor) mockery; scoffing; raillery
kpinkarz [kpeen-kahsh] m. scoffer; giber
kpinkować [kpeen-ko-vahćh] v. make fun (of); poke fun (at); jest;

banter (*repeatedly*)
kpinkowanie [kpeen-ko-**vah**-ńe] n. making fun (of); poking fun (at); jesting; bantering
kra [krah] f. ice flow; ice float
krab [krahp] m. crab
kraby [**krah**-bi] pl. the suborder Brachyura (including crabs)
krabołów [krah-**bo**-woof] m. ship specializing in catching and processing Pacific crabs
krabownik [krah-**bo**-vńeek] m. crab net; crab pot
krach [krahkh] m. crash; slump; smash; collapse; crisis; failure; bankruptcy
kraciak [**kah**-ćhahk] m. checkered texture; check
kraciasty [krah-**ćhahs**-ti] adj.m. checkered; grated
kradnięcie [krahd-**ńan**-ćhe] n. stealing; robbery
kradzenie [krah-**dze**-ńe] n. robbery
kradzież [**krah**-dźhesh] f. theft; robbery; larceny; colloq: stolen object
kradzieżowy [krah-dźhe-**zho**-vi] adj.m. of theft; theft (risk, etc.)
kradziony [krah-**dźho**-ni] adj.m. stolen (object); robbed
kraik [**krah**-eek] m. (small, little) land; region; province; country
kraina [krah-**ee**-nah] f. land; region; province; country
krainka [krah-**een**-kah] f. (small, nice) land; region; province; country; slang: geography class
kraj [krahy] m. country; verge; edge; hem of a garment; land
co kraj to obyczaj [tso krahy to o-bi-chahy] exp.: other countries other laws
kraj rad [krahy raht] exp.: Soviet Union; slang: Russian language class
krajacz [**krah**-yahch] m. cutter
krajać [**krah**-yahćh] v. cut; slice; carve; hack; saw; colloq: use the knife; operate (upon) (*repeatedly*)
krajać się [**krah**-yahćh śhan] v. cut; be cut (*repeatedly*)
serce się kraje [**ser**-tse śhan **krah**-ye] exp.: the heart breaks; the heart aches; it is heart breaking
krajak [**krah**-yahk] m. cutting tool; cutter
krajalnia [krah-**yahl**-ńah] f. cutting room
krajalnica [krah-yahl-**ńee**-tsah] f. cutting machine
krajalniczy [krah-yahl-**ńee**-chi] adj.m. cutting (tool, etc.)
krajalność [krah-**yahl**-nośhćh] f. ease of cutting; resistance to cutting
krajalny [krah-**yahl**-ni] adj.m. cuttable
krajan [**krah**-yahn] m. countryman; compatriot
krajanie [krah-**yah**-ńe] pl. countrymen; compatriots
krajanie [krah-**yah**-ńe] n. cutting; carving
krajanie się [krah-**yah**-ńe śhan] n. cutting oneself
krajanka [krah-**yahn**-kah] f. cuttings; slices (of bread, cakes, etc.); countrywoman; compatriot
krajarka [krah-**yahr**-kah] f. cutter; slicer; (paper) guillotine
krajer [**krah**-yer] m. merchant sailing ship (used before the 19th cent.)
krajka [**krahy**-kah] f. belt; ribbon; selvage; selvedge; border; edge; list; wale; strip (of paper, etc.)
krajniak [**krahy**-ńahk] m. mob slang: trusted gang member; thief
krajnik [**krahy**-ńeek] m. cornice
krajobraz [krah-**yo**-brahs] m. landscape; scenery painting
krajobrazowo [krah-yo-brah-**zo**-vo] adv. as regards the landscape; from the point of view of scenery
krajobrazowy [krah-yo-brah-**zo**-vi] adj.m. landscape (painting, gardening, etc.)
krajowiec [krah-**yo**-vyets] m. native; local inhabitant; aborigine
krajowy [krah-**yo**-vi] adj.m. native; locally made; local; domestic (product, etc.); home (product, etc.); inland (trade, etc.); home-made; indigenous
krajoznawca [krah-yo-**znahf**-tsah] m. tourist; sightseer; excursionist; colloq: hiker
krajoznawczy [krah-yo-**znahf**-chi]

adj.m. hiking; touring
krajoznawstwo [krah-yo-**znahf**-stfo] n. touring; sightseeing
krajuszek [krah-**yoo**-shek] m. brink; the very edge; the last bit; the very end
krakacz [**krah**-kahch] m. croaker; panic-monger
krakać [**krah**-kahćh] v. croak; caw; foretell evil; mob slang: admit to a crime; accuse (*repeatedly*)
krakanie [krah-**kah**-ńe] n. croaks; slang: (court) speech by prosecutor (mob jargon)
krakauer [krah-**kah**-wer] m. colloq: inhabitant of Kraków (Cracow)
krakelura [krah-ke-**loo**-rah] f. cracks (in painting)
krakers [**krah**-kers] m. (a) cracker
kraking [**krah**-kink] m. cracking (process, etc.)
krakingowy [krah-kin-**go**-vi] adj.m. cracking (oil, process, etc.)
kraknąć [**krahk**-nownćh] v. caw; croak
krakowanie [krah-ko-**vah**-ńe] n. cracking
krakowiaczek [krah-ko-**vyah**-chek] m. Cracovian boy; boy dressed in Cracow regional costume
krakowiak [krah-**ko**-vyahk] m. Cracovian; man dressed in Cracow regional costume
krakowian [krah-**ko**-vyahn] m. cracovian matrix
krakowianin [krah-ko-**vyah**-ńeen] m. a Cracovian
krakowianka [krah-ko-**vyahn**-kah] f. a Cracovian (woman, girl)
krakowianowy [krah-ko-vyah-**no**-vi] adj.m. cracovian (calculus, etc.)
krakowski [krah-**ko**-fskee] adj.m. Cracovian; of Cracow; Cracow (history, population, etc.)
krakowski targ [krah-**ko**-fskee tahrk] exp.: splitting the difference
Kraków [**krah**-koof] m. Cracow
kraksa [**krah**-ksah] f. crash; car accident; crash-landing
krakus [**krah**-koos] m. colloq: Cracovian; man dressed in Cracow regional costume
krakuska [krah-**koos**-kah] f. four-cornered cap (as part of Cracovian costume)
krakwa [**krah**-kfah] f. gadwall (duck)
kram [krahm] m. booth; mess; trouble; stall; odds and ends
kramarka [krah-**mahr**-kah] f. (female) huckster; haggler
kramarski [krah-**mahr**-skee] adj.m. huckster's; haggler's; huckstering; haggling
kramarstwo [krah-**mahr**-stfo] n. huckster's trade; haggler' trade
kramarz [**krah**-mahsh] m. huckster; haggler
kramarzenie [krah-mah-**zhe**-ńe] n. huckstering; haggling
kramarzenie się [krah-mah-**zhe**-ńe śhan] n. haggling with one another; delaying one another; fussing with each other
kramarzyć [krah-**mah**-zhićh] v. huckster; haggle; keep a market stall (*repeatedly*)
kramarzyć się [krah-**mah**-zhićh śhan] v. haggle; stall; fuss; mire (*repeatedly*)
kramik [**krah**-meek] m. (little) booth; mess; trouble; stall; odds and ends
kran [krahn] m. tap; faucet; cock; crane; hoist
kraniec [**krah**-ńets] m. border; edge; end; extremity; margin; confines; outskirts; slang: street corner
kranik [**krah**-ńeek] m. (small) tap; faucet; cock; crane; slang; thug's short pipe
kraniolog [krah-**ńo**-log] m. craniologist
kraniologia [krah-ńo-**lo**-gyah] f. craniology
kraniologicznie [krah-ńo-lo-**geech**-ńe] adv. craniologically
kraniologiczny [krah-ńo-lo-**geech**-ni] adj.m. craniological
kraniometr [krah-**ńo**-metr] m. cranial measurement device; craniometer
kraniometria [krah-ńo-**metr**-yah] f. craniometry
kraniometrycznie [krah-ńo-met-**rich**-ńe] adv. craniometrically
kraniometryczny [krah-ńo-met-**rich**-ni] adj.m. craniometrical; craniometric

kranioskopia [krah-ńo-**skop**-yah] f. cranioscopy; methodology of describing the skull
kranioskopowy [krah-ńo-sko-**po**-vi] adj.m. of cranioscopy; of the methodology of describing the skull
kraniotomia [krah-ńo-**tom**-yah] f. craniotomy; the opening of the skull
kranista [krah-**ńee**-stah] m. crane operator; craneman
kranowy [krah-**no**-vi] adj.m. of a tap; of a faucet; crane (hoist, etc.)
kranówa [krah-**noo**-vah] f. colloq: tap water
krańcowo [krahń-**tso**-vo] adv. extremely; excessively; to the extreme degree
krańcowość [krahń-**tso**-vośhćh] f. extremism; extremeness
krańcowy [krahń-**tso**-vi] adj.m. extreme; marginal; excessive
kraplak [**krah**-plahk] m. red dye
kras [krahs] m. Karst (region)
krasa [**krah**-sah] f. colloq: grace; beauty; loveliness; splendor
krasawica [krah-sah-**vee**-tsah] f. beautiful woman
krasić [**krah**-śheećh] v. decorate; season; flavor; add butter (to a dish); add color; colloq: paint (*repeatedly*)
kraska [**krahs**-kah] f. European roller (bird of Coraciidae family)
krasnal [**krahs**-nahl] m. brownie; genie; benevolent goblin
krasnalek [krahs-**nah**-lek] m. (small) brownie; genie; benevolent goblin
krasnodrzew [krahs-**no**-dzhef] m. coca bush
krasnodrzewowaty [krahs-no-dzhe-vo-**vah**-ti] adj.m. of the Erythroxylace family of shrubs
krasnodrzewowate [krahs-no-dzhe-vo-**vah**-te] pl. the Erythroxylace family of shrubs
krasnolicy [krahs-no-**lee**-tsi] adj.m. pretty-faced; lovely; rosy-cheeked
krasnoludek [krahs-no-**loo**-dek] m. brownie; genie; benevolent goblin
krasnopiórka [krahs-no-**pyoor**-kah] f. rudd (fish)
krasnopióry [krahs-no-**pyoo**-ri] adj.m. fine-feathered; red-feathered
krasnorost [krahs-**no**-rost] m. red alga
krasnorosty [krahs-no-**ros**-ti] pl. Rhodophyta family of algae
krasnosok [krahs-**no**-sok] m. coca
krasnosokowaty [krahs-no-so-ko-**vah**-ti] adj.m. erythroxylaceous (shrub, tree)
krasnosokowate [krahs-no-so-ko-**vah**-te] pl. the genus of Erythroxylaceae shrubs and trees
krasny [**krahs**-ni] adj.m. red; colored; colorful; beautiful; lovely
krasomówca [krah-so-**moof**-tsah] m. orator (very eloquent)
krasomówczy [krah-so-**moof**-chi] adj.m. oratorical
krasomówczyni [krah-so-moof-**chi**-ńee] f. (female) orator
krasomówstwo [krah-so-**moof**-stfo] n. oratory; eloquence
krasowacieć [krah-so-**vah**-ćhećh] v. undergo acidic erosion of rocks (*repeatedly*)
krasowieć [krah-**so**-vyećh] v. undergo acidic erosion of rocks (*repeatedly*)
krasowienie [krah-so-**vye**-ńe] n. acidic erosion of rocks
krasowy [krah-**so**-vi] adj.m. of the acidic erosion of rocks; karstic
krasula [krah-**soo**-lah] f. colloq: roan cow
krasy [**krah**-si] adj.m. roan
kraszanka [krah-**shahn**-kah] f. Easter egg painted in a solid color
kraszenie [krah-**she**-ńe] n. decorating; seasoning; flavoring
kraszony [krah-**sho**-ni] adj.m. seasoned with butter
kraść [krahśhćh] v. steal; rob; purloin; pilfer; lift (cattle, etc.); thieve (*repeatedly*)
kraśnieć [**krahśh**-ńećh] v. blush; grow more beautiful; redden (*repeatedly*)
kraśnienie [krahśh-**ńe**-ńe] n. blushing; growing more beautiful; reddening
kraśnik [**krahśh**-ńeek] m. zygaenid (a moth)
kraśniki [krahśh-**ńee**-kee] pl.

Zygaenidae family of moth
kraśny [**krahśh**-ni] adj.m. fat (deer, etc.)
krata [**krah**-tah] f. grate; grill; grating; check; checkered pattern; crate; packing-case
kraty [**krah**-ti] pl. iron bars; checkered pattern; grills
za kratami [zah krah-**tah**-mee] exp.: behind iron bars
krateczka [krah-**tech**-kah] f. (small) grate; grill; grating; check; checkered pattern; crate; packing-case
krategus [krah-**te**-goos] m. hawthorn herb of the genus Crataegous
krater [**krah**-ter] m. crater
kraterowaty [krah-te-ro-**vah**-ti] adj.m. crater-like
kraterowy [krah-te-**ro**-vi] adj.m. crater (lake, etc.)
kratka [**kraht**-kah] f. (small) grate; grill; grating; check; checkered pattern; crate; packing-case
w kratkę [f **kraht**-kan] exp.: squared; in checkered pattern; colloq: irregularly; by fits and starts
kratkować [kraht-**ko**-vahćh] v. rule (paper) in squares; cross-rule; checker; check; square (paper) (*repeatedly*)
kratkowanie [kraht-ko-**vah**-ńe] n. ruling (paper) in squares
kratkowany [kraht-ko-**vah**-ni] adj.m. in squares; in checkered pattern
kratować [krah-**to**-vahćh] v. install a grill; protect (windows, etc.) with iron bars (*repeatedly*)
kratowanie [krah-to-**vah**-ńe] n. installing a grill; protecting (windows, etc.) with iron bars
kratowany [krah-to-**vah**-ni] adj.m. made with latticework
altanka kratowana [ahl-**tahn**-kah krah-to-**vah**-nah] exp.: gazebo made with latticework; trellis
kratownica [krah-tov-**ńee**-tsah] f. grate; grating; latticework; trussing; truss; truss rib
kratownicowy [krah-tov-ńee-**tso**-vi] adj.m. truss (member, stress, bridge, etc.)
kratowy [krah-**to**-vi] adj.m. lattice (frame, girder, etc.); grated (window, etc.)
konstrukcja kratowa [kon-**strook**-tsyah krah-**to**-vah] exp.: latticework
kratówka [krah-**toof**-kah] f. perforated brick
kraul [krahwl] m. crawl (swimming)
kraulista [krahw-**lees**-tah] m. crawler
kraulistka [krahw-**leest**-kah] f. (woman) crawler
krawaciarka [krah-vah-**ćhahr**-kah] f. (woman) tie-maker
krawaciarstwo [krah-vah-**ćhahr**-stfo] n. tie-making
krawaciarz [krah-**vah**-ćhahsh] m. tie-maker; slang: shoplifter; robber; man sentenced to die; death sentence (mob jargon)
krawacik [krah-**vah**-ćheek] m. (small, nice) tie
krawacz [**krah**-vahch] m. shoemaker's paring knife
krawalnik [krah-**vahl**-ńeek] m. shoemaker's paring knife
krawat [**krah**-vaht] m. tie; necktie; slang: neck-hold; choking grip; gallows; death sentence (by hanging) (mob jargon)
krawatka [krah-**vaht**-kah] f. necktie; tie; gorget; ruff; slang: public prosecutor's office (mob jargon)
krawatowy [krah-vah-**to**-vi] adj.m. necktie (material, etc.); tie (fabric, etc.)
krawatówka [krah-vah-**toof**-kah] f. necktie material; tie fabric
krawcowa [krahf-**tso**-vah] f. seamstress; tailor's wife; dressmaker
krawczyna [krahf-**chi**-nah] m. colloq: paltry tailor; contemptible tailor; slang: snip (mob jargon)
krawczyni [krahf-**chi**-ńee] f. seamstress; tailor's wife; dressmaker
krawędziak [krah-**van**-dźhahk] m. square rough timber (4 to 8 inches)
krawędziarka [krah-van-**dźhahr**-kah] f. sheet-metal bending machine; plainer for narrow strips of wood
krawędziować [krah-van-**dźho**-vahćh] v. place metal edges on

skis (*repeatedly*)
krawędziowanie [krah-van-dźho-**vah**-ńe] n. placing of metal edges on skis
krawędziowy [krah-van-**dźho**-vi] adj.m. edge (protector, etc.)
krawędź [krah-vandźh] f. edge; margin; border; brink; verge; shoulder (of a tool); rib; lip (of a pot, etc.); ledge (of a rock, etc.)
krawężnica [krah-vanzh-**ńee**-tsah] f. edge saw; bow saw; roof ridge beam; roof-hip
krawężnik [krah-**vanzh**-ńeek] m. curb (stone); roof-hip
krawiec [**krah**-vyets] m. tailor
krawiecki [krah-**vye**-tskee] adj.m. tailor's; sartorial
po krawiecku [po krah-**vye**-tskoo] exp.: like a qualified tailor
mięsień krawiecki [**myan**-śheń krah-**vye**-tskee] exp.: sartorius; sartorial muscle
krawiectwo [krah-**vye**-tstfo] n. tailoring; sewing
krawieczyzna [krah-vye-**chiz**-nah] f. tailoring; sewing
krąg [krownk] m. ring; vertebra; disc; disk; range; circle; sphere; coil; (prison) slang: pistol; revolver (mob jargon)
kręgiem [**kran**-gem] exp.: in a ring; in a circle; around
w krąg [f krownk] exp.: all around
krąglak [**krowng**-lahk] m. round timber; round log; log cabin
krąglakowy [krowng-lah-**ko**-vi] adj.m. of round timber (logs)
krąglik [**krowng**-leek] m. round extension tube of a brass instrument
krąglizna [krowng-**leez**-nah] f. roundness; round shape
krągławy [krowng-**wah**-vi] adj.m. roundish
krągło [**krowng**-wo] adv. in a circle; in a ring
krągłość [**krowng**-wośhćh] f. roundness
krągłousty [krowng-wo-**oos**-ti] adj.m. craniate (vertebrate
krągłouste [krowng-wo-**oos**-te] pl. the Cyclostomata class
krągły [**krowng**-wi] adj.m. rounded
krąp [krownp] m. fish of the Cyprinidae family
krążek [**krown**-zhek] m. small disk; potter's wheel; pulley; (hockey) puck; block; trolley; slang: disk; record
krążenie [krown-**zhe**-ńe] n. circulation
krążeniowy [krown-zhe-**ńo**-vi] adj.m. of circulation; circulatory
krążkopław [krownsh-**ko**-pwahf] m. scyphozoan jellyfish
krążkopławy [krownsh-ko-**pwah**-vi] pl. the Scyphozoa class of coelenterates (incl. jellyfish)
krążkować [krownsh-**ko**-vahćh] v. roll and finish (metal surface) (*repeatedly*)
krążkowanie [krownsh-ko-**vah**-ńe] n. rolling and finishing (of a metal surface)
krążkownica [krownsh-kov-**ńee**-tsah] f. polishing device for drilled holes
krążkownik [krownsh-**kov**-ńeek] m. polishing lathe attachment for outer surfaces
krążkowy [krownsh-**ko**-vi] adj.m. disk-shaped; pulley (line, rope, etc.)
krążnik [**krownzh**-ńeek] m. giant's-stride; runner; idler; roller; muller
krążownik [krown-**zhov**-ńeek] m. cruiser
krążyć [**krown**-zhićh] v. revolve; circle; make circles; make rings; hover; wheel (in the air); rove; circulate; rotate; wander; stray; spin; cruise (the seas); walk back and forth; go round (from hand to hand); be handed round; go round; go from mouth to mouth; flow (*repeatedly*)
krążyna [krown-**zhi**-nah] f. centering; center; cradling
kreacja [kre-**ah**-tsyah] f. (dress) creation; creation (of a theater part, of a world of fiction, etc.)
kreacjonista [kre-ah-tsyo-**ńees**-tah] m. creationist
kreacjonistyczny [kre-ah-tsyo-ńees-**tich**-ni] adj.m. based on creation
kreacjonizm [kre-ah-**tsyo**-ńeezm] m.

creationism
kreacyjnie [kre-ah-**tsiy**-ńe] adv. creatively
kreacyjność [kre-ah-**tsiy**-nośhćh] f. creativeness; creativity
kreacyjny [kre-ah-**tsiy**-ni] adj.m. creative
kreator [kre-**ah**-tor] m. creator
kreatura [kre-ah-**too**-rah] f. colloq: contemptible person; toad; skunk; creature (a tool of another)
kreatyna [kre-ah-**ti**-nah] f. creatine
kreatynina [kre-ah-ti-**ńee**-nah] f. creatinine
kreatywny [kre-ah-**tiv**-ni] adj.m. creative
krecha [**kre**-khah] f. thick line; stroke of the pen; stroke of the pencil
krechtać [**krekh**-tahćh] v. (wood grouse) call (*repeatedly*)
krechtanie [krekh-**tah**-ńe] n. call (of the wood grouse)
kreci [**kre**-ćhee] adj.m. mole's
krecia robota [**kre**-ćhah ro-**bo**-tah] exp.: colloq: intrigues; scheming; underhand dealings
kreda [**kre**-dah] f. chalk; the Cretaceous (period)
kredencerz [kre-**den**-tsesh] m. cup-bearer
kredens [**kre**-dens] m. china cabinet; cupboard; buffet; butler's pantry; mob slang: trolley; streetcar
kredensik [kre-**den**-śheek] m. (small) china cabinet; cellaret
kredensowy [kre-den-**so**-vi] adj.m. of a china cabinet; of the sideboard; sideboard (keys, etc.)
kredka [**kret**-kah] f. crayon; lipstick; chalk for writing; piece of chalk; colored pencil
kredkowy [kret-**ko**-vi] adj.m. crayon (drawing, etc.)
kredo [**kre**-do] n. credo; creed
kredować [kre-**do**-vahćh] v. chalk; whiten with chalk (*repeatedly*)
kredowanie [kre-do-**vah**-ńe] n. chalking; whitening with chalk
kredowo [kre-**do**-vo] adv. like a chalk
kredowobiały [kre-do-vo-**byah**-wi] adj.m. chalky; white as chalk
kredowy [kre-**do**-vi] adj.m. cretaceous; chalky; made of chalk; white like chalk
kredyt [**kre**-dit] m. credit; credit account
kredyty [kre-**di**-ti] pl. credits; allocation; appropriation
kupować na kredyt [koo-**po**-vahćh nah **kre**-dit] exp.: to buy on credit
udzielić kredytu [oo-**dźhe**-leećh kre-**di**-too] exp.: to sell on credit; to extend a line of (limited) credit to somebody
kredytobiorca [kre-di-to-**byor**-tsah] m. debtor; debtor nation
kredytodawca [kre-di-to-**dahf**-tsah] m. creditor; creditor nation
kredytować [kre-di-**to**-vahćh] v. give credit; sell on credit (*repeatedly*)
kredytowanie [kre-di-to-**vah**-ńe] n. giving credit; the selling on credit (*repeated*)
kredytowy [kre-di-**to**-vi] adj.m. credit (account, bank, etc.)
kredziasty [kre-**dźhahs**-ti] adj.m. chalk (hills, etc.); chalky
kreking [**kre**-king] m. cracking
krekingowy [kre-kin-**go**-vi] adj.m. cracked (gas, etc.)
krektać [**krek**-tahćh] v. call (by the wood grouse) (*repeatedly*)
krektanie [krek-**tah**-ńe] n. calling (by the wood grouse)
krektun [**krek**-toon] m. young wood grouse (male)
krem [krem] m. cream; custard; complexion cream; soup of strained vegetables; mob slang: homosexual intercourse
kremacja [kre-**mah**-tsyah] f. cremation; incineration (of corpses)
kremacyjny [kre-mah-**tsiy**-ni] adj.m. crematory; cremation (oven, etc.)
kremaliera [kre-mahl-**ye**-rah] f. rack; rack-bar; focusing rack
krematorium [kre-mah-**to**-ryoom] n. crematorium; crematory; slang: social rehabilitation center; school (mob jargon)
krematoryjny [kre-mah-to-**riy**-ni] adj.m. crematory
kremik [**kre**-meek] m. (pleasant,

nice) complexion cream
kreml [kreml] m. kremlin; slang: make-up of the court (jargon)
kremogen [kre-**mo**-gen] m. blend of homogenized fruit (refrigerated)
kremowo [kre-**mo**-vo] adv. in cream color; in cream-yellow color
kremowy [kre-**mo**-vi] adj.m. cream (cake, etc.); cream-yellow colored; cream-colored
kremówka [kre-**moof**-kah] f. cream cake
kremplina [kremp-**lee**-nah] f. a synthetic fiber (fluffy)
kremplinowy [kremp-lee-**no**-vi] adj.m. of fluffy synthetic fiber
krenelaż [kre-**ne**-lahsh] m. crenelle; crenel
krenele [kre-**ne**-le] pl. crenelles
krenologia [kre-no-**lo**-gyah] f. geological study of springs
kreodont [kre-**o**-dont] m. creodont (extinct mammal)
kreodonty [kre-o-**don**-ti] pl. Creodonta suborder of extinct mammals (order Carnivora)
Kreol [**kre**-ol] m. creole
kreolina [kre-o-**lee**-nah] f. creolin
kreolizm [kre-**o**-leezm] m. creolism
Kreolka [kre-**ol**-kah] f. (woman) creole
kreolski [kre-**ol**-skee] adj.m. creole (language, cooking, singing, etc.)
kreować [kre-**o**-vahćh] v. create; act (a part); set up (an institution); institute; appoint; nominate (*repeatedly*)
kreowanie [kre-o-**vah**-ńe] n. creation
kreozol [kre-**o**-zol] m. creosol
kreozot [kre-**o**-zot] m. creosote
impregnować kreozotem [eem-pre-**gno**-vahćh kre-o-**zo**-tem] exp.: to creosote
kreozotowy [kre-o-zo-**to**-vi] adj.m. creosote (oil, bush, etc.); creosotic
krepa [**kre**-pah] f. crepe; crape; slang: holdup (mob jargon)
opaska z krepy [o-**pahs**-kah s **kre**-pi] exp.: crepe band
krepdeszyn [krep-**de**-shin] m. crepe de Chine
krepdeszyna [krep-de-**shi**-nah] f. crepe de Chine
krepdeszynowy [krep-de-shi-**no**-vi] adj.m. (frock, etc.) of crepe de Chine
krepina [kre-**pee**-nah] f. crinkled paper; (upholstery) fringe; hair pad
krepinka [kre-**peen**-kah] f. flowers, etc. made of crinkled paper
krepitacja [kre-pee-**tah**-tsyah] f. crepitation
krepon [**kre**-pon] m. crepon
krepować [kre-**po**-vahćh] v. crinkle (paper) (*repeatedly*)
krepowanie [kre-po-**vah**-ńe] n. crinkling
krepowy [kre-**po**-vi] adj.m. crepe (frock, band, etc.); crinkly
kres [kres] m. end; limit; term; verge; aim
kresy [**kre**-si] pl. eastern borderlands of Poland; borderlands
kresa [**kre**-sah] f. (heavy, thick) line; scar
krescent [**kres**-tsent] m. a type of poetic form increasing in the length of verses
kreseczka [kre-**sech**-kah] f. (small) dash (line); hyphen; accent; stroke; hatch
kreska [**kres**-kah] f. dash (line); hyphen; stroke; hatch; scar; accent; mark (on a graduated scale); degree; vote
kreskować [kres-**ko**-vahćh] v. accentuate; put on an accent mark; hatch; cover with lines; shade with lines; hachure a map; crosshatch (*repeatedly*)
kreskowanie [kres-ko-**vah**-ńe] n. lines; hatches (in an engraving, etc.); crosshatching
kreskowanie krzyżowe [kres-ko-**vah**-ńe kshi-**zho**-ve] exp.: crosshatching
kreskowany [kres-ko-**vah**-ni] adj.m. accentuated; with an acute accent; lined; hatched; lineate
kreskownica [kres-kov-**ńee**-tsah] f. drafting device for drawing parallel lines
kreskowy [kres-**ko**-vi] adj.m. line (drawing, etc.)
sztych kreskowy [shtikh kres-**ko**-

vi] exp.: line engraving
kreskówka [kres-**koof**-kah] f. animated cartoons; printed line drawing
kresomózgowie [kre-so-mooz-**go**-vye] n. part of the human brain most developed during phylogeny; telocephalon
kresowiak [kre-**so**-vyahk] m. inhabitant of the borderlands
kresowianin [kre-so-**vyah**-ńeen] m. inhabitant of the borderlands
kresowianka [kre-so-**vyahn**-kah] f. (female) inhabitant of the borderlands
kresowiec [kre-**so**-vyets] m. inhabitant of the borderlands
kresowość [kre-**so**-vośhćh] f. the character of the borderlands
kresowy [kre-**so**-vi] adj.m. of the borderlands; from the borderlands; borderland (population, etc.)
kreślarka [kreśh-**lahr**-kah] f. (woman) designer; tracer; plotter
kreślarnia [kreśh-**lahr**-ńah] f. drafting room; plotting room
kreślarski [kreśh-**lahr**-skee] adj.m. draftsman's; designer's; tracer's; plotter's
kreślarstwo [kreśh-**lahrs**-tfo] n. draftsmanship; drafting; designing; plotting
kreślarz [**kreśh**-lahsh] m. draftsman; designer; tracer; plotter
kreślenie [kreśh-**le**-ńe] n. draftsmanship; drafting; designing; plotting
kreślić [**kreśh**-leećh] v. draft; design; draw; trace; sketch; cross out; describe; depict; picture (*repeatedly*)
kreślić się [**kreśh**-leećh śhan] v. stand out; be outlined against a background; sign oneself; write one's signature (*repeatedly*)
kreślę się z poważaniem [**kreśh**-lan śhan s po-vah-**zhah**-ńem] exp.: I remain, yours very truly
kreślnik [**kreśhl**-ńeek] m. slang: pencil
kret [kret] m. mole; mole fur; mechanical mole; colloq: schemer; mole-sighted person; slang: miner; homosexual; informer (mob jargon)
kretes [**kre**-tes] (only in) exp.:
z kretesem [s kre-**te**-sem] exp.: completely; utterly; hopelessly; altogether; wholly; lock, stock, and barrel; for good and all; neck and crop; toot and branch
kreton [**kre**-ton] m. cretonne
kretonik [kre-**to**-ńeek] m. light cretonne (used for dresses, etc.)
kretonowy [kre-to-**no**-vi] adj.m. cretonne (curtains, etc.)
kretować [kre-**to**-vahćh] v. burrow (*repeatedly*)
kretowanie [kre-to-**vah**-ńe] n. burrowing
kretowina [kre-to-**vee**-nah] f. molehill (made by burrowing)
kretowisko [kre-to-**vees**-ko] n. molehill (made by burrowing)
kretyn [**kre**-tin] m. cretin; imbecile; moron; colloq: idiot; nitwit; imbecile
kretynizm [kre-**ti**-ńeezm] m. cretinism; imbecility; idiotic idea; idiotic thing
kretynka [kre-**tin**-kah] f. (female) cretin; imbecile; moron; colloq: idiot; nitwit; imbecile
kretynowaty [kre-ti-no-**vah**-ti] adj.m. idiotic
kretyński [kre-**tiń**-skee] adj.m. cretinous; imbecile; moronic
kretyństwo [kre-**tiń**-stfo] n. cretinism; imbecility; idiotic idea; idiotic thing
krew [kref] f. blood; race; temperament; nature; blood relationship; descent; stock; lineage; family; slang: red color in cards (mob jargon)
ciałka krwi [**ćhahw**-kah krfee] exp.: blood corpuscles
dawca krwi [**dahf**-tsah krfee] exp.: blood donor
grupa krwi [**groo**-pah krfee] exp.: blood group
krew ci idzie [kref ćhee ee-dźhe] exp.: you are bleeding
krew go zalała [kref go zah-**lah**-wah] exp.: he had a stroke of apoplexy; he burst a blood vessel;

he went wild; he saw red
krew z krwi i kość z kości [kref s krfee ee kośhćh s **kośh**-ćhee] exp.: one's flesh and blood; blood of one's blood; one's worthy son
mrożący krew [mro-**zh**own-tsi kref] exp.: bloodcurdling (event)
psuć krew [psooćh kref] exp.: to exasperate (somebody)
zamordować z zimną krwią [zah-mor-**do**-vahćh z **źheem**-nown krfyown] exp.: to murder in cold blood
krewa [**kre**-vah] f. slang: (a) flop; (prison) slang: red beet soup; death sentence (mob jargon)
kreweta [kre-**ve**-tah] f. shrimp; Paleamon
krewetka [kre-**vet**-kah] f. shrimp
krewetki [kre-**vet**-kee] pl. Natania suborder of shrimp(s)
krewetkowy [kre-vet-**ko**-vi] adj.m. shrimp (salad, dish, etc.)
krewić [**kre**-veećh] v. slang: break one's word; disappoint (mob jargon) (*repeatedly*)
krewki [**kref**-kee] adj.m. rash; quick-tempered; impetuous; irascible; easily provoked; testy; choleric
krewko [**kref**-ko] adv. rashly; in a quick-tempered manner; hastily; impetuously; irascibly; testily
krewkość [**kref**-kośhćh] f. rashness; quick-temper; impetuosity; irascibility
krewna [**krev**-nah] f. (female) relative; kinswoman; connection; blood relation
krewne [**krev**-ne] exp.: (female) kinsfolk
krewniacki [krev-**ńahts**-kee] adj.m. related; of a relative
krewniaczka [krev-**ńahch**-kah] f. (female) related; relative; connection
krewniak [**krev**-ńahk] m. related; relative; connection; mob slang: debtor; indebted person
to nasz krewniak [to nahsh **krev**-ńahk] exp.: he is a relative of ours
krewny [**krev**-ni] m. related; relative; connection
moi krewni [mo-ee **krev**-nee] exp.: my family; my folks
kreza [**kre**-zah] f. ruff; ruche
krezy [**kre**-zi] pl. frilling
krezka [**kres**-kah] f. frill; mesentery (membrane)
krezki [**kres**-kee] pl. tripe (dish)
krezkowy [kres-**ko**-vi] adj.m. mesenteric
krezol [**kre**-zol] m. cresol
krezolowy [kre-zo-**lo**-vi] adj.m. creosotic; cresol (iodide, etc.)
krezus [**kre**-zoos] m. Croesus
krezusowy [kre-zoo-**so**-vi] adj.m. of Croesus
kręcenie [kran-**tse**-ńe] n. twisting (a story, etc.); turning; spinning
kręcenie się [kran-**tse**-ńe śhan] n. stirring; turning oneself
kręcicki [kran-**ćheets**-kee] m. busy body
kręcicka [kran-**ćheets**-kah] f. (female) busy body
kręcić [**kran**-ćheećh] v. twist; turn; shoot film; fuss; boss; roll (cigarettes, etc.); wind; meander; colloq: quibble; prevaricate; shuffle; palter; shift one's ground; slang: live with a woman; trade; lie; cheat; squeal (*repeatedly*)
kręcić się [**kran**-ćheećh śhan] v. go round; turn; revolve; spin; whirl; rotate; gyrate; eddy; bustle; move about; bestir oneself; wind; bend; meander; wreathe; curl; frizzle; roll; busy oneself (about); colloq: fidget; fret; mob slang: be after (something); watch (*repeatedly*)
kręciek [**kran**-ćhek] m. colloq: staggers; craze; fad
dostać kręćka [do-stahćh **kranćh**-kah] exp.: colloq: to go crazy
mieć kręćka [myećh **kranćh**-kah] exp.: colloq: to be crazy
kręciołek [kran-**ćho**-wek] m. colloq: hand-cranked adding machine
kręciołka [kran-**ćhow**-kah] f. colloq: a dance; a party
kręcony [kran-**tso**-ni] adj.m. twisted; curled; winding; spiral
kręcz [kranch] m. cramp
kręcz karku [kranch **kahr**-koo] exp.: stiff-neck; wryneck; cramp

in the neck; torticollis
kręczynka [kran-chin-kah] f. lady's-tresses (an orchid)
kręg [krank] m. vertebra; slang: fingerprint (mob jargon)
kręgarstwo [kran-gahr-stfo] n. chiropractic (practice); chiropraxis
kręgarz [kran-gahsh] m. chiropractor
kręgiel [kran-gel] m. bowling-pin; skittle (Brit.)
kręgle [krang-le] pl. ninepins; skittles (Brit.); bowling; playing the skittles (Brit.); bowling game; game of skittles (Brit.)
kręgielnia [kran-gel-ńah] f. bowling alley; skittle-alley (Brit.)
kręglarski [krang-lahr-skee] adj.m. bowling (game, pin, etc.); bowler's; skittle-player's
kręglarstwo [krang-lahr-stfo] n. bowling; skittles-game (Brit.)
kręglarz [krang-lahsh] m. bowler; skittle-player (Brit.)
kręgosłup [kran-go-swoop] m. vertebral column; spinal column; spine; backbone; colloq: moral rectitude; moral principles; character; willpower
skrzywienie kręgosłupa [skhsi-vye-ńe kran-go-swoo-pah] exp.: spinal curvature
kręgousty [kran-go-oos-ti] adj.m. cyclostomatous (tumor, etc.)
kręgouste [kran-go-oos-te] pl. the cyclostomata tumors containing cysts
kręgowiec [kran-go-vyets] m. vertebrate; animal with spine
kręgowce [kran-gof-tse] pl. vertebrates
kręgowy [kran-go-vi] adj.m. vertebral; spinal
kanał kręgowy [kah-nahw kran-go-vi] exp.: spinal canal
kolumna kręgowa [ko-loom-nah kran-go-vah] exp.: spinal column
rdzeń kręgowy [rdzeń kran-go-vi] exp.: spinal cord
zwierzęta kręgowe [zvye-zhan-tah kran-go-ve] exp.: vertebrates
krępacja [kran-pah-tsyah] f. slang: embarrassment
bez krępacji [bes kran-pah-tsyee] exp.: without ceremony; without embarrassment
krępawo [kran-pah-vo] adv. in a somewhat squatty manner; stockishly
krępawość [kran-pah-vośhćh] f. squatty manner; stockishness
krępawy [kran-pah-vi] adj.m. somewhat squatty; somewhat thickset; somewhat stockish
krępel [kran-pel] m. slang: short, stocky man; penis; tail bone; spine (mob jargon)
krępo [kran-po] adv. in a thickset fashion
krępo zbudowany [kran-po zboo-do-vah-ni] exp.: thickset; stocky; squat; stumpy; square-built
krępować [kran-po-vahćh] v. bind; tie up (somebody); pinion; cramp; trammel; shackle; fetter; cumber; embarrass; hamper; hinder; impede; peg down; cause discomfort; inconvenience; incommode (*repeatedly*)
krępować się [kran-po-vahćh śhan] v. be embarrassed; feel embarrassed; feel constrained; be bashful; feel bashful; stand on ceremony (*repeatedly*)
nie krępować się [ńe kran-po-vahćh śhan] exp.: to be free and easy; to feel at ease; to be unembarrassed; to feel at home; to be unconstrained; to be unceremonious; not to stand on ceremony; act without hesitation
nie krępuj się [ńe kran-pooy śhan] exp.: don't hesitate; feel at ease; don't be bashful; make yourself at home
krępowanie [kran-po-vah-ńe] n. constraint
krępowanie się [kran-po-vah-ńe śhan] n. embarrassment
krępująco [kran-poo-yown-tso] adv. embarrassingly; awkwardly
krępujący [kran-poo-yown-tsi] adj.m. embarrassing; awkward; uneasy; inconvenient
krępulec [kran-poo-lets] m. tourniquet; tongue (of a frame saw)
krępy [kran-pi] adj.m. stocky; thickset; sturdy; short; squat

kręt [kr<u>an</u>t] m. angular moment; angular momentum; colloq: double-dealer; dodger; quibbler; cheat; crooked lawyer; shyster
krętacki [kr<u>an</u>-tah-tskee] adj.m. shifty; shuffling; slippery; colloq: wriggling; prevaricating; pettifogging (lawyer, etc.)
krętactwo [kr<u>an</u>-**tah**-tstfo] n. cheat; foul dealing; prevarication; shuffle; slipperiness; pettifogging (lawyer's behavior); crookedness
krętacz [**kr<u>an</u>**-tahch] m. double-dealer; dodger; quibbler; cheat; crooked lawyer, etc.; slang: fraud; swindler; shyster
krętaczka [kr<u>an</u>-**tahch**-kah] f. (female) double-dealer; dodger; quibbler; cheat; crooked lawyer; shyster; pettifogger
krętak [**kr<u>an</u>**-tahk] m. hand tap; whirligig (a beetle)
krętaki [kr<u>an</u>-**tah**-kee] pl. Gyrinidae family of beetles
krętanina [kr<u>an</u>-tah-**ńee**-nah] f. movement to and fro; comings and goings; confusion; tangle; colloq: cheat; foul dealing; prevarication; shuffle; slipperiness; pettifogging (lawyer's behavior); crookedness
krętarz [**kr<u>an</u>**-tahsh] m. trochanter
krętek [**kr<u>an</u>**-tek] m. spirochaete
krętek blady [**kr<u>an</u>**-tek **blah**-di] exp.: pathogen of syphilis
krętki [**kr<u>an</u>t**-kee] pl. the Spirochaeta genus of bacteria
krętkowy [kr<u>an</u>t-**ko**-vi] adj.m. spirochaetal; spirocheatic
krętlik [**kr<u>an</u>t**-leek] m. chain swivel
krętło [**kr<u>an</u>t**-wo] n. brace (of a drill, etc.)
krętnica [kr<u>an</u>t-**ńee**-tsah] f. ileum (of the small intestine)
kręto [**kr<u>an</u>**-to] adv. tortuously; in a winding manner; spirally; deviously; by devious ways
krętogłów [kr<u>an</u>t-**to**-gwoof] m. wryneck (woodpecker, torticollis)
krętość [**kr<u>an</u>**-tośhćh] f. sinuosity; tortuosity; deviousness; intricacy
krętość włosów [**kr<u>an</u>**-tośhćh **vwo**-soof] exp.: fuzziness of hair
krętowłosek [kr<u>an</u>-to-**vwo**-sek] m. spirochaete
krętu-wętu [**kr<u>an</u>**-too **v<u>an</u>**-too] exp.: colloq: double-dealing; dodging; quibbling; cheating
kręty [**kr<u>an</u>**-ti] adj.m. curved; curly; twisting; winding; spiral; sinuous; tortuous; flexuous; intricate; crooked; indirect; circuitous; devious
kręte schody [**kr<u>an</u>**-te **skho**-di] exp.: winding stairs; spiral stairs
kręte włosy [**kr<u>an</u>**-te **vwo**-si] exp.: fuzzy hair; frizzled hair; wooly hair; friz
krio- [**kree**-yo] prefix: cold-; low temperature
kriofit [kree-**yo**-feet] m. a cold climate plant; arctic plant
kriofity [kree-yo-**fee**-ti] pl. arctic plants
kriofizyka [kree-yo-**fee**-zi-kah] f. cryogenics; physics of low temperatures; cryogeny
kriofor [kree-**yo**-for] m. cryophorus (instrument)
kriogenicznie [kree-yo-ge-**ńeech**-ńe] adv. cryogenically
kriogeniczny [kree-yo-ge-**ńeech**-ni] adj.m. cryogenic
kriogenika [kree-yo-**ge**-ńee-kah] f. cryogenics; cryogeny
kriochirurgia [kree-yo-khee-**roor**-gyah] f. cryosurgery
kriokauter [kree-yo-**kahw**-ter] m. device for cryogenic removal of skin irregularities
kriolit [kree-**yo**-leet] m. cryolite
kriologia [kree-yo-**lo**-gyah] f. study of ice in nature; cryology
kriometr [kree-**yo**-metr] m. cryometer; frigorimeter
kriometria [kree-yo-**me**-tryah] f. cryometry (measuring the temperature of coagulation)
kriometryczny [kree-yo-me-**trich**-ni] adj.m. of a cryometer; of a frigorimeter
krioplankton [kree-yo-**plahnk**-ton] m. cryoplankton
kriosfera [kree-yo-**sfe**-rah] f. the part of hydrosphere which is in solid form
krioskop [kree-**yo**-skop] m. cryoscope

krioskopia [kree-yo-**sko**-pyah] f. cryoscopy
krioskopowy [kree-yo-sko-**po**-vi] adj.m. cryoscopic
kriostat [kree-**yo**-staht] m. cryostat
krioterapia [kree-yo-te-**rah**-pyah] f. cryotherapy
krioturbacja [kree-yo-toor-**bah**-tsyah] f. the geological effect of freezing and thawing
kris [krees] m. crease; kris
kriuki [**kryoo**-kee] pl. Byzantine church music notation
krnąbrnie [krn<u>own</u>**br**-ńe] adv. restively; fractiously; refractorily
krnąbrnieć [krn<u>own</u>br-ńećh] v. grow restive; become unruly; become restive; grow bulky; become insubordinate (*repeatedly*)
krnąbrność [krn<u>own</u>br-nośhćh] f. restiveness; refractoriness; recalcitrance; intractability
krnąbrny [krn<u>own</u>br-ni] adj.m. stubborn; unruly; restive; insubordinate; balky; fractious
kroacki [kro-**ahts**-kee] adj.m. Croatian; Croat
Kroat [**kro**-aht] m. (a) Croat
Kroatka [kro-**aht**-kah] f. (woman) Croat
kroaza [kro-**ah**-zah] f. cotton fabric used for lining
krobnik [**krob**-ńeek] m. a variety of butterfly
krochmal [**krokh**-mahl] m. (wheat, corn, potato) starch; colloq: (laundry) starch; slang: potato
krochmalarka [krokh-mah-**lahr**-kah] f. starch mangle
krochmalarz [krokh-**mah**-lahsh] m. starcher (man)
krochmalenie [krokh-mah-**le**-ńe] n. starching; stiffening
krochmalić [krokh-**mah**-leećh] v. (clear)starch; stiffen; colloq: beat up; lang: speak; lie; slight; not to give a damn (*repeatedly*)
krochmalić się [krokh-**mah**-leećh śh<u>an</u>] v. mob slang: have sex (*repeatedly*)
krochmalnia [krokh-**mahl**-ńah] f. (clear)starching shop
krochmalnictwo [krokh-mahl-**ńeets**-tfo] n. starch industry
krochmalniczy [krokh-mahl-**ńee**-chi] adj.m. of the starch industry; starch (production, etc.)
krochmalowy [krokh-mah-**lo**-vi] adj.m. starch (glue, etc.)
krocie [**kro**-ćhe] pl. thousands; huge sums; enormous quantities
krocień [**kro**-ćheń] m. croton; castor-oil plant
krocionóg [kro-**ćho**-nook] m. multiped; multipede
krociowy [kro-**ćho**-vi] adj.m. enormous; fabulously rich
krocz [kroch] m. (horse's) amble
kroczak [**kro**-chahk] m. ambling horse
krocze [**kro**-che] n. perineum; colloq: crotch; crutch
kroczek [**kro**-chek] m. small step; small carp (fish); bow compass
kroczki [**kroch**-kee] pl. small steps; small fry (of carp)
kroczenie [kro-**che**-ńe] n. pacing
kroczkowy [kroch-**ko**-vi] adj.m. fish (pond, etc.); carp (pond, etc.)
kroczny [**kroch**-ni] adj.m. of jumping (with one foot and landing on the other)
kroczowy [kro-**cho**-vi] adj.m. perineal
kroczyć [**kro**-chićh] v. stride; pace; step; tread; go at foot pace (horse); colloq: advance; progress (*repeatedly*)
-kroć [kroćh] suffix: times
dwakroć [**dvah**-kroćh] adv. twice
krocset [**kroćh**-set] (only in) exp.: **do krocset diabłów!** [do **kroćh**-set **dyahb**-woof] exp.: dammit; hang it!; to hell with it!
krogulczy [kro-**gool**-chi] adj.m. sparrow hawk's; hawk-like
krogulczy nos [kro-**gool**-chi nos] exp.: aquiline nose; hooknose
krogulec [kro-**goo**-lets] m. sparrow hawk
kroić [**kro**-eećh] v. cut; slice; carve; cut out (a garment, etc.); shape: slang: reckon; take (*repeatedly*)
kroić się [**kro**-eećh śh<u>an</u>] v. be afoot; be brewing; be in prospect; about to happen (*repeatedly*)
krojcza [**kroy**-chah] adj.f. (clothes) cutting (machine, etc.); f.

(woman) cutter (of clothes)
krojczy [**kroy**-chi] adj.m. cutting (machine, etc.); m. cutter (of clothes)
krojczyni [kroy-**chi**-ńee] f. (woman) cutter (of clothes)
krojenie [kro-**ye**-ńe] n. cutting (of clothes, garments, etc.)
krojenie się [kro-**ye**-ńe śhan] n. being cut; being afoot; being in prospect
krojownia [kro-**yov**-ńah] f. cloth cutting room
krok [krok] m. step; pace; march; move; footfall; tread; gait; measure; thread (of a screw); colloq: crotch; crutch
kroki [**kro**-kee] pl. steps (legal, etc.); (preventive, etc.) measures; moves
kroki chamskie [**kro**-kee **khahm**-ske] exp.: slang: crude manners; beating (mob jargon)
krokiet [**kro**-ket] m. croquet (game); croquette (dish)
krokietować [kro-ke-**to**-vahćh] v. croquet (*repeatedly*)
krokietowy [kro-ke-**to**-vi] adj.m. croquet (mallet, etc.)
krokiew [**kro**-kef] f. rafter
krokiewka [kro-**kef**-kah] f. small rafter; V-shaped sleeve-mark of noncommissioned officer
krokodyl [kro-**ko**-dil] m. crocodile; split flap (aviation)
krokodylek [kro-ko-**di**-lek] m. small crocodile
krokodyli [kro-ko-**di**-lee] adj.m. crocodile's; crocodilian
krokodylowy [kro-ko-di-**lo**-vi] adj.m. crocodile's; crocodilian
krokomierz [kro-**ko**-myesh] m. pedometer
krokosz [**kro**-kosh] m. safflower
krokoszowy [kro-ko-**sho**-vi] adj.m. safflower (oil, etc.)
krokowy [kro-**ko**-vi] adj.m. crotched
gruczoł krokowy [**groo**-chow kro-**ko**-vi] exp.: prostate (gland)
krokówka [kro-**koof**-kah] f. field-map sketched on the basis of pacing and a compass
kroksztyn [**krok**-shtin] m. corbel; bracket; cantilever; console
kroksztynowy [krok-shti-**no**-vi] adj.m. cantilever (beam, etc.)
krokus [**kro**-koos] m. crocus
krokwiasty [krok-**fyah**-sti] adj.m. raftered (roof)
krokwiowy [krok-**fyo**-vi] adj.m. raftered (roof)
krokydolit [kro-ki-**do**-leet] m. crocidolite (mineral)
krom [krom] prep.: apart from (hist.)
nic krom [ńeets krom] exp.: nothing but
kroma [**kro**-mah] f. hunk (of bread, etc.); big slice (of bread, etc.)
kromanioński [kro-mah-**ńyoń**-skee] adj.m. Cro-Magnon (man, race, period, etc.)
kromeczka [kro-**mech**-kah] f. (small, nice) slice
kromka [**krom**-kah] f. slice
kromlech [**krom**-lekh] m. cromlech (stone circle); Stonehenge
kron [kron] m. crown glass
kronika [**kro**-ńee-kah] f. chronicle; annals; news; report
kronikalny [kro-ńee-**kahl**-ni] adj.m. of (film) chronicle; of narrative
kronikarka [kro-ńee-**kahr**-kah] f. (female) chronicler; annalist; recorder of events
kronikarski [kro-ńee-**kahr**-skee] adj.m. chronicler's; annalist's
po kronikarsku [po kro-ńee-**kahr**-skoo] exp.: in chronicler's style
kronikarsko [kro-ńee-**kahr**-sko] adv. in chronicler's style
kronikarstwo [kro-ńee-**kahr**-stfo] n. chronicler's work; recording of events
kronikarz [kro-**ńee**-kahsh] m. chronicler; annalist; recorder of events
kronselka [kron-**sel**-kah] f. colloq: (French) variety of apple
kronselski [kron-**sel**-skee] adj.m. of a French apple tree; of a French apple
kropa [**kro**-pah] f. large drop; large dot
kropeczka [kro-**pech**-kah] f. dot; spot
kropelka [kro-**pel**-kah] f. droplet; blob
ani kropelki [ah-ńee kro-**pel**-kee]

exp.: not a drop
dodać kropelkę [do-dahćh kro-pel-kan] exp.: to add a drop
po kropelce [po kro-pel-tse] exp.: drop by drop
wypić kropelkę [vi-peećh kro-pel-kan] exp.: to have a drop (of vodka, etc.)
kropelkowy [kro-pel-ko-vi] adj.m. droplet (dispersion, etc.)
kropiasty [krop-yah-sti] adj.m. dotted; spotted
kropić [kro-peećh] v. sprinkle; splash; water (plants); drizzle; colloq: gulp down; drink; dash off; dispatch; expedite; rattle away; beat; strike; lash; shoot; slang: swig (drink alcohol) (mob jargon) (*repeatedly*)
kropić się [kro-peećh śhan] v. sprinkle oneself; colloq: hit each other (*repeatedly*)
kropidełko [kro-pee-dew-ko] n. small sprinkler
kropidlak [kro-peed-lahk] m. aspergillus (a fungus)
kropidlakowy [kro-peed-lah-ko-vi] adj.m. aspergillus (disease, etc.); of aspergillus
kropidło [kro-peed-wo] n. sprinkler; aspergillus; water dropwort; slang: billy club; gas sprayer
kropielnica [kro-pyel-ńee-tsah] f. holy-water basin; slang: mother-in-law (mob jargon)
kropielniczka [kro-pyel-ńeech-kah] f. small holy-water basin
kropienie [krop-ye-ńe] n. sprinkling; covering with dots
kropienie się [kro-pye-ńe śhan] n. sprinkling oneself; colloq: exchanging blows
kropierz [krop-yesh] m. horsecloth; housing
kropka [krop-kah] f. dot; point; speck; punctum; period; full stop; multiplication sign
... i kropka [ee krop-kah] exp.: that's all; that's plain
w kropki [f krop-kee] exp.: dotted; spotted
znaleźć się w kropce [znah-leśhćh śhan f krop-tse] exp.: to be in a fix; to be at one's wit's end; to do the proper thing; to rise to the occasion
kropkować [krop-ko-vahćh] v. dot; speckle; spot; slang: tattoo (mob jargon) (*repeatedly*)
kropkowanie [krop-ko-vah-ńe] n. dots
kropkowany [krop-ko-vah-ni] adj.m. dotted; speckled; guttate; spotted; mottled; powdered
kropla [krop-lah] f. drop; raindrop; teardrop; slang: fingerprint; woman; girl; link in an electric circuit (mob jargon)
krople [krop-le] pl. drops; (vodka) flavoring extract; flavor; guttae
lać po kropli [lahćh po krop-lee] exp.: drip; trickle; dribble; pour drop by drop; pour by drops; pour a drop at a time
kroplan [krop-lahn] m. Aleurites tree (with milky juice)
kroplik [krop-leek] m. Mimulus (herb); monkey flower
kroplisty [krop-lees-ti] adj.m. in heavy drops; in form of drops
kroplomierz [krop-lo-myesh] m. dropping-tube; dropper; stactometer
kroplowy [krop-lo-vi] adj.m. of a drop; of drops; in drops
kroplówka [krop-loof-kah] f. drip (continuous)
kroplówka dożylna [krop-loof-kah do-zhil-nah] exp.: intravenous drip
kropnąć [krop-nownćh] v. colloq: take a swig; slug; hit; come down (pouring); shoot
kropnąć sobie w łeb [krop-nownćh so-bye v wep] exp.: to blow out one's brains
kropnąć się [krop-nownćh śhan] v. colloq: come a cropper; fall flat; run over (to); dash off
kropnąć się spać [krop-nownćh śhan spahćh] exp.: to tumble into bed
kropnąć się za mąż [krop-nownćh śhan zah mownsh] exp.: to get married in a hurry
kropnięcie [krop-ńan-ćhe] n. dashing off; colloq: hitting
kropnięcie się [krop-ńan-ćhe śhan] n. falling flat (on one's face)

kros [kros] m. cross-country race; cross (passing of tennis ball from one corner to the other); slang: cross; cemetery (mob jargon)
krosienko [kro-**śhen**-ko] n. hand loom; small loom
krosno [**kros**-no] n. loom; tambour; embroidery-frame; tabouret; window frame
krosowiec [kro-**so**-vyets] m. contestant in cross-country competition
krosownica [kro-sov-**ńee**-tsah] f. computer mother board
krosowy [kro-**so**-vi] adj.m. cross-country (competition, motorcycle, etc.)
krosta [**kros**-tah] f. pimple; acne
krosteczka [kros-**tech**-kah] f. small pimple
krostka [**krost**-kah] f. pimple; pustule; acne
krostowaty [kros-to-**vah**-ti] adj.m. covered with pimples; acned
krośniak [**krośh**-ńahk] m. cotton fabric
krośniarka [krośh-**ńahr**-kah] f. (woman) loom-weaver
krośniarz [**krośh**-ńahsh] m. loom-weaver
krotnica [krot-**ńee**-tsah] f. device for simultaneous multiple use of a telecommunication channel
krotnik [**krot**-ńeek] m. photoelectric cell for strengthening of current by secondary emission of electrons
krotność [**krot**-nośhćh] f. product
krotny [**krot**-ni] adj.m. multiple (unit of measurement, etc.)
krotochwila [kro-to-**khfee**-lah] f. joke; burlesque; farce
krotochwilny [kro-to-**khfeel**-ni] adj.m. jocular; burlesque; farcical; facetious
krotolaria [kro-to-**lah**-ryah] f. Crotolaria (Indian) plant; Crotolaria fiber
kroton [**kro**-ton] m. croton
krotonowy [kro-to-**no**-vi] adj.m. croton (oil, etc.)
krowa [**kro**-vah] f. cow; colloq: mine thrower; mine; vulg. slang: lumbering clumpy woman
krowi [**kro**-vee] adj.m. cow's
ospa krowia [**os**-pah **kro**-vyah] exp.: cowpox
krowiak [**kro**-vyahk] m. paxillus (agaric)
krowiakowaty [kro-vyah-ko-**vah**-ti] adj.m. of the paxillus family
krowiakowate [kro-vyah-ko-**vah**-te] pl. the Paxiliaceae family of mushrooms
krowianka [kro-**vyahn**-kah] f. cowpox; (cowpox) vaccine
krowiankowaty [kro-vyahn-ko-**vah**-ti] adj.m. characteristic of cowpox
krowiankowy [kro-vyahn-**ko**-vi] adj.m. vaccine (pock, etc.)
krowiarka [kro-**vyahr**-kah] f. dairymaid; cowgirl
krowiarz [**kro**-vyahsh] m. dairy; cowherd; cowboy
krowiasty [kro-**vyahs**-ti] adj.m. cow-like (gait, shape, eyes, etc.)
krowieniec [kro-**vye**-ńets] m. cow manure; cow dung
krowienta [kro-**vyen**-tah] m. & f. clumsy little actress (or actor)
krowieńczak [kro-**vyeń**-chahk] m. dung beetle (Copris lunaris)
krowina [kro-**vee**-nah] f. (pitiful, wretched) cow
krowiziół [kro-**vee**-źhoow] m. cowherb (Vaccaria); cow-fat
króbka [**kroop**-kah] f. set of letters of the same size
krócej [**kroo**-tsey] adv. shorter (time, etc.); a shorter time; in a shorter time; more tersly; more concisely; at a shorter distance
o połowę krócej [o po-**wo**-van **kroo**-tsey] exp.: shorter by half; half as long; in half the time
króciak [**kroo**-ćhahk] m. board three to eight feet long; short steel rod
krócica [kroo-**ćhee**-tsah] f. pistol (used in the 18th, and 19th cent.)
króciec [**kroo**-ćhets] m. stub pipe; connector pipe
króciuchno [kroo-**ćhookh**-no] adv. (cut, etc.) short; a very short time; just a minute; very briefly
króciuchny [kroo-**ćhookh**-ni] adj.m. very short
króciusieńki [kroo-ćhoo-**śheń**-kee]

adj.m. very short
króciusieńko [kroo-ćhoo-śheń-ko] adv. (cut, etc.) short; a very short time; just
króciuteńki [kroo-ćhoo-teń-kee] adj.m. very short
króciuteńko [kroo-ćhoo-teń-ko] adv. (cut, etc.) short; a very short time; just
króciutki [kroo-ćhoot-kee] adj.m. very short
króciutko [kroo-ćhoot-ko] adv. (cut, etc.) short; a very short time; just a minute; very briefly
krój [krooy] m. cut; fashion; style;, cutting technique; typeface; font; coulter (of a plow)
król [krool] m. king; sovereign monarch; rabbit; mob slang: gang leader; chief public prosecutor
król malowany [krool mah-lo-vah-ni] exp.: puppet king; figurehead
królestwo [kroo-le-stfo] n. kingdom; the realms; realm; sphere
królewiak [kroo-le-vyahk] m. inhabitant of Congress Poland
królewiątko [kroo-le-vyownt-ko] n. nice little royal child; borderland lord (in eastern Poland 16th-18th cent.); colloq: petty king; kingling
królewicz [kroo-le-veech] m. crown prince; king's son; Royal Prince
królewiczowski [kroo-le-vee-chof-skee] adj.m. crown prince's
królewięta [kroo-le-vyan-tah] pl. borderland lords (in eastern Poland 16th-18th cent.)
królewna [kroo-lev-nah] f. king's daughter; princess; colloq: sluggish, listless, girl
śpiąca królewna [śhpyown-tsah kroo-lev-nah] exp.: sleeping beauty
królewski [kroo-lef-skee] adj.m. royal; kingly; majestic; king's; queen's; princely; sumptuous
po królewsku [po kroo-lef-skoo] exp.: royally; in a princely manner; in princely fashion
królewsko [kroo-lef-sko] adv. royally; in a princely manner; in princely fashion
królewskość [kroo-lef-skośhćh] f. regal stateliness; majesty; splendor; grandeur
królewszczyzna [kroo-lef-shchiz-nah] f. crown lands; Royal demesne
królica [kroo-lee-tsah] f. doe (of a tame rabbit)
króliczarnia [kroo-lee-chahr-ńah] f. rabbit warren
króliczek [kroo-lee-chek] m. (small, young) rabbit
króliczy [kroo-lee-chi] adj.m. rabbit's (fur, etc.)
królik [kroo-leek] m. rabbit; kingling; kinglet; lordling
królik doświadczalny [kroo-leek do-śhfyaht-chahl-ni] exp.: guinea pig
królikarnia [kroo-lee-kahr-ńah] f. warren; rabbit warren
królobójca [kroo-lo-booy-tsah] m. regicide
królobójczy [kroo-lo-booy-chi] adj.m. regicidal
królobójstwo [kroo-lo-booy-stfo] n. regicide
królowa [kroo-lo-vah] f. queen; belle (of the ball); (chess) queen; queen ant; queen wasp; queen bee
królować [kroo-lo-vahćh] v. reign; rule; dominate; rise (above a region, etc.); overlook (a region); prevail; reign supreme (*repeatedly*)
królowanie [kroo-lo-vah-ńe] n. reign; rule; kinghood; queenhood
królówka [kroo-loof-kah] f. (chess) queen; (card) queen
krótkawy [kroot-kah-vi] adj.m. shortish; somewhat short; just a little too short
krótki [kroot-kee] adj.m. short; brief; terse; concise; curt; of short duration; short-lived; short-term (credit, etc.)
krótka broń [kroot-kah broń] exp.: small arm; revolver; pistol
krótki a gruby [kroot-kee ah groo-bi] exp.: thickset; squat; dumpy; squabby; stubby; squab
krótki oddech [kroot-kee od-dekh] exp.: short wind; shortness of breath
krótkie spięcie [kroot-ke spyan-ćhe] exp.: short circuit

w krótkim czasie [f **kroot**-keem **chah**-śhe] exp.: soon; before long; presently; in a short time; shortly (after)
krótko [**kroot**-ko] adv. short; a short time; briefly; shortly; tersely; (hold) tightly; a short distance
krótko- [kroot-ko] prefix: short-
krótkobieżny [kroot-ko-**byeżh**-ni] adj.m. shuttle (train)
krótkodystansowiec [kroot-ko-dis-tahn-**so**-vyets] m. short-distance runner
krótkodystansowy [kroot-ko-dis-tahn-**so**-vi] adj.m. short-distance (run, etc.)
krótkofalarski [kroot-ko-fah-**lahr**-skee] adj.m. of a shortwave operator(s); of a shortwave transmitter
krótkofalarstwo [kroot-ko-fah-**lahr**-stfo] n. (amateur) operation of shortwave transmitter
krótkofalowiec [kroot-ko-fah-**lo**-vyets] m. amateur-operator of short wave transmitter
krótkofalowy [kroot-ko-fah-**lo**-vi] adj.m. shortwave (transmitter, etc.)
krótkofalówka [kroot-ko-fah-**loof**-kah] f. short wave transmitter; diathermy; slang: telltale (in school)
krótkogłowiec [kroot-ko-**gwo**-vyets] m. brachycephal
krótkogłowość [kroot-ko-**gwo**-vośhćh] f. brachycephalism
krótkogłowy [kroot-ko-**gwo**-vi] adj.m. brachycephalic
krótkometrażowiec [kroot-ko-me-trah-**zho**-vyets] m. short-feature-film specialist
krótkometrażowy [kroot-ko-met-rah-**zho**-vi] adj.m. of up to 600 meters (documentary, etc.) film
krótkometrażowy film [kroot-ko-met-rah-**zho**-vi feelm] exp.: (a) short; short-feature film
krótkometrażówka [kroot-ko-met-rah-**zhoof**-kah] f. (a) short; short-feature film
krótkometrażysta [kroot-ko-met-rah-**zhis**-tah] m. short-feature-film specialist
krótkonogi [kroot-ko-**no**-gee] adj.m. short-legged
krótkonóżka [kroot-ko-**noosh**-kah] f. short-legged hen
krótkoogniskowy [kroot-ko-og-ńees-**ko**-vi] adj.m. short-focus (lens)
krótkoogonkowy [kroot-ko-o-gon-**ko**-vi] adj.m. short-petioled (leaf)
krótkookresowy [kroot-ko-o-kre-**so**-vi] adj.m. short-term (plan, etc.)
krótkopęd [kroot-**ko**-pant] m. dwarf shoot; short stem
krótkopłomienny [kroot-ko-pwo-**myen**-ni] adj.m. short-flame (coal)
krótkorogi [kroot-ko-**ro**-gee] adj.m. shorthorn (cattle)
krótkorunny [kroot-ko-**roon**-ni] adj.m. short-wooled (sheep)
krótkoseryjność [kroot-ko-se-**riy**-nośhćh] f. short-series production
krótkoseryjny [kroot-ko-se-**riy**-ni] adj.m. short-series (production)
krótkosłupkowy [kroot-ko-swoop-**ko**-vi] adj.m. short-pistilled
krótkoszpon [kroot-**ko**-shpon] m. short-claw hawk
krótkość [**kroot**-kośhćh] f. shortness; short duration; conciseness; brevity; terseness
w krótkości [f kroot-**kośh**-ćhee] exp.: in short; in brief; in a few words; briefly
krótkoterminowy [kroot-ko-ter-mee-**no**-vi] adj.m. short; short-term (notice, etc.); short-notice (lease, etc.); short-dated (loan, etc.)
krótkotrwałość [kroot-ko-**trfah**-wośhćh] f. short duration; briefness; transitoriness; evanescence
krótkotrwały [kroot-ko-**trfah**-wi] adj.m. of short duration; transitory; evanescent; ephemeral; short-lived
krótkowąs [kroot-**ko**-vowns] m. a variety of butterfly
krótkowąsy [kroot-ko-**vown**-si] adj.m. having a short mustache
kiełb krótkowąsy [kewp kroot-ko-**vown**-si] exp.: gudgeon
krótkowełniasty [kroot-ko-vew-**ńahs**-ti] adj.m. short-wooled (sheep, etc.)

krótkowełnisty [kroot-ko-vew-**ńees**-ti] adj.m. short-wooled (sheep, etc.)
krótkowidz [kroot-**ko**-veets] m. short-sighted person
krótkowidztwo [kroot-ko-**veets**-tfo] n. short-sightedness
krótkowieczność [kroot-ko-**vyech**-nośhćh] f. short life expectancy
krótkowieczny [kroot-ko-**vyech**-ni] adj.m. short-lived (hope, etc.)
krótkowłosy [kroot-ko-**vwo**-si] adj.m. short-haired
krótkowzrocznie [kroot-ko-**vzroch**-ńe] adv. short-sightedly; without foresight
krótkowzroczność [kroot-ko-**vzroch**-nośhćh] f. short-sightedly; without foresight
krótkowzroczny [kroot-ko-**vzroch**-ni] adj.m. short-sighted; not foreseeing
krótszy [**kroot**-shi] adj.m. shorter
o połowę krótszy [o po-**wo**-van **kroot**-shi] exp.: half as long (as)
o wiele krótszy [o **vye**-le **kroot**-shi] exp.: much shorter; shorter by far
pójść krótszą drogą [pooyśhćh **kroot**-shown **dro**-gown] exp.: to take a shortcut
stawać się krótszym [**stah**-vahćh śhan **kroot**-shim] exp.: to shorten; to grow shorter; to become shorter
krówka [**kroof**-kah] f. (nice, litte) cow; coprophagous beetle
boża krówka [**bo**-zhah **kroof**-kah] exp.: lady-cow; lady-bird; ladybug
krówki [**kroof**-kee] pl. fondants; sweetmeats
krówsko [**kroof**-sko] n. (big, clumsy, run-down) cow
krtaniowy [krtah-**ńo**-vi] adj.m. laryngeal
krtań [krtahń] f. larynx
rozdęcie krtani [roz-**dan**-ćhe **krtah**-ńee] exp.: laryngotomy
zapalenie krtani [zah-pah-**le**-ńe **krtah**-ńee] exp.: laryngitis
kruchciany [krookh-**ćhah**-ni] adj.m. of a vestibule; of a porch
krucho [**kroo**-kho] adv. badly
być krucho z czasem [**bićh kroo**-kho s **chah**-sem] exp.: to be hard pressed for time
krucho ze mną [**kroo**-kho ze mnown] exp.: I am in trouble; I am in a bad way; I am in an evil plight (Brit.)
kruchość [**kroo**-khośhćh] f. fragility; brittleness; friability; crispness; crustiness; frail constitution; colloq: frailty; uncertainty; flimsiness; precariousness
kruchta [**krookh**-tah] f. (church) porch; vestibule
kruchtowy [krookh-**to**-vi] adj.m. of a (church) porch; of a vestibule
kruchusieńki [kroo-khoo-**śheń**-kee] adj.m. (nicely) brittle; frail; tender; crisp; crusty; fragile
kruchuteńki [kroo-khoo-**teń**-kee] adj.m. (nicely) brittle; frail; tender; crisp; crusty; fragile
kruchutki [kroo-**khoot**-kee] adj.m. (very nicely) brittle; frail; tender; crisp; crusty; fragile
kruchy [**kroo**-khi] adj.m. brittle; frail; tender; crisp; crusty; fragile; colloq: weak; frail; uncertain; flimsy; precarious
krucjata [kroots-**yah**-tah] f. crusade; action for some cause
krucjatowy [kroots-yah-**to**-vi] adj.m. crusade (movement, march, etc.)
krucyfiks [kroo-**tsi**-feeks] m. crucifix; cross of Jesus
kruczeć [**kroo**-chećh] v. rumble; call (by flying cranes) (*repeatedly*)
kruczek [**kroo**-chek] m. trick
kruczenie [kroo-**che**-ńe] n. rumbling; calling (by flying cranes)
kruczę [**kroo**-chan] n. young raven
kruczoczarny [kroo-cho-**chahr**-ni] adj.m. raven-black
kruczość [**kroo**-chośhćh] f. blackness (of hair, etc.)
kruczowłosy [kroo-cho-**vwo**-si] adj.m. raven-haired
kruczy [**kroo**-chi] adj.m. jet-black; raven's color; raven (hair, etc.); raven-black; coracoid
kruk [krook] m. raven; slang: priest; judge; guard; physician (treating drug addicts) (mob jargon)
biały kruk [**byah**-wi krook] exp.:

white crow; a rarity
krukać [kroo-kahćh] v. call (by flying cranes) (*repeatedly*)
krukanie [kroo-kah-ńe] n. calling (by flying cranes)
krukowaty [kroo-ko-vah-ti] adj.m. corvine; of the family Corvidae; resembling a crow
krukowate [kroo-ko-vah-te] pl. the family Corvidae of the crows
krukówka [kroo-koof-kah] f. a species of sheep
krup [kroop] m. croup (child disease)
krupa [kroo-pah] f. groat; groats; grits; cereals; granular snow
krupy [kroo-pi] pl. groats
krupy jęczmienne [kroo-pi yanch-myen-ne] exp.: peeled barley
krupy perłowe [kroo-pi per-wo-ve] exp.: pearl barley
krupada [kroo-pah-dah] f. croupade; horse's jump with hind legs well under the belly
krupczatka [kroo-pchah-tkah] f. pure wheaten flour
krupiarnia [kroo-pyah-rńah] f. huller
krupiasty [kroo-pyah-sti] adj.m. gritty
krupić się [kroo-peećh śhan] v. clot; lump (*repeatedly*)
to się krupi na nim [to śhan kroo-pee nah ńeem] exp.: he is the scapegoat; he stands the racket; he bears the consequences
krupiec [kroop-yets] m. crystallized honey
krupienie [kroo-pye-ńe] n. clotting; lumping
krupienie się [kroo-pye-ńe śhan] n. undergoing clotting
krupier [kroo-pyer] m. croupier
krupierski [kroo-pyer-skee] adj.m. croupier's
krupierstwo [kroo-pyer-stfo] n. croupier's occupation
krupka [kroop-kah] f. a grain (of groat, groats, cereals, barley, grits, buckwheat, granular snow)
krupniak [kroop-ńahk] m. sausage of pork, liver, and peeled barley
krupniczek [kroop-ńee-chek] m. (nice) barley soup; spiced hot mead
krupnik [kroop-ńeek] m. barley soup; spiced hot mead
krupniok [kroop-ńok] m. sausage of pork, liver, and peeled barley
krupon [kroo-pon] m. butt; sole-leather
kruponiarka [kroo-po-ńahr-kah] f. machine for removal of hides in slaughterhouses
kruponować [kroo-po-no-vahćh] v. divide (cow, etc.) hides into butt, sides, and neck (*repeatedly*)
kruponowanie [kroo-po-no-vah-ńe] n. dividing of hides into butt, sides, and neck
krupowy [kroo-po-vi] adj.m. croupous; croupy; gritty
kruszarka [kroo-shahr-kah] f. crushing machine; grinding mill; splitter; stamping mill
kruszarnia [kroo-shahr-ńah] f. crushing machine in a coal mine
kruszący [kroo-shown-tsi] adj.m. disrupting (bomb, etc.)
kruszconośny [kroosh-tso-nośh-ni] adj.m. ore-bearing; metalliferous
żyła kruszconośna [zhi-wah kroosh-tso-nośh-nah] exp.: reef
kruszcorodny [kroosh-tso-rod-ni] adj.m. ore-bearing; metalliferous
żyła kruszcorodna [zhi-wah kroosh-tso-rod-nah] exp.: reef
kruszcowy [kroosh-tso-vi] adj.m. metallic
żyła kruszcowa [zhi-wah kroosh-tso-vah] exp.: reef; lode
kruszczyca [kroosh-chi-tsah] f. flower beetle; Cetonia
kruszczyk [kroosh-chik] m. helleborine (orchid)
kruszec [kroo-shets] m. (metal) ore; metal; gold; silver
kruszeć [kroo-shećh] v. crumble; grow brittle; repent (*repeatedly*)
kruszenie [kroo-she-ńe] n. crumbling
kruszenie się [kroo-she-ńe śhan] n. undergoing crumbling
kruszeń [kroo-sheń] m. aggregate
kruszka [kroosh-kah] f. crumbs
krusznica [kroosh-ńee-tsah] f. lichens; Lecanora
kruszność [kroosh-nośhćh] f. crumbliness
kruszon [kroo-shon] m. mulled and

spiced wine; bishop
kruszonka [kroo-**shon**-kah] f. crumble
kruszyć [**kroo**-shićh] v. crush; crumb; destroy; shatter; disrupt; break into pieces; crumble (*repeatedly*)
kruszyć kopie [**kroo**-shićh **kop**-ye] exp.: to tilt; to take up the cudgels (for); to fight (for); to carry on a stubborn fight (for)
kruszyć się [**kroo**-shićh śhan] v. repent; show repentance; become brittle; grow friable; crumble (*repeatedly*)
kruszyna [kroo-**shi**-nah] f. crumb; fragment; alder buckthorn; colloq: sweet little baby; dot; mite
kruszynek [kroo-**shi**-nek] m. a variety of insects useful in insect control
kruszynka [kroo-**shin**-kah] f. crumb; fragment; alder buckthorn; colloq: sweet little baby; dot; mite
kruszynkowaty [kroo-shin-ko-**vah**-ti] adj.m. of the Trichogrammatidae family of insects
kruszynkowate [kroo-shin-ko-**vah**-te] pl. variety of insects useful in insect control
kruszynowa kora [kroo-shi-**no**-vah **ko**-rah] exp.: frangula
kruszywo [kroo-**shi**-vo] n. aggregate
kruż [kroosh] m. prehistoric jar
kruża [**kroo**-zhah] f. prehistoric jar
krużganek [kroozh-**gah**-nek] m. portico; gallery; ambulatory
krużgankowy [kroozh-gahn-**ko**-vi] adj.m. cloistered
krwawiączka [krfah-**vyownch**-kah] f. hemophilia; haemophilia
krwawica [krfah-**vee**-tsah] f. hard won money; toil; labor
krwawicowy [krfah-vee-**tso**-vi] adj.m. of hard won money; of a toil; of a labor
guzy krwawicowe [**goo**-zi krfah-vee-**tso**-ve] exp.: hemorrhoids; bleeding piles
krwawić [**krfah**-veećh] v. bleed; strike till the blood is drawn; inflict bleeding wounds (on); colloq: draw blood; redden; color red (*repeatedly*)
krwawić się [**krfah**-veećh śhan] v. bleed; redden (*repeatedly*)
krwawiec [**krfah**-vyets] m. hemophiliac; hemophilic
krwawienie [krfah-**vye**-ńe] n. bleeding
krwawieniec [krfah-**vye**-ńets] m. hemophiliac; hemophilic
krwawień [**krfah**-vyeń] m. hematite; haematite
krwawnica [krfah-**vńee**-tsah] f. loosestrife; Solicaria (plant)
krwawnice [krfah-**vńee**-tse] pl. hemorrhoids; bleeding piles
krwawnicowaty [krfah-vńee-tso-**vah**-ti] adj.m. lythraceous (plant)
krwawnicowate [krfah-vńee-tso-**vah**-te] pl. the Lythraceae family of plants
krwawniczy [krfah-**vńee**-chi] adj.m. hemorrhoidal
krwawnik [**krfah**-vńeek] m. yarrow (herb); water milfoil; carnelian; cornelian (mineral)
krwawnikowy [krfah-vńee-**ko**-vi] adj.m. carnelian (signet, etc.)
krwawo [**krfah**-vo] adv. bloodily; with blood; in blood; painfully; in a deadly manner; in blood-red hues; in crimson hues
krwawoczerwony [krfah-vo-cher-**vo**-ni] adj.m. blood-red
krwawopurpurowy [krfah-vo-poor-poo-**ro**-vi] adj.m. crimson
krwawosiny [krfah-vo-**śhee**-ni] adj.m. livid
krwawy [**krfah**-vi] adj.m. bloody; bloodthirsty; bloodstained; containing blood; sanguineous; suffused with blood; bleeding; sanguinolent; covered with blood; deadly; blood-red; crimson
krwawa biegunka [**krfah**-vah bye-**goon**-kah] exp.: dysentery
krwawa kiszka [**krfah**-vah **keesh**-kah] exp.: blood sausage; pudding
krwawa plama [**krfah**-vah **plah**-mah] exp.: bloodstain
krwawe łzy [**krfah**-ve wzi] exp.: bitter tears; tears of blood
krwawe odchody [**krfah**-ve ot-**kho**-di] exp.: bloody evacuations; blood in stool
krwawy pot [**krfah**-vi pot] exp.:

bloody sweat
krwiak [krfyahk] m. hematoma
krwinka [**krfeen**-kah] f. blood corpuscle
krwinki [**krfeen**-kee] pl. blood corpuscles
krwinkowiec [krfeen-**ko**-vyets] m. parasite living in red blood corpuscles
krwinkowce [krfeen-**kof**-tse] pl. parasites living in red blood corpuscles
krwiobieg [**krfyo**-byek] m. blood circulation; circulation
krwiodawca [krfyo-**dahf**-tsah] m. blood donor; slang: bribe giver; briber (mob jargon)
krwiodawczyni [krfyo-dahf-**chi**-ńee] f. (female) blood donor
krwiodawstwo [krfyo-**dahf**-stfo] n. blood donations (to blood bank, blood collection station, Red Cross, etc.)
krwiolecznictwo [krfyo-lech-**ńeets**-tfo] n. hemotherapy
krwiomocz [**krfyo**-moch] m. hematuria; red water (of an animal)
krwionośny [krfyo-**nośh**-ni] adj.m. blood (vessel, etc.)
układ krwionośny [**ook**-waht krfyo-**nośh**-ni] exp.: blood-vascular system
krwiopędny [krfyo-**pand**-ni] adj.m. hematopoietic
krwiopijca [krfyo-**peey**-tsah] m. bloodsucker
krwioplucie [krfyo-**ploo**-ćhe] n. hemoptysis; spitting with blood
krwiopochodny [krfyo-po-**khod**-ni] adj.m. blood-born
krwiotoczny [krfyo-**toch**-ni] adj.m. hemorrhagic
krwiotwórczo [krfyo-**tfoor**-cho] adv. in hemogenous manner
krwiotwórczy [krfyo-**tfoor**-chi] adj.m. hemogenous; hemogenic; hematopoietic
krwiozastępczy [krfyo-zahs-**tanp**-chi] adj.m. blood-replacement (serum, etc.)
krwiożerca [krfyo-**zher**-tsah] m. blood-thirster
krwiożerczo [krfyo-**zher**-cho] adv. bloodthirstily
krwiożerczość [krfyo-**zher**-chośhćh] f. bloodthirstiness
krwiożerczy [krfyo-**zher**-chi] adj.m. bloodthirsty; murderous; thirsting for blood; gory (killing, etc.)
krwistek [**krfees**-tek] m. hematoma
krwisto [**krfees**-to] adv. like blood
krwistoczerwony [krfees-to-cher-**vo**-ni] adj.m. blood-red; sanguineous
krwistordzawy [krfees-to-**rdzah**-vi] adj.m. red-rust; blood-rust (color)
krwistość [**krfees**-tośhćh] f. ruddiness
krwisty [**krfees**-ti] adj.m. of blood; sanguineous; blood-red; ruddy; full-blooded
krwiściąg [**krfeeśh**-ćhownk] m. burnet (herb)
krwotoczny [krfo-**toch**-ni] adj.m. hemorrhagic; of heavy bleeding
skaza krwotoczna [**skah**-zah krfo-**toch**-nah] exp.: hemorrhagic diathesis
krwotok [**krfo**-tok] m. hemorrhage; heavy bleeding
krycie [**kri**-ćhe] n. roofing; roof-covering; upholstery; cover
krycie słomiane [**kri**-ćhe swo-**myah**-ne] exp.: thatch
krycie się [**kri**-ćhe śhan] n. hiding; concealment
kryć [kryćh] v. hide; conceal; cover; roof over; shield; mask; guard; protect; keep secret; avoid (somebody); keep hidden; disguise; cloak; veil; screen from sight; inseminate (horses, dogs, etc.) (*repeatedly*)
kryć się [krićh śhan] v. hide (oneself); seek concealment; keep in concealment; lie in hiding; retire; retreat; take cover; keep to oneself; stay covered; nestle; underlie; be behind (words, actions, etc.); cover oneself (with) (*repeatedly*)
kryg [krik] m. affectation
krygi [**kri**-gee] pl. affectations; affected airs; airs and graces; prunes and prisms
krygować się [kri-**go**-vahćh śhan] v. give oneself airs and graces; mince; simper (*repeatedly*)

krygowanie się [kri-go-**vah**-ńe śhan] n. airs and graces; affectations
kryjomy [kri-**yo**-mi] adj.m. secret
po kryjomu [po kri-**yo**-moo] exp.: in secret; on the sly; on the quiet; unbeknown to anyone
kryjówka [kri-**yoof**-kah] f. hiding place; cache; place of concealment; colloq: hideout
krykiet [**kri**-ket] m. cricket (game)
krykietowy [kri-ke-**to**-vi] adj.m. cricket (ball, bat, etc.)
krykucha [kri-**koo**-khah] f. decoy duck
kryl [kril] m. krill; planktonic crustacean larvae
krymek [**kri**-mek] m. a breed of pigeons
kryminalista [kri-mee-nah-**lees**-tah] m. criminal; felon; colloq: criminologist
kryminalistka [kri-mee-nah-**leest**-kah] f. (female) criminal; felon; colloq: criminologist
kryminalistyczny [kri-mee-nah-lees-**tich**-ni] adj.m. criminal
kryminalistyk [kri-mee-nah-**lees**-tik] m. criminologist
kryminalistyka [kri-mee-nah-**lees**-ti-kah] f. (study of) crime detection; criminology
kryminalnie [kri-mee-**nahl**-ńe] adv. criminally; feloniously
kryminalność [kri-mee-**nahl**-nośhćh] f. criminality
kryminalny [kri-mee-**nahl**-ni] adj.m. criminal; felonious; criminous; disgraceful
kryminał [kri-**mee**-nahw] m. jail; prison; crime; felony; thriller; colloq: lockup
kryminałek [kri-mee-**nah**-wek] m. (small) jail; prison; crime; felony; thriller; colloq: lockup
kryminogenność [kri-mee-no-**gen**-nośhćh] f. criminogenesis
kryminogenny [kri-mee-no-**gen**-ni] adj.m. criminogenic
kryminolog [kri-mee-**no**-log] m. criminologist
kryminologia [kri-mee-no-**lo**-gyah] f. criminology
kryminologicznie [kri-mee-no-lo-**geech**-ńe] adv. criminologically
kryminologiczny [kri-mee-no-lo-**geech**-ni] adj.m. criminological
krymka [**krim**-kah] f. skullcap (Crimean style)
krynica [kri-**ńee**-tsah] f. spring; source; fount
krynicznik [kri-**ńeech**-ńeek] m. Nitella (lake) alga; variety of aquatic plants
kryniczny [kri-**ńeech**-ni] adj.m. spring (water, etc.)
krynoid [kri-**no**-eet] m. crinoid; member of the cup-shaped crinoidean class of enchinoderms
krynoidy [kri-no-**ee**-di] pl. the Crinoidean class of enchinoderms
krynoidowy [kri-no-ee-**do**-vi] adj.m. crinoidean
krynolina [kri-no-**lee**-nah] f. crinoline; hoop skirt
krynolinka [kri-no-**leen**-kah] f. (small, nice) crinoline; hoop skirt
krypa [**kri**-pah] f. boat; scow
krypeć [**kri**-pećh] m. moccasin of tree bark; colloq: worn-out shoe
krypta [**krip**-tah] f. crypt; vault
krypto- [**krip**-to] prefix: crypt-; crypto-; hidden; covered
kryptodepresja [krip-to-de-**pre**-syah] f. depression below sea level filled with water
kryptofit [krip-**to**-feet] m. cryptogam
kryptofity [krip-to-**fee**-ti] pl. cryptogamic plants (fern, moss, alga, fungus, etc.)
kryptogam [krip-**to**-gahm] m. cryptogam
kryptogamia [krip-to-**gah**-myah] f. cryptogamia
kryptogamiczny [krip-to-gah-**meech**-ni] adj.m. cryptogamous
kryptograf [krip-**to**-grahf] m. cryptographer
kryptografia [krip-to-**grah**-fyah] f. cryptography
kryptograficznie [krip-to-grah-**feech**-ńe] adv. cryptographically
kryptograficzny [krip-to-grah-**feech**-ni] adj.m. cryptographic
kryptogram [krip-**to**-grahm] m. cryptogram
kryptogramowy [krip-to-grah-**mo**-vi] adj.m. cryptogrammic
kryptokok [krip-**to**-kok] m.

cryptococcus
kryptokokoza [krip-to-ko-**ko**-zah] f. cryptococcosis; fungus infection
kryptol [**krip**-tol] m. kryptol; an electrically insulating powder (based on graphite, etc.)
kryptologia [krip-to-**lo**-gyah] f. cryptology; secret or enigmatic language
kryptolowy [krip-to-**lo**-vi] adj.m. of an electrically insulating powder (based on graphite, etc.)
kryptomeria [krip-to-**me**-ryah] f. Cryptomeria (Japanese cedar tree)
kryptomorficzny [krip-to-mor-**feech**-ni] adj.m. of chemicals which do not form minerals in Earth's crust
krypton [**krip**-ton] m. krypton (atomic number 36)
kryptonim [krip-**to**-ńeem] m. cryptonym; secret name
kryptonimować [krip-to-ńee-**mo**-vahćh] v. sign with a cryptonym; use cryptonyms (*repeatedly*)
kryptonimowanie [krip-to-ńee-mo-**vah**-ńe] n. signing with a cryptonym; using of cryptonyms
kryptonimowo [krip-to-ńee-**mo**-vo] adv. by means of cryptonyms
kryptonimowy [krip-to-ńee-**mo**-vi] adj.m. cryptonymous
kryptonowy [krip-to-**no**-vi] adj.m. of krypton
kryptoportyk [krip-to-**por**-tik] m. secret underground pass (exit)
krysa [**kri**-sah] f. slang: pseudonym; fictitious name (mob jargon)
kryska [**kris**-kah] f. colloq: line (on paper, etc.); defeat
przyszła kryska na niego [**pshish**-wah **kris**-kah nah **ńe**-go] exp.: he must give up
krystalicznie [kris-tah-**leech**-ńe] adv. like a crystal; limpidly
krystaliczność [kris-tah-**leech**-nośhćh] f. crystallinity; limpidity
krystaliczny [kris-tah-**leech**-ni] adj.m. crystalline; limpid
krystalit [kris-**tah**-leet] m. crystallite
krystalizacja [kris-tah-lee-**zah**-tsyah] f. crystallization
krystalizacyjny [kris-tah-lee-zah-**tsiy**-ni] adj.m. crystallization (process, etc.)
krystalizator [kris-tah-lee-**zah**-tor] m. crystallizer
krystalizować [kris-tah-lee-**zo**-vahćh] v. crystallize; shape (*repeatedly*)
krystalizować się [kris-tah-lee-**zo**-vahćh śhan] v. crystallize; take shape (*repeatedly*)
krystalizowanie [kris-tah-lee-zo-**vah**-ńe] n. crystallization; taking shape
krystalizowanie się [kris-tah-lee-zo-**vah**-ńe śhan] n. undergoing crystallization; taking shape
krystalochemia [kri-stah-lo-**khe**-myah] f. crystallochemistry
krystalochemiczny [kri-stah-lo-khe-**meech**-ni] adj.m. crystallochemical
krystalofizyka [kri-stah-lo-**fee**-zi-kah] f. physics of crystallization
krystalograf [kri-stah-**lo**-grahf] m. crystallographer
krystalografia [kri-stah-lo-**grah**-fyah] f. crystallography
krystalograficznie [kri-stah-lo-grah-**feech**-ńe] adv. crystallographically
krystalograficzny [kri-stah-lo-grah-**feech**-ni] adj.m. crystallographical; crystallographic
krystaloid [kris-tah-**lo**-eet] m. crystalloid
krystaloidowy [kris-tah-lo-ee-**do**-vi] adj.m. crystalloid; crystalloidal
krystalomancja [kris-tah-lo-**mahn**-tsyah] f. crystallomancy; divination by crystal gazing
krystalooptyka [kris-tah-lo-**op**-ti-kah] f. optics of crystals
krystiania [krist-**yah**-ńyah] f. christiania (of skis)
krystobalit [kris-to-**bah**-leet] m. mineral of Cristobal (variety of the silicon-oxide); cristobalite
krysz [krish] m. kris; crease; creese
kryształik [krish-**tah**-leek] m. (small, nice) crystal
kryształ [**krish**-tahw] m. crystal; transparent quartz; quality glass
kryształek [krish-**tah**-wek] m. (small, radio) crystal
kryształkowy [krish-tahw-**ko**-vi] adj.m. crystal (detector, set, etc.)

kryształowo [krish-tah-**wo**-vo] adv. like a crystal; crystal (clear, etc.)
kryształowo czysty [krish-tah-**wo**-vo **chis**-ti] exp.: crystal clear
kryształowość [krish-tah-**wo**-vośhćh] f. crystal-like quality (of character, etc.)
kryształowy [krish-tah-**wo**-vi] adj.m. crystal; crystalline; limpid; cut-glass (vase, etc.); upright
kryształowy człowiek [krish-tah-**wo**-vi **chwo**-vyek] exp.: man of spotless integrity
kryterium [kri-**te**-ryoom] n. criterion; touchstone; test; gauge; colloq: acid test; yardstick
krytojad [kri-**to**-yaht] m. cockchafer (eating sugar beets)
kryty [**kri**-ti] adj.m. covered
krytycyzm [kri-**ti**-tsizm] m. critical judgment; criticism; critical philosophy
krytyczka [kri-**tich**-kah] f. (female) critic; reviewer; criticaster; faultfinder
krytycznie [kri-**tich**-ńe] adv. critically
krytycznoliteracki [kri-tich-no-lee-te-**rahts**-kee] adj.m. of book reviewers; literary critic's; critico-literary
krytyczność [kri-**tich**-nośhćh] f. criticality; criticalness; critical character; critical nature
krytyczny [kri-**tich**-ni] adj.m. critical; decisive; crucial
krytyczny wiek [kri-**tich**-ni vyek] exp.: awkward age; critical period
krytyczna sytuacja [kri-**tich**-nah si-too-ah-tsyah] exp.: critical situation; emergency
krytyk [**kri**-tik] m. critic; reviewer; criticaster; faultfinder
krytyka [**kri**-ti-kah] f. criticism; review; censure; critique; critical estimate; condemnation; disprise; literary criticism; reviewing; the reviewers
krytyka historyczna [**kri**-ti-kah khees-to-**rich**-nah] exp.: historical criticism
krytyka tekstu [**kri**-ti-kah **teks**-too] exp.: textual criticism
ostra krytyka [**ost**-rah **kri**-ti-kah] exp.: slashing criticism; severe criticism; stricture
poddać coś krytyce [**pod**-dahćh tsośh **kri**-ti-tse] exp.: to submit something to a critical examination
poniżej wszelkiej krytyki [po-**ńee**-zhey **fshel**-key **kri**-ti-kee] exp.: below criticism; beneath contempt; abominable; vile
wytrzymać krytykę [vi-**tshi**-mahćh **kri**-ti-kan] exp.: to stand the test of criticism
krytykancki [kri-ti-**kahnts**-kee] adj.m. faultfinding
krytykanctwo [kri-ti-**kahnts**-tfo] n. faultfinding
krytykant [kri-**ti**-kahnt] m. faultfinding individual; hypercritical man; carper
krytykomania [kri-ti-ko-**mah**-ńyah] f. a mania for faultfinding
krytykować [kri-ti-**ko**-vahćh] v. criticize; censure; dispraise; damn; pass censure (on); find faults (with); pick holes (in); review (*repeatedly*)
krytykować kogoś za coś [kri-ti-**ko**-vahćh **ko**-gośh zah tsośh] exp.: to take somebody to task for something
ostro krytykować [**ost**-ro kri-ti-**ko**-vahćh] exp.: to criticize severely; colloq: to cut up; to pull to pieces; to flay; to scalp
krytykowanie [kri-ti-ko-**vah**-ńe] n. criticism; censure; faultfinding
kryza [**kri**-zah] f. ruff; ruche; flange; orifice; diaphragm
końcowa kryza [**koń**-tso-vah **kri**-zah] exp.: end flange
kryziasty [kri-**źhahs**-ti] adj.m. ruffed
kryziki [kri-**źhee**-kee] pl. ruffles; frills
kryzka [**kris**-kah] f. (small) ruff; ruche; flange; orifice; diaphragm
kryzować [kri-**zo**-vahćh] v. make frilling; instal orifice; instal flange (*repeatedly*)
kryzowanie [kri-zo-**vah**-ńe] n. making frilling; installing orifice; installing flange
kryzowy [kri-**zo**-vi] adj.m. ruffed; flanged

kryzys [kri-zis] m. crisis; depression; turning point; slump; recession; slang: shortage (of cigarettes in prison, etc.) (mob jargon)
przeżywać kryzys [pshe-zhi-vahćh kri-zis] exp.: to pass through a crisis; to be passing through a crisis
kryzysowy [kri-zi-so-vi] adj.m. of crisis; critical
krzaczasto [kshah-chahs-to] adv. shaggily
krzaczasty [kshah-chahs-ti] adj.m. bushy; shaggy; thick (moustache, etc.); beetle; fruticose (plant)
krzaczek [kshah-chek] m. (small) bush; brushwood
krzaczkowaty [kshahch-ko-vah-ti] adj.m. shaped like a small bush
krzaczysty [kshah-chis-ti] adj.m. bushy; shaggy; thick (moustache, etc.); beetle
krzak [kshahk] m. bush; brushwood
krzaki [kshah-kee] pl. bushes; brushwood; thicket; brake
krzakówka [kshah-koof-kah] f. mob slang: vodka; liquor; moonshine
krząkać [kshown-kahćh] v. colloq: hawk; clear one's throat; hem and haw; grunt (*repeatedly*)
krzątać się [kshown-tahćh śhan] v. bustle (about); busy oneself (with, about); strive (for, after); exert oneself (for); hurtle; stir about; bestir oneself; colloq: rustle (*repeatedly*)
krzątanie się [kshown-tah-ńe śhan] n. bustle; comings and goings; stir; colloq: rustle
krzątanina [kshown-tah-ńee-nah] f. bustle; comings and goings; stir; colloq: rustle
krzeczot [kshe-chot] m. gyrfalcon
krzem [kshem] m. silicone
dwutlenek krzemu [dvoo-tle-nek kshe-moo] exp.: silicon dioxide; silica
krzemek [kshe-mek] m. silicide
krzemki [kshem-kee] pl. silicides
krzemian [kshem-yahn] m. silicate
krzemiany [kshem-yah-ni] pl. silicates
krzemianować [kshem-yah-no-vahćh] v. silicate (*repeatedly*)
krzemianowy [kshem-yah-no-vi] adj.m. siliceous
krzemica [kshe-mee-tsah] f. silicosis
krzemienisty [kshe-mye-ńees-ti] adj.m. flinty
krzemienny [kshe-myen-ni] adj.m. flint (implement, etc.)
grot krzemienny [grot kshe-myen-ni] exp.: flint arrowhead; elf-bolt
krzemień [kshe-myeń] m. flint; silex (mineral)
krzemionka [kshe-myon-kah] f. silicon dioxide; silica
krzemionkowy [kshe-myon-ko-vi] adj.m. siliceous (fireproof products, etc.)
krzemoorganiczny [kshe-mo-or-gah-ńeech-ni] adj.m. of silicon carbide; of silanes
krzemowodór [kshe-mo-vo-door] m. silane
krzemowodory [kshe-mo-vo-do-ri] pl. silanes
krzemowy [kshe-mo-vi] adj.m. silicic (acid, etc.); siliceous; silicon (steel, etc.)
pylica krzemowa [pi-lee-tsah kshe-mo-vah] exp.: silicosis
krzemyk [kshe-mik] m. flint
krzepa [kshe-pah] f. colloq: grit; vim
chłop z krzepą [khwop s kshe-pown] exp.: colloq: guy full of pep; dude full of vim and vigor
krzepiąco [kshe-pyown-tso] adv. in an invigorating manner
krzepiący [kshe-pyown-tsi] adj.m. bracing; refreshing; invigorating; tonic
krzepić [kshe-peećh] v. brace up; refresh; invigorate; fortify; strengthen (*repeatedly*)
krzepić moralnie [kshe-peećh mo-rahl-ńe] exp.: to comfort; to strengthen
krzepić się [kshe-peećh śhan] v. fortify oneself; brace oneself up; refresh oneself; invigorate oneself; gather strength (*repeatedly*)
krzepienie [kshe-pye-ńe] n. bracing; refreshing; invigorating
krzepienie się [kshe-pye-ńe śhan] n. bracing oneself; refreshing oneself; invigorating oneself

krzepki [**kshep**-kee] adj.m. vigorous; lusty; robust; husky; sprightly; hale and hearty; bracing; refreshing; invigorating; tonic

krzepko [**kshep**-ko] adv. vigorously; with vigor

trzymać się krzepko [**tshi**-mahćh śhan **kshep**-ko] exp.: to keep hale and hearty

krzepkość [**kshep**-kośhćh] f. vigor; robustness; lustiness; colloq: vim; sprightliness

krzepliwość [kshep-lee-**vo**śhćh] f. coagulability

krzepliwy [kshep-**lee**-vi] adj.m. coagulable

krzepnąć [**kshep**-nownćh] v. clot; coagulate; gather strength; set; stiffen; find strength; freeze; congeal; solidify; acquire (new) vigor; harden; be fortified (*repeatedly*)

krzepnienie [kshep-**ńe**-ńe] n. coagulation; solidification

krzepnięcie [kshep-**ńan**-ćhe] n. coagulation; solidification

punkt krzepnięcia [poonkt kshep-**ńan**-ćhah] exp.: freezing point

krzesać [**kshe**-sahćh] v. strike fire (out of); strike sparks (*repeatedly*)

krzesak [**kshe**-sahk] m. garden knife

krzesanica [kshe-sah-**ńee**-tsah] f. cliff; precipice; crag; steep rock

krzesanie [kshe-**sah**-ńe] n. striking (fire, sparks, etc.)

krzesany [kshe-**sah**-ni] adj.m. (fire) started with sparks

krzesełko [kshe-**sew**-ko] n. small chair

krzesełkowy [kshe-sew-**ko**-vi] adj.m. chair (lift, etc.); of child's chair

krzesiwko [kshe-**śheef**-ko] n. small tinderbox; flint (and steel)

krzesiwo [kshe-**śhee**-vo] n. tinderbox; flint (and steel); slang: cigarette lighter (mob jargon)

krzeska [**kshes**-kah] f. miner's pick-hammer

krzesło [**kshes**-wo] n. chair

krzesła [**kshes**-wah] pl. chairs; (theater) stalls

krzesło na kołach [**kshes**-wo nah ko-wahkh] exp.: wheelchair

krzesło składane [**kshes**-wo skwah-**dah**-ne] exp.: camp chair; folding chair

krześlisko [ksheśh-**lees**-ko] n. fish hatching device (on water bottom)

krzew [kshef] m. shrub; bush

krzewiasty [kshe-**vyah**-sti] adj.m. shrubby; fruticose; fasciculated

krzewiciel [kshe-**vee**-ćhel] m. propagator; promulgator; promotor

krzewicielka [kshe-vee-**ćhel**-kah] f. (female) propagator; promulgator; promotor

krzewić [**kshe**-veećh] v. spread; propagate; promulgate; teach; graft; inculcate (*repeatedly*)

krzewić się [**kshe**-veećh śhan] v. spread; grow apace (*repeatedly*)

krzewienie [kshe-**vye**-ńe] n. propagation; promulgation

krzewienie się [kshe-**vye**-ńe śhan] n. the spread; growth

krzewina [kshe-**vee**-nah] f. small bush; brushwood; thicket; bushes

krzewinka [kshe-**veen**-kah] f. bush; brushwood; thicket (below two foot high)

krzewinkowaty [kshe-veen-ko-**vah**-ti] adj.m. of brushwood; of thicket; shaped like a small bush

krzewisty [kshe-**vees**-ti] adj.m. shrubby; fruticose; fasciculated

krzewny [**kshev**-ni] adj.m. (growing, etc.) like a bush

krzewostan [kshe-**vo**-stahn] m. growing shrubs

krzewuszka [kshe-**voosh**-kah] f. weigela (shrub)

krzta [kshtah] f. whit; bit; particle; tittle

ani krzty [ah-ńee kshti] exp.: not an ounce (of common sense, etc.); not an atom of (work, etc.); not a scrap (of truth, etc.); not a shred (of evidence, etc.)

do krzty [do kshti] exp.: utterly; thoroughly

krztusić się [**kshtoo**-śheećh śhan] v. choke; stifle; be seized with a fit of coughing; be choking (*repeatedly*)

krztusiec [**kshtoo**-śhets] m. whooping cough

krztuszenie się [kshtoo-**she**-ńe śhan] n. being seized with a fit of coughing; choking
krztuścowy [kshtoośh-**tso**-vi] adj.m. of whooping cough
krztyna [**kshti**-nah] f. a little bit; particle; whit; tittle
krztynę [**kshti**-nan] exp.: just a little bit; just a short while; a little bit; a wee bit
krzyca [**kshi**-tsah] f. a species of rye
krzycząco [kshi-**chown**-tso] adv. flagrantly; outrageously; glaring; blatantly
krzyczący [kshi-**chown**-tsi] adj.m. loud; gaudy; gross; crying; flagrant; outrageous; glaring; blatant
krzyczeć [**kshi**-chećh] v. shout (at); cry; scream; yell; clamor (for, against); vociferate; storm (at) (*repeatedly*)
krzyczenie [kshi-**che**-ńe] n. shouts; clamor; yelling
krzyk [kshik] m. cry; scream; shriek; yell; outcry; call; shout
co to za krzyki? [tso to zah **kshi**-kee] exp.: what is all this noise about?
krzyk bojowy [kshik bo-**yo**-vi] exp.: war cry
ostatni krzyk mody [os-**taht**-ńee kshik **mo**-di] exp.: the latest fashion; the last word in fashion; the last thing; all the go; all the rage
krzykactwo [kshi-**kahts**-tfo] n. stump oratory; tub-thumping; noisy electioneering; political agitation
krzykacz [**kshi**-kahch] m. bawler; crier; shouter; agitator; slang: lawyer; prosecutor (mob jargon)
krzykaczka [kshi-**kahch**-kah] f. (female) bawler; crier; shouter; agitator
krzykała [kshi-**kah**-wah] f. & m. crier; shouter
krzykliwie [kshik-**lee**-vye] adv. noisily; clamorously; loudly; blatantly; garishly; uproariously; vociferously; obstreperously; shrilly
krzykliwość [kshik-**lee**-vośhćh] f. noisiness; clamorousness; showiness; uproariousness; blatancy; garishnes
krzykliwy [kshik-**lee**-vi] adj.m. noisy; clamorous; loud; showy; uproarious; blatant; brawling; gaudy
krzykliwe [kshik-**lee**-ve] pl. the clamatores; noisy (children, etc.)
krzyknąć [**kshik**-nownćh] v. cry out; exclaim; utter a cry; give a cry; shout
krzyknięcie [kshik-**ńan**-ćhe] n. cry; shout; exclamation
krzyna [**kshi**-nah] f. colloq: a little bit; particle; whit; tittle
krzynę [**kshi**-nan] exp.: colloq: just a little bit; short while
krzynka [**kshin**-kah] f. colloq: a little bit; particle; whit; tittle; a wee bit
krzywa [**kshi**-vah] f. curve; flexure; slang: fictitious name (jargon)
krzywa tutka [**kshi**-vah **toot**-kah] exp.: mob slang: prostitute
krzywak [**kshi**-vahk] m. crooked trunk of a tree; plane for cutting concave surfaces; compass plane
krzywawy [kshi-**vah**-vi] adj.m. somewhat warped; somewhat crooked
krzywda [**kshiv**-dah] f. harm; a sense of wrong; wrong; injury; prejudice; detriment; unfair treatment; grievance; injustice; colloq: a raw deal
poczucie krzywdy [po-**choo**-ćhe **kshiv**-di] exp.: a sense of wrong; a sense of injustice
ponieść krzywdę [**po**-ńeśhćh **kshiv**-dan] exp.: to suffer a wrong; to suffer an injustice
wyrządzić komuś krzywdę [vi-**zhown**-dźheećh **ko**-moośh **kshiv**-dan] exp.: to do somebody wrong; to harm somebody; to do somebody an injustice
krzywdować [kshiv-**do**-vahćh] v. colloq: complain (*repeatedly*)
krzywdować sobie [kshiv-**do**-vaćh **so**-bye] exp.: colloq: to resent; to feel mistreated
krzywdząco [kshiv-**dzown**-tso] adv. harmfully; injuriously; unjustly; unfairly

krzywdzący [kshiv-**dzown**-tsi] adj.m. wrongful; harmful; injurious; unjust; unfair; prejudicial; detrimental
krzywdzenie [kshiv-**dzhe**-ńe] n. harm; wrongs
krzywdziciel [kshiv-**dźhee**-ćhel] m. wrongdoer
krzywdzicielka [kshiv-dźhee-**ćhel**-kah] f. (female) wrong doer
krzywdzić [**kshiv**-dźheećh] v. harm; wrong; damage; prejudice; be unfair (to); be unjust (to); be prejudicial (to); be detrimental (to); be injurious (to) (*repeatedly*)
krzywica [kshi-**vee**-tsah] f. rickets; rachitis; turning saw; sweep saw; jigsaw
krzywiczny [kshi-**veech**-ni] adj.m. rickety; of rachitis; of sweep saw; of jigsaw
krzywiczy [kshi-**vee**-chi] adj.m. rickety; of rachitis; rachitic
krzywić [**kshi**-veećh] v. bend; curve; crook; deflect; inflect; colloq: distort; twist; warp (*repeatedly*)
krzywić usta [**kshi**-veećh **oos**-tah] exp.: to make a grimace; to pull a face; to make a wry mouth
krzywić się [**kshi**-veećh śhan] v. make faces; bend; warp; colloq: frown; scowl (at, upon); look askance (at); be ill-disposed (towards) (*repeatedly*)
krzywienie [kshi-**vye**-ńe] n. bending; deflecting; warping
krzywienie ust [kshi-**vye**-ńe oost] exp.: grimace; wry mouth; wry face
krzywienie się [kshi-**vye**-ńe śhan] n. (a) frown; (a) scowl
krzywik [**kshi**-veek] m. French curve; drawing curve
krzywiki [kshi-**vee**-kee] pl. the Incurvariidae family of butterflies
krzywizna [kshi-**veez**-nah] f. curvature; bend; curve; flexure
krzywka [**kshif**-kah] f. cam; French curve; drawing curve; slang: fictitious name (of a criminal, etc.) (mob jargon)
krzywkowy [kshif-**ko**-vi] adj.m. cam (wheel, etc.)
wał krzywkowy [vahw kshif-**ko**-vi] exp.: camshaft
krzywo [**kshi**-vo] adv. crookedly; not straight; out of true; out of (the) perpendicular; aslant; askew; awry; lopsidedly; colloq: disapprovingly; with disapproval; falsely; distortedly
krzywo patrzeć na ... [**kshi**-vo **pah**-tshećh nah] exp.: to look askance at...; to frown at (upon) ...; to scowl at (upon)...
krzywolinijny [kshi-vo-lee-**ńeey**-ni] adj.m. curvilinear; curvilineal (motion, etc.)
krzywoliniowo [kshi-vo-leeń-**yo**-vo] adv. curvilinearly
krzywoliniowość [kshi-vo-leeń-**yo**-vośhćh] f. curvilinearity (of motion, etc.)
krzywoliniowy [kshi-vo-leeń-**yo**-vi] adj.m. curvilinear (motion, etc.)
krzywomierz [kshi-**vo**-myesh] m. device for measuring the length of a line on a map
krzywonogi [kshi-vo-**no**-gee] adj.m. bow-legged; bandy-legged
krzywoprzysiąc [kshi-vo-**pshi**-śhownts] v. foreswear oneself; perjure oneself; commit perjury
krzywoprzysięgać [kshi-vo-pshi-**śhan**-gahćh] v. foreswear oneself; perjure oneself; commit perjury (*repeatedly*)
krzywoprzysięganie [kshi-vo-pshi-śhan-**gah**-ńe] n. perjury
krzywoprzysięgnąć [kshi-vo-pshi-**śhang**-nownćh] v. foreswear oneself; perjure oneself; commit perjury
krzywoprzysięgnięcie [kshi-vo-pshi-śhang-**ńan**-ćhe] n. perjury
krzywoprzysięski [kshi-vo-pshi-**śhans**-kee] adj.m. perjurious
krzywoprzysięstwo [kshi-vo-pshi-**śhan**-stfo] n. perjury
krzywoprzysiężca [kshi-vo-pshi-**śhansh**-tsah] m. perjurer
krzywoprzysiężny [kshi-vo-pshi-**śhanzh**-ni] adj.m. perjurious
krzywość [**kshi**-vośhćh] f. crookedness; distorted state; slant; twist; lopsidedness; warp (in wood, etc.); slang: bad

reputation (among fellow inmates, etc.) (mob jargon)
krzywozębny [kshi-vo-**zanb**-ni] adj.m. with crooked teeth
krzywulec [kshi-**voo**-lets] m. crooked object; deformed person
krzywy [**kshi**-vi] adj.m. crooked; skew; distorted; slanting; twisted; curved; not straight; out of true; out of (the) perpendicular; aslant; askew; awry; lopsided; warped; disapproving
krzywa [**kshi**-vah] f. curve; flexure
krzywe spojrzenie [**kshi**-ve spoy-**zhe**-ńe] exp.: scowl; frown
krzyż [kshish] m. cross; crucifix; troubles; tribulations; afflictions; sign of the cross; military decoration; the small of the back
bóle w krzyżu [**boo**-le f **kshi**-zhoo] exp.: pains in the small of the back
krzyż koński [kshish **koń**-skee] exp.: crupper
krzyż wołowy [kshish vo-**wo**-vi] exp.: rump
na krzyż [nah kshish] exp.: crosswise
przecinać się na krzyż [pshe-**ćhee**-nahćh śhan nah kshish] exp.: to cross; to crisscross
krzyżacki [kshi-**zhahts**-kee] adj.m. of the Teutonic Order (of armed monks); of the Teutonic Knights
zakon krzyżacki [**zah**-kon kshi-**zhahts**-kee] exp.: Teutonic Order (of armed monks)
krzyżactwo [kshi-**zhahts**-tfo] n. Teutonic Order (of armed monks)
krzyżak [**kshi**-zhahk] m. trestle; cross-bit; trestle table; cross (bar); armed monk of the Teutonic Order; cross spider; slang: German
krzyżakowy [kshi-zhah-**ko**-vi] adj.m. trestle (table, etc.); of a cross-bit; of a trestle table
krzyżmo [**kshizh**-mo] n. chrism (consecrated oil)
krzyżodziób [kshi-**zho**-dźhoop] m. loxia (of the crossbills)
krzyżowa [kshi-**zho**-vah] adj.f. sirloin (meat, etc.)
krzyżować [kshi-**zho**-vahćh] v. cross (swords, etc.); frustrate; baffle; traverse; thwart; crucify; intercross; hybridize; interbreed; intersect; cross-fertilize; tack about (at sea, etc.) (*repeatedly*)
krzyżować się [kshi-**zho**-vahćh śhan] v. cross (with swords, etc.); crisscross; hybridize; interbreed; intersect; cross-fertilize; meet (by crossing) (*repeatedly*)
krzyżowanie [kshi-zho-**vah**-ńe] n. crucifixion; hybridization; interbreeding; cross-fertilization; crossbreeding
krzyżowanie się [kshi-zho-**vah**-ńe śhan] n. intersection
krzyżowanie się dróg [kshi-zho-**vah**-ńe śhan drook] exp.: crossroads; intersection
krzyżowe [kshi-**zho**-ve] pl. the Cruciferae family of plants
krzyżowiaczek [kshi-zho-**vyah**-chek] m. variety of butterfly
krzyżowiec [kshi-**zho**-vyets] m. crusader
krzyżownica [kshi-zhov-**ńee**-tsah] f. trestle; frog (rail switch); crisscross; milkwort (plant); rogation flower
krzyżownicowaty [kshi-zhov-ńee-tso-**vah**-ti] adj.m. like milkwort (plant); like rogation flower; polygalaceous
krzyżownicowate [kshi-zhov-ńee-tso-**vah**-te] pl. the Polygaceae family of flowers
krzyżowo [kshi-**zho**-vo] adv. crosswise; across; transversely; by cross-fertilization
przecinać się krzyżowo [pshe-**ćhee**-nahćh śhan kshi-**zho**-vo] exp.: to intersect
krzyżowy [kshi-**zho**-vi] adj.m. placed crosswise; cross; cross-fertilized; cross-shaped; x-shaped; cruciform; decussate; intersecting; transverse; of the (Holy) cross; sacral; crusader's; crusaders'
Droga Krzyżowa [dro-gah kshi-**zho**-vah] exp.: the Way of the Cross; the Stations of the Cross
kość krzyżowa [kośhćh kshi-

zho-vah] exp.: sacrum
kręgi krzyżowe [kran-gee kshi-zho-ve] exp.: sacral vertebrae
krzyżowy ogień pytań [kshi-zho-vi o-geń pi-tahń] exp.: cross-examination
ogień krzyżowy [o-geń kshi-zho-vi] exp.: crossfire; cross fire
sklepienie krzyżowe [skle-pye-ńe kshi-zho-ve] exp.: cross vault
wyprawa krzyżowa [vip-rah-vah kshi-zho-vah] exp.: crusade
krzyżówa [kshi-zhoo-vah] f. slang: vodka (mob jargon)
krzyżówka [kshi-zhoof-kah] f. crossword puzzle; hybrid; (a) cross; sirloin; baron of beef (Brit.); crossing; hybridization; grading; variety of wild duck; mallard; colloq: crossroads
krzyżówka wsteczna [kshi-zhoof-kah fstech-nah] exp.: backcross
krzyżówkowy [kshi-zhoof-ko-vi] adj.m. crossword-puzzle (solution, etc.); hybrid (plant, etc.); mallard's
haft krzyżówkowy [khahft kshi-zhoof-ko-vi] exp.: cross-stitch
krzyżulcowy [kshi-zhool-tso-vi] adj.m. of a cross-brace; of a lattice bar; of a crosshead (of a piston)
krzyżulec [kshi-zhoo-lets] m. cross-brace; lattice bar; crosshead
krzyżyk [kshi-zhik] m. small cross; mark; cross-stitch; (a) sharp (note); colloq: ten years of a person's life; slang: powdered narcotic; headache powder; headache pill (tablet)
krzyżyk biały [kshi-zhik byah-wi] exp.: slang: cocaine (mob jargon)
krzyżyk czerwony [kshi-zhik cher-vo-ni] exp.: mob slang: morphine
krzyżykowy [kshi-zhi-ko-vi] adj.m. of a small cross; of a mark; of cross-stitches
ksantat [ksahn-taht] m. xanthate
ksantofil [ksahn-to-feel] m. xanthophyll
ksantofile [ksahn-to-fee-le] pl. xanthophyllic pigments
ksantofilina [ksahn-to-fee-lee-nah] f. xanthophyll
ksantogenian [ksahn-to-geń-yahn] m. xanthate
ksantyna [ksahn-ti-nah] f. xanthine
ksantypa [ksahn-ti-pah] f. Xanthippe; shrew
ksenofil [kse-no-feel] m. xenophile; xenophilous
ksenofilia [kse-no-feel-yah] f. xenophile attitude
ksenofob [kse-no-fop] m. xenophobe
ksenofobia [kse-no-fob-yah] f. xenophobia
ksenon [kse-non] m. xenon (atomic number 54)
ksenonowy [kse-no-no-vi] adj.m. xenon (lamp, flashtube, etc.)
kserofil [kse-ro-feel] m. xerophilous animal; xerophilous plant
kserofile [kse-ro-fee-le] pl. xerophilous plants
kserofilny [kse-ro-feel-ni] adj.m. xerophilous; xerophile
kserofit [kse-ro-feet] m. xerophyte
kserofity [kse-ro-fee-ti] pl. xerophytic plants
kserofitowo [kse-ro-fee-to-vo] adv. xerophytically
kserofitowy [kse-ro-fee-to-vi] adj.m. xerophytic
kserofityczny [kse-ro-fee-tich-ni] adj.m. xerophytic
kserofityzm [kse-ro-fee-tizm] m. xerophytism
kseroftalmia [kse-rof-tahl-myah] f. xerophthalmia
kseroftalmiczny [kse-rof-tahl-meech-ni] adj.m. xerophthalmic
kserograf [kse-ro-grahf] m. xerographic copier; Xerox (trademark)
kserografia [kse-ro-grah-fyah] f. xerography
kserograficznie [kse-ro-grah-feech-ńe] adv. xerographically
kserograficzny [kse-ro-grah-feech-ni] adj.m. xerographic
kserokopia [kse-ro-ko-pyah] f. xerographic copy
kserokopiarka [kse-ro-ko-pyahr-kah] f. xerographic copier; Xerox (trademark)
kseromorficzny [kse-ro-mor-feech-ni] adj.m. xeromorphic;

xeromorphous
kseromorfizm [kse-ro-**mor**-feezm] m. xeromorphy
kserotermiczny [kse-ro-ter-**meech**-ni] adj.m. xerothermic
kserotyczny [kse-ro-**tich**-ni] adj.m. xeromorphic; xeromorphous
ksiądz [kśhownts] m. priest; clergyman; slang: prosecutor; judge; school principal (jargon)
ksiąstewko [kśhown-**stef**-ko] n. small duchy; small principality
książątko [kśhown-**zhownt**-ko] n. princeling; petty prince; young prince
książczyna [kśhownsh-**chi**-nah] f. worthless book; worn-out book
książeczka [kśhown-**zhech**-kah] f. (small, nice) book
książeczka czekowa [kśhown-**zhech**-kah che-**ko**-vah] exp.: checkbook; cheque book (Brit.)
książeczka oszczędnościowa [kśhown-**zhech**-kah osh-chand-nośh-**ćho**-vah] exp.: pass book; savings book
książeczkowy [kśhown-zhech-**ko**-vi] adj.m. in the shape of a book
książę [**kśhown**-zhan] m. prince; duke; ruler of a duchy
książęco [kśhown-**zhan**-tso] adv. in princely manner
książęcy [kśhown-**zhan**-tsi] adj.m. princely; prince's; duke's
książka [**kśhownsh**-kah] f. book
książka beletrystyczna [**kśhownsh**-kah be-le-tris-**tich**-nah] exp.: book of fiction
książka podręczna [**kśhownsh**-kah pod-**ranch**-nah] exp.: reference book
siedzieć nad książką [**śhe**-dźhećh naht **kśhownsh**-kown] exp.: to pour over a book
książkowo [kśhownsh-**ko**-vo] adv. in form of a book; in bookish manner; bookishly
książkowość [kśhownsh-**ko**-vośhćh] f. bookishness; bookish character (of a literary composition)
książkowy [kśhownsh-**ko**-vi] adj.m. of a book; of books; book (cover, value, etc.); bookish
książnica [kśhownzh-**ńee**-tsah] f. library
ksieni [**kśhe**-ńee] f. abbes; prioress; prelatess
księga [**kśhan**-gah] f. register; large book; volume; tome; chapter; canto
księga magazynowa [**kśhan**-gah mah-gah-zi-**no**-vah] exp.: inventory ledger; warehouse book
księga zamówień [**kśhan**-gah zah-**moo**-vyeń] exp.: order book
księgi [**kśhan**-gee] pl. ruminant's third stomach; omasum; psalterium; books
księgi archiwalne [**kśhan**-gee ahr-khee-**vahl**-ne] exp.: archives
prowadzić księgi [pro-**vah**-dźheećh **kśhan**-gee] exp.: to keep books
złota księga [**zwo**-tah **kśhan**-gah] exp.: roll of honor; honor roll
księgarenka [kśhan-gah-**ren**-kah] f. small bookstore
księgarnia [kśhan-**gahr**-ńah] f. bookstore; books; bookshop
księgarski [kśhan-**gahr**-skee] adj.m. of a bookstore; bookstore owner's; bookseller's; booksellers'
rynek księgarski [ri-nek kśhan-**gahr**-skee] exp.: the book market
stoisko księgarskie [sto-**ees**-ko kśhan-**gahr**-ske] exp.: bookstall
księgarstwo [kśhan-**gahr**-stfo] n. the book trade; book selling
księgarz [**kśhan**-gahsh] m. bookseller; owner of a bookstore
księgosusz [kśhan-**go**-soosh] m. a disease of ruminant animals; rinderpest; cattle plague
księgowa [kśhan-**go**-vah] f. (female) bookkeeper; accountant
księgować [kśhan-**go**-vahćh] v. keep books; enter in books (*repeatedly*)
księgowanie [kśhan-go-**vah**-ńe] n. bookkeeping
księgowość [kśhan-**go**-vośhćh] f. bookkeeping work; bookkeeping department (system, etc.)
księgowość amerykańska [kśhan-**go**-vośhćh ah-me-ri-**kahń**-skah] exp.: American system of

double-entry bookkeeping
księgowy [kśhan-go-vi] m. bookkeeper; accountant; adj.m. bookkeeping (entry, etc.)
dyplomowany księgowy [di-plo-mo-vah-ni kśhan-go-vi] exp.: certified accountant; chartered accountant (Brit.)
księgozbiór [kśhan-go-zbyoor] m. book collection; library
księgoznak [kśhan-go-znahk] m. exlibris; ex libris; bookplate
księgoznawca [kśhan-go-znahf-tsah] m. bibliographer; bibliologist
księgoznawczo [kśhan-go-znahf-cho] adv. bibliographically
księgoznawczy [kśhan-go-znahf-chi] adj.m. bibliographic; bibliographical
księgoznawstwo [kśhan-go-znahf-stfo] n. bibliography; bibliology
księstwo [kśhans-tfo] n. duchy; office of prince; prince and princess; duke and duchess
księżak [kśhan-zhahk] m. inhabitant of the Łowicz district of Poland
księżna [kśhan-zhnah] f. duchess; princess; wife of a prince
księżniczka [kśhanzh-ńeech-kah] f. princess; daughter of a prince
księżowski [kśhan-zhof-skee] adj.m. of a priest; priest's; clergyman's
księżulek [kśhan-zhoo-lek] m. (dear, nice) priest; slang: judge
księży [kśhan-zhi] adj.m. priestly; belonging to a priest; clerical
księży kołnierzyk [kśhan-zhi kow-ńe-zhik] exp.: clerical collar; Roman collar; colloq: dog collar
księżyc [kśhan-zhits] m. moon; the Crescent; the Turkish Empire; moonlight
blask księżyca [blahsk kśhan-zhi-tsah] exp.: moonlight
sierp księżyca [śherp kśhan-zhi-tsah] exp.: crescent
księżycoróg [kśhan-zhi-tso-rook] m. variety of beetles
księżycowy [kśhan-zhi-tso-vi] adj.m. of the moon; moon's; lunar (cycle, eclipse, month, etc.); slang: m. drug addict; moonshine (mob jargon)
blask księżycowy [blahsk kśhan-zhi-tso-vi] exp.: moonlight
lot księżycowy [lot kśhan-zhi-tso-vi] exp.: flight to the moon
nów księżycowy [noof kśhan-zhi-tso-vi] exp.: new moon
księżyna [kśhan-zhi-nah] m. colloq: (run-down) priest
ksiuty [kśhoo-ti] pl. colloq: courting (in the countryside); flirtations
ksobny [ksob-ni] adj.m. adducent
mięsień ksobny [myan-śheń ksob-ni] exp.: adducent muscle; adductor
ksyk [ksik] m. hiss (of a snake, goose, etc.)
ksykać [ksi-kahćh] v. hiss (*repeatedly*)
ksykanie [ksi-kah-ńe] n. hisses
ksyknąć [ksik-nownćh] v. hiss
ksyknięcie [ksik-ńan-ćhe] n. a hiss
ksylamit [ksi-lah-meet] m. a wood preserver
ksylan [ksi-lahn] m. xylan; wood gum
ksylany [ksi-lah-ni] pl. ploysaccharides
ksylem [ksi-lem] m. xylem; woody tissue
ksylen [ksi-len] m. xylene
ksyleny [ksi-le-ni] pl. xylenes
ksylit [ksi-leet] m. an explosive used in World War I
ksylofag [ksi-lo-fahk] m. xylophage
ksylofagi [ksi-lo-fah-gee] pl. xylophagous organisms
ksylofit [ksi-lo-feet] m. tree-like plant
ksylofity [ksi-lo-fee-ti] pl. bushes, trees, and shrubs
ksylofon [ksi-lo-fon] m. xylophone
ksylograf [ksi-lo-grahf] m. xylographer
ksylografia [ksi-lo-grahf-yah] f. xylography
ksylograficznie [ksi-lo-grah-feech-ńe] adv. xylographically
ksylograficzny [ksi-lo-grah-feech-ni] adj.m. xylographical; xylographic
ksylografy [ksi-lo-grah-fi] pl. xylograph; book made of block-printed pages
ksylol [ksi-lol] m. xylol
ksylolit [ksi-lo-leet] m. xylolite

(particle board)
ksylolitowy [ksi-lo-lee-**to**-vi] adj.m. of xylolite
ksylometr [ksi-**lo**-metr] m. xylometer
ksyloza [ksi-**lo**-zah] f. xylose
ksywa [**ksi**-vah] f. colloq: criminal alias; pseudonym; criminal slang; slang: document; certificate of stocks or securities (mob jargon)
kształcąco [kshtahw-**tsown**-tso] adv. instructively
kształcący [kshtahw-**tsown**-tsi] adj.m. instructive
kształcenie [kshtahw-**tse**-ńe] n. instruction; education; training; schooling; cultivation
kształcenie się [kshtahw-**tse**-ńe śhan] n. self-instruction; self-education; self-improvement; formation
kształcić [**kshtahw**-ćheećh] v. educate; train; form; school; teach; discipline; cultivate; nurture; instruct (*repeatedly*)
kształcić się [**kshtahw**-ćheećh śhan] v. be educated; learn; be formed; go to school; school oneself; improve one's mind; develop; be modelled; be fashioned (*repeatedly*)
kształt [kshtahwt] m. form; shape; configuration; figure
  kształty [**kshtahw**-ti] pl. figure; proportions; shape
  na kształt [nah kshtahwt] exp.: like; kind of; similar; as; as if
kształtka [**kshtahwt**-kah] f. molder; moldboard; shaped stone
kształtnie [**kshtahwt**-ńe] adv. shapely; neatly; with nice proportions
kształtność [**kshtahwt**-nośhćh] f. shapeliness; neatness; nice proportions
kształtny [**kshtahwt**-ni] adj.m. shapely; neat; nicely made; well proportioned
kształtować [kshtahw-**to**-vahćh] v. shape; form; mold; fashion; mould; frame (*repeatedly*)
kształtować się [kshtahw-**to**-vahćh śhan] v. be shaped; be formed; be molded; be fashioned; be moulded; be framed; take form; assume form; spring up; arise; trend (upwards, downwards) (*repeatedly*)
kształtowanie [kshtahw-to-**vah**-ńe] n. formation
kształtowanie się [kshtahw-to-**vah**-ńe śhan] n. formation; rise; (a) trend
kształtownik [kshtahw-**tov**-ńeek] m. section; (structural) shape
kształtowy [kshtahw-**to**-vi] adj.m. of a section; of (structural) shape
  żelazo kształtowe [zhe-**lah**-zo kshtahw-**to**-ve] exp.: section iron; (structural) shaped iron
kształtówka [kshtahw-**toof**-kah] f. section iron; (structural) shaped iron
kształtujący [kshtahw-too-**yown**-tsi] adj.m. formative; constitutive
kszyk [kshik] m. snipe (bird)
kto [kto] pron. who; all who; those who; everyone who; somebody; anybody; anyone
  byle kto [**bi**-le kto] exp.: anybody; anyone
  kto? [kto] exp.: who?
  kto bądź [kto bownćh] exp.: anybody; no one; just anyone
  kto inny [kto **een**-ni] exp.: somebody else; someone else
  kto to? [kto to] exp.: who is that?; who is he?; who is she?; who are these people?
  mało kto [**mah**-wo kto] exp.: hardly anyone; hardly anybody
  rzadko kto [**zhaht**-ko kto] exp.: hardly anyone; hardly anybody
ktokolwiek [kto-**kol**-vyek] pron. anybody; anyone (you like); whoever (you like)
  ktokolwiek jesteś [kto-**kol**-vyek **yes**-teśh] exp.: whoever you are
ktoś [ktośh] pron. somebody; someone; anybody; anyone; colloq: m. an unknown person
  ktoś trzeci [ktośh **tshe**-ćhee] exp.: a third person; a third party
  ktoś zapukał [ktośh zah-**poo**-kahw] exp.: somebody has knocked (at the door, etc.)
ktośkolwiek [ktośh-**kol**-vyek] pron. anybody; anyone (you like); whoever (you like)

którędy [ktoo-ran-di] adv. which way?; how to get there?
którędykolwiek [ktoo-ran-di-kol-vyek] pron. any way; in any direction
którędyż [ktoo-ran-dish] pron. (emphatic) which way?; how to get there?
który [ktoo-ri] pron. who; which; that; any; one; various; whichever; which one?
dla którego [dlah ktoo-re-go] exp.: for whom; for which
do którego [do ktoo-re-go] exp.: to whom
którego [ktoo-re-go] exp.: (pron.) whose; of which
którego dzisiaj? [ktoo-re-go dźhee-śhahy] exp.: colloq: which day of the month is it?; what day is it?
którego mamy dzisiaj? [ktoo-re-go mah-mi dźhee-śhahy] exp.: which day of the month is it?; what day is it?
który bądź [ktoo-ri bownćh] exp.: any; either (of two)
od którego [ot ktoo-re-go] exp.: from whom; from which; wherefrom
przez którego [pshes ktoo-re-go] exp.: through whom; by whom
przez który [pshes ktoo-ri] exp.: through which; by which; whereby; wherethrough
rzadko który [zhaht-ko ktoo-ri] exp.: hardly anyone; hardly any man; scarcely any (man, day, etc.)
ten który [ten ktoo-ri] exp.: the one who; such ... as
w którego [f ktoo-re-go] exp.: in which
w którym [f ktoo-rim] exp.: in which; wherein
z którym [s ktoo-rim] exp.: with whom; with which; wherewith
którykolwiek [ktoo-ri-kol-vyek] pron. whichever; whatever; any one (of)
któryś [ktoo-riśh] pron. a; some; some (one, day, man, etc.) or other; one (of)
któregoś dnia [ktoo-re-gośh dńah] exp.: one day (in the past)
któryś z was [ktoo-riśh z vahs] exp.: one of you
któryż [ktoo-rish] pron. = (emphatic) **który**
któż [ktoosh] pron. whichever; whoever; colloq: who on earth
ku [koo] prep. towards; to; in the direction; about; for; -wards
ku dołowi [koo do-wo-vee] exp.: downwards
ku domowi [koo do-mo-vee] exp.: home; towards one's home; homeward(s)
ku górze [koo goo-zhe] exp.: upwards
ku niebu [koo ńe-boo] exp.: to the sky; skyward(s)
ku sobie [koo so-bye] exp.: to oneself
kuandu [koo-ahn-doo] n. Coendu hedgehog
kuban [koo-bahn] m. bribe; golden key; silver key
Kubanka [koo-bahn-kah] f. Cuban (female)
Kubańczyk [koo-bahń-chik] m. Cuban
kubański [koo-bahń-skee] adj.m. Cuban
kubas [koo-bahs] m. large cup
kubatura [koo-bah-too-rah] f. (building) volume; cubature; capacity; cubic content
kubaturowo [koo-bah-too-ro-vo] adv. in respect of cubature; in respect of cubic content
kubaturowy [koo-bah-too-ro-vi] adj.m. capacity (factor, etc.)
kubeba [koo-be-bah] f. cubeb (fruit)
kubeczek [koo-be-chek] m. small cup; goblet
kubeczki smakowe [koo-bech-kee smah-ko-ve] exp.: taste buds; taste goblets
kubecznikowaty [koo-bech-ńee-ko-vah-ti] adj.m. nidulariaceous; m. one of the bird's nest fungi
kubek [koo-bek] m. cup; mug; tumbler; noggin; mugful; tumblerful
kubeł [koo-bew] m. pail; bucket; kibble; slang: mug; big goblet
kubełek [koo-be-wek] m. (small)

pail; bucket; kibble
kubełkowy [koo-bew-**ko**-vi] adj.m. bucket (conveyor, etc.)
kubiczny [koo-**beech**-ni] adj.m. cubic
kubik [**koo**-beek] m. colloq: cubic meter; stere (one cubic meter)
kubista [koo-**bees**-tah] m. cubist
kubistka [koo-**beest**-kah] f. (woman) cubist
kubistycznie [koo-bees-**tich**-ńe] adv. after the manner of cubists; according to the rules of cubism
kubistyczny [koo-bees-**tich**-ni] adj.m. cubist
kubizm [**koo**-beezm] m. cubism
kubizować [koo-bee-**zo**-vahćh] v. paint or make sculptures in the cubist style (*repeatedly*)
kubizowanie [koo-bee-zo-**vah**-ńe] n. painting or making sculptures in the cubist style
kubkowaty [koop-ko-**vah**-ti] adj.m. cup-shaped
kubkowy [koop-**ko**-vi] adj.m. of a cup
komórki kubkowe [ko-**moor**-kee koop-**ko**-ve] exp.: beaker cells; chalice cells
kubłowy [koob-**wo**-vi] adj.m. of a bucket; bucket (handle, etc.)
kubofuturyzm [koo-bo-foo-**too**-rizm] m. combination of cubism and futurism
kubraczek [koob-**rah**-chek] m. (small, nice) doublet
kubraczek żółty [koob-**rah**-chek **zhoow**-ti] exp.: slang: barbiturate used by drug addicts (mob jargon)
kubrak [**koob**-rahk] m. doublet
kubryk [**koob**-rik] m. forecastle
kuc [koots] m. pony
kucać [**koo**-tsahćh] v. squat; crouch (*repeatedly*)
kucanie [koo-**tsah**-ńe] n. squating; crouching
kucany [koo-**tsah**-ni] adj.m. squatting
berek kucany [**be**-rek koo-**tsah**-ni] exp.: tag game combined with squatting
kuch [kookh] m. linseed cake
kuchareczka [koo-khah-**rech**-kah] f. (nice, little) cook
kucharka [koo-**khahr**-kah] f. cook
kucharski [koo-**khahr**-skee] adj.m. cook's; cooks'; of cooking; cooking (utensils, etc.)
książka kucharska [kśhownsh-kah koo-**khahr**-skah] exp.: cookbook; cookery book (Brit.)
kucharstwo [koo-**khahr**-stfo] n. cooking; the art of cooking
kucharz [**koo**-khahsh] m. cook
kucharzenie [koo-khah-**zhe**-ńe] n. cooking
kucharzować [koo-khah-**zho**-vahćh] v. cook; to do the cooking (*repeatedly*)
kucharzyć [koo-**khah**-zhićh] v. cook; to do the cooking (*repeatedly*)
kuchcik [**kookh**-ćheek] m. cook's boy; cook's little helper
kuchenka [koo-**khen**-kah] f. small kitchen; toy kitchen; kitchenette
kuchenka gazowa [koo-**khen**-kah gah-**zo**-vah] exp.: (gas) hot plate; gas-stove
kuchenny [koo-**khen**-ni] adj.m. of the kitchen stove; of the kitchen range; kitchen (floor, salt, etc.)
schody kuchenne [**skho**-di koo-**khen**-ne] exp.: backstairs
kuchmistrz [**kookh**-meestsh] m. head cook
kuchmistrzowski [kookh-mees-**tshof**-skee] adj.m. of the head cook; chef's
kuchnia [**kookh**-ńah] f. kitchen; kitchen stove; cooking range; food; fare; cooking; cuisine
mistrz kuchni [meestsh **kookh**-ńee] exp.: chef
kuchta [**kookh**-tah] f. colloq: skivvy
kucie [**koo**-ćhe] n. horseshoeing; farriery; slang; making a tattoo
kucie matrycowe [**koo**-ćhe maht-ri-**tso**-ve] exp.: drop forging
kucja [**koots**-yah] f. Ukrainian dish of wheat with honey and poppy seeds (served on Christmas Eve)
kucki [**koots**-kee] pl. squatting
siedzieć w kucki [**śhe**-dźhećh f **koots**-kee] exp.: to squat
kucmerka [koots-**mer**-kah] f. a marsh plant with nutritious root
kucnąć [**koots**-nownćh] v. squat down; squat; crouch

kucnięcie [koots-ńan-ćhe] n. squatting down; squatting
kucyk [koo-tsik] m. small pony; nag; cob
kuczka [kooch-kah] f. bower; tent
Kuczki [kooch-kee] pl. exp.: Jewish Feast of Tabernacles
kuczny [kooch-ni] adj.m. squatting (position, etc.)
kuć [kooćh] v. hammer; shoe a horse; forge; colloq: cram lessons; peck; pick; coin (new words, etc.); bruise (metal); pick (axe); mob slang: whack; slosh; put handcuffs (on) (*repeatedly*)
kudełki [koo-dew-kee] pl. shaggy hair; hair locks; hair
kudlić [kood-leećh] v. make shaggy; tousle (*repeatedly*)
kudlić się [kood-leećh śhan] v. become shaggy; get tousled (*repeatedly*)
kudłacenie [kood-wah-tse-ńe] n. making shaggy; making a mop of hair
kudłacić [kood-wah-ćheećh] v. make shaggy; tousle (*repeatedly*)
kudłacić się [kood-wah-ćheećh śhan] v. become shaggy; get tousled (*repeatedly*)
kudłacz [kood-wahch] m. hairy fellow; shaggy man; hirsute man; mop of hair; shaggy animal
kudłać [kood-wahćh] v. make shaggy; tousle (*repeatedly*)
kudłać się [kood-wahćh śhan] v. become shaggy; get tousled (*repeatedly*)
kudłaj [kood-wahy] m. slang: (a) Jew (mob jargon)
kudłaty [kood-wah-ti] adj.m. shaggy; hairy; hirsute
kudły [kood-wi] pl. colloq: shaggy hair; mop of hair; shag
kudu [koo-doo] not declined: koodoo; kudu
kuesta [kwes-tah] f. steep edge; crag; steep rock
kufa [koo-fah] f. vat; small sailing ship; colloq: mug (face); potbelly (man); slang: rear end; behind
kufajka [koo-fahy-kah] f. quilted coat
kufel [koo-fel] m. beer mug; mugful; tankard
kufelek [koo-fe-lek] m. small beer mug; colloq: small mugful
kufer [koo-fer] m. trunk; chest
kuferek [koo-fe-rek] m. small trunk; small chest; box; suitcase; valise
kuficki [koo-feets-kee] adj.m. Cufic; Kufic (writing)
kufika [koo-fee-kah] f. Cufic characters; Kufic ornamentation
kuflowy [koof-lo-vi] adj.m. mug (glass, etc.)
kugiel [koo-gel] m. Jewish festive cake
kuglarka [koog-lahr-kah] f. (female) juggler; conjurer; magician; colloq: thimblerigger; prestidigitator; impostor; fraud; mob slang: cardsharper; cheat
kuglarski [koog-lahr-skee] adj.m. juggling; conjuring; colloq: deceitful; fraudulent
kuglarstwo [koog-lahr-stfo] n. jugglery; hocus-pocus; thimblerig; sleight of hand; prestidigitation; colloq: fraud; deception
kuglarz [koog-lahsh] m. juggler; conjurer; magician; colloq: thimblerigger; prestidigitator; impostor; fraud; slang: cardsharper; cheat (mob jargon)
kugler [koog-ler] m. crystal glass cutter (man)
kuglować [koog-lo-vahćh] v. juggle; beguile; clown; play pranks (*repeatedly*)
kuguar [koo-goo-ahr] m. cougar; puma
kujawiaczek [koo-yah-vyah-chek] m. (small, nice) inhabitant of Kujawy province; folk dance; a melody
kujawiak [koo-yah-vyahk] m. inhabitant of Kujawy province; folk dance; a melody
kujawski [koo-yahf-skee] adj.m. of Kujawy; Kujavian
kujnąć [kooy-nownćh] v. peck; slang: hit
kujnięcie [kooy-ńan-ćhe] n. pecking
kujność [kooy-nośhćh] f. malleability; forgeability; ductility; malleable tenacity
kujny [kooy-ni] adj.m. malleable; forgeable; ductile

kujon [**koo**-yon] m. colloq: crammer; slang: sap; plodder
kujot [**koo**-yot] m. coyote; prairie wolf
kuk [kook] m. ship's cook; slang: eyes
kukać [**koo**-kahćh] v. cuckoo; mob slang: speak; spy; accuse; denounce; admit guilt (*repeatedly*)
kukanie [koo-**kah**-ńe] n. (call of the) cuckoo
kukawka [koo-**kahf**-kah] f. cuckoo (bird)
kukersyt [**koo**-ker-sit] m. a combustible sedimentary rock
kukiełka [koo-**kew**-kah] f. doll; puppet
kukiełkowy [koo-kew-**ko**-vi] adj.m. puppet (show, etc.)
teatr kukiełkowy [**te**-ahtr koo-kew-**ko**-vi] exp.: puppet show
kuklik [**kook**-leek] m. avens (perennial herb); bennet
kukła [**kook**-wah] f. puppet; doll; effigy (of famous or hated person); man of straw; slang: night watchman; juror; girl; woman (mob jargon)
kuknąć [**kook**-nownćh] v. have a look (at); have a squint (at)
kuknięcie [kook-**ńan**-ćhe] n. a squint; a look
kuks [kooks] m. nudge; punch; blow; rap; clout; cuff
kuksać [**kook**-sahćh] v. hit; punch; nudge (*repeatedly*)
kuksanie [kook-**sah**-ńe] n. blows; punches; nudges
kuksaniec [kook-**sah**-ńets] m. rap; nudge; punch; blow; clout; cuff
kuksnąć [**kooks**-nownćh] v. give somebody a punch; poke with the elbow; give somebody a nudge
kuksnięcie [kooks-**ńan**-ćhe] n. a punch; a nudge
kuku [**koo**-koo] not declined: (call of the) cuckoo
a kuku! [ah **koo**-koo] excl.: peekaboo!
mieć kuku na muniu [myećh **koo**-koo nah **moo**-ńoo] exp.: colloq: to be wacky; to have a loose screw; to have a loose tile
kukuczka [koo-**kooch**-kah] f. Gymnadenia (an orchid)
kukułczę [koo-**koow**-chan] n. cuckoo fledgling
kukułczy [koo-**koow**-chi] adj.m. cuckoo's
kukułeczka [koo-koo-**wech**-kah] f. (nice, little) cuckoo
kukułka [koo-**koow**-kah] f. cuckoo bird; cuckoo clock; slang: casing by a thief; prostitute (mob jargon)
zegar z kukułką [**ze**-gahr s koo-**koow**-kown] exp.: cuckoo clock
kukułki [koo-**koow**-kee] pl. the Cuculiformes (parasitic birds)
kukurudza [koo-koo-**roo**-dzah] f. maize; corn; Indian corn
kukuruźnik [koo-koo-**roo**źh-ńeek] m. colloq: a type of Russian scouting aeroplane
kukurydza [koo-koo-**ri**-dzah] f. maize; corn; Indian corn
kukurydzanka [koo-koo-ri-**dzahn**-kah] f. maize flour; corn flour; corn grits; gruel; hominy; samp
kukurydzany [koo-koo-ri-**dzah**-ni] adj.m. corn (harvest, etc.)
kukurydziany [koo-koo-ri-**dźhah**-ni] adj.m. corn (harvest, etc.)
kukurydzowy [koo-koo-ri-**dzo**-vi] adj.m. corn (harvest, etc.)
kukurykać [koo-koo-**ri**-kahćh] v. crow (*repeatedly*)
kukuryknąć [koo-koo-**rik**-nownćh] v. crow
kukuryku [koo-koo-**ri**-koo] not declined: cock-a-doodle-doo; slang: chicken thief; a prison game (mob jargon)
kula [**koo**-lah] f. sphere; bullet; crutch; ball; globe; shot; pommel (of a saddle-bow)
chodzić o kulach [**kho**-dźheećh o **koo**-lahkh] exp.: to walk on crutches
śnieżna kula [**śhńezh**-nah **koo**-lah] exp.: snowball; mob slang: narcotic in an ampule
kulać [**koo**-lahćh] v. roll (a stone, etc.) (*repeatedly*)
kulać się [**koo**-lahćh śhan] v. roll; colloq: keep (start, etc.) rolling (*repeatedly*)
kulanie [koo-**lah**-ńe] n. rolling motion; roll

kulanie się [koo-**lah**-ńe śh<u>an</u>] n. rolling oneself (on the snow, etc.)
kulas [**koo**-lahs] m. colloq: leg; cripple; lame person; scribbled letter
kulawić [koo-**lah**-veećh] v. lame; cripple (a person, an animal) (*repeatedly*)
kulawiec [koo-**lah**-vyets] m. lame fellow; cripple; slang: beginning thief (mob jargon)
kulawieć [koo-**lah**-vyećh] v. become lame; become crippled; hobble; limp (*repeatedly*)
kulawienie [koo-lah-**vye**-ńe] n. becoming lame; becoming crippled; hobbling; limping
kulawizna [koo-lah-**veez**-nah] f. colloq: limp; hobble; a limp; a hobble; lameness
kulawka [koo-**lahf**-kah] f. limp; hobble; a limp; a hobble
kulawo [koo-**lah**-vo] adv. with a limp; lamely; hugger-mugger
iść kulawo [eeśhćh koo-**lah**-vo] exp.: to struggle along; to contend with difficulties
kulawy [koo-**lah**-vi] adj.m. lame; limping; hobbling; faulty; rickety (chair, etc.); game; broken (language, etc.); slang: stupid; m. cripple (mob jargon)
kulbaczenie [kool-bah-**che**-ńe] n. saddling a horse (a mule, etc.)
kulbaczyć [kool-**bah**-chićh] v. saddle (a horse, a pony, etc.); slang: smoke cigarettes (mob jargon) (*repeatedly*)
kulbak [**kool**-bahk] m. halibut (fish)
kulbaki [kool-**bah**-kee] pl. Hippoglossus and Reinhardtius fishes
kulbaka [kool-**bah**-kah] f. saddle
kulbin [**kool**-been] m. Sciaena (fish)
kulbinowaty [kool-bee-no-**vah**-ti] adj.m. of the Sciaena (fish) family
kulbinowate [kool-bee-no-**vah**-te] pl. the Sciaena (fish) family
kulczyba [kool-**chi**-bah] f. St. Ignatius's beam (Strychnos)
kulczyk [**kool**-chik] m. canary-like bird
kulebiak [koo-le-byahk] m. stuffed dumpling; pie with meat, fish or cabbage
kulebiaka [koo-le-**byah**-kah] f. stuffed dumpling; pie with meat, fish or cabbage
kuleczka [koo-**lech**-kah] f. (small) ball; sphere; shot; bullet
kuleczkowaty [koo-lech-ko-**vah**-ti] adj.m. ball-like; spherical
kuleć [**koo**-lećh] v. limp; hobble; dot and go one; colloq: struggle along; contend with difficulties; flag (*repeatedly*)
kulenie [koo-**le**-ńe] n. limping; hobbling; struggling along
kulenie się [koo-**le**-ńe śh<u>an</u>] n. snuggling; nestling; cringing
kulfon [**kool**-fon] m. ill-formed letter; colloq: pudge; squab; humpty-dumpty; dump; slang: blockhead; nose; leg; failing grade (in school)
kulfoniasty [kool-fo-**ńahs**-ti] adj.m. ill-formed (person, etc.); hulking; lumpish
kulić [**koo**-leećh] v. duck (one's head); bend (one's shoulders, etc.) (*repeatedly*)
kulić się [**koo**-leećh śh<u>an</u>] v. snuggle; crouch; cringe; nestle; huddle oneself up (*repeatedly*)
kulig [**koo**-leek] m. (carnival) sledging cavalcade; curlew jack; whimbrel (bird)
kuligowy [koo-lee-**go**-vi] adj.m. of sledging cavalcade
kulik [**koo**-leek] m. curlew jack; whimbrel
kulinarnie [koo-lee-**nahr**-ńe] adv. in respect of cooking; in respect of cuisine
kulinarny [koo-lee-**nahr**-ni] adj.m. culinary; of cooking; of cookery; cooking (ability, etc.); gastronomical
sztuka kulinarna [**shtoo**-kah koo-lee-**nahr**-nah] exp.: gastronomy; art of cooking
kulis [**koo**-lees] m. coolie; cooly
kulisa [koo-**lee**-sah] f. stage decoration
kulisy [koo-**lee**-si] pl. stage decorations; (theater) wings; scenes; slips; coulisses; the inner scenes
za kulisami [zah koo-lee-**sah**-mee]

exp.: behind the scenes
kulisowy [koo-lee-**so**-vi] adj.m. of theater decorations; of link (motion)
kulisto [koo-**lee**-sto] adv. spherically
kulistość [koo-**lee**-stośhćh] f. sphericity; roundness; globosity
kulisty [koo-**lees**-ti] adj.m. spherical; ball-shaped; round; globular; having the shape of a globe
kulisy [koo-**lee**-si] pl. theater scenes; the inner facts; links
za kulisami [zah koo-lee-**sah**-mee] exp.: behind the scenes
kulka [**kool**-kah] f. ball; globule; spherule; pellet; (gun, etc.) shot; ball (of a ball bearing); wooden hook
kulkować [kool-**ko**-vahćh] v. ping (metal); compress (metal); pin down vegetation (to prevent freezing) (*repeatedly*)
kulkowanie [kool-ko-**vah**-ńe] n. pinging (metal); pinning down vegetation
kulkowy [kool-**ko**-vi] adj.m. ball (valve, handle, tap, etc.)
pióro kulkowe [**pyoo**-ro kool-**ko**-ve] exp.: ball-point pen
łożysko kulkowe [wo-**zhis**-ko kool-**ko**-ve] exp.: ball bearing
kulkówka [kool-**koof**-kah] f. sphaerium (a bivalve)
kulm [koolm] m. culm
kulminacja [kool-mee-**nah**-tsyah] f. height; peak; climax; culmination; acme
kulminacyjny [kool-mee-nah-**tsiy**-ni] adj.m. culminant; final; climactic; of a turning point
punkt kulminacyjny [poonkt kool-mee-nah-**tsiy**-ni] exp.: climax
kulminować [kool-mee-**no**-vahćh] v. culminate; reach a climax (*repeatedly*)
kulminowanie [kool-mee-no-**vah**-ńe] n. culmination
kulnąć [**kool**-nownćh] v. roll; slang: pay; bankroll (mob jargon)
kulnąć się [**koo**-nownćh śhan] v. roll
kulnięcie [kool-**ńan**-ćhe] n. rolling
kulnięcie się [kool-**ńan**-ćhe śhan] n. rolling oneself
kulnik [**kool**-ńeek] m. globe daisy
kulnikowaty [kool-ńee-ko-**vah**-ti] adj.m. globulariaceous; of a globe daisy
kulnikowate [kool-ńee-ko-**vah**-te] pl. the Globulariaceae family of flowers
kulochwyt [koo-**lo**-khfit] m. butt; protective earth-embankment against artillery fire
kulomb [**koo**-lomp] m. coulomb
kulombometr [koo-lom-**bo**-metr] m. coulomb meter; coulometer
kulombomierz [koo-lom-**bo**-myesh] m. coulomb meter; coulometer
kulometr [koo-**lo**-metr] m. coulomb meter; coulometer
kulometryczny [koo-lo-met-**rich**-ni] adj.m. of coulomb meter; of coulo-meter
kulomiot [koo-**lo**-myot] m. colloq: machine gun
kulon [**koo**-lon] m. stone curlew; stone plover; large curlew (bird)
kuloodporny [koo-lo-ot-**por**-ni] adj.m. bulletproof (vest, etc.)
kulowy [koo-**lo**-vi] adj.m. of a ball; of a bullet
kruszarka kulowa [kroo-**shahr**-kah koo-**lo**-vah] exp.: gyrosphere crusher
młyn kulowy [mwin koo-**lo**-vi] exp.: grinder; ball mill; preliminary grinder
kulsza [**kool**-shah] f. ischial bone
kulszowy [kool-**sho**-vi] adj.m. sciatic (nerve, artery)
kult [koolt] m. cult; worship; devotion
kult jednostki [koolt yed-**nost**-kee] exp.: personality cult
kultowy [kool-**to**-vi] adj.m. of a cult; of a rite; ritualistic
kultura [kool-**too**-rah] f. culture; good manners; cultivation; high standard of excellence; breeding
kulturalnie [kool-too-**rahl**-ńe] adv. culturally; in gentlemanly fashion; in respect of culture; in mannerly fashion
kulturalny [kool-too-**rahl**-ni] adj.m. cultural; educated; mannerly; well-mannered; culture (stage, center, etc.)

kulturotwórczy [kool-too-ro-**tfoor**-chi] adj.m. culture-generating
kulturowo [kool-too-**ro**-vo] adv. culturally; in respect of culture
kulturowy [kool-too-**ro**-vi] adj.m. cultural; educated; mannerly; well-mannered; culture (stage, center, etc.)
kulturoznawczy [kool-too-ro-**znahf**-chi] adj.m. of cultural anthropology
kulturoznawstwo [kool-too-ro-**znahf**-stfo] n. cultural anthropology
kulturysta [kool-too-**ris**-tah] m. culturist
kulturystka [kool-too-**rist**-kah] f. (female) culturist
kulturystyczny [kool-too-ris-**tich**-ni] adj.m. of physical culture
kulturystyka [kool-too-**ris**-ti-kah] f. physical culture
kultysta [kool-**tis**-tah] m. cultist
kultywacja [kool-ti-**vahts**-yah] f. cultivation
kultywacyjny [kool-ti-vah-**tsiy**-ni] adj.m. of cultivation
kultywator [kool-ti-**vah**-tor] m. cultivator
kultywatorować [kool-ti-vah-to-**ro**-vahćh] v. cultivate the soil with a cultivator (*repeatedly*)
kultywatorowanie [kool-ti-vah-to-ro-**vah**-ńe] n. cultivation of the soil
kultywować [kool-ti-**vo**-vahćh] v. cultivate; improve; develop (knowledge, etc.) (*repeatedly*)
kultywowanie [kool-ti-vo-**vah**-ńe] n. cultivation (of knowledge, etc.)
kultyzm [**kool**-tizm] m. cultism
kuluar [koo-**loo**-ahr] m. lobby; colloq: lobbying
kuluary [koo-loo-**ah**-ri] pl. lobbies
kuluarowy [koo-loo-ah-**ro**-vi] adj.m. of a lobby
rozmowy kuluarowe [roz-**mo**-vi koo-loo-ah-**ro**-ve] exp.: lobbying
kułacki [koo-**wahts**-kee] adj.m. kulak's; kulaks'
kułactwo [koo-**wahts**-tfo] n. the kulaks
kułaczka [koo-**wahch**-kah] f. kulak's wife; well-to-do peasant woman
kułak [**koo**-wahk] m. fist; punch; kulak; well-to-do peasant; slang: lawbreaker (in business deals)
kułan [**koo**-wahn] m. Asiatic wild pony; Equus hemionus
kum [koom] m. godfather; crony
kum, kum [koom koom] exp.: croak, croak (the sound of frogs)
kuma [**koo**-mah] f. fellow sponsor; godmother (in relation to the godfather); colloq: friend; neighbor; crony; mob slang: agreement; prison slang
kumać się [**koo**-mahćh śhan] v. colloq: hobnob (with); be friends (with); be cronies; be on friendly terms; slang: make friends; use prison slang; know how; hear (mob jargon) (*repeatedly*)
kumak [**koo**-mahk] m. toad (of the family Discoglossidae)
kumanie się [koo-**mah**-ńe śhan] n. friendly terms; friendship; fraternization
kumaryna [koo-mah-**ri**-nah] f. coumarin
kumberland [koom-**ber**-lant] m. Cumberland meat sauce
kumcia [**koom**-ćhah] f. (nice) fellow sponsor; godmother (in relation to the godfather); colloq: friend; neighbor; crony
kumka [**koom**-kah] f. toad (of the family Discoglossidae); slang: prison watchtower (mob jargon)
kumkać [**koom**-kahćh] v. croak; slang: sing (*repeatedly*)
kumkanie [koom-**kah**-ńe] n. croak
kumostwo [koo-**most**-fo] n. relationship as between fellow sponsors; fellow sponsors; close friendship
kumoszka [koo-**mosh**-kah] f. busybody; an officious and inquisitive person; gossip
kumoszkowaty [koo-mosh-ko-**vah**-ti] adj.m. gossipy
kumoter [koo-**mo**-ter] m. member of a clique; logroller; confederate; colloq: godfather; crony
kumoterski [koo-mo-**ter**-skee] adj.m. logrolling; of a clique
kumoterstwo [koo-mo-**ters**-tfo] n. favoritism; logrolling
uprawiać kumoterstwo [oo-**prah**-vyahćh koo-mo-**ters**-tfo] exp.: to

have favorites
kumpel [**koom**-pel] m. colloq: pal; chum; mate; buddy; slang: friend
kumpelka [koom-**pel**-kah] f. (female) pal; chum; mate; buddy
kumpelski [koom-**pel**-skee] adj.m. of a pal; of a mate; of a buddy
kumplostwo [koomp-**los**-tfo] n. friendship; camaraderie
kumplować się [koomp-**lo**-vahćh śhan] v. slang: make friends (mob jargon) (*repeatedly*)
kumplowski [koomp-**lof**-skee] adj.m. of a pal; of a mate; of a buddy
po kumplowsku [po koomp-**lof**-skoo] exp.: like a pal; like a mate; like a buddy; in a friendly manner
kumulacja [koo-moo-**lahts**-yah] f. accumulation; merger; fusion
kumulacyjny [koo-moo-lah-**tsiy**-ni] adj.m. (ac)cumulative; accrued
podatek kumulacyjny [po-**dah**-tek koo-moo-lah-**tsiy**-ni] exp.: accumulated tax
kumulatywnie [koo-moo-lah-**tiv**-ńe] adv. cumulatively
kumulatywny [koo-moo-lah-**tiv**-ni] adj.m. cumulative; accrued
kumulen [koo-**moo**-len] m. an unstable compound of carbon
kumuleny [koo-moo-**le**-ni] pl. unstable compounds of carbon
kumulować [koo-moo-**lo**-vahćh] v. accumulate; merge; fuse (*repeatedly*)
kumulować się [koo-moo-**lo**-vahćh śhan] v. accumulate; merge (*repeatedly*)
kumulowanie [koo-moo-lo-**vah**-ńe] n. cumulation; accumulation
kumys [**koo**-mis] m. koumiss; kumiss; mare's milk
kumysowy [koo-mi-**so**-vi] adj.m. of koumiss; of kumiss; of mare's milk
kuna [**koo**-nah] f. marten; holdfast; an instrument of torture; slang: prostitute (mob jargon)
kuny [**koo**-ni] pl. martens; the family Mustelidae; the mustelids; martens (fur)
kundel [**koon**-del] m. mongrel; cur; colloq: tyke; cur
kundelek [koon-**de**-lek] m. (small) mongrel; cur
kundlowatość [koond-lo-**vah**-tośhćh] f. mongreldom; mongrelity; mongrelism; mongrelness
kundlowaty [koond-lo-**vah**-ti] adj.m. like a mongrel; mongrelly; mongrelish
kundys [**koon**-dis] m. mongrel; cur; colloq: tyke; cur
kung-fu [koonk-**foo**] n. kung fu; Chinese art of self-defense; slang: gangland brawl; assault and battery (mob jargon)
kuni [**koo**-ńee] adj.m. marten's; martens'; marten (cat, fur, etc.)
kunktator [koonk-**tah**-tor] m. cunctator; procrastinator
kunktatorski [koonk-tah-**tor**-skee] adj.m. cunctative; procrastinative; delaying; dilatory
kunktatorstwo [koonk-tah-**tor**-stfo] n. procrastination; delay; cunctatorship; dilatoriness
kunowaty [koo-no-**vah**-ti] adj.m. musteline
kunowate [koo-no-**vah**-te] pl. the family Mustelidae
kunszt [koonsht] m. art; skill; artistry; masterly skill; craft
kunsztownie [koon-**shtov**-ńe] adv. artistically; artfully; ingeniously; with masterly skill; minutely; skillfully; with minute precision
kunsztowność [koon-**shtov**-nośhćh] f. artistry; masterly skill; ingenuity
kunsztowny [koon-**shtov**-ni] adj.m. artistic; artful; ingenious; skillful; minute
kupa [**koo**-pah] f. heap; pile; huddle; assemblage; collection; crowd; throng; mob; bunch; gang; set; pack (of thieves, fools, etc.); a lot; excrement; colloq: a lot; lots; skits; oodles (of money); tons (of gold, etc.); vulg.: turd; shit; crap; dung
do kupy [do **koo**-pi] exp.: together
kupami [koo-**pah**-mee] exp.: in heaps; piled up
kupą [**koo**-pown] exp.: all together; as a crowd; in a pack;

in a gang; in large number
na kupę [nah **koo**-pan] exp.: (put) on a heap; (make) a pileup
na kupie [nah **koo**-pye] exp.: heaped up; piled up; huddled together
w kupie [f **koo**-pye] exp.: in a heap; in a pile; piled up; huddled together; together
wziąć się do kupy [vźhownćh śhan do **koo**-pi] exp.: to shake oneself together; to pull oneself together
zwalić na kupę [**zvah**-leećh nah **koo**-pan] exp.: to heap; to pile; to pile up
kupal [**koo**-pahl] m. rolled bimetal of aluminum and copper
kupalnik [koo-**pahl**-ńeek] m. arnica (herb, tincture, liniment, etc.)
kupalny [koo-**pahl**-ni] adj.m. of Midsummer Eve
kupała [koo-**pah**-wah] f. Ukrainian festivities with bonfires on St. John's Eve
kupaż [**koo**-pahsh] m. upgrading beverages by mixing
kupażować [koo-pah-**zho**-vahćh] v. upgrade beverages by mixing (*repeatedly*)
kupażowanie [koo-pah-zho-**vah**-ńe] n. upgrading beverages by mixing
kupcowa [koop-**tso**-vah] f. shopkeeper; shopkeeper's wife
kupczenie [koop-**che**-ńe] n. bargaining; trading; colloq: influence peddling
kupczyć [**koop**-chićh] v. bargain; trade; peddle influence; traffic (in one's influence) (*repeatedly*)
kupczyk [**koop**-chik] m. (small-time) trader; peddler; slang: shoplifter
kupeczka [koo-**pech**-kah] f. (very small) heap; pile
kupela [koo-**pe**-lah] f. cupellation furnace
kupelacja [koo-pe-**lahts**-yah] f. cupellation
kupelacyjny [koo-pe-lah-**tsiy**-ni] adj.m. cupellation (analysis, etc.)
kupelka [koo-**pel**-kah] f. (small) cupellation furnace
kupelować [koo-pe-**lo**-vahćh] v. refine by means of cupellation; cupel; assay; test (*repeatedly*)
kupelowanie [koo-pe-lo-**vah**-ńe] n. cupellation
kupelowy [koo-pe-**lo**-vi] adj.m. cupellation (process, etc.)
kuper [**koo**-per] m. rump; colloq: backside; bottom; behind
kaczy kuper [**kah**-chi **koo**-per] exp.: duck's rump; duck's rear end; duck's bottom; duck's behind
strzelać jak w kaczy kuper [**stshe**-lahćh yahk f **kah**-chi **koo**-per] exp.: to shoot point-blank
zebrać kuper a garść [**zeb**-rahćh **koo**-per v gahrśhćh] exp.: vulg.: to beat it; to be off; to take oneself away
kuperek [koo-**pe**-rek] m. (small) rump
kupić [**koo**-peećh] v. buy; purchase; draw (a card)
dobrze kupić [**dob**-zhe **koo**-peećh] exp.: to get one's money's worth; to get good value for one's money; to make a bargain
Kupido [koo-**pee**-do] m. Cupid
Kupidyn [koo-**pee**-din] m. Cupid
Kupidynek [koo-pee-**di**-nek] m. (small, nice) Cupid
kupiec [**koo**-pyets] m. storekeeper; shopkeeper; merchant; dealer; businessman; buyer; prospective buyer
kupcy [**koop**-tsi] pl. shopkeepers; merchants; tradespeople
kupiecki [koo-**pyets**-kee] adj.m. shopkeeper's; trader's; storekeeper's; merchant's; dealer's; businessman's; shopkeepers'
po kupiecku [po koo-**pyets**-koo] exp.: commercially; like a merchant
kupiecko [koo-**pyets**-ko] adv. commercially
kupiectwo [koo-**pyets**-tfo] n. business; commerce; trade
kupienie [koo-**pye**-ńe] n. purchase
kupka [**koop**-kah] f. (small) heap; pile; huddle; group; cluster; knot (of people, etc.)
kupki [**koop**-kee] pl. sori (of fern)

kupkowo [koop-**ko**-vo] adv. (seed, etc.) by means of little clusters
kupkowy [koop-**ko**-vi] adj.m. (seeding, etc.) in little clusters
kupkówka [koop-**koof**-kah] f. orchard grass; cocksfoot
kupla [**koop**-lah] f. emblem of a miner's guild (hammer and pick)
kuplecik [koo-**ple**-ćheek] m. (nice, little) couplet; verse; cabaret song
kuplecista [koo-ple-**ćhees**-tah] m. singer (of couplets, cabaret songs, music-hall songs, etc.)
kuplet [**koop**-let] m. music-hall song; couplet; verse; cabaret song
kupno [**koop**-no] n. purchase; (a) buy; buying
akt kupna [ahkt **koop**-nah] exp.: purchase deed
cena kupna [**tse**-nah **koop**-nah] exp.: purchase price
dobre kupno [**dob**-re **koop**-no] exp.: bargain; a good buy
siła kupna [**śhee**-wah **koop**-nah] exp.: purchasing power
kupny [**koop**-ni] adj.m. bought; purchased; ready-made; venal; corrupt; purchasing (power, etc.)
kupolak [koo-**po**-lahk] m. cupola (-furnace)
kupon [**koo**-pon] m. coupon; detachable part of a ticket; length of cloth; dividend coupon
kuponik [koo-**po**-ńeek] m. (small, nice) coupon
kuponowy [koo-po-**no**-vi] adj.m. coupon's
kupować [koo-**po**-vahćh] v. buy; purchase; make purchases; do one's shopping; draw (a card) (*repeatedly*)
kupowanie [koo-po-**vah**-ńe] n. purchase; making purchases
kupror [**koop**-ror] m. copper-aluminum alloy; American gold
kuprowy [koop-**ro**-vi] adj.m. of a rump
gruczoł kuprowy [**groo**-chow koop-**ro**-vi] exp.: oil gland
kuprówka [koop-**roof**-kah] f. brown-tail moth
kupryt [**koop**-rit] m. cuprite; red copper ore; ruby copper
kuprytowy [koop-ri-**to**-vi] adj.m. of cuprite; of red copper ore; of ruby copper
kupujący [koo-poo-**yown**-tsi] adj.m. buying; purchasing; m. customer; purchaser; shopper; buyer
kur [koor] m. cock; cockcrow(ing); bullhead; miller's thumb; sculpin (fish); roseola; German measles
czerwony kur [cher-**vo**-ni koor] exp.: fire; conflagration
kura [**koo**-rah] f. hen; hen bird; fowl dish; chicken
jak zmokła kura [yahk **zmok**-wah **koo**-rah] exp.: like a drowned rat
kura karłowata [**koo**-rah kahr-wo-**vah**-tah] exp.: bantam
kuracja [koo-**rah**-tsyah] f. cure; treatment; diet
poddać się kuracji [**pod**-dahćh śhan koo-**rah**-tsyee] exp.: to undergo treatment
kuracjusz [koo-**rah**-tsyoosh] m. patient; visitor at a health resort; bather at a spa
kuracjuszka [koo-rah-**tsyoosh**-kah] f. (female) patient
kuracyjny [koo-rah-**tsiy**-ni] adj.m. curative; therapeutic
kurak [**koo**-rahk] m. cock; chicken; gallinacean; gallinaceous bird
kuraki [koo-**rah**-kee] pl. the Galliformes
kurancik [koo-**rahn**-ćheek] m. (small, nice) carillon chime; peal of bells
kurant [**koo**-rahnt] m. carillon chime; peal of bells
kurantowy [koo-rahn-**to**-vi] adj.m. chiming (clock, etc.)
kurara [koo-**rah**-rah] f. curare
kurarowy [koo-rah-**ro**-vi] adj.m. of curare
kuraryna [koo-rah-**ri**-nah] f. curarine
kuraryzacja [koo-rah-ri-**zahts**-yah] f. curarization
kuraryzować [koo-rah-ri-**zo**-vahćh] v. curarize (*repeatedly*)
kuraryzowanie [koo-rah-ri-zo-**vah**-ńe] n. curarization
kuratela [koo-rah-**te**-lah] f. wardship; guardianship; tutelage
kurator [koo-**rah**-tor] m. school superintendent; guardian; curator; keeper; trustee

kuratorium [koo-rah-**tor**-yoom] n. board of trustees (of schools); school superintendent's office
kuratorka [koo-rah-**tor**-kah] f. (female) school superintendent; guardian; curator; keeper; trustee
kuratorski [koo-rah-**tor**-skee] adj.m. of school board of trustees; of school superintendent's office
kuratorstwo [koo-rah-**tor**-stfo] n. board of trustees (of schools); trusteeship; school superintendence; guardianship
kuratoryjny [koo-rah-to-**riy**-ni] adj.m. of school board of trustees; of a school superintendent
kuraż [**koo**-rahsh] m. colloq: courage
dla kurażu [dlah koo-**rah**-zhoo] exp.: to summon up courage
kurbel [**koor**-bel] m. crank; winch
kurbet [**koor**-bet] m. curvet; colloq: (respectful) bow
kurcz [koorch] m. cramp; shrinking; twitching; colloq: crossbreed; mongrel; monstrosity; eyesore
dostać kurczu [**dos**-tahćh **koor**-choo] exp.: to be seized with cramp
kurczak [**koor**-chahk] m. chicken
kurczatow [koor-**chah**-tof] m. Kurchatov (atomic number 104)
kurcząco [koor-**chown**-tso] adv. shrinkingly
kurczątko [koor-**chownt**-ko] n. chick; mob slang: young whore
kurczenie [koor-**che**-ńe] n. contraction; retraction; shrinking
kurczenie się [koor-**che**-ńe śhan] n. shrinking; growing smaller; diminution
kurczę [**koor**-chan] n. chicken; chick
kurczęcy [koor-**chan**-tsi] adj.m. chicken's; chick's
kurczliwie [koorch-**lee**-vye] adv. by causing contraction; by causing retraction
działać kurczliwie [**dźhah**-wahćh koorch-**lee**-vye] exp.: to cause contraction; to cause retraction
kurczliwość [koorch-**lee**-vośhćh] f. contractility; contractibility; retractability
kurczliwy [koorch-**lee**-vi] adj.m. contractile; contractible; retractile; retractable
kurczowo [koor-**cho**-vo] adv. convulsively; spasmodically; tightly
kurczowy [koor-**cho**-vi] adj.m. convulsive; spasmodic; tonic (spasm)
kurczyć [**koor**-chićh] v. draw in; reduce; contract (muscles, etc.) colloq: lessen; diminish; reduce; shrink (*repeatedly*)
kurczyć się [**koor**-chićh śhan] v. contract; dwindle; lessen; run low; diminish; reduce one's size; shrink; retract (*repeatedly*)
Kurd [koort] m. Kurd
kurdesz [**koor**-desh] m. Turkish folk dance; drinking song
kurdiuczny [koor-**dyooch**-ni] adj.m. of a variety of Asiatic sheep (storing fat in the hind quarters)
kurdiuk [**koor**-dyook] m. fat of Asiatic sheep (stored in animal's hind quarters)
kurdupel [koor-**doo**-pel] m. vulg.: slang: pudge; squab; humpty-dumpty; runt; ass-high; shorty
kurduplowaty [koor-doop-lo-**vah**-ti] adj.m. vulg.: slang: (appearing) pudgy; squabby; humpty-dumpty; runty; ass-high; shorty
kurdyban [koor-**di**-bahn] m. cordovan
kurdybanek [koor-di-**bah**-nek] m. ground ivy
kurdybanowy [koor-di-bah-**no**-vi] adj.m. cordovan (leather, etc.)
kurdyjski [koor-**diy**-skee] adj.m. Kurdish
kureczka [koo-**rech**-kah] f. small hen; water hen
kurek [**koo**-rek] m. tap; (gun) cock; faucet; spigot; sea robin; weather vane
odwodzić kurek [od-**vo**-dźheećh **koo**-rek] exp.: to cock a gun
kurenda [koo-**ren**-dah] f. circular
kureniowy [koo-re-**ńo**-vi] adj.m. of Cossack camp; of a stanitsa; of a Cossack unit; of an Ukrainian partisan unit
kureń [**koo**-reń] m. Cossack camp; stanitsa; Cossack unit; Ukrainian

partisan unit
kurewka [koo-**ref**-kah] f. colloq: (little) harlot; prostitute; whore
kurewski [koo-**ref**-skee] adj.m. vulg.: of a harlot; of a prostitute; whorish; bitchy; excl.: bloody!; goddamned!
kurewstwo [koo-**ref**-stfo] n. vulg.: harlots; prostitutes; whores; prostitution; bitchiness; bitchery
kurhan [**koor**-khahn] m. grave-mound; barrow; tumulus
kurhanek [koor-**khah**-nek] m. (small) grave-mound; barrow; tumulus
kurhanowy [koor-khah-**no**-vi] adj.m. of a grave-mound; of a barrow; of a tumulus
kuria [**koor**-yah] f. curia; electoral group
kurialny [koor-**yahl**-ni] adj.m. curial
kurier [**koor**-yer] m. courier; messenger; dispatch-rider; (daily) newspaper
kuriery [koor-**ye**-ri] pl. daily; express train; mail (coach)
kurierzy [koor-**ye**-zhi] pl. couriers; messengers; dispatch-riders
kurierka [koor-**yer**-kah] f. (female) courier; messenger
kurierski [koor-**yer**-skee] adj.m. courier's; messenger's; of an express train; of a mail (coach)
kuriozum [koor-**yo**-zoom] n. oddity; monstrosity
kurka [**koor**-kah] f. small hen; hen bird
kurka wodna [**koor**-kah **vod**-nah] exp.: gallinule; water hen; moorhen; an edible fungus
kurkowy [koor-**ko**-vi] adj.m. of a water hen
bractwo kurkowe [**brahts**-tfo koor-**ko**-ve] exp.: rifle club
król kurkowy [krool koor-**ko**-vi] exp.: champion shot; president of the rifle club
kurkówka [koor-**koof**-kah] f. hand-cocked (old style) gun
kurkuma [koor-**koo**-mah] f. curcuma; turmeric (plant)
kurkumina [koor-koo-**mee**-nah] f. curcuma (dye)
kurkumowy [koor-koo-**mo**-vi] adj.m. curcuma (paper, etc.); turmeric (paper, etc.)
kurniawa [koor-**ńah**-vah] f. snowstorm; blizzard
kurniczek [koor-**ńee**-chek] m. (small) chicken house; henhouse; hen roost; poultry house; hen cote
kurnik [**koor**-ńeek] m. chicken house; henhouse; hen roost; poultry house; hen cote
kurnosy [koor-**no**-si] adj.m. having a short snub nose; snub-nosed
kurny [**koor**-ni] adj.m. without a chimney
kurna chata [**koor**-nah **khah**-tah] exp.: cabin without chimney; cabin with a hole in the roof for the smoke
kuropatewka [koo-ro-pah-**tef**-kah] f. (young, small) partridge
kuropatwa [koo-ro-**paht**-fah] f. partridge (game bird)
kuropatwi [koo-ro-**paht**-fee] adj.m. partridge's; of a partridge; of partridges
stado kuropatw [**stah**-do koo-**ro**-pahtf] exp.: covey (of partridges)
kuropatwiarz [koo-ro-**paht**-fyahsh] m. pointer dog; setter dog; partridge dog
kurort [**koo**-rort] m. health resort; spa; watering place
kuros [**koo**-ros] m. Greek sculpture of a nude young man (used on graves)
kuroślep [koo-**ro**-śhlep] m. hen-blindness; nyctalopia
kurować [koo-**ro**-vahćh] v. heal; cure; treat for an illness (*repeatedly*)
kurować się [koo-ro-vahćh śhan] v. heal oneself; take a cure; undergo treatment (for an illness) (*repeatedly*)
kurowanie [koo-ro-**vah**-ńe] n. treatment; cure
kurowanie się [koo-ro-**vah**-ńe śhan] n. treating oneself; curing oneself
Kurp [koorp] m. Kurp; inhabitant of the Kurpie province (North-East of Warsaw)
Kurpie [**koor**-pye] pl. the Kurps; Kurpie district (North-East of Warsaw); moccasin of tree bark; a regional dance

kurpiowski [koor-**pyof**-skee] adj.m. of the Kurpie area (North-East of Warsaw)
kurs [koors] m. drive; run; course (of study, etc.); class; rate (of exchange, etc.); market price (of securities); fare; policy; tack; course of action; line of conduct; circulation
ostry kurs [**os**-tri koors] exp.: stringent policy; stringent course of procedure
zmienić kurs [**zmye**-ńeećh koors] exp.: to change (ship's, etc.) course; to tack about; to put about
kursant [**koor**-sahnt] m. student
kursantka [koor-**sahnt**-kah] f. (female) student
kursista [koor-**śhees**-tah] m. student
kursistka [koor-**śheest**-kah] f. (female) student
kurs-konferencja [koors kon-fe-**ren**-tsyah] exp.: teaching conference; symposium
kursograf [koor-**so**-grahf] m. device for automatic plotting of ship's course
kursomierz [koor-**so**-myesh] m. device for automatic measuring of airplane's speed with respect to the ground
kursoryczny [koor-so-**rich**-ni] adj.m. fluent; running (commentary, etc.)
kursować [koor-**so**-vahćh] v. circulate; ferry; run; ply; be in circulation; be legal tender; colloq: be abroad; be about; be afloat; be current; pass from mouth to mouth (*repeatedly*)
kursowanie [koor-so-**vah**-ńe] n. circulation
kursowy [koor-**so**-vi] adj.m. course (protractor, etc.); of fluctuation (of prices, etc.); of the rate of exchange
kursywa [koor-**si**-vah] f. italic (font); running hand; flowing hand (writing)
wydrukować wyraz kursywą [vi-droo-**ko**-vahćh **vi**-rahs koor-**si**-vown] exp.: to italicize a word
kursywny [koor-**siv**-ni] adj.m. cursive; running; flowing
kurta [**koor**-tah] f. jacket
kurtaczek [koor-**tah**-chek] m. pitta; ground thrush (bird)
kurtaczki [koor-**tahch**-kee] pl. the Pittidae family of birds
kurtaż [**koor**-tahsh] m. brokerage
kurteczka [koor-**tech**-kah] f. jacket
kurtka [**koort**-kah] f. jacket; short overcoat; stout jacket; reefer
kurtuazja [koor-too-**ah**-zyah] f. courtesy; civility
brak kurtuazji [brahk koor-too-**ahz**-yee] exp.: lack of politeness; lack of courtesy; impoliteness
kurtuazyjnie [koor-too-ah-**ziy**-ńe] adv. courteously
kurtuazyjny [koor-too-ah-**ziy**-ni] adj.m. courteous
kurtyna [koor-**ti**-nah] f. curtain
żelazna kurtyna [zhe-**lahz**-nah koor-**ti**-nah] exp.: iron curtain; fireproof curtain
kurtyzacja [koor-ti-**zah**-tsyah] f. docking (a horse, a dog, etc.)
kurtyzana [koor-ti-**zah**-nah] f. courtesan
kurtyzować [koor-ti-**zo**-vahćh] v. dock (a horse, a dog, etc.) (*repeatedly*)
kurtyzowanie [koor-ti-zo-**vah**-ńe] n. docking (a horse, a dog, etc.)
kurulny [koo-**rool**-ni] adj.m. curule (chair, etc.)
kurwa [**koor**-vah] f. whore (vulg.); prostitute
kurwiarz [**koor**-vyahsh] m. john; prostitute's client
kurwić się [**koor**-veećh śhan] v. vulg.: to walk the streets; prostitute; whore (*repeatedly*)
kurwisko [koor-**vees**-ko] n. vulg.: (clumsy, big) prostitute; bitch
kurwiszcze [koor-**veesh**-che] n. vulg.: (clumsy, big) prostitute; bitch
kurwiszon [koor-**vee**-shon] m. vulg.: (clumsy, big) prostitute; bitch
kurz [koosh] m. dust
pokryty kurzem [po-**kri**-ti **koo**-zhem] exp.: dusty
tumany kurzu [too-**mah**-ni **koo**-zhoo] exp.: clouds of dust
kurza ślepota [**koo**-

zhah śhle-**po**-tah] exp.: colloq: night blindness
kurzajka [koo-**zhahy**-kah] f. wart
kurzawa [koo-**zhah**-vah] f. whirling cloud of dust; swirl of dust; snowstorm
kurzawka [koo-**zhahf**-kah] f. sandstorm; quicksand; sandwater; driftsand
kurzenie [koo-**zhe**-ńe] n. raising clouds of dust; colloq: smoking; puffing away (cigarette; pipe)
kurzenie się [koo-**zhe**-ńe śhan] n. making dust
kurzeniowy [koo-zhe-**ńo**-vi] adj.m. of a Cossack camp; of stanitsa; of a Cossack unit; of a Ukrainian querrilla unit
kurzeń [**koo**-zheń] m. Cossack camp; stanitsa; Cossack unit; Ukrainian querrilla unit
kurzowiec [koo-**zho**-vyets] m. dustcoat
kurzy [**koo**-zhi] adj.m. hen's; hens'; fowls'
kurza ślepota [**koo**-zhah śhle-**po**-tah] exp.: night blindness
kurzyć [**koo**-zhićh] v. raise clouds of dust; smoke; puff away (cigarette, pipe) (*repeatedly*)
kurzyć się [**koo**-zhićh śhan] v. be enveloped in clouds of dust; smoke; reek (*repeatedly*)
kurzyślad [koo-**zhi**-śhlaht] m. pimpernel (plant)
kurzywo [koo-**zhi**-vo] n. bee smoking flame (no open fire)
kusak [**koo**-sahk] m. rove beetle
kusaki [koo-**sah**-kee] pl. the family of rove beetles; the Tinamiformes (birds)
kusiciel [koo-**śhee**-ćhel] m. seducer; tempter
kusicielka [koo-śhee-**ćhel**-kah] f. (female) seducer; temptress; siren; Jezebel
kusicielski [koo-śhee-**ćhel**-skee] adj.m. tempting; seducing; enticing
kusicielsko [koo-śhee-**ćhel**-sko] adv. seductively; enticingly; invitingly
kusić [**koo**-śheećh] v. tempt; lure; entice; seduce; attract (*repeatedly*)
kusić się [**koo**-śheećh śhan] v. attempt (to do); try one's hand (at) (*repeatedly*)
kusiutki [koo-**śhoot**-kee] adj.m. (very) short; scanty; skimpy; meager
kuskuta [koos-**koo**-tah] f. winnower; winnowing machine (for selection of seed); fan
kuso [**koo**-so] adv. too short; scantily; colloq: bad; badly; ill; lamentably
kustoda [koos-**to**-dah] f. printer's old style guide marks
kustodia [koos-**to**-dyah] f. custodia; guardianship; custodial
kustosz [**koos**-tosh] m. curator; keeper; conservator; guardian
kustoszostwo [koos-to-**sho**-stfo] n. office of a curator; guardianship
kustrzebka [koos-**tshep**-kah] f. an order of fungi
kusy [**koo**-si] adj.m. short; scanty; skimpy; meager; colloq: bob-tailed
kusza [**koo**-shah] f. crossbow; arbalest; ballista
kusząco [koo-**shown**-tso] adv. seductively; invitingly; enticingly
kuszący [koo-**shown**-tsi] adj.m. tempting; seductive; inviting; enticing; luring
kuszenie [koo-**she**-ńe] n. temptation(s)
kuszetka [koo-**shet**-kah] f. sleeping compartment; love seat
kuszetkowy [koo-shet-**ko**-vi] adj.m. of a sleeping compartment; of a love seat
kusznik [**koosh**-ńeek] m. crossbowman
kusztyk, kusztyk [**koosh**-tik **koosh**-tik] exp.: dot and go one
kusztykać [koosh-**ti**-kahćh] v. hobble (along); limp; dot and go one (*repeatedly*)
kusztykanie [koosh-ti-**kah**-ńe] n. hobbling (along); limping
kuśnierka [koośh-**ńer**-kah] f. (female) furrier; fur dealer
kuśnierski [koośh-**ńer**-skee] adj.m. furrier's
kuśnierstwo [koośh-**ńer**-stfo] n. furriery; furrier's trade

kuśnierz [**kooŝh**-ńesh] m. furrier; fur dealer
kuśtyk, kuśtyk [**kooŝh**-tik **kooŝh**-tik] exp.: dot and go one
kuśtykać [kooŝh-**ti**-kahćh] v. hobble (along); limp; dot and go one (*repeatedly*)
kuśtykanie [kooŝh-ti-**kah**-ńe] n. hobbling (along); limping
kutas [**koo**-tahs] m. tassel; vulg.: penis; prick; cock
kutasek [koo-**tah**-sek] m. small tassel
kutasik [koo-**tah**-ŝheek] m. small tassel
kuter [**koo**-ter] m. fishing boat; smack; fish cutter; one mast sailboat; (meat) cutter
kuter ratowniczy [**koo**-ter rah-tov-**ńee**-chi] exp.: rescue cruiser; rescue boat
kuternoga [koo-ter-**no**-gah] f. & m. slang: lame-leg (mob jargon)
kutia [**koo**-tyah] f. a festive Ukrainian Christmas dish (of wheat, poppy seeds, honey, raisins, etc.)
kutikula [koo-tee-**koo**-lah] f. cuticle
kutner [**koot**-ner] m. tomentum; nap (of cloth); fluff (of cloth)
kutnerować [koot-ne-**ro**-vahćh] v. nap (cloth) (*repeatedly*)
kutnerowanie [koot-ne-ro-**vah**-ńe] n. napping (cloth)
kutnerowatość [koot-ne-ro-**vah**-toŝhćh] f. having a fluffy nap
kutnerowaty [koot-ne-ro-**vah**-ti] adj.m. tomantose; tomantous
kutrowy [koot-**ro**-vi] adj.m. of a fishing boat; of a smack; of a fish cutter
kutwa [**koot**-fah] m. & f. miser; hanks; niggard; skinflint; screw
kuty [**koo**-ti] adj.m. forged; shod; colloq: cunning; sly; shrewd; slang: tattooed (mob jargon)
kutykula [koo-ti-**koo**-lah] f. cuticle
kutyna [koo-**ti**-nah] f. cutin
kutynizacja [koo-ti-ńee-**zah**-tsyah] f. cutinization
kuwertura [koo-ver-**too**-rah] f. chocolate cover on candies
kuweta [koo-**ve**-tah] f. flat container used for chemicals
kuziemny [koo-**źhem**-ni] adj.m. directed down (towards the ground)
kuzienny [koo-**źhen**-ni] adj.m. of a smithy; forge (hammer, works, etc.)
kuzyn [**koo**-zin] m. cousin
kuzyneczka [koo-zi-**nech**-kah] f. (nice, little) (female) cousin
kuzynek [koo-**zi**-nek] m. (nice, little) cousin
kuzynka [koo-**zin**-kah] f. (female) cousin
kuzynostwo [koo-zi-**no**-stfo] n. cousinhood; cousinship; cousinage; cousin and his wife; kinfolk; kinship
kuzynowski [koo-zi-**nof**-skee] adj.m. cousin's
kuźnia [**kooźh**-ńah] f. forge; smithy; blacksmith's shop; colloq: hot bed (of sedition, intrigue, etc.)
kuźniarka [kooźh-**ńahr**-kah] f. power hammer
kuźnica [kooźh-**ńee**-tsah] f. ironworks
kuźnictwo [kooźh-**ńeets**-tfo] n. smithcraft; smithing; forging
kuźniczo [kooźh-**ńee**-cho] adv. by means of forging
kuźniczy [kooźh-**ńee**-chi] adj.m. blacksmith's; malleable
młot kuźniczy [mwot kooźh-**ńee**-chi] exp.: forge hammer
piec kuźniczy [pyets kooźh-**ńee**-chi] exp.: forge furnace
kwa, kwa [kfah kfah] exp.: (duck call) quack, quack
kwacz [kfahch] m. mop; swab
kwadra [**kfahd**-rah] f. quarter moon; square
kwadracik [kfah-**drah**-ćheek] m. small square
kwadrans [**kfahd**-rahns] m. quarter of an hour; fifteen minutes
kwadransik [kfah-**drahn**-ŝheek] m. short fifteen minutes; some quarter of an hour
kwadransowy [kfah-drahn-**so**-vi] adj.m. of a quarter of an hour; a quarter-hour (ride, walk, etc.)
kwadrant [**kfahd**-rahnt] m. quadrant
kwadrantowy [kfahd-rahn-**to**-vi]

adj.m. quadrantal (electrometer, etc.)

kwadrat [kfahd-raht] m. square; square of a number; second power; unit of printer's measure

kwadratel [kfah-drah-tel] m. bevelled stove tile

kwadratnica [kfah-draht-ńee-tsah] f. drafting device for drawing squares

kwadratowo [kfah-drah-to-vo] adv. in a square; in squares

kwadratowy [kfah-drah-to-vi] adj.m. square

metr kwadratowy [metr kfah-drah-to-vi] exp.: one square meter

kwadratura [kfah-drah-too-rah] f. quadrature; squaring (of the circle)

kwadrofonia [kfah-droh-fo-ńyah] f. quadruple sound recording

kwadrupleks [kfah-droop-leks] m. simultaneous cable transmission in both directions; quadruplex

kwadryga [kfah-dri-gah] f. quadriga

kwadrygant [kfah-dri-gahnt] m. member of Quadriga group of poets in Warsaw (1926)

kwadrygowiec [kfah-dri-go-vyets] m. member of Quadriga group of poets in Warsaw (1926)

kwadrylion [kfah-dril-yon] m. quadrillion (10^{24})

kwadrywium [kfah-dri-vyoom] n. quadrivium

kwaga [kfah-gah] f. quagga

kwak [kfahk] m. quack (of a duck)

kwakać [kfah-kahćh] v. quack (*repeatedly*)

kwakanie [kfah-kah-ńe] n. quacks

kwakier [kfah-ker] m. Quaker

kwakierka [kfah-ker-kah] f. (female) Quaker

kwakierski [kfah-ker-skee] adj.m. Quaker's; Quakers'; Quaker (preaching, etc.)

kwakierstwo [kfah-ker-stfo] n. Quakers; Quakers' doctrine, etc.

kwakrowski [kfah-krof-skee] adj.m. Quaker's; Quakers'; Quaker (preaching, etc.)

kwaknąć [kfahk-nownćh] v. quack

kwaknięcie [kfahk-ńan-ćhe] n. (a) quack

kwalifikacja [kfah-lee-fee-kah-tsyah] f. qualification; evaluation; estimation; qualifications; competence (for)

kwalifikacje zawodowe [kfah-lee-fee-kah-tsye zah-vo-do-ve] exp.: professional qualification

kwalifikacyjny [kfah-lee-fee-kah-tsiy-ni] adj.m. qualifying (examination, etc.)

kwalifikator [kfah-lee-fee-kah-tor] m. qualifier

kwalifikować [kfah-lee-fee-ko-vahćh] v. qualify; class; appraise; describe; evaluate; estimate (*repeatedly*)

kwalifikować się [kfah-lee-fee-ko-vahćh śhan] v. be qualified (for); be fit (for); be suitable (for); be ripe (for) (*repeatedly*)

kwalifikowanie [kfah-lee-fee-ko-vah-ńe] n. classification; appraisal; description; qualification

kwalifikowanie się [kfah-lee-fee-ko-vah-ńe śhan] n. qualifications

kwalifikowany [kfah-lee-fee-ko-vah-ni] adj.m. qualified; prepared

kwalitatywnie [kfah-lee-tah-tiv-ńe] adv. qualitatively

kwalitatywny [kfah-lee-tah-tiv-ni] adj.m. qualitative

kwant [kfahnt] m. quantum

teoria kwantów [te-or-yah kfahn-toof] exp.: the quantum theory

kwantometr [kfahn-to-metr] m. automatic X-ray spectrograph for analysis of metals

kwantowanie [kfahn-to-vah-ńe] n. quantization

kwantowy [kfahn-to-vi] adj.m. quantum (jump, mechanics, number, etc.)

kwantum [kfahn-toom] n. quantum; quantity; amount; number; sum; bulk

kwantyfikacja [kfahn-ti-fee-kah-tsyah] f. quantification

kwantyfikacyjnie [kfahn-ti-fee-kah-tsiy-ńe] adv. quantificationally

kwantyfikacyjny [kfahn-ti-fee-kah-tsiy-ni] adj.m. quantificational

kwantyfikator [kfahn-ti-fee-kah-tor] m. quantifier

kwantytatywnie [kfahn-ti-tah-tiv-ńe]

adv. quantitatively
kwantytatywny [kfahn-ti-tah-**tiv**-ni] adj.m. quantitative
kwantyzacja [kfahn-ti-**zah**-tsyah] f. quantization; conversion from classical physics to quantum theory
kwapić się [**kfah**-peećh śhan] v. be eager (for); be in a hurry (*repeatedly*)
nie kwapić się [ńe **kfah**-peećh śhan] exp.: to be in no hurry (to do); to be slow in doing; to be backward in doing
kwapienie się [kfah-**pye**-ńe śhan] n. eagerness
kwarantanna [kfah-rahn-**tahn**-nah] f. quarantine; period of isolation
kwarantannowy [kfah-rahn-tahn-**no**-vi] adj.m. quarantine (period, flag, etc.)
kwarc [kfahrts] m. quartz (mineral)
kwarciany [kfahr-**ćhah**-ni] adj.m. of regular Polish army (paid for with the quarter tax)
kwarcowy [kfahr-**tso**-vi] adj.m. quartz (glass, lamp, etc.)
kwarcówka [kfahr-**tsoof**-kah] f. quartz lamp
kwarcyt [**kfahr**-tsit] m. quartzite
kwarcytowy [kfahr-tsi-**to**-vi] adj.m. quartzitic; quartzite (glass, etc.)
kwargiel [**kfahr**-gel] m. kind of home-made moldy cheese
kwark [kfahrk] m. quark
kwarta [**kfahr**-tah] f. quart
kwartalnie [kfahr-**tahl**-ńe] adv. quarterly; quarter-yearly
kwartalnik [kfahr-**tahl**-ńeek] m. (a) quarterly
kwartalny [kfahr-**tahl**-ni] adj.m. quarterly; occurring quarterly
kwartał [**kfahr**-tahw] m. term; quarter; three months
kwartant [**kfahr**-tahnt] m. oversized book
kwartecista [kfahr-te-**ćhees**-tah] m. member of a quartet
kwartet [**kfahr**-tet] m. quartet
kwartetowy [kfahr-te-**to**-vi] adj.m. quartet (performance, composition, etc.)
kwarto [**kfahr**-to] n. (printer's quarter size) quarto
kwartowy [kfahr-**to**-vi] adj.m. of (printer's) quarter size; quart (container, etc.)
kwartyna [kfahr-**ti**-nah] f. quadrain
kwas [kfahs] m. acid; acidity; sourness; leaven; fermenting dough
kwasy [**kfah**-si] pl. discord; bitterness; ill feelings; bad blood; sourness
kwasek [**kfah**-sek] m. slight acidity; slight sourness
kwasek cytrynowy [**kfah**-sek tsi-tri-**no**-vi] exp.: colloq: citric acid
kwasica [kfah-**śhee**-tsah] f. acidosis
kwasić [**kfah**-śheećh] v. subject to fermentation; sour (milk, etc.); leaven (dough, etc.); pickle (cucumber, cabbage, etc.); colloq: sour; embitter (*repeatedly*)
kwasić się [**kfah**-śheećh śhan] v. ferment; sour; pickle; become pickled; colloq: idle; become soured; become embittered (*repeatedly*)
kwasja [**kfahs**-yah] f. Quassia amara tree or shrub
kwaskowato [kfahs-ko-**vah**-to] adv. sourlishly
kwaskowatość [kfahs-ko-**vah**-tośhćh] f. acidity; acidulous content; acidulous taste
kwaskowaty [kfahs-ko-**vah**-ti] adj.m. acrid; sourlish; acidulous
kwaskowy [kfahs-**ko**-vi] adj.m. acidic
kwasochłonny [kfah-so-**khwon**-ni] adj.m. absorbing and neutralizing acids
kwasolubny [kfahs-so-**loob**-ni] adj.m. acidophilic
kwasomierz [kfah-**so**-myesh] m. acidimeter
kwasoodporność [kfah-so-ot-**por**-nośhćh] f. resistance to acids
kwasoodporny [kfah-so-ot-**por**-ni] adj.m. acid-resisting; acid-proof
kwasopłetwy [kfah-so-**pwet**-fi] adj.m. crossopterygian
kwasopłetwe [kfah-so-**pwet**-fe] pl. the Crossopoterygia (fishes); the crossopterygian division of fishes
kwasoród [kfah-**so**-root] m. oxygen
kwasoryt [kfah-**so**-rit] m. etching

made with aquafortis (nitric acid)
kwasorytnictwo [kfah-so-rit-ńeets-tfo] n. the art of etching with aquafortis
kwasota [kfah-**so**-tah] f. acidity
kwasotwórczy [kfah-so-**tfoor**-chi] adj.m. acid-forming
kwasowęglowy [kfah-so-vang-**lo**-vi] adj.m. carbonic-acid (bath, treatment, etc.)
kwasowęglówka [kfah-so-vang-**loof**-kah] f. carbonic-acid bath
kwasowochromowy [kfah-so-vo-khro-**mo**-vi] adj.m. of chromium-acid (dyes, etc.)
kwasowość [kfah-**so**-vośhćh] f. acidity
kwasowy [kfah-**so**-vi] adj.m. acid; acidic
kwasy [**kfah**-si] pl. fusses; bad blood; ill humor; dissent
kwaszarnia [kfah-**shahr**-ńah] f. (cabbage, cucumber) pickling plant
kwaszarnictwo [kfah-shahr-**ńeets**-tfo] n. pickling industry
kwaszeniak [kfah-**she**-ńahk] m. cucumber suitable for pickling
kwaszenie [kfah-**she**-ńe] n. fermentation; souring; acid wash
kwaszenie się [kfah-**she**-ńe śhan] n. getting fermented; getting sour; colloq: being idle; being embittered
kwaszonka [kfah-**shon**-kah] f. silage
kwaśnawo [kfahśh-**nah**-vo] adv. acridly
kwaśnawy [kfahśh-**nah**-vi] adj.m. acrid; acidulous; subacid
kwaśnica [kfahśh-**ńee**-tsah] f. barberry; berberry
kwaśnicowaty [kfahśh-ńee-tso-**vah**-ti] adj.m. like barberry
kwaśnicowate [kfahśh-ńee-tso-**vah**-te] pl. the barberry family
kwaśnieć [**kfahśh**-ńećh] v. ferment; pickle; sour; colloq: become embittered (*repeatedly*)
kwaśnienie [kfahśh-**ńe**-ńe] n. fermentation; pickling; colloq: becoming embittered
kwaśno [**kfahśh**-no] adv. sourly; acidly
pachnieć kwaśno [**pahkh**-ńećh **kfahśh**-no] exp.: to smell sour
kwaśnosłodki [kfahśh-no-**swot**-kee] adj.m. bittersweet; sour-sweet
kwaśnosłony [kfahśh-no-**swo**-ni] adj.m. salty acid
kwaśność [**kfahśh**-nośhćh] f. sourness; acidity
kwaśny [**kfahśh**-ni] adj.m. sour; acid
kwatera [kfah-**te**-rah] f. quarters; lodging; living accommodation
kwaterka [kfah-**ter**-kah] f. quarter of a liter; quarter liter bottle
kwatermistrz [kfah-**ter**-meestsh] m. quartermaster
kwatermistrzostwo [kfah-ter-mees-**tshos**-tfo] n. quartermaster department; logistics
kwatermistrzować [kfah-ter-mees-tsho-vahćh] v. be quartermaster (*repeatedly*)
kwatermistrzowski [kfah-ter-mees-**tshof**-skee] adj.m. quartermaster's; quartermaster (department, etc.)
kwaternion [kfah-**ter**-ńon] m. quaternion
kwaterować [kfah-te-ro-vahćh] v. give living accommodation; lodge; quarter troops; stay; be quartered; be cantoned; colloq: put up (somebody) (*repeatedly*)
kwaterowanie [kfah-te-ro-**vah**-ńe] n. quarters; cantonment
kwaterowy [kfah-te-**ro**-vi] adj.m. of a quarter system (of pastures)
kwaterunek [kfah-te-**roo**-nek] m. state office for the control of living accommodation; housing allocation; living quarters; colloq: digs
kwaterunkowy [kfah-te-roon-**ko**-vi] adj.m. of the state office for the control of living accommodation; of housing allocation; living quarters (allocation, etc.)
kwazar [**kfah**-zahr] m. quasar; quasi-stellar radio source
kwazarowy [kfah-zah-**ro**-vi] adj.m. quasar (radio signal, etc.); of quasi-stellar radio source
kwazary [kfah-**zah**-ri] pl. quasars; quasi-stellar radio sources
kwaziczątstka [kfah-zee-chowns-

tkah] f. quasiparticle
kwazicząstki [kfah-zee-**ch**o**wn**s-tkee] pl. quasiparticles

kweba [**kfe**-bah] f. wooden float supporting a net

kwebracho [kfe-**brah**-cho] n. quebracho; wood of quebracho tree

kwef [kfef] m. Muslim woman's (Turkish) veil; yashmak; wimple

kwercetyna [kfer-tse-**ti**-nah] f. variety of flavone (wool dye)

kwercytron [kfer-**tsi**-tron] m. quercitron; variety of flavone (wool dye)

kwerenda [kfe-**ren**-dah] f. archival research (for a particular item)

kweres [**kfe**-res] m. riot; tumult; confusion

kwerulencja [kfe-roo-**len**-tsyah] f. pettifogging; pettifoggery; chicanery

kwesta [**kfes**-tah] f. collection (for charitable purposes); passing the hat around

kwestarka [kfes-**tahr**-kah] f. collector (of funds for charitable purposes)

kwestarz [**kfes**-tahsh] m. collector (of funds for charitable purposes)

kwestia [**kfes**-tyah] f. question; matter; issue; problem; affair; topic; point; doubt; (stage) lines
kwestia życia i śmierci [**kfes**-tyah **zhi**-ćhah ee **śhmyer**-ćhee] exp.: a matter of life and death
kwestie [**kfes**-tye] pl. difficulties; questions; matters; problems; affairs
otwarta kwestia [ot-**fahr**-tah **kfes**-tyah] exp.: an open question
to nie ulega kwestii [to ńe oo-**le**-gah **kfes**-tyee] exp.: there is no doubt about it; it is beyond all doubt
ważna kwestia [**vahzh**-nah **kfes**-tyah] exp.: an important issue

kwestionariusz [kfes-tyo-**nah**-ryoosh] m. questionnaire; inquiry form (sheet)

kwestionować [kfes-tyo-**no**-vahćh] v. call in question; question; argue (the point); dispute; challenge; contest; gainsay (*repeatedly*)

kwestionowanie [kfes-tyo-no-**vah**-ńe] n. the calling in question (the truth, etc.); challenge; contestation

kwestor [**kfes**-tor] m. bursar; quaestor

kwestować [kfes-**to**-vahćh] v. collect (for charitable purposes); colloq: pass the hat around (*repeatedly*)

kwestowanie [kfes-to-**vah**-ńe] n. collection (for charitable purposes); colloq: passing the hat around

kwestura [kfes-**too**-rah] f. bursary; quaestor's office

kwezal [**kfe**-zahl] m. quetzal; trogon (bird)

kwękać [**kfan**-kahćh] v. be sickly; be forever ailing; complain of ill health; pine; waste away; grouch; slang: grouse (*repeatedly*)

kwękanie [kfan-**kah**-ńe] n. being forever ailing; ill health

kwiaciarka [kfyah-**ćhahr**-kah] f. florist; flower girl; flower vendor

kwiaciarnia [kfyah-**ćhahr**-ńah] f. flower shop; florist's

kwiaciarski [kfyah-**ćhahr**-skee] adj.m. flower (shop, etc.)

kwiaciarstwo [kfyah-**ćhahr**-stfo] n. cultivation of flowers; floriculture; manufacture of artificial flowers

kwiaciarz [**kfyah**-ćhahsh] m. florist; flower grower; floriculturist; artificial flower maker

kwiaciasty [kfyah-**ćhahs**-ti] adj.m. flowery

kwiat [kfyaht] m. flower
kwiat młodości [kfyaht mwo-**dośh**-ćhee] exp.: the bloom of youth; the first flush of youth
kwiat polny [kfyaht **pol**-ni] exp.: wild flower

kwiatek [**kfyah**-tek] m. (small, little) flower

kwiatogłówka [kfyah-to-**gwoof**-kah] f. sprout end flower

kwiaton [**kfyah**-tоń] fleuron; finial

kwiatonośny [kfyah-to-**nośh**-ni] adj.m. flower-bearing (plant, etc.)

kwiatostan [kfyah-**to**-stahn] m. inflorescence

kwiatostanowy [kfyah-to-stah-**no**-vi] adj.m. inflorescent
kwiatowy [kfyah-**to**-vi] adj.m. of a flower; of flowers; flower (garden, bed, grower, etc.); floral (design, etc.)
kwiatuszek [kfyah-**too**-shek] m. (nice, little) flower
kwiczeć [**kfee**-chećh] v. make a shrill cry; squeak; squeal (*repeatedly*)
kwiczenie [kfee-**che**-ńe] n. shrill cry
kwiczoł [**kfee**-chow] m. fieldfare (Turdus pilavis)
kwiecenie się [kfye-**tse**-ńe śhan] n. flowering
kwieciak [**kfye**-ćhahk] m. a variety of blossom beetle
kwieciak jabłkowiec [**kfye**-ćhahk yahp-**ko**-vyets] exp.: apple blossom weevil
kwieciarka [kfye-**ćhahr**-kah] f. florist; flower girl
kwieciarnia [kfye-**ćhahr**-ńah] f. flower shop; florist's
kwieciarski [kfye-**ćhahr**-skee] adj.m. florist's
kwieciarstwo [kfye-**ćhahr**-stfo] n. cultivation of flowers; floriculture; manufacture of artificial flowers
kwieciarz [**kfye**-ćhahsh] m. florist; flower grower; floriculturist; artificial flower maker
kwiecić [**kfye**-ćheećh] v. adorn with flowers; deck with flowers (*repeatedly*)
kwiecić się [**kfye**-ćheećh śhan] v. bloom; blossom (*repeatedly*)
kwiecie [**kfye**-ćhe] n. flowers; blossom; blossoms
kwiecień [**kfye**-ćheń] m. April
kwieciście [kfye-**ćhees**-to] adv. floridly; colorfully; ornately
kwiecistość [kfye-**ćhees**-tośhćh] f. floridness; flowery style
kwiecisty [kfye-**ćhees**-ti] adj.m. flowery; covered with flowers; flowered; florid; colorful; ornate
kwieciście [kfye-**ćheeśh**-ćhe] adv. floridly; colorfully; ornately
kwietnik [**kfyet**-ńeek] m. flower-bed; carpet bed
kwietnikowy [kfyet-ńee-**ko**-vi] adj.m. bedding (plant, geranium, etc.)
kwietniowy [kfyet-**ńo**-vi] adj.m. of April; April (day, showers, etc.)
kwietny [**kfyet**-ni] adj.m. of a flower; of flowers; flower (garden, bed, etc.); floral (design, etc.)
kwietysta [kfye-**tis**-tah] m. quietist
kwietystyczny [kfye-tis-**tich**-ni] adj.m. quietist
kwietyzm [**kfye**-tizm] m. quietism
kwik [kfeek] m. squeal; squeak
kwikać [**kfee**-kahćh] v. make a shrill cry; squeak; squeal (*repeatedly*)
kwikanie [kfee-**kah**-ńe] n. making a shrill cry; squeak; squeal
kwiknąć [**kfeek**-nownćh] v. make a shrill cry; squeak; squeal
kwiknięcie [kfeek-**ńan**-ćhe] n. making a shrill cry; squeak; squeal
kwilaja [kfee-**lah**-yah] f. quillai tree; quillai bark; quillai soap
kwilenie [kfee-**le**-ńe] n. wail; whimper; whine; chirp; twitter; groan
kwilić [**kfee**-leećh] v. whimper; mewl; whine; chirp; chirrup (*repeatedly*)
kwinkunks [**kfeen**-koonks] m. quincunx
kwinta [**kfeen**-tah] f. quint (in fencing, music); fifth (in music)
spuścić nos na kwintę [**spoośh**-ćheećh nos nah **kfeen**-tan] exp.: to make a long face
kwintal [**kfeen**-tahl] m. quintal
kwintesencja [kfeen-te-**sen**-tsyah] f. quintessence; pitch and marrow; essence (of a reasoning, etc.)
kwintet [**kfeen**-tet] m. quintet
kwintylion [kfeen-**til**-yon] m. quintillion (10^{30})
kwiryta [kfee-**ri**-tah] m. (Roman) Quirite
kwit [kfeet] m. receipt
kwity [**kfee**-ti] pl. receipts
być na kwit z kimś [bićh nah kfeet s keemśh] exp.: colloq: to be square with somebody; to be quits with somebody
kwit bagażowy [kfeet bah-gah-**zho**-vi] exp.: luggage receipt;

baggage check; baggage ticket
kwit dłużny [kfeet **dwoozh**-ni] exp.: I.O.U. (I owe you)
kwit lombardowy [kfeet lom-bahr-**do**-vi] exp.: pawn ticket
kwita [**kfee**-tah] f. colloq: enough (of that)!; that will do!
kwita z nami [**kfee**-tah z **nah**-mee] exp.: colloq: we are square; we are quits; we are through
kwita z naszej przyjaźni [**kfee**-tah z nah-shey pshi-**yahźh**-ńee] exp.: colloq: we are through; I'm through with you
kwitariusz [kfee-**tahr**-yoosh] m. receipt-book
kwitek [**kfee**-tek] m. minor receipt
odejść z kwitkiem [o-deyśhćh s **kfeet**-kem] exp.: to go empty-handed; to leave empty-handed
odprawić z kwitkiem [ot-**prah**-veećh s **kfeet**-kem] exp.: to rebuff somebody; to send somebody away empty-handed
kwitnąco [kfeet-**nown**-tso] adv. flourishingly
wyglądać kwitnąco [vig-**lown**-dahćh kfeet-**nown**-tso] exp.: to look the picture of health
kwitnący [kfeet-**nown**-tsi] adj.m. in bloom; blooming; in blossom; prosperous; thriving; flourishing
kwitnąć [**kfeet**-nownćh] v. bloom; be in bloom; effloresce; blossom; grow moldy; look healthy; thrive; prosper; become covered with mold; grow moldy (*repeatedly*)
kwitnienie [kfeet-**ńe**-ńe] n. florescence
kwitnięcie [kfeet-**ńan**-će] n. florescence
kwitować [kfee-**to**-vahćh] v. give receipt; relinquish; forgo; acknowledge receipt (*repeatedly*)
kwitować z czegoś [kfee-**to**-vahćh s **che**-gośh] exp.: to give something up
kwitowanie [kfee-to-**vah**-ńe] n. giving receipt; relinquishing; forgoing; acknowledging receipt
kwitownik [kfee-**tov**-ńeek] m. indicator of the condition of an automatic remote control circuit
kwitowy [kfee-**to**-vi] adj.m. receipt (book, form, etc.)
kwiz [kfees] m. quiz
kwiz telewizyjny [kfees te-le-vee-**ziy**-ni] exp.: television quiz
kwizowy [kfee-**zo**-vi] adj.m. quiz (question, price, etc.)
kwoczenie [kfo-**che**-ńe] n. clucking; colloq: grumbling
kwoczka [**kfoch**-kah] f. little brooding hen; colloq: home-bird; homebody; home-keeping girl
kwocznik [**kfoch**-ńeek] m. suspended cage for teaching hens not to cluck
kwoczy [**kfo**-chi] adj.m. hen (nest, egg, etc.)
kwoczyć [**kfo**-chićh] v. cluck; colloq: grumble (*repeatedly*)
kwoka [**kfo**-kah] f. sitting hen; brooding hen; clucking hen; colloq: grumbler; peevish woman
kwokacz [**kfo**-kahch] m. sandpiper (bird)
kwokać [**kfo**-kahćh] v. cluck; call (by grouse hen); colloq: grumble (*repeatedly*)
kwokanie [kfo-**kah**-ńe] n. clucking; calling (by wood grouse hen); colloq: grumbling
kwoknąć [**kfok**-nownćh] v. cluck (like a hen)
kwoknięcie [kfok-**ńan**-će] n. a cluck
kwoktać [**kfok**-tahćh] v. cluck; call (by grouse hen) (*repeatedly*)
kwoktanie [kfok-**tah**-ńe] n. clucking; calling (by wood grouse hen)
kworum [**kfo**-room] n. quorum
kwota [**kfo**-tah] f. amount; amount of money; sum
kwota ogólna [**kfo**-tah o-**gool**-nah] exp.: sum total
kwota przeznaczona na... [**kfo**-tah pshez-nah-**cho**-nah nah] exp.: allocation (for ...)
kwotowy [kfo-**to**-vi] adj.m. of a sum; of an amount
ryczałt kwotowy [**ri**-chahwt kfo-**to**-vi] exp.: global sum; lump sum
kynologia [ki-no-**log**-yah] f. study of dog anatomy, physiology, food, care, training, etc.
kynologiczny związek [ki-no-lo-**geech**-ni **zvyown**-zek] exp.:

kennel club; kennel association
kysz! [kish] excl.: away!; begone!; avaunt!
a kysz!, a kysz! [ah kish ah kish] excl.: away!; begone! (to chicken, ghosts, etc.)

L

L, l [el] n. the letter "l"; the sound "l" [el]
la [lah] not declined: (syllabic name for musical sound "a")
la, la [lah lah] (word replacement syllables used in singing)
laba [**lah**-bah] f. time free from school; truancy; idleness
labarum [lah-**bah**-room] n. labarum; Roman emperor's standard
labet [**lah**-bet] m. an old-time card game
labializacja [lah-byah-lee-**zah**-tsyah] f. labialization; labialism
labializować [lah-byah-lee-**zo**-vahćh] v. labialize; make labial (*repeatedly*)
labializowanie [lah-byah-lee-zo-**vah**-ńe] n. labialization; labialism
labialnie [lah-**byahl**-ńe] adv. labially
labialny [lah-**byahl**-ni] adj.m. labial (consonant, etc.); uttered with participation of one or both lips
labidzić [lah-**bee**-dźheećh] v. complain; bellyache (*repeatedly*)
labiedzenie [lah-bye-**dze**-ńe] n. complaints; bellyaching
labiedzić [lah-**bye**-dźheećh] v. complain; bellyache (*repeatedly*)
labilność [lah-**beel**-nośhćh] f. lability
labilnie [lah-**beel**-ńe] adv. with lability; without stability
labilny [lah-**beel**-ni] adj.m. labile; unstable
labiodentalny [lah-byo-den-**tahl**-ni] adj.m. labiodental
labiowelarny [lah-byo-ve-**lahr**-ni] adj.m. labiovelar
labirynt [lah-**bee**-rint] m. labyrinth; maze
labiryntodont [lah-bee-rin-**to**-dont] m. labyrinthodont
labiryntowiec [lah-bee-rin-**to**-vyets] m. variety of freshwater fish kept in an aquarium
labiryntowce [lah-bee-rin-**tof**-tse] pl. the order Labyrinthici of fishes
labiryntowo [lah-bee-rin-**to**-vo] adv. labyrinthically
labiryntowy [lah-bee-rin-**to**-vi] adj.m. labyrinthine; labyrinthic; labyrinthical
laboga [lah-**bo**-gah] excl.: colloq: my Goodness!; bless me!
laborancki [lah-bo-**rahn**-tskee] adj.m. laboratory assistant's
laborant [lah-**bo**-rahnt] m. lab technician; assistant chemist; manipulator; laboratory assistant
laborantka [lah-bo-**rahnt**-kah] f. (woman) lab technician; assistant chemist; manipulator; laboratory assistant
laboratorium [lah-bo-rah-**tor**-yoom] n. laboratory; colloq: lab
laboratoryjnie [lah-bo-rah-to-**riy**-ńe] adv. experimentally; in the sphere of laboratory experiments
laboratoryjny [lah-bo-rah-to-**riy**-ni] adj.m. laboratory (equipment, test, worker, etc.)
labrador [lah-**brah**-dor] m. labrador feldspar (mineral)
labradoryt [lah-brah-**do**-rit] m. labradorite (mineral)
labry [**lahb**-ri] pl. labrum
laburzysta [lah-boo-**zhis**-tah] m. laborite; laborist
laburzystowski [lah-boo-zhis-**tof**-skee] adj.m. of a laborite; of a labor party
lach [lahkh] m. dalesman (of Poland)
Lach [lahkh] m. Pole
strachy na Lachy [**strah**-khi nah **lah**-khi] exp.: nothing to be afraid of; nothing to be alarmed at
lacha [**lah**-khah] f. (big) cane; stick; walking stick; rod; bar (of metal, chocolate, etc.); stem; staff; truncheon; slang: failing grade
lacrimoso [lah-kree-**mo**-zo] adv. (Italian) lachrymosely; mournfully (played music)
laczek [**lah**-chek] m. open (back)

slipper
lać [lahćh] v. pour; shed; spill; cast; rain heavily (*repeatedly*)
lać łzy [lahćh wzi] exp.: to shed tears
lać łzy radości [lahćh wzi rah-**dośh**-ćhee] exp.: to weep tears of joy
lać się [lahćh śhan] v. flow; to pour; run (*repeatedly*)
lać się strumieniami [lahćh śhan stroo-mye-ńah-mee] exp.: to stream down
lada [lah-dah] f. counter
lada [lah-dah] part. any; whatever; the least; paltry
lada co [lah-dah tso] exp.: anything; no matter what; a trifle
lada gdzie [lah-dah gdźhe] exp.: anywhere
lada kto [lah-dah kto] exp.: anybody
lada chwila [lah-dah **khfee**-lah] exp.: any moment
lada rok [**lah**-dah rok] exp.: in a year, maybe in two or three
nie lada [ńe lah-dah] exp.: no mean; first-class; of the highest order; first-rate; colloq: tiptop
ladaco [lah-**dah**-tso] m. & n. rascal; rogue; good-for-nothing
ladacznica [lah-dahch-**ńee**-tsah] f. harlot; prostitute; strumpet
lady [**ley**-dee] f. lady
lafirynda [lah-fee-**rin**-dah] f. colloq: wanton; hussy
laga [**lah**-gah] f. colloq: (big) cane; stick; walking stick; rod; bar (of metal, etc.); stem; staff; truncheon
lagier [**lah**-ger] m. Nazi concentration camp
lagrowiec [lah-**gro**-vyets] m. inmate in a Nazi-German concentration camp
lagrowy [lah-**gro**-vi] adj.m. of a Nazi-German concentration camp
laguna [lah-**goo**-nah] f. lagoon
laicki [lah-**ee**-tskee] adj.m. lay (opinion, etc.); unprofessional; amateurish; secular
laickość [lah-**ee**-tskośhćh] f. secularity
laicyzacja [lah-ee-tsi-**zah**-tsyah] f. secularization
laicyzm [lah-**ee**-tsizm] m. secularity
laik [**lah**-eek] m. layman; outsider; person uninitiated (in art, science, etc.); one ignorant; lay brother
laicy [lah-**ee**-tsi] pl. the laity
laikat [lah-**ee**-kaht] m. the laity
lajkonik [lahy-**ko**-ńeek] m. Cracovian anniversary of the repulse of Tartars in the 13th cent.; rider of a hobby-horse in Tartar disguise
lak [lahk] m. sealing wax; wallflower
laka [**lah**-kah] f. lacquer; japan lacquer; lake (red pigment)
lakier [**lah**-ker] m. varnish; (nail) enamel; oil varnish; spirit varnish; patent leather
lakier do paznokci [**lah**-ker do pahz-**nok**-ćhee] exp.: nail polish; nail enamel
lakierek [lah-**ke**-rek] m. patent-leather shoe
lakierkowy [lah-ker-**ko**-vi] adj.m. patent-leather (shoe, etc.)
lakiernia [lah-**ker**-ńah] f. varnish factory; varnisher's workshop
lakiernictwo [lah-ker-**ńeets**-tfo] n. varnish manufacture; varnishing; whitewash; gloss
lakierniczy [lah-ker-**ńee**-chi] adj.m. varnish (brush, trade, etc.); varnisher's (work)
lakiernik [lah-**ker**-ńeek] m. varnish maker; varnisher; japanner
lakierować [lah-ke-**ro**-vahćh] v. varnish; gloss over; whitewash; lacquer; japan (*repeatedly*)
lakierowanie [lah-ke-ro-**vah**-ńe] n. varnishing; whitewash; gloss; japanning
lakierownia [lah-ke-**rov**-ńah] f. varnish factory; varnisher's workshop
lakierowy [lah-ke-**ro**-vi] adj.m. of varnish
lakista [lah-**kees**-tah] m. lake poet
lakmus [**lahk**-moos] m. litmus
lakmusowy [lahk-moo-**so**-vi] adj.m. litmus (paper, etc.)
papierek lakmusowy [pah-**pye**-rek lahk-moo-**so**-vi] exp.: litmus paper
lakolit [lah-**ko**-leet] m. laccolith; laccolite

lakonicznie [lah-ko-**ńeech**-ńe] adv. briefly; tersely; laconically; curtly
lakoniczność [lah-ko-**ńeech**-nośhćh] f. briefness; terseness; laconism; laconicism; curtness
lakoniczny [lah-ko-**ńeech**-ni] adj.m. terse; brief; curt; laconic; stating much in few words
lakonizm [lah-**ko**-ńeezm] m. briefness; terseness; laconism; curtness
lakować [lah-**ko**-vahćh] v. seal (with sealing wax) (*repeatedly*)
lakowanie [lah-ko-**vah**-ńe] n. sealing with wax
lakowy [lah-**ko**-vi] adj.m. of sealing wax; of Chinese (Japanese) lacquer; of sumac varnish
laksacja [lahk-**sah**-tsyah] f. diarrhea
laktacja [lahk-**tah**-tsyah] f. lactation
laktacyjnie [lahk-tah-**tsiy**-ńe] adv. lactationally
laktacyjny [lahk-tah-**tsiy**-ni] adj.m. of lactation; lactational
laktam [**lahk**-tahm] m. lactam
laktamy [lahk-**tah**-mi] pl. lactam amino acids
laktarium [lahk-**tahr**-yoom] n. lactarium
laktaza [lahk-**tah**-zah] f. lactase
laktoalbumina [lahk-to-ahl-boo-**mee**-nah] f. milk protein; lactalbumin
laktodensymetr [lahk-to-den-**si**-metr] m. device for measuring the density of milk; lactometer
laktoflawina [lahk-to-flah-**vee**-nah] f. riboflavin
laktometr [lahk-**to**-metr] m. lactometer; lactodensimeter
lakton [**lahk**-ton] m. lactone
laktoskop [lahk-**tos**-kop] m. lactoscope
laktoza [lahk-**to**-zah] f. lactose; milk sugar
lala [**lah**-lah] f. doll; puppet; colloq: vain, well-dressed woman
jak ta lala [yahk tah **lah**-lah] exp.: nicely; perfectly; superbly; first-rate
pasuje jak ta lala [pah-**soo**-ye yahk tah **lah**-lah] exp.: it fits like a glove; it fits perfectly
pójść do lali [pooyśhćh do **lah**-lee] exp.: to die
lalczyn [**lahl**-chin] adj.m. doll's; dolls'
lalczyny [lahl-**chi**-ni] adj.m. doll's; dolls'
laleczka [lah-**lech**-kah] f. (nice, little) doll
lalemancja [lah-le-**mahn**-tsyah] f. an oily Asiatic plant (Lalemantia iberica)
lalka [**lahl**-kah] f. doll; puppet
lalkarka [lahl-**kahr**-kah] f. (woman) doll maker; toy maker; puppet-show operator
lalkarski [lahl-**kahr**-skee] adj.m. doll-maker's; toy-maker's; of the puppet-show industry
lalkarstwo [lahl-**kahr**-stfo] n. doll manufacture; puppet-show industry
lalkarz [**lahl**-kahsh] m. doll manufacturer; puppet-show operator
lalkowato [lahl-ko-**vah**-to] adv. like a doll; pretty but without facial expression
lalkowaty [lahl-ko-**vah**-ti] adj.m. dollish
lalkowata twarz [lahl-ko-**vah**-tah tfahsh] exp.: doll's face
lalkowy [lahl-**ko**-vi] adj.m. puppet (show, etc.)
lalunia [lah-**loo**-ńah] f. (nice, little) doll
lalusia [lah-**loo**-śhah] f. (nice, little) doll
lalusiowaty [lah-loo-śho-**vah**-ti] adj.m. foppish
laluś [lah-loośh] m. fop; dude; colloq: dandy
lama [**lah**-mah] f. llama; lame (brocaded fabric with gold threads, etc.); m. (Tibetan) lama; a Lamaist monk
klasztor lamów [**klahsh**-tor lah-moof] exp.: lamasery
lamaistyczny [lah-mah-ees-**tich**-ni] adj.m. Lamaist
lamaita [lah-mah-**ee**-tah] m. Lamaist
lamaizm [lah-**mah**-eezm] m. Lamaism
lamarkizm [lah-**mahr**-keezm] m. Lamarckism
lambdacyzm [lahmb-**dah**-tsizm] m. lambdacism; lallation

lambert [**lahm**-bert] m. lambert (unit of brightness)
lambeth-walk [**lam**-bet wok] m. lambeth walk dance
lamblia [**lahmb**-lyah] f. lamblia; Giardia (intestinal parasite)
lamblioza [lahm-**blyo**-zah] f. lambliasis; Giardiasis (intestinal parasite infection)
lambrekin [lahm-**bre**-keen] m. lambrequin; pelmet
lamelka [lah-**mel**-kah] f. electric fuse
lament [**lah**-ment] m. lament; lamentation; wail; elegy; dirge
lamentacja [lah-men-**tah**-tsyah] f. lamentation; wail; elegy; dirge
lamentacyjnie [lah-men-tah-**tsiy**-ńe] adv. lamentedly; lamentably; plaintively
lamentacyjny [lah-men-tah-**tsiy**-ni] adj.m. lamentatory; plaintive; of a lament; of lamentation; of a wail; of an elegy; of a dirge
lamentoso [lah-men-**to**-zo] adv. plaintively (played music)
lamentować [lah-men-**to**-vahćh] v. wail; lament; mourn; bewail; colloq: jammer; croon; sing plaintively (*repeatedly*)
lamentowanie [lah-men-to-**vah**-ńe] n. wailing; lamenting; mourning
lameta [lah-**me**-tah] f. metal (thread) trimming
lamina [lah-**mee**-nah] f. thin sedimentary layer (less than one centimeter thick); lamina
laminarny [lah-mee-**nahr**-ni] adj.m. laminar
laminat [lah-**mee**-naht] m. laminate; laminated plastic
laminatowy [lah-mee-nah-**to**-vi] adj.m. laminate (structure, etc.); laminated (plastic, etc.)
laminować [lah-mee-**no**-vahćh] v. laminate; roll into a thin plate; separate into laminae (*repeatedly*)
laminowanie [lah-mee-no-**vah**-ńe] n. lamination; the process of laminating
lamna [**lahm**-nah] f. shark; porbeagle; Lamna cornubica
lamować [lah-**mo**-vahćh] v. trim; edge; pipe; border (with lace, braid, fur, etc.) (*repeatedly*)
lamowanie [lah-mo-**vah**-ńe] n. trimming; edge; border; piping
lamowy [lah-**mo**-vi] adj.m. lame; brocaded (fabric with golden thread, etc.)
lamówka [lah-**moof**-kah] f. trim; border; edge; trimming; piping
lampa [**lahm**-pah] f. lamp
  lampy [**lahm**-pi] pl. lamps; colloq: wolf's eyes
  lampa błyskowa [**lahm**-pah bwis-**ko**-vah] exp.: flash lamp; photoflash (lamp); flashlight
  lampa jarzeniowa [**lahm**-pah yah-zhe-**ńo**-vah] exp.: fluorescent lamp; glow-tube lamp (Brit.)
  lampa obrazowa [**lahm**-pah o-brah-**zo**-vah] exp.: picture tube; kinescope
  lampa próżniowa [**lahm**-pah proozh-**ńo**-vah] exp.: vacuum tube
  lampa sygnalizacyjna [**lahm**-pah sig-nah-lee-zah-**tsiy**-nah] exp.: flash lamp; signal light
  mówić do lampy [**moo**-veećh do **lahm**-pi] exp.: colloq: to waste one's breath
  przy świetle lampy [pshi **śhfyet**-le **lahm**-pi] exp.: by lamplight
lamparci [lahm-**pahr**-ćhee] adj.m. leopard's; leopard (skin, etc.)
lamparcica [lahm-pahr-**ćhee**-tsah] f. leopardess
lampart [**lahm**-pahrt] m. leopard; panther
lampas [**lahm**-pahs] m. side stripe (on pants); lampas; stripe; frieze
lampeczka [lam-**pech**-kah] f. (very small, nice) lamp; wine glass; glassful
lamperia [lahm-**per**-yah] f. wainscot; panelling
lampiarnia [lahm-**pyahr**-ńah] f. lamp-room (in a coal mine, etc.)
lampiarski [lahm-**pyahr**-skee] adj.m. lamp-maker's (equipment, etc.)
lampiarz [**lahm**-pyahsh] m. lamp-man; lamp-maker; lamp-seller; lamp-trimmer (Brit.); lamplighter
lampion [**lahm**-pyon] m. lampion; Chinese lantern
lampka [**lahmp**-kah] f. night-lamp; ever burning lamp; colloq: wine

glass
lampka wina [lahmp-kah vee-nah] exp.: glass of wine
lampownia [lahm-pov-ńah] f. lamp-room (in a coal mine, etc.)
lampowy [lahm-po-vi] adj.m. of a lamp; tube (set, etc.)
lamprofir [lahm-pro-feer] m. lamprophyre (mineral)
lamus [lah-moos] m. storeroom; granary; lumber room; colloq: junk-room
lanca [lahn-tsah] f. lance; spear
lancet [lahn-tset] m. lancet; fleam; cleaner; lifter
lancetnik [lahn-tset-ńeek] m. lancelet
lancetowaty [lahn-tse-to-vah-ti] adj.m. lanceolate; linear
lancknecht [lahnts-knekht] m. medieval German mercenary
landara [lahn-dah-rah] f. chaise; jalopy; old crate; rumble-tumble; shandrydan; jumbo; (large, enormous, mammoth) object; landau (carriage)
landgraf [lahnd-grahf] m. landgrave
lando [lahn-do] n. landau
landolet [lahn-do-let] m. landolet; landolette
landolfia [lahn-dol-fyah] f. Landolphia; Congo rubber; landolphia (plant, fruit, vine, etc.)
landrat [lahnd-raht] m. district chief in Prussia
landryna [lahn-dri-nah] f. acid drop
landrynek [lahn-dri-nek] m. fruit candy
landrynka [lahn-drin-kah] f. fruit candy
landrynkowaty [lahn-drin-ko-vah-ti] adj.m. like fruit candy
landrynkowy [lahn-drin-ko-vi] adj.m. of fruit candy
landsberski [lahnds-ber-skee] adj.m. of Landsberg; of Gorzów Wielkopolski (apple tree, apple, etc.)
landszaft [lahnt-shahft] m. landscape; colloq: daub
landtag [lahnt-tahg] m. German provincial legislature
landwera [lahnd-ve-rah] f. territorial defense force
landy [lahn-di] pl. sandy moors; heaths
langbajnit [lahng-bahy-ńeet] m. langbanite (mineral)
langusta [lahn-goos-tah] f. spiny lobster
lanie [lah-ńe] n. pouring; casting; beating; thrashing; licking; spanking
oberwać lanie [o-ber-vahćh lah-ńe] exp.: to get a thrashing
lanista [lah-ńees-tah] m. lanista
lanital [lah-ńee-tahl] m. lanital
lanka [lahn-kah] f. ball of solid rubber
lanolina [lah-no-lee-nah] f. lanolin; wool fat (in ointments)
lanolinowy [lah-no-lee-no-vi] adj.m. lanolin (soap, cream, etc.)
lansada [lahn-sah-dah] f. (horse's) gambade; gambado; bounce
lansady [lahn-sah-di] pl. prancing; gait; skips; leaps; bounds; bounces
lansjer [lahn-syer] m. lancer
lansjerzy [lahn-sye-zhi] pl. lancers
lansjerski [lahn-syer-skee] adj.m. lancer's; of a lancer; of lancers
lansjery [lahn-sye-ri] pl. lancers' dance
lansować [lahn-so-vahćh] v. promote; launch; initiate; start; bring out (a film star, etc.); give publicity (to); set the fashion (for) (*repeatedly*)
lansowanie [lahn-so-vah-ńe] n. promotion; initiation
lantan [lahn-tahn] m. lanthanum (atomic number 57)
lantana [lahn-tah-nah] f. Lantana (shrub)
lantanowiec [lahn-tah-no-vyets] m. lanthanide (one of heavy metals)
lantanowce [lahn-tah-nof-tse] pl. lanthanides
lanuszka [lah-noosh-kah] f. lily of the valley
lany [lah-ni] adj.m. cast
z lanego żelaza [z lah-ne-go zhe-lah-zah] exp.: cast-iron
lane ciasto [lah-ne ćhahs-to] exp.: soft egg noodles
laparoskopia [lah-pah-ro-sko-pyah] f. laparoscopy

laparotomia [lah-pah-ro-**to**-myah] f. laparotomy
lapidarium [lah-pee-**dahr**-yoom] n. collection of stones and stone fragments
lapidarnie [lah-pee-**dahr**-ńe] adv. tersely; concisely; crisply; curtly
lapidarność [lah-pee-**dahr**-nośhćh] f. terseness; conciseness; crispness; curtness
lapidarny [lah-pee-**dahr**-ni] adj.m. terse; concise; curt; crisp
lapilli [lah-**peel**-lee] pl. lapilli
lapis [**lah**-pees] m. silver nitrate; lunar caustic
lapis-lazuli [**lah**-pees lah-**zoo**-lee] m. not declined: lapis lazuli
lapisować [lah-pee-**so**-vahćh] v. cauterize with silver nitrate (*repeatedly*)
lapisowanie [lah-pee-so-**vah**-ńe] n. cauterization with silver nitrate
lapnąć [**lahp**-nownćh] v. colloq: rap out; blurt out
Laponka [lah-**pon**-kah] f. Lapp (woman)
laponoid [lah-po-**no**-eed] m. person of Lapponian type
laponoidalny [lah-po-no-ee-**dahl**-ni] adj.m. Lapponian (anthropologic type, stocky build, etc.)
Lapończyk [lah-**poń**-chik] m. Lapp (man)
lapoński [lah-**poń**-skee] adj.m. Lapponian (language, etc.)
po lapońsku [po lah-**poń**-skoo] exp.: in Lappish
lapsus [**lahp**-soos] m. lapse; slip of the tongue; error
laptop [**lahp**-top] m. laptop computer
larghetto [lahr-**get**-to] n. (Italian) larghetto (movement)
largo [**lahr**-go] adj.m. and adv. largo; in a very slow and broad manner (music)
larum [**lah**-room] n. alarm; outcry; clamor; uproar
larwa [**lahr**-vah] f. larva; grub; maggot; ghost; mask
larwalny [lahr-**vahl**-ni] adj.m. larval
larwicyd [lahr-**vee**-tsid] m. larvicide
larwicydy [lahr-vee-**tsi**-di] pl. larvicides
larwicydowy [lahr-vee-tsi-**do**-vi] adj.m. larvicidal
lary [**lah**-ri] pl. lares
lary i penaty [**lah**-ri ee pe-**nah**-ti] exp.: lares and penates; household goods; one's personal effects; one's household goods
laryngalnie [lah-rin-**gahl**-ńe] adv. laryngeally
laryngalny [lah-rin-**gahl**-ni] adj.m. laryngeal (consonant, etc.)
laryngofon [lah-rin-**go**-fon] m. laryngophony; larynx microphone
laryngolog [lah-rin-**go**-log] m. laryngologist; throat specialist; E.N.T. specialist
laryngologia [lah-rin-go-**lo**-gyah] f. laryngology; throat diseases department (ward)
laryngologiczny [lah-rin-go-lo-**geech**-ni] adj.m. laryngologic
laryngoskop [lah-rin-**go**-skop] m. laryngoscope
laryngoskopia [lah-rin-go-**sko**-pyah] f. laryngoscopy
las [lahs] m. wood; forest; thicket
gęsty las [**gan**-sti lahs] exp.: thicket
las iglasty [lahs ee-**glahs**-ti] exp.: coniferous forest
las liściasty [lahs leeśh-**ćhahs**-ti] exp.: leafy forest
lasa [**lah**-sah] f. (sifting) screen; riddle
laseczek [lah-**se**-chek] m. (nice, cozy) wood; grove
laseczka [lah-**sech**-kah] f. down stroke (of a letter); minim; half note
laseczki [lah-**sech**-kee] pl. rod-shaped bacteria
laseczkowaty [lah-sech-ko-**vah**-ti] adj.m. rod-shaped
lasecznik [lah-**sech**-ńeek] m. rod-shaped bacterium; bacillus
laseczniki [lah-sech-**ńee**-kee] pl. rod-shaped bacteria
lasek [**lah**-sek] m. grove; copse; coppice
laser [**lah**-ser] m. laser
laserować [lah-se-**ro**-vahćh] v. scumble; glaze (a painting, etc.) (*repeatedly*)
laserowanie [lah-se-ro-**vah**-ńe] n.

scumbling; glazing
laserowy [lah-se-**ro**-vi] adj.m. of a laser; laser (printer, etc.)
laserunek [lah-se-**roo**-nek] m. scumble; glaze
laserunkowy [lah-se-roon-**ko**-vi] adj.m. scumbling (paints, etc.); glazing (a surface, etc.)
laska [**lahs**-kah] f. cane; stick; walking stick; rod; bar (of metal, chocolate etc.); pointer; down stroke (of a letter); stem; staff; truncheon; thin column; mullion; monial
laskarz [**lahs**-kahsh] m. grass-hockey player
laskonogi [lahs-ko-**no**-gee] adj.m. spindle-legged; spindle-shanked
laskowanie [lahs-ko-**vah**-ńe] n. fluting; reeds
laskowany [lahs-ko-**vah**-ni] adj.m. fluted
laskowy [lahs-**ko**-vi] adj.m. rod-shaped; stick (sulphur); of woods
orzech laskowy [o-zhekh lahs-**ko**-vi] exp.: hazelnut
lasonóg [lah-**so**-noog] m. variety of small shellfish
lasonogi [lah-so-**no**-gee] pl. the family of small marine shellfish
lasostep [lah-**so**-step] m. interphase between forest and steppe
lasotundra [lah-so-**toond**-rah] f. interphase between taiga and tundra
lasować [lah-**so**-vahćh] v. slake (lime) (*repeatedly*)
lasować się [lah-**so**-vahćh śh<u>an</u>] v. slake; become slaked; crumble; disintegrate (*repeatedly*)
lasowanie [lah-so-**vah**-ńe] n. slaking of lime
lasowanie się [lah-so-**vah**-ńe śh<u>an</u>] n. becoming slaked
lasowy [lah-**so**-vi] adj.m. of forestry; forest (trees, etc.); wood (anemone, lark, etc.)
lassalizm [lahs-**sah**-leezm] m. an anti-marxist labor movement
lasso [**lahs**-so] n. lasso
chwytać na lasso [khfi-tahćh nah **lahs**-so] exp.: to lasso; to rope (a horse, etc.)
lastrico [lahs-**tree**-ko] n. terrazzo
lastriko [lahs-**tree**-ko] n. terrazzo
lastrykarski [lahs-tri-**kahr**-skee] adj.m. terrazzo (works, etc.)
lastrykarstwo [lahs-tri-**kahr**-stfo] n. terrazzo work
lastrykarz [lahs-**tri**-kahsh] m. terrazzo installer
lastryko [lahs-**tri**-ko] n. terrazzo
lastrykować [lahs-tri-**ko**-vahćh] v. install terrazzo; cover with terrazzo (*repeatedly*)
lastrykowanie [lahs-tri-ko-**vah**-ńe] n. installation of terrazzo
lastrykowy [lahs-tri-**ko**-vi] adj.m. terrazzo (floor, stairs, etc.); covered with terrazzo
lasza [**lah**-shah] f. (railroad) fish joint; fishplate
Laszka [**lahsh**-kah] f. Polish woman (in East-Slavonic languages)
laszować [lah-**sho**-vahćh] v. release (a glider, etc.) (*repeatedly*)
laszowanie [lah-sho-**vah**-ńe] n. releasing of a glider (from an airplane, etc.)
laszt [lahsht] m. fishing-ship's netting section
lata [**lah**-tah] pl. years
latacz [**lah**-tahch] m. upper triangular foresail
latać [**lah**-tahćh] v. fly; flit; flutter; flitter; be on the wing; wing; be in constant motion; run backwards and forwards; be on the run; run (after) (*repeatedly*)
latający [lah-tah-**y<u>own</u>**-tsi] adj.m. flying; volant; capable of flying
latająca ryba [lah-tah-**y<u>own</u>**-tsah ri-bah] exp.: flying fish
latania [lah-**tah**-ńah] f. fan palm
latanie [lah-**tah**-ńe] n. flying
latanina [lah-tah-**ńee**-nah] f. colloq: comings and goings; fuss; exertions; stir; bustle
latarenka [lah-tah-**ren**-kah] f. small flashlight; (electric) torch; very small lamp
latarka [lah-**tahr**-kah] f. flashlight; (electric) torch; small lamp
latarnia [lah-**tahr**-ńah] f. streetlight; lantern; beacon; lamppost
latarnia morska [lah-**tahr**-ńah **mors**-kah] exp.: lighthouse; beacon

latarnia uliczna [lah-**tahr**-ńah oo-leech-nah] exp.: street lamp
latarnie [lah-**tahr**-ńe] pl. lanterns; colloq: wolf's eyes
latarniany [lah-tahr-**ńah**-ni] adj.m. streetlight (light, etc.)
latarnik [lah-**tahr**-ńeek] m. lighthouse keeper; lamplighter; lantern fly
latarniki [lah-tahr-**ńee**-kee] pl. lantern flies
latarniowiec [lah-tahr-**ńo**-vyets] m. beacon ship; lightship
latarniowy [lah-tahr-**ńo**-vi] adj.m. beacon (ship, etc.); light (post, etc.)
latawica [lah-tah-**vee**-tsah] f. gadabout (woman)
latawiec [lah-**tah**-vyets] m. kite; gliding squirrel (of Asia)
latawce [lah-**tahf**-tse] pl. kites; gliding squirrels (of Asia)
lateks [**lah**-teks] m. latex
lateksowy [lah-tek-**so**-vi] adj.m. of latex; latex (paper etc.)
latensyfikacja [lah-ten-si-fee-**kah**-tsyah] f. latensifiication (a method for an increase of film-sensitivity by special lighting)
lateński [lah-**teń**-skee] adj.m. of the second part of the iron age (ending 2000 years ago)
lateralizacja [lah-te-rah-lee-**zah**-tsyah] f. lateralization; conversion of rock to laterite
lateralny [lah-te-**rahl**-ni] adj.m. (anatomically) lateral
lateryt [lah-**te**-rit] m. laterite (mineral)
laterytowy [lah-te-ri-**to**-vi] adj.m. lateritic; laterite (rock, etc.)
latimeria [lah-tee-**me**-ryah] f. a crossopterygian fish
latko [**laht**-ko] n. (nice, short) summer
lato [**lah**-to] n. summer
w lecie [v **le**-ćhe] exp.: in summer
w pełni lata [f **pew**-ńee **lah**-tah] exp.: in midsummer
całymi latami [tsah-**wi**-mi lah-**tah**-mee] exp.: years and years; for years at a stretch
z biegiem lat [z **bye**-gem laht] exp.: with years; as years passed
dziecięce lata [dźhe-**ćhan**-tse **lah**-tah] exp.: childhood; callowness
latopis [lah-**to**-pees] m. chronicler
latopisarz [lah-to-**pee**-sahsh] m. chronicler
latorośl [lah-**to**-rośhl] f. shoot; scion; spring; sprout; colloq: offspring
latoś [**lah**-tośh] adv. colloq: this year
latować [lah-**to**-vahćh] v. rut; be in heat (*repeatedly*)
latowanie [lah-to-**vah**-ńe] n. rut; heat
latryna [lah-**tri**-nah] f. latrine
latyfundialny [lah-ti-foon-**dyahl**-ni] adj.m. latifundian
latyfundium [lah-ti-**foond**-yoom] n. large complex of farming and town properties centrally owned; latifundium
latynista [lah-ti-**ńees**-tah] m. Latinist
latynizacja [lah-ti-ńee-**zah**-tsyah] f. latinization
latynizm [lah-**ti**-ńeezm] m. Latinism; Latin borrowing
latynizować [lah-ti-ńee-**zo**-vahćh] v. latinize (*repeatedly*)
latynizowanie [lah-ti-ńee-zo-**vah**-ńe] n. latinization
latynoamerykański [lah-ti-no-ah-me-ri-**kahń**-skee] adj.m. Latin-American
latynoski [lah-ti-**nos**-kee] adj.m. Latin-American
latyński [lah-**tiń**-skee] adj.m. Roman (law, etc.); Latin (culture, language, etc.)
latyt [**lah**-tit] m. variety of igneous rock
laubzega [lahwb-**ze**-gah] f. fret saw; jigsaw; scroll saw
laubzegowy [lahwb-ze-**go**-vi] adj.m. fret (work); of fret saw
lauda [**lahw**-dah] f. medieval religious hymn
laudanum [lahw-**dah**-noom] n. laudanum
laufer [**lahw**-fer] m. runner (footman); (chess) bishop
laur [lahwr] m. laurel; bay (tree); laurel wreath
spoczywać na laurach [spo-chi-

vahćh nah **lahw**-rahkh] exp.: to rest on one's laurels
laureat [lahw-**re**-aht] m. laureate; prizewinner; prizeman
laureat nagrody Nobla [lahw-**re**-aht nah-**gro**-di **No**-blah] exp.: Nobel prizewinner
laureatka [lahw-re-**aht**-kah] f. (woman) laureate; prizewinner; prizeman
laurencja [lahw-**ren**-tsyah] f. Laurencia (red alga)
laurka [lah-**oor**-kah] f. congratulatory scroll; colloq: exaggerated prize
laurowiśnia [lahw-ro-**veeśh**-ńah] f. Laurocerasus (shrub)
laurowy [lahw-**ro**-vi] adj.m. of the laurel; of the bay tree; laurel (leaves)
lautal [lah-**oo**-tahl] m. an aluminum alloy
lawa [**lah**-vah] f. volcanic lava; fluid (rock) mass
lawenda [lah-**ven**-dah] f. lavender; lavender water
lawendowy [lah-ven-**do**-vi] adj.m. lavender (water, oil, etc.)
lawerak [lah-**ve**-rahk] m. variety of English setter (dog)
laweta [lah-**ve**-tah] f. gun carriage; heavy artillery gun base
lawina [lah-**vee**-nah] f. avalanche; shover (of words, rock, etc.)
lawiniasty [lah-vee-**ńah**-sti] adj.m. having frequent avalanches
lawinisko [lah-vee-**ńees**-ko] n. snow and rocks of an avalanche; final pileup of avalanche mass
lawinowo [lah-vee-**no**-vo] adv. like an avalanche
lawinowy [lah-vee-**no**-vi] adj.m. avalanche
lawirant [lah-**vee**-rahnt] m. colloq: artful dodger; trimmer; schemer
lawirować [lah-vee-**ro**-vahćh] v. dodge obstacles; scheme successfully; veer; tack; intrigue; shift; take devious ways to achieve one's ends; sail close to the wind (*repeatedly*)
lawirowanie [lah-vee-ro-**vah**-ńe] n. dodging obstacles; scheming successfully; veering
lawować [lah-**vo**-vahćh] v. wash (a drawing with thin watercolor) (*repeatedly*)
lawowanie [lah-vo-**vah**-ńe] n. washing (a drawing with thin watercolor)
lawowy [lah-**vo**-vi] adj.m. of lava; lava (field, etc.)
lawrens [**lahv**-rens] m. lawrencium (atomic number 103)
lawsonia [lahf-**so**-ńyah] f. Lawsonia (shrub)
lazaret [lah-**zah**-ret] m. field hospital (for infections)
lazarysta [lah-zah-**ris**-tah] m. Lazarist monk
lazerunek [lah-ze-**roo**-nek] m. scumble; glaze
lazulit [lah-**zoo**-leet] m. lazulite (mineral)
lazur [**lah**-zoor] m. azure; sky blue; the blue; blue pigment
lazurować [lah-zoo-**ro**-vahćh] v. treat glass with silver and copper salts (before baking) (*repeatedly*)
lazurowanie [lah-zoo-ro-**vah**-ńe] n. treating glass with silver and copper salts (before baking)
lazurowy [lah-zoo-**ro**-vi] adj.m. azure (sky, etc.); blue (eyes, etc.)
lazuryt [lah-**zoo**-rit] m. lazurite (mineral)
ląc się [lownts śhan] v. breed; hatch (*repeatedly*)
ląd [lownd] m. land; mainland; continent
lądy [**lown**-di] pl. lands; countries; continents
ku lądowi [koo lown-**do**-vee] exp.: landward
ląd stały [lownt **stah**-wi] exp.: mainland
lądem [**lown**-dem] exp.: by land; overland
na lądzie [nah **lown**-dźhe] exp.: on land; on shore
zejść na ląd [zeyśhćh nah lownd] exp.: to go ashore; to land; to disembark
lądolód [lown-**do**-lood] m. continental glacier
lądotwórczość [lown-do-**tfoor**-chośhćh] f. epeirogeny
lądotwórczy [lown-do-**tfoor**-chi] adj.m. epeirogenic

lądować [lown-**do**-vahćh] v. land; disembark; go ashore; alight; colloq: save oneself; land (in prison, etc.) (*repeatedly*)
lądowanie [lown-do-**vah**-ńe] n. landing
lot bez lądowania [lot bez lown-do-**vah**-ńah] exp.: nonstop flight
przymusowe lądowanie [pshi-moo-**so**-ve lown-do-**vah**-ńe] exp.: forced landing
lądowisko [lown-do-**vees**-ko] n. landing field; colloq: airfield
lądownik [lown-**dov**-ńeek] m. space vehicle landing capsule
lądowy [lown-**do**-vi] adj.m. continental (climate, etc.); land (army, etc.); terrestrial
klimat lądowy [**klee**-maht lown-**do**-vi] exp.: continental climate
drogą lądową [**dro**-gown lown-**do**-vown] exp.: by land; overland
lądzieniec [lown-**dźhe**-ńets] m. a mite
lądzień [**lown**-dźheń] m. a mite
lądzienie [lown-**dźhe**-ńe] pl. mites; Trombidiidae
ląg [lowng] m. hatching; brood; hatch
leader [**lee**-der] m. leader
leasing [**lee**-zeenk] m. leasing (of equipment, cars, etc.)
leasingowy [lee-zeen-**go**-vi] adj.m. leasing (contract, equipment, etc.)
lebiega [le-**bye**-gah] f. colloq: muff; oaf; lout; duffer
lebioda [le-**byo**-dah] f. pigweed
lebiodka [le-**byot**-kah] f. Origanum; oregano; marjoram
lec [lets] v. lie down; fall
lec jak długi [lets yahkh **dwoo**-gee] exp.: to fall flat; to take a bad fall; to measure one's length on the ground
lec na spoczynek [lets nah spo-**chi**-nek] exp.: to lie down to rest
lechicki [le-**kheets**-kee] adj.m. North-Western Slavonic (languages, etc.); of the Elbe, Oder, and Vistula River Slavs
lecieć [**le**-ćhećh] v. fly; run; hurry; wing; drift; be wafted; soar; rise into the air; drop; go down; sink; fall; flow; rush; tear along; career; pass; go by (*repeatedly*)
lecieć na (kogoś, coś) [**le**-ćhećh nah **ko**-gośh tsośh] exp.: to be sweet on somebody; to run after somebody (something); slang: to be interested in stealing something (mob jargon)
lecieć na całego [**le**-ćhećh nah tsah-**we**-go] exp.: colloq: to decide on (something)
lecę z nóg [**le**-tsan z noog] exp.: I am dog tired; I am exhausted
leciuchno [le-**ćhookh**-no] adv. barely touching; very lightly; very easily
leciuchny [le-**ćhookh**-ni] adj.m. very (extremely, awfully) light
leciusi [le-**ćhoo**-śhee] adj.m. very (extremely, awfully) light
leciusieńki [le-ćhoo-**śheń**-kee] adj.m. very (extremely) light
leciusieńko [le-ćhoo-**śheń**-ko] adv. barely touching; very lightly; very easily
leciusio [le-**ćhoo**-śho] adv. barely touching; very lightly; very easily
leciuśki [le-**ćhoośh**-kee] adj.m. very (extremely, awfully) light
leciuśko [le-**ćhoośh**-ko] adv. barely touching; very lightly; very easily
leciuteńki [le-ćhoo-**teń**-kee] adj.m. very (extremely, awfully) light
leciuteńko [le-ćhoo-**teń**-ko] adv. barely touching; very lightly; very easily
leciutki [le-**ćhoot**-kee] adj.m. very (extremely, awfully) light
leciutko [le-**ćhoot**-ko] adv. barely touching; very lightly; very easily
leciwy [le-**ćhee**-vi] adj.m. up in years; advanced in years; aged; elderly
lecka [**lets**-kah] f. (small) rein
lecytyna [le-tsi-**ti**-nah] f. lecithin
lecytyny [le-tsi-**ti**-ni] pl. lecithins (waxy hygroscopic phosphatides)
lecz [lech] conj. but; however; though
leczenie [le-**che**-ńe] n. healing; cure; treatment
być w leczeniu [bićh v le-**che**-ńoo] exp.: to be under treatment
niewłaściwe leczenie [ńe-vwah-**śhćhee**-ve le-**che**-ńe] exp.:

improper treatment; inadequate treatment; treatment below standard
sprawa o niewłaściwe leczenie [**sprah**-vah o ńe-vwah-**śhćhee**-ve le-**che**-ńe] exp.: malpractice suit
leczenie się [le-**che**-ńe śhan] n. undergoing medical treatment
lecznica [lech-**ńee**-tsah] f. small hospital; clinic; infirmary
lecznica chorób nieuleczalnych [lech-**ńee**-tsah **kho**-roop ńe-oo-le-**chahl**-nikh] exp.: hospitium
lecznica prywatna [lech-**ńee**-tsah pri-**vaht**-nah] exp.: clinic office; private practice
lecznictwo [lech-**ńeets**-tfo] n. therapeutics; medical care; health service
lecznictwo otwarte [lech-**ńeets**-tfo o-**tfahr**-te] exp.: outpatient treatment; medical service
lecznictwo uspołecznione [lech-**ńeets**-tfo oo-spo-wech-**ńo**-ne] exp.: National Health Service; socialized medicine; public health service
lecznictwo zamknięte [lech-**ńeets**-tfo zahm-**kńan**-te] exp.: hospital service; inpatient medical service
leczniczo [lech-**ńee**-cho] adv. therapeutically
działać leczniczo [**dźhah**-wahćh lech-**ńee**-cho] exp.: to have a curative effect; to heal
leczniczy [lech-**ńee**-chi] adj.m. curative; healing; remedial; therapeutic; medicinal (tincture, plant, etc.)
środek leczniczy [**śhro**-dek lech-**ńee**-chi] exp.: remedy; medicine; healing action
zabiegi lecznicze [zah-**bye**-gee lech-**ńee**-che] exp.: medication; treatments
leczo [**le**-cho] n. Hungarian paprika dish
leczyć [**le**-chićh] v. heal; treat (a disease); nurse (a cold, etc.); practice medicine; attend (patients) (*repeatedly*)
leczyć się [**le**-chićh śhan] v. undergo treatment; be treated (for); take a cure (for) (*repeatedly*)
leczyć się samemu [**le**-chićh śhan sah-**me**-moo] exp.: to be one's own doctor
ledwie [**led**-vye] adv. hardly; no sooner; scarcely; barely; almost; nearly; only just; narrowly; with difficulty; just a little
ledwie co [**led**-vye tso] exp.: just as; as soon as
ledwie ledwie [**led**-vye **led**-vye] exp.: just barely
ledwie że [**led**-vye zhe] exp.: just barely
ledwie móc stać [**led**-vye moots stahćh] exp.: to be hardly able to stand; to be scarcely able to stand
ledwie zarabiać na życie [**led**-vye zah-**rah**-byahćh nah **zhi**-ćhe] exp.: to earn a bare living
ledwo [**led**-vo] adv. hardly; no sooner; scarcely; barely; almost; nearly; only just; narrowly; with difficulty; just a little
ledwo że nie [**led**-vo zhe ńe] exp.: almost; nearly; hardly
lega [**le**-gah] f. quire (one twentieth of a ream of sheets)
legacja [le-**gah**-tsyah] f. legation; legacy; bequest
legać [**le**-gahćh] v. lie; recline; stay in bed; be buried; be (at a location); be situated (at) (*repeatedly*)
legalista [le-gah-**lee**-stah] m. legalist
legalistka [le-gah-**leest**-kah] f. (woman) legalist
legalistycznie [le-gah-lees-**tich**-ńe] adv. legalistically
legalistyczny [le-gah-lees-**tich**-ni] adj.m. legalistic
legalizacja [le-gah-lee-**zah**-tsyah] f. legalization; authentication; attestation; certification
legalizacyjny [le-gah-lee-zah-**tsiy**-ni] adj.m. of legalization; legalizing
legalizm [le-**gah**-leezm] m. legalism
legalizować [le-gah-lee-**zo**-vahćh] v. legalize; certify; attest; authenticate (*repeatedly*)
legalizowanie [le-gah-lee-zo-**vah**-ńe] n. legalization
legalnie [le-**gahl**-ńe] adv. legally;

lawfully
legalność [le-**gahl**-nośhćh] f. legality; lawfulness
legalny [le-**gahl**-ni] adj.m. legal; lawful; allowed by law
legalny pieniądz [le-**gahl**-ni **pye**-ńownts] exp.: legal tender
pokrewieństwo legalne [po-kre-**vyeń**-stfo le-**gahl**-ne] exp.: relationship by marriage
legar [**le**-gahr] m. joist; mudsill; ground beam; bed timber; sleeper (timber)
legart [**le**-gahrt] m. setter; pointer
legat [**le**-gaht] m. bequest; papal nuncio; anything bequeathed
legatariusz [le-gah-**tahr**-yoosh] m. beneficiary of a bequest
legato [le-**gah**-to] not declined: legato (music)
legator [le-**gah**-tor] m. person making a bequest
legawiec [le-**gah**-vyets] m. pointer; setter (a large hunting dog)
legawy pies [le-**gah**-vi pyes] exp.: pointer; setter (a hunting dog)
legenda [le-**gen**-dah] f. legend; caption; list of conventional signs; explanation of conventional signs
legendarnie [le-gen-**dahr**-ńe] adv. fabulously; legendarily
legendarność [le-gen-**dahr**-nośhćh] f. legendary nature; fictitious character
legendarny [le-gen-**dahr**-ni] adj.m. legendary; fabulous; storied
legendowy [le-gen-**do**-vi] adj.m. of a legend
leghorn [**lek**-khorn] m. Leghorn fowl
legia [**le**-gyah] f. legion; regiment; multitude
legimatyzacja [le-gee-mah-ti-**zah**-tsyah] f. legitimation; legalization
legion [**leg**-yon] m. legion; host
legiony [leg-**yo**-ni] pl. legions
Polskie Legiony [**pols**-ke leg-**yo**-ni] exp.: Polish Legions (of the Napoleonic wars and of World War I)
legionista [leg-yo-**ńee**-stah] m. legionary; member of the Polish Legions
legionowy [leg-yo-**no**-vi] adj.m. legionary
legislacja [le-gee-**slah**-tsyah] f. legislation
legislacyjnie [le-gee-slah-**tsiy**-ńe] adv. legislatively
legislacyjny [le-gee-slah-**tsiy**-ni] adj.m. legislative (assembly, council, etc.); of legislation
legislatura [le-gee-slah-**too**-rah] f. legislature
legislatywa [le-gee-slah-**ti**-vah] f. legislative branch of the government; the legislature
legityma [le-gee-**ti**-mah] f. a part of inheritance which is reserved by law to close relatives
legitymacja [le-gee-ti-**mah**-tsyah] f. ID card; identification papers; membership card; warrant; legitimation
legitymacyjny [le-gee-ti-mah-**tsiy**-ni] adj.m. of identity; identity (papers, etc.)
legitymista [le-gee-ti-**mees**-tah] m. legitimist
legitymistyczny [le-gee-ti-mees-**tich**-ni] adj.m. legitimist
legitymizm [le-gee-**ti**-meezm] m. legitimism
legitymować [le-gee-ti-**mo**-vahćh] v. check (verify) identity papers; identify; authorize; warrant; justify (*repeatedly*)
legitymować się [le-gee-ti-**mo**-vahćh śhan] v. prove one's identity; identify oneself; give evidence (of); show one's (membership, identity, etc.) papers (*repeatedly*)
legitymowanie [le-gee-ti-mo-**vah**-ńe] n. check of identity papers; identity check; authorization
legitymowanie się [le-gee-ti-mo-**vah**-ńe śhan] n. proving one's identity; identifying oneself; giving evidence (of)
legnąć [**leg**-nownćh] v. fall in battle; perish; lie down
legować [le-**go**-vahćh] v. bequeath (*repeatedly*)
legowisko [le-go-**vees**-ko] n. berth; bedding; encampment; den; pallet; lair; quarters; place for hiding; colloq: digs
legumina [le-goo-**mee**-nah] f.

dessert; sweet dish; legumin
legun [le-goon] m. colloq: legionary
legwan [leg-vahn] m. iguana
leiszmania [leysh-mah-ńyah] f. Leishmania (parasite)
leiwo [le-ee-vo] n. liquid substance
leizna [le-ee-znah] f. cast metal
lej [ley] m. crater; funnel; shell-pit
leja [le-yah] f. lei (unit of Romanian money)
lejarnia [le-yahr-ńah] f. foundry
lejarz [le-yahsh] m. founder
lejba [ley-bah] f. loose dress; lesson
lejbgwardia [leyb-gvahr-dyah] f. bodyguard
lejbik [ley-beek] m. (loose) jacket; bodice
lejc [leyts] m. rein
lejce [ley-tse] pl. (driving) reins
ściągać lejce [śhćhown-gahćh ley-tse] exp.: to rein in
lejcowy [ley-tso-vi] adj.m. rein (leather, etc.); m. lead-horse
lejdejski [ley-dey-skee] adj.m. of Leyden
butelka lejdejska [boo-tel-kah ley-dey-skah] exp.: Leyden jar
lejek [le-yek] m. small funnel; small crater
lejkowato [ley-ko-vah-to] adv. in funnel form
lejkowaty [ley-ko-vah-ti] adj.m. funnel-shaped
lejnia [ley-ńah] f. mold
lejność [ley-nośhćh] f. liquidity
lejny [ley-ni] adj.m. in liquid state; liquid (metal, etc.)
lejowaty [le-yo-vah-ti] adj.m. funnel-shaped
lejowy [le-yo-vi] adj.m. of a funnel; of a crater
lejtmotyw [leyt-mo-tif] m. leitmotiv
lejtnant [leyt-nahnt] m. lieutenant
lek [lek] m. medicine; drug; medicament; remedy (against, for); antidote (against, for, to); monetary unit of Albania
uniwersalny lek [oo-ńee-ver-sahl-ni lek] exp.: panacea; colloq: cure-all; heal-all
lekarka [le-kahr-kah] f. lady (woman) doctor
lekarski [le-kahr-skee] adj.m. medical; medicinal; doctor's; physician's
gabinet lekarski [gah-bee-net le-kahr-skee] exp.: doctor's office
Izba Lekarska [eez-bah le-kahr-skah] exp.: State Board of Medicine
świadectwo lekarskie [śhfyah-dets-tfo le-kahr-ske] exp.: health certificate
wydział lekarski [vi-dźhahw le-kahr-skee] exp.: Faculty of Medicine; Department of Medicine
lekarstwo [le-kahr-stfo] n. drug; medicine
zażywać lekarstwo [zah-zhi-vahćh le-kahr-stfo] exp.: to take medicine
ani na lekarstwo [ah-ńee nah le-kahr-stfo] exp.: not a whit; not a single one; not a soul
na lekarstwo [nah le-kahr-stfo] exp.: very little; hardly any
na to nie ma lekarstwa [nah to ńe mah le-kahr-stfah] exp.: there is no cure for that; that can't be remedied; nothing can be done about it
lekarz [le-kahsh] m. physician; doctor
czas jest najlepszym lekarzem [chahs yest nahy-lep-shim le-kah-zhem] exp.: time is the best healer
lekarz dentysta [le-kahsh den-ti-stah] exp.: dental surgeon
lekarz weterynarii [le-kahsh ve-te-ri-nah-ryee] exp.: veterinary surgeon
lekarz ogólnie praktykujący [le-kahsh o-gool-ńe prahk-ti-koo-yown-tsi] exp.: general practitioner
pójść do lekarza [pooyśhćh do le-kah-zhah] exp.: to go and see a doctor
lekceważąco [lek-tse-vah-zhown-tso] adv. slightingly; carelessly; disrespectfully; superciliously; contemptuously; scornfully; neglectfully; depreciatingly; heedlessly
mówić o kimś lekceważąco [moo-veećh o keemśh lek-tse-vah-zhown-tso] exp.: to

depreciate somebody
lekceważący [lek-tse-vah-**zhown**-tsi] adj.m. disrespectful; slighting; supercilious; contemptuous; scornful; depreciating; neglectful
lekceważenie [lek-tse-vah-**zhe**-ńe] n. disdain; disrespect; scorn; slight; contempt; disregard; superciliousness; neglectfulness
z lekceważeniem kogoś, czegoś [z lek-tse-vah-**zhe**-ńem **ko**-gośh, **che**-gośh] exp.: in defiance of somebody, something
lekceważyć [lek-tse-**vah**-zhićh] v. slight; scorn; neglect; disdain; treat with disregard; treat superciliously; depreciate; make light; set at naught; make little account; disregard (ignore) (*repeatedly*)
lekceważyć niebezpieczeństwa [lek-tse-**vah**-zhićh ńe-bes-pye-**cheń**-stfah] exp.: to brave dangers
lekceważyć zdrowie [lek-tse-**vah**-zhićh **zdro**-vye] exp.: to trifle with one's health
lekcja [lek-tsyah] f. lesson; class; private tuition; object lesson; lection
dać komuś lekcję [dahćh **ko**-moośh **lek**-tsyan] exp.: to lesson somebody; to read somebody a lesson; to give a lesson to somebody
odrabiać lekcje [od-**rah**-byahćh **lek**-tsye] exp.: to do one's lessons; to do one's homework
zadać lekcje [zah-dahćh **lek**-tsye] exp.: to give (somebody) homework
lekcjonarz [lek-**tsyo**-nahsh] m. (religious) lectionary; book of lections
lekcyjny [lek-**tsiy**-ni] adj.m. of a lesson
sala lekcyjna [**sah**-lah lek-**tsiy**-nah] exp.: classroom
lekki [lek-kee] adj.m. light; graceful; delicate; slight; gentle; weak; easy; facile; light-hearted; not serious
lekka odzież [lek-kah **o**-dźhesh] exp.: light clothing
lekka waga [**lek**-kah **vah**-gah] exp.: light weight
lekki przemysł [**lek**-kee **pshe**-misw] exp.: light industry
dość lekki [dośhćh **lek**-kee] exp.: lightish; rather light
lekki chleb [**lek**-kee khlep] exp.: easy gain (profit)
mieć lekką rękę [myećh lek-kown ran-kan] exp.: to be a facile worker
lekkie obyczaje [**lek**-ke o-bi-**chah**-ye] exp.: licentiousness
kobieta lekkich obyczajów [ko-**bye**-tah **lek**-keekh o-bi-**chah**-yoof] exp.: woman of easy virtue; promiscuous woman
z lekka [z **lek**-kah] exp.: adv. slightly; not clearly; superficially; a little bit
lekko [**lek**-ko] adv. easily; lightly; slightly; somewhat; (just) a little; a little bit; gently; negligently; triflingly; light-heartedly; wantonly; with ease
lekko ubrany [**lek**-ko oo-**brah**-ni] exp.: lightly clad
lekko mi się zrobiło na sercu [lek-ko mee śhan zro-**bee**-wo nah **ser**-tsoo] exp.: I felt light-hearted; I felt relieved; it was a weight off my heart
lekko sobie poradzę [**lek**-ko **so**-bye po-**rah**-dzan] exp.: I can well manage it
lekko coś traktować [**lek**-ko tsośh trahk-**to**-vahćh] exp.: to treat something lightly
lekko napomknąć coś [**lek**-ko nah-**pom**-knownćh tsośh] exp.: to give a gentle hint at something
lekkoatleta [lek-ko-aht-**le**-tah] m. athlete; track-and-field athlete
lekkoatletka [lek-ko-aht-**let**-kah] f. (female) athlete; track-and-field athlete
lekkoatletyczny [lek-ko-aht-le-**ti**-chni] adj.m. athletic
lekkoatletyka [lek-ko-aht-**le**-ti-kah] f. track-and-field sports; athletics; sports
lekkociężki [lek-ko-**ćhan**-shkee] adj.m. light heavy-weight (boxer)
lekkoduch [lek-**ko**-dookh] m. trifler;

spark; frivolous (light-minded) person; colloq: playboy
lekkoduchostwo [lek-ko-doo-**kho**-stfo] n. frivolity; light-mindedness
lekkomyślnie [lek-ko-**miśhl**-ńe] adv. rashly; recklessly; thoughtlessly; inconsiderately; hastily; injudiciously; flightily; frivolously; in a flighty manner
lekkomyślność [lek-ko-**miśhl**-nośhćh] f. rashness; recklessness; thoughtlessness; light-headedness; light-mindedness; flightiness; fickleness; frivolity; levity; wantonness
lekkomyślny [lek-ko-**miśhl**-ni] adj.m. careless; thoughtless; reckless; rash; fickle; hasty; hare-brained; inconsiderate; light-headed; light-minded; happy-go-lucky; frivolous; flighty; unwise; injudicious
lekkopółśredni [lek-ko-poow-**śhred**-ńee] adj.m. lower light-middle weight (boxer up to 140 pounds)
lekkostrawny [lek-ko-**strahv**-ni] adj.m. light; easily digestible
lekkość [**lek**-kośhćh] f. lightness; delicacy; ease; wantonness; light-headedness; light-mindedness; flightiness; fickleness; frivolity; levity
lekkość stylu [**lek**-kośhćh **sti**-loo] exp.: lightness of style
lekkość w duszy [**lek**-kośhćh v **doo**-śhi] exp.: a light heart
lekkość w mowie [**lek**-kośhćh v **mo**-vye] exp.: fluency of speech
lekkość obyczajów [**lek**-kośhćh o-bi-**chah**-yoof] exp.: licentiousness
lekkośredni [lek-ko-**śhred**-ńee] adj.m. light-middle weight (boxer up to 156 pounds)
lekkozbrojny [lek-ko-**zbroy**-ni] adj.m. light-armed; m. light-armed soldier
lekkuchno [lek-**kookh**-no] adv. very lightly
lekkuchny [lek-**kookh**-ni] adj.m. very light
lekkusi [lek-**koo**-śhee] adj.m. nice and light
lekkusieńki [lek-koo-**śheń**-kee] adj.m. very light
lekkusieńko [lek-koo-**śheń**-ko] adv. very lightly
lekkuśki [lek-**koośh**-kee] adj.m. nice and light
lekomania [le-ko-**mah**-ńyah] f. habit of taking too much medication
lekospis [le-**ko**-spees] m. pharmacopoeia
lekospisowy [le-ko-spee-**so**-vi] adj.m. officinal
lekoznawstwo [le-ko-**znahf**-stfo] n. pharmacognosy; pharmaceutics
leksem [**lek**-sem] m. lexical element; a word
leksyka [**lek**-si-kah] f. content of a lexicon; content of a dictionary
leksykalizacja [le-ksi-kah-lee-**zah**-tsyah] f. process of development of the lexical meaning of a word
leksykalizować [le-ksi-kah-lee-**zo**-vahćh] v. undergo the process of development of the lexical meaning (*repeatedly*)
leksykalizować się [lek-si-kah-lee-**zo**-vahćh śhan] v. be undergoing the process of development of the lexical meaning (*repeatedly*)
leksykalizowanie [le-ksi-kah-lee-zo-**vah**-ńe] n. process of development of the lexical meaning of a word
leksykalizowanie się [lek-si-kah-lee-zo-**vah**-ńe śhan] n. acquiring of the lexical meaning by a word
leksykalnie [le-ksi-**kahl**-ńe] adv. lexically
leksykalny [le-ksi-**kahl**-ni] adj.m. lexical
leksykograf [le-ksi-**ko**-grahf] m. lexicographer
leksykografia [le-ksi-ko-**grah**-fyah] f. lexicography
leksykograficznie [le-ksi-ko-grah-**feech**-ńe] adv. lexicographically
leksykograficzny [le-ksi-ko-grah-**feech**-ni] adj.m. lexicographical
leksykolog [le-ksi-**ko**-log] m. lexicologist
leksykologia [le-ksi-ko-**lo**-gyah] f. lexicology
leksykologiczny [le-ksi-ko-lo-**geech**-ni] adj.m. lexicological
leksykon [le-**ksi**-kon] m. lexicon;

encyclopedic dictionary
lektor [**lek**-tor] m. reader; lector; lecturer; proofreader's assistant
lektorat [lek-**to**-raht] m. lectorship; post of lector; course (in a foreign language); class; lectorate
lektorium [lek-**to**-ryoom] n. reading room
lektorka [lek-**tor**-kah] f. woman reader; woman lector; woman lecturer
lektorski [lek-**tor**-skee] adj.m. reader's; lector's; lecturer's
lektura [lek-**too**-rah] f. reading matter; reading list; reading
lekturowy [lek-too-**ro**-vi] adj.m. of reading matter; of a reading list; reading (matter, etc.)
lektyka [lek-**ti**-kah] f. litter; sedan chair
lektyka konna [lek-**ti**-kah **kon**-nah] exp.: horse-litter
lekuchno [le-**kookh**-no] adv. very lightly
lekuchny [le-**kookh**-ni] adj.m. very light
lekusi [le-**koo**-śhee] adj.m. nice and light
lekusieńki [le-koo-**śheń**-kee] adj.m. very light
lekusieńko [le-koo-**śheń**-ko] adv. very lightly
lekuśki [le-**koośh**-kee] adj.m. nice and light
lekyt [**le**-kit] m. ancient Greek oil pitcher
lelek [**le**-lek] m. nightjar; goatsucker
lelki [**lel**-kee] pl. nightjars; the goatsucker family of birds
lelingit [le-**leen**-geet] m. löllingite (mineral)
leluja [le-**loo**-yah] f. (stylized) lily
lelum polelum [**le**-loom po-**le**-loom] n. sluggard; adv. sluggishly; slowly; leisurely
leman [**le**-mahn] m. feudal tenant; vassal
lemański [le-**mahń**-skee] adj.m. of Geneva
lemat [**le**-maht] m. lemma
lemiesz [**le**-myesh] m. (plow)share; shear blade; vomer
lemieszowy [le-mye-**sho**-vi] adj.m. of a (plow)share; of a shear blade; vomer (bone, etc.)
leming [**le**-meenk] m. lemming
lemoniada [le-mo-**ńah**-dah] f. lemonade; lemon squash
lemur [**le**-moor] m. lemur
lemury [le-**moo**-ri] pl. the lemurs
len [len] m. flax; flaxseed; linseed; linen
czesanie lnu [che-**sah**-ńe lnoo] exp.: flax dressing
lendler [**lend**-ler] m. Austrian folk dance
lenek [**le**-nek] m. a plant of the flax family
leniak [**le**-ńahk] m. hair shedding mammal
lenicja [le-**ńee**-tsyah] f. weakening of audibility and clarity of a sound
lenić się [**le**-ńeećh śhan] v. laze; dally; dillydally; delay; be lazy; shed hair; slough; molt (*repeatedly*)
leniec [**le**-ńets] m. thesium; bastard toadflax
lenieć [**le**-ńećh] v. shed hair; slough (skin); moult (feathers) (*repeatedly*)
lenienie [le-**ńe**-ńe] n. shedding hair
lenienie się [le-**ńe**-ńe śhan] n. undergoing hair shedding; laziness
leniniana [le-ńee-**ńyah**-nah] pl. Lenin's activities, works, and souvenirs
leninizm [le-**ńee**-ńeezm] m. Leninism; Lenin's system
leninowiec [le-ńee-**no**-vyets] m. Lenin's follower
leninowski [le-ńee-**nof**-skee] adj.m. Lenin's; Leninist
leniowaty [le-ńo-**vah**-ti] adj.m. of the Bibionidae insects
leniowate [le-ńo-**vah**-te] pl. the Bibionidae insects
lenistwo [le-**ńee**-stfo] n. laziness; idleness; sloth; sluggishness
leniuch [**le**-ńookh] m. sluggard; idler; lazybones; slowcoach
leniuchować [le-ńoo-**kho**-vahćh] v. laze; idle one's time away; slack (*repeatedly*)
leniuchowanie [le-ńoo-kho-**vah**-ńe] n. idleness; laziness; idling one's time away
leniuchowaty [le-ńoo-kho-**vah**-ti]

adj.m. somewhat lazy; somewhat sluggish

leniuszek [le-ńoo-shek] m. (little) idler; lazybones

leniwie [le-ńee-vye] adv. lazily; slothfully; sluggishly; slowly; tardily

leniwie spędzać czas [le-ńee-vye span-dzahćh chahs] exp.: to waste one's time in idleness

leniwiec [le-ńee-vyets] m. sloth; colloq: sluggard; idler; lazybones; slowcoach

leniwieć [le-ńee-vyećh] v. become lazy; grow lazy (slothful, sluggish) (*repeatedly*)

leniwienie [le-ńee-vye-ńe] n. becoming lazy; growing lazy

leniwka [le-ńeef-kah] f. micrometer

leniwo [le-ńee-vo] adv. lazily; slothfully; sluggishly; slowly; tardily

leniwy [le-ńee-vi] adj.m. lazy; slothful; indolent; idle; sluggish; slack; slow; tardy

lennictwo [len-ńeets-tfo] n. vassalage

lenniczka [len-ńeech-kah] f. woman vassal

lenniczy [len-ńee-chi] adj.m. feudal; feudatory; liege

lennik [len-ńeek] m. vassal; liegeman

lenno [len-no] n. fief; feud

lennodawca [len-no-dahf-tsah] m. feudal (liege) lord

lenny [len-ni] adj.m. feudal

hołd lenny [howd len-ni] exp.: oath of fealty

lenteks [len-teks] m. variety of woven floor-covering

lentex [len-teks] m. variety of woven floor-covering

lento [len-to] n. lento; in a slow manner (music)

leń [leń] m. lazybones; idler; lazy bum; sluggard

mieć lenia [myećh le-ńah] exp.: colloq: to feel lazy; to be lazy

leonin [le-o-ńeen] m. Leonine (poetry)

leoniny [le-o-ńee-ni] pl. Leonine verses

leoniński [le-o-ńeeń-skee] adj.m. Leonine (verses, etc.)

leopard [le-o-pahrt] m. leopard; panther

lep [lep] m. glue

lep na muchy [lep nah moo-khi] exp.: flypaper

lep na ptaki [lep nah ptah-kee] exp.: birdlime

brać kogoś na lep [brahćh ko-gośh nah lep] exp.: colloq: to ensnare somebody; to beguile somebody

iść na lep czegoś [eeśhćh nah lep che-gośh] exp.: colloq: to be lured by something

lepczyca [lep-chi-tsah] f. madwort

lepianka [le-pyahn-kah] f. mud hut; mud-built cabin

lepić [le-peećh] v. model; fashion; mold; build; construct; stick together; paste; glue (*repeatedly*)

lepić się [le-peećh śhan] v. to be sticky; stick (to, together, on); adhere (*repeatedly*)

lepić się od brudu [le-peećh śhan od broo-doo] exp.: to be covered with grime

lepidodendron [le-pee-do-den-dron] m. lepidodendron

lepiej [le-pyey] adv. better; rather better

lepiej się czuć [le-pyey śhan chooćh] exp.: to be (to feel) better; to be improving

ona się lepiej ubiera [o-nah śhan le-pyey oo-bye-rah] exp.: she dresses with better taste

tak jest lepiej [tahk yest le-pyey] exp.: it's better so

coraz lepiej [tso-rahs le-pyey] exp.: better and better

chodźmy lepiej stąd [khodźh-mi le-pyey stownt] exp.: we better get out of here

milczałbyś lepiej [meel-chahw-biśh le-pyey] exp.: I wish you'd keep quiet; I wish you would not talk

pójdźmy lepiej do kina [pooy-dźhmi le-pyey do kee-nah] exp.: let's rather go to the movies

lepienie [le-pye-ńe] n. stickiness

lepiężnik [le-pyan-zhńeek] m. butterbur; fleadock (plant)

lepik [**le**-peek] m. cement; glue; agglutinant; adhesive (substance)
lepiszcze [le-**peesh**-che] n. an adhesive; binder; binding (cementing) agent
lepki [**lep**-kee] adj.m. sticky; gluey; tenacious; clammy; cloggy
mieć lepkie ręce [myećh **lep**-ke ran-tse] exp.: to have light fingers; to be easily tempted to steal
lepko [**lep**-ko] adv. stickily
lepkościomierz [lep-ko-**śhćho**-myesh] m. viscosimeter
lepkość [**lep**-kośhćh] f. stickiness; viscosity; tack
lepnica [lep-**ńee**-tsah] f. catchfly; flybane
lepnik [**lep**-ńeek] m. stickseed; gluten
leporello [le-po-**rel**-lo] n. advertising print folded like a harmonica
lepować [le-**po**-vahćh] v. glue insecticidal bands on trees (*repeatedly*)
lepowanie [le-po-**vah**-ńe] n. installation of insecticidal bands on trees
lepowy [le-**po**-vi] adj.m. of adhesive bands (for insect control)
lepra [**le**-prah] f. leprosy
leprozorium [le-pro-**zor**-yoom] n. leprosaria; hospital for lepers
lepsze [**lep**-she] adj.n. better (egg, etc.); n. something better; a better future; a better life
a co lepsze [ah tso **lep**-she] exp.: ... better still...; ...and what more ...
w najlepsze [v nahy-**lep**-she] exp.: for good; to the highest degree
lepszość [**lep**-shośhćh] f. superiority; better state; improved state; better quality
lepszy [**lep**-shi] adj.m. better; improved; superior; preferable
iść ku lepszemu [eeśhćh koo lep-**she**-moo] exp.: to take a turn for the better
moja lepsza połowa [mo-yah **lep**-shah po-**wo**-vah] exp.: my better half
obrócić się na lepsze [o-**broo**-ćheećh śhan nah **lep**-she] exp.: to take a turn for the better
pierwszy lepszy głupiec [**pyerf**-shi **lep**-shi **gwoo**-pyets] exp.: any fool
w braku czegoś lepszego [v **brah**-koo **che**-gośh lep-**she**-go] exp.: for lack (for want) of something better
zmiana na lepsze [**zmyah**-nah nah **lep**-she] exp.: a turn for the better
lepta [**lep**-tah] f. Greek cent
leptosomatyk [lep-to-so-**mah**-tik] m. leptosome; asthenic; ectomorphic
leptosomia [lep-to-**so**-myah] f. leptosome condition
leptosomiczny [lep-to-so-**meech**-ni] adj.m. leptosome
leptyt [**lep**-tit] m. leptite (mineral)
lerka [**ler**-kah] f. woodlark
lesbijka [les-**beey**-kah] f. lesbian; homosexual woman
lesbijski [les-**beey**-skee] adj.m. Lesbian
leseferyzm [le-se-**fe**-rizm] m. laissez-faire economics; laissez faire system; laissez faire policies; laissez faire doctrine
leser [**le**-ser] m. colloq: lazybones; sluggard; sloth; idler; slowcoach
leserować [le-se-**ro**-vahćh] v. colloq: be lazybones; be a sloth; be a sluggard; be an idler; be a slowcoach; mob slang: commit forgery; be vagrant (*repeatedly*)
lesistość [le-**śhees**-tośhćh] f. forestage; timber stand
lesisty [le-**śhees**-ti] adj.m. wooded; woody; forested
less [les] m. loess
lessowy [les-**so**-vi] adj.m. of loess; loessal; loessic
lesz [lesh] m. cinders; slag
leszcz [leshch] m. bream (variety of carp) (fish)
leszczyk [**lesh**-chik] m. carp; bream (variety of carp) (fish)
leszczyna [lesh-**chi**-nah] f. hazel; filbert; hazelnut tree; hazel grove
kotki leszczyny [**kot**-kee lesh-**chi**-ni] exp.: lamb's tails
leszczynowy [lesh-chi-**no**-vi] adj.m. of a hazel; of a filbert; hazelnut (tree, etc.); hazel (grove, etc.)
leszować [le-**sho**-vahćh] v. cover

with cinders; spread slag (*repeatedly*)
leszowanie [le-sho-**vah**-ńe] n. covering with cinders; spreading of slag
leszowy [le-**sho**-vi] adj.m. cinder (walkway); slag (heap, etc.)
leśnictwo [leśh-**ńeets**-tfo] n. forestry; forest-range
leśniczanka [leśh-ńee-**chahn**-kah] f. forester's daughter
leśniczostwo [leśh-ńee-**chos**-tfo] n. forestership; post of forester; forester and his wife
leśniczówka [leśh-ńee-**choof**-kah] f. ranger's house
leśniczy [leśh-**ńee**-chi] m. ranger; forest-ranger; forester; adj.m. ranger's; forest-ranger's; forester's
leśniczyna [leśh-ńee-**chi**-nah] f. forester's wife
leśnik [**leśh**-ńeek] m. forester
leśny [**leśh**-ni] adj.m. of a forest; of forestry; forest; wood; m. forest guerilla
gospodarka leśna [gos-po-**dahr**-kah **leśh**-nah] exp.: forest-administration
krajobraz leśny [krahy-**o**-brahs **leśh**-ni] exp.: woodland scenery
szkółka leśna [shkoow-kah **leśh**-nah] exp.: nursery
letalny [le-**tahl**-ni] adj.m. lethal
letarg [**le**-tahrg] m. lethargy; trance; inertness; torpor
letargiczny [le-tahr-**geech**-ni] adj.m. lethargic
letejski [le-**tey**-skee] adj.m. Lethean (water, etc.)
letkiewicz [let-k̲e-veech] m. trifler; spark; colloq: playboy
letkiewiczostwo [let-k̲e-vee-**chos**-tfo] n. frivolity; light-mindedness
letni [**let**-ńee] adj.m. summer (months, residence, etc.); lukewarm; half-hearted; tepid
czas letni [chahs **let**-ńee] exp.: summer daylight-saving time
pora letnia [**po**-rah **let**-ńah] exp.: summertime
letniczka [let-**ńeech**-kah] f. (female) holiday-maker; vacationer; visitor (at a summer resort)
letniczek [let-**ńee**-chek] m. summer dress
letniak [**let**-ńahk] m. summer home; vacation house
na letniaka [nah let-**ńah**-kah] exp.: in summer clothing; lightly dressed
letnik [**let**-ńeek] m. vacationer; visitor (at a summer resort)
letnio [**let**-ńo] adv. (be dressed) lightly; for summer
letnisko [let-**ńees**-ko] n. summer resort; summer vacation spot
letniskowy [let-ńees-**ko**-vi] adj.m. summer-resort (atmosphere, etc.)
leucyna [lew-**tsi**-nah] f. leucine
leucyt [**lew**-tsit] m. leucite (mineral)
leukemia [lew-**ke**-myah] f. leukemia
leukocydyna [lew-ko-tsi-**di**-nah] f. leucocidin
leukocyt [lew-**ko**-tsit] m. leucocyte
leukocyty [lew-ko-**tsi**-ti] pl. leucocyte nucleated blood cells
leukocytoza [lew-ko-tsi-**to**-zah] f. leucocytosis
leukopenia [lew-ko-**pe**-ńyah] f. leukopenia
leukopeniczny [lew-ko-pe-**ńeech**-ni] adj.m. leukopenic
leukoplast [lew-**ko**-plahst] m. leucoplast; sticking-plaster
leukoplasty [lew-ko-**plahs**-ti] pl. leucoplasts
lew [lev] m. lion; unit of Bulgarian money; colloq: lady's man
lew morski [lev **mor**-skee] exp.: sea lion
lewa [**le**-vah] f. (card) trick; left side; unit of Bulgarian money
lewacki [le-**vah**-tskee] adj.m. colloq: radical leftist's (views, etc.)
lewactwo [le-**vah**-tstfo] n. colloq: radical leftist views, programs, etc.
lewak [**le**-vahk] m. colloq: radical leftist
lewant [**le**-vahnt] m. Near East; Levant; colloq: Polish merchant ship serving the Near East
Lewantyńczyk [le-vahn-**tiń**-chik] m. Levantine
lewantyński [le-vahn-**tiń**-skee] adj.m. Levantine
lewar [**le**-vahr] m. lever; jack

podnieść lewarem [pod-ńeśhćh le-**vah**-rem] exp.: to jack up (a car, etc.); siphon; syphon
lewarek [le-**vah**-rek] m. (small) lever; jack; syphon; teeth pulling tool
lewarowy [le-vah-**ro**-vi] adj.m. of a jack; of a syphon
barometr lewarowy [bah-**ro**-metr le-vah-**ro**-vi] exp.: siphon barometer
lewatywa [le-vah-**ti**-vah] f. enema; lavement
lewek [**le**-vek] m. young lion; small lion; lion's cub
lewiatan [le-**vyah**-tahn] m. leviathan
lewica [le-**vee**-tsah] f. the Left; left-hand side; left hand political party, etc.
na lewicy [nah le-**vee**-tsi] exp.: on the left; at somebody's left
lewicować [le-vee-**tso**-vahćh] v. have leftist tendencies (*repeatedly*)
lewicowanie [le-vee-tso-**vah**-ńe] n. leftist tendencies
lewicowiec [le-vee-**tso**-vyets] m. (a) leftist
lewicowość [le-vee-**tso**-vośhćh] f. left leaning tendency; leftist views
lewicowy [le-vee-**tso**-vi] adj.m. leftist
odchylenia lewicowe [ot-khi-**le**-ńah le-vee-**tso**-ve] exp.: leftist deviations
lewirat [le-**vee**-raht] m. obligation to marry brother's widow; levirate
lewita [le-**vee**-tah] m. Levite
lewitacja [le-vee-**tah**-tsyah] f. levitation
lewitować [le-vee-**to**-vahćh] v. levitate (*repeatedly*)
lewizna [le-**veez**-nah] f. colloq: an illegal and profitable possession
lewkonia [lef-**ko**-ńyah] f. stock (gillyflower)
lewo [**le**-vo] adv. left; to the left
iść na lewo [eeśhćh nah **le**-vo] exp.: to go left
na lewo [nah **le**-vo] exp.: to the left; left; colloq: on the crook; illegally
na prawo i na lewo [nah **prah**-vo ee nah **le**-vo] exp.: to the right and left; all over the place
zwrot w lewo [zvrot v le-vo] exp.: left turn
lewobrzeżny [le-vo-**bzhe**-zhni] adj.m. situated on the left bank of a river; left-bank
leworęczność [le-vo-**ranch**-nośhćh] f. left-handedness
leworęczny [le-vo-**ranch**-ni] adj.m. left-handed; m. left-handed man
leworęki [le-vo-**ran**-kee] adj.m. left-handed; m. left-handed man
lewoskręt [le-**vo**-skrant] m. left turn
lewoskrętność [le-vo-**skrant**-nośhćh] f. left-handed rotation
lewoskrętny [le-vo-**skrant**-ni] adj.m. with a left-hand thread; rotating to the left
lewoskrzydłowy [le-vo-skshi-**dwo**-vi] adj.m. left-flank; left-wing (unit, etc.); m. the outside left (ball player)
lewostronny [le-vo-**stron**-ni] adj.m. left-sided
lewuloza [le-voo-**lo**-zah] f. levulose; fruitsugar; fructose
lewy [**le**-vi] adj.m. left; false; sinister; left-hand (side, etc.); verso (of a coin); back; wrong side
lewa [**le**-vah] f. left hand; the left-hand side; the left
wstać lewą nogą [fstahćh **le**-vown **no**-gown] exp.: to get out of bed on the wrong side
na lewą stronę [nah **le**-vown **stro**-nan] exp.: inside out
z lewa [z **le**-vah] exp.: on the left; on the left-hand side
lezginka [lez-**geen**-kah] f. a Caucasian dance
Lezginka [lez-**geen**-kah] f. Caucasian Dagestan woman
leźć [leśhćh] v. crawl; creep; climb; shuffle along; plod one's way; go along; jostle one's way (*repeatedly*)
uważaj, jak leziesz [oo-**vah**-zhahy yahk le-źhesh] exp.: colloq: look where you're going
nie lezie mi do głowy [ńe le-źhe mee do **gwo**-vi] exp.: colloq: I can't get that into my head

leża [**le**-zhah] f. lair; den; lie
leżak [**le**-zhahk] m. folding (canvas) chair; deck chair; lager beer
leżakować [le-zhah-**ko**-vahćh] v. lie in a deck chair; to mellow in storage (*repeatedly*)
leżakowanie [le-zhah-ko-**vah**-ńe] n. open-air rest cure; bed-rest in the open air
leżakownia [le-zhah-**kov**-ńah] f. storage of folding (canvas) chairs (deck chairs)
leżakowy [le-zhah-**ko**-vi] adj.m. of folding (canvas) chairs; of deck chairs
leżalnia [le-**zhahl**-ńah] f. terrace for patients taking an open air rest; room for resting
leżanina [le-zhah-ńee-nah] f. rotten wood on the forest floor
leżanka [le-**zhahn**-kah] f. couch
leżąco [le-**zhown**-tso] adv. lying down; in a recumbent posture
leżący [le-**zhown**-tsi] adj.m. reclining; lying; recumbent; m. lying person
leżący na wznak [le-**zhown**-tsi nah vznahk] exp.: supine
pozycja leżąca [po-**zi**-tsyah le-**zhown**-tsah] exp.: recumbent posture
leżąc twarzą do ziemi [le-**zhownts** **tfah**-zhown do **źhe**-mee] exp.: prone; prostate
leże [**le**-zhe] n. place to lie down; shakedown; pallet; (military) quarters; lair; den; lie
leżeć [le-zhećh] v. lie; recline; be recumbent; stay in bed; keep one's bed; be buried; be (located on); fit; suit; be situated; fail to meet one's contract (in a card game) (*repeatedly*)
leżeć na grypę [le-zhećh nah **gri**-pan] exp.: to be ill (laid up) with the flu
leżeć w szpitalu [le-zhećh f shpee-**tah**-loo] exp.: to be in the hospital
leżeć do góry brzuchem [le-zhećh do **goo**-ri **bzhoo**-khem] exp.: to loll in indolence
kurz leżał na meblach [koosh le-zhahw nah **me**-blahkh] exp.: there was (a layer of) dust on the furniture
leżeć w gruzach [le-zhećh v **groo**-zahkh] exp.: to lie in ruin
leżało mu to na sumieniu [le-**zhah**-wo moo to nah soo-**mye**-ńoo] exp.: it lay heavy on his conscience
leży mi to na sercu [le-zhi mee to nah **ser**-tsoo] exp.: I have it at heart
leży mi to na wątrobie [**le**-zhi mee to nah vown-**tro**-bye] exp.: it is a weight on my mind
pieniądze leżą na ulicach [pye-ńown-dze **le**-zhown nah oo-**lee**-tsahkh] exp.: the streets are paved with gold
to leży w jego usposobieniu [to **le**-zhi v **ye**-go oo-spo-so-**bye**-ńoo] exp.: it is in his nature
to leży na twojej głowie [to **le**-zhi nah **tfo**-yey **gwo**-vye] exp.: it is your responsibility
to leży w twoim interesie [to le-zhi f **tfo**-eem een-te-re-śhe] exp.: it is (it lies) in your interest
nie leży dobrze [ńe le-zhi **do**-bzhe] exp.: it's not a good fit
wina leży po twojej stronie [**vee**-nah **le**-zhi po **tfo**-yey **stro**-ńe] exp.: it's your fault
leżenie [le-**zhe**-ńe] n. recumbent position; failure to make one's contract
leźnia [lezh-ńah] f. transom pole; putlog; rafter plate
leźnik [lezh-ńeek] m. scaffolding floor board
lędźwian [**landźh**-vyahn] m. everlasting pea (plant)
lędźwica [landźh-**vee**-tsah] f. lumbago
lędźwie [**landźh**-vye] pl. loins; lumbus
lędźwiowy [landźh-**vyo**-vi] adj.m. lumbar
lęg [lank] m. hatch; hatching; brood
lęgnąć się [**lang**-nownćh śhan] v. breed; hatch; arise; spring up; come into being (*repeatedly*)
lęgnia [**lang**-ńah] f. oogonium
lęgowisko [lan-go-**vee**-sko] n. breeding ground

lęgowy [lan-**go**-vi] adj.m. of breeding
jama lęgowa [yah-mah lan-**go**-vah] exp.: brood chamber
kanał lęgowy [**kah**-nahw lan-**go**-vi] exp.: brood canal
pora lęgowa [**po**-rah lan-**go**-vah] exp.: breeding season
lęk [lank] m. fear; anxiety; dread; apprehension
lęk przestrzeni [lank pshe-**stshe**-ńee] exp.: agoraphobia; fear of open space
lęk wysokości [lank vi-so-**kośh**-ćhee] exp.: acrophobia; fear of being at a great height
ogarnął go lęk [o-**gahr**-now go lank] exp.: he succumbed to fear; he shied; he felt apprehensive; he had a feeling of dread
bez lęku [bez **lan**-koo] exp.: fearlessly
budzący lęk [boo-**dzown**-tsi lank] exp.: awe-inspiring
z lękiem [z **lan**-kem] exp.: anxiously
lękać się [**lan**-kahćh śhan] v. be afraid; dread; fear (of, for); stand in awe; quail (before); shy (at); be full of anxiety (for); be apprehensive (for) (*repeatedly*)
lękać się kogoś [**lan**-kahćh śhan **ko**-gośh] exp.: to be afraid of somebody
lękanie się [lan-**kah**-ńe śhan] n. fear; dread; apprehension; anxiety
lękliwie [lan-**klee**-vye] adv. timidly; apprehensively; faintheartedly
lękliwość [lan-**klee**-vośhćh] f. timidity; apprehensiveness; faintheartedness
lękliwy [lan-**klee**-vi] adj.m. timid; fainthearted; apprehensive
lękowy [lan-**ko**-vi] adj.m. anxiety (hysteria, neurosis, etc.)
lgnący [**lgnown**-tsi] adj.m. adhesive; sticky; clingy
lgnąć [lgnownćh] v. adhere; sink; stick; be partial; feel attracted; get stuck; cling (*repeatedly*)
lgnięcie [**lgńan**-ćhe] n. stickiness; adhesion; partiality; attraction
li [lee] particle: only; also; suffix: **-li** [lee] whether?; do you?; if
li tylko [lee **til**-ko] exp.: only; exclusively; nothing but; nobody but; nowhere but
znaszli ten kraj? [**znahsh**-lee ten krahy] exp.: do you know the country (where)? (poetic exp.)
liana [**lyah**-nah] f. liana
lias [lyahs] m. lias (Jurassic series)
liasowy [lyah-**so**-vi] adj.m. liassic (limestone, etc.)
libacja [lee-**bah**-tsyah] f. drinking party; drinking bout; revel; carousal; libation
libacyjka [lee-bah-**tsiy**-kah] f. (small) drinking party; drinking bout; revel; carousal; libation
Libańczyk [lee-**bahń**-chik] m. Lebanese
libański [lee-**bahń**-skee] adj.m. Lebanese
libella [lee-**bel**-lah] f. level; bubble
liberalistyczny [lee-be-rah-lees-**tich**-ni] adj.m. liberalistic
liberalizacja [lee-be-rah-lee-**zah**-tsyah] f. liberalization
liberalizm [lee-be-**rah**-leezm] m. liberalism; laissez-faire policy
liberalizować [lee-be-rah-lee-**zo**-vahćh] v. liberalize (*repeatedly*)
liberalizowanie [lee-be-rah-lee-zo-**vah**-ńe] n. liberalization
liberalnie [lee-be-**rahl**-ńe] adv. liberally
liberalność [lee-be-**rahl**-nośhćh] f. liberality
liberalny [lee-be-**rahl**-ni] adj.m. liberal; broad-minded; tolerant
być liberalnym [bićh lee-be-**rahl**-nim] exp.: to live and let live
liberał [lee-**be**-rahw] m. liberal
liberia [lee-**be**-ryah] f. livery; the livery; retainers
szwajcar w liberii [**shfahy**-tsahr v lee-**ber**-yee] exp.: liveried commissionaire; livered footman; levered doorman
libertacja [lee-ber-**tah**-tsyah] f. liberation; exemption (from taxes, etc.)
libertyn [lee-**ber**-tin] m. libertine; freethinker; promiscuous man
libertynizm [lee-ber-**ti**-ńeezm] m. freethinking; libertinism
libertyński [lee-ber-**tiń**-skee] adj.m.

freethinking; libertine
Liberyjczyk [lee-be-**riy**-chik] m. Liberian
liberyjny [lee-be-**riy**-ni] adj.m. livery (colors, etc.); liveried
liberyjski [lee-be-**riy**-skee] adj.m. Liberian
libido [lee-**bee**-do] n. libido
Libijczyk [lee-**beey**-chik] m. Libian
libijski [lee-**beey**-skee] adj.m. Libian
libra [**lee**-brah] f. quire; collection of 24 or 25 identical sheets of paper
libracja [lee-**brah**-tsyah] f. libration
librecista [lee-bre-**ćhee**-stah] m. librettist
libretto [lee-**bret**-to] n. libretto; book (of an opera)
lice [**lee**-tse] n. face; cheek; the right side; evidence (of guilt)
licealista [lee-tse-ah-**lee**-stah] m. high-school student; junior college student
licealistka [lee-tse-ah-**leest**-kah] f. (female) high-school student; junior college student
licealny [lee-tse-**ahl**-ni] adj.m. of a high school; of a junior college
licencja [lee-**tsen**-tsyah] f. license (permission to practice)
licencjat [lee-**tsen**-tsyaht] m. licentiate; graduate of a university
licencjonować [lee-tsen-tsyo-**no**-vahćh] v. license (somebody to do something) (*repeatedly*)
licencjonowanie [lee-tsen-tsyo-no-**vah**-ńe] n. licensing; issuing a license (to somebody to do something)
licencyjny [lee-tsen-**tsiy**-ni] adj.m. license (board, etc.); licensed (sale, etc.); (produced) under license
liceum [lee-**tse**-oom] n. Polish junior college (senior high school)
licha [**lee**-khah] f. big caterpillar
lichawy [lee-**khah**-vi] adj.m. baddish; rather poor
lichenolog [lee-khe-**no**-log] m. lichenologist
lichenologia [lee-khe-no-**lo**-gyah] f. lichenology
lichenologiczny [lee-khe-no-lo-**geech**-ni] adj.m. lichenologic; lichenological
licho [**lee**-kho] adv. poorly; badly; indifferently; scantily; miserably; insufficiently
licho [**lee**-kho] n. evil spirit; devil; the deuce; the dickens; evil; mischief; misfortune; odd
licha wart [**lee**-khah vahrt] exp.: of no earthly use; no good
licho go bierze [**lee**-kho go **bye**-zhe] exp.: he is going mad
licho go nosi [**lee**-kho go **no**-śhee] exp.: he gads about; he is on the go to little purpose
licho go opętało [**lee**-kho go o-p<u>an</u>-**tah**-wo] exp.: he is off his chump; he is off his mind; he is off his rocker
licho nie śpi [**lee**-kho ńe śhpee] exp.: accidents will happen
licho wie [**lee**-kho vye] exp.: goodness knows
licho wie dlaczego [**lee**-kho vye dlah-**che**-go] exp.: for no earthly reason
co my do licha zrobimy? [tso mi do **lee**-khah zro-**bee**-mi] exp.: what ever are we going to do?
gdzie on się do licha podziewa? [gdźhe on śh<u>an</u> do **lee**-khah po-**dźhe**-vah] exp.: where can he possibly be?
po kiego licha on to zrobił? [po <u>k</u>e-go **lee**-khah on to **zro**-beew] exp.: what business had he to do that?; what did he do it for?
niech licho porwie [ńekh **lee**-kho **por**-vye] exp.: hang it all!
lichość [**lee**-khośhćh] f. poor quality; flimsiness; trash; rubbish; trumpery; junk; shoddy; poor stuff
lichota [lee-**kho**-tah] f. trash; poor quality
lichtarz [**leekh**-tahsh] m. candlestick; candelabra
lichtarzowy [leekh-tah-**zho**-vi] adj.m. of a candlestick; of a candelabra
lichtarzyk [leekh-**tah**-zhik] m. (small, nice) candlestick; candelabra
lichtować [leekh-**to**-vahćh] v. move ship's cargo (*repeatedly*)
lichtowanie [leekh-to-**vah**-ńe] n. transferring ship's cargo
lichtuga [leekh-**too**-gah] f. port

service vessel
lichutki [lee-**khoot**-kee] adj.m. (somewhat) petty; flimsy; poor; worthless; inadequate; colloq: rotten
lichutko [lee-**khoot**-ko] adv. (somewhat) pettily; flimsily; poorly; worthlessly; inadequately; colloq: in a rotten manner
lichwa [**lee**-khfah] f. usury
lichwiarka [lee-**khfyahr**-kah] f. woman usurer
lichwiarski [lee-**khfyahr**-skee] adj.m. usurious
lichwiarstwo [lee-**khfyahr**-stfo] n. usury
lichwiarz [**lee**-khfyahsh] m. usurer; loan shark; moneylender (at high interest rate)
lichy [**lee**-khi] adj.m. shoddy; shabby; poor; mean; miserable; inferior; paltry; flimsy; trivial; rotten; wretched; bad; indifferent; petty; insignificant; worthless; inadequate; colloq: rotten
lico [**lee**-tso] n. face; cheek; surface; front; outer part
licować [lee-**tso**-vahćh] v. be in harmony; fit for...; be compatible (with); befit; veneer; face (a wall, etc.) (*repeatedly*)
licowanie [lee-tso-**vah**-ńe] n. veneer; facing (a wall, etc.)
licowy [lee-**tso**-vi] adj.m. right; facing ...; front...(side); zygomatic; malar
kość licowa [kośhćh lee-**tso**-vah] exp.: zygoma; jugal bone
strona licowa [**stro**-nah lee-**tso**-vah] exp.: front side; obverse (of a coin, etc.)
licówka [lee-**tsoof**-kah] f. facing brick; face brick; surface dressing
licujący [lee-tsoo-**yown**-tsi] adj.m. compatible
licytacja [lee-tsi-**tah**-tsyah] f. auction; bidding; the bid; contest; emulation
sprzedawać coś na licytacji [spshe-**dah**-vahćh tsośh nah lee-tsi-**tah**-tsyee] exp.: to sell something by auction
wystawić na licytację [vi-**stah**-veećh nah lee-tsi-**tah**-tsyan] exp.: to put something up for auction
licytacyjny [lee-tsi-tah-**tsiy**-ni] adj.m. auction (house, day, etc.)
licytant [lee-**tsi**-tahnt] m. bidder; offerer
licytator [lee-tsi-**tah**-tor] m. auctioneer
licytować [lee-tsi-**to**-vahćh] v. sell by auction; auction; bid; offer; sell up; call (*repeatedly*)
licytować się [lee-tsi-**to**-vahćh śhan] v. contend with each other (one another); to outbid each other (*repeatedly*)
licytowanie [lee-tsi-to-**vah**-ńe] n. selling by auction; auction; bidding
licytowanie się [lee-tsi-to-**vah**-ńe śhan] n. outbidding each other
liczba [**leedzh**-bah] f. number; figure; integer; group; class
liczba całkowita [**leedzh**-bah tsahw-ko-**vee**-tah] exp.: whole number; integer
liczba nieparzysta [**leedzh**-bah ńe-pah-**zhi**-stah] exp.: odd number
liczba porządkowa [**leedzh**-bah po-zhownt-**ko**-vah] exp.: ordinal (number)
liczba atomowa [**leedzh**-bah ah-to-**mo**-vah] exp.: atomic number
liczba mnoga [**leedzh**-bah **mno**-gah] exp.: plural number
pewna liczba [**pev**-nah **leedzh**-bah] exp.: a certain number
znaczna liczba [**znahch**-nah **leedzh**-bah] exp.: a considerable number
liczbować [leedzh-**bo**-vahćh] v. number (*repeatedly*)
liczbowanie [leedzh-bo-**vah**-ńe] n. numbering
liczbowo [leedzh-**bo**-vo] adv. in numbers; in respect of figures; numerically
liczbowy [leedzh-**bo**-vi] adj.m. numerical; numeral
loteria liczbowa [lo-**te**-ryah leedzh-**bo**-vah] exp.: number lottery
liczbówka [leedzh-**boof**-kah] f. number lottery
liczebnie [lee-**cheb**-ńe] adv. numerically; in number; in respect of numbers

przewyższać liczebnie [pshe-**vish**-shahćh lee-**cheb**-ńe] exp.: to outnumber
liczebnik [lee-**cheb**-ńeek] m. numeral; number
liczebniki główne [lee-cheb-ńee-kee **gwoo**-vne] exp.: cardinal numbers
liczebnikowy [lee-cheb-ńee-**ko**-vi] adj.m. of a numeral; of a number
liczebność [lee-**cheb**-nośhćh] f. numerical force; great number; numbers
zwyciężyć liczebnością [zvi-ćhan-zhićh lee-cheb-**no**-śhćhown] exp.: to win by the force of numbers
liczebny [lee-**cheb**-ni] adj.m. numerical; numerically strong
stan liczebny oddziału wojsk [stahn lee-**cheb**-ni od-**dźhah**-woo voysk] exp.: effective (numerical) force of a unit
liczenie [lee-**che**-ńe] n. count; calculation; computing; numeration
liczenie się [lee-**che**-ńe śhan] n. expecting; taking under consideration
liczko [**leech**-ko] n. grain side (of leather); hair side (of leather); child's face
liczman [**leech**-mahn] m. counter (of shipped items); colloq: substitute; substitution
licznie [**leech**-ńe] adv. numerously; in great number; in force; in crowds
coraz liczniej [tso-rahs **leech**-ńey] exp.: in greater and greater number
licznik [**leech**-ńeek] m. counter; numerator; gas meter; electric meter; taximeter; register
licznikowy [leech-ńee-**ko**-vi] adj.m. meter (box, unit, etc.)
liczny [**leech**-ni] adj.m. numerous; large; abundant; plentiful; frequent
liczyć [lee-chićh] v. count; reckon; compute; calculate; do sums; expect; bank; rely; add up; take into account; include; be composed; comprise; number; estimate; charge (*repeatedly*)
on nie umie liczyć do trzech [on ńe oo-mye **lee**-chićh do tshekh] exp.: he doesn't know anything; colloq: he is ignorant
liczyć, że się coś stanie [lee-chićh zhe śhan tsośh **stah**-ńe] exp.: to expect something to happen
liczyć na coś [lee-chićh nah tsośh] exp.: to look forward to something
liczyć na to, że ktoś coś zrobi [lee-chićh nah to zhe ktośh cośh **zro**-bee] exp.: to leave it to somebody to do something
liczyć na własne siły [lee-chićh nah **vwah**-sne **śhee**-wi] exp.: to depend on oneself
możesz na to liczyć [mo-zhesh nah to **lee**-chićh] exp.: you may depend on it
można ich liczyć na tuziny [mo-zhnah eekh lee-chićh nah too-**źhee**-ni] exp.: they are numbered by the dozen
lekko licząc [lek-ko **lee**-chownts] exp.: at the lowest estimate
liczyć krupy [lee-chićh **kroo**-pi] exp.: to be stingy
nie licząc mnie [ńe **lee**-chownts mńe] exp.: beside myself
liczono go na pół miliona [lee-**cho**-no go nah poow meel-**yo**-nah] exp.: he was estimated to be worth half a million
ile on liczy za wizytę? [ee-le on lee-chi zah vee-**zi**-tan] exp.: how much does he charge for a consultation?
liczyć się [lee-chićh śhan] v. to be counted (*repeatedly*)
liczyć się na dni [lee-chićh śhan nah dńee] exp.: to be a matter of days
on się liczy za dwóch [on śhan **lee**-chi zah dvookh] exp.: he counts for two
to się nie liczy [to śhan ńe **lee**-chi] exp.: that doesn't count
nie liczyć się z kimś [ńe lee-chićh śhan s keemśh] exp.: to ignore somebody
liczyć się z czasem [lee-chićh

śhan s chah-sem] exp.: to watch the clock
liczyć się ze słowami [lee-chićh śhan ze swo-vah-mee] exp.: to mind one's words
liczyć się z każdym groszem [lee-chićh śhan s kahzh-dim gro-shem] exp.: to be careful of every penny one spends
nie licząc się z wydatkami [ńe lee-chownts śhan z vi-daht-kah-mee] exp.: regardless of the expense
nie liczyć się z niczym [ńe lee-chićh śhan z ńee-chim] exp.: to go all lengths
liczydełko [lee-chi-dew-ko] n. (small) abacus; twisted-stalk; counter; register
liczydło [lee-chid-wo] n. abacus; twisted-stalk; counter; register
liczydłowy [lee-chid-wo-vi] adj.m. of an abacus; of a counter; of a register
liczygrosz [lee-chi-grosh] m. miser; niggard; skinflint
liczykrupa [lee-chi-kroo-pah] m. miser; niggard; skinflint
lider [lee-der] m. leader
lido [lee-do] n. lido; a fashionable beach resort
lidyt [lee-dit] m. lydite; Lydian stone; touchstone
lift [leeft] m. a variety of rebound of a tennis ball
lifting [leef-teenk] m. face lifting
liftowany [leef-to-vah-ni] adj.m. rebounded (tennis ball)
liga [lee-gah] f. league; alliance; organization; confederacy; title (of gold, etc.)
ligand [lee-gahnt] m. ligand
ligatura [lee-gah-too-rah] f. ligature; bind; tie (music)
ligawka [lee-gahf-kah] f. old-time pastoral piping instrument
ligaza [lee-gah-zah] f. variety of a basic enzyme
lignifikacja [leeg-ńee-fee-kah-tsyah] f. lignification
lignifikować [leeg-ńee-fee-ko-vahćh] v. lignify (*repeatedly*)
lignifikowanie [leeg-ńee-fee-ko-vah-ńe] n. lignification; conversion into wood
lignina [leeg-ńee-nah] f. lignin; wood-wool
ligninowy [leeg-ńee-no-vi] adj.m. ligneous; of lignin; woody; resembling wood
lignit [leeg-ńeet] m. lignite (mineral)
lignitowy [leeg-ńee-to-vi] adj.m. lignitic
lignofol [leeg-no-fol] m. high quality (lignitic) plywood
lignoston [leeg-no-ston] m. lignitic plate produced under high pressure; compressed wood
lignoza [leeg-no-zah] f. lignose
ligowiec [lee-go-vyets] m. league player
ligowy [lee-go-vi] adj.m. league (football, etc.)
ligroina [lee-groy-nah] f. ligroin
liguryjski [lee-goo-riy-skee] adj.m. Ligurian
ligustr [lee-goostr] m. privet
ligustrowy [lee-goo-stro-vi] adj.m. privet ... (hedge, etc.)
lik [leek] m. lot; leech; edge of a sail
bez liku [bez lee-koo] exp.: countless; innumerable
likier [lee-ker] m. liquor
likierek [lee-ke-rek] m. (nice; small) liquor
likierowy [lee-ke-ro-vi] adj.m. of liquor
liklina [leek-lee-nah] f. edge rope sown into a sail; boltrope
likopodium [lee-ko-po-dyoom] n. lycopodium powder
likować [lee-ko-vahćh] v. sow edge rope on a sail (*repeatedly*)
likowanie [lee-ko-vah-ńe] n. sowing edge rope on a sail
liktor [leek-tor] m. lictor
liktorski [leek-tor-skee] adj.m. lictorian; lictor's
likwacja [leek-fah-tsyah] f. liquation
likwidacja [leek-fee-dah-tsyah] f. liquidation; winding up; closing down (of a business, etc.); suppression; abolition; doing away (with); eradication; extirpation; putting to death (of a tyrant, etc.); extermination (of a race, etc.); the stamping out (of

an epidemic, of heresy, illiteracy, etc.); clearing (of accounts, etc.); settlement (of accounts)
likwidacyjny [leek-fee-dah-**tsiy**-ni] adj.m. clearing (sale, etc.)
termin likwidacyjny [**ter**-meen leek-fee-dah-**tsiy**-ni] exp.: claim registration date mandated by a court in bankruptcy proceedings
likwidator [leek-fee-**dah**-tor] m. receiver; liquidator
likwidatorski [leek-fee-dah-**tor**-skee] adj.m. of a receiver; of a liquidator
likwidatura [leek-fee-dah-**too**-rah] f. payments department
likwidować [leek-fee-**do**-vahćh] v. liquidate; wind up; close down; do away with; suppress; abolish; eradicate; annihilate; extirpate; stamp out; put to death; exterminate; clear (*repeatedly*)
likwidowanie [leek-fee-do-**vah**-ńe] n. suppression; abolition
likwor [**leek**-for] m. liquor (alcoholic)
likworowy [leek-fo-**ro**-vi] adj.m. liquor (candy, etc.)
lila [**lee**-lah] adj.m. (color) pale-violet; lily (color); lilac (blue)
lilak [**lee**-lahk] m. mock-orange (shrub, tree)
lilaróż [lee-lah-**roosh**] m. reddish pink (color)
lilia [**lee**-lyah] f. lily; fleur-de-lis
lilia wodna [**lee**-lyah **vod**-nah] exp.: water lily; nenuphar
lilijka [lee-**leey**-kah] f. lily; scout badge
liliowaty [lee-lyo-**vah**-ti] adj.m. liliaceous
liliowate [lee-lyo-**vah**-te] pl. the lily family
liliowiec [lee-**lyo**-vyets] m. day lily
liliowce [lee-**lyo**-ftse] pl. Hemerocallis (plants); Crinoidea (echinoderms)
liliowieć [lee-**lyo**-vyećh] v. go (become, turn) lilac; assume a lilac hue; appear as a lilac patch (*repeatedly*)
liliowienie [lee-lyo-**vye**-ńe] n. going (becoming, turning) lilac; assuming a lilac hue
liliowo [lee-**lyo**-vo] adv. in lilac color; purple
liliowobiały [lee-lyo-vo-**byah**-wi] adj.m. lily-white
liliowoniebieski [lee-lyo-vo-ńe-**bye**-skee] adj.m. lilac-blue
liliowość [lee-**lyo**-vośhćh] f. lilac color
liliowy [lee-**lyo**-vi] adj.m. lilac (color); lily (white)
lilipuci [lee-lee-**poo**-ćhee] adj.m. Lilliputian; midgety; diminutive; tiny
liliput [lee-**lee**-poot] m. Lilliputian; little; dwarf; midget; pygmy; colloq: tiny object
liliputek [lee-lee-**poo**-tek] m. (small, nice) Lilliputian; little; dwarf; midget; pygmy; colloq: very tiny object
liliputka [lee-lee-**poot**-kah] f. (female) Lilliputian; wife of a Lilliputian; little; dwarf; midget; pygmy; tiny object; bantam hen
limakologia [lee-mah-ko-**lo**-gyah] f. study of snails
liman [**lee**-mahn] m. coastal salt lake
limba [**leem**-bah] f. stone pine; mountain pine
limbowy [leem-**bo**-vi] adj.m. stone-pine (nuts, etc.)
limbus [**leem**-boos] m. limb
limeryk [lee-**me**-rik] m. limerick
limes [**lee**-mes] n. (mathematical) limit
limfa [**leem**-fah] f. lymph; vaccine
limfatycznie [leem-fah-**tich**-ńe] adv. lymphatically
limfatyczny [leem-fah-**tich**-ni] adj.m. lymphatic
gruczoł limfatyczny [**groo**-chow leem-fah-**tich**-ni] exp.: lymphatic gland
naczynie limfatyczne [nah-**chi**-ńe leem-fah-**tich**-ne] exp.: (a) lymphatic vessel
układ limfatyczny [**ook**-wahd leem-fah-**tich**-ni] exp.: lymphatic system
limfocyt [leem-**fo**-tsit] m. lymphocyte
limfocyty [leem-fo-**tsi**-ti] pl. lymphocytes
limfocytowy [leem-fo-tsi-**to**-vi] adj. m. lymphocytic; lymphocytotic

limfocytoza [leem-fo-tsi-**to**-zah] f. lymphocytosis
limfoidalny [leem-fo-ee-**dahl**-ni] adj.m. lymphoid
tkanka limfoidalna [**tkahn**-kah leem-fo-ee-**dahl**-nah] exp.: lymphoid tissue
limit [**lee**-meet] m. limit
limitacja [lee-mee-**tah**-tsyah] f. limitation
limiter [lee-**mee**-ter] m. current limiter
limitować [lee-mee-**to**-vahćh] v. limit (*repeatedly*)
limitowanie [lee-mee-to-**vah**-ńe] n. limitation
limitowy [lee-mee-**to**-vi] adj.m. limiting (factor, etc.); limitary; enclosing
limniczny [leem-**ńeech**-ni] adj.m. limnetic; mid-continental; of fresh water
limnigraf [leem-**ńee**-grahf] m. limnograph
limnolog [leem-**no**-log] m. limnologist
limnologia [leem-no-**lo**-gyah] f. limnology
limnologicznie [leem-no-lo-**geech**-ńe] adv. limnologically
limnologiczny [leem-no-lo-**geech**-ni] adj.m. limnologic
limnoplankton [leem-no-**plahnk**-ton] m. limnoplankton
limonen [lee-**mo**-nen] m. limonene
limoniada [lee-mo-**ńah**-dah] f. lemonade; lemon squash
limonit [lee-**mo**-ńeet] m. limonite
limonitowy [lee-mo-ńee-**to**-vi] adj.m. limonitic
limuzyna [lee-moo-**zi**-nah] f. limousine; pilot's enclosure
lin [leen] m. tench (fish)
lina [**lee**-nah] f. line; rope; cord; steep rope; tightrope
lina holownicza [**lee**-na kho-lov-**ńee**-chah] exp.: towline; towing-line
na linie [nah **lee**-ńe] exp.: in tow; on a tightrope; on a rope
wlec na linie [vlets nah **lee**-ńe] exp.: to tow
lincz [leench] m. lynch (law)
linczować [leen-**cho**-vahćh] v. lynch; kill (by mob) (*repeatedly*)
linczowanie [leen-cho-**vah**-ńe] n. lynching
lindan [**leen**-dahn] m. lindane (insecticide)
linea [lee-**ne**-ahw] m. ruler; straightedge
linearnie [lee-ne-**ahr**-ńe] adv. lineally; linearly
linearność [lee-ne-**ahr**-nośhćh] f. lineality; linearity
linearny [lee-ne-**ahr**-ni] adj.m. lineal; linear
wymiar linearny [**vi**-myahr lee-ne-**ahr**-ni] exp.: lineal measure; linear measure
linearyzm [lee-ne-**ah**-rizm] m. lineament; linearization
linek [**lee**-nek] m. small tench (fish)
linewka [lee-**nef**-kah] f. cord; string; (angling) line; leash
lingwafon [leen-**gvah**-fon] m. linguaphone
lingwetka [leen-**gvet**-kah] f. an under-the-tongue chewing tablet
lingwista [leen-**gvees**-tah] m. linguist (specialist)
lingwistycznie [leen-gvees-**tich**-ńe] adv. linguistically
lingwistyczny [leen-gvees-**tich**-ni] adj.m. linguistic; linguistical
lingwistyka [leen-**gvees**-ti-kah] f. linguistics
linia [**lee**-ńyah] f. line; lane; (woman's) figure; line (of conduct, policy, operation, etc.); front line; line of descent; ruler
linia autobusowa [**lee**-ńyah ahw-to-boo-**so**-vah] exp.: bus line
linia kolejowa [**lee**-ńyah ko-le-**yo**-vah] exp.: railroad line
linia krzywa [**lee**-ńyah **kshi**-vah] exp.: curve (line)
linia lotnicza [**lee**-ńyah lot-**ńee**-chah] exp.: airline; airway; air route
linia magnetyczna [**lee**-ńyah mahg-ne-**tich**-nah] exp.: magnetic curve
linia najmniejszego oporu [**lee**-ńyah nahy-mńey-**she**-go o-**po**-roo] exp.: the path of least resistance
linia partyjna [**lee**-ńyah pahr-**tiy**-nah] exp.: party line; party

platform; party policy
linia powietrzna [**lee**-ńyah po-**vyetsh**-nah] exp.: air line; beeline; a straight direct course
liniał [**lee**-ńyahw] m. ruler; straightedge
liniarka [lee-**ńyahr**-kah] f. ruler; paper ruling machine
liniatura [lee-ńyah-**too**-rah] f. ruling; ruled lines
linieć [**lee**-ńećh] v. molt; shed hair; cast off hair; slough (its) skin; cast off (its) cuticular layer (*repeatedly*)
linienie [lee-**ńe**-ńe] n. molting; shedding of hair; casting off hair; sloughing (its) skin; casting off (its) cuticular layer
linierka [leeń-**yer**-kah] f. paper ruling machine
linierski [leeń-**yer**-skee] adj.m. of a paper ruling machine
linijka [lee-**ńeey**-kah] f. (small) ruler; straightedge; four-wheeled horse-drawn vehicle with a long narrow seat
linijnie [lee-**ńeey**-ńe] adv. linearly
linijność [lee-**ńeey**-nośhćh] f. linearity
linijny [lee-**ńeey**-ni] adj.m. lineal; linear
liniować [lee-**ńyo**-vahćh] v. line (paper, sheet, etc.); rule (paper, sheet, etc.) (*repeatedly*)
liniowanie [lee-ńyo-**vah**-ńe] n. ruling; lining (paper)
liniowiec [lee-**ńyo**-vyets] m. liner (ship); ship of the line; front-line soldier
liniowo [lee-**ńyo**-vo] adv. linearly
liniowy [lee-**ńyo**-vi] adj.m. linear; lineal; m. liner (ship); ship of the line; front-line soldier
okręt liniowy [**ok**-rant lee-**ńyo**-vi] exp.: liner (ship); battleship
papier liniowy [**pah**-pyer lee-**ńyo**-vi] exp.: ruled paper; lined paper
równanie liniowe [roov-**nah**-ńe lee-**ńyo**-ve] exp.: linear equation
widmo liniowe [**veed**-mo lee-**ńyo**-ve] exp.: line spectrum
wojsko liniowe [**voy**-sko lee-**ńyo**-ve] exp.: troops of the line
współczynnik liniowy [fspoow-chin-ńeek lee-**ńyo**-vi] exp.: linear coefficient
linka [**leen**-kah] f. thin line; thin rope; cord; cablet
linkowy [leen-**ko**-vi] adj.m. of a thin line; thin-rope (coil, etc.); of a cord; of a cablet
Linneusza system [leen-ne-**oo**-shah **sis**-tem] exp.: the Linnean system
linociąg [lee-**no**-ćhowng] m. hoist
linoleum [lee-no-**le**-oom] n. linoleum; colloq: lino
linoryt [lee-**no**-rit] m. linoleum-block printing; linoleum print
linorytowy [lee-no-ri-**to**-vi] adj.m. of linoleum-block printing; linoleum print (exhibit, etc.)
linoskoczek [lee-no-**sko**-chek] m. tightrope dancer; acrobat; equilibrist
linotyp [lee-**no**-tip] m. linotype; typesetting machine
linotypista [lee-no-ti-**pees**-tah] m. linotypist; linotyper; linotype operator
linotypowy [lee-no-ti-**po**-vi] adj.m. of a linotype
linownica [lee-nov-**ńee**-tsah] f. horizontal cable mounted hoist
linowy [lee-**no**-vi] adj.m. rope (ladder, etc.); cable (carrier, suspension, etc.)
kolejka linowa [ko-**ley**-kah lee-**no**-vah] exp.: cable car; cable railway; funicular
linter [**leen**-ter] m. linter; machine for removing linters
liofilizacja [lyo-fee-lee-**zah**-tsyah] f. lyophilization; freeze-drying
liofilizacyjny [lyo-fee-lee-zah-**tsiy**-ni] adj.m. of lyophilization; of freeze-drying
liofilizator [lyo-fee-lee-**zah**-tor] m. lyophilizer
liofilizować [lyo-fee-lee-**zo**-vahćh] v. lyophilize; freeze-dry (*repeatedly*)
liofilizowanie [lyo-fee-lee-zo-**vah**-ńe] n. lyophilization; freeze-drying
lipa [**lee**-pah] f. linden tree; lime tree; colloq: fake; cheat; fraud; hum; trash; shoddy
liparyt [lee-**pah**-rit] m. liparite (mineral)
lipaza [lee-**pah**-zah] f. lipase

lipazy [lee-pah-zi] pl. lipases (enzymes)
lipcowy [leep-tso-vi] adj.m. July (day, manifesto, etc.)
lipić [lee-peećh] v. slang: watch; look (mob jargon) (*repeatedly*)
lipid [lee-peet] m. lipid
lipidy [lee-pee-di] pl. lipids
lipidowy [lee-pee-do-vi] adj.m. lipid (compound, etc.); lipidic
lipiec [lee-pyets] m. July; linden honey; mead of linden honey
lipieniowaty [lee-pye-ńo-vah-ti] adj.m. of the graylings (family)
lipieniowate [lee-pye-ńo-vah-te] pl. the graylings' family
lipiennik [lee-pyen-ńeek] m. fen orchid
lipień [lee-pyeń] m. grayling
lipina [lee-pee-nah] f. lindens; linden wood
lipka [leep-kah] f. small linden tree
lipny [leep-ni] adj.m. colloq: snide; faked up (documents, etc.); duff; trashy; shoddy
lipoid [lee-po-eed] m. lipoid
lipoidalny [lee-po-ee-dahl-ni] adj.m. lipoidal
lipoproteid [lee-po-pro-te-eed] m. lipoproteid
lipoproteidy [lee-po-pro-te-ee-di] pl. lipoproteids
lipoproteina [lee-po-pro-te-ee-nah] f. lipoprotein
lipowaty [lee-po-vah-ti] adj.m. tiliaceous; of the linden tree family; colloq: somewhat trashy; somewhat faked
lipowate [lee-po-vah-te] pl. the linden family
lipowy [lee-po-vi] adj.m. linden (wood, etc.); lime (wood, etc.)
napar z kwiatu lipowego [nah-pahr s kfyah-too lee-po-ve-go] exp.: lime-flower tea; tisane
lir [leer] m. lira (Italian monetary unit)
lira [lee-rah] f. lyre
lirnik [leer-ńeek] m. lyrist
lirogon [lee-ro-gon] m. lyrebird
liryczka [lee-rich-kah] f. (woman) lyric poet
lirycznie [lee-rich-ńe] adv. lyrically
liryczność [lee-rich-nośhćh] f. lyricalness
liryczny [lee-rich-ni] adj.m. lyric (poetry, etc.); lyrical (poet, etc.)
liryk [lee-rik] m. lyrical poet; lyricist
liryka [lee-ri-kah] f. lyric poetry; lyrism; lyricism
liryzacja [lee-ri-zah-tsyah] f. giving lyric quality
liryzm [lee-rizm] m. lyrism; lyricism
liryzować [lee-ri-zo-vahćh] v. give lyric quality; render in lyric style (*repeatedly*)
lis [lees] m. fox; colloq: sly man; old fox; fox fur
lisek [lee-sek] m. young fox
lisi [lee-śhee] adj.m. fox's; fox (fur, etc.); volpine; colloq: foxy (man, etc.)
lisiak [lee-śhahk] m. handsaw; compass saw
lisiątko [lee-śhownt-ko] n. whelp
lisica [lee-śhee-tsah] f. vixen; chanterelle; colloq: hand-saw; compass-saw
lisicowaty [lee-śhee-tso-vah-ti] adj.m. of the Agonidae family; like a vixen
lisicowate [lee-śhee-tso-vah-te] pl. the Agonidae family
lisiczka [lee-śheech-kah] f. (small) vixen; chanterelle
lisię [lee-śhan] n. small whelp
lisisko [lee-śhees-ko] n. (big, bad) fox
lisiura [lee-śhoo-rah] f. fox fur; fox-fur red cap; m. (big, old) fox
lisiurka [lee-śhoor-kah] f. (small, nice) fox fur; fox-fur red cap
lisowczyk [lee-sof-chik] m. horseman of 17th cent. Polish light cavalry led by A. Lisowski
lisowczycy [lee-sof-chi-tsi] pl. 17th cent. Polish light cavalry led by A. Lisowski
list [leest] m. letter; note
list gończy [leest goń-chi] exp.: warrant of arrest
list gwarancyjny [leest gvah-rahn-tsiy-ni] exp.: guarantee
list kredytowy [leest kre-di-to-vi] exp.: letter of credit
list obiegowy [leest o-bye-go-vi] exp.: circular
list otwarty [leest ot-fahr-ti] exp.:

open letter
list pasterski [leest pahs-**ter**-skee] exp.: pastoral
list przewozowy [leest pshe-vo-**zo**-vi] exp.: bill of lading
list żelazny [leest zhe-**lahz**-ni] exp.: safe-conduct
lista [**lees**-tah] f. list; roll; register; (attendance, time) record
listeczek [lees-**te**-chek] m. (small, nice) leaf; leaflet
listek [**lees**-tek] m. (little) leaf; leaflet; sepal; pinnule; sheet (of paper)
listera [lees-**te**-rah] f. twayblade
listewka [lees-**tef**-kah] f. (small) slat; batten; skirting-board; baseboard; list; border; selvage; selvedge; ledge; listel; fillet
listewkowy [lees-tef-**ko**-vi] adj.m. slat (work, etc.); border (finish, etc.)
listewnik [lees-**tev**-ńeek] m. letter box; mailbox
listkowaty [leest-ko-**vah**-ti] adj.m. shaped like a leaf
listkowy [leest-**ko**-vi] adj.m. of a little leaf; of a little leaflet
listnienie [leest-**ńe**-ńe] n. covering with leaves; foliation
listny [**leest**-ni] adj.m. leaf (bud, etc.)
kwas listny [kfahs **leest**-ni] exp.: folic acid
listonosz [lees-**to**-nosh] m. postman; mail carrier
listonoszka [lees-to-**nosh**-kah] f. (woman) mail carrier
listopad [lees-**to**-paht] m. November
listopadowy [lees-to-pah-**do**-vi] adj.m. November (day, etc.)
listowie [lees-**to**-vye] n. leaves; foliage; leafage
listownica [lees-tov-**ńee**-tsah] f. Laminaria; deep-sea tangle (edible kelp)
listownie [lees-**tov**-ńe] adv. by letter; by mail
listownik [lees-**tov**-ńeek] m. letter writer (manual)
listowny [lees-**tov**-ni] adj.m. letter (communication, etc.); written; imparted by letter
listowy [lees-**to**-vi] adj.m. letter (paper, etc.)
papier listowy [**pah**-pyer lees-**to**-vi] exp.: notepaper; stationary
skrzynka listowa [**skshin**-kah lees-**to**-vah] exp.: letter box; mailbox
listwa [**lees**-tfah] f. trim
listwować [lees-**tfo**-vahćh] v. batten; skirt; install baseboards (*repeatedly*)
listwowanie [lees-tfo-**vah**-ńe] n. battening; skirting with baseboards
liszaj [**lee**-shahy] m. herpes; lichen; tetter
liszajec [lee-**shah**-yets] m. impetigo
liszajowaty [lee-shah-yo-**vah**-ti] adj.m. lichenoid
liszka [**leesh**-kah] f. caterpillar; vixen; colloq: sly fox
liszkarz [**leesh**-kahsh] m. calsoma (a beetle)
liszkojad [leesh-**ko**-yahd] m. calsoma (a beetle)
liściak [**leeśh**-ćhahk] m. phyllode
liściarka [leeśh-**ćhahr**-kah] f. leafy hay (including small branches)
liściasty [leeśh-**ćhahs**-ti] adj.m. leafed; leafy; foliaceous; leaf-like
drzewo liściaste [**dzhe**-vo leeśh-**ćhahs**-te] exp.: deciduous tree
liściaste [leeśh-**ćhahs**-te] pl. deciduous trees
liściec [**leeśh**-ćhets] m. a tropical phylliform insect
liścieniowy [leeśh-ćhe-**ńo**-vi] adj.m. cotyledonous
liścień [**leeśh**-ćheń] m. cotyledon; seed leaf
liścik [**leeśh**-ćheek] m. (small, nice) note; a note; a line; a few words
liścionogi [leeśh-ćho-**no**-gee] adj.m. phyllopodan
liścionos [leeśh-**ćho**-nos] m. leaf-nosed bat
liścionosy [leeśh-ćho-**no**-si] pl. the leaf-nosed bats
liścionóg [leeśh-**ćho**-noog] m. phyllopod
liścionogi [leeśh-ćho-**no**-gee] pl. the group Phyllopoda
liściowy [leeśh-**ćho**-vi] adj.m. foliaceous; foliar; leaf (base, blade, green, etc.)
pączek liściowy [**pown**-chek

leeśh-ćho-vi] exp.: leaf bud
liściozwój [leeśh-ćho-zvooy] m. leaf curling
liść [leeśhćh] m. leaf; (fern) frond
liście [leeśh-ćhe] pl. leaves; (fern) fronds
liście drzew [leeśh-ćhe dzhef] exp.: foliage
lit [leet] m. lithium (atomic number 3)
litania [lee-tah-ńyah] f. litany
litanijny [lee-tah-ńeey-ni] adj.m. litany (song, etc.)
litaury [lee-tahw-ri] pl. ancient kettledrums
litera [lee-te-rah] f. letter; character
duża litera [doo-zhah lee-te-rah] exp.: capital letter
mała litera [mah-wah lee-te-rah] exp.: small letter
litera prawa [lee-te-rah prah-vah] exp.: letter of the law
przestawienie liter [pshe-stah-vye-ńe lee-ter] exp.: literal error
podać wyraz po jednej literze [po-dahćh vi-rahs po yed-ney lee-te-zhe] exp.: to spell a word
literacina [lee-te-rah-ćhee-nah] m. paltry writer; worthless writer
literacki [lee-te-rahts-kee] adj.m. literary; of letters
po literacku [po lee-te-rahts-koo] exp.: in a literary style
literacko [lee-te-rahts-ko] adv. in a literary style
literackość [lee-te-rahts-kośhćh] f. literary style; literary character (of a composition); literariness
literak [lee-te-rahk] m. letter lichen
literalizm [lee-te-rah-leezm] m. literalism
literalnie [lee-te-rahl-ńe] adv. literally
tłumaczyć literalnie [twoo-mah-chićh lee-te-rahl-ńe] exp.: to translate word for word
literalność [lee-te-rahl-nośhćh] f. literalism; literalness; literality
literalny [lee-te-rahl-ni] adj.m. literal (translation, etc.)
czynić literalnym [chi-ńeećh lee-te-rahl-nim] exp.: to literalize
literat [lee-te-raht] m. writer
literatka [lee-te-raht-kah] f. (female) writer; colloq: wine glass
literatura [lee-te-rah-too-rah] f. literature; writings; literary output; references; bibliography; colloq: history of literature
literatura brukowa [lee-te-rah-too-rah broo-ko-vah] exp.: gutter press; tabloid press
literatura piękna [lee-te-rah-too-rah pyank-nah] exp.: belles-lettres
literaturoznawca [lee-te-rah-too-ro-znahf-tsah] m. literature specialist
literaturoznawczy [lee-te-rah-too-ro-znahf-chi] adj.m. of the theory of literature
literaturoznawstwo [lee-te-rah-too-ro-znahf-stfo] n. theory of literature; literatures
literek [lee-te-rek] m. (nice, little) liter (of vodka, etc.)
litergol [lee-ter-gol] m. liquid rocket fuel
literka [lee-ter-kah] f. (nice, little) letter; small letter
liternictwo [lee-ter-ńeets-tfo] n. letterer's craft
literniczka [lee-ter-ńeech-kah] f. (female) letterer
literniczy [lee-ter-ńee-chi] adj.m. letterer's (pen, etc.)
liternik [lee-ter-ńeek] m. letterer
literować [lee-te-ro-vahćh] v. spell (*repeatedly*)
literowiec [lee-te-ro-vyets] m. contracted word (made up of initials of several words, etc.); contraction
literowy [lee-te-ro-vi] adj.m. literal
wymowa literowa [vi-mo-vah lee-te-ro-vah] exp.: literal pronunciation; exaggerated pronunciation of each letter in a word
literówka [lee-te-roof-kah] f. machine error (misspelling); typewriter error (letters out of order)
litewski [lee-tef-skee] adj.m. & m. Lithuanian; Lithuanian language
po litewsku [po lee-tef-skoo] exp.: in Lithuanian
litkup [leet-koop] m. gifts or treats exchanged at the closing of a sale
lit[illegible]

chromolithography; chromolithograph
litofan [**lee**-to-fahn] m. lithophane
litofania [lee-to-**fah**-ńyah] f. lithophany
litofilny [lee-to-**feel**-ni] adj.m. lithophilous (oxides, etc.)
litogeneza [lee-to-ge-**ne**-zah] f. lithogenesis
litoglifia [lee-to-glee-**fee**-lyah] f. lithoglyphics
litograf [lee-**to**-grahf] m. lithographer
litografia [lee-to-**grah**-fyah] f. lithography; lithograph; lithographic works
litografia rytowana [lee-to-**grah**-fyah ri-to-**vah**-nah] exp.: zincography
litograficzny [lee-to-grah-**feech**-ni] adj.m. lithographic
litografować [lee-to-grah-**fo**-vahćh] v. lithograph; make lithographs (*repeatedly*)
litografowanie [lee-to-grah-fo-**vah**-ńe] n. making lithographs
litoklaz [lee-**to**-klahs] m. lithoclase
litologia [lee-to-**lo**-gyah] f. lithology
litologicznie [lee-to-lo-**geech**-ńe] adv. lithologically
litologiczny [lee-to-lo-**geech**-ni] adj.m. lithologic
litometeor [lee-to-me-**te**-or] m. earth crust particle suspended in the air
litometeory [lee-to-me-te-**o**-ri] pl. earth crust particles suspended in the air
litoptern [lee-**top**-tern] m. an extinct animal similar to llama-vicuna
litopterny [lee-top-**ter**-ni] pl. extinct animals similar to llama-vicuna
litoral [lee-**to**-rahl] m. litoral
litoralny [lee-to-**rahl**-ni] adj.m. litoral; of coastal region
litosfera [lee-to-**sfe**-rah] f. lithosphere
litościwie [lee-tośh-**ćhee**-vye] adv. mercifully; with pity; compassionately
litościwość [lee-tośh-**ćhee**-vośhćh] f. mercifulness; compassion
litościwy [lee-tośh-**ćhee**-vi] adj.m. merciful; pitying; compassionate
litość [**lee**-tośhćh] f. pity; mercy; compassion
bez litości [bez lee-**tośh**-ćhee] exp.: without pity; merciless; pitiless
litości! [lee-**tośh**-ćhee] excl.: mercy!
mieć litość nad... [myećh **lee**-tośhćh nahd] exp.: to take pity on ...; to have mercy on ...
na litość Boską! [nah **lee**-tośhćh **bos**-kown] excl.: for goodness' sake!
z litości [z lee-**tośh**-ćhee] exp.: out of pity; out of charity; for pity's sake
litota [lee-**to**-tah] f. litotes; meisosis
litotamnion [lee-to-**tahm**-ńon] m. variety of sea coral
litotes [lee-**to**-tes] not declined: litotes; meisosis
litotomia [lee-to-**to**-myah] f. lithotomy
litować się [lee-**to**-vahćh śhan] v. have mercy (on); take pity (on); feel pity (for); commiserate with (*repeatedly*)
litowanie się [lee-to-**vah**-ńe śhan] n. mercy; compassion; pity
litowanie się nad samym sobą [lee-to-**vah**-ńe śhan naht **sah**-mim **so**-bown] exp.: self-pity
litowiec [lee-**to**-vyets] m. alkali metal
litowce [lee-**tof**-tse] pl. alkali metals
litr [leetr] m. liter
litraż [**leet**-rahsh] m. capacity in liters
litrowy [lee-**tro**-vi] adj.m. liter (bottle, etc.)
litrówka [lee-**troof**-kah] f. liter bottle
lituanista [lee-twah-**ńees**-tah] m. student of Lithuanian culture and language
lituanistyka [lee-twah-**ńees**-ti-kah] f. study of Lithuanian culture and language
lituanizacja [lee-twah-ńee-**zah**-tsyah] f. Lithuanization
lituanizm [lee-**twah**-ńeezm] m. Lithuanism; borrowing from Lithuanian language
liturgia [lee-**toor**-gyah] f. liturgy;

religious ritual
liturgicznie [lee-toor-**geech**-ńe] adv. liturgically
liturgiczny [lee-toor-**geech**-ni] adj.m. liturgical
liturgika [lee-**toor**-gee-kah] f. liturgics; liturgiology
litwak [**leet**-fahk] m. Lithuanian Jew; colloq: Lithuanian
Litwin [**leet**-feen] m. Lithuanian
Litwinka [leet-**feen**-kah] f. Lithuanian (woman)
litwor [**leet**-for] m. angelica; angelique
litworowy [leet-fo-**ro**-vi] adj.m. angelica (oil, etc.)
lity [**lee**-ti] adj.m. massive; solid; cast; pure; pure stand (of trees)
litycznie [lee-**tich**-ńe] adv. lytically
lityczny [lee-**tich**-ni] adj.m. lytic
liwistonia [lee-vees-**to**-ńyah] f. large fan-leaf palm; Livistona
liwr [leevr] m. livre (monetary unit)
lizaczek [lee-**zah**-chek] m. (nice, small) lollipop
lizać [**lee**-zahćh] v. lick; taste; colloq: dabble (at) (*repeatedly*)
palce lizać [**pahl**-tse **lee**-zahćh] exp.: colloq: first-rate; excellent; crack
lizać się [**lee**-zahćh śhan] v. fawn (upon); cringe (to); colloq: kiss each other in an obscene manner (*repeatedly*)
lizak [**lee**-zahk] m. lollipop; colloq: hand-held stop sign
lizanie [lee-**zah**-ńe] n. licking; tasting
lizanie się [lee-**zah**-ńe śhan] n. licking oneself; licking one another; slang: French kissing
lizawka [lee-**zahf**-kah] f. trough for the mix of salt and minerals for animals; salt lick; deer lick
lizawość [lee-**zah**-vośhćh] f. animal tendency to lick (hair, soil, excrements, etc.)
lizawy [lee-**zah**-vi] adj.m. with an animal tendency to lick (hair, soil, excrements, etc.)
lizena [lee-**ze**-nah] f. pilaster strip
lizeska [lee-**zes**-kah] f. soft robe used over a nightgown
liznąć [**leez**-nownćh] v. lick; taste; colloq: dabble (at)
lizol [**lee**-zol] m. lysol
lizus [**lee**-zoos] m. colloq: toady; lickspitle; reptile; bootlicker; suck-up
lizuska [lee-**zoos**-kah] f. colloq: (female) toady; lickspitle; reptile; bootlicker; suck-up
lizusostwo [lee-zoo-**so**-stfo] n. bootlick; bootlicking
lizusować [lee-zoo-**so**-vahćh] v. bootlick; toady; fawn (on, upon) obsequiously; suck-up (to) (*repeatedly*)
lizusowanie [lee-zoo-so-**vah**-ńe] n. bootlicking
lizusowski [lee-zoo-**sof**-skee] adj.m. bootlicker's; toadying; fawning
lizymetr [lee-**zi**-metr] m. lysimeter
lizyna [lee-**zi**-nah] f. lysin; lysine
lizys [**lee**-zis] m. lysis
liźnięcie [leeźh-**ńan**-ćhe] n. lick; taste; colloq: dabble (at)
lnianka [**lńahn**-kah] f. hurds; coarse refuse of flax, hemp, etc.; Camelina
lnianki [**lńahn**-kee] pl. hurds
lnianowłosy [lńah-no-**vwo**-si] adj.m. flaxen-haired
lniany [**lńah**-ni] adj.m. linen; flax (straw, etc.); flaxen (thread, etc.); linseed (oil, etc.)
lniarski [**lńahr**-skee] adj.m. of flax (trade, cloth, etc.)
lniarstwo [**lńahr**-stfo] n. flax trade
lnica [**lńee**-tsah] f. toadflax
lnicznik [**lńeech**-ńeek] m. Camelina
lnicznik siewny [**lńeech**-ńeek **śhev**-ni] exp.: gold-of-pleasure
lnisko [**lńees**-ko] n. flax field
lnowaty [lno-**vah**-ti] adj.m. linaceous; of the flax family
lnowate [lno-**vah**-te] pl. the flax family
lob [lob] m. (tennis) lob
lobby [**lob**-bi] n. lobby
lobelia [lo-**be**-lyah] f. lobelia
lobelina [lo-be-**lee**-nah] f. lobeline
lobeliowaty [lo-bel-yo-**vah**-ti] adj.m. of the lobelia family
lobeliowate [lo-bel-yo-**vah**-te] pl. the lobelia family
lobo [**lo**-bo] n. variety of apple; variety of apple tree

lobować [lo-**bo**-vahćh] v. lob (tennis) (*repeatedly*)
loch [lokh] m. dungeon; cellar
locha [**lo**-khah] f. sow
lochać się [**lo**-khahćh śhan] v. be in heat (swine) (*repeatedly*)
lochanie się [lo-**khah**-ńe śhan] n. heat (in swine)
locja [**lo**-tsyah] f. pilotage; sailing (pilot's) direction; coast pilot
locman [**lots**-mahn] m. (ship) pilot
loco [**lo**-ko] indecl.: on the spot
loco stacja [**lo**-ko **stah**-tsyah] exp.: free on rail
loco statek [**lo**-ko **stah**-tek] exp.: free on board; F.O.B.; ex ship
lokum [**lo**-koom] n. room; lodgings; living quarters; accommodation
loczek [**lo**-chek] m. lock; curl; ringlet
zalotny loczek [zah-**lot**-ni **lo**-chek] exp.: quiff
loden [**lo**-den] m. coarse, woolen cloth
lodenowy [lo-de-**no**-vi] adj.m. of coarse woolen cloth
lododział [lo-**do**-dźhahw] m. glacial (continental) divide
lodołam [lo-**do**-wahm] m. ice apron
lodołamacz [lo-do-**wah**-mahch] m. icebreaker; ice shield
lodospad [lo-**do**-spahd] m. glacier's breaking edge; icefall
lodoszreń [lo-**do**-shreń] f. frozen layer on top of thick snow
lodowacenie [lo-do-vah-**tse**-ńe] n. freezing; icing up
lodowacieć [lo-do-**vah**-ćhećh] v. freeze; ice up; colloq: stiffen; become frigid (*repeatedly*)
lodować [lo-**do**-vahćh] v. load ice (*repeatedly*)
lodowanie [lo-do-**vah**-ńe] n. loading of ice
lodowato [lo-do-**vah**-to] adv. icily; in icy cold manner
lodowatość [lo-do-**vah**-tośhćh] f. iciness; colloq: icy manners
lodowaty [lo-do-**vah**-ti] adj.m. icy; ice-cold; chilling; frigid
lodowcowo [lo-dof-**tso**-vo] adv. glacially
lodowcowy [lo-dof-**tso**-vi] adj.m. glacial; of a glacier
lodowica [lo-do-**vee**-tsah] f. icy layer on top of the road
lodowiec [lo-**do**-vyets] m. glacier; mass of ice and snow
lodowisko [lo-do-**vees**-ko] n. ice field; skating-rink; ice rink
lodownia [lo-**do**-vńah] f. ice-chamber; ice-cellar; icy cold room
lodownik [lo-**do**-vńeek] m. ice generator; ice-making machine
lodowo [lo-**do**-vo] adv. icily; in icy-cold manner
lodowy [lo-**do**-vi] adj.m. of ice; icy
lodówka [lo-**doof**-kah] f. icebox; refrigerator; ice chest
lodówkowy [lo-doof-**ko**-vi] adj.m. of a refrigerator; of an ice chest
lody [**lo**-di] pl. ice cream
lodziarka [lo-**dźhahr**-kah] f. (woman) ice-cream vendor
lodziarnia [lo-**dźhahr**-ńah] f. ice-cream factory; ice-cream parlor
lodziarski [lo-**dźhahr**-skee] adj.m. ice-cream (parlor, etc.)
lodziarstwo [lo-**dźhahr**-stfo] n. production and sale of ice cream
lodziarz [**lo**-dźhahsh] m. ice-cream vendor
lodżia [**lo**-dzhyah] f. loggia; roofed open gallery
loess [**lo**-es] m. loess (unstratified loamy deposit)
loessowy [lo-es-**so**-vi] adj.m. of loess (loamy wind deposit)
loftka [**loft**-kah] f. large size lead shot; buckshot
loftkowy [loft-**ko**-vi] adj.m. of buckshot
log [log] m. ship's speedometer (automatic, electrical, mechanical, manual, etc.)
logarytm [lo-**gah**-ritm] m. logarithm
logarytmicznie [lo-gah-rit-**meech**-ńe] adv. logarithmically
logarytmiczny [lo-gah-rit-**meech**-ni] adj.m. logarithmic
logarytmować [lo-gah-rit-**mo**-vahćh] v. compute the logarithm of a number or expression; use logarithms (*repeatedly*)
logarytmowanie [lo-gah-rit-mo-**vah**-ńe] n. computation of logarithms
logatom [lo-**gah**-tom] m. nonsense-word
loggia [**lo**-dzhyah] f. loggia; roofed

open gallery
logicyzm [lo-**gee**-tsizm] m. logic as the basis of mathematics
logicznie [lo-**geech**-ńe] adv. logically; consistently; soundly
logiczność [lo-**geech**-nośhćh] f. soundness (of argument, conclusion, etc.); consistency (of conduct, policy, etc.)
logiczny [lo-**geech**-ni] adj.m. logical; consistent; sound
logik [**lo**-geek] m. logician; expert in logic
logika [**lo**-gee-kah] f. logic; reason; common sense; consistency
logistyczny [lo-gees-**tich**-ni] adj.m. logistic; logistical
logistyka [lo-**gees**-ti-kah] f. (military, etc.) logistics; (symbolic) mathematical logic
logizacja [lo-gee-**zah**-tsyah] f. logicalization
logizować [lo-gee-**zo**-vahćh] v. logicalize; make logical (*repeatedly*)
logizowanie [lo-gee-zo-**vah**-ńe] n. logicalization; making logical
loglina [log-**lee**-nah] f. log line
logograf [lo-**go**-grahf] m. logograph
logografia [lo-go-**grah**-fyah] f. logography
logograficznie [lo-go-grah-**feech**-ńe] adv. logographically
logograficzny [lo-go-grah-**feech**-ni] adj.m. logographic
logogryf [lo-**go**-grif] m. logogriph
logogryfowy [lo-go-gri-**fo**-vi] adj.m. logogriphic
logomachia [lo-go-**mah**-khyah] f. logomachy; game of word making; idle discussion about words
logometr [lo-**go**-metr] m. logometer
logopatia [lo-go-**pah**-tyah] f. speech defect; logopedics; logopedia
logopatolog [lo-go-pah-**to**-log] m. specialist in speech defects; specialist in logopedics
logopatologia [lo-go-pah-to-**lo**-gyah] f. study of speech defects; study of logopedics
logopeda [lo-go-**pe**-dah] m. speech defect therapist
logopedia [lo-go-**pe**-dyah] f. speech defects therapy; logopedics
logopedyczny [lo-go-pe-**dich**-ni] adj.m. of speech defects therapy
logorea [lo-go-**re**-ah] f. logorrhea; excessive and incoherent talkativeness
logos [**lo**-gos] m. logos; the rational principle in the universe; the Word of God; the divine wisdom
logotyp [lo-**go**-tip] m. logotype
lojalista [lo-yah-**lees**-tah] m. loyalist (man)
lojalistka [lo-yah-**leest**-kah] f. loyalist (woman)
lojalizm [lo-**yah**-leezm] m. loyalism
lojalka [lo-**yahl**-kah] f. colloq: loyalty oath
lojalnie [lo-**yahl**-ńe] adv. loyally; straightforwardly; staunchly; faithfully; colloq: through thick and thin
lojalność [lo-**yahl**-nośhćh] f. loyalty; uprightness; straightforwardness; allegiance
lojalny [lo-**yahl**-ni] adj.m. loyal; straightforward; staunch; stanch; true (to)
lok [lok] m. lock; curl; coil
lok nad czołem [lok naht **cho**-wem] exp.: forelock
lokacja [lo-**kah**-tsyah] f. location; foundation (of a town); foundation charter; ranging (in navigation)
lokacyjny [lo-kah-**tsiy**-ni] adj.m. foundation (date, etc.)
lokaj [**lo**-kahy] m. lackey; manservant; footman; valet; colloq: flunkey
główny lokaj [**gwoov**-ni **lo**-kahy] exp.: butler
lokajczyk [lo-**kahy**-chik] m. (young) lackey; manservant; footman; valet
lokajski [lo-**kahy**-skee] adj.m. lackey's; manservant's; colloq: servile; fulsome
lokajstwo [lo-**kahy**-stfo] n. post of lackey; flankeyism
lokal [**lo**-kahl] m. premises; rooms; place; restaurant; cafe; bar; colloq: local; pub (Brit.)
lokalik [lo-**kah**-leek] m. (small, nice) place; restaurant; cafe; bar

lokalizacja [lo-kah-lee-**zah**-tsyah] f. localization; location
lokalizacyjny [lo-kah-lee-zah-**tsiy**-ni] adj.m. locational; of location
lokalizator [lo-kah-lee-**zah**-tor] m. locating device (for aircraft, etc.)
lokalizm [lo-**kah**-leezm] m. localism
lokalizować [lo-kah-lee-**zo**-vahćh] v. localize; locate; range (*repeatedly*)
lokalnie [lo-**kahl**-ńe] adv. locally; regionally
lokalność [lo-**kahl**-nośhćh] f. localism; sectionalism
lokalny [lo-**kahl**-ni] adj.m. local; regional; of a place
lokalowy [lo-kah-**lo**-vi] adj.m. of a restaurant; of a cafe; of a bar
lokata [lo-**kah**-tah] f. investment
lokatiwus [lo-kah-**tee**-voos] m. the locative case
lokator [lo-**kah**-tor] m. tenant; occupant; occupier; roomer; lodger; paying guest; guest; device for locating objects, etc.
lokatorka [lo-kah-**tor**-kah] f. (female) tenant
lokatorski [lo-kah-**tor**-skee] adj.m. tenant's; occupant's; occupier's; roomer's; lodger's
lokatywny [lo-kah-**tiv**-ni] adj.m. locative (case, etc.)
lokaut [**lo**-kahwt] m. lockout
loko [**lo**-ko] indecl.: loco; place; on the spot = **loco**
lokomobila [lo-ko-mo-**bee**-lah] f. locomobile
lokomocja [lo-ko-**mo**-tsyah] f. locomotion; communication; vehicle; conveyance
środek lokomocji [**śhro**-dek lo-ko-**mots**-yee] exp.: means of communication; vehicle; conveyance
lokomocyjny [lo-ko-mo-**tsiy**-ni] adj.m. locomotive; motion (sickness, etc.)
lokomotoryczny [lo-ko-mo-to-**rich**-ni] adj.m. locomotive (reaction, etc.)
lokomotywa [lo-ko-mo-**ti**-vah] f. train engine; locomotive
lokomotywka [lo-ko-mo-**ti**-fkah] f. pony engine; shunting locomotive
lokomotywownia [lo-ko-mo-ti-**vov**-ńah] f. train engine shed; locomotive depot
lokomotywowy [lo-ko-mo-ti-**vo**-vi] adj.m. of a train engine; locomotive (depot, etc.)
lokować [lo-**ko**-vahćh] v. place; locate; put (somebody) up; find an accommodation (for); invest (one's capital in) (*repeatedly*)
lokować się [lo-**ko**-vahćh śhan] v. place oneself; locate oneself; sit oneself; find accommodation; find a lodging; take a lodging; put up (somewhere); take one's stand; take one's position; settle oneself (*repeatedly*)
lokowanie [lo-ko-**vah**-ńe] n. placing; locating; putting (somebody) up; finding accommodation (for); investing (one's capital in)
lokowanie się [lo-ko-**vah**-ńe śhan] n. placing oneself
lokówka [lo-**koof**-kah] f. cannon-curl
loksodroma [lok-so-**dro**-mah] f. loxodrome; rhumb line
loksodromiczny [lok-so-dro-**meech**-ni] adj.m. loxodromic; rhumb line
żegluga loksodromiczna [zheg-**loo**-gah lok-so-dro-**meech**-nah] exp.: plane sailing
lokum [**lo**-koom] n. room; lodgings; living quarters; accommodation; see: **locum**
lolitka [lo-**leet**-kah] f. colloq: very young and (sexually) attractive girl
lombard [**lom**-bahrd] m. pawnshop
właściciel lombardu [vwahśh-**ćhee**-ćhel lom-**bahr**-doo] m. pawnbroker
lombardowy [lom-bahr-**do**-vi] adj.m. pawn (ticket, shop, etc.)
lombrozowski [lom-bro-**zof**-skee] adj.m. Lombrosian (school, etc.)
lon [lon] m. colloq: linchpin
londyńczyk [lon-**diń**-chik] m. Londoner
londyński [lon-**diń**-skee] adj.m. London (fog, etc.)
londyński akcent [lon-**diń**-skee **ahk**-tsent] exp.: cockney accent
longplay [**long**-pley] m. long play; long-playing record
lonicera [lo-ńee-**tse**-rah] f. honeysuckle

lont [lont] m. (blasting) fuse; slow match
lonża [**lon**-zhah] f. lunging-rein; lunge
lonżować [lon-**zho**-vahćh] v. train a horse on a lunging-rein (*repeatedly*)
looping [**loo**-peeng] m. looping; the loop
lora [**lo**-rah] f. truck; bowline-knot
loran [**lo**-rahn] m. laran; long range navigational system
lord [lord] m. lord; peer
lordostwo [lor-**do**-stfo] n. peerage; earldom
lordowski [lor-**dof**-skee] adj.m. of a lord; lord's
lordoza [lor-**do**-zah] f. lordosis
lorenc [**lo**-rens] m. unit of velocity equal to speed of light in a the vacuum
lorens [**lo**-rens] m. lawrencium (atomic number 103)
loretański [lo-re-**tahń**-skee] adj.m. of Loretto; of Our Lady of Loretto
lorgnon [**lor**-ńown] m. (French) lorgnon; lorgnette
lori [**lo**-ree] m. loris lemur
lorneta [lor-**ne**-tah] f. big binoculars
lornetka [lor-**net**-kah] f. binoculars
lornetka teatralna [lor-**net**-kah te-ah-**trahl**-nah] exp.: opera glass; opera glasses
lornetka polowa [lor-**net**-kah po-**lo**-vah] exp.: field glass
lornetować [lor-ne-**to**-vahćh] v. observe through binoculars (*repeatedly*)
lornetowanie [lor-ne-to-**vah**-ńe] n. observing through binoculars
lornion [**lor**-ńown] n. lorgnon; lorgnette
los [los] m. lot; fate; destiny; doom; chance; hazard; lottery ticket
borykać się z losem [bo-ri-kahćh śhan z **lo**-sem] exp.: to wrestle with adversity
koleje losu [ko-**le**-ye **lo**-soo] exp.: vicissitudes; ups and downs;
losem [**lo**-sem] exp.: by lot
los tak chciał [los tahk khćhahw] exp.: fate willed it; it was fated
masz ci los! [mahsh ćhee los] excl.: (it's) too bad!; what a nuisance
na los szczęścia [nah los shch**an**śh-ćhah] exp.: at a venture; at all hazards; on the off chance
zły los [zwi los] exp.: adversity; misfortune
losować [lo-**so**-vahćh] v. draw lots; draw cuts; toss up (a coin) (*repeatedly*)
losowanie [lo-so-**vah**-ńe] n. drawing (of lots); toss
losowy [lo-**so**-vi] adj.m. of fate
klęska losowa [kl**an**s-kah lo-**so**-vah] exp.: disaster
loszek [**lo**-shek] m. small dungeon
loszka [**losh**-kah] f. small sow
lot [lot] m. flight; fly; speed; flight feather (of a bird); lead plummet
lotem błyskawicy [**lo**-tem bwis-kah-**vee**-tsi] exp.: in a flash; in a shot
prędkość lotu [pr**an**t-kośhćh **lo**-too] exp.: airspeed
tablica lotów [tah-**blee**-tsah **lo**-toof] exp.: flight schedule; listing of flights
w locie [v **lo**-ćhe] exp.: on the fly; on the wing
w lot [v lot] exp.: in a twinkling
z lotu ptaka [z **lo**-too **ptah**-kah] exp.: from the air
loteria [lo-**te**-ryah] f. lottery
loteria fantowa [lo-**te**-ryah fahn-**to**-vah] exp.: raffle
loteryjka [lo-te-**riy**-kah] f. lotto
loteryjny [lo-te-**riy**-ni] adj.m. lottery (ticket, etc.)
lotka [**lot**-kah] f. flight feather; remex; aileron
lotnia [**lot**-ńah] f. hang glider
lotniarstwo [lot-**ńahr**-stfo] n. hang gliding
lotniarz [**lot**-ńahsh] m. hang glider
lotnictwo [lot-**ńeets**-tfo] n. aviation; aeronautics; air force; aerial fleet; air-force
lotniczka [lot-**ńeech**-kah] f. (female) aviator; airwoman
lotniczy [lot-**ńee**-chi] adj.m. air (base, etc.)
linie lotnicze [**lee**-ńye lot-**ńee**-che] exp.: airlines
poczta lotnicza [**poch**-tah lot-**ńee**-

chah] exp.: air mail
pocztą lotniczą [**poch**-town lot-**ńee**-chown] exp.: by air mail
port lotniczy [port lot-**ńee**-chi] exp.: airport
szlak lotniczy [shlahk lot-**ńee**-chi] exp.: air lane

lotnik [**lot**-ńeek] m. aviator; airman; colloq: flyer

lotnisko [lot-**ńees**-ko] n. airport; airfield; aerodrome

lotniskowiec [lot-ńees-**ko**-vyets] m. aircraft carrier

lotniskowy [lot-ńees-**ko**-vi] adj.m. airport (runway, lights, etc.)

lotność [**lot**-nośhćh] f. volatility; fugacity; lightness; airiness; swiftness; sprightness; buoyancy; vivacity; colloq: sharpness; acuteness; quick wits; quickness (of mind)

lotny [**lot**-ni] adj.m. flight (feather, etc.); flying (conditions, etc.); volatile; aeriform; fugacious; light; airy; swift; sprightly; buoyant; vivacious; colloq: sharp; acute; quick of apprehension; ready witted; subtle
rzut lotny [zhoot **lot**-ni] exp.: flying kick; volley
start lotny [stahrt **lot**-ni] exp.: flying start

lotos [**lo**-tos] m. lotus

lotosowy [lo-to-**so**-vi] adj.m. lotus (flowers, etc.)

lotto [**lot**-to] n. lotto (a game of chance)

lowelas [lo-**ve**-lahs] m. ladies' man; flirt; philanderer

lowelasowski [lo-ve-lah-**sof**-skee] adj.m. of a ladies' man; flirt's; philanderer's

loża [**lo**-zhah] f. (theater) box; lodge
loża masońska [**lo**-zhah mah-**soń**-skah] exp.: shriners' lodge
loża prasowa [**lo**-zhah prah-**so**-vah] exp.: press gallery

lożowy [lo-**zho**-vi] adj.m. of (theater) box; lodge (member, etc.)

lód [loot] m. ice
lody [**lo**-di] pl. ice cream
jak lodu [yahk **lo**-doo] exp.: galore
pójść na lody [pooyśhćh nah **lo**-di] exp.: to go to have some ice cream
suchy lód [**soo**-khi loot] exp.: dry ice

LSD [el-es-de] indecl. LSD; lysergic acid diethylamide (inducing symptoms of schizophrenia)

lśniący [lśhń**own**-tsi] adj.m. shiny; shining; bright; glossy; sleek; lustrous

lśnić [lśhńeećh] v. glitter; shine; gleam; glimmer; shimmer; glisten; sparkle (*repeatedly*)

lśnić się [lśhńeećh śhan] v. be glittering; be shimmering (*repeatedly*)

lśnienie [**lśhńe**-ńe] n. glitter; shine; gleam; glimmer; shimmer; sparkle; glint

lu [loo] colloq: (for sound imitation of) splashing of water; a bang; a sudden start
no to lu! [no to loo] exp.: let us drink! (vodka, etc.)

lub [loop] conj. or; or else
lub też [loop tesh] exp.: or; or else

luba [**loo**-bah] f. sweetheart; darling; one's best girl; girl friend

lubaszka [loo-**bahsh**-kah] f. variety of Asian prune; bullace

lubczyk [**loop**-chik] m. lovage (plant)

lubczykowy [loop-chi-**ko**-vi] adj.m. lovage (oil, etc.)

lubeckit [loo-**be**-keet] m. a mineral containing manganese, copper, and cobalt

lubić [**loo**-beećh] v. like; be fond; enjoy; be partial (to); colloq: be apt (to); be liable (to) (*repeatedly*)

lubić się [**loo**-beećh śhan] v. like each other; be fond of each other (*repeatedly*)

lubienie [loo-**bye**-ńe] n. liking

lubieżnica [loo-byezh-**ńee**-tsah] f. wanton woman; sensualist; voluptuary

lubieżnie [loo-**byezh**-ńe] adv. lustfully; lewdly; lecherously; lasciviously; libidinously

lubieżnik [loo-**byezh**-ńeek] m. sensualist; voluptuary

lubieżność [loo-**byezh**-nośhćh] f. lust; voluptuousness; lewdness;

lechery; lasciviousness
lubieżny [loo-**byezh**-ni] adj.m. lustful; voluptuous; lewd; lecherous; lascivious
lublinit [loo-**blee**-ńeet] m. a variety of calcite
lubo [**loo**-bo] adv. pleasantly; with pleasure; conj.: albeit; though; although
lubość [**loo**-bośhćh] f. delight; pleasure
lubować się [loo-**bo**-vahćh śhan] v. delight (in); take delight (in); find pleasure (in); relish; be fond (of) (*repeatedly*)
lubowanie się [loo-bo-**vah**-ńe śhan] n. delight; pleasure
lubryka [loo-**bri**-kah] f. colloq: red chalk; reddle
luby [**loo**-bi] adj.m. pleasant; dear; beloved; m. sweetheart; darling
lucerna [loo-**tser**-nah] f. lucerne; alfalfa; medick; nonesuch
lucernik [loo-**tser**-ńeek] m. lucerne field
lucyfer [loo-**tsi**-fer] m. Lucifer; the devil
lucyper [loo-**tsi**-per] m. Lucifer; the devil
lud [loot] m. people; nation
ludek [**loo**-dek] m. (small) nation; people
ludnie [**lood**-ńe] adv. multidinously
ludno [**lood**-no] adv. multidinously
ludnościowy [lood-nośh-**ćho**-vi] adj.m. of the population
ludność [**lood**-nośhćh] f. population (of a given territory, city, country, etc.)
ludny [**lood**-ni] adj.m. populous; teeming; crowded
ludobójca [loo-do-**booy**-tsah] m. genocide
ludobójczy [loo-do-**booy**-chi] adj.m. genocidal
ludobójstwo [loo-do-**booy**-stfo] n. genocide; killing of a nation
ludojad [loo-**do**-yahd] m. anthropophagous animal; man-eater; cannibal; orge
ludolfina [loo-dol-**fee**-nah] f. Lupolphian number; Ludolph's number
ludomania [loo-do-**mah**-ńyah] f. excessive enthusiasm for the peasantry
ludowiec [loo-**do**-vyets] m. social worker among peasantry; member of the Peasant Party
ludowładczy [loo-do-**vwaht**-chi] adj.m. democratic
ludowładztwo [loo-do-**vwahts**-tfo] n. democracy
ludowo [loo-**do**-vo] adv. in country style; in regional style
ludowodemokratyczny [loo-do-vo-de-mo-krah-**tich**-ni] adj.m. of a people's democracy (Soviet style)
ludowość [loo-**do**-vośhćh] f. popular character (of a literary work, treatise, etc.)
ludowy [loo-**do**-vi] adj.m. populist; popular; country (style. etc.); folkloristic
ludoznawca [loo-do-**znahf**-tsah] m. folklorist; ethnographer
ludoznawczo [loo-do-**znahf**-cho] adv. ethnographically
ludoznawczy [loo-do-**znahf**-chi] adj.m. folkloric; ethnographic; ethnographical
ludoznawstwo [loo-do-**znahf**-stfo] n. ethnography
ludożerca [loo-do-**zher**-tsah] m. cannibal; man-eater
ludożerczy [loo-do-**zher**-chi] adj.m. cannibalistic; of a man-eater; cannibal (tribe, etc.); anthropophagous
ludożerstwo [loo-do-**zher**-stfo] n. cannibalism; anthropophagy
ludwik [**lood**-veek] m. louis-d'or (coin); Louis' style piece of furniture
ludwikowski [lood-vee-**kof**-skee] adj.m. of the louis-d'or (coin); of Louis' style piece of furniture
ludwisarnia [lood-vee-**sahr**-ńah] f. (bell-)foundry
ludwisarski [lood-vee-**sahr**-skee] adj.m. (bell-)foundry (works, products, etc.)
ludwisarstwo [lood-vee-**sahr**-stfo] n. (bell-)founder's trade
ludwisarz [lood-**vee**-sahsh] m. (bell-) founder
ludyczność [loo-**dich**-nośhćh] f. entertaining character (of a

program, etc.)
ludyczny [loo-**dich**-ni] adj.m. entertaining
ludyzm [**loo**-dizm] m. playfulness; the need for frequent entertainment
ludzie [**loo**-dźhe] pl. people
ludzik [**loo**-dźheek] m. little man
ludziska [loo-**dźhees**-kah] pl. colloq: (common) people
ludzki [**loots**-kee] adj.m. of man; humane; human; man's; people's; benevolent; decent; suitable; proper; passable; tolerable; colloq: servant's (quarters, etc.); other people's; somebody's; somebody else's
po ludzku [po **loots**-koo] exp.: like a human being; kindly; benevolently; decently; suitably; properly; humanely
wyglądać po ludzku [vi-**glown**-dahćh po **loots**-koo] exp.: to be presentable
ludzkość [**loots**-kośhćh] f. mankind; humaneness; humanity; human feelings; kindness
lues [**loo**-es] m. lues; syphilis; slang: venereal disease (mob jargon)
luetyczny [loo-e-**tich**-ni] adj.m. luetic; syphilitic
lufa [**loo**-fah] f. gunbarrel; barrel (of a rifle, etc.); colloq: duffer; slacker; bungler; lubber; muff; slang: bad grade in school; big glass of vodka
gładka lufa [**gwaht**-kah **loo**-fah] exp.: smoothbore (gun)
lufcik [**loof**-ćheek] m. casement; ventilator
luffa [**loof**-fah] f. loofah; luffa; dishcloth gourd
lufka [**loof**-kah] f. gunbarrel; barrel (of a rifle, etc.); cigarette holder
luft [looft] m. chimney flue
do luftu [do **loof**-too] exp.: good-for-nothing; no good; not worth a hoot
lugier [**loo**-ger] m. lugger; drifter; drift boat
lugrotrawler [loog-ro-**trahv**-ler] m. small trawler
lugrowy [loog-**ro**-vi] adj.m. lugger (fleet, sails, etc.)
lugubre [loo-**goob**-re] n. lugubriously (played music); mournfully
luidor [loo-**ee**-dor] m. louis-d'or (coin)
luizyt [loo-**ee**-zit] m. lewisite
luk [look] m. hatch; skylight; (ship's storage) hold
luka [**loo**-kah] f. gap; blank; break; lacuna; vacancy; hiatus; (ship's storage) hold
mieć lukę w załodze [myećh **loo**-kan v zah-**wo**-dze] exp.: to be undermanned; to be short-handed; to be short of hands
zapełnić lukę [zah-**pew**-ńeećh **loo**-kan] exp.: to fill a gap; to bridge a gap
lukarna [loo-**kahr**-nah] f. lucarne; dormer window; attic-window
lukier [**loo**-ker] m. sugar icing; frosting (on a cake)
lukowy [loo-**ko**-vi] adj.m. of a hatch; of a gap; of a ship's storage hold
lukratywnie [loo-krah-**tiv**-ńe] adv. lucratively; profitably
lukratywność [loo-krah-**tiv**-nośhćh] f. lucrativeness
lukratywny [loo-krah-**tiv**-ni] adj.m. lucrative; profitable
lukrecja [loo-**kre**-tsyah] f. liquorice; licorice; colloq: wishy-washy talk; wish-wash
lukrecjowy [loo-kre-**tsyo**-vi] adj.m. liquorice (root, etc.); licorice (root, etc.); colloq: wishy-washy
lukrować [look-**ro**-vahćh] v. ice; frost (with sugar); colloq: varnish (*repeatedly*)
lukrowanie [look-ro-**vah**-ńe] n. icing; frosting (with sugar); colloq: varnish
lukrowy [look-**ro**-vi] adj.m. of icing; of frosting
luks [looks] m. lux
luksemburgizm [loo-ksem-**boor**-geezm] m. subversive theories of Rosa Luxemburg
luksemburski [loo-ksem-**boor**-skee] adj.m. Luxemburgian
luksfer [**looks**-fer] m. translucent glass masonry brick
luksografia [look-so-**grah**-fyah] f. direct printing on light-sensitive surface

luksomierz [look-**so**-myesh] m. variety of light meter
luksosekunda [look-so-se-**koon**-dah] f. one lux of light per second
luksus [**look**-soos] m. luxury
podatek od luksusu [po-**dah**-tek od look-**soo**-soo] exp.: luxury tax
luksusowo [look-soo-**so**-vo] adv. luxuriously; richly; sumptuously; superbly
luksusowy [look-soo-**so**-vi] adj.m. luxurious; rich; sumptuous; superb; deluxe; luxury (article, etc.)
lukubracja [loo-koo-**brah**-tsyah] f. lucubration; meditation
lukullusowy [loo-kool-loo-**so**-vi] adj.m. of Lucullus; Lucullan; lavish; luxurious (feast, etc.)
lulać [loo-lahćh] v. rock to sleep; lull to sleep; sing (a child) to sleep; sleep (*repeatedly*)
lulaj! [**loo**-lahy] excl.: hushaby!; bye-bye!; go to sleep!
lulanie [loo-**lah**-ńe] n. (child's) sleep
lulek [**loo**-lek] m. (black) henbane (plant)
luli [**loo**-lee] exp.: bye-bye; hushaby
lulka [**lool**-kah] f. (tobbaco-)pipe
lulkowy [lool-**ko**-vi] adj.m. of a tobacco-pipe; henbane (leaves, etc.)
lulu [**loo**-loo] exp.: bye-bye; hushaby
lumbago [loom-**bah**-go] n. lumbago
lumen [**loo**-men] m. lumen
lumenometr [loo-me-**no**-metr] m. variety of light meter
lumenomierz [loo-me-**no**-myesh] m. variety of light meter
lumenosekunda [loo-me-no-se-**koon**-dah] f. measurement unit of one lumen per second
luminal [loo-**mee**-nahl] m. luminal (tranquilizer)
luminancja [loo-mee-**nahn**-tsyah] f. luminosity
luminarz [loo-**mee**-nahsh] m. luminary; eminent personage
luminescencja [loo-mee-nes-**tsen**-tsyah] f. luminescence
luminescencyjny [loo-mee-nes-tsen-**tsiy**-ni] adj.m. luminescent
luminizm [loo-**mee**-ńeezm] m. luminism
luminofor [loo-mee-**no**-for] m. luminous substance
luminofory [loo-mee-no-**fo**-ri] pl. luminous substances
lumityp [loo-**mee**-tip] m. photographic printing machine
lump [loomp] m. colloq: drunk; tipper; toper; reveller; carouser; outcast
lumpy [**loom**-pi] pl. tatters (clothes worn in German-Nazi concentration camp)
lumpenproletariacki [loom-pen-pro-le-tahr-**yah**-tskee] adj.m. of the outcasts (of society)
lumpenproletariat [loom-pen-pro-le-**tahr**-yaht] m. outcasts (of society)
lumpenproletariusz [loom-pen-pro-le-**tahr**-yoosh] m. outcast
lumpiarz [**loom**-pyahsh] m. colloq: drunk; tipper; toper; reveller; carouser; outcast
lumpować [loom-**po**-vahćh] v. colloq: booze in bars; tipple in bars; revel; carouse (*repeatedly*)
lumpować się [loom-**po**-vahćh śhan] v. colloq: booze oneself up (in bars) (*repeatedly*)
lumpowanie [loom-po-**vah**-ńe] n. revelry; revelries
lumpowski [loom-**pof**-skee] adj.m. lumpen (proletariat, etc.)
luna [**loo**-nah] f. colloq: moon
lunacja [loo-**nah**-tsyah] f. lunation (29 days, 12 hours, 44 minutes, 2.8 seconds)
lunapark [loo-**nah**-pahrk] m. amusement park
lunatyczka [loo-nah-**tich**-kah] f. (female) somnambulist; sleepwalker; colloq: loony
lunatycznie [loo-nah-**tich**-ńe] adv. like a somnambulist; like a sleepwalker
lunatyczny [loo-nah-**tich**-ni] adj.m. somnambulistic
lunatyk [loo-**nah**-tik] m. sleepwalker; colloq: loony
lunatyzm [loo-**nah**-tizm] m. somnambulism; sleepwalking
lunąć [**loo**-nownćh] v. rain in torrents; lash down in sheets; colloq: whack; fail; flunk
lunch [lahnch] m. lunch

luneta [loo-**ne**-tah] f. fieldglass; spyglass; telescope; lunette
lunetka [loo-**net**-kah] f. (small) fieldglass; spyglass
lunetowy [loo-ne-**to**-vi] adj.m. of a fieldglass; of a spyglass; of a telescope; of a lunette
lunie [**loo**-ńe] exp.: colloq: downpour is coming
lunięcie [loo-**ńan**-ćhe] n. gust (of rain); downpour
lunit [**loo**-ńeet] m. moon surface
lunonauta [loo-no-**nahw**-tah] m. astronaut travelling to the moon
lupa [**loo**-pah] f. magnifying glass; jeweler's glass; reading glass; lens
wziąć (coś) pod lupę [vźhownćh tsośh pod **loo**-pan] exp.: to examine (something) with the aid of a magnifying glass; make a close investigation (of a question, problem, etc.)
lupanar [loo-**pah**-nahr] m. brothel; bawdyhouse; lupanar
lupinoza [loo-pee-**no**-zah] f. sheep's and horses' disease
lupka [**loop**-kah] f. (small) magnifying glass; jeweler's glass; reading glass
lupulina [loo-poo-**lee**-nah] f. lupulin
lura [**loo**-rah] f. colloq: slops; swill; hogwash; swipes; cat-lap; wish-wash
lureks [**loo**-reks] m. variety of artificial fiber
lurka [**loor**-kah] f. colloq: watery coffee; watery tea; slops; swill
lurowaty [loo-ro-**vah**-ti] adj.m. wishy-washy
lustereczko [loos-te-**rech**-ko] n. (small, nice) hand glass; rear-view mirror (in a car); pocket looking-glass
lusterko [loos-**ter**-ko] n. hand glass; rear-view mirror (in a car); pocket looking-glass
lustr [loostr] m. metallic luster; luster
lustracja [loos-**trah**-tsyah] f. inspection; audit
lustracyjny [loos-trah-**tsiy**-ni] adj.m. inspection (sticker, etc.); audit (report, etc.)
lustrator [loos-**trah**-tor] m. inspector; auditor
lustratorka [loos-trah-**tor**-kah] f. (female) inspector; auditor
lustro [**loo**-stro] n. mirror; looking-glass
lustrować [loo-**stro**-vahćh] v. inspect; review; check; audit; survey; scrutinize (*repeatedly*)
lustrować się [loo-**stro**-vahćh śhan] v. inspect each other; scrutinize each other (*repeatedly*)
lustrowanie [loo-stro-**vah**-ńe] n. inspection; audit; survey
lustrowanie się [loo-stro-**vah**-ńe śhan] n. scrutinizing each other
lustryna [loo-**stri**-nah] f. lustrine
lustrzanka [loos-**tshahn**-kah] f. reflex camera
lustrzanka jednoobiektywowa [loos-**tshahn**-kah ye-dno-o-bye-kti-**vo**-vah] exp.: SLR (single lens reflex) camera
lustrzany [loos-**tshah**-ni] adj.m. mirror (glass, etc.); shining; shiny
lustrzeń [**loos**-tsheń] m. mirror carp
luśnia [**loośh**-ńah] f. bracket of a rack wagon
lut [loot] m. solder
lut twardy [loot **tfahr**-di] exp.: bronze weld; brazing solder; hard solder (nonferrous)
luteina [loo-te-**ee**-nah] f. lutein
luter [**loo**-ter] m. Lutheran (church member)
luteranin [loo-te-**rah**-ńeen] m. Lutheran (church member)
luteranizm [loo-te-**rah**-ńeezm] m. Lutheranism
luterański [loo-te-**rahń**-skee] adj.m. Lutheran
lutet [**loo**-tet] m. lutetium; cassiopeium (atomic number 71)
lutnia [**loot**-ńah] f. (stringed) lute
lutnictwo [loot-**ńeets**-tfo] n. violin making; manufacture of stringed musical instruments
lutniczy [loot-**ńee**-chi] adj.m. of violin making; of manufacture of stringed musical instruments
lutnik [**loot**-ńeek] m. violin maker; manufacturer of stringed musical instruments; maker of lutes; lutist; colloq: lute player

lutniowy [loot-ńo-vi] adj.m. of a lute; lute (fingerboard, etc.)
lutnista [loot-**ńees**-tah] m. lutenist
lutnistka [loot-**ńeest**-kah] f. (female) lutenist
lutospawanie [loo-to-spah-**vah**-ńe] n. soldering using blowtorch
lutospawacz [loo-to-**spah**-vahch] m. solderer using blow-torch
lutość [**loo**-tośhćh] f. severity
lutowacz [loo-**to**-vahch] m. specialist solderer
lutować [loo-**to**-vahćh] v. solder (*repeatedly*)
lutować lutowiną twardą [loo-**to**-vahćh loo-to-**vee**-nown **tfahr**-down] exp.: to braze (*repeatedly*)
lutowanie [loo-to-**vah**-ńe] n. soldering
lutowie [loo-**to**-vye] n. solder
lutowina [loo-to-**vee**-nah] f. soldered place; solder
lutownica [loo-tov-**ńee**-tsah] f. soldering gun; soldering tool; soldering iron
lutowniczy [loo-tov-**ńee**-chi] adj.m. soldering (copper, nipple, etc.)
lampa lutownicza [**lahm**-pah loo-tov-ńee-chah] exp.: blowtorch; blow lamp
lutownik [loo-**tov**-ńeek] m. soldering gun; soldering tool; soldering iron; solderer
lutowy [loo-**to**-vi] adj.m. February (frost, etc.)
lutówka [loo-**toof**-kah] f. soldering gun; soldering tool; soldering iron
lutry [**loot**-ri] pl. otters; otter fur
lutunek [loo-**too**-nek] m. soldered joint
luty [**loo**-ti] m. February; adj.m. severe; bleak; grim
lutz [loots] m. a jump in figure skating
luwers [**loo**-vers] m. reinforced opening in a sail
luz [loos] m. clearance; play; colloq: relax; slang: freedom (outside prison) (mob jargon)
biec luzem [byets **loo**-zem] exp.: to run idle
luzem [**loo**-zem] exp.: without load; freely; on the loose
na luzie [nah **loo**-źhe] exp.: freely; without restrain; unabashedly
luzak [**loo**-zahk] m. loose; led horse; (replacement) horse
luzować [loo-**zo**-vahćh] v. replace; relieve; loosen; slacken (a rope, etc.); relay; ease off (a cable, etc.) (*repeatedly*)
luzować się [loo-**zo**-vahćh śhan] v. replace one another; relieve one another; take turns (*repeatedly*)
luzowanie [loo-zo-**vah**-ńe] n. relay; relief
luzowanie się [loo-zo-**vah**-ńe śhan] n. the changeover
luźnie [**looźh**-ńe] adv. loosely
luźno [**looźh**-no] adv. loosely
puszczony luźno [poosh-**cho**-ni **looźh**-no] exp.: free; unrestrained
wisieć luźno [**vee**-śhećh **looźh**-no] exp.: to hang loose
luźność [**looźh**-nośhćh] f. looseness
luźny [**looźh**-ni] adj.m. loose; ample; wide; full; baggy; detached; unfixed; lax; slack; led (horse)
lwi [lvee] adj.m. lion's; lions'
lwia część [lvyah chanśhćh] exp.: the lion's share; the main part; the major part; the bulk
lwia grzywa [lvyah **gzhi**-vah] exp.: mane
lwie serce [lvye **ser**-tse] exp.: lionheart
lwi pazur [lvee **pah**-zoor] exp.: the stamp of genius
lwiarnia [**lvyahr**-ńah] f. the lion's cage; the lion's enclosure (in a zoo)
lwiątko [lvyownt-ko] n. lion's cub; lion's whelp
lwica [**lvee**-tsah] f. lioness
lwię [lvyan] n. lion's cub; lion's whelp
lwisko [**lvees**-ko] n. (big, old) lion
lycra [**lik**-rah] f. elastic polyurethane fiber
lyncz [linch] m. lynch; lynching
lżej [lzhey] adv. lighter; easier; with less weight
lżej ranni [lzhey **rahn**-ńee] exp.: those with minor wounds
jest mi lżej [yest mee lzhey] exp.:

I feel better; I am relieved; it is easier for me now
lżejszy [**lzhey**-shi] adj.m. lighter; easier; not serious
lżenie [**lzhe**-ńe] n. abuse; insults; vituperation
lżenie się [**lzhe**-ńe śhan] n. abusing each other; insulting each other
lżyć [lzhićh] v. abuse; insult; revile; (against); shower abuse (on); rail (against); vituperate (*repeatedly*)
lżyć się [lzhićh śhan] v. abuse one another; insult one another; revile one another (*repeatedly*)
lżywy [**lzhi**-vi] adj.m. abusive; insulting

Ł

Ł, ł [ew] the letter "ł"; the sound [ew]
łabaj [**wah**-bahy] m. slang: hospital for venereal diseases; specialist in venereal diseases; physician; jail
łabędzi [wah-**ban**-dźhee] adj.m. of a swan; swan (lake, etc); of swans
łabędzi śpiew [wah-**ban**-dźhee śhpyef] exp.: swan song
łabędzi puch [wah-**ban**-dźhee pookh] exp.: swan's-down
łabędzia szyja [wah-**ban**-dźhah **shi**-yah] exp.: swan neck
łabędziarnia [wah-ban-**dźhahr**-ńah] f. swannery
łabędzica [wah-ban-**dźhee**-tsah] f. pen (female swan)
łabędziątko [wah-ban-**dźhownt**-ko] n. cygnet
łabędziowaty [wah-ban-dźho-**vah**-ti] adj.m. like a swan; swanny
łabędziowy [wah-ban-**dźho**-vi] adj.m. swan's
łabędź [**wah**-bandźh] m. swan; cob (male swan)
łabuniec [wah-**boo**-ńets] m. a variety of predatory insects
łabuńce [wah-**booń**-tse] pl. the family Gagrellidae of predatory insects
łach [wahkh] m. rag; clout
stare łachy [**stah**-re **wah**-khi] exp.: old rags; old duds
łacha [**wah**-khah] f. sandbank; shoal; hurst; patch (of snow)
łachać [**wah**-khahćh] v. wear to tatters; wear out (one's clothes); colloq: tramp uselessly (*repeatedly*)
łachetka [wah-**khet**-kah] f. slang: whore (mob jargon)
łachman [**wahkh**-mahn] m. rag; clout; tatter; (human) wreck
w łachmanach [v wahkh-**mah**-nahkh] exp.: in rags; tattered
łachmaniarka [wahkh-mah-**ńahr**-kah] f. (woman) ragpicker; beggar; bag lady; bagwoman; homeless woman; ragamuffin
łachmaniarski [wahkh-mah-**ńahr**-skee] adj.m. ragpicker'; ragpickers'; shabby; ragged; run down; dilapidated; wearing badly worn clothing; shameful (behavior)
łachmaniarz [wahkh-**mah**-ńahsh] m. ragpicker; beggar; bagman; homeless man; ragamuffin; shabby man; run-down person
łachmyta [wahkh-**mi**-tah] f. & m. ragamuffin; tatterdemalion; homeless man; slang: clumsy thief (mob jargon)
łachotać [wah-**kho**-tahćh] v. tickle; titillate (*repeatedly*)
łachotki [wah-**khot**-kee] pl. tickles
mieć łachotki [myećh wah-**khot**-kee] exp.: to be ticklish
łachudra [wah-**khood**-rah] m. & f. slang: dirty scoundrel; ragamuffin; lousy scamp; rogue (mob jargon)
łachudrować [wah-khood-**ro**-vahćh] v. slang: steal anything (mob jargon) (*repeatedly*)
łaciarz [**wah**-ćhahsh] m. patcher; patcher-up (of old clothes); cobbler; second-hand dealer; used-clothes salesman; colloq: homeless man; ragamuffin; shabby man; run-down person
łaciasty [wah-**ćhahs**-ti] adj.m. patchy; spotted; speckled; multicolored; particolored; roan (cow); pinto (horse); piebald (horse)

łaciaty [wah-**ćhah**-ti] adj.m. in patches; pinto (horse); piebald (horse); roan (cow); speckled; particolored
łaciasty [wah-**ćhahs**-ti] adj.m. = **łaciaty** [wah-**ćhah**-ti]
łacina [wah-**ćhee**-nah] f. Latin (language, class, lesson, etc.); slang: insulting language; strong language
łacinka [wah-**ćhee**-nkah] f. Latin alphabet; italics
łacinnik [wah-**ćheen**-ńeek] m. Latin scholar; Latinist; member of the Latin Church
łaciński [wah-**ćheeń**-skee] adj.m. Latin; of Latin; lateen (sail)
obrządek łaciński [ob-**zhown**-dek wah-**ćheeń**-skee] exp.: Latin rite
łacińskość [wah-**ćheeń**-skośhćh] f. appurtenance to Latin culture
łacnie [**wahts**-ńe] adv. easily
łacno [**wahts**-no] adv. easily; without effort
ład [waht] m. order; orderliness
nowy ład [no-vi waht] exp.: New Deal; new order
bez ładu [bez **wah**-doo] exp.: pell-mell; in confusion; without rhyme or reason; disorderly
dojść do ładu [doyśhćh do **wah**-doo] exp.: to come to terms; to get straightened out; to make sense
według nowego ładu [**ved**-woog no-**ve**-go **wah**-doo] exp.: after a new fashion; after a new order
ładnie [**wahd**-ńe] adv. nicely; prettily; attractively
ładnie ci w tym [**wahd**-ńe ćhee f tim] exp.: that suits you very well; it's becoming to you
ładnie postąpić [**wahd**-ńe po-**stown**-peećh] exp.: to act nicely; to treat handsomely; to do the handsome thing (by)
ładnieć [**wahd**-ńećh] v. grow pretty; grow (look) prettier; become prettier (*repeatedly*)
ładniuchny [wahd-**ńookh**-ni] adj.m. very nice; very attractive
ładniutki [wahd-**ńoot**-kee] adj.m. very nice; very attractive
ładniutko [wahd-**ńoot**-ko] adv. very nicely; very attractively
ładny [**wahd**-ni] adj.m. nice; pretty; lovely; cute; attractive; good-looking; fair-faced; handsome; seemly; becoming; beautiful; goodly (number, etc.); comfortable (income); fine; shapely (leg, etc.); m. slang: homosexual (mob jargon)
panie ładny! [**pah**-ńe **wahd**-ni] exp.: I say!; look here you!
ładowacz [wah-**do**-vahch] m. loader; stevedore; heaver
ładowaczka [wah-do-**vahch**-kah] f. woman loader; stevedore; loading machine
ładować [wah-**do**-vahćh] v. load; charge (a battery); cram; fill; freight (a ship); ship (goods); slang: invest; have sex (mob jargon) (*repeatedly*)
ładować się [wah-**do**-vahćh śhan] v. get in; force one's way into; crawl in (*repeatedly*)
ładowanie [wah-do-**vah**-ńe] n. shovelling; loading
ładowanie na statek [wah-do-vah-ńe nah **stah**-tek] exp.: loading a ship; embarkation
ładowanie się [wah-do-**vah**-ńe śhan] n. getting in; forcing one's way (into)
ładowarka [wah-do-**vahr**-kah] f. loading machine; loader
ładowarkowy [wah-do-vahr-**ko**-vi] adj.m. loading machine (operator, etc.)
ładownia [wah-**dov**-ńah] f. loading platform
ładownica [wah-dov-**ńee**-tsah] f. cartridge pouch (or belt); battery charger
ładowniczy [wah-dov-**ńee**-chi] adj.m. loading; m. loader
ładownik [wah-**dov**-ńeek] m. loader; charger clip; battery charger
ładowność [wah-**dov**-nośhćh] f. load carrying capacity; cargo capacity
ładowny [wah-**dov**-ni] adj.m. capacious; roomy; loaded
ładuga [wah-**doo**-gah] f. cargo; freight
ładugowy [wah-doo-**go**-vi] adj.m.

loading (capacity, etc.)
linia ładugowa [leeń-yah wah-doo-**go**-vah] exp.: load line
ładunek [wah-**doo**-nek] m. load; cargo; (electr.) charge; shipload; burden; freight; bulk
nadmierny ładunek [nahd-**myer**-ni wah-**doo**-nek] exp.: overload
ostry ładunek [**os**-tri wah-**doo**-nek] exp.: full charge
ślepy ładunek [**śhle**-pi wah-**doo**-nek] exp.: blank charge
ładunkowy [wah-doon-**ko**-vi] adj.m. loading (device, documents, charges, etc.)
dokumenty ładunkowe [do-koo-**men**-ti wah-doon-**ko**-ve] exp.: shipping documents
opłaty ładunkowe [op-**wah**-ti wah-doon-**ko**-ve] exp.: stowage
otwór ładunkowy [**ot**-foor wah-doon-**ko**-vi] exp.: port; porthole
ładzenie [wah-**dze**-ńe] n. colloq: putting in order
ładzić [**wah**-dźheećh] v. colloq: put in order; slang: be on good terms (with) (*repeatedly*)
ładzić się [**wah**-dźheećh śh<u>an</u>] v. colloq: put oneself in order (*repeatedly*)
łagier [**wah**-<u>g</u>er] m. slave-labor camp in the Soviet Union; slang: prison
łagiernik [wah-<u>g</u>er-ńeek] m. inmate in a slave-labor camp in the Soviet Union; slang: prison warden; prison guard (jargon)
łagiew [**wah**-<u>g</u>ef] f. utricle
łagiewka [wah-**<u>g</u>ef**-kah] f. utricle
łagiewkowy [wah-<u>g</u>ef-**ko**-vi] adj.m. utricular; containing a utricle (animal pouch)
łagodnie [wah-**god**-ńe] adv. mildly; with lenience; gently; kindly; softly; quietly; meekly; suavely; blandly; placidly
łagodnieć [wah-**god**-ńećh] v. become mild; soften; grow less severe; tame down; relent; abate; subside; slacken; mellow (*repeatedly*)
łagodniutki [wah-god-**ńoot**-kee] adj.m. (nicely) gentle; mild; soft; meek; easy; tamed down; relent; abated; slack; mellow; tame; good-natured; docile; tractable; lenient; clement; mellow
łagodniutko [wah-god-**ńoot**-ko] adv. (pleasantly) mildly; with lenience; gently; kindly; softly; quietly; meekly; suavely; blandly; placidly
łagodność [wah-**god**-nośhćh] f. gentleness; kindliness; suavity; mildness; placidity; tameness; tractability; meekness; good nature; docility; tractability; leniency; clemency; softness; mellowness; indolence; benignity; mildness of disposition
łagodny [wah-**god**-ni] adj.m. gentle; mild; soft; meek; easy; tamed down; relent; abated; slack; mellow; tame; good natured; docile; tractable; lenient; clement; mellow; indolent; benign; non-corroding
łagodząco [wah-go-**dz<u>own</u>**-tso] adv. soothingly
łagodzący [wah-go-**dz<u>own</u>**-tsi] adj.m. alleviating; extenuating
środek łagodzący [**śhro**-dek wah-go-**dz<u>own</u>**-tsi] exp.: (a) palliative; (a) lenitive; remissive
okoliczności łagodzące [o-ko-leech-**nośh**-ćhe wah-go-**dz<u>own</u>**-tse] exp.: extenuating circumstances
łagodzenie [wah-go-**dze**-ńe] n. appeasement; pacification; assuagement; relief; palliation
łagodzić [wah-**go**-dźheećh] v. soothe; relieve; alleviate; attenuate; mitigate; smooth; tone down; temper; mollify; commute (a sentence); subdue; slacken off; break (the force of a blow); absorb (shocks, etc.); ease (pain, etc.); allay; tame down; deaden (a blow, etc.) (*repeatedly*)
łagodzić się [wah-**go**-dźheećh śh<u>an</u>] v. soften; be appeased; be soothed; be alleviated (*repeatedly*)
łagrowy [wahg-**ro**-vi] adj.m. of a slave-labor camp in Soviet Union
łajać [**wah**-yahćh] v. scold; chide; rate; upbraid; nag; revile; abuse; slang: rag; rail (at) (*repeatedly*)
łajać się [**wah**-yahćh śh<u>an</u>] v. scold one another; chide one

another; revile one another; abuse one another; squabble; nag; rail one another (*repeatedly*)
łajanie [wah-**yah**-ńe] n. scolding; chiding; rating; nagging; reviling; abuse; invectives
łajanie się [wah-**yah**-ńe śhan] n. squabbling with each other; nagging against each other; reviling each other; abusing one another; railing at one another
łajba [**wahy**-bah] f. colloq: (dear, old) boat, ship; slang: fat woman
łajdacki [wahy-**dah**-tskee] adj.m. roguish; villainous; dastardly; rascally; scoundrelly
po łajdacku [po wahy-**dah**-tskoo] exp.: like a scoundrel; like a villain; like a rogue
łajdacko [wahy-**dah**-tsko] adv. like a rogue; like a villain; in a dastardly manner; like a scoundrel
łajdactwo [wahy-**dah**-tstfo] n. rascality; roguery; rascally tricks; piece of roguery; mean trick; scoundrels; rabble; gang of rascals
łajdaczenie się [wahy-dah-**che**-ńe śhan] n. dissolute living; easy virtue; dissipated and immoral living; wenching; rakishness; revelry; revels
łajdaczka [wahy-**dah**-chkah] f. (woman) wretch; scoundrel; rascal; villain; rogue
łajdaczyć się [wahy-**dah**-chićh śhan] v. lead a dissolute life; go wenching; go womanizing; revel; carouse (*repeatedly*)
łajdaczyna [wahy-dah-**chi**-nah] m. miserable wretch; shabby scoundrel
łajdak [**wahy**-dahk] m. scoundrel; rascal; villain; rogue; wretch
łajdus [**wahy**-doos] m. colloq: scoundrel; rascal; villain; rogue; wretch
łajka [**wahy**-kah] f. Siberian spitz dog
łajnić [**wahy**-ńeećh] v. dung (by animals) (*repeatedly*)
łajno [**wahy**-no] n. dung; droppings; vulg.: turd; shit
łajza [**wahy**-zah] f. & m. vagrant; duffer; muff; oaf; slacker
łaknąć [**wahk**-nownćh] v. hunger for; thirst for; crave for; colloq: starve for; long for; pant for (*repeatedly*)
łaknienie [wahk-**ńe**-ńe] n. hunger; thirst; craving (for); colloq: longing
łakocie [wah-**ko**-ćhe] pl. delicacies; sweets; tidbits; candy; bonbons; dainties
łakomczuch [wah-**kom**-chookh] m. glutton; gourmand; greedy eater; greedy child
łakomić się [wah-**ko**-meećh śhan] v. covet; lust; be tempted (by); be greedy (of); be avid (of) (*repeatedly*)
łakomie [wah-**kom**-ye] adv. greedily; gluttonously; avidly; covetously
łakomiec [wah-**kom**-yets] m. glutton; gourmand; greedy eater; greedy child
łakomienie [wah-ko-**mye**-ńe] n. tempting; making greedy
łakomienie się [wah-ko-**mye**-ńe śhan] n. becoming tempted; feeling greedy
łakomstwo [wah-**koms**-tfo] n. greed; gluttony; greediness; gourmandism; covetousness; lickerishness; fondness of sweets
łakomy [wah-**ko**-mi] adj.m. greedy; covetous; avid; fond of sweets; tempting; alluring; coveted
łam [wahm] m. column (of a newspaper)
na łamach gazety [nah wah-mahkh gah-**ze**-ti] exp.: in the columns of a newspaper
łamacz [**wah**-mahch] m. breaker; crusher; smasher; crushing machine
łamacz fal [**wah**-mahch fahl] exp.: breakwater
łamacz lodów [**wah**-mahch **lo**-doof] exp.: icebreaker
łamacze [wah-**mah**-che] pl. crushing teeth of carnivores; breakers; crushers; smashers; crushing machines
łamać [**wah**-mahćh] v. break; crush; quarry; shatter; crack; snap; smash; fracture (a bone);

transgress (the law, etc.); infringe (a rule, etc.) (*repeatedly*)
łamać głowę [**wah**-mahćh **gwo**-van] exp.: to rack one's brains
łamać kamień [**wah**-mahćh **kah**-myeń] exp.: to quarry
łamać się [**wah**-mahćh śhan] v. share; break; smash; be shattered; snap; go snap; crack; go to pieces; come apart; give in; falter; collapse; have a nervous breakdown; grapple; contend (with difficulties); waver (*repeatedly*)
łamać się opłatkiem [**wah**-mahćh śhan o-**pwaht**-kem] exp.: to break the traditional wafer at Christmas (when good wishes are exchanged)
łamać się z sobą [**wah**-mahćh śhan s **so**-bown] exp.: to be perplexed; to be in a quandary; to be on the horns of a dilemma; to waver
łamaga [wah-**mah**-gah] m. & f. bungler; botcher; muff; weakling
łamana [wah-**mah**-nah] f. zigzag made up of straight line segments
łamanie [wah-**mah**-ńe] n. the breaking; the fracturing
łamanie w kościach [wah-**mah**-ńe f **kośh**-ćhahkh] exp.: rheumatic pains
łamanie się ze sobą [wah-**mah**-ńe śhan ze **so**-bown] exp.: perplexity
łamaniec [wah-**mah**-ńets] m. contortion; feat of acrobatics; waffle; goffer; flourish (an ornamental curve)
łamany [wah-**mah**-ni] adj.m. broken
linia łamana [**leeń**-yah wah-**mah**-nah] exp.: broken line
łamana angielszczyzna [wah-**mah**-nah an-gel-**shchiz**-nah] exp.: broken English
łamany dach [wah-**mah**-ni dahkh] exp.: mansard roof
łamarka [wah-**mahr**-kah] f. jaw crusher
łamigłówka [wah-mee-**gwoof**-kah] f. riddle; puzzle; jigsaw puzzle; enigma
łamigłówkowy [wah-mee-gwoof-**ko**-vi] adj.m. of a riddle; of a puzzle; of a jigsaw puzzle; of an enigma
łamistrajk [wah-**mee**-strahyk] m. scab; strikebreaker
łamistrajkowy [wah-mee-strahy-**ko**-vi] adj.m. scab (hiring, etc.); strikebreaker (action, etc.)
łamliwość [wahm-**lee**-vośhćh] f. fragility; brittleness
łamliwy [wahm-**lee**-vi] adj.m. fragile; frail; brittle; breakable
łamulec [wah-**moo**-lets] m. crowbar
łan [wahn] m. feud; fief; stand of wheat; cornfield; standing corn
łani [**wah**-ńee] adj.m. of a hind; of a doe
łania [**wah**-ńah] f. hind; doe
łanowy [wah-**no**-vi] adj.m. of a cornfield; fief (infantry, founded in Poland in 1655)
łańcuch [**wahń**-tsookh] m. chain; range; series; train; succession (of events, etc.)
łańcuch górski [**wahń**-tsookh **goor**-skee] exp.: mountain range
łańcuchowy [wahń-tsoo-**kho**-vi] adj.m. catenary (curve, etc.); chain (coupling, etc.); acyclic
most łańcuchowy [most wahń-tsoo-**kho**-vi] exp.: chain bridge
reakcja łańcuchowa [re-**ahk**-tsyah wahń-tsoo-**kho**-vah] exp.: chain reaction (of nuclear fission)
łańcuchówka [wahń-tsoo-**khoof**-kah] f. a type of village built along a road
łańcuszek [wahń-**tsoo**-shek] m. little chain; watch chain; chainlet; chain stitch
łańcuszkowo [wahń-tsoosh-**ko**-vo] adv. by means of a chain (stitch, etc.)
łańcuszkowy [wahń-tsoosh-**ko**-vi] adj.m. chain (stitch, work, etc.)
łap [wahp] indecl. exp.: with a swoop (snap, snatch, etc.)
łapa [**wah**-pah] f. paw; claw; arm; flipper; flapper; lug
dać w łapę [dahćh v **wah**-pan] exp.: to grease (somebody's) hand
daj łapę [dahy **wah**-pan] exp.: colloq: shake hand
łapa kotwicy [**wah**-pah kot-**fee**-tsi]

exp.: anchor blade; fluke of an anchor; palm of an anchor
łapacz [**wah**-pahch] m. catcher; slime separator; colloq: sleuthhound; police detective
łapać [**wah**-pahćh] v. catch; get hold (of); snatch; grasp; seize; kidnap; round up; catch hold (of); clutch (at); snap (at) (*repeatedly*)
łapać oddech [**wah**-pahćh **od**-dekh] exp.: to catch one's breath; to gasp for breath
łapać w sidła [**wah**-pahćh f **śheed**-wah] exp.: to trap (an animal)
łapać się [**wah**-pahćh śhan] v. catch oneself (doing, etc.); let oneself be caught; resort (to); fall into (traps, nets, etc.) (*repeatedly*)
łapadło [wah-**pahd**-wo] n. catcher; sleuthhound; slime separator; (mine) gripper; cage catcher
łapanie [wah-**pah**-ńe] n. a catch; catches; a snatch; snatches
łapanie się [wah-**pah**-ńe śhan] n. catching oneself (in to a net, etc.); catching each other
łapanka [wah-**pahn**-kah] f. roundup; German-Nazi raid to arrest people (usually in a closed off street); mooring rope; mooring line
łapawica [wah-pah-**vee**-tsah] f. mitten; mitt
łap-cap [wahp tsahp] indecl. exp.: hurry-scurry; helter-skelter; slapdash; in a rough-and-tumble manner
na łap-cap [nah wahp tsahp] exp.: in a hurry; without thinking; sloppily; carelessly
łapcia [**wahp**-ćhah] f. (small) paw
łapciarz [**wahp**-ćhahsh] m. moccasin maker; beggar; ragamuffin; tatterdemalion
łapcie [**wahp**-ćhe] pl. bast sandals; moccasins
łapczywie [wahp-**chi**-vye] adv. greedily; avidly
łapczywie jeść [wahp-**chi**-vye yeśhćh] exp.: to gobble up (one's food); to swallow greedily; to eat greedily
łapczywie pić [wahp-**chi**-vye peećh] exp.: to swill
łapczywość [wahp-**chi**-vośhćh] f. greed; greediness; avidity
łapczywy [wahp-**chi**-vi] adj.m. greedy; money-grubbing; avid; rapacious
łapeczka [wah-**pech**-kah] f. (small, nice) paw
łapeć [**wah**-pećh] m. bast moccasin
łapiduch [wah-**pee**-dookh] m. stretcher-bearer
łapigrosz [wah-**pee**-grosh] m. colloq: money-grubber
łapina [wah-**pee**-nah] f. (small, poor) paw; child's hand
łapka [**wahp**-kah] f. (mouse) trap; little paw
łapka na myszy [**wahp**-kah nah **mi**-shi] exp.: mousetrap
łapownictwo [wah-pov-**ńee**-tstfo] n. bribery; corruption; corruptibility; venality
łapowniczy [wah-pov-**ńee**-chi] adj.m. corrupt
łapownik [wah-**pov**-ńeek] m. grafter; bribe-taker
łapówa [wah-**poo**-vah] f. colloq: (big, fat) bribe; graft
łapówka [wah-**poof**-kah] f. bribe; graft; gratification
dać łapówkę [dahćh wah-**poof**-kan] exp.: to bribe
łapówkarski [wah-poof-**kahr**-skee] adj.m. bribe-taking (habit, etc.); graft (money. etc.)
łapówkarstwo [wah-poof-**kahr**-stfo] n. bribe-taking; graft
łapówkarz [wah-**poof**-kahsh] m. bribe-taker; grafter
łapówkowo [wah-poof-**ko**-vo] adv. by (means of) bribery
łapówkowy [wah-poof-**ko**-vi] adj.m. of bribery
łaps [wahps] indecl. exp.: (meaning:) with a swoop (to snatch, to seize, to snap up, etc.)
łapserdak [wahp-**ser**-dahk] m. rogue; ragamuffin; scoundrel
łapsko [**wahp**-sko] n. (big, fat) hand, paw
łapu-capu [**wah**-poo **tsah**-poo] indecl. exp.: hurry-scurry; helter-skelter; slapdash; in a rough-and-tumble manner

łasica [wah-śhee-tsah] f. weasel
łasice [wah-**śhee**-tse] pl. weasels; colloq: weasel fur
łasicowaty [wah-śhee-tso-**vah**-ti] adj.m. like a weasel; of the Mustelidae family
łasicowate [wah-śhee-tso-**vah**-te] pl. the Mustelidae family
łasiczka [wah-**śheech**-kah] f. small weasel; nice weasel
łasiczy [wah-**śhee**-chi] adj.m. weasel's; weasels'
futro łasicze [**foo**-tro wah-**śhee**-che] exp.: weasel fur
łasić się [**wah**-śheećh śhan] v. fawn; fawn on somebody; toady; flatter (*repeatedly*)
łaska [**wahs**-kah] f. colloq: weasel = **łasica**
łaska [**wahs**-kah] f. grace; good graces; favor; bounty; generosity; mercy; condescension; pity; act of grace; pardon; reprieve; clemency
akt łaski [ahkt **wahs**-kee] exp.: act of grace
być na łasce [bićh nah **wahs**-tse] exp.: to live on (somebody's) generosity
na łasce [nah **wahs**-tse] exp.: at the mercy
prawo łaski [prah-vo **wahs**-kee] exp.: the right of reprieve
stan łaski [stahn **wahs**-kee] exp.: the right to reprieve
w stanie łaski [f **stah**-ńe **wahs**-kee] exp.: in a state of grace
łaskawca [wahs-**kahf**-tsah] m. colloq: would be benefactor
łaskawie [wahs-**kah**-vye] adv. graciously; kindly; generously; partially; magnanimously; condescendingly; favorably
zechciej łaskawie [**zekh**-ćhey wahs-**kah**-vye] exp.: be so kind to ...; have the kindness to...; have the goodness to ...; will you please; would you mind
łaskawość [wahs-**kah**-vośhćh] f. kindness, benevolence; benignity; kindliness; generosity
łaskawy [wahs-**kah**-vi] adj.m. gracious; kind; generous; partial; magnanimous; condescending; favorable; docile (animal)
bądź łaskaw to zrobić [bownćh wahs-kahf to **zro**-beećh] exp.: be so kind as to do it
Łaskawa Pani [wahs-**kah**-vah **pah**-ńee] exp.: Dear Madam; Dear Mrs. X
łaskotać [wah-**sko**-tahćh] v. tickle; titillate; delight (*repeatedly*)
łaskotanie [wahs-ko-**tah**-ńe] n. tickling
łaskotki [wah-**skot**-kee] pl. tickling
łaskotliwie [wah-sko-**tlee**-vye] adv. ticklishly
łaskotliwy [wah-sko-**tlee**-vi] adj.m. ticklish; titillating
łaskotnica [wah-skot-**ńee**-tsah] f. bamboo
łaskun [**wahs**-koon] m. civet cat
łaskuny [wahs-**koo**-ni] pl. the family of civet cats
łasować [wah-**so**-vahćh] v. colloq: steal sweets (from a pantry, etc.) (*repeatedly*)
łasowanie [wah-so-**vah**-ńe] n. colloq: stealing sweets (from a pantry, etc.)
łasuch [**wah**-sookh] m. glutton; greedy eater
łasy [**wah**-si] adj.m. greedy; gourmand; keen; avid; tempting
łasza [**wah**-shah] f. animal of the family Viverridae
łaszczenie się [wahsh-**che**-ńe śhan] n. coveting (something)
łaszczyć się [**wahsh**-chićh śhan] v. covet; lust (*repeatedly*)
łaszek [**wah**-shek] m. colloq: woman's neckerchief; casual garment etc.
łaszenie się [wah-**she**-ńe śhan] n. fawning; courting favor
łaszowaty [wah-sho-**vah**-ti] adj.m. like an animal of the family Viverridae
łaszowate [wah-sho-**vah**-te] pl. animals of the family Viverridae
łaszt [wahsht] m. last (a measure)
łasztem [**wahsh**-tem] exp.: wholesale
łata [**wah**-tah] f. patch; lath (timber); batten; splash of color; speckle; spot; stain; staff; (surveyor's) rod; scantling

brat łata [braht **wah**-tah] exp.: colloq: pal; chum; warm-hearted companion
łata niwelacyjna [**wah**-tah ńee-ve-lah-**tsiy**-nah] exp.: levelling staff; levelling rod
przypiąć łatę [pshi-py<u>own</u>ćh **wah**-t<u>an</u>] exp.: to brand (somebody)
łatacz [**wah**-tahch] m. patcher; cobbler
łatać [**wah**-tahćh] v. patch up; cobble (shoes); repair; tinker up; mend; botch (badly) (*repeatedly*)
łatanie [wah-**tah**-ńe] n. patching
łatanina [wah-tah-**ńee**-nah] f. patchwork; mending; tinkering; patching up; bungled work; botched piece of work
łatek [**wah**-tek] m. mob slang: contemptible person
łatka [**waht**-kah] f. small patch
łatwiutki [waht-**fyoot**-kee] adj.m. very easy; colloq: awfully easy
łatwiutko [waht-**fyoot**-ko] adv. very easily; awfully easily; without the least effort
łatwizna [waht-**feez**-nah] f. easy task; easy shot; soft snap; shallowness; superficiality
łatwo [**waht**-fo] adv. easily; without difficulty; without effort; well; readily; soon
łatwo dostępny [**waht**-fo dos-**t<u>an</u>p**-ni] exp.: of easy access
łatwo się męczę [**waht**-fo śh<u>an</u> **m<u>an</u>**-ch<u>an</u>] exp.: I soon get tired; I tire easily; I get tired easily
łatwo to powiedzieć [**waht**-fo to po-**vye**-dźhećh] exp.: it's easy to say; it's easier said than done
łatwopalność [waht-fo-**pahl**-nośhćh] f. (easy) inflammability; combustibility
łatwopalny [waht-fo-**pahl**-ni] adj.m. (easily) inflammable; combustible
łatwostrawny [wah-tfvo-**strahv**-ni] adj.m. easily digestible
łatwość [**waht**-fośhćh] f. easy; easiness; facility; aptitude; fluency; simplicity; easy manners; lax morals
łatwość mówienia [**waht**-fośhćh moo-**vye**-ńah] exp.: fluency of speech; glibness
z łatwością [z waht-**fośh**-ćh<u>own</u>] exp.: easily; without effort
łatwowiernie [waht-fo-**vyer**-ńe] adv. credulously; confidently
łatwowierność [waht-fo-**vyer**-nośhćh] f. credulity; easiness of belief; gullibility
łatwowierny [waht-fo-**vyer**-ni] adj.m. credulous; gullible; confiding; overtrustful
łatwy [**waht**-fi] adj.m. easy; simple; effortless; light; of easy manners; accessible; superficial (text, etc.); ready (to do something)
ława [**wah**-vah] f. bench; footing; footbridge; stall; layer; bed; sandbank; shelf; shoal; compact mass (of humanity, etc.)
ława piaszczysta [**wah**-vah pyahsh-**chis**-tah] exp.: sandbank
ława przysięgłych [**wah**-vah pshi-**śh<u>an</u>g**-wikh] exp.: jury
ławą [**wah**-v<u>own</u>] exp.: in a mass (of people); as a crowd
kolega z ławy szkolnej [ko-**le**-gah z **wah**-vi **shkol**-ney] exp.: schoolmate
przybyć ławą [**pshi**-bićh **wah**-v<u>own</u>] exp.: to come in a mass; to pour in a stream; to pour out
ławeczka [wah-**vech**-kah] f. footstool; small bench
ławica [wah-**vee**-tsah] f. (fish) shoal; sandbank; shelf; layer
ławica lodowa [wah-**vee**-tsah lo-**do**-vah] exp.: ice-bank
ławicowo [wah-vee-**tso**-vo] adv. in shoals
ławicowy [wah-vee-**tso**-vi] adj.m. of shoals; shoaling (fishes)
ławka [**wahf**-kah] f. pew; bench; school desk; (boat) band; thwart
ławkowiec [wahf-**ko**-vyets] m. wide brush of house-painters
ławkowy [wahf-**ko**-vi] adj.m. of a pew; of a bench
ławniczy [wahv-**ńee**-chi] adj.m. juror's; alderman's; assessor's
ławnik [**wahv**-ńeek] m. juror; alderman; assessor
ławra [**wahv**-rah] f. compound of hermits' dwellings; major

orthodox monastery under a synod
łazanek [wah-**zah**-nek] m. (Polish) noodle
łazanka [wah-**zahn**-kah] f. (Polish) noodle
łazanki [wah-**zahn**-kee] pl. (Polish) noodles
łazarz [**wah**-zahsh] m. poor beggar; object of compassion
łazęga [wah-**zan**-gah] f. dawdling; loitering; sauntering; gadding about; m. & f. loiterer; dawdler; gadabout; slacker
łazęgostwo [wah-zan-**go**-stfo] n. loitering; dawdling
łazęgować [wah-zan-**go**-vahćh] v. colloq: loiter; dawdle (*repeatedly*)
łazęgowanie [wah-zan-go-**vah**-ńe] n. colloq: loitering; dawdling
łazić [**wah**-źheećh] v. crawl; loiter; slouch about; creep; dawdle; saunter; walk (heavily); tread; crawl; climb (*repeatedly*)
łazić po drzewach [**wah**-źheećh po **dzhe**-vahkh] exp.: to climb trees
łazić za [**wah**-źheećh zah] exp.: to dangle after; to seek favor (with, for)
łazidło [wah-**źheed**-wo] n. climbing iron
łaziebna [wah-**źheb**-nah] f. colloq: (female) bath attendant
łaziebny [wah-**źheb**-ni] adj.m. colloq: bath (attendant, etc.); m. colloq: bath attendant
łaziec [**wah**-źhets] m. climbing perch (fish)
łazienka [wah-**źhen**-kah] f. bathroom; toilet; bath
łazienkowy [wah-źhen-**ko**-vi] adj.m. of a bathroom; toilet (paper, etc.); of a bath
łazienna [wah-**źhen**-nah] f. (woman) bathroom attendant
łazienny [wah-**źhen**-ni] m. (man) bathroom attendant
łazik [**wah**-źheek] m. jeep; tramp; loiterer; lazy wastrel
łazikostwo [wah-źhee-**kos**-tfo] n. loitering; lounging; sloping about
łazikować [wah-źhee-**ko**-vahćh] v. loiter; lounge; slope about (*repeatedly*)
łazikowanie [wah-źhee-ko-**vah**-ńe] n. loitering; lounging; sloping about
łaziwo [wah-**źhee**-vo] n. climbing ropes
łaźbić [**wahźh**-beećh] v. remove some combs (of honey and wax) from a hive (*repeatedly*)
łaźcowaty [wahśh-tso-**vah**-ti] adj.m. like the climbing fish; of the Anabantidae family
łaźcowate [wahśh-tso-**vah**-te] pl. the Anabantidae family of climbing fish
łaźnia [**wahźh**-ńah] f. bath
łaźniowy [wahźh-**ńo**-vi] adj.m. of a bath
łażący [wah-**zhown**-tsi] adj.m. dragging; crawling; scansorial
łażący ptak [wah-**zhown**-tsi ptahk] exp.: climber (bird)
łażenie [wah-**zhe**-ńe] n. dawdling; sauntering; loitering; (a) crawl
łączarka [wown-**chahr**-kah] f. machine for sawing knitted fabric
łączący [wown-**chown**-tsi] adj.m. uniting; joining; junctive; connecting
nić łącząca [ńeećh wown-**chown**-tsah] exp.: link; bond; tie
rura łącząca [**roo**-rah wown-**chown**-tsah] exp.: connector (pipe)
tryb łączący [trib wown-**chown**-tsi] (gram.) exp.: subjunctive mood
łącze [**wown**-che] n. (electrical) connection; connector
łączenie [wown-**che**-ńe] n. union; junction; connection; connexion; merger; splice
łączenie się [wown-**che**-ńe śhan] n. union; junction; connection; connexion; combination; association; articulation; joint; contiguity; intercommunication; convergence
łączeniowy [wown-che-**ńo**-vi] adj.m. connecting
łączeń [**wown**-cheń] m. variety of a marsh shrub
łączka [**wownch**-kah] f. small meadow; connector

łączliwość [wownch-lee-vośhćh] f. (phonetic) ability to connect
łączliwy [wownch-**lee**-vi] adj.m. having (phonetic) ability to connect
łącznia [**wownch**-ńah] f. connecting element
łączniarka [wownch-**ńahr**-kah] f. yarn processing machine
łącznica [wownch-**ńee**-tsah] f. telephone relay station; railroad siding; junction; (phone) switchboard; telephone exchange
łącznicowy [wownch-ńee-**tso**-vi] adj.m. of a telephone relay station; of railroad siding
łączniczka [wownch-**ńeech**-kah] f. (woman) liaison officer
łącznie [**wownch**-ńe] adv. together; including; inclusive of; along with; jointly; conjointly; in conjunction
łącznie z kosztami [**wownch**-ńe s kosh-**tah**-mee] exp.: including costs; inclusive of costs
pisane łącznie [pee-**sah**-ne **wownch**-ńe] exp.: spelt in one word; not hyphenated
łącznik [**wownch**-ńeek] m. hyphen; liaison officer; link; tie; bond; connecting (rod, link, word, etc.); fastener; (football) guard; copula
łącznikowy [wownch-ńee-**ko**-vi] adj.m. connecting (link, etc.); liaison (officer, etc.)
łączniowaty [wownch-ńo-**vah**-ti] adj.m. butomaceous (herb)
łączniowate [wownch-ńo-**vah**-te] pl. the family of butomaceous herbs
łącznościowiec [wownch-nośh-**ćho**-vyets] m. (military) communication officer
łącznościowy [wownch-nośh-**ćho**-vi] adj.m. communication (satellite, etc.)
łączność [**wownch**-nośhćh] f. contact; (tele)communication; unity; signal service; connection; communion; liaison
oficer łączności [o-fee-tser wownch-**nośh**-ćhee] exp.: signal officer
nawiązać łączność [nah-**vyown**-zahćh **wownch**-nośhćh] exp.: to establish contact (with)
służba łączności [**swooozh**-bah wownch-**nośh**-ćhee] exp.: Signals Corps; Corps of Signals
środki łączności [**śhrot**-kee wownch-**nośh**-ćhee] exp.: means of communication
łącznotkankowy [wownch-no-tkahn-**ko**-vi] adj.m. of connective tissue
łączny [**wownch**-ni] adj.m. joint; combined; total; global; united; cumulative; connective
łączna suma [**wownch**-nah **soo**-mah] exp.: sum total
pisownia łączna [pee-**sov**-ńah **wownch**-nah] exp.: unhyphened spelling; not hyphenated spelling
tkanka łączna [**tkahn**-kah **wownch**-nah] exp.: connective tissue
łączyć [**wown**-chićh] v. join; unite; merge; link; bind; weld; couple; splice; aggregate; amalgamate; bring together; put together; piece together; cement; knit together; fasten together; mix; mingle; blend; connect; give a connection; wed; marry; join in wedlock; pair; mate (*repeatedly*)
łączyć się [**wown**-chićh śhan] v. unite; combine; be united; be joined; be coupled; come together; merge; be connected; be linked; adjoin; be contiguous; communicate; interconnect; meet; converge; mix; blend; mingle; get a connection; be joined in wedlock; pair; couple; ring up (by telephone); reach by phone; marry; mate; join; combine; associate; coalesce (*repeatedly*)
łączyć się na nowo [**wown**-chićh śhan nah **no**-vo] exp.: to reunite
łączyć się z kimś [**wown**-chićh śhan s keemśh] exp.: to ring somebody up; to get somebody on the phone; to marry; to be joined in wedlock; to come together; to combine; to associate
łąg [wownk] m. marshy meadow
łąka [**wown**-kah] f. meadow; grassland; grass pasture
łąkarski [wown-**kahr**-skee] adj.m.

meadow (cultivation, etc.)
łąkarstwo [wown-**kahr**-stfo] n. cultivation of meadows
łąkarz [**wown**-kahsh] m. meadower; cultivator of meadow land
łąkotka [wown-**kot**-kah] f. meniscus
łąkowy [wown-**ko**-vi] adj.m. of meadow; meadow (grass, etc.)
łąkoznawstwo [wown-ko-**znahf**-stfo] n. study and classification of pastures
łątka [**wownt**-kah] f. puppet; marionette; damsel fly
łbica [**wbee**-tsah] f. cylinder head
łeb [wep] m. head; colloq: pate; top; frontlet; (nail, rivet, hammer, cylinder, etc.) head
łeb w łeb [wep v wep] exp.: (to finish) neck and neck
na łeb, na szyję [nah wep nah **shi**-yan] exp.: headlong; head over heels
nadstawiać łba [naht-**stah**-vyahćh wbah] exp.: to risk one's life
kocie łby [**ko**-ćhe wbi] exp.: cobblestones
łebek [**we**-bek] m. small head; slang: head; person (mob jargon)
od łebka [od **wep**-kah] exp.: per person; per passenger; per head
po łebkach [po **wep**-kahkh] exp.: superficially; cursorily; perfunctorily
łebski [**wep**-skee] adj.m. slang: brainy; clever; cute; smart
łebsko [**wep**-sko] adv. slang: cleverly; cutely; smartly
łechtaczka [wekh-**tahch**-kah] f. clitoris
łechtać [**wekh**-tahćh] v. tickle; colloq: flatter; titillate; colloq: lure (*repeatedly*)
łechtanie [wekh-**tah**-ńe] n. (a) tickle (in the nose, etc.)
łechtliwie [wekh-**tlee**-vye] adv. ticklishly; ticklingly; colloq: alluringly
łechtliwy [wekh-**tlee**-vi] adj.m. ticklish; tickling; colloq: alluring
łejba [**wey**-bah] f. slang: class in school
łepak [**we**-pahk] m. mullet (fish); slang: brainy fellow
łepek [**we**-pek] m. slang: head; person; see: **łebek**
łepetyna [we-pe-**ti**-nah] f. colloq: head; child's head
łepski [**wep**-skee] adj.m. slang: brainy; clever; cute; smart; see: **łebski**
łepsko [**wep**-sko] adv. slang: cleverly; cutely; smartly
łezka [**wes**-kah] f. little tear; colloq: sentimentality; mawkishness; slang: pearl
łezki [**wes**-kee] pl. guttae
z łezką [z **wes**-kown] exp.: mawkish
łęcina [wan-**ćhee**-nah] f. potato stalks
łęg [wank] m. marshy meadow; swampy meadow
łęgowy [wan-**go**-vi] adj.m. marshy; swampy
łęk [wank] m. saddlebow; saddletree; pommel; saddle with pommel and cantle; trough; syncline; arch; bow
łęki [**wan**-kee] pl. saddlebows; saddletrees; pommels; troughs; synclines; arches; bows
łękotka [wan-**kot**-kah] f. meniscus
łękotki [wan-**kot**-kee] pl. meniscuses; menisci
łękowaty [wan-ko-**vah**-ti] adj.m. arched; saddle-backed (animal)
łękowy [wan-**ko**-vi] adj.m. arched
łęt [want] m. potato stalk
łętowina [wan-to-**vee**-nah] f. potato stalk
łgać [wgahćh] v. lie; brag; boast; tell lies (*repeatedly*)
łgać na potęgę [wgahćh nah po-**tan**-gan] exp.: to lie unblushingly; to lie through one's teeth; to lie through one's throat
łgać jak pies [wgahćh yahk pyes] exp.: to lie unblushingly; to lie through one's teeth; to lie through one's throat
łgać jak z nut [wgahćh yahk z noot] exp.: to lie unblushingly; to lie through one's teeth; to lie through one's throat
łganie [**wgah**-ńe] n. lies; lying
łgarski [**wgahr**-skee] adj.m. lying; mendacious

łgarstwo [**wgahr**-stfo] n. lie; falsehood; brag; boasting; mendacity; lies
łgarz [wgahsh] m. liar; braggart; boaster
łkać [wkahćh] v. sob; weep (*repeatedly*)
łkanie [**wkah**-ńe] n. sobs
łoboda [wo-**bo**-dah] f. orach (plant)
łobuz [**wo**-boos] m. bounder; rogue; rascal; scamp; scoundrel; urchin; pickle
łobuz dziewczyna [**wo**-boos dźhef-**chi**-nah] exp.: hoyden
ty stary łobuzie! [ti **stah**-ri wo-**boo**-źhe] exp.: you old son of a gun!
łobuzeria [wo-boo-**zer**-yah] f. scamps; urchins; mischievous boys; slang: gang (bunch, band) of rascals; mischief; pranks; roguery
łobuzerka [wo-boo-**zer**-kah] f. mischief; pranks; roguery
łobuzerski [wo-boo-**zer**-skee] adj.m. mischievous; roguish; raffish; saucy; arch
po łobuzersku [po wo-boo-**zer**-skoo] exp.: mischievously; roguishly; raffishly; saucily
łobuzersko [wo-boo-**zer**-sko] adv. mischievously; roguishly; raffishly; saucily
łobuzerstwo [wo-boo-**zer**-stfo] n. petty villainy; knavery; see: **łobuzeria**
łobuziak [wo-**boo**-źhahk] m. scamp; boisterous girl; tomboy; hoyden
łobuzować [wo-boo-**zo**-vahćh] v. play pranks; be up to mischief (*repeatedly*)
łobuzować się [wo-boo-**zo**-vahćh śhan] v. play pranks; be up to mischief (*repeatedly*)
łobuzowanie [wo-boo-zo-**vah**-ńe] n. pranks; devilment; roguery
łobuzowanie się [wo-boo-zo-**vah**-ńe śhan] n. playing pranks; being up to mischief
łobuzowaty [wo-boo-zo-**vah**-ti] adj.m. scampish; full of mischief
łochynia [wo-**khi**-ńah] f. bog bilberry; European whortleberry
łoczyga [wo-**chi**-gah] f. lapsana; nipplewort
łodyga [wo-**di**-gah] f. stem; stalk; culm; haulm; spire (of grass); colloq: beam of a stag's antler; slang: scrag; skinny dude; lean guy (mob jargon)
łodygowaty [wo-di-go-**vah**-ti] adj.m. coalescent
łodygowy [wo-di-**go**-vi] adj.m. cauline; stem (leaf, etc.)
łodyżka [wo-**dish**-kah] f. small stem
łodzik [**wo**-dźheek] m. navicula alga; nautilus cephalopod
łodzikowaty [wo-dźhee-ko-**vah**-ti] adj.m. of the order Nautiloidea
łodzikowate [wo-dźhee-ko-**vah**-te] pl. the order of Nautiloidea cephalopos
łodziowy [wo-**dźho**-vi] adj.m. of a boat; of boats; boat (deck, etc.)
łogacizna [wo-gah-**ćheez**-nah] f. bone spavin
łogawizna [wo-gah-**veez**-nah] f. bone spavin
łogawy [wo-**gah**-vi] adj.m. spavined
łogowaty [wo-go-**vaht**-ti] adj.m. pediliaceous
łogowate [wo-go-**vaht**-te] pl. the family Pediliaceae
łogowy [wo-**go**-vi] adj.m. of sesame; sesame (oil, etc.)
łoić [**wo**-eećh] v. tallow; curry; colloq: beat up; wallop (*repeatedly*)
łojak [**wo**-yahk] m. steatoma
łojenie [wo-**ye**-ńe] n. currying; treating with tall oil
łojny [**woy**-ni] adj.m. colloq: fat
łojotok [wo-**yo**-tok] m. seborrhea; seborrhagia
łojotokowy [wo-yo-to-**ko**-vi] adj.m. seborrhoeic
łojowaty [wo-yo-**vah**-ti] adj.m. tallowy; suety
łojowy [wo-**yo**-vi] adj.m. sebaceous; tallow (candle, etc.)
gruczoł łojowy [**groo**-chow wo-**yo**-vi] exp.: sebaceous gland
łojówka [wo-**yoof**-kah] f. tallow-candle; tallowy beef; tallowy mutton
łokaś [**wo**-kahśh] m. ground beetle
łokciowy [wok-**ćho**-vi] adj.m. of elbow; ulnar; cubital; anconeal;

yard-long; yard-deep; narrow (goods)
kość łokciowa [kośhćh wok-ćho-vah] exp.: ulna
staw łokciowy [stahf wok-ćho-vi] exp.: elbow joint
towary łokciowe [to-vah-ri wok-ćho-ve] exp.: narrow goods; haberdashery
łokieć [wo-kećh] m. elbow; ell
rozpychać się łokciami [ros-pi-khahćh śhan wok-ćhah-mee] exp.: to elbow one's way
trącać łokciem [trown-tsahćh wok-ćhem] exp.: to nudge
łoktusza [wok-too-shah] f. warp
łom [wom] m. crowbar; scrap; junk; rubble; block (chocolate); quarry; ashlar; jemmy; jimmy; chips; sprigs; twigs
łomianka [wom-yahn-kah] f. a plant of the goosefoot family
łomikost [wo-mee-kost] m. softening of the bones
łomot [wo-mot] m. crash; crack; clatter; thud; rumble; din; racket; clangor; mob slang: beating
łomotać [wo-mo-tahćh] v. clatter; rattle; knock; rumble; batter (at the door); bang; colloq: hit; strike; punch; whack (*repeatedly*)
łomotanie [wo-mo-tah-ńe] n. clatter; rattle; knocking; rumbling
łomotanina [wo-mo-tah-ńee-nah] f. colloq: clatter; rattle; knocking; rumbling
łomotnąć [wo-mot-nownćh] v. clatter; rattle; knock; rumble; batter (at the door); bang; hit; strike; punch; whack
łomotnąć się [wo-mot-nownćh śhan] v. bang oneself up; hit oneself
łomotnięcie [wo-mot-ńan-ćhe] n. clatter; rattle; knock; rumble
łomotnięcie się [wo-mot-ńan-ćhe śhan] n. banging oneself up; hitting oneself
łoni [wo-ńee] adv. colloq: last year
łono [wo-no] n. lap; bosom; womb; pubes; venter
na łonie przyrody [nah wo-ńe pshi-ro-di] exp.: in the open; in the sticks; together with nature; back to nature
łonowy [wo-no-vi] adj.m. pubic
kość łonowa [kośhćh wo-no-vah] exp.: pubic bone
wesz łonowa [vesh wo-no-vah] exp.: pubic louse; crab (louse)
łoński [woń-skee] adj.m. colloq: last year's
łopata [wo-pah-tah] f. spade; shovel; peel; shovelful; spadeful; paddle; (broad) antler; battledore; blade (of a propeller); vane (of a propeller)
łopaty [wo-pah-ti] pl. spades; shovels; peels; paddles; (propeller) blades; (broad) antlers
łopatka [wo-paht-kah] f. little shovel; spatula; omoplate; shoulder blade; (animal's) shoulder
łopatka do śmieci [wo-paht-kah do śhmye-ćhee] exp.: dustpan
łopatkowaty [wo-paht-ko-vah-ti] adj.m. spatula-like; spoon-shaped
łopatkowy [wo-paht-ko-vi] adj.m. spatular; spoon-shaped; scapular
łopatologia [wo-pah-to-log-yah] f. colloq: spoon feeding
łopatologiczny [wo-pah-to-lo-geech-ni] adj.m. of spoon feeding
łopaty [wo-pah-ti] pl. (broad) antlers
łopian [wo-pyahn] m. burdock
łopianowy [wo-pyah-no-vi] adj.m. burdock (roots, etc.)
łopot [wo-pot] m. (sail) flutter; flap; flapping; fluttering; slating
łopotać [wo-po-tahćh] v. flap; flutter (bird's wings, etc.); slat; clatter; rattle; thump (in the heart) (*repeatedly*)
łopotać skrzydłami [wo-po-tahćh skshi-dwah-mee] exp.: to flap the wings
łopotać żaglami [wo-po-tahćh zhah-glah-mee] exp.: to flap the sails
łopotanie [wo-po-tah-ńe] n. flutter
łopuch [wo-pookh] m. burdock; slang: hat (mob jargon)
łopucha [wo-poo-khah] f. variety of radishes
łopuchowy [wo-poo-kho-vi] adj.m. burdock (roots, etc.)
łosi [wo-śhee] adj.m. of elk; elk's;

elk (leather, etc.)
łosia [**wo**-śhah] f. slang: girl; gal
łosica [wo-**śhee**-tsah] f. female elk
łosiczka [wo-**śheech**-kah] f. slang: woman (mob jargon)
łosię [**wo**-śhan] n. young elk
łosina [wo-**śhee**-nah] f. elk meat
łosiowy [wo-**śho**-vi] adj.m. elk's; see: **łosi**
łoskot [**wos**-kot] m. clatter; bang; din; rumble; racket; boom; bluster (of a storm); reverberation; peal (of thunder, etc.); roar (of an airplane)
narobić łoskotu [nah-**ro**-beećh wos-**ko**-too] exp.: to boom; to bluster; to bang; to roar by
łoskotać [wos-**ko**-tahćh] v. clatter; bang; din; rumble; racket; boom; bluster (like a storm); reverberate; peal (of thunder, etc.); roar (*repeatedly*)
łoskotanie [wos-ko-**tah**-ńe] n. clatter
łososiowaty [wo-so-śho-**vah**-ti] adj.m. salmonoid; salmon-like
łososiowate [wo-so-śho-**vah**-te] pl. the family Salmonidae
łososiowy [wo-so-**śho**-vi] adj.m. salmon (season); salmon-(color)
łosoś [**wo**-sośh] m. salmon
dwuletni łosoś [dvoo-**let**-ńee **wo**-sośh] exp.: mort
jednoroczny łosoś [yed-no-**roch**-ni **wo**-sośh] exp.: parr; grilse; smolt
młody łosoś [**mwo**-di **wo**-sośh] exp.: samlet
łosza [**wo**-shah] f. female elk
łoszak [**wo**-shahk] m. young elk
łoszę [**wo**-shan] n. very young horse; colt; filly
łoś [wośh] m. elk; moose
łotewski [wo-**tef**-skee] adj.m. Latvian (language, etc.)
język łotewski [**yan**-zik wo-**tef**-skee] exp.: Lettish; Lett; Latvian language
łotr [wotr] m. scoundrel; knave; rascal; rogue; (Biblical) thief
łotrostwo [wo-**tro**-stfo] n. rascally trick; knavery; roguery
łotrować [wo-**tro**-vahćh] v. colloq: perpetrate rascally tricks; commit knavery; be a rogue (*repeatedly*)
łotrować się [wo-**tro**-vahćh śhan] v. colloq: (emphatic:) perpetrate rascally tricks; commit knavery; be a rogue (*repeatedly*)
łotrowanie [wo-tro-**vah**-ńe] n. colloq: rascally tricks; knavery; roguery
łotrowski [wo-**trof**-skee] adj.m. scoundrelly; rascally; knavish; roguish
po łotrowsku [po wo-**trof**-skoo] exp.: like a scoundrel
łotrzyca [wo-**tshi**-tsah] f. (female) scoundrel; knave; rascal; rogue
łotrzyk [**wot**-shik] m. colloq: small time rogue; little rogue
łotrzykowski [wo-tshi-**kof**-skee] adj.m. picaresque (novel, etc.)
Łotysz [**wo**-tish] m. Latvian; Lett
Łotyszka [wo-**tish**-kah] f. Latvian woman; Lett woman
łowca [**wof**-tsah] m. hunter; huntsman; trapper
łowca głów [**wof**-tsah gwoof] exp.: headhunter; slang: recruiter
łowca niewolników [**wof**-tsah ńe-vol-**ńee**-koof] exp.: slave-hunter
łowca posagów [**wof**-tsah po-sah-goof] exp.: fortune hunter
łowczy [**wof**-chi] adj.m. hunting (grounds, etc.); huntsman's; hunter's; m. Master of the Royal Hunt; master of the chase
łowicki [wo-**veets**-kee] adj.m. of Łowicz; Łowicz (design, etc.)
pasy łowickie [pah-si wo-**veets**-ke] exp.: colored stripes
łowić [**wo**-veećh] v. trap; fish; catch (sounds, game, butterflies, etc.); hunt; chase; be heedful (*repeatedly*)
łowić gapy [**wo**-veećh **gah**-pi] exp.: colloq: to catch absent-minded people; slang: to pick pockets (mob jargon)
łowić ryby [**wo**-veećh **ri**-bi] exp.: to fish
łowiecki [wo-**vye**-tskee] adj.m. hunting (terms, etc.); shooting (grounds, etc.)
rewir łowiecki [**re**-veer wo-**vye**-tskee] exp.: shoot; hunt
prawo łowieckie [**prah**-vo wo-**vye**-tske] exp.: game law
ustawa łowiecka [oos-**tah**-vah

wo-**vye**-tskah] exp.: game law
łowiectwo [wo-**vyets**-tfo] n. hunting; game shooting
łowienie [wo-**vye**-ńe] n. hunting; the hunt; the chase; the game shooting; the angling
łowienie ryb [wo-**vye**-ńe rip] exp.: angling
łowik [**wo**-veek] m. asilid (insect)
łowikowaty [wo-vee-ko-**vah**-ti] adj.m. asilid (insect); of the Asilids
łowikowate [wo-vee-ko-**vah**-te] pl. the Asilids (insects)
łowisko [wo-**vees**-ko] n. hunting ground; fishing-waters; fishery
łowność [**wov**-nośhćh] f. hunting ability; angling ability
łowny [**wov**-ni] adj.m. old enough to be hunted; warrantable (stag); good mouse-catcher; mouser (cat)
zwierzyna łowna [zvye-**zhi**-nah **wov**-nah] exp.: game; beasts of chase
łowy [**wo**-vi] pl. hunt; chase
łoza [**wo**-zah] f. osier; wicker
łozina [wo-**źhee**-nah] f. wicker; sallow; osier; osier-bed
łozinowy [wo-źhee-**no**-vi] adj.m. wicker (basket, chair, etc.)
łozowy [wo-**zo**-vi] adj.m. osier (twigs, etc.)
łozówka [wo-**zoof**-kah] f. olive-colored small bird (Acrocephalus palustris)
łoże [**wo**-zhe] n. bed; cradle
łoże działa [**wo**-zhe **dźhah**-wah] exp.: gun mount
łoże małżeńskie [**wo**-zhe mahw-**zheń**-s<u>k</u>e] exp.: marriage-bed
łoże śmierci [**wo**-zhe **śhmyer**-ćhee] exp.: deathbed
dziecko z nieprawego łoża [**dźhe**-tsko z ńe-prah-**ve**-go **wo**-zhah] exp.: an illegitimate child
łożenie [wo-**zhe**-ńe] n. spending money (on); defraying (costs)
łożnica [wozh-**ńee**-tsah] f. an old fashion bed
łożyć [**wo**-zhićh] v. spend money (on somebody, something); defray (the costs of); pay (large sums, etc.); lay out (*repeatedly*)
łożysko [wo-**zhis**-ko] n. riverbed; (ball) bearing; (gun) stock; bed; pillow block
łożysko kulkowe [wo-**zhis**-ko kool-**ko**-ve] exp.: ball bearing
łożysko rolkowe [wo-**zhis**-ko rol-**ko**-ve] exp.: roller bearing
łożysko toczne [wo-**zhis**-ko **toch**-ne] exp.: rolling bearing
łożyskować [wo-zhis-**ko**-vahćh] v. support on bearings (*repeatedly*)
łożyskowanie [wo-zhis-ko-**vah**-ńe] n. providing support on bearings
łożyskowiec [wo-zhis-**ko**-vyets] m. placental animal
łożyskowce [wo-zhis-**kof**-tse] pl. placentalia
łożyskowy [wo-zhis-**ko**-vi] adj.m. bearing (ring, etc.); placental; of placenta
stop łożyskowy [stop wo-zhis-**ko**-vi] exp.: bearing metal
łódeczka [woo-**dech**-kah] f. very small boat; carina
łódeczkowaty [woo-dech-ko-**vah**-ti] adj.m. of carina; carinal
łódka [**woot**-kah] f. small boat; dinghy; canoe; (balloon) gondola; (weaver's) shuttle; (cartridge) clip
łódkonóg [woot-**ko**-nook] m. marine mollusk (with tapering tubular shell)
łódkonogi [woot-ko-**no**-gee] pl. Scaphopoda
łódkowaty [woot-ko-**vah**-ti] adj.m. boat-shaped; navicular
łódź [woóćh] f. boat; craft; barge; ferryboat; pilot boat
łódź mieszkalna [woóćh myesh-**kahl**-nah] exp.: houseboat
łódź motorowa [woóćh mo-to-**ro**-vah] exp.: motorboat
łódź podwodna [woóćh pod-**vod**-nah] exp.: submarine
łódź wyścigowa [woóćh viśh-ćhee-**go**-vah] exp.: racing-boat
łój [wooy] m. tallow; suet; sebum
łów [woof] m. hunt; chase; hunting; fishing
łóżeczko [woo-**zhech**-ko] n. (child's) bed; small bed
łóżko [**woosh**-ko] n. bed; bunk; sleeping-berth; cot; bedstead
leżeć w łóżku [le-zhećh v **woosh**-koo] exp.: to be in bed; to

keep to one's bed
położyć się do łóżka [po-**wo**-zhićh śhan do **woosh**-kah] exp.: to go to bed
słać łóżko [swahćh **woosh**-ko] exp.: to make the bed
łóżkowy [woosh-**ko**-vi] adj.m. bed (springs, etc.)
łub [woop] m. chip; strip of tree bark; split; splint
łubek [**woo**-bek] m. splint; shin
łubianka [woo-**byahn**-kah] f. chip basket; trug
łubiany [woo-**byah**-ni] adj.m. made of wood strips
łubin [**woo**-been] m. lupin
łubinowy [woo-bee-**no**-vi] adj.m. lupin (seeds, etc.)
łubkowy [woop-**ko**-vi] adj.m. of a splint; of a shin
połączenie łubkowe [po-wown-che-ńe woop-**ko**-ve] exp.: fish joint
łubowy [woo-**bo**-vi] adj.m. of a splint; of a shin
łubu-du [**woo**-boo doo] exp.: colloq: (meaning:) the sound of a bang; the sound of a thump
łuczek [**woo**-chek] m. small arch (ornamental); small bow
łucznictwo [wooch-**ńee**-tstfo] n. archery
łuczniczka [wooch-**ńeech**-kah] f. (female) archer; bowman; bowyer
łuczniczy [wooch-**ńee**-chi] adj.m. of archery; archer's; archers'
łucznik [**wooch**-ńeek] m. archer; bowman; bowyer
łuczywo [woo-**chi**-vo] n. resinous kindling; resinous chips
łudząco [woo-**dzown**-tso] adv. delusively; deceptively; illusively
być łudząco podobnym [bićh woo-**dzown**-tso po-**dob**-nim] exp.: to look exactly alike
łudzący [woo-**dzown**-tsi] adj.m. delusive; deceptive; illusive
łudzenie [woo-**dze**-ńe] n. deception; delusion
łudzenie się [woo-**dze**-ńe śhan] n. delusion
łudzić [**woo**-dźheećh] v. delude; deceive; give false hope; dangle hopes before someone (*repeatedly*)
łudzić się [**woo**-dźheećh śhan] v. be deluded; deceive oneself; cherish illusions (*repeatedly*)
ług [wook] m. lye
ług warzelny [woog vah-**zhel**-ni] exp.: buck
ług żrący [woog **zhrown**-tsi] exp.: alkali lye
ługoodporny [woo-go-ot-**por**-ni] adj.m. lyeproof; alkali-resisting
ługować [woo-**go**-vahćh] v. leach; lixiviate (*repeatedly*)
ługowanie [woo-go-**vah**-ńe] n. leaching; lixiviation
kadź do ługowania [kahdźh do woo-go-**vah**-ńah] exp.: leach; lixiviation vat
ługowaty [woo-go-**vah**-ti] adj.m. lixivial
ługowiny [woo-go-**vee**-ni] pl. lixiviation residue
ługownia [woo-**gov**-ńah] f. leaching plant
ługownik [woo-**gov**-ńeek] m. lye vat; lye extraction apparatus
ługowy [woo-**go**-vi] adj.m. lye (vat, etc.)
łuk [wook] m. bow; arch; bent; curve; vault; flying buttress; arc (electrical, etc.); turn (on ice, on snow, etc.); (musical) slur
łukować [woo-**ko**-vahćh] v. drift around on an anchor line (*repeatedly*)
łukowanie [woo-ko-**vah**-ńe] n. drifting around on an anchor line
łukowato [woo-ko-**vah**-to] adv. archwise; arcuately; in the shape of a bow
łukowato sklepiony [woo-ko-**vah**-to skle-**pyo**-ni] exp.: arched
łukowaty [woo-ko-**vah**-ti] adj.m. arched; curved; bow-shaped
łukowo [woo-**ko**-vo] adv. in the shape of an arch
łukowy [woo-**ko**-vi] adj.m. arched; curved; arc (flame, generator, etc.)
cięcie łukowe [ćhan-ćhe woo-**ko**-ve] exp.: arc cutting
spawanie łukowe [spah-**vah**-ńe woo-**ko**-ve] exp.: arc welding
strop łukowy [strop woo-**ko**-vi]

exp.: vault
łuna [**woo**-nah] f. glow (of light); slang: light (mob jargon)
łuna na niebie [**woo**-nah nah ńe-bye] exp.: afterglow
łunnik [**woon**-ńeek] m. Soviet lunar probe
łunochod [woo-**no**-khot] m. Soviet lunar vehicle
łup [woop] m. booty; spoils; prize; plunder; loot; capture; prey; quarry
łup! [woop] excl.: bang!; whang!
paść łupem [pahśhćh **woo**-pem] exp.: to fall prey (to)
łupa [**woo**-pah] f. peel; chip; chunk
łupacz [**woo**-pahch] m. haddock (fish)
łupać [**woo**-pahćh] v. cleave; split; ache; give shooting pain; hit; knock; bash; chip; fissure; slang: inflict (taxes, fines, etc.); harass (with taxes, etc.) (*repeatedly*)
łupać się [**woo**-pahćh śhan] v. cleave; split; crack; fissure; laminate (*repeatedly*)
łupanica [woo-pah-**ńee**-tsah] f. chip
łupanie [woo-**pah**-ńe] n. cleaving; splitting; shooting pain; shooting pains
łupanie się [woo-**pah**-ńe śhan] n. cleaving; splitting; cracking
łuparka [woo-**pahr**-kah] f. device for splitting wood
łupek [**woo**-pek] m. slate; shale; schist; roof slate
łupiarka [woo-**pyahr**-kah] f. splitting machine (for rock shaping)
łupić [**woo**-peećh] v. plunder; loot; pillage; flay; skin; fleece; peel; strike; bash; beat; slang: shoot (mob jargon) (*repeatedly*)
łupić się [**woo**-peećh śhan] v. steal from one another; slang: take advantage of one another (mob jargon) (*repeatedly*)
łupienie [woo-**pye**-ńe] n. pillage; plunder
łupienie się [woo-**pye**-ńe śhan] n. plundering each other; exploiting each other
łupień [**woo**-pyeń] m. wallop; beating; pasting
łupieski [woo-**pyes**-kee] adj.m. plundering; pillaging; predatory
łupiestwo [woo-**pyes**-stfo] n. plundering; pillaging
łupież [**woo**-pyesh] m. dandruff; mob slang: venereal disease
łupieżca [woo-**pyesh**-tsah] m. plunderer; looter; pillager
łupieżczy [woo-**pyesh**-chi] adj.m. plundering; pillaging; predatory
łupina [woo-**pee**-nah] f. husk; shell; peel; skin; hull; rind; tiny boat; cockleshell; mob slang: skull
łupinka [woo-**pee**-nkah] f. very small husk; very small shell; small hull; very tiny boat
łupinowy [woo-pee-**no**-vi] adj.m. skin (condition, etc.)
łupka [**woop**-kah] f. small husk; small shell; small hull; firewood
łupki [**woop**-kee] pl. firewood; husks; slates
łupkarnia [woop-**kahr**-ńah] f. slate quarry
łupkarz [**woop**-kahsh] m. slate worker
łupkowatość [woop-ko-**vah**-tośhćh] f. slate-like condition
łupkowaty [woop-ko-**vah**-ti] adj.m. slate-like; slaty
łupkowy [woop-**ko**-vi] adj.m. slate (floor, etc.); shale (quarry, etc.); schist (strata, etc.)
łupkoząb [woop-**ko**-zownp] m. sphenodon; Hatteria
łupliwość [woop-**lee**-vośhćh] f. fissility
łupliwy [woop-**lee**-vi] adj.m. fissile; scissile; splintery
łupnąć [**woop**-nownćh] v. ache; cleave; split; give shooting pain; hit; knock; bash; chip; fissure; slang: inflict (taxes, fines, etc.); harass (with taxes, etc.)
łupnąć się [**woop**-nownćh śhan] v. cleave; split; crack; fissure; laminate
łupnięcie [woop-**ńan**-ćhe] n. ache; cleaving; split
łupnięcie się [woop-**ńan**-ćhe śhan] n. hitting oneself; splitting
łupu-cupu [**woo**-poo **tsoo**-poo] exp.: rub-a-dub
łusczarka [woos-**chahr**-kah] f. (female) huller; decorticator;

hulling machine
łuseczka [woo-**sech**-kah] f. (small) scale; husk; shell; pod; flake; rind; bract; cartridge case
łuska [**woos**-kah] f. scale; husk; shell; pod; flake; rind; bract; cartridge case; squama; test
łuska spadła mi z oczu [**woos**-kah **spahd**-wah mee z **o**-choo] exp.: the scale fell from my eyes
rybia łuska [**ri**-byah **woos**-kah] exp.: ichthyosis; fish scale
łuskacz [**woos**-kahch] m. huller
łuskać [**woos**-kahćh] v. scale (almonds, etc.); husk (maize, etc.); peel; hull (rice); shell (nuts, etc.); pod (peas, etc.); scale off in thin pieces (*repeatedly*)
łuskanie [woos-**kah**-ńe] n. scaling; peeling; shelling
łuskarka [woos-**kahr**-kah] f. (female) huller
łuskiewnik [woos-k̲ev-ńeek] m. the genus Latharea; toothwort
łuskodrzew [woos-**ko**-dzhef] m. lepidodendron
łuskonośny [woos-ko-**nośh**-ni] adj.m. squamous; scaly; of the order Squamata
łuskonośne [woos-ko-**nośh**-ne] pl. the order Squamata
łuskoskóry [woos-ko-**skoo**-ri] adj.m. squamous; scaly; of the order Squamata
łuskoskóre [woos-ko-**skoo**-re] pl. the order Squamata
łuskoskrzydlaty [woos-ko-skshid-**lah**-ti] adj.m. resembling a butterfly; papilonaceous of family Fabaceae
łuskoskrzydły [woos-ko-**skshid**-wi] adj.m. having butterfy wings
łuskoskrzydłe [woos-ko-**skshid**-we] pl. family Fabaceae
łuskowato [woos-ko-**vah**-to] adv. with a scale pattern
łuskowaty [woos-ko-**vah**-ti] adj.m. husky; scaly; scaled; squamous
łuskowiec [woos-**ko**-vyets] m. pangolin (mammal); pine grossbeak
łuskowce [woos-**kof**-tse] pl. pangolins; the order of Pholidota; edentate mammals
łuskowy [woos-**ko**-vi] adj.m. husky; scaly; scaled; squamate
łuskwina [woos-**kfee**-nah] f. cartridge of (an apple, etc.) seed
łuszczak [**woosh**-chahk] m. hazelnut
łuszczaki [woosh-**chah**-kee] pl. the family Fringillidae
łuszczarka [woosh-**chahr**-kah] f. huller; decorticator; hulling machine; female huller
łuszczarnia [woosh-**chahr**-ńah] f. (rice) pearling mill
łuszczarski [woosh-**chahr**-skee] adj.m. huller's; decorticator's; of a pearling mill
łuszczarz [**woosh**-chahsh] m. huller; decorticator
łuszczasty [woosh-**chahs**-ti] adj.m. husky; scaly; squamate; loricate
łuszczenie [woos-**che**-ńe] n. scaling; peeling; shelling; fall off in thin pieces
łuszczenie się [woosh-**che**-ńe śh<u>an</u>] n. losing scale; peeling
łuszczka [**wooshch**-kah] f. (grass) lodicule; wood layer for plywood fabrication; veneer
łuszczkowy [woshch-**ko**-vi] adj.m. of a veneer; of a wood layer within plywood; of a lodicule (scale)
łuszczyca [woosh-**chi**-tsah] f. psoriasis (skin condition)
łuszczycowaty [woosh-chi-tso-**vah**-ti] adj.m. psoroid
łuszczycowy [woos-chi-**tso**-vi] adj.m. psoriatic
łuszczyć [**woosh**-chićh] v. peel; pare; decorticate; flake; shell (*repeatedly*)
łuszczyć się [**woosh**-chićh śh<u>an</u>] v. peel off; pare off; flake off; shell off (*repeatedly*)
łuszczyna [woosh-**chi**-nah] f. silique (fruit)
łuszczynka [woosh-**chin**-kah] f. silicle (fruit)
łuszczynowaty [woosh-chi-no-**vah**-ti] adj.m. resembling silique
łut [woot] m. half an ounce; 1/32 of a pound
łut szczęścia [woot **shch<u>an</u>śh**-ćhah] exp.: a little bit of luck
łutówka [woo-**toof**-kah] f. variety of sour cherry tree; sour cherry
łuza [**woo**-zah] f. billiard pocket

łuzowy [woo-**zo**-vi] adj.m. billiard-pocket (content, etc.)
łużycki [woo-**zhi**-tskee] adj.m. Lusatian (language, culture, etc.); of Lusatia (south-east of Berlin, Germany)
łycha [**wi**-khah] f. (big, old) spoon
łyczek [**wi**-chek] m. small sip; colloq: petty bourgeois
łyczko [**wich**-ko] n. (small, nice) bast; bass; inner bark; phloem
łydka [**wit**-kah] f. calf (leg-shank)
łydkowy [wit-**ko**-vi] adj.m. of the calf of the leg; sural
łyk [wik] m. gulp; sip; draft; mouthful; draught; hist.: petty bourgeois; Philistine; slang: water; drink (mob jargon)
jednym łykiem [**yed**-nim **wi**-kem] exp.: at one gulp
łyk powietrza [wik po-**vyet**-shah] exp.: a breath of air
pić wielkimi łykami [peećh vyel-kee-mee wi-**kah**-mee] exp.: to take long draughts; to swig; to quaf; to take big gulps
łykać [**wi**-kahćh] v. swallow; gulp down; sip; bolt; gorge; drink (*repeatedly*)
łykać powietrze [**wi**-kahćh po-**vyet**-she] exp.: to breathe; to inhale air
łykanie [wi-**kah**-ńe] n. swallowing; gulping down; sipping
łykawość [wi-**kah**-vośhćh] f. crib-biting (of a horse)
łykawy [wi-**kah**-vi] adj.m. crib-biting (horse)
łyknąć [**wik**-nownćh] v. swallow; gulp; sip; bolt; gorge; drink
łyknąć wódki [**wik**-nownćh **voot**-kee] exp.: to take a sip of vodka; to have a shot of vodka
łyknięcie [wik-ńan-ćhe] n. draught; sip; mouthful; gulp
łyko [**wi**-ko] n. bast; bass; inner bark; phloem; hist.: bondage; slang: theft in the countryside
w łykach [v **wi**-kahkh] exp.: in bonds
łykodrzewny [wi-ko-**dzhev**-ni] adj.m. of the connecting tissue between the stem and bast
łykowacieć [wi-ko-**vah**-ćhećh] v. become wiry; become tough; become fibrous; become coriariaceous (*repeatedly*)
łykowatość [wi-ko-**vah**-tośhćh] f. toughness; fibrousness
łykowaty [wi-ko-**vah**-ti] adj.m. wiry; tough; fibrous
łykowy [wi-**ko**-vi] adj.m. bass (cells, etc.); phloem (fiber, etc.)
łyp [wip] indecl.: colloq: squint (at somebody); slang: eye (jargon)
łyp, łyp [wip wip] exp.: colloq: to look; to have a quick look
łypać [**wi**-pahćh] v. blink (at); wink (at); leer (at); cast furtive glances (*repeatedly*)
łypanie [wi-**pah**-ńe] n. glances
łypnąć [**wip**-nownćh] v. cast a glance (at); have a sudden look (at); glance suddenly (at)
łypnięcie [wip-ńan-ćhe] n. glance
łysa [**wi**-sah] adj.f. baldheaded (female); f. boldheaded woman
łysawy [wi-**sah**-vi] adj.m. baldish; becoming bald; growing bald; almost devoid of (leaves, vegetation, etc.); almost bare; almost bald
łysek [**wi**-sek] m. colloq: a baldhead; bald man; animal with a blaze; slang: a naked john; behind; the buttocks; a penniless thief (mob jargon)
łysica [wi-**śhee**-tsah] f. bald-pate (duck)
łysiec [**wi**-śhets] m. colloq: bald man
łysieć [**wi**-śhećh] v. become bald; grow bald; lose hair (*repeatedly*)
łysienie [wi-**śhe**-ńe] n. progressing baldness
łysina [wi-**śhee**-nah] f. pate; bald spot; bald head; baldness; blaze (on horse's head)
łysinka [wi-**śheen**-kah] f. (small) pate; bald spot; bald head; baldness
łyska [**wis**-kah] f. blaze (on horses head); bald-faced cow; bald-faced horse; bald coot (bird)
łyskać [**wis**-kahćh] v. flash; slang: (do a) strip-tease; show one's behind; (mob jargon) (*repeatedly*)
łyso [**wi**-so] adv. without hair; with

bald face (tire, etc.)
łysy [**wi**-si] adj.m. bald; bald-faced; bare (of vegetation); m. bald-faced man; bald-faced animal; slang: naked man; penis (jargon)
łysa opona [**wi**-sah o-**po**-nah] exp.: bald tire; worn-out tire
łysy dupek [**wi**-si **doo**-pek] exp.: slang: fool (mob jargon)
łysy jak kolano [**wi**-si yahk ko-**lah**-no] exp.: as bald as a coot
łyszczak [**wish**-chahk] m. species of primrose
łyszczec [**wish**-chets] m. gypsophila; babies'-breath (plant)
łyszczyk [**wish**-chik] m. mica
łyszczykowy [wish-chi-**ko**-vi] adj.m. micaceous
łupek łyszczykowy [**woo**-pek wish-chi-**ko**-vi] exp.: mica-late
łyszczynkowaty [wish-chin-ko-**vah**-ti] adj.m. nitidulid (beetle)
łyszczynkowate [wish-chin-ko-vah-te] pl. the family Nitidulidae of beetles
łyśnięcie [wiśh-**ńan**-ćhe] n. a flash of lightning
łyżeczka [wi-**zhech**-kah] f. teaspoon; dessert spoon; curette; small spoonful
łyżeczka chirurgiczna [wi-**zhech**-kah khee-roor-**geech**-nah] exp.: curette; cruet
łyżeczkować [wi-zhech-**ko**-vahćh] v. scrape with a curette; curette (*repeatedly*)
łyżeczkowanie [wi-zhech-ko-**vah**-ńe] n. scraping with a curette
łyżewka [wi-**zhef**-kah] f. small skate
łyżka [**wish**-kah] f. spoon; spoonful; tablespoonful; scoop (of a backhoe, etc.); slang: crowbar
łyżka do butów [**wish**-kah do **boo**-toof] exp.: shoehorn
łyżka wazowa [**wish**-kah vah-**zo**-vah] exp.: ladle
łyżki [**wish**-kee] pl. spoons; ears of a game animal
łyżkować [wish-**ko**-vahćh] v. scoop (drilling debris in a coal mine, etc.) (*repeatedly*)
łyżkowanie [wish-ko-**vah**-ńe] n. taking out by scoops
łyżkowaty [wish-ko-**vah**-ti] adj.m. spoon-shaped
łyżkowy [wish-**ko**-vi] adj.m. spoon (drilling bit, etc.)
łyżnik [**wizh**-ńeek] m. spoon rack
łyżwa [**wizh**-vah] f. skate; runner (of a sledge); mob slang: whore
łyżwiarka [wizh-**vyahr**-kah] f. (woman) skater
łyżwiarski [wizh-**vyahr**-skee] adj.m. skating (boots, etc.)
łyżwiarstwo [wizh-**vyahr**-stfo] n. skating
łyżwiarz [**wizh**-vyahsh] m. skater
łyżwowy [wizh-**vo**-vi] adj.m of skates; of a sledge runner; pontoon (bridge, etc.)
łza [wzah] f. tear
czysty jak łza [**chi**-sti yahk wzah] exp.: clear as crystal
krokodyle łzy [kro-ko-**di**-le wzi] exp.: crocodile tears
lać gorzkie łzy [lahćh **gosh**-ke wzi] exp.: to shed bitter tears
szkoda łez [**shko**-dah wes] exp.: it's no use crying; it's no use; it's no go
we łzach [ve wzahkh] exp.: in tears
zalewać się łzami [zah-**le**-vahćh śhan **wzah**-mee] exp.: to be all in tears
łzawiący [wzah-**vyown**-tsi] adj.m. watery; running; lachrymatory; tear (gas)
gaz łzawiący [gahs wzah-**vyown**-tsi] exp.: tear gas
łzawica [wzah-**vee**-tsah] f. lachrymal urn; lachrymatory urn
łzawić [**wzah**-veećh] v. water; run (*repeatedly*)
łzawić się [**wzah**-veećh śhan] v. water; run; weep; shed tears; cry (*repeatedly*)
łzawienie [wzah-**vye**-ńe] n. watering; weeping; shedding tears; crying
łzawik [**wzah**-veek] m. slang: tear-gas gun (mob jargon)
łzawka [**wzahf**-kah] f. slang: tear-gas gun (mob jargon)
łzawnica [wzahv-**ńee**-tsah] f. lachrymal urn; lachrymatory urn
łzawnik [**wzahv**-ńeek] m. lachrymal

urn; lachrymatory urn; a subclass of fungi; drip (groove); throating (groove); gorge
łzawo [**wzah**-vo] adv. tearfully
łzawość [**wzah**-vośhćh] f. tearfulness
łzawy [**wzah**-vi] adj.m. tearful; tear-stained; mournful; maudlin; slang: soppy
łzotok [**wzo**-tok] m. epiphora; watering of the eyes
łzowy [**wzo**-vi] adj.m. lacrimal; lachrymal
gruczoł łzowy [groo-chow **wzo**-vi] exp.: lachrymal gland
kanał łzowy [kah-nahw **wzo**-vi] exp.: tear canal; tear duct
przewód łzowy [pshe-voot **wzo**-vi] exp.: lachrymal duct; tear duct
woreczek łzowy [vo-**re**-chek **wzo**-vi] exp.: lachrymal sac; dacryocyst

M

M, m [em] n. indecl. the letter "m"; the sound "m"
ma [mah] pron.f. my; see: **moja**; masculine form see: **mój**
maar [**mah**-ahr] m. geol. volcanic lake
maca [**mah**-tsah] f. matzos; Passover (unleavened) bread
macać [**mah**-tsahćh] v. feel; probe; examine by touch; palate; sound out; try; grope; finger; slang: paw; cuddle (women) (*repeatedly*)
macać po ciemku [**mah**-tsahćh po **ćhem**-koo] exp.: to grope
macać puls [**mah**-tsahćh pools] exp.: to feel a pulse
macać się [**mah**-tsahćh śh<u>an</u>] v. feel one's (pocket, head, chest, hips, etc.) (*repeatedly*)
macanie [mah-**tsah**-ńe] n. feeling; examining by touch
macanie się [mah-**tsah**-ńe śh<u>an</u>] n. feeling oneself; feeling one another
maccartysta [mahk-kahr-**tis**-tah] m. McCarthyite
maccartyzm [mahk-**kahr**-tizm] m. McCarthyism
maceba [mah-**tse**-bah] f. ornate Jewish gravestone
maceracja [mah-tse-**rah**-tsyah] f. maceration
macerat [mah-**tse**-raht] m. macerator
macerować [mah-tse-**ro**-vahćh] v. macerate; steep; soften by soaking in liquid (*repeatedly*)
macewa [mah-**tse**-vah] f. ornate Jewish gravestone
mach [mahkh] m. unit of lineal sound velocity in 15 deg. temp. C. and one atmosphere pressure
ciach-mach i zrobione [ćhahkh mahkh ee zro-**byo**-ne] exp.: colloq: done in a trice; done in a jiffy; done right away
mach-mach i skończone [mahkh mahkh ee skoń-**cho**-ne] exp.: colloq: done in a trice; done in a jiffy; done right away; finished in a jiffy
szach-mach i załatwione [shahkh mahkh ee zah-waht-**fyo**-ne] exp.: colloq: done in a trice; done in a jiffy; done right away; finished in a jiffy
machać [**mah**-khahćh] v. wave; whisk; swing; swish; lash; wag; run; flap; flop; flutter; brandish; slang: dispatch; expedite; go; run; walk; ride; fly; swim (*repeatedly*)
machać drogę [**mah**-khahćh **dro**-g<u>an</u>] exp.: to walk a distance quickly; to make a distance quickly
machać ogonem [**mah**-khahćh o-**go**-nem] exp.: to wag (its) tail
machać ręką [**mah**-khahćh r<u>an</u>-k<u>own</u>] exp.: to wave one's hand
machać ręką na przywitanie [**mah**-khahćh r<u>an</u>-k<u>own</u> nah pshi-vee-**tah**-ńe] exp.: to wave welcome
machać ręką na pożegnanie [**mah**-khahćh r<u>an</u>-k<u>own</u> nah po-zheg-**nah**-ńe] exp.: to wave farewell
machać robotę [**mah**-khahćh ro-**bo**-t<u>an</u>] exp.: to expedite work

machać szablą [mah-khahćh shahb-lown] exp.: to brandish a sabre
machać wachlarzem [mah-khahćh vah-khlah-zhem] exp.: to flirt a fan; to wave a fan
machanie [mah-**khah**-ńe] n. waving (to somebody, etc.)
macher [**mah**-kher] m. trickster; bluffer; humbug; swindler; cheater; master hand (at)
macherka [mah-**kher**-kah] f. swindle; dirty trick
machiaweliczny [mah-khyah-ve-**leech**-ni] adj.m. crafty; deceitful; Machiavellian; see: **makiaweliczny**
machiawelizm [mah-khyah-**ve**-leezm] m. Machiavellism
machina [mah-**khee**-nah] f. (large) machine; bureaucratic machine
machina wojenna [mah-**khee**-nah vo-**yen**-nah] exp.: war machine
machina państwowa [mah-**khee**-nah pahń-**stfo**-vah] exp.: the wheels of State
machinacja [mah-khee-**nah**-tsyah] f. machination; dodge; intrigue; scheming; shady dealing; an evil plot; wirepulling; machinations
machinacje przedwyborcze [mah-khee-**nah**-tsye pshed-vi-**bor**-che] exp.: gerrymandering; tampering; manipulations
machinalnie [mah-khee-**nahl**-ńe] adv. instinctively; mechanically
machinalność [mah-khee-**nahl**-nośhćh] f. instinctive reaction; mechanical movements
machinalny [mah-khee-**nahl**-ni] adj.m. instinctive; mechanical
machista [mah-**khees**-tah] m. follower of philosophy of Ernst Mach
machizm [**mah**-kheezm] m. the philosophy of Ernst Mach
machlojka [mah-**khloy**-kah] f. colloq: swindle; defraudation
machnąć [**mahkh**-nownćh] v. wave; slang: dispatch; expedite; slang: hit; chop; punch (mob jargon) see: **machać**
machnąć na coś ręką [**mahkh**-nownćh nah tsośh **ran**-kown] exp.: to wave something aside; to give up something; to abandon (an effort, etc.)
machnąć sporo roboty [**mahkh**-nownćh **spo**-ro ro-**bo**-ti] exp.: to go through a lot of work
machnąć się [**mahkh**-nownćh śhan] v. colloq: go quickly; take a fast trip; marry in a hurry; drop suddenly on one's bed
machnięcie [mahkh-**ńan**-ćhe] n. a wave (of the hand, etc.); a stroke (of a brush, etc.)
machnięcie się [mahkh-**ńan**-ćhe śhan] n. colloq: going expeditiously (after something); (marrying, etc.) in a hurry
machometr [mah-**kho**-metr] m. airspeed meter
machora [mah-**kho**-rah] f. colloq: shag
machorka [mah-**khor**-kah] f. shag; variety of low-grade tobacco plant
machorkowy [mah-khor-**ko**-vi] adj.m. shag (cigarette, etc.)
macica [mah-**ćhee**-tsah] f. uterus; matrix; womb; screw nut; female screw; tap root; fishing net; grapevine
macica perłowa [mah-**ćhee**-tsah per-**wo**-vah] exp.: mother-of-pearl
maciczny [mah-**ćheech**-ni] adj.m. uterine
maciejka [mah-**ćhey**-kah] f. night-scented stock
maciejówka [mah-ćhe-**yoof**-kah] f. visored cap
Maciek [**mah**-ćhek] m. little Matthew; Matt
maciek [**mah**-ćhek] m. colloq: stork slang: rustic; potbelly; stick; cane
macierz [**mah**-ćhesh] f. mother country; matrix; mother
macierzanka [mah-ćhe-**zhahn**-kah] f. thyme; wild thyme; mint
macierzankowy [mah-ćhe-zhahn-**ko**-vi] adj.m. thyme (aroma, etc.); wild thyme; mint (tea, etc.); of the genus of mints
macierzowy [mah-ćhe-**zho**-vi] adj.m. matrix (computation, etc.)
macierzyński [mah-ćhe-**zhiń**-skee] adj.m. maternal; mother's; motherly; like a mothern

po macierzyńsku [po mah-ćhe-**zhiń**-skoo] exp.: like a mother; maternally; in motherly fashion
macierzyńsko [mah-ćhe-**zhiń**-sko] adv. maternally; in motherly fashion
macierzyństwo [mah-ćhe-**zhiń**-stfo] n. maternity; motherhood; parenthood
macierzystość [mah-ćhe-**zhis**-tośhćh] f. maternal origin; vernacular character
macierzysty [mah-ćhe-**zhis**-ti] adj.m. maternal; parental; motherly; vernacular; maternity (ward, etc.); mother (tongue, etc.)
macierzysty kraj [mah-ćhe-**zhis**-ti krahy] exp.: mother country
macierzysty port [mah-ćhe-**zhis**-ti port] exp.: port of registry; home port
maciora [mah-**ćho**-rah] f. sow
maciorka [mah-**ćho**-rkah] f. sow; small sow; ewe; pistillate (female) flower of hemp
maciupci [mah-**ćhoop**-ćhee] adj.m. very, very small; very tiny
maciupeńki [mah-ćhoo-**peń**-kee] adj.m. very small; very tiny (fingers, etc.)
maciupki [mah-**ćhoop**-kee] adj.m. very small; tiny
macka [**mahts**-kah] f. tentacle; feeler; antenna; horn; palp
macki [**mahts**-kee] pl. calipers; feelers
macnąć [**mahts**-nownćh] v. feel; examine by touch; palate; sound out; probe; try; grope; finger; slang: paw; cuddle (a woman)
macnięcie [mahts-**ńan**-ćhe] n. examining by touch
macocha [mah-**tso**-khah] f. stepmother; not as good as (treating worse than) mother
być od macochy [bićh od mah-**tso**-khi] exp.: to receive worse treatment than others
macoszy [mah-**tso**-shi] adj.m. stepmotherly; novercal; harsh; unfair
po macoszemu [po mah-tso-**she**-moo] exp.: harshly; unfairly; with neglect
maczać [**mah**-chahćh] v. dip in a liquid; dip; soak (*repeatedly*)
maczać palce [**mah**-chahćh **pahl**-tse] exp.: to wet one's fingers; to have a hand (in it, etc.)
maczanka [mah-**chahn**-kah] f. dip; sippet; sop
maczek [**mah**-chek] m. tiny poppy seed; colloq: tiny handwriting; tiny print; drizzle; buckwheat seeds; hundreds and thousands
maczeta [mah-**che**-tah] f. machete (used for cutting sugar cane)
maczuga [mah-**choo**-gah] f. bat; club; bludgeon; cudgel
maczugowaty [mah-choo-go-**vah**-ti] adj.m. bat-shaped; club-shaped; clavate
maczugowiec [mah-choo-**go**-vyets] m. corynebacterium
maczugowce [mah-choo-**gof**-tse] pl. corynebacteria
maczugowy [mah-choo-**go**-vi] adj.m. bludgeon (blow, etc.); of cudgels
mać [mahćh] f. vulg.: mother
psia mać! [pśhah mahćh] excl.: dammit! (vulg.)
mada [**mah**-dah] f. mud; silt
madapolam [mah-dah-**po**-lahm] m. madapollam
madejowy [mah-de-**yo**-vi] adj.m. colloq: uncomfortable (bed, etc.)
madera [mah-**de**-rah] f. Madeira (wine); colloq: waterproof cotton cloth
maderyzacja [mah-de-ri-**zah**-tsyah] f. ripening of wine (in 45-60 degrees centigrade or Celsius)
madison [me-**dee**-son] m. Madison dance (music, step, etc.)
Madonna [mah-**don**-nah] f. Madonna; colloq: woman of delicate and spiritual beauty
madowy [mah-**do**-vi] adj.m. muddy; silty
madrepora [mah-dre-**po**-rah] f. madrepore (coral)
madrepory [mah-dre-**po**-ri] pl. the madrepore corals
madreporowy [mah-dre-po-**ro**-vi] adj.m. of madrepore; madreporic; madrepore (coral, etc.)
madreporyd [mah-dre-**po**-rit] m. madrepore

madrygał [mah-**dri**-gahw] m. madrigal
madrygałowy [mah-dri-gah-**wo**-vi] adj.m. madrigal (love poetry, etc.)
mady [**mah**-di] pl. silts
madziarski [mah-**dźhahr**-skee] adj.m. Magyar; Hungarian
z madziarska [z mah-**dźhahr**-skah] exp.: after the Hungarian fashion
madziaryzacja [mah-dźhah-ri-**zah**-tsyah] f. spreading or acquiring the Hungarian culture
madziaryzować [mah-dźhah-ri-**zo**-vahćh] v. spread the Hungarian culture (*repeatedly*)
madziaryzować się [mah-dźhah-ri-**zo**-vahćh śhan] v. acquire the Hungarian culture (*repeatedly*)
maestria [mah-**es**-tryah] f. masterly skill
maestro [mah-e-stro] m. maestro
mafia [**mah**-fyah] f. Mafia; Maffia; organized crime; colloq: clique, coterie; set
mafijny [mah-**feey**-ni] adj.m. of Mafia; cliquish
mafioso [mah-**fyo**-so] m. mafioso; member of the Mafia
mag [mahg] m. magus; sorcerer
magazyn [mah-**gah**-zin] m. store; warehouse; repository; emporium; house of fashion; magazine (of a rifle)
magazynek [mah-gah-**zi**-nek] m. bullet clip; rifle magazine
magazynier [mah-gah-**zi**-ńer] m. warehouseman; storekeeper
magazynierka [mah-gah-zi-**ńer**-kah] f. (woman) storekeeper
magazynować [mah-gah-zi-**no**-vahćh] v. store up; keep in store; warehouse; accumulate (*repeatedly*)
magazynowanie [mah-gah-zi-no-**vah**-ńe] n. storage; storing up; keeping in store; accumulating; warehousing (*repeated*)
magazynowy [mah-gah-zi-**no**-vi] adj.m. warehouse (buildings, stock, deposit, etc.)
magazynówka [mah-gah-zi-**noof**-kah] f. magazine gun
magdalenka [mahg-dah-**len**-kah] f. nun of the Order of St. Mary Magdalene
magdaleński [mahg-dah-**leń**-skee] adj.m. Magdalenian (period, etc.)
magdeburski [mahg-de-**boor**-skee] adj.m. of Magdeburg
prawo magdeburskie [**prah**-vo mahg-de-**boor**-ske] exp.: law of Magdeburg (a city law used as an example in medieval Poland)
magia [**mah**-gyah] f. sorcery; magic; witchcraft; wizardry; deviltry; enigma
czarna magia [**chahr**-nah **mah**-gyah] exp.: black magic
magicznie [mah-**geech**-ńe] adv. (as if) by magic
magiczność [mah-**geech**-nośhćh] f. magic character
magiczny [mah-**geech**-ni] adj.m. magic; conjuring tricks
magiel [**mah**-gel] m. mangle
magierka [mah-**ger**-kah] f. Magyar cap (used by Polish peasants)
magik [**mah**-geek] m. magician; illusionist; wizard; conjurer; swindler; (Indian) powpow
magister [mah-**gees**-ter] m. master (diplomate); chemist; apothecary; holder of a master's (M.Sc. or M.A.) degree
magisterium [mah-gees-**ter**-yoom] n. (university) master's degree
magisterski [mah-gees-**ter**-skee] adj.m. graduate's
egzamin magisterski [eg-**zah**-meen mah-gees-**ter**-skee] exp.: final (university) examination
praca magisterska [**prah**-tsah mah-gees-**ter**-skah] exp.: Master's thesis
magistracki [mah-gee-**strahts**-kee] adj.m. municipal; of city hall
magistrala [mah-gee-**strah**-lah] f. arterial road; trunk line
magistrala wodna [mah-gee-**strah**-lah **vod**-nah] exp.: water main
magistralny [mah-gee-**strahl**-ni] adj.m. main
magistrancki [mah-gee-**strahn**-tskee] adj.m. master's (program, degree, etc.)
magistrant [mah-**gee**-strahnt] m. candidate for the master's degree
magistrat [mah-**gee**-straht] m. city

hall; municipal authorities
magistratura [mah-gee-strah-**too**-rah] f. colloq: city hall; municipal authorities
maglarka [mah-**glahr**-kah] f. (female) mangle owner; calenderer
maglarnia [mah-**glahr**-ńah] f. mangling room
maglarski [mah-**glahr**-skee] adj.m. calendering (department, etc.)
maglarstwo [mah-**glahr**-stfo] n. mangling; calendering
maglarz [**mah**-glahsh] m. mangle owner; calenderer
maglować [mah-**glo**-vahćh] v. mangle; calender; bother; crush; tire with; harp on (the same string) (*repeatedly*)
maglowanie [mah-glo-**vah**-ńe] n. calendering; mangling
maglownia [mah-**glov**-ńah] f. mangling room; calendering room
maglownica [mah-glov-**ńee**-tsah] f. hand mangle
maglownik [mah-**glov**-ńeek] m. hand mangle roll; mangling protection wrap-cloth
maglowy [mah-**glo**-vi] adj.m. hand mangle (operation, etc.)
magma [**mahg**-mah] f. geol.: magma
magmatyczny [mahg-mah-**tich**-ni] adj.m. magmatic
magmatyzm [mahg-**mah**-tizm] m. magmatic character
magmowy [mahg-**mo**-vi] adj.m. magma (igneous rock, etc.)
magnacki [mahg-**nah**-tskee] adj.m. lordly
magnal [**mahg**-nahl] m. magnalium
magnalium [mahg-**nahl**-yoom] n. magnalium
magnat [**mahg**-naht] m. magnate; lord; baron
magnateria [mahg-nah-**ter**-yah] f. the nobility; the magnates; the baronage
magnatka [mahg-**naht**-kah] f. (woman) magnate; great lady
magnes [**mahg**-nes] m. magnet; lure; attraction; charm
magnesować [mahg-ne-**so**-vahćh] v. magnetize (*repeatedly*)
magnesować się [mahg-ne-**so**-vahćh śhan] v. become magnetized (*repeatedly*)
magnesowanie [mahg-ne-so-**vah**-ńe] n. magnetization
magnesowy [mahg-ne-**so**-vi] adj.m. magnetic
magnesyn [mahg-**ne**-sin] m. electromagnetic converter for remote control of navigational measurements, etc.
magneśnica [mahg-neśh-**ńee**-tsah] f. electromagnet; field magnet (of dynamo)
magneto [mahg-**ne**-to] n. permanent magnet machine; magneto
magneto- [mahg-**ne**-to] prefix: magneto-
magnetochemia [mahg-ne-to-**khe**-myah] f. magnetochemistry
magnetodynamika [mahg-ne-to-di-**nah**-mee-kah] f. study of periodic magnetism
magnetoelektryczny [mahg-ne-to-e-lek-**trich**-ni] adj.m. magnetoelectric
magnetofon [mahg-ne-**to**-fon] m. taperecorder
magnetofonowy [mahg-ne-to-fo-**no**-vi] adj.m. of a taperecorder
magnetograf [mahg-ne-**to**-grahf] m. magnetograph
magnetogram [mahg-ne-**to**-grahm] m. magnetogram
magnetohydrodynamiczny [mahg-ne-to-khid-ro-di-nah-**meech**-ni] adj.m. magnetohydrodynamic
magnetohydrodynamika [mahg-ne-to-khid-ro-di-**nah**-mee-kah] f. hydromagnetics
magnetometr [mahg-ne-**to**-metr] m. magnetometer
magnetometria [mahg-ne-to-**me**-tryah] f. magnetometry
magnetometryczny [mahg-ne-to-me-**trich**-ni] adj.m. magnetometric
magnetomotoryczny [mahg-ne-to-mo-to-**rich**-ni] adj.m. magnetomotive
siła magnetomotoryczna [**śhee**-wah mahg-ne-to-mo-to-**rich**-nah] exp.: magnetomotive force
magneton [mahg-**ne**-ton] m. magneton
magnetooptyczny [mahg-ne-to-op-**tich**-ni] adj.m. magnetooptic;

magnetooptical
magnetooptyka [mahg-ne-to-**op**-ti-kah] f. magnetooptics
magnetosfera [mahg-ne-to-**sfe**-rah] f. magnetosphere
magnetosferyczny [mahg-ne-to-sfe-**rich**-ni] adj.m. magnetospheric
magnetoskop [mahg-ne-**to**-skop] m. magnetoscope (for finding and measuring of magnetic field)
magnetostatyczny [mahg-ne-to-stah-**tich**-ni] adj.m. magnetostatic
magnetostatyka [mahg-ne-to-**stah**-ti-kah] f. magnetostatics
magnetostrykcja [mahg-ne-to-**strik**-tsyah] f. magnetostriction
magnetostrykcyjnie [mahg-ne-to-strik-**tsiy**-ńe] adv. magnetostrictively
magnetostrykcyjny [mahg-ne-to-strik-**tsiy**-ni] adj.m. magnetostrictive
magnetowid [mahg-ne-**to**-veet] m. video recorder (using videotape); VCR
magnetowidowy [mahg-ne-to-vee-**do**-vi] adj.m. of a video recorder
magnetron [mahg-**ne**-tron] m. magnetron
magnetronowy [mahg-ne-tro-**no**-vi] adj.m. of a magnetron
magnetycznie [mahg-ne-**tich**-ńe] adv. magnetically
magnetyczność [mahg-ne-**tich**-nośhćh] f. magnetic nature
magnetyczny [mahg-ne-**tich**-ni] adj.m. magnetic
biegun magnetyczny [**bye**-goon mahg-ne-**tich**-ni] exp.: magnetic pole
południk magnetyczny [po-**wood**-ńeek mahg-ne-**tich**-ni] exp.: magnetic meridian
pole magnetyczne [**po**-le mahg-ne-**tich**-ne] exp.: magnetic field
magnetyk [mahg-**ne**-tik] m. objects with magnetic properties
magnetyka [mahg-**ne**-ti-kah] f. use of magnetic properties for geological surveys
magnetyt [mahg-**ne**-tit] m. magnetite; loadstone; lodestone
magnetytowy [mahg-ne-ti-**to**-vi] adj.m. magnetitic; magnetite (arch, etc.)
magnetyzer [mahg-ne-**ti**-zer] m. colloq: magnetizer; magnetist; hypnotist
magnetyzerka [mahg-ne-ti-**zer**-kah] f. (woman) magnetizer; magnetist; hypnotist
magnetyzm [mahg-**ne**-tizm] m. magnetism; personal charm
magnetyzować [mahg-ne-ti-**zo**-vahćh] v. magnetize; mesmerize (*repeatedly*)
magnez [**mahg**-nes] m. magnesium (metallic element, atomic number 12)
magnezja [mahg-**ne**-zyah] f. magnesia; magnesium
magnezjowy [mahg-ne-**zyo**-vi] adj.m. of magnesia; magnesian
światło magnezjowe [**śhfyaht**-wo mahg-ne-**zyo**-ve] exp.: magnesium light
magnezoorganiczny [mahg-ne-zo-or-gah-**ńeech**-ni] adj.m. of magnesium carbonate
magnezowy [mahg-ne-**zo**-vi] adj.m. magnesian
magnezyt [mahg-**ne**-zit] m. magnesite (mineral)
magnezytowy [mahg-ne-zi-**to**-vi] adj.m. of magnesite
magnificencja [mahg-ńee-fee-**tsen**-tsyah] m. magnificence (title given to heads of universities)
magnifika [mahg-**ńee**-fee-kah] f. colloq: wife; one's better half
magnitola [mahg-ńee-**to**-lah] f. radio receiver and tape recorder combined
magnolia [mahg-**no**-lyah] f. magnolia (bot. Magnolia)
magnoliowaty [mahg-nol-yo-**vah**-ti] adj.m. like magnolia; magnoliaceous
magnoliowate [mahg-nol-yo-**vah**-te] pl. the magnolia family
magnoliowy [mahg-nol-**yo**-vi] adj.m. of a magnolia
magot [**mah**-got] m. magot (monkey)
maharadża [mah-khah-**rah**-dzhah] m. maharajah
żona maharadży [**zho**-nah mah-khah-**rah**-dzhi] exp.: maharanee

mahatma [mah-**khaht**-mah] m. mahatma
Mahatma [mah-**khaht**-mah] m. Mahatma
mahdi [**mahkh**-dee] m. Mahdi (expected messiah of Muslim tradition)
mahometanin [mah-kho-me-**tah**-ńeen] m. Mohammedan; Moslem; follower of Islam
mahometanizm [mah-kho-me-**tah**-ńeezm] m. Mohammedanism; Islam
mahometanka [mah-kho-me-**tahn**-kah] f. (female) Mohammedan; Moslem; follower of Islam
mahometański [mah-kho-me-**tahń**-skee] adj.m. Mohammedan; Islamic
mahonia [mah-**kho**-ńyah] f. mahonia
mahoniowiec [mah-kho-**ńo**-vyets] m. mahogany tree; mahogany wood
mahoniowo [mah-kho-**ńo**-vo] adv. of mahogany (wood) color; in mahogany
mahoniowy [mah-kho-**ńo**-vi] adj.m. of mahogany; of the color of mahogany; mahogany (furniture)
mahoń [**mah**-khoń] m. mahogany (wood); mahogany furniture; mahogany (color)
maić [**mah**-eećh] v. decorate with green leaves (verdure); adorn with verdure (*repeatedly*)
maik [**mah**-eek] m. spring festival; oil beetle
maj [mahy] m. May; verdure
do maja [do **mah**-yah] exp.: endlessly; indefinitely; without end
majaczeć [mah-**yah**-chećh] v. rave; loom; be delirious; be raving; wander in one's mind (*repeatedly*)
majaczeć się [mah-**yah**-chećh śhan] v. loom; appear in delirium; see in one's dreams (*repeatedly*)
majaczenie [mah-yah-**che**-ńe] n. hallucinations; ravings; nightmares; delirium
majaczeniowy [mah-yah-che-**ńo**-vi] adj.m. delirious
majaczyć [mah-**yah**-chićh] v. rave; loom; be delirious; be raving; wander in one's mind (*repeatedly*)
majaczyć się [mah-**yah**-chićh śhan] v. loom; appear in delirium; see in one's dreams (*repeatedly*)
majaczy mi się to [mah-**yah**-chi mee śhan to] exp.: I dream of it; I see it in my dreams
majak [**mah**-yahk] m. hallucination; phantom
majączek [mah-yown-**te**-chek] m. (nice, little) fortune; estate; property
majątek [mah-**yown**-tek] m. fortune; estate; property; wealth; one's (earthly) possessions; riches; assets
majątek dziedziczny [mah-**yown**-tek dźhe-**dźheech**-ni] exp.: inheritance
majątkowo [mah-yownt-**ko**-vo] adv. in respect of property; financially
majątkowy [mah-yownt-**ko**-vi] adj.m. relating to property; property (tax, etc.)
majcher [**mahy**-kher] m. slang: knife; sticker (mob jargon)
majdać [**mahy**-dahćh] v. dandle; swing (one's legs, etc.); tinker at; fool with; monkey about; see: **majtać** (*repeatedly*)
majdan [**mahy**-dahn] m. parade ground; open space; clearing; personal junk; traps; chattels
majdrować [mahy-**dro**-vahćh] v. tinker (*repeatedly*)
majenie [mah-**ye**-ńe] n. decorating with verdure; decking with verdure
majeran [mah-**ye**-rahn] m. marjoram; fragrant plant of the mint family used for cooking
majeranek [mah-ye-**rah**-nek] m. marjoram; fragrant plant of the mint family used for cooking
majerankowy [mah-ye-rahn-**ko**-vi] adj.m. of marjoram; marjoram (flavor, etc.)
majestat [mah-**ye**-staht] m. majesty; kingship; stateliness; sublimity
majestatycznie [mah-ye-stah-**tich**-ńe] adv. majestically; in stately fashion; grandly; sublimely
majestatyczność [mah-ye-stah-**tich**-nośhćh] f. regal stateliness;

grandeur; sublimity
majestatyczny [mah-ye-stah-**tich**-ni] adj.m. majestic; stately; grandiose; commanding; august; sublime
majętnie [mah-**yant**-ńe] adv. with wealth; richly
majętność [mah-**yant**-nośhćh] f. wealth; fortune; property; belongings; (an) estate
majętny [mah-**yant**-ni] adj.m. well to do; wealthy; affluent; rich
sfery majętne [**sfe**-ri mah-**yant**-ne] exp.: the leisured classes
majka [**mahy**-kah] f. lytta; cantharis
majkowaty [mahy-ko-**vah**-ti] adj.m. of the family of blister beetles and oil beetles
majkowate [mahy-ko-**vah**-te] pl. the family of blister beetles and oil beetles
majolika [mah-yo-**lee**-kah] f. majolica; opaque, decorated glaze; an Italian earthenware
majolikowy [mah-yo-lee-**ko**-vi] adj.m. of majolica; majolica (tiles, ware, etc.)
majonez [mah-**yo**-nes] m. mayonnaise; egg yolk dressing
majonezowy [mah-yo-ne-**zo**-vi] adj.m. mayonnaise (sauce, etc.)
major [mah-yor] m. major
majoracki [mah-yo-**rah**-tskee] adj.m. of primogeniture
majorat [mah-**yo**-raht] m. right of primogeniture; entailed estate
majoratowy [mah-yo-rah-**to**-vi] adj.m. of primogeniture
majordom [mah-**yor**-dom] m. mayor-domo; head steward
majordomus [mah-yor-**do**-moos] m. mayor-domo; head steward
majorostwo [mah-yo-**ro**-stfo] n. rank of major; major and his wife
majorowa [mah-yo-**ro**-vah] f. major's wife
majorowy [mah-yo-**ro**-vi] adj.m. major's
majoryzować [mah-yo-ri-**zo**-vahćh] v. outvote; outnumber (*repeatedly*)
majoryzowanie [mah-yo-ri-zo-**vah**-ńe] n. outvoting; outnumbering
majownik [mah-**yo**-vńeek] m. lily-of-the-valley (shrub); Maianthemum bifolium; Convallariacea
majowo [mah-**yo**-vo] adv. as in the month of May; joyfully
majowy [mah-**yo**-vi] adj.m. May (day, etc.)
majówka [mah-**yoof**-kah] f. May outing; picnic; junket
majówkowy [mah-yoof-**ko**-vi] adj.m. May outing (program, etc.); picnic (plans, etc.); junket (arrangement, etc.)
majster [**mahy**-ster] m. qualified craftsman; boss; master (carpenter, baker, etc.); foreman
majster do wszystkiego [**mahy**-ster do fshist-**ke**-go] exp.: jack of all trades
majster klepka [**mahy**-ster **klep**-kah] exp.: bungler; dab; dabster; skilful hand
majsterek [mahy-**ste**-rek] m. colloq: craftsman; tinkerer
majsterka [mahy-**ster**-kah] f. colloq: tinkering
majsterkować [mahy-ster-**ko**-vahćh] v. tinker (*repeatedly*)
majsterkowanie [mahy-ster-ko-**vah**-ńe] n. tinkering
majsterkowicz [mahy-ster-**ko**-vich] m. colloq: tinkerer
majsterski [mahy-**ster**-skee] adj.m. masterly; skilled-craftsman's
majsterstwo [mahy-**ster**-stfo] n. mastery; artistry; expertness
majstersztyk [mahy-**ster**-shtik] m. masterpiece; greatest work
majstrowa [mahy-**stro**-vah] f. wife of a craftsman
majstrować [mahy-**stro**-vahćh] v. colloq: tinker; make (an object); fool with (some object) (*repeatedly*)
majstrowanie [mahy-stro-**vah**-ńe] n. colloq: tinkering; making (an object); fooling with (some object)
majstrowy [mahy-**stro**-vi] adj.m. craftsman's
majtać [**mahy**-tahćh] v. colloq: dangle; swing (one's legs, etc.); wag (its tail, etc.) (*repeatedly*)
majtasy [mahy-**tah**-si] pl. (used, big) panties; knickers

majteczki [mahy-**tech**-kee] pl. small panties; nice panties; small knickers
majtek [**mahy**-tek] m. deck hand
majtki [**mahyt**-kee] pl. panties; knickers; drawers; shorts
majtnąć [**mahyt**-nownćh] v. colloq: dangle; swing (one's legs, etc.); wag (its tail, etc.); slang: throw (at, to) (vulg.)
majufes [mah-**yoo**-fes] m. Jewish religious song
majuskuła [mah-yoos-**koo**-wah] f. capital letter (in print)
majuskułowy [mah-yoos-koo-**wo**-vi] adj.m. of a capital letter (in print)
mak [mahk] m. poppy; poppy seed
jest cicho jak makiem zasiał [yest **ćhee**-kho yahk **mah**-kem **zah**-śhahw] exp.: one might hear a pin drop
mak kalifornijski [mahk kah-lee-for-**ńeey**-skee] exp.: eschscholtzia; California poppy
mak lekarski [mahk le-**kahr**-skee] exp.: opium poppy
mak polny [mahk **pol**-ni] exp.: corn poppy
rozbić w drobny mak [**roz**-beećh v **drob**-ni mahk] exp.: to shatter completely; to break into atoms
makabra [mah-**kah**-brah] f. ghastly sight; horrible scene; gruesome story; hair-raising situation, etc.
makabreska [mah-kah-**bres**-kah] f. small (stage) script including macabre elements and comedy
makabrycznie [mah-kah-**brich**-ńe] adv. horribly; in ghastly fashion
makabryczność [mah-kah-**brich**-nośhćh] f. gruesomeness; ghastly character; horrible nature (of a scene, etc.); macabre character
makabryczny [mah-kah-**brich**-ni] adj.m. macabre; ghastly; gruesome
makabryzm [mah-**kah**-brizm] m. macabre character; ghastly atmosphere; gruesome nature
makadam [mah-**kah**-dahm] m. macadam (roadbed, small broken stone, etc)
makagiga [mah-kah-**gee**-gah] f. sweetmeat of poppy seed, honey, almonds, and nuts
makak [**mah**-kahk] m. monkey of the family Ceropithecidae, genus Macoca
makao [mah-**kah**-o] n. Macao card game
makaron [mah-**kah**-ron] m. pasta in tubular form; macaroni; vermicelli; colloq: macaronicism; macaronic expression; slang: (an) Italian
makaron zapiekany z serem [mah-**kah**-ron zah-pye-**kah**-ni s **se**-rem] exp.: macaroni and cheese
makaroniarnia [mah-kah-ro-**ńahr**-ńah] f. macaroni factory
makaroniarz [mah-kah-**ro**-ńahsh] m. colloq: Italian; slang: Dego
makaroniczny [mah-kah-ro-**ńeech**-ni] adj.m. macaronic (style, etc.)
makaronik [mah-kah-**ro**-ńeek] m. small macaroni; macaroon
makaronista [mah-kah-ro-**ńees**-tah] m. man barbarizing a language
makaronizm [mah-kah-**ro**-ńeezm] m. (exaggerated) borrowing from another language; macaronicism; macaronic expression
makaronizować [mah-kah-ro-ńee-**zo**-vahćh] v. barbarize (a language) (*repeatedly*)
makaronizowanie [mah-kah-ro-ńee-zo-**vah**-ńe] n. barbarizing (a language)
makaronowy [mah-kah-ro-**no**-vi] adj.m. macaroni (flour, etc.)
makartowski [mah-kahr-**tof**-skee] adj.m. dried (flower, etc.)
makata [mah-**kah**-tah] f. tapestry
makatka [mah-**kah**-tkah] f. small (nice) tapestry
makatkowy [mah-kah-**tko**-vi] adj.m. of small tapestry
makatowy [mah-kah-**to**-vi] adj.m. of tapestry
makia [**mah**-kyah] f. thicket of greenery
makiawelicznie [mah-kyah-ve-**leech**-ńe] adv. like Machiavelli
makiaweliczny [mah-kyah-ve-**leech**-ni] adj.m. Machiavellian
makiawelizm [mah-kyah-**ve**-leezm] m. Machiavellism
makiawelski [mah-kyah-**vel**-skee]

adj.m. Machiavellian
makieta [mah-ke-tah] f. model; mock-up; dummy (print, etc.); pattern volume
makietka [mah-ket-kah] f. (small) model; mock-up; dummy (print, etc.); pattern volume
makietować [mah-ke-to-vahćh] v. make a model; make a mock-up (*repeatedly*)
makietowanie [mah-ke-to-vah-ńe] n. making of a model; making of a mock-up
makietowy [mah-ke-to-vi] adj.m. of a model; of a mock-up
makijaż [mah-kee-yahsh] m. make-up
makler [mahk-ler] m. broker; stockbroker
maklerski [mahk-ler-skee] adj.m. stockbroker's (business, etc.); ship brokerage (agency, etc.)
maklerstwo [mahk-ler-stfo] n. stockbroker's business; ship brokerage agency
makolągwa [mah-ko-lown-gvah] f. linnet; colloq: young gal; chick
makowaty [mah-ko-vah-ti] adj.m. like poppy seed; papaverceous; of the poppy family
makowate [mah-ko-vah-te] pl. the poppy family
makowica [mah-ko-vee-tsah] f. capital of a column
makowiec [mah-ko-vyets] m. poppy-seed cake; opium
makownik [mah-ko-vńeek] m. poppy-seed cake; opium; see: **makowiec**
makowy [mah-ko-vi] adj.m. of the poppy; poppy (seed)
makówka [mah-koof-kah] f. poppy-head; pate
makrela [mah-kre-lah] f. mackerel
makrelowaty [mah-kre-lo-vah-ti] adj.m. of the mackerel family; scombroid
makrelowate [mah-kre-lo-vah-te] pl. the mackerel family
makro- [mah-kro] prefix: macro-; long-; large-
makroanaliza [mah-kro-ah-nah-lee-zah] f. chemical analysis on a sample of at least 100 mg
makrobiotyczny [mah-kro-byo-tich-ni] adj.m. macrobiotic
makrobiotyka [mah-kro-byo-ti-kah] f. macrobiotics
makrocefalia [mah-kro-tse-fahl-yah] f. macrocephaly
makrocząsteczka [mah-kro-chownstech-kah] f. macromolecule
makroekonomia [mah-kro-e-ko-no-myah] f. macroeconomics
makroekonomiczny [mah-kro-e-ko-no-meech-ni] adj.m. macroeconomic
makroelement [mah-kro-e-le-ment] m. basic element for life (on earth)
makroewolucja [mah-kro-e-vo-loots-yah] f. long term evolution of species
makrofag [mah-kro-fahg] m. macrophage
makrofagi [mah-kro-fah-gee] pl. the macrophage cells
makrofauna [mah-kro-fahw-nah] f. group of the larger animals in a given environment
makrofizyczny [mah-kro-fee-zich-ni] adj.m. of macrophysics
makrofizyka [mah-kro-fee-zi-kah] f. macrophysics
makrofotografia [mah-kro-fo-to-grah-fyah] f. macrophotography; macrophotograph
makrogameta [mah-kro-gah-me-tah] f. macrogamete
makrogametocyt [mah-kro-gah-me-to-tsit] m. macrogametocyte
makroklimat [mah-kro-klee-maht] m. macroclimate
makroklimatologia [mah-kro-klee-mah-to-lo-gyah] f. macroclimatology
makrokosmicznie [mah-kro-kos-meech-ńe] adj.m. macrocosmically
makrokosmiczny [mah-kro-kos-meech-ni] adj.m. macrocosmic; macrocosmical
makrokosmos [mah-kro-kos-mos] m. macrocosm; macrocosmos
makrokosmosowy [mah-kro-kos-mo-so-vi] adj.m. macrocosmic; macrocosmical
makromolekularny [mah-kro-mo-le-

koo-**lahr**-ni] adj.m. macromolecular
makromolekuła [mah-kro-mo-le-**koo**-wah] f. macromolecule
makron [**mah**-kron] m. macron
makroplankton [mah-kro-**plahnk**-ton] m. macroplankton
makropod [mah-**kro**-pot] m. macropodus
makroregion [mah-kro-**re**-gyon] m. unit in a system of economic regions
makroregionalny [mah-kro-reg-yo-**nahl**-ni] adj.m. of a unit in a system of economic regions
makrorzeźba [mah-kro-**zheźh**-bah] f. prominent geographic features suitable for inclusion in a relief map
makrosejsmiczny [mah-kro-seys-**meech**-ni] adj.m. macroseismic
makrosiedlisko [mah-kro-śhed-**lees**-ko] n. large region of similar climatic and geographic characteristics
makroskala [mah-kro-**skah**-lah] f. macroscale
makroskopia [mah-kro-**sko**-pyah] f. eye-inspection of a metallic surface
makroskopijny [mah-kro-sko-**peey**-ni] adj.m. macroscopic
makroskopowo [mah-kro-sko-**po**-vo] adv. macroscopically; by eye-inspection (of a metallic surface)
makroskopowy [mah-kro-sko-**po**-vi] adj.m. macroscopic; eye-inspection (of a metallic surface)
makrosocjolog [mah-kro-so-**tsyo**-log] m. sociologist of macrostructures
makrosocjologia [mah-kro-so-tsyo-**lo**-gyah] f. sociology of macrostructures
makrospora [mah-kro-**spo**-rah] f. megaspore
makrostruktura [mah-kro-strook-**too**-rah] f. macrostructure
maksi [**mahk**-see] n. colloq: maxi (long skirt; long coat, etc.)
maksimum [mahk-**see**-moom] n. maximum; extreme limit; highest pitch; the most (that can be done, etc.); adv. at the utmost
do maksimum [do mahk-**see**-moom] exp.: to the maximum; to the extreme limit; to the highest pitch; to the max
maksyma [mahk-**si**-mah] f. axiom; maxim; adage; rule of conduct
maksymalista [mahk-si-mah-**lee**-stah] m. maximalist; maximizer
maksymalistyczny [mahk-si-mah-lee-**stich**-ni] adj.m. maximalist (political program, etc.)
maksymalizacja [mahk-si-mah-lee-**zah**-tsyah] f. maximization
maksymalizm [mahk-si-**mah**-leezm] m. maximalism
maksymalizować [mahk-si-mah-lee-**zo**-vahćh] v. maximize (*repeatedly*)
maksymalnie [mahk-si-**mahl**-ńe] adv. to a maximum; in the highest degree; at most; at the utmost; at the outside; maximally
maksymalny [mahk-si-**mahl**-ni] adj.m. maximal; highest; greatest; most (visible, etc.); top (speed, etc.); peak (load, etc.); utmost (degree, efficiency, etc.)
makuch [**mah**-kookh] m. oil cake
makuchowy [mah-koo-**kho**-vi] adj.m. oil-cake (serving, etc.)
makulatura [mah-koo-lah-**too**-rah] f. wastepaper; spoilage; trash; rubbish
makulaturowy [mah-koo-lah-too-**ro**-vi] adj.m. of wastepaper; spoilage (disposal); trash (accumulation, etc.); rubbish (disposal, etc.)
makutra [mah-**koot**-rah] f. mixing bowl (with rough interior)
malachit [mah-**lah**-kheet] m. malachite (mineral, color)
malachitowy [mah-lah-khee-**to**-vi] adj.m. malachite (mineral, color, etc.)
malaga [mah-**lah**-gah] f. Malaga wine; Malaga grape
Malajczyk [mah-**lahy**-chik] m. (a) Malay
Malajka [mah-**lahy**-kah] f. Malay woman
malajski [mah-**lahy**-skee] adj.m. Malay (language, etc.)
język malajski [yan-zik mah-**lahy**-skee] exp.: Malay language
nóż malajski [noosh mah-**lahy**-

skee] exp.: parang; short sword or knife with inlaid designs
malakologia [mah-lah-ko-**lo**-gyah] f. study of shellfish; malacology
malakologiczny [mah-lah-ko-lo-**geech**-ni] adj.m. malacological; of study of the shellfish
malakser [mah-**lah**-kser] m. kitchen aid device for mixing, grinding, and cutting
malaria [mah-**lah**-ryah] f. malaria; paludism
malarka [mah-**lahr**-kah] f. (woman) artist; painter; paintress
malarnia [mah-**lahr**-ńah] f. painting shop
malarski [mah-**lahr**-skee] adj.m. painter's (studio, brushes, palette, etc.); of a painting; pictorial; picturesque
malarsko [mah-**lahr**-sko] adv. in painting; in paints; pictorially; from the painter's point of view
malarskość [mah-**lahr**-skośhćh] f. pictorial quality
malarstwo [mah-**lahr**-stfo] n. painting; pictorial (art); house painting
malaryczny [mah-lah-**rich**-ni] adj.m. malarial; paludal
malarz [**mah**-lahsh] m. painter
malarzyna [mah-lah-**zhi**-nah] m. paltry painter
malatura [mah-lah-**too**-rah] f. painting; manner of painting; paints
malec [**mah**-lets] m. youngster; boy; lad; kid
maleć [**mah**-lećh] v. shrink; dwindle; grow smaller; lessen (*repeatedly*)
maleinowy [mah-le-ee-**no**-vi] adj.m. maleic; of the acid (used for production of synthectic resins)
maleńka [mah-**leń**-kah] f. sweet little baby girl
maleńki [mah-**leń**-kee] adj.m. very small; tiny; insignificant; minute; modest; m. little one; little darling
maleńka chwila [mah-**leń**-kah **khfee**-lah] exp.: a moment; a short while; blink of an eye; colloq: a jiffy
od maleńkiego [od mah-leń-<u>ke</u>-go] exp.: since childhood; from childhood; from a child
maleńko [mah-**leń**-ko] adv. very little
maleńkość [mah-**leń**-końhćh] f. littleness; smallness; (early) youth
maleństwo [mah-**leń**-stfo] n. tiny thing; little one; little mite; tiny tot; little darling
maligna [mah-**lee**-gnah] f. malignant fever
malina [mah-**lee**-nah] f. raspberry
wpuścić kogoś w maliny [**fpoośh**-ćheećh **ko**-gośh v mah-**lee**-ni] exp.: to mislead somebody
maliniak [mah-**lee**-ńahk] m. raspberry patch; raspberry-flavored mead
malinka [mah-**leen**-kah] f. raspberry-shaped candy
malinnik [mah-**leen**-ńeek] m. raspberry plantation
malinowoczerwony [mah-lee-no-vo-cher-**vo**-ni] adj.m. raspberry red
malinowy [mah-lee-**no**-vi] adj.m. raspberry (jam, patch, apple, etc); raspberry red (color, rhubarb, etc.)
malinówka [mah-lee-**noof**-kah] f. raspberry vodka; raspberry apple
malkontencki [mahl-kon-**ten**-tskee] adj.m. grumbling; disgruntled
malkontenctwo [mahl-kon-**ten**-tstfo] n. grumbling; discontent
malkontent [mahl-**kon**-tent] m. malcontent; grumbler; growler
malm [mahlm] m. malm (mineral, epoch)
malonowy [mah-lo-**no**-vi] adj.m. malic (acid)
malować [mah-**lo**-vahćh] v. paint; stain; color; make up; depict; portray; describe; express; be expressive (*repeatedly*)
malować się [mah-**lo**-vahćh śh<u>an</u>] v. make up; do up one's face; put on makeup; be painted; appear; stand out (against a background); be written (on one's face) (*repeatedly*)
malowanie [mah-lo-**vah**-ńe] n. brushwork
malowanie się [mah-lo-**vah**-ńe śh<u>an</u>] n. putting on makeup;

doing one's face
malowanka [mah-lo-**vahn**-kah] f. folkloric ornament; painted figure
malowany [mah-lo-**vah**-ni] adj.m. painted
jak malowany [yahk mah-lo-**vah**-ni] exp.: motionless
malowidło [mah-lo-**veed**-wo] n. painting; picture (painted)
malowniczo [mah-lov-**ńee**-cho] adv. picturesquely; vividly
malowniczość [mah-lov-**ńee**-chośhćh] f. picturesqueness; vividness
malowniczy [mah-lov-**ńee**-chi] adj.m. picturesque; vivid
malstrom [**mahl**-strom] m. Maelstrom
Maltańczyk [mahl-**tahń**-chik] m. (a) Maltese; Knight of Malta; Hospitaler; Maltese dog
maltański [mahl-**tahń**-skee] adj.m. Maltese; of Malta
maltaza [mahl-**tah**-zah] f. maltase
maltazy [mahl-**tah**-zi] pl. maltase enzymes
maltoza [mahl-**to**-zah] f. maltose
maltretować [mahl-tre-**to**-vahćh] v. abuse; mistreat; ill-treat; maltreat; bully; mishandle (*repeatedly*)
maltretowanie [mahl-tre-to-**vah**-ńe] n. abuse; mistreatment; ill-treatment; maltreatment; bullying; rough handling
maltuzjanizm [mahl-tooz-**yah**-ńeezm] m. Malthusianism
maltuzjański [mahl-tooz-**yahń**-skee] adj.m. Malthusian
maluch [**mah**-lookh] m. baby boy; colloq: Fiat model 126p; very small car
maluchny [mah-**lookh**-ni] adj.m. very small
maluczka [mah-**looch**-kah] f. colloq: an average woman (not too bright)
maluczki [mah-**looch**-kee] m. colloq: an average man (not too bright)
maluczko [mah-**looch**-ko] adv. in a very small way; just a little bit (more, etc.)
malunek [mah-**loo**-nek] m. colloq: picture; painting
malusi [**mah-loo**-śhee] adj.m. very little; very tiny; teeny tiny
malusieńki [mah-loo-**śheń**-kee] adj.m. very little; tiny; teeny tiny
malusieńko [mah-loo-**śheń**-ko] adv. in a very small way
maluśka [mah-**loośh**-kah] adj.f. very little (girl); f. very small girl
maluśki [mah-**loośh**-kee] adj.m. very little; very small; tiny; diminutive; minute; m. little
maluśko [mah-**loośh**-ko] adv. in a very small way
maluteńki [mah-loo-**teń**-kee] adj.m. very little; very small; tiny; diminutive; minute; m. little thing; little darling
maluteńko [mah-loo-**teń**-ko] adv. in a very small way; diminutively; minutely
malutka [mah-**loot**-kah] adj.f. very little (girl); f. very small girl
malutki [mah-**loot**-kee] adj.m. very little; very small; tiny; diminutive; minute; m. little thing; little darling
malutko [mah-**loot**-ko] adv. in a very small way; diminutively; minutely
malwa [**mahl**-vah] f. mallow; Malva
malwersacja [mahl-ver-**sah**-tsyah] f. embezzlement; peculation
popełnić malwersację [po-**pew**-ńeećh mahl-ver-**sah**-tsyan] exp.: to embezzle money; to peculate
malwersant [mahl-**ver**-sahnt] m. embezzler; peculator
malwersantka [mahl-ver-**sahnt**-kah] f. (woman) embezzler; peculator
malwowaty [mahl-vo-**vah**-ti] adj.m. malvaceous; of Malva
malwowate [mahl-vo-**vah**-te] pl. the mallow family
malwowy [mahl-**vo**-vi] adj.m. mallow (flower, etc.); of Malva
malwowe [mahl-**vo**-ve] pl. the order Malvales
mała [**mah**-wah] adj.f. small (girl)
małe [**mah**-we] adj.n. & pl.f. small
małgorzatka [mahw-go-**zhaht**-kah] f. summer pear; summer pear tree; loaf of bread with poppy seeds
małmazja [mahw-**mah**-zyah] f. malmsey; sweet wine from the Mediterranean islands
małmazyjski [mahw-mah-**ziy**-skee]

adj.m. malvasian (wine, etc.)
mało [mah-wo] adv. little; few; seldom; lack; not enough; not much; not many; insufficiently; but little; hardly at all
bez mała [bez mah-wah] exp.: almost; pretty nearly; very nearly; nearly
jak mało kto [yahk mah-wo kto] exp.: to a rare degree; uncommonly
jakich mało [yah-keekh mah-wo] exp.: rare
mało co [mah-wo tso] exp.: not much; but little; hardly at all
mało gdzie [mah-wo gdźhe] exp.: hardly anywhere
mało kiedy [mah-wo ke-di] exp.: very seldom
mało kto [mah-wo kto] exp.: hardly anybody
mało który [mah-wo ktoo-ri] exp.: hardly any; hardly a ... but
mało poza tym [mah-wo po-zah tim] exp.: little else; not much else
mało tego [mah-wo te-go] exp.: what is more; and that's not all; too little of it; not enough of it
mało to? [mah-wo to] exp.: is it not enough?
o mało [o mah-wo] exp.: nearly
za mało [zah mah-wo] exp.: too little; too few
za mało, za późno [zah mah-wo zah poožh-no] exp.: too little, too late
mało- [mah-wo] prefix: little-; faint-; few-
małodusznie [mah-wo-doosh-ńe] adv. pusillanimously; faintheartedly; meanly
małoduszność [mah-wo-doosh-nośhćh] f. pusillanimity; faint heart; meanness
małoduszny [mah-wo-doosh-ni] adj.m. pusillanimous; fainthearted; meanspirited; mean; cheap; small-minded
małodzietność [mah-wo-dżhet-nośhćh] f. having few children; having a small family
małodzietny [mah-wo-dżhet-ni] adj.m. of few children; of a small family
małogabarytowy [mah-wo-gah-bah-ri-to-vi] adj.m. small; having small dimensions
małogłowie [mah-wo-gwo-vye] n. microcephaly
małokalibrowy [mah-wo-kah-leeb-ro-vi] adj.m. small caliber (rifle, pistol, etc.)
małokalorycznie [mah-wo-kah-lo-rich-ńe] adv. with small caloric content; with small calorific power
małokaloryczny [mah-wo-kah-lo-rich-ni] adj.m. of small caloric content; of small calorific power
małolat [mah-wo-laht] m. colloq: underage boy
małolata [mah-wo-lah-tah] f. colloq: underage girl
małolatek [mah-wo-lah-tek] m. underage boy; minor; juvenile
małolatka [mah-wo-lah-tkah] f. underage girl; minor; juvenile
małoletni [mah-wo-let-ńee] adj.m. minor; underage; juvenile; immature; young
małoletnia [mah-wo-let-ńah] adj.f. (female) minor; under age; juvenile; immature; young
małoletniość [mah-wo-let-ńośhćh] f. minority
małolitrażowy [mah-wo-lee-trah-zho-vi] adj.m. low-capacity (motor)
małomiasteczkowość [mah-wo-myahs-tech-ko-vośhćh] f. provincial character; parochial nature; provincialism
małomiasteczkowy [mah-wo-myahs-tech-ko-vi] adj.m. provincial; parochial
małomiasteczkowa umysłowość [mah-wo-myahs-tech-ko-vah oo-mi-swo-vośhćh] exp.: provincialism
małomieszczanin [mah-wo-myesh-chah-ńeen] m. a member of the lower middle class
małomieszczański [mah-wo-myesh-chahń-skee] adj.m. of the lower middle class
małomieszczańskość [mah-wo-myesh-chahń-skośhćh] f. characteristics of the lower

middle class
małomieszczaństwo [mah-wo-myesh-**chahń**-stfo] n. lower middle class
małomówność [mah-wo-**moov**-nośhćh] f. taciturnity; reticence
małomówny [mah-wo-**moov**-ni] adj.m. reticent; laconic; taciturn; uncommunicative
małoobrazkowy [mah-wo-ob-rahs-**ko**-vi] adj.m. 35 millimeter (camera, film, etc.)
małopolski [mah-wo-**pol**-skee] adj.m. of Little Poland
małoprocentowy [mah-wo-pro-tsen-**to**-vi] adj.m; of a low interest rate; of a low percentage
małorolny [mah-wo-**rol**-ni] adj.m. petty (farmer); m. petty farmer; small holder
małoseryjny [mah-wo-se-**riy**-ni] adj.m. produced in small numbers
małosolny [mah-wo-**sol**-ni] adj.m. containing a small amount of salt
małostka [mah-**wost**-kah] f. trifle
małostkowo [mah-wost-**ko**-vo] adv. meanly; narrow-mindedly; small-mindedly
małostkowość [mah-wost-**ko**-vośhćh] f. petty-mindedness
małostkowy [mah-wost-**ko**-vi] adj.m. fussy; mean; small-minded; narrow-minded
małość [mah-wośhćh] f. small size; littleness; small quantity
małowartościowość [mah-wo-vahr-to-**śhćho**-vośhćh] f. little worth; little value
małowartościowy [mah-wo-vahr-to-**śhćho**-vi] adj.m. of little worth; of little value
małoważny [mah-wo-**vahzh**-ni] adj.m. unimportant; of little importance; insignificant; trifling; trivial; negligible; minor (detail, etc.); petty (problem, quarrel, etc.)
małoż [mah-wosh] adv. emphatic: **mało**
małpa [**mahw**-pah] f. monkey; colloq: 100-gram vodka bottle
małpa bezogonowa [**mahw**-pah bez-o-go-**no**-vah] exp.: ape
małpy [**mahw**-pi] pl. the simians; monkeys; monkey-skins
małpeczka [mahw-**pech**-kah] f. (nice, little) monkey
małpeczki [mahw-**pech**-kee] pl. the family Callithrichidae
małpi [**mahw**-pee] adj.m. monkey (skin, fur, etc.); monkey's; simian; monkeyish; apish
małpia gęba [**mahw**-pyah gan-bah] exp.: colloq: monkey face
małpie figle [**mahw**-pye **feeg**-le] exp.: monkey business; monkeyish tricks (antics, pranks, etc.); monkeyshine
małpiarnia [mahw-**pyahr**-ńah] f. monkey compound in a zoo
małpiarski [mahw-**pyahr**-skee] adj.m. monkeyish; apish
małpiarstwo [mahw-**pyahr**-stfo] n. apishness
małpiatka [mahw-**pyaht**-kah] f. lemur
małpiatki [mahw-**pyaht**-kee] pl. The Lemurs; the Lemuroidea
małpiątko [mahw-**pyownt**-ko] n. little monkey; little ape; newborn monkey
małpię [**mahw**-pyan] n. little monkey; little ape; very small monkey
małpio [**mahw**-pyo] adv. apishly
małpiszon [mahw-**pee**-shon] m. an ugly (and mean) person
małpka [**mahwp**-kah] f. little monkey; (nice) little ape
małpolud [mahw-**po**-loot] m. ape-man; anthropoid (creature)
małpować [mahw-**po**-vahćh] v. ape; imitate (poorly, blindly, clumsily, ineptly, etc.); trifle (*repeatedly*)
małpowanie [mahw-po-**vah**-ńe] n. aping; imitating
małpozwierz [mahw-**po**-zvyesh] m. lemuroid
mały [**mah**-wi] adj.m. little; small size; low (speed, etc.); modest; slight; insignificant; short; m. little fellow; tot; trifle; a young (animal)
bez mała [bez **mah**-wah] exp.: almost; pretty nearly; very nearly; nearly; practically; as good as
mała chwila [**mah**-wah **khfee**-lah]

exp.: a short while; a moment; colloq: a jiffy
mała kawa [**mah**-wah **kah**-vah] exp.: small coffee
mała waga [**mah**-wah **vah**-gah] exp.: short weight
małe litery [**mah**-we lee-**te**-ri] exp.: small letters; lower case letters
o mały włos [o **mah**-wi vwos] exp.: by a hairbreadth
od małego [od mah-**we**-go] exp.: from a child; from childhood
zacząć od małego [zah-chownćh od mah-**we**-go] exp.: to start from scratch; to make a modest beginning

małż [mahwsh] m. mollusk; mollusc
małże [**mahw**-zhe] pl. the mollusks; the Mollusca

małżeński [mahw-**zheń**-skee] adj.m. matrimonial; conjugal; marital; wedded; connubial; nuptial; hymeneal
para małżeńska [pah-rah mahw-**zheń**-skah] exp.: married couple; bridal pair; newly-married couple
stan małżeński [stahn mahw-**zheń**-skee] exp.: matrimony; wedlock; married state

małżeństwo [mahw-**zheń**-stfo] n. marriage; matrimony; married couple; wedlock
małżeństwo mieszane [mahw-**zheń**-stfo mye-**shah**-ne] exp.: intermarriage
małżeństwo z wyrachowania [mahw-**zheń**-stfo z vi-rah-kho-**vah**-ńah] exp.: marriage of convenience
zawrzeć małżeństwo [**zahv**-zhećh mahw-**zheń**-stfo] exp.: to contract a marriage

małżonek [mahw-**zho**-nek] m. husband; spouse; consort; mate; bedfellow; partner
małżonkowie [mahw-zhon-**ko**-vye] pl. husband and wife; married couple

małżonka [mahw-**zhon**-kah] f. wife; spouse; consort; mate

małżoraczek [mahw-zho-**rah**-chek] m. ostracod; eztracode
małżoraczki [mahw-zho-**rah**-chkee] pl. the freshwater crustacean subclass Ostracoda

małżowina [mahw-zho-**vee**-nah] f. shell
małżowina nosowa [mahw-zho-**vee**-nah no-**so**-vah] exp.: turbinated bone
małżowina uszna [mahw-zho-**vee**-nah **oosh**-nah] exp.: auricle; concha

małżowinowy [mahw-zho-vee-**no**-vi] adj.m. shell-like

mam [mahm] v. I have (see: **mieć**)

mama [**mah**-mah] f. mamma; mother; mum; mummy; mama

mamałyga [mah-mah-**wi**-gah] f. maize gruel; hominy

mambo [**mahm**-bo] n. mambo dance

mamcia [**mahm**-ćhah] f. mummy; mum

mamelucki [mah-me-**loo**-tskee] adj.m. Mameluke (rule, etc.)

mameluk [mah-**me**-look] m. Mameluke; colloq: servile person; blind follower

mamer [**mah**-mer] m. slang: jail; jug; lockup; clink (mob jargon)
w mamrze [v **mahm**-zhe] exp.: in jail; in the jug; in the clink

mamić [**mah**-meećh] v. deceive; delude; beguile; lure; tempt; seduce; entice (*repeatedly*)

mamić się [**mah**-meećh śhan] v. deceive oneself; delude oneself (*repeatedly*)

mamidło [mah-**mee**-dwo] n. illusion; delusion; lure; seduction; enticement; temptation

mamienie [mah-**mye**-ńe] n. delusion; lure; seduction; beguilement

mamin [**mah**-meen] adj.m. mother's; mummy's

maminsynek [mah-meen-**si**-nek] m. spoiled brat; mother's pet; sissy boy

maminy [mah-**mee**-ni] adj.m. mother's; mummy's

mamka [**mahm**-kah] f. wet nurse; foster mother

mamlać [**mahm**-lahćh] v. mumble; mutter; eat in a clumsy way (*repeatedly*)

mamlanie [mahm-**lah**-ńe] n. mumbling; muttering; eating in a

clumsy way
mamleć [**mahm**-lećh] v. mumble; mutter; eat in a clumsy way (*repeatedly*)
mamlenie [mahm-**le**-ńe] n. mumbling; muttering; eating in a clumsy way
mamłać [**mahm**-wahćh] v. mumble (words, food, etc.); mutter (*repeatedly*)
mammografia [mahm-mo-**grah**-fyah] f. mammography; X-ray examination of the breast
mammolog [mahm-**mo**-log] m. mammalogist
mammologia [mahm-mo-**lo**-gyah] f. mammalogy
mammologiczny [mahm-mo-lo-**geech**-ni] adj.m. of mammalogy
mamona [mah-**mo**-nah] f. mammon
mamotrekt [mah-**mo**-trekt] m. dictionary of biblical terms
mamotrept [mah-**mo**-trept] m. dictionary of biblical terms
mamraj [**mahm**-rahy] m. rich clay used in foundry molds
mamrot [**mahm**-rot] m. (a) mumble; gibber
mamrotać [mahm-**ro**-tahćh] v. mutter; mumble; gibber (*repeatedly*)
mamrotanie [mahm-ro-**tah**-ńe] n. mutter; mumble; gibber
mamuci [mah-**moo**-ćhee] adj.m. of a mammoth
mamunia [mah-**moo**-ńah] f. mummy; mum
mamusia [mah-**moo**-śhah] f. mummy; mum
mamusin [mah-**moo**-śheen] adj.m. mummy's; mum's
mamusiny [mah-moo-**śhee**-ni] adj.m. mummy's; mum's
mamut [**mah**-moot] m. mammoth; large size bean; colloq: old fogy
mamutowiec [mah-moo-**to**-vyets] m. giant sequoia; mammoth tree
mamutowy [mah-moo-**to**-vi] adj.m. mammoth (ox, etc.)
manager [me-**ne**-dzher] m. manager
manageryzm [me-ne-**dzhe**-rizm] m. the theory (stage) of managerial control of enterprises (after capitalism)
manat [mah-naht] m. manatee
manaty [mah-**nah**-ti] pl. manatees
manatki [mah-**naht**-kee] pl. colloq: personal belongings; traps; chattels
zwijać manatki [**zvee**-yahćh mah-**naht**-kee] exp.: to pack up one's traps
manca [**mahn**-tsah] f. fishing-net
manczester [mahn-**ches**-ter] m. corduroy
manczesterowy [mahn-ches-te-**ro**-vi] adj.m. corduroy (coat, etc.)
manczesteryzm [mahn-ches-**te**-rizm] m. Manchesterism
manczestrowy [mahn-chest-**ro**-vi] adj.m. corduroy (coat, etc.)
mandaryn [mahn-**dah**-rin] m. mandarin; Chinese dignitary
mandarynat [mahn-dah-**ri**-naht] m. mandarinate
mandarynizm [mahn-dah-**ri**-**ńeezm**] m. mandarinism
mandarynka [mahn-dah-**rin**-kah] f. mandarin orange; tangerine orange
mandarynki [mahn-dah-**rin**-kee] pl. Chinese slippers
mandarynkowy [mahn-dah-rin-**ko**-vi] adj.m. of a mandarin orange
mandaryński [mahn-dah-**riń**-skee] adj.m. mandarinic; mandarin's; mandarin (porcelain, etc.)
mandat [**mahn**-daht] m. mandate; traffic ticket; fine; mandamus
mandat karny [**mahn**-daht **kahr**-ni] exp.: fine
mandat poselski [**mahn**-daht po-**sel**-skee] exp.: seat in parliament
mandatariusz [mahn-dah-**tahr**-yoosh] m. mandatary; trustee; assignee
mandatariuszka [mahn-dah-tahr-**yoosh**-kah] f. (female) mandatary; trustee; assignee
mandatowy [mahn-dah-**to**-vi] adj.m. mandatory (states); mandated (territory)
mandola [mahn-**do**-lah] f. mandola
mandolina [mahn-do-**lee**-nah] f. mandolin with 8 to 10 strings
mandolinista [mahn-do-lee-**ńees**-tah] m. mandolinist
mandolinowy [mahn-do-lee-**no**-vi] adj.m. mandolin (strings, etc.)

mandorla [mahn-**dor**-lah] f. mandorla; vesica piscis
mandragora [mahn-drah-**go**-rah] f. mandragora; mandrake
mandryl [**mahn**-dril] m. mandrill (monkey)
mandżurski [mahn-**dzhoor**-skee] adj.m. Manchurian
manekin [mah-**ne**-keen] m. mannequin; model of human body; dummy; manikin; figurehead; automaton
manela [mah-**ne**-lah] f. bracelet
manele [mah-**ne**-le] pl. colloq: traps
manetka [mah-**net**-kah] f. ignition lever (key); throttle
manewr [**mah**-nevr] m. maneuver; stratagem; artifice
manewry [mah-**ne**-vri] pl. military exercises; maneuvers
manewrować [mah-ne-**vro**-vahćh] v. maneuver; steer; handle; switch; shunt; plot; intrigue; manipulate (*repeatedly*)
manewrowanie [mah-ne-vro-**vah**-ńe] n. manipulation; maneuver; steering; handling; switching; shunting; stratagems; artifices
manewrowy [mah-ne-**vro**-vi] adj.m. maneuvering; m. (railroad) switcher; shunter
maneż [**mah**-nesh] m. riding school; horse-driven thrasher
mangan [**mahn**-gahn] m. manganese (used in alloys; atomic number 25)
manganawy [mahn-gah-**nah**-vi] adj.m. manganous (salts, etc.)
manganian [mahn-**gah**-ńyahn] m. salt with manganese in the form of MnO; manganate; manganite
manganiany [mahn-gah-**ńyah**-ni] pl. manganates
manganin [mahn-**gah**-ńeen] m. manganine
manganit [mahn-**gah**-ńeet] m. manganite
manganometria [mahn-gah-no-**met**-ryah] f. manganometry
manganowiec [mahn-gah-**no**-vyets] m. one of the elements of the manganic group
manganowce [mahn-gah-**no**-ftse] pl. the manganic group
manganowy [mahn-gah-**no**-vi] adj.m. manganic; manganous; manganesian
mango [**mahn**-go] n. mango
mangostan [mahn-**go**-stahn] m. mangosteen (tree, fruit)
mangowiec [mahn-**go**-vyets] m. mango tree
mangowy [mahn-**go**-vi] adj.m. mango (tree, etc.)
mangrowe [mahn-**gro**-ve] pl. mangrove
mangusta [mahn-**goos**-tah] f. viverrid mongoose
mangusty [mahn-**goos**-ti] pl. the Viverridae carnivorous family
mania [**mah**-ńyah] f. mania (for); fad; fixed idea; craze (for); rage (for)
mania prześladowcza [mah-ńyah pshe-śhlah-**dof**-chah] exp.: persecution mania
mania wielkości [**mah**-ńyah vyel-**kośh**-ćhee] exp.: megalomania
maniacki [mah-**ńyah**-tskee] adj.m. manic (depressive, etc.); maniac; maniacal; faddish; crazy
maniacko [mah-**ńyah**-tsko] adv. maniacally; manically
maniactwo [mah-**ńyah**-tstfo] n. faddishness; craziness; mania (for)
maniaczka [mah-**ńyahch**-kah] f. (female) maniac; crank; lunatic; insane woman
maniak [**mah**-ńyahk] m. maniac; crank; insane person; (hunting) decoy; colloq: feed bag
maniakalnie [mah-ńyah-**kahl**-ńe] adv. maniacally; franticly
maniakalny [mahń-yah-**kahl**-ni] adj.m. maniacal; frantic
manicheizm [mah-ńee-**khe**-eezm] m. Manichaeanism; Manichaeism
manichejczyk [mah-ńee-**khey**-chik] m. Manichaean; Manichean
manichejski [mah-ńee-**khey**-skee] adj.m. Manichaean; Manichean
manicure [mah-**ńee**-keer or mah-ńee-**keer**] m. (French) manicure; trimming (polishing, doing, etc.) one's fingernails
manicurzysta [mah-ńee-kyee-**zhi**-

stah] m. manicurist
manicurzystka [mah-ńee-kyee-**zhi**-stkah] f. (female) manicurist
manić [**mah**-ńeećh] v. deceive; tempt; delude; beguile; lure (*repeatedly*)
maniera [mah-**ńe**-rah] f. mannerism; style
maniery [mah-**ńe**-ri] pl. exp.: manners; good breeding
manierka [mah-**ńer**-kah] f. canteen; water bottle
manierować [mah-ńe-**ro**-vahćh] v. render (somebody) manneristic (*repeatedly*)
manierować się [mah-ńe-**ro**-vahćh śh<u>an</u>] v. acquire a mannerism (*repeatedly*)
manierowanie [mah-ńe-ro-**vah**-ńe] n. rendering manneristic; mannerism
manierowanie się [mah-ńe-ro-**vah**-ńe śh<u>an</u>] n. becoming manneristic
manierycznie [mah-ńe-**rich**-ńe] adv. manneristically
maniereczność [mah-ńe-**rich**-nośhćh] f. mannerism
manieryczny [mah-ńe-**rich**-ni] adj.m. manneristic; manneristical
manierysta [mah-ńe-**ris**-tah] m. mannerist
manierystyczny [mah-ńe-ris-**tich**-ni] adj.m. manneristic
manieryzm [mah-**ńe**-rizm] m. mannerism; artificiality; preciosity
manierzysta [mah-ńe-**zhi**-stah] m. mannerist
manifest [mah-**ńee**-fest] m. manifesto; a public declaration; manifest (of ship's cargo, etc.)
manifestacja [mah-ńee-fes-**tah**-tsyah] f. manifestation; demonstration; ostentatious display
manifestacyjnie [mah-ńee-fes-tah-**tsiy**-ńe] adv. manifestatively
manifestacyjny [mah-ńee-fes-tah-**tsiy**-ni] adj.m. manifestative
manifestant [mah-ńee-**fes**-tahnt] m. manifestant; manifester
manifestantka [mah-ńee-fes-**tahnt**-kah] f. (female) manifestant; manifester
manifestować [mah-ńee-fes-**to**-vahćh] v. manifest; demonstrate; stage a demonstration; display (*repeatedly*)
manifestować się [mah-ńee-fes-**to**-vahćh śh<u>an</u>] v. manifest itself; evince itself (*repeatedly*)
manifestowanie [mah-ńee-fes-to-**vah**-ńe] n. manifestation; demonstration
manikiur [mah-**ńee**-kyoor] m. manicure
manikiurzystka [mah-ńee-kyoo-**zhist**-kah] f. manicurist
manila [mah-**ńee**-lah] f. Manila (hemp); abaca (fabric)
manilowy [mah-ńee-**lo**-vi] adj.m.. Manila (hemp) (rope, etc.); of abaca; of Manila hemp
maniok [**mah**-ńyok] m. manioc (plant, flour); cassava
maniokowy [mah-ńyo-**ko**-vi] adj.m. manioc (plant, flour); cassava (bush, etc.)
manipulacja [mah-ńee-poo-**lah**-tsyah] f. manipulation; handling
manipulacje [mah-ńee-poo-**lah**-tsye] pl. procedure
manipulacyjny [mah-ńee-poo-lah-**tsiy**-ni] adj.m. of manipulation; manipulative
koszty manipulacyjne [**kosh**-ti mah-ńee-poo-lah-**tsiy**-ne] exp.: administrative costs
opłaty manipulacyjne [op-**wah**-ti mah-ńee-poo-lah-**tsiy**-ne] exp.: handling charges
manipulant [mah-ńee-**poo**-lahnt] m. manipulator; clerk
manipularz [mah-ńee-**poo**-lahsh] m. maniple
manipulator [mah-ńee-poo-**lah**-tor] m. conjuror; conjurer; manipulator; signalling key
manipulować [mah-ńee-poo-**lo**-vahćh] v. manipulate; handle; tinker (at); manage artfully (*repeatedly*)
manipulowanie [mah-ńee-poo-lo-**vah**-ńe] n. manipulation; procedure
manipuł [mah-**ńee**-poow] m. maniple
mankament [mahn-**kah**-ment] m.

fault; defect; weak point; shortcoming; drawback
bez mankamentów [bez mahn-kah-**men**-toof] exp.: faultless; faultlessly
mankiecik [mahn-k̲e-ćheek] m. (small, nice) cuff; turnup; wristband; ruffle
mankiet [**mahn**-k̲et] m. cuff; turnup; wristband; ruffle
manko [**mahn**-ko] n. (account) shortage; allowance to cashier for errors; cash shortage; shortage (of weight, etc.); wastage; leakage; ullage
manko wagowe [**mahn**-ko vah-**go**-ve] exp.: short weight
mankowicz [mahn-**ko**-veech] m. colloq: cashier (employee) who has produced a (cash) shortage
mankowiczka [mahn-ko-**veech**-kah] f. colloq: (female) cashier (employee) who has produced a (cash) shortage
manlicher [mahn-lee-kher] m. Austrian rifle
manna [**mahn**-nah] f. cream of wheat; a godsend manna; semolina; manna grass; manna lichen
mannica [mahn-ńee-tsah] f. variety of near-shore, salt-resistant grass
mannowy [mahn-**no**-vi] adj.m. like manna (growth, etc.)
manograf [mah-**no**-grahf] m. manograph
manometr [mah-**no**-metr] m. pressure gauge; steam gauge; manometer
manometria [mah-no-**met**-ryah] f. manometry
manometrycznie [mah-no-met-**rich**-ńe] adv. manometrically
manometryczny [mah-no-met-**rich**-ni] adj.m. manometrical; manometric
manowiec [mah-**no**-vyets] m. nowhere; an unknown, distant, or obscure place
manowce [mah-**nof**-tse] pl. misguided direction; roadless area; wrong way
sprowadzić na manowce [spro-**vah**-dźheećh nah mah-**nof**-tse] exp.: to lead astray
zejść na manowce [zeyśhćh nah mah-**nof**-tse] exp.: to go astray
mansarda [mahn-**sahr**-dah] f. attic; garret; mansard roof
mansardka [mahn-**sahrt**-kah] f. (small) attic; garret; mansard roof
mansardowy [mahn-sahr-**do**-vi] adj.m. mansard (roof, etc.)
mansjon [**mahn**-syon] m. building decoration in medieval theater
mansjonarz [mahn-**syo**-nahsh] m. vicar at a cathedral church
manszeta [mahn-**she**-tah] f. bracelet (used in hospitals); blow to fencer's hand; gasket
manto [**mahn**-to] n. indecl.: colloq: beating
dostać manto [**dos**-tahćh **mahn**-to] exp.: colloq: to get a hiding
mantolet [mahn-**to**-let] m. mantelet
mantra [**mahn**-trah] f. mantra (invocation or incantation)
mantyczenie [mahn-ti-**che**-ńe] n. grumbling; fretting
mantyczyć [mahn-**ti**-chićh] v. grumble; fret (*repeatedly*)
mantyka [mahn-**ti**-kah] m. grumbler; growler; f. divination
mantyla [mahn-**ti**-lah] f. mantilla
mantylka [mahn-**ti**-lkah] f. (small, nice) mantilla
mantysa [mahn-**ti**-sah] f. mantissa
manualista [mah-noo-ah-**lees**-tah] m. manualist
manualistyczny [mah-noo-ah-lees-**tich**-ni] adj.m. of manual training; of manualism
manualizm [mah-noo-**ah**-leezm] m. manualism; program of hands-on teaching; teaching by the manual method
manualny [mah-noo-**ahl**-ni] adj.m. manual
manuał [nah-**noo**-ahw] m. manual; organ key
manuałowy [nah-noo-ah-**wo**-vi] adj.m. manual (sound of the organs)
manufaktura [mah-noo-fahk-**too**-rah] f. workshop; manufacture; shop; manual occupation
manufaktury [mah-noo-fahk-**too**-ri] pl. fabrics; textiles
manufakturowy [mah-noo-fahk-too-

ro-vi] adj.m. workshop (production, etc.); manual occupation (classification, etc.)
manuskrypt [mah-**noo**-skript] m. manuscript; (hand or typewritten) document, book, etc.
manuskryptowy [mah-noo-skrip-**to**-vi] adj.m. manuscript (file, etc.)
mańka [mahń-kah] f. left hand
zażyć kogoś z mańki [zah-zhićh ko-gośh z **mahń**-kee] exp.: to fool (to gull, to dupe, to diddle, to finesse) somebody; to take somebody in; to deceive somebody; to get somebody with the left hand
mańkuctwo [mahń-**koo**-tstfo] n. left-handedness
mańkut [**mahń**-koot] m. left-handed person
maoista [mah-o-**ee**-stah] m. Maoist
maoistowski [mah-o-ees-**tof**-skee] adj.m. Maoist
maoizm [mah-**o**-eezm] m. Maoism
Maorys [mah-**o**-ris] m. Maori (language, man, people, etc.)
mapa [**mah**-pah] f. map; chart
mapa drogowa [**mah**-pah dro-**go**-vah] exp.: highway map; road map
mapa fizyczna [**mah**-pah fee-**zich**-nah] exp.: physical map
mapa morska [**mah**-pah **mor**-skah] exp.: nautical chart
mapa samochodowa [**mah**-pah sah-mo-kho-**do**-vah] exp.: motoring map; highway map; road map
mapa sztabowa [mah-pah shtah-**bo**-vah] exp.: ordnance map
mapa sztabu generalnego [**mah**-pah **shtah**-boo ge-ne-rahl-**ne**-go] exp.: ordnance map
mapa ślepa [**mah**-pah **śhle**-pah] exp.: skeleton map
mapa warstwicowa [**mah**-pah vahr-stfee-**tso**-vah] exp.: contour map; chart
mapka [**mahp**-kah] f. (small) map; chart
mapnik [**mahp**-ńeek] m. map-case
mapografia [mah-po-**grah**-fyah] f. cartography
mapować [mah-**po**-vahćh] v. locate (something) on a map; plot on a map (*repeatedly*)
mapowanie [mah-po-**vah**-ńe] n. putting (something) on a map; locating (something) on a map; plotting on a map
mapowy [mah-**po**-vi] adj.m. map (paper, etc.)
mapoznawstwo [mah-po-**znahf**-stfo] n. the science of cartography
mara [**mah**-rah] f. ghost; apparition; nightmare; dream; vision
marabut [mah-**rah**-boot] m. marabout; dervish (in Muslim Africa); marabou; adjutant stork; turkey feather (long, soft)
marakas [mah-**rah**-kahs] m. maraca; rattle (dried gourd with pebbles or seeds used as a percussion instrument)
maral [**mah**-rahl] m. Siberian deer
maranta [mah-**rahn**-tah] f. maranta (an herb); arrowroot
marantowaty [mah-rahn-to-**vah**-ti] adj.m. marantaceous; of the family Marantaceae
marantowate [mah-rahn-to-**vah**-te] pl. the family Marantaceae
maraskino [mah-rah-**skee**-no] n. maraschino
maraton [mah-**rah**-ton] m. the Marathon
maratończyk [mah-rah-**toń**-chik] m. Marathon runner
maratoński [mah-rah-**toń**-skee] adj.m. Marathon (runner, race, etc.)
marazm [**mah**-rahzm] m. torpor; sluggishness; stagnation; marasmus
marblit [**mahr**-bleet] m. opaque glass tile
marblitowy [mahr-blee-**to**-vi] adj.m. of opaque glass tile
marcato [mahr-**kah**-to] n. (Italian) accentuated part of a musical piece
marcepan [mahr-**tse**-pahn] m. marzipan; marchpane
marcepanowy [mahr-tse-pah-**no**-vi] adj.m. marzipan (confection, etc.); marchpane (paste, etc.)
marchew [**mahr**-khef] f. carrot
marchewka [mahr-**khef**-kah] f.

carrot
marchewnik [mahr-**khev**-ńeek] m. carrot leaves; (sweet) cicely
marchewnik anyżowy [mahr-**khev**-ńeek ah-ni-**zho**-vi] exp.: sweet cicely
marchia [**mahr**-khyah] f. margraviate
marchion [**mahr**-khyon] m. margrave
marchwianka [mahr-**khfyahn**-kah] f. carrot soup
marchwiany [mahr-**khfyah**-ni] adj.m. of a carrot; carrot (leaves, etc.)
marchwica [mahr-**khfee**-tsah] f. baldmoney (plant)
marchwisko [mahr-**khfees**-ko] n. carrot field
marcinek [mahr-**ćhee**-nek] m. colloq: variety of flowering shrubs
marcować [mahr-**tso**-vahćh] v. be in heat (cats) (*repeatedly*)
marcowanie [mahr-tso-**vah**-ńe] n. (sexual) heat (of cats)
marcowy [mahr-**tso**-vi] adj.m. March (weather, beer, etc.)
marczak [**mahr**-chahk] m. March hare
marek [**mah**-rek] m. water parsnip
tłuc się jak Marek po piekle [twoots śh<u>an</u> yahk **mah**-rek po **pyek**-le] exp.: colloq: to make a hell of a noise
marena [mah-**re**-nah] f. variety of salmon
marengo [mah-**ren**-go] n. pepper-and-salt cloth; adj. pepper-and-salt (color, etc.)
mareograf [mah-re-**o**-grahf] m. marigraph; tide gauge
margać [**mahr**-gahćh] v. colloq: complain (*repeatedly*)
margnąć [**mahr**-gn<u>own</u>ćh] v. colloq: complain
margaryna [mahr-gah-**ri**-nah] f. margarine; colloq: marge
margarynownia [mahr-gah-ri-**nov**-ńah] f. margarine factory
margarynowy [mahr-gah-ri-**no**-vi] adj.m. margarine (serving, etc.); margaric (acid, etc.)
margerytka [mahr-ge-**rit**-kah] f. daisy
margiel [**mahr**-gel] m. marl
marginalia [mah-gee-**nah**-lyah] pl. marginal notes; things of secondary importance; minor things
marginalizm [mahr-gee-**nah**-leezm] m. political economy using marginal analysis
marginalnie [mahr-gee-**nahl**-ńe] adv. marginally
marginalność [mahr-gee-**nahl**-nośhćh] f. marginality
marginalny [mahr-gee-**nahl**-ni] adj.m. marginal; of secondary importance; of minor importance
margines [mahr-**gee**-nes] m. margin; edge; border; (minor, incidental, secondary) thing
uwaga na marginesie [oo-**vah**-gah nah mahr-gee-**ne**-śhe] exp.: side-note
być na marginesie [bićh nah mahr-gee-**ne**-śhe] exp.: to play a secondary role; to remain in the background
marginesowo [mahr-gee-ne-**so**-vo] adv. marginally; casually; parenthetically; incidentally
marginesowość [mahr-gee-ne-**so**-vośhćh] f. marginality; secondary importance; minor importance
marginesowy [mahr-gee-ne-**so**-vi] adj.m. marginal; of secondary importance; of minor importance; casual; parenthetic; incidental
marglisty [mahr-**glees**-ti] adj.m. marly (soil)
marglować [mahr-**glo**-vahćh] v. marl (the soil) (*repeatedly*)
marglowanie [mahr-glo-**vah**-ńe] n. marling (of the soil)
marglowaty [mahr-glo-**vah**-ti] adj.m. marly
marglowy [mahr-**glo**-vi] adj.m. marlaceous
margrabia [mahr-**grah**-byah] m. margrave
margrabina [mahr-grah-**bee**-nah] f. margravine
margrabiowski [mahr-grah-**byof**-skee] adj.m. margrave's; margravial
margrabstwo [mahr-**grahp**-stfo] n. margraviate
margraf [**mahr**-graf] m. margrave
mariacki [mahr-**yah**-tskee] adj.m. of St. Mary; St. Mary's
marianin [mahr-**yah**-ńeen] m. Marian

monk
mariański [mahr-**yahń**-skee] adj.m. Marian (order, etc.)
mariasz [**mahr**-yahsh] m. card game; king and queen of the same color; marriage; matrimony see: **mariaż**
mariawicki [mahr-yah-**vee**-tskee] adj.m. of a religious sect created in Poland in the 19th century
mariawita [mahr-yah-**vee**-tah] m. member of a religious sect (in Poland)
mariawitka [mahr-yah-**vee**-tkah] f. (female) member of a religious sect (in Poland)
mariawityzm [mahr-yah-**vee**-tizm] m. religious sect created in Poland in the 19th century
mariaż [**mahr**-yahsh] m. marriage; matrimony
marihuana [mah-ree-**khwah**-nah] f. marihuana; marijuana; variety of hashish
marina [mah-**ree**-nah] f. seascape
marines [mah-**ree**-nes] pl. (U.S.) marines
marinizm [mah-**ree**-ńeezm] m. Marinism
marionetka [mah-ryo-**net**-kah] f. puppet; dummy; figurehead
marionetkarz [mah-ryo-**net**-kahsh] m. puppet show operator
marionetkowy [mah-ryo-net-**ko**-vi] adj.m. puppet (show, state, government, ruler, stage, etc.); marionette (stage, etc.)
marka [**mahr**-kah] f. mark; German monetary unit; brand; trade mark; reputation; name (good, bad); colloq: check (number); counter (token); (postal, etc.) stamp
mieć dobrą markę [myećh **do**-brown **mahr**-kan] exp.: to enjoy a good reputation; to be in high repute
markasyt [mahr-**kah**-sit] m. (mineral) marcasite
markazyt [mahr-**kah**-zit] m. (mineral) marcasite
marketing [mahr-**ke**-teeng] m. marketing
marketingowy [mahr-ke-teen-**go**-vi] adj.m. of marketing
markier [**mahr**-ker] m. marker; scorer; tally-keeper; scorekeeper
markieranctwo [mahr-ke-**rahn**-tstfo] n. evading duty; neglecting work; shirking; pretending to work
markierant [mahr-**ke**-rahnt] m. shirker; lazybones; slacker
markierować [mahr-ke-**ro**-vahćh] v. evade duty; neglect work; shirk; pretend to work; be lazy (*repeatedly*)
markietan [mahr-**ke**-tahn] m. sutler; camp follower
markietanka [mahr-ke-**tahn**-kah] f. (female) sutler; camp follower
markietański [mahr-ke-**tahń**-skee] adj.m. sutler's (stores, etc.)
markietaństwo [mahr-ke-**tahń**-stfo] n. sutler's occupation
markieteria [mahr-ke-**te**-ryah] f. sutler's occupation
markietaż [mahr-**ke**-tahsh] m. marquetry; inlaid work
markiz [**mahr**-kees] m. marquis
markiza [mahr-**kee**-zah] f. marchioness; awning; marquee
markizeta [mahr-kee-**ze**-tah] f. marquisette
markizetowy [mahr-kee-ze-**to**-vi] adj.m. marquizette (curtain, etc.)
markizowy [mahr-kee-**zo**-vi] adj.m. of a marquee
markocenie [mahr-ko-**tse**-ńe] n. being gloomy; being sullen; being moody; being morose
markocenie się [mahr-ko-**tse**-ńe śhan] n. being gloomy; being sullen (with somebody); being moody; being morose
markocić [mahr-**ko**-ćheećh] v. be gloomy; be sullen; be moody; be morose (*repeatedly*)
markocić się [mahr-**ko**-ćheećh śhan] v. be gloomy; be sullen (with somebody); be moody; be morose (*repeatedly*)
markotnie [mahr-**kot**-ńe] adv. sadly; in low spirits; in bad humor; gloomily; sullenly; moodily, see: **markotno**
markotnieć [mahr-**kot**-ńećh] v. become gloomy; grow sullen; grow moody (*repeatedly*)
markotnienie [mahr-kot-**ńe**-ńe] n.

becoming gloomy; growing sullen; growing moody
markotno [mahr-**kot**-no] adv. sadly; in low spirits; in bad humor; gloomily; sullenly; moodily
markotność [mahr-**kot**-nośhćh] f. sadness; low spirits; bad humor; gloomy mood; sullen mood; moroseness
markotny [mahr-**kot**-ni] adj.m. peevish; moody; sullen; sad
markować [mahr-**ko**-vahćh] v. work (read, etc.) without stopping; mark; pretend; make believe; feign (illness, etc.); sham (sleep, etc.) (*repeatedly*)
markowanie [mahr-ko-**vah**-ńe] n. working (reading, etc.) without stopping; marking; pretending
markownia [mahr-**kov**-ńah] f. room with a diagram of work stations
markowy [mahr-**ko**-vi] adj.m. brand-name (product, etc.)
marksista [mahr-**kśhees**-tah] m. Marxist
marksistowski [mahr-kśhee-**stof**-skee] adj.m. Marxist (socialist or communist)
po marksistowsku [po mahr-kśhee-**stof**-skoo] exp.: according to Marxism
marksistowsko-leninowski [mahr-kśhee-**stof**-sko le-ńee-**nof**-skee] adj.m. Marxist-Leninist (ideology, etc.)
marksistowsko [mahr-kśhee-**stof**-sko] adv. like a Marxist; according to Marxism
marksizm [**mahr**-kśheezm] m. Marxism; Marxist beliefs
marksizm-leninizm [**mahr**-kśheezm le-**ńee**-ńeezm] m. Marxism-Leninism; Marxist-Leninist beliefs
marksizować [mahr-kśhee-**zo**-vahćh] v. become a fellow-traveller of Marxism (*repeatedly*)
marksowski [mahr-**ksof**-skee] adj.m. Marxian (socialist or communist)
markur [**mahr**-koor] m. wild goat (of India and Afghanistan)
marla [**mahr**-lah] f. half-cotton and half-silk fabric net
marlin [**mahr**-leen] m. marlin (fish)
marlinka [mahr-**leen**-kah] f. marline (line)
marlować [mahr-**lo**-vahćh] v. tie a marline line of a sail (*repeatedly*)
marmit [**mahr**-meet] m. cylindrical erosion of marmit shape
marmelada [mahr-me-**lah**-dah] f. marmalade; jam; slang: shambles; butchery (mob jargon)
marmeladka [mahr-me-**laht**-kah] f. jelly sweet
marmeladkowy [mahr-me-laht-**ko**-vi] adj.m. of marmalade; marmalade (cake, etc.)
marmeladowy [mahr-me-lah-**do**-vi] adj.m. of marmalade; marmalade (cake, etc.)
marmolada [mahr-mo-**lah**-dah] f. marmalade; jam; slang: shambles; butchery (mob jargon)
marmoladka [mahr-mo-**laht**-kah] f. jelly sweet
marmoladkowy [mahr-mo-laht-**ko**-vi] adj.m. of marmalade; marmalade (cake, etc.)
marmoladowy [mahr-mo-lah-**do**-vi] adj.m. of marmalade; marmalade (cake, etc.)
marmoryzacja [mahr-mo-ri-**zah**-tsyah] f. marbleizing; marbling
marmoryzować [mahr-mo-ri-**zo**-vahćh] v. marbleize; marble (*repeatedly*)
marmoryzowanie [mahr-mo-ri-zo-**vah**-ńe] n. marbleizing; marbling
marmur [**mahr**-moor] m. marble (rock, statue, slab, etc.)
marmurek [mahr-**moo**-rek] m. (small, nice) marble (rock, statue, slab, etc.)
marmurkować [mahr-moor-**ko**-vahćh] v. marbleize; marble (*repeatedly*)
marmurkowanie [mahr-moor-ko-**vah**-ńe] n. marbleizing; marbling
marmurkowaty [mahr-moor-ko-**vah**-ti] adj.m. marbled; veined
marmurkowy [mahr-moor-**ko**-vi] adj.m. marbled; veined (paper, etc.)
marmurołom [mahr-moo-**ro**-wom] m. marble quarry
marmurowo [mahr-moo-**ro**-vo] adv. like marble
marmurowy [mahr-moo-**ro**-vi] adj.m.

marble (statue, etc.)
marnie [mahr-ńe] adv. badly; miserably; poorly; indifferently
marnie wyglądać [mahr-ńe vi-glown-dahćh] exp.: to look miserable; to look sick; to look under the weather; to look out of sorts; to look ill; to be in bad condition
skończyć marnie [skoń-chićh mahr-ńe] exp.: to end badly; to end miserably; to come to a bad end; to come to a pitiful end; to end in a disaster; to end in miserable conditions
marnieć [mahr-ńećh] v. deteriorate; waste (away); be wasted; decline; decay; perish; wilt; languish; fade; droop; pine (*repeatedly*)
marnienie [mahr-ńe-ńe] n. deterioration; decay; decline
marniutki [mahr-ńoot-kee] adj.m. (poor, little) worthless (thing, etc.)
marność [mahr-nośhćh] f. futility; flimsiness; wretchedness; uselessness; vanity
marnota [mahr-no-tah] f. poor stuff; something worthless, flimsy, trivial, indifferent
marnotrawca [mahr-no-trahf-tsah] m. spendthrift; wastrel; squanderer
marnotrawić [mahr-no-trah-veećh] v. waste; squander (*repeatedly*)
marnotrawić się [mahr-no-trah-veećh śhan] v. be wasted; be squandered (*repeatedly*)
marnotrawienie [mahr-no-trah-vye-ńe] n. waste; thriftlessness
marnotrawienie się [mahr-no-trah-vye-ńe śhan] n. wasting oneself; squandering one's talents
marnotrawnie [mahr-no-trahv-ńe] adv. wastefully; prodigally; thriftlessly
marnotrawny [mahr-no-trahv-ni] adj.m. wasteful; prodigal
syn marnotrawny [sin mahr-no-trahv-ni] exp.: prodigal son
marnotrawstwo [mahr-no-trahf-stfo] n. prodigality; waste; thriftlessness
marnować [mahr-no-vahćh] v. waste; run to waste; squander; trifle away; fritter away; dissipate; spoil (an opportunity, etc.); make a mess; dawdle away (*repeatedly*)
marnować się [mahr-no-vahćh śhan] v. be wasted; go to waste; be squandered; be dissipated; be useless; bring no profit (*repeatedly*)
marnowanie [mahr-no-vah-ńe] n. waste
marnowanie się [mahr-no-vah-ńe śhan] n. being wasted
marny [mahr-ni] adj.m. poor; meager; sorry; of no value; worthless; trivial; indifferent; mean; miserable; wretched; vain; futile; useless
wszystko poszło na marne [fshist-ko posh-wo nah mahr-ne] exp.: it all dissolved into thin air; it all was wasted; it was all in vain; it all came to nothing
Marokanka [mah-ro-kahn-kah] f. Moroccan (female)
Marokańczyk [mah-ro-kahń-chik] m. Moroccan
marokański [mah-ro-kahń-skee] adj.m. of Morocco (leather, etc.); Moroccan
maron [mah-ron] m. edible chestnut
maronita [mah-ro-ńee-tah] m. Maronite
marowaty [mah-ro-vah-ti] adj.m. of the Caviidae family
marowate [mah-ro-vah-te] pl. the Caviidae family
mars [mahrs] m. Mars (planet); observation point on warships; (sailing:) top; crow's nest (observation point); frown
robić marsa [ro-beećh mahr-sah] exp.: to frown; to knit one's brow
marsala [mahr-sah-lah] f. Marsala (wine)
marsel [mahr-sel] m. (square) topsail
marski [mahr-skee] adj.m. cirrhotic
marskość [mahr-skośhćh] f. cirrhosis
marsowatość [mahr-so-vah-tośhćh] f. sternness

marsowaty [mahr-so-**vah**-ti] adj.m. stern
marsowo [mahr-**so**-vo] adv. sternly; grimly; severely
marsowość [mahr-**so**-vośhćh] f. sternness; grimness; severity
marsowy [mahr-**so**-vi] adj.m. martial; stern; grim; severe
marspikiel [mahr-**spee**-kel] m. a tool for making steel lines
marsreja [mahrs-**re**-yah] f. upper boom (in sailing)
marsylia [mahr-**sil**-yah] f. marsilea fern; the clover fern
Marsylianka [mahr-sil-**yahn**-kah] f. Marseillaise
marsyliowaty [mahr-sil-yo-**vah**-ti] adj.m. marsileaceous (fern)
marsyliowate [mahr-sil-yo-**vah**-te] pl. the family Marsileaceae of ferns
marsylski [mahr-**sil**-skee] adj.m. of Marseilles; Marseilles (soap, etc.)
marsz [mahrsh] m. march; walk; advance; progress; geogr.: salt marsh
marsz! [mahrsh] excl.: (command) forward march!; split!; get out!; off you go!; out!; double!
marsz weselny [mahrsh ve-**sel**-ni] exp.: wedding march
marszałek [mahr-**shah**-wek] m. marshal; Polish Seym (house of representatives) speaker
marszałkostwo [mahr-shahw-**kos**-tfo] n. the office (rank) of a marshal
marszałkowa [mahr-shahw-**ko**-vah] f. marshal's wife
marszałkować [mahr-shahw-**ko**-vahćh] v. preside (*repeatedly*)
marszałkowanie [mahr-shahw-ko-**vah**-ńe] n. presiding
marszałkowski [mahr-shahw-**kof**-skee] adj.m. marshal's (rank, office, etc.)
marszand [**mahr**-shahnt] m. merchant
marszczenie [mahr-**shche**-ńe] n. wrinkling; frowning; creases; folds; plaits
marszczenie brwi [mahr-**shche**-ńe brvee] exp.: frowning
marszcznica [mahr-**shchńee**-tsah] f. a Mediterranean seaweed
marszczyć [**mahr**-shchićh] v. wrinkle; frown; crease; gather in folds; ripple; crimp; ruffle (a lake surface, etc.) (*repeatedly*)
marszczyć brwi [**mahr**-shchićh brvee] exp.: to knit one's brows
marszczyć się [**mahr**-shchićh śhan] v. wrinkle; become wrinkled; frown (upon) (*repeatedly*)
marszobieg [mahr-**sho**-byeg] m. alternate marching and jogging; marching and jogging exercise
marszowy [mahr-**sho**-vi] adj.m. marching (orders, etc.)
szyk marszowy [shik mahr-**sho**-vi] exp.: marching order; order of march
marszruta [mahr-**shroo**-tah] f. route; itinerary; a record of a journey
marszrutowy [mahr-shroo-**to**-vi] adj.m. of a route; itinerary (schedule, etc.); of a record of a journey
marten [**mahr**-ten] m. colloq: open-hearth furnace
martenowski [mahr-te-**nof**-skee] adj.m. open-hearth (furnace, steel, etc.)
martwak [**mahrt**-fahk] m. sequestrum
martwica [mahrt-**fee**-tsah] f. necrosis; sinter; travertine; wool from dead sheep
martwica kości [mahrt-**fee**-tsah **kośh**-ćhee] exp.: necrosed bone
martwica wapienna [mahrt-**fee**-tsah vah-**pyen**-nah] exp.: calcareous sinter; tufa
martwicowy [mahrt-fee-**tso**-vi] adj.m. necrotic
martwiczy [mahrt-**fee**-chi] adj.m. necrotic
martwić [**mahrt**-feećh] v. distress; grieve; vex; worry; sadden; afflict; (cause) trouble; (cause) sorrow; (cause) pain; annoy (*repeatedly*)
martwić się [**mahrt**-feećh śhan] v. worry; be cut up (about); grieve; be grieved; trouble oneself (about); be uneasy (about); fret (about); bother (about); be sorry (about); mortify oneself

(*repeatedly*)
martwieć [mahrt-fyećh] v. grow numb; deaden; undergo necrobiosis (*repeatedly*)
martwienie [mahrt-**fye**-ńe] n. worry; cares; troubles (see: **martwić**); growing numb; necrobiosis (see: **martwieć**)
martwo [**mahrt**-fo] adv. deadly; lifelessly
leżeć martwo [le-zhećh **mahrt**-fo] exp.: to lie lifeless
martwość [mahr-tfośhćh] f. lifelessness; torpor; deadness; inertia; numbness; stiffness
martwota [mahrt-**fo**-tah] f. lifelessness; torpor; deadness; inertia; numbness; stiffness
martwy [**mahrt**-fi] adj.m. dead; lifeless; inanimate; stagnant (economy, etc.); dormant (capital, etc.); m. deceased
martwa cisza [**mahrt**-fah **ćhee**-shah] exp.: dead silence; dead calm (at sea)
martwa litera [**mahrt**-fah lee-**te**-rah] exp.: dead letter
martwa natura [**mahrt**-fah nah-**too**-rah] exp.: still life
martwe ciało [**mahrt**-fe **ćhah**-wo] exp.: dead body
martwy głos [**mahrt**-fi gwos] exp.: dull voice
martwy punkt [**mahrt**-fi poonkt] exp.: deadlock; standstill; a tie score
martwy sezon [**mahrt**-fi **se**-zon] exp.: slack season
wskrzesić z martwych [fskshe-śheećh z **mahrt**-fikh] exp.: to rise from the dead
martyrolog [mahr-ti-**ro**-log] m. martyrologist
martyrologia [mahr-ti-ro-**lo**-gyah] f. martyrology; martyrdom
martyrologiczny [mahr-ti-ro-lo-**geech**-ni] adj.m. of martyrology; of martyrdom
martyrologium [mahr-ti-ro-**lo**-gyoom] n. martyrology; martyrdom; passional
marucha [mah-**roo**-khah] m. colloq: bear
maruda [mah-**roo**-dah] f. and m. dawdler; laggard; slow coach; loss of time
maruder [mah-**roo**-der] m. marauder; straggler; loiterer; dawdler; laggard; slow coach; slacker
maruderski [mah-roo-**der**-skee] adj.m. marauder's; marauders'
maruderstwo [mah-roo-**der**-stfo] n. marauding; dawdling; band of marauders
marudnie [mah-**rood**-ńe] adv. toilsomely; tediously; slothfully; lazily
marudny [mah-**rood**-ni] adj.m. toilsome; hard; tough; tedious; slothful; lazy; indolent; peevish; fretful; querulous
marudzenie [mah-roo-**dze**-ńe] n. dawdling
marudzić [mah-**roo**-dźheećh] v. loiter; grumble; lag behind; dally; linger; be tedious; be peevish; be fretful; find fault (*repeatedly*)
maruna [mah-**roo**-nah] f. pyrethrum; chrysanthemum
mary [**mah**-ri] pl. bier; a coffin together with its stand
maryjny [mah-**riy**-ni] adj.m. devoted to the cult of the Virgin Mary
marynaciarnia [mah-ri-nah-**ćhahr**-ńah] f. pickling plant
marynarczyna [mah-ri-nahr-**chi**-nah] f. (worn-out) jacket; sports coat
marynareczka [mah-ri-nah-**rech**-kah] f. (nice, little) jacket; sports coat
marynarka [mah-ri-**nahr**-kah] f. jacket; sports coat; navy; naval forces; merchant marine
marynarkowy [mah-ri-nahr-**ko**-vi] adj.m. of a jacket; of a sports coat
marynarski [mah-ri-**nahr**-skee] adj.m. sailor's; naval; of navigation
marynarz [mah-**ri**-nahsh] m. mariner; sailor; seaman
marynata [mah-ri-**nah**-tah] f. pickle; marinade; souse
marynista [mah-ri-**ńees**-tah] m. marine painter; seascapist; marine writer
marynistyczny [mah-ri-ńees-**tich**-ni] adj.m. marine (paintings, exhibit, etc.)
marynistyka [mah-ri-**ńees**-ti-kah] f.

seascape painting
marynizm [mah-ri-ńeezm] m. art work depicting the sea
marynować [mah-ri-**no**-vahćh] v. pickle; marinade; slang: sidetrack; keep sidetracked (mob jargon) (*repeatedly*)
marynować się [mah-ri-**no**-vahćh śhan] v. be in a pickle; slang: be sidetracked; be wasted (mob jargon) (*repeatedly*)
marynowanie [mah-ri-no-**vah**-ńe] n. pickling
marynowany [mah-ri-no-**vah**-ni] adj.m. pickled
marzanka [mah-**zhahn**-kah] f. squinancy; sweet woodruff
marzanna [mah-**zhahn**-nah] f. madder
marzanowaty [mah-zhah-no-**vah**-ti] adj.m. rubiaceous; of the madder family
marzanowate [mah-zhah-no-**vah**-te] pl. the madder family
marząco [mah-**zh**own-tso] adv. dreamily
marzący [mah-**zh**own-tsi] adj.m. (one who is) dreaming
marzec [**mah**-zhets] m. March
marzenie [mah-**zhe**-ńe] n. dream; reverie; daydream; pensiveness; daydreaming
oddawać się marzeniom [od-**dah**-vahćh śhan mah-**zhe**-ńom] exp.: to muse; to be lost in reverie
marzenie ściętej głowy [mah-**zhe**-ńe śhćhan-tey **gwo**-vi] exp.: an impossibility
szczyt marzeń [shchit **mah**-zheń] exp.: the climax of one's dreams
marzłoć [**mahr**-zwoćh] f. permafrost
marznąć [**mahr**-znownćh] v. be frozen; freeze; freeze to death (*repeatedly*)
marznięcie [mahr-**zń**an-ćhe] n. freezing
marzyca [mah-**zhi**-tsah] f. the genus Schoenus of sedges
marzyciel [mah-**zhi**-ćhel] m. dreamer; fantast; visionary
marzycielka [mah-zhi-**ćhel**-kah] f. (female) dreamer; fantast; visionary
marzycielski [mah-zhi-**ćhel**-skee] adj.m. dreamy; fanciful; visionary
marzycielsko [mah-zhi-**ćhel**-sko] adv. dreamily
marzycielskość [mah-zhi-**ćhel**-skośhćh] f. dreamy disposition; inclination to daydreaming
marzycielstwo [mah-zhi-**ćhel**-stfo] n. daydreaming
marzyć [**mah**-zhićh] v. dream (*repeatedly*)
szkoda marzyć [**shko**-dah **mah**-zhićh] exp.: it is out of the question; it is not feasible
marzyć się [**mah**-zhićh śhan] v. appear in one's dreams; occupy the thoughts; attract the imagination (*repeatedly*)
marzymięta [mah-zhi-**my**an-tah] f. the genus Elsholtzia of herbs
marża [**mahr**-zhah] f. margin of profit; markup
marżowy [mahr-**zho**-vi] adj.m. of profit margin; markup (size, etc.)
masa [**mah**-sah] f. bulk; mass; accumulation; great quantities; great deal; great numbers; a lot; lots; a heap; heaps; the generality; pulp; substance; filling
masa atomowa [**mah**-sah ah-to-**mo**-vah] exp.: atomic mass
masa cząsteczkowa [**mah**-sah chown-stech-**ko**-vah] exp.: molecular mass
masa drzewna [**mah**-sah **dzhev**-nah] exp.: wood pulp
masa papiernicza [**mah**-sah pah-pyer-**ńee**-chah] exp.: paper-pulp
masa perłowa [**mah**-sah per-**wo**-vah] exp.: mother of pearl
masa upadłościowa [**mah**-sah oo-pah-dwo-**śhćho**-vah] exp.: bankrupt's estate
masami [mah-**sah**-mee] exp.: in great numbers; in great quantities; in masses
masami przybywać [mah-**sah**-mee pshi-**bi**-vahćh] exp.: to pour in great quantities; to pour in great numbers
masę [**mah**-san] exp.: heaps; a lot
mieć masę do roboty [myećh **mah**-san do ro-**bo**-ti] exp.: to have a lot of work to do; to be

swamped by work
masakra [mah-**sahk**-rah] f. massacre; carnage; wholesale slaughter; butchery
masakrować [mah-sah-**kro**-vahćh] v. massacre; slaughter; butcher; hack; mangle (a text, etc.) (*repeatedly*)
masarka [mah-**sahr**-kah] f. (woman) pork-butcher
masarnia [mah-**sahr**-ńah] f. pork-meat (pork butcher's) shop
masarski [mah-**sahr**-skee] adj.m. pork-butcher's
masarstwo [mah-**sahr**-stfo] n. pork-butcher's business
masarz [**mah**-sahsh] m. pork-butcher; pork meat worker; pork sausage maker
masaż [**mah**-sahsh] m. massage
masażysta [mah-sah-**zhis**-tah] m. masseur; rubber
masażystka [mah-sah-**zhist**-kah] f. masseuse
maseczka [mah-**sech**-kah] f. small mask; masker
maseczka kosmetyczna [mah-**sech**-kah kos-me-**tich**-nah] exp.: beauty mask; face mask
maselnica [mah-sel-**ńee**-tsah] f. butter-churn; big butter-dish
maselniczka [mah-sel-**ńeech**-kah] f. butter-dish; small churn
masełko [mah-**sew**-ko] n. (tasty) butter
maser [**mah**-ser] m. maser; device for generating electromagnetic radiation
maserowy [mah-se-**ro**-vi] adj.m. maser (generation of electromagnetic radiation, etc.)
maset [**mah**-set] m. butcher's knife sharpening device
masielnica [mah-śhel-**ńee**-tsah] f. butter-churn; big butter-dish
masielniczka [mah-śhel-**ńeech**-kah] f. butter-dish; small churn
maska [**mahs**-kah] f. mask; masker; face-guard; (car) hood; screen; vizard; disguise
pod maską [pod **mahs**-kown] exp.: under the guise (of); under the cover; under the mask
zedrzeć maskę [ze-dzhećh **mahs**-kan] exp.: to unmask
maska gazowa [**mahs**-kah gah-**zo**-vah] exp.: gas mask
maskarada [mahs-kah-**rah**-dah] f. masquerade
maskaradowo [mahs-kah-rah-**do**-vo] adv. as if masquerading
maskaradowy [mahs-kah-rah-**do**-vi] adj.m. of a masquerade
maskaron [mahs-**kah**-ron] m. mascaron; see: = **maszkaron**
maskonur [mahs-**ko**-noor] m. arctic puffin; Fratrecula arctica
maskota [mahs-**ko**-tah] f. mascot, charm; (somebody's) good luck charm
maskotka [mahs-**kot**-kah] f. (nice, little) mascot; charm
maskować [mahs-**ko**-vahćh] v. disguise; mask; conceal; screen; hide; camouflage; veil; cloak; dissemble (*repeatedly*)
maskować się [mahs-**ko**-vahćh śhan] v. disguise oneself; mask oneself; conceal (one's intentions, feelings, etc.); pretend; hide oneself; dissemble; put on a mask; wear a mask (*repeatedly*)
maskowanie [mahs-ko-**vah**-ńe] n. concealment; pretence
maskowanie się [mahs-ko-**vah**-ńe śhan] n. masking oneself
maskowatość [mahs-ko-**vah**-tośhćh] f. mask-like quality (of expression, etc.)
maskowaty [mahs-ko-**vah**-ti] adj.m. mask-like
maskownica [mahs-kov-**ńee**-tsah] f. printing-mask
maskowniczy [mahs-kov-**ńee**-chi] adj.m. masking (supplies, etc.)
maskowy [mahs-**ko**-vi] adj.m. of a mask
bal maskowy [bahl mahs-**ko**-vi] exp.: masked ball; fancy dress ball; masquerade
maskulinizacja [mah-skoo-lee-ńee-**zah**-tsyah] f. giving masculine characteristics; masculinization
maskulinizm [mah-skoo-**lee**-ńeezm] m. masculineness; masculinity
maskulinizować [mah-skoo-lee-ńee-**zo**-vahćh] v. masculinize (*repeatedly*)

maskulinizować się [mah-skoo-lee-ńee-**zo**-vahćh śhan] v. become masculinized; become masculine (*repeatedly*)
maskulinizowanie [mah-skoo-lee-ńee-zo-**vah**-ńe] n. acquiring masculinity
maskulinizowanie się [mah-skoo-lee-ńee-zo-**vah**-ńe śhan] n. becoming masculine
masło [**mahs**-wo] n. butter
masło maślane [**mahs**-wo mahśh-**lah**-ne] exp.: tautology; pleonasm
masłosz [**mahs**-wosh] m. shea (tree)
masłowaty [mah-swo-**vah**-ti] adj.m. buttery
masłownia [mah-**swov**-ńah] f. butter producing dairy department
masłowy [mah-**swo**-vi] adj.m. butyric (acid, etc.)
masochista [mah-so-**khees**-tah] m. masochist; one who finds pleasure in being abused by a love object
masochistycznie [mah-so-khees-**tich**-ńe] adv. masochistically
masochistyczny [mah-so-khees-**tich**-ni] adj.m. masochistic
masochizm [mah-**so**-kheezm] m. masochism
mason [**mah**-son] m. freemason
masoneria [mah-so-**ne**-ryah] f. freemasonry
masonka [mah-**son**-kah] f. (woman) freemason
masoński [mah-**soń**-skee] adj.m. masonic; freemason's
masować [mah-**so**-vahćh] v. give a massage; massage; rub (*repeatedly*)
masować się [mah-**so**-vahćh śhan] v. take a massage (*repeatedly*)
masowanie [mah-so-**vah**-ńe] n. massage
masowanie się [mah-so-**vah**-ńe śhan] n. massaging oneself
masowiec [mah-**so**-vyets] m. ship for bulk transport
masowo [mah-**so**-vo] adv. wholesale; in a mass; in masses; in great numbers (quantities); in the thousands, etc.
produkować masowo [pro-doo-**ko**-vahćh mah-**so**-vo] exp.: to mass-produce
masowość [mah-**so**-vośhćh] f. large scale character (of riots, etc.)
masowy [mah-**so**-vi] adj.m. of mass; mass; made of plastic; wholesale
produkcja masowa [pro-**dook**-tsyah mah-**so**-vah] exp.: mass production
masówka [mah-**soof**-kah] f. mass meeting
mass media [mahs **me**-dyah] pl. mass media (Engl. borrowing)
mastaba [mahs-**tah**-bah] f. mastaba
master [**mahs**-ter] m. master (of fox chase, etc.)
mastodont [mahs-**to**-dont] m. mastodon; mammoth structure
mastologia [mahs-to-**lo**-gyah] f. mammalogy
masturbacja [mahs-toor-**bah**-tsyah] f. masturbation; erotic self-stimulation
mastyf [**mahs**-tif] m. mastiff
mastyka [**mahs**-ti-kah] f. wood filler
mastyks [**mahs**-tiks] m. mastic; gum mastic
mastyksowy [mahs-tik-**so**-vi] adj.m. mastic (gum, etc.)
maswerk [**mahs**-verk] m. tracery
masykot [mah-**si**-kot] m. massicot
masyw [**mah**-sif] m. massif; solid mass; pile; edifice
masywnie [mah-**siv**-ńe] adv. massively; solidly
masywność [mah-**siv**-nośhćh] f. massiveness; solidity
masywny [mah-**siv**-ni] adj.m. massive; solid; bulky; massy; lumpish; thickset
maszcik [**mahsh**-ćheek] m. small mast
maszczenie [mahsh-**che**-ńe] n. lubrication; oiling; adding gravy
maszerować [mah-she-**ro**-vahćh] v. march; march on; keep marching; advance steadily (*repeatedly*)
maszerowanie [mah-she-ro-**vah**-ńe] n. a march; marches
maszkara [mahsh-**kah**-rah] f. monster; scarecrow; eyesore
maszkaron [mahsh-**kah**-ron] m. mask; mascaron

maszop [**mah**-shop] m. member of fisherman's guild
maszoperia [mah-sho-**pe**-ryah] f. fisherman's guild; fishing cooperative
maszopski [mah-**shop**-skee] adj.m. fisherman's guild (member, etc.)
maszt [mahsht] m. mast; pole; flagstaff
masztalerski [mahsh-tah-**ler**-skee] adj.m. stableman's; groom's
masztalerstwo [mahsh-tah-**ler**-stfo] n. stableman's work; groom's work
masztalerz [mahsh-**tah**-lesh] m. stableman; groom
masztowiec [mahsh-**to**-vyets] m. sailing ship
masztowina [mahsh-to-**vee**-nah] f. mast wood; masts
masztowy [mahsh-**to**-vi] adj.m. of a mast
masztówka [mahsh-**toof**-kah] f. mast support
maszyna [mah-**shi**-nah] f. machine; engine; automaton
maszyna do pisania [mah-**shi**-nah do pee-**sah**-ńah] exp.: typewriter
maszyna do szycia [mah-**shi**-nah do **shi**-ćhah] exp.: sewing machine
maszyna parowa [mah-**shi**-nah pah-**ro**-vah] exp.: steam-engine
pisać na maszynie [pee-sahćh nah mah-**shi**-ńe] exp.: to typewrite; to type
maszyneria [mah-shi-**ne**-ryah] f. machinery; mechanism
maszynista [mah-shi-**ńees**-tah] m. railroad engineer; machinist; tender; stagehand
maszynistka [mah-shi-**ńees**-tkah] f. one who typewrites; typist
maszynka [mah-**shin**-kah] f. device
maszynka do golenia [mah-**shin**-kah do go-**le**-ńah] exp.: safety razor; shaver
maszynka do mięsa [mah-**shin**-kah do **myan**-sah] exp.: mincing-machine
maszynka do strzyżenia [mah-**shin**-kah do stshi-**zhe**-ńah] exp.: clipper
maszynkarz [mah-**shin**-kahsh] m. linotypist
maszynogodzina [mah-shi-no-go-**dźhee**-nah] f. machine-hour
maszynopis [mah-shi-**no**-pees] m. typescript; typewritten copy
maszynownia [mah-shi-**nov**-ńah] f. engine room
maszynowo [mah-shi-**no**-vo] adv. by machine; by machinery
wykonany maszynowo [vi-ko-**nah**-ni mah-shi-**no**-vo] exp.: machine-made
maszynowy [mah-shi-**no**-vi] adj.m. machine (parts, room, etc.); mechanical; automatic; machine-made; typewriter (paper, brush, ribbon, etc.)
karabin maszynowy [kah-**rah**-been mah-shi-**no**-vi] exp.: machine gun; rapid firing automatic gun
papier maszynowy [**pah**-pyer mah-shi-**no**-vi] exp.: typewriter paper; computer paper
maszynoznawstwo [mah-shi-no-**znahf**-stfo] n. science of mechanization; machine-design and building
maścić [**mahśh**-ćheećh] v. oil; grease; butter; put gravy (on a dish); slang: abuse; revile; rail (mob jargon) (*repeatedly*)
maściowy [mahśh-**ćho**-vi] adj.m. ointment (content, color, etc.); of horse color
maść [mahśhćh] f. ointment; horse color; unguent; salve
maślacz [**mah**-śhlahch] m. a specie of edible fungus; type of Hungarian wine
maślak [**mah**-śhlahk] m. a specie of edible fungus
maślanka [mah-**śhlahn**-kah] f. buttermilk; sour liquid (a product of churning butter)
maślany [mah-**śhlah**-ni] adj.m. buttered; buttery; cooked in butter
maślarnia [mah-**śhlahr**-ńah] f. butter-making shop
maślarski [mah-**śhlahr**-skee] adj.m. butter (making, etc.)
maślnica [mahśhl-**ńee**-tsah] f. butter-dish; churn
mat [maht] m. flat color; mat

surface; lusterless color; checkmating (one's opponent); deck noncommissioned officer of the lowest rank; mate
dać mata [dahćh **mah**-tah] exp.: to checkmate
mata [**mah**-tah] f. mat; matting
matacki [mah-**tah**-tskee] adj.m. fraudulent; deceiving; deceptive
matactwo [mah-**tah**-tstfo] n. legal trickery; fraudulence; deceit; subterfuge; deception; stratagem; fraud; hoax; swindle; humbug; scheming; machination
matacz [**mah**-tahch] m. schemer; machinator; prevaricator; humbug
mataczyć [mah-**tah**-chićh] v. colloq: scheme; cheat (*repeatedly*)
matador [mah-**tah**-dor] m. matador; bull fighter; slang: bigwig; big gun; VIP (mob jargon)
matczyn [**maht**-chin] adj.m. maternal (love etc.); mother's
matczyny [maht-**chi**-ni] adj.m. maternal (love etc.); mother's
po matczynemu [po maht-chi-**ne**-moo] exp.: maternally; with motherly love; like a mother
matczysko [maht-**chis**-ko] n. dear old mother
mate [**mah**-te] n. holm oak; holly
mateczka [mah-**tech**-kah] f. dear mummy
matecznik [mah-**tech**-ńeek] m. backwoods; lair; den; hiding-place; queen bee's cell; plant nursery
mateczny [mah-**tech**-ni] adj.m. parent (tree, branch, etc.)
matematyczka [mah-te-mah-**tich**-kah] f. (woman) student of mathematics; mathematician
matematycznie [mah-te-mah-**tich**-ńe] adv. mathematically; with mathematical accuracy
matematyczny [mah-te-mah-**tich**-ni] adj.m. mathematical
umysł matematyczny [**oo**-misw mah-te-mah-**tich**-ni] exp.: mathematical turn of mind
matematyczno-fizyczny [mah-te-mah-**tich**-no fee-**zich**-ni] exp.: mathematico-physical
matematyczno-przyrodniczy [mah-te-mah-**tich**-no pshi-rod-**ńee**-chi] exp.: mathematico-scientific
matematyk [mah-te-**mah**-tik] m. mathematician; student of mathematics
matematyka [mah-te-**mah**-ti-kah] f. mathematics; science of numbers, quantities, forms, etc., and their relationships; colloq: math
matematyzacja [mah-te-mah-ti-**zah**-tsyah] f. mathematization; reduction to mathematical form
matematyzować [mah-te-mah-ti-**zo**-vahćh] v. mathematize; reduce to mathematical form; subject to mathematical treatment (*repeatedly*)
matematyzować się [mah-te-mah-ti-**zo**-vahćh śhan] v. use mathematical methods (*repeatedly*)
matematyzowanie [mah-te-mah-ti-zo-**vah**-ńe] n. mathematization
matematyzowanie się [mah-te-mah-ti-zo-**vah**-ńe śhan] n. acquiring mathematical character
mateńka [mah-**teń**-kah] f. dear mother; colloq: mummy
materac [mah-te-rahts] m. mattress
materacowy [mah-te-rah-**tso**-vi] adj.m. mattress (size, etc.)
materacyk [mah-te-**rah**-tsik] m. (small) mattress
materia [mah-**ter**-yah] f. matter; what a thing is made of; stuff; subject; point; puss; cloth; any specified substance; material; fabric
przemiana materii [pshe-**myah**-nah mah-**ter**-yee] exp.: metabolism
w tej materii [f tey mah-**ter**-yee] exp.: on this subject; on this point; in this matter
materialik [mah-ter-**yah**-leek] m. (small, nice) fabric
materialista [mah-ter-yah-**lees**-tah] m. materialist; money grabber
materialistka [mah-ter-yah-**lees**-tkah] f. materialist; woman money grabber
materialistycznie [mah-ter-yah-lee-**stich**-ńe] adv. materialistically
materialistyczny [mah-ter-yah-lee-**stich**-ni] adj.m. materialistic

(opposite to spiritual)
filozofia materialistyczna [fee-lo-**zo**-fyah mah-ter-yah-lee-**stich**-nah] exp.: materialism
materializacja [mah-ter-yah-lee-**zah**-tsyah] f. materialization
materializm [mah-ter-**yah**-leezm] m. materialism
materializm dialektyczny [mah-ter-**yah**-leezm dyah-lek-**tich**-ni] exp.: dialectical materialism
materializować [mah-ter-yah-lee-**zo**-vahćh] v. materialize; substantialize (*repeatedly*)
materializować się [mah-ter-yah-lee-**zo**-vahćh śhan] v. materialize (*repeatedly*)
materializowanie [mah-ter-yah-lee-zo-**vah**-ńe] n. materializing
materializowanie się [mah-ter-yah-lee-zo-**vah**-ńe śhan] n. becoming materialized
materialnie [mah-ter-**yahl**-ńe] adv. materially; corporeally; financially
popierać materialnie [po-**pye**-rahćh mah-ter-**yahl**-ńe] exp.: to give financial support
materialność [mah-ter-**yahl**-nośhćh] f. materiality; corporeality
materialny [mah-ter-**yahl**-ni] adj.m. material; corporeal; physical; substantial; tangible; financial; pecuniary; worldly (possessions); substantive
środki materialne [**śhrot**-kee mah-ter-**yahl**-ne] exp.: material means; material resources; pecuniary resources
dobra materialne [**do**-brah mah-ter-**yahl**-ne] exp.: material goods
obrona materialna [o-**bro**-nah mah-ter-**yahl**-nah] exp.: substantive defense
prawo materialne [**prah**-vo mah-ter-**yahl**-ne] exp.: substantive law
materiał [mah-**ter**-yahw] m. material; substance; stuff; cloth; fabric; assignment
materiał na prezydenta [mah-**ter**-yahw nah pre-zi-**den**-tah] exp.: presidential timber
materiał dowodowy [mah-**ter**-yahw do-vo-**do**-vi] exp.: evidence (in court, etc.)
materiałochłonność [mah-ter-yah-wo-**khwon**-nośhćh] f. the use of materials; consumption of materials
materiałochłonny [mah-ter-yah-wo-**khwon**-ni] adj.m. material-consuming (production, etc.)
materiałooszczędny [mah-ter-yah-wo-osh-**chand**-ni] adj.m. material-saving (method, plan, etc.)
materiałowo [mah-ter-yah-**wo**-vo] adv. as regards material; in respect of material
materiałowy [mah-ter-yah-**wo**-vi] adj.m. of materials (economy, control, etc.)
pomoc materiałowa [**po**-mots mah-ter-yah-**wo**-vah] exp.: aid in materials
materiałoznawca [mah-ter-yah-wo-**znahf**-tsah] m. expert in commercial materials
materiałoznawstwo [mah-ter-yah-wo-**znahf**-stfo] n. knowledge of commercial materials
maties [**maht**-yes] m. young herring (dish)
matinka [mah-**teen**-kah] f. woman's morning jacket
matka [**maht**-kah] f. mother; dam (of a four-legged animal); Mother Superior; parent; queen (bee, wasp, ant)
matka chrzestna [**maht**-kah **khshes**-tnah] exp.: godmother
matka rodu [**maht**-kah **ro**-doo] exp.: ancestress
przybrana matka [pshi-**brah**-nah **maht**-kah] exp.: foster mother
potrzeba jest matką wynalazków [po-**tshe**-bah yest **maht**-kown vi-nah-**lahs**-koof] exp.: necessity is the mother of invention
matkobójca [maht-ko-**booy**-tsah] m. matricide
matkobójstwo [maht-ko-**booy**-stfo] n. matricide
matkować [maht-**ko**-vahćh] v. mother; be the mother of; be a mother to (*repeatedly*)
matkowanie [maht-ko-**vah**-ńe] n. mothering
matma [**maht**-mah] f. colloq: math;

mathematics
matnia [maht-ńah] f. snare; trap; poke-net; noose; pitfall; entanglement
być w matni [bićh v maht-ńee] exp.: to be at bay; to be entangled; to be ensnared; to be entrapped
wydobyć się z matni [vi-do-bićh śhan z maht-ńee] exp.: to disentangle oneself; colloq: to get out of trouble
złapać w matnię [zwah-pahćh v maht-ńan] exp.: to ensnare; to entrap
matoł [mah-tow] m. imbecile; idiot; see: **matołek**
matołectwo [mah-to-wets-tfo] n. imbecility; idiocy; cretinism; amentia
matołek [mah-to-wek] m. imbecile; idiot; cretin; colloq: insult: idiot; nitwit; fathead
matołkowaty [mah-tow-ko-vah-ti] adj.m. idiotic; imbecile
matołowaty [mah-to-wo-vah-ti] adj.m. idiotic; imbecile
matować [mah-to-vahćh] v. mat; render mat; tarnish (metals); frost (glass); flat (paint); dull (paint); checkmate (*repeatedly*)
matowanie [mah-to-vah-ńe] n. matting; rendering dull; checkmating
matowieć [mah-to-vyećh] v. become dull; become dim; lose gloss; lose luster; tarnish (*repeatedly*)
matowienie [mah-to-vye-ńe] n. becoming mat; becoming tarnished
matowo [mah-to-vo] adv. without gloss; with a dull (finish, etc.); (to sound) flatly, huskily
matowoczerwony [mah-to-vo-cher-vo-ni] adj.m. of a dull red color
matowość [mah-to-vośhćh] f. gloss; dull finish
matowy [mah-to-vi] adj.m. flat color; dull; lackluster
matówka [mah-toof-kah] f. focusing screen
matriarchalnie [mah-tri-yahr-khal-ńe] adv. by matriarchy
matriarchalny [mah-tri-yahr-khal-ni] adj.m. matriarchal
matriarchat [mah-tri-yahr-khaht] m. matriarchate; matriarchy
matrona [mah-tro-nah] f. matron; staid woman
matronimicum [mah-tro-ńee-mee-koom] n. matronymic appellation
matronimik [mah-tro-ńee-meek] m. matronymic
matronowata [mah-tro-no-vah-tah] adj.f. matronly; staid
matronowaty [mah-tro-no-vah-ti] adj.m. matronly
matros [maht-ros] m. colloq: seaman
matryca [mah-tri-tsah] f. matrix; die; type mold; stencil; stamp; swage
matrycować [mah-tri-tso-vahćh] v. take a matrix (of); take a mold (of); plate; swage; stamp; stencil (*repeatedly*)
matrycowanie [mah-tri-tso-vah-ńe] n. taking of a matrix
matrycowy [mah-tri-tso-vi] adj.m. matrix (paper, etc.); stencil (copy, etc.); stamp (mill, etc.); die (caster, etc.)
matrykuła [mah-tri-koo-wah] f. register of university students
matrymonialny [mah-tri-mоń-yahl-ni] adj.m. matrimonial (agency, office, etc.); marital
matuchna [mah-tookh-nah] f. dear mother
matula [mah-too-lah] f. dear mother
matura [mah-too-rah] f. final high-school examination; secondary-school certificate
maturacja [mah-too-rah-tsyah] f. maturation
maturacyjny [mah-too-rah-tsiy-ni] adj.m. maturative; maturational
maturalny [mah-too-rahl-ni] adj.m. of a secondary-school education; of a secondary-school certificate
maturzysta [mah-too-zhis-tah] m. secondary-school graduate
maturzystka [mah-too-zhist-kah] f. (girl) secondary-school graduate
matusia [mah-too-śhah] f. dear mother
matuś [mah-toośh] f. dear mother
matuzal [mah-too-zahl] m.

Methuselah; very old man
matuzalem [mah-too-**zah**-lem] m. colloq: Methuselah; a very old man
matuzalemowy [mah-too-zah-le-**mo**-vi] adj.m. of Methuselah; of a very old man
matuzalowy [mah-too-zah-**lo**-vi] adj.m. of Methuselah; of a very old man; of very old men
maureska [mahw-**res**-kah] f. Moresque ornament
mauretański [mahw-re-**tahń**-skee] adj.m. Moorish; of Moors
mauzer [**mahw**-zer] m. Mauser (rifle, pistol)
mauzoleum [mahw-zo-**le**-oom] n. mausoleum
maworek [mah-**vo**-rek] m. Physarium; Thallopphyte
mawiać [mah-**vyahćh**] v. be accustomed to say; be wont to say; say (often) (*repeatedly*)
mawianie [mah-**vyah**-ńe] n. saying
maxi [**mah**-ksee] not declined: maxi; long skirt; long coat
mazać [mah-**zahćh**] v. smear; defile; scribble; blot; stain; daub; scrawl; wipe out; rub out; efface; atone (*repeatedly*)
mazać się [**mah**-zahćh śh<u>an</u>] v. smear oneself; colloq: snivel; whine; pule (*repeatedly*)
mazagran [mah-**zah**-grahn] m. iced coffee
mazaja [mah-**zah**-yah] f. colloq: colored design (poor, ugly)
mazak [**mah**-zahk] m. shoe dauber; thick painting brush; (wide line) marker
mazanie [mah-**zah**-ńe] n. daub; daubing strokes
mazanie się [mah-**zah**-ńe śh<u>an</u>] n. colloq: crying
mazanina [mah-zah-**ńee**-nah] f. daub; daubing strokes
mazdaizm [mahz-**dah**-eezm] m. Mazdeism; Mazdaism
mazdeizm [mahz-**de**-eezm] m. Mazdeism; Mazdaism
mazepa [mah-**ze**-pah] m. crybaby
mazer [**mah**-zer] m. veined wood; veined design
mazerować [mah-ze-ro-vahćh] v. make a veined design (*repeatedly*)
mazerowanie [mah-ze-ro-**vah**-ńe] n. making veined design
mazerunek [mah-ze-**roo**-nek] m. veined design
mazgaić się [mahz-**gah**-eećh śh<u>an</u>] v. dawdle; dally; snivel; blubber; lament (*repeatedly*)
mazgaj [**mahz**-gahy] m. colloq: crybaby
mazgajenie się [mahz-gah-**ye**-ńe śh<u>an</u>] n. colloq: dawdling; snivelling; blubbering
mazgajowaty [mahz-gah-yo-**vah**-ti] adj.m. colloq: dawdling; snivelling; blubbering
mazgajstwo [mahz-**gahy**-stfo] n. colloq: dawdling; snivelling; blubbering
maziczka [mah-**źheech**-kah] f. tarweed
mazidło [mah-**źhee**-dwo] n. liniment
maziowaty [mah-źho-**vah**-ti] adj.m. clammy; sticky
maziowy [mah-**źho**-vi] adj.m. synovial
błona maziowa [**bwo**-nah mah-**źho**-vah] exp.: synovial membrane
maziówka [mah-**źhoof**-kah] f. synovial membrane
mazisto [mah-**źhees**-to] adv. with grease; stickily
mazistość [mah-**źhees**-tośhćh] f. clamminess; stickiness; greasiness
mazisty [mah-**źhees**-ti] adj.m. clammy; sticky; greasy
maznąć [**mahz**-n<u>own</u>ćh] v. smear; stain; defile; colloq: daub; scribble
mazowiecki [mah-zo-**vyets**-kee] adj.m. Mazovian
mazowizm [mah-**zo**-veezm] m. Mazovian expression, accent, dialect, etc.
mazur [**mah**-zoor] m. mazurka rhythm; Mazurian; Mazovian
mazurek [mah-**zoo**-rek] m. mazurka; a kind of cake
mazurkowy [mah-zoor-**ko**-vi] adj.m. Mazovian (rhythm, etc.)
mazurowy [mah-zoo-**ro**-vi] adj.m. Mazovian (dance figure, etc.)
mazurski [mah-**zoor**-skee] adj.m.

Mazovian
mazurzenie [mah-zoo-**zhe**-ńe] n. a characteristic feature of the pronunciation of Mazovians (consisting in substituting dental stops and affricates for alveolar stops and affricates)
mazurzyć [mah-**zoo**-zhićh] v. pronounce in Mazovian fashion (substitute "s, z, c, dz" for "sz, ż, cz, dż") (*repeatedly*)
mazut [**mah**-zoot] m. mazut (fuel)
mazutowy [mah-zoo-**to**-vi] adj.m. mazut (fuel, oil, etc.)
maź [mahśh] f. grease; tallow; lubricant; cart-grease
maźnica [mahźh-**ńee**-tsah] f. axle-box; grease-box; oil-box; lubricating-box
maźniczy [mahźh-**ńee**-chi] adj.m. grease (gun, etc.); oil (can, etc.); lubricating (instructions, schedule, etc.)
maźnięcie [mahźh-**ńan**-ćhe] n. dab; smear; stroke of the brush
mącenie [mown-**tse**-ńe] n. clouding up; muddying up; blurring
mąciciel [mown-**ćhee**-ćhel] m. disturber of the peace; troublemaker; fomenter of trouble
mącicielski [mown-ćhee-**ćhel**-skee] adj.m. troublemaking (disposition, etc.)
mącić [**mown**-ćheećh] v. blur; ruffle; muddy; cloud; confuse; make turbid; disturb; alloy; mar; create confusion; perplex (*repeatedly*)
mącić się [**mown**-ćheećh śhan] v. be blurred; be ruffled; be muddied; be clouded; be confused; become turbid; be disturbed; become perplexed (*repeatedly*)
mąci mi się w głowie [**mown**-ćhee mee śhan v **gwo**-vye] exp.: my head reels; I feel dizzy; I am confused; I am perplexed
mąciwoda [mown-ćhee-**vo**-dah] m. troublemaker; brawler
mączasty [mown-**chahs**-ti] adj.m. floury; farinose; mealy
mączka [**mownch**-kah] f. fine flour; powder; dust; starch; meal
mączlik [**mownch**-leek] m. a variety of heteropter (insect)
mączniak [**mownch**-ńahk] m. powdery mildew
mącznica [mownch-**ńee**-tsah] f. flour bin; meal-chest; four-hopper; a disease of corn; bearberry
mącznie [**mownch**-ńe] adv. with flour
mącznieć [**mownch**-ńećh] v. become farinaceous; turn into powder (*repeatedly*)
mącznik [**mownch**-ńeek] m. meal worm; beetle
mącznikowaty [mownch-ńee-ko-**vah**-ti] adj.m. tenebrionid; of a darkling beetle
mącznikowate [mownch-ńee-ko-**vah**-te] pl. the darkling beetles; the family Tenebrionidae
mączny [**mownch**-ni] adj.m. of flour; of a meal; mealy; flour (beetle, etc.); meal (moth, etc.); farinaceous (foods, etc.); farinose (substances)
wyroby mączne [vi-**ro**-bi **mownch**-ne] exp.: cereals
mączystość [mown-**chis**-tośhćh] f. floury quality
mączysty [mown-**chis**-ti] adj.m. floury; mealy
mądrala [mown-**drah**-lah] m. know-all; smart aleck; smart-alecky kid; wiseacre; wise guy; know-it-all; colloq: clever kid
mądrość [**mown**-drośhćh] f. wisdom; intelligence; sagacity
mądrości [mown-**drośh**-ćhee] pl. wise sayings
mądrość książkowa [**mown**-drośhćh kśhownsh-**ko**-vah] exp.: book learning
mądrość życiowa [**mown**-drośhćh zhi-**ćho**-vah] exp.: practical wisdom
ząb mądrości [zownp mown-**dro**-śhćhee] exp.: wisdom tooth
mądry [**mownd**-ri] adj.m. wise; clever; intelligent; sensible; judicious; sound; well-advised; keen; shrewd; learned; sharp-witted; smart; perspicacious; sagacious; m. intelligent person; clever person

mądrze [mownd-zhe] adv. wisely; cleverly; intelligently; sensibly; judiciously; learnedly; smartly; sagaciously
mądrze zrobiłeś [mownd-zhe zro-bee-weśh] exp.: you were wise to do that
mądrzeć [mownd-zhećh] v. grow wise; acquire wisdom (*repeatedly*)
mądrzenie [mownd-**zhe**-ńe] n. growing wise
mądrzenie się [mownd-**zhe**-ńe śhan] n. colloq: being the wise guy
mądrzyć się [mownd-zhićh śhan] v. colloq: play the philosopher; be a wise guy (*repeatedly*)
mąka [mown-kah] f. flour; meal; colloq: powder
mąka kartoflana [mown-kah kahr-to-**flah**-nah] exp.: potato flour
mąka ziemniaczana [mown-kah źhem-ńah-**chah**-nah] exp.: potato flour
mąkinia [mown-**kee**-ńah] f. whitebeam
mąkla [mownk-lah] f. a species of lichen
mąt [mownt] m. confusion; muddy liquid
mątew [mown-tef] f. stirring spatula; whisk
mątewka [mown-**tef**-kah] f. (small) stirring spatula; whisk
mątwa [mownt-fah] f. cuttle-fish; sepia
mątwik [mownt-feek] m. eelworm
mątwiki [mownt-**fee**-kee] pl. eelworms
mąż [mownsh] m. husband; man
mąż stanu [mownsh **stah**-noo] exp.: statesman; outstanding politician; outstanding diplomat
mąż zaufania [mownsh zah-oo-**fah**-ńah] exp.: delegate; confidential agent; representative with power of attorney
jak jeden mąż [yahk **ye**-den mownsh] exp.: to a man; as one man; in a body; unanimously
wychodzić za mąż [vi-**kho**-dźheećh zah mownsh] exp.: to marry; to get married
mcholubny [mkho-**loob**-ni] adj.m. of organisms living in moss
mchowaty [mkho-**vah**-ti] adj.m. moss-like
mchowy [**mkho**-vi] adj.m. moss (like, etc.); of moss
mdleć [mdlećh] v. faint; lose consciousness; fail; weaken; go off into a faint; droop; flag; swoon; be failing; wither (*repeatedly*)
mdlejącym głosem [mdle-yown-tsim **gwo**-sem] exp.: in a faint voice
serce mdleje [**ser**-tse **mdle**-ye] exp.: the heart is sinking
mdlenie [**mdle**-ńe] n. fainting; losing consciousness
mdlić [mdleećh] v. nauseate; sicken (*repeatedly*)
mdli mnie [mdlee mńe] exp.: I feel sick; I am queasy; I feel qualmish; I feel nauseated; I sicken (at); my stomach turns (at the sight of)
mdławo [**mdwah**-vo] adv. faintly; dimly; indistinctly; in blurred manner; fuzzily; nauseatingly; in a sickening manner
mdławy [**mdwah**-vi] adj.m. faint; dim; indistinct; blurred; fuzzy; nauseating; sickening
mdło [mdwo] adv. nauseatingly; sickeningly; faintly; fuzzily; indistinctly; dimly; dull
robi mi się mdło [ro-bee mee śhan mdwo] exp.: I sicken; I feel sick; I feel faint
mdłosłodki [mdwo-**swot**-kee] adj.m. sickeningly sweet
mdłość [mdwośhćh] f. nausea; fuzziness; indistinctness
mdły [mdwi] adj.m. insipid; dull; nauseating; sickening; faint; dim; vapid; mawkish; fuzzy; tame; lackadaisical; indistinct; blurred
me [me] pron.: my; mine; see: **mój; moje**
me [me] imitation of the sound of bleating (of sheep)
meander [me-**ahn**-der] m. meander
meandrować [me-ahn-**dro**-vahćh] v. wind (river's way); meander (*repeatedly*)
meandrowanie [me-ahn-dro-**vah**-ńe]

n. winding; meandering
meandrowy [me-ahn-**dro**-vi] adj.m. winding; meander (curve)
meandryczny [me-ahn-**drich**-ni] adj.m. winding; meander (curve)
mebel [**me**-bel] m. piece of furniture
meble [**me**-ble] pl. furniture
mebelek [me-**be**-lek] m. (small, nice) piece of furniture
meblarka [me-**blahr**-kah] f. cabinetmaking; carpentry
meblarnia [me-**blahr**-ńah] f. furniture manufacturing plant
meblarski [me-**blahr**-skee] adj.m. cabinetmaking (shop, etc.)
meblarstwo [me-**blahr**-stfo] n. cabinetmaking; furniture building
meblarz [**me**-blahsh] m. cabinetmaker; furniture maker; colloq: furniture store owner
meblościanka [me-blo-**śhćhahn**-kah] f. (sectional) wall unit; wall entertainment center; sectional partition unit
meblować [me-**blo**-vahćh] v. furnish (a room, etc.) (*repeatedly*)
meblować się [me-**blo**-vahćh śhan] v. furnish one's (room, apartment, flat, etc.) (*repeatedly*)
meblowanie [me-blo-**vah**-ńe] n. furnishing
meblowóz [me-**blo**-voos] m. furniture truck
meblowy [me-**blo**-vi] adj.m. furniture (truck, etc.)
mecenas [me-**tse**-nahs] m. lawyer; Maecenas; art patron
mecenaska [me-tse-**nahs**-kah] f. (female) art patron; patroness
mecenasostwo [me-tse-nah-**sos**-tfo] n. art patronage; lawyer's practice
mecenasowa [me-tse-nah-**so**-vah] f. lawyer's wife
mecenasować [me-tse-nah-**so**-vahćh] v. patronize (art, etc.); act as a patron (*repeatedly*)
mecenasowanie [me-tse-nah-so-**vah**-ńe] n. patronizing (art, etc.); acting as a patron; patronage
mecenasowski [me-tse-nah-**sof**-skee] adj.m. of an art patron; patron's (donations, etc.); patronage (activity, etc.)
mecenat [me-**tse**-naht] m. (art) patronage
mech [mekh] m. moss; down; colloq: silky bristle; light beard
mechacenie [me-khah-**tse**-ńe] n. matting
mechacenie się [me-khah-**tse**-ńe śhan] n. getting matted; becoming matted
mechacić [me-**khah**-ćheećh] v. matt; mat (*repeatedly*)
mechacić się [me-**khah**-ćheećh śhan] v. become matted; form into a tangled mass (*repeatedly*)
mechanicyzm [me-khah-**ńee**-tsizm] m. mechanistic materialism
mechanicznie [me-khah-**ńeech**-ńe] adv. mechanically; by machinery; automatically
mechaniczność [me-khah-**ńeech**-nośhćh] f. mechanical nature; automation (of movements, etc.)
mechaniczny [me-khah-**ńeech**-ni] adj.m. mechanical; automatic; machine (tool, etc.)
mechanik [me-**khah**-ńeek] m. mechanic; fitter; colloq: mechanical engineer; slang: Jack of all trades (mob jargon)
mechanika [me-**khah**-ńee-kah] f. mechanics (practical, political, strategic, etc.)
mechanista [me-khah-**ńee**-stah] m. mechanist
mechanistycznie [me-khah-ńees-**tich**-ńe] adv. mechanistically
mechanistyczny [me-khah-ńees-**tich**-ni] adj.m. mechanistic
mechanizacja [me-khah-ńee-**zah**-tsyah] f. mechanization
mechanizacyjny [me-khah-ńee-zah-**tsiy**-ni] adj.m. of mechanization; mechanizing
mechanizator [me-khah-ńee-**zah**-tor] m. mechanizer
mechanizatorski [me-khah-ńee-zah-**tor**-skee] adj.m. mechanizer's
mechanizm [me-**khah**-ńeezm] m. mechanism; gear; device; contrivance; mechanization
mechanizmowy [me-khah-ńeez-**mo**-vi] adj.m. of mechanism; mechanical
mechanizować [me-khah-ńee-**zo**-

vahćh] v. mechanize (*repeatedly*)
mechanizować się [me-khah-ńee-**zo**-vahćh śhan] v. become mechanized; undergo the process of mechanization; become automatic (*repeatedly*)
mechanizowanie [me-khah-ńee-zo-**vah**-ńe] n. mechanization
mechanizowanie się [me-khah-ńee-zo-**vah**-ńe śhan] n. becoming mechanized
mechanochemia [me-khah-no-**khe**-myah] f. chemistry of mechanical processes; mechanochemistry
mechanochemiczny [me-khah-no-khe-**meech**-ni] adj.m. mechanochemical
mechanogeniczny [me-khah-no-ge-**ńeech**-ni] adj.m. of sedimentary sand strata
mechanolamarkizm [me-khah-no-lah-**mahr**-keezm] m. Lamarckian evolutionism
mechanorecepcja [me-khah-no-re-**tsep**-tsyah] f. mechanoreception
mechanorecepcyjny [me-khah-no-re-tsep-**tsiy**-ni] adj.m. mechanoreceptive
mechanoreceptor [me-khah-no-re-**tsep**-tor] m. mechanoreceptor
mechanoreceptory [me-khah-no-re-tsep-**to**-ri] pl. mechanoreceptors
mechanoskopia [me-khah-no-**sko**-pyah] f. detective study and identification of the weapon of crime
mechanoskopijny [me-khah-no-sko-**peey**-ni] adj.m. of the study and identification of the weapon of crime
mechanoterapeuta [me-khah-no-te-rah-**pew**-tah] m. mechanotherapist
mechanoterapia [me-khah-no-te-**rah**-pyah] f. mechanotherapy
mechaty [me-**khah**-ti] adj.m. mossy; resembling moss
meches [**me**-khes] m. Jew converted to the Christian faith
mechowiec [me-**kho**-vyets] m. variety of saprophyte; mite
mechowce [me-**khof**-tse] pl. Oribatei; wood mites
mechowisko [me-kho-**vees**-ko] n. overgrown moss area; moss-grown spot
mecyja [me-**tsi**-yah] f. colloq: a dainty; a tidbit; stunning good thing; rare thing; stunning thing; rattling thing; kickshaw
mecyje [me-**tsi**-ye] pl. colloq: dainties; tidbits; stunning good things; rare things; stunning things; rattling things; kickshaw
wielkie mi mecyje [**vyel**-ke mee me-**tsi**-ye] exp.: it's as easy as pie; nothing to it
mecz [mech] m. sport match; game; match
mecz sparingowy [mech spah-reen-**go**-vi] exp.: spar
meczbol [**mech**-bol] m. match point; match ball (Brit.) (as in tennis)
meczecik [me-**che**-ćheek] m. small mosque
meczeć [**me**-chećh] v. bleat (*repeatedly*)
meczenie [me-**che**-ńe] n. (a) bleat
meczet [**me**-chet] m. mosque
meczetowy [me-che-**to**-vi] adj.m. of a mosque
meczowy [me-**cho**-vi] adj.m. match (point, etc.); sparring (partner, etc.)
medal [**me**-dahl] m. medal
każdy medal ma dwie strony [**kahzh**-di **me**-dahl mah dvye **stro**-ni] exp.: there are two sides to every coin
na medal [nah **me**-dahl] exp.: perfect; faultless; perfectly; faultlessly
odwrotna strona medalu [od-**vrot**-nah **stro**-nah me-**dah**-loo] exp.: the reverse of the medal; the seamy side; the dark side of a question
medalier [me-**dahl**-yer] m. medal maker; medal designer
medaliernia [me-dahl-**yer**-ńah] f. medalist's workshop
medalierski [me-dahl-**yer**-skee] adj.m. medalist's
medalierstwo [me-dahl-**yer**-stfo] n. medalist's profession; the medalists
medalik [me-**dah**-leek] m. holy medal

medalion [me-**dahl**-yon] m. locket; medallion
medalionik [me-dahl-**yo**-ńeek] m. (small, nice) locket; medallion
medalionowy [me-dahl-yo-**no**-vi] adj.m. locket (design, etc.); medallion (collection, etc.)
medalista [me-dah-**lees**-tah] m. medalist
medalistka [me-dah-**lees**-tkah] f. (woman) medalist
medalowy [me-dah-**lo**-vi] adj.m. of medal; medallic
mediacja [me-**dyah**-tsyah] f. mediation; settling of differences (between persons, nations, etc)
mediacyjny [me-dyah-**tsiy**-ni] adj.m. mediatory; mediative
medialny [me-**dyahl**-ni] adj.m. mediumistic
mediana [me-**dyah**-nah] f. median line; (statistical) median
medianta [me-**dyahn**-tah] f. mediant
mediator [me-**dyah**-tor] m. mediator
mediatorski [me-dyah-**tor**-skee] adj.m. mediatory
mediatorstwo [me-dyah-**tor**-stfo] n. mediation; mediateness
mediatyzacja [me-dyah-ti-**zah**-tsyah] f. mediatization
mediatyzować [me-dyah-ti-**zo**-vahćh] v. mediatize (*repeatedly*)
mediewistyczny [me-dye-vee-**stich**-ni] adj.m. medievalistic
mediewalnie [me-dye-**vahl**-ńe] adv. medievally
mediewalny [me-dye-**vahl**-ni] adj.m. medieval
mediewista [me-dye-**vees**-tah] m. medievalist
mediewistka [me-dye-**veest**-kah] f. (woman) medievalist
mediewalistyczny [me-dye-vah-lees-**tich**-ni] adj.m. medievalistic
mediewistyka [me-dye-**vees**-ti-kah] f. medieval studies
medium [**me**-dyoom] n. (hypnotic) medium; environment; medium
mediumiczny [me-dyoo-**meech**-ni] adj.m. (hypnotic) medium (behavior, etc.)
mediumistyczny [me-dyoo-mees-**tich**-ni] adj.m. (hypnotic) medium (behavior, etc.)
mediumizm [me-**dyoo**-meezm] m. theory and practice of hypnosis
medok [**me**-dok] m. Medoc (wine)
medresa [med-**re**-sah] f. madrasah; medresseh; Islamic school
Meduza [me-**doo**-zah] f. Medusa
meduza [me-**doo**-zah] f. jellyfish
medycejski [me-di-**tsey**-skee] adj.m. Medicean
medycyna [me-di-**tsi**-nah] f. medicine; art of healing
medycyna sądowa [me-di-**tsi**-nah sown-**do**-vah] exp.: forensic medicine
medyczka [me-**dich**-kah] f. girl student of medicine
medycznie [me-**dich**-ńe] adv. medically
medyczny [me-**dich**-ni] adj.m. medical; medicinal
medyk [**me**-dik] m. medical student; medic (physician)
medykament [me-di-**kah**-ment] m. drug; medicine (hist. exp.)
medytacja [me-di-**tahts**-yah] f. meditation; thinking deeply
medytacyjnie [me-di-tah-**tsiy**-ńe] adv. meditatively
medytacyjny [me-di-tah-**tsiy**-ni] adj.m. meditative
medytować [me-di-**to**-vahćh] v. meditate; ponder (*repeatedly*)
medytowanie [me-di-to-**vah**-ńe] n. meditation; pondering
mefistofeliczny [me-fee-sto-fe-**leech**-ni] adj.m. Mephistophelean; colloq: devilish
mefistofelowy [me-fee-sto-fe-**lo**-vi] adj.m. Mephistophelean; colloq: devilish
mega- [**me**-gah] prefix: mega-; large-
megadyna [me-gah-**di**-nah] f. megadyne
megaerg [me-**gah**-erg] m. megaerg
megafon [me-**gah**-fon] m. loudspeaker; megaphone
megafonizować [me-gah-fo-ńee-**zo**-vahćh] v. provide with megaphones (*repeatedly*)
megafonowy [me-gah-fo-**no**-vi] adj.m. megaphonic
megaherc [**me**-gah-**herts**] m. megahertz
megakaloria [me-gah-kah-**lor**-yah] f.

megacalorie; 1,000,000 calories
megalit [me-**gah**-leet] m. megalith
megalityczny [me-gah-lee-**tich**-ni] adj.m. megalithic
megaloman [me-gah-**lo**-mahn] m. megalomaniac; self-appointed boss; self-important person
megalomania [me-gah-lo-**mah**-ńyah] f. megalomania
megalomanka [me-gah-lo-**mahn**-kah] f. (woman) megalomaniac; self-appointed boss; self-important person
megalomański [me-gah-lo-**mahń**-skee] adj.m. megalomanic; megalomaniacal
po megalomańsku [po me-gah-lo-**mahń**-skoo] exp.: megalomaniacally
megalozaurus [me-gah-lo-**zahw**-roos] m. Megalosaurus
megantrop [me-**gahn**-trop] m. pleistocene man
megaom [**me**-gah-**om**] m. 1,000,000 ohms; megohm
megaomomierz [me-gah-o-**mo**-myesh] m. ohmmeter with 1,000,000 ohms scale
megaparsek [me-gah-**pahr**-sek] m. megaparsec; 1,000,000 parsecs
megaplankton [me-gah-**plahnk**-ton] m. the largest plankton
megapond [**me**-gah-**pont**] m. 1,000,000 ponds
megaron [me-**gah**-ron] m. megaron; Mycenaean house
megasam [**me**-gah-**sahm**] m. supermarket
megaskop [me-**gah**-skop] m. megascope; unaided eye
megaskopowy [me-gah-sko-**po**-vi] adj.m. megascopic
megaspora [me-gah-**spo**-rah] f. megaspore
megasporyczny [me-gah-spo-**rich**-ni] adj.m. megasporic
megater [me-**gah**-ter] m. Megatherium; Pleistocene ground sloth
megaterium [me-gah-**ter**-yoom] n. Megatherium
megatona [me-gah-**to**-nah] f. megaton
megawat [me-**gah**-vaht] m. megawatt; 1,000,000 watts
megawolt [me-**gah**-volt] m. megavolt; 1,000,000 volts
megiera [me-**ge**-rah] f. shrew; scold; termagant; vixen; virago
megom [**meg**-om] m. megohm
mejoza [me-**yo**-zah] f. meiosis
mekintosz [me-**keen**-tosh] m. MacIntosh apple
mekka [**mek**-kah] m. mecca; colloq: a place sought as a goal by numerous people
Mekka [**mek**-kah] f. Mecca
meklemburg [**me**-klem-boorg] m. horse of German Meklemburgian breed
meklemburski [me-klem-**boor**-skee] adj.m. Meklemburgian (horse, etc.)
Meksyk [**me**-ksik] m. Mexico
meksyk [**me**-ksik] m. colloq: disorder; confusion; riot
Meksykanin [me-ksi-**kah**-ńeen] m. Mexican
meksykański [mek-si-**kahń**-skee] adj.m. Mexican
melafir [me-**lah**-feer] m. melaphyre (mineral)
melakser [me-**lah**-kser] m. kitchen appliance combining mixer and blender
melamina [me-lah-**mee**-nah] f. melamine
melaminowy [me-lah-mee-**no**-vi] adj.m. melamine (resin, etc.)
melancholia [me-lahn-**kho**-lyah] f. melancholy; the blues; dejection; despondency; low spirits; dumps; melancholia
czarna melancholia [**chahr**-nah me-lahn-**kho**-lyah] exp.: absolute prostration
opanowała go melancholia [o-pah-no-**vah**-wah go me-lahn-**kho**-lyah] exp.: he fell into despondency
melancholiczka [me-lahn-kho-**leech**-kah] f. (woman) melancholiac
melancholiczny [me-lahn-kho-**leech**-ni] adj.m. melancholic; melancholy
melancholijnie [me-lahn-kho-**leey**-ńe] adv. melancholically; dismally
melancholijność [me-lahn-kho-**leey**-nośhćh] f. melancholia;

melancholy
melancholijny [me-lahn-kho-**leey**-ni] adj.m. melancholy; melancholic
być w melancholijnym nastroju [bićh v me-lahn-kho-**leey**-nim nah-**stro**-yoo] exp.: to have the blues
melancholik [me-lahn-**kho**-leek] m. melancholiac
melancholizować [me-lahn-kho-lee-**zo**-vahćh] v. melancholize (*repeatedly*)
melancholizowanie [me-lahn-kho-lee-zo-**vah**-ńe] n. melancholy
melanina [me-lah-**ńee**-nah] f. melanin
melanit [me-**lah**-ńeet] m. melanite (mineral)
melanizm [me-**lah**-ńeezm] m. melanism
melanoma [me-lah-**no**-mah] f. melanoma (malignant tumor containing dark pigment)
melanż [**me**-lahnsh] m. mixture; blend; medley; melange
melanżer [me-**lahn**-zher] m. mixer; mixing machine
melasa [me-**lah**-sah] f. molasses; brown sugar; treacle
melasowy [me-lah-**so**-vi] adj.m. molassy; of molasses
melba [**mel**-bah] f. ice cream "Melba;" (vanilla ice cream with fruits or preserves)
melchior [**mel**-khyor] m. German (nickel) silver
meldometr [mel-**do**-metr] m. meldometer
meldować [mel-**do**-vahćh] v. report; register; announce; inform; notify; give an account (*repeatedly*)
meldować o postępach [mel-**do**-vahćh o pos-t<u>an</u>-pahkh] exp.: to report progress; to make a progress report
meldować się [mel-**do**-vahćh śh<u>an</u>] v. report oneself (at); register (*repeatedly*)
meldować się jako chory [mel-**do**-vahćh śh<u>an</u> **yah**-ko **kho**-ri] exp.: to report oneself sick
meldowanie [mel-do-**vah**-ńe] n. notification
wejść bez meldowania [veyśhćh bez mel-do-**vah**-ńah] exp.: to enter unannounced
meldowanie się [mel-do-**vah**-ńe śh<u>an</u>] n. registration
meldunek [mel-**doo**-nek] m. report; announcement; notification; registration
meldunkowy [mel-doon-**ko**-vi] adj.m. registration (card, form, etc.)
meleks [**me**-leks] m. electric golf cart; small electric car
melex [**me**-leks] m. electric golf cart; small electric car
melicznie [me-**leech**-ńe] adv. lyrically
meliczny [me-**leech**-ni] adj.m. melic, lyric (poet, etc.)
melika [**me**-lee-kah] f. lyric poetry and songs
melina [me-**lee**-nah] f. hideout (of thieves, etc.); den; haunt; colloq: joint; hangout
meliniarka [me-lee-**ńahr**-kah] f. (woman) fence; receiver of stolen goods
meliniarski [me-lee-**ńahr**-skee] adj.m. fence (stolen goods); joint (meeting, etc.)
meliniarz [me-**lee**-ńahsh] m. fence; receiver of stolen goods
melinit [me-**lee**-ńeet] m. melinite (mineral)
melinować [me-lee-**no**-vahćh] v. receive and conceal (stolen goods); harbor (criminals) (*repeatedly*)
melinować się [me-lee-**no**-vahćh śh<u>an</u>] v. conceal oneself; find harbor (for oneself) (*repeatedly*)
melinowanie [me-lee-no-**vah**-ńe] n. receiving and concealing (of stolen goods); harboring (of criminals)
melinowanie się [me-lee-no-**vah**-ńe śh<u>an</u>] n. concealing oneself; finding harbor (for oneself)
melioracja [me-lyo-**rahts**-yah] f. reclamation of land; drainage
melioracyjny [mel-yo-rah-**tsiy**-ni] adj.m. drainage (pipes, etc.)
meliorant [me-**lyo**-rahnt] m. specialist in the reclamation of land and drainage
meliorator [me-lyo-**rah**-tor] m. specialist in the reclamation of

land and drainage
melioratywny [mel-yo-rah-**tiv**-ni] adj.m. meliorative; ameliorative
meliorować [me-lyo-**ro**-vahćh] v. meliorate; drain land; reclaim land (*repeatedly*)
meliorowanie [me-lyo-ro-**vah**-ńe] n. melioration; drainage; reclaiming of land
melioryzacja [me-lyo-ri-**zah**-tsyah] f. melioration; acquisition of positive meaning by words
melisa [me-**lee**-sah] f. melissa
melisa lekarska [me-**lee**-sah le-**kahr**-skah] exp.: lemon balm
melisowy [me-lee-**so**-vi] adj.m. melissa (leaves, etc.)
melit [**me**-leet] m. mellite (mineral)
melizmat [me-**leez**-maht] m. melisma; cadenza
melizmatyczny [me-leez-mah-**tich**-ni] adj.m. melismatic
melodeklamacja [me-lo-de-klah-**mahts**-yah] f. recitation delivered to the accompaniment of music
melodeklamator [me-lo-de-klah-**mah**-tor] m. recitalist speaking to the accompaniment of music
melodia [me-**lod**-yah] f. melody; tune
melodia przyszłości [me-**lod**-yah pshi-**shwośh**-ćhee] exp.: (something) still a long way off
nie mieć melodii do czegoś [ńe myećh me-**lod**-yee do **che**-gośh] exp.: to be in no mind for something
melodramat [me-lo-**drah**-maht] m. melodrama
melodramatycznie [me-lo-drah-mah-**tich**-ńe] adv. melodramatically
melodramatyczność [me-lo-drah-mah-**tich**-nośhćh] f. melodramatics
melodramatyczny [me-lo-drah-mah-**tich**-ni] adj.m. melodramatic
melodramatyzm [me-lo-drah-**mah**-tizm] m. melodramatics
melodramatyzować [me-lo-drah-mah-ti-**zo**-vahćh] v. melodramatize (*repeatedly*)
melodramatyzowanie [me-lo-drah-mah-ti-zo-**vah**-ńe] n. melodramatization
melodycznie [me-lo-**dich**-ńe] adv. melodically
melodyczność [me-lo-**dich**-nośhćh] f. melodic quality; melodic character
melodyczny [me-lo-**dich**-ni] adj.m. melodic (interval, etc.); melodial; melodical
melodyjka [me-lo-**diy**-kah] f. (nice, light) melody
melodyjnie [me-lo-**diy**-ńe] adv. melodiously; harmoniously; tunefully
melodyjność [me-lo-**diy**-nośhćh] f. melodiousness; harmoniousness; tunefulness
melodyjny [me-lo-**diy**-ni] adj.m. melodious; harmonious; sweet; tuneful; dulcet; melody (music, etc.)
melodyka [me-**lo**-di-kah] f. melodics
melodykon [me-**lo**-di-kon] m. melodicon
melodysta [me-lo-**dis**-tah] m. melodist
melofarsa [me-lo-**fahr**-sah] f. farce with vocalist parts
meloman [me-**lo**-mahn] m. music lover; music enthusiast
melomania [me-lo-**mahń**-yah] f. love of music
melomanka [me-lo-**mahn**-kah] f. (woman) music lover; music enthusiast
melomański [me-lo-**mahń**-skee] adj.m. music-lover's; music-enthusiast's
melon [**me**-lon] m. melon; colloq: million zlotys
melonik [me-**lo**-ńeek] m. bowler hat; derby; bowler; billycock
melonowcowaty [me-lo-nof-tso-**vah**-ti] adj.m. caricaceous; of the Caricaceae family
melonowcowate [me-lo-nof-tso-**vah**-te] pl. the Caricaceae family
melonowiec [me-lo-**no**-vyets] m. Carica papaya
melonowy [me-lo-**no**-vi] adj.m. of melon; melon (plantation, transport, etc.)
melopeja [me-lo-**pe**-yah] f. melopoeia
melorecytacja [me-lo-re-tsi-**tahts**-

yah] f. recitation delivered to the accompaniment of music
melotypia [me-lo-**ti**-pyah] f. printing of musical scores with convex characters
meluzyna [me-loo-**zi**-nah] f. Melusina (French legend)
mełamed [me-**wah**-met] m. melamed; melammed; teacher in elementary Hebrew school
membrana [mem-**brah**-nah] f. membrane; diaphragm
membranofon [mem-brah-**no**-fon] m. kettledrum; timpani
membranowy [mem-brah-**no**-vi] adj.m. tympanic
instrumenty membranowe [een-stroo-**men**-ti mem-brah-**no**-ve] exp.: timpani (instruments)
pompa membranowa [**pom**-pah mem-brah-**no**-vah] exp.: diaphragm pump
memento [me-**men**-to] n. memento; reminder
memłać [**mem**-wahćh] v. colloq: chew a long time (*repeatedly*)
memorabilia [me-mo-rah-**bee**-lyah] pl. memorabilia
memorandum [me-mo-**rahn**-doom] n. memorandum; memo
memoriał [me-**mor**-yahw] m. memorial; minutes' journal; written communication
memoriałowy [me-mor-yah-**wo**-vi] adj.m. of a memorial; of a minutes' journal; of written communication
memuar [me-**moo**-ahr] m. diary
memuarystyka [me-moo-ah-**ris**-ti-kah] f. diary writing; memorialist's writing
menada [me-**nah**-dah] f. ecstatic woman; maenad
menaża [me-**nah**-zhah] f. mess (military)
menażer [me-**nah**-zher] m. manager
menażeria [me-nah-**zher**-yah] f. menagerie; animal collection
menażerstwo [me-nah-**zher**-stfo] n. management
menażeryjny [me-nah-zhe-**riy**-ni] adj.m. of management
menażka [me-**nahsh**-kah] f. mess kit; canteen; mess-tin; dixie
menażki [me-**nahsh**-kee] pl. mess kit
menchia [**men**-khyah] f. a plant of the pink family
menda [**men**-dah] f. crab louse; vulg.: despicable person; contemptible person; bore; blighter; see: **mendoweszka**
mendel [**men**-del] m. fifteen (eggs, etc.); shock (of 15 sheaves)
mendelejew [men-de-**le**-yef] m. mendelevium (atomic number 101)
mendelista [men-de-**lees**-tah] m. Mendelist
mendelistyczny [men-de-lees-**tich**-ni] adj.m. Mendelian
mendelizm [men-**de**-leezm] m. Mendelism
mendlować [men-**dlo**-vahćh] v. mendelize; mix according to Mendel's genetic law (*repeatedly*)
mendoweszka [men-do-**vesh**-kah] f. crab louse; vulg.: despicable person; contemptible person; bore; blighter; see: **menda**
menedżer [me-**ne**-dzher] m. manager (of a large firm)
menedżeryzm [me-ne-**dzhe**-rizm] m. managers' age (after capitalism)
menhir [**men**-kheer] m. menhir
menhiry [men-**khee**-ri] pl. crude monoliths; menhirs
menilit [me-**ńee**-leet] m. menilite (mineral)
menilitowy [me-nee-lee-**to**-vi] adj.m. menilite (mineral, etc.)
meningokok [me-ńeen-**go**-kok] m. meningococcus
meningokoki [me-ńeen-go-**ko**-kee] pl. meningococci
menisk [**me**-ńeesk] m. meniscus
mennica [men-**ńee**-tsah] f. mint
mennictwo [men-**ńeets**-tfo] n. minting; mintage; coinage
menniczy [men-**ńee**-chi] adj.m. mint (operation, etc.); coin (gold, silver, etc.)
opłata mennicza [o-**pwah**-tah men-**ńee**-chah] exp.: brassage
meno [**me**-no] n. less intensely, slower playing of music
menonita [me-no-**ńee**-tah] m. Mennonite

menopauza [me-no-**pahw**-zah] f. menopause
menopauzowy [me-no-pahw-**zo**-vi] adj.m. menopausal
menora [me-**no**-rah] f. menorah
mensa [**men**-sah] f. mensa
menstruacja [men-stroo-**ahts**-yah] f. menstruation; menses; period; monthlies
menstruacyjny [men-stroo-ah-**tsiy**-ni] adj.m. menstrual
menstrualny [men-stroo-**ahl**-ni] adj.m. menstrual
mentalizacja [men-tah-lee-**zah**-tsyah] f. mentation; making mental
mentalnie [men-**tahl**-ńe] adv. mentally
mentalność [men-**tahl**-nośhćh] f. mentality; way of thinking; (person's) turn of mind
mentalny [men-**tahl**-ni] adj.m. mental; inner (anguish, etc.)
mentol [**men**-tol] m. menthol
mentolowy [men-to-**lo**-vi] adj.m. mentholated
menton [**men**-ton] m. ketonic terpene; menthene
mentor [**men**-tor] m. mentor; preceptor; moralizer
mentorka [men-**tor**-kah] f. (woman) mentor; preceptor; moralizer
mentorować [men-to-**ro**-vahćh] v. graft young plants (on grown and developed plants) (*repeatedly*)
mentorowanie [men-to-ro-**vah**-ńe] n. grafting of young plants (on grown and developed plants)
mentorski [men-**tor**-skee] adj.m. tutorial; preceptorial
mentorstwo [men-**tor**-stfo] n. tutorial duties; moralizing
menu [**me**-ńyoo or me-**ńee**] n. menu; bill of fare; list of foods served
menuet [me-**noo**-et] m. minuet
menuetowy [me-noo-e-**to**-vi] adj.m. of a minuet dance
menzura [men-**zoo**-rah] f. (musical) measure
menzuralny [men-zoo-**rahl**-ni] adj.m. of musical measure
menzurka [men-**zoo**-rkah] f. burette; measuring glass
mer [mer] m. mayor
mercedes [mer-**tse**-des] m. Mercedes (car)
merceryzacja [mer-tse-ri-**zahts**-yah] f. mercerization
merceryzarka [mer-tse-ri-**zahr**-kah] f. mercerization machine
merceryzować [mer-tse-ri-**zo**-vahćh] v. mercerize (*repeatedly*)
merceryzowanie [mer-tse-ri-zo-**vah**-ńe] n. mercerization
merdać [**mer**-dahćh] v. wag (its) tail (*repeatedly*)
merdanie [mer-**dah**-ńe] n. wagging of the tail
merdnąć [**merd**-nownćh] v. wag (its) tail
merdnięcie [merd-**ńan**-ćhe] n. a wag of the tail
merenga [me-**ren**-gah] f. meringue
mereżka [me-**resh**-kah] f. hemstitch; drawn work
mereżkarka [me-resh-**kahr**-kah] f. hemstitching machine; hemstitching seamstress
mereżkarski [me-resh-**kahr**-skee] adj.m. hemstitching (machine, etc.)
mereżkować [me-resh-**ko**-vahćh] v. hemstitch; embellish with drawn work (*repeatedly*)
mereżkowanie [me-resh-ko-**vah**-ńe] n. hemstitching
mereżkowy [me-resh-**ko**-vi] adj.m. hemstitching (machine, etc.); of drawn work
meritum [me-ree-toom] n. essence (of a matter); merits (of a case)
merkantylista [mer-kahn-ti-**lees**-tah] m. mercantilist
merkantylistyczny [mer-kahn-ti-lees-**tich**-ni] adj.m. mercantilistic
merkantylizacja [mer-kahn-ti-lee-**zah**-tsyah] f. making mercantilistic; depending on mercantilism
merkantylizm [mer-kahn-**ti**-leezm] m. mercantilism
merkantylny [mer-kahn-**til**-ni] adj.m. mercantile; mercantilistic
merkaptan [mer-**kahp**-tahn] m. mercaptan
merla [**mer**-lah] f. gauze
merlan [**mer**-lahn] m. whiting (fish)
merostwo [me-**ros**-tfo] n. mayoralty
merydionalnie [me-ri-dyo-**nahl**-ńe]

adv. meridionally
merydionalny [me-ri-dyo-**nahl**-ni] adj.m. meridional
merynoprekos [me-ri-no-**pre**-kos] m. a cross between a merino and a French sheep
merynos [me-**ri**-nos] m. merino sheep; merino wool, etc.
merynosowy [me-ri-no-**so**-vi] adj.m. merino (sheep, wool, etc.)
merystem [me-**ri**-stem] m. meristem
merystema [me-ri-**ste**-mah] f. meristem
merystemalnie [me-ri-ste-**mahl**-ńe] adv. meristemically
merystemalny [me-ri-ste-**mahl**-ni] adj.m. meristematic
meryterium [me-ri-**ter**-yoom] n. Moeritherium (mammal)
merytorycznie [me-ri-to-**rich**-ńe] adv. essentially; in essence; on the merits of the case
merytoryczny [me-ri-to-**rich**-ni] adj.m. of substance; essential; substantial
rozważać sprawę pod względem merytorycznym [roz-**vah**-zhahćh **sprah**-v<u>an</u> pod **vzgl<u>an</u>**-dem me-ri-to-**rich**-nim] exp.: to consider a matter on its merits
merzyk [**me**-zhik] m. Mnium moss of Mniaceae family
mesa [**me**-sah] f. ship's dining room
mesjanista [me-syah-**ńees**-tah] m. Messianist
mesjanistyczny [me-syah-ńees-**tich**-ni] adj.m. Messianic
mesjanizm [me-**syah**-ńeezm] m. Messianism
mesjański [me-**syahń**-skee] adj.m. Messianic
mesjasz [**mes**-yahsh] m. the Messiah; (a) messiah
meskalina [mes-kah-**lee**-nah] f. mescalin; mescaline
mesmerycznie [mes-me-**rich**-ńe] adv. mesmerically; irresistibly
mesmeryczny [mes-me-**rich**-ni] adj.m. mesmeric; irresistible
mesmerysta [mes-me-**ris**-tah] m. mesmerist; mesmerizer
mesmeryzm [mes-**me**-rizm] m. mesmerism; hypnotism
mesmeryzować [mes-me-ri-**zo**-vahćh] v. mesmerize; hypnotize; spellbind; fascinate (*repeatedly*)
mesmeryzowanie [mes-me-ri-zo-**vah**-ńe] n. mesmerizing; hypnotizing; fascinating (*repeated*)
messa [**mes**-sah] f. mess
messerschmitt [**mes**-ser-shmeet] m. Messerschmitt (plane)
mesz [mesh] m. horse feed mix
meszek [**me**-shek] m. down; nap; fluff; bloom; pubescence
meszka [**mesh**-kah] f. gnat (fly) of Melusinidae family, of Simuliidae family; see: **mustyk**
meszt [mesht] m. slipper
meszta [**mesh**-tah] f. slipper; moccasin
meta [**me**-tah] f. goal; winning post; aim; distance; range; colloq: hangout; hideout (of thieves, etc.); den; haunt; joint
na dalszą metę [nah **dahl**-sh<u>own</u> **me**-t<u>an</u>] exp.: in the long run; at long-range; long-term (policy, plans, development, forecast, etc.)
meta- [**me**-tah] prefix: meta-
metabaza [me-tah-**bah**-zah] f. apostrophe; metabasis
metabioza [me-tah-**byo**-zah] f. metabiosis
metabola [me-tah-**bo**-lah] f. metabolic repetition of the same idea in different words; interchange of syllables or words for better sound; change of rhythm
metabolicznie [me-tah-bo-**leech**-ńe] adv. in a metabolic way; metabolically
metaboliczny [me-tah-bo-**leech**-ni] adj.m. metabolic
metabolit [me-tah-**bo**-leet] m. metabolite; product of metabolism
metabolity [me-tah-bo-**lee**-ti] pl. Metabola (insects)
metabolizm [me-tah-**bo**-leezm] m. metabolism; metamorphosis
metacentrum [me-tah-**tsen**-troom] n. metacenter
metafaza [me-tah-**fah**-zah] f. metaphase
metafilozofia [me-tah-fee-lo-**zo**-fyah] f. theory of philosophy as

independent of history
metafizycznie [me-tah-fee-**zich**-ńe] adv. metaphysically
metafizyczność [me-tah-fee-**zich**-nośhćh] f. abstractness
metafizyczny [me-tah-fee-**zich**-ni] adj.m. metaphysical; supernatural; very abstract; metaphysic
metafizyk [me-tah-**fee**-zik] m. metaphysician
metafizyka [me-tah-**fee**-zi-kah] f. metaphysics (speculative phil.); metaphysic; colloq: sham theories
metafora [me-tah-**fo**-rah] f. metaphor
metaforycznie [me-tah-fo-**rich**-ńe] adv. metaphorically; figuratively
metaforyczność [me-tah-fo-**rich**-nośhćh] f. metaphoric nature
metaforyczny [me-tah-fo-**rich**-ni] adj.m. metaphorical; figurative; metaphoric
metaforyka [me-tah-**fo**-ri-kah] f. the use of metaphors
metaforyzacja [me-tah-fo-ri-**zah**-tsyah] f. metaphorical presentation; figurative presentation
metaforyzować [me-tah-fo-ri-**zo**-vahćh] v. present by means of metaphors (*repeatedly*)
metaforyzowanie [me-tah-fo-ri-zo-**vah**-ńe] n. presentation by means of metaphors
metafraza [me-tah-**frah**-zah] f. metaphrase
metafrazować [me-tah-frah-**zo**-vahćh] v. metaphrase; make a literal translation; alter the wording (*repeatedly*)
metafrazowanie [me-tah-frah-zo-**vah**-ńe] n. metaphrasing; alteration of wording
metageneza [me-tah-ge-**ne**-zah] f. metagenesis
metajęzyk [me-tah-**y<u>an</u>**-zik] m. theoretical, abstract language used in linguistics
metajęzykowy [me-tah-y<u>an</u>-zi-**ko**-vi] adj.m. pertaining to the theoretical, abstract language used in linguistics
metal [**me**-tahl] m. metal
metal łożyskowy [**me**-tahl wo-zhis-**ko**-vi] exp.: bearing metal
metal nieszlachetny [**me**-tahl ńe-shlah-**khet**-ni] exp.: base metal
metal szlachetny [**me**-tahl shlah-**khet**-ni] exp.: noble metal
metaldehyd [me-tahl-**de**-khit] m. product of polymerization of aldehyde; metaldehyde
metalepsja [me-tah-**lep**-syah] f. metalepsis
metalicznie [me-tah-**leech**-ńe] adv. metallically
metaliczność [me-tah-**leech**-nośhćh] f. metallicity
metaliczny [me-tah-**leech**-ni] adj.m. metallic (luster, sound, oxide, etc.)
metalik [me-**tah**-leek] m. metallic color; car painted with metallic color
metalingwistyka [me-tah-leen-**gvees**-ti-kah] f. theory and methodology of linguistics
metalizacja [me-tah-lee-**zah**-tsyah] f. metalization (of a surface)
metalizować [me-tah-lee-**zo**-vahćh] v. metalize; make a metallic surface (*repeatedly*)
metalizowanie [me-tah-lee-zo-**vah**-ńe] n. metalization
metaloceramika [me-tah-lo-tse-**rah**-mee-kah] f. production of metallic powders; use of metallic powders in products
metalochromia [me-tah-lo-**khro**-myah] f. metalochromy
metalogiczny [me-tah-lo-**geech**-ni] adj.m. of theory and methodology of deductive systems
metalogika [me-tah-**lo**-gee-kah] f. theory and methodology of deductive systems
metalograf [me-tah-**lo**-grahf] m. metallograph; metallographic print; metallographist
metalografia [me-tah-lo-**grah**-fyah] f. metallography
metalograficzny [me-tah-lo-grah-**feech**-ni] adj.m. metallographic
metaloid [me-tah-**lo**-eet] m. metalloid
metaloorganiczny [me-tah-lo-or-gah-**ńeech**-ni] adj.m. organometallic
metaloplastyczny [me-tah-lo-plahs-

tich-ni] adj.m. of (artistic) work in metal; metal-work (design, etc.)
metaloplastyk [me-tah-lo-**plahs**-tik] m. artistic worker in metal; artist producing metal-works
metaloplastyka [me-tah-lo-**plahs**-ti-kah] f. (artistic) work in metal; metal-work
metaloryt [me-tah-**lo**-rit] m. metallograph; engraving in metal
metalotechnika [me-tah-lo-**tekh**-ńee-kah] f. colloq: manufacture of metallic products
metalowiec [me-tah-**lo**-vyets] m. metal-worker; worker in metal
metalowy [me-tah-**lo**-vi] adj.m. of metal; metal (industry, works, etc.)
metaloznawca [me-tah-lo-**znahf**-tsah] m. metallurgist
metaloznawstwo [me-tah-lo-**znahf**-stfo] n. science of metallurgy
metalurg [me-**tah**-loorg] m. metallurgist
metalurgia [me-tah-**loor**-gyah] f. metallurgy; science of metals
metalurgicznie [me-tah-loor-**geech**-ńe] adv. metallurgically
metalurgiczny [me-tah-loor-**geech**-ni] adj.m. metallurgical
metamatematyczny [me-tah-mah-te-mah-**tich**-ni] adj.m. metamathematical
metamatematyka [me-tah-mah-te-**mah**-ti-kah] f. metamathematics
metamer [me-**tah**-mer] m. metamere; somite
metamery [me-tah-**me**-ri] pl. metameres; somites; repeating segments of a body (of an insect, etc.)
metameria [me-tah-**mer**-yah] f. metamerism
metamerycznie [me-tah-me-**rich**-ńe] adv. metamerically
metameryczny [me-tah-me-**rich**-ni] adj.m. metameric
metamorficzny [me-tah-mor-**feech**-ni] adj.m. metamorphic (rocks)
metamorfizacja [me-tah-mor-fee-**zahts**-yah] f. metamorphosis; metamorphism
metamorfizm [me-tah-**mor**-feezm] m. metamorphosis; metamorphism
metamorfogeniczny [me-tah-mor-fo-ge-**ńeech**-ni] adj.m. of metamorphic geological processes
metamorfoza [me-tah-mor-**fo**-zah] f. metamorphosis; a change in (form, appearance, condition, character, etc.); metamorphism
ulec metamorfozie [**oo**-lets me-tah-mor-**fo**-źhe] exp.: to metamorphose; to undergo metamorphosis
metan [**me**-tahn] m. methane; marsh gas; fire damp
metanauka [me-tah-**nah**-oo-kah] f. study of scientific theories and methodology
metanit [me-**tah**-ńeet] m. explosive used in coal mines
metanol [me-**tah**-nol] m. methanol; methyl alcohol; methylated spirit
metanomierz [me-tah-**no**-myesh] m. gauge for methane content in the air
metanowy [me-tah-**no**-vi] adj.m. methanated (bacteria, etc.)
metapleks [me-**tah**-pleks] m. super-plastic for windshields, etc. (made in Poland)
metapleksowy [me-tah-plek-**so**-vi] adj.m. super-plastic (windshields, etc.)
metapsychiczny [me-tah-psi-**kheech**-ni] adj.m. metapsychical
metapsychik [me-tah-**psi**-kheek] m. metapsychist
metapsychika [me-tah-**psi**-khee-kah] f. psyche as defined by occultists; metapsychics
metapsychologia [me-tah-psi-kho-**lo**-gyah] f. parapsychology; metapsychology
metastaza [me-tahs-**tah**-zah] f. metastasis; a secondary growth of a malignant cancer
metateza [me-tah-**te**-zah] f. metathesis; transposition of letters or sounds in a word
metatonia [me-tah-**toń**-yah] f. tone transposition
metempsychiczny [me-tem-psi-**kheech**-ni] adj.m. metempsychic; metempsychosal
metempsychoza [me-tem-psi-**kho**-zah] f. metempsychosis

meteonawigacja [me-te-o-nah-vee-**gah**-tsyah] f. meteorologic navigation
meteor [me-**te**-or] m. meteor; fireball; a kind of silk
meteorograf [me-te-o-**ro**-grahf] m. meteorgraph (recording device)
meteorogram [me-te-o-**ro**-grahm] m. record of a meteorgraph
meteorolit [me-te-o-**ro**-leet] m. meteorlite; meteorite
meteorolog [me-te-o-**ro**-log] m. meteorologist
meteorologia [me-te-o-ro-**lo**-gyah] f. meteorology
meteorologiczny [me-te-o-ro-lo-**geech**-ni] adj.m. meteorological
komunikat meteorologiczny [ko-moo-**ńee**-kaht me-te-o-ro-lo-**geech**-ni] exp.: weather-forecast; weather report; colloq: the weather
służba meteorologiczna [**swoozh**-bah me-te-o-ro-lo-**geech**-nah] exp.: weather service
stacja meteorologiczna [**stahts**-yah me-te-o-ro-lo-**geech**-nah] exp.: weather station; weather office; meteorological office
wykres meteorologiczny [**vi**-kres me-te-o-ro-lo-**geech**-ni] exp.: weather-chart
meteoropata [me-te-o-ro-**pah**-tah] m. person allergic to meteoric changes
meteoropatia [me-te-o-ro-**pah**-tyah] f. allergy to meteoric changes
meteoropatologia [me-te-o-ro-pah-to-**lo**-gyah] f. meteoropathology (a study of allergy)
meteorowy [me-te-o-**ro**-vi] adj.m. meteor (dust, etc.)
meteoryczny [me-te-o-**rich**-ni] adj.m. meteoritic
meteoryt [me-te-**o**-rit] m. meteorite; shooting star
meteorytowy [me-te-o-ri-**to**-vi] adj.m. meteoritic; shooting star (observation, etc.)
meteorytyka [me-te-o-**ri**-ti-kah] f. study of meteorites; meteoritics
metka [**met**-kah] f. a variety of sausage; label (including price) sown on garments
metkal [**met**-kahl] m. light cotton fabric used for lining (of clothing and upholstery)
metkować [met-**ko**-vahćh] v. label; stick a label on merchandise (*repeatedly*)
metkownica [met-kov-**ńee**-tsah] f. labeling device for sticking labels on merchandise
metoda [me-**to**-dah] f. method; system of doing or handling; process; tactics
w tym szaleństwie jest metoda [f tim shah-**leń**-stfye yest me-**to**-dah] exp.: there's method in this madness
metodolog [me-to-**do**-log] m. methodologist
metodologia [me-to-do-**lo**-gyah] f. methodology
metodologicznie [me-to-do-lo-**geech**-ńe] adv. methodologically
metodologiczny [me-to-do-lo-**geech**-ni] adj.m. methodological
metodycznie [me-to-**dich**-ńe] adv. methodically; systematically
metodyczność [me-to-**dich**-nośhćh] f. methodism; systematic manner
metodyczny [me-to-**dich**-ni] adj.m. methodical; systematic
metodyk [me-**to**-dik] m. methodologist specializing in education
metodyka [me-**to**-di-kah] f. methodology
metodysta [me-to-**dis**-tah] m. methodist
metodystyczny [me-to-dis-**tich**-ni] adj.m. methodist; methodistic
metodyzm [me-**to**-dizm] m. Methodist denomination
metol [**me**-tol] m. metol
metolowy [me-to-**lo**-vi] adj.m. of metol
metonim [me-**to**-ńeem] m. metonym
metonimia [me-to-**ńee**-myah] f. metonymy
metonimicznie [me-to-ńee-**meech**-ńe] adv. metonymically
metonimiczny [me-to-ńee-**meech**-ni] adj.m. metonymic; metonimical
metopa [me-**to**-pah] f. metope
metr [metr] m. meter; 39.97 in.;

quintal; 100 kilograms; meter-stick; tape measure; colloq: dance teacher; language tutor
metr bieżący [metr bye-zhown-tsi] exp.: running meter
metr liniowy [metr lee-ńyo-vi] exp.: linear meter
metr kwadratowy [metr kfah-drah-to-vi] exp.: square meter
metr sześcienny [metr sheśh-ćhen-ni] exp.: cubic meter
metrampaż [me-trahm-pahsh] m. (printer) clicker; maker-up
metraż [met-rahsh] m. surface in square meters; metric area; measurement; metric volume; living area; house area
metrażowo [met-rah-zho-vo] adv. in terms of square footage; using a metric area
metrażowy [met-rah-zho-vi] adj.m. of square footage
metresa [me-tre-sah] f. colloq: metreza; mistress
metro [met-ro] n. subway; tube
metrolog [me-tro-log] m. metrologue; metrologist
metrologia [me-tro-lo-gyah] f. metrology
metrologicznie [me-tro-lo-geech-ńe] adv. by way of metrology
metrologiczny [me-tro-lo-geech-ni] adj.m. metrological
metron [me-tron] m. smallest unit in computerized experimental metrical information
metronom [me-tro-nom] m. metronome
metronomicznie [me-tro-no-meech-ńe] adv. metronomically
metronomiczny [me-tro-no-meech-ni] adj.m. metronomical; metronomic
metropolia [me-tro-pol-yah] f. metropolis; main large city
metropolita [me-tro-po-lee-tah] m. metropolitan; archbishop
metropolitalny [me-tro-po-lee-tahl-ni] adj.m. metropolitan
metropolitarny [me-tro-po-lee-tahr-ni] adj.m. metropolitan
metrowy [met-ro-vi] adj.m. one-meter long; of one meter
metrówka [met-roof-kah] f. meter-stick; meter measure
metrum [met-room] n. (musical) meter
metryczka [me-trich-kah] f. baby's birth certificate; certificate; specification
metryczny [met-rich-ni] adj.m. metric; of the metrical system
metryka [me-tri-kah] f. birth certificate; the public register; certificate; specification; system of Latin verses
metrykalny [me-tri-kahl-ni] adj.m. of a register
metyl [me-til] m. methyl
metylen [me-ti-len] m. methylene
metylenowy [me-ti-le-no-vi] adj.m. methylene (blue, etc.)
metylowy [me-ti-lo-vi] adj.m. methylic; methyl (alcohol, etc.)
metys [me-tis] m. metis; half-breed
metyska [me-tis-kah] f. (female) half-breed; metisse
metyzacja [me-ti-zahts-yah] f. crossbreeding
mewa [me-vah] f. sea gull
mewy [me-vi] pl. sea gulls; the gulls
mewi [me-vee] adj.m. sea-gull's; of a sea gull
mewka [mef-kah] f. young sea gull; small sea gull; colloq: harlot (in a port-city) (mob jargon)
mezalians [me-zah-lyahns] m. misalliance; improper alliance
mezenchyma [me-zen-khi-mah] f. mesenchyme
mezenchymatyczny [me-zen-khi-mah-tich-ni] adj.m. mesenchymal
mezo- [me-zo] prefix: middle-; average; central
mezoblast [me-zo-blahst] m. mesoblast
mezoderma [me-zo-der-mah] f. mesoderm
mezofil [me-zo-feel] m. mesophyll
mezofit [me-zo-feet] m. mesophyte
mezofity [me-zo-fee-ti] pl. mesophytes
mezofityczny [me-zo-fee-tich-ni] adj.m. mesophytic
mezognatyzm [me-zo-gnah-tizm] m. mesognathism
mezoklimat [me-zo-klee-maht] m. climatic conditions of a specific

region
mezolit [me-**zo**-leet] m. mesolythic period
mezolityczny [me-zo-lee-**tich**-ni] adj.m. mesolythic
mezon [**me**-zon] m. meson (particle)
mezony [me-**zo**-ni] pl. meson group (of unstable particles)
mezonin [me-**zo**-ńeen] m. mezzanine (floor between two stories)
mezonowy [me-zo-**no**-vi] adj.m. mesonic
mezopitek [me-zo-**pee**-tek] m. extinct monkey of the Tertiary period
mezoplankton [me-zo-**plahnk**-ton] m. mesoplankton (of middle depth)
mezosfera [me-zo-**sfe**-rah] f. mesosphere
mezosferyczny [me-zo-sfe-**rich**-ni] adj.m. mesospheric
mezoterma [me-zo-**ter**-mah] f. mesotherm (plants)
mezotermiczny [me-zo-ter-**meech**-ni] adj.m. mesothermal
mezotor [me-**zo**-tor] m. isotope of radium; mesothormium
mezozaur [me-**zo**-zahwr] m. mesosaur; Mesosaurus
mezozoiczny [me-zo-zo-**eech**-ni] adj.m. Mesozoic
mezozoik [me-zo-**zo**-eek] m. Mesozoic era
mezozoikum [me-zo-**zo**-ee-koom] n. Mesozoic era
mezzosopran [me-dzo-**sop**-rahn] m. mezzo-soprano (voice)
mezzosopranistka [me-dzo-sop-rah-**ńeest**-kah] f. mezzo-soprano (female singer)
mezzosopranowy [me-dzo-sop-rah-**no**-vi] adj.m. mezzo-soprano (female singer, voice, etc.)
mezzotinta [me-dzo-**teen**-tah] f. concave printing technique
męczarnia [man-**chahr**-ńah] f. torture; torment; anguish; agony; tribulation; anxiety
męcząco [man-**chown**-tso] adv. painfully; worrisomely
męczący [man-**chown**-tsi] adj.m. painful; tiring; fatiguing; exhausting; strenuous; weary; wearying; wearisome
męczelkowaty [man-chel-ko-**vah**-ti] adj.m. like the ichneumon fly
męczelkowate [man-chel-ko-**vah**-te] pl. the Ichneumonidae family
męczenie [man-**che**-ńe] n. bothering; tormenting
męczenie się [man-**che**-ńe śhan] n. getting tired
męczennica [man-chen-**ńee**-tsah] f. (woman) martyr
męczennicowaty [man-chen-ńee-tso-**vah**-ti] adj.m. of the passion-flower family
męczennicowate [man-chen-ńee-tso-**vah**-te] pl. the passion-flower family
męczennik [man-**chen**-ńeek] m. martyr; sufferer for faith, etc.
męczeński [man-**cheń**-skee] adj.m. martyr's
śmierć męczeńska [śhmyerćh man-**cheń**-skah] exp.: death of torture; martyrdom; martyr's death
męczeńsko [man-**cheń**-sko] adv. like a martyr
męczeństwo [man-**cheń**-stfo] n. martyrdom; torment; torture
męczyć [man-chićh] v. bother; torment; oppress; tire; exhaust; trouble; rack; prey (on); torture; agonize; weary; importune; make tired; fatigue; toil (at) (*repeatedly*)
on mnie męczy [on mńe man-chi] exp.: he bothers me; he makes me sick
męczyć się [man-chićh śhan] v. take pains; exert oneself; labor; rack one's brains; be in pain; suffer; worry (about); be agonized (at); tire (of); get tired; grow tired; become exhausted; drudge (at); give oneself trouble (*repeatedly*)
męczydusza [man-chi-**doo**-shah] m. & f. slang: a pest; a bore
mędlica [mand-**lee**-tsah] f. flax-comb; hackle; scutcher
mędrek [man-drek] m. smart alec(k); know-it-all; wiseacre
mędrkostwo [mandr-**ko**-stfo] n. sophistry; captious reasoning
mędrkować [mandr-**ko**-vahćh] v. play (the philosopher, the wise,

the wit, etc); sophisticate (*repeatedly*)
mędrkowanie [mandr-ko-**vah**-ńe] n. playing the philosopher; playing the wise; playing the wit; sophistication; sophistry
mędrzec [mand-zhets] m. sage; thinker; philosopher
męka [man-kah] f. fatigue; torment; pain; distress; nuisance; suffering; anguish; vexation; pangs (of hunger, death, etc.); misery; tribulation; agony; drudgery; annoyance
co za męka! [tso zah **man**-kah] excl.: how annoying!; what a nuisance!
to istna męka! [to **eest**-nah **man**-kah] exp.: it's a pest!
męski [man-skee] adj.m. masculine; manly; man's; virile; male; gentleman's; manlike; brave; manful; staminate
agresywnie męski [ah-gre-**siv**-ńe man-skee] exp.: aggressively virile; macho
cechy męskie [**tse**-khi **mans**-ke] exp.: virility
chór męski [khoor **mans**-kee] exp.: chorus of men; choir of men; group of male singers
garnitur męski [gahr-**ńee**-toor **mans**-kee] exp.: men's suit
obuwie męskie [o-boo-vye **mans**-ke] exp.: men's boots; men's shoes
po męsku [po **mans**-koo] exp.: like a man; in a manly fashion; manfully
rodzaj męski [ro-dzahy **mans**-kee] exp.: masculine gender
męskoosobowość [mans-ko-o-so-bo-vośhćh] f. the masculine gender (of adjectives, etc.)
męskoosobowy [mans-ko-o-so-**bo**-vi] adj.m. of the masculine gender; masculine
męskość [**mans**-kośhćh] f. manhood; virility; manliness; masculinity
przesadna męskość [pshe-**sahd**-nah **mans**-kośhćh] exp.: an exaggerated assertion of masculinity; machismo
męstwo [mahns-tfo] n. bravery; courage; prowess; fortitude; stalwartness; manfulness; valor
męt [mant] m. lees; dregs; draff; grounds; scum; refuse; underworld; raffle; see: **męty**
mętlik [**mant**-leek] m. topsy-turvy; puddle; muddle; mess; confusion
mętnawy [mant-**nah**-vi] adj.m. not quite clear; filmy
mętniacki [mant-**ńahts**-kee] adj.m. colloq: muddle-headed; wooly; foggy
mętniactwo [mant-**ńahts**-tfo] n. colloq: muddle-headedness; woolliness
mętniak [**mant**-ńahk] m. colloq: muddle-headed fellow
mętnie [**mant**-ńe] adv. turbidly; hazily; dimly; mistily; vaguely; confusedly; indistinctly; ambiguously
mętnieć [**mant**-ńećh] v. become or grow: turbid; hazy; dim; muddy; clouded; misty; vague; confused; indistinct; ambiguous; blurred; dull (*repeatedly*)
mętnienie [mant-**ńe**-ńe] n. becoming or growing: turbid; hazy; dim; muddy; clouded; misty; vague; confused; indistinct; ambiguous; blurred; dull
mętność [**mant**-nośhćh] f. turbidity; opacity; haziness; dimness; mistiness; vagueness; indistinctness; ambiguity; dullness; obscurity
mętny [**mant**-ni] adj.m. turbid; dull; dim; blurred; vague; fishy; confused; dubious
mętwik [**mant**-feek] m. comma bacillus
męty [man-ti] pl. dregs; scum of society; underworld; raffle
mężatka [man-**zhaht**-kah] f. married woman; femme covert
mężczyzna [mansh-**chiz**-nah] m. man (on restrooms: men)
prawdziwy mężczyzna [prahv-**dźhee**-vi mansh-**chiz**-nah] exp.: he-man; macho-man; macho
mężnie [**manzh**-ńe] adv. bravely; with courage; stalwartly;

valiantly; manfully; dauntlessly; high-spiritedly
mężnieć [manzh-ńećh] v. grow manly; muster courage; take heart; grow into a man (*repeatedly*)
mężny [manzh-ni] adj.m. brave; courageous; stalwart; valiant; manly; dauntless; high-spirited
mężobójczyni [man-zho-booy-chi-ńee] f. husband's murderer
mężobójstwo [man-zho-booy-stfo] n. murder of one's husband
mężowski [man-zhof-skee] adj.m. husband's; marital
mężulek [man-zhoo-lek] m. (nice, dear) husband
mężuś [man-zhoośh] m. (sweet, dear) husband
mężysko [man-zhis-ko] m. & n. colloq: (good, old) husband
mgielny [mgel-ni] adj.m. hazy; misty
mgiełka [mgew-kah] f. haze
mglisto [mglees-to] adv. foggily; mistily; dimly; nebulously; vaguely; obscurely; turbidly
jest mglisto [yest mglees-to] exp.: it is foggy; it is misty
mglistość [mglees-tośhćh] f. fog; mist; mistiness; vagueness; turbidity; turbidness; haze; haziness
mglisty [mglees-ti] adj.m. foggy; misty; dim; nebulous; vague
mgliste pojęcie [mglees-te po-yan-ćhe] exp.: vague idea
mgliście [mgleeśh-ćhe] adv. see: **mglisto**
mgła [mgwah] f. fog; mist; cloud (of smoke, etc.); gauziness (of fabric, etc.); dimness; darkness
jest mgła [yest mgwah] exp.: it is foggy
lekka mgła [lek-kah mgwah] exp.: haze
mgły [mgwi] pl. vapors
obłok mgły [ob-wok mgwi] exp.: fog bank
pamiętać jak przez mgłę [pah-myan-tahćh yahk pshez mgwan] exp.: to have a distant recollection (of); to have a hazy recollection (of)
zachodzić mgłą [zah-kho-dźheećh mgwown] exp.: to cloud over; to become misted over
mgławica [mgwah-vee-tsah] f. nebula; cloud; hazy idea; haze
mgławicowość [mgwah-vee-tso-vośhćh] f. nebulous rendition; cloudy condition
mgławicowy [mgwah-vee-tso-vi] adj.m. nebulous; cloudy
mgławy [mgwah-vi] adj.m. hazy; gauzy; dim; rather obscure; rather vague
mgłowy [mgwo-vi] adj.m. fog (signal, etc.)
syrena mgłowa [si-re-nah mgwo-vah] exp.: foghorn
mgnienie [mgńe-ńe] n. blink; twinkle; wink; flash; jiffy; trice; instant; moment; flicker (of the eye)
w mgnieniu oka [v mgńe-ńoo o-kah] exp.: in the twinkling of an eye; in a split second; in a flash; in a jiffy
mi [mee] pron.: me
daj mi [dahy mee] exp.: give me
miał [myahw] m. dust; powder
miałki [myahw-kee] adj.m. fine (sugar, sand, etc.); powdered
miałko [myahw-ko] adv. (crushed) fine
utrzeć na miałko [oo-tshećh nah myahw-ko] exp.: to grind into powder
miałkość [myahw-kośhćh] f. powdery condition
miano [myah-no] n. name; designation; appellation (label); denomination
mianować [myah-no-vahćh] v. appoint; promote; give a title (*repeatedly*)
mianować się [myah-no-vahćh śhan] v. call oneself (something) (*repeatedly*)
mianowanie [myah-no-vah-ńe] n. appointment; designation
mianowanie się [myah-no-vah-ńe śhan] n. calling oneself (something)
mianowicie [myah-no-vee-ćhe] adv. namely; to wit; that is ...
mianownictwo [myah-nov-ńeets-tfo]

n. nomenclature
mianownik [myah-**nov**-ńeek] m. denominator; nominative case; the nominative
mianownikowy [myah-nov-ńee-**ko**-vi] adj.m. nominative (ending, etc.)
miara [**myah**-rah] f. measure; gauge; yardstick; foot rule; amount; measuring rod; limit; size; dimensions; amount; measurements; standard; number; quantity measured out; moderation; bounds; fitting; measuring
bez miary [bez **myah**-ri] exp.: boundlessly; without restraint
w miarę jak ... [v **myah**-ran yahk] exp.: as ...
w pewnej mierze [f **pev**-ney **mye**-zhe] exp.: to some extent; to a certain degree; in some measure; after a sort; after a fashion
brać miarę [brahćh **myah**-ran] exp.: to measure
ubranie na miarę [oo-**brah**-ńe nah **myah**-ran] exp.: custom-made suit; suit to measure
w miarę jak się zbliżał [v **myah**-ran yahk śhan **zblee**-zhahw] exp.: as he was approaching
w jakiej mierze? [v **yah**-key **mye**-zhe] exp.: to what extent?
w miarę możności [v **myah**-ran mozh-**nośh**-ćhee] exp:. as much as possible; to the best of (my) ability
w pewnej mierze [f **pev**-ney **mye**-zhe] exp.: in some measure; to a certain extent
żadną miarą [**zhahd**-nown **myah**-rown] exp.: by no means; not by any means; not in the least
żadną miarą! [**zhahd**-nown **myah**-rown] excl.: far from it!; in no way!; by no means!
miareczka [myah-**rech**-kah] f. small measure
miareczkować [myah-rech-**ko**-vahćh] v. titrate (*repeatedly*)
miareczkowanie [myah-rech-ko-**vah**-ńe] n. titration
miareczkowo [myah-rech-**ko**-vo] adv. titrimetrically
miareczkowy [myah-rech-**ko**-vi] adj.m. titrimetric
miarka [**myahr**-kah] f. gauge; burette
przebrała się miarka [pshe-**brah**-wah śhan **myahr**-kah] exp.: that's too much; that's overdoing it; this is carrying things too far
miarkować [myahr-**ko**-vahćh] v. guess; note; measure out; deal out; gather; understand; see (for oneself); mitigate; check; restrain; moderate; temper (*repeatedly*)
miarkować się [myahr-**ko**-vahćh śhan] v. mitigate oneself; restrain oneself; be under restraint; keep oneself in check; realize (*repeatedly*)
miarkowanie [myahr-ko-**vah**-ńe] n. restraint; moderation
miarkownik [myahr-**kov**-ńeek] m. regulator (of machine-work)
miarodajnie [myah-ro-**dahy**-ńe] adv. authoritatively; competently; conclusively; reliably
miarodajność [myah-ro-**dahy**-nośhćh] f. authoritativeness; competence; conclusiveness
miarodajny [myah-ro-**dahy**-ni] adj.m. authoritative; competent; conclusive; reliable
miarowo [myah-**ro**-vo] adv. rhythmically; steadily; regularly; with cadenced regularity
miarowość [myah-**ro**-vośhćh] f. rhythm; steadiness; regularity; cadence regularity
miarowy [myah-**ro**-vi] adj.m. rhythmical; steady; regular; mensural; graduated; metrical
miarówka [myah-**roof**-kah] f. graduated ruler; burette; graduated glass
miast [myahst] adv. colloq: instead
miasteczko [myah-**stech**-ko] n. borough; small country town
wesołe miasteczko [ve-**so**-we myah-**stech**-ko] exp.: amusement park
żydowskie miasteczko [zhi-**dof**-ske myah-**stech**-ko] exp.: Jewish small town; shtetl
miasteczkowy [myah-stech-**ko**-vi] adj.m. of a country town;

country-town (atmosphere, market place, etc.)

miastenia [myah-**ste**-ńyah] f. myasthenia; muscular debility

miasteniczny [myah-ste-**ńeech**-ni] adj.m. myasthenic

miasto [**myahs**-to] n. town; city; townsfolk; townspeople; municipality; civic government
nie ma go w mieście [ńe mah go v **myeśh**-ćhe] exp.: he is out of town
poza miastem [**po**-zah **myahs**-tem] exp.: outside the town; out of town

miastowy [myahs-**to**-vi] adj.m. urban; town (life, gossip, traffic, etc.)

miau [myahw] m. cat's call: mew

miauczeć [**myahw**-chećh] v. mew; mial; meow; waul; utter a meow (*repeatedly*)

miauczenie [myahw-**che**-ńe] n. (a) mew; (a) mial; (a) meow; (a) waul; (an) uttering of a meow

miauk [myahwk] m. (a) mew; (a) mial; (a) meow; (a) waul; (an) uttering of a meow

miauknąć [**myahwk**-nownćh] v. mew; mial; miaow; waul; utter a miaow

miauknięcie [myahwk-**ńan**-ćhe] n. (a) mew; (a) mial; (a) miaow; (a) waul; (an) uttering of a miaow

miazdra [**myahz**-drah] f. cuticle; epidermis; true skin; corium

miazga [**myahz**-gah] f. pulp; squash; cambium
miazga zębowa [**myahz**-gah zan-**bo**-vah] exp.: dental pulp

miazgowiec [myahz-**go**-vyets] m. Lyctus beetle

miazma [**myahz**-mah] f. miasma; colloq: tobacco smoke
miazmy [**myahz**-mi] pl. miasmata

miazmat [**myahz**-maht] m. miasma; colloq: tobacco smoke

miażdżarka [myahzh-**dzhahr**-kah] f. crusher

miażdżąco [myahzh-**dzhown**-tso] adv. crushingly

miażdżący [myahzh-**dzhown**-tsi] adj.m. crushing; smashing

miażdżenie [myahzh-**dzhe**-ńe] n. crushing; squashing; smashing; grinding; laceration

miażdżyca [myahzh-**dzhi**-tsah] f. sclerosis; an abnormal hardening of body tissues

miażdżycowy [myahzh-dzhi-**tso**-vi] adj.m. sclerotic

miażdżyć [**myahzh**-dzhićh] v. crush; squash; smash; grind; lacerate; reduce to a pulp (*repeatedly*)
miażdżyć ciało [**myahzh**-dzhićh **ćhah**-wo] exp.: lacerate a body; mangle a body

miażdżysty [myahzh-**dzhis**-ti] adj.m. pultaceous

miąć [myownćh] v. crumple; wrinkle; crease; rumple; crush up; crush (*repeatedly*)

miąć się [myownćh śhan] v. crumple; get crumpled (*repeatedly*)

miąższ [myownsh] m. pulp; flesh of fruit; pomace; squash; parenchyma

miąższość [**myown**sh-shośhćh] f. thickness; viscosity

miąższowy [myownsh-**sho**-vi] adj.m. of the pulp; of the flesh; pulposus; pulpy

micela [mee-**tse**-lah] f. micelle

micelarny [mee-tse-**lahr**-ni] adj.m. micellar; of colloidal particle

micha [**mee**-khah] f. large bowl; large bowlful; bowlful

michaelita [mee-khah-e-**lee**-tah] m. member of a monastic order affording protection to orphans

michałek [mee-**khah**-wek] m. Michaelmas daisy; colloq: trifle; triviality

mickiewicziana [meets-ke-vee-**chyah**-nah] pl. the works and life of Adam Mickiewicz

mickiewiczolog [meets-ke-vee-**cho**-lok] m. expert in works and life of Adam Mickiewicz

mickiewiczologia [meets-ke-vee-cho-**lo**-gyah] f. research on the works and life of Adam Mickiewicz

miczman [**meech**-mahn] m. midshipman

miczurinizm [mee-choo-**ree**-ńeezm] m. agrobiology of I. Michurin

miczurinowiec [mee-choo-ree-**no**-vyets] m. adherent of theories of I. Michurin
midasowy [mee-dah-**so**-vi] adj.m. of Midas
midi [**mee**-dee] not declined: half-calf length (of dress, skirt, etc.)
midinetka [mee-dee-**net**-kah] f. French salesgirl in women's fashion store
midynetka [mee-di-**net**-kah] f. French salesgirl in women's fashion store
miech [myekh] m. bellows; sack; bag
miechy [**mye**-khi] pl. slang: lungs
miechera [mye-**khe**-rah] f. moss of the family Neckeraceae
miecherowaty [mye-khe-ro-**vah**-ti] adj.m. of the family Neckeraceae of mosses
miecherowate [mye-khe-ro-**vah**-te] pl. the family Neckeraceae of mosses
miechowaty [mye-kho-**vah**-ti] adj.m. baggy
miechowita [mye-kho-**vee**-tah] m. monk of a medieval monastic order
miechowici [mye-kho-**vee**-ćhee] pl. a medieval monastic order
miechunka [mye-**khoon**-kah] f. winter cherry; Cape gooseberry
miecielica [mye-ćhe-**lee**-tsah] f. snowstorm; blizzard; a folk dance
miecz [myech] m. sword; diagonal brace; drop keel; centerboard; spear side (in a family)
ogniem i mieczem [og-ńem ee **mye**-chem] exp.: by fire and sword
pod groźbą miecza [pod **groźh**-bown **mye**-chah] exp.: at the point of the sword
postawić sprawę na ostrzu miecza [po-**stah**-veećh **sprah**-van nah o-stshoo **mye**-chah] exp.: to bring matters to a head
miecznik [**myech**-ńeek] m. sword-bearer; swordfish
miecznikostwo [myech-ńee-**kos**-tfo] n. sword-bearer's office
mieczogon [mye-**cho**-gon] m. crab; king crab
mieczować [mye-**cho**-vahćh] v. brace (a beam, etc.) (*repeatedly*)
mieczowanie [mye-cho-**vah**-ńe] n. bracing (a beam, etc.); system of braces
mieczowaty [mye-cho-**vah**-ti] adj.m. sword-shaped
mieczowy [mye-**cho**-vi] adj.m. of the sword; of a brace; of a center-board; of a dropkeel
Kawalerowie Mieczowi [kah-vah-le-**ro**-vye mye-**cho**-vee] exp.: Livonian (Latvian) branch of the Teutonic Order of armed monks
wiązanie mieczowe [vyown-**zah**-ńe mye-**cho**-ve] exp.: bracing
mieczyk [**mye**-chik] m. small sword; toy sword; gladiolus; a fish of the family Cyprinodontidae
mieć [myećh] v. have; have got; hold; possess; run; own; keep; have of one's own; have to do (*repeatedly*)
co miałem robić? [tso **myah**-wem **ro**-beećh] exp.: what was I to do?
czy mam to zrobić? [chi mahm to **zro**-beećh] exp.: shall I do it?
ile masz lat? [**ee**-le mahsh laht] exp.: how old are you?
mam trzydzieści lat [mahm tshi-**dźheśh**-ćhee laht] exp.: I am 30 years old
mieć kogoś za coś [myećh **ko**-gośh zah tsośh] exp.: to take somebody for something
mieć zamiar [myećh **zah**-myahr] exp.: to intend; to have the intention
nie ma [ńe mah] exp.: there isn't; there isn't any; there is no; there aren't any; there are no (people, flowers, etc.)
nie ma dokąd pójść [ńe mah **do**-kownt pooyśhćh] exp.: there's no place to go
nie ma jak Zakopane [ńe mah yahk zah-ko-**pah**-ne] exp.: there's nothing like Zakopane
nie ma za co [ńe mah zah tso] exp.: don't mention it; I am glad to do it
mieć się [myećh śhan] v. be; feel (well, sick, etc); be getting on; be

faring; stand; be drawing (*repeatedly*)
jak się masz? [yahk **śhan** mahsh] exp.: how do you do?; how are you?
ma się na deszcz [mah śhan nah deshch] exp.: it is going to rain; it looks like rain
mieć się dobrze [myećh śhan **dob**-zhe] exp.: to be well; to feel well
mieć się ku końcowi [myećh śhan koo koń-**tso**-vee] exp.: to draw to an end
mieć się na baczności [myećh śhan nah bahch-**nośh**-ćhee] exp.: to be on one's guard
mieć się z pyszna [myećh śhan s **pish**-nah] exp.: to be in a sorry plight
nie masz się czego bać [ńe mahsh śhan **che**-go bahćh] exp.: you do not have to be afraid of anything
miednica [myed-**ńee**-tsah] f. hand washtub; pelvis; wash basin
miednicowy [myed-ńee-**tso**-vi] adj.m. pelvic
miedniczka [myed-**ńeech**-kah] f. small hand washtub
miedniczka nerkowa [myed-**ńeech**-kah ner-**ko**-vah] exp.: renal pelvis
zapalenie miedniczek nerkowych [zah-pah-le-ńe myed-**ńee**-chek ner-**ko**-vikh] exp.: pyelitis (renal pelvis lining inflamation)
miedniczkowy [myed-ńeech-**ko**-vi] adj.m. of a small hand washtub; of the renal pelvis
miedniczny [myed-**ńeech**-ni] adj.m. of a pelvis
miedza [**mye**-dzah] f. farm boundary strip; bounds; balk (between cultivated fields)
miedziak [**mye**-dźhahk] m. copper penny; copper coin
miedzianka [mye-**dźhahn**-kah] f. copperhead (viper); smooth snake (Coronella austriaca); copper ore
miedzianobrody [mye-dźhah-no-**bro**-di] adj.m. red-bearded
miedzianoczerwony [mye-dźhah-no-cher-**vo**-ni] adj.m. copper red
miedzianoskóry [mye-dźhah-no-**skoo**-ri] adj.m. coppery
miedzianowłosy [mye-dźhah-no-**vwo**-si] adj.m. copper-headed; red-haired
miedziany [mye-**dźhah**-ni] adj.m. of copper; coppery; of brass
blacha miedziana [**blah**-khah mye-**dźhah**-nah] exp.: copperplate
miedziawy [mye-**dźhah**-vi] adj.m. cupreous
miedzionikiel [mye-dźho-**ńee**-kel] m. copper-nickel
miedzionośny [mye-dźho-**nośh**-ni] adj.m. copper-rich
miedzioryt [mye-**dźho**-rit] m. copperplate engraving; copperplate
miedziorytnictwo [mye-dźho-rit-**ńeets**-tfo] n. copperplate engraving; chalcography
miedziorytniczy [mye-dźho-rit-**ńee**-chi] adj.m. of a copperplate engraving; copper engraver's
miedziorytnik [mye-dźho-**rit**-ńeek] m. copper engraver
miedziorytowy [mye-dźho-ri-**to**-vi] adj.m. copperplate (engraving, etc.)
miedziować [mye-**dźho**-vahćh] v. copper; coat with copper (*repeatedly*)
miedziowanie [mye-dźho-**vah**-ńe] n. coating with copper
miedziowiec [mye-**dźho**-vyets] m. an element of the copper group
miedziowce [mye-**dźhof**-tse] pl. (elements of the) copper group
miedziownia [mye-**dźhov**-ńah] f. copper works
miedziownik [mye-**dźhov**-ńeek] m. copper worker; copper miner
miedziowy [mye-**dźho**-vi] adj.m. copper (steel, etc.); cupric
miedź [myećh] f. copper; copper coins
miejsce [**myeys**-tse] n. place; location; spot; point; room; space; seat; employment; berth; scene; occupation; job
miejscami [myeys-**tsah**-mee] exp.: here and there; in places
miejsce pobytu [**myeys**-tse po-**bi**-too] exp.: residence

miejsce przeznaczenia [myeys-tse pshe-znah-che-ńah] exp.: destination
miejsce siedzące [myeys-tse śhe-dzown-tse] exp.: sitting place
miejsca stojące [myeys-tsah sto-yown-tse] exp.: standing room
miejsce urodzenia [myeys-tse oo-ro-dze-ńah] exp.: birthplace
odmówić z miejsca [od-moo-veećh z myey-stsah] exp.: to refuse point blank
płatne na miejscu [pwaht-ne nah myeys-tsoo] exp.: payable on the spot
jest dużo miejsca [yest doo-zho myeys-tsah] exp.: there is plenty of room
zająć miejsce [zah-yownćh myeys-tse] exp.: to take one's seat
zrobić miejsce [zro-beećh myeys-tse] exp.: to make room
nie na miejscu [ńe nah myeys-tsoo] exp.: out of place
na miejsce [nah myeys-tse] exp.: in place; instead
z miejsca [z myey-stsah] exp.: adv. right off; straightaway; straight off; at once; out of hand

miejscowa [myey-stso-vah] adj.f. (female) local; native; indigenous; f. native woman; local girl

miejscownik [myeys-tsov-ńeek] m. (gram.) locative case; local postmark

miejscownikowy [myeys-tsov-ńee-ko-vi] adj.m. locative

miejscowo [myey-stso-vo] adv. locally; partly; in places

miejscowość [myey-stso-vośhćh] f. locality; place; town; village; spot
miejscowość kąpielowa [myey-stso-vośhćh kown-pye-lo-vah] exp.: spa; watering place
miejscowość kuracyjna [myey-stso-vośhćh koo-rah-tsiy-nah] exp.: health resort
miejscowość letniskowa [myey-stso-vośhćh let-ńees-ko-vah] exp.: summer resort
miejscowość nadmorska [myey-stso-vośhćh nahd-mor-skah] exp.: seaside resort
nazwa miejscowości [nahz-vah myey-stso-vośh-ćhee] exp.: place-name

miejscowy [myey-stso-vi] adj.m. local; native; indigenous; aboriginal; autochthonous; endemic; stationary; partial
człowiek miejscowy [chwo-vyek myey-stso-vi] exp.: a native
język miejscowy [yan-zik myey-stso-vi] exp.: vernacular
znieczulenie miejscowe [zńe-choo-le-ńe myey-stso-ve] exp.: local anesthesia

miejscówka [myey-stsoof-kah] f. colloq: reserved seat ticket

miejski [myey-skee] adj.m. of a town; of a city; urban
czytelnia miejska [chi-tel-ńah myey-skah] exp.: public library
po miejsku [po myeys-koo] exp.: after the manner of townspeople
prawa miejskie [prah-vah myeys-ke] exp.: civic rights; city laws and regulations
rada miejska [rah-dah myeys-kah] exp.: town-council; city council
zarząd miejski [zah-zhownt myey-skee] exp.: municipal government

mielec [mye-lets] m. gizzard; gigerium (dish, etc.)

mielenie [mye-le-ńe] n. grinding; milling; mincing; jabber; prattling incoherently

mielerz [mye-lesh] m. charcoal kiln

mielizna [mye-leez-nah] f. shoal; shallow water; sandbank; shelf
osiąść na mieliźnie [o-śhownśhćh nah mye-leeźh-ńe] exp.: to run aground; to be stranded

mielnica [myel-ńee-tsah] f. Baltic salmon

mielonka [mye-lon-kah] f. groundings; mincings

mielony [mye-lo-ni] adj.m. ground; milled; minced; pulverized; chewed up

mieniak tęczowy [mye-ńahk tan-cho-vi] m. emperor butterfly; purple emperor

mieniać [mye-ńahćh] v. colloq: change; swap; exchange; convert

(*repeatedly*)
mieniać się [**mye**-ńahćh śhan] v. colloq: swap with each other; exchange with each other; convert oneself (*repeatedly*)
mieniący się [mye-**ńown**-tsi śhan] adj.m. shot (silk, etc.); versicolored; iridescent
mienić [**mye**-ńeećh] v. call; glitter; shimmer; change color; show a play of colors (*repeatedly*)
mienić się [**mye**-ńeećh śhan] v. change one's color; glitter; exhibit a play of colors; be iridescent; shimmer; change (into) (*repeatedly*)
mienie [**mye**-ńe] n. property; belongings; estate; effects; possessions
mienienie się [mye-**ńe**-ńe śhan] n. being iridescent
mienszewicki [myen-she-**vee**-tskee] adj.m. Menshevik (party, etc.)
mienszewik [myen-**she**-veek] m. Menshevik
mienszewizm [myen-**she**-veezm] m. Menshevism
miernictwo [myer-**ńeets**-tfo] n. surveying; land measuring
mierniczy [myer-**ńee**-chi] m. surveyor; adj.m. geodetic
miernie [**myer**-ńe] adv. moderately; poorly; indifferently
miernik [**myer**-ńeek] m. measure; gauge; standard; measuring (cup, glass, device, instrument, etc.)
miernikowiec [myer-ńee-**ko**-vyets] m. geometer moth
gąsienica miernikowca [gown-śhe-**ńee**-tsah myer-ńee-**kof**-tsah] exp.: measuring worm; looper
miernikowce [myer-ńee-**kof**-tse] pl. the geometrids
mierność [**myer**-nośhćh] f. mediocrity; average range; moderation; average intelligence; work of no value; insignificant person; slang.: pip-squeak (Brit.)
miernota [myer-**no**-tah] f. average intelligence; mediocrity; work of no value; slang.: pip-squeak (Brit.)
mierny [**myer**-ni] adj.m. mediocre; mean; of moderate means; moderate; indifferent; temperate; well aimed (shot)
mierzalny [mye-**zhahl**-ni] adj.m. measurable
mierzchnąć [**myesh**-khnownćh] v. grow dim; grow dusky; pale; darken (*repeatedly*)
mierzeja [mye-**zhe**-yah] f. sandbar; spit
mierzenie [mye-**zhe**-ńe] n. measurement; mensuration
mierzenie się [mye-**zhe**-ńe śhan] n. competing; measuring oneself
mierzić [**myer**-źheećh] v. be disgusting; disgust; sicken; make (render) unbearable (*repeatedly*)
mierznąć [**myer**-znownćh] v. become disgusting; pall (on somebody) (*repeatedly*)
mierzwa [**myezh**-vah] f. litter; muck; matted straw; farmyard manure
mierzwić [**myezh**-veećh] v. manure a field; tousle; ruffle; mat (*repeatedly*)
mierzwić się [**myezh**-veećh śhan] v. get tousled; get ruffled; get matted (*repeatedly*)
mierzwienie [myezh-**vye**-ńe] n. putting manure on a field; matting
mierzyć [**mye**-zhićh] v. measure; measure out (cloth, etc.); sound (the sea, etc.); judge; try on; aim (at); level a gun (at); tend towards; estimate; evaluate (*repeatedly*)
mierzyć się [**mye**-zhićh śhan] v. match; be a match (for); equal; rival; vie (with); measure oneself; measure one's strength (*repeatedly*)
mierzyć się na szable [**mye**-zhićh śhan nah **shahb**-le] exp.: to measure swords (with somebody)
nie móc się mierzyć z kimś [ńe moots śhan **mye**-zhićh s keeśh] exp.: to be be no match for somebody; to have no chance winning against someone
mierzyn [**mye**-zhin] m. horse of draught
mierzynek [mye-**zhi**-nek] m. (small) horse of draught
miesiąc [**mye**-śhownts] m. month; colloq: moon; lunar month
od dziś za miesiąc [od dźheeśh

zah **mye**-śhownts] exp.: this day month
miesiąc miodowy [**mye**-śhownts myo-**do**-vi] exp.: honeymoon
miesiąc w pełni [**mye**-śhownts f **pew**-ńee] exp.: full moon
za miesiąc [zah **mye**-śhownts] exp.: in a month; a month from today; this day month
miesiączek [mye-**śhown**-chek] m. (nice, little) moon; month
miesiączka [mye-**śhownch**-kah] f. menstruation; monthlies; menses; colloq: period
miesiączkować [mye-śhownch-**ko**-vahćh] v. menstruate; have one's monthlies (*repeatedly*)
miesiączkowanie [mye-śhownch-ko-**vah**-ńe] n. menstruation
miesiącznica [mye-śhownch-**ńee**-tsah] f. satin-flower; honesty (plant)
miesić [**mye**-śheećh] v. massage; knead (dough, clay, etc.); churn (mud) (*repeatedly*)
miesięcznie [mye-**śhanch**-ńe] adv. monthly; every month
płacić komuś miesięcznie [**pwah**-ćheećh **ko**-moośh mye-**śhanch**-ńe] exp.: to pay somebody by the month
miesięcznik [mye-**śhanch**-ńeek] m. monthly paper; monthly
miesięcznikowaty [mye-śhanch-ńee-ko-**vah**-ti] adj.m. menispermaceous
miesięcznikowate [mye-śhanch-ńee-ko-**vah**-te] pl. the moonseed family
miesięczny [mye-**śhanch**-ni] adj.m. monthly; one month's (wages, holiday, etc.); of one month duration; one month old; month old
mieszacz [**mye**-shahch] m. mixer
mieszać [**mye**-shahćh] v. mix; mingle; blend; stir; mix up; agitate; knead; temper; blunge; amalgamate and blend; add; entangle; involve; shuffle; confuse; mistake (one for another); abash; throw into confusion (*repeatedly*)
mieszać karty [**mye**-shahćh **kahr**-ti] exp.: to shuffle the cards
mieszać się [**mye**-shahćh śhan] v. mix; mingle; blend; meddle (with); become (be) confused; interfere (in, with); be mixed up; get mixed up; be put out; lose countenance (*repeatedly*)
nie mieszaj się w to [ńe **mye**-shahy śhan f to] exp.: keep out of this
mieszadełko [mye-shah-**dew**-ko] n. small stirrer
mieszadło [mye-**shah**-dwo] n. stirrer; stirring apparatus; mixer (arm); (steel mill) rabble
mieszak [**mye**-shahk] m. stirrer; stirring tool (device)
mieszalnia [mye-**shahl**-ńah] f. (fodder, etc.) mixing room (or shed)
mieszalnik [mye-**shahl**-ńeek] m. mixing container
mieszalny [mye-**shahl**-ni] adj.m. miscible; mixing (vat, etc.)
mieszałka [mye-**shahw**-kah] f. stirrer
mieszanie [mye-**shah**-ńe] n. agitation; interference (in); confusion
mieszanie się [mye-**shah**-ńe śhan] n. interfering; getting confused
mieszaniec [mye-**shah**-ńets] m. half-breed; hybrid; cross; mongrel
mieszanina [mye-shah-**ńee**-nah] f. mixture; compound; medley; jumble; hotchpotch
mieszanka [mye-**shahn**-kah] f. blend; mix; mixture; miscellany; composition; compound
bogata mieszanka [bo-**gah**-tah mye-**shahn**-kah] exp.: rich mixture
uboga mieszanka [oo-**bo**-gah mye-**shahn**-kah] exp.: lean mixture; weak mixture
mieszany [mye-**shah**-ni] adj.m. hybrid; cross-breed; mongrel; miscellaneous; assorted; compound
mieszańcowy [mye-shahń-**tso**-vi] adj.m. hybrid (features, etc.)
mieszarka [mye-**shahr**-kah] f. blender; mixer; agitator; kneading machine
mieszczanin [myesh-**chah**-ńeen] m. burgher; townsman; citizen;

middle-class man
mieszczanie [myesh-chah-ńe] pl. burghers; townspeople; townsfolk
mieszczanka [myesh-chahn-kah] f. middle-class woman; bourgeois woman; townswoman
mieszczański [myesh-chahń-skee] adj.m. middle-class (mentality, circles, etc.); bourgeois; colloq: narrow-minded; Philistine
stan mieszczański [stahn myesh-chahń-skee] exp.: middle class; bourgeoisie
mieszczańskość [myesh-chahń-skośhćh] f. colloq: philistinism; narrow-mindedness; Babbittry
mieszczaństwo [myesh-chahń-stfo] n. middle class; townspeople; colloq: narrow-mindedness
mieszczenie [myesh-che-ńe] n. placing; storing; holding; situating
mieszczenie się [myesh-che-ńe śhan] n. fitting into (a box, a bed, an apartment, etc.)
mieszczka [myeshch-kah] f. colloq: middle-class woman; bourgeois woman; townswoman
mieszczuch [myesh-chookh] m. derogatory form of: **mieszczanin**
mieszek [mye-shek] m. (small) sack; bag; bellows; follicle; utricle; folliculus; colloq: moneybag
mieszenie [mye-she-ńe] n. kneading; massaging
mieszkać [myesh-kahćh] v. dwell; live; have a flat; have an apartment; stay (with); be staying (with); lodge; reside; inhabit; abide (*repeatedly*)
mieszkać gdzieś [myesh-kahćh gdźheśh] exp.: to stay somewhere
mieszkać u kogoś [myesh-kahćh oo ko-gośh] exp.: to stay with somebody
nie mieszkać [ńe myesh-kahćh] exp.: colloq: not to tarry; not to be late
nie mieszkając [ńe myesh-kah-yownts] exp.: colloq: without delay
mieszkalnictwo [myesh-kahl-ńeets-tfo] n. domestic architecture; housing (term used in socialist city planing)
mieszkalny [myesh-kahl-ni] adj.m. inhabitable; habitable
dom mieszkalny [dom myesh-kahl-ni] exp.: dwelling house; farm house; habitation
mieszkanie [myesh-kah-ńe] n. apartment; rooms; lodgings; home; dwelling place; abode; tenement
dać komuś mieszkanie i utrzymanie [dahćh ko-moośh myesh-kah-ńe ee oo-tshi-mah-ńe] exp.: to give somebody bed and board
wynająć mieszkanie [vi-nah-yownćh myesh-kah-ńe] exp.: to rent an apartment
mieszkaniec [myesh-kah-ńets] m. inhabitant; lodger; resident; occupant; inmate
mieszkaniowiec [myesh-kah-ńo-vyets] m. block of apartments; apartment high-rise; tenement house; specialist in housing problems
mieszkaniowy [myesh-kah-ńo-vi] adj.m. housing (problems, etc.); dwelling (house, etc.)
dzielnica mieszkaniowa [dźhel-ńee-tsah myesh-kah-ńo-vah] exp.: residential district
głód mieszkaniowy [gwood myesh-kah-ńo-vi] exp.: housing shortage
kultura mieszkaniowa [kool-too-rah myesh-kah-ńo-vah] exp.: living habits
problem mieszkaniowy [prob-lem myesh-kah-ńo-vi] exp.: housing problem
urząd mieszkaniowy [oo-zhownd myesh-kah-ńo-vi] exp.: housing office
mieszkaniówka [myesh-kah-ńoof-kah] f. state management of housing construction and assignment
mieszkanka [myesh-kahn-kah] f. (woman) inhabitant; lodger, resident
mieszkanko [myesh-kahn-ko] n. (small, nice) apartment; dwelling
mieszkowy [myesh-ko-vi] adj.m.

provided with bellows; follicular
mieścić [**myeśh**-ćheećh] v. contain; place; set; hold; store (*repeatedly*)
mieścić się [**myeśh**-ćheećh śhan] v. be contained; be situated; have enough room; fit into; be comprised; be included; find enough room (*repeatedly*)
mieścina [myeśh-**ćhee**-nah] f. out-of-the-way paltry place; small town
mieść [myeśhćh] v. sweep; fling; hurl; blow (leaves, etc.) (*repeatedly*)
mietelnik [mye-**tel**-ńeek] m. Kochia shrub
mietlasty [myet-**lahs**-ti] adj.m. shaggy
mietlica [myet-**lee**-tsah] f. bent grass (Agrostis)
miewać [**mye**-vahćh] v. have occasionally; feel sometimes (*repeatedly*)
on miewa bóle głowy [on **mye**-vah **boo**-le **gwo**-vi] exp.: he has occasional headaches
miewać się [**mye**-vahćh śhan] v. feel; be feeling (*repeatedly*)
jak się pan miewa? [yahk śhan pahn **mye**-vah] exp.: how are you feeling?
mięcho [**myan**-kho] n. colloq: meat
mięcie [**myan**-ćhe] n. crumpling; wrinkling
mięciuchno [myan-**ćhookh**-no] adv. softly in a nice way
mięciuchny [myan-**ćhookh**-ni] adj.m. nicely soft
mięciusieńki [myan-ćhoo-**śheń**-kee] adj.m. very nicely soft
mięciusieńko [myan-ćhoo-**śheń**-ko] adv. very softly
mięciuteńki [myan-ćhoo-**teń**-kee] adj.m. very nicely soft
mięciuteńko [myan-ćhoo-**teń**-ko] adv. softly in a very nice way
mięciutki [myan-**ćhoot**-kee] adj.m. nicely soft
mięciutko [myan-**ćhoot**-ko] adv. softly in a nice way
mięczak [**myan**-chahk] m. mollusc; shellfish; colloq: wimp
mięczaki [myan-**chah**-kee] pl. the phylum Mollusca
mięczakowaty [myan-chah-ko-**vah**-ti] adj.m. molluscous
międlak [**myand**-lahk] m. hand swingle; brake
międlarka [myand-**lahr**-kah] f. swingle; brake; staking machine
międlarnia [myand-**lahr**-ńah] f. swingle shop; staking shop
międlenie [myand-**le**-ńe] n. swingle
międlica [myand-**lee**-tsah] f. brake
międlić [**myand**-leećh] v. bruise; hackle; crush; swingle; scutch; hold forth; twaddle (*repeatedly*)
międoła [myan-**do**-wah] m. slang: twaddler
między [**myan**-dzi] preposition: between (us, etc.); among; amongst; in the midst
między innymi [**myan**-dzi een-**ni**-mee] exp.: among other things
między nami [**myan**-dzi **nah**-mee] exp.: among us; in our midst; (strictly) between us
między wierszami [**myan**-dzi vyer-**shah**-mee] exp.: between the lines
ściśle między nami [**śhćhee**-śhle **myan**-dzi **nah**-mee] exp.: between ourselves; between you and me
między- [myan-dzi] prefix: between-; inter-
międzyatomowy [myan-dzi-ah-to-**mo**-vi] adj.m. interatomic
międzybieg [**myan**-dzi-byeg] m. heat (in a race)
międzyczas [myan-**dzi**-chahs] m. intermediate time (during a race)
międzycząsteczkowy [myan-dzi-chown-stech-**ko**-vi] adj.m. intermolecular
międzydzielnicowy [myan-dzi-dźhel-ńee-**tso**-vi] adj.m. interurban; interprovincial
międzygatunkowy [myan-dzi-gah-toon-**ko**-vi] adj.m. interspecific; between species
międzygórski [myan-dzi-**goor**-skee] adj.m. intermontane (terrain, etc.)
międzygórze [myan-dzi-**goo**-zhe] n. intermontane terrain
międzygwiazdowy [myan-dzi-gvyahz-**do**-vi] adj.m. interstellar

międzygwiezdny [myan-dzi-**gvyezd**-ni] adj.m. interstellar
lot międzygwiezdny [lot myan-dzi-**gvyezd**-ni] exp.: interstellar flight
międzyklubowy [myan-dzi-kloo-**bo**-vi] adj.m. interclub (contests, etc.)
międzykomorowy [myan-dzi-ko-mo-**ro**-vi] adj.m. interventricular
międzykomórkowy [myan-dzi-ko-moor-**ko**-vi] adj.m. intercellular
międzykontynentalny [myan-dzi-kon-ti-nen-**tahl**-ni] adj.m. intercontinental
międzykostny [myan-dzi-**kost**-ni] adj.m. interosseous
międzykręgowy [myan-dzi-kran-**go**-vi] adj.m. intervertebral
międzylądowanie [myan-dzi-lown-do-**vah**-ńe] n. airplane landing for refueling and taking additional passengers
międzylekcyjny [myan-dzi-lek-**tsiy**-ni] adj.m. occurring between classes (in school)
międzylodowcowy [myan-dzi-lo-dof-**tso**-vi] adj.m. interglacial
międzyludzki [myan-dzi-**loots**-kee] adj.m. interpersonal; between people
stosunki międzyludzkie [sto-**soon**-kee myan-dzi-**loots**-ke] exp.: mutual relations between people; interpersonal (human) relations
międzymiastowy [myan-dzi-myah-**sto**-vi] adj.m. interurban
(rozmowa) międzymiastowa [roz-**mo**-vah myan-dzi-myah-**sto**-vah] exp.: long-distance call; trunk call (Brit.)
międzymięśniowy [myan-dzi-myan-**śhńo**-vi] adj.m. intermuscular
międzymorski [myan-dzi-**mor**-skee] adj.m. interoceanic
międzymorze [myan-dzi-**mo**-zhe] n. isthmus; narrow strip of land (with water on each side)
międzymózgowie [myan-dzi-mooz-**go**-vye] n. diencephalon
międzymurze [myan-dzi-**moo**-zhe] n. intermural space
międzynarodowiec [myan-dzi-nah-ro-**do**-vyets] m. internationalist; cosmopolitan; cosmopolite
międzynarodowo [myan-dzi-nah-ro-**do**-vo] adv. internationally
międzynarodowościowy [myan-dzi-nah-ro-do-vośh-**ćho**-vi] adj.m. international
międzynarodowy [myan-dzi-nah-ro-**do**-vi] adj.m. international; cosmopolitan
międzynarodówka [myan-dzi-nah-ro-**doof**-kah] f. International; the Internationale (anthem)
międzyosobniczy [myan-dzi-o-sob-**ńee**-chi] adj.m. occurring between individuals; interpersonal
międzypaństwowy [myan-dzi-pahń-**stfo**-vi] adj.m. interstate; between sovereign states
międzyparlamentarny [myan-dzi-pahr-lah-men-**tahr**-ni] adj.m. interparliamentary
międzyplanetarny [myan-dzi-plah-ne-**tahr**-ni] adj.m. interplanetary; of cosmic space; of outer space
międzyplemienny [myan-dzi-ple-**myen**-ni] adj.m. intertribal
międzyplon [myan-**dzi**-plon] m. intercrop; catch crop; aftercrop
międzypokład [myan-dzi-**pok**-waht] m. 'tweendecks; space between decks
międzypokładzie [myan-dzi-pok-**wah**-dźhe] n. space between decks
międzypokoleniowy [myan-dzi-po-ko-le-**ńo**-vi] adj.m. occuring between generations; intergenerational (conflicts, etc.)
międzyresortowy [myan-dzi-re-sor-**to**-vi] adj.m. interdepartmental
międzyrząd [myan-**dzi**-zhownt] m. intercrop
międzyrządowy [myan-dzi-zhown-**do**-vi] adj.m. intergovernmental
międzyrzecze [myan-dzi-**zhe**-che] n. region between two rivers
międzyrzędowy [myan-dzi-zhan-**do**-vi] adj.m. of the space between rows of plants
międzyrzędzie [myan-dzi-**zhan**-dźhe] n. space between rows of plants
międzysamogłoskowy [myan-dzi-sah-mo-gwos-**ko**-vi] adj.m. intervocal; intervocalic
międzysemestralny [myan-dzi-se-mes-**trahl**-ni] adj.m. of the time

between school terms
międzysłupie [myan-dzi-**swoo**-pye] n. (building) bay
międzysojuszniczy [myan-dzi-so-yoosh-**ńee**-chi] adj.m. interallied
międzystanowy [myan-dzi-stah-**no**-vi] adj.m. interstate (within the United States of America) (highway, etc.)
międzyszczękowy [myan-dzi-shchan-**ko**-vi] adj.m. intermaxillar
międzyszkolny [myan-dzi-**shkol**-ni] adj.m. interschool (contest, etc.)
międzytorze [myan-dzi-**to**-zhe] n. inter-track space
międzyuczelniany [myan-dzi-oo-chel-**ńah**-ni] adj.m. intercollegiate
międzywęźle [myan-dzi-**van**-źhle] n. internode
międzywierszowy [myan-dzi-vyer-**sho**-vi] adj.m. between the lines (meaning, reading, etc.)
międzywojenny [myan-dzi-vo-**yen**-ni] adj.m. interwar (period, etc.); between the two World Wars
międzywojewódzki [myan-dzi-vo-ye-**voots**-kee] adj.m. interregional; interprovincial
międzywojnie [myan-dzi-**voy**-ńe] n. interwar period
międzywyrazowy [myan-dzi-vi-rah-**zo**-vi] adj.m. interverbal; between words
międzywyznaniowy [myan-dzi-vi-znah-**ńo**-vi] adj.m. interdenominational; interconfessional
międzyzakładowy [myan-dzi-zah-khwah-**do**-vi] adj.m. interdepartmental; intercompany
międzyzakresowy [myan-dzi-zah-kre-**so**-vi] adj.m. between ranges (of radio transmission, etc.)
międzyzdaniowy [myan-dzi-zdah-**ńo**-vi] adj.m. between sentences (space, etc.)
międzyzwrotnikowy [myan-dzi-zvrot-**ńee**-**ko**-vi] adj.m. intertropical
międzyżebrowy [myan-dzi-zhe-**bro**-vi] adj.m. intercostal
międzyżebrze [myan-dzi-**zhe**-bzhe] n. intercostal region of the rib cage
miękczenie [myank-**che**-ńe] n. palatization (of consonants)
miękczenie się [myank-**che**-ńe śhan] n. getting soft
miękczyć [**myank**-chićh] v. soften; move; touch; palatalize (*repeatedly*)
miękczyć się [**myank**-chićh śhan] v. become soft (*repeatedly*)
miękinia [myan-**kee**-ńah] f. chaff
miękisz [**myan**-keesh] m. pulp
miękiszowy [myan-kee-**sho**-vi] adj.m. pulpy
miękkawy [myank-**kah**-vi] adj.m. softish
miękki [**myank**-kee] adj.m. soft; flabby; flaccid; limp; supple; tender; slack; mild; pliant; yielding; feeble; irresolute; gentle; mellow; palatal (pronunciation, etc.)
miękki w dotyku [**myank**-kee v do-ti-koo] exp.: soft to the touch
miękko [**myank**-ko] adv. softly; gently; tenderly; limply; supply; flabbily; slackly; flaccidly
jajka na miękko [**yahy**-kah nah **myank**-ko] exp.: soft-boiled eggs
miękkopłetwy [myank-ko-**pwet**-fi] adj.m. malacopterygian; soft-finned
miękkopłetwe [myank-ko-**pwet**-fe] pl. the malacopterygians; the soft-finned fishes
miękkopodniebienny [myank-ko-pod-ńe-**byen**-ni] adj.m. velar; of soft palate
miękkość [**myank**-kośhćh] f. softness; flabbiness; slackness; limpness; suppleness; feebleness; irresolution; gentleness; mellowness; pliancy; palatalism; palatality (of pronunciation, etc.)
miękkotematowy [myank-ko-te-mah-**to**-vi] adj.m. of palatal (soft) ending (of a stem of a word)
miękławka [myank-**wahf**-kah] f. Amia clava fish
mięknąć [**myank**-nownćh] v. soften up; relax; relent; yield to compassion; be moved; grow milder; become more gentle (*repeatedly*)
mięknienie [myank-**ńe**-ńe] n. softening

mięknięcie [myank-ńan-ćhe] n. becoming soft
mięsak [myan-sahk] m. sarcoma; malignant tumor in connective tissue
mięsakowy [myan-sah-ko-vi] adj.m. sarcomatous (neoplasm, etc.)
mięsiarz [myan-śhahsh] m. pot-hunter
miesić [myan-śheećh] v. knead; massage (*repeatedly*)
mięsień [myan-śheń] m. muscle; colloq: strength of a muscle; muscular strength
mięśnie [myan-śhńe] pl. brawn; sinews; thews
mięsistość [myan-śhees-tośhćh] f. fleshiness
mięsisty [myan-śhees-ti] adj.m. fleshy; meaty; beefy; succulent; pulpous
mięsiwo [myan-śhee-vo] n. meat dish; dish of meat
mięsko [myans-ko] n. tasty meat (dish)
mięsność [myans-nośhćh] f. fleshiness
mięsny [myans-ni] adj.m. fleshy; meat (products, etc.)
bydło mięsne [bid-wo myans-ne] exp.: colloq: beef cattle
mięso [myan-so] n. flesh; meat
sztuka mięsa [shtoo-kah myan-sah] exp.: boiled beef
mięso armatnie [myan-so ahr-maht-ńe] exp.: cannon fodder
mięsopust [myan-so-poost] m. carnival; Shrovetide
mięsopustny [myan-so-poost-ni] adj.m. carnival (festivities, etc.)
mięsoznawstwo [myan-so-znahf-stfo] n. meat grading specialty
mięsożerca [myan-so-zher-tsah] m. carnivore
mięsożerny [myan-so-zher-ni] adj.m. carnivorous; meat-eating; insect-eating (plants, etc.)
mięsożerne [myan-so-zher-ne] pl. carnivores; carnivora
mięszać (się) [myan-shahćh śhan] v. colloq: see: **mieszać (się)**
mięśniak [myan-śhńahk] m. myoma; a tumor consisting of muscle tissue
mięśniochwat [myan-śhńo-khfaht] m. muscular disease of horses
mięśniowy [myan-śhńo-vi] adj.m. muscular
układ mięśniowy [ook-waht myan-śhńo-vi] exp.: musculature
mięśniówka [myan-śhńoof-kah] f. membrane of muscle tissue; membrane muscularis
mięta [myan-tah] f. mint; peppermint; trifle
czuć miętę do ... [chooćh myan-tan do] exp.: to be keen on ...; to have a crush on (somebody)
miętosić [myan-to-śheećh] v. crumble; knead; crush up (*repeatedly*)
miętosić się [myan-to-śheećh śhan] v. crumble up (*repeatedly*)
miętoszenie [myan-to-she-ńe] n. kneading; crumbling
miętowy [myan-to-vi] adj.m. peppermint (water, etc.)
miętówka [myan-toof-kah] f. peppermint (lozenge); peppermint-flavored vodka
miętus [myan-toos] m. burbot; colloq: peppermint vodka
mig [meeg] m. split second; twinkle; flash; sign language
migiem [mee-gem] exp.: adv. in a flash; in a split second; in a twinkling; in no time
migiem! [mee-gem] excl.: right away!; quickly!; hurry up!; look sharp!
mówić na migi [moo-veećh nah mee-gee] exp.: to speak by signs; to speak in finger language
w mig [v meeg] exp.: adv. in a twinkling; in a flash
migacz [mee-gahch] m. flasher; blinker (light)
migać [mee-gahćh] v. flash; flit by; flash past; whisk past; brush past; flicker; twinkle (*repeatedly*)
migać się [mee-gahćh śhan] v. be flickering; shirk (*repeatedly*)
miganie [mee-gah-ńe] n. using sign language; flickering
migawka [mee-gahf-kah] f. camera shutter; news in brief; nictitating membrane (in an eye); cilium
migawka sektorowa [mee-gahf-

kah sek-to-**ro**-vah] exp.: diaphragm shutter
migawka szczelinowa [mee-**gahf**-kah shche-lee-**no**-vah] exp.: focal-plane shutter
migawkowość [mee-gahf-**ko**-vośhćh] f. instantaneous nature (quality, character, etc.)
migawkowy [mee-gahf-**ko**-vi] adj.m. instantaneous; flashlight (signals, etc.)
zdjęcie migawkowe [**zdyan**-ćhe mee-gahf-**ko**-ve] exp.: snapshot
migdalić się [meeg-**dah**-leećh śhan] v. colloq: neck; smooch; kiss; pet (*repeatedly*)
migdał [**meeg**-dahw] m. almond (tree, shrub); tonsil; good and tasty thing
niebieskie migdały [ńe-**byes**-ke meeg-**dah**-wi] exp.: daydream
zapalenie migdałów [zah-pah-**le**-ńe meeg-**dah**-woof] exp.: tonsillitis
migdałek [meeg-**dah**-wek] m. tonsil; small almond
migdałowaty [meeg-dah-wo-**vah**-ti] adj.m. almond-shaped
migdałowiec [meeg-dah-**wo**-vyets] m. amygdaloid (mineral)
migdałowy [meeg-dah-**wo**-vi] adj.m. almond (kernel, icing, etc.); almond-shaped
migi [mee-gee] pl. sign language
mówić na migi [moo-veećh nah mee-gee] exp.: to communicate using sign language; to speak by (hand-made) signs
migiel [**mee**-gel] m. (only in) exp.: **figle-migle** [feeg-le **meeg**-le] exp.: naughty jokes; practical jokes; mischief
miglanc [**meeg**-lahnts] m. (Yiddish) work dodger
migma [**meeg**-mah] f. plastic magma
migmatyt [meeg-**mah**-tit] m. igneous rock composed of different minerals
mignąć [**meeg**-nownćh] v. flash; flit by; flash past; whisk past; brush past; flicker; twinkle; see: **migać**
mignąć się [meeg-nownćh śhan] v. flash past; flicker
mignięcie [meeg-**ńan**-ćhe] n. flashing
mignon [meeń-**yown**] m. seven point printer's font
migot [**mee**-got] m. gleam; glimmer; glint; sparkle; blink; flicker
migotać [mee-**go**-tahćh] v. waver; twinkle; flicker; whisk; glimmer; shimmer; glitter (*repeatedly*)
migotanie [mee-go-**tah**-ńe] n. twinkle; flicker; flit; glimmer; shimmer; glitter; glisten
migotka [mee-**got**-kah] f. haw (the third eyelid of animals)
migotliwie [mee-got-**lee**-vye] adv. flickeringly; lambently
migotliwość [mee-got-**lee**-vośhćh] f. lambency
migotliwy [mee-got-**lee**-vi] adj.m. wavering; twinkling; flickering; glimmering; lambent shimmering; glittering
migowy [mee-**go**-vi] adj.m. expressed by signs
mowa migowa [**mo**-vah mee-**go**-vah] exp.: speech by signs; sign language; finger language
migracja [mee-**grahts**-yah] f. migration; migrating (of groups of people, birds, etc.)
migracyjny [mee-grah-**tsiy**-ni] adj.m. migrational
migrant [**mee**-grahnt] m. migrant person
migrena [mee-**gre**-nah] f. migraine; sick headache; hemicrania
migrenowy [mee-gre-**no**-vi] adj.m. migrainous
migrenowy ból głowy [mee-gre-**no**-vi bool **gwo**-vi] exp.: migraine headache
migrować [mee-**gro**-vahćh] v. migrate (*repeatedly*)
mijać [**mee**-yahćh] v. go past; pass by; pass away; go by; run by; drive past; fly past; ride past; run past; sail past; go beyond; leave behind; elapse; flow by; roll by; come to an end; cease (*repeatedly*)
mijać się [**mee**-yahćh śhan] v. cross each other; pass each other; miss each other; fail to meet; fail to come together; cross

(*repeatedly*)
mijać się z prawdą [mee-yahćh śhan s prahv-down] exp.: to swerve from the truth; to be untrue
mijanie [mee-**yah**-ńe] n. passage (of time); lapse
mijanie się [mee-**yah**-ńe śhan] n. passing each other
mijanka [mee-**yahn**-kah] f. turnout; loop (of railroad tracks); staggered arrangement
mijankowy [mee-yahn-**ko**-vi] adj.m. staggered
mika [**mee**-kah] f. mica (mineral)
mikado [mee-**kah**-do] m. mikado
mikolog [mee-**ko**-log] m. mycologist
mikologia [mee-ko-**lo**-gyah] f. mycology
mikologicznie [mee-ko-lo-**geech**-ńe] adv. mycologically
mikologiczny [mee-ko-lo-**geech**-ni] adj.m. mycological; mycologic
mikołajek [mee-ko-**wah**-yek] m. sea holly (plant); gingerbread figure of St. Nicholas
mikołajkowy [mee-ko-wahy-**ko**-vi] adj.m. of a sea-holly plant
mikołajowy [mee-ko-wah-**yo**-vi] adj.m. of Nicholas
mikoryza [mee-ko-**ri**-zah] f. mycorrhiza
mikot [**mee**-kot] m. instrument used by huntsmen for enticing deer
mikotać [mee-**ko**-tahćh] v. entice deer by means of a special instrument (*repeatedly*)
mikotroficzność [mee-ko-tro-**feech**-nośhćh] f. mycorhizal feeding
mikowy [mee-**ko**-vi] adj.m. mica
łupek mikowy [**woo**-pek mee-**ko**-vi] exp.: mica schist
mikoza [mee-**ko**-zah] f. mycosis
mikro- [mee-kro] prefix: micro-
mikroamper [mee-kro-**ahm**-per] m. microampere
mikroanalityczny [mee-kro-ah-nah-lee-**tich**-ni] adj.m. microanalytical
mikroanaliza [mee-kro-ah-nah-**lee**-zah] f. microanalysis
mikroatmosfera [mee-kro-aht-mos-**fe**-rah] f. local atmospheric conditions
mikrob [**mee**-krop] m. microbe
mikrobiolog [mee-kro-**byo**-log] m. microbiologist
mikrobiologia [mee-kro-byo-**lo**-gyah] f. microbiology
mikrobiologiczny [mee-kro-byo-lo-**geech**-ni] adj.m. microbiological
mikrobowy [mee-kro-**bo**-vi] adj.m. microbial
mikrobus [mee-**kro**-boos] m. minivan
mikrobusowy [mee-kro-boo-**so**-vi] adj.m. of a minivan
mikrocefalia [mee-kro-tse-**fah**-lyah] f. microcephaly
mikrochemiczny [mee-kro-khe-**meech**-ni] adj.m. microchemical
mikrochirurg [mee-kro-**khee**-roorg] m. microsurgeon; micrurgist
mikrochirurgia [mee-kro-khee-**roor**-gyah] f. microsurgery
mikrochirurgiczny [mee-kro-khee-roor-**geech**-ni] adj.m. microsurgical
mikrocysta [mee-kro-**tsis**-tah] f. microcyst
mikrocząstka [mee-kro-**chownst**-kah] f. micromolecule
mikrocząstki [mee-kro-**chownst**-kee] pl. micromolecules
mikrodruk [mee-**kro**-drook] m. offset print
mikroelektronika [mee-kro-e-lek-**tro**-ńee-kah] f. microelectronics
mikroelement [mee-kro-e-**le**-ment] m. trace element; microorganism
mikroelementy [mee-kro-e-le-**men**-ti] pl. trace elements
mikroewolucja [mee-kro-e-vo-**loots**-yah] f. microevolution
mikroewolucyjny [mee-kro-e-vo-loo-**tsiy**-ni] adj.m. microevolutionary
mikrofag [mee-**kro**-fahg] m. microphage; small phagocyte
mikrofagi [mee-kro-**fah**-gee] pl. microphage group
mikrofala [mee-kro-**fah**-lah] f. microwave
mikrofalowy [mee-kro-fah-**lo**-vi] adj.m. microwave (oven, etc.)
kuchenka mikrofalowa [koo-**khen**-kah mee-kro-fah-**lo**-vah] exp.: microwave oven
mikrofarad [mee-kro-**fah**-raht] m. microfarad
mikrofauna [mee-kro-**fahw**-nah] f.

microfauna
mikrofilm [mee-**kro**-feelm] m. microfilm
mikrofilmować [mee-kro-feel-**mo**-vahćh] v. microfilm (*repeatedly*)
mikrofilmowanie [mee-kro-feel-mo-**vah**-ńe] n. microfilming
mikrofilmowy [mee-kro-feel-**mo**-vi] adj.m. microphotographic
mikrofizyczny [mee-kro-fee-**zich**-ni] adj.m. microphysical
mikrofizyka [mee-kro-**fee**-zi-kah] f. microphysics
mikroflora [mee-kro-**flo**-rah] f. microflora
mikrofon [mee-**kro**-fon] m. microphone; transmitter
występować przed mikrofonem [vi-st<u>an</u>-**po**-vahćh pshed mee-kro-**fo**-nem] exp.: to broadcast
mikrofonizacja [mee-kro-fo-ńee-**zahts**-yah] f. placing of microphones (in a building, etc.)
mikrofonowy [mee-kro-fo-**no**-vi] adj.m. microphonic
mikrofotografia [mee-kro-fo-to-**grah**-fyah] f. microphotography
mikrofotograficzny [mee-kro-fo-to-grah-**feech**-ni] adj.m. microphotographic
mikrofotogram [mee-kro-fo-**to**-grahm] m. microphotograph
mikrofotometr [mee-kro-fo-**to**-metr] m. microphotometer
mikrogameta [mee-kro-gah-**me**-tah] f. microgamete
mikrografia [mee-kro-**grah**-fyah] f. micrography; description of objects seen under a microscope
mikroguma [mee-kro-**goo**-mah] f. composition rubber
mikrokarta [mee-kro-**kahr**-tah] f. Microcard (used in library)
mikrokinematografia [mee-kro-kee-ne-mah-to-**grah**-fyah] f. making of microfilms; microfilming
mikroklimat [mee-kro-**klee**-maht] m. microclimate
mikroklimatologia [mee-kro-klee-mah-to-**lo**-gyah] f. microclimatology
mikroklimatyczny [mee-kro-klee-mah-**tich**-ni] adj.m. microclimatological
mikroklin [mee-**kro**-kleen] m. microcline
mikrokok [mee-**kro**-kok] m. micrococcus
mikrokoki [mee-kro-**ko**-kee] pl. micrococci
mikrokomputer [mee-kro-kom-**poo**-ter] m. microcomputer
mikrokomputerowy [mee-kro-kom-poo-te-**ro**-vi] adj.m. microcomputer (program, etc.)
mikrokosmiczny [mee-kro-kos-**meech**-ni] adj.m. microcosmic
mikrokosmos [mee-kro-**kos**-mos] m. microcosm
mikrokrystaliczny [mee-kro-kris-tah-**leech**-ni] adj.m. microcrystalline (mineral)
mikroksiążka [mee-kro-**kśh**<u>own</u>sh-kah] f. small book produced from microfilm
mikroksiężyc [mee-kro-**kśh**<u>an</u>-zhits] m. artificial satellite of the Earth
mikrolit [mee-**kro**-leet] m. microlith
mikrolityczny [mee-kro-lee-**tich**-ni] adj.m. microlithic
mikrolog [mee-**kro**-log] m. micrologist
mikrologia [mee-kro-**lo**-gyah] f. micrology
mikromania [mee-kro-**mahń**-yah] f. inferiority complex; micromania
mikromanipulator [mee-kro-mah-ńee-poo-**lah**-tor] m. micromanipulator
mikromaszyna [mee-kro-mah-**shi**-nah] f. small electrical (household) appliance
mikromer [mee-**kro**-mer] m. micromere
mikrometeoryt [mee-kro-me-te-**o**-rit] m. micrometeoroid; micrometeorite
mikrometr [mee-**kro**-metr] m. micrometer; caliper
mikrometryczny [mee-kro-me-**trich**-ni] adj.m. micrometrical
mikromierz [mee-**kro**-myesh] m. caliper; micrometer = **mikrometr**
mikrominiaturowy [mee-kro-mee-ńyah-too-**ro**-vi] adj.m. of microminiature
mikrominiaturyzacja [mee-kro-mee-ńyah-too-ri-**zahts**-yah] f.

microminiaturization
mikromodel [mee-kro-**mo**-del] m. micro-model
mikromoduł [mee-kro-**mo**-doow] m. micro-module; microchip
mikron [**mee**-kron] m. micron
mikronawóz [mee-kro-**nah**-voos] m. microfertilizer
mikronika [mee-**kro**-ńee-kah] f. miniaturization technique
mikroorganizm [mee-kro-or-**gah**-ńeezm] m. microorganism
mikroorganizmy [mee-kro-or-gah-**ńeez**-mi] pl. microorganisms
mikropaleontolog [mee-kro-pah-le-on-**to**-log] m. micropaleontologist
mikropaleontologia [mee-kro-pah-le-on-to-**lo**-gyah] f. micropaleontology
mikropaleontologiczny [mee-kro-pah-le-on-to-lo-**geech**-ni] adj.m. micropaleontological
mikropipeta [mee-kro-pee-**pe**-tah] f. micropipette
mikroplankton [mee-kro-**plahnk**-ton] m. microplankton
mikroporowaty [mee-kro-po-ro-**vah**-ti] adj.m. microporous
mikroporyt [mee-kro-**po**-rit] m. rock-wool insulation
mikropowieść [mee-kro-**po**-vyeśhćh] f. small size novel
mikroprocesor [mee-kro-pro-**tse**-sor] m. microprocessor
mikroprogram [mee-kro-**pro**-grahm] m. microprogram
mikropyle [mee-kro-**pi**-le] n. micropyle
mikroregion [mee-kro-**re**-gyon] m. micro-region
mikrorejon [mee-kro-**re**-yon] m. micro-region
mikroreprodukcja [mee-kro-re-pro-**dook**-tsyah] f. microreproduction
mikrosamochód [mee-kro-sah-**mo**-khoot] m. micro-car; subcompact (car)
mikrosejsmiczny [mee-kro-seys-**meech**-ni] adj.m. microseismic
mikrosekunda [mee-kro-se-**koon**-dah] f. microsecond
mikroskala [mee-kro-**skah**-lah] f. microscale
mikroskop [mee-**kro**-skop] m. microscope
mikroskopia [mee-kro-**sko**-pyah] f. microscopy
mikroskopijnie [mee-kro-sko-**peey**-ńe] adv. microscopically
mikroskopijny [mee-kro-sko-**peey**-ni] adj.m. microscopic; minute; tiny
mikroskopowo [mee-kro-sko-**po**-vo] adv. under the microscope; by means of the microscope
mikroskopowy [mee-kro-sko-**po**-vi] adj.m. microscopic; microscope (parts, etc.)
mikrosocjologia [mee-kro-so-tsyo-**lo**-gyah] f. microsociology
mikrosom [mee-**kro**-som] m. microsome
mikrospis [mee-**kro**-spees] m. list of people in a representative sample of the general population
mikrospołeczeństwo [mee-kro-spo-we-**cheń**-stfo] n. local social group
mikrospołeczność [mee-kro-spo-**wech**-nośhćh] f. (professional, village, etc.) social group
mikrospora [mee-kro-**spo**-rah] f. microspore
mikrostruktura [mee-kro-strook-**too**-rah] f. microstructure
mikroślad [mee-**kro**-śhlaht] m. invisible criminological evidence
mikroświat [mee-**kro**-śhfyaht] m. microcosm
mikrotechnika [mee-kro-**tekh**-ńee-kah] f. microtechnic; microtechnique
mikrotektoniczny [mee-kro-tek-to-**ńeech**-ni] adj.m. of small tectonic features
mikrotelefon [mee-kro-te-**le**-fon] m. telephone receiver; handset; microtelephone
mikroterma [mee-kro-**ter**-mah] f. microtherm
mikrotermiczny [mee-kro-ter-**meech**-ni] adj.m. microthermic; of plants requiring temperatures from 0 to +15 degrees Celsius
mikrotom [mee-**kro**-tom] m. microtome
mikrowaga [mee-kro-**vah**-gah] f. microbalance; microchemical balance; very sensitive scales

mikrowat [mee-**kro**-vaht] m. microwatt
mikrovolt [mee-**kro**-volt] m. microvolt
mikrowolt [mee-**kro**-volt] m. microvolt
mikrurgia [meek-**roor**-gyah] f. microsurgery; micrurgy; science or practice of microdissection and microinjection
mikrurgiczny [meek-roor-**geech**-ni] adj.m. microsurgical; micrurgic; micrurgical
mikrus [**meek**-roos] m. midget; midge-car; pillbox
mikrynit [mee-**kri**-ńeet] m. micrinite (mineral)
mikser [**meek**-ser] m. bartender; barman; mixer; disk jockey
mikserski [meek-**ser**-skee] adj.m. mixer's; bartender's; barman's
miksobakteria [meek-so-bahk-**ter**-yah] f. bacteria of the family Myxobacteriaceae
miksować [meek-**so**-vahćh] v. mix drinks; mix food; produce phonic signals; produce television signals (*repeatedly*)
miksowanie [meek-so-**vah**-ńe] n. mixing drinks; mixing food; producing phonic signals; producing television signals
mikst [meekst] m. mixed double game (tennis, ping-pong, etc.)
mikstowy [meek-**sto**-vi] adj.m. mixed (pair, etc.)
mikstura [meek-**stoo**-rah] f. mixture; concoction; compound; medicine
mila [**mee**-lah] f. mile
mila lądowa [mee-lah lown-**do**-vah] exp.: statute mile (1609.35 m., 5,280 ft.)
mila morska [**mee**-lah **mor**-skah] exp.: nautical mile (1853.2 m.)
milady [mee-**ley**-di] f. (Engl.) milady
milanez [mee-**lah**-nes] m. artificial silk knitted in stoking stitch
milanezowy [mee-lah-ne-**zo**-vi] adj.m. of an artificial silk (knitted in stoking stitch)
milcząco [meel-**chown**-tso] adv. in silence; tacitly
milczący [meel-**chown**-tsi] adj.m. silent; reticent; mum; tacit; implicit; unspoken; taciturn
milczeć [**meel**-chećh] v. be silent; hold one's tongue; keep silent (*repeatedly*)
milczeć! [**meel**-chećh] excl.: quit talking!; be quiet!; hold your tongue!; shut up!
milczek [**meel**-chek] m. man of few words; taciturn person
milczkiem [**meelch**-kem] adv. silently; in silence; secretly; on the sly; on the quiet; stealthily
milczenie [meel-**che**-ńe] n. silence; keeping still; stillness
grobowe milczenie [gro-**bo**-ve meel-**che**-ńe] exp.: dead silence
pominąć milczeniem [po-mee-nownćh meel-**che**-ńem] exp.: to pass over in silence
w milczeniu [v meel-**che**-ńoo] exp.: in silence
milczkowatość [meelch-ko-**vah**-tośhćh] f. colloq: taciturn personality
milczkowaty [meelch-ko-**vah**-ti] adj.m. (man) of few words; taciturn
mile [**mee**-le] adv. pleasantly; kindly; warmly; courteously; affably; heartily; in a pleasant manner; agreeably
milenarysta [mee-le-nah-**ris**-tah] m. millenarian
milenarystyczny [mee-le-nah-ris-**tich**-ni] adj.m. millenarian
milenaryzm [mee-le-**nah**-rizm] m. millenarianism
milenijny [mee-le-**ńeey**-ni] adj.m. millenary
milenium [mee-**le**-ńyoom] n. millennium
mili- [mee-lee] prefix: milli-
miliamper [mee-lee-**ahm**-per] m. milliampere
miliamperomierz [mee-lee-ahm-pe-**ro**-myesh] m. milliampere meter
miliard [**meel**-yahrt] m. thousand million; billion (in the USA)
miliarder [meel-**yahr**-der] m. billionaire; multimillionaire
miliarderka [meel-yahr-**der**-kah] f. woman billionaire
miliardowy [meel-yahr-**do**-vi] adj.m. billionth; one-thousand-millionth

(part, etc.)
milibar [mee-**lee**-bahr] m. millibar
milicja [mee-**leets**-yah] f. militia; police; constabulary; voluntary guard
milicjant [mee-**leets**-yahnt] m. policeman; constable
milicjantka [mee-leets-**yahnt**-kah] f. policewoman; constabless
milicyjny [mee-lee-**tsiy**-ni] adj.m. of the police; of the constabulary
miligram [mee-**lee**-grahm] m. milligram; 1/1000 of a gram
miligramowy [mee-lee-grah-**mo**-vi] adj.m. milligram (weight, etc.)
milikiur [mee-**lee**-kyoor] m. millicurie
mililitr [mee-**lee**-leetr] m. milliliter
mililitrowy [mee-lee-lee-**tro**-vi] adj.m. of a milliliter
milimetr [mee-**lee**-metr] m. millimeter
milimetrowy [mee-lee-me-**tro**-vi] adj.m. of a millimeter
milimetrówka [mee-lee-me-**troof**-kah] f. millimeter rule
milimikron [mee-lee-**mee**-kron] m. micromillimeter; bicron
milimol [mee-**lee**-mol] m. millimole
milion [**mee**-lyon] m. million; 1,000,000
milioner [mee-**lyo**-ner] m. millionaire; a person owning at least a million dollars (pounds)
milionerka [mee-lyo-**ner**-kah] f. (woman) millionaire
milionerski [mee-lyo-**ner**-skee] adj.m. millionaire's
milionik [mee-**lyo**-ńeek] m. (nice, little) million (dollars, etc.)
milionkrotny [mee-lyon-**krot**-ni] adj.m. millionfold
milionowy [mee-lyo-**no**-vi] adj.m. one millionth; of one million; numbering millions; countless; amounting to a million (of dollars, etc.)
milionowe miasto [mee-lyo-no-ve **myahs**-to] exp.: city of a million people
milisekunda [mee-lee-se-**koon**-dah] f. millisecond
militaria [mee-lee-**tahr**-yah] pl. military accessories
militarnie [mee-lee-**tahr**-ńe] adv. militarily
militarny [mee-lee-**tahr**-ni] adj.m. military; fit for war
militarysta [mee-lee-tah-**ris**-tah] m. militarist
militarystyczny [mee-lee-tah-ris-**tich**-ni] adj.m. militaristic
militaryzacja [mee-lee-tah-ri-**zahts**-yah] f. militarization
militaryzm [mee-lee-**tah**-rizm] m. militarism
militaryzować [mee-lee-tah-ri-**zo**-vahćh] v. militarize (*repeatedly*)
militaryzować się [mee-lee-tah-ri-**zo**-vahćh śhan] v. become militarized (*repeatedly*)
militaryzowanie [mee-lee-tah-ri-zo-**vah**-ńe] n. militarization
militaryzowanie się [mee-lee-tah-ri-zo-**vah**-ńe śhan] n. becoming militarized
miliwat [mee-**lee**-vaht] m. milliwatt
milivolt [mee-**lee**-volt] m. millivolt
miliwolt [mee-**lee**-volt] m. millivolt
milkliwość [meel-**klee**-vośhćh] f. taciturnity
milkliwy [meel-**klee**-vi] adj.m. taciturn
milknąć [**meelk**-nownćh] v. abate; cease talking; die away; calm down; be hushed; subside into silence; break off talking (*repeatedly*)
milknięcie [meelk-**ńan**-ćhe] n. subsiding into silence
millenarysta [meel-le-nah-**ris**-tah] m. millenarian
millenarystyczny [meel-le-nah-ris-**tich**-ni] adj.m. millenarian
millenaryzm [meel-le-**nah**-rizm] m. millenarianism
millenialny [meel-leń-**yahl**-ni] adj.m. millenary; of millennium
millenium [meel-**leń**-yoom] n. millennium; thousandth anniversary
milord [**mee**-lort] m. milord
milowy [mee-**lo**-vi] adj.m. of a mile
kamień milowy [**kah**-myeń mee-**lo**-vi] exp.: milestone
milrejs [**meel**-reys] m. milreis (coin, etc.)
milszy [**meel**-shi] adj.m. preferable (to); nicer (than)

miluchny [mee-**lookh**-ni] adj.m. very nice
milusi [mee-**loo**-śhee] adj.m. very nice
milusieńki [mee-loo-**śheń**-kee] adj.m. very, very nice
milusińscy [mee-loo-**śheeń**-stsi] pl. the little ones
milusińska [mee-loo-**śheeń**-skah] f. sweet little girl
milusiński [mee-loo-**śheeń**-skee] m. nice little boy
miluśki [mee-**loośh**-kee] adj.m. very nice (little breeze, etc.)
milutki [mee-**loot**-kee] adj.m. very nice; very likable
milutko [mee-**loot**-ko] adv. very pleasantly; in a very likable manner
miła [**mee**-wah] f. loved woman; loved girl
miłek [**mee**-wek] m. phesant's eye; garden pink
miłka [**meew**-kah] f. grass of the genus Eragrostis
miło [**mee**-wo] adv. nicely; pleasantly; agreeably; with pleasure
aż miło! [ash **mee**-wo] exp.: (an exclamation stressing the intensity of an action) it's a real pleasure; it's worth seeing
je aż miło [ye ash **mee**-wo] exp.: he eats very well; he eats a lot
miło to usłyszeć [**mee**-wo to oo-**swi**-shećh] exp.: it's a pleasure to hear
miło poznać [mee-wo **poz**-nahćh] exp.: glad to meet; delighted to meet; nice to meet (you)
miłorząb [mee-**wo**-zhownp] m. maidenhair tree; ginkgo
miłorzębowaty [mee-wo-zhan-bo-**vah**-ti] adj.m. ginkgoaceous
miłorzębowate [mee-wo-zhan-bo-**vah**-te] pl. the genus Ginkgo
miłorzębowy [mee-wo-zhan-**bo**-vi] adj.m. ginkgoaceous
miłorzębowe [mee-wo-zhan-**bo**-ve] pl. the genus Ginkgo
miłosierdzie [mee-wo-**śher**-dźhe] n. charity; mercy; compassion
bez miłosierdzia [bez mee-wo-**śher**-dźhah] exp.: adj.: without pity; pitiless; unmerciful; ruthless; adv. pitilessly; unmercifully; ruthlessly
siostra miłosierdzia [**śhos**-trah mee-wo-**śher**-dźhah] exp.: Sister of Mercy
wołać o miłosierdzie [**vo**-wahćh o mee-wo-**śher**-dźhe] exp.: to crave for mercy
miłosiernie [mee-wo-**śher**-ńe] adv. mercifully; charitably; compassionately; pitifully; beseechingly; imploringly
miłosierny [mee-wo-**śher**-ni] adj.m. merciful; charitable; compassionate; pitiful
Boże miłosierny! [**bo**-zhe mee-wo-**śher**-ni] excl.: good gracious!; gracious me!
miłosna [mee-**wos**-nah] f. Adenostyles (mountain) plant
miłosny [mee-**wos**-ni] adj.m. love; amatory
list miłosny [leest mee-**wos**-ni] exp.: love letter
scena miłosna [**stse**-nah mee-**wos**-nah] exp.: love scene
stosunek miłosny [sto-**soo**-nek mee-**wos**-ni] exp.: liaison; affair
miłostka [mee-**wost**-kah] f. little love affair
miłościwie [mee-wośh-**ćhee**-vye] adv. graciously; mercifully; fondly
miłościw [mee-**wośh**-ćheef] adj.m. gracious; merciful
miłościwy [mee-wośh-**ćhee**-vi] adj.m. gracious; merciful
miłość [**mee**-wośhćh] f. love; affection; fondness; sweetheart; ladylove
miłość własna [**mee**-wośhćh **vwahs**-nah] exp.: self-love; self-respect; self-esteem; amour-propre
na miłość Boską! [nah mee-wośhćh **bos**-kown] excl.: for goodness' sake!
miłośnictwo [me-wo-**shńee**-tstfo] n. love (of art, etc.); amateurism; fondness (for)
miłośniczka [mee-wośh-**ńeech**-kah] f. (woman) fancier; amateur; fan
miłośnie [mee-**wośh**-ńe] adv. lovingly; fondly; affectionately

miłośnik [mee-**wośh**-ńeek] m. fancier; amateur; fan
miłować [mee-**wo**-vahćh] v. love; cherish (*repeatedly*)
miłować się [mee-**wo**-vahćh śhan] v. love each other; be a lover (of); be fond (of) (*repeatedly*)
miłowanie [mee-wo-**vah**-ńe] n. love; loving
miłowanie się [mee-wo-**vah**-ńe śhan] n. loving one another
miły [**mee**-wi] adj.m. pleasant; beloved; likable; nice; enjoyable; prepossessing; attractive; agreeable; palatable; gratifying; dear; lovable
miłe usposobienie [**mee**-we oos-po-so-**bye**-ńe] exp.: good disposition; sweet temper
mim [meem] m. mime; mimic (actor)
mimetyczny [mee-me-**tich**-ni] adj.m. of imitation; of mimesis; of mimicry
mimetyzm [mee-**me**-tizm] m. mimesis; mimicry
mimicznie [mee-**meech**-ńe] adv. imitatively; by gestures
mimiczny [mee-**meech**-ni] adj.m. mimic; imitative; make-believe
mimik [**mee**-meek] m. mimic; actor-imitator
mimika [**mee**-mee-kah] f. mimics; mimic art; mimicry; dumb show; way of mimicking
mimikra [mee-**mee**-krah] f. mimicry (among animals)
mimista [mee-**mees**-tah] m. mimic; actor-imitator
mimo [**mee**-mo] prep. in spite of; notwithstanding; although; though; colloq: tho
mimo trudności [mee-mo trood-**nośh**-ćhee] exp.: in spite of the difficulties; despite the difficulties
mimo woli [**mee**-mo **vo**-lee] exp.: adv. involuntarily; adj. unintentional
mimo wszystko [**mee**-mo **fshist**-ko] exp.: after all; in spite of all; for all you may say; for all that; all the same; even then
przejść mimo [psheyśhćh **mee**-mo] exp.: to walk past
mimo [**mee**-mo] adv. past; by
mimo- [mee-mo] prefix: past-
mimochodem [mee-mo-**kho**-dem] adv. by the way; by way of digression; casually; incidentally
mimodram [mee-**mo**-drahm] m. dramatic pantomime
mimośrodkowo [mee-mo-śhrot-**ko**-vo] adv. eccentrically
mimośrodkowy [mee-mo-śhrot-**ko**-vi] adj.m. eccentric
mimośrodowo [mee-mo-śhro-**do**-vo] adv. bypassing the center
mimośrodowość [mee-mo-śhro-**do**-vośhćh] f. eccentricity
mimośrodowy [mee-mo-śhro-**do**-vi] adj.m. eccentric; without common center
mimośród [mee-**mo**-śhroot] m. eccentric; circular cam; eccentricity
mimowiednie [mee-mo-**vyed**-ńe] adv. not knowingly; unknowingly
mimowiedny [mee-mo-**vyed**-ni] adj.m. not knowing; unknowing
mimowolnie [mee-mo-**vol**-ńe] adv. involuntarily; unintentionally; instinctively; against one's will
mimowolność [mee-mo-**vol**-nośhćh] f. involuntariness
mimowolny [mee-mo-**vol**-ni] adj.m. involuntary; unintentional; unintended; unmeant; instinctive
mimoza [mee-**mo**-zah] f. mimosa; sensitive plant
mimozowatość [mee-mo-zo-**vah**-tośhćh] f. being like mimosa
mimozowaty [me-mo-zo-**vah**-ti] adj.m. sensitive; like mimosa
mimozowate [mee-mo-zo-**vah**-te] pl. the genus Mimosa
mina [mee-nah] f. air; facial expression; look; appearance; (an explosive) mine
kwaśna mina [**kfahśh**-nah **mee**-nah] exp.: wry face
robić miny [ro-beećh **mee**-ni] exp.: to make faces
minarecik [mee-nah-**re**-ćheek] m. small minaret
minaret [mee-**nah**-ret] m. minaret
minaretowy [mee-nah-re-**to**-vi] adj.m. of minaret
minąć [mee-nownćh] v. pass by; go past; elapse; cease

dawno minęła piąta godzina [dahv-no mee-ne-wah pyown-tah go-dźhee-nah] exp.: it is long past 5 o'clock
burza minęła [boo-zhah mee-ne-wah] exp.: the storm is over
minąć się [mee-nownćh śhan] v. pass each other
minąć się z powołaniem [mee-nownćh śhan s po-vo-wah-ńem] exp.: to miss one's calling
miner [mee-ner] m. miner; sapper
mineralizacja [mee-ne-rah-lee-zahts-yah] f. mineralization
mineralizować [mee-ne-rah-lee-zo-vahćh] v. mineralize (*repeatedly*)
mineralizować się [mee-ne-rah-lee-zo-vahćh śhan] v. become mineralized (*repeatedly*)
mineralizowanie [mee-ne-rah-lee-zo-vah-ńe] n. mineralization
mineralizowanie się [mee-ne-rah-lee-zo-vah-ńe śhan] n. becoming mineralized
mineralny [mee-ne-rahl-ni] adj.m. mineral; containing minerals
mineralog [mee-ne-rah-log] m. mineralogist
mineralogia [mee-ne-rah-lo-gyah] f. mineralogy
mineralogiczny [mee-ne-rah-lo-geech-ni] adj.m. mineralogical
minerał [mee-ne-rahw] m. mineral
minerałowy [mee-ne-rah-wo-vi] adj.m. mineral (matter, etc.)
minerski [mee-ner-skee] adj.m. miner's; miners'; sapper's
minerstwo [mee-ner-stfo] n. specialty of military explosives
minezinger [mee-ne-zeen-ger] m. German medieval bard; minnesinger
mini [mee-ńee] indecl. mini; minicar; miniskirt
mini- [mee-ńee] prefix: mini-
minia [mee-ńyah] f. minium; red lead paint base; red lead
miniasty [mee-ńah-sti] adj.m. putting on airs
miniator [mee-ńyah-tor] m. miniaturist; illuminator
miniatorski [mee-ńyah-tor-skee] adj.m. of a miniature painting; of illumination (of manuscripts, etc.)
miniatorstwo [mee-ńyah-tor-stfo] n. art of making miniatures
miniatura [mee-ńyah-too-rah] f. miniature; miniature copy; mini-drama; mini-poetry
w miniaturze [v mee-ńyah-too-zhe] exp.: in miniature
miniaturka [mee-ńyah-too-rkah] f. small miniature; miniature copy; miniature (animal, etc.)
miniaturowo [mee-ńyah-too-ro-vo] adv. in miniature; in a great detail; very precisely
miniaturowość [mee-ńyah-too-ro-vośhćh] f. miniature size
miniaturowy [mee-ńyah-too-ro-vi] adj.m. miniature (copy, etc.); of a miniature painting
miniaturyzacja [mee-ńyah-too-ri-zahts-yah] f. imparting features of a miniature; making a miniature
miniaturyzacyjny [mee-ńyah-too-ri-zah-tsiy-ni] adj.m. of imparting features of a miniature; of reducing to a miniature
miniaturyzować [mee-ńyah-too-ri-zo-vahćh] v. impart features of a miniature; reduce to a miniature (*repeatedly*)
miniaturyzowanie [mee-ńyah-too-ri-zo-vah-ńe] n. imparting features of a miniature; reducing to miniature
miniaturzysta [mee-ńyah-too-zhis-tah] m. miniaturist
miniaturzystka [mee-ńah-too-zhist-kah] f. (woman) miniaturist
minier [mee-ńer] m. miner; sapper; mine laying soldier
minierski [mee-ńer-skee] adj.m. miner's; sapper's; of a mine laying soldier
minięcie [mee-ńan-ćhe] n. passing by; lapse; passage (of time, etc.)
minikalkulator [mee-ńee-kahl-koo-lah-tor] m. (mini)calculator
minikomputer [mee-ńee-kom-poo-ter] m. minicomputer
minikomputerowy [mee-ńee-kom-poo-te-ro-vi] adj.m. of minicomputer
minimalista [mee-ńee-mah-lees-tah] m. minimalist
minimalistycznie [mee-ńee-mah-lees-

tich-ńe] adv. like a minimalist
minimalistyczny [mee-ńee-mah-lees-**tich**-ni] adj.m. of a minimalist
minimalizacja [mee-ńee-mah-lee-**zahts**-yah] f. minimization
minimalizm [mee-ńee-**mah**-leezm] m. minimalism; minimal art
minimalizować [mee-ńee-mah-lee-**zo**-vahćh] v. minimize (*repeatedly*)
minimalizowanie [mee-ńee-mah-lee-zo-**vah**-ńe] n. minimization
minimalnie [mee-ńee-**mahl**-ńe] adv. in a very small degree; to a very small degree; slightly; imperceptibly; infinitesimally; slang: a wee bit
minimalny [mee-ńee-**mahl**-ni] adj.m. minimal; the least possible; infinitesimal; tiny
minimalna legalna płaca [mee-ńee-**mahl**-nah le-**gahl**-nah **pwah**-tsah] exp.: minimum wage; minimum legal wage
minimetr [mee-**ńee**-metr] m. precision measuring device
minimoduł [mee-ńee-**mo**-doow] m. miniature system board (module for a computer, etc.); chip
minimum [**mee**-ńee-moom] n. minimum; adv. at the very least; at the lowest point
minimum egzystencji [**mee**-ńee-moom eg-zis-**ten**-tsyee] exp.: living wage; poverty line
sprowadzić do minimum [spro-**vah**-dźheećh do **mee**-ńee-moom] exp.: to reduce to a minimum; to minimize (something)
minione [mee-**ńo**-ne] n. the past
rzeczy minione [**zhe**-chi mee-**ńo**-ne] exp.: things of the past
miniony [mee-**ńo**-ni] adj.m. bygone; of long ago; olden; past
miniona sława [mee-**ńo**-nah **swah**-vah] exp.: departed glory; past glory
miniować [meeń-**yo**-vahćh] v. apply corrosion resistant paint coat (*repeatedly*)
miniowanie [meeń-yo-**vah**-ńe] n. application of corrosion resistant paint coat
miniowy [meeń-**yo**-vi] adj.m. of corrosion resistant paint
minispódniczka [mee-ńee-spood-**ńeech**-kah] f. miniskirt
minister [mee-**ńees**-ter] m. minister; cabinet member; clergyman
minister bez teki [mee-**ńees**-ter bes **te**-kee] exp.: minister without portfolio
minister handlu [mee-**ńees**-ter **khahn**-dloo] exp.: Secretary of Commerce; President of the Board of Trade
minister oświaty [mee-**ńees**-ter o-**śhfyah**-ti] exp.: Minister of Education; Secretary of Education
minister skarbu [mee-**ńees**-ter **skahr**-boo] exp.: Secretary of the Treasury; Chancellor of the Exchequer (Brit.)
minister spraw wewnętrznych [mee-**ńees**-ter sprahv vev-**nantsh**-nikh] exp.: Home Secretary; Secretary of the Interior
minister spraw zagranicznych [mee-**ńees**-ter sprahv zah-grah-**ńeech**-nikh] exp.: Secretary of State; Foreign Secretary
minister opieki społecznej [mee-**ńees**-ter o-**pye**-kee spo-**wech**-ney] exp.: Minister of Social Welfare
ministerialny [mee-ńees-ter-**yahl**-ni] adj.m. ministerial
teka ministerialna [**te**-kah mee-ńees-te-**ryahl**-nah] exp.: portfolio
ministerstwo [mee-ńees-**ter**-stfo] n. ministry; department under a government minister
ministrant [mee-**ńees**-trahnt] m. choirboy; altar boy; acolyte
ministrantura [mee-ńees-trahn-**too**-rah] f. acolyte's responses; altarboy's responses
ministrostwo [mee-ńee-**stro**-stfo] n. the minister and his wife
ministrowa [mee-ńees-**tro**-vah] f. minister's wife
minisukienka [mee-ńee-soo-**ken**-kah] f. mini dress
minka [**meen**-kah] f. air; look (on somebody's face)
minoderia [mee-no-**der**-yah] f. making faces; making advances
minoderyjnie [mee-no-de-**riy**-ńe] adv. by way of airs and graces

minoderyjność [mee-no-de-**riy**-nośhćh] f. making faces; making advances
minoderyjny [mee-no-de-**riy**-ni] adj.m. of airs and graces
minoga [mee-**no**-gah] f. eel-like water animal with jawless sucking mouth; lamprey
minogi [mee-**no**-gee] pl. lampreys
minogowaty [mee-no-go-**vah**-ti] adj.m. petromyzontoid
minogowate [mee-no-go-**vah**-te] pl. the lampreys
minojski [mee-**noy**-skee] adj.m. Minoan
minor [**mee**-nor] m. minor (musical) scale
minorat [mee-**no**-raht] m. right of inheritance belonging to younger-born
minorka [mee-**nor**-kah] f. Minorca (chicken)
minorowo [mee-no-**ro**-vo] adv. in minor key; dolefully
minorowy [mee-no-**ro**-vi] adj.m. in minor key; low-spirited
minoryta [mee-no-**ri**-tah] m. Friar Minor
minotaur [mee-**no**-tahwr] m. Minotaur
minować [mee-**no**-vahćh] v. mine; lay mines; mine channels in leaves and plant stems (said of larvae of insects) (*repeatedly*)
minowanie [mee-no-**vah**-ńe] n. mining
minowiec [mee-**no**-vyets] m. mine tender (boat)
minowy [mee-**no**-vi] adj.m. mine (field, etc.)
minóg [**mee**-noog] m. lamprey
minstrel [**meen**-strel] m. minstrel
minus [**mee**-noos] m. minus; below zero; drawback; disadvantage; fault; defect; weak point
plus minus [ploos **mee**-noos] exp.: more or less; approximately
minuskuła [mee-noos-**koo**-wah] f. minuscule; small letter
minuskułowy [mee-noos-koo-**wo**-vi] adj.m. minuscule; in small letters
minusowy [mee-noo-**so**-vi] adj.m. negative; minus
minuta [mee-**noo**-tah] f. minute
co do minuty [tso do mee-**noo**-ti] exp.: to the minute; on the dot; on the stroke; exactly on time; precisely on time
lada minuta [**lah**-dah mee-**noo**-tah] exp.: any moment; any time
z minuty na minutę [z mee-**noo**-ti nah mee-**noo**-tan] exp.: from one minute to the next; from one moment to the next
minutka [mee-**noo**-tkah] f. a minute; exp.: just a moment (please)
minutnik [mee-**noot**-ńeek] m. minute hand (of a clock, of a watch)
minutowy [mee-noo-**to**-vi] adj.m. of one minute; one-minute (intervals, etc.)
wskazówka minutowa [fskah-**zoof**-kah mee-noo-**to**-vah] exp.: minute-hand
miocen [**myo**-tsen] m. Miocene
mioceński [myo-**tseń**-skee] adj.m. Miocene
miodarka [myo-**dahr**-kah] f. honey extractor
miodek [**myo**-dek] m. (nice, sweet) honey
miodnik [**myod**-ńeek] m. honey-gland; nectary
miodniki [myod-**ńee**-kee] pl. honey-glands
miodnikowy [myod-ńee-**ko**-vi] adj.m. of the honey-gland; of the nectary
miodny [**myod**-ni] adj.m. honey-like; characteristic of honey
miodobranie [myo-do-**brah**-ńe] n. honey harvest
miododajny [myo-do-**dahy**-ni] adj.m. honey-yielding; melliferous
miodojad [myo-**do**-yaht] m. meliphagous bird
miodojady [myo-do-**yah**-di] pl. the Meliphagidae family of birds
miodokwiat [myo-**do**-kfyaht] m. musk orchis
miodokwiatowy [myo-do-kfyah-**to**-vi] adj.m. melianthaceous
miodokwiatowe [myo-do-kfyah-**to**-ve] pl. the family Melianthaceae
miodonośny [myo-do-**nośh**-ni] adj.m. honey-bearing; nectar bearing (flower, etc.)
miodopłynny [myo-do-**pwin**-ni]

adj.m. mellifluous; honeyed; honey-sweet; honey-yielding; melliferous
miodosytnia [myo-do-**sit**-ńah] f. mead bar; mead brewery; mead cellar; mead vault
miodosytnictwo [myo-do-sit-**ńee**-tstfo] n. mead brewing
miodosytnik [myo-do-**sit**-ńeek] m. mead brewer
miodownik [myo-**dov**-ńeek] m. gingerbread; bastard balm
miodowo [myo-**do**-vo] adv. like honey
pachnieć miodowo [**pahkh**-ńećh myo-**do**-vo] exp.: to emanate a honey-sweet fragrance
miodowy [myo-**do**-vi] adj.m. honey; honeyed; honey-sweet; honey yellow
miesiąc miodowy [**mye**-śhownts myo-**do**-vi] exp.: honeymoon
opieńka miodowa [o-**pyeń**-kah myo-**do**-vah] exp.: honey fungus
miodówka [myo-**doof**-kah] f. jumping plant louse; varieties of apples, pears, and cherries
miodówkowaty [myo-doof-ko-**vah**-ti] adj.m. psylid; like plant louse
miodówkowate [myo-doof-ko-**vah**-te] pl. Psyllidae; plant lice
miodunka [myo-**doon**-kah] f. lungwort
miologia [myo-**lo**-gyah] f. myology; study of muscles
miologiczny [myo-lo-**geech**-ni] adj.m. myologic; myological
mion [myon] m. meson (unstable nuclear particle)
miony [**myo**-ni] pl. mesons (unstable nuclear particles)
miopia [mee-**yo**-pyah] f. myopia
miot [myot] m. throw; cast; litter; brood; animal birth; fling; shooting party
miotacz [**myo**-tahch] m. thrower; putter
miotacz bomb [**myo**-tahch bomp] exp.: bomb-thrower
miotacz min [**myo**-tahch meen] exp.: mine-thrower
miotacz ognia [**myo**-tahch **og**-ńah] exp.: flamethrower
miotaczka [myo-**tahch**-kah] f. (woman) thrower; putter
miotać [**myo**-tahćh] v. throw; fling; toss; hurl; stir; rave; storm; agitate; convulse; sputter (abuse, etc.); belch forth (curses, etc.) (*repeatedly*)
miotać się [**myo**-tahćh śhan] v. be restless; toss about; be raving; be storming (*repeatedly*)
miotać się na falach [**myo**-tahćh śhan nah **fah**-lahkh] exp.: to be tossed on the waves
miotanie [myo-**tah**-ńe] n. throwing; flinging
miotanie się [myo-**tah**-ńe śhan] n. agitation; jactitation
miotarka [myo-**tahr**-kah] f. (sand, etc.) blowing machine; street sweeping machine
miotełka [myo-**tew**-kah] f. feather duster; whisk
miotełkować [myo-tew-**ko**-vahćh] v. cover up (foot steps on snow, etc.) (*repeatedly*)
miotełkowaty [myo-tew-ko-**vah**-ti] adj.m. shaggy
miotełkowy [myo-tew-**ko**-vi] adj.m. broom-like
wyładowanie miotełkowe [vi-wah-do-**vah**-ńe myo-tew-**ko**-ve] exp.: brush discharge
miotlarz [**myot**-lahsh] m. broom-maker
miotlastość [myot-**lahs**-tośhćh] f. broom-like shape
miotlasty [myot-**lahs**-ti] adj.m. shaggy
miotlisko [myot-**lees**-ko] n. (big, old) broom
miotła [**myot**-wah] f. broom; besom; (bushy) tail; bent grass
kij od miotły [keey od **myot**-wi] exp.: broomstick
miozyn [**myo**-zin] m. myosin (fibrous globulin of muscle)
miozyna [myo-**zi**-nah] f. myosin
miód [myoot] m. honey; mead
mir [meer] m. esteem; respect; peace
cieszyć się mirem (u) [**će**-shićh śhan **mee**-rem (oo)] exp.: to be popular (with)
mira [**mee**-rah] f. sighting mark; azimuth mark

mirabela [mee-rah-**be**-lah] f. wild plum
mirabelka [mee-rah-**bel**-kah] f. wild plum
mirabilit [mee-rah-**bee**-leet] m. mirabilite (mineral)
mirakl [**mee**-rahkl] m. medieval miracle play
mirakle [mee-**rah**-kle] pl. miracle plays
miranda [mee-**rahn**-dah] f. wrinkle-free fabric; non-iron fabric
miraż [**mee**-rahsh] m. mirage; fata morgana; illusion
mirażowy [mee-rah-**zho**-vi] adj.m. of mirage; illusory
miriadowy [mee-ryah-**do**-vi] adj.m. myriad
miriady [mee-**ryah**-di] pl. myriads; large numbers (of persons, etc.)
miriagram [mee-**ryah**-grahm] m. 10,000 grams; 10 kilograms; myriagram; myrigramme (Brit.)
mirialitr [mee-**ryah**-leetr] m. 10,000 liters
miriametr [mee-**ryah**-metr] m. 10,000 meters; 10 kilometers
mirmekofolia [meer-me-ko-**fo**-lyah] f. myrmecophily
mirnik [**meer**-ńeek] m. a plant of the family Burseraceae
mirra [**meer**-rah] f. myrrh (gum resin)
mirt [meert] m. myrtle (Myrtus)
mirtowaty [meer-to-**vah**-ti] adj.m. myrtaceous (guava, etc.); (tree or shrub) of the family Myrtaceae
mirtowate [meer-to-**vah**-te] pl. the myrtle family; the family Myrtaceae
mirtowy [meer-**to**-vi] adj.m. of myrtle; myrtle (leaves, berries, etc.)
mirtowe [meer-**to**-ve] pl. the myrtles
mirza [**meer**-zah] m. mirza
misa [**mee**-sah] f. platter; bowl; basin; pan; tureen; dish; dishful; bowlful
miscellanea [mees-tsel-lah-**ne**-ah] pl. miscellanea; miscellany
miseczka [mee-**sech**-kah] f. small bowl; porringer; cupule; small tray
miseczkowaty [mee-sech-ko-**vah**-ti] adj.m. cup-shaped; cupped; cupuliferous
miseczkowate [mee-sech-ko-**vah**-te] pl. the cupuliferous trees
misecznica [mee-sech-**ńee**-tsah] f. foliaceous lichen; the lichen lecanora
misecznicowaty [mee-sech-ńee-tso-**vah**-ti] adj.m. lecanoraceous
misecznicowate [mee-sech-ńee-tso-**vah**-te] pl. the lecanoraceous lichens
misecznik [mee-**sech**-ńeek] m. soft scale insect; Lecanium
miserere [mee-ze-**re**-re] n. (Latin) (musical) miserere; ileus
misić [**mee**-śheećh] v. colloq: castrate; geld (*repeatedly*)
misiek [**mee**-śhek] m. young bear
misio [**mee**-śho] m. (nice, small) bear cub
misiura [mee-**śhoo**-rah] f. casque; basinet
misiurka [mee-**śhoor**-kah] f. (small) casque; basinet
misja [**mees**-yah] f. mission; message; commission; embassy
misjonarski [mees-yo-**nahr**-skee] adj.m. missionary (work, etc.)
misjonarstwo [mees-yo-**nahr**-stfo] n. missionary work
misjonarz [mees-**yo**-nahsh] m. (religious) missionary
miska [**mees**-kah] f. dish; pan; wash-basin; finger bowl; casque
miska klozetowa [**mees**-kah klo-ze-**to**-vah] exp.: toilet bowl
miskowaty [mees-ko-**vah**-ti] adj.m. bowl-shaped
misowaty [mee-so-**vah**-ti] adj.m. shaped like a large bowl
miss [mees] f. miss
mister [**mees**-ter] m. mister
misterium [mees-**ter**-yoom] n. mystery; miracle play; mystery play
misternie [mees-**ter**-ńe] adv. delicately; subtly; cleverly; ingeniously; with minute precision
misterność [mees-**ter**-nośhćh] f. fineness; delicacy; subtlety; cleverness; ingeniousness
misterny [mees-**ter**-ni] adj.m. fine; delicate; subtle; clever; fine-

wrought; ingenious
misteryjny [mees-te-**riy**-ni] adj.m. mystery (play, etc.)
mistral [**mees**-trahl] m. mistral (northerly wind in France)
mistrz [meestsh] m. master; maestro; champion; expert; master hand; record-holder; master craftsman; colloq: boss; foreman
mistrz ceremonii [meestsh tse-re-**moń**-yee] exp.: Master of Ceremonies
mistrzostwo [mees-**tshos**-tfo] n. championship; mastery; expertness; artistry; mastership
mistrzowski [mees-**tshof**-skee] adj.m. masterly; master's; of a master; of an expert; champion's; record-holder's
mistrzowski ruch [mees-**tshof**-skee rookh] exp.: master stroke
po mistrzowsku [po mees-**tshof**-skoo] exp.: expertly; in a masterly manner; like a master
mistrzowsko [mees-**tshof**-sko] adv. masterly
mistrzyni [mees-**tshi**-ńee] f. (woman) record-holder; champion; expert; mistress (of music, etc.)
mistycyzm [mees-**ti**-tsizm] m. mysticism; intuitive knowledge
mistycyzować [mees-ti-tsi-**zo**-vahćh] v. become mystic (*repeatedly*)
mistyczka [mees-**tich**-kah] f. (woman) mystic; a mystic
mistycznie [mees-**tich**-ńe] adv. mystically
mistyczność [mees-**tich**-nośhćh] f. mystical character; occult nature
mistyczny [mees-**tich**-ni] adj.m. mystic; mystical; occult
mistyfikacja [mees-ti-fee-**kahts**-yah] f. mystification; hoax; catch; deception
mistyfikacyjny [mees-ti-fee-kah-**tsiy**-ni] adj.m. of mystification; deceitful; fraudulent; mystifying
mistyfikator [mees-ti-fee-**kah**-tor] m. deceiver; trickster; swindler
mistyfikatorka [mees-ti-fee-kah-**tor**-kah] f. (woman) deceiver; trickster; swindler
mistyfikatorski [mees-ti-fee-kah-**tor**-skee] adj.m. deceitful; fraudulent
mistyfikatorstwo [mees-ti-fee-kah-**tor**-stfo] n. deceitful conduct
mistyfikować [mees-ti-fee-**ko**-vahćh] v. mystify; hoax; deceive; puzzle; perplex (*repeatedly*)
mistyfikowanie [mees-ti-fee-ko-**vah**-ńe] n. mystification; deception
mistyk [**mees**-tik] m. mystic
mistyka [**mees**-ti-kah] f. religious mysticism
misyjny [mee-**siy**-ni] adj.m. missionary (activities, etc.); mission (building, etc.)
miszkulancja [meesh-koo-**lahn**-tsyah] f. mixture; medley; hotchpotch (dish)
miszmasz [**meesh**-mahsh] indecl. mishmash; hotchpotch; pell-mell
miś [meeśh] m. Teddy bear; nylon fur coat or jacket
miśnieński [meśh-**ńeń**-skee] adj.m. of Meissen
mit [meet] m. myth; mythology; fable
mitel [**mee**-tel] m. 14-point English font
mitenka [mee-**ten**-kah] f. mitten
mitochondrion [mee-to-**khon**-dryon] m. mitochondrion
mitochondria [mee-to-**khon**-dryah] pl. mitochondria
mitochondrionowy [mee-to-khon-dryo-**no**-vi] adj.m. mitochondrial
mitolog [mee-**to**-log] m. mythologist
mitologia [mee-to-**lo**-gyah] f. mythology; study of myths
mitologicznie [mee-to-lo-**geech**-ńe] adv. mythologically
mitologiczność [mee-to-lo-**geech**-nośhćh] f. mythologic character
mitologiczny [mee-to-lo-**geech**-ni] adj.m. mythologic
mitologizacja [mee-to-lo-gee-**zahts**-yah] f. making mythologic; mythologizing
mitologizm [mee-to-**lo**-geezm] m. legendary character; mythologic nature
mitologizować [mee-to-lo-gee-**zo**-vahćh] v. mythologize; mythicize (*repeatedly*)
mitologizować się [mee-to-lo-gee-

zo-vahćh śhan] v. become mythologized (*repeatedly*)
mitoman [mee-**to**-man] m. mythomaniac
mitomania [mee-to-**mahń**-yah] f. mythomania
mitomanka [mee-to-**mahn**-kah] f. (woman) mythomaniac
mitomański [mee-to-**mahń**-skee] adj.m. mythomaniac
mitotwórca [mee-to-**tfoor**-tsah] m. mythmaker
mitotwórczy [mee-to-**tfoor**-chi] adj.m. mythmaking
mitotwórstwo [mee-to-**tfoor**-stfo] n. mythmaking
mitoza [mee-**to**-zah] f. mitosis
mitra [**meet**-rah] f. mitre (hat); coronet; episcopal office
mitralieza [mee-trah-**lye**-zah] f. mitrailleuse; multi-barrel machine gun
mitralny [mee-**trahl**-ni] adj.m. mitral
wada mitralna [**vah**-dah mee-**trahl**-nah] exp.: mitral insufficiency
zastawka mitralna [zahs-**tahf**-kah mee-**trahl**-nah] exp.: mitral valve
mitręga [mee-**tran**-gah] f. colloq: delay; waste of time; loss of time; m. & f. dawdler; miser
mitrężenie [mee-tran-**zhe**-ńe] n. waste of time; loss of time
mitrężyć [mee-**tran**-zhićh] v. loiter; waste time; delay; lag; dawdle away; hang around; hang about (*repeatedly*)
mitrowy [mee-**tro**-vi] adj.m. mitred (abbot, etc.)
mitycznie [mee-**tich**-ńe] adv. mythically; fictitiously
mityczność [mee-**tich**-nośhćh] f. mythical character
mityczny [mee-**tich**-ni] adj.m. mythical; mythic; fictitious
mitygować [mee-ti-**go**-vahćh] v. quiet; appease; check; restrain (*repeatedly*)
mitygować się [mee-ti-**go**-vahćh śhan] v. control oneself; restrain oneself (*repeatedly*)
mitygowanie [mee-ti-go-**vah**-ńe] n. moderation; restraint
mitygowanie się [mee-ti-go-**vah**-ńe śhan] n. self-control; self-restraint
mityng [**mee**-ting] m. (mass) meeting; a mass gathering of people; a coming together
mitynka [mee-**tin**-kah] f. mitten
mityzacja [mee-ti-**zah**-tsyah] f. mythmaking
mityzować [mee-ti-**zo**-vahćh] v. mythicize (*repeatedly*)
mizantrop [mee-**zahn**-trop] m. misanthrope; hater of people
mizantropia [mee-zahn-**tro**-pyah] f. misanthropy
mizantropijny [mee-zahn-tro-**peey**-ni] adj.m. misanthropic
mizantropka [mee-zahn-**trop**-kah] f. misanthrope (woman)
mizdra [**meez**-drah] f. rough side (of leather)
mizdrować [meez-**dro**-vahćh] v. scour; skive (leather) (*repeatedly*)
mizdrowanie [meez-dro-**vah**-ńe] n. scouring
mizdrownica [meez-drov-**ńee**-tsah] f. scouring device
mizdrownik [meez-**drov**-ńeek] m. scouring knife (for leather)
mizdrowy [meez-**dro**-vi] adj.m. of the flesh side (of leather)
mizdrowa strona skóry [meez-**dro**-vah **stro**-nah **skoo**-ri] exp.: the flesh (rough) side of leather
mizdrzenie się [meez-**dzhe**-ńe śhan] n. making eyes; cajoling
mizdrzyć się [**meez**-dzhićh śhan] v. ogle; wheedle; make eyes; cajole; coquet; posture (in front of the mirror) (*repeatedly*)
mizer [**mee**-zer] m. (card) misery
mizera [mee-**ze**-rah] f. (card) misery
mizeracki [mee-ze-**rahts**-kee] adj.m. wretched
mizeractwo [mee-ze-**rahts**-tfo] n. poverty; beggary; wretchedness
mizeraczek [mee-ze-**rah**-chek] m. poor little soul; poor little fellow
mizerak [mee-**ze**-rahk] m. poor soul; weakling; poor devil; starveling; poverty-stricken fellow
mizerere [mee-ze-**re**-re] n. (musical) miserere; ileus
mizeria [mee-**ze**-ryah] f. cucumber salad; shabby possessions; traps; misfortune

mizerka [mee-**zer**-kah] f. (card) misery
mizernie [mee-**zer**-ńe] adv. palely; wanly; meagerly; wretchedly; paltrily; poorly
wyglądać mizernie [vi-glown-dahćh mee-**zer**-ńe] exp.: to look poorly; to look haggard; to look shabby
mizernieć [mee-**zer**-ńećh] v. grow meager; grow wan; grow thin; grow lean; lose flesh (*repeatedly*)
mizerniutki [mee-zer-**ńoot**-kee] adj.m. meager (nice, little fellow); ill-looking; wretched; paltry; haggard; poor; gaunt
mizerność [mee-**zer**-nośhćh] f. wanness; poor looks
mizerny [mee-**zer**-ni] adj.m. meager; ill-looking; wretched; paltry; haggard; poor; gaunt
mizerny wygląd [mee-**zer**-ni **vi**-glownt] exp.: poor looks; wanness
mizerota [mee-ze-**ro**-tah] f. misery; poverty; want; rubbish; trash; m. & f. starveling; weakling
mizerykordia [mee-ze-ri-**kord**-yah] f. stiletto; misericord
mizoandria [mee-zo-**ahn**-dryah] f. man-fobia; hatred of men by women; misandry
mizoandryczny [mee-zo-ahn-**drich**-ni] adj.m. man-hating
mizoandryzm [mee-zo-**ahn**-drizm] m. hatred of men by women
mizogamia [mee-zo-**gah**-myah] f. misogamy; hatred of marriage
mizogin [mee-**zo**-geen] m. misogyne; misoginist
mizoginia [mee-zo-**geeń**-yah] f. misogyny; hatred of women
mizoginiczny [mee-zo-gee-**ńeech**-ni] adj.m. misogynistic
mizoginista [mee-zo-gee-**ńees**-tah] m. misogynist; women hater
mizoginistyczny [mee-zo-gee-ńees-**tich**-ni] adj.m. misogynist; misogynistic
mizoginizm [mee-zo-**gee**-ńeezm] m. misogynism; misogyny
mklik [mkleek] m. night moth; Ephetia
mknąć [mknownćh] v. fleet; rush; dash along; dash away; speed; scurry; spin along; spin away; scamper; scud (*repeatedly*)
mknięcie [**mkńan**-ćhe] n. fleeting; dashing along
mlask [mlahsk] m. smack; click; slap
mlaskać [**mlahs**-kahćh] v. lap; smack; click; make smacking noises; plash (*repeatedly*)
mlaskanie [mlahs-**kah**-ńe] n. smacking noises
mlasnąć [**mlahs**-nownćh] v. lap; smack; click; make smacking noises; plash
mlaśnięcie [mlahśh-**ńan**-ćhe] n. smack of the tongue; click of the lips; smacking noises (made when eating)
mlecz [mlech] m. sow thistle; (spinal) marrow; (fish) milt; roe
mleczaj [**mle**-chahy] m. a species of agaric; Lactarious
mleczak [**mle**-chahk] m. suckling; milter; colloq: milk tooth; whippersnapper
mleczan [**mle**-chahn] m. lactate
mleczarka [mle-**chahr**-kah] f. dairywoman; milkmaid
mleczarnia [mle-**chahr**-ńah] f. dairy; creamery; milk bar
mleczarniany [mle-chahr-**ńah**-ni] adj.m. of a milk bar; of a dairy; of a creamery
mleczarski [mle-**chahr**-skee] adj.m. dairyman's; of a creamery
zakład mleczarski [**zah**-kwahd mle-**chahr**-skee] exp.: creamery
mleczarstwo [mle-**chahr**-stfo] n. dairying; dairy work
mleczarz [**mle**-chahsh] m. dairyman
mleczko [**mlech**-ko] n. milk; bee-milk; custard
mlecznik [**mlech**-ńeek] m. sea milkwort
mlecznobiały [mlech-no-**byah**-wi] adj.m. milk-white
mlecznoniebieski [mlech-no-ńe-**bye**-skee] adj.m. pale-blue
mlecznoróżowy [mlech-no-roo-**zho**-vi] adj.m. light pink (color)
mleczność [**mlech**-nośhćh] f. milkiness; milking yield; milking capacity; lactation

mlecznozielony [mlech-no-**źhe**-lo-ni] adj.m. pale-green
mleczny [**mlech**-ni] adj.m. of milk; milk; milky; dairy; lactic; lactescent; milk-white; frosted (glass, etc.)
bar mleczny [bahr **mlech**-ni] exp.: milk bar
Droga Mleczna [**dro**-gah **mlech**-nah] exp.: Milky Way
drzewo mleczne [**dzhe**-vo **mlech**-ne] exp.: latex-yielding tree
gospodarstwo mleczne [gos-po-**dahr**-stfo **mlech**-ne] exp.: dairy farm
gruczoł mleczny [**groo**-chow **mlech**-ni] exp.: lacteal gland
mleczna siostra [**mlech**-nah **śhos**-trah] exp.: foster sister
mleczny brat [**mlech**-ni braht] exp.: foster brother
przewody mleczne [pshe-**vo**-di **mlech**-ne] exp.: lacticifers
szkło mleczne [shkwo **mlech**-ne] exp.: frosted glass; opal glass; opaline glass
ząb mleczny [zownp **mlech**-ni] exp.: milk tooth
żarówka mleczna [zhah-**roof**-kah **mlech**-nah] exp.: frosted (light) bulb
mleć [mlećh] v. grind; mill; mince; munch; chew (*repeatedly*)
mleć językiem [mlećh yan-**zi**-kem] exp.: colloq: to jabber
mleć się [mlećh śhan] v. getting ground up; getting minced (*repeatedly*)
mleko [**mle**-ko] n. milk; latex
dawać mleko [**dah**-vahćh **mle**-ko] exp.: to yield milk
mleko cementowe [**mle**-ko tse-**men**-to-ve] exp.: cement grout
mleko kwaśne [**mle**-ko **kfahśh**-ne] exp.: curdled milk; sour milk
mleko pełnotłuste [**mle**-ko pew-no-**twoo**-ste] exp.: whole milk
mleko prosto od krowy [**mle**-ko **pro**-sto ot **kro**-vi] exp.: milk fresh from the cow
mleko w proszku [**mle**-ko f **prosh**-koo] exp.: powdered milk
mleko zbierane [**mle**-ko zbye-**rah**-ne] exp.: skimmed milk
mleko zsiadłe [**mle**-ko **sśhahd**-we] exp.: curdled milk; sour milk
pełne mleko [**pew**-ne **mle**-ko] exp.: full-cream milk
wydzielanie mleka [vi-dźhe-**lah**-ńe **mle**-kah] exp.: lactation
mlekodajny [mle-ko-**dahy**-ni] adj.m. milch (cow, goat, etc.); milk-producing
mlekopędny [mle-ko-**pand**-ni] adj.m. milk-producing
mlekowaty [mle-ko-**vah**-ti] adj.m. moraceous
mlekowate [mle-ko-**vah**-te] pl. the family Moraceae
mlekowy [mle-**ko**-vi] adj.m. lactic
cukier mlekowy [**tsoo**-ker mle-**ko**-vi] exp.: lactose; milk sugar
kwas mlekowy [kfahs mle-**ko**-vi] exp.: lactic acid
kwasek mlekowy [**kfah**-sek mle-**ko**-vi] exp.: lactic acid
sól kwasu mlekowego [sool **kfah**-soo mle-ko-**ve**-go] exp.: lactate
mlewnik [**mlev**-ńeek] m. (grain grinding) roller mill
mlewo [**mle**-vo] n. grist
młaka [**mwah**-kah] f. slang: marsh; bog; swamp
młocarnia [mwo-**tsahr**-ńah] f. thresher; threshing machine
młocarz [**mwo**-tsahsh] m. thresher
młocek [**mwo**-tsek] m. thresher
młociarz [**mwo**-ćhahsh] m. hammer-thrower
młocka [**mwots**-kah] f. threshing
młockarnia [mwots-**kahr**-ńah] f. threshing machine
młoda [**mwo**-dah] adj.f. young (female); f. young female
młode [**mwo**-de] adj.pl. young; pl. the young; litter; n. cub
młodniak [**mwod**-ńahk] m. young forest (less than 20 years old)
młodnieć [**mwod**-ńećh] v. grow younger; grow young again; feel younger; look younger (*repeatedly*)
młodnik [**mwod**-ńeek] m. young forest (trees 10-20 years old)
młodo [**mwo**-do] adv. (talk, etc.) young; in one's youth; (do, etc.) as a boy or girl
młodocianie [mwo-do-**ćhah**-ńe] adv.

youthfully
wyglądać młodocianie [vi-glown-dahćh mwo-do-**ćhah**-ńe] exp.: to have a juvenile look
młodociany [mwo-do-**ćhah**-ni] adj.m. juvenile; youthful; adolescent; young; immature; early
przestępczość młodocianych [pshe-**stanp**-chośhćh mwo-do-**ćhah**-nikh] exp.: juvenile delinquency
sąd dla młodocianych [sownd dlah mwo-do-**ćhah**-nikh] exp.: juvenile court
młodogramatyk [mwo-do-grah-**mah**-tik] m. German linguist of the Leipzig school
młodopolski [mwo-do-**pol**-skee] adj.m. of neo-romantic Polish literary style
młodopolszczyzna [mwo-do-polsh-**chiz**-nah] f. neo-romantic Polish literary style
młodość [**mwo**-dośhćh] f. youth; early stage
błędy młodości [**bwan**-di mwo-**dośh**-ćhee] exp.: youthful mistakes
już nie pierwszej młodości [yoosh ńe **pyerf**-shey mwo-**dośh**-ćhee] exp.: past one's prime
pierwsza młodość [**pyerf**-shah **mwo**-dośhćh] exp.: prime (of life); early youth
w młodości [v mwo-**dośh**-ćhee] exp.: in one's young days; when young
młodszy [**mwot**-shi] adj.m. younger; junior; green; lower
młodsi [**mwot**-śhee] pl. younger folks
młodszy brat [**mwot**-shi braht] exp.: younger brother
w młodszym wieku [v **mwot**-shim **vye**-koo] exp.: earlier in life
młody [**mwo**-di] adj.m. young; youthful; new (wine, etc.); later; m. young person; cub; pup; kitten
dość młody [dośhćh **mwo**-di] exp.: youngish
młode [**mwo**-de] pl. the young; litter
młode lata [mwo-de **lah**-tah] exp.: youth
młode drzewo [**mwo**-de **dzhe**-vo] exp.: sapling
pan młody [pahn **mwo**-di] exp.: groom
panna młoda [**pahn**-nah **mwo**-dah] exp.: bride
za młodu [zah **mwo**-doo] exp.: in one's young days; in one's youth; when young; early in life
młodziak [**mwo**-dźhahk] m. teenager boy; young stag
młodzian [**mwo**-dźhahn] m. young man; lad (Brit.); youth
młodziczka [mwo-**dźheech**-kah] f. young girl contender in sport competition
młodzieniaszek [mwo-dźhe-**ńah**-shek] m. sprig; stripling; lad (Brit.); youngster; youth
młodzieniec [mwo-**dźhe**-ńets] m. young man; lad (Brit.); youth
złoty młodzieniec [**zwo**-ti mwo-**dźhe**-ńets] exp.: one of the gilded youth; one of the jet set
młodzieńczo [mwo-**dźheń**-cho] adv. youthfully; immaturely
wyglądać młodzieńczo [vi-glown-dahćh mwo-**dźheń**-cho] exp.: to look very young; to look boyish
młodzieńczość [mwo-**dźheń**-chośhćh] f. youthfulness; juvenility
młodzieńczy [mwo-**dźheń**-chi] adj.m. youthful; immature
po młodzieńczemu [po mwo-dźheń-**che**-moo] exp.: in a youthful fashion; youthfully
usposobienie młodzieńcze [oo-spo-so-**bye**-ńe mwo-**dźheń**-che] exp.: youthfulness
wiek młodzieńczy [vyek mwo-**dźheń**-chi] exp.: adolescence
wygląd młodzieńczy [**vi**-glownd mwo-**dźheń**-chi] exp.: youthful appearance
młodzież [**mwo**-dźhesh] f. youth; young generation; young people; boys and girls; the young; teenagers
młodzież szkolna [**mwo**-dźhesh **shkol**-nah] exp.: school children
młodzież uniwersytecka [**mwo**-dźhesh oo-ńee-ver-si-**te**-tskah]

exp.: university students
młodzieżowiec [mwo-dźhe-**zho**-vyets] m. organizer of the young people
młodzieżowo [mwo-dźhe-**zho**-vo] adv. with the young; youthfully
młodzieżowość [mwo-dźhe-**zho**-vośhćh] f. youthful character
młodzieżowy [mwo-dźhe-**zho**-vi] adj.m. juvenile; of the young; youth (organization, etc.)
młodzik [**mwo**-dźheek] m. youngster; teenager; youngling
młodziuchny [mwo-**dźhookh**-ni] adj.m. very young
młodziusieńki [mwo-dźhoo-**śheń**-kee] adj.m. very, very young
młodziuteńki [mwo-dźhoo-**teń**-kee] adj.m. very, very young
młodziutki [mwo-**dźhoot**-kee] adj.m. very young (diminutive of: **młody**)
młodziutko [mwo-**dźhoot**-ko] adv. diminutive of: **młodo**
młodziwo [mwo-**dźhee**-vo] n. colostrum; beestings
młodzizna [mwo-**dźhee**-znah] f. colloq: young folks; children; young plants
młokos [**mwo**-kos] m. kid
młot [mwot] m. sledge; hammer; rammer; stamp; the hammer (sport); colloq: blockhead
między młotem a kowadłem [myan-dzi **mwo**-tem ah ko-**vahd**-wem] exp.: between the hammer and the anvil; between the devil and the deep sea
młot parowy [mwot pah-**ro**-vi] exp.: steam hammer
młot pneumatyczny [mwot pnew-mah-**tich**-ni] exp.: air hammer; pneumatic hammer
młot spadowy [mwot spah-**do**-vi] exp.: drop hammer; tilt hammer (Brit.)
rzut młotem [zhoot **mwo**-tem] exp.: hammer throw
młoteczek [mwo-**te**-chek] m. very small hammer; clapper; malleus
młoteczkować [mwo-tech-**ko**-vahćh] v. hammer with a machine (*repeatedly*)
młoteczkowanie [mwo-tech-ko-**vah**-ńe] n. hammering with a machine
młoteczkowy [mwo-tech-**ko**-vi] adj.m. of a hammering with a machine; of a small hammer
młotek [**mwo**-tek] m. hammer; tack-hammer; clapper
młotkować [mwot-ko-**vah**-vahćh] v. hammer (by hand) (*repeatedly*)
młotkownica [mwot-kov-**ńee**-tsah] f. hammering machine
młotkowy [mwot-**ko**-vi] adj.m. percussion (drill, etc.)
młotnik [**mwot**-ńeek] m. hammering worker
młotować [mwo-**to**-vahćh] v. machine hammer (*repeatedly*)
młotowanie [mwo-to-**vah**-ńe] n. machine hammering
młotowaty [mwo-to-**vah**-ti] adj.m. hammer-like
młotowate [mwo-to-**vah**-te] pl. hammer shark-like fishes; the family Sphyrindae
młotowina [mwo-to-**vee**-nah] f. scale produced by hammering
młotowiny [mwo-to-**vee**-ni] pl. scales produced by hammering
młotownia [mwo-**tov**-ńah] f. shed for hammering machines
młotowy [mwo-**to**-vi] adj.m. of a hammer; of hammers
młócenie [mwoo-**tse**-ńe] n. threshing
młócić [**mwoo**-ćheećh] v. thresh (out); pommel; pound; belabor (*repeatedly*)
młócka [**mwoots**-kah] f. threshing
młódka [**mwoot**-kah] f. young female; fledgling
młódź [mwooćh] f. young people; young folks
młóto [**mwoo**-to] n. malt residue
młyn [mwin] m. (flour-)mill; grinder; grinding-mill
młyn wodny [mwin **vod**-ni] exp.: water mill
młynarczyk [mwi-**nahr**-chik] m. miller's apprentice
młynarek [mwi-**nah**-rek] m. meal worm; meal beetle
młynarka [mwi-**nahr**-kah] f. miller's wife; (woman) miller
młynarski [mwi-**nahr**-skee] adj.m. miller's; milling (machine, etc.)
młynarstwo [mwi-**nahr**-stfo] n.

miller's work; flour-milling
młynarz [**mwi**-nahsh] m. miller
młynarzować [mwi-nah-**zho**-vahćh] v. work as a miller (*repeatedly*)
młynarzyć [mwi-**nah**-zhićh] v. work as a miller (*repeatedly*)
młynek [**mwi**-nek] m. hand-grinder; winnow mill; flay; fan
młynek do kawy [**mwi**-nek do **kah**-vi] exp.: coffee grinder; coffee mill
młyniec [**mwi**-ńets] m. whirl; spin; moulinet (in fencing)
młynkomikser [mwin-ko-**meek**-ser] m. combined mixer and blender (kitchen appliance)
młynkować [mwin-**ko**-vahćh] v. winnow; whirl; spin; twirl (a cane, etc.) (*repeatedly*)
młynkowanie [mwin-ko-**vah**-ńe] n. winnowing (grain)
młynkowy [mwin-**ko**-vi] adj.m. of a mill
młynownia [mwi-**nov**-ńah] f. grinding plant
młynowy [mwi-**no**-vi] adj.m. of a mill
młynówka [mwi-**noof**-kah] f. millrace; leat
młyński [**mwiń**-skee] adj.m. mill (building, etc.); of a mill
kamień młyński [**kah**-myeń **mwiń**-skee] exp.: millstone; grindstone
mnemoneutyka [mne-mo-**new**-ti-kah] f. mnemotechny; a technique for improving the memory; mnemonics
mnemonicznie [mne-mo-**ńeech**-ńe] adv. mnemonically
mnemoniczny [mne-mo-**ńeech**-ni] adj.m. mnemonic (technique for improving of the memory, exercises, etc.)
mnemonika [mne-**mo**-ńee-kah] f. mnemonics; mnemotechny; a technique for improving the memory
mnemotechnicznie [mne-mo-tekh-**ńeech**-ńe] adv. mnemonically
mnemotechniczny [mne-mo-tekh-**ńeech**-ni] adj.m. mnemotechnic
mnemotechnika [mne-mo-**tekh**-ńee-kah] f. mnemonics; mnemonism; mnemotechny; a technique for improving the memory
mnich [mńeekh] m. monk; friar
mnisi [**mńee**-śhee] pl. monks
mniej [mńey] adv. less; fewer; minus
nie mniej niż [ńe mńey ńeesh] exp.: not less than; not fewer than
ni mniej, ni więcej [ńee mńey ńee **vyan**-tsey] exp.: neither more nor less; downright; exactly
mniej więcej [mńey **vyan**-tsey] exp.: more or less; about; around; approximately
mniejszościowy [mńey-shośh-**ćho**-vi] adj.m. minority (party, etc.); of a minority
mniejszość [**mńey**-shośhćh] f. minority; the lesser part
mniejszości narodowe [mńey-**shośh**-ćhee nah-ro-**do**-ve] exp.: national minorities
mniejszy [**mńey**-shi] adj.m. smaller; lesser; minor; slighter; less (intense, acute, etc.); diminished
mniejsza! [**mńey**-shah] excl.: never mind!
mniejsza o to [**mńey**-shah o to] exp.: never mind that
w mniejszym stopniu [v **mńe**-shim **stop**-ńoo] exp.: in a lesser degree; to a smaller extent
mniemać [**mńe**-mahćh] v. suppose; deem; imagine; think; consider; be of opinion; conjecture (*repeatedly*)
mniemanie [mńe-**mah**-ńe] n. opinion; notion; conviction; estimation
czynić coś w błędnym mniemaniu [chi-ńeećh tsośh v **bwand**-nim mńe-**mah**-ńoo] exp.: to do something under a misapprehension
mieć wysokie mniemanie o kimś [myećh vi-**so**-ke mńe-**mah**-ńe o keemśh] exp.: to hold somebody in high esteem; to think highly of somebody
mniemany [mńe-**mah**-ni] adj.m. supposed; would-be
mnisi [**mńee**-śhee] adj.m. monk's; monastic

mniszek [mńee-shek] m. young monk; dandelion; colloq: puffball
mniszka [mńeesh-kah] f. nun; nun moth (Lymantria monacha)
mniszy [mńee-shi] adj.m. of a monk; of monks; monk's
mnoga [mno-gah] num. plural
liczba mnoga [leedzh-bah mno-gah] exp.: plural
mnogi [mno-gee] adj.m. numerous; of the plural
mnogość [mno-gośhćh] f. abundance; plurality; multitude; great number
mnożarka [mno-zhahr-kah] f. multiplication machine
mnożarnia [mno-zhahr-ńah] f. multiplication machine; greenhouse
mnożenie [mno-zhe-ńe] n. multiplication; increase; proliferation; breeding
tabliczka mnożenia [tahb-leech-kah mno-zhe-ńah] exp.: multiplication table
mnożenie się [mno-zhe-ńe śhan] n. multiplication; procreation; breeding; increase
mnożna [mnozh-nah] f. multiplicand
mnożnik [mnozh-ńeek] m. factor; multiplier; coefficient
mnożność [mnozh-nośhćh] f. prolificacy; fertility
mnożny [mnozh-ni] adj.m. prolific; fertile; multiplicative
liczebnik mnożny [lee-cheb-ńeek mnozh-ni] exp.: a multiplicative
mnożyć [mno-zhićh] v. multiply; augment; propagate; reproduce (plants, animals) (*repeatedly*)
mnożyć się [mno-zhićh śhan] v. multiply; increase; grow in number; breed; proliferate (*repeatedly*)
mnóstwo [mnoos-tfo] n. very many; multitude; swarm; large numbers; colloq: loads; heaps; lots
całe mnóstwo ludzi [tsah-we mnoos-tfo loo-dźhee] exp.: lots of people
mnóstwo książek [mnoos-tfo kśhown-zhek] exp.: books galore; great number of books
mnóstwo szczegółów [mnoos-tfo shche-goo-woof] exp.: a wealth of detail
moa [mo-ah] m. moa (Dinornis, ratite bird)
mobil [mo-beel] m. mobile sculpture
mobiliarny [mo-bee-lyahr-ni] adj.m. mobiliary; pertaining to movables; pertaining to mobilization
mobilizacja [mo-bee-lee-zahts-yah] f. mobilization; call-up
mobilizacyjny [mo-bee-lee-zah-tsiy-ni] adj.m. of mobilization; mobilization (order, etc.)
mobilizować [mo-bee-lee-zo-vahćh] v. mobilize; call up; raise (funds, etc.); put forth (efforts, etc.) (*repeatedly*)
mobilizować się [mo-bee-lee-zo-vahćh śhan] v. mobilize oneself (*repeatedly*)
mobilizowanie [mo-bee-lee-zo-vah-ńe] n. mobilization
mobilizowanie się [mo-bee-lee-zo-vah-ńe śhan] n. mobilizing oneself
mobilizująco [mo-bee-lee-zoo-yown-tso] adv. in mobilizing fashion
mobilność [mo-beel-nośhćh] f. mobility; movement
mobilny [mo-beel-ni] adj.m. mobile; moving (picture, etc.)
moc [mots] f. power; might; great-deal; vigor; strength; force; violence; vehemence; efficiency; impressiveness; grip; validity; authority; solidity; intensity; serviceableness; see: **mnóstwo**
być w mocy [bićh v mo-tsi] exp.: to be in force
mieć moc [myećh mots] exp.: to be valid
moc argumentu [mots ahr-goo-men-too] exp.: force of an argument; potency of an argument
moc aut [mots ahwt] exp.: great number of cars
moc wina [mots vee-nah] exp.: body of a wine; headiness of a wine
moc prawna [mots prahv-nah] exp.: legal force
na mocy [nah mo-tsi] exp.: in virtue of; on the strength of

nabrać mocy [nah-brahćh **mo**-tsi] exp.: to take effect
nadać moc [nah-dahćh mots] exp.: to validate; to implement
nie mieć mocy [ńe myećh **mo**-tsi] exp.: to be weak
w mojej mocy [v **mo**-yey **mo**-tsi] exp.: in my power
mocarnie [mo-**tsahr**-ńe] adv. powerfully; strongly; mightily; with great force
mocarność [mo-**tsahr**-nośhćh] f. power; strength
mocarny [mo-**tsahr**-ni] adj.m. mighty; strong; powerful
mocarstwo [mo-**tsahr**-stfo] n. strong country; (world) power
mocarstwowość [mo-tsahr-**stfo**-vośhćh] f. power status
mocarstwowy [mo-tsahr-**stfo**-vi] adj.m. of power status; ranging among the great powers
polityka mocarstwowa [po-**lee**-ti-kah mo-tsahr-**stfo**-vah] exp.: power politics
mocarz [**mo**-tsahsh] m. strong man; potentate; powerful man; pillar of strength; mighty ruler
mocja [**mots**-yah] f. gender-specific ending of a word
mocnica burtowa [mots-**ńee**-tsah boor-**to**-vah] exp.: sheer strake
mocno [**mots**-no] adv. fast; firmly; strongly; mightily; with great might; powerfully; sturdily; vigorously; robustly; greatly; very much; intensely; vividly; in strong terms; in strong language; tight
mocno bić [**mots**-no beećh] exp.: to strike hard
mocno spać [**mots**-no spahćh] exp.: to be fast asleep
mocno stać na nogach [**mots**-no stahćh nah **no**-gahkh] exp.: to stand firm on one's legs
mocno trzymać [**mots**-no **tshi**-mahćh] exp.: to hold tight
mocno przekonany [**mots**-no pshe-ko-**nah**-ni] exp.: firmly convinced
mocno zbudowany [**mots**-no zboo-do-**vah**-ni] exp.: of sturdy build
mocno zobowiązany [**mots**-no zo-bo-vyown-**zah**-ni] exp.: deeply obliged
to siedzi mocno [to **śhe**-dźhee **mots**-no] exp.: it is safe; it is steady; it sits tight
mocny [**mots**-ni] adj.m. strong; powerful; mighty; sinewy; hard; heavy; vigorous; smart; loud; tight; firm; fast; steady; nasty; stiff; substantial; potent; stable; sound; stout; stressed; robust; sturdy; hefty; intense; steadfast; full-bodied; generous; durable; serviceable; solid; tough; safe; vivid; expressive; proficient; versed; well up (in)
mocna głowa [**mots**-nah **gwo**-vah] exp.: one who can stand drink; brainy man; brains
mocna ręka [**mots**-nah ran-kah] exp.: tight grip; firm control; strong hand
mocne przekonanie [**mots**-ne pshe-ko-**nah**-ńe] exp.: strong conviction
mocne słowa [**mots**-ne **swo**-vah] exp.: sharp words; forcible words
mocni [**mots**-ńee] pl. the strong
mocny uścisk dłoni [**mots**-ni oośh-ćheesk **dwo**-ńee] exp.: strong handshake
mocny w pysku [**mots**-ni f **pis**-koo] exp.: vulg.: he has a ready tongue; he is bold in words
mocodawca [mo-tso-**dahf**-tsah] m. mandatary; principal; person giving authorization to represent and act
mocodawczyni [mo-tso-dahf-**chi**-ńee] f. (female) mandatary; principal; woman giving authorization to represent and act
mocować [mo-**tso**-vahćh] v. fasten; fix; make fast (*repeatedly*)
mocować się [mo-**tso**-vahćh śhan] v. wrestle; exert oneself; fight against (disease, etc.); be at grips (with); cope (with); battle (with) (*repeatedly*)
mocowanie [mo-tso-**vah**-ńe] n. coping; fastening
mocowanie się [mo-tso-**vah**-ńe śhan] n. wrestling with one another; wrestling

mocz [moch] m. urine
analiza moczu [ah-nah-**lee**-zah **mo**-choo] exp.: urinalysis
oddawanie moczu [od-dah-**vah**-ńe **mo**-choo] exp.: urination
parcie na mocz [**pahr**-ćhe nah moch] exp.: diuresis
trudne oddawanie moczu [**trood**-ne od-dah-**vah**-ńe **mo**-choo] exp.: dysuria; strangury
zatrzymanie moczu [zah-tshi-**mah**-ńe **mo**-choo] exp.: ischuria
moczan [**mo**-chahn] m. urate
moczany [mo-**chah**-ni] pl. urates
moczanowy [mo-chah-**no**-vi] adj.m. uric
skaza moczanowa [**skah**-zah mo-chah-**no**-vah] exp.: gout
moczar [**mo**-chahr] m. bog; marsh; swamp; morass
moczarka [mo-**chahr**-kah] f. water-thyme; Elodea
moczarnia [mo-**chahr**-ńah] f. wetting facility; place where flax is steeped
moczarowaty [mo-chah-ro-**vah**-ti] adj.m. boggy; marshy
moczarowy [mo-chah-**ro**-vi] adj.m. bog (peat, hay, etc.)
moczenie [mo-**che**-ńe] n. soaking; micturition; wetting; passing water; urination
moczenie **nóg** [mo-**che**-ńe noog] exp.: footbath
moczenie się [mo-**che**-ńe śh<u>an</u>] n. getting wet; getting soaked
mocznica [moch-**ńee**-tsah] f. uremia
mocznicowy [moch-ńee-**tso**-vi] adj.m. uremic
mocznik [**moch**-ńeek] m. urea
mocznikowy [moch-ńee-**ko**-vi] adj.m. ureal; urea (frost, etc.); of the chief solid component of mammalian urine
moczopędnie [mo-cho-**p<u>an</u>d**-ńe] adv. diuretically
moczopędny [mo-cho-**p<u>an</u>d**-ni] adj.m. diuretic
moczopłciowy [mo-cho-**pwćho**-vi] adj.m. urogenital; of organs of excretion and reproduction
narządy moczopłciowe [nah-**zh<u>own</u>**-di mo-cho-**pwćho**-ve] exp.: urogenital tract
moczowo-płciowy [mo-**cho**-vo **pwćho**-vi] adj.m. pertaining to urination and sex organs
moczowód [mo-**cho**-voot] m. ureter
moczowy [mo-**cho**-vi] adj.m. uric; urinary (calculus, etc.); of urine; uretic (medicine, etc.)
cewka moczowa [**tsef**-kah mo-**cho**-vah] exp.: urethra
drogi moczowe [**dro**-gee mo-**cho**-ve] exp.: urinary tracts
pęcherz moczowy [**p<u>an</u>**-khesh mo-**cho**-vi] exp.: urinary bladder
przewód moczowy [**pshe**-voot mo-**cho**-vi] exp.: ureter
moczówka [mo-**choof**-kah] f. diabetes (hist.)
moczówka cukrowa [mo-**choof**-kah tsoo-**kro**-vah] exp.: diabetes mellitus; see: **cukrzyca**
moczówka prosta [mo-**choof**-kah **pros**-tah] exp.: diabetes insipidus
moczyć [**mo**-chićh] v. wet; drench; douse; moisten; steep; soak; urinate; pass urine (*repeatedly*)
moczyć len [**mo**-chićh len] exp.: to ret flax; to dew ret flax
moczyć się [**mo**-chićh śh<u>an</u>] v. wet oneself; douse oneself; be steeped; soak; bathe (*repeatedly*)
moczygęba [mo-chi-**g<u>an</u>**-bah] m. slang: soaker; a drunkard
moczymorda [mo-chi-**mor**-dah] m. slang: soaker; a drunkard
moda [**mo**-dah] f. fashion; style; vogue
mody [**mo**-di] pl. fashions
ostatnia moda [os-**taht**-ńah **mo**-dah] exp.: the latest fashion; the new look
ostatni krzyk mody [os-**taht**-ńee kshik **mo**-di] exp.: the height of fashion
rewia mody [**re**-vyah **mo**-di] exp.: fashion show
wchodzić w modę [**fkho**-dźheećh v **mo**-d<u>an</u>] exp.: to come into fashion
wychodzić z mody [vi-**kho**-dźheećh z **mo**-di] exp.: to grow out of fashion
modalność [mo-**dahl**-nośhćh] f. modality
modalny [mo-**dahl**-ni] adj.m. modal

model [mo-del] m. model; type; pattern; shape; design; mold; cast; style; (artist's) sitter

modelacja [mo-de-lahts-yah] f. modelling; fashioning; shaping; molding

modelarka [mo-de-lahr-kah] f. (woman) patternmaker

modelarnia [mo-de-lahr-ńah] f. pattern-shop

modelarski [mo-de-lahr-skee] adj.m. modelist's; modelists'; of a modelmaker; modelmaker's

gips modelarski [geeps mo-de-lahr-skee] exp.: plaster of Paris

modelarstwo [mo-de-lahr-stfo] n. modelling; modelling-work; patternmaking

modelarz [mo-de-lahsh] m. modeller; patternmaker; modelmaker

modelator [mo-de-lah-tor] m. theater decorator

modelatorka [mo-de-lah-tor-kah] f. (woman) theater decorator

modelatornia [mo-de-lah-tor-ńah] f. theater decorator's studio

modelik [mo-de-leek] m. small model

modelka [mo-del-kah] f. model

modelować [mo-de-lo-vahćh] v. model; shape; mold; fashion (*repeatedly*)

modelowanie [mo-de-lo-vah-ńe] n. working as a model; making models

modelowy [mo-de-lo-vi] adj.m. model (specimen, etc.)

gips modelowy [geeps mo-de-lo-vi] exp.: plaster of Paris

modelunek [mo-de-loo-nek] m. molding; plasticity

modelunkowy [mo-de-loon-ko-vi] adj.m. of molding; of plasticity

moderacja [mo-de-rah-tsyah] f. moderation

moderato [mo-de-rah-to] n. moderato (in music)

moderator [mo-de-rah-tor] m. moderator; regulator

moderna [mo-der-nah] f. literary style of the end of modernism

modernista [mo-der-ńees-tah] m. modernist

modernistyczny [mo-der-ńees-tich-ni] adj.m. modernist; modernistic

modernizacja [mo-der-ńee-zah-tsyah] f. modernization

modernizacyjny [mo-der-ńee-zah-tsiy-ni] adj.m. modernizing

modernizator [mo-der-ńee-zah-tor] m. modernizer

modernizm [mo-der-ńeezm] m. modernism

modernizować [mo-der-ńee-zo-vahćh] v. modernize; bring up to date; make modern (*repeatedly*)

modernizować się [mo-der-ńee-zo-vahćh śhan] v. be modernized (*repeatedly*)

modernizowanie [mo-der-ńee-zo-vah-ńe] n. modernization

modernizowanie się [mo-der-ńee-zo-vah-ńe śhan] n. modernizing oneself

moderunek [mo-de-roo-nek] m. soldier's equipment; harness; gear (of a draught animal)

modlić się [mod-leećh śhan] v. pray; say one's prayer (*repeatedly*)

modlić się za [mod-leećh śhan zah] exp.: pray for; say one's prayer on behalf of

módl się [moodl śhan] exp.: (please) say your prayers

modligroszek [mod-lee-gro-shek] m. jequirity; Arbus precatorius

modliszka [mod-leesh-kah] f. Mantis religiosa insect; mantis

modliszki [mod-leesh-kee] pl. genus Mantis (of insects)

modliszkowate [mod-leesh-ko-vah-te] pl. the family Mantidae

modlitewnie [mod-lee-tev-ńe] adv. in prayer; beseechingly

modlitewnik [mod-lee-tev-ńeek] m. prayer-book

modlitewny [mod-lee-tev-ni] adj.m. prayer (rug, etc.); beseeching

modlitwa [mod-leet-fah] f. prayer; grace (at meal time)

dom modlitwy [dom mod-leet-fi] exp.: house of prayer; place of worship

modlitwy [mod-leet-fi] pl. prayers

modła [mod-wah] f. mold; standard; fashion; model; pattern; distinctive character

na modłę [nah mod-wan] exp.:

after the fashion
modły [**mod**-wi] pl. prayers; invocations
modniarka [mod-**ńahr**-kah] f. milliner; modiste; hat maker
modniarski [mod-**ńahr**-skee] adj.m. milliner's
modniarstwo [mod-**ńahr**-stfo] n. millinering; milliner's work
modnie [**mod**-ńe] adv. fashionably; in modern style; in fashion; in vogue; stylishly; up to date; according to prevailing fashion
modnisia [mod-**ńee**-śhah] f. slave of fashion; dressy woman; woman of fashion
modnisiostwo [mod-ńee-**śho**-stfo] n. dandyism; foppishness; foppery; coxcombry; dressiness
modniś [**mod**-ńeeśh] m. dandy; fop; coxcomb
modny [**mod**-ni] adj.m. fashionable; in fashion; in vogue; stylish; up to date
modrak [**mod**-rahk] m. bluebottle (fly); Centaurea cyanus
modrak morski [**mod**-rahk **mor**-skee] exp.: sea kale; Crambe maritima
modraszek [mod-**rah**-shek] m. large blue butterfly; Lycaena
modrawy [mod-**rah**-vi] adj.m. bluish
modro [**mod**-ro] adv. in deep-blue (color)
modrooki [mod-ro-**o**-kee] adj.m. blue-eyed
modrość [**mod**-rośhćh] f. deep blue
modrozielony [mod-ro-źhe-**lo**-ni] adj.m. green-blue
modry [**mod**-ri] adj.m. azure-blue; deep blue; cerulean blue
modrzew [**mo**-dzhef] m. larch; larch wood
modrzewina [mo-dzhe-**vee**-nah] f. larch; larch wood
modrzewiowy [mo-dzhe-**vyo**-vi] adj.m. larch (cones, etc.); of squared larch trunks
modrzewnica [mo-dzhev-**ńee**-tsah] f. andromeda
modulacja [mo-doo-**lah**-tsyah] f. modulation; inflexion; transition
modulacyjny [mo-doo-lah-**tsiy**-ni] adj.m. modular; modulatory; modulative; inflectional (languages); inflective
modularny [mo-doo-**lahr**-ni] adj.m. modular
modulator [mo-doo-**lah**-tor] m. modulator
modulować [mo-doo-**lo**-vahćh] v. modulate; inflect; regulate (*repeatedly*)
modulowanie [mo-doo-lo-**vah**-ńe] n. modulation; inflection; transition
moduł [**mo**-doow] m. module; modulus
moduł liczby [**mo**-doow **leedzh**-bi] exp.: modulus of a number; absolute value of a number
moduł sprężystości [**mo**-doow spran-zhi-**stośh**-ćhee] exp.: modulus of elasticity
modułowy [mo-doo-**wo**-vi] adj.m. modular
modus [**mo**-doos] m. variable characteristic
modyfikacja [mo-di-fee-**kah**-tsyah] f. modification; alteration
modyfikator [mo-di-fee-**kah**-tor] m. modifier
modyfikować [mo-di-fee-**ko**-vahćh] v. modify; alter; qualify; change partially (*repeatedly*)
modyfikować się [mo-di-fee-**ko**-vahćh śhan] v. modify oneself; change oneself partially (*repeatedly*)
modyfikowanie [mo-di-fee-ko-**vah**-ńe] n. modification; alteration
modyfikowanie się [mo-di-fee-ko-**vah**-ńe śhan] n. modifying oneself
modylion [mo-**dil**-yon] m. modillion
modylon [mo-**di**-lon] m. artificial fiber; fluffed up nylon (or other artificial fiber)
modylonowy [mo-di-lo-**no**-vi] adj.m. of fluffed up nylon (or other artificial fiber)
modystka [mo-**dist**-kah] f. modiste; milliner; hat maker
modzel [**mo**-dzel] m. callus
modzelowatość [mo-dze-lo-**vah**-tośhćh] f. callosity; tylosis
modzelowaty [mo-dze-lo-**vah**-ti] adj.m. callous

mofety [mo-**fe**-ti] pl. cool volcanic gases
mogący [mo-**gown**-tsi] adj.m. able; capable; competent
mogę [**mo**-gan] v. I can; I may (*repeatedly*)
mogilnik [mo-**geel**-ńeek] m. burial ground
mogilno [mo-**geel**-no] n. place of tombs; place of (old) burials
mogilny [mo-**geel**-ni] adj.m. of the grave; sepulchral; tumular
kopiec mogilny [**ko**-pyets mo-**geel**-ni] exp.: tumulus; barrow; mound over a grave
mogiła [mo-**gee**-wah] f. tomb; grave; tumulus; mound
mogiła zbiorowa [mo-**gee**-wah zbyo-**ro**-vah] exp.: common grave
mogoł [**mo**-gow] m. mogul
moher [**mo**-kher] m. mohair
moherowy [mo-khe-**ro**-vi] adj.m. mohair (sweater, etc.)
Mohikanin [mo-khee-**kah**-ńeen] m. Mahican
ostatni Mohikanin [os-**taht**-ńee mo-khee-**kah**-ńeen] exp.: the last of the Mahicans
moi [**mo**-ee] pl. my people; my folks; my friends
moiściewy [mo-eeśh-**ćhe**-vi] excl.: gee!; you don't say!
moja [**mo**-yah] pron.f. my (girl, mother, etc.)
moje [**mo**-ye] pron. n. & pl. my (baby, girls, horses, etc.)
mojr [moyr] m. colloq: fear (Hebrew)
mojra [**moy**-rah] f. colloq: fate; destiny; act of God
mojżeszowy [moy-zhe-**sho**-vi] adj.m. Mosaic; of Moses
wyznanie mojżeszowe [vi-**znah**-ńe moy-zhe-**sho**-ve] exp.: Jewish faith
mokasyn [mo-**kah**-sin] m. moccasin
mokiet [**mo**-ket] m. a plush fabric
mokietowy [mo-ke-**to**-vi] adj.m. plush (fabric, etc.)
mokka [**mok**-kah] f. natural coffee; mocha; Mocha coffee
moknąć [**mok**-nownćh] v. get wet; get soaked; drenched; be soaked; be steeped; be out in the rain (*repeatedly*)
moknięcie [mok-**ńan**-ćhe] n. getting wet; being in the rain
mokradło [mo-**krahd**-wo] n. bog; morass; marsh; swamp; marshy ground; wetland
mokrawo [mo-**krah**-vo] adv. rather wet; pretty wet
mokrawy [mo-**krah**-vi] adj.m. moist; damp; humid
mokro [**mok**-ro] adv. wet
czesać się na mokro [**che**-sahćh śhan nah **mok**-ro] exp.: to comb one's hair wet
jest mokro [yest **mok**-ro] exp.: it is wet outside
mokry [**mok**-ri] adj.m. wet; moist; watery; rainy; sweaty
mokrzuteńki [mok-shoo-**teń**-kee] adj.m. wet through; soaking wet; wringing wet; dripping wet; very sweaty
mokrzyca [mok-**shi**-tsah] f. Minuartia plant of the pink family
mokrzycznik baldaszkowy [mok-**shich**-ńeek bahl-dahsh-**ko**-vi] m. jagged chickweed
mol [mol] m. mole; gram molecule
molarny [mo-**lahr**-ni] adj.m. molar
roztwór molarny [**ros**-tfoor mo-**lahr**-ni] exp.: molar solution
roztwór molowy [**ros**-tfoor mo-**lo**-vi] exp.: molar solution
molasa [mo-**lah**-sah] f. Molasse; sandstone
molekularny [mo-le-koo-**lahr**-ni] adj.m. molecular; of molecule
fizyka molekularna [fee-zi-kah mo-le-koo-**lahr**-nah] exp.: molecular physics
molekuła [mo-le-**koo**-wah] f. molecule (smallest particle)
moleskin [mo-**les**-keen] m. moleskin
molestować [mo-les-**to**-vahćh] v. molest; annoy; vex; trouble; pester; importune; worry (*repeatedly*)
molestowanie [mo-les-to-**vah**-ńe] n. pestering; molesting
moleta [mo-**le**-tah] f. muller; knurling tool
moletować [mo-le-**to**-vahćh] v. shape with a knurling tool; press designs in sheet metal

(*repeatedly*)
moletowanie [mo-le-to-**vah**-ńe] n. shaping with a knurling tool; pressing designs in sheet metal
molibden [mo-**leeb**-den] m. molybdenum (atomic number 42)
molibdenian [mo-leeb-**deń**-yahn] m. molybdate; salt of molybdic acid
molibdeniany [mo-leeb-deń-**yah**-ni] pl. salts of molybdic acid
molibdenit [mo-leeb-**de**-ńeet] m. molybdenite (mineral)
molibdenowy [mo-leeb-de-**no**-vi] adj.m. molybdic; molybdenum (steel, fertilizer, acids, compounds, etc.)
molierowski [mol-ye-**rof**-skee] adj.m. of Moliere; Moliere's
molik [**mo**-leek] m. Ephestia nocturnal moth
molinizm [mo-**lee**-ńeezm] m. Molinism
molino [mo-**lee**-no] n. soft cotton fabric (used for bed sheets, etc.)
moll [mol] indecl.: minor (in music)
mollowy [mol-**lo**-vi] adj.m. minor (scale, etc.)
molo [**mo**-lo] n. pier; mole; jetty; breakwater; quay
moloch [**mo**-lokh] m. insatiable demon; Moloch
moloodporny [mo-lo-ot-**por**-ni] adj.m. mothproof
molowy [mo-**lo**-vi] adj.m. gram-molecular
molto [**mol**-to] not declined: (Italian) molto; much; very (in music)
molton [**mol**-ton] m. duffel (fabric)
moltopren [mol-**to**-pren] m. polyurethane foam
moltoprenowy [mol-to-pre-**no**-vi] adj.m. polyurethane-foam (sponge, etc.)
molwa [**mol**-vah] f. ling (fish)
momencik [mo-**men**-ćheek] m. short while; jiffy; half a sec; two ticks; jiff; a very short time
moment [**mo**-ment] m. moment; instant; point; consideration; factor; (bending, etc.) moment
moment bezwładności [**mo**-ment bez-vwahd-**nośh**-ćhee] exp.: moment of inertia
w momencie gdy ...[v mo-**men**-ćhe gdi] exp.: just as ...
momentalnie [mo-men-**tahl**-ńe] adv. instantaneously; immediately; in a moment; in a jiffy; in no time; at once
momentalny [mo-men-**tahl**-ni] adj.m. instantaneous; immediate; momentary; momentaneous
momot [**mo**-mot] m. colloq.: duff; slack
monacyt [mo-**nah**-tsit] m. monazite (mineral)
monada [mo-**nah**-dah] f. monad
monadologia [mo-nah-do-**lo**-gyah] f. monadism; monadology
monadyczny [mo-nah-**dich**-ni] adj.m. monadic
monarcha [mo-**nahr**-khah] m. monarch; sovereign; king
monarchia [mo-**nahr**-khyah] f. monarchy
monarchicznie [mo-nahr-**kheech**-ńe] adv. monarchically
monarchiczność [mo-nahr-**kheech**-nośhćh] f. monarchic character
monarchiczny [mo-nahr-**kheech**-ni] adj.m. monarchic; monarchial
monarchini [mo-nahr-**khee**-ńee] f. woman monarch
monarchista [mo-nahr-**khees**-tah] m. monarchist; royalist
monarchistyczny [mo-nahr-khees-**tich**-ni] adj.m. monarchist
monarchizm [mo-**nahr**-kheezm] m. monarchism
monarszy [mo-**nahr**-shi] adj.m. regal; monarchial
monaster [mo-**nahs**-ter] m. Eastern monastery
monastyr [mo-**nahs**-tir] m. Eastern monastery
monel [**mo**-nel] m. monel; Monel metal
monergol [mo-**ner**-gol] m. rocket liquid fuel including oxidizer
moneta [mo-**ne**-tah] f. coin; chink
przyjmować za dobrą monetę [pshiy-**mo**-vahćh zah **dob**-rown mo-**ne**-tan] exp.: to accept at face value
moneta brzęcząca [mo-ne-tah bzhan-**chown**-tsah] exp.: hard cash; coins
monetarny [mo-ne-**tahr**-ni] adj.m.

monetary
monetka [mo-**net**-kah] f. small coin; small snail; Cypraea moneta
mongolista [mon-go-**lees**-tah] m. specialist in Mongolian studies
mongolistyka [mon-go-**lees**-ti-kah] f. Mongolian studies
mongolizm [mon-**go**-leezm] m. Mongolism
mongoloid [mon-**go**-loyt] m. Mongoloid
mongoloidalny [mon-go-loy-**dahl**-ni] adj.m. Mongoloid (features, etc.)
mongolski [mon-**gol**-skee] adj.m. Mongol; of Mongolia
mongolskość [mon-**gol**-skośhćh] f. Mongolian character
Mongoł [**mon**-gow] m. Mongolian
mongołowatość [mon-go-wo-**vah**-tośhćh] f. Mongoloid character
moniak [**mo**-ńahk] m. colloq: small value coin
monilioza [mo-ńee-**lyo**-zah] f. moniliaceus disease of fruit trees
monista [mo-**ńees**-tah] m. monist
monistycznie [mo-ńees-**tich**-ńe] adv. monistically
monistyczny [mo-ńees-**tich**-ni] adj.m. monistic; monistical
monit [**mo**-ńeet] m. (official) dunning letter; dun; insistent demand for payment
monitor [mo-**ńee**-tor] m. monitor
monitować [mo-ńee-**to**-vahćh] v. admonish; monitor; check on (a person or timing) (*repeatedly*)
monitowanie [mo-ńee-to-**vah**-ńe] n. monitoring; admonishing
moniuszkowski [mo-ńoosh-**kof**-skee] adj.m. Moniuszko's (compositions, etc.)
monizm [**mo**-ńeezm] m. monism; a view that there is only one kind of ultimate substance
mono [**mo**-no] n. mono; monophonic
mono- [**mo**-no] prefix: mono-; alone-; single-
monocentryzm [mo-no-**tsen**-trizm] m. principle of central leadership (global and local)
monochord [mo-**no**-khort] m. monochord
monochrom [mo-**no**-khrom] m. monochrome
monochromator [mo-no-khro-**mah**-tor] m. monochromator
monochromatycznie [mo-no-khro-mah-**tich**-ńe] adv. monochromatically
monochromatyczność [mo-no-khro-mah-**tich**-nośhćh] f. monochromatic character
monochromatyczny [mo-no-khro-mah-**tich**-ni] adj.m. monochromatic
monochromatyzm [mo-no-khro-**mah**-tizm] m. monochromatism
monochromia [mo-no-**khro**-myah] f. painting (photograph, drawing, etc.) in a single hue
monochromiczny [mo-no-khro-**meech**-ni] adj.m. monochromic
monocukier [mo-no-**tsoo**-ker] m. monosaccharide
monocykl [mo-**no**-tsikl] m. monocycle
monocyt [mo-**no**-tsit] m. monocyte
monocyty [mo-no-**tsi**-ti] pl. monocytes (cytoplasm)
monodia [mo-**no**-dyah] f. monody (music)
monodram [mo-**no**-drahm] m. monodrama (by a single person)
monodramat [mo-no-**drah**-maht] m. monodrama
monodramatyczny [mo-no-drah-mah-**tich**-ni] adj.m. monodramatic
monodyczny [mo-no-**dich**-ni] adj.m. monodic (music)
monofag [mo-**no**-fahg] m. monophagous animal (eating only one kind of food)
monofagi [mo-no-**fah**-gee] pl. monotrophic animals
monofagiczny [mo-no-fah-**geech**-ni] adj.m. monophagous
monofagizm [mo-no-**fah**-geezm] m. monophagy
monofiletyczny [mo-no-fee-le-**tich**-ni] adj.m. monophyletic
monofiletyzm [mo-no-fee-**le**-tizm] m. monophyletism
monofizyta [mo-no-fee-**zi**-tah] m. Monophysite
monofobia [mo-no-**fo**-byah] f. fear of being alone
monofonia [mo-no-**fo**-ńyah] f. monophonous technique (of

broadcasting, etc.)
monofoniczny [mo-no-fo-ńeech-ni] adj.m. monophonic
monofoto [mo-no-fo-to] n. printer's camera with automatic device for handling camera-ready text
monoftong [mo-nof-tong] m. monophthong; clear single vowel sound (formed superglottally)
monoftongiczny [mo-nof-ton-geech-ni] adj.m. monophthongal
monoftongizacja [mo-nof-ton-gee-zahts-yah] f. monophthongization
monogamia [mo-no-gah-myah] f. monogamy
monogamiczny [mo-no-gah-meech-ni] adj.m. monogamic; monogamous
monogamista [mo-no-gah-mees-tah] m. monogamist
monogeneza [mo-no-ge-ne-zah] f. monogenesis
monogeniczny [mo-no-ge-ńeech-ni] adj.m. monogenetic; monogenic
monogenizm [mo-no-ge-ńeezm] m. monogenism
monoginia [mo-no-geeń-yah] f. condition of having but one pistil or style
monogonia [mo-no-goń-yah] f. monogony; asexual reproduction
monografia [mo-no-grah-fyah] f. monograph
monograficznie [mo-no-grah-feech-ńe] adv. monographically
monograficzny [mo-no-grah-feech-ni] adj.m. monographic
monografista [mo-no-grah-fees-tah] m. monographer; monographist
monografistyka [mo-no-grah-fees-ti-kah] f. monography; monographic literature; monographic output
monogram [mo-no-grahm] m. monogram; initials in a design
podpisać się monogramem [pot-pi-sahćh śhan mo-no-grah-mem] exp.: to initial (something)
monohydrat [mo-no-hi-draht] m. monohydrate
monoidea [mo-no-ee-de-ah] f. single dominating thought; monoideic condition; monodeistic (hypnotic) absorption in a single idea
monoideizm [mo-no-ee-de-eezm] m. monoideism; monoideic trance
monokarpiczny [mo-no-kahr-peech-ni] adj.m. monocarpic; bearing fruit but once
roślina monokarpiczna [rośh-lee-nah mo-no-kahr-peech-nah] exp.: monocarp
monokl [mo-nokl] m. eyeglass
monoklina [mo-no-klee-nah] f. monoclinal fold
monoklinalny [mo-no-klee-nahl-ni] adj.m. monoclinal
monokrystaliczny [mo-no-kris-tah-leech-ni] adj.m. single-crystal (laser, fiber, etc.)
monokryształ [mo-no-krish-tahw] m. single crystal
monokultura [mo-no-kool-too-rah] f. monoculture (in agriculture)
monokulturowy [mo-no-kool-too-ro-vi] adj.m. monocultural
monolit [mo-no-leet] m. monolith
monolitowość [mo-no-lee-to-vośhćh] f. monolithic nature
monolitowy [mo-no-lee-to-vi] adj.m. monolithic
monolitycznie [mo-no-lee-tich-ńe] adv. like a monolith
monolityczność [mo-no-lee-tich-nośhćh] f. monolithic nature
monolityczny [mo-no-lee-tich-ni] adj.m. monolithic
monolog [mo-no-log] m. monologue; soliloquy of one actor; skit for one actor only; monolog
monologista [mo-no-lo-gees-tah] m. monologuist; monologist
monologizować [mo-no-lo-gee-zo-vahćh] v. monologize; soliloquize (*repeatedly*)
monologizowanie [mo-no-lo-gee-zo-vah-ńe] n. monologizing
monologować [mo-no-lo-go-vahćh] v. soliloquize; monologize (*repeatedly*)
monologowanie [mo-no-lo-go-vah-ńe] n. monology
monologowy [mo-no-lo-go-vi] adj.m. monologic; monological
monoman [mo-no-mahn] m. monomaniac
monomania [mo-no-mahń-yah] f. monomania
monomer [mo-no-mer] m. monomer

monomentalizm [mo-no-men-**tah**-leezm] m. monomentallism
monometalizm [mo-no-me-**tah**-leezm] m. monometallism
monomorficzny [mo-no-mor-**feech**-ni] adj.m. monomorphic
mononukleoza [mo-no-noo-kle-**o**-zah] f. mononucleosis
monopartia [mo-no-**pahrt**-yah] f. single party in power
monopodia [mo-no-**pod**-yah] f. monopody
monopol [mo-**no**-pol] m. monopoly; exclusive control
monopolista [mo-no-po-**lees**-tah] m. monopolizer
monopolistycznie [mo-no-po-lees-**tich**-ńe] adv. monopolistically
monopolistyczny [mo-no-po-lees-**tich**-ni] adj.m. monopolistic
monopolizacja [mo-no-po-lee-**zahts**-yah] f. monopolization
monopolizować [mo-no-po-lee-**zo**-vahćh] v. monopolize (*repeatedly*)
  monopolizować handel [mo-no-po-lee-**zo**-vahćh **khahn**-del] exp.: to monopolize trade
  monopolizować rozmowę [mo-no-po-lee-**zo**-vahćh roz-**mo**-van] exp.: to monopolize the conversation; to engross the conversation
monopolizowanie [mo-no-po-lee-zo-**vah**-ńe] n. monopolization
monopolka [mo-no-**pol**-kah] f. slang: pure vodka (mob jargon)
monopolowa [mo-no-po-**lo**-vah] f. slang: pure vodka (mob jargon)
monopolowy [mo-no-po-**lo**-vi] adj.m. monopolistic; m. liqueur store
monopolówka [mo-no-po-**loof**-kah] f. slang: pure vodka (mob jargon)
monopter [mo-**nop**-ter] m. monopteral building with a row of pillars
monorym [mo-**no**-rim] m. monorhyme
monosacharyd [mo-no-sah-**khah**-rit] m. monosaccharide
  monosacharydy [mo-no-sah-khah-**ri**-di] pl. monosaccharides
monoskop [mo-**no**-skop] m. monoscope
monospermia [mo-no-**sper**-myah] f. monospermy
monospermiczny [mo-no-sper-**meech**-ni] adj.m. monospermal; monospermous
monostrofa [mo-no-**stro**-fah] f. monostrophe
monostroficzny [mo-no-stro-**feech**-ni] adj.m. monostrophic
monostych [mo-**no**-stikh] m. monostich
monostychiczny [mo-no-sti-**kheech**-ni] adj.m. monostichous
monosylaba [mo-no-si-**lah**-bah] f. monosyllable
  mówić monosylabami [**moo**-veećh mo-no-si-lah-**bah**-mee] exp.: to speak in monosyllables
monosylabiczność [mo-no-si-lah-**beech**-nośhćh] f. monosyllabic character
monosylabiczny [mo-no-si-lah-**beech**-ni] adj.m. monosyllabic
monoteista [mo-no-te-**ees**-tah] m. monotheist
monoteistyczny [mo-no-te-ees-**tich**-ni] adj.m. monotheistic; monotheistical
monoteizm [mo-no-**te**-eezm] m. monotheism; belief in one god
monoteleta [mo-no-te-**le**-tah] m. Monothelete
monotematyczność [mo-no-te-mah-**tich**-nośhćh] f. single theme
monotematyczny [mo-no-te-mah-**tich**-ni] adj.m. having a single theme
monotonia [mo-no-**to**-ńyah] f. monotony; tiresome sameness; lack of variety
monotoniczny [mo-no-to-**ńeech**-ni] adj.m. monotonic
monotonnie [mo-no-**ton**-ńe] adv. monotonously; dully; in a humdrum manner
  mówić monotonnie [**moo**-veećh mo-no-**ton**-ńe] exp.: to speak monotonously; to drone; to speak in a sing-song voice
  żyć monotonnie [zhićh mo-no-**ton**-ńe] exp.: to live a monotonous (drab) life
monotonność [mo-no-**ton**-nośhćh] f. monotony
monotonny [mo-no-**ton**-ni] adj.m. monotonous; drab; dull

monotonny głos [mo-no-**ton**-ni gwos] exp.: drone; singsong
monotyp [mo-**no**-tip] m. monotype
monotypia [mo-no-**ti**-pyah] f. monotype technique
monotypista [mo-no-ti-**pees**-tah] m. printer working with monotype
monotypowy [mo-no-ti-**po**-vi] adj.m. of monotype
monsinior [mon-**see**-ńor] m. monsignor
monstrancja [mon-**strahnts**-yah] f. monstrance; a receptacle for displaying consecrated host
monstrualnie [mon-stroo-**ahl**-ńe] adv. monstrously; horribly
monstrualność [mon-stroo-**ahl**-nośhćh] f. monstrosity
monstrualny [mon-stroo-**ahl**-ni] adj.m. monstrous; horrible
monstrum [**mon**-stroom] n. monster; monstrosity
monsun [**mon**-soon] m. monsoon
monsunowy [mon-soo-**no**-vi] adj.m. monsoonal
montanowy [mon-tah-**no**-vi] adj.m. montan (wax, shoe polish, etc.)
montaż [**mon**-tahsh] m. mounting; assembling; installation; set-up; assembly; laying down (of cables, etc.); fitting up (of parts, etc.); mounting; staging (of a play, etc.); editing (of a film, etc.)
montażownia [mon-tah-**zhov**-ńah] f. assembly shop; fitting shop
montażowy [mon-tah-**zho**-vi] adj.m. assembly (room, etc.)
stół montażowy [stoow mon-tah-**zho**-vi] exp.: film cutting bench; assembly table
montażysta [mon-tah-**zhis**-tah] m. film editor; editor of radio programs; worker erecting prefabricated buildings
montażystka [mon-tah-**zhist**-kah] f. (woman) film editor; editor of radio programs
montejus [mon-**te**-yoos] m. montejus
monter [**mon**-ter] m. mechanic; fitter; installer; electrician
monterka [mon-**ter**-kah] f. fitting work; plumbing work; (woman) mechanic; fitter; installer; electrician
monterski [mon-**ter**-skee] adj.m. mechanic's; fitter's; installer's; electrician's
montmorylonit [mont-mo-ri-**lo**-ńeet] m. montmorillonite (mineral)
montować [mon-**to**-vahćh] v. install; put together; put up; assemble; erect; set up; fit up; lay down (cables, etc.); organize; stage; mount; set on foot (*repeatedly*)
montowanie [mon-to-**vah**-ńe] n. assembly; installation; set up (of parts, etc.)
montownia [mon-**tov**-ńah] f. assembly shop; fitting shop
monument [mo-**noo**-ment] m. monument
monumentalizm [mo-noo-men-**tah**-leezm] m. monumentality
monumentalizować [mo-noo-men-tah-lee-**zo**-vahćh] v. monumentalize (*repeatedly*)
monumentalizowanie [mo-noo-men-tah-lee-zo-**vah**-ńe] n. making monumental
monumentalnie [mo-noo-men-**tahl**-ńe] adv. in monumental style; in the manner of a monument
monumentalność [mo-noo-men-**tahl**-nośhćh] f. monumentality
monumentalny [mo-noo-men-**tahl**-ni] adj.m. monumental
monzonit [mon-**zo**-ńeet] m. monzonite (igneous rock)
mopan [**mo**-pahn] m. colloq: Sir; Mister; Esquire
mopanek [mo-**pah**-nek] m. colloq: (funny, droll) Sir; Mister; Esquire
moped [**mo**-pet] m. variety of motorcycle; moped
mopek [**mo**-pek] m. variety of bat; Barbastella
mops [mops] m. pugdog
nudzić się jak mops [**noo**-dźheećh śh<u>an</u> yahk mops] exp.: to be bored stiff
mopsi [**mop**-śhee] adj.m. of a pugdog
mopsica [mop-**śhee**-tsah] f. pugdog bitch
mopsik [**mop**-śheek] m. small pugdog

mopsowaty [mop-so-**vah**-ti] adj.m. puggy; puggish
mora [**mo**-rah] f. moire; tabby; mora (unit of measure in quantitative verse)
morale [mo-**rah**-le] n. indecl.: morale
moralista [mo-rah-**lees**-tah] m. moralist
moralistka [mo-rah-**lees**-tkah] f. (woman) moralist
moralistyczny [mo-rah-lees-**tich**-ni] adj.m. moralistic
moralistyka [mo-rah-**lees**-ti-kah] f. moralizing
moralitet [mo-rah-**lee**-tet] m. morality; medieval moral play
moralitetowy [mo-rah-lee-te-**to**-vi] adj.m. of morality; of a medieval moral play
moralizacja [mo-rah-lee-**zahts**-yah] f. moralization
moralizator [mo-rah-lee-**zah**-tor] m. moralizer
moralizatorka [mo-rah-lee-zah-**tor**-kah] f. (woman) moralizer
moralizatorski [mo-rah-lee-zah-**tor**-skee] adj.m. moralistic; moralizing
moralizatorsko [mo-rah-lee-zah-**tor**-sko] adv. moralistically; explaining morally
moralizatorstwo [mo-rah-lee-zah-**tor**-stfo] n. moralization
moralizm [mo-**rah**-leezm] m. moralism
moralizować [mo-rah-lee-**zo**-vahćh] v. moralize; discuss moral questions (tediously) (*repeatedly*)
moralizowanie [mo-rah-lee-zo-**vah**-ńe] n. moralization
moralnie [mo-**rahl**-ńe] adv. morally; ethically
moralność [mo-**rahl**-nośhćh] f. morals; morality; ethics
brak moralności [brahk mo-rahl-**nośh**-ćhee] exp.: immorality
nauka moralności [nah-oo-kah mo-rahl-**nośh**-ćhee] exp.: moral teaching
świadectwo moralności [śhfyah-**dets**-tfo mo-rahl-**nośh**-ćhee] exp.: certificate of conduct
upadek moralności [oo-**pah**-dek mo-rahl-**nośh**-ćhee] exp.: corruption of morals, manners
zasady moralności [zah-**sah**-di mo-rahl-**nośh**-ćhee] exp.: moral principles
moralny [mo-**rahl**-ni] adj.m. moral; ethical; of good (sexual) conduct or character
odpowiedzialność moralna [ot-po-vye-**dźhahl**-nośhćh mo-**rahl**-nah] exp.: moral responsibility
sens moralny [sens mo-**rahl**-ni] exp.: the moral
morał [**mo**-rahw] m. moral lesson
prawić morały [**prah**-veećh mo-**rah**-wi] exp.: to moralize; to preachify
moratorium [mo-rah-**to**-ryoom] n. moratorium; legalized delay
moratoryjny [mo-rah-to-**riy**-ni] adj.m. moratory (law, etc.)
morawianie [mo-rah-**vyah**-ńe] pl. Moravian brothers
morawski [mo-**rahf**-skee] adj.m. Moravian
mord [mort] m. murder; unlawful killing; slaughter
popełnić mord [po-**pew**-ńeećh mort] exp.: to commit murder
morda [**mor**-dah] f. snout; muzzle, vulg.: mug; kisser; puss; phiz
zamknij mordę! [zahm-kńeey **mor**-dan] excl.: (vulg.) shut up!
mordeczka [mor-**dech**-kah] f. darling little face
mordent [**mor**-dent] m. mordent (music)
morderca [mor-**der**-tsah] m. murderer; assassin; cutthroat
morderczo [mor-**der**-cho] adv. (funny, etc.) in a killing manner; in a captivating way; irresistibly (amusing, etc.)
morderczy [mor-**der**-chi] adj.m. murderous; cutthroat; deadly
morderczyni [mor-der-**chi**-ńee] f. murderess
morderstwo [mor-**der**-stfo] n. murder; assassination
mordęga [mor-**dan**-gah] f. toil; drudge; moil; fag; strain
mordka [**mort**-kah] f. small mouth (of an animal)
mordobicie [mor-do-**bee**-ćhe] n. colloq: bashing somebody's face; smashing somebody's head;

bashing one another's faces; punching one another's head
mordować [mor-**do**-vahćh] v. murder; kill; torment; harass; toil; sweat; worry; assassinate (*repeatedly*)
mordować się [mor-**do**-vahćh śhan] v. kill oneself with work; toil; sweat (over); drudge; murder one another (*repeatedly*)
mordowanie [mor-do-**vah**-ńe] n. murder; assassination
mordowanie się [mor-do-**vah**-ńe śhan] n. colloq: drudgery; strain; fag
mordownia [mor-**dov**-ńah] f. deathtrap; murdering; slaughter; colloq: toil; drudge; moil; fag; strain; mob slang: drinking den
morduchna [mor-**dookh**-nah] f. nice little animal's face
morejna [mo-**rey**-nah] m. rich Jew
morela [mo-**re**-lah] f. apricot
morelarnia [mo-re-**lahr**-ńah] f. hothouse for the cultivation of apricots
morelowy [mo-re-**lo**-vi] adj.m. apricot (jam, etc.); apricot-colored
morelówka [mo-re-**loof**-kah] f. apricot liqueur
morena [mo-**re**-nah] f. moraine
morena czołowa [mo-**re**-nah cho-**wo**-vah] exp.: frontal moraine; terminal moraine
morenowaty [mo-re-no-**vah**-ti] adj.m. like moraine; morainal; morainic
morenowy [mo-re-**no**-vi] adj.m. morainic
mores [**mo**-res] m. manners; good breeding; disciplined behavior
nauczyć moresu [nah-**oo**-chićh mo-**re**-soo] exp.: to teach good manners
znać mores [znahćh **mo**-res] exp.: to know one's place; to keep one's place
moreska [mo-**res**-kah] f. Moresque
moręgowaty [mo-ran-go-**vah**-ti] adj.m. brindled; having a gray or tawny coat marked with darker streaks
morfem [**mor**-fem] m. morpheme; the smallest meaningful language unit, as an affix
morfemowy [mor-fe-**mo**-vi] adj.m. morphemical; morphemic
Morfeusz [mor-**fe**-oosh] m. Morpheus
morfina [mor-**fee**-nah] f. morphine (derivative of opium)
morfinista [mor-fee-**ńees**-tah] m. morphine addict; morphinist
morfinistka [mor-fee-**ńeest**-kah] f. (woman) morphine addict; morphinist
morfinizm [mor-**fee**-ńeezm] m. morphinism
morfinizować się [mor-fee-ńee-**zo**-vahćh śhan] v. be addicted to morphine; take morphine (*repeatedly*)
morfinizowanie się [mor-fee-ńee-zo-**vah**-ńe śhan] n. being addicted to morphine; the morphine habit
morfinowy [mor-fee-**no**-vi] adj.m. morphinic
morfogenetyczny [mor-fo-ge-ne-**tich**-ni] adj.m. morphogenetic
morfogeneza [mor-fo-ge-**ne**-zah] f. morphogenesis
morfografia [mor-fo-**grah**-fyah] f. morphography
morfolog [mor-**fo**-log] m. morphologist
morfologia [mor-fo-**lo**-gyah] f. morphology; science of forms; composition of the blood
morfologicznie [mor-fo-lo-**geech**-ńe] adv. morphologically
morfologiczny [mor-fo-lo-**geech**-ni] adj.m. morphological
morfologizacja [mor-fo-lo-gee-**zahts**-yah] f. combining phonetic characteristics with grammatical forms
morfometria [mor-fo-**met**-ryah] f. morphometry
morfometryczny [mor-fo-met-**rich**-ni] adj.m. morphometrical
morfonem [mor-**fo**-nem] m. one of the alternate phonemes producing the same morpheme in different phonetic forms
morga [**mor**-gah] f. Polish acre = 5600 sq. meters = approx. 1.5 acre
morganatycznie [mor-gah-nah-**tich**-ńe] adv. morganatically

morganatyczny [mor-gah-nah-**tich**-ni] adj.m. morganatic; left-handed; secret; secretly wedded
morganit [mor-**gah**-ńeet] m. Morganite
morgowy [mor-**go**-vi] adj.m. of a Polish acre; of 5600 sq. meters; of one and a half acre
morion [**mor**-yon] m. morion; variety of helmet; black quartz (mineral)
morka [**mor**-kah] f. sea wind
morlesz [**mor**-lesh] m. bream (sunfish)
mormon [**mor**-mon] m. Mormon
mormonizm [mor-**mo**-ńeezm] m. Mormonism
mormorando [mor-mo-**rahn**-do] n. mormorando (song)
moroszka [mo-**rosh**-kah] f. cloudberry; herbaceous raspberry
morowiec [mo-**ro**-vyets] m. slang: slyboots; clever guy; tricky person cunning in an engaging way; sly tricky guy
morowo [mo-**ro**-vo] adv. first-rate; mightily; hard; like the devil; very pleasantly; wonderfully; very well; on moire surface paper
morowy [mo-**ro**-vi] adj.m. pestilential; clever; first-rate; m. good buddy; fine fellow
morowe powietrze [mo-**ro**-ve po-**vyet**-she] exp.: pestilence
morowy chłop [mo-**ro**-vi khwop] exp.: a brave man; regular fellow
mors [mors] m. walrus; Morse code
alfabet Morsa [al-**fah**-bet **mor**-sah] exp.: Morse alphabet; dot-and-dash code
morski [**mor**-skee] adj.m. maritime; sea; nautical; naval
bitwa morska [**beet**-fah **mor**-skah] exp.: sea-battle; sea fight
brzeg morski [bzhek **mor**-skee] exp.: seacoast
morska choroba [**mor**-skah kho-**ro**-bah] exp.: seasickness; dizziness
podróż morska [**pod**-roosh **mor**-skah] exp.: sea-voyage; cruise; pl. seafaring
morsować [mor-**so**-vahćh] v. signal by Morse code (*repeatedly*)
morsowy [mor-**so**-vi] adj.m. walrus (tusk, etc.)
morszczuk [**morsh**-chook] m. hake (fish)
morszczyn [**morsh**-chin] m. fucus; rockweed; seaweed; alga
morszczyna [morsh-**chi**-nah] f. seaweeds; algae; Permian fossilized seaweeds
morszczynowate [morsh-chi-no-**vah**-te] pl. a family of marine algae
morszczyzna [morsh-**chi**-znah] f. seaweeds; algae; Permian fossilized seaweeds
morświn [**morśh**-feen] m. porpoise; dolphin
mortadela [mor-tah-**de**-lah] f. a type of sausage
mortus [**mor**-toos] m. colloq: hard times; ill luck
morula [mo-**roo**-lah] f. early stage of human embryo
morus [**mo**-roos] m. colloq: sloven; slyboots; clever guy
morusać [mo-**roo**-sahćh] v. dirty; soil; smudge (*repeatedly*)
morusać się [mo-**roo**-sahćh śhan] v. get dirty; get soiled; smudge oneself; smudge one's hands (face, etc.) (*repeatedly*)
morusanie się [mo-roo-**sah**-ńe śhan] n. getting dirty; getting soiled; smudging oneself; smudging one's hands (etc.)
morwa [**mor**-vah] f. mulberry
morwowaty [mor-vo-**vah**-ti] adj.m. like mulberry; of the family Moraceae
morwowate [mor-vo-**vah**-te] pl. the family Moraceae
morwowy [mor-**vo**-vi] adj.m. mulberry (shrub, etc.); cream-colored
jedwabnik morwowy [yed-**vahb**-ńeek mor-**vo**-vi] exp.: silkworm
morze [**mo**-zhe] n. sea; ocean; a sea (of troubles, etc.); floods (of tears, etc.)
kropla w morzu [**krop**-lah v **mo**-zhoo] exp.: a drop in the bucket; a drop in the ocean
ku morzu [koo **mo**-zhoo] exp.: seawards; seaward; towards the sea
na morzu [nah **mo**-zhoo] exp.: at sea

na pełnym morzu [nah pew-nim mo-zhoo] exp.: on the high seas
nad morzem [nahd mo-zhem] exp.: at the seaside
za morzem [zah mo-zhem] exp.: overseas

morzenie [mo-zhe-ńe] n. harassment

morzenie się [mo-zhe-ńe śhan] n. starving oneself

morzyć [mo-zhićh] v. starve; harass (*repeatedly*)
sen go morzył [sen go mo-zhiw] exp.: he suffered from the lack of sleep

morzyć się [mo-zhićh śhan] v. starve oneself (*repeatedly*)
morzyć się głodem [mo-zhićh śhan gwo-dem] exp.: to starve oneself

morzysko [mo-zhis-ko] n. gripes; colic

mosiądz [mo-śhownts] m. brass

mosiądzować [mo-śhown-dzo-vahćh] v. braze (*repeatedly*)

mosiądzowanie [mo-śhown-dzo-vah-ńe] n. brazing

mosiężnictwo [mo-śhanzh-ńee-tstfo] n. brasswork; brazing

mosiężnik [mo-śhanzh-ńeek] m. brazier

mosiężny [mo-śhanzh-ni] adj.m. brass; brazen; brassy

moskalik [mos-kah-leek] m. pickled herring

moskiewski [mos-kef-skee] adj.m. of Moscow; Russian
po moskiewsku [po mos-kef-skoo] exp.: in Russian
z moskiewska [z mos-kef-skah] exp.: with a Russian accent; after the Russian manner

moskit [mos-keet] m. mosquito
ukąszenie moskita [oo-kown-she-ńe mos-kee-tah] exp.: mosquito-bite

moskitiera [mos-kee-tye-rah] f. mosquito net; (window) screen

moskwicz [mos-kfeech] m. Moskvich (a Russian car)

mospan [mos-pahn] m. colloq: Sir; Mister; Esquire

mospanek [mos-pah-nek] m. colloq: (funny, droll) Sir; Mister; Esquire

most [most] m. bridge
most łańcuchowy [most wahń-tsoo-kho-vi] exp.: chain-bridge
most obrotowy [most ob-ro-to-vi] exp.: swing bridge
most pontonowy [most pon-to-no-vi] exp.: pontoon bridge
most wiszący [most vee-shown-tsi] exp.: suspension bridge
most zwodzony [most zwo-dzo-ni] exp.: drawbridge
mosty [mos-ti] pl. bridges
prosto z mostu [pros-to z mos-too] exp.: right of the bat; outright; without mincing

mosteczek [mos-te-chek] m. small bridge

mostek [mos-tek] m. little bridge; footbridge; sternum; bridge

mostownica [mos-tov-ńee-tsah] f. railroad tie

mostowy [mos-to-vi] adj.m. of a bridge; bridge (pillar, etc.)
mostowe [mos-to-ve] exp.: bridge-toll

moszcz [moshch] m. grape-juice; must; stum; raw juice

moszczenie [mosh-che-ńe] n. cushioning

moszczenie się [mosh-che-ńe śhan] n. making oneself comfortable

moszna [mosh-nah] f. scrotum; the pouch of skin containing the testicles

mosznowy [mosh-no-vi] adj.m. scrotal
przepuklina mosznowa [pshe-poo-klee-nah mosh-no-vah] exp.: scrotal hernia; inguinal hernia (descending to the scrotum)

mościć [mośh-ćheećh] v. pad (a nest); make a bed of straw; cushion (a seat, etc.) (*repeatedly*)

mościć się [mośh-ćheećh śhan] v. lie comfortably down to sleep; make oneself comfortable for the night (*repeatedly*)

mościwy [mo-śhćhee-vi] adj.m. colloq: gracious; merciful

mość [mośhćh] f. Your (Majesty, Highness, Lordship, etc.)
Wasza Królewska Mość [vah-shah kroo-lef-skah mośhćh] exp.: Your Royal Highness; Your Majesty

motacz [mo-tahch] m. reeler; spooler; intriguer
motać [mo-tahćh] v. reel; embroil; entangle; intrigue; spool; involve in difficulty (*repeatedly*)
motać się [mo-tahćh śhan] v. getting entangled (*repeatedly*)
motak [mo-tahk] m. reeling machine; reel; spool
motanie [mo-**tah**-ńe] n. intriguing; embroiling; involving in difficulty
motanie się [mo-**tah**-ńe śhan] n. getting entangled
motarka [mo-**tahr**-kah] f. wool reeling machine
motek [mo-tek] m. reel; ball; spool; hand; skein
motel [mo-tel] m. motel
motela [mo-**te**-lah] f. a fish of the family Gadidae
motelowy [mo-te-**lo**-vi] adj.m. of a motel; motel (room, etc.)
motet [mo-tet] m. motet (music)
motłoch [**mot**-wokh] m. mob; rabble; riffraff
motocross [mo-**to**-kros] m. motorcycle race on closed course
motocrossowy [mo-to-kro-**so**-vi] adj.m. of a motorcycle race on a closed course
motocykl [mo-**to**-tsikl] m. motorcycle; motor bike
motocyklista [mo-to-tsi-**klees**-tah] m. motorcyclist
motocyklistka [mo-to-tsi-**kleest**-kah] f. (female) motorcyclist
motocyklowy [mo-to-tsi-**klo**-vi] adj.m. motorcycle (wheel, etc.)
motodrom [mo-**to**-drom] m. motordrome
motogodzina [mo-to-go-**dźhee**-nah] f. one hour of engine's work
motokros [mo-**to**-kros] m. motorcycle race on closed course
motokrosowy [mo-to-kro-**so**-vi] adj.m. of motorcycle race on closed course
motopiryna [mo-to-pee-**ri**-nah] f. variety of aspirin
motopompa [mo-to-**pom**-pah] f. fire department's pump
motor [**mo**-tor] m. motor; engine; motive power; motor bike
motorek [mo-**to**-rek] m. small motor; small engine
motorniczy [mo-tor-**ńee**-chi] m. motor driver; motorman
motorower [mo-to-**ro**-ver] m. bicycle with a small engine; motorized bicycle
motorowerowy [mo-to-ro-ve-**ro**-vi] adj.m. of a bicycle with a small engine
motorowerzysta [mo-to-ro-ve-**zhis**-tah] m. rider on a bicycle with a small engine
motorowiec [mo-to-**ro**-vyets] m. motor ship
motorowodniak [mo-to-ro-**vod**-ńahk] m. motorboat racer
motorowodny [mo-to-ro-**vod**-ni] adj.m. motorboat (races, etc.)
motorowy [mo-to-**ro**-vi] adj.m. motor (traction, vehicle, etc.); motor driver; motorman
motorówka [mo-to-**roof**-kah] f. motorboat
motoryczny [mo-to-**rich**-ni] adj.m. motor (nerve, etc.)
siła motoryczna [**śhee**-wah mo-to-**rich**-nah] exp.: motive power
motoryka [mo-**to**-ri-kah] f. ability to move and make movements
motorynka [mo-to-**rin**-kah] f. (home made) small motorvehicle
motoryzacja [mo-to-ri-**zah**-tsyah] f. motorization; mechanization; development of motor transport
motoryzacyjny [mo-to-ri-zah-**tsiy**-ni] adj.m. of motorization
motoryzować [mo-to-ri-**zo**-vahćh] v. motorize; mechanize (*repeatedly*)
motoryzować się [mo-to-ri-**zo**-vahćh śhan] v. get motorized (*repeatedly*)
motoryzowanie [mo-to-ri-zo-**vah**-ńe] n. motorization
motoryzowanie się [mo-to-ri-zo-**vah**-ńe śhan] n. getting motorized
motorzysta [mo-to-**zhis**-tah] m. designer of motors; motor-specialist; motorist
motoskuter [mo-to-**skoo**-ter] m. motor scooter
motoszybowcowy [mo-to-shi-bof-**tso**-vi] adj.m. of a motor glider
motoszybowiec [mo-to-shi-**bo**-vyets] m. motor glider

motowidło [mo-to-**veed**-wo] n. reeling-machine; reel; spool
motto [**mot**-to] n. motto
motyczenie [mo-ti-**che**-ńe] n. hoeing
motyczka [mo-**tich**-kah] f. small hoe
motyczkować [mo-tich-**ko**-vahćh] v. hoe (*repeatedly*)
motyczkowanie [mo-tich-ko-**vah**-ńe] n. turning soil with a hoe
motyczyć [mo-**ti**-chićh] v. hoe (*repeatedly*)
motyka [mo-**ti**-kah] f. hoe
ciężka motyka [**ćhansh**-kah mo-**ti**-kah] exp.: grub hoe
z motyką na słońce [z mo-**ti**-kown nah **swoń**-tse] exp.: on a wild-goose chase; on an impossible mission (task)
motykować [mo-ti-**ko**-vahćh] v. hoe (*repeatedly*)
motykowanie [mo-ti-ko-**vah**-ńe] n. turning soil with a hoe
motyl [**mo**-til] m. butterfly; spinnaker sail
motyle [mo-**ti**-le] pl. butterflies; the order Lepidoptera
motylek [mo-**ti**-lek] m. butterfly (swimming) stroke; butterfly-nut; small butterfly
motyli [mo-**ti**-lee] adj.m. butterfly's
motylica [mo-ti-**lee**-tsah] f. fluke; trematode; mechanism for rolling shutters
motylica wątrobowa [mo-ti-**lee**-tsah vown-tro-**bo**-vah] exp.: fluke disease; distomiasis
motyliczka [mo-ti-**leech**-kah] f. trematode; trematoditis
motyliczy [mo-ti-**lee**-chi] adj.m. of a fluke; of a trematode
motylkowaty [mo-til-ko-**vah**-ti] adj.m. resembling a butterfly
motylkowate [mo-til-ko-**vah**-te] pl. the family Papilionaceae
motylkowy [mo-til-**ko**-vi] adj.m. of a butterfly; papilonaceous
krawat motylkowy [**krah**-vaht mo-til-**ko**-vi] exp.: bow tie
nakrętka motylkowa [nah-**krant**-kah mo-til-**ko**-vah] exp.: butterfly-nut
motylowy [mo-ti-**lo**-vi] adj.m. of a butterfly
motyw [**mo**-tif] m. motif; motive; theme; reason
motywacja [mo-ti-**vahts**-yah] f. statement of reasons (for); statement of grounds (for); justification (for); warrant (for); motivation
motywacyjny [mo-ti-vah-**tsiy**-ni] adj.m. motivational; of an argument for (something)
motywować [mo-ti-**vo**-vahćh] v. give reasons; explain; justify; adduce reasons (for); account (for); warrant (an action, etc.) (*repeatedly*)
motywowanie [mo-ti-vo-**vah**-ńe] n. giving reasons; explaining; justifying; adducing reasons (for); accounting (for); warranting (an action, etc.)
mowa [**mo**-vah] f. speech; talk; language; tongue; address; parlance; mention; reference (to); discourse; oration; words; manner of speaking; slang: lingo
była mowa o ... [**bi**-wah **mo**-vah o] exp.: there was talk of...; reference was made to...; mention was made of...
mowa! [**mo**-vah] exp.: of course!; naturally!; certainly!
mowa niezależna [**mo**-vah ńe-zah-**lezh**-nah] exp.: direct speech
mowa ojczysta [**mo**-vah oy-**chis**-tah] exp.: mother tongue
mowa zależna [**mo**-vah zah-**lezh**-nah] exp.: indirect speech
o tym nie ma mowy [o tim ńe mah **mo**-vi] exp.: that's out of the question
wygłosić mowę [vi-**gwo**-śheećh **mo**-van] exp.: to make a speech
mowny [**mov**-ni] adj.m. verbose; talkative; of speech
mozaika [mo-**zahy**-kah] f. mosaic; inlay; tessera (used in mosaic work); diversity of colors
mozaikowatość [mo-zahy-ko-**vah**-tośhćh] f. similarity to a mosaic
mozaikowaty [mo-zahy-ko-**vah**-ti] adj.m. similar to a mosaic
mozaikowo [mo-zahy-**ko**-vo] adv. like a mosaic
mozaikowość [mo-zahy-**ko**-vośhćh] f. similarity to a mosaic

mozaikowy [mo-zahy-**ko**-vi] adj.m. mosaic (colors, etc.)
mozaista [mo-zah-**ees**-tah] m. Mosaist
mozaistyczny [mo-zah-ees-**tich**-ni] adj.m. Mosaic
mozaizm [mo-**zah**-eezm] m. Mosaism
mozazaur [mo-**zah**-zahwr] m. Mosasaurus; mosasauroid
mozga [**moz**-gah] f. canary grass
mozolenie się [mo-zo-**le**-ńe śhan] n. exerting oneself; taking pains
mozolić się [mo-**zo**-leećh śhan] v. toil; take pains; exert oneself; drudge; strain one's wits (over); rake one's brains (for a solution, etc.) (*repeatedly*)
mozolnie [mo-**zol**-ńe] adv. with great effort; with pains; with difficulty; strenuously; arduously; laboriously; painfully
mozolny [mo-**zol**-ni] adj.m. toilsome; strenuous; arduous; laborious
mozół [**mo**-zoow] m. exertion; toil; labor; uphill work
z mozołem [z mo-**zo**-wem] exp.: with great effort; with pains; with difficulty; strenuously; arduously; laboriously; painfully
moździerz [**moźh**-dźhesh] m. mortar; mine thrower
moździerzowy [moźh-dźhe-**zho**-vi] adj.m. mortar (shell, etc.)
moździerzyk [moźh-**dźhe**-zhik] m. small mortar
możdżeń [**mozh**-dzheń] m. bony core (of an animal's horn)
może [**mo**-zhe] adv. perhaps; maybe; very likely; how about?; suppose...?; what would you say to ...?; v. (he, she) can (do something)
być może [bićh **mo**-zhe] exp.: maybe; possibly; perhaps, very likely; see: **może być**
może być [**mo**-zhe bićh] exp.: maybe; perhaps; very likely; possibly; it is O.K.; it is okay
może być i tak [**mo**-zhe bićh ee tahk] exp.: that may be; it is possible
może byś ...? [**mo**-zhe biśh] exp.: would you mind ...?
może byś przestał? [**mo**-zhe biśh **pshes**-tahw] exp.: wish you would stop
może coś zjesz? [**mo**-zhe tsośh zyesh] exp.: would you like something to eat?; won't you have something to eat?
może już jest [**mo**-zhe yoosh yest] exp.: he may be here by now; it may be here by now
nie może być! [ńe **mo**-zhe bićh] excl.: impossible!; you don't say so!; go on!; I don't believe it!
możebność [mo-**zheb**-nośhćh] f. possibility; chance; contingency; capabilities; power; potentiality; prospect; vista
możliwe [mozh-**lee**-ve] n. whatever is possible
wszystko co możliwe [**fshist**-ko tso mozh-**lee**-ve] exp.: everything possible; every possible thing
możliwie [mozh-**lee**-vye] adv. if possible; possibly; colloq: tolerably
możliwie najwyższa cena [mozh-lee-vye nahy-**vish**-shah **tse**-nah] exp.: the highest possible price
możliwość [mozh-**lee**-vośhćh] f. possibility; chance; contingency; capabilities; power; potentiality; prospect; vista
istnieje możliwość [eest-**ńe**-ye mozh-**lee**-vośhćh] exp.: there is a possibility
możliwości [mozh-lee-**vośh**-ćhee] pl. scope; vistas; capabilities; chances; power; prospects
możliwy [mozh-**lee**-vi] adj.m. possible; fairly good; passable; acceptable; colloq: feasible; practicable
możliwe [mozh-lee-ve] exp.: n. whatever is possible
możliwy kandydat [mozh-**lee**-vi kahn-**di**-daht] exp.: a likely candidate
wszystko co możliwe [**fshist**-ko tso mozh-**lee**-ve] exp.: everything; every possible thing
można [**mozh**-nah] v. imp. it is possible; one may; one can
czy można..? [chi **mozh**-nah]

exp.: may I...?

gdzie można [gdźhe **mozh**-nah] exp.: wherever possible; wherever you can

ile można [**ee**-le **mozh**-nah] exp.: as much as possible; as much as you can

jak można najlepiej [yahk **mozh**-nah nahy-le-pyey] exp.: as well as possible

jak tylko można [yahk **til**-ko **mozh**-nah] exp.: by all possible means; however you can; however one can

jeśli można [**yeśh**-lee **mozh**-nah] exp.: if possible

jeśli tylko można [**yeśh**-lee **til**-ko **mozh**-nah] exp.: if at all possible

kiedy można [**ke**-di **mozh**-nah] exp.: whenever possible; whenever you can

można by ... [**mozh**-nah bi] exp.: it would be possible to...; one could; one would; we could; we would; you could; you would; he could; he would, etc.

można by to zrobić [**mozh**-nah bi to **zro**-beećh] exp.: it might be done

nie można [ńe **mozh**-nah] exp.: one cannot; you cannot; it is impossible (to)

możni [**mozh**-ńee] pl. the oligarchy; magnates

możność [**mozh**-nośhćh] f. possibility; power; freedom to; free choice to; ability; opportunity; occasion; chance

mieć możność [myećh **mozh**-nośhćh] exp.: to have the possibility of (doing, etc.); to be in position to (do, read, etc.); to be free to (go, etc.)

w miarę możności [v **myah**-ran mozh-**nośh**-ćhe] exp.: as far as possible

możnowładca [mozh-no-**vwaht**-tsah] m. potentate; magnate

możnowładczy [mozh-no-**vwaht**-chi] adj.m. potentate's; magnate's

możnowładztwo [mozh-no-**vwahts**-tfo] n. the magnates

możny [**mozh**-ni] adj.m. potent; powerful; mighty; convincing

możni [**mozh**-ńee] pl. the oligarchy; magnates

możylinek [mo-zhi-**lee**-nek] m. moehryngia; a low herb of chickweed family

móc [moots] v. be free to; to be able; be capable of (doing); be allowed (to do); be likely (to happen); may; be liable (to take place) (*repeatedly*)

być może [bićh **mo**-zhe] exp.: maybe; perhaps; likely

może być [**mo**-zhe bićh] exp.: maybe; perhaps; likely

nie może być [ńe **mo**-zhe bićh] exp.: impossible

nie móc [ńe moots] exp.: not to be able (to)

mógł [moogw] v. (he) could

będę mógł [**ban**-dan moogw] exp.: I shall be able (to)

będziesz mógł [**ban**-dźhesh moogw] exp.: you will be able

mógłbyś trochę uważać [**moogw**-biśh **tro**-khan oo-**vah**-zhahćh] exp.: I wish you would be more careful; I wish you might be more careful

mój [mooy] pron. my (father, etc.); mine

ma [mah] exp.: my (mother, etc.)

me [me] exp.: my (baby, etc.)

moi [**mo**-ee] exp.: my people; my folks

moja [**mo**-yah] exp.: my (mother, book, cow, etc.)

moje [**mo**-ye] exp.: my (baby)

po mojemu [po mo-**ye**-moo] exp.: to my mind; as I see it; that's how I do it; the way I do it

mól [mool] m. moth; tineid; worry

on ma swojego mola [on mah sfo-**ye**-go **mo**-lah] exp.: he has his own worries

mól książkowy [mool kśhownsh-**ko**-vi] exp.: bookworm

mór [moor] m. pestilence; epidemic; plague; pest; murrain

mórg [moorg] m. Polish acre; 1.5 American acre; 5600 sq. meters; see: **morga**

mówca [**moof**-tsah] m. speaker; orator

mówca uliczny [**moof**-tsah oo-

leech-ni] exp.: soapbox orator
mówczyni [moof-chi-ńee] f. speaker
mówiąca [moo-vyown-tsah] adj.f. (female) speaking
mówiący [moo-vyown-tsi] adj.m. (male) speaking
mówić [moo-veećh] v. speak; talk; say; tell; say things; carry on a conversation; refer (to); mention (*repeatedly*)
mądrze mówić [mownd-zhe moo-veećh] exp.: to speak wisely; to talk sense
mówić dalej [moo-veećh dah-ley] exp.: to go on speaking; to continue one's talk; to resume one's talk; to resume one's conversation
mówić szeptem [moo-veećh shep-tem] exp.: to whisper; to talk in a whisper
nie ma o czym mówić [ńe mah o chim moo-veećh] exp.: nothing to speak of; there is nothing to say
wiem, co mówię [vyem tso moo-vyan] exp.: I know what I'm talking about
mówienie [moo-vye-ńe] n. speech
zdolność mówienia [zdol-nośhćh moo-vye-ńah] exp.: the faculty of speech
mówka [moof-kah] f. colloq: small oration
mównica [moov-ńee-tsah] f. pulpit; rostrum; speaker's platform
mózg [moozg] m. brain; mind; brains; intellect; cerebrum
trust mózgów [troost mooz-goof] exp.: brains trust
wstrząs mózgu [fstshowns mooz-goo] exp.: concussion of the brain
zapalenie mózgu [zah-pah-le-ńe mooz-goo] exp.: brain fever; encephalitis
mózgoczaszka [mooz-go-chahsh-kah] f. cerebral cranium
mózgordzeniowy [mooz-go-rdze-ńo-vi] adj.m. cerebrospinal
opony mózgordzeniowe [o-po-ni mooz-go-rdze-ńo-ve] exp.: meninges
płyn mózgordzeniowy [pwin mooz-go-rdze-ńo-vi] exp.: cerebrospinal fluid
mózgowie [mooz-go-vye] n. cerebrum
mózgowiec [mooz-go-vyets] m. colloq: egghead; intellectual; scientist; highbrow
mózgownica [mooz-go-vńee-tsah] f. slang: brains; head; mind
ciasna mózgownica [ćhahs-nah mooz-go-vńee-tsah] exp.: slang: narrow mind; slow wit
mózgowo-rdzeniowy [mooz-go-vo-rdze-ńo-vi] adj.m. cerebrospinal
mózgowy [mooz-go-vi] adj.m. cerebral; of the brain; encephalic
móżdżek [moozh-dzhek] m. small brains; cerebellum
móżdżkowy [mooshch-ko-vi] adj.m. cerebellar
mroczek [mro-chek] m. slight dimness; scotoma; dimness of vision; blind spot in the field of vision; bat (Vesperugo)
mroczki [mroch-kee] pl. scotomas
mrocznawy [mroch-nah-vi] adj.m. darkish
mrocznie [mroch-ńe] adv. darkly
mrocznieć [mroch-ńećh] v. darken; grow dark; grow darker (*repeatedly*)
mroczno [mroch-no] adv. darkly; duskly; duskily; gloomily; obscurely
było mroczno [bi-wo mroch-no] exp.: it was dark
mroczność [mroch-nośhćh] f. darkness; obscurity; duskness; dimness; duskiness
mroczny [mroch-ni] adj.m. dusky; gloomy; obscure; dark; dim; dismal; murky
mroczne wieki [mroch-ne vye-kee] exp.: the dark ages
mroczyć [mro-chićh] v. darken; shroud in gloom; grow dusky; grow darker; grow dim (*repeatedly*)
sen go mroczył [sen go mro-chiw] exp.: he was overcome with sleep
mroczyć się [mro-chićh śhan] v. grow dark; get dark; grow dusk; grow dusky (hist.) (*repeatedly*)
mrok [mrok] m. dusk; twilight;

dimness; obscurity; gloom; murk; darkness
zapada mrok [zah-**pah**-dah mrok] exp.: it gets dark
mrowić się [**mro**-veećh śhan] v. swarm; teem; be alive (with people, with insects, etc.) (*repeatedly*)
mrowie [**mro**-vye] n. swarm; tingle; gooseflesh; creeps; multitude
mrowienie [mro-**vye**-ńe] n. formication; prickly feeling; crawly feeling; tingling sensation; prickling sensation; pins and needles
mrowisko [mro-**vees**-ko] n. anthill; ants' nest
ludzkie mrowisko [**loots**-ke mro-**vees**-ko] exp.: swarm
wsadzić kij w mrowisko [**fsah**-dźheećh keey v mro-**vees**-ko] exp.: colloq: to cause a stir; to set people agog
mrozek [**mro**-zek] m. light frost
mrozić [**mro**-źheećh] v. freeze; congeal; refrigerate; chill; ice (*repeatedly*)
mrozik [**mro**-źheek] m. slight frost
mrozoodporność [mro-zo-ot-**por**-nośhćh] f. frost-proof quality; frost-resisting characteristic
mrozoodporny [mro-zo-ot-**por**-ni] adj.m. frost-proof; frost-resisting; frost-hardy (plant)
mrozowisko [mro-zo-**vees**-ko] n. area of cold air draining
mrozowy [mro-**zo**-vi] adj.m. frost (signal, crack, etc.)
pęknięcie mrozowe [pank-**ńan**-ćhe mro-**zo**-ve] exp.: frost-crack
mroźnia [**mroźh**-ńah] f. freezer truck; refrigerator
mroźnie [**mroźh**-ńe] adv. frostily
mroźno [**mroźh**-no] adv. frostily
mroźny [**mroźh**-ni] adj.m. frosty; icy; freezing
mrożenie [mro-**zhe**-ńe] n. freezing; chilling
mrożonka [mro-**zhon**-kah] f. frozen vegetable; chilled vegetable
mrożonki [mro-**zhon**-kee] pl. frozen food; frozen vegetables; frozen fruits; chilled fruits
mrówczan [**mroof**-chahn] m. formate
mrówczany [mroof-**chah**-ni] pl. formates
mrówczo [**mroof**-cho] adv. like an ant
mrówczy [**mroof**-chi] adj.m. ant's; ants'; unremitting (work, etc.); unflagging (efforts, etc.)
mrówka [**mroof**-kah] f. ant; emmet; pismire
mrówki [**mroof**-kee] pl. ants
mrówki chodzą mi po krzyżach [**mroof**-kee **kho**-dzown mee po **kshi**-zhahkh] exp.: my spine tingles; I have the creeps; I have a creepy feeling
mrówkojad [mroof-**ko**-yaht] m. ant bear
mrówkolew [mroof-**ko**-lef] m. antlion
mrówkolubny [mroof-ko-**loob**-ni] adj.m. myrmecophytic
roślina mrówkolubna [ro-**śhlee**-nah mroof-ko-**loob**-nah] exp.: myrmecophyte (plant)
mrówkowiec [mroof-**ko**-vyets] m. colloq: multistory, large apartment building
mrówkowy [mroof-**ko**-vi] adj.m. formic (acid, etc.)
mrównik [**mroov**-ńeek] m. aardvark; Orycteropus of the order Tubulidentata
mróz [mroos] m. frost; the cold; hoarfrost; shudder; temperature below freezing point
biały mróz [**byah**-wi mroos] exp.: white frost
dwa stopnie mrozu [dvah **stop**-ńe **mro**-zoo] exp.: two degrees below freezing
siwy mróz [**śhee**-vi mroos] exp.: white frost
sześć stopni mrozu [sheśhćh **stop**-ńee **mro**-zoo] exp.: six degrees below freezing
mróz po nim przeszedł [mroos po ńeem **pshe**-shedw] exp.: a shudder run down his spine; his blood ran cold
mruczando [mroo-**chahn**-do] n. colloq: mormorando; murmuring
śpiewać mruczando [**śhpye**-vahćh mroo-**chahn**-do] exp.: to hum

mruczeć [mroo-chećh] v. mumble; mutter; purr; murmur; grumble; growl; grunt (*repeatedly*)
mruczek [mroo-chek] m. blindman's buff (a kind of game)
mruczenie [mroo-che-ńe] n. a murmur; murmur
mudżahedin [moo-dzhah-khe-deen] m. Muslim religious freedom fighter; mujaheddin
mrugać [mroo-gahćh] v. twinkle; blink; wink; flicker; flinch (*repeatedly*)
szkoda mrugać! [shko-dah mroo-gahćh] exp.: colloq: nothing doing!
mruganie [mroo-gah-ńe] n. flicker (of a light); flutter (of the eyelids)
mrugliwy [mroog-lee-vi] adj.m. twinkling; blinking
mrugnąć [mroog-nownćh] v. twinkle; blink; wink
mrugnąć na znak zgody [mroog-nownćh nah znahk zgo-di] exp.: to wink assent
nie mrugnąć okiem [ńe mroog-nownćh o-kem] exp.: not to lift a finger; never to bat an eyelid; not to turn a hair; to do nothing
nie mrugnąwszy okiem [ńe mroog-nown-fshi o-kem] exp.: without flinching; unshrinkingly
mrugnięcie [mroog-ńan-ćhe] n. (a) wink; (a) twinkle
mruk [mrook] m. mumbler; man of few words; growler
mrukliwie [mroo-klee-vye] adv. mutteringly; in a mutter; gruffly; churlishly; sulkily; indistinctly
mrukliwość [mroo-klee-vośhćh] f. gruffness; taciturnity; churlishness
mrukliwy [mroo-klee-vi] adj.m. mumbling; sulky; gruff; taciturn; speaking indistinctly
mruknąć [mrook-nownćh] v. purr; growl; grunt; murmur; grumble; mumble; mutter
mruknięcie [mrook-ńan-ćhe] n. murmur; growl; grunt
mrukowatość [mroo-ko-vah-tośhćh] f. gruffness; taciturnity; churlishness
mrukowaty [mroo-ko-vah-ti] adj.m. mumbling; sulky; gruff; taciturn; speaking indistinctly; churlish
mru-mru [mroo mroo] (only in) exp.: **ani mru-mru** [ah-ńee mroo-mroo] exp.: not a word of this to anybody; mum's the word
mrużenie [mroo-zhe-ńe] n. squinting (one's eyes)
mrużenie się [mroo-zhe-ńe śhan] n. blinking (one's eyes)
mrużyć [mroo-zhićh] v. wink; blink; squint; hold the eyes half-shut (*repeatedly*)
mrużyć się [mroo-zhićh śhan] v. blink (*repeatedly*)
mrzeć [mzhećh] v. die; perish (*repeatedly*)
mrzeżna [mzhezh-nah] f. a type of fishing net
mrzonka [mzhon-kah] f. illusion; fantasy; daydream; fancy; reverie; imagination; an impossible dream
mrzyk [mzhik] m. buffalo bug; carpet beetle
msza [mshah] f. mass (in church)
odprawiać mszę [ot-prah-vyahćh mshan] exp.: to say mass
mszak [mshahk] m. phylum of Bryophyta plant
mszaki [mshah-kee] pl. the phylum of Bryophyta plants
mszalik [mshah-leek] m. abbreviated missal
mszalny [mshahl-ni] adj.m. for mass; of the mass (in the church)
mszał [mshahw] m. missal
mszar [mshahr] m. bog; morass; variety of moss
mszarny [mshahr-ni] adj.m. of a morass
mszczenie [mshche-ńe] n. vengeance; retaliation
mszczenie się [mshche-ńe śhan] n. taking vengeance
mszyca [mshi-tsah] f. plant louse; aphis; mite
mszyce [mshi-tse] pl. plant lice; mites
mszysty [mshis-ti] adj.m. moss-grown; flocculent; wooly; mossy
mszywioł [mshi-vyow] m. bryozoan
mszywioły [mshi-vyo-wi] pl. bryozoan aquatic invertebrate animals; the Bryozoa

mszywiołowy [mshi-vyo-**wo**-vi] adj.m. of bryozoan aquatic invertebrate animals; bryozoan
mściciel [**mśhćhee**-ćhel] m. avenger; retaliator
mścicielka [mśhćhee-**ćhel**-kah] f. (female) avenger; retaliator
mścicielski [mśhćhee-**ćhel**-skee] adj.m. avenging; avenger's
mścić [mśhćheećh] v. take vengeance (for); avenge; retaliate; revenge oneself; requite (*repeatedly*)
mścić się [mśhćheećh śhan] v. revenge oneself; take revenge; wreak one's rage; have evil consequences (*repeatedly*)
mściwie [**mśhćhee**-vye] adv. vindictively; vengefully; with a vengeance
mściwość [**mśhćhee**-vośhćh] f. vindictiveness; vengefulness
mściwy [**mśhćhee**-vi] adj.m. vindictive; vengeful
mu [moo] pron. him; for him
muc [moots] m. pony; chain dog; colloq: growler
mucha [**moo**-khah] f. fly; colloq: trifle
mucha końska [moo-khah **koń**-skah] exp.: horse fly; breeze
mucha nie siada [moo-khah ńe **śhah**-dah] exp.: colloq: first-rate
padać jak muchy [**pah**-dahćh yahk **moo**-khi] exp.: to die like flies; to die in their thousands
muchar [moo-khahr] m. a poisonous fungus
muchołapka [moo-kho-**wahp**-kah] f. fly trap
muchołówka [moo-kho-**woof**-kah] f. flytrap; Venus flytrap; fly catcher
muchołówki [moo-kho-**woof**-kee] pl. the family of Venus flytraps; Dionaea muscipula; fly catchers; the Muscicapidae
muchołówkowate [moo-kho-woof-ko-**vah**-te] pl. the family Muscicapidae
muchomor [moo-**kho**-mor] m. flybane; fly agaric; toadstool
muchomór [moo-**kho**-moor] m. flybane; fly agaric; toadstool
muchotrzew [moo-**kho**-tshef] m. sand spurry
muchowaty [moo-kho-**vah**-ti] adj.m. of the family Muscidae
muchowate [moo-kho-**vah**-te] pl. the family Muscidae
muchówka [moo-**khoof**-kah] f. an insect of the order Diptera
muchówki [moo-**khoof**-kee] pl. the order Diptera
muchówkowy [moo-khoof-**ko**-vi] adj.m. dipterous
muchy [**moo**-khi] pl. flies
mucyk [**moo**-tsik] m. pony (hist.)
mucyna [moo-**tsi**-nah] f. mucin
mucyny [moo-**tsi**-ni] pl. mucins; mucoproteins
muczeć [**moo**-chećh] v. moo (*repeatedly*)
muczenie [moo-**che**-ńe] n. mooing
muezin [moo-**e**-zeen] m. muezzin
mufa [**moo**-fah] f. muff; coupler; coupling; coupling-box; sleeve
mufka [**moof**-kah] f. muff
mufla [**moof**-lah] f. muffle
muflarz [**moof**-lahsh] m. muffler; muffle-man
muflon [**moof**-lon] m. mouflon; mufflon (wild sheep); Ovis musimon
muflonowy [moof-lo-**no**-vi] adj.m. of mufflon
muflowy [moof-**lo**-vi] adj.m. muffle (furnace; etc.)
mukoid [moo-**ko**-eet] m. mucoid
mukoproteid [moo-ko-pro-**te**-eet] m. mucoprotein
mukoproteidy [moo-ko-pro-te-ee-di] pl. mucoproteins
mularstwo [moo-**lahr**-stfo] n. masonry
mularz [**moo**-lahsh] m. mason
mulasty [moo-**lahs**-ti] adj.m. muddy; oozy; slimy; sludgy
mulat [**moo**-laht] m. mulatto; slang: blockhead (mob jargon)
mulatka [moo-**laht**-kah] f. mulatto woman; mulatto girl
mulątko [moo-**lownt**-ko] n. mule's foal; hinny's foal
mulda [**mool**-dah] f. ski run dip
muleta [moo-**le**-tah] f. matador's muleta
muli [**moo**-lee] adj.m. of a mule
mulica [moo-**lee**-tsah] f. hinny

mulić [moo-leećh] v. cover with slime; silt up; obstruct with slime (*repeatedly*)
mulina [moo-**lee**-nah] f. embroidery floss
mulisko [moo-**lees**-ko] n. accumulated slime
mulistość [moo-**lees**-tośhćh] f. slimishness
mulisty [moo-**lees**-ti] adj.m. muddy; oozy; slimy; sludgy
mulit [**moo**-leet] m. raw material for fireproof bricks
mulitowy [moo-lee-**to**-vi] adj.m. of raw material for fireproof bricks
mulnik [**mool**-ńeek] m. mule-driver; muleteer
multan [**mool**-tahn] m. broadsword
multanka [mool-**tahn**-kah] f. bagpipe
multanki [mool-**tahn**-kee] pl. bagpipes
multi- [mool-tee] prefix: multi-
multicyklon [mool-tee-**tsik**-lon] m. air cleaning device (removing dust)
multilateralizm [mool-tee-lah-te-**rah**-leezm] m. multilateral nature
multilateralnie [mool-tee-lah-te-**rahl**-ńe] adv. multilaterally
multilateralny [mool-tee-lah-te-**rahl**-ni] adj.m. multilateral
multimilioner [mool-tee-mee-**lyo**-ner] m. multimillionaire
multipleks [mool-**tee**-pleks] m. multiplex telegraphic connection
multiplet [mool-**tee**-plet] m. multiplet
multiplikator [mool-tee-plee-**kah**-tor] m. multiplier
multiwitamina [mool-tee-vee-tah-**mee**-nah] f. multiple vitamin pill
multograf [mool-**to**-grahf] m. duplicator
multum [**mool**-toom] indecl. huge number; multitude; host; swarm; lots
multyplikator [mool-ti-plee-**kah**-tor] m. multiplier; intensifier
muł [moow] m. ooze; slime; silt; mud; sludge; mule; slang: blockhead; fool; sad sack; quiet guy; nurse (mob jargon)
muł płuczkowy [moow pwooch-**ko**-vi] exp.: (mine) slurry
muł rudny [moow **rood**-ni] exp.: pulp
muł wiertniczy [moow vyert-**ńee**-chi] exp.: (drilling) slum; drilling mud
mułek [**moo**-wek] m. quartz rich sedimentary rock
mułkowy [moow-**ko**-vi] adj.m. of quartz rich sedimentary rock
mułła [**moow**-wah] m. mullah
mułowaty [moo-wo-**vah**-ti] adj.m. mule like; mulish muddy; oozy; slimy; sludgy; slang: stupid; see: **mulisty**
mułowiec [moo-**wo**-vyets] m. mudstone (mineral)
mułowy [moo-**wo**-vi] adj.m. mulelike; mulish
mułowy [moo-**wo**-vi] adj.m. muddy; oozy; slimy; sludgy
złoża mułowe [**zwo**-zhah moo-**wo**-ve] exp.: alluvial silt
mułówka [moo-**woof**-kah] f. mud baths
mumia [**moo**-myah] f. mummy; mummy fruit
mumifikacja [moo-mee-fee-**kahts**-yah] f. mummification
mumifikować [moo-mee-fee-**ko**-vahćh] v. mummify (*repeatedly*)
mumifikowanie [moo-mee-fee-ko-**vah**-ńe] n. mummification
mumiowaty [moo-myo-**vah**-ti] adj.m. dried-up
mundial [**moon**-dyahl] m. world soccer championships; world cup
mundur [**moon**-door] m. uniform
mundur polowy [**moon**-door po-**lo**-vi] exp.: battle-dress
mundur roboczy [**moon**-door ro-**bo**-chi] exp.: fatigue-dress
mundurek [moon-**doo**-rek] m. school uniform
mundurować [moon-doo-**ro**-vahćh] v. clothe in uniform (*repeatedly*)
mundurować się [moon-doo-**ro**-vahćh śhan] v. provide oneself with a uniform (*repeatedly*)
mundurowanie [moon-doo-ro-**vah**-ńe] n. clothing in uniforms
mundurowanie się [moon-doo-ro-**vah**-ńe śhan] n. providing oneself with a uniform
mundurowy [moon-doo-**ro**-vi] adj.m. uniform (cap, etc.)
mundżak [**moon**-dzhahk] m.

muntjak; muntjac (deer)
mungo [**moon**-go] n. mungo (wool)
municypalizacja [moo-ńee-tsi-pah-lee-**zahts**-yah] f. municipalization
municypalny [moo-ńee-tsi-**pahl**-ni] adj.m. municipal
municypium [moo-ńee-**tsi**-pyoom] n. municipium; municipality
munio [**moo**-ńo] m. (only in) colloq: exp.:
mieć kuku na muniu [myećh **koo**-koo nah **moo**-ńoo] exp.: colloq: to be crazy; to be retarded
munsztuk [**moon**-shtook] m. (bridle) bit; mouthpiece
mur [moor] m. brick wall; wall
mur oporowy [moor o-po-**ro**-vi] exp.: buttress; retaining wall
mur pruski [moor **proos**-kee] exp.: brick-nogged timber wall; post and pan
mury obronne [**moo**-ri o-**bron**-ne] exp.: city walls
przyprzeć do muru [pshi-pshećh do **moo**-roo] exp.: to drive (somebody) into a corner
w murach [v **moo**-rahkh] exp.: within the walls
murarka [moo-**rahr**-kah] f. brickwork; bricklaying; masonry; (woman) bricklayer; see: **murarstwo** [moo-**rahr**-stfo]
murarski [moo-**rahr**-skee] adj.m. mason's; bricklayer's
murarstwo [moo-**rahr**-stfo] n. masonry; bricklaying; brickwork
murarz [**moo**-rahsh] m. bricklayer; mason
murator [moo-**rah**-tor] m. colloq: builder; architect
murawa [moo-**rah**-vah] f. lawn; grass; the green; greensward
murek [**moo**-rek] m. small masonry wall; low wall; mantelpiece
murena [moo-**re**-nah] f. morey fish
murenowaty [moo-re-no-**vah**-ti] adj.m. of the moray family of fishes
murenowate [moo-re-no-**vah**-te] pl. the moray family of fishes
murga [**moor**-gah] m. colloq: churl; lout; simpleton
murgrabia [moor-**grah**-byah] m. colloq: margrave
murłat [**moor**-waht] m. rafter plate; wall plate
murłata [moor-**wah**-tah] f. rafter plate; wall plate
murować [moo-**ro**-vahćh] v. lay bricks; build in brick (in stone); colloq: stonewall (*repeatedly*)
murowanie [moo-ro-**vah**-ńe] n. bricklaying
murowanie [moo-ro-**vah**-ńe] adv. for certain; for sure; without fail; you can bet your life; as sure as heaven above
murowanie, będzie na czas [moo-ro-**vah**-ńe **ban**-dźhe nah chahs] exp.: he is sure to be on time
murowany [moo-ro-**vah**-ni] adj.m. of bricks; of stone; absolutely certain
dom murowany [dom moo-ro-**vah**-ni] exp.: house of stone
to murowane [to moo-ro-**vah**-ne] exp.: it's a cinch; it's dead certain
murowy [moo-**ro**-vi] adj.m. made with bricks; of a brick wall
mursz [moorsh] m. dryrot; rotting wood; boggy soil
murszeć [**moor**-shećh] v. rot (*repeatedly*)
murszenie [moor-**she**-ńe] n. rotting; rot
murszowy [moor-**sho**-vi] adj.m. boggy (soil, etc.)
murza [**moor**-zah] m. mirza
Murzyn [**moo**-zhin] m. Negro; Black
Murzynek [moo-**zhi**-nek] m. young Negro; Negro child; Black child; black roan horse; black coffee with whipped cream
Murzyniątko [moo-zhi-**ńownt**-ko] n. very young Negro; small Negro child
Murzynka [moo-**zhin**-kah] f. Negro woman; Negress; Black woman
murzyński [moo-**zhiń**-skee] adj.m. Negro's; Negroes'; Negro (songs, etc.)
pieśni murzyńskie [**pyeśh**-ńee moo-**zhiń**-ske] exp.: Negro religious songs; Negro spirituals; plantation songs
mus [moos] m. necessity; compulsion; constraint

z musu [z **moo**-soo] exp.: of necessity; forcibly; under constraint; on compulsion
mus [moos] m. froth; mousse; whipped cream
musical [myoo-**zee**-kahl] m. musical; musical comedy
musicalowy [myoo-zee-kah-**lo**-vi] adj.m. musical
music-hall [**myoo**-zeek hol] m. music hall
musieć [**moo**-śhećh] v. be obliged to; have to; be forced; must do; got to have it; want; be compelled; must; will; want badly; must have it; be sure; be certain; be bound to (*repeatedly*)
czy muszę to robić [chi **moo**-shan to **ro**-beećh] exp.: must I do it?; do I have to do it?; need I do it?
on musi to mieć [on **moo**-śhee to myećh] exp.: he must have it; he's got to have it; he is obliged to have it
to musi być naprawione [to **moo**-śhee bićh nah-prah-**vyo**-ne] exp.: this must be repaired; this needs mending; this wants mending; this has to be repaired
muskać [**moos**-kahćh] v. touch lightly; skim (a surface, etc.); brush (by, against, past); graze (by, against); shave; stroke; preen; prink (*repeatedly*)
muskać się [**moos**-kahćh śhan] v. stroke one's (moustache, etc.); preen oneself up; prink oneself up; trick oneself up (*repeatedly*)
muskanie [moos-**kah**-ńe] n. stroking
muskanie się [moos-**kah**-ńe śhan] n. stroking oneself
muskaryna [moos-kah-**ri**-nah] f. muscarine
muskowit [moos-**ko**-veet] m. muscovite (mineral)
muskularnie [moos-koo-**lahr**-ńe] adv. muscularly
muskularność [moos-koo-**lahr**-nośhćh] f. muscularity
muskularny [moos-koo-**lahr**-ni] adj.m. muscular; strong; hefty; sinewy; beefy; brawny
muskulatura [moos-koo-lah-**too**-rah] f. musculature
muskuł [**moos**-koow] m. muscle
musnąć [**moos**-nownćh] v. skim; brush; graze; see: **muskać**
musować [moo-**so**-vahćh] v. foam; froth; bubble; fizz; sparkle; effervesce (*repeatedly*)
musowanie [moo-so-**vah**-ńe] n. bubbling; sparkling
musowo [moo-**so**-vo] adv. slang: willy-nilly; there's no getting out of it; there's no help for it; by hook or by crook (mob jargon)
mustang [**moos**-tahng] m. mustang
mustra [**moos**-trah] f. drill; exercise; see: **musztra**
mustrować [moos-**tro**-vahćh] v. drill (soldiers, etc.); teach (manners, etc.); rebuke; reprimand (*repeatedly*)
mustrowanie [moos-tro-**vah**-ńe] n. drill; exercise
mustyk [**moos**-tik] m. simulid
mustyki [moos-**ti**-kee] pl. the family Simulidae; the simulids
mustykowaty [moos-ti-ko-**vah**-ti] adj.m. of the family Simulidae; simulid
mustykowate [moos-ti-ko-**vah**-te] pl. the family Simulidae; the simulids
musujący [moo-soo-**yown**-tsi] adj.m. gassy; effervescent; bubbly; fizzy; sparkling
muszelka [moo-**shel**-kah] f. small shell; scallop; cockleshell
muszelkowy [moo-shel-**ko**-vi] adj.m. of a shell; of cockleshells
muszka [**moosh**-kah] f. fly; gunbead; face skin-spot; bow tie; midge; dry fly; patch (on the face); spot; gun foresight; muzzle sight
wziąć na muszkę [vźhownćh nah **moosh**-kan] exp.: to draw a bead on
muszkat [**moosh**-kaht] m. nutmeg; muscatel (wine); geranium
muszkatel [moosh-**kah**-tel] m. muscatel (a sweet desert wine); geranium
muszkatołowiec [moosh-kah-to-**wo**-vyets] m. nutmeg tree; mystrica
muszkatołowy [moosh-kah-to-**wo**-vi]

adj.m. muscat (grape, vine, etc.); myristicaceous
gałka muszkatołowa [**gahw**-kah moosh-kah-to-**wo**-vah] exp.: nutmeg
muszkatowiec [moosh-kah-**to**-vyets] m. nutmeg tree; mystrica
muszkiet [**moosh**-ket] m. musket; smoothbore firearm
muszkieter [moosh-**ke**-ter] m. musketeer
muszkietowy [moosh-ke-**to**-vi] adj.m. of a musket; of muskets
muszla [**moosh**-lah] f. shell; conch; scallop; band shell; shell roof
muszla klozetowa [**moosh**-lah klo-ze-**to**-vah] exp.: lavatory pan
muszla małżowiny usznej [**moosh**-lah mahw-zho-**vee**-ni **oosh**-ney] exp.: external ear; auricular conch; auricular concha
muszlowaty [moosh-lo-**vah**-ti] adj.m. shell-shaped
muszlowy [moosh-**lo**-vi] adj.m. of a shell
musztarda [moosh-**tahr**-dah] f. mustard (seasoning)
musztardniczka [moosh-tahrd-**ńeech**-kah] f. mustard-pot; mustard-dish
musztardowy [moosh-tahr-**do**-vi] adj.m. mustard (gas, etc.)
musztardówka [moosh-tahr-**doof**-kah] f. slang: empty mustard jar
musztra [**moosh**-trah] f. training; exercise; (military) drill
musztrować [moosh-**tro**-vahćh] v. drill; teach manners; rebuke; reprimand (*repeatedly*)
musztrowanie [moosh-tro-**vah**-ńe] n. drill; exercise
muszy [**moo**-shi] adj.m. of a fly; fly's; flies'
muszyca [moo-**shi**-tsah] f. horse fly
muszyca skórna [moo-**shi**-tsah **skoor**-nah] exp.: myiasis
muszysko [moo-**shis**-ko] n. nasty fly; big fly
muślin [**mooś**h-leen] m. muslin (of India)
muślinowy [moośh-lee-**no**-vi] adj.m. of muslin; muslin (dress, curtains, etc.)
muśnięcie [moośh-**ń**an-ćhe] n. a brush; a graze; a shave; peck (on a cheek)
muśnięcie się [moośh-**ń**an-ćhe śhan] n. brushing oneself
mutacja [moo-**tah**-tsyah] f. mutation; (voice) change; breaking of a voice; variation
mutacjonizm [moo-tah-**tsyo**-ńeezm] m. mutationism
mutacyjny [moo-tah-**tsiy**-ni] adj.m. mutative; mutational
mutagen [moo-**tah**-gen] m. mutagen
mutant [**moo**-tahnt] m. mutant; a mutate
muterka [moo-**ter**-kah] f. (bolt) nut; female screw; a small metal block with a threaded hole, for screwing onto a bolt
muton [**moo**-ton] m. mouton; roche moutonee (geol.)
mutować [moo-**to**-vahćh] v. mutate; change; undergo mutation; undergo voice change; undergo breaking of a voice (*repeatedly*)
mutowanie [moo-to-**vah**-ńe] n. change; mutation; undergo breaking of voice
mutra [**moot**-rah] f. (bolt) nut; female screw; a metal block with a threaded hole for screwing onto a threaded rod
mutualizm [moo-too-**ah**-leezm] m. mutualism
muza [**moo**-zah] f. Muse; muse
muzealia [moo-ze-**ah**-lyah] pl. museum collections
muzealnictwo [moo-ze-ahl-**ńeets**-tfo] n. museum management; of museology
muzealniczy [moo-ze-ahl-**ńee**-chi] adj.m. of a museum
muzealnik [moo-ze-**ahl**-ńeek] m. museum management expert; museologist
muzealny [moo-ze-**ahl**-ni] adj.m. of a museum; of museums; museum (piece, value, etc.)
muzealny przedmiot [moo-ze-**ahl**-ni **pshed**-myot] exp.: museum piece
muzeobus [moo-ze-**o**-boos] m. mobile museum
muzeograf [moo-ze-**o**-grahf] m.

museographer
muzeografia [moo-ze-o-**grah**-fyah] f. museography
muzeograficzny [moo-ze-o-grah-**feech**-ni] adj.m. of museography
muzeolog [moo-ze-**o**-log] m. museologist
muzeologia [moo-ze-o-**lo**-gyah] f. museology
muzeologiczny [moo-ze-o-lo-**geech**-ni] adj.m. of museology
muzeum [moo-**ze**-oom] n. museum; exhibition building
muzułman [moo-**zoow**-mahn] m. colloq: Moslem; Muslim; follower of Islam (Mussulman)
muzułmanin [moo-zoow-**mah**-ńeen] m. Moslem; Muslim; follower of Islam (Mussulman)
muzułmanizm [moo-zoow-**mah**-ńeezm] m. Islam; Mussulmanism; Mohammedanism
muzułmanka [moo-zoow-**mahn**-kah] f. (woman) Moslem; Muslim; follower of Islam (Mussulman)
muzułmański [moo-zoow-**mahń**-skee] adj.m. Moslem; Islamic; Muslim; Mohammedan
muzyczka [moo-**zich**-kah] f. light music
muzycznie [moo-**zich**-ńe] adv. musically; in the sphere of music
muzyczność [moo-**zich**-nośhćh] f. musicalness
muzyczny [moo-**zich**-ni] adj.m. musical; set to music
muzyk [**moo**-zik] m. musician; performer; composer; instrumentalist
muzyka [**moo**-zi-kah] f. music; melody; slang: band; dance
muzyka kameralna [**moo**-zi-kah kah-me-**rahl**-nah] exp.: chamber music
muzykalia [moo-zi-**kahl**-yah] pl. musical requisites
muzykalnie [moo-zi-**kahl**-ńe] adv. musically
muzykalność [moo-zi-**kahl**-nośhćh] f. ear for music; love for music; musicalness; talent for music; melodiousness
muzykalny [moo-zi-**kahl**-ni] adj.m. having an ear for music; gifted for music; music-loving; musical; melodious
człowiek muzykalny [**chwo**-vyek moo-zi-**kahl**-ni] exp.: man with an ear for music
muzykant [moo-**zi**-kahnt] m. low class musician; bandsman; instrumentalist
muzykanci [moo-zi-**kahn**-ćhee] pl. the band
muzykantka [moo-zi-**kahnt**-kah] f. (woman) low class musician; instrumentalist; member of a band
muzykograf [moo-zi-**ko**-grahf] m. musicographer
muzykografia [moo-zi-ko-**grah**-fyah] f. musicography
muzykolog [moo-zi-**ko**-log] m. musicologist
muzykologia [moo-zi-ko-**lo**-gyah] f. musicology
muzykologiczny [moo-zi-ko-lo-**geech**-ni] adj.m. musicological
muzykoman [moo-zi-**ko**-mahn] m. colloq: music-lover
muzykomania [moo-zi-ko-**mah**-ńyah] f. colloq: love of music
muzykować [moo-zi-**ko**-vahćh] v. play music; practice music; perform music; listen to music (*repeatedly*)
muzykoterapia [moo-zi-ko-te-**rah**-pyah] f. musicotherapy
muzykus [moo-**zi**-koos] m. colloq: low grade musician; paltry musician
my [mi] pron. we; us
my, ty i ja [mi, ti ee yah] pron. we, you, and I
u nas [oo nahs] exp.: in our house; at home; in our family; in our country; back home
już po nas [yoosh po nahs] exp.: we are done for; we are lost
myca [mi-tsah] f. skullcap
mycie [mi-ćhe] n. washing
mycie się [mi-ćhe śhan] n. washing oneself
mycka [**mits**-kah] f. skullcap
myczeć [mi-chećh] v. moo
myczenie [mi-**che**-ńe] n. mooing (like a cow)
myć [mićh] v. wash (*repeatedly*)

myć się [mićh śhan] v. wash; wash oneself (*repeatedly*)
mydelnica [mi-del-ńee-tsah] f. soap dish; soap-holder
mydelniczka [mi-del-ńeech-kah] f. soap dish; soap-holder
mydełko [mi-dew-ko] n. (small) cake of soap
mydlany [mid-lah-ni] adj.m. soap (powder, etc.); soapy
bańka mydlana [bahń-kah mid-lah-nah] exp.: soap-bubble
płatki mydlane [pwaht-kee mid-lah-ne] exp.: soap-flakes
puszczać bańki mydlane [poo-shchahćh bahń-kee mid-lah-ne] exp.: to blow soap bubbles
mydlarka [mi-dlahr-kah] f. (female) soap boiler
mydlarnia [mi-dlahr-ńah] f. soap store; soap works; perfumery
mydlarski [mi-dlahr-skee] adj.m. soap boiler's; soap (industry, etc.)
mydlarstwo [mi-dlahr-stfo] n. soap-making; soap-boiling
mydlarz [mid-lahsh] m. soap-maker; soap boiler
mydlasty [mi-dlahs-ti] adj.m. soapy
mydlenie [mi-dle-ńe] n. soaping
mydlenie oczu [mi-dle-ńe o-choo] exp.: colloq: bluff; sham; window dressing; eyewash; pulling wool over people's eyes; throwing dust into people's eyes
mydlenie się [mi-dle-ńe śhan] n. putting soap on oneself; producing soap bubbles
mydlić [mid-leećh] v. soap; froth; dress someone down (*repeatedly*)
mydlić oczy [mid-leećh o-chi] exp.: to pull wool over eyes
mydlić sobie ręce [mid-leećh so-bye ran-tse] exp.: to soap one's hands
mydlić się [mid-leećh śhan] v. froth; lather; soap oneself (*repeatedly*)
mydlik [mid-leek] m. soapwort
mydliny [mid-lee-ni] pl. soapsuds; lather
mydlnica [midl-ńee-tsah] f. soapwort
mydłek [mid-wek] m. whippersnapper
mydłkowaty [midw-ko-vah-ti] adj.m. colloq: contemptible; not serious
mydło [mid-wo] n. soap; soft soap; cake of soap; soap-ball; toilet soap; cake of soap; double blank (in domino)
mydłodrzew [mid-wo-dzhef] m. soaptree; Quillaja tree
mygła [mig-wah] f. pile of barked trees
myjak [mi-yahk] m. wash cloth
myjka [miy-kah] f. washing-glove; wash-cloth
myjnia [miy-ńah] f. bottle-washer
myk! [mik] excl. rush!; run away!
myknąć [mik-nownćh] v. speed; rush; dash along; dash away; fleet; scurry
mykwa [mik-fah] f. Jewish ritual bath
mylenie [mi-le-ńe] n. misleading
mylenie się [mi-le-ńe śhan] n. making errors; getting confused
mylić [mi-leećh] v. mislead; misguide; confuse; deceive; lead astray; be deceitful; mistake for (somebody else); mix up (with somebody else) (*repeatedly*)
mylić się [mi-leećh śhan] v. be mistaken; make a mistake; be wrong; err; trip; blunder (*repeatedly*)
mylnie [mil-ńe] adv. wrong; wrongly; erroneously; faultily; falsely; fallaciously; incorrectly; by mistake; by error; mistakenly
mylność [mil-nośhćh] f. erroneousness; falsity; fallacy
mylny [mil-ni] adj.m. wrong; erroneous; faulty; false; fallacious; incorrect
mylna informacja [mil-nah een-for-mah-tsyah] exp.: wrong information; misinformation
mylny pogląd [mil-ni pog-lownt] exp.: mistaken opinion; misconception; misbelief
mylonit [mi-lo-ńeet] m. mylonite (mineral)
myłka [miw-kah] f. mistake; error
myrra [mir-rah] f. myrrh
mysi [mi-śhee] adj.m. of mice; mice's; mouse's; mouse-gray (color)

mysikrólik [mi-śhee-kroo-leek] m. kinglet
mysiurek [mi-śhoo-rek] m. mousetail; Mysorous minimus
mysz [mish] f. mouse; computer mouse; computer entering device
myszy [mi-shi] pl. mice
myszaty [mi-shah-ti] adj.m. mouse-colored; mouse-gray
myszka [mish-kah] f. small mouse; birthmark; aroma; bouquet; nose
myszkować [mish-ko-vahćh] v. covertly explore; trace scent; poke about; poke and pry; ferret; burrow; prowl (*repeatedly*)
myszkowanie [mish-ko-vah-ńe] n. poking about
myszołów [mi-sho-woof] m. buzzard
myszopłoch [mi-sho-pwokh] m. butcher's broom; Jew's myrtle; knee-holly
myszowaty [mi-sho-vah-ti] adj.m. mouse-colored; mouse-dun; mouse-gray
myszowate [mi-sho-vah-te] pl. the family Muridae
myszy [mi-shi] pl. mice; adj.m. of a mouse; see: **mysi**
myśl [miśhl] f. thought; idea; mind; notion; opinion; view; suggestion; intention; intent
być dobrej myśli [bićh dob-rey miśh-lee] exp.: to be of good cheer
dobra myśl [dob-rah miśhl] exp.: bright idea
mieć na myśli [myećh nah miśh-lee] exp.: to mean; to have in mind
na samą myśl [nah sah-mown miśhl] exp.: at the mere thought
po mojej myśli [po mo-yey miśh-lee] exp.: after my heart
przychodzi mi na myśl [pshi-kho-dźhee mee nah miśhl] exp.: it occurs to me
w dobrej myśli [v dob-rey miśh-lee] exp.: with good intent; with the best of intention
w myśl ... [v miśhl] exp.: in accordance with ...; in agreement with ...; according to ... (something)
z myślą o [z miśh-lown o] exp.: with a view to something
myślący [miśh-lown-tsi] adj.m. thoughtful; reflective; thinking; reasoning; indicative of thought
myśleć [miśh-lećh] v. think; ponder; be of opinion; suppose; expect; bear in mind; care (for); be thinking (of doing); intend (to do); contemplate (doing) (*repeatedly*)
co o tym myślisz? [tso o tim miśh-leesh] exp.: what do you think of it?
głośno myśleć [gwośh-no miśh-lećh] exp.: to think aloud
myślę, że tak [miśh-lan zhe tahk] exp.: I think so; I suppose so; I expect so; I am afraid so; probably so; in all likelihood
nie myślę tego robić [ńe miśh-lan te-go ro-beećh] exp.: I do not mean to do it; I do not want to do it; I haven't the slightest intention of doing that
o czym myślisz? [o chim miśh-leesh] exp.: what are you thinking about?
myślenie [miśh-le-ńe] n. reflection; thinking
myśliciel [miśh-lee-ćhel] m. thinker; one who thinks a lot
myślicielstwo [miśh-lee-ćhel-stfo] n. philosophy; cogitations
myśliczek [miśh-lee-chek] m. shooting jacket; hunting vest
myślistwo [miśh-lees-tfo] n. hunting; game shooting; stalking; chase
myśliwiec [miśh-lee-vyets] m. fighter plane; fighter pilot
myśliwski [miśh-leef-skee] adj.m. hunting; hunter's; of a hunter; of hunters
domek myśliwski [do-mek miśh-leef-skee] exp.: hunting lodge
karta myśliwska [kahr-tah miśh-leef-skah] exp.: hunting license
kurta myśliwska [koor-tah miśh-leef-skah] exp.: hunting jacket
pies myśliwski [pyes miśh-leef-skee] exp.: retriever; hunting dog
teren myśliwski [te-ren miśh-leef-skee] exp.: hunting grounds
torba myśliwska [tor-bah miśh-

leef-skah] exp.: game bag
myśliwy [miśh-**lee**-vi] m. hunter; huntsman
myślnik [**miśhl**-ńeek] m. dash (mark); hyphen
myślowo [miśh-**lo**-vo] adv. mentally; in thought; intellectually; inwardly
myślowy [miśh-**lo**-vi] adj.m. mental; reflective; intellectual; inward; notional
mytnik [**mit**-ńeek] m. tollkeeper; toll collector
myto [**mi**-to] n. toll; tollgate; toll bar; tollhouse
mżawka [**mzhahf**-kah] f. drizzle; drizzling rain
mżenie [**mzhe**-ńe] n. drizzle
mżyć [mzhićh] v. drizzle; mizzle (*repeatedly*)
mżyć się [mzhićh śhan] v. be dimly visible; loom; glimmer (*repeatedly*)
mżysty [**mzhis**-ti] adj.m. drizzly

N

n [en] the letter "n"; the sound "n" [en]
na [nah] prep. on; upon; at; for; by; in; to; towards; against; into; like; after; with; from; of; in the name of; per
(Note: for verbs with prefix "na" NOT INCLUDED HERE: PLEASE, CHECK WITHOUT THE PREFIX "na")
na całe życie [nah **tsah**-we **zhi**-ćhe] exp.: for life
na chleb [nah khlep] exp.: for one's daily bread; colloq: for a living; for one's livelihood
na co to? [nah tso to] exp.: what is that for?
na czyjś rozkaz [nah chiyśh **ros**-kahs] exp.: at somebody's command; on somebody's order
na dole [nah **do**-le] exp.: down; below; at the bottom
na dworze [nah **dvo**-zhe] exp.: out of doors; outdoors; outside; in the open
na górze [nah **goo**-zhe] exp.: up; above; on top; at the top
na jednego [nah yed-**ne**-go] exp.: per person; colloq: for a quick one; for a quick drink
na kolanach [nah ko-**lah**-nahkh] exp.: kneeling down; on one's knees; in a state of defeat
na konferencji [nah kon-fe-**ren**-tsyee] exp.: at a conference
na końcu [nah **koń**-tsoo] exp.: at the end (of the road, etc.)
na krótko [nah **kroot**-ko] exp.: for a while; for a short time
na Litwie [nah **leet**-fye] exp.: in Lithuania
na moją prośbę [nah **mo**-yown **proźh**-ban] exp.: at my request
na modłę włoską [na **mod**-wan **vwos**-kown] exp.: after the Italian fashion
na mój koszt [nah mooy kosht] exp.: at my expense
na myśl o tym [nah miśhl o tim] exp.: at the thought of it
na pamięć [nah **pah**-myanćh] exp.: by heart; by rote
na pierwszy rzut oka [nah **pyerf**-shi zhoot **o**-kah] exp.: at first sight; at first glance
na piśmie [nah **peeśh**-mye] exp.: in writing; in black and white
na początku [nah po-**chownt**-koo] exp.: at the beginning
na podziw [nah **po**-dźheef] exp.: to perfection
na pokrycie kosztów [nah po-**kri**-ćhe **kosh**-toof] exp.: towards the cost; to cover the costs
na północ [nah **poow**-nots] exp.: to the North; towards the North
na setki [nah **set**-kee] exp.: by the hundreds
na sprzedaż [nah **spshe**-dahsh] exp.: for sale
na stare lata [nah **stah**-re **lah**-tah] exp.: in one's old age
na strzępy [nah **stshan**-pi] exp.: (tear) to shreds
na śmierć [nah śhmyerćh] exp.: (sentenced, etc.) to death
na ten widok [nah ten **vee**-dok]

exp.: at the sight
na ulicy [nah oo-lee-tsi] exp.: in the street
na wierzchu [nah **vyesh**-khoo] exp.: at the top; on top
na wiosnę [nah **vyos**-nan] exp.: in spring
na wypadek nieszczęścia [nah vi-**pah**-dek ńesh-**chanśh**-ćhah] exp.: in case of misfortune
na zawsze [nah **zahf**-she] exp.: forever; in perpetuity
na znak [nah znahk] exp.: at a signal; on (somebody's) order
dwóch na jednego [dvookh nah yed-**ne**-go] exp.: two to one
chorować na odrę [kho-**ro**-vahćh nah **od**-ran] exp.: to be sick with measles
cierpieć na ból głowy [ćher-pyećh nah bool **gwo**-vi] exp.: to suffer from (a) headache
cóż ty na to? [tsoosh ti nah to] exp.: what do you say to this?
funt na osobę [foont nah o-**so**-ban] exp.: one pound per person
iść na wroga [eeśhćh nah **vro**-gah] exp.: to march (to advance) against the enemy
lekarstwo na bezsenność [le-**kahr**-stfo nah bes-**sen**-nośhćh] exp.: a medicine for insomnia
pokój sześć na sześć metrów [po-kooy sheśhćh nah sheśhćh **me**-troof] exp.: room six by six meters
raz na sto lat [rahs nah sto laht] exp.: once in a hundred years
raz na tydzień [rahs nah **ti**-dźheń] exp.: once a week
głęboki na dwa metry [gwan-**bo**-kee nah dvah **met**-ri] exp.: two meters deep
głuchy na lewe ucho [**gwoo**-khi nah **le**-ve **oo**-kho] exp.: deaf in his left ear
iść na obiad [eeśhćh nah o-byaht] exp.: to go to dinner
iść na spacer [eeśhćh nah **spah**-tser] exp.: to go for a walk
pięć na siedem [pyanćh nah **śhe**-dem] exp.: five by seven (meters, feet, etc.)
sprzedawać na funty [spshe-**dah**-vahćh nah **foon**-ti] exp.: to sell by the pound
umrzeć na tyfus [oom-zhećh nah **ti**-foos] exp.: to die of typhus; to die of typhoid fever
wyglądać na artystę [vi-**glown**-dahćh nah ahr-**tis**-tan] exp.: to look like an artist

na- [nah] prefix: on-; in-
nabab [**nah**-bahp] m. nabob; very rich and important man
nabajać [nah-**bah**-yahćh] v. tell (some, plenty of) gossip, lies
nabajdurzyć [nah-bahy-**doo**-zhićh] v. talk no end of nonsense; talk a lot of nonsense
na bakier [nah **bah**-ker] exp.: aslant; tilted; at odds (with); at loggerheads (with); cocked
wszystko poszło na bakier [fshist-ko **posh**-wo nah **bah**-ker] exp.: everything went wrong; things took a wrong turn
nabałaganić [nah-bah-wah-**gah**-ńeećh] v. make a mess; mess up
nabałamucić [nah-bah-wah-**moo**-ćheećh] v. have carried on flirtations; colloq: mislead
nabarłożyć [nah-bahr-**wo**-zhićh] v. litter
nabawiać [nah-**bah**-vyahćh] v. be the cause (of); cause (anxiety, etc.) (*repeatedly*)
nabawiać się [nah-**bah**-vyahćh śhan] v. get (into trouble, etc.); get (a cold, etc.); contract (an illness, etc.); develop (a fever, etc.); let oneself in (for trouble, etc.); have plenty of fun; have no end of fun; play to one's heart's content (*repeatedly*)
nabawić [nah-**bah**-veećh] v. be the cause of; bring (shame upon, etc.)
nabawić strachu [nah-**bah**-veećh **strah**-khoo] exp.: to frighten
nabawić się [nah-**bah**-veećh śhan] v. bring upon oneself; incur; contract; catch (cold, etc.); let oneself in for (trouble, etc.); play to one's heart's content; have plenty of fun
nabawić się choroby [nah-**bah**-veećh śhan kho-**ro**-bi] exp.: to

contract a disease
nabawić się kłopotów [nah-**bah**-veećh śh<u>an</u> kwo-**po**-toof] exp.: to get into trouble
nabazgrać [nah-**bahz**-grahćh] v. make a very rough sketch; make a pitiful drawing; scrawl; scribble; concoct (a story, etc.)
nabesztać [nah-**besh**-tahćh] v. give a rough scolding; scold
nabiadać się [nah-**byah**-dahćh śh<u>an</u>] v. colloq: complain a lot; whine a lot; slang: bitch a lot
nabiał [nah-byahw] m. dairy produce including eggs
nabiałowy [nah-byah-**wo**-vi] adj.m. dairy (produce, etc.)
sklep nabiałowy [sklep nah-byah-**wo**-vi] exp.: dairy
nabić [nah-beećh] v. beat; whack; slaughter (a mass of); kill (a lot of); pack (with); fill (with); load (a gun, etc.); charge (a battery, etc.); stud (with); tap (a heel); insert; fix; hoop (a wheel, etc.); stick (on a fork, etc.)
nabić kogoś w butelkę [nah-beećh **ko**-gość v boo-**tel**-k<u>an</u>] exp.: to dupe someone
nabić komuś guza [nah-beećh ko-moośh **goo**-zah] exp.: to punch someone in the head
nabić rewolwer [nah-beećh re-**vol**-ver] exp.: to load a revolver; to load a handgun
nabić się [nah-beećh śh<u>an</u>] v. get stuck (on); get impaled
nabiec [nah-byets] v. swell (with); fill (with); be injected (with); flush (with); see: **nabiegać**
nabiedować się [nah-bye-**do**-vahćh śh<u>an</u>] v. go through hard times; live in want; have a hard time
nabiedzić się [nah-**bye**-dźheećh śh<u>an</u>] v. have a lot of trouble (with); see: **nabiedować się**
nabiegać [nah-**bye**-gahćh] v. swell; be injected (with); fill (with); flush (with anger, etc.) (*repeatedly*)
nabiegły krwią [nah-**byeg**-wi krfy<u>own</u>] exp.: bloodshot; injected with blood
nabiegać się [nah-**bye**-gahćh śh<u>an</u>] v. run a lot; exert oneself; run about a great deal; give oneself a lot of trouble
nabiegnąć [nah-**byeg**-n<u>own</u>ćh] v. swell; be injected (with); fill (with); flush (with anger, etc.)
nabiegunnik [nah-bye-**goon**-ńeek] m. pole shoe
nabieracz [nah-**bye**-rahch] m. cheat; swindler
nabierać [nah-**bye**-rahćh] v. take; take in; tease; cheat; amass (*repeatedly*)
nabierać się [nah-**bye**-rahćh śh<u>an</u>] v. be taken in; be hoaxed; be duped; amass (a lot of loot, etc.) (*repeatedly*)
nabieranie [nah-bye-**rah**-ńe] n. hoax; amassing (a lot of loot, etc.)
nabieżnik [nah-**byezh**-ńeek] m. leading mark (on pavement, etc.)
nabieżniki [nah-byezh-**ńee**-kee] pl. leading marks (on a runway, etc.)
nabieżnikowy [nah-byezh-ńee-**ko**-vi] adj.m. of leading mark (on pavement, etc.)
nabijacz [nah-**bee**-yahch] m. loader
nabijać [nah-**bee**-yahćh] v. stud; load (a gun, etc.) (*repeatedly*)
nabijać sobie głowę czymś [nah-**bee**-yahćh **so**-bye **gwo**-v<u>an</u> chimśh] exp.: to get an idea into one's head; to stuff some notion into one's head
nabijać w butelkę [nah-**bee**-yahćh v boo-**tel**-k<u>an</u>] exp.: to make a fool (of); slang: to spoof; to deceive
nabijać strzelbę [nah-**bee**-yahćh **stshel**-b<u>an</u>] exp.: to load a gun
nabijać się [nah-**bee**-yahćh śh<u>an</u>] v. make fun of (somebody); colloq: pull (somebody's) leg (*repeatedly*)
nabijanie [ńah-bee-**yah**-ńe] n. loading (a gun, etc.); studding
nabijanie się [nah-bee-**yah**-ńe śh<u>an</u>] n. making fun of; colloq: leg pulling
nabiodrek [nah-**byod**-rek] m. cuisse; defensive plate; thigh armor
nabity [nah-**bee**-ti] adj.m. crowded; crammed; compact; close-knit; close (woven); thickset; solid
nablagować [nah-blah-**go**-vahćh] v.

tell a lot of lies; invent lies; exaggerate with lies

nablagować się [nah-blah-**go**-vahćh śhan] v. have told plenty of stories

nabluzgać [nah-**bloo**-zgahćh] v. colloq: curse (somebody) out; swear at (somebody)

nabłądzić [nah-**bwown**-dźheećh] v. make a lot of mistakes

nabłądzić się [nah-**bwown**-dźheećh śhan] v. be on a wild-goose chase; roam; wander

nabłąkać się [nah-**bwown**-kahćh śhan] v. be on a wild-goose chase; roam; wander; keep losing one's way

nabłonek [nah-**bwo**-nek] m. epithelium

nabłoniak [nah-**bwo**-ńahk] m. epithelioma (benign or malignant tumor)

nabłonkowaty [nah-bwon-ko-**vah**-ti] adj.m. epithelioid

nabłonkowy [nah-bwon-**ko**-vi] adj.m. epithelial

nabłotny [nah-**bwot**-ni] adj.m. marshlands (vegetation, etc.)

nabłyszczać [nah-**bwish**-chahćh] v. polish up; glaze (paper, etc.) (*repeatedly*)

nabłyszczanie [nah-bwish-**chah**-ńe] n. polishing; glazing (*repeated*)

nabłyszczenie [nah-bwish-**che**-ńe] n. polishing; glazing

nabłyszczyć [nah-**bwish**-chićh] v. polish up; glaze (paper, etc.)

naboczny [nah-**boch**-ni] adj.m. lateral; side (line, etc.)

naboda [nah-**bo**-dah] f. myrobalan; tanning ingredient; cherry plum

nabojowy [nah-bo-**yo**-vi] adj.m. of a cartridge; cartridge (case, etc.)

na bok! [nah bok] excl.: make room!; move to the side!; stand aside! exp.: aside; apart; aslant

na boku [nah **bo**-koo] exp.: on the side; aside; apart

naborykać się [nah-bo-ri-kahćh śhan] v. have struggled a lot

na bosaka [nah bo-**sah**-kah] exp.: barefoot; without shoes and stockings

nabożeństwo [nah-bo-**zheń**-stfo] n. church service; devotion; liking for; unction

godziny nabożeństw [go-**dźhee**-ni nah-**bo**-zheństf] exp.: hours of worship

książeczka do nabożeństwa [kśhown-**zhech**-kah do nah-bo-**źheń**-stfah] exp.: prayer book

nabożeństwo żałobne [nah-bo-**zheń**-stfo zhah-**wob**-ne] exp.: requiem mass

odprawiać nabożeństwo [ot-**prah**-vyahćh nah-bo-**zheń**-stfo] exp.: to celebrate a mass

z nabożeństwem [z nah-bo-**zheń**-stfem] exp.: devoutly; with reverence

nabożnie [nah-**bozh**-ńe] adv. piously; with religious care; with reverence; devoutly; religiously

nabożnisia [nah-bozh-**ńee**-śhah] f. colloq: (woman) bigot; sanctimonious woman

nabożniś [nah-**bozh**-ńeeśh] m. (man) bigot; sanctimonious man

nabożny [nah-**bozh**-ni] adj.m. pious; religious; godly; devoutly; devotional (hymn)

słuchać w nabożnym skupieniu [**swoo**-khahćh v nah-**bozh**-nim skoo-**pye**-ńoo] exp.: to listen devoutly; to listen with reverence

nabój [**nah**-booy] m. charge; cartridge; round of ammunition

ostry nabój [**os**-tri **nah**-booy] exp.: live bullet (ammunition); ball-cartridge

ślepy nabój [**śhle**-pi **nah**-booy] exp.: blank cartridge

nabór [**nah**-boor] m. conscription; enlistment; levy; recruits

nabrać [**nahb**-rahćh] v. take (a great deal); take in; tease; cheat; gather; swell; fork (hay, etc.); draw in; inhale (air, etc.); leak (water, etc.); become flooded; buy a lot (on credit); gather (speed, etc.); acquire (habit, etc.); develop (a taste, etc., for); become (certain, etc.); grow in strength, etc.); fill (with water, etc.); colloq: hoax; dupe; gather (pus, etc.); slang: kid

nabrać benzyny [**nahb**-rahćh ben-

zi-ni] exp.: to fill up (the gas tank); to take a fill of petrol (Brit.)
nabrać doświadczenia [nahb-rahćh do-śhfyaht-che-ńah] exp.: to get experience; to acquire experience
nabrać ochoty [nahb-rahćh o-kho-ti] exp.: to be encouraged
nabrać pewności [nahb-rahćh pev-nośh-ćhee] exp.: to become certain
nabrać przekonania [nahb-rahćh pshe-ko-nah-ńah] exp.: to become convinced
nabrać wody w usta [nahb-rahćh vo-di v oos-tah] exp.: to become dumb; to take a mouthful of water; to say nothing
nabrać się [nahb-rahćh śhan] v. be taken in; be hoaxed; be duped; amass (a lot of loot, etc.)
dać się nabrać [dahćh śhan nahb-rahćh] exp.: to be taken; to be taken in; to be hoaxed; to be duped
nabranie [nah-brah-ńe] n. cheat; swindle; fraud; trick; a take in; piece of humbug
nabrechać [nah-bre-khahćh] v. colloq: tell a lot of lies
nabroić [nah-bro-eećh] v. do a lot of mischief; frolic a good deal
nabrudzić [nah-broo-dźheećh] v. make a mess; make dirty
nabruździć [nah-broośh-dźheećh] v. be a great hindrance; thwart many a plan
nabrzeże [nah-bzhe-zhe] n. wharf; jetty; embankment; landing pier
nabrzeżny [nah-bzhe-zhni] adj.m. of a seashore; of a riverside; coastal
nabrzeżowy [nah-bzhe-zho-vi] adj.m. of a river front (dock)
nabrzękać [nah-bzhan-kahćh] v. swell (*repeatedly*)
nabrzęknąć [nah-bzhank-nownćh] v. swell
nabrzęknięcie [nah-bzhank-ńan-ćhe] n. a swelling; swelling
nabrzmiałość [nah-bzhmyah-wośhćh] f. swelling; a swelling
nabrzmiały [nah-bzhmyah-wi] adj.m. swollen; distended
nabrzmieć [nah-bzhmyećh] v. swell; see: **nabrzmiewać**
nabrzmienie [nah-bzhmye-ńe] n. swelling; distension
nabrzmiewać [nah-bzhmye-vahćh] v. swell; plump up; plump out; distend; grow big (*repeatedly*)
nabrzmiewanie [nah-bzhmye-vah-ńe] n. swelling; edema; tumefaction; state of puffiness
nabudować [nah-boo-do-vahćh] v. build a great quantity
nabudować się [nah-boo-do-vahćh śhan] v. build plenty; get tired (of) building
nabujać [nah-boo-yahćh] v. tell lies
nabujać się [nah-boo-yahćh śhan] v. tell plenty of lies
nabuntować [nah-boon-to-vahćh] v. instigate insubordination; foment sedition
nabuntować się [nah-boon-to-vahćh śhan] v. mutiny; revolt many times
nabuńczuczyć się [nah-booń-choo-chićh śhan] v. fume; storm
naburczeć [nah-boor-chećh] v. go about growling; go about grumbling
naburczeć się [nah-boor-chećh śhan] v. grumble without restraint
naburmuszenie się [nah-boor-moo-she-ńe śhan] n. sulks; bad humor; sulky face; sour face
naburmuszony [nah-boor-moo-sho-ni] adj.m. sulky; bad humored
naburmuszyć się [nah-boor-moo-shićh śhan] v. grow gloomy; grow fussy; make a wry face; look black; bristle up
nabuzować [nah-boo-zo-vahćh] v. put a strong fire in a stove
nabuzować się [nah-boo-zo-vahćh śhan] v. colloq: booze; get drunk
nabuzowany [nah-boo-zo-vah-ni] adj.m. colloq: full of anger; upset; slang: boozed up; drunk; drunken
nabycie [nah-bi-ćhe] n. acquisition; purchase; acquirement; obtention
nabyć [nah-bićh] v. buy; make a purchase; purchase; get; obtain; procure; acquire (experience, etc.); develop (a habit, etc.)
nabyć się [nah-bićh śhan] v. stay

a long time
nabytek [nah-**bi**-tek] m. acquisition; purchase; new recruit (new employee)
nabyty [nah-**bi**-ti] adj.m. acquired (knowledge, etc.)
nabywać [nah-**bi**-vahćh] v. buy; acquire; obtain; gain; procure; purchase; get; develop (a habit) (*repeatedly*); see: **nabyć**
nabywać doświadczenia [nah-**bi**-vahćh do-śhfyaht-**che**-ńah] exp.: to get experience; to acquire experience
nabywać przyzwyczajenia [nah-bi-vahćh pshiz-vi-chah-**ye**-ńah] exp.: to acquire a habit; to get into a habit
nabywać wprawy [nah-**bi**-vahćh **fprah**-vi] exp.: to become proficient
nabywanie [nah-bi-**vah**-ńe] n. acquisition; obtainment; obtention
nabywca [nah-**bif**-tsah] m. buyer; purchaser
nabywczy [nah-**bif**-chi] adj.m. purchasing
siła nabywcza [**śhe**-wah nah-**bif**-chah] exp.: purchasing power
nabywczyni [nah-bif-**chi**-ńee] f. (female) buyer; purchaser
nabzdurzyć [nah-**bzdoo**-zhićh] v. talk a lot of nonsense
nabzdyczać się [nah-**bzdi**-chahćh śh<u>an</u>] v. colloq: show displeasure; show an angry face; frown (*repeatedly*)
nabzdyczony [nah-bzdi-**cho**-ni] adj.m. colloq: displeased; gloomy; frowning
nabzdyczyć się [nah-**bzdi**-chićh śh<u>an</u>] v. colloq: show angry face; show displeasure; frown
na całego [nah tsah-**we**-go] exp.: colloq: the whole hog; to go all the way; the whole nine yards
nacałować się [nah-tsah-**wo**-vahćh śh<u>an</u>] v. kiss enough; kiss plenty
nacechować [nah-tse-**kho**-vahćh] v. mark; characterize; be characteristic (of); be a distinctive feature; stamp; gauge
nacechowany [nah-tse-kho-**vah**-ni] adj.m. marked; characterized
być nacechowanym czymś [bićh nah-tse-kho-**vah**-nim chimśh] exp.: to bear a stamp (of); to be characterized (by)
nacedzić [nah-**tse**-dźheećh] v. strain (a lot); pass through a sieve
nachalnie [nah-**khahl**-ńe] adv. impudently; brazenly; insolently
nachalność [nah-**khahl**-nośhćh] f. impudence; effrontery; insolence
nachalny [nah-**khahl**-ni] adj.m. impudent; brazen; insolent
nachalstwo [nah-**khahl**-stfo] n. impudence; effrontery; insolence; see: **nachalność**
nachapać [nah-**khah**-pahćh] v. snatch plenty; grab plenty (of)
nachlapać [nah-**khlah**-pahćh] v. splash; stray; mess up with fluid
nachłeptać się [nah-**khwep**-tahćh śh<u>an</u>] v. lap up one's fill (of)
nachmurzyć [nah-**khmoo**-zhićh] v. darken; cloud (the brow, etc.)
nachmurzyć się [nah-**khmoo**-zhićh śh<u>an</u>] v. frown; lour; scowl; lower; cloud over; cloud up
nachodzić [nah-**kho**-dźheećh] v. intrude; (abstraction:) haunt; see: **najść** (*repeatedly*)
nachodzić się [nah-**kho**-dźheećh śh<u>an</u>] v. walk plenty; get tired of walking
nachorować się [nah-kho-**ro**-vahćh śh<u>an</u>] v. go through a long illness; have no end of illnesses
nachrapek [nah-**khrah**-pek] m. noseband
nachuchać [nah-**khoo**-khahćh] v. exhale upon; blow on; pamper
nachwalić się [nah-**khfah**-leećh śh<u>an</u>] v. extol; praise to the skies; boast; brag without restraint
nachwyt [nah-khfit] m. overhand grip
nachwytać [nah-**khfi**-tahćh] v. grab a lot (of); catch a great quantity (of)
na chybcika [nah khip-**ćhee**-kah] exp.: colloq: in a hurry; in haste; with speed; rushing
nachylać [nah-**khi**-lahćh] v. stoop; bend; incline; lean; tilt; slant

(*repeatedly*)
nachylać się [nah-khi-lahćh śhan] v. bow; incline; stoop; lean forward; have a slant; slope (*repeatedly*)
nachylenie [nah-khi-le-ńe] n. inclination; slope
nachylenie się [nah-khi-le-ńe śhan] n. stooping down; becoming inclined
nachylić [nah-khi-leećh] v. stoop; bend; incline; lean; tilt; slant; see: **nachylać**
nachylić się [nah-khi-leećh śhan] v. stoop down; bend down; tilt oneself; lean forward
nachylony [nah-khi-lo-ni] adj.m. inclined; sloping; slanting (forward, backward, etc.); aslant; oblique
naciąć [nah-ćhownćh] v. cut a great deal; cut plenty; notch; incise; make an incision; score; nick; scarify; trick; hoax; dupe; play a trick on
naciąć się [nah-ćhownćh śhan] v. be taken in; be duped; be hoaxed
naciąg [nah-ćhowng] m. stringing (of a tennis racket, etc.); spring (of ski binding); tension; tensioning; tightening (of a rope, cable, etc.)
naciągacz [nah-ćhown-gahch] m. trickster; fraud; tightening tool; stretcher
naciągaczka [nah-ćhown-gahch-kah] f. (woman) trickster; fraud
naciągać [nah-ćhown-gahćh] v. stretch; draw; strain; slip on; colloq: stretch the truth; strain an interpretation; pull one's leg; take (somebody) in; infuse (*repeatedly*)
naciągać się [nah-ćhown-gahćh śhan] v. stretch oneself; strain oneself; tighten oneself (*repeatedly*)
naciąganie [nah-ćhown-gah-ńe] n. trickery; hoax; take-in; infusion
naciągnąć [nah-ćhowng-nownćh] v. stretch; draw; strain; slip on; colloq: stretch the truth; strain an interpretation; pull one's leg; take (somebody) in; infuse; see: **naciągać**
naciągnąć się [nah-ćhowng-nownćh śhan] v. stretch oneself; strain oneself; tighten oneself
naciągnięcie [nah-ćhowng-ńan-ćhe] n. trickery; hoax; take-in; infusion
naciągnięty [nah-ćhowng-ńan-ti] adj.m. tight; stretched; bent; strung; strained; taut; far-fetched
naciągowy [nah-ćhown-go-vi] adj.m. tightening (nut, knob, lever, etc.)
nacichać [nah-ćhee-khahćh] v. calm down; subside; abate; be hushed; be lulled (*repeatedly*)
nacichnąć [nah-ćheekh-nownćh] v. calm down; subside; abate; be hushed; be lulled
naciec [nah-ćhets] v. gather by leaking; gather by pouring; gather by dripping; gather by trickling; infiltrate
nacieczenie [nah-ćhe-che-ńe] n. infiltration
naciek [nah-ćhek] m. swelling; gathering (of a fluid); drip-stone; infiltration
naciekać [nah-ćhe-kahćh] v. gather by leaking; gather by pouring; gather by dripping; gather by trickling; infiltrate (*repeatedly*); see: **naciec**
naciekąć [nah-ćhek-nownćh] v. gather by leaking; gather by pouring; gather by dripping; gather by trickling; infiltrate
naciekowiec [nah-ćhe-ko-vyets] m. travertine
naciekowo [nah-ćhe-ko-vo] adv. by infiltration
naciekowy [nah-ćhe-ko-vi] adj.m. travertine (formation, etc.); infiltrating; infiltrative
nacieniować [nah-ćhe-ńo-vahćh] v. shade; put a shade in (drawing, graph, etc.)
nacierać [nah-ćhe-rahćh] v. rub; give a rubdown; rub down; embrocate; wax (a floor, etc.); attack; assail; charge (an enemy, etc.); rush (at); dash (at); demand; harass (*repeatedly*)
nacierać się [nah-ćhe-rahćh śhan] v. rub oneself; put a lotion

(cream, etc.) on oneself (*repeatedly*)

nacieranie [nah-ćhe-**rah**-ńe] n. rub; rubdown; rubbing-down; friction; embrocation

nacieranie się [nah-ćhe-**rah**-ńe śhan] n. rubbing oneself down

nacierpieć się [nah-**ćher**-pyećh śhan] v. suffer a great deal; go through a great deal of suffering

nacieszyć [nah-**ćhe**-shićh] v. gladden (one's eyes, heart, etc.)

nacieszyć się [nah-**ćhe**-shićh śhan] v. enjoy to the full

nacięcie [nah-**ćhan**-ćhe] n. cut; incision; notch; nick; score; indentation; scarification

nacinać [nah-**ćhee**-nahćh] v. cut a great deal; notch; score; nick; scarify; hoax; dupe; see: **naciąć** (*repeatedly*)

nacinać się [nah-**ćhee**-nahćh śhan] v. be taken in; be duped; cut oneself (shaving, etc.) (*repeatedly*)

nacinak [nah-**ćhee**-nahk] m. cutter

nacinanie [nah-ćhee-**nah**-ńe] n. incision; indentation; scarification

nacios [nah-ćhos] m. notch; nick; blaze

naciosać [nah-**ćho**-sahćh] v. hew a lot; hew a great quantity; see: **naciąć**

naciosać się [nah-**ćho**-sahćh śhan] v. hew a great deal; get tired of hewing

naciosywać [nah-ćho-**si**-vahćh] v. hew a lot; hew a great quantity (*repeatedly*)

naciowy [nah-**ćho**-vi] adj.m. of leaves of vegetables; of vegetable tops

nacisk [nah-ćheesk] m. pressure; stress; accent; thrust; push; accentuation; emphasis (on); insistence (on); influence; compulsion; constraint

kłaść nacisk [kwahśhćh **nah**-ćheesk] exp.: to stress; to lay stress (on something)

pod naciskiem [pod nah-**ćhees**-kem] exp.: under the pressure (of circumstances, etc.)

wywierać nacisk [vi-**vye**-rahćh nah-ćheesk] exp.: to press (somebody, something)

z naciskiem [z nah-**ćhees**-kem] exp.: emphatically

naciskać [nah-**ćhees**-kahćh] v. press; urge; bear on; push (the enemy, etc.); exert pressure; apply weight; bring pressure to bear; throw (stones, etc.) (*repeatedly*)

naciskanie [nah-ćhees-**kah**-ńe] n. pressure

nacisnąć [nah-**ćhees**-nownćh] v. press; urge; bear on; push (the enemy, etc.); exert pressure; apply weight; bring pressure to bear; throw (stones, etc.); see: **naciskać**

nacisnąć się [nah-**ćhees**-nownćh śhan] v. press oneself; put oneself under pressure

naciśnięcie [nah-ćheeśh-**ńan**-ćhe] n. a push; a press; push; press

za naciśnięciem guzika [zah nah-ćheeśh-**ńan**-ćhem goo-**źhee**-kah] exp.: at one push of the button

naciułać [nah-**ćhoo**-wahćh] v. slang: store up (a sum of money)

naciupać [nah-**ćhoo**-pahćh] v. chop up

nacja [nah-tsyah] f. nation; a people

nacjonalista [nah-tsyo-nah-**lees**-tah] m. nationalist

nacjonalistyczny [nah-tsyo-nah-lees-**tich**-ni] adj.m. nationalist; nationalistic

nacjonalizacja [nah-tsyo-nah-lee-**zahts**-yah] f. nationalization

nacjonalizacyjny [nah-tsyo-nah-lee-zah-**tsiy**-ni] adj.m. of nationalization

nacjonalizm [nah-tsyo-**nah**-leezm] m. nationalism

nacjonalizować [nah-tsyo-nah-lee-**zo**-vahćh] v. nationalize (*repeatedly*)

nacjonalizowanie [nah-tsyo-nah-lee-zo-**vah**-ńe] n. nationalization

nacmokać się [nah-**tsmo**-kahćh śhan] v. smack one's fill

nacysta [nah-tsis-tah] m. Nazi

nacystowski [nah-tsis-**tof**-skee] adj.m. Hitlerite

nacyzm [nah-tsizm] m. Nazism
na czczo [nah chcho] adv. on an empty stomach; unfed; fasting; see: **czczo**
naczalstwo [nah-chahl-stfo] n. colloq: the establishment; the big wigs; the management; the higher-ups; superior officials
naczekać się [nah-che-kahćh śhan] v. wait too long; get tired of waiting; wait indefinitely
na czele [nah che-le] exp.: at the head
naczelnictwo [nah-chel-ńee-tstfo] n. authority; management; command; leadership; direction; control; those in authority
naczelniczka [nah-chel-ńeech-kah] f. (female) manager; chief; head; master
naczelnik [nah-chel-ńeek] m. manager; chief; head; master
naczelnik stacji [nah-chel-ńeek stah-tsyee] exp.: stationmaster
naczelnikostwo [nah-chel-ńee-kos-tfo] n. direction; management; leadership; manager and his wife
naczelnikowa [nah-chel-ńee-ko-vah] f. manager's wife; chief's wife; slang: red beet soup (mob jargon)
naczelnikowski [nah-chel-ńee-kof-skee] adj.m. manager's; chief's
naczelny [nah-chel-ni] adj.m. leading; foremost; chief; head; paramount; primary; principal; main; front (ranks, etc.); frontal
naczelne [nah-chel-ne] pl. (biol.) primates
naczelne dowództwo [nah-chel-ne do-voots-tfo] exp.: High Command; supreme command
naczelny dowódca [nah-chel-ni do-voot-tsah] exp.: commander in chief
redaktor naczelny [re-dahk-tor nah-chel-ni] exp.: editor in chief
naczepa [nah-che-pah] f. trailer
naczepiać [nah-che-pyahćh] v. hook a lot (of things, etc.) (*repeatedly*)
naczepiać się [nah-che-pyahćh śhan] v. hang on (to something) (*repeatedly*)
naczerpać [nah-cher-pahćh] v. dip up; draw (fluid); scoop up (grain, etc.)
naczesać [nah-che-sahćh] v. gather by combing
naczesywać [nah-che-si-vahćh] v. gather by combing (*repeatedly*)
naczółek [nah-choo-wek] m. headstall; pediment; ice apron (on a pillar)
naczółkowy [nah-choow-ko-vi] adj.m. of an ice apron (on river bridge pillars, etc.)
naczulić [nah-choo-leećh] v. sensitize
naczulić się [nah-choo-leećh śhan] v. fondle; caress (a lot)
nie mogą naczulić się [ńe mo-gown nah-choo-leećh śhan] exp.: they are never tired of caresses
naczupirzyć się [nah-choo-pee-zhićh śhan] v. slang: put a flashy dress on; trick oneself out; perk oneself out; assume a pugnacious attitude; assume a cocky attitude
naczupurzyć się [nah-choo-poo-zhićh śhan] v. slang: assume a pugnacious attitude; assume a cocky attitude; assume a stern attitude
na czworakach [nah chfo-rah-kahkh] exp.: on all fours; on one's hands and knees
naczyniak [nah-chi-ńahk] m. angioma
naczyniasty [nah-chi-ńahs-ti] adj.m. vascular
naczynie [nah-chi-ńe] n. vessel; vase; dish; receptacle; container; holder; trachea; tool; instrument; boat
naczynia [nah-chi-ńah] pl. pot and pans; vessels; dishes
naczynia gliniane [nah-chi-ńah glee-ńah-ne] exp.: earthenware; pottery
naczynia krwionośne [nah-chi-ńah krfyo-nośh-ne] exp.: blood vessels
naczynia kuchenne [nah-chi-ńah koo-khen-ne] exp.: kitchen utensils; colloq: pots and pans
naczynia włosowate [nah-chi-ńah vwo-so-vah-te] exp.: capillary vessels

zmywać naczynia [zmi-vahćh nah-**chi**-ńah] exp.: to wash dishes
naczynioruchowy [nah-chi-ńo-roo-**kho**-vi] adj.m. vasomotor (nerve, drug, etc.)
naczyniowy [nah-chi-**ńo**-vi] adj.m. vascular
naczyniówka [nah-chi-**ńoof**-kah] f. choroid (of eye); pia mater (of brain)
naczyniówkowy [nah-chi-ńoof-**ko**-vi] adj.m. choroidal (of an eye); of pia mater (of the brain)
naczyńko [nah-**chiń**-ko] n. (small) vessel; vase; dish; receptacle; container; holder; trachea; tool; instrument
naczytać się [nah-**chi**-tahćh śhan] v. read a great deal; get tired of reading
naczytać się książek [nah-**chi**-tahćh śhan **kśhown**-zhek] exp.: to read plenty of books; to read no end of books
nać [nahćh] f. top (of vegetables); tops; leaves (pl.)
nad [naht or nahd] prep. over; above; on; upon; beyond; at; of; for; than
cenniejszy nad złoto [tsen-**ńey**-shi nahd **zwo**-to] exp.: more precious than gold
dach nad głową [dahkh nahd **gwo**-vown] exp.: roof over (above) one's head
Londyn leży nad Tamizą [lon-din le-zhi naht tah-**mee**-zown] exp.: London is situated on the Thames
nad chmurami [naht khmoo-**rah**-mee] exp.: above the clouds
nad miarę [nahd **myah**-ran] exp.: beyond measure
nad morzem [nahd **mo**-zhem] exp.: at the seaside
nad ranem [nahd **rah**-nem] exp.: at daybreak
niebo jest nad naszymi głowami [**ńe**-bo yest nahd nah-**shi**-mee gwo-**vah**-mee] exp.: the sky is over our heads
skandal nad skandale [**skahn**-dahl naht skahn-**dah**-le] exp.: scandal without precedent
ślęczeć nad książką [**śhlan**-chećh naht **kśhownsh**-kown] exp.: to get tired reading; to slave over a book
nad- [naht or nahd] prefix: over-; above-
nadać [**nah**-dahćh] v. confer; bestow; give; grant; endow; christen; invest; vest; offer; cause; broadcast; transmit; register (a letter, etc.); make (appear, etc.); colloq: order; procure; see: **nadawać**
diabli nadali! [**dyahb**-lee nah-**dah**-lee] excl.: to hell with it!; devil sent it!; dammit!
nadać imię [**nah**-dahćh **ee**-myan] exp.: to name
nadać tytuł [**nah**-dahćh ti-toow] exp.: to title; to give a title
nadać się [**nah**-dahćh śhan] v. be suitable (for); be adapted (to); suit; match (with); be serviceable; be fit for use; suit a purpose; be fitted (for); be competent (for); be qualified (for); come in handy; fit
nadajnik [nah-**dahy**-ńeek] m. transmitter; feeder
nadal [**nah**-dahl] adv. still; in future; continue (to do); as before; as in the past; as formerly; as hitherto; as heretofore
nadal być [**nah**-dahl bićh] exp.: to have remained (a bachelor, in Gdańsk, etc.)
nadal robić [**nah**-dahl **ro**-beećh] exp.: to continue to do
próbuj nadal [**proo**-booy **nah**-dahl] exp.: keep trying; go on trying
nadanie [nah-**dah**-ńe] n. conferment (of); investiture (with); sending (of mail, etc.); registration (of a letter, etc.); charter; grant; endowment
nadaremnie [nah-dah-**rem**-ńe] adv. in vain; unsuccessfully; to no purpose; without result; fruitlessly
nadaremno [nah-dah-**rem**-no] adv. unsuccessfully; to no purpose; without result; fruitlessly; see: **nadaremnie**
nadaremny [nah-dah-**rem**-ni] adj.m. fruitless; vain; unsuccessful
nadarzać [nah-**dah**-zhahćh] v. give opportunity (*repeatedly*)

nadarzać się [nah-**dah**-zhahćh śhan] v. happen; occur; turn up; present itself; offer (of) (*repeatedly*)
nadarzyć [nah-**dah**-zhićh] v. give opportunity; send (something somebody's way)
nadarzyć się [nah-**dah**-zhićh śhan] v. happen; occur; turn up; present itself; offer (of)
nadarzyła się okazja [nah-dah-**zhi**-wah śhan o-**kah**-zyah] exp.: an opportunity presented itself; an occasion arose
nadawa [nah-**dah**-vah] f. the feed; feed
nadawać [nah-**dah**-vahćh] v. confer; bestow; grant; endow; christen; invest; vest; offer; cause; broadcast; transmit; register (a letter, etc.); make (appear, etc.); colloq: order; procure; talk a lot; not let the others put a word in edgewise see: **nadać** (*repeatedly*)
nadawać wygląd [nah-**dah**-vahćh **vig**-lownt] exp.: to make (someone) look like (a sailor, etc.)
nadawać się [nah-**dah**-vahćh śhan] v. be fit; be fitted (for); be suited; be suitable (for); be adapted (to); suit; match (with); be serviceable; be fit for use; suit a purpose; be competent (for); be qualified (for); come in handy; fit; see: **nadać się** (*repeatedly*)
ja się do tego nie nadaję [yah śhan do **te**-go ńe nah-**dah**-yan] exp.: I am no good for it; it's not for me; I don't feel up to it
nadawać się do czytania [nah-dah-vahćh śhan do chi-**tah**-ńah] exp.: to make a good reading; to be a good reading
nie nadawać się do użytku [ńe nah-**dah**-vahćh śhan do oo-**zhit**-koo] exp.: to be of no use; to be useless; colloq: to be no good
nadawanie [nah-dah-**vah**-ńe] n. transmission
nadawanie się [nah-dah-**vah**-ńe śhan] n. fitness (for)
nadawca [nah-**dahf**-tsah] m. sender; broadcaster; consignor; grantor
nadawczy [nah-**dahf**-chi] adj.m. sending; broadcasting (station, etc.); transmitting (station, etc.); (deed) of conferment, grant, bestowal, etc.
aparat nadawczy [ah-**pah**-raht nah-**dahf**-chi] exp.: transmitter
nadawczyni [nah-dahf-**chi**-ńee] f. (woman) sender; broadcaster; consignor; grantor
nadawnictwo [nah-dahv-**ńeets**-tfo] n. right of investiture
nadawstwo [nah-**dahf**-stfo] n. right of investiture
nadąć [**nah**-downćh] v. puff up; inflate; fill (a balloon, etc.); puff out; blow out; bulge out; pump up; pout (one's lips); swell (sails, etc.)
nadąć się [**nah**-downćh śhan] v. puff oneself up; inflate oneself (with); draw in air; fill out (like a balloon, etc.); puff oneself out; assume a sullen air; assume a sulky air; pout (one's lips); swell out; blow up (with pride, etc.); put on an air
nadąsać się [nah-**down**-sahćh śhan] v. assume a sullen air; assume a sulky air; pout (one's lips); sulk and sulk; keep sulking
nadąsanie [nah-down-**sah**-ńe] n. sulky mood
z nadąsaniem [z nah-down-**sah**-ńem] exp.: sulkily
nadąsany [nah-down-**sah**-ni] adj.m. sulky; sullen; stuffy; pouting
być nadąsanym [bićh nah-down-**sah**-nim] exp.: to sulk; to be in the sulks; to be in the pouts; to pout
nadążać [nah-**down**-zhahćh] v. keep up with; cope with; keep pace; not (to) lag behind; follow (*repeatedly*)
nadążyć [nah-**down**-zhićh] v. keep up with; cope with; keep pace; not (to) lag behind; follow
nadbagaż [nahd-**bah**-gahsh] m. excess baggage
nadbałtycki [nahd-bahw-**tits**-kee] adj.m. on the Baltic; Baltic (States)
nadbić [**nahd**-beećh] v. chip (a

plate, etc.); bruise (fruit, etc.); crack (eggs, etc.); nail additionally
nadbiec [**nahd**-byets] v. come running up; hasten up; run up; approach; come near
nadbieg [**nahd**-byeg] m. overdrive; gear advantage in (car) gearbox
nadbiegać [nahd-**bye**-gahćh] v. run up; come running; hasten up; come near; approach; be heard (*repeatedly*)
nadbiegnąć [nahd-**byeg**-nownćh] v. run up; come running; hasten up; come near; approach; be heard
nadbierać [nahd-**bye**-rahćh] v. take a little; broach; overdraw; take too much (*repeatedly*)
nadbijać [nahd-**bee**-yahćh] v. chip (a plate, etc.); bruise (fruit, etc.); crack (eggs, etc.); nail (on top of, additionally, etc.); see: **nadbić** (*repeatedly*)
nadbitka [nahd-**beet**-kah] f. offprint; extra printed (sheet, etc.)
nadbłotny [nahd-**bwot**-ni] adj.m. marshland (fowl, etc.)
nadboran [nahd-**bo**-rahn] m. perborate
nadbrodnik [nahd-**brod**-ńeek] m. plant of the family Orchidaceae
nadbrzeże [nahd-**bzhe**-zhe] n. shore; coast; littoral; riverside; lakeside; see: **nabrzeże**
nadbrzeżny [nahd-**bzhezh**-ni] adj.m. coastal; seashore (homes, etc.); waterside (village, etc.); riverside (location, etc.); riparian
miasto nadbrzeżne [**myahs**-to nahd-**bzhezh**-ne] exp.: riverside town; seaside town
nadbrzusze [nahd-**bzhoo**-she] n. epigastrium
nadbudowa [nahd-boo-**do**-vah] f. superstructure; added floor
nadbudować [nahd-boo-**do**-vahćh] v. build on; add an upper floor
nadbudowywać [nahd-boo-do-**vi**-vahćh] v. build on; add an upper floor (*repeatedly*)
nadbudówka [nahd-boo-**doof**-kah] f. additional story; added story; superstructure; quarter-deck
nadbudżetowy [nahd-boo-dzhe-**to**-vi] adj.m. not provided for in the budget
nadburcie [nahd-**boor**-ćhe] n. (boat-deck) rail
nadburmistrz [nahd-**boor**-meestsh] m. senior town manager
nadbutwieć [nahd-**boot**-fyećh] v. rot slightly; be affected by rot
nadchloran [naht-**khlo**-rahn] m. perchlorate
nadchodzący [naht-kho-**dzown**-tsi] adj.m. oncoming; approaching; at hand; forthcoming; imminent
nadchodzenie [naht-kho-**dze**-ńe] n. the approach; approach
nadchodzić [naht-**kho**-dźheećh] v. walk up; approach; arrive; come near (to); be forthcoming; be imminent; come on; be near; be nearing; close in; draw near; draw nearer; draw closer (to); be coming; be setting in (*repeatedly*)
nadchodzi zima [naht-**kho**-dźhee **źhee**-mah] exp.: winter is drawing on
nadszedł pociąg [**naht**-shedw **po**-ćhowng] exp.: the train is in
nadchrapnik [naht-**khrahp**-ńeek] m. noseband (of a horse)
nadciąć [**naht**-ćhownćh] v. make a slight cut (in); make a slight incision (in); notch; scotch; nick; score
nadciągać [naht-**ćhown**-gahćh] v. draw near; be nearing; be imminent; be setting in; come; be coming; approach (*repeatedly*)
nadciągający [naht-ćhown-gah-**yown**-tsi] adj.m. oncoming; approaching; drawing near; imminent
nadciąganie [naht-ćhown-**gah**-ńe] n. the approach; oncoming; being imminent
nadciągnąć [naht-**ćhowng**-nownćh] v. set in; arrive; come; be coming; approach
nadciągnięcie [naht-ćhowng-**ńan**-ćhe] n. the arrival; arrival
nadciekłość [naht-**ćhek**-wośhćh] f. superfluidity
nadcięcie [naht-**ćhan**-ćhe] n. incision; cut; notch; scotch; nick; score

nadcinać [naht-ćhee-nahćh] v. make a slight cut (in); make a slight incision (in); notch; scotch; nick; score; see: **nadciąć** (*repeatedly*)
nadcinanie [naht-ćhee-nah-ńe] n. cutting partially; making incisions
nadciśnienie [naht-ćheeśh-ńe-ńe] n. hypertension; excess pressure
nadciśnieniowiec [naht-ćheeśh-ńe-ńo-vyets] m. hypertensive (person); person suffering from excessive blood pressure
nadciśnieniowy [naht-ćheeśh-ńe-ńo-vi] adj.m. hypertensive
nadczerpać [naht-cher-pahćh] v. scoop a little of the top surface
nadczerstwieć [naht-cherst-fyećh] v. become slightly stale
nadczłowieczeństwo [naht-chwo-vye-cheń-stfo] n. supermanliness; overmanliness
nadczłowiek [naht-chwo-vyek] m. superman; superhuman man; overman
nadludzie [nahd-loo-dźhe] pl. supermen
nadczułość [naht-choo-wośhćh] f. hypersensitivity; hypersensitiveness; oversensitiveness; sentimentality
nadczuły [naht-choo-wi] adj.m. hypersensitive; oversensitive; sentimental
nadczynność [naht-chin-nośhćh] f. hyperactivity; excessive activity
nadczynność tarczycy [naht-chin-nośhćh tahr-chi-tsi] exp.: hyperthyroidism
nadczynny [naht-chin-ni] adj.m. hyperactive
naddać [nahd-dahćh] v. lengthen; piece out; widen; give more than necessary
naddarcie [nahd-dahr-ćhe] n. slight tear
naddatek [nahd-dah-tek] m. surplus; overmeasure; (theater) encore
odebrać z naddatkiem [o-deb-rahćh z nahd-daht-kem] exp.: to recover with interest; to get back with interest
naddawać [nahd-dah-vahćh] v. lengthen; piece out; widen; give more than necessary (*repeatedly*)
naddruk [nahd-drook] m. excess printing
naddunajski [nahd-doo-nahy-skee] adj.m. Danubian; of the shores of the Danube
naddział [nahd-dźhahw] m. special bequest in a testament
naddziałowy [nahd-dźhah-wo-vi] adj.m. of a special bequest in a testament
naddzierać [nahd-dźhe-rahćh] v. make a slight tear; tear a part off; see: **nadedrzeć** (*repeatedly*)
naddziobać [nahd-dźho-bahćh] v. peck at; peck a little
naddźwiękowiec [nahd-dźhvyan-ko-vyets] m. supersonic aircraft
naddźwiękowy [nahd-dźhvyan-ko-vi] adj.m. supersonic
nade [nah-de] prep. see: **nad**
nade mną [nah-de mnown] exp.: above me; over me
nade dniem [nah-de dńem] exp.: at daybreak
nade wszystko [nah-de fshist-ko] exp.: above everything else; above all
nade- [nah-de] prefix: over-; above
nadebrać [nah-de-brahćh] v. take a little; broach; overdraw; take too much; see: **nadbierać**
nadecznik [nah-dech-ńeek] m. spongillid; siliceous freshwater sponge
nadedrzeć [nah-de-dzhećh] v. make a slight tear; tear a part off
nadejście [nah-dey-śhćhe] n. coming; arrival; oncoming
nadejść [nah-deyśhćh] v. set in; approach; arrive; come; be forthcoming; be imminent; come on; be near; be nearing; close in; draw near; draw closer (to); be coming; be setting in; see: **nadchodzić**
nadenerwować [nah-de-ner-vo-vahćh] v. make (somebody) very nervous; vex very much; irritate beyond measure
nadenerwować się [nah-de-ner-vo-vahćh śhan] v. fret a lot; be exasperated; become very nervous; be vexed very much;

become irritated beyond measure; be annoyed by petty provocation
nadeń [**nah**-deń] exp.: above him; better than him
nadepnąć [nah-**dep**-nownćh] v. step on; tread on (crushing); see: **nadeptać**
nadepnąć komuś na odcisk [nah-**dep**-nownćh **ko**-moośh nah **ot**-ćheesk] exp.: to tread on somebody's corns
nadepnięcie [nah-dep-ńan-ćhe] n. stepping on (somebody's foot, etc.)
nadeptać [nah-**dep**-tahćh] v. tread on; step on; crush under foot
nadeptać się [nah-**dep**-tahćh śhan] v. get tired from walking (after errands, etc.]
nadeptany [nah-dep-**tah**-ni] adj.m. crushed under foot
nadeptywać [nah-dep-**ti**-vahćh] v. tread on; step on; crush under foot (*repeatedly*)
nadeptywać komuś na pięty [nah-dep-**ti**-vahćh **ko**-moośh nah **pyan**-ti] exp.: to be at somebody's heels
nader [**nah**-der] adv. greatly; excessively; highly; most (tasteful, etc.); exceedingly; extremely
naderwać [nah-**der**-vahćh] v. tear partly; tear off a part; strain (a muscle, etc.); overstrain
naderwać się [nah-**der**-vahćh śhan] v. overstrain
naderwanie [nah-der-**vah**-ńe] n. overstrain
naderwany [nah-der-**vah**-ni] adj.m. partially torn
naderwane ścięgno [nah-der-**vah**-ne **śhćhang**-no] exp.: torn tendon
naderznąć [nah-**dezh**-nownćh] v. cut a piece off; cut a fragment off; make a slight cut in
naderżnąć [nah-**der**-zhnownćh] v. cut a piece off; cut a fragment off; make a slight cut in
nadesłać [nah-**de**-swahćh] v. send in; forward; remit (a sum, etc.)
nadetatowo [nahd-e-tah-**to**-vo] adv. as a supernumerary employee; not permanently
nadetatowy [nahd-e-tah-**to**-vi] adj.m. supernumerary; not permanent; not on a permanent basis
nade wszystko [**nah**-de **fshist**-ko] exp.: adv. above all; above everything else
nadeżreć [nah-**de**-zhrećh] v. damage with corrosion; damage partly; devour partly
nadętość [nah-**dan**-tośhćh] f. uppishness; conceitedness; pompousness; pomposity; bombast; stiltedness; artificial formality
nadęty [nah-**dan**-ti] adj.m. puffed up; inflated; (acting) superior; sulky; sullen; pompous; stilted; bombastic
nadfiolet [naht-**fyo**-let] m. ultraviolet rays
nadfioletowy [naht-fyo-le-**to**-vi] adj.m. ultra-violet; see: **nadfiołkowy**
nadfiołkowy [naht-fyow-**ko**-vi] adj.m. ultraviolet
nadforteca [naht-for-**te**-tsah] f. superfortress
nadfrunąć [naht-**froo**-nownćh] v. come flying
nadfruwać [naht-**froo**-vahćh] v. come flying (like a bird) (*repeatedly*)
nadganiać [nahd-**gah**-ńahćh] v. catch up (with) (*repeatedly*)
nadgarstek [nahd-**gahrs**-tek] m. wrist; carpus
nadgarstkowy [nahd-gahrst-**ko**-vi] adj.m. of wrist; carpal
staw nadgarstkowy [stahf nahd-gahrst-**ko**-vi] exp.: wrist-joint
nadgarstnik [nahd-**gahrst**-ńeek] m. wristband; wrist brace
nadgnić [**nahd**-gńeećh] v. rot slightly; rot partly; be somewhat affected by rot
nadgniły [nahd-**gńee**-wi] adj.m. slightly affected with rot; somewhat affected with putrefaction
nadgniwać [nahd-**gńee**-vahćh] v. rot slightly; rot partly; be somewhat affected by rot; see: **nadgnić** (*repeatedly*)

nadgodzina [nahd-go-**dźhee**-nah] f. hour of extra work
nadgodzinowy [nahd-go-dźhee-**no**-vi] adj.m. of overtime
nadgodziny [nahd-go-**dźhee**-ni] pl. overtime
nadgonić [nahd-**go**-ńeećh] v. catch up (with); see: **nadganiać**
nadgorliwiec [nahd-gor-**lee**-vyets] m. overzealous man; meddlesome man; officious man; highhanded man
nadgorliwość [nahd-gor-**lee**-vośhćh] f. overzeal; officiousness
nadgorliwy [nahd-gor-**lee**-vi] adj.m. overzealous; meddlesome; officious; colloq: gung ho
nadgórnik [nahd-**goor**-ńeek] m. senior miner
nadgraniczny [nahd-grah-**ńeech**-ni] adj.m. near-border; frontier (town, etc.)
nadgrobny [nahd-**grob**-ni] adj.m. of a tomb; of a grave (hist.) **kamień nadgrobny** [**kah**-myehń nahd-**grob**-ni] exp.: tombstone
nadgryzać [nahd-**gri**-zahćh] v. gnaw at; damage slightly with corrosion (*repeatedly*)
nadgryziony [nahd-gri-**źho**-ni] adj.m. partially eaten (by corrosion, etc.) **nadgryziony zębem czasu** [nahd-gri-**źho**-ni z<u>an</u>-bem **chah**-soo] exp.: timeworn
nadgryźć [nahd-griśhćh] v. gnaw (at); affect (by corrosion, etc.)
nadinspektor [nad-een-**spek**-tor] m. senior inspector
nadir [nah-deer] m. nadir (opposite to the zenith and directly below the observer)
nadjadać [nahd-**yah**-dahćh] v. bite (into); eat a part (of); see: **nadjeść** (*repeatedly*)
nadjaźń [nahd-yahźhń] f. superego
nadjechać [nahd-**ye**-khahćh] v. drive up; come up; arrive; drive in
nadjeść [**nahd**-yeśhćh] v. bite (into); eat a part (of)
nadjeziorny [nahd-ye-**źhor**-ni] adj.m. lake-side (hotel, reeds, etc.)
nadjeżdżać [nahd-**yezh**-dzhahćh] v. approach (by car, on a horse, etc., but not on foot) (*repeatedly*) see: **nadjechać**
nadkład [**naht**-kwaht] m. cap rock; cap stone
nadkładać [naht-**kwah**-dahćh] v. add in excess of what is necessary (*repeatedly*)
nadkole [naht-**ko**-le] n. plastic lining of fender; fender
nadkomisarz [naht-ko-**mee**-sahsh] m. police superintendent
nadkomplet [naht-**kom**-plet] m. redundance; superfluity; extra (pieces, etc.)
nadkrajać [naht-**krah**-yahćh] v. cut into (*repeatedly*)
nadkrawać [naht-**krah**-vahćh] v. cut into (*repeatedly*)
nadkręcić [naht-**kr**<u>an</u>-ćheećh] v. loosen by turning; give a turn or two
nadkroić [naht-**kro**-eećh] v. cut into
nadkruszyć [naht-**kroo**-shićh] v. damage by crumbling; impair by crumbling
nadkruszyć się [naht-**kroo**-shićh śh<u>an</u>] v. show some damage by crumbling; show signs of deterioration
nadkwasota [naht-kfah-**so**-tah] f. hyperacidity
nadkwaśność [naht-**kfah**śh-nośhćh] f. hyperacidity
nadkwaśny [naht-**kfah**śh-ni] adj.m. hyperacid
nadlać [**nahd**-lahćh] v. pour some liquid off
nadlatywać [nahd-lah-**ti**-vahćh] v. fly in; arrive (drive up) in a hurry (*repeatedly*)
nadlecieć [nahd-**le**-ćhećh] v. fly in; arrive (drive up) in a hurry
nadległy [nahd-**leg**-wi] adj.m. overlaying
nadleśnictwo [nahd-leśh-**ńeets**-tfo] n. forest inspectorate; rangers' command post
nadleśniczówka [nahd-leśh-ńee-**choof**-kah] f. office of forest inspectorate; rangers' command post
nadleśniczy [nahd-leśh-**ńee**-chi] m. chief ranger; forest inspector; head (chief) of rangers

nadlew [**nahd**-lef] m. nob; top; (hydraulic, etc.) head; deadhead; feedhead
nadlewać [nahd-**le**-vahćh] v. pour off (some of the liquid) (*repeatedly*)
nadlewek [nahd-**le**-vek] m. nob; top; (hydraulic, etc.) head; deadhead; feedhead
nadliczbowo [nahd-leedzh-**bo**-vo] adv. additionally
nadliczbowy [nahd-leedzh-**bo**-vi] adj.m. additional; supernumerary
godziny nadliczbowe [go-**dźhee**-ni nahd-leedzh-**bo**-ve] exp.: overtime hours
praca nadliczbowa [**prah**-tsah nahd-leedzh-**bo**-vah] exp.:overtime work
nadliczbówka [nahd-leech-**boof**-kah] f. overtime work
nadlina [nahd-**lee**-nah] f. heavy (towing, etc.) line
nadludzie [nahd-**loo**-dźhe] pl. supermen; superhumans
nadludzki [nahd-**loots**-kee] adj.m. superhuman; divine; unearthly; terrific; enormous
nadludzko [nahd-**loots**-ko] adv. superhumanly; divinely; unearthly; enormously
nadlufka [nahd-**loof**-kah] f. double-barreled gun (with one barrel above the other)
nadłamać [nahd-**wah**-mahćh] v. break off slightly; crack; cause a slight break (in); fracture; break
nadłamanie [nahd-wah-**mah**-ńe] n. incomplete fracture; infraction
nadłamywać [nahd-wah-**mi**-vahćh] v. break off slightly; crack; cause a slight break (in); fracture; break (*repeatedly*)
nadłączny [nahd-**wownch**-ni] adj.m. lying near a meadow; located near the meadow
nadłożyć [nahd-**wo**-zhićh] v. add too much (of distance travelled, etc.); give in excess of what is due
nadłożyć drogi [nahd-**wo**-zhićh **dro**-gee] exp.: to take a roundabout way
nadłożyć milę drogi [nahd-**wo**-zhićh **mee**-lan **dro**-gee] exp.: to go one mile out of one's way
nadłubać [nah-**dwoo**-bahćh] v. hollow out; scoop out
nadłupać [nahd-**woo**-pahćh] v. break off a bit; break off a part; split (partly); crack
nadłupywać [nahd-woo-**pi**-vahćh] v. break off a bit; break off a part; split; crack (*repeatedly*)
nadmanganian [nahd-mahn-**gahń**-yahn] m. permanganate
nadmanganiany [nahd-mahn-gahń-**yah**-ni] pl. permanganates
nadmanganowy [nahd-mahn-gah-**no**-vi] adj.m. permanganic (acid, etc.)
nadmarszczyć [nahd-**mahrsh**-chićh] v. crease somewhat; crumple somewhat
nadmarzać [nahd-**mahr**-zahćh] v. be frostbitten; partly freeze (*repeatedly*)
nadmarznąć [nahd-**mahr**-znownćh] v. be frostbitten; partly freeze
nadmarznięty [nahd-mahr-**zńan**-ti] adj.m. frostbitten; partly frozen
nadmetraż [nahd-**me**-trahsh] m. excess of space in living quarters (above allowable, above rationing, etc.)
nadmiar [**nahd**-myahr] m. excess; surplus; glut; overabundance; surfeit; redundance
w nadmiarze [v nahd-**myah**-zhe] exp.: in excess; to excess; enough and to spare
nad miarę [nahd **myah**-ran] exp.: in excess; beyond measure
nadmiarowość [nahd-myah-**ro**-vośhćh] f. presbyopia
nadmiarowo [nahd-myah-**ro**-vo] adv. redundantly
nadmiarowy [nahd-myah-**ro**-vi] adj.m. redundant; presbyopic
nadmieniać [nahd-**mye**-ńahćh] v. mention; add; hint; allude; see: **nadmienić** (*repeatedly*)
nadmienianie [nahd-mye-**ńah**-ńe] n. mentioning; (a) mention
nadmienić [nahd-**mye**-ńeećh] v. mention; add; hint; allude
nadmienienie [nahd-mye-**ńe**-ńe] n. mention
nadmiernie [nahd-**myer**-ńe] adv. in

excess; to excess; excessively; overmuch; inordinately; unduly
nadmierność [nahd-**myer**-nośhćh] f. excess; superfluity; surfeit; redundance
nadmierny [nahd-**myer**-ni] adj.m. excessive; inordinate; undue; unconscionable; unreasonable; exorbitant; immoderate; extravagant
nadmorski [nahd-**mor**-skee] adj.m. seaside (resort); maritime
nadmuch [**nah**-dmookh] m. blow of air (into fire, etc.)
nadmuchać [nah-**dmoo**-khahćh] v. inflate; blow up with air; blow air into
nadmuchiwać [nah-dmoo-**khee**-vahćh] v. inflate; blow up with air; blow air into (*repeatedly*)
nadmuchiwanie [nah-dmoo-khee-**vah**-ńe] n. inflation (with air, etc.)
nadmuchiwany [nah-dmoo-khee-**vah**-ni] adj.m. inflated (with air, etc.)
nadmuchiwany materac [nah-dmoo-khee-**vah**-ni mah-**te**-rahts] exp.: air mattress
nadmurować [nahd-moo-**ro**-vahćh] v. rise (a brick wall)
nadmurowanie [nahd-moo-ro-**vah**-ńe] n. addition to a brick wall
nadmurowywać [nahd-moo-ro-**vi**-vahćh] v. rise (a brick wall) (*repeatedly*)
nadmurszeć [nahd-**moor**-shećh] v. rot partly
nadnaturalnie [nahd-nah-too-**rahl**-ńe] adv. supernaturally
nadnaturalność [nahd-nah-too-**rahl**-nośhćh] f. supernaturalism
nadnaturalny [nahd-nah-too-**rahl**-ni] adj.m. supernatural
nadnerczak [nahd-**ner**-chahk] m. suprarenal metastatic cancer; clear-cell hypernephroma
nadnercze [nahd-**ner**-che] n. suprarenal gland; suprarenal body; adrenal gland
nadnerkowy [nahd-ner-**ko**-vi] adj.m. adrenal; suprarenal
nadniebny [nahd-**ńeb**-ni] adj.m. supernatural; heavenly; firmamental
nadniszczyć [nahd-**ńeesh**-chićh] v. impair; damage slightly
nadobłoczny [nahd-ob-**woch**-ni] adj.m. cloud-kissing; located above clouds
nadobny [nah-**dob**-ni] adj.m. handsome; comely; pretty
płeć nadobna [pwećh nah-**dob**-nah] exp.: the fair sex
nadobojczykowy [nahd-o-boy-chi-**ko**-vi] adj.m. supraclavicular
nadobowiązkowo [nahd-o-bo-vyown-**sko**-vo] adv. optionally
nadobowiązkowy [nahd-o-bo-vyown-**sko**-vi] adj.m. optional; elective; voluntary
na dobre [nah **dob**-re] exp.: for good; for good and all; for keeps
nadobrót [nahd-**ob**-root] m. highest permissible r.p.m. (revolution per minute)
nadobroty [nahd-ob-**ro**-ti] pl. highest permissible number of revolutions per minute
nadocznica [nahd-och-**ńee**-tsah] f. brow antler
nadoczodołowy [nahd-o-cho-do-**wo**-vi] adj.m. supraorbital
na dodatek [nah do-**dah**-tek] exp.: for a good measure; in excess
nadoić [nah-**do**-eećh] v. milk (a pailful, etc.)
nadoić się [nah-**do**-eećh śhan] v. weary with milking; drink one's fill
nadokiennik [nahd-o-**ken**-ńeek] m. drip; label mold; window mold
nadokienny [nahd-o-**ken**-ni] adj.m. window (moldings, etc.)
nadoknie [nahd-**ok**-ńe] n. wall above the window
nadokuczać [nah-do-**koo**-chahćh] v. cause a great deal of annoyance
nadolbrzym [nahd-**ol**-bzhim] m. giant
na domiar [nah **do**-myahr] exp.: in excess
nadopiekuńczość [nahd-o-pye-**kooń**-chośhćh] f. excessive mothering (of a child, etc.)
nadopiekuńczy [nahd-o-pye-**kooń**-chi] adj.m. excessively mothering (father, system, etc.)
nadorganiczny [nahd-or-gah-**ńeech**-ni] adj.m. superorganic
nadoskwierać [nah-dos-**kfye**-rahćh]

v. cause a great deal of annoyance
nadowiadywać się [nah-do-vyah-**di**-vahćh śhan] v. learn all sorts of things; hear all sorts of things
na dół [nah doow] exp.: down; downstairs; downwards
nadpalać [naht-**pah**-lahćh] v. burn in part (*repeatedly*)
nadpalać się [naht-**pah**-lahćh śhan] v. get burned in part; burn oneself somewhat (*repeatedly*)
nadpalić [naht-**pah**-leećh] v. burn in part
nadpalić się [naht-**pah**-leećh śhan] v. have caught fire (but did not burn entirely)
nadpartyjny [naht-pahr-**tiy**-ni] adj.m. above-partisan (point of view, etc.)
nadpełzać [naht-**pew**-zahćh] v. crawl up (*repeatedly*)
nadpełznąć [naht-**pewz**-nownćh] v. crawl up
nadpękać [naht-**pan**-kahćh] v. crack (a little, etc.); have a small crack; begin cracking (*repeatedly*)
nadpęknąć [naht-**pank**-nownćh] v. crack (a little, etc.); have a small crack
nadpęknięcie [naht-pank-**ńan**-ćhe] n. (a) slight crack
nadpić [**naht**-peećh] v. take a sip; start an overfilled drink
nadpijać [naht-**pee**-yahćh] v. take a sip (often, many times, etc.) (*repeatedly*)
nadpiłować [naht-pee-**wo**-vahćh] v. saw (into); start cutting with a saw
nadpiłowywać [naht-pee-wo-**vi**-vahćh] v. saw (into); start cutting with a saw (*repeatedly*)
nadpis [**naht**-pees] m. title; superscription
nadpisać [naht-**pee**-sahćh] v. superinscribe
nadpisywać [naht-pee-**si**-vahćh] v. superinscribe (*repeatedly*)
nadplanowy [naht-plah-**no**-vi] adj.m. in excess of the plan (produced, delivered, sold, etc.)
nadpleśnieć [naht-**pleśh**-ńećh] v. be tainted with mildew
nadpłacać [naht-**pwah**-tsahćh] v. overpay; make an excessive payment (*repeatedly*)
nadpłacić [naht-**pwah**-ćheećh] v. overpay; make an excessive payment
nadpłata [naht-**pwah**-tah] f. excess payment; overpayment
nadpłowieć [naht-**pwo**-vyećh] v. become slightly discolored; bleach slightly
nadpłynąć [naht-**pwi**-nownćh] v. sail in; swim in; arrive (by boat, etc.)
nadpłynięcie [naht-pwi-**ńan**-ćhe] n. arrival (by boat, etc.)
nadpłynność [naht-**pwin**-nośhćh] f. superfluidity
nadpływać [naht-**pwi**-vahćh] v. sail in; swim in; arrive (by boat, etc.) (*repeatedly*)
nadpobudliwość [naht-po-bood-**lee**-vośhćh] f. hyperactivity
nadpobudliwy [naht-po-bood-**lee**-vi] adj.m. hyperactive
nadpodaż [naht-**po**-dahsh] f. oversupply
nad podziw [naht **po**-dźheef] exp.: admirably; wonderfully
nadpowietrzny [naht-po-**vyetsh**-ni] adj.m. of outer space
nadpracować [naht-prah-**tso**-vahćh] v. work ahead of the time
nadprodukcja [naht-pro-**dook**-tsyah] f. excess production; surplus production; overproduction
nadprogram [naht-**pro**-grahm] m. supplement
nadprogramowo [naht-pro-grah-**mo**-vo] adv. additionally; as a supplement
nadprogramowy [naht-pro-grah-**mo**-vi] adj.m. extra; additional; supplementary
praca nadprogramowa [**prah**-tsah naht-pro-grah-**mo**-vah] exp.: extra work
nadprokurator [naht-pro-koo-**rah**-tor] m. Attorney General
nadproże [naht-**pro**-zhe] n. lintel; transom; platband
nadpróchnieć [naht-**prookh**-ńećh] v. be slightly affected with rot
nadpruć [**naht**-proośh] v. unsew a

few stitches (of)
nadpruć się [naht-proo**ćh** **ś**h<u>an</u>] v. become partly unsewn
nadprzewodnictwo [naht-pshe-vod-**ńeets**-tfo] n. superconductivity
nadprzewodnik [naht-pshe-**vod**-ńeek] m. superconductor
nadprzewodnikowy [naht-pshe-vod-ńee-**ko**-vi] adj.m. superconductive
nadprzyrodzoność [naht-pshi-ro-**dzo**-nośhćh] f. supernaturalness; the supernatural
nadprzyrodzony [naht-pshi-ro-**dzo**-ni] adj.m. supernatural; miraculous
nadpsucie [naht-**psoo**-ćhe] n. partial decay; partial deterioration
nadpsuć [**naht**-psooćh] v. impair; cause some decay; cause some damage (to)
nadpsuć się [**naht**-psooćh śh<u>an</u>] v. begin to decay; begin to deteriorate; spoil somewhat; taint somewhat
nadpsuty [naht-**psoo**-ti] adj.m. partly spoiled; impaired; partly tainted
nadrabiać [nahd-**rah**-byahćh] v. catch up with; make up (for lost time, etc.); work ahead of schedule; compensate for (a deficiency); outdo; eke out; piece on; affect (courteousness, etc.); exceed (*repeatedly*)
nadrabiać brak [nahd-**rah**-byahćh brahk] exp.: to make up for the want of; to compensate for
nadrabiać czas [nahd-**rah**-byahćh chahs] exp.: to make up for lost time
nadrabiać miną [nahd-**rah**-byahćh **mee**-n<u>own</u>] exp.: to put on a good face to a bad business
nadrabiać zaległości [nahd-rah-byahćh zah-leg-**wośh**-ćhee] exp.: to make up arrears (of work)
nadrabianie [nahd-rah-**byah**-ńe] n. making up deficiencies
nadradca [nahd-**raht**-tsah] m. senior counsellor
nadrąbać [nahd-**r<u>own</u>**-bahćh] v. chop into (a tree, etc.)
nadrdzewieć [nahd-**rdze**-vyećh] v. get a little rusty
nadrealista [nahd-re-ah-**lees**-tah] m. surrealist
nadrealistycznie [nahd-re-ah-lees-**tich**-ńe] adv. surrealistically
nadrealistyczny [nahd-re-ah-lees-**tich**-ni] adj.m. surrealistic
nadrealizm [nahd-re-**ah**-leezm] m. surrealism
nadreptać się [nah-**drep**-tahćh śh<u>an</u>] v. mince one's steps too long
nadręczyć [nah-**dr<u>an</u>**-chićh] v. cause a great deal of torment (worry, annoyance, etc.)
nadręczyć się [nah-**dr<u>an</u>**-chićh śh<u>an</u>] v. worry more than enough
nadrobić [nahd-**ro**-beećh] v. crumble; catch up with; make up (for lost time, etc.); work ahead of schedule; compensate for (a deficiency); outdo; eke out; piece on; affect (courteousness, etc.); exceed; see: **nadrabiać**
nadrostek [nahd-**ros**-tek] m. epiphysis; bone ossification into pineal body
nadrożny [nah-**drozh**-ni] adj.m. laying on the road; wayside (trees, etc.)
nadrujnować [nahd-rooy-**no**-vahćh] v. cause partial deterioration (of)
nadrujnowany [nahd-rooy-no-**vah**-ni] adj.m. impaired; deteriorating; crumbling
nadruk [**nah**-drook] m. overprint
nadrukować [nah-droo-**ko**-vahćh] v. print; overprint; surprint
nadrukowywać [nah-droo-ko-**vi**-vahćh] v. print; overprint; surprint (*repeatedly*)
nadrwić [**nah**-drveećh] v. deride; scoff
nadrwić się [**nah**-drveećh śh<u>an</u>] v. deride without restraint; scoff at without restraint
nadrywać [nahd-**ri**-vahćh] v. tear partly; tear off a part; strain (a muscle, etc.); overstrain (*repeatedly*)
nadrywanie [nahd-ri-**vah**-ńe] n. strain; partial tear; partial interruption
nadrząd [**nahd**-zh<u>ownt</u>] m. (zoological) superorder
nadrzecze [nahd-**zhe**-che] n. riverside

nadrzeczny [nahd-**zhech**-ni] adj.m. riverside (cottage etc.); riverine (plant, etc.)
nadrzeć [**nah**-dzhećh] v. tear a lot; tear no end; tear out a lot; tear out no end; tear up a lot; tear up no end; wear into shreds
nadrzeć się [**nah**-dzhećh śhan] v. colloq: shout more than enough; shout oneself hoarse
nadrzemać się [nah-**dzhe**-mahćh śhan] v. doze away much of the time
nadrzewny [nah-**dzhev**-ni] adj.m. arboreal
nadrzędnie [nahd-**zhand**-ńe] adv. by superior authority
nadrzędnik [nahd-**zhand**-ńeek] m. (a) primary language, etc.
nadrzędność [nahd-**zhand**-nośhćh] f. superiority; primary status; precedence; superior authority
nadrzędny [nahd-**zhand**-ni] adj.m. superior; primary; precedent
nadrzynać [nahd-**zhi**-nahćh] v. cut a piece off; make a slight cut; see: **naderznąć** (*repeatedly*)
nadrzynanie [nahd-zhi-**nah**-ńe] n. making of a slight cut; making of an incision
nadscenie [naht-**stse**-ńe] n. (theater) fly
nadsiarczan [naht-**śhahr**-chahn] m. persulphate
nadsiębierny [naht-śhan-**byer**-ni] adj.m. overshot (water-mill wheel)
nadsięwłom [naht-**śhan**-vwom] m. climbing (coal) mine work front
nadskakiwacz [naht-skah-**kee**-vahch] m. flunkey; toady; flatterer
nadskakiwać [naht-skah-**kee**-vahćh] v. try to ingratiate oneself; curry favor (with) (*repeatedly*)
nadskakiwanie [naht-skah-kee-**vah**-ńe] n. servility; flunkeyism; obsequiousness
nadskakująco [naht-skah-koo-**yown**-tso] adv. servilely; fawningly; obsequiously
nadskakujący [naht-skah-koo-**yown**-tsi] adj.m. servile; fawning; obsequious
nadskarpie [naht-**skahr**-pye] n. land overlooking a cliff
nadskronie [naht-**skro**-ńe] n. supratemporal bone
nadskubać [naht-**skoo**-bahćh] v. pluck
nadsłuchiwać [naht-swoo-**khee**-vahćh] v. strain to listen; keep one's ears open; strain one's ears (*repeatedly*)
nadsłuchiwanie [naht-swoo-khee-**vah**-ńe] n. keeping one's ears open
nadsłupie [naht-**swoo**-pye] n. architrave
nadspodziewanie [naht-spo-dźhe-**vah**-ńe] adv. unexpectedly; beyond expectation; above all expectations
nadspodziewany [naht-spo-dźhe-**vah**-ni] adj.m. unexpected; unhoped for
nadstawiać [naht-**stah**-vyahćh] v. expose; risk; hold out; cock; prick up; strain (*repeatedly*)
  nadstawiać karku [naht-**stah**-vyahćh **kahr**-koo] exp.: to risk one's neck
  nadstawiać uszu [naht-**stah**-vyahćh **oo**-shoo] exp.: to prick up one's ears
nadstawiać się [naht-**stah**-vyahćh śhan] v. expose oneself to risk; run risks (*repeatedly*)
nadstawianie [naht-stah-**vyah**-ńe] n. holding out; straining (one's ears, etc.)
nadstawić [naht-**stah**-veećh] v. expose; risk; hold out; cock; prick up; strain
nadstawić się [naht-**stah**-veećh śhan] v. expose oneself; take a risk
nadstawka [naht-**stahf**-kah] f. level riser (in a hive, etc.)
  nadstawka ula [naht-**stahf**-kah **oo**-lah] exp.: superhive
nadsterowność [naht-ste-**rov**-nośhćh] f. oversteering (steering defect in a car)
nadstępka [naht-**stanp**-kah] f. keelson
nadstop [**naht**-stop] m. super-alloy
nadsyłać [naht-**si**-wahćh] v. send; forward (*repeatedly*)
nadsyłanie [naht-si-**wah**-ńe] n.

sending; forwarding

nadsypać [naht-**si**-pahćh] v. discharge (dry material, sand, etc.); overheap

nadsypywać [naht-si-**pi**-vahćh] v. discharge (dry material, sand, etc.); overheap (*repeatedly*)

nadszargać [naht-**shahr**-gahćh] v. dirty

nadszargany [naht-shahr-**gah**-ni] adj.m. somewhat bedraggled; somewhat dirty

nadszarpać [naht-**shahr**-pahćh] v. impair (health, etc.); reduce (wealth, etc.)

nadszarpnąć [naht-**shahrp**-nownćh] v. impair (health, etc.); reduce (wealth, etc.)

nadszarpywać [naht-shahr-**pi**-vahćh] v. impair (health, etc.); reduce (wealth, etc.) (*repeatedly*) (imperfect form of:) **nadszarpać** and **nadszarpnąć**

nadszczerbić [naht-**shcher**-beećh] v. nick (a knife, etc.); chip (crockery, etc.)

nadsztukować [naht-shtoo-**ko**-vahćh] v. lengthen; piece out; piece down

nadsztukowywać [naht-shtoo-ko-**vi**-vahćh] v. lengthen; piece out; piece down (*repeatedly*)

nadsztygar [naht-**shti**-gahr] m. mining engineer in charge of a mine (or mine section)

nadszybie [naht-**shi**-bye] n. drilling tower; pithead; shaft top

nadślemię [naht-**śhle**-myan] n. upper window in a two-window group

nadśródziemnomorski [naht-śhrood-źhem-no-**mor**-skee] adj.m. Mediterranean

nadświetle [naht-**śhfye**-tle] n. transom window

nadtaczać [naht-**tah**-chahćh] v. tap; draw (beer, etc.); start boring (into wood, etc.) (*repeatedly*)

nadtapiać [naht-**tah**-pyahćh] v. cause to begin to melt; cause to start melting (*repeatedly*)

nadtapiać się [naht-**tah**-pyahćh śhan] v. begin to melt; start melting (*repeatedly*)

nadtarczyczność [naht-tahr-**chich**-nośhćh] f. hyperthyroidism

nadtlenek [naht-**tle**-nek] m. peroxide

nadtlenki [naht-**tlen**-kee] pl. peroxides

nadtlenowy [naht-tle-**no**-vi] adj.m. peroxidic

nadtłuc [**naht**-twoots] v. notch; indent; crack (partly)

nadtłuczenie [naht-twoo-**che**-ńe] n. a chip; a notch; an indentation

nadtłukiwać [naht-twoo-**kee**-vahćh] v. notch; indent; crack (*repeatedly*)

nadto [**naht**-to] adv. moreover; furthermore; nor; besides; too; too much; too many

aż nadto [ahsh **naht**-to] exp.: too much; more than enough; amply; enough and to spare

nadtoczyć [naht-**to**-chićh] v. tap; draw (beer, etc.); start boring (into wood, etc.); roll (a barrel, etc.); start machining on a lathe

nadtopić [naht-**to**-peećh] v. cause to begin to melt; cause to start melting

nadtopić się [naht-**to**-peećh śhan] v. begin to melt; start melting

nadtopienie [naht-to-**pye**-ńe] n. partial melting; partial fusion

nadtrawiać [naht-**trah**-vyahćh] v. keep corroding slightly; keep affecting slightly (*repeatedly*)

nadtrawić [naht-**trah**-veećh] v. corrode slightly; affect slightly

nadtytuł [nath-**ti**-toow] m. superscription

nadusić [nah-**doo**-śheećh] v. press; press out; stew (meat, vegetables, etc.)

nadusić się [nah-**doo**-śheećh śhan] v. suffer from pressure (in a crowd, etc.); press oneself; stew for a long time

nadusić się pieniędzy [nah-**doo**-śheećh śhan pye-**ńan**-dzi] exp.: to scrape up some money

nadużycia [nahd-oo-**zhi**-ćhah] pl. corrupt practices

nadużycie [nahd-oo-**zhi**-ćhe] n. abuse; excess; misuse (of a word, etc.)

nadużycie kasowe [nahd-oo-**zhi**-

ćhe kah-**so**-ve] exp.: embezzlement; misappropriation of funds
nadużycie władzy [nahd-oo-**zhi**-ćhe **vwah**-dzi] exp.: abuse of power; use of undue authority
nadużyć [nahd-**oo**-zhićh] v. abuse; take advantage; strain (relations); misuse
nadużywać [nahd-oo-**zhi**-vahćh] v. keep on: abusing, taking advantage, straining (relations), misusing (*repeatedly*)
nadużywać alkoholu [nahd-oo-**zhi**-vahćh ahl-ko-**kho**-loo] exp.: to indulge too freely in alcohol; to drink too much of alcohol
nadużywanie [nahd-oo-zhi-**vah**-ńe] n. abuse; misuse
nadwachta [nahd-**vahkh**-tah] f. next watch (on a ship); next shift
nadwaga [nahd-**vah**-gah] f. overweight; allowance of extra weight (in travel)
nadwartość [nahd-**vahr**-tośhćh] f. overvalue (in economics)
nadważkość [nahd-**vahsh**-kośhćh] f. increase of weight due to acceleration
nadważyć [nahd-**vah**-zhićh] v. give overweight (of merchandise, etc.)
nadwątlać [nahd-**vownt**-lahćh] v. keep on: weakening, impairing, damaging (*repeatedly*)
nadwątlanie [nahd-vownt-**lah**-ńe] n. weakened state (*repeated*)
nadwątleć [nahd-**vownt**-lećh] v. weaken; be damaged; get weakened
nadwątlenie [nahd-vownt-**le**-ńe] n. weakened state
nadwątlić [nahd-**vownt**-leećh] v. weaken; impair; damage
nadwerężać [nahd-ve-**ran**-zhahćh] v. impair; weaken; damage; injure; vitiate; strain; tax (*repeatedly*)
nadwerężać się [nahd-ve-**ran**-zhahćh śhan] v. strain oneself; tax oneself; injure oneself; damage oneself (*repeatedly*)
nadwerężanie [nahd-ve-ran-**zhah**-ńe] n. impairment; strain; tax (on something)
nadwerężenie [nahd-ve-ran-**zhe**-ńe] n. impairment; strain (on)
nadwerężyć [nahd-ve-**ran**-zhićh] v. impair; weaken; damage; injure; vitiate; strain; tax (energies, resources, etc.)
nadwerężyć się [nahd-ve-**ran**-zhićh śhan] v. sprain
nadwichnąć [nahd-**veekh**-nownćh] v. sprain (to some extent)
nadwieczorny [nahd-vye-**chor**-ni] adj.n. of late afternoon
nadwiesić [nahd-**vye**-śheećh] v. overhang
nadwieszać [nahd-**vye**-shahćh] v. overhang (*repeatedly*)
nadwieszenie [nahd-vye-**she**-ńe] n. overhang
nadwiędnąć [nahd-**vyand**-nownćh] v. become slightly: faded, withered, wasted; weakened; grow slightly: faded, withered
nadwiślański [nahd-veeśh-**lahń**-skee] adj.m. on the Vistula
nadwodnik [nahd-**vod**-ńeek] m. a plant of the family Elatinaceae
nadwodnikowaty [nahd-vod-ńee-ko-**vah**-ti] adj.m. elatinaceous
nadwodnikowate [nahd-vod-ńee-ko-**vah**-te] pl. the waterwort family
nadwodny [nahd-**vod**-ni] adj.m. near water; riverside; aquatic
nadwodzie [nahd-**vo**-dźhe] n. above-water body (of a ship)
nadworny [nah-**dvor**-ni] adj.m. court (official, etc.)
nadworny dostawca [nah-**dvor**-ni dos-**tahf**-tsah] exp.: court-purveyor; purveyor by appointment (in ordinary)
nadwozie [nahd-**vo**-źhe] n. car body; body of a car or truck
nadwoziowy [nahd-vo-**źho**-vi] adj.m. (car) body (parts, paint, etc.)
nadwoziownia [nahd-vo-**źhov**-ńah] f. (car) body shop; body assembly department
nadwrażliwie [nahd-vrahzh-**lee**-vye] adv. with oversensitivity; with hypersensitivity; with allergy (to)
nadwrażliwiec [nahd-vrahzh-**lee**-vyets] m. colloq: oversensitive

person; hypersensitive person
nadwrażliwość [nahd-vrahzh-**lee**-vośhćh] f. oversensitivity; hypersensitiveness; allergy (to)
nadwrażliwy [nahd-vrahzh-**lee**-vi] adj.m. oversensitive; hypersensitive; allergic (to)
nad wyraz [nahd **vi**-rahs] exp.: very good; superb; extraordinary
nadwyrężać [nahd-vi-**ran**-zhahćh] v. colloq: impair; strain; weaken (*repeatedly*)
nadwyrężyć [nahd-vi-**ran**-zhićh] v. colloq: impair; strain; weaken
nadwyżka [nahd-**vish**-kah] f. surplus; excess (luggage weight, etc.); excess amount; leftover
nadwyżka kasowa [nahd-**vish**-kah kah-**so**-vah] exp.: cash surplus
stanowić nadwyżkę [stah-**no**-veećh nahd-**vish**-kan] exp.: to be in excess; to be left over
nadwyżkowy [nahd-vish-**ko**-vi] adj.m. surplus (cash); excess
nadwzroczność [nahd-**vzroch**-nośhćh] f. hyperopia; farsightedness
nadwzroczny [nahd-**vzroch**-ni] adj.m. farsighted; hyperopic
nadyktować [nah-dik-**to**-vahćh] v. dictate (a good many letters, etc.)
nadymać [nah-**di**-mahćh] v. puff up; inflate; swell out; fill out; bulge; blow out; pump up; distend; colloq: put on airs (*repeatedly*)
nadymać się [nah-**di**-mahćh śhan] v. swell; puff oneself up (*repeatedly*)
nadymanie [nah-di-**mah**-ńe] n. inflation (with air, etc.)
nadymanie się [nah-di-**mah**-ńe śhan] n. conceit; airs; swagger; sulks
nadymany [nah-di-**mah**-ni] adj.m. inflated (with air, etc.)
nadymić [nah-**di**-meećh] v. fill (a room) with smoke; make a lot of smoke
nadziać [**nah**-dźhahćh] v. stuff; fill (sausages, etc.); stick (on a fork, etc.); fix (on); pierce (with); impale (on a sharp stake, etc.)
nadziać na widelec [nah-dźhahćh nah vee-**de**-lets] exp.: to stick (fix) on a fork
nadziać na rożen [**nah**-dźhahćh nah **ro**-zhen] exp.: to stick (fix) on a larding pin
nadziać się [**nah**-dźhahćh śhan] v. stuff oneself; fill oneself (with); stick oneself; pierce oneself (with); come up (against)
nadział [**nah**-dźhahw] m. apportionment (of land, etc.); portion
nadzianie [nah-**dźhah**-ńe] n. stuffing (into); fixing (on); piercing
nadzianie się [nah-**dźhah**-ńe śhan] n. stuffing oneself; piercing oneself; coming up against
nadziany [nah-**dźhah**-ni] adj.m. stuffed (turkey, etc.); colloq: rich
nadziąślak [nah-**dźhownśh**-lahk] m. gumboil
nadzieja [nah-**dźhe**-yah] f. hope
mieć nadzieję [myećh nah-**dźhe**-yan] exp.: to hope; to have good hope
mam nadzieję, że nie [mahm nah-**dźhe**-yan zhe ńe] exp.: I hope not
mam nadzieję, że tak [mahm nah-**dźhe**-yan zhe tahk] exp.: I hope so
nie tracić nadziei [ńe **trah**-ćheećh nah-**dźhe**-ee] exp.: to hope against hope
pełen nadziei [pe-wen nah-**dźhe**-ee] exp.: hopeful; full of hope (that)
pokładać nadzieje w kimś [po-**kwah**-dahćh nah-**dźhe**-ye f keemśh] exp.: to set (all) one's hope on somebody
pokładać nadzieje w czymś [po-**kwah**-dahćh nah-**dźhe**-ye f chimśh] exp.: to set (all) one's hope on something
przy nadziei [pshi nah-**dźhe**-ee] exp.: in the family way (in pregnancy)
słaba nadzieja [**swah**-bah nah-**dźhe**-yah] exp.: a faint hope; an off chance
nadzielać [nah-**dźhe**-lahćh] v. apportion (*repeatedly*)

nadzielanie [nah-dźhe-**lah**-ńe] n. apportionment (of land, etc.)
nadzielić [nah-**dźhe**-leećh] v. apportion (land, etc.)
nadziemny [nahd-**źhem**-ni] adj.m. above-ground (work, etc.); overland (mail, etc.)
przewody nadziemne [pshe-**vo**-di nahd-**źhem**-ne] exp.: overhead wires
nadziemski [nahd-**źhem**-skee] adj.m. celestial; heavenly; divine; superterrestrial
nadziemsko [nahd-**źhem**-sko] adv. celestially; divinely; superterrestrially
nadzienie [nah-**dźhe**-ńe] n. stuffing (of fowl, etc.); filling; forcemeat
nadziewać [nah-**dźhe**-vahćh] v. stuff; fill (sausages, etc.); stick (on a fork, etc.); fix (on); pierce (with) (*repeatedly*)
nadziewać się [nah-**dźhe**-vahćh śhan] v. stuff oneself; fill oneself (with); stick oneself; pierce oneself (with); come up against (*repeatedly*)
nadziewanie [nah-dźhe-**vah**-ńe] n. stuffing; filling (sausages, etc.); sticking (on a fork, etc.); fixing (on); piercing (with); impaling (on a sharp stake, etc.)
nadziewarka [nah-dźhe-**vahr**-kah] f. sausage making machine; sausage stuffing machine
nadziewka [nah-**dźhef**-kah] f. stuffing (of fowl, etc.); filling; forcemeat
nadziękować się [nah-dźhan-**ko**-vahćh śhan] v. thank a lot; thank many times
nadziurkować [nah-dźhoor-**ko**-vahćh] v. perforate
nadziwić się [nah-**dźhee**-veećh śhan] v. be amazed (at)
nie móc się nadziwić [ńe moots śhan nah-**dźhee**-veećh] exp.: to be amazed; to express surprise (at)
nadzmysłowo [nahd-zmi-**swo**-vo] adv. transcendentally; supernaturally
nadzmysłowość [nahd-zmi-**swo**-vośhćh] f. transcendentalism; supernaturalism
nadzmysłowy [nahd-zmi-**swo**-vi] adj.m. transcendental; supernatural
nadzorca [nahd-**zor**-tsah] m. overseer; superintendent; supervisor (of work, workers, etc.)
nadzorczy [nahd-**zor**-chi] adj.m. of an overseer; of a superintendent; supervisory
rada nadzorcza [**rah**-dah nahd-**zor**-chah] exp.: Board of Directors
nadzorczyni [nahd-zor-**chi**-ńee] f. (woman) overseer; superintendent; supervisor (of work, workers, etc.)
nadzorować [nahd-zo-**ro**-vahćh] v. superintend; supervise; inspect; keep an eye on (somebody, etc.) (*repeatedly*)
nadzorowanie [nahd-zo-ro-**vah**-ńe] n. superintendence; supervision; inspection
nadzorujący [nahd-zo-roo-**yown**-tsi] m. supervisor; overseer; foreman
nadzór [**nahd**-zoor] m. supervision; inspection; superintendence; superintendents
mieć nadzór nad [myećh **nahd**-zoor naht] exp.: to superintend; to supervise; to inspect
nadzór policyjny [**nahd**-zoor po-lee-**tsiy**-ni] exp.: police control; surveillance
sprawować nadzór nad [sprah-**vo**-vahćh **nahd**-zoor naht] exp.: to superintend; to supervise; to inspect
nadzwyczaj [nahd-**zvi**-chahy] adv. unusually; extremely; exceedingly; intensely; immensely; extraordinarily; exceptionally; most (kindly, etc.)
nadzwyczajnie [nahd-zvi-**chahy**-ńe] adv. unusually; extremely; exceedingly; intensely; immensely; extraordinarily; exceptionally; most (kindly, etc.)
nadzwyczajność [nahd-zvi-**chahy**-nośhćh] f. uncommonness; extraordinariness; uncommon occurrence; extraordinary phenomenon

nadzwyczajny [nahd-zvi-**chahy**-ni] adj.m. extraordinary; extreme; exceptional; remarkable; uncommon; unusual; special
profesor nadzwyczajny [pro-**fe**-sor nahd-zvi-**chahy**-ni] exp.: assistant professor
poseł nadzwyczajny [**po**-sew nahd-zvi-**chahy**-ni] exp.: envoy extraordinary
wydanie nadzwyczajne [vi-**dah**-ńe nahd-zvi-**chahy**-ne] exp.: extra edition; special edition; extra-special

nadźwiękawianie [nah-dźhvyan-kah-**vyah**-ńe] n. installation of microphones, speakers, and audio system

nadźwigać [na-**dźhvee**-gahćh] v. carry a lot; carry a great quantity (of)

nadźwigać się [na-**dźhvee**-gahćh śhan] v. get tired of carrying; carry great loads

nadżarcie [nahd-**zhahr**-ćhe] n. (partial) corrosion

nadżelazian [nahd-zhe-**lah**-źhahn] m. ferrate

nadżerać [nahd-**zhe**-rahćh] v. affect with corrosion (*repeatedly*)

nadżeranie [nahd-zhe-**rah**-ńe] n. corrosion; decay

nadżerka [nahd-**zher**-kah] f. erosion

nadżerkowy [nahd-zher-**ko**-vi] adj.m. erosion (changes, conditions, etc.)

naelektryzować [nah-e-lek-tri-**zo**-vahćh] v. electrify

naelektryzować się [nah-e-lek-tri-**zo**-vahćh śhan] v. become electrified

nafabrykować [nah-fahb-ri-**ko**-vahćh] v. fabricate a lot; produce plenty (of junk, shabby articles, etc.)

nafałdować [nah-fahw-**do**-vahćh] v. make many folds; make many pleats (creases)

nafantazjować [nah-fahn-tah-**zyo**-vahćh] v. fantasize a lot; fantasize plenty (of nonsense, etc.)

nafaszerować [nah-fah-she-**ro**-vahćh] v. stuff a lot; stuff plenty

nafciany [nahf-**ćhah**-ni] adj.m. oil (fields, equipment, etc.)

nafciarski [nahf-**ćhahr**-skee] adj.m. oil exploiter's; mineral-oil (industry, drilling equipment, pipeline, etc.)

nafciarstwo [nahf-**ćhahrs**-tfo] n. mineral-oil industry

nafciarz [**nahf**-ćhahsh] m. oil exploiter; workman in the mineral-oil industry

nafosforować [nah-fos-fo-**ro**-vahćh] v. phosphorate

nafosforyzować [nah-fos-fo-ri-**zo**-vahćh] v. phosphorate

nafta [**nahf**-tah] f. petroleum; paraffin oil; lamp-oil; kerosene; mineral oil

naftalen [nahf-**tah**-len] m. naphthalene; naphthaline

naftalenowy [nahf-tah-le-**no**-vi] adj.m. naphthalene (oil, etc.)

naftalina [nahf-tah-**lee**-nah] f. naphthalene (moth repellent)

naftalinowy [nahf-tah-lee-**no**-vi] adj.m. of naphthalene; naphthalene (products)
kulki naftalinowe [**kool**-kee nahf-tah-lee-**no**-ve] exp.: mothballs

nafteny [nahf-**te**-ni] pl. naphthenes

naftociąg [nahf-**to**-ćhowng] m. oil pipeline

naftodajny [nahf-to-**dahy**-ni] adj.m. petroliferous; oil-yielding

naftol [**nahf**-tol] m. naphtol; naphthol

naftonośny [nahf-to-**nośh**-ni] adj.m. petroliferous; oil-yielding

naftopochodny [nahf-to-po-**khod**-ni] adj.m. of crude oil derivatives
naftopochodne [nahf-to-po-**khod**-ne] pl. crude oil derivatives

naftować [nahf-**to**-vahćh] v. paraffin; impregnate with paraffin (*repeatedly*)

naftowanie [nahf-to-**vah**-ńe] n. impregnation with paraffin; spraying with paraffin

naftowiec [nahf-**to**-vyets] m. oil exploiter; workman in the mineral-oil industry

naftownictwo [nahf-tov-**ńeets**-tfo] n. exploration and production of crude oil and gas

naftowy [nahf-**to**-vi] adj.m. oil (industry, worker, etc.); kerosene (lamp, etc.); paraffin (candle)
maszynka naftowa [mah-**shin**-kah nahf-**to**-vah] exp.: oil-cooker; (small) oil-stove
pole naftowe [**po**-le nahf-**to**-ve] exp.: oil field
ropa naftowa [**ro**-pah nahf-**to**-vah] exp.: mineral oil
szyb naftowy [ship nahf-**to**-vi] exp.: oil well; oil drilling rig
zagłębie naftowe [zah-**gwan**-bye nahf-**to**-ve] exp.: oil fields
naftówka [nahf-**toof**-kah] f. paraffin-lamp
nagabnąć [nah-**gahb**-nownćh] v. annoy; accost; trouble; molest; importune (with); solicit; urge; press; tout (for orders, etc.)
nagabnięcie [nah-gahb-**ńan**-ćhe] n. annoyance; urging; molestation
nagabywać [nah-gah-**bi**-vahćh] v. annoy; accost; trouble; molest; importune (with); solicit; urge; press; tout (for) (*repeatedly*)
nagabywać pytaniami [nah-gah-**bi**-vahćh pi-tah-**ńah**-mee] exp.: beset (somebody) with questions
nagabywanie [nah-gah-bi-**vah**-ńe] n. annoyance; accosting; troubling; molesting (with); soliciting; urging; pressing; touting (for)
nagadać [nah-**gah**-dahćh] v. say; tell (with emphasis); backbite; rate; give a piece of mind; give a talking-to
nagadać głupstw [nah-**gah**-dahćh gwoopstf] exp.: to talk a lot of nonsense
nagadać na kogoś [nah-**gah**-dahćh nah **ko**-gośh] exp.: to backbite
nagadać się [nah-**gah**-dahćh śhan] v. talk to one's heart's content; talk at pleasure; talk at will
nagadywać [nah-gah-**di**-vahćh] v. say; tell (emphatically); backbite; rate; give a piece of mind; give a talking-to (*repeatedly*)
nagan [**nah**-gahn] m. type of revolver
nagana [nah-**gah**-nah] f. reprimand; reproof; rebuke; blame; disease caused by the tsetse flies
udzielić nagany [oo-**dźhe**-leećh nah-**gah**-ni] exp.: to reprimand; to reproof; to rebuke
naganiacz [nah-**gah**-ńahch] m. man who solicits (clients, business deals, etc.) for someone else; beater; tout
naganiać [nah-**gah**-ńahćh] v. drive (cattle, workers, etc.); head back (game, etc.) (*repeatedly*)
naganiać do roboty [nah-**gah**-ńahćh do ro-**bo**-ti] exp.: to compel to work
naganiać się [nah-**gah**-ńahćh śhan] v. run a lot; get tired running
naganka [nah-**gahn**-kah] f. campaign (against); dead set (at); battue
nagannie [nah-**gahn**-ńe] adv. in a blameworthy way; deserving censure; reprehensively; reproachfully
naganność [nah-**gahn**-nośhćh] f. blameworthiness
naganny [nah-**gahn**-ni] adj.m. blameworthy; censurable; reprehensive; reproachful; m. bad mark for conduct
nagapić się [nah-**gah**-peećh śhan] v. stare at pleasure; stare at will
nagar [**nah**-gahr] m. carbon deposit
nagarbować [nah-gahr-**bo**-vahćh] v. tan
nagardłować się [nah-gahr-**dwo**-vahćh śhan] v. colloq: clamor a lot; declaim a lot; clamor plenty (for)
nagarnąć [nah-**gahr**-nownćh] v. rake together; sweep together; heap
nagarniacz [nah-**gahr**-ńahch] m. scoop
nagarniać [nah-**gahr**-ńahćh] v. rake together; sweep together; heap (*repeatedly*)
nagarnięcie [nah-gahr-**ńan**-ćhe] n. heap
nagawędzić się [nah-gah-**van**-dźheećh śhan] v. chat at will; chat at pleasure; chat to one's heart's content
nagazować [nah-gah-**zo**-vahćh] v. fill with gas
nagderać [nahg-**de**-rahćh] v.

grumble and grumble
nagderać się [nahg-de-rahćh śhan] v. grumble at will; colloq: grouch and grouch at will
nagi [nah-gee] adj.m. naked; in the buff; bare; nude; bald; empty
do naga [do nah-gah] exp.: to the skin
nagie fakty [nah-ge fahk-ti] exp.: bare facts; crude facts
nagi jak go Pan Bóg stworzył [nah-gee yahk go pahn book stfo-zhiw] exp.: stark naked
nagie fakty [nah-ge fahk-ti] exp.: bare facts; crude facts
nagiąć [nah-gyownćh] v. bend down; submit to; adapt; bow
nagiąć się [nah-gyownćh śhan] v. bend oneself down; submit to; adapt oneself; incline oneself; bow oneself
nagietek [nah-ge-tek] m. marigold; Calendula
nagietka [nah-get-kah] f. marigold; Calendula
nagięcie [nah-gyan-ćhe] n. a bend; bend; inclination
nagimnastykować się [nah-geem-nahs-ti-ko-vahćh śhan] v. exercise a lot; get tired exercising
naginać [nah-gee-nahćh] v. bend down; submit to; adapt; bow (*repeatedly*)
naginać się [nah-gee-nahćh śhan] v. bend; bow; incline; colloq: adopt oneself (to); accommodate oneself (to) (*repeatedly*)
na glanc [nah glahnts] exp.: (to polish something) to high gloss; to high shine
na glans [nah glahns] exp.: to high gloss; to high shine
nagląco [nah-glown-tso] adv. urgently
naglący [nah-glown-tsi] adj.m. urgent; pressing; instant; imperative; imperious
nagle [nahg-le] adv. suddenly; all of a sudden; at once; abruptly; without a moment's warning; hastily; swiftly; precipitately; in a flash
stanąć nagle [stah-nownćh nahg-le] exp.: to stop short
naglenie [nahg-le-ńe] n. urgency; pressure
naglić [nahg-leećh] v. urge; press; hasten (*repeatedly*)
czas nagli [chahs nahg-lee] exp.: time presses
nic nie nagli [ńeets ńe nahg-lee] exp.: there is no haste
naglinować [nah-glee-no-vahćh] v. calorize
nagład [nah-gwaht] m. flatfish of the family Pleuronectidae
nagłaśniać [nah-gwahśh-ńahćh] v. install a quality audio system (*repeatedly*)
nagłaśnianie [nah-gwahśh-ńah-ńe] n. installation of audio system
nagłodować się [nah-gwo-do-vahćh śhan] v. hunger; starve
nagłos [nah-gwos] m. pronunciation: initial sound; anlaut
nagłosowy [nah-gwo-so-vi] adj.m. of initial sound; of anlaut
nagłość [nahg-wośhćh] f. urgency; suddenness; instancy; abruptness; immediacy
nagłość potrzeby [nahg-wośhćh po-tshe-bi] exp.: urgency of a need
nagłośnia [nah-gwośh-ńah] f. epiglottis
nagłośniać [nah-gwośh-ńahćh] v. install a quality audio system (*repeatedly*)
nagłośnić [nah-gwośh-ńeećh] v. install a quality audio system
nagłośnienie [nah-gwośh-ńe-ńe] n. quality audio system
nagłośnieniowy [nah-gwośh-ńe-ńo-vi] adj.m. of an audio system
nagłośniowy [nah-gwośh-ńo-vi] adj.m. epiglottal
nagłowić się [nah-gwo-veećh śhan] v. puzzle a good bit (over); beat one's brains out
nagłowny [nah-gwov-ni] adj.m. (miner's) head (lamp); (worn) on the head
nagłówek [nah-gwoo-vek] m. heading; caption; title; headline; (horse's) headstall
nagłówek listu [nah-gwoo-vek lees-too] exp.: letterhead
sążniste nagłówki [sownzh-ńees-

te nah-**gwoof**-kee] exp.: big headlines
nagłówkowy [nah-gwoof-**ko**-vi] adj.m. of a heading; of a caption; title (page, etc.); headline (size, etc.)
nagły [**nahg**-wi] adj.m. sudden; urgent; instant; abrupt; pressing; unexpected; immediate; instantaneous
nagła krew go zalała [**nahg**-wah kref go zah-**lah**-wah] exp.: he had a stroke; he went wild; he saw red (vulg.)
w nagłym wypadku [v **nahg**-wim vi-**paht**-koo] exp.: in case of emergency
z nagła [z **nahg**-wah] exp.: adv. suddenly; all of a sudden; all at once; abruptly; unexpectedly
nagminnie [nah-**gmeen**-ńe] adv. commonly; usually; currently; generally
nagminność [nah-**gmeen**-nośhćh] f. common place occurrence; common place manners, etc.
nagminny [nah-**gmeen**-ni] adj.m. universal; usual; current; general; epidemic; enzootic
nagnać [nah-gnahćh] v. drive; beat up (game); head back (cattle, etc.)
nagnajać [nah-**gnah**-yahćh] v. fertilize; manure (land) (*repeatedly*)
nagniatać [nah-**gńah**-tahćh] v. press (in); indent; crush (a quantity of something, etc.) (*repeatedly*)
nagnieciony [nah-gńe-**ćho**-ni] adj.m. partly pressed; crushed to some extent
nagnieść [**nah**-gńeśhćh] v. press (in); indent; crush (a quantity, etc.)
nagnieść się [**nah**-gńeśhćh śh<u>an</u>] v. press a great quantity; get tired of crushing
nagniotek [nah-**gńo**-tek] m. (skin) corn; callus (on the skin)
nagnoić [nah-**gno**-eećh] v. fertilize; manure (land)
nago [**nah**-go] adv. nakedly; with no clothes on; in the nude; crude
do naga [do **nah**-gah] exp.: to the bare skin; with no clothes on; to the skin
rozebrany do naga [ro-ze-**brah**-ni do **nah**-gah] exp.: nude; completely undressed
zupełnie nago [zoo-**pew**-ńe **nah**-go] exp.: stark nakedly
nagodzić [nah-**go**-dźheećh] v. reconcile; hire (workers, etc.)
nagolenica [nah-go-le-**ńee**-tsah] f. shin guard; kneepad; greave
nagolennik [nah-go-**len**-ńeek] m. shin guard; kneepad; greave
nagonasienny [nah-go-nah-**śhen**-ni] adj.m. gymnospermous
nagonasienne [nah-go-nah-**śhen**-ne] pl. the gymnosperms
nagonić [nah-**go**-ńeećh] v. drive; beat up (game); head back (cattle, etc.)
nagonka [nah-**gon**-kah] f. campaign against; hue and cry against; dead set (at)
nagosz [**nah**-gosh] m. a species of moss; Gymnostomum
nagość [**nah**-gośhćh] f. nudity; nakedness; starkness; bareness; baldness; crudity
nagotować [nah-go-**to**-vahćh] v. cook a whole lot; prepare (a lot of food, etc.)
nagotować się [nah-go-**to**-vahćh śh<u>an</u>] v. cook a good many times
nagozalążkowy [nah-go-zah-l<u>own</u>sh-**ko**-vi] adj.m. gymnospermous
nagozalążkowe [nah-go-zah-l<u>own</u>sh-**ko**-ve] pl. the gymnosperms
nagrabić [nah-**grah**-beećh] v. rake up (some hay, etc.); amass by plunder; amass by robbery
nagrabić się [nah-**grah**-beećh śh<u>an</u>] v. have robbed plenty; get tired of raking; get tired of plundering
nagrać [**nah**-grahćh] v. record (a song, etc.); register (on tape, etc.)
nagrać się [**nah**-grahćh śh<u>an</u>] v. play a great deal; play a great many times; be recorded
nagradzać [nah-**grah**-dzahćh] v. reward; give a prize; recompense; indemnify; make up for; requite;

repay (*repeatedly*)
nagradzanie [nah-grah-**dzah**-ńe] n. giving prizes; rewarding
nagranie [nah-**grah**-ńe] n. recording
nagraniowy [nah-grah-**ńo**-vi] adj.m. of a recording; recording (session, studio, etc.)
nagrobek [nah-**gro**-bek] m. tombstone; monument; epitaph
nagrobkarstwo [nah-grop-**kahr**-stfo] n. tombstone making
nagrobkowy [nah-grop-**ko**-vi] adj.m. sepulchral (stone, etc.)
nagrobny [nah-**grob**-ni] adj.m. sepulchral (stone, etc.)
nagroda [nah-**gro**-dah] f. reward; recompense; retribution; requital; prize; award; compensation; indemnity
nagroda pieniężna [nah-**gro**-dah pye-ńanzh-nah] exp.: remuneration; purse; money prize
nagroda pocieszenia [nah-**gro**-dah po-ćhe-**she**-ńah] exp.: consolation prize
przyznać nagrodę [pshiz-nahćh nah-**gro**-dan] exp.: award (somebody) a prize
w nagrodę za coś [v nah-**gro**-dan zah tsośh] exp.: in reward for something; in requital for something
zdobyć nagrodę [**zdo**-bićh nah-**gro**-dan] exp.: to be awarded a prize
nagrodowy [nah-gro-**do**-vi] adj.m. of an award; (object, etc.) to be awarded
nagrodzenie [nah-gro-**dze**-ńe] n. reward; recompense; retribution; requital
nagrodzić [nah-**gro**-dźeećh] v. reward; recompense; indemnify; make up for; requite; repay; reciprocate
nagrodzony [nah-gro-**dzo**-ni] adj.m. prize (bull, stallion, etc.); m. prizewinner
nagromadzać [nah-gro-**mah**-dzahćh] v. accumulate; congregate; amass; heap up (*repeatedly*)
nagromadzać się [nah-gro-**mah**-dzahćh śhan] v. accumulate; congregate; amass; assemble; agglomerate; heap up (*repeatedly*)
nagromadzenie [nah-gro-mah-**dze**-ńe] n. amassment; accumulation; collection; agglomeration; congeries; mass; heap; huddle (of junk, etc.)
nagromadzenie się [nah-gro-mah-**dze**-ńe śhan] n. huddling together
nagromadzić [nah-gro-**mah**-dźheećh] v. accumulate; congregate; amass; heap up
nagromadzić się [nah-gro-**mah**-dźheećh śhan] v. accumulate; congregate; amass; heap up
nagrymasić [nah-gri-**mah**-śheećh] v. be fussy a lot; keep on being fastidious; be very choosy; be fretful a lot
nagrywać [nah-**gri**-vahćh] v. record (song, etc.); register (on a tape, on a disk, etc.) (*repeatedly*)
nagrywać się [nah-**gri**-vahćh śhan] v. play a great deal; play a great many times; be recorded (*repeatedly*)
nagryzać [nah-**gri**-zahćh] v. corrode; bite; gnaw; chew on with the teeth; wear away by persistent nibbling; erode (*repeatedly*)
nagryzmolić [nah-griz-**mo**-leećh] v. scribble; scrawl; make a rough sketch
nagryźć [**nah**-griśhćh] v. corrode; bite; gnaw; chew on with the teeth
nagryźć się [**nah**-griśhćh śhan] v. worry more than enough; worry in great plenty; cause plenty of annoyance; quarrel many a time
nagrzać [nah-gzhahćh] v. warm up; heat up; preheat
nagrzać się [**nah**-gzhahćh śhan] v. get warm; get hot
nagrzanie [nah-**gzhah**-ńe] n. warming up
nagrzbietnik [nah-**gzhbyet**-ńeek] m. back strip of horse's harness
nagrzeszyć [nah-**gzhe**-shićh] v. sin a great deal
nagrzewacz [nah-**gzhe**-vahch] m. warmer; heater; radiator
nagrzewać [nah-**gzhe**-vahćh] v.

warm up; heat up; preheat (*repeatedly*)
nagrzewać się [nah-**gzhe**-vahćh śh<u>an</u>] v. get warm; get hot (*repeatedly*)
nagrzewanie [nah-gzhe-**vah**-ńe] n. warming up
nagrzewanie się [nah-gzhe-**vah**-ńe śh<u>an</u>] n. warming oneself up
nagrzewarka [nah-gzhe-**vahr**-kah] f. electrical spot heater used in metal works
nagrzewnica [nah-gzhev-**ńee**-tsah] f. (secondary) heater
nagrzewnica dmuchu [nah-gzhev-ńee-tsah **dmoo**-khoo] exp.: hot-blast stove
nagubić [nah-**goo**-beećh] v. loose a great deal of; loose a great many; cause ruin of many; cause death of many; bring about ruin; bring about death
nagumować [nah-goo-**mo**-vahćh] v. rubberize; gum
nagus [**nah**-goos] m. naked person
na nagusa [nah nah-**goo**-sah] exp.: with no clothes on; in buff
nagusek [nah-**goo**-sek] m. naked baby; naked doll
nagusieńki [nah-goo-**śheń**-kee] adj.m. stark naked
nagusieńko [nah-goo-**śheń**-ko] adv. without a shred of clothing
nagusy [nah-**goo**-si] pl. naked people
na gwałt [nah gvahwt] exp.: adv. in all haste; at once; instantly; this instant; urgently; helter-skelter
nagwarzyć się [nah-**gvah**-zhićh śh<u>an</u>] v. chat at pleasure; chat at will; chat to one's heart's content
nagwiazdka [nah-**gvyahst**-kah] f. shrub or tree of the family Malpighiaceae
nagwiazdkowaty [nah-gvyahst-ko-**vah**-ti] adj.m. malpighiaceous
nagwiazdkowate [nah-gvyahst-ko-**vah**-te] pl. the family Malpighiaceae
nagwintować [nah-gveen-**to**-vahćh] v. tap a screw; tap a nut; rifle (a gun barrel)
nagwożdżenie [nah-gvozh-**dzhe**-ńe] n. pulled-out nail; picked-up nail
nahaftować [nah-khahf-**to**-vahćh] v. embroider; decorate with embroidery
nahaj [**nah**-khahy] m. whip; lash
nahajka [nah-**khahy**-kah] f. whip; lash
nahałasować [nah-khah-wah-**so**-vahćh] v. make a great deal of noise; make a lot of noise
nahałasować się [nah-khah-wah-**so**-vahćh śh<u>an</u>] v. be as noisy as one pleases; make as much noise as one pleases
naharować się [nah-khah-**ro**-vahćh śh<u>an</u>] v. toil as much as one can stand; sweat a lot; drudge as much as one can stand
nahulać się [nah-**khoo**-lahćh śh<u>an</u>] v. revel a lot; be on a spree a lot; run riot; know no restraints; commit the worst outrages; pillage a lot; indulge oneself
naia [**nah**-yah] f. the genus Naja
naigrawać [nah-ee-**grah**-vahćh] v. mock; scoff; deride; ridicule (*repeatedly*)
naigrawać się [nah-ee-**grah**-vahćh śh<u>an</u>] v. ridicule; deride; taunt; sneer at; scoff at; gibe at; mock; make fun of (*repeatedly*)
naigrawanie [nah-ee-grah-**vah**-ńe] n. ridicule; derision; sneers; gibes; taunts
naigrawanie się [nah-ee-grah-**vah**-ńe śh<u>an</u>] n. ridicule; derision; sneers; gibes; taunts
naigrawnik [nah-ee-**grahv**-ńeek] m. the genus Marcgravia
naigrawnikowaty [nah-ee-grahv-ńee-ko-**vah**-ti] adj.m. marcgraviaceous
naigrawnikowate [nah-ee-grahv-ńee-ko-**vah**-te] pl. the family Marcgraviacae
naindyczony [nah-een-di-**cho**-ni] adj.m. colloq: sullen; with anger on his face
naindyczyć się [nah-een-**di**-chićh śh<u>an</u>] v. look sullen; mope; sulk; show bad humor; show anger; make an unpleasant face
nairytować [nah-ee-ri-**to**-vahćh] v. vex; irritate; annoy
nairytować się [nah-ee-ri-**to**-vahćh śh<u>an</u>] v. be vexed; be irritated;

be annoyed
naiwna [nah-**eev**-nah] f. the first simple part of a beginning actress
naiwniactwo [nah-eev-**ńahts**-tfo] n. slang: simple-mindedness
naiwniaczek [nah-eev-**ńah**-chek] m. slang: little gull; greenhorn; simpleton; poor fool; mug; dupe
naiwniaczka [nah-eev-**ńahch**-kah] f. slang: (woman) little gull; greenhorn; simpleton; poor fool; mug; dupe
naiwniak [nah-**eev**-ńahk] m. slang: simple-minded man; gull; greenhorn; simpleton; poor fool; mug; dupe
naiwnie [nah-**eev**-ńe] adv. naively; artlessly; in an unsophisticated way; simple-heartedly; simple-mindedly; ingenuously; credulously; gullibly
naiwniutki [nah-eev-**ńoot**-kee] adj.m. simple-hearted (nice little person)
naiwność [nah-**eev**-nośhćh] f. naivety; artlessness; simple-heartedness; simple-mindedness; ingenuousness; credulity; gullibility; silly remark; artless opinion
naiwny [nah-**eev**-ni] adj.m. naive; artless; unsophisticated; simple-hearted; simple-minded; ingenuous; credulous; gullible
naj- [nahy] prefix: very-; the best; the most
najada [nah-**yah**-dah] f. naiad
najady [nah-**yah**-di] pl. naiads
najadać się [nah-**yah**-dahćh śhan] v. eat a lot; eat a great quantity; eat one's fill; appease one's hunger; suffer (indignities, etc.); experience (unpleasantness, etc.) (*repeatedly*)
najazd [nah-yahst] m. invasion; incursion; inroad; foray; raid; irruption
dokonać najazdu [do-**ko**-nahćh nah-**yahz**-doo] exp.: to invade (a country, etc.)
najazdowy [nah-yahz-**do**-vi] adj.m. inertial (break of a trailor, etc.); invasive (character, etc.)
nająć [nah-yownćh] v. hire; engage; take on (workers, etc.); rent (a house, etc.); lease (land, etc.)
nająć się [**nah**-yownćh śhan] v. be hired; engage oneself; take a job; take work
nająć się do pracy [**nah**-yownćh śhan do **prah**-tsi] exp.: to be hired; to take work; to take a job; to engage oneself; colloq: to hire out for work
najądrze [nah-**yown**-dzhe] n. epididymis (of the testis)
najbardziej [nahy-**bahr**-dźhey] adv. most; most of all
jak najbardziej [yahk nahy-**bahr**-dźhey] exp.: as much as possible
najbliżej [nahy-**blee**-zhey] adv. nearest (to); next (to)
jak najbliżej [yahk nahy-**blee**-zhey] exp.: as near as possible
najbliższy [nahy-**bleesh**-shi] adj.m. nearest (to); next (to); next (of kin, etc.)
najbliżsi [nahy-**bleesh**-śhee] pl. one's family and closest friends
najbliższy krewny [nahy-**bleesh**-shi **krev**-ni] exp.: next of kin
przy najbliższej sposobności [pshi nahy-**bleesh**-shey spo-sob-**nośh**-ćhee] exp.: as soon as the occasion arises; as soon as the occasion presents itself; as soon as I get a chance; as soon as I have a chance
najczęściej [nahy-**chanśh**-ćhey] adv. most often; generally; predominantly; as often as not; nine times out of ten; mostly; for the most part; most of the time
najdalej [nahy-**dah**-ley] adv. at the longest; at the least; at the latest; at the outmost; at the uttermost; most remotely; outermost; farthest of all; furthest of all; at the farthest
najdalszy [nahy-**dahl**-shi] adj.m. farthest; furthest; utmost; extreme
najdonioślejszy [nahy-do-ńo-**śhley**-shi] adj.m. paramount
najechać [nah-**ye**-khahćh] v. override (a country, etc.); make an incursion into; make an inroad

into; overrun; invade; run into; ram; crowd; run over; crush into; rundown; ram into; knock against; dash against
samochód najechał na drzewo [sah-**mo**-khoot nah-**ye**-khahw nah **dzhe**-vo] exp.: the car has stricken against a tree; a car run into a tree
najechać się [nah-**ye**-khahćh śhan] v. come together in great number; assemble; crowd; come (to a place, etc.)
najedzony [nah-ye-**dzo**-ni] adj.m. full (of food); satiated
najem [nah-yem] m. hire; renting; hiring; leasing; letting
najemca [nah-**yem**-tsah] m. hirer; tenant; lessee
najemnica [nah-yem-**ńee**-tsah] f. charwoman; cleaning woman
najemnictwo [nah-yem-**ńeets**-tfo] n. hiring of manpower; wage-earning
najemniczy [nah-yem-**ńee**-chi] adj.m. mercenary's; hired man's; wage earner's
najemnik [nah-**yem**-ńeek] m. hireling; mercenary; free lance; soldier of fortune; wage earner
najemny [nah-**yem**-ni] adj.m. wage-earning; mercenary; hired (labor, etc.); venal; corrupt
praca najemna [**prah**-tsah nah-**yem**-nah] exp.: hired labor
żołnierz najemny [**zhow**-ńesh nah-**yem**-ni] exp.: mercenary
najeść się [**nah**-yeśhćh śhan] v. eat plenty of; eat a lot
najeść się strachu [nah-yeśhćh śhan **strah**-khoo] exp.: to be in deadly fear
najezdniczy [nah-yezd-**ńee**-chi] adj.m. predatory; invasive; incursive
najezdny [nah-**yezd**-ni] adj.m. passing (scene, etc.); invading (sea, etc.)
najeździć się [nah-**yeźh**-dźheećh śhan] v. travel a good deal; be tired of travelling; ski a great deal; ski a lot; ski at will; skate a lot; skate at will; ride a great deal; ride a lot; ride at will; drive a great deal; drive a lot; drive at will
najeźdźca [nah-**yeśhćh**-tsah] m. invader; assailant; violator
najeźdźczy [nah-**yeśhćh**-chi] adj.m. invasive
najeżać [nah-**ye**-zhahćh] v. bristle up; ruffle (feathers); rise; set on end (*repeatedly*)
najeżać się [nah-**ye**-zhahćh śhan] v. bristle up; get one's back up; stand on end; start bristling; ruffle (it's) feathers; bristle (it's) hair (*repeatedly*)
najeżdżać [nah-**yezh**-dzhahćh] v. invade; run into; attack; ram (*repeatedly*)
najeżony [nah-ye-**zho**-ni] adj.m. bristling (with bayonets, pikes, etc.); bristly; beset (with difficulties, etc.)
najeżyć [nah-**ye**-zhićh] v. bristle up; ruffle (feathers); rise; set on end
najeżyć się [nah-**ye**-zhićh śhan] v. bristle up; get one's back up; stand on end; start bristling; ruffle (it's) feathers; bristle (it's) hair
najęczeć się [nah-**yan**-chećh śhan] v. moan endlessly; groan endlessly; lament endlessly
najęcie [nah-**yan**-ćhe] n. hire; lease; rent; retainer
najęty [nah-**yan**-ti] adj.m. hired
kłamać jak najęty [**kwah**-mahćh yahk nah-**yan**-ti] exp.: colloq: to lie a lot; to lie plenty; to lie madly; to tell a lot of lies
wrzeszczeć jak najęty [**vzhesh**-chećh yahk nah-**yan**-ti] exp.: to scream like one possessed; to scream madly
najgłębszy [nahy-**gwanp**-shi] adj.m. inmost; innermost; deepest
najgorsze [nahy-**gor**-she] n. the worst; the worst of all
najgorsze to to, że ... [nahy-**gor**-she to to zhe] exp.: the worst of it is that ...
najgorszy [nahy-**gor**-shi] adj.m. the worst; the worst of all
w najgorszym wypadku [v nahy-**gor**-shim vi-**paht**-koo] exp.: if it comes to the worst; if the worst

comes to the worst
najgorzej [nahy-**go**-zhey] adv. worst of all; worst possible; worst
najjaśniejszy [nahy-yahśh-**ńey**-shi] adj.m. the brightest; the most luminous; the clearest; the most resplendent; the most serene; the most lucid; the most explicit
Najjaśniejszy Panie [nahy-yahśh-**ńey**-shi **pah**-ńe] exp.: Your Majesty
najlepiej [nahy-**le**-pyey] adv. best; best of all
najlepsze [nahy-**lep**-she] n. the best thing; the very best
wszystkiego najlepszego! [fshist-ke-go nahy-lep-**she**-go] excl.: the best of luck!; many happy returns!
najlepszy [nahy-**lep**-shi] adj.m. best; best of all; best possible; the very best
w najlepszym razie [v nahy-**lep**-shim **rah**-źhe] exp.: at best
najłatwiejszy [nahy-waht-**fyey**-shi] adj.m. the easiest; easiest
najmita [nahy-**mee**-tah] m. colloq: hireling; mercenary; seasonal farm worker
najmitka [nahy-**meet**-kah] f. (female) hireling; seasonal farm worker
najmniej [**nahy**-mńey] adv. least of all; fewest of all; the very least; nothing less than; at the lowest estimate
co najmniej [tso **nahy**-mńey] exp.: at least
jak najmniej [yahk **nahy**-mńey] exp.: at the very least
najmniejszy [nahy-**mńey**-shi] adj.m. least; smallest; least of all; the least
nie ma najmniejszej szansy [ńe mah nahy-**mńey**-shey **shahn**-si] exp.: there isn't the slightest chance; there isn't the ghost of a chance; see **mały**
najmobiorca [nahy-mo-**byor**-tsah] m. tenant; lessee
najmodawca [nahy-mo-**dahf**-tsah] m. lessor
najmować [nahy-mo-vahćh] v. rent; hire; engage; lease (*repeatedly*)
najmować się [nahy-mo-vahćh śhan] v. get hired; take work (*repeatedly*)
najniższy [nahy-**ńeesh**-shi] adj.m. lowest; lowermost; undermost; nethermost; rock-bottom (price, etc.); (see **niski**)
najnowszy [nahy-**nof**-shi] adj.m. the latest; the last (thing, etc.); see: **nowy**
najnowszy fason [nahy-**nof**-shi **fah**-son] exp.: the latest fashion; the latest fad
najnowszy wynalazek [nahy-**nof**-shi vi-nah-**lah**-zek] exp.: the latest thing; the latest fad; the latest notion
najoczywiściej [nahy-o-chi-**veeśh**-ćhey] adv. most clearly; clearly; unmistakably; obviously; evidently; see **oczywiście**
najodleglejszy [nahy-od-leg-**ley**-shi] adj.m. farthest; furthest; farthermost; furthermost
najpewniej [nahy-**pev**-ńey] adv. very likely; very like; as likely as not; like enough
najpierw [**nahy**-pyerf] adv. first of all; in the first place; at first; first and foremost; to begin with; to start with
najpóźniej [nahy-**pooźh**-ńey] adv. latest of all; at the very latest; see **późno**
najprawdopodobniej [nahy-prahv-do-po-**dob**-ńey] adv. most likely; very likely; in all likelihood; see **prawdopodobnie**
najprędzej [nahy-**pran**-dzey] adv. at the earliest; see **prędko**
jak najprędzej [yahk nahy-**pran**-dzey] exp.: as soon as possible
najprzedniejszy [nahy-pshed-**ńey**-shi] adj.m. superfine; of the best quality; see **przedni**
najprzód [**nahy**-pshoot] adv. first of all; in the first place; at first; first and foremost; to begin with; to start with; see: **najpierw**
najrozmaiciej [nahy-roz-mah-**ee**-ćhey] adv. in many different ways; in various ways; in all possible ways
najrozmaitszy [nahy-roz-mah-**eet**-shi] adj.m. of all possible sorts; of all

possible kinds; various; different
najsampierw [nahy-**sahm**-pyerf] adv. colloq: first of all; in the very first place; at first; first and foremost; to begin with; to start with
najskromniej licząc [nahy-**skrom**-ńey lee-chownts] exp.: at the lowest estimate
najskrytszy [nahy-**skrit**-shi] adj.m. inmost; innermost; the most intimate
najspieszniej [nahy-**spyesh**-ńey] adv. in the greatest hurry; with utmost haste
jak najspieszniej [yahk nahy-**spyesh**-ńey] exp.: as quickly as possible
najstarszy [nahy-**stahr**-shi] adj.m. the oldest (brother, son, etc.)
najście [**nahy**-śhćhe] n. intrusion; inroad; invasion; incursion; irruption; encroachment
najść [nahyśhćh] v. intrude (upon); importune (on); thrust oneself (on); invade (into); make an incursion; make an inroad; fill; pervade; saturate; come across
najść się [nahyśhćh śhan] v. invade each other's country; go about from place to place; tramp up and down; get tired of running from place to place
najświeższy [nahy-**śhfyesh**-shi] adj.m. the latest; the freshest; see: **świeży**
najświętszy [nahy-**śhfyant**-shi] adj.m. the holiest; sacred; holy; see: **święty**
Najświętsza Panna [nahy-**śhfyant**-shah **pahn**-nah] exp.: Our Lady
najtajniejszy [nahy-tahy-**ńey**-shi] adj.m. most intimate; most secret; innermost; see **tajny**
najtyczanka [nahy-ti-**chahn**-kah] f. type of britzka (carriage)
najważniejszy [nahy-vahzh-**ńey**-shi] adj.m. main; chief; leading; paramount; prime; most important; see: **ważny**
najwcześniej [nahy-**fcheśh**-ńey] adv. at the earliest; earliest; see: **wcześnie**
najwięcej [nahy-**vyan**-tsey] adv. most of all
bać się najwięcej ... [bahćh śhan nahy-**vyan**-tsey] exp.: to fear worst of all
największy [nahy-**vyan**-kshi] adj.m. biggest; largest; extreme; utmost; maximum; supreme; see: **wielki, duży**
największa część [nahy-**vyan**-kshah chanśhćh] exp.: the best part (of); the largest part (of)
po największej części [po nahy-**vyan**-kshey **chanśh**-ćhee] exp.: for the most part
sprawa największej wagi [**sprah**-vah nahy-**vyank**-shey **vah**-gee] exp.: matter of utmost importance; matter of the greatest importance
najwyraźniej [nahy-vi-**rahźh**-ńey] adv. most clearly; clearly; evidently; see: **wyraźnie**
najwyżej [nahy-**vi**-zhey] adv. highest; at the very most; at the outside; at the outmost
najwyżej odmówi [nahy-**vi**-zhey od-**moo**-vee] exp.: he can only say "no"
najwyższy [nahy-**vish**-shi] adj.m. highest; top; utmost; extreme; uppermost; chief; outstanding; paramount; maximum; superlative (degree); sublime; see: **wysoki**
najwyższy czas [nahy-**vish**-shi chahs] exp.: high time
stopień najwyższy [**sto**-pyeń nahy-**vish**-shi] grammatical exp.: superlative degree
w najwyższym stopniu [v nahy-**vish**-shim **stop**-ńoo] exp.: extremely
z najwyższą uwagą [z nahy-**vish**-shown oo-**vah**-gown] exp.: with rapt attention
najzupełniej [nahy-zoo-**pew**-ńey] adv. most fully; most completely; see: **zupełnie**
najzupełniej nic [nahy-zoo-**pew**-ńey ńeets] exp.: absolutely nothing
nakadzić [nah-kah-**dźheećh**] v. burn a lot of incense; fill with (tobacco) smoke; vulg.: fart a lot; poison the air; fill (a room) with

stench
nakaleczyć [nah-kah-**le**-chićh] v. maim
nakapać [nah-**kah**-pahćh] v. drip (a liquid); let (a liquid) drip
nakarbować [nah-kahr-**bo**-vahćh] v. notch; nick; indent; curl (hair)
nakarcznik [nah-**kahrch**-ńeek] m. neck part of horse's harness
nakarmić [nah-**kahr**-meećh] v. feed (population); give food and drink; appease hunger; fodder (cattle)
nakarmić się [nah-**kahr**-meećh śhan] v. take food; eat one's fill
nakaz [**nah**-kahs] m. order; writ; demand; command; injunction; warrant; rule; dictate
jest nakazem chwili [yest nah-kah-zem **khfee**-lee] exp.: it is imperative (to)
nakazać [nah-**kah**-zahćh] v. order; give orders; demand; command; issue injunction; issue warrant; rule; dictate; enjoin to do; require
nakazanie [nah-kah-**zah**-ńe] n. order; command; injunction
nakazowy [nah-kah-**zo**-vi] adj.m. of the nature of a command
nakazująco [nah-kah-zoo-**yown**-tso] adv. peremptorily; imperatively
nakazujący [nah-kah-zoo-**yown**-tsi] adj.m. peremptory; imperative; compelling; imperious
nakazywać [nah-kah-**zi**-vahćh] v. order; give orders; demand; command; issue injunction; issue warrant; rule; dictate; enjoin to do; require (*repeatedly*)
nakazywanie [nah-kah-zi-**vah**-ńe] n. the giving of orders
nakichać [nah-**kee**-khahćh] v. sneeze; slang: give up (on something, etc.) (mob jargon)
nakichać się [nah-**kee**-khahćh śhan] v. keep sneezing; sneeze and sneeze
nakiełczarka [nah-kew-**chahr**-kah] f. drilling machine for making the center hole in a rod or plate to be machined
nakiełek [nah-**ke**-wek] m. the center hole in a rod or plate to be machined; colloq: center drill
nakierować [nah-ke-**ro**-vahćh] v. direct (to, towards); point at; aim at; level (a firearm) at
nakierowanie [nah-ke-ro-**vah**-ńe] n. direction
nakipieć [nah-**kee**-pyećh] v. boil over (on)
nakiwać [nah-**kee**-vahćh] v. swing to and fro; beck to; give a dressing down; fool; dodge
nakiwać się [nah-**kee**-vahćh śhan] v. swing to and fro a lot; fool a lot; dodge a lot; get tired of dodging
nakląć [**nah**-klownćh] v. curse; swear at
nakląć się [**nah**-klownćh śhan] v. keep on cursing; keep on swearing (at)
naklecić [nah-**kle**-ćheećh] v. botch; jerry-build; concoct
naklecić się [nah-**kle**-ćheećh śhan] v. botch a lot; jerry-build a lot; concoct a lot
nakleić [nah-**kle**-eećh] v. stick on; paste up; mount; post
naklejać [nah-**kle**-yahćh] v. stick; paste; post (posters, etc.); mount (photos, etc.) (*repeatedly*)
naklejanie [nah-kle-**yah**-ńe] n. sticking; pasting; posting (posters, etc.); mounting (photos, etc.)
naklejanka [nah-kle-**yahn**-kah] f. cutout of colored paper used in villages as adornment on a wall
naklejka [nah-**kley**-kah] f. label; sticker
naklepać [nah-**kle**-pahćh] v. hammer; planish (sheet-metal surface); toughen by hammering; beat to a sharp edge; blab; prattle
naklepywać [nah-kle-**pi**-vahćh] v. hammer; planish (metal); toughen by hammering; beat to a sharp edge; blab; prattle (*repeatedly*)
nakluczyć [nah-**kloo**-chićh] v. dodge; weave
nakluczyć się [nah-**kloo**-chićh śhan] v. dodge a lot; weave a lot
nakład [**nah**-kwaht] m. outlay; cost; expenditure (of money, work, energy, time, etc.); circulation (of a paper, etc.); edition; issue; impression

nakładem wydawnictwa... [nah-kwah-dem vi-dahv-ńeets-tfah] exp.: published by the firm of ...; edited by the company of ...
własnym nakładem [vwahs-nim nah-kwah-dem] exp.: author-publisher
nakładacz [nah-**kwah**-dahch] m. layer-on; stoker-in; feeder
nakładaczka [nah-kwah-**dahch**-kah] f. (woman) layer-on; stoker-in; feeder
nakładać [nah-**kwah**-dahćh] v. lay on; put on (garment, etc.); place; set (on); fix (on); spread; smear; impose (taxes, etc.); put on; go (a roundabout way) (*repeatedly*)
nakładać karę [nah-kwah-dahćh kah-ran] exp.: to assess a penalty (on); to inflict a penalty (on somebody)
nakładać na talerz [nah-kwah-dahćh nah tah-lesh] exp.: to give (somebody) a helping of (something); to serve (something) on a plate
nakładać podatek [nah-kwah-dahćh po-dah-tek] exp.: to impose a tax
nakładać rękawiczki [nah-kwah-dahćh ran-kah-veech-kee] exp.: to pull on (one's) gloves
nakładać się [nah-**kwah**-dahćh śhan] v. overlap (*repeatedly*)
nakładanie [nah-kwah-**dah**-ńe] n. placing; putting on; imposing; spreading
nakładanie kary [nah-kwah-dah-ńe kah-ri] exp.: infliction of a punishment
nakładanie podatków [nah-kwah-dah-ńe po-daht-koof] exp.: imposition of taxes
nakładany [nah-kwah-**dah**-ni] adj.m. placed on; sewn on; imposed on
nakładarka [nah-kwah-**dahr**-kah] f. machine for making bast tape
nakładca [nah-**kwaht**-tsah] m. publisher (of printed work)
nakładczy [nah-**kwaht**-chi] adj.m. publishing (firm, etc.)
nakładka [nah-**kwaht**-kah] f. splice; lap
nakładowy [nah-kwah-**do**-vi] adj.m. publishing (firm, etc.)
nakładzenie [nah-kwah-**dze**-ńe] n. fill; a full supply
nakłamać [nah-**kwah**-mahćh] v. lie a lot; tell a lot of lies
nakłaniać [nah-**kwah**-ńahćh] v. persuade; induce; bring to do; get to do; urge; incite to do; incline to do; prevail to do; incline; bend (*repeatedly*)
nakłaniać się [nah-**kwah**-ńahćh śhan] v. bend; incline; stoop; be inclined to do; have an inclination (for) (*repeatedly*)
nakłanianie [nah-kwah-**ńah**-ńe] n. inducement; incitement; persuasion
nakłaść [**nah**-kwahśhćh] v. put on (plenty of ...); pile up a lot (of); fill (with); give (an earful, etc.); slang: beat up (mob jargon)
nakłonić [nah-**kwo**-ńeećh] v. persuade; induce; bring to do; get to do; urge; incite to do; incline to do; prevail to do; incline; bend
nakłonić się [nah-**kwo**-ńeećh śhan] v. bend; incline; stoop; be inclined to do; have an inclination (for)
nakłopotać [nah-kwo-**po**-tahćh] v. cause a great deal of concern; cause a lot of worry
nakłopotać się [nah-kwo-**po**-tahćh śhan] v. cause oneself a great deal of concern; cause oneself a lot of worry
nakłócić się [nah-**kwoo**-ćheećh śhan] v. have endless quarrels; quarrel a lot
nakłucie [nah-**kwoo**-ćhe] n. prick; puncture
nakłuć [**nah**-kwooćh] v. prick; cover with pricks; puncture; tap; fix on a spike; stab; transfix; pierce
nakłuć się [**nah**-kwooćh śhan] v. prick oneself; impale oneself; stab a lot; pierce in plenty
nakłuwacz [nah-**kwoo**-vahch] m. spike-file; pricker; stylus; pick
nakłuwać [nah-**kwoo**-vahćh] v. prick; cover with pricks; puncture; tap; fix on a spike; stab; transfix; pierce (*repeatedly*)

nakłuwać się [nah-**kwoo**-vahćh śh<u>an</u>] v. prick oneself; impale oneself; stab a lot; pierce in plenty (*repeatedly*)
nakłuwanie [nah-kwoo-**vah**-ńe] n. pricking; puncturing
naknocić [nah-**kno**-ćheećh] v. slang: bungle; botch
naknocić co niemiara [nah-**kno**-ćheećh tso ńe-**myah**-rah] exp.: slang: to bungle a lot; to botch no end
nako [**nah**-ko] n. patent leather
nakolanek [nah-ko-**lah**-nek] m. kneecap; kneepad; kneepiece (of armor)
nakolannik [nah-ko-**lahn**-ńeek] m. kneepad; knee-protector
nakołatać się [nah-ko-**wah**-tahćh śh<u>an</u>] v. get tired of begging; get tired of petitioning; roam about a great deal; wander about a great deal
nakombinować się [nah-kom-bee-no-vahćh śh<u>an</u>] v. give a great deal of thought; contrive a lot
nakompromitować [nah-kom-pro-mee-**to**-vahćh] v. compromise (many people)
na koniec [nah **ko**-ńets] exp.: finally; at the (very) end
nakopać [nah-**ko**-pahćh] v. kick; give kicks; dig up; excavate; extract (coal, etc.)
nakopać się [nah-**ko**-pahćh śh<u>an</u>] v. dig a lot; get tired of digging
nakopcić [nah-**kop**-ćheećh] v. puff out clouds of tobacco smoke; dirty with soot
nakopcić się [nah-**kop**-ćheećh śh<u>an</u>] v. smoke a lot; have smoked more than enough
nakosić [nah-**ko**-śheećh] v. mow (grass, hay, etc.)
nakosić się [nah-**ko**-śheećh śh<u>an</u>] v. have enough of mowing; get tired of mowing
nakostniak [nah-**kost**-ńahk] m. ankle pad
nakostnik [nah-**kost**-ńeek] m. ankle pad
nakpić [**nah**-kpeećh] v. scoff a lot (at); gibe in plenty (at); jeer in plenty (at); poke fun a lot (at)
nakpić się [**nah**-kpeećh śh<u>an</u>] v. scoff a lot (at); gibe a lot (at); jeer in plenty (at); poke fun a lot (at)
nakrajać [nah-**krah**-yahćh] v. cut many slices (of ham, bread, etc.)
nakrajany [nah-krah-**yah**-ni] adj.m. sliced
nakrajany chleb [nah-krah-**yah**-ni khlep] exp.: sliced bread; slices of bread
nakrakać [nah-**krah**-kahćh] v. caw; predict all sorts of disasters
nakrapiać [nah-**krah**-pyahćh] v. moisten; sprinkle; spray (*repeatedly*)
nakrapiać się [nah-**krah**-pyahćh śh<u>an</u>] v. spray oneself; sprinkle oneself (*repeatedly*)
nakrapianie [nah-krah-**pyah**-ńe] n. spraying; moistening; sprinkling (*repeated*)
nakrapiany [nah-krah-**pyah**-ni] adj.m. spotted; dappled; freckled
nakraść [**nah**-krahśhćh] v. steal a lot; rob a lot; thieve a lot
nakraść się [**nah**-krahśhćh śh<u>an</u>] v. steal in great plenty; rob a great amount; thieve very much
nakremować [nah-kre-**mo**-vahćh] v. put a cream (on something)
nakremować się [nah-kre-**mo**-vahćh śh<u>an</u>] v. put a cream (on one's face, etc.)
nakres [**nah**-kres] m. graph of radar reading (of ships at sea); plot
nakreślacz [nah-**kreśh**-lahch] m. protractor; plotter; station pointer
nakreślać [nah-**kreśh**-lahćh] v. delineate; sketch; draft; write (*repeatedly*)
nakreślenie [nah-kreśh-**le**-ńe] n. delineation; outline; a sketch; a draft; sketching; drafting; outlining; delineating
nakreślić [nah-**kreśh**-leećh] v. delineate; sketch; draft; write
nakręcać [nah-**kr<u>an</u>**-tsahćh] v. wind up; dial; shoot (movie); turn; direct; set on; cheat; swindle (*repeatedly*)
nakręcać się [nah-**kr<u>an</u>**-tsahćh śh<u>an</u>] v. wind oneself up; set oneself on; bustle about

(*repeatedly*)
nakręcanie [nah-kran-**tsah**-ńe] n. winding on; setting on; dialing on (*repeated*)
nakręcenie [nah-kran-**tse**-ńe] n. winding on; setting on; dialing on
nakręcić [nah-**kran**-ćheećh] v. wind up; dial; shoot (movie); turn; direct; set on; cheat; swindle
nakręcić scenę [nah-**kran**-ćheećh **stse**-nan] exp.: to shoot a scene
nakręcić zegar [nah-**kran**-ćheećh **ze**-gahr] exp.: to wind up a clock
nakręcić się [nah-**kran**-ćheećh śhan] v. wind oneself up; set oneself on; bustle about
nakręcony [nah-kran-**tso**-ni] adj.m. wound up; coiled (on)
jak nakręcony [yahk nah-kran-**tso**-ni] exp.: like an automaton; mechanically; like a robot
nakrętka [nah-**krant**-kah] f. (screw) nut; female screw; jam nut; stopper; screw cap; screw top
nakrętka kołpakowa [nah-**krant**-kah kow-pah-**ko**-vah] exp.: cap-nut
nakrętka motylkowa [nah-**krant**-kah mo-til-**ko**-vah] exp.: butterfly-nut
nakrętka rzymska [nah-**krant**-kah **zhim**-skah] exp.: turnbuckle
nakrętka skrzydełkowa [nah-**krant**-kah skshi-dew-**ko**-vah] exp.: wing nut
nakrochmalić [nah-krokh-**mah**-leećh] v. starch; stiffen
nakrochmalony [nah-krokh-mah-**lo**-ni] adj.m. starchy; stiff
nakroić [nah-**kro**-eećh] v. cut many slices (of ham, bread, etc.)
nakrojenie [nah-kro-**ye**-ńe] n. cut
nakrojony [nah-kro-**yo**-ni] adj.m. sliced
nakropić [nah-**kro**-peećh] v. moisten; sprinkle; spray
nakropić się [nah-**kro**-peećh śhan] v. spray oneself; sprinkle oneself
nakropienie [nah-kro-**pye**-ńe] n. moistening; sprinkling; spraying
nakruszyć [nah-**kroo**-shićh] v. crumb; leave crumbs of bread behind one
nakrycie [nah-**kri**-ćhe] n. cover; overlay; shelter; tableware
nakrycie głowy [nah-**kri**-ćhe **gwo**-vi] exp.: headgear; head-cover; hat
nakryć [**nah**-krićh] v. cover; overspread; overlay; set the table; slang: nab; catch red-handed; disclose (theft, etc.) (mob jargon)
nakryć się [**nah**-krićh śhan] v. cover oneself
nakryć się nogami [**nah**-krićh śhan no-**gah**-mee] exp.: to fall head over heels
nakrywa [nah-**kri**-vah] f. lid; cover; covering
nakrywać [nah-**kri**-vahćh] v. cover; overspread; overlay; set the table; slang: nab; catch red-handed; disclose (theft, etc.) (*repeatedly*)
nakrywać do stołu [nah-**kri**-vahćh do **sto**-woo] exp.: to set the table
nakrywać się [nah-**kri**-vahćh śhan] v. cover oneself (*repeatedly*)
nakrywanie [nah-kri-**vah**-ńe] n. covering; covering up; slang: catching red-handed (mob jargon)
nakrywka [nah-**krif**-kah] f. small lid
nakrywkowy [nah-krif-**ko**-vi] adj.m. covering
nakrzątać się [nah-**kshown**-tahćh śhan] v. bustle about
nakrzemować [nah-kshe-**mo**-vahćh] v. protect metal surface with silicon
nakrzemowywać [nah-kshe-mo-**vi**-vahćh] v. protect metal surface with silicon (*repeatedly*)
nakrzyczeć [nah-**kshi**-chećh] v. shout; bawl; bellow; scold; rate; storm (at)
nakrzyczeć się [nah-**kshi**-chećh śhan] v. shout a lot; get tired of shouting
nakrzywdzić [nah-**kshiv**-dźheećh] v. wrong lots of people
na krzyż [nah kshish] exp.: crosswise; as a crisscross
na kształt [nah kshtahwt] exp.: in form of...; in shape of; a kind of...
naktuz [**nahk**-toos] m. binnacle
na kupę [nah **koo**-pan] exp.: into a pile; into a heap
rzucić na kupę [zhoo-ćheećh

nah **koo**-pan] exp.: to pile up; to pile; to heap
nakupić [nah-**koo**-peećh] v. buy a lot; buy a great quantity
na kupie [nah **koo**-pye] exp.: heaped up; piled up
nakupować [nah-koo-**po**-vahćh] v. buy a lot; buy a great quantity
nakurzyć [nah-**koo**-zhićh] v. raise a lot of dust; puff out clouds of tobacco smoke
nakwasić [nah-**kfah**-śheećh] v. pickle a lot (of cucumbers, etc.)
nakwękać się [nah-**kfan**-kahćh śhan] v. groan and moan unceasingly
nalać [**nah**-lahćh] v. pour in; pour on (liquid only, no sand, etc.); pour into; fill (with); pour (over); spill (over); swell
nalać się [**nah**-lahćh śhan] v. fill; swell
nalamentować się [nah-lah-men-**to**-vahćh śhan] v. lament endlessly; be forever lamenting
nalanie [nah-**lah**-ńe] n. spilled fluid
nalany [nah-**lah**-ni] adj.m. obese; fat; bloated; puffy
nalana twarz [nah-**lah**-nah tfahsh] exp.: suety face; pudding face
nalatać się [nah-**lah**-tahćh śhan] v. fly about a great deal; make many flights; slang: chase around; hunt about; have a lively time; roam about
nalatywać [nah-lah-**ti**-vahćh] v. drift; come by air; throng; flock; come in swarms (*repeatedly*)
naleciałość [nah-le-**ćhah**-wośhćh] f. accretion; borrowing (of foreign words, expressions, habits, etc.)
naleciałość językowa [nah-le-ćhah-wośhćh yan-zi-**ko**-vah] exp.: loan word; borrowing; denizen
nalecieć [nah-**le**-ćhećh] v. drift; come by air; throng; flock; come in swarms; assail; attack from the air
nalegać [nah-**le**-gahćh] v. insist; urge; press (*repeatedly*)
nalegał na mnie, żebym to zrobił [nah-**le**-gahw nah mńe **zhe**-bim to **zro**-beew] exp.: he urged me to do this
nalegająco [nah-le-gah-**yown**-tso] adv. insistently
nalegający [nah-le-gah-**yown**-tsi] adj.m. insistent
naleganie [nah-le-**gah**-ńe] n. insistence; urgent demand
nalepa [nah-**le**-pah] f. old-style bed adjacent to stove
nalepiacz [nah-**le**-pyahch] m. billsticker; billposter
nalepiać [nah-**le**-pyahćh] v. stick on; paste on; mount; glue on (*repeatedly*)
nalepianie [nah-le-**pyah**-ńe] n. pasting on; gluing; sticking on; mounting
nalepić [nah-**le**-peećh] v. stick on; paste on; mount; glue on
nalepić się [nah-**le**-peećh śhan] v. stick a lot; get tired of sticking; paste a lot; stick (on something)
nalepka [nah-**lep**-kah] f. sticker; label
naleśnik [nah-**leśh**-ńeek] m. pancake wrapped around stuffing; flapjack
naleśnikowy [nah-leśh-ńee-**ko**-vi] adj.m. of a pancake
ciasto naleśnikowe [**ćhahs**-to nah-leśh-ńee-**ko**-ve] exp.: batter
na letniaka [nah let-**ńah**-kah] exp.: in summer fashion; in summer (dress, etc.)
nalew [**nah**-lef] m. emulsion; filling
nalewać [nah-**le**-vahćh] v. pour in; pour on (liquid only, no sand, etc.); pour into; fill (with); pour (over); spill (over); swell (*repeatedly*)
nalewać się [nah-le-vahćh śhan] v. fill; swell (*repeatedly*)
nalewanie [nah-le-**vah**-ńe] n. pouring (in, into, over); filling (with); spilling (over)
nalewka [nah-**lef**-kah] f. infusion (of herbs, etc.) steeped in alcohol; tincture
nalewkowaty [nah-lef-ko-**vah**-ti] adj.m. arytenoid
nalewkowy [nah-lef-**ko**-vi] adj.m. arytenoid
na lewo [nah **le**-vo] exp.: to the left; go to the left

naleźć [nah-leśhćh] v. importune; barge (in); flock together; overlap
należałoby [nah-le-zhah-**wo**-bi] exp.: one ought to; one should; one rightfully must; it is proper; it is rightful
należeć [nah-**le**-zhećh] v. belong; rest with; lie with (*repeatedly*)
należeć do czyichś obowiązków [nah-**le**-zhećh do **chi**-eekhśh o-bo-**vy**owns-koof] exp.: to come within somebodies duties
należeć do organizacji [nah-**le**-zhećh do or-gah-ńee-**zah**-tsyee] exp.: to belong to an organization
nie należeć do najgorszych [ńe nah-**le**-zhećh do nahy-**gor**-shikh] exp.: to be none of the worst
zrobić, co do kogoś należy [**zro**-beećh, tso do **ko**-gośh nah-**le**-zhi] exp.: to do one's bit; to do one's part
należeć się [nah-**le**-zhećh śhan] v. be due; be owing; be due to; fall by right to; deserve (*repeatedly*); lie (in bed) at will
ile się należy? [ee-le śhan nah-**le**-zhi] exp.: how much do I owe?
należało mu się [nah-le-**zhah**-wo moo śhan] exp.: he deserved (it)
należenie [nah-le-**zhe**-ńe] n. being a part of
należność [nah-**lezh**-nośhćh] f. dues; ration; charge; fee; amount due; sum due
cała moja należność [**tsah**-wah **mo**-yah nah-**lezh**-nośhćh] exp.: the whole amount due to me
należność nadal nie uregulowana [nah-**lezh**-nośhćh **nah**-dahl ńe oo-re-goo-lo-**vah**-nah] exp.: the arrears still outstanding; unpaid debt
ściągnąć należność [**śhćh**owng-nownćh nah-**lezh**-nośhćh] exp.: to collect a debt; to collect one's dues
należny [nah-**lezh**-ni] adj.m. due; owing; rightful; proper
należy [nah-**le**-zhi] exp.: one ought to; one should; one rightfully must; it is proper; it is rightful
należy być ostrożnym [nah-**le**-zhi bićh os-**trozh**-nim] exp.: one should be careful; one should act with prudence
należy przeprosić [nah-**le**-zhi pshe-**pro**-śheećh] exp.: one must apologize; you are to beg to be excused
nie należy mówić takich rzeczy [ńe nah-**le**-zhi **moo**-veećh **tah**-keekh **zhe**-chi] exp.: you should not say such things
należycie [nah-le-**zhi**-ćhe] adv. properly; duly; suitably; in due form; adequately; appropriately; rightly
należytość [nah-le-**zhi**-tośhćh] f. amount due; dues; charge; fee
należyty [nah-le-**zhi**-ti] adj.m. proper; right; appropriate; suitable; adequate
naliczać [nah-**lee**-chahćh] v. count (up to); compute; reckon (Brit.) (*repeatedly*)
naliczek [nah-**lee**-chek] m. visor
naliczyć [nah-**lee**-chićh] v. count (up to); compute; reckon (Brit.)
naliczyć się [nah-**lee**-chićh śhan] v. count a lot; get tired of counting
nalistny [nah-**leest**-ni] adj.m. epiphytic
nalot [**nah**-lot] m. air raid; (skin) rush; coating; deposit; coat; incursion; blitz
dokonać nalotu [do-**ko**-nahćh nah-**lo**-too] exp.: to air-ride (a town, etc.)
nalutować [nah-loo-**to**-vahćh] v. solder on; solder (many objects)
na luzie [nah **loo**-źhe] exp.: (to be) relaxed; idling; without load
naładować [nah-wah-**do**-vahćh] v. load; charge; cram; freight
naładować się [nah-wah-**do**-vahćh śhan] v. get tired of loading; weary with loading; cram oneself with food
naładowanie [nah-wah-do-**vah**-ńe] n. loading; cramming; charging (a battery, etc.)
naładowywać [nah-wah-do-**vi**-vahćh] v. load; charge; cram; freight (*repeatedly*)
naładowywać się [nah-wah-do-**vi**-vahćh śhan] v. get tired of loading; weary with loading; cram

oneself with food (*repeatedly*)
naładunek [nah-wah-**doo**-nek] m. loading; freightage
nałamać [nah-**wah**-mahćh] v. break a lot (of branches, etc.)
nałamać sobie głowy nad [nah-**wah**-mahćh **so**-bye **gwo**-vi naht] exp.: to puzzle a great deal (over something); to beat one's brains out (over something)
nałamać się [nah-**wah**-mahćh śhan] v. inure oneself; work hard; break a large quantity
nałamywać [nah-wah-**mi**-vahćh] v. break a lot (of branches, etc.); (*repeatedly*)
nałamywać się [nah-wah-**mi**-vahćh śhan] v. inure oneself; work hard; break a large quantity (*repeatedly*)
nałapać [nah-**wah**-pahćh] v. catch a lot (of mice, etc.)
nałapać się [nah-**wah**-pahćh śhan] v. get tired of catching
nałatać [nah-**wah**-tahćh] v. patch a lot (of garments, etc.)
nałazić [nah-**wah**-źheećh] v. importune; barge (in); flock together; overlap (*repeatedly*)
nałazić się [nah-**wah**-źheećh śhan] v. colloq: get tired of walking; loiter at will
nałęcz [**nah**-wanch] m. sash; kerchief
nałgać [**nahw**-gahćh] v. lie a lot
nałogowiec [nah-wo-**go**-vyets] m. addict; chain-smoker; drunkard
nałogowo [nah-wo-**go**-vo] adv. inveterately; habitually
pić nałogowo [peećh nah-wo-**go**-vo] exp.: to be an intemperate drunkard; to suffer from the alcoholic disease
nałogowość [nah-wo-go-vośhćh] f. inveteracy; addiction
nałogowy [nah-wo-**go**-vi] adj.m. addicted; inveterate; habitual
nałogowy pijak [nah-wo-**go**-vi **pee**-yahk] exp.: alcoholic; drunkard
nałoić [nah-**wo**-eećh] v. tallow; grease with tallow; slang: give a beating (mob jargon)
nałokieć [nah-**wo**-kećh] m. elbow-pad; elbow guard
nałokietnik [nah-wo-**ket**-ńeek] m. sleeve protector; elbow-pad
nałowić [nah-**wo**-veećh] v. catch plenty (of fish, etc.)
nałowić się [nah-**wo**-veećh śhan] v. catch at will; catch as much as one could wish
nałożenie [nah-wo-**zhe**-ńe] n. imposition (of taxes, etc.)
nałożnica [nah-wozh-**ńee**-tsah] f. colloq: concubine
nałożnictwo [nah-wozh-**ńeets**-tfo] n. concubinage
nałożyć [nah-**wo**-zhićh] v. lay on; put on (garment, etc.); place; set (on); fix (on); spread; smear; impose (taxes, etc.); go (a roundabout way)
nałożyć się [nah-**wo**-zhićh śhan] v. overlap
nałóg [**nah**-woog] m. addiction; bad habit
popaść w nałóg [**po**-pahśhćh v **nah**-woog] exp.: to drop into a habit; to acquire a habit; to become addicted
pozbyć się nałogu [**poz**-bićh śhan nah-**wo**-goo] exp.: to get rid of an addiction; to free oneself from an addiction; to grow out of a habit
przez nałóg [pshez **nah**-woog] exp.: out of habit; from force of habit
rzucić nałóg [**zhoo**-ćheećh **nah**-woog] exp.: to get rid of an addiction
nałupać [nah-**woo**-pahćh] v. split (wood, logs, etc.)
nałupić [nah-**woo**-peećh] v. plunder; rob
nałuskać [nah-**woos**-kahćh] v. shell (nuts, etc.); husk (maize, etc.); pod (peas, etc.)
nałuszczyć [nah-**woosh**-chićh] v. shell (nuts, etc.); pod (peas, etc.); husk (maize, etc.)
nałykać się [nah-**wi**-kahćh śhan] v. gorge oneself; breathe in (no end of smoke, dust, etc.)
nałykać się kurzu [nah-**wi**-kahćh śhan **koo**-zhoo] exp.: to breathe no end of dust

namacać [nah-**mah**-tsahćh] v. find by feeling; feel (under fingers); spot
namacalnie [nah-mah-**tsahl**-ńe] adv. tangibly; substantially; palpably
namacalność [nah-mah-**tsahl**-nośhćh] f. tangibility; substantiality; palpability
namacalny [nah-mah-**tsahl**-ni] adj.m. tangible; substantial; palpable
namachać się [nah-**mah**-khahćh śhan] v. wave energetically; swing fiercely; shake violently; swing till one is tired; colloq: get tired working (physically)
namaczalnik nah-mah-**chahl**-ńeek] m. vat
namagnesować [nah-mahg-ne-**so**-vahćh] v. magnetize
namagnesować się [nah-mahg-ne-so-vahćh śhan] v. become magnetized
namagnesowanie [nah-mahg-ne-so-**vah**-ńe] n. magnetization
namagnesowywać [nah-mahg-ne-so-**vi**-vahćh] v. magnetize (*repeatedly*)
namagnesowywać się [nah-mahg-ne-so-**vi**-vahćh śhan] v. become magnetized (*repeatedly*)
namakać [nah-**mah**-kahćh] v. soak; became saturated (*repeatedly*)
namakanie [nah-mah-**kah**-ńe] n. soaking; becoming saturated
namalować [nah-mah-**lo**-vahćh] v. paint; picture; depict; describe; represent
na marne [nah **mahr**-ne] exp.: futile; useless; in vain; into waste; see: **marny**
namarnować [nah-mahr-**no**-vahćh] v. waste a lot; spoil a lot
namarszczenie [nah-mahrsh-**che**-ńe] n. pleats; folds
namarszczenie się [nah-mahrsh-**che**-ńe śhan] n. frowning; knitting one's brow
namarszczyć [nah-**mahrsh**-chićh] v. pleat; gather into folds; knit (one's brow)
namarszczyć się [nah-**mahrsh**-chićh śhan] v. frown; knit one's brow
namartwić [nah-**mahrt**-feećh] v. worry; give cause for worry
namartwić się [nah-**mahrt**-feećh śhan] v. fret; worry
namarzać [nah-**mahr**-zahćh] v. be covered with ice (*repeatedly*)
namarzać się [nah-**mahr**-zahćh śhan] v. freeze (*repeatedly*)
namarznąć [nah-**mahr**-znownćh] v. be covered with ice
namarznąć się [nah-**mahr**-znownćh śhan] v. freeze; suffer from cold
namarzyć się [nah-**mah**-zhićh śhan] v. indulge in endless dreams; dream at will
namaszczać [nah-**mahsh**-chahćh] v. anoint; apply holy oil; grease; smear (*repeatedly*)
namaszczać się [nah-**mahsh**-chahćh śhan] v. rub oneself with cream (oil, etc.) (*repeatedly*)
namaszczanie [nah-mahsh-**chah**-ńe] n. rubbing (with oil, etc.); giving a rub
namaszczenie [nah-mahsh-**che**-ńe] n. solemnity; anointing
ostatnie namaszczenie [os-**taht**-ńe nah-mahsh-**che**-ńe] exp.: Extreme Unction; anointing of the sick; last rites
z namaszczeniem [z nah-mahsh-**che**-ńem] exp.: solemnly; with unction
namaszczony [nah-mahsh-**cho**-ni] adj.m. solemn; anointed; grave; unctuous
namaścić [nah-**mahśh**-ćheećh] v. anoint; apply holy oil; grease; smear
namaścić się [nah-**mahśh**-ćheećh śhan] v. put cream on; apply oil to one's skin
namawiać [nah-**mah**-vyahćh] v. persuade; prompt; urge; exhort; instigate; encourage; egg on (to do); talk into doing; get to do (*repeatedly*)
namawiać się [nah-**mah**-vyahćh śhan] v. plot; conspire; prompt each other (*repeatedly*)
namawianie [nah-mah-**vyah**-ńe] n. persuasion; instigation; encouragement; incitement; inducement; egging on (to do); talking (someone) into doing
namaz [nah-mahs] m. Islamic prayer

repeated five times daily
namazać [nah-**mah**-zahćh] v. daub; anoint; scrawl; scribble
namazywać [nah-mah-**zi**-vahćh] v. daub; anoint; scrawl; scribble (*repeatedly*)
namącić [nah-**mown**-ćheećh] v. colloq: cause confusion; disturb the peace
namedytować się [nah-me-di-**to**-vahćh śhan] v. spend much time in meditations
nameczyć [nah-**man**-chićh] v. torment; harass trouble; worry; tire out
nameczyć się [nah-**man**-chićh śhan] v. give oneself a great deal of pain; tire oneself out
namiar [**nah**-myahr] m. bearings; bearing; batch; (furnace, etc.) charge
namiarowy [nah-myah-**ro**-vi] adj.m. batch (measure, container, etc.); charge (weight, etc.)
namiastka [nah-**myahst**-kah] f. substitute; ersatz; stopgap; makeshift
namiatać [nah-**myah**-tahćh] v. drift (into a pile, etc.); sweep; sweep up; sweep together (*repeatedly*)
namiernik [nah-**myer**-ńeek] m. direction finder; pelorus
namierzać [nah-**mye**-zhahćh] v. measure out; take one's bearings (*repeatedly*)
namierzyć [nah-**mye**-zhićh] v. measure out; take one's bearings
namierzyć się [nah-**mye**-zhićh śhan] v. measure many times; get tired measuring
namiestnictwo [nah-myest-**ńeets**-tfo] n. regency; governorship; office of a deputy
namiestniczy [nah-myest-**ńee**-chi] adj.m. vicarious; viceregent's; governor's; deputy's
namiestnik [nah-**myest**-ńeek] m. regent; governor; viceroy; deputy; viceregent
namiestnikowski [nah-myest-ńee-**kof**-skee] adj.m. regent's; governor's; viceroy's; deputy's; viceregent's
namieszać [nah-**mye**-shahćh] v. mix; blend
namieść [nah-myeśhćh] v. drift (into a pile, etc.); sweep; sweep up; sweep together
namiękać [nah-**myan**-kahćh] v. soften (*repeatedly*)
namięknąć [nah-**myank**-nownćh] v. soften
namiętnie [nah-**myant**-ńe] adv. passionately; keenly; ardently; lustfully; vehemently; sensually; fervently; inveterately
namiętnostka [nah-myant-**nost**-kah] f. fleeting passion; infatuation
namiętność [nah-**myant**-nośhćh] f. passion; infatuation; fervor; keenness; inveteracy
namiętny [nah-**myant**-ni] adj.m. passionate; keen; ardent; lusty; vehement; impassioned; lustful; fervent; confirmed
namilczeć się [nah-**meel**-chećh śhan] v. keep silent (for a long time); keep one's mouth shut
namiocik [nah-**myo**-ćheek] m. small tent; small booth
namiot [**nah**-myot] m. tent; booth
rozbić namiot [**roz**-beećh **nah**-myot] exp.: to pitch a tent
pod namiotem [pod nah-**myo**-tem] exp.: under a tent
namiotka [nah-**myot**-kah] f. colloq: kerchief
namiotnik [nah-**myot**-ńeek] m. apple moth; ermine moth; Hyponomeuta
namiotnikowiec [nah-myot-ńee-**ko**-vyets] m. apple moth; ermine moth; Hyponomeuta
namiotnikowce [nah-myot-ńee-**kof**-tse] pl. the family Hyponomeutidae
namiotowisko [nah-myo-to-**vees**-ko] n. camping ground; tent camp
namiotowy [nah-myo-**to**-vi] adj.m. tent (cloth, etc.)
dach namiotowy [dahkh nah-myo-**to**-vi] exp.: pavilion roof; tent roof; polygonal roof
namleć [**nahm**-lećh] v. grind (corn, etc.); jabber; prate
namłócić [nah-**mwoo**-ćheećh] v. thresh (a certain quantity of corn); trounce (the enemy, etc.)
namłócić się [nah-**mwoo**-ćheećh

śhan] v. thresh oneself tired
namnożyć [nah-**mno**-zhićh] v. multiply great quantities; breed a lot
namnożyć się [nah-**mno**-zhićh śhan] v. multiply; proliferate; breed
namoczyć [nah-**mo**-chićh] v. wet; soak; steep; drench
namoczyć się [nah-**mo**-chićh śhan] v. get wet; get soaked; absorb moisture; get drenched; become wet
namok [**nah**-mok] m. a soak; a steep; infusion; tincture
namoknąć [nah-**mok**-nownćh] v. get soaked; become saturated
namoknąć się [nah-**mok**-nownćh śhan] v. get soaked a lot; get wet for a long time
namoknięcie [nah-mok-ńan-ćhe] n. getting soaked; becoming saturated; getting wet
namoknięty [nah-mok-ńan-ti] adj.m. saturated; soaked; thoroughly wet
namolny [nah-**mol**-ni] adj.m. colloq: importunate; persistent in asking or demanding
namordować [nah-mor-**do**-vahćh] v. kill (lots of people, animals, etc.); tire out
namordować się [nah-mor-**do**-vahćh śhan] v. get tired of killing (lots of people, animals, etc.); tire oneself out; weary of killing
namorzyn [nah-**mo**-zhin] m. mangrove
namorzyny [nah-mo-**zhi**-ni] pl. the genus Rhizophora
namorzynowy [nah-mo-zhi-**no**-vi] adj.m. mangrove (swamps, etc.)
namościć [nah-**mośh**-ćheećh] v. pad (seats, etc.); cushion; strew (with hay, straw, etc.)
namotać [nah-**mo**-tahćh] v. wind (on a reel, etc.); reel; spool; intrigue; scheme; plot
namowa [nah-**mo**-vah] f. instigation; suggestion; persuasion; promoting; incitement
za namową [zah nah-**mo**-vown] exp.: on persuasion; at instigation
ulec namowom [**oo**-lets nah-mo-vom] exp.: to yield to persuasion
namozolić się [nah-mo-**zo**-leećh śhan] v. take great pains; give oneself a great deal of trouble; tire oneself out
namówić [nah-**moo**-veećh] v. persuade; prompt; urge; exhort; instigate; encourage; egg on (to do); talk into doing; get to do
namówić się [nah-**moo**-veećh śhan] v. plot; conspire; prompt each other
namówienie [nah-moo-**vye**-ńe] n. incitement; persuasion; instigation
namulać [nah-**moo**-lahćh] v. slime up; silt up; mud up; ooze up; cover with slime; warp; make callous (*repeatedly*)
namulać się [nah-**moo**-lahćh śhan] v. become covered with mud (slime, ooze, silt, etc.) (*repeatedly*)
namulić [nah-**moo**-leećh] v. slime up; silt up; mud up; ooze up; cover with slime; warp; make callous
namulić się [nah-**moo**-leećh śhan] v. become covered with mud (slime, ooze, silt, etc.)
namulisko [nah-moo-**lees**-ko] n. silt; mud; ooze; warp; silt-covered land
namuliskowy [nah-moo-lees-**ko**-vi] adj.m. of silt-covered land
namulisty [nah-moo-**lees**-ti] adj.m. mud-covered land; silt-covered land
namulizna [nah-moo-**leez**-nah] f. silt; mud; ooze; warp; silt-covered land
namulnik [nah-**mool**-ńeek] m. mudweed; Limosella
namuł [**nah**-moow] m. silt; ooze; mud; warp; alluvion
namurnica [nah-moor-**ńee**-tsah] f. crown beam on top of masonry; wall plate; rafter plate
namydlać [nah-**mid**-lahćh] v. soap up; put soap lather on (*repeatedly*)
namydlać się [nah-**mid**-lahćh śhan] v. soap oneself; lather (one's chin, etc.) (*repeatedly*)
namydlić [nah-**mid**-leećh] v. soap

up; put soap lather on (something)
namydlić się [nah-**mid**-leećh śh<u>an</u>] v. soap oneself; lather (one's chin, etc.)
namysł [**nah**-misw] m. reflection; consideration; serious thought
bez namysłu [bez nah-**mis**-woo] exp.: inconsiderately; without thinking
czas do namysłu [chahs do nah-**mis**-woo] exp.: time for reflection
po namyśle [po nah-**miśh**-le] exp.: after due consideration
namyślać się [nah-**mi**-śhlahćh śh<u>an</u>] v. ponder; reflect; think over; make up one's mind (*repeatedly*)
namyślanie się [nah-mi-**śhlah**-ńe śh<u>an</u>] n. reflection; thinking over; making up one's mind
namyśleć się [nah-**miśh**-lećh śh<u>an</u>] v. think a lot; get tired thinking
namyślić się [nah-**mi**-śhleećh śh<u>an</u>] v. ponder; reflect; think over; make up one's mind
namyw [**nah**-mif] m. mud bank formed by stream at the exit of a canyon
nandu [**nahn**-doo] (not declined) m. nandu; rhea; Rhea americana
nanercz [**nah**-nerch] m. Anacardium (tree, bush, fruit)
nanerczowaty [nah-ner-cho-**vah**-ti] adj.m. Anacardiaceous
nanerczowate [nah-ner-cho-**vah**-te] pl. the family Anacardiaceae
na niby [nah **ńee**-bi] exp.: make-believe; pseudo
na nic [nah ńeets] exp.: completely useless; useless; no good; of no use; of no avail; to no purpose; no use; in vain; of no earthly use
na nice [nah **ńee**-tse] exp.: to be turned inside out, wrong side out, topsy-turvy
na niepewne [nah ńe-**pev**-ne] exp.: at a risk; at a venture
naniesienie [nah-ńe-**śhe**-ńe] n. mark (on a map); written (correction, etc.)
nanieść [**nah**-ńeśhćh] v. bring; deposit; lay (quantity of eggs); plot; track (mud); drift; mark (on a map); write in (corrections, etc.)
naniszczyć [nah-**ńeesh**-chićh] v. spoil a lot; ruin a quantity
nanizać [nah-**ńee**-zahćh] v. thread (beads, pearls, etc.)
nankin [**nahn**-keen] m. nankeen (cotton fabric)
nankinowy [nahn-kee-**no**-vi] adj.m. nankeen (trousers, etc.)
nanometr [nah-**no**-metr] m. one billionth of a meter
nanoplankton [nah-no-**plahnk**-ton] m. nannoplankton; nanoplankton
nanos [**nah**-nos] m. silt; mud; ooze; drift (brought by flood, etc.)
nanosekunda [nah-no-se-**koon**-dah] f. nanosecond
nanosić [nah-**no**-śheećh] v. bring; deposit; plot; track (mud); drift; mark (on a map) (*repeatedly*)
nanosić się [nah-**no**-śheećh śh<u>an</u>] v. be weary of carrying; bring (large quantities)
nanoszenie [nah-no-**she**-ńe] n. plotting (on maps, etc.); tracking (of mud, etc.); drifting; depositing
na nowo [nah **no**-vo] exp.: anew
nansuk [**nahn**-sook] m. nainsook (cotton fabric)
nansukowy [nahn-soo-**ko**-vi] adj.m. nainsook (blouse, dress, etc.)
nań [nahń] exp.: (look) at him; at her; at it
naobcinać [nah-op-**ćhee**-nahćh] v. cut off great quantities
naobiecywać [nah-o-bye-**tsi**-vahćh] v. promise a lot; make all sorts of promises
naobierać [nah-o-**bye**-rahćh] v. peel (a lot); pick out (lots of people, etc.); elect many people
naobijać [nah-o-**bee**-yahćh] v. upholster a lot (of chairs, etc.)
naobijać się [nah-o-**bee**-yahćh śh<u>an</u>] v. hit oneself many times; colloq: wonder a lot; loiter a lot
naocznie [nah-**och**-ńe] adv. by eye; visually; clearly; distinctly; in person; personally; with one's own eyes
przekonać się naocznie [pshe-**ko**-nahćh śh<u>an</u> nah-**och**-ńe] exp.: to

see for oneself
naoczny [nah-**och**-ni] adj.m. visual; ocular
naoczny świadek [nah-**och**-ni **śhfyah**-dek] exp.: eyewitness
na odchodne [nah ot-**khod**-ne] exp.: by way of farewell; when parting; when taking one's leave
na odchodnym [nah ot-**khod**-nim] exp.: when parting; when taking one's leave; by way of farewell
na odczepne [nah ot-**chep**-ne] exp.: in order to get rid; in order to shake off
na odczepnego [nah ot-chep-**ne**-go] exp.: see: **na odczepne**
na odjezdne [nah od-**yezd**-ne] exp.: when driving off; when parting; by way of farewell; when riding off
na odjezdnym [nah od-**yezd**-nim] exp.: when parting; when taking one's leave; by way of farewell
naodkładać [nah-ot-**kwah**-dahćh] v. save a lot
naodkładać się [nah-ot-**kwah**-dahćh śhan] v. get tired of putting off; get tired of delaying
na odlew [nah **od**-lef] exp.: with all one's might; with a (return) swing; back-handedly; with the back edge of a saber
na odwrót [nah **od**-vroot] exp.: inversely; the other way round; directly opposite
na ogół [nah **o**-goow] exp.: adv. in general; generally; on the whole; not specifically
na oklep [nah **ok**-lep] exp.: adv. on the bare back of a horse; without a saddle
naokolusieńko [nah-o-ko-loo-**śheń**-ko] adv. round and round
naokoluteńko [nah-o-ko-loo-**teń**-ko] adv. round and round
naokoło [nah-o-**ko**-wo] prep. all around; round; about; on all sides; adv. in a ring; all the way round; on all sides; in all directions; all over a place
naokół [nah-o-koow] see: **naokoło**
naoliwiać [nah-o-lee-vyahćh] v. oil; grease (*repeatedly*)
naoliwić [nah-o-lee-veećh] v. oil; grease; lubricate; make slippery; make smooth; apply oil
naonczas [nah-**on**-chahs] adv. at that time; then; in those days
na opak [nah **o**-pahk] exp.: adv. the wrong way; awry; contrariwise; upside down; wrong side up; counter; against; backwards; perversely
naopowiadać [nah-o-po-**vyah**-dahćh] v. relate without end; tell all sorts of things
naopowiadać się [nah-o-po-**vyah**-dahćh śhan] v. relate as much as one cares; tell all sorts of things; go on endlessly telling (about it)
naorać [nah-**o**-rahćh] v. plow
naorać się [nah-**o**-rahćh śhan] v. be weary with plowing; work very hard; toil
na ostatek [nah o-**stah**-tek] exp.: adv. finally; in the end; at last
na ostatku [nah o-**staht**-koo] exp.: finally; in the end; eventually; at last
naostrzyć [nah-**o**-stshićh] v. sharpen up; become sharp
naoszukiwać [nah-o-shoo-**kee**-vahćh] v. cheat no end; swindle a lot; deceive no end
na oścież [nah **ośh**-ćhesh] exp.: wide open; opened all the way
otwarty na oścież [ot-**fahr**-ti nah **ośh**-ćhesh] exp.: wide open
otworzyć na oścież [ot-**fo**-zhićh nah **ośh**-ćhesh] exp.: to fling wide open
na oślep [nah **ośh**-lep] exp.: adv. blindly; full tilt; headlong; precipitately; at haphazard; at random; blindfold; thoughtlessly
strzelać na oślep [**stshe**-lahćh nah **ośh**-lep] exp.: to shoot wild; to shoot without aiming; to shoot blindly; to shoot without seeing the target
naowocnia [nah-o-**vots**-ńah] f. pericarp
naówczas [nah **oof**-chahs] adv. at that time; then; in those days
napa [**nah**-pah] f. zipper; snap fastner
napaćkać [nah-**pahćh**-kahćh] v. stain; smear; scrawl; daub

napad [**nah**-paht] m. assault; fit; attempt; attack; outburst; invective; outbreak; onset; aggression; inroad; raid; paroxysm; access
dokonać napadu [do-**ko**-nahćh nah-**pah**-doo] exp.: to assault; to hold up; to assail
napad na bank [**nah**-paht nah bahnk] exp.: bank robbery; holdup of a bank
napad rabunkowy [**nah**-paht rah-boon-**ko**-vi] exp.: robbery by assault
napad z bronią w ręku [**nah**-paht z **bro**-ńown v **ran**-koo] exp.: armed robbery
napadać [nah-**pah**-dahćh] v. assail; attack; assault; make inroads; fall upon; raid; rob; turn against; lash at (*repeatedly*)
napadanie [nah-pah-**dah**-ńe] n. aggression
napadowy [nah-pah-**do**-vi] adj.m. paroxysmal
napakować [nah-pah-**ko**-vahćh] v. cram full; pack full; crowd together; crowd into
napakować się [nah-pah-**ko**-vahćh śhan] v. gorge oneself; cram full till one is tired; pack till one is tired; be weary with packing
napakowany [nah-pah-ko-**vah**-ni] adj.m. crammed; packed full
napalać [nah-**pah**-lahćh] v. make a fire (in); burn great quantities (of); fill (a room) with tobacco smoke (*repeatedly*)
napalić [nah-**pah**-leećh] v. make a fire (in); burn great quantities (of); fill (a room) with tobacco smoke
napalić w piecu [nah-**pah**-leećh f **pye**-tsoo] exp.: to make a fire in the stove
napalić się [nah-**pah**-leećh śhan] v. smoke at will; colloq: want badly
napalić się na kupno [nah-**pah**-leećh śhan nah **koop**-no] exp.: to be excited about a purchase; to want to buy (an item) very much
napalm [**nah**-pahlm] m. napalm
napalmowy [nah-pahl-**mo**-vi] adj.m. of napalm
napalony [nah-pah-**lo**-ni] adj.m. colloq: excited (about a woman, a purchase, etc.)
napalowisko [nah-pah-lo-**vees**-ko] n. palofitte (a type of archaeologic artifact)
napar [**nah**-pahr] m. infusion; brew; a beverage brewed
naparować [nah-pah-**ro**-vahćh] v. steam
naparowywać [nah-pah-ro-**vi**-vahćh] v. steam (*repeatedly*)
naparstek [nah-**pahr**-stek] m. thimble; dram; thimblefull
naparstnica [nah-pahrst-**ńee**-tsah] f. foxglove; digitalis
naparstnik [nah-**pahrst**-ńeek] m. archer's glove
napartaczyć [nah-pahr-**tah**-chićh] v. bungle a lot; bungle (various jobs)
napartolić [nah-pahr-**to**-leećh] v. bungle a lot; bungle (various jobs)
naparzać [nah-**pah**-zhahćh] v. infuse; slang: fight; beat up (badly) (mob jargon) (*repeatedly*)
naparzać się [nah-**pah**-zhahćh śhan] v. slang: hit one another (*repeatedly*)
naparzanie [nah-pah-**zhah**-ńe] n. infusion
naparzyć [nah-**pah**-zhićh] v. infuse; slang: fight; beat up (badly)
naparzyć się [nah-**pah**-zhićh śhan] v. infuse; slang: fight; beat up (badly) (mob jargon)
napasać [nah-**pah**-sahćh] v. feed (cattle); graze; give cattle plenty of pasture (*repeatedly*)
napasać się [nah-**pah**-sahćh śhan] v. eat plenty of feed; have plenty of pasture; eat one's fill; have plenty of food (*repeatedly*)
napasiony [nah-pah-**śho**-ni] adj.m. well-fed
napaskudzić [nah-pahs-**koo**-dźheećh] v. soil up; make a mess; dirty; foul; make trouble
napastliwie [nah-pahs-**tlee**-vye] adv. aggressively; bitterly; maliciously
napastliwość [nah-pahs-**tlee**-vośhćh] f. aggressiveness; bitterness; malice
napastliwy [nah-pahs-**tlee**-vi] adj.m. aggressive; malicious; bitter; quarrelsome

napastniczka [nah-pahst-**ńeech**-kah] f. (woman) aggressor; assailant
napastniczość [nah-pahst-**ńee**-chośhćh] f. aggressiveness; hostility
napastniczy [nah-pahst-**ńee**-chi] adj.m. aggressive; hostile; invasive
wojna napastnicza [**voy**-nah nah-pahst-**ńee**-chah] exp.: war of aggression; war of conquest
napastnik [nah-**pahst**-ńeek] m. aggressor; assailant; forward, forward center (sport)
środkowy napastnik [śhrot-**ko**-vi nah-**pahst**-ńeek] exp.: forward center (in soccer)
napastować [nah-pahs-**to**-vahćh] v. pester; attack; molest; worry; assail; persecute; fall upon; plague; importune; beset; try to pick a fight (with); thrust oneself upon; come upon (*repeatedly*); wax (floor, etc.); put paste on
napastować się [nah-pahs-**to**-vahćh śhan] v. molest one another (*repeatedly*); put paste on oneself
napastowanie [nah-pahs-to-**vah**-ńe] n. pestering; attacking; molestation; assault; persecution; invasion; inroad; inroads; waxing (floors, etc.)
napaść [**nah**-pahśhćh] v. assault; assail; attack; make inroads; fall upon; raid; rob; turn against; lash (at someone, etc.); see: **napadać**
napaść [**nah**-pahśhćh] f. assault; invective; assailing; attack; making inroads; falling upon; raiding; robbery; turning against; lashing at; outbreak; fit
napaść [**nah**-pahśhćh] v. feed (cattle); graze; give cattle plenty of pasture
napaść oczy [**nah**-pahśhćh **o**-chi] exp.: to feast one's eyes (on something)
napaść się [**nah**-pahśhćh śhan] v. eat plenty of feed; have plenty of pasture; eat one's fill; have plenty of food
napaść się widokiem [nah-pahśhćh śhan vee-**do**-kem] exp.: to feast one's eyes on ...
napataczać się [nah-pah-**tah**-chahćh śhan] v. turn up; crop up; come across; come up (against) (*repeatedly*)
na patataj [nah pah-**tah**-tahy] exp.: colloq: just any way; any old way, but quickly; helter-skelter; hurry-scurry; slapdash; in a rough-and-tumble manner
napatoczyć się [nah-pah-**to**-chićh śhan] v. turn up; crop up; come across; come up (against)
napatrzeć się [nah-**pah**-tshećh śhan] v. have a good look (at); see as much as one could wish
nie móc się napatrzeć [ńe moots śhan nah-**pah**-tshećh] exp.: not to be able to take one's eyes off it; never to tire looking at it; to have one's eyes glued to it
napatrzyć się [nah-**pah**-tshićh śhan] v. have a good look (at); see as much as one could wish; see enough; see a lot of
napawać [nah-**pah**-vahćh] v. fill up (with feelings, panic, wonder); imbibe; imbue (*repeatedly*)
napawać lękiem [nah-**pah**-vahćh lan-kem] exp.: to strike somebody with terror; to fill somebody with fear
napawać oczy czymś [nah-**pah**-vahćh **o**-chi chimśh] exp.: to feast one's eyes on something; to regale one's eyes with something
napawać się [nah-**pah**-vahćh śhan] v. become imbued; delight (in); gloat (over) (*repeatedly*)
napawanie [nah-pah-**vah**-ńe] n. striking (with panic)
napawanie się [nah-pah-**vah**-ńe śhan] n. delighting (in); gloating (over)
napawarka [nah-pah-**vahr**-kah] f. fabric soaking device; fabric impregnation device
napchać [**nah**-pkhahćh] v. cram; pack; fill; crowd; stow; gorge; stuff
napchać się [**nah**-pkhahćh śhan] v. gorge oneself; stuff oneself (with food)
napchany [nah-**pkhah**-ni] adj.m. replete (with); stuffed full; full up;

cram-full
napełniacz [nah-**pew**-ńahch] m. filler
napełniać [nah-**pew**-ńahćh] v. fill up; inspire; imbue; pervade (*repeatedly*)
napełniać po brzegi [nah-**pew**-ńahćh po **bzhe**-gee] exp.: to fill to the brim
napełniać ponownie [nah-**pew**-ńahćh po-**nov**-ńe] exp.: to refill
napełniać się [nah-**pew**-ńahćh śhan] v. fill; become filled (*repeatedly*)
napełnianie [nah-pew-**ńah**-ńe] n. filling; pervading
napełnić [nah-**pew**-ńeećh] v. fill up; inspire; imbue; pervade
napełnić ponownie [nah-**pew**-ńeećh po-**nov**-ńe] exp.: to refill
napełnić się [nah-**pew**-ńeećh śhan] v. fill; become filled
naperfumować [nah-per-foo-**mo**-vahćh] v. scent (one's handkerchief, etc.); put perfume on; perfume
naperfumować się [nah-per-foo-**mo**-vahćh śhan] v. spray oneself with scent; perfume oneself
na pewniaka [nah pev-**ńah**-kah] exp.: slang: unfailingly; safely; surely; for certain; certainly; for sure; without fail; with utmost assurance; confidently
na pewno [nah **pev**-no] exp.: adv. surely; certainly; for sure; without fail; with assurance
napęcznieć [nah-**panch**-ńećh] v. fill out; distend; swell (with pride, etc.)
napęd [nah-pant] m. propulsion; drive; force; driving gear; mechanical power
napęd bezpośredni [nah-pand bes-pośh-**red**-ńee] exp.: direct drive
napęd elektryczny [nah-pand e-lek-**trich**-ni] exp.: electric drive; electromotion; electromotive force
napęd odrzutowy [nah-pand od-zhoo-**to**-vi] exp.: jet propulsion
napędowy [nah-pan-**do**-vi] adj.m. motive; driving; impulsive; propulsive
koło napędowe [**ko**-wo nah-pan-**do**-ve] exp.: flywheel; drive wheel; traction wheel; main wheel (in a watch)
mechanizm napędowy [me-**khah**-ńeezm nah-pan-**do**-vi] exp.: driving mechanism
pas napędowy [pahs nah-pan-**do**-vi] exp.: drive belt
siła napędowa [**śhee**-wah nah-pan-**do**-vah] exp.: motive power
wał napędowy [vahw nah-pan-**do**-vi] exp.: drive shaft
napędzać [nah-**pan**-dzahćh] v. chase in; propel; round up; drift in; carry along; egg on; bring in; goad; incite; impel (*repeatedly*)
napędzać strachu [nah-**pan**-dzahćh **strah**-khoo] exp.: frighten
napędzany [nah-pan-**dzah**-ni] adj.m. driven
napędzany mechanicznie [nah-pan-**dzah**-ni me-khah-**ńeech**-ńe] exp.: power driven
napędzany ręcznie [nah-pan-**dzah**-ni **ranch**-ńe] exp.: hand driven
napędzić [nah-**pan**-dźheećh] v. chase in; propel; round up; drift in; carry along; egg on; bring in; goad; incite; impel
napędzić strachu [nah-**pan**-dźheećh **strah**-khoo] exp.: to frighten
napiąć [**nah**-pyownćh] v. strain; stretch; draw (a bow, etc.); tighten (a rope); string (a bow, etc.); brace (a drum, etc.); tense (the muscles); start (the end-game)
napiąć się [**nah**-pyownćh śhan] v. become strained; tighten (oneself); tense
napić się [**nah**-peećh śhan] v. have a drink; quench one's thirst; have (something) to drink
napić się kawy [**nah**-peećh śhan **kah**-vi] exp.: to have a cup of coffee
napiec [**nah**-pyets] v. bake a lot (of bread, etc.); roast a lot (of meat, etc.)
napiec się [**nah**-pyets śhan] v. clamor (for)
na piechotę [nah pye-**kho**-tan] exp.: (to travel, etc.) on foot

napierać [nah-pye-rahćh] v. press forward; advance; press on; press to do; urge to do; insist (on) (*repeatedly*)

napierać się [nah-pye-rahćh śhan] v. insist; claim; clamor for (*repeatedly*)

napieranie [nah-pye-rah-ńe] n. an advance; pressing (for); insistence; claim; claims; claiming; clamor

napierśnik [nah-pyerśh-ńeek] m. bib; apron-top; breastplate; plastron (in medieval armor)

napieścić się [nah-pyeśh-ćheećh śhan] v. caress at will; fondle at will; pet at will; caress to one's heart's content; delight (in)

napieścić się z dziewczyną [nah-pyeśh-ćheećh śhan z dźhef-chi-nown] exp.: to share caresses with a girl; to caress a girl to one's heart's content

napięcie [nah-pyan-ćhe] n. tension; tenseness; tensity; tightness; tautness; tone; strain; voltage; intensity; intentness; stress; stretch

linia wysokiego napięcia [leeń-yah vi-so-ke-go nah-pyan-ćhah] exp.: high tension line

napięcie powierzchniowe [nah-pyan-ćhe po-vyesh-khńo-ve] exp.: surface tension

pod napięciem [pod nah-pyan-ćhem] exp.: live (wire)

w napięciu [v nah-pyan-ćhoo] exp.: under stress

z napięciem [z nah-pyan-ćhem] exp.: with fascination

napięciowy [nah-pyan-ćho-vi] adj.m. tensional

napięstek [nah-pyans-tek] m. wrist; carpus

napiętek [nah-pyan-tek] m. heel; talus

napiętnik [nah-pyant-ńeek] m. (shoe) quarter

napiętnować [nah-pyant-no-vahćh] v. brand; stigmatize; censure; condemn as being very bad; stamp

napiętnowanie [nah-pyant-no-vah-ńe] n. censure

godny napiętnowania [god-ni nah-pyant-no-vah-ńah] exp.: censurable

napięty [nah-pyan-ti] adj.m. tense; taut; strained; tight

napięta uwaga [nah-pyan-tah oo-vah-gah] exp.: close attention; rapt attention

słabo napięty [swah-bo nah-pyan-ti] exp.: slack; sagging

napinacz [nah-pee-nahch] m. tensor; stretcher; tightener; take-up

napinać [nah-pee-nahćh] v. strain; stretch; draw (a bow, etc.); tighten (a rope); string (a bow, etc.); brace (a drum, etc.); tense (the muscles); start (the end-game) (*repeatedly*)

napinać się [nah-pee-nahćh śhan] v. strain oneself (*repeatedly*)

napinanie [nah-pee-nah-ńe] n. straining; tensioning; drawing (a bow, etc.)

napis [nah-pees] m. inscription; legend; lettering; caption; subtitle

napisać [nah-pee-sahćh] v. write; write down; drop a line; type

napisać się [nah-pee-sahćh śhan] v. write a lot; get tired of writing

napisanie [nah-pee-sah-ńe] n. writing

na piśmie [nah peeśh-mye] exp.: in writing

napitek [nah-pee-tek] m. drink; beverage; liquor

napity [nah-pee-ti] adj.m. slang: drunk; tipsy; intoxicated; screwed; tight (mob jargon)

napiwek [nah-pee-vek] m. tip; gratuity; perquisite

napIądrować [nah-plown-dro-vahćh] v. amass loot; plunder

naplecznik [nah-plech-ńeek] m. backplate; back-piece

naplenić [nah-ple-ńeećh] v. produce great quantities; produce a lot (of)

naplenić się [nah-ple-ńeećh śhan] v. proliferate; breed (a lot)

napleść [nah-pleśhćh] v. plait (baskets); tell (a lot); prate (all sorts of nonsense, gossip, etc.)

napletek [nah-ple-tek] m. foreskin; prepuce

naplotkować [nah-plot-**ko**-vahćh] v. make gossip
naplotkować się [nah-plot-**ko**-vahćh śhan] v. gossip at will; get tired of gossiping
napluć [**nah**-plooćh] v. spit on
napłakać [nah-**pwah**-kahćh] v. shed (torrents of tears); weep a lot
tyle co kot napłakał [**ti**-le tso kot nah-**pwah**-kahw] exp.: next to nothing; as good as nothing
napłakać się [nah-**pwah**-kahćh śhan] v. shed torrents of tears; weep oneself out; have a hearty weep
na płask [nah pwahsk] exp.: adv. flatwise
napłatać [nah-**pwah**-tahćh] v. slice; chop; make practical jokes; make mischief
napłodzić [nah-**pwo**-dźheećh] v. beget (numerous offspring, etc.); produce (a lot)
napłynąć [nah-**pwi**-nownćh] v. flow in; gush forth; well up; arrive (by boat, etc.); come (by ship, etc.); glide along; approach; arise; flow; flock; pour in; come (in great numbers); be suffused
krew napłynęła mu do głowy [kref nah-pwi-**ne**-wah moo do **gwo**-vi] exp.: the blood rushed to his head
łzy napłynęły mi do oczu [wzi nah-pwi-**ne**-wi mee do **o**-choo] exp.: tears rose to my eyes
napływ [**nah**-pwif] m. influx
napływać [nah-**pwi**-vahćh] v. flow in; gush forth; well up; arrive (by boat, etc.); come (by ship, etc.); glide along; approach; arise; flow; flock; pour in; come (in great numbers); be suffused (*repeatedly*)
napływać się [nah-**pwi**-vahćh śhan] v. swim plenty; get tired of swimming
napływający [nah-pwi-vah-**yown**-tsi] adj.m. flowing-in; pouring-in; going-in (fluid, etc.)
napływowy [nah-pwi-**vo**-vi] adj.m. alluvial; immigrant; alien; extraneous; foreign
napocić się [nah-**po**-ćheećh śhan] v. sweat profusely; exert oneself; strain; tire oneself out
napocząć [nah-**po**-chownćh] v. start up; cut into (a loaf, etc.); open (a jar, etc.); broach; tap (a cask, etc.)
na poczekaniu [nah po-che-**kah**-ńoo] exp.: adv. off-hand; out of hand; on the spot; then and there; extempore; straight off
napoczęcie [nah-po-**chan**-ćhe] n. starting up; cutting into (a loaf, etc.); opening (a jar, etc.); disturbing (the whole of)
napoczynać [nah-po-**chi**-nahćh] v. start up; cut into (a loaf, etc.); open (a jar, etc.); broach; tap (a cask, etc.) (*repeatedly*)
na podorędziu [nah po-do-**ran**-dźhoo] exp.: adv. at hand; within one's reach
napodróżować się [nah-po-droo-**zho**-vahćh śhan] v. travel a great deal; travel as much as one could wish
na pohybel [nah po-**khi**-bel] exp.: (wishing) confusion to (somebody, etc.); misery; perishing; destruction; loss; undoing
napoić [nah-**po**-eećh] v. water (cattle, etc.); give water to drink
napoić się [nah-**po**-eećh śhan] v. drink enough; drink to their (cattle's, etc.) fill
napojenie [nah-po-**ye**-ńe] n. watering (of animals, cattle, horses, etc.)
na pokaz [nah **po**-kahs] exp.: masterly; for show; for the sake of appearances
napokładowy [nah-po-kwah-**do**-vi] adj.m. on board; (seamen, etc.) on deck
napokostować [nah-po-kos-**to**-vahćh] v. varnish
napokutować się [nah-po-koo-**to**-vahćh śhan] v. expiate; suffer for
napoleon [nah-po-**le**-on] m. (a) napoleon (coin)
napoleondor [nah-po-le-**on**-dor] m. (a) napoleon (gold coin)
napoleonista [nah-po-le-o-**ńees**-tah]

m. Napoleonist
napoleonizm [nah-po-le-o-ńeezm] m. Napoleonism
napoleonka [nah-po-le-on-kah] f. napoleon (cake)
napoleoński [nah-po-le-oń-skee] adj.m. Napoleonic (wars, etc.)
po napoleońsku [po nah-po-le-oń-skoo] exp.: after the manner of Napoleon
napolować się [nah-po-lo-vahćh śhan] v. hunt a lot; get tired of hunting
na poły [nah po-wi] exp.: half (done, etc.); pretty nearly; almost
napomadować [nah-po-mah-do-vahćh] v. put pomade on
napomadować się [nah-po-mah-do-vahćh śhan] v. put pomade on oneself
napominać [nah-po-mee-nahćh] v. admonish; reprimand; rebuke; exhort (*repeatedly*)
napominanie [nah-po-mee-nah-ńe] n. admonition; exhortation; (a) reprimand; (a) rebuke
napomknąć [nah-pomk-nownćh] v. hint at; give a hint; drop a hint; allude to; make an allusion; mention; intimate; make a reference to
napomknienie [nah-pomk-ńe-ńe] n. hint at; allusion to; reference to; intimation
napomknięcie [nah-pom-kńan-ćhe] n. (a) hint; (an) allusion
napomnieć [nah-pom-ńećh] v. admonish; reprimand; rebuke; exhort
napomnienie [nah-pom-ńe-ńe] n. admonition; reprimand; rebuke
na pomoc! [nah po-mots] excl.: help!; give help!; please, help!
napompować [nah-pom-po-vahćh] v. pump up; inflate (a tire, etc.); blow up
napomykać [nah-po-mi-kahćh] v. hint at; give a hint; drop a hint; allude to; make an allusion; mention; intimate; make a reference to (*repeatedly*)
naponiewierać [nah-po-ńe-vye-rahćh] v. mistreat (a lot of people, etc.); brutalize (somebody many times)
naponiewierać się [nah-po-ńe-vye-rahćh śhan] v. mistreat oneself; get mistreated a lot
na poprzek [nah po-pshek] exp.: crosswise; transversely; across; athwart
naporowy [nah-po-ro-vi] adj.m. of pressure
turbina naporowa [toor-bee-nah nah-po-ro-vah] exp.: reaction turbine
napościć się [nah-pośh-ćheećh śhan] v. keep a long fast; fast many times; have fasted quite enough; be tired of fasting
na potem [nah po-tem] exp.: for later; for the future; for a future occasion
na potęgę [nah po-tan-gan] exp.: adv. mightily; a lot
napotkać [nah-pot-kahćh] v. come across; happen upon; light upon; hit upon; be faced with; be confronted with; encounter; meet with; run across; find (in a text, etc.)
napotkanie [nah-pot-kah-ńe] n. encounter; meeting (with)
napotnie [nah-pot-ńe] adv. inducing perspiration
działać napotnie [dźhah-wahćh nah-pot-ńe] exp.: to induce perspiration
napotny [nah-pot-ni] adj.m. perspiratory; diaphoretic; sudorific; sudatory
środek napotny [śhro-dek nah-pot-ni] exp.: (a) sudorific; (a) diaphoretic
napotykać [nah-po-ti-kahćh] v. run in; come across; be faced with; happen; be confronted with; happen upon; light upon; hit upon; encounter; meet with; run across; find (in a text, etc.) (*repeatedly*)
napotykanie [nah-po-ti-kah-ńe] n. coming across; encountering
napowietrzać [nah-po-vyet-shahćh] v. air; ventilate; clear of carbon dioxide; entrain air (into concrete, etc.) (*repeatedly*)
napowietrzny [nah-po-vyetsh-ni]

adj.m. aerial; overhead (wires, etc.)
napowietrzyć [nah-po-**vyet**-shićh] v. air; ventilate; clear of carbon dioxide; entrain air (into)
na powrót [nah **po**-vroot] exp.: adv. return; again; on the way back
na pozór [nah **po**-zoor] exp.: adv. apparently; on the face of it
napożyczać [nah-po-**zhi**-chahćh] v. lend many times (to); lend considerable sums (to); borrow many times (from); borrow considerable sums (from)
napój [**nah**-pooy] m. drink; beverage; potion; draught
napój alkoholowy [nah-pooy ahl-ko-kho-**lo**-vi] exp.: strong drink; alcoholic beverage (liquor)
napój bezalkoholowy [**nah**-pooy bez-ahl-ko-kho-**lo**-vi] exp.: soft drink
napój chłodzący [nah-pooy khwo-dzown-tsi] exp.: refreshing drink
napoje wyskokowe [nah-**po**-ye vis-ko-**ko**-ve] exp.: alcoholic beverages
na pół [nah poow] exp.: adv. in half
napór [**nah**-poor] m. pressure; stress; onrush; inrush; onset; thrust
napór hydrodynamiczny [**nah**-poor khi-dro-di-nah-**meech**-ni] exp.: hydrodynamic head; pressure of flow
napór lodu [nah-poor **lo**-doo] exp.: ice thrust; ice pressure
napór wiatru [nah-poor **vyaht**-roo] exp.: wind load; wind pressure
nappa [**nahp**-pah] f. thin leather (for gloves, etc.)
napracować się [nah-prah-**tso**-vahćh śhan] v. work very hard; toil a lot; work awfully hard
darmo się napracować [**dahr**-mo śhan nah-prah-**tso**-vahćh] exp.: to work in vain; to labor in vain
naprać [**nah**-prahćh] v. get a lot of washing done; colloq: beat up (a lot of people)
naprać się [nah-prahćh śhan] v. be weary of washing; colloq: hit each other hard; fight like a deuce
napraszać się [nah-**prah**-shahćh śhan] v. importune; implore; intrude upon; thrust oneself upon (*repeatedly*)
napraszanie [nah-prah-**shah**-ńe] n. solicitation; solicitations; intrusion; intrusions
napraszanie się [nah-prah-**shah**-ńe śhan] n. solicitation(s); intrusion(s)
naprawa [nah-**prah**-vah] f. repair; redress; renovation; reform; repairing; reparation; improvement
muszę dać zegarek do naprawy [moo-shan dahćh ze-**gah**-rek do nah-**prah**-vi] exp.: I must have my watch repaired
naprawa ekspresowa [nah-**prah**-vah eks-pre-**so**-vah] exp.: emergency repair
naprawa gwarancyjna [nah-**prah**-vah gvah-rahn-**tsiy**-nah] exp.: service; servicing
w naprawie [v nah-**prah**-vye] exp.: under repair; undergoing repairs
naprawczy [nah-**prahf**-chi] adj.m. of reparation
warsztat naprawczy [**vahrsh**-taht nah-**prahf**-chi] exp.: repair shop; repair-works
naprawdę [nah-**prahv**-dan] adv. indeed; really; truly; positively; in ernest
naprawdę? [nah-**prahv**-dan] excl.: really?; indeed?; is that so?; colloq: do you mean it?
naprawiacz [nah-**prah**-vyahch] m. repairman; repairer; mender; reformer; renovator
naprawiać [nah-**prah**-vyahćh] v. repair; fix; mend; rectify; reform; set right; put right; put in repair; renovate; service; better; redress; remedy; retrieve; make good; make amends (*repeatedly*)
naprawiać krzywdę [nah-**prah**-vyahćh **kshiv**-dan] exp.: to redress the wrong
naprawiać się [nah-**prah**-vyahćh śhan] v. take a turn for the better; improve (*repeatedly*)
naprawianie [nah-prah-**vyah**-ńe] n. mending; repairing; fixing;

reforming; renovating (*repeated*)
naprawić [nah-**prah**-veećh] v. repair; fix; mend; rectify; reform; set right; put right; put in repair; renovate; service; better; redress; remedy; retrieve; make good; make amends
naprawić błąd [nah-**prah**-veećh bwownt] exp.: to correct an error
naprawić krzywdę [nah-**prah**-veećh **kshiv**-dan] exp.: to redress the wrong
naprawić się [nah-**prah**-veećh śhan] v. take a turn for the better; improve; come right
naprawienie [nah-prah-**vye**-ńe] n. mending; repairing; fixing; reforming; renovating
nie do naprawienia [ńe do nah-prah-**vye**-ńah] exp.: beyond repair; not repairable
na prawo [nah **prah**-vo] exp.: adv. to the right; go to the right
naprędce [nah-**prant**-tse] adv. hastily; in a hurry; slapdash; in all haste; at short notice
naprężacz [nah-**pran**-zhahch] m. tightener; erector-muscle
naprężać [nah-**pran**-zhahćh] v. tighten; stretch; strain; string (a bow, etc.) (*repeatedly*)
naprężać się [nah-**pran**-zhahćh śhan] v. stretch; become strained; tighten (*repeatedly*)
naprężenie [nah-pran-**zhe**-ńe] n. tension; strain; tautness; stretch; tenseness; stress
naprężnik [nah-**pranzh**-ńeek] m. tension regulator
naprężony [nah-pran-**zho**-ni] adj.m. tense; taut; strained; erect; stretched; strung up
naprężyć [nah-**pran**-zhićh] v. tighten; stretch; strain; string (a bow, etc.)
naprężyć się [nah-**pran**-zhićh śhan] v. stretch; become strained; tighten
naprodukować [nah-pro-doo-**ko**-vahćh] v. produce a lot (of); produce great quantities (of)
napromieniać [nah-pro-**mye**-ńahćh] v. irradiate (*repeatedly*)
napromienić [nah-pro-**mye**-ńeećh] v. irradiate
napromienienie [nah-pro-mye-**ńe**-ńe] n. irradiation
napromieniować [nah-pro-mye-**ńo**-vahćh] v. irradiate; submit to radiation
napromieniowanie [nah-pro-mye-ńo-**vah**-ńe] n. irradiation
napromieniowywać [nah-pro-mye-ńo-**vi**-vahćh] v. irradiate; submit to radiation (*repeatedly*)
naprosić [nah-**pro**-śheećh] v. invite a lot (of people, etc.)
naprosić się [nah-**pro**-śheećh śhan] v. plead (with); entreat; press; urge
na prost [nah prost] exp.: colloq: straight on; ahead; opposite
naprostować [nah-pros-**to**-vahćh] v. straighten; straighten out; erect; right; put straight; adjust; correct
naprostowywać [nah-pros-to-**vi**-vahćh] v. straighten; straighten out; erect; right; put straight; adjust; correct (*repeatedly*)
naprowadzać [nah-pro-**vah**-dzahćh] v. lead in; direct to; point out to; advise; suggest (*repeatedly*)
naprowadzenie [nah-pro-vah-**dze**-ńe] n. lead; direction; pointing out to; advise; suggestion
naprowadzić [nah-pro-**vah**-dźheećh] v. lead in; direct to; point out to; advise; suggest
naprowadzić na trop [nah-pro-**vah**-dźheećh nah trop] exp.: to lay (the hounds, etc.) on the scent; to put (somebody) on track
naproże [nah-**pro**-zhe] n. head-rail
na próżno [nah **proozh**-no] exp.: adv. in vain; uselessly; to no avail
naprząść [nah-pshownśhćh] v. spin (a quantity of yarn)
na przebój [nah **pshe**-booy] exp.: adv. by sheer force; aggressively; combatively; pugnaciously
naprzeciw [nah-**pshe**-ćheef] adv. opposite; vis-a-vis; across the street; over the way; facing; colloq: compared with; compared to
stać naprzeciw [stahćh nah-**pshe**-ćheef] exp.: to face
wyjść komuś naprzeciw

[viyśhćh **ko**-moośh nah-**pshe**-ćheef] exp.: to (go and) meet somebody
naprzeciwko [nah-pshe-**ćheef**-ko] adv. opposite; vis-a-vis; across the street; over the way; facing; compared with; compared to
z naprzeciwka [z nah-pshe-**ćheef**-kah] exp.: from the opposite side
naprzeciwlegle [nah-pshe-ćheev-**leg**-le] adv. alternately
naprzeciwległy [nah-pshe-ćheev-**leg**-wi] adj.m. opposite
naprzeć [**nah**-pshećh] v. press; urge; press hard; insist on
naprzeć się [**nah**-pshećh śhan] v. demand; press for (something)
na przedzie [nah **pshe**-dźhe] exp.: at the head; up front; ahead; in front; in the foreground
na przekór [nah **pshe**-koor] exp.: adv. in despite; just to spite; to spite; in spite
na przełaj [nah **pshe**-wahy] exp.: adv. shortcut (across obstacles); diagonally
bieg na przełaj [byek nah **pshe**-wahy] exp.: cross-country foot-race (run)
na przemian [nah **pshe**-myahn] exp.: adv. alternately; by turns; turn and turn about
naprzemianlegle [nah-pshe-myahn-**leg**-le] adv. alternately
naprzemianległy [nah-pshe-myahn-**leg**-wi] adj.m. alternate; alternating
kąty naprzemianległe [**kown**-ti nah-pshe-myahn-**leg**-we] exp.: opposite angles (in a crossing); alternate angles
liście naprzemianległe [**leeśh**-ćhe nah-pshe-myahn-**leg**-we] exp.: alternate leaves
naprzemianręczny [nah-pshe-myahn-**ranch**-ni] adj.m. double overarum
na przestrzał [nah **pshes**-tshahw] exp.: through and through; right through
na przodzie [nah **psho**-dźhe] exp.: at the head; up front; ahead; in front; in the foreground
naprzód [**nah**-pshoot] adv. in front; forwards; first; in the first place; forward; onward; ahead; on; foremost; first of all; in advance; ahead of time; in anticipation; firstly; primarily
krok naprzód [krok **nah**-pshoot] exp.: a step forward
naprzód! [**nah**-pshoot] excl.: forward!
na przychodne [nah pshi-**khod**-ne] exp.: as a nonresident (servant, housekeeper, etc.)
naprzyglądać się [nah-pshi-**glown**-dahćh śhan] v. look over a lot; get tired of looking
naprzyjmować [nah-pshiy-**mo**-vahćh] v. receive a lot (of people); engage a lot (of people to work, etc)
na przykład [nah **pshi**-kwaht] exp.: for instance; for example
naprzykrzać się [nah-**pshik**-shahćh śhan] v. bother; molest; pester; obtrude oneself (on); make a nuisance of oneself (*repeatedly*)
naprzykrzanie się [nah-pshik-**shah**-ńe śhan] n. bothering; molestation; obtrusion (on); pestering; making a nuisance of oneself
naprzykrzony [nah-pshik-**sho**-ni] adj.m. troublesome; pestering; importunate
naprzykrzyć się [nah-**pshik**-shićh śhan] v. bother; molest; pester; obtrude oneself (on); make a nuisance of oneself
naprzynosić [nah-pshi-**no**-śheećh] v. bring a lot; bring plenty
naprzytaczać [nah-pshi-**tah**-chahćh] v. cite many times; quote many times
naprzywozić [nah-pshi-**vo**-źheećh] v. bring a lot (by car, etc.); bring plenty (by truck, etc.)
napsioczyć [nah-**pśho**-chićh] v. growl at; complain of; grumble about; grumble over
napsocić [nah-**pso**-ćheećh] v. play all sorts of pranks; make all sorts of mischief
napstrzyć [**nah**-pstshićh] v. deck out; speck
napsuć [**nah**-psooćh] v. spoil a lot; damage a lot; impair a lot

napsuć komuś krwi [nah-psooćh ko-moośh krfee] exp.: to try somebody's patience
napuchły [nah-poo-khwi] adj.m. swollen; bulging; distended
napuchnąć [nah-poo-khnownćh] v. swell; become swollen
napuchnięcie [nah-poo-khńan-ćhe] n. swelling; swollen cheek (arm, etc.)
napudrować [nah-pood-ro-vahćh] v. powder (one's nose, etc.)
napustoszyć [nah-poos-to-shićh] v. lay waste
napuszać [nah-poo-shahćh] v. ruffle (feathers); bristle (hair) (*repeatedly*)
napuszać się [nah-poo-shahćh śhan] v. ruffle (feathers); bristle up; puff oneself up (*repeatedly*)
napuszczać [nah-poosh-chahćh] v. set up; impregnate; let in; fill; pour; saturate; imbue; set on; set one against another (*repeatedly*)
napuszczać wody do wanny [nah-poosh-chahćh vo-di do vahn-ni] exp.: to fill a bathtub with water
napuszczanie [nah-poosh-chah-ńe] n. setting up; impregnating; letting in; filling; pouring; saturating
napuszczenie [nah-poosh-che-ńe] n. saturation; impregnation; colloq: setting on (one against an other)
napuszczony [nah-poosh-cho-ni] adj.m. filled; impregnated; colloq: set on (somebody, something)
napuszoność [nah-poo-sho-nośhćh] f. conceitedness; pompousness; bombast; turgidity; rotundity
napuszony [nah-poo-sho-ni] adj.m. puffed up; bristling; ruffled; conceited; pompous; bombastic; turgid; grandiloquent; rotund
napuszyć [nah-poo-shićh] v. ruffle (feathers); bristle (hair)
napuszyć się [nah-poo-shićh śhan] v. ruffle (feathers); bristle up; puff oneself up
napuścić [nah-poośh-ćheećh] v. set up; impregnate; let in; fill; pour; saturate; imbue; set on; set one against another
napychać [nah-pi-khahćh] v. stuff; cram; fill; pack; crowd; stow; line one's purse; gorge (*repeatedly*)
napychać się [nah-pi-khahćh śhan] v. stuff oneself; line one's purse; gorge oneself (*repeatedly*)
napylać [nah-pi-lahćh] v. spray with dust (*repeatedly*)
napylić [nah-pi-leećh] v. spray with (metal, etc.) dust
napyskować [nah-pis-ko-vahćh] v. bawl; carp (at)
napyskować się [nah-pis-ko-vahćh śhan] v. carp a lot; get tired carping; bawl a lot; get tired of bawling
napytać [nah-pi-tahćh] v. bring
napytać sobie biedy [nah-pi-tahćh so-bye bye-di] exp.: to bring misfortune on oneself
napytać się [nah-pi-tahćh śhan] v. bring on oneself; catch (a disease, etc.); ask a great many questions; ask a lot
narachować [nah-rah-kho-vahćh] v. count up; arrive at an amount; reckon (Brit.)
narachować się [nah-rah-kho-vahćh śhan] v. count a lot; get tired counting
narada [nah-rah-dah] f. consultation; council; conference; meeting; deliberations
odbywać naradę [od-bi-vahćh nah-rah-dan] exp.: to hold a conference
tajna narada [tahy-nah nah-rah-dah] exp.: secret session
zwołać naradę [zwo-wahćh nah-rah-dan] exp.: to call a meeting together; to call a conference together
naradka [nah-raht-kah] f. rock jasmine; Androsace
naradzać się [nah-rah-dzahćh śhan] v. consult on; confer with; deliberate; hold a council (*repeatedly*)
naradzanie się [nah-rah-dzah-ńe śhan] n. consultation; deliberation
naradzić się [nah-rah-dźheećh śhan] v. consult on; confer with;

deliberate; hold a council

naraić [nah-**rah**-eećh] v. procure (for); get (for); find (for)

narajać [nah-**rah**-yahćh] v. procure (for); get (for); find (for) (*repeatedly*)

narajenie [nah-rah-**ye**-ńe] n. procuring

naramiennik [nah-rah-**myen**-ńeek] m. epaulet; shoulder strap

naramienny [nah-rah-**myen**-ni] adj.m. shoulder (knot, strap, etc.)

mięsień naramienny [**my<u>an</u>**-śheń nah-rah-**myen**-ni] exp.: deltoid muscle

narastać [nah-**rah**-stahćh] v. grow on; increase; accumulate; accrete; accrue (interest); gather; augment (*repeatedly*)

narastający [nah-rah-stah-**y<u>own</u>**-tsi] adj.m. growing; increasing; cumulative

narastanie [nah-rah-**stah**-ńe] n. growth; increase; accumulation; accretion

na raty [nah **rah**-ti] exp.: (pay, etc.) in (by) installments; by deferred payments

naraz [**nah**-rahs] adv. suddenly; all of a sudden; all at once; at the same time; at a time; together

narazić [nah-**rah**-źheećh] v. expose to (danger, ridicule, etc.); endanger; imperil; jeopardize; compromise (reputation, etc.)

narazić na niebezpieczeństwo [nah-**rah**-źheećh nah ne-bes-pye-**cheń**-stfo] exp.: to expose to danger; to endanger; to imperil; to jeopardize (one's reputation, health, etc.); to compromise (one's good name, etc.)

narazić na przykrości [nah-**rah**-źheećh nah pshi-**krośh**-ćhee] exp.: to cause (somebody) trouble

narazić na szwank [nah-**rah**-źheećh nah shfahnk] exp.: to damage

narazić się [nah-rah-źheećh śh<u>an</u>] v. expose oneself (to); risk; run the risk

narazić się komuś [nah-**rah**-źheećh śh<u>an</u> **ko**-moośh] exp.: to incur somebody's displeasure; to expose oneself to somebody's displeasure; to incur somebody's ill will; to offend; to anger

narazić się na pewną zgubę [nah-**rah**-źheećh śh<u>an</u> nah **pev**-n<u>own</u> **zgoo**-b<u>an</u>] exp.: to risk a certain death; to kamikaze; to ride to a fall (Brit.); to sacrifice (one's life)

na razie [nah **rah**-źhe] exp.: adv. for the time being; for the present

narażać [nah-**rah**-zhahćh] v. expose to (danger, ridicule, etc.); endanger; imperil; jeopardize; compromise (reputation, etc.) (*repeatedly*)

narażać na niebezpieczeństwo [nah-**rah**-zhahćh nah ńe-bes-pye-**cheń**-stfo] exp.: to endanger; to imperil

narażać na niewygody [nah-rah-zhahćh nah ńe-vi-**go**-di] exp.: to put to inconvenience

narażać się [nah-**rah**-zhahćh śh<u>an</u>] v. risk; run the risk; invite (failure, etc.); lay oneself open (to); incur danger (*repeatedly*)

narażać się na kłopoty [nah-rah-zhahćh śh<u>an</u> nah kwo-**po**-ti] exp.: to ask for trouble; to get oneself into trouble; to lay oneself open; to expose oneself

narażać się komuś [nah-rah-zhahćh śh<u>an</u> **ko**-moośh] exp.: to incur somebody's displeasure

narażenie [nah-rah-**zhe**-ńe] n. risk; venture; exposure

z narażeniem życia [z nah-rah-**zhe**-ńem **zhi**-ćhah] exp.: at the risk of one's life; at the peril of one's life

narażony [nah-rah-**zho**-ni] adj.m. subject to: risk, exposure, temptations, damage, etc.

narąbać [nah-**r<u>own</u>**-bahćh] v. chop; chop a lot (of wood, etc.)

narąbać się [nah-**r<u>own</u>**-bahćh śh<u>an</u>] v. chop a lot; get tired of chopping

narciarka [nahr-**ćhahr**-kah] f. (woman) skier; colloq: ski cap

narciarki [nahr-**ćhahr**-kee] pl. colloq: ski boots

narciarnia [nahr-**ćhahr**-ńah] f.

storage room for skies
narciarski [nahr-**ćhahr**-skee] adj.m. ski (cap, sport, boot, etc.)
narciarstwo [nahr-**ćhahrs**-tfo] n. skiing (sport); gliding on skis
narciarz [nahr-ćhahsh] m. skier
narcystyczny [nahr-tsi-**stich**-ni] adj.m. narcissistic
narcyz [**nahr**-tsis] m. narcissus; narcissist; narcist
narcyzm [**nahr**-tsizm] m. narcissism; narcism
narcyzowaty [nahr-tsi-zo-**vah**-ti] adj.m. narcissist; narcissine
nard [nahrt] m. nard (Nardus); spikenard (oil)
narecznica [nah-rech-**ńee**-tsah] f. shield fern (Dryopteris)
naregulować [nah-re-goo-**lo**-vahćh] v. regulate; adjust
naregulowanie [nah-re-goo-lo-**vah**-ńe] n. regulation; adjustment
nareperować [nah-re-pe-**ro**-vahćh] v. repair; fix; mend
nareszcie [nah-**resh**-ćhe] adv. at last; finally; at long last; ultimately; at length
nareszcie! [nah-**resh**-ćhe] excl.: well!
naręcz [nah-r<u>an</u>ch] f. armful; see: **naręcze**
naręczak [nah-r<u>an</u>-chahk] m. brassart
naręcze [nah-r<u>an</u>-che] n. armful
naręczny [nah-r<u>an</u>**ch**-ni] adj.m. of an armful (sold by a street peddlar, etc.); out of hand
nargile [nahr-**gee**-le] pl. narghile; hookah
narkoman [nahr-**ko**-mahn] m. drug addict
narkomania [nahr-ko-**mahń**-yah] f. the drug habit
narkomanka [nahr-ko-**mahn**-kah] f. (woman) drug addict
narkotycznie [nahr-ko-**tich**-ńe] adv. narcotically
narkotyczny [nahr-ko-**tich**-ni] adj.m. narcotic
narkotyk [nahr-**ko**-tik] m. narcotic; drug (for sleep, relief, etc.); opiate; dope
handel narkotykami [**khahn**-del nahr-ko-ti-**kah**-mee] exp.: drug traffic
zażywać narkotyki [zah-**zhi**-vahćh nahr-ko-**ti**-kee] exp.: to take dope; to indulge in drugs; to be on narcotics
narkotyna [nahr-ko-**ti**-nah] f. narcotine; narcotia; narcotina; narcotin
narkotyzacja [nahr-ko-ti-**zahts**-yah] f. anaesthetizing; drugging; the drug habit
narkotyzer [nahr-ko-**ti**-zer] m. anaesthetist
narkotyzować [nahr-ko-ti-**zo**-vahćh] v. narcotize; drug; anaesthetize (*repeatedly*)
narkotyzować się [nahr-ko-ti-**zo**-vahćh śh<u>an</u>] v. take drugs; use drugs; narcotize oneself; indulge in drugs; take dope; be addicted to the drug habit; be a drug addict (*repeatedly*)
narkotyzowanie [nahr-ko-ti-zo-**vah**-ńe] n. narcotization
narkotyzowanie się [nahr-ko-ti-zo-**vah**-ńe śh<u>an</u>] n. taking drugs; drug addiction
narkotyzująco [nahr-ko-ti-zoo-**y<u>own</u>**-tso] adv. with narcotizing effect
działać narkotyzująco [**dźhah**-wahćh nahr-ko-ti-zoo-**y<u>own</u>**-tso] exp.: to have a narcotic effect; to anaesthetize
narkoza [nahr-**ko**-zah] f. anesthesia; loss of sense of pain, touch, etc.; anaesthetization
dać narkozę [dahćh nahr-**ko**-z<u>an</u>] exp.: to anesthetize
operacja pod narkozą [o-pe-**rahts**-yah pod nahr-**ko**-z<u>own</u>] exp.: surgery under anaesthesia
narobić [nah-**ro**-beećh] v. make a lot; make many objects; mess up; cause a nuisance; make a mess; cause a lot of (trouble)
narobić długów [nah-ro-beećh **dwoo**-goof] exp.: to get into debts
narobić hałasu [nah-ro-beećh khah-**wah**-soo] exp.: to make a noise; to kick up a row
narobić kłopotu [nah-ro-beećh kwo-**po**-too] exp.: to cause trouble; to cause inconvenience

narobić sobie kłopotu [nah-ro-beećh so-bye kwo-po-too] exp.: to get oneself into trouble
narobić zamieszania [nah-ro-beećh zah-mye-shah-ńah] exp.: to make a trouble; to kick up a fuss
narobić się [nah-ro-beećh śhan] v. toil a lot; have worked hard
narodnictwo [nah-rod-ńeets-tfo] n. 19th century Russian democratic movement
narodnik [nah-rod-ńeek] m. member of the 19th century Russian democratic movement
narodowiec [nah-ro-do-vyets] m. nationalist; member of the Nationalist Party
narodowo [nah-ro-do-vo] adv. nationally
narodowo-demokratyczny [nah-ro-do-vo de-mo-krah-tich-ni] adj.m. national-democratic (party, etc.)
narodowościowo [nah-ro-do-vośh-ćho-vo] adv. nationalistically; in respect of nationality
narodowościowy [nah-ro-do-vośh-ćho-vi] adj.m. national; concerning nationality
pod względem narodowościowym [pod vzglan-dem nah-ro-do-vośh-ćho-vim] exp.: in respect of nationality
narodowość [nah-ro-do-vośhćh] f. nationality; national status (attachment)
narodowowyzwoleńczy [nah-ro-do-vo-viz-vo-leń-chi] adj.m. of national liberation; of national independence
narodowy [nah-ro-do-vi] adj.m. national; of national character
narodzenie [nah-ro-dze-ńe] n. birth; being born; the beginning
Boże Narodzenie [bo-zhe nah-ro-dze-ńe] exp.: Christmas; Xmas; Nativity
narodzenie się [nah-ro-dze-ńe śhan] n. being born; one's birth
narodzić [nah-ro-dźheećh] v. bear (children); give birth
narodzić się [nah-ro-dźheećh śhan] v. be born; originate; arise; come into existence
narodziny [nah-ro-dźhee-ni] pl. birth; origin; the beginning; nativity
narodzony [nah-ro-dzo-ni] adj.m. born
czuć się jak nowo narodzony [chooćh śhan yahk no-vo nah-ro-dzo-ni] exp.: to feel restored to life
narolny [nah-rol-ni] adj.m. placed on the soil
droga narolna [dro-gah nah-rol-na] exp.: dirt road; unpaved road
narosnąć [nah-ros-nownćh] v. grow on; increase; accumulate; accrete; accrue (interest); gather; augment
narosły [nah-ros-wi] adj.m. accrued; grown
narosłe odsetki [nah-ros-we ot-set-kee] exp.: accumulated interest
narost [nah-rost] m. tumor; growth; excrescence; wart
narosty [nah-ros-ti] pl. epiphytes; accretion; (metal) bear; sow; tumors; warts
na roścież [nah rośh-ćhesh] exp.: adv. wide (open); see: **na oścież**
narośl [nah-rośhl] f. tumor; growth; excrescence; wart
narośnięcie [nah-rośh-ńan-ćhe] n. growth; increase; accumulation; accretion; expansion
narowić [nah-ro-veećh] v. make restive; render vicious (*repeatedly*)
narowić się [nah-ro-veećh śhan] v. be restive; become vicious (*repeatedly*)
narowienie [nah-ro-vye-ńe] n. restiveness; viciousness; skittishness
narowisty [nah-ro-vees-ti] adj.m. restive; vicious; skittish
narowiście [nah-ro-veeśh-ćhe] adv. restively; viciously; skittishly
narozbijać [nah-roz-bee-yahćh] v. break up a lot; break up plenty
narozbijać się [nah-roz-bee-yahćh śhan] v. travel a lot; get tired of traveling
na rozcież [nah ros-ćhesh] exp.: adv. wide (open); see: **na oścież**

narozlewać [nah-roz-**le**-vahćh] v. spill a lot (of liquid, etc.)
narozlewać krwi [nah-roz-le-vahćh krfee] exp.: to spill much blood
narozrabiać [nah-roz-**rah**-byahćh] v. temper a lot; mix a lot; knead a great quantity; make a lot of mischief; create many disturbances
naroztrząsać [nah-ros-**tshown**-sahćh] v. scatter a lot
naroże [nah-**ro**-zhe] n. corner; angle; crossroads; gusset; quoin
naroże dachu [nah-**ro**-zhe **dah**-khoo] exp.: roof hip
narożnica [nah-rozh-**ńee**-tsah] f. angle rafter
narożnik [nah-**rozh**-ńeek] m. corner; angle; crossroads; gusset; quoin; corner brick; corner house; corner room; L-shaped corner sofa; corner tile
narożnikowy [nag-rozh-ńee-**ko**-vi] adj.m. corner (room, etc.)
narożny [nah-**rozh**-ni] adj.m. corner (store, etc.); at the street corner
narożny dom [nah-**rozh**-ni dom] exp.: corner-house
naród [nah-root] m. nation; people; the nation; colloq: crowd; people
Liga Narodów [lee-gah nah-**ro**-doof] exp.: The League of Nations
naród polski [**nah**-root **pol**-skee] exp.: the people of Poland; the Polish nation
narów [nah-roof] m. vice (restiveness); bad habit; fault
na równi [anh **roov**-ńee] exp.: adv. on a level; on a par; on an equal footing; in common; slang: equally
naróżować [nah-roo-**zho**-vahćh] v. put on rouge
narracja [nahr-**rahts**-yah] f. narrative; narration; story
narracyjnie [nahr-rah-**tsiy**-ńe] adv. narratively
narracyjny [nahr-rah-**tsiy**-ni] adj.m. narrative
narrator [nahr-**rah**-tor] m. narrator; (story) teller
narratorka [nahr-rah-**tor**-kah] f. (female) narrator; (story) teller
narratorski [nahr-rah-**tor**-skee] adj.m. narrative
narta [**nahr**-tah] f. ski; sleigh
pójść (pojechać) na narty [pooyśhćh (po-**ye**-khahćh) nah **nahr**-ti] exp.: to go skiing
jazda na nartach [**yahz**-dah nah **nahr**-tahkh] exp.: skiing
narty wodne [**nahr**-ti **vod**-ne] exp.: water skis; surfboards
narteks [**nahr**-teks] m. narthex
nartnik [**nahrt**-ńeek] m. insect of the family Gerridae and Hydrometriidae
nartniki [nahrt-**ńee**-kee] pl. the family Gerridae and Hydrometriidae of insects
nartorolki [nahr-to-**rol**-kee] pl. roller skis for training without snow
nartosanki [nahr-to-**sahn**-kee] pl. variety of sled
nartostrada [nahr-to-**strah**-dah] f. ski trail
narty [**nahr**-ti] pl. skis; a pair of skis
jeździć na nartach [**yeźh**-dźheećh nah **nahr**-tahkh] exp.: to ski
naruszać [nah-**roo**-shahćh] v. disturb; violate; injure; harm; cut into; break into; derange; spoil; transgress; intrude upon; encroach on (territory, etc.) (*repeatedly*)
naruszać czyjeś interesy [nah-roo-shahćh **chi**-yeśh een-te-**re**-si] exp.: to prejudice somebody's interests
naruszać czyjeś prawa [nah-roo-shahćh **chi**-yeśh **prah**-vah] exp.: to encroach on (upon) somebody's rights
naruszać porządek publiczny [nah-**roo**-shahćh po-**zhown**-dek poob-**leech**-ni] exp.: to create a disturbance
naruszać prawo [nah-**roo**-shahćh **prah**-vo] exp.: to offend against the law; to break the law
naruszać przepisy [nah-roo-shahćh pshe-**pee**-si] exp.: to break the rules
naruszać regulamin [nah-roo-shahćh re-goo-**lah**-meen] exp.: to offend against the rules; to break

the rules
naruszać równowagę [nah-roo-shahćh roov-no-vah-gan] exp.: to upset the (existing) balance; to throw (something) out of balance; to unbalance something
naruszać spokój [nah-roo-shahćh spo-kooy] exp.: to disturb the peace
naruszać tajemnicę [nah-roo-shahćh tah-yem-ńee-tsan] exp.: to disclose a secret
naruszać terytorium [nah-roo-shahćh te-ri-to-ryoom] exp.: to encroach on (upon) a territory

naruszenie [nah-roo-she-ńe] n. offense; disturbance; breach
naruszenie czyjejś reputacji [nah-roo-she-ńe chi-yeyśh re-poo-tah-tsyee] exp.: prejudice to somebody's reputation
naruszenie porządku publicznego [nah-roo-she-ńe po-zhownt-koo poob-leech-ne-go] exp.: breach of the peace
naruszenie prawa [nah-roo-she-ńe prah-vah] exp.: offence against the law; breaking of the law

naruszyciel [nah-roo-shi-ćhel] m. violator; disturber (of the peace, etc.)

naruszyć [nah-roo-shićh] v. disturb; violate; injure; harm; cut into; break into; derange; spoil; transgress; intrude upon; encroach on (territory, etc.)

narwać [nah-rvahćh] v. pluck; pick; gather

narwać się [nah-rvahćh śhan] v. incur ill will; expose oneself to danger; pluck a lot; pick at will; get tired of picking

narwal [nahr-vahl] m. narwhal; unicorn whale; unicorn fish
narwale [nahr-vah-le] pl. the family of Monodon monoceros

narwaniec [nahr-vah-ńets] m. madcap; crank; hothead

narwany [nahr-vah-ni] adj.m. hotheaded; reckless; rash; fitful; erratic

nary [nah-ri] pl. plank bed

narybek [nah-ri-bek] m. small fry; coming generation

narybić [nah-ri-beećh] v. stock with fish

narychtować [nah-rikh-to-vahćh] v. aim; train; prepare; get ready; fix

naryczeć się [nah-ri-chećh śhan] v. colloq: cry a lot; get tired of crying

narys [nah-ris] m. scratch; sketch; rough plan; outline

narysować [nah-ri-so-vahćh] v. draw; trace; delineate; portray; give a picture (of)

narysować się [nah-ri-so-vahćh śhan] v. appear; stand out (against a background); be outlined

narywać [nah-ri-vahćh] v. pluck; pick; gather (*repeatedly*)

narywać się [nah-ri-vahćh śhan] v. incur ill will; expose oneself to danger; pluck a lot; pick at will; get tired of picking (*repeatedly*)

narywanie [nah-ri-vah-ńe] n. gathering; plucking; picking

narywanie się [nah-ri-vah-ne śhan] n. exposing oneself to danger

narząd [nah-zhownt] m. organ

narządowy [nah-zhown-do-vi] adj.m. of a bodily organ

narządzać [nah-zhown-dzahćh] v. prepare; adjust; get ready; mend; fix (*repeatedly*)

narządzanie [nah-zhown-dzah-ńe] n. preparation; getting ready

narządzić [nah-zhown-dźheećh] v. prepare; adjust; get ready; mend; fix

narządzić się [nah-zhown-dźheećh śhan] v. govern a lot; get tired of governing

narzecze [nah-zhe-che] n. (primitive) dialect

narzeczeni [nah-zhe-che-ńee] pl. engaged couple

narzeczeński [nah-zhe-cheń-skee] adj.m. of betrothal

narzeczeństwo [nah-zhe-cheń-stfo] n. period of betrothal; betrothal; engagement; engaged couple

narzeczona [nah-zhe-cho-nah] f. fiancee; an engaged woman

narzeczony [nah-zhe-cho-ni] m. fiance; an engaged man

narzekać [nah-zhe-kahćh] v.

complain (of); grumble at; grumble about; lament; slang: kick at; kick against (*repeatedly*)
cierpieć nie narzekając [**ćher**-pyećh ńe nah-zhe-**kah**-yownts] exp.: to suffer without complaint
narzekający [nah-zhe-kah-**yown**-tsi] adj.m. querulous; peevish; full of complaints
narzekanie [nah-zhe-**kah**-ńe] n. complaints; slang: kick; bitching
bez narzekania [bez nah-zhe-**kah**-ńah] exp.: without complaints
ustawiczne narzekanie [oos-tah-**veech**-ne nah-zhe-**kah**-ńe] exp.: constant complaining; querulousness
narzędnik [nah-**zhand**-ńeek] m. (gram.) instrumental case; ablative
narzędnikowy [nah-zhand-ńee-**ko**-vi] adj.m. of the instrumental case
narzędziarnia [nah-zhan-**dźhahr**-ńah] f. tool-storage; toolhouse; toolshed; toolroom
narzędziarstwo [nah-zhan-**dźhahr**-stfo] n. toolmaking; science of tools
narzędziarz [nah-**zhan**-dźhahsh] m. toolmaker
narzędzie [nah-**zhan**-dźhe] n. tool; utensil; implement; instrument
narzędziowiec [nah-zhan-**dźho**-vyets] m. toolmaker
narzędziownia [nah-zhan-**dźhov**-ńah] f. toolroom; toolhouse
narzędziowy [nah-zhan-**dźho**-vi] adj.m. tool (steel, etc.); m. toolmaker
narzępik [nah-**zhan**-peek] m. horse tick; forest fly
narzępikowaty [nah-zhan-pee-ko-**vah**-ti] adj.m. of horse flies; of the genus of Hippobosca equina
narzępikowate [nah-zhan-pee-ko-**vah**-te] pl. horse flies; the genus of Hippobosca equina
narznąć [**nah**-zhnownćh] v. notch; make incisions; cut (chaff); slaughter a lot
narzucać [nah-**zhoo**-tsahćh] v. throw over; shovel on; fling on; slip on (a coat, etc.); impose (taxes, etc.); force upon; press upon; intrude upon; boss; overrule; force somebody's hand; thrust upon (*repeatedly*)
narzucać swoją wolę [nah-**zhoo**-tsahćh **sfo**-yown **vo**-lan] exp.: to impose one's will; colloq: to boss somebody; to get one's way
narzucać swoje zdanie [nah-**zhoo**-tsahćh **sfo**-ye **zdah**-ńe] exp.: to force one's opinion upon
narzucać warunki [nah-**zhoo**-tsahćh vah-**roon**-kee] exp.: to impose one's terms (conditions)
narzucać się [nah-**zhoo**-tsahćh śhan] v. obtrude oneself; thrust oneself; throw oneself (*repeatedly*)
to się samo narzuca [to śhan **sah**-mo nah-**zhoo**-tsah] exp.: it suggests itself; it is the obvious thing to do
narzucający się [nah-zhoo-tsah-**yown**-tsi śhan] adj.m. officious; obtrusive; intrusive
narzucanie [nah-zhoo-**tsah**-ńe] n. imposition (of conditions, etc.)
narzucanie się [nah-zhoo-**tsah**-ńe śhan] n. obtrusion; intrusion; officiousness
narzucić [nah-**zhoo**-ćheećh] v. throw over; shovel on; fling on; slip on (a coat, etc.); impose (taxes, etc.); force upon; press upon; intrude upon; boss; overrule; force somebody's hand; thrust upon
narzucić się [nah-**zhoo**-ćheećh śhan] v. obtrude oneself; thrust oneself; throw oneself
narzucony [nah-zhoo-**tso**-ni] adj.m. imposed
narzucony samemu sobie [nah-zhoo-**tso**-ni sah-**me**-moo **so**-bye] exp.: self-imposed
narzut [**nah**-zhoot] m. surcharge; coating (with plaster); floating (coat of plaster)
narzuta [nah-**zhoo**-tah] f. cover; bedspread; overlay; coverlet
narzutka [nah-**zhoot**-kah] f. cape; mantle
narzutniak [nah-**zhoot**-ńahk] m. erratic rock
narzutnica [nah-zhoot-**ńee**-tsah] f.

wall plastering machine
narzutowiec [nah-zhoo-**to**-vyets] m. erratic bolder
narzutowy [nah-zhoo-**to**-vi] adj.m. erratic (rock, sand, etc.)
głaz narzutowy [gwahs nah-zhoo-**to**-vi] exp.: erratic bolder
narzynać [nah-**zhi**-nahćh] v. notch; make incisions; cut (chaff); slaughter a lot (*repeatedly*)
narzynka [nah-**zhin**-kah] f. threading die; die nut
narżnąć [**nahr**-zhnownćh] v. notch; make incisions; cut (chaff); slaughter a lot
narżnica [nahr-**zhńee**-tsah] f. dovetail (joint) saw
nas [nahs] pron. us
nasad [**nah**-saht] m. handle; horizontal timber in a ranch wagon
nasada [nah-**sah**-dah] f. base; bottom; root
nasadka [nah-**saht**-kah] f. socket; adapter; cap; cover; thimble; ferrule; trap; snare; brooder; brooding hen; lens cap
nasadkowy [nah-saht-**ko**-vi] adj.m. adapting; supplementary (lens, etc.)
soczewka nasadkowa [so-**chef**-kah nah-saht-**ko**-vah] exp.: supplementary lens
nasadnik [nah-**sahd**-ńeek] m. impost
nasadowy [nah-sah-**do**-vi] adj.m. basal
nasadzać [nah-**sah**-dzahćh] v. fix; set; put; place; helve; haft; mount; plant; accumulate; put in ambush; hire (an assassin, etc.) (*repeatedly*)
nasadzanie [nah-sah-**dzah**-ńe] n. mounting; fixing
nasadzić [nah-**sah**-dźheećh] v. fix; set; put; place; helve; mount; plant; accumulate; put in ambush; hire (an assassin, etc.)
nasalać [nah-**sah**-lahćh] v. salt (meat, fish, etc.); colloq: make improper; make indecent; make suggestive remarks (*repeatedly*)
nasamprzód [nah-**sahm**-pshoot] adv. first (of all); at first; first and foremost; in the first place; to begin with; to start with; see: **najpierw**
nasączać [nah-**sown**-chahćh] v. drip; trickle; saturate; soak (full of liquid, etc.) (*repeatedly*)
nasączać się [nah-**sown**-chahćh śhan] v. get saturated (*repeatedly*)
nasączyć [nah-**sown**-chićh] v. drip; trickle; saturate; soak (full of liquid, etc.)
nasączyć się [nah-**sown**-chićh śhan] v. get saturated
naschodzić się [nah-**skho**-dźheećh śhan] v. meet (in large numbers); gather in a crowd
na schwał [nah skhfahw] exp.: splendid; magnificent; wonderful; beyond all expression
chłop na schwał [khwop nah skhfahw] exp.: hale fellow well met; hale and hearty fellow; strapping man; a strong man; man of powerful build; a great guy; a wonderful fellow
nasennie [nah-**sen**-ńe] adv. soporifically; in sleep-inducing way; narcotically
nasenny [nah-**sen**-ni] adj.m. soporific; sleep-inducing; sleep-producing
pigułka nasenna [pee-**goow**-kah nah-**sen**-nah] exp.: sleeping pill
środek nasenny [**śhro**-dek nah-**sen**-ni] exp.: sleeping pill; a soporific; sleep inducing drug
nasercowy [nah-ser-**tso**-vi] adj.m. cordial; heart (medication, etc.)
środek nasercowy [**śhro**-dek nah-ser-**tso**-vi] exp.: a cordial; cardiac medication
na serio [nah **ser**-yo] exp.: in earnest; in real ernest; really; honestly; sincerely
nasępiać [nah-**san**-pyahćh] v. knit (one's brow) (*repeatedly*)
nasępiać się [nah-**san**-pyahćh śhan] v. cloud over; scowl; look sullen (*repeatedly*)
nasępić [nah-**san**-peećh] v. knit (one's brow)
nasępić się [nah-**san**-peećh śhan] v. cloud over; scowl; look sullen
nasępiony [nah-san-**pyo**-ni] adj.m.

gloomy; scowling; sullen
nasiać [nah-śhahćh] v. sow
nasiad [nah-śhaht] m. brood case (for hens)
nasiadać [nah-śhah-dahćh] v. brood (*repeatedly*)
nasiadka [nah-śhaht-kah] f. brooding hen; brooder
nasiadowy [nah-śhah-do-vi] adj.m. of a hip-bath
kąpiel nasiadowa [kown-pyel nah-śhah-do-vah] exp.: hip-bath; sitz bath
nasiadówka [nah-śhah-doof-kah] f. sitz bath; hip-bath
nasianie [nah-śhah-ńe] n. sowing
nasiany [nah-śhah-ni] adj.m. self-sown
nasiąkać [nah-śhown-kahćh] v. soak up; become saturated; imbibe; soak in; become imbibed; be imbibed (with ideas, etc.); be saturated; be impregnated (*repeatedly*)
nasiąkanie [nah-śhown-kah-ńe] n. absorbing; soaking; imbibing
nasiąkliwość [nah-śhown-klee-vośhćh] f. absorbability; impregnability
nasiąkliwy [nah-śhown-klee-vi] adj.m. absorbable
nasiąknąć [nah-śhownk-nownćh] v. soak up; become saturated; imbibe; soak in; become imbibed; be imbibed (with ideas, etc.); be saturated; be impregnated
nasiąść [nah-śhownśhćh] v. brood
nasiec [nah-śhets] v. cut; chop up; hash (meat, etc.); mow (grass, etc.); kill; cut to pieces; flog
nasieczony [nah-śhe-cho-ni] adj.m. chopped up; cut to pieces
nasiedzieć się [nah-śhe-dźhećh śhan] v. sit a long time; be weary of sitting; stay long enough (in prison, etc.)
nasiekać [nah-śhe-kahćh] v. cut; chop up; hash (meat, etc.); mow (grass, etc.); kill; cut to pieces; flog
nasiekanie [nah-śhe-kah-ńe] n. cutting; chopping; mowing; killing; flogging
nasieniak [nah-śhe-ńahk] m. malignant cancer of the testicles
nasienie [nah-śhe-ńe] n. seed; sperm; semen; posterity
diabelskie nasienie [dyah-bel-ske nah-śhe-ńe] exp.: spawn of the devil
hodowca nasion [kho-dof-tsah nah-śhon] exp.: seed producer
nasiona traw siennych [nah-śho-nah trahf śhen-nikh] exp.: hayseed
wyhodować z nasienia [vi-kho-do-vahćh z nah-śhe-ńah] exp.: to rise from the seed
nasieniodajny [nah-śhe-ńo-dahy-ni] adj.m. seed (plant, etc.)
nasieniotok [nah-śhe-ńo-tok] m. spermatorrhea
nasieniowód [nah-śhe-ńo-voot] m. spermatic duct
nasiennia [nah-śhen-ńah] f. pericarp
nasiennictwo [nah-śhen-ńeets-tfo] n. seed production
nasienniczy [nah-śhen-ńee-chi] adj.m. of seed production
firma nasiennicza [feer-mah nah-śhen-ńee-chah] exp.: seed firm
nasiennik [nah-śhen-ńeek] m. spermatin; seedling; seed-tree
nasienny [nah-śhen-ni] adj.m. seminal; seminiferous
las nasienny [lahs nah-śhen-ni] exp.: seedling forest
płyn nasienny [pwin nah-śhen-ni] exp.: semen
roślina nasienna [rośh-lee-nah nah-śhen-nah] exp.: seed plant
torebka nasienna [to-rep-kah nah-śhen-nah] exp.: seed bag
nasierdzie [nah-śher-dźhe] n. pericardium
nasiewać [nah-śhe-vahćh] v. sow; plant; seed (*repeatedly*)
nasiewanie [nah-śhe-vah-ńe] n. sowing; planting; seeding
nasiębierny [nah-śhan-byer-ni] adj.m. overshot (mill wheel, water wheel)
nasiężrzal [nah-śhanźh-zhahw] m. fern Ophioglossum
nasiężrzałowaty [nah-śhanźh-zhah-wo-vah-ti] adj.m. of the family Ophioglossaceae

nasiężrzałowate [nah-śhanźh-zhah-wo-vah-te] pl. the family Ophioglossaceae

nasilać się [nah-śhee-lahćh śhan] v. grow intense; intensify; become intense; grow stronger; increase; swell (*repeatedly*)

nasilenie [nah-śhee-le-ńe] n. intensification; intensity; increase; growth; force; strength; volume (of sound); exacerbation

nasilić się [nah-śhee-leećh śhan] v. grow intense; intensify; become intense; grow stronger; increase; swell

nasionko [nah-śhon-ko] n. small seed; small grain; a seed; a grain

nasionnica [nah-śhon-ńee-tsah] f. acalyptrate muscoid fly

nasionnice [nah-śhon-ńee-tse] pl. the family Trypetidae of acalyptrate muscoid flies

nasiono [nah-śho-no] n. kernel

nasionoznawstwo [nah-śho-no-znahf-stfo] n. science of seeds

nasiusiać [nah-śhoo-śhahćh] v. colloq: urinate

naskakać się [nah-skah-kahćh śhan] v. jump a lot; get tired of jumping

naskakiwać [nah-skah-kee-vahćh] v. jump upon; get reset (in a joint, etc.); collide with; colloq: attack; hit; accuse (somebody); accuse falsely (*repeatedly*)

naskalny [nah-skahl-ni] adj.m. lichenaceous

porosty naskalne [po-ros-ti nah-skahl-ne] exp.: lichens

naskałka [nah-skahw-kah] f. a plant of the heath family; Loiseleuria

naskamlać się [nah-skahm-lahćh śhan] v. whine a lot; get tired of whining; implore a lot; get tired of imploring

naskarżyć [nah-skahr-zhićh] v. lodge a complaint (against); inform (against); sneak (on); tell tales (on); complain (of)

naskarżyć się [nah-skahr-zhićh śhan] v. pour out complaints (about)

naskładać [nah-skwah-dahćh] v. accumulate; collect; gather; pile up; heap up; save up

naskoczyć [nah-sko-chićh] v. jump upon; get reset (in a joint, etc.); collide with; colloq: attack; hit; accuse (somebody); accuse falsely

naskorupienie [nah-sko-roo-pye-ńe] n. incrustation; scab; crustification

na skos [nah skos] exp.: adv. aslant; obliquely; slantwise; on the bias; askew

naskórek [nah-skoo-rek] m. outer skin; epidermis; cuticle

naskórkowaty [nah-skoor-ko-vah-ti] adj.m. epidermal

naskórkowość [nah-skoor-ko-vośhćh] f. skin effect

naskórkowy [nah-skoor-ko-vi] adj.m. epidermic; epidermal

naskórniak [nah-skoor-ńahk] m. external parasite (of animals)

naskórny [nah-skoor-ni] adj.m. endermic; cutaneous

naskrobać [nah-skro-bahćh] v. scrape (carrots, etc.); scrawl

naskrobać się [nah-skro-bahćh śhan] v. scrape a lot; get tired scraping

na skroś [nah skrośh] exp.: adv. right through; all the way across; from end to end; completely; utterly; fundamentally

na skutek [nah skoo-tek] exp.: as a result (of); in consequence; on account (of); owing (to); due (to); consequently; hence; therefore; through (an illness, etc.)

nasłać [nah-swahćh] v. incite (against); hire (an assassin, etc.); send (someone to badger, pester, etc.); strew; bed; litter (for horses, etc.)

nasłanie [nah-swah-ńe] n. sending (an assassin, etc.)

nasłoneczniać [nah-swo-nech-ńahćh] v. expose to the sun's rays; insolate; heat (*repeatedly*)

nasłoneczniać się [nah-swo-nech-ńahćh śhan] v. take a sun bath; get sun tan (*repeatedly*)

nasłonecznić [nah-swo-nech-ńeećh] v. expose to sun's rays; insolate; heat

nasłonecznić się [nah-swo-**nech**-ńeećh śhan] v. take a sun bath; get a sun tan
nasłonecznianie [nah-swo-nech-**ńah**-ńe] n. insolation
nasłonecznianie się [nah-swo-nech-**ńah**-ńe śhan] n. getting a sun tan; exposing oneself to sunshine
nasłonecznienie [nah-swo-nech-**ńe**-ńe] n. insolation
nasłoneczniony [nah-swo-nech-**ńo**-ni] adj.m. sun tanned
strona nasłoneczniona [**stro**-nah nah-swo-nech-**ńo**-nah] exp.: sunny side
nasłoneczny [nah-swo-**nech**-ni] adj.m. sunlit; sunny (side, etc.)
nasłuch [**nah**-swookh] m. monitoring
nasłuchać się [nah-**swoo**-khahćh śhan] v. hear plenty (of complaints, etc.)
nasłuchiwać [nah-swoo-**khee**-vahćh] v. monitor (radio); listen; be on the watch for; listen intently (*repeatedly*)
nasłuchiwanie [nah-swoo-khee-**vah**-ńe] n. monitoring
nasłuchowiec [nah-swoo-**kho**-vyets] m. (radio) monitor
nasłuchowy [nah-swoo-**kho**-vi] adj.m. (radio) monitoring
nasłupny [nah-**swoop**-ni] adj.m. pillared (on pillars)
nasłużyć się [nah-**swoo**-zhićh śhan] v. serve a lot; get tired of serving
nasmarować [nah-smah-**ro**-vahćh] v. smear over; grease; oil; lubricate; rub with ointment; butter; scrawl
nasmarować się [nah-smah-**ro**-vahćh śhan] v. smear over oneself; rub oneself with ointment; get dirty
nasmażyć [nah-**smah**-zhićh] v. fry (food, etc.); candy; make jam
nasmolić [nah-**smo**-leećh] v. dirty; blacken with soot
nasmołować [nah-smo-**wo**-vahćh] v. tar; coat with tar
nasnuć [**nah**-snooćh] v. reel (yarn); dream up (plans, etc.)
nasnuć się [**nah**-snooćh śhan] v. gather; cover the sky; drift over (with smoke, clouds, etc.); dream up a lot
nasnuwać [nah-**snoo**-vahćh] v. reel (yarn); dream up (plans, etc.) (*repeatedly*)
nasnuwać się [nah-**snoo**-vahćh śhan] v. gather; cover the sky; drift over (with smoke, clouds, etc.); dream up a lot (*repeatedly*)
nasobaczyć [nah-so-**bah**-chićh] v. curse a lot
nasolenie [nah-so-**le**-ńe] n. saltiness
nasolić [nah-**so**-leećh] v. salt (fish, etc.); make improper; make indecent; make suggestive remarks
naspraszać [nah-**sprah**-shahćh] v. invite (a lot of people)
nasprowadzać [nah-spro-**vah**-dzahćh] v. buy a lot; order a lot; get a lot; bring together (many people, etc.); call together; summon
nasrożać [nah-**sro**-zhahćh] v. give a stern look; give a severe appearance (to); bristle (*repeatedly*)
nasrożać się [nah-**sro**-zhahćh śhan] v. assume a stern look; look severe; appear stern; scowl (*repeatedly*)
nasrożony [nah-sro-**zho**-ni] adj.m. stern in appearance; severe
nasrożyć [nah-**sro**-zhićh] v. give a stern look; give a severe appearance (to); bristle
nasrożyć się [nah-**sro**-zhićh śhan] v. assume a stern look; look severe; appear stern; scowl
nassać [**nahs**-sahćh] v. suck in; draw
nassać się [**nahs**-sahćh śhan] v. suck one's fill
nastać [nah-**stahćh**] v. set in; enter; occur; come about; supervene; come after; follow; ensue; start (a watch, service, etc.); take over
nastała noc [nah-**stah**-wah nots] exp.: night came; night set in
nastał czas, kiedy... [**nah**-stahw chahs **ke**-di] exp.: there came a time when
nastało milczenie [nah-**stah**-wo

meel-**che**-ńe] exp.: a silence ensued

nastać się [nah-**stahćh** śh<u>an</u>] v. stand a lot; get tired of standing

nastalać [nah-**stah**-lahćh] v. acierate; convert into steel (*repeatedly*)

nastalić [nah-**stah**-leećh] v. acierate; convert into steel

na stałe [nah **stah**-we] exp.: for good

przyjechać na stałe [pshi-**ye**-khahćh nah **stah**-we] exp.: to come for good; to come to stay

nastały [nah-**stah**-wi] adj.m. ensuing; subsequent

nastanie [nah-**stah**-ńe] n. arrival; setting in; advent; coming

nastarczać [nah-**stahr**-chahćh] v. supply enough; keep pace with; cope with the demand; cope with; meet the demand (*repeatedly*)

nastarczyć [nah-**stahr**-chićh] v. supply enough; keep pace with; cope with the demand; cope with; meet the demand

nastarczyć potrzebom [nah-**stahr**-chićh po-**tshe**-bom] exp.: to meet the needs

nastawa [nah-**stah**-vah] f. topmast

nastawać [nah-**stah**-vahćh] v. insist; start service; be against; set in; enter; occur; come about; supervene; come after; follow; ensue; start (a watch, etc.); take over; seek (to ruin, kill, etc.) (*repeatedly*)

nastawać na kogoś [nah-**stah**-vahćh nah **ko**-gośh] exp.: to press someone

nastawać na czyjąś zgubę [nah-stah-vahćh nah chi-y<u>own</u>śh **zgoo**-b<u>an</u>] exp.: to seek somebody's ruin

nastawanie [nah-stah-**vah**-ńe] n. insistence

nastawczy [nah-**stahf**-chi] adj.m. adjustable; accomodational

zdolność nastawcza oka [zdol-nośhćh nah-**stahf**-chah **o**-kah] exp.: accommodation of the eye

nastawiacz [nah-**stah**-vyahch] m. setter; tuner; adjuster

nastawiać [nah-**stah**-vyahćh] v. set up; set right; tune in; point; put; place; stand lots of (furniture, etc.) (*repeatedly*)

nastawiać uszu [nah-**stah**-vyahćh oo-shoo] exp.: to prick up one's ears

nastawiać się [nah-**stah**-vyahćh śh<u>an</u>] v. expose oneself; turn towards; assume an attitude towards; incline to; get ready for; prepare for; make ready for; compose one's thoughts for; compose oneself to do (*repeatedly*)

nastawiać się wrogo do kogoś (czegoś) [nah-**stah**-vyahćh śh<u>an</u> **vro**-go do **ko**-gośh (**che**-gośh)] exp.: to turn against somebody (something)

nastawialny [nah-stah-**vyahl**-ni] adj.m. adjustable

nastawianie [nah-stah-**vyah**-ńe] n. tuning-in; adjusting; setting

nastawić [nah-**stah**-veećh] v. set up; set right; tune in; point; put; place; stand lots of (furniture, etc.); adapt

nastawić aparat [nah-**stah**-veećh ah-**pah**-raht] exp.: to point a camera

nastawić budzik [nah-**stah**-veećh boo-dźheek] exp.: to set an alarm clock

nastawić kogoś wrogo [nah-**stah**-veećh **ko**-gośh **vro**-go] exp.: to set somebody against; to make somebody antagonistic; to antagonize somebody

nastawić pułapkę [nah-**stah**-veećh poo-**wahp**-k<u>an</u>] exp.: to set a trap; to set a snare

nastawić radio na jakąś stację [nah-**stah**-veećh **rah**-dyo nah **yah**-k<u>own</u>śh **stah**-tsy<u>an</u>] exp.: to tune in to a station

nastawić wodę na herbatę [nah-**stah**-veećh **vo**-d<u>an</u> nah kher-**bah**-t<u>an</u>] exp.: to put the kettle on

nastawić zegarek [nah-**stah**-veećh ze-**gah**-rek] exp.: to set one's watch

nastawić złamaną kość [nah-**stah**-veećh zwah-**mah**-n<u>own</u>

košhćh] exp.: to set a broken bone
nastawić zwichnięty staw [nah-**stah**-veećh zveekh-ńan-ti stahf] exp.: to reduce a displaced joint; to reset a displaced joint
nastawić się [nah-**stah**-veećh šhan] v. expose oneself; turn towards; assume an attitude towards; incline to; get ready for; prepare for; make ready for; compose one's thoughts for; compose oneself to do
nastawienie [nah-stah-**vye**-ńe] n. attitude; bias; disposition; inclination; adjustment; regulation; setting (of broken bones, etc.)
negatywne nastawienie [ne-gah-**tiv**-ne nah-stah-**vye**-ńe] exp.: negative attitude
przychylne nastawienie [pshi-**khil**-ne nah-stah-**vye**-ńe] exp.: friendly attitude
wrogie nastawienie [**vro**-ge nah-stah-**vye**-ńe] exp.: bias against
nastawienie się [nah-stah-**vye**-ńe šhan] n. assuming an attitude
nastawiony [nah-stah-**vyo**-ni] adj.m. disposed (towards)
nastawiony pokojowo [nah-stah-**vyo**-ni po-ko-**yo**-vo] exp.: peaceful
wrogo nastawiony [**vro**-go nah-stah-**vyo**-ni] exp.: hostile
nastawka [nah-**stahf**-kah] f. adjustment device (a part of an apparatus for measuring, etc.)
nastawnia [nah-**stahv**-ńah] f. control room; signal box; control station
nastawnica [nah-stahv-**ńee**-tsah] f. control room; control station; (railroad, etc.) signal box; central control (of air conditioning, etc.)
nastawniczy [nah-stahv-**ńee**-chi] m. switchman; pointsman
nastawnik [nah-**stahv**-ńeek] m. controller; regulating unit
nastawność [nah-**stahv**-nošhćh] f. accomodation
nastawny [nah-**stahv**-ni] adj.m. adjustable
śrubka nastawna [**šhroop**-kah nah-**stahv**-nah] exp.: adjusting screw
nastąpić [nah-**stown**-peećh] v. tread on; step on; follow; come after; succeed; come next; ensue; supervence; come about; take place; set in; happen; occur; take over; launch (an attack, etc.)
nastąpiła śmierć [nah-stown-**pee**-wah šhmyerćh] exp.: death ensued; death followed
nastąpiły mrozy [nah-stown-**pee**-wi **mro**-zi] exp.: frost came
nastąpić się [nah-**stown**-peećh šhan] v. step aside
nastąpienie [nah-stown-**pye**-ńe] n. stepping on; ascending (the throne, etc.)
nastecznik [nah-**stech**-ńeek] m. spider wasp
nasteczniki [nah-stech-**ńee**-kee] pl. spider wasps; the family Pompilidae of spider wasps
następ [**nah**-stanp] m. pedal
następca [nah-**stanp**-tsah] m. successor; heir (to the throne)
następca tronu [nah-**stanp**-tsah **tro**-noo] exp.: Crown prince
następczość [nah-**stanp**-chošhćh] f. sequence
następczy [nah-**stanp**-chi] adj.m. sequent; consequent
następczyni [nah-stanp-**chi**-ńee] f. (female) successor; heiress
następnie [nah-**stanp**-ńe] adv. next; then; subsequently
a następnie [ah nah-**stanp**-ńe] exp.: whereupon; whereafter
następnik [nah-**stanp**-ńeek] m. consequent clause; apodosis; (musical) consequent
następny [nah-**stanp**-ni] adj.m. next; the next; the following; m. successor
następne pokolenia [nah-**stanp**-ne po-ko-**le**-ńah] exp.: subsequent generations
następnego dnia [nah-stanp-**ne**-go dńah] exp.: the next day; the day after
następnym razem [nah-**stanp**-nim **rah**-zem] exp.: next time
następny rangą [nah-**stanp**-ni rahn-gown] exp.: next in rank
w następnym tygodniu [v nahs-**tanp**-nim ti-**god**-ńoo] exp.: during

the next week
następować [nah-stan-**po**-vahćh] v. follow; tread; come after; ensue; step on; take place; succeed; come next; supervence; come about; set in; happen; occur; take over; launch (an attack, etc.) (*repeatedly*)
co następuje [tso nah-stan-**poo**-ye] exp.: what follows; the following
jak następuje [yahk nah-stan-**poo**-ye] exp.: as follows
następować bezpośrednio po czymś [nah-stan-**po**-vahćh bes-po-**śhred**-ńo po chimśh] exp.: to follow immediately after something; to tread on the heels of something
następować się [nah-stan-**po**-vahćh śhan] v. step aside (*repeatedly*)
następowanie [nah-stan-po-**vah**-ńe] n. succession
następstwo [nah-**stanp**-stfo] n. result; succession; upshot; consequence; outcome; sequel; corollary; aftereffects; sequence; order; heirdom
być następstwem czegoś [bićh nah-**stanp**-stfem **che**-gośh] exp.: to be the result of something
następstwo czasów [nah-**stanp**-stfo **chah**-soof] exp.: sequence of tenses
w następstwie czegoś [v nah-**stanp**-stfye **che**-gośh] exp.: as a result of something
następująco [nah-stan-poo-**yown**-tso] adv. successively; as follows; in the following terms
następujący [nah-stan-poo-**yown**-tsi] adj.m. (the) successive; the following; the next
nastia [**nah**-styah] f. nastic movement
na stojaka [nah sto-**yah**-kah] exp.: adv. standing (on the bus, etc.)
nastolatek [nah-sto-**lah**-tek] m. teenager
nastolatka [nah-sto-**laht**-kah] f. (girl) teenager
nastolatki [nah-sto-**laht**-kee] pl. the teenagers
nastoletni [nah-sto-**let**-ńee] adj.m. teenager (fashion, etc.)
nastopny [nah-**stop**-ni] adj.m. plantigrade
zwierzęta nastopne [zvye-**zhan**-tah nah-**stop**-ne] exp.: the plantigrada
nastój [**nah**-stooy] m. infusion; tincture
nastrajać [nah-**strah**-yahćh] v. attune; tune up; tune; dispose to (*repeatedly*)
nastrajać się [nah-**strah**-yahćh śhan] v. adopt a mood (of solemnity, etc.) (*repeatedly*)
nastrajanie [nah-strah-**yah**-ńe] n. tuning; attuning (an instrument, etc.)
nastrajanie się [nah-strah-**yah**-ńe śhan] n. putting oneself in a mood; adopting a mood
nastraszyć [nah-**strah**-shićh] v. frighten; intimidate; scare; alarm; startle
nastraszyć się [nah-**strah**-shićh śhan] v. be frightened; take fright (at); get scared; be alarmed; be startled
nastręczać [nah-**stran**-chahćh] v. afford; offer; procure; recommend; present (difficulties, etc.) (*repeatedly*)
nastręczać się [nah-**stran**-chahćh śhan] v. occur; be present; present itself; arise; crop up; come to one's mind (*repeatedly*)
nastręczyć [nah-**stran**-chićh] v. afford; recommend; present (difficulties, etc.); offer; procure
nastręczyć się [nah-**stran**-chićh śhan] v. occur; be present; present itself; arise; crop up; come to one's mind
nastroić [nah-**stro**-eećh] v. attune; tune up; tune; dispose to
nastroić się [nah-**stro**-eećh śhan] v. adopt a mood (of solemnity, etc.)
nastrojenie [nah-stro-**ye**-ńe] n. tuning up; disposition (to); mood
nastrojony [nah-stro-**yo**-ni] adj.m. in tune; in a mood (for)
nastrojowiec [nah-stro-**yo**-vyets] m. moody person; person given to moods

nastrojowo [nah-stro-**yo**-vo] adv. romantically; in a poetic vein
nastrojowość [nah-stro-**yo**-vośhćh] f. romantic atmosphere; poetic feeling
nastrojowy [nah-stro-**yo**-vi] adj.m. romantic; conducive to dreams; moody; full of feelings; pathetic; stirring; poetic
nastrosz [**nah**-strosh] m. epacris plant; plant of the Epacris family
nastroszać [nah-**stro**-shahćh] v. bristle up; perk up; heap up; rise; erect; ruffle (feathers); cock (ears, etc.) (*repeatedly*)
nastroszać się [nah-**stro**-shahćh śhan] v. bristle up; stand erect; assume a pugnacious attitude; become stern (*repeatedly*)
nastroszony [nah-stro-**sho**-ni] adj.m. erect; bristling; colloq: defensive
nastroszowaty [nah-stro-sho-**vah**-ti] adj.m. epacridaceous; epacrid
nastroszowate [nah-stro-sho-**vah**-te] pl. the Epacris family
nastroszyć [nah-**stro**-shićh] v. bristle up; perk up; heap up; rise; erect; ruffle (feathers); cock (ears, etc.)
nastroszyć się [nah-**stro**-shićh śhan] v. bristle up; stand erect; assume a pugnacious attitude; become stern
nastrój [**nah**-strooy] m. mood; humor; state of mind; frame of mind; atmosphere; public feeling
mieć nastrój do czegoś [myećh nah-strooy do **che**-gośh] exp.: to be in the mood for something
nastroje pokojowe [nah-**stro**-ye po-ko-**yo**-ve] exp.: peaceful atmosphere
nastroje wojenne [nah-**stro**-ye vo-**yen**-ne] exp.: warlike atmosphere
nie mieć nastroju [ńe myećh nah-**stro**-yoo] exp.: to be in no mood; to have no mood (for)
popsuć nastrój w towarzystwie [**po**-psoośh **nah**-strooy f to-vah-**zhis**-tfye] exp.: to cast a damper over the company; to sour the atmosphere
w dobrym nastroju [v **dob**-rim nah-**stro**-yoo] exp.: in high spirits
nastrzelać [nah-**stshe**-lahćh] v. shoot a lot
nastrzelać byków [nah-**stshe**-lahćh **bi**-koof] exp.: colloq: to make a lot of mistakes
nastrzelać się [nah-**stshe**-lahćh śhan] v. shoot at will; get tired of shooting
nastrzępiać [nah-**stshan**-pyahćh] v. fray; tear edges; erect; bristle; ruffle (*repeatedly*)
nastrzępiać się [nah-**stshan**-pyahćh śhan] v. bristle up (*repeatedly*)
nastrzępić [nah-**stshan**-peećh] v. fray; tear edges; erect; bristle; ruffle
nastrzępić się [nah-**stshan**-peećh śhan] v. bristle up
nastrzępiony [nah-stshan-**pyo**-ni] adj.m. with torn edges
nastrzyc [**nah**-stshits] v. cut a lot (of paper, hair, etc.)
na stu [nah stoo] exp.: per hundred (men, etc.)
nastu [**nah**-stoo] exp.: colloq: between ten and twenty (men, etc.)
nasturcja [nah-**stoor**-tsyah] f. nasturtium; lark-heel
nasturcjowaty [nah-stoor-tsyo-**vah**-ti] adj.m. tropaeolaceous
nasturcjowate [nah-stoor-tsyo-**vah**-te] pl. the nasturtium family
nastyczny [nah-**stich**-ni] adj.m. nastic (plant)
ruchy nastyczne [**roo**-khi nah-**stich**-ne] exp.: nastic movements
nasunąć [nah-**soo**-nownćh] v. shove up; draw over; afford; overthrust; offer (possibilities, etc.)
nasunąć myśl [nah-**soo**-nownćh miśhl] exp.: to suggest; to bring something to mind
nasunąć wątpliwości [nah-soo-nownćh vownt-plee-**vośh**-ćhee] exp.: to raise doubts
nasunąć się [nah-**soo**-nownćh śhan] v. occur; arise; creep; glide; emerge; present (itself); suggest (itself to ...)
nasunąć się komuś [nah-soo-nownćh śhan **ko**-moośh] exp.: to come to somebody's head; to

occur to somebody; to suggest itself to somebody; to come to one's mind
nasunąć się na siebie [nah-soo-nownćh śhan nah śhe-bye] exp.: to overlap
nasunięcie [nah-soo-ńan-ćhe] n. overlap; overfold
nasuszyć [nah-soo-shićh] v. dry a quantity (of flowers, etc.)
nasuw [nah-soof] m. overlap; overfold
nasuwać [nah-soo-vahćh] v. shove up; draw over; afford; overthrust; offer (possibilities, etc.); (*repeatedly*)
nasuwać wątpliwości [nah-soo-vahćh vownt-plee-vośh-ćhee] exp.: to raise doubts
nasuwać się [nah-soo-vahćh śhan] v. occur; arise; creep; glide; emerge; present itself; suggest itself (to) (*repeatedly*)
nasuwanie [nah-soo-vah-ńe] n. drawing over; offering; overthrusting
nasuwka [nah-soof-kah] f. muff; nipple; sleeve
nasycać [nah-si-tsahćh] v. satiate; satisfy; sate; saturate; appease; fill; prevade; imbue; impregnate; soak; steep; charge; glut (*repeatedly*)
nasycać się [nah-si-tsahćh śhan] v. eat one's fill; eat enough; be saturated; appease one's hunger; enjoy to the full; gratify one's desire (for); be impregnated (with); be imbued (with); imbibe (*repeatedly*)
nasycalnia [nah-si-tsahl-ńah] f. (wood) treating plant
nasycalnia drewna [nah-si-tsahl-ńah drev-nah] exp.: wood treating plant; timber preserving plant
nasycalnik [nah-si-tsahl-ńeek] m. saturator
nasycalny [nah-si-tsahl-ni] adj.m. saturable
nasycanie [nah-si-tsah-ńe] n. saturation
nasycarka [nah-si-tsahr-kah] f. impregnating machine
nasycenie [nah-si-tse-ńe] n. satiation; satisfaction; gratification; saturation; impregnation; permeation
nasycenie barwy [nah-si-tse-ńe bahr-vi] exp.: saturation of color
nasycić [nah-si-ćheećh] v. satiate; satisfy; sate; saturate; appease; fill; prevade; imbue; impregnate; soak; steep; charge; glut
nasycić głód [nah-si-ćheećh gwoot] exp.: to appease one's hunger; to satisfy one's hunger
nasycić się [nah-si-ćheećh śhan] v. eat one's fill; eat enough; be saturated; appease one's hunger; enjoy to the full; gratify one's desire (for); be impregnated (with); be imbued (with); imbibe
nasycony [nah-si-tso-ni] adj.m. satiated; saturated; replete
nasyłać [nah-si-wahćh] v. send on (to pester, badger, kill, etc.) (*repeatedly*)
nasyp [nah-sip] m. embankment; bank; mound
nasypać [nah-si-pahćh] v. pour in; spread up; pour; heap; strew (dry powder, etc.) (does not apply to any liquid)
nasypanie [nah-si-pah-ńe] n. spreading; heaping (of dry powders, etc.)
nasypisko [nah-si-pees-ko] n. mound; hillock
nasypywać [nah-si-pi-vahćh] v. pour in; spread up; pour; heap; strew (dry powder, etc. - does not apply to any liquid) (*repeatedly*)
nasz [nahsh] pron. our; ours
dobra nasza! [dob-rah nah-shah] excl.: hurray!
po naszemu [po nah-she-moo] exp.: according to our custom; after our fashion; as we do it; Polish fashion; in our language
naszarpać [nah-shahr-pahćh] v. tear apart; tear a lot (of something)
naszarpać się [nah-shahr-pahćh śhan] v. tear a lot; get tired tearing up
naszatkować [nah-shaht-ko-vahćh]

v. shred a lot; shred plenty
naszczekać [nah-**shche**-kahćh] v. bark; slang: abuse; revile; slander
naszczekiwać [nah-shche-**kee**-vahćh] v. bark (off and on, from time to time) (*repeatedly*)
naszczekiwanie [nah-shche-kee-**vah**-ńe] n. barking from time to time
naszczeknąć [nah-**shchek**-nownćh] v. bark; slang: abuse; revile; slander (mob jargon)
naszczepić [nah-**shche**-peećh] v. vaccinate (a lot); inoculate (a lot); graft (a lot of plants, etc.)
naszczuć [nah-shchooćh] v. set (a dog at someone, a person against another, etc.)
naszczytnik [nah-**shchit**-ńeek] m. decorative element at the top of an (architectual) elevation; acroterium
naszelnik [nah-**shel**-ńeek] m. part of draft horse's harness; trace
naszeptać [nah-**shep**-tahćh] v. whisper (into somebody's ear, etc.); whisper a lot
naszkicować [nah-shkee-**tso**-vahćh] v. sketch; make a sketch of; outline; draw up (a plan, etc.)
naszkicować plan [nah-shkee-**tso**-vahćh plahn] exp.: to draft a plan; to draw up a plan
naszkliwny [nah-**shklee**-vni] adj.m. enamel (painting)
naszkodzić [nah-**shko**-dźheećh] v. cause a lot of damage; prejudice
naszły [nah-shwi] adj.m. saturated
naszpikować [nah-shpee-**ko**-vahćh] v. lard; stuff; interlard
naszpikować się [nah-shpee-**ko**-vahćh śhan] v. swallow a lot (pills, etc.)
na sztorc [nah shtorts] exp.: upright; endwise; endways; end on; on end
naszukać się [nah-**shoo**-kahćh śhan] v. search a lot; spend a lot of time searching
naszycie [nah-**shi**-ćhe] n. trimmings
naszycie się [nah-**shi**-ćhe śhan] n. getting tired of sewing
naszyć [nah-shićh] v. sew on; trim (with fur, ribbons, etc.)
naszyć się [nah-shićh śhan] v. sew plenty; get tired of sewing
naszyjnik [nah-**shiy**-ńeek] m. necklace; neck jewelry
naszykować [nah-shi-**ko**-vaćh] v. get ready; prepare
naszywać [nah-**shi**-vahćh] v. sew on; trim (with fur, ribbons, etc.) (*repeatedly*)
naszywanie [nah-shi-**vah**-ńe] n. trimming
naszywanka [nah-shi-**vahn**-kah] f. trimming
naszywany [nah-shi-**vah**-ni] adj.m. sewn on
kieszeń naszywana [ke-sheń nah-shi-**vah**-nah] exp.: patch pocket
naszywka [nah-**shif**-kah] f. stripe; band
naści! [nahśh-ćhee] excl.: colloq: take this!; here you are!; just take it!
naściągać [nah-**śhćhown**-gahćh] v. assemble; gather; collect; drag together; steal a lot; pinch
naście [nahśh-ćhe] exp.: colloq: between ten and twenty (horses, etc.)
naścielać [nah-**śhćhe**-wahćh] v. strew; litter (*repeatedly*)
na ścieżaj [nah **śhćhe**-zhahy] exp.: wide open
naścinać [nah-**śhćhee**-nahćh] v. cut plenty (of flowers, etc.)
naśladować [nah-śhlah-**do**-vahćh] v. imitate; mimic; reproduce; copy; forge; mime; follow in somebody's footsteps; play the ape; ape; counterfeit (*repeatedly*)
naśladowanie [nah-śhlah-do-**vah**-ńe] n. imitation; copy
godny naśladowania [**god**-ni nah-śhlah-do-**vah**-ńah] exp.: deserving of imitation
naśladowca [nah-śhlah-**dof**-tsah] m. imitator
naśladowczy [nah-śhlah-**dof**-chi] adj.m. imitative
naśladowczyni [nah-śhlah-dof-**chi**-ńee] f. (woman) imitator
naśladownictwo [nah-śhlah-dov-**ńee**-tstfo] n. imitation; counterfeit; forgery; mimicry
naśladownictwo dźwiękowe [nah-śhlah-dov-**ńeets**-tfo

dźhvyan-**ko**-ve] exp.: onomatopeia

naśladownik [nah-śhlah-**dov**-ńeek] m. simulator

na ślepo [nah **śhle**-po] exp.: blindly

naślęczeć [nah-**śhlan**-chećh] v. work tediously; peg away

naślęczeć się [nah-**śhlan**-chećh śhan] v. peg away (at); work long (at); get tired pegging away

naślinić [nah-**śhlee**-ńeećh] v. moisten with saliva; lick (stamps, etc.); drivel; slaver; drool

naśmiać się [nah-**śhmyahćh** śhan] v. laugh at; deride; laugh to the full; poke fun (at); have a good laugh

naśmiecić [nah-**śhmye**-ćheećh] v. make a mess; leave rubbish behind one; litter

naśmiewać się [nah-**śhmye**-vahćh śhan] v. laugh at; deride; laugh to the full (*repeatedly*)

naśnieżny [nah-**śhńezh**-ni] adj.m. living in the snow; living in a cold environment

naświetlać [nah-**śhfye**-tlahćh] v. explain; irradiate; expose; show in a certain light; throw some light; shed some light; elucidate (*repeatedly*)
naświetlać sprawę [nah-**śhfye**-tlahćh **sprah**-van] exp.: to clarify a matter; to shed light on a question; to elucidate

naświetlać się [nah-**śhfye**-tlahćh śhan] v. expose oneself to irradiation (*repeatedly*)

naświetlanie [na-śhfye-**tlah**-ńe] n. elucidation; irradiation; exposure; light shed upon (a question, etc.)

naświetlenie [nah-śhfye-**tle**-ńe] n. elucidation; irradiation; exposure; light shed upon (a question, etc.)

naświetlenie się [nah-śhfye-**tle**-ńe śhan] n. (taking) a sun bath; exposure to X-rays; exposure to irradiation

naświetlić [nah-**śhfye**-tleećh] v. explain; irradiate; expose; show in a certain light; throw some light; shed some light; elucidate

naświetlić się [nah-**śhfye**-tleećh śhan] v. expose oneself to irradiation; take a sun bath; expose oneself to X-rays

naświnić [nah-**śhfee**-ńeećh] v. make a mess; leave litter behind one; be a great hindrance; play a dirty trick (to)

natańczyć się [nah-**tahń**-chićh śhan] v. dance at will; be weary with dancing

natapiać [nah-**tah**-pyahćh] v. melt; drown (many people, etc.); sink (many ships, boats, etc.) (*repeatedly*)

natapirować [nah-tah-pee-**ro**-vahćh] v. make a ruffled up hairdo

natarcie [nah-**tahr**-ćhe] n. a rub; rubbing; onslaught; attack; offensive; advance

natarczywie [nah-tahr-**chi**-vye] adv. insistently; pressingly; urgently; importunately; obtrusively

natarczywość [nah-tahr-**chi**-vośhćh] f. insistence; obtrusiveness; urgency; pressure; importunity

natarczywy [nah-tahr-**chi**-vi] adj.m. insistent; pressing; urgent; obtrusive; importunate

nataskać [nah-**tahs**-kahćh] v. carry a lot; bring a lot (of wood, etc.)

nataskać się [nah-**tahs**-kahćh śhan] v. carry a lot; get tired of carrying

nataszczyć [nah-**tahsh**-chićh] v. carry a lot; bring a lot (of wood, etc.)

natchnąć [**naht**-khnownćh] v. inspire; infuse; penetrate (with feelings, etc.); breathe; instill
natchnąć kogoś jakimś uczuciem [naht-khnownćh **ko**-gośh **yah**-keemśh oo-**choo**-ćhem] exp.: to inspire somebody with a feeling

natchnienie [naht-**khńe**-ńe] n. inspiration; brain wave; impulse; afflation; happy thought
znajdować w czymś natchnienie [znahy-do-vahćh f chimśh naht-**khńe**-ńe] exp.: to be inspired by something

natchniony [naht-**khńo**-ni] adj.m. inspired

natenczas [nah-**ten**-chahs] adv.

then; at that time; as
natęsknić się [nah-tansk-ńeećh śhan] v. long a lot; get tired of longing (for)
natężać [nah-tan-zhahćh] v. strain; intensify; strengthen; exert; heighten; enhance (*repeatedly*)
natężać się [nah-tan-zhahćh śhan] v. strain oneself; exert oneself; put one's back into a task; become intesified; become strengthened (*repeatedly*)
natężenie [nah-tan-zhe-ńe] n. tension; strain; effort; pitch
natężenie dźwięku [nah-tan-zhe-ńe dźhvyan-koo] exp.: volume of sound
natężenie pola magnetycznego [nah-tan-zhe-ńe po-lah mahg-ne-tich-ne-go] exp.: field strength
natężenie prądu [nah-tan-zhe-ńe prown-doo] exp.: current intensity
z natężeniem [z nah-tan-zhe-ńem] exp.: with effort; exerting oneself
natężony [nah-tan-zho-ni] adj.m. intense; strained; concentrated
natężyć [nah-tan-zhićh] v. strain; intensify; strengthen; exert; heighten; enhance
natężyć się [nah-tan-zhićh śhan] v. strain oneself; exert oneself; put one's back into a task; become intesified; become strengthened
natka [nah-tkah] f. leaves of vegetables
natkać [nah-tkahćh] v. weave a lot; cram into; stick into
natknąć [naht-knownćh] v. butt; stick; stud; lard
natknąć się [naht-knownćh śhan] v. come across; butt against; come up against; fall in (with); happen upon; chance upon
natleniać [nah-tle-ńahćh] v. provide oxygen (*repeatedly*)
natleniać się [nah-tle-ńahćh śhan] v. provide oneself with oxygen (*repeatedly*)
natlenić [nah-tle-ńeećh] v. provide oxygen
natlenić się [nah-tle-ńeećh śhan] v. provide oneself with oxygen
natlenienie [nah-tle-ńe-ńe] n. oxygenation; oxidation
natlenienie się [nah-tle-ńe-ńe śhan] n. oxygenation
natleniony [nah-tle-ńo-ni] adj.m. oxygenized; oxidized
natłoczka [nah-twoch-kah] f. cup leather packing
natłoczka skórzana [nah-twoch-kah skoo-zhah-nah] exp.: leather gasket
natłoczony [nah-two-cho-ni] adj.m. crowded; packed; huddled; cram-full
natłoczyć [nah-two-chićh] v. cram; pack; crowd; huddle
natłoczyć się [nah-two-chićh śhan] v. crowd together; be crowded; be huddled
natłok [nah-twok] m. crowd; throng; pressure; accumulation; affluence; crush
w natłoku zajęć [v nah-two-koo zah-yanćh] exp.: under pressure of business
natłuc [nah-twoots] v. pound; break a lot (of glass, etc.); punch; batter (a man, etc.); kill (lots of people, etc.); slaughter (lots of animals, etc.)
natłuc się [nah-twoots śhan] v. get broken (in great quantities); get bruised a lot; be weary of travelling; have wandered more than enough
natłuczony [nah-twoo-cho-ni] adj.m. bruised
natłumaczyć [nah-twoo-mah-chićh] v. translate a lot
natłumaczyć się [nah-twoo-mah-chićh śhan] v. give endless excuses; give endless explanations; keep persuading not to do (something)
natłuszczać [nah-twoosh-chahćh] v. grease; oil; lubricate (*repeatedly*)
natłuszczenie [nah-twoosh-che-ńe] n. lubrication
natłuszczony [nah-twoosh-cho-ni] adj.m. lubricated
natłuścić [nah-twoośh-ćheećh] v. grease; oil; lubricate; supply a lubricant

natoczyć [nah-to-chićh] v. draw (wine out of a barrel, etc.); turn (on a lathe)
natomiast [nah-to-myahst] adv. however; yet; on the contrary; on the other hand; while
natopić [nah-to-peećh] v. melt; drown (many people, etc.); sink (many ships, boats, etc.)
natorfowy [nah-tor-fo-vi] adj.m. peaty
natracić [nah-trah-ćheećh] v. waste a lot (of money, etc.) sacrifice a lot (of soldiers, people, etc.)
natrafiać [nah-trah-fyahćh] v. encounter; come across; find; happen upon; hit upon; stumble upon (*repeatedly*)
natrafić [nah-trah-feećh] v. encounter; come across; find; happen upon; hit upon; stumble upon
natrafić na przeszkodę [nah-trah-feećh nah pshesh-ko-dan] exp.: to run into an obstacle
natręctwo [nah-trants-tfo] n. intrusiveness; obtrusiveness; meddlesomeness; obtrusion; intrusion
natręctwo myślowe [nah-trants-tfo miśh-lo-ve] exp.: obsession
natręt [nah-trant] m. intruder; interloper; bore
natrętnie [nah-tran-tńe] adv. intrusively; troublesomely; persistently; importunately; obtrusively; obsesively
natrętny [nah-tran-tni] adj.m. intrusive; bothersome; troublesome; meddlesome; persistent; importune; obtrusive; obsessive
natron [nah-tron] m. natron
natronowy [nah-tro-no-vi] adj.m. natron (ceramic paste, etc.)
natroskać się [nah-tros-kahćh śhan] v. have a lot of worries; have a lot of cares
natrudzić [nah-troo-dźheećh] v. put to hard work; make a lot of trouble
natrudzić się [nah-troo-dźheećh śhan] v. exert oneself; work hard; go to a lot of trouble; take great pains
natrysk [nah-trisk] m. shower bath; shower; spraying; spray
natrysk cementowy [nah-trisk tse-men-to-vi] exp.: gunite; tintocrete
natryskiwacz [nah-tris-kee-vahch] m. spray gun; air-brush
natryskiwać [nah-tris-kee-vahćh] v. spray; shower (*repeatedly*)
natryskiwanie [nah-tris-kee-vah-ńe] n. spraying; showering
natryskownia [nah-tris-kov-ńah] f. shower bath
natryskownica [nah-tris-kov-ńee-tsah] f. spray gun; sprayer
natryskowy [nah-tris-ko-vi] adj.m. of spraying; of a sprayer
kąpiel natryskowa [kown-pyel nah-tris-ko-vah] exp.: shower
pistolet natryskowy [pees-to-let nah-tris-ko-vi] exp.: air-brush
natryt [nah-trit] m. mineral sodium
natrząsać [nah-tshown-sahćh] v. shake down (fruits, etc.) (*repeatedly*)
natrząsać się [nah-tshown-sahćh śhan] v. scoff at; sneer at; poke fun at; hold in derision; make a laughing stock of; jeer at; gibe at (*repeatedly*)
natrząsanie się [nah-tshown-sah-ńe śhan] n. sneers; derision; scoffs; jeers; gibes
natrząść [nah-tshownśhćh] v. shake down (fruits, etc.)
natrząść się [nah-tshownśhćh śhan] v. get tired shaking down (fruits, etc.); get tired shaking in a rickety railroad car
natrzeć [nah-tshećh] v. rub; attack; harass; scold; rate
natrzeć komuś uszu [nah-tshećh ko-moośh oo-shoo] exp.: colloq: to scold (rate) somebody
natrzeć się [nah-tshećh śhan] v. rub oneself (with an ointment, a cream, etc.)
natrzęsiony [nah-tshan-śho-ni] adj.m. shaken down (fruit, etc.)
natura [nah-too-rah] f. nature; natural state; constitution; disposition; temper; cast of mind; (mining) tribute; (payment in) kind

być przeciwnym czyjejś naturze [bićh pshe-ćheev-nim chi-yeyśh nah-too-zhe] exp.: to be contrary to somebody's nature
martwa natura [mahrt-fah nah-too-rah] exp.: still life
natura ludzka [nah-too-rah loots-kah] exp.: human nature
płacić w naturze [pwah-ćheećh v nah-too-zhe] exp.: to pay in kind
prawa natury [prah-vah nah-too-ri] exp.: laws of nature; natural laws
przyzwyczajenie jest drugą naturą [pshi-zvi-chah-ye-ńe yest droo-gown nah-too-rown] exp.: habit is a second nature
sprawy natury finansowej [sprah-vi nah-too-ri fee-nahn-so-vey] exp.: financial matter; matter of a financial nature
taką już mam naturę [tah-kown yoosh mahm nah-too-ran] exp.: colloq: that's the way I am
z natury [z nah-too-ri] exp.: by nature; from nature

naturalia [nah-too-rah-lyah] pl. farm products; agricultural produce
naturalista [nah-too-rah-lees-tah] m. naturalist
naturalistka [nah-too-rah-lees-tkah] f. (woman) naturalist
naturalistycznie [nah-too-rah-lees-tich-ńe] adv. naturalistically
naturalistyczny [nah-too-rah-lees-tich-ni] adj.m. naturalistic
naturalizacja [nah-too-rah-lee-zah-tsyah] f. naturalization
naturalizm [nah-too-rah-leezm] m. naturalism
naturalizować [nah-too-rah-lee-zo-vahćh] v. naturalize (*repeatedly*)
naturalizować się [nah-too-rah-lee-zo-vahćh śhan] v. naturalize; become naturalized (*repeatedly*)
naturalnie [nah-too-rahl-ńe] adv. naturally; of course; by nature; without affection; unaffectedly; unconstrainedly
naturalnie! [nah-too-rahl-ńe] excl.: most certainly!; certainly!
naturalność [nah-too-rahl-nośhćh] f. naturalness; natural state; unaffectedness; unconstraint
naturalny [nah-too-rahl-ni] adj.m. natural; true to life; inborn; native; untutored (talent, etc.); life-size; matter-of-course; simple; plain; artless; unconstrained; unaffected; paid in kind (of farm products)
bogactwa naturalne [bo-gahts-tfah nah-too-rahl-ne] exp.: natural resources
dobór naturalny [do-boor nah-too-rahl-ni] exp.: natural selection
liczby naturalne [leedzh-bi nah-too-rahl-ne] exp.: natural numbers
przyrost naturalny [pshi-rost nah-too-rahl-ni] exp.: birth rate
rzecz naturalna [zhech nah-too-rahl-nah] exp.: matter of course
portret naturalnej wielkości [por-tret nah-too-rahl-ney vyel-kośh-ćhee] exp.: life-size portrait
umrzeć śmiercią naturalną [oom-zhećh śhmyer-ćhown nah-too-rahl-nown] exp.: to die of natural causes; to die a natural death
załatwić potrzebę naturalną [zah-waht-feećh po-tshe-ban nah-too-rahl-nown] exp.: to relieve oneself; to go to the bathroom
naturszczyk [nah-toor-shchik] m. natural (not trained) film actor
naturysta [nah-too-ris-tah] m. nudist
naturystka [nah-too-ris-tkah] f. (female) nudist
naturyzm [nah-too-rizm] m. nudism
natworzyć [nah-tfo-zhićh] v. create a lot (of things, problems, etc.)
natychmiast [nah-tikh-myahst] adv. at once; instantly; right away; immediately; forthwith; straight off; on the spot; out of hand; straight away; right off
płatne natychmiast [pwaht-ne nah-tikh-myahst] exp.: cash on the spot; spot cash (Brit.); to be paid immediately
natychmiastowy [nah-tikh-myahs-to-vi] adj.m. instantaneous; instant; immediate; prompt; on the spot
natykać [nah-ti-kahćh] v. butt; stick; stud; lard (*repeatedly*)
natykać się [nah-ti-kahćh śhan] v. come across; butt against; come up against; fall in (with); happen

upon; chance upon (*repeatedly*)
natykany [nah-ti-**kah**-ni] adj.m. studded (with); larded (with); stuck (with)
natylnik [nah-**til**-ńeek] m. rear part of a horse harness
natyrać się [nah-**ti**-rahćh śhan] v. toil; sweat; be jaded; be worn out with hard work; colloq: slave
natywista [nah-ti-**vees**-tah] m. nativist
natywistyczny [nah-ti-vees-**tich**-ni] adj.m. nativistic
natywizm [nah-**ti**-veezm] m. nativism
naubijać się [nah-oo-**bee**-yahćh śhan] v. compact a lot; get tired of compacting
naubliżać [nah-oob-**lee**-zhahćh] v. abuse; revile; rail at
nauczać [nah-**oo**-chahćh] v. teach; instruct; tutor; train; give instruction; be a teacher (*repeatedly*)
nauczanie [nah-oo-**chah**-ńe] n. teaching; instruction
prywatne nauczanie [pri-**vaht**-ne nah-oo-**chah**-ńe] exp.: private schooling; private tutoring; private tuition
nauczenie [nah-oo-**che**-ńe] n. teaching
nauczenie się [nah-oo-**che**-ńe śhan] n. learning
nauczka [nah-**ooch**-kah] f. (pointed) lesson (unpleasant)
dać nauczkę [dahćh nah-**ooch**-kan] exp.: to teach (someone) a lesson
masz nauczkę! [mahsh nah-**ooch**-kan] exp.: let it be a lesson!; it serves you right!
nauczony [nah-oo-**cho**-ni] adj.m. taught; educated; trained
nauczony doświadczeniem [nah-oo-**cho**-ni do-śhfyaht-**che**-ńem] exp.: having learned a lesson of experience
nauczyciel [nah-oo-**chi**-ćhel] m. teacher; instructor; schoolmaster
nauczycielka [nah-oo-chi-**ćhel**-kah] f. (female) teacher; instructress; schoolmistress
nauczycielski [nah-oo-chi-**ćhel**-skee] adj.m. teacher's; teachers'; tutorial
grono nauczycielskie [**gro**-no nah-oo-chi-**ćhel**-ske] exp.: teaching staff; teaching faculty
pokój nauczycielski [**po**-kooy nah-oo-chi-**ćhel**-skee] exp.: teacher's office; teacher's conference room
seminarium nauczycielskie [se-mee-**nahr**-yoom nah-oo-chi-**ćhel**-ske] exp.: teacher's seminary
nauczycielstwo [nah-oo-chi-**ćhel**-stfo] n. teachership; mastership; teachers; schoolmasters
nauczyć [nah-**oo**-chićh] v. teach; instruct; tutor; train
nauczyć kogoś rozumu [nah-oo-chićh **ko**-gośh ro-**zoo**-moo] exp.: to teach somebody a lesson; to bring somebody to his senses; to bring somebody to reason
nauczyć się [nah-**oo**-chićh śhan] v. learn; come to know
na udry [nah **ood**-ri] exp.: adv. with hostility; in a hostile manner; at loggerheads (with); at odds (with)
iść z kimś na udry [eeśhćh s keemśh nah **ood**-ri] exp.: to quarrel with somebody; to be at loggerheads with somebody; to be at odds with somebody; to be at variance with somebody
udry na udry [**ood**-ri nah **ood**-ri] exp.: adv. tit for tat
nauganiać się [nah-oo-**gah**-ńahćh śhan] v. chase around; hunt about
nauka [nah-oo-kah or nah-**oo**-kah] f. science; research work; learning; study; teaching; knowledge; lesson; education; schooling; school; apprenticeship; sermon
nauka jazdy [nah-**oo**-kah **yahz**-di] exp.: driving lesson
nauka moralna [nah-**oo**-kah mo-**rahl**-nah] exp.: (a) moral
nauka nie poszła w las [nah-**oo**-kah ńe **posh**-wah v lahs] exp.: the lesson has not been forgotten
nauki humanistyczne [**nah**-oo-kee khoo-mah-ńees-**tich**-ne] exp.: humanities
nauki matematyczne [**nah**-oo-kee mah-te-mah-**tich**-ne] exp.:

mathematics
nauki polityczne [nah-oo-kee po-lee-tich-ne] exp.: political science
nauki przyrodnicze [nah-oo-kee pshi-rod-ńee-che] exp.: natural sciences
nauki ścisłe [nah-oo-kee śhćhees-we] exp.: exact sciences
nauki wyzwolone [nah-oo-kee viz-vo-lo-ne] exp.: liberal arts
skończyć naukę [skoń-chićh nah-oo-kan] exp.: to graduate
naukładać [nah-oo-kwah-dahćh] v. heap up
na ukos [nah oo-kos] exp.: adv. obliquely; aslant; on the bias; diagonally
naukowiec [nah-oo-ko-vyets] m. scientist; scholar; researcher
naukowo [nah-oo-ko-vo] adv. scientifically; in scholarly fashion; in the field of research; in respect of research
naukowość [nah-oo-ko-vośhćh] f. erudition; scholarship; learning; scientific nature
naukowy [nah-oo-ko-vi] adj.m. scientific; scholarly; academic; educational
praca naukowa [prah-tsah nah-oo-ko-vah] exp.: research work
stopień naukowy [sto-pyeń nah-oo-ko-vi] exp.: academic degree
towarzystwo naukowe [to-vah-zhis-tfo nah-oo-ko-ve] exp.: learned society
naukoznawca [nah-oo-ko-znahf-tsah] m. specialist in scientism and methodology of science
naukoznawczy [nah-oo-ko-znahf-chi] adj.m. of scientism and methodology of science
naukoznawstwo [nah-oo-ko-znahf-stfo] n. the study of the progress of human knowledge; scientism
naumieć się [nah-oo-myećh śhan] v. colloq: teach oneself; instruct oneself; train oneself; become proficient (in doing something)
na umór [nah oo-moor] exp.: to the bitter end; head over hills
pić na umór [peećh nah oo-moor] exp.: to drink oneself dead drunk
naumyślnie [nah-oo-miśhl-ńe] adv. on purpose; of set purpose; deliberately; intentionally; purposely
na upartego [nah oo-pahr-te-go] exp.: in the last resort; if the worse comes to the worse
naurągać [nah-oo-rown-gahćh] v. revile; abuse; insult
nausznica [nah-oosh-ńee-tsah] f. earring; eardrop
nausznik [nah-oosh-ńeek] m. earflap; earlap; ear protector; earpiece; ear plate
nauszniki [nah-oosh-ńee-kee] pl. earflaps; ear laps; ear protectors; earpiece; earmuffs
nauszny [nah-oosh-ni] adj.m. auricular
nautilus [nah-oo-tee-loos] m. nautilus; nautilus vase
nautofon [nahw-to-fon] m. (electric) fog signal
nautologia [nahw-to-lo-gyah] f. history of navigation, ports, and shipyards
nautyczny [nahw-tich-ni] adj.m. nautical
nautyka [nahw-ti-kah] f. nautics
nauwijać się [nah-oo-vee-yahćh śhan] v. bustle a lot; bestir oneself
naużerać się [nah-oo-zhe-rahćh śhan] v. bicker; squabble (a lot)
naużywać [nah-oo-zhi-vahćh] v. use a lot (of paper towels, etc.)
naużywać się [nah-oo-zhi-vahćh śhan] v. use a lot; get tired of using a lot of (garments, etc.)
nawa [nah-vah] f. nave; aisle; vessel
nawa boczna [nah-vah boch-nah] exp.: (side) aisle
nawa główna [nah-vah gwoov-nah] exp.: nave; the main aisle
nawa państwowa [nah-vah pahń-stfo-vah] exp.: the ship of the State
nawadniać [nah-vahd-ńahćh] v. irrigate; saturate with water; hydrate; moisten (*repeatedly*)
nawadnianie [nah-vahd-ńah-ńe] n. irrigation
nawaga [nah-vah-gah] f. a gadid;

Eleginus navaga
nawalacz [nah-**vah**-lahch] m. slang: bungler; good-for-nothing; rotter
nawalać [nah-**vah**-lahćh] v. pile up; heap up; soil; dirty; fail; bungle; break down; mob slang: steal; pilfer; pinch; conk out; (tires) go flat; blow out (*repeatedly*)
nawalanka [nah-vah-**lahn**-kah] f. slang: bungling; bungled work; letdown (mob jargon)
nawalcować [nah-vahl-**tso**-vahćh] v. roll a lot; mill a lot; laminate a lot
nawalcowywać [nah-vahl-tso-**vi**-vahćh] v. roll a lot; mill a lot; laminate a lot (*repeatedly*)
nawalenie [nah-vah-**le**-ńe] n. crowding together; heaping up; letting down; bungle; breakdown
na waleta [nah vah-**le**-tah] exp.: head to tail (two on one bed, etc.)
nawalić [nah-**vah**-leećh] v. pile up; heap up; soil; dirty; fail; bungle; break down; slang: steal; pilfer; pinch; conk out; (tires) go flat; blow out (jargon)
nawalić się [nah-**vah**-leećh śhan] v. crowd together; come in shoals; mob slang: get drunk
nawalny [nah-**vahl**-ni] adj.m. tempestuous; violent
nawalony [nah-vah-**lo**-ni] adj.m. out of whack; broken down; drunk
nawał [nah-vahw] m. no end of; an overwhelming amount; multitude; host; heaps; lots
nawał zajęć [nah-vahw **zah**-yanćh] exp.: being swamped; being overloaded; having too much to do; lot of commitments; pressure of business
nawał pracy [nah-vahw **prah**-tsi] exp.: being swamped; avalanche of work; multitude of jobs; pile of work; spate of work (Brit.)
nawała [nah-**vah**-wah] f. overwhelming mass; swarms; onslaught; onset; enormous amount; an overwhelming amount; multitude; host; heaps; lots
nawała ogniowa [nah-**vah**-wah og-ńo-vah] exp.: onslaught of artillery fire; time on target salvo (of many cannons)
nawałnica [nah-vahw-**ńee**-tsah] f. tempest; storm; hurricane; torrential rain; rainstorm; blizzard; onset; onrush; onslaught
nawałnicowy [nah-vahw-ńee-**tso**-vi] adj.m. storm (warning, etc.)
nawałnik [nah-**vahw**-ńeek] m. stormy petrel (bird) of the family Hydrobatidae
nawałowy [nah-vah-**wo**-vi] adj.m. overwhelming (artillery fire, etc.)
nawaniać [nah-**vah**-ńahćh] v. add warning scent to gas (*repeatedly*)
nawanianie [nah-vah-**ńah**-ńe] n. addition of warning scent to gas
nawapniacz [nah-**vahp**-ńahch] m. device for treating (sugar beets, etc.) with lime
nawapniać [nah-**vahp**-ńahćh] v. treat (sugar beets, etc.) with lime (*repeatedly*)
nawapnianie [nah-vahp-**ńah**-ńe] n. treatment (of sugar beets, etc.) with lime
nawar [**nah**-vahr] m. incrustation; sinter
nawarstwiać [nah-**vahr**-stfyahćh] v. stratify; arrange in layers (*repeatedly*)
nawarstwiać się [nah-**vahr**-stfyahćh śhan] v. stratify; accumulate in layers (*repeatedly*)
nawarstwianie [nah-vahr-**stfyah**-ńe] n. stratification
nawarstwianie się [nah-vahr-**stfyah**-ńe śhan] n. piling up (of strata); forming stratification (*repeatedly*)
nawarstwić [nah-**vahr**-stfeećh] v. stratify; arrange in layers
nawarstwić się [nah-**vahr**-stfeećh śhan] v. stratify; accumulate in layers
nawarstwienie [nah-vahr-**stfye**-ńe] n. stratification
nawarstwienie się [nah-vahr-**stfye**-ńe śhan] n. piling up (of strata); forming stratification
nawarzyć [nah-**vah**-zhićh] v. brew; cook; concoct; get into (trouble, jam, etc.); cause (trouble, etc.)
nawarzyć piwa [nah-**vah**-zhićh

pee-vah] exp.: to cause trouble
naważyć [nah-**vah**-zhićh] v. weigh out (some apples, etc.)
naważyć się [nah-**vah**-zhićh śhan] v. weigh a lot; get tired weighing
nawąchać się [nah-**vown**-khahćh śhan] v. breathe in (enough nasty smells); smell (the fragrance of ...)
nawąchać się prochu [nah-**vown**-khahćh śhan **pro**-khoo] exp.: do quite enough soldiering
nawbijać [nah-**vbee**-yahćh] v. drive a lot (of nails, etc.) into; hammer no end (of nails, etc.) into
nawerbować [nah-ver-**bo**-vahćh] v. recruit; enlist
naweselić się [nah-ve-**se**-leećh śhan] v. enjoy oneself to the full
nawet [**nah**-vet] adv. even
nawet nie [**nah**-vet ńe] exp.: adv. not even; not so much as; never; not yet
nawet gdyby [**nah**-vet **gdi**-bi] exp.: adv. even if; even though; even
nawęd [**nah**-vant] m. angler fish; Lophious piscatorius
nawędrować się [nah-van-**dro**-vahćh śhan] v. wander a lot; roam a lot; get tired of wandering
nawęglać [nah-**vang**-lahćh] v. face-harden; carbonize; acierate (*repeatedly*)
nawęglanie [nah-vang-**lah**-ńe] n. carbonization (*repeated*)
nawęglenie [nah-vang-**le**-ńe] n. carbonization
nawęglić [nah-**vang**-leećh] v. face-harden; carbonize; acierate
nawiać [**nah**-vyahćh] v. blow (snow, etc.); drift (sand, etc.); drive (leaves, etc.); carry (clouds, etc.); bring (smoke, etc.); blow on; colloq: escape; desert
nawiany [nah-**vyah**-ni] adj.m. windblown (snow, sand, etc.)
nawias [**nah**-vyahs] m. parenthesis; bracket; the pale
nawiasem mówiąc [nah-**vyah**-sem **moo**-vyownts] exp.: incidentally; by and by; by the way; by way of digression; speaking parenthetically
nawias klamrowy [**nah**-vyahs klahm-**ro**-vi] exp.: brace
nawias kwadratowy [**nah**-vyahs kfah-drah-**to**-vi] exp.: square bracket
nawias okrągły [**nah**-vyahs o-**krowng**-wi] exp.: round bracket
poza nawiasem społeczeństwa [**po**-zah nah-**vyah**-sem spo-we-**cheń**-stfah] exp.: ouside of the pale of society
w nawiasach [v nah-**vyah**-sahkh] exp.: in parentheses; in brackets; bracketed
wyrzucony poza nawias [vi-zhoo-**tso**-ni **po**-zah **nah**-vyahs] exp.: not needed any more
wziąć w nawias [vźhownćh v **nah**-vyahs] exp.: to bracket (a word, etc.)
nawiasem [nah-**vyah**-sem] adv. incidentally; by way of digression; by the way
nawiasem mówiąc [nah-**vyah**-sem **moo**-vyownts] exp.: incidentally; by the way; by way of digression
nawiasowo [nah-vyah-**so**-vo] adv. parenthetically; incidentally; digressively
nawiasowość [nah-vyah-**so**-vośhćh] f. parenthetical nature
nawiasowy [nah-vyah-**so**-vi] adj.m. parenthetical; incidental; digressive
nawiązać [nah-**vyown**-zahćh] v. tie to; refer to; enter in; tie; bind; attach; fasten; connect; link (with); revert; turn back
nawiązać do czegoś [nah-**vyown**-zahćh do **che**-gośh] exp.: to refer to something
nawiązać kontakt [nah-**vyown**-zahćh **kon**-tahkt] exp.: to get in touch (with); to establish contact (with the enemy, etc.)
nawiązać korespondencję [nah-**vyown**-zahćh ko-res-pon-**den**-tsyan] exp.: to enter into correspondence
nawiązać rozmowę [nah-**vyown**-zahćh roz-**mo**-van] exp.: to engage in conversation
nawiązać stosunki [nah-**vyown**-zahćh sto-**soon**-kee] exp.: to

enter into relations
nawiązać znajomość [nah-**vyown**-zahćh znah-**yo**-mośhćh] exp.: to strike up an acquaintance
nawiązać się [nah-**vyown**-zahćh śhan] v. become tied; become attached; become linked
nawiązanie [nah-vyown-**zah**-ńe] n. connection; reference to; tie; bridle strap
w nawiązaniu do czegoś [v nah-vyown-**zah**-ńoo do **che**-gośh] exp.: with reference to something
nawiązka [nah-**vyowns**-kah] f. sum paid over and above the amount due; vindictive damages
z nawiązką [z nah-**vyowns**-kown] exp.: with interest; with usury; with a vengeance
nawiązywać [nah-vyown-**zi**-vahćh] v. tie to; refer to; enter in; tie; bind; attach; fasten; connect; link (with); revert; turn back (*repeatedly*)
nawiązywać się [nah-vyown-**zi**-vahćh śhan] v. become tied; become attached; become linked (*repeatedly*)
nawiedzać [nah-**vye**-dzahćh] v. visit; haunt; afflict; obsess; come upon; smite (*repeatedly*)
nawiedzenie [nah-vye-**dze**-ńe] n. visitation
nawiedzić [nah-**vye**-dźheećh] v. visit; haunt; afflict; obsess; come upon; smite
nawiedzony [nah-vye-**dzo**-ni] adj.m. stricken (with pestilence, etc.); colloq: blindly following (a cult, etc.); fanatical
nawiercać [nah-**vyer**-tsahćh] v. bore (a number of holes, etc.) (*repeatedly*)
nawiercić [nah-**vyer**-ćheećh] v. bore (a number of holes, etc.)
nawiertak [nah-**vyer**-tahk] m. countersink
nawierzchnia [nah-**vyesh**-khńah] f. surface (finish); pavement
nawierzchniowy [nah-vyesh-**khńo**-vi] adj.m. surface (dressing, finish, etc.)
nawietrzna [nah-**vyetsh**-nah] f. windward (side, etc.)
po nawietrznej [po nah-**vyetsh**-ney] exp.: to the windward
nawietrzny [nah-**vyetsh**-ni] adj.m. windward
nawiew [**nah**-vyef] m. blowing of air
nawiewać [nah-**vye**-vahćh] v. blow (snow, etc.); drift (sand, etc.); drive (leaves, etc.); carry (clouds, etc.); bring (smoke, etc.); blow on (*repeatedly*)
nawiewnik [nah-**vyev**-ńeek] m. ventilator
nawiewny [nah-**vyev**-ni] adj.m. blowing; air-compressing
nawiewowy [nah-vye-**vo**-vi] adj.m. blowing; air-compressing
nawieźć [nah-vyeśhćh] v. bring; cart; truck (goods, etc.); fill (a ditch, etc.) with (sand, etc.); fertilize; manure; dung; dress
nawigacja [nah-vee-**gahts**-yah] f. navigation; sailing
nawigacja powietrzna [nah-vee-**gahts**-yah po-**vyetsh**-nah] exp.: air navigation
nawigacyjnie [nah-vee-gah-**tsiy**-ńe] adv. by means of navigation
nawigacyjny [nah-vee-gah-**tsiy**-ni] adj.m. navigational
mapa nawigacyjna [**mah**-pah nah-vee-gah-**tsiy**-nah] exp.: chart; sea map
światła nawigacyjne [**śhfyaht**-wah nah-vee-gah-**tsiy**-ne] exp.: position lights; sea lights
znaki nawigacyjne [**znah**-kee nah-vee-gah-**tsiy**-ne] exp.: sea signs; navigational markings
nawigator [nah-vee-**gah**-tor] m. navigator
nawigator lotniczy [nah-vee-**gah**-tor lot-**ńee**-chi] exp.: air navigator
nawigować [nah-vee-**go**-vahćh] v. navigate (*repeatedly*)
nawigowanie [nah-vee-go-**vah**-ńe] n. navigation
nawijacz [nah-**vee**-yahch] m. winder
nawijaczka [nah-vee-**yahch**-kah] f. (woman) winder
nawijać [nah-**vee**-yahćh] v. wind up; reel; roll up; spool; coil; colloq: keep on talking without interruption; prattle; prate; babble (*repeatedly*)

nawijać się [nah-**vee**-yahćh śhan] v. be reeled; be spooled; come into sight; turn up; show up; present (oneself, itself, etc.); appear suddenly (*repeatedly*)
nawijadło [nah-vee-**yahd**-wo] n. winder
nawijak [nah-**vee**-yahk] m. reeling tool
nawijalnia [nah-vee-**yahl**-ńah] f. winding shop
nawijanie [nah-vee-**yah**-ńe] n. winding; reeling; putting on a spool
nawijarka [nah-vee-**yahr**-kah] f. winder; reeler
nawilgacać [nah-veel-**gah**-tsahćh] v. humidify (*repeatedly*)
nawilgacanie [nah-veel-gah-**tsah**-ńe] n. humidification
nawilgać [nah-**veel**-gahćh] v. moisten; become moist; absorb moisture (*repeatedly*)
nawilgatniacz [nah-veel-**gaht**-ńahch] m. humidifier; moistener; damper
nawilgnąć [nah-**veelg**-nownćh] v. moisten; become moist; absorb moisture
nawilgocenie [nah-veel-go-**tse**-ńe] n. humidification
nawilgocić [nah-veel-**go**-ćheećh] v. humidify
nawilgocony [nah-veel-go-**tso**-ni] adj.m. humidified
nawilżacz [nah-**veel**-zhahch] m. humidifier; moistener; damper
nawilżać [nah-**veel**-zhahćh] v. humidify; moisten; dampen (*repeatedly*)
nawilżarka [nah-veel-**zhahr**-kah] f. cloth dampening machine (in preparation for ironing)
nawilżyć [nah-**veel**-zhićh] v. humidify; moisten; dampen; damp
nawinąć [nah-**vee**-nownćh] v. wind up; reel; roll up; spool; coil
nawinąć się [nah-**vee**-nownćh śhan] v. be reeled; be spooled; come into sight; turn up; show up; present (oneself, itself, etc.); offer
wszystko, co mu się nawinie pod rękę [**fshist**-ko tso moo śhan nah-**vee**-ńe pod ran-kan] exp.: whatever he lays his hands on
nawis [**nah**-vees] m. overhang; brow (of a hill, etc.)
nawisać [nah-**vee**-sahćh] v. hang over (*repeatedly*)
nawisanie [nah-vee-**sah**-ńe] n. hanging over
nawisły [nah-**vees**-wi] adj.m. overhanging
nawisnąć [nah-**vees**-nownćh] v. hang over
nawitaminować [nah-vee-tah-mee-**no**-vahćh] v. vitaminize
nawlec [**nah**-vlets] v. thread; string; pass through the eye of a needle; slip on; slip over
nawlec igłę [**nah**-vlets **eeg**-wan] exp.: to thread a needle
nawleczenie [nah-vle-**che**-ńe] n. threading (through); pulling over
nawleczenie igły [nah-vle-**che**-ńe **eeg**-wi] exp.: threading of a needle
nawleczka [nah-**vlech**-kah] f. pillowcase
nawlekać [nah-**vle**-kahćh] v. thread; string; slip on; slip over; pass through the eye of a needle (*repeatedly*)
nawlekanie [nah-vle-**kah**-ńe] n. threading; pulling over
nawłoć [**nah**-vwoćh] f. golden rod; Solidago (plant)
nawłoka [nah-**vwo**-kah] f. cord; rope
nawłóczyć [nah-**vwoo**-chićh] v. drag others (on a wild-goose chase, etc.); get tired of dragging others; thread; string; pass through the eye of a needle; slip on; slip over
nawłóczyć się [nah-**vwoo**-chićh śhan] v. roam at will; wander at will; gad about; tramp at will
nawodniać [nah-**vod**-ńahćh] v. irrigate; water; saturate with water; hydrate; moisten (*repeatedly*)
nawodnić [nah-**vod**-ńeećh] v. irrigate; water; saturate with water; hydrate; moisten
nawodnienie [nah-vod-**ńe**-ńe] n. irrigation; saturation with water; washing out (a cavity)
nawodnieniowy [nah-vod-ńe-**ńo**-vi]

adj.m. irrigational; irrigation (project, etc.)
nawodny [nah-**vod**-ni] adj.m. aquatic; waterside (trees, etc.); offshore (structure, etc.)
ptactwo nawodne [**ptah**-tstfo nah-**vod**-ne] exp.: waterfowl
nawojować się [nah-vo-**yo**-vahćh śh<u>an</u>] v. spent a long time at war; be in a lot of battles; to have fought enough; to be tired of fighting
nawojowy [nah-vo-**yo**-vi] adj.m. insulated coil (wire, etc.)
nawołujący [nah-vo-woo-**<u>yown</u>**-tsi] adj.m. urging (call, etc.)
nawoływać [nah-vo-**wi**-vahćh] v. call; hail; exhort; urge; lure; incite; halloo (*repeatedly*)
nawoływać się [nah-vo-**wi**-vahćh śh<u>an</u>] v. call one another; urge each other; exhort one another (*repeatedly*)
nawoływanie [nah-vo-wi-**vah**-ńe] n. call (of a dog, an animal, etc.); exhortation; urge; incitement
nawoskować [nah-vos-**ko**-vahćh] v. wax (furniture, etc.)
nawowy [nah-**vo**-vi] adj.m. of a nave
nawozić [nah-**vo**-źheećh] v. fertilize; manure; truck; cart; fill (a ditch); bring (gravel) (*repeatedly*)
nawozić się [nah-**vo**-źheećh śh<u>an</u>] v. truck a lot; cart a lot; get tired of trucking; get tired of carting
nawozowy [nah-vo-**zo**-vi] adj.m. fertilizing
siewnik nawozowy [**śhev**-ńeek nah-vo-**zo**-vi] exp.: fertilizer-sower
wapno nawozowe [**vahp**-no nah-vo-**zo**-ve] exp.: soil lime
nawożenie [nah-vo-**zhe**-ńe] n. fertilization
nawożenie pogłówne [nah-vo-**zhe**-ne po-**gwoov**-ne] exp.: top dressing
nawój [**nah**-vooy] m. (weaver's) beam; warp
nawój nadawczy [**nah**-vooy nah-**dahf**-chi] exp.: yarn beam
nawój odbiorczy [**nah**-vooy od-**byor**-chi] exp.: fore beam
nawóz [**nah**-voos] m. manure; dung; muck; fertilizer
sztuczny nawóz [**shtooch**-ni **nah**-voos] exp.: fertilizer
na wpół [nah fpoow] exp.: adv. half; semi (finished); half (boiled)
na wprost [nah fprost] adv. straight on; ahead; opposite
nawracać [nah-**vrah**-tsahćh] v. turn around; convert; turn back; wheel around; wheel about (*repeatedly*)
nawracać się [nah-**vrah**-tsahćh śh<u>an</u>] v. be converted; become a convert; be reformed; mend one's ways; return; turn around; convert; turn back; wheel around; wheel about (*repeatedly*)
nawracanie [nah-vrah-**tsah**-ńe] n. proselytism
nawrot [**nah**-vrot] m. gromwell; Lithospermum
nawrotami [nah-vro-**tah**-mee] exp.: repeatedly; again and again
nawrotnik [nah-**vrot**-ńeek] m. lady's mantle; Alchemillia
nawrotny [nah-**vrot**-ni] adj.m. recurrent; reversible
nawrotowy [nah-vro-**to**-vi] adj.m. recurrent
nawrócenie [nah-vroo-**tse**-ńe] n. conversion; being converted
nawrócić [nah-**vroo**-ćheećh] v. turn around; convert; turn back; wheel around; wheel about
nawrócić się [nah-**vroo**-ćheećh śh<u>an</u>] v. be converted; become a convert; be reformed; mend one's ways; return; turn around; convert; turn back; wheel around; wheel about
nawrócić się na chrześcijaństwo [nah-**vroo**-ćheećh śh<u>an</u> nah khsheśh-ćhee-**yahń**-stfo] exp.: to convert to Christianity
nawrócić się na katolicyzm [nah-**vroo**-ćheećh śh<u>an</u> nah kah-to-**lee**-tsizm] exp.: to convert to Catholicism
nawrót [**nah**-vroot] m. return; relapse; recurrence; setback; reversion; regression; regress; recrudescence
za każdym nawrotem [zah **kahzh**-dim nah-**vro**-tem] exp.: each time

nawrzeszczeć [nah-**vzhesh**-chećh] v. colloq: shout a lot
nawrzeszczeć się [nah-**vzhesh**-chećh śhan] v. colloq: shout a lot; get tired of shouting; shout at will
nawrzucać [nah-**vzhoo**-tsahćh] v. throw in (many items, etc.); colloq: curse (somebody) out; berate (somebody); insult (somebody)
na **wskroś** [nah fskrośh] exp.: adv. throughout; from end to end
na **wspak** [nah fspahk] exp.: adv. backwards; upside down; the wrong way; the wrong way; contrariwise; topsyturvy
nawściekać się [nah-**fśhćhe**-kahćh śhan] v. colloq: get mad a lot; get tired of being mad
nawtrajać się [nah-**ftrah**-yahćh śhan] v. colloq: eat a lot; eat at will; get tired of eating
nawtykać [nah-**fti**-kahćh] v. stick a lot (of flowers in the hair, etc.); colloq: berate (somebody); scold (somebody)
nawychwalać [nah-vikh-**fah**-lahćh] v. praise to the skies; sing the praises
nawychwalać się [nah-vikh-**fah**-lahćh śhan] v. praise adequately
nawyczka [nah-**vich**-kah] f. habit
nawyczyniać [nah-vi-**chi**-ńahćh] v. colloq: misbehave a lot; misbehave plenty; carry on
nawydziwiać [nah-vi-**dźhee**-vyahćh] v. colloq: act up a lot; talk a lot of nonsense
nawygadywać [nah-vi-gah-**di**-vahćh] v. talk a lot of nonsense; say a lot of nasty things
nawygrażać [nah-vi-**grah**-zhaćh] v. threaten a lot; make a lot of threats
nawygrażać się [nah-vi-**grah**-zhahćh śhan] v. threaten with violence
nawyk [**nah**-vik] m. habit; wont; custom; mannerism; trick
z nawyku [z nah-**vi**-koo] exp.: out of habit
nawykać [nah-**vi**-kahćh] v. accustom; fall into a habit; acquire a habit; become accustomed; get used to; become used to (*repeatedly*)
nawykły [nah-**vik**-wi] adj.m. accustomed; used to (do, etc.)
nawyknąć [nah-**vi**-knownćh] v. accustom; fall into a habit; acquire a habit; become accustomed; get used to; become used to
nawyknienie [nah-vik-**ńe**-ńe] n. habit; custom
nawykowy [nah-vi-**ko**-vi] adj.m. habitual
na **wylot** [nah **vi**-lot] exp.: adv. right through; through and through
nawyłudzać [nah-vi-**woo**-dzahćh] v. extort a lot; extort many times
nawymyślać [nah-vi-**miśh**-lahćh] v. revile; abuse; insult; invent
nawymyślać komuś od ostatnich [nah-vi-**miśh**-lahćh **ko**-moośh od os-**taht**-ńeekh] exp.: to curse somebody out; to revile somebody in the most insulting words
na **wynos** [nah **vi**-nos] exp.: (serve, etc.) off the premises
na **wyprzódki** [nah vi-**pshoot**-kee] exp.: competitively; in competition; colloq: racing each other; in emulation of each other
nawyrabiać [nah-vi-**rah**-byahćh] v. misbehave a lot; be naughty; do lot of harm
nawyrabiać się [nah-vi-**rah**-byahćh śhan] v. (strange things, etc.) happen a lot
na **wyrost** [nah **vi**-rost] exp.: allowing for growth; with room to grow; with room for growth
na **wyrywki** [nah vi-**rif**-kee] exp.: adv. at random; haphazardly
nawyszukiwać [nah-vi-shoo-**kee**-vahćh] v. find a lot (in a library, in archives, etc.)
nawytwarzać [nah-vi-**tfah**-zhahćh] v. make a lot; produce a lot
na **wywrót** [nah **viv**-root] exp.: inside out; the wrong side out
nawzajem [nah-**vzah**-yem] adv. mutually; same to you; each other; one another; reciprocally; in return

oddziaływać na siebie nawzajem [od-dźhah-**wi**-vahćh nah **śhe**-bye nah-**vzah**-yem] exp.: to interact
na wznak [nah vznahk] exp.: adv. on one's back; supine
nazabijać [nah-zah-**bee**-yahćh] v. kill (many people); slaughter (much cattle)
na zabój [nah **zah**-booy] exp.: adv. immoderately; without measure
nazad [**nah**-zaht] adv. back
nazad! [**nah**-zaht] excl.: back! (command for horses)
tam i nazad [tahm ee **nah**-zaht] exp.: backwards and forwards; this way and that
nazajutrz [nah-**zah**-yootsh] adv. the day after; the following day; the next day
nazalizacja [nah-zah-lee-**zahts**-yah] f. twang; nasalization
nazalizować [nah-zah-lee-**zo**-vahćh] v. twang; nasalize (*repeatedly*)
nazaretanka [nah-zah-re-**tahn**-kah] f. nun of the order of the Holy Family of Nazareth
na zawołanie [nah zah-vo-**wah**-ńe] exp.: (to be called) any time; (to be at service) always; at hand; in readiness; at moment's notice
na zawsze [nah **zahf**-she] exp.: forever; for all times; for good
nazbierać [nah-**zbye**-rahćh] v. gather up; collect; assemble
nazbierać się [nah-**zbye**-rahćh śhan] v. gather up; collect in a great number; assemble in a considerable number
nazabijać [nah-zah-**bee**-yahćh] v. kill a lot (of people, animals, etc.)
nazbijać [nah-**zbee**-yahćh] v. nail together a lot; knock off a lot; throw down a lot
nazbyt [**nahz**-bit] adv. too much; too; overmuch; beyond measure; excessively
aż nazbyt [ahsh **nahz**-bit] exp.: only too
nie nazbyt [ńe **nahz**-bit] exp.: not too; none too; not so very
na zewnątrz [nah **zev**-nowntsh] exp.: adv. out; outward; outside
nazewnictwo [nah-zev-**ńeets**-tfo] n. giving of names; naming; onomastics; onomatology
nazewniczy [nah-zev-**ńee**-chi] adj.m. name giving; onomastic
nazębny [nah-**zanb**-ni] adj.m. on teeth
kamień nazębny [**kah**-myeń nah-**zanb**-ni] exp.: tartar; scale (on teeth)
nazgromadzać [nah-zgro-**mah**-dzahćh] v. bring together a lot (of people, things, etc.)
nazi [**nah**-zee or **nah**-tsee] indecl. Nazi
naziemny [nah-**źhem**-ni] adj.m. ground (cover, etc.); overground (mail, etc.); terrestial (problems, etc.)
obsługa naziemna [op-**swoo**-gah nah-**źhem**-nah] exp.: ground crew; ground staff
roboty naziemne [ro-**bo**-ti nah-**źhem**-ne] exp.: earthwork
nazimek [nah-**źhee**-mek] m. animal less than one year old
nazista [nah-**źhees**-tah] m. a Nazi
nazistowski [nah-źhees-**tof**-skee] adj.m. Nazi
nazizm [**nah**-źheezm] m. nazism
nazjeżdżać [nah-**zyezh**-dzhahćh] v. come in great numbers; arrive in great numbers
nazjeżdżać się [nah-**zyezh**-dzhahćh śhan] v. come in great numbers; arrive in great numbers; slide down at will; slide down to one's heart's content
nazlatywać się [nah-zlah-**ti**-vahćh śhan] v. (birds, etc.) fly in in great numbers
nazłazić się [nah-**zwah**-źheećh śhan] v. come in in great numbers
nazłorzeczyć [nah-zwo-**zhe**-chićh] v. utter countless curses
nazmyślać [nah-**zmi**-śhlahćh] v. tell all sorts of lies; invent (endless gossip, etc.)
naznaczać [nah-**znah**-chahćh] v. mark; fix; appoint; outline; stamp; indicate; trace; draw; delineate; set; scar (*repeatedly*)
naznaczać się [nah-**znah**-chahćh śhan] v. mark oneself (with a tatoo, etc.) (*repeatedly*)

naznaczyć [nah-**znah**-chićh] v. mark; fix; appoint; outline; stamp; indicate; trace; draw; delineate; set; scar

naznaczyć się [nah-**znah**-chićh śhan] v. mark oneself (with a tatoo, etc.)

naznosić [nah-**zno**-śheećh] v. bring a lot; gather a lot

nazrywać [nah-**zri**-vahćh] v. pick a lot; pluck a lot

nazwa [**nahz**-vah] f. designation; name; appellation; title
być czymś tylko z nazwy [bićh chimśh **til**-ko z **nahz**-vi] exp.: to be something in the name only

nazwać [**nahz**-vahćh] v. call; designate; name; term; denominate; give a name; christen; label

nazwać się [**nahz**-vahćh śhan] v. be called; name oneself; answer to the name; be termed; be designated

nazwanie [nahz-**vah**-ńe] n. name

nazwisko [nahz-**vees**-ko] n. family name; surname; reputation
nazwiskiem Smith [nahz-**vees**-kem Smith] exp.: Smith by name; by the name of Smith

nazwozić [nah-**zvo**-źheećh] v. bring a lot (by truck, etc.)

nazywać [nah-**zi**-vahćh] v. call; name; term; denominate; label; christen; give a name (*repeatedly*)
nazywać kogoś osłem [nah-**zi**-vahćh **ko**-gośh **os**-wem] exp.: to call somebody a nitwit (a dupe)
nazywać rzeczy po imieniu [nah-**zi**-vahćh **zhe**-chi po ee-**mye**-ńoo] exp.: to speak plainly; to call a spade a spade

nazywać się [nah-**zi**-vahćh śhan] v. be called; be named; name oneself; answer to the name; be termed; be designated (*repeatedly*)
nazywam się Smith [nah-**zi**-vahm śhan Smith] exp.: my name is Smith
jak się nazywasz? [yahk śhan nah-**zi**-vahsh] exp.: what is your name?
jak się pan nazywa? [yahk śhan pahn nah-**zi**-vah] exp.: what is your name, Sir?
to się nazywa szczęście! [to śhan nah-**zi**-vah **shchan**śh-ćhe] exp.: that's really good luck!

na żarty [nah **zhahr**-ti] exp.: adv. in jest; in play; in sport
nie na żarty [ńe nah **zhahr**-ti] exp.: in good ernest; in ernest; seriously; with a vengeance

nażarty [nah-**zhahr**-ti] adj.m. gorged; stuffed (greedily)

nażąć [**nah**-zhownćh] v. reap (a quantity of rye, etc.)

nażąć się [**nah**-zhownćh śhan] v. reap a lot; reap a quantity; get tired of reaping; work hard while reaping

nażłopać się [nah-**zhwo**-pahćh śhan] v. slang: drink one's fill; guzzle one's fill (vulg.)

nażreć się [**nah**-zhrećh śhan] v. eat its's (animal's) fill; vulg.: gorge; stuff oneself; have a blowout; eat as an animal

nażyć się [**nah**-zhićh śhan] v. enjoy life to the full; spend a good part of one's life with (wife, parents, etc.)

neandertalczyk [ne-ahn-der-**tahl**-chik] m. Neanderthal man

neandertalski [ne-ahn-der-**tahl**-skee] adj.m. Neanderthal (race, etc.)

nearktyczny [ne-ahrk-**tich**-ni] adj.m. Nearctic

nearktyka [ne-**ahrk**-ti-kah] f. Nearctica

nefelin [ne-**fe**-leen] m. nephelin

nefelometr [ne-fe-**lo**-metr] m. nephelometer

nefelometria [ne-fe-lo-**metr**-yah] f. nephelometry

nefoskop [ne-**fo**-skop] m. nephoscope

nefrolog [ne-**fro**-log] m. nephrologist

nefrologia [ne-fro-**lo**-gyah] f. nephrology

nefrologiczny [ne-fro-lo-**geech**-ni] adj.m. nephrologic

nefron [**nef**-ron] m. nephron

nefrotomia [ne-fro-**to**-myah] f. nephrotomy

nefroza [ne-**fro**-zah] f. nephrosis

nefryt [**nef**-rit] m. nephrite (mineral)

negacja [ne-**gahts**-yah] f. negation; opposite of positive
negaton [ne-**gah**-ton] m. negaton
negatyw [ne-**gah**-tif] m. negative
negatywista [ne-gah-ti-**vees**-tah] m. negativist
negatywistyczny [ne-gah-ti-vees-**tich**-ni] adj.m. negativistic
negatywizm [ne-gah-**ti**-veezm] m. negativism
negatywnie [ne-gah-**tiv**-ńe] adv. negatively
być nastawionym negatywnie do czegoś [bićh nah-stah-**vyo**-nim ne-gah-**tiv**-ńe do **che**-gośh] exp.: to disapprove of something
odpowiedzieć negatywnie [ot-po-**vye**-dźhećh ne-gah-**tiv**-ńe] exp.: to answer in negative
prośbę załatwiono negatywnie [**prożh**-ban zah-wah-**tfyo**-no ne-gah-**tiv**-ńe] exp.: the request was rejected
negatywny [ne-gah-**tiv**-ni] adj.m. negative; saying "no"
odpowiedź negatywna [ot-**po**-vyećh ne-gah-**tiv**-nah] exp.: negative answer
wynik negatywny [vi-ńeek ne-gah-**tiv**-ni] exp.: negative diagnosis; negative result
negatywowy [ne-gah-ti-**vo**-vi] adj.m. of a (photographic) negative
negliż [**neg**-leesh] m. undress; morning dress; dishabille
w negliżu [v neg-**lee**-zhoo] exp.: in undress; in dishabille
negliżować [neg-lee-**zho**-vahćh] v. neglect; ignore (*repeatedly*)
negliżować się [neg-lee-**zho**-vahćh śhan] v. be in undress; be in dishabille (*repeatedly*)
negliżowy [neg-lee-**zho**-vi] adj.m. unceremonious (attire, etc.)
negocjacja [ne-go-**tsyah**-tsyah] f. negotiation
negocjacje [ne-go-**tsyah**-tsye] pl. negotiations; settling a treaty
negocjacyjny [ne-go-tsyah-**tsiy**-ni] adj.m. of negotiation
negocjator [ne-go-**tsyah**-tor] m. negotiator
negocjować [ne-go-**tsyo**-vahćh] v. negotiate (*repeatedly*)
negować [ne-**go**-vahćh] v. deny; negate (*repeatedly*)
negowanie [ne-go-**vah**-ńe] n. negation
Negr [negr] m. colloq: Negro
negroid [neg-**ro**-eet] m. Negroid
negroidzi [neg-ro-**ee**-dźhee] pl. Negroids
negroidalny [neg-ro-ee-**dahl**-ni] adj.m. Negroid
negus [**ne**-goos] m. negus
nekrobioza [ne-kro-**byo**-zah] f. necrobiosis
nekrofag [ne-**kro**-fahg] m. necrophagous
nekrofagi [ne-kro-**fah**-gee] pl. necrophaga
nekrofil [ne-**kro**-feel] m. necrophyle
nekrofilia [ne-kro-**fee**-lyah] f. necrophilia
nekrofilski [ne-kro-**feel**-skee] adj.m. nercophilic
nekrofobia [ne-kro-**fo**-byah] f. necrophobia
nekrolatria [ne-kro-**lah**-tryah] f. necrolatry
nekrolog [ne-**kro**-log] m. obituary notice; obituary
nekromancja [ne-kro-**mahn**-tsyah] f. necromancy
nekromanta [ne-kro-**mahn**-tah] m. necromancer
nekropola [ne-kro-**po**-lah] f. necropolis
nekropolia [ne-kro-**po**-lyah] f. necropolis
nekroskopia [ne-kro-**sko**-pyah] f. necroscopy
nekrotyczny [ne-kro-**tich**-ni] adj.m. necrotic
nekroza [ne-**kro**-zah] f. necrosis
nektar [**nek**-tahr] m. nectar
nektarium [nek-**tahr**-yoom] n. nectary
nektaria [nek-**tahr**-yah] pl. nectaries
nektarnik [nek-**tahr**-ńeek] m. sunbird (of the family Nectariniidae)
nektarniki [nek-tahr-**ńee**-kee] pl. the family Nectariniidae
nektarowy [nek-tah-**ro**-vi] adj.m. nectarous
nektaryna [nek-tah-**ri**-nah] f. nectarine (tree, fruit)

nektarynka [nek-tah-**rin**-kah] f. (small) nectarine
nekton [**nek**-ton] m. nekton
nektoniczny [nek-to-**ńeech**-ni] adj.m. nectonic
nelson [**nel**-son] m. half-nelson (the use of leverage against an arm, neck, and head of an opponent)
podwójny nelson [pod-**vooy**-ni **nel**-son] exp.: full nelson
nelsoński [nel-**soń**-skee] adj.m. of Nelson
po nelsońsku [po nel-**soń**-skoo] exp.: in Nelson style; (collops) a la Nelson
zrazy po nelsońsku [**zrah**-zi po nel-**soń**-skoo] exp.: collops Nelson style
nemezis [ne-**me**-zees] indecl.: nemesis; goddess of fate
nemezys [ne-**me**-zis] indecl.: nemesis; goddess of fate
nenia [**ne**-ńyah] f. Roman funeral song
nemrod [**nem**-rot] m. Nimrod
nenufar [ne-**noo**-fahr] m. water lily; nenuphar
neo- [ne-o] prefix: new (compound, etc.); recent; new and different; new and abnormal; latest (period)
neoanarchizm [ne-o-ah-**nahr**-kheezm] m. neoanarchism (of the new left, etc.)
neobarok [ne-o-**bah**-rok] m. neo-baroque style (of 19th. cent.)
neobehawioryzm [ne-o-be-khah-**vyo**-rizm] m. neobehaviorism
neodarwinista [ne-o-dahr-vee-**ńees**-tah] m. neo-Darwinian
neodarwinistyczny [ne-o-dahr-vee-ńees-**tich**-ni] adj.m. neo-Darwinian
neodarwinizm [ne-o-dahr-**vee**-ńeezm] m. neo-Darwinism
neodym [ne-**o**-dim] m. neodymium (atomic number 60)
neoewolucjonizm [ne-o-e-vo-loo-**tsyo**-ńeezm] m. neo-evolutionism
neofaszysta [ne-o-fah-**shis**-tah] m. neo-fascist
neofaszystowski [ne-o-fah-shis-**tof**-skee] adj.m. neo-fascist
neofaszyzm [ne-o-**fah**-shizm] m. neo-fascism
neoficki [ne-o-**feets**-kee] adj.m. neophitic
neofilolog [ne-o-fee-**lo**-log] m. specialist in modern languages and literature
neofilologia [ne-o-fee-lo-**lo**-gyah] f. philology of modern languages
neofilologiczny [ne-o-fee-lo-lo-**geech**-ni] adj.m. of philology of modern languages
neofita [ne-o-**fee**-tah] m. convert; neophyte; proselyte
neofitka [ne-o-**feet**-kah] f. (female) convert; neophyte; proselyte
neofityzm [ne-o-**fee**-tizm] m. neophytism
neogea [ne-o-**ge**-ah] f. Neogaea
neogen [ne-**o**-gen] m. Neogene
neogeniczny [ne-o-ge-**ńeech**-ni] adj.m. neogenetic
neogotycki [ne-o-go-**tits**-kee] adj.m. neo-Gothic
neogotyk [ne-o-**go**-tik] m. neo-Gothic
neografia [ne-o-**grah**-fyah] f. neography
neogramatyk [ne-o-grah-**mah**-tik] m. neo-grammarian
neohegelianizm [ne-o-khe-ge-**lyah**-ńeezm] m. neo-Hegelianism
neoheglizm [ne-o-**heg**-leezm] m. neo-Hegelianism
neoheglowski [ne-o-heg-**lof**-skee] adj.m. neo-Hegelian
neohellenista [ne-o-hel-le-**ńees**-tah] m. neo-Hellenist
neohellenizm [ne-o-hel-**le**-ńeezm] m. neo-Hellenism
neohitleryzm [ne-o-hit-**le**-rizm] m. neo-Hitlerism
neohumanizm [ne-o-hoo-**mah**-ńeezm] m. neo-humanism
neoimpresjonizm [ne-o-eem-pre-**syo**-ńeezm] m. neo-impressionism
neokantysta [ne-o-kahn-**tis**-tah] m. neo-Kantian
neokantyzm [ne-o-**kahn**-tizm] m. neo-Kantianism
neoklasycyzm [ne-o-klah-**si**-tsizm] m. neo-classicism
neoklasyczny [ne-o-klah-**sich**-ni] adj.m. neo-classic
neoklasyk [ne-o-**klah**-sik] m. neo-classicist

neokolonialista [ne-o-ko-lo-ńyah-**lees**-tah] m. neocolonialist
neokolonializm [ne-o-ko-lo-**ńyah**-leezm] m. neocolonialism
neokolonialny [ne-o-ko-lo-**ńyahl**-ni] adj.m. neocolonial
neokom [ne-**o**-kom] m. the Neocomian
neolamarkizm [ne-o-lah-**mahr**-keezm] m. neo-Lamarckism
neoliberalizm [ne-o-lee-be-**rah**-leezm] m. neoliberalism
neolit [ne-**o**-lit] m. Neolithic age
neolityczny [ne-o-lee-**tich**-ni] adj.m. Neolithic
neologizm [ne-o-**lo**-geezm] m. neologism; new word; new meaning; new-coined word
neomaltuzjanizm [ne-o-mahl-tooz-**yah**-ńeezm] m. neo-Malthusianism
neomerkantylizm [ne-o-mer-kahn-**ti**-leezm] m. neomercantilism
neon [**ne**-on] m. neon light; neon sign; neon lamp; neon tube; neon
neonacysta [ne-o-nah-**tsis**-tah] m. neonazi
neonacystowski [ne-o-nah-tsis-**tof**-skee] adj.m. neonazi (movement, propaganda, etc.)
neonacyzm [ne-o-**nah**-tsizm] m. Neo-Nazism
neonazista [ne-o-nah-**źhees**-tah] m. neonazi
neonazistowski [ne-o-nah-źhees-**tof**-skee] adj.m. neonazi
neonazizm [ne-o-**nah**-źheezm] m. Neo-Nazism
neonek [ne-**o**-nek] m. an aquarium fish
neonik [ne-**o**-ńeek] m. small neon lamp
neonowy [ne-o-**no**-vi] adj.m. neon (lamp, sign, etc.)
neonówka [ne-o-**noof**-kah] f. neon lamp; neon sign
neontologia [ne-on-to-**lo**-gyah] f. the opposite of paleontology
neoplatonik [ne-o-plah-**to**-ńeek] m. neo-Platonist
neoplatonizm [ne-o-plah-**to**-neezm] m. neo-Platonism
neoplatończyk [ne-o-plah-**toń**-chik] m. neo-Platonist
neoplatoński [ne-o-plah-**toń**-skee] adj.m. neo-Platonic
neopozytywista [ne-o-po-zi-ti-**vees**-tah] m. neo-positivist
neopozytywistyczny [ne-o-po-zi-ti-vees-**tich**-ni] adj.m. neo-positivistic
neopozytywizm [ne-o-po-zi-**ti**-veezm] m. neo-positivism
neorealista [ne-o-re-ah-**lees**-tah] m. neo-realist
neorealistyczny [ne-o-re-ah-lees-**tich**-ni] adj.m. neo-realistic
neorealizm [ne-o-re-**ah**-leezm] m. neo-realism
neoromanizm [ne-o-ro-**mah**-ńeezm] m. Neo-Roman style
neoromantyczny [ne-o-ro-mahn-**tich**-ni] adj.m. neo-romantic
neoromantyk [ne-o-ro-**mahn**-tik] m. neo-romanticist
neoromantyzm [ne-o-ro-**mahn**-tizm] m. neo-romanticism
neoscholastyczny [ne-o-skho-lahs-**tich**-ni] adj.m. Neo-Scholastic
neoscholastyk [ne-o-skhko-**lahs**-tik] m. Neo-Scholasticist
neoscholastyka [ne-o-skho-**lahs**-ti-kah] f. Neo-Scholasticism
neosemantyzm [ne-o-se-**mahn**-tizm] m. neo-semantism
neotektonika [ne-o-tek-**to**-ńee-kah] f. neo-tectonics
neotenia [ne-o-**teń**-yah] f. neotenia
neotomista [ne-o-to-**mees**-tah] m. Neo-Tomist
neotomistyczny [ne-o-to-mees-**tich**-ni] adj.m. Neo-Tomistic
neotomizm [ne-o-**to**-meezm] m. Neo-Tomism
neozoiczny [ne-o-zo-**eech**-ni] adj.m. neozoic
nepotysta [ne-po-**tis**-tah] m. nepotist
nepotyzm [ne-**po**-tizm] m. nepotism; favoritism shown to relatives in securing jobs, etc.
neptek [**nep**-tek] m. colloq: muff; oaf; lout; duffer
neptun [**nep**-toon] m. neptunium (atomic number 93)
neptuniczny [nep-too-**ńeech**-ni] adj.m. neptunian (rock)
neptunizm [nep-**too**-ńeezm] m. neptunism
nera [**ne**-rah] f. (big, old) kidney

nerczyca [ner-**chi**-tsah] f. nephrosis
nerczycowy [ner-chi-**tso**-vi] adj.m. nephrotic
nereczka [ne-**rech**-kah] f. (small) kidney
nerecznica [ne-rech-**ńee**-tsah] f. shield fern; Dryopteris fern of the polypody family
nereida [ne-**rey**-dah] f. nereid
nerka [**ner**-kah] f. kidney; kidney-shaped (pool, etc.)
nerka wędrująca [**ner**-kah vand-roo-**yown**-tsah] exp.: floating kidney
zapalenie nerek [zah-pah-**le**-ńe **ne**-rek] exp.: nephritis
nerki [**ner**-kee] pl. kidneys
nerkowato [ner-ko-**vah**-to] adv. in a kidney-shape
nerkowaty [ner-ko-**vah**-ti] adj.m. kidney-shaped; reniform
nerkowiec [ner-**ko**-vyets] m. cashew tree; cashew nut
nerkowy [ner-**ko**-vi] adj.m. renal; nephritic; kidney (trouble, etc.)
kamienie nerkowe [kah-**mye**-ńe ner-**ko**-ve] exp.: kidney stones; stones in the kidneys
piasek nerkowy [**pyah**-sek ner-**ko**-vi] exp.: gravel
nerkówka [ner-**koof**-kah] f. loin of veal
nerpa [**ner**-pah] f. seal; Phoca vitulina
nerw [nerf] m. nerve; vigor; ardor; coolness in danger; ability; skill
działać na nerwy [**dźhah**-wahćh nah **ner**-vi] exp.: to get on somebody's nerves
kłębek nerwów [**kwan**-bek **ner**-voof] exp.: a bundle of nerves
nerw pisarski [nerf pee-**sahr**-skee] exp.: literary ability
nerwy odmówiły mu posłuszeństwa [**ner**-vi od-moo-**vee**-wi moo pos-woo-**sheń**-stfah] exp.: his nerves broke down; he had a nervous breakdown
panować nad nerwami [pah-**no**-vahćh naht ner-**vah**-mee] exp.: to keep cool
stalowe nerwy [stah-**lo**-ve **ner**-vi] exp.: nerves of steel
szarpiący nerwy [shahr-**pyown**-tsi **ner**-vi] exp.: nerve-racking
zapalenie nerwu [zah-pah-**le**-ńe **ner**-voo] exp.: neuritis
z nerwem [z **ner**-vem] exp.: with vigor
nerwacja [ner-**vah**-tsyah] f. nervation
nerwiak [**ner**-vyahk] m. neuroma
nerwica [ner-**vee**-tsah] f. neurosis; nervous disturbance
nerwicowiec [ner-vee-**tso**-vyets] m. neurotic; emotionally unstable person
nerwicowy [ner-vee-**tso**-vi] adj.m. neurotic
nerwisty [ner-**vees**-ti] adj.m. nervate
nerwoból [ner-**vo**-bool] m. neuralgia; severe pain along a nerve; neuralgy
nerwowiec [ner-**vo**-vyets] m. excitable person; jumpy person; edgy person
nerwowo [ner-**vo**-vo] adv. nervously; fretfully; restlessly; feverishly; neurotically
nie wytrzymać nerwowo [ńe vi-**tshi**-mahćh ner-**vo**-vo] exp.: to lose one's nerve
rozstrojony nerwowo [ros-stro-**yo**-ni ner-**vo**-vo] exp.: with shattered nerves
wyczerpany nerwowo [vi-cher-**pah**-ni ner-**vo**-vo] exp.: nervously exhausted; in a state of nervous prostration
załamać się nerwowo [zah-**wah**-mahćh śhan ner-**vo**-vo] exp.: to have a nervous breakdown
nerwowość [ner-**vo**-vośhćh] f. nervosity; nervous disorder; irritability; fidgets; restlessness; feverishness; fidgetiness
nerwowy [ner-**vo**-vi] adj.m. nervous (breakdown, etc.); made up of nerves; fearful; fretful; fidgety; ; restless; excitable; edgy; jumpy; nerve (center, fiber, cell, etc.)
atak nerwowy [ah-tahk ner-**vo**-vi] exp.: fit of nerves
specjalista chorób nerwowych [spets-yah-**lees**-tah **kho**-roop ner-**vo**-vikh] exp.: neurologist
załamanie nerwowe [zah-wah-**mah**-ńe ner-**vo**-ve] exp.: nervous

breakdown
nerwówa [ner-**voo**-vah] f. hectic, nervously exhausting work (at home, in an office, etc.)
nerwówka [ner-**voof**-kah] f. hectic and nervous atmosphere (before examination, etc.)
nerwus [**ner**-voos] m. excitable person; jumpy person; edgy person
nerwy [**ner**-vi] pl. the nerves
działać na nerwy [**dźhah**-wahćh nah **ner**-vi] exp.: to irritate
kłębek nerwów [**kwan**-bek **ner**-voof] exp.: a bundle of nerves
nerwy odmówiły mu posłuszeństwa [**ner**-vi od-moo-**vee**-wi moo pos-woo-**sheń**-stfah] exp.: his nerves broke down
panować nad nerwami [pah-**no**-vahćh naht ner-**vah**-mee] exp.: to keep cool
stalowe nerwy [stah-**lo**-ve **ner**-vi] exp.: nerves of steel
szarpiący nerwy [shahr-**pyown**-tsi **ner**-vi] exp.: irritating
nerytyczny [ne-ri-**tich**-ni] adj.m. neurotic
neseser [ne-**se**-ser] m. dressing case; make-up case; toilet-case
neseserek [ne-se-**se**-rek] m. (small) dressing case; make-up case; toilet-case
neska [**nes**-kah] f. Nescafe; instant coffee
nestor [**nes**-tor] m. Nestor; senior
nestorianizm [nes-to-**ryah**-ńeezm] m. Nestorianism
nestorka [nes-**tor**-kah] f. (female) Nestor
net [net] m. net (in tennis)
neta [**ne**-tah] f. a type of fishing net
netto [**net**-to] (not declined) net (cost, price, profit, weight, result)
neuma [**new**-mah] f. neueme
neumy [**new**-mi] pl. neuemes
neuralgia [new-**rahl**-gyah] f. neuralgia
neuralgiczny [new-rahl-**geech**-ni] adj.m. neuralgic; see: **newralgiczny**
neurastenia [new-rah-**ste**-ńyah] f. neurasthenia
neurasteniczny [new-rah-ste-**ńeech**-ni] adj.m. neurasthenic
neurastenik [new-rah-**ste**-ńeek] m. neurasthenic
neuro- [new-ro] prefix: neuro-
neuroblast [new-**ro**-blahst] m. neuroblast
neurochirurg [new-ro-**khee**-roorg] m. neurosurgeon
neurochirurgia [new-ro-khee-**roor**-gyah] f. neurosurgery
neurochirurgiczny [new-ro-khee-roor-**geech**-ni] adj.m. neurosurgical
neurofizjolog [new-ro-feez-**yo**-log] m. neurophysiologist
neurofizjologia [new-ro-feez-yo-**lo**-gyah] f. neurophysiology
neurofizjologiczny [new-ro-feez-yo-lo-**geech**-ni] adj.m. neurophysiologic
neurogenicznie [new-ro-ge-**ńeech**-ńe] adv. neurogenically
neurogeniczny [new-ro-ge-**ńeech**-ni] adj.m. neurogenic
neurogenny [new-ro-**gen**-ni] adj.m. neurogenic
neuroleptyczny [new-ro-lep-**tich**-ni] adj.m. neuroleptic
neuroleptyk [new-ro-**lep**-tik] m. neuroleptic
neurolog [new-**ro**-log] m. neurologist
neurologia [new-ro-**log**-yah] f. neurology
neurologiczny [new-ro-lo-**geech**-ni] adj.m. neurological
neuron [**new**-ron] m. neuron
neuropata [new-ro-**pah**-tah] m. neuropath
neuropatia [new-ro-**pah**-tyah] f. neuropathy
neuropatolog [new-ro-pah-**to**-log] m. neuropathologist
neuropatologia [new-ro-pah-to-**lo**-gyah] f. neuropathology
neuropatyczny [new-ro-pah-**tich**-ni] adj.m. neuropathic
neuropsychiatria [new-ro-psi-**khyah**-tryah] f. neuropsychiatry
neuropsychiatryczny [new-ro-psi-khyah-**trich**-ni] adj.m. neuropsychiatric
neuropsychologia [new-ro-psi-kho-**lo**-gyah] f. neuropsychology
neuropsychologiczny [new-ro-psi-kho-lo-**geech**-ni] adj.m.

neuropsychologic
neurotyczny [new-ro-**tich**-ni] adj.m. neurotic
neurotyk [new-**ro**-tik] m. neurotic
neuroza [new-**ro**-zah] f. neurosis
neuryna [new-**ri**-nah] f. neurine
neuryt [**new**-rit] m. neurite
neutralizacja [ne-oo-trah-lee-**zahts**-yah] f. neutralization
neutralizacyjny [ne-oo-trah-lee-zah-**tsiy**-ni] adj.m. neutralizing
neutralizator [ne-oo-trah-lee-**zah**-tor] m. neutralizer
neutralizm [ne-oo-**trah**-leezm] m. neutralism
neutralizować [ne-oo-trah-lee-**zo**-vahćh] v. neutralize (*repeatedly*)
neutralizować się [ne-oo-trah-lee-**zo**-vahćh śhan] v. become neutralized (*repeatedly*)
neutralizowanie [ne-oo-trah-lee-zo-**vah**-ńe] n. neutralization
neutralizowanie się [ne-oo-trah-lee-zo-**vah**-ńe śhan] n. becoming neutralized
neutralnie [ne-oo-**trahl**-ńe] adv. neutrally; indifferently; impartially
zachowywać się neutralnie [zah-kho-**vi**-vahćh śhan ne-oo-**trahl**-ńe] exp.: to observe neutrality; to remain neutral; to stand neutral; colloq: to sit on the fence
neutralność [ne-oo-**trahl**-nośhćh] f. neutrality; neutral status; impartiality
zachować neutralność [zah-**kho**-vahćh ne-oo-**trahl**-nośhćh] exp.: to observe neutrality; to remain neutral
zbrojna neutralność [**zbroy**-nah ne-oo-**trahl**-nośhćh] exp.: armed neutrality
neutralny [ne-oo-**trahl**-ni] adj.m. neutral; indifferent; impartial
być neutralnym [bićh ne-oo-**trahl**-nim] exp.: to stand neutral; to remain neutral; to observe neutrality; to sit on the fence
pozostać neutralnym [po-**zos**-tahćh ne-oo-**trahl**-nim] exp.: to observe neutrality; to remain neutral
neutrino [ne-oo-**tree**-no] n. neutrino
neutrofil [ne-oo-**tro**-feel] m. neutrophile
neutron [ne-**oo**-tron] m. neutron
neutronowy [ne-oo-tro-**no**-vi] adj.m. neutron (bomb, etc.)
newralgia [nev-**rahl**-gyah] f. neuralgia; pain along a nerve
newralgicznie [nev-rahl-**geech**-ńe] adv. neuralgically
newralgiczny [nev-rahl-**geech**-ni] adj.m. neuralgic (pain along a nerve, etc.)
bóle newralgiczne [**boo**-le nev-rahl-**geech**-ne] exp.: growing pains
punkt newralgiczny [poonkt nev-rahl-**geech**-ni] exp.: sore point
newroza [nev-**ro**-zah] f. neurosis
nęcąco [nan-**tsown**-tso] adv. alluringly; enticingly; temptingly; invitingly; seductively; tantalizingly
nęcący [nan-**tsown**-tsi] adj.m. alluring; enticing; tempting; inviting; seductive; tantalizing
nęcenie [nan-**tse**-ńe] n. lure; seduction
nęcić [**nan**-ćheećh] v. entice; court; allure; tempt; be seductive; be inviting; tantalize (*repeatedly*)
nęcisko [nan-**ćhees**-ko] n. (animal) alluring area (for hunting)
nędza [**nan**-dzah] f. misery; extreme poverty; indigence; penury; destitution; the destitute; trash; refuse; worthless stuff
cierpieć nędzę [**ćher**-pyećh **nan**-dzan] exp.: to be poverty-stricken; to be in want
doprowadzić do nędzy [do-pro-**vah**-dźheećh do **nan**-dzi] exp.: to reduce to destitution; to reduce to beggary
w skrajnej nędzy [f **skrahy**-ney **nan**-dzi] exp.: down and out; in abject poverty
nędzarka [nan-**dzahr**-kah] f. bag lady; destitute wretch; beggar-woman; pauper; homeless woman
nędzarski [nan-**dzahr**-skee] adj.m. beggarly
nędzarz [**nan**-dzahsh] m. destitute wretch; beggar; pauper; homeless man; tatterdemalion
nędznica [nandz-**ńee**-tsah] f.

(woman) villain; rascal; rogue; scoundrel; wretch

nędznie [nandz-ńe] adv. poorly; wretchedly; squalidly; in squalor; shabbily; pitifully; stingily; scantily; incompetently; indolently; negligently; carelessly

nędznieć [nandz-ńećh] v. decline; waste away; become sickly (*repeatedly*)

nędznik [nandz-ńeek] m. villain; rascal; rogue; scoundrel; wretch

nędzny [nandz-ni] adj.m. wretched; miserable; shabby; sorry; beggarly; abject; trashy; paltry; sorry; despicable; base; mean; sordid; ignoble; sad; worthless; indigent; poverty-stricken; emaciated; starved; frail; more dead than alive; slang: measly

nękać [nan-kahćh] v. molest; harry; torment; harass; annoy; worry; gnaw; press hard (the enemy, etc.) (*repeatedly*)

nękać nieprzyjaciela [nan-kahćh ńe-pshi-yah-**ćhe**-lah] exp.: to press the enemy hard

nękać się [nan-kahćh śhan] v. torment oneself (with thoughts, etc.) (*repeatedly*)

nękanie [nan-**kah**-ńe] n. pinch (of hunger, etc.); stress (of poverty, etc.)

nękany [nan-**kah**-ni] adj.m. hard pressed; compelled; constrained

ni [ńee] conj. nor; no; neither; not even

ni mniej, ni więcej [ńee mńey ńee **vyan**-tsey] exp.: imagine; just fancy; would you believe

ni... ni... [ńee... ńee...] exp.: neither ... nor ...

ni stąd, ni z owąd [ńee stownt ńee z o-vownt] exp.: without any reason; suddenly; for no reason whatever; unexpectedly

ni to, ni owo [ńee to ńee **o**-vo] exp.: adv. neither this nor that

ni to, ni sio [ńee to ńee śho] exp.: neither this nor that; neither fish, flesh nor good red herring (Brit.)

ni to ... ni to [ńee to ńee to] exp.: cannot be said for certain

ni widu, ni słychu [ńee **vee**-doo ńee **swi**-khoo] exp.: no trace whatever

ni w pięć, ni w dziewięć [ńee f pyanćh ńee v **dźhe**-vyanćh] exp.: without rhyme or reason; out of place; most inappropriately

niania [ńah-ńah] f. (baby's) nurse; nanny; dry nurse

niańczenie [ńahń-**che**-ńe] n. nursing

niańczyć [ńahń-chićh] v. nurse; dandle (*repeatedly*)

niańczyny [ńahń-**chi**-ni] adj.m. nurse's; nanny's

niańka [ńahń-kah] f. nurse; nurserymaid; nanny; nursemaid

niby [ńee-bi] adv. as if; pretending; as it were; like; a sort of; as though; supposedly; kind of; sort of; of a kind; of a sort; of sorts

na niby [nah **ńee**-bi] exp.: pretending; make-believe

niby doktor [ńee-bi **dok**-tor] exp.: sham doctor; would-be doctor; professing to be a doctor

niby przypadkiem [ńee-bi pshi-**paht**-kem] exp.: by would-be accident; as if by chance; as though by chance

niby- [ńee-bi] prefix: as if; as though; like; as it were; supposedly; kind of; sort of; of a kind; colloq: of sorts

nibygwiazda [ńee-bi-**gvyahz**-dah] f. quasi-stellar object; quasi-stellar radio source; quasar

nibyjagoda [ńee-bi-yah-**go**-dah] f. true berry

nibynóżka [ńee-bi-**noosh**-kah] f. pseudopodium

nibynóżki [ńee-bi-**noosh**-kee] pl. pseudopodia

nic [ńeets] pron. nothing at all; not a bit; nothing whatever; n. a mere nothing; something of no value; nobody; a man of no account

a on nic [ah on ńeets] exp.: all to no purpose; he did nothing

a tu nic [ah too ńeets] exp.: all to no purpose; nothing happened

a wy nic [ah vi ńeets] exp.: all to no purpose; you (all) did nothing

bez niczego [bez ńee-**che**-go] exp.: without anything on; with nothing on; penniless
do niczego [do ńee-**che**-go] exp.: useless; no good; good-for-nothing; (to feel) like nothing on earth; fit for nothing
jak nic [yahk ńeets] exp.: as easy as anything; without the least effort; for sure
mieć kogoś za nic [myećh **ko**-gośh zah ńeets] exp.: to think little of somebody
mnie nic do tego [mńe ńeets do **te**-go] exp.: it is no business of mine
na nic [nah ńeets] exp.: for nothing; to no purpose
na niczym się skończyć [nah ńee-chim śhan **skoń**-chićh] exp.: to come to nothing
nic a nic [ńeets ah ńeets] exp.: nothing at all; nothing whatever; colloq: not a bit
nic dobrego [ńeets dob-**re**-go] exp.: trash; colloq: good-for-nothing (man)
nic dziwnego [ńeets dźheev-**ne**-go] exp.: no wonder
nic mi nie jest [ńeets mee ńe yest] exp.: I am OK; I am all right; nothing is the matter with me
nic mi po tym [ńeets mee po tim] exp.: I have no use for it
nic mu się nie stało [ńeets moo śhan ńe **stah**-wo] exp.: nothing hapened to him
nic nie gorszy [ńeets ńe **gor**-shi] exp.: every bit as good
nic nie lepszy [ńeets ńe **lep**-shi] exp.: not a bit better
nic nie szkodzi [ńeets ńe **shko**-dźhee] exp.: does not matter; do not mention it!
nic podobnego [ńeets po-dob-**ne**-go] exp.: nothing of the sort
nic szczególnego [ńeets shche-gool-**ne**-go] exp.: nothing particular
nic ważnego [ńeets vahzh-**ne**-go] exp.: nothing of importance; nothing of value
nic wcale [ńeets **ftsah**-le] exp.: nothing at all; nothing whatever; colloq: not a bit; no
nic więcej [ńeets **vyan**-tsey] exp.: nothing else; nothing more
nic zgoła [ńeets **zgo**-wah] exp.: nothing at all; nothing whatever; colloq: not a bit; no
nic z tego [ńeets s **te**-go] exp.: no use; to no purpose; to no avail; no use for it
nie mam nic więcej do powiedzenia [ńe mahm ńeets **vyan**-tsey do po-vye-**dze**-ńah] exp.: I have no more to say
odejść z niczym [**o**-deyśhćh z **ńee**-chim] exp.: to go away empty-handed
skończyć na niczym [**skoń**-chićh nah **ńee**-chim] exp.: to come to nothing
to ci nic nie pomoże [to ćhee ńeets ńe po-**mo**-zhe] exp.: it won't help you a bit
to jest na nic [to yest nah ńeets] exp.: that will never do
to na nic [to nah ńeets] exp.: it's no use
to nic [to ńeets] exp.: it doesn't matter; never mind; it's of no consequence
to nic nie jest [to ńeets ńe yest] exp.: it's nothing
tyle co nic [**ti**-le tso ńeets] exp.: next to nothing; as good as nothing; practically nothing
w niczym [v **ńee**-chim] exp.: in no respect
za nic [zah ńeets] exp.: for nothing
za nic na świecie [zah ńeets nah **śhfye**-ćhe] exp.: not for anything
z niczego [z ńee-**che**-go] exp.: out of nothing
z niczym [z **ńee**-chim] exp.: empty-handed

nice [**ńee**-tse] pl. meringues; wrong side (of a garment); colloq: changing something (radically)
nicejski [ńee-**tsey**-skee] adj.m. of Nice; Nice (oil, etc.)
nicenie [ńee-**tse**-ńe] n. riveting
nicennica [ńee-tsen-**ńee**-tsah] f. herb of the genus Filago
nicestwić [ńee-**tses**-tfeećh] v.

annihilate (*repeatedly*)
nicestwieć [ńee-tses-tfyećh] v. vanish (*repeatedly*)
nicestwienie [ńee-tses-**tfye**-ńe] n. vanishing; annihilation
nicestwo [ńee-**tses**-tfo] n. nothingness
nichrom [**ńee**-khrom] m. nichrome; chrome-nickel
nici [**ńee**-ćhee] pl. threads; nothing; exp.: nothing of it
nici będą z tego [**ńee**-ćhee **ban**-down s **te**-go] exp.: it will come to nothing; it will do no good
nicianka [ńee-**ćhahn**-kah] f. cotton-threaded lace
niciany [ńee-**ćhah**-ni] adj.m. of thread
niciane rękawiczki [ńee-**ćhah**-ne ran-kah-**veech**-kee] exp.: fabric gloves
niciarka [ńee-**ćhahr**-kah] f. riveting machine; (woman) haberdasher; book sewer; sewing machine
niciarnia [ńee-**ćhahr**-ńah] f. plant producing threads
niciarz [**ńee**-ćhahsh] m. haberdasher; riveter
nicielnica [ńee-ćhel-**ńee**-tsah] f. perforated plate used in thread production; harness
nicienica [ńee-ćhe-**ńee**-tsah] f. perforated plate used in thread production; harness
nicieniobójczy [ńee-ćhe-ńo-**booy**-chi] adj.m. nematode-killing (spray, etc.); round-worm-killing (spray, etc.)
nicień [**ńee**-ćheń] m. nematode; round worm
nicienie [ńee-**ćhe**-ńe] pl. nematodes
niciowaty [ńee-ćho-**vah**-ti] adj.m. thread-like
nicość [**ńee**-tsośhćh] f. nothingness; oblivion; nihility; nonentity; a mere nothing
rozpływać się w nicości [ros-pwi-vahćh śhan v ńee-**tsośh**-ćhee] exp.: to vanish
nicować [ńee-**tso**-vahćh] v. turn (a garment inside out); pick to pieces; carp at; distort; falsify (*repeatedly*)
nicowanie [ńee-tso-**vah**-ńe] n. turning clothes inside out
nicpoń [**ńeets**-poń] m. good-for-nothing; "nogoodnik"; scamp; bad egg; bad lot
niczego [ńee-**che**-go] exp.: not bad; quite good; not unsightly
bez niczego [bez ńee-**che**-go] exp.: without anything on; without nothing on; penniless
do niczego [do ńee-**che**-go] exp.: useless; no good; good for nothing
niczego sobie [ńee-**che**-go **so**-bye] exp.: not bad; good looking
niczyj [**ńee**-chiy] pron. nobody's; no one's; ownerless
niczym [**ńee**-chim] exp.: like
nić [ńeećh] f. thread
dojść po nici do kłębka [doyśhćh po **ńee**-ćhee do **kwanp**-kah] exp.: to unravel a plot; to solve an enigma
nici z tego będą [**ńee**-ćhee s **te**-go **ban**-down] exp.: it will come to nothing; it will end in smoke
to jest grubymi nićmi szyte [to yest groo-**bi**-mee **ńeećh**-mee **shi**-te] exp.: it is a thin disguise; it's a crude scheme; it's an obvious scheme; it's a crude setup
niderlandzki [ńee-der-**lahn**-tskee] adj.m. Netherlandic; Dutch
język niderlandzki [yan-zik ńee-der-lahn-tskee] exp.: Netherlandish; Dutch (hist.)
nie [ńe] part; no; not (any); prefix: un-; non-; mis-; -less
ależ nie! [ah-lesh ńe] excl.: no, no!; oh, no!; definitely not!
co to, to nie [tso to to ńe] exp.: absolutely not; no way; out of the question; by no means not
czemu nie? [**che**-moo ńe] exp.: why not?; why shoudn't I? (he, you, we, etc.)
... czy nie? [chi ńe] exp.: ... or not; no?; ... isn't it?
czy wiesz, czy nie? [chi vyesh chi ńe] exp.: do you know or don't you?
ja tego także nie wiem [yah **te**-go **tahg**-zhe ńe vyem] exp.: I do not know it either

jeszcze nie [**yesh**-che ńe] exp.: not yet; not for a long time
już nie [yoosh ńe] exp.: no more
kto jak nie on [kto yahk ńe on] exp.: who but he; who but him
nie bez [ńe bes] exp.: not without (effort, etc.)
nie brak ...[ńe brahk] exp.: there is no lack of
nie całkiem [ńe **tsahw**-kem] exp.: not quite
nie do pojęcia [ńe do po-**yan**-ćhah] exp.: incomprehensible; impossible to understand
nie do uratowania [ńe do oo-rah-to-**vah**-ńah] exp.: past recovery
nie do złamania [ńe do zwah-**mah**-ńah] exp.: unbreakable
nie kto inny, jak tylko on [ńe kto **een**-ni yahk **til**-ko on] exp.: none but he; none but him
nie mniej [ńe mńey] exp.: no less
nie wiem [ńe vyem] exp.: I don't know
nie więcej [ńe **vyan**-tsey] exp.: no more
no nie? [no ńe] exp.: don't you think so?
tak albo nie? [tahk **ahl**-bo ńe] exp.: either it is or it isn't; either you do or you don't
tak czy nie? [tahk chi ńe] exp.: yes or no?
także nie [**tahg**-zhe ńe] exp.: neither, not ... either
wcale nie [**ftsah**-le ńe] exp.: not at all
nie- [ńe] prefix: non-; mis-; -less
nieadekwatny [ńe-ah-dek-**faht**-ni] adj.m. inadequate
nieagresja [ńe-ah-**gre**-syah] f. nonaggression
pakt o nieagresji [pahkt o ńe-ah-**gre**-syee] exp.: nonaggression pact (or treaty)
nieaktualny [ńe-ahk-too-**ahl**-ni] adj.m. out of date; off the map; no longer considered; stale
nieaktywny [ńe-ahk-**tiv**-ni] adj.m. inactive
nieambitny [ńe-ahm-**beet**-ni] adj.m. unambitious; not ambitious
nieantagonistyczny [ńe-ahn-tah-go-ńees-**tich**-ni] adj.m. not antagonistic
nieapetycznie [ńe-ah-pe-**tich**-ńe] adv. unappetizingly; uninvitingly
nieapetyczny [ńe-ah-pe-**tich**-ni] adj.m. unappetizing; uninviting
nieartykułowany [ńe-ahr-ti-koo-wo-**vah**-ni] adj.m. inarticulate
nieartystyczny [ńe-ahr-tis-**tich**-ni] adj.m. inartistic
nieatrakcyjnie [ńe-ah-trahk-**tsiy**-ńe] adv. inattractively
nieatrakcyjność [ńe-ah-trahk-**tsiy**-nośhćh] f. inattractiveness
nieatrakcyjny [ńe-ah-trahk-**tsiy**-ni] adj.m. inattractive; uninteresting; not attractive; plain; dull
nieautentycznie [ńe-ahw-ten-**tich**-ńe] adv. not authentically
nieautentyczność [ńe-ahw-ten-**tich**-nośhćh] f. inauthenticity; spuriousness
nieautentyczny [ńe-ahw-ten-**tich**-ni] adj.m. not genuine; inauthentic; spurious; unauthentic
nieautomatyczny [ńe-ahw-to-mah-**tich**-ni] adj.m. nonautomatic
niebacznie [ńe-**bahch**-ńe] adv. imprudently; rashly; inconsiderately; incautiously; inadvertently
niebaczny [ńe-**bahch**-ni] adj.m. imprudent; rash; inconsiderate; incautious; inadvertent; unguarded
niebadawczy [ńe-bah-**dahf**-chi] adj.m. inquisitive
niebagatelny [ńe-bah-gah-**tel**-ni] adj.m. not trifling; not trivial; by no means trival
niebakteryjny [ńe-bahk-te-**riy**-ni] adj.m. nonbacterial
niebanalnie [ńe-bah-**nahl**-ńe] adv. not in commonplace fashion
niebanalny [ńe-bah-**nahl**-ni] adj.m. not commonplace; original
niebarwny [ńe-**bahrv**-ni] adj.m. not colored; colorless
niebawem [ńe-**bah**-vem] adv. by and by; before long; soon; presently; directly; shortly after; anon; at another time
niebeletrystyczny [ńe-be-le-tri-**stich**-ni] adj.m. nonfiction (work, etc.)
niebezpieczeństwo [ńe-bes-pye-

cheń-stfo] n. danger; peril; menace; jeopardy
narazić na niebezpieczeństwo [nah-**rah**-źheećh nah ńe-bes-pye-**cheń**-stfo] exp.: to endanger; to imperil; to expose to danger
niebezpiecznie [ńe-bes-**pyech**-ńe] adv. dangerously; perilously; riskily; trickily; unsafely; hazardously
niebezpieczny [ńe-bes-**pyech**-ni] adj.m. dangerous; risky; tricky; unsafe; hazardous; vicious (horse); breakneck (speed); treacherous
niebezpieczny zakręt [ńe-bes-**pyech**-ni **zahk**-rant] exp.: danderous curve
niebezpośredni [ńe-bes-po-**śhred**-ńee] adj.m. indirect
niebezużyteczny [ńe-bez-oo-zhi-**tech**-ni] adj.m. not useless
niebiałkowy [ńe-byahw-**ko**-vi] adj.m. protein-free
niebianin [ńe-**byah**-ńeen] m. heavenly being
niebianka [ńe-**byahn**-kah] f. (woman) heavenly being
niebiański [ńe-**byahń**-skee] adj.m. heavenly; divine
niebiańsko [ńe-**byahń**-sko] adv. heavenly
niebiańskość [ńe-**byahń**-skośhćh] f. heavenliness
niebiednie [ńe-**byed**-ńe] adv. not without money; not without funds; richly; not inexpensively
niebiedny [ńe-**byed**-ni] adj.m. not badly off; not without money; not impecunious
niebiegły [ńe-**byeg**-wi] adj.m. unskilled; unversed (in); incompetent
niebielistka [ńe-bye-**leest**-kah] f. a plant of the family Gentianaceae
niebieskawo [ńe-bye-**skah**-vo] adv. in a bluish tint
niebieskawość [ńe-bye-**skah**-vośhćh] f. bluish tint
niebieskawy [ńe-bye-**skah**-vi] adj.m. bluish; off blue
niebieski [ńe-**byes**-kee] adj.m. blue; heavenly; of the sky; of the firmament; celestial; divine
ciało niebieskie [**ćhah**-wo ńe-**byes**-ke] exp.: celestial body
królestwo niebieskie [kroo-**les**-tfo ńe-**byes**-ke] exp.: the Kingdom of Heaven
niebieski lis [ńe-**byes**-kee lees] exp.: arctic fox; blue fox
niebieski ptak [ńe-**byes**-kee ptahk] exp.: sponger; sponge; freeloader
niebiesko [ńe-**byes**-ko] adv. in blue (color)
niebiesko- [ńe-byes-ko] prefix: blue-
niebieskolila [ńe-byes-ko-**lee**-lah] adj.m. or adj.f. in lilac-blue (color)
niebieskooki [ńe-byes-ko-**o**-kee] adj.m. blue-eyed
niebieskoszary [ńe-byes-ko-**shah**-ri] adj.m. blue-gray
niebieskość [ńe-**byes**-kośhćh] f. blue color
niebieskozielony [ńe-byes-ko-źhe-**lo**-ni] adj.m. blue-green; glaucous
niebieszczeć [ńe-**byesh**-chećh] v. become blue; grow blue; turn blue; acquire a blue tint; show blue; appear in blue patches (*repeatedly*)
niebieszczenie [ńe-byesh-**che**-ńe] n. blueing
niebieszczyć [ńe-**byesh**-chićh] v. tint blue; paint in a blue shade; dye in a blue color (*repeatedly*)
niebieszczyć się [ńe-**byesh**-chićh śhan] v. display blue color (*repeatedly*)
niebieścić [ńe-**byeśh**-ćheećh] v. make (something) blue; paint blue (*repeatedly*)
niebieścić się [ńe-**byeśh**-ćheećh śhan] v. display blue color (*repeatedly*)
niebieścieć [ńe-**byeśh**-ćhećh] v. display blue color; tint blue; paint blue; dye blue (*repeatedly*)
niebiosa [ńe-**byo**-sah] pl. Heavens; the visible sky
o niebiosa! [o ńe-**byo**-sah] excl.: Heavens above!
wychwalać coś pod niebiosa [vi-**khfah**-lahćh tsośh pod ńe-**byo**-sah] exp.: to praise something to the skies; to extol something to the skies; colloq: to crack

something up; to crack somebody up
niebliski [ńe-**blees**-kee] adj.m. not so very near; distant
niebliśko [ńe-**blees**-ko] adv. not so very near; pretty far; some way off
niebłahy [ńe-**bwah**-khi] adj.m. not trifling; not trivial; by no means trivial; not unimportant
niebo [**ńe**-bo] n. sky; Heaven; the firmament; paradise; heavens
być w siódmym niebie [bićh f **śhood**-mim **ńe**-bye] exp.: to be in the seventh heaven
na niebie [nah **ńe**-bye] exp.: in the sky
o niebo lepszy [o **ńe**-bo **lep**-shi] exp.: better by far
pod gołym niebem [pod **go**-wim **ńe**-bem] exp.: under the open sky
poruszyć niebo i ziemię [po-**roo**-shićh **ńe**-bo ee **źhe**-myan] exp.: to move heaven and earth; to leave no stone unturned
spaść z nieba [spahśhćh z **ńe**-bah] exp.: to come as a godsend; to be off the wall (to be in a strange condition)
to niebo i ziemia [to **ńe**-bo ee **źhe**-myah] exp.: they are not to be compared
wielkie nieba! [**vyel**-ke **ńe**-bah] excl.: good heavens!; heavens above!
w niebie [v **ńe**-bye] exp.: in heaven
z nieba spadły [z **ńe**-bah **spahd**-wi] exp.: off the wall
nieboga [ńe-**bo**-gah] f. poor dear; poor thing; sweetheart
niebogato [ńe-bo-**gah**-to] adv. as not rich (person, people, etc.)
niebogaty [ńe-bo-**gah**-ti] adj.m. not rich
niebojaźliwie [ńe-bo-yah-**źhlee**-vye] adv. fearlessly
niebojaźliwy [ńe-bo-yah-**źhlee**-vi] adj.m. fearless; unafraid
niebojowy [ńe-bo-**yo**-vi] adj.m. unaggressive; without fighting spirit
niebolesny [ńe-bo-**les**-ni] adj.m. painless; not painful
niebolešnie [ńe-bo-**leśh**-ńe] adv. painlessly
nieboractwo [ńe-bo-**rahts**-tfo] n. poor soul; poor creature
nieboraczek [ńe-bo-**rah**-chek] m. poor devil; poor creature; poor thing; poor soul
nieboraczka [ńe-bo-**rahch**-kah] f. (woman) poor devil; poor creature; poor thing; poor soul
nieboradka [ńe-bo-**raht**-kah] f. ageratum; Ageratum herb of the thistle family
nieborak [ńe-**bo**-rahk] m. poor soul; poor devil; poor creature; poor thing
niebosiężny [ńe-bo-**śhanzh**-ni] adj.m. sky-high; sky-reaching; soaring; towering; cloud-capped
nieboski [ńe-**bos**-kee] adj.m. ungodly
jak nieboskie stworzenie [yahk ńe-**bos**-ke stfo-**zhe**-ńe] exp.: dreadfully; terribly; awfully; in a disagreeable manner
nieboskłon [ńe-bo-skwon] m. horizon
nieboszczka [ńe-**boshch**-kah] f. (female) deceased; dead woman; dead; defunct; departed; the late (mother, etc.)
nieboszczyk [ńe-**bosh**-chik] m. dead person; deceased; dead; defunct; departed; the late (father, etc.)
jego ojciec nieboszczyk [ye-go **oy**-ćhets ńe-**bosh**-chik] exp.: his late father
udawać nieboszczyka [**oo-dah**-vahćh ńe-bosh-**chi**-kah] exp.: to play possum
niebotycznie [ńe-bo-**tich**-ńe] adv. sky-high
niebotyczność [ńe-bo-**tich**-nośhćh] f. sky-high elevation
niebotyczny [ńe-bo-**tich**-ni] adj.m. sky-high; sky-reaching
niebożątko [ńe-bo-**zhownt**-ko] n. poor little creature; poor soul; poor thing; poor devil
niebożę [ńe-**bo**-zhan] n. poor soul; poor thing; poor devil
niebrzydki [ńe-**bzhit**-kee] adj.m. not unsightly; rather good looking; not unpleasing; prettyish; colloq:

not bad; tolerable; passable
niebrzydko [ńe-**bzhit**-ko] adv. in not unsightly fashion
niebujny [ńe-**booy**-ni] adj.m. not luxuriant; not exuberant
nie byle jak [ńe **bi**-le yahk] exp.: adv. not just any way; not carelessly; unusually well; in no mean fashion; like the dickens; like the duece; not just anyhow
nie byle jaki [ńe **bi**-le **yah**-kee] exp.: adj.m. no mean (player, etc.); considerable; of no mean importance
niebyły [ńe-**bi**-wi] adj.m. null and void; nonexistent; unexisting; cancelled; to be forgotten
uważać coś za niebyłe [oo-**vah**-zhahćh tsośh zah ńe-**bi**-we] exp.: to consider something null and void
niebyt [**ńe**-bit] m. nonentity; nonexistence
niebywale [ńe-bi-**vah**-le] adv. unusually; exceptionally; uncommonly; exceedingly; extremely
niebywały [ńe-bi-**vah**-wi] adj.m. unheard-of; unusual; uncommon; unparalleled; exceptional
niecałkowicie [ńe-tsahw-ko-**vee**-ćhe] adv. not altogether; not completely; incompletely; not quite
niecałkowity [ńe-tsahw-ko-**vee**-ti] adj.m. incomplete; not complete; deficient; defective; fragmentary; fractional
niecały [ńe-**tsah**-wi] adj.m. not the whole (thing); not all; incomplete; defective; deficient; fragmentary
niecała **godzina** [ńe-**tsah**-wah go-**dźhee**-nah] exp.: a short hour
niecałe dziesięć minut [ńe-**tsah**-we **dźhe**-śhanćh **mee**-noot] exp.: a short ten minutes
niecałe pół arkusza [ńe-**tsah**-we poow ahr-**koo**-shah] exp.: not so much as half a sheet
niecelnie [ńe-**tsel**-ńe] adv. without accuracy of aim; wide of the mark
niecelny [ńe-**tsel**-ni] adj.m. inaccurate (of aim)
niecelowość [ńe-tse-**lo**-vośhćh] f. futility; inexpedience; inexpediency
niecelowy [ńe-tse-**lo**-vi] adj.m. futile; inexpedient; of no avail; aimless; superfluous
niecenie [ńe-**tse**-ńe] n. stirring up; rousing
niecenzuralnie [ńe-tsen-zoo-**rahl**-ńe] adv. indecently; unprintably; suggestively; coarsely; broadly
niecenzuralność [ńe-tsen-zoo-**rahl**-nośhćh] f. unprintable nature
niecenzuralny [ńe-tsen-zoo-**rahl**-ni] adj.m. indecent; unprintable; obscene; suggestive; coarse; broad; ribald
nieceremonialnie [ńe-tse-re-mo-**ńyahl**-ńe] adv. unceremoniously; informally; without ceremony
nieceremonialność [ńe-tse-re-mo-**ńyahl**-nośhćh] f. unceremoniousness
nieceremonialny [ńe-tse-re-mo-**ńyahl**-ni] adj.m. unceremonial; informal
niech [ńekh] part. let; suppose; supposing; say (used with the imperative form)
a niech ci się nie uda? [ah ńekh ćhee śhan ńe **oo**-dah] exp.: supposing you fail?; what if you fail?
niech ci będzie! [ńekh ćhee **ban**-dźhe] excl.: all right!; OK!
niech się dzieje co chce! [ńekh śhan **dźhe**-ye tso khtse] excl.: come what may!
niech sobie idzie [ńekh so-bye **ee**-dźhe] exp.: let him go
niech tam! [ńekh tahm] excl.: let it be!; never mind!
niech żyje! [ńekh **zhi**-ye] excl.: three cheers for...; hip, hip, hurrah!; long live!
niechaj [**ńe**-khahy] part. let; suppose; supposing; say; emphatic: **niech**
niechajże [ńe-**khahy**-zhe] exp.: part. let; suppose; supposing; say; emphatic: **niech**
niechby [**ńekh**-bi] part. even if; even though; suppose; supposing
niechby się ludzie dowiedzieli

[ńekh-bi śhan loo-dźhe do-vye-dźhe-lee] exp.: supposing people get to know
niechcąco [ńekh-tsown-tso] adv. unintentionally; involuntarily; unwittingly; unawares; accidentally; by accident; without meaning to
niechcący [ńekh-tsown-tsi] adv. unintentionally; unawares; involuntarily; unwittingly; accidentally; by accident; without meaning to
niechcenie [ńe-khtse-ńe] n. unwillingness
od niechcenia [od ńe-khtse-ńah] exp.: by mere chance; accidentally; involuntarily; casually; nonchalantly; carelessly; unwillingly; perfunctorily; easily; without effort; faintly
niechęć [ńe-khanćh] f. disinclination (for); aversion (to); ill will (towards); indisposition (for); reluctance (to do); repugnance (to); unwillingness (to do); distaste (for); dislike (for); antipathy (to); animosity (against); malice (to)
czuć niechęć do kogoś [chooćh ńe-khanćh do ko-gośh] exp.: to dislike somebody; to bear somebody a grudge (Brit.)
z niechęcią [z ńe-khan-ćhown] exp.: unwillingly; reluctantly; grudgingly; with a bad grace; unfavorably; with aversion; in an unfriendly way; malevolently; with animosity
żywić niechęć [zhi-veećh ńe-khanćh] exp.: to bear animosity; to bear ill will; to bear malice
niechętnie [ńe-khant-ńe] adv. unwillingly; reluctantly; grudgingly; with a bad grace; unfavorably; with aversion; in an unfriendly way; malevolently; with animosity
niechętny [ńe-khant-ni] adj.m. unwilling; reluctant; averse; disinclined (for, to); loath; tardy (in doing); ill-disposed (towards); unfavorable; unfriendly; malevolent
być komuś niechętnym [bićh ko-moośh ńe-khant-nim] exp.: to be unfriendly towards somebody
niechlubnie [ńe-khloob-ńe] adv. ingloriously; discreditably; disgracefully
niechlubny [ńe-khloob-ni] adj.m. inglorious; discreditable; disgraceful
niechluj [ńe-khlooy] m. grub; sloppy; dirty; sloven; pig; slut; slattern; draggletail
niechlujnie [ńekh-looy-ńe] adv. in slovenly fashion; in an unkempt manner; grubbily; piggishly; slatternly; slipshod; sloppily; untidily; disorderly; messily; carelessly
niechlujnie pracować [ńekh-looy-ńe prah-tso-vahćh] exp.: to be slovenly in one's work
niechlujnie wyglądać [ńekh-looy-ńe vi-glown-dahćh] exp.: to be unkempt; to be grubby; to be piggish; to be sluttish; to be slatternly
niechlujnie wykonany [ńekh-looy-ńe vi-ko-nah-ni] exp.: slipshod; sloppy
niechlujność [ńekh-looy-nośhćh] f. slovenliness; grubbiness; piggishness; sloppiness; untidiness; messiness; unkempt appearance
niechlujny [ńekh-looy-ni] adj.m. dirty; slovenly; unkempt; frowzy; grubby; piggish; slatternly; sluttish; slipshod; sloppy; untidy; disorderly; messy
niechlujstwo [ńekh-looy-stfo] n. slovenliness; grubbiness; piggishness; sloppiness; untidiness; messiness; unkempt appearance
niechodliwy [ńe-khod-lee-vi] adj.m. not in demand; unsaleable (article, etc.)
niechodliwy towar [ńe-khod-lee-vi to-vahr] exp.: a drag on the market; hard to sell merchandise
niechrześcijański [ńe-khshe-śhćhee-yahń-skee] adj.m. non-Christian; unchristian
niechwalebny [ńe-khfah-leb-ni]

adj.m. inglorious; discreditable; disgraceful; censurable
niechybnie [ńe-**khib**-ńe] adv. without fail; for sure; for certain; unerringly; unavoidably; inescapably; as sure as death; no mistake; sure to happen
niechybny [ńe-**khib**-ni] adj.m. without fail; certain; unerring (aim); unavoidable; inescapable
niechże [**ńekh**-zhe] part. let; suppose; supposing; say; emphatic **niech**
a niechże to! [ah **ńekh**-zhe to] excl.: what a nuisance!; what a bother!
nieciągły [ńe-**ćhowng**-wi] adj.m. discontinuous
funkcja nieciągła [**foonk**-tsyah ńe-**ćhowng**-wah] exp.: discontinuous function
niecić [**ńe**-ćheećh] v. kindle; stir up; light (a fire); rouse (passions, etc.) (*repeatedly*)
niecić się [**ńe**-ćheećh śhan] v. kindle; take fire (*repeatedly*)
nieciecz [**ńe**-ćhech] f. old riverbed
nieciekawie [ńe-ćhe-**kah**-vye] adv. blankly; in an uninteresting manner; in an unentertaining manner; in a way void of interest
wypaść nieciekawie [vi-pahśhćh ńe-ćhe-**kah**-vye] exp.: to be dull; to be commonplace; to fail to arouse interest
nieciekawy [ńe-ćhe-**kah**-vi] adj.m. blank; uninterested; unentertaining; of no interest; void of interest; commonplace; dull; humdrum
niecielesny [ńe-ćhe-**les**-ni] adj.m. incorporeal
niecienki [ńe-**ćhen**-kee] adj.m. pretty thick
niecierpek [ńe-**ćher**-pek] m. touch-me-not; noli-me-tangere; Impatiens
niecierpkowaty [ńe-ćherp-ko-**vah**-ti] adj.m. balsaminaceous
niecierpkowate [ńe-ćherp-ko-**vah**-te] pl. the family Balsaminaceae of annual plants
niecierpliwić [ńe-ćher-**plee**-veećh] v. make impatient; put out of patience; provoke; make restless (*repeatedly*)
niecierpliwić się [ńe-ćher-**plee**-veećh śhan] v. be impatient; grow impatient; become impatient; get impatient; get restless (*repeatedly*)
niecierpliwie [ńe-ćher-**plee**-vye] adv. impatiently; restlessly
niecierpliwienie [ńe-ćher-plee-**vye**-ńe] n. making (somebody) impatient
niecierpliwienie się [ńe-ćher-plee-**vye**-ńe śhan] n. getting impatient
niecierpliwość [ńe-ćher-**plee**-vośhćh] f. impatience
z niecierpliwością [z ńe-ćher-plee-**vośh**-ćhown] exp.: impatiently; restlessly
niecierpliwy [ńe-ćher-**plee**-vi] adj.m. impatient; restless; intolerant of delay; anxious (to see his girl)
niecka [**ńe**-tskah] f. kneading trough; panful; pan; syncline
nieckowato [ńe-tsko-**vah**-to] adv. in form of a channel
nieckowaty [ńe-tsko-**vah**-ti] adj.m. channelled
nieckowy [ńe-**tsko**-vi] adj.m. like a channel; channel-shaped
niecnie [**ńe**-tsńe] adv. infamously; ignominiously; disgracefully; shabbily; dishonorably
niecnota [ńe-**tsno**-tah] m. & f. scamp; rogue; rascal; f. roguery; infamy; foul deed; knavery
niecny [**ńe**-tsni] adj.m. vile; infamous; ignoble; ignominious; disgraceful; shabby; dishonorable; disreputable; iniquitous; foul (deed, etc.)
nieco [**ńe**-tso] adv. somewhat; a little; a trifle; slightly; in some measure; to a certain degree; to some extent; rather
co nieco [tso **ńe**-tso] exp.: a little (of)
niecodziennie [ńe-tso-**dźhen**-ńe] adv. uncommonly; unusually
niecodzienność [ńe-tso-**dźhen**-nośhćh] f. uncommon nature (of an event); unusual (character, etc.)
niecodzienny [ńe-tso-**dźhen**-ni]

adj.m. uncommon; unusual; out of the ordinary; out of the common
niecodzienne wydarzenie [ńe-tso-**dźhen**-ne vi-dah-**zhe**-ńe] exp.: unusual occurence; not an everyday occurence
niecoś [**ńe**-tsośh] adv. somewhat; a little; a trifle; slightly; in some measure; to a certain degree; to some extent; rather; emphatic **nieco**
coś niecoś [tsośh **ńe**-tsośh] exp.: something; a thing or two
niecukier [ńe-**tsoo**-ker] m. nonsugary substance in sugar beets and sugar cane; nonsugar
niecukry [ńe-**tsoo**-kri] pl. nonsugary substances in sugar beets and sugar cane; nonsugars
niecywilizowany [ńe-tsi-vee-lee-zo-**vah**-ni] adj.m. uncivilized; savage; barbarous
nieczesany [ńe-che-**sah**-ni] adj.m. unkempt; disorderly
nieczęsto [ńe-**chan**-sto] adv. infrequently; not frequently; at long intervals; not often
nieczęsty [ńe-**chan**-sti] adj.m. infrequent; not frequent; not of everyday occurence
nieczujny [ńe-**chooy**-ni] adj.m. incautious; imprudent
nieczule [ńe-**choo**-le] adv. callously; heartlessly; insensibly; insensitively; cold-bloodedly
nieczułość [ńe-**choo**-wośhćh] f. insensibility; callousness; heartlessness; frigidity; hard-heartedness; insusceptibility; obduracy; impassiveness; numbness; unresponsiveness; insensitivity
nieczuły [ńe-**choo**-wi] adj.m. unaffectionate; unfeeling; callous; heartless; frigid; insensible; hard-hearted; obdurate; impassive; numb; hardened; unresponsive; insensitive
nieczynność [ńe-**chin**-nośhćh] f. inertness; inactivity
nieczynny [ńe-**chin**-ni] adj.m. inert; inactive; out of order; inoperative; closed down; out of gear; "no performance"
gaz nieczynny [gahs ńe-**chin**-ni] exp.: inert gas
nieczysto [ńe-**chis**-to] adv. dirtily; unfairly; out of tune
nieczystości [ńe-chis-**tośh**-ćhee] pl. impurities
wywozić nieczystości [vi-**vo**-źheećh ńe-chis-**tośh**-ćhee] exp.: to scavange; to cleanse
nieczystość [ńe-**chis**-tośhćh] f. uncleanness; impurity; unchastity; dirt; filth; slovenliness; rubbish; litter
grzech nieczystości [gzhekh ńe-chis-**tośh**-ćhee] exp.: sin of flesh
nieczysty [ńe-**chis**-ti] adj.m. unclean; polluted; dirty; shady; dishonest; impure; unchaste
duch nieczysty [dookh ńe-**chis**-ti] exp.: the Devil; Satan; the Evil One
nieczyste sumienie [ńe-**chis**-te soo-**mye**-ńe] exp.: bad conscience; guilty conscience
nieczytelnie [ńe-chi-**tel**-ńe] adv. illegibly
pisać nieczytelnie [**pee**-sahćh ńe-chi-**tel**-ńe] exp.: to scribble; to write an illegible hand
nieczytelność [ńe-chi-**tel**-nośhćh] f. illegibility
nieczytelny [ńe-chi-**tel**-ni] adj.m. illegible; cramped; crabbed; undecipherable
nieczytelne pismo [ńe-chi-**tel**-ne **pees**-mo] exp.: a scribble
podpis nieczytelny [**pot**-pees ńe-chi-**tel**-ni] exp.: illegible signature; undecipherable signature
niedaleki [ńe-dah-**le**-kee] adj.m. near; not distant; at hand; not far away; nearby; coming; approaching
niedaleki od doskonałości [ńe-dah-le-kee od dos-ko-nah-**wośh**-ćhee] exp.: nearly perfect; not far removed from perfection
w niedalekiej przyszłości [v ńe-dah-le-key pshi-**shwośh**-ćhee] exp.: in the near future
z niedaleka [z ńe-dah-**le**-kah] exp.: from close; from near; from near by; from close by

niedaleko [ńe-dah-**le**-ko] adv. near; not far; a short way off; close by; a little way; soon; pretty soon
niedaleko pada jabłko od jabłoni [ńe-dah-**le**-ko **pah**-dah **yahp**-ko od yahb-**wo**-ńee] exp.: a chip off the old block; like father like son
nie darmo [ńe **dahr**-mo] exp.: adv. not free of charge; not for nothing; not in vain; not gratuitously
niedawno [ńe-**dahv**-no] adv. recently; not long ago; newly; freshly; a short while ago; only just
niedawno temu [ńe-**dahv**-no **te**-moo] exp.: not long ago
niedawny [ńe-**dahv**-ni] adj.m. recent; fresh
do niedawna [do ńe-**dahv**-nah] exp.: until quite lately; till recently
od niedawna [od ńe-**dahv**-nah] exp.: since a short time; recently
niedbale [ńed-**bah**-le] adv. neglectfully; carelessly; casually; nonchalantly; heedlessly; negligently; perfunctorily; in a sloppy manner
niedbalstwo [ńed-**bahl**-stfo] n. negligence; laxity; carelessness; nonchalance
niedbaluch [ńed-**bah**-lookh] m. bungler; careless pupil; sloven; slattern; slut
niedbałość [ńed-**bah**-wośhćh] f. negligence; laxity; carelessness; nonchalance
niedbały [ńed-**bah**-wi] adj.m. negligent; untidy; lax; careless; unkempt; disorderly; slack; remiss; perfunctory; slapdash; sloppy; slipshod; nonchalant; airy; slouching
w niedbałej pozie [v ńed-**bah**-wey **po**-źhe] exp.: slouching
niedelikatnie [ńe-de-lee-**kaht**-ńe] adv. indelicately; tactlessly; rudely; coarsely
niedelikatność [ńe-de-lee-**kaht**-nośhćh] f. indelicacy; tactlessness; rudeness; coarseness
niedelikatny [ńe-de-lee-**kaht**-ni] adj.m. indelicate; tactless; rude; coarse; rough
niedialektyczny [ńe-dyah-lek-**tich**-ni] adj.m. nondialectical
niedługi [ńe-**dwoo**-gee] adj.m. short; not long; brief; curt
niedługo [ńe-**dwoo**-go] adv. soon; not long; before long; by and by; a short time; shortly
to potrwa niedługo [to **po**-trfah ńe-**dwoo**-go] exp.: it won't last long; it won't take long
to się niedługo skończy [to śhan ńe-**dwoo**-go **skoń**-chi] exp.: it will end before long
niedługoletni [ńe-dwoo-go-**let**-ńee] adj.m. of not many years' duration; not to last many years
niedługotrwały [ńe-dwoo-go-**trfah**-wi] adj.m. of short duration; short
niedługowieczny [ńe-dwoo-go-**vyech**-ni] adj.m. short-lived
niedo- [ńe-do] prefix: under-
niedobitek [ńe-do-**bee**-tek] m. survivor
niedobitki [ńe-do-**beet**-kee] pl. survivors; routed soldiers; remains
niedobór [ńe-**do**-boor] m. deficit; shortage; scarcity; loss; defficiency; insufficiency
niedobór kasowy [ńe-**do**-boor kah-**so**-vi] exp.: cash shortage
niedobrany [ńe-do-**brah**-ni] adj.m. ill-suited; ill-matched; ill-assorted; inappropriate; discordant; unharmonious
niedobry [ńe-**do**-bri] adj.m. no-good; bad; wicked; nasty; naughty; unkind; unfriendly; ill-disposed; wrong; improper; not too good; unpleasant
niedobrze [ńe-**dob**-zhe] adv. not well; badly; wrong; improperly; the wrong way; not the right way; unwell; ill; unfavorably; in a nasty manner; horridly
czuć się niedobrze [chooćh śhan ńe-**dob**-zhe] exp.: to feel sick
jest mi niedobrze [yest mee ńe-**dob**-zhe] exp.: I don't feel well; I feel sick
jest z nim niedobrze [yest z ńeem ńe-**dob**-zhe] exp.: he is in a bad way; his affairs are in a bad way
mieć niedobrze w głowie [myećh

ńe-**dob**-zhe v **gwo**-vye] exp.: to have a screw loose
robi mi się niedobrze na samą myśl o tym [ro-bee mee śhan ńe-**dob**-zhe nah **sah**-mown miśhl o tim] exp.: it makes me sick to think of it; I get nauseated at the very idea of it
zrobiło mi się niedobrze [zro-**bee**-wo mee śhan ńe-**dob**-zhe] exp.: I felt sick
nie doceniać [ńe do-**tse**-ńahćh] v. underestimate; estimate too low; set too low an estimate (*repeatedly*)
niedochodowy [ńe-do-kho-**do**-vi] adj.m. unprofitable
niedociągnięcie [ńe-do-ćhown-gńan-ćhe] n. shortcoming; failing; defect; deficiency; down side; bad side (of a plan, etc.)
niedocieczony [ńe-do-ćhe-**cho**-ni] adj.m. unfathomable; inscrutable; impenetrable; mysterious; enigmatic; incomprehensible
niedociśnienie [ńe-do-ćheeśh-**ńe**-ńe] n. low blood pressure
niedocukrzenie [ńe-do-tsook-**she**-ńe] n. hypoglycemia
niedoczas [ńe-**do**-chahs] m. lack of time (in chess game, sport, etc.)
niedoczekanie [ńe-do-che-**kah**-ńe] n. waiting not long enough
niedoczekanie twoje! [ńe-do-che-**kah**-ńe **tfo**-ye] excl.: you'l never make it!; never, never!
niedoczynność [ńe-do-**chin**-nośhćh] f. hypofunction
niedodma [ńe-**dod**-mah] f. atelectasis; collapse of the lung
niedogodnie [ńe-do-**god**-ńe] adv. awkwardly; inconveniently
niedogodność [ńe-do-**god**-nośhćh] f. inconvenience; drawback; lack of comfort
niedogodny [ńe-do-**god**-ni] adj.m. awkward; inconvenient; undesirable; causing bother; inopportune
niedogon [ńe-**do**-gon] m. fusel (oil); amyl alcohol
niedogony [ńe-do-**go**-ni] pl. fusel oils
niedogotowany [ńe-do-go-to-**vah**-ni] adj.m. underdone; half-cooked; half-raw
niedojadać [ńe-do-**yah**-dahćh] v. not finish eating; not eat enough; leave food not eaten (*repeatedly*)
niedojadanie [ńe-do-yah-**dah**-ńe] n. undernourishment; insufficient food; not finishing eating
niedojadek [ńe-do-**yah**-dek] m. starveling; scrap of food
niedojda [ńe-**doy**-dah] m. & f. nitwit; bungler; fumbler; lout; duffer; bumpkin; slacker
niedojdowaty [ńe-doy-do-**vah**-ti] adj.m. colloq: like a nitwit; like a bungler; like a fumbler; like a lout; like a duffer; like a bumpkin
niedojrzale [ńe-doy-**zhah**-le] adv. immaturely
niedojrzałość [ńe-doy-**zhah**-wośhćh] f. immaturity; unripe state; unripeness
niedojrzały [ńe-doy-**zhah**-wi] adj.m. unripe; immature; underage; green; raw; half grown; of tender age
niedokładnie [ńe-do-**kwahd**-ńe] adv. inaccurately; inexactly; incorrectly; incompletely; deficiently; not precisely (stated)
niedokładność [ńe-do-**kwahd**-nośhćh] f. inaccuracy; inexactitude
niedokładny [ńe-do-**kwahd**-ni] adj.m. inaccurate; inexact; incorrect; incomplete; deficient; not precisely stated
niedokonaność [ńe-do-ko-**nah**-nośhćh] f. imperfect state; imperfect condition
niedokonany [ńe-do-ko-**nah**-ni] adj.m. (gram.) imperfect (tense); verb describing repeated activity, state, or condition
niedokończony [ńe-do-końń-**cho**-ni] adj.m. unfinished; incomplete; uncompleted
niedokos [ńe-**do**-kos] m. hay partly not cut on a pasture
niedokrwienie [ńe-do-**krfye**-ńe] n. local anemia; ischemia
niedokrwistość [ńe-do-**krfees**-tośhćh] f. anaemia; anemia
niedokrwistość złośliwa [ńe-do-

krfees-tośhćh zwo-śhlee-vah] exp.: pernicious anemia
niedokrwisty [ńe-do-**krfees**-ti] adj.m. anemic; anaemic
niedokształcenie [ńe-do-kshtahw-**tse**-ńe] n. incomplete education; malformation
niedokszkałcony [ńe-do-kshtahw-**tso**-ni] adj.m. not fully educated; of incomplete (professional) education; malformed
niedokuczliwy [ńe-do-kooch-**lee**-vi] adj.m. not malignant; not vexing
niedokwasota [ńe-do-kfah-**so**-tah] f. hypoacidity
niedokwaśność [ńe-do-kfahśh-nośhćh] f. hypoacidity
niedola [ńe-**do**-lah] f. adversity; distress; misery
niedolew [ńe-**do**-lef] m. incomplete casting; misrun; short run casting
niedolisek [ńe-do-**lee**-sek] m. young fox
niedołęga [ńe-do-**wan**-gah] m. & f. blunderer; cripple; duffer; oaf; lout; muff
niedołęstwo [ńe-do-**wans**-tfo] n. physical unfitness; awkwardness; inefficiency; infirmity; impotence; indolence; incompetence; clumsiness
niedołęstwo starcze [ńe-do-**wans**-tfo **stahr**-che] exp.: decreptitude; senility
niedołęstwo umysłowe [ńe-do-**wans**-tfo oo-mis-**wo**-ve] exp.: mental deterioration; dementia
niedołężnie [ńe-do-**wanzh**-ńe] adv. awkwardly; inefficiently; infirmly; impotently; indolently; incompetently; clumsily
niedołężnieć [ńe-do-**wanzh**-ńećh] v. grow awkward; become inefficient; grow incompetent; become clumsy; grow decrepit (*repeatedly*)
niedołężnienie [ńe-do-wanzh-**ńe**-ńe] n. loss of physical fitness; loss of efficiency; loss of competence
niedołężny [ńe-do-**wanzh**-ni] adj.m. awkward; inefficient; infirm; impotent; indolent; incompetent; decrepit; clumsy
niedomagać [ńe-do-**mah**-gahćh] v. be unwell; be ailing; be ill; be suffering; be indisposed; waste away; feel unwell; be faulty; be wrong; be amiss (*repeatedly*)
niedomagać na serce [ńe-do-**mah**-gahćh nah **ser**-tse] exp.: to have heart trouble; to have an affected heart; to have a weak heart
niedomagający [ńe-do-mah-gah-**yown**-tsi] adj.m. unwell; ailing; ill; suffering; indisposed
niedomaganie [ńe-do-mah-**gah**-ńe] n. indisposition; defect; imperfection; deficiency; illness; shortcoming
niedomaganie silnika [ńe-do-mah-**gah**-ńe śheel-**ńee**-kah] exp.: engine trouble
niedomiar [ńe-**do**-myahr] m. insufficiency
niedomknięty [ńe dom-**kńan**-ti] adj.m. ajar; slightly open
niedomoga [ńe-do-**mo**-gah] f. asthenia; insufficiency
niedomoga mięśniowa [ńe-do-**mo**-gah myanśh-**ńo**-vah] exp.: myasthenia
niedomowy [ńe-do-**mo**-vi] adj.m. wild; not domesticated
niedomówienie [ńe-do-moo-**vye**-ńe] n. vague hint; insinuation; sudden pause
niedomykalność [ńe-do-mi-**kahl**-nośhćh] f. being slightly open; lagophthalmos (of the eyes); valvular insufficiency (in the heart)
niedomykalność powiek [ńe-do-mi-**kahl**-nośhćh **po**-vyek] exp.: lagophthalmos
niedomykalność zastawek serca [ńe-do-mi-**kahl**-nośhćh zahs-**tah**-vek **ser**-tsah] exp.: valvular insufficiency
niedomyślnie [ńe-do-**miśhl**-ńe] adv. with lack of perspicacity
niedomyślność [ńe-do-**miśhl**-nośhćh] f. dull-brains; lack of perspicacity
niedomyślny [ńe-do-**miśhl**-ni] adj.m. slow thinking; dull-brained; lacking perspicacity
niedonoszony [ńe-do-no-**sho**-ni]

adj.m. premature (fetus)
niedopałek [ńe-do-**pah**-wek] m. (cigarette) butt; stub; ember; brand
niedopałek papierosa [ńe-do-**pah**-wek pah-pye-**ro**-sah] exp.: cigarette butt; cigarette stub
niedopałek świecy [ńe-do-**pah**-wek **śhfye**-tsi] exp.: candle stub
niedopatrzenie [ńe-do-pah-**tshe**-ńe] n. oversight; neglect; inadvertence; want of care
przez niedopatrzenie [pshez ńe-do-pah-**tshe**-ńe] exp.: through oversight
niedopełnienie [ńe-do-pew-**ńe**-ńe] n. nonfulfillment
niedopieczony [ńe-do-pye-**cho**-ni] adj.m. underdone (roast); slack-baked (bread)
niedopity [ńe-do-**pee**-ti] adj.m. colloq: half-drunk (man who did not yet drink enough to be drunk)
niedopłata [ńe-do-**pwah**-tah] f. unpaid due
niedopłetwe [ńe-do-**pwet**-fe] pl. the order Apodes anguilliformes
niedopowiedzenie [ńe-do-po-vye-**dze**-ńe] n. vague hint; insinuation; sudden pause; see: **niedomówienie**
niedoprzęd [ńe-**do**-pshant] m. roving
niedopuszczalnie [ńe-do-poosh-**chahl**-ńe] adv. inadmissibly
niedopuszczalność [ńe-do-poosh-**chahl**-nośhćh] f. inadmissibility
niedopuszczalny [ńe-do-poosh-**chahl**-ni] adj.m. inadmissible; not to be tolerated
to jest niedopuszczalne [to yest ńe-do-poosh-**chahl**-ne] exp.: this is inadmissible; this cannot be tolerated; this shall not be tolerated
niedopuszczenie [ńe-do-poosh-**che**-ńe] n. exclusion
niedorajda [ńe-do-**rahy**-dah] m. & f. oaf; lout; duffer; muff; slacker
niedorąb [ńe-**do**-rownp] m. trees remaining in the forest after cutting
niedoręczenie [ńe-do-ran-**che**-ńe] n. nondelivery; miscarriage
w razie niedoręczenia [v **rah**-źhe ńe-do-ran-**che**-ńah] exp.: if undelivered
niedorosłość [ńe-do-**ros**-wośhćh] f. minority; tender age
niedorosły [ńe-do-**ros**-wi] adj.m. minor; underage; immature
niedorostek [ńe-do-**ros**-tek] m. stripling; greenhorn
niedorozwinięty [ńe-do-roz-vee-**ńan**-ti] adj.m. underdeveloped; mentally retarded; not fully developed; weak-minded; imbecile
niedorozwinięty umysłowo [ńe-do-roz-vee-**ńan**-ti oo-mis-**wo**-vo] exp.: mentally retarded
niedorozwój [ńe-do-**roz**-vooy] m. underdevelopment; undergrowth; mental defficiency; malformation
niedorozwój umysłowy [ńe-do-**roz**-vooy oo-mis-**wo**-vi] exp.: mental retardation
niedoróbka [ńe-do-**roop**-kah] f. colloq: that which remains to be finished (in the job in progress)
niedorzecznie [ńe-do-**zhech**-ńe] adv. absurdly; ridiculously; nonsensically; preposterously
mówić niedorzecznie [**moo**-veećh ńe-do-**zhech**-ńe] exp.: to talk absurdly; to talk nonsensically
niedorzeczność [ńe-do-**zhech**-nośhćh] f. pure nonsense; piece of nonsense; an absurdity; preposterousness
prawić niedorzeczności [**prah**-veećh ńe-do-zhech-**nośh**-ćhee] exp.: to talk nonsense
to jest niedorzeczność [to yest ńe-do-**zhech**-nośhćh] exp.: it is pure nonsense; it is absurd; it is ludicrous; it is ridiculous
niedorzeczny [ńe-do-**zhech**-ni] adj.m. absurd; ridiculous; ludicrous; nonsensical; preposterous
niedorzeczny projekt [ńe-do-**zhech**-ni **pro**-yekt] exp.: wild scheme; hairbrained scheme; colloq: half-assed project
niedosięgły [ńe-do-**śhang**-wi] adj.m. unattainable; inaccessible; out of reach
niedosiężny [ńe-do-**śhanzh**-ni] adj.m. unattainable; inaccessible;

out of reach
niedoskonale [ńe-do-sko-**nah**-le] adv. imperfectly
niedoskonałość [ńe-do-sko-**nah**-wośhćh] f. imperfection; deficiency
niedoskonały [ńe-do-sko-**nah**-wi] adj.m. imperfect; deficient; faulty
niedosłyszalnie [ńe-do-swi-**shahl**-ńe] adv. inaudibly
niedosłyszalny [ńe-do-swi-**shahl**-ni] adj.m. inaudible
niedosłyszeć [ńe-do-**swi**-shećh] v. be hard of hearing (*repeatedly*)
niedosłyszenie [ńe-do-swi-**she**-ńe] n. partial deafness; being hard of hearing
niedosmażony [ńe-do-smah-**zho**-ni] adj.m. underdone
niedosolony [ńe-do-so-**lo**-ni] adj.m. insufficiently salted
nie dospać [ńe **dos**-pahćh] v. sleep too short time
niedostatecznie [ńe-do-stah-**tech**-ńe] adv. insufficiently; scantily; unsatisfactorily; inadequately
niedostateczność [ńe-do-stah-**tech**-nośhćh] f. insufficiency; scantiness
niedostateczny [ńe-do-stah-**tech**-ni] adj.m. insufficient; scanty; short; tight; unsatisfactory; inadequate
stopień niedostateczny [**sto**-pyeń ńe-do-stah-**tech**-ni] exp.: bad mark; failure
niedostatek [ńe-do-**stah**-tek] m. shortage; indigence; poverty; want; privation; distress; lack; insufficiency; shortcoming; defect; strained circumstances
cierpieć niedostatek [ćher-pyećh ńe-do-**stah**-tek] exp.: to be in need; to be in distress; to be in difficulties
niedostawać [ńe-do-**stah**-vahćh] v. lack; be lacking; be wanting; be in short supply (*repeatedly*)
niedostępnie [ńe-do-**st<u>an</u>p**-ńe] adv. inaccessibly; unaccessibly
niedostępność [ńe-do-**st<u>an</u>p**-nośhćh] f. inaccessibility
niedostępny [ńe-do-**st<u>an</u>**-pni] adj.m. inaccessible; out of reach; unattainable; impenetrable; unapproachable; prohibited; unobtainable; slang: un-get-at-able
niedostosowanie [ńe-do-sto-so-**vah**-ńe] n. maladjustment
niedostrojenie [ńe-do-stro-**ye**-ńe] n. being out of tune; lacking conformation
niedostrzegalnie [ńe-do-stshe-**gahl**-ńe] adv. imperceptibly; unnoticeably; invisibly
niedostrzegalność [ńe-do-stshe-**gahl**-nośhćh] f. imperceptibility
niedostrzegalny [ńe-do-stshe-**gahl**-ni] adj.m. imperceptible; unnoticeable; invisible
niedostrzeganie [ńe-do-stshe-**gah**-ńe] n. lack of perception
niedostrzeżenie [ńe-do-stshe-**zhe**-ńe] adv. imperceptibly; unnoticeably; invisibly
niedosypiać [ńe-do-**si**-pyahćh] v. not to have enough sleep; to have insufficient sleep (*repeatedly*)
niedosypianie [ńe-do-si-**pyah**-ńe] n. insufficient sleep
niedosyt [ńe-**do**-sit] m. insufficiency; deficiency; lack; unsatisfied need; hunger for; thirst for; voracious appetite; insatiable appetite; bulimia
niedoszły [ńe-**dosh**-wi] adj.m. unrealized; not attained; would-be; might-have-been
niedościgle [ńe-do-**śhćheeg**-le] adv. matchlessly; inimitably; peerlessly; uniquely; unfathomably
niedościgłość [ńe-do-**śhćheeg**-wośhćh] f. matchlessness; inimitability; inimitableness; peerlessness; uniqueness
niedościgły [ńe-do-**śhćheeg**-wi] adj.m. matchless; inimitable; peerless; unique; unfathomable; inscrutable; unequalled
niedościgniony [ńe-do-śhćheeg-**ńo**-ni] adj.m. swift; light-footed; winged; matchless; inimitable; peerless; unique; unfathomable; inscrutable; unequalled
nie dość [ńe dośhćh] exp.: adv. not enough; insufficient

nie dość, że [ńe dośhćh zhe] exp.: not only
niedośpiałek [ńe-do-**śhpyah**-wek] m. herb of the genus Centunculus
niedoświadczenie [ńe-do-śhfyaht-**che**-ńe] n. inexperience; lack of experience
niedoświadczony [ńe-do-śhfyaht-**cho**-ni] adj.m. inexperienced; raw; fresh; green; untrained; new (to)
niedoświetlenie [ńe-do-śhfyet-le-ńe] n. underexposure
niedoświetlony [ńe-do-śhfyet-lo-ni] adj.m. underexposed; thin
niedotarty [ńe-do-**tahr**-ti] adj.m. not rubbed sufficiently; not run-in; running-in
niedotlenienie [ńe-do-tle-**ńe**-ńe] n. insufficient oxygenation
niedotlenienie krwi [ńe-do-tle-**ńe**-ńe krfee] exp.: anoxemia; anoxia
niedotrenowanie [ńe-do-tre-no-**vah**-ńe] n. insufficient training
niedotykalny [ńe-do-ti-**kahl**-ni] adj.m. intangible; untouchable; unpalatable (food, etc.)
niedotykalska [ńe-do-ti-**kahl**-skah] adj.f. with a chip on her shoulder; untouchable
niedotykalski [ńe-do-ti-**kahl**-skee] adj.m. colloq: with a chip on his shoulder; untouchable
niedouczek [ńe-do-**oo**-chek] m. half-educated man; undereducated man; smatterer; one of smattering knowledge
niedouczenie [ńe-do-oo-**che**-ńe] n. lack of education; lack of training
niedouczony [ńe-do-oo-**cho**-ni] adj.m. half-educated; undereducated
niedouk [ńe-**do**-ook] m. half-educated man; undereducated man; smatterer
niedowaga [ńe-do-**vah**-gah] f. underweight; short weight
niedowarzenie [ńe-do-vah-**zhe**-ńe] n. half-boiling; immaturity; half-learning
niedowarzony [ńe-do-vah-**zho**-ni] adj.m. half-boiled; rough; immature; half-learned; undereducated
niedowcipny [ńe-dof-**ćheep**-ni] adj.m. unwitty; unamusing; with no sense of humor
niedowiarek [ńe-do-**vyah**-rek] m. unbeliever; atheist; skeptic
niedowiarstwo [ńe-do-**vyahr**-stfo] n. unbelief; atheism; skepticism; incredulity; mistrust
niedowidzenie [ńe-do-vee-**dze**-ńe] n. short-sightedness; amblyopia; dimness of vision
niedowidzieć [ńe-do-**vee**-dźhećh] v. be short-sighted (*repeatedly*)
niedowierzać [ńe do-**vye**-zhahćh] v. distrust; disbelieve (*repeatedly*)
niedowierzająco [ńe-do-vye-zhah-**yown**-tso] adv. distrustfully; mistrustfully; incredulously
niedowierzanie [ńe-do-vye-**zhah**-ńe] n. distrust; mistrust; incredulity; disbelief
uśmiechać się z niedowierzaniem [oośh-**mye**-khahćh śhan z ńe-do-vye-**zhah**-ńem] exp.: to smile incredulously
niedowład [ńe-**do**-vwaht] m. partial paralysis; paresis
niedowołanie [ńe-do-vo-**wah**-ńe] n. underdevelopment (of a photograph, etc.)
niedowołany [ńe-do-vo-**wah**-ni] adj.m. underdeveloped (photograph, etc.)
niedozwolony [ńe-do-zvo-**lo**-ni] adj.m. not allowed; illicit; forbidden; prohibited; unlawful; foul (in sport)
niedożywianie [ńe-do-zhi-**vyah**-ńe] n. underfeeding
niedożywienie [ńe-do-zhi-**vye**-ńe] n. undernutrition; want of food
niedożywiony [ńe-do-zhi-**vyo**-ni] adj.m. underfed; undernourished
niedramatyczny [ńe-drah-mah-**tich**-ni] adj.m. nondramatic
niedrapieżny [ńe-drah-**pyezh**-ni] adj.m. nonpredatory
niedrobny [ńe-**drob**-ni] adj.m. not little; not tiny; considerable
niedrogi [ńe-**dro**-gee] adj.m. cheap; inexpensive; low priced
niedrogo [ńe-**dro**-go] adv. cheap
niedrogo zapłaciłem [ńe-**dro**-go zah-pwah-**ćhee**-wem] exp.: I paid a reasonable price; colloq: I got a

bargain
niedrożność [ńe-**drozh**-nośhćh] f. occlusion
niedrożność jelit [ńe-**drozh**-nośhćh **ye**-leet] exp.: intestinal occlusion
niedrożny [ńe-**drozh**-ni] adj.m. choked; impervious; occluded
niedrzewny [ńe-**dzhev**-ni] adj.m. wood-free
niedużo [ńe-**doo**-zho] adv. not much; not many
nieduży [ńe-**doo**-zhi] adj.m. small; little; not big; not tall; smallish; somewhat short; rather short
niedwuznacznie [ńe-dvoo-**znahch**-ńe] adv. unequivocally; clearly; distinctly; unmistakably
niedwuznaczność [ńe-dvoo-**znahch**-nośhćh] f. clearness; distinctness
niedwuznaczny [ńe-dvoo-**znahch**-ni] adj.m. unequivocal; clear; distinct; unmistakable; straightforward; unambiguous; flat; pointed (remark, etc.); broad (hint)
niedychawiczny [ńe-di-khah-**veech**-ni] adj.m. short-winded
niedyftongiczny [ńe-dif-ton-**geech**-ni] adj.m. nondiphthongal
niedyplomatycznie [ńe-di-plo-mah-**tich**-ńe] adv. impolitically; undiplomatically; injudiciously; unwisely; awkwardly; impolitely
niedyplomatyczny [ńe-di-plo-mah-**tich**-ni] adj.m. impolitic; undiplomatic; injudicious; unwise; awkward
niedyskrecja [ńe-dis-**krets**-yah] f. indiscreetness; indiscretion; an indelicacy
popełnić niedyskrecję [po-**pew**-ńeećh ńe-dis-**krets**-yan] exp.: to commit an indiscretion; to be guilty of an indiscretion
niedyskretnie [ńe-dis-**kret**-ńe] adv. indiscreetly; indelicately
niedyskretny [ńe-dis-**kret**-ni] adj.m. indiscreet; indelicate; tactless; incontinent of secrets; leaky
niedyskursywny [ńe-dis-koor-**siv**-ni] adj.m. intuitive; undiscursive
niedysponowany [ńe-dis-po-no-**vah**-ni] adj.m. indisposed; unwell; unfit (for); seedy; off color; out of sorts
niedyspozycja [ńe-dis-po-zi-tsyah] f. indisposition; ill-health
niedziecięcy [ńe-dźhe-**ćh**an-tsi] adj.m. not infantile; not child-like
niedziedziczny [ńe-dźhe-**dźheech**-ni] adj.m. nonhereditary
niedziela [ńe-**dźhe**-lah] f. Sunday
co niedziela [tso ńe-**dźhe**-lah] exp.: on Sundays; of a Sunday; every Sunday
w każdą niedzielę [f **kahzh**-down ńe-**dźhe**-lan] exp.: on Sundays; of a Sunday; every Sunday
w przyszłą niedzielę [f **pshish**-wown ńe-**dźhe**-lan] exp.: next Sunday
w ubiegłą niedzielę [v oo-**byeg**-wown ńe-**dźhe**-lan] exp.: last Sunday
w zeszłą niedzielę [v **zesh**-wown ńe-**dźhe**-lan] exp.: last Sunday
niedzielnie [ńe-**dźhel**-ńe] adv. like for a Sunday; like for a holiday; in Sunday attire; in one's Sunday best
niedzielny [ńe-**dźhel**-ni] adj.m. Sunday (rest, program, etc.)
niedzielny odpoczynek [ńe-**dźhel**-ni ot-po-chi-nek] exp.: the Sabbath; Sunday rest
po niedzielnemu [po ńe-dźhel-**ne**-moo] exp.: in Sunday attire; in one's Sunday best
niedzierżawczość [ńe-dźher-**zhahf**-chośhćh] f. lack of (grammatical) possessiveness
niedzierżawczy [ńe-dźher-**zhahf**-chi] adj.m. lacking a possessive form
niedzisiejszy [ńe-dźhee-**śhey**-shi] adj.m. not-today's; old-time (customs, etc.); not modern; old-fashioned; outmoded; antiquated; behind the times
niedziurawy [ńe-dźhoo-**rah**-vi] adj.m. not leaky; without holes
niedźwiadek [ńedźh-**vyah**-dek] m. bear's cub; Teddy bear; young bear
niedźwiadki [ńedźh-**vyaht**-kee] pl. bear cubs; the order Scorpionida
niedźwiadkowy [ńedźh-vyaht-**ko**-vi]

adj.m. bear's; bear (trap, etc.)
niedźwiedzi [ńedźh-**vye**-dźhee] adj.m. bear's; ursine; bearish; gruff; rough in manners
niedźwiedzia łapa [ńedźh-**vye**-dźhah **wah**-pah] exp.: cow parsnip; Heracleum sphondylium; colloq: clumsy hand
niedźwiedzia przysługa [ńedźh-**vye**-dźhah pshi-**swoo**-gah] exp.: an ill turn; (to do) damage
niedźwiedzie grono [ńedźh-**vye**-dźhe **gro**-no] exp.: bearberry
niedźwiedziątko [ńedźh-vye-**dźhownt**-ko] n. bear's cub; whelp
niedźwiedzica [ńedźh-vye-**dźhee**-tsah] f. female bear; she-bear
Mała Niedźwiedzica [**mah**-wah ńedźh-vye-**dźhee**-tsah] exp.: Ursa Minor; the Little bear
Wielka Niedźwiedzica [**vyel**-kah ńedźh-vye-**dźhee**-tsah] exp.: Great Bear; Ursa Major
niedźwiedzina [ńedźh-vye-**dźhee**-nah] f. bear's meat
niedźwiedziowato [ńedźh-vye-dźho-**vah**-to] adv. bearishly
niedźwiedziowaty [ńedźh-vye-dźho-**vah**-ti] adj.m. bearish
niedźwiedziówka [ńedźh-vye-**dźhoof**-kah] f. arctiid; tiger moth
niedźwiedziówki [ńedźh-vye-**dźhoof**-kee] pl. tiger moths
niedźwiedzisko [ńedźh-vye-**dźhees**-ko] n. colloq: big old bear
niedźwiedź [**ńedźh**-vyećh] m. bear; bearskin; bear's pelt; colloq: clumsy man; clumsy lout; galoot
dzielić skórę na niedźwiedziu [**dźhe**-leećh **skoo**-ran nah ńedźh-**vye**-dźhoo] exp.: to sell proceeds before earning them; to draw too early conclusions; to count the chickens before they hatch
niedźwiedzie [ńedźh-**vye**-dźhe] pl. the bears
niedźwiedź brunatny [**ńedźh**-vyećh broo-**naht**-ni] exp.: brown bear
niedźwiedź jaskiniowy [**ńedźh**-vyećh yahs-kee-**ńo**-vi] exp.: cave bear
niedźwiedź polarny [**ńedźh**-vyećh po-**lahr**-ni] exp.: polar bear
niedźwiedź szary [**ńedźh**-vyećh **shah**-ri] exp.: grizzly bear
niedźwięczny [ńe-**dźhvyanch**-ni] adj.m. dull; muffled; unharmonious; unvoiced; voiceless
nieefektownie [ńe-e-fek-**tov**-ńe] adv. unattractively; ineffectively; modestly; plainly
nieefektowny [ńe-e-fek-**tov**-ni] adj.m. unattractive; ineffective; modest; plain
nieegoistyczny [ńe-e-go-ees-**tich**-ni] adj.m. unselfish
nieekonomicznie [ńe-e-ko-no-**meech**-ńe] adv. uneconomically
nieekonomiczność [ńe-e-ko-no-**meech**-nośhćh] f. uneconomical management
nieekonomiczny [ńe-e-ko-no-**meech**-ni] adj.m. uneconomic; thriftless
nieelastyczny [ńe-e-lah-**stich**-ni] adj.m. inelastic; inflexible
nieelegancki [ńe-e-le-**gahnts**-kee] adj.m. inelegant; lacking smartness; lacking style
nieelegancko [ńe-e-le-**gahnts**-ko] adv. inelegantly; without style
nieelektrolit [ńe-e-lek-**tro**-leet] m. nonelectrolyte
nieemocjonalny [ńe-e-mots-yo-**nahl**-ni] adj.m. unemotional; stolid
nieenergicznie [ńe-e-ner-**geech**-ńe] adv. without energy
nieenergiczny [ńe-e-ner-**geech**-ni] adj.m. without energy
nieestetycznie [ńe-es-te-**tich**-ńe] adv. unesthetically; in bad taste; offensively; shockingly
nieestetyczny [ńe-es-te-**tich**-ni] adj.m. unaesthetic; in bad taste; offensive; shocking
nieetatowy [ńe-e-tah-**to**-vi] adj.m. part-time; supernumerary; not foreseen in the budget
nieetycznie [ńe-e-**tich**-ńe] adv. unethically; immorally
nieetyczny [ńe-e-**tich**-ni] adj.m. unethical; immoral
nieeuklidesowy [ńe-e-oo-kli-de-**so**-vi] adj.m. non-Euclidean
nieeuropejski [ńe-e-oo-ro-**pey**-skee] adj.m. non-European
niefachowiec [ńe-fah-**kho**-vyets] m.

layman; amateur
niefachowo [ńe-fah-**kho**-vo] adv. incompetently; inexpertly; unprofessionally; amateurishly; clumsily
niefachowość [ńe-fah-**kho**-vośhćh] f. inexpertness
niefachowy [ńe-fah-**kho**-vi] adj.m. incompetent; inexpert; unprofessional; amateurish; unqualified; unworkmanlike
niefałszywy [ńe-fahw-**shi**-vi] adj.m. truthful; genuine; authentic
niefart [**ńe**-fahrt] m. colloq: bad luck; adversity; unexpected difficulties
niefartowny [ńe-fahr-**tov**-ni] adj.m. colloq: unlucky; unfortunate
niefiguratywny [ńe-fee-goo-rah-**tiv**-ni] adj.m. abstract (art, etc.)
nieforemnie [ńe-fo-**rem**-ńe] adv. misshapenly
nieforemność [ńe-fo-**rem**-nośhćh] f. shapelessness; deformity; malformation
nieforemny [ńe-fo-**rem**-ni] adj.m. shapeless; deformed
nieformalnie [ńe-for-**mahl**-ńe] adv. informally; illegally
nieformalność [ńe-for-**mahl**-nośhćh] f. informality; irregularity; illegality
nieformalny [ńe-for-**mahl**-ni] adj.m. not formal; informal; irregular; illegal
niefortunnie [ńe-for-**toon**-ńe] adv. unluckily; regrettably; unfortunately; haplessly; awkwardly
niefortunnie wypaść [ńe-for-**toon**-ńe **vi**-pahśhćh] exp.: to go amiss; to take a bad turn
niefortunny [ńe-for-**toon**-ni] adj.m. unlucky; regrettable; unfortunate; unhappy; hapless; awkward; infelicitous; ill-timed
niefrasobliwie [ńe-frah-so-**blee**-vye] adv. in a carefree way; light-heartedly; jauntily; unconcernedly; with unconcern
niefrasobliwość [ńe-frah-so-**blee**-vośhćh] f. jauntiness; light-heartedness; unconcern
niefrasobliwy [ńe-frah-so-**blee**-vi] adj.m. carefree; jaunty; light-hearted; easygoing; happy-go-lucky; unconcerned; unpreoccupied
niefunkcjonalny [ńe-foonk-tsyo-**nahl**-ni] adj.m. useless
niegadatliwy [ńe-gah-daht-**lee**-vi] adj.m. sparing with words; reticent; reserved
niegasnący [ńe-gahs-**nown**-tsi] adj.m. unextinguished; unfading; undying; constant
niegaszony [ńe-gah-**sho**-ni] adj.m. unslaked (lime)
wapno niegaszone [**vahp**-no ńe-gah-**sho**-ne] exp.: quick lime
niegatunkowy [ńe-gah-toon-**ko**-vi] adj.m. nonquality
niegdysiejszy [ńeg-di-**śhey**-shi] adj.m. (gentleman, etc.) of old
niegdyś [**ńeg**-diśh] adv. formerly; once; at one time; in bygone days
niegęsto [ńe-**gans**-to] adv. thinly; loosely; at intervals
niegęsty [ńe-**gans**-ti] adj.m. rather thin; loose; not close
niegiętki [ńe-**gant**-kee] adj.m. inflexible; stiff-necked
niegiętkość [ńe-**gant**-kośhćh] f. inflexibility
niegładki [ńe-**gwaht**-kee] adj.m. uneven; rough; not smooth; unpolished; uncourtly; uncourteous
niegładko [ńe-**gwaht**-ko] adv. unevenly; roughly
niegładkość [ńe-**gwaht**-kośhćh] f. unevenness; asperity
niegładzica [ńe-gwah-**dźhee**-tsah] f. a fish of family Pleuronectidae
niegłęboki [ńe-gwan-**bo**-kee] adj.m. rather shallow; pretty shallow; not deep; not profound; not intense; superficial; trivial
niegłęboko [ńe-gwan-**bo**-ko] adv. not deeply; not profoundly; superficially
niegłodny [ńe-**gwod**-ni] adj.m. not hungry
niegłośno [ńe-**gwośh**-no] adv. not loud; not loudly; without noise; noiselessly; in a low voice
niegłośny [ńe-**gwośh**-ni] adj.m. scarcely audible; gentle; soft;

discreet
niegłupi [ńe-**gwoo**-pee] adj.m. sensible; not stupid; pretty clever
niegłupio [ńe-**gwoo**-pyo] adv. sensibly
niegodnie [ńe-**god**-ńe] adv. vilely; basely; in a base manner; discreditably; shamefully; disgracefully
niegodny [ńe-**god**-ni] adj.m. unworthy; undignified; vile; base; discreditable; shameful
jestem niegodny tego zaszczytu [**yes**-tem ńe-**god**-ni **te**-go zahsh-**chi**-too] exp.: I do not deserve this honor
niegodny uwagi [ńe-**god**-ni oo-**vah**-gee] exp.: unworthy of notice
niegodzenie się [ńe-go-**dze**-ńe śhan] n. disagreement
niegodzien [ńe-**go**-dźhen] adj.m. unworthy; see: **niegodny**
niegodziwie [ńe-go-**dźhee**-vye] adv. wickedly; vilely; basely; meanly; unscrupulously; ignobly; dishonorably; shabbily; scurvily
niegodziwiec [ńe-go-**dźhee**-vyets] m. scoundrel; rogue; knave; wretch
niegodziwość [ńe-go-**dźhee**-vośhćh] f. wickedness; villainy
niegodziwy [ńe-go-**dźhee**-vi] adj.m. wicked; vile; base; mean; foul; unscrupulous; ignoble; dishonorable; shabby; scurvy
niegorący [ńe-go-**rown**-tsi] adj.m. not particularly hot; not hot; not ardent
niegorliwy [ńe-gor-**lee**-vi] adj.m. not zealous
niegospodarczy [ńe-gos-po-**dahr**-chi] adj.m. uneconomical; thriftless
niegospodarnie [ńe-gos-po-**dahr**-ńe] adv. uneconomically; thriftily
niegospodarność [ńe-gos-po-**dahr**-nośhćh] f. uneconomical management; thriftlessness
niegospodarny [ńe-gos-po-**dahr**-ni] adj.m. uneconomical; thriftless; improvident
niegościnnie [ńe-gośh-**ćheen**-ńe] adv. inhospitably
niegościnność [ńe-gośh-**ćheen**-nośhćh] f. inhospitality; forbidding aspect; bleakness
niegościnny [ńe-gośh-**ćheen**-ni] adj.m. inhospitable; desolate; forbidding; bleak
niegotowy [ńe-go-**to**-vi] adj.m. not ready; not finished; not done; not executed
niegotów [ńe-**go**-toof] adj.m. not ready; not finished; not done; not executed
niegramatycznie [ńe-grah-mah-**tich**-ńe] adv. ungrammatically; incorrectly
niegramatyczność [ńe-grah-mah-**tich**-nośhćh] f. bad grammar; incorrectness
niegramatyczny [ńe-grah-mah-**tich**-ni] adj.m. ungrammatical; incorrect
niegroźnie [ńe-**groźh**-ńe] adv. not dangerously; not seriously
niegroźnie chory [ńe-**groźh**-ńe **kho**-ri] exp.: not seriously ill
niegroźny [ńe-**groźh**-ni] adj.m. not dangerous; not serious
niegroźna operacja [ńe-**groźh**-nah o-pe-**rahts**-yah] exp.: light surgery
niegroźny konkurent [ńe-**groźh**-ni kon-**koo**-rent] exp.: weak competitor
niegruby [ńe-**groo**-bi] adj.m. not thick; rather thin; not big; not very big; not stout
niegrzecznie [ńe-**gzhech**-ńe] adv. rudely; impolitely; unkindly; unmannerly; discourteously; like a naughty child
niegrzecznie się zachowywać [ńe-**gzhech**-ńe śhan zah-kho-**vi**-vahćh] exp.: to be impolite; to be rude; to be naughty
niegrzeczność [ńe-**gzhech**-nośhćh] f. unkindness; impoliteness; naughtiness; rude behavior; incivility
niegrzeczny [ńe-**gzhech**-ni] adj.m. rude; impolite; unkind; bad; unmannerly; discourteous; uncivil; naughty
być niegrzecznym [bićh ńe-**gzhech**-nim] exp.: to misbehave; to be naughty
niegustownie [ńe-goo-**stov**-ńe] adv.

tastelessly; in bad taste; inelegantly
niegustowność [ńe-goo-**stov**-nośhćh] f. bad taste
niegustowny [ńe-goo-**stov**-ni] adj.m. tasteless; in bad taste; inelegant
niegwałtowny [ńe-gvahw-**tov**-ni] adj.m. not violent; gentle; mild
niegwiaździsty [ńe-gvyahźh-**dźhees**-ti] adj.m. starless
niehałaśliwy [ńe-khah-wah-**śhlee**-vi] adj.m. noiseless
nieharmonicznie [ńe-khahr-mo-**ńeech**-ńe] adv. inharmoniously
nieharmoniczny [ńe-khahr-mo-**ńeech**-ni] adj.m. nonharmonic; inharmonic
nieharmonijnie [ńe-khahr-mo-**ńeey**-ńe] adv. inharmoniously
nieharmonijny [ńe-khahr-mo-**ńeey**-ni] adj.m. unharmonious; discordant
niehartowany [ńe-khahr-to-**vah**-ni] adj.m. not hardened (to the cold, etc.); untempered (steel, etc.); unhardened (to the cold, etc.)
niehartowny [ńe-khahr-**tov**-ni] adj.m. untempered (steel, etc.); unhardened (to the cold, etc.)
nieherbowny [ńe-kher-**bov**-ni] adj.m. not of noble birth
nieherbowy [ńe-kher-**bo**-vi] adj.m. not of noble birth
nieheroiczny [ńe-khe-ro-**eech**-ni] adj.m. unheroic; not heroic
niehigienicznie [ńe-khee-ge-**ńeech**-ńe] adv. insanitary; unhygienically
niehigieniczność [ńe-khee-ge-ńeech-nośhćh] f. lack of hygiene
niehigieniczny [ńe-khee-ge-**ńeech**-ni] adj.m. insanitary; unhygienic
niehigroskopijny [ńe-kheeg-ro-sko-**peey**-ni] adj.m. nonhygroscopic
niehistoryczny [ńe-khees-to-**rich**-ni] adj.m. nonhistorical; unhistorical
niehomogeniczny [ńe-kho-mo-ge-**ńeech**-ni] adj.m. heterogenous
niehonor [ńe-**kho**-nor] m. colloq: dishonorable deed
niehonorowo [ńe-kho-no-**ro**-vo] adv. dishonorably; unfairly; in ungentlemanly manner
niehonorowość [ńe-kho-no-ro-vośhćh] f. dishonorable conduct; ungentlemanly conduct
niehonorowy [ńe-kho-no-**ro**-vi] adj.m. dishonorable; unfair; foul; ungentlemanly
nieidentyczny [ńe-ee-den-**tich**-ni] adj.m. not identical
nieingerencja [ńe-een-ge-**ren**-tsyah] f. nonintervention (into internal affairs of another state, etc.)
nieinteligentnie [ńe-een-te-lee-**gent**-ńe] adv. unintelligently; injudiciously; without sense; dully
nieinteligentny [ńe-een-te-lee-**gent**-ni] adj.m. unintelligent; not very clever; injudicious; senseless; dull
nieinteresująco [ńe-een-te-re-soo-**yown**-tso] adv. in an uninteresting manner; in a dull manner; not entertainingly
nieinteresujący [ńe-een-te-re-soo-**yown**-tsi] adj.m. uninteresting; dull; unamusing
nieinterwencja [ńe-een-ter-**ven**-tsyah] f. nonintervention
polityka nieinterwencji [po-lee-**ti**-kah ńe-een-ter-**ven**-tsyee] exp.: policy of nonintervention
polityka nieinterwencji rządowej w handlu [po-lee-**ti**-kah ńe-een-ter-**ven**-tsyee zhown-**do**-vey f **khahn**-dloo] exp.: laissez faire
nieistniejący [ńe-eest-ńe-**yown**-tsi] adj.m. nonexistent; nonexistant
nieistnienie [ńe-eest-**ńe**-ńe] n. nonexistence
nieistotnie [ńe-ee-**stot**-ńe] adv. not essentially; immaterially unsubstantially; insignificantly
nieistotny [ńe-ee-**stot**-ni] adj.m. inessential; immaterial; unessential; nonessential; unsubstantial; insignificant
sprawy nieistotne [**sprah**-vi ńe-ees-**tot**-ne] exp.: the unessentials
niejadalny [ńe-yah-**dahl**-ni] adj.m. inedible; uneatable; tasteless
niejadek [ńe-**yah**-dek] m. poor eater
niejadowity [ńe-yah-do-**vee**-ti] adj.m. nonpoisonous
niejaki [ńe-**yah**-kee] adj.m. a; one; certain; some; slight
niejaki pan Smith [ńe-**yah**-kee pahn Smith] exp.: a certain Mr. Smith; a Mr. Smith

od niejakiego czasu [od ńe-yah-ke-go chah-soo] exp.: for some time past
z niejaką trudnością [z ńe-yah-kown trood-nośh-ćhown] exp.: with some difficulty
niejako [ńe-**yah**-ko] adv. so to say; as it were; to some extent; in some measure
niejasno [ńe-**yahs**-no] adv. dimly; vaguely; ambiguously; darkly; obscurely; indistinctly; hazily; foggily
niejasność [ńe-**yahs**-nośhćh] f. dimness; vagueness; obscurity
niejasny [ńe-**yahs**-ni] adj.m. dim; unclear; indistinct; vague; obscure; ambiguous; hazy; foggy; abstruse; dark
niejawnie [ńe-**yahv**-ńe] adv. secretly
niejawny [ńe-**yahv**-ni] adj.m. secret
posiedzenie niejawne [po-śhe-**dze**-ńe ńe-**yahv**-ne] exp.: closed session
niejeden [ńe-**ye**-den] m. many a; quite a number; not a few
niejeden z nas [ńe-**ye**-den z nahs] exp.: not a few of us; quite a number of us
niejedna [ńe-**yed**-nah] f. many a; quite a number; not a few (of female gender)
niejedna dobra książka [ńe-**yed**-nah **dob**-rah **kśhownsh**-kah] exp.: many a good book
niejednaki [ńe-yed-**nah**-kee] adj.m. not alike; different; diverse
niejednako [ńe-yed-**nah**-ko] adv. not alike; differently; diversely
niejednakowo [ńe-yed-nah-**ko**-vo] adv. not alike; differently; diversely
niejednakowość [ńe-yed-nah-**ko**-vośhćh] f. diversity; lack of similarity
niejednakowy [ńe-yed-nah-**ko**-vi] adj.m. not alike; different; diverse
niejedno [ńe-**yed**-no] n. many; quite a number; not a few (babies, etc.)
niejednoczesność [ńe-yed-no-**ches**-nośhćh] f. lack of simultaneity
niejednoczesny [ńe-yed-no-**ches**-ni] adj.m. not simultaneous
niejednokrotnie [ńe-yed-no-**krot**-ńe] adv. recurrently; more than once; repeatedly
niejednokrotność [ńe-yed-no-**krot**-nośhćh] f. recurrence
niejednokrotny [ńe-yed-no-**krot**-ni] adj.m. repeated; recurrent
niejednolicie [ńe-yed-no-**lee**-ćhe] adv. not uniformly; not always in the same manner; variously; without uniformity
niejednolitość [ńe-yed-no-**lee**-tośhćh] f. absence of uniformity; diversity; heterogeneity
niejednolity [ńe-yed-no-**lee**-ti] adj.m. not uniform; not always alike; various; diversified; heterogenous
niejednomyślny [ńe-yed-no-**miśhl**-ni] adj.m. not unanimous
niejednorodnie [ńe-yed-no-**rod**-ńe] adv. heterogeneously
niejednorodność [ńe-yed-no-**rod**-nośhćh] f. heterogeneity
niejednorodny [ńe-yed-no-**rod**-ni] adj.m. heterogenous
niejednostajnie [ńe-yed-no-**stahy**-ńe] adv. not uniformly; unevenly; irregularly
niejednostajność [ńe-yed-no-**stahy**-nośhćh] f. lack of uniformity; unevenness; absence of regularity
niejednostajny [ńe-yed-no-**stahy**-ni] adj.m. not uniform; uneven; irregular
niejednoznacznie [ńe-yed-no-**znahch**-ńe] adv. with more than one meaning
niejednoznaczność [ńe-yed-no-**znahch**-nośhćh] f. diversity of meaning
niejednoznaczny [ńe-yed-no-**znahch**-ni] adj.m. not synonymous (with); having more than one meaning
niekaligraficznie [ńe-kah-lee-grah-**feech**-ńe] adv. (written) in poor penmanship
niekaligraficzny [ńe-kah-lee-grah-**feech**-ni] adj.m. (written) in poor penmanship; scribbled
niekanonicznie [ńe-kah-no-**ńeech**-ńe] adv. uncanonically
niekanoniczny [ńe-kah-no-**ńeech**-ni] adj.m. uncanonical

niekapitalistyczny [ńe-kah-pee-tah-lees-**tich**-ni] adj.m. noncapitalistic
niekaralność [ńe-kah-**rahl**-nośhćh] f. unpunishedness; unpunishing; impunity
niekaralny [ńe-kah-**rahl**-ni] adj.m. unpunishable
nie karany [ńe kah-**rah**-ni] adj.m. with a clean record; not convicted before
niekarnie [ńe-**kahr**-ńe] adv. insubordinately; with disregard of discipline
niekarność [ńe-**kahr**-nośhćh] f. undiscipline; insubordination
niekarny [ńe-**kahr**-ni] adj.m. undisciplined
niekatolicki [ńe-kah-to-**lee**-tskee] adj.m. non-Catholic
niekiedy [ńe-**ke**-di] adv. now and then; sometimes; at times
nieklarowny [ńe-klah-**rov**-ni] adj.m. not limpid; unclear; not clarified
nieklasyczny [ńe-klah-**sich**-ni] adj.m. unclassical
nieklawo [ńe-**klah**-vo] adv. colloq: badly; poorly
nieklawy [ńe-**klah**-vi] adj.m. colloq: bad; poor; dull; no good
niekłamanie [ńe-kwah-**mah**-ńe] adv. unfeignably; unfeignedly; genuinely; wholeheartedly
niekłamany [ńe-kwah-**mah**-ni] adj.m. unfeigned; genuine
niekłopotliwy [ńe-kwo-po-**tlee**-vi] adj.m. not inconveniencing; convenient; not troubling; easy to get along
niekłótliwy [ńe-kwoot-**lee**-vi] adj.m. not quarrelsome
niekobiecy [ńe-ko-**bye**-tsi] adj.m. unwomanly
niekoleżeński [ńe-ko-le-**zheń**-skee] adj.m. aloof; uncooperative; uncomradely (Brit.); unobliging (Brit.)
niekoleżeńskość [ńe-ko-le-**zheń**-skośhćh] f. being aloof
niekompetencja [ńe-kom-pe-**ten**-tsyah] f. incompetence; incompetency
niekompetentny [ńe-kom-pe-**ten**-tni] adj.m. incompetent; unqualified
niekompletnie [ńe-kom-**plet**-ńe] adv. incompletely
niekompletność [ńe-kom-**plet**-nośhćh] f. incompleteness; deficiency
niekompletny [ńe-kom-**plet**-ni] adj.m. incomplete; deficient
niekonformista [ńe-kon-for-**mees**-tah] m. nonconformist
niekonformistyczny [ńe-kon-for-mees-**tich**-ni] adj.m. nonconformist (tendencies, etc.)
niekoniecznie [ńe-ko-**ńech**-ńe] adv. not necessarily; not exclusively; not quite
niekonieczny [ńe-ko-**ńech**-ni] adj.m. unnecessary
niekonsekwencja [ńe-kon-se-**kfen**-tsyah] f. inconsistency
niekonsekwentnie [ńe-kon-se-**kfent**-ńe] adv. inconsistently; inconsequentially
niekonsekwentny [ńe-kon-se-**kfent**-ni] adj.m. inconsistent
niekonstytucyjny [ńe-kon-sti-too-**tsiy**-ni] adj.m. unconstitutional
niekontrastowy [ńe-kon-trahs-**to**-vi] adj.m. without contrast; lacking of contrast; not contrasty (photograph, etc.)
niekonwencjonalny [ńe-kon-ven-tsyo-**nahl**-ni] adj.m. unconventional
niekoronowany [ńe-ko-ro-no-**vah**-ni] adj.m. uncrowned; respected; very popular
niekorzystnie [ńe-ko-**zhist**-ńe] adv. unfavorably; undesirably; inconveniently
niekorzystny [ńe-ko-**zhist**-ni] adj.m. disadvantageous; unprofitable
być w niekorzystnej sytuacji [bićh v ńe-ko-**zhist**-ney si-too-ah-tsyee] exp.: to be at a disadvantage
niekorzyść [ńe-**ko**-zhiśhćh] f. disadvantage; detriment
na niekorzyść [nah ńe-**ko**-zhiśhćh] exp.: to the detriment
rozstrzygnąć sprawę na czyjąś niekorzyść [ros-**stshig**-nownćh **sprah**-van nah **chi**-yownśh ńe-**ko**-zhiśhćh] exp.: to decide a case against somebody
niekosztownie [ńe-kosh-**tov**-ńe]

adv. inexpensively; at small cost; cheap; cheaply
niekosztowny [ńe-kosh-**tov**-ni] adj.m. inexpensive; cheap
niekowalny [ńe-ko-**vahl**-ni] adj.m. not malleable; not ductile
niekrępujący [ńe-kran-poo-**yown**-tsi] adj.m. convenient
niekrótki [ńe-**kroot**-kee] adj.m. longish
niekrwawy [ńe-**krfah**-vi] adj.m. bloodless
niekrystaliczny [ńe-kris-tah-**leech**-ni] adj.m. noncrystalline
niekryty [ńe-**kri**-ti] adj.m. open; roofless (building, etc.)
niekrytycznie [ńe-kri-**tich**-ńe] adv. uncritically
niekrytyczny [ńe-kri-**tich**-ni] adj.m. uncritical
niekrzepliwość [ńe-kshe-**plee**-vośhćh] f. noncoagulability
niekrzepliwy [ńe-kshe-**plee**-vi] adj.m. noncoagulable
nieksiążkowy [ńe-kśhownsh-**ko**-vi] adj.m. nonliterary
niekształtnie [ńe-**kshtahwt**-ńe] adv. not in shapely fashion; clumsily
niekształtność [ńe-**kshtahwt**-nośhćh] f. lack of shapeliness; clumsiness; deformity
niekształtny [ńe-**kshtahwt**-ni] adj.m. unshapely; formless
niektóre [ńe-**ktoo**-re] pron. & pl. (f.m.n.) some; one here and there
niektóry [ńe-**ktoo**-ri] pron. m. some; one here and there
niektórzy [ńe-**ktoo**-zhi] pl. some men
niekulisty [ńe-koo-**lees**-ti] adj.m. nonspherical
niekulturalnie [ńe-kool-too-**rahl**-ńe] adv. without culture; in an uncultivated manner; not in gentlemanly manner
niekulturalny [ńe-kool-too-**rahl**-ni] adj.m. uncultured
niekurczliwy [ńe-koorch-**lee**-vi] adj.m. shrink-proof; unshrinkable
niekwaśny [ńe-**kfahśh**-ni] adj.m. nonacid
nie lada [ńe **lah**-dah] exp.: first-class; no mean; first-rate; of the highest order; colloq: tiptop
nieleczniczy [ne-lech-**ńee**-chi] adj.m. nonmedical
nieledwie [ńe-**led**-vye] adv. all but; almost; practically
nieledwo [ńe-**led**-vo] adv. all but; almost; practically
nielegalnie [ńe-le-**gahl**-ńe] adv. illegally; unlawfully
nielegalność [ńe-le-**gahl**-nośhćh] f. illegality; illicitness
nielegalny [ńe-le-**gahl**-ni] adj.m. illegal; unlawful; illicit
nielekki [ńe-**lek**-kee] adj.m. not light; rather heavy
nielekko [ńe-**lek**-ko] adv. not lightly
nieleśny [ńe-**leśh**-ni] adj.m. unforested
nieletni [ńe-**let**-ńee] adj.m. under age; juvenile; minor; pl. minors **sąd dla nieletnich** [sownd dlah ńe-**let**-ńeekh] exp.: juvenile court **zatrudnianie nieletnich** [zah-trood-ńah-ńe ńe-**let**-ńeekh] exp.: child labor; juvenile labor
nieletnia [ńe-**let**-nah] f. an underage girl
nieletniość [ńe-**let**-ńośhćh] f. minority; nonage; lack of maturity
nielękliwie [ńe-lan-**klee**-vye] adv. fearlessly; without fear
nielękliwość [ńe-lan-**klee**-vośhćh] f. fearlessness
nielękliwy [ńe-lan-**klee**-vi] adj.m. unafraid; fearless
nielicho [ńe-**lee**-kho] adv. not so bad; quite well
nielichy [ńe-**lee**-khi] adj.m. colloq: not (at all) bad; quite good; awfully good; not a little
nieliczbowany [ńe-leedzh-bo-**vah**-ni] adj.m. not numbered; bearing no number
nieliczni [ńe-**leech**-ńee] pl. some few; rare
nielicznie [ńe-**leech**-ńe] adv. in small numbers
nieliczny [ńe-**leech**-ni] adj.m. not numerous; scarce; rare; small **nieliczne wyjątki** [ńe-**leech**-ne vi-**yownt**-kee] exp.: a few exceptions
nieliniowy [ńe-leeń-**yo**-vi] adj.m. nonlinear; non-front-line (soldier, etc.)

nieliteracki [ńe-lee-te-**rahts**-kee] adj.m. nonliterary
wyraz nieliteracki [**vi**-rahs ńe-lee-te-**rahts**-kee] exp.: vulgarism
nieliterowy [ńe-lee-te-**ro**-vi] adj.m. letterless; without letters
nielitościwie [ńe-lee-tośh-**ćhee**-vye] adv. mercilessly; pitilessly; relentlessly
nielitościwy [ńe-lee-tośh-**ćhee**-vi] adj.m. unmerciful; pitiless; ruthless
niello [**ńel**-lo] n. niello (alloy, decoration, etc.)
nielogicznie [ńe-lo-**geech**-ńe] adv. illogically; nonsensically; inconsistently
nielogiczność [ńe-lo-**geech**-nośhćh] f. illogicality; nonsense
nielogiczny [ńe-lo-**geech**-ni] adj.m. illogical; nonsensical; inconsistent
nielojalnie [ńe-lo-**yahl**-ńe] adv. disloyally; unfairly
nielojalność [ńe-lo-**yahl**-nośhćh] f. disloyalty; disaffection
nielojalny [ńe-lo-**yahl**-ni] adj.m. disloyal; disaffected; unfair
nielot [**ńe**-lot] m. kiwi (bird)
nielotny [ńe-**lot**-ni] adj.m. fixed; nonvolatile; flightless; colloq: slow-witted; slow in the uptake
nielubienie [ńe-loo-**bye**-ńe] n. dislike
nieludzki [ńe-**loots**-kee] adj.m. inhuman; atrocious; ruthless
nieludzko [ńe-**loots**-ko] adv. inhumanly; atrociously; ruthlessly
nieludzko zmęczony [ńe-**loots**-ko zman-**cho**-ni] exp.: dead tired
nieludzkość [ńe-**loots**-kośhćh] f. inhumanity
nieład [**ńe**-waht] m. disorder; disarray; confusion; mess
w nieładzie [v ńe-**wah**-dźhe] exp.: untidy; messy; in disorder
nieładnie [ńe-**wahd**-ńe] adv. not nicely; unattractively; wrongly; not pleasingly; improperly
to nieładnie [to ńe-**wahd**-ńe] exp.: it is not nice
nieładny [ńe-**wahd**-ni] adj.m. plain; not handsome; unsightly; improper
niełamliwość [ńe-wahm-**lee**-vośhćh] f. unbreakable nature; toughness
niełamliwy [ńe-wahm-**lee**-vi] adj.m. not brittle; unbreakable; tough
niełapczywy [ńe-wahp-**chi**-vi] adj.m. not greedy
niełaska [ńe-**wahs**-kah] f. disgrace; disfavor; loss of respect
popaść w niełaskę [**po**-pahśhćh v ńe-**wahs**-kan] exp.: to fall into disgrace; to fall out of favor
w niełasce [v ńe-**wahs**-tse] exp.: out of favor
niełaskaw [ńe-**wahs**-kahf] adj.m. unkind; unfavorable
niełaskawie [ńe-wahs-**kah**-vye] adv. unkindly; with disfavor
niełaskawy [ńe-wahs-**kah**-vi] adj.m. unkind; unfavorable
niełatwo [ńe-**waht**-fo] adv. not easily
niełatwo mi przychodzi... [ńe-**waht**-fo mee pshi-**kho**-dźhee] exp.: I find it difficult...; I find it pretty hard (to)
niełatwy [ńe-**waht**-fi] adj.m. not easy; fairly difficult; pretty tough
niełaz [**ńe**-wahs] m. marsupial mammal
niełazy [ńe-**wah**-zi] pl. Dasyuridae
niełowny [ńe-**wov**-ni] adj.m. not game; not good at catching
niełowny kot [ńe-**wov**-ni kot] exp.: cat which is not good at catching mice
niełupka [ńe-**woop**-kah] f. achene
nie ma [ńe mah] exp.: there is no
niema [**ńe**-mah] f. speechless (woman)
niemacalny [ńe-mah-**tsahl**-ni] adj.m. intangible; not palpable
niemagnetyczność [ńe-mahg-ne-**tich**-nośhćh] f. lack of magnetism
niemagnetyczny [ńe-mahg-ne-**tich**-ni] adj.m. nonmagnetic
niemajętny [ńe-mah-**yant**-ni] adj.m. not rich; not wealthy
niemal [**ńe**-mahl] adv. almost; nearly; pretty nearly; well-nigh
niemalże [ńe-**mahl**-zhe] adv. almost; nearly; pretty nearly; well-nigh; emphatic: **niemal**
niemalejący [ńe-mah-le-**yown**-tsi] adj.m. nondecreasing (function,

etc.)
niemało [ńe-**mah**-wo] adv. not a few; pretty much; not a little
niemały [ńe-**mah**-wi] adj.m. pretty big; fair-sized; goodly; no mean; of considerable size
niemała liczba [ńe-**mah**-wah **leedzh**-bah] exp.: a good number
niemałym kosztem [ńe-**mah**-wim **kosh**-tem] exp.: at considerable expense
niematerialność [ńe-mah-te-**ryahl**-nośhćh] f. immateriality; incorporeality
niematerialny [ńe-mah-ter-**yahl**-ni] adj.m. immaterial
niemądry [ńe-**mown**-dri] adj.m. unwise; ill-judged; silly; stupid
niemądrze [ńe-**mownd**-zhe] adv. unwisely; stupidly; like a fool
niemczeć [**ńem**-chećh] v. become Germanized (*repeatedly*)
niemczenie [ńem-**che**-ńe] n. Germanization
niemczyć [**ńem**-chićh] v. Germanize (under pressure) (*repeatedly*)
niemczyć się [**ńem**-chićh śhan] v. become Germanized (*repeatedly*)
niemczyzna [ńem-**chiz**-nah] f. the German language; German culture; German way of life; things German
niemedalowy [ńe-me-dah-**lo**-vi] adj.m. not earning a medal (in competition, etc.)
niemelodyjny [ńe-me-lo-**diy**-ni] adj.m. not melodious; unmelodious; tuneless; not harmonious; inharmonious
niemetal [ńe-**me**-tahl] m. nonmetal
niemetale [ńe-me-**tah**-le] pl. nonmetals
niemetaliczny [ńe-me-tah-**leech**-ni] adj.m. nonmetallic
niemetalowy [ńe-me-tah-**lo**-vi] adj.m. nonmetallic
niemetodycznie [ńe-me-to-**dich**-ńe] adv. unmethodically; without method; not methodically
niemetodyczny [ńe-me-to-**dich**-ni] adj.m. unmethodical; having no method; not methodical
niemetryczny [ńe-me-**trich**-ni] adj.m. nonmetrical
niemęcząco [ńe-man-**chown**-tso] adv. without causing fatigue
niemęski [ńe-**man**-skee] adj.m. unmanly (without nerve, etc.)
niemęsko [ńe-**man**-sko] adv. in unmanly fashion
niemęskoosobowy [ńe-man-sko-o-so-**bo**-vi] adj.m. not masculine
niemęskość [ńe-**man**-skośhćh] f. lack of masculinity
niemętny [ńe-**mant**-ni] adj.m. not turbid; clear
niemianowany [ńe-myah-no-**vah**-ni] adj.m. abstract (number, etc.)
liczba niemianowana [**leedzh**-bah ńe-myah-no-**vah**-nah] exp.: abstract number
wielkość niemianowana [**vyel**-kośhćh ńe-myah-no-**vah**-nah] exp.: abstract entity
niemiara [ńe-**myah**-rah] f. lack of measure
co niemiara [tso ńe-**myah**-rah] exp.: no end; numberless; countless; without limit
kłopotu co niemiara [kwo-**po**-too tso ńe-**myah**-rah] exp.: a world of trouble; no end of trouble; endless trouble
niemiarodajny [ńe-myah-ro-**dahy**-ni] adj.m. not authoritative; incompetent
niemiarowość [ńe-myah-**ro**-vośhćh] f. irregularity; absence of rhythm; lack of rhythm; arrythmia (of the heart)
niemiarowy [ńe-myah-**ro**-vi] adj.m. unrhythmical; irregular
Niemiec [**ńe**-myets] m. German
niemiec [**ńe**-myets] m. colloq: German teacher; German (lesson, language, etc.)
niemiecczyzna [ńe-myets-**chiz**-nah] f. the German language; German culture; German way of life; things German
niemiecki [ńe-**myets**-kee] adj.m. German; German language
po niemiecku [po ńe-**myets**-koo] exp.: in German
z niemiecka [z ńe-**myets**-kah] exp.: after the German fashion
niemieckość [ńe-**myets**-kośhćh] f.

German character; German origin
niemieć [ńe-myećh] v. grow speechless; grow dumb; become dumb; lose the faculty of speech (*repeatedly*)
niemienie [ńe-**mye**-ńe] n. becoming dumb
niemieszkalny [ńe-myesh-**kahl**-ni] adj.m. uninhabitable
niemile [ńe-**mee**-le] adv. unpleasantly; disagreeably
być niemile dotkniętym [bićh ńe-mee-le dot-**kńan**-tim] exp.: to feel hurt (by); to be much affected (by)
niemiło [ńe-**mee**-wo] adv. unpleasantly; disagreeably
być niemiło dotkniętym [bićh ńe-mee-wo dot-**kńan**-tim] exp.: to feel hurt (by); to be much affected (by)
niemiłosiernie [ńe-mee-wo-**śher**-ńe] adv. unmercifully; without pity; ruthlessly
niemiłosierność [ńe-mee-wo-**śher**-nośhćh] f. ruthlessness
niemiłosierny [ńe-mee-wo-**śher**-ni] adj.m. unmerciful; merciless
niemiły [ńe-**mee**-wi] adj.m. unpleasant; unsightly; harsh; surly; disagreeable; offensive
niemłody [ńe-**mwo**-di] adj.m. no longer young; past one's prime; colloq: oldish
niemnący [ńe-**mnown**-tsi] adj.m. colloq: not wrinkly; crease-resistant; not crushable
niemniej [ńem-ńey] adv. however; still; all the same
niemniej jednak [ńem-ńey **yed**-nahk] exp.: nevertheless
niemo [ńe-mo] adv. dumbly; in silence
patrzyli niemo [pah-**tshi**-lee **ńe**-mo] exp.: they looked on speechless
niemoc [**ńe**-mots] f. impotence; faintness; prostration; languor
niemoc płciowa [ńe-mots **pwćho**-vah] exp.: impotence
popaść w niemoc [po-pahśhćh v **ńe**-mots] exp.: to go into decline; to sink into feebleness
złożony niemocą [zwo-**zho**-ni ńe-mo-tsown] exp.: powerless; in a decline; sick in bed
niemocno [ńe-**mots**-no] adv. feebly
niemocny [ńe-**mots**-ni] adj.m. faint; weak; infirm
niemodnie [ńe-**mod**-ńe] adv. not fashionably
niemodnie ubrana [ńe-**mod**-ńe oob-**rah**-nah] exp.: (woman) not fashionably dressed; in outmoded dress
niemodny [ńe-**mod**-ni] adj.m. outmoded; out of fashion
niemoralnie [ńe-mo-**rahl**-ńe] adv. immorally
niemoralność [ńe-mo-**rahl**-nośhćh] f. immorality
niemoralny [ńe-mo-**rahl**-ni] adj.m. immoral; dishonest; depraved
niemota [ńe-**mo**-tah] f. dumbness; m. or f. colloq: retardate; dumb; oaf; slang: close-tongued man
niemowa [ńe-**mo**-vah] m. & f. mute; dumb; speechless
niemowlak [ńe-**mov**-lahk] m. baby; infant in arms
niemowlę [ńe-**mov**-lan] n. baby
od niemowlęcia [od ńe-mov-**lan**-ćhah] exp.: from babyhood; from the cradle
niemowlęctwo [ńe-mov-**lants**-tfo] n. babyhood; infancy
niemowlęcy [ńe-mov-**lan**-tsi] adj.m. infantile; infantine
być w okresie niemowlęcym [bićh v o-**kre**-śhe ńe-mov-**lan**-tsim] exp.: to be in infancy
niemożebnie [ńe-mo-**zheb**-ńe] adv. impossibly; terribly; dreadfully; shockingly
niemożebny [ńe-mo-**zheb**-ni] adj.m. impossible; unfeasible; awful; shocking; unreasonable; colloq: very bad; dreadful
niemożliwe! [ńe-mozh-**lee**-ve] exp.: impossible!; bless my soul! (Brit.); just fancy!; I'll be darned!; I'll be!
niemożliwie [ńe-mozh-**lee**-vye] adv. impossibly; terribly; dreadfully; shockingly
niemożliwość [ńe-mozh-**lee**-vośhćh] f. impossibility
do niemożliwości [do ńe-mozh-lee-**vośh**-ćhee] exp.: extremely;

excessively; beyond all bounds
jest niemożliwością... [yest ńe-mozh-lee-**vośh**-ćhown] exp.: it is impossible (to) ...
niemożliwy [ńe-mo-**zhlee**-vi] adj.m. impossible; unfeasible
niemożliwe! [ńe-mozh-**lee**-ve] excl.: impossible!; bless my soul! (Brit.); just fancy!; I'll be darned!; I'll be!
niemożliwy do opanowania [ńe-mo-**zhlee**-vi do o-pah-no-**vah**-ńah] exp.: uncontrollable
niemożliwy do opisania [ńe-mo-**zhlee**-vi do o-pee-**sah**-ńah] exp.: indescribable
rzecz niemożliwa [zhech ńe-mozh-**lee**-vah] exp.: an impossibility
niemożność [ńe-**mozh**-nośhćh] f. impossibility; inability (to do)
niemrawiec [ńe-**mrah**-vyets] m. sluggard; oaf; lout; duff; muff; lubber
niemrawo [ńe-**mrah**-vo] adv. sluggishly; torpidly; indolently
niemrawość [ńe-**mrah**-vośhćh] f. sluggishness; torpor; indolence
niemrawy [ńe-**mrah**-vi] adj.m. sluggish; tardy; indolent
niemroźny [ńe-**mroźh**-ni] adj.m. not frosty
niemuzykalność [ńe-moo-zi-**kahl**-nośhćh] f. lack of ear for music
niemuzykalny [ńe-moo-zi-**kahl**-ni] adj.m. unmusical
jestem niemuzykalny [**yes**-tem ńe-moo-zi-**kahl**-ni] exp.: I have no ear for music
niemy [**ńe**-mi] adj.m. dumb; mute
niema litera [**ńe**-mah lee-**te**-rah] exp.: mute letter
niema samogłoska [**ńe**-mah sah-mo-**gwos**-kah] exp.: mute vowel
niema spółgłoska [**ńe**-mah spoow-**gwos**-kah] exp.: mute consonant
niemy film [**ńe**-mi feelm] exp.: silent film
niemy świadek [**ńe**-mi **śhfyah**-dek] exp.: tacit spectator
nienadaremnie [ńe-nah-dah-**rem**-ńe] adv. not in vain; not for nothing
nienadążanie [ńe-nah-down-**zhah**-ńe] n. not keeping up; not keeping pace; having no time (to do); not being in time
nienadzwyczajnie [ńe-nahd-zvi-**chahy**-ńe] adv. not extraordinarily; not particularly
nienadzwyczajny [ńe-nahd-zvi-**chahy**-ni] adj.m. not extraordinary; not specially good
nic nadzwyczajnego [ńeets nahd-zvi-chahy-**ne**-go] exp.: nothing particular
nienagannie [ńe-nah-**gahn**-ńe] adv. faultlessly; impeccably
nienaganność [ńe-nah-**gahn**-nośhćh] f. faultlessness; impeccability
nienaganny [ńe-nah-**gahn**-ni] adj.m. blameless; faultless
nienależny [ńe-nah-**lezh**-ni] adj.m. undue
nienależycie [ńe-nah-le-**zhi**-ćhe] adv. inadequately; improperly
nienależyty [ńe-nah-le-**zhi**-ti] adj.m. inadequate; improper; unsuitable
nienamacalny [ńe-nah-mah-**tsahl**-ni] adj.m. intangible; unsubstantial; impalpable
nienamiętnie [ńe-nah-**myant**-ńe] adv. dispassionately; impassionately
nienamiętny [ńe-nah-**myant**-ni] adj.m. dispassionate; impassionate
nienapastliwy [ńe-nah-pahst-**lee**-vi] adj.m. not aggressive; unaggressive
nienarodowy [ńe-nah-ro-**do**-vi] adj.m. nonnational; unnational
nienaruszalnie [ńe-nah-roo-**shahl**-ńe] adv. inviolably; sacredly; infrangibly
nienaruszalność [ńe-nah-roo-**shahl**-nośhćh] f. inviolability; infrangibility
nienaruszalny [ńe-nah-roo-**shahl**-ni] adj.m. inviolable; sacred
nienaruszalny przepis [ńe-nah-roo-**shahl**-ni **pshe**-pees] exp.: standing rule; hard and fast rule
nienaruszenie [ńe-nah-roo-**she**-ńe] n. not disturbing the whole (of); without transgression; without infraction

nienaruszony [ńe-nah-roo-**sho**-ni] adj.m. intact; undisturbed
nienasiąkliwy [ńe-nah-śhownk-**lee**-vi] adj.m. unimbibing
nienasienny [ńe-nah-**śhen**-ni] adj.m. seedless
nienastawialny [ńe-nah-stah-**vyahl**-ni] adj.m. not adjustable; unadjustable
nienasycenie [ńe-nah-si-**tse**-ńe] n. insatiability; adv. insatiably; unquenchably
nienasycony [ńe-nah-si-**tso**-ni] adj.m. insatiable; voracious; (chem.) unsaturated; hungry; unsatiated
para nienasycona [pah-rah ńe-nah-si-**tso**-nah] exp.: unsaturated steam
roztwór nienasycony [**ros**-tfoor ńe-nah-si-**tso**-ni] exp.: unsaturated solution
nienatarczywie [ńe-nah-tahr-**chi**-vye] adv. unobtrusively; unimportunately
nienatarczywy [ńe-nah-tahr-**chi**-vi] adj.m. unobtrusive; unimportunate
nienatrętny [ńe-nah-**trant**-ni] adj.m. unobtrusive
nienaturalnie [ńe-nah-too-**rahl**-ńe] adv. unnaturally; with affectation; artificially
nienaturalność [ńe-nah-too-**rahl**-nośhćh] f. unnaturalness; affectation; artificiality
nienaturalny [ńe-nah-too-**rahl**-ni] adj.m. unnatural; insincere
nienaukowo [ńe-nah-oo-**ko**-vo] adv. not scientifically; unscientifically
nienaukowość [ńe-nah-oo-**ko**-vośhćh] f. unscientific approach; unscientific treatment
nienaukowy [ńe-nah-oo-**ko**-vi] adj.m. unscientific
nienaumyślnie [ńe-nah-oo-**miśhl**-ńe] adv. not willingly; unintentionally; without meaning it; unwillingly
nienawidzenie [ńe-nah-vee-**dze**-ńe] n. hatred
nienawidzenie się [ńe-nah-vee-**dze**-ńe śhan] n. hating one another
nienawidzić [ńe-nah-**vee**-dźheećh] v. hate; detest (*repeatedly*)
nienawidzić się [ńe-nah-**vee**-dźheećh śhan] v. hate each other; detest one another (*repeatedly*)
nienawistnie [ńe-nah-**veest**-ńe] adv. with hatred; hatefully; odiously
nienawistny [ńe-nah-**veest**-ni] adj.m. hateful; full of hatred
nienawiść [ńe-**nah**-veeśhćh] f. hate; abomination; detestation
czuć do kogoś nienawiść [choośh do **ko**-gośh ńe-nah-veeśhćh] exp.: to harbor hatred of somebody
ziać nienawiścią [źhahćh ńe-nah-**veeśh**-ćhown] exp.: to breathe hatred
nienawykły [ńe-nah-**vik**-wi] adj.m. not accustomed (to)
nienazwany [ńe-nahz-**vah**-ni] adj.m. unnamed
nienażarty [ńe-nah-**zhahr**-ti] adj.m. voracious; gluttonous; greedy; colloq: piggish
nienormalnie [ńe-nor-**mahl**-ńe] adv. abnormally
nienormalność [ńe-nor-**mahl**-nośhćh] f. abnormality
nienormalny [ńe-nor-**mahl**-ni] adj.m. abnormal; insane
nienosowy [ńe-no-**so**-vi] adj.m. nonnasal (vowel, etc.)
nienowoczesność [ńe-no-vo-**ches**-nośhćh] f. antiquation; lack of modernity
nienowoczesny [ńe-no-vo-**ches**-ni] adj.m. not modern; unmodern; antiquated
nienowy [ńe-**no**-vi] adj.m. not new
nieobcy [ńe-**op**-tsi] adj.m. familiar
nieobce mi to jest [ńe-**op**-tse mee to yest] exp.: I have experienced that; I am familiar with that
nieobecni [ńe-o-**bets**-ńee] pl. the missing
nieobecność [ńe-o-**bets**-nośhćh] f. absence; nonattendance; truancy
pod nieobecność [pod ńe-o-**bets**-nośhćh] exp.: in (somebody's) absence
w razie nieobecności [v rah-źhe ńe-o-bets-**nośh**-ćhee] exp.: in case of absence
nieobecny [ńe-o-**bets**-ni] adj.m.

absent; not present; not in; missing; m. absentee; the absent one
być nieobecnym myślami [bićh ńe-o-**bets**-nim miśh-**lah**-mee] exp.: to have thoughts far away
nieobecne spojrzenie [ńe-o-**bets**-ne spoy-**zhe**-ńe] exp.: distant gaze
nieobecni [ńe-o-**bets**-ńee] pl. the missing
nieobelżywy [ńe-o-bel-**zhi**-vi] adj.m. nonabusive; not insulting
nieobeschły [ńe-o-**bes**-khwi] adj.m. not dry; (still) wet
nieobeznanie [ńe-o-bez-**nah**-ńe] n. ignorance (of); lack of acquaintance (with)
nieobeznany [ńe-o-bez-**nah**-ni] adj.m. uninformed; ignorant
nieobfity [ńe-op-**fee**-ti] adj.m. not abundant; rather scarce
nieobliczalnie [ńe-ob-lee-**chahl**-ńe] adv. incalculably; irresponsibly
nieobliczalność [ńe-ob-lee-**chahl**-nośhćh] f. irresponsibility
nieobliczalny [ńe-ob-lee-**chahl**-ni] adj.m. unreliable; incalculable; irresponsible; unpredictable
on jest nieobliczalny [on yest ńe-ob-lee-**chahl**-ni] exp.: he is irresponsible; he is unreliable
nieobojętny [ńe-o-bo-**yant**-ni] adj.m. not indifferent (to); not unimportant
nieobopólny [ńe-o-bo-**pool**-ni] adj.m. not mutual
nieobowiązkowość [ńe-o-bo-vyowns-**ko**-vośhćh] f. lack of conscientiousness; negligence
nieobowiązkowy [ńe-o-bo-vyowns-**ko**-vi] adj.m. optional; negligent
nieobowiązująco [ńe-o-bo-vyown-zoo-**yown**-tso] adv. not in compulsory manner; optionally; voluntarily
nieobronność [ńe-ob-**ron**-nośhćh] f. indefensibility
nieobronny [ńe-ob-**ron**-ni] adj.m. unfortified
nieobrotny [ńe-ob-**rot**-ni] adj.m. not resourceful; shiftless; not ingenious
nieobrotowy [ńe-ob-ro-**to**-vi] adj.m. not revolving; nonrevolving
nieobszerny [ńe-op-**sher**-ni] adj.m. not spacious
nieobycie [ńe-o-**bi**-ćhe] n. lack of good breeding; crudeness
nieobyczajnie [ńe-o-bi-**chahy**-ńe] adv. in ill-mannered fashion; indecently; immorally
nieobyczajność [ńe-o-bi-**chahy**-nośhćh] f. immorality; ill manners
nieobyczajny [ńe-o-bi-**chahy**-ni] adj.m. immoral; ill-mannered
nieobyty [ńe-o-**bi**-ti] adj.m. ill-mannered; unfamiliar (with); with poor manners
nieobywatelski [ńe-o-bi-vah-**tel**-skee] adj.m. unsocial; lacking civic virtues
nieoceniony [ńe-o-tse-**ńo**-ni] adj.m. inestimable; priceless; invaluable
nieochoczo [ńe-o-**kho**-cho] adv. reluctantly
nieochoczy [ńe-o-**kho**-chi] adj.m. reluctant
nieoczekiwanie [ńe-o-che-kee-**vah**-ńe] adv. unexpectedly; without notice
nieoczekiwany [ńe-o-che-kee-**vah**-ni] adj.m. unexpected; unforeseen
nieoczekiwane odwiedziny [ńe-o-che-kee-**vah**-ne od-vye-**dźhee**-ni] exp.: surprise visit
rzeczy nieoczekiwane [**zhe**-chi ńe-o-che-kee-**vah**-ne] exp.: the unexpected
nieodczuwalny [ńe-ot-choo-**vahl**-ni] adj.m. not sensible; imperceptible
nieoddanie [ńe-od-**dah**-ńe] n. failure to return
pożyczyć na wieczne nieoddanie [po-**zhi**-chićh nah **vyech**-ne ńe-od-**dah**-ńe] exp.: lend for keeps; borrow for keeps
nieodgadniony [ńe-od-gahd-**ńo**-ni] adj.m. inscrutable; mysterious
nieodgadniona tajemnica [ńe-od-gahd-**ńo**-nah tah-yem-**ńee**-tsah] exp.: impenetrable mystery
nieodkształcalny [ńe-ot-kshtahw-**tsahl**-ni] adj.m. not deformable
nieodległy [ńe-od-**leg**-wi] adj.m. not distant; located not far (from)
nieodłącznie [ńe-od-**wownch**-ńe]

adv. inseparably
nieodłączny [ńe-od-**wownch**-ni] adj.m. inseparable; inherent
stanowić nieodłączną część [stah-**no**-veećh ńe-od-**wownch**-nown chanśhćh] exp.: to be part and parcel (of something)
nieodmiennie [ńe-od-**myen**-ńe] adv. invariably; unvaryingly; unalterably
nieodmienność [ńe-od-**myen**-nośhćh] f. invariability
nieodmienny [ńe-od-**myen**-ni] adj.m. invariable; undeclinable
nieodparcie [ne-ot-**pahr**-ćhe] adv. irrefutably; irresistibly; unavertibly
nieodparty [ńe-ot-**pahr**-ti] adj.m. irrefutable; compelling; irresistible; unavertible; cogent
nieodpłatnie [ńe-ot-**pwaht**-ńe] adv. gratuitously
nieodpłatność [ńe-ot-**pwaht**-nośhćh] f. gratuitousness
nieodpłatny [ńe-ot-**pwaht**-ni] adj.m. gratuitous
nieodporny [ńe-ot-**por**-ni] adj.m. not resistant; not inured; not proof
nieodporny na mróz [ńe-ot-**por**-ni nah mroos] exp.: half-hardy; not resistant to freezing (frost)
nieodpowiedni [ńe-ot-po-**vyed**-ńee] adj.m. inadequate; inappropriate; improper; inopportune; unbecoming; incongruous; wrong (moment, etc.); failing (grade)
nieodpowiednio [ńe-ot-po-**vyed**-ńo] adv. inadequately; inappropriately; unsuitably; improperly
nieodpowiedniość [ńe-ot-po-**vyed**-ńośhćh] f. inadequacy; inappropriateness; impropriety; incongruity
nieodpowiedzialnie [ńe-ot-po-vye-**dźyahl**-ńe] adv. irresponsibly
nieodpowiedzialność [ńe-ot-po-vye-**dźhahl**-nośhćh] f. irresponsibility
nieodpowiedzialny [ńe-ot-po-vye-**dźhahl**-ni] adj.m. irresponsible; unpredictable
nieodrodny [ńe-od-**rod**-ni] adj.m. true (offshoot of a noble stock, etc.); worthy (scion, etc.)
nieodrodne dziecko swej epoki [ńe-od-**rod**-ne **dźhets**-ko sfey e-**po**-kee] exp.: true child of his time
nieodstępnie [ńe-ot-**stanp**-ńe] adv. inseparably
nieodstępny [ńe-ot-**stanp**-ni] adj.m. inseparable
nieodwołalnie [ńe-od-vo-**wahl**-ńe] adv. irrevocably; irreversibly
nieodwołalność [ńe-od-vo-**wahl**-nośhćh] f. irrevocability; finality; peremptoriness
nieodwołalny [ńe-od-vo-**wahl**-ni] adj.m. irrevocable; final; irreversible; beyond recall; peremptory
to jest nieodwołalne [to yest ńe-od-vo-**wahl**-ne] exp.: this is beyond recall; this is past recall
nieodwracalnie [ńe-od-vrah-**tsahl**-ńe] adv. irreversibly; indivertibly
nieodwracalność [ńe-od-vrah-**tsahl**-nośhćh] f. irreversibility
nieodwracalny [ńe-od-vrah-**tsahl**-ni] adj.m. irreversible
nieodzownie [ńe-od-**zov**-ńe] adv. inevitably; absolutely
nieodzowność [ńe-od-**zov**-nośhćh] f. indispensability; irrevocability
nieodzowny [ńe-od-**zov**-ni] adj.m. indispensable; irrevocable
nieodżałowany [ńe-od-zhah-wo-**vah**-ni] adj.m. never enough regretted; much regretted
nieodżałowanej pamięci [ńe-od-zhah-wo-**vah**-ney pah-**myan**-ćhee] exp.: the late lamented
nieoficjalnie [ńe-o-fee-**tsyahl**-ńe] adv. unofficially; informally; privately
nieoficjalny [ńe-o-fee-**tsyahl**-ni] adj.m. unofficial; informal; private
nieogarnięty [ńe-o-gahr-**ńan**-ti] adj.m. boundless; limitless
nieogarniony [ne-o-gahr-**ńo**-ni] adj.m. limitless; infinite; inconceivable
nieoględnie [ńe-o-**gland**-ńe] adv. inconsiderately; rashly; recklessly
nieoględność [ńe-o-**gland**-nośhćh] f. inconsideration
nieoględny [ńe-o-**gland**-ni] adj.m. inconsiderate; reckless; rash; heedless; too hasty
nieograniczenie [ńe-o-grah-ńee-**che**-

ńe] adv. unrestrictedly; freely; infinitely
nieograniczoność [ńe-o-grah-ńee-**cho**-nośhćh] f. limitlessness; boundlessness; nonrestrictedness
nieograniczony [ńe-o-grah-ńee-**cho**-ni] adj.m. infinite; boundless; unrestricted; unstinted; unlimited; indefinite; absolute
nieokazale [ńe-o-kah-**zah**-le] adv. unostentatiously; inconspicuously; modestly
nieokazały [ńe-o-kah-**zah**-wi] adj.m. unostentatious; inconspicuous; modest
nieokiełznany [ńe-o-kew-**znah**-ni] adj.m. unbridled; rampant; reinless; uncontrollable
nieokresowy [ńe-o-kre-**so**-vi] adj.m. aperiodic; irrational (fraction, etc.)
nieokreślenie [ńe-o-kre-**śhle**-ńe] adv. indefinitely; undefinably; uncertainly; without definition
nieokreśloność [ńe-o-kre-**śhlo**-nośhćh] f. indefinableness; vagueness; indefinite character
nieokreślony [ńe-o-kre-**śhlo**-ni] adj.m. indefinite; undetermined; nondescript; uncertain
na czas nieokreślony [nah chahs ńe-o-kre-**śhlo**-ni] exp.: indefinitely
nieokrzesanie [ńe-o-kshe-**sah**-ńe] n. crudeness; coarseness; bad manners
nieokrzesany [ńe-o-kshe-**sah**-ni] adj.m. rude; crude; ill-mannered; coarse; uncouth
człowiek nieokrzesany [**chwo**-vyek ńe-o-kshe-**sah**-ni] exp.: lout; bumpkin
nieomal [ńe-o-mahl] adv. almost; pretty nearly; practically
nieomal nie [ńe-**o**-mahl ńe] exp.: almost; pretty nearly; practically
nie omieszkać [ńe o-**myesh**-kahćh] v. not fail; not omit; not neglect; do without fail; be sure (to do something)
nieomylnie [ńe-o-**mil**-ńe] adv. unerringly; infallibly
nieomylność [ńe-o-**mil**-nośhćh] f. infallibility
nieomylny [ńe-o-**mil**-ni] adj.m. infallible; unerring; sure
nie ma ludzi nieomylnych [ńe mah **loo**-dźhee ńe-o-**mil**-nikh] exp.: it is human to fail
nieopanowanie [ńe-o-pah-no-**vah**-ńe] n. lack of self-control
nieopanowany [ńe-o-pah-no-**vah**-ni] adj.m. vehement; impetuous; unruled; uncontrollable; unrestrained
nieopatrznie [ńe-o-**pahtsh**-ńe] adv. inconsiderately; recklessly
nieopatrzność [ńe-o-**pahtsh**-nośhćh] f. improvidence; inconsideration
nieopatrzny [ńe-o-**pahtsh**-ni] adj.m. unguarded; inconsiderate; reckless
nieopisanie [ńe-o-pee-**sah**-ńe] adv. indescribably; extremely; inexpressibly; unutterably
nieopisany [ńe-o-pee-**sah**-ni] adj.m. indescribable; excessive; extreme; inexpressible; unutterable
nieopłacalnie [ńe-o-pwah-**tsahl**-ńe] adv. unprofitably
nieopłacalność [ńe-o-pwah-**tsahl**-nośhćh] f. lack of profitability; lacking cost-effectiveness; unprofitableness; unremunerativeness
nieopłacalny [ńe-o-pwah-**tsahl**-ni] adj.m. unprofitable; unremunerative; not cost-effective
nieopłacony [ńe-o-pwah-**tso**-ni] adj.m. unpaid; not paid for
nie opodal [ńe o-**po**-dahl] adv. nearby; close at hand; next door
nieoprawiony [ńe-o-prah-**vyo**-ni] adj.m. unbound
nieoprawny [ńe-o-**prahv**-ni] adj.m. unframed (picture, etc.); unset (diamond, etc.); not set; not fixed (in a setting); not mounted; unmounted (diamond, etc.); unbound
nieorganiczny [ńe-or-gah-**ńeech**-ni] adj.m. inorganic (compound); inanimate
chemia nieorganiczna [**khe**-myah ńe-or-gah-**ńeech**-nah] exp.: inorganic chemistry
związki nieorganiczne [**zvyowns**-kee ńe-or-gah-**ńeech**-ne] exp.:

inorganic compounds
nieortograficznie [ńe-or-to-grah-**feech**-ńe] adv. in bad spelling; in incorrect spelling
nieortograficznie napisane [ńe-or-to-grah-**feech**-ńe nah-pee-**sah**-ne] exp.: misspelt; incorrectly spelt
nieortograficzny [ńe-or-to-grah-**feech**-ni] adj.m. incorrectly spelt; misspelt
nieoryginalność [ńe-o-ri-gee-**nahl**-nośhćh] f. lack of originality; unoriginality; lack of authenticity; unauthenticity
nieoryginalny [ńe-o-ri-gee-**nahl**-ni] adj.m. unoriginal; not genuine
nieosiadły [ńe-o-**śhahd**-wi] adj.m. unsettled; nomadic; migrating
nieosiągalność [ńe-o-śhown-**gahl**-nośhćh] f. unattainableness
nieosiągalny [ńe-o-śhown-**gahl**-ni] adj.m. unattainable; unobtainable
nieosłonięty [ńe-o-swo-**ńan**-ti] adj.m. uncovered; unshielded
nieosobisty [ńe-o-so-**bees**-ti] adj.m. not personal
nieosobliwie [ńe-o-so-**blee**-vye] adv. not particularly well; none too well
nieosobliwy [ńe-o-so-**blee**-vi] adj.m. not particularly good; none too good
nieosobowo [ńe-o-so-**bo**-vo] adv. not personally; impersonally
nieosobowy [ńe-o-so-**bo**-vi] adj.m. impersonal; not personal
nieostatni [ńe-os-**taht**-ńee] adj.m. not the worst; quite good; tolerable
nieostrość [ńe-**os**-trośhćh] f. bluntness; dullness
nieostrość obrazu [ńe-**os**-trośhćh ob-**rah**-zoo] exp.: image blurring
nieostrość zdjęcia [ńe-**os**-trośhćh **zdyan**-ćhah] exp.: blurring of a photograph; want of clear detail; lack of focus
nieostrożnie [ńe-o-**strozh**-ńe] adv. incautiously; carelessly
nieostrożność [ńe-o-**strozh**-nośhćh] f. lack of caution; inadvertence
nieostrożny [ńe-o-**strozh**-ni] adj.m. careless; imprudent
nieostry [ńe-**os**-tri] adj.m. not sharp; blunt; dull; mild; out of focus
nieoswojony [ńe-o-sfo-**yo**-ni] adj.m. untamed; unfamiliar; wild
nieoszacowany [ńe-o-shah-tso-**vah**-ni] adj.m. inestimable; incalculable
nieoszczędny [ńe-osh-**chand**-ni] adj.m. uneconomical; thriftless
nieoświecony [ńe-o-śhfye-**tso**-ni] adj.m. dark; ignorant
nieozdobny [ńe-oz-**dob**-ni] adj.m. unadorned
nieoznaczony [ńe-oz-nah-**cho**-ni] adj.m. indefinite; unmarked
nieożywiony [ńe-o-zhi-**vyo**-ni] adj.m. inanimate
przyroda nieożywiona [pshi-**ro**-dah ńe-o-zhi-**vyo**-nah] exp.: inanimate nature
niepakowny [ńe-pah-**kov**-ni] adj.m. not capacious; lacking of capacity
niepalatalny [ńe-pah-lah-**tahl**-ni] adj.m. nonpalatal
niepalący [ńe-pah-**lown**-tsi] adj.m. not smoking; nonsmoking; m. nonsmoker
jestem niepalący [**yes**-tem ńe-pah-**lown**-tsi] exp.: I don't smoke
przedział dla niepalących [**pshe**-dźhahw dlah ńe-pah-**lown**-tsikh] exp.: nonsmoking compartment
niepalność [ńe-**pahl**-nośhćh] f. noncombustibility
niepalny [ńe-**pahl**-ni] adj.m. incombustible; uninflammable
niepamięć [ńe-**pah**-myanćh] f. oblivion; forgetfulness; unconsciousness; negligence
pójść w niepamięć [pooyśhćh v ńe-**pah**-myanćh] exp.: to sink into oblivion; to go out of mind
puścić coś w niepamięć [**poośh**-ćheećh tsośh v ńe-**pah**-myanćh] exp.: to consign something to oblivion; to be willing to forget something
niepamiętliwy [ńe-pah-myan-**tlee**-vi] adj.m. forgiving; not rancorous; not vindictive
niepamiętnie [ńe-pah-**myant**-ńe] adv. immemorially
niepamiętny [ńe-pah-**myant**-ni] adj.m. forgetful; immemorial; the

greatest within living memory; the most extraordinary within living memory
od niepamiętnych czasów [od ńe-pah-**myant**-nikh **chah**-soof] exp.: from times immemorial
niepaństwowy [ńe-pahń-**stfo**-vi] adj.m. not belonging to the state; not run by the state; not administered by the state
niepańszczyźniany [ńe-pahńsh-chiźh-**ńah**-ni] adj.m. not of serfdom; not of socage
nieparka [ńe-**pahr**-kah] f. gypsy moth
brudnica nieparka [brood-**ńee**-tsah ńe-**pahr**-kah] exp.: gypsy moth
nieparlamentarnie [ńe-pahr-lah-men-**tahr**-ńe] adv. colloq: in vulgar language
nieparlamentarny [ńe-pahr-lah-men-**tahr**-ni] adj.m. rough (language); using vulgar words
nieparzystokopytny [ńe-pah-zhis-to-ko-**pit**-ni] adj.m. perissodactylous
nieparzystokopytne [ńe-pah-zhis-to-ko-**pit**-ne] pl. the Perissodactyla
nieparzystość [ńe-pah-**zhis**-tośhćh] f. oddness (of a number)
nieparzysty [ńe-pah-**zhis**-ti] adj.m. odd; uneven; unpaired
nieparzyście [ńe-pah-**zhiśh**-ćhe] adv. unevenly
niepedagogiczny [ńe-pe-dah-go-**geech**-ni] adj.m. against the principles of teaching
niepełno [ńe-**pew**-no] adv. not brimfull; not to fullness
nalej niepełno [**nah**-ley ńe-**pew**-no] exp.: don't fill the glass brimfull
niepełnoletni [ńe-pew-no-**let**-ńee] adj.m. minor; underage
niepełnoletniość [ńe-pew-no-**let**-ńośhćh] f. minority
niepełnoletność [ńe-pew-no-**let**-nośhćh] f. minority
niepełnoprawność [ńe-pew-no-**prahv**-nośhćh] f. incomplete (legal) status (of a citizen, etc.)
niepełnoprawny [ńe-pew-no-**prahv**-ni] adj.m. not full-fledged (lawyer, etc.)
niepełnosprawny [ńe-pew-no-**sprahv**-ni] adj.m. deficient (in development, performance, etc.); disabled (physically, mentally, etc.)
niepełność [ńe-**pew**-nośhćh] f. incompleteness
niepełnowartościowy [ńe-pew-no-vahr-tośh-**ćho**-vi] adj.m. defective; deficient
niepełny [ńe-**pew**-ni] adj.m. incomplete
nieperiodyczny [ńe-per-yo-**dich**-ni] adj.m. nonperiodical
niepewien [ńe-**pe**-vyen] adj.m. uncertain; insecure; unsafe; chancy; unsettled; hesitant; doubtful; unsteady; shaky
niepewnie [ńe-**pev**-ńe] adv. without certainty; hesitantly; dubiously; unsteadily
niepewność [ńe-**pev**-nośhćh] f. uncertainty; incertitude
być w niepewności [bićh v ńe-pev-**nośh**-ćhee] exp.: to be in doubt
niepewność jutra [ńe-**pev**-nośhćh **yoo**-trah] exp.: uncertain future
stan niepewności [stahn ńe-pev-**nośh**-ćhee] exp.: suspense
trzymać kogoś w niepewności [tshi-mahćh **ko**-gośh v ńe-pev-**nośh**-ćhee] exp.: to keep somebody in suspense; to keep somebody guessing
niepewny [ńe-**pev**-ni] adj.m. uncertain; insecure; unsafe; chancy; unsettled; hesitant; doubtful; unsteady; shaky
chodzić po niepewnym gruncie [kho-dźheećh po ńe-**pev**-nim **groon**-ćhe] exp.: to skate on thin ice
iść na niepewne [eeśhćh nah ńe-**pev**-ne] exp.: to run a risk; to run risks
mówić niepewnym głosem [moo-veećh ńe-**pev**-nim **gwo**-sem] exp.: to falter; to speak falteringly
na niepewne [nah ńe-**pev**-ne] exp.: at a venture
to jest rzecz niepewna [to yest zhech ńe-**pev**-nah] exp.: it is uncertain

z niepewną miną [z ńe-**pev**-nown **mee**-nown] exp.: unassured; in uncertain way; insecure
niepieniężny [ńe-pye-**ńanzh**-ni] adj.m. nonpecuniary; (transaction) without money changing hands
niepierwotny [ńe-pyer-**vot**-ni] adj.m. nonprimary; secondary
niepierwszy [ńe-**pyerf**-shi] adj.m. not fresh; not used for the first time
niepierwszej czystości [ńe-**pyerf**-shey chis-**tośh**-ćhee] exp.: not fresh from the laundry; colloq: not really clean
niepierwszej młodości [ńe-**pyerf**-shey mwo-**dośh**-ćhee] exp.: no longer in the prime of life; no longer in the pink of youth
niepierwszy raz [ńe-**pyerf**-shi rahs] exp.: not for the first time
niepięknie [ńe-**pyank**-ńe] adv. not nicely; unattractively; wrongly; not pleasingly; improperly
niepiękny [ńe-**pyank**-ni] adj.m. plain; uncomely; unsightly; improper
niepijący [ńe-pee-**yown**-tsi] adj.m. abstinent; m. abstainer; teetotaller
niepilny [ńe-**peel**-ni] adj.m. not urgent; not diligent; not industrious; not studious; not watchful; not hard-working
niepisany [ńe-pee-**sah**-ni] adj.m. unwritten; not in writing
niepiśmienny [ńe-peeśh-**myen**-ni] adj.m. illiterate; unlettered
nieplanowo [ńe-plah-**no**-vo] adv. without a plan
nieplanowy [ńe-plah-**no**-vi] adj.m. unplanned
nieplatoniczny [ńe-plah-to-**ńeech**-ni] adj.m. not Platonic
niepłacący [ńe-pwah-**tsown**-tsi] adj.m. nonpaying
niepłaski [ńe-**pwahs**-kee] adj.m. nonplane; out-of-flat
niepłatny [ńe-**pwaht**-ni] adj.m. unpaid; gratuitous
niepłochliwy [ńe-pwokh-**lee**-vi] adj.m. tame; not shy
niepłodność [ńe-**pwod**-nośhćh] f. sterility
niepłodny [ńe-**pwod**-ni] adj.m. sterile; barren; infertile
niepłonny [ńe-**pwon**-ni] adj.m. well-founded; motivated
niepłynnie [ńe-**pwin**-ńe] adv. not in liquid form; not fluently
niepłynność [ńe-**pwin**-nośhćh] f. unavailability (of assets, etc.)
niepłynny [ńe-**pwin**-ni] adj.m. not liquid; not fluent; unavailable (capital, etc.)
niepobłażliwie [ńe-pob-wahzh-**lee**-vye] adv. unindulgently; without leniency
niepobłażliwość [ńe-pob-wahzh-**lee**-vośhćh] f. intolerance; lack of leniency; lack of indulgence
niepobłażliwy [ńe-pob-wahzh-**lee**-vi] adj.m. intolerant; not indulgent
niepobożny [ńe-po-**bozh**-ni] adj.m. impious; ungodly
niepobudliwy [ńe-po-bood-**lee**-vi] adj.m. nonexcitable
niepochlebnie [ńe-po-**khleb**-ńe] adv. unflatteringly; detractively
niepochlebnie o kimś mówić [ńe-po-**khleb**-ńe o keemśh **moo**-veećh] exp.: to speak of somebody in uncomplimentary terms
niepochlebny [ńe-po-**khleb**-ni] adj.m. unfavorable; unflattering; detractive; belittling; disparaging
mieć o kimś niepochlebne zdanie [myećh o keemśh ńe-po-**khleb**-ne **zdah**-ńe] exp.: to hold a low opinion of somebody; to have a low opinion of somebody
niepochopny [ńe-po-**khop**-ni] adj.m. not very eager; slow (in doing something)
niepociągający [ńe-po-ćhyown-gah-**yown**-tsi] adj.m. unattractive
niepocieszający [ńe-po-ćhe-shah-**yown**-tsi] adj.m. not cheerful; causing sadness
niepocieszony [ńe-po-ćhe-**sho**-ni] adj.m. desolate; disconsolate
byłbym niepocieszony, gdyby... [**biw**-bim ńe-po-ćhe-**sho**-ni **gdi**-bi] exp.: I should be very unhappy if...; I should be very disappointed if...; it would break my heart if ...
niepoczciwy [ńe-poch-**ćhee**-vi] adj.m. wicked; unkind

niepoczesny [ńe-po-**ches**-ni] adj.m. inconspicuous; scrubby; modest; humble; colloq: shabby; paltry
niepocześnie [ńe-po-**cheśh**-ńe] adv. inconspicuously; modestly; humbly; colloq: shabbily
niepocześnie wyglądać [ńe-po-**cheśh**-ńe vig-**lown**-dahćh] exp.: to be inconspicuous; to be scrubby
niepoczytalnie [ńe-po-chi-**tahl**-ńe] adv. insanely; irresponsibly
niepoczytalność [ńe-po-chi-**tahl**-nośhćh] f. irresponsibility
niepoczytalny [ńe-po-chi-**tahl**-ni] adj. m. irresponsible; insane; lunatic
niepoczytność [ńe-po-**chit**-nośhćh] f. limited popularity; limited circulation
niepoczytny [ńe-po-**chit**-ni] adj.m. of limited popularity; of limited circulation
niepodatność [ńe-po-**daht**-nośhćh] f. intractability; inurement (to fatigue, to the cold); insusceptibility (to disease)
niepodatny [ńe-po-**daht**-ni] adj.m. intractable (material, soil); unreceptive; inured (to fatigue; to the cold, etc.); insusceptible (to disease, etc.)
niepodatny na choroby [ńe-po-**daht**-ni nah kho-**ro**-bi] exp.: insusceptible to disease
niepodejrzanie [ńe-po-dey-**zhah**-ńe] adv. unsuspectedly
niepodejrzany [ńe-po-dey-**zhah**-ni] adj.m. unsuspected
niepodejrzliwy [ńe-po-dey-**zhlee**-vi] adj.m. unsuspicious; unsuspecting
niepodlegle [ńe-pod-**leg**-le] adv. independently; with independence
niepodległościowiec [ńe-pod-leg-wośh-**ćho**-vyets] m. advocate of independence; advocate of sovereignty
niepodległościowy [ńe-pod-leg-wośh-**ćho**-vi] adj.m. favoring independence (of a state, etc.)
ruch niepodległościowy [rookh ńe-pod-leg-wośh-**ćho**-vi] exp.: struggle for independence
niepodległość [ńe-pod-leg-wośhćh] f. independence; sovereignty (of state, ruler)
niepodległy [ńe-pod-**leg**-wi] adj.m. independent; sovereign
niepodniebienny [ńe-pod-ńe-**byen**-ni] adj.m. nonpalatal
niepodobieństwo [ńe-po-do-**byeń**-stfo] n. impossibility; dissimilarity
być niepodobieństwem [bićh ńe-po-do-**byeń**-stfem] exp.: to represent an impossibility
dokonać niepodobieństwa [do-**ko**-nahćh ńe-po-do-**byeń**-stfah] exp.: to achieve the impossible
do niepodobieństwa [do ńe-po-do-**byeń**-stfah] exp.: beyond measure
niepodobna [ńe-po-**dob**-nah] exp.: it's impossible; there is no way; one cannot possibly
niepodobny [ńe-po-**dob**-ni] adj.m. (altogether) unlike; unlikely; (quite) dissimilar
oni są do siebie niepodobni [o-ńee sown do **śhe**-bye ńe-po-**dob**-ńee] exp.: they are dissimilar; they are unlike each other
niepodważalność [ńe-pod-vah-**zhahl**-nośhćh] f. unshakable nature
niepodważalny [ńe-pod-vah-**zhahl**-ni] adj.m. unmovable (authority, etc.); unshakable
niepodzielnie [ńe-po-**dźhel**-ńe] adv. indivisibly
niepodzielność [ńe-po-**dźhel**-nośhćh] f. indivisibility
niepodzielny [ńe-po-**dźhel**-ni] adj.m. indivisible; undivided
niepodzielna całość [ńe-po-**dźhel**-nah **tsah**-wośhćh] exp.: indivisible entity
niepodzielna własność [ńe-po-**dźhel**-nah **vwahs**-nośhćh] exp.: indivisible property
niepoetycki [ńe-po-e-**tits**-kee] adj.m. nonpoetic
niepoetyczny [ńe-po-e-**tich**-ni] adj.m. nonpoetic; unpoetic
niepogoda [ńe-po-**go**-dah] f. bad weather; foul weather
mimo niepogody [**mee**-mo ńe-po-**go**-di] exp.: in spite of bad weather
wskutek niepogody [fskoo-tek ńe-

po-**go**-di] exp.: because of bad weather; under the stress of weather
niepogodny [ńe-po-**go**-dni] adj.m. rainy; stormy; cloudy; cheerless
niepogwałcony [ńe-po-gvahw-**tso**-ni] adj.m. inviolate
niepohamowanie [ńe-po-khah-mo-**vah**-ńe] adv. uncontrollably; irresistibly; violently; without restraint
niepohamowany [ńe-po-khah-mo-**vah**-ni] adj.m. unrestrained; uncontrollable; violent; immoderate
niepohamowany gniew [ne-po-khah-mo-**vah**-ni gńef] exp.: rage; uncontrollable anger
niepojęcie [ńe-po-**y**an-ćhe] adv. inconceivably
niepojętność [ńe-po-**y**ant-nośhćh] f. dullness; stupidity
niepojętny [ńe-po-**y**ant-ni] adj.m. dull (man); stupid
niepojęty [ńe-po-**y**an-ti] adj.m. inconceivable; incomprehensible; unimaginable; beyond understanding
niepokalanek [ńe-po-kah-**lah**-nek] m. chaste tree; agnus castus
niepokalanie [ńe-po-kah-**lah**-ńe] adv. immaculately
niepokalanka [ńe-po-kah-**lahn**-kah] f. nun of the Order of the Immaculate Conception
niepokalany [ńe-po-kah-**lah**-ni] adj.m. immaculate; faultless
niepokaźnie [ńe-po-**kahźh**-ńe] adv. inconspicuously; modestly; humbly
wyglądać niepokaźnie [vig-**lown**-dahćh ńe-po-**kahźh**-ńe] exp.: colloq: to look shabby; to look paltry; not to amount to much
niepokaźność [ńe-po-**kahźh**-nośhćh] f. inconspicuousness; modest appearance; humble appearance; colloq: shabby appearance
niepokaźny [ńe-po-**kahźh**-ni] adj.m. inconspicuous; modest; plain; shabby; wretched
niepokoić [ńe-po-**ko**-eećh] v. disturb; trouble; annoy; pester; bother (*repeatedly*)
niepokoić się [ńe-po-**ko**-eećh śhan] v. be alarmed; feel uneasy (*repeatedly*)
niepokojąco [ńe-po-ko-**yown**-tso] adv. alarmingly; distressingly; disquietingly
niepokojący [ńe-po-ko-**yown**-tsi] adj.m. alarming; distressing; disquieting
niepokojenie [ńe-po-ko-**ye**-ńe] n. trouble; bother; intrusion; disturbance
niepokojenie się [ńe-po-ko-**ye**-ńe śhan] n. worry; alarm; uneasiness
niepokonalny [ńe-po-ko-**nahl**-ni] adj.m. invincible; impossible to overcome; impossible to defeat; unsurmountable; unbreakable (record, score, etc.)
niepokonany [ńe-po-ko-**nah**-ni] adj.m. invincible; irresistible; unsurmountable; uncontrollable; unbroken (record, etc.)
niepokój [ńe-**po**-kooy] m. anxiety; unrest; trouble; agitation; concern; worry; disquiet
niepokoje [ńe-po-**ko**-ye] pl. unrest; agitation
niepokupny [ne-po-**koop**-ni] adj.m. not much in demand
niepoliczony [ńe-po-lee-**cho**-ni] adj.m. uncounted; not counted
niepolitycznie [ńe-po-lee-**tich**-ńe] adv. not diplomatically; impolitically; impolitely; improperly; indecorously
niepolityczny [ńe-po-lee-**tich**-ni] adj.m. impolitical; inexpedient; improper; impolitic; nonpolitical; injudicious
niepolski [ńe-**pol**-skee] adj.m. non-Polish
niepomiernie [ńe-po-**myer**-ńe] adv. extremely; exceedingly; excessively; beyond measure
niepomierny [ńe-po-**myer**-ni] adj.m. excessive; extreme
niepomny [ńe-**pom**-ni] adj.m. forgetful; oblivious
niepomyślnie [ńe-po-**miśhl**-ńe] adv. unfavorably; adversely; unsuccessfully

niepomyślność [ńe-po-**mishl**-noshćh] f. adversity; unsuccess; misfortune; failure
niepomyślny [ńe-po-**mishl**-ni] adj.m. adverse; unlucky; unfortunate; unhappy; unsuccessful
niepomyślne wiadomości [ńe-po-**mishl**-ne vyah-do-**mosh**-ćhee] exp.: bad news; sad news
nieponętnie [ńe-po-**nant**-ńe] adv. unattractively
nieponętny [ńe-po-**nant**-ni] adj.m. unattractive
niepopłatność [ńe-po-**pwaht**-noshćh] f. unprofitableness
niepopłatny [ńe-po-**pwaht**-ni] adj.m. unprofitable; unrewarding
niepoprawnie [ńe-po-**prahv**-ńe] adv. incorrectly; defectively
mówić niepoprawnie [moo-veećh ńe-po-**prahv**-ńe] exp.: to speak incorrectly
pisać niepoprawnie [pee-sahćh ńe-po-**prahv**-ne] exp.: to make mistakes in spelling
niepoprawność [ńe-po-**prahv**-noshćh] f. incorrigibility; incorrectness; mistake; error
niepoprawny [ńe-po-**prahv**-ni] adj.m. incorrigible; incorrect; defective
niepoprawny gramatycznie [ńe-po-**prahv**-ni grah-mah-**tich**-ńe] exp.: ungrammatical
zakład dla niepoprawnych [zahk-wahd dlah ńe-po-**prahv**-nikh] exp.: reformatory
niepopularność [ńe-po-poo-**lahr**-noshćh] f. unpopularity
niepopularny [ńe-po-poo-**lahr**-ni] adj.m. unpopular
nieporadnie [ńe-po-**rahd**-ńe] adv. helplessly; unpractically; awkwardly
nieporadność [ńe-po-**rahd**-noshćh] f. helplessness; lack of resources; lack of skill
nieporadny [ńe-po-**rahd**-ni] adj.m. awkward; helpless; unskillful
nieporęcznie [ńe-po-**ranch**-ńe] adv. inconveniently; awkwardly
nieporęcznie mi było to powiedzieć [ńe-po-**ranch**-ńe mee bi-wo to po-**vye**-dźhećh] exp.: I found it awkward to say that
nieporęczność [ńe-po-**ranch**-noshćh] f. inconvenience
nieporęczny [ńe-po-**ranch**-ni] adj.m. cumbersome; unhandy; awkward; inconvenient; unwieldy
nieporowaty [ńe-po-ro-**vah**-ti] adj.m. nonporous
nieporozumienie [ńe-po-ro-zoo-**mye**-ńe] n. misunderstanding; misconception; misapprehension
niech nie będzie co do tego żadnych nieporozumień [ńekh ńe **ban**-dźhe tso do **te**-go **zhahd**-nikh ńe-po-ro-**zoo**-myeń] exp.: and let there be no mistake about this
nieporównanie [ńe-po-roov-**nah**-ńe] adv. incomparably; matchlessly; without comparison; extremely
nieporównany [ńe-po-roov-**nah**-ni] adj.m. incomparable; matchless; perfect; peerless
nieporównywalnie [ńe-po-roov-ni-**vahl**-ńe] adv. incomparably; matchlessly; without comparison; extremely
nieporównywalność [ńe-po-roov-ni-**vahl**-noshćh] f. incomparable condition
nieporównywalny [ńe-po-roov-ni-**vahl**-ni] adj.m. incomparable
nieporuszenie [ńe-po-roo-**she**-ńe] adv. immovably; firmly
nieporuszony [ńe-po-roo-**sho**-ni] adj.m. immovable; firm
nieporządek [ńe-po-**zhown**-dek] m. disorder; mess; untidiness
narobić nieporządku [nah-**ro**-beećh ńe-po-**zhownt**-koo] exp.: colloq: to make a mess; to mess up (one's room, etc.)
w nieporządku [v ńe-po-**zhownt**-koo] exp.: in disorder; untidy; messy
nieporządnie [ńe-po-**zhownd**-ńe] adv. in disorderly fashion; unmethodically; chaotically; in slovenly fashion
nieporządny [ńe-po-**zhownd**-ni] adj.m. disorderly; untidy; messy; slipshod; chaotic
nieposkromiony [ńe-pos-kro-**myo**-ni] adj.m. uncontrollable; indomitable; unrestrained; unchecked;

unsubdued
nieposłuszeństwo [ńe-po-swoo-**sheń**-stfo] n. disobedience; indocility; insubordination
nieposłusznie [ńe-po-**swoosh**-ńe] adv. lacking subordination; disobediently; in unruly fashion
nieposłuszny [ńe-po-**swoosh**-ni] adj.m. disobedient; unruly; insubordinate
niepospiesznie [ńe-pos-**pyesh**-ńe] adv. without haste
niepospieszny [ńe-pos-**pyesh**-ni] adj.m. not hasty; slow (train, etc.)
niepospolicie [ńe-pos-po-**lee**-ćhe] adv. uncommonly; exceptionally; extremely
niepospolitość [ńe-pos-po-**lee**-tośhćh] f. uncommonness
niepospolity [ńe-pos-po-**lee**-ti] adj.m. uncommon; rare; exceptional; extraordinary
niepostępowy [ńe-pos-tan-**po**-vi] adj.m. unprogressive
niepostrzegalny [ńe-pos-tshe-**gahl**-ni] adj.m. imperceptible
niepostrzeżenie [ńe-pos-tshe-**zhe**-ńe] adv. imperceptibly; without being noticed
odejść niepostrzeżenie [o-deyśhćh ńe-pos-tshe-**zhe**-ńe] exp.: to slip out; to take French leave
zrobić coś niepostrzeżenie [zro-beećh tsośh ńe-pos-tshe-**zhe**-ńe] exp.: to do something unseen; to do something unobserved; to do something unnoticed; to do something without being noticed
nieposzanowanie [ńe-po-shah-no-**vah**-ńe] n. disrespect; irreverence (towards somebody, something); disregard (of somebody, something)
nieposzlakowanie [ńe-po-shlah-ko-**vah**-ńe] adv. irreproachably; unimpeachably
nieposzlakowany [ńe-po-shlah-ko-**vah**-ni] adj.m. unblemished; unspotted; irreproachable; unimpeachable
mieć nieposzlakowaną opinię [myećh ńe-po-shlah-ko-**vah**-nown o-**pee**-ńyan] exp.: to have an excellent reputation
nieposzlakowanej uczciwości [ńe-po-shlah-ko-**vah**-ney ooch-ćhee-**vośh**-ćhee] exp.: of unimpeachable integrity
niepośledni [ńe-pośh-**led**-ńee] adj.m. no mean (writer, etc.); not unimportant; not inconsiderable; not unworthy of notice
niepoślednio [ńe-pośh-**led**-ńo] adv. not insignificantly; in no slight measure; not inconsiderably
niepośpiesznie [ńe-pośh-**pyesh**-ńe] adv. without haste
niepośpieszny [ńe-pośh-**pyesh**-ni] adj.m. not hasty; slow (train, etc.)
nie potrzeba [ńe po-**tshe**-bah] exp.: there is no need (for); it is not necessary
niepotrzebnie [ńe-po-**tsheb**-ńe] adv. unnecessarily; needlessly; redundantly
niepotrzebność [ńe-po-**tsheb**-nośhćh] f. redundancy; uselessness; superfluousness
niepotrzebny [ńe-po-**tsheb**-ni] adj.m. unnecessary; useless; redundant
niepowabny [ńe-po-**vahb**-ni] adj.m. unenticing; unattractive
niepoważnie [ńe-po-**vahzh**-ńe] adv. not seriously
niepoważny [ńe-po-**vahzh**-ni] adj.m. not serious; not to be taken seriously
niepowetowanie [ńe-po-ve-to-**vah**-ńe] adv. irreparably; irretrievably; irremediably
niepowetowany [ńe-po-ve-to-**vah**-ni] adj.m. irreparable; lamentable; much regretted
niepowierzchownie [ńe-po-vyesh-**khov**-ńe] adv. deeply; thoroughly; precisely; with insight
niepowierzchowny [ńe-po-vyesh-**khov**-ni] adj.m. deep; thorough; precise
niepowodzenie [ńe-po-vo-**dze**-ńe] n. failure; adversity
doznać niepowodzenia [doz-nahćh ńe-po-vo-**dze**-ńah] exp.: to fail; to come to grief; to be unsuccessful

niepowołany [ńe-po-vo-**wah**-ni] adj.m. uncalled for; incompetent; unfit; undesirable; wrong
dostać się w niepowołane ręce [**dos**-tahćh śhan v ńe-po-vo-**wah**-ne **ran**-tse] exp.: to get into the wrong hands
ludzie niepowołani [**loo**-dźhe ńe-po-vo-**wah**-ńee] exp.: the wrong people
niepowrotnie [ńe-pov-**rot**-ńe] adv. irrevocably; beyond recall
niepowrotny [ńe-pov-**rot**-ni] adj.m. irrevocable; irrecoverable; beyond recall; irretrievable
niepowstrzymanie [ńe-pof-stshi-**mah**-ńe] adv. irresistibly; uncontrollably
niepowstrzymany [ńe-pof-stshi-**mah**-ni] adj.m. irresistible; uncontrollable; unrestrained
niepowszedni [ńe-pof-**shed**-ńee] adj.m. uncommon; unusually good; exceptional
niepowszednio [ńe-pof-**shed**-ńo] adv. uncommonly; exceptionally; rarely
niepowszedniość [ńe-pof-**shed**-ńośhćh] f. exceptional character
niepowściągliwie [ńe-pof-śhćhowng-**lee**-vye] adv. without moderation; intemperately; uncontrollably; irresistibly; irrepressibly; immoderately
niepowściągliwość [ńe-pof-śhćhowng-**lee**-vośhćh] f. incontinence; lack of moderation
niepowściągliwy [ńe-pof-śhćhowng-**lee**-vi] adj.m. intemperate; uncontrollable; irresistible; unrestrained
niepowtarzalność [ńe-pof-tah-**zhahl**-nośhćh] f. uniqueness; unique character; nonrepetition; nonrecurrence
niepowtarzalny [ńe-pof-tah-**zhahl**-ni] adj.m. unrepeatable; unique
niepozbywalny [ńe-poz-bi-**vahl**-ni] adj.m. inalienable; unalienable
niepoznaka [ńe-poz-**nah**-kah] f. (only in) exp.:
dla niepoznaki [dlah ńe-po-**znah**-kee] exp.: to avoid recognition; to make oneself unrecognizable; to cover up one's tracks; to draw off attention
do niepoznaki [do ńe-po-**znah**-kee] exp.: beyond recognition
niepoznanie [ńe-poz-**nah**-ńe] n. failure to recognize
do niepoznania [do ńe-poz-**nah**-ńah] exp.: beyond recognition
niepoznawalność [ńe-poz-nah-**vahl**-nośhćh] f. inscrutability; unknowableness
niepoznawalny [ńe-po-znah-**vahl**-ni] adj.m. unknowable; inscrutable
rzeczy niepoznawalne [**zhe**-chi ńe-poz-nah-**vahl**-ne] exp.: the Unknowable
niepozornie [ńe-po-**zor**-ńe] adv. inconspicuously; modestly
wyglądać niepozornie [vig-**lown**-dahćh ńe-po-**zor**-ńe] exp.: to look inconspicuous; to be inconspicuous
niepozorność [ńe-po-**zor**-nośhćh] f. inconspicuous appearance
niepozorny [ńe-po-**zor**-ni] adj.m. inconspicuous; modest
niepożądany [ńe-po-zhown-**dah**-ni] adj.m. undesirable; unwanted; objectionable
niepożyteczność [ńe-po-zhi-**tech**-nośhćh] f. uselessness
niepożyteczny [ńe-po-zhi-**tech**-ni] adj.m. useless; unprofitable; to no purpose
niepożyty [ńe-po-**zhi**-ti] adj.m. indefatigable; hardy; robust; indestructible; imperishable (hist.)
niepożywny [ńe-po-**zhiv**-ni] adj.m. not nutritious; innutritious
niepracowity [ńe-prah-tso-**vee**-ti] adj.m. indolent; lazy
niepraktycznie [ńe-prahk-**tich**-ńe] adv. unpractically
niepraktyczność [ńe-prahk-**tich**-nośhćh] f. impracticality
niepraktyczny [ńe-prahk-**tich**-ni] adj.m. impractical; unwieldy; unhandy
niepraktykujący [ńe-prahk-ti-koo-**yown**-tsi] adj.m. noncommunicant; retired (professional)
nieprawda [ńe-**prahv**-dah] f. untruth; falsehood; lie; exp.:

impossible!; isn't that so?
nieprawda! [ńe-**prahv**-dah] excl.: impossible!; don't tell me!
nieprawda? [ńe-**prahv**-dah] exp.: isn't that so; don't you think (so)?
to nieprawda [to ńe-**prahv**-dah] exp.: this is not true
nieprawdaż? [ńe-**prahv**-dahsh] exp.: isn't that so; don't you think (so)?
nieprawdomówny [ńe-prahv-do-**moov**-ni] adj.m. untruthful
nieprawdopodobieństwo [ńe-prahv-do-po-do-**byeń**-stfo] n. improbability; unlikelihood; incredibility
nieprawdopodobieństwem jest, żeby [ńe-prahv-do-po-do-**byeń**-stfem yest **zhe**-bi] exp.: it is improbable that...
nieprawdopodobnie [ńe-prahv-do-po-**dob**-ńe] adv. improbably; incredibly
nieprawdopodobny [ńe-prahv-do-po-**dob**-ni] adj.m. improbable; unlikely; incredible; not credible; impossible; unheard of
nieprawdziwie [ńe-prahv-**dźhee**-vye] adv. untruthfully; fictitiously; falsely; not genuinely; artificially
nieprawdziwość [ńe-prahv-**dźhee**-vośhćh] f. untruth; fallacy; unreality; falseness; artificiality
nieprawdziwy [ńe-prahv-**dźhee**-vi] adj.m. untrue; false; bogus; faked; fictitious; unreal
nieprawidłowo [ńe-prah-vee-**dwo**-vo] adv. irregularly; abnormally; incorrectly
nieprawidłowość [ńe-prah-vee-**dwo**-vośhćh] f. anomaly; irregularity; falsity; incorrectness; abnormality; faultiness
nieprawidłowy [ńe-prah-vee-**dwo**-vi] adj.m. anomalous; irregular; contrary to the rules
nieprawnie [ńe-**prahv**-ńe] adv. unlawfully; illegally
nieprawność [ńe-**prahv**-nośhćh] f. illegality; infringement of the law; misdeed
nieprawny [ńe-**prahv**-ni] adj.m. illegal; unlawful; invalid
nieprawomocny [ńe-prah-vo-**mo**-tsni] adj.m. invalid
nieprawomyślność [ńe-prah-vo-**miśhl**-nośhćh] f. unorthodoxy; disloyalty
nieprawomyślny [ńe-prah-vo-**miśhl**-ni] adj.m. unorthodox; disloyal; unfaithful; not loyal
nieprawość [ńe-**prah**-vośhćh] f. iniquity
nieprawowierność [ńe-prah-vo-**vyer**-nośhćh] f. nonconformity; unorthodoxy
nieprawowierny [ńe-prah-vo-**vyer**-ni] adj.m. nonconformist; unorthodox
nieprawowity [ńe-prah-vo-**vee**-ti] adj.m. illegal; illegitimate
nieprawy [ńe-**prah**-vi] adj.m. unrighteous; adulterous; bastard; unlawful; illegitimate; illicit; unauthorized; unfathered (child)
z nieprawego łoża [z ńe-prah-**ve**-go **wo**-zhah] exp.: born out of wedlock
nieprecyzyjnie [ńe-pre-tsi-**ziy**-ńe] adv. inexactly; inaccurately; without great precision
nieprecyzyjny [ńe-pre-tsi-**ziy**-ni] adj.m. inaccurate; inexact
nieprędki [ńe-**prant**-kee] adj.m. not quick; not hasty; rather sluggish
nieprędko [ńe-**prant**-ko] adv. not soon; not immediately; not at once; without haste
nieprodukcyjny [ńe-pro-dook-**tsiy**-ni] adj.m. unconnected with production; unproductive; unprofitable
nieproduktywnie [ńe-pro-dook-**tiv**-ńe] adv. unproductively; uselessly
nieproduktywny [ńe-pro-dook-**tiv**-ni] adj.m. unproductive; unprofitable
nieprofesjonalista [ńe-pro-fes-yo-nah-**lees**-tah] m. layman
nieprofesjonalny [ńe-pro-fes-yo-**nahl**-ni] adj.m. unprofessional; not professional
nieproletariacki [ńe-pro-le-tahr-**yahts**-kee] adj.m. nonproletarian
nieproliferacja [ńe-pro-lee-fe-**rahts**-yah] f. nonproliferation
nieproporcjonalnie [ńe-pro-por-tsyo-**nahl**-ńe] adv. disproportionately; out of proportion

nieproporcjonalność [ńe-pro-por-tsyo-**nahl**-nośhćh] f. lack of proportion
nieproporcjonalny [ńe-pro-por-tsyo-**nahl**-ni] adj.m. disproportional; out of proportion
nieprosty [ńe-**pros**-ti] adj.m. not straight; not simple
nieproszony [ńe-pro-**sho**-ni] adj.m. uncalled for; self-invited; unwelcome (guest)
nieprotestowy [ńe-pro-tes-**to**-vi] adj.m. nontrading (day)
niepróżny [ńe-**proozh**-ni] adj.m. not empty; not futile; not unavailing
nieprzebaczalny [ńe-pshe-bah-**chahl**-ni] adj.m. unpardonable; inexcusable
nieprzebity [ńe-pshe-**bee**-ti] adj.m. impenetrable (darkness, etc.); impassable (forest, etc.)
nieprzebłagany [ńe-pshe-bwah-**gah**-ni] adj.m. implacable
nieprzebrany [ńe-pshe-**brah**-ni] adj.m. inexhaustible; countless
nieprzebyty [ńe-pshe-**bi**-ti] adj.m. impassable; impenetrable
nieprzechodni [ńe-pshe-**khod**-ńee] adj.m. (gram.) intransitive
nieprzeciętnie [ńe-pshe-**ćhant**-ńe] adv. uncommonly; extraordinarily
nieprzeciętny [ńe-pshe-**ćhant**-ni] adj.m. uncommon; above the average; of superior grade
nieprzedawnienie [ńe-pshe-dahv-**ńe**-ńe] n. not subject to legal limitation (in time)
nieprzedstawiający [ńe-pshet-stah-vyah-**yown**-tsi] adj.m. unrepresentative; not representative
nieprzejednanie [ńe-pshe-yed-nah-ńe] adv. irreconcilably; uncompromisingly; implacably; relentlessly
nieprzejednany [ńe-pshe-yed-**nah**-ni] adj.m. irreconcilable; uncompromising; implacable; relentless
nieprzejezdny [ńe-pshe-**yezd**-ni] adj.m. impassable
nieprzejrzany [ńe-pshey-**zhah**-ni] adj.m. boundless; immeasurable; impenetrable
nieprzejrzysty [ńe-pshey-**zhis**-ti] adj.m. not clear; opaque; not transparent
nieprzejrzyście [ńe-pshey-**zhiśh**-ćhe] adv. opaquely; not clearly
nieprzekładalność [ńe-pshe-kwah-**dahl**-nośhćh] f. untranslatable character
nieprzekładalny [ńe-pshe-kwah-**dahl**-ni] adj.m. untranslatable
nieprzekonująco [ńe-pshe-ko-noo-**yown**-tso] adv. unconvincingly
nieprzekonujący [ńe-pshe-ko-noo-**yown**-tsi] adj.m. unconvincing
nieprzekonywająco [ńe-pshe-ko-ni-vah-**yown**-tso] adv. unconvincingly
nieprzekonywający [ńe-pshe-ko-ni-vah-**yown**-tsi] adj.m. unconvincing
nieprzekraczalny [ńe-pshe-krah-**chahl**-ni] adj.m. impassable; untraversable
nieprzekraczalny termin [ńe-pshe-krah-**chahl**-ni **ter**-meen] exp.: deadline; final date
nieprzekupność [ńe-pshe-**koop**-nośhćh] f. incorruptibility
nieprzekupny [ńe-pshe-**koop**-ni] adj.m. unbribable; incorruptible; refusing to take bribes
nieprzeliczony [ńe-pshe-lee-**cho**-ni] adj.m. countless; innumerable
nieprzemakalność [ńe-pshe-mah-**kahl**-nośhćh] f. impermeability; watertightness
nieprzemakalny [ńe-pshe-mah-**kahl**-ni] adj.m. waterproof; impermeable
płaszcz nieprzemakalny [pwahshch ńe-pshe-mah-**kahl**-ni] exp.: raincoat
ubranie nieprzemakalne [oob-**rah**-ńe ńe-pshe-mah-**kahl**-ne] exp.: oilskins; waterproof clothing
nieprzemijający [ńe-pshe-mee-yah-**yown**-tsi] adj.m. lasting; permanent; imperishable; of lasting value
nieprzemijalny [ńe-pshe-mee-**yahl**-ni] adj.m. lasting; permanent; imperishable; of lasting value
nieprzemożony [ńe-pshe-mo-**zho**-ni] adj.m. irresistible; overpowering; overwhelming; invincible;

unconquerable
nieprzenikalny [ńe-pshe-ńee-**kahl**-ni] adj.m. inscrutable; impermeable; undiscerning; impervious
nieprzenikliwość [ńe-pshe-ńee-**klee**-vośhćh] f. impermeability; lack of discernment; imperviousness
nieprzenikliwy [ńe-pshe-ńee-**klee**-vi] adj.m. impermeable; undiscerning; impervious
nieprzenikniony [ńe-pshe-ńeek-**ńo**-ni] adj.m. impenetrable; impassable (area); inscrutable
nieprzenośny [ńe-pshe-**nośh**-ni] adj.m. not figurative; not portable; untransferable
nieprzeparcie [ńe-pshe-**pahr**-ćhe] adv. irresistibly; overpoweringly
nieprzeparty [ńe-pshe-**pahr**-ti] adj.m. irresistible; overpowering
nieprzepisowo [ńe-pshe-pee-**so**-vo] adv. by breaking the rules
nieprzepisowy [ńe-pshe-pee-**so**-vi] adj.m. contrary to the rules
nieprzepisowa gra [ńe-pshe-pee-so-vah grah] exp.: foul play
nieprzepuszczalność [ńe-pshe-poosh-**chahl**-nośhćh] f. impenetrability
nieprzepuszczalność (dla) cieczy [ne-pshe-poosh-**chahl**-noshćh dlah **ćhe**-chi] exp.: impermeability; imperviousness
nieprzepuszczalność (dla) światła [ńe-pshe-poosh-**chahl**-nośhćh (dlah) **śhfyaht**-wah] exp.: opacity
nieprzepuszczalny [ńe-pshe-poosh-**chahl**-ni] adj.m. impervious; impenetrable
nieprzepuszczalny dla cieczy [ńe-pshe-poosh-**chahl**-ni (dlah) **ćhe**-chi] exp.: impervious; waterproof
nieprzepuszczalny dla światła [ńe-pshe-poosh-**chahl**-ni dlah **śhfyaht**-wah] exp.: opaque
nieprzerwanie [ńe-psher-**vah**-ńe] adv. uninterruptedly; continuously; constantly
nieprzerwany [ńe-psher-**vah**-ni] adj.m. continuous; ceaseless; consecutive
nieprzestępny [ńe-pshes-**t**<u>an</u>**p**-ni] adj.m. not leap(-year); not bissextile (year); not a transcendental (function); not criminal (deed, etc.)
nieprzestrzeganie [ńe-pshes-tshe-**gah**-ńe] n. nonobservance
nieprześcigniony [ńe-psheśh-ćheeg-**ńo**-ni] adj.m. unsurpassable; unexcelled
nieprzetłumaczalność [ńe-pshe-twoo-mah-**chahl**-nośhćh] f. untranslatable character
nieprzetłumaczalny [ńe-pshe-twoo-mah-**chahl**-ni] adj.m. untranslatable
nieprzewidzianie [ńe-pshe-vee-**dźhah**-ńe] adv. in an unexpected fashion; in an unlooked for way
nieprzewidziany [ńe-pshe-vee-**dźhah**-ni] adj.m. unforeseen; unlooked for; unexpected
nieprzewidziane wydatki [ńe-pshe-vee-**dźhah**-ne vi-**daht**-kee] exp.: unexpected expenses
nieprzewodnik [ńe-pshe-**vod**-ńeek] m. nonconductor
nieprzezornie [ńe-pshe-**zor**-ńe] adv. improvidently
nieprzezorność [ńe-pshe-**zor**-nośhćh] f. improvidence
nieprzezorny [ńe-pshe-**zor**-ni] adj.m. improvident; unforseeing; wanting of foresight
nieprzezroczystość [ńe-pshez-ro-**chis**-tośhćh] f. opacity; nontransparency
nieprzezroczysty [ńe-pshez-ro-**chis**-ti] adj.m. opaque; nontransparent
nieprzezwyciężony [ńe-pshez-vi-ćh<u>an</u>-**zho**-ni] adj.m. invincible; insurmountable
nieprzeźroczysty [ńe-psheźh-ro-**chis**-ti] adj.m. opaque; not transparent; nontranslucent
nieprzychylnie [ńe-pshi-**khil**-ńe] adv. unfavorably; disapprovingly
nieprzychylnie nastawiony do czegoś [ńe-pshi-**khil**-ńe nahs-tah-**vyo**-ni do **che**-gośh] exp.: unfavorable to something
nieprzychylność [ńe-pshi-**khil**-nośhćh] f. disfavor; prejudice; disapproval
nieprzychylny [ńe-pshi-**khil**-ni]

adj.m. unfriendly; prejudiced; unfavorable
nieprzychylne okoliczności [ńe-pshi-**khil**-ne o-ko-leech-**nośh**-ćhee] exp.: adverse circumstances; unfavorable circumstances
nieprzydatność [ńe-pshi-**daht**-nośhćh] f. uselessness
nieprzydatny [ńe-pshi-**daht**-ni] adj.m. useless; unserviceable
nieprzygotowany [ńe-pshi-go-to-**vah**-ni] adj.m. unprepared
nieprzyjaciel [ńe-pshi-**yah**-ćhel] m. enemy; foe; ill-wisher
nieprzyjacielski [ńe-pshi-yah-**ćhel**-skee] adj.m. enemy; hostile; enemy's (tanks, guns, etc.)
działanie nieprzyjacielskie [dźhah-**wah**-ńe ńe-pshi-yah-**ćhel**-ske] exp.: hostilities
siły nieprzyjacielskie [**śhee**-wi ńe-pshi-yah-**ćhel**-ske] exp.: enemy forces
nieprzyjaciółka [ńe-pshi-yah-**ćhoow**-kah] f. (female) enemy; foe; ill-wisher
nieprzyjazny [ńe-pshi-**yahz**-ni] adj.m. unfriendly; inimical; inhospitable
nieprzyjaźnie [ńe-pshi-**yahźh**-ńe] adv. hostilely; in unfriendly fashion; inimically; adversely
nieprzyjaźń [ńe-**pshi**-yahźhń] f. hostility; unfriendliness
nieprzyjemnie [ńe-pshi-**yem**-ńe] adv. unpleasantly; disagreeably
było mi nieprzyjemnie [**bi**-wo mee ńe-pshi-**yem**-ńe] exp.: I felt uneasy; I felt uncomfortable
nieprzyjemność [ńe-pshi-**yem**-nośhćh] f. unpleasantness
nieprzyjemności [ńe-pshi-yem-**nośh**-ćhee] pl. trouble; unpleasantness; difficulties
nieprzyjemny [ńe-pshi-**yem**-ni] adj.m. unpleasant; disagreeable; distasteful; annoying; nasty; obnoxious; repulsive
nieprzymiotnikowy [ńe-pshi-myot-ńee-**ko**-vi] adj.m. nonadjectival
nieprzymuszony [ńe-pshi-moo-**sho**-ni] adj.m. unconstrained; voluntary; uncoerced
z własnej nieprzymuszonej woli [z **vwahs**-ney ńe-pshi-moo-**sho**-ney **vo**-lee] exp.: of one's own free will
nieprzypadkowo [ńe-pshi-paht-**ko**-vo] adv. not by accident
nieprzypadkowy [ńe-pshi-paht-**ko**-vi] adj.m. not accidental
nieprzystawalność [ńe-pshis-tah-**vahl**-nośhćh] f. noncongruence
nieprzystawalny [ńe-pshis-tah-**vahl**-ni] adj.m. noncongruent
nieprzystępnie [ńe-pshis-**tanp**-ńe] adv. inaccessibly; unapproachably
nieprzystępność [ńe-pshis-**tanp**-nośhćh] f. inaccessibility; grumpiness
nieprzystępny [ńe-pshis-**tanp**-ni] adj.m. inaccessible; grumpy; unapproachable
nieprzystojnie [ńe-pshis-**toy**-ńe] adv. improperly; indecently
nieprzystojny [ńe-pshis-**toy**-ni] adj.m. improper; indecent; objectionable; demoralizing
nieprzystosowanie [ńe-pshis-to-so-**vah**-ńe] n. nonadaptation; lack of accommodation; lack of adjustment
nieprzystosowany [ńe-pshis-to-so-**vah**-ni] adj.m. non-adapted; not getting along; not adequate
nieprzyswajalny [ńe-pshis-fah-**yahl**-ni] adj.m. inassimilable
nieprzytomnie [ńe-pshi-**tom**-ńe] adv. unconsciously; senselessly
mówić nieprzytomnie [**moo**-veećh ńe-pshi-**tom**-ńe] exp.: to speak incoherently; to rave
nieprzytomnie pijany [ńe-pshi-**tom**-ńe pee-**yah**-ni] exp.: dead drunk
patrzeć nieprzytomnie [**pah**-tshećh ńe-pshi-**tom**-ńe] exp.: to stare vacantly
nieprzytomność [ńe-pshi-**tom**-nośhćh] f. unconsciousness; absentmindedness; senselessness; foolishness
do nieprzytomności [do ńe-pshi-tom-**nośh**-ćhee] exp.: franticly; madly; wildly
pobić kogoś do nieprzytomności [**po**-beećh **ko**-gośh do ńe-pshi-tom-**nośh**-ćhee] exp.: to beat

somebody unconscious
upić się do nieprzytomności [oo-peećh śh<u>an</u> do ńe-pshi-tom-**nośh**-ćhee] exp.: to drink oneself unconscious; to get dead drunk
nieprzytomny [ńe-pshi-**tom**-ni] adj.m. unconscious; absent-minded; frantic; mad; wild
nieprzytomne spojrzenie [ńe-pshi-**tom**-ne spoy-**zhe**-ńe] exp.: vacant stare; haggard look; faraway look
nieprzytomny wzrok [ńe-pshi-**tom**-ni vzrok] exp.: vacant stare; haggard look; far-away look
nieprzytulnie [ńe-pshi-**tool**-ńe] adv. not cozily
nieprzytulność [ńe-pshi-**tool**-nośhćh] f. lack of coziness
nieprzytulny [ńe-pshi-**tool**-ni] adj.m. not cozy; not snug
nieprzywiedlny [ńe-pshi-**vyedl**-ni] adj.m. irreducible (equation)
równanie nieprzywiedlne [roov-nah-ńe ńe-pshi-**vyedl**-ne] exp.: irreducible equation
nieprzywykły [ńe-pshi-**vik**-wi] adj.m. unaccustomed (to); not accustomed (to)
nieprzyzwoicie [ńe-pshi-zvo-**ee**-ćhe] adv. indecently; improperly
zachowywać się nieprzyzwoicie [zah-kho-**vi**-vahćh śh<u>an</u> ńe-pshi-zvo-**ee**-ćhe] exp.: to forget one's manners; to behave improperly
nieprzyzwoitość [ńe-pshi-zvo-**ee**-tośhćh] f. indecency; impropriety
nieprzyzwoity [ńe-pshi-zvo-**ee**-ti] adj.m. indecent; obscene; improper
nieprzyzwyczajenie [ńe-pshiz-vi-chah-**ye**-ńe] n. lack of habit; unaccustomedness
nieprzyzwyczajony [ńe-pshiz-vi-chah-**yo**-ni] adj.m. not accustomed to; unaccustomed
niepublicznie [ńe-poob-**leech**-ńe] adv. not in public
niepubliczny [ńe-poob-**leech**-ni] adj.m. not public
niepunktualnie [ńe-poonk-too-**ahl**-ńe] adv. not punctually
niepunktualność [ńe-poon-ktoo-**ahl**-nośhćh] f. unpunctuality; lack of punctuality
niepunktualny [ńe-poon-ktoo-**ahl**-ni] adj.m. unpunctual; late
niepylak [ńe-**pi**-lahk] m. Apollo butterfly
niepyszny [ńe-**pish**-ni] adj.m. exp.:
jak niepyszny [yahk ńe-**pish**-ni] exp.: crestfallen; shamefaced; with his tail between his legs
nieracjonalnie [ńe-rah-tsyo-**nahl**-ńe] adv. unreasonably; irrationally
nieracjonalność [ńe-rah-tsyo-**nahl**-nośhćh] f. unreasonableness; irrationality; irrationalness
nieracjonalny [ńe-rah-tsyo-**nahl**-ni] adj.m. unreasonable; irrational
nierad [**ńe**-raht] adj.m. unwilling; annoyed; adv. unwillingly; reluctantly
nierad komuś [**ńe**-raht **ko**-moośh] exp.: annoyed to see somebody
rad nierad [rahd **ńe**-raht] exp.: willy-nilly
nierasowy [ńe-rah-**so**-vi] adj.m. not purebred
nieraz [**ńe**-rahs] adv. often; again and again; many a time
nieraźnie [ńe-**rahźh**-ńe] adv. uncomfortably; awkwardly
nieraźno [ńe-**rahźh**-no] adv. uncomfortably; awkwardly
szło mi nieraźno [shwo mee ńe-**rahźh**-no] exp.: I was clumsy; I was awkward
zrobiło mi się nieraźno [zro-**bee**-wo mee śh<u>an</u> ńe-**rahźh**-no] exp.: I felt ill at ease; I felt uncomfortable
nierdzewność [ńe-**rdzev**-nośhćh] f. stainless quality; stainlessness
nierdzewny [ńe-**rdzev**-ni] adj.m. rustproof; stainless; rustless; corrosion proof
nierealistyczny [ńe-re-ah-lees-**tich**-ni] adj.m. unrealistic
nierealność [ńe-re-**ahl**-nośhćh] f. unreality
nierealny [ńe-re-**ahl**-ni] adj.m. imaginary; unreal; unrealizable; wild; visionary
nieregularnie [ńe-re-goo-**lahr**-ńe] adv. irregularly; erratically
nieregularność [ńe-re-goo-**lahr**-nośhćh] f. irregularity;

unshapedness; unshapenness
nieregularny [ńe-re-goo-**lahr**-ni] adj.m. irregular; erratic
wiersz nieregularny [vyersh ńe-re-goo-**lahr**-ni] exp.: irregular verse
wojska nieregularne [**voy**-skah ńe-re-goo-**lahr**-ne] exp.: irregulars
niereligijność [ńe-re-lee-**geey**-nośhćh] f. lack of piety; impiety
niereligijny [ńe-re-lee-**geey**-ni] adj.m. not religious; profane; impious; irreligious
nierentownie [ńe-ren-**tov**-ńe] adv. unprofitably; unremuneratively
nierentowność [ńe-ren-**tov**-nośhćh] f. unprofitableness; unremunerativeness
nierentowny [ńe-ren-**tov**-ni] adj.m. unprofitable; unremunerative
nierewolucyjny [ńe-re-vo-loo-**tsiy**-ni] adj.m. nonrevolutionary
nierodzinny [ńe-ro-**dźheen**-ni] adj.m. nondomestic
nierogacizna [ńe-ro-gah-**ćheez**-nah] f. swines; hogs
nierogaty [ńe-ro-**gah**-ti] adj.m. hornless
nierolniczy [ńe-rol-**ńee**-chi] adj.m. nonagricultural
nieromantycznie [ńe-ro-mahn-**tich**-ńe] adv. nonromantically; unromantically
nieromantyczny [ńe-ro-mahn-**tich**-ni] adj.m. not romantic; unromantic
nierozciągliwy [ńe-ros-ćhown-**glee**-vi] adj.m. inextensible
nierozdzielnie [ńe-roz-**dźhel**-ńe] adv. inseparably; indissolubly
nierozdzielność [ńe-roz-**dźhel**-nośhćh] f. inseparability
nierozdzielny [ńe-roz-**dźhel**-ni] adj.m. inseparable
nierozegrana [ńe-ro-ze-**grah**-nah] f. tie; tie game
nierozerwalnie [ńe-ro-zer-**vahl**-ńe] adv. indissolubly; inseparably
nierozerwalność [ńe-ro-zer-**vahl**-nośhćh] f. indissolubility
nierozerwalność węzła małżeńskiego [ńe-ro-zer-**vahl**-nośhćh **vanz**-wah mahw-zheń-**ske**-go] exp.: the indissolubility of marriage
nierozerwalny [ńe-ro-zer-**vahl**-ni] adj.m. indissoluble
nierozeznanie [ńe-ro-ze-**znah**-ńe] n. lack of discernment
nierozgarnięcie [ńe-roz-gahr-**ńan**-ćhe] n. slow wits; lack of perspicacity
nierozgarnięty [ńe-roz-gahr-**ńan**-ti] adj.m. dull; dim-witted
nierozgłośny [ńe-roz-**gwośh**-ni] adj.m. quiet (wedding, etc.)
nierozkładalny [ńe-ros-kwah-**dahl**-ni] adj.m. indecomposable; not resolvable into elements
nierozległy [ńe-roz-**le**-gwi] adj.m. inextensive; not extensive
nierozłączka [ńe-roz-**wownch**-kah] f. budgerigar (Australian parrot)
nierozłącznie [ńe-roz-**wownch**-ńe] adv. inseparably
nierozłączność [ńe-roz-**wownch**-nośhćh] f. inseparability
nierozłączny [ńe-roz-**wownch**-ni] adj.m. inseparable
nierozmowność [ńe-roz-**mov**-nośhćh] f. reticence; reserve in speech; uncommunicativeness
nierozmowny [ńe-roz-**mov**-ni] adj.m. uncommunicative; reserved
nierozmyślnie [ńe-roz-**miśhl**-ńe] adv. unintentionally
nierozmyślny [ńe-roz-**miśhl**-ni] adj.m. unpremeditated; unintentional
nierozpoznawalny [ńe-ros-poz-nah-**vahl**-ni] adj.m. undistinguishable
nierozpryskowy [ńe-ros-pris-**ko**-vi] adj.m. splinter-proof
szkło nierozpryskowe [shkwo ńe-ros-pris-**ko**-ve] exp.: safety glass
nierozpuszczalność [ńe-ros-poo-**shchahl**-nośhćh] f. indissolubility
nierozpuszczalny [ńe-ros-poo-**shchahl**-ni] adj.m. indissoluble
nierozrośnięty [ńe-roz-rośh-**ńan**-ti] adj.m. physically undeveloped
nierozsądek [ńe-ros-**sown**-dek] m. unwisdom; unreasonableness
nierozsądnie [ńe-ros-**sownd**-ńe] adv. unwisely; unreasonably
nierozsądny [ńe-ros-**sownd**-ni] adj.m. unreasonable; imprudent; silly
nierozstrzygalny [ńe-ros-stshi-**gahl**-ni] adj.m. unsolvable

nieroztropnie [ńe-ros-**trop**-ńe] adv. unwisely; injudiciously; rashly; senselessly; inadvisably
nieroztropność [ńe-ros-**trop**-nośhćh] f. unwisdom; rashness; impolicy
nieroztropny [ńe-ros-**trop**-ni] adj.m. unwise; rash; imprudent; undiplomatic
nierozumnie [ńe-ro-**zoom**-ńe] adv. unreasonably; foolishly
nierozumny [ńe-ro-**zoom**-ni] adj.m. unreasonable; foolish
nierozwaga [ńe-roz-**vah**-gah] f. inconsiderateness; imprudence; thoughtlessness; hastiness
nierozważnie [ńe-roz-**vahzh**-ńe] adv. inconsiderately; rashly; hastily
nierozważny [ńe-roz-**vahzh**-ni] adj.m. inconsiderate; imprudent; hasty
nierozważny czyn [ńe-roz-**vahzh**-ni chin] exp.: indiscretion
nierozwiązalność [ńe-roz-vyown-**zahl**-nośhćh] f. insolubility; insolvability (of a problem, etc.)
nierozwiązalny [ńe-roz-vyown-**zahl**-ni] adj.m. insoluble; irresolvable
nierozwiązywalny [ńe-roz-vyown-zi-**vahl**-ni] adj.m. impossible to solve; having no solution
nierozwijalny [ńe-roz-vee-**yahl**-ni] adj.m. irresolvable (math.)
nierozwikłanie [ńe-roz-vee-**kwah**-ńe] adv. inextricably
nierozwikłany [ńe-roz-vee-**kwah**-ni] adj.m. inextricable
nierozwinięty [ńe-roz-vee-**ńan**-ti] adj.m. undeveloped; backward
nierozwlekle [ńe-roz-**vle**-kle] adv. concisely
nierozwlekły [ńe-roz-**vle**-kwi] adj.m. concise
nierozwojowy [ńe-roz-vo-**yo**-vi] adj.m. not developing; not progressive
nierób [**ńe**-roop] m. idler; loafer
nieróbstwo [ńe-**roop**-stfo] n. loafing; idleness; inactivity
nieródka [ńe-**root**-kah] f. nullipara
nierównie [ńe-**roov**-ńe] adv. incomparably; beyond comparison; by far
nierówno [ńe-**roov**-no] adv. not straight; crookedly; unevenly
nierównoboczny [ńe-roov-no-**boch**-ni] adj.m. inequilateral; unequal-sided
trójkąt nierównoboczny [**trooy**-kownt ńe-roov-no-**boch**-ni] exp.: scalene triangle
nierównoległy [ńe-roov-no-**leg**-wi] adj.m. not parallel
nierównomiernie [ńe-roov-no-**myer**-ńe] adv. unequally; irregularly; unevenly
nierównomierność [ńe-roov-no-**myer**-nośhćh] f. inequality; irregularity
nierównomierny [ńe-roov-no-**myer**-ni] adj.m. unequal; irregular; uneven
nierównosylabowość [ńe-roov-no-si-lah-**bo**-vośhćh] f. imparisyllabic condition; not having the same number of syllables
nierównosylabowy [ńe-roov-no-si-lah-**bo**-vi] adj.m. imparisyllabic
nierówność [ńe-**roov**-nośhćh] f. inequality; unevenness; irregularity
nierówności [ńe-roov-**nośh**-ćhee] pl. inequalities
nierówności społeczne [ńe-roov-**nośh**-ćhee spo-**wech**-ne] exp.: social inequalities
usunąć nierówności [oo-**soo**-nownćh ńe-roov-**nośh**-ćhee] exp.: to plane down the irregularities; to plane away the irregularities
znak nierówności [znahk ńe-roov-**nośh**-ćhee] exp.: inequality sign
nierównowaga [ńe-roov-no-**vah**-gah] f. lack of equilibrium; lack of stability; lack of balance; wobbliness
nierównozgłoskowy [ńe-roov-no-zgwos-**ko**-vi] adj.m. imparisyllabic
nierówny [ńe-**roov**-ni] adj.m. unequal; uneven; crooked; hilly; irregular; misshapen; erratic
nieruchawo [ńe-roo-**khah**-vo] adv. sluggishly; torpidly; indolently; awkwardly; clumsily
nieruchawość [ńe-roo-**khah**-vośhćh] f. sluggishness;

torpidity; indolence; awkwardness; clumsiness
nieruchawy [ńe-roo-**khah**-vi] adj.m. sluggish; torpid; indolent; awkward; clumsy
nieruchliwość [ńe-rookh-**lee**-vośhćh] f. ponderousness; unwieldiness
nieruchliwy [ńe-rookh-**lee**-vi] adj.m. slow; impassive; ponderous
nieruchomieć [ńe-roo-**kho**-myećh] v. cease moving; come to a standstill; become motionless (*repeatedly*)
nieruchomienie [ńe-roo-kho-**mye**-ńe] n. cessation of motion
nieruchomo [ńe-roo-**kho**-mo] adv. without motion
nieruchomość [ńe-roo-**kho**-mośhćh] f. immobility; real estate; property
nieruchomości [ńe-roo-kho-**mośh**-ćhee] pl. immovables
nieruchomy [ńe-roo-**kho**-mi] adj.m. immovable; motionless; still
majątek nieruchomy [mah-**yown**-tek ńe-roo-**kho**-mi] exp.: real estate
oś nieruchoma [ośh ńe-roo-**kho**-mah] exp.: dead axle
nierybny [ńe-**rib**-ni] adj.m. lacking fish; not a variety of fish
nierycerski [ńe-ri-**tser**-skee] adj.m. unchivalrous; uncourteous
nierycersko [ńe-ri-**tser**-sko] adv. unchivalrously; uncourteously; with lack of courtesy
nierychliwy [ńe-rikh-**lee**-vi] adj.m. tardy; sluggish
Pan Bóg nierychliwy, ale sprawiedliwy [pahn book ńe-rikh-**lee**-vi ah-le sprah-vyed-**lee**-vi] exp.: God's mill grinds slow but sure
nierychło [ńe-**rikh**-wo] adv. slowly; distantly; not readily
nierychły [ńe-**rikh**-wi] adj.m. unready; not ready; slow; distant; not forthcoming
nierytmicznie [ńe-rit-**meech**-ńe] adv. without rhythm
nierytmiczność [ńe-rit-**meech**-nośhćh] f. lack of rhythm
nierytmiczny [ńe-rit-**meech**-ni] adj.m. unrhythmic; unrythmical
nierzadki [ńe-**zhaht**-kee] adj.m. not infrequent; not uncommon; pretty dense; thickish
nierzadko [ńe-**zhaht**-ko] adv. often; not infrequently; not seldom; from time to time
nierząd [**ńe**-zhownt] m. prostitution; anarchy
dom nierządu [dom ńe-**zhown**-doo] exp.: whorehouse
uprawiać nierząd [oop-**rah**-vyahćh **ńe**-zhownt] exp.: to walk the streets; to work as a prostitute
nierządnica [ńe-zhownd-**ńee**-tsah] f. prostitute; harlot
nierządny [ńe-**zhownd**-ni] adj.m. of prostitution; illegal (sex)
nierzeczownikowy [ńe-zhe-chov-ńee-**ko**-vi] adj.m. nonsubstantival
nierzeczowy [ńe-zhe-**cho**-vi] adj.m. pointless; not to the point
nierzeczywistość [ńe-zhe-chi-**vees**-tośhćh] f. unreality; fiction
nierzeczywisty [ńe-zhe-chi-**vees**-ti] adj.m. unreal; fictitious
nierzetelnie [ńe-zhe-**tel**-ńe] adv. unconscientiously; dishonestly
nierzetelność [ńe-zhe-**tel**-nośhćh] f. dishonesty; lack of conscientiousness
nierzetelny [ńe-zhe-**tel**-ni] adj.m. dishonest; unreliable; slippery
niesalonowy [ńe-sah-lo-**no**-vi] adj.m. rude; inelegant; offensive (language, etc.)
niesamodzielnie [ńe-sah-mo-**dźhel**-ńe] adv. independently; without self-reliance
niesamodzielność [ńe-sah-mo-**dźhel**-nośhćh] f. lack of self-reliance
niesamodzielny [ńe-sah-mo-**dźhel**-ni] adj.m. not self-reliant; not done independently; done with assistance
niesamoistność [ńe-sah-mo-**eest**-nośhćh] f. lack of self subsistence; absence of self-subsistence
niesamoistny [ńe-sah-mo-**eest**-ni] adj.m. not self-subsistent
niesamolubnie [ńe-sah-mo-**loob**-ńe]

adv. unegoistically; not egoistically
niesamolubny [ńe-sah-mo-**loob**-ni] adj.m. unegoistical
niesamowicie [ńe-sah-mo-**vee**-ćhe] adv. uncommonly; weirdly; strangely
niesamowitość [ńe-sah-mo-**vee**-tośhćh] f. strangeness; weirdness
niesamowity [ńe-sah-mo-**vee**-ti] adj.m. uncanny; strange; uncommon; weird
niesamożywny [ńe-sah-mo-**zhiv**-ni] adj.m. heterotrophic
niesądowy [ńe-sown-**do**-vi] adj.m. nonjudicial
niesceniczność [ńe-stse-**ńeech**-nośhćh] f. quality not fit for theater
niesceniczny [ńe-stse-**ńeech**-ni] adj.m. (play, etc.) not fit for theater
nieschludny [ńe-**skhlood**-ni] adj.m. untidy; not neat
niesentymentalny [ńe-sen-ti-men-**tahl**-ni] adj.m. unsentimental
nieserdeczny [ńe-ser-**dech**-ni] adj.m. showing no cordiality
niesfornie [ńe-**sfor**-ńe] adv. turbulently; refractorily
niesforność [ńe-**sfor**-nośhćh] f. unruliness; indocility; turbulence
niesforny [ńe-**sfor**-ni] adj.m. unruly; indocile; intractable; turbulent; refractory
nieskalanie [ńe-skah-**lah**-ńe] adv. immaculately; in stainless fashion; spotlessly; without blemish
nieskalany [ńe-skah-**lah**-ni] adj.m. immaculate; stainless; spotless
nieskazitelnie [ńe-skah-źhee-**tel**-ńe] adv. immaculately; spotlessly; without blemish
nieskazitelność [ńe-skah-źhee-**tel**-nośhćh] f. spotlessness; integrity; immaculacy; unimpeachable character
nieskazitelny [ńe-skah-źhee-**tel**-ni] adj.m. unblemished; stainless; immaculate; spotless; untainted
nieskażony [ńe-skah-**zho**-ni] adj.m. unpolluted; unstinted; undefiled
nieskąpo [ńe-**skown**-po] adv. unstintedly; not in stingy manner
nieskąpy [ńe-**skown**-pi] adj.m. liberal; unstinted; profuse
nieskł**adnie** [ńe-**skwahd**-ńe] adv. inharmoniously; discordantly; awkwardly
szło mu to nieskładnie [shwo moo to ńe-**skwahd**-ńe] exp.: he was clumsy at it
nieskładność [ńe-**skwahd**-nośhćh] f. awkwardness; clumsiness
nieskładny [ńe-**skwahd**-ni] adj.m. awkward; inharmonious; clumsy
nieskł**onny** [ńe-**skwon**-ni] adj.m. indisposed; disinclined
nieskomplikowany [ńe-skom-plee-ko-**vah**-ni] adj.m. not complicated
nieskończenie [ńe-skoń-**che**-ńe] adv. infinitely; endlessly; everlastingly
nieskończenie mały [ńe-skoń-**che**-ńe **mah**-wi] exp.: infinitesimal
nieskończoność [ńe-skoń-**cho**-nośhćh] f. infinity; immensity; endless time; vastitude of space
do nieskończoności [do ńe-skoń-cho-**nośh**-ćhee] exp.: to infinity; endlessly; without limit
trwający w nieskończoność [trfah-**yown**-tsi v ńe-skoń-**cho**-nośhćh] exp.: interminable
w nieskończoność [v ńe-skoń-**cho**-nośhćh] exp.: endlessly; to infinity; without limit
nieskończony [ńe-skoń-**cho**-ni] adj.m. infinite; endless; never-ending
nieskoordynowanie [ńe-sko-or-di-no-**vah**-ńe] n. incoordination; lack of coordination
nieskoordynowany [ńe-sko-or-di-no-**vah**-ni] adj.m. incoordinate
nieskory [ńe-**sko**-ri] adj.m. not eager; indisposed; not inclined
nieskory do rozmów [ńe-**sko**-ri do **roz**-moof] exp.: coy of speech; (man) of few words
nieskracalny [ńe-skrah-**tsahl**-ni] adj.m. irreducible
nieskromnie [ńe-**skrom**-ńe] adv. immodestly; indecently
nieskromność [ńe-**skrom**-nośhćh] f. immodesty; indecency
nieskromny [ńe-**skrom**-ni] adj.m.

immodest; indecent
nieskutecznie [ńe-skoo-**tech**-ńe] adv. ineffectively
nieskuteczność [ńe-skoo-**tech**-nośhćh] f. inefficacy
nieskuteczny [ńe-skoo-**tech**-ni] adj.m. ineffective; futile
nieskwapliwie [ńe-skfah-**plee**-vye] adv. not eagerly
nieskwapliwy [ńe-skfah-**plee**-vi] adj.m. not eager; indisposed; not inclined
niesłabnący [ńe-swahb-**nown**-tsi] adj.m. unabated; unflagging
niesława [ńe-**swah**-vah] f. infamy; disgrace; shame
okryty niesławą [o-**kri**-ti ńe-**swah**-vown] exp.: disgraced; infamous
niesławnie [ńe-**swahv**-ńe] adv. ingloriously; disgracefully
niesławny [ńe-**swahv**-ni] adj.m. infamous; inglorious; disgraceful; having a bad reputation
niesłodki [ńe-**swot**-kee] adj.m. not sweet; unsweetened
niesłodko [ńe-**swot**-ko] adv. colloq: roughly
niesłony [ńe-**swo**-ni] adj.m. unsalted
niesłowiański [ńe-swo-**vyahń**-skee] adj.m. non-Slavic
niesłowiańskość [ńe-swo-**vyahń**-skośhćh] f. non-Slavic character
niesłowność [ńe-**swov**-nośhćh] f. unreliability; undependableness
niesłowny [ńe-**swov**-ni] adj.m. unreliable; undependable
być niesłownym [bićh ńe-**swov**-nim] exp.: to break one's word
niesłusznie [ńe-**swoosh**-ńe] adv. unjustly; wrongly; groundlessly
niesłusznie sądzisz, że... [ńe-**swoosh**-ńe sown-dźheesh zhe] exp.: you are wrong to think that...
niesłuszność [ńe-**swoosh**-nośhćh] f. injustice; unfairness; groundlessness
niesłuszny [ńe-**swoosh**-ni] adj.m. unjust; wrong; groundless; unfair
niesłuszny zarzut [ńe-**swoosh**-ni **zah**-zhoot] exp.: undeserved accusation; groundless charge
niesłychanie [ńe-swi-**khah**-ńe] adv. extremely; excessively; outrageously
niesłychany [ńe-swi-**khah**-ni] adj.m. unheard of; unprecedented; outrageous; unparalleled
to niesłychane! [to ńe-swi-**khah**-ne] exp.: this is incredible!
niesłyszalnie [ńe-swi-**shahl**-ńe] adv. inaudibly
niesłyszalność [ńe-swi-**shahl**-nośhćh] f. inaudibility
niesłyszalny [ńe-swi-**shahl**-ni] adj.m. inaudible
niesmacznie [ńe-**smahch**-ńe] adv. unpalatably; tastelessly; without taste
niesmaczny [ńe-**smahch**-ni] adj.m. tasteless; unsavory; unseemly; unpalatable; coarse
niesmak [**ńe**-smahk] m. bad taste; disgust; repugnance; nasty taste (in the mouth)
miałem uczucie niesmaku [**myah**-wem oo-**choo**-ćhe ńe-**smah**-koo] exp.: I had a feeling of disgust
niesnaska [ńes-**nahs**-kah] f. discord
niesnaski [ńes-**nahs**-kee] pl. dissension; discord; quarrels
niesnaski rodzinne [ńes-**nahs**-kee ro-**dźheen**-ne] exp.: family quarrels
niesnujowate [ńe-snoo-yo-**vah**-te] pl. Pamphilidae wasps, bees, sawflies, etc. with membranous wings
niesolidarnie [ńe-so-lee-**dahr**-ńe] adv. without solidarity
niesolidarność [ńe-so-lee-**dahr**-nośhćh] f. lack of solidarity
niesolidarny [ńe-so-lee-**dahr**-ni] adj.m. disloyal; not solidary
niesolidnie [ńe-so-**leed**-ńe] adv. unreliably; unconscientiously
niesolidność [ńe-so-**leed**-nośhćh] f. unreliability; unconscientious behavior
niesolidność w pracy [ńe-so-**leed**-nośhćh f **prah**-tsi] exp.: sloppy work; unreliable attitude towards work
niesolidny [ńe-so-**leed**-ni] adj.m. unreliable; unconscientious
niespanie [ńe-**spah**-ńe] n. lack of sleep; sleeplessness
niespawalny [ńe-spah-**vahl**-ni]

adj.m. unweldable; not weldable; not fit for welding
niespecjalista [ńe-spe-tsyah-**lees**-tah] m. layman; nonspecialist
niespecjalistyczny [ńe-spe-tsyah-lees-**tich**-ni] adj.m. outside of specialty
niespecjalnie [ńe-spe-**tsyahl**-ńe] adv. not especially
niespecjalny [ńe-spe-**tsyahl**-ni] adj.m. not special
niespełna [ńe-**spew**-nah] adv. nearly; not all; not quite; about; somewhat less than
niespełna rozumu [ńe-**spew**-nah ro-**zoo**-moo] exp.: crackbrained
w niespełna dwie godziny [v ńe-**spew**-nah dvye go-**dźhee**-ni] exp.: inside two hours
niespieralny [ńe-spye-**rahl**-ni] adj.m. not washable (color, etc.)
niespiesznie [ńe-**spyesh**-ńe] adv. without haste; deliberately; in a leisurely manner
niespieszny [ńe-**spyesh**-ni] adj.m. deliberate; leisurely
niesplik [**ńe**-spleek] m. medlar fruit; medlar tree (of the rose family)
niespłacalny [ńe-spwah-**tsahl**-ni] adj.m. unpayable
niespodzianie [ńe-spo-**dźhah**-ńe] adv. unexpectedly; unawares
niespodzianka [ńe-spo-**dźhahn**-kah] f. surprise; surprise gift
a to niespodzianka! [ah to ńe-spo-**dźhahn**-kah] exp.: what a surprise!
być przygotowanym na niespodzianki [bićh pshi-go-to-**vah**-nim nah ńe-spo-**dźhahn**-kee] exp.: to be ready for the unexpected
zrobić komuś niespodziankę [zro-beećh **ko**-moośh ńe-spo-**dźhahn**-kan] exp.: to give somebody a surprise
niespodziany [ńe-spo-**dźhah**-ni] adj.m. unexpected; unlooked for; unforeseen
niespodziewanie [ńe-spo-dźhe-**vah**-ńe] adv. unexpectedly; unawares
niespodziewany [ńe-spo-dźhe-**vah**-ni] adj.m. unexpected; unlooked for; unforeseen
niespodziewane odwiedziny [ńe-spo-dźhe-**vah**-ne od-vye-**dźhee**-ni] exp.: surprise visit
niespokojnie [ńe-spo-**koy**-ńe] adv. restlessly; uneasily; nervously
w okolicy jest niespokojnie [v o-ko-**lee**-tsi yest ńe-spo-**koy**-ńe] exp.: there is a restlessness in the neighborhood
niespokojny [ńe-spo-**koy**-ni] adj.m. restless; fussy; upset; fretful; turbulent; ill at ease
niespokojne czasy [ńe-spo-**koy**-ne **chah**-si] exp.: stormy days
niespokojne sumienie [ńe-spo-**koy**-ne soo-**mye**-ńe] exp.: guilty conscience
niespokojny koń [ńe-spo-**koy**-ni koń] exp.: skittish horse
niespokojny sen [ńe-spo-**koy**-ni sen] exp.: restless sleep
niespołeczny [ńe-spo-**wech**-ni] adj.m. unsocial; not communally owned
niesporczak [ńe-**spor**-chahk] m. tardigrade microscopic arthropod
niesporczaki [ńe-spor-**chah**-kee] pl. the Tardigrad arthropods; the phylum Tardigrada
niesporny [ńe-**spor**-ni] adj.m. undisputable; incontestable; not under dispute; not in litigation
niesporo [ńe-**spo**-ro] adv. slowly; sluggishly; torpidly
idzie mi niesporo [ee-dźhe mee ńe-**spo**-ro] exp.: I am progressing with difficulty; I am not doing very well
nie sposób [ńe **spo**-soop] exp.: it's impossible; by no means
niespostrzeżenie [ńe-spos-tshe-**zhe**-ńe] adv. imperceptibly; unnoticeably
niespotykany [ńe-spo-ti-**kah**-ni] adj.m. unheard-of; without parallel; nonexisting
niespożyty [ńe-spo-**zhi**-ti] adj.m. durable; indefatigable
niespójność [ńe-**spooy**-nośhćh] f. lack of cohesion
niespójny [ńe-**spooy**-ni] adj.m. incoherent; cohesionless
niesprawdzalność [ńe-sprahv-**dzahl**-nośhćh] f. lack of verifiableness;

lack of verifiability; impossibility to verify; impossibility to confirm
niesprawdzalny [ńe-sprahv-**dzahl**-ni] adj.m. unascertainable
niesprawiedliwie [ńe-sprah-vyed-**lee**-vye] adv. unjustly; wrongly; unfairly; inequitably
niesprawiedliwość [ńe-sprah-vyed-**lee**-vośhćh] f. injustice
niesprawiedliwy [ńe-sprah-vyed-**lee**-vi] adj.m. unjust; unfair; inequitable
być niesprawiedliwym [bićh ńe-sprah-vyed-**lee**-vim] exp.: to be unjust; to wrong (somebody)
niesprawnie [ńe-**sprahv**-ńe] adv. inefficiently
niesprawność [ńe-**sprahv**-nośhćh] f. inefficiency
niesprawny [ńe-**sprahv**-ni] adj.m. ineffective; inefficient
niesprężysty [ńe-spr<u>an</u>-**zhi**-sti] adj.m. not resilient; inelastic; inflexible
niesprzeciwianie się [ńe-spshe-ćhee-**vyah**-ńe śh<u>an</u>] n. passive submission; nonresistance
niesprzeczność [ńe-**spshech**-nośhćh] f. consistency
niesprzeczny [ńe-**spshech**-ni] adj.m. consistent
niesprzedajność [ńe-spshe-**dahy**-nośhćh] f. incorruptibility
niesprzedajny [ńe-spshe-**dahy**-ni] adj.m. incorruptible
niesprzedażny [ńe-spshe-**dahzh**-ni] adj.m. not for sale; unsalable
nie sprzyjający [ńe spshi-yah-**y<u>own</u>**-tsi] adj.m. adverse
niesrogi [ńe-**sro**-gee] adj.m. not severe; lenient; mild
niestabilny [ńe-stah-**beel**-ni] adj.m. unstable; wobbly
niestacjonarny [ńe-stah-tsyo-**nahr**-ni] adj.m. not stationary; nonstationary
niestale [ńe-**stah**-le] adv. irregularly; not constantly
niestałość [ńe-**stah**-wośhćh] f. inconstancy; instability
niestały [ńe-**stah**-wi] adj.m. shaky; unsteady; inconsistent; variable; fickle; wavery; shifting; wobbly
ludność niestała [**lood**-nośhćh ńe-**stah**-wah] exp.: floating population
niestała pogoda [ńe-**stah**-wah po-**go**-dah] exp.: unsettled weather
niestanowczość [ńe-stah-**nof**-chośhćh] f. lack of decisiveness; indecision; lack of finality
niestanowczy [ńe-stah-**nof**-chi] adj.m. lacking decision; undecided; indecisive
niestarannie [ńe-stah-**rahn**-ńe] adv. carelessly; neglectfully; slapdash
niestaranność [ńe-stah-**rahn**-nośhćh] f. carelessness; neglectfulness
niestaranny [ńe-stah-**rahn**-ni] adj.m. careless; sloppy; dowdy; neglectful; slapdash
niestarty [ńe-**stahr**-ti] adj.m. indelible
niestary [ńe-**stah**-ri] adj.m. not yet old; still full of vigor
niestatecznie [ńe-stah-**tech**-ńe] adv. unsedately; unstaidly; flightily; not steadily
niestateczność [ńe-stah-**tech**-nośhćh] f. instability; unstaidness; unsedatedness; flightiness; lack of steadiness
niestateczny [ńe-stah-**tech**-ni] adj.m. unstable; fickle; flighty; unstaid; unsedate; not steady
niestawiennictwo [ńe-stah-vyen-**ńeets**-tfo] n. nonappearance; absence
niestety [ńe-**ste**-ti] adv. alas; unfortunately; exp.: I am sorry
muszę niestety powiedzieć [moo-sh<u>an</u> ńe-**ste**-ti po-**vye**-dźhećh] exp.: I am sorry to say
niestety nie [ńe-**ste**-ti ńe] exp.: I am afraid not
niestety nie mogę [ńe-**ste**-ti ńe mo-g<u>an</u>] exp.: I'm sorry I can't do it
niestety on nie wróci [ńe-**ste**-ti on ńe **vroo**-ćhee] exp.: I'm afraid he will not come back
niestety tak [ńe-**ste**-ti tahk] exp.: I am afraid so
niestosownie [ńe-sto-**sov**-ńe] adv. unfittingly; unsuitably; inappropriately; tactlessly
zachować się niestosownie [zah-

kho-vahćh śhan ńe-sto-**sov**-ńe] exp.: to forget one's manners
niestosowność [ńe-sto-**sov**-nośhćh] f. unsuitableness; inappropriateness; irrelevancy; incorrectness
niestosowny [ńe-sto-**sov**-ni] adj.m. improper; unsuitable; unfit; inappropriate; out of place
niestrachliwy [ńe-strahkh-**lee**-vi] adj.m. not shy; not timid; unafraid
niestrawność [ńe-**strahv**-nośhćh] f. indigestion; dyspepsia; difficulty in digesting
cierpiący na niestrawność [ćher-**pyown**-tsi nah ńe-**strahv**-nośhćh] exp.: dyspeptic
niestrawny [ńe-**strahv**-ni] adj.m. indigestible; stodgy; dull
niestrojny [ńe-**stroy**-ni] adj.m. not dressy; unadorned; untrimmed
niestrudzenie [ńe-stroo-**dze**-ńe] adv. indefatigably; untiringly
niestrudzoność [ńe-stroo-**dzo**-nośhćh] f. diligence; tirelessness (at work, etc.)
niestrudzony [ńe-stroo-**dzo**-ni] adj.m. indefatigable; untiring
niestrzęp [**ńe**-stshanp] m. a butterfly of the family Pieridae
niestrzęp głogowiec [**ńe**-stshanp gwo-**go**-vyets] exp.: a butterfly of the family Pieridae
niestworzony [ńe-stfo-**zho**-ni] adj.m. unreal; nonsense; unbelievable
opowiadać niestworzone rzeczy [o-po-**vyah**-dahćh ńe-stfo-**zho**-ne **zhe**-chi] exp.: tell tall stories; tell tall tales
niestylowy [ńe-sti-**lo**-vi] adj.m. not stylish; unstylish
niesubiektywny [ńe-soo-byek-**tiv**-ni] adj.m. nonsubjective
niesubordynacja [ńe-soo-bor-di-**nahts**-yah] f. insubordination; lack of discipline; disobedience
niesubtelny [ńe-soop-**tel**-ni] adj.m. not subtle; unsubtle
niesumiennie [ńe-soo-**myen**-ńe] adv. unconscientiously; carelessly
niesumienność [ńe-soo-**myen**-nośhćh] f. dishonesty; unscrupulousness
niesumienny [ńe-soo-**myen**-ni] adj.m. unscrupulous; unconscientious; unreliable; careless
niesumienna robota [ńe-soo-**myen**-nah ro-**bo**-tah] exp.: sloppy work
nieswobodny [ńe-sfo-**bod**-ni] adj.m. not free; constrained
nieswoisty [ńe-sfo-**ees**-ti] adj.m. unspecific
nieswojo [ńe-**sfo**-yo] adv. uneasily; strangely; qualmishly
czuć się nieswojo [choośh śhan ńe-**sfo**-yo] exp.: to feel uneasy
nieswojski [ńe-**sfoy**-skee] adj.m. strange; foreign; not of one's native land
nieswojsko [ńe-**sfoy**-sko] adv. strangely
nieswój [**ńe**-sfooy] adj.m. ill at ease; uncomfortable; seedy; strange; off color
jestem (jakiś) nieswój [**yes**-tem (**yah**-keeśh) **ńe**-sfooy] exp.: I am not myself (altogether)
niesylabiczny [ńe-si-lah-**beech**-ni] adj.m. nonsyllabic; unsyllabic
niesymetrycznie [ńe-si-met-**rich**-ńe] adv. not symmetrically
niesymetryczność [ńe-si-met-**rich**-nośhćh] f. asymmetry
niesymetryczny [ńe-si-met-**rich**-ni] adj.m. asymmetrical
niesympatycznie [ńe-sim-pah-**tich**-ńe] adv. uncongenially; unpleasantly; in unfriendly manner
niesympatyczny [ńe-sim-pah-**tich**-ni] adj.m. unpleasant; unlikable; unengaging
niesystematycznie [ńe-sis-te-mah-**tich**-ńe] adv. not systematically; not methodically; haphazardly
niesystematyczność [ńe-sis-te-mah-**tich**-nośhćh] f. not systematical behavior; not methodical behavior
niesystematyczny [ńe-sis-te-mah-**tich**-ni] adj.m. not systematical; not methodical; haphazard
niesyty [ńe-**si**-ti] adj.m. unsated; unsatiated
nieszablonowo [ńe-shahb-lo-**no**-vo] adv. not tritely; in no

commonplace manner
nieszablonowość [ńe-shahb-lo-**no**-vośhćh] f. not commonplace feature
nieszablonowy [ńe-shahb-lo-**no**-vi] adj.m. not trite; not commonplace
nieszczególnie [ńe-shche-**gool**-ńe] adv. not particularly well; indifferently
wyglądać nieszczególnie [vig-**lown**-dahćh ńe-shche-**gool**-ńe] exp.: not to be at one's best; to look unattractive
nieszczególny [ńe-shche-**gool**-ni] adj.m. mediocre; so-so; not particularly good
nieszczelnie [ńe-**shchel**-ńe] adv. not hermetically; not tight
nieszczelność [ńe-**shchel**-nośhćh] f. lack of tightness; leak; escape (of gas, etc.)
nieszczelność drzwi [ńe-**shchel**-nośhćh dzhvee] exp.: draftiness of doors
w statku powstała nieszczelność [f **staht**-koo pof-**stah**-wah ńe-shchel-nośhćh] exp.: the ship sprang a leak
nieszczelny [ńe-**shchel**-ni] adj.m. leaky; not shut tight
nieszczelne drzwi [ńe-**shchel**-ne dzhvee] exp.: drafty door
nieszczelne okna [ńe-**shchel**-ne **ok**-nah] exp.: drafty windows
nieszczerość [ńe-**shche**-rośhćh] f. insincerity; double-dealing
nieszczery [ńe-**shche**-ri] adj.m. insincere; double-dealing; hypocritical; uncandid
nieszczery uśmiech [ńe-**shche**-ri **oośh**-myekh] exp.: constrained smile; insincere smile
nieszczerze [ńe-**shche**-zhe] adv. insincerely; uncandidly; falsely
nieszczęsny [ńe-**shchans**-ni] adj.m. miserable; ill-fated
nieszczęście [ńe-**shchanśh**-ćhe] n. misfortune; disaster; adversity; bad luck; misery; distress
na moje nieszczęście [nah **mo**-ye ńe-**shchanśh**-ćhe] exp.: to my misfortune
na nieszczęście [nah ńe-**shchanśh**-ćhe] exp.: unfortunately; unluckily
nieszczęścia chodzą parami [ńe-**shchanśh**-ćhah **kho**-dzown pah-**rah**-mee] exp.: it never rains but it pours
nieszczęściem [ńe-**shchanśh**-ćhem] exp.: by bad luck
seria nieszczęść [**ser**-yah ńe-shchanśhćh] exp.: a series of mishaps; a series of misfortunes
wyglądać jak nieszczęście [vig-**lown**-dahćh yahk ńe-**shchanśh**-ćhe] exp.: to look the very picture of misery
nieszczęśliwie [ńe-shchan-**śhlee**-vye] adv. unhappily; pitifully; miserably
tak się nieszczęśliwie złożyło [tahk śhan ńe-shchan-**śhlee**-vye zwo-**zhi**-wo] exp.: thus, an unhappy situation occurred
nieszczęśliwiec [ńe-shchan-**śhlee**-vyets] m. see: **nieszczęśnik**
nieszczęśliwy [ńe-shchan-**śhlee**-vi] adj.m. unhappy; ill-starred; ill-fated; luckless; wretched; ill-omened; distressed; unfortunate; miserable; unsuccessful; doomed
mieć nieszczęśliwą minę [myećh ńe-shchan-**śhlee**-vown **mee**-nan] exp.: to look wretched
mieć nieszczęśliwy wypadek [myećh ńe-shchan-**śhlee**-vi vi-**pah**-dek] exp.: to meet with an accident; to have an accident
nieszczęśliwa miłość [ńe-shchan-**śhlee**-vah **mee**-wośhćh] exp.: unhappy love
nieszczęśnica [ńe-shchanśh-**ńee**-tsah] f. unfortunate woman; wretched woman
nieszczęśnie [ńe-**shchanśh**-ńe] adv. unhappily; unfortunately; unluckily
nieszczęśnik [ńe-**shchanśh**-ńeek] m. (poor) wretch; poor devil; unfortunate fellow; ill-starred creature
nieszkodliwie [ńe-shko-**dlee**-vye] adv. harmlessly; not seriously
nieszkodliwość [ńe-shko-**dlee**-vośhćh] f. harmlessness; inoffensiveness
nieszkodliwy [ńe-shko-**dlee**-vi]

adj.m. harmless; not grave; inoffensive; innoxious
nieszlachcic [ńe-**shlahkh**-ćheets] m. commoner (not a noble)
nieszlachecki [ńe-shlah-**khets**-kee] adj.m. not of noble stock; not of noble birth
nieszlachetnie [ńe-shlah-**khet**-ńe] adv. basely; meanly; degradingly
nieszlachetność [ńe-shlah-**khet**-nośhćh] f. baseness; meanness
nieszlachetny [ńe-shlah-**khet**-ni] adj.m. base; mean; dishonorable
metale nieszlachetne [me-**tah**-le ńe-shlah-**khet**-ne] exp.: base metals
nieszpetnie [ńe-**shpet**-ńe] adv. handsomely; prettily
nieszpetny [ńe-**shpet**-ni] adj.m. fairly good-looking
nieszpory [ńe-**shpo**-ri] pl. vespers; evening prayers
dzwon na nieszpory [dzvon nah ńe-**shpo**-ri] exp.: vesper bell
nieszpory sycylijskie [ńe-**shpo**-ri si-tsi-**leey**-ske] exp.: Sicilian vespers
nieszpułka [ńe-**shpoow**-kah] f. medlar
niesztowica [ńe-shto-**vee**-tsah] f. ecthyma (cutaneous eruption)
niesztowice [ńe-shto-**vee**-tse] pl. ecthymata (skin disease)
niesztuczny [ńe-**shtooch**-ni] adj.m. not artificial; genuine
niesztywny [ńe-**shtiv**-ni] adj.m. not stiff; flexible; elastic
nieszykownie [ńe-shi-**kov**-ńe] adv. not smartly; without style; not in elegant manner
nieszykowny [ńe-shi-**kov**-ni] adj.m. inelegant; without style; not smart
nieściągalność [ńe-śhćhown-**gahl**-nośhćh] f. uncollectability (of a sum due)
nieściągalny [ńe-śhćhown-**gahl**-ni] adj.m. uncollectible
długi nieściągalne [dwoo-gee ńe-śhćhown-**gahl**-ne] exp.: bad debts; irrecoverable debts
nieścieralny [ńe-śhćhe-**rahl**-ni] adj.m. ineffaceable; indelible
nieścisłość [ńe-**śhćhees**-wośhćh] f. inexactitude; inaccuracy; error; want of precision; misstatement; incoherence
nieścisły [ńe-**śhćhees**-wi] adj.m. inexact; inaccurate; faulty; imprecise; incoherent
nieściśle [ńe-**śhćheeśh**-le] adv. in inaccurate manner (of reporting, etc.); not in a compact manner
nieściśliwość [ńe-śhćheeśh-**lee**-vośhćh] f. incompressibility
nieściśliwy [ńe-śhćheeśh-**lee**-vi] adj.m. incompressible
nieść [ńeśhćh] v. carry; bring; bear; lay; afford; drive; bear along; give as a sacrifice (*repeatedly*)
nieść komuś pomoc [ńeśhćh **ko**-moośh **po**-mots] exp.: to come to somebody's help
nieść pociechę [ńeśhćh po-**ćhe**-khan] exp.: to bring relief
wieść niesie, że [vyeśhćh ńe-śhe zhe] exp.: it is rumored that; a rumor is afloat that
nieść się [ńeśhćh śhan] v. speed along; spin along; flow; be borne; make headway; fly; wing one's way; be diffused; be wafted; drift; lay eggs (*repeatedly*)
nieślubny [ńe-**śhloob**-ni] adj.m. illegitimate; born out of wedlock; natural; unwedded
nieśmiało [ńe-**śhmyah**-wo] adv. shyly; bashfully; timidly; timorously
nieśmiałość [ńe-**śhmyah**-wośhćh] f. shyness; bashfulness; timidity; sheepishness; faint heart; coyness
nieśmiały [ńe-**śhmyah**-wi] adj.m. coy; shy; timid; fainthearted; bashful; sheepish
nieśmiertelnie [ńe-śhmyer-**tel**-ńe] adv. immortally; everlastingly; undyingly
nieśmiertelnik [ńe-śhmyer-**tel**-ńeek] m. an everlasting; xeranthemum (annual herb)
nieśmiertelność [ńe-śhmyer-**tel**-nośhćh] f. immortality; life everlasting
nieśmiertelny [ńe-śhmyer-**tel**-ni] adj.m. immortal; everlasting;

undying; imperishable
nieśmiertelni [ńe-śhmyer-tel-ńee] pl. the immortals
nieśna [ńeśh-nah] adj.f. laying (hen)
nieśna kura [ńeśh-nah koo-rah] exp.: laying hen
nieśność [ńeśh-nośhćh] f. egg laying
kontrola nieśności [kon-tro-lah ńeśh-nośh-ćhee] exp.: egg-laying test
nieśpiesznie [ńe-śhpyesh-ńe] adv. without haste; in leisurely manner; deliberately
nieśpiesznie mi [ńe-śhpyesh-ńe mee] exp.: I am in no hurry
nieśpieszny [ńe-śhpyesh-ni] adj.m. leisurely; deliberate
nieśpiewność [ńe-śhpyev-nośhćh] f. unmelodiousness
nieświadom [ńe-śhfyah-dom] adj.m. ignorant (of); unaware; unknowing (of); involuntary
nieświadomie [ńe-śhfyah-do-mye] adv. unknowingly; unconsciously; unawares; unwittingly
robić coś nieświadomie [ro-beećh tsośh ńe-śhfyah-do-mye] exp.: to be unconscious of doing something
nieświadomość [ńe-śhfyah-do-mośhćh] f. unconsciousness; ignorance; unawareness
nieświadomy [ńe-śhfyah-do-mi] adj.m. ignorant (of); unaware; unknowing (of); involuntary
nieświąteczny [ńe-śhfyown-tech-ni] adj.m. working (day)
dzień nieświąteczny [dźheń ńe-śhfyown-tech-ni] exp.: weekday
nieświetny [ńe-śhfyet-ni] adj.m. not outstandingly good; indifferent; nothing to boast about; nothing to boast of
nieświeżo [ńe-śhfye-zho] adv. in a stale manner; not freshly
nieświeżość [ńe-śhfye-zhośhćh] f. staleness; lack of freshness
nieświeży [ńe-śhfye-zhi] adj.m. not fresh; stale; bad; outdated
nietakt [ńe-tahkt] m. lack of tact; slip; tactlessness; indelicacy
nietaktownie [ńe-tahk-tov-ńe] adv. tactlessly
nietaktowność [ńe-tahk-tov-nośhćh] f. lack of tact; want of tact; slip; tactlessness; indelicacy
nietaktowny [ńe-tahk-tov-ni] adj.m. tactless; indelicate
nietaktyczny [ńe-tahk-tich-ni] adj.m. impolitic
nieterminowość [ńe-ter-mee-no-vośhćh] f. lack of punctuality
nieterminowy [ńe-ter-mee-no-vi] adj.m. unpunctual
nietęgi [ńe-tan-gee] adj.m. not very strong; wanting in strength; not particularly good; mediocre; indifferent
nietęgo [ńe-tan-go] adv. not particularly well; not quite satisfactorily; indifferently; poorly
nietknięty [ńe-tkńan-ti] adj.m. intact; virgin; untouched; unharmed
nietknięty ludzką stopą [ńe-tkńan-ti loots-kown sto-pown] exp.: untrodden; not touched by human foot
nietłukący [ńe-twoo-kown-tsi] adj.m. unbreakable
nietłusty [ńe-twoo-sti] adj.m. fat-free; oil-less
nietłuszczowy [ńe-twoosh-cho-vi] adj.m. fatless
nietoksyczny [ńe-tok-sich-ni] adj.m. nontoxic
nietolerancja [ńe-to-le-rahn-tsyah] f. intolerance
nietolerancyjnie [ńe-to-le-rahn-tsiy-ńe] adv. intolerantly; without toleration
nietolerancyjność [ńe-to-le-rahn-tsiy-nośhćh] f. lack of toleration
nietolerancyjny [ńe-to-le-rahn-tsiy-ni] adj.m. intolerant
nietoperz [ńe-to-pesh] m. bat; hurricane lantern
nietoperze [ńe-to-pe-zhe] pl. the order Chiroptera; bats
nietoperzowy [ńe-to-pe-zho-vi] adj.m. bat's; chiropterous
nietopliwość [ńe-to-plee-vośhćh] f. infusibility
nietopliwy [ńe-to-plee-vi] adj.m. infusible; nonmelting
nietota [ńe-to-tah] f. club moth

nietowarzyski [ńe-to-vah-**zhis**-kee] adj.m. unsociable
nietrafnie [ńe-**trahf**-ńe] adv. ineptly; inappropriately; not to the point
nietrafność [ńe-**trahf**-nośhćh] f. inaptness; inaptitude; inaccuracy; erroneousness; ineptitude
nietrafny [ńe-**trahf**-ni] adj.m. wrong; missing the mark
nietragiczny [ńe-trah-**geech**-ni] adj.m. not tragic
nietreściwy [ńe-treśh-**ćhee**-vi] adj.m. unsubstantial; trivial
nietrudno [ńe-**trood**-no] adv. easily; without difficulty
nietrudno zgadnąć [ńe-**trood**-no **zgahd**-nownćh] exp.: it is easy to guess
nietrudny [ńe-**trood**-ni] adj.m. not difficult; not hard; easy
nietrwale [ńe-**trfah**-le] adv. impermanently; not durably; unstably
nietrwałość [ńe-**trfah**-wośhćh] f. impermanence; lack of durability; transitoriness; instability; lability
nietrwały [ńe-**trfah**-wi] adj.m. impermanent; not durable; unstable
nietrwożnie [ńe-**trfozh**-ńe] adv. fearlessly
nietrwożny [ńe-**trfozh**-ni] adj.m. fearless
nietrzeźwość [ńe-**tsheźh**-vośhćh] f. intoxication
nietrzeźwy [ńe-**tsheźh**-vi] adj.m. drank; tipsy; unsound
w stanie nietrzeźwym [f **stah**-ńe ńe-**tsheźh**-vim] exp:. under the influence of drink
nietutejszy [ńe-too-**tey**-shi] adj.m. stranger; nonresident
nietuzinkowy [ńe-too-źheen-**ko**-vi] adj.m. not trite; not commonplace; not banal; above the ordinary
nietwardy [ńe-**tfahr**-di] adj.m. not hard; soft
nietwórczy [ńe-**tfoor**-chi] adj.m. uncreative; uninventive
nietykalność [ńe-ti-**kahl**-nośhćh] f. inviolability; privilege; immunity
nietykalność osobista [ńe-ti-**kahl**-nośhćh o-so-**bees**-tah] exp.: personal immunity
nietykalność poselska [ńe-ti-**kahl**-nośhćh po-**sel**-skah] exp.: parliamentary privilege
naruszenie nietykalności cielesnej [nah-roo-**she**-ńe ńe-ti-kahl-**nośh**-ćhee ćhe-**les**-ney] exp.: battery
nietykalny [ńe-ti-**kahl**-ni] adj.m. immune; inviolable; untouchable
nie tyle [ńe **ti**-le] exp.: not so much; not exactly; but; rather
nie tylko [ńe **til**-ko] exp.: not only; anything but; not merely
nietypowo [ńe-ti-**po**-vo] adv. not typically
nietypowość [ńe-ti-**po**-vośhćh] f. nontypical character; nontypicalness
nietypowy [ńe-ti-**po**-vi] adj.m. nontypical; untypical
nietzscheanizm [ńee-che-**ah**-ńeezm] m. Nietzscheism
nietzscheański [ńee-che-**ahń**-skee] adj.m. Nietzschean
nieubłagalny [ńe-oo-bwah-**gahl**-ni] adj.m. implacable; irrevocable
nieubłaganie [ńe-oo-bwah-**gah**-ńe] adv. relentlessly; implacably
nieubłagany [ńe-oo-bwah-**gah**-ni] adj.m. relentless; implacable; irrevocable
nieubogi [ńe-oo-**bo**-gee] adj.m. not badly off; not without money; not without funds; not impecunious
nieubogo [ńe-oo-**bo**-go] adv. not inexpensively; not without money; richly
nieuchronnie [ne-oo-**khron**-ńe] adv. inevitably; unavoidably
nieuchronność [ńe-oo-**khron**-nośhćh] f. inevitability; inescapableness
nieuchronny [ńe-oo-**khron**-ni] adj.m. inevitable; inescapable; unavoidable
nieuchronny los [ńe-oo-**khron**-ni los] exp.: fate; destiny; fatality
nieuchwytnie [ńe-oo-**khfit**-ńe] adv. elusively; unattainably; imperceptibly
nieuchwytność [ńe-oo-**khfit**-nośhćh] f. elusiveness; evasiveness; inaudibility; imperceptibility

nieuchwytny [ńe-oo-**khfit**-ni] adj.m. elusive; evasive; inaudible; imperceptible
nieuciążliwy [ńe-oo-ćhyown-**zhlee**-vi] adj.m. not burdensome; not troublesome
nieuctwo [ńe-**oots**-tfo] n. lack of education; ignorance
nieuczciwie [ńe-ooch-**ćhee**-vye] adv. dishonestly; fraudulently
nieuczciwie postąpić wobec kogoś [ńe-ooch-**ćhee**-vye po-**stown**-peećh **vo**-bets **ko**-gośh] exp.: to cheat somebody
nieuczciwiec [ńe-ooch-**ćhee**-vyets] m. (a) fraud
nieuczciwość [ńe-ooch-**ćhee**-vośhćh] f. dishonesty; fraud
nieuczciwy [ńe-ooch-**ćhee**-vi] adj.m. dishonest; foul; unfair
nieuczciwa konkurencja [ńe-ooch-**ćhee**-vah kon-koo-**ren**-tsyah] exp.: unfair competition
uzyskać coś w nieuczciwy sposób [oo-**zis**-kahćh tsośh v ńe-ooch-**ćhee**-vi **spo**-soop] exp.: to get something by dishonest means
nieuczenie [ńe-oo-**che**-ńe] adv. artlessly; in a simple manner
nieuczenie się [ńe-oo-**che**-ńe śhan] n. refusal to study
nieuczony [ńe-oo-**cho**-ni] adj.m. artless; unschooled; unlettered; unsophisticated
nieuczynny [ńe-oo-**chin**-ni] adj.m. unobliging; disobliging
nieudacznik [ńe-oo-**dahch**-ńeek] m. colloq: oaf; muff; milksop (Brit.); stick; slang: thief, who changed his specialty (mob jargon)
nieudały [ńe-oo-**dah**-wi] adj.m. unsuccessful; abortive; unhappy; infelicitous; colloq: puny
nieudany [ńe-oo-**dah**-ni] adj.m. unsuccessful; abortive; unhappy; infelicitous; colloq: puny
nieudany człowiek [ńe-oo-**dah**-ni **chwo**-vyek] exp.: (a) failure; (a) washout
nieudolnie [ńe-oo-**dol**-ńe] adv. inefficiently; ineffectively; fecklessly
nieudolnie coś załatwić [ńe-oo-**dol**-ńe tsośh zah-**wah**-tfeećh] exp.: to bungle something
nieudolnie posuwać się naprzód [ńe-oo-**dol**-ńe po-**soo**-vahćh śhan **nah**-pshoot] exp. to blunder along
nieudolność [ńe-oo-**dol**-nośhćh] f. inability; incompetence; clumsiness; ineffectiveness; inaptitude; incapacity; decrepitude
nieudolny [ńe-oo-**dol**-ni] adj.m. awkward; clumsy; decrepit; inefficient; ineffective
nieudolna administracja [ńe-oo-**dol**-nah ahd-mee-ńees-**trahts**-yah] exp.: maladministration
nieudolne starania [ńe-oo-**dol**-ne stah-**rah**-ńah] exp.: (a) flounder
nieufnie [ńe-**oof**-ńe] adv. distrustfully; suspiciously
nieufność [ńe-**oof**-nośhćh] f. mistrust
wotum nieufności [**vo**-toom ńe-oof-**nośh**-ćhee] exp.: vote of censure
nieufny [ńe-**oof**-ni] adj.m. distrustful; suspicious
nieugaszony [ńe-oo-gah-**sho**-ni] adj.m. unextinguished; unquenchable; unsuppressible
nieugięcie [ńe-oo-**gyan**-ćhe] adv. inflexibly; unyieldingly; relentlessly
nieugiętość [ńe-oo-**gyan**-tośhćh] f. inflexibility; relentlessness
nieugięty [ńe-oo-**gyan**-ti] adj.m. inflexible; unyielding; relentless
nieujarzmiony [ńe-oo-yahzh-**myo**-ni] adj.m. unsubdued
nieuk [ńe-ook] m. know-nothing
nieukładność [ńe-oo-**kwahd**-nośhćh] f. unmannerliness; uncouthness
nieukładny [ńe-oo-**kwahd**-ni] adj.m. unmannered; stiff
nieukojony [ńe-oo-ko-**yo**-ni] adj.m. inconsolable (grief, etc.)
nieuleczalnie [ńe-oo-le-**chahl**-ńe] adv. incurably
nieuleczalnie chory [ńe-oo-le-**chahl**-ńe **kho**-ri] exp.: incurable
nieuleczalność [ńe-oo-le-**chahl**-nośhćh] f. incurability
nieuleczalny [ńe-oo-le-**chahl**-ni] adj.m. incurable

nieulękły [ńe-oo-lank-wi] adj.m. fearless; undaunted
nieułomek [ńe-oo-**wo**-mek] m. not a weakling; rather strong man; colloq: well-built fellow
nieułomny [ńe-oo-**wom**-ni] adj.m. not crippled; rather handsome
nieumiarkowanie [ńe-oo-myahr-ko-**vah**-ńe] adv. immoderately; excessively; beyond measure; without restraint; n. immoderation; unrestraint; intemperance
nieumiarkowanie w piciu [ńe-oo-myahr-ko-**vah**-ńe f **pee**-ćhoo] exp.: intemperance
nieumiarkowany [ńe-oo-myahr-ko-**vah**-ni] adj.m. intemperate; immoderate; excessive; unrestrained
nieumiarkowany w piciu [ńe-oo-myahr-ko-**vah**-ni f **pee**-ćhoo] exp.: intemperate
nieumiejętnie [ńe-oo-mye-**yant**-ńe] adv. incompetently; unskillfully
nieumiejętność [ńe-oo-mye-**yant**-nośhćh] f. inability; unskillfulness
nieumiejętny [ńe-oo-mye-**yant**-ni] adj.m. inexpert; unskilled; incompetent
nieumyślnie [ńe-oo-**miśhl**-ńe] adv. unintentionally; inadvertently
nieumyślny [ńe-oo-**miśhl**-ni] adj.m. unintentional; accidental
nieunikniony [ńe-oo-ńeek-**ńo**-ni] adj.m. unavoidable; inevitable
wypadki są nieuniknione [vi-**paht**-kee sown ńe-oo-ńeek-**ńo**-ne] exp.: accidents will happen
nieuprawny [ńe-oo-**prahv**-ni] adj.m. uncultivated; untilled; waste (land)
nieuprzedzony [ńe-oo-pshe-**dzo**-ni] adj.m. unbiased; not forewarned; not prejudiced
nieuprzejmie [ńe-oo-**pshey**-mye] adv. impolitely; discourteously; unkindly; without compassion
nieuprzejmość [ńe-oo-**pshey**-mośhćh] f. impoliteness
nieuprzejmy [ńe-oo-**pshey**-mi] adj.m. impolite; discourteous; unkind; lacking compassion
nieurodzaj [ńe-oo-**ro**-dzahy] m. bad harvest; bad crops; scarcity (of crops, etc.)
nieurodzajność [ńe-oo-ro-**dzahy**-nośhćh] f. infertility; barrenness
nieurodzajny [ńe-oo-ro-**dzahy**-ni] adj.m. infertile; barren
nieurodzajny rok [ńe-oo-ro-**dzahy**-ni rok] exp.: lean year
nieurodziwy [ńe-oo-ro-**dźhee**-vi] adj.m. homely; not handsome; plain; uncomely; ill-favored (Brit.)
nieurzędowy [ńe-oo-zhan-**do**-vi] adj.m. unofficial; informal
nieusłuchany [ńe-oo-swoo-**khah**-ni] adj.m. disobedient
nieusłużny [ńe-oo-**swoozh**-ni] adj.m. disobliging
nieuspołeczniony [ńe-oo-spo-wech-**ńo**-ni] adj.m. privately owned; (man) devoid of civic spirit
nieusprawiedliwiony [ńe-oo-sprah-vye-dlee-**vyo**-ni] adj.m. unexcused; unjustified
nieustający [ńe-oos-tah-**yown**-tsi] adj.m. continual; steady; permanent; incessant; constant
nieustannie [ńe-oos-**tahn**-ńe] adv. incessantly; continually; perpetually
nieustanny [ńe-oos-**tahn**-ni] adj.m. constant; perpetual; unceasing; continual; incessant
nieustanny deszcz [ńe-oos-**tahn**-ni deshch] exp.: unceasing rain
nieustawny [ńe-oos-**tahv**-ni] adj.m. incommodious; awkward to furnish; cumbersome; unwieldy
nieustępliwie [ńe-oos-tan-**plee**-vye] adv. uncompromisingly; inflexibly
nieustępliwość [ńe-oos-tan-**plee**-vośhćh] f. uncompromising attitude; inflexibility; unyieldingness
nieustępliwy [ńe-oos-tan-**plee**-vi] adj.m. uncompromising; inflexible
nieustraszenie [ńe-oos-trah-**she**-ńe] adv. intrepidly; fearlessly
nieustraszoność [ńe-oos-trah-**sho**-nośhćh] f. intrepidity
nieustraszony [ńe-oos-trah-**sho**-ni] adj.m. fearless; intrepid
nieusuwalność [ńe-oo-soo-**vahl**-nośhćh] f. irremovability; permanence (of a judge, etc.)

nieusuwalny [ńe-oo-soo-**vahl**-ni] adj.m. immovable (object); irremovable (from office)
nieuszanowanie [ńe-oo-shah-no-**vah**-ńe] n. disrespect; disregard (of the law, etc.)
nie uszkodzony [**ńe** oosh-ko-**dzo**-ni] adj.m. unhurt; not hurt; undamaged; not damaged
nieutulony [ńe-oo-too-**lo**-ni] adj.m. inconsolable; broken-hearted; sick at heart; disconsolate
pozostali w nieutulonym żalu [po-zo-**stah**-lee v ńe-oo-too-**lo**-nim **zhah**-loo] exp.: the bereaved
nieuwaga [ńe-oo-**vah**-gah] f. inattention; absent-mindedness
chwila nieuwagi [**khfee**-lah ńe-oo-**vah**-gee] exp.: unguarded moment
przez nieuwagę [pshes ńe-oo-**vah**-gan] exp.: through inadvertence; by oversight
nieuważnie [ńe-oo-**vahzh**-ńe] adv. inattentively; inadvertently; carelessly; neglectfully
nieuważny [ńe-oo-**vahzh**-ni] adj.m. inattentive; careless
nieuzasadniony [ńe-oo-zah-sahd-**ńo**-ni] adj.m. unfounded; unjustified; groundless
nieuzbrojony [ńe-ooz-bro-**yo**-ni] adj.m. unarmed; disarmed
nieuzdolniony [ńe-ooz-dol-**ńo**-ni] adj.m. untalented; skill-less
nieużytecznie [ńe-oo-zhi-**tech**-ńe] adv. uselessly
nieużyteczność [ńe-oo-zhi-**tech**-nośhćh] f. uselessness
nieużyteczny [ńe-oo-zhi-**tech**-ni] adj.m. useless; superfluous
nieużytek [ńe-oo-**zhi**-tek] m. (a) barren; useless object
nieużytki [ńe-oo-**zhit**-kee] pl. waste land
nieużyty [ńe-oo-**zhi**-ti] adj.m. unused; not worn; uncooperative; disobliging
człowiek nieużyty [**chwo**-vyek ńe-oo-**zhi**-ti] exp.: uncooperative person; colloq: hedgehog
niewart [**ńe**-vahrt] adj.m. not worth; unworthy (of reward, praise, etc.); not deserving
gra niewarta świeczki [grah ńe-**vahr**-tah **śhfyech**-kee] exp.: the game is not worth the candle
niewart funta kłaków [**ńe**-vahrt **foon**-tah **kwah**-koof] exp.: not worth a hoot; not worth a rush (Brit.)
nie warto [ńe **vahr**-to] exp.: adv. not worth (talking about it); not worthwhile (considering it)
nieważki [ńe-**vahsh**-kee] adj.m. imponderable; trivial; trifling
nieważkość [ńe-**vahsh**-kośhćh] f. weightlessness
nieważnie [ńe-**vahzh**-ńe] adv. unimportantly; unessentially; triflingly; invalidly; without validity
nieważność [ńe-**vahzh**-nośhćh] f. invalidity; triviality
nieważny [ńe-**vahzh**-ni] adj.m. invalid; trivial; null and void; unimportant
niewąski [ńe-**vowns**-kee] adj.m. colloq: very big; extraordinary; not just any
niewąsko [ńe-**vowns**-ko] adv. colloq: on a grand scale; in a big way
niewątpliwie [ńe-vownt-**plee**-vye] adv. undoubtedly; no doubt
niewątpliwy [ńe-vownt-**plee**-vi] adj.m. sure; doubtless; unquestionable
niewczas [**ńe**-fchahs] m. untimeliness
po niewczasie [po ńe-**fchah**-śhe] exp.: too late; after the event
niewczesność [ńe-**fches**-nośhćh] f. untimeliness; unseasonableness
niewczesny [ńe-**fches**-ni] adj.m. untimely; late; ill-timed; inopportune; premature
niewdzięcznica [ńe-vdźhanch-**ńee**-tsah] f. ungrateful woman (girl)
niewdzięcznie [ńe-**vdźhanch**-ńe] adv. ungratefully; thanklessly
niewdzięcznik [ńe-**vdźhanch**-ńeek] m. ungrateful fellow
niewdzięczność [ńe-**vdźhanch**-nośhćh] f. ingratitude
czarna niewdzięczność [**chahr**-nah ńe-**vdźhanch**-nośhćh] exp.: black ingratitude
niewdzięczny [ńe-**vdźhanch**-ni]

adj.m. ungrateful; thankless
niewdzięczna robota [ńe-vdźh**an**ch-nah ro-**bo**-tah] exp.: unrewarding task
niewdzięczny wiek [ńe-vdźh**an**ch-ni vyek] exp.: the awkward age
niewerbalny [ńe-ver-**bahl**-ni] adj.m. nonverbal
niewesoło [ńe-ve-**so**-wo] adv. without joy; sadly
sytuacja wyglądała niewesoło [si-too-**ah**-tsyah vi-gl**own**-**dah**-wah ńe-ve-**so**-wo] exp.: things looked pretty bad
niewesoły [ńe-ve-**so**-wi] adj.m. sad; joyless; pretty bad
niewesoła mina [ńe-ve-**so**-wah mee-nah] exp.: a long face
niewiadoma [ńe-vyah-**do**-mah] f. (math.) unknown quantity
niewiadome [ńe-vyah-**do**-me] n. the unknown
w niewiadome [v ńe-vyah-**do**-me] exp.: into the unknown
niewiadomy [ńe-vyah-**do**-mi] adj.m. unknown (direction, origin, quantity, reason, etc.)
niewiara [ńe-**vyah**-rah] f. disbelief (in); mistrust (of); unbelief
niewiara we własne siły [ńe-**vyah**-rah ve **vwahs**-ne **śhee**-wi] exp.: diffidence; self-distrust
niewiarogodnie [ńe-vyah-ro-**god**-ńe] adv. incredibly; unbelievably
niewiarogodność [ńe-vyah-ro-**god**-nośhćh] f. lack of credibility
niewiarogodny [ńe-vyah-ro-**god**-ni] adj.m. incredible; unbelievable
niewiarygodnie [ńe-vyah-ri-**god**-ńe] adv. incredibly; unbelievably
niewiarygodność [ńe-vyah-ri-**god**-nośhćh] f. lack of credibility
niewiarygodny [ńe-vyah-ri-**god**-ni] adj.m. incredible; unbelievable
to jest wprost niewiarygodne [to yest fprost ńe-vyah-ri-**god**-ne] exp.: it is past all belief
niewiasta [ńe-**vyahs**-tah] f. woman
niewiązany [ńe-vy**own**-**zah**-ni] adj.m. in prose; not tied together
mowa niewiązana [**mo**-vah ńe-vy**own**-**zah**-nah] exp.: prose
niewidka [ńe-**veet**-kah] f. in exp.:
czapka niewidka [**chahp**-kah ńe-**veet**-kah] exp.: cap of invisibility
niewidocznie [ńe-vee-**doch**-ńe] adv. invisibly; imperceptibly
niewidoczny [ńe-vee-**doch**-ni] adj.m. invisible; unseen
być niewidocznym [bićh ńe-vee-**doch**-nim] exp.: to be out of sight; to be out of eyeshot
niewidoma [ńe-vee-**do**-mah] adj.f. & f. (female) blind; lacking sight
niewidomy [ńe-vee-**do**-mi] adj.m. & m. blind; lacking sight
niewidomi [ńe-vee-**do**-mee] pl. the blind
niewidząco [ńe-vee-**dzown**-tso] adv. without seeing
patrzeć niewidząco [**pah**-tshećh ńe-vee-**dzown**-tso] exp.: to look with unseeing eyes
niewidzenie [ńe-vee-**dze**-ńe] n. failure to see; failure to notice; overlooking (of); shutting one's eyes (to)
niewidzenie się [ńe-vee-**dze**-ńe śh**an**] n. separation
niewidzialnie [ńe-vee-**dźhahl**-ńe] adv. invisibly
niewidzialność [ńe-vee-**dźhahl**-nośhćh] f. invisibility
niewidzialny [ńe-vee-**dźhahl**-ni] adj.m. invisible; obscure
promienie niewidzialne [pro-**mye**-ńe ńe-vee-**dźhahl**-ne] exp.: obscure rays
niewidziany [ńe-vee-**dźhah**-ni] adj.m. unseen; unprecedented; extraordinary
niewiedza [ńe-**vye**-dzah] f. ignorance (of); unawareness
niewiele [ńe-**vye**-le] adv. not much; not many; little; few
niewiele brakowało, żeby go zabiło [ńe-**vye**-le brah-ko-**vah**-wo **zhe**-bi go zah-**bee**-wo] exp.: he very nearly got killed
niewiele myśląc [ńe-**vye**-le **miśh**-l**own**ts] exp.: immediately; quick as a flash
niewielki [ńe-**vyel**-kee] adj.m. small; little; unimportant
niewielka nadzieja [ńe-**vyel**-kah nah-**dźhe**-yah] exp.: slender hope
niewielka rzecz [ńe-**vyel**-kah

zhech] exp.: a trifle
niewielkiego wzrostu [ńe-vyel-k̲e-go **vzros**-too] exp.: rather short of statue
niewielkim kosztem [ńe-**vyel**-keem **ko**-shtem] exp.: at no great expense
niewielu [ńe-**vye**-loo] num. not much; not many; little; few
niewielu nas było [ńe-**vye**-loo nahs **bi**-wo] exp.: we were few; there were not many of us
niewiernie [ńe-**vyer**-ńe] adv. not faithfully; inaccurately
niewierność [ńe-**vyer**-nośhćh] f. unfaithfulness; faithlessness; disloyalty; infidelity
niewierny [ńe-**vyer**-ni] adj.m. disloyal; infidel; unfaithful; inaccurate
niewierna żona [ńe-**vyer**-nah **zho**-nah] exp.: unfaithful wife
niewierny mąż [ńe-**vyer**-ni mownsh] exp.: unfaithful husband
niewierny Tomasz [ńe-**vyer**-ni **to**-mahsh] exp.: doubting Thomas
niewierząca [ńe-vye-**zhown**-tsah] f. & adj.f. unbelieving; not religious
niewierzący [ńe-vye-**zhown**-tsi] m. & adj.m. unbelieving; unreligious
niewieści [ńe-**vyeśh**-ćhee] adj.m. womanly; feminine
niewieścieć [ńe-**vyeśh**-ćhećh] v. become effeminate; acquire female characteristics (*repeatedly*)
niewieściuch [ńe-**vyeśh**-ćhookh] m. effeminate man; sissy; pantywaist; mollycoddle (Brit.)
niewiniątko [ńe-vee-**nownt**-ko] n. (an) innocent; infant
rzeź niewiniątek [zheśh ńe-vee-**ńown**-tek] exp.: Massacre of the Innocents
niewinnie [ńe-**veen**-ńe] adv. innocently; guiltlessly; harmlessly
niewinnie wyglądający [ńe-**veen**-ńe vig-**lown**-dah-**yown**-tsi] exp.: innocent-looking
niewinność [ńe-**veen**-nośhćh] f. innocence; purity; chastity; unsophistication
niewinny [ńe-**veen**-ni] adj.m. not guilty; innocent; harmless
przybrać niewinną minę [pshi-brahćh ńe-**veen**-nown **mee**-nan] exp.: to put on an innocent air
niewiotki [ńe-**vyot**-kee] adj.m. inflexible
niewładny [ńe-**vwahd**-ni] adj.m. torpid; palsied; unable to move
niewłaściwie [ńe-vwahśh-**ćhee**-vye] adv. unsuitably; inappropriately; wrongly
niewłaściwość [ńe-vwahśh-**ćhee**-vośhćh] f. impropriety; unsuitableness
niewłaściwość sądu [ńe-vwahśh-**ćhee**-vośhćh **sown**-doo] exp.: improper jurisdiction
niewłaściwy [ńe-vwahśh-**ćhee**-vi] adj.m. improper; unsuitable; wrong; inappropriate
niewłaściwy wyraz [ńe-vwahśh-**ćhee**-vi **vi**-rahs] exp.: the wrong word
pójść niewłaściwą drogą [pooyśhćh ńe-vwahśh-**ćhee**-vown **dro**-gown] exp.: to go wrong; to take the wrong way
ułamek niewłaściwy [oo-**wah**-mek ńe-vwahśh-**ćhee**-vi] exp.: improper fraction
niewłóknisty [ńe-vwook-**ńees**-ti] adj.m. not fibered; not fibrous
niewodny [ńe-**vod**-ni] adj.m. anhydrous
niewojenny [ńe-vo-**yen**-ni] adj.m. peaceful; peacetime (activities, etc.)
niewojowniczy [ńe-vo-yov-**ńee**-chi] adj.m. unwarlike; not bellicose; peaceful
niewojskowy [ńe-voy-**sko**-vi] adj.m. not military; civil (aviation, etc.); civilian
niewola [ńe-**vo**-lah] f. captivity; bondage; servitude; slavery
dostać się do niewoli [**dos**-tahćh śhan do ńe-**vo**-lee] exp.: to be taken prisoner
wziąć kogoś do niewoli [vźhownćh **ko**-gośh do ńe-**vo**-lee] exp.: to take somebody prisoner
niewolący [ńe-vo-**lown**-tsi] adj.m. irresistible
niewolenie [ńe-vo-**le**-ńe] n. restraint; compulsion; oppression

niewolić [ńe-**vo**-leećh] v. enslave; compel; oppress; constrain (*repeatedly*)
niewolnica [ńe-vol-**ńee**-tsah] f. (female) slave; serf; war-prisoner
niewolnica mody [ńe-vol-**ńee**-tsah **mo**-di] exp.: slave of fashion
niewolnictwo [ńe-vol-**ńee**-tstfo] n. slavery
niewolniczo [ńe-vol-**ńee**-cho] adv. slavishly; servilely
niewolniczość [ńe-vol-**ńee**-chośhćh] f. slavery
niewolniczy [ńe-vol-**ńee**-chi] adj.m. slavish
niewolnik [ńe-**vol**-ńeek] m. slave; serf; prisoner of war
handel niewolnikami [**khahn**-del ńe-vol-ńee-**kah**-mee] exp.: slave trade
niewolnik mody [ńe-**vol**-ńeek **mo**-di] exp.: slave of fashion
poganiacz niewolników [po-**gah**-ńahch ńe-vol-**ńee**-koof] exp.: slave driver
statek do przewozu niewolników [stah-tek do pshe-**vo**-zoo ńe-vol-**ńee**-koof] exp.: slave ship
uczynić kogoś niewolnikiem [oo-chi-ńeećh **ko**-gośh ńe-vol-**ńee**-kem] exp.: to enslave somebody
zrobić z kogoś niewolnika [**zro**-beećh s **ko**-gośh ńe-vol-**ńee**-kah] exp.: to enslave somebody
nie wolno [ńe **vol**-no] exp.: not allowed; not permitted
niewolny [ńe-**vol**-ni] adj.m. enslaved; m. bondsman; slave; serf
niewonny [ńe-**von**-ni] adj.m. odorless; colloq: fetid
niewód [**ńe**-voot] m. dragnet
niewprawnie [**ńe-fprahv**-ńe] adv. ineptly; inexpertly; incompetently; clumsily; awkwardly; inefficiently
niewprawność [ńe-**fprahv**-nośhćh] f. ineptness; ineptitude; lack of skill; inefficiency; awkwardness
niewprawny [ńe-**fprahv**-ni] adj.m. unversed; unskilled; inexpert; incompetent; clumsy; awkward; inefficient; inept
niewrażliwość [ńe-vrahzh-**lee**-vośhćh] f. insensibility (to); stolidity
niewrażliwy [ńe-vrahzh-**lee**-vi] adj.m. insensible; unemotional
niewskazany [ńe-fskah-**zah**-ni] adj.m. inadvisable
niewspółczesność [ńe-fspoow-**ches**-nośhćh] f. not a contemporary character; uncontemporariness
niewspółczesny [ńe-fspoow-**ches**-ni] adj.m. uncontemporary; not contemporary; uncontemporaneous
niewspółcześnie [ńe-fspoow-**cheśh**-ńe] adv. in uncontemporary fashion
niewspółmiernie [ńe-fspoow-**myer**-ńe] adv. incommensurably; incomparably
niewspółmierność [ńe-fspoow-**myer**-nośhćh] f. incommensurability
niewspółmierny [ńe-fspoow-**myer**-ni] adj.m. incommensurable; out of proportion
odcinki niewspółmierne [ot-**ćheen**-kee ńe-fspoow-**myer**-ne] exp.: incommensurable segments
niewspółosiowy [ńe-fspoow-o-**śho**-vi] adj.m. noncoaxial
niewspółrzędny [ńe-fspoow-**zhand**-ni] adj.m. noncoordinate
niewspółśrodkowy [ńe-fspoow-śhrot-**ko**-vi] adj.m. nonconcentric
niewstrzemięźliwie [ńe-fstshe-myanźh-**lee**-vye] adv. immoderately; unrestrainedly
niewstrzemięźliwość [ńe-fstshe-myanźh-**lee**-vośhćh] f. lack of moderation; lack of restraint; intemperance
niewstrzemięźliwy [ne-fstshe-myanźh-**lee**-vi] adj.m. immoderate; unrestrained; intemperate
nie wtajemniczony [ńe ftah-yem-ńee-**cho**-ni] adj.m. uninitiated; uninformed; not privy
niewulkaniczny [ńe-vool-kah-**ńeech**-ni] adj.m. nonvolcanic
niewybaczalny [ńe-vi-bah-**chahl**-ni] adj.m. unpardonable; inexcusable
niewybredność [ńe-vi-**bred**-nośhćh] f. indiscrimination; lack

of discrimination; absence of fastidiousness; unrefined taste
niewybredny [ńe-vi-**bred**-ni] adj.m. easy to please; indiscriminate; not choosy; not fastidious
niewybuch [ńe-**vi**-bookh] m. dud; a bomb or missile that fails to explode
niewyczerpalny [ńe-vi-cher-**pahl**-ni] adj.m. inexhaustible; unfailing; never-failing
niewyczerpany [ńe-vi-cher-**pah**-ni] adj.m. inexhaustible; unfailing; never-failing
niewyczuwalny [ńe-vi-choo-**vahl**-ni] adj.m. imperceptible; impalpable
niewydajnie [ńe-vi-**dahy**-ńe] adv. inefficiently
niewydajność [ńe-vi-**dahy**-nośhćh] f. inefficiency; lack of productivity
niewydajny [ńe-vi-**dahy**-ni] adj.m. inefficient; unproductive
niewydarzony [ńe-vi-dah-**zho**-ni] adj.m. unsuccessful; incompetent
niewydolność [ńe-vi-**dol**-nośhćh] f. incapacity; inefficiency
niewydolność lewokomorowa [ńe-vi-**dol**-nośhćh le-vo-ko-mo-**ro**-vah] exp.: dyspnoeic heart failure
niewydolny [ńe-vi-**dol**-ni] adj.m. inefficient
niewygadany [ńe-vi-gah-**dah**-ni] adj.m. close-tongued; voluble (talker)
niewygasły [ńe-vi-**gahs**-wi] adj.m. unextinguished; unexpired; inextinguishable
niewygoda [ńe-vi-**go**-dah] f. discomfort; trouble; hardship; inconvenience
narażać kogoś na niewygodę [ńah-**rah**-zhahćh **ko**-gośh nah ńe-vi-**go**-dan] exp.: to put somebody to inconvenience
znosić niewygody [**zno**-śheećh ńe-vi-**go**-di] exp.: to suffer hardships; colloq: to rough it
niewygodnie [ńe-vi-**god**-ńe] adv. uncomfortably; inconveniently
niewygodny [ńe-vi-**god**-ni] adj.m. uncomfortable; awkward; inconvenient
znaleźć się w niewygodnym położeniu [**znah**-leśhćh śhan v ńe-vi-**god**-nim po-wo-**zhe**-ńoo] exp.: to be awkwardly situated
niewykluczone [ńe-vi-kloo-**cho**-ne] exp.: possibly; probably
niewykluczone, że przyjdzie [ńe-vi-kloo-**cho**-ne zhe **pshiy**-dźhe] exp.: it is very likely that he will come
niewykluczony [ńe-vi-kloo-**cho**-ni] adj.m. possible; probable
niewykonalność [ńe-vi-ko-**nahl**-nośhćh] f. impracticability; infeasibility
niewykonalny [ńe-vi-ko-**nahl**-ni] adj.m. unfeasible; unworkable; impracticable
niewykształcony [ńe-vi-kshtahw-**tso**-ni] adj.m. uneducated; untaught
niewykwalifikowany [ńe-vi-kfah-lee-fee-ko-**vah**-ni] adj.m. not qualified
niewykwintny [ńe-vi-**kfeent**-ni] adj.m. inelegant; unrefined
niewymagający [ńe-vi-mah-gah-yown-tsi] adj.m. easygoing (teacher, etc.); lenient; not strict
niewymawialny [ńe-vi-mah-**vyahl**-ni] adj.m. unpronounceable; colloq: unmentionable
niewymienny [ńe-vi-**myen**-ni] adj.m. noninterchangeable; unconvertible
niewymienny na złoto [ńe-vi-**myen**-ni nah **zwo**-to] exp.: irredeemable
niewymierny [ńe-vi-**myer**-ni] adj.m. irrational; surd
liczba niewymierna [**leedzh**-bah ńe-vi-**myer**-nan] exp.: irrational number (a number that cannot be expressed as the quotient of two integers: a surd, the pi, etc.)
niewymierzalny [ńe-vi-mye-**zhahl**-ni] adj.m. incommensurable
niewymownie [ńe-vi-**mov**-ńe] adv. unutterably; inexpressibly; ineffably
niewymowny [ńe-vi-**mov**-ni] adj.m. unspeakable; inexpressible; unutterable; ineffable; ineloquent
niewymowne [ńe-vi-**mov**-ne] pl. unmentionables; underwear
niewymuszoność [ńe-vi-moo-**sho**-nośhćh] f. lack of constraint;

naturalness
niewymuszony [ńe-vi-moo-**sho**-ni] adj.m. unconstrained; voluntary; natural; unaffected
niewymyślnie [ńe-vi-**miśhl**-ńe] adv. not fastidiously; plainly; simply
niewymyślny [ńe-vi-**miśhl**-ni] adj.m. unsophisticated; plain; not choosy; easy to please; simple
niewyobrażalny [ńe-vi-ob-rah-**zhahl**-ni] adj.m. unimaginable
niewypał [ńe-**vi**-pahw] m. dud; misfire; blind shell
usuwanie niewypałów [oo-soo-**vah**-ńe ńe-vi-**pah**-woof] exp.: bomb disposal
niewyparzony [ńe-vi-pah-**zho**-ni] adj.m. foul (language, etc.)
mieć niewyparzoną gębę [myećh ńe-vi-pah-**zho**-nown **gan**-ban] exp.: to be foulmouthed; to be foul-tongued
niewypłacalność [ńe-vi-pwah-**tsahl**-nośhćh] f. insolvency
ogłosić niewypłacalność [o-**gwo**-śheećh ńe-vi-pwah-**tsahl**-nośhćh] exp.: to declare oneself insolvent
niewypłacalny [ńe-vi-pwah-**tsahl**-ni] adj.m. insolvent
niewypłacalny dłużnik [ńe-vi-pwah-**tsahl**-ni **dwoozh**-ńeek] exp.: (an) insolvent
niewypowiedzianie [ńe-vi-po-vye-**dźhah**-ńe] adv. inexpressibly; unutterably; ineffably; beyond words
niewypowiedziany [ńe-vi-po-vye-**dźhah**-ni] adj.m. untold; unspeakable; inexpressible
niewyprawny [ńe-vi-**prahv**-ni] adj.m. untanned; not tanned; crude
niewyrazistość [ńe-vi-rah-**źhees**-tośhćh] f. inexpressiveness
niewyrazisty [ńe-vi-rah-**źhees**-ti] adj.m. inexpressive
niewyraźnie [ńe-vi-**rahźh**-ńe] adv. indistinctly; seedily
mówić niewyraźnie [**moo**-veećh ńe-vi-**rahźh**-ńe] exp.: to speak indistinctly
czuć się niewyraźnie [chooćh śhan ńe-vi-**rahźh**-ńe] exp.: to feel not assured; not to feel well
niewyraźność [ńe-vi-**rahźh**-nośhćh] f. indistinctness; vagueness
niewyraźny [ńe-vi-**rahźh**-ni] adj.m. queer; indistinct; faint; dim; obscure; vague; inexplicit
niewyraźna mowa [ńe-vi-**rahźh**-nah **mo**-vah] exp.: mumble
z niewyraźną miną [z ńe-vi-**rahźh**-nown **mee**-nown] exp.: lacking self-confidence; lacking self-assurance
niewyrażalny [ńe-vi-rah-**zhahl**-ni] adj.m. inexpressible
niewyrobienie [ńe-vi-ro-**bye**-ńe] n. immaturity; rawness; inexperience
niewyrobiony [ńe-vi-ro-**byo**-ni] adj.m. raw; inexperienced; immature; untrained
niewyrozumiałość [ńe-vi-ro-zoo-**myah**-wośhćh] f. lack of forbearance; strictness
niewyrozumiały [ńe-vi-ro-zoo-**myah**-wi] adj.m. intolerant; strict; not forbearing
niewysłowienie [ńe-vi-swo-**vye**-ńe] adv. ineffably; inexpressibly; unspeakably; unutterably
niewysłowienie się [ńe-vi-swo-**vye**-ńe śhan] n. failure to verbalize
niewysłowiony [ńe-vi-swo-**vyo**-ni] adj.m. ineffable; inexpressible; unspeakable; unutterable
niewysoki [ńe-vi-**so**-kee] adj.m. not very high; rather low
niewysoko [ńe-vi-**so**-ko] adv. not very highly; rather low
niewyspany [ńe-vis-**pah**-ni] adj.m. sleepy (one that did not have enough sleep); heavy with sleep
jestem niewyspany [**yes**-tem ńe-vis-**pah**-ni] exp.: I am sleepy; I have not slept enough
niewystarczająco [ńe-vis-tahr-chah-**yown**-tso] adv. inadequately; insufficiently; unsatisfactorily
niewystarczający [ńe-vis-tahr-chah-**yown**-tsi] adj.m. insufficient; inadequate
niewystarczalność [ńe-vis-tahr-**chahl**-nośhćh] f. insufficiency; inadequacy
niewystawny [ńe-vis-**tahv**-ni] adj.m. frugal; modest; simple

niewysuwalny [ńe-vi-soo-**vahl**-ni] adj.m. immovable; fixed
niewyszukany [ńe-vi-shoo-**kah**-ni] adj.m. homely; simple; unsophisticated
niewytłumaczalny [ńe-vi-twoo-mah-**chahl**-ni] adj.m. inexplicable; incomprehensible
niewytłumaczony [ńe-vi-twoo-mah-**cho**-ni] adj.m. inexplicable; incomprehensible
niewytrawny [ńe-vi-**trahv**-ni] adj.m. inexperienced; not dry (wine)
niewytrwały [ńe-vi-**trfah**-wi] adj.m. not persistent
niewytrzymały [ńe-vi-tshi-**mah**-wi] adj.m. not enduring; not resistant; sensitive
niewytworność [ńe-vi-**tfor**-nośhćh] f. inelegance; lack of style; lack of refinement
niewytworny [ńe-vi-**tfor**-ni] adj.m. inelegant; unrefined
niewywłaszczalny [ńe-vi-vwahsh-**chahl**-ni] adj.m. not subject to expropriation
niewywrotny [ńe-vi-**vrot**-ni] adj.m. stable; not capsizeable; self-righting; not to be overturned
niewyzbywalny [ńe-vi-zbi-**vahl**-ni] adj.m. unrelinquishable
niewyznaczalny [ńe-vi-znah-**chahl**-ni] adj.m. undeterminable
niewyżyty [ńe-vi-**zhi**-ti] adj.m. unappeased
niewzajemność [ńe-vzah-**yem**-nośhćh] f. unreciprocated feeling; unreciprocated sentiment
niewzajemny [ńe-vzah-**yem**-ni] adj.m. unreciprocated
niewzruszalność [ńe-vzroo-**shahl**-nośhćh] f. immovability; imperturbability; firmness
niewzruszalny [ńe-vzroo-**shahl**-ni] adj.m. immovable; imperturbable; firm
niewzruszenie [ńe-vzroo-**she**-ńe] adv. unchangeably; firmly; without motion; invariably
niewzruszoność [ńe-vzroo-**sho**-nośhćh] f. rigidity; inflexibility; imperturbability; impassivity; uninfringeability; immovability; unyieldingness; inexorability; inexorableness
niewzruszony [ńe-vzroo-**sho**-ni] adj.m. unmoved; rigid; inflexible; imperturbable; uninfringeable; immovable; unyielding; impassive; inexorable; insensitive
niezaangażowanie [ńe-zah-ahn-gah-zho-**vah**-ńe] n. disengagement
niezaangażowany [ńe-zah-ahn-gah-zho-**vah**-ni] adj.m. not engaged; not interested; not involved
niezabawnie [ńe-zah-**bahv**-ńe] adv. unamusingly; in dull fashion
niezabawny [ńe-zah-**bahv**-ni] adj.m. unamusing; uninteresting; dull
niezabudka [ńe-zah-**boot**-kah] f. forget-me-not; myosote
niezachwianie [ńe-zah-**khfyah**-ńe] adv. in an unshaken manner; in an undeterred manner; in an unwavering manner
niezachwiany [ńe-zah-**khfyah**-ni] adj.m. unshaken; undeterred; unwavering
niezadługo [ńe-zah-**dwoo**-go] adv. soon; in a short time
niezadowalający [ńe-zah-do-vah-lah-**yown**-sti] adj.m. unsatisfactory
niezadowolenie [ńe-zah-do-vo-**le**-ńe] n. discontent; displeasure
niezadowolony [ńe-zah-do-vo-**lo**-ni] adj.m. dissatisfied; displeased (with); unsatisfied; discontented (with); disgruntled
ustawicznie niezadowolony [oos-tah-**veech**-ńe ńe-zah-do-vo-**lo**-ni] exp.: querulous
wiecznie niezadowolony [vyech-ńe ńe-zah-do-vo-**lo**-ni] exp.: querulous
niezakłócony [ńe-zah-kwoo-**tso**-ni] adj.m. undisturbed; unmarred
niezakrzepły [ńe-zah-**kshep**-wi] adj.m. uncoagulated
niezależnie [ńe-zah-**lezh**-ńe] adv. independently; irrespective; beside
niezależność [ńe-zah-**lezh**-nośhćh] f. independence; self-sufficiency
niezależność materialna [ńe-zah-**lezh**-nośhćh mah-ter-**yahl**-nah] exp.: self-sufficiency
niezależność osobista [ńe-zah-**lezh**-nośhćh o-so-**bees**-tah] exp.:

self-dependence
niezależność sądu [ńe-zah-**lezh**-nośhćh **sown**-doo] exp.: detachment
niezależny [ńe-zah-**lezh**-ni] adj.m. independent; self-contained; self-sufficient
być niezależnym [bićh ńe-zah-**lezh**-nim] exp.: to depend on oneself
mowa niezależna [mo-vah ńe-zah-**lezh**-nah] exp.: direct speech
niezależny dziennikarz [ńe-zah-**lezh**-ni dźhen-ńe-kahsh] exp.: free lance
przypadek niezależny [pshi-**pah**-dek ńe-zah-**lezh**-ni] exp.: nominative (case)
zdanie niezależne [**zdah**-ńe ńe-zah-**lezh**-ne] exp.: main clause
zmienna niezależna [**zmyen**-nah ńe-zah-**lezh**-nah] exp.: independent variable
z powodów niezależnych [s po-**vo**-doof ńe-zah-**lezh**-nikh] exp.: for reasons beyond our control
niezamącony [ńe-zah-mown-**tso**-ni] adj.m. undisturbed; unruffled
niezamężna [ńe-zah-**manzh**-nah] adj.f. unmarried; single
kobieta niezamężna [ko-**bye**-tah ńe-zah-**manzh**-nah] exp.: single woman; unmarried woman
niezamienny [ńe-zah-**myen**-ni] adj.m. inconvertible; incommutable
niezamieszkalny [ńe-zah-mye-**shkahl**-ni] adj.m. uninhabitable
niezamieszkały [ńe-zah-mye-**shkah**-wi] adj.m. uninhabited; untenanted
niezamożnie [ńe-zah-**mozh**-ńe] adv. in indigence; as an indigent
niezamożność [ńe-zah-**mozh**-nośhćh] f. indigence
niezamożny [ńe-zah-**mozh**-ni] adj.m. poor; indigent; unpropertied
niezapalny [ńe-zah-**pahl**-ni] adj.m. uninflammable
niezapłacenie [ńe-zah-pwah-**tse**-ńe] n. default; failure to pay; unpayment (Brit.)
w razie niezapłacenia [v **rah**-źhe ńe-zah-pwah-**tse**-ńah] exp.: failing payment
niezapobiegliwość [ńe-zah-po-bye-**glee**-vośhćh] f. improvidence
niezapobiegliwy [ńe-zah-po-bye-**glee**-vi] adj.m. improvident
niezapominajka [ńe-zah-po-mee-**nahy**-kah] f. forget-me-not
niezapominajkowy [ńe-zah-po-mee-nahy-**ko**-vi] adj.m. of forget-me-not
kolor niezapominajkowy [**ko**-lor ńe-zah-po-mee-nahy-**ko**-vi] exp.: forget-me-not blue
niezapomniany [ńe-zah-pom-**ńah**-ni] adj.m. not-to-be-forgotten; unforgettable; memorable
niezaprzeczalnie [ńe-zah-pshe-**chahl**-ńe] adv. undeniably; incontestably; indisputably
niezaprzeczalny [ńe-zah-pshe-**chahl**-ni] adj.m. undeniable; undisputable; incontestable
niezaprzeczenie [ńe-zah-pshe-**che**-ńe] adv. undeniably; incontestably; indisputably
niezaprzeczony [ńe-zah-pshe-**cho**-ni] adj.m. undeniable; undisputable; incontestable
niezaradnie [ńe-zah-**rad**-ńe] adv. resourcelessly; shiftlessly
niezaradność [ńe-zah-**rahd**-nośhćh] f. lack of resources; shiftlessness; resourcelessness
niezaradny [ńe-zah-**rahd**-ni] adj.m. helpless; shiftless
niezasadny [ńe-zah-**sahd**-ni] adj.m. baseless; groundless
niezasłużenie [ńe-zah-swoo-**zhe**-ńe] adv. undeservedly; unjustly
niezasłużony [ńe-zah-swoo-**zho**-ni] adj.m. undeserved
niezasobność [ńe-zah-**sob**-nośhćh] f. scantiness; poverty; penury
niezasobny [ńe-zah-**sob**-ni] adj.m. scantily provided (with); poor; penurious; of limited means
niezastąpiony [ńe-zah-stown-**pyo**-ni] adj.m. irreplaceable; indispensable
niezastygły [ńe-zah-**stig**-wi] adj.m. not yet set; not yet jellied
niezaszczytnie [ńe-zah-**shchit**-ńe] adv. ingloriously; shamefully
niezaszczytny [ńe-zah-**shchit**-ni] adj.m. inglorious; shameful

niezatapialny [ńe-zah-tah-**pyahl**-ni] adj.m. buoyant; unsinkable
niezatarty [ńe-zah-**tahr**-ti] adj.m. indelible; ineffaceable; memorable
niezatarte wrażenia [ńe-zah-**tahr**-te vrah-**zhe**-ńah] exp.: lasting impression; unforgettable impression
niezauważalnie [ńe-zah-oo-vah-**zhahl**-ńe] adv. without being noticed; unnoticeably
niezauważalny [ńe-zah-oo-vah-**zhahl**-ni] adj.m. imperceptible; unnoticeable
niezauważenie [ńe-zah-oo-vah-**zhe**-ńe] adv. unnoticeably
wyszedł niezauważenie [**vi**-shedw ńe-zah-oo-vah-**zhe**-ńe] exp.: he went out unnoticed
niezawile [ńe-zah-**vee**-le] adv. without complications
niezawiły [ńe-zah-**vee**-wi] adj.m. uncomplicated
niezawisłość [ńe-zah-**vees**-wośhćh] f. independence
niezawisły [ńe-zah-**vees**-wi] adj.m. independent; self-reliant; self-governing; free
niezawiśle [ńe-zah-**veeśh**-le] adv. independently
niezawodnie [ńe-zah-**vod**-ńe] adv. surely; without fail; infallibly; unfailingly
niezawodność [ńe-zah-**vod**-nośhćh] f. sureness; steadfastness; reliability; safeness; infallibility
niezawodny [ńe-zah-**vod**-ni] adj.m. sure; never-failing; safe; unerring; steadfast; reliable; true as steel; sterling; infallible
nieząbkowany [ńe-zownp-ko-**vah**-ni] adj.m. imperforate
niezbadany [ńe-zbah-**dah**-ni] adj.m. unexplorable; inscrutable; unfathomable
niezbędnie [ńe-**zband**-ńe] adv. indispensably
niezbędnie potrzebny [ńe-**zband**-ńe po-**tsheb**-ni] exp.: indispensable
niezbędnik [ńe-**zband**-ńeek] m. combination of spoon and fork
niezbędność [ńe-**zband**-nośhćh] f. indispensability; absolute necessity
niezbędny [ńe-**zband**-ni] adj.m. indispensable; essential; necessary
jest rzeczą niezbędną, żebyśmy... [yest **zhe**-chown ńe-**zband**-nown zhe-**biśh**-mi] exp.: it is essential that we should...; it is vital that we should...; it is imperative that we should...
niezbicie [ńe-**zbee**-ćhe] adv. irrefutably; incontrovertibly
niezbity [ńe-**zbee**-ti] adj.m. irrefutable; incontrovertible
niezborność [ńe-**zbor**-nośhćh] f. astigmatism
niezborny [ńe-**zbor**-ni] adj.m. astigmatic
niezbożność [ńe-**zbozh**-nośhćh] f. lack of religion; impious act
niezbrojny [ńe-**zbroy**-ni] adj.m. unarmed
niezbyt [**ńe**-zbit] adv. not very (much); none too; not too; not overmuch
niezbyt dobrze [**ńe**-zbit **dob**-zhe] exp.: none too well
niezbywalność [ńe-zbi-**vahl**-nośhćh] f. lack of transferability
niezbywalny [ńe-zbi-**vahl**-ni] adj.m. not transferable
niezdara [ńe-**zdah**-rah] f. or m. oaf; duffer; muff; lubber; galoot; all-thumbs
niezdarnie [ńe-**zdahr**-ńe] adv. clumsily; awkwardly
niezdarność [ńe-**zdahr**-nośhćh] f. clumsiness; awkwardness
niezdarny [ńe-**zdahr**-ni] adj.m. clumsy; awkward; bungled
niezdarzony [ńe-zdah-**zho**-ni] adj.m. unsuccessful; botched; bungled
niezdatność [ńe-**zdaht**-nośhćh] f. unfitness; incompetence; disability
niezdatny [ńe-**zdaht**-ni] adj.m. unfit (for use); unqualified (for doing); unserviceable
woda niezdatna do picia [**vo**-dah ńe-**zdaht**-nah do **pee**-ćhah] exp.: water unfit to drink
niezdatny do użytku [ńe-**zdaht**-ni do oo-**zhit**-koo] exp.: unfit for use

niezdecydowanie [ńe-zde-tsi-do-**vah**-ńe] n. indecision; irresolution; hesitancy; wavering; vacillation; shilly-shally; adv. irresolutely; hesitantly; waveringly
niezdecydowanie się [ńe-zde-tsi-do-**vah**-ńe śhan] n. lack of decision; lack of commitment
niezdecydowany [ńe-zde-tsi-do-**vah**-ni] adj.m. undecided; hesitant; irresolute
być niezdecydowanym [bićh ńe-zde-tsi-do-**vah**-nim] exp.: to hesitate; to vacillate; to waver; not to know one's own mind
niezdobyty [ńe-zdo-**bi**-ti] adj.m. impregnable; unconquerable
niezdolność [ńe-**zdol**-nośhćh] f. inability; unfitness
niezdolność do działań prawnych [ńe-**zdol**-nośhćh do **dźhah**-wahń prahv-nikh] exp.: incapacity
niezdolność do pracy [ńe-**zdol**-nośhćh do **prah**-tsi] exp.: incapacity for work
niezdolny [ńe-**zdol**-ni] adj.m. incapable; unable; unfit; dull
niezdolny do pracy [ńe-**zdol**-ni do **prah**-tsi] exp.: incapable of work
niezdolny do służby wojskowej [ńe-**zdol**-ni do **swoozh**-bi voy-**sko**-vey] exp:. unfit for military service
niezdrowo [ńe-**zdro**-vo] adv. unhealthily
to niezdrowo [to ńe-**zdro**-vo] exp.: it is bad for you; it is unwholesome
wyglądać niezdrowo [vi-**glown**-dahćh ńe-**zdro**-vo] exp.: to look ill
niezdrowotny [ńe-zdro-**vot**-ni] adj.m. harmful to health; insalubrious; unhealthy; unwholsome
niezdrowy [ńe-**zdro**-vi] adj.m. unhealthy; unwell; ill; sickly
niezdrów [ne-zdroof] adj.m. unhealthy; unwell; ill; sickly
niezdyscyplinowanie [ńe-zdis-tsi-plee-no-**vah**-ńe] n. undiscipline; unruliness
niezdyscyplinowany [ńe-zdis-tsi-plee-no-**vah**-ni] adj.m. undisciplined; unruly
niezespołowo [ńe-zes-po-**wo**-vo] adv. not collectively; individually
niezginalny [ńe-zgee-**nahl**-ni] adj.m. unbendable
niezgłębiony [ńe-zgwan-**byo**-ni] adj.m. inscrutable; abyssal; bottomless
niezgłębiona tajemnica [ńe-zgwan-**byo**-nah tah-yem-**ńee**-tsah] exp.: impenetrable mystery
niezgłoskotwórczy [ńe-zgwos-ko-**tfoor**-chi] adj.m. nonsyllabic
niezgoda [ńe-**zgo**-dah] f. discord; disagreement; dissension
być w niezgodzie [bićh v ńe-**zgo**-dźhe] exp.: to be in conflict; to be at variance; to disagree (with)
jabłko niezgody [**yahp**-ko ńe-**zgo**-di] exp.: apple of discord
kość niezgody [kośhćh ńe-**zgo**-di] exp.: bone of contention
siać niezgodę [śhahćh ńe-**zgo**-dan] exp.: to bring discord (into)
niezgodnie [ńe-**zgod**-ńe] adv. incompatibly; inconsistently; discordantly; disharmoniously
niezgodność [ńe-**zgod**-nośhćh] f. inconsistency; incompatibility; disagreement; discordance
niezgodność charakterów [ńe-**zgod**-nośhćh khah-rahk-**te**-roof] exp.: incompatibility of temper; incompatibility of personalities
niezgodny [ńe-**zgod**-ni] adj.m. discordant; incompatible; inconsistent; out of accord
niezgorszy [ńe-**zgor**-shi] adj.m. tolerable; passable; fairly good; of some size; of considerable size
niezgorzej [ńe-**zgo**-zhey] adv. tolerably; passably; fairly well; pretty hard; not a little; quite a lot
niezgraba [ńe-**zgrah**-bah] m. or f. all-thumbs; duffer; muff; oaf; lubber; galoot (Brit.)
niezgrabiasz [ńe-**zgrah**-byahsh] m. duffer; muff; oaf; lubber; galoot (Brit.)
niezgrabnie [ńe-**zgrahb**-ńe] adv. clumsily; awkwardly; shapelessly
niezgrabność [ńe-**zgrahb**-nośhćh] f. clumsiness; awkwardness; ungainliness; uncouthness;

gawkishness; left-handedness; unshapeliness
niezgrabny [ńe-**zgrahb**-ni] adj.m. unhandy; clumsy; shapeless
niezgrabstwo [ńe-**zgrahp**-stfo] n. clumsiness; awkwardness; ungainliness; uncouthness; gawkishness; left-handedness; unshapeliness
niezguła [ńe-**zgoo**-wah] f. or m. duffer; muff; oaf; lubber; galoot (Brit.)
niezielony [ńe-źhe-**lo**-ni] adj.m. destitute of chlorophyll
nieziemski [ńe-**źhem**-skee] adj.m. unearthly; unworldly; celestial; heavenly; angelic; supermundane
nieziemsko [ńe-**źhem**-sko] adv. divinely
nieziemskość [ńe-**źhem**-skośhćh] f. divine nature
nieziszczalność [ńe-zeesh-**chahl**-nośhćh] f. unrealizability
nieziszczalny [ńe-zeesh-**chahl**-ni] adj.m. unattainable; unrealizable
niezjadliwy [ńe-zyahd-**lee**-vi] adj.m. nonvirulent; nonvenomous; colloq: unedible; distasteful
niezliczoność [ńe-zlee-**cho**-nośhćh] f. innumerableness; infinity
niezliczony [ńe-zlee-**cho**-ni] adj.m. uncountable; countless; numberless
niezliczoną ilość razy [ńe-zlee-**cho**-nown **ee**-lośhćh **rah**-zi] exp.: times out of number
niezliczone bogactwo [ńe-zlee-**cho**-ne bo-**gahts**-tfo] exp.: untold wealth
niezliczone mnóstwo [ńe-zlee-**cho**-ne **mnoos**-tfo] exp.: infinitude; infinity
niezłomnie [ńe-**zwom**-ńe] adv. steadfastly; unshakenly
niezłomność [ńe-**zwom**-nośhćh] f. steadfastness; firmness; inflexibility
niezłomny [ńe-**zwom**-ni] adj.m. inflexible; firm; steadfast
niezłośliwy [ne-zwośh-**lee**-vi] adj.m. devoid of malice
nowotwór niezłośliwy [no-**vo**-tfoor ńe-zwośh-**lee**-vi] exp.: benign neoplasm; benign tumor
niezłożony [ńe-zwo-**zho**-ni] adj.m. uncomplicated; simple
niezły [**ńe**-zwi] adj.m. quite nice; tolerably good; passable; tolerable; quite good; quite profitable; pretty big; of considerable size
niezły numer [**ńe**-zwi **noo**-mer] exp.: spoiled brat; a fine bit of a knave (Brit.)
niezmazalny [ńe-zmah-**zahl**-ni] adj.m. indelible; ineffaceable; unobliterated
niezmazany [ńe-zmah-**zah**-ni] adj.m. indelible; ineffaceable; unobliterated
niezmącony [ńe-zmown-**tso**-ni] adj.m. unruffled; undisturbed
niezmęczenie [ńe-zman-**che**-ńe] adv. untiringly
niezmiarka [ńe-**zmyahr**-kah] f. fly of the family Chloropidae
niezmiarka paskowana [ńe-**zmyahr**-kah pahs-ko-**vah**-nah] exp.: gout fly
niezmiarki [ńe-**zmyahr**-kee] pl. the family Chloropidae
niezmiarkowaty [ńe-zmyahr-ko-**vah**-ti] adj.m. of the family Chloropidae
niezmiarkowate [ńe-zmyahr-ko-**vah**-te] pl. the family Chloropidae
niezmiennie [ńe-**zmyen**-ńe] adv. unalterably; constantly; invariably
niezmiennik [ńe-**zmyen**-ńeek] m. (math.) constant; invariant
niezmienność [ńe-**zmyen**-nośhćh] f. immutability; constancy; permanency
niezmiennotematowy [ńe-zmyen-no-te-mah-**to**-vi] adj.m. (verb) of an unchanging stem
niezmienny [ńe-**zmyen**-ni] adj.m. invariable; constant; fixed; unchanging; permanent
niezmiernie [ńe-**zmyer**-ńe] adv. extremely; exceedingly; immensely
niezmierność [ńe-**zmyer**-nośhćh] f. immensity; vastness
niezmierny [ńe-**zmyer**-ni] adj.m. immense; vast; boundless
niezmierzony [ńe-zmye-**zho**-ni] adj.m. immeasurable

niezmordowanie [ńe-zmor-do-**vah**-ńe] adv. unwearyingly; indefatigably; tirelessly; untiringly; unflaggingly
niezmordowany [ńe-zmor-do-**vah**-ni] adj.m. indefatigable; tireless; untiring; unflagging
niezmożony [ńe-zmo-**zho**-ni] adj.m. invincible; indefatigable; untiring; overpowering; overwhelming
niezmysłowy [ńe-zmis-**wo**-vi] adj.m. not sensual; platonic
niezmyty [ńe-**zmi**-ti] adj.m. indelible; ineffaceable
niezmywalny [ńe-zmi-**vahl**-ni] adj.m. indelible
nieznacznie [ńe-**znahch**-ńe] adv. insensibly; slightly; insignificantly
nieznaczny [ńe-**znahch**-ni] adj.m. trivial; insignificant; inconsiderable; slight
nieznaczna większość głosów [ńe-**znahch**-nah **vyank**-shośhćh **gwo**-soof] exp.: narrow majority
nieznajoma [ńe-znah-**yo**-mah] f. & adj.f. strange (female)
nieznajoma osoba [ńe-znah-**yo**-mah o-**so**-bah] exp.: stranger
nieznajomość [ńe-znah-**yo**-mośhćh] f. ignorance; lack of acquaintance; unawareness
nieznajomy [ńe-znah-**yo**-mi] adj.m. unknown (man, etc.); strange (man, etc.); m. stranger
nieznajomy człowiek [ńe-znah-**yo**-mi **chwo**-vyek] exp.: stranger
nieznane [ńe-**znah**-ne] n. the unknown
podróż w nieznane [**pod**-roosh v ńe-**znah**-ne] exp.: trip into the unknown
nieznany [ńe-**znah**-ni] adj.m. unknown; unfamiliar; obscure; strange
Grób Nieznanego Żołnierza [groop ńe-znah-**ne**-go zhow-**ńe**-zhah] exp.: tomb of the Unknown Soldier
nieznikomy [ńe-zńee-**ko**-mi] adj.m. not perishing; lasting
niezniszczalność [ńe-zńeesh-**chahl**-nośhćh] f. imperishableness; indestructibility
niezniszczalny [ńe-zńeesh-**chahl**-ni] adj.m. imperishable; indestructible
nieznośnie [ńe-**znośh**-ńe] adv. unbearably; intolerably; provokingly
nieznośny [ńe-**znośh**-ni] adj.m. unbearable; annoying; nasty; pesky; intolerable
nieznużenie [ńe-znoo-**zhe**-ńe] adv. unwearyingly; indefatigably; tirelessly; untiringly; unflaggingly
nieznużony [ńe-znoo-**zho**-ni] adj.m. unwearying; indefatigable; tireless; untiring; unflagging
niezrażony [ńe-zrah-**zho**-ni] adj.m. undeterred; undiscouraged
niezręcznie [ńe-**zranch**-ńe] adv. clumsily; awkwardly; inconveniently; tactlessly
niezręczność [ńe-**zranch**-nośhćh] f. awkwardness; clumsiness; indiscretion
niezręczny [ńe-**zranch**-ni] adj.m. awkward; clumsy; tactless
niezrozumiale [ńe-zro-zoo-**myah**-le] adv. incomprehensibly; unintelligibly
niezrozumiałość [ńe-zro-zoo-**myah**-wośhćh] f. incomprehensibility; abstruseness; obscureness; reconditeness; inexplicability; unaccountableness
niezrozumiały [ńe-zro-zoo-**myah**-wi] adj.m. unintelligible; incomprehensible
niezrozumiała mowa [ńe-zro-zoo-**myah**-wah **mo**-vah] exp.: jargon
to dla mnie jest niezrozumiałe [to dlah mńe yest ńe-zro-zoo-**myah**-we] exp.: I can't make it out
w sposób niezrozumiały [f **spo**-soop ńe-zro-zoo-**myah**-wi] exp.: unaccountably
niezrozumienie [ńe-zro-zoo-**mye**-ńe] n. lack of understanding; incomprehension
niezrozumienie się [ńe-zro-zoo-**mye**-ńe śhan] n. misunderstanding of one another; mutual lack of understanding
niezrównanie [ńe-zroov-**nah**-ńe] adv. incomparably; extremely; surpassingly; colloq: in a grand style
niezrównany [ńe-zroov-**nah**-ni]

adj.m. matchless; incomparable; peerless; unique; grand; beyond compare; unrivalled
niezrównany człowiek [ńe-zroov-nah-ni **chwo**-vyek] exp.: nonesuch
on jest niezrównany! [on yest ńe-zroov-**nah**-ni] exp.: he is great!; he is the greatest!
niezrównoważenie [ńe-zroov-no-vah-**zhe**-ńe] n. lack of balance; lack of poise
niezrównoważony [ńe-zroov-no-vah-**zho**-ni] adj.m. unbalanced; unpoised; ill-balanced
niezupełnie [ńe-zoo-**pew**-ńe] adv. not quite; not altogether; incompletely
niezupełność [ńe-zoo-**pew**-nośhćh] f. incompleteness
niezupełny [ńe-zoo-**pew**-ni] adj.m. incomplete; imperfect; defective
kwiat niezupełny [kfyaht ńe-zoo-**pew**-ni] exp.: imperfect flower
przeobrażenie niezupełne [pshe-o-brah-**zhe**-ńe ńe-zoo-**pew**-ne] exp.: imperfect metamorphosis
zdanie niezupełne [**zdah**-ńe ńe-zoo-**pew**-ne] exp.: elliptical sentence
niezwalczony [ńe-zvahl-**cho**-ni] adj.m. undefeated; unconquerable; invincible
niezwłocznie [ńe-**zvwoch**-ńe] adv. immediately; without delay
niezwłoczny [ńe-**zvwoch**-ni] adj.m. instant; prompt; immediate
niezwrotność [ńe-**zvrot**-nośhćh] f. unwieldiness; nonrepayability
niezwrotny [ńe-**zvrot**-ni] adj.m. unwieldy; not repayable
niezwyciężalny [ńe-zvi-ćhan-**zhahl**-ni] adj.m. not to be defeated; unconquerable; invincible
niezwyciężony [ńe-zvi-ćhan-**zho**-ni] adj.m. invincible
niezwyczajnie [ńe-zvi-**chahy**-ńe] adv. uncommonly; unusually; extraordinarily
niezwyczajny [ńe-zvi-**chahy**-ni] adj.m. uncommon; unusual; extraordinary
niezwykle [ńe-**zvik**-le] adv. extraordinarily; extremely; not as usual; oddly
niezwykłość [ńe-**zvik**-wośhćh] f. singularity; unusualness; extraordinariness; oddity; uncommonness
niezwykły [ńe-**zvik**-wi] adj.m. unusual; extreme; rare; odd; uncommon; singular
niezwykłej piękności [ńe-**zvik**-wey pyank-**nośh**-ćhee] exp.: of extraordinary beauty; of singular beauty
niezżycie się [ńez-**zhi**-ćhe śhan] n. failure to get on well together; lack of team spirit; absence of teamwork; failure to get along
nieźle [**ńe**-źhle] adv. pretty fairly; pretty tolerably; pretty well
nieźle by było [**ńe**-źhle bi **bi**-wo] exp.: it wouldn't be a bad thing; you might do worse; we might do worse
nieżartobliwy [ńe-zhahr-tob-**lee**-vi] adj.m. not humorous; unhumorous
nieżeglowny [ńe-zheg-**lov**-ni] adj.m. unnavigable
nieżelazny [ńe-zhe-**lahz**-ni] adj.m. nonferrous (metals)
nieżonaty [ńe-zho-**nah**-ti] adj.m. unmarried; single; m. bachelor
nieżyciowo [ńe-zhi-**ćho**-vo] adv. impracticably; fancifully (scheming, etc.)
nieżyciowość [ńe-zhi-**ćho**-vośhćh] f. impracticability; fanciful character
nieżyciowy [ńe-zhi-**ćho**-vi] adj.m. impracticable; fanciful (scheme, etc.)
nieżyczliwie [ńe-zhi-**chlee**-vye] adv. unkindly; malevolently
usposobiony nieżyczliwie [oos-po-so-**byo**-ni ńe-zhi-**chlee**-vye] exp.: ill-disposed (towards somebody)
nieżyczliwość [ńe-zhi-**chlee**-vośhćh] f. unfriendliness; unkindness
nieżyczliwy [ńe-zhi-**chlee**-vi] adj.m. unfriendly; ill-disposed; unkind
nieżyjący [ńe-zhi-**yown**-tsi] adj.m. dead; deceased; late
nieżyt [**ńe**-zhit] m. inflammation; catarrh; hay fever; colitis

nieżyt kiszek [ńe-zhit **kee**-shek] exp.: colitis
nieżyt oskrzeli [ńe-zhit os-**kshe**-lee] exp.: bronchitis
nieżyt sienny [ńe-zhit **śhen**-ni] exp.: hay fever
nieżyt żołądka [ńe-zhit zho-wownt-kah] exp.: gastritis
nieżytowy [ńe-zhi-**to**-vi] adj.m. catarrhal
nieżywiczny [ńe-zhi-**veech**-ni] adj.m. nonresinous
nieżywotność [ńe-zhi-**vot**-nośhćh] f. inanimateness
nieżywotny [ńe-zhi-**vot**-ni] adj.m. inanimate
nieżywy [ńe-**zhi**-vi] adj.m. dead; lifeless; inanimate
nieżyzny [ńe-**zhiz**-ni] adj.m. unfertile; barren
nigdy [**ńeeg**-di] adv. never
jak gdyby nigdy nic [yahg **gdi**-bi **neeg**-di ńeets] exp.: as if nothing had happened
jak nigdy [yahk **ńeeg**-di] exp.: as never before
na święty nigdy [nah **śhfyan**-ti ńeeg-di] exp.: at the Greek calends; on the Greek calends
nigdy przedtem [**ńeeg**-di **pshet**-tem] exp.: never before
nigdy więcej [**ńeeg**-di **vyan**-tsey] exp.: never again
nigdy w życiu [**ńeeg**-di v **zhi**-ćhoo] exp.: never before; nothing of the kind!; I should say not!
nigdzie [**ńeeg**-dźhe] adv. nowhere; anywhere (after negation)
nihilista [ńee-khee-**lees**-tah] m. nihilist
nihilistyczny [ńee-khee-lees-**tich**-ni] adj.m. nihilistic
nihilizm [ńee-**khee**-leezm] m. nihilism
nijak [**ńee**-yahk] adv. nowise
nijaki [ńee-**yah**-kee] adj.m. none; neuter (gender); indistinct
rodzaj nijaki [ro-dzahy ńee-**yah**-kee] exp.: neuter; neutral gender
nijako [ńee-**yah**-ko] adv. indeterminately; vaguely; awkwardly
czuć się nijako [chooćh śhan ńee-**yah**-ko] exp.: to feel queer
nijako mi było zwrócić mu uwagę [ńee-**yah**-ko mee **bi**-wo **zvroo**-ćheećh moo oo-**vah**-gan] exp.: it was awkward for me to tell him (about it)
nijakość [ńee-**yah**-kośhćh] f. vagueness
nikczemnić [ńeek-**chem**-ńeećh] v. debase; degrade; disgrace; dishonor (*repeatedly*)
nikczemnie [ńeek-**chem**-ńe] adv. basely; meanly; abjectly; despicably; infamously; shabbily
nikczemnieć [ńeek-**chem**-ńećh] v. degenerate; abase oneself; sink into degradation (*repeatedly*)
nikczemnienie [ńeek-chem-**ńe**-ńe] n. abasement; degradation
nikczemnik [ńeek-**chem**-ńeek] m. villain; scoundrel; wretch
nikczemność [ńeek-**chem**-nośhćh] f. villainy; meanness; baseness; sordidness
nikczemny [ńeek-**chem**-ni] adj.m. vile; abject; despicable; base; shabby; mean; dirty; dishonorable
nikiel [**ńee**-kel] m. nickel
nikielin [ńee-**ke**-leen] m. nickeline; niccolite; nickel-brass (alloy)
nikielina [ńee-ke-**lee**-nah] f. nickel-copper-zinc alloy
nikielinowy [ńee-ke-lee-**no**-vi] adj.m. of nickel-brass alloy
nikla [**ńeek**-lah] f. woody pea herb
nikla indyjska [**ńeek**-lah een-**diy**-skah] exp.: pigeon pea (seed)
niklawy [ńeek-**lah**-vi] adj.m. nickelous (hydroxide, etc.)
nikle [**ńeek**-le] adv. dimly; faintly; minutely
nikle wyglądać [**ńeek**-le vig-**lown**-dahćh] exp.: to look minute; to seem minute
niklować [ńeek-**lo**-vahćh] v. nickel-plate; coat with nickel (*repeatedly*)
niklowanie [ńeek-lo-**vah**-ńe] n. nickel-plating
niklownia [ńeek-**lov**-ńah] f. nickel-plating shop (plant)
niklowy [**ńeek**-lo-vi] adj.m. nickelic; nickel (coin, etc.)
nikło [**ńeek**-wo] adv. dimly; faintly; minutely

nikłość [ńeek-wośhćh] f. minuteness; dimness; glimmer
nikły [**ńeek**-wi] adj.m. scanty; dim; faint; glimmering
niknąć [**ńeek**-nownćh] v. vanish; dwindle; waste away; decay (*repeatedly*)
niknąć w oczach [**ńeek**-nownćh v **o**-chahkh] exp.: to vanish before one's eyes; to sink fast
niknienie [ńeek-**ńe**-ńe] n. vanishing; dwindling; decaying
niknięcie [ńeek-**ńan**-ćhe] n. vanishing; dwindling; decaying
nikogusieńko [ńee-ko-goo-**śheń**-ko] pron. exp.: colloq: not a soul
nikoguteńko [ńee-ko-goo-**teń**-ko] pron. exp.: colloq: not a soul
nikol [**ńee**-kol] m. nicol
nikotyna [ńee-ko-**ti**-nah] f. nicotine; poisonous tobacco extract causing nicotinism
zatrucie nikotyną [zah-**troo**-ćhe ńee-ko-ti-nown] exp.: nicotinism
nikotynizm [ńee-ko-ti-ńeezm] m. nicotinism
nikotynizować się [ńee-ko-ti-ńee-**zo**-vahćh śhan] v. drug oneself with nicotine (*repeatedly*)
nikotynizowanie się [ńee-ko-ti-ńee-zo-**vah**-ńe śhan] n. drugging oneself with nicotine
nikotynowy [ńee-ko-ti-**no**-vi] adj.m. nicotinic (acid, etc.); nicotine (sulfate, etc.)
nikt [ńeekt] pron. nobody; anybody; anyone
nikt a nikt [ńeekt ah ńeekt] exp.: nobody whatsoever
nikt inny [ńeekt **een**-ni] exp.: nobody else
nikt prócz [ńeekt prooch] exp.: nobody except
nikt z nas [ńeekt z nahs] exp.: none of us
nim [ńeem] conj. before; till
nimb [ńeemp] m. halo; aureole
nimbostratus [ńeem-bo-**strah**-toos] m. nimbostratus; a low dark rainy cloud layer
nimbus [**ńeem**-boos] m. nimbus
nimfa [**ńeem**-fah] f. nymph
nimfa leśna [**ńeem**-fah **leśh**-nah] exp.: wood nymph
nimfa morska [**ńeem**-fah **mor**-skah] exp.: sea nymph; nereid
nimfetka [ńeem-**fet**-kah] f. (small, young) nymph; colloq: young sexy girl
nimfomania [ńeem-fo-**mahń**-yah] f. nymphomania (excessive sexual desire by a female)
nimfomanka [ńeem-fo-**mahn**-kah] f. (female) nymphomaniac
niniejszy [ńee-**ńey**-shi] adj.m. this; present; the present; this here; this indeed
do niniejszego [do ńee-ńey-**she**-go] exp.: hereto; hereunto
niniejsza sprawa [ńee-**ńey**-shah **sprah**-vah] exp.: the matter under consideration; the matter under discussion
niniejszym [ńee-**ńey**-shim] exp.: hereby
niniejszym oświadczam [ńee-**ńey**-shim o-**śhfyaht**-chahm] exp.: I hereby testify
wraz z niniejszym [vrahz z ńee-**ńey**-shim] exp.: herewith
niob [ńop] m. niobium; columbium (atomic number 41)
nioska [**ńos**-kah] f. laying hen; layer
nirwana [ńeer-**vah**-nah] f. nirvana; final beatitude
niskawy [ńees-**kah**-vi] adj.m. lowish; pretty low; rather low; shortish (man, etc.); not very tall
niski [**ńees**-kee] adj.m. low; short; of short statue; humble; base; mean; abject; vile; deep
na niskim poziomie [nah **ńees**-keem po-**źho**-mye] exp.: at a low level; on a low level
niskiego pochodzenia [ńees-ke-go po-kho-**dze**-ńah] exp.: low born; of humble birth
niskie progi [ńees-ke **pro**-gee] exp.: our humble roof
niski i gruby [**ńees**-kee ee **groo**-bi] exp.: podgy; pudgy
niski i szeroki [**ńees**-kee ee she-**ro**-kee] exp.: squat
niski ukłon [**ńees**-kee **ook**-won] exp.: deep bow; low bow
nisko [**ńees**-ko] adv. low
dolar stoi nisko [do-lahr **sto**-ee **ńees**-ko] exp.: the rate of

exchange of the dollar is low
nisko kłaniać się [ńees-ko **kwah**-ńahćh śhan] exp.: to bow low
nisko mierzyć [ńees-ko **mye**-zhićh] exp.: to aim low
nisko- [ńees-ko] prefix: low-
niskoalkoholowy [ńees-ko-ahl-ko-kho-**lo**-vi] adj.m. low-proof (wine, etc.); of low alcohol content
niskobiałkowy [ńees-ko-byahw-**ko**-vi] adj.m. of low protein content
niskociśnieniowiec [ńees-ko-ćheeśh-ńe-**ńo**-vyets] m. person with low blood pressure
niskociśnieniowy [ńees-ko-ćheeśh-ńe-**ńo**-vi] adj.m. of low pressure
niskogatunkowy [ńees-ko-gah-toon-**ko**-vi] adj.m. poor-quality
niskokaloryczny [ńees-ko-kah-lo-**rich**-ni] adj.m. of low calorie content
niskolotny [ńees-ko-**lot**-ni] adj.m. low-flying
niskonapięciowy [ńees-ko-nah-pyan-**ćho**-vi] adj.m. low-voltage (line, etc.)
niskooktanowy [ńees-ko-ok-tah-**no**-vi] adj.m. of low octane
niskopączkowy [ńees-ko-pownch-**ko**-vi] adj.m. low blossoming (plants, etc.)
niskopączkowe [ńees-ko-pownch-**ko**-ve] pl. the genus of low-blossoming plants
niskopienny [ńees-ko-**pyen**-ni] adj.m. dwarf (apple, etc.); coppice (shoot, etc.)
niskopodwoziowy [ńees-ko-pod-vo-**źho**-vi] adj.m. (car, trailer, etc.) of low road clearance
niskoprężny [ńees-ko-**pranzh**-ni] adj.m. low-pressure (boiler, etc.)
niskoprocentowy [ńees-ko-pro-tsen-**to**-vi] adj.m. low-standard; low-grade; low-interest
niskorosły [ńees-ko-**ros**-wi] adj.m. dwarfish; short-statured
niskostopowy [ńees-ko-sto-**po**-vi] adj.m. base-alloy (metal)
niskość [**ńees**-kośhćh] f. lowness; low degree; low standard; low stature; baseness; meanness; abjectness
niskotopliwy [ńees-ko-to-**plee**-vi] adj.m. of low melting point
niskowartościowy [ńees-ko-vahr-tośh-**ćho**-vi] adj.m. of small value
niskowęglowy [ńees-ko-van-**glo**-vi] adj.m. of low carbon content
niskowitaminowy [ńees-ko-vee-tah-mee-**no**-vi] adj.m. of small vitamin content
niskowodny [ńees-ko-**vod**-ni] adj.m. low-water (bridge submersible at flood stage)
niskowrzący [ńees-ko-**vzhown**-tsi] adj.m. of low boiling point
nisza [**ńee**-shah] f. niche; recess
niszcząco [ńeesh-**chown**-tso] adv. destructively; disruptively; ruinously
niszczący [ńeesh-**chown**-tsi] adj.m. destructive; disruptive; ruinous
niszczeć [**ńeesh**-chećh] v. waste away; deteriorate; get wasted; decay; go to ruin (*repeatedly*)
niszczenie [ńeesh-**che**-ńe] n. deterioration; decay; ruin; waste; devastation; destruction; ravage
niszczenie się [ńeesh-**che**-ńe śhan] n. wasting away; going to ruin; getting wasted
niszczuka [ńeesh-**choo**-kah] f. gar (pike); Lepisosteus
niszczyciel [ńeesh-**chi**-ćhel] m. devastator; destroyer; waster
niszczycielka [ńeesh-chi-**ćhel**-kah] f. (female) devastator; destroyer; waster
niszczycielski [ńeesh-chi-**ćhel**-skee] adj.m. destructive; ruinous; devastating; ravaging; all-consuming (fire, etc.)
niszczycielstwo [ńeesh-chi-**ćhel**-stfo] n. destruction; ruin; devastation; ravages; ravage
niszczyć [**ńeesh**-chićh] v. destroy; spoil; ruin; wreck; damage; demolish; lay waste; wear out (*repeatedly*)
niszczyć się [**ńeesh**-chićh śhan] v. spoil; deteriorate; wear (*repeatedly*)
nit [ńeet] m. rivet
nitarka [nee-**tahr**-kah] f. riveter; riveting machine
niteczka [ńee-**tech**-kah] f. (thin) thread

niter [ńee-ter] m. riveter
niterka [ńee-**ter**-kah] f. riveting work
niterski [ńee-**ter**-skee] adj.m. riveter's (work, etc.)
nitka [**ńeet**-kah] f. thread
  nitki [**ńeet**-kee] pl. threads
  (dojść) po nitce do kłębka [(doyśhćh) po ńeet-tse do **kwanp**-kah] exp.: to unravel a plot; to solve an enigma
  nie zostawić na kimś suchej nitki [ńe zos-**tah**-veećh nah keemśh **soo**-khey **ńeet**-kee] exp.: to pick somebody to pieces
  wisieć na nitce [**vee**-śhećh nah **ńeet**-tse] exp.: to hang by a thread
  wyciągnąć nitkę z igły [vi-**ćhown**-gnownćh **ńeet**-kan z **ee**-gwi] exp.: to unthread a needle
  zmoknąć do nitki [**zmok**-nownćh do **ńeet**-kee] exp.: to be soaking wet; to be soaked; to be drenched to the skin
nitkować [ńeet-**ko**-vahćh] v. twist into threads; throw (silk, etc.) (*repeatedly*)
nitkowanie [ńeet-ko-**vah**-ńe] n. twisting into threads
nitkowato [ńeet-ko-**vah**-to] adv. like a thread; thread-like
nitkowatość [ńeet-ko-**vah**-tośhćh] f. thread-like appearance
nitkowaty [ńeet-ko-**vah**-ti] adj.m. filiform; thread-like; filamentous; thready
  tętno nitkowate [**tant**-no ńeet-ko-**vah**-te] exp.: thready pulse
nitkowiec [ńeet-**ko**-vyets] m. filaria (parasite)
nitkowy [ńeet-**ko**-vi] adj.m. filamentous
niton [**ńee**-ton] m. niton
nitowacz [ńee-**to**-vahch] m. riveter
nitować [ńee-**to**-vahćh] v. rivet (*repeatedly*)
nitowanie [ńee-to-**vah**-ńe] n. riveting
nitownica [ńee-tov-**ńee**-tsah] f. riveter; riveting machine
nitowniczy [ńee-tov-**ńee**-chi] adj.m. of riveting
nitownik [ńee-**tov**-ńeek] m. riveter (tool)
nitowy [ńee-**to**-vi] adj.m. rivet (forge, connection, joint, etc.)
nitratyn [ńee-**trah**-tin] m. saltpetre; potassium nitrate; chile saltpeter
nitro- [**ńeet**-ro] prefix: nitro-
nitrobakterie [ńeet-ro-bahk-**te**-rye] pl. nitrobacteria
nitrobenzen [ńeet-ro-**ben**-zen] m. nitrobenzene
nitrobenzol [ńeet-ro-**ben**-zol] m. nitrobenzene
nitroceluloza [ńeet-ro-tse-loo-**lo**-zah] f. nitrocellulose
nitrocelulozowy [ńeet-ro-tse-loo-lo-**zo**-vi] adj.m. nitrocellulose (paint, etc.)
nitrofil [ńeet-**ro**-feel] m. nitrophyte
nitrofilny [ńeet-ro-**feel**-ni] adj.m. nitrophilous (plant)
nitrofit [ńeet-**ro**-feet] m. nitrophyte
  nitrofity [ńeet-ro-**fee**-ti] pl. nitrophytic plants
nitrofob [ńeet-**ro**-fop] m. plant growing on nitrogen poor soils
  nitrofoby [ńeet-ro-**fo**-bi] pl. plants growing on nitrogen poor soils
nitrogenaza [ńeet-ro-ge-**nah**-zah] f. nitrogenase
nitrogliceryna [ńeet-ro-glee-tse-**ri**-nah] f. nitroglycerin(e)
nitrokultura [ńeet-ro-kool-**too**-rah] f. nitration; nitrification
nitrolakier [ńeet-ro-**lah**-ker] m. nitrocellulose varnish
nitrować [ńeet-**ro**-vahćh] v. nitrate (*repeatedly*)
nitrowanie [ńeet-ro-**vah**-ńe] n. nitration
nitrowy [ńeet-**ro**-vi] adj.m. nitric
nitrozobakterie [ńeet-ro-zo-bahk-**te**-rye] pl. nitrosobacteria
nitrozwiązek [ńeet-ro-**zvyown**-zek] m. nitro-compound
nitryfikacja [ńeet-ri-fee-**kahts**-yah] f. nitrification
nitryfikacyjny [ńeet-ri-fee-kah-**tsiy**-ni] adj.m. nitrifying
nitryfikator [ńeet-ri-fee-**kah**-tor] m. nitrifier
  nitryfikatory [ńeet-ri-fee-kah-**to**-ri] pl. nitrifiers
nitryfikować [ńeet-ri-fee-**ko**-vahćh] v. nitrify (*repeatedly*)
nitryfikowanie [ńeet-ri-fee-ko-**vah**-

ńe] n. nitrification
nitryt [ńeet-rit] m. nitrite
niuans [ńyoo-ahns] m. nuance; shade of difference
niuansik [ńyoo-ahn-śheek] m. (nice, little) nuance
niuch [ńookh] m. pinch (of snuff)
mieć niucha [myećh ńoo-khah] exp.: colloq: to have a flair (for)
niuchać [ńoo-khahćh] v. take (snuff); sniff; colloq: nose about (*repeatedly*)
niuchanie [ńoo-khah-ńe] n. taking snuff; sniffing
niuchnąć [ńookh-nownćh] v. take a pinch of snuff
niuchnięcie [ńookh-ńan-ćhe] n. taking a pinch of snuff
niuton [ńyoo-ton] m. newton
niwa [ńee-vah] f. field; soil; colloq: realm; sphere; (professional, etc.) field
niwacja [ńee-vah-tsyah] f. nivation
niwalny [ńee-vahl-ni] adj.m. nival
niweczenie [ńee-ve-che-ńe] n. annihilation; frustration; destruction
niwecznik [ńee-vech-ńeek] m. antibody
niweczyć [ńee-ve-chićh] v. destroy; annihilate; lay waste; wreck (*repeatedly*)
niweczyć czyjeś nadzieje [ńee-ve-chićh chi-yeśh nah-dźhe-ye] exp.: to shatter somebody's hopes; to dash somebody's hopes
niweczyć czyjeś plany [ńee-ve-chićh chi-yeśh plah-ni] exp.: to frustrate somebody's plans; to baffle somebody's plans; to foil somebody's plans
niweczyć czyjeś zamiary [ńee-ve-chićh chi-yeśh zah-myah-ri] exp.: to frustrate somebody's plans; to spoil somebody's designs; to foil somebody's plans
niwelacja [ńee-ve-lahts-yah] f. levelling; survey; surveying
niwelacyjny [ńee-ve-lah-tsiy-ni] adj.m. surveying (equipment, etc.); of levelling
niwelator [ńee-ve-lah-tor] m. leveller
niweleta [ńee-ve-le-tah] f. grade line
niwelować [ńee-ve-lo-vahćh] v. make level; demolish; survey (*repeatedly*)
niwelować się [ńee-ve-lo-vahćh śhan] v. become levelled; be levelled (*repeatedly*)
niwelowanie [ńee-ve-lo-vah-ńe] n. surveying; levelling
nizać [ńee-zahćh] v. thread; string (*repeatedly*)
nizanie [ńee-zah-ńe] n. stringing (beads, etc.); threading (pearls, etc.)
nizina [ńee-źhee-nah] f. lowland; valley
nizinny [ńee-źheen-ni] adj.m. low-lying; lowland (vegetation, etc.)
torf nizinny [torf ńee-źheen-ni] exp.: low-moor peat
nizinowy [ńee-źhee-no-vi] adj.m. low-lying; lowland (vegetation, etc.)
niziuchny [ńee-źhookh-ni] adj.m. very short
niziusieńki [ńee-źhoo-śheń-kee] adj.m. very, very short
niziuśki [ńee-źhoośh-kee] adj.m. nice and short
niziuteńki [ńee-źhoo-teń-kee] adj.m. very, very short
niziuteńko [ńee-źhoo-teń-ko] adv. very low; very lowly
niziutki [ńee-źhoot-kee] adj.m. very short
niziutko [ńee-źhoot-ko] adv. nice and low; very low
niźli [ńeeźh-lee] conj. (rather) than
niźliby [ńeeźh-lee-bi] exp.: than
niż [ńeesh] m. lowland; depression; atmospheric low; low
niż [ńeesh] conj. than
niżby [ńeezh-bi] conj. (rather) than
lepiej niżbym się spodziewał [le-pyey ńeezh-bim śhan spo-dźhe-vahw] exp.: better than I should (would) have expected
niżej [ńee-zhey] adv. lower; below; down; further down
niżej podpisany [ńee-zhey pot-pee-sah-ni] exp.: the undersigned
niżej wymieniony [ńee-zhey vi-mye-ńo-ni] exp.: stated below; mentioned below; stated hereafter; mentioned hereafter
niżeli [ńee-zhe-lee] conj. (rather)

than
niżeliby [ńee-zhe-lee-bi] conj. than
niżowy [ńee-zho-vi] adj.m. lowland (area, etc.); depression (area, etc.)
niższość [ńeesh-shośhćh] f. inferiority
kompleks niższości [kom-pleks ńeesh-shośh-ćhee] exp.: inferiority complex
poczucie niższości [po-choo-ćhe ńeesh-shośh-ćhee] exp.: feeling of one's inferiority; awarness of one's inferiority
niższy [ńeesh-shi] adj.m. lower; inferior; shorter; subordinate
niższa izba parlamentu [ńeesh-shah eez-bah pahr-lah-men-too] exp.: lower house; lower chamber
no [no] part. why; well; now; then; just; there; there now!
dawaj no, to! [dah-vahy no to] exp.: give me that quick!
no? [no] exp.: what?; and?; well?
no, nie wiem [no ńe vyem] exp.: I am not sure
no, no! [no no] exp.: well, well!
no to co? [no to tso] exp.: so what?
nobel [no-bel] m. nobelium (atomic number 102)
nobil [no-beel] m. Roman patrician; nobleman
nobilitacja [no-bee-lee-tah-tsyah] f. ennoblement; the raising to the rank of nobility
nobilitacyjny [no-bee-lee-tah-tsiy-ni] adj.m. of ennoblement
nobilitet [no-bee-lee-tet] m. Roman patriciate
nobilitować [no-bee-lee-to-vahćh] v. ennoble; raise to the rank of nobility (*repeatedly*)
nobilitować się [no-bee-lee-to-vahćh śhan] v. ennoble oneself (*repeatedly*)
nobilitowanie [ńo-bee-lee-to-vah-ńe] n. ennobling
nobilitowanie się [no-bee-lee-to-vah-ńe śhan] n. ennobling oneself
noblista [no-blees-tah] m. Nobel prize laureate
nobliwie [no-blee-vye] adv. with refinement; with elegance
wyglądać nobliwie [vig-lown-dahćh nob-lee-vye] exp.: to look refined
nobliwy [no-blee-vi] adj.m. refined; elegant
noc [nots] f. night
białe noce [byah-we no-tse] exp.: white nights
całą noc [tsah-wown nots] exp.: all night long
co noc [tso nots] exp.: nightly; every night; night after night
czarny jak noc [chahr-ni yahk nots] exp.: night-black; raven black
dziś w nocy [dźheeśh v no-tsi] exp.: tonight
nocą [no-tsown] exp.: by night; at night
noc polarna [nots po-lahr-nah] exp.: polar night
noc świętojańska [nots śhfyan-to-yahń-skah] exp.: (beginning of summer) Saint John's night after summer solstice, June 22; night of 23/24 of June (the shortest)
od świtu do nocy [ot śhfee-too do no-tsi] exp.: whole day long
pod osłoną nocy [pod os-wo-nown no-tsi] exp.: under cover of night
po nocy [po no-tsi] exp.: during the night
poprzedniej nocy [po-pshed-ńey no-tsi] exp.: last night
przed nocą [pshed no-tsown] exp.: before dark; before nightfall
przez noc [pshez nots] exp.: overnight
ubiegłej nocy [oo-byeg-wey no-tsi] exp.: last night
w ciemną noc [f ćhem-nown nots] exp.: at the dead of night; in the depth of night
wczoraj w nocy [fcho-rahy v no-tsi] exp.: last night
w nocy z soboty na niedzielę [v no-tsi s so-bo-ti nah ńe-dźhe-lan] exp.: the night from Saturday to Sunday
z nastaniem nocy [z nah-stah-ńem no-tsi] exp.: at nightfall
nocek [no-tsek] m. a bat of the family Vespertilionidae

nochal [no-khahl] m. big nose; slang: snout; beezer; boko; conk
nocka [**nots**-kah] f. (short) night
nocleg [**nots**-leg] m. place to sleep; night's lodging; accommodation
znaleźć nocleg w hotelu [**znah**-leśhćh **nots**-lek f ho-**te**-loo] exp.: to put up at a hotel
noclegownia [nots-le-**go**-vńah] f. (overnight) shelter
noclegowy [nots-le-**go**-vi] adj.m. of a place to sleep; of a night's lodging; of an accommodation
dom noclegowy [dom nots-le-**go**-vi] adj.m. hostel; common lodging house
nocnica [nots-**ńee**-tsah] f. an herb of the family Nyctaginaceae
nocnicowate [nots-ńee-tso-**vah**-te] pl. the family Nyctaginaceae of herbs
nocnicówka [nots-ńee-**tsoof**-kah] f. moth of the family Noctudiae
nocnicówki [nots-ńee-**tsoof**-kee] pl. the family Noctudiae of moths
nocniczek [nots-**ńee**-chek] m. small chamber pot
nocnik [**nots**-ńeek] m. chamber pot
nocny [**nots**-ni] adj.m. nocturnal; night (shift, etc.)
ciemności nocne [ćhem-**nośh**-ćhee **nots**-ne] exp.: the darkness of night; the dark
koszula nocna [ko-**shoo**-lah **nots**-nah] exp.: nightshirt
nocna bielizna [**nots**-nah bye-**leez**-nah] exp.: night clothes; bed clothes
nocny lokal [**nots**-ni **lo**-kahl] exp.: night club
nocny marek [**nots**-ni **mah**-rek] exp.: man, who goes late to bed; night owl
nocny ptak [**nots**-ni ptahk] exp.: night bird
służba nocna [**swoozh**-bah **nots**-nah] exp.: night-duty
spoczynek nocny [spo-**chi**-nek **nots**-ni] exp.: night's rest
stolik nocny [**sto**-leek **nots**-ni] exp.: nightstand
stróż nocny [stroosh **nots**-ni] exp.: night watchman
nocoświetlik [no-tso-**śhfyet**-leek] m. noctiluca (marine bioluminescent flagellate)
nocować [no-**tso**-vahćh] v. spend the night; stay overnight (regularly); sleep (*repeatedly*)
noga [**no**-gah] f. leg; foot; colloq: man
być cały dzień na nogach [bićh **tsah**-wi dźheń nah **no**-gahkh] exp.: to be on the run all day; to be on foot all day; to be astir all day
być na nogach [bićh nah **no**-gahkh] exp.: to be up
być jedną nogą na tamtym świecie [bićh **yed**-nown **no**-gown nah **tahm**-tim **śhfye**-ćhe] exp.: to have one foot in the grave
być kulą u nogi [bićh **koo**-lown oo **no**-gee] exp.: to be a burden
dać nogę [dahćh **no**-gan] exp.: colloq: to run away
do góry nogami [do **goo**-ri no-**gah**-mee] exp.: upside down
do nogi [do **no**-gee] exp.: to a man
do nogi! [do **no**-gee] exp.: to heel!; heel!
do nogi broń! [do **no**-gee broń] exp.: order arms!; ground arms! (Brit.)
grunt pali mu się pod nogami [groont **pah**-lee moo śhan pod no-**gah**-mee] exp.: he is in hot water; he is in trouble; he is a wanted man
(ledwo) powłóczyć nogami [(**led**-vo) po-**vwoo**-chićh no-**gah**-mee] exp.: to (barely) drag one's feet
moja noga więcej tam nie postanie [mo-yah no-gah **vyan**-tsey tahm ńe pos-**tah**-ńe] exp.: I shall never set foot there again
nie ruszyłem się nogą z domu [ńe roo-**shi**-wem śhan **no**-gown z **do**-moo] exp.: I did not leave home for a moment
noga za nogą [**no**-gah zah **no**-gown] exp.: at a snail's pace
padać z nóg [**pah**-dahćh z noog] exp.: to fall off one's feet
pies z kulawą nogą nie przyjdzie [pyes s koo-**lah**-vown **no**-gown ńe **pshiy**-dźhe] exp.: no one will

come; not a soul will come
pod nogami [pod no-**gah**-mee] exp.: under foot
podstawić komuś nogę [pot-**stah**-veećh **ko**-moośh **no**-gan] exp.: to trip somebody up
suchą nogą [**soo**-khown **no**-gown] exp.: without getting mud on one's feet; without wetting one's feet
ściąć kogoś z nóg [śhćhownćh **ko**-gośh z nook] exp.: to knock somebody of his feet; to knock somebody down
wstać lewą nogą [fstahćh **le**-vown **no**-gown] exp.: to get up on a wrong foot; to get up on the wrong side of the bed
wyciągnąć nogi [vi-**ćh**owng-nownćh **no**-gee] exp.: slang: to kick the bucket; to turn up one's toes (Brit.)
wziąć nogi za pas [vźhownćh **no**-gee zah pahs] exp.: to bolt; to take to one's heels
zerwać się na równe nogi [**zer**-vahćh śhan nah **roov**-ne **no**-gee] exp.: to jump up

nogawica [no-gah-**vee**-tsah] f. legging; trouser leg
nogawka [no-**gahf**-kah] f. legging; trouser leg
nogietek [no-**ge**-tek] m. marigold; Calendula
nogogłaszczek [no-go-**gwahsh**-chek] m. pedipalpus
nogogłaszczki [no-go-**gwahshch**-kee] pl. pedipalpi
nogopłetwe [no-go-**pwet**-fe] pl. the order pediculate (Pediculati) of fishes
nohajec [no-**khah**-yets] m. Nogai (Tartar)
nok [nok] m. nock; notch
nokaut [**no**-kahwt] m. knockout
nokautować [no-kahw-**to**-vahćh] v. knock out; tire out; exhaust (*repeatedly*)
nokdaun [**nok**-dahwn] m. knockdown; a striking down and overwhelming blow (in boxing)
noks [noks] m. unit of light intensity (0.1 lux)
noktambulik [nok-tahm-**boo**-leek] m. sleepwalker; somnambulist
noktambulista [nok-tahm-boo-**lees**-tah] m. sleepwalker; somnambulist
noktambulizm [nok-tahm-**boo**-leezm] m. sleepwalking; somnambulism; noctambulism
noktowizja [nok-to-**veez**-yah] f. night vision; infrared vision
noktowizor [nok-to-**vee**-zor] m. noctovisor; night vision goggles
noktowizyjny [nok-to-vee-**ziy**-ni] adj.m. of night vision; of infrared vision
nokturn [**nok**-toorn] m. nocturne
nomada [no-**mah**-dah] m. nomad
nomadyczny [no-mah-**dich**-ni] adj.m. nomadic
nomadyzm [no-**mah**-dizm] m. nomadism
nomarcha [no-**mahr**-khah] m. nomarch
nomarchia [no-**mahr**-khyah] f. nomarchy
nomenklator [no-men-**klah**-tor] m. Roman nomenclator
nomenklatura [no-men-klah-**too**-rah] f. nomenclature; terminology; group of people designated (by the Communist party) to occupy the leading posts in state administration and institutions
podwójna nomenklatura [po-**dvooy**-nah no-men-klah-**too**-rah] exp.: binomial system; binomial nomenclature

nomenklaturowy [no-men-klah-too-**ro**-vi] adj.m. of nomenclature; of the group of people designated (by the Communist party) to occupy the leading posts in state administration and institutions
nominacja [no-mee-**nahts**-yah] f. appointment; nomination
dostać nominację na stanowisko [**do**-stahćh no-mee-**nah**-tsyan nah stah-no-**vees**-ko] exp.: to be appointed to a post

nominacyjny [no-mee-nah-**tsiy**-ni] adj.m. of appointment; of nomination
nominalista [no-mee-nah-**lees**-tah] m. nominalist
nominalistyczny [no-mee-nah-lees-

tich-ni] adj.m. nominalistic
nominalizm [no-mee-nah-leezm] m. nominalism
nominalnie [no-mee-nahl-ńe] adv. nominally; in name only
nominalny [no-mee-nahl-ni] adj.m. nominal; (face) value
wartość nominalna [vahr-tośhćh no-mee-nahl-nah] exp.: face value; book value; nominal value
nominalna zapłata [no-mee-nahl-nah zah-pwah-tah] exp.: token payment
nominał [no-mee-nahw] m. nominal value (of stock, etc.)
nominat [no-mee-naht] m. nominee
nominatiwus [no-mee-nah-tee-voos] m. nominative (form in naming a noun)
nominatywny [no-mee-nah-tiv-ni] adj.m. nominative
nomografia [no-mo-grah-fyah] f. nomography
nomograficzny [no-mo-grah-feech-ni] adj.m. nomographical; nomographic
nomogram [no-mo-grahm] m. nomogram
nomokanon [no-mo-kah-non] m. nomocanon
nomokracja [no-mo-krahts-yah] f. nomocracy
nomologia [no-mo-lo-gyah] f. nomology
nomologiczny [no-mo-lo-geech-ni] adj.m. nomological
nomotetyczny [no-mo-te-tich-ni] adj.m. nomothetic; nomothetical
nona [no-nah] f. (music) ninth; none
nonajron [non-ahy-ron] m. non-iron (fabric)
nonajronowy [non-ahy-ro-no-vi] adj.m. of a non-iron (fabric)
nonet [no-net] m. (music) nonet
non-iron [non-ahy-ron] m. non-iron (fabric)
non-ironowy [non-ahy-ro-no-vi] adj.m. of a non-iron (fabric)
noniusz [noń-yoosh] m. nonius; vernier
nonkonformista [non-kon-for-mees-tah] m. nonconformist
nonkonformiści [non-kon-for-meeśh-ćhee] pl. the nonconformists
nonkonformistyczny [non-kon-for-mees-tich-ni] adj.m. nonconformist
nonkonformizm [non-kon-for-meezm] m. nonconformism
nonowy [no-no-vi] adj.m. ninth
akord nonowy [ah-kort no-no-vi] exp.: ninth chord
nonparel [non-pah-rel] m. nonpareil (font)
drukowany nonparelem [droo-ko-vah-ni non-pah-re-lem] exp.: printed in nonpareil
nonparelowy [non-pah-re-lo-vi] adj.m. of nonpareil
nonsens [non-sens] m. nonsense; absurdity
ależ to nonsens! [ah-lesh to non-sens] exp.: nonsense!; how absurd!
to jest kompletny nonsens! [to yest kom-plet-ni non-sens] exp.: it's sheer nonsense!; it's pure rubbish!; it's sheer stupidity!
nonsensowność [non-sen-sov-nośhćh] f. a piece of nonsense; (an) absurdity
nonsensowny [non-sen-sov-ni] adj.m. nonsensical; absurd
non stop [non stop] exp.: nonstop (flight, etc.)
nonszalancja [non-shah-lahn-tsyah] f. nonchalance; unconcern; careless behavior
z nonszalancją [z non-shah-lahn-tsyown] exp.: nonchalantly; without concern; disrespectfully
nonszalancki [non-shah-lahn-tskee] adj.m. nonchalant; unconcerned; disrespectful
nonszalancko [non-shah-lahn-tsko] adv. nonchalantly; without concern; disrespectfully
nopal [no-pahl] m. nopal; a genus of cacti
nora [no-rah] f. burrow; den
nora borsucza [no-rah bor-soo-chah] exp.: badger's set
nora lisa [no-rah lee-sah] exp.: fox's den
norbertanin [nor-ber-tah-ńeen] m. Norbertine monk
norbertanka [nor-ber-tahn-kah] f.

Norbertine nun
norbertański [nor-ber-**tahń**-skee] adj.m. Premonstratensian
norbid [**nor**-beet] m. norbide
nordowy [nor-**do**-vi] adj.m. colloq: of the North
wiatr nordowy [vyahtr nor-**do**-vi] exp.: North wind
nordycki [nor-**dits**-kee] adj.m. Nordic
nordyczny [nor-**dich**-ni] adj.m. Nordic
nordyjski [nor-**diy**-skee] adj.m. Nordic
nordyjczyk [nor-**diy**-chik] m. a Nordic
nordyk [**nor**-dik] m. a Nordic
nordyzacja [nor-di-**zahts**-yah] f. Nordicisation
noria [**nor**-yah] f. noria; an undershot water wheel
norka [**nor**-kah] f. mink
norma [**nor**-mah] f. standard; norm; rule; general principle
wrócić do normy [**vroo**-ćheećh do **nor**-mi] exp.: to be back to normal
normalizacja [nor-mah-lee-**zahts**-yah] f. normalization; standardiztion
normalizacyjny [nor-mah-lee-zah-**tsiy**-ni] adj.m. normalizing; standardizing; of normalization; of standardization
normalizator [nor-mah-lee-**zah**-tor] m. normalizer
normalizować [nor-mah-lee-**zo**-vahćh] v. normalize (metal); standardize; make standard (*repeatedly*)
normalizować się [nor-mah-lee-**zo**-vahćh śhan] v. become normalized; conform to standards (*repeatedly*)
normalizowanie [nor-mah-lee-zo-**vah**-ńe] n. normalization; standardization
normalizowanie się [ńor-mah-lee-zo-**vah**-ńe śhan] n. becoming normalized; conforming to standards
normalka [nor-**mahl**-kah] f. colloq: normalcy (of an event, situation, phenomenon, etc.); slang: obviousness; evidence; the usual; normalcy; normality
normalna [nor-**mahl**-nah] f. perpendicular; normal
normalnie [nor-**mahl**-ńe] adv. normally; in the ordinary course
normalnieć [nor-**mahl**-ńećh] v. become normal; recuperate back to normal condition (*repeatedly*)
normalność [nor-**mahl**-nośhćh] f. normalcy; normality
normalnotorowy [nor-mahl-no-to-**ro**-vi] adj.m. standard-gauge (rail track, raliroad, etc.)
normalny [nor-**mahl**-ni] adj.m. normal; standard; ordinary
niecałkiem normalny [ńe-**tsahw**-kem nor-**mahl**-ni] exp.: subnormal; a little retarded; somewhat strange; irregular
w normalnych warunkach [v nor-**mahl**-nikh vah-**roon**-kahkh] exp.: in normal circumstances; under normal circumstances; in normal conditions; under normal conditions
normand [**nor**-mahnt] m. horse of Normandy breed
normański [nor-**mahń**-skee] adj.m. Norman
normatyw [nor-**mah**-tif] m. norm; standard
normatywista [nor-mah-ti-**vees**-tah] m. normalizer of laws
normatywistyczny [nor-mah-ti-vees-**tich**-ni] adj.m. of a normalizer of laws; of normalization of laws
normatywizm [nor-mah-**ti**-veezm] m. normalization of laws
normatywnie [nor-mah-**tiv**-ńe] adv. normatively
normatywność [nor-mah-**tiv**-nośhćh] f. normativeness
normatywny [nor-mah-**tiv**-ni] adj.m. normative; prescribing laws; standard
nauki normatywne [nah-oo-kee nor-mah-**tiv**-ne] exp.: normative science
normować [nor-**mo**-vahćh] v. regulate; standardize; make standard or uniform; normalize (*repeatedly*)
normować się [nor-**mo**-vahćh śhan] v. accept standards (*repeatedly*)

normowanie [nor-mo-**vah**-ńe] n. standardization
normowanie się [nor-mo-**vah**-ńe śhan] n. becoming standardized
nornica [nor-**ńee**-tsah] f. mole; Clethrionomys
nornik [nor-ńeek] m. field mole
norniki [nor-**ńee**-kee] pl. field moles; the family Microtidae
norweg [nor-veg] m. horse of Norwegian breed
Norweg [nor-veg] m. Norwegian
norweski [nor-**ves**-kee] adj.m. Norwegian
po norwesku [po nor-**ves**-koo] exp.: in Norwegian (language, style, etc.)
noryt [**no**-rit] m. norite (mineral)
nos [nos] m. nose; snout; having a sharp nose; colloq: toe cap
chustka do nosa [**khoost**-kah do **no**-sah] exp.: handkerchief
dostać po nosie [**dos**-tahćh po **no**-śhe] exp.: to get snubbed
idzie jak krew z nosa [**ee**-dźhe yahk kref z **no**-sah] exp.: I am making no headway
kręcić nosem [**kran**-ćheećh **no**-sem] exp.: to pick and choose
mieć kogoś (coś) w nosie [myećh **ko**-gośh (tsośh) v **no**-śhe] exp.: to ignore somebody (something); to snap one's fingers at somebody
mieć mleko pod nosem [myećh **mle**-ko pod **no**-sem] exp.: to have milk on one's chin; to be immature; to be green
mieć nosa [myećh **no**-sah] exp.: to have a flair (for something); to have a scent (for something)
mówić przez nos [**moo**-veećh pshez nos] exp.: to nasalize; to snuffle; to speak through the nose
mruczeć pod nosem [**mroo**-chećh pod **no**-sem] exp.: to mumble; to mutter
nie widzieć dalej niż koniec własnego nosa [ńe **vee**-dźhećh **dah**-ley ńeesh **ko**-ńets vwahs-**ne**-go **no**-sah] exp.: not to see beyond the tip of one's nose
pilnować swego nosa [peel-**no**-vahćh **sfe**-go **no**-sah] exp.: to mind one's own business
pocałuj psa w nos [po-**tsah**-wooy psah v nos] exp.: get lost
pociągać nosem [po-**ćhown**-gahćh **no**-sem] exp.: to sniff; to sniffle
podsuwać coś komuś pod nos [pot-**soo**-vahćh tsośh **ko**-moośh pod nos] exp.: to shove something under somebody's nose
powiedzieć coś komuś prosto w nos [po-**vye**-dźhećh tsośh **ko**-moośh **pros**-to v nos] exp.: to say something to somebody's face
sprzatnąć komuś coś sprzed nosa [**spshownt**-nownćh **ko**-moośh tsośh spshed **no**-sah] exp.: colloq: to steal something from under somebody's nose
(tuż) pod nosem [(toosh) pod **no**-sem] exp.: (just) under (somebody's) nose
uśmiechać się pod nosem [oo-**śhmye**-khahćh śhan pod **no**-sem] exp.: to laugh in one's sleeve
utrzeć komuś nosa [**oo**-tshećh **ko**-moośh **no**-sah] exp.: to put somebody in his place; to take somebody down a peg; to cut somebody's comb (Brit.)
wodzić za nos [**vo**-dźheećh zah nos] exp.: to lead by the nose
wtykać nos w nieswoje sprawy [**fti**-kahćh nos v ńe-**sfo**-ye **sprah**-vi] exp.: to meddle into somebody else's business
wycierać nos [vi-**ćhe**-rahćh nos] exp.: to blow one's nose
wyczuć pismo nosem [**vi**-chooćh **pees**-mo **no**-sem] exp.: to smell a rat
zadzierać nosa [zah-**dźhe**-rahćh **no**-sah] exp.: to put up one's nose high
zatrzasnąć komuś drzwi przed nosem [zah-**tshah**-snownćh **ko**-moośh dzhvee pshed **no**-sem] exp.: to slam the door in somebody's face
zwiesić nos na kwintę [zvye-

śheećh nos nah **kfeen**-tan] exp.: colloq: to make a long face
nosacizna [nosah-**ćheez**-nah] f. (med.) glanders
nosacz [**no**-sahch] m. man with a big nose; monkey Nasalis larvatus
nosal [**no**-sahl] m. man with a big nose
nosaty [no-**sah**-ti] adj.m. nosy
noseczek [no-**se**-chek] m. very small nose
nosek [**no**-sek] m. small nose; cog; nib; pane; peen
nosiciel [no-**śhee**-ćheel] m. carrier; wearer
nosicielka [no-śhee-**ćhel**-kah] f. (female) carrier; wearer
nosicielstwo [no-śhee-**ćhel**-stfo] n. germ carrying
nosić [**no**-śheećh] v. carry; wear; bear; have about one (*repeatedly*)
diabli gdzieś kogoś noszą [**dyahb**-lee gdźheśh **ko**-gośh **no**-shown] exp.: somebody is gone, God knows where
nosić brodę [no-śheećh **bro**-dan] exp.: to have a beard
nosić koszulę w zębach [no-śheećh ko-**shoo**-lan v **zan**-bahkh] exp.: to be green; to be inexperienced; to have milk on one's chin
nosić na barana [no-śheećh nah bah-**rah**-nah] exp.: to carry piggyback
nosić nazwisko [no-śheećh nahz-**vees**-ko] exp.: to bear a name
nosić żałobę [no-śheećh zhah-**wo**-ban] exp.: to be in mourning
nosić się [**no**-śheećh śhan] v. wear (*repeatedly*)
nosić się z myślą [no-śheećh śhan z **miśh**-lown] exp.: to entertain an idea
nosić się z zamiarem [no-śheećh śhan z zah-**myah**-rem] exp.: to intend (doing); to contemplate (doing)
nosidło [no-**śheed**-wo] n. yoke
nosidła [no-**śheed**-wah] pl. yokes
nosidełko [no-śhee-**dew**-ko] n. harness for carrying a baby; mob slang: brassiere; bra
nosiłki [no-**śheew**-kee] pl. handbarrow
nosisko [no-**śhees**-ko] n. colloq: huge nose; enormous nose; ugly big nose
nosiwoda [no-śhee-**vo**-dah] m. water carrier
nosorożec [no-so-**ro**-zhets] m. rhinoceros
nosowo [no-**so**-vo] adv. nasally
nosowość [no-**so**-vośhćh] f. nasal quality; nasality
nosowy [no-**so**-vi] adj.m. nasal
głoska nosowa [**gwos**-kah no-**so**-vah] exp.: a nasal
nosówka [no-**soof**-kah] f. a nasal syllable; canine distemper
nosówkowy [no-soof-**ko**-vi] adj.m. nasalized; (symptoms, etc.) of canine distemper
nostalgia [no-**stahl**-gyah] f. nostalgia; homesickness
cierpieć na nostalgię [**ćher**-pyećh nah no-**stahl**-gyan] exp.: to be homesick; to suffer from homesickness; to suffer from nostalgia
nostalgicznie [no-stahl-**geech**-ńe] adv. nostalgically
nostalgiczny [no-stahl-**geech**-ni] adj.m. nostalgic
nostryfikacja [no-stri-fee-**kah**-tsyah] f. nostrification
nostryfikacyjny [no-stri-fee-kah-**tsiy**-ni] adj.m. of nostrification
nostryfikować [no-stri-fee-**ko**-vahćh] v. nostrificate; accept as equal to one's own (foreign diploma, etc.) (*repeatedly*)
nostryfikowanie [no-stri-fee-ko-**vah**-ńe] n. nostrification
nostrzyk [**no**-stshik] m. melilot; Melilotus plant
nostrzykowy [no-stshi-**ko**-vi] adj.m. melilot (leaves, raceme, etc.)
nosze [**no**-she] pl. stretchers
noszenie [no-**she**-ńe] n. wearing
do noszenia na co dzień [do no-she-ńah nah tso dźheń] exp.: for everyday wear
noszenie się [no-**she**-ńe śhan] n. the manner in which one bears or comports oneself
noszowa [no-**sho**-vah] f. (female) stretcher-bearer

noszowy [no-**sho**-vi] m. stretcher-bearer
nośnik [**nośh**-ńeek] m. carrier; conveyor
nośnik ciepła [**nośh**-ńeek **ćhep**-wah] exp.: heat carrier; heat medium
nośność [**nośh**-nośhćh] f. carrying capacity
nośność łożyska [**nośh**-nośhćh wo-**zhis**-kah] exp.: bearing capacity
nośność statku [**nośh**-nośhćh **staht**-koo] exp.: deadweight (capacity)
nośny [**nośh**-ni] adj.m. (load) bearing
kura nośna [**koo**-rah **nośh**-nah] exp.: laying hen
płaszczyzna nośna samolotu [pwahsh-**chiz**-nah **nośh**-nah sah-mo-**lo**-too] exp.: bearing surface of an airplane
sezon nośny [**se**-zon **nośh**-ni] exp.: (egg-)laying sezon; laying period
siła nośna [**śhee**-wah **nośh**-nah] exp.: carrying capacity
nota [**no**-tah] f. note; grade
notabene [no-tah-**be**-ne] indecl. by and by; by the way; incidentally
notable [no-**tahb**-le] pl. the notables
notacja [no-**tahts**-yah] f. (musical) notation
notarialnie [no-tahr-**yahl**-ńe] adv. before a notary
poświadczony notarialnie [po-śhfyaht-**ćho**-ni no-tahr-**yahl**-ńe] exp.: authenticated by a notary
notarialny [no-tahr-**yahl**-ni] adj.m. notarial (acts, charges, etc.)
akt notarialny [ahkt no-tahr-**yahl**-ni] exp.: notarized deed
notariat [no-**tahr**-yaht] m. notariate; notary's office
notariusz [no-**tahr**-yoosh] m. notary public
notariuszostwo [no-tahr-yoo-**shos**-tfo] n. notariate; notary's office
notatka [no-**taht**-kah] f. note
notatka dziennikarska [no-**taht**-kah dźhen-ńee-**kahr**-skah] exp.: paragraph; colloq: par
robić notatki z czegoś [**ro**-beećh no-**taht**-kee s **che**-gośh] exp.: to take notes of something
notatkowy [no-taht-**ko**-vi] adj.m. on a note; of notes
notatnik [no-**taht**-ńeek] m. notebook; diary; notes
notes [**no**-tes] m. pocket notebook; small notebook
notesik [no-**te**-śheek] m. (small, nice) notebook; diary; notes
notka [**not**-kah] f. footnote
notorycznie [no-to-**rich**-ńe] adv. notoriously
notoryczność [no-to-**rich**-nośhćh] f. notoriety
notoryczny [no-to-**rich**-ni] adj.m. notorious; flagrant; arrant
notoryjny [no-to-**riy**-ni] adj.m. (legally) notorious
notować [no-**to**-vahćh] v. make notes; take notes; write down (*repeatedly*)
być notowanym przez policję [bićh no-to-**vah**-nim pshes po-**leets**-yan] exp.: to have a (bad, police) record
być źle notowanym [bićh źhle no-to-**vah**-nim] exp.: to have a bad record; to have a bad reputation
notować coś w pamięci [no-to-vahćh tsośh f pah-**myan**-ćhee] exp.: to make a mental note of something
notowanie [no-to-**vah**-ńe] n. quotation; record (of facts)
notyfikacja [no-ti-fee-**kahts**-yah] f. notification; announcement; intimation
notyfikacyjny [no-ti-fee-kah-**tsiy**-ni] adj.m. of notification; of announcement; of intimation
notyfikować [no-ti-fee-**ko**-vahćh] v. notify (somebody of something); intimate (something to somebody) (*repeatedly*)
notyfikowanie [no-ti-fee-ko-**vah**-ńe] n. notification; announcement; intimation
noumen [**now**-men] m. noumenon; an unknowable object (as the soul) apprehended by thought
noumenon [now-**me**-non] m. noumenon

novum [**no**-voom] n. (Lat.) a novelty
nowa [**no**-vah] f. new female (in an office, etc.)
nowacja [no-**vahts**-yah] f. (legal) novation
nowalgina [no-vahl-**gee**-nah] f. novaldin
nowalia [no-**vah**-lyah] f. early vegetable; forced fruit
nowalijka [no-vah-**leey**-kah] f. (small) early vegetable; forced fruit
nowator [no-**vah**-tor] m. innovator
nowatorka [no-vah-**tor**-kah] f. (female) innovator
nowatorski [no-vah-**tor**-skee] adj.m. innovatory
po nowatorsku [po no-vah-**tor**-skoo] exp.: like an innovator
nowatorstwo [no-vah-**tor**-stfo] n. innovatory activities; the urge to innovate; innovation; novelty
nowe [**no**-ve] n. the new; the modern; the progressive; progress
nowela [no-**ve**-lah] f. short story; amendment (to a constitution)
noweleta [no-ve-**le**-tah] f. novelette
nowelista [no-ve-**lees**-tah] m. short-story writer
nowelistka [no-ve-**leest**-kah] f. (female) short-story writer
nowelistycznie [no-ve-lees-**tich**-ńe] adv. in short-story style
nowelistyczny [no-ve-lees-**tich**-ni] adj.m. short-story (style, etc.)
nowelistyka [no-ve-**lees**-ti-kah] f. short-story writing
nowelizacja [no-ve-lee-**zahts**-yah] f. amendments (to a bill)
nowelizacyjny [no-ve-lee-zah-**tsiy**-ni] adj.m. amendment (procedure in parliament, etc.)
nowelizator [no-ve-lee-**zah**-tor] m. amendment originator
nowelizować [no-ve-lee-**zo**-vahćh] v. amend (*repeatedly*)
nowelka [no-**vel**-kah] f. (little) short story
nowelowy [no-ve-**lo**-vi] adj.m. short story (plot, etc.)
nowenna [no-**ven**-nah] f. novena
nowicjat [no-**vee**-tsyaht] m. novitiate; period of being a novice
nowicjusz [no-**veets**-yoosh] m. novice; beginner; freshman
jestem tu nowicjuszem [**yes**-tem too no-veets-**yoo**-shem] exp.: I am strange to this; I am a stranger here
nowicjuszka [no-veets-**yoosh**-kah] f. (female) novice; beginner; freshman
nowicjuszostwo [no-veets-yoo-**shos**-tfo] n. freshman characteristics
nowicjuszowski [no-veets-yoo-**shof**-skee] adj.m. beginner's (luck, etc.)
nowik [**no**-veek] m. one of the Closterium spindle-shaped demids
nowina [no-**vee**-nah] f. piece of news; a piece of gossip; colloq: untilled land; new soil; virgin soil
nowiny [no-**vee**-ni] pl. news
dla mnie to nowina [dlah mńe to no-**vee**-nah] exp.: that's news to me
kradzież dla niego nie nowina [**krah**-dźhesh dlah **ńe**-go ńe no-**vee**-nah] exp.: he is no new hand in stealing
smutna nowina [**smoot**-nah no-**vee**-nah] exp.: sad news
nowinka [no-**veen**-kah] f. fad; novelty; innovation; a piece of gossip; colloq: early vegetable; forced fruit
nowinkarski [no-veen-**kahr**-skee] adj.m. innovatory
nowinkarstwo [no-veen-**kahr**-stfo] n. innovating; introducing novelties; gossip mongering
nowinkarz [no-**veen**-kahsh] m. gossip monger; person fond of novelty
nowiuchny [no-**vyookh**-ni] adj.m. brand-new; spick-and-span
nowiusieńki [no-vyoo-**śheń**-kee] adj.m. brand-new; spick-and-span
nowiuśki [no-**vyoośh**-kee] adj.m. brand-new; spick-and-span
nowiuteńki [no-vyoo-**teń**-kee] adj.m. brand-new; spick-and-span
nowiutki [no-**vyoot**-kee] adj.m. brand-new; spick-and-span
nowizna [no-**veez**-nah] f. untilled land; new soil; virgin soil
nowo [**no**-vo] adv. newly; anew; afresh; re-(done, etc.)

na nowo [nah **no**-vo] exp.: again; anew; afresh; once more; once again; from the beginning; from the start
wciąż na nowo [fćhownsh nah **no**-vo] exp.: again and again
nowo- [no-vo] prefix: re-; new-
nowobogacka [no-vo-bo-**gahts**-kah] f. newly rich woman; woman upstart
nowobogacki [no-vo-bo-**gahts**-kee] adj.m. newly enriched; m. upstart; nouveau riche
nowobogaccy [no-vo-bo-**gahts**-tsi] pl. the new rich
nowochrzczeniec [no-vo-**khshche**-ńets] m. convert; neophyte; Anabaptist
nowoczesność [no-vo-**ches**-nośhćh] f. modernity; modernness; up-to-datedness; novelty
nowoczesny [no-vo-**ches**-ni] adj.m. modern; up-to-date; present-day; newest; progressive
nowocześnie [no-vo-**cheśh**-ńe] adv. in up-to-date style; in an up-to-date manner; according to present-day requirements; in a modern manner
nowocześnieć [no-vo-**cheśh**-ńećh] v. become modern (*repeatedly*)
nowodruk [no-**vo**-drook] m. re-edition
nowofalowy [no-vo-fah-**lo**-vi] adj.m. of a new wave (of style, etc.); of the recent style
nowofundlandczyk [no-vo-foond-lahnt-chik] m. Newfoundland dog
Nowofundlandczyk [no-vo-foond-lahnt-chik] m. Newfoundlander
nowogrecki [no-vo-**grets**-kee] adj.m. of modern Greece
nowokaina [no-vo-kah-**ee**-nah] f. novocaine
nowokrytyczny [no-vo-kri-**tich**-ni] adj.m. neo-Kantian
nowołaciński [no-vo-wah-**ćheeń**-skee] adj.m. neo-Latin
nowomiejski [no-vo-**myey**-skee] adj.m. of a new urban area; of a new town
nowomodnie [no-vo-**mod**-ńe] adv. in the newest style; according to the latest fashion
nowomodny [no-vo-**mod**-ni] adj.m. up-to-date; progressive; new-fashion; colloq: newfangled
nowomowa [no-vo-**mo**-vah] f. newspeak; doublespeak; double-talk; propagandistic language marked by ambiguity and contradictions used in Communist countries by the government and mass media
nowonabywca [no-vo-nah-**bif**-tsah] m. new proprietor
nowonarodzony [**no**-vo nah-ro-**dzo**-ni] adj.m. newborn
czuć się jak nowo narodzony [chooćh śhan yahk **no**-vo nah-ro-**dzo**-ni] exp.: to feel young again
nowoprzybyła [**no**-vo pshi-**bi**-wah] f. (female) newly arrived; new-come; f. newcomer
nowoprzybyły [**no**-vo pshi-**bi**-wi] adj.m. newly arrived; new-come; m. newcomer
noworoczny [no-vo-**roch**-ni] adj.m. New Year's; of New Year
noworodek [no-vo-**ro**-dek] m. newborn child; baby; infant
nowosiedliny [no-vo-śhed-**lee**-ni] pl. housewarming; housewarming party
nowość [**no**-vośhćh] f. novelty; newness; strangeness; recency; new fashion, style, craze, etc.
nowości [no-**vośh**-ćhee] pl. news; tidings
nowotestamentowy [no-vo-tes-tah-men-**to**-vi] adj.m. of (from, in) the New Testament
nowotworowy [no-vo-tfo-**ro**-vi] adj.m. neoplastic; tumorous
nowotwór [no-**vo**-tfoor] m. tumor; newly-coined word; morbid growth
nowowystępujący [**no**-vo vi-stan-poo-**yown**-tsi] adj.m. entrant
nowozaciężny [**no**-vo zah-**ćhanzh**-ni] adj.m. newly enlisted (soldier, etc.); m. recruit; conscript; enlisted man
nowożeniec [no-vo-**zhe**-ńets] m. bridegroom
nowożeńcy [no-vo-**zheń**-tsi] pl. the newlywed; bride and groom;

the newly married couple
nowożytny [no-vo-**zhit**-ni] adj.m. (of) modern (period)
nowy [**no**-vi] adj.m. new; fresh; unfamiliar
co nowego? [tso no-**ve**-go] exp.: what's new?; what news?
dla mnie to coś nowego [dlah mńe to tsośh no-**ve**-go] exp.: that's something new to me; that's new to me
jak nowy [yahk **no**-vi] exp.: as good as new
na nowo [nah **no**-vo] exp.: again; anew; afresh; once more; once again; from the beginning; from the start
nic nowego [ńeets no-**ve**-go] exp.: nothing new
nowe [no-ve] pl. the new; n. something new; (a) novelty
Nowy Rok [no-vi rok] exp.: New Year
Nowy Świat [no-vi śhfyaht] exp.: New World
Nowy Testament [ńo-vi tes-**tah**-ment] exp.: New Testament
od nowa [od **no**-vah] exp.: again; anew; afresh; from the beginning
po nowemu [po no-**ve**-moo] exp.: in a new manner; according to the new fashion; colloq: in a new-fangled way
nozdrze [**noz**-dzhe] n. nostril
nozologia [no-zo-**lo**-gyah] f. description of diseases
nożęta [no-**zhan**-tah] pl. small baby's feet
nożny [**nozh**-ni] adj.m. foot (specialist, control, etc.); pedal (cords, ganglion, lathe, etc.)
hamulec nożny [khah-**moo**-lets **nozh**-ni] exp.: foot break
piłka nożna [**peew**-kah **nozh**-nah] exp.: soccer; football (Brit.)
rozrusznik nożny [roz-**roosh**-ńeek **nozh**-ni] exp.: kick starter
nożowaty [no-zho-**vah**-ti] adj.m. cultrate; sharp-edged and pointed
nożowiec [no-**zho**-vyets] m. cutthroat; gangster
nożownictwo [no-zhov-**ńeets**-tfo] n. brigandage
nożowniczy [no-zhov-**ńee**-chi] adj.m. cutthroat's; gangster's; cutler's; cutlery (trade, etc.)
nożownik [no-**zhov**-ńeek] m. knifer; cutthroat; gangster
nożowy [no-**zho**-vi] adj.m. knife (tool, etc.); knife-shaped; knife-like
wyłącznik nożowy [vi-**wownch**-ńeek no-**zho**-vi] exp.: knife switch
nożyce [no-**zhi**-tse] pl. shears; clippers; large shears
nożyce cen [no-**zhi**-tse tsen] exp.: price scissors; price cutting
nożyce do cięcia drutu [no-**zhi**-tse do ćhan-ćhah **droo**-too] exp.: wire cutter
nożyce ręczne do blach [no-**zhi**-tse ranch-ne do blahkh] exp.: snips
uderz w stół a nożyce się odezwą [oo-desh f stoow ah no-zhi-tse śhan o-**dez**-vown] exp.: a guilty conscience will out; guilty conscience will reveal itself
nożycować [no-zhi-**tso**-vahćh] v. do the shears (jumping) (*repeatedly*)
nożycowanie [no-zhi-tso-**vah**-ńe] n. doing the shears
nożycowaty [no-zhi-tso-**vah**-ti] adj.m. scissors-shaped
nożycowo [no-zhi-**tso**-vo] adv. like scissors; scissor-fashion
nożycowy [no-zhi-**tso**-vi] adj.m. scissors (blade, motion, etc.)
nożyczki [no-**zhich**-kee] pl. scissors; small scissors
nożyk [no-zhik] m. pocketknife
nożyna [no-**zhi**-nah] f. poor little (baby's) foot
nożysko [no-**zhis**-ko] n. big old foot
nów [noof] m. new moon
nówka [noof-kah] f. colloq: new car; slang: beginning whore; new set of cards (mob jargon)
nózia [**noo**-źhah] f. pretty little foot
nóż [noosh] m. knife; cutter
nóż chirurgiczny [noosh khee-roor-**geech**-ni] exp.: lancet; scalpel
nóż ogrodniczy [noosh o-grod-ńee-chi] exp.: pruning knife
dostać nożem [dos-tahćh **no**-zhem] exp.: to get knifed

skończyć pod nożem [skoń-chićh pod no-zhem] exp.: to die on the operating table
mieć nóż na gardle [myećh noosh nah gahr-dle] exp.: to be in a tight corner; to be in a hopeless situation
wbić komuś nóż w plecy [vbeećh ko-moośh noosh f ple-tsi] exp.: to stab somebody in the back

nóżęta [noo-zhan-tah] pl. pretty little feet
nóżka [noosh-kah] f. little foot; child's foot
nóżki wieprzowe [noosh-kee vyep-sho-ve] exp.: pig-trotters
nóżki cielęce w galarecie [noosh-kee ćhe-lan-tse v gah-lah-re-ćhe] exp.: calve's foot jelly

nóżkarka [noosh-kahr-kah] f. stem machine (for electric valves)
Nubijczyk [noo-beey-chik] m. (a) Nubian
nubijski [noo-beey-skee] adj.m. Nubian
nucenie [noo-tse-ńe] n. humming
nucić [noo-ćheećh] v. hum; croon (*repeatedly*)
nuda [noo-dah] f. boredom; tedium; monotony; something tedious
robić coś z nudy [ro-beećh tsośh z noo-di] exp.: to do something just to pass the time (to kill time)
umierać z nudów [oo-mye-rahćh z noo-doof] exp.: to be bored stiff; to be bored to death

nudnawo [nood-nah-vo] adv. somewhat dully; rather dully; in an uninteresting manner
nudnawy [nood-nah-vi] adj.m. somewhat dull
nudnie [nood-ńe] adv. dully; monotonously
nudno [nood-no] adv. dully; monotonously
było nudno [bi-wo nood-no] exp.: it was (somewhat) dull
było mi nudno [bi-wo mee nood-no] exp.: I was bored

nudność [nood-nośhćh] f. dullness; tediousness; monotony; tedium
nudności [nood-nośh-ćhee] pl. nausea; a stomach distress and an urge to vomit
dostawać nudności na widok czegoś [dos-tah-vahćh nood-nośh-ćhee nah vee-dok che-gośh] exp.: to nauseate at the sight of something
mieć nudności [myećh nood-nośh-ćhee] exp.: to be nauseated; to feel sick

nudny [nood-ni] adj.m. boring; tedious; nauseating; dull; sickening
nudny jak flaki z olejem [nood-ni yahk flah-kee z o-le-yem] exp.: dull as ditch water; dry as dust; very uninteresting; colloq: dull as hell

nudysta [noo-dis-tah] m. nudist
nudystyczny [noo-dis-tich-ni] adj.m. nudist
nudyzm [noo-dizm] m. nudism
nudzenie [noo-dze-ńe] n. boring
nudzenie się [noo-dze-ńe śhan] n. getting bored
nudziara [noo-dźhah-rah] f. & m. colloq: (a) bore; tiresome person
nudziarski [noo-dźhahr-skee] adj.m. boring; tedious; nauseating; dull; sickening
nudziarstwo [noo-dźhahr-stfo] n. boredom; dullness; tediousness; monotony; tedium; boring talk; uninteresting occupation
nudziarz [noo-dźhahsh] m. bore
to skończony nudziarz [to skoń-cho-ni noo-dźhahsh] exp.: he is a perfect nuisance

nudzić [noo-dźheećh] v. bore (*repeatedly*)
nie nudź! [ńe noo ćh] exp.: stop it!; quit bothering me!
nudzi mnie to [noo-dźhee mńe to] exp.: I am tired of this

nudzić się [noo-dźheećh śhan] v. be bored; be tedious (*repeatedly*)
nudzić się jak mops [noo-dźheećh śhan yahk mops] exp.: to be getting bored stiff

nugat [noo-gaht] m. nougat
nuklearny [noo-kle-ahr-ni] adj.m. nuclear
broń nuklearna [broń noo-kle-ahr-

nah] exp.: nuclear weapon(s)
rozbrojenie nuklearne [roz-bro-**ye**-ńe noo-kle-**ahr**-ne] exp.: nuclear disarmament
nukleinowy [noo-kle-ee-**no**-vi] adj.m. nucleic (acid)
nukleon [noo-**kle**-on] m. nucleon; nuclear particle
nukleoniczny [noo-kle-o-**ńeech**-ni] adj.m. nucleonic
nukleonika [noo-kle-**o**-ńee-kah] f. nucleonics
nukleoproteid [noo-kle-o-pro-**te**-eet] m. nucleoprotein (as a DNA)
nukleoproteidy [noo-kle-o-pro-te-**ee**-di] pl. nucleoproteins
nukleotyd [noo-kle-**o**-tit] m. nucleotide
nukleotydy [noo-kle-o-**ti**-di] pl. nucleotides (basic structural units in DNA and RNA)
nuklid [**noo**-kleed] m. nuclide
nuklidowy [noo-klee-**do**-vi] adj.m. nuclidic
nulka [**nool**-kah] f. rotating compasses; drop compasses
nullifikacja [nool-lee-fee-**kahts**-yah] f. nullification; act of nullifying
numer [**noo**-mer] m. number; size
numer kolejny [noo-mer ko-**ley**-ni] exp.: consecutive number
numer rejestracyjny (samochodu) [**noo**-mer re-yes-trah-**tsiy**-ni (sah-mo-**kho**-doo)] exp.: (car) license plate number; (car) registration number
numer seryjny [**noo**-mer se-**riy**-ni] exp.: serial number
stary numer czasopisma [**stah**-ri **noo**-mer chah-so-**pees**-mah] exp.: an old issue of a magazine
te buty są o dwa numery za duże [te **boo**-ti sown o dvah noo-**me**-ri zah **doo**-zhe] exp.: these shoes are two sizes too large
ten numer nie przejdzie [ten **noo**-mer ńe **pshey**-dźhe] exp.: nothing doing!; that won't do!
to dobry numer! [to **dob**-ri **noo**-mer] exp.: fine fellow!; good trick!
wykręcić numer telefonu [vi-**kran**-ćheećh **noo**-mer te-le-**fo**-noo] exp.: to dial a telephone number
numeracja [noo-me-**rah**-tsyah] f. numeration
numeracja arkuszy [noo-me-**rahts**-yah ahr-**koo**-shi] exp.: foliation
numerator [noo-me-**rah**-tor] m. numberer; numbering stamp
numerek [noo-**me**-rek] m. check; ticket
numerowa [noo-me-**ro**-vah] f. hotel waitress
numerować [noo-me-**ro**-vahćh] v. number; give a number to (*repeatedly*)
numerowanie [noo-me-ro-**vah**-ńe] n. numbering; numeration; foliation of sheets in a book
numerowy [noo-me-**ro**-vi] m. porter; bellboy; hotel waiter; adj.m. number (plate, lottery, etc.)
numerycznie [noo-me-**rich**-ńe] adv. numerically
numeryczny [noo-me-**rich**-ni] adj.m. numerical
numeryk [noo-**me**-rik] m. specialist in numerical methods
numizmat [noo-**meez**-maht] m. numismatic coin
numizmatyczny [noo-meez-mah-**tich**-ni] adj.m. numismatic
numizmatyk [noo-meez-**mah**-tik] m. numismatist
numizmatyka [noo-meez-**mah**-ti-kah] f. numismatics; study (or collection) of coins, medals, etc.
numulit [noo-**moo**-leet] m. numulite
numulity [noo-moo-**lee**-ti] pl. numulitic limestones
numulitowy [noo-moo-lee-**to**-vi] adj.m. numulitic (limestones); of numulite
numulityczny [noo-moo-lee-**tich**-ni] adj.m. numulitic (limestones)
nunatak [noo-**nah**-tahk] m. nunatak
nuncjatura [noon-tsyah-**too**-rah] f. nunciature
nuncjusz [**noon**-tsyoosh] m. nuncio; papal ambassador
nur [noor] m. (a) dive; plunge; loon; Gavia bird
dać nura [dahćh **noo**-rah] exp.: to dive; colloq: to bolt; to duck; to dive (into a crowd, etc.)
nurek [**noo**-rek] m. diver
dać nurka [dahćh **noor**-kah] exp.:

to dive; colloq: to bolt; to duck; to dive (into a crowd, etc.)
płynąć nurkiem [**pwi**-nownćh noor-kem] exp.: to swim under water
nurka [**noor**-kah] f. mink
nurkarstwo [nooor-**kahr**-stfo] n. diving work; scuba diving
nurkować [noor-**ko**-vahćh] v. dive; plunge; duck; nose-dive (*repeatedly*)
nurkowanie [noor-ko-**vah**-ńe] n. diving; nose dive
nurkowiec [noor-**ko**-vyets] m. dive bomber
nurkownictwo [noor-kov-**ńeets**-tfo] n. diving work
nurkowy [noor-**ko**-vi] adj.m. diving (attack, etc.); mink (coat, etc.)
lot nurkowy [lot noor-**ko**-vi] exp.: nose dive
nurnik [**noor**-ńeek] m. plunger; ram; Cephus grylle bird
nurnikowy [noor-ńee-**ko**-vi] adj.m. plunger (pump, etc.)
nurogęś [noo-**ro**-ganśh] f. merganser (bird); Mergus
nurt [noort] m. current (flowing); stream; trend; wake
nurty [**noor**-ti] pl. currents; waters; billows
płynąć z nurtem [pwi-nownćh z **noor**-tem] exp.: to flow down the stream; to flow downstream
nurtować [noor-**to**-vahćh] v. fret; penetrate; pervade; ferment in; rankle; pray on (*repeatedly*)
to mnie nurtuje [to mńe noor-**too**-ye] exp.: I feel uneasy about it
nurtowanie [noor-to-**vah**-ne] n. pervasion
nurzać [noo-zhahćh] v. dip; welter in; plunge into; wallow in; immerse in; steep into (*repeatedly*)
nurzać się [noo-zhaćh śhan] v. plunge; welter (*repeatedly*)
nurzanie [noo-**zhah**-ńe] n. plunging
nurzanie się [noo-**zhah**-ńe śhan] n. wallowing; getting steeped; becoming immersed
nurzaniec [noo-**zhah**-ńets] m. tape grass
nurzyk [noo-zhik] m. guillemot; Uria
nurzyk drobny [**noo**-zhik **drob**-ni] exp.: rotche; Allealle
nurzyk podbielały [**noo**-zhik pod-bye-**lah**-wi] m. common guillemot
nut [noot] m. mortise; mortice; groove
nuta [**noo**-tah] f. (sound) note
kłamać jak z nut [**kwah**-mahćh yahk z noot] exp.: to lie like a gas meter (Brit.); to lie a lot
pulpit na nuty [**pool**-peet nah **noo**-ti] exp.: music stand
uderzyć we właściwa nutę [oo-**de**-zhićh ve vwahśh-**ćhee**-vown noo-tan] exp.: to touch the right chord
nutacja [noo-**tahts**-yah] f. nutation
nutacyjny [noo-tah-**tsiy**-ni] adj.m. nutational
nutka [**noot**-kah] f. small (musical) note
nutowy [noo-**to**-vi] adj.m. note (part, etc.)
papier nutowy [**pah**-pyer noo-**to**-vi] exp.: music-paper
nutria [nootr-yah] f. coypu; nutria
nutriety [nootr-**ye**-ti] pl. dyed sheepskins
nuty [**noo**-ti] pl. written music; printed music; music score
nuworysz [noo-**vo**-rish] m. newly rich; upstart; nouveau riche
nuż [noosh] exp.: if; and if
a nuż [ah noosh] exp.: and if
a nuż mi się uda? [a noosh mee śhan **oo**-dah] exp.: what if I succeed?
a nuż przyjdzie [a noosh **pshiy**-dźhe] exp.: suppose he comes
a nuż wygram [a noosh **vig**-rahm] exp.: what if I win?
nużąco [noo-zhown-tso] adv. in wearying manner; tiresomely
nużący [noo-**zhown**-tsi] adj.m. tiring; tiresome; wearisome
nuże [**noo**-zhe] exp.: colloq: come on!
nużenie [noo-**zhe**-ńe] n. tiring; wearing
nużeniec [noo-**zhe**-ńets] m. follicle mite; Demodex
nużeńcowaty [noo-zheń-tso-**vah**-ti] adj.m. of the Demodex family of mites

nużeńcowate [noo-zheń-tso-vah-te] pl. the Demodex family of mites

nużyca [noo-zhi-tsah] f. infection caused by follicle mite

nużyć [noo-zhićh] v. tire; weary; make tired; oppress (*repeatedly*)

nużyć się [noo-zhićh śh<u>an</u>] v. grow weary; get tired (*repeatedly*)

nygus [ni-goos] m. colloq: lazybones

nygusostwo [ni-goo-sos-tfo] n. colloq: laziness; loafing

nygusować [ni-goo-so-vahćh] v. colloq: lounge about; loiter; loaf (*repeatedly*)

nygusować się [ni-goo-so-vahćh śh<u>an</u>] v. colloq: laze one's time (*repeatedly*)

nygusowanie [ni-goo-so-vah-ńe] n. colloq: loafing; laziness

nygusowanie się [ni-goo-so-vah-ńe śh<u>an</u>] n. colloq: being lazy

nygusowski [ni-goo-sof-skee] adj.m. colloq: loafer's

nylon [ni-lon] m. nylon

nylony [ni-lo-ni] pl. nylon stockings

nylonowy [ni-lo-no-vi] adj.m. nylon (stockings, etc.)

nysa [ni-sah] f. Nysa car

nywka [nif-kah] f. breed of pigeons

nyża [ni-zhah] f. niche; alcove

nyżowy [ni-zho-vi] adj.m. niche (recess, etc.)

POGONOWSKI PHONETIC SYMBOLS

Polish vowels:

A, a as in: father, car;
in the phonetic guide: **a**

E, e as in: let, met, get;
in the phonetic guide: **e**

I, i as in: feel, keel;
in the phonetic guide: **ee**

O, o as in: bought, not;
in the phonetic guide: **o**

U,u,Ó,ó as in: hook, too;
in the phonetic guide: **oo**

Y, y as in: it, big, bib;
in the phonetic guide: **i**

Polish Palatal Consonants

Speech organ diagram for Polish palatal consonants:

ś = śh, ź = źh
ć = ćh, dź = dźh

The two Polish nasalized vowels:

Ą, ą as in: *French sound of "on"*;
in the phonetic guide: **own**

Ę, ę as in: *French sound of "vin"*;
in the phonetic guide: **an**

Note: for detailed discussion of Polish phonetics see text page xxix in Vol. I